Business Law and the Legal Environment

Version 2.0

Don Mayer, Daniel M. Warner, George J. Siedel, and
Jethro K. Lieberman

FlatWorld

9781453383902

Business Law and the Legal Environment
Version 2.0

Don Mayer, Daniel M. Warner, George J. Siedel, and Jethro K. Lieberman

Published by:

FlatWorld
175 Portland Street
Boston, MA 02114

Brief Contents

Contents

About the Authors

Don Mayer

Professor Don Mayer

Don Mayer teaches law, ethics, public policy, and sustainability at the Daniels College of Business, University of Denver, where he is Professor of the Practice of Business Ethics and Legal Studies. His research focuses on the role of business in creating a more just, sustainable, and productive world. With James O'Toole, Professor Mayer has co-edited and contributed content to *Good Business: Exercising Effective and Ethical Leadership* (Routledge, 2010). He is also coauthor of *International Business Law: Cases and Materials*, in its sixth edition with Pearson Publishing Company. He has taught business ethics at St. Mary's College of California, the University of Michigan, Manchester Global Business School, the University of Iowa, and Oakland University (Michigan).

After earning a philosophy degree from Kenyon College and a law degree from Duke University Law School, Professor Mayer served as a Judge Advocate General's (JAG) Corps officer in the United States Air Force during the Vietnam conflict and went into private practice in North Carolina. In 1985, he earned his LL.M. in international and comparative law at the Georgetown University Law Center. Later that year, he began his academic career at Western Carolina University and proceeded to become a full professor at Oakland University in Rochester, Michigan, where he taught for many years before moving to the University of Denver.

Professor Mayer has won numerous awards from the Academy of Legal Studies in Business, including the Hoeber Award for best article in the *American Business Law Journal*, the Maurer Award for best article on business ethics (twice), and the Ralph Bunche Award for best article on international business law (three times). His work has been published in many journals and law reviews but most often in *American Business Law Journal*, the *Journal of Business Ethics*, and the *Business Ethics Quarterly*.

Daniel M. Warner

Professor Daniel Warner

Photo courtesy of Western Washington University College of Business

Daniel M. Warner is a magna cum laude graduate of the University of Washington, where–following military service–he also attended law school. In 1978, after several years of criminal and then civil practice, he joined the faculty at the College of Business and Economics at Western Washington University, where he is now a professor of business legal studies in the Accounting Department. He has published extensively, exploring the intersection of popular culture and the law, and has received the College of Business Dean's Research Award six times for "distinguished contributions in published research." Professor Warner served on the Whatcom County Council for eight years (two years as its chair). He has served on the Faculty Senate and on various university and college committees, including as chairman of the University Master Plan Committee. Professor Warner has also been active in state bar association committee work and in local politics, where he has served on numerous boards and commissions for over thirty years. He is currently president of his local water association.

George J. Siedel

Professor George Siedel

George J. Siedel completed graduate studies at the University of Michigan and Cambridge University. Following graduation from law school, he worked as an attorney in a professional corporation before joining the faculty at the University of Michigan. Professor Siedel has been admitted to practice before the United States Supreme Court and in Michigan, Ohio, and Florida. He has also served on several boards of directors and as Associate Dean of the Ross School of Business at the University of Michigan.

Professor Siedel was a Visiting Professor at Stanford University and Harvard University, a Visiting Scholar at Berkeley, and a Parsons Fellow at the University of Sydney. He has been elected a Visiting Fellow at Cambridge University's Wolfson College and a Life Fellow of the Michigan State Bar Foundation. As a Fulbright Scholar in Eastern Europe, he held a Distinguished Chair in the Humanities and Social Sciences.

The author of numerous books and articles, Professor Siedel is the recipient of research awards from the University of Michigan (the Faculty Recognition Award) and the Academy of Legal Studies in Business (the Hoeber Award, the Ralph Bunche Award and the Maurer Award). The Center for International Business Education and Research selected a case written by Professor Siedel for its annual International Case Writing Award. He has also received many teaching awards, including the 2014 Executive Program Professor of the Year Award from a consortium of thirty-six leading universities committed to international education.

Jethro K. Lieberman

Jethro K. Lieberman is Martin Professor Emeritus at New York Law School, where for many years he served as dean for academic affairs. He taught in law schools for 33 years, at NYLS and at Fordham University School of Law. Before that , he was vice president at what is now the International Institute for Conflict Prevention and Resolution (CPR) in New York. For nearly ten years, he was legal affairs editor of Business Week magazine. He practiced antitrust and trade regulation law at a large Washington law firm and was on active duty as a member of the Navy's Judge Advocate General's (JAG) Corps during the Vietnam era. He earned his BA in politics and economics from Yale University, his JD from Harvard Law School, and his PhD in political science from Columbia University. He is the author of The Litigious Society (Basic Books), winner of the American Bar Association's top literary prize, the Silver Gavel. Among his many other books are Liberalism Undressed (Oxford University Press) and A Practical Companion to the Constitution: How the Supreme Court Has Ruled on Issues from Abortion to Zoning (University of California Press).

He is a long-time letterpress printer and proprietor of The Press at James Pond, a private press, and owner of the historic Kelmscott-Goudy Press, an Albion handpress that was used to print the Kelmscott Press edition of Geoffrey Chaucer's *Canterbury Tales* in the 1890s. For a complete bibliography, see www.jethrolieberman.com.

Professor Jethro Lieberman

Acknowledgments

The authors would like to thank the following colleagues who have reviewed the text and provided comprehensive feedback and suggestions for improving the material:

- Jennifer Barger Johnson, University of Central Oklahoma
- Dawn M. Bradanini, Lincoln College
- Larry Bumgardner, Pepperdine University
- Michael Edward Chaplin, California State University–Northridge
- Nigel Cohen, University of Texas–Pan American
- Mark Edison, North Central College
- Gideon Mark, University of Maryland
- Henry J. Hastings, Eastern Michigan University
- Henry Lowenstein, Coastal Carolina University
- Tanya Marcum, Bradley University
- Harry McCracken, California Lutheran University
- Robert Miller, Dominican University
- Leo Moerson, George Washington University
- Tonia Hap Murphy, University of Notre Dame
- Bart Pachino, California State University–Northridge
- Kimber J. Palmer, Texas A&M University–International
- Lawrence Price, Saint Mary's University of Minnesota
- Kurt Saunders, California State University–Northridge
- Ron Washburn, Bryant University
- Ruth Weatherly, Simpson College
- Eric Yordy, Northern Arizona University

The authors would also like to thank Vicki Brentnall of FlatWorld, without whose patience and graceful prodding this version would not be published.

Preface

Our goal is to provide students with a textbook that is up to date and comprehensive in its coverage of legal and regulatory issues—and organized to permit instructors to tailor the materials to their particular approach. This book engages students by relating law to everyday events with which they are already familiar (or with which they are familiarizing themselves in other business courses) and by its clear, concise, and readable style. (An earlier business law text by authors Lieberman and Siedel was hailed "the best written text in a very crowded field.")

This textbook provides context and essential concepts across the entire range of legal issues with which managers and business executives must grapple. The text provides the vocabulary and legal acumen necessary for businesspeople to talk in an educated way to their customers, employees, suppliers, government officials—and to their own lawyers. This second edition retains the lauded features of the first, and updates the text to incorporate new laws and—while keeping the favorite cases—new cases.

Traditional publishers often create confusion among customers in the text selection process by offering a huge array of publications. Once a text is selected, customers might still have to customize the text to meet their needs. For example, publishers usually offer books that include either case summaries or excerpted cases, but some instructors prefer to combine case summaries with a few excerpted cases so that students can experience reading original material. Likewise, the manner in which most conventional texts incorporate video is cumbersome because the videos are contained in a separate library, which makes access more complicating for instructors and students.

The FlatWorld Knowledge model eliminates the need for "families" of books (such as the ten Miller texts mentioned below) and greatly simplifies text selection. Instructors have only to select between our *Business Law and Legal Environment* volumes of the text and then click on the features they want (as opposed to trying to compare the large number of texts and packages offered by other publishers). In addition to the features inherent in any FlatWorld publication, this book offers these unique features:

- Cases are available in excerpted and summarized format, thus enabling instructors to easily "mix and match" excerpted cases with case summaries.
- Links to forms and uniform laws are embedded in the text. For example, the chapters on contract law incorporate discussion of various sections of the Uniform Commercial Code, which is available at http://www.law.cornell.edu/ucc/ucc.table.html.
- Likewise, many sample legal forms are readily available online. For example, the chapter on employment law refers to the type of terms commonly found in a standard employment agreement, examples of which can be found at http://bit.ly/2lhgsKT.
- Every chapter contains overviews that include the organization and coverage, a list of key terms, chapter summaries, and self-test questions in multiple-choice format (along with answers) that are followed by additional problems with answers available in the Instructors' Manual.
- In addition to standard supplementary materials offered by other texts, students have access to electronic flash cards, proactive quizzes, and audio study guides.

What's New in Version 2.0?

This 2.0 version reflects changes in the law as relevant. For example, there are updated sections on some aspects of commercial paper and banking (regarding computer "apps" that make possible instantaneous deposits and withdrawals from bank accounts); and there is a new section presenting regulations affecting consumer credit transactions (the federal Consumer Finance Protection Agency). This version combines two previous chapters on labor law and employment law into one chapter. A new chapter on accountants' professional liability has been added. New cases are presented, but only if they illustrate the legal point more clearly than the previous cases—old favorites are retained and there is no change merely for the sake of change.

Student feedback caused us to recognize that, in some places, the text could be clarified. Some of the cases have been edited to reduce their length, and extraneous text has been deleted, while new charts and illustrations have been added. In addition, monetary denominations are more regularly noted both as stated in the cases and in current U.S. dollars (for example, a contract made in 1960 for $500 doesn't seem worth much litigation until your realize that would be about $4,200 in current dollars).

The Instructor's Manuals have been updated and improved. Many cases are briefed the "old fashioned way": facts, procedure, issue, holding, reason. We hope this makes it easier for instructors to read the briefs themselves. And the Manuals also include some tips for teaching the material garnered from authors' own use of the text: where do students have problems? What is useful to mention in Chapter 8, for example, that students will encounter again in Chapter 17? PowerPoint slides have also been updated and improved, as have the test file questions.

In short, we are proud to present an updated and improved text. We thank our colleagues who have offered suggestions, and of course we thank our students for their input and (usually) their enthusiasm. It is very gratifying for the instructor when it becomes apparent that the "light has gone on" for the students studying this material. Keep those cards and letters coming!

CHAPTER 1

Introduction to Law and Legal Systems

Learning Objectives

After reading this chapter, you should be able to do the following:

1. Distinguish different philosophies of law—schools of legal thought—and explain their relevance.
2. Identify the various aims that a functioning legal system can serve.
3. Explain how politics and law are related.
4. Identify the sources of law and which laws have priority over other laws.
5. Understand some basic differences between the US legal system and other legal systems.

Law has different meanings as well as different functions. Philosophers have considered issues of justice and law for centuries, and several different approaches, or schools of legal thought, have emerged. In this chapter, we will look at those different meanings and approaches and will consider how social and political dynamics interact with the ideas that animate the various schools of legal thought. We will also look at typical sources of "positive law" in the United States and how some of those sources have priority over others, and we will set out some basic differences between the US legal system and other legal systems.

1.1 What Is Law?

Learning Objectives

1. State a definition of "law" that you find to be accurate.
2. List and describe the various functions of the law.
3. Explain the relationship between law and politics.

Law is a word that can mean many different things. *Black's Law Dictionary* says that law is "a body of rules of action or conduct prescribed by controlling authority, and having binding legal force. That which must be obeyed and followed by citizens subject to sanctions or legal consequence is a law."[1]

Functions of the Law

In a nation, the law can serve to (1) keep the peace, (2) maintain the status quo, (3) preserve individual rights, (4) protect minorities against majorities, (5) promote social justice, and (6) provide for orderly social change. Some legal systems serve these purposes better than others. Although a nation ruled by an authoritarian government may keep the peace and maintain the status quo, it may also oppress minorities or political opponents (e.g., North Korea, Zimbabwe, or Iraq under Saddam Hussein). Under colonialism, European nations often imposed peace in countries whose borders were somewhat arbitrarily created by those same European nations. Over several centuries prior to the twentieth century, empires were built by Spain, Portugal, Britain, Holland, France, Germany, Belgium, and Italy. With regard to the functions of the law, each empire may have kept the peace—largely with force—but it changed the status quo and seldom promoted the native peoples' rights or social justice within the colonized nation.

In nations that were former colonies of European nations, various ethnic and tribal factions have frequently made it difficult for a single, united government to rule effectively. In Rwanda, for example, power struggles between Hutus and Tutsis resulted in genocide of the Tutsi minority. (Genocide is the deliberate and systematic killing or displacement of one group of people by another group. In 1948, the international community formally condemned the crime of genocide.) In nations of the former Soviet Union, the withdrawal of a central power created power vacuums that were exploited by ethnic leaders. When Yugoslavia broke up, the different ethnic groups—Croats, Bosnians, and Serbians—fought bitterly for territorial control rather than share power. A more recent example is Iraq, where Sunni and Shiite sectarian differences have proven to be a major barrier to maintaining a united government.

Law and Politics

In the United States, legislators, judges, administrative agencies, governors, and presidents make law, with substantial input from corporations, lobbyists, and a diverse group of nongovernment organizations (NGOs) such as the American Petroleum Institute, the Sierra Club, and the National Rifle Association. In the fifty states, judges are often appointed by governors or elected by the people. The process of electing state judges has become more and more politicized in the past fifteen years, with growing campaign contributions from those who would seek to seat judges with similar political leanings.

In the federal system, judges are appointed by an elected official (the president) and confirmed by other elected officials (the Senate). If the president is from one party and the other party holds a majority of Senate seats, political conflicts may come up during the judges' confirmation processes. Such a division has been fairly frequent over the past fifty years.

In most **nation-states** (as countries are called in international law), knowing who has power to make and enforce the laws is a matter of knowing who has political power; in many places, the people or groups that have military power can also command political power to make and enforce the laws. Revolutions are difficult and contentious, but each year there are revolts against existing political-legal authority; an aspiration for democratic rule, or greater "rights" for citizens, is a recurring theme in politics and law.

nation-states

The basic entities that comprise the international legal system. *Countries*, *states*, and *nations* are all roughly synonymous. *State* can also be used to designate the basic units of federally united states, such as in the United States of America, which is a nation-state.

Key Takeaway

Law is the result of political action, and the political landscape is vastly different from nation to nation. Unstable or authoritarian governments often fail to serve the principal functions of law.

Exercises

1. Consider North Korea. What political rights do you have that the average North Korean citizen does not?
2. What is a nongovernment organization, and what does it have to do with government? Do you contribute to (or are you active in) a nongovernment organization? What kind of rights do they espouse, what kind of laws do they support, and what kind of laws do they oppose?

1.2 Schools of Legal Thought

Learning Objectives

1. Distinguish different philosophies of law—schools of legal thought—and explain their relevance.
2. Explain why natural law relates to the rights that the founders of the U.S. political-legal system found important.
3. Describe legal positivism and explain how it differs from natural law.
4. Differentiate critical legal studies and ecofeminist legal perspectives from both natural law and legal positivist perspectives.

There are different schools (or philosophies) concerning what law is all about. Philosophy of law is also called **jurisprudence**, and the two main schools are **legal positivism** and **natural law**. Although there are others (see Section 2), these two are the most influential in how people think about the law.

jurisprudence

The philosophy of law. There are many philosophies of law and thus many different jurisprudential views.

legal positivism

A jurisprudence that focuses on the law as it is—the command of the sovereign.

natural law

A jurisprudence that emphasizes a law that transcends positive laws (human laws) and points to a set of principles that are universal in application.

Legal Positivism: Law as Sovereign Command

sovereign

The authority within any nation-state. Sovereignty is what sovereigns exercise. This usually means the power to make and enforce laws within the nation-state.

statutes

Legislative directives, having the form of general rules that are to be followed in the nation-state or its subdivisions. Statutes are controlling over judicial decisions or common law, but are inferior to (and controlled by) constitutional law.

As legal philosopher John Austin concisely put it, "Law is the command of a sovereign." Law is only law, in other words, if it comes from a recognized authority and can be enforced by that authority, or **sovereign**—such as a king, a president, or a dictator—who has power within a defined area or territory. Positivism is a philosophical movement that claims that science provides the only knowledge precise enough to be worthwhile. But what are we to make of the social phenomena of laws?

We could examine existing **statutes**—executive orders, regulations, or judicial decisions—in a fairly precise way to find out what the law says. For example, we could look at the posted speed limits on most US highways and conclude that the "correct" or "right" speed is no more than fifty-five miles per hour. Or we could look a little deeper and find out how the written law is usually applied. Doing so, we might conclude that sixty-one miles per hour is generally allowed by most state troopers, but that occasionally someone gets ticketed for doing fifty-seven miles per hour in a fifty-five miles per hour zone. Either approach is empirical, even if not rigorously scientific. The first approach, examining in a precise way what the rule itself says, is sometimes known as the "positivist" school of legal thought. The second approach—which relies on social context and the actual behavior of the principal actors who enforce the law—is akin to the "legal realist" school of thought (see Section 2).

Positivism has its limits and its critics. New Testament readers may recall that King Herod, fearing the birth of a Messiah, issued a decree that all male children below a certain age be killed. Because it was the command of a sovereign, the decree was carried out (or, in legal jargon, the decree was "executed"). Suppose a group seizes power in a particular place and commands that women cannot attend school and can only be treated medically by women, even if their condition is life-threatening and women doctors are few and far between. Suppose also that this command is carried out, just because it is the law and is enforced with a vengeance. People who live there will undoubtedly question the wisdom, justice, or goodness of such a law, but it is law nonetheless and is generally carried out. To avoid the law's impact, a citizen would have to flee the country entirely. During the Taliban rule in Afghanistan, from which this example is drawn, many did flee.

The positive-law school of legal thought would recognize the lawmaker's command as legitimate; questions about the law's morality or immorality would not be important. In contrast, the natural-law school of legal thought would refuse to recognize the legitimacy of laws that did not conform to natural, universal, or divine law. If a lawmaker issued a command that was in violation of natural law, a citizen would be morally justified in demonstrating civil disobedience. For example, in refusing to give up her seat to a white person, Rosa Parks believed that she was refusing to obey an unjust law.

Natural Law

The natural-law school of thought emphasizes that law should be based on a universal moral order. Natural law was "discovered" by humans through the use of reason and by choosing between that which is good and that which is evil. Here is the definition of natural law according to the *Cambridge Dictionary of Philosophy*: "Natural law, also called the law of nature in moral and political philosophy, is an objective norm or set of objective norms governing human behavior, similar to the positive laws of a human ruler, but binding on all people alike and usually understood as involving a superhuman legislator."[2]

Both the US Constitution and the United Nations (UN) Charter have an affinity for the natural-law outlook, as it emphasizes certain objective norms and rights of individuals and nations. The U.S. Declaration of Independence embodies a natural-law philosophy. The following short extract should provide some sense of the deep beliefs in natural law held by those who signed the document.

The Unanimous Declaration of the Thirteen United States of America

July 4, 1776

> *When in the Course of human events, it becomes necessary for one people to dissolve the political bands which have connected them with another, and to assume among the powers of the earth, the separate and equal station to which the Laws of Nature and of Nature's God entitle them, a decent respect to the opinions of mankind requires that they should declare the causes which impel them to the separation.*
>
> *We hold these truths to be self-evident, that all men are created equal, that they are endowed by their Creator with certain unalienable Rights, that among these are Life, Liberty and the Pursuit of Happiness. That to secure these rights, Governments are instituted among Men, deriving their just powers from the consent of the governed....*

The natural-law school has been very influential in American legal thinking. The idea that certain rights, for example, are "unalienable" (as expressed in the Declaration of Independence and in the writings of John Locke) is consistent with this view of the law. Individuals may have "God-given" or "natural" rights that government cannot legitimately take away. Government only by consent of the governed is a natural outgrowth of this view.

Civil disobedience—in the tradition of Henry Thoreau, Mahatma Gandhi, or Martin Luther King Jr.—becomes a matter of morality over "unnatural" law. For example, in his "Letter from Birmingham Jail," Martin Luther King Jr. claims that obeying an unjust law is not moral and that deliberately disobeying an unjust law is in fact a moral act that expresses "the highest respect for law": "An individual who breaks a law that conscience tells him is unjust, and who willingly accepts the penalty of imprisonment in order to arouse the conscience of the community over its injustice, is in reality expressing the highest respect for law. ... One who breaks an unjust law must do so openly, lovingly, and with a willingness to accept the penalty."[3]

Legal positivists, on the other hand, would say that we cannot know with real confidence what "natural" law or "universal" law is. In studying law, we can most effectively learn by just looking at what the written law says, or by examining how it has been applied. In response, natural-law thinkers would argue that if we care about justice, every law and every legal system must be held accountable to some higher standard, however hard that may be to define.

It is easier to know what the law "is" than what the law "should be." Equal employment laws, for example, have specific statutes, rules, and decisions about racial discrimination. There are always difficult issues of interpretation and decision, which is why courts will resolve differing views. But how can we know the more fundamental "ought" or "should" of human equality? For example, how do we *know* that "all men are created equal" (from the Declaration of Independence)? Setting aside for the moment questions about the equality of women, or that of slaves, who were not counted as men with equal rights at the time of the declaration—can the statement be empirically proven, or is it simply a matter of a priori knowledge? (*A priori* means "existing in the mind prior to and independent of experience.") Or is the statement about equality a matter of faith or belief, not really provable either scientifically or rationally? The dialogue between natural-law theorists and more empirically oriented theories of "what law is" will raise similar questions. In this book, we will focus mostly on the law as it is, but not without also raising questions about what it could or should be.

Other Schools of Legal Thought

The historical school of law believes that societies should base their legal decisions today on the examples of the past. Precedent would be more important than moral arguments.

The legal realist school flourished in the 1920s and 1930s as a reaction to the historical school. Legal realists pointed out that because life and society are constantly changing, certain laws and doctrines have to be altered or modernized in order to remain current. The social context of law was more important to legal realists than the formal application of precedent to current or future legal disputes. Rather than suppose that judges inevitably acted objectively in applying an existing rule to a set of facts, legal realists observed that judges had their own beliefs, operated in a social context, and would give legal decisions based on their beliefs and their own social context.

The legal realist view influenced the emergence of the critical legal studies (CLS) school of thought. The "Crits" believe that the social order (and the law) is dominated by those with power, wealth, and influence. Some Crits are clearly influenced by the economist Karl Marx and also by distributive justice theory (see Chapter 2). The CLS school believes the wealthy have historically oppressed or exploited those with less wealth and have maintained social control through law. In so doing, the wealthy have perpetuated an unjust distribution of both rights and goods in society. Law is politics and is thus not neutral or value-free. The CLS movement would use the law to overturn the hierarchical structures of domination in the modern society.

Related to the CLS school, yet different, is the ecofeminist school of legal thought. This school emphasizes—and would modify—the long-standing domination of men over both women and the rest of the natural world. Ecofeminists would say that the same social mentality that leads to exploitation of women is at the root of man's exploitation and degradation of the natural environment. They would say that male ownership of land has led to a "dominator culture," in which man is not so much a steward of the existing environment or those "subordinate" to him but is charged with making all that he controls economically "productive." Wives, children, land, and animals are valued as economic resources, and legal systems (until the nineteenth century) largely conferred rights only to men with land. Ecofeminists would say that even with increasing civil and political rights for women (such as the right to vote) and with some nations' recognizing the rights of children and animals and caring for the environment, the legacy of the past for most nations still confirms the preeminence of "man" and his dominance of both nature and women.

Key Takeaway

Each of the various schools of legal thought has a particular view of what a legal system is or what it should be. The natural-law theorists emphasize the rights and duties of both government and the governed. Positive law takes as a given that law is simply the command of a sovereign, the political power that those governed will obey. Recent writings in the various legal schools of thought emphasize long-standing patterns of domination of the wealthy over others (the CLS school) and of men over women (ecofeminist legal theory).

Exercises

1. Vandana Shiva draws a picture of a stream in a forest. She says that in our society the stream is seen as unproductive if it is simply there, fulfilling the need for water of women's families and communities, until engineers come along and tinker with it, perhaps damming it and using it for generating hydropower. The same is true of a forest, unless it is replaced with a monoculture plantation of a commercial species. A forest may very well be productive—protecting groundwater; creating oxygen; providing fruit, fuel, and craft materials for nearby inhabitants; and creating a habitat for animals that are also a valuable resource. She criticizes the view that if there is no monetary amount that can contribute to gross domestic

product, neither the forest nor the river can be seen as a productive resource. Which school of legal thought does her criticism reflect?

2. Anatole France said, "The law, in its majesty, forbids rich and poor alike from sleeping under bridges." Which school of legal thought is represented by this quote?
3. Adolf Eichmann was a loyal member of the National Socialist Party in the Third Reich and worked hard under Hitler's government during World War II to round up Jewish people for incarceration—and eventual extermination—at labor camps like Auschwitz and Buchenwald. After an Israeli "extraction team" took him from Argentina to Israel, he was put on trial for "crimes against humanity." His defense was that he was "just following orders." Explain why Eichmann was not an adherent of the natural-law school of legal thought.

1.3 Basic Concepts and Categories of US Positive Law

Learning Objectives

1. In a general way, differentiate contract law from tort law.
2. Consider the role of law in supporting ethical norms in our society.
3. Understand the differing roles of state law and federal law in the US legal system.
4. Know the difference between criminal cases and civil cases.

Most of what we discuss in this book is positive law—US positive law in particular. We will also consider the laws and legal systems of other nations. But first, it will be useful to cover some basic concepts and distinctions.

Law: The Moral Minimums in a Democratic Society

The law does not correct (or claim to correct) every wrong that occurs in society. At a minimum, it aims to curb the worst kind of wrongs, the kinds of wrongs that violate what might be called the "moral minimums" that a community demands of its members. These include not only violations of criminal law (see Chapter 6) but also torts (see Chapter 7) and broken promises (see Chapter 8). Thus it may be wrong to refuse to return a phone call from a friend, but that wrong will not result in a viable lawsuit against you. But if a phone (or the Internet) is used to libel or slander someone, a tort has been committed, and the law may allow the defamed person to be compensated.

There is a strong association between what we generally think of as ethical behavior and what the laws require and provide. For example, contract law upholds society's sense that promises—in general—should be kept. Promise-breaking is seen as unethical. The law provides remedies for broken promises (in breach of contract cases) but not for all broken promises; some excuses are accepted when it would be reasonable to do so. For tort law, harming others is considered unethical. If people are not restrained by law from harming one another, orderly society would be undone, leading to anarchy. Tort law provides for compensation when serious injuries or harms occur. As for property law issues, we generally believe that private ownership of property is socially useful and generally desirable, and it is generally protected (with some exceptions) by laws. You can't throw a party at my house without my permission, but my right to do whatever I want on my own property may be limited by law; I can't, without the public's permission, operate an incinerator on my property and burn heavy metals, as toxic ash may be deposited throughout the neighborhood.

The Common Law: Property, Torts, and Contracts

precedent

A prior judicial decision that is either binding or persuasive, and as such, provides a rule useful in making a decision in the case at hand.

stare decisis

Latin, for "let the decision stand." By keeping within the rule of a prior judicial decision, a court follows "precedent" by letting the prior decision govern the result in the case at hand.

Even before legislatures met to make rules for society, disputes happened and judges decided them. In England, judges began writing down the facts of a case and the reasons for their decision. They often resorted to deciding cases on the basis of prior written decisions. In relying on those prior decisions, the judge would reason that since a current case was pretty much like a prior case, it ought to be decided the same way. This is essentially reasoning by analogy. Thus the use of **precedent** in common-law cases came into being, and a doctrine of **stare decisis** (pronounced STAR-ay-de-SIGH-sus) became accepted in English courts. *Stare decisis* means, in Latin, "let the decision stand."

Most judicial decisions that don't apply legislative acts (known as statutes) will involve one of three areas of law—property, contract, or tort. Property law deals with the rights and duties of those who can legally own land (real property), how that ownership can be legally confirmed and protected, how property can be bought and sold, what the rights of tenants (renters) are, and what the various kinds of "estates" in land are (e.g., fee simple, life estate, future interest, easements, or rights of way). Contract law deals with what kinds of promises courts should enforce. For example, should courts enforce a contract where one of the parties was intoxicated, underage, or insane? Should courts enforce a contract where one of the parties seemed to have an unfair advantage? What kind of contracts would have to be in writing to be enforced by courts? Tort law deals with the types of cases that involve some kind of harm and or injury between the plaintiff and the defendant when no contract exists. Thus if you are libeled or a competitor lies about your product, your remedy would be in tort, not contract.

The thirteen original colonies had been using English common law for many years, and they continued to do so after independence from England. Early cases from the first states are full of references to already-decided English cases. As years went by, many precedents were established by US state courts, so that today a judicial opinion that refers to a seventeenth- or eighteenth-century English common-law case is quite rare.

Courts in one state may look to common-law decisions from the courts of other states where the reasoning in a similar case is persuasive. This will happen in "cases of first impression," a fact pattern or situation that the courts in one state have never seen before. But if the supreme court in a particular state has already ruled on a certain kind of case, lower courts in that state will almost always follow the rule set forth by its highest court.

State Courts and the Domain of State Law

In the early years of our nation, federal courts were not as active or important as state courts. States had jurisdiction (the power to make and enforce laws) over the most important aspects of business life. The power of state law has historically included governing the following kinds of issues and claims:

- Contracts, including sales, commercial paper, letters of credit, and secured transactions
- Torts
- Property, including real property, bailments of personal property (such as when you check your coat at a theater or leave your clothes with a dry cleaner), trademarks, copyrights, and the estates of decedents (dead people)
- Corporations
- Partnerships
- Domestic matters, including marriage, divorce, custody, adoption, and visitation
- Securities law
- Environmental law
- Agency law, governing the relationship between principals and their agents.

- Banking
- Insurance

Over the past eighty years, however, federal law has become increasingly important in many of these areas, including banking, securities, and environmental law.

Civil versus Criminal Cases

Most of the cases we will look at in this textbook are civil cases. Criminal cases are certainly of interest to business, especially as companies may break criminal laws. A criminal case involves a governmental decision—whether state or federal—to prosecute someone (named as a defendant) for violating society's laws. The law establishes a moral minimum and does so especially in the area of criminal laws; if you break a criminal law, you can lose your freedom (in jail) or your life (if you are convicted of a capital offense). In a civil action, you would not be sent to prison; in the worst case, you can lose property (usually money or other assets), such as when Ford Motor Company lost a personal injury case and the judge awarded $295 million to the plaintiffs or when Pennzoil won a $10.54 billion verdict against Texaco (see Chapter 7).

Some of the basic differences between **civil law** and **criminal law** cases are illustrated in Table 1.1.

civil law

In contrast to criminal law, the law that governs noncriminal disputes, such as in lawsuits (as opposed to prosecutions) over contract disputes and tort claims. In contrast to common law, civil law is part of the continental European tradition dating back to Roman law.

criminal law

That body of law in any nation-state that defines offenses against society as a whole, punishable by fines, forfeitures, or imprisonment.

TABLE 1.1 Differences between Civil and Criminal Cases

	Civil Cases	Criminal Cases
Parties	Plaintiff brings case; defendant must answer or lose by default	Prosecutor brings case; defendant may remain silent
Proof	Preponderance of evidence	Beyond a reasonable doubt
Reason	To settle disputes peacefully, usually between private parties	To maintain order in society
		To punish the most blameworthy
		To deter serious wrongdoing
Remedies	Money damages (legal remedy)	Fines, jail, and forfeitures
	Injunctions (equitable remedy)	
	Specific performance (equity)	

Regarding plaintiffs and prosecutors, you can often tell a civil case from a criminal case by looking at the caption of a case going to trial. If the government appears first in the caption of the case (e.g., *U.S. v. Lieberman*), it is likely that the United States is prosecuting on behalf of the people. The same is true of cases prosecuted by state district attorneys (e.g., *State v. Seidel*). But this is not a foolproof formula. Governments will also bring civil actions to collect debts from or settle disputes with individuals, corporations, or other governments. Thus *U.S. v. Mayer* might be a collection action for unpaid taxes, or *U.S. v. Canada* might be a boundary dispute in the International Court of Justice. Governments can be sued, as well; people occasionally sue their state or federal government, but they can only get a trial if the government waives its sovereign immunity and allows such suits. *Warner v. U.S.*, for example, could be a claim for a tax refund wrongfully withheld or for damage caused to the Warner residence by a sonic boom from a US Air Force jet flying overhead.

Substance versus Procedure

Many rules and regulations in law are substantive, and others are procedural. We are used to seeing laws as substantive; that is, there is some rule of conduct or behavior that is called for or some action that is proscribed (prohibited). The substantive rules tell us how to act with one another and with the government. For example, all of the following are substantive rules of law and provide a kind of command or direction to citizens:

- Drive not more than fifty-five miles per hour where that speed limit is posted.
- Do not conspire to fix prices with competitors in the US market.
- Do not falsely represent the curative effects of your over-the-counter herbal remedy.
- Do not drive your motor vehicle through an intersection while a red traffic signal faces the direction you are coming from.
- Do not discriminate against job applicants or employees on the basis of their race, sex, religion, or national origin.
- Do not discharge certain pollutants into the river without first getting a discharge permit.

In contrast, procedural laws are the rules of courts and administrative agencies. They tell us how to proceed if there is a substantive-law problem. For example, if you drive fifty-three miles per hour in a forty mile-per-hour zone on Main Street on a Saturday night and get a ticket, you have broken a substantive rule of law (the posted speed limit). Just how and what gets decided in court is a matter of procedural law. Is the police officer's word final, or do you get your say before a judge? If so, who goes first, you or the officer? Do you have the right to be represented by legal counsel? Does the hearing or trial have to take place within a certain time period? A week? A month? How long can the state take to bring its case? What kinds of evidence will be relevant? Radar? (Does it matter what kind of training the officer has had on the radar device? Whether the radar device had been tested adequately?) The officer's personal observation? (What kind of training has he had, how is he qualified to judge the speed of a car, and other questions arise.) What if you unwisely bragged to a friend at a party recently that you went a hundred miles an hour on Main Street five years ago at half past three on a Tuesday morning? (If the prosecutor knows of this and the "friend" is willing to testify, is it relevant to the charge of fifty-three in a forty-mile-per-hour zone?)

In the United States, all state procedural laws must be fair, since the due process clause of the Fourteenth Amendment directs that no state shall deprive any citizen of "life, liberty, or property," without due process of law. A state court's criminal fine of $200 plus court costs is designed to deprive you of property (in the form of money) if you violate the speed limit. Federal laws must also be fair, because the Fifth Amendment to the US Constitution has the same due process language as the Fourteenth Amendment. This suggests that some laws are more powerful or important than others, which is true. The next section looks at various types of positive law and their relative importance.

Key Takeaway

In most legal systems, like that in the United States, there is a fairly firm distinction between criminal law (for actions that are offenses against the entire society) and civil law (usually for disputes between individuals or corporations). Basic ethical norms for promise-keeping and not harming others are reflected in the civil law of contracts and torts. In the United States, both the states and the federal government have roles to play, and sometimes these roles will overlap, as in environmental standards set by both states and the federal government.

Exercises

1. Jenna gets a ticket for careless driving after the police come to investigate a car accident she had with you on Hanover Boulevard. Your car is badly damaged through no fault of your own. Is Jenna likely to face criminal charges, civil charges, or both?
2. Jenna's ticket says that she has thirty days in which to respond to the charges against her. The thirty days conforms to a state law that sets this time limit. Is the thirty-day limit procedural law or substantive law?

1.4 Sources of Law and Their Priority

Learning Objectives

1. Describe the different sources of law in the US legal system and the principal institutions that create those laws.
2. Explain in what way a statute is like a treaty, and vice versa.
3. Explain why the Constitution is "prior" and has priority over the legislative acts of a majority, whether in the US Congress or in a state legislature.
4. Describe the origins of the common-law system and what common law means.

Sources of Law

In the United States today, there are numerous sources of law. The main ones are (1) constitutions—both state and federal, (2) statutes and agency regulations, and (3) judicial decisions. In addition, chief executives (the president and the various governors) can issue executive orders that have the effect of law.

In international legal systems, sources of law include **treaties** (agreements between states or countries) and what is known as customary international law (usually consisting of judicial decisions from national court systems where parties from two or more nations are in a dispute).

treaties

Formal agreements concluded between nation-states.

As you might expect, these laws sometimes conflict: a state law may conflict with a federal law, or a federal law might be contrary to an international obligation. One nation's law may provide one substantive rule, while another nation's law may provide a different, somewhat contrary rule to apply. Not all laws, in other words, are created equal. To understand which laws have priority, it is essential to understand the relationships between the various kinds of law.

Constitutions

constitutions

The founding documents of any nation-state's legal system.

Constitutions are the foundation for a state or nation's other laws, providing the country's legislative, executive, and judicial framework. Among the nations of the world, the United States has the oldest constitution still in use. It is difficult to amend, which is why there have only been seventeen amendments following the first ten in 1789; two-thirds of the House and Senate must pass amendments, and three-fourths of the states must approve them.

The nation's states also have constitutions. Along with providing for legislative, executive, and judicial functions, state constitutions prescribe various rights of citizens. These rights may be different from, and in addition to, rights granted by the US Constitution. Like statutes and judicial decisions, a constitution's specific provisions can provide people with a "cause of action" on which to base a lawsuit (see Section 4 on "causes of action"). For example, California's constitution provides that the citizens of that state have a right of privacy. This has been used to assert claims against businesses that invade an employee's right of privacy. In the case of Virginia Rulon-Miller, her employer, International Business Machines (IBM), told her to stop dating a former colleague who went to work for a competitor. When she refused, IBM terminated her, and a jury fined the company for $300,000 in damages. As the California court noted, "While an employee sacrifices some privacy rights when he enters the workplace, the employee's privacy expectations must be balanced against the employer's interests....[T]he point here is that privacy, like the other unalienable rights listed first in our Constitution...is unquestionably a fundamental interest of our society."[4]

Statutes and Treaties in Congress

In Washington, DC, the federal legislature is known as Congress and has both a House of Representatives and a Senate. The House is composed of representatives elected every two years from various districts in each state. These districts are established by Congress according to population as determined every ten years by the census, a process required by the Constitution. Each state has at least one district; the most populous state (California) has fifty-two districts. In the Senate, there are two senators from each state, regardless of the state's population. Thus Delaware has two senators and California has two senators, even though California has far more people. Effectively, less than 20 percent of the nation's population can send fifty senators to Washington.

Many consider this to be antidemocratic. The House of Representatives, on the other hand, is directly proportioned by population, though no state can have less than one representative.

Each Congressional legislative body has committees for various purposes. In these committees, proposed bills are discussed, hearings are sometimes held, and bills are either reported out (brought to the floor for a vote) or killed in committee. If a bill is reported out, it may be passed by majority vote. Because of the procedural differences between the House and the Senate, bills that have the same language when proposed in both houses are apt to be different after approval by each body. A conference committee will then be held to try to match the two versions. If the two versions differ widely enough, reconciliation of the two differing versions into one acceptable to both chambers (House and Senate) is more difficult.

If the House and Senate can agree on identical language, the reconciled bill will be sent to the president for signature or veto. The Constitution prescribes that the president will have veto power over any legislation. But the two bodies can override a presidential veto with a two-thirds vote in each chamber.

In the case of treaties, the Constitution specifies that only the Senate must ratify them. When the Senate ratifies a treaty, it becomes part of federal law, with the same weight and effect as a statute passed by the entire Congress. The statutes of Congress are collected in codified form in the US Code. The code is available online at http://uscode.house.gov.

Delegating Legislative Powers: Rules by Administrative Agencies

Congress has found it necessary and useful to create government agencies to administer various laws (see Chapter 5). The Constitution does not expressly provide for administrative agencies, but the US Supreme Court has upheld the delegation of power to create federal agencies.

Examples of administrative agencies would include the Occupational Safety and Health Administration (OSHA), the Environmental Protection Agency (EPA), and the Federal Trade Commission (FTC).

It is important to note that Congress does not have unlimited authority to delegate its lawmaking powers to an agency. It must delegate its authority with some guidelines for the agency and cannot altogether avoid its constitutional responsibilities (see Chapter 5).

Agencies propose rules in the Federal Register, published each working day of the year. Rules that are formally adopted are published in the *Code of Federal Regulations*, or CFR, available online at http://www.access.gpo.gov/nara/cfr/cfr-table-search.html.

State Statutes and Agencies: Other Codified Law

Statutes are passed by legislatures and provide general rules for society. States have legislatures (sometimes called assemblies), which are usually made up of both a senate and a house of representatives. Like the federal government, state legislatures will agree on the provisions of a bill, which is then sent to the governor (acting like the president for that state) for signature. Like the president, governors often have a veto power. The process of creating and amending, or changing, laws is filled with political negotiation and compromise.

On a more local level, counties and municipal corporations or townships may be authorized under a state's constitution to create or adopt ordinances. Examples of ordinances include local building codes, zoning laws, and misdemeanors or infractions such as littering or jaywalking. Most of the more unusual laws that are in the news from time to time are local ordinances. For example, in Logan County, Colorado, it is illegal to kiss a sleeping woman; in Indianapolis, Indiana, and Eureka, Nebraska, it is a crime to kiss if you have a mustache. Most of these laws are eventually repealed, but not all. Reportedly, Kentucky law proclaims that every person in the state must take a bath at least once a year, and failure to do so is illegal.

Judicial Decisions: The Common Law

Common law consists of decisions by courts (judicial decisions) that do not involve interpretation of statutes, regulations, treaties, or the Constitution. Courts make such interpretations, but many cases are decided where there is no statutory or other codified law or regulation to be interpreted. For example, a state court deciding what kinds of witnesses are required for a valid will in the absence of a rule (from a statute) is making common law.

> **common law**
>
> Judicial decisions that do not involve interpretation of statutes, regulations, treaties, or the Constitution.

United States law comes primarily from the tradition of English common law. By the time England's American colonies revolted in 1776, English common-law traditions were well established in the colonial courts. English common law was a system that gave written judicial decisions the force of law throughout the country. Thus if an English court delivered an opinion as to what constituted the common-law crime of burglary, other courts would stick to that decision, so that a common body of law developed throughout the country. Common law is essentially shorthand for the notion that a common body of law, based on past written decisions, is desirable and necessary.

In England and in the laws of the original thirteen states, common-law decisions defined crimes such as arson, burglary, homicide, and robbery. As time went on, US state legislatures either adopted or modified common-law definitions of most crimes by putting them in the form of codes or statutes. This legislative ability—to modify or change common law into judicial law—points to an important phenomenon: the priority of statutory law over common law. As we will see in the next section, constitutional law will have priority over statutory law.

Priority of Laws

The Constitution as Preemptive Force in US Law

The US Constitution takes precedence over all statutes and judicial decisions that are inconsistent. For example, if Michigan were to decide legislatively that students cannot speak ill of professors in state-sponsored universities, that law would be void, since it is inconsistent with the state's obligation under the First Amendment to protect free speech. Or if the Michigan courts were to allow a professor to bring a lawsuit against a student who had said something about him that was derogatory but not defamatory, the state's judicial system would not be acting according to the First Amendment. (As we will see in Chapter 7, free speech has its limits; defamation was a cause of action at the time the First Amendment was added to the Constitution, and it has been understood that the free speech rights in the First Amendment did not negate existing common law.)

Statutes and Cases

Statutes generally have priority, or take precedence, over case law (judicial decisions). Under common-law judicial decisions, employers could hire young children for difficult work, offer any wage they wanted, and not pay overtime work at a higher rate. But various statutes changed that. For example, the federal Fair Labor Standards Act (1938) forbid the use of oppressive child labor and established a minimum pay wage and overtime pay rules.

Treaties as Statutes: The "Last in Time" Rule

A treaty or convention is considered of equal standing to a statute. Thus when Congress ratified the North American Free Trade Agreement (NAFTA), any judicial decisions or previous statutes that were inconsistent—such as quotas or limitations on imports from Mexico that were opposite to NAFTA commitments—would no longer be valid. Similarly, US treaty obligations under the General Agreement on Tariffs and Trade (GATT) and obligations made later through the World Trade Organization (WTO) would override previous federal or state statutes.

One example of treaty obligations overriding, or taking priority over, federal statutes was the tuna-dolphin dispute between the United States and Mexico. The Marine Mammal Protection Act amendments in 1988 spelled out certain protections for dolphins in the Eastern Tropical Pacific, and the United States began refusing to allow the importation of tuna that were caught using "dolphin-unfriendly" methods (such as purse seining). This was challenged at a GATT dispute panel in Switzerland, and the United States lost. The discussion continued at the WTO under its dispute resolution process. In short, US environmental statutes can be ruled contrary to US treaty obligations.

Under most treaties, the United States can withdraw, or take back, any voluntary limitation on its sovereignty; participation in treaties is entirely elective. That is, the United States may "unbind" itself whenever it chooses. But for practical purposes, some limitations on sovereignty may be good for the nation. The argument goes something like this: if free trade in general helps the United States, then it makes some sense to be part of a system that promotes free trade; and despite some temporary setbacks, the WTO decision process will (it is hoped) provide far more benefits than losses in the long run. This argument invokes utilitarian theory (that the best policy does the greatest good overall for society) and David Ricardo's theory of comparative advantage.

Ultimately, whether the United States remains a supporter of free trade and continues to participate as a leader in the WTO will depend upon citizens electing leaders who support the process.

Had Ross Perot been elected in 1992, for example, NAFTA would have been politically (and legally) dead during his term of office. The Trans-Pacific Trade Partnership Agreement negotiated in 2015 may not withstand US political divisions in 2016 to gain Congressional approval.

Causes of Action, Precedent, and *Stare Decisis*

No matter how wrong someone's actions may seem to you, the only wrongs you can right in a court are those that can be tied to one or more **causes of action**. Positive law is full of cases, treaties, statutes, regulations, and constitutional provisions that can be made into causes of action. For example, if you have an agreement with Harold Hill that he will purchase seventy-six trombones from you and he fails to pay for them after you deliver, you will probably feel wronged, but a court will only act favorably on your complaint if you can show that his behavior gives you a cause of action based on some part of your state's contract law. This case would give you a cause of action under the laws of most states; unless Harold Hill had some legal excuse recognized by the applicable state's contract law—such as his legal incompetence, his being less than eighteen years of age, his being drunk at the time the agreement was made, or his claim that the instruments were trumpets rather than trombones or that they were delivered too late to be of use to him—you could expect to recover some compensation for his breaching of your agreement with him.

causes of action

In a complaint, a legal basis on which a claim is predicated. The legal basis can be a Constitutional law, a statute, a regulation, or a prior judicial decision that creates a precedent to be followed.

An old saying in the law is that the law does not deal in trifles, or unimportant issues (in Latin, *de minimis non curat lex*). Not every wrong you may suffer in life will be a cause to bring a court action. If you are stood up for a Saturday night date and feel embarrassed or humiliated, you cannot recover anything in a court of law in the United States, as there is no cause of action (no basis in the positive law) that you can use in your complaint. If you are engaged to be married and your spouse-to-be bolts from the wedding ceremony, there are some states that do provide a legal basis on which to bring a lawsuit. "Breach of promise to marry" is recognized in several states, but most states have abolished this cause of action, either by judicial decision or by legislation. Whether a runaway bride or groom gives rise to a valid cause of action in the courts depends on whether the state courts still recognize and enforce this rapidly disappearing cause of action.

Your cause of action is thus based on existing laws, including decided cases. How closely your case "fits" with a prior decided case raises the question of precedent.

As noted earlier in this chapter, the English common-law tradition placed great emphasis on precedent and what is called ***stare decisis.*** A court considering one case would feel obliged to decide that case in a way similar to previously decided cases. Written decisions of the most important cases had been spread throughout England (the common "realm"), and judges hoped to establish a somewhat predictable, consistent group of decisions.

The English legislature (Parliament) was not in the practice of establishing detailed statutes on crimes, torts, contracts, or property. Thus definitions and rules were left primarily to the courts. By their nature, courts could only decide one case at a time, but in doing so they would articulate holdings, or general rules, that would apply to later cases.

Suppose that one court had to decide whether an employer could fire an employee for no reason at all. Suppose that there were no statutes that applied to the facts: there was no contract between the employer and the employee, but the employee had worked for the employer for many years, and now a younger person was replacing him. The court, with no past guidelines, would have to decide whether the employee had stated a "cause of action" against the employer. If the court decided that the case was not legally actionable, it would dismiss the action. Future courts would then treat similar cases in a similar way. In the process, the court might make a holding that employers could fire employees for any reason or for no reason. This rule could be applied in the future should similar cases come up.

But suppose that an employer fired an employee for not committing perjury (lying on the witness stand in a court proceeding); the employer wanted the employee to cover up the company's criminal or unethical act. Suppose that, as in earlier cases, there were no applicable statutes and no contract of employment. Courts relying on a holding or precedent that "employers may fire employees for any reason or no reason" might rule against an employee seeking compensation for being fired for telling the truth on the witness stand. Or it might make an exception to the general rule, such as, "Employers may generally discharge employees for any reason or for no reason without incurring legal liability; however, employers will incur legal liability for firing an employee who refuses to lie on behalf of the employer in a court proceeding."

In each case (the general rule and its exception), the common-law tradition calls for the court to explain the reasons for its ruling. In the case of the general rule, "freedom of choice" might be the major reason. In the case of the perjury exception, the efficiency of the judicial system and the requirements of citizenship might be used as reasons. Because the court's "reasons" will be persuasive to some and not to others, there is inevitably a degree of subjectivity to judicial opinions. That is, reasonable people will disagree as to the persuasiveness of the reasoning a court may offer for its decision.

Written judicial opinions are thus a good playing field for developing critical thinking skills by identifying the issue in a case and examining the reasons for the court's previous decision(s), or holding. What *has* the court actually decided, and why? Remember that a court, especially the US Supreme Court, is not only deciding one particular case but also setting down guidelines (in its holdings) for federal and state courts that encounter similar issues. Note that court cases often raise a variety of issues or questions to be resolved, and judges (and attorneys) will differ as to what the real issue in a case is. A holding is the court's complete answer to an issue that is critical to deciding the case and thus gives guidance to the meaning of the case as a precedent for future cases.

Beyond the decision of the court, it is in looking at the court's *reasoning* that you are most likely to understand what facts have been most significant to the court and what theories (schools of legal thought) each trial or appellate judge believes in. Because judges do not always agree on first principles (i.e., they subscribe to different schools of legal thought), there are many divided opinions in appellate opinions and in each US Supreme Court term.

Key Takeaway

There are different sources of law in the US legal system. The US Constitution is foundational; US statutory and common law cannot be inconsistent with its provisions. Congress creates statutory law (with the signature of the president), and courts will interpret constitutional law and statutory law. Where there is neither constitutional law nor statutory law, the courts function in the realm of common law. The same is true of law within the fifty states, each of which also has a constitution, or foundational law.

Both the federal government and the states have created administrative agencies. An agency only has the power that the legislature gives it. Within the scope of that power, an agency will often create regulations (see Chapter 5), which have the same force and effect as statutes. Treaties are never negotiated and concluded by states, as the federal government has exclusive authority over relations with other nation-states. A treaty, once ratified by the Senate, has the same force and effect as a statute passed by Congress and signed into law by the president.

Constitutions, statutes, regulations, treaties, and court decisions can provide a legal basis in the positive law. You may believe you have been wronged, but for you to have a right that is enforceable in court, you must have something in the positive law that you can point to that will support a cause of action against your chosen defendant.

Exercises

1. Give one example of where common law was overridden by the passage of a federal statute.
2. How does common law change or evolve without any action on the part of a legislature?
3. Lindsey Paradise is not selected for her sorority of choice at the University of Kansas. She has spent all her time rushing that particular sorority, which chooses some of her friends but

not her. She is disappointed and angry and wants to sue the sorority. What are her prospects of recovery in the legal system? Explain.

1.5 Legal and Political Systems of the World

Learning Objective

1. Describe how the common-law system differs from the civil-law system.

Other legal and political systems are very different from the US system, which came from English common-law traditions and the framers of the US Constitution. Our legal and political traditions are different both in what kinds of laws we make and honor and in how disputes are resolved in court.

Comparing Common-Law Systems with Other Legal Systems

The common-law tradition is unique to England, the United States, and former colonies of the British Empire. Although there are differences among common-law systems (e.g., most nations do not permit their judiciaries to declare legislative acts unconstitutional; some nations use the jury less frequently), all of them recognize the use of precedent in judicial cases, and none of them relies on the comprehensive, legislative codes that are prevalent in civil-law systems.

Civil-Law Systems

The main alternative to the common-law legal system was developed in Europe and is based in Roman and Napoleonic law. A civil-law or code-law system is one where all the legal rules are in one or more comprehensive legislative enactments. During Napoleon's reign, a comprehensive book of laws—a code—was developed for all of France. The code covered criminal law, criminal procedure, noncriminal law and procedure, and commercial law. The rules of the code are still used today in France and in other continental European legal systems. The code is used to resolve particular cases, usually by judges without a jury. Moreover, the judges are not required to follow the decisions of other courts in similar cases. As George Cameron of the University of Michigan has noted, "The law is in the code, not in the cases." He goes on to note, "Where several cases all have interpreted a provision in a particular way, the French courts may feel bound to reach the same result in future cases, under the doctrine of *jurisprudence constante*. The major agency for growth and change, however, is the legislature, not the courts."

Civil-law systems are used throughout Europe as well as in Central and South America. Some nations in Asia and Africa have also adopted codes based on European civil law. Germany, Holland, Spain, France, and Portugal all had colonies outside of Europe, and many of these colonies adopted the legal practices that were imposed on them by colonial rule, much like the original thirteen states of the United States, which adopted English common-law practices.

One source of possible confusion at this point is that we have already referred to US civil law in contrast to criminal law. But the European civil law covers both civil and criminal law.

There are also legal systems that differ significantly from the common-law and civil-law systems. The communist legal systems that remain (e.g., in China and North Korea) operate on very different assumptions than those of either English common law or European civil law. Islamic and other religion-based systems of law bring different values and assumptions to social and commercial relations.

Key Takeaway

Legal systems vary widely in their aims and in the way they process civil and criminal cases. Common-law systems use juries, have one judge, and adhere to precedent. Civil-law systems decide cases without a jury, often use three judges, and often render shorter opinions without reference to previously decided cases.

Exercise

1. Use the Internet to identify some of the better-known nations with civil-law systems. Which Asian nations came to adopt all or part of civil-law traditions, and why?

1.6 A Sample Case

Preliminary Note to Students

Title VII of the Civil Rights Act of 1964 is a federal statute that applies to all employers whose workforce exceeds fifteen people. The text of Title VII says that

> *(a) it shall be an unlawful employment practice for an employer—*
>
> *(1) to fail or refuse to hire or to discharge any individual, or otherwise to discriminate against any individual with respect to his compensation, terms, conditions, or privileges of employment, because of such individual's race, color, religion, sex, or natural origin.*

At common law—where judges decide cases without reference to statutory guidance—employers were generally free to hire and fire on any basis they might choose, and employees were generally free to work for an employer or quit an employer on any basis they might choose (unless the employer and the employee had a contract). This rule has been called "employment at will." State and federal statutes that prohibit discrimination on any basis (such as the prohibitions on discrimination because of race, color, religion, sex, or national origin in Title VII) are essentially legislative exceptions to the common-law employment-at-will rule.

In the 1970s, many female employees began to claim a certain kind of sex discrimination: sexual harassment. Some women were being asked to give sexual favors in exchange for continued employment or promotion (*quid pro quo* sexual harassment) or found themselves in a working environment that put their chances for continued employment or promotion at risk. This form of sexual discrimination came to be called "hostile working environment" sexual harassment.

Notice that the statute itself says nothing about sexual harassment but speaks only in broad terms about discrimination "because of" sex (and four other factors). Having set the broad policy, Congress left it to employees, employers, and the courts to fashion more specific rules through the process of civil litigation.

The following is a case from our federal court system, which had a trial or hearing in the federal district court, an appeal to the Sixth Circuit Court of Appeals, and a final appeal to the US Supreme

Court. Teresa Harris, having lost at both the district court and the Sixth Circuit Court of Appeals, here has petitioned for a writ of certiorari (asking the court to issue an order to bring the case to the Supreme Court). Petitions for certiorari are granted less than 2% of he time. The Supreme Court, in other words, chooses its cases very carefully. Here, the court wanted to resolve a difference of opinion among the various circuit courts of appeal as to whether or not a plaintiff in a hostile-working-environment claim could recover damages without showing "severe psychological injury."

Harris v. Forklift Systems
510 U.S. 17 (U.S. Supreme Court 1992)

JUDGES: O'CONNOR, J., delivered the opinion for a unanimous Court. SCALIA, J., and GINSBURG, J., filed concurring opinions.

JUSTICE O'CONNOR delivered the opinion of the Court.

In this case we consider the definition of a discriminatorily "abusive work environment" (also known as a "hostile work environment") under Title VII of the Civil Rights Act of 1964, 78 Stat. 253, as amended, 42 U.S.C. § 2000e et seq. (1988 ed., Supp. III).

I

Teresa Harris worked as a manager at Forklift Systems, Inc., an equipment rental company, from April 1985 until October 1987. Charles Hardy was Forklift's president.

The Magistrate found that, throughout Harris' time at Forklift, Hardy often insulted her because of her gender and often made her the target of unwanted sexual innuendoes. Hardy told Harris on several occasions, in the presence of other employees, "You're a woman, what do you know" and "We need a man as the rental manager"; at least once, he told her she was "a dumbass woman." Again in front of others, he suggested that the two of them "go to the Holiday Inn to negotiate [Harris's] raise." Hardy occasionally asked Harris and other female employees to get coins from his front pants pocket. He threw objects on the ground in front of Harris and other women, and asked them to pick the objects up. He made sexual innuendoes about Harris' and other women's clothing.

In mid-August 1987, Harris complained to Hardy about his conduct. Hardy said he was surprised that Harris was offended, claimed he was only joking, and apologized. He also promised he would stop, and based on this assurance Harris stayed on the job. But in early September, Hardy began anew: While Harris was arranging a deal with one of Forklift's customers, he asked her, again in front of other employees, "What did you do, promise the guy...some [sex] Saturday night?" On October 1, Harris collected her paycheck and quit.

Harris then sued Forklift, claiming that Hardy's conduct had created an abusive work environment for her because of her gender. The United States District Court for the Middle District of Tennessee, adopting the report and recommendation of the Magistrate, found this to be "a close case," but held that Hardy's conduct did not create an abusive environment. The court found that some of Hardy's comments "offended [Harris], and would offend the reasonable woman," but that they were not "so severe as to be expected to seriously affect [Harris's] psychological well-being. A reasonable woman manager under like circumstances would have been offended by Hardy, but his conduct would not have risen to the level of interfering with that person's work performance.

"Neither do I believe that [Harris] was subjectively so offended that she suffered injury....Although Hardy may at times have genuinely offended [Harris], I do not believe that he created a working environment so poisoned as to be intimidating or abusive to [Harris]."

In focusing on the employee's psychological well-being, the District Court was following Circuit precedent. See Rabidue v. Osceola Refining Co., 805 F.2d 611, 620 (CA6 1986), cert. denied, 481 U.S.

1041, 95 L. Ed. 2d 823, 107 S. Ct. 1983 (1987). The United States Court of Appeals for the Sixth Circuit affirmed in a brief unpublished decision...reported at 976 F.2d 733 (1992).

We granted certiorari, 507 U.S. 959 (1993), to resolve a conflict among the Circuits on whether conduct, to be actionable as "abusive work environment" harassment (no quid pro quo harassment issue is present here), must "seriously affect [an employee's] psychological well-being" or lead the plaintiff to "suffer injury." Compare Rabidue (requiring serious effect on psychological well-being); Vance v. Southern Bell Telephone & Telegraph Co., 863 F.2d 1503, 1510 (CA11 1989) (same); and Downes v. FAA, 775 F.2d 288, 292 (CA Fed. 1985) (same), with Ellison v. Brady, 924 F.2d 872, 877–878 (CA9 1991) (rejecting such a requirement).

II

Title VII of the Civil Rights Act of 1964 makes it "an unlawful employment practice for an employer...to discriminate against any individual with respect to his compensation, terms, conditions, or privileges of employment, because of such individual's race, color, religion, sex, or national origin." 42 U.S.C. § 2000e-2(a)(1). As we made clear in Meritor Savings Bank, FSB v. Vinson, 477 U.S. 57 (1986), this language "is not limited to 'economic' or 'tangible' discrimination. The phrase 'terms, conditions, or privileges of employment' evinces a congressional intent 'to strike at the entire spectrum of disparate treatment of men and women' in employment," which includes requiring people to work in a discriminatorily hostile or abusive environment. Id., at 64, quoting Los Angeles Dept. of Water and Power v. Manhart, 435 U.S. 702, 707, n.13, 55 L. Ed. 2d 657, 98 S. Ct. 1370 (1978). When the workplace is permeated with "discriminatory intimidation, ridicule, and insult," 477 U.S. at 65, that is "sufficiently severe or pervasive to alter the conditions of the victim's employment and create an abusive working environment," Title VII is violated.

This standard, which we reaffirm today, takes a middle path between making actionable any conduct that is merely offensive and requiring the conduct to cause a tangible psychological injury. As we pointed out in Meritor, "mere utterance of an...epithet which engenders offensive feelings in an employee," does not sufficiently affect the conditions of employment to implicate Title VII. Conduct that is not severe or pervasive enough to create an objectively hostile or abusive work environment—an environment that a reasonable person would find hostile or abusive—is beyond Title VII's purview. Likewise, if the victim does not subjectively perceive the environment to be abusive, the conduct has not actually altered the conditions of the victim's employment, and there is no Title VII violation.

But Title VII comes into play before the harassing conduct leads to a nervous breakdown. A discriminatorily abusive work environment, even one that does not seriously affect employees' psychological well-being, can and often will detract from employees' job performance, discourage employees from remaining on the job, or keep them from advancing in their careers. Moreover, even without regard to these tangible effects, the very fact that the discriminatory conduct was so severe or pervasive that it created a work environment abusive to employees because of their race, gender, religion, or national origin offends Title VII's broad rule of workplace equality. The appalling conduct alleged in Meritor, and the reference in that case to environments "'so heavily polluted with discrimination as to destroy completely the emotional and psychological stability of minority group workers,'" Id., at 66, quoting Rogers v. EEOC, 454 F.2d 234, 238 (CA5 1971), cert. denied, 406 U.S. 957,32 L. Ed. 2d 343, 92 S. Ct. 2058 (1972), merely present some especially egregious examples of harassment. They do not mark the boundary of what is actionable.

We therefore believe the District Court erred in relying on whether the conduct "seriously affected plaintiff's psychological well-being" or led her to "suffer injury." Such an inquiry may needlessly focus the fact finder's attention on concrete psychological harm, an element Title VII does not require. Certainly Title VII bars conduct that would seriously affect a reasonable person's psychological well-being, but the statute is not limited to such conduct. So long as the environment would reasonably be perceived, and is perceived, as hostile or abusive, Meritor, supra, at 67, there is no need for it also to be psychologically injurious.

This is not, and by its nature cannot be, a mathematically precise test. We need not answer today all the potential questions it raises, nor specifically address the Equal Employment Opportunity Commission's new regulations on this subject, see 58 Fed. Reg. 51266 (1993) (proposed 29 CFR §§ 1609.1, 1609.2); see also 29 CFR § 1604.11 (1993). But we can say that whether an environment is "hostile" or "abusive" can be determined only by looking at all the circumstances. These may include the frequency of the discriminatory conduct; its severity; whether it is physically threatening or humiliating, or a mere offensive utterance; and whether it unreasonably interferes with an employee's work performance. The effect on the employee's psychological well-being is, of course, relevant to determining whether the plaintiff actually found the environment abusive. But while psychological harm, like any other relevant factor, may be taken into account, no single factor is required.

III

Forklift, while conceding that a requirement that the conduct seriously affect psychological well-being is unfounded, argues that the District Court nonetheless correctly applied the Meritor standard. We disagree. Though the District Court did conclude that the work environment was not "intimidating or abusive to [Harris]," it did so only after finding that the conduct was not "so severe as to be expected to seriously affect plaintiff's psychological well-being," and that Harris was not "subjectively so offended that she suffered injury," ibid. The District Court's application of these incorrect standards may well have influenced its ultimate conclusion, especially given that the court found this to be a "close case."

We therefore reverse the judgment of the Court of Appeals, and remand the case for further proceedings consistent with this opinion.

So ordered.

Note to Students

This was only the second time that the Supreme Court had decided a sexual harassment case. Many feminist legal studies scholars feared that the court would raise the bar and make hostile-working-environment claims under Title VII more difficult to win. That did not happen. When the question to be decided is combined with the court's decision, we get the holding of the case. Here, the question that the court poses, plus its answer, yields a holding that "An employee need not prove severe psychological injury in order to win a Title VII sexual harassment claim." This holding will be true until such time as the court revisits a similar question and answers it differently. This does happen, but happens rarely.

Case Questions

1. Is this a criminal case or a civil-law case? How can you tell?
2. Is the court concerned with making a procedural rule here, or is the court making a statement about the substantive law?
3. Is this a case where the court is interpreting the Constitution, a federal statute, a state statute, or the common law?
4. In *Harris v. Forklift*, what if the trial judge does not personally agree that women should have any rights to equal treatment in the workplace? Why shouldn't that judge dismiss the case even before trial? Or should the judge dismiss the case after giving the female plaintiff her day in court?
5. What was the employer's argument in this case? Do you agree or disagree with it? What if those who legislated Title VII gave no thought to the question of seriousness of injury at all?

1.7 Summary and Exercises

Summary

There are differing conceptions of what law is and of what law should be. Laws and legal systems differ worldwide. The legal system in the United States is founded on the US Constitution, which is itself inspired by natural-law theory and the idea that people have rights that cannot be taken by government but only protected by government. The various functions of the law are done well or poorly depending on which nation-state you look at. Some do very well in terms of keeping order, while others do a better job of allowing civil and political freedoms. Social and political movements within each nation greatly affect the nature and quality of the legal system within that nation.

This chapter has familiarized you with a few of the basic schools of legal thought, such as natural law, positive law, legal realism, and critical legal studies. It has also given you a brief background in common law, including contracts, torts, and criminal law. The differences between civil and criminal cases, substance and procedure, and the various sources of law have also been reviewed. Each source has a different level of authority, starting with constitutions, which are primary and will negate any lower-court laws that are not consistent with its principles and provisions. The basic differences between the common law and civil law (continental, or European) systems of law are also discussed.

Exercises

1. What is the common law? Where do the courts get the authority to interpret it and to change it?
2. After World War II ended in 1945, there was an international tribunal at Nuremberg that prosecuted various officials in Germany's Third Reich who had committed "crimes against humanity." Many of them claim that they were simply "following orders" of Adolf Hitler and his chief lieutenants. What law, if any, have they violated?
3. What does *stare decisis* mean, and why is it so basic to common-law legal tradition?
4. In the following situations, which source of law takes priority, and why?
    a. The state statute conflicts with the common law of that state.
    b. A federal statute conflicts with the U.S. Constitution.
    c. A common-law decision in one state conflicts with the U.S. Constitution.
    d. A federal statute conflicts with a state constitution.

Self-Test Questions

1. The source of law that is foundational in the US legal system is
    a. the common law
    b. statutory law
    c. constitutional law
    d. administrative law
2. "Law is the command of a sovereign" represents what school of legal thought?
    a. civil law
    b. constitutional law
    c. natural law

d. ecofeminist law
e. positive law

3. Which of the following kinds of law are most often found in state law rather than federal law?
   a. torts and contracts
   b. bankruptcy
   c. maritime law
   d. international law
4. Where was natural law discovered?
   a. in nature
   b. in constitutions and statutes
   c. in the exercise of human reason
   d. in the *Wall Street Journal*
5. Wolfe is a state court judge in California. In the case of *Riddick v. Clouse*, which involves a contract dispute, Wolfe must follow precedent. She establishes a logical relationship between the Riddick case and a case decided by the California Supreme Court, *Zhu v. Patel Enterprises, Inc.* She compares the facts of Riddick to the facts in Zhu and to the extent the facts are similar, applies the same rule to reach her decision. This is
   a. deductive reasoning
   b. faulty reasoning
   c. linear reasoning
   d. reasoning by analogy
6. Moore is a state court judge in Colorado. In the case of *Cassidy v. Seawell*, also a contract dispute, there is no Colorado Supreme Court or court of appeals decision that sets forth a rule that could be applied. However, the California case of *Zhu v. Patel Enterprises, Inc.* is "very close" on the facts and sets forth a rule of law that could be applied to the Cassidy case. What process must Moore follow in considering whether to use the Zhu case as precedent?
   a. Moore is free to decide the case any way he wants, but he may not look at decisions and reasons in similar cases from other states.
   b. Moore must wait for the Colorado legislature and the governor to pass a law that addresses the issues raised in the Cassidy case.
   c. Moore must follow the California case if that is the best precedent.
   d. Moore may follow the California case if he believes that it offers the best reasoning for a similar case.

Self-Test Answers

1. c
2. e
3. a
4. c
5. d
6. d

Endnotes

1. *Black's Law Dictionary*, 6th ed., s.v. "law."
2. *Cambridge Dictionary of Philosophy*, s.v. "natural law."

3. Martin Luther King Jr., "Letter from Birmingham Jail."
4. *Rulon-Miller v. International Business Machines Corp.*, 162 Cal. App.3d 241, 255 (1984).

CHAPTER 2

Corporate Social Responsibility and Business Ethics

A great society is a society in which [leaders] of business think greatly about their functions.
— Alfred North Whitehead

Learning Objectives

After reading this chapter, you should be able to do the following:

1. Define ethics and explain the importance of good ethics for business people and business organizations.
2. Understand the principal philosophies of ethics, including utilitarianism, duty-based ethics, and virtue ethics.
3. Distinguish between the ethical merits of various choices by using an ethical decision model.
4. Explain the difference between shareholder and stakeholder models of ethical corporate governance.
5. Explain why it is difficult to establish and maintain an ethical corporate culture in a business organization.

Few subjects are more contentious or important as the role of business in society, particularly, whether corporations have social responsibilities that are distinct from maximizing shareholder value. While the phrase "business ethics" is not oxymoronic (i.e., a contradiction in terms), there is abundant evidence that many businesspeople and firms seek profit only for themselves, and could care less about others, or society generally. But business organizations ignore the ethical and social expectations of consumers, employees, the media, nongovernment organizations (NGOs), government officials, and socially responsible investors at their peril. Legal compliance alone no longer serves the long-term interests of many companies, who find that sustainable profitability requires thinking about people and the planet as well as profits.

This chapter has a fairly modest aim: to introduce potential businesspeople to the differences between legal compliance and ethical excellence by reviewing some of the philosophical perspectives that apply to business, businesspeople, and the role of business organizations in society.

2.1 What Is Ethics?

Learning Objectives

1. Explain how both individuals and institutions can be viewed as ethical or unethical.
2. Explain how law and ethics are different, and why a good reputation can be more important than legal compliance.

Most of those who write about ethics do not make a clear distinction between ethics and morality. The question of what is "right" or "morally correct" or "ethically correct" or "morally desirable" in any situation is variously phrased, but all of the words and phrases are after the same thing: what act is "better" in a moral or ethical sense than some other act? People sometimes speak of morality as something personal but view ethics as having wider social implications. Others see morality as the subject of a field of study, that field being ethics. Ethics would be morality as applied to any number of subjects, including journalistic ethics, business ethics, or the ethics of professionals such as doctors, attorneys, and accountants. We will venture a definition of *ethics*, but for our purposes, *ethics* and *morality* will be used as equivalent terms.

People often speak about the ethics or morality of individuals and also about the morality or ethics of corporations and nations. There are clearly differences in the kind of moral responsibility that we can fairly ascribe to corporations and nations; we tend to see individuals as having a soul, or at least a conscience, but there is no general agreement that nations or corporations have either. Still, our ordinary use of language does point to something significant: if we say that some nations are "evil" and others are "corrupt," then we make moral judgments about the quality of actions undertaken by the governments or people of that nation. For example, if North Korea is characterized by the US president as part of an "axis of evil," or if we conclude that WorldCom or Enron acted "unethically" in certain respects, then we are making judgments that their collective actions are morally deficient.

In talking about morality, we often use the word *good*; but that word can be confusing. If we say that Microsoft is a "good company," we may be making a statement about the investment potential of Microsoft stock, or their preeminence in the market, or their ability to win lawsuits or appeals or to influence administrative agencies. Less likely, though possibly, we may be making a statement about the civic virtue and corporate social responsibility of Microsoft. In the first set of judgments, we use the word *good* but mean something other than ethical or moral; only in the second instance are we using the word *good* in its ethical or moral sense.

A word such as *good* can embrace ethical or moral values but also nonethical values. If I like Daniel and try to convince you what a "good guy" he is, you may ask all sorts of questions: Is he good-looking? Well-off? Fun to be with? Humorous? Athletic? Smart? I could answer all of those questions with a yes, yet you would still not know any of his moral qualities. But if I said that he was honest, caring, forthright, and diligent, volunteered in local soup kitchens, or tithed to the church, many people would see Daniel as having certain ethical or moral qualities. If I said that he keeps the Golden Rule as well as anyone I know, you could conclude that he is an ethical person. But if I said that he is "always in control" or "always at the top of his game," you would probably not make inferences or assumptions about his character or ethics.

There are three key points here:

1. Although morals and ethics are not precisely measurable, people generally have similar reactions about what actions or conduct can rightly be called ethical or moral.
2. As humans, we need and value ethical people and want to be around them.
3. Saying that someone or some organization is law-abiding does not mean the same as saying a person or company is ethical.

Here is a cautionary note: for individuals, it is far from easy to recognize an ethical problem, have a clear and usable decision-making process to deal it, and then have the moral courage to do what's right. All of that is even more difficult within a business organization, where corporate employees vary in their motivations, loyalties, commitments, and character. There is no universally accepted way for developing an organization where employees feel valued, respected, and free to openly disagree; where the actions of top management are crystal clear; and where all the employees feel loyal and accountable to one another.

Before talking about how ethics relates to law, we can conclude that ethics is the study of morality—"right" and "wrong"—in the context of everyday life, organizational behaviors, and even how society operates and is governed.

How Do Law and Ethics Differ?

There is a difference between legal compliance and moral excellence. Few would choose a professional service, health care or otherwise, because the provider had a record of perfect legal compliance, or always following the letter of the law. There are many professional ethics codes, primarily because people realize that law prescribes only a minimum of morality and does not provide purpose or goals that can mean excellent service to customers, clients, or patients.

Business ethicists have talked for years about the intersection of law and ethics. Simply put, what is legal is not necessarily ethical. Conversely, what is ethical is not necessarily legal. There are lots of legal maneuvers that are not all that ethical; the well-used phrase "legal loophole" suggests as much.

Here are two propositions about business and ethics. Consider whether they strike you as true or whether you would need to know more in order to make a judgment.

- Individuals and organizations have reputations. (For an individual, moral reputation is most often tied to others' perceptions of his or her character: is the individual honest, diligent, reliable, fair, and caring? The reputation of an organization is built on the goodwill that suppliers, customers, the community, and employees feel toward it. Although an organization is not a person in the usual sense, the goodwill that people feel about the organization is based on their perception of its better qualities by a variety of stakeholders: customers or clients, suppliers, investors, employees, government officials).
- The goodwill of an organization is to a great extent based on the actions it takes and on whether the actions are favorably viewed. (This goodwill is usually specifically counted in the sale of a business as an asset that the buyer pays for. While it is difficult to place a monetary value on goodwill, a firm's good reputation will generally call for a higher evaluation in the final accounting before the sale. Legal troubles or a reputation for having legal troubles will only lessen the price for a business and will even lessen the value of the company's stock as bad legal news comes to the public's attention.)

Another reason to think about ethics in connection with law is that the laws themselves are meant to express some moral view. If there are legal prohibitions against cheating the Medicare program, it is because people (legislators or their agents) have collectively decided that cheating Medicare is wrong. If there are legal prohibitions against assisting someone to commit suicide, it is because there has been a group decision that doing so is immoral. Thus the law provides some important cues as to what society regards as right or wrong.

Finally, important policy issues that face society are often resolved through law, but it is important to understand the moral perspectives that underlie public debate—as, for example, in the continuing controversies over stem-cell research, medical use of marijuana, and abortion. Some ethical perspectives focus on rights, some on social utility, some on virtue or character, and some on social justice. People consciously (or, more often, unconsciously) adopt one or more of these perspectives, and even if they completely agree on the facts with an opponent, they will not change their views. Fundamentally, the difference comes down to incompatible moral perspectives, a clash of basic values. These are hot-button issues because society is divided, not so much over facts, but over basic values. Understanding the varied moral perspectives and values in public policy debates is a clarifying benefit in following or participating in these important discussions.

Why Should an Individual or a Business Entity Be Ethical?

The usual answer is that good ethics is good business. In the long run, businesses that pay attention to ethics as well as law do better; they are viewed more favorably by customers. But this is a difficult claim to measure scientifically, because "the long run" is an indistinct period of time and because there are as yet no generally accepted criteria by which ethical excellence can be measured. In addition, life is still lived in the short run, and there are many occasions when something short of perfect conduct is a lot more profitable.

Some years ago, Royal Dutch/Shell (one of the world's largest companies) found that it was in deep trouble with the public for its apparent carelessness with the environment and human rights. Consumers were boycotting and investors were getting frightened, so the company took a long, hard look at its ethic of short-term profit maximization. Since then, changes have been made. The CEO told one group of business ethicists that the uproar had taken them by surprise; they thought they had done everything right, but it seemed there was a "ghost in the machine." That ghost was consumers, NGOs, and the media, all of whom objected to the company's seeming lack of moral sensitivity.

The market does respond to unethical behavior. In Section 4, you will read about the Sears Auto Centers case. The loss of goodwill toward Sears Auto Centers was real, even though the total amount of money lost cannot be clearly accounted for. Years later, there are people who will not go near a Sears Auto Center; the customers who lost trust in the company will never return, and many of their children may avoid Sears Auto Centers as well.

The Arthur Andersen story is even more dramatic. A major accounting firm, Andersen worked closely with Enron in hiding its various losses through creative accounting measures. Suspiciously, Andersen's Houston office also did some shredding around the clock, appearing to cover up what it was doing for Enron. A criminal case based on this shredding resulted in a conviction, later overturned by the Supreme Court. But it was too late. Even before the conviction, many clients had found other accounting firms that were not under suspicion, and the Supreme Court's reversal came too late to save the company. Even without the conviction, Andersen would have lost significant market share.

The irony of Andersen as a poster child for overly aggressive accounting practices is that the man who founded the firm built it on integrity and straightforward practices. "Think straight, talk straight" was the company's motto. Andersen established the company's reputation for integrity over a hundred years ago by refusing to play numbers games for a potentially lucrative client.

Maximizing profits while being legally compliant is not a very inspiring goal for a business. People in an organization need some quality or excellence to strive for. By focusing on pushing the edge of what is legal, by looking for loopholes in the law that would help create short-term financial gain, companies have often learned that in the long term they are not actually satisfying the market, the shareholders, the suppliers, or the community generally.

Key Takeaway

Legal compliance is not the same as acting ethically. Your reputation, individually or corporately, depends on how others regard your actions. Goodwill is hard to measure or quantify, but it is real nonetheless and can best be protected by acting ethically.

Exercises

1. Think of a person who did something morally wrong, at least to your way of thinking. What was it? Explain to a friend of yours—or a classmate—why you think it was wrong. Does your friend agree? Why or why not? What is the basic principle that forms the basis for your judgment that it was wrong?
2. Think of a person who did something morally right, at least to your way of thinking. (This is not a matter of finding something they did well, like efficiently changing a tire, but something good.) What was it? Explain to a friend of yours—or a classmate—why you think it was right. Does your friend agree? Why or why not? What is the basic principle that forms the basis for your judgment that it was right?
3. Think of an action by a business organization (sole proprietor, partnership, or corporation) that was legal but still strikes you as wrong. What was it? Why do you think it was wrong?
4. Think of an act by an individual or a corporation that is ethical but not legal. Compare your answer with those of your classmates: were you more likely to find an example from individual action or corporate action? Do you have any thoughts as to why?

2.2 Major Ethical Perspectives

Learning Objectives

1. Describe the various major theories about ethics in human decision making.
2. Begin considering how the major theories about ethics apply to difficult choices in life and business.

There are several well-respected ways of looking at ethical issues. Some of them have been around for centuries. It is important to know that many who think a lot about business and ethics have deeply held beliefs about which perspective is best. Others would recommend considering ethical problems from a variety of different perspectives. Here, we take a brief look at (1) utilitarianism, (2) deontology, (3) social justice and social contract theory, and (4) virtue theory. We are leaving out some important perspectives, such as general theories of justice and "rights" and feminist thought about ethics and patriarchy. We also leave out an increasingly important aspect of business ethics: the growing influence of behavioral psychology, a field which has revealed significant gaps in our ability as individuals and business firms to make rational decisions.[1]

Utilitarianism

utilitarianism

The theory that the "right" moral act is the one that produces the greatest good for society.

Utilitarianism is a prominent perspective on ethics, one that is well aligned with economics and the free-market outlook that has come to dominate much current thinking about business, management, and economics. Jeremy Bentham is often considered the founder of utilitarianism, though John Stuart Mill (who wrote *On Liberty* and *Utilitarianism*) and others promoted it as a guide to what is good. Utilitarianism emphasizes not rules but results. An action (or set of actions) is generally deemed good or right if it maximizes happiness or pleasure throughout society. Originally intended as a guide for legislators charged with seeking the greatest good for society, the utilitarian outlook may also be practiced individually and by corporations.

Bentham believed that the most promising way to obtain agreement on the best policies for a society would be to look at the various policies a legislature could pass and compare the good and bad consequences of each. The right course of action from an ethical point of view would be to choose the policy that would produce the greatest amount of utility, or usefulness. In brief, the utilitarian principle holds that an action is right if and only if the sum of utilities produced by that action is greater than the sum of utilities from any other possible act.

This statement describes "act utilitarianism"—which action among various options will deliver the greatest good to society? "Rule utilitarianism" is a slightly different version; it asks, what rule or principle, if followed regularly, will create the greatest good?

Notice that the emphasis is on finding the best possible results and that the assumption is that we can measure the utilities involved. (This turns out to be more difficult that you might think.) Notice also that "the sum total of utilities" clearly implies that in doing utilitarian analysis, we cannot be satisfied if an act or set of acts provides the greatest utility to us as individuals or to a particular corporation; the test is, instead, whether it provides the greatest utility to society as a whole. Notice that the theory does not tell us what kinds of utilities may be better than others or how much better a good today is compared with a good a year from today.

Whatever its difficulties, utilitarian thinking is alive and well in US law and business. It is found in such diverse places as cost-benefit analysis in administrative and regulatory rules and calculations, environmental impact studies, the majority vote, product comparisons for consumer information, marketing studies, tax laws, and strategic planning. In management, people will often employ a form of utility reasoning by projecting costs and benefits for plan X versus plan Y. But the issue in most of these cost-benefit analyses is usually (1) put exclusively in terms of money and (2) directed to the benefit of the person or organization doing the analysis and not to the benefit of society as a whole.

An individual or a company that consistently uses the test "What's the greatest good for me or the company?" is not following the utilitarian test of the greatest good overall. Another common failing is to see only one or two options that seem reasonable. The following are some frequent mistakes that people make in applying what they think are utilitarian principles in justifying their chosen course of action:

1. Failing to come up with lots of options that seem reasonable and then choosing the one that has the greatest benefit for the greatest number. Often, a decision maker seizes on one or two alternatives without thinking carefully about other courses of action. If the alternative does more good than harm, the decision maker assumes it's ethically okay.
2. Assuming that the greatest good for you or your company is in fact the greatest good for all—that is, looking at situations subjectively or with your own interests primarily in mind.
3. Underestimating the costs of a certain decision to you or your company. The now-classic Ford Pinto case demonstrates how Ford Motor Company executives greatly underestimated the legal costs of not correcting a feature on their Pinto models that they knew could cause death or injury. General Motors learned a similar lesson in its failure to fix an ignition switch that sometimes shut off cars moving along roads and highways, leading to significant injuries to drivers and occupants.

4. Underestimating the cost or harm of a certain decision to someone else or some other group of people.
5. Favoring short-term benefits, even though the long-term costs are greater.
6. Assuming that all values can be reduced to money. In comparing the risks to human health or safety against, say, the risks of job or profit losses, cost-benefit analyses will often try to compare "apples to oranges" and put arbitrary numerical values on human health and safety.

Rules and Duty: Deontology

In contrast to the utilitarian perspective, the deontological view presented in the writings of Immanuel Kant purports that having a moral intent and following the right rules is a better path to ethical conduct than achieving any particular result that seems "good." A deontologist like Kant is likely to believe that ethical action arises from doing one's duty, those duties that are defined by rational thought. Duties, according to Kant, are not specific to particular kinds of human beings but are owed universally to all human beings. Kant therefore uses "universalizing" as a form of rational thought that assumes the inherent equality of all human beings. It considers all humans as equal, not in the physical, social, or economic sense, but equal before God, whether they are male, female, Pygmy, Eskimoan, Islamic, Christian, gay, straight, healthy, sick, young, or old.

For Kantian thinkers, this basic principle of equality means that we should be able to universalize any particular law or action to determine whether it is ethical. **Deontology** requires that we put duty first, act rationally, and give moral weight to the inherent equality of all human beings. Kant has two notable formulations of what he calls "the categorical imperative." The first one is:

Deontology

A theory that judges the morality of choices not by results (or "goods") but by adherence to duty discerned by rational thought. The duty to act in accord with these norms is one that bears no relation to the expected consequences of the action.

Act only according to that maxim whereby you can, at the same time, will that it should become a universal law.

The second version of the categorical imperative is:

Act in such a way that you treat humanity, whether in your own person or in the person of any other, never merely as a means to an end, but always at the same time as an end.

There is considerable scholarly discussion on whether these two formulations amount to the same basic duty. For the sake of brevity, and the enjoyment of application, let's consider each one in turn.

Let's say you are thinking about misrepresenting yourself on a resume for a particular job you really wanted, as you are convinced that doing so would get you that job, and since this is your "dream job," you might be very tempted to do so. ("What harm would it be?" you might very well ask yourself. "When I have the job, I can prove that I am perfect for it, and no one is hurt, so both the employer and I are clearly better off as a result!") The behavioral ethicist would answer that you are obviously biased in your calculations, but Kantian ethicists would have a duty-based reply: that your chosen course of action should be a universal one—a course of action that would be good for all persons at all times. Using Kant's first categorical imperative, there are two requirements for a rule of action to be universal: consistency and reversibility. Consider reversibility: reversibility requires you to actively imagine both that you were the employer in this situation and that you were another well-qualified applicant who lost the job because someone else padded his resume with false accomplishments. If the consequences of such an exercise of the imagination are not appealing to you, your action is probably not ethical.

The second requirement for an action to be universal is the search for consistency. This is more abstract. A deontologist would say that since you know you are telling a lie, you must be willing to say that lying, as a general, universal phenomenon, is acceptable. But if everyone lied, then there would be no point to lying, since no one would believe anyone. It is only because honesty works well for society as a whole and is generally practiced that lying even becomes useful to the liar! That is, lying cannot be universalized, for it depends on the preexistence of honesty.

Similar demonstrations can be made for actions such as polluting, breaking promises, and committing most crimes, including rape, murder, and theft. But these are the easy cases for Kantian thinkers. In the gray areas of life as it is lived, the consistency test is often difficult to apply. If breaking a promise would save a life, then Kantian thought becomes difficult to apply. If some amount of pollution can allow employment and the harm is minimal or distant, Kantian thinking is not all that helpful. Finally, we should note that the well-known Golden Rule, "Do unto others as you would have them do unto you," emphasizes the easier of the two universalizing requirements: practicing reversibility ("How would I like it if someone did this to me?").

Taking the same example and looking at Kant's second formulation of the categorical imperative, we can see that you would be treating others (the employer and other applicants, among others) as mere means to your own ends. Full respect for the humanity of those others would urge honesty, so that others might choose wisely and well.

In short, deontology requires that we put duty first, act rationally, and give moral weight to the inherent equality of all human beings.

Social Justice Theory and Social Contract Theory

Social justice theorists worry about "distributive justice"—that is, what is the fair way to distribute goods among a group of people? Marxist thought emphasizes that members of society should be given goods to according to their needs. But this redistribution would require a governing power to decide who gets what and when. Capitalist thought takes a different approach, rejecting any giving that is not voluntary. Certain economists, such as the late Milton Friedman (see the sidebar in Section 4) also reject the notion that a corporation has a duty to give to unmet needs in society, believing that the government should play that role. Even the most dedicated free-market capitalist will often admit the need for some government and some forms of welfare—Social Security, Medicare, assistance to flood-stricken areas, help for AIDs patients—along with some public goods (such as defense, education, highways, parks, and support of key industries affecting national security).

public goods

Goods that are useful to society (parks, education, national defense, highways) that would ordinarily not be produced by private enterprise. Public goods require public revenues (taxes) and political support to be adequately maintained.

social contract

The idea that people in a civil society have voluntarily given up some of their freedoms to have ordered liberty with the assistance of a government that will support that liberty. Hobbes and Locke are generally regarded as the preeminent social contract theorists.

People who do not see the need for **public goods** (including laws, court systems, and the government goods and services just cited) often question why there needs to be a government at all. One response might be, "Without government, there would be no corporations." Thomas Hobbes believed that people in a "state of nature" would rationally choose to have some form of government. He called this the **social contract**, where people give up certain rights to government in exchange for security and common benefits. In your own lives and in this course, you will see an ongoing balancing act between human desires for freedom and human desires for order; it is an ancient tension. Some commentators also see a kind of social contract between corporations and society; in exchange for perpetual duration and limited liability, the corporation has some corresponding duties toward society. Also, if a corporation is legally a "person," as the Supreme Court reaffirmed in 2010, then some would argue that if this corporate person commits three felonies, it should be locked up for life and its corporate charter revoked!

Modern social contract theorists, such as Thomas Donaldson and Thomas Dunfee (*Ties that Bind*, 1999), observe that various communities, not just nations, make rules for the common good. Your college or school is a community, and there are communities within the school (fraternities, sororities, the folks behind the counter at the circulation desk, the people who work together at the university radio station, the sports teams, the faculty, the students generally, the gay and lesbian alliance, etc.) that have rules, norms, or standards that people can buy into or not. If not, they can exit from that community, just as we are free (though not without cost) to reject US citizenship and take up residence in another country. The fate of Syrian refugees in 2015 demonstrates just how fragile national communities can be and how difficult a right of exit can become.

Donaldson and Dunfee's integrative social contracts theory stresses the importance of studying the rules of smaller communities along with the larger social contracts made in states (such as

Colorado or California) and nation-states (such as the United States or Germany). Our Constitution can be seen as a fundamental social contract.

It is important to realize that a social contract can be changed by the participants in a community, just as the US Constitution can be amended. Social contract theory is thus dynamic—it allows for structural and organic changes. Ideally, the social contract struck by citizens and the government allows for certain fundamental rights such as those we enjoy in the United States, but it need not. People can give up freedom-oriented rights (such as the right of free speech or the right to be free of unreasonable searches and seizures) to secure order (freedom from fear, freedom from terrorism). For example, many citizens in Russia now miss the days when the Kremlin was all powerful; there was less crime and more equality and predictability to life in the Soviet Union, even if there was less freedom.

Thus the rights that people have—in positive law—come from whatever social contract exists in the society. This view differs from that of the deontologists and that of the natural-law thinkers such as Gandhi, Jesus, or Martin Luther King Jr., who believed that rights come from God or, in less religious terms, from some transcendent moral order.

Another important movement in ethics and society is the communitarian outlook. Communitarians emphasize that rights carry with them corresponding duties; that is, there cannot be a right without a duty. Interested students may wish to explore the work of Amitai Etzioni. Etzioni was a founder of the Communitarian Network, which is a group of individuals who have come together to bolster the moral, social, and political environment. It claims to be nonsectarian, nonpartisan, and international in scope.

The relationship between rights and duties—in both law and ethics—calls for some explanations:

1. If you have a right of free expression, the government has a duty to respect that right but can put reasonable limits on it. For example, you can legally say whatever you want about the US president, but you can't get away with threatening the president's life. Even if your criticisms are strong and insistent, you have the right (and our government has the duty to protect your right) to speak freely. In Singapore during the 1990s, even indirect criticisms—mere hints—of the political leadership were enough to land you in jail or at least silence you with a libel suit.
2. Rights and duties exist not only between people and their governments but also between individuals. Your right to be free from physical assault is protected by the law in most states, and when someone walks up to you and punches you in the nose, your rights—as set forth in the positive law of your state—have been violated. Thus other people have a duty to respect your rights and to not punch you in the nose.
3. Your right in legal terms is only as good as your society's willingness to provide legal remedies through the courts and political institutions of society.

A distinction between basic rights and nonbasic rights may also be important. Basic rights may include such fundamental elements as food, water, shelter, and physical safety. Another distinction is between positive rights (the right to bear arms, the right to vote, the right of privacy) and negative rights (the right to be free from unreasonable searches and seizures, the right to be free of cruel or unusual punishments). Yet another is between economic or social rights (adequate food, work, and environment) and political or civic rights (the right to vote, the right to equal protection of the laws, the right to due process). The 1948 Universal Declaration of Human Rights lists all kinds of rights, but those rights can only be manifested through the positive law of various nation-states or by agreement among nation-states.

Aristotle and Virtue Theory

virtue ethics

Aristotle's perspective on finding happiness through the application of reason in human affairs advises continual practice to develop habits of virtuous moral character. In a modern setting, deliberating on core values and their application to individual and corporate ethical dilemmas and adhering to the recommendations of core values analysis would provide similar practice.

Virtue theory, or virtue ethics, has received increasing attention over the past twenty years, particularly in contrast to utilitarian and deontological approaches to ethics. Virtue theory emphasizes the value of virtuous qualities rather than formal rules or useful results. Aristotle is often recognized as the first philosopher to advocate the ethical value of certain qualities, or virtues, in a person's character. As LaRue Hosmer has noted, Aristotle saw the goal of human existence as the active, rational search for excellence, and excellence requires the personal virtues of honesty, truthfulness, courage, temperance, generosity, and high-mindedness. This pursuit is also termed "knowledge of the good" in Greek philosophy.[2]

Aristotle believed that all activity was aimed at some goal or perceived good and that there must be some ranking that we do among those goals or goods. Happiness may be our ultimate goal, but what does that mean, exactly? Aristotle rejected wealth, pleasure, and fame and embraced reason as the distinguishing feature of humans, as opposed to other species. And since a human is a reasoning animal, happiness must be associated with reason. Thus happiness is living according to the active (rather than passive) use of reason. The use of reason leads to excellence, and so happiness can be defined as the active, rational pursuit of personal excellence, or virtue.

Aristotle named fourteen virtues: (1) courage, particularly in battle; (2) temperance, or moderation in eating and drinking; (3) liberality, or spending money well; (4) magnificence, or living well; (5) pride, or taking pleasure in accomplishments and stature; (6) high-mindedness, or concern with the noble rather than the petty; (7) unnamed virtue, which is halfway between ambition and total lack of effort; (8) gentleness, or concern for others; (9) truthfulness; (10) wit, or pleasure in group discussions; (11) friendliness, or pleasure in personal conduct; (12) modesty, or pleasure in personal conduct; (13) righteous indignation, or getting angry at the right things and in the right amounts; and (14) justice.

From a modern perspective, some of these virtues seem old-fashioned or even odd. Magnificence, for example, is not something we commonly speak of. Three issues emerge: (1) How do we know what a virtue is these days? (2) How useful is a list of agreed-upon virtues anyway? (3) What do virtues have to do with companies, particularly large ones where various groups and individuals may have little or no contact with other parts of the organization?

As to the third question, whether corporations can "have" virtues or values is a matter of lively debate. A corporation is obviously not the same as an individual. But there seems to be growing agreement that organizations do differ in their practices and that these practices are value driven. If all a company cares about is the bottom line, other values will diminish or disappear. Quite a few books have been written in the past twenty years that emphasize the need for businesses to define their values in order to be competitive in today's global economy.[3]

As to the first two questions regarding virtues, a look at Michael Josephson's core values may prove helpful.

Josephson's Core Values Analysis and Decision Process

Michael Josephson, a noted American ethicist, believes that a current set of *core values* has been identified and that the values can be meaningfully applied to a variety of personal and corporate decisions.

To simplify, let's say that there are ethical and nonethical qualities among people in the United States. When you ask people what kinds of qualities they admire in others or in themselves, they may say wealth, power, fitness, sense of humor, good looks, intelligence, musical ability, or some other quality. They may also value honesty, caring, fairness, courage, perseverance, diligence, trustworthiness, or integrity. The qualities on the second list have something in common—they are distinctively ethical characteristics. That is, they are commonly seen as moral or ethical qualities, unlike the qualities on the first list. You can be, like the Athenian Alcibiades, brilliant but unprincipled, or, like some political leaders today, powerful but dishonest, or wealthy but uncaring. You can, in short, have a number of admirable qualities (brilliance, power, wealth) that are not per se virtuous. Just because Harold is rich or good-looking or has a good sense of humor does not mean that he is ethical. But if Harold is honest and caring (whether he is rich or poor, humorous or humorless), people are likely to see him as ethical.

Among the virtues, are any especially important? Studies from the Josephson Institute of Ethics in Marina del Rey, California, have identified six **core values** in our society, values that almost everyone agrees are important to them. When asked what values people hold dear, what values they wish to be known by, and what values they wish others would exhibit in their actions, six values consistently turn up: (1) trustworthiness, (2) respect, (3) responsibility, (4) fairness, (5) caring, and (6) citizenship.

core values

Values that are generally recognized as positive ethical characteristics of an individual or a business organization. People may have strong views about other kinds of ethical values, but core values are more widely accepted.

Note that these values are distinctly ethical. While many of us may value wealth, good looks, and intelligence, having wealth, good looks, and intelligence does not automatically make us virtuous in our character and habits. But being more trustworthy (by being honest and by keeping promises) does make us more virtuous, as does staying true to the other five core values.

Notice also that these six core values share something in common with other ethical values that are less universally agreed upon. Many values taught in the family or in places of worship are not generally agreed on, practiced, or admired by all. Some families and individuals believe strongly in the virtue of saving money or in abstaining from alcohol or sex prior to marriage. Others clearly do not, or at least don't act on their beliefs. Moreover, it is possible to have and practice core ethical values even if you take on heavy debt, knock down several drinks a night, or have frequent premarital sex. Some would dispute this, saying that you can't really lead a virtuous life if you get into debt, drink heavily, or engage in premarital sex. But the point here is that since people do disagree in these areas, the ethical traits of thrift, temperance, and sexual abstinence do not have the unanimity of approval that the six core values do.

The importance of an individual's having these consistent qualities of character is well known. Often we remember the last bad thing a person did far more than any or all previous good acts. For example, Eliot Spitzer and Bill Clinton are more readily remembered by people for their last, worst acts than for any good they accomplished as public servants. As for a company, its good reputation also has an incalculable value that when lost takes a great deal of time and work to recover. Shell, Nike, and other companies have discovered that there is a market for morality, however difficult to measure, and that not paying attention to business ethics often comes at a serious price. In the past fifteen years, the career of ethics and compliance officer has emerged, partly as a result of criminal proceedings against companies but also because major companies have found that reputations cannot be recovered retroactively but must be pursued proactively. For individuals, Aristotle emphasized the practice of virtue to the point where virtue becomes a habit. Companies are gradually learning the same lesson.

Key Takeaway

Throughout history, people have pondered what it means "to do what is right." Some of the main answers have come from the differing perspectives of utilitarian thought; duty-based, or deontological, thought; social contract theory; and virtue ethics.

Exercises

XYZ Motor Corporation begins to get customer complaints about two models of its automobiles. Customers have had near-death experiences from sudden acceleration; they would be driving along a highway at normal speed when suddenly the car would begin to accelerate, and efforts to stop the acceleration by braking fail to work. Drivers could turn off the ignition and come to a safe stop, but XYZ does not instruct buyers of its cars to do so, nor is this a common reaction among drivers who experience sudden acceleration.

Internal investigations of half a dozen accidents in U.S. locations come to the conclusion that the accidents are not being caused by drivers who mistake the gas pedal for the brake pedal. In fact, there appears to be a possible flaw in both models, perhaps in a semiconductor chip, that makes sudden acceleration happen. Interference by floor mats and poorly designed gas pedals do not seem to be the problem.

It is voluntary to report these incidents to the National Highway Traffic and Safety Administration (NHTSA), but the company decides that it will wait awhile and see if there are more complaints. Recalling the two models so that local dealers and their mechanics could examine them is also an option, but it would be extremely costly. Company executives are aware that quarterly and annual profit-and-loss statements, on which their bonuses depend, could be decisively worse with a recall. They decide that on a cost-benefit basis, it makes more sense to wait until there are more accidents and more data. After a hundred or more accidents and nearly fifteen fatalities, the company institutes a selective recall, still not notifying NHTSA, which has its own experts and the authority to order XYZ to do a full recall of all affected models.

Experts have advised XYZ that standard failure-analysis methodology requires that the company obtain absolutely every XYZ vehicle that has experienced sudden acceleration, using microscopic analysis of all critical components of the electronic system. The company does not wish to take that advice, as it would be—as one top executive put it—"too time-consuming and expensive."

1. Can XYZ's approach to this problem be justified under utilitarian theory? If so, how? If not, why not?
2. What would Kant advise XYZ to do? Explain.
3. What would the "virtuous" approach be for XYZ in this situation?

2.3 An Ethical Decision Model

Learning Objective

1. Understand one model for ethical decision making: a process to arrive at the most ethical option for an individual or a business organization, using a virtue ethics approach combined with some elements of stakeholder analysis and utilitarianism.

Josephson's Core Values Model

Once you recognize that there is a decision that involves ethical judgment, Michael Josephson would first have you ask as many questions as are necessary to get a full background on the relevant facts. Then, assuming you have all the needed information, the decision process is as follows:

1. Identify the stakeholders. That is, who are the potential gainers and losers in the various decisions that might be made here?
2. Identify several likely or reasonable decisions that could be made.
3. Consider which stakeholders gain or lose with each decision.
4. Determine which decision satisfies the greatest number of core values.
5. If there is no decision that satisfies the greatest number of core values, try to determine which decision delivers the greatest good to the various stakeholders.

It is often helpful to identify who (or what group) is the most important stakeholder, and why. In Milton Friedman's view, it will always be the shareholders. In the view of John Mackey, the CEO of Whole Foods Market, the long-term viability and profitability of the organization may require that customers come first, or, at times, some other stakeholder group (see "Conscious Capitalism" in Section 4).

The Core Values

Here are the core values and their subcomponents as developed by the Josephson Institute of Ethics.

Trustworthiness: Be honest—*tell the truth, the whole truth, and nothing but the truth; be sincere, forthright; don't deceive, mislead, or be tricky with the truth; don't cheat or steal, and don't betray a trust.* Demonstrate integrity—*stand up for what you believe, walk the walk as well as talking the talk; be what you seem to be; show commitment and courage.* Be loyal—*stand by your family, friends, co-workers, community, and nation; be discreet with information that comes into your hands; don't spread rumors or engage in harmful gossip; don't violate your principles just to win friendship or approval; don't ask a friend to do something that is wrong.* Keep promises—*keep your word, honor your commitments, and pay your debts; return what you borrow.*

Respect: *Judge people on their merits, not their appearance; be courteous, polite, appreciative, and accepting of differences; respect others' right to make decisions about their own lives; don't abuse, demean, mistreat anyone; don't use, manipulate, exploit, or take advantage of others.*

Responsibility: *Be accountable—think about the consequences on yourself and others likely to be affected before you act; be reliable; perform your duties; take responsibility for the consequences of your choices; set a good example and don't make excuses or take credit for other people's work. Pursue excellence: Do your best, don't quit easily, persevere, be diligent, make all you do worthy of pride. Exercise self-restraint—be disciplined, know the difference between what you have a right to do and what is right to do.*

Fairness: *Treat all people fairly, be open-minded; listen; consider opposing viewpoints; be consistent; use only appropriate considerations; don't let personal feelings improperly interfere with decisions; don't take unfair advantage of mistakes; don't take more than your fair share.*

Caring: *Show you care about others through kindness, caring, sharing, compassion, and empathy; treat others the way you want to be treated; don't be selfish, mean, cruel, or insensitive to others' feelings.*

Citizenship: *Play by the rules, obey laws; do your share, respect authority, stay informed, vote, protect your neighbors, pay your taxes; be charitable, help your community; protect the environment, conserve resources.*

When individuals and organizations confront ethical problems, the core values decision model offered by Josephson generally works well (1) to clarify the gains and losses of the various stakeholders, which then raises ethical awareness on the part of the decision maker and (2) to provide a fairly reliable guide as to what the most ethical decision would be. In many situations, step 5 in the decision process is not needed.

That said, it does not follow that students (or managers) would necessarily act in accordance with the results of the core values decision process. There are many psychological pressures and organizational constraints that place limits on people, both individually and in organizations. These pressures and constraints tend to compromise ideal or the most ethical solutions for individuals and for organizations. For a business, a recurring problem is that companies may intentionally avoid "doing the right thing" where it is likely to cost the organization money or resources in the short term, regardless of reputational effects. Max Bazerman and Ann Tenbrusel have pointed out that businesses often fail to do the right things because of ill-conceived goals, motivated blindness, and valuing outcomes over processes.[4] Finally, a legal system that consistently fails to keep companies from polluting, cheating, bribing, colluding with competition, or avoiding their fair share of taxes will make it seem as though being ethical only allows competitors an advantage.[5]

In summary, a firm doing the most ethical thing will intentionally be rejected, as it may seem antithetical to short-term company goals, or may be overlooked because of "blind spots," or seen as pointless since others' will simply take advantage of their higher standards.

Key Takeaway

Having a step-by-step process to analyze difficult moral dilemmas is useful. One such process is offered here, based on the core values of trustworthiness, caring, respect, fairness, responsibility, and citizenship. Because of organizational blind spots, coming to a rational conclusion as to what is most ethical is seldom simple, and companies may rationalize against doing the right thing.

Exercise

1. Consider XYZ in the exercises for Section 2 and use the core values decision-making model. What are XYZ's options when they first notice that two of their models are causing sudden acceleration incidents that put their customers at risk? Who are the stakeholders? What options most clearly meet the criteria for each of the core values?

2.4 Corporations and Corporate Governance

Learning Objectives

1. Explain the basic structure of the typical corporation and how the shareholders own the company and elect directors to run it.
2. Understand how the shareholder profit-maximization model is different from stakeholder theory.
3. Discern and describe the ethical challenges for corporate cultures.
4. Explain what conscious capitalism is and how it differs from stakeholder theory.

Legal Organization of the Corporation

FIGURE 2.1 Corporate Legal Structure

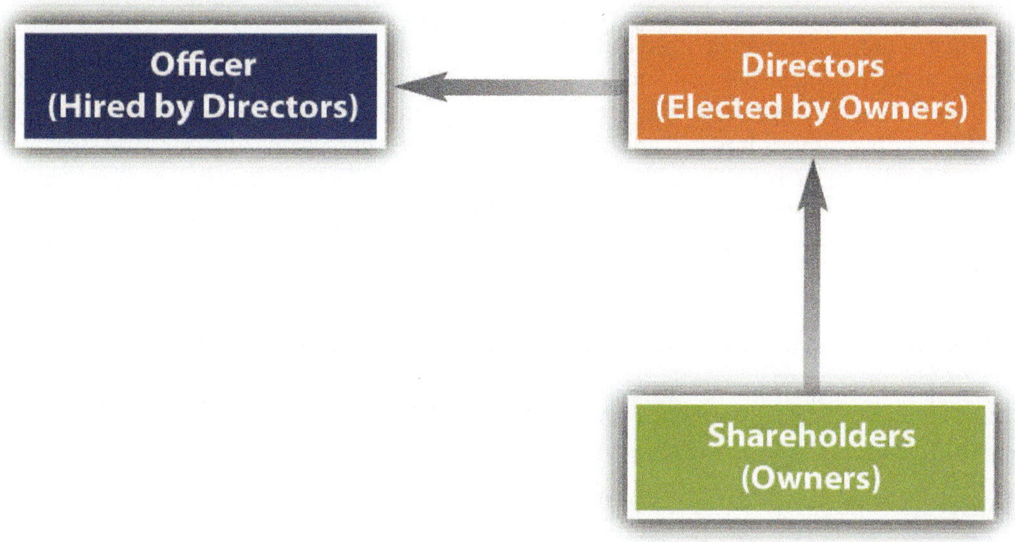

Figure 2.1, though somewhat oversimplified, shows the basic legal structure of a corporation under Delaware law and the laws of most other states in the United States. Shareholders elect directors, who then hire officers to manage the company. From this structure, some very basic realities follow. Because the directors of a corporation do not meet that often, it's possible for the officers hired (top management, or the "C-suite") to be selective of what the board knows about, and directors are not always ready and able to provide the oversight that the shareholders would like. Nor does the law require officers to be shareholders, so that officers' motivations may not align with the best interests of the company. This is the "agency problem" often discussed in corporate governance: how to get officers and other top management to align their own interests with those of the shareholders. For example, a CEO might trade insider information to the detriment of the company's shareholders. Even board members are susceptible to misalignment of interets; for example, board members might resist hostile takeover bids because they would likely lose their perks (short for *perquisites*) as directors, even though the tender offer would benefit stockholders. Among other attempted realignments, the use of stock options was an attempt to make managers more attentive to the value of company stock, but the law of unintended consequences was in full force; managers tweaked and managed earnings in the bubble of the 1990s bull market, and "managing by numbers" became an epidemic in corporations organized under US corporate law. The rights of shareholders can be bolstered by changes in state and federal law, and there have been some attempts to do that since the late 1990s. Ultimately, shareholders do have the power to replace nonperforming or underperforming directors, which usually results in changes at the C-suite level as well.

Shareholders and Stakeholders

There are two main views about what the corporation's duties are. The first view—maximizing profits—is a long-prevailing view among business managers and in business schools. This view assumes that the sole duty of a manager is to maximize return on investment to the owners. Officers and directors do have legally prescribed duties of due care and fidelity to the "owners," although in today's equities markets, the "owners" often vary in their own loyalty and tenure to the firm: many "owners" are merely traders who have no interest in the long-term success of the firm. Still, the officers and directors are legally required to avoid conflicts of interest and to act as "fiduciaries" with respect to the firm. While acknowledging that managers must obey the law and follow ethical customs, economist Milton Friedman emphasized the primacy of maximizing profits in his writings on corporations and social responsibility.

Maximizing Profits: Milton Friedman

Economist Milton Friedman is often quoted as having said that the only moral duty a corporation has is to make the most possible money, or to maximize profits, for its stockholders. Friedman's beliefs are noted at length (see sidebar on Friedman's article from the *New York Times*), but he asserted in a now-famous 1970 article that in a free society, "there is one and only one social responsibility of business: to use its resources and engage in activities designed to increase its profits as long as it stays within the rules of the game, which is to say, engages in open and free competition without deception and fraud." What follows is a major portion of what Friedman had to say in 1970.

"The Social Responsibility of Business Is to Increase Its Profits"

Milton Friedman, *New York Times Magazine*, September 13, 1970

> *What does it mean to say that "business" has responsibilities? Only people can have responsibilities. A corporation is an artificial person and in this sense may have artificial responsibilities, but "business" as a whole cannot be said to have responsibilities, even in this vague sense....*
>
> *Presumably, the individuals who are to be responsible are businessmen, which means individual proprietors or corporate executives....In a free enterprise, private-property system, a corporate executive is an employee of the owners of the business. He has direct responsibility to his employers. That responsibility is to conduct the business in accordance with their desires, which generally will be to make as much money as possible while conforming to the basic rules of the society, both those embodied in law and those embodied in ethical custom....*
>
> *...[T]he manager is that agent of the individuals who own the corporation or establish the eleemosynary institution, and his primary responsibility is to them...*
>
> *Of course, the corporate executive is also a person in his own right. As a person, he may have other responsibilities that he recognizes or assumes voluntarily—to his family, his conscience, his feeling of charity, his church, his clubs, his city, his country. He may feel impelled by these responsibilities to devote part of his income to causes he regards as worthy, to refuse to work for particular corporations, even to leave his job...But in these respects he is acting as a principal, not an agent; he is spending his own money or time or energy, not the money of his employers or the time or energy he has contracted to devote to their purposes. If these are "social responsibilities," they are the social responsibilities of individuals, not of business.*
>
> *What does it mean to say that the corporate executive has a "social responsibility" in his capacity as businessman? If this statement is not pure rhetoric, it must mean that he has to act in some way that is not in the interest of his employers. For example, that he is to refrain from increasing the price of the product in order to contribute to the social objective of preventing inflation, even though a price increase would be in the best interests of the corporation. Or that he is to make expenditures on reducing pollution beyond the amount that is in the best interests of the corporation or that is required by law in order to contribute to the social objective of improving the environment. Or that, at the expense of corporate profits, he is to hire "hardcore" unemployed instead of better qualified available workmen to contribute to the social objective of reducing poverty.*
>
> *In each of these cases, the corporate executive would be spending someone else's money for a general social interest. Insofar as his actions...reduce returns to stockholders, he is spending their money. Insofar as his actions raise the price to customers, he is spending the customers' money. Insofar as his actions lower the wages of some employees, he is spending their money.*
>
> *This process raises political questions on two levels: principle and consequences. On the level of political principle, the imposition of taxes and the expenditure of tax proceeds are governmental functions. We have established elaborate constitutional, parliamentary, and judicial provisions to control these functions, to assure that taxes are imposed so far as possible in accordance with the preferences and desires of the public....*

Others have challenged the notion that corporate managers have no real duties except toward the owners (shareholders). By changing two letters in *shareholder*, stakeholder theorists widened the range of people and institutions that a corporation should pay moral consideration to. Thus they contend that a corporation, through its management, has a set of responsibilities toward non-shareholder interests.

Stakeholder Theory

Stakeholders of a corporation include its employees, suppliers, customers, and the community. Stakeholder is a deliberate play on the word *shareholder*, to emphasize that corporations have obligations that extend beyond the bottom-line aim of maximizing profits. A stakeholder is anyone who most would agree is significantly affected (positively or negatively) by the decision of another moral agent.

There is one vital fact about corporations: the corporation is a creation of the law. Without law (and government), corporations would have no existence. The key concept for corporations is the legal fact of limited liability. The benefit of limited liability for shareholders of a corporation means that larger pools of capital could be aggregated for larger enterprises; shareholders could only lose their investments should the venture fail in any way, and there would be no personal liability and thus no potential loss of personal assets other than the value of the corporate stock. Before New Jersey and Delaware competed to make incorporation as easy as possible and beneficial to the incorporators and founders, those who wanted the benefits of incorporation had to go to legislatures—usually among the states—to show a public purpose that the company would serve.

In the late 1800s, New Jersey and Delaware changed their laws to make incorporating relatively easy. These two states allowed incorporation "for any legal purpose," rather than requiring some public purpose. Thus it is government (and its laws) that makes limited liability happen through the corporate form. That is, only through the consent of the state and armed with the charter granted by the state can a corporation's shareholders have limited liability. This is a right granted by the state, a right granted for good and practical reasons for encouraging capital and innovation. But with this right comes a related duty, not clearly stated at law, but assumed when a charter is granted by the state: that the corporate form of doing business is legal because the government feels that it socially useful to do so.

stakeholder theory

The view that all stakeholders to a corporate decision deserve some kind of moral consideration and that corporations that keep all stakeholders in mind will, over the long term, deliver superior results to shareholders.

Implicitly, then, there is a social contract between governments and corporations: as long as corporations are considered socially useful, they can exist. But do they have explicit social responsibilities? Milton Friedman's position suggests that having gone along with legal duties, the corporation can ignore any other social obligations. But there are others (such as advocates of **stakeholder theory**) who would say that a corporation's social responsibilities go beyond just staying within the law and go beyond the corporation's shareholders to include a number of other important stakeholders, those whose lives can be affected by corporate decisions.

According to stakeholder theorists, corporations (and other business organizations) must pay attention not only to the bottom line but also to their overall effect on the community. Public perception of a company's unfairness, uncaring, disrespect, or lack of trustworthiness often leads to long-term failure, whatever the short-term successes or profits may be. A socially responsible corporation is likely to consider the impact of its decisions on a wide range of stakeholders, not just shareholders. As Table 2.1 indicates, stakeholders have very different kinds of interests ("stakes") in the actions of a corporation.

TABLE 2.1 The Stakes of Various Stakeholders

Ownership	The value of the organization has a direct impact on the wealth of these stakeholders.	Managers
		Directors who own stock
		Shareholders
Economic Dependence	Stakeholders can be economically dependent without having ownership. Each of these stakeholders relies on the corporation in some way for financial well-being.	Salaried managers
		Creditors
		Suppliers
		Employees
		Local communities
Social Interests	These stakeholders are not directly linked to the organization but have an interest in making sure the organization acts in a socially responsible manner.	Communities
		Government
		Media

Corporate Culture and Codes of Ethics

A corporation is a "person" capable of suing, being sued, and having rights and duties in our legal system. (It is a legal or juridical person, not a natural person, according to our Supreme Court.) Moreover, many corporations have distinct cultures and beliefs that are lived and breathed by its members. Often, the culture of a corporation is the best defense against individuals within that firm who may be tempted to break the law or commit serious ethical misdeeds.

What follows is a series of observations about corporations, ethics, and corporate culture.

Ethical Leadership Is Top-Down

People in an organization tend to watch closely what the top managers do and say. Regardless of managers' talk about ethics, employees quickly learn what speech or actions are in fact rewarded. If the CEO is firm about acting ethically, others in the organization will take their cues from him or her. People at the top tend to set the target, the climate, the beliefs, and the expectations that fuel behavior.

Accountability Is Often Weak

Clever managers can learn to shift blame to others, take credit for others' work, and move on before "funny numbers" or other earnings management tricks come to light.[6] Again, we see that the manager is often an agent for himself or herself and will often act more in his or her self-interest than for the corporate interest.

Killing the Messenger

Where organizations no longer function, inevitably some employees are unhappy. If they call attention to problems that are being covered up by coworkers or supervisors, they bring bad news. Managers like to hear good news and discourage bad news. Intentionally or not, those who told on others, or blew the whistle, have rocked the boat and become unpopular with those whose defalcations they report on and with the managers who don't really want to hear the bad news. In many organizations, "killing the messenger" solves the problem. Consider James Alexander at Enron Corporation, who was deliberately shut out after bringing problems to CEO Ken Lay's attention.[7] When Sherron Watkins sent Ken Lay a letter warning him about Enron's accounting practices, CFO Andrew Fastow tried to fire her.[8]

Ethics Codes

Without strong leadership and a willingness to listen to bad news as well as good news, managers do not have the feedback necessary to keep the organization healthy. Ethics codes have been put in place—partly in response to federal sentencing guidelines and partly to encourage feedback loops to top management. The best ethics codes are aspirational, or having an ideal to be pursued, not legalistic or compliance driven. The Johnson & Johnson ethics code predated the Tylenol scare and the company's oft-celebrated corporate response.[9] The corporate response was consistent with that code, which was lived and modeled by the top of the organization.

It's often noted that a code of ethics is only as important as top management is willing to make it. If the code is just a document that goes into a drawer or onto a shelf, it will not effectively encourage good conduct within the corporation. The same is true of any kind of training that the company undertakes, whether it be in racial sensitivity or sexual harassment. If the message is not continuously reinforced, or (worse yet) if the message is undermined by management's actions, the real message to employees is that violations of the ethics code will not be taken seriously, or that efforts to stop racial discrimination or sexual harassment are merely token efforts, and that the important things are profits and performance. The ethics code at Enron seems to have been one of those "3-P" codes that wind up sitting on shelves—"Print, Post, and Pray." Worse, the Enron board twice suspended the code in 1999 to allow outside partnerships to be led by a top Enron executive who stood to gain financially from them.[10]

Ethics Hotlines and Federal Sentencing Guidelines

The federal sentencing guidelines were enacted in 1991. The original idea behind these guidelines was for Congress to correct the lenient treatment often given to white-collar, or corporate, criminals. The guidelines require judges to consider "aggravating and mitigating" factors in determining sentences and fines. (While corporations cannot go to jail, its officers and managers certainly can, and the corporation itself can be fined. Many companies will claim that it is one bad apple that has caused the problem; the guidelines invite these companies to show that they are in fact tending their orchard well. They can show this by providing evidence that they have (1) a viable, active code of ethics; (2) a way for employees to report violations of law or the ethics code; and (3) an ethics ombudsman, or someone who oversees the code.

In short, if a company can show that it has an ongoing process to root out wrongdoing at all levels of the company, the judge is allowed to consider this as a major mitigating factor in the fines the company will pay. Most Fortune 500 companies have ethics hotlines and processes in place to find legal and ethical problems within the company.

Managing by the Numbers

If you manage by the numbers, there is a temptation to lie about those numbers, based on the need to get stock price ever higher. At Enron, "15 percent a year or better earnings growth" was the mantra. Jeffrey Pfeffer, professor of organizational behavior at Stanford University, observes how the belief that "stock price is all that matters" has been hardwired into the corporate psyche. It dictates not only how people judge the worth of their company but also how they feel about themselves and the work that they are doing. And, over time, it has clouded judgments about what is acceptable corporate behavior.[11]

Managing by Numbers: The Sears Auto Center Story

If winning is the most important thing in your life, then you must be prepared to do anything to win.

—Michael Josephson

Most people want to be winners or associate with winners. As humans, our desire to associate with those who have status provides plenty of incentive to glorify winners and ignore losers. But if an individual, a team, or a company does whatever it takes to win, then all other values are thrown out in the goal to win at all costs. The desire of some people within Sears & Roebuck Company's auto repair division to win by gaining higher profits resulted in the situation portrayed here.

Sears Roebuck & Company was a fixture in American retailing throughout the twentieth century. At one time, people in rural America could order virtually anything (including a house) from Sears. Not without some accuracy, the company billed itself as "the place where Americans shop." But in 1992, Sears was charged by California authorities with gross and deliberate fraud in many of its auto centers.

The authorities were alerted by a 50 percent increase in consumer complaints over a three-year period. New Jersey's division of consumer affairs also investigated Sears Auto Centers and found that all six visited by investigators had recommended unnecessary repairs. California's department of consumer affairs found that Sears had systematically overcharged by an average of $223 for repairs and routinely billed for work that was not done. Sears Auto Centers were the largest providers of auto repair services in the state.

The scam was a variant on the old bait-and-switch routine. Customers received coupons in the mail inviting them to take advantage of hefty discounts on brake jobs. When customers came in to redeem their coupons, sales staffers would convince them to authorize additional repairs. As a management tool, Sears had also established quotas for each of their sales representatives to meet.

Ultimately, California got Sears to settle a large number of lawsuits against it by threatening to revoke Sears' auto repair license. Sears agreed to distribute $50 coupons to nearly a million customers nationwide who had obtained certain services between August 1, 1990, and January 31, 1992. Sears also agreed to pay $3.5 million to cover the costs of various government investigations and to contribute $1.5 million annually to conduct auto mechanic training programs. It also agreed to abandon its repair service quotas. The entire settlement cost Sears $30 million. Sears Auto Center sales also dropped about 15 to 20 percent after news of the scandal broke.

Note that in boosting sales by performing unnecessary services, Sears suffered very bad publicity. Losses were incalculable. The short-term gains were easy to measure; long-term consequences seldom are. The case illustrates a number of important lessons:

- People generally choose short-term gains over potential long-term losses.

- People often justify the harm to others as being minimal or "necessary" to achieve the desired sales quota or financial goal.
- In working as a group, we often form an "us versus them" mentality. In the Sears case, it is likely that Sears "insiders" looked at customers as "outsiders," effectively treating them (in Kantian terms) as means rather than ends in themselves. In short, outsiders were used for the benefit of insiders.
- The long-term losses to Sears are difficult to quantify, while the short-term gains were easy to measure and (at least for a brief while) quite satisfying financially.
- Sears' ongoing rip-offs were possible only because individual consumers lacked the relevant information about the service being offered. This lack of information is a market failure, since many consumers were demanding more of Sears Auto Center services than they would have (and at a higher price) if relevant information had been available to them earlier. Sears, like other sellers of goods and services, took advantage of a market system, which, in its ideal form, would not permit such information distortions.
- People in the organization probably thought that the actions they took were necessary.

Noting this last point, we can assume that these key people were motivated by maximizing profits and had lost sight of other goals for the organization.

The emphasis on doing whatever is necessary to win is entirely understandable, but it is not ethical. The temptation will always exist—for individuals, companies, and nations—to dominate or to win and to write the history of their actions in a way that justifies or overlooks the harm that has been done. In a way, this fits with the notion that "might makes right," or that power is the ultimate measure of right and wrong.

Conscious Capitalism

conscious capitalism

Companies that practice conscious capitalism embrace the idea that profit and prosperity can and must go hand in hand with social justice and environmental stewardship.

One effort to integrate the two viewpoints of stakeholder theory and shareholder primacy is the conscious capitalism movement. Companies that practice **conscious capitalism** embrace the idea that profit and prosperity can and must go hand in hand with social justice and environmental stewardship. They operate with a holistic or systems view. This means that they understand that all stakeholders are connected and interdependent. They reject false trade-offs between stakeholder interests and strive for creative ways to achieve win-win-win outcomes for all.[12]

The "conscious business" has a purpose that goes beyond maximizing profits. It is designed to maximize profits but is focused more on its higher purpose and does not fixate solely on the bottom line. To do so, it focuses on delivering value to all its stakeholders, harmonizing as best it can the interests of consumers, partners, investors, the community, and the environment. This requires that company managers take a "servant leadership" role, serving as stewards to the company's deeper purpose and to the company's stakeholders.

Conscious business leaders serve as such stewards, focusing on fulfilling the company's purpose, delivering value to its stakeholders, and facilitating a harmony of interests, rather than on personal gain and self-aggrandizement. Why is this refocusing needed? Within the standard profit-maximizing model, corporations have long had to deal with the "agency problem." Actions by top-level managers—acting on behalf of the company—should align with the shareholders, but in a culture all about winning and money, managers sometimes act in ways that are self-aggrandizing and that do not serve the interests of shareholders. Laws exist to limit such self-aggrandizing, but the remedies are often too little and too late and often catch only the most egregious overreaching. Having a culture of servant leadership is a much better way to see that a company's top management works to ensure a harmony of interests.

Key Takeaway

The corporation sits at the center of a variety of stakeholders, all of whom require managerial attention to different degrees. Thinking ethically as a corporate manager means giving due deliberation to long-term reputation and legal risks.

Exercises

1. Think of a corporation that has recently had a legal or regulatory issue that resulted in lawsuits, government fines, and/or loss of reputation. Do some in-depth reading on that company and list the ways in which its corporate governance for ethics was lacking.

2.5 Summary and Exercises

Summary

Doing good business requires attention to ethics as well as law. Understanding the long-standing perspectives on ethics—utilitarianism, deontology, social contract, and virtue ethics—is helpful in sorting out the ethical issues that face us as individuals and businesses. Each business needs to create or maintain a culture of ethical excellence, where there is ongoing dialogue not only about the best technical practices but also about the company's ethical challenges and practices. A firm that has purpose and passion beyond profitability is best poised to meet the needs of diverse stakeholders and can best position itself for long-term, sustainable success for shareholders and other stakeholders as well.

Exercises

1. Consider again Milton Friedman's article.
    a. What does Friedman mean by "ethical custom"?
    b. If the laws of the society are limiting the company's profitability, would the company be within its rights to disobey the law?
    c. What if the law is "on the books," but the company could count on a lack of enforcement from state officials who were overworked and underpaid? Should the company limit its profits? Suppose that it could save money by discharging a pollutant into a nearby river, adversely affecting fish and, potentially, drinking water supplies for downstream municipalities. In polluting against laws that aren't enforced, is it still acting "within the rules of the game"? What if almost all other companies in the industry were saving money by doing similar acts?
2. Consider again the *Harris v. Forklift* case at the end of Chapter 1. The Supreme Court ruled that Ms. Harris was entitled to be heard again by the federal district court, which means that there would be a trial on her claim that Mr. Hardy, owner of Forklift Systems, had created a "hostile working environment" for Ms. Harris. Apart from the legal aspects, did he really do anything unethical? How can you tell?
    a. Which of his actions, if any, were contrary to utilitarian thinking?
    b. If Kant were his second-in-command and advising him on ethical matters, would he have approved of Mr. Hardy's behavior? Why or why not?

3. Consider the behaviors alleged by Ms. Harris and assume for a moment that they are all true. In terms of core values, which of these behaviors are not consistent with the core values Josephson points to? Be specific.
4. Assume that Forklift Systems is a large public corporation and that the CEO engages in these kinds of behaviors. Assume also that the board of directors knows about it. What action should the board take, and why?
5. Assume that the year is 1963, prior to the passage of the Civil Rights Act of 1964 and the Title VII provisions regarding equal employment opportunity that prohibit discrimination based on sex. So, Mr. Hardy's actions are not illegal, fraudulent, or deceitful. Assume also that he heads a large public company and that there is a large amount of turnover and unhappiness among the women who work for the company. No one can sue him for being sexist or lecherous, but are his actions consistent with maximizing shareholder returns? Should the board be concerned?

   Notice that this question is really a stand-in for any situation faced by a company today regarding its CEO, where the actions are not illegal but are ethically questionable. What would conscious capitalism tell a CEO or a board to do where some group of its employees are regularly harassed or disadvantaged by top management?

Self-Test Questions

1. Milton Friedman would have been most likely to agree to which of the following statements?
   a. The purpose of the corporation is to find a path to sustainable corporate profits by paying careful attention to key stakeholders.
   b. The business of business is business.
   c. The CEO and the board should have a single-minded focus on delivering maximum value to shareholders of the business.
   d. All is fair in love, war, and business.
2. Milton Friedman meant (using the material quoted in this chapter) that companies should
   a. Find a path to sustainable profits by looking at the interconnected needs and desires of all the stakeholders.
   b. Always remember that the business of business is business.
   c. Remind the CEO that he or she has one duty: to maximize shareholder wealth by any means possible.
   d. Maximize shareholder wealth by engaging in open competition without fraud or deceit.
3. What are some key drawbacks to utilitarian thinking at the corporate level?
   a. The corporation may do a cost-benefit analysis that puts the greatest good of the firm above all other considerations.
   b. It is difficult to predict future consequences; decision makers in for-profit organizations will tend to overestimate the upside of certain decisions and underestimate the downside.
   c. Short-term interests will often be favored over long-term consequences.
   d. all of the above
   e. a and b only
4. Which ethical perspective would allow that under certain circumstances, it might be ethical to lie to a liar?
   a. deontology
   b. virtue ethics
   c. utilitarianism
   d. all of the above
5. Under conscious capitalism,

a. Virtue ethics is ignored.
b. Shareholders, whether they be traders or long-term investors, are always the first and last consideration for the CEO and the board.
c. Maximizing profits comes from a focus on higher purposes and harmonizing the interests of various stakeholders.
d. Kantian duties take precedence over cost-benefit analyses.

Self-Test Answers

1. c
2. d
3. d
4. c
5. c

Endnotes

1. See Drumwright, M., Prentice, R. and Biasucci, C. (2015), Behavioral Ethics and Teaching Ethical Decision Making. *Decision Sciences Journal of Innovative Education*, 13: 431–458. doi: 10.1111/dsji.12071
2. LaRue Tone Hosmer, *Moral Leadership in Business* (Chicago: Irwin Professional Publishing, 1994), 72.
3. James O'Toole and Don Mayer, eds., *Good Business: Exercising Effective and Ethical Leadership* (London: Routledge, 2010).
4. Max H. Bazerman and Ann E. Tenbrunsel, *Blind Spots: Why We Fail to Do What's Right and What to Do about It*, (Princeton University Press, 2011).
5. In game theory, the "prisoner's dilemma" has application here. In a 2x2 matrix, the possibilities include variations of cooperation vs. defection. There is a rich literature on game theory, the prisoner's dilemma, and issues of cooperation vs. defection in life and in business. See the Stanford Encyclopedia of Philosophy for a fairly thorough discussion. http://plato.stanford.edu/entries/prisoner-dilemma/
6. See Robert Jackall, *Moral Mazes: The World of Corporate Managers* (New York: Oxford University Press, 1988).
7. John Schwartz, "An Enron Unit Chief Warned, and Was Rebuffed," *New York Times*, February 20, 2002.
8. Warren Bennis, "A Corporate Fear of Too Much Truth," *New York Times*, February 17, 2002.
9. University of Oklahoma Department of Defense Joint Course in Communication, *Case Study: The Johnson & Johnson Tylenol Crisis*, accessed April 5, 2011.
10. FindLaw, *Report of Investigation by the Special Investigative Committee of the Board of Directors of Enron Corp.*, February 1, 2002, accessed April 5, 2011, http://news.findlaw.com/wsj/docs/enron/sicreport.
11. Steven Pearlstein, "Debating the Enron Effect," *Washington Post*, February 17, 2002.
12. Milton Friedman, John Mackey, and T. J. Rodgers, "Rethinking the Social Responsibility of Business," Reason.com, October 2005, http://reason.com/archives/2005/10/01/rethinking-the-social-responsi.

CHAPTER 3

Courts and the Legal Process

Learning Objectives

After reading this chapter, you should be able to do the following:

1. Describe the two different court systems in the United States, and explain why some cases can be filed in either court system.
2. Explain the importance of subject matter jurisdiction and personal jurisdiction and know the difference between the two.
3. Describe the various stages of a civil action: from pleadings, to discovery, to trial, and to appeals.
4. Describe two alternatives to litigation: mediation and arbitration.

In the United States, law and government are interdependent. The Constitution establishes the basic framework of government and imposes certain limitations on the powers of government. In turn, the various branches of government are intimately involved in making, enforcing, and interpreting the law. Today, much of the law comes from Congress and the state legislatures. But it is in the courts that legislation is interpreted and prior case law is interpreted and applied.

As we go through this chapter, consider the case of Harry and Kay Robinson. In which court should the Robinsons file their action? Can the Oklahoma court hear the case and make a judgment that will be enforceable against all of the defendants? Which law will the court use to come to a decision? Will it use New York law, Oklahoma law, federal law, or German law?

Robinson v. Audi

Harry and Kay Robinson purchased a new Audi automobile from Seaway Volkswagen, Inc. (Seaway), in Massena, New York, in 1976. The following year the Robinson family, who resided in New York, left that state for a new home in Arizona. As they passed through Oklahoma, another car struck their Audi in the rear, causing a fire that severely burned Kay Robinson and her two children. Later on, the Robinsons brought a products-liability action in the District Court for Creek County, Oklahoma, claiming that their injuries resulted from the defective design and placement of the Audi's gas tank and fuel system. They sued numerous defendants, including the automobile's manufacturer, Audi NSU Auto Union Aktiengesellschaft (Audi); its importer, Volkswagen of America, Inc. (Volkswagen); its regional distributor, World-Wide Volkswagen Corp. (World-Wide); and its retail dealer, Seaway.

Should the Robinsons bring their action in state court or in federal court? Over which of the defendants will the court have personal jurisdiction?

3.1 The Relationship between State and Federal Court Systems in the United States

Learning Objectives

1. Understand the different but complementary roles of state and federal court systems.
2. Explain why it makes sense for some courts to hear and decide only certain kinds of cases.
3. Describe the difference between a trial court and an appellate court.

Although it is sometimes said that there are two separate court systems, the reality is more complex. There are, in fact, fifty-two court systems: those of the fifty states, the local court system in the District of Columbia, and the federal court system. At the same time, these are not entirely separate; they all have several points of contact.

State and local courts must honor both federal law and the laws of the other states. First, state courts must honor federal law where state laws are in conflict with federal laws (under the supremacy clause of the Constitution; see Chapter 4). Second, claims arising under federal statutes can often be tried in the state courts, where the Constitution or Congress has not explicitly required that only federal courts can hear that kind of claim. Third, under the full faith and credit clause, each state court is obligated to respect the final judgments of courts in other states. Thus a contract dispute resolved by an Arkansas court cannot be relitigated in North Dakota when the plaintiff wants to collect on the Arkansas judgment in North Dakota. Fourth, state courts often must consider the laws of other states in deciding cases involving issues where two states have an interest, such as when drivers from two different states collide in a third state. Under these circumstances, state judges will consult their own state's case decisions involving conflicts of laws and sometimes decide that they must apply another state's laws to decide the case (see Table 3.1).

As state courts are concerned with federal law, so federal courts are often concerned with state law and with what happens in state courts. Federal courts will consider state-law-based claims when a case involves claims using both state and federal law. Claims based on federal laws will permit the federal court to take jurisdiction over the whole case, including any state issues raised. In those cases, the federal court is said to exercise "pendent jurisdiction" over the state claims. Also, the Supreme Court will occasionally take appeals from a state supreme court where state law raises an important issue of federal law to be decided. For example, a convict on death row may claim that the state's chosen method of execution using the injection of drugs is unusually painful and involves "cruel and unusual punishment," raising a federal issue from the Eighth Amendment of the U.S. Constitution.

There is also a broad category of cases heard in federal courts that concern only state legal issues—namely, cases that arise between citizens of different states. The federal courts are permitted to hear these cases under their so-called **diversity of citizenship jurisdiction** (or diversity jurisdiction). A citizen of New Jersey may sue a citizen of New York over a contract dispute in federal court, but if both were citizens of New Jersey, the plaintiff would be limited to the state courts. The Constitution established diversity jurisdiction because it was feared that local courts would be hostile toward people from other states and that they would need separate courts. In 2009, nearly a third of all lawsuits filed in federal court were based on diversity of citizenship. In these cases, the federal courts were applying state law, rather than taking **federal question jurisdiction**, where federal law provided the basis for the lawsuit or where the United States was a party (as plaintiff or defendant).

diversity of citizenship jurisdiction

Subject matter jurisdiction in federal court where the plaintiff is a citizen of one state, no defendant is also a citizen of that state, and the amount in controversy exceeds $75,000.

federal question jurisdiction

Federal court subject matter jurisdiction based on a complaint that uses a federal statutory, regulatory, or constitutional law as a cause of action.

Why are there so many diversity cases in federal courts? Defense lawyers believe that there is sometimes a "home-court advantage" for an in-state plaintiff who brings a lawsuit against a nonresident in his local state court. The defense attorney is entitled to ask for **removal** to a federal court where there is diversity. This fits with the original reason for diversity jurisdiction in the Constitution—the concern that judges in one state court would favor the in-state plaintiff rather than a nonresident defendant. Another reason there are so many diversity cases is that plaintiffs' attorneys know that removal is common and that it will move the case along faster by filing in federal court to begin with. Some plaintiffs' attorneys also find advantages in pursuing a lawsuit in federal court. Federal court procedures are often more efficient than state court procedures, and federal dockets are often less crowded. This means a case will get to trial faster, and many lawyers enjoy the higher status that comes in practicing before the federal bench. In some federal districts, judgments for plaintiffs may be higher, on average, than in local state courts. In short, not only law but also legal strategy factor into the popularity of diversity cases in federal courts.

removal

The right of a defendant to remove a case from state to federal court.

State Court Systems

The vast majority of civil lawsuits in the United States are filed in state courts. Two aspects of civil lawsuits are common to all state courts: trials and appeals. A court exercising a trial function has **original jurisdiction**—that is, jurisdiction to determine the facts of the case and apply the law to them. A court that hears appeals from the trial court is said to have **appellate jurisdiction**—it must accept the facts as determined by the trial court and limit its review to the lower court's theory of the applicable law.

original jurisdiction

The jurisdiction that a judge has to hear witnesses and receive evidence in a trial proceeding.

appellate jurisdiction

The jurisdiction of an appellate court to review whether the parties received a fair trial in accordance with applicable law. Appellate jurisdiction does not include hearing witnesses or receiving new evidence.

Limited Jurisdiction Courts

In most large urban states and many smaller states, there are four and sometimes five levels of courts. The lowest level is that of the limited jurisdiction courts. These are usually county or municipal courts with original jurisdiction to hear minor criminal cases (petty assaults, traffic offenses, and breach of peace, among others) and small claims civil cases involving monetary amounts up to a fixed ceiling (up to $25,000 in Tennessee, with limits of $5,000 to $10,000 being most common, and a low of $3,000 in Alabama and Ohio). The advantage of the small claims court is that its procedures are informal, it is often located in a neighborhood outside the business district, it is usually open after business hours, and it is speedy. Lawyers are not necessary to present the case and in some states are not allowed to appear in court.

General Jurisdiction Courts

All other civil and criminal cases are heard in the general trial courts, or courts of general jurisdiction. These go by a variety of names: superior, circuit, district, or common pleas court (New York calls its general trial court the supreme court). These are the courts in which people seek redress for incidents such as automobile accidents and injuries, or breaches of contract. These state courts also prosecute those accused of murder, rape, robbery, and other serious crimes. The fact finder in these general jurisdiction courts is not a judge, as in the lower courts, but a jury of citizens.

Although courts of general jurisdiction can hear all types of cases, in most states more than half involve family matters (divorce, child custody disputes, and the like). A third were commercial cases, and slightly over 10 percent were devoted to car accident cases and other torts (as discussed in Chapter 7).

Most states have specialized courts that hear only a certain type of case, such as landlord-tenant disputes or probate of wills. Decisions by judges in specialized courts are usually final, although any party dissatisfied with the outcome may be able to get a new trial in a court of general jurisdiction. Because there has been one trial already, this is known as a trial *de novo*. It is not an appeal, since the case essentially starts over.

Appellate Courts

The losing party in a general jurisdiction court can almost always appeal to either one or two higher courts. These intermediate appellate courts—usually called courts of appeal—have been established in forty states. They do not retry the evidence, but rather determine whether the trial was conducted in a procedurally correct manner and whether the appropriate law was applied. For example, the appellant (the losing party who appeals) might complain that the judge wrongly instructed the jury on the meaning of the law, or improperly allowed testimony of a particular witness, or misconstrued the law in question. The appellee (who won in the lower court) will ask that the appellant be denied—usually this means that the appellee wants the lower-court judgment affirmed. The appellate court has quite a few choices: it can affirm, modify, reverse, or reverse and remand the lower court (return the case to the lower court for retrial).

writ of certiorari

The writ issued by a higher court that grants review of the decision of a lower court. In the United States, the Supreme Court's *writ of certiorari* is highly sought by those who would have the court review a state supreme court judgment or that of a federal circuit court of appeals. Most of the cases heard by the Supreme Court are through the granting of a petitioner's appeal to have the writ issued.

The last type of appeal within the state courts system is to the highest court, the state supreme court, which is composed of a single panel of between five and nine judges and is usually located in the state capital. (The intermediate appellate courts are usually composed of panels of three judges and are situated in various locations around the state.) In a few states, the highest court goes by a different name: in New York, it is known as the court of appeals. In certain cases, appellants to the highest court in a state have the right to have their appeals heard, but more often the supreme court selects the cases it wishes to hear. For most litigants, the ruling of the state supreme court is final. In a relatively small class of cases—those in which federal constitutional claims are made—appeal to the US Supreme Court to issue a **writ of certiorari** remains a possibility.

The Federal Court System

District Courts

The federal judicial system is uniform throughout the United States and consists of three levels. At the first level are the federal district courts, which are the trial courts in the federal system. Every state has one or more federal districts; the less populous states have one, and the more populous states (California, Texas, and New York) have four. The federal court with the heaviest commercial docket is the US District Court for the Southern District of New York (Manhattan). There are forty-four district judges and fifteen magistrates in this district. The district judges throughout the United States commonly preside over all federal trials, both criminal and civil.

Courts of Appeal

Cases from the district courts can then be appealed to the circuit courts of appeal, of which there are thirteen (Figure 3.1). Each circuit oversees the work of the district courts in several states. For example, the US Court of Appeals for the Second Circuit hears appeals from district courts in New York, Connecticut, and Vermont. The US Court of Appeals for the Ninth Circuit hears appeals from district courts in California, Oregon, Nevada, Montana, Washington, Idaho, Arizona, Alaska, Hawaii, and Guam. The US Court of Appeals for the District of Columbia Circuit hears appeals from the district court in Washington, DC, as well as from numerous federal administrative agencies (see Chapter 5). The US Court of Appeals for the Federal Circuit, also located in Washington, hears appeals in patent and customs cases. Appeals are usually heard by three-judge panels, but sometimes there will be a rehearing at the court of appeals level, in which case all judges sit to hear the case "en banc."

There are also several specialized courts in the federal judicial system. These include the US Tax Court, the Court of Customs and Patent Appeals, and the Court of Claims.

United States Supreme Court

Overseeing all federal courts is the US Supreme Court, in Washington, DC. It consists of nine justices—the chief justice and eight associate justices. (This number is not constitutionally required; Congress can establish any number. It has been set at nine since after the Civil War.) The Supreme Court has selective control over most of its docket. By law, the cases it hears represent only a tiny fraction of the cases that are submitted. In 2008, the Supreme Court had numerous petitions (over 7,000, not including thousands of petitions from prisoners) but heard arguments in only 87 cases. The Supreme Court does not sit in panels. All the justices hear and consider each case together, unless a justice has a conflict of interest and must withdraw from hearing the case.

FIGURE 3.1 The Federal Judicial Circuits

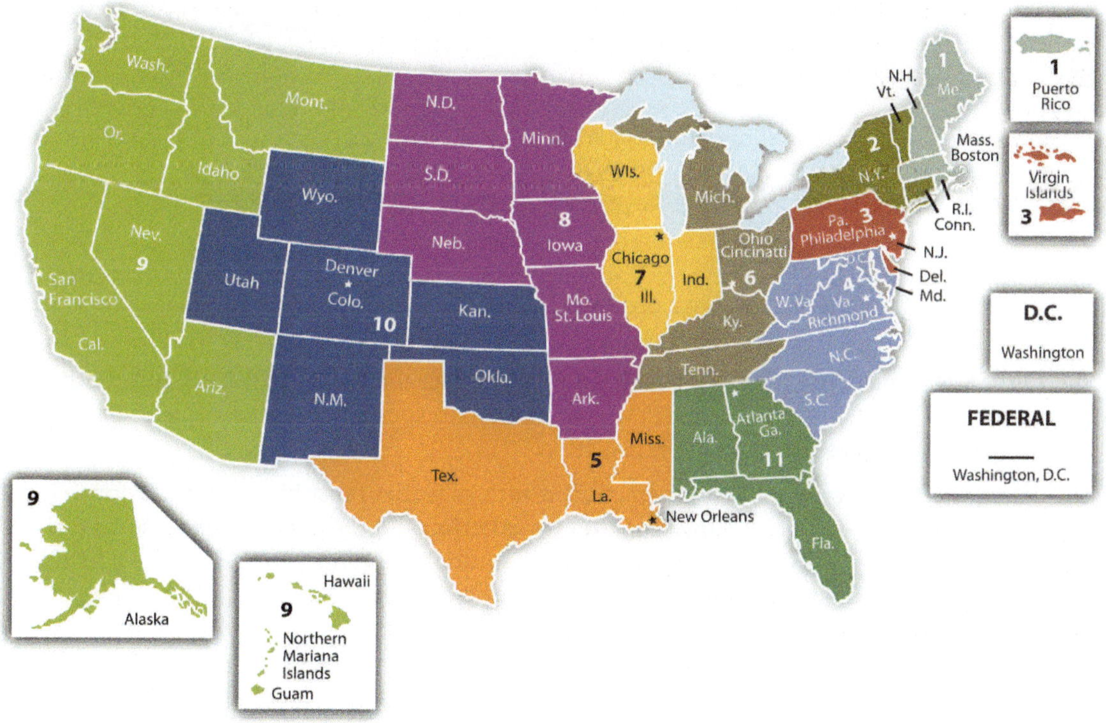

Federal judges—including Supreme Court justices—are nominated by the president and must be confirmed by the Senate. Unlike state judges, who are usually elected and preside for a fixed term of years, federal judges sit for life unless they voluntarily retire or are impeached.

Exercises

1. Why all of this complexity? Why don't state courts hear only claims based on state law, and federal courts only federal-law-based claims?
2. Why would a plaintiff in Iowa with a case against a New Jersey defendant prefer to have the case heard in Iowa?
3. James, a New Jersey resident, is sued by Jonah, an Iowa resident. After a trial in which James appears and vigorously defends himself, the Iowa state court awards Jonah $136,750 dollars in damages for his tort claim. In trying to collect from James in New Jersey, Jonah must have the New Jersey court certify the Iowa judgment. Why, ordinarily, must the New Jersey court do so?

Key Takeaway

Trial courts and appellate courts have different functions. State trial courts sometimes hear cases with federal law issues, and federal courts sometimes hear cases with state law issues. Within both state and federal court systems, it is useful to know the different kinds of courts and what cases they can decide.

3.2 The Problem of Jurisdiction

Learning Objectives

1. Explain the concept of subject matter jurisdiction and distinguish it from personal jurisdiction.
2. Understand how and where the US Constitution provides a set of instructions as to what federal courts are empowered by law to do.
3. Know which kinds of cases must be heard in federal courts only.
4. Explain diversity of citizenship jurisdiction and be able to decide whether a case is eligible for diversity jurisdiction in the federal courts.

Jurisdiction is an essential concept in understanding courts and the legal system. Jurisdiction is a combination of two Latin words: *juris* (law) and *diction* (to speak). Which court has the power "to speak the law" is the basic question of jurisdiction.

subject matter jurisdiction

Legal authority to hear and decide a case or controversy.

There are two questions about jurisdiction in each case that must be answered before a judge will hear a case: the question of **subject matter jurisdiction** and the question of personal jurisdiction. We will consider the question of subject matter jurisdiction first, because judges do; if they determine, on the basis of the initial documents in the case (the "pleadings"), that they have no power to hear and decide that kind of case, they will dismiss it.

The Federal-State Balance: Federalism

State courts have their origins in colonial era courts. After the American Revolution, state courts functioned (with some differences) much like they did in colonial times. The big difference after 1789 was that state courts coexisted with federal courts. **Federalism** was the system devised by the nation's founders in which power is shared between states and the federal government. This sharing requires a division of labor between the states and the federal government. It is Article III of the US Constitution that spells out the respective spheres of authority (jurisdiction) between state and federal courts.

federalism

The idea, originating with the Constitution's Founding Fathers, that the United States legal and political system would be one of governance shared between the states and the federal government.

Take a close look at Article III of the Constitution. (You can find the Constitution at constitution.findlaw.com). Article III makes it clear that federal courts are courts of limited power or jurisdiction. Notice that the only kinds of cases federal courts are authorized to deal with have strong federal connections. For example, federal courts have jurisdiction when a federal law is being used by the plaintiff or prosecutor (a "federal question" case) or the case arises "in admiralty" (meaning that the problem arose not on land but on sea, beyond the territorial jurisdiction of any state, or in navigable waters within the United States). Implied in this list is the clear notion that states would continue to have their own laws, interpreted by their own courts, and that federal courts are needed only where the issues raised by the parties had a clear federal connection. The exception to this is diversity jurisdiction, discussed later.

The Constitution was constructed with the idea that state courts would continue to deal with basic kinds of claims such as tort, contract, or property claims. Since states sanction marriages and divorce, state courts would deal with "domestic" (family) issues. Since states deal with birth and death records, it stands to reason that paternity suits, probate disputes, and the like usually wind up in state courts. You wouldn't go to the federal building or courthouse to get a marriage license, ask for a divorce, or probate a will: these matters have traditionally been dealt with by the states (and the thirteen original colonies before them). Matters that have historically been settled in state courts under state law include not only domestic and probate matters but also law relating to corporations, partnerships, agency, contracts, property, torts, and commercial dealings generally. You cannot get married or divorced in federal court, because federal courts have no jurisdiction over matters that are historically (and are still exclusively) within the domain of state law.

In terms of subject matter jurisdiction, then, state courts will typically deal with the kinds of disputes just cited. Thus if you are Michigan resident and have an auto accident in Toledo with an Ohio resident and you each blame each other for the accident, the state courts would ordinarily resolve the matter if the dispute cannot otherwise be settled. Why state courts? Because when you blame one another and allege that it's the other person's fault, you have the beginnings of a tort case, with negligence as a primary element of the claim, and state courts have routinely dealt with this kind of claim, from British colonial times through Independence and to the present. (See also Chapter 7 of this text.) People have had a need to resolve this kind of dispute long before our federal courts were created, and you can tell from Article III that the founders did not specify that tort or negligence claims should be handled by the federal courts. Again, federal courts are courts of limited jurisdiction, limited to the kinds of cases specified in Article III. If the case before the federal court does not fall within one of those categories, the federal court cannot constitutionally hear the case because it does not have subject matter jurisdiction.

personal jurisdiction

Each court must have subject matter jurisdiction and personal jurisdiction over at least one named defendant. If the defendant is a nonresident where the lawsuit is filed, there may be constitutional issues of personal jurisdiction arising from the due process clause of the Fourteenth Amendment. One state should not claim personal jurisdiction over a nonresident unless various tests are met, such as minimum contacts and the "purposeful availment" test.

statute of limitations

Each state and the federal government has legislated certain time periods beyond which plaintiffs are not allowed to file civil lawsuits. (There are some statutes of limitations for some kinds of criminal offenses, as well.)

Always remember: a court must have subject matter jurisdiction to hear and decide a case. Without it, a court cannot address the merits of the controversy or even take the next jurisdictional step of figuring out which of the defendants can be sued in that court. The question of which defendants are appropriately before the court is a question of **personal jurisdiction**.

Because there are two court systems, it is important for a plaintiff to file in the right court to begin with: one that has subject matter jurisdiction over the case—that is, the power to hear and decide the kind of case that is filed. A court must dismiss a case over which it has no subject matter jurisdiction, and if the dismissal comes after the filing period imposed by an applicable **statute of limitations**, it will be too late to refile in the correct court system. Such cases will be routinely dismissed, regardless of how deserving the plaintiff might be in his quest for justice. (The plaintiff's only remedy at that point would be to sue the lawyer for filing in the wrong court, but then the plaintiff would have to prove that s/he would have recovered if it had been filed and litigated, a difficult proof indeed.)

Exclusive Jurisdiction in Federal Courts

With two court systems, a plaintiff (or the plaintiff's attorney, most likely) must decide whether to file a case in the state court system or the federal court system. Federal courts have exclusive jurisdiction over certain kinds of cases. The reason for this comes directly from the Constitution. Article III of the US Constitution provides the following:

> *The judicial Power shall extend to all Cases, in Law and Equity, arising under this Constitution, the Laws of the United States, and Treaties made, or which shall be made, under their Authority; to all Cases affecting Ambassadors, other public Ministers and Consuls; to all Cases of admiralty and maritime Jurisdiction; to Controversies to which the United States shall be a Party; to Controversies between two or more States; between a State and Citizens of another State; between Citizens of different States; between Citizens of the same State claiming Lands under Grants of different States, and between a State, or the Citizens thereof, and foreign States, Citizens or Subjects.*

By excluding diversity cases, we can assemble a list of the kinds of cases that can only be heard in federal courts. The list looks like this:

1. *Suits between states.* Cases in which two or more states are a party.
2. *Cases involving ambassadors and other high-ranking public figures.* Cases arising between foreign ambassadors and other high-ranking public officials.
3. *Federal crimes.* Crimes defined by or mentioned in the US Constitution or those defined or punished by federal statute. Such crimes include treason against the United States, piracy, counterfeiting, crimes against the law of nations, and crimes relating to the federal government's authority to regulate interstate commerce. However, most crimes are state matters.
4. *Bankruptcy.* The statutory procedure, usually triggered by insolvency, by which a person is relieved of most debts and undergoes a judicially supervised reorganization or liquidation for the benefit of the person's creditors.
5. *Patent, copyright, and trademark cases*
    a. *Patent.* The exclusive right to make, use, or sell an invention for a specified period (usually seventeen years), granted by the federal government to the inventor if the device or process is novel, useful, and nonobvious.
    b. *Copyright.* The body of law relating to a property right in an original work of authorship (such as a literary, musical, artistic, photographic, or film work) fixed in any tan-

gible medium of expression, giving the holder the exclusive right to reproduce, adapt, distribute, perform, and display the work.

   c. *Trademark*. A word, phrase, logo, or other graphic symbol used by a manufacturer or seller to distinguish its product or products from those of others.

6. *Admiralty*. The system of laws that has grown out of the practice of admiralty courts: courts that exercise jurisdiction over all maritime contracts, torts, injuries, and offenses.
7. *Antitrust*. Federal laws designed to protect trade and commerce from restraining monopolies, price fixing, and price discrimination.
8. *Securities and banking regulation*. The body of law protecting the public by regulating the registration, offering, and trading of securities and the regulation of banking practices.
9. *Other cases specified by federal statute*. Any other cases specified by a federal statute where Congress declares that federal courts will have exclusive jurisdiction.

Concurrent Jurisdiction

When a plaintiff takes a case to state court, it will be because state courts typically hear that kind of case (i.e., there is subject matter jurisdiction). If the plaintiff's main cause of action comes from a certain state's constitution, statutes, or court decisions, the state courts have subject matter jurisdiction over the case. If the plaintiff's main cause of action is based on federal law (e.g., Title VII of the Civil Rights Act of 1964), the federal courts have subject matter jurisdiction over the case. But federal courts will also have subject matter jurisdiction over certain cases that have only a state-based cause of action; those cases are ones in which the plaintiff(s) and the defendant(s) are from different states and the amount in controversy is more than $75,000. State courts can have subject matter jurisdiction over certain cases that have only a federal-based cause of action. The Supreme Court has now made clear that state courts have **concurrent jurisdiction** of any federal cause of action unless Congress has given exclusive jurisdiction to federal courts.

concurrent jurisdiction

When both state and federal courts have subject matter jurisdiction of a case, there is concurrent jurisdiction. Only one court will hear the case between the parties and will hear all causes of action, whether based on state or federal law.

In short, a case with a federal question can be often be heard in either state or federal court, and a case that has parties with a diversity of citizenship can be heard in state courts or in federal courts where the tests of complete diversity and amount in controversy are met. (See "Summary of Rules on Subject Matter Jurisdiction".)

Whether a case will be heard in a state court or moved to a federal court will depend on the parties. If a plaintiff files a case in state trial court where concurrent jurisdiction applies, a defendant may (or may not) ask that the case be removed to federal district court.

Summary of Rules on Subject Matter Jurisdiction

1. A court must always have subject matter jurisdiction, and personal jurisdiction over at least one defendant, to hear and decide a case.
2. A state court will have subject matter jurisdiction over any case that is not required to be brought in a federal court.

   Some cases can *only* be brought in federal court, such as bankruptcy cases, cases involving federal crimes, patent cases, and Internal Revenue Service tax court claims. The list of cases for exclusive federal jurisdiction is fairly short. That means that almost any state court will have subject matter jurisdiction over almost any kind of case. If it's a case based on state law, a state court will always have subject matter jurisdiction.
3. A federal court will have subject matter jurisdiction over any case that is either based on a federal law (statute, case, or US Constitution)

   OR

A federal court will have subject matter jurisdiction over any case based on state law where the parties are (1) from different states and (2) the amount in controversy is at least $75,000.

(1) The different states requirement means that no plaintiff can have permanent residence in a state where any defendant has permanent residence—there must be complete diversity of citizenship as between all plaintiffs and defendants.

(2) The amount in controversy requirement means that a good-faith estimate of the amount the plaintiff may recover is at least $75,000.01.

NOTE: For purposes of permanent residence, a corporation is considered a resident where it is incorporated AND where it has a principal place of business.

1. In diversity cases, the following rules apply.

   (1) Federal civil procedure rules apply to how the case is conducted before and during trial and any appeals, but

   (2) State law will be used as the basis for a determination of legal rights and responsibilities.

   (a) This "choice of law" process is interesting but complicated. Basically, each state has its own set of judicial decisions that resolve conflict of laws. For example, just because A sues B in a Texas court, the Texas court will not necessarily apply Texas law. Anna and Bobby collide and suffer serious physical injuries while driving their cars in Roswell, New Mexico. Both live in Austin, and Bobby files a lawsuit in Austin. The court there could hear it (having subject matter jurisdiction and personal jurisdiction over Bobby) but would apply New Mexico law, which governs motor vehicle laws and accidents in New Mexico. Why would the Texas judge do that?

   (b) The Texas judge knows that which state's law is chosen to apply to the case can make a decisive difference in the case, as different states have different substantive law standards. For example, in a breach of contract case, one state's version of the Uniform Commercial Code may be different from another's, and which one the court decides to apply is often exceedingly good for one side and dismal for the other. In *Anna v. Bobby*, if Texas has one kind of comparative negligence statute and New Mexico has a different kind of comparative negligence statute, who wins or loses, or how much is awarded, could well depend on which law applies. Because both were under the jurisdiction of New Mexico's laws at the time, it makes sense to apply New Mexico law.

   (3) Why do some nonresident defendants prefer to be in federal court?

   (a) In the state court, the judge is elected, and the jury may be familiar with or sympathetic to the "local" plaintiff.

   (b) The federal court provides a more neutral forum, with an appointed, life-tenured judge and a wider pool of potential jurors (drawn from a wider geographical area).

   (4) If a defendant does not want to be in state court and there is diversity, what is to be done?

   (a) Make a motion for removal to the federal court.

   (b) The federal court will not want to add to its caseload, or docket, but must take the case unless there is *not* complete diversity of citizenship or the amount in controversy is *less than* $75,000.01.

To better understand subject matter jurisdiction in action, let's take an example. Wile E. Coyote wants a federal judge to hear his products-liability action against Acme, Inc., even though the action is based on state law. Mr. Coyote's attorney wants to "make a federal case" out of it, thinking that the jurors in the federal district court's jury pool will understand the case better and be more likely to deliver a "high value" verdict for Mr. Coyote. Mr. Coyote resides in Arizona, and Acme is incorporated in the state of Delaware and has its principal place of business in Chicago, Illinois. The federal court in Arizona can hear and decide Mr. Coyote's case (i.e., it has subject matter jurisdiction over the case) because of diversity of citizenship. If Mr. Coyote was injured by one of Acme's defective products while chasing a roadrunner in Arizona, the federal district court judge would hear his action—using federal procedural law—and decide the case based on the substantive law of Arizona on product liability.

But now change the facts only slightly: Acme is incorporated in Delaware but has its principal place of business in Phoenix, Arizona. Unless Mr. Coyote has a federal law he is using as a basis for his claims against Acme, his attempt to get a federal court to hear and decide the case will fail. It will fail because there is not complete diversity of citizenship between the plaintiff and the defendant.

Robinson v. Audi

Now consider Mr. and Mrs. Robinson and their products-liability claim against Seaway Volkswagen and the other three defendants. There is no federal products-liability law that could be used as a cause of action. They are most likely suing the defendants using products-liability law based on common-law negligence or common-law strict liability law, as found in state court cases. They were not yet Arizona residents at the time of the accident, and their accident does not establish them as Oklahoma residents, either. They bought the vehicle in New York from a New York–based retailer. None of the other defendants is from Oklahoma.

They file in an Oklahoma state court, but how will they (their attorney or the court) know if the state court has subject matter jurisdiction? Unless the case is *required* to be in a federal court (i.e., unless the federal courts have exclusive jurisdiction over this kind of case), *any* state court system will have subject matter jurisdiction, including Oklahoma's state court system. But if their claim is for a significant amount of money, they cannot file in small claims court, probate court, or any court in Oklahoma that does not have statutory jurisdiction over their claim. They will need to file in a court of general jurisdiction. In short, even filing in the right court system (state versus federal), the plaintiff must be careful to find the court that has subject matter jurisdiction.

If they wish to go to federal court, can they? There is no federal question presented here (the claim is based on state common law), and the United States is not a party, so the only basis for federal court jurisdiction would be diversity jurisdiction. If enough time has elapsed since the accident and they have established themselves as Arizona residents, they could sue in federal court in Oklahoma (or elsewhere), but only if none of the defendants—the retailer, the regional Volkswagen company, Volkswagen of North America, or Audi (in Germany) are incorporated in or have a principal place of business in Arizona. The federal judge would decide the case using federal civil procedure but would have to make the appropriate choice of state law. In this case, the choice of conflicting laws would most likely be Oklahoma, where the accident happened, or New York, where the defective product was sold.

TABLE 3.1 Sample Conflict-of-Law Principles

Substantive Law Issue	Law to be Applied
Liability for injury caused by tortious conduct	State in which the injury was inflicted
Real property	State where the property is located
Personal Property: inheritance	Domicile of deceased (not location of property)
Contract: validity	State in which contract was made
Contract: breach	State in which contract was to be performed*
*Or, in many states, the state with the most significant contacts with the contractual activities	
Note: Choice-of-law clauses in a contract will ordinarily be honored by judges in state and federal courts.	

Legal Procedure, Including Due Process and Personal Jurisdiction

In this section, we consider how lawsuits are begun and how the court knows that it has both subject matter jurisdiction and personal jurisdiction over at least one of the named defendants.

The courts are not the only institutions that can resolve disputes. In Section 8, we will discuss other dispute-resolution forums, such as arbitration and mediation. For now, let us consider how courts make decisions in civil disputes. Judicial decision making in the context of litigation (civil lawsuits) is a distinctive form of dispute resolution.

First, to get the attention of a court, the plaintiff must make a claim based on existing laws. Second, courts do not reach out for cases. Cases are brought to them, usually when an attorney files a case with the right court in the right way, following the various laws that govern all civil procedures in a state or in the federal system. (Most US states' procedural laws are similar to the federal procedural code.)

Once at the court, the case will proceed through various motions (motions to dismiss for lack of jurisdiction, for example, or insufficient service of process), the proofs (submission of evidence), and the arguments (debate about the meaning of the evidence and the law) of contesting parties.

This is at the heart of the adversary system, in which those who oppose each other may attack the other's case through proofs and cross-examination. Every person in the United States who wishes to take a case to court is entitled to hire a lawyer. The lawyer works for his client, not the court, and serves him as an advocate, or supporter. The client's goal is to persuade the court of the accuracy and justness of his position. The lawyer's duty is to shape the evidence and the argument—the line of reasoning about the evidence—to advance his client's cause and persuade the court of its rightness. The lawyer for the opposing party will be doing the same thing, of course, for her client. The judge (or, if one is sitting, the jury) must sort out the facts and reach a decision from this cross-fire of evidence and argument.

The method of adjudication—the act of making an order or judgment—has several important features. First, it focuses the conflicting issues. Other, secondary concerns are minimized or excluded altogether. Relevance is a key concept in any trial. The judge is required to decide the questions presented at the trial, not to talk about related matters. Second, adjudication requires that the judge's decision be reasoned, and that is why judges write opinions explaining their decisions (an opinion may be omitted when the verdict comes from a jury). Third, the judge's decision must not only be reasoned but also be responsive to the case presented: the judge is not free to say that the case is unimportant and that he therefore will ignore it. Unlike other branches of government that are free to ignore problems pressing upon them, judges *must* decide cases. (For example, a legislature need not enact a law, no matter how many people petition it to do so.) Fourth, the court must respond in a certain way. The judge must pay attention to the parties' arguments and his decision must result from their proofs and arguments. Evidence that is not presented and legal arguments that are not made cannot be the basis for what the judge decides. Also, judges are bound by standards of weighing evidence: the burden of proof in a civil case is generally a "preponderance of the evidence."

In all cases, the plaintiff—the party making a claim and initiating the lawsuit (in a criminal case the plaintiff is the prosecution)—has the burden of proving his case. If he fails to prove it, the defendant—the party being sued or prosecuted—will win.

Criminal prosecutions carry the most rigorous burden of proof: the government must prove its case against the defendant *beyond a reasonable doubt*. That is, even if it seems very likely that the defendant committed the crime, as long as there remains some reasonable doubt—perhaps he was not clearly identified as the culprit, perhaps he has an alibi that could be legitimate—the jury must vote to acquit rather than convict.

By contrast, the burden of proof in ordinary civil cases—those dealing with contracts, personal injuries, and most of the cases in this book—is a *preponderance of the evidence*, which means that the plaintiff's evidence must outweigh whatever evidence the defendant can muster that casts doubts on the plaintiff's claim. This is not merely a matter of counting the number of witnesses or of the length of time that they talk: the judge in a trial without a jury (a bench trial), or the jury where one is impaneled, must apply the preponderance of evidence test by determining which side has the greater weight of credible, relevant evidence.

Adjudication and the adversary system imply certain other characteristics of courts. Judges must be impartial; those with a personal interest in a matter must refuse to hear it. The ruling of a court, after all appeals are exhausted, is final. This principle is known as **res judicata** (Latin for "the thing is decided"), and it means that the same parties may not take up the same dispute in another court at another time. Finally, a court must proceed according to a public set of formal procedural rules; a judge cannot make up the rules as he goes along. To these rules we now turn.

res judicata

"The matter has been adjudicated." The same case or controversy cannot be heard and concluded in one court and relitigated in another. The same parties may have different issues and disputes, but a final judgment in a court that has jurisdiction over the case or controversy forever settles the matter.

How a Case Proceeds

Complaint and Summons

Beginning a lawsuit is simple and is spelled out in the rules of procedure by which each court system operates. In the federal system, the plaintiff begins a lawsuit by filing a complaint—a document clearly explaining the grounds for suit—with the clerk of the court. The court's agent (usually a sheriff, for state trial courts, or a US deputy marshal, in federal district courts) will then serve the defendant with the complaint and a summons. The summons is a court document stating the name of the plaintiff and his attorney and directing the defendant to respond to the complaint within a fixed time period.

The timing of the filing can be important. Almost every possible legal complaint is governed by a federal or state statute of limitations, which requires a lawsuit to be filed within a certain period of time. For example, in many states a lawsuit for injuries resulting from an automobile accident must be filed within two years of the accident or the plaintiff forfeits his right to proceed. As noted earlier, making a correct initial filing in a court that has subject matter jurisdiction is critical to avoiding statute of limitations problems.

Jurisdiction and Venue

The place of filing is equally important, and there are two issues regarding location. The first is subject matter jurisdiction, as already noted. A claim for breach of contract, in which the amount at stake is $1 million, cannot be brought in a local county court with jurisdiction to hear cases involving sums of up to only $1,000. Likewise, a claim for copyright violation cannot be brought in a state superior court, since federal courts have exclusive jurisdiction over copyright cases.

The second consideration is venue—the proper geographic location of the court. For example, every county in a state might have a superior court, but the plaintiff is not free to pick any county. Again, a statute will spell out to which court the plaintiff must go (e.g., the county in which the plaintiff resides or the county in which the defendant resides or maintains an office).

Service of Process and Personal Jurisdiction

The defendant must be "served"—that is, must receive notice that he has been sued. Service can be done by physically presenting the defendant with a copy of the summons and complaint. But sometimes the defendant is difficult to find (or deliberately avoids the marshal or other process server). The rules spell out a variety of ways by which individuals and corporations can be served. These include using US Postal Service certified mail or serving someone already designated to receive service of process. A corporation or partnership, for example, is often required by state law to designate a "registered agent" for purposes of getting public notices or receiving a summons and complaint.

One of the most troublesome problems is service on an out-of-state defendant. The personal jurisdiction of a state court over persons is clear for those defendants found within the state. If the plaintiff claims that an out-of-state defendant injured him in some way, must the plaintiff go to the defendant's home state to serve him? Unless the defendant had some significant contact with the plaintiff's state, the plaintiff may indeed have to. For instance, suppose a traveler from Maine stopped at a roadside diner in Montana and ordered a slice of homemade pie that was tainted and caused him to be sick. The traveler may not simply return home and mail the diner a notice that he is suing it in a Maine court. But if out-of-state defendants have some contact with the plaintiff's state of residence, there might be grounds to bring them within the jurisdiction of the plaintiff's state courts. In *Burger King v. Rudzewicz*, Section 9, the federal court in Florida had to consider whether it was constitutionally permissible to exercise personal jurisdiction over a Michigan franchisee.

Again, recall that even if a court has subject matter jurisdiction, it must also have personal jurisdiction over each defendant against whom an enforceable judgment can be made. Often this is not a problem; you might be suing a person who lives in your state or regularly does business in your state. Or a nonresident may answer your complaint without objecting to the court's "in personam" (personal) jurisdiction. But many defendants who do not reside in the state where the lawsuit is filed would rather not be put to the inconvenience of contesting a lawsuit in a distant forum. Fairness—and the due process clause of the Fourteenth Amendment—dictates that nonresidents should not be required to defend lawsuits far from their home base, especially where there is little or no contact or connection between the nonresident and the state where a lawsuit is brought.

Summary of Rules on Personal Jurisdiction

1. Once a court determines that it has subject matter jurisdiction, it must find at least one defendant over which it is "fair" (i.e., in accord with due process) to exercise personal jurisdiction.
2. If a plaintiff sues five defendants and the court has personal jurisdiction over just one, the case can be heard, but the court cannot make a judgment against the other four.

    2.1. But if the plaintiff loses against defendant 1, he can go elsewhere (to another state or states) and sue defendants 2, 3, 4, or 5.

    2.2. The court's decision in the first lawsuit (against defendant 1) does not determine the liability of the nonparticipating defendants.

    This involves the principle of res judicata, which means that you can't bring the same action against the same person (or entity) twice. It's like the civil side of double jeopardy. *Res* means "thing," and *judicata* means "adjudicated." Thus the "thing" has been "adjudicated" and should not be judged again. But, as to nonparticipating parties, it is not over. If you have a *different* case against the same defendant—one that arises out of a completely different situation—that case is not barred by res judicata.
3. Service of process is a necessary (but not sufficient) condition for getting personal jurisdiction over a particular defendant (see rule 4).

    3.1. In order to get a judgment in a civil action, the plaintiff must serve a copy of the complaint and a summons on the defendant.

    3.2. There are many ways to do this.

    - The process server personally serves a complaint on the defendant.
    - The process server leaves a copy of the summons and complaint at the residence of the defendant, in the hands of a competent person.

- The process server sends the summons and complaint by certified mail, return receipt requested.
- The process server, if all other means are not possible, notifies the defendant by publication in a newspaper having a minimum number of readers (as may be specified by law).

4. In addition to successfully serving the defendant with process, a plaintiff must convince the court that exercising personal jurisdiction over the defendant is consistent with due process and any statutes in that state that prescribe the jurisdictional reach of that state (the so-called long-arm statutes). The Supreme Court has long recognized various bases for judging whether such process is fair.
   4.1. Consent. The defendant agrees to the court's jurisdiction by coming to court, answering the complaint, and having the matter litigated there.
   4.2. Domicile. The defendant is a permanent resident of that state.
   4.3. Event. The defendant did something in that state, related to the lawsuit, that makes it fair for the state to say, "Come back and defend!"
   4.4. Service of process within the state will effectively provide personal jurisdiction over the nonresident.

Again, let's consider Mrs. Robinson and her children in the Audi accident. She could file a lawsuit anywhere in the country. She could file a lawsuit in Arizona after she establishes residency there. But while the Arizona court would have subject matter jurisdiction over any products-liability claim (or any claim that was not required to be heard in a federal court), the Arizona court would face an issue of "*in personam* jurisdiction," or personal jurisdiction: under the due process clause of the Fourteenth Amendment, each state must extend due process to citizens of all of the other states. Because fairness is essential to due process, the court must consider whether it is fair to require an out-of-state defendant to appear and defend against a lawsuit that could result in a judgment against that defendant.

Almost every state in the United States has a statute regarding personal jurisdiction, instructing judges when it is permissible to assert personal jurisdiction over an out-of-state resident. These are called long-arm statutes. But no state can reach out beyond the limits of what is constitutionally permissible under the Fourteenth Amendment, which binds the states with its proviso to guarantee the due process rights of the citizens of every state in the union. The "minimum contacts" test in *Burger King v. Rudzewicz* (Section 9) tries to make the fairness mandate of the due process clause more specific. So do other tests articulated in the case (such as "does not offend traditional notions of fair play and substantial justice"). These tests are posed by the Supreme Court and heeded by all lower courts in order to honor the provisions of the Fourteenth Amendment's due process guarantees. These tests are *in addition to* any state long-arm statute's instructions to courts regarding the assertion of personal jurisdiction over nonresidents.

Choice of Law and Choice of Forum Clauses

In a series of cases, the Supreme Court has made clear that it will honor contractual choices of parties in a lawsuit. Suppose the parties to a contract wind up in court arguing over the application of the contract's terms. If the parties are from two different states, the judge may have difficulty determining which law to apply (see Table 3.1). But if the contract says that a particular state's law will be applied if there is a dispute, then ordinarily the judge will apply that state's law as a rule of decision in the case. For example, Kumar Patel (a Missouri resident) opens a brokerage account with Goldman, Sachs and Co., and the contractual agreement calls for "any disputes arising under this agreement" to be determined "according to the laws of the state of New York." When Kumar claims in a Missouri court that his broker is "churning" his account, and, on the other hand, Goldman, Sachs claims that Kumar has failed to meet his margin call and owes $38,568.25 (plus interest and attorney's fees), the judge in Missouri will apply New York law based on the contract between Kumar and Goldman, Sachs.

Ordinarily, a choice-of-law clause will be accompanied by a choice-of-forum clause. In a choice-of-forum clause, the parties in the contract specify which court they will go to in the event of a dispute arising under the terms of contract. For example, Harold (a resident of Virginia) rents a car from Alamo at the Denver International Airport. He does not look at the fine print on the contract. He also waives all collision and other insurance that Alamo offers at the time of his rental. While driving back from Telluride Bluegrass Festival, he has an accident in Idaho Springs, Colorado. His rented Nissan Altima is badly damaged. On returning to Virginia, he would like to settle up with Alamo, but his insurance company and Alamo cannot come to terms. He realizes, however, that he has agreed to hear the dispute with Alamo in a specific court in San Antonio, Texas. In the absence of fraud or bad faith, any court in the United States is likely to uphold the choice-of-form clause and require Harold (or his insurance company) to litigate in San Antonio, Texas.

Key Takeaway

There are two court systems in the United States. It is important to know which system—the state court system or the federal court system—has the power to hear and decide a particular case. Once that is established, the Constitution compels an inquiry to make sure that no court extends its reach unfairly to out-of-state residents. The question of personal jurisdiction is a question of fairness and due process to nonresidents.

Exercises

1. The Constitution specifies that federal courts have exclusive jurisdiction over admiralty claims. Mr. and Mrs. Shute have a claim against Carnival Cruise lines for the negligence of the cruise line. Mrs. Shute sustained injuries as a result of the company's negligence. Mr. and Mrs. Shute live in the state of Washington. Can they bring their claim in state court? Must they bring their claim in federal court?
2. Congress passed Title VII of the Civil Rights Act of 1964. In Title VII, employers are required not to discriminate against employees on the basis of race, color, sex, religion, or national origin. In passing Title VII, Congress did not require plaintiffs to file only in federal courts. That is, Congress made no statement in Title VII that federal courts had "exclusive jurisdiction" over Title VII claims. Mrs. Harris wishes to sue Forklift Systems, Inc. of Nashville, Tennessee, for sexual harassment under Title VII. She has gone through the Equal Employment Opportunity Commission process and has a right-to-sue letter, which is required before a Title VII action can be brought to court. Can she file a complaint that will be heard by a state court?
3. Mrs. Harris fails to go to the Equal Employment Opportunity Commission to get her right-to-sue letter against Forklift Systems, Inc. She therefore does not have a viable Title VII cause of action against Forklift. She does, however, have her rights under Tennessee's equal employment statute and various court decisions from Tennessee courts regarding sexual harassment. Forklift is incorporated in Tennessee and has its principal place of business in Nashville. Mrs. Harris is also a citizen of Tennessee. Explain why, if she brings her employment discrimination and sexual harassment lawsuit in a federal court, her lawsuit will be dismissed for lack of subject matter jurisdiction.
4. Suppose Mr. and Mrs. Robinson find in the original paperwork with Seaway Volkswagen that there is a contractual agreement with a provision that says "all disputes arising between buyer and Seaway Volkswagen will be litigated, if at all, in the county courts of Westchester County, New York." Will the Oklahoma court take personal jurisdiction over Seaway Volkswagen, or will it require the Robinsons to litigate their claim in New York?

3.3 Motions and Discovery

Learning Objectives

1. Explain how a lawsuit can be dismissed prior to any trial.
2. Understand the basic principles and practices of discovery before a trial.

The early phases of a civil action are characterized by many different kinds of motions and a complex process of mutual fact-finding between the parties that is known as discovery. A lawsuit will start with the **pleadings** (complaint and answer in every case, and in some cases a counterclaim by the defendant against the plaintiff and the plaintiff's reply to the defendant's counterclaim). After the pleadings, the parties may make various **motions**, which are requests to the judge. Motions in the early stages of a lawsuit usually aim to dismiss the lawsuit, to have it moved to another venue, or to compel the other party to act in certain ways during the discovery process.

pleadings

The initial documents filed by parties in a lawsuit.

motions

Written requests made to a presiding judge. These include motions to dismiss, motions for summary judgment, motions to direct an opposing party to divulge more in discovery, motions for a directed verdict, motions for judgment n.o.v., and many others.

Initial Pleadings, and Motions to Dismiss

The first papers filed in a lawsuit are called the pleadings. These include the plaintiff's complaint and then (usually after thirty or more days) the answer or response from the defendant. The answer may be coupled with a counterclaim against the plaintiff. (In effect, the defendant becomes the plaintiff for the claims she has against the original plaintiff.) The plaintiff may reply to any counterclaim by the defendant.

State and federal rules of civil procedure require that the complaint must state the nature of the plaintiff's claim, the jurisdiction of the court, and the nature of the relief that is being asked for (usually an award of money, but sometimes an injunction, or a declaration of legal rights). In an answer, the defendant will often deny all the allegations of the complaint or will admit to certain of its allegations and deny others.

A complaint and subsequent pleadings are usually quite general and give little detail. Cases can be decided on the pleadings alone in the following situations: (1) If the defendant fails to answer the complaint, the court can enter a default judgment, awarding the plaintiff what he seeks. (2) The defendant can move to dismiss the complaint on the grounds that the plaintiff failed to "state a claim on which relief can be granted," or on the basis that there is no subject matter jurisdiction for the court chosen by the plaintiff, or on the basis that there is no personal jurisdiction over the defendant. The defendant is saying, in effect, that even if all the plaintiff's allegations are true, they do not amount to a legal claim that can be heard by the court. For example, a claim that the defendant induced a woman to stop dating the plaintiff (a so-called alienation of affections cause of action) is no longer actionable in US state courts, and any court will dismiss the complaint without any further proceedings. (This type of dismissal is occasionally still called a demurrer.)

A third kind of dismissal can take place on a motion for **summary judgment**. If there is no triable question of fact or law, there is no reason to have a trial. For example, the plaintiff sues on a promissory note and, at deposition (an oral examination under oath), the defendant admits having made no payment on the note and offers no excuse that would be recognizable as a reason not to pay. There is no reason to have a trial, and the court should grant summary judgment.

summary judgment

As in a directed verdict, when a judge grants summary judgment, she has concluded that there are no matters of law or fact on which reasonable people would disagree. Summary judgment is a final order, and it is appealable.

Discovery

If there is a factual dispute, the case will usually involve some degree of discovery, where each party tries to get as much information out of the other party as the rules allow. Until the 1940s, when discovery became part of civil procedure rules, a lawsuit was frequently a game in which each party hid as much information as possible and tried to surprise the other party in court.

Beginning with a change in the Federal Rules of Civil Procedure adopted by the Supreme Court in 1938 and subsequently followed by many of the states, the parties are entitled to learn the facts of the case before trial. The basic idea is to help the parties determine what the evidence might be, who the potential witnesses are, and what specific issues are relevant. Discovery can proceed by several methods. A party may serve an interrogatory on his adversary—a written request for answers to specific questions. Or a party may depose the other party or a witness. A deposition is a live question-and-answer session at which the witness answers questions put to him by one of the parties' lawyers. His answers are recorded verbatim and may be used at trial. Each party is also entitled to inspect books, documents, records, and other physical items in the possession of the other. This is a broad right, as it is not limited to just evidence that is admissible at trial. Discovery of physical evidence means that a plaintiff may inspect a company's accounts, customer lists, assets, profit-and-loss statements, balance sheets, engineering and quality-control reports, sales reports, and virtually any other document.

The lawyers, not the court, run the discovery process. For example, one party simply makes a written demand, stating the time at which the deposition will take place or the type of documents it wishes to inspect and make copies of. A party unreasonably resisting discovery methods (whether depositions, written interrogatories, or requests for documents) can be challenged, however, and judges are often brought into the process to push reluctant parties to make more disclosure or to protect a party from irrelevant or unreasonable discovery requests. For example, the party receiving the discovery request can apply to the court for a protective order if it can show that the demand is for privileged material (e.g., a party's lawyers' records are not open for inspection) or that the demand was made to harass the opponent. In complex cases between companies, the discovery of documents can run into tens of millions of pages and can take years. Depositions can consume days or even weeks of an executive's time.

Key Takeaway

Many cases never get to trial. They are disposed of by motions to dismiss or are settled after extensive discovery makes clear to the parties the strengths and weaknesses of the parties to the dispute.

Exercises

1. Suppose Mrs. Robinson (in the Volkswagen Audi case) never establishes residency in Arizona, returns to New York, and files her case in federal district court in New York state against the dealer, alleging diversity jurisdiction, even though she only spent a few months in Arizona and never voted or owned property there. Assume that the defendants do not want to have the case heard in federal court. What motion will they make?
2. Under contributory negligence, the negligence of any plaintiff that causes or contributes to the injuries a plaintiff complains of will be grounds for dismissal. Suppose that in discovery, Mr. Ferlito in *Ferlito v. Johnson & Johnson* (Section 9) admits that he brought the cigarette lighter dangerously close to his costume, saying, "Yes, you could definitely say I was being careless; I had a few drinks under my belt." Also, Mrs. Ferlito admits that she never reads product instructions from manufacturers. If the case is brought in a state where contributory negligence is the law, on what basis can Johnson & Johnson have the case dismissed before trial?

3.4 The Pretrial and Trial Phase

Learning Objectives

1. Understand how judges can push parties into pretrial settlement.
2. Explain the meaning and use of directed verdicts.
3. Distinguish a directed verdict from a judgment n.o.v. ("notwithstanding the verdict").

After considerable discovery, one of the parties may believe that there is no triable issue of law or fact for the court to consider and may file a motion with the court for summary judgment. Unless it is very clear, the judge will deny a summary judgment motion, because that ends the case at the trial level; it is a "final order" in the case that tells the plaintiff "no" and leaves no room to bring another lawsuit against the defendant for that particular set of facts (res judicata). If the plaintiff successfully appeals a summary judgment motion, the case will come back to the trial court.

Prior to the trial, the judge may also convene the parties in an effort to investigate the possibilities of settlement. Usually, the judge will explore the strengths and weaknesses of each party's case with the attorneys. The parties may decide that it is more prudent or efficient to settle than to risk going to trial.

Pretrial Conference

At various times during the discovery process, depending on the nature and complexity of the case, the court may hold a pretrial conference to clarify the issues and establish a timetable. The court may also hold a settlement conference to see if the parties can work out their differences and avoid trial altogether. Once discovery is complete, the case moves on to trial if it has not been settled. Most cases are settled before this stage; perhaps 85 percent of all civil cases end before trial, and more than 90 percent of criminal prosecutions end with a guilty plea.

Trial

At trial, the first order of business is to select a jury. (In a civil case of any consequence, either party can request one, based on the Sixth Amendment to the US Constitution.) The judge and sometimes the lawyers are permitted to question the jurors to be sure that they are unbiased. This questioning is known as the voir dire (pronounced vwahr-DEER). This is an important process, and a great deal of thought goes into selecting the jury, especially in high-profile cases. A jury panel can be as few as six persons, or as many as twelve, with alternates selected and sitting in court in case one of the jurors is unable to continue. In a long trial, having alternates is essential; even in shorter trials, most courts will have at least two alternate jurors.

In both criminal and civil trials, each side has opportunities to challenge potential jurors for cause. For example, in the Robinsons' case against Audi, the attorneys representing Audi will want to know if any prospective jurors have ever owned an Audi, what their experience has been, and if they had a similar problem (or worse) with their Audi that was not resolved to their satisfaction. If so, the defense attorney could well believe that such a juror has a potential for a bias against her client. In that case, she could use a challenge for cause, explaining to the judge the basis for her challenge. The judge, at her discretion, could either accept the for-cause reason or reject it.

Even if an attorney cannot articulate a for-cause reason acceptable to the judge, he may use one of several peremptory challenges that most states (and the federal system) allow. A trial attorney with many years of experience may have a sixth sense about a potential juror and, in consultation with the client, may decide to use a peremptory challenge to avoid having that juror on the panel.

After the jury is sworn and seated, the plaintiff's lawyer makes an opening statement, laying out the nature of the plaintiff's claim, the facts of the case as the plaintiff sees them, and the evidence that the lawyer will present. The defendant's lawyer may also make an opening statement or may reserve his right to do so at the end of the plaintiff's case.

The plaintiff's lawyer then calls witnesses and presents the physical evidence that is relevant to her proof. The direct testimony at trial is usually far from a smooth narration. The rules of evidence (that govern the kinds of testimony and documents that may be introduced at trial) and the question-and-answer format tend to make the presentation of evidence choppy and difficult to follow.

Anyone who has watched an actual televised trial or a television melodrama featuring a trial scene will appreciate the nature of the trial itself: witnesses are asked questions about a number of issues that may or may not be related, the opposing lawyer will frequently object to the question or the form in which it is asked, and the jury may be sent from the room while the lawyers argue at the bench before the judge.

After direct testimony of each witness is over, the opposing lawyer may conduct cross-examination. This is a crucial constitutional right; in criminal cases it is preserved in the Constitution's Sixth Amendment (the right to confront one's accusers in open court). The formal rules of direct testimony are then relaxed, and the cross-examiner may probe the witness more informally, asking questions that may not seem immediately relevant. This is when the opposing attorney may become harsh, casting doubt on a witness's credibility, trying to trip her up and show that the answers she gave are false or not to be trusted. This use of cross-examination, along with the requirement that the witness must respond to questions that are at all relevant to the questions raised by the case, distinguishes common-law courts from those of authoritarian regimes around the world.

Following cross-examination, the plaintiff's lawyer may then question the witness again: this is called redirect examination and is used to demonstrate that the witness's original answers were accurate and to show that any implications otherwise, suggested by the cross-examiner, were unwarranted. The cross-examiner may then engage the witness in re-cross-examination, and so on. The process usually stops after cross-examination or redirect.

During the trial, the judge's chief responsibility is to see that the trial is fair to both sides. One big piece of that responsibility is to rule on the admissibility of evidence. A judge may rule that a particular question is out of order—that is, not relevant or appropriate—or that a given document is irrelevant. Where the attorney is convinced that a particular witness, a particular question, or a particular document (or part thereof) is critical to her case, she may preserve an objection to the court's ruling by saying "exception," in which case the court stenographer will note the exception; on appeal, the attorney may cite any number of exceptions as adding up to the lack of a fair trial for her client and may request a court of appeals to order a retrial.

For the most part, courts of appeal will not reverse and remand for a new trial unless the trial court judge's errors are "prejudicial," or "an abuse of discretion." In short, neither party is entitled to a perfect trial, but only to a fair trial, one in which the trial judge has made only "harmless errors" and not prejudicial ones.

At the end of the plaintiff's case, the defendant presents his case, following the same procedure just outlined. The plaintiff is then entitled to present rebuttal witnesses, if necessary, to deny or argue with the evidence the defendant has introduced. The defendant in turn may present "surrebuttal" witnesses.

When all testimony has been introduced, either party may ask the judge for a **directed verdict**—a verdict decided by the judge without advice from the jury. This motion may be granted if the plaintiff has failed to introduce evidence that is legally sufficient to meet her burden of proof or if the defendant has failed to do the same on issues on which she has the burden of proof. (For example, the plaintiff alleges that the defendant owes him money and introduces a signed promissory note. The defendant cannot show that the note is invalid. The defendant must lose the case unless he can show that the debt has been paid or otherwise discharged.)

directed verdict

At the close of one party's evidence, the other party may move for a directed verdict, or renew that motion at the close of all parties' evidence. A judge will direct a verdict if there is no real issue of fact for reasonable jurors to consider and if the law as applied to the facts in evidence clearly favors the party who requests the directed verdict.

The defendant can move for a directed verdict at the close of the plaintiff's case, but the judge will usually wait to hear the entire case until deciding whether to do so. Directed verdicts are not usually granted, since it is the jury's job to determine the facts in dispute.

If the judge refuses to grant a directed verdict, each lawyer will then present a closing argument to the jury (or, if there is no jury, to the judge alone). The closing argument is used to tie up the loose ends, as the attorney tries to bring together various seemingly unrelated facts into a story that will make sense to the jury.

After closing arguments, the judge will instruct the jury. The purpose of jury instruction is to explain to the jurors the meaning of the law as it relates to the issues they are considering and to tell the jurors what facts they must determine if they are to give a verdict for one party or the other. Each lawyer will have prepared a set of written instructions that she hopes the judge will give to the jury. These will be tailored to advance her client's case. Many a verdict has been overturned on appeal because a trial judge has wrongly instructed the jury. The judge will carefully determine which instructions to give and often will use a set of pattern instructions provided by the state bar association or the supreme court of the state. These pattern jury instructions are often safer because they are patterned after language that appellate courts have used previously, and appellate courts are less likely to find reversible error in the instructions.

After all instructions are given, the jury will retire to a private room and discuss the case and the answers requested by the judge for as long as it takes to reach a unanimous verdict. Some minor cases do not require a unanimous verdict. If the jury cannot reach a decision, this is called a hung jury, and the case will have to be retried. When a jury does reach a verdict, it delivers it in court with both parties and their lawyers present. The jury is then discharged, and control over the case returns to the judge. (If there is no jury, the judge will usually announce in a written opinion his findings of fact and how the law applies to those facts. Juries just announce their verdicts and do not state their reasons for reaching them.)

Posttrial Motions

The losing party is allowed to ask the judge for a new trial or for a judgment notwithstanding the verdict (often called a **judgment n.o.v.**, from the Latin *non obstante veredicto*). A judge who decides that a directed verdict is appropriate will usually wait to see what the jury's verdict is. If it is favorable to the party the judge thinks should win, she can rely on that verdict. If the verdict is for the other party, he can grant the motion for judgment n.o.v. This is a safer way to proceed because if the judge is reversed on appeal, a new trial is not necessary. The jury's verdict always can be restored, whereas without a jury verdict (as happens when a directed verdict is granted before the case goes to the jury), the entire case must be presented to a new jury. *Ferlito v. Johnson & Johnson* (Section 9) illustrates the judgment n.o.v. process in a case where the judge allowed the case to go to a jury that was overly sympathetic to the plaintiffs.

judgment n.o.v.

Judgment "notwithstanding the verdict" may be awarded after the jury returns a verdict that the judge believes no rational jury could have come to. Judgment n.o.v. reverses the verdict and awards judgment to the party against whom the jury's verdict was made.

Rule 50(b) of the Federal Rules of Civil Procedure provides the authorization for federal judges making a judgment contrary to the judgment of the jury. Most states have a similar rule.

Rule 50(b) says,

Whenever a motion for a directed verdict made at the close of all the evidence is denied or for any reason is not granted, the court is deemed to have submitted the action to the jury subject to a later determination of the legal questions raised by the motion. Not later than 10 days after entry of judgment, a party who has moved for a directed verdict may move to have the verdict and any judgment entered thereon set aside and to have judgment entered in accordance with the party's motion for a directed verdict....[A] new trial may be prayed for in the alternative. If a verdict was returned the court may allow the judgment to stand or may reopen the judgment and either order a new trial or direct the entry of judgment as if the requested verdict had been directed.

Key Takeaway

The purpose of a trial judge is to ensure justice to all parties to the lawsuit. The judge presides, instructs the jury, and may limit who testifies and what they testify about what. In all of this, the judge will usually commit some errors; occasionally these will be the kinds of errors that seriously compromise a fair trial for both parties. Errors that do seriously compromise a fair trial for both parties are prejudicial, as opposed to harmless. The appeals court must decide whether any errors of the trial court judge are prejudicial or not.

If a judge directs a verdict, that ends the case for the party who hasn't asked for one; if a judge grants judgment n.o.v., that will take away a jury verdict that one side has worked very hard to get. Thus a judge must be careful not to unduly favor one side or the other, regardless of his or her sympathies.

Exercises

1. What if there was not a doctrine of res judicata? What would the legal system be like?
2. Why do you think cross-examination is a "right," as opposed to a "good thing"? What kind of judicial system would not allow cross-examination of witnesses as a matter of right?

3.5 Judgment, Appeal, and Execution

Learning Objectives

1. Understand the posttrial process—how appellate courts process appeals.
2. Explain how a court's judgment is translated into relief for the winning party.

Judgment or Order

At the end of a trial, the judge will enter an order that makes findings of fact (often with the help of a jury) and conclusions of law. The judge will also make a judgment as to what relief or remedy should be given. Often it is an award of money damages to one of the parties. The losing party may ask for a new trial at this point or within a short period of time following. Once the trial judge denies any such request, the judgment—in the form of the court's order—is final.

Appeal

If the loser's motion for a new trial or a judgment n.o.v. is denied, the losing party may appeal but must ordinarily post a bond sufficient to ensure that there are funds to pay the amount awarded to the winning party. In an appeal, the appellant aims to show that there was some prejudicial error committed by the trial judge. There will be errors, of course, but the errors must be significant (i.e., not harmless). The basic idea is for an appellate court to ensure that a reasonably fair trial was provided to both sides. Enforcement of the court's judgment—an award of money, an injunction—is usually stayed (postponed) until the appellate court has ruled. As noted earlier, the party making the appeal is called the appellant, and the party defending the judgment is the appellee (or in some courts, the petitioner and the respondent).

During the trial, the losing party may have objected to certain procedural decisions by the judge. In compiling a record on appeal, the appellant needs to show the appellate court some examples of mistakes made by the judge—for example, having erroneously admitted evidence, having failed to admit proper evidence that should have been admitted, or having wrongly instructed the jury. The appellate court must determine if those mistakes were serious enough to amount to prejudicial error.

Appellate and trial procedures are different. The appellate court does not hear witnesses or accept evidence. It reviews the *record* of the case—the transcript of the witnesses' testimony and the documents received into evidence at trial—to try to find a legal error on a specific request of one or both of the parties. The parties' lawyers prepare briefs (written statements containing the facts in the case), the procedural steps taken, and the argument or discussion of the meaning of the law and how it applies to the facts. After reading the briefs on appeal, the appellate court may dispose of the appeal without argument, issuing a written opinion that may be very short or many pages. Often, though, the appellate court will hear oral argument. (This can be months, or even more than a year after the briefs are filed.) Each lawyer is given a short period of time, usually no more than thirty minutes, to present his client's case. The lawyer rarely gets a chance for an extended statement because he is usually interrupted by questions from the judges. Through this exchange between judges and lawyers, specific legal positions can be tested and their limits explored.

Depending on what it decides, the appellate court will *affirm* the lower court's judgment, *modify* it, *reverse* it, or *remand* it to the lower court for retrial or other action directed by the higher court. The appellate court itself does not take specific action in the case; it sits only to rule on contested issues of law. The lower court must issue the final judgment in the case. As we have already seen, there is the possibility of appealing from an intermediate appellate court to the state supreme court in twenty-nine states and to the US Supreme Court from a ruling from a federal circuit court of appeal. In cases raising constitutional issues, there is also the possibility of appeal to the Supreme Court from the state courts.

Like trial judges, appellate judges must follow previous decisions, or precedent. But not every previous case is a precedent for every court. Lower courts must respect appellate court decisions, and courts in one state are not bound by decisions of courts in other states. State courts are not bound by decisions of federal courts, except on points of federal law that come from federal courts within the state or from a federal circuit in which the state court sits. A state supreme court is not bound by case law in any other state. But a supreme court in one state with a type of case it has not previously dealt with may find persuasive reasoning in decisions of other state supreme courts.

Federal district courts are bound by the decisions of the court of appeals in their circuit, but decisions by one circuit court are not precedents for courts in other circuits. Federal courts are also bound by decisions of the state supreme courts within their geographic territory in diversity jurisdiction cases. All courts are bound by decisions of the US Supreme Court, except the Supreme Court itself, which seldom reverses itself but on occasion has overturned its own precedents.

Not everything a court says in an opinion is a precedent. Strictly speaking, only the exact holding is binding on the lower courts. A holding is the theory of the law that applies to the particular circumstances presented in a case. The courts may sometimes declare what they believe to be the law with regard to points that are not central to the case being decided. These declarations are called dicta (the singular, *dictum*), and the lower courts do not have to give them the same weight as holdings.

Judgment and Order

When a party has no more possible appeals, it usually pays up voluntarily. If not voluntarily, then the losing party's assets can be seized or its wages or other income garnished to satisfy the judgment. If the final judgment is an injunction, failure to follow its dictates can lead to a contempt citation, with a fine or jail time imposed.

Key Takeaway

The process of conducting a civil trial has many aspects, starting with pleadings and continuing with motions, discovery, more motions, pretrial conferences, and finally the trial itself. At all stages, the rules of civil procedure attempt to give both sides plenty of notice, opportunity to be heard, discovery of relevant information, cross-examination, and the preservation of procedural objections for purposes of appeal. All of these rules and procedures are intended to provide each side with a fair trial.

Exercises

1. Mrs. Robinson has a key witness on auto safety that the judge believes is not qualified as an expert. The judge examines the witness while the jury is in the jury room and disqualifies him from testifying. The jury does not get to hear this witness. Her attorney objects. She loses her case. What argument would you expect Mrs. Robinson's attorney to make in an appeal?
2. Why don't appellate courts need a witness box for witnesses to give testimony under oath?
3. A trial judge in Nevada is wondering whether to enforce a surrogate motherhood contract. Penelope Barr, of Reno, Nevada, has contracted with Reuben and Tina Goldberg to bear the in vitro fertilized egg of Mrs. Goldberg. After carrying the child for nine months, Penelope gives birth, but she is reluctant to give up the child, even though she was paid $20,000 at the start of the contract and will earn an additional $20,000 on handing over the baby to the Goldbergs. (Barr was an especially good candidate for surrogate motherhood: she had borne two perfect children and at age 28 drinks no wine, does not smoke or use drugs of any kind, practices yoga, and maintains a largely vegetarian diet with just enough meat to meet the needs of the fetus within.)

   The Goldbergs have asked the judge for an order compelling Penelope to give up the baby, who was five days old when the lawsuit was filed. The baby is now a month old as the judge looks in vain for guidance from any Nevada statute, federal statute, or any prior case in Nevada that addressed the issue of surrogate motherhood. He does find several well-reasoned cases, one from New Jersey, one from Michigan, and one from Oregon. Are any of these "precedent" that he must follow? May he adopt the reasoning of any of these courts, if he should find that reasoning persuasive?

3.6 When Can Someone Bring a Lawsuit?

Learning Objectives

1. Explain the requirements for standing to bring a lawsuit in US courts.
2. Describe the process by which a group or class of plaintiffs can be certified to file a class action case.

Almost anyone can bring a lawsuit, assuming they have the filing fee and the help of an attorney. But the court may not hear it, for a number of reasons. There may be no case or controversy, there may be no law to support the plaintiff's claim, it may be in the wrong court, too much time might have lapsed (a statute of limitations problem), or the plaintiff may not have standing.

Case or Controversy: Standing to Sue

Article III of the US Constitution provides limits to federal judicial power. For some cases, the Supreme Court has decided that it has no power to adjudicate because there is no "case or controversy." For example, perhaps the case has settled or the "real parties in interest" are not before the court. In such a case, a court might dismiss the case on the grounds that the plaintiff does not have "standing" to sue.

For example, suppose you see a sixteen-wheel moving van drive across your neighbor's flower bed, destroying her beloved roses. You have enjoyed seeing her roses every summer, for years. She is forlorn and tells you that she is not going to raise roses there anymore. She also tells you that she has decided not to sue, because she has made the decision to never deal with lawyers if at all possible. Incensed, you decide to sue on her behalf. But you will not have standing to sue because your person or property was not directly injured by the moving van. Standing means that only the person whose interests are directly affected has the legal right to sue.

The standing doctrine is easy to understand in straightforward cases such as this but is often a fairly complicated matter. For example, can fifteen or more state attorneys general bring a lawsuit for a declaratory judgment that the health care legislation passed in 2010 is unconstitutional? What particular injury have they (or the states) suffered? Are they the best set of plaintiffs to raise this issue? Time—and the Supreme Court—will tell.

Class Actions

Most lawsuits concern a dispute between two people or between a person and a company or other organization. But it can happen that someone injures more than one person at the same time. A driver who runs a red light may hit another car carrying one person or many people. If several people are injured in the same accident, they each have the right to sue the driver for the damage that he caused them. Could they sue as a group? Usually not, because the damages would probably not be the same for each person, and different facts would have to be proved at the trial. Plus, the driver of the car that was struck might have been partially to blame, so the defendant's liability toward him might be different from his liability toward the passengers.

If, however, the potential plaintiffs were all injured in the same way, whether at the same time (an airplane accident caused by the airline's negligence, for example) or even at different times, a single lawsuit might be a far more efficient way of determining liability and deciding financial responsibility than many individual lawsuits.

How could such a suit be brought? All the injured parties could hire the same lawyer, and she could present a common case. With a group numbering more than a handful of people, it could become exceedingly complicated, yet many individuals suing alone in many different jurisdictions for the same civil wrongs can frustrate the orderly and fair resolution of the common dispute. In revising the Federal Rules of Civil Procedure in 1966, Congress tried to create a rule for "class actions" that would serve the interests not only of a large "class" of plaintiffs, but also be manageable by the courts and fair to defendants.

Thus, the class action was provided for in the Federal Rules of Civil Procedure (Rule 23) and in the separate codes of civil procedure in the states. These rules can differ and are often complex, but in general anyone can file a class action in an appropriate case, subject to approval of the court. Once the class is "certified," or judged to be a legally adequate group with common injuries, the lawyers for the named plaintiffs become, in effect, lawyers for the entire class.

Usually a person who doesn't want to be in the class can decide to leave. If she does, she will not be included in an eventual judgment or settlement. But a potential plaintiff who is included in the class cannot, after a final judgment is awarded, seek to relitigate the issue if she is dissatisfied with the outcome, even though she did not participate at all in the legal proceeding.

Key Takeaway

Anyone can file a lawsuit, with or without the help of an attorney, but only those lawsuits where a plaintiff has standing will be heard by the courts. Standing has become a complicated question and is used by the courts to ensure that civil cases heard are being pursued by those with tangible and particular injuries. Class actions are a way of aggregating claims that are substantially similar and arise out of the same facts and circumstances.

Exercise

1. Fuchs Funeral Home is carrying the body of Charles Emmenthaler to its resting place at Forest Lawn Cemetery. Charles's wife, Chloe, and their two children, Chucky and Clarice, are following the hearse when the coffin falls on the street, opens, and the body of Charles Emmenthaler falls out. The wife and children are shocked and aggrieved and later sue in civil court for damages. Assume that this is a viable cause of action based on "negligent infliction of emotional distress" in the state of California and that Charles's brother, sister-in-law, and multiple cousins also were in the funeral procession and saw what happened. The brother of Charles, Kingston Emmenthaler, also sees his brother's body on the street, but his wife, their three children, and some of Charles's other cousins do not.

   Charles was actually emotionally closest to Kingston's oldest son, Nestor, who was studying abroad at the time of the funeral and could not make it back in time. He is as emotionally distraught at his uncle's passing as anyone else in the family and is especially grieved over the description of the incident and the grainy video shot by one of the cousins on his cell phone. Who has standing to sue Fuchs Funeral Home, and who does not?

3.7 Relations with Lawyers

Learning Objectives

1. Understand the various ways that lawyers charge for services.

2. Describe the contingent fee system in the United States.
3. Know the difference between the American rule and the British rule with regard to who pays attorneys' fees.

Legal Fees

Lawyers charge for their services in one of three different ways: flat rate, hourly rate, and contingent fee. A flat rate is used usually when the work is relatively routine and the lawyer knows in advance approximately how long it will take her to do the job. Drawing a will or doing a real estate closing are examples of legal work that is often paid a flat rate. The rate itself may be based on a percentage of the worth of the matter—say, 1 percent of a home's selling price.

Lawyers generally charge by the hour for courtroom time and for ongoing representation in commercial matters. Virtually every sizable law firm bills its clients by hourly rates, which in large cities can range from $300 for an associate's time to $500 and more for a senior partner's time.

A contingent fee is one that is paid only if the lawyer wins—that is, it is contingent, or depends upon, the success of the case. This type of fee arrangement is used most often in personal injury cases (e.g., automobile accidents, products liability, and professional malpractice). Although used quite often, the contingent fee is controversial. Trial lawyers justify it by pointing to the high cost of preparing for such lawsuits. A typical automobile accident case can cost at least ten thousand dollars to prepare, and a complicated products-liability case can cost tens of thousands of dollars. Few people have that kind of money or would be willing to spend it on the chance that they might win a lawsuit. Corporate and professional defendants complain that the contingent fee gives lawyers a license to go big game hunting, or to file suits against those with deep pockets in the hopes of forcing them to settle.

Trial lawyers respond that the contingent fee arrangement forces them to screen cases and weed out cases that are weak, because it is not worth their time to spend the hundreds of hours necessary on such cases if their chances of winning are slim or nonexistent.

Costs

In England and in many other countries, the losing party must pay the legal expenses of the winning party, including attorneys' fees. That is not the general rule in this country. Here, each party must pay most of its own costs, including (and especially) the fees of lawyers. (Certain relatively minor costs, such as filing fees for various documents required in court, are chargeable to the losing side, if the judge decides it.) This type of fee structure is known as the American rule (in contrast to the British rule).

There are two types of exceptions to the American rule. By statute, Congress and the state legislatures have provided that the winning party in particular classes of cases may recover its full legal costs from the loser—for example, the federal antitrust laws so provide and so does the federal Equal Access to Justice Act. The other exception applies to litigants who either initiate lawsuits in bad faith, with no expectation of winning, or who defend them in bad faith, in order to cause the plaintiff great expense. Under these circumstances, a court has the discretion to award attorneys' fees to the winner. But this rule is not infinitely flexible, and courts do not have complete freedom to award attorneys' fees in any amount, but only "reasonable" attorney's fees.

Key Takeaway

Litigation is expensive. Getting a lawyer can be costly, unless you get a lawyer on a contingent fee. Not all legal systems allow contingent fees. In many legal systems, the loser pays attorneys' fees for both parties.

Exercises

1. Mrs. Robinson's attorney estimates that they will recover a million dollars from Volkswagen in the Audi lawsuit. She has Mrs. Robinson sign a contract that gives her firm one-third of any recovery after the firm's expenses are deducted. The judge does in fact award a million dollars, and the defendant pays. The firm's expenses are $100,000. How much does Mrs. Robinson get?
2. Harry Potter brings a lawsuit against Draco Malfoy in Chestershire, England, for slander, a form of defamation. Potter alleges that Malfoy insists on calling him a mudblood. Ron Weasley testifies, as does Neville Chamberlain. But Harry loses, because the court has no conception of wizardry and cannot make sense of the case at all. In dismissing the case, however, who (under English law) will bear the costs of the attorneys who have brought the case for Potter and defended the matter for Malfoy?

3.8 Alternative Means of Resolving Disputes

Learning Objectives

1. Understand how arbitration and mediation are frequently used alternatives to litigation.
2. Describe the differences between arbitration and mediation.
3. Explain why arbitration is final and binding.

Disputes do not have to be settled in court. No law requires parties who have a legal dispute to seek judicial resolution if they can resolve their disagreement privately or through some other public forum. In fact, the threat of a lawsuit can frequently motivate parties toward private negotiation. Filing a lawsuit may convince one party that the other party is serious. Or the parties may decide that they will come to terms privately rather than wait the three or four years it can frequently take for a case to move up on the court calendar.

Arbitration

Beginning around 1980, a movement toward alternative dispute resolution began to gain force throughout the United States. Bar associations, other private groups, and the courts themselves wanted to find quicker and cheaper ways for litigants and potential litigants to settle certain types of quarrels than through the courts. As a result, neighborhood justice centers or dispute resolution centers have sprung up in communities. These are where people can come for help in settling disputes, of both civil and criminal nature, that should not consume the time and money of the parties or courts in lengthy proceedings.

These alternative forums use a variety of methods, including arbitration, mediation, and conciliation, to bring about agreement or at least closure of the dispute. These methods are not all alike, and their differences are worth noting.

Arbitration is a type of adjudication. The parties use a private decision maker, the arbitrator, and the rules of procedure are considerably more relaxed than those that apply in the courtroom. Arbitrators might be retired judges, lawyers, or anyone with the kind of specialized knowledge and training that would be useful in making a final, binding decision on the dispute. In a contractual relationship, the parties can decide even before a dispute arises to use arbitration when the time comes. Or parties can decide after a dispute arises to use arbitration instead of litigation. In a pre-dispute arbitration agreement (often part of a larger contract), the parties can spell out the rules of procedure to be used and the method for choosing the arbitrator. For example, they may name the specific person or delegate the responsibility of choosing to some neutral person, or they may each designate a person and the two designees may jointly pick a third arbitrator.

arbitration

A process agreed to by disputing parties, involving an arbitrator or arbitral panel (usually three), in which a final and binding award is made, enforceable through the courts if necessary.

Many arbitrations take place under the auspices of the American Arbitration Association, a private organization headquartered in New York, with regional offices in many other cities. The association uses published sets of rules for various types of arbitration (e.g., labor arbitration or commercial arbitration); parties who provide in contracts for arbitration through the association are agreeing to be bound by the association's rules. Similarly, the National Association of Securities Dealers provides arbitration services for disputes between clients and brokerage firms. International commercial arbitration often takes place through the auspices of the International Chamber of Commerce. A multilateral agreement known as the Convention on the Recognition and Enforcement of Arbitral Awards provides that agreements to arbitrate—and arbitral awards—will be enforced across national boundaries.

Arbitration has two advantages over litigation. First, it is usually much quicker, because the arbitrator does not have a backlog of cases and because the procedures are simpler. Second, in complex cases, the quality of the decision may be higher, because the parties can select an arbitrator with specialized knowledge.

Under both federal and state law, arbitration is favored, and a decision rendered by an arbitrator is binding by law and may be enforced by the courts. The arbitrator's decision is final and binding, with very few exceptions (such as fraud or manifest disregard of the law by the arbitrator or panel of arbitrators). Saying that arbitration is favored means that if you have agreed to arbitration, you can't go to court if the other party wants you to arbitrate. Under the Federal Arbitration Act, the other party can go to court and get a stay against your litigation and also get an order compelling you to go to arbitration.

Mediation

Unlike adjudication, **mediation** gives the neutral party no power to impose a decision. The mediator is a go-between who attempts to help the parties negotiate a solution. The mediator will communicate the parties' positions to each other, will facilitate the finding of common ground, and will suggest outcomes. But the parties have complete control: they may ignore the recommendations of the mediator entirely, settle in their own way, find another mediator, agree to binding arbitration, go to court, or forget the whole thing!

mediation

A process where disputing parties agree to bring their differences to an experienced mediator, knowledgeable about the type of dispute involved, and in which the mediator's recommendations may be accepted or rejected by either or both parties.

Key Takeaway

Litigation is not the only way to resolve disputes. Informal negotiation between the disputants usually comes first, but both mediation and arbitration are available. Arbitration, though, is final and binding. Once you agree to arbitrate, you will have a final, binding arbitral award that is enforceable through the courts, and courts will almost never allow you to litigate after you have agreed to arbitrate.

Exercises

1. When Mrs. Robinson buys her Audi from Seaway, there is a paragraph in the bill of sale, which both the dealer and Mrs. Robinson sign, that says, "In the event of any complaint by customer/buyer against Seaway regarding the vehicle purchased herein, such complaint shall not be litigated, but may only be arbitrated under the rules of the American Arbitration Association and in accordance with New York law." Mrs. Robinson did not see the provision, doesn't like it, and wants to bring a lawsuit in Oklahoma against Seaway. What do you think is the result?
2. Hendrik Koster (Netherlands) contracts with Automark, Inc. (a U.S. company based in Illinois) to supply Automark with a large quantity of valve cap gauges. He does, and Automark fails to pay. Koster thinks he is owed $66,000. There is no agreement to arbitrate or mediate. Can Koster make Automark mediate or arbitrate?
3. Suppose that there is an agreement between Koster and Automark to arbitrate. It says, "The parties agree to arbitrate any dispute arising under this agreement in accordance with the laws of the Netherlands and under the auspices of the International Chamber of Commerce's arbitration facility." The International Chamber of Commerce has arbitration rules and will appoint an arbitrator or arbitral panel in the event the parties cannot agree on an arbitrator. The arbitration takes place in Geneva. Koster gets an arbitral award for $66,000 plus interest. Automark does not participate in any way. Will a court in Illinois enforce the arbitral award?

3.9 Cases

Burger King v. Rudzewicz

Burger King Corp. v. Rudzewicz
471 U.S. 462 (U.S. Supreme Court 1985)

Summary

Burger King Corp. is a Florida corporation with principal offices in Miami. It principally conducts restaurant business through franchisees. The franchisees are licensed to use Burger King's trademarks and service marks in standardized restaurant facilities. Rudzewicz is a Michigan resident who, with a partner (MacShara) operated a Burger King franchise in Drayton Plains, Michigan. Negotiations for setting up the franchise occurred in 1978 largely between Rudzewicz, his partner, and a regional office of Burger King in Birmingham, Michigan, although some deals and concessions were made by Burger King in Florida. A preliminary agreement was signed in February of 1979. Rudzewicz and MacShara assumed operation of an existing facility in Drayton Plains and

MacShara attended prescribed management courses in Miami during the four months following Feb. 1979.

Rudzewicz and MacShara bought $165,000 [about $553,000 in 2017 dollars] worth of restaurant equipment from Burger King's Davmor Industries division in Miami. But before the final agreements were signed, the parties began to disagree over site-development fees, building design, computation of monthly rent, and whether Rudzewicz and MacShara could assign their liabilities to a corporation they had formed. Negotiations took place between Rudzewicz, MacShara, and the Birmingham regional office; but Rudzewicz and MacShara learned that the regional office had limited decision-making power and turned directly to Miami headquarters for their concerns. The final agreement was signed by June 1979 and provided that the franchise relationship was governed by Florida law, and called for payment of all required fees and forwarding of all relevant notices to Miami headquarters.

The Drayton Plains restaurant did fairly well at first, but a recession in late 1979 caused the franchisees to fall far behind in their monthly payments to Miami. Notice of default was sent from Miami to Rudzewicz, who nevertheless continued to operate the restaurant as a Burger King franchise. Burger King sued in federal district court for the southern district of Florida. Rudzewicz contested the court's personal jurisdiction over him, since he had never been to Florida.

The federal court looked to Florida's long arm statute and held that it did have personal jurisdiction over the non-resident franchisees, and awarded Burger King a quarter of a million dollars in contract damages and enjoined the franchisees from further operation of the Drayton Plains facility. Franchisees appealed to the 11th Circuit Court of Appeals and won a reversal based on lack of personal jurisdiction. Burger King petitioned the Supreme Ct. for a *writ of certiorari.*

Justice Brennan delivered the opinion of the court.

The Due Process Clause protects an individual's liberty interest in not being subject to the binding judgments of a forum with which he has established no meaningful "contacts, ties, or relations." International Shoe Co. v. Washington. By requiring that individuals have "fair warning that a particular activity may subject [them] to the jurisdiction of a foreign sovereign," the Due Process Clause "gives a degree of predictability to the legal system that allows potential defendants to structure their primary conduct with some minimum assurance as to where that conduct will and will not render them liable to suit." * * *

Where a forum seeks to assert specific jurisdiction over an out-of-state defendant who has not consented to suit there, this "fair warning" requirement is satisfied if the defendant has "purposefully directed" his activities at residents of the forum, and the litigation results from alleged injuries that "arise out of or relate to" those activities, Thus "[t]he forum State does not exceed its powers under the Due Process Clause if it asserts personal jurisdiction over a corporation that delivers its products into the stream of commerce with the expectation that they will be purchased by consumers in the forum State" and those products subsequently injure forum consumers. Similarly, a publisher who distributes magazines in a distant State may fairly be held accountable in that forum for damages resulting there from an allegedly defamatory story. * * *

[T]he constitutional touchstone remains whether the defendant purposefully established "minimum contacts" in the forum State....In defining when it is that a potential defendant should "reasonably anticipate" out-of-state litigation, the Court frequently has drawn from the reasoning of Hanson v. Denckla, 357 U.S. 235, 253 (1958):

> *The unilateral activity of those who claim some relationship with a nonresident defendant cannot satisfy the requirement of contact with the forum State. The application of that rule will vary with the quality and nature of the defendant's activity, but it is essential in each case that there be some act by which the defendant purposefully avails itself of the privilege of conducting activities within the forum State, thus invoking the benefits and protections of its laws.*

This "purposeful availment" requirement ensures that a defendant will not be haled into a jurisdiction solely as a result of "random," "fortuitous," or "attenuated" contacts, or of the "unilateral activity of another party or a third person," [Citations] Jurisdiction is proper, however, where the contacts proximately result from actions by the defendant himself that create a "substantial connection" with the forum State. [Citations] Thus where the defendant "deliberately" has engaged in significant activities within a State, or has created "continuing obligations" between himself and residents of the forum, he manifestly has availed himself of the privilege of conducting business there, and because his activities are shielded by "the benefits and protections" of the forum's laws it is presumptively not unreasonable to require him to submit to the burdens of litigation in that forum as well.

Jurisdiction in these circumstances may not be avoided merely because the defendant did not physically enter the forum State. Although territorial presence frequently will enhance a potential defendant's affiliation with a State and reinforce the reasonable foreseeability of suit there, it is an inescapable fact of modern commercial life that a substantial amount of business is transacted solely by mail and wire communications across state lines, thus obviating the need for physical presence within a State in which business is conducted. So long as a commercial actor's efforts are "purposefully directed" toward residents of another State, we have consistently rejected the notion that an absence of physical contacts can defeat personal jurisdiction there.

Once it has been decided that a defendant purposefully established minimum contacts within the forum State, these contacts may be considered in light of other factors to determine whether the assertion of personal jurisdiction would comport with "fair play and substantial justice." International Shoe Co. v. Washington, 326 U.S., at 320. Thus courts in "appropriate case[s]" may evaluate "the burden on the defendant," "the forum State's interest in adjudicating the dispute," "the plaintiff's interest in obtaining convenient and effective relief," "the interstate judicial system's interest in obtaining the most efficient resolution of controversies," and the "shared interest of the several States in furthering fundamental substantive social policies." These considerations sometimes serve to establish the reasonableness of jurisdiction upon a lesser showing of minimum contacts than would otherwise be required. [Citations] Applying these principles to the case at hand, we believe there is substantial record evidence supporting the District Court's conclusion that the assertion of personal jurisdiction over Rudzewicz in Florida for the alleged breach of his franchise agreement did not offend due process....

In this case, no physical ties to Florida can be attributed to Rudzewicz other than MacShara's brief training course in Miami. Rudzewicz did not maintain offices in Florida and, for all that appears from the record, has never even visited there. Yet this franchise dispute grew directly out of "a contract which had a substantial connection with that State." Eschewing the option of operating an independent local enterprise, Rudzewicz deliberately "reach[ed] out beyond" Michigan and negotiated with a Florida corporation for the purchase of a long-term franchise and the manifold benefits that would derive from affiliation with a nationwide organization. Upon approval, he entered into a carefully structured 20-year relationship that envisioned continuing and wide-reaching contacts with Burger King in Florida. In light of Rudzewicz' voluntary acceptance of the long-term and exacting regulation of his business from Burger King's Miami headquarters, the "quality and nature" of his relationship to the company in Florida can in no sense be viewed as "random," "fortuitous," or "attenuated." Rudzewicz' refusal to make the contractually required payments in Miami, and his continued use of Burger King's trademarks and confidential business information after his termination, caused foreseeable injuries to the corporation in Florida. For these reasons it was, at the very least, presumptively reasonable for Rudzewicz to be called to account there for such injuries.

...Because Rudzewicz established a substantial and continuing relationship with Burger King's Miami headquarters, received fair notice from the contract documents and the course of dealing that he might be subject to suit in Florida, and has failed to demonstrate how jurisdiction in that forum would otherwise be fundamentally unfair, we conclude that the District Court's exercise of jurisdiction pursuant to Fla. Stat. 48.193(1)(g) (Supp. 1984) did not offend due process. The judgment of the Court of Appeals is accordingly reversed, and the case is remanded for further proceedings consistent with this opinion.

It is so ordered.

Case Questions

1. Why did Burger King sue in Florida rather than in Michigan?
2. If Florida has a long-arm statute that tells Florida courts that it may exercise personal jurisdiction over someone like Rudzewicz, why is the court talking about the due process clause?
3. Why is this case in federal court rather than in a Florida state court?
4. If this case had been filed in state court in Florida, would Rudzewicz be required to come to Florida? Explain.

Ferlito v. Johnson & Johnson

Ferlito v. Johnson & Johnson Products, Inc.

771 F. Supp. 196 (U.S. District Ct., Eastern District of Michigan 1991)

Gadola, J.

Plaintiffs Susan and Frank Ferlito, husband and wife, attended a Halloween party in 1984 dressed as Mary (Mrs. Ferlito) and her little lamb (Mr. Ferlito). Mrs. Ferlito had constructed a lamb costume for her husband by gluing cotton batting manufactured by defendant Johnson & Johnson Products ("JJP") to a suit of long underwear. She had also used defendant's product to fashion a headpiece, complete with ears. The costume covered Mr. Ferlito from his head to his ankles, except for his face and hands, which were blackened with Halloween paint. At the party Mr. Ferlito attempted to light his cigarette by using a butane lighter. The flame passed close to his left arm, and the cotton batting on his left sleeve ignited. Plaintiffs sued defendant for injuries they suffered from burns which covered approximately one-third of Mr. Ferlito's body.

Following a jury verdict entered for plaintiffs November 2, 1989, the Honorable Ralph M. Freeman entered a judgment for plaintiff Frank Ferlito in the amount of $555,000 [about $1.1 million in 2017 dollars] and for plaintiff Susan Ferlito in the amount of $ 70,000 [about $138,000 in 2017 dollars]. Judgment was entered November 7, 1989. Subsequently, on November 16, 1989, defendant JJP filed a timely motion for judgment notwithstanding the verdict pursuant to Fed.R.Civ.P. 50(b) or, in the alternative, for new trial. Plaintiffs filed their response to defendant's motion December 18, 1989; and defendant filed a reply January 4, 1990. Before reaching a decision on this motion, Judge Freeman died. The case was reassigned to this court April 12, 1990.

Motion for judgment notwithstanding the verdict ["j.n.o.v."]

Defendant JJP filed two motions for a directed verdict, the first on October 27, 1989, at the close of plaintiffs' proofs, and the second on October 30, 1989, at the close of defendant's proofs. Judge Freeman denied both motions without prejudice. Judgment for plaintiffs was entered November 7, 1989; and defendant's instant motion, filed November 16, 1989, was filed in a timely manner.

The standard for determining whether to grant a j.n.o.v. is identical to the standard for evaluating a motion for directed verdict:

In determining whether the evidence is sufficient, the trial court may neither weigh the evidence, pass on the credibility of witnesses nor substitute its judgment for that of the jury. Rather, the evidence must be viewed in the light most favorable to the party against whom the motion is made, drawing from that evidence all reasonable inferences in his favor. If after reviewing the evidence...the trial court is of the opinion that reasonable minds could not come to the result reached by the jury, then the motion for j.n.o.v. should be granted.

To recover in a "failure to warn" product liability action, a plaintiff must prove each of the following four elements of negligence: (1) that the defendant owed a duty to the plaintiff, (2) that the defendant violated that duty, (3) that the defendant's breach of that duty was a proximate cause of the damages suffered by the plaintiff, and (4) that the plaintiff suffered damages.

To establish a *prima facie case* that a manufacturer's breach of its duty to warn was a proximate cause of an injury sustained, a plaintiff must present evidence that the product would have been used differently had the proffered warnings been given.[1] [Citations omitted] In the absence of evidence that a warning would have prevented the harm complained of by altering the plaintiff's conduct, the failure to warn cannot be deemed a proximate cause of the plaintiff's injury as a matter of law. [In accordance with procedure in a diversity of citizenship case, such as this one, the court cites Michigan case law as the basis for its legal interpretation.] * * *

A manufacturer has a duty "to warn the purchasers or users of its product about dangers associated with intended use." Conversely, a manufacturer has no duty to warn of a danger arising from an unforeseeable misuse of its product. [Citation] Thus, whether a manufacturer has a duty to warn depends on whether the use of the product and the injury sustained by it are foreseeable. Gootee v. Colt Industries Inc., 712 F.2d 1057, 1065 (6th Cir. 1983); Owens v. Allis-Chalmers Corp., 414 Mich. 413, 425, 326 N.W.2d 372 (1982). Whether a plaintiff's use of a product is foreseeable is a legal question to be resolved by the court. Trotter, *supra*. Whether the resulting injury is foreseeable is a question of fact for the jury.[2] Thomas v. International Harvester Co., 57 Mich. App. 79, 225 N.W.2d 175 (1974).

In the instant action no reasonable jury could find that JJP's failure to warn of the flammability of cotton batting was a proximate cause of plaintiffs' injuries because plaintiffs failed to offer any evidence to establish that a flammability warning on JJP's cotton batting would have dissuaded them from using the product in the manner that they did.

Plaintiffs repeatedly stated in their response brief that plaintiff Susan Ferlito testified that "she would never again use cotton batting to make a costume. * * * However, a review of the trial transcript reveals that plaintiff Susan Ferlito never testified that she would never again use cotton batting to make a costume. More importantly, the transcript contains no statement by plaintiff Susan Ferlito that a flammability warning on defendant JJP's product would have dissuaded her from using the cotton batting to construct the costume in the first place. At oral argument counsel for plaintiffs conceded that there was no testimony during the trial that either plaintiff Susan Ferlito or her husband, plaintiff Frank J. Ferlito, would have acted any different if there had been a flammability warning on the product's package. The absence of such testimony is fatal to plaintiffs' case; for without it, plaintiffs have failed to prove proximate cause, one of the essential elements of their negligence claim.

In addition, both plaintiffs testified that they knew that cotton batting burns when it is exposed to flame. Susan Ferlito testified that she knew at the time she purchased the cotton batting that it would burn if exposed to an open flame. Frank Ferlito testified that he knew at the time he appeared at the Halloween party that cotton batting would burn if exposed to an open flame. His additional testimony that he would not have intentionally put a flame to the cotton batting shows that he recognized the risk of injury of which he claims JJP should have warned. Because both plaintiffs were already aware of the danger, a warning by JJP would have been superfluous. Therefore, a reasonable jury could not have found that JJP's failure to provide a warning was a proximate cause of plaintiffs' injuries.

The evidence in this case clearly demonstrated that neither the use to which plaintiffs put JJP's product nor the injuries arising from that use were foreseeable. Susan Ferlito testified that the idea for the costume was hers alone. As described on the product's package, its intended uses are for cleansing, applying medications, and infant care. Plaintiffs' showing that the product may be used on occasion in classrooms for decorative purposes failed to demonstrate the foreseeability of an adult male encapsulating himself from head to toe in cotton batting and then lighting up a cigarette.

ORDER

NOW, THEREFORE, IT IS HEREBY ORDERED that defendant JJP's motion for judgment notwithstanding the verdict is GRANTED.

IT IS FURTHER ORDERED that the judgment entered November 2, 1989, is SET ASIDE.

IT IS FURTHER ORDERED that the clerk will enter a judgment in favor of the defendant JJP.

Case Questions

1. The opinion focuses on proximate cause. As we will see in Chapter 7, a negligence case cannot be won unless the plaintiff shows that the defendant has breached a duty and that the defendant's breach has actually and proximately caused the damage complained of. What, exactly, is the alleged breach of duty by the defendant here?
2. Explain why Judge Gadola reasoning that JJP had no duty to warn in this case. After this case, would they then have a duty to warn, knowing that someone might use their product in this way?

American Express v. Italian Colors

American Express v. Italian Colors
570 U.S. (U.S. Supreme Court, 2013)

Summary: Italian Colors Restaurant (the respondents here, but plaintiff at the trial court level) accepts American Express cards. Their contract with American Express contained a clause that requires all disputes between the parties to be resolved by arbitration. The contract also provided that "[t]here shall be no right or authority for any Claims to be arbitrated on a class action basis." As plaintiffs, Italian Colors brought a class action lawsuit against American Express for violations of the federal antitrust laws. Italian Colors alleged that American Express had used its monopoly power in the market for charge cards to force merchants to accept credit cards at rates approximately 30% higher than the fees for competing credit cards.

As defendants, American Express (Petitioners before the Supreme Court) moved the trial court to compel individual arbitration under the Federal Arbitration Act (FAA), 9 U.S.C. §§1 et seq. (The FAA became law in 1925.) (This motion, if accepted by the trial court, would effectively bar Italian Colors from bringing any kind of lawsuit, whether individually or as a lead plaintiff in a class action.)

Respondents countered this motion by submitting a "declaration" in the form of proposed testimony from an economist who estimated that the cost of an expert analysis necessary to prove the antitrust claims would be "at least several hundred thousand dollars, and might exceed $1 million," while the maximum recovery for an individual plaintiff would be $12,850, or $38,549 when trebled under damages allowed by the Clayton Antitrust Act. (The courts and American Express assumed for the sake of argument that these numbers are generally correct, and did not disagree that that the restaurant's costs of pursuing their antitrust claims could greatly exceed their potential recovery from defendants/respondents.)

The District Court granted the motion to compel arbitration and dismissed the lawsuit. But the Court of Appeals reversed and remanded for further proceedings. It held that because respondents had established that "they would incur prohibitive costs if compelled to arbitrate under the class action waiver," the waiver was un-enforceable and the arbitration could not proceed. *In re American Express Merchants' Litigation*, 554 F. 3d 300, 315–316 (CA2 2009).

The Supreme Court granted certiorari, vacated the judgment, and remanded for further consideration in light of *Stolt-Nielsen S. A. v. Animal Feeds Int'l Corp., 559 U.S. 772 (2010)*, which held that a party may not be compelled to submit to class arbitration absent an agreement to do so. The Court of Appeals stood by its reversal, stating that its earlier ruling did not compel class arbitration. *In re American Express Merchants' Litigation*, 634 F. 3d 187, 200 (CA2 2011)... The Supreme Court granted certiorari to consider the question "[w]hether the Federal Arbitration Act permits courts . . . to invalidate arbitration agreements on the ground that they do not permit class arbitration of a federal-law claim." Notice that the issue could also have been phrased, "Can a credit card firm exercise its monopoly power to charge excessive fees and effectively prevent retailers and merchants from suing collectively under U.S. antitrust laws or, if the credit card company insists on arbitration rather than litigation, can it by contract preclude retailers and merchants from using class arbitration?"

Majority opinion, Justice Scalia: (Joined by Justices Kennedy, Thomas, Alito, and Roberts)

Congress enacted the FAA in response to widespread judicial hostility to arbitration. As relevant here, the Act provides:

"A written provision in any maritime transaction or contract evidencing a transaction involving commerce to settle by arbitration a controversy thereafter arising out of such contract or transaction . . . shall be valid, irrevocable, and enforceable, save upon such grounds as exist at law or in equity for the revocation of any contract." 9 U.S.C. §2.

This text reflects the overarching principle that arbitration is a matter of contract. And consistent with that text, courts must "rigorously enforce" arbitration agreements according to their terms, including terms that "specify *with whom* [the parties] choose to arbitrate their disputes," and "the rules under which that arbitration will be conducted," *Volt Information Sciences, Inc.* v. *Board of Trustees of Leland Stanford Junior Univ.*, 489 U.S. 468, 479 (1989). That holds true for claims that allege a violation of a federal statute, unless the FAA's mandate has been " 'overridden by a contrary congressional command.' " *CompuCredit Corp.* v. *Greenwood*, 565 U. S.95 (2012).

No contrary congressional command requires us to reject the waiver of class arbitration here. Respondents argue that requiring them to litigate their claims individually—as they contracted to do—would contravene the policies of the antitrust laws. But the antitrust laws do not guarantee an affordable procedural path to the vindication of every claim. Congress has taken some measures to facilitate the litigation of antitrust claims—for example, it enacted a multiplied-damages remedy. See 15 U.S.C. §15 (treble damages). In enacting such measures, Congress has told us that it is willing to go, in certain respects, beyond the normal limits of law in advancing its goals of deterring and remedying unlawful trade practice. But to say that Congress must have intended whatever departures from those normal limits advance antitrust goals is simply irrational. "[N]o legislation pursues its purposes at all costs." *Rodriguez* v. *United States, 480 U.S. 522-526 (1987)*.

The antitrust laws do not "evinc[e] an intention to preclude a waiver" of class-action procedure. *Mitsubishi Motors Corp.* v. *Soler Chrysler-Plymouth, Inc.*, 473 U.S. 614, 473 (1985). The Sherman and Clayton Acts make no mention of class actions. In fact, they were enacted decades before the advent of Federal Rule of Civil Procedure 23, which was "designed to allow an exception to the usual rule that litigation is conducted by and on behalf of the individual named parties only." *Califano* v. *Yamasaki*, 442 U.S. 682-701 (1979). The parties here agreed to arbitrate pursuant to that "usual rule," and it would be remarkable for a court to erase that expectation. * * *

Our finding of no "contrary congressional command" does not end the case. Respondents invoke a judge-made exception to the FAA which, they say, serves to harmonize competing federal policies by allowing courts to invalidate agreements that prevent the "effective vindication" of a federal statutory right. Enforcing the waiver of class arbitration bars effective vindication, respondents contend, because they have no economic incentive to pursue their antitrust claims individually in arbitration.

But the fact that it is not worth the expense involved in *proving* a statutory remedy does not constitute the elimination of the *right to pursue* that remedy. The class-action waiver merely limits arbitration to the two contracting parties. It no more eliminates those parties' right to pursue their statutory remedy than did federal law before its adoption of the class action for legal relief in 1938, see Fed. Rule Civ. Proc. 23 * * * Or, to put it differently, the individual suit that was considered adequate to assure "effective vindication" of a federal right before adoption of class-action procedures did not suddenly become "ineffective vindication" upon their adoption.

In *Gilmer v. Interstate Johnson Lane*, 500 U.S. 20 (1991), we had no qualms in enforcing a class waiver in an arbitration agreement even though the federal statute at issue, the Age Discrimination in Employment Act, expressly permitted collective actions. We said that statutory permission did " 'not mean that individual attempts at conciliation were intended to be barred.'" *[Citations], where* we held that requiring arbitration in a foreign country was compatible with the federal Carriage of Goods by Sea Act. That legislation prohibited any agreement "relieving" or "lessening" the liability of a carrier for damaged goods, [Citations]—which is close to codification of an "effective vindication" exception. The Court rejected the argument that the "inconvenience and costs of proceeding" abroad "lessen[ed]" the defendants' liability, stating that "[i]t would be unwieldy and unsupported by the terms or policy of the statute to require courts to proceed case by case to tally the costs and burdens to particular plaintiffs in light of their means, the size of their claims, and the relative burden on the carrier." [Citation]. Such a "tally[ing] [of] the costs and burdens" is precisely what the dissent would impose upon federal courts here.

The regime established by the Court of Appeals' decision would require—before a plaintiff can be held to contractually agreed bilateral arbitration—that a federal court determine (and the parties litigate) the legal requirements for success on the merits claim-by-claim and theory-by-theory, the evidence necessary to meet those requirements, the cost of developing that evidence, and the damages that would be recovered in the event of success. Such a preliminary litigating hurdle would undoubtedly destroy the prospect of speedy resolution that arbitration in general and bilateral arbitration in particular was meant to secure. The FAA does not sanction such a judicially created superstructure.

The judgement of the Court of Appeals is reversed.

It is so ordered.

Justice Sotomayor took no part in the consideration or decision of this case.

Justice Kagan, with whom Justice Ginsburg and Justice Breyer join, dissenting.

Here is the nutshell version of this case, unfortunately obscured in the Court's decision. The owner of a small restaurant (Italian Colors) thinks that American Express (Amex) has used its monopoly power to force merchants to accept a form contract violating the antitrust laws. The restauranteur wants to challenge the allegedly unlawful provision (imposing a tying arrangement), but the same contract's arbitration clause prevents him from doing so. That term imposes a variety of procedural bars that would make pursuit of the antitrust claim a fool's errand. So, if the arbitration clause is enforceable, Amex has insulated itself from antitrust liability—even if it has in fact violated the law. The monopolist gets to use its monopoly power to insist on a contract, effectively depriving its victims of all legal recourse.

And here is the nutshell version of today's opinion, admirably flaunted rather than camouflaged: Too darn bad.

That answer is a betrayal of our precedents, and of federal statutes like the antitrust laws. Our decisions have developed a mechanism—called the effective-vindication rule—to prevent arbitration clauses from choking off a plaintiff's ability to enforce congressionally created rights. That doctrine bars applying such a clause when (but only when) it operates to confer immunity from potentially meritorious federal claims. In so doing, the rule reconciles the Federal Arbitration Act (FAA) with all the rest of federal law—and indeed, promotes the most fundamental purposes of the FAA itself. As applied here, the rule would ensure that Amex's arbitration clause does not foreclose Italian Colors from vindicating its right to redress antitrust harm.

The majority barely tries to explain why it reaches a contrary result. It notes that we have not decided this exact case before—neglecting that the principle we have established fits this case hand in glove. And it concocts a special exemption for class-arbitration waivers—ignoring that this case concerns much more than that. Throughout, the majority disregards our decisions' central tenet: An arbitration clause may not thwart federal law, irrespective of exactly how it does so. Because the Court today prevents the effective vindication of federal statutory rights, I respectfully dissent.

Start with an uncontroversial proposition: We would refuse to enforce an exculpatory clause insulating a company from antitrust liability—say, "Merchants may bring no Sherman Act claims"—even if that clause were contained in an arbitration agreement. Congress created the Sherman Act's private cause of action not solely to compensate individuals, but to promote "the public interest in vigilant enforcement of the antitrust laws." *Lawlor v. National Screen Service Corp.*, 349 U.S. 322 (1955). Accordingly, courts will not enforce a prospective waiver of the right to gain redress for an antitrust injury, whether in an arbitration agreement or any other contract. See *Mitsubishi Motors Corp. v. Soler Chrysler-Plymouth, Inc.* 473 U.S. 614 (1985). The same rule applies to other important federal statutory rights. See *Penn Plaza LLC v. Pyett* 556 U.S. 247, 273 (2009). (Age Discrimination in Employment Act). But its necessity is nowhere more evident than in the antitrust context. Without the rule, a company could use its monopoly power to protect its monopoly power, by coercing agreement to contractual terms eliminating its antitrust liability.

If the rule were limited to baldly exculpatory provisions, however, a monopolist could devise numerous ways around it. Consider several alternatives that a party drafting an arbitration agreement could adopt to avoid antitrust liability, each of which would have the identical effect. On the front end: The agreement might set outlandish filing fees or establish an absurd (e.g., one-day) statute of limitations, thus preventing a claimant from gaining access to the arbitral forum. On the back end: The agreement might remove the arbitrator's authority to grant meaningful relief, so that a judgment gets the claimant nothing worthwhile. And in the middle: The agreement might block the claimant from presenting the kind of proof that is necessary to establish the defendant's liability—say, by prohibiting any economic testimony (good luck proving an antitrust claim without that!). Or else the agreement might appoint as an arbitrator an obviously biased person—say, the CEO of Amex. The possibilities are endless—all less direct than an express exculpatory clause, but no less fatal. So the rule against prospective waivers of federal rights can work only if it applies not just to a contract clause explicitly barring a claim, but to others that operate to do so.

And sure enough, our cases establish this proposition: An arbitration clause will not be enforced if it prevents the effective vindication of federal statutory rights, however it achieves that result. The rule originated in Mitsubishi, where we held that claims brought under the Sherman Act and other federal laws are generally subject to arbitration. Mitsubishi, 473 U.S., at 628. By agreeing to arbitrate such a claim, we explained, "a party does not forgo the substantive rights afforded by the statute; it only submits to their resolution in an arbitral, rather than a judicial, forum." But crucial to our decision was a limiting principle, designed to safeguard federal rights: An arbitration clause will be enforced only "so long as the prospective litigant effectively may vindicate its statutory cause of action in the arbitral forum." Id., at 637. If an arbitration provision "operated . . . as a prospective waiver of a party's right to pursue statutory remedies," we emphasized, we would "condemn[ ]" it. Id., at 637, n. 19. Similarly, we stated that such a clause should be "set aside" if "proceedings in the contractual forum will be so gravely difficult" that the claimant "will for all practical purposes be deprived of his day in court." Id., at 632 And in the decades since Mitsubishi, we have repeated its admonition time and again, instructing courts not to enforce an arbitration agreement that effectively (even if not explicitly) forecloses a plaintiff from remedying the violation of a federal statutory right. See [Citations] * * *

Applied as our precedents direct, the effective-vindication rule furthers the purposes not just of laws like the Sherman Act, but of the FAA itself. That statute reflects a federal policy favoring actual arbitration—that is, arbitration as a streamlined "method of resolving disputes," not as a foolproof way of killing off valid claims. Rodriguez de Quijas v. Shearson/American Express, Inc., 490 U.S. 477, 481 (1989). Put otherwise: What the FAA prefers to litigation is arbitration, not de facto immunity. The effective-vindication rule furthers the statute's goals by ensuring that arbitration remains a real, not faux, method of dispute resolution. With the rule, companies have good reason to adopt arbitral procedures that facilitate efficient and accurate handling of complaints. Without it, companies have every incentive to draft their agreements to extract backdoor waivers of statutory rights, making arbitration unavailable or pointless. So down one road: More arbitration, better enforcement of federal statutes. And down the other: Less arbitration, poorer enforcement of federal statutes. Which would you prefer? Or still more aptly: Which do you think Congress would? * * *

And this is just the kind of case the rule was meant to address. Italian Colors, as I have noted, alleges that Amex used its market power to impose a tying arrangement in violation of the Sherman Act. The antitrust laws, all parties agree, provide the restaurant with a cause of action and give it the chance to recover treble damages. Here, that would mean Italian Colors could take home up to $38,549. But a problem looms. As this case comes to us, the evidence shows that Italian Colors cannot prevail in arbitration without an economic analysis defining the relevant markets, establishing Amex's monopoly power, showing anticompetitive effects, and measuring damages. And that expert report would cost between several hundred thousand and one million dollars.[1] So the expense involved in proving the claim in arbitration is ten times what Italian Colors could hope to gain, even in a best-case scenario. That counts as a "prohibitive" cost, in Randolph's terminology, if anything does. No rational actor would bring a claim worth tens of thousands of dollars if doing so meant incurring costs in the hundreds of thousands.

An arbitration agreement could manage such a mismatch in many ways, but Amex's disdains them all. As the Court makes clear, the contract expressly prohibits class arbitration. But that is only part of the problem.[2] The agreement also disallows any kind of joinder or consolidation of claims or parties. And more: Its confidentiality provision prevents Italian Colors from informally arranging with other merchants to produce a common expert report. And still more: The agreement precludes any shifting of costs to Amex, even if Italian Colors prevails. And beyond all that: Amex refused to enter into any stipulations that would obviate or mitigate the need for the economic analysis. In short, the agreement as applied in this case cuts off not just class arbitration, but any avenue for sharing, shifting, or shrinking necessary costs. Amex has put Italian Colors to this choice: Spend way, way, way more money than your claim is worth, or relinquish your Sherman Act rights.

So contra the majority, the court below got this case right. Italian Colors proved what the plaintiff in Randolph could not—that a standard-form agreement, taken as a whole, renders arbitration of a claim "prohibitively expensive." 531 U.S., at 92. The restaurant thus established that the contract "operate[s] . . . as a prospective waiver," and prevents the "effective[ ] . . . vindicat[ion]" of Sherman Act rights. Mitsubishi, 473 U.S., at 637, andn. 19. I would follow our precedents and decline to compel arbitration. * * *

The Court today mistakes what this case is about. To a hammer, everything looks like a nail. And to a Court bent on diminishing the usefulness of Rule 23, everything looks like a class action, ready to be dismantled. So the Court does not consider that Amex's agreement bars not just class actions, but "other forms of cost-sharing . . . that could provide effective vindication." Majority opinion, at 7, n. 4. In short, the Court does not consider—and does not decide—Italian Colors's (and similarly situated litigants') actual argument about why the effective-vindication rule precludes this agreement's enforcement.

As a result, Amex's contract will succeed in depriving Italian Colors of any effective opportunity to challenge monopolistic conduct allegedly in violation of the Sherman Act. The FAA, the majority says, so requires. Do not be fooled. Only the Court so requires; the FAA was never meant to produce this outcome. The FAA conceived of arbitration as a "method of resolving disputes"—a way of using tailored and streamlined procedures to facilitate redress of injuries. Rodriguez de Quijas, 490 U.S., at 481 (emphasis added). In the hands of today's majority, arbitration threatens to become more nearly the opposite—a mechanism easily made to block the vindication of meritorious federal claims and insulate wrongdoers from liability. The Court thus undermines the FAA no less than it does the Sherman Act and other federal statutes providing rights of action. I respectfully dissent.

Case Questions

1. How can Supreme Court justices, or any judge, know what Congress meant or "intended" in 1925?
2. From the case, it's clear that the Justices have made many interpretations of the FAA in recent decades, and that they very much tend to favor the arbitration process. Why do you think they do?
3. These many interpretations add meaning and content to the FAA so that the public (and business, in particular) understands what kinds of contractual agreements to arbitrate will be upheld by the courts. Could Congress invalidate these interpretations if they chose to do so?
4. Here's a hoary Latin phrase for you: *Ubi Jus Ibi Remedium*. It means, For every wrong, the law provides a remedy. This was a principle of Roman law, known to the common law, and part of "equity" jurisprudence (that is, where the law courts in England did not provide a remedy, the equity courts did). Law and equity rules and principles are now merged in U.S. law. Which opinion, majority or dissent, takes this principle more seriously?

Endnotes

1. By "prima facie case," the court means a case in which the plaintiff has presented all the basic elements of the cause of action alleged in the complaint. If one or more elements of proof are missing, then the plaintiff has fallen short of establishing a prima facie case, and the case should be dismissed (usually on the basis of a directed verdict).
2. Note the division of labor here: questions of law are for the judge, while questions of "fact" are for the jury. Here, "foreseeability" is a fact question, while the judge retains authority over questions of law. The division between questions of fact and questions of law is not an easy one, however.

CHAPTER 4
Constitutional Law and US Commerce

Learning Objectives

After reading this chapter, you should be able to do the following:

1. Explain the historical importance and basic structure of the US Constitution.
2. Know what judicial review is and what it represents in terms of the separation of powers between the executive, legislative, and judicial branches of government.
3. Locate the source of congressional power to regulate the economy under the Constitution, and explain what limitations there are to the reach of congressional power over interstate commerce.
4. Describe the different phases of congressional power over commerce, as adjudged by the US Supreme Court over time.
5. Explain what power the states retain over commerce, and how the Supreme Court may sometimes limit that power.
6. Describe how the Supreme Court, under the supremacy clause of the Constitution, balances state and federal laws that may be wholly or partly in conflict.
7. Explain how the Bill of Rights relates to business activities in the United States.

The US Constitution is the foundation for all of US law. Business and commerce are directly affected by the words, meanings, and interpretations of the Constitution. Because it speaks in general terms, its provisions raise all kinds of issues for scholars, lawyers, judges, politicians, and commentators. For example, arguments still rage over the nature and meaning of "federalism," the concept that there is shared governance between the states and the federal government. The US Supreme Court is the ultimate arbiter of those disputes, and as such it has a unique role in the legal system. It has assumed the power of **judicial review**, unique among federal systems globally, through which it can strike down federal or state statutes that it believes violate the Constitution and can even void the president's executive orders if they are contrary to the Constitution's language. No knowledgeable citizen or businessperson can afford to be ignorant of its basic provisions.

judicial review

The power the Supreme Court has to say what the US Constitution means. Because the Constitution speaks in broad terms, the interpretations of the Supreme Court as to the meaning of its provisions define what the Constitution means. The Constitution can only be changed by amendment or by further interpretation by the Supreme Court.

4.1 Basic Aspects of the US Constitution

Learning Objectives

1. Describe the American values that are reflected in the US Constitution.
2. Know what federalism means, along with separation of powers.
3. Explain the process of amending the Constitution and why judicial review is particularly significant.

The Constitution as Reflecting American Values

In the US, the one document to which all public officials and military personnel pledge their unswerving allegiance is the Constitution. If you serve, you are asked to "support and defend" the Constitution "against all enemies, foreign and domestic." The oath usually includes a statement that you swear that this oath is taken freely, honestly, and without "any purpose of evasion." This loyalty oath may be related to a time—fifty years ago—when "un-American" activities were under investigation in Congress and the press; the fear of communism (seen as contrary to American values and principles, or at least the values of capitalism) was paramount. As you look at the Constitution and how it affects the legal environment of business, please consider what basic values it may impart to us and what makes it uniquely American and worth defending "against all enemies, foreign and domestic."

In Article I, the Constitution places the legislature first and prescribes the ways in which representatives are elected to public office. Article I balances influence in the federal legislature between large states and small states by creating a Senate in which the smaller states (by population) as well as the larger states have two votes. In Article II, the Constitution sets forth the powers and responsibilities of the branch—the presidency—and makes it clear that the president should be the commander in chief of the armed forces. Article II also gives states rather than individuals (through the Electoral College) a clear role in the election process. Article III creates the federal judiciary, and the Bill of Rights, adopted in 1791, makes clear that individual rights must be preserved against activities of the federal government. In general, the concept of "unalienable" rights—rights that cannot be waived or sacrificed to government—is particularly strong.

The Constitution itself speaks of rights in fairly general terms, and the judicial interpretation of various rights has been in flux. The "right" of a person to own another person was notably affirmed by the Supreme Court in the *Dred Scott* decision in 1857.[1] The "right" of a child to freely contract for long, tedious hours of work was upheld by the court in *Hammer v. Dagenhart* in 1918. Both decisions were later repudiated, just as the decision that a woman has a "right" to an abortion in the first trimester of pregnancy could later be repudiated if *Roe v. Wade* is overturned by the Supreme Court.[2]

General Structure of the Constitution

Look at the Constitution. Notice that there are seven articles, starting with Article I (legislative powers), Article II (executive branch), and Article III (judiciary). Notice that there is no separate article for administrative agencies, sometimes erroneously referred to as "the Fourth Branch" of government. The Constitution also declares that it is "the supreme Law of the Land" (Article VI). Article VII allowed for ratification by 9 of the 13 states under the Articles of Confederation. Following Article VII are the ten amendments adopted in 1791 that are referred to as the Bill of Rights. Notice also that in 1868, a new amendment, the Fourteenth, was adopted, requiring states to provide "due process" and "equal protection of the laws" to citizens of the United States.

Federalism

The partnership created in the Constitution between the states and the federal government is called **federalism**. The Constitution is a document created by the states in which certain powers are delegated to the national government, and other powers are reserved to the states. This is made explicit in the Tenth Amendment.

federalism

The idea, built into the structure of the Constitution, that states and the federal government have concurrent powers. In effect, federalism is the concept of shared governance between the states and the federal government.

Separation of Powers and Judicial Review

Because the Founding Fathers wanted to ensure that no single branch of the government, especially the executive branch, would be ascendant over the others, they created various checks and balances to ensure that each of the three principal branches had ways to limit or modify the power of the others. This is known as the **separation of powers**. Thus the president retains veto power, but the House of Representatives is entrusted with the power to initiate spending bills.

separation of powers

In the original design of the Constitution, the executive, legislative, and judicial branches were all given powers that could modify or limit the powers of the other branches of government. For example, the president wields a veto power over congressional legislation.

Power sharing was evident in the basic design of Congress, the federal legislative branch. The basic power imbalance was between the large states (with greater population) and the smaller ones (such as Delaware). The smaller ones feared a loss of sovereignty if they could be outvoted by the larger ones, so the federal legislature was constructed to guarantee two Senate seats for every state, no matter how small. The Senate was also given great responsibility in ratifying treaties and judicial nominations. The net effect of this today is that senators from a very small number of states can block treaties and other important legislation. The power of small states is also magnified by the Senate's cloture rule, which currently requires sixty out of one hundred senators to vote to bring a bill to the floor for an up-or-down vote. The cloture rule is often referred to in the context of a "filibuster."[3]

Because the Constitution often speaks in general terms (with broad phrases such as "due process" and "equal protection"), reasonable people have disagreed as to how those terms apply in specific cases. The United States is unique among industrialized democracies in having a Supreme Court that reserves for itself an exclusive power to interpret what the Constitution means. The famous case of *Marbury v. Madison* began that tradition in 1803, when the Supreme Court had marginal importance in the new republic. The decision in *Bush v. Gore*, decided in December of 2000, illustrates the power of the court to shape our destiny as a nation. In that case, the court overturned a ruling by the Florida Supreme Court regarding the way to proceed on a recount of the Florida vote for the presidency. The court's ruling was purportedly based on the "equal protection of the laws" provision in the Fourteenth Amendment.

From *Marbury* to the present day, the Supreme Court has articulated the view that the US Constitution sets the framework for all other US laws, whether statutory or judicially created. Thus, any statute (or portion thereof) or legal ruling (judicial or administrative) in conflict with the Constitution is not enforceable. And as the *Bush v. Gore* decision indicates, the states are not entirely free to do what they might choose; their own sovereignty is limited by their union with the other states into the federal sovereignty.

If the Supreme Court makes a "bad decision" as to what the Constitution means or how it may apply to important federal or state legislation, it is not easily overturned. Either the court must change its mind (which it seldom does) or two-thirds of Congress and three-fourths of the states must make an amendment (Article V). In recent years, constitutional challenges to the Affordable Care Act (also known as "Obamacare") have been numerous, but the Court has (by the thinnest of margins) upheld the constitutionality of the legislation thus far.

Because the Supreme Court has this power of judicial review, there have been many arguments about how it should be exercised and what kind of "philosophy" a Supreme Court justice should have. President Richard Nixon often said that a Supreme Court justice should "strictly construe" the Constitution and not add to its language. For Nixon, finding "new law" in the Constitution was "judicial activism" rather than "judicial restraint." Republican presidents since Nixon have announced their intention to only appoint Supreme Court justices who are "strict constructionists." The general philosophy behind the call for "strict constructionist" justices is that legislatures make laws in accord with the wishes of the majority, and so unelected judges should not make law according to their own views and values. Nixon had in mind the 1960s Warren court, which "found" rights in the Constitution that were not specifically mentioned—the right of privacy, for example. *Roe v. Wade* (1973) is often pointed to as a prime example of judicial activism for using a "right of privacy" to create a woman's right to make determinations about abortion in the first trimester without undue government interference.

In later years, critics of the Rehnquist court would charge that more conservative courts, such as the Rehnquist court, also created newly-found rights that were not specifically mentioned in the Constitution, such as the right of states to be free from federal anti-discrimination laws. See, for example, *Kimel v. Florida Board of Regents*, or the *Citizens United v. Federal Election Commission* case (Section 6), which held that corporations are "persons" with "free speech rights" that include spending unlimited amounts of money in campaign donations and political advocacy.[4]

Because *Roe v. Wade* has been so controversial, this chapter includes a seminal case on "the right of privacy," *Griswold v. Connecticut*, Section 6. Was the court correct in recognizing a "right of privacy" in Griswold? This may not seem like a "business case," but consider: the manufacture and distribution of birth control devices is a highly profitable (and legal) business in every US state. Moreover, Griswold illustrates another important and much-debated concept in US constitutional law: substantive due process (see Section 5). The problem of judicial review and its proper scope is brought into sharp focus in the abortion controversy. Abortion became a lucrative service business after *Roe v. Wade* was decided in 1973. That has gradually changed, with state laws that have limited rather than overruled *Roe v. Wade* and with persistent anti-abortion protests, killings of abortion doctors, and efforts to publicize the human nature of the fetuses being aborted. The key here is to understand that there is no *explicit* mention in the Constitution of any right of privacy. As Justice Harry Blackmun argued in his majority opinion in *Roe v. Wade*,

> *The Constitution does not explicitly mention any right of privacy. In a line of decisions, however, the Court has recognized that a right of personal privacy or a guarantee of certain areas or zones of privacy, does exist under the Constitution....[T]hey also make it clear that the right has some extension to activities relating to marriage...procreation...contraception...family relationships...and child rearing and education....The right of privacy...is broad enough to encompass a woman's decision whether or not to terminate her pregnancy.*

In short, US Supreme Court Justices, appointed not elected, wield enormous power through judicial review. In deciding that the right of privacy applied to a woman's decision to abort in the first trimester, the Supreme Court did not act on the basis of a popular mandate or clear and unequivocal language in the Constitution, and it made illegal any state or federal legislative or executive action contrary to its interpretation. Only a constitutional amendment or the court's repudiation of *Roe v. Wade* as a precedent could change that interpretation.

Key Takeaway

The Constitution gives voice to the idea that people have basic rights and that a civilian president is also the commander in chief of the armed forces. It gives instructions as to how the various branches of government must share power and also tries to balance power between the states and the federal government. It does not expressly allow for judicial review, but the Supreme Court's ability to declare what laws are (or are not) constitutional has given the judicial branch a kind of power not seen in other industrialized democracies.

Exercises

1. Suppose the Supreme Court declares that Congress and the president cannot authorize the indefinite detention of terrorist suspects without a trial of some sort, whether military or civilian. Suppose also that the people of the United States favor such indefinite detention and that Congress wants to pass a law rebuking the court's decision. What kind of law would have to be passed, by what institutions, and by what voting percentages?
2. When does a prior decision of the Supreme Court deserve overturning? Name one decision of the Supreme Court that you think is no longer "good law." Does the court have to wait one hundred years to overturn its prior case precedents?

4.2 The Commerce Clause

Learning Objectives

1. Name the specific clause through which Congress has the power to regulate commerce. What, specifically, does this clause say?
2. Explain how early decisions of the Supreme Court interpreted the scope of the commerce clause and how that impacted the legislative proposals and programs of Franklin Delano Roosevelt during the Great Depression.
3. Describe both the wider use of the commerce clause from World War II through the 1990s and the limitations the Supreme Court imposed in *Lopez* and other cases.

First, turn to Article I, Section 8. The **commerce clause** gives Congress the exclusive power to make laws relating to foreign trade and to commerce among the various states. Most of the federally created legal environment springs from this one clause: if Congress is not authorized in the Constitution to make certain laws, then it acts unconstitutionally and its actions may be ruled unconstitutional by the Supreme Court. Over the past 20 years, the Supreme Court has been more active in ruling that certain acts of Congress are unconstitutional.

commerce clause

Article I, Section 8, of the US Constitution is generally regarded as the legal authority by which the federal government can make law that governs commerce among the states and with foreign nations.

Here are the first five parts of Article I, Section 8, which sets forth the powers of the federal legislature. The commerce clause is in boldface. It is short, but most federal legislation affecting business depends on this very clause:

Section 8
[Clause 1] The Congress shall have Power To lay and collect Taxes, Duties, Imposts and Excises, to pay the Debts and provide for the common Defence and general Welfare of the United States; but all Duties, Imposts and Excises shall be uniform throughout the United States;

[Clause 2] To borrow Money on the credit of the United States;

[Clause 3] To regulate Commerce with foreign Nations, and among the several States, and with the Indian Tribes[5];

[Clause 4] To establish a uniform Rule of Naturalization, and uniform Laws on the subject of Bankruptcies throughout the United States;

[Clause 5] To coin Money, regulate the Value thereof, and of foreign Coin, and fix the Standard of Weights and Measures;

Early Commerce Clause Cases

For many years, the Supreme Court was very strict in applying the commerce clause: Congress could only use it to legislate aspects of the movement of goods from one state to another. Anything else was deemed local rather than national. For example, In *Hammer v. Dagenhart*, decided in 1918, a 1916 federal statute had barred transportation in interstate commerce of goods produced in mines or factories employing children under fourteen or employing children fourteen and above for more than eight hours a day. A complaint was filed in the US District Court for the Western District of North Carolina by a father in his own behalf and on behalf of his two minor sons, one under the age of fourteen years and the other between fourteen and sixteen years, who were employees in a cotton mill in Charlotte, North Carolina. The father's lawsuit asked the court to enjoin (block) the enforcement of the act of Congress intended to prevent interstate commerce in the products of child labor.

The Supreme Court saw the issue as whether Congress had the power under the commerce clause to control interstate shipment of goods made by children under the age of fourteen. The Court found that Congress did not. The Court cited several cases that had considered what interstate commerce could be constitutionally regulated by Congress. In *Hipolite Egg Co. v. United States*, the Supreme Court had sustained the power of Congress to pass the Pure Food and Drug Act, which prohibited the introduction into the states by means of interstate commerce impure foods and drugs.[6] In *Hoke v. United States*, the Supreme Court had sustained the constitutionality of the so-called White Slave Traffic Act of 1910, whereby the transportation of a woman in interstate commerce for the purpose of prostitution was forbidden. In that case, the court said that Congress had the power to protect the channels of interstate commerce: "If the facility of interstate transportation can be taken away from the demoralization of lotteries, the debasement of obscene literature, the contagion of diseased cattle or persons, the impurity of food and drugs, the like facility can be taken away from the systematic enticement to, and the enslavement in prostitution and debauchery of women, and, more insistently, of girls."[7]

In each of those instances, the Supreme Court said, "[T]he use of interstate transportation was necessary to the accomplishment of harmful results." In other words, although the power over interstate transportation was to regulate commerce, that could only be accomplished by prohibiting the use of the *facilities* of interstate commerce to effect the evil intended. But in *Hammer v. Dagenhart*, that essential element was lacking. The law passed by Congress aimed to standardize among all the states the ages at which children could be employed in mining and manufacturing, while the goods themselves are harmless. Once the labor is done and the articles have left the factory, the "labor of their production is over, and the mere fact that they were intended for interstate commerce transportation does not make their production subject to federal control under the commerce power."

In short, the early use of the commerce clause was limited to the movement of physical goods (or people) between states. Just because something might enter the channels of interstate commerce later on does not make it a fit subject for national regulation. The production of articles intended for interstate commerce is a matter of local regulation. The court therefore upheld the result from the district and circuit court of appeals; the application of the federal law was enjoined. Goods produced by children under the age of fourteen could be shipped anywhere in the United States without violating the federal law.

From the New Deal to the New Frontier and the Great Society: 1930s–1970

During the global depression of the 1930s, the US economy saw jobless rates of a third of all workers, and President Roosevelt's New Deal program required more active federal legislation. Included in the New Deal program was the recognition of a right to form labor unions without undue interference from employers. Congress created the National Labor Relations Board (NLRB) in 1935 to investigate and to enjoin employer practices that violated this right.

In *NLRB v. Jones & Laughlin Steel Corporation*, a union dispute with management at a large steel-producing facility near Pittsburgh, Pennsylvania led to litigation. In this case, the NLRB had charged the Jones & Laughlin Steel Corporation with discriminating against employees who were union members. The company's position was that the law authorizing the NLRB was unconstitutional, exceeding Congress's powers. The Court held that the act was narrowly constructed so as to regulate industrial activities that had the potential to restrict interstate commerce. The earlier decisions under the commerce clause to the effect that labor relations had only an indirect effect on commerce were effectively reversed. Since the ability of employees to engage in collective bargaining (one activity protected by the act) is "an essential condition of industrial peace," the national government was justified in penalizing corporations engaging in interstate commerce that "refuse to confer and negotiate" with their workers. This was, however, a close decision, and the switch of one Justice made this ruling possible. Without this switch, the New Deal agenda would have been effectively derailed.[8]

The Substantial Effects Doctrine: World War II to the 1990s

Subsequent to *NLRB v. Jones & Laughlin Steel Corporation*, Congress and the courts generally accepted that even modest impacts on interstate commerce were "reachable" by federal legislation. For example, the case of *Wickard v. Filburn*, from 1942, represents a fairly long reach for Congress in regulating what appear to be very local economic decisions (Section 6).

Wickard established that "substantial effects" in interstate commerce could be so local that one farming family's consumption of wheat withheld from "the channels of interstate commerce" could be regulated by Congress. But commerce clause challenges in the nature of "this is too local" for federal regulation continued. The Civil Rights Act of 1964 was quickly challenged on the ground that Congress lacked the power under the commerce clause to regulate what was otherwise fairly local conduct. For example, Title II of the act prohibited racial discrimination in public accommodations (such as hotels, motels, and restaurants), leading to the famous case of *Katzenbach v. McClung* (1964).

Ollie McClung's barbeque place in Birmingham, Alabama, allowed "colored" people to buy take-out at the back of the restaurant but not to sit down with "white" people inside. The US attorney sought a court order to require Ollie to serve all races and colors, but Ollie resisted on commerce clause grounds: the federal government had no business regulating a purely local establishment. Indeed, Ollie did not advertise nationally, or even regionally, and had customers only from the local area. But the court found that some 42 percent of the supplies for Ollie's restaurant had moved in the channels of interstate commerce. This was enough to sustain federal regulation based on the commerce clause.[9]

For nearly thirty years following, it was widely assumed that Congress could almost always find some interstate commerce connection for any law it might pass. It thus came as surprise to many in 1995 when the Rehnquist court decided *U.S. v. Lopez*. Lopez had been convicted under a federal law that prohibited possession of firearms within 1,000 feet of a school. The law was part of a twenty-year trend (roughly 1970 to 1990) for senators and congressmen to pass laws that were "tough on crime." Lopez's lawyer admitted that Lopez had had a gun within 1,000 feet of a San Antonio school yard but challenged the law itself, arguing that Congress exceeded its authority under the commerce clause in passing this legislation. The US government's Solicitor General argued on behalf of the Department of Justice to the Supreme Court that Congress was within its constitutional rights under the commerce clause because education of the future workforce was the foundation for a sound economy and because guns at or near school yards detracted from students' education. The court rejected this analysis, noting that with the government's analysis, an interstate commerce connection could be conjured from almost anything. Lopez could not be convicted under a federal criminal statute that lacked constitutional basis under the commerce clause.

Congress made no attempt to pass similar legislation after the case was decided. But in passing subsequent legislation, Congress was often careful to make a record as to why it believed it was addressing a problem that related to interstate commerce. In 1994, Congress passed the Violence Against Women Act (VAWA), but only after holding hearings to establish why violence against women on a local level would impair interstate commerce. In 1994, while enrolled at Virginia Polytechnic Institute (Virginia Tech), Christy Brzonkala alleged that Antonio Morrison and James Crawford, both students and varsity football players at Virginia Tech, had raped her. In 1995, Brzonkala filed a complaint against Morrison and Crawford under Virginia Tech's sexual assault policy. After a hearing, Morrison was found guilty of sexual assault and sentenced to immediate suspension for two semesters. Crawford was not punished. A second hearing again found Morrison guilty. After an appeal through the university's administrative system, Morrison's punishment was set aside, as it was found to be "excessive." Brzonkala dropped out of the university. She then sued Morrison, Crawford, and Virginia Tech in federal district court, alleging that Morrison's and Crawford's attack violated 42 USC Section 13981 (part of the VAWA), which provides a federal civil remedy for the victims of gender-motivated violence. Morrison and Crawford moved to dismiss Brzonkala's suit on the ground that Section 13981's civil remedy was unconstitutional. In dismissing the complaint, the district court found that Congress lacked authority to enact Section 13981 under either the commerce clause or the Fourteenth Amendment, which Congress had explicitly identified as the sources of federal authority for the VAWA. Ultimately, the court of appeals affirmed, as did the Supreme Court.

The Supreme Court held that Congress lacked the authority to enact a statute under the commerce clause or the Fourteenth Amendment because the statute did not regulate an activity that substantially affected interstate commerce nor did it redress harm caused by the state. Chief Justice William H. Rehnquist wrote for the court that "under our federal system that remedy must be provided by the Commonwealth of Virginia, and not by the United States." Dissenting, Justice Stephen G. Breyer argued that the majority opinion "illustrates the difficulty of finding a workable judicial Commerce Clause touchstone." Justice David H. Souter, dissenting, noted that VAWA contained a "mountain of data assembled by Congress...showing the effects of violence against women on interstate commerce."

The absence of a workable judicial commerce clause touchstone remains. In 1996, California voters passed the Compassionate Use Act, legalizing marijuana for medical use. California's law conflicted with the federal Controlled Substances Act (CSA), which banned possession of marijuana. After the Drug Enforcement Administration (DEA) seized doctor-prescribed marijuana from a patient's home, a group of medical marijuana users sued the DEA and US Attorney General John Ashcroft in federal district court.

The medical marijuana users argued that the CSA—which Congress passed using its constitutional power to regulate interstate commerce—exceeded Congress's commerce clause power. The district court ruled against the group, but the Ninth Circuit Court of Appeals reversed and ruled the CSA unconstitutional because it applied to medical marijuana use solely within one state. In doing so, the Ninth Circuit relied on *U.S. v. Lopez* (1995) and *U.S. v. Morrison* (2000) to say that using medical marijuana did not "substantially affect" interstate commerce and therefore could not be regulated by Congress.

But by a 6–3 majority, the Supreme Court held that the commerce clause gave Congress authority to prohibit the local cultivation and use of marijuana, despite state law to the contrary. Justice John Paul Stevens argued that the court's precedents established Congress's commerce clause power to regulate purely local activities that are part of a "class of activities" with a substantial effect on interstate commerce. The majority argued that Congress could ban local marijuana use because it was part of such a class of activities: the national marijuana market. Local use affected supply and demand in the national marijuana market, making the regulation of intrastate use "essential" to regulating the drug's national market.

Notice how similar this reasoning is to the court's earlier reasoning in *Wickard v. Filburn* (Section 6). In contrast, the court's conservative wing was adamant that federal power had been exceeded. Justice Clarence Thomas's dissent in *Gonzalez v. Raich* stated that Raich's local cultivation and consumption of marijuana was not "Commerce...among the several States." Representing the "originalist" view that the Constitution should mostly mean what the Founders meant it to mean, he also said that in the early days of the republic, it would have been unthinkable that Congress could prohibit the local cultivation, possession, and consumption of marijuana.

Key Takeaway

The commerce clause is the basis on which the federal government regulates interstate economic activity. The phrase "interstate commerce" has been subject to differing interpretations by the Supreme Court over the past one hundred years. There are certain matters that are essentially local or intrastate, but the range of federal involvement in local matters is still considerable.

Exercises

1. Why would Congress have power under the Civil Rights Act of 1964 to require restaurants and hotels to not discriminate against interstate travelers on the basis of race, color, sex, religion, or national origin? Suppose the Holiday Restaurant near I-80 in Des Moines, Iowa, has a sign that says, "We reserve the right to refuse service to any Muslim or person of Middle Eastern descent." Suppose also that the restaurant is very popular locally and that only 40 percent of its patrons are travelers on I-80. Are the owners of the Holiday Restaurant in violation of the Civil Rights Act of 1964? What would happen if the owners resisted enforcement by claiming that Title II of the act (relating to "public accommodations" such as hotels, motels, and restaurants) was unconstitutional?
2. If the Supreme Court were to go back to the days of *Hammer v. Dagenhart* and rule that only goods and services involving interstate movement could be subject to federal law, what kinds of federal programs might be lacking a sound basis in the commerce clause? "Obamacare"? Medicare? Homeland security? Social Security?

4.3 Dormant Commerce Clause

Learning Objectives

1. Understand that when Congress does not exercise its powers under the commerce clause, the Supreme Court may still limit state legislation that discriminates against interstate commerce or places an undue burden on interstate commerce.
2. Distinguish between "discrimination" dormant-commerce-clause cases and "undue burden" dormant-commerce-clause cases.

Congress has the power to legislate under the commerce clause and often does legislate. For example, Congress might say that trucks moving on interstate highways must not be more than seventy feet in length. But if Congress does not exercise its powers and regulate in certain areas (such as the size and length of trucks on interstate highways), states may make their own rules. States may do so under the so-called historic police powers of states that were never yielded up to the federal government.

dormant commerce clause

Even when the federal government does not act to make rules to govern matters of interstate commerce, the states may (using their police powers), but they may not do so in ways that unduly burden or discriminate against interstate commerce.

These police powers can be broadly exercised by states for purposes of health, education, welfare, safety, morals, and the environment. But the Supreme Court has reserved for itself the power to determine when state action is excessive, even when Congress has not used the commerce clause to regulate. This power is claimed to exist in the **dormant commerce clause**.

There are two ways that a state may violate the dormant commerce clause. If a state passes a law that is an "undue burden" on interstate commerce or that "discriminates" against interstate commerce, it will be struck down. *Kassel v. Consolidated Freightways* (in Section 4.6, Cases) is an example of a case where Iowa imposed an undue burden on interstate commerce by prohibiting double trailers on its highways.[10] Iowa's prohibition was judicially declared void when the Supreme Court judged it to be an undue burden.

Discrimination cases such as *Hunt v. Washington Apple Advertising Commission* (Section 4.6 "Cases") pose a different standard. The court has been fairly inflexible here: if one state discriminates in its treatment of any article of commerce based on its state of origin, the court will strike down the law. For example, in *Oregon Waste Systems v. Department of Environmental Quality*, the state wanted to place a slightly higher charge on waste coming from out of state.[11] The state's reasoning was that in-state residents had already contributed to roads and other infrastructure and that tipping fees at waste facilities should reflect the prior contributions of in-state companies and residents. Out-of-state waste handlers who wanted to use Oregon landfills objected and won their dormant commerce clause claim that Oregon's law discriminated "on its face" against interstate commerce. Under the Supreme Court's rulings, anything that moves in channels of interstate commerce is "commerce," even if someone is paying to get rid of something instead of buying something.

Thus the states are bound by Supreme Court decisions under the dormant commerce clause to do nothing that differentiates between articles of commerce that originate from within the state from those that originate elsewhere. If Michigan were to let counties decide for themselves whether to take garbage from outside of the county or not, this could also be a discrimination based on a place of origin outside the state. (Suppose, for instance, each county were to decide not to take waste from outside the county; then all Michigan counties would effectively be excluding waste from outside of Michigan, which is discriminatory.)[12]

The Supreme Court probably would uphold any solid waste requirements that did not differentiate on the basis of origin. If, for example, all waste had to be inspected for specific hazards, then the law would apply equally to in-state and out-of-state garbage. Because this is the dormant commerce clause, Congress could still act (i.e., it could use its broad commerce clause powers) to say that states are free to keep out-of-state waste from coming into their own borders. But Congress has declined to do so. What follows is a statement from one of the US senators from Michigan, Carl Levin, in 2003, regarding the significant amounts of waste that were coming into Michigan from Toronto, Canada.

Dealing with Unwelcome Waste

Senator Carl Levin, January 2003

Michigan is facing an intolerable situation with regard to the importation of waste from other states and Canada.

Canada is the largest source of waste imports to Michigan. Approximately 65 truckloads of waste come in to Michigan per day from Toronto alone, and an estimated 110–130 trucks come in from Canada each day.

This problem isn't going to get any better. Ontario's waste shipments are growing as the Toronto area signs new contracts for waste disposal here and closes its two remaining landfills. At the beginning of 1999, the Toronto area was generating about 2.8 million tons of waste annually, about 700,000 tons of which were shipped to Michigan. By early this year, barring unforeseen developments, the entire 2.8 million tons will be shipped to Michigan for disposal.

Why can't Canada dispose of its trash in Canada? They say that after 20 years of searching they have not been able to find a suitable Ontario site for Toronto's garbage. Ontario has about 345,000 square miles compared to Michigan's 57,000 square miles. With six times the land mass, that argument is laughable.

The Michigan Department of Environmental Quality estimates that, for every five years of disposal of Canadian waste at the current usage volume, Michigan is losing a full year of landfill capacity. The environmental impacts on landfills, including groundwater contamination, noise pollution and foul odors, are exacerbated by the significant increase in the use of our landfills from sources outside of Michigan.

I have teamed up with Senator Stabenow and Congressman Dingell to introduce legislation that would strengthen our ability to stop shipments of waste from Canada.

We have protections contained in a 17 year-old international agreement between the U.S. and Canada called the Agreement Concerning the Transboundary Movement of Hazardous Waste. The U.S. and Canada entered into this agreement in 1986 to allow the shipment of hazardous waste across the U.S./Canadian border for treatment, storage or disposal. In 1992, the two countries decided to add municipal solid waste to the agreement. To protect both countries, the agreement requires notification of shipments to the importing country and it also provides that the importing country may withdraw consent for shipments. Both reasons are evidence that these shipments were intended to be limited. However, the agreement's provisions have not been enforced by the United States.

Canada could not export waste to Michigan without the 1986 agreement, but the U.S. has not implemented the provisions that are designed to protect the people of Michigan. Although those of us that introduced this legislation believe that the Environmental Protection Agency has the authority to enforce this agreement, they have not done so. Our bill would require the EPA [Environmental Protection Agency] to enforce the agreement.

In order to protect the health and welfare of the citizens of Michigan and our environment, we must consider the impact of the importation of trash on state and local recycling efforts, landfill capacity, air emissions, road deterioration resulting from increased vehicular traffic and public health and the environment.

Our bill would require the EPA to consider these factors in determining whether to accept imports of trash from Canada. It is my strong view that such a review should lead the EPA to say "no" to the status quo of trash imports.

Key Takeaway

Where Congress does not act pursuant to its commerce clause powers, the states are free to legislate on matters of commerce under their historic police powers. However, the Supreme Court has set limits on such powers. Specifically, states may not impose undue burdens on interstate commerce and may not discriminate against articles in interstate commerce.

Exercises

1. Suppose that the state of New Jersey wishes to limit the amount of hazardous waste that enters into its landfills. The general assembly in New Jersey passes a law that specifically forbids any hazardous waste from entering into the state. All landfills are subject to tight regulations that will allow certain kinds of hazardous wastes originating in New Jersey to be put in New Jersey landfills but that impose significant criminal fines on landfill operators that accept out-of-state hazardous waste. The Baldessari Brothers Landfill in Linden, New Jersey, is fined for taking hazardous waste from a New York State transporter and appeals that ruling on the basis that New Jersey's law is unconstitutional. What is the result?
2. The state of Arizona determines through its legislature that trains passing through the state cannot be longer than seventy cars. There is some evidence that in Eastern U.S. states longer trains pose some safety hazards. There is less evidence that long trains are a problem in Western states. Several major railroads find the Arizona legislation costly and burdensome and challenge the legislation after applied-for permits for longer trains are denied. What kind of dormant commerce clause challenge is this, and what would it take for the challenge to be successful?

4.4 Preemption: The Supremacy Clause

Learning Objectives

1. Understand the role of the supremacy clause in the balance between state and federal power.
2. Give examples of cases where state legislation is preempted by federal law and cases where state legislation is not preempted by federal law.

When Congress does use its power under the commerce clause, it can expressly state that it wishes to have exclusive regulatory authority. For example, when Congress determined in the 1950s to promote nuclear power ("atoms for peace"), it set up the Nuclear Regulatory Commission and provided a limitation of liability for nuclear power plants in case of a nuclear accident. The states were expressly told to stay out of the business of regulating nuclear power or the movement of nuclear materials. Thus Rochester, Minnesota, or Berkeley, California, could declare itself a nuclear-free zone, but the federal government would have preempted such legislation. If Michigan wished to set safety standards at Detroit Edison's Fermi II nuclear reactor that were more stringent than the federal Nuclear Regulatory Commission's standards, Michigan's standards would be preempted and thus be void.

Even where Congress does not expressly preempt state action, such action may be impliedly pre-empted. States cannot constitutionally pass laws that interfere with the accomplishment of the purposes of the federal law. Suppose, for example, that Congress passes a comprehensive law that sets standards for foreign vessels to enter the navigable waters and ports of the United States. If a state creates a law that sets standards that conflict with the federal law or sets standards so burdensome that they interfere with federal law, the doctrine of preemption will (in accordance with the supremacy clause) void the state law or whatever parts of it are inconsistent with federal law.

But Congress can allow what might appear to be inconsistencies; the existence of federal statutory standards does not always mean that local and state standards cannot be more stringent. If California wants cleaner air or water than other states, it can set stricter standards—nothing in the Clean Water Act or Clean Air Act forbids the state from setting stricter pollution standards. As the auto industry well knows, California has set stricter standards for auto emissions. Since the 1980s, most automakers have made both a federal car and a California car, because federal Clean Air Act emissions restrictions do not preempt more rigorous state standards.

Large industries and companies actually prefer regulation at the national level. It is easier for a large company or industry association to lobby in Washington, DC, than to lobby in fifty different states. Accordingly, industry often asks Congress to put preemptive language into its statutes. The tobacco industry is a case in point.

The cigarette warning legislation of the 1960s (where the federal government required warning labels on cigarette packages) effectively preempted state negligence claims based on failure to warn. When the family of a lifetime smoker who had died sued in New Jersey court, one cause of action was the company's failure to warn of the dangers of its product. The Supreme Court reversed the jury's award based on the federal preemption of failure to warn claims under state law.[13]

The Supremacy Clause

Article VI

> *This Constitution, and the Laws of the United States which shall be made in Pursuance thereof; and all Treaties made, or which shall be made, under the Authority of the United States, shall be the supreme Law of the Land; and the Judges in every State shall be bound thereby, any Thing in the Constitution or Laws of any State to the Contrary notwithstanding.*

preemption

Based on the supremacy clause, the preemption doctrine holds that state and federal laws that conflict must yield to the superior law, which is federal law.

The **preemption** doctrine derives from the supremacy clause of the Constitution, which states that the "Constitution and the Laws of the United States...shall be the supreme Law of the Land...any Thing in the Constitutions or Laws of any State to the Contrary notwithstanding." This means of course, that *any* federal law—even a regulation of a federal agency—would control over *any* conflicting state law.

Preemption can be either express or implied. When Congress chooses to expressly preempt state law, the only question for courts becomes determining whether the challenged state law is one that the federal law is intended to preempt. Implied preemption presents more difficult issues. The court has to look beyond the express language of federal statutes to determine whether Congress has "occupied the field" in which the state is attempting to regulate, or whether a state law directly conflicts with federal law, or whether enforcement of the state law might frustrate federal purposes.

Federal "occupation of the field" occurs, according to the court in *Pennsylvania v. Nelson* (1956), when there is "no room" left for state regulation. Courts are to look to the pervasiveness of the federal scheme of regulation, the federal interest at stake, and the danger of frustration of federal goals in making the determination as to whether a challenged state law can stand.

In *Silkwood v. Kerr-McGee* (1984), the court, voting 5–4, found that a $10 million punitive damages award (in a case litigated by famed attorney Gerry Spence) against a nuclear power plant was not impliedly preempted by federal law. Even though the court had recently held that state regulation of the safety aspects of a federally licensed nuclear power plant was preempted, the court drew a different conclusion with respect to Congress's desire to displace state tort law—even though the tort actions might be premised on a violation of federal safety regulations.

Cipollone v. Liggett Group (1993) was a closely watched case concerning the extent of an express preemption provision in two cigarette labeling laws of the 1960s. The case was a wrongful death action brought against tobacco companies on behalf of Rose Cipollone, a lung cancer victim who had started smoking cigarette in the 1940s. The court considered the preemptive effect on state law of a provision in the federal labeling law that stated, "No requirement based on smoking and health shall be imposed under state law with respect to the advertising and promotion of cigarettes." The court concluded that several types of state tort actions were preempted by the provision but allowed other types to go forward.

In recent years, several states have passed laws for medical and recreational marijuana that are inconsistent with the federal Controlled Substances Act. In 1970, Congress (at the urging of President Nixon as part of his "law and order" agenda) enacted the federal Controlled Substances Act (CSA) and placed the plant cannabis, referred to in the CSA as *marihuana*, into Schedule I—the most restrictive schedule. Schedule I substances are the most tightly controlled of the CSA's five classifications. Schedule I substances are said to have "a high potential for abuse," "no currently accepted medical use in treatment in the United States," and "lack accepted safety for use under medical supervision." Both medical marijuana and recreational marijuana are treated by this federal law as criminal. In *Gonzales v. Raich*, the Supreme Court affirmed the primacy of federal law over California state law, even where the federal law was allegedly violated by wholly intrastate cultivation and possession of a few marijuana plants prescribed for medical use in total compliance with federal law. The advent of legal recreational marijuana in Colorado and Washington may test the inherent federal-state tensions here; during the Obama Administration (2008–2016), the Department of Justice did not press the conflict, but a future administration might.[14]

Key Takeaway

In cases of conflicts between state and federal law, federal law will preempt (or control) state law because of the supremacy clause. Preemption can be express or implied. In cases where preemption is implied, the court usually finds that compliance with both state and federal law is not possible or that a federal regulatory scheme is comprehensive (i.e., "occupies the field") and should not be modified by state actions.

Exercises

1. For many years, the United States engaged in discussions with friendly nations as to the reciprocal use of ports and harbors. These discussions led to various multilateral agreements between the nations as to the configuration of oceangoing vessels and how they would be piloted. At the same time, concern over oil spills in Puget Sound led the state of Washington to impose fairly strict standards on oil tankers and requirements for the training of oil tanker pilots. In addition, Washington's state law imposed many other requirements that went above and beyond agreed-upon requirements in the international agreements negotiated by the federal government. Are the Washington state requirements preempted by federal law?
2. The Federal Arbitration Act of 1925 requires that all contracts for arbitration be treated as any other contract at common law. Suppose that the state of Alabama wishes to protect its citizens from a variety of arbitration provisions that they might enter into unknowingly. Thus the legislation provides that all predispute arbitration clauses be in bold print, that they be

of twelve-point font or larger, that they be clearly placed within the first two pages of any contract, and that they have a separate signature line where the customer, client, or patient acknowledges having read, understood, and signed the arbitration clause in addition to any other signatures required on the contract. Is the Alabama law preempted by the Federal Arbitration Act?

4.5 Business and the Bill of Rights

Learning Objectives

1. Understand and describe which articles in the Bill of Rights apply to business activities and how they apply.
2. Explain the application of the Fourteenth Amendment—including the due process clause and the equal protection clause—to various rights enumerated in the original Bill of Rights.

We have already seen the Fourteenth Amendment's application in *Burger King v. Rudzewicz* (Chapter 3.9). In general, any and all of the Amendments to the Constitution have a pre-emptive effect on inconsistent state laws. In *Rudzewicz*, the court considered whether it was constitutionally correct for a court in Florida to assert personal jurisdiction over a nonresident (from Michigan). The states cannot constitutionally award a judgment against a nonresident if doing so would offend "traditional notions of fair play and substantial justice" found by the Supreme Court in the Fourteenth Amendment. Even if the state's long-arm statute says it would allow such a judgment, the federal courts will not recognize it, and other states should not give it full faith and credit (see Article V of the Constitution). In short, a state's long-arm statute cannot confer personal jurisdiction that the state cannot constitutionally claim, and both states and businesses must comply with the commands of the Constitution, where they apply.

The Bill of Rights (the first ten amendments to the Constitution) was originally meant to apply to federal actions only. During the twentieth century, the court began to apply selected rights to state action as well. So, for example, federal agents were prohibited from using evidence seized in violation of the Fourth Amendment, but state agents were not, until *Mapp v. Ohio* (1960), when the court applied the guarantees (rights) of the Fourth Amendment to state action as well. In this and in similar cases, the Fourteenth Amendment's due process clause was the basis for the court's action. The due process clause commanded that states provide due process in cases affecting the life, liberty, or property of US citizens, and the court saw in this command certain "fundamental guarantees" that states would have to observe. Over the years, most of the important guarantees in the Bill of Rights came to apply to state as well as federal action. The court refers to this process as selective incorporation.

Here are some very basic principles to remember:

1. The guarantees of the Bill of Rights apply *only* to state and federal government action. They do not limit what a company or person in the private sector may do. For example, states may not impose censorship on the media or limit free speech in a way that offends the First Amendment, but your boss (in the private sector) may order you not to talk to the media.
2. In some cases, a private company may be regarded as participating in "state action." For example, a private defense contractor that gets 90 percent of its business from the federal government has been held to be public for purposes of enforcing the constitutional right to free speech (the company had a rule barring its employees from speaking out in public against its corporate position). It has even been argued that public regulation of private activity is sufficient to convert the private into public activity, thus subjecting it to the requirements of due process. But the Supreme Court rejected this extreme view in 1974 when it refused to require

private power companies, regulated by the state, to give customers a hearing before cutting off electricity for failure to pay the bill.[15]

3. States have rights, too. While "states rights" was a battle cry of Southern states before the Civil War, the question of what balance to strike between state sovereignty and federal union has never been simple. In *Kimel v. Florida*, for example, the Supreme Court found in the words of the Eleventh Amendment a basis for declaring that states may not have to obey certain federal statutes.

First Amendment

In part, the First Amendment states that "Congress shall make no law...abridging the freedom of speech, or of the press." The Founding Fathers believed that democracy would work best if people (and the press) could talk or write freely, without governmental interference. But the First Amendment was also not intended to be as absolute as it sounded. Oliver Wendell Holmes's famous dictum that the law does not permit you to shout "Fire!" in a crowded theater where there is no fire has seldom been answered with the question, "But why not?" And no one in 1789 thought that defamation laws (tort actions for slander and libel) had been made unconstitutional. Moreover, because the apparent purpose of the First Amendment was to make sure that the nation had a continuing, vigorous debate over matters political, political speech has been given the highest level of protection over such other forms of speech as (1) "commercial speech," (2) speech that can and should be limited by reasonable "time, place, and manner" restrictions, or (3) obscene speech.

Because of its higher level of protection, political speech can be false, malicious, mean-spirited, or even a pack of lies. (You may even have noticed this in election campaigns, past and present!) A public official in the United States must be prepared to withstand all kinds of false accusations and cannot succeed in an action for defamation unless the defendant has acted with "malice" and "reckless disregard" of the truth. Public figures, such as CEOs of the largest US companies, must also be prepared to withstand accusations that are false. In any defamation action, truth is a defense, but a defamation action brought by a public figure or public official must prove that the defendant not only has his facts wrong but also lies to the public in a malicious way with reckless disregard of the truth. Celebrities such as Lindsay Lohan, Kanye West, or Steven Colbert have the same burden to go forward with a defamation action. It is for this reason that the *National Enquirer* writes exclusively about public figures, public officials, and celebrities; it is possible to say many things that aren't completely true and still have the protection of the First Amendment.

Political speech is so highly protected that the court has recognized the right of people to support political candidates through campaign contributions and thus promote the particular viewpoints and speech of those candidates. Fearing the influence of money on politics, Congress has from time to time placed limitations on corporate contributions to political campaigns. But the Supreme Court has had mixed reactions over time. Initially, the court recognized the First Amendment right of a corporation to donate money, subject to certain limits.[16] In another case, *Austin v. Michigan Chamber of Commerce* (1990), the Michigan Campaign Finance Act prohibited corporations from using treasury money for independent expenditures to support or oppose candidates in elections for state offices. But a corporation could make such expenditures if it set up an independent fund designated solely for political purposes. The law was passed on the assumption that "the unique legal and economic characteristics of corporations necessitate some regulation of their political expenditures to avoid corruption or the appearance of corruption."

The Michigan Chamber of Commerce wanted to support a candidate for Michigan's House of Representatives by using general funds to sponsor a newspaper advertisement and argued that as a nonprofit organization, it was not really like a business firm. The court disagreed and upheld the Michigan law. Justice Marshall found that the chamber was akin to a business group, given its activities, linkages with community business leaders, and high percentage of members (over 75 percent) that were business corporations. Furthermore, Justice Marshall found that the statute was narrowly crafted and implemented to achieve the important goal of maintaining integrity in the political process. But as you will see in *Citizens United v. Federal Election Commission* (Section 4.

6 "Cases"), *Austin* was overruled; corporations are recognized as "persons" with First Amendment political speech rights that cannot be impaired by Congress or the states without some compelling governmental interest with restrictions on those rights that are "narrowly tailored."

Fourth Amendment

The Fourth Amendment says, "all persons shall be secure in their persons, houses, papers, and effects from unreasonable searches and seizures, and no warrants shall issue, but upon probable cause, before a magistrate and upon Oath, specifically describing the persons to be searched and places to be seized."

The court has read the Fourth Amendment to prohibit only those government searches or seizures that are "unreasonable." Because of this, businesses that are in an industry that is "closely regulated" can be searched more frequently and can be searched without a warrant. In one case, an auto parts dealer at a junkyard was charged with receiving stolen auto parts. Part of his defense was to claim that the search that found incriminating evidence was unconstitutional. But the court found the search reasonable, because the dealer was in a "closely regulated industry."

In the 1980s, Dow Chemical objected to an overflight by the US Environmental Protection Agency (EPA). The EPA had rented an airplane to fly over the Midland, Michigan, Dow plant, using an aerial mapping camera to photograph various pipes, ponds, and machinery that were not covered by a roof. Because the court's precedents allowed governmental intrusions into "open fields," the EPA search was ruled constitutional. Because the literal language of the Fourth Amendment protected "persons, houses, papers, and effects," anything searched by the government in "open fields" was reasonable. (The court's opinion suggested that if Dow had really wanted privacy from governmental intrusion, it could have covered the pipes and machinery that were otherwise outside and in open fields.)

The Supreme Court justified the EPA's search at least partially on the basis that the EPA had used a commercial technology available to anyone. That is, anyone could have rented a private plane and used an expensive (but available) aerial mapping camera to look at Dow's Midland facility. In *Kyllo v. United States*, 533 U.S. 27 (2001), however, the use of a thermal imaging device from a public vantage point to monitor the amount of heat radiation was deemed a search that required a prior warrant. The object of the authorities' search was an indoor marijuana operation. But the Court was divided, 5–4, and the decision hinged at least partly on the thermal imaging device being not commercially available to the public.

Note again that constitutional guarantees like the Fourth Amendment only apply to governmental action. Your employer or any private enterprise is not bound by constitutional limits. For example, if drug testing of all employees every week is done by a government agency, the employees may have a cause of action to object based on the Fourth Amendment. However, if a private employer begins the same kind of routine drug testing, employees have no constitutional arguments to make; they can simply leave that employer, or they may pursue whatever statutory or common law remedies are available.

The Fourth Amendment has significant application to the ongoing efforts to thwart those who would conduct attacks in the U.S. to promote the aims of Al Qaeda or ISIL. Courts and legislatures have tried to balance security concerns with privacy concerns, and some Fourth Amendment issues have been raised where the Executive branch has carried out warrantless surveillance for national security purposes; these have been settled in favor of surveillance in several circuit courts. The business application is this: for continued governmental surveillance of individuals who use cellphones and computers, the federal government has wanted to enlist the help of U.S. companies in "Silicon Valley," yet some of these companies are reluctant to share everything with the federal government in order to protect the "privacy" rights and interests of their customers.[17]

Fifth Amendment

The Fifth Amendment states, "No person shall be...deprived of life, liberty, or property, without due process of law; nor shall private property be taken for public use, without just compensation."

The Fifth Amendment has three principal aspects: **procedural due process**, the **takings clause**, and **substantive due process**. In terms of procedural due process, the amendment prevents government from arbitrarily taking the life of a criminal defendant. In civil lawsuits, it is also constitutionally essential that the proceedings be fair. This is why, for example, the defendant in *Burger King v. Rudzewicz* had a serious constitutional argument, even though he lost.

The takings clause of the Fifth Amendment ensures that the government does not take private property without just compensation. In the international setting, governments that take private property engage in what is called expropriation. The standard under customary international law is that when governments do that, they must provide prompt, adequate, and effective compensation. This does not always happen, especially where foreign owners' property is being expropriated. The guarantees of the Fifth Amendment (incorporated against state action by the Fourteenth Amendment) are available to property owners where state, county, or municipal government uses the power of eminent domain to take private property for public purposes. Just what is a public purpose is a matter of some debate. For example, if a city were to condemn economically viable businesses or neighborhoods to construct a baseball stadium with public money to entice a private enterprise (the baseball team) to stay, is a public purpose being served?

In *Kelo v. City of New London*, Mrs. Kelo and other residents fought the city of New London, in its attempt to use powers of eminent domain to create an industrial park and recreation area that would have Pfizer & Co. as a principal tenant.[18] The city argued that increasing its tax base was a sufficient public purpose. In a very close decision, the Supreme Court determined that New London's actions did not violate the takings clause. However, political reactions in various states resulted in a great deal of new state legislation that would limit the scope of public purpose in eminent domain takings and provide additional compensation to property owners in many cases.

In addition to the takings clause and aspects of procedural due process, the Fifth Amendment is also the source of what is called substantive due process. During the first third of the twentieth century, the Supreme Court often nullified state and federal laws using substantive due process. In 1905, for example, in *Lochner v. New York*, the Supreme Court voided a New York statute that limited the number of hours that bakers could work in a single week. New York had passed the law to protect the health of employees, but the court found that this law interfered with the basic constitutional right of private parties to freely contract with one another. Over the next thirty years, dozens of state and federal laws were struck down that aimed to improve working conditions, secure social welfare, or establish the rights of unions. However, in 1934, during the Great Depression, the court reversed itself and began upholding the kinds of laws it had struck down earlier.

Since then, the court has employed a two-tiered analysis of substantive due process claims. Under the first tier, legislation on economic matters, employment relations, and other business affairs is subject to minimal judicial scrutiny. This means that a law will be overturned only if it serves no rational government purpose. Under the second tier, legislation concerning fundamental liberties is subject to "heightened judicial scrutiny," meaning that a law will be invalidated unless it is "narrowly tailored to serve a significant government purpose."

The Supreme Court has identified two distinct categories of fundamental liberties. The first category includes most of the liberties expressly enumerated in the Bill of Rights. Through a process known as selective incorporation, the court has interpreted the due process clause of the Fourteenth Amendment to bar states from denying their residents the most important freedoms guaranteed in the first ten amendments to the federal Constitution. Only the Third Amendment right (against involuntary quartering of soldiers) and the Fifth Amendment right to be indicted by a grand jury have not been made applicable to the states. Because these rights are still not applicable to state governments, the Supreme Court is often said to have "selectively incorporated" the Bill of Rights into the due process clause of the Fourteenth Amendment.

procedural due process

In matters of civil or criminal procedure, the Constitution requires that both states and the federal government provide fair process (or due process) to all parties, especially defendants who are accused of a crime or, in a civil case, defendants who are served with a summons and complaint in a state other than their residence.

takings clause

In the Fifth Amendment, the government is required to provide compensation to the owner for any taking of private property. The same requirement is imposed on states through the due process clause of the Fourteenth Amendment (under selective incorporation).

substantive due process

A doctrine of the Supreme Court that negated numerous laws in the first third of the 20th century. Its use in the past 80 years is greatly diminished, but it survives in terms of protecting substantive liberties not otherwise enumerated in the Constitution.

The second category of fundamental liberties includes those liberties that are not expressly stated in the Bill of Rights but that can be seen as essential to the concepts of freedom and equality in a democratic society. These unstated liberties come from Supreme Court precedents, common law, moral philosophy, and deeply rooted traditions of US legal history. The Supreme Court has stressed that he word *liberty* cannot be defined by a definitive list of rights; rather, it must be viewed as a rational continuum of freedom through which every aspect of human behavior is protected from arbitrary impositions and random restraints. In this regard, as the Supreme Court has observed, the due process clause protects abstract liberty interests, including the right to personal autonomy, bodily integrity, self-dignity, and self-determination.

These liberty interests often are grouped to form a general right to privacy, which was first recognized in *Griswold v. Connecticut* (Section 6), where the Supreme Court struck down a state statute forbidding married adults from using, possessing, or distributing contraceptives on the ground that the law violated the sanctity of the marital relationship. According to Justice Douglas's plurality opinion, this penumbra of privacy, though not expressly mentioned in the Bill of Rights, must be protected to establish a buffer zone or breathing space for those freedoms that are constitutionally enumerated.

But substantive due process has seen fairly limited use since the 1930s. During the 1990s, the Supreme Court was asked to recognize a general right to die under the doctrine of substantive due process. Although the court stopped short of establishing such a far-reaching right, certain patients may exercise a constitutional liberty to hasten their deaths under a narrow set of circumstances. In *Cruzan v. Missouri Department of Health*, the Supreme Court ruled that the due process clause guarantees the right of competent adults to make advanced directives for the withdrawal of life-sustaining measures should they become incapacitated by a disability that leaves them in a persistent vegetative state.[19] Once it has been established by clear and convincing evidence that a mentally incompetent and persistently vegetative patient made such a prior directive, a spouse, parent, or other appropriate guardian may seek to terminate any form of artificial hydration or nutrition.

Fourteenth Amendment: Due Process and Equal Protection Guarantees

The Fourteenth Amendment (1868) requires that states treat citizens of other states with due process. This can be either an issue of procedural due process (as in Chapter 3.9, *Burger King v. Rudzewicz*) or an issue of substantive due process. For substantive due process, consider what happened in an Alabama court not too long ago.[20]

The plaintiff, Dr. Ira Gore, bought a new BMW for $40,000 from a dealer in Alabama. He later discovered that the vehicle's exterior had been slightly damaged in transit from Europe and had therefore been repainted by the North American distributor prior to his purchase. The vehicle was, by best estimates, worth about 10 percent less than he paid for it. The distributor, BMW of North America, had routinely sold slightly damaged cars as brand new if the damage could be fixed for less than 3 percent of the cost of the car. In the trial, Dr. Gore sought $4,000 in compensatory damages and also punitive damages. The Alabama trial jury considered that BMW was engaging in a fraudulent practice and wanted to punish the defendant for a number of frauds it estimated at somewhere around a thousand nationwide. The jury awarded not only the $4,000 in compensatory damages but also $4 million in punitive damages, which was later reduced to $2 million by the Alabama Supreme Court. On appeal to the US Supreme Court, the court found that punitive damages may not be "grossly excessive." If they are, then they violate substantive due process. Whatever damages a state awards must be limited to what is reasonably necessary to vindicate the state's legitimate interest in punishment and deterrence.

"Equal protection of the laws" is a phrase that originates in the Fourteenth Amendment, adopted in 1868. The amendment provides that no state shall "deny to any person within its jurisdiction the equal protection of the laws." This is the equal protection clause. It means that, generally speaking, governments must treat people equally. Unfair classifications among people or corporations will not be permitted. A well-known example of unfair classification would be race discrimination: requiring white children and black children to attend different public schools or requiring "separate but equal" public services, such as water fountains or restrooms. Yet despite the clear intent of the 1868 amendment, "separate but equal" was the law of the land until *Brown v. Board of Education* (1954).[21]

Governments make classifications every day, so not all classifications can be illegal under the equal protection clause. People with more income generally pay a greater percentage of their income in taxes. People with proper medical training are licensed to become doctors; people without that training cannot be licensed and commit a criminal offense if they do practice medicine. To know what classifications are permissible under the Fourteenth Amendment, we need to know what is being classified. The court has created three classifications, and the outcome of any equal protection case can usually be predicted by knowing how the court is likely to classify the case:

- Minimal scrutiny: economic and social relations. Government actions are usually upheld if there is a rational basis for them.
- Intermediate scrutiny: gender. Government classifications are sometimes upheld.
- Strict scrutiny: race, ethnicity, and fundamental rights. Classifications based on any of these are almost never upheld.

Under minimal scrutiny for economic and social regulation, laws that regulate economic or social issues are presumed valid and will be upheld if they are rationally related to legitimate goals of government. So, for example, if the city of New Orleans limits the number of street vendors to some rational number (more than one but fewer than the total number that could possibly fit on the sidewalks), the local ordinance would not be overturned as a violation of equal protection.

Under intermediate scrutiny, the city of New Orleans might limit the number of street vendors who are men. For example, suppose that the city council decreed that all street vendors must be women, thinking that would attract even more tourism. A classification like this, based on sex, will have to meet a sterner test than a classification resulting from economic or social regulation. A law like this would have to substantially relate to important government objectives. Increasingly, courts have nullified government sex classifications as societal concern with gender equality has grown. (See Shannon Faulkner's case against The Citadel, an all-male state school.)[22]

Suppose, however, that the city of New Orleans decided that no one of Middle Eastern heritage could drive a taxicab or be a street vendor. That kind of classification would be examined with strict scrutiny to see if there was any compelling justification for it. As noted, classifications such as this one are almost never upheld. The law would be upheld only if it were necessary to promote a compelling state interest. Very few laws that have a racial or ethnic classification meet that test.

The strict scrutiny test will be applied to classifications involving racial and ethnic criteria as well as classifications that interfere with a fundamental right. In *Palmore v. Sidoti*, the state refused to award custody to the mother because her new spouse was racially different from the child.[23] This practice was declared unconstitutional because the state had made a racial classification; this was presumptively invalid, and the government could not show a compelling need to enforce such a classification through its law. An example of government action interfering with a fundamental right will also receive strict scrutiny. When New York State gave an employment preference to veterans who had been state residents at the time of entering the military, the court declared that veterans who were new to the state were less likely to get jobs and that therefore the statute interfered with the right to travel, which was deemed a fundamental right.[24]

Key Takeaway

The Bill of Rights, through the Fourteenth Amendment, largely applies to state actions. The Bill of Rights has applied to federal actions from the start. Both the Bill of Rights and the Fourteenth Amendment apply to business in various ways, but it is important to remember that the rights conferred are rights against governmental action and not the actions of private enterprise.

Exercises

1. John Hanks works at ProLogis. The company decides to institute a drug-testing policy. John is a good and longtime employee but enjoys smoking marijuana on the weekends. The drug testing will involve urine samples and, semiannually, a hair sample. It is nearly certain that the drug-testing protocol that ProLogis proposes will find that Hanks is a marijuana user. The company has made it clear that it will have zero tolerance for any kind of nonprescribed controlled substances. John and several fellow employees wish to go to court to challenge the proposed testing as "an unreasonable search and seizure." Can he possibly succeed?
2. Larry Reed, majority leader in the Senate, is attacked in his reelection campaign by a series of ads sponsored by a corporation (Global Defense, Inc.) that does not like his voting record. The corporation is upset that Reed would not write a special provision that would favor Global Defense in a defense appropriations bill. The ads run constantly on television and radio in the weeks immediately preceding election day and contain numerous falsehoods. For example, in order to keep the government running financially, Reed found it necessary to vote for a bill that included a last-minute rider that defunded a small government program for the handicapped, sponsored by someone in the opposing party that wanted to privatize all programs for the handicapped. The ad is largely paid for by Global Defense and depicts a handicapped child being helped by the existing program and large letters saying "Does Larry Reed Just Not Care?" The ad proclaims that it is sponsored by Citizens Who Care for a Better Tomorrow. Is this protected speech? Why or why not? Can Reed sue for defamation? Why or why not?

4.6 Cases

Griswold v. Connecticut

Griswold v. Connecticut

381 U.S. 479 (U.S. Supreme Court 1965)

A nineteenth-century Connecticut law made the use, possession, or distribution of birth control devices illegal. The law also prohibited anyone from giving information about such devices. The executive director and medical director of a planned parenthood association were found guilty of giving out such information to a married couple that wished to delay having children for a few years. The directors were fined $100 each [about $800 in 2017 dollars].

They appealed throughout the Connecticut state court system, arguing that the state law violated (infringed) a basic or fundamental right of privacy of a married couple: to live together and have sex together without the restraining power of the state to tell them they may legally have intercourse but not if they use condoms or other birth control devices. At each level (trial court, court of appeals, and Connecticut Supreme Court), the Connecticut courts upheld the constitutionality of the convictions.

Plurality Opinion by Justice William O. Douglass

We do not sit as a super legislature to determine the wisdom, need, and propriety of laws that touch economic problems, business affairs, or social conditions. The [Connecticut] law, however, operates directly on intimate relation of husband and wife and their physician's role in one aspect of that relation.

[Previous] cases suggest that specific guarantees in the Bill of Rights have penumbras, formed by emanations from those guarantees that help give them life and substance....Various guarantees create zones of privacy. The right of association contained in the penumbra of the First Amendment is one....The Third Amendment in its prohibition against the quartering of soldiers "in any house" in time of peace without the consent of the owner is another facet of that privacy. The Fourth Amendment explicitly affirms the "right of the people to be secure in their persons, houses, papers and effects, against unreasonable searches and seizures." The Fifth Amendment in its Self-Incrimination Clause enables the citizen to create a zone of privacy which the government may not force him to surrender to his detriment. The Ninth Amendment provides: "The enumeration in the Constitution, of certain rights, shall not be construed to deny or disparage others retained by the people."

The Fourth and Fifth Amendments were described...as protection against all governmental invasions "of the sanctity of a man's home and the privacies of life." We recently referred in *Mapp v. Ohio*...to the Fourth Amendment as creating a "right to privacy, no less important than any other right carefully and particularly reserved to the people."

[The law in question here], in forbidding the *use* of contraceptives rather than regulating their manufacture or sale, seeks to achieve its goals by having a maximum destructive impact on [the marital] relationship. Such a law cannot stand....Would we allow the police to search the sacred precincts of marital bedrooms for telltale signs of the use of contraceptives? The very idea is repulsive to the notions of privacy surrounding the marital relationship.

We deal with a right of privacy older than the Bill of Rights—older than our political parties, older than our school system. Marriage is a coming together for better or for worse, hopefully enduring, and intimate to the degree of being sacred. It is an association that promotes a way of life, not causes; a harmony in living, not political faiths; a bilateral loyalty, not commercial or social projects. Yet it is an association for as noble a purpose as any involved in our prior decisions.

Mr. Justice Stewart, whom Mr. Justice Black joins, dissenting.

Since 1879 Connecticut has had on its books a law which forbids the use of contraceptives by anyone. I think this is an uncommonly silly law. As a practical matter, the law is obviously unenforceable, except in the oblique context of the present case. As a philosophical matter, I believe the use of contraceptives in the relationship of marriage should be left to personal and private choice, based upon each individual's moral, ethical, and religious beliefs. As a matter of social policy, I think professional counsel about methods of birth control should be available to all, so that each individual's choice can be meaningfully made. But we are not asked in this case to say whether we think this law is unwise, or even asinine. We are asked to hold that it violates the United States Constitution. And that I cannot do.

In the course of its opinion the Court refers to no less than six Amendments to the Constitution: the First, the Third, the Fourth, the Fifth, the Ninth, and the Fourteenth. But the Court does not say which of these Amendments, if any, it thinks is infringed by this Connecticut law. * * *

As to the First, Third, Fourth, and Fifth Amendments, I can find nothing in any of them to invalidate this Connecticut law, even assuming that all those Amendments are fully applicable against the States. It has not even been argued that this is a law "respecting an establishment of religion, or prohibiting the free exercise thereof." And surely, unless the solemn process of constitutional adjudication is to descend to the level of a play on words, there is not involved here any abridgment of "the freedom of speech, or of the press; or the right of the people peaceably to assemble, and to petition the Government for a redress of grievances." No soldier has been quartered in any house. There has been no search, and no seizure. Nobody has been compelled to be a witness against himself.

The Court also quotes the Ninth Amendment, and my Brother Goldberg's concurring opinion relies heavily upon it. But to say that the Ninth Amendment has anything to do with this case is to turn somersaults with history. The Ninth Amendment, like its companion the Tenth, which this Court held "states but a truism that all is retained which has not been surrendered," *United States v. Darby*, 312 U.S. 100, 124, was framed by James Madison and adopted by the States simply to make clear that the adoption of the Bill of Rights did not alter the plan that the *Federal* Government was to be a government of express and limited powers, and that all rights and powers not delegated to it were retained by the people and the individual States. Until today no member of this Court has ever suggested that the Ninth Amendment meant anything else, and the idea that a federal court could ever use the Ninth Amendment to annul a law passed by the elected representatives of the people of the State of Connecticut would have caused James Madison no little wonder.

What provision of the Constitution, then, does make this state law invalid? The Court says it is the right of privacy "created by several fundamental constitutional guarantees." With all deference, I can find no such general right of privacy in the Bill of Rights, in any other part of the Constitution, or in any case ever before decided by this Court.

At the oral argument in this case we were told that the Connecticut law does not "conform to current community standards." But it is not the function of this Court to decide cases on the basis of community standards. We are here to decide cases "agreeably to the Constitution and laws of the United States." It is the essence of judicial duty to subordinate our own personal views, our own ideas of what legislation is wise and what is not. If, as I should surely hope, the law before us does not reflect the standards of the people of Connecticut, the people of Connecticut can freely exercise their true Ninth and Tenth Amendment rights to persuade their elected representatives to repeal it. That is the constitutional way to take this law off the books.

Case Questions

1. Which opinion is the strict constructionist opinion here—Justice Douglas's or that of Justices Stewart and Black?
2. What would have happened if the Supreme Court had allowed the Connecticut Supreme Court decision to stand and followed Justice Black's reasoning? Is it likely that the citizens of Connecticut would have persuaded their elected representatives to repeal the law challenged here?

Wickard v. Filburn

Wickard v. Filburn

317 U.S. 111 (U.S. Supreme Court 1942)

Mr. Justice Jackson delivered the opinion of the Court.

Mr. Filburn for many years past has owned and operated a small farm in Montgomery County, Ohio, maintaining a herd of dairy cattle, selling milk, raising poultry, and selling poultry and eggs. It has been his practice to raise a small acreage of winter wheat, sown in the Fall and harvested in the following July; to sell a portion of the crop; to feed part to poultry and livestock on the farm, some of which is sold; to use some in making flour for home consumption; and to keep the rest for the following seeding.

His 1941 wheat acreage allotment was 11.1 acres and a normal yield of 20.1 bushels of wheat an acre. He sowed, however, 23 acres, and harvested from his 11.9 acres of excess acreage 239 bushels, which under the terms of the Act as amended on May 26, 1941, constituted farm marketing excess, subject to a penalty of 49 cents a bushel, or $117.11 in all.

The general scheme of the Agricultural Adjustment Act of 1938 as related to wheat is to control the volume moving in interstate and foreign commerce in order to avoid surpluses and shortages and the consequent abnormally low or high wheat prices and obstructions to commerce. [T]he Secretary of Agriculture is directed to ascertain and proclaim each year a national acreage allotment for the next crop of wheat, which is then apportioned to the states and their counties, and is eventually broken up into allotments for individual farms.

It is urged that under the Commerce Clause of the Constitution, Article I, § 8, clause 3, Congress does not possess the power it has in this instance sought to exercise. The question would merit little consideration since our decision in United States v. Darby, 312 U.S. 100, sustaining the federal power to regulate production of goods for commerce, except for the fact that this Act extends federal regulation to production not intended in any part for commerce but wholly for consumption on the farm.

Case Questions

1. Why would Congress want to regulate the price and supply of wheat? Why did it not let the free market decide?
2. If Congress can control what a person can grow and consume on his or her own land, are there any limits to the power of the federal government?

Kassel v. Consolidated Freightways Corp.

Kassel v. Consolidated Freightways Corp.
450 U.S. 662 (U.S. Supreme Court 1981)

JUSTICE POWELL announced the judgment of the Court and delivered an opinion, in which JUSTICE WHITE, JUSTICE BLACKMUN, and JUSTICE STEVENS joined.

The question is whether an Iowa statute that prohibits the use of certain large trucks within the State unconstitutionally burdens interstate commerce.

I

Appellee Consolidated Freightways Corporation of Delaware (Consolidated) is one of the largest common carriers in the country: it offers service in 48 States under a certificate of public convenience and necessity issued by the Interstate Commerce Commission. Among other routes, Consolidated carries commodities through Iowa on Interstate 80, the principal east-west route linking New York, Chicago, and the west coast, and on Interstate 35, a major north-south route.

Consolidated mainly uses two kinds of trucks. One consists of a three-axle tractor pulling a 40-foot two-axle trailer. This unit, commonly called a single, or "semi," is 55 feet in length overall. Such trucks have long been used on the Nation's highways. Consolidated also uses a two-axle tractor pulling a single-axle trailer which, in turn, pulls a single-axle dolly and a second single-axle trailer. This combination, known as a double, or twin, is 65 feet long overall. Many trucking companies, including Consolidated, increasingly prefer to use doubles to ship certain kinds of commodities. Doubles have larger capacities, and the trailers can be detached and routed separately if necessary. Consolidated would like to use 65-foot doubles on many of its trips through Iowa.

The State of Iowa, however, by statute, restricts the length of vehicles that may use its highways. Unlike all other States in the West and Midwest, Iowa generally prohibits the use of 65-foot doubles within its borders.

...

Because of Iowa's statutory scheme, Consolidated cannot use its 65-foot doubles to move commodities through the State. Instead, the company must do one of four things: (i) use 55-foot singles; (ii) use 60-foot doubles; (iii) detach the trailers of a 65-foot double and shuttle each through the State separately; or (iv) divert 65-foot doubles around Iowa. Dissatisfied with these options, Consolidated filed this suit in the District Court averring that Iowa's statutory scheme unconstitutionally burdens interstate commerce. Iowa defended the law as a reasonable safety measure enacted pursuant to its police power. The State asserted that 65-foot doubles are more dangerous than 55-foot singles and, in any event, that the law promotes safety and reduces road wear within the State by diverting much truck traffic to other states.

In a 14-day trial, both sides adduced evidence on safety and on the burden on interstate commerce imposed by Iowa's law. On the question of safety, the District Court found that the "evidence clearly establishes that the twin is as safe as the semi." 475 F.Supp. 544, 549 (SD Iowa 1979). For that reason, "there is no valid safety reason for barring twins from Iowa's highways because of their configuration....The evidence convincingly, if not overwhelmingly, establishes that the 65-foot twin is as safe as, if not safer than, the 60-foot twin and the 55-foot semi...."

"Twins and semis have different characteristics. Twins are more maneuverable, are less sensitive to wind, and create less splash and spray. However, they are more likely than semis to jackknife or upset. They can be backed only for a short distance. The negative characteristics are not such that they render the twin less safe than semis overall. Semis are more stable, but are more likely to 'rear-end' another vehicle."

In light of these findings, the District Court applied the standard we enunciated in *Raymond Motor Transportation, Inc. v. Rice*, 434 U.S. 429 (1978), and concluded that the state law impermissibly burdened interstate commerce: "[T]he balance here must be struck in favor of the federal interests. The *total effect* of the law as a safety measure in reducing accidents and casualties is so slight and problematical that it does not outweigh the national interest in keeping interstate commerce free from interferences that seriously impede it."

The Court of Appeals for the Eighth Circuit affirmed. 612 F.2d 1064 (1979). It accepted the District Court's finding that 65-foot doubles were as safe as 55-foot singles. *Id.* at 1069. Thus, the only apparent safety benefit to Iowa was that resulting from forcing large trucks to detour around the State, thereby reducing overall truck traffic on Iowa's highways. The Court of Appeals noted that this was not a constitutionally permissible interest. It also commented that the several statutory exemptions identified above, such as those applicable to border cities and the shipment of livestock, suggested that the law, in effect, benefited Iowa residents at the expense of interstate traffic. *Id.* at 1070-1071. The combination of these exemptions weakened the presumption of validity normally accorded a state safety regulation. For these reasons, the Court of Appeals agreed with the District Court that the Iowa statute unconstitutionally burdened interstate commerce.

Iowa appealed, and we noted probable jurisdiction. 446 U.S. 950 (1980). We now affirm.

II

It is unnecessary to review in detail the evolution of the principles of Commerce Clause adjudication. The Clause is both a "prolific ' of national power and an equally prolific source of conflict with legislation of the state[s]." *H. P. Hood & Sons, Inc. v. Du Mond*, 336 U.S. 525, 336 U.S. 534 (1949). The Clause permits Congress to legislate when it perceives that the national welfare is not furthered by the independent actions of the States. It is now well established, also, that the Clause itself is "a limitation upon state power even without congressional implementation." *Hunt v. Washington Apple Advertising Comm'n*, 432 U.S. 333 at 350 (1977). The Clause requires that some aspects of trade generally must remain free from interference by the States. When a State ventures excessively into the regulation of these aspects of commerce, it "trespasses upon national interests," *Great A&P Tea Co. v. Cottrell*, 424 U.S. 366, 424 U.S. 373 (1976), and the courts will hold the state regulation invalid under the Clause alone.

The Commerce Clause does not, of course, invalidate all state restrictions on commerce. It has long been recognized that, "in the absence of conflicting legislation by Congress, there is a residuum of power in the state to make laws governing matters of local concern which nevertheless in some measure affect interstate commerce or even, to some extent, regulate it." *Southern Pacific Co. v. Arizona*, 325 U.S. 761 (1945).

The extent of permissible state regulation is not always easy to measure. It may be said with confidence, however, that a State's power to regulate commerce is never greater than in matters traditionally of local concern. *Washington Apple Advertising Comm'n, supra* at 432 U.S. 350. For example, regulations that touch upon safety—especially highway safety—are those that "the Court has been most reluctant to invalidate." *Raymond, supra* at 434 U.S. 443 (and other cases cited). Indeed, "if safety justifications are not illusory, the Court will not second-guess legislative judgment about their importance in comparison with related burdens on interstate commerce." *Raymond, supra* at 434 U.S. at 449. Those who would challenge such bona fide safety regulations must overcome a "strong presumption of validity." *Bibb v. Navajo Freight Lines, Inc.*, 359 U.S. 520 at (1959).

But the incantation of a purpose to promote the public health or safety does not insulate a state law from Commerce Clause attack. Regulations designed for that salutary purpose nevertheless may further the purpose so marginally, and interfere with commerce so substantially, as to be invalid under the Commerce Clause. In the Court's recent unanimous decision in *Raymond* we declined to "accept the State's contention that the inquiry under the Commerce Clause is ended without a weighing of the asserted safety purpose against the degree of interference with interstate commerce." This "weighing" by a court requires—and indeed the constitutionality of the state regulation depends on—"a sensitive consideration of the weight and nature of the state regulatory concern in light of the extent of the burden imposed on the course of interstate commerce." *Id.* at 434 U.S. at 441; *accord, Pike v. Bruce Church, Inc.*, 397 U.S. 137 at 142 (1970); *Bibb, supra*, at 359 U.S. at 525-530.

III

Applying these general principles, we conclude that the Iowa truck length limitations unconstitutionally burden interstate commerce.

In *Raymond Motor Transportation, Inc. v. Rice*, the Court held that a Wisconsin statute that precluded the use of 65-foot doubles violated the Commerce Clause. This case is *Raymond* revisited. Here, as in *Raymond*, the State failed to present any persuasive evidence that 65-foot doubles are less safe than 55-foot singles. Moreover, Iowa's law is now out of step with the laws of all other Midwestern and Western States. Iowa thus substantially burdens the interstate flow of goods by truck. In the absence of congressional action to set uniform standards, some burdens associated with state safety regulations must be tolerated. But where, as here, the State's safety interest has been found to be illusory, and its regulations impair significantly the federal interest in efficient and safe interstate transportation, the state law cannot be harmonized with the Commerce Clause.

A

Iowa made a more serious effort to support the safety rationale of its law than did Wisconsin in *Raymond*, but its effort was no more persuasive. As noted above, the District Court found that the "evidence clearly establishes that the twin is as safe as the semi." The record supports this finding. The trial focused on a comparison of the performance of the two kinds of trucks in various safety categories. The evidence showed, and the District Court found, that the 65-foot double was at least the equal of the 55-foot single in the ability to brake, turn, and maneuver. The double, because of its axle placement, produces less splash and spray in wet weather. And, because of its articulation in the middle, the double is less susceptible to dangerous "off-tracking," and to wind.

None of these findings is seriously disputed by Iowa. Indeed, the State points to only three ways in which the 55-foot single is even arguably superior: singles take less time to be passed and to clear intersections; they may back up for longer distances; and they are somewhat less likely to jackknife.

The first two of these characteristics are of limited relevance on modern interstate highways. As the District Court found, the negligible difference in the time required to pass, and to cross intersections, is insignificant on 4-lane divided highways, because passing does not require crossing into oncoming traffic lanes, *Raymond*, 434 U.S. at 444, and interstates have few, if any, intersections. The concern over backing capability also is insignificant, because it seldom is necessary to back up on an interstate. In any event, no evidence suggested any difference in backing capability between the 60-foot doubles that Iowa permits and the 65-foot doubles that it bans. Similarly, although doubles tend to jackknife somewhat more than singles, 65-foot doubles actually are less likely to jackknife than 60-foot doubles.

Statistical studies supported the view that 65-foot doubles are at least as safe overall as 55-foot singles and 60-foot doubles. One such study, which the District Court credited, reviewed Consolidated's comparative accident experience in 1978 with its own singles and doubles. Each kind of truck was driven 56 million miles on identical routes. The singles were involved in 100 accidents resulting in 27 injuries and one fatality. The 65-foot doubles were involved in 106 accidents resulting in 17 injuries and one fatality. Iowa's expert statistician admitted that this study provided "moderately strong evidence" that singles have a higher injury rate than doubles. Another study, prepared by the Iowa Department of Transportation at the request of the state legislature, concluded that "[s]ixty-five foot twin trailer combinations have *not* been shown by experiences in other states to be less safe than 60-foot twin trailer combinations *or* conventional tractor-semitrailers."

In sum, although Iowa introduced more evidence on the question of safety than did Wisconsin in *Raymond*, the record as a whole was not more favorable to the State.

B

Consolidated, meanwhile, demonstrated that Iowa's law substantially burdens interstate commerce. Trucking companies that wish to continue to use 65-foot doubles must route them around Iowa or detach the trailers of the doubles and ship them through separately. Alternatively, trucking companies must use the smaller 55-foot singles or 65-foot doubles permitted under Iowa law. Each of these options engenders inefficiency and added expense. The record shows that Iowa's law added about $12.6 million each year to the costs of trucking companies.

Consolidated alone incurred about $2 million per year in increased costs.

In addition to increasing the costs of the trucking companies (and, indirectly, of the service to consumers), Iowa's law may aggravate, rather than, ameliorate, the problem of highway accidents. Fifty-five-foot singles carry less freight than 65-foot doubles. Either more small trucks must be used to carry the same quantity of goods through Iowa or the same number of larger trucks must drive longer distances to bypass Iowa. In either case, as the District Court noted, the restriction requires more highway miles to be driven to transport the same quantity of goods. Other things being equal, accidents are proportional to distance traveled. Thus, if 65-foot doubles are as safe as 55-foot singles, Iowa's law tends to increase the number of accidents and to shift the incidence of them from Iowa to other States.

[IV. Omitted]

V

In sum, the statutory exemptions, their history, and the arguments Iowa has advanced in support of its law in this litigation all suggest that the deference traditionally accorded a State's safety judgment is not warranted. *See Raymond, supra* at 434 U.S. at 444-447. The controlling factors thus are the findings of the District Court, accepted by the Court of Appeals, with respect to the relative safety of the types of trucks at issue, and the substantiality of the burden on interstate commerce.

Because Iowa has imposed this burden without any significant countervailing safety interest, its statute violates the Commerce Clause. The judgment of the Court of Appeals is affirmed.

It is so ordered.

Case Questions

1. Under the Constitution, what gives Iowa the right to make rules regarding the size or configuration of trucks upon highways within the state?
2. Did Iowa try to exempt trucking lines based in Iowa, or was the statutory rule nondiscriminatory as to the origin of trucks that traveled on Iowa highways?

Hunt v. Washington Apple Advertising Commission

Hunt v. Washington Apple Advertising Commission

432 U.S. 33 (U.S. Supreme Court 1977)

MR. CHIEF JUSTICE BURGER delivered the opinion of the Court.

In 1973, North Carolina enacted a statute which required, *inter alia*, all closed containers of apples sold, offered for sale, or shipped into the State to bear "no grade other than the applicable U.S. grade or standard."...Washington State is the Nation's largest producer of apples, its crops accounting for approximately 30% of all apples grown domestically and nearly half of all apples shipped in closed containers in interstate commerce. [Because] of the importance of the apple industry to the State, its legislature has undertaken to protect and enhance the reputation of Washington apples by establishing a stringent, mandatory inspection program [that] requires all apples shipped in interstate commerce to be tested under strict quality standards and graded accordingly. In all cases, the Washington State grades [are] the equivalent of, or superior to, the comparable grades and standards adopted by the [U.S. Dept. of] Agriculture (USDA).

[In] 1972, the North Carolina Board of Agriculture adopted an administrative regulation, unique in the 50 States, which in effect required all closed containers of apples shipped into or sold in the State to display either the applicable USDA grade or a notice indicating no classification. State grades were expressly prohibited. In addition to its obvious consequence—prohibiting the display of Washington State apple grades on containers of apples shipped into North Carolina—the regulation presented the Washington apple industry with a marketing problem of potentially nationwide significance. Washington apple growers annually ship in commerce approximately 40 million closed containers of apples, nearly 500,000 of which eventually find their way into North Carolina, stamped with the applicable Washington State variety and grade. [Compliance] with North Carolina's unique regulation would have required Washington growers to obliterate the printed labels on containers shipped to North Carolina, thus giving their product a damaged appearance. Alternatively, they could have changed their marketing practices to accommodate the needs of the North Carolina market, i.e., repack apples to be shipped to North Carolina in containers bearing only the USDA grade, and/or store the estimated portion of the harvest destined for that market in such special containers. As a last resort, they could discontinue the use of the preprinted containers entirely. None of these costly and less efficient options was very attractive to the industry. Moreover, in the event a number of other States followed North Carolina's lead, the resultant inability to display the Washington grades could force the Washington growers to abandon the State's expensive inspection and grading system which their customers had come to know and rely on over the 60-odd years of its existence....

Unsuccessful in its attempts to secure administrative relief [with North Carolina], the Commission instituted this action challenging the constitutionality of the statute. [The] District Court found that the North Carolina statute, while neutral on its face, actually discriminated against Washington State growers and dealers in favor of their local counterparts [and] concluded that this discrimination [was] not justified by the asserted local interest—the elimination of deception and confusion from the marketplace—arguably furthered by the [statute].

...

[North Carolina] maintains that [the] burdens on the interstate sale of Washington apples were far outweighed by the local benefits flowing from what they contend was a valid exercise of North Carolina's [police powers]. Prior to the statute's enactment,...apples from 13 different States were shipped into North Carolina for sale. Seven of those States, including [Washington], had their own grading systems which, while differing in their standards, used similar descriptive labels (e.g., fancy, extra fancy, etc.). This multiplicity of inconsistent state grades [posed] dangers of deception and confusion not only in the North Carolina market, but in the Nation as a whole. The North Carolina statute, appellants claim, was enacted to eliminate this source of deception and confusion. [Moreover], it is contended that North Carolina sought to accomplish this goal of uniformity in an evenhanded manner as evidenced by the fact that its statute applies to all apples sold in closed containers in the State without regard to their point of origin.

[As] the appellants properly point out, not every exercise of state authority imposing some burden on the free flow of commerce is invalid, [especially] when the State acts to protect its citizenry in matters pertaining to the sale of foodstuffs. By the same token, however, a finding that state legislation furthers matters of legitimate local concern, even in the health and consumer protection areas, does not end the inquiry. Rather, when such state legislation comes into conflict with the Commerce Clause's overriding requirement of a national "common market," we are confronted with the task of effecting an accommodation of the competing national and local interests. We turn to that task.

As the District Court correctly found, the challenged statute has the practical effect of not only burdening interstate sales of Washington apples, but also discriminating against them. This discrimination takes various forms. The first, and most obvious, is the statute's consequence of raising *the costs* of doing business in the North Carolina market for Washington apple growers and dealers, while leaving those of their North Carolina counterparts unaffected. [This] disparate effect results from the fact that North Carolina apple producers, unlike their Washington competitors, were not forced to alter their marketing practices in order to comply with the statute. They were still free to market their wares under the USDA grade or none at all as they had done prior to the statute's enactment. Obviously, the increased costs imposed by the statute would tend to shield the local apple industry from the competition of Washington apple growers and dealers who are already at a competitive disadvantage because of their great distance from the North Carolina market.

Second, the statute has the effect of *stripping away* from the Washington apple industry the competitive and economic advantages it has earned for itself through its expensive inspection and grading system. The record demonstrates that the Washington apple-grading system has gained nationwide acceptance in the apple trade. [The record] contains numerous affidavits [stating a] preference [for] apples graded under the Washington, as opposed to the USDA, system because of the former's greater consistency, its emphasis on color, and its supporting mandatory inspections. Once again, the statute had no similar impact on the North Carolina apple industry and thus operated to its benefit.

Third, by *prohibiting* Washington growers and dealers from marketing apples under their State's grades, the statute has a *leveling effect* which insidiously operates to the advantage of local apple producers. [With] free market forces at work, Washington sellers would normally enjoy a distinct market advantage vis-à-vis local producers in those categories where the Washington grade is superior. However, because of the statute's operation, Washington apples which would otherwise qualify for and be sold under the superior Washington grades will now have to be marketed under their inferior USDA counterparts. Such "downgrading" offers the North Carolina apple industry the very sort of protection against competing out-of-state products that the Commerce Clause was designed to prohibit. At worst, it will have the effect of an embargo against those Washington apples in the superior grades as Washington dealers withhold them from the North Carolina market. At best, it will deprive Washington sellers of the market premium that such apples would otherwise command.

Despite the statute's facial neutrality, the Commission suggests that its discriminatory impact on interstate commerce was not an unintended by-product, and there are some indications in the record to that effect. The most glaring is the response of the North Carolina Agriculture Commissioner to the Commission's request for an exemption following the statute's passage in which he indicated that before he could support such an exemption, he would "want to have the sentiment from our apple producers *since they were mainly responsible for* this *legislation being passed.*" [Moreover], we find it somewhat suspect that North Carolina singled out only closed containers of apples, the very means by which apples are transported in commerce, to effectuate the statute's ostensible consumer protection purpose when apples are not generally sold at retail in their shipping containers. However, we need not ascribe an economic protection motive to the North Carolina Legislature to resolve this case; we conclude that the challenged statute cannot stand insofar as it prohibits the display of Washington State grades even if enacted for the declared purpose of protecting consumers from deception and fraud in the marketplace.

...

Finally, we note that any potential for confusion and deception created by the Washington grades was not of the type that led to the statute's enactment. Since Washington grades are in all cases equal or superior to their USDA counterparts, they could only "deceive" or "confuse" a consumer to his benefit, hardly a harmful result.

In addition, it appears that nondiscriminatory alternatives to the outright ban of Washington State grades are readily available. For example, North Carolina could effectuate its goal by permitting out-of-state growers to utilize state grades only if they also marked their shipments with the applicable USDA label. In that case, the USDA grade would serve as a benchmark against which the consumer could evaluate the quality of the various state grades....

[The court affirmed the lower court's holding that the North Carolina statute was unconstitutional.]

Case Questions

1. Was the North Carolina law discriminatory on its face? Was it, possibly, an undue burden on interstate commerce? Why wouldn't it be?
2. What evidence was there of discriminatory intent behind the North Carolina law? Did that evidence even matter? Why or why not?

Citizens United v. Federal Election Commission

Citizens United v. Federal Election Commission
588 U.S. 310; 130 S.Ct. 876 (U.S. Supreme Court 2010)

Justice Kennedy delivered the opinion of the Court.

Federal law prohibits corporations and unions from using their general treasury funds to make independent expenditures for speech defined as an "electioneering communication" or for speech expressly advocating the election or defeat of a candidate. 2 U.S.C. §441b. Limits on electioneering communications were upheld in *McConnell v. Federal Election Comm'n*, 540 U.S. 93, 203–209 (2003). The holding of *McConnell* rested to a large extent on an earlier case, *Austin v. Michigan Chamber of Commerce*, 494 U.S. 652 (1990). *Austin* had held that political speech may be banned based on the speaker's corporate identity.

In this case we are asked to reconsider *Austin* and, in effect, *McConnell*. It has been noted that "*Austin* was a significant departure from ancient First Amendment principles," *Federal Election Comm'n v. Wisconsin Right to Life, Inc.*, 551 U.S. 449, 490 (2007) (*WRTL*) (Scalia, J., concurring in part and concurring in judgment). We agree with that conclusion and hold that *stare decisis* does not compel the continued acceptance of *Austin*. The Government may regulate corporate political speech through disclaimer and disclosure requirements, but it may not suppress that speech altogether. We turn to the case now before us.

I

A

Citizens United is a nonprofit corporation. It has an annual budget of about $12 million. Most of its funds are from donations by individuals; but, in addition, it accepts a small portion of its funds from for-profit corporations.

In January 2008, Citizens United released a film entitled *Hillary: The Movie*. We refer to the film as *Hillary*. It is a 90-minute documentary about then-Senator Hillary Clinton, who was a candidate in the Democratic Party's 2008 Presidential primary elections. *Hillary* mentions Senator Clinton by name and depicts interviews with political commentators and other persons, most of them quite critical of Senator Clinton....

In December 2007, a cable company offered, for a payment of $1.2 million, to make *Hillary* available on a video-on-demand channel called "Elections '08."...Citizens United was prepared to pay for the video-on-demand; and to promote the film, it produced two 10-second ads and one 30-second ad for *Hillary*. Each ad includes a short (and, in our view, pejorative) statement about Senator Clinton, followed by the name of the movie and the movie's Website address. Citizens United desired to promote the video-on-demand offering by running advertisements on broadcast and cable television.

B

Before the Bipartisan Campaign Reform Act of 2002 (BCRA), federal law prohibited—and still does prohibit—corporations and unions from using general treasury funds to make direct contributions to candidates or independent expenditures that expressly advocate the election or defeat of a candidate, through any form of media, in connection with certain qualified federal elections....BCRA §203 amended §441b to prohibit any "electioneering communication" as well. An electioneering communication is defined as "any broadcast, cable, or satellite communication" that "refers to a clearly identified candidate for Federal office" and is made within 30 days of a primary or 60 days of a general election. §434(f)(3)(A). The Federal Election Commission's (FEC) regulations further define an electioneering communication as a communication that is "publicly distributed." 11 CFR §100.29(a)(2) (2009). "In the case of a candidate for nomination for President...*publicly distributed* means" that the communication "[c]an be received by 50,000 or more persons in a State where a primary election...is being held within 30 days." 11 CFR §100.29(b)(3)(ii). Corporations and unions are barred from using their general treasury funds for express advocacy or electioneering communications. They may establish, however, a "separate segregated fund" (known as a political action committee, or PAC) for these purposes. 2 U.S.C. §441b(b)(2). The moneys received by the segregated fund are limited to donations from stockholders and employees of the corporation or, in the case of unions, members of the union. *Ibid.*

C

Citizens United wanted to make *Hillary* available through video-on-demand within 30 days of the 2008 primary elections. It feared, however, that both the film and the ads would be covered by §441b's ban on corporate-funded independent expenditures, thus subjecting the corporation to civil and criminal penalties under §437g. In December 2007, Citizens United sought declaratory and injunctive relief against the FEC. It argued that (1) §441b is unconstitutional as applied to *Hillary*; and (2) BCRA's disclaimer and disclosure requirements, BCRA §§201 and 311, are unconstitutional as applied to *Hillary* and to the three ads for the movie.

The District Court denied Citizens United's motion for a preliminary injunction, and then granted the FEC's motion for summary judgment.

...

The court held that §441b was facially constitutional under *McConnell*, and that §441b was constitutional as applied to *Hillary* because it was "susceptible of no other interpretation than to inform the electorate that Senator Clinton is unfit for office, that the United States would be a dangerous place in a President Hillary Clinton world, and that viewers should vote against her." 530 F. Supp. 2d, at 279. The court also rejected Citizens United's challenge to BCRA's disclaimer and disclosure requirements. It noted that "the Supreme Court has written approvingly of disclosure provisions triggered by political speech even though the speech itself was constitutionally protected under the First Amendment." *Id.* at 281.

II

[Omitted: the court considers whether it is possible to reject the BCRA without declaring certain provisions unconstitutional. The court concludes it cannot find a basis to reject the BCRA that does not involve constitutional issues.]

III

The First Amendment provides that "Congress shall make no law...abridging the freedom of speech." Laws enacted to control or suppress speech may operate at different points in the speech process....The law before us is an outright ban, backed by criminal sanctions. Section 441b makes it a felony for all corporations—including nonprofit advocacy corporations—either to expressly advocate the election or defeat of candidates or to broadcast electioneering communications within 30 days of a primary election and 60 days of a general election. Thus, the following acts would all be felonies under §441b: The Sierra Club runs an ad, within the crucial phase of 60 days before the general election, that exhorts the public to disapprove of a Congressman who favors logging in national forests; the National Rifle Association publishes a book urging the public to vote for the challenger because the incumbent U.S. Senator supports a handgun ban; and the American Civil Liberties Union creates a Web site telling the public to vote for a Presidential candidate in light of that candidate's defense of free speech. These prohibitions are classic examples of censorship.

Section 441b is a ban on corporate speech notwithstanding the fact that a PAC created by a corporation can still speak. PACs are burdensome alternatives; they are expensive to administer and subject to extensive regulations. For example, every PAC must appoint a treasurer, forward donations to the treasurer promptly, keep detailed records of the identities of the persons making donations, preserve receipts for three years, and file an organization statement and report changes to this information within 10 days.

And that is just the beginning. PACs must file detailed monthly reports with the FEC, which are due at different times depending on the type of election that is about to occur....

PACs have to comply with these regulations just to speak. This might explain why fewer than 2,000 of the millions of corporations in this country have PACs. PACs, furthermore, must exist before they can speak. Given the onerous restrictions, a corporation may not be able to establish a PAC in time to make its views known regarding candidates and issues in a current campaign.

Section 441b's prohibition on corporate independent expenditures is thus a ban on speech. As a "restriction on the amount of money a person or group can spend on political communication during a campaign," that statute "necessarily reduces the quantity of expression by restricting the number of issues discussed, the depth of their exploration, and the size of the audience reached." *Buckley v. Valeo*, 424 U.S. 1 at 19 (1976)....

Speech is an essential mechanism of democracy, for it is the means to hold officials accountable to the people. See *Buckley, supra*, at 14–15 ("In a republic where the people are sovereign, the ability of the citizenry to make informed choices among candidates for office is essential.") The right of citizens to inquire, to hear, to speak, and to use information to reach consensus is a precondition to enlightened self-government and a necessary means to protect it. The First Amendment "'has its fullest and most urgent application' to speech uttered during a campaign for political office."

For these reasons, political speech must prevail against laws that would suppress it, whether by design or inadvertence. Laws that burden political speech are "subject to strict scrutiny," which requires the Government to prove that the restriction "furthers a compelling interest and is narrowly tailored to achieve that interest."

...

The Court has recognized that First Amendment protection extends to corporations. This protection has been extended by explicit holdings to the context of political speech. Under the rationale of these precedents, political speech does not lose First Amendment protection "simply because its source is a corporation." *First National Bank of Boston v. Bellotti*, 435 U.S. 765, at 784. The Court has thus rejected the argument that political speech of corporations or other associations should be treated differently under the First Amendment simply because such associations are not "natural persons."

The purpose and effect of this law is to prevent corporations, including small and nonprofit corporations, from presenting both facts and opinions to the public. This makes *Austin*'s antidistortion rationale all the more an aberration. "[T]he First Amendment protects the right of corporations to petition legislative and administrative bodies." *Bellotti*, 435 U.S., at 792, n. 31....

Even if §441b's expenditure ban were constitutional, wealthy corporations could still lobby elected officials, although smaller corporations may not have the resources to do so. And wealthy individuals and unincorporated associations can spend unlimited amounts on independent expenditures. See, e.g., *WRTL*, 551 U.S., at 503–504 (opinion of Scalia, J.) ("In the 2004 election cycle, a mere 24 individuals contributed an astounding total of $142 million to [26 U.S.C. §527 organizations]"). Yet certain disfavored associations of citizens—those that have taken on the corporate form—are penalized for engaging in the same political speech.

When Government seeks to use its full power, including the criminal law, to command where a person may get his or her information or what distrusted source he or she may not hear, it uses censorship to control thought. This is unlawful. The First Amendment confirms the freedom to think for ourselves.

What we have said also shows the invalidity of other arguments made by the Government. For the most part relinquishing the anti-distortion rationale, the Government falls back on the argument that corporate political speech can be banned in order to prevent corruption or its appearance....

When Congress finds that a problem exists, we must give that finding due deference; but Congress may not choose an unconstitutional remedy. If elected officials succumb to improper influences from independent expenditures; if they surrender their best judgment; and if they put expediency before principle, then surely there is cause for concern. We must give weight to attempts by Congress to seek to dispel either the appearance or the reality of these influences. The remedies enacted by law, however, must comply with the First Amendment; and, it is our law and our tradition that more speech, not less, is the governing rule. An outright ban on corporate political speech during the critical preelection period is not a permissible remedy. Here Congress has created categorical bans on speech that are asymmetrical to preventing *quid pro quo* corruption.

Our precedent is to be respected unless the most convincing of reasons demonstrates that adherence to it puts us on a course that is sure error. "Beyond workability, the relevant factors in deciding whether to adhere to the principle of *stare decisis* include the antiquity of the precedent, the reliance interests at stake, and of course whether the decision was well reasoned." [citing prior cases]

These considerations counsel in favor of rejecting *Austin*, which itself contravened this Court's earlier precedents in *Buckley* and *Bellotti*. "This Court has not hesitated to overrule decisions offensive to the First Amendment." *WRTL*, 551 U.S., at 500 (opinion of Scalia, J.). "*[S]tare decisis* is a principle of policy and not a mechanical formula of adherence to the latest decision." *Helvering* v. *Hallock*, 309 U.S. 106 at 119 (1940).

Austin is undermined by experience since its announcement. Political speech is so ingrained in our culture that speakers find ways to circumvent campaign finance laws. See, *e.g.*, *McConnell*, 540 U.S., at 176–177 ("Given BCRA's tighter restrictions on the raising and spending of soft money, the incentives...to exploit [26 U.S.C. §527] organizations will only increase"). Our Nation's speech dynamic is changing, and informative voices should not have to circumvent onerous restrictions to exercise their First Amendment rights. Speakers have become adept at presenting citizens with sound bites, talking points, and scripted messages that dominate the 24-hour news cycle. Corporations, like individuals, do not have monolithic views. On certain topics corporations may possess valuable expertise, leaving them the best equipped to point out errors or fallacies in speech of all sorts, including the speech of candidates and elected officials.

Rapid changes in technology—and the creative dynamic inherent in the concept of free expression—counsel against upholding a law that restricts political speech in certain media or by certain speakers. Today, 30-second television ads may be the most effective way to convey a political message. Soon, however, it may be that Internet sources, such as blogs and social networking Web sites, will provide citizens with significant information about political candidates and issues. Yet, §441b would seem to ban a blog post expressly advocating the election or defeat of a candidate if that blog were created with corporate funds. The First Amendment does not permit Congress to make these categorical distinctions based on the corporate identity of the speaker and the content of the political speech.

Due consideration leads to this conclusion: *Austin* should be and now is overruled. We return to the principle established in *Buckley* and *Bellotti* that the Government may not suppress political speech on the basis of the speaker's corporate identity. No sufficient governmental interest justifies limits on the political speech of nonprofit or for-profit corporations.

[IV. Omitted]

V

When word concerning the plot of the movie *Mr. Smith Goes to Washington* reached the circles of Government, some officials sought, by persuasion, to discourage its distribution. See Smoodin, "Compulsory" Viewing for Every Citizen: *Mr. Smith* and the Rhetoric of Reception, 35 Cinema Journal 3, 19, and n. 52 (Winter 1996) (citing Mr. Smith Riles Washington, Time, Oct. 30, 1939, p. 49); Nugent, Capra's Capitol Offense, N. Y. Times, Oct. 29, 1939, p. X5. Under *Austin*, though, officials could have done more than discourage its distribution—they could have banned the film. After all, it, like *Hillary*, was speech funded by a corporation that was critical of Members of Congress. *Mr. Smith Goes to Washington* may be fiction and caricature; but fiction and caricature can be a powerful force.

Modern day movies, television comedies, or skits on YouTube.com might portray public officials or public policies in unflattering ways. Yet if a covered transmission during the blackout period creates the background for candidate endorsement or opposition, a felony occurs solely because a corporation, other than an exempt media corporation, has made the "purchase, payment, distribution, loan, advance, deposit, or gift of money or anything of value" in order to engage in political speech. 2 U.S.C. §431(9)(A)(i). Speech would be suppressed in the realm where its necessity is most evident: in the public dialogue preceding a real election. Governments are often hostile to speech, but under our law and our tradition it seems stranger than fiction for our Government to make this political speech a crime. Yet this is the statute's purpose and design.

Some members of the public might consider *Hillary* to be insightful and instructive; some might find it to be neither high art nor a fair discussion on how to set the Nation's course; still others simply might suspend judgment on these points but decide to think more about issues and candidates. Those choices and assessments, however, are not for the Government to make. "The First Amendment underwrites the freedom to experiment and to create in the realm of thought and speech. Citizens must be free to use new forms, and new forums, for the expression of ideas. The civic discourse belongs to the people, and the Government may not prescribe the means used to conduct it." *McConnell*, *supra*, at 341 (opinion of Kennedy, J.).

The judgment of the District Court is reversed with respect to the constitutionality of 2 U.S.C. §441b's restrictions on corporate independent expenditures. The case is remanded for further proceedings consistent with this opinion.

It is so ordered.

Case Questions

1. What does the case say about disclosure? Corporations have a right of free speech under the First Amendment and may exercise that right through unrestricted contributions of money to political parties and candidates. Can the government condition that right by requir-

ing that the parties and candidates disclose to the public the amount and origin of the contribution? What would justify such a disclosure requirement?

2. Are a corporation's contributions to political parties and candidates tax deductible as a business expense? Should they be?
3. How is the donation of money equivalent to speech? Is this a strict construction of the Constitution to hold that it is?

Brown v. Entertainment Merchants Association

Brown v. Entertainment Merchants Association, et al.
564 U.S. 786, (U.S. Supreme Court 2011).

Justice Scalia delivered the opinion of the Court.

We consider whether a California law imposing restrictions on violent video games comports with the First Amendment.

I

California Assembly Bill 1179 (2005), prohibits the sale or rental of "violent video games" to minors, and requires their packaging to be labeled "18." The Act covers games "in which the range of options available to a player includes killing, maiming, dismembering, or sexually assaulting an image of a human being, if those acts are depicted" in a manner that "[a] reasonable person, considering the game as a whole, would find appeals to a deviant or morbid interest of minors," that is "patently offensive to prevailing standards in the community as to what is suitable for minors," and that "causes the game, as a whole, to lack serious literary, artistic, political, or scientific value for minors." Violation of the Act is punishable by a civil fine of up to $1,000.

Respondents, representing the video-game and software industries, brought a pre-enforcement challenge to the Act in the United States District Court for the Northern District of California. That court concluded that the Act violated the First Amendment and permanently enjoined its enforcement. The Court of Appeals affirmed, and we granted *certiorari*.

II

California correctly acknowledges that video games qualify for First Amendment protection. The Free Speech Clause exists principally to protect discourse on public matters, but we have long recognized that it is difficult to distinguish politics from entertainment, and dangerous to try. "Everyone is familiar with instances of propaganda through fiction. What is one man's amusement, teaches another's doctrine." *Winters v. New York*, 333 U.S. 507, 510 (1948). Like the protected books, plays, and movies that preceded them, video games communicate ideas—and even social messages—through many familiar literary devices (such as characters, dialogue, plot, and music) and through features distinctive to the medium (such as the player's interaction with the virtual world). That suffices to confer First Amendment protection. Under our Constitution, "esthetic and moral judgments about art and literature ... are for the individual to make, not for the Government to decree, even with the mandate or approval of a majority." (case precedent cited). And whatever the challenges of applying the Constitution to ever-advancing technology, "the basic principles of freedom of speech and the press, like the First Amendment's command, do not vary" when a new and different medium for communication appears. (case precedent cited).

The most basic of those principles is this: "[A]s a general matter, ... government has no power to restrict expression because of its message, its ideas, its subject matter, or its content." *Ashcroft v. American Civil Liberties Union*, 535 U.S. 564, 573 (2002), (internal quotation marks omitted). There are of course exceptions. (case precedents cited, including obscenity, incitement, fighting words, defamation, etc.) which represent "well-defined and narrowly limited classes of speech, the prevention and punishment of which have never been thought to raise any Constitutional problem," *id.*, at 571–572.

Last term in *United States* v. *Stevens*, 559 U. S. 460, (2010) we held that new categories of unprotected speech may not be added to the list by a legislature that concludes certain speech is too harmful to be tolerated. *Stevens* concerned a federal statute purporting to criminalize the creation, sale, or possession of certain depictions of animal cruelty. See 18 U.S.C. §48 (amended 2010). The statute covered depictions "in which a living animal is intentionally maimed, mutilated, tortured, wounded, or killed" if that harm to the animal was illegal where the "the creation, sale, or possession t[ook] place," §48(c)(1). A saving clause largely borrowed from our obscenity jurisprudence (see *Miller* v. *California*, 413 U.S. 15, 24 (1973)), exempted depictions with "serious religious, political, scientific, educational, journalistic, historical, or artistic value," §48(b). *(Note to readers of this Flatworld text: a "saving clause" here means that the California legislature added a clause that was intended to save the legislation from being deemed unconstitutional.)*

We held that statute to be an impermissible content-based restriction on speech. There was no American tradition of forbidding the *depiction of* animal cruelty—though States have long had laws against *committing* it.

The Government argued in *Stevens* that lack of a historical warrant did not matter; that it could create new categories of unprotected speech by applying a "simple balancing test" that weighs the value of a particular category of speech against its social costs and then punishes that category of speech if it fails the test. We emphatically rejected that "startling and dangerous" proposition. *Ibid.* "Maybe there are some categories of speech that have been historically unprotected, but have not yet been specifically identified or discussed as such in our case law." *Id.* But without persuasive evidence that a novel restriction on content is part of a long . . .tradition of proscription, a legislature may not revise the "judgment [of] the American people," embodied in the First Amendment, "that the benefits of its restrictions on the Government outweigh the costs." *Id.*

That holding controls this case. As in *Stevens*, California has tried to make violent-speech regulation look like obscenity regulation by appending a saving clause required for the latter. That does not suffice. Our cases have been clear that the obscenity exception to the First Amendment does not cover whatever a legislature finds shocking, but only depictions of "sexual conduct," *Miller*, *supra*, at 24.

. . . .

California does not argue that it is empowered to prohibit selling offensively violent works *to adults* —and it is wise not to, since that is but a hair's breadth from the argument rejected in *Stevens*. Instead, it wishes to create a wholly new category of content-based regulation that is permissible only for speech directed at children.

That is unprecedented and mistaken. "[M]inors are entitled to a significant measure of First Amendment protection, and only in relatively narrow and well-defined circumstances may government bar public dissemination of protected materials to them." (Case cited) No doubt a State possesses legitimate power to protect children from harm, *Ginsberg* v. *New York*, 390 U.S. 629, 640-41 (1968); *Prince* v. *Massachusetts*, 321 U.S. 158, 165 (1944), but that does not include a free-floating power to restrict the ideas to which children may be exposed. "Speech that is neither obscene as to youths nor subject to some other legitimate proscription cannot be suppressed solely to protect the young from ideas or images that a legislative body thinks unsuitable for them." *Erznoznik v. Jacksonville*, 422 U.S. 205, 212-13 (1975).

California's argument would fare better if there were a longstanding tradition in this country of specially restricting children's access to depictions of violence, but there is none. Certainly the *books* we give children to read—or read to them when they are younger—contain no shortage of gore. Grimm's Fairy Tales, for example, are grim indeed. As her just deserts for trying to poison Snow White, the wicked queen is made to dance in red hot slippers "till she fell dead on the floor, a sad example of envy and jealousy." The Complete Brothers Grimm Fairy Tales, 198 (2006 ed.). Cinderella's evil stepsisters have their eyes pecked out by doves. *Id.*at 95. And Hansel and Gretel (children!) kill their captor by baking her in an oven. *Id.* at 54.

High-school reading lists are full of similar fare. Homer's Odysseus blinds Polyphemus the Cyclops by grinding out his eye with a heated stake. *The Odyssey of Homer*, Book IX, p. 125 (S. Butcher & A. Lang translations, 1909) ("Even so did we seize the fiery-pointed brand and whirled it round in his eye, and the blood flowed about the heated bar. And the breath of the flame singed his eyelids and brows all about, as the ball of the eye burnt away, and the roots thereof crackled in the flame"). In the Inferno, Dante and Virgil watch corrupt politicians struggle to stay submerged beneath a lake of boiling pitch, lest they be skewered by devils above the surface. Canto XXI, pp. 187–189 *(etc., with other examples from "classic literature").*

. . .

California claims that video games present special problems because they are "interactive," in that the player participates in the violent action on screen and determines its outcome. The latter feature is nothing new: Since at least the publication of *The Adventures of You: Sugarcane Island* in 1969, young readers of choose-your-own-adventure stories have been able to make decisions that determine the plot by following instructions about which page to turn to. Cf. *Interactive Digital Software Assn. v. St. Louis County*, 329 F. 3d 954, 957–958 (2003). (*Note: referencing an 8th Circuit Court of Appeals decision*)

III

Because the Act imposes a restriction on the content of protected speech, it is invalid unless California can demonstrate that it passes strict scrutiny—that is, unless it is justified by a compelling government interest and is narrowly drawn to serve that interest. The State must specifically identify an "actual problem" in need of solving, *Playboy*, 529 U. S. 803, at 822–823, and the curtailment of free speech must be actually necessary to the solution..... That is a demanding standard. "It is rare that a regulation restricting speech because of its content will ever be permissible." *Playboy, supra*, at 818.

California cannot meet that standard. At the outset, it acknowledges that it cannot show a direct causal link between violent video games and harm to minors. Rather, relying upon our decision in *Turner Broadcasting System, Inc. v. FCC*, 512 U.S. 622 (1994), the State claims that it need not produce such proof because the legislature can make a predictive judgment that such a link exists, based on competing psychological studies. But reliance on *Turner Broadcasting* is misplaced. That decision applied *intermediate scrutiny* to a content-neutral regulation. *Id.* at 661–662. California's burden is much higher, and because it bears the risk of uncertainty, see *Playboy, supra*, at 816–817, ambiguous proof will not suffice.

The State's evidence is not compelling. California relies primarily on the research of Dr. Craig Anderson and a few other research psychologists whose studies purport to show a connection between exposure to violent video games and harmful effects on children. These studies have been rejected by every court to consider them, and with good reason: They do not prove that violent video games *cause* minors to *act* aggressively (which would at least be a beginning). Instead, "[n]early all of the research is based on correlation, not evidence of causation, and most of the studies suffer from significant, admitted flaws in methodology." *Video Software Dealers Assn.* 556 F. 3d, at 964. They show at best some correlation between exposure to violent entertainment and minuscule real-world effects, such as children's feeling more aggressive or making louder noises in the few minutes after playing a violent game than after playing a nonviolent game.

Even taking for granted Dr. Anderson's conclusions that violent video games produce some effect on children's feelings of aggression, those effects are both small and indistinguishable from effects produced by other media. In his testimony in a similar lawsuit, Dr. Anderson admitted that the "effect sizes" of children's exposure to violent video games are "about the same" as that produced by their exposure to violence on television. And he admits that the *same* effects have been found when children watch cartoons starring Bugs Bunny or the Road Runner, or when they play video games like Sonic the Hedgehog that are rated "E" (appropriate for all ages), or even when they "vie[w] a picture of a gun."

Of course, California has (wisely) declined to restrict Saturday morning cartoons, the sale of games rated for young children, or the distribution of pictures of guns. The consequence is that its regulation is wildly under-inclusive when judged against its asserted justification, which in our view is alone enough to defeat it. Under-inclusiveness raises serious doubts about whether the government is in fact pursuing the interest it invokes, rather than disfavoring a particular speaker or viewpoint. (cases cited). Here, California has singled out the purveyors of video games for disfavored treatment—at least when compared to booksellers, cartoonists, and movie producers—and has given no persuasive reason why.

The Act is also seriously under-inclusive in another respect—and a respect that renders irrelevant the contentions of the concurrence and the dissents that video games are qualitatively different from other portrayals of violence. The California Legislature is perfectly willing to leave this dangerous, mind-altering material in the hands of children so long as one parent (or even an aunt or uncle) says it's OK. And there are not even any requirements as to how this parental or avuncular relationship is to be verified; apparently the child's or putative parent's, aunt's, or uncle's say-so suffices. That is not how one addresses a serious social problem.

California claims that the Act is justified in aid of parental authority: By requiring that the purchase of violent video games can be made only by adults, the Act ensures that parents can decide what games are appropriate. At the outset, we note our doubts that punishing third parties for conveying protected speech to children *just in case* their parents disapprove of that speech is a proper governmental means of aiding parental authority. Accepting that position would largely vitiate the rule that "only in relatively narrow and well-defined circumstances may government bar public dissemination of protected materials to [minors]." *Erznoznik*, 422 U. S., at 212–213.

But leaving that aside, California cannot show that the Act's restrictions meet a substantial need of parents who wish to restrict their children's access to violent video games but cannot do so. The video-game industry has in place a voluntary rating system designed to inform consumers about the content of games. The system, implemented by the Entertainment Software Rating Board (ESRB), assigns age-specific ratings to each video game submitted: EC (Early Childhood); E (Everyone); E10+ (Everyone 10 and older); T (Teens); M (17 and older); and AO (Adults Only—18 and older). The Video Software Dealers Association encourages retailers to prominently display information about the ESRB system in their stores; to refrain from renting or selling adults-only games to minors; and to rent or sell "M" rated games to minors only with parental consent. In 2009, the Federal Trade Commission (FTC) found that, as a result of this system, "the video game industry outpaces the movie and music industries" in "(1) restricting target-marketing of mature-rated products to children; (2) clearly and prominently disclosing rating information; and (3) restricting children's access to mature-rated products at retail." FTC, Report to Congress, Marketing Violent Entertainment to Children 30 (Dec. 2009). This system does much to ensure that minors cannot purchase seriously violent games on their own, and that parents who care about the matter can readily evaluate the games their children bring home. Filling the remaining modest gap in concerned-parents' control can hardly be a compelling state interest.

And finally, the Act's purported aid to parental authority is vastly over-inclusive. Not all of the children who are forbidden to purchase violent video games on their own have parents who *care* whether they purchase violent video games. While some of the legislation's effect may indeed be in support of what some parents of the restricted children actually want, its entire effect is only in support of what the State thinks parents *ought* to want. This is not the narrow tailoring to "assisting parents" that restriction of First Amendment rights requires.

* * *

California's effort to regulate violent video games is the latest episode in a long series of failed attempts to censor violent entertainment for minors. While we have pointed out above that some of the evidence brought forward to support the harmfulness of video games is unpersuasive, we do not mean to demean or disparage the concerns that underlie the attempt to regulate them—concerns that may and doubtless do prompt a good deal of parental oversight. We have no business passing judgment on the view of the California Legislature that violent video games (or, for that matter, any other forms of speech) corrupt the young or harm their moral development. Our task is only to say whether or not such works constitute a "well-defined and narrowly limited clas[s] of speech, the prevention and punishment of which have never been thought to raise any Constitutional problem," *Chaplinsky v. New Hampshire*, 315 U.S. 568, at 571–572 (1942) (the answer plainly is no); and if not, whether the regulation of such works is justified by that high degree of necessity we have described as a compelling state interest (it is not). Even where the protection of children is the object, the constitutional limits on governmental action apply.

California's legislation straddles the fence between (1) addressing a serious social problem and (2) helping concerned parents control their children. Both ends are legitimate, but when they affect First Amendment rights they must be pursued by means that are neither seriously under-inclusive nor seriously over-inclusive. See *Church of Lukumi Babalu Aye, Inc. v. Hialeah*, 508 U.S. 520, 546 (1993). As a means of protecting children from portrayals of violence, the legislation is seriously under-inclusive, not only because it excludes portrayals other than video games, but also because it permits a parental or avuncular veto. And as a means of assisting concerned parents it is seriously over-inclusive because it abridges the First Amendment rights of young people whose parents (and aunts and uncles) think violent video games are a harmless pastime. And the overbreadth in achieving one goal is not cured by the underbreadth in achieving the other. Legislation such as this, which is neither fish nor fowl, cannot survive strict scrutiny.

We affirm the judgment below.

Justice Thomas, dissenting.

The Court's decision today does not comport with the original public understanding of the First Amendment. The majority strikes down, as facially unconstitutional, a state law that prohibits the direct sale or rental of certain video games to minors because the law "abridg[es] the freedom of speech." U. S. Const., Amendment 1. But I do not think the First Amendment stretches that far. The practices and beliefs of the founding generation establish that "the freedom of speech," as originally understood, does not include a right to speak to minors (or a right of minors to access speech) without going through the minors' parents or guardians. I would hold that the law at issue is not facially unconstitutional under the First Amendment and reverse and remand for further proceedings.

When interpreting a constitutional provision, "the goal is to discern the most likely public understanding of [that] provision at the time it was adopted." *McDonald v. Chicago*, 561 U. S. 742, (2010) Because the Constitution is a written instrument, "its meaning does not alter." *McIntyre v. Ohio Elections Comm'n*, 514 U.S. 334 (1995), (Thomas, J., concurring in judgment). "That which it meant when adopted, it means now." *Ibid.*

As originally understood, the First Amendment protection against laws "abridging the freedom of speech" did not extend to *all* speech. "There are certain well-defined and narrowly limited classes of speech, the prevention and punishment of which have never been thought to raise any Constitutional problem." *Chaplinsky v. New Hampshire*, 315 U.S. 568, 571-72 (1942); see also *United States v. Stevens*, 559 U.S. 460, (2010) (slip op., at 5–6). Laws regulating such speech do not "abridg[e] the freedom of speech" because such speech is understood to fall outside "the freedom of speech." See *Ashcroft v. Free Speech Coalition*, 535 U.S. 234, 245-246 (2002).

In my view, the "practices and beliefs held by the Founders" reveal another category of excluded speech: speech to minor children bypassing their parents. *McIntyre, supra*, at 360. The historical evidence shows that the founding generation believed parents had absolute authority over their minor children and expected parents to use that authority to direct the proper development of their children. It would be absurd to suggest that such a society understood "the freedom of speech" to include a right to speak to minors (or a corresponding right of minors to access speech) without going through the minors' parents. Cf. Brief for Common Sense Media as *Amicus Curiae* 12–15. The founding generation would not have considered it an abridgment of "the freedom of speech" to support parental authority by restricting speech that bypasses minors' parents.

Justice Breyer wrote a separate dissent. He stated that the majority's opinion conflicted with prior decisions in *Ginsberg* and *Miller*. He asked what sense it made to forbid selling an image of a nude woman but allow violent video games: "But what sense does it make to forbid selling to a 13-year-old boy a magazine with an image of a nude woman, while protecting a sale to that 13 year-old of an interactive video game in which he actively, but virtually, binds and gags the woman, then tortures and kills her?" Breyer saw the case as less about censorship and the First Amendment and more about education, and that "California's law imposes no more than a modest restriction on expression." As to the industry's voluntary program of labelling video games, he noted that self-regulation of the industry still allowed for 20% of minors to purchase mature video games, and as high as 50% in the case of one nationwide chain, based on the 2011 FTC study.

The Court's decision today does not comport with the original public understanding of the First Amendment. The majority strikes down, as facially unconstitutional, a state law that prohibits the direct sale or rental of certain video games to minors because the law "abridg[es] the freedom of speech." U.S. Const., Amendment 1. But I do not think the First Amendment stretches that far. The practices and beliefs of the founding generation establish that "the freedom of speech," as originally understood, does not include a right to speak to minors (or a right of minors to access speech) without going through the minors' parents or guardians. I would hold that the law at issue is not facially unconstitutional under the First Amendment and reverse and remand for further proceedings.

Case Questions

1. What about the distinction the Court makes between depictions of sexual conduct and depictions of violence? Is the majority actually saying that the First Amendment law's exception for "obscenity" (*Miller v. California*, holding that some depictions and descriptions are beyond First Amendment protection) does not apply to depictions and descriptions and interactive "acts" of killing, maiming, dismembering, or sexually assaulting an image of a human being, if those acts are depicted" in a manner that "[a] reasonable person, considering the game as a whole, would find appeals to a deviant or morbid interest of minors?
2. What would a "strict constructionist" say? Does the express language of the First Amendment resolve the case in any straightforward way?
3. What do you make of Justice Breyer's dissent, and that of Justice Thomas? To what extent should the First Amendment, or any other Amendment, be set forth and interpreted only in the sense that the Framers would have understood it?

4.7 Summary and Exercises

Summary

The U.S. Constitution sets the framework for all other laws of the United States, at both the federal and the state level. It creates a shared balance of power between states and the federal government (federalism) and shared power among the branches of government (separation of powers), establishes individual rights against governmental action (Bill of Rights), and provides for federal oversight of matters affecting interstate commerce and commerce with foreign nations. Knowing the contours of the U.S. legal system is not possible without understanding the role of the U.S. Constitution.

The Constitution is difficult to amend. Thus when the Supreme Court uses its power of judicial review to determine that a law is unconstitutional, it actually shapes what the Constitution means. New meanings that emerge must do so by the process of amendment or by the passage of time and new appointments to the court. Because justices serve for life, the court changes its philosophical outlook slowly.

The Bill of Rights is an especially important piece of the Constitutional framework. It provides legal causes of action for infringements of individual rights by government, state or federal. Through the due process clause of the Fifth Amendment and the Fourteenth Amendment, both procedural and (to some extent) substantive due process rights are given to individuals.

Exercises

1. For many years, the Supreme Court believed that "commercial speech" was entitled to less protection than other forms of speech. One defining element of commercial speech is that its dominant theme is to propose a commercial transaction. This kind of speech is protected by the First Amendment, but the government is permitted to regulate it more closely than other forms of speech. However, the government must make reasonable distinctions, must narrowly tailor the rules restricting commercial speech, and must show that government has a legitimate goal that the law furthers.

   Edward Salib owned a Winchell's Donut House in Mesa, Arizona. To attract customers, he displayed large signs in store windows. The city ordered him to remove the signs because they violated the city's sign code, which prohibited covering more than 30 percent of a store's windows with signs. Salib sued, claiming that the sign code violated his First Amendment rights. What was the result, and why?
2. Jennifer is a freshman at her local public high school. Her sister, Jackie, attends a nearby private high school. Neither school allows them to join its respective wrestling team; only boys can wrestle at either school. Do either of them have a winning case based on the equal protection clause of the Fourteenth Amendment?
3. The employees of the U.S. Treasury Department that work the border crossing between the United States and Mexico learned that they will be subject to routine drug testing. The customs bureau, which is a division of the treasury department, announces this policy along with its reasoning: since customs agents must routinely search for drugs coming into the United States, it makes sense that border guards must themselves be completely drug-free. Many border guards do not use drugs, have no intention of using drugs, and object to the invasion of their privacy. What is the constitutional basis for their objection?
4. Happy Time Chevrolet employs Jim Bydalok as a salesman. Bydalek takes part in a Gay Pride March in Los Angeles, is interviewed by a local news camera crew, and reports that he is gay and proud of it. His employer is not, and he is fired. Does he have any constitutional causes of action against his employer?
5. You begin work at the Happy-Go-Lucky Corporation on Halloween. On your second day at work, you wear a political button on your coat, supporting your choice for U.S. senator in the upcoming election. Your boss, who is of a different political persuasion, looks at the button and says, "Take that stupid button off or you're fired." Has your boss violated your constitutional rights?
6. David Lucas paid $975,000 for two residential parcels on the Isle of Palms near Charleston, South Carolina. His intention was to build houses on them. Two years later, the South Carolina legislature passed a statute that prohibited building beachfront properties. The purpose was to leave the dunes system in place to mitigate the effects of hurricanes and strong storms. The South Carolina Coastal Commission created the rules and regulations with substantial input from the community and from experts and with protection of the dune system primarily in mind. People had been building on the shoreline for years, with harmful results to localities and the state treasury. When Lucas applied for permits to build two houses near the shoreline, his permits were rejected. He sued, arguing that the South Carolina legislation had effectively "taken" his property. At trial, South Carolina conceded that because of the legislation, Lucas's property was effectively worth zero. Has there been a taking under the Fifth Amendment (as incorporated through the Fourteenth Amendment), and if so, what should the state owe to Lucas? Suppose that Lucas could have made an additional $1 million by building a house on each of his parcels. Is he entitled to recover his original purchase price or his potential profits?

Self-Test Questions

1. Harvey filed a suit against the state of Colorado, claiming that a Colorado state law violates the commerce clause. The court will agree if the statute
   a. places an undue burden on interstate commerce
   b. promotes the public health, safety, morals, or general welfare of Colorado
   c. regulates economic activities within the state's borders
   d. a and b
   e. b and c
2. The state legislature in Maine enacts a law that directly conflicts with a federal law. Mapco Industries, located in Portland, Maine, cannot comply with both the state and the federal law.
   a. Because of federalism, the state law will have priority, as long as Maine is using its police powers.
   b. Because there's a conflict, both laws are invalid; the state and the federal government will have to work out a compromise of some sort.
   c. The federal law preempts the state law.
   d. Both laws govern concurrently.
3. Hannah, who lives in Ada, is the owner of Superior Enterprises, Inc. She believes that certain actions in the state of Ohio infringe on her federal constitutional rights, especially those found in the Bill of Rights. Most of these rights apply to the states under
   a. the supremacy clause
   b. the protection clause
   c. the due process clause of the Fourteenth Amendment
   d. the Tenth Amendment
4. Minnesota enacts a statute that bans all advertising that is in "bad taste," "vulgar," or "indecent." In Michigan, Aaron Calloway and his brother, Clarence "Cab" Calloway, create unique beer that they decide to call Old Fart Ale. In their marketing, the brothers have a label in which an older man in a dirty T-shirt is sitting in easy chair, looking disheveled and having a three-day growth of stubble on his chin. It appears that the man is in the process of belching. He is also holding a can of Old Fart Ale. The Minnesota liquor commission orders all Minnesota restaurants, bars, and grocery stores to remove Old Fart Ale from their shelves. The state statute and the commission's order are likely to be held by a court to be
   a. a violation of the Tenth Amendment
   b. a violation of the First Amendment
   c. a violation of the Calloways' right to equal protection of the laws
   d. a violation of the commerce clause, since only the federal laws can prevent an article of commerce from entering into Minnesota's market
5. Raunch Unlimited, a Virginia partnership, sells smut whenever and wherever it can. Some of its material is "obscene" (meeting the Supreme Court's definition under *Miller v. California*) and includes child pornography. North Carolina has a statute that criminalizes obscenity. What are possible results if a store in Raleigh, North Carolina, carries Raunch merchandise?
   a. The partners could be arrested in North Carolina and may well be convicted.
   b. The materials in Raleigh may be the basis for a criminal conviction.
   c. The materials are protected under the First Amendment's right of free speech.
   d. The materials are protected under state law.
   e. a and b

Self-Test Answers

1. a
2. c
3. c
4. b
5. e

Endnotes

1. In *Scott v. Sanford* (the Dred Scott decision), the court states that Scott should remain a slave, that as a slave he is not a citizen of the United States and thus not eligible to bring suit in a federal court, and that as a slave he is personal property and thus has never been free.
2. *Roe v. Wade*, 410 US 113 (1973).
3. The U.S. Senate.gov page provides an intriguing history on the cloture rule.
4. *Kimel v. Florida Board of Regents*, 528 US 62 (2000).
5. Up until the mid-1970s "Indian Law" was a quiet legal backwater, not considered very important. In 1974 a federal judge in Washington state ruled that the state was abusing Native Americans' treaty rights, from treaties made with tthe US in 1855, by denying them access to fishing grounds and prohibiting them from using certain types of fishing gear. The decison was affirmed by the 9th Circuit Court of Appeals, and the US Supreme Court declined to hear it. The consequence has been, as the non-Indian capitalists see it, that the Indians are interfering with Growth and Progress by denying non-Indians the "right" to exploit natural resources, including fish, water, minerals, and access to land for laying pipe.
6. *Hipolite Egg Co. v. United States*, 220 US 45 (1911).
7. *Hoke v. United States*, 227 US 308 (1913).
8. As FDR has a "court packing plan" that would add more Justices to the Supreme Court (there was nothing in the Constitution that mandated only 9 Justices), the switch of Justice Owen Roberts has been called "the switch in time that saved nine."
9. *Katzenbach v. McClung*, 379 US 294 (1964).
10. *Kassell v. Consolidated Freightways*, 450 US 662 (1981).
11. *Oregon Waste Systems v. Department of Environmental Quality*, 511 US 93 (1994).
12. *Fort Gratiot Sanitary Landfill v. Michigan Dep't of Natural Resources*, 504 US 353 (1992).
13. *Cippolone v. Liggett Group*, 505 US 504 (1993).
14. See Bradley Steinman, The Medical Use of Marijuana v. The Use of Marijuana for Medical Purposes http://www.americanbar.org/publications/tyl/topics/health-law/medical-use-marijuana-versus-use-marijuana-medical-purposes.html
15. *Jackson v. Metropolitan Edison Co.*, 419 US 345 (1974).
16. *Buckley v. Valeo*, 424 US 1 (1976).
17. Cybersecurity Summit Exposes Silicon Valley's Privacy Fears, *Wall Street Journal*, Feb. 13, 2015. ww.wsj.com/articles/cybersecurity-summit-exposes-silicon-valleys-privacy-fears-1423862917.
18. *Kelo v. City of New London*, 545 US 469 (2005).
19. *Cruzan v. Missouri Department of Health*, 497 US 261 (1990).
20. *BMW of North America, Inc. v. Gore*, 517 U.S. 559 (1996).
21. *Plessy v. Ferguson*, 163 US 537 (1896).
22. *United States v. Virginia*, 518 US 515 (1996).
23. *Palmore v. Sidoti*, 466 US 429 (1984).
24. *Atty. Gen. of New York v. Soto-Lopez*, 476 US 898 (1986).

CHAPTER 5

Administrative Law

Learning Objectives

After reading this chapter, you should be able to do the following:

1. Understand the purpose served by federal administrative agencies.
2. Know the difference between executive branch agencies and independent agencies.
3. Understand the political control of agencies by the president and Congress.
4. Describe how agencies make rules and conduct hearings.
5. Describe how courts can be used to challenge administrative rulings.

Administrative agencies, with all of their laws and their procedures, have virtually remade our government and much of private life. Every day, business must deal with rules and decisions of state and federal administrative agencies. Informally, such rules are often called regulations, and they differ (only in their source) from laws passed by Congress and signed into law by the president. The rules created by agencies are voluminous: thousands of new regulations pour forth each year. The ongoing political question of whether there is too much regulation of business—or the wrong kind of regulation—is a most important one but well beyond the scope of this chapter. Here, we merely offer an essential overview of the purpose of administrative agencies, their structure, and their impact on business.

5.1 Administrative Agencies: Their Structure and Powers

Learning Objectives

1. Explain the reasons why we have federal administrative agencies.
2. Explain the difference between executive branch agencies and independent agencies.
3. Describe the constitutional issue that questions whether administrative agencies could have authority to make enforceable rules that affect business.

Why Have Administrative Agencies?

The US Constitution mentions only three branches of government: legislative, executive, and judicial (Articles I, II, and III). There is no mention of agencies in the Constitution, even though federal agencies are sometimes referred to as "the fourth branch of government." The Supreme Court has recognized the legitimacy of federal **administrative agencies** to make rules that have the same binding effect as statutes by Congress.

administrative agencies

Governmental units, either state or federal, that have specialized expertise and authority over some area of the economy.

Most commentators note that having agencies with rule-making power is a practical necessity: (1) Congress does not have the expertise or continuity to develop specialized knowledge in various areas (e.g., communications, the environment, aviation). (2) Because of this, it makes sense for Congress to set forth broad statutory guidance to an agency and delegate authority to the agency to propose rules that further the statutory purposes. (3) As long as Congress makes this delegating guidance sufficiently clear, it is not delegating improperly. If Congress's guidelines are too vague or undefined, it is (in essence) giving away its constitutional power to some other group, and this it cannot do.

Why Regulate the Economy at All?

The market often does not work properly, as economists often note. Monopolies, for example, happen in the natural course of human events but are not always desirable. To fix this, well-conceived and objectively enforced competition law (what is called antitrust law in the United States) is needed.

Negative externalities must be "fixed," as well. For example, as we see in tort law (Chapter 7), people and business organizations often do things that impose costs (damages) on others, and the legal system will try—through the award of compensatory damages—to make fair adjustments. In terms of the ideal conditions for a free market, think of tort law as the legal system's attempt to compensate for negative externalities: those costs imposed on people who have not voluntarily consented to bear those costs.

In terms of freedoms to enter or leave the market, the US constitutional guarantees of equal protection can prevent local, state, and federal governments from imposing discriminatory rules for commerce that would keep minorities, women, and gay people from full participation in business. For example, if the small town of Xenophobia, Colorado, passed a law that required all business owners and their employees to be Christian, heterosexual, and married, the equal protection clause (as well as numerous state and federal equal opportunity employment laws) would empower plaintiffs to go to court and have the law struck down as unconstitutional.

Knowing that information is power, we will see many laws administered by regulatory agencies that seek to level the playing field of economic competition by requiring disclosure of the most pertinent information for consumers (consumer protection laws), investors (securities laws), and citizens (e.g., the toxics release inventory laws in environmental law).

Ideal Conditions for a Free Market

1. There are many buyers and many sellers, and none of them has a substantial share of the market.
2. All buyers and sellers in the market are free to enter the market or leave it.
3. All buyers and all sellers have full and perfect knowledge of what other buyers and sellers are up to, including knowledge of prices, quantity, and quality of all goods being bought or sold.
4. The goods being sold in the market are similar enough to each other that participants do not have strong preferences as to which seller or buyer they deal with.
5. The costs and benefits of making or using the goods that are exchanged in the market are borne only by those who buy or sell those goods and not by third parties or people "external" to the market transaction. (That is, there are no "externalities.")
6. All buyers and sellers are utility maximizers; each participant in the market tries to get as much as possible for as little as possible.
7. There are no parties, institutions, or governmental units regulating the price, quantity, or quality of any of the goods being bought and sold in the market.

In short, some forms of legislation and regulation are needed to counter a tendency toward consolidation of economic power (Chapter 48) and discriminatory attitudes toward certain individuals and groups (Chapter 50) and to insist that people and companies clean up their own messes and not hide information that would empower voluntary choices in the free market.

But there are additional reasons to regulate. For example, in economic systems, it is likely for natural monopolies to occur. These are where one firm can most efficiently supply all of the good or service. Having duplicate (or triplicate) systems for supplying electricity, for example, would be inefficient, so most states have a public utilities commission to determine both price and quality of service. This is direct regulation.

Sometimes destructive competition can result if there is no regulation. Banking and insurance are good examples of this. Without government regulation of banks (setting standards and methods), open and fierce competition would result in widespread bank failures. This would erode public confidence in banks and business generally. The current situation (circa 2016) of six major banks that are "too big to fail" is, however, an example of destructive *noncompetition*.

Other market imperfections can yield a demand for regulation. For example, there is a need to regulate frequencies for public broadcast on radio, television, and other wireless transmissions (for police, fire, national defense, etc.). Many economists would also list an adequate supply of public goods as something that must be created by government. On its own, for example, the market would not provide public goods such as education, a highway system, lighthouses, a military for defense.

True laissez-faire capitalism—a market free from any regulation—would not try to deal with market imperfections and would also allow people to freely choose products, services, and other arrangements that historically have been deemed socially unacceptable. These would include making enforceable contracts for the sale and purchase of persons (slavery), sexual services, "street drugs" such as heroin or crack cocaine, votes for public office, grades for this course in business law, and even marriage partnership.

Thus, the free market in actual terms—and not in theory—consists of commerce legally constrained by what is economically desirable and by what is socially desirable as well. Public policy objectives in the social arena include ensuring equal opportunity in employment, protecting employees from unhealthy or unsafe work environments, preserving environmental quality and resources, and protecting consumers from unsafe products. Sometimes these objectives are met by giving individuals statutory rights that can be used in bringing a complaint (e.g., Title VII of the Civil Rights Act of 1964, for employment discrimination), and sometimes they are met by creating agencies with the right to investigate, monitor, and enforce statutory law and regulations created to enforce such law (e.g., the Environmental Protection Agency, for bringing a lawsuit against a polluting company or setting enforceable standards for greenhouse gas emissions).

History of Federal Agencies

Through the commerce clause in the US Constitution, Congress has the power to regulate trade between the states and with foreign nations. The first federal agency, the Interstate Commerce Commission (ICC), was created in 1887 and dealt with trucking and railroads, to set the rules of the road (literally) for interstate commerce. Congress delegated to the ICC the power to enforce federal laws against railroad rate discrimination and other unfair pricing practices. By the early part of the 20th century, the ICC had gained the power to fix rates. From the 1970s through 1995, however, Congress passed deregulatory measures, and the ICC was formally abolished in 1995, with some of its powers transferred to the Surface Transportation Board.

Beginning with the Federal Trade Commission (FTC) in 1914, Congress has created numerous other agencies, many of them familiar actors in American government, such as the Securities and Exchange Commission, the Federal Aviation Authority, and the Federal Communications Commission. Today, more than eighty-five federal agencies have jurisdiction to regulate some form of private activity. Most were created since 1930, and more than a third have been created since 1960. A similar growth has occurred at the state level. Most states now have dozens of regulatory agencies, many of them overlapping in function with federal bodies.

Classification of Agencies

Independent agencies are different from federal executive departments and other executive agencies by their structural and functional characteristics. Most executive departments have a single director, administrator, or secretary appointed by the president of the United States. Independent agencies almost always have a commission or board consisting of five to seven members who share power over the agency. The president appoints the commissioners or board subject to Senate confirmation, but they often serve with staggered terms and often for longer terms than a usual four-year presidential term. They cannot be removed except for "good cause." This means that most presidents will not get to appoint all the commissioners of a given independent agency. Most independent agencies have a statutory requirement of bipartisan membership on the commission.

In addition to the ICC and the FTC, the major independent agencies are the Federal Communications Commission (1934), Securities and Exchange Commission (1934), National Labor Relations Board (1935), and Environmental Protection Agency (1970). See "Ideal Conditions for a Free Market" in the sidebar.

By contrast, members of executive branch agencies serve at the pleasure of the president and are therefore far more amenable to political control. One consequence of this distinction is that the rules that independent agencies promulgate may not be reviewed by the president or his staff—only Congress may directly overrule them—whereas the White House or officials in the various cabinet departments may oversee the work of the agencies contained within them (unless specifically denied the power by Congress).

Powers of Agencies

Agencies have a variety of powers. Many of the original statutes that created them, like the Federal Communications Act, gave them licensing power. No party can enter into the productive activity covered by the act without prior license from the agency—for example, no utility can start up a nuclear power plant unless first approved by the Nuclear Regulatory Commission. Many agencies also have the authority to set the rates charged by companies, subject to the agency's jurisdiction. Finally, the agencies can regulate business practices. The FTC has general jurisdiction over all business in interstate commerce to monitor and root out "unfair acts" and "deceptive practices." The Securities and Exchange Commission (SEC) oversees the issuance of corporate securities and other investments and monitors the practices of the stock exchanges.

Unlike courts, administrative agencies are charged with the responsibility of carrying out specific assignments or reaching a goal or set of goals. They are not to remain neutral on the various issues of the day; they must act. They have been given legislative (rule-making) powers because in a society growing ever more complex, Congress does not know how to legislate with the kind of detail that is necessary, nor would it have the time to approach all the sectors of society even if it tried. Precisely because they are to do what general legislative bodies cannot do, agencies are specialized bodies. Through years of experience in dealing with similar problems they accumulate a body of knowledge that they can apply to accomplish their statutory duties.

All administrative agencies have two different sorts of personnel. The heads, whether a single administrator or a collegial body of commissioners, are political appointees and serve for relatively limited terms. Below them is a more or less permanent staff—the bureaucracy. Much policy making occurs at the staff level, because these employees are in essential control of gathering facts and presenting data and argument to the commissioners, who wield the ultimate power of the agencies.

The Constitution and Agencies

Congress can establish an agency through legislation. When Congress gives powers to an agency, the legislation is known as an **enabling act**. The concept that Congress can delegate power to an agency is known as the **delegation doctrine**. Usually, the agency will have all three kinds of power: executive, legislative, and judicial. (That is, the agency can set the rules that business must comply with, can investigate and prosecute those businesses, and can hold administrative hearings for violations of those rules. They are, in effect, rule maker, prosecutor, and judge.) Because agencies have all three types of governmental powers, important constitutional questions were asked when Congress first created them. The most important question was whether Congress was giving away its legislative power. Was the separation of powers violated if agencies had power to make rules that were equivalent to legislative statutes?

enabling act

The legislative act that establishes an agency's authority in a particular area of the economy.

delegation doctrine

As a matter of constitutional law, the delegation doctrine declares that an agency can only exercise that power delegated to it by a constitutional authority.

In 1935, in *Schechter Poultry Corp. v. United States*, the Supreme Court overturned the National Industrial Recovery Act on the ground that the congressional delegation of power was too broad.[1] Under the law, industry trade groups were granted the authority to devise a code of fair competition for the entire industry, and these codes became law if approved by the president. No administrative body was created to scrutinize the arguments for a particular code, to develop evidence, or to test one version of a code against another. The Supreme Court found it unconstitutional for the Congress to transfer all of its legislative powers to an agency. In later decisions, it was made clear that Congress could delegate some of its legislative powers, but only if the delegation of authority was not overly broad.

Still, some congressional enabling acts are very broad, such as the enabling legislation for the Occupational Safety and Health Administration (OSHA), which is given the authority to make rules to provide for safe and healthful working conditions in US workplaces. Such a broad initiative power gives OSHA considerable discretion. But, as noted in Section 2, there are both executive and judicial controls over administrative agency activities, as well as ongoing control by Congress through funding and the continuing oversight of agencies, both in hearings and through subsequent statutory amendments.

Key Takeaway

Congress creates administrative agencies through enabling acts. In these acts, Congress must delegate authority by giving the agency some direction as to what it wants the agency to do. Agencies are usually given broad powers to investigate, set standards (promulgating regulations), and enforce those standards. Most agencies are executive branch agencies, but some are independent.

Exercises

1. Explain why Congress needs to delegate rule-making authority to a specialized agency.
2. Explain why there is any need for interference in the market by means of laws or regulations.

5.2 Controlling Administrative Agencies

Learning Objectives

1. Understand how the president controls administrative agencies.
2. Understand how Congress controls administrative agencies.
3. Understand how the courts can control administrative agencies.

During the course of the past seventy years, a substantial debate has been conducted, often in shrill terms, about the legitimacy of administrative lawmaking. One criticism is that agencies are "captured" by the industry they are directed to regulate. Another is that they overregulate, stifling individual initiative and the ability to compete. During the 1960s and 1970s, a massive outpouring of federal law created many new agencies and greatly strengthened the hands of existing ones. In the late 1970s during the Carter administration, Congress began to deregulate American society, and deregulation increased under the Reagan administration. But the accounting frauds of WorldCom, Enron, and others led to the Sarbanes-Oxley Act of 2002, and the financial meltdown of 2008 has led to increased regulation of the financial sector in the Dodd-Frank Act. It remains to be seen whether the *Deepwater Horizon* oil blowout of 2010 will lead to more environmental regulations or a rethinking on how to make agencies more effective regulators. The Obama administration's regulation of greenhouse gases and the EPA's efforts to regulate emissions of coal-burning utility companies has been controversial, but is in keeping with US commitments at COP-21 in 2016.

Administrative agencies are often a focal point of controversy because they are policy-making bodies, incorporating facets of legislative, executive, and judicial power in a hybrid form that fits uneasily at best in the framework of American government (see Figure 5.1). They are necessarily at the center of tugging and hauling by the legislature, the executive branch, and the judiciary, each of which has different means of exercising political control over them. In early 1990, for example, the Bush administration approved a Food and Drug Administration regulation that limited disease-prevention claims by food packagers, reversing a position by the Reagan administration in 1987 permitting such claims.

FIGURE 5.1 Major Administrative Agencies of the United States

The major independent regulatory agencies

- Consumer Product Safety Commission
- Environmental Protection Agency
- Equal Employment Opportunity Commission
- Federal Communications Commission
- Federal Energy Regulatory Commission
- Federal Reserve Commission
- Federal Trade Commission
- National Labor Relations Board
- Occupational Safety and Health Administration
- Securities ad Exchange Commission

The major agencies within the Executive Branch*

- **Department of Agriculture**
  - Farmers Home Administration
  - Forest Service
  - Food Safety and Inspection Service
  - Rural Electrification Administration
- **Department of Commerce**
  - Bureau of the Census
  - Bureau of Export Administration
  - Patent and Trademark Office
  - National Institute of Standards
- **Department of Defense**
  - Army, Air Force, Navy, Marines
- **Department of Education**
- **Department of Energy**
- **Department of Health and Human Services**
- **Department of Homeland Security**
  - Transportation Security Administration
  - U.S. Customs and Border Protection
  - U.S. Citizenship and Immigration Services
  - United States Coast Guard
  - United States Secret Service
- **Department of Housing and Urban Development**
- **Department of the Interior**
  - U.S. Fish and Wildlife Service
  - National Park Service
  - Bureau of Indian Affairs
  - Minerals Management Service
- **Department of Justice**
  - F.B.I. (Federal Bureau of Investigation)
  - Antitrust Division
  - Civil Division
  - Criminal Division
  - Civil Rights Division
  - Drug Enforcement Administration
- **Department of Labor**
- **Department of State**
- **Department of Transportation**
  - Federal Aviation Administration
  - Federal Highway Administration
  - Federal Railroad Administration
  - National Highway Traffic Safety Administration
  - United States Coast Guard
- **Department of Treasury**
  - Bureau of Alcohol, Tobacco, and Firearms
  - Internal Revenue Service
  - United States Mint
  - Bureau of Engraving and Printing

* With selected well-known sub-departments.

Legislative Control

Congress can always pass a law repealing a regulation that an agency promulgates. Because this is a time-consuming process that runs counter to the reason for creating administrative bodies, it happens rarely. Another approach to controlling agencies is to reduce or threaten to reduce their appropriations. By retaining ultimate control of the purse strings, Congress can exercise considerable informal control over regulatory policy. For example, Congress threatened to cut funds to the Securities and Exchange Commission during the latter years of the Clinton administration when Chairman Arthur Levitt proposed that corporations should expense stock options to CEOs.[2]

Executive Control

The president (or a governor, for state agencies) can exercise considerable control over agencies that are part of his cabinet departments and that are not statutorily defined as independent. Federal agencies, moreover, are subject to the fiscal scrutiny of the Office of Management and Budget (OMB), subject to the direct control of the president. Agencies are not permitted to go directly to Congress for increases in budget; these requests must be submitted through the OMB, giving the president indirect leverage over the continuation of administrators' programs and policies.

Judicial Review of Agency Actions

Administrative agencies are creatures of law and like everyone else must obey the law. The courts have jurisdiction to hear claims that the agencies have overstepped their legal authority or have acted in some unlawful manner.

Courts are unlikely to overturn administrative actions, believing in general that the agencies are better situated to judge their own jurisdiction and are experts in rulemaking for those matters delegated to them by Congress. Some agency activities are not reviewable, for a number of reasons.

However, after a business (or some other interested party) has exhausted all administrative remedies, it may seek judicial review of a final agency decision. The reviewing court is often asked to strike down or modify agency actions on several possible bases (see Section 5 on "Strategies for Obtaining Judicial Review").

Key Takeaway

Administrative agencies are given unusual powers: to legislate, investigate, and adjudicate. But these powers are limited by executive and legislative controls and by judicial review.

Exercises

1. Find the website of the Consumer Product Safety Commission (CPSC). Identify from that site a product that has been banned by the CPSC for sale in the United States. What reasons were given for its exclusion from the U.S. market?
2. What has Congress told the CPSC to do in its enabling act? Is this a clear enough mandate to guide the agency? What could Congress do if the CPSC does something that may be outside of the scope of its powers? What can an affected business do?

5.3 The Administrative Procedure Act

Learning Objectives

1. Understand why the Administrative Procedure Act was needed.
2. Understand how hearings are conducted under the act.
3. Understand how the act affects rulemaking by agencies.

Administrative Procedure Act (APA)
The federal act that governs all agency procedures in both hearings and rulemaking.

In 1946, Congress enacted the **Administrative Procedure Act (APA)**. This fundamental statute detailed for all federal administrative agencies how they must function when they are deciding cases or issuing regulations, the two basic tasks of administration. At the state level, the Model State Administrative Procedure Act, issued in 1946 and revised in 1961, has been adopted in twenty-eight states and the District of Columbia; three states have adopted the 1981 revision. The other states have statutes that resemble the model state act to some degree.

Trial-Type Hearings

administrative law judge
The primary hearing officer in an administrative agency, who provides the initial ruling of the agency (often called an order) in any contested proceeding.

Deciding cases is a major task of many agencies. For example, the Federal Trade Commission (FTC) is empowered to charge a company with having violated the Federal Trade Commission Act. Perhaps a seller is accused of making deceptive claims in its advertising. Proceeding in a manner similar to a court, staff counsel will prepare a case against the company, which can defend itself through its lawyers. The case is tried before an **administrative law judge** (ALJ), formerly known as an administrative hearing examiner. The change in nomenclature was made in 1972 to enhance the prestige of ALJs and more accurately reflect their duties. Although not appointed for life as federal judges are, the ALJ must be free of assignments inconsistent with the judicial function and is not subject to supervision by anyone in the agency who carries on an investigative or prosecutorial function.

The accused parties are entitled to receive notice of the issues to be raised, to present evidence, to argue, to cross-examine, and to appear with their lawyers. *Ex parte* (eks-PAR-tay) communications—contacts between the ALJ and outsiders or one party when both parties are not present—are prohibited. However, the usual burden-of-proof standard followed in a civil proceeding in court does not apply: the ALJ is not bound to decide in favor of that party producing the more persuasive evidence. The rule in most administrative proceedings is "substantial evidence," evidence that is not flimsy or weak, but is not necessarily overwhelming evidence, either. The ALJ in most cases will write an opinion. That opinion is not the decision of the agency, which can be made only by the commissioners or agency head. In effect, the ALJ's opinion is appealed to the commission itself.

Certain types of agency actions that have a direct impact on individuals need not be filtered through a full-scale hearing. Safety and quality inspections (grading of food, inspection of airplanes) can be made on the spot by skilled inspectors. Certain licenses can be administered through tests without a hearing (a test for a driver's license), and some decisions can be made by election of those affected (labor union elections).

Rulemaking

Trial-type hearings generally impose on particular parties liabilities based on past or present facts. Because these cases will serve as precedents, they are a partial guide to future conduct by others. But they do not directly apply to nonparties, who may argue in a subsequent case that their conduct does not fit within the holding announced in the case. Agencies can affect future conduct far more directly by announcing rules that apply to all who come within the agency's jurisdiction.

The acts creating most of the major federal agencies expressly grant them authority to engage in rulemaking. This means, in essence, authority to legislate. The outpouring of federal regulations has been immense. The APA directs agencies about to engage in rulemaking to give notice in the ***Federal Register*** of their intent to do so. The *Federal Register* is published daily, Monday through Friday, in Washington, DC, and contains notice of various actions, including announcements of proposed rulemaking and regulations as adopted. The notice must specify the time, place, and nature of the rulemaking and offer a description of the proposed rule or the issues involved. Any interested person or organization is entitled to participate by submitting written "data, views or arguments." Agencies are not legally required to air debate over proposed rules, though they often do so.

Federal Register

The *Federal Register* is where all proposed administrative regulations are first published, usually inviting comment from interested parties.

The procedure just described is known as "informal" rulemaking. A different procedure is required for "formal" rulemaking, defined as those instances in which the enabling legislation directs an agency to make rules "on the record after opportunity for an agency hearing." When engaging in formal rulemaking, agencies must *hold* an adversary hearing.

Administrative regulations are not legally binding unless they are published. Agencies must publish in the *Federal Register* the text of final regulations, which ordinarily do not become effective until thirty days later. Every year the annual output of regulations is collected and reprinted in the ***Code of Federal Regulations* (CFR)**, a multivolume paperback series containing all federal rules and regulations keyed to the fifty titles of the US Code (the compilation of *all* federal statutes enacted by Congress and grouped according to subject).

***Code of Federal Regulations* (CFR)**

A compilation of all final agency rules. The CFR has the same legal effect as a bill passed by Congress and signed into law by the president.

Key Takeaway

Agencies make rules that have the same effect as laws passed by Congress and the president. But such rules (regulations) must allow for full participation by interested parties. The Administrative Procedure Act (APA) governs both rulemaking and the agency enforcement of regulations, and it provides a process for fair hearings.

Exercises

1. Go to http://www.regulations.gov/search/Regs/home.html#home. Browse the site. Find a topic that interests you, and then find a proposed regulation. Notice how comments on the proposed rule are invited.
2. Why would there be a trial by an administrative agency? Describe the process.

5.4 Administrative Burdens on Business Operations

Learning Objectives

1. Describe the paperwork burden imposed by administrative agencies.
2. Explain why agencies have the power of investigation, and what limits there are to that power.
3. Explain the need for the Freedom of Information Act and how it works in the U.S. legal system.

The Paperwork Burden

The administrative process is not frictionless. The interplay between government agency and private enterprise can burden business operations in a number of ways. Several of these are noted in this section.

Deciding whether and how to act are not decisions that government agencies reach out of the blue. They rely heavily on information garnered from business itself. Dozens of federal agencies require corporations to keep hundreds of types of records and to file numerous periodic reports. The Commission on Federal Paperwork, established during the Ford administration to consider ways of reducing the paperwork burden, estimated in its final report in 1977 that the total annual cost of federal paperwork amounted to $50 billion and that the 10,000 largest business enterprises spent $10 billion annually on paperwork alone. The paperwork involved in licensing a single nuclear power plant, the commission said, costs upward of $15 million.

Not surprisingly, therefore, businesses have sought ways of avoiding requests for data. Since the 1940s, the Federal Trade Commission (FTC) has collected economic data on corporate performance from individual companies for statistical purposes. As long as each company engages in a single line of business, data are comparable. When the era of conglomerates began in the 1970s, with widely divergent types of businesses brought together under the roof of a single corporate parent, the data became useless for purposes of examining the competitive behavior of different industries. So the FTC ordered dozens of large companies to break out their economic information according to each line of business that they carried on. The companies resisted, but the US Court of

Appeals for the District of Columbia Circuit, where much of the litigation over federal administrative action is decided, directed the companies to comply with the commission's order, holding that the Federal Trade Commission Act clearly permits the agency to collect information for investigatory purposes.[3]

In 1980, responding to cries that businesses, individuals, and state and local governments were being swamped by federal demands for paperwork, Congress enacted the Paperwork Reduction Act. It gives power to the federal Office of Management and Budget (OMB) to develop uniform policies for coordinating the gathering, storage, and transmission of all the millions of reports flowing in each year to the scores of federal departments and agencies requesting information. These reports include tax and Medicare forms, financial loan and job applications, questionnaires of all sorts, compliance reports, and tax and business records. The OMB was given the power also to determine whether new kinds of information are needed. In effect, any agency that wants to collect new information from outside must obtain the OMB's approval.

Inspections

No one likes surprise inspections. A section of the Occupational Safety and Health Act of 1970 empowers agents of the Occupational Safety and Health Administration (OSHA) to search work areas for safety hazards and for violations of OSHA regulations. The act does not specify whether inspectors are required to obtain search warrants, required under the Fourth Amendment in criminal cases. For many years, the government insisted that surprise inspections are not unreasonable and that the time required to obtain a warrant would defeat the surprise element. The Supreme Court finally ruled squarely on the issue in 1978. In *Marshall v. Barlow's, Inc.*, the court held that no less than private individuals, businesses are entitled to refuse police demands to search the premises unless a court has issued a search warrant.[4]

But where a certain type of business is closely regulated, surprise inspections are the norm, and no warrant is required. For example, businesses with liquor licenses that might sell to minors are subject to both overt and covert inspections (e.g., an undercover officer may "search" a liquor store by sending an underage patron to the store). Or a junkyard that specializes in automobiles and automobile parts may also be subject to surprise inspections, on the rationale that junkyards are highly likely to be active in the resale of stolen autos or stolen auto parts.[5]

It is also possible for inspections to take place without a search warrant and without the permission of the business. For example, the Environmental Protection Agency (EPA) wished to inspect parts of the Dow Chemical facility in Midland, Michigan, without the benefit of warrant. When they were refused, agents of the EPA obtained a fairly advanced aerial mapping camera and rented an airplane to fly over the Dow facility. Dow went to court for a restraining order against the EPA and a request to have the EPA turn over all photographs taken. But the Supreme Court ruled that the areas photographed were "open fields" and not subject to the protections of the Fourth Amendment.[6]

Access to Business Information in Government Files

In 1966, Congress enacted the Freedom of Information Act (FOIA), opening up to the citizenry many of the files of the government. (The act was amended in 1974 and again in 1976 to overcome a tendency of many agencies to stall or refuse access to their files.) Under the FOIA, any person has a legally enforceable right of access to all government documents, with nine specific exceptions, such as classified military intelligence, medical files, and trade secrets and commercial or financial information if "obtained from a person and privileged or confidential." Without the trade-secret and financial-information exemptions, business competitors could, merely by requesting it, obtain highly sensitive competitive information sitting in government files.

A federal agency is required under the FOIA to respond to a document request within ten days. But in practice, months or even years may pass before the government actually responds to an

FOIA request. Requesters must also pay the cost of locating and copying the records. Moreover, not all documents are available for public inspection. Along with the trade-secret and financial-information exemptions, the FOIA specifically exempts the following:

- records required by executive order of the president to be kept secret in the interest of national defense or public policy
- records related solely to the internal personnel rules and practice of an agency
- records exempted from disclosure by another statute
- interagency memos or decisions reflecting the deliberative process
- personnel files and other files that if disclosed, would constitute an unwarranted invasion of personal privacy
- information compiled for law enforcement purposes
- geological information concerning wells

Note that the government may provide such information but is not required to provide such information; it retains discretion to provide information or not.

Regulated companies are often required to submit confidential information to the government. For these companies, submitting such information presents a danger under the FOIA of disclosure to competitors. To protect information from disclosure, the company is well advised to mark each document as privileged and confidential so that government officials reviewing it for a FOIA request will not automatically disclose it. Most agencies notify a company whose data they are about to disclose. But these practices are not legally required under the FOIA.

Key Takeaway

Government agencies, in order to do their jobs, collect a great deal of information from businesses. This can range from routine paperwork (often burdensome) to inspections, those with warrants and those without. Surprise inspections are allowed for closely regulated industries but are subject to Fourth Amendment requirements in general. Some information collected by agencies can be accessed using the Freedom of Information Act.

Exercises

1. Give two examples of a closely regulated industry. Explain why some warrantless searches would be allowed.
2. Find out why FOIA requests often take months or years to accomplish.

5.5 The Scope of Judicial Review

Learning Objectives

1. Describe the "exhaustion of remedies" requirement.
2. Detail various strategies for obtaining judicial review of agency rules.
3. Explain under what circumstances it is possible to sue the government.

Neither an administrative agency's adjudication nor its issuance of a regulation is necessarily final. Most federal agency decisions are appealable to the federal circuit courts. To get to court, the appellant must overcome numerous complex hurdles. He or she must have standing—that is, be in some sense directly affected by the decision or regulation. The case must be ripe for review; administrative remedies such as further appeal within the agency must have been exhausted. Finally, anyone challenging an agency rule or process must convince a court that the agency's interpretation of the law that delegates power to it is a reasonable interpretation, deserving of "judicial deference." The Court insists that agencies may choose among reasonable interpretations of a statute, but does not permit agencies to pick and choose provisions it likes and ignore those it does not.

Exhaustion of Administrative Remedies

Before you can complain to court about an agency's action, you must first try to get the agency to reconsider its action. Generally, you must have asked for a hearing at the hearing examiner level, there must have been a decision reached that was unfavorable to you, and you must have appealed the decision to the full board. The full board must rule against you, and only then will you be heard by a court. The broadest exception to this **exhaustion of administrative remedies** requirement is if the agency had no authority to issue the rule or regulation in the first place, if exhaustion of remedies would be impractical or futile, or if great harm would happen should the rule or regulation continue to apply. Also, if the agency is not acting in good faith, the courts will hear an appeal without exhaustion.

exhaustion of administrative remedies

A requirement that anyone wishing to appeal an agency action must wait until the agency has taken final action.

Strategies for Obtaining Judicial Review

Once administrative remedies are exhausted, the court may look at one of a series of claims. The appellant might assert that the agency's action was *ultra vires* (UL-truh VI-reez)—beyond the scope of its authority as set down in the statute. This attack can be successful, and often hinges on the question of whether the agency's interpretation of ambiguous statutory language is reasonable or not. Another avenue of relief from administrative rules may be traveled successfully if the agency did not abide by its own procedures or those imposed upon it by the Administrative Procedure Act. The question of whether the agency's interpretation of statutory language is reasonable or not is discussed at length in *Michigan v. E.P.A.* (Cases, Section 5.6).

In formal rule-making, the appellant also might insist that the agency lacked substantial evidence for the determination that it made. In *Aqua Slide 'n Dive v. Consumer Product Safety Commission*, 569 F. 2d 831 (1978), the CPSC made some final rules about swimming pool slides that the court found were not adequately grounded in empirical studies. The effectiveness of mandated signs and chains on the ladders to the top of the swimming pool slides were not at all clear, even if the CPSC had reason to regulate on behalf of consumer safety: a significant cases of paraplegia and quadriplegia were associated with head-first uses of such slides. The case represents the relatively rare instance where there is little or no evidence to support the agency's findings; in such cases, the court may reverse.

Likewise, there has long been a presumption that when an agency issues a regulation, it has the authority to do so: those opposing the regulation must bear a heavy burden in court to upset it. This is not a surprising rule, for otherwise courts, not administrators, would be the authors of regulations. Nevertheless, regulations cannot exceed the scope of the authority conferred by Congress on the agency. In an important 1981 case before the Supreme Court, the issue was whether the secretary of labor, acting through the Occupational Health and Safety Administration (OSHA), could lawfully issue a standard limiting exposure to cotton dust in the workplace without first undertaking a cost-benefit analysis. A dozen cotton textile manufacturers and the American Textile Manufacturers Institute, representing 175 companies, asserted that the cotton dust standard was unlawful because it did not rationally relate the benefits to be derived from the standard to the costs that the standard would impose. See Section 6, *American Textile Manufacturers Institute v. Donovan*.(1980).

While Donovan was a 1980 case, the costs vs. benefits issue continues to be litigated. Businesses and their trade associations seldom like to have profits impaired by government rules and regulations. In *Michigan v. E.P.A*, **in Chapter 5, Section 6 "Cases,"** the Supreme Court chastened the E.P.A. for not performing an adequate "cost benefit analysis" in promulgating final rules affecting emissions of mercury and other hazardous pollutants from coal and oil-fired power plants. The case is important because it represents a decreased level of judicial deference to agency findings and procedures. It may also signal a willingness to hold, as Justice Scalia suggested, that no regulation may be legally "appropriate" if it does significantly more harm than good. The Supreme Court majority has not so held, but a conservative Court skeptical of agency rule-making could be tempted to do so, and a pro-business Congress would be unlikely to pass legislation that directed less judicial oversight on "cost-benefit analysis" by agencies.

In summary, then, an individual or a company may (after exhaustion of administrative remedies) challenge agency action where such action is the following:

- not in accordance with the agency's scope of authority
- not in accordance with the US Constitution or the Administrative Procedure Act
- not in accordance with the substantial evidence test
- unwarranted by the facts
- arbitrary, capricious, an abuse of discretion, or otherwise not in accord with the law

Section 706 of the Administrative Procedure Act sets out those standards. While it is difficult to show that an agency's action is arbitrary and capricious, there are cases that have so held. For example, after the Reagan administration set aside a Carter administration rule from the National Highway Traffic and Safety Administration on passive restraints in automobiles, State Farm and other insurance companies challenged the reversal as arbitrary and capricious. Examining the record, the Supreme Court found that the agency had failed to state enough reasons for its reversal and required the agency to review the record and the rule and provide adequate reasons for its reversal. State Farm and other insurance companies thus gained a legal benefit by keeping an agency rule that placed costs on automakers for increased passenger safety and potentially reducing the number of injury claims from those it had insured.[7]

Suing the Government

In the modern administrative state, the range of government activity is immense, and administrative agencies frequently get in the way of business enterprise. Often, bureaucratic involvement is wholly legitimate, compelled by law; sometimes, however, agencies or government officials may overstep their bounds, in a fit of zeal or spite. What recourse does the private individual or company have?

Mainly for historical reasons, it has always been more difficult to sue the government than to sue private individuals or corporations. For one thing, the government has long had recourse to the doctrine of sovereign immunity as a shield against lawsuits. Yet in 1976, Congress amended the Administrative Procedure Act to waive any federal claim to sovereign immunity in cases of injunctive or other nonmonetary relief. Earlier, in 1946, in the Federal Tort Claims Act, Congress had waived sovereign immunity of the federal government for most tort claims for money damages, although the act contains several exceptions for specific agencies (e.g., one cannot sue for injuries resulting from fiscal operations of the Treasury Department or for injuries stemming from activities of the military in wartime). The act also contains a major exception for claims "based upon [an official's] exercise or performance or the failure to exercise or perform a discretionary function or duty." This exception prevents suits against parole boards for paroling dangerous criminals who then kill or maim in the course of another crime and suits against officials whose decision to ship explosive materials by public carrier leads to mass deaths and injuries following an explosion en route.[8]

In recent years, the Supreme Court has been stripping away the traditional immunity enjoyed by many government officials against personal suits. Some government employees—judges, prosecutors, legislators, and the president, for example—have absolute immunity against suit for official actions. But many public administrators and government employees have at best a qualified immunity. Under a provision of the Civil Rights Act of 1871 (so-called Section 1983 actions), *state* officials can be sued in federal court for money damages whenever "under color of any state law" they deprive anyone of his rights under the Constitution or federal law. In *Bivens v. Six Unknown Federal Narcotics Agents*, the Supreme Court held that *federal* agents may be sued for violating the plaintiff's Fourth Amendment rights against an unlawful search of his home.[9] Subsequent cases have followed this logic to permit suits for violations of other constitutional provisions. This area of the law is in a state of flux, and it is likely to continue to evolve.

Sometimes damage is done to an individual or business because the government has given out erroneous information. For example, suppose that Charles, a bewildered, disabled navy employee, is receiving a federal disability annuity. Under the regulations, he would lose his pension if he took a job that paid him in each of two succeeding years more than 80 percent of what he earned in his old navy job. A few years later, Congress changed the law, making him ineligible if he earned more than 80 percent in anyone year. For many years, Charles earned considerably less than the ceiling amount. But then one year he got the opportunity to make some extra money. Not wishing to lose his pension, he called an employee relations specialist in the US Navy and asked how much he could earn and still keep his pension. The specialist gave him erroneous information over the telephone and then sent him an out-of-date form that said Charles could safely take on the extra work. Unfortunately, as it turned out, Charles did exceed the salary limit, and so the government cut off his pension during the time he earned too much. Charles sues to recover his lost pension. He argues that he relied to his detriment on false information supplied by the navy and that in fairness the government should be estopped from denying his claim.

Unfortunately for Charles, he will lose his case. In *Office of Personnel Management v. Richmond*, the Supreme Court reasoned that it would be unconstitutional to permit recovery.[10] The appropriations clause of Article I says that federal money can be paid out only through an appropriation made by law. The law prevented this particular payment to be made. If the court were to make an exception, it would permit executive officials in effect to make binding payments, even though unauthorized, simply by misrepresenting the facts. The harsh reality, therefore, is that mistakes of the government are generally held against the individual, not the government, unless the law specifically provides for recompense (as, for example, in the Federal Tort Claims Act just discussed).

Key Takeaway

After exhausting administrative remedies, there are numerous grounds for seeking judicial review of an agency's order or of a final rule. While courts defer to agencies to some degree, an agency must follow its own rules, comply with the Administrative Procedure Act, act within the scope of its delegated authority, avoid acting in an arbitrary manner, and make final rules that are supported by substantial evidence.

Exercises

1. Why would U.S. courts require that someone seeking judicial review of an agency order first exhaust administrative remedies?
2. On the Internet, find a case where someone has successfully sued the U.S. government under the Federal Tort Claims Act. What kind of case was it? Did the government argue sovereign immunity? Does sovereign immunity even make sense to you?

5.6 Cases

Marshall v. Barlow's, Inc.

Marshall v. Barlow's, Inc.
436 U.S. 307 (U.S. Supreme Court 1978)

MR. JUSTICE WHITE delivered the opinion of the Court.

Section 8(a) of the Occupational Safety and Health Act of 1970 (OSHA or Act) empowers agents of the Secretary of Labor (Secretary) to search the work area of any employment facility within the Act's jurisdiction. The purpose of the search is to inspect for safety hazards and violations of OSHA regulations. No search warrant or other process is expressly required under the Act.

On the morning of September 11, 1975, an OSHA inspector entered the customer service area of Barlow's, Inc., an electrical and plumbing installation business located in Pocatello, Idaho. The president and general manager, Ferrol G. "Bill" Barlow, was on hand; and the OSHA inspector, after showing his credentials, informed Mr. Barlow that he wished to conduct a search of the working areas of the business. Mr. Barlow inquired whether any complaint had been received about his company. The inspector answered no, but that Barlow's, Inc., had simply turned up in the agency's selection process. The inspector again asked to enter the nonpublic area of the business; Mr. Barlow's response was to inquire whether the inspector had a search warrant.

The inspector had none. Thereupon, Mr. Barlow refused the inspector admission to the employee area of his business. He said he was relying on his rights as guaranteed by the Fourth Amendment of the United States Constitution.

Three months later, the Secretary petitioned the United States District Court for the District of Idaho to issue an order compelling Mr. Barlow to admit the inspector. The requested order was issued on December 30, 1975, and was presented to Mr. Barlow on January 5, 1976. Mr. Barlow again refused admission, and he sought his own injunctive relief against the warrantless searches assertedly permitted by OSHA....The Warrant Clause of the Fourth Amendment protects commercial buildings as well as private homes. To hold otherwise would belie the origin of that Amendment, and the American colonial experience.

An important forerunner of the first 10 Amendments to the United States Constitution, the Virginia Bill of Rights, specifically opposed "general warrants, whereby an officer or messenger may be commanded to search suspected places without evidence of a fact committed." The general warrant was a recurring point of contention in the Colonies immediately preceding the Revolution. The particular offensiveness it engendered was acutely felt by the merchants and businessmen whose premises and products were inspected for compliance with the several parliamentary revenue measures that most irritated the colonists....

This Court has already held that warrantless searches are generally unreasonable, and that this rule applies to commercial premises as well as homes. In *Camara v. Municipal Court*, we held:

> *[E]xcept in certain carefully defined classes of cases, a search of private property without proper consent is 'unreasonable' unless it has been authorized by a valid search warrant.*
>
> *On the same day, we also ruled: As we explained in* Camara*, a search of private houses is presumptively unreasonable if conducted without a warrant. The businessman, like the occupant of a residence, has a constitutional right to go about his business free from unreasonable official entries upon his private commercial property. The businessman, too, has that right placed in jeopardy if the decision to enter and inspect for violation of regulatory laws can be made and enforced by the inspector in the field without official authority evidenced by a warrant. These same cases also held that the Fourth Amendment prohibition against unreasonable searches protects against warrantless intrusions during civil as well as criminal investigations. The reason is found in the "basic purpose of this Amendment...[which] is to safeguard the privacy and security of individuals against arbitrary invasions by governmental officials." If the government intrudes on a person's property, the privacy interest suffers whether the government's motivation is to investigate violations of criminal laws or breaches of other statutory or regulatory standards....*

[A]n exception from the search warrant requirement has been recognized for "pervasively regulated business[es]," *United States v. Biswell*, 406 U.S. 311, 316 (1972), and for "closely regulated" industries "long subject to close supervision and inspection," *Colonnade Catering Corp. v. United States*, 397 U.S. 72, 74, 77 (1970). These cases are indeed exceptions, but they represent responses to relatively unique circumstances. Certain industries have such a history of government oversight that no reasonable expectation of privacy could exist for a proprietor over the stock of such an enterprise. Liquor (*Colonnade*) and firearms (*Biswell*) are industries of this type when an entrepreneur embarks upon such a business, he has voluntarily chosen to subject himself to a full arsenal of governmental regulation. * * *

The clear import of our cases is that the closely regulated industry of the type involved in *Colonnade* and *Biswell* is the exception. The Secretary would make it the rule. Invoking the Walsh-Healey Act of 1936, 41 U.S.C. § 35 et *seq.*, the Secretary attempts to support a conclusion that all businesses involved in interstate commerce have long been subjected to close supervision of employee safety and health conditions. But...it is quite unconvincing to argue that the imposition of minimum wages and maximum hours on employers who contracted with the Government under the Walsh-Healey Act prepared the entirety of American interstate commerce for regulation of working conditions to the minutest detail. Nor can any but the most fictional sense of voluntary consent to later searches be found in the single fact that one conducts a business affecting interstate commerce. Under current practice and law, few businesses can be conducted without having some effect on interstate commerce. * * *

The critical fact in this case is that entry over Mr. Barlow's objection is being sought by a Government agent. Employees are not being prohibited from reporting OSHA violations. What they observe in their daily functions is undoubtedly beyond the employer's reasonable expectation of privacy. The Government inspector, however, is not an employee. Without a warrant he stands in no better position than a member of the public. What is observable by the public is observable, without a warrant, by the Government inspector as well. The owner of a business has not, by the necessary utilization of employees in his operation, thrown open the areas where employees alone are permitted to the warrantless scrutiny of Government agents. That an employee is free to report, and the Government is free to use, any evidence of noncompliance with OSHA that the employee observes furnishes no justification for federal agents to enter a place of business from which the public is restricted and to conduct their own warrantless search. * * *

[The District Court judgment is affirmed.]

Case Questions

1. State, as briefly and clearly as possible, the argument that Barlow's is making in this case.
2. Why would some industries or businesses be "closely regulated"? What are some of those businesses?
3. The Fourth Amendment speaks of "people" being secure in their "persons, houses, papers, and effects." Why would the Fourth Amendment apply to a business, which is not in a "house"?
4. If the Fourth Amendment does not distinguish between closely regulated industries and those that are not, why does the court do so?

American Textile Manufacturers Institute v. Donovan

American Textile Manufacturers Institute v. Donovan

452 U.S. 490 (1981)

JUSTICE BRENNAN delivered the opinion of the Court.

Congress enacted the Occupational Safety and Health Act of 1970 (Act) "to assure so far as possible every working man and woman in the Nation safe and healthful working conditions...."The Act authorizes the Secretary of Labor to establish, after notice and opportunity to comment, mandatory nationwide standards governing health and safety in the workplace. In 1978, the Secretary, acting through the Occupational Safety and Health Administration (OSHA), promulgated a standard limiting occupational exposure to cotton dust, an airborne particle byproduct of the preparation and manufacture of cotton products, exposure to which produces a "constellation of respiratory effects" known as "byssinosis." This disease was one of the expressly recognized health hazards that led to passage of the Act.

Petitioners in these consolidated cases representing the interests of the cotton industry, challenged the validity of the "Cotton Dust Standard" in the Court of Appeals for the District of Columbia Circuit pursuant to § 6 (f) of the Act, 29 U.S.C. § 655 (f). They contend in this Court, as they did below, that the Act requires OSHA to demonstrate that its Standard reflects a reasonable relationship between the costs and benefits associated with the Standard. Respondents, the Secretary of Labor and two labor organizations, counter that Congress balanced the costs and benefits in the Act itself, and that the Act should therefore be construed not to require OSHA to do so. They interpret the Act as mandating that OSHA enact the most protective standard possible to eliminate a significant risk of material health impairment, subject to the constraints of economic and technological feasibility.

The Court of Appeals held that the Act did not require OSHA to compare costs and benefits.

We granted certiorari, 449 U.S. 817 (1980), to resolve this important question, which was presented but not decided in last Term's *Industrial Union Dept. v. American Petroleum Institute*, 448 U.S. 607 (1980), and to decide other issues related to the Cotton Dust Standard. * * *

* * *

Not until the early 1960s was byssinosis recognized in the United States as a distinct occupational hazard associated with cotton mills. In 1966, the American Conference of Governmental Industrial Hygienists (ACGIH), a private organization, recommended that exposure to total cotton dust be limited to a "threshold limit value" of 1,000 micrograms per cubic meter of air (1,000 g/m^3.) averaged over an 8-hour workday. See 43 Fed. Reg. 27351, col. 1 (1978). The United States Government first regulated exposure to cotton dust in 1968, when the Secretary of Labor, pursuant to the Walsh-Healey Act, 41 U.S.C. 35 (e), promulgated airborne contaminant threshold limit values, applicable to public contractors, that included the 1,000 g/m^3 limit for total cotton dust. 34 Fed. Reg. 7953 (1969). Following passage of the Act in 1970, the 1,000 g/m^3. standard was adopted as an "established Federal standard" under 6 (a) of the Act, 84 Stat. 1593, 29 U.S.C. 655 (a), a provision designed to guarantee immediate protection of workers for the period between enactment of the statute and promulgation of permanent standards.

That same year, the Director of the National Institute for Occupational Safety and Health (NIOSH), pursuant to the Act, 29 U.S.C. §§ 669(a)(3), 671 (d)(2), submitted to the Secretary of Labor a recommendation for a cotton dust standard with a permissible exposure limit (PEL) that "should be set at the lowest level feasible, but in no case at an environmental concentration as high as 0.2 mg lint-free cotton dust/cu m," or 200 g/m^3. of lint-free respirable dust. Several months later, OSHA published an Advance Notice of Proposed Rulemaking, 39 Fed.Reg. 44769 (1974), requesting comments from interested parties on the NIOSH recommendation and other related matters. Soon thereafter, the Textile Worker's Union of America, joined by the North Carolina Public Interest Research Group, petitioned the Secretary, urging a more stringent PEL of 100 g/m^3.

On December 28, 1976, OSHA published a proposal to replace the existing federal standard on cotton dust with a new permanent standard, pursuant to § 6(b)(5) of the Act, 29 U.S.C. § 655(b)(5). 41 Fed.Reg. 56498. The proposed standard contained a PEL of 200 g/m^3 of vertical elutriated lint-free respirable cotton dust for all segments of the cotton industry. *Ibid.* It also suggested an implementation strategy for achieving the PEL that relied on respirators for the short term and engineering controls for the long-term. OSHA invited interested parties to submit written comments within a 90-day period. * * *

* * *

The starting point of our analysis is the language of the statute itself. Section 6(b)(5) of the Act, 29 U.S.C. § 655(b)(5) (emphasis added), provides:

> *The Secretary, in promulgating standards dealing with toxic materials or harmful physical agents under this subsection, shall set the standard which most adequately assures,* **to the extent feasible**, *on the basis of the best available evidence, that no employee will suffer material impairment of health or functional capacity even if such employee has regular exposure to the hazard dealt with by such standard for the period of his working life. Although their interpretations differ, all parties agree that the phrase "to the extent feasible" contains the critical language in § 6(b)(5) for purposes of these cases.*

The plain meaning of the word "feasible" supports respondents' interpretation of the statute. According to Webster's Third New International Dictionary of the English Language 831 (1976), "feasible" means "capable of being done, executed, or effected." In accord, the Oxford English Dictionary 116 (1933) ("Capable of being done, accomplished or carried out"); Funk & Wagnalls New "Standard" Dictionary of the English Language 903 (1957) ("That may be done, performed or effected"). Thus, § 6(b)(5) directs the Secretary to issue the standard that "most adequately assures...that no employee will suffer material impairment of health," limited only by the extent to which this is "capable of being done." In effect then, as the Court of Appeals held, Congress itself defined the basic relationship between costs and benefits, by placing the "benefit" of worker health above all other considerations save those making attainment of this "benefit" unachievable. Any standard based on a balancing of costs and benefits by the Secretary that strikes a different balance than that struck by Congress would be inconsistent with the command set forth in § 6(b)(5). Thus, cost-benefit analysis by OSHA is not required by the statute because feasibility analysis is.

When Congress has intended that an agency engage in cost-benefit analysis, it has clearly indicated such intent on the face of the statute. One early example is the Flood Control Act of 1936, 33 U.S.C. § 701:

> *[T]he Federal Government should improve or participate in the improvement of navigable waters or their tributaries, including watersheds thereof, for flood control purposes if the* **benefits to whomsoever they may accrue are in excess of the estimated costs**, *and if the lives and social security of people are otherwise adversely affected. (emphasis added)*

A more recent example is the Outer Continental Shelf Lands Act Amendments of 1978, providing that offshore drilling operations shall use the best available and safest technologies which the Secretary determines to be economically *feasible*, wherever failure of equipment would have a significant effect on safety, health, or the environment, except where the Secretary determines that the *incremental benefits are clearly insufficient to justify the incremental costs of using such technologies*.

These and other statutes demonstrate that Congress uses specific language when intending that an agency engage in cost-benefit analysis. Certainly in light of its ordinary meaning, the word "feasible" cannot be construed to articulate such congressional intent. We therefore reject the argument that Congress required cost-benefit analysis in § 6(b)(5).

Case Questions

1. What is byssinosis? Why should byssinosis be anything that the textile companies are responsible for, ethically or legally? If it is well-known that textile workers get cotton dust in their systems and develop brown lung, don't they nevertheless choose to work there and assume the risk of all injuries?
2. By imposing costs on the textile industry, what will be the net effect on US textile manufacturing jobs?
3. How is byssinosis a "negative externality" that is not paid for by either the manufacturer or the consumer of textile products? How should the market, to be fair and efficient, adjust for these negative externalities *other* than by setting a reasonable standard that shares the burden between manufacturers and their employees? Should *all* the burden be on the manufacturer?

Michigan et al., v. E.P.A.

Michigan et al., v. E.P.A.

576 U.S. ______ (2015)

JUSTICE SCALIA delivered the opinion of the Court.

The Clean Air Act directs the Environmental Protection Agency to regulate emissions of hazardous air pollutants from power plants if the Agency finds regulation "appropriate and necessary." We must decide whether it was reasonable for EPA to refuse to consider cost when making this finding.

I

The Clean Air Act establishes a series of regulatory programs to control air pollution from stationary sources (such as refineries and factories) and moving sources (such as cars and airplanes). One of these is the National Emissions Standards for Hazardous Air Pollutants Program—the hazardous-air-pollutants program, for short. Established in its current form by the Clean Air Act Amendments of 1990, this program targets . . . more than 180 specified "hazardous air pollutants." §7412(b).

For stationary sources in general, the applicability of the program depends in part on how much pollution the source emits. A source that emits more than 10 tons of a single pollutant or more than 25 tons of a combination of pollutants per year is called a major source. EPA is required to regulate all major sources under the program. A source whose emissions do not cross the just-mentioned thresholds is called an area source. The Agency is required to regulate an area source under the program if it "presents a threat of adverse effects to human health or the environment . . . warranting regulation." §7412(c)(3).

At the same time, Congress established a unique procedure to determine the applicability of the program to fossil-fuel-fired power plants. . . . Congress directed the Agency to "perform a study of the hazards to public health reasonably anticipated to occur as a result of emissions by [power plants] of [hazardous air pollutants] after imposition of the requirements of this chapter." §7412(n)(1)(A). If the Agency "finds . . . regulation is appropriate and necessary after considering the results of the study," it "shall regulate [power plants] under [§7412]." EPA has interpreted the Act to mean that power plants become subject to regulation on the same terms as ordinary major and area sources, see 77 Fed. Reg. 9330 (2012), and we assume without deciding that it was correct to do so.

EPA completed the study required by §7412(n)(1)(A) *in 1998, 65 Fed. Reg. 79826 (2000)*, and concluded that regulation of coal- and oil-fired power plants was "appropriate and necessary" in 2000 . . . In 2012, it reaffirmed the appropriate-and-necessary finding, divided power plants into subcategories, and promulgated floor standards. The Agency found regulation "appropriate" because (1) power plants' emissions of mercury and other hazardous air pollutants posed risks to human health and the environment and (2) controls were available to reduce these emissions. 77 Fed. Reg. 9363. It found regulation "necessary" because the imposition of the Act's other requirements did not eliminate these risks. EPA concluded that "costs should not be considered" when deciding whether power plants should be regulated under §7412. Id. at 9326.

In accordance with Executive Order, the Agency issued a "Regulatory Impact Analysis" alongside its regulation. This analysis estimated that the regulation would force power plants to bear costs of $9.6 billion per year. Id. at 9306. The Agency could not fully quantify the benefits of reducing power plants' emissions of hazardous air pollutants; to the extent it could, it estimated that these benefits were worth $4 to $6 million per year. The costs to power plants were thus between 1,600 and 2,400 times as great as the quantifiable benefits from reduced emissions of hazardous air pollutants. The Agency continued that its regulations would have ancillary benefits—including cutting power plants' emissions of particulate matter and sulfur dioxide, substances that are not covered by the hazardous-air-pollutants program. Although the Agency's appropriate-and-necessary finding did not rest on these ancillary effects, the regulatory impact analysis took them into account, increasing the Agency's estimate of the quantifiable benefits of its regulation to $37 to $90 billion per year, Id. at 9306. *EPA concedes that the regulatory impact analysis "played no role" in its appropriate-and-necessary finding. Brief for Federal Respondents 14.*

Petitioners (who include 23 States) sought review of EPA's rule in the Court of Appeals for the D. C. Circuit. As relevant here, they challenged the Agency's refusal to consider cost when deciding whether to regulate power plants. The Court of Appeals upheld the Agency's decision not to consider cost. We granted certiorari.

II

Federal administrative agencies are required to engage in "reasoned decision-making." (case cited) "Not only must an agency's decreed result be within the scope of its lawful authority, but the process by which it reaches that result must be logical and rational."

EPA's decision to regulate power plants under §7412 allowed the Agency to reduce power plants' emissions of hazardous air pollutants and thus to improve public health and the environment. But the decision also ultimately cost power plants, according to the Agency's own estimate, nearly $10 billion a year. EPA refused to consider whether the costs of its decision outweighed the benefits. The Agency gave cost no thought at all, because it considered cost irrelevant to its initial decision to regulate.

EPA's disregard of cost rested on its interpretation of §7412(n)(1)(A), which, to repeat, directs the Agency to regulate power plants if it "finds such regulation is appropriate and necessary." The Agency accepts that it could have interpreted this provision to mean that cost is relevant to the decision to add power plants to the program. But it chose to read the statute to mean that cost makes no difference to the initial decision to regulate.

We review this interpretation under the standard set out in *Chevron U.S.A. Inc. v. Natural Resources Defense Council, Inc.*, 467 U.S. 837 (1984). Chevron directs courts to accept an agency's reasonable resolution of an ambiguity in a statute that the agency administers. Id. at 842-843. Even under this deferential standard, however, "agencies must operate within the bounds of reasonable interpretation." *Utility Air Regulatory Group v. EPA*, 573 U. S. ___, ___ (2014). EPA strayed far beyond those bounds when it read §7412(n)(1) to mean that it could ignore cost when deciding whether to regulate power plants.

A

The Clean Air Act treats power plants differently from other sources for purposes of the hazardous-air-pollutants program. Elsewhere in §7412, Congress established . . . criteria for EPA to apply when deciding whether to include sources in the program. It required the Agency to regulate sources whose emissions exceed specified numerical thresholds (major sources). It also required the Agency to regulate sources whose emissions fall short of these thresholds (area sources) if they "presen[t] a threat of adverse effects to human health or the environment . . . warranting regulation." §7412(c)(3). In stark contrast, Congress instructed EPA to add power plants to the program if (but only if) the Agency finds regulation "appropriate and necessary." §7412(n)(1)(A). One does not need to open up a dictionary in order to realize the capaciousness of this phrase. In particular, "appropriate" is "the classic broad and all-encompassing term that naturally and traditionally includes consideration of all the relevant factors." 748 F. 3d, at 1266 (opinion of Kavanaugh, J.). Although this term leaves agencies with flexibility, an agency may not "entirely fai[l] to consider an important aspect of the problem" when deciding whether regulation is appropriate.

Read naturally in the present context, the phrase "appropriate and necessary" requires at least some attention to cost. One would not say that it is even rational, never mind "appropriate," to impose billions of dollars in economic costs in return for a few dollars in health or environmental benefits. In addition, "cost" includes more than the expense of complying with regulations; any disadvantage could be termed a cost. EPA's interpretation precludes the Agency from considering any type of cost—including, for instance, harms that regulation might do to human health or the environment. The Government concedes that if the Agency were to find that emissions from power plants do damage to human health, but that the technologies needed to eliminate these emissions do even more damage to human health, it would still deem regulation appropriate. No regulation is "appropriate" if it does significantly more harm than good.

There are undoubtedly settings in which the phrase "appropriate and necessary" does not encompass cost. But this is not one of them. * * *

Statutory context reinforces the relevance of cost. The procedures governing power plants that we consider today appear in §7412(n)(1), which bears the caption "Electric utility steam generating units." In subparagraph (A), the part of the law that has occupied our attention so far, Congress required EPA to study the hazards to public health posed by power plants and to determine whether regulation is appropriate and necessary. But in subparagraphs (B) and (C), Congress called for two additional studies. One of them, a study into mercury emissions from power plants and other sources, must consider "the health and environmental effects of such emissions, technologies which are available to control such emissions, and the costs of such technologies." §7412(n)(1)(B) (emphasis added). This directive to EPA to study cost is a further indication of the relevance of cost to the decision to regulate.

. . .

EPA has not explained why §7412(n)(1)(B)'s reference to "environmental effects . . . and . . . costs" provides "direct evidence that Congress was concerned with environmental effects," but not "direct evidence" that it was concerned with cost. *Chevron* allows agencies to choose among competing reasonable interpretations of a statute; it does not license interpretive gerrymanders under which an agency keeps parts of statutory context it likes while throwing away parts it does not.

B

EPA identifies a handful of reasons to interpret §7412(n)(1)(A) to mean that cost is irrelevant to the initial decision to regulate. We find those reasons unpersuasive.

EPA points out that other parts of the Clean Air Act expressly mention cost, while §7412(n)(1)(A) does not. But this observation shows only that §7412(n)(1)(A)'s broad reference to appropriateness encompasses multiple relevant factors (which include but are not limited to cost); other provisions' specific references to cost encompass just cost. It is unreasonable to infer that, by expressly making cost relevant to other decisions, the Act implicitly makes cost irrelevant to the appropriateness of regulating power plants. * * *

Along similar lines, EPA seeks support in this Court's decision in *Whitman v. American Trucking Assns., Inc.*, 531 U.S. 457 (2001). There, the Court addressed a provision of the Clean Air Act requiring EPA to set ambient air quality standards at levels "requisite to protect the public health" with an "adequate margin of safety." 42 U. S. C. §7409(b). Read naturally, that discrete criterion does not encompass cost; it encompasses health and safety. The Court refused to read that provision as carrying with it an implicit authorization to consider cost, in part because authority to consider cost had "elsewhere, and so often, been expressly granted." 531 U.S. at 467. American Trucking thus establishes the modest principle that where the Clean Air Act expressly directs EPA to regulate on the basis of a factor that on its face does not include cost, the Act normally should not be read as implicitly allowing the Agency to consider cost anyway. That principle has no application here. "Appropriate and necessary" is a far more comprehensive criterion than "requisite to protect the public health"; read fairly and in context, as we have explained, the term plainly subsumes consideration of cost.

Our reasoning so far establishes that it was unreasonable for EPA to read §7412(n)(1)(A) to mean that cost is irrelevant to the initial decision to regulate power plants. The Agency must consider cost—including, most importantly, cost of compliance—before deciding whether regulation is appropriate and necessary. We need not and do not hold that the law unambiguously required the Agency, when making this preliminary estimate, to conduct a formal cost-benefit analysis in which each advantage and disadvantage is assigned a monetary value. It will be up to the Agency to decide (as always, within the limits of reasonable interpretation) how to account for cost. * * *

We hold that EPA interpreted §7412(n)(1)(A) unreasonably when it deemed cost irrelevant to the decision to regulate power plants. We reverse the judgment of the Court of Appeals for the D. C. Circuit and remand the cases for further proceedings consistent with this opinion.

JUSTICE KAGAN, with whom JUSTICE GINSBURG, JUSTICE BREYER, and JUSTICE SOTOMAYOR join, dissenting.

The Environmental Protection Agency placed emissions limits on coal and oil power plants following a lengthy regulatory process during which the Agency carefully considered costs. At the outset, EPA determined that regulating plants' emissions of hazardous air pollutants is "appropriate and necessary" given the harm they cause, and explained that it would take costs into account in developing suitable emissions standards. Next, EPA divided power plants into groups based on technological and other characteristics bearing significantly on their cost structures. It required plants in each group to match the emissions levels already achieved by the best-performing members of the same group--benchmarks necessarily reflecting those plants' own cost analyses. EPA then adopted a host of measures designed to make compliance with its proposed emissions limits less costly for plants that needed to catch up with their cleaner peers. And with only one narrow exception, EPA decided not to impose any more stringent standards (beyond what some plants had already achieved on their own) because it found that doing so would not be cost-effective. After all that, EPA conducted a formal cost-benefit study which found that the quantifiable benefits of its regulation would exceed the costs up to nine times over--by as much as $80 billion each year. Those benefits include as many as 11,000 fewer premature deaths annually, along with a far greater number of avoided illnesses.

Despite that exhaustive consideration of costs, the Court strikes down EPA's rule on the ground that the Agency "unreasonably . . . deemed cost irrelevant." On the majority's theory, the rule is invalid because EPA did not explicitly analyze costs at the very first stage of the regulatory process, when making its "appropriate and necessary" finding. And that is so even though EPA later took costs into account again and again and . . . so on. The majority thinks entirely immaterial, and so entirely ignores, all the subsequent times and ways EPA considered costs in deciding what any regulation would look like.

That is a peculiarly blinkered way for a court to assess the lawfulness of an agency's rulemaking. I agree with the majority—let there be no doubt about this—that EPA's power plant regulation would be unreasonable if "[t]he Agency gave cost no thought at all." But that is just not what happened here. Over more than a decade, EPA took costs into account at multiple stages and through multiple means as it set emissions limits for power plants. And when making its initial "appropriate and necessary" finding, EPA knew it would do exactly that—knew it would thoroughly consider the cost-effectiveness of emissions standards later on. That context matters. The Agency acted well within its authority in declining to consider costs at the opening bell of the regulatory process given that it would do so in every round thereafter—and given that the emissions limits finally issued would depend crucially on those accountings. Indeed, EPA could not have measured costs at the process's initial stage with any accuracy. And the regulatory path EPA chose parallels the one it has trod in setting emissions limits, at Congress's explicit direction, for every other source of hazardous air pollutants over two decades. The majority's decision that EPA cannot take the same approach here—its micromanagement of EPA's rulemaking, based on little more than the word "appropriate"—runs counter to Congress's allocation of authority between the Agency and the courts. Because EPA reasonably found that it was "appropriate" to decline to analyze costs at a single stage of a regulatory proceeding otherwise imbued with cost concerns, I respectfully dissent.

Case Questions

1. What is the actual result here? Is the EPA's rule "thrown out" entirely? Or, does the agency just "go back to the drawing board" to do a cost-benefit analysis to justify its rule?

2. What kinds of costs, and what kinds of benefits, do you think should go into the EPA's cost/benefit analysis?

3. The majority and the dissent view the same facts differently, or, one side has chosen to emphasize certain facts, while others will "see it differently." How can you, or the most diligent observer, tell what's really going on?

5.7 Summary and Exercises

Summary

Administrative rules and regulations constitute the largest body of laws that directly affect business. These regulations are issued by dozens of federal and state agencies that regulate virtually every aspect of modern business life, including the natural environment, corporate finance, transportation, telecommunications, energy, labor relations, and trade practices. The administrative agencies derive their power to promulgate regulations from statutes passed by Congress or state legislatures.

The agencies have a variety of powers. They can license companies to carry on certain activities or prohibit them from doing so, lay down codes of conduct, set rates that companies may charge for their services, and supervise various aspects of business.

Exercises

1. The Equal Employment Opportunity Commission seeks data about the racial composition of Terrific Textiles' labor force. Terrific refuses on the grounds that inadvertent disclosure of the numbers might cause certain "elements" to picket its factories. The EEOC takes Terrific to court to get the data. What is the result?
2. In order to police the profession, the state legislature has just passed a law permitting the State Plumbers' Association the power to hold hearings to determine whether a particular plumber has violated the plumbing code of ethics, written by the association. Sam, a plumber, objects to the convening of a hearing when he is accused by Roger, a fellow plumber, of acting unethically by soliciting business from Roger's customers. Sam goes to court, seeking to enjoin the association's disciplinary committee from holding the hearing. What is the result? How would you argue Sam's case? The association's case?
3. Assume that the new president of the United States was elected overwhelmingly by pledging in his campaign to "do away with bureaucrats who interfere in your lives." The day he takes the oath of office he determines to carry out his pledge. Discuss which of the following courses he may lawfully follow: (a) Fire all incumbent commissioners of federal agencies in order to install new appointees. (b) Demand that all pending regulations being considered by federal agencies be submitted to the White House for review and redrafting, if necessary. (c) Interview potential nominees for agency positions to determine whether their regulatory philosophy is consistent with his.
4. Dewey owned a mine in Wisconsin. He refused to allow Department of Labor agents into the mine to conduct warrantless searches to determine whether previously found safety violations had been corrected. The Federal Mine Safety and Health Amendments Act of 1977 authorizes four warrantless inspections per year. Is the provision for warrantless inspections by this agency constitutional?[11]
5. In determining the licensing requirements for nuclear reactors, the Nuclear Regulatory Commission (NRC) adopted a zero-release assumption: that the permanent storage of certain nuclear waste would have no significant environmental impact and that potential storage leakages should not be a factor discussed in the appropriate environmental impact statement (EIS) required before permitting construction of a nuclear power plant. This assumption is based on the NRC's belief that technology would be developed to isolate the wastes from the environment, and it was clear from the record that the NRC had "digested a massive material and disclosed all substantial risks" and had considered that the zero-release assumption was uncertain. There was a remote possibility of contamination by water leakage into the storage facility. An environmental NGO sued, asserting that the NRC had violated the regulations governing the EIS by arbitrarily and capriciously ignoring the potential contamination. The court of appeals agreed, and the power plant appealed. Had the NRC acted arbitrarily and capriciously?[12]

Self-Test Questions

1. Most federal administrative agencies are created by
    a. an executive order by the president
    b. a Supreme Court decision
    c. the passage of enabling legislation by Congress, signed by the president
    d. a and c
2. The Federal Trade Commission, like most administrative agencies of the federal government, is part of
    a. the executive branch of government
    b. the legislative branch of government
    c. the judicial branch of government
    d. the administrative branch of government
3. In the Clean Water Act, Congress sets broad guidelines, but it is the Environmental Protection Agency that proposes rules to regulate industrial discharges. Where do proposed rules originally appear?
    a. in the Congressional record
    b. in the *Federal Register*
    c. in the *Code of Federal Regulations*
    d. in the United States code service
4. The legal basis for all administrative law, including regulations of the Federal Trade Commission, is found in
    a. the Administrative Procedure Act
    b. the US Constitution
    c. the commerce clause
    d. none of the above
5. The Federal Trade Commission, like other administrative agencies, has the power to
    a. issue proposed rules
    b. undertake investigations of firms that may have violated FTC regulations
    c. prosecute firms that have violated FTC regulations
    d. none of the above
    e. all of the above

Self-Test Answers

1. c
2. a
3. b
4. b
5. e

Endnotes

1. *Schechter Poultry Corp. v. United States*, 295 US 495 (1935).
2. See Frontline, Bigger than Enron (2001), http://www.pbs.org/wgbh/pages/frontline/shows/regulation/ The entire video may be available on You Tube, and describes the political process that can undermine effective agency regulation.

3. *In re FTC Line of Business Report Litigation*, 595 F.2d 685 (D.C. Cir. 1978).
4. *Marshall v. Barlow's, Inc.*, 436 US 307 (1978).
5. *New York v. Burger*, 482 US 691 (1987).
6. *Dow Chemical Co. v. United States Environmental Protection Agency*, 476 US 227 (1986).
7. *Motor Vehicle Manufacturers' Assn. v. State Farm Mutual Ins.*, 463 US 29 (1983).
8. *Dalehite v. United States*, 346 US 15 (1953).
9. *Bivens v. Six Unknown Federal Narcotics Agents*, 403 US 388 (1971).
10. *Office of Personnel Management v. Richmond*, 110 S. Ct. 2465 (1990).
11. *Donovan v. Dewey*, 452 US 594 (1981).
12. *Baltimore Gas and Electric Co. v. Natural Resources Defense Council Inc.*, 462 US 87 (1983).

CHAPTER 6

Criminal Law

Learning Objectives

After reading this chapter, you should be able to do the following:

1. Explain how criminal law differs from civil law.
2. Categorize the various types of crimes and define the most serious felonies.
3. Discuss and question the criminal "intent" of a corporation.
4. Explain basic criminal procedure and the rights of criminal defendants.

At times, unethical behavior by businesspeople can be extreme enough that society will respond by criminalizing certain kinds of activities. Ponzi schemes, arson, various kinds of fraud, embezzlement, racketeering, foreign corrupt practices, tax evasion, and insider trading are just a few. A corporation can face large fines, and corporate managers can face both fines and jail sentences for violating criminal laws. This chapter aims to explain how criminal law differs from civil law, to discuss various types of crimes, and to relate the basic principles of criminal procedure.

6.1 The Nature of Criminal Law

Learning Objectives

1. Explain why crimes concern the entire society, not just individuals who are harmed by criminal actions.
2. Describe which bodies or institutions have defined various crimes over the past 500 years.
3. Explain how Constitutional law matters in criminal cases.

Criminal law is the most ancient branch of the law. Many wise observers have tried to define and explain it, but the explanations often include many complex and subtle distinctions. A traditional criminal law course would include a lot of discussions on criminal intent, the nature of criminal versus civil responsibility, and the constitutional rights accorded the accused. But in this chapter, we will consider only the most basic aspects of intent, responsibility, and constitutional rights.

Unlike civil actions, where plaintiffs seek compensation or other remedies for themselves, crimes involve "the state" (the federal government, a state government, or some subunit of state government). This is because crimes involve some "harm to society" and not just harm to certain individuals. But "harm to society" is not always evident in the act itself. For example, two friends of yours at a party argue, take the argument outside, and blows are struck; one has a bloody nose and immediately goes home. The crimes of assault and battery have been committed, even though no one else knows about the fight and the friends later make up. By contrast, suppose a major corporation publicly announces that it is closing operations in your community and moving operations to Southeast Asia. There is plenty of harm to society as the plant closes down and no new jobs take the place of the company's jobs. Although the effects on society are greater in the second example, only the first example is a crime.

Crimes are generally defined by legislatures, in statutes; the statutes describe in general terms the nature of the conduct they wish to criminalize. For government punishment to be fair, citizens must have clear notice of what is criminally prohibited. Ex post facto laws—laws created "after the fact" to punish an act that was legal at the time—are expressly prohibited by the US Constitution. Overly vague statutes can also be struck down by courts under a constitutional doctrine known as "void for vagueness."

What is considered a crime will also vary from society to society and from time to time. For example, while cocaine use was legal in the United States at one time, it is now a controlled substance, and unauthorized use is now a crime. Medical marijuana was not legal fifty years ago when its use began to become widespread, and in some states its use or possession was a felony. Now, some states make it legal to use or possess it under some circumstances. In the United States, you can criticize and make jokes about the president of the United States without committing a crime, but in many countries it is a serious criminal act to criticize a public official.

Attitudes about appropriate punishment for crimes will also vary considerably from nation to nation. Uganda has decreed long prison sentences for homosexuals and death to repeat offenders. In Saudi Arabia, the government has proposed to deliberately paralyze a criminal defendant who criminally assaulted someone and unintentionally caused the victim's paralysis. Limits on punishment are set in the United States through the Constitution's prohibition on "cruel or unusual punishments."

It is often said that ignorance of the law is no excuse. But there are far too many criminal laws for anyone to know them all. Also, because most people do not actually read statutes, the question of "criminal intent" comes up right away: if you don't know that the legislature has made driving without a seat belt fastened a misdemeanor, you cannot have intended to harm society. You might even argue that there is no harm to anyone but yourself!

The usual answer to this is that the phrase "ignorance of the law is no excuse" means that society (through its elected representatives) gets to decide what is harmful to society, not you. Still, you may ask, "Isn't it my choice whether to take the risk of failing to wear a seat belt? Isn't this a victimless crime? Where is the harm to society?" A policymaker or social scientist may answer that your injuries, statistically, are generally going to be far greater if you don't wear one and that your choice may actually impose costs on society. For example, you might not have enough insurance, so that a public hospital will have to take care of your head injuries, injuries that would likely have been avoided by your use of a seat belt.

But, as just noted, it is hard to know the meaning of some criminal laws. Teenagers hanging around the sidewalks on Main Street were sometimes arrested for "loitering." The constitutional void-for-vagueness doctrine has led the courts to overturn statutes that are not clear. For example, "vagrancy" was long held to be a crime, but US courts began some forty years ago to overturn vagrancy and "suspicious person" statutes on the grounds that they are too vague for people to know what they are being asked not to do.

This requirement that criminal statutes not be vague does not mean that the law always defines crimes in ways that can be easily and clearly understood. Many statutes use terminology developed by the common-law courts. For example, a California statute defines murder as "the unlawful killing of a human being, with malice aforethought." If no history backed up these words, they would be unconstitutionally vague. But there is a rich history of judicial decisions that provides meaning for much of the arcane language like "malice aforethought" strewn about in the statute books.

Because a crime is an act that the legislature has defined as socially harmful, the parties involved cannot agree among themselves to forget a particular incident, such as a barroom brawl, if the authorities decide to prosecute. This is one of the critical distinctions between criminal and civil law. An assault is both a crime and a tort. The person who was assaulted may choose to forgive his assailant and not to sue him for damages. But he cannot stop the prosecutor from bringing an indictment against the assailant. (However, because of crowded dockets, a victim that declines to press charges may cause a busy prosecutor to choose to not to bring an indictment.)

A crime consists of an act defined as criminal—an actus reus—and the requisite "criminal intent." Someone who has a burning desire to kill a rival in business or romance and who may actually intend to murder but does not act on his desire has not committed a crime. He may have a "guilty mind"—the translation of the Latin phrase mens rea—but he is guilty of no crime. A person who is forced to commit a crime at gunpoint is not guilty of a crime, because although there was an act defined as criminal—an actus reus—there was no criminal intent.

Key Takeaway

Crimes are usually defined by statute and constitute an offense against society. In each case, there must be both an act and some mens rea (criminal intent).

Exercises

1. Other than deterring certain kinds of conduct, what purpose does the criminal law serve?
2. Why is ignorance of the law no excuse? Why shouldn't it be an excuse, when criminal laws can be complicated and sometimes ambiguous?

6.2 Types of Crimes

Learning Objectives

1. Categorize various types of crimes.
2. Name and define the major felonies in criminal law.
3. Explain how white-collar crime differs from other crimes.
4. Define a variety of white-collar crimes.

Most classifications of crime turn on the seriousness of the act. In general, seriousness is defined by the nature or duration of the punishment set out in the statute. A **felony** is a crime punishable (usually) by imprisonment of more than one year or by death. (Crimes punishable by death are sometimes known as capital crimes; they are increasingly rare in the United States.) The major felonies include murder, rape, kidnapping, armed robbery, embezzlement, insider trading, fraud, and racketeering. All other crimes are usually known as **misdemeanors**, petty offenses, or infractions. Another way of viewing crimes is by the type of social harm the statute is intended to prevent or deter, such as offenses against the person, offenses against property, and white-collar crime.

felony

A serious kind of crime, usually involving potential imprisonment of six months or more.

misdemeanors

Crimes that are less serious than a felony, usually involving punishment of six months in prison or less.

Offenses against the Person

Homicide

homicide

The killing of one person by another without legal excuse.

justifiable homicide

When the law permits one person to kill another.

Homicide is the killing of one person by another. Not every killing is criminal. When the law permits one person to kill another—for example, a soldier killing an enemy on the battlefield during war, or a killing in self-defense—the death is considered the result of **justifiable homicide**. An *excusable homicide*, by contrast, is one in which death results from an accident in which the killer is not at fault.

All other homicides are criminal. The most severely punished form is murder, defined as homicide committed with "malice aforethought." This is a term with a very long history. Boiled down to its essentials, it means that the defendant had the intent to kill. A killing need not be premeditated for any long period of time; the premeditation might be quite sudden, as in a bar fight that escalates in that moment when one of the fighters reaches for a knife with the intent to kill.

Sometimes a homicide can be murder even if there is no intent to kill; an intent to inflict great bodily harm can be murder if the result is the death of another person. A killing that takes place while a felony (such as armed robbery) is being committed is also murder, whether or not the killer intended any harm. This is the so-called felony murder rule. Examples are the accidental discharge of a gun that kills an innocent bystander or the asphyxiation death of a fireman from smoke resulting from a fire set by an arsonist. The felony murder rule is more significant than it sounds, because it also applies to the accomplices of one who does the killing. Thus the driver of a getaway car stationed a block away from the scene of the robbery can be convicted of murder if a gun accidentally fires during the robbery and someone is killed. Manslaughter is an act of killing that does not amount to murder. Voluntary manslaughter is an intentional killing, but one carried out in the "sudden heat of passion" as the result of some provocation. An example is a fight that gets out of hand. Involuntary manslaughter entails a lesser degree of willfulness; it usually occurs when someone has taken a reckless action that results in death (e.g., a death resulting from a traffic accident in which one driver recklessly runs a red light).

Assault and Battery

battery

The unlawful application of force to another person. The force need not be violent.

Ordinarily, we would say that a person who has struck another has "assaulted" him. Technically, that is a **battery**—the unlawful application of force to another person. The force need not be violent. Indeed, a man who kisses a woman is guilty of a battery if he does it against her will. The other person may consent to the force. That is one reason why surgeons require patients to sign consent forms, giving the doctor permission to operate. In the absence of such a consent, an operation is a battery. That is also why football players are not constantly being charged with battery. Those who agree to play football agree to submit to the rules of the game, which of course include the right to tackle. But the consent does not apply to all acts of physical force: a hockey player who hits an opponent over the head with his stick can be prosecuted for the crime of battery.

assault

An attempt to commit a battery, or the deliberate placing of another in fear of receiving an immediate battery.

Criminal **assault** is an *attempt* to commit a battery or the deliberate placing of another in fear of receiving an immediate battery. If you throw a rock at a friend, but he manages to dodge it, you have committed an assault. Some states limit an assault to an attempt to commit a battery by one who has a "present ability" to do so. Pointing an unloaded gun and threatening to shoot would not be an assault, nor, of course, could it be a battery. The modem tendency, however, is to define an assault as an attempt to commit a battery by one with an *apparent* ability to do so.

Assault and battery may be excused. For example, a bar owner (or her agent, the bouncer) may use reasonable force to remove an unruly patron. If the use of force is excessive, the bouncer can be found guilty of assault and battery, and a civil action could arise against the bar owner as well.

Offenses against Property

Theft: Larceny, Robbery, Embezzlement, False Pretenses

The concept of theft is familiar enough. Less familiar is the way the law has treated various aspects of the act of stealing. Criminal law distinguishes among many different crimes that are popularly known as theft. Many technical words have entered the language—burglary, larceny, robbery—but are often used inaccurately. Brief definitions of the more common terms are discussed here.

The basic crime of stealing personal property is **larceny**. By its old common-law definition, still in use today, larceny is the wrongful "taking and carrying away of the personal property of another with intent to steal the same."

larceny

The wrongful taking and carrying away of the personal property of another with intent to steal the same.

The separate elements of this offense have given rise to all kinds of difficult cases. Take the theft of fruit, for example, with regard to the essential element of "personal property." If a man walking through an orchard plucks a peach from a tree and eats it, he is not guilty of larceny because he has not taken away *personal* property (the peach is part of the land, being connected to the tree). But if he picks up a peach lying on the ground, he is guilty of larceny. Or consider the element of "taking" or "carrying away." Sneaking into a movie theater without paying is not an act of larceny (though in most states it is a criminal act). Taking electricity by tapping into the power lines of an electric utility was something that baffled judges late in the nineteenth century because it was not clear whether electricity is a "something" that can be taken. Modern statutes have tended to make clear that electricity can be the object of larceny. Or consider the element of an "intent to steal the same." If you borrow your friend's BMW without his permission in order to go to the grocery store, intending to return it within a few minutes and then do return it, you have not committed larceny. But if you meet another friend at the store who convinces you to take a long joyride with the car and you return hours later, you may have committed larceny.

A particular form of larceny is **robbery**, which is defined as larceny from a person by means of violence or intimidation.

robbery

Larceny from a person by means of violence or intimidation.

Larceny involves the taking of property from the possession of another. Suppose that a person legitimately comes to possess the property of another and wrongfully appropriates it—for example, an automobile mechanic entrusted with your car refuses to return it, or a bank teller who is entitled to temporary possession of cash in his drawer takes it home with him. The common law had trouble with such cases because the thief in these cases already had possession; his crime was in assuming ownership. Today, such wrongful conversion, known as **embezzlement**, has been made a statutory offense in all states.

embezzlement

A form of larceny in which a person entrusted with someone else's property wrongfully takes sole possession or has the intent to take sole possession.

Statutes against larceny and embezzlement did not cover all the gaps in the law. A conceptual problem arises in the case of one who is tricked into giving up his title to property. In larceny and embezzlement, the thief gains possession or ownership without any consent of the owner or custodian of the property. Suppose, however, that an automobile dealer agrees to take his customer's present car as a trade-in. The customer says that he has full title to the car. In fact, the customer is still paying off an installment loan and the finance company has an interest in the old car. If the finance company repossesses the car, the customer—who got a new car at a discount because of his false representation—cannot be said to have taken the new car by larceny or embezzlement. Nevertheless, he tricked the dealer into selling, and the dealer will have lost the value of the repossessed car. Obviously, the customer is guilty of a criminal act; the statutes outlawing it refer to this trickery as the crime of **false pretenses**, defined as obtaining ownership of the property of another by making untrue representations of fact with intent to defraud.

false pretense

A form of larceny in which the rightful owner is tricked into giving up title to his or her property.

A number of problems have arisen in the judicial interpretation of false-pretense statutes. One concerns whether the taking is permanent or only temporary. The case of *State v. Mills* (Section 7) shows the subtle questions that can be presented and the dangers inherent in committing "a little fraud."

In the *Mills* case, the claim was that a mortgage instrument dealing with one parcel of land was used instead for another. This is a false representation of fact. Suppose, by contrast, that a person misrepresents his state of mind: "I will pay you back tomorrow," he says, knowing full well that he does not intend to. Can such a misrepresentation amount to false pretenses punishable as a criminal offense? In most jurisdictions it cannot. A false-pretense violation relates to a past event or existing fact, not to a statement of intention. If it were otherwise, anyone failing to pay a debt might find himself facing criminal prosecution, and business would be less prone to take risks.

The problem of proving intent is especially difficult when a person has availed himself of the services of another without paying. A common example is someone leaving a restaurant without paying for the meal. In most states, this is specifically defined in the statutes as *theft of services*.

Receiving Stolen Property

receiving stolen property

Depending on the value of the property, if you receive property from another person, knowing that it has been stolen, you have committed either a misdemeanor or a felony.

One who engages in **receiving stolen property** with knowledge that it is stolen is guilty of a felony or misdemeanor, depending on the value of the property. The receipt need not be personal; if the property is delivered to a place under the control of the receiver, then he is deemed to have received it. "Knowledge" is construed broadly: not merely actual knowledge, but (correct) belief and suspicion (strong enough not to investigate for fear that the property will turn out to have been stolen) are sufficient for conviction.

Forgery

forgery

False writing of a document of legal significance (or apparent legal significance) with intent to defraud.

Forgery is false writing of a document of legal significance (or apparent legal significance!) with intent to defraud. It includes the making up of a false document or the alteration of an existing one. The writing need not be done by hand but can be by any means—typing, printing, and so forth. Documents commonly the subject of forgery are negotiable instruments (checks, money orders, and the like), deeds, receipts, contracts, and bills of lading. The forged instrument must itself be false, not merely contain a falsehood. If you fake your neighbor's signature on one of his checks made out to cash, you have committed forgery. But if you sign a check of your own that is made out to cash, knowing that there is no money in your checking account, the instrument is not forged, though the act may be criminal if done with the intent to defraud.

The mere making of a forged instrument is unlawful. So is the "uttering" (or presentation) of such an instrument, whether or not the one uttering it actually forged it. The usual example of a false signature is by no means the only way to commit forgery. If done with intent to defraud, the backdating of a document, the modification of a corporate name, or the filling in of lines left blank on a form can all constitute forgery.

Extortion

extortion

The wrongful collection of money or something else of value by anyone by means of a threat.

Under common law, **extortion** could only be committed by a government official, who corruptly collected an unlawful fee under color of office. A common example is a salaried building inspector who refuses to issue a permit unless the permittee pays him. Under modern statutes, the crime of extortion has been broadened to include the wrongful collection of money or something else of value by anyone by means of a threat (short of a threat of immediate physical violence, for such a threat would make the demand an act of robbery). This kind of extortion is usually called blackmail. The blackmail threat commonly is to expose some fact of the victim's private life or to make a false accusation about him.

Offenses against Habitation and Other Offenses

Burglary

Burglary is not a crime against property. It is defined as "the breaking and entering of the dwelling of another in the nighttime with intent to commit a felony." The intent to steal is not an issue: a man who sneaks into a woman's home intent on raping her has committed a burglary, even if he does not carry out the act. The student doing critical thinking will no doubt notice that the definition provides plenty of room for argument. What is "breaking"? (The courts do not require actual destruction; the mere opening of a closed door, even if unlocked, is enough.) What is entry? When does night begin? What kind of intent? Whose dwelling? Can a landlord burglarize the dwelling of his tenant? (Yes.) Can a person burglarize his own home? (No.)

burglary

The crime of breaking and entering the dwelling place of another with intent to commit a felony therein.

Arson

Under common law, **arson** was the malicious burning of the dwelling of another. Burning one's own house for purposes of collecting insurance was not an act of arson under common law. The statutes today make it a felony intentionally to set fire to any building, whether or not it is a dwelling and whether or not the purpose is to collect insurance.

arson

The intentional setting of a fire to any building, whether commercial or residential, and whether or not for the purpose of collecting insurance proceeds.

Bribery

Bribery is a corrupt payment (or receipt of such a payment) for official action. The payment can be in cash or in the form of any goods, intangibles, or services that the recipient would find valuable. Under common law, only a public official could be bribed. In most states, bribery charges can result from the bribe of anyone performing a public function.

Bribing a public official in government procurement (contracting) can result in serious criminal charges. Bribing a public official in a foreign country to win a contract can result in charges under the Foreign Corrupt Practices Act.

bribery

A secret payment to another to get them to favor the payer of the bribe, or his business organization. A bribe could offered in a commercial transaction, which usually raises ethical issues, or could be offered to get a public official to act (or ignore a criminal act) in favor of the person or firm paying. Bribery of a state or federal public official is generally a criminal offense, both for the bribe payer and the official accepting the bribe.

Perjury

Perjury is the crime of giving a false oath, either orally or in writing, in a judicial or other official proceeding (lies made in proceedings other than courts are sometimes termed "false swearing"). To be perjurious, the oath must have been made corruptly—that is, with knowledge that it was false or without sincere belief that it was true. An innocent mistake is not perjury. A statement, though true, is perjury if the maker of it believes it to be false. Statements such as "I don't remember" or "to the best of my knowledge" are not sufficient to protect a person who is lying from conviction for perjury. To support a charge of perjury, however, the false statement must be "material," meaning that the statement is relevant to whatever the court is trying to find out.

perjury

The crime of giving a false oath, either orally or in writing, in a judicial or other official proceeding.

White-Collar Crime

White-collar crime, as distinguished from "street crime," refers generally to fraud-related acts carried out in a nonviolent way, usually connected with business. Armed bank robbery is not a white-collar crime, but embezzlement by a teller or bank officer is. Many white-collar crimes are included within the statutory definitions of embezzlement and false pretenses. Most are violations of state law. Depending on how they are carried out, many of these same crimes are also violations of federal law.

white-collar crime

Any number of crimes, usually involving a business context; any illegal act committed by nonviolent means to obtain a personal or business advantage.

Any act of fraud in which the United States postal system is used or which involves interstate phone calls or Internet connections is a violation of federal law. Likewise, many different acts around the buying and selling of securities can run afoul of federal securities laws. Other white-collar crimes include tax fraud; price fixing; violations of food, drug, and environmental laws; corporate bribery of foreign companies; and—the newest form—computer fraud. Some of these are discussed here; others are covered in later chapters.

Mail and Wire Fraud

Federal law prohibits the use of the mails or any interstate electronic communications medium for the purpose of furthering a "scheme or artifice to defraud." The statute is broad, and it is relatively easy for prosecutors to prove a violation. The law also bans attempts to defraud, so the prosecutor need not show that the scheme worked or that anyone suffered any losses. "Fraud" is broadly construed: anyone who uses the mails or telephone to defraud anyone else of virtually anything, not just of money, can be convicted under the law. In one case, a state governor was convicted of mail fraud when he took bribes to influence the setting of racing dates. The court's theory was that he defrauded the citizenry of its right to his "honest and faithful services" as governor.[1]

Violations of Antitrust Law

In Chapter 48 we consider the fundamentals of antitrust law, which for the most part affects the business enterprise civilly. But violations of Section 1 of the Sherman Act, which condemns activities in "restraint of trade" (including price fixing), are also crimes.

Violations of the Food and Drug Act

The federal Food, Drug, and Cosmetic Act prohibits any person or corporation from sending into interstate commerce any adulterated or misbranded food, drug, cosmetics, or related device. For example, in a 2010 case, Allergen had to pay a criminal fine for marketing Botox as a headache or pain reliever, a use that had not been approved by the Food and Drug Administration. Unlike most criminal statutes, willfulness or deliberate misconduct is not an element of the act. As the *United States v. Park* case (Section 7) shows, an executive can be held criminally liable even though he may have had no personal knowledge of the violation.

Environmental Crimes

Many federal environmental statutes have criminal provisions. These include the Federal Water Pollution Control Act (commonly called the Clean Water Act); the Rivers and Harbors Act of 1899 (the Refuse Act); the Clean Air Act; the Federal Insecticide, Fungicide, and Rodenticide Act (FIFRA); the Toxic Substances Control Act (TSCA); and the Resource Conservation and Recovery Act (RCRA). Under the Clean Water Act, for example, wrongful discharge of pollutants into navigable waters carries a fine ranging from $2,500 to $25,000 per day and imprisonment for up to one year. "Responsible corporate officers" are specifically included as potential defendants in criminal prosecutions under the act. They can include officers who have responsibility over a project where subcontractors and their employees actually caused the discharge.[2]

Violations of the Foreign Corrupt Practices Act

As a byproduct of Watergate, federal officials at the Securities and Exchange Commission and the Internal Revenue Service uncovered many instances of bribes paid by major corporations to officials of foreign governments to win contracts with those governments. Congress responded in 1977 with the Foreign Corrupt Practices Act, which imposed a stringent requirement that the disposition of assets be accurately and fairly accounted for in a company's books and records. The act also made illegal the payment of bribes to foreign officials or to anyone who will transmit the money to a foreign official to assist the payor (the one offering and delivering the money) in getting business.

Violations of the Racketeering Influenced and Corrupt Organizations Act

In 1970 Congress enacted the Racketeering Influenced and Corrupt Organizations Act (RICO), aimed at ending organized crime's infiltration into legitimate business. The act tells courts to construe its language broadly "to effectuate its remedial purpose," and many who are not part of organized crime have been successfully prosecuted under the act. It bans a "pattern of racketeering," defined as the commission of at least two acts within ten years of any of a variety of already-existing crimes, including mail, wire, and securities fraud. The act thus makes many types of fraud subject to severe penalties.

Computer Crime

Computer crime generally falls into four categories: (1) theft of money, financial instruments, or property; (2) misappropriation of computer time; (3) theft of programs; and (4) illegal acquisition of information. The main federal statutory framework for many computer crimes is the Computer Fraud and Abuse Act (CFAA; see Table 6.1). Congress only prohibited computer fraud and abuse where there was a federal interest, as where computers of the government were involved or where the crime was interstate in nature.

computer crime

Any crime (usually theft of some sort, or sabotage) committed with the aid of a computer.

TABLE 6.1 Summary of Provisions of the Computer Fraud and Abuse Act

Obtaining national security information	Sec. (a)(1)	10 years maximum (20 years second offense)
Trespassing in a government computer	Sec. (a)(3)	1 year (5)
Compromising the confidentiality of a computer	Sec. (a)(2)	1 year (10)
Accessing a computer to defraud and obtain value	Sec. (a)4	5 years (10)
Intentional access and reckless damage	(a)(5)(A)(ii)	5 years (20)
Trafficking in passwords	(a)(6)	1 year (10)

Key Takeaway

Offenses can be against persons, against property, or against public policy (as when you bribe a public official, commit perjury, or use public goods such as the mails or the Internet to commit fraud, violate antitrust laws, or commit other white-collar crimes).

Exercises

1. Which does more serious harm to society: street crimes or white-collar crimes?
2. Why are various crimes so difficult to define precisely?
3. Hungry Harold goes by the home of Juanita Martinez. Juanita has just finished baking a cherry pie and sets it in the open windowsill to cool. Harold smells the pie from the sidewalk.

It is twilight; while still light, the sun has officially set. Harold reaches into the window frame and removes the pie. Technically, has Harold committed burglary? What are the issues here based on the definition of burglary?

4. What is fraud? How is it different from dishonesty? Is being dishonest a criminal offense? If so, have you been a criminal already today?

6.3 The Nature of a Criminal Act

Learning Objectives

1. Understand how it is possible to commit a criminal act without actually doing anything that you think might be criminal.
2. Analyze and explain the importance of intention in criminal law and criminal prosecutions.
3. Explain how a corporation can be guilty of a crime, even though it is a corporation's agents that commit the crime.

To be guilty of a crime, you must have acted. Mental desire or intent to do so is insufficient. But what constitutes an act? This question becomes important when someone begins to commit a crime, or does so in association with others, or intends to do one thing but winds up doing something else.

Attempt

It is not necessary to commit the intended crime to be found guilty of a criminal offense. An *attempt* to commit the crime is punishable as well, though usually not as severely. For example, Brett points a gun at Ashley, intending to shoot her dead. He pulls the trigger but his aim is off, and he misses her heart by four feet. He is guilty of an attempt to murder. Suppose, however, that earlier in the day, when he was preparing to shoot Ashley, Brett had been overheard in his apartment muttering to himself of his intention, and that a neighbor called the police. When they arrived, he was just snapping his gun into his shoulder holster.

At that point, courts in most states would not consider him guilty of an attempt because he had not passed beyond the stage of *preparation*. After having buttoned his jacket he might have reconsidered and put the gun away. Determining when the accused has passed beyond mere preparation and taken an actual step toward *perpetrating* the crime is often difficult and is usually for the jury to decide.

Impossibility

What if a defendant is accused of attempting a crime that is factually impossible? For example, suppose that men believed they were raping a drunken, unconscious woman, and were later accused of attempted rape, but defended on the grounds of factual impossibility because the woman was actually dead at the time sexual intercourse took place? Or suppose that a husband intended to poison his wife with strychnine in her coffee, but put sugar in the coffee instead? The "mens rea" or criminal intent was there, but the act itself was not criminal (rape requires a live victim, and murder by poisoning requires the use of poison). States are divided on this, but thirty-seven states have ruled out factual impossibility as a defense to the crime of attempt.

Legal impossibility is different, and is usually acknowledged as a valid defense. If the defendant completes all of his intended acts, but those acts do not fulfill all the required elements of a crime, there could be a successful "impossibility" defense. If Barney (who has poor sight), shoots at a tree stump, thinking it is his neighbor, Ralph, intending to kill him, has he committed an attempt? Many courts would hold that he has not. But the distinction between factual impossibility and legal impossibility is not always clear, and the trend seems to be to punish the intended attempt.

Conspiracy

Under both federal and state laws, it is a separate offense to work with others toward the commission of a crime. When two or more people combine to carry out an unlawful purpose, they are engaged in a conspiracy. The law of conspiracy is quite broad, especially when it is used by prosecutors in connection with white-collar crimes. Many people can be swept up in the net of conspiracy, because it is unnecessary to show that the actions they took were sufficient to constitute either the crime or an attempt. Usually, the prosecution needs to show only (1) an agreement and (2) a single overt act in furtherance of the conspiracy. Thus if three people agree to rob a bank, and if one of them goes to a store to purchase a gun to be used in the holdup, the three can be convicted of conspiracy to commit robbery. Even the purchase of an automobile to be used as the getaway car could support a conspiracy conviction.

The act of any one of the conspirators is imputed to the other members of the conspiracy. It does not matter, for instance, that only one of the bank robbers fired the gun that killed a guard. All can be convicted of murder. That is so even if one of the conspirators was stationed as a lookout several blocks away and even if he specifically told the others that his agreement to cooperate would end "just as soon as there is shooting."

Agency and Corporations

A person can be guilty of a crime if he acts through another. Again, the usual reason for "imputing" the guilt of the actor to another is that both were engaged in a conspiracy. But imputation of guilt is not limited to a conspiracy. The agent may be innocent even though he participates. A corporate officer directs a junior employee to take a certain bag and deliver it to the officer's home. The employee reasonably believes that the officer is entitled to the bag. Unbeknownst to the employee, the bag contains money that belongs to the company, and the officer wishes to keep it. This is not a conspiracy. The employee is not guilty of larceny, but the officer is, because the agent's act is imputed to him.

Since intent is a necessary component of crime, an agent's intent cannot be imputed to his principal if the principal did not share the intent. The company president tells her sales manager, "Go make sure our biggest customer renews his contract for next year"—by which she meant, "Don't ignore our biggest customer." Standing before the customer's purchasing agent, the sales manager threatens to tell the purchasing agent's boss that the purchasing agent has been cheating on his expense account, unless he signs a new contract. The sales manager could be convicted of blackmail, but the company president could not.

Can a corporation be guilty of a crime? For many types of crimes, the guilt of individual employees may be imputed to the corporation. Thus the antitrust statutes explicitly state that the corporation may be convicted and fined for violations by employees. This is so even though the shareholders are the ones who ultimately must pay the price—and who may have had nothing to do with the crime nor the power to stop it. The law of corporate criminal responsibility has been changing in recent years. The tendency is to hold the corporation liable under criminal law if the act has been directed by a responsible officer or group within the corporation (the president or board of directors).

Key Takeaway

Although proving the intent to commit a crime (the mens rea) is essential, the intent can be established by inference (circumstantially). Conspirators may not actually commit a crime, for example, but in preparing for a criminal act, they may be guilty of the crime of conspiracy. Certain corporate officers, as well, may not be directly committing criminal acts but may be held criminally responsible for acts of their agents and contractors.

Exercises

1. Give an example of how someone can intend to commit a crime but fail to commit one.
2. Describe a situation where there is a conspiracy to commit a crime without the crime actually taking place.
3. Create a scenario based on current events where a corporation could be found guilty of committing a crime even though the CEO, the board of directors, and the shareholders have not themselves done a criminal act.

6.4 Responsibility

Learning Objectives

1. Explain why criminal law generally requires that the defendant charged with a crime have criminal "intent."
2. Know and explain the possible excuses relating to responsibility that are legally recognized by courts, including lack of capacity.

In General

The mens rea requirement depends on the nature of the crime and all the circumstances surrounding the act. In general, though, the requirement means that the accused must in some way have intended the criminal consequences of his act. Suppose, for example, that Charlie gives Gabrielle a poison capsule to swallow. That is the act. If Gabrielle dies, is Charlie guilty of murder? The answer depends on what his state of mind was. Obviously, if he gave it to her intending to kill her, the act was murder.

What if he gave it to her knowing that the capsule was poison but believing that it would only make her mildly ill? The act is still murder, because we are all liable for the consequences of any intentional act that may cause harm to others. But suppose that Gabrielle had asked Harry for aspirin, and he handed her two pills that he reasonably believed to be aspirin (they came from the aspirin bottle and looked like aspirin) but that turned out to be poison, the act would not be murder, because he had neither intent nor a state of knowledge from which intent could be inferred.

Not every criminal law requires criminal intent as an ingredient of the crime. Many regulatory codes dealing with the public health and safety impose strict requirements. Failure to adhere to such requirements is a violation, whether or not the violator had mens rea. The *United States v. Park* case, Section 7, a decision of the US Supreme Court, shows the different considerations involved in mens rea.

Excuses That Limit or Overcome Responsibility

Mistake of Fact and Mistake of Law

Ordinarily, ignorance of the *law* is not an excuse. If you believe that it is permissible to turn right on a red light but the city ordinance prohibits it, your belief, even if reasonable, does not excuse your violation of the law. Under certain circumstances, however, ignorance of law will be excused. If a statute imposes criminal penalties for an action taken without a license, and if the government official responsible for issuing the license formally tells you that you do not need one (though in fact you do), a conviction for violating the statute cannot stand. In rare cases, a lawyer's advice, contrary to the statute, will be held to excuse the client, but usually the client is responsible for his attorney's mistakes. Otherwise, as it is said, the lawyer would be superior to the law.

Ignorance or mistake of *fact* more frequently will serve as an excuse. If you take a coat from a restaurant, believing it to be yours, you cannot be convicted of larceny if it is not. Your honest mistake of fact negates the requisite intent. In general, the rule is that a mistaken belief of fact will excuse criminal responsibility if (1) the belief is honestly held, (2) it is reasonable to hold it, and (3) the act would not have been criminal if the facts were as the accused supposed them to have been.

Entrapment

One common technique of criminal investigation is the use of an undercover agent or decoy—the policeman who poses as a buyer of drugs from a street dealer or the elaborate "sting" operations in which ostensibly stolen goods are "sold" to underworld "fences." Sometimes these methods are the only way by which certain kinds of crime can be rooted out and convictions secured.

But a rule against **entrapment** limits the legal ability of the police to play the role of criminals. The police are permitted to use such techniques to detect criminal activity; they are not permitted to do so to instigate crime. The distinction is usually made between a person who intends to commit a crime and one who does not. If the police provide the former with an opportunity to commit a criminal act—the sale of drugs to an undercover agent, for example—there is no defense of entrapment. But if the police knock on the door of one not known to be a drug user and persist in a demand that he purchase drugs from them, finally overcoming his will to resist, a conviction for purchase and possession of drugs can be overturned on the ground of entrapment.

entrapment

When a police officer or other government agent entices people to commit crimes they were not disposed to commit without the government agent's suggestions and inducements.

Other Excuses

A number of other circumstances can limit or excuse criminal liability. These include compulsion (a gun pointed at one's head by a masked man who apparently is unafraid to use the weapon and who demands that you help him rob a store), honest consent of the "victim" (the quarterback who is tackled), adherence to the requirements of legitimate public authority lawfully exercised (a policeman directs a towing company to remove a car parked in a tow-away zone), the proper exercise of domestic authority (a parent may spank a child, within limits), and defense of self, others, property, and habitation. Each of these excuses is a complex subject in itself.

Lack of Capacity

A further defense to criminal prosecution is the lack of mental capacity to commit the crime. Infants and children are considered incapable of committing a crime; under common law any child under the age of seven could not be prosecuted for any act. That age of incapacity varies from state to state and is now usually defined by statutes. Likewise, insanity or mental disease or defect can be a complete defense. Intoxication can be a defense to certain crimes, but the mere fact of drunkenness is not ordinarily sufficient.

Key Takeaway

In the United States, some crimes can be committed by not following strict regulatory requirements for health, safety, or the environment. The law does provide excuses from criminal liability for mistakes of fact, entrapment, and lack of capacity.

Exercises

1. Describe several situations in which compulsion, consent, or other excuses take away criminal liability.
2. Your employee is drunk on the job and commits the crime of assault and battery on a customer. He claims lack of capacity as an excuse. Should the courts accept this excuse? Why or why not?

6.5 Procedure

Learning Objectives

1. Describe the basic steps in pretrial criminal procedure that follow a government's determination to arrest someone for an alleged criminal act.
2. Describe the basic elements of trial and posttrial criminal procedure.

The procedure for criminal prosecutions is complex. Procedures will vary from state to state. A criminal case begins with an arrest if the defendant is caught in the act or fleeing from the scene; if the defendant is not caught, a warrant for the defendant's arrest will issue. The warrant is issued by a judge or a magistrate upon receiving a complaint detailing the charge of a specific crime against the accused. It is not enough for a police officer to go before a judge and say, "I'd like you to arrest Bonnie because I think she's just murdered Clyde." She must supply enough information to satisfy the magistrate that there is probable cause (reasonable grounds) to believe that the accused committed the crime. The warrant will be issued to any officer or agency that has power to arrest the accused with warrant in hand.

The accused will be brought before the magistrate for a preliminary hearing. The purpose of the hearing is to determine whether there is sufficient reason to hold the accused for trial. If so, the accused can be sent to jail or be permitted to make bail. Bail is a sum of money paid to the court to secure the defendant's attendance at trial. If he fails to appear, he forfeits the money. Constitutionally, bail can be withheld only if there is reason to believe that the accused will flee the jurisdiction.

Once the arrest is made, the case is in the hands of the prosecutor. In the fifty states, prosecution is a function of the district attorney's office. These offices are usually organized on a county-by-county basis. In the federal system, criminal prosecution is handled by the office of the US attorney, one of whom is appointed for every federal district.

Following the preliminary hearing, the prosecutor must either file an **information** (a document stating the crime of which the person being held is accused) or ask the **grand jury** for an **indictment**. The grand jury consists of twenty-three people who sit to determine whether there is sufficient evidence to warrant a prosecution. It does not sit to determine guilt or innocence. The indictment is the grand jury's formal declaration of charges on which the accused will be tried. If indicted, the accused formally becomes a defendant.

The defendant will then be arraigned, that is, brought before a judge to answer the accusation in the indictment. The defendant may plead guilty or not guilty. If he pleads not guilty, the case will be tried before a jury (sometimes referred to as a petit jury). The jury cannot convict unless it finds the defendant guilty **beyond a reasonable doubt**.

The defendant might have pleaded guilty to the offense or to a lesser charge (often referred to as a "lesser included offense"—simple larceny, for example, is a lesser included offense of robbery because the defendant may not have used violence but nevertheless stole from the victim). Such a plea is usually arranged through **plea bargaining** with the prosecution. In return for the plea, the prosecutor promises to recommend to the judge that the sentence be limited. The judge most often, but not always, goes along with the prosecutor's recommendation.

The defendant is also permitted to file a plea of nolo contendere (no contest) in prosecutions for certain crimes. In so doing, he neither affirms nor denies his guilt. He may be sentenced as though he had pleaded guilty, although usually a nolo plea is the result of a plea bargain. Why plead nolo? In some offenses, such as violations of the antitrust laws, the statutes provide that private plaintiffs may use a conviction or a guilty plea as proof that the defendant violated the law. This enables a plaintiff to prove liability without putting on witnesses or evidence and reduces the civil trial to a hearing about the damages to plaintiff. The nolo plea permits the defendant to avoid this, so that any plaintiff will have to not only prove damages but also establish civil liability.

Following a guilty plea or a verdict of guilt, the judge will impose a sentence after presentencing reports are written by various court officials (often, probation officers). Permissible sentences are spelled out in statutes, though these frequently give the judge a range within which to work (e.g., twenty years to life). The judge may sentence the defendant to imprisonment, a fine, or both, or may decide to suspend sentence (i.e., the defendant will not have to serve the sentence as long as he stays out of trouble).

Sentencing usually comes before appeal. As in civil cases, the defendant, now convicted, has the right to take at least one appeal to higher courts, where issues of procedure and constitutional rights may be argued.

information

A formal charge that a less serious crime has been committed.

grand jury

A group of citizens that hear the state's evidence and determine whether a reasonable basis (probable cause) exists for believing that a crime has been committed and thus that a criminal proceeding should be brought against a defendant.

indictment

A formal charge that a serious crime has been committed; where a grand jury is convened, an indictment may issue if probable cause is found.

beyond a reasonable doubt

The prosecutor must prove how each element of the offense charged is "beyond a reasonable doubt."

plea bargaining

A defendant's plea of guilty, given in exchange for a recommendation from the prosecutor to the judge for a limited or lesser sentence for the defendant.

Key Takeaway

Criminal procedure in US courts is designed to provide a fair process to both criminal defendants and to society. The grand jury system, prosecutorial discretion, plea bargains, and appeals for lack of a fair trial are all part of US criminal procedure.

Exercises

1. Harold is charged with the crime of assault with a deadly weapon with intent to kill or inflict serious bodily injury. It is a more serious crime than simple assault. Harold's attorney wants the prosecutor to give Harold a break, but Harold is guilty of at least simple assault and may also have had the intent to kill. What is Harold's attorney likely to do?
2. Kumar was driving his car, smoking marijuana, and had an accident with another vehicle. The other driver was slightly injured. When the officer arrived, she detected a strong odor of marijuana in Kumar's car and a small amount of marijuana in the glove compartment. The other driver expects to bring a civil action against Kumar for her injuries after Kumar's crim-

inal case. What should Kumar plead in the criminal case—careless driving or driving under the influence?

6.6 Constitutional Rights of the Accused

Learning Objectives

1. Describe the most significant constitutional rights of defendants in US courts, and name the source of these rights.
2. Explain the Exclusionary rule and the reason for its existence.

Search and Seizure

The rights of those accused of a crime are spelled out in four of the ten constitutional amendments that make up the Bill of Rights (Amendments Four, Five, Six, and Eight). For the most part, these amendments have been held to apply to both the federal and the state governments. The Fourth Amendment says in part that "the right of the people to be secure in their persons, houses, papers, and effects, against unreasonable searches and seizures, shall not be violated." Although there are numerous and tricky exceptions to the general rule, ordinarily the police may not break into a person's house or confiscate his papers or arrest him unless they have a warrant to do so. This means, for instance, that a policeman cannot simply stop you on a street corner and ask to see what is in your pockets (a power the police enjoy in many other countries), nor can your home be raided without probable cause to believe that you have committed a crime. What if the police do search or seize unreasonably?

exclusionary rule

Evidence obtained in violation of constitutional rights from the Fourth, Fifth, and Sixth Amendments are generally not admissible at trial.

The courts have devised a remedy for the use at trial of the fruits of an unlawful search or seizure. Evidence that is unconstitutionally seized is excluded from the trial. This is the so-called exclusionary rule, first made applicable in federal cases in 1914 and brought home to the states in 1961. The **exclusionary rule** is highly controversial, and there are numerous exceptions to it. But it remains generally true that the prosecutor may not use evidence willfully taken by the police in violation of constitutional rights generally, and most often in the violation of Fourth Amendment rights. (The fruits of a coerced confession are also excluded.)

Double Jeopardy

The Fifth Amendment prohibits the government from prosecuting a person twice for the same offense. The amendment says that no person shall be "subject for the same offence to be twice put in jeopardy of life or limb." If a defendant is acquitted, the government may not appeal. If a defendant is convicted and his conviction is upheld on appeal, he may not thereafter be reprosecuted for the same crime.

Self-Incrimination

The Fifth Amendment is also the source of a person's right against self-incrimination (no person "shall be compelled in any criminal case to be a witness against himself"). The debate over the limits of this right has given rise to an immense literature. In broadest outline, the right against self-incrimination means that the prosecutor may not call a defendant to the witness stand during trial and may not comment to the jury on the defendant's failure to take the stand. Moreover, a defendant's confession must be excluded from evidence if it was not voluntarily made (e.g., if the police beat the person into giving a confession). In *Miranda v. Arizona*, the Supreme Court ruled that no confession is admissible if the police have not first advised a suspect of his constitutional rights, including the right to have a lawyer present to advise him during the questioning.[3] These so-called Miranda warnings have prompted scores of follow-up cases that have made this branch of jurisprudence especially complex.

Speedy Trial

The Sixth Amendment tells the government that it must try defendants speedily. How long a delay is too long depends on the circumstances in each case. In 1975, Congress enacted the Speedy Trial Act to give priority to criminal cases in federal courts. It requires all criminal prosecutions to go to trial within seventy-five days (though the law lists many permissible reasons for delay).

Cross-Examination

The Sixth Amendment also says that the defendant shall have the right to confront witnesses against him. No testimony is permitted to be shown to the jury unless the person making it is present and subject to cross-examination by the defendant's counsel.

Assistance of Counsel

The Sixth Amendment guarantees criminal defendants the right to have the assistance of defense counsel. During the eighteenth century and before, the British courts frequently refused to permit defendants to have lawyers in the courtroom during trial. The right to counsel is much broader in this country, as the result of Supreme Court decisions that require the state to pay for a lawyer for indigent defendants in most criminal cases.

Cruel and Unusual Punishment

Punishment under the common law was frequently horrifying. Death was a common punishment for relatively minor crimes. In many places throughout the world, punishments still persist that seem cruel and unusual, such as the practice of stoning someone to death. The guillotine, famously in use during and after the French Revolution, is no longer used, nor are defendants put in stocks for public display and humiliation. In pre-Revolutionary America, an unlucky defendant who found himself convicted could face brutal torture before death.

The Eighth Amendment banned these actions with the words that "cruel and unusual punishments [shall not be] inflicted." Virtually all such punishments either never were enacted or have been eliminated from the statute books in the United States. Nevertheless, the Eighth Amendment has become a source of controversy, first with the Supreme Court's ruling in 1976 that the death penalty, as haphazardly applied in the various states, amounted to cruel and unusual punishment. Later Supreme Court opinions have made it easier for states to administer the death penalty. As of 2010, there were 3,300 defendants on death row in the United States. Of course, no corporation is on death row, and no corporation's charter has ever been revoked by a US state, even though some corporations have repeatedly been indicted and convicted of criminal offenses.

Presumption of Innocence

The most important constitutional right in the US criminal justice system is the presumption of innocence. The Supreme Court has repeatedly cautioned lower courts in the United States that juries must be properly instructed that the defendant is innocent until proven guilty. This is the origin of the "beyond all reasonable doubt" standard of proof and is an instruction given to juries in each criminal case. The Fifth Amendment notes the right of "due process" in federal proceedings, and the Fourteenth Amendment requires that each state provide "due process" to defendants.

Key Takeaway

The US Constitution provides several important protections for criminal defendants, including a prohibition on the use of evidence that has been obtained by unconstitutional means. This would include evidence seized in violation of the Fourth Amendment and confessions obtained in violation of the Fifth Amendment.

Exercises

1. Do you think it is useful to have a presumption of innocence in criminal cases? What if there were not a presumption of innocence in criminal cases?
2. Do you think public humiliation, public execution, and unusual punishments would reduce the amount of crime? Why do you think so?
3. "Due process" is another phrase for "fairness." Why should the public show fairness toward criminal defendants?

6.7 Cases

False Pretenses

State v. Mills

96 Ariz. 377, 396 P.2d 5 (Ariz. 1964)

LOCKWOOD, VICE CHIEF JUSTICE

Defendants appeal from a conviction on two counts of obtaining money by false pretenses in violation of AR.S. §§ 13-661.A3. and 13-663.A1. The material facts, viewed "...in the light most favorable to sustaining the conviction," are as follows: Defendant William Mills was a builder and owned approximately 150 homes in Tucson in December, 1960. Mills conducted his business in his home. In 1960 defendant Winifred Mills, his wife, participated in the business generally by answering the telephone, typing, and receiving clients who came to the office.

In December 1960, Mills showed the complainant, Nathan Pivowar, a house at 1155 Knox Drive and another at 1210 Easy Street, and asked Pivowar if he would loan money on the Knox Drive house. Pivowar did not indicate at that time whether he would agree to such a transaction. Later in the same month Nathan Pivowar told the defendants that he and his brother, Joe Pivowar, would loan $5,000 and $4,000 on the two houses. Three or four days later Mrs. Mills, at Pivowar's request, showed him these homes again.

Mills had prepared two typed mortgages for Pivowar. Pivowar objected to the wording, so in Mills' office Mrs. Mills retyped the mortgages under Pivowar's dictation. After the mortgages had been recorded on December 31, 1960, Pivowar gave Mills a bank check for $5,791.87 [about $48,000 in 2017 dollars], some cash, and a second mortgage formerly obtained from Mills in the approximate sum of $3,000. In exchange Mills gave Pivowar two personal notes in the sums of $5,250.00 and $4,200.00 and the two mortgages as security for the loan.

Although the due date for Mills' personal notes passed without payment being made, the complainant did not present the notes for payment, did not demand that they be paid, and did not sue upon them. In 1962 the complainant learned that the mortgages which he had taken as security in the transaction were not first mortgages on the Knox Drive and Easy Street properties. These mortgages actually covered two vacant lots on which there were outstanding senior mortgages. On learning this, Pivowar signed a complaint charging the defendants with the crime of theft by false pretenses.

On appeal defendants contend that the trial court erred in denying their motion to dismiss the information. They urge that a permanent taking of property must be proved in order to establish the crime of theft. Since the complainant had the right to sue on the defendants' notes, the defendants assert that complainant cannot be said to have been deprived of his property permanently. Defendants misconceive the elements of the crime of theft by false pretenses. Stated in a different form, their argument is that although the complainant has parted with his cash, a bank check, and a second mortgage, the defendants intend to repay the loan.

Defendants admit that the proposition of law which they assert is a novel one in this jurisdiction. Respectable authority in other states persuades us that their contention is without merit. A creditor has a right to determine for himself whether he wishes to be a secured or an unsecured creditor. In the former case, he has a right to know about the security. If he extends credit in reliance upon security which is falsely represented to be adequate, he has been defrauded even if the debtor intends to repay the debt. His position is now that of an unsecured creditor. At the very least, an unreasonable risk of loss has been forced upon him by reason of the deceit. This risk which he did not intend to assume has been imposed upon him by the intentional act of the debtor, and such action constitutes an intent to defraud. * * *

* * *

The cases cited by defendants in support of their contention are distinguishable from the instant case in that they involved theft by larceny. Since the crime of larceny is designed to protect a person's possessory interest in property whereas the crime of false pretenses protects one's title interest, the requirement of a permanent deprivation is appropriate to the former. Accordingly, we hold that an intent to repay a loan obtained on the basis of a false representation of the security for the loan is no defense.

* * *

Affirmed in part, reversed in part, and remanded for resentencing.

Case Questions

1. False pretenses is a crime of obtaining ownership of property of another by making untrue representations of fact with intent to defraud. What were the untrue representations of fact made by Mills?
2. Concisely state the defendant's argument as to why Pivowar has not been deprived of any property.
3. If Pivowar had presented the notes and Mills had paid, would a crime have been committed?

White-Collar Crimes

United States v. Park
421 U.S. 658 (1975)

MR. CHIEF JUSTICE BURGER delivered the opinion of the Court.

We granted certiorari to consider whether the jury instructions in the prosecution of a corporate officer under § 301 (k) of the Federal Food, Drug, and Cosmetic Act, 52 Stat. 1042, as amended, 21 U.S.C. § 331 (k), were appropriate under *United States v. Dotterweich*, 320 U.S. 277 (1943). Acme Markets, Inc., is a national retail food chain with approximately 36,000 employees, 874 retail outlets, 12 general warehouses, and four special warehouses. Its headquarters, including the office of the president, respondent Park, who is chief executive officer of the corporation, are located in Philadelphia, Pennsylvania. In a five-count information filed in the United States District Court for the District of Maryland, the Government charged Acme and respondent with violations of the Federal Food, Drug, and Cosmetic Act. Each count of the information alleged that the defendants had received food that had been shipped in interstate commerce and that, while the food was being held for sale in Acme's Baltimore warehouse following shipment in interstate commerce, they caused it to be held in a building accessible to rodents and to be exposed to contamination by rodents. These acts were alleged to have resulted in the food's being adulterated within the meaning of 21 U.S.C. §§ 342 * * *, in violation of 21 U.S.C. § 331 (k).

Acme pleaded guilty to each count of the information. Respondent pleaded not guilty. The evidence at trial demonstrated that in April 1970 the Food and Drug Administration (FDA) advised respondent by letter of insanitary conditions in Acme's Philadelphia warehouse. In 1971 the FDA found that similar conditions existed in the firm's Baltimore warehouse. An FDA consumer safety officer testified concerning evidence of rodent infestation and other insanitary conditions discovered during a 12-day inspection of the Baltimore warehouse in November and December 1971. He also related that a second inspection of the warehouse had been conducted in March 1972. On that occasion the inspectors found that there had been improvement in the sanitary conditions, but that "there was still evidence of rodent activity in the building and in the warehouses and we found some rodent-contaminated lots of food items."

The Government also presented testimony by the Chief of Compliance of the FDA's Baltimore office, who informed respondent by letter of the conditions at the Baltimore warehouse after the first inspection. There was testimony by Acme's Baltimore division vice president, who had responded to the letter on behalf of Acme and respondent and who described the steps taken to remedy the insanitary conditions discovered by both inspections. The Government's final witness, Acme's vice president for legal affairs and assistant secretary, identified respondent as the president and chief executive officer of the company and read a bylaw prescribing the duties of the chief executive officer. He testified that respondent functioned by delegating "normal operating duties" including sanitation, but that he retained "certain things, which are the big, broad, principles of the operation of the company and had "the responsibility of seeing that they all work together."

At the close of the Government's case in chief, respondent moved for a judgment of acquittal on the ground that "the evidence in chief has shown that Mr. Park is not personally concerned in this Food and Drug violation." The trial judge denied the motion, stating that *United States v. Dotterweich*, 320 U.S. 277 (1943), was controlling.

Respondent was the only defense witness. He testified that, although all of Acme's employees were in a sense under his general direction, the company had an "organizational structure for responsibilities for certain functions" according to which different phases of its operation were "assigned to individuals who, in turn, have staff and departments under them." He identified those individuals responsible for sanitation, and related that upon receipt of the January 1972 FDA letter, he had conferred with the vice president for legal affairs, who informed him that the Baltimore division vice president "was investigating the situation immediately and would be taking corrective action and would be preparing a summary of the corrective action to reply to the letter." Respondent stated that he did not "believe there was anything [he] could have done more constructively than what [he] found was being done."

On cross-examination, respondent conceded that providing sanitary conditions for food offered for sale to the public was something that he was "responsible for in the entire operation of the company" and he stated that it was one of many phases of the company that he assigned to "dependable subordinates." Respondent was asked about and, over the objections of his counsel, admitted receiving, the April 1970 letter addressed to him from the FDA regarding insanitary conditions at Acme's Philadelphia warehouse. He acknowledged that, with the exception of the division vice president, the same individuals had responsibility for sanitation in both Baltimore and Philadelphia. Finally, in response to questions concerning the Philadelphia and Baltimore incidents, respondent admitted that the Baltimore problem indicated the system for handling sanitation "wasn't working perfectly" and that as Acme's chief executive officer he was "responsible for any result which occurs in our company."

At the close of the evidence, respondent's renewed motion for a judgment of acquittal was denied. The relevant portion of the trial judge's instructions to the jury challenged by respondent is set out in the margin. Respondent's counsel objected to the instructions on the ground that they failed fairly to reflect our decision in *United States v. Dotterweich supra*, and to define "'responsible relationship.'" The trial judge overruled the objection. The jury found respondent guilty on all counts of the information, and he was subsequently sentenced to pay a fine of $50 on each count. The Court of Appeals reversed the conviction and remanded for a new trial. * * *

The question presented by the Government's petition for certiorari in *United States v. Dotterweich*, and the focus of this Court's opinion, was whether the manager of a corporation, as well as the corporation itself, may be prosecuted under the Federal Food, Drug, and Cosmetic Act of 1938 for the introduction of misbranded and adulterated articles into interstate commerce. In *Dotterweich*, a jury had disagreed as to the corporation, a jobber purchasing drugs from manufacturers and shipping them in interstate commerce under its own label, but had convicted Dotterweich, the corporation's president and general manager. The Court of Appeals reversed the conviction on the ground that only the drug dealer, whether corporation or individual, was subject to the criminal provisions of the Act, and that where the dealer was a corporation, an individual connected therewith might be held personally only if he was operating the corporation as his 'alter ego.'

In reversing the judgment of the Court of Appeals and reinstating Dotterweich's conviction, this Court looked to the purposes of the Act and noted that they "touch phases of the lives and health of people which, in the circumstances of modern industrialism, are largely beyond self-protection. It observed that the Act is of "a now familiar type" which "dispenses with the conventional requirement for criminal conduct-awareness of some wrongdoing: In the interest of the larger good it puts the burden of acting at hazard upon a person otherwise innocent but standing in responsible relation to a public danger. Central to the Court's conclusion that individuals other than proprietors are subject to the criminal provisions of the Act was the reality that the only way in which a corporation can act is through the individuals, who act on its behalf.

The Court recognized that, because the Act dispenses with the need to prove "consciousness of wrongdoing," it may result in hardship even as applied to those who share "responsibility in the business process resulting in" a violation....The rule that corporate employees who have "a responsible share in the furtherance of the transaction which the statute outlaws" are subject to the criminal provisions of the Act was not formulated in a vacuum. Cf. *Morissette v. United States*, 342 U.S. 246, 258 (1952). Cases under the Federal Food and Drugs Act of 1906 reflected the view both that knowledge or intent were not required to be proved in prosecutions under its criminal provisions, and that responsible corporate agents could be subjected to the liability thereby imposed. * * *

The rationale of the interpretation given the Act in *Dotterweich*...has been confirmed in our subsequent cases. Thus, the Court has reaffirmed the proposition that the public interest in the purity of its food is so great as to warrant the imposition of the highest standard of care on distributors.

Thus *Dotterweich* and the cases which have followed reveal that in providing sanctions which reach and touch the individuals who execute the corporate mission—and this is by no means necessarily confined to a single corporate agent or employee—the Act imposes not only a positive duty to seek out and remedy violations when they occur but also, and primarily, a duty to implement measures that will insure that violations will not occur. The requirements of foresight and vigilance imposed on responsible corporate agents are beyond question demanding, and perhaps onerous, but they are no more stringent than the public has a right to expect of those who voluntarily assume positions of authority in business enterprises whose services and products affect the health and well-being of the public that supports them. * * *

* * *

Reading the entire charge satisfies us that the jury's attention was adequately focused on the issue of respondent's authority with respect to the conditions that formed the basis of the alleged violations. Viewed as a whole, the charge did not permit the jury to find guilt solely on the basis of respondent's position in the corporation; rather, it fairly advised the jury that to find guilt it must find respondent "had a responsible relation to the situation," and "by virtue of his position...had...authority and responsibility" to deal with the situation.

The situation referred to could only be "food...held in unsanitary conditions in a warehouse with the result that it consisted, in part, of filth or...may have been contaminated with filth."

Our conclusion that the Court of Appeals erred in its reading of the jury charge suggests as well our disagreement with that court concerning the admissibility of evidence demonstrating that respondent was advised by the FDA in 1970 of insanitary conditions in Acme's Philadelphia warehouse. We are satisfied that the Act imposes the highest standard of care and permits conviction of responsible corporate officials who, in light of this standard of care, have the power to prevent or correct violations of its provisions. * * *

Reversed.

Case Questions

1. Did Park have criminal intent to put adulterated food into commerce? If not, how can Park's conduct be criminalized?
2. To get a conviction, what does the prosecutor have to show, other than that Park was the CEO of Acme and therefore responsible for what his company did or didn't do?

6.8 Summary and Exercises

Summary

Criminal law is that branch of law governing offenses against society. Most criminal law requires a specific intent to commit the prohibited act (although a very few economic acts, made criminal by modern legislation, dispense with the requirement of intent). In this way, criminal law differs from much of civil law—for example, from the tort of negligence, in which carelessness, rather than intent, can result in liability.

Major crimes are known as felonies. Minor crimes are known as misdemeanors. Most people have a general notion about familiar crimes, such as murder and theft. But conventional knowledge does not suffice for understanding technical distinctions among related crimes, such as larceny, robbery, and false pretenses. These distinctions can be important because an individual can be found guilty not merely for committing one of the acts defined in the criminal law but also for attempting or conspiring to commit such an act. It is usually easier to convict someone of attempt or conspiracy than to convict for the main crime, and a person involved in a conspiracy to commit a felony may find that very little is required to put him into serious trouble.

Of major concern to the business executive is white-collar crime, which encompasses a host of offenses, including bribery, embezzlement, fraud, restraints of trade, and computer crime. Anyone accused of crime should know that they always have the right to consult with a lawyer and should always do so.

Exercises

1. Bill is the chief executive of a small computer manufacturing company that desperately needs funds to continue operating. One day a stranger comes to Bill to induce him to take part in a cocaine smuggling deal that would net Bill millions of dollars. Unbeknownst to Bill, the stranger is an undercover policeman. Bill tells the stranger to go away. The stranger persists, and after five months of arguing and cajoling, the stranger wears down Bill's will to resist. Bill agrees to take delivery of the cocaine and hands over a down payment of $10,000 to the undercover agent, who promptly arrests him for conspiracy to violate the narcotics laws. What defenses does Bill have?
2. You are the manager of a bookstore. A customer becomes irritated at having to stand in line and begins to shout at the salesclerk for refusing to wait on him. You come out of your office and ask the customer to calm down. He shouts at you. You tell him to leave. He refuses. So you and the salesclerk pick him up and shove him bodily out the door. He calls the police to have you arrested for assault. Should the police arrest you? Assuming that they do, how would you defend yourself in court?
3. Marilyn is arrested for arson against a nuclear utility, a crime under both state and federal law. She is convicted in state court and sentenced to five years in jail. Then the federal government decides to prosecute her for the same offense. Does she have a double-jeopardy defense against the federal prosecution?
4. Tectonics, a U.S. corporation, is bidding on a project in Nigeria, and its employee wins the bid by secretly giving $100,000 to the Nigerian public official that has the most say about which company will be awarded the contract. The contract is worth $80 million, and Tectonics expects to make at least $50 million on the project. Has a crime under U.S. law been committed?
5. Suppose that the CEO of Tectonics, Ted Nelson, is not actually involved in bribery of the Nigerian public official Adetutu Adeleke. Instead, suppose that the CFO, Jamie Skillset, is very accomplished at insulating both top management and the board of directors from some of the "operational realities" within the company. Skillset knows that Whoopi Goldmine, a Nigerian employee of Tectonics, has made the deal with Adeleke and secured the contract for Tectonics. Is it possible that Nelson, as well as Skillset, can be found guilty of a crime?

6. You have graduated from college and, after working hard for ten years, have scraped enough money together to make a down payment on a forty-acre farm within driving distance to the small city where you work in Colorado. In town at lunch one day, you run into an old friend from high school, Hayley Mills, who tells you that she is saving her money to start a high-end consignment shop in town. You allow her to have a room in your house for a few months until she has enough money to go into business. Over the following weeks, however, you realize that old acquaintances from high school are stopping by almost daily for short visits. When you bring this up to Hayley, she admits that many old friends are now relying on her for marijuana. She is not a licensed caregiver in Colorado and is clearly violating the law. Out of loyalty, you tell her that she has three weeks to move out, but you do not prevent her from continuing sales while she is there. What crime have you committed?
7. The Center Art Galleries—Hawaii sells artwork, and much of it involves art by the famous surrealist painter Salvador Dali. The federal government suspected the center of selling forged Dali artwork and obtained search warrants for six locations controlled by the center. The warrants told the executing officer to seize any items that were "evidence of violations of federal criminal law." The warrants did not describe the specific crime suspected, nor did the warrants limit the seizure of items solely to Dali artwork or suspected Dali forgeries. Are these search warrants valid?[4]

Self-Test Questions

1. Jared has made several loans to debtors who have declared bankruptcy. These are unsecured claims. Jared "doctors" the documentation to show amounts owed that are higher than the debtors actually owe. Later, Jared is charged with the federal criminal offense of filing false claims. The standard (or "burden") of proof that the US attorney must meet in the prosecution is
    a. beyond all doubt
    b. beyond a reasonable doubt
    c. clear and convincing evidence
    d. a preponderance of the evidence
2. Jethro, a businessman who resides in Atlanta, creates a disturbance at a local steakhouse and is arrested for being drunk and disorderly. Drunk and disorderly is a misdemeanor under Georgia law. A misdemeanor is a crime punishable by imprisonment for up to
    a. one year
    b. two years
    c. five years
    d. none of the above
3. Yuan is charged with a crime. To find him guilty, the prosecutor must show
    a. actus reus and mens rea
    b. mens rea only
    c. the performance of a prohibited act
    d. none of the above
4. Kira works for Data Systems Ltd. and may be liable for larceny if she steals
    a. a competitor's trade secrets
    b. company computer time
    c. the use of Data Systems' Internet for personal business
    d. any of the above
5. Candace is constructing a new office building that is near its completion. She offers Paul $500 to overlook certain things that are noncompliant with the city's construction code. Paul accepts the money and overlooks the violations. Later, Candace is charged with the crime of bribery. This occurred when

a. Candace offered the bribe.
b. Paul accepted the bribe.
c. Paul overlooked the violations.
d. none of the above

Self-Test Answers

1. b
2. a
3. a
4. d
5. a

Endnotes

1. *United States v. Isaacs*, 493 F.2d 1124 (7th Cir. 1974), cert. denied, 417 US 976 (1974).
2. *U.S. v. Hanousek*, 176 F.3d 1116 (9th Cir. 1999).
3. *Miranda v. Arizona*, 384 US 436 (1966).
4. *Center Art Galleries—Hawaii, Inc. v. United States*, 875 F.2d 747 (9th Cir. 1989).

CHAPTER 7

Introduction to Tort Law

Learning Objectives

After reading this chapter, you should be able to do the following:

1. Know why most legal systems have tort law.
2. Identify the three kinds of torts.
3. Explain how tort law relates to criminal law and contract law.
4. Understand negligent torts and defenses to claims of negligence.
5. Understand strict liability torts and the reasons for them in the US legal system.

In U.S. civil litigation, contract and tort claims are by far the most numerous. The law tries to compensate for harms done to individuals and firms by awarding damages to plaintiffs who can demonstrate that the defendant was the cause of the plaintiff's losses. Torts can be intentional torts, negligent torts, or strict liability torts. Employers must be aware that in many circumstances, their employees may create liability in tort. This chapter explains the different kind of torts, as well as available defenses to tort claims.

7.1 Purpose of Tort Laws

Learning Objectives

1. Explain why a sound market system requires tort law.
2. Define a tort and give two examples.
3. Explain the moral basis of tort liability.
4. Understand the purposes of damage awards in tort.

Definition of *Tort*

The term *tort* is the French equivalent of the English word *wrong*. The word *tort* is also derived from the Latin word *tortum*, which means twisted, crooked, or wrong, in contrast to the word *rectum*, which means straight (*rectitude* uses that Latin root). Thus, conduct that is not straight ("twisted" or "crooked") is a tort. The term was introduced into the English law by the Norman jurists from France. Roman Law and subsequently European law ("civil" or "continental" law) recognized "torts" as actionable in public courts.

Long ago, *tort* was used in everyday speech; today it is left to the legal system. A judge will instruct a jury that a tort is usually defined as a wrong for which the law will provide a remedy, most often in the form of money damages. The law does not remedy all "wrongs." There are wrongs in the moral sphere that are not remedied in the legal sphere. For example, the law will not provide a remedy for saying something false and cruel to someone directly, while it may provide a remedy for "defaming" someone (saying something false about them, orally or in writing).

Although the word is no longer in general use, tort suits are the stuff of everyday headlines. More and more people injured by exposure to a variety of risks now seek "redress" (that is, some sort of remedy through the courts). Headlines boast of multi-million dollar jury awards against doctors who bungled operations, against newspapers and other media that have libeled people or invaded their privacy, and against oil companies that devastate entire ecosystems. All are examples of tort suits.

The law of torts developed almost entirely in the common-law courts; that is, plaintiffs would rely on the common law (judicial decisions) rather than statutes passed by legislatures. Through contracts, individuals can craft their own rights and responsibilities toward each other. Over many years, the courts have fashioned a series of rules that govern the conduct of individuals in their non-contractual dealings with each other. In the absence of contracts, tort law holds individuals legally accountable for the consequences of their actions. Those who suffer losses at the hands of others can be compensated.

Many acts (like homicide) are both criminal and tortious. But torts and crimes are different. A crime is an act against society as a whole. In a criminal case, society punishes the murderer; it does not usually compensate the family of the homicide victim. In contrast, tort law views the death as a private wrong for which damages are owed. In a civil case, the tort victim or his family, not the state, brings the action. The judgment against a defendant in a civil tort suit is usually expressed in monetary terms, not in terms of prison times or fines, and is the legal system's way of trying to make up for the victim's loss.

Kinds of Torts

There are three kinds of torts: intentional torts, negligent torts, and strict liability torts. Intentional torts arise from intentional acts, whereas unintentional torts often result from carelessness (e.g., when you are momentarily distracted with a cellphone text message and rear-end a car that has suddenly stopped in front of you). Both intentional torts and negligent torts imply some kind of fault on the part of the defendant. In strict liability torts, by contrast, there may be no fault at all, but the law will sometimes require a defendant to make up for the victim's losses even where the defendant was not careless and did not intend to do harm.

Dimensions of Tort Liability

There is a clear moral basis for recovery through the legal system where the defendant has been careless (negligent) or has intentionally caused harm. Using the concepts that we are free and autonomous beings with basic rights, we can see that when others interfere with either our freedom or our autonomy, we will usually react negatively. As the old saying goes, "Your right to swing your arm ends at the tip of my nose." The law takes this even one step further: under intentional tort law, if you frighten someone by swinging your arms toward the tip of her nose, you may have committed the tort of assault, even if there is no actual touching (battery).

Under a capitalist market system, rational economic rules also call for a minimum amount of negative externalities, and preferably none. That is, actions of individuals, either alone or in concert with others, should not negatively impact innocent, non-participating third parties. The law will try to compensate third parties who are harmed by your actions, even as it knows that money judgments most often cannot fully mend badly injured victims.

FIGURE 7.1 Dimensions of Tort Liability

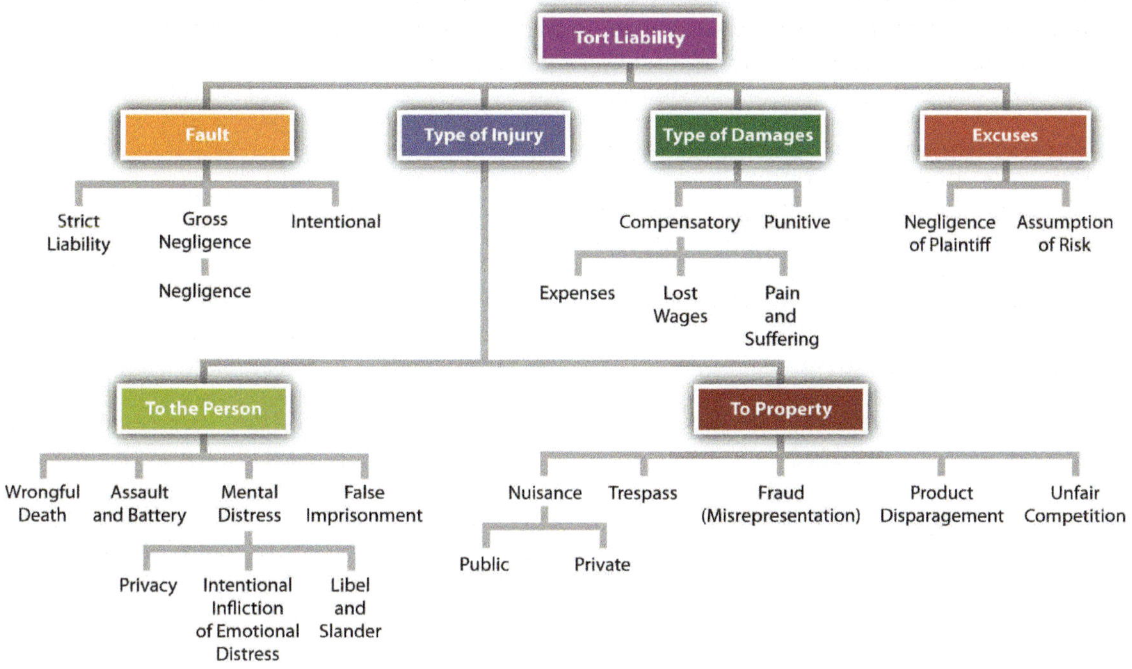

Dimensions of Tort: Fault

Tort principles can be viewed along different dimensions. One is the **fault** dimension. Like criminal law, tort law requires a wrongful act by a defendant for the plaintiff to recover. Unlike criminal law, however, there need not be a specific intent. Since tort law focuses on injury to the plaintiff, it is less concerned than criminal law about either the reasons for the defendant's actions or his mental state. An innocent act or a relatively innocent one may still provide the basis for liability. Nevertheless, tort law—except for strict liability—relies on standards of fault, or blameworthiness.

The most obvious standard is willful conduct. If the defendant (often called the **tortfeasor**—i.e., the one committing the tort) intentionally injures another, there is little argument about tort liability. Thus all crimes resulting in injury to a person or property (murder, assault, arson, etc.) are also torts, and the plaintiff may bring a separate lawsuit to recover damages for injuries to his person, family, or property.

tortfeasor

A person or legal entity that commits a tort.

Most tort suits do not rely on *intentional* fault. They are instead based on negligent conduct that, under the circumstances, is careless or poses unreasonable risks of causing damage. Most automobile accident and medical malpractice suits are examples of negligence suits.

The fault dimension is a continuum. At one end is the deliberate desire to do injury. The middle ground is occupied by careless conduct. At the other end is conduct that most would consider morally blameless. The defendant may have observed all possible precautions and yet still be held liable. This is called **strict liability**. An example is that incurred by the manufacturer of a defective product that is placed on the market despite all possible precautions, including quality-control inspection. In many states, if the product causes injury, the manufacturer will be held liable.

strict liability

Liability without fault. This may arise when the defendant engages in ultrahazardous activities or where defective product creates an unreasonable risk of injury to consumers or others.

Dimensions of Tort: Nature of Injury

Tort liability varies by the type of injury caused. The most obvious type is physical harm to the person (assault, battery, infliction of emotional distress, negligent exposure to toxic pollutants, wrongful death) or property (trespass, nuisance, arson, interference with contract). Mental suffering can be redressed if it is a result of physical injury (e.g., shock and depression following an automobile accident). A few states now permit recovery for mental distress alone (a mother's shock at seeing her son injured by a car while both were crossing the street). Other protected interests include a person's reputation (injured by defamatory statements or writings), privacy (injured by those who divulge secrets of his personal life), and economic interests (misrepresentation to secure an economic advantage, certain forms of unfair competition).

Dimensions of Tort: Excuses

A third element in the law of torts is the excuse for committing an apparent wrong. The law does not condemn every act that ultimately results in injury.

assumption of risk

A defense to a plaintiff's action in tort where the plaintiff has knowingly and voluntarily entered into a risky activity that results in injury.

One common rule of exculpation is **assumption of risk**. A baseball fan who sits along the third base line close to the infield assumes the risk that a sizzling line drive foul ball may strike him. He will not be permitted to complain in court that the batter should have been more careful or that management should have either warned him or put up a protective barrier. (This is the traditional rule; some baseball stadiums, however, are putting up additional protective nets beyond the net directly behind home plate.)

Another excuse is negligence of the plaintiff. If two drivers are careless and hit each other on the highway, some states will refuse to permit either to recover from the other. Still another excuse is consent: two boxers in the ring presumably consent to being struck with fists (but not to being bitten on the ear or kicked in the groin).

Damages

compensatory damages

An award of money damages to make the plaintiff whole, as opposed to additional damages (punitive) that punish the defendant or make an example of defendant.

punitive damages

Punitive damages are awarded in cases where the conduct of the defendant is deemed to be so outrageous that justice is only served by adding a penalty over and above compensatory damages.

Since the purpose of tort law is to compensate the victim for harm actually done, damages are usually measured by the extent of the injury. Expressed in money terms, these include replacement of property destroyed, compensation for lost wages, reimbursement for medical expenses, and dollars that are supposed to approximate the pain that is suffered. Damages for these injuries are called **compensatory damages**.

In certain instances, the courts will permit an award of **punitive damages**. As the word *punitive* implies, the purpose is to punish the defendant's actions. Because a punitive award (sometimes called exemplary damages) is at odds with the general purpose of tort law, it is allowable only in aggravated situations. The law in most states permits recovery of punitive damages only when the defendant has deliberately committed a wrong with malicious intent or has otherwise done something outrageous.

Punitive damages are rarely allowed in negligence cases for that reason. But if someone sets out intentionally and maliciously to hurt another person, punitive damages may be appropriate. Punitive damages are intended not only to punish the wrongdoer, by exacting an additional and sometimes heavy payment (the exact amount is left to the discretion of jury and judge), but also to deter others from similar conduct. The punitive damage award has been subject to heavy criticism in recent years, especially in cases in which it has been awarded against manufacturers and retailers. One fear is that huge damage awards on behalf of a multitude of victims could swiftly bankrupt the defendant. Unlike compensatory damages, punitive damages are taxable.

Key Takeaway

There are three kinds of torts, and in two of them (negligent torts and strict liability torts), damages are usually limited to making the victim whole through an enforceable judgment for money damages. These compensatory damages awarded by a court accomplish only approximate justice for the injuries or property damage caused by a tortfeasor. Tort laws go a step further toward deterrence, beyond compensation to the plaintiff, in occasionally awarding punitive damages against a defendant. These are almost always in cases where an intentional tort has been committed.

Exercises

1. Why is deterrence needed for intentional torts (where punitive damages are awarded) rather than negligent torts?
2. Why are costs imposed on others without their consent a problem for a market economy? What if the law did not try to reimpose the victim's costs onto the tortfeasor?

7.2 Intentional Torts

Learning Objectives

1. Distinguish intentional torts from other kinds of torts.
2. Give three examples of an intentional tort—one that causes injury to a person, one that causes injury to property, and one that causes injury to a reputation.

The analysis of most intentional torts is straightforward and parallels the substantive crimes already discussed in Chapter 6. When physical injury or damage to property is caused, there is rarely debate over liability if the plaintiff deliberately undertook to produce the harm. Certain other intentional torts are worth noting for their relevance to business.

Assault and Battery

One of the most obvious intentional torts is assault and battery. Both criminal law and tort law serve to restrain individuals from using physical force on others. Assault is (1) the threat of immediate harm or offense of contact or (2) any act that would arouse reasonable apprehension of imminent harm. Battery is unauthorized and harmful or offensive physical contact with another person that causes injury.

Often an assault results in battery, but not always. In *Western Union Telegraph Co. v. Hill*, for example, the defendant did not touch the plaintiff's wife, but the case presented an issue of possible assault even without an actual battery; the defendant employee attempted to kiss a customer across the countertop, couldn't quite reach her, but nonetheless created actionable fear (or, as the court put it, "apprehension") on the part of the plaintiff's wife. It is also possible to have a battery without an assault. For example, if someone hits you on the back of the head with a skateboard and you didn't see it coming, there is a battery but no assault. Likewise, if Andrea passes out from drinking too much at the fraternity party and a stranger (Andre) kisses her on the lips while she is passed out, she would not be aware of any threat of offensive contact and would have no apprehension of any harm. But even if there has been no assault, she could allege the tort of battery. (The question of what damages might be awarded, if any, might be an interesting argument.)

Under the doctrine of transferred intent, if Draco aims his wand at Harry but Harry ducks just in time and the impact is felt by Hermione instead, English law (and American law) would transfer Draco's intent from the target to the actual victim of the act. Thus Hermione could sue Draco for battery for any damages she had suffered.

False Imprisonment

The tort of false imprisonment originally implied a locking up, as in a prison, but today it can occur if a person is restrained in a room or a car or even if his or her movements are restricted while walking down the street. People have a right to be free to go as they please, and anyone who without cause deprives another of personal freedom has committed a tort. Damages are allowed for time lost, discomfort and resulting ill health, mental suffering, humiliation, loss of reputation or business, and expenses such as attorneys' fees incurred as a result of the restraint (such as a false arrest). But as the case of *Lester v. Albers Super Markets, Inc.* (Section 5) shows, the defendant must be shown to have restrained the plaintiff in order for damages to be allowed.

Intentional Infliction of Emotional Distress

Until recently, the common-law rule was that there could be no recovery for acts, even though intentionally undertaken, that caused purely mental or emotional distress. For a case to go to the jury, the courts required that the mental distress result from some physical injury. In recent years, many courts have overthrown the older rule and now recognize the so-called new tort. In an employment context, however, it is rare to find a case where a plaintiff is able to recover. The most difficult hurdle is proving that the conduct was "extreme" or "outrageous."

In an early California case, bill collectors came to the debtor's home repeatedly and threatened the debtor's pregnant wife. Among other things, they claimed that the wife would have to deliver her child in prison. The wife miscarried and had emotional and physical complications. The court found that the behavior of the collection company's two agents was sufficiently outrageous to prove the tort of intentional infliction of emotional distress. In *Roche v. Stern* (New York), the famous cable television talk show host Howard Stern had tastelessly discussed the remains of Deborah Roche, a topless dancer and cable access television host.[1] The remains had been brought to Stern's show by a close friend of Roche, Chaunce Hayden, and a number of crude comments by Stern and Hayden about the remains were videotaped and broadcast on a national cable television station. Roche's sister and brother sued Howard Stern and Infinity broadcasting and were able to get past the defendant's motion to dismiss so that a jury could consider their claim.

A plaintiff's burden in these cases is to show that the mental distress is severe. Many states require that this distress must result in physical symptoms such as nausea, headaches, ulcers, or, as in the case of the pregnant wife, a miscarriage. Other states have not required physical symptoms, finding that shame, embarrassment, fear, and anger constitute severe mental distress. Freedom of speech, as protected in the First Amendment, can create interesting conflicts between tort law and Constitutional law. *Hustler* magazine printed a false advertisement showing Reverend Jerry Falwell, describing him as having lost his virginity to his mother in an outhouse while he was drunk. Suing for intentional infliction of emotional distress, he won at the trial court, but the Supreme Court overturned, holding that parodies of public figures was protected under the First Amendment.[2] The "public figure" standard also applies to defamation lawsuits. See *N.Y. Times v. Sullivan*, infra.)

Trespass and Nuisance

Trespass is intentionally going on land that belongs to someone else or putting something on someone else's property and refusing to remove it. This part of tort law shows how strongly the law values the rights of property owners. The right to enjoy your property without interference from others is also found in common law of nuisance. There are limits to property owners' rights, however. In *Katko v. Briney*, for example, the plaintiff was injured by a spring gun while trespassing on the defendant's property.[3] The defendant had set up No Trespassing signs after ten years of trespassing and housebreaking events, with the loss of some household items. Windows had been broken, and there was "messing up of the property in general." The defendants had boarded up the windows and doors in order to stop the intrusions and finally had set up a shotgun trap in the north bedroom of the house. One defendant had cleaned and oiled his 20-gauge shotgun and taken it to the old house where it was secured to an iron bed with the barrel pointed at the bedroom door. "It was rigged with wire from the doorknob to the gun's trigger so would fire when the door was opened." The angle of the shotgun was adjusted to hit an intruder in the legs. The spring could not be seen from the outside, and no warning of its presence was posted.

The plaintiff, Katko, had been hunting in the area for several years and considered the property abandoned. He knew it had long been uninhabited. He and a friend had been to the house and found several old bottles and fruit jars that they took and added to their collection of antiques. When they made a second trip to the property, they entered by removing a board from a porch window. When the plaintiff opened the north bedroom door, the shotgun went off and struck him in the right leg above the ankle bone. Much of his leg was blown away. While Katko knew he had no right to break and enter the house with intent to steal bottles and fruit jars, the court held that a property owner could not protect an unoccupied boarded-up farmhouse by using a spring gun capable of inflicting death or serious injury.

In *Katko*, there is an intentional tort. But what if someone who is trespassing is injured by the negligence of the landowner? States have differing rules about trespass and negligence. In some states, a trespasser is only protected against the gross negligence of the landowner. In other states, trespassers may be owed the duty of due care on the part of the landowner. The burglar who falls into a drained swimming pool, for example, may have a case against the homeowner unless the courts or legislature of that state have made it clear that trespassers are owed only the limited duty to avoid gross negligence. Or a very small child may wander off his own property and fall into a gravel pit on a nearby property and suffer death or serious injury; if the owner of the gravel pit (in the exercise of due care) should have filled in the pit or had some barrier erected around it, then there was negligence. But if the state law holds that the duty to trespassers is only to avoid gross negligence, the child's family would lose, unless the state law makes an exception for very young trespassers. In general, guests, licensees, and invitees are owed a duty of due care; a trespasser may not be owed such a duty, but states have different rules on this.

Intentional Interference with Contractual Relations

Tortious interference with a contract can be established by proving four elements:

1. There was a contract between the plaintiff and a third party.
2. The defendant knew of the contract.
3. The defendant improperly induced the third party to breach the contract or made performance of the contract impossible.
4. There was injury to the plaintiff.

In a famous case of contract interference, Texaco was sued by Pennzoil for interfering with an agreement that Pennzoil had with Getty Oil. After complicated negotiations between Pennzoil and Getty, a takeover share price was struck, a memorandum of understanding was signed, and a press release announced the agreement in principle between Pennzoil and Getty. Texaco's lawyers, however, believed that Getty oil was "still in play," and before the lawyers for Pennzoil and Getty could complete the paperwork for their agreement, Texaco announced it was offering Getty shareholders an additional $12.50 per share over what Pennzoil had offered.

Texaco later increased its offer to $228 per share, and the Getty board of directors soon began dealing with Texaco instead of Pennzoil. Pennzoil decided to sue in Texas state court for tortious interference with a contract. After a long trial, the jury returned an enormous verdict against Texaco: $7.53 billion in actual damages and $3 billion in punitive damages. The verdict was so large that it would have bankrupted Texaco. Appeals from the verdict centered on an obscure rule of the Securities and Exchange Commission (SEC), Rule 10(b)-13, and Texaco's argument was based on that rule and the fact that the contract had not been completed. If there was no contract, Texaco could not have legally interfered with one. After the SEC filed a brief that supported Texaco's interpretation of the law, Texaco agreed to pay $3 billion to Pennzoil to dismiss its claim of tortious interference with a contract.

Malicious Prosecution

Malicious prosecution is the tort of causing someone to be prosecuted for a criminal act, knowing that there was no probable cause to believe that the plaintiff committed the crime. The plaintiff must show that the defendant acted with malice or with some purpose other than bringing the guilty to justice. A mere complaint to the authorities is insufficient to establish the tort, but any official proceeding will support the claim—for example, a warrant for the plaintiff's arrest. The criminal proceeding must terminate in the plaintiff's favor in order for his suit to be sustained.

A related cause of action if for **abuse of process**. A majority of U.S. courts permit a suit for wrongful civil proceedings. Civil litigation is usually costly and burdensome, and someone who forces another to defend himself against baseless accusations should not be permitted to impose the costs of defending against such accusation. But because civil litigation is a socially favored way to vindicate legal rights, a plaintiff in an abuse of process case must meet a heavy burden. The mere dismissal of the original lawsuit against the plaintiff is not sufficient proof that the suit was unwarranted. The plaintiff in a suit for wrongful civil proceedings must show that the defendant (who was the plaintiff in the original suit) filed the action for an improper purpose and had no reasonable belief that his cause was legally or factually well grounded.

However, because, as a matter of public policy, litigation is favored as the means by which legal rights can be vindicated—indeed, the Supreme Court has even ruled that individuals have a constitutional right to litigate—the plaintiff must meet a heavy burden in proving his case. The mere dismissal of the original lawsuit against the plaintiff is not sufficient proof that the suit was unwarranted. The plaintiff in a suit for wrongful civil proceedings must show that the defendant (who was the plaintiff in the original suit) filed the action for an improper purpose and had no reasonable belief that his cause was legally or factually well grounded.

Conversion and Fraud

Conversion

Taking or using someone else's personal property without their consent.

Conversion is the taking or using of someone else's property without their consent. Personal property is discussed in detail in Chapter 31. But in brief, personal property is any tangible or intangible thing that is not a physical structure, such as a house or building ("real property"), and is not attached to real property. Priya's cellphone, Justin's backpack, or even your roommate's six pack that was left in the refrigerator—all of these are personal property that can be "converted." Conversion is the tort counterpart to the crime of theft. But recall that with any tort, proving a criminal intent to permanently deprive the owner of the use and possession of her personal property is not required. The person converting may intend only to "borrow" the item before losing or damaging it.

In practice, the one whose property is stolen or borrowed is unlikely to bring an action for conversion unless the item is one of considerable value. The costs of hiring an attorney would likely exceed the value of many items of personal property. But note that personal property can be intangible as well: software codes, designs, customer lists, trade secrets, and intellectual property (copyrights, trademarks, and patents) can all be taken and used by others, depriving the owner of exclusive use. (See Chapter 32, Intellectual Property).

Fraud is a tortious injury to another by deliberate deception. Fraud is actionable in civil courts for a variety of misrepresentations, without the need to demonstrate criminal "mens rea" or criminal intent. The types of fraud are as varied as human nature. Phony checks, online misrepresentations, phone solicitations for free cruises to the Bahamas, organizations that pretend to be charities but aren't, Ponzi schemes (such as chain letters), and many more. Securities fraud—a particularly important aspect of how law deals with fraud—will be covered in Chapter 46.

Defamation

Defamation is injury to a person's good name or reputation. In general, if the harm is done through the spoken word—one person to another, by telephone, by radio, or on television—it is called slander. If the defamatory statement is published in written form, it is called libel.

The Restatement (Second) of Torts defines a defamatory communication as one that "so tends to harm the reputation of another as to lower him in the estimation of the community or to deter third persons from associating or dealing with him."[4]

A statement is not defamatory unless it is false. Truth is an absolute defense to a charge of libel or slander. Moreover, the statement must be "published"—that is, communicated to a third person. You cannot be libeled by one who sends you a letter full of false accusations and scurrilous statements about you unless a third person opens it first (your roommate, perhaps). Any living person is capable of being defamed, but the dead are not. Corporations, partnerships, and other forms of associations can also be defamed, if the statements tend to injure their ability to do business or to garner contributions.

The statement must have reference to a particular person, but he or she need not be identified by name. A statement that "the company president is a crook" is defamatory, as is a statement that "the major network weathermen are imposters." The company president and the network weathermen could show that the words were aimed at them. But statements about large groups will not support an action for defamation (e.g., "all doctors are butchers" is not defamatory of any particular doctor).

The law of defamation is largely built on strict liability. That a person did not intend to defame is ordinarily no excuse; a typographical error that converts a true statement into a false one in a newspaper, magazine, or corporate brochure can be sufficient to make out a case of libel. Even the exercise of due care is usually no excuse if the statement is in fact communicated. Repeating a libel is itself a libel; a libel cannot be justified by showing that you were quoting someone else. Though a plaintiff may be able to prove that a statement was defamatory, he is not necessarily entitled to an award of damages. That is because the law contains a number of privileges that excuse the defamation.

Publishing false information about another business's product constitutes the tort of slander of quality, or trade libel. In some states, this is known as the tort of product disparagement. It may be difficult to establish damages, however. A plaintiff must prove that actual damages proximately resulted from the slander of quality and must show the extent of the economic harm as well.

Absolute Privilege

Statements made during the course of judicial proceedings are absolutely privileged, meaning that they cannot serve as the basis for a defamation suit. Accurate accounts of judicial or other proceedings are absolutely privileged; a newspaper, for example, may pass on the slanderous comments of a judge in court. "Judicial" is broadly construed to include most proceedings of administrative bodies of the government. The Constitution exempts members of Congress from suits for libel or slander for any statements made in connection with legislative business. The courts have constructed a similar privilege for many executive branch officials.

Qualified Privilege

Absolute privileges pertain to those in the public sector. A narrower privilege exists for private citizens. In general, a statement that would otherwise be actionable is held to be justified if made in a reasonable manner and for a reasonable purpose. Thus, you may warn a friend to beware of dealing with a third person, and if you had reason to believe that what you said was true, you are privileged to issue the warning, even though false. Likewise, an employee may warn an employer about the conduct or character of a fellow or prospective employee, and a parent may complain to a school board about the competence or conduct of a child's teacher. Although many employers fear to give accurate accounts of their experiences with ex-employees to other employers, they do have a qualified privilege if the statements are made in good faith and the publication is limited to those who have a legitimate interest in the communications. There is a line to be drawn, however, and a defendant with nothing but an idle interest in the matter must take the risk that his information is wrong.

public figures

Based on the First Amendment of the US Constitution, a public figure cannot recover in a defamation case unless the plaintiff's defamation was done with actual malice.

The "public figure" exception as a kind of qualified privilege is by now well established. In 1964, the Supreme Court handed down its historic decision in *New York Times v. Sullivan*, holding that under the First Amendment a libel judgment brought by a public official against a newspaper cannot stand unless the plaintiff has shown "actual malice," which in turn was defined as "knowledge that [the statement] was false or with a reckless disregard of whether it was false or not."[5] In subsequent cases, the court extended the constitutional doctrine further, applying it not merely to government officials but to **public figures**, people who voluntarily place themselves in the public eye or who involuntarily find themselves the objects of public scrutiny. This would include politicians, entertainers, professional athletes, and others who are in the public eye. Whether a private person is or is not a public figure is a difficult question that has so far eluded rigorous definition and has been answered only from case to case. A CEO of a private corporation ordinarily will be considered a private figure unless he puts himself in the public eye—for example, by starring in the company's television commercials. Former Secretary of Labor Robert Reich labels himself as a "public figure" on his blog, and Kim Kardashian is a public figure because of her desire to put herself in the public eye.

Invasion of Privacy

The right of privacy—the right "to be let alone"—did not receive judicial recognition until the twentieth century, and its legal formulation is still evolving. In fact there is no single right of privacy. Courts and commentators have discerned at least four different types of interests: (1) the right to control the appropriation of your name and picture for commercial purposes, (2) the right to be free of intrusion on your "personal space" or seclusion, (3) freedom from public disclosure of embarrassing and intimate facts of your personal life, and (4) the right not to be presented in a "false light."

Appropriation of Name or Likeness

The earliest privacy interest recognized by the courts was appropriation of name or likeness: someone else placing your photograph on a billboard or cereal box as a model or using your name as endorsing a product or in the product name. A New York statute makes it a misdemeanor to use the name, portrait, or picture of any person for advertising purposes or for the purposes of trade (business) without first obtaining written consent. The law also permits the aggrieved person to sue and to recover damages for unauthorized profits and also to have the court enjoin (judicially block) any further unauthorized use of the plaintiff's name, likeness, or image. This is particularly useful to celebrities.

Because the publishing and advertising industries are concentrated heavily in New York, the statute plays an important part in advertising decisions made throughout the country. Deciding what "commercial" or "trade" purposes are is not always easy. Thus a newsmagazine may use a baseball player's picture on its cover without first obtaining written permission, but a chocolate manufacturer could not put the player's picture on a candy wrapper without consent.

Personal Space

One form of intrusion upon a person's solitude—trespass—has long been actionable under common law. Physical invasion of home or other property is not a new tort. But in recent years, the notion of intrusion has been broadened considerably. Now, taking photos of someone else with your cell phone in a locker room could constitute invasion of the right to privacy. Reading someone else's mail or e-mail could also constitute an invasion of the right to privacy. Photographing someone on a city street is not tortious, but subsequent use of the photograph could be. Whether the invasion is in a public or private space, the amount of damages will depend on how the image or information is disclosed to others.

Public Disclosure of Embarrassing Facts

Circulation of false statements that do injury to a person are actionable under the laws of defamation. What about true statements that might be every bit as damaging—for example, disclosure of someone's income tax return, revealing how much he earned? The general rule is that if the facts are truly private and of no "legitimate" concern to the public, then their disclosure is a violation of the right to privacy. But a person who is in the public eye cannot claim the same protection.

Media companies now pay close attention to this aspect of privacy law. In a case against Gawker Media, Terry Gene Bollea (known generally by his professional wrestling name, "Hulk Hogan") sued for invasion of privacy and infliction of emotional distress when Gawker published 2 minutes of a 30-minute video showing consensual sexual acts by Hulk Hogan with the wife of radio personality "Bubba the Love Sponge." In March of 2016, a state jury awarded Bollea $115 million in damages, including $60 million for emotional distress and $25 million in punitive damages. While Gawker appealed the judgment and the amounts, it also filed for bankruptcy within three months.

False Light

A final type of privacy invasion is that which paints a false picture in a publication. Though false, it might not be libelous, since the publication need contain nothing injurious to reputation. Indeed, the publication might even glorify the plaintiff, making him seem more heroic than he actually is. Subject to the First Amendment requirement that the plaintiff must show intent or extreme recklessness, statements that put a person in a false light, like a fictionalized biography, are actionable.

Key Takeaway

There are many kinds of intentional torts. Some of them involve harm to the physical person or to his or her property, reputation or feelings, or economic interests. In each case of intentional tort, the plaintiff must show that the defendant intended harm, but the intent to harm does not need to be directed at a particular person and need not be malicious, as long as the resulting harm is a direct consequence of the defendant's actions.

Exercises

1. Name two kinds of intentional torts that could result in damage to a business firm's bottom line.
2. Name two kinds of intentional torts that are based on protection of a person's property.
3. Why are intentional torts more likely to result in a verdict not only for compensatory damages but also for punitive damages?

7.3 Negligence

Learning Objectives

1. Understand how the duty of due care relates to negligence.
2. Distinguish between actual and proximate cause.
3. Explain the primary defenses to a claim of negligence.

Elements of Negligence

Physical harm need not be intentionally caused. A pedestrian knocked over by an automobile does not hurt less because the driver intended no wrong but was merely careless. The law imposes a duty of care on all of us in our everyday lives. Accidents caused by negligence are actionable.

negligence

A breach of the duty of due care.

Determining **negligence** is not always easy. If a driver runs a red light, we can say that he is negligent because a driver must always be careful to ascertain whether the light is red and be able to stop if it is. Suppose that the driver was carrying a badly injured person to a nearby hospital and that after slowing down at an intersection, went through a red light, blowing his horn, whereupon a driver to his right, seeing him, drove into the intersection anyway and crashed into him. Must one always stop at a red light? Is proof that the light was red always proof of negligence? Usually, but not always: negligence is an abstract concept that must always be applied to concrete and often widely varying sets of circumstances. Whether someone was or was not negligent is almost always a question of fact for a jury to decide. Rarely is it a legal question that a judge can settle.

The tort of negligence has four elements: (1) a duty of due care that the defendant had, (2) the **breach of the duty of due care**, (3) connection between cause and injury, and (4) actual damage or loss. Even if a plaintiff can prove each of these aspects, the defendant may be able to show that the law excuses the conduct that is the basis for the tort claim. We examine each of these factors below.

breach of the duty of due care

Any act that fails to meet a standard of the person's duty of due care toward others. The standard is usually described as the standard of behavior that is expected of a hypothetical "reasonable person" under the circumstances. Certain professionals, however, may be held to a higher standard than the ordinary person.

Standard of Care

Not every unintentional act that causes injury is negligent. If you brake to a stop when you see a child dart out in front of your car, and if the noise from your tires gives someone in a nearby house a heart attack, you have not acted negligently toward the person in the house. The purpose of the negligence standard is to protect others against the risk of injury that would foreseeably ensue from unreasonably dangerous conduct.

Given the infinite variety of human circumstances and conduct, no general statement of a reasonable standard of care is possible. Nevertheless, the law has tried to encapsulate it in the form of the famous standard of "the reasonable person." This fictitious person "of ordinary prudence" is the model that juries are instructed to use in assessing whether those defendants have acted negligently. Analysis of this mythical personage has baffled several generations of commentators. How much knowledge must she have of events in the community, of technology, of cause and effect? With what physical attributes, courage, or wisdom is this nonexistent person supposedly endowed? If the defendant is a person with specialized knowledge, like a doctor or an automobile designer, must the jury also treat the "reasonable man" as having this knowledge, even though the average person in the community will not? (Answer: in most cases, yes.)

Despite the many difficulties, the concept of the reasonable person is one on which most negligence cases ultimately turn. If a defendant has acted "unreasonably under the circumstances" and his conduct posed an unreasonable risk of injury, then he is liable for injury caused by his conduct. Perhaps in most instances, it is not difficult to divine what the reasonable person would do. The reasonable person stops for traffic lights and always drives at reasonable speeds, does not throw baseballs through windows, performs surgical operations according to the average standards of the medical profession, ensures that the floors of his grocery store are kept free of fluids that would cause a patron to slip and fall, takes proper precautions to avoid spillage of oil from his supertanker, and so on. The "reasonable person" standard imposes hindsight on the decisions and actions of people in society; the circumstances of life are such that courts may sometimes impose a standard of due care that many people might not find reasonable.

Duty of Care and Its Breach

The law does not impose on us a duty to care for every person. If the rule were otherwise, we would all, in this interdependent world, be our brothers' keepers, constantly unsure whether any action we took might subject us to liability for its effect on someone else. The law copes with this difficulty by limiting the number of people toward whom we owe a duty to be careful.

In general, the law imposes no obligation to act in a situation to which we are strangers. We may pass the drowning child without risking a lawsuit. But if we do act, then the law requires us to act carefully. The law of negligence requires us to behave with due regard for the foreseeable consequences of our actions in order to avoid unreasonable risks of injury.

During the course of the twentieth century, the courts have constantly expanded the notion of "foreseeability," so that today many more people are held to be within the zone of injury than was once the case. For example, it was once believed that a manufacturer or supplier owed a duty of care only to immediate purchasers, not to others who might use the product or to whom the product might be resold. This limitation was known as the rule of privity. And users who were not immediate purchasers were said not to be in privity with a supplier or manufacturer. In 1916, Judge Benjamin N. Cardozo, then on the New York Court of Appeals, penned an opinion in a celebrated case that exploded the theory of privity, though it would take half a century before the last state—Mississippi in 1966—would fall in line.

Determining a duty of care can be a vexing problem. Physicians, for example, are bound by principles of medical ethics to respect the confidences of their patients. Suppose a patient tells a psychiatrist that he intends to kill his girlfriend. Does the physician then have a higher legal duty to warn prospective victim? The California Supreme Court has said yes.[6]

negligence per se

An act of the defendant that violates a statute regulation or ordinance can be used to establish a breach of the duty of due care.

Establishing a breach of the duty of due care where the defendant has violated a statute or municipal ordinance is eased considerably with the doctrine of **negligence per se**, a doctrine common to all US state courts. If a legislative body sets a minimum standard of care for particular kinds of acts to protect a certain set of people from harm and a violation of that standard causes harm to someone in that set, the defendant is negligent per se. If Harvey is driving sixty-five miles per hour in a fifty-five-mile-per-hour zone when he crashes into Haley's car and the police accident report establishes that or he otherwise admits to going ten miles per hour over the speed limit, Haley does not have to prove that Harvey has breached a duty of due care. She will only have to prove that the speeding was an actual and proximate cause of the collision and will also have to prove the extent of the resulting damages to her.

Causation: Actual Cause and Proximate Cause

actual cause (causation in fact)

The actual cause of negligence is sometimes called the "but for" event that is a breach of duty on the part of the defendant.

proximate cause

Sometimes known as legal cause, proximate cause must be shown as well as actual cause, so that an act of the defendant will not result in liability if the consequences of the negligent act are too remote or unforeseeable.

"For want of a nail, the kingdom was lost," as the old saying has it. Virtually any cause of an injury can be traced to some preceding cause. The problem for the law is to know when to draw the line between causes that are immediate and causes too remote for liability reasonably to be assigned to them. In tort theory, there are two kinds of causes that a plaintiff must prove: actual cause and proximate cause. **Actual cause (causation in fact)** can be found if the connection between the defendant's act and the plaintiff's injuries passes the "but for" test: if an injury would not have occurred "but for" the defendant's conduct, then the defendant is the cause of the injury. Still, this is not enough causation to create liability. The injuries to the plaintiff must also be foreseeable, or not "too remote," for the defendant's act to create liability. This is **proximate cause**: a cause that is not too remote or unforseeable.

Suppose that the person who was injured was not one whom a reasonable person could have expected to be harmed. Such a situation was presented in one of the most famous US tort cases, *Palsgraf v. Long Island Railroad* (Section 5), which was decided by Judge Benjamin Cardozo. Although Judge Cardozo persuaded four of his seven brethren to side with his position, the closeness of the case demonstrates the difficulty that unforeseeable consequences and unforeseeable plaintiffs present.

Damages

For a plaintiff to win a tort case, she must allege and prove that she was injured. The fear that she might be injured in the future is not a sufficient basis for a suit. This rule has proved troublesome in medical malpractice and industrial disease cases. A doctor's negligent act or a company's negligent exposure of a worker to some form of contamination might not become manifest in the body for years. In the meantime, the tort statute of limitations might have run out, barring the victim from suing at all. An increasing number of courts have eased the plaintiff's predicament by ruling that the statute of limitations does not begin to run until the victim discovers that she has been injured or contracted a disease.

The law allows an exception to the general rule that damages must be shown when the plaintiff stands in danger of immediate injury from a hazardous activity. If you discover your neighbor experimenting with explosives in his basement, you could bring suit to enjoin him from further experimentation, even though he has not yet blown up his house—and yours.

Problems of Proof

The plaintiff in a tort suit, as in any other, has the burden of proving his allegations.

He must show that the defendant took the actions complained of as negligent, demonstrate the circumstances that make the actions negligent, and prove the occurrence and extent of injury. Factual issues are for the jury to resolve. Since it is frequently difficult to make out the requisite proof, the law allows certain presumptions and rules of evidence that ease the plaintiff's task, on the ground that without them substantial injustice would be done. One important rule goes by the Latin phrase **res ipsa loquitur**, meaning "the thing speaks for itself." The best evidence is always the most direct evidence: an eyewitness account of the acts in question. But eyewitnesses are often unavailable, and in any event they frequently cannot testify directly to the reasonableness of someone's conduct, which inevitably can only be inferred from the circumstances.

res ipsa loquitur

Literally, "the thing speaks for itself." In tort cases, res ipsa loquitur creates a presumption that the defendant was negligent because he or she was in exclusive control of the situation and that the plaintiff would not have suffered injury but for someone's negligence. Res ipsa loquitur shifts the burden to the defendant to prove that he or she was not negligent.

In many cases, therefore, **circumstantial evidence** (evidence that is indirect) will be the only evidence or will constitute the bulk of the evidence. Circumstantial evidence can often be quite telling: though no one saw anyone leave the building, muddy footprints tracing a path along the sidewalk are fairly conclusive. Res ipsa loquitur is a rule of circumstantial evidence that permits the jury to draw an inference of negligence. A common statement of the rule is the following: "There must be reasonable evidence of negligence but where the thing is shown to be under the management of the defendant or his servants, and the accident is such as in the ordinary course of things does not happen if those who have the management use proper care, it affords reasonable evidence, in the absence of explanation by the defendants, that the accident arose from want of care."[7]

circumstantial evidence

Evidence that is not "direct" but that provides judges and juries with facts that tend to show legal liability.

If a barrel of flour rolls out of a factory window and hits someone, or a soda bottle explodes, or an airplane crashes, courts in every state permit juries to conclude, in the absence of contrary explanations by the defendants, that there was negligence. The plaintiff is not put to the impossible task of explaining precisely how the accident occurred. A defendant can always offer evidence that he acted reasonably—for example, that the flour barrel was securely fastened and that a bolt of lightning, for which he was not responsible, broke its bands, causing it to roll out the window. But testimony by the factory employees that they secured the barrel, in the absence of any further explanation, will not usually serve to rebut the inference. That the defendant was negligent does not conclude the inquiry or automatically entitle the plaintiff to a judgment. Tort law provides the defendant with several excuses, some of which are discussed briefly in the next section.

Excuses

There are more excuses (defenses) than are listed here, but contributory negligence or comparative negligence, assumption of risk, and act of God are among the principal defenses that will completely or partially excuse the negligence of the defendant.

Contributory and Comparative Negligence

contributory negligence

Actions of a plaintiff that contribute to his or her own injuries. In a few states, comparative negligence is a complete bar to the plaintiff's recovery.

comparative negligence

In most states, the negligence of the plaintiff is weighed against the negligence of the defendant, and where the defendant's negligence outweighs the plaintiff's, the plaintiff can recover against the defendant even though the plaintiff has caused some of his or her own injuries.

At common law, it was ordinarily a complete defense to show that the plaintiff in a negligence suit was himself negligent. Even if the plaintiff was only a little bit negligent, with most of the fault being chargeable to the defendant, the court would dismiss the suit if the plaintiff's conduct contributed to his injury. In a few states today, this rule of **contributory negligence** is still in effect. This rule operated to defeat many claims where the defendant's negligence greatly outweighed the plaintiff's, and most states, either by statute or judicial decision, have changed to some version of **comparative negligence**. Under the rule of comparative negligence, damages are apportioned according to the defendant's degree of culpability. For example, if the plaintiff has sustained a $100,000 injury, and the defendant is 80% responsible and the plaintiff is 20 percent responsible in the jury's formal estimation, the defendant will be liable for $80,000 in damages. In a state where contributory negligence remains the operative doctrine, the plaintiff's negligence will cause her to lose the case and recover nothing.

Assumption of Risk

Risk of injury pervades the modern world, and plaintiffs should not win a lawsuit simply because they took a risk and lost. The law provides, therefore, that when a person knowingly takes a risk, he or she must suffer the consequences.

The assumption of risk doctrine comes up in three ways. The plaintiff may have formally agreed with the defendant before entering a risky situation that he will relieve the defendant of liability should injury occur. ("You can borrow my car if you agree not to sue me if the brakes fail, because they're worn and I haven't had a chance to replace them.") Or the plaintiff may have entered into a relationship with the defendant knowing that the defendant is not in a position to protect him from known risks (the fan who is hit by a line drive in a baseball park). Or the plaintiff may act in the face of a risky situation known in advance to have been created by the defendant's negligence (getting into an automobile when the driver is known to be drunk).

The difficulty in many cases is to determine what the injured party knew or should have known. If the plaintiff had no actual knowledge of the risk, he cannot be held to have assumed it. On the other hand, it is easy to claim that you did not appreciate the danger, and the courts will apply an objective standard of community knowledge in some situations (a test more like "but you should have known"). But when the plaintiff has no real alternative, assumption of risk fails as a defense (e.g., a landlord who negligently fails to light the exit to the street cannot claim that his tenants assumed the risk of using it).

At the turn of the century, courts applied assumption of risk in industrial cases to bar relief to workers injured on the job. They were said to assume the risk of dangerous conditions or equipment. This rule has been abolished by workers' compensation statutes in most states.

Act of God

Technically, the rule that no one is responsible for an "act of God," or *force majeure* as it is sometimes called, is not an excuse but a defense premised on a lack of causation. If a force of nature caused the harm, then the defendant was not negligent in the first place. A marina, obligated to look after boats moored at its dock, is not liable if a sudden and fierce storm against which no precaution was possible destroys someone's vessel. However, if it is foreseeable that harm will flow from a negligent condition triggered by a natural event, then there is liability. For example, a work crew failed to remove residue explosive gas from an oil barge. Lightning hit the barge, exploded the gas, and injured several workmen. The plaintiff recovered damages against the company because the negligence consisted in the failure to guard against any one of a number of chance occurrences that could ignite the gas.[8]

Vicarious Liability

Liability for negligent acts does not always end with the one who was negligent. Under certain circumstances, the liability is imputed to others. For example, an employer is responsible for the negligence of his employees if they were acting in the scope of employment. This rule of vicarious liability is often called *respondeat superior*, meaning that the higher authority must respond to claims brought against one of its agents. *Respondeat superior* is not limited to the employment relationship but extends to a number of other agency relationships as well.

Legislatures in many states have enacted laws that make people vicariously liable for acts of certain people with whom they have a relationship, though not necessarily one of agency. It is common, for example, for the owner of an automobile to be liable for the negligence of one to whom the owner lends the car. So-called dram shop statutes place liability on bar and tavern owners and others who serve too much alcohol to one who, in an intoxicated state, later causes injury to others. In these situations, although the injurious act of the drinker stemmed from negligence, the one whom the law holds vicariously liable (the bartender) is not himself necessarily negligent—the law is holding him *strictly liable*, and to this concept we now turn.

Key Takeaway

The most common tort claim is based on the negligence of the defendant. In each negligence claim, the plaintiff must establish by a preponderance of the evidence that (1) the defendant had a duty of due care, (2) the defendant breached that duty, (3) that the breach of duty both actually and approximately has caused harm to the plaintiff, and (4) that the harm is measurable in money damages.

It is also possible for the negligence of one person to be imputed to another, as in the case of respondeat superior, or in the case of someone who loans his automobile to another driver who is negligent and causes injury. There are many excuses (defenses) to claims of negligence, including assumption of risk and comparative negligence. In those few jurisdictions where contributory negligence has not been modified to comparative negligence, plaintiffs whose negligence contributes to their own injuries will be barred from any recovery.

Exercises

1. Explain the difference between comparative negligence and contributory negligence.
2. How is actual cause different from probable cause?
3. What is an example of assumption of risk?
4. How does res ipsa loquitur help a plaintiff establish a case of negligence?

7.4 Strict Liability

Learning Objectives

1. Understand how strict liability torts differ from negligent torts.
2. Understand the historical origins of strict liability under common law.

3. Be able to apply strict liability concepts to liability for defective products.
4. Distinguish strict liability from absolute liability, and understand the major defenses to a lawsuit in products-liability cases.

Historical Basis of Strict Liability: Animals and Ultrahazardous Activities

To this point, we have considered principles of liability that in some sense depend upon the "fault" of the tortfeasor. This fault does not always imply serious moral blame, especially with negligence lawsuits, but some moral blame is part and parcel of intentional torts. There is, however, no ascription of moral blame where "strict liability" torts are involved. The earliest examples of strict liability at common law involved animals; an owner of any animal that escaped from its pastures and caused damage to neighboring property may be liable, even if the reason for their escape was beyond the power of the owner to stop (e.g., a fire started by lightning that burns open a barn door). Another well-established common law principle is that those who engage in ultrahazardous (sometimes termed "abnormally dangerous") activities are liable for damage that they cause, even though they have taken every possible precaution to avoid harm to others.

In such cases, the courts invoke the principle of strict liability, or, as it is sometimes called, liability without fault. The reason for the rule is explained in *Klein v. Pyrodyne Corporation* (Section 5).

Strict Liability for Products

Because of the importance of products liability, this text devotes an entire chapter to it (Chapter 20). Strict liability may also apply as a legal standard for products, even those that are not ultrahazardous. In some national legal systems, strict liability is not available as a cause of action to plaintiffs seeking to recover a judgment of products liability against a manufacturer, wholesaler, distributor, or retailer. (Some states limit liability to the manufacturer.) But it is available in the United States and initially was created by a California Supreme Court decision in the 1962 case of *Greenman v. Yuba Power Products, Inc.*

In *Greenman*, the plaintiff had used a home power saw and bench, the Shopsmith, designed and manufactured by the defendant. He was experienced in using power tools and was injured while using the approved lathe attachment to the Shopsmith to fashion a wooden chalice. The case was decided on the premise that Greenman had done nothing wrong in using the machine but that the machine had a defect that was "latent" (not easily discoverable by the consumer). Rather than decide the case based on warranties, or requiring that Greenman prove how the defendant had been negligent, Justice Traynor found for the plaintiff based on the overall social utility of strict liability in cases of defective products. According to his decision, the purpose of such liability is to ensure that the "cost of injuries resulting from defective products is borne by the manufacturers...rather than by the injured persons who are powerless to protect themselves."

Today, the majority of US states recognize strict liability for defective products, although some states limit strict liability actions to damages for personal injuries rather than property damage. Injured plaintiffs have to prove the product caused the harm but do not have to prove exactly how the manufacturer was careless. Purchasers of the product, as well as injured guests, bystanders, and others with no direct relationship with the product, may sue for damages caused by the product.

The Restatement of the Law of Torts, Section 402(a), was originally issued in 1964. It is a widely accepted statement of the liabilities of sellers of goods for defective products. The Restatement specifies six requirements, all of which must be met for a plaintiff to recover using strict liability for a product that the plaintiff claims is defective:

1. The product must be in a defective condition when the defendant sells it.
2. The defendant must normally be engaged in the business of selling or otherwise distributing the product.
3. The product must be unreasonably dangerous to the user or consumer because of its defective condition.
4. The plaintiff must incur physical harm to self or to property by using or consuming the product.
5. The defective condition must be the proximate cause of the injury or damage.
6. The goods must not have been substantially changed from the time the product was sold to the time the injury was sustained.

Section 402(a) also explicitly makes clear that a defendant can be held liable even though the defendant has exercised "all possible care." Thus in a strict liability case, the plaintiff does not need to show "fault" (or negligence).

For defendants, who can include manufacturers, distributors, processors, assemblers, packagers, bottlers, retailers, and wholesalers, there are a number of defenses that are available, including assumption of risk, product misuse and comparative negligence, commonly known dangers, and the knowledgeable-user defense. We have already seen assumption of risk and comparative negligence in terms of negligence actions; the application of these is similar in products-liability actions.

Under product misuse, a plaintiff who uses a product in an unexpected and unusual way will not recover for injuries caused by such misuse. For example, suppose that someone uses a rotary lawn mower to trim a hedge and that after twenty minutes of such use loses control because of its weight and suffers serious cuts to his abdomen after dropping it. Here, there would be a defense of product misuse, as well as contributory negligence. Consider the urban (or Internet) legend of Merv Grazinski, who supposedly put his Winnebago on autopilot to go back and make coffee in the kitchen, and then recovered millions after his Winnebago turned over and he suffered serious injuries. There are multiple defenses to this alleged action; these would include the defenses of contributory negligence, comparative negligence, and product misuse. (There was never any such case, and certainly no such recovery; it is not known who started this legend, or why.)

Another defense against strict liability as a cause of action is the knowledgeable user defense. If the parents of obese teenagers bring a lawsuit against McDonald's, claiming that its fast-food products are defective and that McDonald's should have warned customers of the adverse health effects of eating its products, a defense based on the knowledgeable user is available. In one case, the court found that the high levels of cholesterol, fat, salt, and sugar in McDonald's food is well known to users. The court stated, "If consumers know (or reasonably should know) the potential ill health effects of eating at McDonald's, they cannot blame McDonald's if they, nonetheless, choose to satiate their appetite with a surfeit of supersized McDonald's products."[9]

Key Takeaway

Common-law courts have long held that certain activities are inherently dangerous and that those who cause damage to others by engaging in those activities will be held strictly liable. More recently, courts in the United States have applied strict liability to defective products. Strict liability, however, is not absolute liability, as there are many defenses available to defendants in lawsuits based on strict liability, such as comparative negligence and product abuse.

Exercises

1. Someone says, "Strict liability means that you're liable for whatever you make, no matter what the consumer does with your product. It's a crazy system." Respond to and refute this statement.
2. What is the essential difference between strict liability torts and negligent torts? Should the U.S. legal system even allow strict liability torts? What reasons seem persuasive to you?

7.5 Cases

Intentional Torts: False Imprisonment

Lester v. Albers Super Markets, Inc.

94 Ohio App. 313, 114 N.E.2d 529 (Ohio 1952)

Facts: The plaintiff, carrying a bag of rolls purchased at another store, entered the defendant's grocery store to buy some canned fruit. Seeing her bus outside, she stepped out of line and put the can on the counter. The store manager intercepted her and repeatedly demanded that she submit the bag to be searched. Finally she acquiesced; he looked inside and said she could go. She testified that several people witnessed the scene, which lasted about fifteen minutes, and that she was humiliated. The jury awarded her $800 [about $7400 in 2017 dollars[. She also testified that no one laid a hand on her or made a move to restrain her from leaving by any one of numerous exits. * * *

MATTHEWS, JUDGE.

As we view the record, it raises the fundamental question of what is imprisonment. Before any need for a determination of illegality arises there must be proof of imprisonment. In [a legal encyclopedia], it is said: "Submission to the mere verbal direction of another, unaccompanied by force or by threats of any character, cannot constitute a false imprisonment, and there is no false imprisonment where an employer interviewing an employee declines to terminate the interview if no force or threat of force is used and false imprisonment may not be predicated on a person's unfounded belief that he was restrained."

Many cases are cited in support of the text. * * *

In *Fenn v. Kroger Grocery & Baking Co.*, Mo. Sup., 209 S.W. 885, 887, the court said:

> *A case was not made out for false arrest. The plaintiff said she was intercepted as she started to leave the store; that Mr. Krause stood where she could not pass him in going out. She does not say that he made any attempt to intercept her. She says he escorted her back to the desk, that he asked her to let him see the change.*
>
> *...She does not say that she went unwillingly...Evidence is wholly lacking to show that she was detained by force or threats. It was probably a disagreeable experience, a humiliating one to her, but she came out victorious and was allowed to go when she desired with the assurance of Mr. Krause that it was all right. The demurrer to the evidence on both counts was properly sustained.*

The result of the cases is epitomized in [a legal encyclopedia], as follows:

> *A customer or patron who apparently has not paid for what he has received may be detained for a reasonable time to investigate the circumstances, but upon payment of the demand, he has the unqualified right to leave the premises without restraint, so far as the proprietor is concerned, and it is false imprisonment for a private individual to detain one for an unreasonable time, or under unreasonable circumstances, for the purpose of investigating a dispute over the payment of a bill alleged to be owed by the person detained for cash services.* * * *

* * *

For these reasons, the judgment is reversed and final judgment entered for the defendant-appellant.

Case Questions

1. The court begins by saying what false imprisonment is not. What is the legal definition of false imprisonment?
2. What kinds of detention are permissible for a store to use in accosting those that may have been shoplifting?
3. Jody broke up with Jeremy and refused to talk to him. Jeremy saw Jody get into her car near the business school and parked right behind her so she could not move. He then stood next to the driver's window for fifteen minutes, begging Jody to talk to him. She kept saying, "No, let me leave!" Has Jeremy committed the tort of false imprisonment?

Negligence: Duty of Due Care

> *Whitlock v. University of Denver*
>
> *744 P.2d 54 (Supreme Court of Colorado, 1987)*

On June 19, 1978, at approximately 10:00 p.m., plaintiff Oscar Whitlock suffered a paralyzing injury while attempting to complete a one-and-three-quarters front flip on a trampoline. The injury rendered him a quadriplegic. The trampoline was owned by the Beta Theta Pi fraternity (the Beta house) and was situated on the front yard of the fraternity premises, located on the University campus. At the time of his injury, Whitlock was twenty years old, attended the University of Denver, and was a member of the Beta house, where he held the office of acting house manager. The property on which the Beta house was located was leased to the local chapter house association of the Beta Theta Pi fraternity by the defendant University of Denver.

Whitlock had extensive experience jumping on trampolines. He began using trampolines in junior high school and continued to do so during his brief tenure as a cadet at the United States Military Academy at West Point, where he learned to execute the one-and-three-quarters front flip. Whitlock testified that he utilized the trampoline at West Point every other day for a period of two months. He began jumping on the trampoline owned by the Beta house in September of 1977. Whitlock recounted that in the fall and spring prior to the date of his injury, he jumped on the trampoline almost daily. He testified further that prior to the date of his injury, he had successfully executed the one-and-three-quarters front flip between seventy-five and one hundred times.

During the evening of June 18 and early morning of June 19, 1978, Whitlock attended a party at the Beta house, where he drank beer, vodka and scotch until 2:00 a.m. Whitlock then retired and did not awaken until 2:00 p.m. on June 19. He testified that he jumped on the trampoline between 2:00 p.m. and 4:00 p.m., and again at 7:00 p.m. At 10:00 p.m., the time of the injury, there again was a party in progress at the Beta house, and Whitlock was using the trampoline with only the illumination from the windows of the fraternity house, the outside light above the front door of the house, and two street lights in the area. As Whitlock attempted to perform the one-and-three-quarters front flip, he landed on the back of his head, causing his neck to break.

Whitlock brought suit against the manufacturer and seller of the trampoline, the University, the Beta Theta Pi fraternity and its local chapter, and certain individuals in their capacities as representatives of the Beta Theta Pi organizations. Whitlock reached settlements with all of the named defendants except the University, so only the negligence action against the University proceeded to trial. The jury returned a verdict in favor of Whitlock, assessing his total damages at $ 7,300,000 [about $25 million in 2017 dollars]. The jury attributed twenty-eight percent of causal negligence to the conduct of Whitlock and seventy-two percent of causal negligence to the conduct of the University. The trial court accordingly reduced the amount of the award against the University to $ 5,256,000 [about $17 million in 2017 dollars].

The University moved for judgment notwithstanding the verdict, or, in the alternative, a new trial. The trial court granted the motion for judgment notwithstanding the verdict, holding that as a matter of law, no reasonable jury could have found that the University was more negligent than Whitlock, and that the jury's monetary award was the result of sympathy, passion or prejudice.

A panel of the court of appeals reversed...by a divided vote. *Whitlock v. University of Denver*, 712 P.2d 1072 (Colo. App. 1985). The court of appeals held that the University owed Whitlock a duty of due care to remove the trampoline from the fraternity premises or to supervise its use....The case was remanded to the trial court with orders to reinstate the verdict and damages as determined by the jury. The University then petitioned for certiorari review, and we granted that petition.

II.

A negligence claim must fail if based on circumstances for which the law imposes no duty of care upon the defendant for the benefit of the plaintiff. [Citations] Therefore, if Whitlock's judgment against the University is to be upheld, it must first be determined that the University owed a duty of care to take reasonable measures to protect him against the injury that he sustained.

Whether a particular defendant owes a legal duty to a particular plaintiff is a question of law. [Citations] "The court determines, as a matter of law, the existence and scope of the duty—that is, whether the plaintiff's interest that has been infringed by the conduct of the defendant is entitled to legal protection." [Citations] In *Smith v. City & County of Denver*, 726 P.2d 1125 (Colo. 1986), we set forth several factors to be considered in determining the existence of duty in a particular case:

> *Whether the law should impose a duty requires consideration of many factors including, for example, the risk involved, the foreseeability and likelihood of injury as weighed against the social utility of the actor's conduct, the magnitude of the burden of guarding against injury or harm, and the consequences of placing the burden upon the actor.*

* * * A court's conclusion that a duty does or does not exist is "an expression of the sum total of those considerations of policy which lead the law to say that the plaintiff is [or is not] entitled to protection." * * *

We believe that the fact that the University is charged with negligent failure to act rather than negligent affirmative action is a critical factor that strongly militates against imposition of a duty on the University under the facts of this case. In determining whether a defendant owes a duty to a particular plaintiff, the law has long recognized a distinction between action and a failure to act—"that is to say, between active misconduct working positive injury to others [misfeasance] and passive inaction or a failure to take steps to protect them from harm [nonfeasance]." W. Keeton, § 56, at 373. Liability for nonfeasance was slow to receive recognition in the law. "The reason for the distinction may be said to lie in the fact that by 'misfeasance' the defendant has created a new risk of harm to the plaintiff, while by 'nonfeasance' he has at least made his situation no worse, and has merely failed to benefit him by interfering in his affairs." *Id.* The *Restatement (Second) of Torts* § 314 (1965) summarizes the law on this point as follows:

> *The fact that an actor realizes or should realize that action on his part is necessary for another's aid or protection does not of itself impose upon him a duty to take such action.*

Imposition of a duty in all such cases would simply not meet the test of fairness under contemporary standards.

In nonfeasance cases the existence of a duty has been recognized only during the last century in situations involving a limited group of special relationships between parties. Such special relationships are predicated on "some definite relation between the parties, of such a character that social policy justifies the imposition of a duty to act." W. Keeton, § 56, at 374. Special relationships that have been recognized by various courts for the purpose of imposition of a duty of care include common carrier/passenger, innkeeper/guest, possessor of land/invited entrant, employer/employee, parent/child, and hospital/patient. *See Restatement (Second) of Torts* § 314 A (1965); 3 Harper and James, § 18.6, at 722–23. The authors of the *Restatement (Second) of Torts* § 314 A, comment b (1965), state that "the law appears...to be working slowly toward a recognition of the duty to aid or protect in any relation of dependence or of mutual dependence."

...

III.

The present case involves the alleged negligent failure to act, rather than negligent action. The plaintiff does not complain of any affirmative action taken by the University, but asserts instead that the University owed to Whitlock the duty to assure that the fraternity's trampoline was used only under supervised conditions comparable to those in a gymnasium class, or in the alternative to cause the trampoline to be removed from the front lawn of the Beta house....If such a duty is to be recognized, it must be grounded on a special relationship between the University and Whitlock. According to the evidence, there are only two possible sources of a special relationship out of which such a duty could arise in this case: the status of Whitlock as a student at the University, and the lease between the University and the fraternity of which Whitlock was a member. We first consider the adequacy of the student-university relationship as a possible basis for imposing a duty on the University to control or prohibit the use of the trampoline, and then examine the provisions of the lease for that same purpose.

A.

The student-university relationship has been scrutinized in several jurisdictions, and it is generally agreed that a university is not an insurer of its students' safety. [Citations] The relationship between a university and its students has experienced important change over the years. At one time, college administrators and faculties stood in loco parentis to their students, which created a special relationship "that imposed a duty on the college to exercise control over student conduct and, reciprocally, gave the students certain rights of protection by the college." *Bradshaw,* 612 F.2d at 139. However, in modern times there has evolved a gradual reapportionment of responsibilities from the universities to the students, and a corresponding departure from the in loco parentis relationship. *Id.* at 139–40. Today, colleges and universities are regarded as educational institutions rather than custodial ones. *Beach,* 726 P.2d at 419 (contrasting colleges and universities with elementary and high schools). * * *

...By imposing a duty on the University in this case, the University would be encouraged to exercise more control over private student recreational choices, thereby effectively taking away much of the responsibility recently recognized in students for making their own decisions with respect to private entertainment and personal safety. Such an allocation of responsibility would "produce a repressive and inhospitable environment, largely inconsistent with the objectives of a modern college education." *Beach,* 726 P.2d at 419.

The evidence demonstrates that only in limited instances has the University attempted to impose regulations or restraints on the private recreational pursuits of its students, and the students have not looked to the University to assure the safety of their recreational choices. Nothing in the University's student handbook, which contains certain regulations concerning student conduct, reflects an effort by the University to control the risk-taking decisions of its students in their private recreation....Indeed, fraternity and sorority self-governance with minimal supervision appears to have been fostered by the University. * * *

...

Aside from advising the Beta house on one occasion to put the trampoline up when not in use, there is no evidence that the University officials attempted to assert control over trampoline use by the fraternity members. We conclude from this record that the University's very limited actions concerning safety of student recreation did not give Whitlock or the other members of campus fraternities or sororities any reason to depend upon the University for evaluation of the safety of trampoline use....Therefore, we conclude that the student-university relationship is not a special relationship of the type giving rise to a duty of the University to take reasonable measures to protect the members of fraternities and sororities from risks of engaging in extra-curricular trampoline jumping.

The plaintiff asserts, however, that we should recognize a duty of the University to take affirmative action to protect fraternity members because of the foreseeability of the injury, the extent of the risks involved in trampoline use, the seriousness of potential injuries, and the University's superior knowledge concerning these matters. The argument in essence is that a duty should spring from the University's natural interest in the welfare and safety of its students, its superior knowledge of the nature and degree of risk involved in trampoline use, and its knowledge of the use of trampolines on the University campus. The evidence amply supports a conclusion that trampoline use involves risks of serious injuries and that the potential for an injury such as that experienced by Whitlock was foreseeable. It shows further that prior injuries resulting from trampoline accidents had been reported to campus security and to the student clinic, and that University administrators were aware of the number and severity of trampoline injuries nationwide.

The record, however, also establishes through Whitlock's own testimony that he was aware of the risk of an accident and injury of the very nature that he experienced....

We conclude that the relationship between the University and Whitlock was not one of dependence with respect to the activities at issue here, and provides no basis for the recognition of a duty of the University to take measures for protection of Whitlock against the injury that he suffered.

B.

We next examine the lease between the University and the fraternity to determine whether a special relationship between the University and Whitlock can be predicated on that document. The lease was executed in 1929, extends for a ninety-nine year term, and gives the fraternity the option to extend the term for another ninety-nine years. The premises are to be occupied and used by the fraternity "as a fraternity house, clubhouse, dormitory and boarding house, and generally for religious, educational, social and fraternal purposes." Such occupation is to be "*under control of the tenant*." (emphasis added) The annual rental at all times relevant to this case appears from the record to be one dollar. The University has the obligation to maintain the grounds and make necessary repairs to the building, and the fraternity is to bear the cost of such maintenance and repair. * * *

We conclude that the lease, and the University's actions pursuant to its rights under the lease, provide no basis of dependence by the fraternity members upon which a special relationship can be found to exist between the University and the fraternity members that would give rise to a duty upon the University to take affirmative action to assure that recreational equipment such as a trampoline is not used under unsafe conditions.

IV.

Considering all of the factors presented, we are persuaded that under the facts of this case the University of Denver had no duty to Whitlock to eliminate the private use of trampolines on its campus or to supervise that use. There exists no special relationship between the parties that justifies placing a duty upon the University to protect Whitlock from the well-known dangers of using a trampoline. Here, a conclusion that a special relationship existed between Whitlock and the University sufficient to warrant the imposition of liability for nonfeasance would directly contravene the competing social policy of fostering an educational environment of student autonomy and independence.

We reverse the judgment of the court of appeals and return this case to that court with directions to remand it to the trial court for dismissal of Whitlock's complaint against the University.

Case Questions

1. How are comparative negligence numbers calculated by the trial court? How can the jury say that the university is 72 percent negligent and that Whitlock is 28 percent negligent?
2. Why is this not an assumption of risk case?
3. Is there any evidence that Whitlock was contributorily negligent? If not, why would the court engage in comparative negligence calculations?

Negligence: Proximate Cause

Palsgraf v. Long Island R.R.
248 N.Y. 339,162 N.E. 99 (N.Y. 1928)

CARDOZO, Chief Judge

Plaintiff was standing on a platform of defendant's railroad after buying a ticket to go to Rockaway Beach. A train stopped at the station, bound for another place. Two men ran forward to catch it. One of the men reached the platform of the car without mishap, though the train was already moving. The other man, carrying a package, jumped aboard the car, but seemed unsteady as if about to fall. A guard on the car, who had held the door open, reached forward to help him in, and another guard on the platform pushed him from behind. In this act, the package was dislodged, and fell upon the rails. It was a package of small size, about fifteen inches long, and was covered by a newspaper. In fact it contained fireworks, but there was nothing in its appearance to give notice of its contents. The fireworks when they fell exploded. The shock of· the explosion threw down some scales at the other end of the platform many feet away. The scales struck the plaintiff, causing injuries for which she sues.

The conduct of the defendant's guard, if a wrong in its relation to the holder of the package, was not a wrong in its relation to the plaintiff, standing far away. Relatively to her it was not negligence at all. Nothing in the situation gave notice that the falling package had in it the potency of peril to persons thus removed. Negligence is not actionable unless it involves the invasion of a legally protected interest, the violation of a right. "Proof of negligence in the air, so to speak, will not do.... If no hazard was apparent to the eye of ordinary vigilance, an act innocent and harmless, at least to outward seeming, with reference to her, did not take to itself the quality of a tort because it happened to be a wrong, though apparently not one involving the risk of bodily insecurity, with reference to someone else.... The plaintiff sues in her own right for a wrong personal to her, and not as the vicarious beneficiary of a breach of duty to another.

A different conclusion will involve us, and swiftly too, in a maze of contradictions. A guard stumbles over a package which has been left upon a platform.

It seems to be a bundle of newspapers. It turns out to be a can of dynamite. To the eye of ordinary vigilance, the bundle is abandoned waste, which may be kicked or trod on with impunity. Is a passenger at the other end of the platform protected by the law against the unsuspected hazard concealed beneath the waste? If not, is the result to be any different, so far as the distant passenger is concerned, when the guard stumbles over a valise which a truckman or a porter has left upon the walk? ... The orbit of the danger as disclosed to the eye of reasonable vigilance would be the orbit of the duty. One who jostles one's neighbor in a crowd does not invade the rights of others standing at the outer fringe when the unintended contact casts a bomb upon the ground. The wrongdoer as to them is the man who carries the bomb, not the one who explodes it without suspicion of the danger. Life will have to be made over, and human nature transformed, before prevision so extravagant can be accepted as the norm of conduct, the customary standard to which behavior must conform.

The argument for the plaintiff is built upon the shifting meanings of such words as "wrong" and "wrongful" and shares their instability. For what the plaintiff must show is a "wrong" to herself; i.e., a violation of her own right, and not merely a "wrong" to someone else, nor conduct "wrongful" because unsocial, but not a "wrong" to anyone. We are told that one who drives at reckless speed through a crowded city street is guilty of a negligent act and therefore of a wrongful one, irrespective of the consequences.

Negligent the act is, and wrongful in the sense that it is unsocial, but wrongful and unsocial in relation to other travelers, only because the eye of vigilance perceives the risk of damage. If the same act were to be committed on a speedway or a race course, it would lose its wrongful quality. The risk reasonably to be perceived defines the duty to be obeyed, and risk imports relation; it is risk to another or to others within the range of apprehension. This does not mean, of course, that one who launches a destructive force is always relieved of liability, if the force, though known to be destructive, pursues an unexpected path. . . . Some acts, such as shooting are so imminently dangerous to anyone who may come within reach of the missile however unexpectedly, as to impose a duty of prevision not far from that of an insurer. Even today, and much oftener in earlier stages of the law, one acts sometimes at one's peril. . . . These cases aside, wrong-is defined in terms of the natural or probable, at least when unintentional. . . . Negligence, like risk, is thus a term of relation.

Negligence in the abstract, apart from things related, is surely not a tort, if indeed it is understandable at all. . . . One who seeks redress at law does not make out a cause of action by showing without more that there has been damage to his person. If the harm was not willful, he must show that the act as to him had possibilities of danger so many and apparent as to entitle him to be protected against the doing of it though the harm was unintended. * * *

The judgment of the Appellate Division and that of the Trial Term should be reversed, and the complaint dismissed, with costs in all courts.

Case Questions

1. Is there actual cause in this case? How can you tell?
2. Why should Mrs. Palsgraf (or her insurance company) be made to pay for injuries that were caused by the negligence of the Long Island Rail Road?
3. How is this accident *not* foreseeable?

Klein v. Pyrodyne Corporation

Klein v. Pyrodyne Corporation
810 P.2d 917 (Supreme Court of Washington, 1991)

Pyrodyne Corporation (Pyrodyne) is a licensed fireworks display company that contracted to display fireworks at the Western Washington State Fairgrounds in Puyallup, Washington, on July 4,1987. During the fireworks display, one of the mortar launchers discharged a rocket on a horizontal trajectory parallel to the earth. The rocket exploded near a crowd of onlookers, including Danny Klein. Klein's clothing was set on fire, and he suffered facial burns and serious injury to his eyes. Klein sued Pyrodyne for strict liability to recover for his injuries. Pyrodyne asserted that the Chinese manufacturer of the fireworks was negligent in producing the rocket and therefore Pyrodyne should not be held liable. The trial court applied the doctrine of strict liability and held in favor of Klein. Pyrodyne appealed.

Section 519 of the Restatement (Second) of Torts provides that any party carrying on an "abnormally dangerous activity" is strictly liable for ensuing damages. The public display of fireworks fits this definition. The court stated: "Any time a person ignites rockets with the intention of sending them aloft to explode in the presence of large crowds of people, a high risk of serious personal injury or property damage is created. That risk arises because of the possibility that a rocket will malfunction or be misdirected." Pyrodyne argued that its liability was cut off by the Chinese manufacturer's negligence. The court rejected this argument, stating, "Even if negligence may properly be regarded as an intervening cause, it cannot function to relieve Pyrodyne from strict liability."

The Washington Supreme Court held that the public display of fireworks is an abnormally dangerous activity that warrants the imposition of strict liability.

Affirmed.

Case Questions

1. Why would certain activities be deemed ultrahazardous or abnormally dangerous so that strict liability is imposed?
2. If the activities are known to be abnormally dangerous, did Klein assume the risk?
3. Assume that the fireworks were negligently manufactured in China. Should Klein's only remedy be against the Chinese company, as Pyrodyne argues? Why or why not?

7.6 Summary and Exercises

Summary

The principles of tort law pervade modern society because they spell out the duties of care that we owe each other in our private lives. Tort law has had a significant impact on business because modern technology poses significant dangers and the modern market is so efficient at distributing goods to a wide class of consumers.

Unlike criminal law, tort law does not require the tortfeasor to have a specific intent to commit the act for which he or she will be held liable to pay damages. Negligence—that is, carelessness—is a major factor in tort liability. In some instances, especially in cases involving injuries caused by products, a no-fault standard called strict liability is applied.

What constitutes a legal injury depends very much on the circumstances. A person can assume a risk or consent to the particular action, thus relieving the person doing the injury from tort liability. To be liable, the tortfeasor must be the proximate cause of the injury, not a remote cause. On the other hand, certain people are held to answer for the torts of another—for example, an employer is usually liable for the torts of his employees, and a bartender might be liable for injuries caused by someone to whom he sold too many drinks. Two types of statutes—workers' compensation and no-fault automobile insurance—have eliminated tort liability for certain kinds of accidents and replaced it with an immediate insurance payment plan.

Among the torts of particular importance to the business community are wrongful death and personal injury caused by products or acts of employees, misrepresentation, defamation, and interference with contractual relations.

Exercises

1. What is the difference in objectives between tort law and criminal law?
2. A woman fell ill in a store. An employee put the woman in an infirmary but provided no medical care for six hours, and she died. The woman's family sued the store for wrongful death. What arguments could the store make that it was not liable? What arguments could the family make? Which seem the stronger arguments? Why?
3. The signals on a railroad crossing are defective. Although the railroad company was notified of the problem a month earlier, the railroad inspector has failed to come by and repair them. Seeing the all-clear signal, a car drives up and stalls on the tracks as a train rounds the bend.

For the past two weeks the car had been stalling, and the driver kept putting off taking the car to the shop for a tune-up. As the train rounds the bend, the engineer is distracted by a conductor and does not see the car until it is too late to stop. Who is negligent? Who must bear the liability for the damage to the car and to the train?

4. Suppose in the *Katko v. Briney* case (Section 2) that instead of setting such a device, the defendants had simply let the floor immediately inside the front door rot until it was so weak that anybody who came in and took two steps straight ahead would fall through the floor and to the cellar. Will the defendant be liable in this case? What if they invited a realtor to appraise the place and did not warn her of the floor? Does it matter whether the injured person is a trespasser or an invitee?
5. Plaintiff's husband died in an accident, leaving her with several children and no money except a valid insurance policy by which she was entitled to $5,000. Insurance Company refused to pay, delaying and refusing payment and meanwhile "inviting" Plaintiff to accept less than $5,000, hinting that it had a defense. Plaintiff was reduced to accepting housing and charity from relatives. She sued the insurance company for bad-faith refusal to settle the claim and for the intentional infliction of emotional distress. The lower court dismissed the case. Should the court of appeals allow the matter to proceed to trial?

Self-Test Questions

1. Catarina falsely accuses Jeff of stealing from their employer. The statement is defamatory only if
   a. a third party hears it
   b. Nick suffers severe emotional distress as a result
   c. the statement is the actual and proximate cause of his distress
   d. the statement is widely circulated in the local media and on Twitter
2. Garrett files a suit against Colossal Media Corporation for defamation. Colossal has said that Garrett is a "sleazy, corrupt public official" (and provided some evidence to back the claim). To win his case, Garrett will have to show that Colossal acted with
   a. malice
   b. ill will
   c. malice aforethought
   d. actual malice
3. Big Burger begins a rumor, using social media, that the meat in Burger World is partly composed of ground-up worms. The rumor is not true, as Big Burger well knows. Its intent is to get some customers to shift loyalty from Burger World to Big Burger. Burger World's best cause of action would be
   a. trespass on the case
   b. nuisance
   c. product disparagement
   d. intentional infliction of emotional distress
4. Wilfred Phelps, age 65, is driving his Nissan Altima down Main Street when he suffers the first seizure of his life. He loses control of his vehicle and runs into three people on the sidewalk. Which statement is true?
   a. He is liable for an intentional tort.
   b. He is liable for a negligent tort.
   c. He is not liable for a negligent tort.
   d. He is liable under strict liability, because driving a car is abnormally dangerous.
5. Jonathan carelessly bumps into Amanda, knocking her to the ground. He has committed the tort of negligence
   a. only if Amanda is injured

b. only if Amanda is not injured
c. whether or not Amanda is injured

Self-Test Answers

1. a
2. d
3. c
4. c
5. a

Endnotes

1. *Roche v. Stern*, 675 N.Y.S.2d 133 (1998).
2. *Hustler Magazine, Inc. v. Falwell*, 485 U.S. 46, 108 S.Ct. 876 (1988).
3. *Katko v. Briney*, 183 N.W.2d 657 (Iowa 1971).
4. Restatement (Second) of Torts, Section 559 (1965).
5. *Times v. Sullivan*, 376 US 254 (1964).
6. *Tarasoff v. Regents of University of California*, 551 P.2d 334 (Calif. 1976).
7. *Scott v. London & St. Katherine Docks Co.*, 3 H. & C. 596, 159 Eng.Rep. 665 (Q.B. 1865).
8. *Johnson v. Kosmos Portland Cement Co.*, 64 F.2d 193 (6th Cir. 1933).
9. *Pellman v. McDonald's Corp.*, 237 F.2d 512 (S.D.N.Y. 2003).

CHAPTER 8

Introduction to Contract Law

Learning Objectives

After reading this chapter, you should understand the following:

1. Why and how contract law has developed.
2. What a contract is.
3. What topics will be discussed in the contracts chapter of this book.
4. What the sources of contract law are.
5. How contracts are classified (basic taxonomy).

8.1 General Perspectives on Contracts

Learning Objectives

1. Explain contract law's cultural roots: how it has evolved as capitalism has evolved.
2. Understand that contracts serve essential economic purposes.
3. Define contract.
4. Understand the basic issues in contract law.

The Role of Contracts in Modern Society

Contract is probably the most familiar legal concept in our society because it is so central to the essence of our political, economic, and social life. In common parlance, contract is used interchangeably with *agreement*, *bargain*, *undertaking*, or *deal*. Whatever the word, the concept it embodies is our notion of freedom to pursue our own lives together with others. Contract is central because it is the means by which a free society orders what would otherwise be a jostling, frenetic anarchy.

So commonplace is the concept of contract—and our freedom to make contracts with each other—that it is difficult to imagine a time when contracts were rare, when people's everyday associations with one another were not freely determined. Yet in historical terms, it was not so long ago that contracts were rare, entered into if at all by very few: that affairs should be ordered based on mutual assent was mostly unknown. In primitive societies and in feudal Europe, relationships among people were largely fixed; traditions spelled out duties that each person owed to family, tribe, or manor. People were born into an ascribed position—a status (not unlike the caste system still existing in India)—and social mobility was limited. Sir Henry Maine, a nineteenth-century British historian, wrote that "the movement of the progressive societies has...been a movement from status to contract."[1] This movement was not accidental—it developed with the emerging industrial order. From the fifteenth to the nineteenth century, England evolved into a booming mercantile economy, with flourishing trade, growing cities, an expanding monetary system, the commercialization of agriculture, and mushrooming manufacturing. With this evolution, contract law was created of necessity.

Contract law did not develop according to a conscious plan, however. It was a response to changing conditions, and the judges who created it frequently resisted, preferring the imagined quieter pastoral life of their forefathers. Not until the nineteenth century, in both the United States and England, did a full-fledged law of contracts arise together with, and help create, modern capitalism.

Modern capitalism, indeed, would not be possible without contract law. So it is that in planned economies, like those of the former Soviet Union and precapitalistic China, the contract did not determine the nature of an economic transaction. That transaction was first set forth by the state's planning authorities; only thereafter were the predetermined provisions set down in a written contract. Modern capitalism has demanded new contract regimes in Russia and China; the latter adopted its Revised Contract Law in 1999.

Contract law may be viewed economically as well as culturally. In *An Economic Analysis of Law*, Judge Richard A. Posner (a former University of Chicago law professor) suggests that contract law performs three significant economic functions. First, it helps maintain incentives for individuals to exchange goods and services efficiently. Second, it reduces the costs of economic transactions because its very existence means that the parties need not go to the trouble of negotiating a variety of rules and terms already spelled out. Third, the law of contracts alerts the parties to troubles that have arisen in the past, thus making it easier to plan the transactions more intelligently and avoid potential pitfalls.[2]

The Definition of *Contract*

contract

A legally enforceable set of promises.

As usual in the law, the legal definition of **contract** is formalistic. The Restatement (Second) of Contracts (Section 1) says, "A contract is a promise or a set of promises for the breach of which the law gives a remedy, or the performance of which the law in some way recognizes as a duty." Similarly, the Uniform Commercial Code says, "'Contract' means the total legal obligation which results from the parties' agreement as affected by this Act and any other applicable rules of law."[3] As operational definitions, these two are circular; in effect, a contract is defined as an agreement that the law will hold the parties to.

Most simply, a contract is a legally enforceable promise. This implies that not every promise or agreement creates a binding contract; if every promise did, the simple definition set out in the preceding sentence would read, "A contract is a promise." But—again—a contract is not simply a promise: it is a legally enforceable promise. The law takes into account the way in which contracts are made, by whom they are made, and for what purposes they are made. For example, in many states, a wager is unenforceable, even though both parties "shake" on the bet. We will explore these issues in the chapters to come.

Overview of the Contracts Chapter

Although contract law has many wrinkles and nuances, it consists of four principal inquiries, each of which will be taken up in subsequent chapters:

1. Did the parties create a valid contract? Four elements are necessary for a valid contract:
   a. Mutual assent (i.e., offer and acceptance), Chapter 9
   b. Real assent (no duress, undue influence, misrepresentation, mistake, or incapacity), Chapter 10

   c. Consideration, Chapter 11
   d. Legality, Chapter 12
2. What does the contract mean, and is it in the proper form to carry out this meaning? Sometimes contracts need to be in writing (or evidenced by some writing), or they can't be enforced. Sometimes it isn't clear what the contract means, and a court has to figure that out. These problems are taken up in Chapter 13.
3. Do persons other than the contracting parties have rights or duties under the contract? Can the right to receive a benefit from the contract be assigned, and can the duties be delegated so that a new person is responsible? Can persons not a party to the contract sue to enforce its terms? These questions are addressed in Chapter 14.
4. How do contractual duties terminate, and what remedies are available if a party has breached the contract? These issues are taken up in Chapter 15 and Chapter 16.

Together, the answers to these four basic inquiries determine the rights and obligations of contracting parties.

Key Takeaway

Contract law developed when the strictures of feudalism dissipated, when a person's position in society came to be determined by personal choice (by mutual agreement) and not by status (by how a person was born). Capitalism and contract law have developed together, because having choices in society means that people decide and agree to do things with and to each other, and those agreements bind the parties; the agreements must be enforceable.

Exercises

1. Why is contract law necessary in a society where a person's status is not predetermined by birth?
2. Contract law serves some economic functions. What are they?

8.2 Sources of Contract Law

Learning Objectives

1. Understand that contract law comes from two sources: judges (cases) and legislation.
2. Know what the Restatement of Contracts is.
3. Recognize the Convention on Contracts for the International Sale of Goods.

The most important sources of contract law are state case law and state statutes (though there are also many federal statutes governing how contracts are made by and with the federal government).

Case Law

case law

Law decided by judges as recorded in cases and published.

Law made by judges is called **case law**. Because contract law was made up in the common-law courtroom by individual judges as they applied rules to resolve disputes before them, it grew over time to formidable proportions. By the early twentieth century, tens of thousands of contract disputes had been submitted to the courts for resolution, and the published opinions, if collected in one place, would have filled dozens of bookshelves. Clearly this mass of material was too unwieldy for efficient use. A similar problem also had developed in the other leading branches of the common law.

Restatement of the Law of Contracts

An organized codification of the common law of contracts.

Disturbed by the profusion of cases and the resulting uncertainty of the law, a group of prominent American judges, lawyers, and law teachers founded the American Law Institute (ALI) in 1923 to attempt to clarify, simplify, and improve the law. One of the ALI's first projects, and ultimately one of its most successful, was the drafting of the **Restatement of the Law of Contracts**, completed in 1932. A revision—the Restatement (Second) of Contracts—was undertaken in 1964 and completed in 1979. Hereafter, references to "the Restatement" pertain to the Restatement (Second) of Contracts.

The Restatements—others exist in the fields of torts, agency, conflicts of laws, judgments, property, restitution, security, and trusts—are detailed analyses of the decided cases in each field. These analyses are made with an eye to discerning the various principles that have emerged from the courts, and to the maximum extent possible, the Restatements declare the law as the courts have determined it to be. The Restatements, guided by a reporter (the director of the project) and a staff of legal scholars, go through several so-called tentative drafts—sometimes as many as fifteen or twenty—and are screened by various committees within the ALI before they are eventually published as final documents.

The Restatement (Second) of Contracts won prompt respect in the courts and has been cited in innumerable cases. The Restatements are not authoritative, in the sense that they are not actual judicial precedents; but they are nevertheless weighty interpretive texts, and judges frequently look to them for guidance. They are as close to "black letter" rules of law as exist anywhere in the American common-law legal system.

Common law, case law (the terms are synonymous), governs contracts for the sale of real estate and services. "Services" refer to acts or deeds (like plumbing, drafting documents, driving a car) as opposed to the sale of property.

Statutory Law: The Uniform Commercial Code

Uniform Commercial Code (UCC)

The modern American state statutory law governing commercial transactions.

Article 2

That part of the Uniform Commercial Code dealing with the sale of goods.

Common-law contract principles govern contracts for real estate and services. Because of the historical development of the English legal system, contracts for the sale of goods came to be governed by a different body of legal rules. In its modern American manifestation, that body of rules is an important statute: the **Uniform Commercial Code (UCC)**, especially **Article 2**, which deals with the sale of goods.

History of the UCC

A bit of history is in order. Before the UCC was written, commercial law varied, sometimes greatly, from state to state. This first proved a nuisance and then a serious impediment to business as the American economy became nationwide during the twentieth century. Although there had been some uniform laws concerned with commercial deals—including the Uniform Sales Act, first published in 1906—few were widely adopted and none nationally. As a result, the law governing sales of goods, negotiable instruments, warehouse receipts, securities, and other matters crucial to doing business in an industrial market economy was a crazy quilt of untidy provisions that did not mesh well from state to state.

The UCC is a model law developed by the ALI and the National Conference of Commissioners on Uniform State Laws; it has been adopted in one form or another by the legislatures in all fifty states, the District of Columbia, and the American territories. It is a "national" law not enacted by Congress—it is not federal law but uniform state law.

Initial drafting of the UCC began in 1942 and was ten years in the making, involving the efforts of hundreds of practicing lawyers, law teachers, and judges. A final draft, promulgated by the ALI, was endorsed by the American Bar Association and published in 1951. Various revisions followed in different states, threatening the uniformity of the UCC. The ALI responded by creating a permanent editorial board to oversee future revisions. In one or another of its various revisions, the UCC has been adopted in whole or in part in all American jurisdictions. The UCC is now a basic law of relevance to every business and business lawyer in the United States, even though it is not entirely uniform because different states have adopted it at various stages of its evolution—an evolution that continues still.

Organization of the UCC

The UCC consists of nine major substantive articles; each deals with separate though related subjects. The articles are as follows:

- Article 1: General Provisions
- Article 2: Sales
- Article 2A: Leases
- Article 3: Commercial Paper
- Article 4: Bank Deposits and Collections
- Article 4A: Funds Transfers
- Article 5: Letters of Credit
- Article 6: Bulk Transfers
- Article 7: Warehouse Receipts, Bills of Lading, and Other Documents of Title
- Article 8: Investment Securities
- Article 9: Secured Transactions

Article 2 deals only with the sale of goods, which the UCC defines as "all things...which are movable at the time of identification to the contract for sale other than the money in which the price is to be paid."[4] The only contracts and agreements covered by Article 2 are those relating to the present or future sale of goods.

Article 2 is divided in turn into six major parts: (1) Form, Formation, and Readjustment of Contract; (2) General Obligation and Construction of Contract; (3) Title, Creditors, and Good Faith Purchasers; (4) Performance; (5) Breach, Repudiation, and Excuse; and (6) Remedies. These topics will be discussed in Chapter 17, Chapter 18, Chapter 19, Chapter 20, and Chapter 21.

FIGURE 8.1 Sources of Law

	Source of Law	
Type of Contract	Common Law	UCC
Real Estate	✓	
Services	✓	
Sale of Goods		✓

International Sales Law

The Convention on Contracts for the International Sale of Goods

Convention on Contracts for the International Sale of Goods (CISG)

An international body of contract law.

A **Convention on Contracts for the International Sale of Goods (CISG)** was approved in 1980 at a diplomatic conference in Vienna. (A convention is a preliminary agreement that serves as the basis for a formal treaty.) The CISG has been adopted by more than forty countries, including the United States.

The CISG is significant for three reasons. First, it is a uniform law governing the sale of goods—in effect, an international Uniform Commercial Code. The major goal of the drafters was to produce a uniform law acceptable to countries with different legal, social, and economic systems. Second, although provisions in the CISG are generally consistent with the UCC, there are significant differences. For instance, under the CISG, consideration (discussed in Chapter 11) is not required to form a contract, and there is no Statute of Frauds (a requirement that certain contracts be evidenced by a writing). Third, the CISG represents the first attempt by the US Senate to reform the private law of business through its treaty powers, for the CISG preempts the UCC. The CISG is not mandatory: parties to an international contract for the sale of goods may choose to have their agreement governed by different law, perhaps the UCC, or perhaps, say, Japanese contract law. The CISG does not apply to contracts for the sale of (1) ships or aircraft, (2) electricity, or (3) goods bought for personal, family, or household use, nor does it apply (4) where the party furnishing the goods does so only incidentally to the labor or services part of the contract.

Key Takeaway

Judges have made contract law over several centuries by deciding cases that create, extend, or change the developing rules affecting contract formation, performance, and enforcement. The rules from the cases have been abstracted and organized in the Restatements of Contracts. To facilitate interstate commerce, contract law for many commercial transactions—especially the sale of goods—not traditionally within the purview of judges has been developed by legal scholars and presented for the states to adopt as the Uniform Commercial Code. There is an analogous Convention on Contracts for the International Sale of Goods, to which the United States is a party.

Exercises

1. How do judges make contract law?
2. What is the Restatement of the Law of Contracts, and why was it necessary?
3. Why was the Uniform Commercial Code developed, and by whom?
4. Who adopts the UCC as governing law?
5. What is the Convention on Contracts for the International Sale of Goods?

8.3 Basic Taxonomy of Contracts

Learning Objectives

1. Understand that contracts are classified according to the criteria of explicitness, mutuality, enforceability, and degree of completion and that some noncontract promises are nevertheless enforceable under the doctrine of promissory estoppel.
2. Keep your eyes (and ears) alert to the use of suffixes (word endings) in legal terminology that express relationships between parties.

Some contracts are written, some oral; some are explicit, some not. Because contracts can be formed, expressed, and enforced in a variety of ways, a taxonomy of contracts has developed that is useful in grouping together like legal consequences. In general, contracts are classified along four different dimensions: explicitness, mutuality, enforceability, and degree of completion. Explicitness is the degree to which the agreement is manifest to those not party to it. Mutuality takes into account whether promises are given by two parties or only one. Enforceability is the degree to which a given contract is binding. Completion considers whether the contract is yet to be performed or whether the obligations have been fully discharged by one or both parties. We will examine each of these concepts in turn.

Explicitness

Express Contract

An **express contract** is one in which the terms are spelled out directly. The parties to an express contract, whether it is written or oral, are conscious that they are making an enforceable agreement. For example, an agreement to purchase your neighbor's car for $5,500 and to take title next Monday is an express contract.

express contract

A contract in words, orally or in writing.

Implied Contract (Implied in Fact)

An **implied contract** is one that is inferred from the actions of the parties. When parties have not discussed terms, an implied contract exists if it is clear from the conduct of both parties that they intended there be one. A delicatessen patron who asks for a turkey sandwich to go has made a contract and is obligated to pay when the sandwich is made. By ordering the food, the patron is implicitly agreeing to the price, whether posted or not.

implied contract

A contract that is not expressed but is inferred from the actions of the parties.

The distinction between express and implied contracts has received a degree of notoriety in the so-called palimony cases, in which one member of an unmarried couple seeks a division of property after a long-standing live-together relationship has broken up. When a married couple divorces, their legal marriage contract is dissolved, and financial rights and obligations are spelled out in a huge body of domestic relations statutes and judicial decisions. No such laws exist for unmarried couples. However, about one-third of the states recognize common-law marriage, under which two people are deemed to be married if they live together with the intent to be married, regardless of their failure to have obtained a license or gone through a ceremony. Although there is no actual contract of marriage (no license), their behavior implies that the parties intended to be treated as if they were married.

Quasi-Contract

quasi-contract (implied in law)

A contract imposed on a party when there was none, to avoid unjust enrichment.

A **quasi-contract (implied in law)** is—unlike both express and implied contracts, which embody an actual agreement of the parties—an obligation said to be "imposed by law" in order to avoid unjust enrichment of one person at the expense of another. A quasi-contract is not a contract at all; it is a fiction that the courts created to prevent injustice. Suppose, for example, that the local lumberyard mistakenly delivers a load of lumber to your house, where you are repairing your deck. It was a neighbor on the next block who ordered the lumber, but you are happy to accept the load for free; since you never talked to the lumberyard, you figure you need not pay the bill. Although it is true there is no contract, the law implies a contract for the value of the material: of course you will have to pay for what you got and took. The existence of this implied contract does not depend on the intention of the parties.

Mutuality

Bilateral Contract

bilateral contract

A contract in which each party makes a promise to the other.

The typical contract is one in which the parties make mutual promises. Each is both promisor and promisee; that is, each pledges to do something, and each is the recipient of such a pledge. This type of contract is called a **bilateral contract**.

Unilateral Contract

unilateral contract

A contract that is accepted by performance of the requested action, not by a promise.

Mutual promises are not necessary to constitute a contract. **Unilateral contracts**, in which one party performs an act in exchange for the other party's promise, are equally valid. An offer of a reward—for catching a criminal or for returning a lost cat—is an example of a unilateral contract: there is an offer on one side, and the other side accepts by taking the action requested.

FIGURE 8.2 Bilateral and Unilateral Contracts

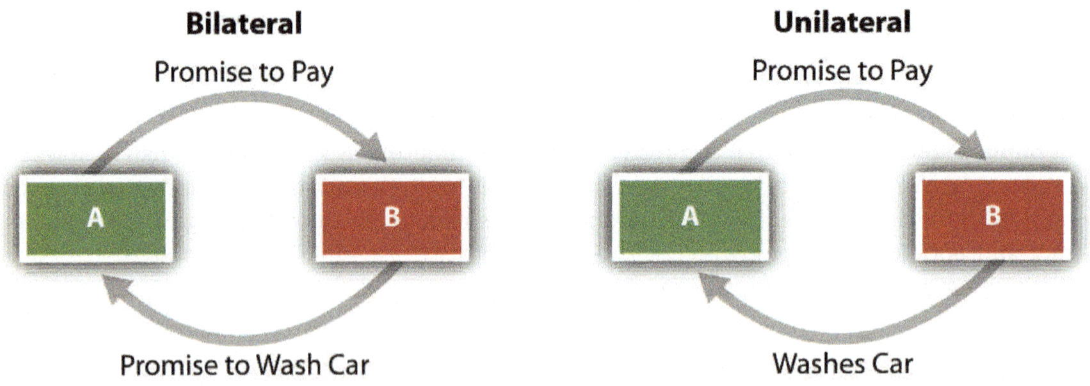

Enforceability

Void

void contract

An agreement that never was a contract.

Not every agreement between two people is a binding contract. An agreement that is lacking one of the legal elements of a contract is said to be a **void contract**—that is, not a contract at all. An agreement that is illegal—for example, a promise to commit a crime in return for a money payment—is void. Neither party to a void "contract" may enforce it.

Voidable

By contrast, a **voidable contract** is one that may become unenforceable by one party but can be enforced by the other. For example, a minor (any person under eighteen, in most states) may "avoid" a contract with an adult; the adult may not enforce the contract against the minor if the minor refuses to carry out the bargain. But the adult has no choice if the minor wishes the contract to be performed. (A contract may be voidable by both parties if both are minors.)

voidable contract

A contract that is capable of being annulled.

Ordinarily, the parties to a voidable contract are entitled to be restored to their original condition. Suppose you agree to buy your seventeen-year-old neighbor's car. He delivers it to you in exchange for your agreement to pay him next week. He has the legal right to terminate the deal and recover the car, in which case you will of course have no obligation to pay him. If you have already paid him, he still may legally demand a return to the status quo ante (previous state of affairs). You must return the car to him; he must return the cash to you.

A voidable contract remains a valid contract until it is voided. Thus a contract with a minor remains in force unless the minor decides he or she does not wish to be bound by it. When the minor reaches majority, he or she may "ratify" the contract—that is, agree to be bound by it—in which case the contract will no longer be voidable and will thereafter be fully enforceable.

Unenforceable

An **unenforceable contract** is one that some rule of law bars a court from enforcing. For example, Tom owes Pete money, but Pete has waited too long to collect it and the statute of limitations has run out. The contract for repayment is unenforceable and Pete is out of luck, unless Tom makes a new promise to pay or actually pays part of the debt. (However, if Pete is holding collateral as security for the debt, he is entitled to keep it; not all rights are extinguished because a contract is unenforceable.) A debt becomes unenforceable, too, when the debtor declares bankruptcy.

unenforceable contract

A contract for which the nonbreaching party has no remedy for its breach.

promissory estoppel

To be prohibited from denying a promise when another subsequently has relied on it.

A bit more on enforceability is in order. A promise or what seems to be a promise is usually enforceable only if it is otherwise embedded in the elements necessary to make that promise a contract. Those elements are mutual assent, real assent, consideration, capacity, and legality. Sometimes, though, people say things that seem like promises, and on which another person relies. In the early twentieth century, courts began, in some circumstances, to recognize that insisting on the existence of the traditional elements of contract to determine whether a promise is enforceable could work an injustice where there has been reliance. Thus developed the equitable doctrine of **promissory estoppel**, which has become an important adjunct to contract law. The Restatement (Section 90) puts it this way: "A promise which the promisor should reasonably expect to induce action or forbearance on the party of the promisee or a third person and which does induce such action or forbearance is binding if injustice can be avoided only by enforcement of the promise. The remedy granted for breach may be limited as justice requires."

To be "estopped" means to be prohibited from denying now the validity of a promise you made before.

The doctrine has an interesting background. In 1937, High Trees House Ltd. (a British corporation) leased a block of London apartments from Central London Properties. As World War II approached, vacancy rates soared because people left the city. In 1940 the parties agreed to reduce the rent rates by half, but no term was set for how long the reduction would last. By mid-1945, as the war was ending, occupancy was again full, and Central London sued for the full rental rates from June on. The English court, under Judge Alfred Thompson Denning (1899–1999), had no difficulty finding that High Trees owed the full amount once full occupancy was again achieved, but Judge Denning went on. In an aside (called a dicta—a statement "by the way"—that is, not necessary as part of the decision), he mused about what would have happened if in 1945 Central London had sued for the full-occupancy rate back to 1940. Technically, the 1940 amendment to the 1937 contract was not binding on Central London—it lacked consideration—and Central London could have reached back to demand full-rate payment. But Judge Denning said that High Trees would certainly have relied on Central London's promise that a reduced-rate rent would be acceptable, and that would have been enough to bind it, to prevent it from acting inconsistently with the promise. He wrote, "The courts have not gone so far as to give a cause of action in damages for the breach of such a promise, but they have refused to allow the party making it to act inconsistently with it."[5]

In the years since, though, courts *have* gone so far as to give a cause of action in damages for various non-contract promises. Contracts protect agreements; promissory estoppel protects reliance, and that's a significant difference. The law of contracts continues to evolve.

Degree of Completion

executory contract

A contract that has yet to be completed.

partially executed contract

A contract in which one party has performed, or partly performed, and the other party has not.

executed contract

A contract that has been completed.

An agreement consisting of a set of promises is called an **executory contract** before any promises are carried out. Most executory contracts are enforceable. If John makes an agreement to deliver wheat to Humphrey and does so, the contract is called a **partially executed contract**: one side has performed, the other has not. When John pays for the wheat, the contract is fully performed. A contract that has been carried out fully by both parties is called an **executed contract**.

Terminology: Suffixes Expressing Relationships

Although not really part of the taxonomy of contracts (i.e., the orderly classification of the subject), an aspect of contractual—indeed, legal—terminology should be highlighted here. *Suffixes* (the end syllables of words) in the English language are used to express relationships between parties in legal terminology. Here are examples:

- **Offeror.** One who makes an offer.
- **Offeree.** One to whom an offer is made.
- **Promisor.** One who makes a promise.
- **Promisee.** One to whom a promise is made.
- **Obligor.** One who makes and has an obligation.
- **Obligee.** One to whom an obligation is made.
- **Transferor.** One who makes a transfer.
- **Transferee.** One to whom a transfer is made.

Key Takeaway

Contracts are described and thus defined on the basis of four criteria: explicitness (express, implied, or quasi-contracts), mutuality (bilateral or unilateral), enforceability (void, voidable, unenforceable), and degree of completion (executory, partially executed, executed). Legal terminology in English often describes relationships between parties by the use of suffixes, to which the eye and ear must pay attention.

Exercises

1. Able *writes* to Baker: "I will mow your lawn for $20." If Baker accepts, is this an express or implied contract?
2. Able *telephones* Baker: "I will mow your lawn for $20." Is this an express or implied contract?
3. What is the difference between a void contract and a voidable one?

4. Carr staples this poster to a utility pole: "$50 reward for the return of my dog, Argon." Describe this in contractual terms regarding explicitness, mutuality, enforceability, and degree of completion.
5. Is a voidable contract always unenforceable?
6. Contractor bids on a highway construction job, incorporating Guardrail Company's bid into its overall bid to the state. Contractor cannot accept Guardrail's offer until it gets the nod from the state. Contractor gets the nod from the state, but before it can accept Guardrail's offer, the latter revokes it. Usually a person can revoke an offer any time before it is accepted. Can Guardrail revoke its offer in this case?

8.4 Cases

Explicitness: Implied Contract

Roger's Backhoe Service, Inc. v. Nichols

681 N.W.2d 647 (Iowa 2004)

Carter, J.

Defendant, Jeffrey S. Nichols, is a funeral director in Muscatine. * * * In early 1998 Nichols decided to build a crematorium on the tract of land on which his funeral home was located. In working with the Small Business Administration, he was required to provide drawings and specifications and obtain estimates for the project. Nichols hired an architect who prepared plans and submitted them to the City of Muscatine for approval. These plans provided that the surface water from the parking lot would drain onto the adjacent street and alley and ultimately enter city storm sewers. These plans were approved by the city.

Nichols contracted with Roger's [Backhoe Service, Inc.] for the demolition of the foundation of a building that had been razed to provide room for the crematorium and removal of the concrete driveway and sidewalk adjacent to that foundation. Roger's completed that work and was paid in full.

After construction began, city officials came to the job site and informed Roger's that the proposed drainage of surface water onto the street and alley was unsatisfactory. The city required that an effort be made to drain the surface water into a subterranean creek, which served as part of the city's storm sewer system. City officials indicated that this subterranean sewer system was about fourteen feet below the surface of the ground. * * * Roger's conveyed the city's mandate to Nichols when he visited the job site that same day.

It was Nichols' testimony at trial that, upon receiving this information, he advised * * * Roger's that he was refusing permission to engage in the exploratory excavation that the city required. Nevertheless, it appears without dispute that for the next three days Roger's did engage in digging down to the subterranean sewer system, which was located approximately twenty feet below the surface. When the underground creek was located, city officials examined the brick walls in which it was encased and determined that it was not feasible to penetrate those walls in order to connect the surface water drainage with the underground creek. As a result of that conclusion, the city reversed its position and once again gave permission to drain the surface water onto the adjacent street and alley.

[T]he invoices at issue in this litigation relate to charges that Roger's submitted to Nichols for the three days of excavation necessary to locate the underground sewer system and the cost for labor and materials necessary to refill the excavation with compactable materials and attain compaction by means of a tamping process. * * * The district court found that the charges submitted on the * * * invoices were fair and reasonable and that they had been performed for Nichols' benefit and with his tacit approval. * * *

The court of appeals * * * concluded that a necessary element in establishing an implied-in-fact contract is that the services performed be beneficial to the alleged obligor. It concluded that Roger's had failed to show that its services benefited Nichols. * * *

In describing the elements of an action on an implied contract, the court of appeals stated in [Citation], that the party seeking recovery must show:

> *(1) the services were carried out under such circumstances as to give the recipient reason to understand:*
>
> *(a) they were performed for him and not some other person, and*
>
> *(b) they were not rendered gratuitously, but with the expectation of compensation from the recipient; and*
>
> (2) the services were beneficial to the recipient.

In applying the italicized language in [Citation] to the present controversy, it was the conclusion of the court of appeals that Roger's' services conferred no benefit on Nichols. We disagree. There was substantial evidence in the record to support a finding that, unless and until an effort was made to locate the subterranean sewer system, the city refused to allow the project to proceed. Consequently, it was necessary to the successful completion of the project that the effort be made. The fact that examination of the brick wall surrounding the underground creek indicated that it was unfeasible to use that source of drainage does not alter the fact that the project was stalemated until drainage into the underground creek was fully explored and rejected. The district court properly concluded that Roger's' services conferred a benefit on Nichols. * * *

Decision of court of appeals vacated; district court judgment affirmed.

Case Questions

1. What facts must be established by a plaintiff to show the existence of an implied contract?
2. What argument did Nichols make as to why there was no implied contract here?
3. How would the facts have to be changed to make an express contract?

Mutuality of Contract: Unilateral Contract

SouthTrust Bank v. Williams

775 So.2d 184 (Ala. 2000)

Cook, J.

SouthTrust Bank ("SouthTrust") appeals from an order denying its motion to compel arbitration of an action against it by checking-account customers Mark Williams and Bessie Daniels. We reverse and remand.

Daniels and Williams began their relationships with SouthTrust in 1981 and 1995, respectively, by executing checking-account "signature cards." The signature card each customer signed contained a "change-in-terms" clause. Specifically, when Daniels signed her signature card, she "agree[d] to be subject to the Rules and Regulations as may now or *hereafter* be adopted by the Bank." (Emphasis added) * * * [Later,] SouthTrust added paragraph 33 to the regulations:

> *ARBITRATION OF DISPUTES. You and we agree that the transactions in your account involve 'commerce' under the Federal Arbitration Act ('FAA'). ANY CONTROVERSY OR CLAIM BETWEEN YOU AND US...WILL BE SETTLED BY BINDING ARBITRATION UNDER THE FAA.* * * *

This action * * * challenges SouthTrust's procedures for paying overdrafts, and alleges that SouthTrust engages in a "uniform practice of paying the largest check(s) before paying multiple smaller checks * * * [in order] to generate increased service charges for [SouthTrust] at the expense of [its customers]."

SouthTrust filed a "motion to stay [the] lawsuit and to compel arbitration." It based its motion on paragraph 33 of the regulations. [T]he trial court...entered an order denying SouthTrust's motion to compel arbitration. SouthTrust appeals. * * *

Williams and Daniels contend that SouthTrust's amendment to the regulations, adding paragraph 33, was ineffective because, they say, they did not *expressly assent* to the amendment. In other words, they object to submitting their claims to arbitration because, they say, when they opened their accounts, neither the regulations nor any other relevant document contained an arbitration provision. They argue that "mere failure to object to the addition of a material term cannot be construed as an acceptance of it." * * * They contend that SouthTrust could not unilaterally insert an arbitration clause in the regulations and make it binding on depositors like them.

SouthTrust, however, referring to its change-of-terms clause, insists that it "notified" Daniels and Williams of the amendment in January 1997 by enclosing in each customer's "account statement" a complete copy of the regulations, as amended. Although it is undisputed that Daniels and Williams never affirmatively assented to these amended regulations, SouthTrust contends that their assent was evidenced by their failure to close their accounts after they received notice of the amendments. * * * Thus, the disposition of this case turns on the legal effect of Williams and Daniels's continued use of the accounts after the regulations were amended.

Williams and Daniels argue that "[i]n the context of contracts between merchants [under the UCC], a written confirmation of an acceptance may modify the contract *unless* it adds a *material* term, and arbitration clauses are material terms."

Williams and Daniels concede—as they must—...that Article 2 governs "transactions in goods," and, consequently, that it is not applicable to the transactions in this case. Nevertheless, they argue:

> *It would be astonishing if a Court were to consider the addition of an arbitration clause a material alteration to a contract between merchants, who by definition are sophisticated in the trade to which the contract applies, but not hold that the addition of an arbitration clause is a material alteration pursuant to a change-of-terms clause in a contract between one sophisticated party, a bank, and an entire class of less sophisticated parties, its depositors....*

In response, SouthTrust states that "because of the 'at-will' nature of the relationship, banks by necessity must contractually reserve the right to amend their deposit agreements from time to time." In so stating, SouthTrust has precisely identified the fundamental difference between the transactions here and those transactions governed by [Article 2].

Contracts for the purchase and sale of goods are essentially *bilateral* and executory in nature. See [Citation] "An agreement whereby one party promises to sell and the other promises to buy a thing at a later time...is a bilateral promise of sale or contract to sell." * * * "[A] unilateral contract results from an exchange of a promise for an act; a bilateral contract results from an exchange of promises." * * * Thus, "in a unilateral contract, there is no bargaining process or exchange of promises by parties as in a bilateral contract." [Citation] "[O]nly one party makes an offer (or promise) which invites performance by another, and performance constitutes both acceptance of that offer and consideration." Because "a 'unilateral contract' is one in which no promisor receives promise as consideration for his promise," only one party is bound. * * * The difference is not one of semantics but of substance; it determines the rights and responsibilities of the parties, including the time and the conditions under which a cause of action accrues for a breach of the contract.

This case involves at-will, commercial relationships, based upon a series of unilateral transactions. Thus, it is more analogous to cases involving insurance policies, such as [Citations]. The common thread running through those cases was the *amendment* by one of the parties to a business relationship of a document underlying that relationship—without the express assent of the other party—to require the arbitration of disputes arising after the amendment. * * *

The parties in [the cited cases], like Williams and Daniels in this case, took no action that could be considered inconsistent with an assent to the arbitration provision. In each case, they continued the business relationship after the interposition of the arbitration provision. In doing so, they implicitly assented to the addition of the arbitration provision. * * *

Reversed and remanded.

Case Questions

1. Why did the plaintiffs think they should not be bound by the arbitration clause?
2. The court said this case involved a unilateral contract. What makes it that, as opposed to a bilateral contract?
3. What should the plaintiffs have done if they didn't like the arbitration requirement?

Unilateral Contract and At-Will Employment

Woolley v. Hoffmann-La Roche, Inc.

491 A.2d 1257 (N.J. 1985)

Wilntz, C. J.

Plaintiff, Richard Woolley, was hired by defendant, Hoffmann-La Roche, Inc., in October 1969, as an Engineering Section Head in defendant's Central Engineering Department at Nutley. There was no written employment contract between plaintiff and defendant. Plaintiff began work in mid-November 1969. Sometime in December, plaintiff received and read the personnel manual on which his claims are based.

[The company's personnel manual had eight pages;] five of the eight pages are devoted to "termination." In addition to setting forth the purpose and policy of the termination section, it defines "the types of termination" as "layoff," "discharge due to performance," "discharge, disciplinary," "retirement" and "resignation." As one might expect, layoff is a termination caused by lack of work, retirement a termination caused by age, resignation a termination on the initiative of the employee, and discharge due to performance and discharge, disciplinary, are both terminations for cause. There is no category set forth for discharge without cause. The termination section includes "Guidelines for discharge due to performance," consisting of a fairly detailed procedure to be used before an employee may be fired for cause. Preceding these definitions of the five categories of termination is a section on "Policy," the first sentence of which provides: "It is the policy of Hoffmann-La Roche to retain to the extent consistent with company requirements, the services of all employees who perform their duties efficiently and effectively."

In 1976, plaintiff was promoted, and in January 1977 he was promoted again, this latter time to Group Leader for the Civil Engineering, the Piping Design, the Plant Layout, and the Standards and Systems Sections. In March 1978, plaintiff was directed to write a report to his supervisors about piping problems in one of defendant's buildings in Nutley. This report was written and submitted to plaintiff's immediate supervisor on April 5, 1978. On May 3, 1978, stating that the General Manager of defendant's Corporate Engineering Department had lost confidence in him, plaintiff's supervisors requested his resignation. Following this, by letter dated May 22, 1978, plaintiff was formally asked for his resignation, to be effective July 15, 1978.

Plaintiff refused to resign. Two weeks later defendant again requested plaintiff's resignation, and told him he would be fired if he did not resign. Plaintiff again declined, and he was fired in July.

Plaintiff filed a complaint alleging breach of contract. * * * The gist of plaintiff's breach of contract claim is that the express and implied promises in defendant's employment manual created a contract under which he could not be fired at will, but rather only for cause, and then only after the procedures outlined in the manual were followed. Plaintiff contends that he was not dismissed for good cause, and that his firing was a breach of contract.

Defendant's motion for summary judgment was granted by the trial court, which held that the employment manual was not contractually binding on defendant, thus allowing defendant to terminate plaintiff's employment at will. The Appellate Division affirmed. We granted certification.

The employer's contention here is that the distribution of the manual was simply an expression of the company's "philosophy" and therefore free of any possible contractual consequences. The former employee claims it could reasonably be read as an explicit statement of company policies intended to be followed by the company in the same manner as if they were expressed in an agreement signed by both employer and employees. * * *

This Court has long recognized the capacity of the common law to develop and adapt to current needs. * * * The interests of employees, employers, and the public lead to the conclusion that the common law of New Jersey should limit the right of an employer to fire an employee at will.

In order for an offer in the form of a promise to become enforceable, it must be accepted. Acceptance will depend on what the promisor bargained for: he may have bargained for a return promise that, if given, would result in a bilateral contract, both promises becoming enforceable. Or he may have bargained for some action or non-action that, if given or withheld, would render his promise enforceable as a unilateral contract. In most of the cases involving an employer's personnel policy manual, the document is prepared without any negotiations and is voluntarily distributed to the workforce by the employer. It seeks no return promise from the employees. It is reasonable to interpret it as seeking continued work from the employees, who, in most cases, are free to quit since they are almost always employees at will, not simply in the sense that the employer can fire them without cause, but in the sense that they can quit without breaching any obligation. Thus analyzed, the manual is an offer that seeks the formation of a unilateral contract—the employees' bargained-for action needed to make the offer binding being their continued work when they have no obligation to continue.

The unilateral contract analysis is perfectly adequate for that employee who was aware of the manual and who continued to work intending that continuation to be the action in exchange for the employer's promise; it is even more helpful in support of that conclusion if, but for the employer's policy manual, the employee would have quit. See generally [Citation] (judicial use of unilateral contract analysis in employment cases is widespread).

* * * All that this opinion requires of an employer is that it be fair. It would be unfair to allow an employer to distribute a policy manual that makes the workforce believe that certain promises have been made and then to allow the employer to renege on those promises. What is sought here is basic honesty: if the employer, for whatever reason, does not want the manual to be capable of being construed by the court as a binding contract, there are simple ways to attain that goal. All that need be done is the inclusion in a very prominent position of an appropriate statement that there is no promise of any kind by the employer contained in the manual; that regardless of what the manual says or provides, the employer promises nothing and remains free to change wages and all other working conditions without having to consult anyone and without anyone's agreement; and that the employer continues to have the absolute power to fire anyone with or without good cause.

Reversed and remanded for trial.

Case Questions

1. What did Woolley do to show his acceptance of the terms of employment offered to him?
2. In part of the case not included here, the court notes that Mr. Woolley died "before oral arguments on this case." How can there be any damages if the plaintiff has died? Who now has any case to pursue?
3. The court here is changing the law of employment in New Jersey. It is making case law, and the rule here articulated governs similar future cases in New Jersey. Why did the court make this change? Why is it relevant that the court says it would be easy for an employer to avoid this problem?

8.5 Summary and Exercises

Summary

Contract law developed as the status-centered organization of feudal society faded and people began to make choices about how they might order their lives. In the capitalistic system, people make choices about how to interact with others, and—necessarily—those choices expressed as promises must be binding and enforceable.

The two fundamental sources of contract law are (1) the common law as developed in the state courts and as summarized in the Restatement (Second) of Contracts and (2) the Uniform Commercial Code for the sale of goods. In general, the UCC is more liberal than the common law in upholding the existence of a contract.

Types of contracts can be distinguished by four criteria: (1) express and implied, including quasi-contracts implied by law; (2) bilateral and unilateral; (3) enforceable and unenforceable; and (4) completed (executed) and uncompleted (executory). To understand contract law, it is necessary to master these distinctions and their nuances.

Exercises

1. a. Mr. and Mrs. Smith, an elderly couple, had no relatives. When Mrs. Smith became ill, the Smiths asked a friend, Henrietta, to help with various housekeeping chores, including cleaning and cooking. Although the Smiths never promised to pay her, Henrietta performed the chores for eighteen months. Henrietta now claims that she is entitled to the reasonable value of the services performed. Is she correct? Explain.

   b. Assume instead that the Smiths asked Mrs. Smith's sister, Caroline, who lived nearby, to help with the housekeeping. After eighteen months, Caroline claims she is entitled to the reasonable value of the services performed. Is she correct? Explain.

2. A letter from Bridge Builders Inc. to the Allied Steel Company stated, "We offer to purchase 10,000 tons of No. 4 steel pipe at today's quoted price for delivery two months from today. Your acceptance must be received in five days." Does Bridge Builders intend to create a bilateral or a unilateral contract? Why?

3. Roscoe's barber persuaded him to try a new hair cream called Sansfree, which the barber applied to Roscoe's hair and scalp. The next morning Roscoe had a very unpleasant rash along his hairline. Upon investigation he discovered that the rash was due to an improper chemical compound in Sansfree. If Roscoe filed a breach of contract action against the barber, would the case be governed by the Uniform Commercial Code or common law? Explain.

4. Rachel entered into a contract to purchase a 2004 Dodge from Hanna, who lived in the neighboring apartment. When a dispute arose over the terms of the contract, Hanna argued that, because neither she nor Rachel was a merchant, the dispute should be decided under general principles of common law. Rachel, on the other hand, argued that Hanna was legally considered to be a merchant because she sold the car for profit and that, consequently, the sale was governed by the Uniform Commercial Code. Who is correct? Explain.

5. Lee and Michelle decided to cohabit. When they set up house, Michelle gave up her career, and Lee promised to share his earnings with her on a fifty-fifty basis. Several years later they ended their relationship, and when Lee failed to turn over half of his earnings, Michelle filed suit on the basis of Lee's promise. What kind of contract would Michelle allege that Lee had breached? Explain.

6. Harry and Wilma were divorced in 2008, and Harry was ordered in the divorce decree to pay his ex-wife $10,000. In 2009 and 2010, Harry was hospitalized, incurring $3,000 in bills. He and Wilma discussed the matter, and Wilma agreed to pay the bill with her own money, even though Harry still owed her $5,000 from the divorce decree. When Harry died in late 2010, Wilma made a claim against his estate for $8,000 (the $3,000 in medical bills and the $5,000 from the decree), but the estate was only willing to pay the $5,000 from the decree, claiming she had paid the hospital bill voluntarily and had no contract for repayment. Is the estate correct? Explain.

7. Louie, an adult, entered into a contract to sell a case of scotch whiskey to Leroy, a minor. Is the contract void or voidable? Explain.

8. James Mann owned a manufacturing plant that assembled cell phones. A CPA audit determined that several phones were missing. Theft by one or more of the workers was suspected. Accordingly, under Mann's instructions, the following sign was placed in the employees' cafeteria:

   > Reward. *We are missing phones. I want all employees to watch for thievery. A reward of $500 will be paid for information given by any employee that leads to the apprehension of employee thieves.*
   >
   > *—James Mann*

   Waldo, a plant employee, read the notice and immediately called Mann, stating, "I accept your offer. I promise to watch other employees and provide you with the requested information." Has a contract been formed? Explain.

9. Almost every day Sally took a break at lunch and went to the International News Stand—a magazine store—to browse the newspapers and magazines and chat with the owner, Conrad. Often she bought a magazine. One day she went there, browsed a bit, and took a magazine off the rack. Conrad was busy with three customers. Sally waved the magazine at Conrad and left the store with it. What kind of a contract, if any, was created?
10. Joan called Devon Sand & Gravel and ordered two "boxes" (dump-truck loads) of gravel to be spread on her rural driveway by the "shoot and run" method: the tailgate is partially opened, the dump-truck bed is lifted, and the truck moves down the driveway spreading gravel as it goes. The driver mistakenly graveled the driveway of Joan's neighbor, Watson, instead of Joan's. Is Devon entitled to payment by Watson? Explain.

Self-Test Questions

1. An implied contract
    a. must be in writing
    b. is one in which the terms are spelled out
    c. is one inferred from the actions of the parties
    d. is imposed by law to avoid an unjust result
    e. may be avoided by one party
2. The Convention on Contracts for the International Sale of Goods is
    a. an annual meeting of international commercial purchasing agents.
    b. contract law used in overseas US federal territories
    c. a customary format or template for drafting contracts
    d. a kind of treaty setting out international contract law, to which the United States is a party
    e. the organization that develops uniform international law
3. An unenforceable contract is
    a. void, not a contract at all
    b. one that a court will not enforce for either side because of a rule of law
    c. unenforceable by one party but enforceable by the other
    d. one that has been performed by one party but not the other
    e. too indefinite to be valid
4. Betty Baker found a bicycle apparently abandoned near her house. She took it home and spent $150 repairing and painting it, after which Carl appeared and proved his ownership of it. Under what theory is Betty able to get reimbursed for her expenditures?
    a. express contract
    b. implied contract
    c. apparent or quasi-contract
    d. executory contract
    e. none: she will not get reimbursed
5. Alice discusses with her neighbor Bob her plan to hire Woodsman to cut three trees on her side of their property line, mentioning that she can get a good deal because Woodsman is now between jobs. Bob says, "Oh, don't do that. My brother is going to cut some trees on my side, and he can do yours too for free." Alice agrees. But Bob's brother is preoccupied and never does the job. Three weeks later Alice discovers Woodsman's rates have risen prohibitively. Under what theory does Alice have a cause of action against Bob?
    a. express contract
    b. promissory estoppel
    c. quasi-contract

d. implied contract
e. none: she has no cause of action against Bob

Self-Test Answers

1. c
2. d
3. c
4. c
5. b

Endnotes

1. Sir Henry Maine, *Ancient Law* (1869), 180–82.
2. Richard A. Posner, *Economic Analysis of Law* (New York: Aspen, 1973).
3. Uniform Commercial Code, Section 1-201(11).
4. Uniform Commercial Code, Section 2-105.
5. *Central London Property Trust Ltd. v. High Trees House Ltd.* (1947) KB 130.

CHAPTER 9

The Agreement

Learning Objectives

After reading this chapter, you should understand the following:

1. What a contract offer is, and what proposals are not offers.
2. How an offer is communicated.
3. How definite the offer needs to be.
4. How long an offer is good for.
5. How an offer is accepted, who can accept it, and when acceptance is effective.

In this chapter, we begin the first of the four broad inquiries of contract law mentioned in Chapter 8: Did the parties create a valid contract? The answer is not always obvious; the range of factors that must be taken into account can be large, and their relationships subtle. Since businesspeople frequently conduct contract negotiations without the assistance of a lawyer, it is important to attend to the nuances in order to avoid legal trouble at the outset. Whether a contract has been formed depends in turn on whether:

1. the parties reached an agreement (the focus of this chapter);
2. consideration was present;
3. the agreement was legal; and
4. the parties entered into the contract of their own free will, with knowledge of the facts, and with the capacity to make a contract.

Factors 2, 3, and 4 are the subjects of subsequent chapters.

9.1 The Agreement in General

Learning Objectives

1. Recognize that not all agreements or promises are contracts.
2. Understand that whether a contract exists is based on an objective analysis of the parties' interaction, not on a subjective one.

The Significance of Agreement

The core of a legal contract is the agreement between the parties. This is not a necessary ingredient; in Communist nations, contracts were (or are, in the few remaining Communist countries) routinely negotiated between parties who had the terms imposed on them. But in the West, and especially in the United States, agreement is of the essence. That is not merely a matter of convenience; it is at the heart of our philosophical and psychological beliefs. As the great student of contract law Samuel Williston put it, "It was a consequence of the emphasis laid on the ego and the individual will that the formation of a contract should seem impossible unless the wills of the parties concurred. Accordingly we find at the end of the eighteenth century, and the beginning of the nineteenth century, the prevalent idea that there must be a 'meeting of the minds' (a new phrase) in order to form a contract."[1]

Although agreements may take any form, including unspoken conduct between the parties, they are usually structured in terms of an offer and an acceptance.[2] These two components will be the focus of our discussion. Note, however, that not every agreement, in the broadest sense of the word, need consist of an offer and an acceptance, and that it is entirely possible, therefore, for two persons to reach agreement without forming a contract. For example, people may agree that the weather is pleasant or that it would be preferable to go out for Chinese food rather than to see a foreign film; in neither case has a contract been formed. One of the major functions of the law of contracts is to sort out those agreements that are legally binding—those that are contracts—from those that are not.

The Objective Test

objective standard

Judging something as an outsider would understand it; not subjective.

In interpreting agreements, courts generally apply an **objective standard** (outwardly, as an observer would interpret; not subjectively). The Restatement (Second) of Contracts defines *agreement* as a "manifestation of mutual assent by two or more persons to one another."[3] The Uniform Commercial Code defines *agreement* as "the bargain of the parties in fact as found in their language or by implication from other circumstances including course of dealing or usage of trade or course of performance."[4] The critical question is what the parties said or did, not what they thought they said or did, or not what impression they thought they were making.

The distinction between objective and subjective standards crops up occasionally when one person claims he spoke in jest. The vice president of a company that manufactured punchboards, used in gambling, testified to the Washington State Gambling Commission that he would pay $100,000 to anyone who found a "crooked board." Barnes, a bartender, who had purchased two boards that were crooked some time before, brought one to the company office and demanded payment. The company refused, claiming that the statement was made in jest (the audience at the commission hearing had laughed when the offer was made). The court disagreed, holding that it was reasonable to interpret the pledge of $100,000 as a means of promoting punchboards:

> *[I]f the jest is not apparent and a reasonable hearer would believe that an offer was being made, then the speaker risks the formation of a contract which was not intended. It is the objective manifestations of the offeror that count and not secret, unexpressed intentions. If a party's words or acts, judged by a reasonable standard, manifest an intention to agree in regard to the matter in question, that agreement is established, and it is immaterial what may be the real but unexpressed state of the party's mind on the subject.*[5]

Lucy v. Zehmer (Section 4 at the end of the chapter) illustrates that a party's real state of mind must be expressed to the other party, rather than in an aside to one's spouse.

Key Takeaway

Fundamentally, a contract is a legally binding "meeting of the minds" between the parties. It is not the unexpressed intention in the minds of the parties that determines whether there was "a meeting." The test is objective: how would a reasonable person interpret the interaction?

Exercises

1. For the purposes of determining whether a party had a contractual intention, why do courts employ an objective rather than a subjective test?
2. What is the relationship between "the emphasis laid on the ego and the individual will" in modern times (Williston) and the concept of the contractual agreement?

9.2 The Offer

Learning Objectives

1. Know the definition of *offer*.
2. Recognize that some proposals are not offers.
3. Understand the three essentials of an offer: intent, communication, and definiteness.
4. Know when an offer expires and can no longer be accepted.

Offer and acceptance may seem to be straightforward concepts, as they are when two people meet face-to-face. But in a commercial society, the ways of making offers and accepting them are nearly infinite. A retail store advertises its merchandise in the newspaper. A seller makes his offer by mail or over the Internet. A telephone caller states that his offer will stand for ten days. An offer leaves open a crucial term. An auctioneer seeks bids. An offeror gives the offeree a choice. All these situations can raise tricky questions, as can corresponding situations involving acceptances.

The Definition of *Offer*

The Restatement defines **offer** as "the manifestation of willingness to enter into a bargain, so made as to justify another person in understanding that his assent to that bargain is invited and will conclude it."[6] Two key elements are implicit in that definition: the offer must be communicated, and it must be definite. Before considering these requirements, we examine the threshold question of whether an offer was intended. Let us look at proposals that may look like, but are not, offers.

offer

The proposal upon which the contract is based.

Proposals That Are Not Offers

Advertisements

Most advertisements, price quotations, and invitations to bid are not construed as offers. A notice in the newspaper that a bicycle is on sale for $800 is normally intended only as an invitation to the public to come to the store to make a purchase. Similarly, a statement that a seller can "quote" a unit price to a prospective purchaser is not, by itself, of sufficient definiteness to constitute an offer; quantity, time of delivery, and other important factors are missing from such a statement. Frequently, in order to avoid construction of a statement about price and quantity as an offer, a seller or buyer may say, "Make me an offer." Such a statement obviously suggests that no offer has yet been made. This principle usually applies to invitations for bids (e.g., from contractors on a building project). Many forms used by sales representatives as contracts indicate that by signing, the customer is making an offer to be accepted by the home office and is not accepting an offer made by the sales representative.

Although advertisements, price quotations, and the like are generally not offers, the facts in each case are important. Under the proper circumstances, an advertised statement can be construed as an offer, as shown in the well-known *Lefkowitz* case (Section 4 at the end of the chapter), in which the offended customer acted as his own lawyer and pursued an appeal to the Minnesota Supreme Court against a Minneapolis department store that took back its advertised offer.

Despite the common-law rule that display advertisements (but not classified-ad types) are normally to be considered invitations rather than offers, legislation and government regulations may offer redress. For many years, retail food stores have been subject to a rule, promulgated by the Federal Trade Commission (FTC), that goods advertised as "specials" must be available and must be sold at the price advertised. It is unlawful for a retail chain not to have an advertised item in each of its stores and in sufficient quantity, unless the advertisement specifically states how much is stocked and which branch stores do not carry it. Many states have enacted consumer protection statutes that parallel the FTC rule.

Invitations to Bid

Invitations to bid are also not generally construed as offers. An auctioneer does not make offers but solicits offers from the crowd: "May I have an offer?—$500? $450? $450! I have an offer for $450. Do I hear $475? May I have an offer?"

Communication

A contract is an agreement in which each party assents to the terms of the other party. Without mutual assent there cannot be a contract, and this implies that the assent each person gives must be with reference to that of the other. If Toni places several alternative offers on the table, only one of which can be accepted, and invites Sandy to choose, no contract is formed if Sandy says merely, "I accept your terms." Sandy must specify which offer she is assenting to.

From this general proposition, it follows that no contract can be legally binding unless an offer is in fact communicated to the offeree. If you write an e-mail to a friend with an offer to sell your car for a certain sum and then get distracted and forget to send it, no offer has been made. If your friend coincidentally e-mails you the following day and says that she wants to buy your car and names the same sum, no contract has been made. Her e-mail to you is not an acceptance, since she did not know of your offer; it is, instead, an offer or an invitation to make an offer. Nor would there have been a contract if you had sent your communication and the two e-mails crossed in cyberspace. Both e-mails would be offers, and for a valid contract to be formed, it would still be necessary for one of you to accept the other's offer. An offer is not effective until it is received by the offeree (and that's also true of a revocation of the offer, and a rejection of the offer by the offeree).

The requirement that an offer be communicated does not mean that every term must be communicated. You call up your friend and offer to sell him your car. You tell him the price and start to tell him that you will throw in the snow tires but will not pay for a new inspection, and that you expect to keep the car another three weeks. Impatiently, he cuts you off and says, "Never mind about all that; I'll accept your offer on whatever terms you want." You and he have a contract.

These principles apply to unknown offers of reward. An offer of a reward constitutes a unilateral contract that can be made binding only by performing the task for which the reward is offered.

Suppose that Bonnie posts on a tree a sign offering a reward for returning her missing dog. If you saw the sign, found the dog, and returned it, you would have fulfilled the essentials of the offer. But if you chanced upon the dog, read the tag around its neck, and returned it without ever having been aware that a reward was offered, then you have not responded to the offer, even if you acted in the hope that the owner would reward you. There is no contractual obligation.

In many states, a different result follows from an offer of a reward by a governmental entity. Commonly, local ordinances provide that a standing reward of, say, $1,000 will be paid to anyone providing information that leads to the arrest and conviction of arsonists. To collect the reward, it is not necessary for a person who does furnish local authorities with such information to know that a reward ordinance exists. In contract terms, the standing reward is viewed as a means of setting a climate in which people will be encouraged to act in certain ways in the expectation that they will earn unknown rewards. It is also possible to view the claim to a reward as noncontractual; the right to receive it is guaranteed, instead, by the local ordinance.

Although a completed act called for by an unknown private offer does not give rise to a contract, partial performance usually does. Suppose Apex Bakery posts a notice offering a one-week bonus to all bakers who work at least six months in the kitchen. Charlene works two months before discovering the notice on the bulletin board. Her original ignorance of the offer will not defeat her claim to the bonus if she continues working, for the offer serves as an inducement to complete the performance called for.

Definiteness

The common law reasonably requires that an offer spell out the essential proposed terms with sufficient **definiteness**—a certainty of terms that enables a court to order enforcement or measure damages in the event of a breach. As it has often been put, "The law does not make contracts for the parties; it merely enforces the duties which they have undertaken." Thus, a supposed promise to sell "such coal as the promisor may wish to sell" is not an enforceable term because the seller, the coal company, undertakes no duty to sell anything unless it wishes to do so. Essential terms certainly include price and the work to be done. But not every omission is fatal; for example, as long as a missing term can be fixed by referring to some external standard—such as "no later than the first frost"—the offer is sufficiently definite.

definiteness

The requirement that contracts be certain enough to determine liabilities.

In major business transactions involving extensive negotiations, the parties often sign a preliminary "agreement in principle" before a detailed contract is drafted. These preliminary agreements may be definite enough to create contract liability even though they lack many of the terms found in a typical contract. For example, in a famous 1985 case, a Texas jury concluded that an agreement made "in principle" between the Pennzoil Company and the Getty Oil Company and not entirely finished was binding and that Texaco had unlawfully interfered with their contract. As a result, Texaco was held liable for over $10 billion, which was settled for $3 billion after Texaco went into bankruptcy.

Offers that state alternatives are definitive if each alternative is definite. David offers Sheila the opportunity to buy one of two automobiles at a fixed price, with delivery in two months and the choice of vehicle left to David. Sheila accepts. The contract is valid. If one of the cars is destroyed in the interval before delivery, David is obligated to deliver the other car. Sometimes, however, what appears to be an offer in the alternative may be something else. Charles makes a deal to sell his business to Bernie. As part of the bargain, Charles agrees not to compete with Bernie for the next two years, and if he does, to pay $25,000. Whether or not this is an alternative contract depends on the circumstances and intentions of the parties. If it is, then Charles is free to compete as long as he pays Bernie $25,000. On the other hand, the intention might have been to prevent Charles from competing in any event; hence a court could order payment of the $25,000 as damages for a breach and still order Charles to refrain from competition until the expiration of the two-year period.

The UCC Approach

The Uniform Commercial Code (UCC) is generally more liberal in its approach to definiteness than is the common law—at least as the common law was interpreted in the heyday of classical contract doctrine. Section 2-204(3) states the rule: "Even though one or more terms are left open, a contract for sale does not fail for indefiniteness if the parties have intended to make a contract and there is a reasonably certain basis for giving an appropriate remedy."

The drafters of the UCC sought to give validity to as many contracts as possible and grounded that validity on the intention of the parties rather than on formalistic requirements. As the official comment to Section 2-204(3) notes, "If the parties intend to enter into a binding agreement, this subsection recognizes that agreement as valid in law, despite missing terms, if there is any reasonably certain basis for granting a remedy. * * * Commercial standards on the point of 'indefiniteness' are intended to be applied." Other sections of the UCC spell out rules for filling in such open provisions as price, performance, and remedies.[7]

One of these sections, Section 2-306(1), provides that a contract term under which a buyer agrees to purchase the seller's entire output of goods (an "outputs contract") or a seller agrees to meet all the buyer's requirements (a "requirements" or "needs" contract) means output or requirements that occur in good faith. A party to such a contract cannot offer or demand a quantity that is "unreasonably disproportionate" to a stated estimate or past quantities.

Duration of Offer

An offer need not be accepted on the spot. Because there are numerous ways of conveying an offer and numerous contingencies that may be part of the offer's subject matter, the offeror might find it necessary to give the offeree considerable time to accept or reject the offer. By the same token, an offer cannot remain open forever, so that once given, it never lapses and cannot be terminated. The law recognizes seven ways by which the offer can expire (besides acceptance, of course): revocation, rejection by the offeree, counteroffer, acceptance with counteroffer, lapse of time, death or insanity of a person or destruction of an essential term, and illegality. We will examine each of these in turn.

Revocation

People are free to make contracts and, in general, to revoke them.

Revocability

revocation

The withdrawal of an offer by the offeror.

The general rule, both in common law and under the UCC, is that the offeror may revoke his or her offer at any time before acceptance, even if the offer states that it will remain open for a specified period of time. Neil offers Arlene his car for $5,000 and promises to keep the offer open for ten days. Two days later, Neil calls Arlene to revoke the offer. The offer is terminated, and Arlene's acceptance thereafter, though within the ten days, is ineffective. But if Neil had sent his **revocation** (the taking back of an offer before it is accepted) by mail, and if Arlene, before she received it, had telephoned her acceptance, there would be a contract, since revocation is effective only when the offeree actually receives it. There is an exception to this rule for offers made to the public through newspaper or like advertisements. The offeror may revoke a public offering by notifying the public by the same means used to communicate the offer. If no better means of notification is reasonably available, the offer is terminated even if a particular offeree had no actual notice.

Revocation may be communicated indirectly. If Arlene had learned from a friend that Neil had sold his car to someone else during the ten-day period, she would have had sufficient notice. Any attempt to accept Neil's offer would have been futile.

Irrevocable Offers

Not every type of offer is revocable. One type of offer that cannot be revoked is the **option contract** (the promisor explicitly agrees for consideration to limit his right to revoke). Arlene tells Neil that she cannot make up her mind in ten days but that she will pay him $25 to hold the offer open for thirty days. Neil agrees. Arlene has an option to buy the car for $5,000; if Neil should sell it to someone else during the thirty days, he will have breached the contract with Arlene. Note that the transactions involving Neil and Arlene consist of two different contracts. One is the promise of a thirty-day option for the promise of $25. It is this contract that makes the option binding and is independent of the original offer to sell the car for $5,000. The offer can be accepted and made part of an independent contract during the option period.

option contract
A promise to keep an offer open for some time; must be supported by consideration.

Partial performance of a unilateral contract creates an option. Although the option is not stated explicitly, it is recognized by law in the interests of justice. Otherwise, an offeror could induce the offeree to go to expense and trouble without ever being liable to fulfill his or her part of the bargain. Before the offeree begins to carry out the contract, the offeror is free to revoke the offer. But once performance begins, the law implies an option, allowing the offeree to complete performance according to the terms of the offer. If, after a reasonable time, the offeree does not fulfill the terms of the offer, then it may be revoked.

Revocability under the UCC

The UCC changes the common-law rule for offers by merchants. Under Section 2-205, a **firm offer** (a written and signed promise by a merchant to hold an offer to buy or sell goods for some period of time) is irrevocable. That is, an option is created, but no consideration is required. The offer must remain open for the time period stated or, if no time period is given, for a reasonable period of time, which may not exceed three months.

firm offer
A UCC option made in writing and signed by a merchant, promising to keep an offer open; needs no consideration.

Irrevocability by Law

By law, certain types of offers may not be revoked (statutory irrevocability), despite the absence of language to that effect in the offer itself. One major category of such offers is that of the contractor submitting a bid to a public agency. The general rule is that once the period of bidding opens, a bidder on a public contract may not withdraw his or her bid unless the contracting authority consents. The contractor who purports to withdraw is awarded the contract based on the original bid and may be sued for damages for nonperformance.

Rejection by the Offeree

Rejection (a manifestation of refusal to agree to the terms of an offer) of the offer is effective when the offeror receives it. A subsequent change of mind by the offeree cannot revive the offer. Donna calls Chuck to reject Chuck's offer to sell his lawn mower. Chuck is then free to sell it to someone else. If Donna changes her mind and calls Chuck back to accept after all, there still is no contract, even if Chuck has made no further effort to sell the lawn mower. Having rejected the original offer, Donna, by her second call, is not accepting but making an offer to buy. Suppose Donna had written Chuck to reject, but on changing her mind, decided to call to accept before the rejection letter arrived. In that case, the offer would have been accepted.

Rejection
A manifestation of refusal to agree to the terms of an offer.

Counteroffer

counteroffer

A response to an offer that changes its terms.

A **counteroffer**, a response that varies the terms of an offer, is a rejection. Jones offers Smith a small parcel of land for $10,000 and says the offer will remain open for one month. Smith responds ten days later, saying he will pay $5,000. Jones's original offer has thereby been rejected. If Jones now declines Smith's counteroffer, may Smith bind Jones to his original offer by agreeing to pay the full $10,000? He may not, because once an original offer is rejected, all the terms lapse. However, an inquiry by Smith as to whether Jones would consider taking less is not a counteroffer and would not terminate the offer.

Acceptance with Counteroffer

mirror image rule

Common-law rule that the acceptance must be the same as the offer.

This is not really an acceptance at all but is a counteroffer: an acceptance that changes the terms of the offer is a counteroffer and terminates the offer. The common law imposes a **mirror image rule**: the acceptance must match the offer in all its particulars or the offer is rejected. However, if an acceptance that requests a change or an addition to the offer does not require the offeror's assent, then the acceptance is valid. The broker at Friendly Real Estate offers you a house for $320,000. You accept but include in your acceptance "the vacant lot next door." Your "acceptance" is a counteroffer, which serves to terminate the original offer. If, instead, you had said, "It's a deal, but I'd prefer it with the vacant lot next door," then there is a contract because you are not demanding that the broker abide by your request. If you had said, "It's a deal, and I'd also like the vacant lot next door," you have a contract, because the request for the lot is a separate offer, not a counteroffer rejecting the original proposal.

The UCC and Counteroffers

The UCC is more liberal than the common law in allowing contracts to be formed despite counteroffers and in incorporating the counteroffers into the contracts. This UCC provision is necessary because the use of routine forms for contracts is very common, and if the rule were otherwise, much valuable time would be wasted by drafting clauses tailored to the precise wording of the routine printed forms. A buyer and a seller send out documents accompanying or incorporating their offers and acceptances, and the provisions in each document rarely correspond precisely. Indeed, it is often the case that one side's form contains terms favorable to it but inconsistent with terms on the other side's form. Section 2-207 of the UCC attempts to resolve this "battle of the forms" by providing that additional terms or conditions in an acceptance operate as such unless the acceptance is conditioned on the offeror's consent to the new or different terms. The new terms are construed as offers but are automatically incorporated in any contract between merchants for the sale of goods unless "(a) the offer expressly limits acceptance to the terms of the offer; (b) [the terms] materially alter it; or (c) notification of objection to them has already been given or is given within a reasonable time after notice of them is received."

An example of terms that become part of the contract without being expressly agreed to are clauses providing for interest payments on overdue bills. Examples of terms that would materially alter the contract and hence need express approval are clauses that negate the standard warranties that sellers give buyers on their merchandise.

Frequently, parties use contract provisions to prevent the automatic introduction of new terms. A typical seller's provision is as follows:

> *Amendments*
>
> *Any modification of this document by the Buyer, and all additional or different terms included in Buyer's purchase order or any other document responding to this offer, are hereby objected to. BY ORDERING THE GOODS HERE FOR SHIPMENT, BUYER AGREES TO ALL THE TERMS AND CONDITIONS CONTAINED ON BOTH SIDES OF THIS DOCUMENT.*

Section 2-207 of the UCC, liberalizing the mirror image rule, is pervasive, covering all sorts of contracts, from those between industrial manufacturers to those between friends.

Lapse of Time

Offers are not open-ended; they lapse after some period of time. An offer may contain its own specific time limitation—for example, "until close of business today."

In the absence of an expressly stated time limit, the common-law rule is that the offer expires at the end of a "reasonable" time. Such a period is a factual question in each case and depends on the particular circumstances, including the nature of the service or property being contracted for, the manner in which the offer is made, and the means by which the acceptance is expected to be made. Whenever the contract involves a speculative transaction—the sale of securities or land, for instance—the time period will depend on the nature of the security and the risk involved. In general, the greater the risk to the seller, the shorter the period of time. Karen offers to sell Gary a block of oil stocks that are fluctuating rapidly hour by hour. Gary receives the offer an hour before the market closes; he accepts by fax two hours after the market has opened the next morning and after learning that the stock has jumped up significantly. The time period has lapsed if Gary was accepting a fixed price that Karen set, but it may still be open if the price is market price at time of delivery. (Under Section 41 of the Restatement, an offer made by mail is "seasonably accepted if an acceptance is mailed at any time before midnight on the day on which the offer is received.")

For unilateral contracts, both the common law and the UCC require the offeree to notify the offeror that he has begun to perform the terms of the contract. Without notification, the offeror may, after a reasonable time, treat the offer as having lapsed.

Death or Insanity of the Offeror or Offeree

The death or insanity of the offeror prior to acceptance terminates the offer; the offer is said to die with the offeror. (Notice, however, that the death of a party to a *contract* does not necessarily terminate the contract: the estate of a deceased person may be liable on a contract made by the person before death.)

Destruction of Subject Matter Essential to the Offer

Destruction of something essential to the contract also terminates the offer. You offer to sell your car, but the car is destroyed in an accident before your offer is accepted; the offer is terminated.

Post-offer Illegality

A statute making unlawful the object of the contract will terminate the offer if the statute takes effect after the offer was made. Thus, an offer to sell a quantity of herbal weight-loss supplements will terminate if the Food and Drug Administration outlaws the sale of such supplements.

Key Takeaway

An offer is a manifestation of willingness to enter into a contract, effective when received. It must be communicated to the offeree, be made intentionally (according to an objective standard), and be definite enough to determine a remedy in case of breach. An offer terminates in one of seven ways: revocation before acceptance (except for option contracts, firm offers under the UCC, statutory irrevocability, and unilateral offers where an offeree has commenced performance); rejection; counteroffer; acceptance with counteroffer; lapse of time (as stipulated or after a reasonable time); death or insanity of the offeror before acceptance or destruction of subject matter essential to the offer; and postoffer illegality.

Exercises

1. Why is it said an offer is a "manifestation" of willingness to enter into a contract? How could willingness be "manifested"?
2. Which kind of standard is used to determine whether a person has made an offer—subjective or objective?
3. If Sandra posts a written notice offering "to the kitchen staff at Coldwater Bay (Alaska) transportation to Seattle at the end of the fishing season," and if David, one of the maintenance workers, says to her, "I accept your offer of transportation to Seattle," is there a contract?
4. What are the seven ways an offer can terminate?

9.3 The Acceptance

Learning Objectives

1. Define *acceptance*.
2. Understand who may accept an offer.
3. Know when the acceptance is effective.
4. Recognize when silence is acceptance.

General Definition of *Acceptance*

acceptance

Assent to the terms of the offer.

To result in a legally binding contract, an offer must be accepted by the offeree. Just as the law helps define and shape an offer and its duration, so the law governs the nature and manner of **acceptance**. The Restatement defines acceptance of an offer as "a manifestation of assent to the terms thereof made by the offeree in a manner invited or required by the offer."[8] The assent may be either by the making of a mutual promise or by performance or partial performance. If there is doubt about whether the offer requests a return promise or a return act, the Restatement, Section 32, provides that the offeree may accept with either a promise or performance. The Uniform Commercial Code (UCC) also adopts this view; under Section 2-206(1)(a), "an offer to make a contract shall be construed as inviting acceptance in any manner and by any medium reasonable in the circumstances" unless the offer unambiguously requires a certain mode of acceptance.

Who May Accept?

The identity of the offeree is usually clear, even if the name is unknown. The person to whom a promise is made is ordinarily the person whom the offeror contemplates will make a return promise or perform the act requested. But this is not invariably so. A promise can be made to one person who is not expected to do anything in return. The consideration necessary to weld the offer and acceptance into a legal contract can be given by a third party. Under the common law, whoever is invited to furnish consideration to the offeror is the offeree, and only an offeree may accept an offer. A common example is sale to a minor. George promises to sell his automobile to Bartley, age seventeen, if Bartley's father will promise to pay $3,500 to George. Bartley is the promisee (the person to whom the promise is made) but not the offeree; Bartley cannot legally accept George's offer. Only Bartley's father, who is called on to pay for the car, can accept, by making the promise requested. And notice what might seem obvious: a *promise* to perform as requested in the offer is itself a binding acceptance.

When Is Acceptance Effective?

As noted previously, an offer, a revocation of the offer, and a rejection of the offer are not effective until received. The same rule does not always apply to the acceptance.

Instantaneous Communication

Of course, in many instances the moment of acceptance is not in question: in face-to-face deals or transactions negotiated by telephone, the parties extend an offer and accept it instantaneously during the course of the conversation. But problems can arise in contracts negotiated through correspondence.

Stipulations as to Acceptance

One common situation arises when the offeror stipulates the mode of acceptance (e.g., return mail, fax, or carrier pigeon). If the offeree uses the stipulated mode, then the acceptance is deemed effective when sent. Even though the offeror has no knowledge of the acceptance at that moment, the contract has been formed. Moreover, according to the Restatement, Section 60, if the offeror says that the offer can be accepted only by the specified mode, that mode must be used. (It is said that "the offeror is the master of the offer.")

If the offeror specifies no particular mode, then acceptance is effective when transmitted, as long as the offeree uses a reasonable method of acceptance. It is implied that the offeree can use the same means used by the offeror or a means of communication customary to the industry.

The "Mailbox Rule"

The use of the postal service is customary, so acceptances are considered effective when mailed, regardless of the method used to transmit the offer. Indeed, the so-called **mailbox rule** has a lineage tracing back more than one hundred years to the English courts.[9]

mailbox rule

Common-law rule that acceptance is effective when dropped in mail.

The mailbox rule may seem to create particular difficulties for people in business, since the acceptance is effective even though the offeror is unaware of the acceptance, and even if the letter is lost and never arrives. But the solution is the same as the rationale for the rule. In contracts negotiated through correspondence, there will always be a burden on one of the parties. If the rule were that the acceptance is not effective until received by the offeror, then the offeree would be on tenterhooks, rather than the other way around, as is the case with the present rule. As between the two, it seems fairer to place the burden on the offeror, since he or she alone has the power to fix the moment of effectiveness. All the offeror need do is specify in the offer that acceptance is not effective until received.

In all other cases—that is, when the offeror fails to specify the mode of acceptance and the offeree uses a mode that is not reasonable—acceptance is deemed effective only when received.

Acceptance "Outruns" Rejection

When the offeree sends a rejection first and then later transmits a superseding acceptance, the "effective when received" rule also applies. Suppose a seller offers a buyer two cords of firewood and says the offer will remain open for a week. On the third day, the buyer writes the seller, rejecting the offer. The following evening, the buyer rethinks his firewood needs, and on the morning of the fifth day, he sends an e-mail accepting the seller's terms. The previously mailed letter arrives the following day. Since the letter had not yet been received, the offer had not been rejected. For there to be a valid contract, the e-mailed acceptance must arrive before the mailed rejection. If the e-mail were hung up in cyberspace, although through no fault of the buyer, so that the letter arrived first, the seller would be correct in assuming the offer was terminated—even if the e-mail arrived a minute later. In short, where "the acceptance outruns the rejection" the acceptance is effective. See Figure 9.1.

FIGURE 9.1
When Is Communication Effective?

	When Sent	When Received
1. Offer		✓
2. Revocation of Offer		✓
3. Rejection		✓
4. Acceptance	If reasonable or by specified mode	If unreasonable or mode not specified or after rejection sent

Electronic Communications

Uniform Electronic Transactions Act (UETA)

A US law generally making electronic contracting valid and the contracts enforceable.

Electronic communications have, of course, become increasingly common. Many contracts are negotiated by e-mail, and accepted and "signed" electronically. Generally speaking, this does not change the rules. The **Uniform Electronic Transactions Act (UETA)** was promulgated (i.e., disseminated for states to adopt) in 1999. It is one of a number of uniform acts, like the Uniform Commercial Code. As of June 2015, only three states have not adopted the UETA (Illinois, New York, and Washington—they have their own equivalents). The introduction to the act provides that "the purpose of the UETA is to remove barriers to electronic commerce by validating and effectuating electronic records and signatures."[10] In general, the UETA provides the following:

a. A record or signature may not be denied legal effect or enforceability solely because it is in electronic form.
b. A contract may not be denied legal effect or enforceability solely because an electronic record was used in its formation.
c. If a law requires a record to be in writing, an electronic record satisfies the law.
d. If a law requires a signature, an electronic signature satisfies the law.

The UETA, though, doesn't address all the problems with electronic contracting. Clicking on a computer screen may constitute a valid acceptance of a contractual offer, but only if the offer is clearly communicated. In *Specht v. Netscape Communications Corp.*, customers who had downloaded a free online computer program complained that it effectively invaded their privacy by inserting into their machines "cookies"; they wanted to sue, but the defendant said they were bound to arbitration.[11] They had clicked on the Download button, but hidden below it were the licensing terms, including the arbitration clause. The federal court of appeals held that there was no valid acceptance. The court said, "We agree with the district court that a reasonably prudent Internet user in circumstances such as these would not have known or learned of the existence of the license terms before responding to defendants' invitation to download the free software, and that defendants therefore did not provide reasonable notice of the license terms. In consequence, the plaintiffs' bare act of downloading the software did not unambiguously manifest assent to the arbitration provision contained in the license terms."

If a faxed document is sent but for some reason not received or not noticed, the emerging law is that the mailbox rule does not apply. A court would examine the circumstances with care to determine the reason for the nonreceipt or for the offeror's failure to notice its receipt. A person has to have fair notice that his or her offer has been accepted, and modern communication makes the old-fashioned mailbox rule—that acceptance is effective upon dispatch—problematic.[12]

Silence as Acceptance

General Rule: Silence Is Not Acceptance

Ordinarily, for there to be a contract, the offeree must make some positive manifestation of assent to the offeror's terms. The offeror cannot usually word his offer in such a way that the offeree's failure to respond can be construed as an acceptance.

Exceptions

The Restatement, Section 69, gives three situations, however, in which silence can operate as an acceptance. The first occurs when the offeree avails himself of services proffered by the offeror, even though he could have rejected them and had reason to know that the offeror offered them expecting compensation. The second situation occurs when the offer states that the offeree may accept without responding and the offeree, remaining silent, intends to accept. The third situation is that of previous dealings, in which only if the offeree intends not to accept is it reasonable to expect him to say so.

As an example of the first type of acceptance by silence, assume that a carpenter happens by your house and sees a collapsing porch. He spots you in the front yard and points out the deterioration. "I'm a professional carpenter," he says, "and between jobs. I can fix that porch for you. Somebody ought to." You say nothing. He goes to work. There is an implied contract, with the work to be done for the carpenter's usual fee.

To illustrate the second situation, suppose that a friend has left her car in your garage. The friend sends you a letter in which she offers you the car for $4,000 and adds, "If I don't hear from you, I will assume that you have accepted my offer." If you make no reply, with the intention of accepting the offer, a contract has been formed.

The third situation is illustrated by Section 4, a well-known decision made by Justice Oliver Wendell Holmes Jr. when he was sitting on the Supreme Court of Massachusetts.

Key Takeaway

Without an acceptance of an offer, no contract exists, and once an acceptance is made, a contract is formed. If the offeror stipulates how the offer should be accepted, so be it. If there is no stipulation, any reasonable means of communication is good. Offers and revocations are usually effective upon receipt, while an acceptance is effective on dispatch. The advent of electronic contracting has caused some modification of the rules: courts are likely to investigate the facts surrounding the exchange of offer and acceptance more carefully than previously. But the nuances arising because of the mailbox rule and acceptance by silence still require close attention to the facts.

Exercises

1. Rudy puts this poster, with a photo of his dog, on utility poles around his neighborhood: "$50 reward for the return of my lost dog." Carlene doesn't see the poster, but she finds the dog and, after looking at the tag on its collar, returns the dog to Rudy. As she leaves his house, her eye falls on one of the posters, but Rudy declines to pay her anything. Why is Rudy correct that Carlene has no legal right to the reward?
2. How has the UCC changed the common law's mirror image rule, and why?
3. When is an offer generally said to be effective? A rejection of an offer? A counteroffer?
4. How have modern electronic communications affected the law of offer and acceptance?
5. When is silence considered an acceptance?

9.4 Cases

Objective Intention

Lucy v. Zehmer

84 S.E.2d 516 (Va. 1954)

Buchanan, J.

This suit was instituted by W. O. Lucy and J. C. Lucy, complainants, against A. H. Zehmer and Ida S. Zehmer, his wife, defendants, to have specific performance of a contract by which it was alleged the Zehmers had sold to W. O. Lucy a tract of land owned by A. H. Zehmer in Dinwiddie county containing 471.6 acres, more or less, known as the Ferguson farm, for $50,000. J. C. Lucy, the other complainant, is a brother of W. O. Lucy, to whom W. O. Lucy transferred a half interest in his alleged purchase.

The instrument sought to be enforced was written by A. H. Zehmer on December 20, 1952, in these words: "We hereby agree to sell to W. O. Lucy the Ferguson farm complete for $50,000.00, title satisfactory to buyer," and signed by the defendants, A. H. Zehmer and Ida S. Zehmer.

The answer of A. H. Zehmer admitted that at the time mentioned W. O. Lucy offered him $50,000 cash for the farm, but that he, Zehmer, considered that the offer was made in jest; that so thinking, and both he and Lucy having had several drinks, he wrote out "the memorandum" quoted above and induced his wife to sign it; that he did not deliver the memorandum to Lucy, but that

Lucy picked it up, read it, put it in his pocket, attempted to offer Zehmer $5 to bind the bargain, which Zehmer refused to accept, and realizing for the first time that Lucy was serious, Zehmer assured him that he had no intention of selling the farm and that the whole matter was a joke. Lucy left the premises insisting that he had purchased the farm....

In his testimony Zehmer claimed that he "was high as a Georgia pine," and that the transaction "was just a bunch of two doggoned drunks bluffing to see who could talk the biggest and say the most." That claim is inconsistent with his attempt to testify in great detail as to what was said and what was done. * * *

If it be assumed, contrary to what we think the evidence shows, that Zehmer was jesting about selling his farm to Lucy and that the transaction was intended by him to be a joke, nevertheless the evidence shows that Lucy did not so understand it but considered it to be a serious business transaction and the contract to be binding on the Zehmers as well as on himself. The very next day he arranged with his brother to put up half the money and take a half interest in the land. The day after that he employed an attorney to examine the title. The next night, Tuesday, he was back at Zehmer's place and there Zehmer told him for the first time, Lucy said, that he wasn't going to sell and he told Zehmer, "You know you sold that place fair and square." After receiving the report from his attorney that the title was good he wrote to Zehmer that he was ready to close the deal.

Not only did Lucy actually believe, but the evidence shows he was warranted in believing, that the contract represented a serious business transaction and a good faith sale and purchase of the farm.

In the field of contracts, as generally elsewhere, "We must look to the outward expression of a person as manifesting his intention rather than to his secret and unexpressed intention. The law imputes to a person an intention corresponding to the reasonable meaning of his words and acts" [Citation].

At no time prior to the execution of the contract had Zehmer indicated to Lucy by word or act that he was not in earnest about selling the farm. They had argued about it and discussed its terms, as Zehmer admitted, for a long time. Lucy testified that if there was any jesting it was about paying $50,000 that night. The contract and the evidence show that he was not expected to pay the money that night. Zehmer said that after the writing was signed he laid it down on the counter in front of Lucy. Lucy said Zehmer handed it to him. In any event there had been what appeared to be a good faith offer and a good faith acceptance, followed by the execution and apparent delivery of a written contract. Both said that Lucy put the writing in his pocket and then offered Zehmer $5 to seal the bargain. Not until then, even under the defendants' evidence, was anything said or done to indicate that the matter was a joke. Both of the Zehmers testified that when Zehmer asked his wife to sign he whispered that it was a joke so Lucy wouldn't hear and that it was not intended that he should hear.

The mental assent of the parties is not requisite for the formation of a contract. If the words or other acts of one of the parties have but one reasonable meaning, his undisclosed intention is immaterial except when an unreasonable meaning which he attaches to his manifestations is known to the other party.

"* * * The law, therefore, judges of an agreement between two persons exclusively from those expressions of their intentions which are communicated between them. * * *." [Citation]

An agreement or mutual assent is of course essential to a valid contract but the law imputes to a person an intention corresponding to the reasonable meaning of his words and acts. If his words and acts, judged by a reasonable standard, manifest an intention to agree, it is immaterial what may be the real but unexpressed state of his mind.

So a person cannot set up that he was merely jesting when his conduct and words would warrant a reasonable person in believing that he intended a real agreement.

Whether the writing signed by the defendants and now sought to be enforced by the complainants was the result of a serious offer by Lucy and a serious acceptance by the defendants, or was a serious offer by Lucy and an acceptance in secret jest by the defendants, in either event it constituted a binding contract of sale between the parties....

Reversed and remanded.

Case Questions

1. What objective evidence was there to support the defendants' contention that they were just kidding when they agreed to sell the farm?
2. Suppose the defendants really did think the whole thing was a kind of joke. Would that make any difference?
3. As a matter of public policy, why does the law use an objective standard to determine the seriousness of intention, instead of a subjective standard?
4. It's 85 degrees in July and 5:00 p.m., quitting time. The battery in Mary's car is out of juice, again. Mary says, "Arrgh! I will sell this stupid car for $50!" Jason, walking to his car nearby, whips out his checkbook and says, "It's a deal. Leave your car here. I'll give you a ride home and pick up your car after you give me the title." Do the parties have a contract?

Advertisements as Offers

Lefkowitz v. Great Minneapolis Surplus Store

86 N.W.2d 689 (Minn. 1957)

Murphy, Justice.

This is an appeal from an order of the Municipal Court of Minneapolis denying the motion of the defendant for amended findings of fact, or, in the alternative, for a new trial. The order for judgment awarded the plaintiff the sum of $138.50 as damages for breach of contract.

This case grows out of the alleged refusal of the defendant to sell to the plaintiff a certain fur piece which it had offered for sale in a newspaper advertisement. It appears from the record that on April 6, 1956, the defendant published the following advertisement in a Minneapolis newspaper:

Saturday 9 A.M. Sharp

3 Brand New Fur Coats Worth to $100.00

First Come

First Served

$1 Each

[The $100 coat would be worth about $880 in 2016 dollars.] On April 13, the defendant again published an advertisement in the same newspaper as follows:

Saturday 9 A.M.
2 Brand New Pastel Mink 3-Skin Scarfs
Selling for $89.50
Out they go Saturday. Each...$1.00
1 Black Lapin Stole Beautiful, worth $139.50...$1.00
First Come First Served

The record supports the findings of the court that on each of the Saturdays following the publication of the above-described ads the plaintiff was the first to present himself at the appropriate counter in the defendant's store and on each occasion demanded the coat and the stole so advertised and indicated his readiness to pay the sale price of $1. On both occasions, the defendant refused to sell the merchandise to the plaintiff, stating on the first occasion that by a "house rule" the offer was intended for women only and sales would not be made to men, and on the second visit that plaintiff knew defendant's house rules.

The trial court properly disallowed plaintiff's claim for the value of the fur coats since the value of these articles was speculative and uncertain. The only evidence of value was the advertisement itself to the effect that the coats were "Worth to $100.00," how much less being speculative especially in view of the price for which they were offered for sale. With reference to the offer of the defendant on April 13, 1956, to sell the "1 Black Lapin Stole * * * worth $139.50 * * *" the trial court held that the value of this article was established and granted judgment in favor of the plaintiff for that amount less the $1 quoted purchase price.

The defendant contends that a newspaper advertisement offering items of merchandise for sale at a named price is a "unilateral offer" which may be withdrawn without notice. He relies upon authorities which hold that, where an advertiser publishes in a newspaper that he has a certain quantity or quality of goods which he wants to dispose of at certain prices and on certain terms, such advertisements are not offers which become contracts as soon as any person to whose notice they may come signifies his acceptance by notifying the other that he will take a certain quantity of them. Such advertisements have been construed as an invitation for an offer of sale on the terms stated, which offer, when received, may be accepted or rejected and which therefore does not become a contract of sale until accepted by the seller; and until a contract has been so made, the seller may modify or revoke such prices or terms.

* * * On the facts before us we are concerned with whether the advertisement constituted an offer, and, if so, whether the plaintiff's conduct constituted an acceptance. There are numerous authorities which hold that a particular advertisement in a newspaper or circular letter relating to a sale of articles may be construed by the court as constituting an offer, acceptance of which would complete a contract. [Citations] The test of whether a binding obligation may originate in advertisements addressed to the general public is "whether the facts show that some performance was promised in positive terms in return for something requested." [Citation.]

The authorities above cited emphasize that, where the offer is clear, definite, and explicit, and leaves nothing open for negotiation, it constitutes an offer, acceptance of which will complete the contract. * * * Whether in any individual instance a newspaper advertisement is an offer rather than an invitation to make an offer depends on the legal intention of the parties and the surrounding circumstances. [Citations] We are of the view on the facts before us that the offer by the defendant of the sale of the Lapin fur was clear, definite, and explicit, and left nothing open for negotiation. The plaintiff having successfully managed to be the first one to appear at the seller's place of business to be served, as requested by the advertisement, and having offered the stated purchase price of the article, he was entitled to performance on the part of the defendant. We think the trial court was correct in holding that there was in the conduct of the parties a sufficient mutuality of obligation to constitute a contract of sale.

The defendant contends that the offer was modified by a "house rule" to the effect that only women were qualified to receive the bargains advertised. The advertisement contained no such restriction. This objection may be disposed of briefly by stating that, while an advertiser has the right at any time before acceptance to modify his offer, he does not have the right, after acceptance, to impose new or arbitrary conditions not contained in the published offer. [Citations]

Affirmed.

Case Questions

1. If the normal rule is that display advertisements in newspapers and the like are not offers, but rather invitations to make an offer, why was this different? Why did the court hold that this was an offer?
2. What is the rationale for the rule that a display ad is usually not an offer?
3. If a newspaper display advertisement reads, "This offer is good for two weeks," is it still only an invitation to make an offer, or is it an offer?
4. Is a listing by a private seller for the sale of a trailer on Craigslist or in the weekly classified advertisements an offer or an invitation to make an offer?

Silence as Acceptance

Hobbs v. Massasoit Whip Co.

33 N.E. 495 (Mass. 1893)

Holmes, J.

This is an action for the price of eel skins sent by the plaintiff to the defendant, and kept by the defendant some months, until they were destroyed. It must be taken that the plaintiff received no notice that the defendant declined to accept the skins. The case comes before us on exceptions to an instruction to the jury that, whether there was any prior contract or not, if skins are sent to the defendant, and it sees fit, whether it has agreed to take them or not, to lie back, and to say nothing, having reason to suppose that the man who has sent them believes that it is taking them, since it says nothing about it, then, if it fails to notify, the jury would be warranted in finding for the plaintiff.

Standing alone, and unexplained, this proposition might seem to imply that one stranger may impose a duty upon another, and make him a purchaser, in spite of himself, by sending goods to him, unless he will take the trouble, and bear the expense, of notifying the sender that he will not buy. The case was argued for the defendant on that interpretation. But, in view of the evidence, we do not understand that to have been the meaning of the judge and we do not think that the jury can have understood that to have been his meaning. The plaintiff was not a stranger to the defendant, even if there was no contract between them. He had sent eel skins in the same way four or five times before, and they had been accepted and paid for. On the defendant's testimony, it was fair to assume that if it had admitted the eel skins to be over 22 inches in length, and fit for its business, as the plaintiff testified and the jury found that they were, it would have accepted them; that this was understood by the plaintiff; and, indeed, that there was a standing offer to him for such skins.

In such a condition of things, the plaintiff was warranted in sending the defendant skins conforming to the requirements, and even if the offer was not such that the contract was made as soon as skins corresponding to its terms were sent, sending them did impose on the defendant a duty to act about them; and silence on its part, coupled with a retention of the skins for an unreasonable time, might be found by the jury to warrant the plaintiff in assuming that they were accepted, and thus to amount to an acceptance. [Citations] The proposition stands on the general principle that conduct which imports acceptance or assent is acceptance or assent, in the view of the law, whatever may have been the actual state of mind of the party—a principle sometimes lost sight of in the cases. [Citations]

Exceptions overruled.

Case Questions

1. What is an eel, and why would anybody make a whip out of its skin? Look up the verb "to sniggle" and the noun "sniggler."
2. Why did the court here deny the defendant's assertion that it never accepted the plaintiff's offer?
3. If it reasonably seems that silence is acceptance, does it make any difference what the offeree really intended?

9.5 Summary and Exercises

Summary

Whether a legally valid contract was formed depends on a number of factors, including whether the parties reached agreement, whether consideration was present, and whether the agreement was legal. Agreement may seem like an intuitive concept, but intuition is not a sufficient guide to the existence of agreement in legal terms. The most common way of examining an agreement for legal sufficiency is by determining whether a valid offer and acceptance were made.

An offer is a manifestation of willingness to enter into a bargain such that it would be reasonable for another individual to conclude that assent to the offer would complete the bargain. Offers must be communicated and must be definite; that is, they must spell out terms to which the offeree can assent.

An important aspect of the offer is its duration. An offer can expire in any one of several ways: (1) rejection, (2) counteroffer, (3) acceptance with counteroffer, (4) lapse of time, (5) death or insanity of the offeror or destruction of an essential term, (6) illegality, and (7) revocation. No understanding of agreement is complete without a mastery of these conditions.

To constitute an agreement, an offer must be accepted.

The offeree must manifest his assent to the terms of the offer in a manner invited or required by the offer. Complications arise when an offer is accepted indirectly through correspondence. Although offers and revocations of offers are not effective until received, an acceptance is deemed accepted when sent if the offeree accepts in the manner specified by the offeror. But the nuances that arise because of the mailbox rule and acceptance by silence require close attention to the circumstances of each agreement.

Exercises

1. Sarah's student apartment was unfurnished. She perused Doug's List, an online classified ad service (for nonmerchants), and saw this advertisement: "Moving. For sale: a very nice brown leather couch, almost new, $600." There was an accompanying photo and contact

information. Sarah e-mailed the contact, saying she wanted to buy the couch. Does Sarah have a contract with the seller? Explain.

2. Seller called Buyer on the telephone and offered to sell his used stereo. Buyer agreed to buy it without asking the price. The next day Buyer changed her mind and attempted to back out of the agreement. Do the parties have a contract? Explain.
3. On August 1, Ernie wrote to Elsie offering to sell Elsie his car for $7,600, and he promised to hold the offer open for ten days. On August 4, Ernie changed his mind; he sent Elsie a letter revoking the offer. On August 5, Elsie e-mailed Ernie, accepting the offer. Ernie's letter of revocation arrived on August 6. Is there a contract? Explain.
4. On August 1, Grover visited a local electronics shop to purchase a new television. He saw one he liked but wasn't sure if he could afford the $750. The store owner agreed to write up and sign an offer stating that it would be held open for ten days, which he did. On August 2, the owner changed his mind and sent Grover an e-mail revoking the offer, which Grover received immediately. On August 3, Grover sent a reply e-mail accepting the original offer. Is there a contract? Explain.
5. Acme Corporation sent the following letter, here set out in its entirety:

> *January 2, 2012*
>
> *Acme Corporation*
>
> *We hereby offer you 100 Acme golden widgets, size 6. This offer will be good for 10 days.*
>
> *[Signed] Roberta Acme*
>
> *Owner, Acme Corporation*

Is this offer irrevocable for the time stated? Explain.

6. On November 26, Joe wrote to Kate offering to purchase a farm that she owned. Upon receiving the letter on November 28, Kate immediately sent Joe a letter of acceptance. However, shortly after mailing the letter, Kate had second thoughts and called Joe to advise him that she was rejecting his offer. The call was made before Joe received the letter of acceptance. Has a contract been formed? Why?
7. On a busy day just before April 15, Albert Accountant received a call from a local car dealer. The dealer said, "Hi, Mr. Accountant. Now, while you have income from doing clients' taxes, I have an excellent offer for you. You can buy a new Buick Century automobile completely loaded for $36,000. Al, I know you're busy. If I don't hear from you by the end of the day, I'll assume you want the car." Albert, distracted, did not respond immediately, and the dealer hung up. Then followed an exhausting day of working with anxiety-ridden tax clients. Albert forgot about the conversation. Two days later a statement arrived from the dealer, with instructions on how Albert should pick up the car at the dealership. Is there a contract? Explain.
8. Mr. and Mrs. Mitchell, the owners of a small secondhand store, attended an auction where they bought a used safe for $50. The safe, part of the Sumstad estate, had a locked compartment inside, a fact the auctioneer mentioned. After they bought the safe, the Mitchells had a locksmith open the interior compartment; it contained $32,000 in cash. The locksmith called the police, who impounded the safe, and a lawsuit ensued between the Mitchells and the Sumstad estate to determine the ownership of the cash. Who should get it, and why?
9. Ivan Mestrovic, an internationally renowned artist, and his wife lived for years in a house in Indiana. Ivan died in 1982. His widow remained in the house for some years; upon her death the contents of the house were willed to her children. When the Wilkens bought the house from the estate, it was very cluttered. A bank representative (the executor of the estate) said, "You can clean it yourself and keep whatever items you want, or we—as executor of Mrs. Mestrovic's estate—will hire a rubbish removal service to dispose of it." The Wilkens opted to clean it up themselves, and amid the mess, behind sofas and in odd closets, were six

apparently valuable paintings by Mestrovic. The estate claimed them; the Wilkens claimed them. Who gets the paintings, and why?

10. David Kidd's dog bit Mikaila Sherrod. On June 14, 2010, the Kidds offered to settle for $32,000. On July 12, the Sherrods sued the Kidds. On July 20 the Kidds bumped their offer up to $34,000. The suit was subject to mandatory arbitration, which proceeded on April 28, 2011. On May 5, the arbitrator awarded the Sherrods $25,000. On May 9, the Sherrods wrote to the Kidds and purported to accept their last offer of $34,000, made the year before. The Sherrods' attorney moved to enforce that purported $34,000 "settlement agreement." The court concluded that the offer was properly accepted because it had not been withdrawn and entered judgment against the Kidds for $34,000. The Kidds appealed. What result should obtain on appeal, and why?[13]

Self-Test Questions

1. In interpreting agreements for the purpose of establishing whether a valid contract exists, courts generally apply
    a. subjective standards
    b. objective standards
    c. either a subjective or an objective standard
    d. none of the above
2. A valid offer must be
    a. written
    b. written and intended
    c. communicated by letter
    d. communicated and definite
3. An offer
    a. must specify time, place, and manner of acceptance
    b. must be accepted immediately to be valid
    c. need not be accepted immediately
    d. can only be accepted by the same means it was made
4. An offer generally
    a. is rejected by a counteroffer
    b. can be revoked if the offeror changes his or her mind
    c. can lapse after a reasonable period of time
    d. involves all of the above
5. An acceptance is generally considered effective
    a. when a letter is received by the offeror
    b. when a letter is mailed
    c. when the offeree is silent
    d. only when the acceptance is transmitted in writing

Self-Test Answers

1. b
2. d
3. c

4. d
5. b

Endnotes

1. Samuel Williston, "Freedom of Contract," *Cornell Law Quarterly* 6 (1921), 365.
2. Uniform Commercial Code, Section 2-204(1).
3. Uniform Commercial Code, Section 3.
4. Uniform Commercial Code, Section 1-201(3).
5. *Barnes v. Treece*, 549 P.2d 1152 (Wash. App. 1976).
6. Restatement (Second) of Contracts, Section 24.
7. Chiefly, Uniform Commercial Code, Sections 2-305 through 2-310.
8. Restatement (Second) of Contracts, Section 24.
9. *Adams v. Lindsell*, 1 Barnewall & Alderson 681 (K.B. 1818).
10. The National Conference of Commissioners on Uniform State Laws, *Uniform Electronic Transactions Act (1999)* (Denver: National Conference of Commissioners on Uniform State Laws, 1999), accessed March 29, 2011, http://www.law.upenn.edu/bll/archives/ulc/fnact99/1990s/ueta99.pdf.
11. *Specht v. Netscape Communications Corp.*, 306 F.3d 17 (2d Cir. 2002).
12. See, for example, *Clow Water Systems Co. v. National Labor Relations Board*, 92 F.3d 441 (6th Cir. 1996).
13. *Sherrod ex rel. Cantone v. Kidd*, 155 P.3d 976 (Wash. Ct. App., 2007).

CHAPTER 10

Free Will, Knowledge, and Capacity (Real Assent)

Learning Objectives

After reading this chapter, you should understand the following:

1. Contracts require "a meeting of the minds" between competent parties, and if there is no such "meeting," the agreement is usually voidable.
2. Parties must enter the contract voluntarily, without duress or undue influence.
3. Misrepresentation or fraud, when proven, vitiates a contract.
4. A mistake may make a contract voidable.
5. A party who lacks legal capacity—who is an infant, intoxicated, or insane—may usually avoid the contract made.

We turn to the second of the four requirements for a valid contract. In addition to manifestation of assent, a party's assent must be real; he or she must consent to the contract freely, with adequate knowledge, and must have capacity. The requirement of real assent raises the following major questions:

1. Did the parties enter into the contract of their own free will, or was one forced to agree under duress or undue influence?
2. Did the parties enter into the contract with full knowledge of the facts, or was one or both led to the agreement through fraud or mistake?
3. Did both parties have the capacity to make a contract?

10.1 Duress and Undue Influence

Learning Objectives

1. Recognize that if a person makes an agreement under duress (being forced to enter a contract against his or her will), the agreement is void.
2. Understand what undue influence is and what the typical circumstances are when it arises to make a contract voidable.

Duress

When a person is forced to do something against his or her will, that person is said to have been the victim of **duress**—compulsion. There are two types of duress: physical duress and duress by improper threat. A contract induced by physical violence is void.

duress

A threat of improper action to induce a person to make a contract.

Physical Duress

physical duress

The threat of physical harm that wrongfully induces a party to contract.

If a person is forced into entering a contract on threat of physical bodily harm, he or she is the victim of **physical duress**. It is defined by the Restatement (Second) of Contracts in Section 174: "If conduct that appears to be a manifestation of assent by a party who does not intend to engage in that conduct is physically compelled by duress, the conduct is not effective as a manifestation of assent."

Comment (a) to Section 174 provides in part, "This Section involves an application of that principle to those *relatively rare situations in which actual physical force* has been used to compel a party to appear to assent to a contract. * * * The essence of this type of duress is that a party is compelled by physical force to do an act that he has no intention of doing. He is, it is sometimes said, 'a mere mechanical instrument.' The result is that there is no contract at all, or a 'void contract' as distinguished from a voidable one" (emphasis added).

The Restatement is undoubtedly correct that there are "relatively rare situations in which actual physical force" is used to compel assent to a contract. Extortion is a crime.

There is a very interesting incidence of duress—famous in English law and history. By 1206 King John of England had lost most of his—England's — historically claimed provinces of Normandy, Anjou, and Maine (these are parts of France today). To take them back he needed money, and he so pressed the barons (nobility) for funding that they rebelled. Negotiations failed; civil war broke out in May of 1215. When the rebels seized London, John was forced to negotiate for peace. At Runnymede in June of 1215 John—really at swordpoint—was compelled to accept the terms of the Magna Carta, which limited royal power and proclaimed for the first time that the king was subordinate to the rule of law just like his subjects were. But John later renounced the Magna Carta, claiming it was signed under duress. Civil war broke out again, but John's death in 1216 enabled a compromise peace. John's son Henry III became king.[1]

Duress by Threat

The second kind of duress is ***duress by threat***; it is more common than physical duress. Here the perpetrator threatens the victim, who feels there is no reasonable alternative but to assent to the contract. It renders the contract voidable. This rule contains a number of elements.

First, the threat must be improper. Second, there must be no reasonable alternative. If, for example, a supplier threatens to hold up shipment of necessary goods unless the buyer agrees to pay more than the contract price, this would not be duress if the buyer could purchase identical supplies from someone else. Third, the test for inducement is subjective. It does not matter that the person threatened is unusually timid or that a reasonable person would not have felt threatened. The question is whether the threat in fact induced assent by the victim. Such facts as the victim's belief that the threatener had the ability to carry out the threat and the length of time between the threat and assent are relevant in determining whether the threat did prompt the assent.

There are many types of improper threats that might induce a party to enter into a contract: threats to commit a crime or a tort (e.g., bodily harm or taking of property), to instigate criminal prosecution, to instigate civil proceedings when a threat is made in bad faith, to breach a "duty of good faith and fair dealing under a contract with the recipient," or to disclose embarrassing details about a person's private life.

Jack buys a car from a local used-car salesman, Mr. Olson, and the next day realizes he bought a lemon. He threatens to break windows in Olson's showroom if Olson does not buy the car back for $2,150, the purchase price. Mr. Olson agrees. The agreement is voidable, even though the underlying deal is fair (that is, it is fair for Jack to insist that Mr. Olson re-purchase the car), if Olson feels he has no reasonable alternative and is frightened into agreeing. Suppose Jack knows that Olson has been tampering with his cars' odometers, a federal offense, and threatens to have Olson prosecuted if he will not repurchase the car. Even though Olson may be guilty, this threat makes the repurchase contract voidable, because it is a misuse for personal ends of a power (to go to the police) given each of us for other purposes. If these threats failed, suppose Jack then tells Olson, "I'm going to haul you into court and sue your pants off." If Jack means he will sue for his purchase price, this is not an improper threat, because everyone has the right to use the courts to gain what they think is rightfully theirs. But if Jack meant that he would fabricate damages done him by a (falsely) claimed odometer manipulation, that would be an improper threat. Although Olson could defend against the suit, his reputation would suffer in the meantime from his being accused of odometer tampering.

A threat to breach a contract that induces the victim to sign a new contract could be improper. Suppose that as part of the original purchase price, Olson agrees to make all necessary repairs and replace all failed parts for the first ninety days. At the end of one month, the transmission dies, and Jack demands a replacement. Olson refuses to repair the car unless Jack signs a contract agreeing to buy his next car from Olson. Whether or not this threat is improper depends on whether Jack has a reasonable alternative; if a replacement transmission is readily available and Jack has the funds to pay for it, he might have an alternative in suing Olson in small claims court for the cost. But if Jack needs the car immediately and he is impecunious, then the threat would be improper and the contract voidable. A threat to breach a contract is not necessarily improper, however. It depends on whether the new contract is fair and equitable because of unanticipated circumstances. If, for example, Olson discovers that he must purchase a replacement transmission at three times the anticipated cost, his threat to hold up work unless Jack agrees to pay for it might be reasonable.

Undue Influence

The Restatement of Contracts (Second) characterizes **undue influence** as "unfair persuasion."[2] It is a milder form of duress than physical harm or threats. The unfairness does not lie in any misrepresentation; rather, it occurs when the victim is under the domination of the persuader or is one who, in view of the relationship between them, is warranted in believing that the persuader will act in a manner detrimental to the victim's welfare if the victim fails to assent. It is the improper use of trust or power to deprive a person of free will and substitute instead another's objective. Usually the fact pattern involves the victim being isolated from receiving advice except from the persuader. Falling within this rule are situations where, for example, a child takes advantage of an infirm parent, a doctor takes advantage of an ill patient, or a lawyer takes advantage of an unknowledgeable client. If there has been undue influence, the contract is voidable by the party who has been unfairly persuaded. Whether the relationship is one of domination and the persuasion is unfair is a factual question. The answer hinges on a host of variables, including "the unfairness of the resulting bargain, the unavailability of independent advice, and the susceptibility of the person persuaded."[3] See Section 5, *Hodge v. Shea*.

undue influence

Improper use of power or trust in a way that deprives a person of free will and substitutes another's objective.

Key Takeaway

A contract induced by physical duress—threat of bodily harm—is void; a contract induced by improper threats—another type of duress—is voidable. Voidable also are contracts induced by undue influence, where a weak will is overborne by a stronger one.

Exercises

1. What are the two types of duress?
2. What are the elements necessary to support a claim of undue influence?

10.2 Misrepresentation

Learning Objectives

1. Understand the two types of misrepresentation: fraudulent and nonfraudulent.
2. Distinguish between fraudulent misrepresentation in the execution and fraudulent misrepresentation in the inducement.
3. Know the elements necessary to prove fraudulent and nonfraudulent misrepresentation.
4. Recognize the remedies for misrepresentation.

General Description and Taxonomy

The two types of misrepresentation are fraudulent and nonfraudulent. Within the former are fraud in the execution and fraud in the inducement. Within the latter are negligent misrepresentation and innocent misrepresentation.

Misrepresentation

A false or misleading statement or impression given that induces a party to contract.

Fraud in the execution

Causing a person to sign a legal document while that person believes he or she is signing some other type of document.

Misrepresentation is a statement of fact that is not consistent with the truth. If misrepresentation is intentional, it is fraudulent misrepresentation; if it is not intentional, it is nonfraudulent misrepresentation, which can be either negligent or innocent.

In further taxonomy, courts distinguish between fraud in the execution and fraud in the inducement. **Fraud in the execution** is defined by the Restatement as follows: "If a misrepresentation as to the character or essential terms of a proposed contract induces conduct that appears to be a manifestation of assent by one who neither knows nor has reasonable opportunity to know of the character or essential terms of the proposed contract, his conduct is not effective as a manifestation of assent."[4] For example, Alphonse and Gaston decide to sign a written contract incorporating terms to which they have agreed. It is properly drawn up, and Gaston reads it and approves it. Before he can sign it, however, Alphonse shrewdly substitutes a different version to which Gaston has not agreed. Gaston signs the substitute version. There is no contract. There has been fraud in the execution.

Fraud in the inducement

Deceit or trick to cause someone to contract to his or her disadvantage.

Fraud in the inducement is more common. It involves some misrepresentation about the subject of the contract that induces assent. Alphonse tells Gaston that the car Gaston is buying from Alphonse has just been overhauled—which pleases Gaston—but it has not been. This renders the contract voidable.

Fraudulent Misrepresentation

fraudulent misrepresentation

Misrepresentation with the intention to deceive.

Necessary to proving **fraudulent misrepresentation** (usually just "fraud," though technically "fraud" is the crime and "fraudulent misrepresentation" is the civil wrong) is a misstatement of fact that is intentionally made and justifiably relied upon.

Misstatement of Fact

Again, generally, any statement not in accord with the facts (a fact is something amenable to testing as true) is a misrepresentation. Falsity does not depend on intent. A typist's unnoticed error in a letter (inadvertently omitting the word "not," for example, or transposing numbers) can amount to a misrepresentation on which the recipient may rely (it is not fraudulent misrepresentation). A half-truth can amount to a misrepresentation, as, for example, when the seller of a hotel says that the income is from both permanent and transient guests but fails to disclose that the bulk of the income is from single-night stopovers by sailors using the hotel as a brothel.[5]

Concealment

Another type of misrepresentation is concealment. It is an act that is equivalent to a statement that the facts are to the contrary and that serves to prevent the other party from learning the true statement of affairs; it is hiding the truth. A common example is painting over defects in a building—by concealing the defects, the owner is misrepresenting the condition of the property. The act of concealment need not be direct; it may consist of sidetracking the other party from gaining necessary knowledge by, for example, convincing a third person who has knowledge of the defect not to speak. Concealment is always a misrepresentation.

Nondisclosure

A more passive type of concealment is nondisclosure. Although generally the law imposes no obligation on anyone to speak out, nondisclosure of a fact can operate as a misrepresentation under certain circumstances. This occurs, for example, whenever the other party has erroneous information, or, as *Reed v. King* (Section 5) shows, where the nondisclosure amounts to a failure to act in good faith, or where the party who conceals knows or should know that the other side cannot, with reasonable diligence, discover the truth.

In a remarkable 1991 case out of New York, a New York City stockbroker bought an old house in upstate New York (basically anyplace north of New York City) in the village of Nyack, and then wanted out of the deal when he discovered—the defendant seller had not told him—that it was "haunted." The court summarized the facts: "Plaintiff, to his horror, discovered that the house he had recently contracted to purchase was widely reputed to be possessed by poltergeists [ghosts], reportedly seen by defendant seller and members of her family on numerous occasions over the last nine years. Plaintiff promptly commenced this action seeking rescission of the contract of sale. Supreme Court reluctantly dismissed the complaint, holding that plaintiff has no remedy at law in this jurisdiction."

The high court of New York ruled he could rescind the contract because the house was "haunted as a matter of law": the defendant herself had promoted it as such on village tours and in *Reader's Digest*. She had concealed it, and no reasonable buyer's inspection would have revealed the "fact." The dissent basically hooted, saying, "The existence of a poltergeist is no more binding upon the defendants than it is upon this court."[6]

Statement Made False by Subsequent Events

If a statement of fact is made false by later events, it must be disclosed as false. For example, in idle chatter one day, Alphonse tells Gaston that he owns thirty acres of land. In fact, Alphonse owns only twenty-seven, but he decided to exaggerate a little. He meant no harm by it, since the conversation had no import. A year later, Gaston offers to buy the "thirty acres" from Alphonse, who does not correct the impression that Gaston has. The failure to speak is a nondisclosure—presumably intentional, in this situation—that would allow Gaston to rescind a contract induced by his belief that he was purchasing thirty acres.

Statements of Opinion

An opinion, of course, is not a fact; neither is sales puffery. For example, the statements "In my opinion this apple is very tasty" and "These apples are the best in the county" are not facts; they are not expected to be taken as true. Reliance on opinion is hazardous and generally not considered justifiable.

If Jack asks what condition the car is in that he wishes to buy, Mr. Olson's response of "Great!" is not ordinarily a misrepresentation. As the Restatement puts it: "The propensity of sellers and buyers to exaggerate the advantages to the other party of the bargains they promise is well recognized, and to some extent their assertions must be discounted."[7] Vague statements of quality, such as that a product is "good," ought to suggest nothing other than that such is the personal judgment of the opinion holder.

Despite this general rule, there are certain exceptions that justify reliance on opinions and effectively make them into facts. Merely because someone is less astute than the one with whom she is bargaining does not give rise to a claim of justifiable reliance on an unwarranted opinion. But if the person is inexperienced and susceptible or gullible to blandishments, the contract can be voided, as illustrated in *Vokes v. Arthur Murray, Inc.* in Section 5.

Misstatement of Law

Incorrect assertions of law usually do not give rise to any relief, but sometimes they do. An assertion that "the city has repealed the sales tax" or that a court has cleared title to a parcel of land is a statement of fact; if such assertions are false, they are governed by the same rules that govern misrepresentations of fact generally. An assertion of the legal consequences of a given set of facts is generally an opinion on which the recipient relies at his or her peril, especially if both parties know or assume the same facts. Thus, if there is a lien on a house, the seller's statement that "the courts will throw it out, you won't be bothered by it" is an opinion. A statement that "you can build a five-unit apartment on this property" is not actionable because, at common law, people are supposed to know what the local and state laws are, and nobody should rely on a layperson's statement about the law. However, if the statement of law is made by a lawyer or real estate broker, or some other person on whom a layperson may justifiably rely, then it may be taken as a fact and, if untrue, as the basis for a claim of misrepresentation. (Assertions about foreign laws are generally held to be statements of fact, not opinion.)

Assertions of Intention

Usually, assertions of intention are not considered facts. The law allows considerable leeway in the honesty of assertions of intention. The Restatement talks in terms of "a misrepresentation of intention...consistent with reasonable standards of fair dealing."[8] The right to misstate intentions is useful chiefly in the acquisition of land; the cases permit buyers to misrepresent the purpose of the acquisition so as not to arouse the suspicion of the seller that the land is worth considerably more than his asking price. To be a misrepresentation that will permit rescission, an assertion of intention must be false at the time made; that is, the person asserting an intention must not then have intended it. That later he or she does not carry out the stated intention is not proof that there was no intention at the time asserted. Moreover, to render a contract voidable, the false assertion of intention must be harmful in some way to other interests of the recipient. Thus, in the common example, the buyer of land tells the seller that he intends to build a residence on the lot, but he actually intends to put up a factory and has lied because he knows that otherwise the seller will not part with it because her own home is on an adjacent lot. The contract is voidable by the seller. So a developer says, as regards the picturesque old barn on the property, "I'll sure try to save it," but after he buys the land he realizes it would be very expensive (and in the way), so he does not try to save it. No misrepresentation.

Intentionally Made Misrepresentation

The second element necessary to prove fraud is that the misrepresentation was intentionally made. A misrepresentation is intentionally made "if the maker intends his assertion to induce a party to manifest his assent and the maker (a) knows or believes that the assertion is not in accord with the facts, or (b) does not have the confidence that he states or implies in the truth of the assertion, or (c) knows that he does not have the basis that he states or implies for the assertion."[9]

The question of intent often has practical consequences in terms of the remedy available to the plaintiff. If the misrepresentation is fraudulent, the plaintiff may, as an alternative to avoiding the contract, recover damages. Some of this is discussed in Section 2 and more fully in Chapter 16, where we see that some states would force the plaintiff to elect one of these two remedies, whereas other states would allow the plaintiff to pursue both remedies (although only one type of recovery would eventually be allowed). If the misrepresentation is not intentional, then the common law allowed the plaintiff only the remedy of rescission. But the Uniform Commercial Code (UCC), Section 2-721, allows both remedies in contracts for the sale of goods, whether the misrepresentation is fraudulent or not, and does not require election of remedies.

Reliance

The final element necessary to prove fraud is reliance by the victim. He or she must show that the misrepresentation induced assent—that is, he or she relied on it. The reliance need not be solely on the false assertion; the defendant cannot win the case by demonstrating that the plaintiff would have assented to the contract even without the misrepresentation. It is sufficient to avoid the contract if the plaintiff weighed the assertion as one of the important factors leading him to make the contract, and he believed it to be true. The person who asserts reliance to avoid a contract must have acted in good faith and reasonably in relying on the false assertion. Thus if the victim failed to read documents given him that truly stated the facts, he cannot later complain that he relied on a contrary statement, as, for example, when the purchaser of a car dealership was told the inventory consisted of new cars, but the supporting papers, receipt of which he acknowledged, clearly stated how many miles each car had been driven. If Mr. Olson tells Jack that the car Jack is interested in is "a recognized classic," and if Jack doesn't care a whit about that but buys the car because he likes its tail fins, he will have no case against Mr. Olson when he finds out the car is not a classic: it didn't matter to him, and he didn't rely on it.

Ordinarily, the person relying on a statement need not verify it independently. However, if verification is relatively easy, or if the statement is one that concerns matters peculiarly within the person's purview, he or she may not be held to have justifiably relied on the other party's false assertion. Moreover, usually the rule of reliance applies to statements about past events or existing facts, not about the occurrence of events in the future.

Nonfraudulent Misrepresentation

Nonfraudulent misrepresentation may also be grounds for some relief. There are two types: negligent misrepresentation and innocent misrepresentation.

Negligent Misrepresentation

Where representation is caused by carelessness, it is **negligent misrepresentation**. To prove it, a plaintiff must show a negligent misstatement of fact that is material and justifiably relied upon.

negligent misrepresentation

A false or misleading statement or impression made because of carelessness.

Negligent

As an element of misrepresentation, "negligent" here means the party who makes the representation was careless. A potential buyer of rural real estate asks the broker if the neighborhood is quiet. The broker assures her it is. In fact, the neighbors down the road have a whole kennel of hunting hounds that bark a lot. The broker didn't know that; she just assumed the neighborhood was quiet. That is negligence: failure to use appropriate care.

Misstatement of Fact

Whether a thing is a fact may be subject to the same general analysis used in discussing fraudulent misrepresentation. (A person could negligently conceal a fact, or negligently give an opinion, as in legal malpractice.)

Materiality

A material misrepresentation is one that "would be likely to induce a reasonable person to manifest his assent" or that "the maker knows...would be likely to induce the recipient to do so."[10] An honestly mistaken statement that the house for sale was built in 1922 rather than 1923 would not be the basis for avoiding the contract because it is not material unless the seller knew that the buyer had sentimental or other reasons for purchasing a house built in 1922.

We did not mention materiality as an element of fraud; if the misrepresentation is fraudulent, technically the victim can avoid the contract, no matter the significance of the misrepresentation. So although materiality is not technically required for fraudulent misrepresentation, it is usually a crucial factor in determining whether the plaintiff did rely. Obviously, the more immaterial the false assertion, the less likely it is that the victim relied on it to his detriment. This is especially the case when the defendant knows that he does not have the basis that he states for an assertion but believes that the particular point is unimportant and therefore immaterial. And of course it is usually not worth the plaintiff's while to sue over an immaterial fraudulent misrepresentation. Consequently, for practical purposes, materiality is an important consideration in most cases. *Reed v. King* (Section 5) discusses materiality (as well as nondisclosure). The court there rather confuses fraudulent misrepresentation and negligent misrepresentation in its analysis.

Justifiable Reliance

The issues here for negligent misrepresentation are the same as those set out for fraudulent misrepresentation.

Negligent misrepresentation implies culpability and is usually treated the same as fraudulent misrepresentation; if the representation is not fraudulent, however, it cannot be the basis for rescission unless it is also material.

Innocent Misrepresentation

innocent misrepresentation

A misrepresentation made by one who believes it is true.

The elements necessary to prove **innocent misrepresentation** are, reasonably enough, based on what we've looked at so far, as follows: an innocent misstatement of fact that is material and justifiably relied upon.

It is not necessary here to go over the elements in detail. The issues are the same as previously discussed, except now the misrepresentation is innocent. The plaintiffs purchased the defendants' eighteen-acre parcel on the defendants' representation that the land came with certain water rights for irrigation, which they believed was true. It was not true. The plaintiffs were entitled to rescission on the basis of innocent misrepresentation.[11]

Remedies

Remedies will be taken up in Chapter 16, but it is worth noting the difference between remedies for fraudulent misrepresentation and remedies for nonfraudulent misrepresentation.

Fraudulent misrepresentation has traditionally given the victim the right to rescind the contract promptly (return the parties to the before-contract status) *or* affirm it and bring an action for damages caused by the fraud, but not both.[12] As noted earlier, the UCC (Section 2-721) has rejected the "election of remedies" doctrine; it allows cumulative damages, such that the victim can both return the goods and sue for damages. And this is the modern trend for fraudulent misrepresentation: victims may first seek damages, and if that does not make them whole, they may seek rescission.[13] In egregious cases of fraud where the defendant has undertaken a pattern of such deceit, the rare civil remedy of punitive damages may be awarded against the defendant.

One further note: the burden of proof for fraudulent misrepresentation is that it must be proved not just "by a preponderance of the evidence," as in the typical civil case, but rather "by clear, cogent, and convincing evidence"; the fact finder must believe the claim of fraud is *very* probably true.[14]

Key Takeaway

Misrepresentation may be of two types: fraudulent (in the execution or in the inducement) and nonfraudulent (negligent or innocent). Each type has different elements that must be proved, but in general there must be a misstatement of fact by some means that is intentionally made (for fraud), material (for nonfraudulent), and justifiably relied upon.

Exercises

1. Distinguish between fraudulent misrepresentation and nonfraudulent misrepresentation, between fraud in the execution and fraud in the inducement, and between negligent and innocent misrepresentation.
2. List the elements that must be shown to prove the four different types of misrepresentation noted in Exercise 1.
3. What is the difference between the traditional common-law approach to remedies for fraud and the UCC's approach?

10.3 Mistake

Learning Objectives

1. Recognize under what circumstances a person may be relieved of a unilateral mistake.
2. Recognize when a mutual mistake will be grounds for relief, and the types of mutual mistakes.

In discussing fraud, we have considered the ways in which trickery by the other party makes a contract void or voidable. We now examine the ways in which the parties might "trick" themselves by making assumptions that lead them mistakenly to believe that they have agreed to something they have not. A mistake is "a belief about a fact that is not in accord with the truth."[15]

Mistake by One Party

Unilateral Mistake

unilateral mistake

A mistake made by one party to a contract; relief is not usually granted.

Where one party makes a mistake, it is a **unilateral mistake**. The rule: ordinarily, a contract is not voidable because one party has made a mistake about the subject matter (e.g., the truck is not powerful enough to haul the trailer; the dress doesn't fit).

Exceptions

If one side *knows or should know* that the other has made a mistake, he or she may not take advantage of it. A person who makes the mistake of not reading a written document will usually get no relief, nor will relief be afforded to one whose mistake is caused by negligence (a contractor forgets to add in the cost of insulation) unless the negligent party would suffer unconscionable hardship if the mistake were not corrected. Courts will allow the correction of drafting errors in a contract ("reformation") in order to make the contract reflect the parties' intention.[16]

Mutual Mistake

mutual mistake

Erroneous belief shared and relied on by both parties to a contract for which a court often grants relief.

In the case of **mutual mistake**—both parties are wrong about the subject of the contract—the general rule is that relief may be granted.

The Restatement sets out three requirements for successfully arguing mutual mistake.[17] The party seeking to avoid the contract must prove that

1. the mistake relates to a "basic assumption on which the contract was made,"
2. the mistake has a material effect on the agreed exchange of performances,
3. the party seeking relief does not bear the risk of the mistake.

Basic assumption is probably clear enough. In the famous "cow case," the defendant sold the plaintiff a cow—Rose of Abalone—believed by both to be barren and thus of less value than a fertile cow (a promising young dairy cow in 2016 might sell for $1,800, while a young beef cow—not suitable for milking of course, might go for $1000).[18] Just before the plaintiff was to take Rose from the defendant's barn, the defendant discovered she was "large with calf"; he refused to go on with the contract. The court held this was a mutual mistake of fact—"a barren cow is substantially a different creature than a breeding one"—and ruled for the defendant. That she was infertile was "a basic assumption," but—for example—that hay would be readily available to feed her inexpensively was not, and had hay been expensive, that would not have vitiated the contract.

Material Effect on the Agreed-to Exchange of Performance

"Material effect on the agreed—to exchange of performance" means that because of the mutual mistake, there is a significant difference between the value the parties thought they were exchanging compared with what they would exchange if the contract were performed, given the standing facts. Again, in the cow case, had the seller been required to go through with the deal, he would have given up a great deal more than he anticipated, and the buyer would have received an unagreed-to windfall.

Party Seeking Relief Does Not Bear the Risk of the Mistake

This is where mutual mistake does *not* give rise to relief—the exception. Assume a weekend browser sees a painting sitting on the floor of an antique shop. The owner says, "That old thing? You can have it for $100." The browser takes it home, dusts it off, and hangs it on the wall. A year later a visitor, an expert in art history, recognizes the hanging as a famous lost El Greco worth $1 million. The story is headlined; the antique dealer is chagrined and claims the contract for sale should be voided because both parties mistakenly thought they were dickering over an "old, worthless" painting. The contract is valid. The owner is said to bear the risk of mistake because he contracted with conscious awareness of his ignorance: he knew he didn't know what the painting's possible value might be, but he didn't feel it worthwhile to have it appraised. He gambled it wasn't worth much, and lost.

Key Takeaway

A mistake may be unilateral, in which case no relief will be granted unless the other side knows of the mistake and takes advantage of it. A mistake may be mutual, in which case relief may be granted if it is about a basic assumption on which the contract was made, if the mistake has a material effect on the agreed-to exchange, and if the person adversely affected did not bear the risk of the mistake.

Exercises

1. Why is relief usually not granted for unilateral mistakes? When is relief granted for them?
2. If there is a mutual mistake, what does the party seeking relief have to show to avoid the contract?

10.4 Capacity

Learning Objectives

1. Understand that infants may avoid their contracts, with limitations.
2. Understand that insane or intoxicated people may avoid their contracts, with limitations.
3. Understand the extent to which contracts made by mentally ill persons are voidable, void, or effectively enforceable.
4. Recognize that contracts made by intoxicated persons may be voidable.

A contract is a meeting of minds. If someone lacks mental capacity to understand what she is assenting to—or that she is assenting to anything—it is unreasonable to hold her to the consequences of her act. At common law there are various classes of people who are presumed to lack the requisite capacity. These include infants (minors), the mentally ill, and the intoxicated.

Minors (or "Infants")

The General Rule

minors

Basically synonymous with *infant*: a young person who may avoid contracts on that account.

infants

A person who has not reached the age of majority and who may (usually) avoid contracts on that account.

age of majority

When a person is old enough to make his or her contracts unavoidable on account of age.

The general rule is this: **minors** (or more legalistically "**infants**") are in most states persons younger than 18 years old; they can avoid their contracts, up to and within a reasonable time after reaching majority, subject to some exceptions and limitations. The rationale here is that infants do not have mental capacity equal to adults, and it is unfair to require them to abide by contracts made when they have immature judgment.

The words *minor* and *infant* are mostly synonymous, but not exactly, necessarily. In a state where the legal age to drink alcohol is twenty-one, a twenty-year-old would be a minor, but not an infant, because infancy is under eighteen. A seventeen-year-old may avoid contracts (usually), but an eighteen-year-old, while legally bound to his contracts, cannot legally drink alcohol. Strictly speaking, the better term for one who may avoid his contracts is *infant*, even though, of course, in normal speaking we think of an infant as a baby.

The **age of majority** (when a person is no longer an infant) was lowered in all states except during the 1970s (to correspond to the Twenty-Sixth Amendment, ratified in 1971, guaranteeing the right to vote at eighteen) from twenty-one to either eighteen or nineteen. Legal rights for those under twenty-one remain ambiguous, however. Although eighteen-year-olds may assent to binding contracts, not all creditors and landlords believe it, and they may require parents to cosign. There is as yet no uniform set of rules.

The exact day on which the disability of minority vanishes also varies. The old common-law rule put it on the day before the twenty-first birthday. Many states have changed this rule so that majority commences on the day of the eighteenth birthday.

An infant's contract is voidable, not void. An infant wishing to avoid the contract need do nothing positive to disaffirm, and the disaffirmance can be express or implied (it would be implied if an infant, having contracted to sell a car to Able instead sells it to Baker; the sale to Baker would be an implied disaffirmance of the previous sale to Able). If the infancy defense is raised by the infant, the adult cannot enforce the contract, but the infant can (which—again—is why it is said to be voidable, not void).

Exceptions and Complications

There are exceptions and complications here. We call out seven of them.

Necessities

First, as an exception to the general rule, infants are generally liable for the reasonable cost of necessities (for the reason that denying them the right to contract for necessities would harm them, not protect them). At common law, a necessity was defined as food, medicine, clothing, or shelter. In recent years, however, the courts have expanded the concept, so that in many states today, necessities include property and services that will enable the infant to earn a living and to provide for those dependent on him. If the contract is executory, the infant can simply disaffirm. If the contract has been executed, however, the infant must face more onerous consequences. Although he will not be required to perform under the contract, he will be liable under a theory of "quasi-contract" for the reasonable value of the necessity. In *Gastonia Personnel Corp. v. Rogers*, an emancipated infant, nineteen years old (before the age of minority was reduced), needed employment; he contracted with a personnel company to find him a job, for which it would charge him a fee.[19] The company did find him a job, and when he attempted to disaffirm his liability for payment on the grounds of infancy, the North Carolina court ruled against him, holding that the concepts of necessities "should be enlarged to include such ... services as are reasonable and necessary to enable the infant to earn the money required to provide the necessities of life for himself" and his dependents.

Nonvoidable Contracts

Second, state statutes variously prohibit disaffirmation for such contracts as insurance, education or medical care, bonding agreements, stocks, or bank accounts. In addition, an infant will lose her power to avoid the contract if the rights of third parties intervene. Roberta, an infant, sells a car to Oswald; Oswald, in turn, shortly thereafter sells it to Byers, who knows nothing of Roberta. May Roberta—still an infant—recover it from Byers? No: the rights of the third party have intervened. To allow the infant seller recovery in this situation would undermine faith in commercial transactions (UCC 2-403). However, in the case of the sale of real estate, an infant may disaffirm a deed of conveyance even against a third party who bought the land without any knowledge that the third party's seller had bought it from an infant. This alarming circumstance is not very common, and there's an odd quirk in real estate transaction by way of exception: an infant who sells real estate cannot avoid the contract until *after* she or he reaches majority. That turns the usual rule for infants avoiding their contracts on its head (again, usually the infant must disaffirm before or within a reasonable time after reaching majority).

Misrepresentation of Age

A third exception involves misrepresentation of age. Certainly, that the adult reasonably believed the infant was an adult is of no consequence in a contract suit. In many states, an infant may misrepresent his age and disaffirm in accordance with the general rule. But it depends. If an infant affirmatively lies about his age, the trend is to deny disaffirmation. A Michigan statute, for instance, prohibits an infant from disaffirming if he has signed a "separate instrument containing only the statement of age, date of signing and the signature." And some states estop him from claiming to be an infant even if he less expressly falsely represented himself as an adult. Estoppel is a refusal by the courts on equitable grounds to allow a person to escape liability on an otherwise valid defense; unless the infant can return the consideration, the contract will be enforced. It is a question of fact how far a nonexpressed (an implied) misrepresentation will be allowed to go before it is considered so clearly misleading as to range into the prohibited area. Some states hold the infant liable for damages for the tort of misrepresentation, but others do not. As William Prosser, the noted torts scholar, said of cases paying no attention to an infant's lying about his age, "The effect of the decisions refusing to recognize tort liability for misrepresentation is to create a privileged class of liars who are a great trouble to the business world."[20]

Ratification

Fourth, when the infant becomes an adult, she has two choices: she may ratify the contract or disaffirm it. She may ratify explicitly; nothing further is necessary. She may also do so by implication—for instance, by continuing to make payments or retaining goods for an unreasonable period of time. If the child has not disaffirmed the contract while still an infant, she may do so within a reasonable time after reaching majority; what is a "reasonable time" depends on the circumstances. The ratification is irrevocable, and it must be total: the infant cannot ratify only part of the contract and avoid the rest. For example, an infant, upon selling an automobile, cannot retain by ratification the $3000 he got for it and then attempt to disaffirm the transfer of the car; he can't keep the money and also get the car back.

Duty to Return Consideration Received

Fifth, in most cases of disavowal, the infant's only obligation is to return the goods (if he still has them) or repay the consideration (unless it has been dissipated); he does not have to account for what he wasted, consumed, or damaged during the contract. But since the age of majority has been lowered to eighteen or nineteen, when most young people have graduated from high school, some courts require, if appropriate to avoid injustice to the adult, that the infant account for what he got. (In *Dodson v. Shrader*, the supreme court of Tennessee held that an infant would—if the contract was fair—have to pay for the pickup truck he bought and wrecked.)[21]

Tort Connected with a Contract

Sixth, the general rule is that infants are liable for their torts (e.g., assault, trespass, nuisance, negligence) unless the tort suit is only an indirect method of enforcing a contract. Henry, age seventeen, holds himself out to be a competent mechanic. He is paid $500 to overhaul Baker's engine, but he does a careless job and the engine is seriously damaged. He offers to return the $500 but disaffirms any further contractual liability. Can Baker sue him for his negligence, a tort? No, because such a suit would be to enforce the contract.

Contracts for the Sale of Real Estate

Finally, one last (rather odd) exception, touched on previously. A contract by a minor to sell real estate can *not* be disaffirmed until *after* she reaches majority. The theory is apparently that the sale of real estate confers on the buyer a special expectation that the he gets title, and the contract cannot be avoided by the infant until she has judgment mature enough to realize the significance of what she is doing—divesting a person of title to real estate is significant.

Persons Who Are Mentally Ill or Intoxicated

Mentally Ill Persons

The general rule is that a contract made by person who is mentally ill is voidable by the person when she regains her sanity, or, as appropriate, by a guardian. If, though, a guardian has been legally appointed for a person who is mentally ill, *any* contract made by the mentally ill person is void, but may nevertheless be ratified by the ward (the incompetent person who is under a guardianship) upon regaining sanity or by the guardian.[22]

However, if the contract was for a necessity, the other party may have a valid claim against the estate of the one who is mentally ill in order to prevent unjust enrichment. In other cases, whether a court will enforce a contract made with a person who is mentally ill depends on the circumstances. Only if the mental illness impairs the competence of the person in the particular transaction can the contract be avoided; the test is whether the person understood the nature of the business at hand. Upon avoidance, the person must return any property in her possession. And if the contract was fair and the other party had no knowledge of the mental illness, the court has the power to order other relief.

Intoxicated Persons

If a person is so drunk that he has no awareness of his acts, and if the other person knows this, there is no contract. The intoxicated person is obligated to refund the consideration to the other party unless he dissipated it during his drunkenness. If the other person is unaware of his intoxicated state, however, an offer or acceptance of fair terms manifesting assent is binding.

If a person is only partially inebriated and has some understanding of his actions, "avoidance depends on a showing that the other party induced the drunkenness or that the consideration was inadequate or that the transaction departed from the normal pattern of similar transactions; if the particular transaction is one which a reasonably competent person might have made, it cannot be avoided even though entirely executory."[23] A person who was intoxicated at the time he made the contract may nevertheless subsequently ratify it. Thus, where Mervin Hyland, several times involuntarily committed for alcoholism, executed a promissory note in an alcoholic stupor but later, while sober, paid the interest on the past-due note, he was denied the defense of intoxication; the court said he had ratified his contract.[24] In any event, intoxicated is a disfavored defense on public policy grounds.

Key Takeaway

Infants may generally disaffirm their contracts up to majority and within a reasonable time afterward, but the rule is subject to some exceptions and complications: necessities, contracts made nonvoidable by statute, misrepresentation of age, extent of duty to return consideration, ratification, and a tort connected with the contract are among these exceptions.

Contracts made by insane or intoxicated people are voidable when the person regains competency. A contract made by a person under guardianship is void, but the estate will be liable for necessities. A contract made while insane or intoxicated may be ratified.

Exercises

1. Ivar, an infant, bought a used car—not a necessity—for $9,500. Seller took advantage of Ivar's infancy: the car was really worth only $5,500. Can Ivar keep the car but disclaim liability for the $4,000 difference?
2. If Ivar bought the car and it was a necessity, could he disclaim liability for the $4,000?
3. Alice Ace found her adult son's Christmas stocking; Mrs. Ace herself had made it fifty years before. It was considerably deteriorated. Isabel, sixteen, handy with knitting, agreed to reknit it for $100, which Mrs. Ace paid in advance. Isabel, regrettably, lost the stocking. She returned the $100 to Mrs. Ace, who was very upset. May Mrs. Ace now sue Isabel for the loss of the stocking (conversion) and emotional distress?
4. Why is voluntary intoxication a disfavored defense?

10.5 Cases

Undue Influence

Hodge v. Shea

168 S.E.2d 82 (S.C. 1969)

Brailsford, J.

In this equitable action the circuit court decreed specific performance of a contract for the sale of land, and the defendant has appealed. The plaintiff is a physician, and the contract was prepared and executed in his medical office on August 19, 1965. The defendant had been plaintiff's patient for a number of years. On the contract date, he was seventy-five years of age, was an inebriate of long standing, and was afflicted by grievous chronic illnesses, including arteriosclerosis, cirrhosis of the liver, neuritises, arthritis of the spine and hip and varicose veins of the legs. These afflictions and others required constant medication and frequent medical attention, and rendered him infirm of body and mind, although not to the point of incompetency to contract.

During the period immediately before and after August 19, 1965, George A. Shea, the defendant, was suffering a great deal of pain in his back and hip and was having difficulty in voiding. He was attended professionally by the plaintiff, Dr. Joseph Hodge, either at the Shea home, at the doctor's office or in the hospital at least once each day from August 9 through August 26, 1965, except for August 17. The contract was signed during the morning of August 19. One of Dr. Hodge's frequent house calls was made on the afternoon of that day, and Mr. Shea was admitted to the hospital on August 21, where he remained until August 25.

Mr. Shea was separated from his wife and lived alone. He was dependent upon Dr. Hodge for house calls, which were needed from time to time. His relationship with his physician, who sometimes visited him as a friend and occasionally performed non-professional services for him, was closer than ordinarily arises from that of patient and physician. * * *

"Where a physician regularly treats a chronically ill person over a period of two years, a confidential relationship is established, raising a presumption that financial dealings between them are fraudulent." [Citation]

A 125-acre tract of land near Mr. Shea's home, adjacent to land which was being developed as residential property, was one of his most valuable and readily salable assets. In 1962, the developer of this contiguous land had expressed to Mr. Shea an interest in it at $1,000.00 per acre [about $4,800 in 2015]. A firm offer of this amount was made in November, 1964, and was refused by Mr. Shea on the advice of his son-in-law that the property was worth at least $1,500.00 per acre. Negotiations between the developer and Mr. Ransdell commenced at that time and were in progress when Mr. Shea, at the instance of Dr. Hodge and without consulting Mr. Ransdell or anyone else, signed the contract of August 19, 1965. Under this contract Dr. Hodge claims the right to purchase twenty choice acres of the 125-acre tract for a consideration calculated by the circuit court to be the equivalent of $361.72 per acre [$2,900 in 2015]. The market value of the land on the contract date has been fixed by an unappealed finding of the master at $1,200.00 per acre [about $9,300 in 2015]. * * *

The consideration was expressed in the contract between Dr. Hodge and Mr. Shea as follows:

> *The purchase price being (Cadillac Coupe DeVille $6,600 [about $47,500 in 2015 dollars) & $4,000.00 [about $29,000 in 2015 dollars] Dollars, on the following terms: Dr. Joseph Hodge to give to Mr. George Shea a new $6,600 Coupe DeVille Cadillac, which is to be registered in the name of Mr. George A. Shea at absolutely no cost to him. In return, Mr. Shea will give to Dr. Joe Hodge his 1964 Cadillac Coupe DeVille and shall transfer title of this vehicle to Dr. Hodge. Further, Dr. Joseph Hodge will pay to Mr. George A. Shea the balance of $4,000.00 for the 20 acres of land described above subject to survey, title check, less taxes on purchase of vehicle.*

Dr. Hodge was fully aware of Mr. Shea's financial troubles, the liens on his property and his son-in-law's efforts in his behalf. He was also aware of his patient's predilection for new Cadillacs. Although he was not obligated to do so until the property was cleared of liens, which was not accomplished until the following June, Dr. Hodge hastened to purchase a 1965 Cadillac Coupe DeVille and delivered it to Mr. Shea on the day after his discharge from the hospital on August 25, 1965. If he acted in haste in an effort to fortify what he must have realized was a dubious contract, he has so far succeeded....

The case at hand is attended by gross inadequacy of consideration, serious impairment of the grantor's mentality from age, intemperance, and disease, and a confidential relationship between the grantee and grantor. Has the strong presumption of vitiating unfairness arising from this combination of circumstances been overcome by the evidence? We must conclude that it has not. The record is devoid of any evidence suggesting a reason, compatible with fairness, for Mr. Shea's assent to so disadvantageous a bargain. Disadvantageous not only because of the gross disparity between consideration and value, but because of the possibility that the sale would impede the important negotiations in which Mr. Ransdell was engaged. Unless his memory failed him, Mr. Shea knew that his son-in-law expected to sell the 125 acre tract for about $1,500.00 per acre as an important step toward raising sufficient funds to satisfy the tax and judgment liens against the Shea property. These circumstances furnish strong evidence that Mr. Shea's assent to the contract, without so much as notice to Mr. Ransdell, was not the product of a deliberate exercise of an informed judgment. * * *

Finally, on this phase of the case, it would be naive not to recognize that the 1965 Cadillac was used to entice a highly susceptible old man into a hard trade. Mr. Shea was fatuously fond of new Cadillacs, but was apparently incapable of taking care of one. His own 1964 model (he had also had a 1963 model) had been badly abused. According to Dr. Hodge, it 'smelled like a toilet. * * * had several fenders bumped, bullet holes in the top and the car was just filthy * * *. It was a rather foul car.'...Knowing the condition of Mr. Shea's car, his financial predicament and the activities of his son-in-law in his behalf, Dr. Hodge used the new automobile as a means of influencing Mr. Shea to agree to sell. The means was calculated to becloud Mr. Shea's judgment, and, under the circumstances, its use was unfair....

Reversed and remanded.

Case Questions

1. Why is it relevant that Mr. Shea was separated from his wife and lived alone?
2. Why is it relevant that it was his doctor who convinced him to sell the real estate?
3. Why did the doctor offer the old man a Cadillac as part of the deal?
4. Generally speaking, if you agree to sell your real estate for less than its real value, that's just a unilateral mistake and the courts will grant no relief. What's different here?

Misrepresentation by Concealment

Reed v. King

193 Cal. Rptr. 130 (Calif. Ct. App. 1983)

Blease, J.

In the sale of a house, must the seller disclose it was the site of a multiple murder? Dorris Reed purchased a house from Robert King. Neither King nor his real estate agents (the other named defendants) told Reed that a woman and her four children were murdered there ten years earlier. However, it seems "truth will come to light; murder cannot be hid long." (Shakespeare, *Merchant of Venice*, Act II, Scene II.) Reed learned of the gruesome episode from a neighbor after the sale. She sues, seeking rescission and damages. King and the real estate agent defendants successfully demurred to her first amended complaint for failure to state a cause of action. Reed appeals the ensuing judgment of dismissal. We will reverse the judgment.

Facts

We take all issuable facts pled in Reed's complaint as true. King and his real estate agent knew about the murders and knew the event materially affected the market value of the house when they listed it for sale. They represented to Reed the premises were in good condition and fit for an "elderly lady" living alone. They did not disclose the fact of the murders. At some point King asked a neighbor not to inform Reed of that event. Nonetheless, after Reed moved in neighbors informed her no one was interested in purchasing the house because of the stigma. Reed paid $76,000 [about $215,000 in 2016], but [alleged] the house is only worth $65,000 because of its past.

Discussion

Does Reed's pleading state a cause of action? Concealed within this question is the nettlesome problem of the duty of disclosure of blemishes on real property that are not physical defects or legal impairments to use.

Numerous cases have found non-disclosure of physical defects and legal impediments to use of real property are material. [Citation] However, to our knowledge, no prior real estate sale case has faced an issue of non-disclosure of the kind presented here. Should this variety of ill-repute be required to be disclosed? Is this a circumstance where "non-disclosure of the fact amounts to a failure to act in good faith and in accordance with reasonable standards of fair dealing [?]" (Rest.2d Contracts, § 161, subd. (b).)

The paramount argument against an affirmative conclusion is it permits the camel's nose of unrestrained irrationality admission to the tent. If such an "irrational" consideration is permitted as a basis of rescission the stability of all conveyances will be seriously undermined. Any fact that might disquiet the enjoyment of some segment of the buying public may be seized upon by a disgruntled purchaser to void a bargain. In our view, keeping this genie in the bottle is not as difficult a task as these arguments assume. We do not view a decision allowing Reed to survive a demurrer in these unusual circumstances as endorsing the materiality of facts predicating peripheral, insubstantial, or fancied harms.

The murder of innocents is highly unusual in its potential for so disturbing buyers they may be unable to reside in a home where it has occurred. This fact may foreseeably deprive a buyer of the intended use of the purchase. Murder is not such a common occurrence that *buyers* should be charged with anticipating and discovering this disquieting possibility. Accordingly, the fact is not one for which a duty of inquiry and discovery can sensibly be imposed upon the buyer.

Reed alleges the fact of the murders has a quantifiable effect on the market value of the premises. We cannot say this allegation is inherently wrong and, in the pleading posture of the case, we assume it to be true. If information known or accessible only to the seller has a significant and measurable effect on market value and, as is alleged here, the seller is aware of this effect, we see no principled basis for making the duty to disclose turn upon the character of the information. Physical usefulness is not and never has been the sole criterion of valuation. Stamp collections and gold speculation would be insane activities if utilitarian considerations were the sole measure of value.

Reputation and history can have a significant effect on the value of realty. "George Washington slept here" is worth something, however physically inconsequential that consideration may be. Ill-repute or "bad will" conversely may depress the value of property. Failure to disclose such a negative fact where it will have a forseeably depressing effect on income expected to be generated by a business is tortious. [Citation] Some cases have held that *unreasonable* fears of the potential buying public that a gas or oil pipeline may rupture may depress the market value of land and entitle the owner to incremental compensation in eminent domain.

Whether Reed will be able to prove her allegation the decade-old multiple murder has a significant effect on market value we cannot determine. If she is able to do so by competent evidence she is entitled to a favorable ruling on the issues of materiality and duty to disclose. Her demonstration of objective tangible harm would still the concern that permitting her to go forward will open the floodgates to rescission on subjective and idiosyncratic grounds. * * *

The judgment is reversed.

Case Questions

1. Why is it relevant that the plaintiff was "an elderly lady living alone"?
2. How did Mrs. Reed find out about the gruesome fact here?
3. Why did the defendants conceal the facts?
4. What is the concern about opening "floodgates to rescission on subjective and idiosyncratic grounds"?
5. Why *did* George Washington sleep in so many places during the Revolutionary War?
6. Did Mrs. Reed get to rescind her contract and get out of the house as a result of this case?

Misrepresentation by Assertions of Opinion

Vokes v. Arthur Murray, Inc.

212 S.2d. 906 (Fla. 1968)

Pierce, J.

This is an appeal by Audrey E. Vokes, plaintiff below, from a final order dismissing with prejudice, for failure to state a cause of action, her fourth amended complaint, hereinafter referred to as plaintiff's complaint.

Defendant Arthur Murray, Inc., a corporation, authorizes the operation throughout the nation of dancing schools under the name of "Arthur Murray School of Dancing" through local franchised operators, one of whom was defendant J. P. Davenport whose dancing establishment was in Clearwater.

Plaintiff Mrs. Audrey E. Vokes, a widow of 51 years and without family, had a yen to be "an accomplished dancer" with the hopes of finding "new interest in life." So, on February 10, 1961, a dubious fate, with the assist of a motivated acquaintance, procured her to attend a "dance party" at Davenport's "School of Dancing," where she whiled away the pleasant hours, sometimes in a private room, absorbing his accomplished sales technique, during which her grace and poise were elaborated upon and her rosy future as "an excellent dancer" was painted for her in vivid and glowing colors. As an incident to this interlude, he sold her eight 1/2-hour dance lessons to be utilized within one calendar month therefrom, for the sum of $14.50 cash in hand paid, obviously a baited "come-on."

Thus she embarked upon an almost endless pursuit of the terpsichorean art during which, over a period of less than sixteen months, she was sold fourteen "dance courses" totaling in the aggregate 2,302 hours of dancing lessons for a total cash outlay of $31,090.45 [about $240,000 in 2016 dollars] all at Davenport's dance emporium. All of these fourteen courses were evidenced by execution of a written "Enrollment Agreement-Arthur Murray's School of Dancing" with the addendum in heavy black print, "No one will be informed that you are taking dancing lessons. Your relations with us are held in strict confidence," setting forth the number of "dancing lessons" and the "lessons in rhythm sessions" currently sold to her from time to time, and always of course accompanied by payment of cash of the realm.

These dance lesson contracts and the monetary consideration therefore of over $31,000 were procured from her by means and methods of Davenport and his associates, which went beyond the unsavory, yet legally permissible, perimeter of "sales puffing" and intruded well into the forbidden area of undue influence, the suggestion of falsehood, the suppression of truth, and the free exercise of rational judgment, if what plaintiff alleged in her complaint was true. From the time of her first contact with the dancing school in February, 1961, she was influenced unwittingly by a constant and continuous barrage of flattery, false praise, excessive compliments, and panegyric encomiums, to such extent that it would be not only inequitable, but unconscionable, for a Court exercising inherent chancery power to allow such contracts to stand.

She was incessantly subjected to overreaching blandishment and cajolery. She was assured she had "grace and poise"; that she was "rapidly improving and developing in her dancing skill"; that the additional lessons would "make her a beautiful dancer, capable of dancing with the most accomplished dancers"; that she was "rapidly progressing in the development of her dancing skill and gracefulness," etc., etc. She was given "dance aptitude tests" for the ostensible purpose of "determining" the number of remaining hours of instructions needed by her from time to time.

At one point she was sold 545 additional hours of dancing lessons to be entitled to an award of the "Bronze Medal" signifying that she had reached "the Bronze Standard," a supposed designation of dance achievement by students of Arthur Murray, Inc. * * * At another point, while she still had over 1,000 unused hours of instruction she was induced to buy 151 additional hours at a cost of $2,049.00 to be eligible for a "Student Trip to Trinidad," at her own expense as she later learned. * * *

Finally, sandwiched in between other lesser sales promotions, she was influenced to buy an additional 481 hours of instruction at a cost of $6,523.81 in order to "be classified as a Gold Bar Member, the ultimate achievement of the dancing studio."

All the foregoing sales promotions, illustrative of the entire fourteen separate contracts, were procured by defendant Davenport and Arthur Murray, Inc., by false representations to her that she was improving in her dancing ability, that she had excellent potential, that she was responding to instructions in dancing grace, and that they were developing her into a beautiful dancer, whereas in truth and in fact she did not develop in her dancing ability, she had no "dance aptitude," and in fact had difficulty in "hearing that musical beat." The complaint alleged that such representations to her "were in fact false and known by the defendant to be false and contrary to the plaintiff's true ability, the truth of plaintiff's ability being fully known to the defendants, but withheld from the plaintiff for the sole and specific intent to deceive and defraud the plaintiff and to induce her in the purchasing of additional hours of dance lessons." It was averred that the lessons were sold to her "in total disregard to the true physical, rhythm, and mental ability of the plaintiff." In other words, while she first exulted that she was entering the "spring of her life," she finally was awakened to the fact there was "spring" neither in her life nor in her feet.

The complaint prayed that the Court decree the dance contracts to be null and void and to be cancelled, that an accounting be had, and judgment entered against, the defendants "for that portion of the $31,090.45 not charged against specific hours of instruction given to the plaintiff." The Court held the complaint not to state a cause of action and dismissed it with prejudice. We disagree and reverse.

It is true that "generally a misrepresentation, to be actionable, must be one of fact rather than of opinion." [Citations] But this rule has significant qualifications, applicable here. It does not apply where there is a fiduciary relationship between the parties, or where there has been some artifice or trick employed by the representor, or where the parties do not in general deal at "arm's length" as we understand the phrase, or where the representee does not have equal opportunity to become apprised of the truth or falsity of the fact represented. [Citation] As stated by Judge Allen of this Court in [Citation]:

"* * * A statement of a party having * * * superior knowledge may be regarded as a statement of fact although it would be considered as opinion if the parties were dealing on equal terms."...

In [Citation] it was said that "* * * what is plainly injurious to good faith ought to be considered as a fraud sufficient to impeach a contract."... [Reversed.]

Case Questions

1. What was the motivation of the "motivated acquaintance" in this case?
2. Why is it relevant that Mrs. Vokes was a "widow of 51 years and without family"?
3. How did the defendant J. P. Davenport entice her into spending a lot of money on dance lessons?
4. What was the defendants' defense as to why they should not be liable for misrepresentation, and why was that defense not good?
5. Would you say the court here is rather condescending to Mrs. Vokes, all things considered? How could an apparently competent—and apparently rich—51 year old woman be taken for such a ride?

Mutual Mistake

Konic International Corporation v. Spokane Computer Services, Inc.,
708 P.2d 932 (Idaho 1985)

The magistrate found the following facts. David Young, an employee of Spokane Computer, was instructed by his employer to investigate the possibility of purchasing a surge protector, a device which protects computers from damaging surges of electrical current. Young's investigation turned up several units priced from $50 to $200, none of which, however, were appropriate for his employer's needs. Young then contacted Konic. After discussing Spokane Computer's needs with a Konic engineer, Young was referred to one of Konic's salesmen. Later, after deciding on a certain unit, Young inquired as to the price of the selected item. The salesman responded, "fifty-six twenty." The salesman meant $5,620 [about $13,000 in 2015]. Young in turn thought $56.20.

The salesman for Konic asked about Young's authority to order the equipment and was told that Young would have to get approval from one of his superiors. Young in turn prepared a purchase order for $56.20 and had it approved by the appropriate authority. Young telephoned the order and purchase order number to Konic, who then shipped the equipment to Spokane Computer. However, because of internal processing procedures of both parties the discrepancy in prices was not discovered immediately. Spokane Computer received the surge protector and installed it in its office. The receipt and installation of the equipment occurred while the president of Spokane Computer was on vacation. Although the president's father, who was also chairman of the board of Spokane Computer, knew of the installation, he only inquired as to what the item was and who had ordered it. The president came back from vacation the day after the surge protector had been installed and placed in operation and was told of the purchase. He immediately ordered that power to the equipment be turned off because he realized that the equipment contained parts which alone were worth more than $56 in value. Although the president then told Young to verify the price of the surge protector, Young failed to do so. Two weeks later, when Spokane Computer was processing its purchase order and Konic's invoice, the discrepancy between the amount on the invoice and the amount on the purchase order was discovered. The president of Spokane Computer then contacted Konic, told Konic that Young had no authority to order such equipment, that Spokane Computer did not want the equipment, and that Konic should remove it. Konic responded that Spokane Computer now owned the equipment and if the equipment was not paid for, Konic would sue for the price. Spokane Computer refused to pay and this litigation ensued.

Basically what is involved here is a failure of communication between the parties. A similar failure to communicate arose over 100 years ago in the celebrated case of *Raffles v. Wichelhaus,*

[Citation] which has become better known as the case of the good ship *Peerless*. In *Peerless*, the parties agreed on a sale of cotton which was to be delivered from Bombay by the ship *Peerless*. In fact, there were two ships named *Peerless* and each party, in agreeing to the sale, was referring to a different ship. Because the sailing time of the two ships was materially different, neither party was willing to agree to shipment by the "other" *Peerless*. The court ruled that, because each party had a different ship in mind at the time of the contract, there was in fact no binding contract. The *Peerless* rule later was incorporated into section 71 of the Restatement of Contracts and has now evolved into section 20 of Restatement (Second) of Contracts (1981). Section 20 states in part:

> *(1) There is no manifestation of mutual assent to an exchange if the parties attach materially different meanings to their manifestations and*
>
> *(a) neither knows or has reason to know the meaning attached by the other.*

Comment (c) to Section 20 further explains that "even though the parties manifest mutual assent to the same words of agreement, there may be no contract because of a material difference of understanding as to the terms of the exchange." Another authority, Williston, discussing situations where a mistake will prevent formation of a contract, agrees that "where a phrase of contract...is reasonably capable of different interpretations ... there is no contract." [Citation]

In the present case, both parties attributed different meanings to the same term, "fifty-six twenty." Thus, there was no meeting of the minds of the parties. With a hundred fold difference in the two prices, obviously price was a material term. Because the "fifty-six twenty" designation was a material term expressed in an ambiguous form to which two meanings were obviously applied, we conclude that no contract between the parties was ever formed. Accordingly, we do not reach the issue of whether Young had authority to order the equipment.

[Affirmed.]

Case Questions

1. Why is it reasonable to say that no contract was made in this case?
2. A discrepancy in price of one hundred times is, of course, enormous. How could such an egregious mistake have occurred by both parties? In terms of running a sensible business, how could this kind of mistake be avoided before it resulted in expensive litigation?

10.6 Summary and Exercises

Summary

No agreement is enforceable if the parties did not enter into it (1) of their own free will, (2) with adequate knowledge of the terms, and (3) with the mental capacity to appreciate the relationship.

Contracts coerced through duress will void a contract if actually induced through physical harm and will make the contract voidable if entered under the compulsion of many types of threats. The threat must be improper and leave no reasonable alternative, but the test is subjective—that is, what did the person threatened actually fear, not what a more reasonable person might have feared.

Misrepresentations may render an agreement void or voidable. Among the factors to be considered are whether the misrepresentation was deliberate and material; whether the promisee relied on the misrepresentation in good faith; whether the representation was of fact, opinion, or intention; and whether the parties had a special relationship.

Similarly, mistaken beliefs, not induced by misrepresentations, may suffice to avoid the bargain. Some mistakes on one side only make a contract voidable. More often, mutual mistakes of facts will show that there was no meeting of the minds.

Those who lack capacity are often entitled to avoid contract liability. Although it is possible to state the general rule, many exceptions exist—for example, in contracts for necessities, infants will be liable for the reasonable value of the goods purchased.

Exercises

1. Eulrich, an auto body mechanic who had never operated a business, entered into a Snap-On Tools franchise agreement. For $22,000 invested from his savings and the promise of another $22,000 from the sale of inventory, he was provided a truck full of tools. His job was to drive around his territory and sell them. The agreement allowed termination by either party; if Eulrich terminated, he was entitled to resell to Snap-On any new tools he had remaining. When he complained that his territory was not profitable, his supervisors told him to work it harder, that anybody could make money with Snap-On's marketing system. (In fact, the evidence was the system made money for the supervisors and little for dealers; dealers quickly failed and were replaced by new recruits.) Within several months Eulrich was out of money and desperate. He tried to "check in" his truck to get money to pay his household bills and uninsured medical bills for his wife; the supervisors put him off for weeks. On the check-in day, the exhausted Eulrich's supervisors berated him for being a bad businessman, told him no check would be forthcoming until all the returned inventory was sold, and presented him with a number of papers to sign, including a "Termination Agreement" whereby he agreed to waive any claims against Snap-On; he was not aware that was what he had signed. He sued to rescind the contract and for damages. The defendants held up the waiver as a defense. Under what theory might Eulrich recover?[25]
2. Chauncey, a college student, worked part-time in a restaurant. After he had worked for several months, the owner of the restaurant discovered that Chauncey had stolen $2,000 from the cash register. The owner called Chauncey's parents and told them that if they did not sign a note for $2,000, he would initiate criminal proceedings against Chauncey. The parents signed and delivered the note to the owner but later refused to pay. May the owner collect on the note? Why?
3. A restaurant advertised a steak dinner that included a "juicy, great-tasting steak, a fresh crisp salad, and a warm roll." After reading the ad, Clarence visited the restaurant and ordered the steak dinner. The steak was dry, the lettuce in the salad was old and limp with brown edges, and the roll was partly frozen. May Clarence recover from the restaurant on the basis of misrepresentation? Why?
4. Bert purchased Ernie's car. Before selling the car, Ernie had stated to Bert, "This car runs well and is reliable. Last week I drove the car all the way from Seattle to San Francisco to visit my mother and back again to Seattle." In fact, Ernie was not telling the truth: he had driven the car to San Francisco to visit his paramour, not his mother. Upon discovery of the truth, may Bert avoid the contract? Why?
5. Randolph enrolled in a business law class and purchased a new business law textbook from the local bookstore. He dropped the class during the first week and sold the book to his friend Scott. Before making the sale, Randolph told Scott that he had purchased the book new and had owned it for one week. Unknown to either Randolph or Scott, the book was in fact a used one. Scott later discovered some underlining in the middle of the book and attempted to avoid the contract. Randolph refused to refund the purchase price, claiming that he had not intentionally deceived his friend. May Scott avoid the contract? Why?
6. Langstraat was seventeen when he purchased a motorcycle. When applying for insurance, he signed a "Notice of Rejection," declining to purchase uninsured motorist coverage. He

was involved in an accident with an uninsured motorist and sought to disaffirm his rejection of the uninsured motorist coverage on the basis of infancy. May he do so?

7. Waters was attracted to Midwest Supply by its advertisements for doing federal income taxes. The ads stated "guaranteed accurate tax preparation." Waters inquired about amending past returns to obtain refunds. Midwest induced him to apply for and receive improper refunds. When Waters was audited, he was required to pay more taxes, and the IRS put tax liens on his wages and bank accounts. In fact, Midwest hired people with no knowledge about taxes at all; if a customer inquired about employees' qualifications, Midwest's manual told the employees to say, "Midwest has been preparing taxes for twenty years." The manual also instructed office managers never to refer to any employee as a "specialist" or "tax expert," but never to correct any news reporters or commentators if they referred to employees as such. What cause of action has Waters, and for what remedies?
8. Mutschler Grain Company (later Jamestown Farmers Elevator) agreed to sell General Mills 30,000 bushels of barley at $1.22 per bushel. A dispute arose: Mutschler said that transportation was to be by truck but that General Mills never ordered any trucks to pick up the grain; General Mills said the grain was to be shipped by rail (railcars were in short supply). Nine months later, after Mutschler had delivered only about one-tenth the contracted amount, the price of barley was over $3.00 per bushel. Mutschler defaulted on, and then repudiated, the contract. Fred Mutschler then received this telephone call from General Mills: "We're General Mills, and if you don't deliver this grain to us, why we'll have a battery of lawyers in there tomorrow morning to visit you, and then we are going to the North Dakota Public Service (Commission); we're going to the Minneapolis Grain Exchange and we're going to the people in Montana and there will be no more Mutschler Grain Company. We're going to take your license."

   Mutchsler then shipped 22,000 bushels of barley at the $1.22 rate and sued General Mills for the difference between that price and the market price of over $3.00. Summary judgment issued for General Mills. Upon what basis might Mutschler Grain appeal?
9. Duke decided to sell his car. The car's muffler had a large hole in it, and as a result, the car made a loud noise. Before showing the car to potential buyers, Duke patched the hole with muffler tape to quiet it. Perry bought the car after test-driving it. He later discovered the faulty muffler and sought to avoid the contract, claiming fraud. Duke argued that he had not committed fraud because Perry had not asked about the muffler and Duke had made no representation of fact concerning it. Is Duke correct? Decide and explain.
10. At the end of the term at college, Jose, talking in the library with his friend Leanne, said, "I'll sell you my business law notes for $25." Leanne agreed and paid him the money. Jose then realized he'd made a mistake in that he had offered his notes when he meant to offer his book. Leanne didn't want the book; she had a book. She wanted the notes. Would Leanne have a cause of action against Jose if he refused to deliver the notes? Decide and explain.

Self-Test Questions

1. Misrepresentation that does not go to the core of a contract is
   a. fraud in the execution
   b. fraud in the inducement
   c. undue influence
   d. an example of mistake
2. In order for a misrepresentation to make a contract voidable,
   a. it must have been intentional
   b. the party seeking to void must have relied on the misrepresentation
   c. it must always be material
   d. none of the above is required
3. A mistake by one party will not invalidate a contract unless
   a. the other party knew of the mistake

   b. the party making the mistake did not read the contract closely
   c. the parties to the contract had never done business before
   d. the party is mistaken about the law

4. Upon reaching the age of majority, a person who entered into a contract to purchase goods while a minor may
   a. ratify the contract and keep the goods without paying for them
   b. disaffirm the contract and keep the goods without paying for them
   c. avoid paying for the goods by keeping them without ratifying or disaffirming the contract
   d. none of these

5. Seller does not disclose to Buyer that the foundation of a house is infested with termites. Upon purchasing the house and remodeling part of the basement, Buyer discovers the termites. Has Buyer a cause of action against Seller?
   a. yes
   b. no

Self-Test Answers

1. a
2. d
3. a
4. e
5. b

Endnotes

1. BBC, King John. At http://www.bbc.co.uk/history/historic_figures/john.shtml.
2. Restatement (Second) of Contracts, Section 177.
3. Restatement (Second) of Contracts, Section 177(b).
4. Restatement (Second) of Contracts, Section 163.
5. *Ikeda v. Curtis*, 261 P.2d 684 (Wash. 1951).
6. *Stambovsky v. Ackley*, 169 A.D.2d 254 (N.Y. 1991).
7. Restatement (Second) of Contracts, Section 168(d).
8. Restatement (Second) of Contracts, Section 171(1).
9. Restatement (Second) of Contracts, Section 162(1).
10. Restatement (Second) of Contracts, Section 162(2).
11. *Lesher v. Strid*, 996 P.2d 988 (Or. Ct. App. 2000).
12. *Merritt v. Craig*, 753 A.2d 2 (Md. Ct. App. 2000).
13. *Ehrman v. Mann*, 979 So.2d 1011 (Fla. Ct. App. 2008).
14. *Kirkham v. Smith*, 23 P.3d 10 (Wash. Ct. App. 2001).
15. Restatement (Second) of Contracts, Section 151.
16. *Sikora v. Vanderploeg*, 212 S.W.3d 277 (Tenn. Ct. App. 2006).
17. Restatement (Second) of Contracts, Section 152.
18. *Sherwood v. Walker*, 33 N.W. 919 (1887).
19. *Gastonia Personnel Corp. v. Rogers*, 172 S.E.2d 19 (N.C. 1970).
20. William L. Prosser, *Handbook of the Law of Torts*, 4th ed. (St. Paul, MN: West, 1971), 999.
21. *Dodson v. Shrader*, 824 S.W.2d 545 (Tenn. 1992).
22. Restatement (Second) of Contracts, Section 13.
23. Restatement (Second) of Contracts, Section 16(b).
24. *First State Bank of Sinai v. Hyland*, 399 N.W.2d 894 (S.D. 1987).
25. *Eulrich v. Snap-On Tools Corp.*, 853 P.2d 1350 (Or. Ct. App. 1993).

CHAPTER 11

Consideration

Learning Objectives

After reading this chapter, you should understand the following:

1. What "consideration" is in contract law, what it is not, and what purposes it serves.
2. How the sufficiency of consideration is determined.
3. In what common situations an understanding of consideration is important.
4. What promises are enforceable without consideration.

11.1 General Perspectives on Consideration

Learning Objectives

1. Understand what "consideration" is in contract law.
2. Recognize what purposes the doctrine serves.
3. Understand how the law determines whether consideration exists.
4. Know the elements of consideration.

The Purpose of Consideration

This chapter continues our inquiry into whether the parties created a valid contract. In Chapter 9 we saw that the first requisite of a valid contract is an agreement: offer and acceptance. In this chapter, we assume that agreement has been reached and concentrate on one of its crucial aspects: the existence of consideration. Which of the following, if any, is a contract?

1. Betty offers to give a book to Lou. Lou accepts.
2. Betty offers Lou the book in exchange for Lou's promise to pay twenty-five dollars. Lou accepts.
3. Betty offers to give Lou the book if Lou promises to pick it up at Betty's house. Lou agrees.

In American law, only the second situation is a binding contract, because only that contract contains **consideration**, a set of mutual promises in which each party agrees to give up something to the benefit of the other. This chapter will explore the meaning and rationale of that statement.

consideration

The surrender of any legal right (a detriment) in return for the promise of some benefit in return.

The question of what constitutes a binding contract has been answered differently throughout history and in other cultures. For example, under Roman law, a contract without consideration was binding if certain formal requirements were met. And in the Anglo-American tradition, the presence of a seal—the wax impression affixed to a document—was once sufficient to make a contract binding without any other consideration. The seal is no longer a substitute for consideration, although in some states it creates a presumption of consideration; in forty-nine states, the Uniform

Commercial Code (UCC) has abolished the seal on contracts for the sale of goods. (Louisiana has not adopted UCC Article 2.)

Whatever its original historical purposes, and however apparently arcane, the doctrine of consideration serves some still-useful purposes. It provides objective evidence for asserting that a contract exists; it distinguishes between enforceable and unenforceable bargains; and it is a check against rash, unconsidered action, against thoughtless promise making.[1]

Some wags (a "wag" is a witty person, a joker) have suggested that consideration remains viable in American law (the concept is by no means universal) in part because most people—not having been exposed to it—don't understand it very well. Therefore, they need lawyers to help them, and there are a lot of lawyers in most legislatures. They have no particular interest in abolishing the doctrine of consideration, something about which they have specialized and possibly valuable knowledge.

A Definition of *Consideration*

legal detriment

The giving up by a person of that which he or she had a right to retain.

legal benefit

The receipt by one person of something legal he or she had no preexisting right to.

Consideration is said to exist when the promisor receives some benefit for his promise and the promisee gives up something in return; it is the bargained-for price you pay for what you get. That may seem simple enough. But as with much in the law, the complicating situations are never very far away. The "something" that is promised or delivered cannot be just anything, such as a feeling of pride, warmth, amusement, or friendship; it must be something known as a **legal detriment**—an act, forbearance, or a promise of such from the promisee. The detriment need not be an actual detriment; it may in fact be a benefit to the promisee, or at least not a loss. The detriment to one side is usually a **legal benefit** to the other, but the detriment to the promisee need not confer a tangible benefit on the promisor; the promisee can agree to forego something without that something being given to the promisor. Whether consideration is legally sufficient has nothing to do with whether it is morally or economically adequate to make the bargain a fair one. Moreover, legal consideration need not even be certain; it can be a promise contingent on an event that may never happen. Consideration is a legal concept, and it centers on the giving up of a legal right or benefit.

Consideration has two elements. The first, as just outlined, is whether the promisee has incurred a legal detriment—given up something, paid some "price," though it may be, for example, the promise to do something, like paint a house. (Some courts—although a minority—take the view that a bargained-for legal benefit to the promisor is sufficient consideration.) The second element is whether the legal detriment was *bargained* for: did the promisor specifically intend the act, forbearance, or promise in return for his promise? Applying this two-pronged test to the three examples given at the outset of the chapter, we can easily see why only in the second is there legally sufficient consideration. In the first, Lou incurred no legal detriment; he made no pledge to act or to forbear from acting, nor did he in fact act or forbear from acting. In the third example, what might appear to be such a promise is not really so. Betty made a promise on a condition that Lou comes to her house; the intent clearly is to make a gift.

Key Takeaway

Consideration is—with some exceptions—a required element of a contract. It is the bargained-for giving up of something of legal value for something in return. It serves the purposes of making formal the intention to contract and reducing rash promise making.

Exercises

1. Alice promises to give her neighbor a blueberry bush; the neighbor says, "Thank you!" Subsequently, Alice changes her mind. Is she bound by her promise?
2. Why, notwithstanding its relative antiquity, does consideration still serve some useful purposes?
3. Identify the exchange of consideration in this example: A to B, "I will pay you $800 if you paint my garage." B to A, "Okay, I'll paint your garage for $800."

11.2 Legal Sufficiency

Learning Objectives

1. Know in general what "legal sufficiency" means when examining consideration.
2. Recognize how the concept operates in such common situations as threat of litigation, and accord and satisfaction.
3. Understand why illusory promises are unenforceable, and how courts deal with needs, outputs, and exclusive dealings contracts.

The Concept of Legal Sufficiency

As suggested in Section 1, what is required in contract is the bargained-for exchange of a legal detriment and a legal benefit; if that happens, the consideration is said to have **legal sufficiency**.

legal sufficiency

Something of value enough to constitute consideration.

Actual versus Legal Detriment

Suppose Phil offers George $500 if George will quit smoking for one year. Is Phil's promise binding? Because George is presumably benefiting by making and sticking to the agreement—surely his health will improve if he gives up smoking—how can his act be considered a legal *detriment*? The answer is that there is forbearance on George's part: George is legally entitled to smoke, and by contracting not to, he suffers a loss of his legal right to do so. This is a legal detriment; consideration does not require an actual detriment.

Adequacy of Consideration

Scrooge offers to buy Caspar's motorcycle, worth $700, for $10 and a shiny new fountain pen (worth $5). Caspar agrees. Is this agreement supported by adequate consideration? Yes, because both have agreed to give up something that is theirs: Scrooge, the cash and the pen; Caspar, the motorcycle. Courts are not generally concerned with the economic adequacy of the consideration but instead with whether it is present. As Judge Richard A. Posner puts it, "To ask whether there is consideration is simply to inquire whether the situation is one of exchange and a bargain has been struck. To go further and ask whether the consideration is adequate would require the court to do what . . . it is less well equipped to do than the parties—decide whether the price (and other essential terms) specified in the contract are reasonable."[2] In short, "courts do not inquire into the adequacy of consideration."

Of course, normally, parties to contracts will not make such a one-sided deal as Scrooge and Caspar's. But there is a common class of contracts in which nominal consideration—usually one dollar—is recited in printed forms. Usually these are option contracts, in which "in consideration of one dollar in hand paid and receipt of which is hereby acknowledged" one party agrees to hold open the right of the other to make a purchase on agreed terms. The courts will enforce these contracts if the dollar is intended "to support a short-time option proposing an exchange on fair terms."[3] If, however, the option is for an unreasonably long period of time and the underlying bargain is unfair (the Restatement gives as an example a ten-year option permitting the optionee to take phosphate rock from a widow's land at a per-ton payment of only one-fourth the prevailing rate), then the courts are unlikely to hold that the nominal consideration makes the option irrevocable.

Because the consideration on such option contracts is nominal, its recital in the written instrument is usually a mere formality, and it is frequently never paid; in effect, the recital of nominal consideration is false. Nevertheless, the courts will enforce the contract—precisely because the recital has become a formality and nobody objects to the charade. Moreover, it would be easy enough to upset an option based on nominal consideration by falsifying oral testimony that the dollar was never paid or received. In a contest between oral testimonies where the incentive to lie is strong and there is a written document clearly incorporating the parties' agreement, the courts prefer the latter. However, as Section 4, *Board of Control of Eastern Michigan University v. Burgess*, demonstrates, the state courts are not uniform on this point, and it is a safe practice always to deliver the consideration, no matter how nominal.

Applications of the Legal Sufficiency Doctrine

This section discusses several common circumstances where the issue of whether the consideration proffered (offered up) is adequate.

Threat of Litigation: Covenant Not to Sue

covenant not to sue

An agreement not to pursue legal action.

Because every person has the legal right to file suit if he or she feels aggrieved, a promise to refrain from going to court is sufficient consideration to support a promise of payment or performance. In *Dedeaux v. Young*, Dedeaux purchased property and promised to make certain payments to Young, the broker.[4] But Dedeaux thereafter failed to make these payments, and Young threatened suit; Young filed papers in court, the transfer of title to Dedeaux could have been blocked. To keep Young from suing, Dedeaux promised to pay a 5 percent commission if Young would stay out of court. Dedeaux later resisted paying on the ground that he had never made such a promise and that even if he had, it did not amount to a contract because there was no consideration from Young. The court disagreed, holding that the evidence supported Young's contention that Dedeaux had indeed made such a promise and upholding Young's claim for the commission because "a request to forbear to exercise a legal right has been generally accepted as sufficient consideration to support a contract." If Young had had no grounds to sue—for example, if he had threatened to sue a stranger, or if it could be shown that Dedeaux had no obligation to him originally—then there would have been no consideration because Young would not have been giving up a legal right. A promise to forebear suing in return for settlement of a dispute is called a **covenant not to sue** (*covenant* is another word for agreement).

Accord and Satisfaction Generally

Frequently, the parties to a contract will dispute the meaning of its terms and conditions, especially the amount of money actually due. When the dispute is genuine (and not the unjustified attempt of one party to avoid paying a sum clearly due), it can be settled by the parties' agreement on a fixed sum as the amount due. This second agreement, which substitutes for the disputed first agreement, is called an accord, and when the payment or other term is discharged, the completed second contract is known as an **accord and satisfaction.** A suit brought for an alleged breach of the original contract could be defended by citing the later accord and satisfaction.

accord and satisfaction

An agreement to substitute a new contract for a disputed one; when executed, the accord is satisfied.

An accord is a contract and must therefore be supported by consideration. Suppose Jan owes Andy $7,000, due November 1. On November 1, Jan pays only $3,500 in exchange for Andy's promise to release Jan from the remainder of the debt. Has Andy (the promisor) made a binding promise? He has not, because there is no consideration for the accord. Jan has incurred no detriment; she has received something (release of the obligation to pay the remaining $3,500), but she has given up nothing. But if Jan and Andy had agreed that Jan would pay the $3,500 on October 25, then there would be consideration; Jan would have incurred a legal detriment by obligating herself to make a payment earlier than the original contract required her to. If Jan had paid the $3,500 on November 11 and had given Andy something else agreed to—a pen, a keg of beer, a peppercorn—the required detriment would also be present.

Let's take a look at some examples of the accord and satisfaction principle. The dispute that gives rise to the parties' agreement to settle by an accord and satisfaction may come up in several typical ways: where there is an unliquidated debt; a disputed debt; an "in-full-payment check" for less than what the creditor claims is due; unforeseen difficulties that give rise to a contract modification, or a novation; or a composition among creditors. But no obligation ever arises—and no real legal dispute can arise—where a person promises a benefit if someone will do that which he has a preexisting obligation to, or where a person promises a benefit to someone not to do that which the promisee is already disallowed from doing, or where one makes an illusory promise.

Settling an Unliquidated Debt

An **unliquidated debt** is one that is uncertain in amount. Such debts frequently occur when people consult professionals in whose offices precise fees are rarely discussed, or where one party agrees, expressly or by implication, to pay the customary or reasonable fees of the other without fixing the exact amount. It is certain that a debt is owed (a **liquidated debt**, on the other hand, is one that is fixed in amount, certain), but it is not certain how much debt can be liquidated by being written down in unambiguous terms—"IOU $100"—or by being mathematically ascertainable—$1 per pound of ice ordered and 60 pounds delivered; hence the liquidated debt is $60.

unliquidated debt

A money obligation the amount of which is unknown.

liquidated debt

A money obligation the value of which is known.

Here is how the matter plays out: Assume a patient goes to the hospital for a gallbladder operation. The cost of the operation has not been discussed beforehand in detail, although the cost in the metropolitan area is normally around $8,000. After the operation, the patient and the surgeon agree on a bill of $6,000. The patient pays the bill; a month later the surgeon sues for another $2,000. Who wins? The patient: the surgeon has forgone his right to challenge the reasonableness of the fee by agreeing to a fixed amount payable at a certain time. The agreement liquidating the debt is an accord and is enforceable. If, however, the patient and the surgeon had agreed on an $8,000 fee before the operation, and if the patient arbitrarily refused to pay this liquidated debt unless the surgeon agreed to cut her fee in half, then the surgeon would be entitled to recover the other half in a lawsuit, because the patient would have given no consideration—given up nothing, "suffered no detriment"—for the surgeon's subsequent agreement to cut the fee.

Settling a Disputed Debt

A **disputed debt** arises where the parties *did* agree on (liquidated) the price or fee but subsequently get into a dispute about its fairness, and then settle. When this dispute is settled, the parties have given consideration to an agreement to accept a fixed sum as payment for the amount due. Assume that in the gallbladder case the patient agrees in advance to pay $8,000. Eight months after the operation and as a result of nausea and vomiting spells, the patient undergoes a second operation; the surgeons discover a surgical sponge embedded in the patient's intestine. The patient refuses to pay the full sum of the original surgeon's bill; they settle on $6,000, which the patient pays. This is a binding agreement because subsequent facts arose to make legitimate the patient's quarrel over his obligation to pay the full bill. As long as the dispute is based in fact and is not trumped up, as long as the promisee is acting in good faith, then consideration is present when a disputed debt is settled. The surgeon gives up $2,000 (detriment), but gets the dispute resolved (benefit); the patient gives up the right to demand any further discount (detriment), and gets the dispute resolved (benefit).

The "In-Full-Payment" Check Situation

To discharge his liquidated debt for $8,000 to the surgeon, the patient sends a check for $6,000 marked "payment in full." The surgeon cashes it. There is no dispute. May the surgeon sue for the remaining $2,000? This may appear to be an accord: by cashing the check, the surgeon seems to be agreeing with the patient to accept the $6,000 in full payment. But consideration is lacking. Because the surgeon is owed more than the face amount of the check, she gets no benefit and the patient incurs no legal detriment by accepting the check. If the rule were otherwise, debtors could easily tempt hard-pressed creditors to accept less than the amount owed by presenting immediate cash. The key to the enforceability of a "payment in full" legend is the character of the debt. If unliquidated, or if there is a dispute, then "payment in full" can serve as accord and satisfaction when written on a check that is accepted for payment by a creditor. But if the debt is liquidated and undisputed, there is no consideration when the check is for a lesser amount. (However, it is arguable that if the check is considered to be an agreement modifying a sales contract, no consideration is necessary under Uniform Commercial Code (UCC) Section 2-209.)

Unforeseen Difficulties

unforeseen difficulty

Problems in executing a contract so great as to warrant the assumption that the contract is modified.

novation

A new contract substituting for an old one, or a new party to a contract replacing a former party.

An **unforeseen difficulty** arising after a contract is made may be resolved by an accord and satisfaction, too. Difficulties that no one could foresee can sometimes serve as catalyst for a further promise that may appear to be without consideration but that the courts will enforce nevertheless. Suppose Peter contracts to build Jerry a house for $390,000. While excavating, Peter unexpectedly discovers quicksand, the removal of which will cost an additional $10,000. To ensure that Peter does not delay, Jerry promises to pay Peter $10,000 more than originally agreed. But when the house is completed, Jerry reneges on his promise. Is Jerry liable? Logically perhaps not: Peter has incurred no legal detriment in exchange for the $10,000; he had already contracted to build the house. But most courts would allow Peter to recover on the theory that the original contract was terminated, or modified, either by mutual agreement or by an implied condition that the original contract would be discharged if unforeseen difficulties developed. In short, the courts will enforce the parties' own mutual recognition that the unforeseen conditions had made the old contract unfair. The parties either have modified their original contract (which requires consideration at common law) or have given up their original contract and made a new one (called a **novation**).

It is a question of fact whether the new circumstance is new and difficult enough to make a preexisting obligation into an unforeseen difficulty. Obviously, if Peter encounters only a small pocket of quicksand—say two gallons' worth—he would have to deal with it as part of his already-agreed-to job. If he encounters as much quicksand as would fill an Olympic-sized swimming pool, that's clearly unforeseen, and he should get extra to deal with it. Some place between the two quantities of quicksand there is enough of the stuff so that Peter's duty to remove it is outside the original agreement and new consideration would be needed in exchange for its removal.

Creditors' Composition

A **creditors' composition** may give rise to debt settlement by an accord and satisfaction. It is an agreement whereby two or more creditors of a debtor consent to the debtor's paying them pro rata shares of the debt due in full satisfaction of their claims. A composition agreement can be critically important to a business in trouble; through it, the business might manage to stave off bankruptcy. Even though the share accepted is less than the full amount due and is payable after the due date so that consideration appears to be lacking, courts routinely enforce these agreements. The promise of each creditor to accept a lesser share than that owed in return for getting something is taken as consideration to support the promises of the others. A debtor has $3,000 on hand. He owes $3,000 each to A, B, and C. A, B, and C agree to accept $1,000 each and discharge the debtor. Each creditor has given up $2,000 but in return has at least received something, the $1,000. Without the composition, one might have received the entire amount owed her, but the others would have received nothing.

creditors' composition

An agreement among creditors, each accepting less than full payment from a debtor so that each gets something.

Preexisting Duty

Not amenable to settlement by an accord and satisfaction is the situation where a party has a **preexisting duty** and he or she is offered a benefit to discharge it. When the only consideration offered the promisor is an act or promise to act to carry out a preexisting duty, there is no valid contract. As *Denney v. Reppert* (Section 4) makes clear, the promisee suffers no legal detriment in promising to undertake that which he is already obligated to do. Where a person is promised a benefit not to do that which he is already disallowed from doing, there is no consideration. David is sixteen years old; his uncle promises him $50 if he will refrain from smoking. The promise is not enforceable: legally, David already must refrain from smoking, so he has promised to give up nothing to which he had a legal right. As noted previously, the difficulty arises where it is unclear whether a person has a preexisting obligation or whether such unforeseen difficulties have arisen as to warrant the recognition that the parties have modified the contract or entered into a novation. What if Peter insists on additional payment to remove one wheelbarrow full of quicksand from the excavation? Surely that's not enough "unforeseen difficulty." How much quicksand is enough?

Illusory Promises

Not every promise is a pledge to do something. Sometimes it is an **illusory promise**, where the terms of the contract really bind the promisor to give up nothing, to suffer no detriment. For example, Lydia offers to pay Juliette $10 for mowing Lydia's lawn. Juliette promises to mow the lawn if she feels like it. May Juliette enforce the contract? No, because Juliette has incurred no legal detriment; her promise is illusory, since by doing nothing she still falls within the literal wording of her promise. The doctrine that such bargains are unenforceable is sometimes referred to as the rule of mutuality of obligation: if one party to a contract has not made a binding obligation, neither is the other party bound. Thus if A contracts to hire B for a year at $6,000 a month, reserving the right to dismiss B at any time (an "option to cancel" clause), and B agrees to work for a year, A has not really promised anything; A is not bound to the agreement, and neither is B.

illusory promise

The promisor actually gives up no consideration, as in "I will paint your house in June if I feel like it."

The illusory promise presents a special problem in agreements for exclusive dealing, outputs, and needs contracts.

Exclusive Dealing Agreement

exclusive dealing agreement

A contract—as between buyer and seller—where the parties agree only to deal with each other.

In an **exclusive dealing agreement**, one party (the franchisor) promises to deal solely with the other party (the franchisee)—for example, a franchisor-designer agrees to sell all of her specially designed clothes to a particular department store (the franchisee). In return, the store promises to pay a certain percentage of the sales price to the designer. On closer inspection, it may appear that the store's promise is illusory: it pays the designer only if it manages to sell dresses, but it may sell none. The franchisor-designer may therefore attempt to back out of the deal by arguing that because the franchisee (the store) is not obligated to do anything, there was no consideration for her promise to deal exclusively with the store.

Courts, however, have upheld exclusive dealing contracts on the theory that the franchisee has an obligation to use reasonable efforts to promote and sell the product or services. This obligation may be spelled out in the contract or implied by its terms. In the classic statement of this concept, Judge Benjamin N. Cardozo, then on the New York Court of Appeals, in upholding such a contract, declared:

> *It is true that [the franchisee] does not promise in so many words that he will use reasonable efforts to place the defendant's endorsements and market her designs. We think, however, that such a promise is fairly to be implied. The law has outgrown its primitive stage of formalism when the precise word was the sovereign talisman, and every slip was fatal. It takes a broader view today. A promise may be lacking, and yet the whole writing may be "instinct with an obligation," imperfectly expressed....His promise to pay the defendant one-half of the profits and revenues resulting from the exclusive agency and to render accounts monthly was a promise to use reasonable efforts to bring profits and revenues into existence.*[5]

The UCC follows the same rule. In the absence of language specifically delineating the seller's or buyer's duties, an exclusive dealing contract under Section 2-306(2) imposes "an obligation by the seller to use best efforts to supply the goods and by the buyer to use best efforts to promote their sale."

Outputs Contracts and Needs Contracts

outputs contract

An agreement to sell all of one's goods or services to a single person.

needs contract

An agreement to buy all of one's requirements (of goods or services) from a single source.

A similar issue arises with outputs contracts and needs contracts. In an **outputs contract**, the seller—say a coal company—agrees to sell its entire yearly output of coal to an electric utility. Has it really agreed to produce and sell any coal at all? What if the coal-mine owner decides to shut down production to take a year's vacation—is that a violation of the agreement? Yes. The law imposes upon the seller here a duty to produce and sell a reasonable amount (or, if the owner doesn't want to operate the mine, then the owner will have pay the buyer the difference in price between what they had agreed the buyer would pay and what the buyer had to pay to get coal on the spot market). Similarly, if the electric utility contracted to buy all its requirements of coal from the coal company—a **needs contract**—could it decide to switch to natural gas and take no coal at all? Certainly anybody has the *power* to breach a contract, but not the right. The electric company can refuse to take coal, but it must answer in damages to the coal company for the latter's loss of profits.

Key Takeaway

Courts do not inquire into the adequacy of consideration, but (with some exceptions) do require the promisor to incur a legal detriment (the surrender of any legal right he or she possesses—to give up something) in order to receive the bargained-for benefit. The surrender of the right to sue is a legal detriment, and the issue arises in analyzing various kinds of dispute settlement agreements (accord and satisfaction): the obligation to pay the full amount claimed by a creditor on a liquidated debt, an unliquidated debt, and a disputed debt. Where unforeseen difficulties arise, an obligor will be entitled to additional compensation (consideration) to resolve them either because the contract is modified or because the parties have entered into a novation, but no additional consideration is owing to one who performs a preexisting obligation or forbears from performing that which he or she is under a legal duty not to perform. If a promisor gives an illusory promise, he or she gives no consideration and no contract is formed; but exclusive dealing agreements, needs contracts, and outputs contracts are not treated as illusory.

Exercises

1. What is meant by "legally sufficient" consideration?
2. Why do courts usually not "inquire into the adequacy of consideration"?
3. How can it be said there is consideration in the following instances: (a) settlement of an unliquidated debt? (b) settlement of a disputed debt? (c) a person agreeing to do more than originally contracted for because of unforeseen difficulties? (d) a creditor agreeing with other creditors for each of them to accept less than they are owed from the debtor?
4. Why is there no consideration where a person demands extra compensation for that which she is already obligated to do, or for forbearing to do that which she already is forbidden from doing?
5. What is the difference between a contract modification and a novation?
6. How do courts resolve the problem that a needs or outputs contract apparently imposes no detriment—no requirement to pass any consideration to the other side—on the promisor?

11.3 Promises Enforceable without Consideration

Learning Objective

1. Understand the exceptions to the requirement of consideration.

For a variety of policy reasons, courts will enforce certain types of promises even though consideration may be absent. Some of these are governed by the Uniform Commercial Code (UCC); others are part of the established common law.

Promises Enforceable without Consideration at Common Law

Past Consideration

past consideration

A promise subsequent to a promisee's act, not bargained for; it does not count as consideration.

Ordinarily, **past consideration** is not sufficient to support a promise. By past consideration, the courts mean an act that could have served as consideration if it had been bargained for at the time but that was not the subject of a bargain. For example, Mrs. Ace's dog Fluffy escapes from her mistress's condo at dusk. Robert finds Fluffy, sees Mrs. Ace, who is herself out looking for her pet, and gives Fluffy to her. She says, "Oh, thank you for finding my dear dog. Come by my place tomorrow morning and I'll give you fifty dollars as a reward." The next day, Robert stops by Mrs. Ace's condo, but she says, "Well, I don't know. Fluffy soiled the carpet again last night. I think maybe a twenty-dollar reward would be plenty." Robert cannot collect the fifty dollars. Even though Mrs. Ace might have a moral obligation to pay him and honor her promise, there was no consideration for it. Robert incurred no legal detriment; his contribution—finding the dog—was paid out *before* her promise, and his past consideration is invalid to support a contract. There was no bargained-for exchange.

Fluffy soiled the carpet again last night. I think maybe a twenty-dollar reward would be plenty." Robert cannot collect the fifty dollars. Even though Mrs. Ace might have a moral obligation to pay him and honor her promise, there was no consideration for it. Robert incurred no legal detriment; his contribution—finding the dog—was paid out *before* her promise, and his past consideration is invalid to support a contract. There was no bargained-for exchange.

However, a valid consideration, given in the *past* to support a promise, can be the basis for another, later contract under certain circumstances. These occur when a person's duty to act for one reason or another has become no longer binding. If the person then makes a new promise based on the unfulfilled past duty, the new promise is binding without further consideration. Three types of cases follow.

Promise Revived after Statute of Limitations Has Passed

statute of limitations

The law stipulating how long after a cause of action arises that a person has to sue on it.

A **statute of limitations** is a law requiring a lawsuit to be filed within a specified period of years. For example, in many states a contract claim must be sued on within six years; if the plaintiff waits longer than that, the claim will be dismissed, regardless of its merits. When the time period set forth in the statute of limitations has lapsed, the statute is said to have "run." If a debtor renews a promise to pay or acknowledges a debt after the running of a statute of limitations, then at common law the promise is binding, although there is no consideration in the usual sense. In many states, this promise or acknowledgment must be in writing and signed by the debtor. Also, in many states, the courts will imply a promise or acknowledgment if the debtor makes a partial payment after the statute has run.

Voidable Duties

Some promises that might otherwise serve as consideration are voidable by the promisor, for a variety of reasons, including infancy, fraud, duress, or mistake. But a voidable contract does not automatically become void, and if the promisor has not avoided the contract but instead thereafter renews his promise, it is binding. For example, Mr. Melvin sells his bicycle to Seth, age thirteen. Seth promises to pay Mr. Melvin one hundred dollars. Seth may repudiate the contract, but he does not. When he turns eighteen, he renews his promise to pay the one hundred dollars. This promise is binding. (However, a promise made up to the time he turned eighteen would not be binding, since he would still have been a minor.)

Promissory Estoppel

We examined the meaning of this forbidding phrase in Chapter 8 (recall the English *High Trees* case). It represents another type of promise that the courts will enforce without consideration. Simply stated, **promissory estoppel** here means that the courts will stop the promisor from claiming that there was no consideration—the courts will stop the promisor from denying the validity of her promise. The doctrine of promissory estoppel is invoked in the interests of justice when three conditions are met: (1) the promise is one that the promisor should reasonably expect to induce the promisee to take action or forbear from taking action of a definite and substantial character; (2) the action or forbearance is taken; and (3) injustice can be avoided only by enforcing the promise. (The complete phraseology is "promissory estoppel with detrimental reliance.")

promissory estoppel

To be prohibited from denying a promise when another subsequently has relied on it.

Timko served on the board of trustees of a school. He recommended that the school purchase a building for a substantial sum of money, and to induce the trustees to vote for the purchase, he promised to help with the purchase and to pay at the end of five years the purchase price less the down payment. At the end of four years, Timko died. The school sued his estate, which defended on the ground that there was no consideration for the promise. Timko was promised or given nothing in return, and the purchase of the building was of no direct benefit to him (which would have made the promise enforceable as a unilateral contract). The court ruled that under the three-pronged promissory estoppel test, Timko's estate was liable.[6]

Cases involving pledges of charitable contributions have long been troublesome to courts. Recognizing the necessity to charitable institutions of such pledges, the courts have also been mindful that a mere pledge of money to the general funds of a hospital, university, or similar institution does not usually induce substantial action but is, rather, simply a promise without consideration. When the pledge does prompt a charitable institution to act, promissory estoppel is available as a remedy. In about one-quarter of the states, another doctrine is available for cases involving simple pledges: the "mutual promises" theory, whereby the pledges of many individuals are taken as consideration for each other and are binding against each promisor. This theory was not available to the plaintiff in *Timko* because his was the only promise.

Moral Obligation

The Restatement allows, under some circumstances, the enforcement of past-consideration contracts. It provides as follows in Section 86, "Promise for Benefit Received":

> *A promise made in recognition of a benefit previously received by the promisor from the promisee is binding to the extent necessary to prevent injustice.*
>
> *A promise is not binding under Subsection (1)*
>
> *if the promisee conferred the benefit as a gift or for other reasons the promisor has not been unjustly enriched; or*
>
> *to the extent that its value is disproportionate to the benefit.*

Promises Enforceable without Consideration by Statute

We have touched on several common-law exceptions to the consideration requirement. Some also are provided by statute.

Under the UCC

waiver

An informed choice wherein one surrenders the right to pursue some otherwise available legal remedy.

renunciation

A formal rejection of something, as a contract.

firm offer

A signed promise made by a merchant to hold an offer open.

reservation of rights

A statement that one is intentionally retaining all or some legal rights, so as to warn others of those rights.

The UCC permits one party to discharge, without consideration, a claim or right arising out of an alleged breach of contract by the other party. This is accomplished by delivering to the other party a signed written **waiver** or **renunciation**.[7] This provision applies to any contract governed by the UCC and is not limited to the sales provisions of Article 2.

The UCC also permits a party to discharge the other side without consideration when there is no breach, and it permits parties to modify their Article 2 contract without consideration.[8] The official comments to the UCC section add the following: "However, modifications made thereunder must meet the test of good faith imposed by this Act. The effective use of bad faith to escape performance on the original contract terms is barred, and the extortion of a 'modification' without legitimate commercial reason is ineffective as a violation of the duty of good faith."

Seller agrees to deliver a ton of coal within seven days. Buyer needs the coal sooner and asks Seller to deliver within four days. Seller agrees. This promise is binding even though Seller received no additional consideration beyond the purchase price for the additional duty agreed to (the duty to get the coal to Buyer sooner than originally agreed). The UCC allows a merchant's **firm offer**, signed, in writing, to bind the merchant to keep the offer to buy or sell open without consideration.[9] This is the UCC's equivalent of a common-law option, which, as you recall, does require consideration.

Section 1-207 of the UCC allows a party a **reservation of rights** while performing a contract. This section raises a difficult question when a debtor issues an in-full-payment check in payment of a disputed debt. As noted earlier in this chapter, because under the common law the creditor's acceptance of an in-full-payment check in payment of a disputed debt constitutes an accord and satisfaction, the creditor cannot collect an amount beyond the check. But what if the creditor, in cashing the check, reserves the right (under Section 1-207) to sue for an amount beyond what the debtor is offering? The courts are split on the issue: regarding the sale of goods governed by the UCC, some courts allow the creditor to sue for the unpaid debt notwithstanding the check being marked "paid in full," and others do not.

Bankruptcy

reaffirmation

To confirm again the validity of a promise that was discharged, as in bankruptcy.

Bankruptcy is, of course, federal statutory law. The rule here regarding a promise to pay after the obligation is discharged is similar to that governing statutes of limitations. Traditionally, a promise to repay debts after a bankruptcy court has discharged them makes the debtor liable once again. This traditional rule gives rise to potential abuse: after undergoing the rigors of bankruptcy, a debtor could be badgered by creditors into **reaffirmation**, putting him in a worse position than before, since he must wait six years before being allowed to avail himself of bankruptcy again.

The federal Bankruptcy Act includes certain procedural protections to ensure that the debtor knowingly enters into a reaffirmation of his debt. Among its provisions, the law requires the debtor to have reaffirmed the debt before the debtor is discharged in bankruptcy; he then has sixty days to rescind his reaffirmation. If the bankrupt party is an individual, the law also requires that a court hearing be held at which the consequences of his reaffirmation must be explained, and reaffirmation of certain consumer debts is subject to court approval if the debtor is not represented by an attorney.

International Contracts

Contracts governed by the Convention on Contracts for the International Sale of Goods (as mentioned in Chapter 8) do not require consideration to be binding. It is obvious that an entire contract regime could exist—does exist—that eschews the whole concept of consideration.

Key Takeaway

There are some exceptions to the consideration requirement. At common law, past consideration doesn't count, but no consideration is necessary in these cases: where a promise barred by the statute of limitations is revived, where a voidable duty is reaffirmed, where there has been detrimental reliance on a promise (i.e., promissory estoppel), or where a court simply finds the promisor has a moral obligation to keep the promise.

Under statutory law, the UCC has several exceptions to the consideration requirement. No consideration is needed to revive a debt discharged in bankruptcy, and none is called for under the Convention on Contracts for the International Sale of Goods.

Exercises

1. Melba began work for Acme Company in 1975 as a filing clerk. Thirty years later, she had risen to be comptroller. At a thirty-year celebration party, her boss, Mr. Holder, said, "Melba, I hope you work here for a long time, and you can retire at any time, but if you decide to retire, on account of your years of good service, the company will pay you a monthly pension of $2,000." Melba continued to work for another two years, then retired. The company paid the pension for three years and then, in an economic downturn, stopped. When Melba sued, the company claimed it was not obligated to her because the pension was of past consideration. What will be the result?
2. What theories are used to enforce charitable subscriptions?
3. What are the elements necessary for the application of the doctrine of promissory estoppel?
4. Under what circumstances does the Restatement employ moral obligation as a basis for enforcing an otherwise unenforceable contract?
5. Promises unenforceable because barred by bankruptcy or by the running of the statute of limitations can be revived without further consideration. What do the two circumstances have in common?
6. Under the UCC, when is no consideration required where it would be in equivalent situations at common law?

11.4 Cases

Consideration for an Option

Board of Control of Eastern Michigan University v. Burgess

206 N.W.2d 256 (Mich. 1973)

Burns, J.

On February 15, 1966, defendant signed a document which purported to grant to plaintiff a 60-day option to purchase defendant's home. That document, which was drafted by plaintiff's agent, acknowledged receipt by defendant of "One and no/100 ($1.00) Dollar and other valuable consideration." Plaintiff concedes that neither the one dollar nor any other consideration was ever paid or even tendered to defendant. On April 14, 1966, plaintiff delivered to defendant written notice of its intention to exercise the option. On the closing date defendant rejected plaintiff's tender of the purchase price. Thereupon, plaintiff commenced this action for specific performance.

At trial defendant claimed that the purported option was void for want of consideration, that any underlying offer by defendant had been revoked prior to acceptance by plaintiff, and that the agreed purchase price was the product of fraud and mutual mistake. The trial judge concluded that no fraud was involved, and that any mutual mistake was not material. He also held that defendant's acknowledgment of receipt of consideration bars any subsequent contention to the contrary. Accordingly, the trial judge entered judgment for plaintiff.

Options for the purchase of land, if based on valid consideration, are contracts which may be specifically enforced. [Citations] Conversely, that which purports to be an option, but which is not based on valid consideration, is not a contract and will not be enforced. [Citations] One dollar is valid consideration for an option to purchase land, provided the dollar is paid or at least tendered. [Citations] In the instant case defendant received no consideration for the purported option of February 15, 1966.

A written acknowledgment of receipt of consideration merely creates a rebuttable presumption that consideration has, in fact, passed. Neither the parol evidence rule nor the doctrine of estoppel bars the presentation of evidence to contradict any such acknowledgment. [Citation]

It is our opinion that the document signed by defendant on February 15, 1966, is not an enforceable option, and that defendant is not barred from so asserting.

The trial court premised its holding to the contrary on *Lawrence v. McCalmont*...(1844). That case is significantly distinguishable from the instant case. Mr. Justice Story held that '(t)he guarantor acknowledged the receipt of one dollar, and is now estopped to deny it.' However, in reliance upon the guaranty substantial credit had been extended to the guarantor's sons. The guarantor had received everything she bargained for, save one dollar. In the instant case defendant claims that she never received any of the consideration promised her.

That which purports to be an option for the purchase of land, but which is not based on valid consideration, is a simple offer to sell the same land. [Citation] An option is a contract collateral to an offer to sell whereby the offer is made irrevocable for a specified period. [Citation] Ordinarily, an offer is revocable at the will of the offeror. Accordingly, a failure of consideration affects only the collateral contract to keep the offer open, not the underlying offer.

A simple offer may be revoked for any reason or for no reason by the offeror at any time prior to its acceptance by the offeree. [Citation] Thus, the question in this case becomes, "Did defendant effectively revoke her offer to sell before plaintiff accepted that offer?"

Defendant testified that within hours of signing the purported option she telephoned plaintiff's agent and informed him that she would not abide by the option unless the purchase price was increased. Defendant also testified that when plaintiff's agent delivered to her on April 14, 1966, plaintiff's notice of its intention to exercise the purported option, she told him that "the option was off."

Plaintiff's agent testified that defendant did not communicate to him any dissatisfaction until sometime in July, 1966.

If defendant is telling the truth, she effectively revoked her offer several weeks before plaintiff accepted that offer, and no contract of sale was created. If plaintiff's agent is telling the truth, defendant's offer was still open when plaintiff accepted that offer, and an enforceable contract was created. The trial judge thought it unnecessary to resolve this particular dispute. In light of our holding the dispute must be resolved.

An appellate court cannot assess the credibility of witnesses. We have neither seen nor heard them testify. [Citation] Accordingly, we remand this case to the trial court for additional findings of fact based on the record already before the court. * * *

Reversed and remanded for proceedings consistent with this opinion. Costs to defendant.

Case Questions

1. Why did the lower court decide the option given by the defendant was valid?
2. Why did the appeals court find the option invalid?
3. The case was remanded. On retrial, how could the plaintiff (the university) still win?
4. It was not disputed that the defendant signed the purported option. Is it right that she should get out of it merely because she didn't really get the $1.00?

Consideration: Preexisting Obligation

Denney v. Reppert
432 S.W.2d 647 (Ky. 1968)

R. L. Myre, Sr., Special Commissioner.

The sole question presented in this case is which of several claimants is entitled to an award for information leading to the apprehension and conviction of certain bank robbers. * * *

On June 12th or 13th, 1963, three armed men entered the First State Bank, Eubank, Kentucky, and with a display of arms and threats robbed the bank of over $30,000 [about $209,000 in 2016 dollars]. Later in the day they were apprehended by State Policemen Garret Godby, Johnny Simms and Tilford Reppert, placed under arrest, and the entire loot was recovered. Later all of the prisoners were convicted and Garret Godby, Johnny Simms and Tilford Reppert appeared as witnesses at the trial.

The First State Bank of Eubank was a member of the Kentucky Bankers Association which provided and advertised a reward of $500.00 for the arrest and conviction of each bank robber. Hence the outstanding reward for the three bank robbers was $1,500.00 [about $11,000 in 2010 dollars]. Many became claimants for the reward and the Kentucky State Bankers Association being unable to determine the merits of the claims for the reward asked the circuit court to determine the merits of the various claims and to adjudge who was entitled to receive the reward or share in it. All of the claimants were made defendants in the action.

At the time of the robbery the claimants Murrell Denney, Joyce Buis, Rebecca McCollum and Jewell Snyder were employees of the First State Bank of Eubank and came out of the grueling situation with great credit and glory. Each one of them deserves approbation and an accolade. They were vigilant in disclosing to the public and the peace officers the details of the crime, and in describing the culprits, and giving all the information that they possessed that would be useful in capturing the robbers. Undoubtedly, they performed a great service. It is in the evidence that the claimant Murrell Denney was conspicuous and energetic in his efforts to make known the robbery, to acquaint the officers as to the personal appearance of the criminals, and to give other pertinent facts.

The first question for determination is whether the employees of the robbed bank are eligible to receive or share in the reward. The great weight of authority answers in the negative. [Citation] states the rule thusly:

> *"To the general rule that, when a reward is offered to the general public for the performance of some specified act, such reward may be claimed by any person who performs such act, is the exception of agents, employees and public officials who are acting within the scope of their employment or official duties."* * * *

At the time of the robbery the claimants Murrell Denney, Joyce Buis, Rebecca McCollum, and Jewell Snyder were employees of the First State Bank of Eubank. They were under duty to protect and conserve the resources and moneys of the bank, and safeguard every interest of the institution furnishing them employment. Each of these employees exhibited great courage, and cool bravery, in a time of stress and danger. The community and the county have recompensed them in commendation, admiration and high praise, and the world looks on them as heroes. But in making known the robbery and assisting in acquainting the public and the officers with details of the crime and with identification of the robbers, they performed a duty to the bank and the public, for which they cannot claim a reward.

The claims of Corbin Reynolds, Julia Reynolds, Alvie Reynolds and Gene Reynolds also must fail. According to their statements they gave valuable information to the arresting officers. However, they did not follow the procedure as set forth in the offer of reward in that they never filed a claim with the Kentucky Bankers Association. It is well established that a claimant of a reward must comply with the terms and conditions of the offer of reward. [Citation]

State Policemen Garret Godby, Johnny Simms and Tilford Reppert made the arrest of the bank robbers and captured the stolen money. All participated in the prosecution. At the time of the arrest, it was the duty of the state policemen to apprehend the criminals. Under the law they cannot claim or share in the reward and they are interposing no claim to it.

This leaves the defendant, Tilford Reppert the sole eligible claimant. The record shows that at the time of the arrest he was a deputy sheriff in Rockcastle County, but the arrest and recovery of the stolen money took place in Pulaski County. He was out of his jurisdiction, and was thus under no legal duty to make the arrest, and is thus eligible to claim and receive the reward. In [Citation] it was said:

> *"It is * * * well established that a public officer with the authority of the law to make an arrest may accept an offer of reward or compensation for acts or services performed outside of his bailiwick or not within the scope of his official duties."* * * *....

It is manifest from the record that Tilford Reppert is the only claimant qualified and eligible to receive the reward. Therefore, it is the judgment of the circuit court that he is entitled to receive payment of the $1,500.00 reward now deposited with the Clerk of this Court.

The judgment is affirmed.

Case Questions

1. Why did the Bankers Association put the resolution of this matter into the court's hands?
2. Several claimants came forward for the reward; only one person got it. What was the difference between the person who got the reward and those who did not?

Consideration: Required for Contract Modification

Gross v. Diehl Specialties International, Inc.
776 S.W.2d 879 (Missouri Ct. App. 1989)

Smith, J.

Plaintiff appeals from a jury verdict and resultant judgment for defendant in a breach of employment contract case....

Plaintiff was employed under a fifteen year employment contract originally executed in 1977 between plaintiff and [Dairy Specialties, Inc. which] was a company in the business of formulating ingredients to produce non-dairy products for use by customers allergic to cow's milk. Plaintiff successfully formulated [Vitamite] * * * for that usage.

Thereafter, on August 24, 1977, plaintiff and [Dairy Specialties] entered into an employment contract employing plaintiff as general manager of defendant for fifteen years. Compensation was established at $14,400 annually plus cost of living increases [about $57,000 in 2016 dollars]. In addition, when 10% of defendant's gross profits exceeded the annual salary, plaintiff would receive an additional amount of compensation equal to the difference between his compensation and 10% of the gross profits for such year. On top of that plaintiff was to receive a royalty for the use of each of his inventions and formulae of 1% of the selling price of all of the products produced by defendant using one or more of plaintiff's inventions or formulae during the term of the agreement. That amount was increased to 2% of the selling price following the term of the agreement. The contract further provided that during the term of the agreement the inventions and formulae would be owned equally by plaintiff and defendant and that following the term of the agreement the ownership would revert to plaintiff. During the term of the agreement defendant had exclusive rights to use of the inventions and formulae and after the term of agreement a non-exclusive right of use.

At the time of the execution of the contract, sales had risen from virtually nothing in 1976 to $750,000 annually from sales of Vitamite [Google "Vitamite" to see what it is] and a chocolate flavored product formulated by plaintiff called Chocolite. [Dairy's owner] was in declining health and in 1982 desired to sell his company. At that time yearly sales were $7,500,000. [Owner sold Dairy Specialties] to the Diehl family enterprises for 3 million dollars.

Prior to sale Diehl insisted that a new contract between plaintiff and defendant be executed or Diehl would substantially reduce the amount to be paid for [the company]. A new contract was executed August 24, 1982. It reduced the expressed term of the contract to 10 years, which provided the same expiration date as the prior contract. It maintained the same base salary of $14,400 effective September 1982, thereby eliminating any cost of living increases incurred since the original contract. The 10% of gross profit provision remained the same. The new contract provided that plaintiff's inventions and formula were exclusively owned by defendant during the term of the contract and after its termination. The 1% royalty during the term of the agreement remained the same, but no royalties were provided for after the term of the agreement. No other changes were made in the agreement. Plaintiff received no compensation for executing the new contract. He was not a party to the sale of the company by [Owner] and received nothing tangible from that sale.

After the sale plaintiff was given the title and responsibilities of president * * * with additional duties but no additional compensation. In 1983 and 1984 the business of the company declined severely and in October 1984, plaintiff's employment with defendant was terminated by defendant. This suit followed. * * *

We turn now to the court's holding that the 1982 agreement was the operative contract. Plaintiff contends this holding is erroneous because there existed no consideration for the 1982 agreement. We agree. A modification of a contract constitutes the making of a new contract and such new contract must be supported by consideration. [Citation] Where a contract has not been fully performed at the time of the new agreement, the substitution of a new provision, resulting in a modification of the obligations on *both* sides, for a provision in the old contract still unperformed is sufficient consideration for the new contract. While consideration may consist of either a detriment to the promisee or a benefit to the promisor, a promise to carry out an already existing contractual duty does not constitute consideration. [Citation]

Under the 1982 contract defendant assumed no detriment it did not already have. The term of the contract expired on the same date under both contracts. Defendant undertook no greater obligations than it already had. Plaintiff on the other hand received less than he had under the original contract. His base pay was reduced back to its amount in 1977 despite the provision in the 1977 contract for cost of living adjustments. He lost his equal ownership in his formulae during the term of the agreement and his exclusive ownership after the termination of the agreement. He lost all royalties after termination of the agreement and the right to use and license the formulae subject to defendant's right to non-exclusive use upon payment of royalties. In exchange for nothing, defendant acquired exclusive ownership of the formulae during and after the agreement, eliminated royalties after the agreement terminated, turned its non-exclusive use after termination into exclusive use and control, and achieved a reduction in plaintiff's base salary. Defendant did no more than promise to carry out an already existing contractual duty. There was no consideration for the 1982 agreement.

Defendant asserts that consideration flowed to plaintiff because the purchase of defendant by the Diehls might not have occurred without the agreement and the purchase provided plaintiff with continued employment and a financially viable employer. There is no evidence to support this contention. Plaintiff had continued employment with the same employer under the 1977 agreement. Nothing in the 1982 agreement provided for any additional financial protection to plaintiff. The essence of defendant's position is that [the Owner-seller] received more from his sale of the company because of the new agreement than he would have without it. We have difficulty converting [the owner's] windfall into a benefit to plaintiff.

[Remanded to determine how much plaintiff should receive.]

Case Questions

1. Why did the court determine that Plaintiff's postemployment benefits should revert to those in his original contract instead being limited to those in the modified contract?
2. What argument did Defendant make as to why the terms of the modified contract should be valid?

11.5 Summary and Exercises

Summary

Most agreements—including contract modification at common law (but not under the Uniform Commercial Code [UCC])—are not binding contracts in the absence of what the law terms "consideration." Consideration is usually defined as a "legal detriment"—an act, forbearance, or a promise. The act can be the payment of money, the delivery of a service, or the transfer of title to property. Consideration is a legal concept in that it centers on the giving up of a legal right or benefit.

An understanding of consideration is important in many commonplace situations, including those in which (1) a debtor and a creditor enter into an accord that is later disputed, (2) a duty is preexisting, (3) a promise is illusory, and (4) creditors agree to a composition.

Some promises are enforceable without consideration. These include certain promises under the UCC and other circumstances, including (1) contracts barred by the statute of limitations, (2) promises by a bankrupt to repay debts, and (3) situations in which justice will be served by invoking the doctrine of promissory estoppel. Determining whether an agreement should be upheld despite the lack of consideration, technically defined, calls for a diligent assessment of the factual circumstances.

Exercises

1. Hornbuckle purchased equipment from Continental Gin (CG) for $6,300. However, after some of the equipment proved defective, Hornbuckle sent CG a check for $4,000 marked "by endorsement this check is accepted in full payment," and CG endorsed and deposited the check. May CG force Hornbuckle to pay the remaining $2,300? Why?
2. Joseph Hoffman alleged that Red Owl Stores promised him that it would build a store building in Chilton, Wisconsin, and stock it with merchandise for Hoffman to operate in return for Hoffman's investment of $18,000. The size, cost, design, and layout of the store building was not discussed, nor were the terms of the lease as to rent, maintenance, and purchase options. Nevertheless, in reliance on Red Owl's promise, the Hoffmans sold their bakery and grocery store business, purchased the building site in Chilton, and rented a residence there for the family. The deal was never consummated: a dispute arose, Red Owl did not build the store, and it denied liability to Hoffman on the basis that its promise to him was too indefinite with respect to all details for a contract to have resulted. Is Hoffman entitled to some relief? On what theory?
3. Raquel contracted to deliver one hundred widgets to Sam on December 15, for which he would pay $4,000. On November 25, Sam called her and asked if she could deliver the widgets on December 5. Raquel said she could, and she promised delivery on that day. Is her promise binding? Why?
4. Richard promised to have Darlene's deck awning constructed by July 10. On June 20, Darlene called him and asked if he could get the job done by July 3, in time for Independence Day. Richard said he could, but he failed to do so, and Darlene had to rent two canopies at some expense. Darlene claims that because Richard breached his promise, he is liable for the cost of awning rental. Is she correct—was his promise binding? Why?
5. Seller agreed to deliver gasoline to Buyer at $3.15 per gallon over a period of one year. By the sixth month, gasoline had increased in price over a dollar a gallon. Although Seller had gasoline available for sale, he told Buyer the price would have to increase by that much or he would be unable to deliver. Buyer agreed to the increase, but when billed, refused to pay the additional amount. Is Buyer bound by the promise? Explain.
6. Montbanks's son, Charles, was seeking an account executive position with Dobbs, Smith & Fogarty, Inc., a large brokerage firm. Charles was independent and wished no interference by his well-known father. The firm, after several weeks' deliberation, decided to hire Charles. They made him an offer on April 12, 2010, and Charles accepted. Montbanks, unaware that

his son had been hired and concerned that he might not be, mailed a letter to Dobbs on April 13 in which he promised to give the brokerage firm $150,000 in commission business if the firm would hire his son. The letter was received by Dobbs, and the firm wishes to enforce it against Montbanks. May Dobbs enforce the promise? Why?

7. In 1869, William E. Story promised his nephew, William E. Story II (then sixteen years old), $5,000 (about $120,000 in today's money) if "Willie" would abstain from drinking alcohol, smoking, swearing, and playing cards or billiards for money until the nephew reached twenty-one years of age. All of these were legally permissible activities for the teenager at that time in New York State. Willie accepted his uncle's promise and did refrain from the prohibited acts until he turned twenty-one. When the young man asked for the money, his uncle wrote to him that he would honor the promise but would rather wait until Willie was older before delivering the money, interest added on. Willie agreed. Subsequently, Willie assigned the right to receive the money to one Hamer (Willie wanted the money sooner), and Story I died without making any payment. The estate, administered by Franklin Sidway, refused to pay, asserting there was no binding contract due to lack of consideration: the boy suffered no "detriment," and the uncle got no benefit. The trial court agreed with the estate, and the plaintiff appealed. Should the court on appeal affirm or reverse? Explain.
8. Harold Pearsall and Joe Alexander were friends for over twenty-five years. About twice a week, they bought what they called a package: a half-pint of vodka, orange juice, two cups, and two lottery tickets. They went to Alexander's house to watch TV, drink screwdrivers, and scratch the lottery tickets. The two had been sharing tickets and screwdrivers since the Washington, DC, lottery began. On the evening in issue, Pearsall bought the package and asked Alexander, "Are you in on it?" Alexander said yes. Pearsall asked for his half of the purchase price, but Alexander had no money. A few hours later, Alexander, having come by some funds of his own, bought another package. He handed one ticket to Pearsall, and they both scratched the tickets; Alexander's was a $20,000 winner. When Pearsall asked for his share, Alexander refused to give him anything. Are the necessary elements of offer, acceptance, and consideration present here so as to support Pearsall's assertion the parties had a contract?
9. Defendant, Lee Taylor, had assaulted his wife, who took refuge in the house of Plaintiff, Harrington. The next day, Taylor gained access to the house and began another assault upon his wife. Mrs. Taylor knocked him down with an axe and was on the point of cutting his head open or decapitating him while he was lying on the floor when Plaintiff intervened and caught the axe as it was descending. The blow intended for Defendant fell upon Harrington's hand, mutilating it badly, but saving Defendant's life. Subsequently, Defendant orally promised to pay Plaintiff her damages but, after paying a small sum, failed to pay anything more. Is Harrington entitled to enforce Taylor's entire promise?
10. White Sands Forest Products (Defendant) purchased logging equipment from Clark Corporation (Plaintiff) under an installment contract that gave Plaintiff the right to repossess and resell the equipment if Defendant defaulted on the contract. Defendant did default and agreed to deliver the equipment to Plaintiff if Plaintiff would then discharge Defendant from further obligation. Plaintiff accepted delivery and resold the equipment, but the sale left a deficiency (there was still money owing by Defendant). Plaintiff then sued for the deficiency, and Defendant set up as a defense the accord and satisfaction. Is the defense good?

Self-Test Questions

1. Consideration
    a. can consist of a written acknowledgment of some benefit received, even if in fact the benefit is not delivered
    b. cannot be nominal in amount
    c. is a bargained-for act, forbearance, or promise from the promisee
    d. is all of the above
2. An example of valid consideration is a promise
    a. by a seventeen-year-old to refrain from drinking alcohol

   b. to refrain from going to court
   c. to cook dinner if the promisor can get around to it
   d. to repay a friend for the four years of free legal advice he had provided

3. An unliquidated debt is a debt
   a. one is not able to pay
   b. not yet paid
   c. of uncertain amount
   d. that is unenforceable debt
4. The rule that if one party to a contract has not made a binding obligation, the other party is not bound is called
   a. revocation
   b. mutuality of obligation
   c. accord and satisfaction
   d. estoppel
5. Examples of promises enforceable without consideration include
   a. an agreement modifying a sales contract
   b. a promise to pay a debt after the statute of limitations has run
   c. a debtor's promise to repay a debt that has been discharged in bankruptcy
   d. all of the above

Self-Test Answers

1. c
2. b
3. c
4. b
5. d

Endnotes

1. Lon L. Fuller, "Consideration and Form," *Columbia Law Review* 41 (1941): 799.
2. Richard A. Posner, *Economic Analysis of Law* (New York: Aspen, 1973), 46.
3. Restatement (Second) of Contracts, Section 87(b).
4. *Dedeaux v. Young*, 170 So.2d 561 (1965).
5. *Otis F. Wood v. Lucy, Lady Duff-Gordon*, 118 N.E. 214 (1917).
6. *Estate of Timko v. Oral Roberts Evangelistic Assn.*, 215 N.W.2d 750 (Mich. App. 1974).
7. Uniform Commercial Code, Section 1-107.
8. Uniform Commercial Code, Sections 2-209(4) and 2-209(1).
9. Uniform Commercial Code, Section 2-205.

CHAPTER 12
Legality

Learning Objectives

After reading this chapter, you should understand the following:

1. The types of contracts (bargains) that are deemed illegal.
2. How courts deal with disputes concerning illegal contracts.
3. Under what circumstances courts will enforce otherwise illegal contracts.

12.1 General Perspectives on Illegality

Learning Objectives

1. Understand why courts refuse to enforce illegal agreements.
2. Recognize the rationale behind exceptions to the rule.

We have discussed the requirements of mutual assent, real assent, and consideration. We now turn to the fourth of the five requirements for a valid contract: the legality of the underlying bargain. The basic rule is that courts will not enforce an illegal bargain. (The term *illegal bargain* is better than *illegal contract* because a contract is by definition a legal agreement, but the latter terminology prevails in common usage.) Why should this be? Why should the courts refuse to honor contracts made privately by people who presumably know what they are doing—for example, a wager on the World Series or a championship fight? Two reasons are usually given. One is that refusal to enforce helps discourage unlawful behavior; the other is that honoring such contracts would demean the judiciary. Are these reasons valid? Yes and no, in the opinion of one contracts scholar:

> *[D]enying relief to parties who have engaged in an illegal transaction . . . helps to effectuate the public policy involved by discouraging the conduct that is disapproved. Mere denial of contractual and quasi-contractual remedy [however] rarely has a substantial effect in discouraging illegal conduct. A man who is hired to perform a murder is not in the least deterred by the fact that the courts are not open to him to collect his fee. Such a man has other methods of enforcement, and they are in fact more effective than legal process. The same is true in varying degrees where less heinous forms of illegal conduct are involved. Even in the matter of usury it was found that mere denial of enforcement was of little value in the effort to eliminate the loan shark. And restraints of trade were not curbed to an appreciable extent until contracts in restraint of trade were made criminal.*
>
> *In most instances, then, the protection of the good name of the judicial institution must provide the principal reason for the denial of a remedy to one who has trafficked in the forbidden. This is, moreover, a very good reason. The first duty of an institution is to preserve itself, and if the courts to any appreciable extent busied themselves with "justice among thieves," the community . . . would be shocked and the courts would be brought into disrepute.*[1]

Strictly enforced, the rule prohibiting courts from ordering the parties to honor illegal contracts is harsh. It means that a promisee who has already performed under the contract can neither obtain performance of the act for which he bargained nor recover the money he paid or the value of the performance he made. The court will simply leave the parties where it finds them, meaning that one of the parties will have received an uncompensated benefit.

restitution

The return or restoration of some specific thing to its rightful owner or status.

Not surprisingly, the severity of the rule against enforcement has led courts to seek ways to moderate it, chiefly by modifying the agreement according to the principle of **restitution**. In general, restitution requires that one who has conferred a benefit or suffered a loss should not unfairly be denied compensation.

Pursuing this notion, the courts have created several exceptions to the general rule. Thus a party who is excusably ignorant that her promise violates public policy and a party who is not equally in the wrong may recover. Likewise, when a party "would otherwise suffer a forfeiture that is disproportionate in relation to the contravention of public policy involved," restitution will be allowed.[2] Other exceptions exist when the party seeking restitution withdraws from the transaction contemplated in the contract before the illegal purpose has been carried out and when "allowing the claim would put an end to a continuing situation that is contrary to the public interest."[3] An example of the latter situation occurs when two bettors place money in the hands of a stakeholder. If the wager is unlawful, the loser of the bet has the right to recover his money from the stakeholder before it is paid out to the winner.

Though by and large courts enforce contracts without considering the worth or merits of the bargains they incorporate, freedom of contract can conflict with other public policies. Tensions arise between the desire to let people pursue their own ends and the belief that certain kinds of conduct should not be encouraged. Thus a patient may agree to be treated by an herbalist, but state laws prohibit medical care except by licensed physicians. Law and public policies against usury, gambling, obstructing justice, bribery, corrupt influence, perjury, restraint of trade, impairment of domestic relations, and fraud all significantly affect the authority and willingness of courts to enforce contracts.

In this chapter, we will consider two types of illegality: (1) that which results from a bargain that violates a statute and (2) that which the courts deem contrary to public policy, even though not expressly set forth in statutes.

Key Takeaway

Courts refuse to enforce illegal bargains notwithstanding the basic concept of freedom to contract because they do not wish to reward illegal behavior or sully themselves with adjudication of that which is forbidden to undertake. However, fairness sometimes compels courts to make exceptions.

Exercises

1. Why is *illegal contract* a contradiction in terms?
2. Why do courts refuse to enforce contracts (or bargains) made by competent adults if the contracts harm no third party but are illegal?

12.2 Agreements in Violation of Statute

Learning Objectives

1. Understand that various types of bargains may be made illegal by statute, including gambling, some service-for-fee agreements involving unlicensed practitioners, and usury.
2. Recognize that while gambling contracts are often illegal, some agreements that might appear to involve gambling are not.

Overview

Any bargain that violates the criminal law—including statutes that govern extortion, robbery, embezzlement, forgery, some gambling, licensing, and consumer credit transactions—is illegal. Thus determining whether contracts are lawful may seem to be an easy enough task. Clearly, whenever the statute itself explicitly forbids the making of the contract or the performance agreed upon, the bargain (such as a contract to sell drugs) is unlawful. But when the statute does not expressly prohibit the making of the contract, courts examine a number of factors, as discussed in Section 5 involving the apparently innocent sale of a jewelry manufacturing firm whose real business was making marijuana-smoking paraphernalia.

Types of Bargains Made Illegal by Statute

Gambling Contracts

All states have regulations affecting gambling (wagering) contracts because gambling tends to be an antiutilitarian activity most attractive to those who can least afford it, because gambling tends to reinforce fatalistic mind-sets fundamentally incompatible with capitalism and democracy, because gambling can be addictive, and because gambling inevitably attracts criminal elements lured by readily available money. With the spread of anti-tax enthusiasms over the last forty plus years, however, some kinds of gambling have been legalized and regulated, including state-sponsored lotteries. Gambling is betting on an outcome of an event over which the bettors have no control, where the purpose is to play with the risk.

But because the outcome is contingent on events that lie outside the power of the parties to control does not transform a bargain into a wager. For example, if a gardener agrees to care for the grounds of a septuagenarian for life in return for an advance payment of $10,000, the uncertainty of the date of the landowner's death does not make the deal a wager. The parties have struck a bargain that accurately assesses, to the satisfaction of each, the risks of the contingency in question. Likewise, the fact that an agreement is phrased in the form of a wager does not make it one. Suppose a father says to his daughter, "I'll bet you can't get an A in organic chemistry. If you do, I'll give you $50." This is a unilateral contract, the consideration to the father being the daughter's achieving a good grade, a matter over which she has complete control.

Despite the general rule against enforcing wagers, there are exceptions, most statutory but some rooted in the common law. The common law permits the sale or purchase of securities: Sally invests $6,000 in stock in Acme Company, hoping the stock will increase in value, though she has no control over the firm's management. It is not called gambling; it is considered respectable risk taking in the capitalist system, or "entrepreneurialism." (It really is gambling, though, similar to horse-race gambling.) But because there are speculative elements to some agreements, they are subject to state and federal regulation.

Insurance contracts are also speculative, but unless one party has no insurable interest (a concern for the person or thing insured) in the insured, the contract is not a wager. Thus, if you took out a life insurance contract on the life of someone whose name you picked out of the phone book, the agreement would be void because you and the insurance company would have been gambling on a contingent event. (You bet that the person would die within the term of the policy, the insurance company that she would not.) If, however, you insure your spouse, your business partner, or your home, the contingency does not make the policy a wagering agreement because you will have suffered a direct loss should it occur, and the agreement, while compensating for a possible loss, does not create a new risk just for the "game."

Sunday Contracts

At common law, contracts entered into on Sundays, as well as other commercial activities, were valid and enforceable. But a separate, religious tradition that traces to the Second Commandment frowned on work performed on "the Lord's Day." In 1781, a New Haven city ordinance banning Sunday work was printed on blue paper, and since that time such laws have been known as blue laws. The first statewide blue law was enacted in the United States in 1788; it prohibited travel, work, sports and amusements, and the carrying on of any business or occupation on Sundays. The only exceptions in most states throughout most of the nineteenth century were mutual promises to marry and contracts of necessity or charity. As the Puritan fervor wore off, and citizens were, more and more, importuned to consider themselves "consumers" in a capitalistic economic system, the laws have faded in importance and are mostly repealed, moribund, or unenforced. Washington State, up until 2008, completely prohibited hard alcohol sales on Sunday, and all liquor stores were closed, but subsequently the state—desperate for tax revenue—relaxed the prohibition.

Usury

usury

Charging interest in excess of the legal limit.

A usury statute is one that sets the maximum allowable interest that may be charged on a loan; **usury** is charging illegal interest rates. Formerly, such statutes were a matter of real importance because the penalty levied on the lender—ranging from forfeiture of the interest, or of both the principal and the interest, or of some part of the principal—was significant. But usury laws, like Sunday contract laws, have been relaxed to accommodate an ever-more-frenzied consumer society. There are a number of transactions to which the laws do not apply, varying by state: small consumer loans, pawn shop loans, payday loans, and corporate loans. In *Marquette v. First Omaha*

Service Corp., the Supreme Court ruled that a national bank could charge the highest interest rate allowed in its home state to customers living anywhere in the United States, including states with restrictive interest caps.[4] Thus it was that in 1980 Citibank moved its credit card headquarters from cosmopolitan New York City to the somewhat less cosmopolitan Sioux Falls, South Dakota. South Dakota had recently abolished its usury laws, and so, as far as credit-card interest rates, the sky was the limit. That appealed to Citibank and a number of other financial institutions, and to the state: it became a major player in the US financial industry, garnering many jobs.[5]

Licensing Statutes

To practice most professions and carry on the trade of an increasing number of occupations, states require that providers of services possess licenses—hairdressers, doctors, plumbers, real estate brokers, and egg inspectors are among those on a long list. As sometimes happens, though, a person may contract for the services of one who is unlicensed either because he is unqualified and carrying on his business without a license or because for technical reasons (e.g., forgetting to mail in the license renewal application) he does not possess a license at the moment. Robin calls Paul, a plumber, to install the pipes for her new kitchen. Paul, who has no license, puts in all the pipes and asks to be paid. Having discovered that Paul is unlicensed, Robin refuses to pay. May Paul collect?

To answer the question, a three-step analysis is necessary. First, is a license required? Some occupations may be performed without a license (e.g., lawn mowing). Others may be performed with or without certain credentials, the difference lying in what the professional may tell the public. (For instance, an accountant need not be a certified public accountant to carry on most accounting functions.) Let us assume that the state requires everyone who does any sort of plumbing for pay to have a valid license.

The second step is to determine whether the licensing statute explicitly bars recovery by someone who has performed work while unlicensed. Some do; many others contain no specific provision on the point. Statutes that do bar recovery must of course govern the courts when they are presented with the question.

If the statute is silent, courts must, in the third step of the analysis, distinguish between "regulatory" and "revenue" licenses. A **regulatory license** is intended to protect the public health, safety, and welfare. To obtain these licenses, the practitioner of the art must generally demonstrate his or her abilities by taking some sort of examination, like the bar exam for lawyers or the medical boards for doctors. A plumber's or electrician's licensing requirement might fall into this category. A "revenue license" (something of a misnomer: "registration license" would be better) generally requires no such examination and is imposed for the sake of raising revenue and to ensure that practitioners register their address so they can be found if a disgruntled client wants to serve them legal papers for a lawsuit. Some revenue licenses, in addition to requiring registration, require practitioners to demonstrate that they have insurance. A license to deliver milk, open to anyone who applies and pays the fee, would be an example of a revenue license. (In some states, plumbing licenses are for revenue purposes only.)

regulatory license

A license to practice a trade or profession that requires a competency test to obtain.

Generally speaking, failure to hold a regulatory license bars recovery, but the absence of a revenue or registration license does not—the person may obtain the license and then move to recover. See Section 5 for an example of a situation in which the state statute demands practitioners be licensed.

Key Takeaway

Gambling, interest rates, and Sunday contracts are among the types of contracts that have, variously, been subject to legislative illegality. Laws may require certain persons to have licenses in order to practice a trade or profession. Whether an unlicensed person is barred from recovering a fee for service depends on the language of the statute and the purpose of the requirement: if it is a mere revenue-raising or registration statute, recovery will often be allowed. If the practitioner is required to prove competency, no recovery is possible for an unlicensed person.

Exercises

1. List the typical kinds of contracts made illegal by statute.
2. Why are some practitioners completely prohibited from collecting a fee for service if they don't have a license, and others allowed to collect the fee after they get the license?
3. If no competency test is required, why do some statutes require the practitioner to be licensed?

12.3 Bargains Made Illegal by Common Law

Learning Objective

1. Understand what contracts or bargains have been declared illegal by courts.

Overview

Public policy is expressed by courts as well as legislatures. In determining whether to enforce a contract where there is no legislative dictate, courts must ordinarily balance the interests at stake. To strike the proper balance, courts must weigh the parties' expectations, the forfeitures that would result from denial of enforcement, and the public interest favoring enforcement against these factors: the strength of the policy, whether denying enforcement will further the policy, the seriousness and deliberateness of the violation, and how direct the connection is between the misconduct and the contractual term to be enforced.[6]

Types of Bargains Made Illegal by Common Law

Common-Law Restraint of Trade

One of the oldest public policies evolved by courts is the common-law prohibition against restraint of trade. From the early days of industrialism, the courts took a dim view of ostensible competitors who agreed among themselves to fix prices or not to sell in each other's territories. Since 1890, with the enactment of the Sherman Act, the law of restraint of trade has been absorbed by federal and state antitrust statutes. But the common-law prohibition still exists. Though today it is concerned almost exclusively with promises not to compete in sales of businesses and employment contracts, it can arise in other settings. For example, George's promise to Arthur never to sell the parcel of land that Arthur is selling to him is void because it unreasonably restrains trade in the land.

The general rule is one of reason: not every restraint of trade is unlawful; only unreasonable ones are. As the Restatement puts it, "Every promise that relates to business dealings or to a professional or other gainful occupation operates as a restraint in the sense that it restricts the promisor's future activity. Such a promise is not, however, unenforceable, unless the restraint that it imposes is unreasonably detrimental to the smooth operation of a freely competitive private economy."[7] An agreement that restrains trade will be construed as unreasonable unless it is ancillary to a legitimate business interest and is no greater than necessary to protect the legitimate interest. Common-law estraint-of-trade cases usually arise in two settings: (1) the sale of a business and an attendant agreement not to compete with the purchasers and (2) an employee's agreement not to compete with the employer should the employee leave for any reason.

Sale of a Business

A first common area where a restraint-of-trade issue may arise is with the sale of a business. Regina sells her lingerie store to Victoria and promises not to establish a competing store in town for one year. Since Victoria is purchasing Regina's goodwill (the fact that customers are used to shopping at her store), as well as her building and inventory, there is clearly a property interest to be protected. And the geographical limitation ("in town") is reasonable if that is where the store does business. But if Regina had agreed not to engage in any business in town, or to wait ten years before opening up a new store, or not to open up a new store anywhere within one hundred miles of town, she could avoid the noncompetition terms of the contract because the restraint in each case (nature, duration, and geographic area of restraint) would have been broader than necessary to protect Victoria's interest. Whether the courts will uphold an agreement not to compete depends on all the circumstances of the particular case.

Employment Noncompete Agreements

A second common restraint-of-trade issue arises with regard to **noncompete agreements** in employment contracts. As a condition of employment by the research division of a market research firm, Bruce, a product analyst, is required to sign an agreement in which he promises, for a period of one year after leaving the company, not to "engage, directly or indirectly, in any business competing with the company and located within fifty miles of the company's main offices." The principal reason recited in the agreement for this covenant not to compete is that by virtue of the employment, Bruce will come to learn a variety of internal secrets, including client lists, trade or business secrets, reports, confidential business discussions, ongoing research, publications, computer programs, and related papers. Is this agreement a lawful restraint of trade?

noncompete agreements

One party agrees not to pursue a similar profession or trade in competition against another party.

Here both the property interest of the employer and the extent of the restraint are issues. Certainly an employer has an important competitive interest in seeing that company information not walk out the door with former employees. Nevertheless, a promise by an employee not to compete with his or her former employer is scrutinized carefully by the courts, and an **injunction** (an order directing a person to stop doing what he or she should not do) will be issued cautiously, partly because the prospective employee is usually confronted with a **contract of adhesion** (take it or leave it) and is in a weak bargaining position compared to the employer, and partly because an injunction might cause the employee's unemployment. Many courts are not enthusiastic about employment noncompete agreements. The California Business and Professions Code provides that "every contract by which anyone is restrained from engaging in a lawful profession, trade, or business of any kind is to that extent void."[8] To promote entrepreneurial robustness, California courts typically interpret the statute broadly and refuse to enforce noncompete agreements. Other states are less stingy, and employers have attempted to avoid the strictures of no-enforcement state rulings by providing in the contract that their employment agreement will be interpreted according to the law of a state where noncompetes are favorably viewed.

injunction

A judicial order directing a person to stop doing that which he or she should not do

contract of adhesion

A contract presented to the offeree to take or leave without bargaining.

If a covenant not to compete is ruled unlawful, the courts can pursue one of three courses by way of remedy. A court can refuse to enforce the entire covenant, freeing the employee to compete thenceforth. The court could delete from the agreement only that part that is unreasonable and enforce the remainder (the "blue pencil" rule). In some states, the courts have moved away from this rule and have actually taken to rewriting the objectionable clause themselves. Since the parties intended that there be some form of restriction on competition, a reasonable modification would achieve a more just result.[9]

Unconscionable Contracts

unconscionable contract

A contract so unfair as to be unenforceable.

Courts may refuse to enforce **unconscionable contracts**, those that are very one-sided, unfair, the product of unequal bargaining power, or oppressive; a court may find the contract divisible and enforce only the parts that are not unconscionable.

The common-law rule is reflected in Section 208 of the Restatement: "If a contract or term thereof is unconscionable at the time the contract is made a court may refuse to enforce the contract, or may enforce the remainder of the contract without the unconscionable term, or may so limit the application of any unconscionable term as to avoid any unconscionable result."

And the Uniform Commercial Code (UCC) (again, of course, a statute, not common law) provides a similar rule in Section 2-302(1): "If the court as a matter of law finds the contract or any clause of the contract to have been unconscionable at the time it was made the court may refuse to enforce the contract, or it may enforce the remainder of the contract without the unconscionable clause, or it may so limit the application of any unconscionable clause as to avoid any unconscionable result."

Unconscionable is not defined in the Restatement or the UCC, but cases have given gloss to the meaning, as in Section 5, *Williams v. Walker-Thomas Furniture Co.*, a well-known early interpretation of the section by the DC Court of Appeals.

Unconscionability may arise procedurally or substantively. A term is procedurally unconscionable if it is imposed upon the "weaker" party because of fine or inconspicuous print, unexpected placement in the contract, lack of opportunity to read the term, lack of education or sophistication that precludes understanding, or lack of equality of bargaining power. Substantive unconscionability arises where the affected terms are oppressive and harsh, where the term deprives a party of any real remedy for breach. Most often—but not always—courts find unconscionable contracts in the context of consumer transactions rather than commercial transactions. In the latter case, the assumption is that the parties tend to be sophisticated businesspeople able to look out for their own contract interests.

Exculpatory Clauses

Exculpatory clauses

A term in a contract by which one party relieves itself in advance of liability.

The courts have long held that public policy disfavors attempts to contract out of tort liability. **Exculpatory clauses** that exempt one party from tort liability to the other for harm caused intentionally or recklessly are unenforceable without exception. A contract provision that exempts a party from tort liability for negligence is unenforceable under two general circumstances: (1) when it "exempts an employer from liability to an employee for injury in the course of his employment" or (2) when it exempts one charged with a duty of public service and who is receiving compensation from liability to one to whom the duty is owed.[10] Contract terms with offensive exculpatory clauses may be considered somewhat akin to unconscionability.

Put shortly, exculpatory clauses are OK if they are reasonable. Put not so shortly, exculpatory clauses will generally be held valid if (1) the agreement does not involve a business generally thought suitable for public regulation (a twenty-kilometer bicycle race, for example, is probably not one thought generally suitable for public regulation, whereas a bus line is); (2) the party seeking exculpation is not performing a business of great importance to the public or of practical necessity for some members of the public; (3) the party does not purport to be performing the service to just anybody who comes along (unlike the bus line); (4) the parties are dealing at arms' length, able to bargain about the contract; (5) the person or property of the purchaser is not placed under control of the seller, subject to his or his agent's carelessness; or (6) the clause is conspicuous and clear.[11]

Obstructing the Administration of Justice or Violating a Public Duty

It is well established under common law that contracts that would interfere with the administration of justice or that call upon a public official to violate a public duty are void and unenforceable. Examples of such contracts are numerous: to conceal or compound a crime, to pay for the testimony of a witness in court contingent on the court's ruling, to suppress evidence by paying a witness to leave the state, or to destroy documents. Thus, in an unedifying case in Arkansas, a gambler sued a circuit court judge to recover $1,675 allegedly paid to the judge as protection money, and the Arkansas Supreme Court affirmed the dismissal of the suit, holding, "The law will not aid either party to the alleged illegal and void contract . . . 'but will leave them where it finds them, if they have been equally cognizant of the illegality.'"[12] Also in this category are bribes, agreements to obstruct or delay justice (jury tampering, abuse of the legal process), and the like.

Family Relations

Another broad area in which public policy intrudes on private contractual arrangements is that of undertakings between couples, either prior to or during marriage. Marriage is quintessentially a relationship defined by law, and individuals have limited ability to change its scope through legally enforceable contracts. Moreover, marriage is an institution that public policy favors, and agreements that unreasonably restrain marriage are void. Thus a father's promise to pay his twenty-one-year-old daughter $100,000 if she refrains from marrying for ten years would be unenforceable. However, a promise in a **postnuptial (after marriage) agreement** that if the husband predeceases the wife, he will provide his wife with a fixed income for as long as she remains unmarried is valid because the offer of support is related to the need. (Upon remarriage, the need would presumably be less pressing.) Property settlements before, during, or upon the breakup of a marriage are generally enforceable, since property is not considered to be an essential incident of marriage. But agreements in the form of property arrangements that tend to be detrimental to marriage are void—for example, a **prenuptial (premarital) contract** in which the wife-to-be agrees on demand of the husband-to-be to leave the marriage and renounce any claims upon the husband-to-be at any time in the future in return for which he will pay her $100,000. Separation agreements are not considered detrimental to marriage as long as they are entered after or in contemplation of immediate separation; but a separation agreement must be "fair" under the circumstances, and judges may review them upon challenge. Similarly, child custody agreements are not left to the whim of the parents but must be consistent with the best interest of the child, and the courts retain the power to examine this question.

postnuptial (after marriage) agreement

A contract made by spouses after marriage in which they agree on property division.

prenuptial (premarital) contract

A premartial contract by which spouses agree on property division.

The types of contracts or bargains that might be found illegal are innumerable, limited only by the ingenuity of those who seek to overreach.

Key Takeaway

Courts will not enforce contracts that are, broadly speaking, contrary to public policy. These include some noncompete agreements, exculpatory clauses, unconscionable bargains, contracts to obstruct the public process or justice, and contracts interfering with family relations.

Exercises

1. Why are employment noncompete agreements viewed less favorably than sale-of-business noncompete agreements?

2. Can a person by contract exculpate herself from liability for gross negligence? For ordinary negligence?
3. A parking lot agreement says the parking lot is "not responsible for loss of contents or damage to the vehicle." Is that acceptable? Explain.
4. A valet parking lot agreement—where the car owner gives the keys to the attendant who parks the car—has the same language as that for the lot in Exercise 3. Is that acceptable? Explain.

12.4 Effect of Illegality and Exceptions

Learning Objectives

1. Recognize that courts will not enforce illegal bargains.
2. Know that there are exceptions to that rule.

Effect of Illegality

The general rule is this: courts will not enforce illegal bargains. The parties are left where the court found them, and no relief is granted: it's a hands-off policy. The illegal agreement is void, and that a wrongdoer has benefited to the other's detriment does not matter.

For example, suppose a specialty contractor, statutorily required to have a license, constructs a waterslide for Plaintiff, when the contractor knew or should have known he was unlicensed. Plaintiff discovers the impropriety and refuses to pay the contractor $80,000 remaining on the deal. The contractor will not get paid.[13] In another example, a man held himself out to be an architect in a jurisdiction requiring that architects pass a test to be licensed. He was paid $80,000 to design a house costing $900,000. The project was late and over budget, and the building violated relevant easement building-code rules. The unlicensed architect was not allowed to keep his fee.[14]

Exceptions

As always in the law, there are exceptions. Of relevance here are situations where a court might permit one party to recover: party withdrawing before performance, party protected by statute, party not equally at fault, excusable ignorance, and partial illegality.

Party Withdrawing before Performance

Samantha and Carlene agree to bet on a soccer game and deliver their money to the stakeholder. Subsequently, but before the payout, Carlene decides she wants out; she can get her money from the stakeholder. Ralph hires Jacob for $5,000 to arrange a bribe of a juror. Ralph has a change of heart; he can get his money from Jacob.

Party Protected by Statute

An airline pilot, forbidden by federal law from working overtime, nevertheless does so; she would be entitled to payment for the overtime worked. Securities laws forbid the sale or purchase of unregistered offerings—such a contract is illegal; the statute allows the purchaser rescission (return of the money paid). An attorney (apparently unwittingly) charged his client beyond what the statute allowed for procuring for the client a government pension; the pensioner could get the excess from the attorney.

Party Not Equally at Fault

One party induces another to make an illegal contract by undue influence, fraud, or duress; the victim can recover the consideration conveyed to the miscreant if possible.

Excusable Ignorance

A woman agrees to marry a man not knowing that he is already married; bigamy is illegal, the marriage is void, and she may sue him for damages. A laborer is hired to move sealed crates, which contain marijuana; it is illegal to ship, sell, or use marijuana, but the laborer is allowed payment for his services.

Partial Illegality

A six-page employment contract contains two paragraphs of an illegal noncompete agreement. The illegal part is thrown out, but the legal parts are enforceable.

Key Takeaway

There are a number of exceptions to the general rule that courts give no relief to either party to an illegal contract. The rule may be relaxed in cases where justice would be better served than by following the stricture of hands off.

Exercises

1. When, in general, will a court allow a party relief from an illegal contract (or bargain)?
2. A and B engage in a game of high-stakes poker under circumstances making the game illegal in the jurisdiction. A owes B $5,000 when A loses. When A does not pay, B sues. Does B get the money? What if A had paid B the $5,000 and then sued to get it back?

12.5 Cases

Extension of Statutory Illegality Based on Public Policy

Bovard v. American Horse Enterprises

247 Cal. Rptr. 340 (Calif. 1988)

[Bovard sued Ralph and American Horse Enterprises (a corporation) to recover on promissory notes that were signed when Ralph purchased the corporation, ostensibly a jewelry-making business. The trial court dismissed Bovard's complaint.]

Puglia, J.

The court found that the corporation predominantly produced paraphernalia used to smoke marijuana [roach clips and bongs] and was not engaged significantly in jewelry production, and that Bovard had recovered the corporate machinery through self-help [i.e., he had repossessed it]. The parties do not challenge these findings. The court acknowledged that the manufacture of drug paraphernalia was not itself illegal in 1978 when Bovard and Ralph contracted for the sale of American Horse Enterprises, Inc. However, the court concluded a public policy against the manufacture of drug paraphernalia was implicit in the statute making the possession, use and transfer of marijuana unlawful. The trial court held the consideration for the contract was contrary to the policy of express law, and the contract was therefore illegal and void. Finally, the court found the parties were in pari delicto [equally at fault] and thus with respect to their contractual dispute should be left as the court found them.

The trial court concluded the consideration for the contract was contrary to the policy of the law as expressed in the statute prohibiting the possession, use and transfer of marijuana. Whether a contract is contrary to public policy is a question of law to be determined from the circumstances of the particular case. Here, the critical facts are not in dispute. Whenever a court becomes aware that a contract is illegal, it has a duty to refrain from entertaining an action to enforce the contract. Furthermore the court will not permit the parties to maintain an action to settle or compromise a claim based on an illegal contract. * * *

[There are several] factors to consider in analyzing whether a contract violates public policy: "Before labeling a contract as being contrary to public policy, courts must carefully inquire into the nature of the conduct, the extent of public harm which may be involved, and the moral quality of the conduct of the parties in light of the prevailing standards of the community [Citations]"

These factors are more comprehensively set out in the Restatement Second of Contracts section 178:

(1) A promise or other term of an agreement is unenforceable on grounds of public policy if legislation provides that it is unenforceable or the interest in its enforcement is clearly outweighed in the circumstances by a public policy against the enforcement of such terms.

(2) In weighing the interest in the enforcement of a term, account is taken of

(a) the parties' justified expectations,

(b) any forfeiture that would result if enforcement were denied, and

(c) any special public interest in the enforcement of the particular term.

(3) In weighing a public policy against enforcement of a term, account is taken of

(a) the strength of that policy as manifested by legislation or judicial decisions,

(b) the likelihood that a refusal to enforce the term will further that policy,

(c) the seriousness of any misconduct involved and the extent to which it was deliberate, and

(d) the directness of the connection between that misconduct and the term.

Applying the Restatement test to the present circumstances, we conclude the interest in enforcing this contract is very tenuous. Neither party was reasonably justified in expecting the government would not eventually act to geld American Horse Enterprises, a business harnessed to the production of paraphernalia used to facilitate the use of an illegal drug. Moreover, although voidance of the contract imposed a forfeiture on Bovard, he did recover the corporate machinery, the only assets of the business which could be used for lawful purposes, i.e., to manufacture jewelry. Thus, the forfeiture was significantly mitigated if not negligible. Finally, there is no special public interest in the enforcement of this contract, only the general interest in preventing a party to a contract from avoiding a debt.

On the other hand, the Restatement factors favoring a public policy against enforcement of this contract are very strong. As we have explained, the public policy against manufacturing paraphernalia to facilitate the use of marijuana is strongly implied in the statutory prohibition against the possession, use, etc., of marijuana, a prohibition which dates back at least to 1929. * * * Obviously, refusal to enforce the instant contract will further that public policy not only in the present circumstances but by serving notice on manufacturers of drug paraphernalia that they may not resort to the judicial system to protect or advance their business interests. Moreover, it is immaterial that the business conducted by American Horse Enterprises was not expressly prohibited by law when Bovard and Ralph made their agreement since both parties knew that the corporation's products would be used primarily for purposes which were expressly illegal. We conclude the trial court correctly declared the contract contrary to the policy of express law and therefore illegal and void.

Case Questions

1. Why did the court think it was significant that Bovard had repossessed the jewelry-making equipment?
2. What did Bovard want in this case?
3. If it was not illegal to make bongs and roach clips, why did the court determine that this contract should not be enforced?

Unlicensed Practitioner Cannot Collect Fee

Venturi & Company v. Pacific Malibu Development Corp.
172 Cal.App.4th 1417 (Calif. Ct. App. 2009)

Rubin, J.

In June 2003, plaintiff Venturi & Company LLC and defendant Pacific Malibu Development Corp. entered into a contract involving development of a high-end resort on undeveloped property on the Bahamian island of Little Exuma. Under the contract, plaintiff agreed to serve as a financial advisor and find financing for the Little Exuma project. * * * [P]laintiff was entitled to some payment under the contract even if plaintiff did not secure financing for the project [called a success fee].

After signing the contract, plaintiff contacted more than 60 potential sources of financing for the project. * * * [I]n the end, defendants did not receive financing from any source that plaintiff had identified.

Defendants terminated the contract in January 2005. Two months earlier, however, defendants had signed a [financing agreement] with the Talisker Group. Plaintiff was not involved in defendants' negotiations with the Talisker Group. * * * Nevertheless, plaintiff claimed the contract's provision for a success fee entitled plaintiff to compensation following the [Talisker agreement]. When defendants refused to pay plaintiff's fee, plaintiff sued defendants for the fee and for the reasonable value of plaintiff's services.

Defendants moved for summary judgment. They argued plaintiff had provided the services of a real estate broker by soliciting financing for the Little Exuma project yet did not have a broker's license. Thus, defendants asserted * * * the Business and Professions Code barred plaintiff from receiving any compensation as an unlicensed broker. * * * Plaintiff opposed summary judgment. It argued that one of its managing principals, Jane Venturi, had a real estate sales license and was employed by a real estate broker (whom plaintiff did not identify) [thus plaintiff had a] right to a fee.

The court entered summary judgment for defendants. The court found plaintiff had acted as a real estate broker when working on the Little Exuma project. The court pointed to plaintiff's lack of evidence that Jane Venturi's unnamed broker had employed or authorized her to work on the project. * * * [Summary judgment was issued in favor of defendants, denying plaintiff any recovery.] This appeal followed.

The court correctly ruled plaintiff could not receive compensation for providing real estate broker services to defendants because plaintiff was not a licensed broker. (Section 11136 [broker's license required to collect compensation for broker services].) But decisions such as *Lindenstadt* [Citation] establish that the court erred in denying plaintiff compensation to the extent plaintiff's services were not those of a real estate broker. In *Lindenstadt*, the parties entered into 25 to 30 written agreements in which the plaintiff promised to help the defendant find businesses for possible acquisition. After the plaintiff found a number of such businesses, the defendant refused to compensate the plaintiff. The defendant cited the plaintiff's performance of broker's services without a license as justifying its refusal to pay. On appeal, the appellate court rejected the defendant's sweeping contention that the plaintiff's unlicensed services for *some* business opportunities meant the plaintiff could not receive compensation for *any* business opportunity. Rather, the appellate court directed the trial court to examine individually each business opportunity to determine whether the plaintiff acted as an unlicensed broker for that transaction or instead provided only services for which it did not need a broker's license.

Likewise here, the contract called for plaintiff to provide a range of services, some apparently requiring a broker's license, others seemingly not. * * * Thus, triable issues existed involving the extent to which plaintiff provided either unlicensed broker services or, alternatively, non-broker services for which it did not need a license. (Accord: [Citation] [severability allowed partial enforcement of employment contract when license required for some, but not all, services rendered under the contract].)

[T]he contract here envisioned plaintiff directing its efforts toward many potential sources of financing. As to some of those sources, plaintiff may have crossed the line into performing broker services. But for other sources, plaintiff may have provided only financial and marketing advice for which it did not need a broker's license. (See, e.g., [Citation] [statute barring unlicensed contractor from receiving fees for some services did not prohibit recovery for work not within scope of licensing statute].) * * * Whether plaintiff crossed the line into providing broker services is thus a triable issue of fact that we cannot resolve on summary judgment.

Plaintiff * * * did not have a broker's license, and therefore was not entitled to compensation for broker's services. Plaintiff contends it was properly licensed because one of its managers, Jane Venturi, obtained a real estate sales license in February 2004. Thus, she, and plaintiff claims by extension itself, were licensed when defendants purportedly breached the contract by refusing to pay plaintiff months later. * * * Jane Venturi's sales license was not, however, sufficient; only a licensed broker may provide broker services. A sales license does not permit its holder to represent another unless the salesperson acts under a broker's authority.

The judgment for defendants is vacated, and the trial court is directed to enter a new order denying defendants' motion for summary judgment.

Case Questions

1. Why did the plaintiff think it should be entitled to full recovery under the contract, including for services rendered as a real estate broker? Why did the court deny that?
2. Even if the plaintiff were not a real estate broker, why would that mean it could not recover for real estate services provided to the defendant?
3. The appeals court remanded the case; what did it suggest the plaintiff should recover on retrial?

Unconscionability

Williams v. Walker-Thomas Furniture Co.

350 F.2d 445 (D.C. Ct. App. 1965)

Wright, J.

Appellee, Walker-Thomas Furniture Company, operates a retail furniture store in the District of Columbia. During the period from 1957 to 1962 each appellant in these cases purchased a number of household items from Walker-Thomas, for which payment was to be made in installments. The terms of each purchase were contained in a printed form contract which set forth the value of the purchased item and purported to lease the item to appellant for a stipulated monthly rent payment. The contract then provided, in substance, that title would remain in Walker-Thomas until the total of all the monthly payments made equaled the stated value of the item, at which time appellants could take title. In the event of a default in the payment of any monthly installment, Walker-Thomas could repossess the item.

The contract further provided that "the amount of each periodical installment payment to be made by (purchaser) to the Company under this present lease shall be inclusive of and not in addition to the amount of each installment payment to be made by (purchaser) under such prior leases, bills or accounts; and all payments now and hereafter made by (purchaser) shall be credited pro rata on all outstanding leases, bills and accounts due the Company by (purchaser) at the time each such payment is made." The effect of this rather obscure provision was to keep a balance due on every item purchased until the balance due on all items, whenever purchased, was liquidated. As a result, the debt incurred at the time of purchase of each item was secured by the right to repossess all the items previously purchased by the same purchaser, and each new item purchased automatically became subject to a security interest arising out of the previous dealings.

On May 12, 1962, appellant Thorne purchased an item described as a daveno, three tables, and two lamps, having total stated value of $391.11 [about $3,100 in 2016 dollars]. Shortly thereafter, he defaulted on his monthly payments and appellee sought to replevy [repossess] all the items purchased since the first transaction in 1958. Similarly, on April 17, 1962, appellant Williams bought a stereo set of stated value of $514.95 [about $4,900 in 2011 dollars]. She too defaulted shortly thereafter, and appellee sought to replevy all the items purchased since December, 1957. The Court of General Sessions granted judgment for appellee. The District of Columbia Court of Appeals affirmed, and we granted appellants' motion for leave to appeal to this court.

Appellants' principal contention, rejected by both the trial and the appellate courts below, is that these contracts, or at least some of them, are unconscionable and, hence, not enforceable. [In its opinion the lower court said:]

> *The record reveals that prior to the last purchase appellant had reduced the balance in her account to $164. The last purchase, a stereo set, raised the balance due to $678. Significantly, at the time of this and the preceding purchases, appellee was aware of appellant's financial position. The reverse side of the stereo contract listed the name of appellant's social worker and her $218 monthly stipend from the government. Nevertheless, with full knowledge that appellant had to feed, clothe, and support both herself and seven children on this amount, appellee sold her a $514 stereo set.*
>
> *We cannot condemn too strongly appellee's conduct. It raises serious questions of sharp practice and irresponsible business dealings. A review of the legislation in the District of Columbia affecting retail sales and the pertinent decisions of the highest court in this jurisdiction disclose, however, no ground upon which this court can declare the contracts in question contrary to public policy. We note that were the Maryland Retail Installment Sales Act...or its equivalent, in force in the District of Columbia, we could grant appellant appropriate relief. We think Congress should consider corrective legislation to protect the public from such exploitive contracts as were utilized in the case at bar.*

We do not agree that the court lacked the power to refuse enforcement to contracts found to be unconscionable. In other jurisdictions, it has been held as a matter of common law that unconscionable contracts are not enforceable. While no decision of this court so holding has been found, the notion that an unconscionable bargain should not be given full enforcement is by no means novel. * * *

Since we have never adopted or rejected such a rule, the question here presented is actually one of first impression. * * * [W]e hold that where the element of unconscionability is present at the time a contract is made, the contract should not be enforced.

Unconscionability has generally been recognized to include an absence of meaningful choice on the part of one of the parties together with contract terms which are unreasonably favorable to the other party. Whether a meaningful choice is present in a particular case can only be determined by consideration of all the circumstances surrounding the transaction. In many cases the meaningfulness of the choice is negated by a gross inequality of bargaining power. The manner in which the contract was entered is also relevant to this consideration. Did each party to the contract, considering his obvious education or lack of it, have a reasonable opportunity to understand the terms of the contract, or were the important terms hidden in a maze of fine print and minimized by deceptive sales practices? Ordinarily, one who signs an agreement without full knowledge of its terms might be held to assume the risk that he has entered a one-sided bargain. But when a party of little bargaining power, and hence little real choice, signs a commercially unreasonable contract with little or no knowledge of its terms, it is hardly likely that his consent, or even an objective manifestation of his consent, was ever given to all the terms. In such a case the usual rule that the terms of the agreement are not to be questioned should be abandoned and the court should consider whether the terms of the contract are so unfair that enforcement should be withheld. * * *

In determining reasonableness or fairness, the primary concern must be with the terms of the contract considered in light of the circumstances existing when the contract was made. The test is not simple, nor can it be mechanically applied. The terms are to be considered 'in the light of the general commercial background and the commercial needs of the particular trade or case.' Corbin suggests the test as being whether the terms are 'so extreme as to appear unconscionable according to the mores and business practices of the time and place.' We think this formulation correctly states the test to be applied in those cases where no meaningful choice was exercised upon entering the contract. So ordered.

Danaher, J. (dissenting):

[The lower] court...made no finding that there had actually been sharp practice. Rather the appellant seems to have known precisely where she stood.

There are many aspects of public policy here involved. What is a luxury to some may seem an outright necessity to others. Is public oversight to be required of the expenditures of relief funds? A washing machine, e.g., in the hands of a relief client might become a fruitful source of income. Many relief clients may well need credit, and certain business establishments will take long chances on the sale of items, expecting their pricing policies will afford a degree of protection commensurate with the risk. Perhaps a remedy when necessary will be found within the provisions of the D.C. "Loan Shark" law, [Citation].

I mention such matters only to emphasize the desirability of a cautious approach to any such problem, particularly since the law for so long has allowed parties such great latitude in making their own contracts. I dare say there must annually be thousands upon thousands of installment credit transactions in this jurisdiction, and one can only speculate as to the effect the decision in these cases will have.

Case Questions

1. Did the court here say that cross-collateral contracts are necessarily unconscionable?
2. Why is it relevant that the plaintiff had seven children and was on welfare?
3. Why did the defendant have a cross-collateral clause in the contract? What would happen if no such clauses were allowed (the dissent "can only speculate)?
4. What are the elements of unconscionability that the court articulates?
5. What argument did the dissent make as to why this contract should be okay.

12.6 Summary and Exercises

Summary

In general, illegal contracts are unenforceable. The courts must grapple with two types of illegalities: (1) statutory violations and (2) violations of public policy not expressly declared unlawful by statute. The former include gambling contracts, contracts with unlicensed professionals, and Sunday contracts.

Contracts that violate public policy include many types of covenants not to compete. No general rule for determining their legality can be given, except to say that the more rigid their restrictions against working or competing, the less likely they will withstand judicial scrutiny. Other types of agreements that may violate public policy and hence are unenforceable include provisions that waive tort liability and contracts that interfere with family relationships.

The exceptions to the rule that illegal agreements will not be enforced and that courts leave the parties where they are generally involve situations where the hands-off approach would lead to an unfair result: where the parties are not equally at fault, where one is excusably ignorant or withdraws before performance, or where one is protected by a statute. A court may sometimes divide a contract, enforcing the legal part and not the illegal part.

Exercises

1. Henrioulle was an unemployed widower with two children who received public assistance from the Marin County (California) Department of Social Services. There was a shortage of housing for low-income residents in Marin County. He entered into a lease agreement on a printed form, by which the landlord disclaimed any liability for any injury sustained by the tenants anywhere on the property. Henrioulle fractured his wrist when he tripped on a rock on the common stairs in the apartment building. The landlord had been having a hard time keeping the area clean. Is the disclaimer valid? Explain.
2. Albert Bennett, an amateur cyclist, entered a bicycle race sponsored by the United States Cycling Federation. He signed a release exculpating the federation for liability: "I further understand that serious accidents occasionally occur during bicycle racing and that participants in bicycle racing occasionally sustain mortal or serious personal injuries, and/or property damage, as a consequence thereof. Knowing the risks of bicycle racing, nevertheless I hereby agree to assume those risks and to release and hold harmless all the persons or entities mentioned above who (through negligence or carelessness) might otherwise be liable to me (or my heirs or assigns) for damages."

   During the race, Bennett was hit by an automobile that had been allowed on the otherwise blocked-off street by agents of the defendant. Bennett sued; the trial court dismissed the case on summary judgment. Bennett appealed. What was the decision on appeal?
3. Ramses owned an industrial supply business. He contracted to sell the business to Tut. Clause VI of their Agreement of Sale provided as follows: "In further consideration for the purchase, Ramses agrees that he shall not compete, either directly or indirectly, in the same business as is conducted by the corporation in its established territory."

   Two months after the sale, Ramses opened a competing business across the street from the business now owned by Tut, who brought suit, asking the court to close Ramses's business on the basis of Clause VI. What should the court decide? Why?
4. After taking a business law class at State U, Elke entered into a contract to sell her business law book to a classmate, Matthew, for $45. As part of the same contract, she agreed to prepare a will for Matthew's mother for an additional $110. Elke prepared the will and sent the book to Matthew, but he refused to pay her. Is she entitled to any payment? Explain.
5. Elmo, a door-to-door salesman, entered into a contract to sell the Wilson family $320 worth of household products on credit. The Wilsons later learned that Elmo had failed to purchase a city license to make door-to-door sales and refused to pay him. May Elmo collect from the Wilsons? Why?
6. Gardner purchased from Singer a sewing machine ($700) and three vacuums (about $250 each), one after the other, on Singer's "1 to 36 month plan." Gardner defaulted after paying a total of $400 on account, and Singer sued to repossess all the purchases. Gardner defended by claiming the purchase plan was unconscionable and pointed to the *Williams* case (Section 5) as controlling law (that cross-collateral contracts are unconscionable). The trial court ruled for Gardner; Singer appealed. What was the result on appeal?
7. Blubaugh leased a large farm combine from John Deere Leasing by signing an agreement printed on very lightweight paper. The back side of the form was "written in such fine, light print as to be nearly illegible....The court was required to use a magnifying glass." And the wording was "unreasonably complex," but it contained terms much in John Deere's favor. When Blubaugh defaulted, John Deere repossessed the combine, sold it for more than he had paid, and sued him for additional sums in accordance with the default clauses on the back side of the lease. Blubaugh defended by asserting the clauses were unconscionable. Is this a case of procedural, substantive, or no unconscionability? Decide.
8. Sara Hohe, a fifteen-year-old junior at Mission Bay High School in San Diego, was injured during a campus hypnotism show sponsored by the PTSA as a fund-raiser for the senior class. Hypnotism shows had been held annually since 1980, and Sara had seen the previous year's show. She was selected at random from a group of many volunteers. Her participation in the "Magic of the Mind Show" was conditioned on signing two release forms. Hohe's father signed a form entitled "Mission Bay High School PTSA Presents Dr. Karl Santo." Hohe and her father both signed a form titled "Karl Santo Hypnotist," releasing Santo and the school district from all liability. During the course of the show, while apparently hypnotized, Hohe slid from her chair and also fell to the floor about six times, and was injured. She,

through her father, then sued the school district. The Hohes claimed the release was contrary to public policy; the trial court dismissed the suit on summary judgment. Was the release contrary to public policy? Decide.

9. In 1963, the Southern Railway Company was disturbed by an order issued by the Interstate Commerce Commission, a federal agency, which would adversely affect the firm's profit by some $13 million [about $90 million in 2011 dollars]. Southern hired a lawyer, Robert Troutman, who was a friend of President John F. Kennedy, to lobby the president that the latter might convince the attorney general, Robert Kennedy, to back Southern's position in a lawsuit against the ICC. It worked; Southern won. Southern then refused to pay Troutman's bill in the amount of $200,000 [about $14 million in 2011 dollars] and moved for summary judgment dismissing Troutman's claim, asserting—among other things—that contracts whereby one person is hired to use his influence with a public official are illegal bargains. Should summary judgment issue? Decide.
10. Buyer, representing himself to be experienced in timber negotiations, contracted to buy the timber on Seller's land. The first $11,500 would go to Buyer, the next $2,000 would go to Seller, and the rest would be divided fifty-fifty after costs of removal of the timber. Buyer said the timber would be worth $18,000–$20,000. When Seller discovered the timber was in fact worth more than $50,000, he sued, claiming the contract was unconscionable. How should the court rule?

Self-Test Questions

1. Gambling contracts are
    a. always unenforceable
    b. enforceable if written
    c. in effect enforceable in certain situations involving the sale of securities
    d. always enforceable when made with insurance companies
2. In State X, plumbers must purchase a license but do not have to pass an examination. This is an example of
    a. a regulatory license
    b. a revenue license
    c. both a and b
    d. neither a nor b
3. A contract to pay a lobbyist to influence a public official is generally illegal.
    a. true
    b. false
4. Exculpatory clauses are sometimes enforceable when they relieve someone from liability for
    a. an intentional act
    b. recklessness
    c. negligence
    d. all of the above
5. An employee's promise not to compete with the employer after leaving the company
    a. is never enforceable because it restrains trade
    b. is always enforceable if in writing
    c. is always enforceable
    d. is enforceable if related to the employer's property interests

Self-Test Answers

1. c
2. b
3. b
4. c
5. d

Endnotes

1. Harold C. Havighurst, review of *Corbin on Contracts*, by Arthur L. Corbin, *Yale Law Journal* 61 (1952): 1143, 1144–45.
2. Restatement (Second) of Contracts, Section 197(b).
3. Restatement (Second) of Contracts, Section 197(b).
4. *Marquette v. First Omaha Service Corp.*, 439 US 299 (1978).
5. See Thomas M. Reardon, "T. M. Reardon's first-hand account of Citibank's move to South Dakota," *NorthWestern Financial Review*, September 15, 2004, accessed March 1, 2011, http://www.highbeam.com/doc/1P3-708279811.html. Mr. Reardon was a member of the South Dakota Bankers' Association.
6. Restatement (Second) of Contracts, Section 178.
7. Restatement (Second) of Contracts, Section 186(a).
8. California Business and Professions Code, Section 16600.
9. *Raimondo v. Van Vlerah*, 325 N.E.2d 544 (Ohio 1975).
10. Restatement (Second) of Contracts, Section 195.
11. *Henrioulle v. Marin Ventures, Inc.*, 573 P.2d 465 (Calif. 1978).
12. *Womack v. Maner*, 301 S.W.2d 438 (Ark. 1957).
13. *Pacific Custom Pools, Inc. v. Turner Construction*, 94 Cal. Rptr. 2d 756 (Calif. 2000).
14. *Ransburg v. Haase*, 586 N.E. 2d 1295 (Ill. Ct. App. 1992).

CHAPTER 13

Form and Meaning

Learning Objectives

After reading this chapter, you should understand the following:

1. What kinds of contracts must be evidenced by some writing under the Statute of Frauds, what the exceptions to the requirements are, and what satisfies a writing requirement.
2. What effect prior or contemporaneous "side" agreements have on a written contract.
3. How a contract is to be interpreted if its meaning is disputed.

In four chapters, we have focused on the question of whether the parties created a valid contract and have examined the requirements of (1) agreement (offer and acceptance), (2) real consent (free will, knowledge, and capacity), (3) consideration, and (4) legality. Assuming that these requirements have been met, we now turn to the form and meaning of the contract itself. Does the contract have to be in a written form, and—if there is a dispute—what does the contract mean?

13.1 The Statute of Frauds

Learning Objectives

1. Know which contracts are required to be evidenced by some writing to be enforceable.
2. Understand the exceptions to that requirement.
3. Recognize what the writing requirement means.
4. Understand the effect of noncompliance with the Statute of Frauds.

Overview of the Statute of Frauds

The general rule is this: a contract need not be in writing to be enforceable. An oral agreement to pay a high-fashion model $2 million to pose for photographs is as binding as if the language of the deal were printed on vellum and signed in the presence of twenty bishops. For three centuries, however, a large exception grew up around the Statute of Frauds, first enacted in England in 1677 under the formal name "An Act for the Prevention of Frauds and Perjuries." The **Statute of Frauds** requires that some oral agreements be evidenced by a writing, signed by the party to be bound, or there is no enforceable agreement at all. The English statute's two sections dealing with contracts read as follows:

Statute of Frauds

A rule requiring that certain contracts be evidenced by a writing, signed by the party to be bound, to be enforceable.

[Sect. 4]...no action shall be brought

1. *whereby to charge any executor or administrator upon any special promise, to answer damages out of his own estate;*
2. *or whereby to charge the defendant upon any special promise to answer for the debt, default or miscarriages of another person;*
3. *or to charge any person upon any agreement made upon consideration of marriage;*
4. *or upon any contract or sale of lands, tenements or hereditaments, or any interest in or concerning them;*
5. *or upon any agreement that is not to be performed within the space of one year from the making thereof;*

unless the agreement upon which such action shall be brought, or some memorandum or note thereof, shall be in writing, and signed by the party to be charged therewith, or some other person thereunto by him lawfully authorized.

[Sect. 17]...no contract for the sale of any goods, wares and merchandizes, for the price of ten pounds sterling or upwards, shall be allowed to be good, except the buyer shall accept part of the goods so sold, and actually receive the same, or give something in earnest to bind the bargain or in part of payment, or that some note or memorandum in writing of the said bargain be made and signed by the parties to be charged by such contract, or their agents thereunto lawfully authorized.

As may be evident from the title of the act and its language, the general purpose of the law is to provide evidence, in areas of some complexity and importance, that a contract was actually made. To a lesser degree, the law serves to caution those about to enter a contract and "to create a climate in which parties often regard their agreements as tentative until there is a signed writing."[1] Notice, of course, that this is a *statute*; it is a legislative intrusion into the common law of contracts. The name of the act is somewhat unfortunate: insofar as it deals with fraud at all, it does not deal with fraud as we normally think of it. It tries to avoid the fraud that occurs when one person attempts to impose on another an oral agreement that never was made.

The Statute of Frauds has been enacted in form similar to the seventeenth-century act in every state but Maryland and New Mexico, where judicial decisions have given it legal effect, and Louisiana. With minor exceptions in Minnesota, Wisconsin, North Carolina, and Pennsylvania, the laws all embrace the same categories of contracts that are required to be in writing. Early in the twentieth century, Section 17 was replaced by a section of the Uniform Sales Act, and this in turn has now been replaced by provisions in the Uniform Commercial Code (UCC).

FIGURE 13.1 Contracts Required to Be in Writing

Statute of Frauds	UCC Sales of Contracts
1. Promises to Pay Debt of Another 2. Agreements of Executor or Administrator 3. Marriage Promises 4. Sale of Land 5. Contracts Not to be Performed Within One Year	1. Sale of Goods for $500 or More 2. Sale of Securities 3. Other Sales Exceedings $5000

However ancient, the Statute of Frauds is alive and well in the United States. Today it is used as a technical defense in many contract actions, often with unfair results: it can be used by a person to wriggle out of an otherwise perfectly fine oral contract (it is said then to be used "as a sword instead of a shield"). Consequently, courts interpret the law strictly and over the years have enunciated a host of exceptions—making what appears to be simple quite complex. Indeed, after more than half a century of serious scholarly criticism, the British Parliament repealed most of the statute in 1954. As early as 1885, a British judge noted that "in the vast majority of cases [the statute's] operation is simply to enable a man to break a promise with impunity because he did not write it down with sufficient formality." A proponent of the repeal said on the floor of the House of Commons that "future students of law will, I hope, have their labours lightened by the passage of this measure." In the United States, students have no such reprieve from the Statute of Frauds, to which we now turn for examination.

Here is the short of it: if the plaintiff, say, wishes to prove the existence of an oral agreement in those areas affected by the statute, and the other side resists, the plaintiff needs to have something in writing, showing a contractual intention, signed by the other side. (But no oral agreement ever needs to be evidenced by a writing if both sides are willing to perform.) And notice too at common law, that even if the defendant *admits* the existence of the oral agreement, she can still avoid it and not be bound! The statute says, no agreement is enforceable unless the "agreement upon which such action shall be brought, or some memorandum or note thereof, shall be in writing, and signed by the party to be charged therewith." Of course, getting out of an oral agreement because it is not in writing is very impolite, at least; it would not be conducive to maintaining a good reputation, and might be considered bad faith.

Types of Contracts Required in Writing and the Exceptions

Before we go further, note that although we discuss the necessity of a "writing," under the **Uniform Electronic Transaction Act (UETA)**, which has been adopted by almost all states, electronic signatures and contracts cannot be denied enforcement because of the Statute of Frauds. In other words, electronic "signatures" count as "written." More about the UETA is presented below.

Promises to Pay the Debt of Another

The rule: a promise to pay the debt of another person must be evidenced by some writing (or be in proper electronic form) if it is a "**collateral promise** of suretyship (or 'guaranty')." A collateral promise is one secondary or ancillary to some other promise. A **surety** or **guarantor** (the terms are essentially synonymous) is one who promises to perform upon the default of another. Consider this:

A and B agree to pay C.

Here, both A and B are making a direct promise to pay C. Although A is listed first, both are promising to pay C. Now consider this:

B agrees to pay C if A does not.

collateral promise

A promise ancillary to an original promise, not made for the benefit of the party making it, that must be in writing to be enforceable.

surety

One who promises to act or pay upon the default of another: a guarantor.

guarantor

One who promises to pay or perform a contract obligation upon the default of another; a surety.

Here it is clear that there must be another agreement somewhere for A to pay C, but that is not contained in this promise. Rather, B is making an agreement with C that is *collateral*—on the side—to the promise A is making to C. Sometimes the other agreement somewhere for A to pay C is actually in the same document as B's promise to pay C if A does not. That does not make B's promise a direct promise as opposed to a collateral one.

Suppose Lydia wishes to purchase on credit a coat at Miss Juliette's Fine Furs. Juliette thinks Lydia's creditworthiness is somewhat shaky. So Lydia's friend Jessica promises Miss Juliette's that if the store will extend Lydia credit, Jessica will pay whatever balance is due should Lydia default. Jessica is a surety for Lydia, and the agreement is subject to the Statute of Frauds; an oral promise will not be enforceable.[2] Suppose Jessica very much wants Lydia to have the coat, so she calls the store and says, "Send Lydia the fur, and I will pay for it." This agreement does not create a suretyship, because Jessica is primarily liable: she is making a direct promise to pay. To fall within the Statute of Frauds, the surety must back the debt of another person to a third-party promisee (also known as the obligee of the principal debtor). The "debt," incidentally, need not be a money obligation; it can be any contractual duty. If Lydia had promised to work as a cashier on Saturdays at Miss Juliette's in return for the coat, Jessica could become surety to that obligation by agreeing to work in Lydia's place if she failed to show up. Such a promise would need to be in writing to be enforceable.

main purpose doctrine

A promise to pay the debt of another need not be in writing to be enforceable if the promisor was motivated by a desire for advantage or benefit.

The exception: the **main purpose doctrine**. The main purpose doctrine is a major exception to the surety provision of the Statute of Frauds. It holds that if the promisor's principal reason for acting as surety is to secure her own economic advantage, then the agreement is not bound by the Statute of Frauds writing requirement. Suppose, in the previous example, that Jessica is really the one who wants the fur coat but cannot, for reasons of prudence, let it be known that she has bought one. So she proposes that Lydia "buy" it for her and that she will guarantee Lydia's payments. Since the main purpose of Jessica's promise is to advance her own interests, an oral agreement is binding. Normally, the main purpose rule comes into play when the surety desires a financial advantage to herself that cannot occur unless she provides some security. For example, the board chairman of a small company, who also owns all the voting stock, might guarantee a printer that if his company defaulted in paying the bill for desperately needed catalogs, he would personally pay the bill. If his main purpose in giving the guarantee was to get the catalogs printed in order to stave off bankruptcy, and thus to preserve his own interest in the company, he would be bound by an oral agreement.[3] The same principle can be used to bind other creditors to oral agreements, as the bank discovered in Section 4 *Wilson Floors*.

Agreements of Executor or Administrator

The rule: the promise by an executor or administrator of an estate to answer personally for the debt or other duty of the deceased is analogous to the surety provision—it must be evidenced by some writing if it is to be enforced over an objection by the would-be obligor. For an agreement to be covered by the statute, there must have been an obligation before the decedent's death. Thus, if the executor arranges for a funeral and guarantees payment should the estate fail to pay the fee, an oral contract is binding, because there was no preexisting obligation. If, however, the decedent has made his own arrangements and signed a note obligating his estate to pay, the executor's promise to guarantee payment would be binding only if written.

The exception: the main purpose exception to the surety provision applies to this section of the Statute of Frauds as well as to the "promises to pay the debts of another" section, noted earlier.

The Marriage Provision

The rule: if any part of the marriage or the promise to marry consists also of a promise to exchange some consideration, the Statute of Frauds requires that part to be evidenced by some writing (or be in proper electronic form).[4] Mutual promises to marry are not within the rule. John and Sally exchange promises to marry; the promise would not be unenforceable for failure to be evidenced by some writing. (Of course courts are not going to force anybody to keep a promise to marry; the point is, the Statute of Frauds doesn't apply). But if Sally understands John to say, "If you marry me, I will deed to you my property in the Catskill Mountains," the part about the property would need to be evidenced by some writing to be enforced over John's denial. The Statute of Frauds governs such promises regardless of who makes them. Suppose John's father had said, "If you marry Sally and settle down, I will give you $1 million," and John agrees and marries Sally. The father's promise is not enforceable unless written, if he denies it.

Sometimes couples—especially rich people like movie stars—execute written property settlement agreements to satisfy the statute, stipulating how their assets will be treated upon marriage or upon divorce or death. If done before marriage, they are called **prenuptial (premarital) agreements**; if after marriage, **postnuptial (after marriage) agreements** ("prenupts" and "postnupts" in lawyer lingo).

prenuptial (premarital) agreements

A premarital agreement between parties concerning division or ownership of their property.

postnuptial (after marriage) agreements

An agreement after marriage between spouses concerning division or ownership of their property.

The exception: there is no "named" exception here, but courts are free to make equitable adjustments of property of the marriage to avoid an injustice.

> *The factors to be considered in the division of the marital estate are set forth at [Citation], which states, inter alia [among other things], that the court shall finally and equitably apportion the property of the parties, however and whenever acquired. The statute vests wide discretion in the district court. [Citation]. The court is free to adopt any reasonable valuation of marital property which is supported by the record.*[5]

Contracts Affecting an Interest in Real Estate

The rule: almost all contracts involving an interest in real estate are subject to the Statute of Frauds. "An interest in land" is a broad description, including the sale, mortgaging, and leasing of real property (including homes and buildings); profits from the land; the creation of easements; and the establishment of other interests through restrictive covenants and agreements concerning use. Short-term leases, usually for a term of one year or less, are exempt from the provision.

The exception: the **part performance doctrine**. The name here is a misnomer, because it is a doctrine of reliance, and the acts taken in reliance on the contract are not necessarily partial performances under it. As in all such cases, the rationale is that it is unjust not to give the promisee specific performance if he or she acted in reasonable reliance on the contract and the promisor has continued to manifest assent to its terms. An oral contract to sell land is not binding simply because the buyer has paid the purchase price; payment is not by itself reliance, and if the seller refuses to transfer title, the buyer may recover the purchase price. However, if the buyer has taken possession and made improvements on the property, courts will usually say the case is out of the statute, and the party claiming an oral contract can attempt to prove the existence of the oral contract.

part performance doctrine

Equitable exception to Statute of Frauds dispensing with writing requirement when one party performed his or her part of the contract.

The One-Year Rule

The rule: any agreement that cannot be performed within one year from its making must be evidenced by some writing (or be in proper electronic form) to be enforceable. The purpose of this part is perhaps more obvious than most of the statute's provisions: memories fade regarding the terms of oral contracts made long ago; people die; disputes are not uncommon. Notice the critical time frame is not how long it will take to perform the contract, but how long from the time it is made until performance is complete. If a contract is made on January 1 for a house to be constructed starting on June 1 and to be completed on February 1 of the next year, the performance will be completed in eight months from the time it was begun, but thirteen months from the time the contract was made. It falls within the statute.

possibility test

Exception to Statute of Frauds' one-year rule: if at its making, a contract could have been performed in one year, no writing is required.

The exception: the **possibility test**. The statute's one-year rule has been universally interpreted to mean a contract that is impossible to be fully performed within one year; if there is even the slightest chance of carrying out the agreement completely within the year, an oral contract is enforceable. Thus an oral agreement to pay a sum of money on a date thirteen months hence is within the statute and not enforceable, but one calling for payment "within thirteen months" would be enforceable, since it is possible under the latter contract to pay in less than a year. Because in many cases strict application of the statute would dictate harsh results, the courts often strain for an interpretation that finds it possible to perform the agreement within the year. Courts will even hold that because any person may die within the year, a contract without a fixed term may be fully performed in under a year and does not, therefore, fall within the statute.

Under the UCC

The rule: contracts for the sale of goods in an amount greater than $500 must be evidenced by some writing (or, guess what? be in proper electronic form) to be enforceable. Section 2-201 of the UCC requires all contracts for the sale of goods for the price of $500 or more to be in writing, but oral agreements for the sale of goods valued at less than $500 are fully enforceable without exception. The $500 amount has been the same for many years and should be adjusted to account for inflation.

Other Writing Requirements

In addition to these requirements, the UCC provides that agreements for the sale of securities (e.g., most stocks and bonds) usually need to be evidenced by a writing, and agreements for property not included in the sales or securities articles of the UCC that exceed $5,000 in value need to be so evidenced.[6] Included here would be intangible property such as rights to royalties and to mortgage payments, and other rights created by contract. And in many states, other statutes require a writing for several different kinds of contracts. These include agreements to pay commissions to real estate brokers, to make a will, to pay debts already discharged in bankruptcy, to arbitrate rather than litigate, to make loans, and to make installment contracts.

Exceptions under the UCC

There are four exceptions to the UCC's Statute of Frauds requirement that are relevant here.

The Ten-Day-Reply Doctrine

This provides that, as between merchants, if an oral agreement is reached and one party sends the other a written statement confirming it, the other party has ten days to object in writing or the agreement is enforceable.[7]

"Specially Manufactured Goods"

This exception provides that a seller who has manufactured goods to the buyer's specifications or who has made "either a substantial beginning of their manufacture or commitments for their procurement" will not be stuck if the buyer repudiates, assuming that the goods are unsuitable for sale to others.[8]

The "Admission" Exception

This exception arises—reasonably enough (but again, it does not apply at common law)—when the party against whom enforcement is sought admits in testimony or legal papers that a contract was in fact made.[9] However, the admission will not permit enforcement of all claimed terms of the contract; enforcement is limited to the quantity of goods admitted.

The "Payment or Delivery and Acceptance" Exception

The UCC provides that an oral contract for goods in excess of $500 will be upheld if payment has already been made and accepted, or if the goods have been received and accepted.[10] This is a kind of admission, really.

Sufficiency of the Required Writing

At Common Law

We have been careful *not* to say "the contract needs to be in writing." We have said, "a contractual intention must be evidenced by some writing, signed by the party to be bound." A signed contract is not required. What is required in most states, following the wording of the original statute, is that there be at least some memorandum or note concerning the agreement—a logical consequence of the statute's purpose to evidence the making of the contract. The words need not appear in a formal document; they are sufficient in any form in a will, or on a check or receipt, or in longhand on the back of an envelope—so long as the document is signed by the party to be charged (i.e., the party being sued on the contract). (Did we mention electronic contracts, if properly formed, satisfy the statute? Yes, we did.)

Although the writing need not contain every term, it must recite the subject matter of the contract. It need not do so, however, in terms comprehensible to those who were not party to the negotiations; it is enough if it is understandable in context. A written agreement to buy a parcel of land is usually sufficiently definitive if it refers to the parcel in such a way that it could be mistaken for no other—for example, "seller's land in Tuscaloosa," assuming that the seller owned only one parcel there. Beyond the subject matter, the essential terms of promises to be performed must be written out; all details need not be. If an essential term is missing, it cannot be enforced, unless it can be inferred or imposed by rule of law. A written contract for the sale of land containing every term but the time for payment, which the parties orally agreed would be upon delivery of the deed, is sufficient. (A contract that omitted the selling price would not be.)

The parties must be named in the writing in a manner sufficient to identify them. Their whole names need not be given if initials or some other reference makes it inescapable that the writing does concern the actual parties. Reference to the agent of a party identifies the party. Possession of the writing may even be sufficient: if a seller gives a memorandum of an oral agreement for the sale of his land, stating all the terms, to the buyer, the latter may seek specific performance even though the writing omits to name or describe him or his agent.[11]

In a few states, consideration for the promise must be stated in writing, even if the consideration has already been given. Consequently, written contracts frequently contain such language as "for value received." But in most states, failure to refer to consideration already given is unnecessary: "the prevailing view is that error or omission in the recital of past events does not affect the sufficiency of a memorandum."[12] The situation is different, however, when the consideration is a return promise yet to be performed. Usually the return promise is an essential term of the agreement, and failure to state it will vitiate the writing.

Under the UCC

In contracts for the sale of goods, the writing must be signed by the party to be charged (or be in proper electronic form), and the parties must be sufficiently identified.[13] But consideration, including the selling price, need not be set forth for the memorandum to meet the requirements of the UCC ("a writing is not insufficient because it omits or incorrectly states a term agreed upon"), though obviously it makes sense to do so whenever possible. By contrast, UCC Sections 1-206 and 3-319 concerning intangible personal property and investment securities require "a defined or stated price."

Electronic Communications

One of the primary purposes of the Electronic Signatures in Global and National Commerce Act, S. 761, popularly referred to as ESign, is to repeal state law requirements for written instruments as they apply to electronic agreements and to make almost anything reasonably indicative of a signature good enough electronically.[14] It provides the following:

> *Notwithstanding any statute, regulation, or other rule of law [other than subsequent parts of this same statute], with respect to any transactions in or affecting interstate or foreign commerce—*
>
> 1. *a signature, contract, or other record relating to such transaction may not be denied legal effect, validity or enforceability solely because it is in electronic form; and*
> 2. *a contract relating to such transaction may not be denied legal effect, validity or enforceability solely because an electronic signature or electronic record was used in its formation....*
>
> *The term "transaction" means an action or set of actions relating to the conduct of a business, consumer or commercial affairs between two or more persons, including any of the following types of conduct—*
>
> A. *the sale, lease, exchange, or other disposition of [personal property and intangibles]*
>
> B. *the sale, lease, exchange or other disposition of any interest in real property, or any combination thereof.*
>
> *The term "electronic signature" means an electronic sound, symbol, or process, attached to or logically associated with a contract or other record and executed or adopted by a person with the intent to sign the record.*

Effect of Noncompliance and Exceptions; Oral Rescission

The basic rule is that agreements governed by the Statute of Frauds are unenforceable if they are not sufficiently written down. If the agreement contains several promises, the unenforceability of one will generally render the others unenforceable also.

The Statute of Frauds can work injustices. In addition to the exceptions already noted, there are some general exceptions.

Full Performance

First, certainly, if the contract has been performed fully by both sides, its unenforceability under the statute is moot. Having fulfilled its function (neither side having repudiated the contract), the agreement cannot be rescinded on the grounds that it should have been, but was not, reduced to writing.

Detrimental Reliance

Second, some relief may be granted to one who has relied on an oral contract to her detriment (similar to the part performance doctrine mentioned already). For a partially performed contract unenforceable under the Statute of Frauds, restitution may be available. Suppose George agrees orally to landscape Arthur's fifteen acres, in return for which George is to receive title to one acre at the far end of the lot. George is not entitled to the acre if Arthur defaults, but he may recover for the reasonable value of the services he has performed up to the time of repudiation. Somewhat related, if one side has reasonably and foreseeably relied upon a promise in such a way that injustice can only be avoided by enforcing it, some courts will use promissory estoppel to preclude the necessity of a writing, but the connection between the alleged oral contract and the detrimental reliance must be convincing.

Oral Rescission

Third, most contracts required to be in writing may be rescinded orally. The new agreement is treated in effect as a modification of the old one, and since a complete rescission will not usually trigger any action the statute requires to be in writing, the rescission becomes effective in the absence of any signed memorandum.

Some agreements, however, may not be rescinded orally. Those that by their terms preclude oral rescission are an obvious class. Under the UCC, certain agreements for the sale of goods may not be orally rescinded, depending on the circumstances. For instance, if title has already passed to the buyer under a written agreement that satisfies the statute, the contract can be rescinded only by a writing. Contracts for the sale of land are another class of agreements that generally may not be orally rescinded. If title has already been transferred, or if there has been a material change of position in reliance on the contract, oral agreements to rescind are unenforceable. But a contract that remains wholly executory, even though enforceable because in writing, may be rescinded orally in most states.

Contract Modification

Fourth, contracts governed by the Statute of Frauds may be modified orally if the resulting contract, taken as a whole, falls outside the statute. The same rule applies under the UCC.[15] Thus a written contract for the sale of a new bicycle worth $1,200 may be orally modified by substituting the sale of a used bicycle worth $450, but not by substituting the sale of a used bike worth $600. The modified contract effectively rescinds the original contract.

Key Takeaway

The Statute of Frauds, an ancient legislative intrusion into common-law contracts, requires that certain contracts be evidenced by some writing, signed by the party to be bound, to be enforceable (more recent legislation allows electronic contracts to satisfy the statute). Among those affected by the statute are contracts for an interest in real estate, contracts that by their terms cannot be performed within one year, contracts whereby one person agrees to pay the debt of another, contracts involving the exchange of consideration upon promise to marry (except mutual promises to marry), and, under the UCC, contracts in an amount greater than $500. For each contract affected by the statute, there are various exceptions intended to prevent the statute from being used to avoid oral contracts when it is very likely such were in fact made.

The writing need not be a contract; anything in writing, signed by the person to be bound, showing adequate contractual intention will take the matter out of the statute and allow a party to attempt to show the existence of the oral contract.

There may be relief under restitution or promissory estoppel. Contracts affected by the statute can usually be orally rescinded. Any contract can be modified or rescinded; if the new oral contract as modified does not fall within the statute, the statute does not apply.

Exercises

1. What is the purpose of the Statute of Frauds?
2. What common-law contracts are affected by it, and what are the exceptions?
3. How does the UCC deal with the Statute of Frauds?
4. How is the requirement of the statute satisfied?
5. Contracts can always be modified. How does the Statute of Frauds play with contract modification?

13.2 The Parol Evidence Rule

Learning Objectives

1. Understand the purpose and operation of the parol evidence rule, including when it applies and when it does not.
2. Know how the Uniform Commercial Code (UCC) deals with evidence to show a contract's meaning.

The Purpose of the Rule

Unlike Minerva sprung forth whole from the brow of Zeus in Greek mythology, contracts do not appear at a stroke memorialized on paper. Almost invariably, negotiations of some sort precede the concluding of a deal. People write letters, talk by telephone, meet face-to-face, send e-mails, and exchange thoughts and views about what they want and how they will reciprocate. They may even lie and cajole in duplicitous ways, making promises they know they cannot or will not keep in order not to kill the contract talks. In the course of these discussions, they may reach tentative agreements, some of which will ultimately be reflected in the final contract, some of which will be discarded along the way, and some of which perhaps will not be included in the final agreement but will nevertheless not be contradicted by it. Whether any weight should be given to these prior agreements is a problem that frequently arises.

Parol Evidence at Common-Law

The Rule

The rule at common law is this: a written contract intended to be the parties' complete understanding discharges all prior or contemporaneous promises, statements, or agreements that add to, vary, or conflict with it. In short, if there is a dispute about the meaning or interpretation of a written agreement, the writing—"the four corners of the written paper"—controls.

The **parol evidence rule** (*parol* means oral; it is related to *parliament* and *parly*—talking) is a substantive rule of law that operates to bar the introduction of evidence intended to show that the parties had agreed to something different from what they finally arrived at and wrote down. It applies to prior written as well as oral discussions that don't make it into the final written agreement. Though its many apparent exceptions make the rule seem difficult to apply, its purposes are simple: to give freedom to the parties to negotiate without fear of being held to the consequences of asserting preliminary positions, and to give finality to the contract.

parol evidence rule

Under this rule, where there is a written contract, extrinsic (parol) evidence cannot usually change the express terms laid down in that document.

The rule applies to all written contracts, whether or not the Statute of Frauds requires them to be in writing. The Statute of Frauds applies where there is a dispute about whether there was an enforceable oral agreement at all (and again, there is if there's something in writing, signed by the party to be bound showing a contractual intention); the parol evidence rule says, granted there *was* a written contract, does it express the parties' understanding? But the rule is concerned only with events that transpired before (or while) the contract in dispute was signed. It has no bearing on agreements reached subsequently that may alter the terms of an existing contract.

The Exemptions and Exceptions

Despite its apparent stringency, the parol evidence rule does not negate all prior agreements or statements, nor preclude their use as evidence. A number of situations fall outside the scope of the rule and hence are not technically exceptions to it, so they are better phrased as exemptions (something not within the scope of a rule).

Not an Integrated Contract

If the parties never intended the written contract to be their full understanding—if they intended it to be partly oral—then the rule does not apply. If the document is fully integrated (all the intended terms are in there), no extrinsic evidence will be permitted to modify the terms of the agreement, even if the modification is in addition to the existing terms, rather than a contradiction of them. If the contract is partially integrated, prior consistent additional terms may be shown. It is the duty of the party who wants to exclude the parol evidence to show the contract was intended to be integrated. That is not always an easy task. To prevent a party later from introducing extrinsic evidence to show that there were prior agreements, the contract itself can recite that there were none. Here, for example, is the final clause in the National Basketball Association Uniform Player Contract: "This agreement contains the entire agreement between the parties and there are no oral or written inducements, promises or agreements except as contained herein." Such a clause is known as a **merger clause**. (Of course further difficulties arise where parties use form contracts containing boiler-plate merger clauses. Sometimes courts hold that a merger clause, also called "integration clauses" or "complete agreement clauses" are not iron-clad evidence that there were no enforceable terms not contained in the writing. Sometimes courts hold that such a clause only cre-

merger clause

A contract term stating that the written agreement contains—merges—the parties' full understanding and intent.

ates a rebuttable presumption that the contract as written reflects the parties' complete understanding.)

Void or Voidable Contracts

Parol evidence is admissible to show the existence of grounds that would cause the contract to be void. Such grounds include illegality, fraud, duress, mistake, and lack of consideration. And parol evidence is allowed to show evidence of lack of contractual capacity. Evidence of infancy, incompetency, and so on would not change the terms of the contract at all but would show it was voidable or void.

Contracts Subject to a Condition Precedent

condition precedent

A term in a contract that something has to happen before the obligation to perform the contract ripens.

When the parties orally agree that a written contract is contingent on the occurrence of an event or some other condition (a **condition precedent**), the contract is not integrated and the oral agreement may be introduced. The classic case is that of an inventor who sells in a written contract an interest in his invention. Orally, the inventor and the buyer agree that the contract is to take effect only if the buyer's engineer approves the invention. (The contract was signed in advance of approval so that the parties would not need to meet again.) The engineer did not approve it, and in a suit for performance, the court permitted the evidence of the oral agreement because it showed "that in fact there never was any agreement at all."[16] Note that the oral condition does not contradict a term of the written contract; it negates it. The parol evidence rule will not permit evidence of an oral agreement that is inconsistent with a written term, for as to that term the contract is integrated.

Untrue Recital or Errors

reformation

The correction of a contract containing errors.

The parol evidence rule does not prevent a showing that a fact stated in a contract is untrue. The rule deals with prior agreements; it cannot serve to choke off inquiry into the facts. Thus the parol evidence rule will not bar a showing that one of the parties is a minor, even if the contract recites that each party is over eighteen. Nor will it prevent a showing that a figure in the contract had a typographical error—for example, a recital that the rate charged will be the plumber's "usual rate of $6 per hour" when both parties understood that the usual rate was in fact $60 per hour. A court would allow **reformation** (correction) of such errors.

Ambiguity

To enforce a contract, its terms must be understood, so parol evidence would be allowed to clarify ambiguities, but a claim of ambiguity cannot be used to alter, vary, or change the contract's meaning.

Postcontract Modification

The rule does not apply to post-contract mutual modifications or recessions because they do not impugn the integrity of the written contract. Buyer purchases Seller's business on a contract; as part of the agreement, Seller agrees to stay on for three weeks to help Buyer "learn the ropes." Buyer realizes she is not yet prepared to go on her own. She and Seller then agree that Seller will stay on as a salaried employee for five more weeks. Buyer cannot use the parol evidence rule to preclude evidence of the new agreement: it is a postcontract modification supported by new consideration. Similarly, parties could choose to rescind a previously made contract, and the parol evidence rule would not bar evidence of that.

The UCC Approach

Under Section 2-202 of the UCC, a course of dealing, a usage of trade, or a course of performance can be introduced as evidence to explain or supplement any written contract for the sale of goods. A **course of dealing** is defined as "a sequence of previous conduct between the parties to a particular transaction which is fairly to be regarded as establishing a common basis of understanding for interpreting their expressions and other conduct." A **usage of trade** is "any practice or method of dealing having such regularity of observance in a place, vocation or trade as to justify an expectation that it will be observed with respect to the transaction in question." A **course of performance** is the conduct of a party in response to a contract that calls for repeated action (e.g., a purchase agreement for a factory's monthly output, or an undertaking to wash a neighbor's car weekly).

course of dealing

A pattern of behavior between parties showing how they intend their relationship to work.

usage of trade

Customary way of doing business that may be used to inform the parties' contractual intentions.

course of performance

Systematic and uniform conduct in which parties engage after they enter into a contract.

Key Takeaway

The parol evidence rule is intended to preserve "the four corners" of the contract: it generally prohibits the introduction of contemporaneous oral or written elements of negotiation that did not get included in the written contract, subject to a number of exemptions.

The UCC allows evidence of course of dealing, course of performance, or usage of trade to give meaning to the contract.

Exercises

1. What is the purpose of the parol evidence rule?
2. How does it operate to crystallize the intention of the contracting parties?
3. To what kinds of contract issues does the rule not apply?
4. What "help" does the UCC give to fleshing out the parties' contractual understanding?

13.3 Interpretation of Agreements: Practicalities versus Legalities

Learning Objectives

1. Understand the purpose of contractual interpretation.
2. Know the tools courts use to interpret contracts.
3. Recognize that in everyday life, businesspeople tolerate oral contracts or poorly written ones, but a writing remains useful.

The General Problem and the Purpose of Contractual Interpretation

The General Problem

As any reader knows, the meaning of words depends in part on context and in part on the skill and care of the writer. As Justice Oliver Wendell Holmes Jr. once succinctly noted, "A word is not a crystal, transparent and unchanged; it is the skin of a living thought and may vary greatly in color and content according to the circumstances and the time in which it is used."[17] Words and phrases can be ambiguous, either when they stand alone or when they take on a different coloration from words and phrases near them. A writer can be careless and contradict himself without intending to; people often read hurriedly and easily miss errors that a more deliberate perusal might catch. Interpretation difficulties can arise for any of a number of reasons: a form contract might contain language that is inconsistent with provisions specifically annexed; the parties might use jargon that is unclear; they might forget to incorporate a necessary term; assumptions about prior usage or performance, unknown to outsiders like judges, might color their understanding of the words they do use. Because ambiguities do arise, courts are frequently called on to figure out what the parties meant in their agreement.

The Basic Rule of Interpretation

Courts attempt to give meaning to the parties' understanding when they wrote the contract.

The intention of the parties governs, and if their purpose in making the contract is known or can be ascertained from all the circumstances, it will be given great weight in determining the meaning of an obscure, murky, or ambiguous provision or a pattern of conduct. A father tells the college bookstore that in consideration of its supplying his daughter, a freshman, with books for the coming year, he will guarantee payment of up to $350. His daughter purchases books totaling $400 the first semester, and he pays the bill. Midway through the second semester, the bookstore presents him with a bill for an additional $100, and he pays that. At the end of the year, he refuses to pay a third bill for $150. A court could construe his conduct as indicating a purpose to ensure that his daughter had whatever books she needed, regardless of cost, and interpret the contract to hold him liable for the final bill.

Tools of Interpretation

The policy of uncovering purpose has led to a number of tools of judicial interpretation:

- More specific terms or conduct are given more weight than general terms or unremarkable conduct. Thus a clause that is separately negotiated and added to a contract will be counted as more significant than a standard term in a form contract.
- A writing is interpreted as a whole, without undue attention to one clause.
- Common words and terms are given common meaning; technical terms are given their technical meaning.
- In the range of language and conduct that helps in interpretation, the courts prefer the following items in the order listed: express terms, course of performance, course of dealing, and usage of trade.
- If an amount is given in words and figures that differ, the words control.
- Writing controls over typing; typing controls over printed forms.
- Ambiguities are construed against the party that wrote the contract.

In this chapter, we have considered a set of generally technical legal rules that spell out the consequences of contracts that are wholly or partially oral or that, if written, are ambiguous or do not contain every term agreed upon. These rules fall within three general headings: the Statute of Frauds, the parol evidence rule, and the rules of interpretation. Obviously, the more attention paid to the contract before it is formally agreed to, the fewer the unforeseen consequences. In general, the conclusion is inescapable that a written contract will avoid a host of problems. Writing down an agreement is not always sensible or practical, but it can probably be done more often than it is. Writing over fifty years ago—and it is still true—a law professor studying business practices noted the following:

> *Businessmen often prefer to rely on "a man's word" in a brief letter, a handshake or "common honesty and decency"—even when the transaction involves exposure to serious risks. Seven lawyers from law firms with business practices were interviewed. Five thought that businessmen often entered contracts with only a minimal degree of advanced planning. They complained that businessmen desire to "keep it simple and avoid red tape" even where large amounts of money and significant risks are involved....Another said that businessmen when bargaining often talk only in pleasant generalities, think they have a contract, but fail to reach agreement on any of the hard, unpleasant questions until forced to do so by a lawyer.*[18]

Written contracts do not, to be sure, guarantee escape from disputes and litigation. Sometimes ambiguities are not seen; sometimes they are necessary if the parties are to reach an agreement at all. Rather than back out of the deal, it may be worth the risk to one or both parties deliberately to go along with an ambiguous provision and hope that it never arises to be tested in a dispute that winds up in court.

Nevertheless, it is generally true that a written contract has at least three benefits over oral ones, even those that by law are not required to be in writing. (1) The written contract usually avoids ambiguity. (2) It can serve both as a communications device and as a device for the allocation of power, especially within large companies. By alerting various divisions to its formal requirements, the contract requires the sales, design, quality-control, and financial departments to work together. By setting forth requirements that the company must meet, it can place the power to take certain actions in the hands of one division or another. (3) Finally, should a dispute later arise, the written contract can immeasurably add to proof both of the fact that a contract was agreed to and of what its terms were.

Key Takeaway

It is not uncommon for the meaning of a contract to be less than entirely clear. When called upon to interpret the meaning of a contract, courts try to give it the meaning the parties intended when they made it. Various tools of interpretation are used.

Businesspeople usually do not like to seem overbearing; they do not wish to appear untrusting; they often dislike unpleasantries. Therefore it is not uncommon for even big deals to be sealed with a handshake. But it's a trade-off, because a written contract has obvious benefits, too.

Exercises

1. Why do courts fairly frequently have to interpret the meaning of contracts?
2. What is the purpose of contractual interpretation?
3. What tools do the courts use in interpreting contracts?
4. What is the social "cost" of insisting upon a written contract in a business setting? What are the benefits of the contract?

13.4 Cases

The Statute of Frauds' Main Purpose Doctrine

Wilson Floors Co. v. Sciota Park, Ltd., and Unit, Inc.
377 N.E.2d 514 (Ohio 1978)

Sweeny, J.

In December of 1971, Wilson Floors Company (hereinafter "Wilson") entered into a contract with Unit, Inc. (hereinafter "Unit"), a Texas corporation to furnish and install flooring materials for "The Cliffs" project, a development consisting of new apartments and an office building to be located in Columbus, Ohio. Unit...was the general manager for the project. The Pittsburgh National Bank (hereinafter the bank), as the construction lender for the project, held mortgages on The Cliffs property security for construction loans which the bank had made to Unit.

As the work progressed on the project Unit fell behind in making payments to Wilson for its completed work in the spring of 1973. At that time, the project was approximately two-thirds completed, the first mortgage money of seven million dollars having been fully dispersed by the bank to Unit. Appellant [Wilson] thereupon stopped work in May of 1973 and informed Unit that it would not continue until payments were forthcoming. On May 15, 1973, the bank conducted a meeting with the subcontractors in The Cliffs project, including Wilson.

At the meeting, the bank sought to determine whether it would be beneficial at that stage of the project to lend more money to Unit, foreclose on the mortgage and hire a new contractor to complete the work, or do nothing. Subcontractors were requested to furnish the bank an itemized account of what Unit owed them, and a cost estimate of future services necessary to complete their job contracts. Having reviewed the alternatives, the bank determined that it would be in its best interest to provide additional financing for the project. The bank reasoned that to foreclose on the mortgage and hire a new contractor at this stage of construction would result in higher costs.

There is conflicting testimony in regard to whether the bank made assurances to Wilson at this meeting that it would be paid for all work to be rendered on the project. However, after the May meeting, Wilson, along with the other subcontractors, did return to work.

Payments from Unit again were not forthcoming, resulting in a second work stoppage. The bank then arranged another meeting to be conducted on June 28, 1973.

At this second meeting, there is conflicting testimony concerning the import of the statements made by the bank representative to the subcontractors. The bank representative who spoke at the meeting testified at trial that he had merely advised the subcontractors that adequate funds would be available to complete the job. However, two representatives of Wilson, also in attendance at the meeting, testified that the bank representative had assured Wilson that if it returned to work, it would be paid.

After the meeting, Wilson returned to work and continued to submit its progress billings to Unit for payment. Upon completion of its portion of The Cliffs project, Wilson submitted its final invoice of $15,584.50 to Unit. This amount was adjusted downward to $15,443.06 [about $91,600 in 2016 dollars] upon agreement of Unit and Wilson. However, Wilson was not paid this amount.

As a result of nonpayment, Wilson filed suit...against Unit and the bank to recover the $15,443.06 [about $60,700 in 2010 dollars]. On September 26, 1975, Wilson and Unit stipulated that judgment for the sum of $15,365.84, plus interest, be entered against Unit. When Unit failed to satisfy the judgment, appellant proceeded with its action against the bank. [The trial court decided in favor of Wilson, but the intermediate appellate court reversed the trial court decision.] * * * [The Ohio statute of frauds provides]:

> *No action shall be brought whereby to charge the defendant, upon a special promise, to answer for the debt, default, or miscarriage of another person...unless the agreement...or some memorandum thereof, is in writing and signed by the party to be charged....*

In paragraph one of *Crawford v. Edison* [an 1887 Ohio case], however, this court stated:

> *When the leading object of the promisor is, not to answer for another, but to subserve some pecuniary or business purpose of his own, involving a benefit to himself...his promise is not within the statute of frauds, although it may be in form a promise to pay the debt of another and its performance may incidentally have the effect of extinguishing that liability....*

So long as the promisor undertakes to pay the subcontractor whatever his services are worth irrespective of what he may owe the general contractor and so long as the main purpose of the promisor is to further his own business or pecuniary interest, the promise is enforceable. * * *

The facts in the instant case reflect that the bank made its guarantee to Wilson to subserve its own business interest of reducing costs to complete the project. Clearly, the bank induced Wilson to remain on the job and rely on its credit for future payments. To apply the statute of frauds and hold that the bank had no contractual duty to Wilson despite its oral guarantees would not prevent the wrong which the statute's enactment was to prevent, but would in reality effectuate a wrong.

Therefore, this court affirms the finding of the Court of Common Pleas that the verbal agreement made by the bank is enforceable by Wilson, and reverses the judgment of the Court of Appeals.

Case Questions

1. The exception to the Statute of Frauds in issue here is the main purpose doctrine. How does this doctrine relate to the concept of promissory estoppel?
2. What was the main purpose behind the bank's purported promise?

The Statute of Frauds' One-Year Rule

Iacono v. Lyons

16 S.W.3d 92 (Texas Ct. App. 2000)

O'Connor, J.

Mary Iacono, the plaintiff below and appellant here, appeals from a take-nothing summary judgment rendered in favor of Carolyn Lyons, the defendant below and appellee here. We reverse and remand.

The plaintiff [Iacono] and defendant [Lyons] had been friends for almost 35 years. In late 1996, the defendant invited the plaintiff to join her on a trip to Las Vegas, Nevada. There is no dispute that the defendant paid all the expenses for the trip, including providing money for gambling.

The plaintiff contended she was invited to Las Vegas by the defendant because the defendant thought the plaintiff was lucky. Sometime before the trip, the plaintiff had a dream about winning on a Las Vegas slot machine. The plaintiff's dream convinced her to go to Las Vegas, and she accepted the defendant's offer to split "50-50" any gambling winnings.

In February 1997, the plaintiff and defendant went to Las Vegas. They started playing the slot machines at Caesar's Palace. The plaintiff contends that, after losing $47, the defendant wanted to leave to see a show. The plaintiff begged the defendant to stay, and the defendant agreed on the condition that she (the defendant) put the coins into the machines because doing so took the plaintiff too long. (The plaintiff, who suffers from advanced rheumatoid arthritis, was in a wheelchair.) The plaintiff agreed, and took the defendant to a dollar slot machine that looked like the machine in her dream. The machine did not pay on the first try. The plaintiff then said, "Just one more time," and the defendant looked at the plaintiff and said, "This one's for you, Puddin."

The slot machine paid $1,908,064 [about $2.8 million in 2016 dollars]. The defendant refused to share the winnings with the plaintiff, and denied they had an agreement to split any winnings. The defendant told Caesar's Palace she was the sole winner and to pay her all the winnings.

The plaintiff sued the defendant for breach of contract. The defendant moved for summary judgment on the grounds that any oral agreement was unenforceable under the statute of frauds or was voidable for lack of consideration. The trial court rendered summary judgment in favor of the defendant. * * *

[Regarding the "consideration" argument:] The defendant asserted the agreement, if any, was voidable because there was no consideration. The defendant contended the plaintiff's only contribution was the plaintiff's dream of success in Las Vegas and her "luck." The plaintiff asserted the defendant bargained with her to go to Las Vegas in return for intangibles that the defendant thought the plaintiff offered (good luck and the realization of the dream). The plaintiff said she gave up her right to remain in Houston in return for the agreement to split any winnings. The plaintiff also asserted the agreement was an exchange of promises.

* * * The plaintiff alleged she promised to share one-half of her winnings with the defendant in exchange for the defendant's promise to share one-half of her winnings with the plaintiff. These promises, if made, represent the respective benefits and detriments, or the bargained for exchange, necessary to satisfy the consideration requirement. *See* [Citation] (when no other consideration is shown, mutual obligations by the parties to the agreement will furnish sufficient consideration to constitute a binding contract)....[Regarding the Statute of Frauds argument:] The defendant asserted the agreement, if any, was unenforceable under the statute of frauds because it could not be performed within one year. There is no dispute that the winnings were to be paid over a period of 20 years. * * *

[The statute] does not apply if the contract, from its terms, could possibly be performed within a year—however improbable performance within one year may be. [Citations] [It bars] only oral contracts that cannot be completed within one year. [Citation] (If the agreement, either by its terms or by the nature of the required acts, cannot be performed within one year, it falls within the statute of frauds and must be in writing).

To determine the applicability of the statute of frauds with indefinite contracts, this Court may use any reasonably clear method of ascertaining the intended length of performance. [Citation] The method is used to determine the parties' intentions at the time of contracting. The fact that the entire performance within one year is not required, or expected, will not bring an agreement within the statute. *See* [Citations].

Assuming without deciding that the parties agreed to share their gambling winnings, such an agreement possibly could have been performed within one year. For example, if the plaintiff and defendant had won $200, they probably would have received all the money in one pay-out and could have split the winnings immediately. Therefore, the defendant was not entitled to summary judgment based on her affirmative defense of the statute of frauds.

We reverse the trial court's judgment and remand for further proceedings.

Case Questions

1. The defendant contended there was no consideration to support her alleged promise to split the winnings fifty-fifty. What consideration did the court find here?
2. The defendant contended that the Statute of Frauds' one-year rule prohibited the plaintiff from attempting to prove the existence of the alleged oral contract to split the winnings. What reasoning did the court give here as to why the statute did not apply?
3. After this case, the court remanded the matter to the lower court. What has to happen there before plaintiff gets her money?

The Parol Evidence Rule: Resolving Ambiguities

Conway v. Conway, 111 So. 3d 925 (Florida District Court of Appeals, 2013).

Van Nortwick, J.

Elizabeth Ann Conway, the Former Wife, appeals the trial court's Final Order awarding her [only] $31,850.85 in additional alimony. * * * As explained below, we affirm the additional alimony award. * * *

The Former Wife filed a motion to enforce the terms of a Marital Settlement Agreement (MSA) that was incorporated in the Final Judgment of Dissolution of Marriage between her and Michael Warren Conway, the Former Husband, entered in September 2004. Under the MSA, the Former Husband was required to pay the Former Wife 30% of "any bonuses he receives" in 2004, and 20% of any bonuses received each year thereafter as long as his alimony obligation persisted.

Here, the parties agree that resolution of the case is largely determined by what the parties meant in using the terms "bonus" and "receives" in the MSA. The MSA does not provide whether the Former Wife's share of the Former Husband's bonuses should be calculated from his gross or net bonus. The Former Wife argues that "bonus" refers to the gross, pre-tax compensation the Former Husband was paid by his employer, and that "receives" means the gross, pre-tax bonus earned by the Former Husband. By calculating her share from the net bonuses, the Former Wife argues that the Former Husband had significantly underpaid her. The Former Husband argues that "bonus" refers to his net, after-tax remuneration, and that "receives" relates to the money that actually reaches his pocket, because he does not "receive" the amounts withheld from his bonus, which are transferred directly to the government.* * *

When interpreting a contract, a court should ascribe terms their plain meaning and attempt to place itself as close as possible to the position occupied by the parties at the time the contract was executed, keeping in mind the goal to be accomplished by the agreement. This court has stated that a latent ambiguity occurs in a contract when "the language employed is clear and intelligible and suggests but a single meaning, but some extrinsic fact or extraneous evidence creates a necessity for interpretation or a choice among two or more possible meanings." [Citation] Furthermore, we have observed that a contract's silence on the parties' rights can create a latent ambiguity. [Citation]

Parol evidence may be admitted to "explain, clarify, or elucidate the ambiguous term." [Citation] Once it is determined that parol evidence is necessary to establish the parties' intent, the court's finding as to intent is a question of fact. [Citation] A trial court's findings of fact are reviewed to determine whether they are supported by competent substantial evidence. [Citation] When evaluating intent as to an ambiguous portion of a contract, the court must look to the parties' "subsequent acts, and the circumstances existing at the time of entering into the contract or the modification." [Citation]

Although the MSA appears straightforward and clear after initial reading, the parties' conflicting interpretations indicate an unanticipated ambiguity. [Citation] Therefore, the trial court acted appropriately in looking to parol evidence to determine the proper construction in accord with the parties' original intent.

The trial court heard testimony and argument from both parties as to their intent in drafting the MSA. The trial court also looked to the parties' conduct following their divorce. After weighing all the evidence, the trial court found that the parties intended that the Former Wife's share of the Former Husband's bonuses be deducted from his net bonus. There was competent substantial evidence to support this finding, such as testimony that the Former Wife took the checks provided to her without protest for many years. The record also contains evidence that for at least two of the years, the Former Wife was in possession of documentation as to the Former Husband's gross and net bonus amounts, as well as the check representing her additional alimony. Thus, it can reasonably be inferred that she could have ascertained how her additional alimony was being calculated relatively easily, and object to the method if she thought it did not comport with her understanding of the MSA.

There was also competent substantial evidence that the Former Husband underpaid the Former Wife $23,140.85 in additional alimony. The record also reflects that the Former Husband received a $65,000 bonus in 2006 from which he should have paid the Former Wife $8,710, although he actually paid her nothing. The sum of these two amounts is $31,850.85, the amount the trial court ordered the Former Husband to pay the Former Wife. Thus, we affirm the trial court's interpretation of the MSA, as well as the amount of the additional alimony awarded to the Former Wife.* * *

We AFFIRM the trial court's award of additional alimony to the Former Wife. * * *

LEWIS and SWANSON, JJ., concur.

Case Questions

1. How did an apparently unambiguous contract get labeled "ambiguous"?
2. What evidence did the court use to determine the parties' intention here?
3. What difference does it make to the Former Wife whether her payments are calculated based on the Former Husband's gross income or net income?
4. What was the "additional alimony" the Former Wife was awarded?

13.5 Summary and Exercises

Summary

In an economic system mostly governed by contract, parties may not only make the kinds of deals they wish but may make them in any form they wish—with some significant exceptions. The most significant issue of form in contract law is whether the contract must be written or may be oral and still be enforceable. The question can be answered by paying close attention to the Statute of Frauds and court decisions interpreting it. In general, as we have seen, the following types of contracts must be in writing: interests in real property, promises to pay the debt of another, certain agreements of executors and administrators, performances that cannot be completed within one year, sale of goods for $500 or more, and sale of securities. There are exceptions to all these rules.

Another significant rule that permeates contract law is the parol evidence rule: prior statements, agreements, or promises, whether oral or written, made during the negotiation process are often discharged by a subsequent written agreement. No matter what you were promised before you signed on the dotted line, you are stuck if you sign an integrated agreement without the promise. Again, of course, exceptions lie in wait for the unwary: Is the agreement only partially integrated? Are there grounds to invalidate the entire agreement? Is the contract subject to an oral condition? Is a fact recited in the contract untrue?

Contracts are not always clear and straightforward. Often they are murky and ambiguous. Interpreting them when the parties disagree is for the courts. To aid them in the task, the courts over the years have developed a series of guidelines such as these: Does the agreement have a plain meaning on its face? If there is an ambiguity, against whom should it be construed? Are there usages of trade or courses of dealing or performance that would help explain the terms?

Exercises

1. Plaintiff's and Defendant's cars crashed. Plaintiff hired an attorney, who negotiated with Defendant's insurance adjuster. Plaintiff's attorney claimed he and the adjuster reached an oral settlement, but the insurance company refused to honor it and filed for summary judgment, raising the Statute of Frauds' suretyship provision as a defense: a promise by one person (the insurance company here) to pay the debts of another (the insured) must be evidenced by some writing, and there was no writing. Is the defense good? Explain.
2. Plaintiff Irma Kozlowski cohabited with Defendant Thaddeus Kozlowski for fifteen years without marriage. She repeatedly asked him specifically about her financial situation should he predecease her, and he assured her—she said—that he would arrange to provide for her for the rest of her life. She had provided the necessary household services and emotional support to permit him to successfully pursue his business career; she had performed housekeeping, cleaning, and shopping services and had run the household and raised the children, her own as well as his. When they separated and she was "literally forced out of the house," she was sixty-three years old and had no means or wherewithal for survival. When she sued, he raised the Statute of Frauds' one-year rule as a defense. Is the defense good?[19]
3. Carlson purchased a parcel of real estate that was landlocked. Carlson called his neighbor, Peterson, and asked if he could use an abandoned drive on Peterson's property to travel to his (Carlson's) property from the highway. Peterson said, "Sure, anytime." Later the two became engaged in a dispute, and Peterson blocked the drive. May Carlson enforce Peterson's promise that he could use the drive "anytime"? Why?
4. Silverman, who was elderly and somewhat disabled, lived alone on a farm. Silverman called Burch and said, "Burch, if you will move in with me and help me take care of the farm, it will be yours when I die." Burch did as Silverman requested and on Silverman's death two years later, claimed the farm on the basis of their oral agreement, but the estate resisted. Is Burch entitled to the farm? Why?

5. On February 12, Sally was hired to manage a company for a period of one year. She reported for work on February 26 but was fired two weeks later. She sued the owner of the company for breach of their one-year oral contract. May she recover? Why?
6. Baker entered into an oral contract to sell her car to Clyde for $8,600. She delivered the car to Clyde; Clyde inspected it, found no problems, kept it for three days, but then refused to pay and now wants to return the car. Is the contract enforceable? Why?
7. Wayne, a building contractor, built a new house and offered it for sale. A young couple accepted the offer, and the parties entered into an oral agreement covering all the terms of sale. The couple later tried to back out of the agreement. Wayne filed suit, and during the trial, the couple admitted making the contract. Is the contract enforceable? Why?
8. Plaintiff leased commercial space from Defendant for a florist shop. After the lease was signed, Plaintiff learned that the county code allowed only one freestanding sign on the property, and one was already up, advertising Defendant's business. Plaintiff claimed Defendant breached the lease by not providing them space for a sign; Defendant pointed to the lease, paragraph 16 of which provided that "Tenant shall not erect or install any sign...without written consent of the Landlord." But Plaintiff claimed Defendant said during negotiations he could have a sign, evidence Defendant objected to based on the parol evidence rule. Defendant admitted that during negotiations he told Plaintiff that despite paragraph 16, he could have a sign (but not freestanding); that despite language in the lease requiring renovation plans to be in writing, they did not have to be. Defendant also testified that the written form lease he used was not drafted specifically for this property, and that although the lease required attachments of exhibits, there were no attachments. Is Plaintiff barred by the parol evidence rule from showing that Defendant said he could have a freestanding sign?
9. On March 1, 2010, Milton talked to Harriet and, as Harriet claimed, said, "I will hire you as sales manager for one year at a salary of $57,000. You start next Monday, March 8." Harriet agreed. Four months later Milton discharged Harriet and she sued, claiming breach of employment contract. Is the alleged contract enforceable?
10. Al Booth's Inc. sued Boyd-Scarp (a contractor) and James Rathmann for nonpayment following delivery of various appliances to Rathmann's new home being built by Boyd-Scarp. Booth's was aware that Boyd-Scarp was having financial problems and allegedly contacted Rathmann prior to delivery, asking him to guarantee payment. Evidence was adduced that Rathmann orally promised to pay in the event the builder did not and that the goods were then delivered. Rathmann denied any such promise, raising the Statute of Frauds, and Al Booth's sued. Will Al Booth's prevail?

Self-Test Questions

1. As a general rule
    a. contracts do not have to be in writing to be enforceable
    b. contracts that can be performed in one year must be in writing
    c. all oral contracts are unenforceable
    d. a suretyship agreement need not be in writing to be enforceable
2. An exception to the UCC Statute of Frauds provision is
    a. the one-year rule
    b. the reply doctrine
    c. executor agreements
    d. all of the above
3. Rules that require certain contracts to be in writing are found in
    a. state statutory law
    b. the UCC
    c. the Statute of Frauds
    d. all of the above

4. The parol evidence rule
    a. applies only when contracts must be in writing
    b. does not apply to real estate contracts
    c. states that a written contract discharges all prior or contemporaneous promises that add to, vary, or conflict with it
    d. is designed to hold parties to promises they made during negotiations
5. A merger clause
    a. is required when goods are sold for $500 or more
    b. is used when two parcels of real estate are sold in the same contract
    c. invalidates a contract for the sale of securities
    d. evidences an intention that the written contract is the parties' full understanding

Self-Test Answers

1. a
2. b
3. d
4. c
5. d

Endnotes

1. Restatement (Second) of Contracts, Chapter 5, statutory note.
2. Of course, if Jessica really *did* orally promise Miss Juliette's to pay in case Lydia didn't, it would be bad faith to lie about it. The proper course for Jessica is not to say, "Ha, ha, I promised, but it was only oral, so I'm not bound." Jessica should say, "I raise the Statute of Frauds as a defense."
3. *Stuart Studio, Inc. v. National School of Heavy Equipment, Inc.*, 214 S.E.2d 192 (N.C. 1975).
4. Restatement (Second) of Contracts, Section 125.
5. *In re Marriage of Rada*, 402, 869 P.2d 254 (Mont. 1994).
6. Uniform Commercial Code, Sections 8-319 and 1-206.
7. Uniform Commercial Code, Section 2-201(2).
8. Uniform Commercial Code, Section 2-201(3)(a).
9. Uniform Commercial Code, Section 2-201(3)(b).
10. Uniform Commercial Code, Section 2-20l(3)(c).
11. Restatement (Second) of Contracts, Section 207(f).
12. Restatement (Second) of Contracts, Section 207(h).
13. Uniform Commercial Code, Section 2-210(1).
14. Electronic Signatures in Global and National Commerce Act, 15 U.S.C. § 96, 106th Congress (2000).
15. Uniform Commercial Code, Section 2-209(3).
16. *Pym v. Campbell*, 119 Eng. Rep. 903 (Q.B. 1856).
17. *Towne v. Eisner*, 245 US 418, 425 (1917).
18. Stewart Macaulay, "Non-contractual Relations in Business: A Preliminary Study," *American Sociological Review* 28, no. 1 (1963): 58–59.
19. *Kozlowski v. Kozlowski*, 395 A.2d 913 (N.J. 1978).

CHAPTER 14

Third-Party Rights

Learning Objectives

After reading this chapter, you should understand the following:

1. How an assignment of contract rights is made and how it operates.
2. What a delegation of duties is and how it operates.
3. Under what circumstances a person not a party to a contract can enforce it.

To this point, we have focused on the rights and duties of the two parties to the contract. In this chapter, we turn our attention to contracts in which outsiders acquire rights or duties or both. Three types of outsiders merit examination:

1. Assignees (outsiders who acquire rights after the contract is made)
2. Delegatees (outsiders who acquire duties after the contract is made)
3. Third-party beneficiaries (outsiders who acquire rights when the original contract is made)

14.1 Assignment of Contract Rights

Learning Objectives

1. Understand what an assignment is and how it is made.
2. Recognize the effect of the assignment.
3. Know when assignments are not allowed.
4. Understand the concept of assignor's warranties.

The Concept of a Contract Assignment

assignment

The passing or delivering by one person to another of the right to a contract benefit.

obligee

One to whom an obligation is owed.

obligor

One who owes an obligation.

assignee

One to whom the right to receive benefit of a contract is passed or delivered.

assignor

One who agrees to allow another to receive the benefit of a contract.

factor

A person who pays money to receive another's executory contractual benefits.

Contracts create rights and duties. By an **assignment**, an **obligee** (one who has the right to receive a contract benefit) transfers a right to receive a contract benefit owed by the **obligor** (the one who has a duty to perform) to a third person (**assignee**); the obligee then becomes an **assignor** (one who makes an assignment).

The Restatement (Second) of Contracts defines an assignment of a right as "a manifestation of the assignor's intention to transfer it by virtue of which the assignor's right to performance by the obligor is extinguished in whole or in part and the assignee acquires the right to such performance."[1] The one who makes the assignment is both an obligee and a transferor. The assignee acquires the right to receive the contractual obligations of the promisor, who is referred to as the obligor (see Figure 14.1). The assignor may assign any right unless (1) doing so would materially change the obligation of the obligor, materially burden him, increase his risk, or otherwise diminish the value to him of the original contract; (2) statute or public policy forbids the assignment; or (3) the contract itself precludes assignment. The common law of contracts and Articles 2 and 9 of the Uniform Commercial Code (UCC) govern assignments. Assignments are an important part of business financing, such as factoring. A **factor** is one who purchases the right to receive income from another.

FIGURE 14.1 Assignment of Rights

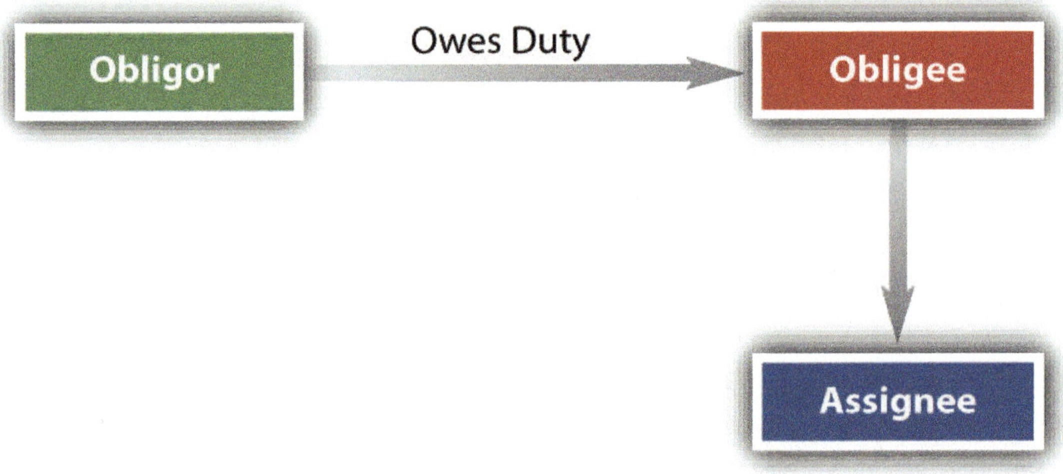

This figure shows that the obligor (upper left) owes a contractual duty to the obligee (upper right); the obligee may assign the right to receive the benefit of the duty to an assignee (lower right).

Method of Assignment

Manifesting Assent

To effect an assignment, the assignor must make known his intention to transfer the rights to the third person. The assignor's intention must be that the assignment is effective without need of any further action or any further manifestation of intention to make the assignment. In other words, the assignor must intend and understand himself to be making the assignment then and there; he is not promising to make the assignment sometime in the future.

Under the UCC, any assignments of rights in excess of $5,000 must be in writing, but otherwise, assignments can be oral and consideration is not required: the assignor could assign the right to the assignee for nothing (not likely in commercial transactions, of course). Mrs. Franklin has the right to receive $750 a month from the sale of a house she formerly owned; she assigns the right to receive the money to her son Jason, as a gift. The assignment is good, though such a gratuitous assignment is usually revocable, which is not the case where consideration has been paid for an assignment.

Acceptance and Revocation

For the assignment to become effective, the assignee must manifest his acceptance under most circumstances. This is done automatically when, as is usually the case, the assignee has given consideration for the assignment (i.e., there is a contract between the assignor and the assignee in which the assignment is the assignor's consideration), and then the assignment is not revocable without the assignee's consent. Problems of acceptance normally arise only when the assignor intends the assignment as a gift. Then, for the assignment to be irrevocable, either the assignee must manifest his acceptance or the assignor must notify the assignee in writing of the assignment.

Notice

Notice to the obligor is not required, but an obligor who renders performance to the assignor without notice of the assignment (that performance of the contract is to be rendered now to the assignee) is discharged. Obviously, the assignor cannot then keep the consideration he has received; he owes it to the assignee. But if notice is given to the obligor and she performs to the assignor anyway, the assignee can recover from either the obligor or the assignee, so the obligor could have to perform twice, as in Exercise 2 at the chapter's end, *Aldana v. Colonial Palms Plaza*. Of course, an obligor who receives notice of the assignment from the assignee will want to be sure the assignment has really occurred. After all, anybody could waltz up to the obligor and say, "I'm the assignee of your contract with the bank. From now on, pay me the $500 a month, not the bank." The obligor is entitled to verification of the assignment.

Effect of Assignment

General Rule

An assignment of rights effectively makes the assignee **stand in the shoes of** the assignor. He gains all the rights against the obligor that the assignor had, but no more. An obligor who could avoid the assignor's attempt to enforce the rights could avoid a similar attempt by the assignee. Likewise, under UCC Section 9-318(1), the assignee of an account is subject to all terms of the contract between the debtor and the creditor-assignor. Suppose Dealer sells a car to Buyer on a contract where Buyer is to pay $300 per month and the car is warranted for 50,000 miles. If the car goes on the fritz before then and Dealer won't fix it, Buyer could fix it for, say, $250 and deduct that $250 from the amount owed Dealer on the next installment (called a setoff). Now, if Dealer assigns the contract to Assignee, Assignee stands in Dealer's shoes, and Buyer could likewise deduct the $250 from payment to Assignee.

stand in the shoes of

An assignee takes no greater rights than his assignor had.

Exceptions

The "shoe rule" does not apply to two types of assignments. First, it is inapplicable to the sale of a negotiable instrument to a holder in due course (covered in detail Chapter 23). Second, the rule may be waived: under the UCC and at common law, the obligor may agree in the original contract not to raise defenses against the assignee that could have been raised against the assignor.[2] While a **waiver of defenses** makes the assignment more marketable from the assignee's point of view, it is

waiver of defenses

Surrender by a party of legal rights otherwise available to him or her.

a situation fraught with peril to an obligor, who may sign a contract without understanding the full import of the waiver. Under the waiver rule, for example, a farmer who buys a tractor on credit and discovers later that it does not work would still be required to pay a credit company that purchased the contract; his defense that the merchandise was shoddy would be unavailing (he would, as used to be said, be "having to pay on a dead horse").

consumer transactions

A contract for household or domestic purposes, not commercial purposes.

For that reason, there are various rules that limit both the holder in due course and the waiver rule. Certain defenses, the so-called real defenses (infancy, duress, and fraud in the execution, among others), may always be asserted. Also, the waiver clause in the contract must have been presented in good faith, and if the assignee has actual notice of a defense that the buyer or lessee could raise, then the waiver is ineffective. Moreover, in consumer transactions, the UCC's rule is subject to state laws that protect consumers (people buying things used primarily for personal, family, or household purposes), and many states, by statute or court decision, have made waivers of defenses ineffective in such **consumer transactions**. Federal Trade Commission regulations also affect the ability of many sellers to pass on rights to assignees free of defenses that buyers could raise against them. Because of these various limitations on the holder in due course and on waivers, the "shoe rule" will not govern in consumer transactions and, if there are real defenses or the assignee does not act in good faith, in business transactions as well.

When Assignments Are Not Allowed

The general rule—as previously noted—is that most contract rights are assignable. But there are exceptions. Five of them are noted here.

Material Change in Duties of the Obligor

When an assignment has the effect of materially changing the duties that the obligor must perform, it is ineffective. Changing the party to whom the obligor must make a payment is not a material change of duty that will defeat an assignment, since that, of course, is the purpose behind most assignments. Nor will a minor change in the duties the obligor must perform defeat the assignment.

Several residents in the town of Centerville sign up on an annual basis with the Centerville *Times* to receive their morning paper. A customer who is moving out of town may assign his right to receive the paper to someone else within the delivery route. As long as the assignee pays for the paper, the assignment is effective; the only relationship the obligor has to the assignee is a routine delivery in exchange for payment. Obligors can consent in the original contract, however, to a subsequent assignment of duties. Here is a clause from the World Team Tennis League contract: "It is mutually agreed that the Club shall have the right to sell, assign, trade and transfer this contract to another Club in the League, and the Player agrees to accept and be bound by such sale, exchange, assignment or transfer and to faithfully perform and carry out his or her obligations under this contract as if it had been entered into by the Player and such other Club." Consent is not necessary when the contract does not involve a personal relationship.

Assignment of Personal Rights

personal right

The right or duty of a particular person to perform or receive contract duties or benefits; cannot be assigned.

When it matters to the obligor who receives the benefit of her duty to perform under the contract, then the receipt of the benefit is a **personal right** that cannot be assigned. For example, a student seeking to earn pocket money during the school year signs up to do research work for a professor she admires and with whom she is friendly. The professor assigns the contract to one of his colleagues with whom the student does not get along. The assignment is ineffective—the student is not obligated to work for the substitute—because it matters to the student (the obligor) who the person of the assignee is. An insurance company provides auto insurance covering Mohammed Kareem, a sixty-five-year-old man who drives very carefully. Kareem cannot assign the contract to his seventeen-year-old grandson because it matters to the insurance company who the person insured is. Tenants usually cannot assign (sublet) their tenancies without the landlord's permission because it matters to the landlord who their tenant is. Section 4, *Nassau Hotel Co. v. Barnett & Barse Corp.*, is an example of the nonassignability of a personal right. A student who is awarded a scholarship cannot assign her right to receive it to another person: the right is personal to the awardee.

Assignment Forbidden by Statute or Public Policy

Various federal and state laws prohibit or regulate some contract assignment. The assignment of future wages is regulated by state and federal law to protect people from improvidently denying themselves future income because of immediate present financial difficulties. And even in the absence of statute, public policy might prohibit some assignments.

Contracts That Prohibit Assignment

Assignability of contract rights is useful, and prohibitions against it are not generally favored. Many contracts contain general language that prohibits assignment of rights or of "the contract." Both the Restatement and UCC Section 2-210(3) declare that in the absence of any contrary circumstances, a provision in the agreement that prohibits assigning "the contract" bars "only the delegation to the assignee of the assignor's duty of performance."[3] In other words, unless the contract specifically prohibits assignment of any of its terms, a party is free to assign anything except his or her own duties. Also, most courts hold that a contractual prohibition against assignment is really only a promise not to assign; if the benefit is assigned, the obligor has a right to damages for the breach of the no-assignment clause, but the assignment is still valid.

Even if a contractual provision explicitly prohibits it, a right to damages for breach of the whole contract is assignable under UCC Section 2-210(2) in contracts for goods. Likewise, UCC Section 9-318(4) invalidates any contract provision that prohibits assigning sums already due or to become due. Indeed, in some states, at common law, a clause specifically prohibiting assignment will fail. For example, the buyer and the seller agree to the sale of land and to a provision barring assignment of the rights under the contract. The buyer pays the full price, but the seller refuses to convey. The buyer then assigns to her friend the right to obtain title to the land from the seller. The latter's objection that the contract precludes such an assignment will fall on deaf ears in some states; the assignment is effective, and the friend may sue for the title.

Future Contracts

The law distinguishes between assigning future rights under an existing contract and assigning rights that will arise from a future contract. Rights contingent on a future event can be assigned in exactly the same manner as existing rights, as long as the contingent rights are already incorporated in a contract. Ben has a long-standing deal with his neighbor, Mrs. Robinson, to keep the latter's walk clear of snow at twenty dollars a snowfall. Ben is saving his money for a new printer, but when he is eighty dollars shy of the purchase price, he becomes impatient and cajoles a friend into loaning him the balance. In return, Ben assigns his friend the earnings from the next four snowfalls. The assignment is effective. However, a right that will arise from a future contract cannot be the subject of a present assignment.

Partial Assignments

An assignor may assign part of a contractual right, but only if the obligor can perform that part of his contractual obligation separately from the remainder of his obligation. Assignment of part of a payment due is always enforceable. However, if the obligor objects, neither the assignor nor the assignee may sue him unless both are party to the suit. Mrs. Robinson owes Ben one hundred dollars. Ben assigns fifty dollars of that sum to his friend. Mrs. Robinson is perplexed by this assignment and refuses to pay until the situation is explained to her satisfaction. The friend brings suit against Mrs. Robinson. The court cannot hear the case unless Ben is also a party to the suit. This ensures all parties to the dispute are present at once and avoids multiple lawsuits.

Successive Assignments

It may happen that an assignor assigns the same interest twice (see Figure 14.2). With certain exceptions, the first assignee takes precedence over any subsequent assignee. One obvious exception is when the first assignment is ineffective or revocable. A subsequent assignment has the effect of revoking a prior assignment that is ineffective or revocable. Another exception: if in good faith the subsequent assignee gives consideration for the assignment and has no knowledge of the prior assignment, he takes precedence whenever he obtains payment from, performance from, or a judgment against the obligor, or whenever he receives some tangible evidence from the assignor that the right has been assigned (e.g., a bank deposit book or an insurance policy).

Some states follow the different English rule: the first assignee to give notice to the obligor has priority, regardless of the order in which the assignments were made. Furthermore, if the assignment falls within the filing requirements of UCC Article 9 (see Chapter 28), the first assignee to file will prevail.

FIGURE 14.2 Successive Assignments

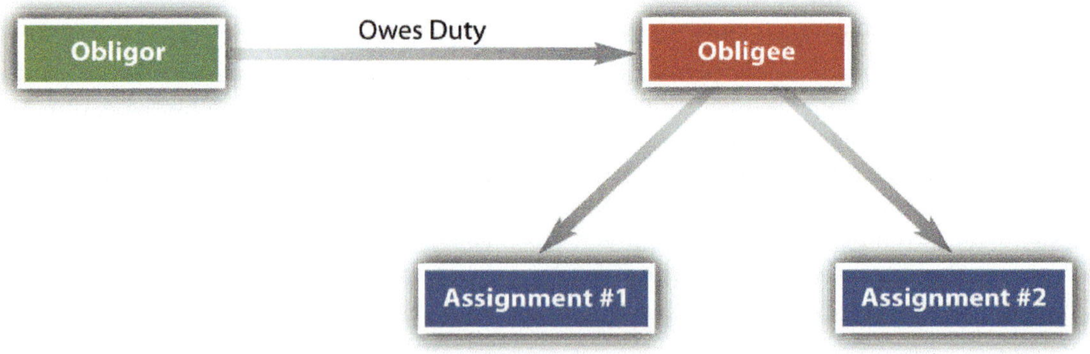

This figure shows that the obligee (on the upper right) of a duty owed by the obligor (on the upper left) may make two assignments of the right owed to her. The assignees are shown in the lower right.

Assignor's Warranties

assignor's warranties

Promises, express or implied, made by an assignor to the assignee about the merits of the assignment.

An assignor has legal responsibilities in making assignments. She cannot blithely assign the same interests pell-mell and escape liability. Unless the contract explicitly states to the contrary, a person who assigns a right for value makes certain **assignor's warranties** to the assignee: that he will not upset the assignment, that he has the right to make it, and that there are no defenses that will defeat it. However, the assignor does not guarantee payment; assignment does not by itself amount to a warranty that the obligor is solvent or will perform as agreed in the original contract. Mrs. Robinson owes Ben fifty dollars. Ben assigns this sum to his friend. Before the friend collects, Ben releases Mrs. Robinson from her obligation. The friend may sue Ben for the fifty dollars. Or again, if Ben represents to his friend that Mrs. Robinson owes him (Ben) fifty dollars and assigns his friend that amount, but in fact Mrs. Robinson does not owe Ben that much, then Ben has breached his assignor's warranty. The assignor's warranties may be express or implied.

Key Takeaway

Generally, it is OK for an obligee to assign the right to receive contractual performance from the obligor to a third party. The effect of the assignment is to make the assignee stand in the shoes of the assignor, taking all the latter's rights and all the defenses against nonperformance that the obligor might raise against the assignor. But the obligor may agree in advance to waive defenses against the assignee, unless such waiver is prohibited by law.

There are some exceptions to the rule that contract rights are assignable. Some, such as personal rights, are not circumstances where the obligor's duties would materially change, cases where assignability is forbidden by statute or public policy, or, with some limits, cases where the contract itself prohibits assignment. Partial assignments and successive assignments can happen, and rules govern the resolution of problems arising from them.

When the assignor makes the assignment, that person makes certain warranties, express or implied, to the assignee, basically to the effect that the assignment is good and the assignor knows of no reason why the assignee will not get performance from the obligor.

Exercises

1. If Able makes a valid assignment to Baker of his contract to receive monthly rental payments from Tenant, how is Baker's right different from what Able's was?
2. Able made a valid assignment to Baker of his contract to receive monthly purchase payments from Carr, who bought an automobile from Able. The car had a 180-day warranty, but the car malfunctioned within that time. Able had quit the auto business entirely. May Carr withhold payments from Baker to offset the cost of needed repairs?
3. Assume in the case in Exercise 2 that Baker knew Able was selling defective cars just before his (Able's) withdrawal from the auto business. How, if at all, does that change Baker's rights?
4. Why are leases generally not assignable? Why are insurance contracts not assignable?

14.2 Delegation of Duties

Learning Objectives

1. Know what a delegation of duty is.
2. Recognize how liability remains on the delegator following a delegation.
3. Understand what duties may not be delegated.

Basic Rules Regarding Delegation

General Rule

delegation

The passing or delivering by one person to another of the duty to perform a contract.

delegator

One who delegates.

delegatee

One to whom the duty to perform a contract is delegated.

To this point, we have been considering the assignment of the assignor's rights (usually, though not solely, to money payments). But in every contract, a right connotes a corresponding duty, and these may be delegated. A **delegation** is the transfer to a third party of the duty to perform under a contract. The one who delegates is the **delegator**. Because most obligees are also obligors, most assignments of rights will simultaneously carry with them the delegation of duties. Unless public policy or the contract itself bars the delegation, it is legally enforceable.

In most states, at common law, duties must be expressly delegated. Under Uniform Commercial Code (UCC) Section 2-210(4) and in a minority of states at common law (as illustrated in Section 4, *Rose v. Vulcan Materials Co.*), an assignment of "the contract" or of "all my rights under the contract" is not only an assignment of rights but also a delegation of duties to be performed; by accepting the assignment, the **delegatee** (one to whom the delegation is made) implies a promise to perform the duties. (See Figure 14.3)

FIGURE 14.3 Delegation of Duties

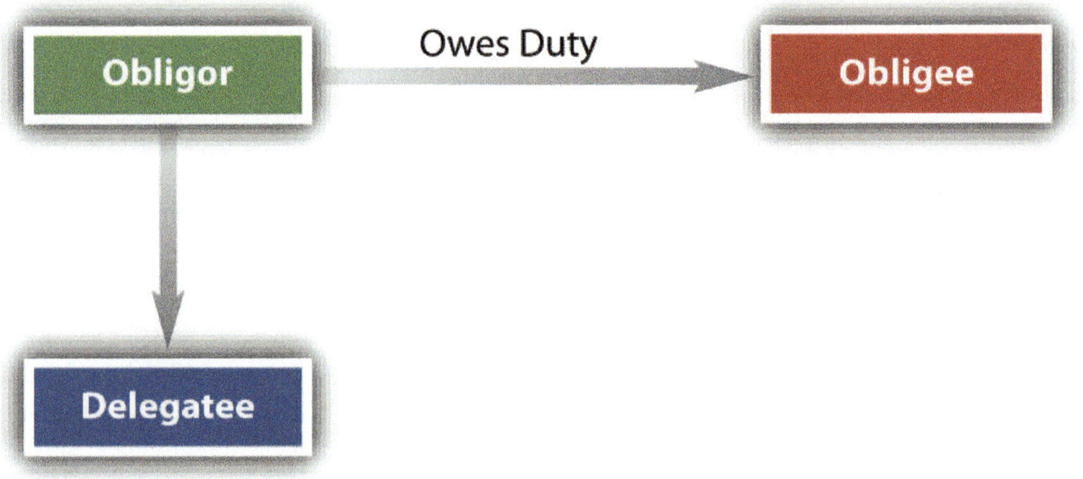

This figure shows how a person who owes a duty—the obligor, on the upper left—may delegate the duty to the delegatee (lower left), who then will perform to the obligee (upper right) in the obligor's stead.

Effect on Obligor

novation

A new contract substituting for an old one, or a new party to a contract replacing a former party.

An obligor who delegates a duty (and becomes a delegator) does not thereby escape liability for performing the duty himself. The obligee of the duty may continue to look to the obligor for performance unless the original contract specifically provides for substitution by delegation. This is a big difference between assignment of contract rights and delegation of contract duties: in the former, the assignor is discharged (absent breach of assignor's warranties); in the latter, the delegator remains liable. The obligee (again, the one to whom the duty to perform flows) may also, in many cases, look to the delegatee, because the obligee becomes an intended beneficiary of the contract between the obligor and the delegatee, as discussed in Section 3. Of course, the obligee may subsequently agree to accept the delegatee and discharge the obligor from any further responsibility for performing the duty. A contract among three persons having this effect is called a **novation**; it is a new contract. Fred sells his house to Lisa, who assumes his mortgage. Fred, in other words, has delegated the duty to pay the bank to Lisa. If Lisa defaults, Fred continues to be liable to the bank, unless in the original mortgage agreement a provision specifically permitted any purchaser to be substituted without recourse to Fred, or unless the bank subsequently accepts Lisa and discharges Fred.

Nondelegable Duties

Personal Services

Personal services are not delegable. If the contract is such that the promisee expects the obligor personally to perform the duty, the obligor may not delegate it. Suppose the Catskill Civic Opera Association hires a famous singer to sing in its production of *Carmen* and the singer delegates the job to her understudy. The delegation is ineffective, and performance by the understudy does not absolve the famous singer of liability for breach. Whether or not a contract calls for personal services is a question of fact.

Many duties may be delegated, however. Indeed, if they could not be delegated, much of the world's work would not get done. If you hire a construction company and an architect to design and build your house to certain specifications, the contractor may in turn hire individual craftspeople—plumbers, electricians, and the like—to do these specialized jobs, and as long as they are performed to specification, the contract terms will have been met. If you hired an architecture firm, though, you might not be contracting for the specific services of a particular individual in that firm.

Public Policy

Public policy may prohibit certain kinds of delegations. A public official, for example, may not delegate the duties of her office to private citizens, although various statutes generally permit the delegation of duties to her assistants and subordinates.

Delegations Barred by Contract

As we have already noted, the contract itself may bar assignment. The law generally disfavors restricting the right to assign a benefit, but it will usually uphold a contract provision that prohibits delegation of a duty. Thus, as we have seen, UCC Section 2-210(3) states that in a contract for sale of goods, a provision against assigning "the contract" is to be construed only as a prohibition against delegating the duties.

Key Takeaway

The duty to perform a contractual obligation may usually be delegated to a third party. Such delegation, however, does not discharge the delegator, who remains liable on the contract absent a novation.

Some duties may not be delegated: personal services cannot be, and public policy or the contract itself may bar delegation.

Exercises

1. What is the difference between an assignment and a delegation?
2. Under what circumstances is the delegator discharged from liability on the contract?

14.3 Third-Party Beneficiaries

Learning Objectives

1. Know what a third-party beneficiary is, and what the types of such beneficiaries are.
2. Recognize the rights obtained by third-party beneficiaries.
3. Understand when the public might be a third-party beneficiary of government contracts.

The fundamental issue with third-party beneficiaries gets to this: can a person who is not a party to a contract sue to enforce its terms?

The General Rule

privity

The relationship of the immediate parties to a contract, a "private" relationship, as between retailer and customer.

The general rule is this: persons not a party to a contract cannot enforce its terms; they are said to lack **privity**, a private, face-to-face relationship with the contracting parties. But if the persons are *intended* to benefit from the performance of a contract between others, then they can enforce it: they are intended beneficiaries.

Two Types of Third-Party Intended Beneficiaries

intended beneficiary

A person not a party to a contract who was intended to benefit from it and who may sue to enforce its terms.

In the vocabulary of the Restatement, a third person whom the parties to the contract intend to benefit is an **intended beneficiary**—that is, one who is entitled under the law of contracts to assert a right arising from a contract to which he or she is not a party. There are two types of intended beneficiaries.

Creditor Beneficiary

creditor beneficiary

One whom the party paying for the other's performance intends to benefit as payment for a debt or obligation.

A **creditor beneficiary** is one to whom the promisor agrees to pay a debt or perform an obligation owed to the promisee. For example, a father is bound by law to support his child. If the child's uncle (the promisor) contracts with the father (the promisee) to furnish support for the child, the child is a creditor beneficiary and could sue the uncle. Or again, suppose Customer pays Ace Dealer for a new car, and Ace delegates the duty of delivery to Beta Dealer. Ace is now a debtor: he owes Customer something: a car. Customer is a creditor; she is owed something: a car. When Beta performs under its delegated contract with Ace, Beta is discharging the debt Ace owes to Customer. Customer is a creditor beneficiary of Dealers' contract and could sue either one for nondelivery. She could sue Ace because she made a contract with it, and she could sue Beta because—again—she was intended to benefit from the performance of Dealers' agreement.

Donee Beneficiary

The second type of intended beneficiary is a **donee beneficiary**. When the promisee is not indebted to the third person but intends for him or her to have the benefit of the promisor's performance, the third person is a donee beneficiary (and the promise is sometimes called a gift promise). For example, an insurance company (the promisor) promises to its policyholder (the promisee), in return for a premium, to pay $100,000 to his wife on his death; this makes the wife a donee beneficiary (see Figure 14.1). The wife could sue to enforce the contract although she was not a party to it. Or if Able makes a contract with Woodsman for the latter to cut the trees in Able's backyard as a Christmas gift to Able's uphill Neighbor (so that Neighbor will have a view), Neighbor could sue Woodsman for breach of the contract.

donee beneficiary

A person not a party to a contract who is intended, as a gift, to benefit from its performance.

If a person is not an intended beneficiary—not a creditor or donee beneficiary—then he or she is said to be only an **incidental beneficiary**, and that person has no rights. So if Able makes the contract with Woodsman not to benefit Neighbor but for Able's own benefit, the fact that the tree removal would benefit Neighbor does not make Neighbor an intended beneficiary.

incidental beneficiary

A person not a party to a contract who benefits from its performance but was not intended to specifically.

The beneficiary's rights are always limited by the terms of the contract. A failure by the promisee to perform his part of the bargain will terminate the beneficiary's rights if the promisee's lapse terminates his own rights, absent language in the contract to the contrary. If Able makes the contract as a gift to Neighbor but doesn't make the required down payment to Woodsman, Neighbor's claim fails. In a suit by the beneficiary, the promisor may avail himself of any defense he could have asserted against the promisee. Woodsman may defend himself against Neighbor's claim that Woodsman did not do the whole job by showing that Able didn't make full payment for the work.

Modification of the Beneficiary's Rights

Conferring rights on an intended beneficiary is relatively simple. Whether his rights can be modified or extinguished by subsequent agreement of the promisor and promisee is a more troublesome issue. The general rule is that the beneficiary's rights may be altered as long as there has been no **vesting of rights** (the rights have not taken effect). The time at which the beneficiary's rights vest differs among jurisdictions: some say immediately, some say when the beneficiary assents to the receipt of the contract right, some say the beneficiary's rights don't vest until she has detrimentally relied on the right. The Restatement says that unless the contract provides that its terms cannot be changed without the beneficiary's consent, the parties may change or rescind the benefit unless the beneficiary has sued on the promise, has detrimentally relied, or has assented to the promise at the request of one of the parties.[4] Some contracts provide that the benefit never vests; for example, standard insurance policies today reserve to the insured the right to substitute beneficiaries, to borrow against the policy, to assign it, and to surrender it for cash.

vesting of rights

The time at which the benefit of a contract is fixed in the beneficiary.

Government Contracts

The general rule is that members of the public are only incidental beneficiaries of contracts made by the government with a contractor to do public works. It is not illogical to see a contract between the government and a company pledged to perform a service on behalf of the public as one creating rights in particular members of the public, but the consequences of such a view could be extremely costly because everyone has some interest in public works and government services.

A restaurant chain, hearing that the county was planning to build a bridge that would reroute commuter traffic, might decide to open a restaurant on one side of the bridge; if it let contracts for construction only to discover that the bridge was to be delayed or canceled, could it sue the county's contractor? In general, the answer is that it cannot. A promisor under contract to the government is not liable for the consequential damages to a member of the public arising from its failure to perform (or from a faulty performance) unless the agreement specifically calls for such liability or unless the promisee (the government) would itself be liable and a suit directly against the promisor would be consistent with the contract terms and public policy. When the government retains control over litigation or settlement of claims, or when it is easy for the public to insure itself against loss, or when the number and amount of claims would be excessive, the courts are less likely to declare individuals to be intended beneficiaries. But the service to be provided can be so tailored to the needs of particular persons that it makes sense to view them as intended beneficiaries—in the case, for example, of a service station licensed to perform emergency road repairs, as in Section 4, *Kornblut v. Chevron Oil Co.*

Key Takeaway

Generally, a person who is not a party to a contract cannot sue to enforce its terms. The exception is if the person is an intended beneficiary, either a creditor beneficiary or a donee beneficiary. Such third parties can enforce the contract made by others but only get such rights as the contract provides, and beneficiaries are subject to defenses that could be made against their benefactor.

The general rule is that members of the public are not intended beneficiaries of contracts made by the government, but only incidental beneficiaries.

Exercises

1. What are the two types of intended beneficiaries?
2. Smith contracted to deliver a truck on behalf of Truck Sales to Byers, who had purchased it from Truck Sales. Smith was entitled to payment by Byers for the delivery. The truck was defective. May Byers withhold payment from Smith to offset the repair costs?
3. Why is the public not usually considered an intended beneficiary of contracts made by the government?

14.4 Cases

Nonassignable Rights

Nassau Hotel Co. v. Barnett & Barse Corporation

147 N.Y.S. 283 (1914)

McLaughlin, J.

Plaintiff owns a hotel at Long Beach, L. I., and on the 21st of November, 1912, it entered into a written agreement with the individual defendants Barnett and Barse to conduct the same for a period of years. * * * Shortly after this agreement was signed, Barnett and Barse organized the Barnett & Barse Corporation with a capital stock of $10,000 [about $240,000 in 2016], and then assigned the agreement to it. Immediately following the assignment, the corporation went into possession and assumed to carry out its terms. The plaintiff thereupon brought this action to cancel the agreement and to recover possession of the hotel and furniture therein, on the ground that the agreement was not assignable. [Summary judgment in favor of the plaintiff, defendant corporation appeals.]

The only question presented is whether the agreement was assignable. It provided, according to the allegations of the complaint, that the plaintiff leased the property to Barnett and Barse with all its equipment and furniture for a period of three years, with a privilege of five successive renewals of three years each. It expressly provided:

"'That said lessees...become responsible for the operation of the said hotel and for the upkeep and maintenance thereof and of all its furniture and equipment in accordance with the terms of this agreement and the said lessees shall have the exclusive possession, control and management thereof. * * * The said lessees hereby covenant and agree that they will operate the said hotel at all times in a first-class business-like manner, keep the same open for at least six (6) months of each year, * * * and in lieu of rental the lessor and lessees hereby covenant and agree that the gross receipts of such operation shall be, as received, divided between the parties hereto as follows: (a) Nineteen per cent. (19%) to the lessor. * * * In the event of the failure of the lessees well and truly to perform the covenants and agreements herein contained, they [will] be liable in the sum of $50,000 [about $1.2 million in 2016] as liquidated damages. That in consideration and upon condition that the said lessees shall well and faithfully perform all the covenants and agreements by them to be performed without evasion or delay the said lessor for itself and its successors, covenants and agrees that the said lessees, their legal representatives and assigns may at all times during said term and the renewals thereof peaceably have and enjoy the said demised premises. This agreement shall inure to the benefit of and bind the respective parties hereto, their personal representatives, successors and assigns."

The complaint further alleges that the agreement was entered into by plaintiff in reliance upon the financial responsibility of Barnett and Barse, their personal character, and especially the experience of Barnett in conducting hotels; that, though he at first held a controlling interest in the Barnett & Barse Corporation, he has since sold all his stock to the defendant Barse, and has no interest in the corporation and no longer devotes any time or attention to the management or operation of the hotel.

* * * [C]learly * * * the agreement in question was personal to Barnett and Barse and could not be assigned by them without the plaintiff's consent. By its terms the plaintiff not only entrusted them with the care and management of the hotel and its furnishings—valued, according to the allegations of the complaint, at more than $1,000,000—but agreed to accept as rental or compensation a percentage of the gross receipts. Obviously, the receipts depended to a large extent upon the management, and the care of the property upon the personal character and responsibility of the persons in possession. When the whole agreement is read, it is apparent that the plaintiff relied, in making it, upon the personal covenants of Barnett and Barse. They were financially responsible. As already said, Barnett had had a long and successful experience in managing hotels, which was undoubtedly an inducing cause for plaintiff's making the agreement in question and for personally obligating them to carry out its terms.

It is suggested that because there is a clause in the agreement to the effect that it should "inure to the benefit of and bind the respective parties hereto, their personal representatives and assigns," that Barnett and Barse had a right to assign it to the corporation. But the intention of the parties is to be gathered, not from one clause, but from the entire instrument [Citation] and when it is thus read it clearly appears that Barnett and Barse were to personally carry out the terms of the agreement and did not have a right to assign it. This follows from the language used, which shows that a personal trust or confidence was reposed by the plaintiff in Barnett and Barse when the agreement was made.

In [Citation] it was said: "Rights arising out of contract cannot be transferred if they * * * involve a relation of personal confidence such that the party whose agreement conferred those rights must have intended them to be exercised only by him in whom he actually confided."

This rule was applied in [Citation] the court holding that the plaintiff—the assignee—was not only technically, but substantially, a different entity from its predecessor, and that the defendant was not obliged to entrust its money collected on the sale of the presses to the responsibility of an entirely different corporation from that with which it had contracted, and that the contract could not be assigned to the plaintiff without the assent of the other party to it.

The reason which underlies the basis of the rule is that a party has the right to the benefit contemplated from the character, credit, and substance of him with whom he contracts, and in such case he is not bound to recognize * * * an assignment of the contract.

The order appealed from, therefore, is affirmed.

Case Questions

1. The corporation created to operate the hotel was apparently owned and operated by the same two men the plaintiff leased the hotel to in the first place. What objection would the plaintiff have to the corporate entity—actually, of course, a legal fiction—owning and operating the hotel?
2. The defendants pointed to the clause about the contract inuring to the benefit of the parties "and assigns." So the defendants assigned the contract. How could that *not* be allowed by the contract's own terms?
3. What is the controlling rule of law upon which the outcome here depends?

Assignment Includes Delegation

Rose v. Vulcan Materials Co.
194 S.E.2d 521 (N.C. 1973)

Huskins, J.

Plaintiff [Rose], after leasing his quarry to J. E. Dooley and Son, Inc., promised not to engage in the rock-crushing business within an eight-mile radius of [the city of] Elkin for a period of ten years. In return for this promise, J. E. Dooley and Son, Inc., promised, among other things, to furnish plaintiff stone f.o.b. the quarry site at Cycle, North Carolina, at stipulated prices for ten years. * * *

By a contract effective 23 April 1960, Vulcan Materials Company, a corporation, * * * purchased the stone quarry operations and the assets and obligations of J. E. Dooley and Son, Inc. * * * [Vulcan sent Rose a letter, part of which read:]

> *Mr. Dooley brought to us this morning the contracts between you and his companies, copies of which are attached. This is to advise that Vulcan Materials Company assumes all phases of these contracts and intends to carry out the conditions of these contracts as they are stated.*

In early 1961 Vulcan notified plaintiff that it would no longer sell stone to him at the prices set out in [the agreement between Rose and Dooley] and would thereafter charge plaintiff the same prices charged all of its other customers for stone. Commencing 11 May 1961, Vulcan raised stone prices to the plaintiff to a level in excess of the prices specified in [the Rose-Dooley agreement].

At the time Vulcan increased the prices of stone to amounts in excess of those specified in [the Rose-Dooley contract], plaintiff was engaged in his ready-mix cement business, using large quantities of stone, and had no other practical source of supply. Advising Vulcan that he intended to sue for breach of contract, he continued to purchase stone from Vulcan under protest. * * *

The total of these amounts over and above the prices specified in [the Rose-Dooley contract] is $25,231.57, [about $201,000 in 2010 dollars] and plaintiff seeks to recover said amount in this action.

The [Rose-Dooley] agreement was an executory bilateral contract under which plaintiff's promise not to compete for ten years gained him a ten-year option to buy stone at specified prices. In most states, the assignee of an executory bilateral contract is not liable to anyone for the nonperformance of the assignor's duties thereunder unless he expressly promises his assignor or the other contracting party to perform, or 'assume,' such duties. * * * These states refuse to imply a promise to perform the duties, but if the assignee expressly promises his assignor to perform, he is liable to the other contracting party on a third-party beneficiary theory. And, if the assignee makes such a promise directly to the other contracting party upon a consideration, of course he is liable to him thereon. [Citation]

A minority of states holds that the assignee of an executory bilateral contract under a general assignment becomes not only assignee of the rights of the assignor but also delegatee of his duties; and that, absent a showing of contrary intent, the assignee impliedly promises the assignor that he will perform the duties so delegated. This rule is expressed in Restatement, Contracts, s 164 (1932) as follows:

> *(1) Where a party under a bilateral contract which is at the time wholly or partially executory on both sides purports to assign the whole contract, his action is interpreted, in the absence of circumstances showing a contrary intention, as an assignment of the assignor's rights under the contract and a delegation of the performance of the assignor's duties.*
>
> *(2) Acceptance by the assignee of such an assignment is interpreted, in the absence of circumstances showing a contrary intention, as both an assent to become an assignee of the assignor's rights and as* **a promise to the assignor to assume the performance of the assignor's duties**.*' (emphasis added)*

We adopt the Restatement rule and expressly hold that the assignee under a general assignment of an executory bilateral contract, in the absence of circumstances showing a contrary intention, becomes the delegatee of his assignor's duties and impliedly promises his assignor that he will perform such duties.

The rule we adopt and reaffirm here is regarded as the more reasonable view by legal scholars and textwriters. Professor Grismore says:

> *It is submitted that the acceptance of an assignment in this form does presumptively import a tacit promise on the part of the assignee to assume the burdens of the contract, and that this presumption should prevail in the absence of the clear showing of a contrary intention. The presumption seems reasonable in view of the evident expectation of the parties. The assignment on its face indicates an intent to do more than simply to transfer the benefits assured by the contract. It purports to transfer the contract as a whole, and since the contract is made up of both benefits and burdens both must be intended to be included.... Grismore, Is the Assignee of a Contract Liable for the Nonperformance of Delegated Duties? 18 Mich.L.Rev. 284 (1920).*

In addition, with respect to transactions governed by the Uniform Commercial Code, an assignment of a contract in general terms is a delegation of performance of the duties of the assignor, and its acceptance by the assignee constitutes a promise by him to perform those duties. Our holding in this case maintains a desirable uniformity in the field of contract liability.

We further hold that the other party to the original contract may sue the assignee as a third-party beneficiary of his promise of performance which he impliedly makes to his assignor, under the rule above laid down, by accepting the general assignment. *Younce v. Lumber Co.*, [Citation] (1908), holds that where the assignee makes an express promise of performance to his assignor, the other contracting party may sue him for breach thereof. We see no reason why the same result should not obtain where the assignee breaches his promise of performance implied under the rule of Restatement s 164. "That the assignee is liable at the suit of the third party where he expressly assumes and promises to perform delegated duties has already been decided in a few cases (citing Younce). If an express promise will support such an action it is difficult to see why a tacit promise should not have the same effect." Grismore, supra. Parenthetically, we note that such is the rule under the Uniform Commercial Code, [2-210].

We now apply the foregoing principles to the case at hand. The contract of 23 April 1960, between defendant and J. E. Dooley and Son, Inc., under which, as stipulated by the parties, "the defendant purchased the assets and obligations of J. E. Dooley and Son, Inc.," was a general assignment of all the assets and obligations of J. E. Dooley and Son, Inc., including those under [the Rose-Dooley contract]. When defendant accepted such assignment it thereby became delegatee of its assignor's duties under it and impliedly promised to perform such duties.

When defendant later failed to perform such duties by refusing to continue sales of stone to plaintiff at the prices specified in [the Rose-Dooley contract], it breached its implied promise of performance and plaintiff was entitled to bring suit thereon as a third-party beneficiary.

The decision is reversed with directions that the case be certified to the Superior Court of Forsyth County for reinstatement of the judgment of the trial court in accordance with this opinion.

Case Questions

1. Why did Rose need the crushed rock from the quarry he originally leased to Dooley?
2. What argument did Vulcan make as to why it should not be liable to sell crushed rock to Rose at the price set out in the Rose-Dooley contract?
3. What rule did the court here announce in deciding that Vulcan was required to sell rock at the price set out in the Rose-Dooley contract? That is, what is the controlling rule of law in this case?

Third party Beneficiaries and Foreseeable Damages

Kornblut v. Chevron Oil Co.
62 A.D.2d 831 (N.Y. 1978)

Hopkins, J.

The plaintiff-respondent has recovered a judgment after a jury trial in the sum of $519,855.98 [about $3.5 million in 2016 dollars] including interest, costs and disbursements, against Chevron Oil Company (Chevron) and Lawrence Ettinger, Inc. (Ettinger) (hereafter collectively referred to as defendants) for damages arising from the death and injuries suffered by Fred Kornblut, her husband. The case went to the jury on the theory that the decedent was the third-party beneficiary of a contract between Chevron and the New York State Thruway Authority and a contract between Chevron and Ettinger.

On the afternoon of an extremely warm day in early August, 1970 the decedent was driving northward on the New York State Thruway. Near Sloatsburg, New York, at about 3:00 p.m., his automobile sustained a flat tire. At the time the decedent was accompanied by his wife and 12-year-old son. The decedent waited for assistance in the 92 degree temperature.

After about an hour a State Trooper, finding the disabled car, stopped and talked to the decedent. The trooper radioed Ettinger, which had the exclusive right to render service on the Thruway under an assignment of a contract between Chevron and the Thruway Authority. Thereafter, other State Troopers reported the disabled car and the decedent was told in each instance that he would receive assistance within 20 minutes.

Having not received any assistance by 6:00 p.m., the decedent attempted to change the tire himself. He finally succeeded, although he experienced difficulty and complained of chest pains to the point that his wife and son were compelled to lift the flat tire into the trunk of the automobile. The decedent drove the car to the next service area, where he was taken by ambulance to a hospital; his condition was later diagnosed as a myocardial infarction [heart attack]. He died 28 days later.

Plaintiff sued, *inter alia*, Chevron and Ettinger alleging in her complaint causes of action sounding in negligence and breach of contract. We need not consider the issue of negligence, since the Trial Judge instructed the jury only on the theory of breach of contract, and the plaintiff has recovered damages for wrongful death and the pain and suffering only on that theory.

We must look, then, to the terms of the contract sought to be enforced. Chevron agreed to provide "rapid and efficient roadside automotive service on a 24-hour basis from each gasoline service station facility for the areas * * * when informed by the authority or its police personnel of a disabled vehicle on the Thruway." Chevron's vehicles are required "to be used and operated in such a manner as will produce adequate service to the public, as determined in the authority's sole judgment and discretion." Chevron specifically covenanted that it would have "sufficient roadside automotive service vehicles, equipment and personnel to provide roadside automotive service to disabled vehicles within a maximum of thirty (30) minutes from the time a call is assigned to a service vehicle, subject to unavoidable delays due to extremely adverse weather conditions or traffic conditions." * * *

In interpreting the contract, we must bear in mind the circumstances under which the parties bargained. The New York Thruway is a limited access toll highway, designed to move traffic at the highest legal speed, with the north and south lanes separated by green strips. Any disabled vehicle on the road impeding the flow of traffic may be a hazard and inconvenience to the other users. The income realized from tolls is generated from the expectation of the user that he will be able to travel swiftly and smoothly along the Thruway. Consequently, it is in the interest of the authority that disabled vehicles will be repaired or removed quickly to the end that any hazard and inconvenience will be minimized. Moreover, the design and purpose of the highway make difficult, if not impossible, the summoning of aid from garages not located on the Thruway. The movement of a large number of vehicles at high speed creates a risk to the operator of a vehicle who attempts to make his own repairs, as well as to the other users. These considerations clearly prompted the making of contracts with service organizations which would be located at points near in distance and time on the Thruway for the relief of distressed vehicles.

Thus, it is obvious that, although the authority had an interest in making provision for roadside calls through a contract, there was also a personal interest of the user served by the contract. Indeed, the contract provisions regulating the charges for calls and commanding refunds be paid directly to the user for overcharges, evince a protection and benefit extended to the user only. Hence, in the event of an overcharge, the user would be enabled to sue on the contract to obtain a recovery. * * * Here the contract contemplates an individual benefit for the breach running to the user. * * *

By choosing the theory of recovery based on contract, it became incumbent on the plaintiff to show that the injury was one which the defendants had reason to foresee as a probable result of the breach, under the ancient doctrine of *Hadley v. Baxendale* [Citation], and the cases following it * * * in distinction to the requirement of proximate cause in tort actions. * * *

The death of the decedent on account of his exertion in the unusual heat of the midsummer day in changing the tire cannot be said to have been within the contemplation of the contracting parties as a reasonably foreseeable result of the failure of Chevron or its assignee to comply with the contract. * * *

The case comes down to this, then, in our view: though the decedent was the intended beneficiary to sue under certain provisions of the contract—such as the rate specified for services to be rendered—he was not the intended beneficiary to sue for consequential damages arising from personal injury because of a failure to render service promptly. Under these circumstances, the judgment must be reversed and the complaint dismissed, without costs or disbursements.

[Martuscello, J., concurred in the result but opined that the traveling public was not an intended beneficiary of the contract.]

Case Questions

1. Chevron made two arguments as to why it should not be liable for Mr. Kornblut's death. What were they?
2. Obviously, when Chevron made the contract with the New York State Thruway Authority, it did not know Mr. Kornblut was going to be using the highway. How could he, then, be an intended beneficiary of the contract?
3. Why was Chevron not found liable for Mr. Kornblut's death when, clearly, had it performed the contract properly, he would not have died?

14.5 Summary and Exercises

Summary

The general rule that the promisee may assign any right has some exceptions—for example, when the promisor's obligation would be materially changed. Of course the contract itself may prohibit assignment, and sometimes statutes preclude it. Knowing how to make the assignment effective and what the consequences of the assignment are on others is worth mastering. When, for example, does the assignee not stand in the assignor's shoes? When may a future right be assigned?

Duties, as well as rights, may be transferred to third parties. Most rights (promises) contained in contracts have corresponding duties (also expressed as promises). Often when an entire contract is assigned, the duties go with it; the transferee is known, with respect to the duties, as the delegatee. The transferor himself does not necessarily escape the duty, however. Moreover, some duties are nondelegable, such as personal promises and those that public policy require to be carried out by a particular official. Without the ability to assign rights and duties, much of the modern economy would grind to a halt.

The parties to a contract are not necessarily the only people who acquire rights or duties under it. One major category of persons acquiring rights is third-party beneficiaries. Only intended beneficiaries acquire rights under the contract, and these are of two types: creditor and donee beneficiaries. The rules for determining whether rights have been conferred are rather straightforward; determining whether rights can subsequently be modified or extinguished is more troublesome. Generally, as long as the contract does not prohibit change and as long as the beneficiary has not relied on the promise, the change may be made.

Exercises

1. The Dayton Country Club offered its members various social activities. Some members were entitled, for additional payment, to use the golf course, a coveted amenity. Golfing memberships could not be transferred except upon death or divorce, and there was a long waiting list in this special category; if a person at the top of the list declined, the next in line was eligible. Golfing membership rules were drawn up by a membership committee. Magness and Redman were golfing members. They declared bankruptcy, and the bankruptcy trustee sought, in order to increase the value of their debtors' estates, to assume and sell the golfing memberships to members on the waiting list, other club members, or the general public, provided the persons joined the club. The club asserted that under relevant state law, it was "excused from rendering performance to an entity other than the debtor"—that is, it could not be forced to accept strangers as members. Can these memberships be assigned?
2. Tenant leased premises in Landlord's shopping center, agreeing in the lease "not to assign, mortgage, pledge, or encumber this lease in whole or in part." Under the lease, Tenant was entitled to a construction allowance of up to $11,000 after Tenant made improvements for its uses. Prior to the completion of the improvements, Tenant assigned its right to receive the first $8,000 of the construction allowance to Assignee, who, in turn, provided Tenant $8,000 to finance the construction. Assignee notified Landlord of the assignment, but when the construction was complete, Landlord paid Tenant anyway; when Assignee complained, Landlord pointed to the nonassignment clause. Assignee sued Landlord. Who wins?[5]
3. Marian contracted to sell her restaurant to Billings for $400,000. The contract provided that Billings would pay $100,000 and sign a note for the remainder. Billings sold the restaurant to Alice, who agreed to assume responsibility for the balance due on the note held by Marian. But Alice had difficulties and declared bankruptcy. Is Billings still liable on the note to Marian?
4. Yellow Cab contracted with the Birmingham Board of Education to transport physically handicapped students. The contract provided, "Yellow Cab will transport the physically handicapped students of the School System . . . and furnish all necessary vehicles and personnel and will perform all maintenance and make all repairs to the equipment to keep it in a safe and efficient operating condition at all times."

   Yellow Cab subcontracted with Metro Limousine to provide transportation in connection with its contract with the board. Thereafter, Metro purchased two buses from Yellow Cab to use in transporting the students. DuPont, a Metro employee, was injured when the brakes on the bus that he was driving failed, causing the bus to collide with a tree. DuPont sued Yellow Cab, alleging that under its contract with the board, Yellow Cab had a non-delegable duty to properly maintain the bus so as to keep it in a safe operating condition; that that duty flowed to him as an intended third-party beneficiary of the contract; and that Yellow Cab had breached the contract by failing to properly maintain the bus. Who wins?[6]
5. Joan hired Groom to attend to her herd of four horses at her summer place in the high desert. The job was too much for Groom, so he told Tony that he (Groom) would pay Tony, who claimed expertise in caring for horses, to take over the job. Tony neglected the horses in hot weather, and one of them needed veterinarian care for dehydration. Is Groom liable?
6. Rensselaer Water Company contracted with the city to provide water for business, domestic, and fire-hydrant purposes. While the contract was in effect, a building caught on fire; the fire spread to Plaintiff's (Moch Co.'s) warehouse, destroying it and its contents. The company knew of the fire but was unable to supply adequate water pressure to put it out. Is the owner of the warehouse able to maintain a claim against the company for the loss?
7. Rusty told Alice that he'd do the necessary overhaul on her classic car for $5,000 during the month of May, and that when the job was done, she should send the money to his son, Jim, as a graduation present. He confirmed the agreement in writing and sent a copy to Jim. Subsequently, Rusty changed his mind. What right has Jim?
8. Fox Brothers agreed to convey to Clayton Canfield Lot 23 together with a one-year option to purchase Lot 24 in a subdivision known as Fox Estates. The agreement contained no prohibitions, restrictions, or limitations against assignments. Canfield paid the $20,000 and took title to Lot 23 and the option to Lot 24. Canfield thereafter assigned his option rights in Lot 24 to the Scotts. When the Scotts wanted to exercise the option, Fox Brothers refused to convey the property to them. The Scotts then brought suit for specific performance. Who wins?

9. Rollins sold Byers, a businessperson, a flatbed truck on a contract. Rollins assigned the contract to Frost, and informed Byers of the assignment. Rollins knew the truck had problems, which he did not reveal to Byers. When the truck needed $3,200 worth of repairs and Rollins couldn't be found, Byers wanted to deduct that amount from payments owed to Frost, but Frost insisted he had a right to payment. Upon investigation, Byers discovered that four other people in the state had experienced similar situations with Rollins and with Frost as Rollins's assignee. What recourse has Byers?
10. Merchants and resort owners in the San Juan Islands in Washington State stocked extra supplies, some perishable, in anticipation of the flood of tourists over Labor Day. They suffered inconvenience and monetary damage due to the union's Labor Day strike of the state ferry system, in violation of its collective bargaining agreement with the state and of a temporary restraining order. The owners sued the union for damages for lost profits, attorney fees, and costs, claiming the union should be liable for intentional interference with contractual relations (the owners' relations with their would-be customers). Do the owners have a cause of action?

Self-Test Questions

1. A creditor beneficiary is
    a. the same as a donee beneficiary
    b. a third-party beneficiary
    c. an incidental beneficiary
    d. none of the above
2. Assignments are not allowed
    a. for rights that will arise from a future contract
    b. when they will materially change the duties that the obligor must perform
    c. where they are forbidden by public policy
    d. for any of the above
3. When an assignor assigns the same interest twice,
    a. the subsequent assignee generally takes precedence
    b. the first assignee generally takes precedence
    c. the first assignee always takes precedence
    d. the assignment violates public policy
4. Factoring
    a. is an example of delegation of duties
    b. involves using an account receivable as collateral for a loan
    c. involves the purchase of a right to receive income from another
    d. is all of the above
5. Personal promises
    a. are always delegable
    b. are generally not delegable
    c. are delegable if not prohibited by public policy
    d. are delegable if not barred by the contract

Self-Test Answers

1. b

2. d
3. b
4. c
5. b

Endnotes

1. Restatement (Second) of Contracts, Section 317(1).
2. Uniform Commercial Code, Section 9-206.
3. Restatement (Second) of Contracts, Section 322.
4. Restatement (Second) of Contracts, Section 311.
5. *Aldana v. Colonial Palms Plaza, Inc.*, 591 So.2d 953 (Fla. Ct. App., 1991).
6. *DuPont v. Yellow Cab Co. of Birmingham, Inc.*, 565 So.2d 190 (Ala. 1990).

CHAPTER 15
Discharge of Obligations

Learning Objectives

After reading this chapter, you should understand the following:

1. What is meant by discharge of contract obligations.
2. How contract obligations are discharged.

15.1 Discharge of Contract Duties

Learning Objectives

1. Understand how performance, partial performance, or no performance may discharge contractual obligations.
2. Recognize what rights accrue to the nonbreaching party when the other side announces, before the time for performance, that performance will not be forthcoming—anticipatory breach.
3. Understand the concept of the right to adequate assurances, and the consequences if no such assurances are forthcoming.

A person is liable to perform agreed-to contract duties until or unless he or she is discharged. If the person fails to perform without being discharged, liability for damages arises. Here we deal with the second-to-the-last of the four broad themes of contract law: how contract duties are discharged.

Discharge by Performance (or Nonperformance) of the Duty

A contract can be discharged by complete performance or material nonperformance of the contractual duty. Note, in passing, that the modern trend at common law (and explicit under the Uniform Commercial Code [UCC], Section 1-203) is that the parties have a **good-faith duty** to perform to each other. There is in every contract "an implied covenant of good faith" (honesty in fact in the transaction) that the parties will deal fairly, keep their promises, and not frustrate the other party's reasonable expectations of what was given and what received.

good-faith duty

The duty to act with honesty in fact in commercial transactions.

Full Performance

Full performance of the contractual obligation discharges the duty. If Ralph does a fine job of plumbing Betty's new bathroom, she pays him. Both are discharged.

Nonperformance, Material Breach

If Ralph doesn't do any work at all on Betty's bathroom, or almost none, then Betty owes him nothing. She—the nonbreaching party—is discharged, and Ralph is liable for breach of contract.

cancellation

The termination of a contract by one party in response to its material breach by the other.

termination

The lawful right to end the contract other than for breach.

Under UCC Section 2-106(4), a party that ends a contract breached by the other party is said to have effected a **cancellation**. The cancelling party retains the right to seek a remedy for breach of the whole contract or any unperformed obligation. The UCC distinguishes cancellation from **termination**, which occurs when either party exercises a lawful right to end the contract other than for breach. When a contract is terminated, all executory duties are discharged on both sides, but if there has been a partial breach, the right to seek a remedy survives.[1]

Substantial Performance

substantial performance

At common law, the idea that a promisee should not be denied all payment under a contract when his or her performance was imperfect if significant benefit has been conferred on the promisor, who must pay for the value received.

Logically, anything less than full performance, even a slight deviation from what is owed, is sufficient to prevent the duty from being discharged and can amount to a breach of contract. So if Ralph does all the plumbing for Betty's new bathroom *except* hook up the toilet feed, he has not really "plumbed the new bathroom." He has only plumbed part of it. At classic common law, that was it: either you did the thing you promised completely or you had materially breached. But under modern theories, an ameliorative doctrine has developed, called **substantial performance**: if one side has substantially, but not completely, performed, so that the other side has received a benefit, the nonbreaching party owes something for the value received. The Restatement (Second) of Contracts puts it this way:[2]

> *Substantial performance. In an important category of disputes over failure of performance, one party asserts the right to payment on the ground that he has completed his performance, while the other party refuses to pay on the ground that there is an uncured material failure of performance. . . . In such cases it is common to state the issue . . . in terms of whether there has been substantial performance. . . . If there has been substantial although not full performance, the building contractor has a claim for the unpaid balance and the owner has a claim only for damages. If there has not been substantial performance, the building contractor has no claim for the unpaid balance, although he may have a claim in restitution.*[3]

The contest here is between the one who claims discharge by the other's material breach (failure to perform) and the one who asserts there has been substantial performance. What constitutes substantial performance is a question of fact, as illustrated in Section 2, *TA Operating Corp. v. Solar Applications Engineering, Inc.* The doctrine has no applicability where the breaching party willfully failed to follow the contract, as where a plumber substitutes a different faucet for the one ordered; installation of the incorrect faucet is a breach, even if it is of equal or greater value than the one ordered.

perfect tender

The precise performance of a contractual obligation.

Under the UCC, there is no such thing as substantial performance. Section 2-601 requires that the goods delivered according to the contract be the exact things ordered—that there be a **perfect tender** (unless the parties agree otherwise).

Anticipatory Breach and Demand for Reasonable Assurances

When a promisor announces before the time his performance is due that he will not perform, he is said to have committed an **anticipatory breach (or repudiation)**. Of course a person cannot fail to perform a duty before performance is due, but the law allows the promisee to treat the situation as a material breach that gives rise to a claim for damages and discharges the obligee from performing duties required of him under the contract. The common-law rule was first recognized in the well-known 1853 British case *Hochster v. De La Tour*. In April, De La Tour hired Hochster as his courier, the job to commence in June. In May, De La Tour changed his mind and told Hochster not to bother to report for duty. Before June, Hochster secured an appointment as courier to Lord Ashburton, but that job was not to begin until July. Also in May, Hochster sued De La Tour, who argued that he should not have to pay Hochster because Hochster had not stood ready and willing to begin work in June, having already agreed to work for Lord Ashburton. The court ruled for the plaintiff Hochster:

anticipatory breach (or repudiation)

A communication that informs a party that the obligations of the original contract will not be fulfilled when due; gives rise to an immediate right to sue.

> *[I]t is surely much more rational, and more for the benefit of both parties, that, after the renunciation of the agreement by the defendant, the plaintiff should be at liberty to consider himself absolved from any future performance of it, retaining his right to sue for any damage he has suffered from the breach of it. Thus, instead of remaining idle and laying out money in preparations which must be useless, he is at liberty to seek service under another employer, which would go in mitigation of the damages to which he would otherwise be entitled for a breach of the contract. It seems strange that the defendant, after renouncing the contract, and absolutely declaring that he will never act under it, should be permitted to object that faith is given to his assertion, and that an opportunity is not left to him of changing his mind.*[4]

Another type of anticipatory breach consists of any voluntary act by a party that destroys, or seriously impairs, that party's ability to perform the promise made to the other side. If a seller of land, having agreed to sell a lot to one person at a date certain, sells it instead to a third party before that time, there is an anticipatory breach. If Carpenter announces in May that instead of building Owner's deck in July, as agreed, he is going on a trip to Europe, there is an anticipatory breach. In the first instance, there would be no point to showing up at the lawyer's office when the date arrives to await the deed, so the law gives a right to sue when the land is sold to the other person. In the second instance, there would be no point to waiting until July, when indeed Carpenter does not do the job, so the law gives the right to sue when the future nonperformance is announced.

These same general rules prevail for contracts for the sale of goods under UCC Section 2-610.

Related to the concept of anticipatory breach is the idea that the obligee has a right to demand reasonable assurances from the obligor that contractual duties will be performed. If the obligee makes such a **demand for reasonable assurances** and no adequate assurances are forthcoming, the obligee may assume that the obligor will commit an anticipatory breach, and consider it so. That is, after making the contract, the obligee may come upon the disquieting news that the obligor's ability to perform is shaky. A change in financial condition occurs, an unknown claimant to rights in land appears, a labor strike arises, or any of a number of situations may crop up that will interfere with the carrying out of contractual duties. Under such circumstances, the obligee has the right to a demand for reasonable assurance that the obligor will perform as contractually obligated. The general reason for such a rule is given in UCC Section 2-609(1), which states that a contract "imposes an obligation on each party that the other's expectation of receiving due performance will not be impaired." Moreover, an obligee would be foolish not to make alternative arrangements, if possible, when it becomes obvious that his original obligor will be unable to perform. The obligee must have reasonable grounds to believe that the obligor will breach. The fear must be that of a failure of performance that would amount to a total breach; a minor defect that

demand for reasonable assurances

A demand to be reassured that contractual performance will be forthcoming when reasonable grounds for insecurity arise with respect to the performance of the other party; failure to get such is an anticipatory breach.

can be cured and that at most would give rise to an offset in price for damages will not generally support a demand for assurances.

Under UCC Section 2-609(1), the demand must be in writing, but at common law the demand may be oral if it is reasonable in view of the circumstances. If the obligor fails within a reasonable time to give adequate assurance, the obligee may treat the failure to do so as an anticipatory repudiation, or she may wait to see if the obligor might change his mind and perform.

Key Takeaway

Contracts can be discharged by performance: complete performance discharges both sides; material breach discharges the nonbreaching party, who has a right to claim damages; substantial performance obligates the promisee to pay something for the benefit conferred but is a breach. A party may demand reasonable assurances of performance, which, if not forthcoming, may be treated as an anticipatory breach (or repudiation).

Exercises

1. What types of performance discharge a contractual obligation?
2. Under the UCC, what is the difference between cancellation and termination of a contract?
3. What is an anticipatory breach, and under what circumstances can a party claim it?

Discharge by Conditions

Learning Objectives

1. Understand the concept of conditions in a contract.
2. Recognize that conditions can be classified on the basis of how they are created, their effect on the duty to perform, the essentialness of timely performance, or performance to someone's satisfaction.

Usually contracts consist of an exchange of promises—a pledge or commitment by each party that somebody will or will not do something. Andy's promise to cut Anne's lawn "over the weekend" in return for Anne's promise to pay twenty-five dollars is a commitment to have the lawn mowed by Sunday night or Monday morning. Andy's promise "not to tell anyone what I saw you doing Saturday night" in return for Anne's promise to pay one hundred dollars is a commitment that an event (the revealing of a secret) will not occur. These promises are known as independent or absolute or unconditional, because their performance does not depend on any outside event. Such promises, if contractually binding, create a present duty to perform (or a duty to perform at the time stated).

However, it is common that the obligation to perform a contract is conditioned (or conditional). A **condition** is an event, the happening or nonhappening of which gives rise to a duty to perform (or discharges a duty to perform). Conditions may be express or implied; they may also be precedent, concurrent, subsequent, or to the satisfaction of a party.

condition

An uncertain future act or event whose occurrence or nonoccurrence determines the rights or obligations of a party under a legal instrument, especially a contract.

Conditions Classified Based on How They Are Created

Express conditions are stated in words in the contract, orally or written. Andy promises to mow Anne's lawn "provided it doesn't rain." "Provided it doesn't rain" is an express condition. If rain comes, there is no duty to cut the lawn, and Andy's failure to do so is not a breach of promise. Express conditions are usually introduced by language such as "provided that," "if," "when," "assuming that," "as soon as," "after," and the like. **Implied conditions** are unexpressed but understood to be part of the contract. If Mr. Olson guarantees Jack's used car for ninety days, it is implied that his obligation to fix any defects doesn't arise until Jack lets him know the car is defective. If Ralph is hired to plumb Betty's new bathroom, it is implied that Betty's duty to pay is conditioned on Ralph's completion of the job.

Express conditions

A condition in words, oral or in writing.

Implied conditions

A provision not explicitly stated in an agreement but considered an important item.

Conditions Classified Based on Their Effect on Duty to Perform

A condition precedent is a term in a contract (express or implied) that requires performance only in the event something else happens first. Jack will buy a car from Mr. Olson if Jack gets financing. "If Jack gets financing" is a condition precedent. A **concurrent condition** arises when the duty to perform the contract is simultaneous: the promise of a landowner to transfer title to the purchaser and the purchaser to tender payment to the seller. The duty of each to perform is conditioned on the performance by the other. (As a practical matter, of course, somebody has to make the first move, proffering deed or tendering the check.) A condition that terminates an already existing duty of performance is known as a **condition subsequent**. Ralph agrees to do preventive plumbing maintenance on Deborah Dairy's milking equipment for as long as David Dairy, Deb's husband, is stationed overseas. When David returns, Ralph's obligation to do the maintenance (and Deb's duty to pay him) terminates.

concurrent condition

A condition that is to be fulfilled by one party at the same time that a mutual condition is to be fulfilled by another party.

condition subsequent

An event that terminates an existing duty of performance.

Condition of Timeliness

If, as often occurs, it does not matter a great deal whether a contract is performed exactly on time, failure to do so is not a material breach, and the promisee has to accept the performance and deduct any losses caused by the delay. If, though, it makes a difference to the promisee whether the promisor acts on time, then it is said that "**time is of the essence**." Time as a condition can be made explicit in a clause reciting that time is of the essence. If there is no express clause, the courts will read it in when the purpose of the contract was clearly to provide for performance at or by a certain time, and the promisee will gain little or nothing from late performance. But even express clauses are subject to a rule of reason, and if the promisor would suffer greatly by enforcement of the clause (and the promisee would suffer only slightly or not at all from a refusal to invoke it), the courts will generally excuse the untimely performance, as long as it was completed within a reasonable time. A builder's failure to finish a house by July 1 will not discharge the buyer's obligation to pay if the house is finished a week or even a month later, although the builder will be liable to the buyer for expenses incurred because of the lateness (storage charges for furniture, costs for housing during the interim, extra travel, and the like).

time is of the essence

A clause asserting that any tardy performance is a material breach, discharging the nonbreaching party.

Condition That a Party Must Be Satisfied

"You must be satisfied or your money back" is a common advertisement. A party to a contract can require that he need not pay or otherwise carry out his undertaking unless satisfied by the obligor's performance, or unless a third party is satisfied by the performance.

Parties may contract to perform to one side's personal satisfaction. Andy tells Anne, a prospective client, that he will cut her hair better than her regular hairdresser, and that if she is not satisfied, she need not pay him. Andy cuts her hair, but Anne frowns and says, "I don't like it." Assume that Andy's work is excellent. Whether Anne must pay depends on the standard for judging to be employed—a standard of objective or subjective satisfaction. The objective standard is that which would satisfy the reasonable purchaser. Most courts apply this standard when the contract involves the performance of a mechanical job or the sale of a machine whose performance is capable of objective measurement. So even if the obligee requires performance to his "personal satisfaction," the courts will hold that the obligor has performed if the service performed or the goods produced are in fact satisfactory. By contrast, if the goods or services contracted for involve personal judgment and taste, the duty to pay will be discharged if the obligee states personal (subjective) dissatisfaction. No reason at all need be given, but it must be for a good-faith reason, not just to escape payment.

The duty to make a contract payment may be conditioned on the satisfaction of a third party. Building contracts frequently make the purchaser's duty to pay conditional on the builder's receipt of an architect's certificate of compliance with all contractual terms; road construction contracts often require that the work be done "to the satisfaction of the County Engineer." These conditions can be onerous. The builder has already erected the structure and cannot "return" what he has done. Nevertheless, because the purchaser wants assurance that the building (obviously a major purchase) or road meets his specifications, the courts will hold the contractor to the condition unless it is impossible to provide a certificate (e.g., architect may have died) or the architect has acted in bad faith, or the purchaser has somehow prevented the certificate from issuing. The third party's refusal to issue a certificate needs to be reasonable.

Key Takeaway

Parties may, expressly or implicitly, condition the requirement for contractual performance on the happening or nonhappening of an event, or on timeliness. They may condition performance on satisfaction to one of the parties to the contract or to the satisfaction of a third party; in any event, dissatisfaction must be in good faith.

Exercises

1. What is "conditioned" by a condition in a contract?
2. What conditions are based on how they are made?
3. What conditions are based on their effect on the duty of performance?
4. What typical situations involve performance to a party's satisfaction?

Discharge by Agreement of the Parties

Learning Objective

1. Recognize that there are various ways the parties may agree between themselves to terminate mutual obligations under the contract.

Parties are free to agree to almost any contract they want, and they are free to agree to end the contract whenever they want. There are several ways this is done.

Mutual Rescission

The parties may agree to give up the duties to perform, called **mutual rescission**. This may be by a formal written **release** saying the obligor is discharged upon delivery of the writing or upon occurrence of a condition. Or an obligation may be discharged by a contract not to sue about it.

mutual rescission

The giving up by both sides of the right to demand contract performance.

release

A contractual discharge of obligation by one side to another.

The Restatement terms this an agreement of rescission.[5] An agreement to rescind will be given effect even though partial performance has been made or one or both parties have a claim for partial breach. The agreement need not be in writing or even expressed in words. By their actions, such as failure to take steps to perform or enforce, the parties may signal their mutual intent to rescind. Andy starts to mow Anne's lawn as they agreed. He begins the job, but it is unbearably hot. She sees how uncomfortable he is and readily agrees with him when he says, "Why don't we just forget the whole thing?" Andy's duty to finish mowing is discharged, as is Anne's duty to pay Andy, either for the whole job or for the part he has done.

Business executives live by contracts, but they do not necessarily die by them. A sociologist who studied business behavior under contract discovered a generation ago—and it is still valid—that in the great majority of cases in which one party wishes to "cancel an order," the other party permits it without renegotiation, even though the cancellation amounts to a repudiation of a contract. As one lawyer was quoted as saying,

> *Often business[people] do not feel they have "a contract"—rather they have an "order." They speak of "cancelling the order" rather than "breaching our contract." When I began practice I referred to order cancellations as breaches of contract, but my clients objected since they do not think of cancellation as wrong. Most clients, in heavy industry at least, believe that there is a right to cancel as part of the buyer-seller relationship. There is a widespread attitude that one can back out of any deal within some very vague limits. Lawyers are often surprised by this attitude.*[6]

This attitude is understandable. People who depend for their economic survival on continuing relationships will be loath to react to every change in plans with a lawsuit. The legal consequences of most of these cancellations are an agreement of rescission. Under UCC Section 2-720, the use of a word like "cancellation" or "rescission" does not by itself amount to a renunciation of the right to sue for breach of a provision that occurred before the rescission. If the parties mean to discharge each other fully from all duties owed, they must say so explicitly. Actions continue to speak more loudly than words, however, and in law, so can inactions. Legal rights under contracts may be lost by both parties if they fail to act; by abandoning their claims, they can effect rescission.

Waiver

A second means of discharge is by **waiver**, whereby a party voluntarily gives up a right she has under a contract but doesn't give up the entire right to performance by the other side. Tenant is supposed to pay rent on the first of the month, but because his employer pays on the tenth, Tenant pays Landlady on that day. If Landlady accepts the late payment without objection, she has waived her right to insist on payment by the first of the month, unless the lease provides that no waiver occurs from the acceptance of any late payments. See Section 2, *Minor v. Chase Auto Finance Corporation*. A "waiver" is permission to deviate from the contract; a "release" means to let go of the whole thing.

waiver

The surrender of a legal right.

Substituted Agreement

novation

The replacement of one obligation by another by mutual agreement of both parties; usually the replacement of one of the original parties to a contract with the consent of the remaining party.

substituted agreement

A new agreement between original parties who have given up rights under the old agreement.

accord and satisfaction

The settlement of a dispute by offering up less consideration than demanded in exchange for extinguishing the obligation. The original obligation remains viable until the accord is performed.

Discharge by substituted agreement is a third way of mutual rescission. The parties may enter into a **novation**, either a new contract or one whereby a new person is substituted for the original obligor, and the latter is discharged. If Mr. Olson is obligated to deliver a car to Jack, Jack and Mr. Olson may agree that Dewey Dealer should deliver the car to Jack instead of Mr. Olson; the latter is discharged by this novation. A **substituted agreement** may also simply replace the original one between the original parties.

Accord and Satisfaction

Discharge by **accord and satisfaction** is a fourth way of mutual rescission. Here the parties to a contract (usually a disputed one) agree to substitute some performance different from what was originally agreed, and once this new agreement (the "accord") is executed, the original contract (as well as the more recent accord) is satisfied. But before then, the original agreement is only suspended: if the obligor does not satisfy the accord, the other side can sue on the original obligation or on the accord.

Key Takeaway

Parties to a contract may agree to give it up. This may be by mutual rescission, release, waiver, novation, substituted agreement, or accord and satisfaction.

Exercises

1. How does mutual rescission discharge a common-law contract without apparent new consideration?
2. What is the difference between a substituted agreement and a novation?
3. What happens if the parties negotiate an accord and satisfaction and one side fails to perform it?
4. If an obligee accepts performance from the obligor that deviates from the contract, under what circumstances can the obligee nevertheless insist on strict compliance in the future?

Discharge When Performance Becomes Impossible or Very Difficult

Learning Objective

1. Recognize that there are several circumstances when performance of the contract becomes variously impossible, very difficult, or useless, and that these may give rise to discharge.

There are at least five circumstances in which parties may be discharged from contractual obligations because performance is impossible, difficult, or useless.

Overview

Every contract contains some element of risk: the buyer may run out of money before he can pay; the seller may run out of goods before he can deliver; the cost of raw materials may skyrocket, throwing off the manufacturer's fine financial calculations. Should the obligor's luck run out, he is stuck with the consequences—or, in the legal phrase, his liability is strict: he must either perform or risk paying damages for breach of contract, even if his failure is due to events beyond his control. Of course, an obligor can always limit his liability through the contract itself. Instead of obligating himself to deliver one million units, he can restrict his obligation to "one million units or factory output, whichever is less." Instead of guaranteeing to finish a job by a certain date, he can agree to use his "best efforts" to do so. Similarly, damages in the event of breach can be limited. A party can even include a clause canceling the contract in the event of an untoward happening. But if these provisions are absent, the obligor is generally held to the terms of his bargain.

Exceptions include the concepts of impossibility, impracticability, and frustration of purpose.

Impossibility

If performance is impossible, the duty is discharged. The categories here are death or incapacity of a personal services contractor, destruction of a thing necessary for performance, and performance prohibited by government order.

Death or Incapacity of a Personal Services Contractor

If Buyer makes a contract to purchase a car and dies before delivery, Buyer's estate could be held liable; it is not impossible (for the estate) to perform. But the estate of a painter hired to do a portrait cannot be sued for damages because the painter died before she could complete the work.

Destruction or Deterioration of a Thing Necessary for Performance

When a specific object is necessary for the obligor's performance, its destruction or deterioration making its use impracticable (or its failure to come into existence) discharges the obligor's duty. Diane's Dyers contracts to buy the annual wool output of the Sheepish Ranch, but the sheep die of an epidemic disease before they can be shorn. Since the specific thing for which the contract was made has been destroyed, Sheepish is discharged from its duty to supply Diane's with wool, and Diane's has no claim against the Ranch. However, if the contract had called for a quantity of wool, without specifying that it was to be from Sheepish's flock, the duty would not be discharged; since wool is available on the open market, Sheepish could buy that and resell it to Diane's.

Performance Prohibited by Government Regulation or Order

When a government promulgates a rule after a contract is made, and the rule either bars performance or will make it impracticable, the obligor's duty is discharged. An obligor is not required to break the law and risk the consequences. Financier Bank contracts to sell World Mortgage Company certain collateralized loan instruments. The federal government, in a bank reform measure, prohibits such sales. The contract is discharged. If the Supreme Court later declared the prohibition unconstitutional, World Mortgage's duty to buy (or Financier Bank's to sell) would not revive.

Impracticability

Less entirely un-doable than impossibility, but still grounds for discharge, are common-law impracticability and its relative, commercial impracticability.

Common-Law Impracticability

Impracticability

An excuse for nonperformance of a duty where it has become unexpectedly difficult or expensive for the party who was to perform.

Impracticability is said to exist when there is a radical departure from the circumstances that the parties reasonably contemplated would exist at the time they entered into the contract; on such facts, the courts might grant relief. They will do so when extraordinary circumstances (often called "acts of God" or "force majeure") make it unjust to hold a party liable for performance. Although the justification for judicial relief could be found in an implied condition in all contracts that extraordinary events shall not occur, the Restatement eschews so obvious a bootstrap logic and adopts the language of UCC Section 2-615(a), which states that the crux of the analysis is whether the nonoccurrence of the extraordinary circumstance was "a basic assumption on which the contract was made."[7] If it was—if, that is, the parties assumed that the circumstance would not occur—then the duty is discharged if the circumstance later does occur.

In one well-known case, *Autry v. Republic Productions*, the famous cowboy movie star Gene Autry had a contract to perform to the defendant movie studio. He was drafted into the army in 1942; it was temporarily, at least, impossible for him to perform his movie contractual obligations incurred prior to his service. When he was discharged in 1945, he sued to be relieved of the prewar obligations. The court took notice that there had been a long interruption in Autry's career and of "the great decrease in the purchasing power of the dollar"—postwar inflation—and determined that to require him to perform under the old contract's terms would work a "substantial hardship" on him. A world war is an extraordinary circumstance. In 1945 it was not impossible for Autry to perform, but the war-time temporary impossibility had morphed into impracticability.[8]

objectively impracticable

Impossible.

Impracticability refers to the performance, not to the party doing it. Only if the performance is impracticable is the obligor discharged. The distinction is between "the thing cannot be done" and "I cannot do it." The former refers to that which is **objectively impracticable**, and the latter to that which is subjectively impracticable. That a duty is subjectively impracticable does not excuse it if the circumstances that made the duty difficult are not extraordinary. A buyer is liable for the purchase price of a house, and his inability to raise the money does not excuse him or allow him to escape from a suit for damages when the seller tenders the deed.[9] If Andy promises to transport Anne to the football stadium for ten dollars, he cannot wriggle out of his agreement because someone smashed into his car (rendering it inoperable) a half hour before he was due to pick her up. He could rent a car or take her in a taxi, even though that will cost considerably more than the sum she agreed to pay him. But if the agreement was that he would transport her in his car, then the circumstances make his performance **objectively impracticable**—the equivalent of impossible—and he is excused.

Commercial Impracticability

commercial impracticability

Relief from contract obligations may be granted when performance has been rendered excessively difficult, expensive, or harmful by an unforeseen contingency.

This common-law concept of impracticability has been adopted by the UCC.[10] When performance cannot be undertaken except with extreme difficulty or at highly unreasonable expense, it might be excused on the theory of **commercial impracticability**. However, "impracticable" (the action is impossible) is not the same as "impractical" (the action would yield an insufficient return or would have little practical value). The courts allow a considerable degree of fluctuation in market prices, inflation, weather, and other economic and natural conditions before holding that an extraordinary circumstance has occurred. A manufacturer that based its selling price on last year's costs for raw materials could not avoid its contracts by claiming that inflation within the historical range had made it difficult or unprofitable to meet its commitments. Examples of circumstances that could excuse might be severe limitations of supply due to war, embargo, or a natural disaster. Thus, a shipowner who contracted with a purchaser to carry goods to a foreign port would be excused if an earthquake destroyed the harbor or if war broke out and the military authorities threatened to sink all vessels that entered the harbor. But if the shipowner had planned to steam through a canal that is subsequently closed when a hostile government seizes it, his duty is not discharged if another route is available, even if the route is longer and consequently more expensive.

Frustration of Purpose

If the parties made a basic assumption, express or implied, that certain circumstances would not arise, but they do arise, then a party is discharged from performing his duties if his principal purpose in making the contract has been "substantially frustrated." This is not a rule of objective impossibility. It operates even though the parties easily might be able to carry out their contractual duties. The **frustration of purpose** doctrine comes into play when circumstances make the value of one party's performance virtually worthless to the other. This rule does not permit one party to escape a contract simply because he will make less money than he had planned or because one potential benefit of the contract has disappeared. The purpose that is frustrated must be the core of the contract, known and understood by both parties, and the level of frustration must be severe; that is, the value of the contract to the party seeking to be discharged must be destroyed or nearly destroyed.

frustration of purpose

A defense to contractual nonperformance that occurs when an unforeseen event undermines a party's principal purpose for entering into a contract, and both parties knew of this principal purpose at the time the contract was made.

The classic illustration of frustration of purpose is the litigation that gave birth to the rule: the so-called coronation cases. In 1902, when King Edward VII was due to be crowned following the death of his mother Queen Victoria, a parade route was announced for the coronation. Scores of people rented rooms in buildings that lined the streets of the route to watch the grand spectacle. But the king fell ill with appendicitis, and the procession was postponed. Many expectant viewers failed to pay, and the building owners took them to court; many lessees who had paid took the owners to court to seek refunds. The court declared that the lessees were not liable because the purpose of the contract had been frustrated by the king's illness (see http://en.wikipedia.org/wiki/Coronation_of_King_Edward_VII_and_Queen_Alexandra).

Supervening government regulations (though here different from illegality), floods that destroy buildings in which an event was to take place, and business failures may all contribute to frustration of purpose. But there can be no general rule: the circumstances of each case are determinative. Suppose, for example, that a manufacturer agrees to supply a crucial circuit board to a computer maker who intends to sell his machine and software to the government for use in the international space station's ventilation systems. After the contract is made but before the circuit boards are delivered, the government decides to scrap that particular space station module. The computer manufacturer writes to the circuit board maker, canceling the contract. Whether the manufacturer is discharged depends on the commercial prospects for the computer and the circuit board. If the circuit board can be used only in the particular computer, and it in turn is only of use on the space station, the duty to take the boards is discharged. But if the computer can be sold elsewhere, or the circuit boards can be used in other computers that the manufacturer makes, it is liable for breach of contract, since its principal purpose—selling computers—is not frustrated.

As before, the parties can provide in the contract that the duty is absolute and that no supervening event shall give rise to discharge by reason of frustration of purpose.

Key Takeaway

The obligations to perform under a contract cannot be dismissed lightly, but a person's duty to perform a contract duty may be discharged if it becomes impossible or very difficult to do it. This includes impossibility, common-law impracticability, commercial impracticability under the UCC, and frustration of purpose.

Exercises

1. If it is possible to perform a contract, why might a party be excused because of frustration of purpose?
2. What is the difference between impractical and impracticable?
3. How would supervening government regulation be different from supervening illegality?

Other Methods of Discharge

Learning Objectives

1. Recognize when alteration, power of avoidance, the statute of limitations, and bankruptcy discharge parties from contracts.
2. In addition to performance (or lack of it), agreement of the parties, the happening or nonhappening of conditions, and variations on the theme of impossibility, there are several other ways contract duties may be discharged.

Cancellation, Destruction, or Surrender

An obligee may unilaterally discharge the obligor's duty toward him by canceling, destroying, or surrendering the written document embodying the contract or other evidence of the duty. No consideration is necessary; in effect, the obligee is making a gift of the right that he possesses. No particular method of cancellation, destruction, or surrender is necessary, as long as the obligee manifests his intent that the effect of his act is to discharge the duty. The entire document can be handed over to the obligor with the words, "Here, you don't owe me anything." The obligee can tear the paper into pieces and tell the obligor that he has done so because he does not want anything more. Or he can mutilate the signatures or cross out the writing. This assumes, certainly, that the cancellation or destruction is intentional, not accidental.

Power of Avoidance

A contractual duty can be discharged if the obligor has the right to avoid the contractual obligation. As discussed in Chapter 10, a contract is either void or can be avoided if one of the parties lacked capacity (infancy, insanity); if there has been duress, undue influence, misrepresentation, or mistake; or the contract is determined to be unconscionable. Where a party has a **power of avoidance** and exercises it, that party is discharged from further obligation.

power of avoidance

A party's right to terminate performance of a contract—to avoid it (e.g., a minor has power of avoidance).

Statute of Limitations

When an obligor has breached a contract, the obligee has the right to sue in court for a remedy. But that right does not last forever. Every state has statutes of limitations that establish time periods within which the suit must be brought (different time periods are spelled out for different types of legal wrongs: contract breach, various types of torts, and so on). The time period for contract actions under most statutes of limitations ranges between two and six years. The UCC has a four-year **statute of limitations**.[11] The period begins to run from the day on which the suit could have been filed in court—for example, from the moment of contract breach. An obligee who waits until after the statute has run—that is, does not seek legal relief within the period prescribed by the statute of limitations—is barred from going to court thereafter (unless she is under some incapacity like infancy), but the obligor is not thereby discharged. The effect is simply that the obligee has no legal remedy. If the parties have a continuing relationship, the obligee might be able to recoup—for example, by applying a payment for another debt to the one barred by the statute, or by offsetting a debt the obligee owes to the obligor.

statute of limitations

The law stating how long people have to bring a lawsuit after the cause of action arises.

Bankruptcy

Under the federal bankruptcy laws as discussed in Chapter 30, certain obligations are discharged once a court declares a debtor to be bankrupt. The law spells out the particular types of debts that are canceled upon bankruptcy.

Key Takeaway

Contract duties may be discharged by cancellation, destruction, or surrender of the written contract; by the running of the statute of limitations; or by bankruptcy.

Exercises

1. Sarah has a $3,000 promissory note from Richard. Inadvertently, while cleaning out a desk drawer, Sarah scoops up the note and burns it as fire starter. Sarah tells Richard, who responds, "Destruction of the note discharges me." Is Richard correct? Explain.
2. Sarah has Richard's promissory note for $3,000, due in 2010; it is unpaid. In 2019 Sarah buys a car from Richard, promising to pay him $3,000. Can Sarah refuse to pay Richard the $3,000, and use that non-payment as an offset for the amount he owes her on the old debt?

15.2 Cases

Substantial Performance; Conditions Precedent

TA Operating Corp. v. Solar Applications Engineering, Inc.

191 S.W.3d 173 (Tex. Ct. App. 2005)

TA Operating Corporation, a truck stop travel center company, contracted with Solar Applications Engineering, Inc. to construct a prototype multi-use truck stop in San Antonio for a fixed price of $3,543,233. * * *

[When the project was near] completion, TA sent Solar a "punch list" of items that needed to be finished to complete the building. Solar disputed several items on the list and delivered a response to TA listing the items Solar would correct. * * * Solar began work on the punch list items and filed a lien affidavit [a property that carries a lien can be forced into sale by the creditor in order to collect what is owed] against the project on October 2, 2000 in the amount of $472,392.77. TA understood the lien affidavit to be a request for final payment.

On October 18, 2000, TA sent notice to Solar that Solar was in default for not completing the punch list items, and for failing to keep the project free of liens. TA stated in the letter that Solar was not entitled to final payment until it completed the remainder of the punch list items and provided documentation that liens filed against the project had been paid .... Solar acknowledged at least two items on the punch list had not been completed, and submitted a final application for payment in the amount of $472,148,77. * * * TA refused to make final payment, however, contending that Solar had not complied with section 14.07 of the contract, which expressly made submission of a [lien-release] affidavit a condition precedent to final payment: * * *

The final Application for Payment shall be accompanied by: ... complete and legally effective releases or waivers ... of all lien rights arising out of or liens filed in connection with the work.

Although Solar did not comply with this condition precedent to final payment, Solar sued TA for breach of contract under the theory of substantial performance. * * * TA [asserts that] the doctrine of substantial performance does not excuse Solar's failure to comply with an express condition precedent to final payment. * * *

The first issue we must resolve is whether the doctrine of substantial performance excuses the breach of an express condition precedent to final payment that is unrelated to completion of the building. TA acknowledges that Solar substantially performed its work on the project, but contends its duty to pay was not triggered until Solar pleaded or proved it provided TA with documentation of complete and legally effective releases or waivers of all liens filed against the project. * * * TA contends that when the parties have expressly conditioned final payment on submission of [a liens-release] affidavit, the owner's duty to pay is not triggered until the contractor pleads or proves it complied with the condition precedent.

Solar contends that although it did not submit [a liens-release] affidavit in accordance with the contract, it may still recover under the contract pursuant to the substantial performance doctrine. Solar argues that to hold otherwise would bring back the common law tradition that the only way for a contractor to recover under a contract is full, literal performance of the contract's terms. * * *

While the common law did at one time require strict compliance with the terms of a contract, this rule has been modified for building or construction contracts by the doctrine of substantial performance. "Substantial performance" was defined by the Texas [court] in [Citation]:

> *To constitute substantial compliance the contractor must have in good faith intended to comply with the contract, and shall have substantially done so in the sense that the defects are not pervasive, do not constitute a deviation from the general plan contemplated for the work, and are not so essential that the object of the parties in making the contract and its purpose cannot without difficulty, be accomplished by remedying them. Such performance permits only such omissions or deviation from the contract as are inadvertent and unintentional, are not due to bad faith, do not impair the structure as a whole, and are remediable without doing material damage to other parts of the building in tearing down and reconstructing.*

* * * The doctrine of substantial performance recognizes that the contractor has not completed construction, and therefore is in breach of the contract. Under the doctrine, however, the owner cannot use the contractor's failure to complete the work as an excuse for non-payment. "By reason of this rule a contractor who has in good faith substantially performed a building contract is permitted to sue under the contract, substantial performance being regarded as full performance, so far as a condition precedent to a right to recover thereunder is concerned." [Citation] * * *

Solar argues that by agreeing substantial performance occurred, TA acknowledged that Solar was in "full compliance" with the contract and any express conditions to final payment did not have to be met. [Citation]: "[a] finding that a contract has been substantially completed is the legal equivalent of full compliance, less any offsets for remediable defects." Solar argues that TA may not expressly provide for substantial performance in its contract and also insist on strict compliance with the conditions precedent to final payment. We disagree. While the substantial performance doctrine permits contractors to sue under the contract, it does not ordinarily excuse the non-occurrence of an express condition precedent:

> *The general acceptance of the doctrine of substantial performance does not mean that the parties may not expressly contract for literal performance of the contract terms .... Stated otherwise, if the terms of an agreement make full or strict performance an express condition precedent to recovery, then substantial performance will not be sufficient to enable recovery under the contract.*

15 Williston on Contracts § 44.53 (4th Ed.2000) (citing Restatement (Second) of Contracts, § 237, cmt. d (1981))....

TA, seeking protection from double liability and title problems, expressly conditioned final payment on Solar's submission of a [liens-release] affidavit. Solar did not dispute that it was contractually obligated to submit the affidavit as a condition precedent to final payment, and it was undisputed at trial that $246,627.82 in liens had been filed against the project. Though the doctrine of substantial performance permitted Solar to sue under the contract, Solar did not plead or prove that it complied with the express condition precedent to final payment. Had Solar done so, it would have been proper to award Solar the contract balance minus the cost of remediable defects. While we recognize the harsh results occasioned from Solar's failure to perform this express condition precedent, we recognize that parties are free to contract as they choose and may protect themselves from liability by requesting literal performance of their conditions for final payment. * * *

[T]he trial court erred in awarding Solar the contract balance [as] damages, and we render judgment that Solar take nothing on its breach of contract claim.

Case Questions

1. Why did Solar believe it was entitled to the contract balance here?
2. Why did the court determine that Solar should not have been awarded the contract damages that it claimed, even though it substantially complied?
3. How has the common law changed in regard to demanding strict compliance with a contract?

Waiver of Contract Rights; Nonwaiver Provisions

Minor v. Chase Auto Finance Corporation
—S.W.3d——, 2010 WL 2006401 (Ark. 2010)

Sheffield, J.

We have been asked to determine whether non-waiver and no-unwritten-modifications clauses in a [contract] preclude a creditor from waiving future strict compliance with the agreement by accepting late payments. * * *

Appellant Mose Minor (Minor) entered into a Simple Interest Motor Vehicle Contract and Security Agreement with Appellee Chase Auto Finance Corporation (Chase) to finance the purchase of a 2003 Toyota Tundra. By the terms of the agreement, Minor was to make sixty-six payments of $456.99 on the fourteenth of each month. * * * The agreement also included the following relevant provisions:

> *G. Default: If you...default in the performance of any promise you make in this contract or any other contract you have with us, including, but not limited to, failing to make any payments when due, or become insolvent, or file any proceeding under the U.S. Bankruptcy Code,... we may at our option and without notice or demand (1) declare all unpaid sums immediately due and payable subject to any right of reinstatement as required by law (2) file suit against you for all unpaid sums (3) take immediate possession of the vehicle (4) exercise any other legal or equitable remedy.... Our remedies are cumulative and taking of any action shall not be a waiver or prohibit us from pursuing any other remedy. You agree that upon your default we shall be entitled to recover from you our reasonable collection costs, including, but not limited to, any attorney's fee. In addition, if we repossess the vehicle, you grant to us and our agents permission to enter upon any premises where the vehicle is located. Any repossession will be performed peacefully....*
>
> *J. Other Agreements of Buyer:... (2) You agree that if we accept moneys in sums less than those due or make extensions of due dates of payments under this contract, doing so will not be a waiver of any later right to enforce the contract terms as written.... (12) All of the agreements between us and you are set forth in this contract and no modification of this contract shall be valid unless it is made in writing and signed by you and us....*
>
> *K. Delay in Enforcement: We can delay or waive enforcement of any of our rights under this contract without losing them.*

Minor's first payment was late, as were several subsequent payments. At times he failed to make any payment for months. Chase charged a late fee for each late payment, and sent several letters requesting payment and offering to assist Minor with his account. Chase also warned Minor that continued failure to make payments would result in Chase exercising its legal options available under the agreement, including repossession of the vehicle. * * * At one point, Minor fell so far behind in his payments that Chase was on the verge of repossessing the vehicle. However * * * the parties agreed to a two-month extension of the agreement. * * * The extension agreement indicated that all other terms and conditions of the original contract would remain the same.

On November 2, 2004, Minor filed for bankruptcy [after which] Chase sent Minor a letter acknowledging that Minor's debt to Chase had been discharged in bankruptcy. The letter further stated that Chase still had a valid lien on the vehicle, and if Minor wished to keep the vehicle, he would have to continue to make payments to Chase. Otherwise, Chase would repossess the vehicle. * * *

On September 28, 2006, a repossession agent * * * arrived at Minor's home some time in the afternoon to repossess the vehicle. * * * [Notwithstanding Minor's insistence that the agent stop] the agent removed Minor's possessions from the vehicle and towed it away. Chase sold the vehicle. The amount of the purchase price was reflected on Minor's account. * * *

On January 7, 2008, Minor filed a complaint against Chase [alleging] that, during the course of the contract, the parties had altered the provisions of the contract regarding Chase's right to repossess the vehicle and Chase had waived the right to strictly enforce the repossession clause. Minor further claimed that the repossession agent committed trespass and repossessed the vehicle forcibly, without Minor's permission, and through trickery and deceit, in violation of [state law]. Also, Minor asserted that he was not in default on his payments, pursuant to the repayment schedule, at the time Chase authorized repossession. Therefore, according to Minor, Chase committed conversion, and breached the Arkansas Deceptive Trade Practices Act [Citation], and enhanced by Arkansas Code Annotated section 4-88-202, because Minor is an elderly person. Minor sought compensatory and punitive damages. * * *

After hearing these arguments, the circuit court ruled that Minor had presented no evidence that the conduct of Chase or the repossession agent constituted grounds for punitive damages; that by the express terms of the contract Chase's acceptance of late payments did not effect a waiver of its rights in the future; that at the time of repossession, Minor was behind in his payments and in breach of the contract; that Chase had the right under the contract to repossess the vehicle and did not commit conversion; and that there was no evidence to support a claim that Chase had violated the Arkansas Deceptive Trade Practices Act. * * *

[W]e affirm our previous decisions that when a contract does not contain a non-waiver and a no-unwritten-modification provision and the creditor has established a course of dealing in accepting late payments from the debtor, the creditor waives its right to insist on strict compliance with the contract and must give notice to the debtor that it will no longer accept late payments before it can declare default of the debt. However, we announce today that, if a contract includes non-waiver and no-unwritten-modification clauses, the creditor, in accepting late payments, does not waive its right under the contract to declare default of the debt, and need not give notice that it will enforce that right in the event of future late payments. * * *

In arriving at this conclusion, we adhere to the principle that "a [contract] is effective according to its terms between the parties." * * * We have long held that non-waiver clauses are legal and valid. *See* [Citations] Also, [the Arkansas UCC 2-209(2)] declares that no-unwritten-modification provisions are binding.

We acknowledge that there is a difference of opinion amongst the courts in other jurisdictions over the effect of non-waiver and no-unwritten-modification clauses. * * *

We concur with the Supreme Court of Indiana's decision in [Citation], that a rule providing that non-waiver clauses could themselves be waived by the acceptance of late payments is "illogical, since the very conduct which the [non-waiver] clause is designed to permit[,] acceptance of late payment[,] is turned around to constitute waiver of the clause permitting the conduct." We also agree that the approach of jurisdictions that require creditors who have accepted late payments in the past to notify debtors that they expect strict compliance in the future, despite the existence of a non-waiver provision in the contract, is not "sound." Such a rule, we recognize, "begs the question of validity of the non-waiver clause." Finally, our holding is in line with the Indiana Supreme Court's ruling that it would enforce the provisions of the contract, since the parties had agreed to them, and that it would not require the creditor to give notice, because the non-waiver clause placed the [creditor] in the same position as one who had never accepted a late payment. [Citations] * * *

Certified question answered; remanded to court of appeals.

Case Questions

1. What is a nonwaiver clause?
2. Why did Minor think his late payments were not grounds for repossession of his truck?
3. Why would a creditor accept late payments instead of immediately repossessing the collateral?
4. Why did Minor lose?

Impossibility as a Defense

Parker v. Arthur Murray, Inc.

295 N.E.2d 487 (Ill. Ct. App. 1973)

Stamos, J.

The operative facts are not in dispute. In November, 1959 plaintiff went to the Arthur Murray Studio in Oak Park to redeem a certificate entitling him to three free dancing lessons. At that time he was a 37 year-old college-educated bachelor who lived alone in a one-room attic apartment in Berwyn, Illinois. During the free lessons the instructor told plaintiff he had "exceptional potential to be a fine and accomplished dancer" and generally encouraged further participation. Plaintiff thereupon signed a contract for 75 hours of lessons at a cost of $1,000. At the bottom of the contract were the bold-type words, "NON-CANCELABLE, NEGOTIABLE CONTRACT." This initial encounter set the pattern for the future relationship between the parties. Plaintiff attended lessons regularly. He was praised and encouraged regularly by the instructors, despite his lack of progress. Contract extensions and new contracts for additional instructional hours were executed. Each written extension contained the bold-type words, "NON-CANCELABLE CONTRACT," and each written contract contained the bold-type words, "NON-CANCELABLE NEGOTIABLE CONTRACT." Some of the agreements also contained the bold-type statement, "I UNDERSTAND THAT NO REFUNDS WILL BE MADE UNDER THE TERMS OF THIS CONTRACT."

On September 24, 1961 plaintiff was severely injured in an automobile collision, rendering him incapable of continuing his dancing lessons. At that time he had contracted for a total of 2,734 hours of lessons, for which he had paid $24,812.80 [about $178,000 in 2016 dollars]. Despite written demand defendants refused to return any of the money, and this suit in equity ensued. At the close of plaintiff's case the trial judge dismissed the fraud count (Count II), describing the instructors' sales techniques as merely "a matter of pumping salesmanship." At the close of all the evidence a decree was entered under Count I in favor of plaintiff for all prepaid sums, plus interest, but minus stipulated sums attributable to completed lessons.

Plaintiff was granted rescission on the ground of impossibility of performance. The applicable legal doctrine is expressed in the Restatement of Contracts, s 459, as follows:

> *A duty that requires for its performance action that can be rendered only by the promisor or some other particular person is discharged by his death or by such illness as makes the necessary action by him impossible or seriously injurious to his health, unless the contract indicates a contrary intention or there is contributing fault on the part of the person subject to the duty....*

Defendants do not deny that the doctrine of impossibility of performance is generally applicable to the case at bar. Rather they assert that certain contract provisions bring this case within the Restatement's limitation that the doctrine is inapplicable if "the contract indicates a contrary intention." It is contended that such bold type phrases as "'NON-CANCELABLE CONTRACT," "'NON-CANCELABLE NEGOTIABLE CONTRACT" and "I UNDERSTAND THAT NO REFUNDS WILL BE MADE UNDER THE TERMS OF THIS CONTRACT" manifested the parties' mutual intent to waive their respective rights to invoke the doctrine of impossibility. This is a construction which we find unacceptable. Courts engage in the construction and interpretation of contracts with the sole aim of determining the intention of the parties. We need rely on no construction aids to conclude that plaintiff never contemplated that by signing a contract with such terms as "'NON-CANCELABLE" and "NO REFUNDS" he was waiving a remedy expressly recognized by Illinois courts. Were we also to refer to established tenets of contractual construction, this conclusion would be equally compelled. An ambiguous contract will be construed most strongly against the party who drafted it. [Citation] Exceptions or reservations in a contract will, in case of doubt or ambiguity, be construed least favorably to the party claiming the benefit of the exceptions or reservations. Although neither party to a contract should be relieved from performance on the ground that good business judgment was lacking, a court will not place upon language a ridiculous construction. We conclude that plaintiff did not waive his right to assert the doctrine of impossibility.

Plaintiff's Count II, which alleged fraud and sought punitive damages, was dismissed by the trial judge at the close of plaintiff's case. It is contended on appeal that representations to plaintiff that he had "exceptional potential to be a fine and accomplished dancer," that he had "exceptional potential" and that he was a "natural born dancer" and a "terrific dancer" fraudulently induced plaintiff to enter into the contracts for dance lessons.

Generally, a mere expression of opinion will not support an action for fraud. [Citation] In addition, misrepresentations, in order to constitute actionable fraud, must pertain to present or pre-existing facts, rather than to future or contingent events, expectations or probabilities. [Citation] Whether particular language constitutes speculation, opinion or averment of fact depends upon all the attending facts and circumstances of the case. [Citation] Mindful of these rules, and after carefully considering the representations made to plaintiff, and taking into account the business relationship of the parties as well as the educational background of plaintiff, we conclude that the instructors' representations did not constitute fraud. The trial court correctly dismissed Count II. We affirm.

Affirmed.

Case Questions

1. Why is it relevant that the plaintiff was "a bachelor who lived alone in a one-room attic apartment"?
2. The contract here contained a "no cancellation" clause; how did the court construe the contract to allow cancellation?
3. Plaintiff lost on his claim of fraud (unlike Mrs. Vokes in the similar case in Chapter 10 against another franchisee of Arthur Murray, Inc.). What defense was successful?
4. What is the controlling rule of law here?

15.3 Summary and Exercises

Summary

The law of contracts has various rules to determine whether obligations have been discharged. Of course, if both parties have fully performed the contract, duties will have terminated. But many duties are subject to conditions, including conditions precedent and subsequent, conditions requiring approval of the promisee or someone else, and clauses that recite time to be of the essence.

A contract obligation may be discharged if the promisor has not received the benefit of the promisee's obligation. In some cases, failure to carry out the duty completely will discharge the corresponding obligation (material breach); in other cases, the substantial performance doctrine will require the other party to act.

A contract may have terminated because one of the parties tells the other in advance that he will not carry out his obligations; this is called anticipatory breach. The right to adequate assurance allows one party to determine whether the contract will be breached by the other party.

There are other events, too, that may excuse performance: impracticability (including the UCC rules governing impracticability in contracts for the sale of goods), death or incapacity of the obligor, destruction of the thing necessary for the performance, government prohibition, frustration of purpose, and power of avoidance.

Finally, note that not all obligations are created by contract, and the law has rules to deal with discharge of duties in general. Thus, in the appropriate cases, the obligee may cancel or surrender a written contract, may enter into an accord, may agree to rescind the agreement, or may release the obligor. Or the obligor may show a material alteration in the contract, may become bankrupt, or may plead the statute of limitations—that is, plead that the obligee waited too long to sue. Or the parties may, by word or deed, mutually abandon the agreement. In all these ways, duties may be discharged.

Exercises

1. Theresa hired Contractor to construct a large office building. Theresa's duty to pay Contractor was conditioned on receipt of a statement from her architect that the building complied with the terms of the contract. Contractor completed the building but used the wrong color fixtures in the bathrooms. The architect refused to approve the work, but under state law, Contractor was considered to have substantially performed the contract. Is he entitled to payment, less damages for the improper fixtures? Explain.
2. In early 1987, Larry McLanahan submitted a claim to Farmers Insurance for theft of his 1985 Lamborghini while it was on consignment for sale in the Los Angeles area. The car had sustained extensive damage, which McLanahan had his mechanic document. The insurance policy contained this language: "Allow us to inspect and appraise the damaged vehicle before its repair or disposal." But after considerable delay by Farmers, McLanahan sold the car to a cash buyer without notifying Farmers. He then sued Farmers for its refusal to pay for damages to his car. Upon what legal theory did Farmers get a summary judgment in its favor?
3. Plaintiff sold a tavern to Defendants. Several months later, Defendants began to experience severe problems with the septic tank system. They informed Plaintiff of the problem and demanded the return of their purchase money. Plaintiff refused. Defendants took no formal action against Plaintiff at that time, and they continued to operate the tavern and make their monthly payments under the contract. Some months later, Defendants met with state officials from the Departments of Environmental Quality, Health, and Liquor Control Commission. The officials warned Defendants that because of the health hazards posed by the septic tank problems, Defendants' licenses might not be renewed. As a result, Defendants decided to close the tavern and attempt to reopen when the septic tank was repaired. Defendants advertised a going-out-of-business sale. The purpose of the sale was to deplete the tavern's

inventory before closing. Plaintiff learned about the sale and discovered that Defendants had removed certain personal property from the tavern. He sued the Defendants, claiming, among other things, that they had anticipatorily breached their contract with him, though he was receiving payments on time. Did the Defendants' actions amount to an anticipatory breach?[12]

4. Julius, a manufacturer of neckties, contracted to supply neckties to a wholesaler. When Julius's factory burned, he failed to supply any, and the wholesaler sued. Is Julius excused from performance by impossibility?
5. The Plaintiff (a development corporation) contracted to buy Defendant's property for $1.8 million. A term in the contract read: "The sale...shall be closed at the office of Community Title Company on May 16th at 10:00 am....Time is of the essence in this contract." Defendant appeared at the office at 10:00 a.m. on the day designated, but the Plaintiff's agent was not there. Defendant waited for twenty minutes, then left. Plaintiff's agent arrived at 10:30 a.m. and announced that he would not have funds for payment until 1:30 p.m., but Defendant refused to return; she had already made other arrangements to finance her purchase of other real estate. Plaintiff sued Defendant for specific performance. Who wins, and why?
6. A contract between the Koles and Parker-Yale provided for completion of the Koles's condominium unit within 180 days. It also authorized the Koles to make written changes in the plans and specifications. Construction was not completed within the 180-day period, and the Koles, prior to completion, sent a letter to Parker-Yale rescinding the contract. Were the Koles within their rights to rescind the contract?
7. Defendant contracted to buy Plaintiff's commercial property for $1,265,000. Under the terms of the agreement, Defendant paid $126,000 as an earnest-money deposit, which would be retained by Plaintiff as liquidated damages if Defendant failed to close by the deadline. Defendant's husband died four days before the closing deadline, and she was not able to close by the deadline. She was relying on her husband's business to assist her in obtaining the necessary financing to complete the purchase, and after his death, she was not able to obtain it. Plaintiff sued for the $126,000; Defendant argued that the purpose of the contract was frustrated due to the untimely death of her husband. Is this a good argument?
8. Buyer contracted to buy Seller's house for $290,000; the contract included a representation by Buyer "that he has sufficient cash available to complete this purchase." Buyer was a physician who practiced with his uncle. He had received assurances from his uncle of a loan of $200,000 in order to finance the purchase. Shortly after the contract was executed, the uncle was examined by a cardiologist, who found his coronary arteries to be dangerously clogged. As a result, the uncle immediately had triple bypass surgery. After the operation, he told Buyer that his economic future was now uncertain and that therefore it was impossible for him to finance the house purchase. Meanwhile, Seller, who did not know of Buyer's problem, committed herself to buy a house in another state and accepted employment there as well. Buyer was unable to close; Seller sued. Buyer raised as a defense impossibility or impracticability of performance. Is the defense good?
9. Pursuant to a contract for the repair and renovation of a swimming pool owned by Defendant (City of Fort Lauderdale), Plaintiff commenced the work, which included resurfacing the inside of the pool, and had progressed almost to completion. Overnight, vandals damaged the work Plaintiff had done inside the pool, requiring that part of the work be redone. Plaintiff proceeded to redo the work and billed Defendant, who paid the contract price but refused to pay for the additional work required to repair the damage. Did the damage constitute destruction of subject matter discharging Plaintiff from his obligation to complete the job without getting paid extra?
10. Apache Plaza (the landlord) leased space to Midwest Savings to construct a bank building in Apache's shopping mall, based on a prototype approved by Apache. Midwest constructed the building and used it for twelve years until it was destroyed by a tornado. Midwest submitted plans for a new building to Apache, but Apache rejected the plans because the new building was larger and had less glass than the old building or the prototype. Midwest built it anyway. Its architect claimed that certain changes in the structure of the new building were required by new regulations and building codes, but he admitted that a building of the stipulated size could have been constructed in compliance with the applicable codes. Apache claimed $210,000 in damages over the term of the lease because the new building consumed more square feet of mall space and required more parking. Midwest claimed it had substantially complied with the lease requirements. Is this a good defense?[13]

Self-Test Questions

1. A condition precedent
   a. is a condition that terminates a duty
   b. is always within the control of one of the parties
   c. is an event giving rise to performance
   d. is a condition that follows performance
2. If Al and Betty have an executory contract, and if Betty tells Al that she will not be fulfilling her side of the bargain,
   a. Al must wait until the date of performance to see if Betty in fact performs
   b. Al can sue immediately for full contract damages
   c. Al can never sue because the contract was executory when Betty notified him of non-performance
   d. none of the above
3. Jack contracts with Anne to drive her to the airport Wednesday afternoon in his specially designed stretch limousine. On Wednesday morning Jack's limousine is hit by a drunken driver, and Jack is unable to drive Anne. This is an example of
   a. impossibility of performance
   b. frustration of purpose
   c. discharge by merger
   d. none of the above
4. Jack is ready and willing to drive Anne to the airport. But Anne's flight is cancelled, and she refuses to pay. This is an example of
   a. impracticability of performance
   b. frustration of purpose
   c. discharge of merger
   d. none of the above
5. Rescission is
   a. the discharge of one party to a contract through substitution of a third person
   b. an agreement to settle for substitute performance
   c. a mutual agreement between parties to a contract to discharge each other's contractual duties
   d. none of the above

Self-Test Answers

1. c
2. b
3. a
4. b
5. c

Endnotes

1. Uniform Commercial Code, Section 2-106(3).
2. Restatement (Second) of Contracts, Section 237(d).

3. Restatement (Second) of Contracts, Section 237(d).
4. *Hochster v. De La Tour*, 2 Ellis & Blackburn 678 (Q.B. 1853).
5. Restatement (Second) of Contracts, Section 283.
6. Stewart Macaulay, "Non-contractual Relations in Business: A Preliminary Study," *American Sociological Review* 28, no. 1 (1963): 55, 61.
7. Restatement (Second) of Contracts, Section 261.
8. *Autry v. Republic Productions*, 180 P.2d 144 (Calif. 1947).
9. *Christy v. Pilkinton*, 273 S.W.2d 533 (Ark. 1954).
10. Uniform Commercial Code, Section 2-615.
11. Uniform Commercial Code, Section 2-725.
12. *Crum v. Grant*, 692 P.2d 147 (Or. App., 1984).
13. *Apache Plaza, Ltd. v. Midwest Sav. Ass'n*, 456 N.W.2d 729 (Minn. App. 1990).

CHAPTER 16
Remedies

Learning Objectives

After reading this chapter, you should understand the following:

1. The basic theory of contract remedies, and why courts don't just order the promisor to perform as promised.
2. The interests that are protected by contract remedies.
3. The types of legal remedies.
4. The types of equitable remedies.
5. The limitations on remedies.

We come at last to the question of remedies. A valid common-law contract has been made, the promisor's duties have not been discharged; he or she has breached the contract. When one party has failed to perform, what are the rights of the parties? Or when the contract has been avoided because of incapacity or misrepresentation and the like, what are the rights of the parties after disaffirmation? These questions form the focus of this chapter. Remedies for breach of contracts for the sale of *goods* will be considered separately, in Chapter 18.

16.1 Theory of Contract Remedies

Learning Objectives

1. Understand the basic purpose of remedies.
2. Recognize that there are two general categories of remedies: legal and equitable.
3. See that courts do not simply order obligors to keep their promise but instead allow them to breach and the nonbreaching party to have remedies for that breach.

Purpose of Remedies

The fundamental purpose of remedies in noncriminal (civil) cases is not to punish the breaching party but—if possible—to put the nonbreaching party in the position he or she would have been in had there been no breach. Or, as is said, the purpose is to make the nonbreaching party whole.

damages

Money paid by one party to another to satisfy a liability.

specific performance

An order directing a person to deliver the unique thing contracted for by the other party.

injunction

A judicial order directing a person to stop doing that which he or she should not do.

restitution

Restoration; returning goods or money to put the nonbreaching party in the condition as if the contract had not been made.

There are two general categories of remedies—legal and equitable. In the category of legal remedies are **damages**. Damages are money paid by one party to another; there are several types of damages. In the category of equitable remedies are these three: **specific performance**, which means a person is ordered to deliver a unique thing (land or a unique personal property, such as a painting or an antique car); **injunction**, a judicial order directing a person to stop doing what he or she should not do (such as competing with a former employer in violation of a noncompete agreement); and **restitution**, which means putting the parties back into the position they were in before the contract was made.

Parties Have the Power—but Not the Right—to Breach

In view of the importance given to the intention of the parties in forming and interpreting contracts, it may seem surprising that the remedy for every breach is not a judicial order that the obligor carry out his or her undertakings. But it is not. Of course, some duties cannot be performed after a breach, because time and circumstances will have altered their purpose and rendered many worthless. Still, there are numerous occasions on which it would be theoretically possible for courts to order the parties to carry out their contracts, yet the courts will not do it. In 1897, Justice Oliver Wendell Holmes Jr. declared in a famous line that "the duty to keep a contract at common law means a prediction that you must pay damages if you do not keep it." By that he meant simply that the common law looks more toward compensating the promisee for his or her loss than toward compelling the promisor to perform. Indeed, the law of remedies often provides the parties with an incentive to break the contract. In short, the promisor has a choice: perform or pay.

The logic of this position is clear in many typical cases. The computer manufacturer orders specially designed circuit boards, then discovers before the circuits are made that a competitor has built a better machine and destroyed his market. The manufacturer cancels the order. It would make little economic sense for the circuit board maker to fabricate the boards if they could not be used elsewhere. A damage remedy to compensate the maker for out-of-pocket loss or lost profits is sensible; a judicial decree forcing the computer manufacturer to pay for and take delivery of the boards would be wasteful.

In general and if possible, the fundamental purpose of contract remedies is to put the nonbreaching party in the position it would have been in had there been no breach.

Key Takeaway

Remedies are intended to make the nonbreaching party whole. The two categories of remedies for breach of contract are legal and equitable. In the legal category are damages; in the equitable category are specific performance, injunctions, and restitution. The law does not force a party to perform; he or she always has the power (though not the right) to breach, and may do so if it is economically more advantageous to breach and suffer the consequence than to perform. Remedies, though, are not (usually) intended to punish the breaching party.

Exercises

1. Remedies are not supposed to punish the breaching party, generally. In what circumstances might punishment be a remedy, and what is that called?
2. What is the difference between legal and equitable remedies?
3. Why shouldn't people be forced to perform as they contracted, instead of giving them the power to breach and then be required to pay damages?

16.2 Promisee's Interests Protected by Contract

Learning Objective

1. Understand that the nonbreaching party to a contract has certain expectations that contract remedies seek to fulfill to make the nonbreaching party whole.

Contract remedies serve to protect three different interests: an expectation interest, a reliance interest, and a restitution interest. A promisee will have one of these and may have two or all three.

An **expectation interest** is the benefit for which the promisee bargained, and the remedy is to put him in a position as good as that which he would have been in had the contract been performed. A **reliance interest** is the loss suffered by relying on the contract and taking actions consistent with the expectation that the other party will abide by it; the remedy is reimbursement that restores the promisee to his position before the contract was made. A **restitution interest** is that which restores to the promisee any benefit he conferred on the promisor. These interests do not dictate the outcome according to a rigid formula; circumstances and the nature of the contract, as usual, will play a large role. But in general, specific performance is a remedy that addresses the expectation interest, monetary damages address all three interests, and, not surprisingly, restitution addresses the restitution interest.

expectation interest

The interest of a party to a breached contract in receiving the benefit of the bargain by being put in a position as good as he or she would have been in had there been no breach.

reliance interest

Compensation for the nonbreaching party as a consequence of relying on the breaching party's promise to perform.

restitution interest

The nonbreaching party's interest in being returned to the position it would have been in had the promises never been made. Where this is not possible, then restitution disgorges any unjust enrichment.

Consider some simple examples. A landowner repudiates an executory contract with a builder to construct a garage on her property for $100,000. The builder had anticipated a $10,000 profit (the garage would have cost him $90,000 to build). What can he expect to recover in a lawsuit against the owner? The court will not order the garage to be built; such an order would be wasteful, since the owner no longer wants it and may not be able to pay for it. Instead, the court will look to the builder's three possible interests. Since the builder has not yet started his work, he has given the owner nothing, and therefore has no restitution interest. Nor has he any reliance interest, since we are assuming that he has not paid out any money for supplies, hired a work crew, or advanced money to subcontractors. But he anticipated a profit, and so he has an expectation interest of $10,000.

Now suppose that the builder had dug out the foundation and poured concrete, at a cost of $15,000. His expectation interest has become $25,000 (the difference between $100,000 and $75,000, the money he will save by not having to finish the job). His reliance interest is $15,000, because this is the amount he has already spent. He may also have a restitution interest, depending on how much the foundation of the house is worth to the owner. (The value could be more or less than the sum of money actually expended to produce the foundation; for example, the builder might have had to pay his subcontractors for a greater share of the job than they had completed, and those sums therefore would not be reflected in the worth of the foundation.)

Normally, the promisee will choose which of the three interests to pursue. As is to be expected, the choice hinges on the circumstances of the case, his feelings, and the amount at stake.

Key Takeaway

A nonbreaching party might have one or more interests that the law seeks to realize: expectation, reliance, and restitution.

Exercises

1. What is the expectation interest? The reliance interest? The restitution interest?
2. How are these concepts useful in understanding contract remedies?

16.3 Legal Remedies: Damages

Learning Objectives

1. Understand what is meant when it is said that damages are a legal remedy (as opposed to an equitable remedy).
2. Understand the names and purposes of the six types of remedies.
3. Know when liquidated damages will be allowed.
4. Recognize the circumstances that might allow punitive damages.

Overview

The promisee, whom we will hereafter refer to as the non-breaching party, has the right to damages (a money award), if that is required to make her whole, whenever the other party has breached the contract, unless, of course, the contract itself or other circumstances suspend or discharge that right. **Damages** refers to money paid by one side to the other; it is a legal remedy. For historical and political reasons in the development of the English legal system, the courts of law were originally only able to grant monetary relief. If a petitioner wanted something other than money, recourse to a separate system of equity was required. The courtrooms and proceedings for each were separate. That actual separation is long gone, but the distinction is still recognized; a judge may be said to be "sitting in law" or "sitting in equity," or a case may involve requests for both money and some action. We take up the legal remedies of damages first.

Types of Damages

There are six different types of damages: compensatory, incidental, consequential, nominal, liquidated, and (sometimes) punitive.

Compensatory Damages

Damages paid to directly compensate the non-breaching party for the value of what was not done or performed are **compensatory damages**. Sometimes calculating that value of the promisor's performance is easy—for example, when the non-breaching party has ascertainable costs and profits, as in the case of the builder who would have earned $10,000 profit on a $100,000 house. When the performance is a service, a useful measure of loss is what it would cost to substitute performance by someone else. But the calculation is frequently difficult, especially when the performance is a service that is not easily duplicated. If Rembrandt breached a contract to paint your portrait, the loss could not be measured simply by inquiring how much Van Gogh would charge to do the same thing. Nevertheless, in theory, whatever net value would ultimately have been conferred on the nonbreaching party is the proper measure of compensatory damages. An author whose publisher breaches its contract to publish the book and who cannot find another publisher is entitled to lost royalties (if ascertainable) plus the value that would have accrued from her enhanced reputation.

compensatory damages

In contract, damages paid to compensate the nonbreaching party for the direct loss suffered.

Since the nonbreaching party usually has obligations under the contract also, a breach by the other party discharges his duty to perform and may result in savings. Or he may have made substitute arrangements and realized at least a partial profit on the substitution. Or, as in the case of the builder, he may have purchased goods intended for the job that can be used elsewhere. In all these situations, the losses he has avoided—savings, profits, or value of goods—are subtracted from the losses incurred to arrive at the net damages. The nonbreaching party may recover his actual losses, not more. Suppose an employer breaches a contract with a prospective employee who was to begin work for a year at a salary of $65,000. The employee quickly finds other, similar work at a salary of $60,000. Aside from whatever she might have had to spend searching for the job (incidental damages), her compensatory damages are limited to $5,000, the difference between what she would have earned and what he is earning.

Lost volume can be a troublesome problem in calculating damages. This problem arises when the non-breaching party, a supplier of goods or services, enters a second contract when the buyer repudiates. The question is whether the second contract is a substituted performance or an additional one. If it is substituted, damages may be little or nothing; if additional, the entire expectation interest may be recovered. An automobile dealer contracts to sell a car in his inventory. Shortly before the deal is closed, the buyer calls up and repudiates the contract. The dealer then sells the car to someone else. If the dealer can show that he could have sold an identical car to the second purchaser regardless of what the first purchaser did, then the second sale stands on its own and cannot be used to offset the net profit recoverable from the first purchaser. The factual inquiry in lost volume cases is whether the non-breaching party would have engaged in the second transaction if the breach had never occurred.

Lost volume

Damages for loss of profits on an item of inventory.

Incidental Damages

In addition to compensatory damages, the nonbreaching party may recover **incidental damages**. Incidental loss includes expenditures that the nonbreaching party incurs in attempting to minimize the loss that flows from the breach. To arrange for substitute goods or services, the nonbreaching party might have to pay a premium or special fees to locate another supplier or source of work.

incidental damages

Compensation for commercially reasonable expenses incurred as a result of the other party's breach.

Consequential Damages

consequential damages

Those losses or injuries which are a result of a breach of contract but are not direct and immediate.

A consequential loss is addressed with **consequential damages**. These are damages incurred by the nonbreaching party without action on his part because of the breach. For example, if Ralph does a poor job of plumbing Betty's bathroom and the toilet leaks, damaging the floor, the downstairs ceiling, and the downstairs rug, Ralph would owe for those loses in consequential damages. Or, again, lost sales stemming from a failure to fix a manufacturer's machine in time or physical and property injury due to a defective machine sold by the promisor would be addressed with consequential damages. Note, however, that one obvious, and often large, expenditure occasioned by a breach—namely, legal expenses in bringing a lawsuit to remedy the particular breach—is not an element of damages, unless the contract explicitly states that it is, and cannot be charged to the defendant. There is one situation, however, in which legal costs can be added to damages: when the breach causes the nonbreaching party to be involved in a lawsuit with someone else. Consequential damages will not be allowed if those damages are not foreseeable. This issue is taken up in Section 5.

Nominal Damages

nominal damages

Damages in name only, as where actual damages are nonexistent or cannot be proved.

In the situation where there has been a breach but the nonbreaching party has really suffered no loss or cannot prove what his loss is, he is entitled to **nominal damages**. Ricardo contracts to buy a new car from a dealer; the dealer breaches the contract. Ricardo finds and buys the same car from another dealer at the same price that the first one was to sell it for. Ricardo has suffered nominal damages: five dollars, perhaps. (Prudent people do not bring lawsuits to recover only nominal damages—it's not worth it.)

Liquidated Damages

liquidated damages

Damages agreed to in the contract that are payable in case of breach.

Precisely because damages are sometimes difficult to assess, the parties themselves may specify how much should be paid in the event of a breach. Courts will enforce a **liquidated damages** provision as long as the actual amount of damages is difficult to ascertain (if it is not difficult to ascertain, then proof of it is simply made at trial) and the sum is reasonable in light of the expected or actual harm. If the liquidated sum is unreasonably large, the excess is termed a penalty and is said to be against public policy and unenforceable. Section 6, *Watson v. Ingram*, illustrates liquidated damages.

Punitive Damages

Punitive damages

Damages to punish the breaching party.

Punitive damages are those awarded for the purpose of punishing a defendant in a civil action. They are proper in cases in which the defendant has acted willfully and maliciously and are thought to deter others from acting similarly. Since the purpose of contract law is compensation, not punishment, punitive damages have not traditionally been awarded, with one exception—when the breach of contract is also a tort for which punitive damages may be recovered. Punitive damages are permitted in the law of torts (in all but four states) when the behavior is malicious or willful (reckless conduct causing physical harm, deliberate defamation of one's character, a knowingly unlawful taking of someone's property), and some kinds of contract breach are also tortious. For example, when a creditor holding collateral as security under a contract for a loan sells the collateral to a good-faith purchaser for value even though the debtor was not in default, he has breached the contract and committed the tort of conversion; punitive damages may be awarded, assuming the behavior was willful and not merely mistaken.

Punitive damages are not fixed by law. The judge or jury may award at its discretion whatever sum is believed necessary to redress the wrong or deter like conduct in the future. This means that a richer person may be slapped with much heavier punitive damages than a poorer one in the appropriate case. But the judge in all cases may remit (reduce) some or all of a punitive damage award if he or she considers it excessive.

Key Takeaway

As the purpose of contract remedies is, in general, to make the nonbreaching party whole, the law allows several types of damages (money paid) to reflect the losses suffered by the nonbreaching party. Compensatory damages compensate for the special loss suffered; consequential damages compensate for the foreseeable consequences of the breach; incidental damages compensate for the costs of keeping any more damages from occurring; nominal damages are awarded if the actual amount cannot be shown or there are no actual damages; liquidated damages are agreed to in advance where the actual amount is difficult to ascertain, and they are allowed if not a penalty; and punitive damages may sometimes be allowed if the breaching party's behavior is an egregious tort, an outrage.

Exercises

1. What is the difference between a legal remedy and an equitable remedy?
2. What types of remedies are there, and what purpose does each serve?
3. What must be shown if liquidated damages are to be allowed?
4. Under what circumstances may punitive damages be allowed?

16.4 Equitable Remedies

Learning Objectives

1. Know when equitable (as opposed to legal) remedies will be allowed.
2. Understand the different types of equitable remedies: specific performance, injunction, and restitution.

Overview

Really the only explanation for the differences between law and equity is to be found in the history and politics of England dating to the twelfth century (1300s), but in practical terms, the distinctions are notable. First, juries are not used in equitable cases. Second, equity relies less on precedent and more on the sense that justice should be served. Third, and of most significance, where what is sought by the non-breaching party is not money—that is, where there is no adequate legal remedy—equity may afford relief. In equity a person may get a judge to order the breaching party to deliver some actual property, or to stop doing something that he should not do, or to return the consideration the non-breaching party gave so as to return the parties to the precontract status (specific performance, injunction, and restitution, respectively).

Types of Remedies in Equity

There are three types of equitable remedies: specific performance, injunction, and restitution.

Specific Performance

Specific performance is a judicial order to the promisor that he undertake the performance to which he obligated himself in a contract. Specific performance is an alternative remedy to damages and may be issued at the discretion of the court, subject to a number of exceptions. Emily signs a contract to sell Charlotte a gold samovar, a Russian antique of great sentimental value because it once belonged to Charlotte's mother. Emily then repudiates the contract while still executory. A court may properly grant Charlotte an order of specific performance against Emily.

Once students understand the basic idea of specific performance, they often want to pounce upon it as the solution to almost any breach of contract. It seems reasonable that the non-breaching party could ask a court to simply require the promisor to do what she promised she would. But specific performance is a very limited remedy: it is *only* available for breach of contract to sell a unique item, that is, a unique item of personal property (the samovar), or a parcel of real estate (all real estate is unique). But if the item is not unique, so that the non-breaching party can go out and buy another one, then the legal remedy of money damages will solve the problem. And specific performance will never be used to force a person to perform services against his will, which would be involuntary servitude (slavery). A person may be forced to *stop doing* that which she should not do (injunction), but not forced to do what she will not do.

Injunction

An **injunction** is the second type of equitable remedy available in contract (it is also available in tort). It is a court order directing a person to stop doing that which she should not do. For example, if an employer has a valid noncompete contract with an employee, and the employee, in breach of that contract, nevertheless undertakes to compete with his former employer, a court may enjoin (issue an order of injunction), directing the former employee to stop such competition. A promise by a person not to do something—in this example, not to compete—is called a **negative covenant** (a covenant is a promise in a contract, itself a contract). Or if Seller promises to give Buyer the right of first refusal on a parcel of real estate or a unique work of art, but Seller, in breach of a written promise, offers the thing to a third party, a court may enjoin Seller from selling it to the third party. If a person violates an injunction, he may be held in contempt of court and put in jail for a while. *Madison Square Garden v. Carnera Corporation*, Section 6, is a classic case involving injunctions for breach of contract.

Restitution

The third type of equitable relief is **restitution**. Restitution is a remedy applicable to several different types of cases: those in which the contract was avoided because of incapacity or misrepresentation, those in which the other party breached, and those in which the party seeking restitution breached. As the word implies, *restitution* is a restoring to one party of what he gave to the other. Therefore, only to the extent that the injured party conferred a benefit on the other party may the injured party be awarded restitution. The point is, a person who breaches a contract should not suffer a punishment, and the non-breaching party should not be unjustly enriched.

Total Nonperformance by Breaching Party

The non-breaching party is always entitled to restitution in the event of total breach by nonperformance or repudiation, unless both parties have performed all duties except for payment by the other party of a definite sum of money for the injured party's performance.[1] Calhoun, a contractor, agrees to build $3,000 worth of fence for only $2,000 and completes the construction. Arlene, the landowner, refuses to pay. Calhoun's only right is to get the $2,000; he does not have a restitution right to $2,500, the market price of his services (or $3,000, the amount by which her property increased in value); he is entitled, instead, only to $2,000, his contract price. Had Arlene repudiated prior to completion, however, Calhoun would then have been entitled to restitution based either on the market price of the work or on the amount by which he enhanced her property. If the one party breaches, the non-breaching party is generally entitled to restitution of property that can be returned. Arlene gives Calhoun a valuable Ming vase in return for his promise to construct the fences. Upon Calhoun's breach, Arlene is entitled to specific restitution of the vase—she gets the vase back.

Measuring restitution interest can be problematic. The courts have considerable discretion to award either what it would have cost to hire someone else to do the work that the non-breaching party performed (generally, the market price of the service) or the value that was added to the property of the party in breach by virtue of the claimant's performance. Calhoun, the contractor, agrees to construct ten fences around Arlene's acreage at the market price of $25,000. After erecting three, Calhoun has performed services that would cost $7,500, market value. Assume that he has increased the value of Arlene's grounds by $8,000. If Arlene repudiated, there are two measures of Calhoun's restitution interest: $8,000, the value by which the property was enhanced, or $7,500, the amount it would have cost Arlene to hire someone else to do the work. Which measure to use depends on who repudiated the contract and for what reason. In some cases, the enhancement of property or wealth measurement could lead to an award vastly exceeding the market price for the service. In such cases, the smaller measure is used. For a doctor performing lifesaving operations on a patient, restitution would recover only the market value of the doctor's services—not the monetary value of the patient's life.

Part Performance and Then Breach

A party who has substantially performed and then breached is entitled to restitution of a benefit conferred on the injured party, if the injured party has refused (even though justifiably) to complete his own performance owing to the other's breach. Since the party in breach is liable to the injured party for damages for loss, this rule comes into play only when the benefit conferred is greater than the amount the nonbreaching party has lost. Arlene agrees to sell her property to Calhoun for $120,000, and Calhoun makes a partial payment of $30,000. He then repudiates. Arlene turns around and sells the property to a third party for $110,000. Calhoun—the breaching party—can get his money back, less the damages Arlene suffered as a result of his breach. He gets $30,000 minus the $10,000 loss Arlene incurred. He gets $20,000 in restitution. Otherwise Arlene would be enriched by Calhoun's breach: she'd get $140,000 in total for real estate worth $120,000. But if he gets $20,000 of his $30,000 back, she receives $110,000 from the third party and $10,000 from Calhoun, so she gets $120,000 total (plus, we hope, incidental damages, at least).

Restitution in Other Cases

Upon repudiation of an oral contract governed by the Statute of Frauds, the nonbreaching party is not entitled to her expectation interest, but she may recover in restitution unless the purpose of the statute would be frustrated. When one party avoids a contract owing to lack of capacity, mistake, misrepresentation, duress, or the like, she is entitled to restitution for benefit conferred on the other party. Restitution is also available if a contract duty is discharged or never arises because (1) performance was impracticable, (2) the purpose of the contract was frustrated, (3) a condition did not occur, or (4) a beneficiary disclaimed his benefit.

Key Takeaway

Equitable remedies for breach of contract are available when legal remedies won't make the nonbreaching party whole. The equitable remedies are specific performance (an order directing a person to deliver to the buyer the unique thing the seller contracted to sell), injunction (an order directing a person to stop doing that which he should not do), and restitution (the return by one party of the benefit conferred on him when the contract is not performed, to the extent necessary to avoid imposing a penalty on the breaching party).

Exercises

1. Buyer contracts to buy a 1941 four-door Cadillac convertible from Seller for $75,000. Seller, having found a Third Party who will pay $85,000 for the car, refuses to sell to Buyer. What is Buyer's remedy?
2. Assume Third Party had paid the $85,000 and Seller was ordered to sell to Buyer. What is Third Party's remedy?
3. Professor Smith contracts to teach business law at State University for the academic year. After the first term is over, she quits. Can State University get an order of specific performance or an injunction requiring Professor Smith to return for the second term?
4. Now suppose that the reason Professor Smith quit work at State University is because she got a better job at Central University, fifteen miles away. Can State University get an injunction prohibiting her from teaching at Central University?

16.5 Limitations on Contract Remedies

Learning Objectives

1. Understand that there are various rules that limit recovery for the nonbreaching party in a contract case.
2. Know how these concepts serve to limit contract remedies: foreseeability, mitigation of damages, certainty of damages, loss of power of avoidance, election of remedies, and agreement of the parties.

Overview

We have observed that the purpose of remedies in contract law is, where possible, to put the non-breaching party in as good a position as she would have been in had there been no breach. There are, however, several limitations or restrictions affecting when a person can claim remedies, in both law (damages) and equity. Of course the contract itself may—if not unconscionable—limit remedies. Beyond that, the non-breaching party must be able to articulate with some degree of certainty what her damages are; the damages must be foreseeable; the non-breaching party must have made a reasonable effort to mitigate the damages; she must sometime elect to go with one remedy and forgo another; she cannot seek to avoid a contract if she has lost the power to do so. We turn to these points.

Foreseeability

If the damages that flow from a breach of contract lack **foreseeability**, they will not be recoverable. Failures to act, like acts themselves, have consequences. As the old fable has it, "For want of a nail, the kingdom was lost." To put a non-breaching party in the position he would have been in had the contract been carried out could mean, in some cases, providing compensation for a long chain of events. In many cases, that would be unjust, because a person who does not anticipate a particular event when making a contract will not normally take steps to protect himself (either through limiting language in the contract or through insurance). The law is not so rigid; a loss is not compensable to the non-breaching party unless the breaching party, at the time the contract was made, understood the loss was foreseeable as a probable result of his breach.

foreseeability

In contract, the requirement that damages from a breach be proximately caused by the breach.

Of course, the loss of the contractual benefit in the event of breach is always foreseeable. A company that signs an employment contract with a prospective employee knows full well that if it breaches, the employee will have a legitimate claim to lost salary. But it might have no reason to know that the employee's holding the job for a certain length of time was a condition of his grandfather's gift of $1 million.

The leading case, perhaps the most studied case in all the common law is *Hadley v. Baxendale*, decided in England in 1854. Joseph and Jonah Hadley were proprietors of a flour mill in Gloucester. In May 1853, the shaft of the milling engine broke, stopping all milling. An employee went to Pickford and Company, a common carrier, and asked that the shaft be carried by railroad as quickly as possible to a Greenwich foundry that would use the old shaft as a model to construct a new one. The carrier's agent promised delivery within two days. But through an error, the shaft was shipped by canal rather than by rail and did not arrive in Greenwich for seven days. The Hadleys sued Joseph Baxendale, managing director of Pickford, for the profits they lost because of the delay. In ordering a new trial, the Court of Exchequer ruled that Baxendale was not liable because he had had no notice that the mill was stopped:

> *Where two parties have made a contract which one of them has broken, the damages which the other party ought to receive in respect of such breach of contract should be such as may fairly and reasonably be considered either arising naturally, i.e., according to the usual course of things, from such breach of contract itself, or such as may reasonably be supposed to have been in the contemplation of both parties, at the time they made the contract, as the probable result of the breach of it.*[2]

Thus when the party in breach has not known and has had no reason to know that the contract entailed a special risk of loss, the burden must fall on the non-breaching party. As we have seen, damages attributable to losses that flow from events that do not occur in the ordinary course of events are known as consequential or special damages. The exact amount of a loss need not be foreseeable; it is the nature of the event that distinguishes between claims for ordinary or consequential damages. A repair shop agrees to fix in a timely fashion a machine that it knows is intended to be resold. Because it delays, the sale is lost. The repair shop, knowing why timeliness of performance was important, is liable for the lost profit, as long as it was reasonable. It would not be liable for an extraordinary profit that the seller could have made because of circumstances peculiar to the particular sale unless they were disclosed.

The special circumstances need not be recited in the contract. It is enough for the party in breach to have actual knowledge of the loss that would occur through his breach. Moreover, the parol evidence rule (Chapter 13) does not bar introduction of evidence bearing on the party's knowledge before the contract was signed. So the lesson to a promisee is that the reason for the terms he bargains for should be explained to the promisor—although too much explanation could kill a contract. A messenger who is paid twenty dollars to deliver a letter across town is not likely to undertake the mission if he is told in advance that his failure for any reason to deliver the letter will cost the sender $1 million, liability to be placed on the messenger.

Actual knowledge is not the only criterion, because the standard of foreseeability is objective, not subjective. That means that if the party had reason to know—if a reasonable person would have understood—that a particular loss was probable should he breach, then he is liable for damages. What one has reason to know obviously depends on the circumstances of the case, the parties' prior dealings, and industry custom. A supplier selling to a wholesaler should know that the commodity will be resold and that delay or default may reduce profits, whereas delay in sale to an end user might not. If it was foreseeable that the breach might cause the non-breaching party to be sued, the other party is liable for legal fees and a resulting judgment or the cost of a settlement.

Even though the breaching party may have knowledge, the courts will not always award full consequential damages. In the interests of fairness, they may impose limitations if such an award would be manifestly unfair. Such cases usually crop up when the parties have dealt informally and there is a considerable disproportion between the loss caused and the benefit the non-breaching party had agreed to confer on the party who breached. The messenger may know that a huge sum of money rides on his prompt delivery of a letter across town, but unless he explicitly contracted to bear liability for failure to deliver, it is unlikely that the courts would force him to ante up $1 million when his fee for the service was only twenty dollars.

EBWS, LLC v. Britly Corp., Section 6, is a case that represents a modern application of the rule of *Hadley v. Baxendale* on the issue of foreseeability of consequential damages.

Mitigation of Damages

mitigation of damages

The plaintiff's duty to take reasonable steps to minimize his or her damages or losses and to attempt to prevent further damage.

Contract law encourages the non-breaching party to avoid loss wherever possible; this is called **mitigation of damages**. The concept is a limitation on damages in law, so there can be no recovery if the non-breaching party had an opportunity to avoid or limit losses and failed to take advantage of it. Such an opportunity exists as long as it does not impose, in the Restatement's words, an "undue risk, burden or humiliation."[3] The effort to mitigate need not be successful. As long as the non-breaching party makes a reasonable, good-faith attempt to mitigate his losses, damages are recoverable.

Mitigation crops up in many circumstances. Thus, a non-breaching party who continues to perform after notice that the promisor has breached or will breach may not recover for expenses incurred in continuing to perform. And losses from the use of defective goods delivered in breach of contract are not compensable if the non-breaching party knew before use that they were defective. Often the non-breaching party can make substitute arrangements—find a new job or a new employee, buy substitute goods or sell them to another buyer—and his failure to do so will limit the amount of damages he will recover from the party who breaches. Under the general rule, failure to mitigate when possible permits the promisor to deduct from damages the amount of the loss that the non-breaching party could have avoided. When there is a readily ascertainable market price for goods, damages are equal to the difference between the contract price and the market price.

A substitute transaction is not just any possible arrangement; it must be suitable under the circumstances. Factors to be considered include the similarity, time, and place of performance, and whether the difference between the contracted-for and substitute performances can be measured and compensated. A prospective employee who cannot find substitute work within her field need not mitigate by taking a job in a wholly different one. An advertising salesperson whose employment is repudiated need not mitigate by taking a job as a taxi driver. When the only difference between the original and the substitute performances is price, the non-breaching party must mitigate, even if the substitute performer is the original promisor.

The non-breaching party must make reasonable efforts to mitigate in timely fashion, but each case is different. If it is clear that the promisor has unconditionally repudiated before performance is due, the non-breaching party must begin to mitigate as soon as practicable and should not wait until the day performance is due to look for an alternative.

As long as the non-breaching party makes a reasonable effort to mitigate, the success of that effort is not an issue in assessing damages. If a film producer's original cameraman breaches the contract, and if the producer had diligently searched for a substitute cameraman, who cost $150 extra per week, and it later came to light that the producer could have hired a cameraman for $100, the company is entitled nevertheless to damages based on the higher figure. *Shirley MacLaine v. Twentieth Century-Fox Corporation*, Section 6, is a well-known case involving mitigation of damages.

Certainty of Damages

A party can recover only that amount of damage in law which can be proved with reasonable certainty. Especially troublesome in this regard are lost profits and loss of goodwill. Alf is convinced that next spring the American public will be receptive to polka-dotted belts with his name monogrammed in front. He arranges for a garment factory to produce 300,000 such belts, but the factory, which takes a large deposit from him in advance, misplaces the order and does not produce the belts in time for the selling season. When Alf discovers the failure, he cannot raise more money to go elsewhere, and his project fails. He cannot recover damages for lost profits because the number is entirely speculative; no one can prove how much he would have made, if anything. He can, instead, seek restitution of the monies advanced. If he had rented a warehouse to store the belts, he would also be able to recover his reliance interest.

Proof of lost profits is not always difficult: a seller can generally demonstrate the profit he would have made on the sale to the buyer who has breached. The problem is more difficult, as Alf's case demonstrates, when it is the seller who has breached. A buyer who contracts for but does not receive raw materials, supplies, and inventory cannot show definitively how much he would have netted from the use he planned to make of them. But he is permitted to prove how much money he has made in the past under similar circumstances, and he may proffer (offer up) financial and market data, surveys, and expert testimony to support his claim. When proof of profits is difficult or impossible, the courts may grant a nonmonetary award, such as specific performance.

Loss of Power of Avoidance

You will recall that there are several circumstances when a person may avoid a contract: duress, undue influence, misrepresentation (fraudulent, negligent, or innocent), infancy, or mistake. But a party may lose the right to avoid, and thus the right to any remedy, in several ways.

Delay

If a party is the victim of fraud, she must act promptly to rescind at common law, or she will lose the right and her remedy will be limited to damages in tort. (This is discussed a bit more in Section 5.)

Affirmation

An infant who waits too long to disaffirm will have ratified the contract, as will one who—notwithstanding being the victim of duress, undue influence, mistake, or any other grounds for avoidance—continues to operate under the contract with full knowledge of her right to avoid. Of course the disability that gave rise to the power of avoidance must have passed before affirmation works (the infant must come of age before she can be said to have ratified her contract).

Rights of Third Parties

The intervening rights of third parties may terminate the power to avoid. For example, Michelle, a minor, sells her watch to Betty Buyer. Up to and within a reasonable time after reaching majority, Michelle could avoid—disaffirm—the contract. But if, before that time, Betty sells the watch to a third party, Michelle cannot get it back from the third party. Similarly, Salvador Seller sells his car to Bill Buyer, who pays for it with a bad check. If the check bounces, Salvador can rescind the deal—Bill's consideration (the money represented by the check) has failed: Salvador could return the check and get his car back. But if, before the check from Bill bounces, Bill in turn sells the car to Pat Purchaser, Salvador cannot avoid the contract. Pat gets to keep the car. There are some exceptions to this rule.

Agreement of the Parties Limiting Remedies

Certainly it is the general rule that parties are free to enter into any kind of a contract they want, so long as it is not illegal or unconscionable. The inclusion into the contract of a liquidated damages clause—mentioned previously—is one means by which the parties may make an agreement affecting damages. But beyond that, as we saw in Chapter 12, it is very common for one side to limit its liability, or for one side to agree that it will pursue only limited remedies against the other in case of breach. Such agreed-to limitations on the availability of remedies are generally okay provided they are conspicuous, bargained-for, and not unconscionable. In consumer transactions, courts are more likely to find a contracted-for limitation of remedies unconscionable than in commercial transactions, and under the Uniform Commercial Code (UCC) there are further restrictions on contractual remedy limitations.

For example, Juan buys ten bags of concrete to make a counter and stand for his expensive new barbecue. The bags have this wording in big print: "Attention. Our sole liability in case this product is defective will be to provide you with a like quantity of nondefective material. We will not be liable for any other damages, direct or indirect, express or implied." That's fine. If the concrete is defective, the concrete top breaks, and Juan's new barbecue is damaged, he will get nothing but some new bags of good concrete. He could have shopped around to find somebody who would deliver concrete with no limitation on liability. As it is, his remedies are limited by the agreement he entered into.

Election of Remedies

At Common Law

election of remedies

The situation of a plaintiff in a civil lawsuit having multiple causes of action from which to choose as to how the defendant's wrong may be righted.

Another limitation on remedies—at common law—is the concept of **election of remedies**. The nature of a loss resulting from a contract breach may be such as to entitle one party to a choice among two or more means to redress the grievance, where the choices are mutually exclusive.

At classic common law, a person who was defrauded had an election of remedies: she could, immediately upon discovering the fraud, rescind, or she could retain the item (real estate or personal property) and attempt to remedy the fraudulently defective performance by suing for damages, but not both. Buyer purchases real estate from Seller for $300,000 and shortly discovers that Seller fraudulently misrepresented the availability of water. Buyer spends $60,000 trying to drill wells. Finally he gives up and sues Seller for fraud, seeking $360,000. Traditionally at common law, he would not get it. He should have rescinded upon discovery of the fraud. Now he can only get $60,000 in damages in tort.[4] The purpose of the election of remedies doctrine is to prevent the victim of fraud from getting a double recovery, but it has come under increasing criticism. Here is one court's observation: "A host of commentators support elimination of the election of remedies doctrine. A common theme is that the doctrine substitutes labels and formalism for inquiry into whether double recovery results in fact. The rigid doctrine goes to the other extreme, actually resulting in the under compensation of fraud victims and the protection of undeserving wrongdoers."[5]

Under the UCC

The doctrine of election of remedy has been rejected by the UCC, which means that the remedies are cumulative in nature. According to Section 2-703(1): "Whether the pursuit of one remedy bars another depends entirely on the facts of the individual case." UCC, Section 2-721, provides that neither demand for rescission of the contract in the case of misrepresentation or fraud, nor the return or rejection of goods, bars a claim for damages or any other remedy permitted under the UCC for nonfraudulent breach (we will examine remedies for breach of sales contracts in Chapter 18).

Tort versus Contract

Frequently a contract breach may also amount to tortious conduct. A physician warrants her treatment as perfectly safe but performs the operation negligently, scarring the patient for life. The patient could sue for malpractice (tort) or for breach of warranty (contract). The choice involves at least four considerations:

1. Statute of limitations. Most statutes of limitations prescribe longer periods for contract than for tort actions.
2. Allowable damages. Punitive damages are more often permitted in tort actions, and certain kinds of injuries are compensable in tort but not in contract suits—for example, pain and suffering.
3. Expert testimony. In most cases, the use of experts would be the same in either tort or contract suits, but in certain contract cases, the expert witness could be dispensed with, as, for example, in a contract case charging that the physician abandoned the patient.
4. Insurance coverage. Most policies do not cover intentional torts, so a contract theory that avoids the element of willfulness would provide the plaintiff with a surer chance of recovering money damages.

Legal versus Extralegal Remedies

A party entitled to a legal remedy is not required to pursue it. Lawsuits are disruptive not merely to the individuals involved in the particular dispute but also to the ongoing relationships that may have grown up around the parties, especially if they are corporations or other business enterprises. Buyers must usually continue to rely on their suppliers, and sellers on their buyers. Not surprisingly, therefore, many businesspeople refuse to file suits even though they could, preferring to settle their disputes privately or even to ignore claims that they might easily press. Indeed, the decision whether or not to sue is not one for the lawyer but for the client, who must analyze a number of pros and cons, many of them not legal ones at all.

Key Takeaway

There are several limitations on the right of an aggrieved party to get contract remedies for a breach besides any limitations fairly agreed to by the parties. The damages suffered by the nonbreaching party must be reasonably foreseeable. The nonbreaching party must make a reasonable effort to mitigate damages, or the amount awarded will be reduced by the damages that could have been avoided. The party seeking damages must be able to explain within reason how much loss he has suffered as a result of the breach. If he cannot articulate with any degree of certainty—if the damages are really speculative—he will be entitled to nominal damages and that's all. There are circumstances in which a party who could have got out of a contractual obligation—avoided it—loses the power to do so, and her remedy of avoidance is lost. Not infrequently, a person will enter into a contract for services or goods that contains a limitation on her right to damages in case the other side breaches. That's all right unless the limitation is unconscionable. Sometimes parties are required to make an election of remedies: to choose among two or more possible bases of recovery. If the remedies are really mutually exclusive and one is chosen, the aggrieved party loses the right to pursue the others. And of course a person is always free not to pursue any remedy at all for breach of contract; that may be strategically or economically smart in some circumstances.

Exercises

1. When one party to a contract breaches, what duty, if any, is then imposed on the other party?
2. A chef who has never owned her own restaurant sues a contractor who failed to finish building the chef's first restaurant on time. She presents evidence of the profits made by similar restaurants that have been in business for some time. Is this good evidence of the damages she has suffered by the delay? To what damages is she entitled?
3. Rebecca, seventeen years and ten months old, buys a party dress for $300. She wears it to the junior prom but determines it doesn't look good on her. She puts it in her closet and forgets about it until six months later, when she decides to return it to the store. Is she now entitled to the remedy of rescission?
4. What is the difference between *rescission* and *restitution*?
5. Why are parties sometimes required to make an election of remedies?

16.6 Cases

Consequential Damages

EBWS, LLC v. Britly Corp.

928 A.2d 497 (Vt. 2007)

Reiber, C.J.

The Ransom family owns Rock Bottom Farm in Strafford, Vermont, where Earl Ransom owns a dairy herd and operates an organic dairy farm. In 2000, the Ransoms decided to build a creamery on-site to process their milk and formed EBWS, LLC to operate the dairy-processing plant and to market the plant's products. In July 2000, Earl Ransom, on behalf of EBWS, met with Britly's president to discuss building the creamery. * * * In January 2001, EBWS and Britly entered into a contract requiring Britly to construct a creamery building for EBWS in exchange for $160,318. * * * The creamery was substantially completed by April 15, 2001, and EBWS moved in soon afterward. On June 5, 2001, EBWS notified Britly of alleged defects in construction. [EBWS continued to use the creamery pending the necessity to vacate it for three weeks when repairs were commenced].

On September 12, 2001, EBWS filed suit against Britly for damages resulting from defective design and construction. * * *

Following a three-day trial, the jury found Britly had breached the contract and its express warranty, and awarded EBWS: (1) $38,020 in direct damages, and (2) $35,711 in consequential damages. * * *

The jury's award to EBWS included compensation for both direct and consequential damages that EBWS claimed it would incur while the facility closed for repairs. Direct damages [i.e., compensatory damages] are for "losses that naturally and usually flow from the breach itself," and it is not necessary that the parties actually considered these damages. [Citation]. In comparison, special or consequential damages "must pass the tests of causation, certainty and foreseeability, and, in addition, be reasonably supposed to have been in the contemplation of both parties at the time they made the contract."

* * * The court ruled that EBWS could not recover for lost profits because it was not a going concern at the time the contract was entered into, and profits were too speculative. The court concluded, however, that EBWS could submit evidence of other business losses, including future payment for unused milk and staff wages. * * *

At trial, Huyffer, the CEO of EBWS, testified that during a repairs closure the creamery would be required to purchase milk from adjacent Rock Bottom Farm, even though it could not process this milk. She admitted that such a requirement was self-imposed as there was no written output contract between EBWS and the farm to buy milk. In addition, Huyffer testified that EBWS would pay its employees during the closure even though EBWS has no written contract to pay its employees when they are not working. The trial court allowed these elements of damages to be submitted to the jury, and the jury awarded EBWS consequential damages for unused milk and staff wages.

On appeal, Britly contends that because there is no contractual or legal obligation for EBWS to purchase milk or pay its employees, these are not foreseeable damages. EBWS counters that it is common knowledge that cows continue to produce milk, even if the processing plant is not working, and thus it is foreseeable that this loss would occur. We conclude that these damages are not the foreseeable result of Britly's breach of the construction contract and reverse the award. * * *

[W]e conclude that * * * it is not reasonable to expect Britly to foresee that its failure to perform under the contract would result in this type of damages. While we are sympathetic to EBWS's contention that the cows continue to produce milk, even when the plant is closed down, this fact alone is not enough to demonstrate that buying and dumping milk is a foreseeable result of Britly's breach of the construction contract. Here, the milk was produced by a separate and distinct entity, Rock Bottom Farm, which sold the milk to EBWS. * * *

Similarly, EBWS maintained no employment agreements with its employees obligating it to pay wages during periods of closure for repairs, dips in market demand, or for any other reason. Any losses EBWS might suffer in the future because it chooses to pay its employees during a plant closure for repairs would be a voluntary expense and not in Britly's contemplation at the time it entered the construction contract. It is not reasonable to expect Britly to foresee losses incurred as a result of agreements that are informal in nature and carry no legal obligation on EBWS to perform. "[P]arties are not presumed to know the condition of each other's affairs nor to take into account contracts with a third party that is not communicated." [Citation] While it is true that EBWS may have business reasons to pay its employees even without a contractual obligation, for example, to ensure employee loyalty, no evidence was introduced at trial by EBWS to support a sound rationale for such considerations. Under these circumstances, this business decision is beyond the scope of what Britly could have reasonably foreseen as damages for its breach of contract. * * *

In addition, the actual costs of the wages and milk are uncertain. * * * [T]he the milk and wages here are future expenses, for which no legal obligation was assumed by EBWS, and which are separate from the terms of the parties' contract. We note that at the time of the construction contract EBWS had not yet begun to operate as a creamery and had no history of buying milk or paying employees. See [Citation] (explaining that profits for a new business are uncertain and speculative and not recoverable). Thus, both the cost of the milk and the number and amount of wages of future employees that EBWS might pay in the event of a plant closure for repairs are uncertain.

Award for consequential damages is reversed. * * *

Case Questions

1. Why, according to EBWS's CEO, would EBWS be required to purchase milk from adjacent Rock Bottom Farm, even though it could not process this milk?
2. Surely it is well known in Vermont dairy country that dairy farmers can't simply stop milking cows when no processing plant is available to take the milk—the cows will soon stop producing. Why was EBWS then not entitled to those damages which it will certainly suffer when the creamery is down for repairs?
3. Britly (the contractor) must have known EBWS had employees that would be idled when the creamery shut down for repairs. Why was it not liable for their lost wages?
4. What could EBWS have done at the time of contracting to protect itself against the damages it would incur in the event the creamery suffered downtime due to faulty construction?

Liquidated Damages

Watson v. Ingram

881 P.2d 247 (Wash. 1994)

Johnson, J.

* * * In the summer of 1990, Wayne Watson offered to buy James Ingram's Bellingham [Washington state] home for $355,000 [about $640,000 in 2015 dollars] with a $15,000 [about $29,000 in 2016 dollars] earnest money deposit....

Under the agreement, the entire amount of the purchase price was due in cash on or before December 3, 1990. * * * The agreement required Watson to pay a $15,000 earnest money deposit into escrow at Kelstrup Realty, and provided that "[i]n the event of default by Buyer, earnest money shall be forfeited to Seller as liquidated damages, unless Seller elects to seek actual damages or specific performance. Lastly, the agreement contained a provision entitled "BUYER'S REPRESENTATIONS," which stated, "Buyer represents that buyer has sufficient funds available to close this sale in accordance with this agreement, and is not relying on any contingent source of funds unless otherwise set forth in this agreement." * * *

On November 10, 1990, Watson sent a written proposal to Ingram seeking to modify the original agreement. The proposed modification would have allowed Watson to defer paying $54,000 of the $355,000 sale price for between 6 and 12 months after the scheduled December closing date. In exchange, Ingram would receive a second lien position on certain real estate Watson owned.

According to Ingram, the November 10 proposal was the first time he realized Watson did not have financing readily available for the purchase of the house. Ingram notified Watson on November 12, 1990, that he would not agree to modify the original agreement and intended to strictly enforce its terms. Ingram was involved in a child custody suit in California and wanted to move to that state as soon as possible. * * * [Further efforts by Ingram to sell to third parties and by Watson to get an extension from Ingram failed.]

In September 1991, Ingram finally sold the house to a third party for $355,000 [about $650,000 in 2016 dollars], the same price that Watson had agreed to pay in December 1990.

Ingram and Watson each sought to recover the $15,000 earnest money held in escrow. On December 4, 1990, Ingram wrote to Kelstrup Realty, indicating he was entitled to the $15,000 earnest money in escrow because Watson had defaulted. In January 1991, Watson filed this action to recover the earnest money, alleging it amounted to a penalty and Ingram had suffered no actual damages. * * *

The trial court found the earnest money "was clearly intended by both parties to be nonrefundable" if Watson defaulted and determined $15,000 was "a reasonable forecast by [Ingram and Watson] of damages that would be incurred by [Ingram] if [Watson] failed to complete the purchase." The court entered judgment in favor of Ingram for the amount of the earnest money plus interest. The court also awarded Ingram his attorney fees pursuant to the parties' agreement. The Court of Appeals, Division One, affirmed. Watson now appeals to this court.

This case presents a single issue for review: whether the parties' contract provision requiring Watson to forfeit a $15,000 nonrefundable earnest money deposit is enforceable as liquidated damages. Liquidated damages clauses are favored in Washington, and courts will uphold them if the sums involved do not amount to a penalty or are otherwise unlawful. [Citation] To determine whether liquidated damages clauses are enforceable, Washington courts have applied a 2-part test from the Restatement of Contracts. * * * Liquidated damages clauses are upheld if the following two factors are satisfied:

> *First, the amount fixed must be a reasonable forecast of just compensation for the harm that is caused by the breach. Second, the harm must be such that it is incapable or very difficult of ascertainment.*

The question before this court is whether this test is to be applied as of the time of contract formation (prospectively) or as of the time of trial (retrospectively). We have previously held, the "[r]easonableness of the forecast will be judged as of the time the contract was entered." [Citations]

In contrast, a prior Division One opinion relied upon by Petitioner held the reasonableness of the estimate of damages and the difficulty of ascertainment of harm should be measured as of the time of trial, and earnest money agreements should not be enforceable as liquidated damages if the nonbreaching party does not suffer actual damage. [Citations]

We * * * adopt the date of contract formation as the proper timeframe for evaluating the Restatement test. The prospective approach concentrates on whether the liquidated sum represents a reasonable prediction of the harm to the seller if the buyer breaches the agreement, and ignores actual damages except as evidence of the reasonableness of the estimate of potential damage.

We believe this approach better fulfills the underlying purposes of liquidated damages clauses and gives greater weight to the parties' expectations. Liquidated damages permit parties to allocate business and litigation risks. Even if the estimates of damages are not exact, parties can allocate and quantify those risks and can negotiate adjustments to the contract price in light of the allocated risks. Under the prospective approach, courts will enforce the parties' allocation of risk so long as the forecasts appear reasonable when made. [Citations]

In addition to permitting parties to allocate risks, liquidated damages provisions lend certainty to the parties' agreements and permit parties to resolve disputes efficiently in the event of a breach. Rather than litigating the amount of actual damages, the non-breaching party must only establish the reasonableness of the agreement. The prospective approach permits parties to rely on their stipulated amounts without having to precisely establish damages at trial. In contrast, if the reasonableness of the amount is judged retrospectively, against the damage actually suffered, the "parties must fully litigate (at great expense and delay) that which they sought not to litigate." [Citation]

Petitioner argues the prospective approach treats buyers unfairly because it permits sellers to retain earnest money deposits even when the seller suffers no actual damage, and this violates the principle that contract damages should be compensatory only. He further contends that by evaluating parties' liquidated damages agreements against actual damages established at trial, courts can most effectively determine whether such agreements were reasonable and fair.

We disagree. As this court has previously explained, "[w]e are loath to interfere with the rights of parties to contract as they please between themselves. [Citations] It is not the role of the court to enforce contracts so as to produce the most equitable result. The parties themselves know best what motivations and considerations influenced their bargaining, and, while, "[t]he bargain may be an unfortunate one for the delinquent party, * * * it is not the duty of courts of common law to relieve parties from the consequences of their own improvidence." * * * [Citations]

The retrospective approach fails to give proper weight to the parties' negotiations. At the time of contract formation, unpredictable market fluctuations and variations in possible breaches make it nearly impossible for contracting parties to predict "precisely or within a narrow range the amount of damages that would flow from breach." [Citations] However, against this backdrop of uncertainty, the negotiated liquidated damages sum represents the parties' best estimate of the value of the breach and permits the parties to allocate and incorporate these risks in their negotiations. Under the prospective approach, a court will uphold the parties' agreed upon liquidated sum so long as the amount represents a reasonable attempt to compensate the non-breaching party. On the other hand, if the reasonableness of a liquidated damages provision is evaluated under a retrospective approach, the parties cannot confidently rely on their agreement because the liquidated sum will not be enforced if, at trial, it is not a close approximation of the damage suffered or if no actual damages are proved. * * *

Having adopted the date of contract formation as the proper timeframe for evaluating the Restatement test, the Restatement's second requirement loses independent significance. The central inquiry is whether the specified liquidated damages were reasonable at the time of contract formation. * * *

We also agree with the Court of Appeals that in the context of real estate agreements, a requirement that damages be difficult to prove at trial would undermine the very purposes of the liquidated damage provision: "certainty, assurance that the contract will be performed, and avoidance of litigation." [Citation] It would "encourage litigation in virtually every case in which the sale did not close, regardless of whether the earnest money deposit was a reasonable estimate of the seller's damages." [Citation]

In sum, so long as the agreed upon earnest money agreement, viewed prospectively, is a reasonable prediction of potential damage suffered by the seller, the agreement should be enforced "without regard to the retrospective calculation of actual damages or the ease with which they may be proved." The prospective difficulty of estimating potential damage is a factor to be used in assessing the reasonableness of the earnest money agreement. * * *

The decision of the Court of Appeals is affirmed.

Case Questions

1. What does the court here mean when it says that liquidated damages clauses allow the parties to "allocate and incorporate the risks [of the transaction] in their negotiations"?
2. Why is it relevant that the plaintiff Ingram was engaged in a child-custody dispute and wanted to move to California as soon as possible?
3. What, in plain language, is the issue here?
4. How does the court's resolution of the issue seem to the court the better analysis?
5. Why did the plaintiff get to keep the $15,000 when he really suffered no damages?
6. Express the controlling rule of law out of this case.

Injunctions and Negative Covenants

Madison Square Garden Corporation v. Carnera

52 F.2d 47 (2d Cir. Ct. App. 1931)

Chase, J.

On January 13, 1931, the plaintiff and defendant by their duly authorized agents entered into the following agreement in writing:

> *1. Carnera agrees that he will render services as a boxer in his next contest (which contest, hereinafter called the "First Contest."*
>
> *9. Carnera shall not, pending the holding of the First Contest, render services as a boxer in any major boxing contest, without the written permission of the Garden in each case had and obtained. A major contest is understood to be one with Sharkey, Baer, Campolo, Godfrey, or like grade heavyweights, or heavyweights who shall have beaten any of the above subsequent to the date hereof. If in any boxing contest engaged in by Carnera prior to the holding of the First Contest, he shall lose the same, the Garden shall at its option, to be exercised by a two weeks' notice to Carnera in writing, be without further liability under the terms of this agreement to Carnera. Carnera shall not render services during the continuance of the option referred to in paragraph 8 hereof for any person, firm or corporation other than the Garden. Carnera shall, however, at all times be permitted to engage in sparring exhibitions in which no decision is rendered and in which the heavy weight championship title is not at stake, and in which Carnera boxes not more than four rounds with any one opponent.*

Thereafter the defendant, without the permission of the plaintiff, written or otherwise, made a contract to engage in a boxing contest with the Sharkey mentioned in paragraph 9 of the agreement above quoted, and by the terms thereof the contest was to take place before the first contest mentioned in the defendant's contract with the plaintiff was to be held.

The plaintiff then brought this suit to restrain the defendant from carrying out his contract to box Sharkey, and obtained the preliminary injunction order, from which this appeal was taken. Jurisdiction is based on diversity of citizenship and the required amount is involved.

The District Court has found on affidavits which adequately show it that the defendant's services are unique and extraordinary. A negative covenant in a contract for such personal services is enforceable by injunction where the damages for a breach are incapable of ascertainment. [Citations]

The defendant points to what is claimed to be lack of consideration for his negative promise, in that the contract is inequitable and contains no agreement to employ him. It is true that there is no promise in so many words to employ the defendant to box in a contest with Stribling or Schmeling, but the agreement read as a whole binds the plaintiff to do just that, provided either Stribling or Schmeling becomes the contestant as the result of the match between them and can be induced to box the defendant. The defendant has agreed to 'render services as a boxer' for the plaintiff exclusively, and the plaintiff has agreed to pay him a definite percentage of the gate receipts as his compensation for so doing. The promise to employ the defendant to enable him to earn the compensation agreed upon is implied to the same force and effect as though expressly stated. [Citations] The fact that the plaintiff's implied promise is conditioned, with respect to the contest with the winner of the Stribling-Schmeling match, upon the consent of that performer, does not show any failure of consideration for the defendant's promise [Citation].

As we have seen, the contract is valid and enforceable. It contains a restrictive covenant which may be given effect. Whether a preliminary injunction shall be issued under such circumstances rests in the sound discretion of the court. [Citation] The District Court, in its discretion, did issue the preliminary injunction. * * *

Order affirmed.

Case Questions

1. Why did the plaintiff not want the defendant to engage in any boxing matches until and except the ones arranged by the plaintiff?
2. What assertion did the defendant make as to why his promise was not enforceable? Why wasn't that argument accepted by the court?
3. If the defendant had refused to engage in a boxing match arranged by the plaintiff, would a court force him to do what he had promised?

Check out Primo Carnera here: https://en.wikipedia.org/wiki/Primo_Carnera

Limitation on Damages: Mitigation of Damages

Shirley MacLaine Parker v. Twentieth Century-Fox Film Corporation

474 P.2d 689 (Cal. 1970)

Burke, Justice.

Defendant Twentieth Century-Fox Film Corporation appeals from a summary judgment granting to plaintiff the recovery of agreed compensation under a written contract for her services as an actress in a motion picture. As will appear, we have concluded that the trial court correctly ruled in plaintiff's favor and that the judgment should be affirmed.

Plaintiff is well known as an actress. * * * Under the contract, dated August 6, 1965, plaintiff was to play the female lead in defendant's contemplated production of a motion picture entitled "Bloomer Girl." The contract provided that defendant would pay plaintiff a minimum "guaranteed compensation" of $53,571.42 per week for 14 weeks commencing May 23, 1966, for a total of $750,000 [about $5,400,000 in 2016 dollars]. Prior to May 1966 defendant decided not to produce the picture and by a letter dated April 4, 1966, it notified plaintiff of that decision and that it would not "comply with our obligations to you under" the written contract.

By the same letter and with the professed purpose "to avoid any damage to you," defendant instead offered to employ plaintiff as the leading actress in another film tentatively entitled "Big Country, Big Man" (hereinafter, "Big Country"). The compensation offered was identical, as were 31 of the 34 numbered provisions or articles of the original contract. Unlike "Bloomer Girl," however, which was to have been a musical production, "Big Country" was a dramatic "western type" movie. "Bloomer Girl" was to have been filmed in California; "Big Country" was to be produced in Australia. Also, certain terms in the proffered contract varied from those of the original. Plaintiff was given one week within which to accept; she did not and the offer lapsed. Plaintiff then commenced this action seeking recovery of the agreed guaranteed compensation.

The complaint sets forth two causes of action. The first is for money due under the contract; the second, based upon the same allegations as the first, is for damages resulting from defendant's breach of contract. Defendant in its answer admits the existence and validity of the contract, that plaintiff complied with all the conditions, covenants and promises and stood ready to complete the performance, and that defendant breached and "anticipatorily repudiated" the contract. It denies, however, that any money is due to plaintiff either under the contract or as a result of its breach, and pleads as an affirmative defense to both causes of action plaintiff's allegedly deliberate failure to mitigate damages, asserting that she unreasonably refused to accept its offer of the leading role in "Big Country."

Plaintiff moved for summary judgment. * * * [T]he motion was granted * * * for $750,000 plus interest * * * in plaintiff's favor. This appeal by defendant followed. * * *

The general rule is that the measure of recovery by a wrongfully discharged employee is the amount of salary agreed upon for the period of service, less the amount which the employer affirmatively proves the employee has earned or with reasonable effort might have earned from other employment. [Citation] However, before projected earnings from other employment opportunities not sought or accepted by the discharged employee can be applied in mitigation, the employer must show that the other employment was comparable, or substantially similar, to that of which the employee has been deprived; the employee's rejection of or failure to seek other available employment of a different or inferior kind may not be resorted to in order to mitigate damages. [Citations]

In the present case defendant has raised no issue of reasonableness of efforts by plaintiff to obtain other employment; the sole issue is whether plaintiff's refusal of defendant's substitute offer of "Big Country" may be used in mitigation. Nor, if the "Big Country" offer was of employment different or inferior when compared with the original "Bloomer Girl" employment, is there an issue as to whether or not plaintiff acted reasonably in refusing the substitute offer. Despite defendant's arguments to the contrary, no case cited or which our research has discovered holds or suggests that reasonableness is an element of a wrongfully discharged employee's option to reject, or fail to seek, different or inferior employment lest the possible earnings therefrom be charged against him in mitigation of damages.

Applying the foregoing rules to the record in the present case, with all intendments in favor of the party opposing the summary judgment motion—here, defendant—it is clear that the trial court correctly ruled that plaintiff's failure to accept defendant's tendered substitute employment could not be applied in mitigation of damages because the offer of the "Big Country" lead was of employment both different and inferior, and that no factual dispute was presented on that issue. The mere circumstance that "Bloomer Girl" was to be a musical review calling upon plaintiff's talents as a dancer as well as an actress, and was to be produced in the City of Los Angeles, whereas "Big Country" was a straight dramatic role in a "Western Type" story taking place in an opal mine in Australia, demonstrates the difference in kind between the two employments; the female lead as a dramatic actress in a western style motion picture can by no stretch of imagination be considered the equivalent of or substantially similar to the lead in a song-and-dance production.

Additionally, the substitute "Big Country" offer proposed to eliminate or impair the director and screenplay approvals accorded to plaintiff under the original "Bloomer Girl" contract, and thus constituted an offer of inferior employment. No expertise or judicial notice is required in order to hold that the deprivation or infringement of an employee's rights held under an original employment contract converts the available "other employment" relied upon by the employer to mitigate damages, into inferior employment which the employee need not seek or accept. [Citation]

The judgment is affirmed.

Case Questions

1. Why did Ms. MacLaine refuse to accept the employment opportunity offered by the defendant?

2. Why did the defendant think it should not be liable for any damages as a result of its admitted breach of the original contract?
3. Who has the burden of proof on mitigation issues—who has to show that no mitigation occurred?
4. Express the controlling rule of law out of this case.

Check out Shirley MacLaine here: https://en.wikipedia.org/wiki/Shirley_MacLaine

16.7 Summary and Exercises

Summary

Contract remedies serve to protect three different interests: an expectation interest (the benefit bargained for), a reliance interest (loss suffered by relying on the contract), and a restitution interest (benefit conferred on the promisor). In broad terms, specific performance addresses the expectation interest, monetary damages address all three, and restitution addresses the restitution interest.

The two general categories of remedies are legal and equitable. In the former category are compensatory, consequential, incidental, nominal, liquated, and (rarely) punitive damages. In the latter category—if legal remedies are inadequate—are specific performance, injunction, and restitution.

There are some limitations or restrictions on the availability of damages: they must pass the tests of foreseeability and certainty. They must be reasonably mitigated, if possible. And liquidated damages must be reasonable—not a penalty. In some situations, a person can lose the remedy of rescission—the power to avoid a contract—when the rights of third parties intervene. In some cases a person is required to make an election of remedies: to choose one remedy among several, and when the one is chosen, the others are not available any more.

Exercises

1. Owner of an auto repair shop hires Contractor to remodel his shop but does not mention that two days after the scheduled completion date, Owner is to receive five small U.S. Army personnel carrier trucks for service, with a three-week deadline to finish the job and turn the trucks over to the army. The contract between Owner and the Army has a liquidated damages clause calling for $300 a day for every day truck not operable after the deadline. Contractor is five days late in finishing the remodel. Can Owner claim the $1,500 as damages against Contractor as a consequence of the latter's tardy completion of the contract? Explain.
2. Inventor devised an electronic billiard table that looked like a regular billiard table, but when balls dropped into the pocket, various electronic lights and scorekeeping devices activated. Inventor contracted with Contractor to manufacture ten prototypes and paid him $50,000 in advance, on a total owing of $100,000 ($10,000 for each completed table). After the tables were built to accommodate electronic fittings, Inventor repudiated the contract. Contractor broke the ten tables up, salvaged $1,000 of wood for other billiard tables, and used the rest for firewood. The ten intact tables, without electronics, could have been sold for $500 each ($5,000 total). Contractor then sued Inventor for the profit Contractor would have made had Inventor not breached. To what, if anything, is Contractor entitled by way of damages and why?
3. Calvin, a promising young basketball and baseball player, signed a multiyear contract with a professional basketball team after graduating from college. After playing basketball for one year, he decided he would rather play baseball and breached his contract with the basketball team. What remedy could the team seek?

4. Theresa leased a one-bedroom apartment from Landlady for one year at $500 per month. After three months, she vacated the apartment. A family of five wanted to rent the apartment, but Landlady refused. Three months later—six months into what would have been Theresa's term—Landlady managed to rent the apartment to Tenant for $400 per month. How much does Theresa owe, and why?
5. Plaintiff, a grocery store, contracted with Defendant, a burglar alarm company, for Defendant to send guards to Plaintiff's premises and to notify the local police if the alarm was activated. The contract had this language: "It is agreed that the Contractor is not an insurer, that the payments here are based solely on the value of the service in the maintenance of the system described, that it is impracticable and extremely difficult to fix the actual damages, if any, which may proximately result from a failure to perform its services, and in case of failure to perform such services and a resulting loss, its liability shall be limited to $500 as liquidated damages, and not as a penalty, and this liability shall be exclusive."

   A burglary took place and the alarm was activated, but Defendant failed to respond promptly. The burglars left with $330,000. Is the liquidated damages clause—the limitation on Plaintiff's right to recover—valid?
6. The decedent, father of the infant Plaintiff, was killed in a train accident. Testimony showed he was a good and reliable man. Through a representative, the decedent's surviving child, age five, recovered judgment against the railroad (Defendant). Defendant objected to expert testimony that inflation would probably continue at a minimum annual rate of 5 percent for the next thirteen years (until the boy attained his majority), which was used to calculate the loss in support money caused by the father's death. The calculations, Defendant said, were unreasonably speculative and uncertain, and damages must be proven with reasonable certainty. Is the testimony valid?
7. Plaintiff produced and directed a movie for Defendant, but contrary to their agreement, Plaintiff was not given screen credit in the edited film (his name was not shown). The film was screened successfully for nearly four years. Plaintiff then sued (1) for damages for loss of valuable publicity or advertising because his screen credits were omitted for the years and (2) for an injunction against future injuries. The jury awarded Plaintiff $25,000 on the first count. On the second count, the court held Plaintiff should be able to "modify the prints in his personal possession to include his credits." But Plaintiff appealed, claiming that Defendant still had many unmodified prints in its possession and that showing those films would cause future damages. What remedy is available to Plaintiff?[6]
8. In 1929, Kerr Steamship Company, Inc. (Plaintiff), delivered to Defendant, the Radio Corporation of America (RCA), a fairly long telegram—in code—to be transmitted to Manila, Philippine Islands, with instructions about loading one of Kerr's ships. By mistake, the telegraph was mislaid and not delivered. As a result of the failure to transmit it, the cargo was not loaded and the freight was lost in an amount of $6,675.29 [about $84,000 in 2010 dollars], profit that would have been earned if the message had been carried. Plaintiff said that because the telegram was long and because the sender was a ship company, RCA personnel should have known it was important information dealing with shipping and therefore RCA should be liable for the consequential damages flowing from the failure to send it. Is RCA liable?
9. Defendant offered to buy a house from Plaintiff. She represented, verbally and in writing, that she had $15,000 to $20,000 of equity in another house and would pay this amount to Plaintiff after selling it. She knew, however, that she had no such equity. Relying on these intentionally fraudulent representations, Plaintiff accepted Defendant's offer to buy, and the parties entered into a land contract. After taking occupancy, Defendant failed to make any of the contract payments. Plaintiff's investigation then revealed the fraud. Based on the fraud, Plaintiff sought rescission, ejectment, and recovery for five months of lost use of the property and out-of-pocket expenses. Defendant claimed that under the election of remedies doctrine, Plaintiff seller could not both rescind the contract and get damages for its breach. How should the court rule?
10. Buyers contracted to purchase a house being constructed by Contractor. The contract contained this clause: "Contractor shall pay to the owners or deduct from the total contract price $100.00 per day as liquidated damages for each day after said date that the construction is not completed and accepted by the Owners and Owners shall not arbitrarily withhold acceptance." Testimony established the rental value of the home at $400–$415 per month. Is the clause enforceable?

Self-Test Questions

1. Contract remedies protect
    a. a restitution interest
    b. a reliance interest
    c. an expectation interest
    d. all of the above
2. A restitution interest is
    a. the benefit for which the promisee bargained
    b. the loss suffered by relying on the contract
    c. that which restores any benefit one party conferred on the other
    d. none of the above
3. When breach of contract caused no monetary loss, the plaintiff is entitled to
    a. special damages
    b. nominal damages
    c. consequential damages
    d. no damages
4. Damages attributable to losses that flow from events that do not occur in the ordinary course of events are
    a. incidental damages
    b. liquidated damages
    c. consequential damages
    d. punitive damages
5. Restitution is available
    a. when the contract was avoided because of incapacity
    b. when the other party breached
    c. when the party seeking restitution breached
    d. all of the above

Self-Test Answers

1. d
2. c
3. b
4. c
5. d

Endnotes

1. Restatement (Second) of Contracts, Section 373.
2. *Hadley v. Baxendale* (1854), 9 Ex. 341, 354, 156 Eng.Rep. 145, 151.
3. Restatement (Second) of Contracts, Section 350.
4. *Merritt v. Craig*, 746 A.2d 923 (Md. 2000).
5. *Head & Seemann, Inc. v. Gregg*, 311 N.W.2d 667 (Wis. App. 1981).
6. *Tamarind Lithography Workshop v. Sanders*, 193 Cal. Rptr. 409 (Calif. Ct. App., 1983).

CHAPTER 17
Introduction to Sales and Leases

Learning Objectives

After reading this chapter, you should understand the following:

1. Why the law of commercial transactions is separate from the common law.
2. What is meant by "commercial transactions" and how the Uniform Commercial Code (UCC) deals with them in general.
3. The scope of Article 2, Article 2A, and the Convention on Contracts for the International Sale of Goods.
4. What obligations similar to the common law's are imposed on parties to a UCC contract, and what obligations different from the common law's are imposed.
5. The difference between a consumer lease and a finance lease.

17.1 Commercial Transactions: the Uniform Commercial Code

Learning Objectives

1. Understand why there is a separate body of law governing commercial transactions.
2. Be aware of the scope of the Uniform Commercial Code.
3. Have a sense of this text's presentation of the law of commercial transactions.

History of the UCC

In Chapter 8 we introduced the Uniform Commercial Code. As we noted, the UCC has become a national law, adopted by every state—although Louisiana has not enacted Article 2, and differences in the law exist from state to state. Of all the uniform laws related to commercial transactions, the UCC is by far the most successful, and its history goes back to feudal times.

In a mostly agricultural, self-sufficient society there is little need for trade, and almost all law deals with things related to land (real estate): its sale, lease, and devising (transmission of ownership by inheritance); services performed on the land; and damages to the land or to things related to it or to its productive capacity (torts). Such trade as existed in England before the late fourteenth century was dominated by foreigners. But after the pandemic of the Black Death in 1348–49 (when something like 30 percent to 40 percent of the English population died), the self-sufficient feudal manors began to break down. There was a shortage of labor. People could move off the manors to find better work, and no longer tied immediately to the old estates, they migrated to towns. Urban centers—cities—began to develop. Urbanization inevitably reached the point where citizens' needs could not be met locally. Enterprising people recognized that some places had a surplus of a product and that other places were in need of that surplus and had a surplus of their own to exchange for it. So then, by necessity, people developed the means to transport the surpluses. Enter ships, roads, some medium of exchange, standardized weights and measures, accountants, lawyers, and rules governing merchandising. And enter merchants.

> *The power of merchants was expressed through franchises obtained from the government which entitled merchants to create their own rules of law and to enforce these rules through their own courts. Franchises to hold fairs [retail exchanges] were temporary; but the franchises of the staple cities, empowered to deal in certain basic commodities [and to have mercantile courts], were permanent. . . . Many trading towns had their own adaptations of commercial law. . . . The seventeenth century movement toward national governments resulted in a decline of separate mercantile franchises and their courts. The staple towns . . . had outlived their usefulness. When the law merchant became incorporated into a national system of laws enforced by national courts of general jurisdiction, the local codes were finally extinguished. But national systems of law necessarily depended upon the older codes for their stock of ideas and on the changing customs of merchants for new developments.*[1]

When the American colonies declared independence from Britain, they continued to use British law, including the laws related to commercial transactions. By the early twentieth century, the states had inconsistent rules, making interstate commerce difficult and problematic. Several uniform laws affecting commercial transactions were floated in the late nineteenth century, but few were widely adopted. In 1942, the American Law Institute (ALI)[2] hired staff to begin work on a rationalized, simplified, and harmonized national body of modern commercial law. The ALI's first draft of the UCC was completed in 1951. The UCC was adopted by Pennsylvania two years later, and other states followed in the 1950s and 1960s.

In the 1980s and 1990s, the leasing of personal property became a significant factor in commercial transactions, and although the UCC had some sections that were applicable to leases, the law regarding the sale of goods was inadequate to address leases. Article 2A governing the leasing of goods was approved by the ALI in 1987. It essentially repeats Article 2 but applies to leases instead of sales. In 2001, amendments to Article 1—which applies to the entire UCC—were proposed and subsequently have been adopted by over half the states. No state has yet adopted the modernizing amendments to Article 2 and 2A that the ALI proposed in 2003.

That's the short history of why the body of commercial transaction law is separate from the common law.

Scope of the UCC and This Text's Presentation of the UCC

The UCC embraces the law of commercial transactions, a term of some ambiguity. A commercial transaction may seem to be a series of separate transactions; it may include, for example, the making of a contract for the sale of goods, the signing of a check, the endorsement of the check, the shipment of goods under a bill of lading, and so on. However, the UCC presupposes that each of these transactions is a facet of one single transaction: the lease or sale of, and payment for, goods. The code deals with phases of this transaction from start to finish. These phases are organized according to the following articles:

- Sales (Article 2)
- Leases (Article 2A)
- Commercial Paper (Article 3)

- Bank Deposits and Collections (Article 4)
- Funds Transfers (Article 4A)
- Letters of Credit (Article 5)
- Bulk Transfers (Article 6)
- Warehouse Receipts, Bills of Lading, and Other Documents of Title (Article 7)
- Investment Securities (Article 8)
- Secured Transactions; Sales of Accounts and Chattel Paper (Article 9)

Although the UCC comprehensively covers commercial transactions, it does not deal with every aspect of commercial law. Among the subjects not covered are the sale of real property, mortgages, insurance contracts, suretyship transactions (unless the surety is party to a negotiable instrument), and bankruptcy. Moreover, common-law principles of contract law that were examined in previous chapters continue to apply to many transactions covered in a particular way by the UCC. These principles include capacity to contract, misrepresentation, coercion, and mistake. Many federal laws supersede the UCC; these include the Bills of Lading Act, the Consumer Credit Protection Act, the warranty provisions of the Magnuson-Moss Act, and other regulatory statutes.

We follow the general outlines of the UCC in this chapter and in Chapter 18 and Chapter 19. In this chapter, we cover the law governing sales (Article 2) and make some reference to leases (Article 2A), though space constraints preclude an exhaustive analysis of leases. The use of documents of title to ship and store goods is closely related to sales, and so we cover documents of title (Article 7) as well as the law of bailments in Chapter 21.

In Chapter 22, Chapter 23, Chapter 24, and Chapter 25, we cover the giving of a check, draft, or note (commercial paper) for part or all of the purchase price and the negotiation of the commercial paper (Article 3). Related matters, such as bank deposits and collections (Article 4), funds transfers (Article 4A), and letters of credit (Article 5), are also covered there.

In Chapter 28 we turn to acceptance of security by the seller or lender for financing the balance of the payment due. Key to this area is the law of secured transactions (Article 9), but other types of security (e.g., mortgages and suretyship) not covered in the UCC will also be discussed in Chapter 29. Chapter 27 covers consumer credit transactions and Chapter 30 covers bankruptcy law; these topics are important for all creditors, even those lacking some form of security.

Finally, the specialized topic of Article 8, investment securities (e.g., corporate stocks and bonds), is treated in Chapter 43.

We now turn our attention to the sale—the first facet, and the cornerstone, of the commercial transaction.

Key Takeaway

In the development of the English legal system, commercial transactions were originally of such little importance that the rules governing them were left to the merchants themselves. They had their own courts and adopted their own rules based on their customary usage. By the 1700s, the separate courts had been absorbed into the English common law, but the distinct rules applicable to commercial transactions remained and have carried over to the modern UCC. The UCC treats commercial transactions in phases, and this text basically traces those phases.

Exercises

1. Why were medieval merchants compelled to develop their own rules about commercial transactions?
2. Why was the UCC developed, and when was the period of its initial adoption by states?

17.2 Introduction to Sales and Lease Law, and the Convention on Contracts for the International Sale of Goods

Learning Objectives

1. Understand that the law of sales not only incorporates many aspects of common-law contract but also addresses some distinct issues that do not occur in contracts for the sale of real estate or services.
2. Understand the scope of Article 2 and the definitions of *sale* and *goods*.
3. Learn how courts deal with hybrid situations: mixtures of the sale of goods and of real estate, mixtures of goods and services.
4. Recognize the scope of Article 2A and the definitions of *lease*, *consumer lease*, and *finance lease*.
5. Learn about the Convention on Contracts for the International Sale of Goods and why it is relevant to our discussion of Article 2.

Scope of Articles 2 and 2A and Definitions

In dealing with any statute, it is of course very important to understand the statute's scope or coverage.

Article 2 does not govern all commercial transactions, only sales. It does not cover all sales, only the sale of goods. Article 2A governs leases, but only of personal property (goods), not real estate. The Convention on Contracts for the International Sale of Goods (CISG)—kind of an international Article 2—"applies to contracts of sale of goods between parties whose places of business are in different States [i.e., countries]" (CISG, Article 1). So we need to consider the definitions of *sale*, *goods*, and *lease*.

Definition of *Sale*

sale

An arrangement whereby the lessee comes to own the leased goods after the term of the lease for little additional consideration.

A **sale** "consists in the passing of title from the seller to the buyer for a price."[3]

Sales are distinguished from gifts, bailments, leases, and secured transactions. Article 2 sales should be distinguished from gifts, bailments, leases, and secured transactions. A **gift** is the transfer of title without consideration, and a "contract" for a gift of goods is unenforceable under the Uniform Commercial Code (UCC) or otherwise (with some exceptions). A **bailment** is the transfer of possession but not title or use; parking your car in a commercial garage often creates a bailment with the garage owner. A lease (see the formal definition later in this chapter) is a fixed-term arrangement for possession and use of something—computer equipment, for example—and does not transfer title. In a **secured transaction**, the owner-debtor gives a security interest in collateral to a creditor that allows the creditor to repossess the collateral if the owner defaults.

gift

A thing bestowed on another gratuitously as a present.

bailment

The rightful possession of goods by one not their owner.

secured transaction

A mortgage on personal property so that the creditor may repossess it in case the debtor-owner defaults.

goods

Under the UCC, all things movable at the time of the contract.

Definition of *Goods*

Even if the transaction is considered a sale, the question still remains whether the contract concerns the sale of goods. Article 2 applies only to goods; sales of real estate and services are governed by non-UCC law. Section 2-105(1) of the UCC defines **goods** as "all things...which are movable at the time of identification to the contract for sale other than the money in which the price is to be paid." Money can be considered goods subject to Article 2 if it is the object of the contract—for example, foreign currency.

In certain cases, the courts have difficulty applying this definition because the item in question can also be viewed as realty or service. Most borderline cases raise one of two general questions:

1. Is the contract for the sale of the real estate, or is it for the sale of goods?
2. Is the contract for the sale of goods, or is it for services?

Real Estate versus Goods

The dilemma is this: A landowner enters into a contract to sell crops, timber, minerals, oil, or gas. If the items have already been detached from the land—for example, timber has been cut and the seller agrees to sell logs—they are goods, and the UCC governs the sale. But what if, at the time the contract is made, the items are still part of the land? Is a contract for the sale of uncut timber governed by the UCC or by real estate law?

The UCC governs under either of two circumstances: (1) if the contract calls for the seller to sever the items or (2) if the contract calls for the buyer to sever the items and if the goods can be severed without material harm to the real estate.[4] The second provision specifically includes growing crops and timber. By contrast, the law of real property governs if the buyer's severance of the items will materially harm the real estate; for example, the removal of minerals, oil, gas, and structures by the buyer will cause the law of real property to govern. (See Figure 17.1.)

FIGURE 17.1 Governing Law

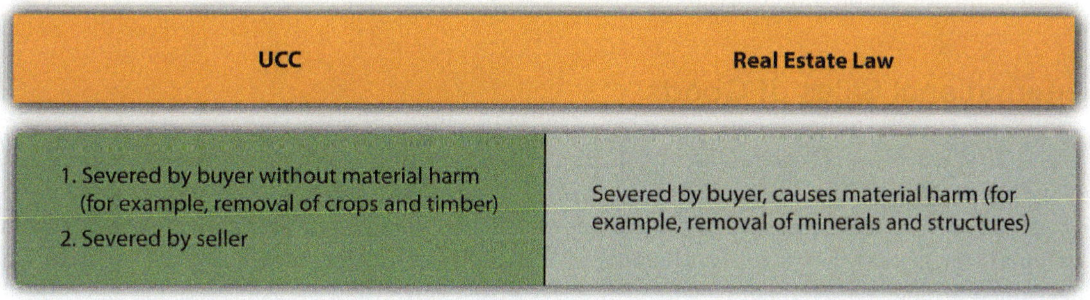

Goods versus Services

Distinguishing goods from services is the other major difficulty that arises in determining the nature of the object of a sales contract. The problem: how can goods and services be separated in contracts calling for the seller to deliver a combination of goods and services? That issue is examined in Section 5 (*Pittsley v. Houser*), where the court applied the common "predominant factor" (also sometimes "predominate purpose" or "predominant thrust") test—that is, it asked whether the transaction was predominantly a contract for goods or for services. However, the results of this analysis are not always consistent. Compare *Epstein v. Giannattasio*, in which the court held that no sale of goods had been made because the plaintiff received a treatment in which the cosmetics were only incidentally used, with *Newmark v. Gimble's, Inc.*, in which the court said "[i]f the permanent wave lotion were sold...for home consumption...unquestionably an implied warranty of fitness for that purpose would have been an integral incident of the sale."[5] The New Jersey court rejected the defendant's argument that by actually applying the lotion to the patron's head, the salon lessened the liability it otherwise would have had if it had simply sold her the lotion.

In two areas, state legislatures have taken the goods-versus-services issue out of the courts' hands and resolved the issue through legislation. Food sold in restaurants is a sale of goods, whether it is to be consumed on or off the premises. Blood transfusions (really the sale of blood) in hospitals have been legislatively declared a service, not a sale of goods, in more than forty states, thus relieving the suppliers and hospitals of an onerous burden for liability from selling blood tainted with the undetectable hepatitis virus.

Definition of *Lease*

Section 2A-103(j) of the UCC defines a **lease** as "a transfer of the right to possession and use of goods for a term in return for consideration." The **lessor** is the one who transfers the right to possession to the **lessee**. If Alice rents a party canopy from Equipment Supply, Equipment Supply is the lessor and Alice is the lessee.

lease

The transfer of right of possession and use for a price.

lessor

One who gives possession of leased goods to another for a price.

lessee

One who takes possession of and uses leased goods for a price.

consumer lease

A lease of goods by a lessor to a lessee for household uses.

finance lease

A lease by a lessor who buys or obtains the goods from a supplier for the purpose of leasing them to a commercial lessee.

Two Types of Leases

The UCC recognizes two kinds of leases: consumer leases and finance leases. A **consumer lease** is used when a lessor leases goods to "an individual...primarily for personal, family, or household purposes," where total lease payments are less than $25,000.[6] The UCC grants some special protections to consumer lessees. A **finance lease** is used when a lessor "acquires the goods or the right to [them]" and leases them to the lessee.[7] The person from whom the lessor acquires the goods is a supplier, and the lessor is simply financing the deal. Jack wants to lease a boom lift (personnel aerial lift, also known as a cherry picker) for a commercial roof renovation. First Bank agrees to buy (or itself lease) the machine from Equipment Supply and in turn lease it to Jack. First Bank is the lessor, Jack is the lessee, and Equipment Supply is the supplier.

International Sales of Goods

The UCC is, of course, American law, adopted by the states of the United States—it is not federal law. The reason it has been adopted is because of the inconvenience of doing interstate business when each state had a different law for the sale of goods. The same problem presents itself in international transactions. As a result, the United Nations Commission on International Trade Law developed an international equivalent of the UCC, the Convention on Contracts for the International Sale of Goods (CISG), first mentioned in Chapter 8. It was promulgated in Vienna in 1980. As of December 2015, the convention (a type of treaty) has been adopted by eighty-four countries, including the United States and all its major trading partners except the United Kingdom. One commentator opined on why the United Kingdom is an odd country out: it is "perhaps because of pride in its longstanding common law legal imperialism or in its long-treasured feeling of the superiority of English law to anything else that could even challenge it."[8]

The CISG is interesting for two reasons. First, assuming globalization continues, the CISG will become increasingly important around the world as the law governing international sale contracts. Its preamble states, "The adoption of uniform rules which govern contracts for the international sale of goods and take into account the different social, economic and legal systems [will] contribute to the removal of legal barriers in international trade and promote the development of international trade." Second, it is interesting to compare the legal culture informing the common law to that informing the CISG, which is not of the English common-law tradition. Throughout our discussion of Article 2, we will make reference to the CISG, the complete text of which is available online.[9] References to the CISG are in bold.

As to the CISG's scope, CISG Article 1 provides that it "applies to contracts of sale of goods between parties whose places of business are in different States [i.e., countries]; it "governs only the formation of the contract of sale and the rights and obligations of the seller and the buyer arising from such a contract," and has nothing to do "with the validity of the contract or of any of its provisions or of any usage" (Article 4). It excludes sales (a) of goods bought for personal, family or household use, unless the seller, at any time before or at the conclusion of the contract, neither knew nor ought to have known that the goods were bought for any such use; (b) by auction; (c) on execution or otherwise by authority of law; (d) of stocks, shares, investment securities, negotiable instruments or money; (e) of ships, vessels, hovercraft or aircraft; (f) of electricity (Article 2).

Parties are free to exclude the application of the Convention or, with a limited exception, vary the effect of any of its provisions (Article 6).

Key Takeaway

Article 2 of the UCC deals with the sale of goods. *Sale* and *goods* have defined meanings. Article 2A of the UCC deals with the leasing of goods. *Lease* has a defined meaning, and the UCC recognizes two types of leases: consumer leases and finance leases. Similar in purpose to the UCC of the United States is the Convention on Contracts for the International Sale of Goods, which has been widely adopted around the world.

Exercises

1. Why is there a separate body of statutory law governing contracts for the sale of goods as opposed to the common law, which governs contracts affecting real estate and services?
2. What is a consumer lease? A finance lease?
3. What is the Convention on Contracts for the International Sale of Goods?

17.3 Sales Law Compared with Common-Law Contracts and the CISG

Learning Objective

1. Recognize the differences and similarities among the Uniform Commercial Code (UCC), common-law contracts, and the CISG as related to the following contract issues:
    - Offer and acceptance
    - Revocability
    - Consideration
    - The requirement of a writing and contractual interpretation (form and meaning)

Sales law deals with the sale of goods. Sales law is a special type of contract law, but the common law informs much of Article 2 of the UCC—with some differences, however. Some of the similarities and differences were discussed in previous chapters that covered common-law contracts, but a review here is appropriate, and we can refer briefly to the CISG's treatment of similar issues.

Mutual Assent: Offer and Acceptance

Definiteness of the Offer

open terms

Under the UCC, a term that has not been expressed in the contract.

The common law requires more definiteness than the UCC. Under the UCC, a contractual obligation may arise even if the agreement has **open terms**. Under Section 2-204(3), such an agreement for sale is not voidable for indefiniteness, as in the common law, if the parties have intended to make a contract and the court can find a reasonably certain basis for giving an appropriate remedy. Perhaps the most important example is the open price term.

The open price term is covered in detail in Section 2-305. At common law, a contract that fails to specify price or a means of accurately ascertaining price will almost always fail. This is not so under the UCC provision regarding open price terms. If the contract says nothing about price, or if it permits the parties to agree on price but they fail to agree, or if it delegates the power to fix price to a third person who fails to do so, then Section 2-305(1) "plugs" the open term and decrees that the price to be awarded is a "reasonable price at the time for delivery." When one party is permitted to fix the price, Section 2-305(2) requires that it be fixed in good faith. However, if the parties *intend* not to be bound unless the price is first fixed or agreed on, and it is not fixed or agreed on, then no contract results.[10]

Another illustration of the open term is in regard to particulars of performance. Section 2-311(1) provides that a contract for sale of goods is not invalid just because it leaves to one of the parties the power to specify a particular means of performing. However, "any such specification must be made in good faith and within limits set by commercial reasonableness." (Performance will be covered in greater detail in Chapter 18.)

The CISG (Article 14) provides the following: **"A proposal for concluding a contract addressed to one or more specific persons constitutes an offer if it is sufficiently definite and indicates the intention of the offeror to be bound in case of acceptance. A proposal is sufficiently definite if it indicates the goods and expressly or implicitly fixes or makes provision for determining the quantity and the price."**

Acceptance Varying from Offer: Battle of the Forms

The concepts of offer and acceptance are basic to any agreement, but the UCC makes a change from the common law in its treatment of an acceptance that varies from the offer (this was discussed in Chapter 8). At common law, where the "mirror image rule" reigns, if the acceptance differs from the offer, no contract results. If that were the rule for sales contracts, with the pervasive use of form contracts—where each side's form tends to favor that side—it would be very problematic.

Section 2-207 of the UCC attempts to resolve this "battle of the forms" by providing that additional terms or conditions in an acceptance operate as such unless the acceptance is conditioned on the offeror's consent to the new or different terms. The new terms are construed as offers but are automatically incorporated in any contract between merchants for the sale of goods unless "(a) the offer expressly limits acceptance to the terms of the offer; (b) [the terms] materially alter it; or (c) notification of objection to them has already been given or is given within a reasonable time after notice of them is received." In any case, Section 2-207 goes on like this: "Conduct by both parties which recognizes the existence of a contract is sufficient to establish a contract for sale although the writings of the parties do not otherwise establish a contract. In such case the terms of the particular contract consist of those terms on which the writings of the parties agree, together with any supplementary terms incorporated under any other provisions of this Act."[11]

As to international contracts, the CISG says this about an acceptance that varies from the offer (Article 19), and it's pretty much the same as the UCC:

(1) A reply to an offer which purports to be an acceptance but contains additions, limitations or other modifications is a rejection of the offer and constitutes a counter-offer.

(2) However, a reply to an offer which purports to be an acceptance but contains additional or different terms which do not materially alter the terms of the offer constitutes an acceptance, unless the offeror, without undue delay, objects orally to the discrepancy or dispatches a notice to that effect. If he does not so object, the terms of the contract are the terms of the offer with the modifications contained in the acceptance.

(3) Additional or different terms relating, among other things, to the price, payment, quality and quantity of the goods, place and time of delivery, extent of one party's liability to the other or the settlement of disputes are considered to alter the terms of the offer materially.

Revocation of Offer

Under both common law and the UCC, an offer can be revoked at any time prior to acceptance unless the offeror has given the offeree an option (supported by consideration); under the UCC, an offer can be revoked at any time prior to acceptance unless a merchant gives a "**firm offer**" (for which no consideration is needed). The CISG (Article 17) provides that an offer is revocable before it is accepted unless, however, "it indicates…that it is irrevocable" or if the offeree reasonably relied on its irrevocability.

firm offer

A promise by a merchant to buy or sell goods in a signed (or "authenticated") writing that is not revocable during the time stated or for a reasonable time not to exceed six months (UCC 2-205).

Reality of Consent

There is no particular difference between the common law and the UCC on issues of duress, misrepresentation, undue influence, or mistake. As for international sales contracts, the CISG provides (Article 4(a)) that it "governs only the formation of the contract of sale and the rights and obligations of the seller and the buyer arising from such a contract and is not concerned with the validity of the contract or of any of its provisions."

Consideration

The UCC

The UCC requires no consideration for modification of a sales contract made in good faith; at common law, consideration is required to modify a contract.[12] The UCC requires no consideration if one party wants to forgive another's breach by written waiver or renunciation signed and delivered by the aggrieved party; under common law, consideration is required to discharge a breaching party.[13] The UCC requires no consideration for a "firm offer"—a writing signed by a merchant promising to hold an offer open for some period of time; at common law an option requires consideration. (Note, however, the person can give an option under either common law or the code.)

Under the CISG (Article 29), "A contract may be modified or terminated by the mere agreement of the parties." No consideration is needed.

Form and Meaning

Requirement of a Writing

The common law is affected by the Statute of Frauds, and there is a writing requirement too, under the UCC. It requires a writing to enforce a contract for the sale of goods worth $500 or more, with some exceptions, as discussed in Chapter 13.[14]

The CISG provides (Article 11), "A contract of sale need not be concluded in or evidenced by writing and is not subject to any other requirement as to form. It may be proved by any means, including witnesses." But Article 29 provides, "A contract in writing which contains a provision requiring any modification or termination by agreement to be in writing may not be otherwise modified or terminated by agreement."

Parol Evidence

Section 2-202 of the UCC provides pretty much the same as the common law: if the parties have a writing intended to be their final agreement, it "may not be contradicted by evidence of any prior agreement or of a contemporaneous oral agreement." However, it may be explained by "course of dealing or usage of trade or by course of performance" and "by evidence of consistent additional terms."

The CISG provides (Article 8) the following: "In determining the intent of a party or the understanding a reasonable person would have had, due consideration is to be given to all relevant circumstances of the case including the negotiations, any practices which the parties have established between themselves, usages and any subsequent conduct of the parties."

Key Takeaway

The UCC modernizes and simplifies some common-law strictures. Under the UCC, the mirror image rule is abolished: an acceptance may sometimes differ from the offer, and the UCC can "plug" open terms in many cases. No consideration is required under the UCC to modify or terminate a contract or for a merchant's "firm offer," which makes the offer irrevocable according to its terms. The UCC has a Statute of Frauds analogous to the common law, and its parol evidence rule is similar as well. The CISG compares fairly closely to the UCC.

Exercises

1. Why does the UCC change the common-law mirror image rule, and how?
2. What is meant by "open terms," and how does the UCC handle them?
3. The requirement for consideration is relaxed under the UCC compared with common law. In what circumstances is no consideration necessary under the UCC?
4. On issues so far discussed, is the CISG more aligned with the common law or with the UCC? Explain your answer.

17.4 General Obligations under UCC Article 2

Learning Objectives

1. Know that the Uniform Commercial Code (UCC) imposes a general obligation to act in good faith and that it makes unconscionable contracts or parts of a contract unenforceable.
2. Recognize that though the UCC applies to all sales contracts, merchants have special obligations.
3. See that the UCC is the "default position"—that within limits, parties are free to put anything they want to in their contract.

Article 2 of the UCC of course has rules governing the obligations of parties specifically as to the offer, acceptance, performance of sales contracts, and so on. But it also imposes some general obligations on the parties. Two are called out here: one deals with unfair contract terms, and the second with obligations imposed on merchants.

Obligation of Good-Faith Dealings in General

Under the UCC

Section 1-203 of the UCC provides, "Every contract or duty within this Act imposes an obligation of good faith in its performance or enforcement." *Good faith* is defined at Section 2-103(j) as "honesty in fact and the observance of reasonable commercial standards of fair dealing." This is pretty much the same as what is held by common law, which "imposes a duty of good faith and fair dealing upon the parties in performing and enforcing the contract."[15]

The UCC's good faith in "performance or enforcement" of the contract is one thing, but what if the terms of the contract itself are unfair? Under Section 2-302(1), the courts may tinker with a contract if they determine that it is particularly unfair. The provision reads as follows: "If the court as a matter of law finds the contract or any clause of the contract to have been unconscionable at the time it was made the court may refuse to enforce the contract, or it may enforce the remainder of the contract without the unconscionable clause, or it may so limit the application of any unconscionable clause as to avoid any unconscionable result."

The court thus has considerable flexibility. It may refuse to enforce the entire contract, strike a particular clause or set of clauses, or limit the application of a particular clause or set of clauses.

And what does "unconscionable" mean? The UCC provides little guidance on this crucial question. According to Section 2-302(1), the test is "whether, in the light of the general commercial background and the commercial needs of the particular trade or case, the clauses involved are so one-sided as to be unconscionable under the circumstances existing at the time of the making of the contract.... The principle is one of the prevention of oppression and unfair surprise and not of disturbance of allocation of risks because of superior bargaining power."

procedural unconscionability

Unfairness in the process of contract making, as when the contract is in such fine print it cannot be read.

substantive unconscionability

Contract terms so harsh and one-sided as to be unacceptably unfair.

The definition is somewhat circular. For the most part, judges have had to develop the concept with little help from the statutory language. Unconscionability is much like US Supreme Court Justice Potter Stewart's famous statement about obscenity: "I can't define it, but I know it when I see it." In the leading case, *Williams v. Walker-Thomas Furniture Co.* (Chapter 12.5, set out in Chapter 12), Judge J. Skelly Wright attempted to develop a framework for analysis. He refined the meaning of unconscionability by focusing on "absence of meaningful choice" (often referred to as **procedural unconscionability**) and on terms that are "unreasonably favorable" (commonly referred to as **substantive unconscionability**). An example of procedural unconscionability is the salesperson who says, "Don't worry about all that little type on the back of this form." Substantive unconscionability is the harsh term—the provision that permits the "taking of a pound of flesh" if the contract is not honored.

Despite its fuzziness, the concept of unconscionability has had a dramatic impact on American law. In many cases, in fact, the traditional notion of *caveat emptor* (Latin for "buyer beware") has changed to *caveat venditor* ("let the seller beware"). So important is this provision that courts in recent years have applied the doctrine in cases not involving the sale of goods.

Under the CISG, Article 7: "Regard is to be had...to the observance of good faith in international trade."

Obligations Owed by Merchants

"Merchant" Sellers

Although the UCC applies to all sales of goods (even when you sell your used car to your neighbor), merchants often have special obligations or are governed by special rules.

As between Merchants

The UCC assumes that merchants should be held to particular standards because they are more experienced and have or should have special knowledge. Rules applicable to professionals ought not apply to the casual or inexperienced buyer or seller. For example, we noted previously that the UCC relaxes the mirror image rule and provides that as "between merchants" additional terms in an acceptance become part of the contract, and we have discussed the "ten-day-reply doctrine" that says that, again "as between merchants," a writing signed and sent to the other binds the recipient as an exception to the Statute of Frauds.[16] There are other sections of the UCC applicable "as between merchants," too.

Article 1 of the CISG abolishes any distinction between merchants and nonmerchants: "Neither the nationality of the parties nor the civil or commercial character of the parties or of the contract is to be taken into consideration in determining the application of this Convention."

Merchant to Nonmerchant

In addition to duties imposed between merchants, the UCC imposes certain duties on a merchant when she sells to a nonmerchant. A merchant who sells her merchandise makes an important **implied warranty of merchantability**. That is, she promises that goods sold will be fit for the purpose for which such goods are normally intended. A nonmerchant makes no such promise, nor does a merchant who is not selling merchandise—for example, a supermarket selling a display case is not a "merchant" in display cases.

implied warranty of merchantability

An unexpressed promise that goods bought from a merchant are suitable for the purposes for which such goods are normally intended.

In *Sheeskin v. Giant Foods, Inc.*, the problem of whether a merchant made an implied warranty of merchantability was nicely presented. Mr. Seigel, the plaintiff, was carrying a six-pack carton of Coca-Cola from a display bin to his shopping cart when one or more of the bottles exploded. He lost his footing and was injured. When he sued the supermarket and the bottler for breach of the implied warranty of fitness, the defendants denied there had been a sale: he never paid for the soda pop, thus no sale by a merchant and thus no warranty. The court said that Mr. Seigel's act of reaching for the soda to put it in his cart was a "reasonable manner of acceptance" (quoting UCC, Section 2-206(1)).[17]

Who Is a Merchant?

Section 2-104(1) of the UCC defines a merchant as one "who deals in goods of the kind or otherwise by his occupation holds himself out as having knowledge or skill peculiar to the practices or goods involved in the transaction." A phrase that recurs throughout Article 2—"between merchants"—refers to any transaction in which both parties are chargeable with the knowledge or skill of merchants.[18] Not every businessperson is a merchant with respect to every possible transaction. But a person or institution normally not considered a merchant can be one under Article 2 if he employs an agent or broker who holds himself out as having such knowledge or skill. (Thus a university with a purchasing office can be a merchant with respect to transactions handled by that department.)

Determining whether a particular person operating a business is a merchant under Article 2-104 is a common problem for the courts. *Goldkist, Inc. v. Brownlee*, Section 5, shows that making the determination is difficult and contentious, with significant public policy implications.

Obligations May Be Determined by Parties

Under the UCC

Under the UCC, the parties to a contract are free to put into their contract pretty much anything they want. Article 1-102 states that "the effect of provisions of this Act may be varied by agreement...except that the obligations of good faith, diligence, reasonableness and care prescribed by this Act may not be disclaimed by agreement but the parties may by agreement determine the standards by which the performance of such obligations is to be measured if such standards are not manifestly unreasonable." Thus the UCC is the "default" position: if the parties want the contract to operate in a specific way, they can provide for that. If they don't put anything in their agreement about some aspect of their contract's operation, the UCC applies. For example, if they do not state where "delivery" will occur, the UCC provides that term. (Section 2-308 says it would be at the "seller's place of business or if he has none, his residence.")

Article 6 of the CISG similarly gives the parties freedom to contract. It provides, "The parties may exclude the application of this Convention or . . . vary the effect of any of its provisions."

Key Takeaway

The UCC imposes some general obligations on parties to a sales contract. They must act in good faith, and unconscionable contracts or terms thereof will not be enforced. The UCC applies to any sale of goods, but sometimes special obligations are imposed on merchants. While the UCC imposes various general (and more specific) obligations on the parties, they are free, within limits, to make up their own contract terms and obligations; if they do not, the UCC applies. The CISG tends to follow the basic thrust of the UCC.

Exercises

1. What does the UCC say about the standard duty parties to a contract owe each other?
2. Why are merchants treated specially by the UCC in some circumstances?
3. Give an example of a merchant-to-merchant duty imposed by the UCC and of a merchant-to-nonmerchant duty.
4. What does it mean to say the UCC is the "default" contract term?

17.5 Cases

Mixed Goods and Services Contracts: The "Predominant Factor" Test

Pittsley v. Houser

875 P.2d 232 (Idaho App. 1994)

Swanstrom, J.

In September of 1988, Jane Pittsley contracted with Hilton Contract Carpet Co. (Hilton) for the installation of carpet in her home. The total contract price was $4,402 [about $8,800 in 2016 dollars]. Hilton paid the installers $700 to put the carpet in Pittsley's home. Following installation, Pittsley complained to Hilton that some seams were visible, that gaps appeared, that the carpet did not lay flat in all areas, and that it failed to reach the wall in certain locations. Although Hilton made various attempts to fix the installation, by attempting to stretch the carpet and other methods, Pittsley was not satisfied with the work. Eventually, Pittsley refused any further efforts to fix the carpet. Pittsley initially paid Hilton $3,500 on the contract, but refused to pay the remaining balance of $902.

Pittsley later filed suit, seeking rescission of the contract, return of the $3,500 and incidental damages. Hilton answered and counterclaimed for the balance remaining on the contract. The matter was heard by a magistrate sitting without a jury. The magistrate found that there were defects in the installation and that the carpet had been installed in an unworkmanlike manner. The magistrate also found that there was a lack of evidence on damages. The trial was continued to allow the parties to procure evidence on the amount of damages incurred by Pittsley. Following this continuance, Pittsley did not introduce any further evidence of damages, though witnesses for Hilton estimated repair costs at $250.

Although Pittsley had asked for rescission of the contract and a refund of her money, the magistrate determined that rescission, as an equitable remedy, was only available when one party committed a breach so material that it destroyed the entire purpose of the contract. Because the only estimate of damages was for $250, the magistrate ruled rescission would not be a proper remedy. Instead, the magistrate awarded Pittsley $250 damages plus $150 she expended in moving furniture prior to Hilton's attempt to repair the carpet. On the counterclaim, the magistrate awarded Hilton the $902 remaining on the contract. Additionally, both parties had requested attorney fees in the action. The magistrate determined that both parties had prevailed and therefore awarded both parties their attorney fees.

Following this decision, Pittsley appealed to the district court, claiming that the transaction involved was governed by the Idaho Uniform Commercial Code (UCC), [Citation]. Pittsley argued that if the UCC had been properly applied, a different result would have been reached. The district court agreed with Pittsley's argument, reversing and remanding the case to the magistrate to make additional findings of fact and to apply the UCC to the transaction. * * *

Hilton now appeals the decision of the district court. Hilton claims that Pittsley failed to allege or argue the UCC in either her pleadings or at trial. Even if application of the UCC was properly raised, Hilton argues that there were no defects in the goods that were the subject of the transaction, only in the installation, making application of the UCC inappropriate. * * *

The single question upon which this appeal depends is whether the UCC is applicable to the subject transaction. If the underlying transaction involved the sale of "goods," then the UCC would apply. If the transaction did not involve goods, but rather was for services, then application of the UCC would be erroneous.

Idaho Code § 28–2-105(1) defines "goods" as "all things (including specially manufactured goods) which are movable at the time of identification to the contract for sale. . . ." Although there is little dispute that carpets are "goods," the transaction in this case also involved installation, a service. Such hybrid transactions, involving both goods and services, raise difficult questions about the applicability of the UCC. Two lines of authority have emerged to deal with such situations.

The first line of authority, and the majority position, utilizes the "predominant factor" test. The Ninth Circuit, applying the Idaho Uniform Commercial Code to the subject transaction, restated the predominant factor test as:

> *The test for inclusion or exclusion is not whether they are mixed, but, granting that they are mixed, whether their predominant factor, their thrust, their purpose, reasonably stated, is the rendition of service, with goods incidentally involved (e.g., contract with artist for painting) or is a transaction of sale, with labor incidentally involved (e.g., installation of a water heater in a bathroom).*

[Citations]. This test essentially involves consideration of the contract in its entirety, applying the UCC to the entire contract or not at all.

The second line of authority, which Hilton urges us to adopt, allows the contract to be severed into different parts, applying the UCC to the goods involved in the contract, but not to the non-goods involved, including services as well as other non-goods assets and property. Thus, an action focusing on defects or problems with the goods themselves would be covered by the UCC, while a suit based on the service provided or some other non-goods aspect would not be covered by the UCC. * * *

We believe the predominant factor test is the more prudent rule. Severing contracts into various parts, attempting to label each as goods or non-goods and applying different law to each separate part clearly contravenes the UCC's declared purpose "to simplify, clarify and modernize the law governing commercial transactions." I.C. § 28–1–102(2)(a). As the Supreme Court of Tennessee suggested in [Citation], such a rule would, in many contexts, present "difficult and in some instances insurmountable problems of proof in segregating assets and determining their respective values at the time of the original contract and at the time of resale, in order to apply two different measures of damages."

Applying the predominant factor test to the case before us, we conclude that the UCC was applicable to the subject transaction. The record indicates that the contract between the parties called for "175 yds Masterpiece # 2122-Installed" for a price of $4,319.50 [about $8,700 in 2016 dollars]. There was an additional charge for removing the existing carpet. The record indicates that Hilton paid the installers $700 for the work done in laying Pittsley's carpet. It appears that Pittsley entered into this contract for the purpose of obtaining carpet of a certain quality and color. It does not appear that the installation, either who would provide it or the nature of the work, was a factor in inducing Pittsley to choose Hilton as the carpet supplier. On these facts, we conclude that the sale of the carpet was the predominant factor in the contract, with the installation being merely incidental to the purchase. Therefore, in failing to consider the UCC, the magistrate did not apply the correct legal principles to the facts as found. We must therefore vacate the judgment and remand for further findings of fact and application of the UCC to the subject transaction.

Case Questions

1. You may recall in Chapter 15 the discussion of the "substantial performance" doctrine. It says that if a common-law contract is not completely, but still "substantially," performed, the nonbreaching party still owes something on the contract. And it was noted there that under the UCC, there is no such doctrine. Instead, the "perfect tender" rule applies: the goods delivered by the seller must be exactly right. Does the distinction between the substantial performance doctrine and the perfect tender rule shed light on what difference applying the common law or the UCC would make in this case?
2. If Pittsley won on remand, what would she get?
3. In discussing the predominant factor test, the court here quotes from the Ninth Circuit, a *federal* court of appeals. What is a federal court doing making rules for a state court (the UCC is state law)?

"Merchants" under the UCC

Goldkist, Inc. v. Brownlee

355 S.E.2d 773 (Ga. App. 1987)

Beasley, J.

The question is whether the two defendant farmers, who as a partnership both grew and sold their crops, were established by the undisputed facts as not being "merchants" as a matter of law, according to the definition in [Georgia UCC 2-104(1)]. * * *

Appellees admit that their crops are "goods" as defined in [2-105]. The record establishes the following facts. The partnership had been operating the row crop farming business for 14 years, producing peanuts, soybeans, corn, milo, and wheat on 1,350 acres, and selling the crops.

It is also established without dispute that Barney Brownlee, whose deposition was taken, was familiar with the marketing procedure of "booking" crops, which sometimes occurred over the phone between the farmer and the buyer, rather than in person, and a written contract would be signed later. He periodically called plaintiff's agent to check the price, which fluctuated. If the price met his approval, he sold soybeans. At this time the partnership still had some of its 1982 crop in storage, and the price was rising slowly. Mr. Brownlee received a written confirmation in the mail concerning a sale of soybeans and did not contact plaintiff to contest it but simply did nothing. In addition to the agricultural business, Brownlee operated a gasoline service station. * * *

In dispute are the facts with respect to whether or not an oral contract was made between Barney Brownlee for the partnership and agent Harrell for the buyer in a July 22 telephone conversation. The plaintiff's evidence was that it occurred and that it was discussed soon thereafter with Brownlee at the service station on two different occasions, when he acknowledged it, albeit reluctantly, because the market price of soybeans had risen. Mr. Brownlee denies booking the soybeans and denies the nature of the conversations at his service station with Harrell and the buyer's manager....

Whether or not the farmers in this case are "merchants" as a matter of law, which is not before us, the evidence does not demand a conclusion that they are outside of that category which is excepted from the requirement of a signed writing to bind a buyer and seller of goods. * * * To allow a farmer who deals in crops of the kind at issue, or who otherwise comes within the definition of "merchant" in [UCC] 2-104(1), to renege on a confirmed oral booking for the sale of crops, would result in a fraud on the buyer. The farmer could abide by the booking if the price thereafter declined but reject it if the price rose; the buyer, on the other hand, would be forced to sell the crop following the booking at its peril, or wait until the farmer decides whether to honor the booking or not.

Defendants' narrow construction of "merchant" would, given the booking procedure used for the sale of farm products, thus guarantee to the farmers the best of both possible worlds (fulfill booking if price goes down after booking and reject it if price improves) and to the buyers the worst of both possible worlds. On the other hand, construing "merchants" in [UCC] 2-104(1) as not excluding as a matter of law farmers such as the ones in this case, protects them equally as well as the buyer. If the market price declines after the booking, they are assured of the higher booking price; the buyer cannot renege, as [UCC]2-201(2) would apply.

In giving this construction to the statute, we are persuaded by [Citation], supra, and the analyses provided in the following cases from other states: [Citations]. By the same token, we reject the narrow construction given in other states' cases: [Citations]. We believe this is the proper construction to give the two statutes, [UCC 2-104(1) and 2-201(2)], as taken together they are thus further branches stemming from the centuries-old simple legal idea *pacta servanda sunt*—agreements are to be kept. So construed, they evince the legislative intent to enforce the accepted practices of the marketplace among those who frequent it.

Judgment reversed. [Four justices concurred with Justice Beasley].

Benham, J., dissenting.

Because I cannot agree with the majority's conclusion that appellees are merchants, I must respectfully dissent.

* * * The validity of [plaintiff's] argument, that sending a confirmation within a reasonable time makes enforceable a contract even though the statute of frauds has not been satisfied, rests upon a showing that the contract was "[b]etween merchants." "Between merchants" is statutorily defined in the Uniform Commercial Code as meaning "any transaction with respect to which both parties are chargeable with the knowledge or skill of merchants" [2-104(3)]. "'Merchant' means a person [1] who deals in goods of the kind or [2] otherwise by his occupation holds himself out as having knowledge or skill peculiar to the practices or goods involved in the transaction or [3] to whom such knowledge or skill may be attributed by his employment of an agent or broker or other intermediary who by his occupation holds himself out as having such knowledge or skill" [Citation]. Whether [plaintiff] is a merchant is not questioned here; the question is whether, under the facts in the record, [defendant]/farmers are merchants. * * *

The Official Comment to § 2-104 of the U.C.C. (codified in Georgia)...states: "This Article assumes that transactions between professionals in a given field require special and clear rules which may not apply to a casual or inexperienced seller or buyer. * * * This section lays the foundation of this policy by defining those who are to be regarded as professionals or 'merchants' and by stating when a transaction is deemed to be 'between merchants.' The term 'merchant' as defined here roots in the 'law merchant' concept of a professional in business." As noted by the Supreme Court of Kansas in [Citation] (1976): "The concept of professionalism is heavy in determining who is a merchant under the statute. The writers of the official UCC comment virtually equate professionals with merchants—the casual or inexperienced buyer or seller is not to be held to the standard set for the professional in business. The defined term 'between merchants,' used in the exception proviso to the statute of frauds, contemplates the knowledge and skill of professionals on each side of the transaction." The Supreme Court of Iowa [concurs in cases cited]. Where, as here, the undisputed evidence is that the farmer's sole experience in the marketplace consists of selling the crops he has grown, the courts of several of our sister states have concluded that the farmer is not a merchant. [Citations]. Just because appellee Barney Brownlee kept "conversant with the current price of [soybeans] and planned to market it to his advantage does not necessarily make him a 'merchant.' It is but natural for anyone who desires to sell anything he owns to negotiate and get the best price obtainable. If this would make one a 'merchant,' then practically anyone who sold anything would be deemed a merchant, hence would be an exception under the statute[,] and the need for a contract in writing could be eliminated in most any kind of a sale." [Citation]

It is also my opinion that the record does not reflect that appellees "dealt" in soybeans, or that through their occupation, they held themselves out as having knowledge or skill peculiar to the practices or goods involved in the transaction. See [UCC] 2-104(1). "[A]lthough a farmer may well possess special knowledge or skill with respect to the production of a crop, the term 'merchant,' as used in the Uniform Commercial Code, contemplates special knowledge and skill associated with the marketplace. As to the area of farm crops, this special skill or knowledge means, for instance, special skill or knowledge associated with the operation of the commodities market. It is inconceivable that the drafters of the Uniform Commercial Code intended to place the average farmer, who merely grows his yearly crop and sells it to the local elevator, etc., on equal footing with the professional commodities dealer whose sole business is the buying and selling of farm commodities" [Citations]. If one who buys or sells something on an annual basis is a merchant, then the annual purchaser of a new automobile is a merchant who need not sign a contract for the purchase in order for the contract to be enforceable. * * *

If these farmers are not merchants, a contract signed by both parties is necessary for enforcement. If the farmer signs a contract, he is liable for breach of contract if he fails to live up to its terms. If he does not sign the contract, he cannot seek enforcement of the terms of the purchaser's offer to buy. * * *

Because I find no evidence in the record that appellees meet the statutory qualifications as merchants, I would affirm the decision of the trial court. I am authorized to state that [three other justices] join in this dissent.

Case Questions

1. How is the UCC's ten-day-reply doctrine in issue here?
2. Five justices thought the farmers here should be classified as "merchants," and four of them thought otherwise. What argument did the majority have against calling the farmers "merchants"? What argument did the dissent have as to why they should not be called merchants?
3. Each side marshaled persuasive precedent from other jurisdictions to support its contention. As a matter of public policy, is one argument better than another?
4. What does the court mean when it says the defendants are not excluded from the definition of merchants "as a matter of law"?

Unconscionability in Finance Lease Contracts

Info. Leasing Corp. v. GDR Investments, Inc.
787 N.E.2d 652 (Ohio App. 2003)

Gorman, J.

The plaintiff-appellant, Information Leasing Corporation ("ILC"), appeals from the order of the trial court rendering judgment in favor of the defendants-appellees ... GDR Investments, Inc. [defendant Arora's corporation], Pinnacle Exxon, and Avtar S. Arora, in an action to recover $15,877.37 on a five-year commercial lease of an Automated Teller Machine ("ATM"). ...

This is one of many cases involving ILC that have been recently before this court. ILC is an Ohio corporation wholly owned by the Provident Bank. ILC is in the business of leasing ATMs through a third party, or vendor. In all of these cases, the vendor has been...Credit Card Center ("CCC"). CCC was in the business of finding lessees for the machines and then providing the services necessary to operate them, offering the lessees attractive commissions. Essentially, CCC would find a customer, usually a small business interested in having an ATM available on its premises, arrange for its customer to sign a lease with ILC, and then agree to service the machine, keeping it stocked with cash and paying the customer a certain monthly commission. Usually, as in the case of [defendants], the owner of the business was required to sign as a personal guarantor of the lease. The twist in this story is that CCC soon went bankrupt, leaving its customers stuck with ATMs under the terms of leases with ILC but with no service provider. Rather than seeking to find another company to service the ATMs, many of CCC's former customers, like [defendants], simply decided that they no longer wanted the ATMs and were no longer going to make lease payments to ILC. The terms of each lease, however, prohibited cancellation. The pertinent section read,

LEASE NON-CANCELABLE AND NO WARRANTY. THIS LEASE CANNOT BE CANCELED BY YOU FOR ANY REASON, INCLUDING EQUIPMENT FAILURE, LOSS OR DAMAGE. YOU MAY NOT REVOKE ACCEPTANCE OF THE EQUIPMENT. YOU, NOT WE, SELECTED THE EQUIPMENT AND THE VENDOR. WE ARE NOT RESPONSIBLE FOR EQUIPMENT FAILURE OR THE VENDOR'S ACTS. YOU ARE LEASING THE EQUIPMENT 'AS IS', [sic] AND WE DISCLAIM ALL WARRANTIES, EXPRESS OR IMPLIED. WE ARE NOT RESPONSIBLE FOR SERVICE OR REPAIRS.

Either out of a sense of fair play or a further desire to make enforcement of the lease ironclad, ILC put a notice on the top of the lease that stated,

NOTICE: THIS IS A NON-CANCELABLE, BINDING CONTRACT. THIS CONTRACT WAS WRITTEN IN PLAIN LANGUAGE FOR YOUR BENEFIT. IT CONTAINS IMPORTANT TERMS AND CONDITIONS AND HAS LEGAL AND FINANCIAL CONSEQUENCES TO YOU. PLEASE READ IT CAREFULLY; FEEL FREE TO ASK QUESTIONS BEFORE SIGNING BY CALLING THE LEASING COMPANY AT 1-513-421-9191.

Arora, the owner of [defendant corporation], was a resident alien with degrees in commerce and economics from the University of Delhi, India. Arora wished to have an ATM on the premises of his Exxon station in the hope of increasing business. He made the mistake of arranging acquisition of the ATM through CCC. According to his testimony, a representative of CCC showed up at the station one day and gave him "formality papers" to sign before the ATM could be delivered. Arora stated that he was busy with other customers when the CCC representative asked him to sign the papers. He testified that when he informed the CCC representative that he needed time to read the documents before signing them, he was told not to worry and…that the papers did not need his attention and that his signature was a mere formality. Arora signed the ILC lease, having never read it.

Within days, CCC went into bankruptcy. Arora found himself with an ATM that he no longer wanted.…According to his testimony, he tried unsuccessfully to contact ILC to take back the ATM. Soon Arora suffered a mild heart attack, the gas station went out of business, and the ATM, which had been in place for approximately eighteen days, was left sitting in the garage, no longer in use until ILC came and removed it several months later.

Unfortunately for Arora, the lease also had an acceleration clause that read,

DEFAULT. If you fail to pay us or perform as agreed, we will have the right to (i) terminate this lease, (ii) sue you for all past due payment AND ALL FUTURE PAYMENTS UNDER THIS LEASE, plus the Residual Value we have placed on the equipment and other charges you owe us, (iii) repossess the equipment at your expense and (iv) exercise any other right or remedy which may be available under applicable law or proceed by court act.

The trial court listened to the evidence in this case, which was awkwardly presented due in large part to Arora's decision to act as his own trial counsel. Obviously impressed with Arora's honesty and sympathetic to his situation, the trial court found that Arora owed ILC nothing. In so ruling, the court stated that ILC "ha[d] not complied with any of its contractual obligations and that [Arora] appropriately canceled any obligations by him, if there really were any." The court also found that ILC, "if they did have a contract, failed to mitigate any damages by timely picking up the machine after [Arora] gave them notice to pick up the machine."…

ILC contends, and we do not disagree, that the lease in question satisfied the definition of a "finance lease" under [UCC 2A-407]. A finance lease is considerably different from an ordinary lease in that it adds a third party, the equipment supplier or manufacturer (in this case, the now defunct CCC). As noted by White and Summers, "In effect, the finance lessee * * * is relying upon the manufacturer * * * to provide the promised goods and stand by its promises and warranties; the [lessee] does not look to the [lessor] for these. The [lessor] is only a finance lessor and deals largely in paper, rather than goods." [Citation].

One notorious feature of a finance lease is its typically noncancelable nature, which is specifically authorized by statute [UCC 2A-407]. [UCC 2A-407(1)] provides in the case of a finance lease that is not a consumer lease, "[T]he lessee's promises under the lease contract become irrevocable and independent upon the lessee's acceptance of the goods." The same statutory section also makes clear that the finance lease is "not subject to cancellation, termination, modification, repudiation, excuse, or substitution without the consent of the party to whom it runs." [Citation]

Because of their noncancelable nature, finance leases enjoy somewhat of a reputation. The titles of law review articles written about them reveal more than a little cynicism regarding their fairness: [Citations].

…As described by Professors White and Summers, "The parties can draft a lease agreement that carefully excludes warranty and promissory liability of the finance lessor to the lessee, and that sets out what is known in the trade as a 'hell or high water clause,' namely, a clause that requires the lessee to continue to make rent payments to the finance lessor even though the [equipment] is unsuitable, defective, or destroyed."…"The lessor's responsibility is merely to provide the money, not to instruct the lessee like a wayward child concerning a suitable purchase * * *. Absent contrary agreement, even if [, for example, a finance-leased] Boeing 747 explodes into small pieces in flight and is completely uninsured, lessee's obligation to pay continues."

...Some people complain about being stuck with the bill; Arora's complaint was that he was stuck with the ATM....

To begin the proper legal analysis, we note first that this was not a "consumer lease" expressly excepted from [UCC 2A-407]. A "consumer lease" is defined in [UCC 2A-103(e)] as one in which the lessee is "an individual and who takes under the lease primarily for a personal, family, or household purpose." This would definitely not apply here, where the ATM was placed on the business premises of the Exxon station, and where the lessee was [Arora's corporation] and not Arora individually. (Arora was liable individually as the personal guarantor of [his corporation]'s obligations under the lease.)...

Certain defenses do remain, however. First, the UCC expressly allows for the application of the doctrine of unconscionability to finance leases, both consumer and commercial. [Citation] authorizes the trial court to find "any clause of a lease contract to have been unconscionable at the time it was made * * *." If it so finds, the court is given the power to "refuse to enforce the lease contract, * * * enforce the remainder of the lease contract without the unconscionable clause, or * * * limit the application of the unconscionable clause as to avoid any unconscionable result." [Citation]

In this case, the trial court made no findings as to whether the finance lease was unconscionable. The primary purpose of the doctrine of unconscionability is to prevent oppression and unfair surprise. [Citation] "Oppression" refers to substantive unconscionability and arises from overly burdensome or punitive terms of a contract, whereas "unfair surprise" refers to procedural unconscionability and is implicated in the formation of a contract, when one of the parties is either overborne by a lack of equal bargaining power or otherwise unfairly or unjustly drawn into a contract. [Citation]

It should be pointed that, although harsh, many characteristics of a finance lease are not inherently unconscionable and, as we have discussed, are specifically authorized by statute. Simply because a finance lease has a "hell or high water clause" does not make it unconscionable. As noted, a finance lease is a separate animal—it is supposed to secure minimal risk to the lessor. At least one court has rejected the argument that an acceleration clause in a commercial finance lease is punitive and unconscionable in the context of parties of relatively equal bargaining power. See [Citation]

At the heart of Arora's defense in this case was his claim that he was misled into signing the finance lease by the CCC representative and was unfairly surprised to find himself the unwitting signatory of an oppressive lease. This is clearly an argument that implicated procedural unconscionability. His claim of being an unwitting signatory, however, must be carefully balanced against the law in Ohio that places upon a person a duty to read any contract before signing it, a duty that is not excused simply because a person willingly gives into the encouragement to "just go ahead and sign." See [Citation]

Moreover, we note that courts have also recognized that the lessor may give, through word or conduct, the lessee consent to cancel an otherwise noncancelable lease. [UCC 2A-40792)(b)] makes a finance lease "not subject to cancellation, termination, modification, repudiation, excuse, or substitution *without the consent of the party to whom it runs*." (Emphasis supplied.) As noted by the court in *Colonial Court* [Citation], the UCC does not say anything with respect to the form or content of the consent. The *Colonial Pacific* court concluded, therefore, "that the consent may be oral and may be established by conduct that reasonably manifests an intent. * * * Any manifestations that the obligation of the lessee will not be enforced independently of the obligation that runs to the consenting party is sufficient." The question whether consent has been given to a cancellation is a question of fact for the trier of fact.

We raise this point because the evidence indicates that there was some communication between Arora and ILC before ILC retrieved the ATM. It is unclear whether ILC removed the ATM at Arora's request, or whether the company was forcibly repossessing the equipment pursuant to the default provision of the lease. In view of the murkiness of the testimony, it is unclear when the ATM was taken back and when the final lease payment was made. One interesting question that arises from ILC's retrieval of the ATM, not addressed in the record, is what ILC did with the equipment afterward. Did ILC warehouse the equipment for the next four and one-half years (conduct that would appear unprofitable and therefore unlikely) or did the company then turn around and lease the ATM to someone else? If there was another lease, was ILC actually seeking a double recovery on the ATM's rental value? In this regard, we note that the trial court ruled that ILC had failed to mitigate its damages, a finding that is not supported by the current record, but may well prove to be true upon further trial of the matter.

In sum, this is a case that requires a much more elaborate presentation of evidence by the parties, and much more detailed findings of fact and conclusions of law than those actually made by the trial court. We sustain ILC's assignment of error upon the basis that the trial court did not apply the correct legal analysis, and that the evidence of record did not mandate a judgment in Arora's favor. Because of the number of outstanding issues and unresolved factual questions, we reverse the trial court's judgment and remand this case for a new trial consistent with the law set forth in this opinion.

Judgment reversed and cause remanded.

Case Questions

1. Why would a finance lease have such an iron-clad, "hell or high water" noncancellation clause as is apparently common and demonstrated here?
2. On what basis did the lower court rule in the defendant's favor?
3. What is an acceleration clause?
4. What was Mr. Arora's main defense? What concern did the court have with it?
5. The appeals court helpfully suggested several arguments the defendant might make on remand to be relieved of his contract obligations. What were they?

17.6 Summary and Exercises

Summary

Sales law is a special type of contract law, governed by Article 2 of the Uniform Commercial Code (UCC), adopted in every state but Louisiana. Article 2 governs the sale of goods only, defined as things movable at the time of identification to the contract for sale. Article 2A, a more recent offering, deals with the leasing of goods, including finance leases and consumer leases. The Convention on Contracts for the International Sale of Goods (CISG) is an international equivalent of Article 2.

Difficult questions sometimes arise when the subject of the contract is a hybrid of goods and real estate or goods and services. If the seller is called on to sever crops, timber, or minerals from the land, or the buyer is required to sever and can do so without material harm to the land, then the items are goods subject to Article 2. When the goods are "sold" incidental to a service, the "predominant factor" test is used, but with inconsistent results. For two categories of goods, legislation specifically answers the question: foodstuffs served by a restaurant are goods; blood supplied for transfusions is not.

Although they are kin, in some areas Article 2 differs from the common law. As regards mutual assent, the UCC abolishes the mirror image rule; it allows for more indefiniteness and open terms. The UCC does away with some requirements for consideration. It sometimes imposes special obligations on merchants (though defining a merchant is problematic), those who deal in goods of the kind, or who by their occupations hold themselves out as experts in the use of the goods as between other merchants and in selling to nonmerchants. Article 2 gives courts greater leeway than under the common law to modify contracts at the request of a party, if a clause is found to have been unconscionable at the time made.

Exercises

1. Ben owns fifty acres of timberland. He enters into a contract with Bunyan under which Bunyan is to cut and remove the timber from Ben's land. Bunyan enters into a contract to sell the logs to Log Cabin, Inc., a homebuilder. Are these two contracts governed by the UCC? Why?
2. Clarence agreed to sell his farm to Jud in exchange for five antique cars owned by Jud. Is this contract governed by the UCC? Why?
3. Professor Byte enters into a contract to purchase a laptop computer from Ultra-Intelligence Inc. He also enters into a contract with a graduate student, who is to write programs that will be run on the computer. Are these two contracts governed by the UCC? Why?
4. Pat had a skin problem and went to Dr. Pore, a dermatologist, for treatment. Dr. Pore applied a salve obtained from a pharmaceutical supplier, which made the problem worse. Is Dr. Pore liable under Article 2 of the UCC? Why?
5. Zanae visited the Bonita Burrito restaurant and became seriously ill after eating tainted food. She was rushed to a local hospital, where she was given a blood transfusion. Zanae developed hepatitis as a result of the transfusion. When she sued the restaurant and the hospital, claiming remedies under the UCC, both defended the suit by arguing that they were providing services, not goods. Are they correct? Why?
6. Bill, the owner of Bill's Used Books, decided to go out of business. He sold two of his bookcases to Ned. Ned later discovered that the bookcases were defective and sued Bill on the theory that, as a merchant, he warranted that the bookcases were of fair, average quality. Will Ned prevail on this theory? Why?
7. Rufus visited a supermarket to purchase groceries. As he moved past a display of soda pop and perhaps lightly brushed it, a bottle exploded. Rufus sustained injury and sued the supermarket, claiming breach of warranty under the UCC. Will Rufus win? Why?
8. Carpet Mart bought carpet from Collins & Aikman (Defendant) represented to be 100 percent polyester fiber. When Carpet Mart discovered in fact the carpet purchased was composed of cheaper, inferior fiber, it sued for compensatory and punitive damages. Defendant moved for a stay pending arbitration, pointing to the language of its acceptance form: "The acceptance of your order is subject to all the terms and conditions on the face and reverse side hereof, including arbitration, all of which are accepted by buyer; it supersedes buyer's order form."

   The small print on the reverse side of the form provided, among other things, that all claims arising out of the contract would be submitted to arbitration in New York City. The lower court held that Carpet Mart was not bound by the arbitration agreement appearing on the back of Collins & Aikman's acknowledgment form, and Defendant appealed. How should the appeals court rule?

9. Plaintiff shipped to Defendant—Pizza Pride Inc. of Jamestown, North Carolina—an order of mozzarella cheese totaling $11,000. That same day, Plaintiff mailed Defendant an invoice for the order, based on Plaintiff's understanding that an oral contract existed between the parties whereby Defendant had agreed to pay for the cheese. Defendant was engaged in the real estate business at this time and had earlier been approached by Pizza Pride Inc. to discuss that company's real estate investment potential. Defendant denied ever guaranteeing payment for the cheese and raised the UCC's Statute of Frauds, Section 2-201, as an affirmative defense. The Plaintiff contended that because Defendant was in the business of buying and selling real estate, she possessed knowledge or skill peculiar to the practices involved in the transaction here. After hearing the evidence, the court concluded as a matter of law that Defendant did agree to pay for the cheese and was liable to Plaintiff in the amount of $11,000. Defendant appealed. How should the appeals court rule?
10. Seller offered to sell to Buyer goods at an agreed price "to be shipped to Buyer by UPS." Buyer accepted on a form that included this term: "goods to be shipped FedEx, Buyer to pay freight." Seller then determined not to carry on with the contract as the price of the goods had increased, and Seller asserted that because the acceptance was different from the offer, there was no contract. Is this correct?

Self-Test Questions

1. Among subjects the UCC does not cover are
    a. letters of credit
    b. service contracts
    c. sale of goods
    d. bank collections
2. When a contract is unconscionable, a court may
    a. refuse to enforce the contract
    b. strike the unconscionable clause
    c. limit the application of the unconscionable clause
    d. take any of the above approaches
3. Under the UCC, the definition of *merchant* is limited to
    a. manufacturers
    b. retailers
    c. wholesalers
    d. none of the above
4. For the purpose of sales law, *goods*
    a. always include items sold incidental to a service
    b. include things movable at the time of identification to the contract
    c. include blood supplied for transfusions
    d. include all of the above
5. Article 2 differs from the common law of contracts
    a. in no substantial way
    b. by disallowing parties to create agreements with open terms
    c. by obligating courts to respect all terms of the contract
    d. by imposing special obligations on merchants

Self-Test Answers

1. a
2. d
3. d
4. b
5. d

Endnotes

1. Frederick G. Kempin Jr., *Historical Introduction to Anglo-American Law* (Eagan, MN: West, 1973), 217–18, 219–20, 221.
2. American Law Insitute, "ALI Overview," accessed March 1, 2011, http://www.ali.org/index.cfm?fuseaction=about.overview.
3. Uniform Commercial Code, Section 2-106.
4. Uniform Commercial Code, Section 2-107.
5. *Epstein v. Giannattasio* 197 A.2d 342 (Conn. 1963); *Newmark v. Gimble's, Inc.*, 258 A.2d 697 (N.J. 1969).
6. Uniform Commercial Code, Section 2A-103(e).
7. Uniform Commercial Code, Section 2A-103(g).
8. A. F. M. Maniruzzaman, quoted by Albert H. Kritzer, Pace Law School Institute of International Commercial Law, *CISG: Table of Contracting States*, accessed March 1, 2011, http://www.cisg.law.pace.edu/cisg/countries/cntries.html.
9. Pace Law School, "United Nations Convention on Contracts for the International Sale of Goods (1980) [CISG]" *CISG Database*, accessed March 1, 2011, http://www.cisg.law.pace.edu/cisg/text/treaty.html.
10. Uniform Commercial Code, Section 2-305(4).
11. This section of the UCC is one of the most confusing and fiercely litigated sections; Professor Grant Gilmore once called it a "miserable, bungled, patched-up job" and "arguably the greatest statutory mess of all time." Mark E. Roszkowski, "Symposium on Revised Article 2 of the Uniform Commercial Code—Section-by-Section Analysis," *SMU Law Review* 54 (Spring 2001): 927, 932, quoting Professor Grant Gilmore to Professor Robert Summers, Cornell University School of Law, September 10, 1980, in *Teaching Materials on Commercial and Consumer Law*, ed. Richard E. Speidel, Robert S Summers, and James J White, 3rd ed. (St. Paul, MN: West. 1981), pp. 54–55. In 2003 the UCC revisioners presented an amendment to this section in an attempt to fix Section 2-207, but no state has adopted this section's revision. See Commercial Law, "UCC Legislative Update," March 2, 2010, accessed March 1, 2011, http://ucclaw.blogspot.com/2010/03/ucc-legislative-update.html.
12. Uniform Commercial Code, Section 2-209(1).
13. Uniform Commercial Code, Section 1–107.
14. Proposed amendments by UCC revisioners presented in 2003 would have raised the amount of money—to take into account inflation since the mid-fifties—to $5,000, but no state has yet adopted this amendment; Uniform Commercial Code, Section 2-201.
15. Restatement (Second) of Contracts, Section 205.
16. Uniform Commercial Code, Sections 2-205 and 2A–205.
17. *Sheeskin v. Giant Food, Inc.*, 318 A.2d 874 (Md. Ct. App. 1974).
18. Uniform Commercial Code, Section 2-104(3).

CHAPTER 18

Title and Risk of Loss

Learning Objectives

After reading this chapter, you should understand the following:

1. Why title is important and at what point in the contracting relationship the buyer acquires title.
2. Why risk of loss is important, when risk of loss passes to the buyer, and when the buyer acquires an insurable interest.
3. Under what circumstances the buyer can obtain title when a nonowner sells the goods.

Parties to a sales contract will usually agree on the obvious details of a sales transaction—the nature of goods, the price, and the delivery time, as discussed in the next chapter. But there are two other issues of importance lurking in the background of every sale:

1. When does the title pass to the buyer? This question arises more in cases involving third parties, such as creditors and tax collectors. For instance, a creditor of the seller will not be allowed to take possession of goods in the seller's warehouse if the title has already passed to the buyer.
2. If goods are damaged or destroyed, who must bear the loss? The answer has obvious financial significance to both parties. If the seller must bear the loss, then in most cases he must pay damages or send the buyer another shipment of goods. A buyer who bears the loss must pay for the goods even though they are unusable. In the absence of a prior agreement, loss can trigger litigation between the parties.

18.1 Transfer of Title

Learning Objectives

1. Understand why it is important to know who has title in a sales transaction.
2. Be able to explain when title shifts.
3. Understand when a person who has no title can nevertheless pass good title on to a buyer.

Why It Is Important When Title Shifts

There are three reasons why it is important when title shifts from seller to buyer—that is, when the buyer gets title.

It Affects Whether a Sale Has Occurred

First, a sale cannot occur without a shift in title. You will recall that a sale is defined by the Uniform Commercial Code (UCC) as a "transfer of title from seller to buyer for a price." Thus if there is no shift of title, there is no sale. And there are several consequences to there being no sale, one of which is—concerning a merchant-seller—that no implied warranty of merchantability arises. (Again, as discussed in the previous chapter, an implied warranty provides that when a merchant-seller sells goods, the goods are suitable for the ordinary purpose for which such goods are used.) In a lease, of course, title remains with the lessor.

Creditors' Rights

Second, title is important because it determines whether creditors may take the goods. If Creditor has a right to seize Debtor's goods to satisfy a judgment or because the parties have a security agreement (giving Creditor the right to repossess Debtor's goods), obviously it won't do at all for Creditor to seize goods when Debtor doesn't have title to them—they are somebody else's goods, and seizing them would be conversion, a tort (the civil equivalent of a theft offense).

Insurable Interest

Third, title is related to who has an **insurable interest**. A buyer cannot legally obtain insurance unless he has an insurable interest in the goods. Without an insurable interest, the insurance contract would be an illegal gambling contract. For example, if you attempt to take out insurance on a ship with which you have no connection, hoping to recover a large sum if it sinks, the courts will construe the contract as a wager you have made with the insurance company that the ship is not seaworthy, and they will refuse to enforce it if the ship should sink and you try to collect. Thus this question arises: under the UCC, at what point does the buyer acquire an insurable interest in the goods? Certainly a person has insurable interest if she has title, but the UCC allows a person to have insurable interest with less than full title. The argument here is often between two insurance companies, each *denying* that its insured had insurable interest as to make it liable.

Goods Identified to the Contract

The Identification Issue

Identification to the contract

Segregating specific goods from the mass as the ones for the immediate contract.

The UCC at Section 2-401 provides that "title to goods cannot pass under a contract for sale prior to their identification to the contract." (In a lease, of course, title to the leased goods does not pass at all, only the right to possession and use for some time in return for consideration.[1]) So identification to the contract has to happen before title can shift. **Identification to the contract** here means that the seller in one way or another picks the goods to be sold out of the mass of inventory so that they can be delivered or held for the buyer.

Article 67 of the CISG says the same thing: "[T]he risk does not pass to the buyer until the goods are clearly identified to the contract, whether by markings on the goods, by shipping documents, by notice given to the buyer or otherwise."

When are goods "identified"? There are two possibilities as to when identification happens.

Parties May Agree

Section 2-501(1) of the UCC says "identification can be made at any time and in any manner explicated agreed to by the parties."

UCC Default Position

If the parties do not agree on when identification happens, the UCC default kicks in. Section 2-501(1) of the UCC says identification occurs

a. when the contract is made if it is for the sale of goods already existing and identified;
b. if the contract is for the sale of future goods other than those described in paragraph c., when goods are shipped, marked, or otherwise identified by the seller as goods to which the contract refers;
c. when crops are planted or otherwise become growing crops or the young are conceived if the contract is for the sale of unborn young to be born within twelve months after contract or for the sale of corps to be harvested within twelve months or the next normal harvest seasons after contracting, whichever is longer.

Thus if Very Fast Food Inc.'s purchasing agent looks at a new type of industrial sponge on Delta Sponge Makers' store shelf for restaurant supplies, points to it, and says, "I'll take it," identification happens then, when the contract is made. But if the purchasing agent wants to purchase sponges for her fast-food restaurants, sees a sample on the shelf, and says, "I want a gross of those"—they come in boxes of one hundred each—identification won't happen until one or the other of them chooses the gross of boxes of sponges out of the warehouse inventory.

When Title Shifts

Parties May Agree

Assuming identification is done, when does title shift? The law begins with the premise that the agreement of the parties governs. Section 2-401(1) of the UCC says that, in general, "title to goods passes from the seller to the buyer in any manner and on any conditions explicitly agreed on by the parties." Many companies specify in their written agreements at what moment the title will pass; here, for example, is a clause that appears in sales contracts of Dow Chemical Company: "Title and risk of loss in all goods sold hereunder shall pass to Buyer upon Seller's delivery to carrier at shipping point." Thus Dow retains title to its goods only until it takes them to the carrier for transportation to the buyer.

Because the UCC's default position (further discussed later in this chapter) is that title shifts when the seller has completed delivery obligations, and because the parties may agree on delivery terms, they also may, by choosing those terms, effectively agree when title shifts (again, they also can agree using any other language they want). So it is appropriate to examine some delivery terms at this juncture. There are three possibilities: shipment contracts, destination contracts, and contracts where the goods are not to be moved.

Shipment Contracts

In a **shipment contract**, the seller's obligation is to send the goods to the buyer, but not to a particular destination. The typical choices are set out in the UCC at Section 2-319:

shipment contract

Seller must see goods are on board vehicle of transportation.

F.O.B. [place of shipment]

Seller must see goods are on board vehicle of transportation at place of shipment.

F.A.S. [named port]

Seller must see goods are on dock for loading on ship at named port.

C.I.F.

Cost of goods includes insurance and freight.

C. & F.

Cost of goods includes freight only.

- **F.O.B. [place of shipment]** (the place from which the goods are to be shipped goes in the brackets, as in "F.O.B. Seattle"). F.O.B. means "free on board"; the seller's obligation, according to Section 2-504 of the UCC, is to put the goods into the possession of a carrier and make a reasonable contract for their transportation, to deliver any necessary documents so the buyer can take possession, and promptly notify the buyer of the shipment.
- **F.A.S. [named port]** (the name of the seaport from which the ship is carrying the goods goes in the brackets, as in "F.A.S. Long Beach"). F.A.S means "free alongside ship"; the seller's obligation is to at his "expense and risk deliver the goods alongside the vessel in the manner usual in that port" and to provide the buyer with pickup instructions.[2]
- **C.I.F.** and **C. & F.** These are actually not, directly, abbreviations for delivery terms, but rather they describe who pays insurance and freight. "C.I.F" means "cost, insurance, and freight"—if this term is used, it means that the contract price "includes in a lump sum the cost of the goods and the insurance and freight to the named destination."[3] "C. & F." means that "the price so includes cost and freight to the named destination."[4] However, the term C.I.F. has delivery significance.
    - Unless otherwise agreed, the term requires the seller to put the goods into the possession of a carrier and obtain a negotiable bill of lading; to load the goods and get a receipt from the carrier; to obtain insurance to cover the goods; to prepare an invoice; to forward all documents in due form necessary to perfect the buyer's rights.
    - Note: the drafters of Article 2 have, in the 2003 amendments, recommended that the parts of the Code about C.I.F. be repealed. Because no states adopted the amendments and, due to industry opposition, none were likely to, in 2011 the sponsors withdrew the amendments. [5]

Destination Contracts

destination contract

Seller's obligation is to get goods to a specific destination.

F.O.B. [destination]

Seller's obligation is to get goods to specific destination.

ex-ship

Seller's obligation is to get goods off-loaded from the ship.

no arrival, no sale

Seller must ship conforming goods but assumes no obligation that they arrive.

In a **destination contract**, the seller's obligation is to see to it that the goods actually arrive at the destination. Here again, the parties may employ the use of abbreviations that indicate the seller's duties. See the following from the UCC, Section 2-319:

- **F.O.B. [destination]** means the seller's obligation is to "at his own expense and risk transport the goods to that place and there tender delivery of them" with appropriate pickup instructions to the buyer.
- **Ex-ship** "is the reverse of the F.A.S. term."[6] It means "from the carrying vessel"—the seller's obligation is to make sure the freight bills are paid and that "the goods leave the ship's tackle or are otherwise properly unloaded."
- **No arrival, no sale** means the "seller must properly ship conforming goods and if they arrive by any means he must tender them on arrival but he assumes no obligation that the goods will arrive unless he has caused the non-arrival."[7] If the goods don't arrive, or if they are damaged or deteriorated through no fault of the seller, the buyer can either treat the contract as avoided, or pay a reduced amount for the damaged goods, with no further recourse against the seller.[8]

Goods Not to Be Moved

document of title

Paper representing ownership interest in goods.

It is not uncommon for contracting parties to sell and buy goods stored in a grain elevator or warehouse without physical movement of the goods. There are two possibilities:

1. Goods with documents of title. A first possibility is that the ownership of the goods is manifested by a **document of title**—"bill of lading, dock warrant, dock receipt, warehouse receipt or order for the delivery of goods, and also any other document which in the regular course of business or financing is treated as adequately evidencing that the person in possession of it is entitled to receive, hold and dispose of the document and the goods it covers."[9] In that case,

the UCC, Section 2-401(3)(a), says that title passes "at the time when and the place where" the documents are delivered to the buyer.

2. Goods without documents of title. If there is no physical transfer of the goods and no documents to exchange, then UCC, Section 2-401(3)(b), provides that "title passes at the time and place of contracting."

Here are examples showing how these concepts work.

Suppose the contract calls for Delta Sponge Makers to "ship the entire lot of industrial grade Sponge No. 2 by truck or rail" and that is all that the contract says about shipment. That's a "shipment contract," and the UCC, Section 2-401(2)(a), says that title passes to Very Fast Foods at the "time and place of shipment." At the moment that Delta turns over the 144 cartons of 1,000 sponges each to a trucker—perhaps Easy Rider Trucking comes to pick them up at Delta's own factory—title has passed to Very Fast Foods.

Suppose the contract calls for Delta to "deliver the sponges on June 10 at the Maple Street warehouse of Very Fast Foods Inc." This is a destination contract, and the seller "completes his performance with respect to the physical delivery of the goods" when it pulls up to the door of the warehouse and tenders the cartons.[10] "Tender" means that the party—here Delta Sponge Makers—is ready, able, and willing to perform and has notified its obligor of its readiness. When the driver of the delivery truck knocks on the warehouse door, announces that the gross of industrial grade Sponge No. 2 is ready for unloading, and asks where the warehouse foreman wants it, Delta has tendered delivery, and title passes to Very Fast Foods.

Suppose Very Fast Foods fears that the price of industrial sponges is about to soar; it wishes to acquire a large quantity long before it can use them all or even store them all. Delta does not store all of its sponges in its own plant, keeping some of them instead at Central Warehousing. Central is a **bailee**, one who has rightful possession but not title. (A parking garage often is a bailee of its customers' cars; so is a carrier carrying a customer's goods.) Now assume that Central has issued a **warehouse receipt** (a document of title that provides proof of ownership of goods stored in a warehouse) to Delta and that Delta's contract with Very Fast Foods calls for Delta to deliver "document of title at the office of First Bank" on a particular day. When the goods are not to be physically moved, that title passes to Very Fast Foods "at the time when and the place where" Delta delivers the document.

bailee

One rightfully possessing goods not hers.

warehouse receipt

A written document for items warehoused, serving as evidence of title to the stored goods.

Suppose the contract did not specify physical transfer or exchange of documents for the purchase price. Instead, it said, "Seller agrees to sell all sponges stored on the north wall of its Orange Street warehouse, namely, the gross of industrial Sponge No. 2, in cartons marked B300–B444, to Buyer for a total purchase price of $14,000, payable in twelve equal monthly installments, beginning on the first of the month beginning after the signing of this agreement." Then title passes at the time and place of contracting—that is, when Delta Sponge Makers and Very Fast Foods sign the contract.

So, as always under the UCC, the parties may agree on the terms they want when title shifts. They can do that directly by just saying when—as in the Dow Chemical example—or they can indirectly agree when title shifts by stipulating delivery terms: shipment, destination, goods not to be moved. If they don't stipulate, the UCC default kicks in.

UCC Default Provision

If the parties do not stipulate by any means when title shifts, Section 2-401(2) of the UCC provides that "title passes to the buyer at the time and place at which seller completes his performance with reference to the physical delivery of the goods." And if the parties have no term in their contract about delivery, the UCC's default delivery term controls. It says "the place for delivery is the seller's place of business or if he has none his residence," and delivery is accomplished at the place when the seller "put[s] and hold[s] conforming goods at the buyer's disposition and give[s] the buyer any notification reasonably necessary to enable him to take delivery."[11]

Key Takeaway

Title is important for three reasons: it determines whether a sale has occurred, it determines rights of creditors, and it affects who has an insurable interest. Parties may explicitly agree when title shifts, or they may agree indirectly by settling on delivery terms (because absent explicit agreement, delivery controls title passage). Delivery terms to choose from include shipment contracts, destination contracts, and delivery without the goods being moved (with or without documents of title). If nothing is said about when title shifts, and the parties have not indirectly agreed by choosing a delivery term, then title shifts when delivery obligations under the contract are complete, and if there are no delivery terms, delivery happens when the seller makes the goods available at seller's place of business (or if seller has no place of business, goods will be made available at seller's residence)—that's when title shifts.

Exercises

1. Why does it matter who has title?
2. If the parties do not otherwise agree, when does title shift from seller to buyer?
3. Why does the question of delivery terms arise in examining when title shifts?
4. When does title shift for goods stored in a warehouse that are not to be moved?

18.2 Title from Nonowners

Learning Objective

1. Understand when and why a nonowner can nevertheless pass title on to a purchaser.

The Problem of Title from Nonowners

conversion

The civil wrong of taking property without its owner's consent.

We have examined when title transfers from buyer to seller, and here the assumption is, of course, that seller had good title in the first place. But what title does a purchaser acquire when the seller has no title or has at best only a voidable title? This question has often been difficult for courts to resolve. It typically involves a type of eternal triangle with a three-step sequence of events, as follows (see Figure 18.1): (1) The nonowner obtains possession, for example, by loan or theft; (2) the nonowner sells the goods to an innocent purchaser for cash; and (3) the nonowner then takes the money and disappears, goes into bankruptcy, or ends up in jail. The result is that two innocent parties battle over the goods, the owner usually claiming that the purchaser is guilty of **conversion** (i.e., the unlawful assumption of ownership of property belonging to another) and claiming damages or the right to recover the goods.

FIGURE 18.1 Sales by Nonowners

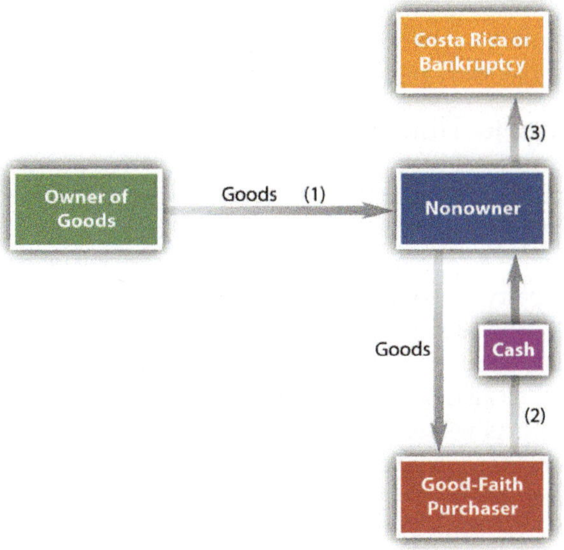

The Response to the Problem of Title from Nonowners

The Basic Rule

To resolve this dilemma, we begin with a basic policy of jurisprudence: a person cannot transfer better title than he or she had. (The Uniform Commercial Code [UCC] notes this policy in Sections 2-403, 2A-304, and 2A-305.) This policy would apply in a sale-of-goods case in which the nonowner had a void title or no title at all. For example, if a nonowner stole the goods from the owner and then sold them to an innocent purchaser, the owner would be entitled to the goods or to damages. Because the thief had no title, he had no title to transfer to the purchaser. A person cannot get good title to goods from a thief, nor does a person have to retain physical possession of her goods at all times to retain their ownership—people are expected to leave their cars with a mechanic for repair or to leave their clothing with a dry cleaner.

If thieves could pass on good title to stolen goods, there would be a hugely increased traffic in stolen property; that would be unacceptable. In such a case, the owner can get her property back from whomever the thief sold it to in an action called **replevin** (an action to recover personal property unlawfully taken). On the other hand, when a buyer in good faith buys goods from an apparently reputable seller, she reasonably expects to get good title, and that expectation cannot be dashed with impunity without faith in the market being undermined. Therefore, as between two innocent parties, sometimes the original owner does lose, on the theory that (1) that person is better able to avoid the problem than the downstream buyer, who had absolutely no control over the situation, and (2) faith in commercial transactions would be undermined by allowing original owners to claw back their property under all circumstances.

replevin

An action to recover possession of goods wrongfully held.

So the basic legal policy that a person cannot pass on better title than he had is subject to a number of exceptions. In Chapter 24, for instance, we discuss how certain purchasers of commercial paper ("holders in due course") will obtain greater rights than the sellers possessed. And in Chapter 28, we examine how a buyer in the ordinary course of business is allowed to purchase goods free of security interests that the seller has given to creditors. Likewise, the law governing the sale of goods contains exceptions to the basic legal policy. These usually fall within one of two categories: sellers with voidable title and entrustment.

The Exceptions

As noted, there are exceptions to the law governing the sale of goods.

Sellers with a Voidable Title

Under the UCC, a person with a voidable title has the power to transfer title to a good-faith purchaser for value (see Figure 18.2). The UCC defines *good faith* as "honesty in fact in the conduct or transaction concerned."[12] A "purchaser" is not restricted to one who pays cash; any taking that creates an interest in property, whether by mortgage, pledge, lien, or even gift, is a purchase for purposes of the UCC. And "value" is not limited to cash or goods; a person gives value if he gives any consideration sufficient to support a simple contract, including a binding commitment to extend credit and security for a preexisting claim. Recall from Chapter 9 that a "voidable" title is one that, for policy reasons, the courts will cancel on application of one who is aggrieved. These reasons include fraud, undue influence, mistake, and lack of capacity to contract. When a person has a voidable title, title can be taken away from her, but if it is not, she can transfer better title than she has to a good-faith purchaser for value. (See Section 4 at the end of this chapter.)

Rita, sixteen years old, sells a video game to her neighbor Annie, who plans to give the game to her nephew. Since Rita is a minor, she could rescind the contract; that is, the title that Annie gets is voidable: it is subject to be avoided by Rita's rescission. But Rita does not rescind. Then Annie discovers that her nephew already has that video game, so she sells it instead to an office colleague, Donald. He has had no notice that Annie bought the game from a minor and has only a voidable title. He pays cash. Should Rita—the minor—subsequently decide she wants the game back, it would be too late: Annie has transferred good title to Donald even though Annie's title was voidable.

FIGURE 18.2 Voidable Title

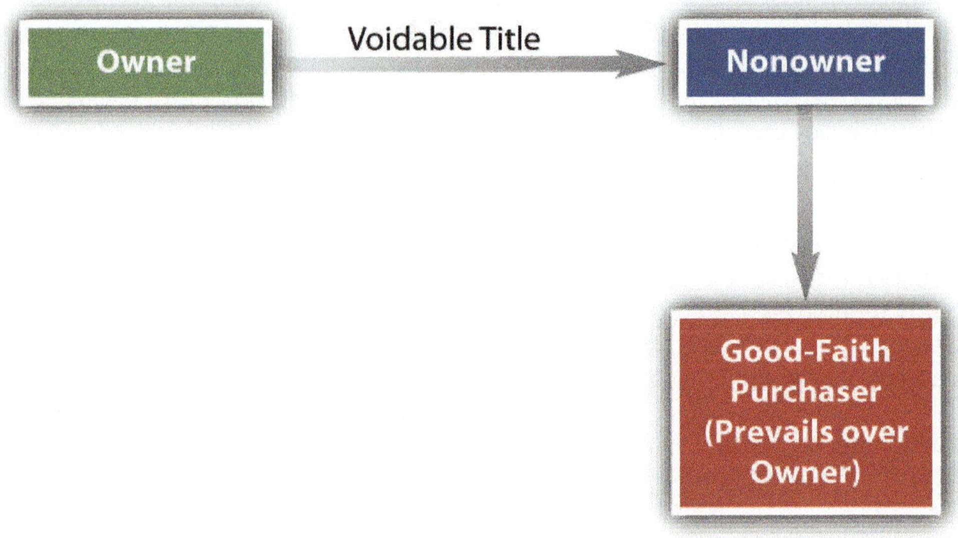

Suppose Rita was an adult and Annie paid her with a check that later bounced, but Annie sold the game to Donald before the check bounced. Does Donald still have good title? The UCC says he does, and it identifies three other situations in which the good-faith purchaser is protected: (1) when the original transferor was deceived about the identity of the purchaser to whom he sold the goods, who then transfers to a good-faith purchaser; (2) when the original transferor was supposed to but did not receive cash from the intermediate purchaser; and (3) when "the delivery was procured through fraud punishable as larcenous under the criminal law."[13]

This last situation may be illustrated as follows: Dimension LLC leased a Volkswagen to DK Inc. The agreement specified that DK could use the Volkswagen solely for business and commercial purposes and could not sell it. Six months later, the owner of DK, Darrell Kempf, representing that the Volkswagen was part of DK's used-car inventory, sold it to Edward Seabold. Kempf embezzled the proceeds from the sale of the car and disappeared. When DK defaulted on its payments for the Volkswagen, Dimension attempted to repossess it. Dimension discovered that Kempf had executed a release of interest on the car's title by forging the signature of Dimension's manager. The Washington Court of Appeals, applying the UCC, held that Mr. Seabold should keep the car. The car was not stolen from Dimension; instead, by leasing the vehicle to DK, Dimension transferred possession of the car to DK voluntarily, and because Seabold was a good-faith purchaser, he won.[14]

Entrustment

A merchant who deals in particular goods has the power to transfer all rights of one who entrusts to him goods of the kind to a "buyer in the ordinary course of business" (see Figure 18.3).[15] The UCC defines such a buyer as a person who buys goods in an ordinary transaction from a person in the business of selling that type of goods, as long as the buyer purchases in "good faith and without knowledge that the sale to him is in violation of the ownership rights or security interest of a third party in the goods."[16] Bess takes a pearl necklace, a family heirloom, to Wellborn's Jewelers for cleaning; as the **entrustor**, she has entrusted the necklace to an **entrustee**. The owner of Wellborn's—perhaps by mistake—sells it to Clara, a buyer, in the ordinary course of business. Bess cannot take the necklace back from Clara, although she has a cause of action against Wellborn's for conversion. As between the two innocent parties, Bess and Clara (owner and purchaser), the latter prevails. Notice that the UCC only says that the entrustee can pass *whatever title the entrustor had* to a good-faith purchaser, not necessarily good title. If Bess's cleaning woman borrowed the necklace, soiled it, and took it to Wellborn's, which then sold it to Clara, Bess could get it back because the cleaning woman had no title to transfer to the entrustee, Wellborn's.

entrustor

One who puts something into another's possession for its care.

entrustee

One to whom something is put for its care.

FIGURE 18.3 Entrustment

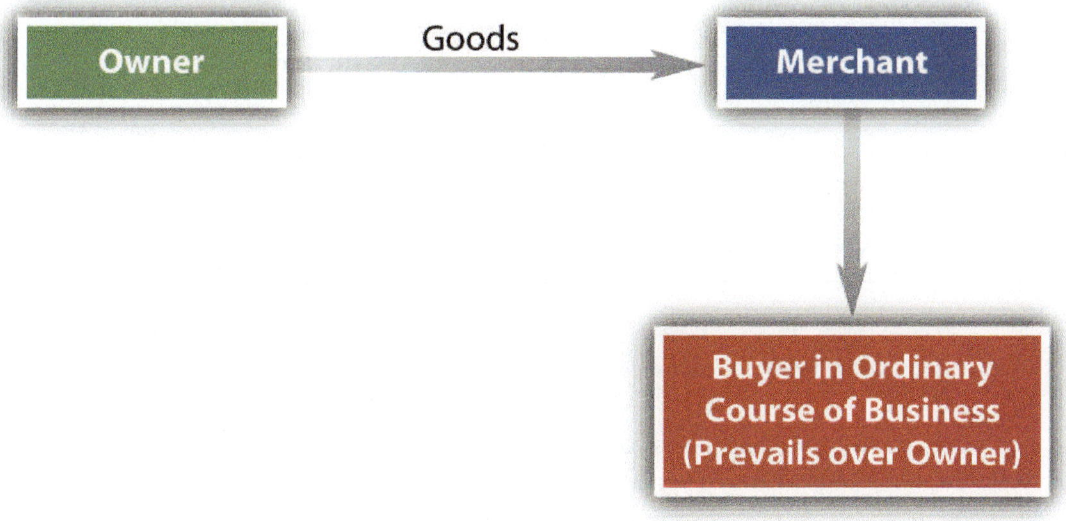

Entrustment is based on the general principle of estoppel: "A rightful owner may be estopped by his own acts from asserting his title. If he has invested another with the usual evidence of title, or an apparent authority to dispose of it, he will not be allowed to make claim against an innocent purchaser dealing on the faith of such apparent ownership."[17]

Larceny (being conned)

Suppose (this is based on Exercise 10 at the chapter end) Seller allows Potential Buyer (PB) to test drive a car, so that PB can see if he likes it. PB takes the car and never returns; PB sells the car to Good Faith Buyer (GFB), based on forged registration papers. The police find the car. Can Seller get it back? It would seem that PB is a thief, and certainly Seller can get it back. But actually PB is not a thief, he (or she) is committing larceny: he has taken (wrongful) possession of that which was voluntarily given up to him. He didn't steal the car, which usually implies the possibility of a breach of the peace. Seller has been conned. He's out of luck.

UCC 2-403 provides that "If goods have been delivered under a transaction of purchase, the purchaser has" power to transfer title "even if the delivery was procured through criminal fraud." In the example here, PB is a "purchaser" (or was supposed to have been such), and the delivery of the car to him was procured through criminal fraud, but not through thievery. So PB can pass on good title to GFB. Why? Because it was a darn foolish thing that Seller did. He acted imprudently, and as between him and the good-faith purchaser, the Code says the GFP should prevail so that such GFP's may have confidence in the integrity of commercial transactions.

Key Takeaway

The general rule—for obvious reasons—is that nobody can pass on better title to goods than he or she has: a thief cannot pass on good title to stolen goods to anybody. But in balancing that policy against the reasonable expectations of good-faith buyers that they will get title, the UCC has made some exceptions. A person with voidable title can pass on good title to a good-faith purchaser, and a merchant who has been entrusted with goods can pass on title of the entrustor to a good-faith purchaser, and a con-artist can pass on good title to a good-faith purchaser.

Exercises

1. Why is it the universal rule that good title to goods cannot be had from a thief?
2. What is the "voidable title" exception to the universal rule? Why is the exception made?
3. What is the "entrusting" exception to the general rule?

18.3 Risk of Loss

Learning Objectives

1. Understand why who has the risk of loss is important.
2. Know how parties may agree on when the risk of loss shifts.
3. Know when the risk of loss shifts if there is no breach, and if there is a breach.
4. Recognize what "insurable interest" is, why it is important, and how it attaches.

Why Risk of Loss Is Important

"Risk of loss" means who has to pay—who bears the risk—if the goods are lost or destroyed *without the fault of either party*. It is obvious why this issue is important: Buyer contracts to purchase a new car for $35,000. While the car is in transit to Buyer, it is destroyed in a landslide. Who takes the $35,000 hit?

The CISG, Article 66, provides as follows: "Loss of or damage to the goods after the risk has passed to the buyer does not discharge him from his obligation to pay the price, unless the loss or damage is due to an act or omission of the seller."

When Risk of Loss Passes

The Parties May Agree

Just as title passes in accordance with the parties' agreement, so too can the parties fix the risk of loss on one or the other. They may even devise a formula to divide the risk between themselves.[18]

The parties can use any language they want to stipulate who bears the risk. Common terms by which parties set out their delivery obligations that then affect when title shifts (F.O.B., F.A.S., ex-ship, and so on) were discussed earlier in this chapter. Similarly, parties may use common terms to set out which party has the risk of loss; these situation arise with trial sales. That is, sometimes the seller will permit the buyer to return the goods even though the seller had conformed to the contract. When the goods are intended primarily for the buyer's use, the transaction is said to be "sale on approval." When they are intended primarily for resale, the transaction is said to be "sale or return." When the "buyer" is really only a sales agent for the "seller," it is a consignment sale.

Sale on Approval

Under a **sale-on-approval contract**, risk of loss (and title) remains with the seller until the buyer accepts, and the buyer's trial use of the goods does not in itself constitute acceptance. If the buyer decides to return the goods, the seller bears the risk and expense of return, but a merchant buyer must follow any reasonable instructions from the seller. Very Fast Foods asks Delta for some sample sponges to test on approval; Delta sends a box of one hundred sponges. Very Fast plans to try them for a week, but before that, through no fault of Very Fast, the sponges are destroyed in a fire. Delta bears the loss.[19]

sale-on-approval contract

An agreement whereby a buyer receives goods for examination. Risk of loss and title remains with the seller until the buyer indicates his or her approval of the goods (or after a reasonable time).

Sale or Return

The buyer might take the goods with the expectation of reselling them—as would a women's wear shop buy new spring fashions, expecting to sell them. But if the shop doesn't sell them before summer wear is in vogue, it could arrange with the seller to return them for credit. In contrast to sale-on-approval contracts, **sale-or-return contracts** have risk of loss (and title too) passing to the buyer, and the buyer bears the risk and expense of returning the goods.

Occasionally the question arises whether the buyer's other creditors may claim the goods when the sales contract lets the buyer retain some rights to return the goods. The answer seems straightforward: in a sale-on-approval contract, where title remains with the seller until acceptance, the buyer does not own the goods—hence they cannot be seized by his creditors—unless he accepts them, whereas they are the buyer's goods (subject to his right to return them) in a sale-or-return contract and may be taken by creditors if they are in his possession.

sale-or-return contracts

An agreement whereby the buyer (usually a retailer) accepts goods from a seller for resale. Risk of loss and title transfer to the buyer them, but if the goods do not sell, they may be returned to the seller, at the buyer's risk and expense.

Consignment Sales

In a consignment situation, the seller is a bailee and an agent for the owner who sells the goods for the owner and takes a commission. Under the Uniform Commercial Code (UCC), this is considered a sale or return, thus the consignee (at whose place the goods are displayed for sale to customers) is considered a buyer and has the risk of loss and title.[20] The consignee's creditors can take the goods; that is, unless the parties comply "with an applicable law providing for a consignor's interest or the like to be evidenced by a sign, or where it is established that the person conducting the business is generally known by his creditors to be substantially engaged in selling the goods of others" (or complies with secured transactions requirements under Article 9, discussed in a later chapter).[21]

The UCC Default Position

If the parties fail to specify how the risk of loss is to be allocated or apportioned, the UCC again supplies the answers. A generally applicable rule, though not explicitly stated, is that risk of loss passes when the seller has completed obligations under the contract. Notice this is *not* the same as when title passes: title passes when seller has completed *delivery* obligations under the contract, risk of loss passes when *all* obligations are completed. (Thus a buyer could get good title to nonconforming goods, which might be better for the buyer than not getting title to them: if the seller goes bankrupt, at least the buyer has something of value.)

Risk of Loss in Absence of a Breach

If the goods are *conforming*, then risk of loss would indeed pass when delivery obligations are complete, just as with title. And the analysis here would be the same as we looked at in examining shift of title.

A shipment contract. The contract requires Delta to ship the sponges by carrier but does not require Delta to deliver them to a particular destination. In this situation, risk of loss passes to Very Fast Foods when the goods are delivered to the carrier. This is 2-509: "risk of loss passes to the buyer when the goods are duly delivered to the carrier."

The CISG—pretty much like the UCC—provides as follows (Article 67):

> **If the contract of sale involves carriage of the goods and the seller is not bound to hand them over at a particular place, the risk passes to the buyer when the goods are handed over to the first carrier for transmission to the buyer in accordance with the contract of sale. If the seller is bound to hand the goods over to a carrier at a particular place, the risk does not pass to the buyer until the goods are handed over to the carrier at that place.**

A destination contract. If the contract agreement calls for Delta to deliver the sponges by carrier to a particular location, Very Fast Foods assumes the risk of loss only when Delta's carrier tenders them at the specified place. 2-509 again: if the deal is that the seller is to deliver the goods to a particular destination, "risk of loss passes to the buyer when the goods are there so tendered as to enable the buyer to take delivery."

The CISG provides for basically the same thing (Article 69): "If the contract is for something other than shipment, the risk passes to the buyer when he takes over the goods or, if he does not do so in due time, from the time when the goods are placed at his disposal and he commits a breach of contract by failing to take delivery."

Goods not to be moved. If Delta sells sponges that are stored at Central Warehousing to Very Fast Foods, and the sponges are not to be moved, Section 2-509(2) of the UCC sets forth three possibilities for transfer of the risk of loss:

1. The buyer receives a negotiable document of title covering the goods. A document of title is negotiable if by its terms goods are to be delivered to the bearer of the document or to the order of a named person.

2. The bailee acknowledges the buyer's right to take possession of the goods. Delta signs the contract for the sale of sponges and calls Central to inform it that a buyer has purchased 144 cartons and to ask it to set aside all cartons on the north wall for that purpose. Central does so, sending notice to Very Fast Foods that the goods are available. Very Fast Foods assumes risk of loss upon receipt of the notice.
3. When the seller gives the buyer a nonnegotiable document of title or a written direction to the bailee to deliver the goods and the buyer has had a reasonable time to present the document or direction.

All other cases. In any case that does not fit within the rules just described, the risk of loss passes to the buyer only when the buyer actually receives the goods. Cases that come within this section generally involve a buyer who is taking physical delivery from the seller's premises. A merchant who sells on those terms can be expected to insure his interest in any goods that remain under his control. The buyer is unlikely to insure goods not in his possession. The *Ramos* case (Section 4 in this chapter) demonstrates how this risk-of-loss provision applies when a customer pays for merchandise but never actually receives his purchase because of a mishap.

Risk of Loss Where Breach Occurs

The general rule for risk of loss was set out as this: risk of loss shifts when seller has completed obligations under the contract. We said if the goods are conforming, the only obligation left is delivery, so then risk of loss would shift upon delivery. But if the goods are nonconforming, then the rule would say the risk doesn't shift. And that's correct, though it's subject to one wrinkle having to do with insurance. Let's examine the two possible circumstances: breach by seller and breach by buyer.

First, suppose the *seller* breaches the contract by proffering nonconforming goods, and the buyer *rejects* them—never takes them at all. Then the goods are lost or damaged. Under Section 2-510(1) of the UCC, the loss falls on seller and remains there until seller cures the breach or until buyer accepts despite the breach. Suppose Delta is obligated to deliver a gross of industrial No. 2 sponges; instead it tenders only one hundred cartons or delivers a gross of industrial No. 3 sponges. The risk of loss falls on Delta because Delta has not completed its obligation under the contract and Very Fast Foods doesn't have possession of the goods. Or suppose Delta has breached the contract by tendering to Very Fast Foods a defective document of title. Delta cures the defect and gives the new document of title to Very Fast Foods, but before it does so the sponges are stolen. Delta is responsible for the loss.

Now suppose that a seller breaches the contract by proffering nonconforming goods and that the buyer, not having discovered the nonconformity, *accepts* them—the nonconforming goods are in the buyer's hands. The buyer has a right to revoke acceptance, but before the defective goods are returned to the seller, they are destroyed while in the buyer's possession. The seller breached, but here's the wrinkle: the UCC says that the seller bears the loss only to the extent of any deficiency in the buyer's insurance coverage.[22] Very Fast Foods had taken delivery of the sponges and only a few days later discovered that the sponges did not conform to the contract. Very Fast has the right to revoke and announces its intention to do so. A day later its warehouse burns down and the sponges are destroyed. It then discovers that its insurance was not adequate to cover all the sponges. Who stands the loss? The seller does, again, to the extent of any deficiency in the buyer's insurance coverage.

Second, what if the *buyer* breaches the contract? Here's the scenario: Suppose Very Fast Foods calls two days before the sponges identified to the contract are to be delivered by Delta and says, "Don't bother; we no longer have a need for them." Subsequently, while the lawyers are arguing, Delta's warehouse burns down and the sponges are destroyed. Under the rules, risk of loss does not pass to the buyer until the seller has delivered, which has not occurred in this case. Nevertheless, responsibility for the loss here has passed to Very Fast Foods, to the extent that the seller's insurance does not cover it. Section 2-510(3) of the UCC permits the seller to treat the risk of loss as resting on the buyer for a "commercially reasonable time" when the buyer repudiates the contract before risk of loss has passed to him. This transfer of the risk can take place only when the goods are identified to the contract. The theory is that if the buyer had taken the goods as per the contract, the goods would not have been in the warehouse and thus would not have been burned up.

Insurable Interest

Why It Matters

We noted at the start of this chapter that who has title is important for several reasons, one of which is because it affects who has an insurable interest. (You can't take out insurance in something you have no interest in: if you have no title, you may not have an insurable interest.) And it was noted that the rules on risk of loss are affected by insurance. (The theory is that a businessperson is likely to have insurance, which is a cost of business, and if she has insurance and also has possession of goods—even nonconforming ones—it is reasonable to charge her insurance with loss of the goods; thus she will have cause to take care of them in her possession, else her insurance rates increase.) So in commercial transactions insurance is important, and when goods are lost or destroyed, the frequent argument is between the buyer's and the seller's insurance companies, neither of which wants to be responsible. They want to deny that their insured had an insurable interest. Thus it becomes important who has an insurable interest.

Insurable Interest of the Buyer

It is not necessary for the buyer to go all the way to having title in order for him to have an insurable interest. The buyer obtains a "special property and insurable interest in goods by identification of existing goods as goods to which the contract refers."[23] We already discussed how "identification" of the goods can occur. The parties can do it by branding, marking, tagging, or segregating them—and they can do it at any time. We also set out the rules for when goods will be considered identified to the contract under the UCC if the parties don't do it themselves (Section 1).

Insurable Interest of the Seller

As long as the seller retains title to or any security interest in the goods, he has an insurable interest.

Other Rights of the Buyer

The buyer's "special property" interest that arises upon identification of goods gives the buyer rights other than that to insure the goods. For example, under Section 2-502 of the UCC, the buyer who has paid for unshipped goods may take them from a seller who becomes insolvent within ten days after receipt of the whole payment or the first installment payment. Similarly, a buyer who has not yet taken delivery may sue a third party who has in some manner damaged the property.

Key Takeaway

Knowing who has the risk of loss in a contract for the sale of goods is important for obvious reasons: it is not uncommon for goods to be lost or stolen between the time they leave the seller's possession and before the buyer gets them. The parties are certainly free to agree on when the risk of loss shifts; if they do not, the UCC says it shifts when the seller has completed obligations under the contract. Thus if there is no breach, the risk of loss shifts upon delivery. If there is a breach, the UCC places the risk of loss on the breaching party, with this caveat: where the nonbreaching party is in control of the goods, the UCC places the risk of loss on that party to the extent of her insurance coverage. So if there is a breach by the seller (delivery of nonconforming goods), the risk of loss never shifts except if the buyer has taken possession of the nonconforming goods; in that case, the buyer does have the risk of loss insofar as her insurance covers the loss. If the buyer breaches by repudiating before the risk of loss passes to him (by the goods' delivery), the UCC permits the seller to treat the risk of loss as resting on the buyer for a commercially reasonable time as to goods identified to the contract.

Insurable interest becomes important when goods suffer a casualty loss because—among other reasons—often neither the seller's nor the buyer's insurance company wants *its* insured to have an interest in the goods: each side denies it. The seller retains an insurable interest if he has title to or any security interest in the goods, and the buyer obtains an insurable interest by identification of existing goods as goods to which the contract refers. A person has an insurable interest in any property owned or in the person's possession.

Exercises

1. Which is more important in determining who has the risk of loss, the agreement of the parties or the UCC's default provisions?
2. When does the risk of loss shift to the buyer if the parties have no agreement on the issue?
3. Why does the UCC impose the risk of loss to the extent of his insurance on a nonbreaching party if that party has control of the goods?
4. Why can a person not take out insurance for goods in which the person has no interest? How does a seller retain an insurable interest? When does the buyer get an insurable interest?

18.4 Cases

Transfer of Title: Destination Contracts

Sam and Mac, Inc. v. Treat

783 N.E.2d 760 (Ind. App. 2003)

Anthony L. Gruda and Sharon R. Gruda (the "Grudas") owned and operated Gruda Enterprises, Inc. (Gruda Enterprises), which in turn operated The Kitchen Works, a kitchen supply business. On March 5, 1998, Gruda Enterprises contracted to sell a set of kitchen cabinets to Sam and Mac, Inc. [SMI], a commercial construction and contracting corporation. Gruda Enterprises was also to deliver and install the cabinets. Because it did not have the cabinets in stock, Gruda Enterprises ordered them from a manufacturer. On March 14, 1998, nine days after placing the order, SMI prepaid Gruda Enterprises for the cabinet order.

On May 14, 1998, prior to delivery and installation of the cabinets, the Grudas ceased operation of Gruda Enterprises and filed for personal bankruptcy. Gruda Enterprises did not file for bankruptcy and was not dissolved. Instead, the Grudas' stock in Gruda Enterprises became part of their bankruptcy estate. * * * When no cabinets were delivered or installed, and the Grudas ceased operation of Gruda Enterprises, SMI asked Treat, who was the landlord of Gruda Enterprises, to open the business premises and permit SMI to remove cabinets from the property. Treat declined, stating that he feared he would incur liability to Gruda Enterprises if he started giving away its inventory.

Treat and other secured creditors sued Gruda Enterprises, which owed them money. [Summary judgment was for Treat, SMI appeals.]

SMI contends that there was a completed sale between SMI, as the buyer, and Gruda Enterprises, as the seller. Specifically, SMI maintains that title to the cabinets under [UCC] 2-401(3)(b) passed to SMI when the contract for sale was [made]. * * * Therefore, SMI argues that the trial court improperly granted summary judgment in favor of Treat because [SMI] held title and, thus, a possessory interest in the cabinets. * * *

[T]he contract is governed by the * * * Indiana Uniform Commercial Code (UCC). 2-401 establishes the point in time at which title passes from seller to buyer. Specifically, 2-401(2) provides, in pertinent part, that unless explicitly agreed, title passes to the buyer at the time and place at which the seller completes his performance with respect to the physical delivery of goods. * * *

Moreover, the record indicates that SMI and Gruda Enterprises did not have an explicit agreement to pass title at any other time, or at any time prior to actual delivery of the cabinets. SMI argues that title passed to it under 2-401(3)(b) ["where delivery is to be made without moving the goods, . . . if the goods are at the time of contacting already identified and no documents are to be delivered, title passes at the time and place of contacting."]. . . . However, the record reflects that SMI admitted that the terms of the contract required Gruda Enterprises to not only order the cabinets, but to deliver and install them at the location specified by SMI (i.e., the house that SMI was building). 2-403(3) applies to purchases of goods where delivery is to be made without moving the goods. SMI argues that since the cabinets were identified at the time of contracting and no documents needed delivery, title passed at the time and place of contracting. * * *

[T]itle to goods cannot pass under a contract for sale prior to their identification in the contract. *See* 2-401(1). This does not mean that title passes when the goods are identified. It only means that identification is merely the earliest possible opportunity for title to pass. * * * [I]dentification does not, in and of itself, confer either ownership or possessory rights in the goods. [UCC] 2-401(2)(b) states that "[i]f the contract requires delivery at destination, title passes on tender there." In the present case, tender did not occur when Gruda Enterprises called SMI to notify it that the cabinets were in and ready to be delivered and installed. SMI requested that the cabinets remain at the warehouse until the house it was building was ready for the cabinets to be installed. * * * [W]e find that SMI and Gruda Enterprises agreed to a destination point, *i.e.* the house that SMI was building. Accordingly, we find that 2-401(2)(b) is also applicable. The title to the cabinets did not pass to SMI because the cabinets were not delivered and installed at the agreed upon destination. Therefore, we conclude that SMI does not have a possessory interest in the cabinets.

Based on the foregoing, we conclude that the trial court properly granted summary judgment in favor of Treat. * * * Affirmed.

Case Questions

1. One argument made by the plaintiff was that because the plaintiff had paid for the goods and they had been identified to the contract, title passed to the plaintiff. Why did the court disagree with this contention?
2. When would title to the cabinets have shifted to the plaintiff?
3. This is footnote 2 (it was not included in the parts of the case set out above): "We note that Treat owned Kitchen Wholesalers, Inc., from approximately 1987 to approximately June 20, 1996. On or about June 20, 1996, Kitchen Wholesalers, Inc. sold its assets, inventory, equipment, and business to Gruda Enterprises. The Grudas executed an Agreement for Sale of Assets, Lease, and Security Agreement, as well as a Promissory Note in which they agreed to pay $45,000 for the assets, inventory, equipment, and business, and to pay monthly rent of $1,500 for the premises where the business was located, and secured their obligations with inventory, equipment, and proceeds therefrom, of the business which they were purchasing. Treat filed and perfected a security interest in the accounts receivable, inventory,

and equipment of The Kitchen Works on August 28, 1998. The Grudas currently owe Treat $61,794.99."

This means that when the Grudas failed to pay Treat, he had a right to repossess all assets *belonging to them*, including the cabinets—Treat was a creditor of the Grudas. SMI, of course, contended it had title to the cabinets. Based on the court's analysis, who is going to get the cabinets?

Defrauding Buyer Sells to Good-Faith Purchaser for Value

Marlow v. Conley

787 N.E.2d 490, (Ind. App. 2003)

Donald E. Marlow appeals the trial court's judgment in favor of Robert L. Medley and Linda L. Medley (collectively, the "Medleys") on Marlow's complaint for replevin. Marlow raises [this issue], * * * whether the Medleys obtained good title to a truck pursuant to Indiana UCC 2-403(1). We affirm.

The relevant facts follow. On May 21, 2000, Robert Medley attended a car show in Indianapolis. Henderson Conley attended the same car show and was trying to sell a 1932 Ford Truck ("Truck"). Conley told Robert that he operated a "buy here, pay here car lot," and Robert saw that the Truck had a dealer license plate. Robert purchased the Truck for $7,500.00 as a gift for Linda. Conley gave Robert the Truck's certificate of title, which listed the owner as Donald Marlow. When Robert questioned Conley about the owner of the Truck, Conley responded that Marlow had signed the title as part of a deal Conley had made with him. After purchasing the Truck, Robert applied to the Bureau of Motor Vehicles for a certificate of title in Linda's name.

On December 18, 2000, Marlow filed a complaint against Conley and the Medleys. * * * At the bench trial, Marlow testified that he had met Conley at a car show in Indianapolis on May 19, 2000, and Conley had told him that Conley owed a "car lot" on the west side of Indianapolis. Marlow also testified that Conley came to his house that night, but he "didn't let him in." Rather, Marlow testified that Conley "[came] over [his] fence...a big high fence." According to Marlow, Conley asked him to invest in Conley's business that night. Marlow gave Conley $500.00. Marlow testified that Conley came back the next day and Marlow gave him an additional $4,000.00. Marlow then testified that Conley stole the certificate of title for the Truck from Marlow's house and stole the Truck from his garage. According to Marlow, he told Conley later in the day to bring his Truck back and Conley told him that it had caught on fire. Marlow testified that he then called the police. However, in the May 30, 2000 police report, which was admitted into evidence at trial, the police officer noted the following:

The deal was [Conley] gets $4,500.00, plus an orange 1932 Ford truck. In return, [Marlow] would get a 1994 Ford flatbed dump truck and an 1989 Ford Bronco. [Marlow] stated that he has not received the vehicles and that [Conley] keeps delaying getting the vehicles for him. [Conley] gave [Marlow] several titles of vehicles which are believed to be junk. [Conley] told [Marlow] that he has a car lot at 16th and Lafayette Road.

[The trial court determined that Conley bought the truck from Marlow, paying Marlow $4,500 plus a Ford flatbed truck and Ford Bronco.]

The issue is whether the Medleys obtained good title to the Truck pursuant to Indiana UCC 2-403(1) [voidable title passed on to good-faith purchaser]. We first note that UCC 2-401(2) provides that "[u]nless otherwise explicitly agreed, title passes to the buyer at the time and place at which the seller completes his performance with reference to the physical delivery of the goods." Further, 2-403(1) provides as follows: "A purchaser of goods acquires all title which his transferor had or had power to transfer.... A person with voidable title has power to transfer a good title to a good faith purchaser for value. When goods have been delivered under a transaction of purchase, the purchaser has such power even though:... (d) the delivery was procured through fraud punishable as theft under the criminal law."

Thus, Conley, as purchaser of the goods, acquired all title to the Truck that Marlow, as transferor, had or had power to transfer. Additionally, even if Conley had "voidable title," he had the power to transfer good title to the Medleys if they were "good faith purchasers for value." Consequently, we must determine whether Conley had voidable title and, if so, whether the Medleys were good faith purchasers for value.

A. Voidable Title

We first determine whether Conley had voidable title to the Truck. * * * [T]he UCC does not define "voidable title." However, we have held that Indiana's UCC 2-403 is consistent with Indiana's common law, which provided that "legal title passes to a defrauding buyer. This title is not void; it is voidable, which means that when title gets into the hands of a bona fide purchaser for value then he will prevail over the defrauded seller." [Citation] Thus, a "defrauding buyer" obtains voidable title. However, a thief obtains void title. See, e.g., [Citation] holding that a renter who stole a motor home had void title, not voidable title, and could not convey good title). * * *

Here, Marlow argues that Conley stole the Truck and forged his name on the certificate of title. However, the trial court was presented with conflicting evidence regarding whether Conley stole the Truck and the certificate of title or whether Conley and Marlow had a business deal and Conley failed to comply with the agreement. The trial court found that:

> *Evidence presented concerning [Marlow's] complaint to the Indianapolis Police Department on May 30, 2000 casts doubt on the credibility of [Marlow's] trial testimony as the report states the truck and title were obtained by Conley in exchange for a 1994 Ford Flatbed Dump Truck and a 1989 Ford Bronco plus the payment of $4,500.00 by [Marlow]. Apparently, [Marlow] was complaining to the police concerning Conley's failure to deliver the two Ford vehicles.*

* * * The trial court did not find Marlow's testimony regarding the theft of the Truck and the certificate of title to be credible. * * * [B]ased upon the trial court's findings of fact, we must assume that the police report accurately describes the circumstances under which Conley obtained possession of the Truck and its signed certificate of title. Consequently, we assume that Marlow gave Conley $4,500.00 and the Truck in exchange for two other vehicles. Although Conley gave Marlow the certificates of title for the two vehicles, he never delivered the vehicles.

Conley's title is voidable if "the delivery was procured through fraud punishable as theft under the criminal law" under 2-403(1)(d). * * * Assuming that Conley knew that he would not deliver the two vehicles to Marlow, the delivery of the Truck to Conley was procured through fraud punishable as theft. Consequently, Marlow was defrauded, and Conley obtained voidable title to the Truck. * * *

B. Good Faith Purchasers for Value

Having determined that Conley obtained voidable title to the Truck, we must now determine whether the Medleys were good faith purchasers for value. Marlow does not dispute that the Medleys were purchasers for value. Rather, Marlow questions their "good faith" because they purchased the Truck from someone other than the person listed on the Truck's certificate of title. [UCC 1-201919] defines good faith as "honesty in fact in the conduct or transaction concerned." Marlow argues that Robert did not purchase the Truck in good faith because, although Robert purchased the vehicle from Conley, he was aware that the certificate of title was signed by Marlow.

* * * Here, the sole evidence presented by Marlow regarding the Medleys' lack of good faith is the fact that the certificate of title provided by Conley was signed by Marlow. Robert testified that he thought Conley was a licensed dealer and operated a "buy here, pay here" car lot. The Truck had a dealer license plate. Robert questioned Conley about the certificate of title. Conley explained that Marlow had signed the title as part of a deal Conley had made with him. Robert also testified that he had previously purchased vehicles at car shows and had previously purchased a vehicle from a dealer where the certificate of title had the previous owner's name on it. * * *

The Medleys' failure to demand a certificate of title complying with [the Indiana licensing statute] does not affect their status as good faith purchasers in this case. * * * The statute does not void transactions that violate the statute. [Citations] Although the failure to comply with [the licensing statute] may, combined with other suspicious circumstances, raise questions about a purchaser's good faith, we find no such circumstances here. Consequently, the Medleys were good faith purchasers for value, * * *

Lastly, Marlow also argues that the Medleys violated [licensing statutes] by providing false information to the Bureau of Motor Vehicles because the Medleys allegedly listed the seller of the Truck as Marlow rather than Conley. We noted above that legal title to a vehicle is governed by the sales provisions of the UCC rather than the Indiana Certificate of Title Act. Thus, although false statements to the Bureau of Motor Vehicles under Ind. Code § 9-18-2-2 could result in prosecution for perjury, such false statements do not affect legal title to the vehicle.

In summary, we conclude that, as a defrauding buyer, Conley possessed voidable title and transferred good title to the Medleys as good faith purchasers for value. * * * Thus, legal title to the Truck passed to the Medleys at the time Conley delivered the Truck to them. See UCC 2-401(2) ("[T]itle passes to the buyer at the time and place at which the seller completes his performance with reference to the physical delivery of the goods."). This result is consistent with the policy behind 2-403.

Section 2-403 was intended to determine the priorities between the two innocent parties: (1) the original owner who parts with his goods through fraudulent conduct of another and (2) an innocent third party who gives value for the goods to the perpetrator of the fraud without knowledge of the fraud. By favoring the innocent third party, the Uniform Commercial Code endeavors to promote the flow of commerce by placing the burden of ascertaining and preventing fraudulent transactions on the one in the best position to prevent them, the original seller. The policy behind the UCC is to favor the Medleys because, as between the Medleys and Marlow, Marlow was in the best position to prevent the fraudulent transaction.

For the foregoing reasons, we affirm the trial court's judgment for the Medleys. Affirmed.

Case Questions

1. The court determined Marlow was defrauded by Conley. How did Conley defraud Marlow?
2. What is the rationale, here expressed, for the UCC's provision that a defrauding purchaser (Conley) can pass on title to a good-faith purchaser for value?

3. Why did Marlow think the Medleys should not be considered good-faith purchasers?
4. Why would the UCC prevail over the state's certificate of title act?

Risk of Loss, Seller a Merchant

Ramos v. Wheel Sports Center
409 N.Y.S.2d 505 (N.Y. Civ. Ct. 1978)

Mercorella, J.

In this non-jury action plaintiff/purchaser is seeking to recover from defendant/vendor the sum of $893 [about $3,300 in 2010 dollars] representing the payment made by plaintiff for a motorcycle.

The parties entered into a sales contract wherein defendant agreed to deliver a motorcycle to plaintiff by June 30, 1978, for the agreed price of $893. The motorcycle was subsequently stolen by looters during the infamous power blackout of July 11, 1977.

It is uncontroverted that plaintiff paid for the motorcycle in full; was given the papers necessary for registration and insurance and did in fact register the cycle and secure liability insurance prior to the loss although license plates were never affixed to the vehicle. It is also conceded that the loss occurred without any negligence on defendant's part.

Plaintiff testified that defendant's salesman was informed that plaintiff was leaving on vacation and plaintiff would come for the cycle when he returned. He further testified that he never saw or rode the vehicle. From the evidence adduced at trial it is apparent that plaintiff never exercised dominion or control over the vehicle.

Defendant's president testified that he had no knowledge of what transpired between his salesman and plaintiff nor why the cycle was not taken prior to its loss.

The sole issue presented to the Court is which party, under the facts disclosed, bears the risk of loss?

It is the opinion of this Court that defendant must bear the risk of loss under the provisions of Section 2-509(3) of the Uniform Commercial Code.

This section provides that "...the risk of loss passes to the buyer on his receipt of the goods if the seller is a merchant...." Section 2-103(1)(c) states that receipt of goods means taking physical possession of them. [Authors' note: UCC revisions have changed the rule so that risk of loss passes to the buyer on his receipt of the goods *irrespective* of whether the seller is a merchant or not. It is still 2-509(3), however.]

The provision tends more strongly to hold risk of loss on the seller than did the former Uniform Sales Act. Whether the contract involves delivery at the seller's place of business or at the situs of the goods, a merchant seller cannot transfer risk of loss and it remains on him until actual receipt by the buyer, even though full payment has been made and the buyer notified that the goods are at his disposal. The underlying theory is that a merchant who is to make physical delivery at his own place continues meanwhile to control the goods and can be expected to insure his interest in them.

The Court is also of the opinion that no bailee/bailor relationship, constructive or otherwise, existed between the parties.

Accordingly, let judgment be entered in favor of plaintiff for the sum of $893, together with interest, costs and disbursements.

Case Questions

1. What caused the loss here, through no fault of either party?
2. What is the rationale for holding the merchant-seller liable in this circumstance?
3. Suppose instead that Ramos had purchased the motorcycle at a garage sale from an acquaintance and the same loss occurred. Who would bear the risk then?

For information about the famous 1977 New York City blackout, look at https://en.wikipedia.org/wiki/New_York_City_blackout_of_1977

18.5 Summary and Exercises

Summary

Two significant questions lurk in the background of any sale: (1) when does title pass? and (2) who must bear the risk of loss if the goods are destroyed or damaged through no fault of either party?

In general, title passes when the buyer and the seller agree that it passes. If the buyer and the seller fail to specify the time at which title passes, Article 2 lays down four rules: (1) under a shipment contract, title passes when the seller places the goods with the carrier; (2) under a destination contract, title passes when the goods are tendered at the place of delivery; (3) under a contract calling for delivery of documents of title, title passes when the seller tenders documents of title, even if the goods are not physically moved; and (4) when no physical delivery or exchange of documents is called for, title passes when the contract is signed.

The buyer and the seller may also specify who must bear the risk of loss. But if they do not, Article 2 sets out these four rules: (1) when the seller must ship by carrier but not to any particular destination, risk passes to the buyer when the seller delivers the goods to the carrier; (2) when the goods must be transported to a particular destination, risk passes when the carrier tenders them at that destination; (3) if the goods are held by a bailee who has issued a negotiable document of title, risk passes when the buyer receives the document; (4) in other cases, risk of loss turns on whether the seller is a merchant. If he is a merchant, risk passes when the buyer receives the goods; if he is not a merchant, risk passes when the seller tenders the goods. These rules are modified when either of the parties breaches the contract. In general, unless the breach is cured, the risk of uninsured losses lies on the party who breached.

Either party may insure the goods if it has an insurable interest in them. The buyer has an insurable interest in goods identified to the contract—for example, by marking them in some manner. The seller has an insurable interest as long as he retains title or a security interest.

In fixing passage of title and risk of loss, the parties often use shorthand terminology whose meaning must be mastered to make sense of the contract. These terms include F.O.B.; F.A.S.; ex-ship; C.I.F.; C.F.; no arrival, no sale; sale on approval; and sale or return. Use of these terms in a contract can have a significant effect on title and risk of loss.

Sometimes goods are sold by nonowners. A person with voidable title has the power to transfer title to a good-faith purchaser for value. A merchant who deals in particular goods has the power to transfer all rights of one who entrusts to him goods of the kind. And a rightful owner may be estopped by his own acts from asserting title against an innocent purchaser.

Exercises

1. Betty from Baltimore contracts to purchase one hundred purple llama figurines from Sam of Syracuse. Sam is to send the goods by carrier and is not required to deliver them to Betty's Boutique, their destination. He ships them by train, which unfortunately crashes in Delaware. All the figurines are destroyed. Whose loss is it? Why?
2. In Exercise 1, assume that the train did not crash but that Sam's creditors attempted to seize the goods before their arrival. May the creditors do so? Why?
3. Hattie's Head Shop signed a written agreement with the Tangerine Computer Company to supply a Marilyn, a supercomputer with bubble memory, to total up its orders and pay its foreign agents. The contract provided that the computer was to be specially built and that Tangerine would deliver it by carrier to Hattie's ready to install no later than June 1. Tangerine engineers worked feverishly to comply with the contract terms. On May 25, the computer stood gleaming in Tangerine's shipping department. That night, before the trucks could depart, a tornado struck the factory and destroyed the computer intended for Hattie's. Whose loss is it? Why?
4. In Exercise 3, assume that the tornado did not strike but that Tangerine's creditors attempted to seize the computer. May they? Why?
5. On February 18, Clancy, who was in debt, took his stereo to Lucy's repair shop. Because Lucy and Clancy were old friends, Lucy didn't give him a receipt. On February 19, hounded by creditors, Clancy sold the stereo on credit to Grover, who was to pick it up on February 21 at Lucy's, pay Lucy the repair bill, and pay the balance of the purchase price to Clancy. Who is entitled to the radio if, on February 20, Clancy's creditor appears with the sheriff to seize the stereo from Lucy? Why?
6. Assume in Exercise 5 that, instead of the attempted seizure of the stereo by the creditor, Lucy's shop and the stereo are destroyed by fire on February 20. Must Grover still pay Clancy for the stereo? Why?
7. Cleo's Close-Outs, a wholesaler of discounted merchandise, offered Randy's Retailers a chance to buy all the contents of a shipment of bathtub toys just received. Cleo estimated that she had between five hundred and six hundred rubber ducks and wrote on October 21 offering them to Randy for only one dollar each if Randy would pick them up at Cleo's. Randy received the letter in the mail the next day and mailed his acceptance immediately. In the wee hours of the following morning, October 23, a fire consumed Cleo's warehouse, melting the ducks into an uneven soup. Assuming that Cleo was a merchant, who bears the loss? Why?
8. Plaintiff, a manufacturer of men's clothing in Los Angeles, contracted to sell a variety of clothing items to Defendant, Harrison's clothing store in Westport, Connecticut, "F.O.B. Los Angeles." Plaintiff delivered the goods to Trucking Company and received a bill of lading. When the goods arrived at Defendant's store about two weeks later, Mrs. Harrison, Defendant's wife, who was in charge of the store at the time, requested the truck driver to deliver the goods inside the door of the shop. The driver refused and ultimately drove away. The goods were lost. Defendant refused to pay for the goods and raised as a defense that "the Plaintiff refused to deliver the merchandise into the Defendant's place of business." Who wins and why?[24]
9. Jackson owned a number of guns and asked his friend Willard, who ran a country store, if Willard would let Jackson display the guns in the store for sale on consignment. Willard would get some compensation for his trouble. Willard agreed. Subsequently Willard's creditors seized assets of the store, including the guns. Jackson protested that they were his guns, not Willard's, and that the latter's creditors should keep their hands off them. Given no other facts, who wins?
10. Plaintiff advertised his car for sale. Roberts stopped by to look at it. He took it for a short test drive, returned to Plaintiff's house, and said, "I like it, but my wife needs to look at it before I buy it. I'll be back in less than half an hour." Roberts took the car and never returned. Plaintiff called the police, who later found the car in a neighboring state. Defendant had bought it from Roberts, who had presented him with forged registration papers. Plaintiff then sued Defendant to get the car back. Who wins?

Self-Test Questions

1. In a sale-on-approval contract
    a. the goods are intended primarily for the buyer's use
    b. the goods are intended primarily for resale
    c. the risk of loss is on the buyer
    d. the buyer obtains title upon receipt of the goods
2. As a general rule
    a. goods cannot be sold by persons with voidable title
    b. a rightful owner cannot be estopped from asserting title against an innocent purchaser
    c. a merchant cannot transfer the rights of a person who entrusts goods to him
    d. a person with voidable title has the power to transfer title to a good-faith purchaser for value
3. In general, title passes
    a. to a buyer when the contract is signed
    b. when the buyer and the seller agree that it passes
    c. to a buyer when the seller receives payment for goods
    d. under none of the above conditions
4. When a destination contract does not specify when title is to pass, it passes
    a. when the goods are shipped
    b. when the contract is signed
    c. when the buyer pays for the goods
    d. when the seller tenders delivery
5. In a C.I.F. contract
    a. the seller must obtain insurance
    b. the buyer must obtain insurance
    c. the seller has fewer duties than with a C.F. contract
    d. title passes to the buyer when the seller tenders delivery

Self-Test Answers

1. a
2. d
3. b
4. d
5. a

Endnotes

1. Uniform Commercial Code, Section 2A-103(1)(j).
2. Uniform Commercial Code, Section 2-319(2).
3. Uniform Commercial Code, Section 2-320.
4. Uniform Commercial Code, Section 2-320.
5. https://en.wikipedia.org/wiki/Uniform_Commercial_Code
6. Uniform Commercial Code, Section 2-322.
7. Uniform Commercial Code, Section 2-324.

8. Uniform Commercial Code, Section 2-613.
9. Uniform Commercial Code, Section 1-201(15).
10. Uniform Commercial Code, Section 2-401(2)(b).
11. Uniform Commercial Code, Sections 2-308 and 2-503.
12. Uniform Commercial Code, Section 1-201(19).
13. Uniform Commercial Code, Sections 2-403(1), 2-403(1), 2A-304, and 2A-305.
14. *Dimension Funding, L.L.C. v. D.K. Associates, Inc.*, 191 P.3d 923 (Wash. App. 2008).
15. Uniform Commercial Code, Sections 2-403(2), 2A-304(2), and 2A-305(2).
16. Uniform Commercial Code, Section 1-201(9).
17. *Zendman v. Harry Winston, Inc.*, 111 N.E. 2d 871 (N.Y. 1953).
18. Uniform Commercial Code, Section 2-303.
19. Uniform Commercial Code, Section 2-327(1)(a).
20. Uniform Commercial Code, Section 2-326(3).
21. Uniform Commerical Code, Section 2-326.
22. Uniform Commercial Code, Section 2-510(2).
23. Uniform Commercial Code, Section 2-501(1).
24. *Ninth Street East, Ltd. v. Harrison*, 259 A.2d 772 (Conn. 1968).

CHAPTER 19
Performance and Remedies

Learning Objectives

After reading this chapter, you should understand the following:

1. What performance is expected of the seller in a sales contract.
2. What performance is expected of the buyer in a sales contract.
3. What rights and duties the buyer has if there is a nonconforming delivery.
4. How, in general, the UCC approaches remedies.
5. What the seller's remedies are for breach by the buyer.
6. What the buyer's remedies are for breach by the seller.
7. What excuses the UCC provides for nonperformance.

Elsewhere we examined contract performance and remedies under common law. In this chapter, we examine performance and remedies under Article 2, the law of sales, of the Uniform Commercial Code (UCC). In the next chapter, we cover special remedies for those damaged or injured by defective products.

The parties often set out in their contracts the details of performance. These include price terms and terms of delivery—where the goods are to be delivered, when, and how. If the parties fail to list these terms, the rules studied in this chapter will determine the parties' obligations: the parties may agree; if they do not, the UCC rules kick in as the default. In any event, the parties have an obligation to act in good faith.

19.1 Performance by the Seller

Learning Objective

1. Understand what is meant when it is said the seller has a duty to "make a timely delivery of conforming goods."

The Seller's Duty in General

The general duty of the seller is this: to make a timely delivery of conforming goods.[1]

The CISG, Article 30, says, "The seller must deliver the goods, hand over any documents relating to them and transfer the property in the goods, as required by the contract and this Convention."

Analysis of the Seller's Duty

Timing

By agreement or stipulation, the parties may fix the time when delivery is to be made by including statements in contracts such as "Delivery is due on or before July 8" or "The first of 12 installments is due on or before July 8." Both statements are clear.

If the parties do not stipulate in their contract when delivery is to occur, the UCC fills the gap. Section 2-309 of the UCC says, "The time for shipment or any other action under a contract if not provided for in this Article or agreed upon shall be a reasonable time." And what is a "reasonable time" is addressed by comment 1 to this section:

> *It thus turns on the criteria as to "reasonable time" and on good faith and commercial standards set forth in Sections 1-202, 1-203 and 2-103. It...depends on what constitutes acceptable commercial conduct in view of the nature, purposes and circumstances of the action to be taken.*

The CISG (Article 33) provides as follows:

> **The seller must deliver the goods**
>
> **(a) if a date is fixed by or determinable from the contract, on that date;**
>
> **(b) if a period of time is fixed by or determinable from the contract, at any time within that period unless circumstances indicate that the buyer is to choose a date; or**
>
> **(c) in any other case, within a reasonable time after the conclusion of the contract.**

Delivery

The parties may agree as to how delivery shall be accomplished; if they do not, the UCC fills the gap.

The CISG (Article 31) says this:

> **If the seller is not bound to deliver the goods at any other particular place, his obligation to deliver consists**
>
> **(a) if the contract of sale involves carriage of the goods—in handing the goods over to the first carrier for transmission to the buyer;**
>
> **(b) if, in cases not within the preceding subparagraph...in placing the goods at the buyer's disposal at that place [where the goods are];**
>
> **(c) in other cases—in placing the goods at the buyer's disposal at the place where the seller had his place of business at the time of the conclusion of the contract.**

By Agreement

The parties may use any language they want to agree on delivery terms.

If There Is No Agreement

If the parties do not stipulate delivery terms or if their agreement is incomplete or merely formulaic, the UCC describes the seller's obligations or gives meaning to the formulaic language. (Because form contracts are prevalent, formulaic language is customary.) You recall the discussion in Chapter 18 about when title shifts: we said title shifts when the seller has completed delivery obligations under the contract, and we ran through how those obligations are usually expressed. A quick review here is appropriate.

The contract may be either a *shipment* contract, a *destination* contract, or a contract where the *goods are not to be moved* (being held by a bailee). In any case, unless otherwise agreed, the delivery must be at a reasonable time and the **tender** (the offer to make delivery) must be kept open for a reasonable time; the buyer must furnish facilities "reasonably suited to the receipt of the goods."[2]

tender

Offer of money or performance to satisfy a debt.

In a shipment contract, the seller has four duties: (1) to deliver the goods to a carrier; (2) to deliver the goods with a reasonable contract for their transportation; (3) to deliver them with proper documentation for the buyer; and (4) to promptly notify the buyer of the shipment (UCC, Section 2-504). The contract may set out the seller's duties using customary abbreviations, and the UCC interprets those: "F.O.B [insert place where goods are to be shipped from]" means "free on board"—the seller must see to it that the goods are loaded on the vehicle of conveyance at the place of shipment. "F.A.S. [port of shipment inserted here]" means the seller must see to it that the goods are placed along the ship on the dock ready to be loaded (Section 2-319). If it is clear from the contract that the seller is supposed to ship the goods (i.e., the buyer is not going to the seller's place to get them) but not clear whether it is a shipment or a destination contract, the UCC presumes it is a shipment contract.[3]

If it is a destination contract, the seller has two duties: to get the goods to the destination at the buyer's disposal and to provide appropriate documents of delivery.[4] The contract language could be "F.O.B. [place of destination inserted here]," which obligates the seller to deliver to that specific location; "ex-ship," which obligates the seller to unload the goods from the vehicle of transportation at the agreed location (e.g., load the goods onto the dock); or it could be "no arrival, no sale," where the buyer is not liable for failure of the goods to arrive, unless she caused it.[5]

If the goods are in the possession of a bailee and are not to be moved—and the parties don't stipulate otherwise—the UCC, Section 2-503 says delivery is accomplished when the seller gives the buyer a negotiable document of title, or if none, when the bailee acknowledges the buyer's right to take the goods.

If nothing at all is said about delivery, the place for delivery is the seller's place of business or his residence if he has no place of business.[6]

Conforming Goods

As always, the parties may put into the contract whatever they want about the goods as delivered. If they don't, the UCC fills the gaps.

By Agreement

The parties may agree on what "conforming goods" means. An order will specify "large grade A eggs," and that means something in the trade. Or an order might specify "20 gross 100-count boxes No. 8 × 3/8 × 32 Phillips flathead machine screws." That is a screw with a designated diameter, length, number of threads per inch, and with a unique, cruciform head insert to take a particular kind of driver. The buyer might, for example, agree to purchase "seconds," which are goods with some flaw, such as clothes with seams not sewed quite straight or foodstuffs past their pull date. The parties may also agree in the contract what happens if nonconforming goods are delivered, as we'll see later in this chapter.

If There Is No Agreement

perfect tender

The UCC's requirement that the seller tender exactly what was contracted for.

If nothing is said in the contract about what quality of goods conform to the contract, then the UCC default rule kicks in. The seller is to make a **perfect tender**: what is delivered must in every respect conform to the contract.[7] And if what is delivered doesn't conform to the contract, the buyer is not obligated to accept the goods.

The CISG has no perfect tender rule. Article 46 provides this:

> **If the goods do not conform with the contract, the buyer may require delivery of substitute goods only if the lack of conformity constitutes a fundamental breach of contract and a request for substitute goods is made either in conjunction with notice given under article 39 or within a reasonable time thereafter. If the goods do not conform with the contract, the buyer may require the seller to remedy the lack of conformity by repair, unless this is unreasonable having regard to all the circumstances. A request for repair must be made either in conjunction with notice given under article 39 or within a reasonable time thereafter.**

Installment Contracts

Unless otherwise agreed, all goods should be delivered at one time, and no payment is due until tender. But where circumstances permit either party to make or demand delivery in lots, Section 2-307 of the UCC permits the seller to demand payment for each lot if it is feasible to apportion the price." What if the contract calls for delivery in installment, and one installment is defective—is that a material breach of the whole contract? No. Section 2-612 of the UCC says this:

> *(2) The buyer may reject any installment which is non-conforming if the non-conformity substantially impairs the value of that installment and cannot be cured or if the non-conformity is a defect in the required documents; but if the non-conformity does not fall within subsection (3) and the seller gives adequate assurance of its cure the buyer must accept that installment.*
>
> *(3) Whenever non-conformity or default with respect to one or more installments substantially impairs the value of the whole contract there is a breach of the whole.*

Cure for Improper Delivery

Failure to make a perfect tender, unless otherwise agreed, is a material breach of the sales contract. However, before the defaulting seller is in complete default, she has a right to cure—there is some wiggle room. Here's what the UCC says in Section 2-508:

> *(1) Where any tender or delivery by the seller is rejected because non-conforming and the time for performance has not yet expired, the seller may seasonably notify the buyer of his intention to cure and may then within the contract time make a conforming delivery.*
>
> *(2) Where the buyer rejects a non-conforming tender which the seller had reasonable grounds to believe would be acceptable with or without money allowance the seller may if he seasonably notifies the buyer have a further reasonable time to substitute a conforming tender.*

Buyer orders Santa Claus candles deliverable November 5; on October 25 the goods are delivered, but they're not right: they're Christmas *angel* candles instead. But the seller still has eleven days to cure, and the buyer must allow that. Buyer places an order exactly the same as the first order, and the order arrives on November 5 in the original manufacturer's packaging, but they're not right. "Well," says the seller, "I thought they'd be OK right out of the package. I'll get the correct ones to you right away." And the buyer would have a duty to allow that, if "right away" is a "further reasonable time."

Article 48 of the CISG says this:

> **The seller may, even after the date for delivery, remedy at his own expense any failure to perform his obligations, if he can do so without unreasonable delay and without causing the buyer unreasonable inconvenience or uncertainty of reimbursement by the seller of expenses advanced by the buyer. However, the buyer retains any right to claim damages as provided for in this Convention. If the seller requests the buyer to make known whether he will accept performance and the buyer does not comply with the request within a reasonable time, the seller may perform within the time indicated in his request. The buyer may not, during that period of time, resort to any remedy which is inconsistent with performance by the seller.**

So, again, the seller's duty is to make a timely delivery of conforming goods. Let's take a look now at the buyer's duties.

Key Takeaway

The seller's obligation under the UCC is to make a timely delivery of conforming goods. For each element of the duty—timely, delivery, conforming goods—the parties may agree in their contract. If they do not, the UCC fills in default rules.

Exercises

1. If the parties do not specify a time for delivery, what is the UCC's default position?
2. What are the seller's obligations in an F.O.B. shipment contract? In an F.O.B. destination contract?
3. Compare the UCC's perfect tender rule to the common-law substantial performance doctrine.

19.2 Performance by Buyer

Learning Objectives

1. Understand what the general duties of the buyer are.
2. Recognize what rights the buyer has if the seller tenders a nonconforming delivery.

General Duties of Buyer

The general duty of the buyer is this: inspection, acceptance, and payment.[8] But the buyer's duty does not arise unless the seller tenders delivery.

Inspection

Under Sections 2-513(1) and (2) of the Uniform Commercial Code (UCC), the buyer has a qualified right to inspect goods. That means the buyer must be given the chance to look over the goods to determine whether they conform to the contract. If they do not, he may properly reject the goods and refuse to pay. The right to inspect is subject to three exceptions:

1. The buyer waives the right. If the parties agree that payment must be made before inspection, then the buyer must pay (unless the nonconformity is obvious without inspection). Payment under these circumstances does not constitute acceptance, and the buyer does not lose the right to inspect and reject later.
2. The delivery is to be made C.O.D. (cash on delivery).
3. Payment is to be made against documents of title (e.g., when the document represents the ownership interest of goods stored at a place distant from where the buyer is).

If the buyer fails to inspect, or fails to discover a defect that an inspection would have revealed, she cannot later revoke her acceptance, subject to some exceptions.

Acceptance

Acceptance is clear enough: it means the buyer takes the goods. But the buyer's options on improper delivery need to be examined, because that's often a problem area.

The buyer may accept goods by words, silence, or action. Section 2-606(1) of the UCC defines acceptance as occurring in any one of three circumstances:

1. **Words.** The buyer, after a reasonable opportunity to inspect, tells the seller either that the goods conform or that he will keep them despite any nonconformity.
2. **Silence.** The buyer fails to reject, after a reasonable opportunity to inspect.
3. **Action.** The buyer does anything that is inconsistent with the seller's ownership, such as using the goods (with some exceptions) or selling the goods to someone else.

Once the buyer accepts, she is obligated to pay at the contract rate and loses the right to reject the goods.[9] She is stuck, subject to some exceptions.

Payment

The parties may specify in their contract what *payment* means and when it is to be made. If they don't, the UCC controls the transaction.[10]

A Buyer's Right on Nonconforming Delivery

Obviously if the delivery is defective, the disappointed buyer does not have to accept the goods: the buyer may (a) reject the whole, (b) accept the whole, or (c) accept any commercial unit and reject the rest (2-601, 2A-509), or (d)—in two situations—revoke an acceptance already made.

Rejection and a Buyer's Duties after Rejection

Under UCC, Section 2-601(a), rejection is allowed if the seller fails to make a perfect tender. The rejection must be made within a reasonable time after delivery or tender. Once it is made, the buyer may not act as the owner of the goods. If he has taken possession of the goods before he rejects them, he must hold them with reasonable care to permit the seller to remove them. If the buyer is a merchant, then the buyer has a special duty to follow reasonable instructions from the seller for disposing of the rejected goods; if no instructions are forthcoming and the goods are perishable, then he must try to sell the goods for the seller's account and is entitled to a commission for his efforts. Whether or not he is a merchant, a buyer may store the goods, reship them to the seller, or resell them—and charge the seller for his services—if the seller fails to send instructions on the goods' disposition. Such storage, reshipping, and reselling are not acceptance or conversion by the buyer.

Acceptance of a Nonconforming Delivery

The buyer need not reject a nonconforming delivery. She may accept it with or without allowance for the nonconformity.

Acceptance of Part of a Nonconforming Delivery

The buyer may accept any commercial unit and reject the rest if she wants to. A **commercial unit** means "such a unit of goods as by commercial usage is a single whole for purposes of sale and division of which materially impairs its character or value on the market or in use. A commercial unit may be a single article (as a machine), a set of articles (as a suite of furniture or an assortment of sizes), a quantity (as a bale, gross, or carload), or any other unit treated in use or in the relevant market as a single whole."[11]

commercial unit

A unit of goods as by usage is a single whole for sale and division.

Installment Sales

A contract for an installment sale complicates the answer to the question, "What right does the buyer have to accept or reject when the seller fails to deliver properly?" (An **installment contract** is one calling for delivery of goods in separate lots with separate acceptance for each delivery.) The general answer is found in the UCC at Section 2-612, which permits the buyer to reject any nonconforming installment if the nonconformity cannot be cured if it substantially impairs the value of that particular installment. However, the seller may avoid rejection by giving the buyer adequate assurances that he will cure the defect, unless the particular defect substantially impairs the value of the whole contract.

installment contract

A contract where payment or performance is in discrete units.

Suppose the Corner Gas Station contracts to buy 12,000 gallons of regular gasoline from Gasoline Seller, deliverable in twelve monthly installments of 1,000 gallons on the first of each month, with a set price payable three days after delivery. In the third month, Seller is short and can deliver only 500 gallons immediately and will not have the second 500 gallons until mid-month. May Corner Gas reject this tender? The answer depends on the circumstances. The nonconformity clearly cannot be cured, since the contract calls for the full 1,000 on a particular day. But the failure to make full delivery does not necessarily impair the value of that installment; for example, Corner Gas may know that it will not use up the 500 gallons until mid-month. However, if the failure will leave Corner Gas short before mid-month and unable to buy from another supplier unless it agrees to take a full 1,000 (more than it could hold at once if it also took Seller's 500 gallons), then Corner Gas is entitled to reject Seller's tender.

Is Corner Gas entitled to reject the entire contract on the grounds that the failure to deliver impairs the value of the contract as a whole? Again, the answer depends on whether the impairment was substantial. Suppose other suppliers are willing to sell only if Corner Gas agrees to buy for a year. If Corner Gas needed the extra gasoline right away, the contract would have been breached as whole, and Corner Gas would be justified in rejecting all further attempted tenders of delivery from Seller. Likewise, if the spot price of gasoline were rising so that month-to-month purchases from other suppliers might cost it more than the original agreed price with Seller, Corner Gas would be justified in rejecting further deliveries from Seller and fixing its costs with a supply contract from someone else. Of course, Corner Gas would have a claim against Seller for the difference between the original contract price and what it had to pay another supplier in a rising market (as you'll see later in this chapter).

Revocation

revocation

The withdrawal of an offer by the offeror.

A **revocation** of acceptance means that although the buyer has accepted and exercised ownership of the goods, he can return the goods and get his money back. There are two circumstances in which the buyer can revoke an acceptance if the nonconformity "substantially impairs its value to him":[12]

a. if the buyer reasonably thought the nonconformity would be cured and it is not within a reasonable time; or
b. if the acceptance was due to a latent defect that could not reasonably have been discovered before acceptance.

Consider two examples illustrated in the next paragraph. The first deals with the first point (buyer thought nonconformity would be cured and it was not within a reasonable time), and the second gets to point "b" (latent defect).

In August 1983, the Borsages purchased a furnished mobile home on the salesperson's assertion that it was "the Cadillac of mobile homes." But when they moved in, the Borsages discovered defects: water leaks, loose moldings, a warped dishwasher door, a warped bathroom door, holes in walls, defective heating and cooling systems, cabinets with chips and holes, furniture that fell apart, mold and mildew in some rooms, a closet that leaked rainwater, and defective doors and windows. They had not seen these defects at the time of purchase because they looked at the mobile home at night and there were no lights on in it. The Borsages immediately complained. Repairmen came by but left, only promising to return again. Others did an inadequate repair job by cutting a hole in the bottom of the home and taping up the hole with masking tape that soon failed, causing the underside of the home to pooch out. Yet more repairmen came by but made things worse by inadvertently poking a hole in the septic line and failing to fix it, resulting in a permanent stench. More repairmen came by, but they simply left a new dishwasher door and countertop at the home, saying they didn't have time to make the repairs. In June 1984, the Borsages provided the seller a long list of uncorrected problems; in October they stopped making payments. Nothing happened. In March 1986—thirty-one months after buying the mobile home—they told the seller to pick up the mobile home: they revoked their acceptance and sued for the purchase price. The defendant seller argued that the Borsages' failure to move out of the house for so long constituted acceptance. But they were repeatedly assured the problems would be fixed, and moreover they had no place else to live, and no property to put another mobile home on if they abandoned the one they had. The court had no problem validating the Borsages' revocation of acceptance, under the section noted earlier, if they ever had accepted it. The seller might have a right to some rental value, though.[13]

In April 1976, Clarence Miller ordered a new 1976 Dodge Royal Monaco station wagon from plaintiff Colonial Dodge. The car included a heavy-duty trailer package with wide tires. The evening of the day the Millers picked up the new car, Mrs. Miller noticed that there was no spare tire. The following morning, the defendant notified the plaintiff that he insisted on a spare tire, but when he was told there were no spare tires available (because of a labor strike), Mr. Miller told the plaintiff's salesman that he would stop payment on the check he'd given them and that the car could be picked up in front of his house. He parked it there, where it remained until the temporary registration sticker expired and it was towed by the police to an impound yard. Plaintiff sued for the purchase price, asserting that the missing spare tire did not "substantially impair the value of the goods to the buyer." On appeal to the Michigan Supreme Court, the plaintiff lost. "In this case the defendant's concern with safety is evidenced by the fact that he ordered the special package which included spare tires. The defendant's occupation demanded that he travel extensively, sometimes in excess of 150 miles per day on Detroit freeways, often in the early morning hours.... He was afraid of a tire going flat ... at 3 a.m. Without a spare, he would be helpless until morning business hours. The dangers attendant upon a stranded motorist are common knowledge, and Mr. Miller's fears are not unreasonable." The court observed that although he had accepted the car before he discovered the nonconformity, that did not preclude revocation: the spare tire storage space was under a fastened panel, concealed from view.[14]

Key Takeaway

The duty of the buyer in a sales contract is to inspect, accept, and pay. Failure to discover a defect that an inspection would have revealed is a waiver of right to complain. Normally the goods are conforming and the buyer accepts them, but upon discovery of a defect the buyer may reject the whole nonconforming delivery, part of it (the buyer has some duties if she has possession of the rejected goods), or in some cases reject one installment of an installment sale or, if one defective installment is serious enough to vitiate the whole contract, the buyer may consider the contract terminated. If goods have been accepted because the seller promised to fix defects or because the defects were latent, then the buyer may revoke the acceptance where the nonconformity substantially impairs the value of the contract to the buyer.

Exercises

1. If a buyer takes possession of goods and shortly thereafter discovers they are nonconforming, what duty does the nonmerchant buyer have with respect to the goods? What duty does the merchant buyer have with respect to the goods?
2. What is the difference between rejection and revocation?
3. Under what circumstances will a defective installment allow the buyer to reject that installment? Under what circumstances would a defective installment allow the buyer to terminate the contract?

19.3 Remedies

Learning Objectives

1. Understand what purpose remedies serve under the UCC.
2. Be able to see when the parties' agreements as to limited remedies fail under the UCC.
3. Recognize what the seller's remedies are.
4. Recognize what the buyer's remedies are.

Remedies in General

General Policy

The general policy of the Uniform Commercial Code (UCC) is to put the aggrieved party in a good position as if the other party had fully performed—as if there had been a timely delivery of conforming goods. The UCC provisions are to be read liberally to achieve that result if possible. Thus the seller has a number of potential remedies when the buyer breaches, and likewise the buyer has a number of remedies when the seller breaches.

The CISG provides, at Article 74:

Damages for breach of contract by one party consist of a sum equal to the loss, including loss of profit, suffered by the other party as a consequence of the breach. Such damages may not exceed the loss which the party in breach foresaw or ought to have foreseen at the time of the conclusion of the contract, in the light of the facts and matters of which he then knew or ought to have known, as a possible consequence of the breach of contract.

Specifying Remedies

We have emphasized how the UCC allows people to make almost any contract they want (as long as it's not unconscionable). Just as the parties may specify details of performance in the contract, so they may provide for and limit remedies in the event of breach.[15] The following would be a typical limitation of remedy: "Seller's sole obligation in the event goods are deemed defective by the seller is to replace a like quantity of non-defective goods." A remedy is optional unless it is expressly agreed that it is the exclusive remedy.[16]

But the parties are not free to eliminate all remedies. As the UCC comment to this provision puts it, "If the parties intend to conclude a contract for sale within this Article they must accept the legal consequence that there be at least a fair quantum of remedy for breach of the obligations or duties outlined in the contract." In particular, the UCC lists three exemptions from the general rule that the parties are free to make their contract up any way they want as regards remedies:

1. When the circumstances cause the agreed-to remedy to fail or be ineffective, the default UCC remedy regime works instead.[17]
2. Consequential damages may be limited or excluded unless the limitation or exclusion is unconscionable. Limitation of consequential damages for injury to the person in the case of

consumer goods is prima facie unconscionable, but limitation of damages where the loss is commercial is not.[18]

3. The parties may agree to liquidated damages: "Damages for breach by either party may be liquidated in the agreement but only at an amount which is reasonable in the light of the anticipated or actual harm caused by the breach, the difficulties of proof of loss, and the inconvenience or nonfeasibility of otherwise obtaining an adequate remedy. A term fixing unreasonably large liquidated damages is void as a penalty."[19] The Code's equivalent position on *leases* is interestingly slightly different. UCC 2A-504(1) says damages may be liquidated "but only at an amount or by a formula that is reasonable in light of the then anticipated harm caused" by the breach. It leaves out anything about difficulties of proof or inconvenience of obtaining another adequate remedy.

Statute of Limitations

The UCC statute of limitations for breach of any sales contract is four years. The parties may "reduce the period of limitation to not less than one year but may not extend it."[20] Article 2A-506(1) is similar, but omits the prohibition against extending the limitation. Article 2-725(2) goes on: "A cause of action accrues when the breach occurs, regardless of the aggrieved party's lack of knowledge of the breach. A breach of warranty occurs when tender of delivery is made, except that where a warranty explicitly extends to future performance of the goods and discovery of the breach must await the time of such performance the cause of action accrues when the breach is or should have been discovered."

Article 2A-506(2) is similar to 2-725(2).

Seller's Remedies

Article 2 in General

Article 2-703 of the UCC lists the four things the buyer can do by way of default, and it lists—here slightly paraphrased—the seller's remedies (2A-523(1) is similar for leases):

> *Where the buyer wrongfully rejects or revokes acceptance of goods or fails to make a payment due on or before delivery or repudiates with respect to a part or the whole, then with respect to any goods directly affected and, if the breach is of the whole contract, then also with respect to the whole undelivered balance, the aggrieved seller may:*
>
> *(1) withhold delivery of such goods;*
>
> *(2) stop delivery by any bailee;*
>
> *(3) identify to the contract conforming goods not already identified;*
>
> *(4) reclaim the goods on the buyer's insolvency;*
>
> *(5) resell and recover damages;*
>
> *(6) recover damages for non-acceptance or repudiation;*
>
> *(7) or in a proper case recover the price;*
>
> *(8) cancel.*

Items (1)–(4) address the seller's rights to deal with the goods; items (5)–(7) deal with the seller's rights as regards the price, and item (8) deals with the continued existence of the contract.

The CISG's take is similar. Article 61 and following state,

> **If the buyer fails to perform any of his obligations under the contract or this Convention, the seller may:...(a) require the buyer to pay the price. (b) Fix an additional period of time of reasonable length for performance by the buyer of his obligations; unless the seller has received notice from the buyer that he will not perform within the period so fixed, the seller may not, during that period, resort to any remedy for breach of contract. (c) Declare the contract avoided if the failure by the buyer to perform any of his obligations under the contract or this Convention amounts to a fundamental breach of contract or if the buyer does not, within the additional period of time fixed by the seller [above], perform his obligation to pay the price or take delivery of the goods, or if he declares that he will not do so within the period so fixed. (d) The seller also has the right to damages.**

To illustrate the UCC's remedy provision, in this and the following section, we assume these facts: Howard, of Los Angeles, enters into a contract to sell and ship one hundred prints of a Pieter Bruegel painting, plus the original, to Bunker in Dallas. Twenty-five prints have already been delivered to Bunker, another twenty-five are en route (having been shipped by common carrier), another twenty-five are finished but haven't yet been shipped, and the final twenty-five are still in production. The original is hanging on the wall in Howard's living room. We will take up the seller's remedies if the buyer breaches and if the buyer is insolvent.

Remedies on Breach

Bunker, the buyer, breaches the contract. He sends Howard an e-mail stating that he won't buy and will reject the goods if delivery is attempted. Howard has the following cumulative remedies; election is not required.

Withhold Further Delivery

Howard may refuse to send the third batch of twenty-five prints that are awaiting shipment.

Stop Delivery

Howard may also stop the shipment. If Bunker is insolvent, and Howard discovers it, Howard would be permitted to stop any shipment in the possession of a carrier or bailee. If Bunker is not insolvent, the UCC permits Howard to stop delivery only of carload, truckload, planeload, or larger shipment. The reason for limiting the right to bulk shipments in the case of noninsolvency is that stopping delivery burdens the carrier and requiring a truck, say, to stop and the driver to find a small part of the contents could pose a sizable burden.

Identify to the Contract Goods in Possession

Howard could "identify to the contract" the twenty-five prints in his possession. Section 2-704(1) of the UCC permits the seller to denote conforming goods that were not originally specified as the exact objects of the contract, if they are under his control or in his possession at the time of the breach. Assume that Howard had five hundred prints of the Bruegel painting. The contract did not state which one hundred of those prints he was obligated to sell, but once Bunker breached, Howard could declare that those particular prints were the ones contemplated by the contract. He has this right whether or not the identified goods could be resold. Moreover, Howard may complete production of the twenty-five unfinished prints and identify them to the contract, too, if in his "reasonable commercial judgment" he could better avoid loss—for example, by reselling them. If continued production would be expensive and the chances of resale slight, the seller should cease manufacture and resell for scrap or salvage value.

Resell

Howard could resell the seventy-five prints still in his possession as well as the original. As long as he proceeds in good faith and in a commercially reasonable manner, per Section 2-706(2) and Section 2A-527(3), he is entitled to recover the difference between the resale price and the contract price, plus incidental damages (but less any expenses saved, like shipping expenses). "Incidental damages" include any reasonable charges or expenses incurred because, for example, delivery had to be stopped, new transportation arranged, storage provided for, and resale commissions agreed on.

The seller may resell the goods in virtually any way he desires as long as he acts reasonably. He may resell them through a public or private sale. If the resale is public—at auction—only identified goods can be sold, unless there is a market for a public sale of futures in the goods (as there is in agricultural commodities, for example). In a public resale, the seller must give the buyer notice unless the goods are perishable or threaten to decline in value speedily. The goods must be available for inspection before the resale, and the buyer must be allowed to bid or buy.

The seller may sell the goods item by item or as a unit. Although the goods must relate to the contract, it is not necessary for any or all of them to have exited or to have been identified at the time of breach.

The seller does not owe the buyer anything if resale or re-lease results in a profit for the buyer.[21]

Recover Damages

The seller may recover damages equal to the difference between the market price (measured at the time and place for tender of delivery) and the unpaid contract price, plus incidental damages, but less any expenses saved because of the buyer's breach. Suppose Howard's contract price was $100 per print plus $10,000 for the original and that the market price on the day Howard was to deliver the seventy-five prints was $75 (plus $8,000 for the original). Suppose too that the shipping costs (including insurance) that Howard saved when Bunker repudiated were $2,000 and that to resell them Howard would have to spend another $750. His damages, then, would be calculated as follows: original contract price ($17,500) less market price ($13,625) = $3,875 less $2,000 in saved expenses = $1,875 plus $750 in additional expenses = $2,625 net damages recoverable by Howard, the seller.

The CISG puts it similarly in Article 75: "If the contract is avoided and if, in a reasonable manner and within a reasonable time after avoidance, the buyer has bought goods in replacement or the seller has resold the goods, the party claiming damages may recover the difference between the contract price and the price in the substitute transaction as well as any further damages recoverable."

If the formula would not put the seller in as good a position as performance under the contract, then the measure of damages is lost profits—that is, the profit that Howard would have made had Bunker taken the original painting and prints at the contract price (again, deducting expenses saved and adding additional expenses incurred, as well as giving credit for proceeds of any resale).[22] This provision becomes especially important for so-called lost volume sellers. Howard may be able to sell the remaining seventy-five prints easily and at the same price that Bunker had agreed to pay. Then why isn't Howard whole? The reason is that the second buyer was not a *substitute* buyer but an *additional* one; that is, Howard would have made that sale even if Bunker had not reneged on the contract. So Howard is still short a sale and is out a profit that he would have made had Bunker honored the contract.

Recover the Price

Howard—the seller—could recover from Bunker for the price of the twenty-five prints that Bunker holds. Or suppose they had agreed to a shipment contract, so that the risk of loss passed to Bunker when Howard placed the other prints with the trucker and that the truck crashed en route and the cargo destroyed. Howard could recover the price. Or suppose there were no market for the remaining seventy-five prints and the original. Howard could identify these prints to the contract and recover the contract price. If Howard did resell some prints, the proceeds of the sale would have to be credited to Bunker's account and deducted from any judgment. Unless sold, the prints must be held for Bunker and given to him upon his payment of the judgment.

Cancel the Contract

When Bunker repudiated, Howard could declare the contract cancelled. This would also apply if a buyer fails to make a payment due on or before delivery. Cancellation entitles the non-breaching party to any remedies for the breach of the whole contract or for any unperformed balance. That is what happens when Howard recovers damages, lost profits, or the price.[23]

Again, the CISG is similar. Article 64 provides that the seller may declare the contract avoided "if the failure by the buyer to perform any of his obligations under the contract or this Convention amounts to a fundamental breach of contract; or if the buyer does not, within the additional period of time fixed by the seller perform his obligation to pay the price or take delivery of the goods, or if he declares that he will not do so within the period so fixed."

Note again that these UCC remedies are cumulative. That is, Howard could withhold future delivery *and* stop delivery en route, *and* identify to the contract goods in his possession, *and* resell, *and* recover damages, *and* cancel.

Remedies on Insolvency

The remedies apply when the buyer *breaches* the contract. In addition to those remedies, the seller has remedies when he learns that the buyer is insolvent, even if the buyer has not breached. Insolvency results, for example, when the buyer has "ceased to pay his debts in the ordinary course of business," or the buyer "cannot pay his debts as they become due."[24]

Upon learning of Bunker's insolvency, Howard could refuse to deliver the remaining prints, unless Bunker pays cash not only for the remaining prints but for those already delivered. If Howard learned of Bunker's insolvency within ten days of delivering the first twenty-five prints, he could make a demand to reclaim them. If within three months prior to delivery, Bunker had falsely represented that he was solvent, the ten-day limitation would not cut off Howard's right to reclaim. If he does seek to reclaim, Howard will lose the right to any other remedy with respect to those particular items. However, Howard cannot reclaim goods already purchased from Bunker by a customer in the ordinary course of business. The customer does not risk losing her print purchased several weeks before Bunker has become insolvent.[25]

In the lease situation, of course, the goods belong to the lessor—the lessor has title to them—so the lessor can repossess them if the lessee defaults.[26]

Buyer's Remedies

In this section, let us assume that Howard, rather than Bunker, breaches, and all other circumstances are the same. That is, Howard had delivered twenty-five prints, twenty-five more were en route, the original painting hung in Howard's living room, another twenty-five prints were in Howard's factory, and the final twenty-five prints were in production.

In General

The buyer can do the following three things by way of defaulting: repudiate the contract, fail to deliver the goods, or deliver or tender nonconforming goods. Section 2-711 of the UCC provides the following remedies for the buyer:

Where the seller fails to make delivery or repudiates, or the buyer rightfully rejects or justifiably revokes, then with respect to any goods involved, and with respect to the whole if the breach goes to the whole contract, the buyer may

(1) cancel the contract, and

(2) recover as much of the price as has been paid; and

(3) "cover" and get damages; and

(4) recover damages for nondelivery.

Where the seller fails to deliver or repudiates, the buyer may also:

(5) if the goods have been identified recover them; or

(6) in a proper case obtain specific performance or

(7) replevy the goods.

On rightful rejection or justifiable revocation of acceptance, a buyer:

(8) has a security interest in goods in his possession or control for any payments made on their price and any expenses reasonably incurred in their inspection, receipt, transportation, care and custody and may hold such goods and resell them in like manner as an aggrieved seller.

If the buyer has accepted non-conforming goods and notified seller of the non-conformity, buyer can

(9) recover damages for the breach;[27]

and in addition the buyer may

(10) recover incidental damages and

(11) recover consequential damages.[28]

Thus the buyer's remedies can be divided into two general categories: (1) remedies for goods that the buyer does not receive or accept, when he has justifiably revoked acceptance or when the seller repudiates, and (2) remedies for goods accepted.

The CISG provides similar remedies at Articles 45–51:

If the seller fails to perform any of his obligations under the contract, buyer may (1) declare the contract avoided if the seller's breach is fundamental; or (2) require performance by the seller of his obligations unless the buyer has resorted to a remedy which is inconsistent with this requirement; (3) require delivery of substitute goods if the non-conformity constitutes a fundamental breach of contract; (4) may require the seller to remedy the lack of conformity by repair, unless this is unreasonable having regard to all the circumstances; (5) may fix an additional period of time of reasonable length for performance by the seller of his obligations and unless the buyer has received notice from the seller that he will not perform within the period so fixed, the buyer may not, during that period, resort to any remedy for breach of contract; (6) in case of non-conforming delivery, reduce the price in the same proportion as the value that the goods actually delivered had at the time of the delivery bears to the value that conforming goods would have had at that time.

Goods Not Received

The UCC sets out buyer's remedies if goods are not received or if they are rightfully rejected or acceptance is rightfully revoked.

Cancel

If the buyer has not yet received or accepted the goods (or has justifiably rejected or revoked acceptance because of their nonconformity), he may cancel the contract and—after giving notice of his cancellation—he is excused from further performance.[29]

Recover the Price

Whether or not the buyer cancels, he is entitled to recover the price paid above the value of what was accepted.

Cover

In the example case, Bunker—the buyer—may "cover" and have damages: he may make a good-faith, reasonable purchase of substitute goods. He may then recover damages from the seller for the difference between the cost of cover and the contract price. This is the buyer's equivalent of the seller's right to resell. Thus Bunker could try to purchase seventy-five additional prints of the Bruegel from some other manufacturer. But his failure or inability to do so does not bar him from any other remedy open to him.

Sue for Damages for Nondelivery

Bunker could sue for damages for nondelivery. Under Section 2-713 of the UCC, the measure of damages is the difference between the market price at the time when the buyer learned of the breach and the contract price (plus incidental damages, less expenses saved). Suppose Bunker could have bought seventy-five prints for $125 on the day Howard called to say he would not be sending the rest of the order. Bunker would be entitled to $1,875—the market price ($9,375) less the contract price ($7,500). This remedy is available even if he did not in fact purchase the substitute prints. Suppose that at the time of breach, the original painting was worth $15,000 (Howard having just sold it to someone else at that price). Bunker would be entitled to an additional $5,000, which would be the difference between his contract price and the market price.

For leases, the UCC, Section 2A-519(1), provides the following: "the measure of damages for nondelivery or repudiation by the lessor or for rejection or revocation of acceptance by the lessee is the present value, as of the date of the default, of the then market rent minus the present value as of the same date of the original rent, computed for the remaining lease term of the original lease agreement, together with incidental and consequential damages, less expenses saved in consequence of the lessor's default."

Recover the Goods

If the goods are unique—as in the case of the original Bruegel—Bunker is entitled to specific performance—that is, recovery of the painting. This section is designed to give the buyer rights comparable to the seller's right to the price and modifies the old common-law requirement that courts will not order specific performance except for unique goods. It permits specific performance "in other proper circumstances," and these might include particular goods contemplated under output or requirements contracts or those peculiarly available from one market source.[30]

Even if the goods are not unique, the buyer is entitled to *replevy* them if they are identified to the contract and after good-faith effort he cannot recover them. **Replevin** is the name of an ancient common-law action for recovering goods that have been unlawfully taken; in effect it is not different from specific performance, and the UCC makes no particular distinction between them in Section 2-716. Section 2A-521 holds the same for leases. In our case, Bunker could replevy the twenty-five prints identified and held by Howard.

Replevin

An action to recover possession of goods wrongfully held.

Bunker also has the right to recover the goods should it turn out that Howard is insolvent. Under UCC, Section 2-502, if Howard were to become insolvent within ten days of the day on which Bunker pays the first installment of the price due, Bunker would be entitled to recover the original and the prints, as long as he tendered any unpaid portion of the price.

For security interest in goods rightfully rejected, if the buyer rightly rejects nonconforming goods or revokes acceptance, he is entitled to a security interest in any goods in his possession. In other words, Bunker need not return the twenty-five prints he has already received unless Howard reimburses him for any payments made and for any expenses reasonably incurred in their inspection, receipt, transportation, care, and custody. If Howard refuses to reimburse him, Bunker may resell the goods and take from the proceeds the amount to which he is entitled.[31]

Goods Accepted

The buyer does not have to reject nonconforming goods. She may accept them anyway or may effectively accept them because the time for revocation has expired. In such a case, the buyer is entitled to remedies as long as she notifies the seller of the breach within a reasonable time.[32] In our example, Bunker can receive three types of damages, all of which are outlined here.

Compensatory Damages

Bunker may recover damages for any losses that in the ordinary course of events stem from the seller's breach. Suppose Howard had used inferior paper that was difficult to detect, and within several weeks of acceptance the prints deteriorated. Bunker is entitled to be reimbursed for the price he paid.

Consequential Damages

Bunker is also entitled to consequential damages.[33] These are losses resulting from general or particular requirements of the buyer's needs, which the seller had reason to know and which the buyer could not reasonably prevent by cover or otherwise. Suppose Bunker is about to make a deal to resell the twenty-five prints that he has accepted, only to discover that Howard used inferior ink that faded quickly. Howard knew that Bunker was in the business of retailing prints and therefore he knew or should have known that one requirement of the goods was that they be printed in long-lasting ink. Because Bunker will lose the resale, he is entitled to the profits he would have made. (If Howard had not wished to take the risk of paying for consequential damages, he could have negotiated a provision limiting or excluding this remedy.) The buyer has the burden or proving consequential damages, but the UCC does not require mathematical precision. Suppose customers come to Bunker's gallery and sneer at the faded colors. If he can show that he would have sold the prints were it not for the fading ink (perhaps by showing that he had sold Bruegels in the past), he would be entitled to recover a reasonable estimate of his lost profits.

In *De La Hoya v. Slim's Gun Shop* the plaintiff purchased a handgun from the defendant, a properly licensed dealer. While the plaintiff was using it for target shooting, he was questioned by a police officer, who traced the serial number of the weapon and determined that—unknown to either the plaintiff or the defendant—it had been stolen. The plaintiff was arrested for possession of stolen property and incurred, in 2016 dollars, $3,200 in attorney fees to extricate himself from the criminal charges. He sued the defendant for breach of the implied warranty of title and was awarded the amount of the attorney fees as consequential damages. On appeal the California court held it foreseeable that the plaintiff would get arrested for possessing a stolen gun, and "once the foreseeability of the arrest is established, a natural and usual consequence is that the [plaintiff] would incur attorney's fee."[34] Compare with *In re Stem* in the exercises later in this chapter.

Incidental Damages

Section 2-715 of the UCC allows incidental damages, which are "damages resulting from the seller's breach including expenses reasonably incurred in inspection, receipt, transportation and care and custody of goods rightfully rejected, any commercially reasonable charges, expenses or commissions in connection with effecting cover and any other reasonable expense incident to the delay or other breach." Section 2A-520(1) of the UCC is similar for leases.

Key Takeaway

Parties to a contract for the sale of goods may specify what the remedies will be in case of breach. They may limit or exclude remedies, but the UCC insists that there be some remedies; if the parties agree to liquidated damages, the amount set cannot be a penalty.

If the parties do not agree to different remedies for the seller in case the buyer defaults, the UCC sets out remedies. As to the seller's obligation, he may cancel the contract. As to the goods, he may withhold or stop delivery, identify conforming goods to the contract, or reclaim goods upon the buyer's insolvency. As to money, he may resell and recover damages or lost profits and recover the price. Unless they are inconsistent, these remedies are cumulative. The point of the range of remedies is, as much as possible, to put the nonbreaching seller in the position she would have been in had there been no breach. The aggrieved lessor is entitled to similar remedies as the seller.

The UCC also provides a full panoply of remedies available to a buyer if the seller fails to deliver goods or if the buyer rightfully rejects them or revokes her acceptance. As to the buyer's obligations, she may cancel the contract. As to the goods, she may claim a security interest in those rightfully rejected, recover goods identified if the seller is insolvent, or replevy or seek specific performance to get goods wrongfully withheld. As to money, she may recover payments made or cover and recover damages for nondelivery. If the buyer accepts nonconforming goods, she is entitled to damages for breach of warranty. These remedies are cumulative, so the aggrieved buyer may pursue any of them, unless the remedies are mutually exclusive. The Article on leases provides basically the same remedies for the aggrieved lessee (UCC 2A 520–523).

Exercises

1. What are the four things a breaching seller could do to cause the buyer grief, commercially speaking?
2. If the buyer breaches, what rights does the seller have in regard to the goods?
3. In regard to the money owed to her?
4. In regard to the continued existence of the contract?
5. What are the four things a breaching buyer could do to cause the seller grief, commercially speaking?
6. If the seller breaches, what rights does the buyer have in regard to the goods?
7. In regard to the money owed to him?
8. In regard to the continued existence of the contract?

19.4 Excuses for Nonperformance

Learning Objectives

1. Recognize how parties are discharged if the goods are destroyed.
2. Determine what defenses are valid when it becomes very difficult or impossible to perform.
3. Understand the UCC's position on the right to adequate assurances and anticipatory repudiation.

In contracts for the sale of goods, as in common law, things can go wrong. What then?

Casualty to Identified Goods

As always, the parties may agree what happens if the goods are destroyed before delivery. The default is Sections 2-613 and 2A-221(a) of the Uniform Commercial Code (UCC). The UCC says that "where the contract requires for its performance goods identified when the contract is made, and the goods suffer casualty without fault of either party before the risk of loss passes to the buyer, ... then (a) if the loss is total the contract is avoided; and (b) if the loss is partial the buyer may nevertheless accept them with due allowance for the goods' defects." Thus, if Howard ships the original Bruegel to Bunker but the painting is destroyed, through no fault of either party, before delivery occurs, the parties are discharged. If the frame is damaged, Bunker could, if he wants, take the painting anyway, but at a discount.

The UCC's Take on Issues Affecting "Impossibility"

Although this matter was touched on in Chapter 15, it is appropriate to mention briefly again the UCC's treatment of variations on the theme of "impossibility."

Impracticability

Sections 2-614(1) and 2A-404(1) of the UCC require reasonable substitution for berthing, loading, and unloading facilities that become unavailable. They also require reasonable substitution for transportation and delivery systems that become "commercially impracticable"; if a practical alternative exists, "performance must be tendered and accepted." If Howard agreed to send the prints by rail, but a critical railroad bridge is unusable and no trains can run, delivery by truck would be required.

Section 2-615 of the UCC says that the failure to deliver goods is not a breach of the seller's duty "if performance as agreed has become impracticable by the occurrence of a contingency the non-occurrence of which was a basic assumption on which the contract was made or by compliance in good faith with any applicable foreign or domestic government regulation or order whether or not it later proves to be invalid." Section 2A-405(b) of the UCC is similar for leases.

The CISG provides something similar at Article 79: "A party is not liable for a failure to perform any of his obligations if he proves that the failure was due to an impediment beyond his control and that he could not reasonably be expected to have taken the impediment into account at the time of the conclusion of the contract or to have avoided or overcome it or its consequences."

Right to Adequate Assurances of Performance

Section 2-609, Comment 1, of the UCC observes that "the essential purpose of a contract... is actual performance [but] a continuing sense of reliance and security that the promised performance will be forthcoming when due is an important feature of the bargain." Thus the UCC says that if one party has "reasonable grounds for insecurity arise... either party may in writing demand adequate assurance and until he receives such assurance may if commercially reasonable suspend [his own] performance[.]"

The CISG has a similar take at Article 71: "A party may suspend the performance of his obligations if, after the conclusion of the contract, it becomes apparent that the other party will not perform a substantial part of his obligations. A party suspending performance, whether before or after dispatch of the goods, must immediately give notice of the suspension to the other party and must continue with performance if the other party provides adequate assurance of his performance."

Anticipatory Repudiation

Obviously, if a person repudiates the contract it's clear she will not perform, but what if she repudiates before time for performance is due? Does the other side have to wait until nonperformance actually happens, or can he sue in anticipation of the other's default? Sections 2-610 and 2A-402 of the UCC say the aggrieved party can do either: wait for performance or "resort to any remedy for breach." Under the UCC, Sections 2-611 and 2A-403, the one who has anticipatorily repudiated can "retract his repudiation unless the aggrieved party has since the repudiation cancelled or materially changed his position[.]"

Suppose that Howard has cause to suspect that if he does deliver the goods, Bunker won't pay. Howard may write to Bunker and demand—not request—assurances of adequate performance. If such assurances are not adequately forthcoming, Howard may assume that Bunker has repudiated the contract and have remedies.

Article 72 of the CISG is pretty much the same: "If prior to the date for performance of the contract it is clear that one of the parties will commit a fundamental breach of contract, the other party may declare the contract avoided."

Key Takeaway

If, through no fault of either party, the goods are destroyed before the risk of loss has passed from the seller to the buyer, the parties are both discharged. If the expected means of performance is impossible, but an alternative is available, the alternative must be utilized. If performance becomes impracticable because of an unexpected contingency, failure to deliver the goods is excused. But a party who has concerns whether the other side will perform is entitled to adequate assurances of performance; if they are not forthcoming, the worried party may suspend performance. Where a party repudiates a contract before performance is due, the other side may sue immediately (anticipatory repudiation) or may wait until the time performance comes due and then sue.

Exercises

1. Suppose Plaintiff sues Defendant for breach of contract, and Defendant successfully raises an excuse for nonperformance. What liability does Defendant have now?
2. The contract read that the goods would be "shipped F.O.B. Seattle, by Burlington Northern Rail to the buyer in Vancouver, B.C." Due to heavy rain and mudslides, the rail line between Seattle and points north was impassable. Buyer insists Seller is obligated to send the goods by motor truck; Seller insists her performance has become impossible or at least that shipment must await the rail-line clearance. Who is correct? Explain.
3. Buyer manufactured ceramic insulators and ordered the dies into which the liquid ceramic would be poured for hardening and finishing from Seller, to be delivered April 15. The first test batch of a dozen dies arrived on February 15; these dies were defective. Buyer wrote inquiring whether the defects could be remedied in time for the final delivery. Seller responded, "We are working to address the problems here." Buyer again inquired; Seller responded, "As I said, we are working on the problems." Buyer fretted that the deadline—two months in the future—would not be met. What remedy, if any, does Buyer have now?

19.5 Cases

Limitations of Remedy Results in No Remedy

Hartzell v. Justus Co., Inc.
693 F.2d 770 (8th Cir. S.D. 1982)

Arnold, J.

This is a diversity case arising out of the purchase by Dr. Allan Hartzell of Sioux Falls, South Dakota, of a log home construction kit manufactured by the defendant Justus Homes. Dr. Hartzell purchased the package in 1977 for $38,622 [about $153,000 in 2016 dollars] from Del Carter, who was Justus Homes' dealer for the Sioux Falls area. He also hired Carter's construction company, Natural Wood Homes, to build the house. Hartzell, who testified that the home eventually cost about $150,000, was dissatisfied with the house in many respects. His chief complaints were that knotholes in the walls and ceiling leaked rain profusely, and that the home was not weather tight because flashings were not included in the roofing materials and because the timbers were not kiln-dried and therefore shrank. He also complained that an undersized support beam, which eventually cracked, was included in the package. This latter defect was alleged to have resulted in cracks in the floor and inside doors that would not close. Hartzell further alleged that these structural defects were only partially remediable, and that the fair market value of the house was reduced even after all practicable repairs had been made. Alleging breach of implied and express warranties and negligence, he sought damages for this loss in value and for the cost of repairs. After a two-day trial, the jury returned a plaintiff's verdict for $34,794.67 [about $137,000 in 2016 dollars].

Justus Homes contends the District Court erred in failing to instruct the jury on a limitation-of-remedies clause contained in its contract with the plaintiff. The defendants rely on Clause 10c of the contract, which says Justus *will repair or replace defective materials*, and Clause 10d, which states that *this limited repair or replacement clause is the exclusive remedy available against Justus* [emphasis added]. These agreements, Justus asserts, are valid under the Uniform Commercial Code 2-719(1). Section 2-719(1) states:

> *(1) Subject to the provisions of subsections (2) and (3) of this section and of § 57A-2-718 on liquidation and limitation of damages,*
>
> *(a) The agreement may provide for remedies in addition to or in substitution for those provided in this chapter and may limit or alter the measure of damages recoverable under this chapter, as by limiting the buyer's remedies to return of the goods and repayment of the price or to repair and replacement of nonconforming goods or parts; and*
>
> *(b) Resort to a remedy as provided is optional unless the remedy is expressly agreed to be exclusive, in which case it is the sole remedy.*

Subsection (1) of section 2-719 is qualified by subsection (2): "Where circumstances cause an exclusive or limited remedy to fail of its essential purpose, remedy may be had as provided in this title."

The jury's verdict for the plaintiff in an amount almost exactly equal to the plaintiff's evidence of cost of repairs plus diminution in market value means it must have found that the structural defects were not entirely remediable. Such a finding necessarily means that the limited warranty failed of its essential purpose.

Two of our recent cases support this conclusion. In *Soo Line R.R. v. Fruehauf Corp.*, 547 F.2d 1365 (8th Cir.1977), the defendant claimed, relying on a limitation-of-remedies clause similar to the one involved here, that the plaintiff's damages should be limited to the reasonable cost of repairing the railroad cars that plaintiff had bought from defendant. The jury verdict included, among other things, an award for the difference between the value of the cars as actually manufactured, and what they would have been worth if they had measured up to the defendant's representations. This Court affirmed the verdict for the larger amount. We held, construing the Minnesota U.C.C., which is identical to § 2-719 as adopted in South Dakota, that the limitation-of-remedies clause was ineffective because the remedy as thus limited failed of its essential purpose. The defendant, though called upon to make the necessary repairs, had refused to do so, and the repairs as performed by the plaintiff itself "did not fully restore the cars to totally acceptable operating conditions."

Here, Justus Homes attempted to help with the necessary repairs, which is more than Fruehauf did in the *Soo Line* case, but after the repairs had been completed the house was still, according to the jury verdict, not what Justus had promised it would be. The purpose of a remedy is to give to a buyer what the seller promised him—that is, a house that did not leak. If repairs alone do not achieve that end, then to limit the buyer's remedy to repair would cause that remedy to fail of its essential purpose. * * *

An analogous case is *Select Pork, Inc. v. Babcock Swine, Inc.* [Citation], applying § 2-719 as adopted in Iowa. The defendant had promised to deliver to plaintiff certain extraordinary pigs known as Midwestern Gilts and Meatline Boars. Instead, only ordinary pigs were delivered. Plaintiff sued for breach of warranty, and defendant claimed that its damages, if any, should be limited to a return of the purchase price by an express clause to that effect in the contract. The District Court held that the clause was unenforceable because it was unconscionable, see § 2-719(3), and because it failed of its essential purpose. We affirmed: "Having failed to deliver the highly-touted special pigs, defendants may not now assert a favorable clause to limit their liability." So here, where the house sold was found by the jury to fall short of the seller's promises, and where repairs could not make it right, defendant's liability cannot be limited to the cost of repairs. If the repairs had been adequate to restore the house to its promised condition, and if Dr. Hartzell had claimed additional consequential damages, for example, water damage to a rug from the leaky roof, the limitation-of-remedies clause would have been effective. But that is not this case.

There was no double recovery here: the verdict was not for cost of repair plus the entire decrease in market value, but rather for cost of repair plus the decrease in market value that still existed after all the repairs had been completed.

[T]he evidence in the record all demonstrate[s] that the repair or replacement clause was a failure under the circumstances of this case. Some of the house's many problems simply could not be remedied by repair or replacement. The clause having failed of its essential purpose, that is, effective enjoyment of implied and express warranties, the plaintiff was entitled, under UCC § 2-719(2), to any of the buyer's remedies provided by the Code. Among these remedies are consequential damages as provided in §§ 2-714 and 2-715(2).

The judgment is affirmed.

Case Questions

1. What did the seller here limit itself to do in case of defects? What was the limitation of remedy?
2. Did Justus Homes disclaim implied and expressed warranties with its contract language regarding limitation of remedies?
3. Was the essential purpose of the limitation of remedy to protect the party benefiting from it—here, the seller of the log home kit—or was the essential purpose of the limitation of remedy, as the court said, "effective enjoyment of implied and expressed warranties"?
4. In a part of the opinion excised, the court wrote, "A finding of unconscionability is, as a matter of logic, simply unnecessary in cases where § 2-719(2) applies." Would it be easier simply to say that the limitation of liability here was unconscionable?

Cure for Improper Delivery

Wilson v. Scampoli

228 A.2d 848 (D.C. App. 1967)

Myers, J.

This is an appeal from an order of the trial court granting rescission of a sales contract for a color television set and directing the return of the purchase price plus interest and costs.

Appellee [Mrs. Kolley's father] purchased the set in question on November 4, 1965, paying the total purchase price in cash. The transaction was evidenced by a sales ticket showing the price paid and guaranteeing ninety days' free service and replacement of any defective tube and parts for a period of one year. Two days after purchase the set was delivered and uncrated, the antennae adjusted and the set plugged into an electrical outlet to "cook out." When the set was turned on however, it did not function properly, the picture having a reddish tinge. Appellant's delivery man advised the buyer's daughter, Mrs. Kolley, that it was not his duty to tune in or adjust the color but that a service representative would shortly call at her house for that purpose. After the departure of the delivery men, Mrs. Kolley unplugged the set and did not use it.

On November 8, 1965, a service representative arrived, and after spending an hour in an effort to eliminate the red cast from the picture advised Mrs. Kolley that he would have to remove the chassis from the cabinet and take it to the shop as he could not determine the cause of the difficulty from his examination at the house. He also made a written memorandum of his service call, noting that the television "Needs Shop Work (Red Screen)." Mrs. Kolley refused to allow the chassis to be removed, asserting she did not want a "repaired" set but another "brand new" set. Later she demanded the return of the purchase price, although retaining the set. Appellant refused to refund the purchase price, but renewed his offer to adjust, repair, or, if the set could not be made to function properly, to replace it. Ultimately, appellee instituted this suit against appellant seeking a refund of the purchase price. After a trial, the court ruled that "under the facts and circumstances the complaint is justified. Under the equity powers of the Court I will order the parties put back in their original status, let the $675 [about $5,100 in 2010 dollars] be returned, and the set returned to the defendant."

Appellant does not contest the jurisdiction of the trial court to order rescission in a proper case, but contends the trial judge erred in holding that rescission here was appropriate. He argues that he was always willing to comply with the terms of the sale either by correcting the malfunction by minor repairs or, in the event the set could not be made thereby properly operative, by replacement; that as he was denied the opportunity to try to correct the difficulty, he did not breach the contract of sale or any warranty thereunder, expressed or implied.

[The District of Columbia UCC 2-508] provides:

> *(1) Where any tender or delivery by the seller is rejected because non-conforming and the time for performance has not yet expired, the seller may seasonably notify the buyer of his intention to cure and may then within the contract time make a conforming delivery.*
>
> *(2) Where the buyer rejects a nonconforming tender which the seller had reasonable grounds to believe would be acceptable with or without money allowance the seller may if he seasonably notifies the buyer have a further reasonable time to substitute a conforming tender.*

...

Removal of a television chassis for a short period of time in order to determine the cause of color malfunction and ascertain the extent of adjustment or correction needed to effect full operational efficiency presents no great inconvenience to the buyer. In the instant case, appellant's expert witness testified that this was not infrequently necessary with new televisions. Should the set be defective in workmanship or parts, the loss would be upon the manufacturer who warranted it free from mechanical defect. Here the adamant refusal of Mrs. Kolley, acting on behalf of appellee, to allow inspection essential to the determination of the cause of the excessive red tinge to the picture defeated any effort by the seller to provide timely repair or even replacement of the set if the difficulty could not be corrected. The cause of the defect might have been minor and easily adjusted or it may have been substantial and required replacement by another new set—but the seller was never given an adequate opportunity to make a determination.

We do not hold that appellant has no liability to appellee, but as he was denied access and a reasonable opportunity to repair, appellee has not shown a breach of warranty entitling him either to a brand new set or to rescission. We therefore reverse the judgment of the trial court granting rescission and directing the return of the purchase price of the set.

Reversed.

Case Questions

1. Why did the seller "have reasonable grounds to believe [the television] would be acceptable"?
2. What did Mrs. Kolley want?
3. Does this case require a buyer to accept patchwork goods or substantially repaired articles in lieu of flawless merchandise?

Seller's Remedies When Buyer Defaults

Santos v. DeBellis
901 N.Y.S.2d 457 (N.Y. Sup.App. 2010)

Molia, J.

On March 1, 2008 and March 11, 2008, plaintiff made payments to defendant of $3,000 each, in connection with the purchase of a mobile home located in Fort Pierce, Florida. Thereafter, on March 13, 2008, plaintiff and defendant signed an agreement which had been prepared by defendant. The agreement described the subject property by its location, recorded the fact that plaintiff had paid defendant deposits totaling $6,000, set forth a closing date of March 25, 2008, and specified that "the remaining $27,000.00" was payable at closing to defendant by a guaranteed financial instrument. Plaintiff never paid the outstanding balance and brought this action to recover the $6,000 deposit she paid to defendant. Following a nonjury trial, judgment was awarded in favor of defendant dismissing the complaint.

Because the sale of a mobile home constitutes a contract for the sale of goods rather than of real property [Citations], the parties' agreement was governed by the Uniform Commercial Code. The agreement, which was made after plaintiff had made the two $3,000 "deposit" payments, constituted a memorandum in confirmation of an oral agreement and, even though it omitted some terms, was sufficient to satisfy the statute of frauds [Citations].

Section 2-718 of the Uniform Commercial Code specifies that in the absence of a contractual provision with respect to the liquidation or limitation of damages and the return of deposits,

(2) Where the seller justifiably withholds delivery of goods because of the buyer's breach, the buyer is entitled to restitution of any amount by which the sum of his payments exceeds...

(b) [in the absence of contractually fixed terms] twenty per cent of the value of the total performance for which the buyer is obligated under the contract or $500, whichever is smaller.

(3) The buyer's right to restitution under subsection (2) is subject to offset to the extent that the seller establishes

(a) a right to recover damages under the provisions of this Article other than subsection (1), and

(b) the amount or value of any benefits received by the buyer directly or indirectly by reason of the contract.

Here, notwithstanding the fact that plaintiff, as buyer, had breached the contract, defendant failed to demonstrate any damages resulting therefrom; nor did defendant establish that plaintiff had received any benefits directly or indirectly by reason of the parties' agreement (*see* UCC 2-718[3]). Therefore, pursuant to UCC 2-718(2), plaintiff was entitled to the return of all but $500 of her deposit.

The order of the District Court dismissing the complaint is accordingly reversed, and judgment is awarded to plaintiff in the principal sum of $5,500.

Case Questions

1. If the plaintiff had been a dealer in mobile homes and the unit here had been part of his inventory, he would be entitled to claim lost profits on the sale of one unit. Here, apparently, the plaintiff seller was a private party. Why was he not entitled to any damages greater than $500?
2. New York adopted the UCC in 1964. Five hundred dollars in 1964 would be worth about $3,500 in 2010. Why isn't the change in the dollar's value recognized here?

Buyer's Remedies When Seller Breaches

[Note: this case is slightly edited by the authors.]

Furlong v. Alpha Chi Omega Sorority
657 N.E.2d 866 (Ohio Mun. 1993)

Bachman, J.

In late September through mid-October 1992, plaintiff Johnathan James Furlong ("Furlong") contacted defendant Alpha Chi Omega Sorority ("AXO"), by phoning the chairperson of its social committee, Emily Lieberman ("Emily"), between a dozen and a dozen and a half times.

Ultimately (about the first week in October), Furlong received Emily's order for one hundred sixty-eight imprinted sweaters at $21.50 each (plus one free sweater) for delivery on Friday, October 23, 1992, so as to arrive in time for AXO's Midnight Masquerade III on the evening of Saturday, October 24, 1992.

The price was to be $3,612, [about $6,100 in 2016 dollars] payable as follows: $2,000 down payment when the contract was made, and $1,612 balance when the sweaters were delivered.

An oral contract for the sale of goods (the imprinted sweaters) was made between Furlong and AXO, at a definite price and with specified dates for payment and for delivery.

At some point in those phone calls with Furlong, Emily said that the sweaters were to be custom designed with the following specified design: namely, with three colors (hunter green letters on top of maroon letters outlined in navy blue, and hunter green masks). Furlong promised to have them so imprinted (by a third party whom he would select). * * * Thereafter, he delivered to Emily an Ohio Wesleyan sweater with maroon letters to show her the maroon color. * * * Additionally, he faxed to Emily a two-page description of the sweaters, which not only included the designs for the fronts and the backs of the sweaters, but also included arrows showing where each of the three colors would go (hunter green letters on top of maroon letters outlined in navy blue, and hunter green masks).

Furlong and Emily created an express warranty by each of the above three statutory means: namely, by affirmation of fact (his initial phone calls); by sample (the maroon sweater) by description (the fax). This express warranty became part of the contract. Each of the three methods of showing the express warranty was not in conflict with the other two methods, and thus they are consistent and cumulative, and constitute the warranty [2-317].

The design was a "dickered" aspect of the individual bargain and went clearly to the essence of that. Thus, the express warranty was that the sweaters would be in accordance with the above design (including types of colors for the letters and the mask, and the number of colors for the same). Further, the express warranty became part of the contract.

On October 13, 1992, AXO mailed Furlong a $2,000 check for the down payment; he deposited it in his bank account on October 16, 1992. Thereafter, as discussed below, Furlong had the sweaters imprinted (on Thursday, October 22) and delivered to AXO (on Friday, October 23). Upon receipt of the delivery, AXO gave a check to Furlong's agent in the amount of $1,612 for the balance of the purchase price. However, later on that day, AXO inspected the sweaters, discovered the design changes (mentioned below), caused AXO's bank to stop payment on the check, and stated AXO's objections in a phone call with Furlong. AXO has never paid Furlong that balance on the purchase price.

Furlong's obligation as the seller was to transfer and deliver the goods in accordance with the contract. AXO's obligation was to accept and pay in accordance with that contract. [2-301] We will now discuss whether it legally did so.

Furlong was a jobber for Argento Bros., Inc. ("Argento") and had Argento print the sweaters. In doing so, Furlong worked with Argento's artists. Early in the morning of Thursday (October 22, 1992), the artist(s) began to prepare the art work and recommended changes to the design. Furlong authorized the artist(s) to change the design without the knowledge or consent of AXO. Argento spent about eight hours printing the sweaters all day Thursday. Furlong did not phone AXO about the changes until the next day, Friday (October 23), after the sweaters were printed with those changes. Here are the five design changes that he made:

- The *first change* was to delete the agreed-upon outline for the letters (namely, the navy blue outline).
- The *second change* was to reduce the agreed-upon number of colors for the fronts and the backs (from three colors per side to two colors per side).
- The *third change* was to alter one of the agreed-upon colors (from maroon to red).
- The *fourth change* was to alter the agreed-upon scheme of colors for the letters on the fronts and the backs (namely, both sides were to have the same two colors of maroon and hunter green; whereas in fact the backs had neither of those colors, and instead had a navy blue color for the letters).
- The *fifth change* was to alter the agreed-upon color of the masks (from hunter green to maroon—actually red).

The court specifically finds that the color was *red* (actually, scarlet) and was *not maroon* (like the maroon-colored letters on the Ohio Wesleyan sweater).

The sweaters did not conform to the contract (specifically, the express warranty in the contract). Thus (in the words of the statute), the sweaters did "fail in any respect to conform to the contract." Actually, the sweaters failed in at least five respects. [2-601] Further, not only did they "fail in any respect," they failed in a substantial respect. In either event, they were a nonconforming tender of goods. [2-601]

On Friday morning (October 23), Furlong picked up the five to six boxes of sweaters from Argento and had a friend deliver them from Columbus to Bowling Green. The boxes arrived at the AXO house around midday. Sometime thereafter on the same day, Emily inspected one of them and screamed her dismay upon discovering that the sweaters were not what AXO had ordered.

The court rejects Furlong's assertion that he did all that he could do under the circumstances. The obvious answer is that he did not do enough. He should have gotten AXO's prior consent to the changes. He could have done this by providing for more lead time-between the time that Argento prepared the art work and the time that it printed the sweaters. Instead, he had both done at the same time (Thursday morning).

Finally, and alternatively, plaintiff should have entered into a contract that gave him discretion to make design changes without AXO's consent. We must remember that "these sweaters," as Furlong himself admits (and describes), were to be "custom-designed" for AXO. Thus, they were to be printed according to AXO's specifications, and not according to Furlong's discretion.

Next, Furlong asserts that AXO—after learning of the changes—should have agreed to his offer of compromise: namely, that he would reduce the unit price of the sweaters in exchange for AXO's keeping them and paying the reduced price. Also, Furlong asserts that AXO should have communicated his compromise offer to AXO's members and pledges. In both respects, the court disagrees: Although the law allowed AXO to do so, it did not require AXO to do. Instead, AXO did exactly what the law allowed: AXO rejected the nconforming goods in whole.

About 4:00 p.m. on the same day that the sweaters arrived at the AXO house (Friday, October 23), Amy—as the AXO president—phoned Furlong. She said that the sweaters were not what AXO had ordered. She stated the specifics as to why the sweaters were not as ordered. She offered to return the sweaters to him, but he said "No." AXO still has possession or custody of the boxes of sweaters.

[The UCC] provides: "Rejection of goods must be within a reasonable time after their delivery. * * * It is ineffective unless the buyer seasonably notifies the seller." [2-602] AXO did what this statute requires.

That statute further provides: "[I]f the buyer has before rejection taken physical possession of goods, * * * he is under a duty after rejection to hold them with reasonable care at the seller's disposition for a time sufficient to permit the seller to remove them[.]" [2-602(2)(b)] AXO has done this, too. From the above, it is seen that AXO legally rejected the sweaters on the same day that AXO received physical possession of them.

The court disagrees with Furlong's assertion that AXO accepted the sweaters. He is confusing a layman's understanding of the term *accept* ("to receive a thing [with a consenting mind])," *Webster's Collegiate Dictionary* (5 Ed.1947), at 6, with the statutory meaning of the term. The mere fact that AXO took physical possession of the sweaters does not, by itself, mean that AXO legally "accepted" them.

In regard to seller's remedies, Furlong has no legal remedies because AXO did not breach the contract. Thus, he is not entitled to an award for the $1,612 balance that he claims is due on the contract price.

As concluded above, AXO rightfully rejected the sweaters, after having paid part of the purchase price: namely, $2,000. AXO is entitled to cancel the contract and to recover the partial payment of the purchase price. [2-606]

Also, as concluded above, AXO still has rightful possession or control of the sweaters. AXO has a security interest in the sweaters in its possession or control for the part payment made on the purchase price—but when reimbursed for that part payment AXO must return the sweaters to Furlong.

The court will prepare, file, and serve a judgment entry as follows: dismissing with prejudice Furlong's claim against all defendants; dismissing with prejudice Emily Lieberman's and Amy Altomondo's counterclaims against Furlong; granting AXO's counterclaim (for $2,000, plus ten percent per annum postjudgment interest and costs).

Further, that entry will order AXO's attorney (Mr. Reddin) to retain possession of the sweaters either until further court order or until AXO's judgment is satisfied in full (whereupon he shall surrender the sweaters to Furlong if Furlong picks them up within thirty days thereafter, or, if Furlong does not, he may then dispose of them as abandoned property without any liability).

Judgment accordingly.

Case Questions

1. Surely the plaintiff could not have thought that the radically altered design would be acceptable for the young women's masquerade ball. On what basis did he think he would be entitled to the full payment contracted for?
2. Whether Amy Altomondo knew it or not, she did what the UCC says a buyer should do when nonconforming goods are delivered. What are those steps?
3. What does it mean that AXO has a security interest in the sweaters? Security for what?

19.6 Summary and Exercises

Summary

As with most of the Uniform Commercial Code (UCC), the parties may specify the terms of their performance. Only if they fail to do so does Article 2 (and 2A) provide the terms for them. The seller's duty is to make a timely delivery of conforming goods. In the absence of agreement, the time for delivery is a reasonable one, and the place of delivery is the seller's place of business. All goods must be tendered in a single delivery, unless circumstances permit either party the right to make or demand delivery in lots.

If the seller ships nonconforming goods but has time to meet his contractual obligations or if he reasonably believed the goods would be suitable, he may notify the buyer of his intention to cure, and if he does so in a timely manner the buyer must pay.

The buyer's general obligation is to inspect, accept, and pay. If an inspection reveals that the goods are nonconforming, the buyer may reject them; if he has accepted because defects were latent or because he received assurances that the defects would be cured, and they are not, the buyer may revoke his acceptance. He then has some duties concerning the goods in his possession. The buyer must pay for any conforming goods; payment may be in any manner consistent with current business customs. Payment is due at the time and place at which the buyer will ultimately receive the goods.

The general policy of the UCC is to put an aggrieved party in as good a position as she would have been had the other party fully performed. The parties may specify or limit certain remedies, but they may not eliminate all remedies for a breach. However, if circumstances make an agreed-on remedy inadequate, then the UCC's other remedies apply; parties may not unconscionably limit consequential damages; they may agree to liquidated damages, but not to unreasonable penalties.

In general, the seller may pursue the following remedies: withhold further delivery, stop delivery, identify to the contract goods in her possession, resell the goods, recover damages or the price, or cancel the contract. In addition, when it becomes apparent that the buyer is insolvent, the seller may, within certain time periods, refuse to deliver the remaining goods or reclaim goods already delivered.

The buyer, in general, has remedies. For goods not yet received, she may cancel the contract; recover the price paid; cover the goods and recover damages for the difference in price; or recover the specific goods if they are unique or in "other proper circumstances." For goods received and accepted, the buyer may recover ordinary damages for losses that stem from the breach and consequential damages if the seller knew of the buyer's particular needs and the buyer could not reasonably cover.

The UCC provides some excuses for nonperformance: casualty of the goods, through no fault of either party; the nonhappening of presupposed conditions that were a basic assumption of the contract; substituted performance if the agreed-on methods of performance become impracticable; right to adequate assurances of performance when reasonable grounds for insecurity of performance arise; anticipatory repudiation and resort to any remedy, before time for performance is due, is allowed if either party indicates an unwillingness to perform.

Exercises

1. Anne contracted to sell one hundred cans of yellow tennis balls to Chris, with a delivery to be made by June 15.
    a. On June 8, Anne delivered one hundred cans of white tennis balls, which were rejected by Chris. What course of action would you recommend for Anne, and why?
    b. Assume Ann had delivered the one hundred cans of white balls on June 15; these were rejected by Chris. Under what circumstances might Anne be allowed additional time to perform the contract?
    c. If the contract did not specify delivery, when must Anne deliver the tennis balls?
2.
    a. When Anne delivers the tennis balls, does Chris have a right to inspect them? If Chris accepts the white tennis balls, may the acceptance be revoked?
    b. Assume Chris decided she could use twenty-five cans of the white balls. Could she accept twenty-five cans and reject the rest?
    c. Suppose Anne delivered white tennis balls because a fire at her warehouse destroyed her entire stock of yellow balls. Does the fire discharge Anne's contractual duties?
    d. If Chris rejected the white tennis balls and Anne refused to deliver yellow ones, may Chris recover damages? If so, how would they be calculated?
3. In 1961, Dorothy and John Wilson purchased a painting from Hammer Galleries titled *Femme Debout*. It cost $11,000 (about $78,000 in 2010 dollars) and came with this promise: "The authenticity of this picture is guaranteed." In 1984, an expert deemed the painting a fake. The district court held that the Wilsons' suit for breach of warranty, filed in February 1987—twenty-one years after its purchase—was barred by the UCC's four-year statute of limitations. The Wilsons argued, however, that the Code's exception to the four-year rule applied:[35] "A breach of warranty occurs when tender of delivery is made, except where a warranty explicitly extends to future performance and discovery must await the time of such performance the cause of action accrues when the breach is or should have been discovered."

    They said the painting "performed" by being an authentic Vuillard—a French artist—and that the warranty of authenticity not only guaranteed the present "being" of the painting but also extended, as required by 2-725(2), to the future existence as a Vuillard. Therefore, they contended, explicit words warranting future performance would be superfluous: a warranty that promises authenticity "now and at all times in the future" would be redundant. How should the court rule?
4. Speedi Lubrication Centers Inc. and Atlas Match Corp. entered into a contract that provided for Speedi to buy 400,000 advertising matchbooks from Atlas, to be paid for within thirty days of delivery of each shipment. Orders for such matches required artwork, artists' commissions, and printing plates. Atlas sent twenty-two cases of matches to Speedi with an invoice showing $2,100 owed. Almost ninety days later, Speedi sent Atlas a check for $1,000, received the same day Atlas sent Speedi a letter declaring Speedi to be in material breach of the contract. A second check for $1,100 was later received; it bounced but was later replaced by a cashier's check. The contract provided that an untimely payment was a breach, and it included these provisions related to liquidated damages:

> *Atlas shall have the right to recover from Purchaser the price of all matchbooks and packaging delivered and/or identified to this agreement at the time of Purchaser's breach hereof and shall be additionally entitled to recover fifty percent (50%) of the contract price of matchbooks and/or packaging ordered hereby, but not delivered or identified to this Agreement at the time of Purchaser's breach. Purchaser agrees that the percentage as specified hereinabove...will be reasonable and just compensation for such breach, and Purchaser hereby promises to pay such sum as liquidated damages, not as penalty in the event of any such breach.*

On appeal, Speedi complained that the liquidated damages clause was a penalty. Is the matter settled by the contract saying the liquidated damages are reasonable? On what criteria would a court determine whether liquidated damages are reasonable?

5. Mrs. Kaiden made a $5,000 deposit on the purchase of new 1973 Rolls-Royce automobile. Lee Oldsmobile, the seller, confirmed the request by transmitting a regular order form, which Mrs. Kaiden signed and returned. The price was $29,500.00 [about $150,000 in 2010 dollars]. Some of the correspondence and a notation on Mrs. Kaiden's check indicated that delivery was expected in November. The order form, however, specified no delivery date. Further, it contained a disclaimer of liability for delay in delivery beyond the dealer's control, and it provided that the dealer had the right, upon failure of the purchaser to accept delivery, to retain as liquidated damages any cash deposit made. On November 21, 1973, Mrs. Kaiden notified Lee by telephone that she had purchased another Rolls-Royce elsewhere. She told the salesman to cancel her order. On November 29, Lee Oldsmobile notified Mrs. Kaiden that the car was ready for delivery. She refused delivery and demanded the return of her deposit. The dealer refused. In January 1974, the dealer—without notice to the Kaidens—sold the Rolls-Royce to another purchaser for $26,495. Mrs. Kaiden sued Lee Oldsmobile for the $5,000 deposit. The dealer carefully itemized its losses on the Kaiden deal—$5,080.07. On what basis did the court dismiss the liquidated damages clause? What is the consequence of the dealer's failure to give notice of the private sale under UCC, Section 2-706(3)?
6. Hemming saw an advertisement for a Cadillac convertible once owned by the famous early rock 'n' roll singer Elvis Presley. He contracted to buy it from Whitney for $350,000 and sent Whitney $10,000 as a deposit. But, after some delay, Whitney returned the $10,000 and informed Hemming that the car had been sold to another purchaser. What remedy does Hemming have?
7. Murrey manufactured and sold pool tables. He was approached by Madsen, who had an idea for a kind of electronic pool table that would light up and make sounds like a pinball machine. Madsen made a $70,000 deposit on an order for one hundred tables but then encountered difficulties and notified Murrey that he would be unable to accept delivery of the tables. Murrey broke the tables up, salvaging materials worth about $15,000 and using the rest for firewood. The evidence was that the tables, if completed by Murrey, could have been sold for $45,000 as regular pool tables. Madsen gets his deposit back less expenses incurred by Murrey. But what principle affects Murrey's measure of damages, his right to claim expenses incurred?
8. In January 1992, Joseph Perna bought an eleven-year-old Oldsmobile at a New York City police auction sale for $1,800 plus towing fees. It had been impounded by the police for nonpayment of parking tickets. The bill of sale from the police to Perna contained this language: "subject to the terms and conditions of any and all chattel mortgages, rental agreements, liens, conditional bills of sale, and encumbrances that may be on the motor vehicle of the [its original owner]." About a year later Perna sold the car to a coworker, Elio Marino, for $1,200. Marino repaired and improved the car by replacing the radiator, a gasket, and door locks. Ten months after his father bought the car, Marino's son was stopped by police and arrested for driving a stolen vehicle; Mario paid $600 to a lawyer to get that matter resolved, and he never got the car back from the police. Is Perna liable to Marino for the value of the car? Is

Perna liable for the consequential damages—the attorney's fees? The relevant UCC sections are 2-312(2) and 2-714.

9. William Stem bought a used BMW from Gary Braden for $6,600 on Braden's assertion that as far as he knew the car had not been wrecked and it was in good condition. Less than a week later Stem discovered a disconnected plug; when connected the oil-sensor warning light glowed. Mechanics informed Stem that the car was made up of the front end of a 1979 BMW and the rear end of a 1975 BMW, and the front half had 100,000 more miles on it than Stem thought. Six weeks after he purchased the car, Stem wrote Braden a letter that he refused the car and intended to rescind the sale. Braden did not accept return of the car or refund the money, and Braden continued to drive it for seven months and nearly 9,000 miles before suing. He had no other car and needed to transport his child. These issues were before the Alabama Supreme Court, construing UCC, Section 2-608: did Stem's use of the car, notwithstanding his letter of rescission, constitute such use of it as to be an acceptance? And if not, does Stem owe Braden anything for its use?
10. Donnelly ordered a leather motorcycle jacket from Leathers Inc. The jacket was specially designed according to Donnelly's instructions: it had a unique collar, various chromed studs throughout, and buckles, and he required an unusually large size. The coat cost $6,000. Donnelly paid $1,200 as a deposit, but after production was nearly complete, he telephoned Leathers Inc. and repudiated the contract. What should Leathers do now?

Self-Test Questions

1. In the absence of agreement, the place of delivery is
   a. the buyer's place of business
   b. the seller's place of business
   c. either the buyer's place of business or the buyer's residence
   d. any of the above
2. The UCC's statute of limitations is
   a. two years
   b. three years
   c. four years
   d. none of the above
3. Under the UCC, if the buyer breaches, the seller can
   a. withhold further delivery
   b. resell the goods still in the seller's possession
   c. recover damages
   d. do all of the above
4. If the seller breaches, the buyer can generally
   a. recover the goods, even when the goods have not been identified to the contract and the seller is not insolvent
   b. purchase substitute goods and recover their cost
   c. purchase substitute goods and recover the difference between their cost and the contract price
   d. recover punitive damages
5. Following a seller's breach, the buyer can recover the price paid
   a. if the buyer cancels the contract
   b. only for goods the buyer has accepted
   c. for all the goods the buyer was to have received, whether or not they were accepted
   d. under none of the above conditions

Self-Test Answers

1. b
2. c
3. d
4. c
5. d

Endnotes

1. Uniform Commercial Code, Sections 2-301and 2-309.
2. Uniform Commercial Code, Section 2-503.
3. Uniform Commercial Code, Section 2-503(5).
4. Uniform Commercial Code, Section 2-503.
5. Uniform Commercial Code, Sections 2-319, 2-322, and 2-324.
6. Uniform Commercial Code, Section 2-308.
7. Uniform Commercial Code, Section 2-601.
8. Uniform Commercial Code, Sections 2-301 and 2-513.
9. Uniform Commercial Code, Section 2-607.
10. Uniform Commercial Code, Sections 2-511 and 2-512.
11. Uniform Commercial Code, Sections 2-105 and 2A103(1).
12. Uniform Commercial Code, Section 2-608.
13. *North River Homes, Inc., v. Borsage, Mississippi* (1992).
14. *Colonial Dodge v. Miller*, 362 N.W.2d 704 (Mich. 1984).
15. Uniform Commercial Code, Sections 2-719(1) and 2A-503(1).
16. Uniform Commercial Code, Sections 2-719(1)(b) and 2A-503(2).
17. Uniform Commercial Code, Sections 2-719(2) and 2A-503(2).
18. Uniform Commercial Code, Sections 2-719(3) and 2A-503(2).
19. Uniform Commercial Code, Section 2-718.
20. Uniform Commercial Code, Section 2-725.
21. Uniform Commercial Code, Sections 2-706 and 2A-527.
22. Uniform Commercial Code, Section 2-708(2); Section 2A-528(2) is similar.
23. Uniform Commercial Code, Sections 2-703(f) and 2A-524(1)(a).
24. Uniform Commercial Code, Section 1-201(23).
25. Uniform Commercial Code, Section 2-702 (3).
26. Uniform Commercial Code, Section 2A-525(2).
27. Uniform Commercial Code, Section 2-714.
28. Uniform Commercial Code, Section 2-715.
29. Uniform Commercial Code, Sections 2-711(1), 2-106, 2A-508(1)(a), and 2A-505(1).
30. Uniform Commercial Code, Sections 2-716(1) and 2A-521(1).
31. Uniform Commercial Code, Sections 2-711(3), 2-706, 2A-508(5), and 2A-527(5).
32. Uniform Commercial Code, Sections 2-714(1) and 2A-519(3).
33. Uniform Commercial Code, Sections 2-714(3), 2-715, and 2A-519(3).
34. *De La Hoya v. Slim's Gun Shop*, 146 Cal. Rptr. 68 (Super. 1978).
35. Uniform Commercial Code, Section 2-725(2).

CHAPTER 20
Products Liability

Learning Objectives

After reading this chapter, you should understand the following:

1. How products-liability law allocates the costs of a consumer society.
2. How warranty theory works in products liability, and what its limitations are.
3. How negligence theory works, and what its problems are.
4. How strict liability theory works, and what its limitations are.
5. What efforts are made to reform products-liability law, and why.

20.1 Introduction: Why Products-Liability Law Is Important

Learning Objectives

1. Understand why products-liability law underwent a revolution in the twentieth century.
2. Recognize that courts play a vital role in policing the free enterprise system by adjudicating how the true costs of modern consumer culture are allocated.
3. Know the names of the modern causes of action for products-liability cases.

In previous chapters, we discussed remedies generally. In this chapter, we focus specifically on remedies available when a defective product causes personal injury or other damages. Products liability describes a type of claim, not a separate theory of liability. Products liability has strong emotional overtones—ranging from the prolitigation position of consumer advocates to the conservative perspective of the manufacturers.

History of Products-Liability Law

The theory of caveat emptor—let the buyer beware—that pretty much governed consumer law from the early eighteenth century until the early twentieth century made some sense. A horse-drawn buggy is a fairly simple device: its workings are apparent; a person of average experience in the 1870s would know whether it was constructed well and made of the proper woods. Most foodstuffs 150 years ago were grown at home and "put up" in the home kitchen or bought in bulk from a local grocer, subject to inspection and sampling; people made home remedies for coughs and colds and made many of their own clothes. Houses and furnishings were built of wood, stone, glass, and plaster—familiar substances. Entertainment was a book or a piano. The state of technology was such that the things consumed were, for the most part, comprehensible and—very important—mostly locally made, which meant that the consumer who suffered damages from a defective product could confront the product's maker directly. Local reputation is a powerful influence on behavior.

The free enterprise system confers great benefits, and no one can deny that: materialistically, compare the image sketched in the previous paragraph with circumstances today. But those benefits come with a cost, and the fundamental political issue always is who has to pay. Consider the following famous passage from Upton Sinclair's great novel *The Jungle*. It appeared in 1906. He wrote it to inspire labor reform; to his dismay, the public outrage focused instead on consumer protection reform. Here is his description of the sausage-making process in a big Chicago meatpacking plant:

> *There was never the least attention paid to what was cut up for sausage; there would come all the way back from Europe old sausage that had been rejected, and that was moldy and white—it would be dosed with borax and glycerin, and dumped into the hoppers, and made over again for home consumption. There would be meat that had tumbled out on the floor, in the dirt and sawdust, where the workers had tramped and spit uncounted billions of consumption germs. There would be meat stored in great piles in rooms; and the water from leaky roofs would drip over it, and thousands of rats would race about on it. It was too dark in these storage places to see well, but a man could run his hand over these piles of meat and sweep off handfuls of the dried dung of rats. These rats were nuisances, and the packers would put poisoned bread out for them; they would die, and then rats, bread, and meat would go into the hoppers together. This is no fairy story and no joke; the meat would be shoveled into carts, and the man who did the shoveling would not trouble to lift out a rat even when he saw one—there were things that went into the sausage in comparison with which a poisoned rat was a tidbit. There was no place for the men to wash their hands before they ate their dinner, and so they made a practice of washing them in the water that was to be ladled into the sausage. There were the butt-ends of smoked meat, and the scraps of corned beef, and all the odds and ends of the waste of the plants, that would be dumped into old barrels in the cellar and left there.*
>
> *Under the system of rigid economy which the packers enforced, there were some jobs that it only paid to do once in a long time, and among these was the cleaning out of the waste barrels. Every spring they did it; and in the barrels would be dirt and rust and old nails and stale water—and cartload after cartload of it would be taken up and dumped into the hoppers with fresh meat, and sent out to the public's breakfast. Some of it they would make into "smoked" sausage—but as the smoking took time, and was therefore expensive, they would call upon their chemistry department, and preserve it with borax and color it with gelatin to make it brown. All of their sausage came out of the same bowl, but when they came to wrap it they would stamp some of it "special," and for this they would charge two cents more a pound.*[1]

It became clear from Sinclair's exposé that associated with the marvels of then-modern meatpacking and distribution methods was food poisoning: a true cost became apparent. When the true cost of some money-making enterprise (e.g., cigarettes) becomes inescapably apparent, there are two possibilities. First, the legislature can in some way mandate that the manufacturer itself pay the cost; with the meatpacking plants, that would be the imposition of sanitary food-processing standards. Typically, Congress creates an administrative agency and gives the agency some marching orders, and then the agency crafts regulations dictating as many industry-wide reform measures as are politically possible. Second, the people who incur damages from the product (1) suffer and die or (2) access the machinery of the legal system and sue the manufacturer. If plaintiffs win enough lawsuits, the manufacturer's insurance company raises rates, forcing reform (as with high-powered muscle cars in the 1970s, which insurance companies effectively kiboshed); the business goes bankrupt; or the legislature is pressured to act, either for the consumer or for the manufacturer.

If the industry has enough clout to blunt—by various means—a robust pro-consumer legislative response so that government regulation is too lax to prevent harm, recourse is had through the legal system. Thus for all the talk about the need for tort reform (discussed later in this chapter), the courts play a vital role in policing the free enterprise system by adjudicating how the true costs of modern consumer culture are allocated.

Obviously the situation has improved enormously in a century, but one does not have to look very far to find terrible problems today. Consider the following, which occurred in 2009–10:

- In the United States, Toyota recalled 412,000 passenger cars, mostly the Avalon model, for steering problems that reportedly led to three accidents.
- Portable baby recliners that are supposed to help fussy babies sleep better were recalled after the death of an infant: the Consumer Product Safety Commission announced the recall of 30,000 Nap Nanny recliners made by Baby Matters of Berwyn, Pennsylvania.
- More than 70,000 children and teens go to the emergency room each year for injuries and complications from medical devices. Contact lenses are the leading culprit, the first detailed national estimate suggests.
- Smith and Noble recalled 1.3 million Roman shades and roller shades after a child was nearly strangled: the Consumer Product Safety Commission says a five-year-old boy in Tacoma, Washington, was entangled in the cord of a roller shade in May 2009.[2]
- The Consumer Product Safety Commission reported that 4,521 people were killed in the United States in consumer-product-related incidences in 2009, and millions of people visited hospital emergency rooms from consumer-product-related injuries.[3]
- Reports about the possibility that cell-phone use causes brain cancer continue to be hotly debated. Critics suggest that the studies minimizing the risk were paid for by cell-phone manufacturers.[4]

Products liability can also be a life-or-death matter from the manufacturer's perspective. In 2009, Bloomberg *BusinessWeek* reported that the costs of product safety for manufacturing firms can be enormous: "Peanut Corp., based in Lynchberg, Va., has been driven into bankruptcy since health officials linked tainted peanuts to more than 600 illnesses and nine deaths. Mattel said the first of several toy recalls it announced in 2007 cut its quarterly operating income by $30 million. Earlier this decade, Ford Motor spent roughly $3 billion replacing 10.6 million potentially defective Firestone tires."[5] Businesses complain, with good reason, about the expenses associated with products-liability problems.

Current State of the Law

Although the debate has been heated and at times simplistic, the problem of products liability is complex and most of us regard it with a high degree of ambivalence. We are all consumers, after all, who profit greatly from living in an industrial society. In this chapter, we examine the legal theories that underlie products-liability cases that developed rapidly in the twentieth century to address the problems of product-caused damages and injuries in an industrial society.

In the typical products-liability case, three legal theories are asserted—a contract theory and two tort theories. The contract theory is **warranty**, governed by the UCC, and the two tort theories are **negligence** and **strict products liability**, governed by the common law. See Figure 20.1.

warranty

A guarantee.

negligence

The legal theory imposing liability on a person for the proximate consequences of her carelessness.

strict products liability

Liability imposed on a merchant-seller of defective goods without fault.

FIGURE 20.1 Major Products Liability Theories

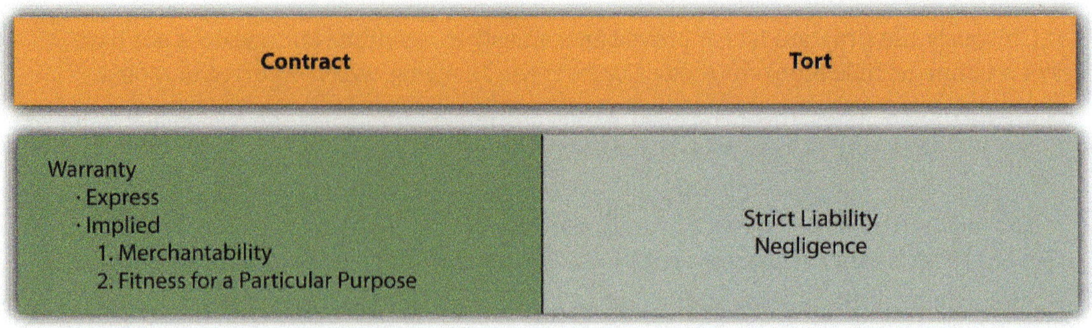

Key Takeaway

As products became increasingly sophisticated and potentially dangerous in the twentieth century, and as the separation between production and consumption widened, products liability became a very important issue for both consumers and manufacturers. Millions of people every year are adversely affected by defective products, and manufacturers and sellers pay huge amounts for products-liability insurance and damages. The law has responded with causes of action that provide a means for recovery for products-liability damages.

Exercises

1. How does the separation of production from consumption affect products-liability issues?
2. What other changes in production and consumption have caused the need for the development of products-liability law?
3. How can it be said that courts adjudicate the allocation of the costs of a consumer-oriented economy?

20.2 Warranties

Learning Objectives

1. Recognize a UCC express warranty and how it is created.
2. Understand what is meant under the UCC by implied warranties, and know the main types of implied warranties: merchantability, fitness for a particular purpose, and title.
3. Know that there are other warranties: against infringement and as may arise from usage of the trade.
4. See that there are difficulties with warranty theory as a cause of action for products liability; a federal law has addressed some of these.

The UCC governs express warranties and various implied warranties, and for many years it was the only statutory control on the use and meanings of warranties. In 1975, after years of debate, Congress passed and President Gerald Ford signed into law the Magnuson-Moss Act, which imposes certain requirements on manufacturers and others who warrant their goods. We will examine both the UCC and the Magnuson-Moss Act.

Types of Warranties

Express Warranties

An **express warranty** is created whenever the seller affirms that the product will perform in a certain manner. Formal words such as "warrant" or "guarantee" are not necessary. A seller may create an express warranty as part of the basis for the bargain of sale by means of (1) an affirmation of a fact or promise relating to the goods, (2) a description of the goods, or (3) a sample or model. Any of these will create an express warranty that the goods will conform to the fact, promise, description, sample, or model. Thus a seller who states that "the use of rustproof linings in the cans would prevent discoloration and adulteration of the Perform solution" has given an express warranty, whether he realized it or not.[6] Claims of breach of express warranty are, at base, claims of misrepresentation.

express warranty

Any manifestation of the nature or quality of goods that becomes a basis of the bargain.

But the courts will not hold a manufacturer to every statement that could conceivably be interpreted to be an express warranty. Manufacturers and sellers constantly "puff" their products, and the law is content to let them inhabit that gray area without having to make good on every claim. UCC 2-313(2) says that "an affirmation merely of the value of the goods or a statement purporting to be merely the seller's opinion or commendation of the goods does not create a warranty." Facts do.

It is not always easy, however, to determine the line between an express warranty and a piece of puffery. A salesperson who says that a strawberry huller is "great" has probably puffed, not warranted, when it turns out that strawberries run through the huller look like victims of a massacre. But consider the classic cases of the defective used car and the faulty bull. In the former, the salesperson said the car was in "A-1 shape" and "mechanically perfect." In the latter, the seller said not only that the bull calf would "put the buyer on the map" but that "his father was the greatest living dairy bull." The car, carrying the buyer's seven-month-old child, broke down while the buyer was en route to visit her husband in the army during World War II. The court said that the salesperson had made an express warranty.[7] The bull calf turned out to be sterile, putting the farmer on the judicial rather than the dairy map. The court said the seller's spiel was trade talk, not a warranty that the bull would impregnate cows.[8]

Is there any qualitative difference between these decisions, other than the quarter century that separates them and the different courts that rendered them? Perhaps the most that can be said is that the more specific and measurable the statement's standards, the more likely it is that a court will hold the seller to a warranty, and that a written statement is easier to construe as a warranty than an oral one. It is also possible that courts look, if only subliminally, at how reasonable the buyer was in relying on the statement, although this ought not to be a strict test. A buyer may be unreasonable in expecting a car to get 100 miles to the gallon, but if that is what the seller promised, that ought to be an enforceable warranty.

The CISG (Article 35) provides, "The seller must deliver goods which are of the quantity, quality and description required by the contract and which are contained or packaged in the manner required by the contract. [And the] goods must possess the qualities of goods which the seller has held out to the buyer as a sample or model."

Implied Warranties

Express warranties are those over which the parties dickered—or could have. Express warranties go to the essence of the bargain. An **implied warranty**, by contrast, is one that circumstances alone, not specific language, compel reading into the sale. In short, an implied warranty is one created by law, acting from an impulse of common sense.

implied warranty

A warranty imposed by law that comes along with a product automatically.

Implied Warranty of Merchantability

implied warranty of merchantability

Merchant-seller's implied warranty that goods are suitable for the goods' normal uses.

Section 2-314 of the UCC lays down the fundamental rule that goods carry an **implied warranty of merchantability** if sold by a merchant-seller. What is merchantability? Section 2-314(2) of the UCC says that merchantable goods are those that conform at least to the following six characteristics:

1. Pass without objection in the trade under the contract description
2. In the case of fungible goods, are of fair average quality within the description
3. Are fit for the ordinary purposes for which such goods are used
4. Run, within the variations permitted by the agreement, of even kind, quality, and quantity within each unit and among all units involved
5. Are adequately contained, packaged, and labeled as the agreement may require
6. Conform to the promise or affirmations of fact made on the container or label if any

For the purposes of Section 2-314(2)(c) of the UCC, selling and serving food or drink for consumption on or off the premises is a sale subject to the implied warranty of merchantability—the food must be "fit for the ordinary purposes" to which it is put. The problem is common: you bite into a cherry pit in the cherry-vanilla ice cream, or you choke on the clam shells in the chowder. Is such food fit for the ordinary purposes to which it is put? There are two schools of thought. One asks whether the food was natural as prepared. This view adopts the seller's perspective. The other asks what the consumer's reasonable expectation was.

The first test is sometimes said to be the "natural-foreign" test. If the substance in the soup is natural to the substance—as bones are to fish—then the food is fit for consumption. The second test, relying on reasonable expectations, tends to be the more commonly used test.

The Convention provides (Article 35) that "unless otherwise agreed, the goods sold are fit for the purposes for which goods of the same description would ordinarily be used."

Fitness for a Particular Purpose

implied warranty of fitness for particular purpose

A seller's implied warranty that the goods will be suitable for the buyer's expressed need.

Section 2-315 of the UCC creates another implied warranty. Whenever a seller, at the time she contracts to make a sale, knows or has reason to know that the buyer is relying on the seller's skill or judgment to select a product that is suitable for the particular purpose the buyer has in mind for the goods to be sold, there is an implied warranty that the goods are fit for that purpose. For example, you go to a hardware store and tell the salesclerk that you need a paint that will dry overnight because you are painting your front door and a rainstorm is predicted for the next day. The clerk gives you an oil-based paint that takes two days to dry. The store has breached an **implied warranty of fitness for particular purpose**.

Note the distinction between "particular" and "ordinary" purposes. Paint is made to color and when dry to protect a surface. That is its ordinary purpose, and had you said only that you wished to buy paint, no implied warranty of fitness would have been breached. It is only because you had a particular purpose in mind that the implied warranty arose. Suppose you had found a can of paint in a general store and told the same tale, but the proprietor had said, "I don't know enough about that paint to tell you anything beyond what's on the label; help yourself." Not every seller has the requisite degree of skill and knowledge about every product he sells to give rise to an implied warranty. Ultimately, each case turns on its particular circumstances.

"The Convention provides (Article 35): [The goods must be] fit for any particular purpose expressly or impliedly made known to the seller at the time of the conclusion of the contract, except where the circumstances show that the buyer did not rely, or that it was unreasonable for him to rely, on the seller's skill and judgment."

Other Warranties

Article 2 contains other warranty provisions, though these are not related specifically to products liability. Thus, under UCC, Section 2-312, unless explicitly excluded, the seller warrants he is conveying *good title* that is rightfully his and that the goods are transferred free of any security interest or other lien or encumbrance. In some cases (e.g., a police auction of bicycles picked up around campus and never claimed), the buyer should know that the seller does not claim title in himself, nor that title will necessarily be good against a third party, and so subsection (2) excludes warranties in these circumstances. But the circumstances must be so obvious that no reasonable person would suppose otherwise.

In *Menzel v. List*, an art gallery sold a painting by Marc Chagall that it purchased in Paris.[9] The painting had been stolen by the Germans when the original owner was forced to flee Belgium in the 1930s. Now in the United States, the original owner discovered that a new owner had the painting and successfully sued for its return. The customer then sued the gallery, claiming that it had breached the implied warranty of title when it sold the painting. The court agreed and awarded damages equal to the appreciated value of the painting. A good-faith purchaser who must surrender stolen goods to their true owner has a claim for breach of the implied warranty of title against the person from whom he bought the goods.

A second implied warranty, related to title, is that the merchant-seller warrants the goods are *free of any rightful claim by a third person* that the seller has infringed his rights (e.g., that a gallery has not infringed a copyright by selling a reproduction). This provision only applies to a seller who regularly deals in goods of the kind in question. If you find an old print in your grandmother's attic, you do not warrant when you sell it to a neighbor that it is free of any valid infringement claims.

A third implied warranty in this context involves the course of dealing or usage of trade. Section 2-314(3) of the UCC says that unless modified or excluded implied warranties may arise from a course of dealing or usage of trade. If a certain way of doing business is understood, it is not necessary for the seller to state explicitly that he will abide by the custom; it will be implied. A typical example is the obligation of a dog dealer to provide pedigree papers to prove the dog's lineage conforms to the contract.

Problems with Warranty Theory

In General

It may seem that a person asserting a claim for breach of warranty will have a good chance of success under an express warranty or implied warranty theory of merchantability or fitness for a particular purpose. In practice, though, claimants are in many cases denied recovery. Here are four general problems:

- The claimant must prove that there was a sale.
- The sale was of goods rather than real estate or services.
- The action must be brought within the four-year statute of limitations under Article 2-725, when the tender of delivery is made, not when the plaintiff discovers the defect.
- Under UCC, Section 2-607(3)(a) and Section 2A-516(3)(a), which covers leases, the claimant who fails to give notice of breach within a reasonable time of having accepted the goods will see the suit dismissed, and few consumers know enough to do so, except when making a complaint about a purchase of spoiled milk or about paint that wouldn't dry.

In addition to these general problems, the claimant faces additional difficulties stemming directly from warranty theory, which we take up later in this chapter.

Exclusion or Modification of Warranties

The UCC permits sellers to exclude or disclaim warranties in whole or in part. That's reasonable, given that the discussion here is about contract, and parties are free to make such contracts as they see fit. But a number of difficulties can arise.

Exclusion of Express Warranties

The simplest way for the seller to exclude express warranties is not to give them. To be sure, Section 2-316(1) of the UCC forbids courts from giving operation to words in fine print that negate or limit express warranties if doing so would unreasonably conflict with express warranties stated in the main body of the contract—as, for example, would a blanket statement that "this contract excludes all warranties express or implied." The purpose of the UCC provision is to prevent customers from being surprised by unbargained for language.

Exclusion of Implied Warranties in General

Implied warranties can be excluded easily enough also, by describing the product with language such as "as is" or "with all faults." Nor is exclusion simply a function of what the seller says. The buyer who has either examined or refused to examine the goods before entering into the contract may not assert an implied warranty concerning defects an inspection would have revealed.

The Convention provides a similar rule regarding a buyer's rights when he has failed to inspect the goods (Article 35): "The seller is not liable ... for any lack of conformity of the goods if at the time of the conclusion of the contract the buyer knew or could not have been unaware of such lack of conformity."

Implied Warranty of Merchantability

Section 2-316(2) of the UCC permits the seller to disclaim or modify the implied warranty of merchantability, as long as the statement actually mentions "merchantability" and, if it is written, is "conspicuous." Note that the disclaimer need not be in writing, and—again—all implied warranties can be excluded as noted.

Implied Warranty of Fitness

Section 2-316(2) of the UCC permits the seller also to disclaim or modify an implied warranty of fitness. This disclaimer or modification must be in writing, however, and must be conspicuous. It need not mention fitness explicitly; general language will do. The following sentence, for example, is sufficient to exclude all implied warranties of fitness: "There are no warranties that extend beyond the description on the face of this contract."

Here is a standard disclaimer clause found in a Dow Chemical Company agreement: "Seller warrants that the goods supplied here shall conform to the description stated on the front side hereof, that it will convey good title, and that such goods shall be delivered free from any lawful security interest, lien, or encumbrance. SELLER MAKES NO WARRANTY OF MERCHANTABILITY OR FITNESS FOR A PARTICULAR USE. NOR IS THERE ANY OTHER EXPRESS OR IMPLIED WARRANTY."

Conflict between Express and Implied Warranties

Express and implied warranties and their exclusion or limitation can often conflict. Section 2-317 of the UCC provides certain rules for deciding which should prevail. In general, all warranties are to be construed as consistent with each other and as cumulative. When that assumption is unreasonable, the parties' intention governs the interpretation, according to the following rules: (a) exact or technical specifications displace an inconsistent sample or model or general language of description; (b) a sample from an existing bulk displaces inconsistent general language of description; (c) express warranties displace inconsistent implied warranties other than an implied warranty of fitness for a particular purpose. Any inconsistency among warranties must always be resolved in favor of the implied warranty of fitness for a particular purpose. This doesn't mean that warranty cannot be limited or excluded altogether. The parties may do so. But in cases of doubt whether it or some other language applies, the implied warranty of fitness will have a superior claim.

The Magnuson-Moss Act and Phantom Warranties

After years of debate over extending federal law to regulate warranties, Congress enacted the Magnuson-Moss Federal Trade Commission Warranty Improvement Act (more commonly referred to as the Magnuson-Moss Act) and President Ford signed it in 1975. The act was designed to clear up confusing and misleading warranties, where—as Senator Magnuson put it in introducing the bill—"purchasers of consumer products discover that their warranty may cover a 25-cent part but not the $100 labor charge or that there is full coverage on a piano so long as it is shipped at the purchaser's expense to the factory.... There is a growing need to generate consumer understanding by clearly and conspicuously disclosing the terms and conditions of the warranty and by telling the consumer what to do if his guaranteed product becomes defective or malfunctions." The Magnuson-Moss Act only applies to consumer products (for household and domestic uses); commercial purchasers are presumed to be knowledgeable enough not to need these protections, to be able to hire lawyers, and to be able to include the cost of product failures into the prices they charge.

The act has several provisions to meet these consumer concerns; it regulates the content of warranties and the means of disclosing those contents. The act gives the Federal Trade Commission (FTC) the authority to promulgate detailed regulations to interpret and enforce it. Under FTC regulations, any written warranty for a product costing a consumer more than ten dollars must disclose in a single document and in readily understandable language the following nine items of information:

1. The identity of the persons covered by the warranty, whether it is limited to the original purchaser or fewer than all who might come to own it during the warranty period.
2. A clear description of the products, parts, characteristics, components, or properties covered, and where necessary for clarity, a description of what is excluded.
3. A statement of what the warrantor will do if the product fails to conform to the warranty, including items or services the warranty will pay for and, if necessary for clarity, what it will not pay for.
4. A statement of when the warranty period starts and when it expires.
5. A step-by-step explanation of what the consumer must do to realize on the warranty, including the names and addresses of those to whom the product must be brought.
6. Instructions on how the consumer can be availed of any informal dispute resolution mechanism established by the warranty.
7. Any limitations on the duration of implied warranties—since some states do not permit such limitations, the warranty must contain a statement that any limitations may not apply to the particular consumer.

8. Any limitations or exclusions on relief, such as consequential damages—as above, the warranty must explain that some states do not allow such limitations.
9. The following statement: "This warranty gives you specific legal rights, and you may also have other rights which vary from state to state."

full warranty

Under the Magnuson-Moss Act, a complete promise of satisfaction limited only in duration.

limited warranty

Under the Magnuson-Moss Act, a less-than-full warranty.

In addition to these requirements, the act requires that the warranty be labeled either a full or limited warranty. A **full warranty** means (1) the defective product or part will be fixed or replaced for free, including removal and reinstallation; (2) it will be fixed within a reasonable time; (3) the consumer need not do anything unreasonable (like shipping the piano to the factory) to get warranty service; (4) the warranty is good for anyone who owns the product during the period of the warranty; (5) the consumer gets money back or a new product if the item cannot be fixed within a reasonable number of attempts. But the full warranty may not cover the whole product: it may cover only the hard drive in the computer, for example; it must state what parts are included and excluded. A **limited warranty** is less inclusive. It may cover only parts, not labor; it may require the consumer to bring the product to the store for service; it may impose a handling charge; it may cover only the first purchaser. Both full and limited warranties may exclude consequential damages.

Disclosure of the warranty provisions prior to sale is required by FTC regulations; this can be done in a number of ways. The text of the warranty can be attached to the product or placed in close conjunction to it. It can be maintained in a binder kept in each department or otherwise easily accessible to the consumer. Either the binders must be in plain sight or signs must be posted to call the prospective buyer's attention to them. A notice containing the text of the warranty can be posted, or the warranty itself can be printed on the product's package or container.

Phantom warranties are addressed by the Magnuson-Moss Act. As we have seen, the UCC permits the seller to disclaim implied warranties. This authority often led sellers to give what were called phantom warranties—that is, the express warranty contained disclaimers of implied warranties, thus leaving the consumer with fewer rights than if no express warranty had been given at all. In the words of the legislative report of the act, "The bold print giveth, and the fine print taketh away." The act abolished these phantom warranties by providing that if the seller gives a written warranty, whether express or implied, he cannot disclaim or modify implied warranties. However, a seller who gives a limited warranty can limit implied warranties to the duration of the limited warranty, if the duration is reasonable.

A seller's ability to disclaim implied warranties is also limited by state law in two ways. First, by amendment to the UCC or by separate legislation, some states prohibit disclaimers whenever consumer products are sold.[10] Second, the UCC at 2-302 provides that unconscionable contracts or clauses will not be enforced. UCC 2-719(3) provides that limitation of damages for personal injury in the sale of "consumer goods is prima facie unconscionable, but limitation of damages where the loss is commercial is not." (Unconscionability was discussed in Chapter 12.)

A first problem with warranty theory, then, is that it's possible to disclaim or limit the warranty. The worst abuses of manipulative and tricky warranties are eliminated by the Magnuson-Moss Act, but there are several other reasons that warranty theory is not the panacea for claimants who have suffered damages or injuries as a result of defective products.

Privity

privity

The relationship between two contracting parties.

A second problem with warranty law (after exclusion and modification of warranties) is that of **privity**. Privity is the legal term for the direct connection between the seller and buyer, the two contracting parties. For decades, the doctrine of privity has held that one person can sue another only if they are in privity. That worked well in the days when most commerce was local and the connection between seller and buyer was immediate. But in a modern industrial (or postindustrial) economy, the product is transported through a much larger distribution system, as depicted in Figure 20.2. Two questions arise: (1) Is the manufacturer or wholesaler (as opposed to the retailer) liable to the buyer under warranty theory? and (2) May the buyer's family or friends assert warranty rights?

FIGURE 20.2 Chain of Distribution

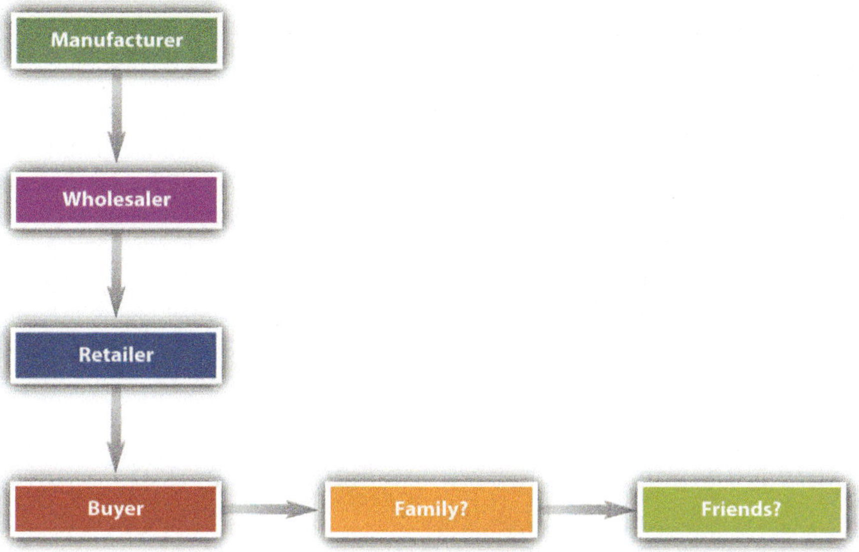

Horizontal Privity

Suppose Carl Consumer buys a new lamp for his family's living room. The lamp is defective: Carl gets a serious electrical shock when he turns it on. Certainly Carl would be covered by the implied warranty of merchantability: he's in direct privity with the seller. But what if Carl's spouse Carlene is injured? She didn't buy the lamp; is she covered? Or suppose Carl's friend David, visiting for an afternoon, gets zapped. Is David covered? This gets to **horizontal privity**, noncontracting parties who suffer damages from defective goods, such as nonbuyer users, consumers, and bystanders. Horizontal privity determines to whose benefit the warranty "flows"—who can sue for its breach. In one of its rare instances of nonuniformity, the UCC does not dictate the result. It gives the states three choices, labeled in Section 2-318 as Alternatives A, B, and C.

horizontal privity

The relationship between the original supplier of a product and an ultimate user or a bystander affected by it.

Alternative A says that a seller's warranty extends "to any natural person who is in the family or household of his buyer or who is a guest in his home" provided (1) it is reasonable to expect the person suffering damages to use, consume, or be affected by the goods and (2) the warranty extends only to damages for personal injury.

Alternative B "extends to any natural person who may reasonably be expected to use, consume, or be affected by the goods, and who is injured in person by breach of the warranty." It is less restrictive than the first alternative: it extends protection to people beyond those in the buyer's home. For example, what if Carl took the lamp to a neighbor's house to illuminate a poker table: under Alternative B, anybody at the neighbor's house who suffered injury would be covered by the warranty. But this alternative does not extend protection to organizations; "natural person" means a human being.

Alternative C is the same as B except that it applies not only to any "natural person" but "to any person who is injured by breach of the warranty." This is the most far-reaching alternative because it provides redress for damage to *property* as well as for *personal* injury, and it extends protection to corporations and other institutional buyers.

One may incidentally note that having three different alternatives for when third-party nonpurchasers can sue a seller or manufacturer for breach of warranty gives rise to unintended consequences. First, different outcomes are produced among jurisdictions, including variations in the common law. Second, the great purpose of the Uniform Commercial Code in promoting national uniformity is undermined. Third, battles over choice of law—where to file the lawsuit—are generated.

UCC, Section 2A-216, provides basically the same alternatives as applicable to the leasing of goods.

Vertical Privity

vertical privity

Privity between parties (manufacturer and retailer) occupying adjoining levels in product distribution systems.

The traditional rule was that remote selling parties were not liable: lack of privity was a defense by the manufacturer or wholesaler to a suit by a buyer with whom these entities did not themselves contract. The buyer could recover damages from the retailer but not from the original manufacturer, who after all made the product and who might be much more financially able to honor the warranty. The UCC takes no position here, but over the last fifty years the judicial trend has been to abolish this **vertical privity** requirement. (See Figure 20.2; the entities in the distribution chain are those in vertical privity to the buyer.) It began in 1958, when the Michigan Supreme Court overturned the old theory in an opinion written by Justice John D. Voelker (who also wrote the novel *Anatomy of a Murder*, under the pen name Robert Traver).[11]

Contributory Negligence, Comparative Negligence, and Assumption of Risk

After disclaimers and privity issues are resolved, other possible impediments facing the plaintiff in a products-liability warranty case are issues of assumption of the risk, contributory negligence, and comparative negligence (discussed in Chapter 7 on torts).

Courts uniformly hold that assumption of risk is a defense for sellers against a claim of breach of warranty, while there is a split of authority over whether comparative and contributory negligence are defenses. However, the courts' use of this terminology is often conflicting and confusing. The ultimate question is really one of causation: was the seller's breach of the warranty the cause of the plaintiff's damages?

The UCC is not markedly helpful in clearing away the confusion caused by years of discussion of assumption of risk and contributory negligence. Section 2-715(2)(b) of the UCC says that among the forms of consequential damage for which recovery can be sought is "injury to person or property *proximately* resulting from any breach of warranty" (emphasis added). But "proximately" is a troublesome word. Indeed, ultimately it is a circular word: it means nothing more than that the defendant must have been a direct enough cause of the damages that the courts will impose liability. Comment 5 to this section says, "Where the injury involved follows the use of goods without discovery of the defect causing the damage, the question of 'proximate' turns on whether it was reasonable for the buyer to use the goods without such inspection as would have revealed the defects. If it was not reasonable for him to do so, or if he did in fact discover the defect prior to his use, the injury would not proximately result from the breach of warranty."

Obviously if a sky diver buys a parachute and then discovers a few holes in it, his family would not likely prevail in court when they sued to recover for his death because the parachute failed to function after he jumped at 5,000 feet. But the general notion that it must have been reasonable for a buyer to use goods without inspection can make a warranty case difficult to prove.

Key Takeaway

A first basis of recovery in products-liability theory is breach of warranty. There are two types of warranties: express and implied. Under the implied category are three major subtypes: the implied warranty of merchantability (only given by merchants), the implied warranty of fitness for a particular purpose, and the implied warranty of title. There are a number of problems with the use of warranty theory: there must have been a sale of the goods; the plaintiff must bring the action within the statute of limitations; and the plaintiff must notify the seller within a reasonable time. The seller may—within the constraints of the Magnuson-Moss Act—limit or exclude express warranties or limit or exclude implied warranties. Privity, or lack of it, between buyer and seller has been significantly eroded as a limitation in warranty theory, but lack of privity may still affect the plaintiff's recovery; the plaintiff's assumption of the risk in using defective goods may preclude recovery.

Exercises

1. What are the two main types of warranties and the important subtypes?
2. Who can make each type of warranty?
3. What general problems does a plaintiff have in bringing a products-liability warranty case?
4. What problems are presented concerning exclusion or manipulative express warranties, and how does the Magnuson-Moss Act address them?
5. How are implied warranties excluded?
6. What is the problem of lack of privity, and how does modern law deal with it?

20.3 Negligence

Learning Objectives

1. Recognize how the tort theory of negligence may be of use in products-liability suits.
2. Understand why negligence is often not a satisfactory cause of action in such suits: proof of it may be difficult, and there are powerful defenses to claims of negligence.

Negligence is the second theory raised in the typical products-liability case. It is a tort theory (as compared to breach of warranty, which is of course a contract theory), and it does have this advantage over warranty theory: privity is never relevant. A pedestrian is struck in an intersection by a car whose brakes were defectively manufactured. Under no circumstances would breach of warranty be a useful cause of action for the pedestrian—there is no privity at all. Negligence is considered in detail in the Chapter 7 on torts; it basically means lack of due care.

Typical Negligence Claims: Design Defects and Inadequate Warnings

Negligence theory in products liability is most useful in two types of cases: defective design and defective warnings.

Design Defects

Manufacturers can be, and often are, held liable for injuries caused by products that were defectively designed. The question is whether the designer used reasonable care in designing a product reasonably safe for its foreseeable use. The concern over reasonableness and standards of care are elements of negligence theory.

Defective-design cases can pose severe problems for manufacturing and safety engineers. More safety means more cost. Designs altered to improve safety may impair functionality and make the product less desirable to consumers. At what point safety comes into reasonable balance with performance, cost, and desirability (see Figure 20.3) is impossible to forecast accurately, though some factors can be taken into account. For example, if other manufacturers are marketing comparable products whose design are intrinsically safer, the less-safe products are likely to lose a test of reasonableness in court.

FIGURE 20.3 The Reasonable Design Balance

Warning Defects

We noted that a product may be defective if the manufacturer failed to warn the user of potential dangers. Whether a warning should have been affixed is often a question of what is reasonably foreseeable, and the failure to affix a warning will be treated as negligence. The manufacturer of a weed killer with poisonous ingredients is certainly acting negligently when it fails to warn the consumer that the contents are potentially lethal.

The law governing the necessity to warn and the adequacy of warnings is complex. What is reasonable turns on the degree to which a product is likely to be misused and, as the disturbing *Laaperi* case (Section 6) illustrates, whether the hazard is obvious.

Problems with Negligence Theory

Negligence is an ancient cause of action and, as was discussed in the torts chapter, it carries with it a number of well-developed defenses. Two categories may be mentioned: common-law defenses and preemption.

Common-Law Defenses against Negligence

Among the problems confronting a plaintiff with a claim of negligence in products-liability suits (again, these concepts are discussed in the torts chapter) are the following:

- Proving negligence at all: just because a product is defective does not necessarily prove the manufacturer breached a duty of care.
- Proximate cause: even if there was some negligence, the plaintiff must prove her damages flowed proximately from that negligence.
- Contributory and comparative negligence: the plaintiff's own actions contributed to the damages.
- Subsequent alteration of the product: generally the manufacturer will not be liable if the product has been changed.
- Misuse or abuse of the product: using a lawn mower to trim a hedge or taking too much of a drug are examples.
- Assumption of the risk: knowingly using the product in a risky way.

Preemption

Preemption (or "pre-emption") is illustrated by this problem: suppose there is a federal standard concerning the product, and the defendant manufacturer meets it, but the standard is not really very protective. (It is not uncommon, of course, for federal standard makers of all types to be significantly influenced by lobbyists for the industries being regulated by the standards.) Is it enough for the manufacturer to point to its satisfaction of the standard so that such satisfaction preempts (takes over) any common-law negligence claim? "We built the machine to federal standards: we can't be liable. Our compliance with the federal safety standard is an affirmative defense."

Preemption

The theory that a federal law supersedes any inconsistent state law or regulation.

Preemption is typically raised as a defense in suits about (1) cigarettes, (2) FDA-approved medical devices, (3) motor-boat propellers, (4) pesticides, and (5) motor vehicles. This is a complex area of law. Questions inevitably arise as to whether there was federal preemption, express or implied. Sometimes courts find preemption and the consumer loses; sometimes the courts don't find preemption and the case goes forward. According to one lawyer who works in this field, there has been "increasing pressure on both the regulatory and congressional fronts to preempt state laws." That is, the usual defendants (manufacturers) push Congress and the regulatory agencies to state explicitly in the law that the federal standards preempt and defeat state law,[12] and defeat the consumer (the whole point).

Key Takeaway

Negligence is a second possible cause of action for products-liability claimants. A main advantage is that no issues of privity are relevant, but there are often problems of proof; there are a number of robust common-law defenses, and federal preemption is a recurring concern for plaintiffs' lawyers.

Exercises

1. What two types of products-liability cases are most often brought under negligence?
2. How could it be said that merely because a person suffers injury as the result of a defective product, proof of negligence is not necessarily made?
3. What is "preemption" and how is it used as a sword to defeat products-liability plaintiffs?

20.4 Strict Liability in Tort

Learning Objectives

1. Know what "strict products liability" means and how it differs from the other two products-liability theories.
2. Understand the basic requirements to prove strict products liability.
3. See what obstacles to recovery remain with this doctrine.

The warranties grounded in the Uniform Commercial Code (UCC) are often ineffective in assuring recovery for a plaintiff's injuries. The notice requirements and the ability of a seller to disclaim the warranties remain bothersome problems, as does the privity requirement in those states that continue to adhere to it.

Negligence as a products-liability theory obviates any privity problems, but negligence comes with a number of familiar defenses and with the problems of preemption.

To overcome the obstacles, judges have gone beyond the commercial statutes and the ancient concepts of negligence. They have fashioned a tort theory of products liability based on the principle of **strict products liability**. One court expressed the rationale for the development of the concept as follows: "The rule of strict liability for defective products is an example of necessary paternalism judicially shifting risk of loss by application of tort doctrine because [the UCC] scheme fails to adequately cover the situation. Judicial paternalism is to loss shifting what garlic is to a stew—sometimes necessary to give full flavor to statutory law, always distinctly noticeable in its result, overwhelmingly counterproductive if excessive, and never an end in itself."[13] Paternalism or not, strict liability has become a very important legal theory in products-liability cases.

Strict Liability Defined

The formulation of strict liability that most courts use is Section 402A of the Restatement of Torts (Second), set out here in full:

> *(1) One who sells any product in a defective condition unreasonably dangerous to the user or consumer or to his property is subject to liability for physical harm thereby caused to the ultimate user or consumer, or to his property, if*
>
> *(a) the seller is engaged in the business of selling such a product, and*
>
> *(b) it is expected to and does reach the user or consumer without substantial change in the condition in which it is sold.*
>
> *(2) This rule applies even though*
>
> *(a) the seller has exercised all possible care in the preparation and sale of his product, and*
>
> *(b) the user or consumer has not bought the product from or entered into any contractual relation with the seller.*

Section 402A of the Restatement avoids the warranty booby traps. It states a rule of law not governed by the UCC, so limitations and exclusions in warranties will not apply to a suit based on the Restatement theory. And the consumer is under no obligation to give notice to the seller within a reasonable time of any injuries. Privity is not a requirement; the language of the Restatement says it applies to "the user or consumer," but courts have readily found that bystanders in various situations are entitled to bring actions under Restatement, Section 402A. The formulation of strict liability, though, is limited to physical harm. Many courts have held that a person who suffers economic loss must resort to warranty law.

Strict liability avoids some negligence traps, too. No proof of negligence is required. See Figure 20.4.

FIGURE 20.4 Major Difference between Warranty and Strict Liability

	Warranty	Strict Liability
1. Notice of Defect from Buyer to Seller Required?	Yes	No
2. Disclaimer Possible?	Yes	No
3. Privity Required?	Sometimes	No

Section 402A Elements

Product in a Defective Condition

Sales of goods but not sales of services are covered under the Restatement, Section 402A. Furthermore, the plaintiff will not prevail if the product was safe for normal handling and consumption when sold. A glass soda bottle that is properly capped is not in a defective condition merely because it can be broken if the consumer should happen to drop it, making the jagged glass dangerous. Chocolate candy bars are not defective merely because you can become ill by eating too many of them at once. On the other hand, a seller would be liable for a product defectively packaged, so that it could explode or deteriorate and change its chemical composition. A product can also be in a defective condition if there is danger that could come from an anticipated wrongful use, such as a drug that is safe only when taken in limited doses. Under those circumstances, failure to place an adequate dosage warning on the container makes the product defective.

The plaintiff bears the burden of proving that the product is in a defective condition, and this burden can be difficult to meet. Many products are the result of complex feats of engineering. Expert witnesses are necessary to prove that the products were defectively manufactured, and these are not always easy to come by. This difficulty of proof is one reason why many cases raise the failure to warn as the dispositive issue, since in the right case that issue is far easier to prove. The *Anderson* case (detailed in the exercises at the end of this chapter) demonstrates that the plaintiff cannot prevail under strict liability merely because he was injured. It is not the fact of injury that is dispositive but the defective condition of the product.

Unreasonably Dangerous

The product must be not merely dangerous but unreasonably dangerous. Most products have characteristics that make them dangerous in certain circumstances. As the Restatement commentators note, "Good whiskey is not unreasonably dangerous merely because it will make some people drunk, and is especially dangerous to alcoholics; but bad whiskey, containing a dangerous amount of fuel oil, is unreasonably dangerous. Good butter is not unreasonably dangerous merely because, if such be the case, it deposits cholesterol in the arteries and leads to heart attacks; but bad butter, contaminated with poisonous fish oil, is unreasonably dangerous."[14] Under Section 402A, "the article sold must be dangerous to an extent beyond that which would be contemplated by the ordinary consumer who purchases it, with the ordinary knowledge common to the community as to its characteristics."

Even high risks of danger are not necessarily unreasonable. Some products are unavoidably unsafe; rabies vaccines, for example, can cause dreadful side effects. But the disease itself, almost always fatal, is worse. A product is unavoidably unsafe when it cannot be made safe for its intended purpose given the present state of human knowledge. Because important benefits may flow from the product's use, its producer or seller ought not to be held liable for its danger.

However, the failure to warn a potential user of possible hazards can make a product defective under Restatement, Section 402A, whether unreasonably dangerous or even unavoidably unsafe. The dairy farmer need not warn those with common allergies to milk, because it will be presumed that the person with an allergic reaction to common foodstuffs will be aware of them. But when the product contains an ingredient that could cause toxic effects in a substantial number of people and its danger is not widely known (or if known, is not an ingredient that would commonly be supposed to be in the product), the lack of a warning could make the product unreasonably dangerous within the meaning of Restatement, Section 402A. Many of the suits brought by asbestos workers charged exactly this point; "The utility of an insulation product containing asbestos may outweigh the known or foreseeable risk to the insulation workers and thus justify its marketing. The product could still be unreasonably dangerous, however, if unaccompanied by adequate warnings. An insulation worker, no less than any other product user, has a right to decide whether to expose himself to the risk."[15] This rule of law came to haunt the Manville Corporation: it was so burdened with lawsuits, brought and likely to be brought for its sale of asbestos—a known carcinogen—that it declared Chapter 11 bankruptcy in 1982 and shucked its liability.[16]

Engaged in the Business of Selling

Restatement, Section 402A(1)(a), limits liability to sellers "engaged in the business of selling such a product." The rule is intended to apply to people and entities engaged in business, not to casual one-time sellers. The business need not be solely in the defective product; a movie theater that sells popcorn with a razor blade inside is no less liable than a grocery store that does so. But strict liability under this rule does not attach to a private individual who sells his own automobile. In this sense, Restatement, Section 402A, is analogous to the UCC's limitation of the warranty of merchantability to the merchant.

The requirement that the defendant be in the business of selling gets to the rationale for the whole concept of strict products liability: businesses should shoulder the cost of injuries because they are in the best position to spread the risk and distribute the expense among the public. This same policy has been the rationale for holding bailors and lessors liable for defective equipment just as if they had been sellers.[17]

Reaches the User without Change in Condition

Restatement, Section 402A(1)(b), limits strict liability to those defective products that are expected to and do reach the user or consumer without substantial change in the condition in which the products are sold. A product that is safe when delivered cannot subject the seller to liability if it is subsequently mishandled or changed. The seller, however, must anticipate in appropriate cases that the product will be stored; faulty packaging or sterilization may be the grounds for liability if the product deteriorates before being used.

Liability Despite Exercise of All Due Care

Strict liability applies under the Restatement rule even though "the seller has exercised all possible care in the preparation and sale of his product." This is the crux of "strict liability" and distinguishes it from the conventional theory of negligence. It does not matter how reasonably the seller acted or how exemplary is a manufacturer's quality control system—what matters is whether the product was defective and the user injured as a result. Suppose an automated bottle factory manufactures 1,000 bottles per hour under exacting standards, with a rigorous and costly quality-control program designed to weed out any bottles showing even an infinitesimal amount of stress. The plant is "state of the art," and its computerized quality-control operation is the best in the world. It regularly detects the one out of every 10,000 bottles that analysis has shown will be defective. Despite this intense effort, it proves impossible to weed out every defective bottle; one out of one million, say, will still escape detection. Assume that a bottle, filled with soda, finds its way into a consumer's home, explodes when handled, sends glass shards into his eye, and blinds him. Under negligence, the bottler has no liability; under strict liability, the bottler will be liable to the consumer.

Liability without Contractual Relation

Under Restatement, Section 402A(2)(b), strict liability applies even though the user has not purchased the product from the seller nor has the user entered into any contractual relation with the seller. In short, privity is abolished and the injured user may use the theory of strict liability against manufacturers and wholesalers as well as retailers. Here, however, the courts have varied in their approaches; the trend has been to allow bystanders recovery. The Restatement explicitly leaves open the question of the bystander's right to recover under strict liability.

Problems with Strict Liability

Strict liability is liability without proof of negligence and without privity. It would seem that strict liability is the "holy grail" of products-liability lawyers: the complete answer. Well, no, it's not the holy grail. It is certainly true that 402A abolishes the contractual problems of warranty. Restatement, Section 402A, Comment *m*, says,

> *The rule stated in this Section is not governed by the provisions of the Uniform Commercial Code, as to warranties; and it is not affected by limitations on the scope and content of warranties, or by limitation to "buyer" and "seller" in those statutes. Nor is the consumer required to give notice to the seller of his injury within a reasonable time after it occurs, as provided by the Uniform Act. The consumer's cause of action does not depend upon the validity of his contract with the person from whom he acquires the product, and it is not affected by any disclaimer or other agreement, whether it be between the seller and his immediate buyer, or attached to and accompanying the product into the consumer's hands. In short, "warranty" must be given a new and different meaning if it is used in connection with this Section. It is much simpler to regard the liability here stated as merely one of strict liability in tort.*

Inherent in the Restatement's language is the obvious point that if the product has been altered, losses caused by injury are not the manufacturer's liability. Beyond that there are still some limitations to strict liability.

Disclaimers

Comment *m* specifically says the cause of action under Restatement, Section 402A, is not affected by disclaimer. But in *non-consumer* cases, courts have allowed clear and specific disclaimers. In 1969, the Ninth Circuit observed: "In *Kaiser Steel Corp.* the [California Supreme Court] court upheld the dismissal of a strict liability action when the parties, dealing from positions of relatively equal economic strength, contracted in a commercial setting to limit the defendant's liability. The court went on to hold that in this situation the strict liability cause of action does not apply at all. In reaching this conclusion, the court in *Kaiser* reasoned that strict liability "is designed to encompass situations in which the principles of sales warranties serve their purpose 'fitfully at best.' [Citation]" It concluded that in such commercial settings the UCC principles work well and "to apply the tort doctrines of products liability will displace the statutory law rather than bring out its full flavor."[18]

Plaintiff's Conduct

Conduct by the plaintiff herself may defeat recovery in two circumstances.

Assumption of Risk

Courts have allowed the defense of assumption of the risk in strict products-liability cases. A plaintiff assumes the risk of injury, thus establishing defense to claim of strict products liability, when he is aware the product is defective, knows the defect makes the product unreasonably dangerous, has reasonable opportunity to elect whether to expose himself to the danger, and nevertheless proceeds to make use of the product. The rule makes sense.

Misuse or Abuse of the Product

Where the plaintiff does not know a use of the product is dangerous but nevertheless uses for an incorrect purpose, a defense arises, but only if such misuse was not foreseeable. If it was, the manufacturer should warn against that misuse. In *Eastman v. Stanley Works*, a carpenter used a framing hammer to drive masonry nails; the claw of the hammer broke off, striking him in the eye.[19] He sued. The court held that while a defense does exist "where the product is used in a capacity which is unforeseeable by the manufacturer and completely incompatible with the product's design . . . misuse of a product suggests a use which was unanticipated or unexpected by the product manufacturer, or unforeseeable and unanticipated [but] it was not the case that reasonable minds could only conclude that appellee misused the [hammer]. Though the plaintiff's use of the hammer might have been *unreasonable*, unreasonable use is not a defense to a strict product-liability action or to a negligence action."

Limited Remedy

The Restatement says recovery under strict liability is limited to "physical harm thereby caused to the ultimate user or consumer, or to his property," but not other losses and not economic losses. In *Atlas Air v. General Electric*, a New York court held that the "economic loss rule" (no recovery for economic losses) barred strict products-liability and negligence claims by the purchaser of a used airplane against the airplane engine manufacturer for damage to the plane caused by an emergency landing necessitated by engine failure, where the purchaser merely alleged economic losses with respect to the plane itself, and not damages for personal injury (recovery for damage to the engine was allowed).[20]

But there are exceptions. In *Duffin v. Idaho Crop Imp. Ass'n*, the court recognized that a party generally owes no duty to exercise due care to avoid purely economic loss, but if there is a "special relationship" between the parties such that it would be equitable to impose such a duty, the duty will be imposed.[21] "In other words, there is an extremely limited group of cases where the law of negligence extends its protections to a party's economic interest."

The Third Restatement

The law develops. What seemed fitting in 1964 when the Restatement (Second) announced the state of the common-law rules for strict liability in Section 402A seemed, by 1997, not to be tracking common law entirely closely. The American Law Institute came out with the Restatement (Third) in that year. The Restatement changes some things. Most notably it abolishes the "unreasonably dangerous" test and substitutes a "risk-utility test." That is, a product is not defective unless its riskiness outweighs its utility. More important, the Restatement (Third), Section 2, now requires the plaintiff to provide a reasonable alternative design to the product in question. In advancing a reasonable alternative design, the plaintiff is not required to offer a prototype product. The plaintiff must only show that the proposed alternative design exists and is superior to the product in question. The Restatement (Third) also makes it more difficult for plaintiffs to sue drug companies successfully. One legal scholar commented as follows on the Restatement (Third):

> *The provisions of the Third Restatement, if implemented by the courts, will establish a degree of fairness in the products liability arena. If courts adopt the Third Restatement's elimination of the "consumer expectations test," this change alone will strip juries of the ability to render decisions based on potentially subjective, capricious and unscientific opinions that a particular product design is unduly dangerous based on its performance in a single incident. More important, plaintiffs will be required to propose a reasonable alternative design to the product in question. Such a requirement will force plaintiffs to prove that a better product design exists other than in the unproven and untested domain of their experts' imaginations.*[22]

Of course some people put more faith in juries than is evident here. The new Restatement has been adopted by a few jurisdictions and some cases the adopting jurisdictions incorporate some of its ideas, but courts appear reluctant to abandon familiar precedent.

Key Takeaway

Because the doctrines of breach of warranty and negligence did not provide adequate relief to those suffering damages or injuries in products-liability cases, beginning in the 1960s courts developed a new tort theory: strict products liability, restated in the Second Restatement, section 402A. Basically the doctrine says that if goods sold are unreasonably dangerous or defective, the merchant-seller will be liable for the immediate property loss and personal injuries caused thereby. But there remain obstacles to recovery even under this expanded concept of liability: disclaimers of liability have not completely been dismissed, the plaintiff's conduct or changes to the goods may limit recovery, and—with some exceptions—the remedies available are limited to personal injury (and damage to the goods themselves); economic loss is not recoverable. Almost forty years of experience with the Second Restatement's section on strict liability has seen changes in the law, and the Third Restatement introduces those, but it has not been widely accepted yet.

Exercises

1. What was perceived to be inadequate about warranty and negligence theories that necessitated the development of strict liability?
2. Briefly describe the doctrine.
3. What defects in goods render their sellers strictly liable?
4. Who counts as a liable seller?
5. What obstacles does a plaintiff have to overcome here, and what limitations are there to recovery?

20.5 Tort Reform

Learning Objectives

1. See why tort reform is advocated, why it is opposed, and what interests take each side.
2. Understand some of the significant state reforms in the last two decades.
3. Know what federal reforms have been instituted.

The Cry for Reform

In 1988, The Conference Board published a study that resulted from a survey of more than 500 chief executive officers from large and small companies regarding the effects of products liability on their firms. The study concluded that U.S. companies are less competitive in international business because of these effects and that products-liability laws must be reformed. The reform effort has been under way ever since, with varying degrees of alarms and finger-pointing as to who is to blame for the "tort crisis," if there even is one. Business and professional groups beat the drums for tort reform as a means to guarantee "fairness" in the courts as well as spur U.S. economic competitiveness in a global marketplace, while plaintiffs' attorneys and consumer advocates claim that businesses simply want to externalize costs by denying recovery to victims of greed and carelessness.

Each side vilifies the other in very unseemly language: pro-business advocates call consumer-oriented states "judicial hell-holes" and complain of "well-orchestrated campaign[s] by tort lawyer lobbyists and allies to undo years of tort reform at the state level,"[23] while pro-plaintiff interests claim that there is "scant evidence" of any tort abuse. [24] It would be more amusing if it were not so shrill and partisan. Perhaps the most one can say with any certainty is that peoples' perceptions of reality are highly colored by their self-interests. In any event, there have been reforms (or, as the detractors say, "deforms").

State Reforms

Prodded by astute lobbying by manufacturing and other business trade associations, state legislatures responded to the cries of manufacturers about the hardships that the judicial transformation of the products-liability lawsuit ostensibly worked on them. Most state legislatures have enacted at least one of some three dozen "reform" proposals pressed on them over the last two decades. Some of these measures do little more than affirm and clarify case law. Among the most that have passed in several states are outlined in the next sections.

Statutes of Repose

statute of repose

A statute limiting the time that a product manufacturer can be liable for its defects.

Perhaps nothing so frightens the manufacturer as the occasional reports of cases involving products that were fifty or sixty years old or more at the time they injured the plaintiff. Many states have addressed this problem by enacting the so-called **statute of repose**. This statute establishes a time period, generally ranging from six to twelve years; the manufacturer is not liable for injuries caused by the product after this time has passed.

State-of-the-Art Defense

Several states have enacted laws that prevent advances in technology from being held against the manufacturer. The fear is that a plaintiff will convince a jury a product was defective because it did not use technology that was later available. Manufacturers have often failed to adopt new advances in technology for fear that the change will be held against them in a products-liability suit. These new statutes declare that a manufacturer has a valid defense if it would have been technologically impossible to have used the new and safer technology at the time the product was manufactured.

Failure to Warn

Since it is often easier to prove that an injury resulted because the manufacturer failed to warn against a certain use than it is to prove an injury was caused by a defective design, manufacturers are subjected to a considerable degree of hindsight. Some of the state statutes limit the degree to which the failure to warn can be used to connect the product and the injury. For example, the manufacturer has a valid defense if it would have been impossible to foresee that the consumer might misuse the product in a certain way.

Comparative Fault for Consumer Misuse

Contributory negligence is generally not a defense in a strict liability action, while assumption of risk is. In states that have enacted so-called comparative fault statutes, the user's damages are pegged to the percentage of responsibility for the injury that the defendant bears. Thus, if the consumer's misuse of the product is assessed as having been 20 percent responsible for the accident (or for the extent of the injuries), the consumer is entitled to only 80 percent of damages, the amount for which the defendant manufacturer is responsible.

Criminal Penalties

Not all state reform is favorable to manufacturers. Under the California Corporate Criminal Liability Act, which took effect twenty years ago, companies and managers must notify a state regulatory agency if they know that a product they are selling in California has a safety defect, and the same rule applies under certain federal standards, as Toyota executives were informed by their lawyers following alarms about sudden acceleration in some Toyota automobiles. Failure to provide notice may result in corporate and individual criminal liability.

Federal Reform

Piecemeal reform of products-liability law in each state has contributed to the basic lack of uniformity from state to state, giving it a crazy-quilt effect. In the nineteenth century, this might have made little difference, but today most manufacturers sell in the national market and are subjected to the varying requirements of the law in every state. For years there has been talk in and out of Congress of enacting a federal products-liability law that would include reforms adopted in many states, as discussed earlier. So far, these efforts have been without much success.

Congressional tort legislation is not the only possible federal action to cope with products-related injuries. In 1972, Congress created the Consumer Product Safety Commission (CPSC) and gave the commission broad power to act to prevent unsafe consumer products. The CPSC can issue mandatory safety standards governing design, construction, contents, performance, packaging, and labeling of more than 10,000 consumer products. It can recall unsafe products, recover costs on behalf of injured consumers, prosecute those who violate standards, and require manufacturers to issue warnings on hazardous products. It also regulates four federal laws previously administered by other departments: the Flammable Fabrics Act, the Hazardous Substances Act, the Poison Prevention Packaging Act, and the Refrigerator Safety Act. In its early years, the CPSC issued standards for bicycles, power mowers, television sets, architectural glass, extension cords, book matches, pool slides, and space heaters. But the list of products is long, and the CPSC's record is mixed: it has come under fire for being short on regulation and for taking too long to promulgate the relatively few safety standards it has issued in a decade.

Key Takeaway

Business advocates claim the American tort system—products-liability law included—is broken and corrupted by grasping plaintiffs' lawyers; plaintiffs' lawyers say businesses are greedy and careless and need to be smacked into recognition of its responsibilities to be more careful. The debate rages on, decade after decade. But there have been some reforms at the state level, and at the federal level the Consumer Product Safety Act sets out standards for safe products and requires recalls for defective ones. It is regularly castigated for (1) being officious and meddling or (2) being too timid.

Exercises

1. Why is it so difficult to determine if there really is a "tort crisis" in the United States?
2. What reforms have been made to state tort law?
3. What federal legislation affects consumer safety?

20.6 Cases

Implied Warranty of Merchantability and the Requirement of a "Sale"

Sheeskin v. Giant Food, Inc.

318 A.2d 874 (Md. App. 1974)

Davidson, J.

Every Friday for over two years Nathan Seigel, age 73, shopped with his wife at a Giant Food Store. This complex products liability case is before us because on one of these Fridays, 23 October 1970, Mr. Seigel was carrying a six-pack carton of Coca-Cola from a display bin at the Giant to a shopping cart when one or more of the bottles exploded. Mr. Seigel lost his footing, fell to the floor and was injured.

In the Circuit Court for Montgomery County, Mr. Seigel sued both the Giant Food, Inc., and the Washington Coca-Cola Bottling Company, Inc., for damages resulting from their alleged negligence and breach of an implied warranty. At the conclusion of the trial Judge Walter H. Moorman directed a verdict in favor of each defendant. * * *

In an action based on breach of warranty it is necessary for the plaintiff to show the existence of the warranty, the fact that the warranty was broken and that the breach of warranty was the proximate cause of the loss sustained. [UCC] 2-314. * * * The retailer, Giant Food, Inc., contends that appellant failed to prove that an implied warranty existed between himself and the retailer because he failed to prove that there was a sale by the retailer to him or a contract of sale between the two. The retailer maintains that there was no sale or contract of sale because at the time the bottles exploded Mr. Seigel had not yet paid for them. We do not agree.

[UCC] 2-314(1) states in pertinent part:

> *Unless excluded or modified, a warranty that the goods shall be merchantable is implied* ***in a contract for their sale*** *if the seller is a merchant with respect to goods of that kind.*[25] *(emphasis added)*

Thus, in order for the implied warranties of 2-314 to be applicable there must be a "contract for sale." In Maryland it has been recognized that neither a completed 'sale' nor a fully executed contract for sale is required. It is enough that there be in existence an executory contract for sale. * * *

Here, the plaintiff has the burden of showing the existence of the warranty by establishing that at the time the bottles exploded there was a contract for their sale existing between himself and Giant. [Citation] Mr. Titus, the manager of Giant, testified that the retailer is a "self-service" store in which "the only way a customer can buy anything is to select it himself and take it to the checkout counter." He stated that there are occasions when a customer may select an item in the store and then change his mind and put the item back. There was no evidence to show that the retailer ever refused to sell an item to a customer once it had been selected by him or that the retailer did not consider himself bound to sell an item to the customer after the item had been selected. Finally, Mr. Titus said that an employee of Giant placed the six-pack of Coca-Cola selected by Mr. Seigel on the shelf with the purchase price already stamped upon it. Mr. Seigel testified that he picked up the six-pack with the intent to purchase it.

We think that there is sufficient evidence to show that the retailer's act of placing the bottles upon the shelf with the price stamped upon the six-pack in which they were contained manifested an intent to offer them for sale, the terms of the offer being that it would pass title to the goods when Mr. Seigel presented them at the check-out counter and paid the stated price in cash. We also think that the evidence is sufficient to show that Mr. Seigel's act of taking physical possession of the goods with the intent to purchase them manifested an intent to accept the offer and a promise to take them to the checkout counter and pay for them there.

[UCC] 2-206 provides in pertinent part:

> *(1) Unless otherwise unambiguously indicated by the language or circumstances*
>
> *(a) An offer to make a contract shall be construed as inviting acceptance in any manner and by any medium reasonable in the circumstances....*

The Official Comment 1 to this section states:

> *Any reasonable manner of acceptance is intended to be regarded as available unless the offeror has made quite clear that it will not be acceptable.*

In our view the manner by which acceptance was to be accomplished in the transaction herein involved was not indicated by either language or circumstances. The seller did not make it clear that acceptance could not be accomplished by a promise rather than an act. Thus it is equally reasonable under the terms of this specific offer that acceptance could be accomplished in any of three ways: 1) by the act of delivering the goods to the check-out counter and paying for them; 2) by the promise to pay for the goods as evidenced by their physical delivery to the check-out counter; and 3) by the promise to deliver the goods to the check-out counter and to pay for them there as evidenced by taking physical possession of the goods by their removal from the shelf.

The fact that customers, having once selected goods with the intent to purchase them, are permitted by the seller to return them to the shelves does not preclude the possibility that a selection of the goods, as evidenced by taking physical possession of them, could constitute a reasonable mode of acceptance. Section 2-106(3) provides:

> *"Termination" occurs when either party pursuant to a power created by agreement or law puts an end to the contract otherwise then for its breach. On "termination" all obligations which are still executory on both sides are discharged but any right based on prior breach or performance survives.*

Here the evidence that the retailer permits the customer to "change his mind" indicates only an agreement between the parties to permit the consumer to end his contract with the retailer irrespective of a breach of the agreement by the retailer. It does not indicate that an agreement does not exist prior to the exercise of this option by the consumer. * * *

Here Mr. Seigel testified that all of the circumstances surrounding his selection of the bottles were normal; that the carton in which the bottles came was not defective; that in lifting the carton from the shelf and moving it toward his basket the bottles neither touched nor were touched by anything other than his hand; that they exploded almost instantaneously after he removed them from the shelf; and that as a result of the explosion he fell injuring himself. It is obvious that Coca-Cola bottles which would break under normal handling are not fit for the ordinary use for which they were intended and that the relinquishment of physical control of such a defective bottle to a consumer constitutes a breach of warranty. Thus, the evidence was sufficient to show that when the bottles left the retailer's control they did not conform to the representations of the warranty of merchantability, and that this breach of the warranty was the cause of the loss sustained. * * *

[Judgment in favor of Giant Foods is reversed and the case remanded for a new trial. Judgment in favor of the bottler is affirmed because the plaintiff failed to prove that the bottles were defective when they were delivered to the retailer.]

Case Questions

1. What warranty did the plaintiff complain was breached here?
2. By displaying the soda pop, the store made an offer to its customers. How did the court say such offers might be accepted?
3. Why did the court get into the discussion about "termination" of the contract?
4. What is the controlling rule of law applied in this case?

Strict Liability and Bystanders

Embs v. Pepsi-Cola Bottling Co. of Lexington, Kentucky, Inc.
528 S.W.2d 703 (Ky. 1975)

Jukowsky, J.

On the afternoon of July 25, 1970 plaintiff-appellant entered the self-service retail store operated by the defendant-appellee, Stamper's Cash Market, Inc., for the purpose of "buying soft drinks for the kids." She went to an upright soft drink cooler, removed five bottles and placed them in a carton. Unnoticed by her, a carton of Seven-Up was sitting on the floor at the edge of the produce counter about one foot from where she was standing. As she turned away from the cooler she heard an explosion that sounded "like a shotgun." When she looked down she saw a gash in her leg, pop on her leg, green pieces of a bottle on the floor and the Seven-Up carton in the midst of the debris. She did not kick or otherwise come into contact with the carton of Seven-Up prior to the explosion. Her son, who was with her, recognized the green pieces of glass as part of a Seven-Up bottle.

She was immediately taken to the hospital by Mrs. Stamper, a managing agent of the store. Mrs. Stamper told her that a Seven-Up bottle had exploded and that several bottles had exploded that week. Before leaving the store Mrs. Stamper instructed one of her children to clean up the mess. Apparently, all of the physical evidence went out with the trash. The location of the Seven-Up carton immediately before the explosion was not a place where such items were ordinarily kept. * * *

When she rested her case, the defendants-appellees moved for a directed verdict in their favor. The trial court granted the motion on the grounds that the doctrine of strict product liability in tort does not extend beyond users and consumers and that the evidence was insufficient to permit an inference by a reasonably prudent man that the bottle was defective or if it was, when it became so.

In [Citation] we adopted the view of strict product liability in tort expressed in Section 402 A of the American Law Institute's Restatement of Torts 2d.

402 A. Special Liability of Seller of Product for Physical Harm to User or Consumer
(1) One who sells any product in a defective condition unreasonably dangerous to the user or to his property is subject to liability for physical harm thereby caused to the ultimate user or consumer, or to his property, if

(a) the seller is engaged in the business of selling such a product, and

(b) it is expected to and does reach the user or consumer without substantial change in the condition in which it was sold.

(2) The rule stated in Subsection (1) applies although

(a) the seller has exercised all possible care in the preparation and sale of his product, and

(b) the user or consumer has not bought the product from or entered into any contractual relation with the seller.

Comment *f* on that section makes it abundantly clear that this rule applies to any person engaged in the business of supplying products for use or consumption, including any manufacturer of such a product and any wholesale or retail dealer or distributor.

Comment *c* points out that on whatever theory, the justification for the rule has been said to be that the seller, by marketing his product for use and consumption, has undertaken and assumed a special responsibility toward any member of the consuming public who may be injured by it; that the public has the right to and does expect that reputable sellers will stand behind their goods; that public policy demands that the burden of accidental injuries caused by products intended for consumption be placed upon those who market them, and be treated as a cost of production against which liability insurance can be obtained; and that the consumer of such products is entitled to the maximum of protection at the hands of someone, and the proper persons to afford it are those who market the products.

The caveat to the section provides that the Institute expresses no opinion as to whether the rule may not apply to harm to persons other than users or consumers. Comment on caveat *o* states the Institute expresses neither approval nor disapproval of expansion of the rule to permit recovery by casual bystanders and others who may come in contact with the product, and admits there may be no essential reason why such plaintiffs should not be brought within the scope of protection afforded, other than they do not have the same reasons for expecting such protection as the consumer who buys a marketed product, and that the social pressure which has been largely responsible for the development of the rule has been a consumer's pressure, and there is not the same demand for the protection of casual strangers. * * *

The caveat articulates the essential point: Once strict liability is accepted, bystander recovery is fait accompli.

Our expressed public policy will be furthered if we minimize the risk of personal injury and property damage by charging the costs of injuries against the manufacturer who can procure liability insurance and distribute its expense among the public as a cost of doing business; and since the risk of harm from defective products exists for mere bystanders and passersby as well as for the purchaser or user, there is no substantial reason for protecting one class of persons and not the other. The same policy requires us to maximize protection for the injured third party and promote the public interest in discouraging the marketing of products having defects that are a menace to the public by imposing strict liability upon retailers and wholesalers in the distributive chain responsible for marketing the defective product which injures the bystander. The imposition of strict liability places no unreasonable burden upon sellers because they can adjust the cost of insurance protection among themselves in the course of their continuing business relationship.

We must not shirk from extending the rule to the manufacturer for fear that the retailer or middleman will be impaled on the sword of liability without regard to fault. Their liability was already established under Section 402 A of the Restatement of Torts 2d. As a matter of public policy the retailer or middleman as well as the manufacturer should be liable since the loss for injuries resulting from defective products should be placed on those members of the marketing chain best able to pay the loss, who can then distribute such risk among themselves by means of insurance and indemnity agreements. [Citation] * * *

The result which we reach does not give the bystander a "free ride." When products and consumers are considered in the aggregate, bystanders, as a class, purchase most of the same products to which they are exposed as bystanders. Thus, as a class, they indirectly subsidize the liability of the manufacturer, middleman and retailer and in this sense do pay for the insurance policy tied to the product. * * *

For the sake of clarity we restate the extension of the rule. The protections of Section 402 A of the Restatement of Torts 2d extend to bystanders whose injury from the defective product is reasonably foreseeable. * * *

The judgment is reversed and the cause is remanded to the Clark Circuit Court for further proceedings consistent herewith.

Stephenson, J. (dissenting):

I respectfully dissent from the majority opinion to the extent that it subjects the seller to liability. Every rule of law in my mind should have a rational basis. I see none here.

Liability of the seller to the user, or consumer, is based upon warranty. Restatement, Second, Torts s 403A. To extend this liability to injuries suffered by a bystander is to depart from any reasonable basis and impose liability by judicial fiat upon an otherwise innocent defendant. I do not believe that the expression in the majority opinion which justifies this rule for the reason that the seller may procure liability insurance protection is a valid legal basis for imposing liability without fault. I respectfully dissent.

Case Questions

1. Why didn't the plaintiff here use warranty as a theory of recovery, as Mr. Seigel did in the previous case?
2. The court offers a rationale for the doctrine of strict products liability. What is it?
3. Restatement, Section 402A, by its terms extends protection "to the ultimate user or consumer," but Mrs. Embs [plaintiff-appellant] was not that. What rationale did the court give for expanding the protection here?
4. Among the entities in the vertical distribution chain—manufacturer, wholesaler, retailer—who is liable under this doctrine?
5. What argument did Judge Stephenson have in dissent? Is it a good one?
6. What is the controlling rule of law developed in this case?

Failure to Warn

Laaperi v. Sears, Roebuck & Co., Inc.

787 F.2d 726 C.A.1 (Mass. 1986)

Campbell, J.

In March 1976, plaintiff Albin Laaperi purchased a smoke detector from Sears. The detector, manufactured by the Pittway Corporation, was designed to be powered by AC (electrical) current. Laaperi installed the detector himself in one of the two upstairs bedrooms in his home.

Early in the morning of December 27, 1976, a fire broke out in the Laaperi home. The three boys in one of the upstairs bedrooms were killed in the blaze. Laaperi's 13-year-old daughter Janet, who was sleeping in the other upstairs bedroom, received burns over 12 percent of her body and was hospitalized for three weeks.

The uncontroverted testimony at trial was that the smoke detector did not sound an alarm on the night of the fire. The cause of the fire was later found to be a short circuit in an electrical cord that was located in a cedar closet in the boys' bedroom. The Laaperi home had two separate electrical circuits in the upstairs bedrooms: one which provided electricity to the outlets and one which powered the lighting fixtures. The smoke detector had been connected to the outlet circuit, which was the circuit that shorted and cut off. Because the circuit was shorted, the AC-operated smoke detector received no power on the night of the fire. Therefore, although the detector itself was in no sense defective (indeed, after the fire the charred detector was tested and found to be operable), no alarm sounded.

Laaperi brought this diversity action against defendants Sears and Pittway, asserting negligent design, negligent manufacture, breach of warranty, and negligent failure to warn of inherent dangers. The parties agreed that the applicable law is that of Massachusetts. Before the claims went to the jury, verdicts were directed in favor of defendants on all theories of liability other than failure to warn. * * *

Laaperi's claim under the failure to warn theory was that he was unaware of the danger that the very short circuit which might ignite a fire in his home could, at the same time, incapacitate the smoke detector. He contended that had he been warned of this danger, he would have purchased a battery-powered smoke detector as a back-up or taken some other precaution, such as wiring the detector to a circuit of its own, in order better to protect his family in the event of an electrical fire.

The jury returned verdicts in favor of Laaperi in all four actions on the failure to warn claim. The jury assessed damages in the amount of $350,000 [$1.5 million in 2016 dollars] for each of the three actions brought on behalf of the deceased sons [about, or about $4.5 million, total, in 2016 dollars], and $750,000 [about $3.15 million in 2016 dollars] in the action brought on behalf of Janet Laaperi. The defendants' motions for directed verdict and judgment notwithstanding the verdict were denied, and defendants appealed.

Defendants ask us to declare that the risk that an electrical fire could incapacitate an AC-powered smoke detector is so obvious that the average consumer would not benefit from a warning. This is not a trivial argument; in earlier—some might say sounder—days, we might have accepted it. * * * Our sense of the current state of the tort law in Massachusetts and most other jurisdictions, however, leads us to conclude that, today, the matter before us poses a jury question; that "obviousness" in a situation such as this would be treated by the Massachusetts courts as presenting a question of fact, not of law. To be sure, it would be obvious to anyone that an electrical outage would cause this smoke detector to fail. But the average purchaser might not comprehend the specific danger that a fire-causing electrical problem can simultaneously knock out the circuit into which a smoke detector is wired, causing the detector to fail at the very moment it is needed. Thus, while the failure of a detector to function as the result of an electrical malfunction due, say, to a broken power line or a neighborhood power outage would, we think, be obvious as a matter of law, the failure that occurred here, being associated with the very risk—fire—for which the device was purchased, was not, or so a jury could find. * * *

Finally, defendants contend that the award of $750,000 [$3.15 million in 2016 dollars] in damages to Janet Laaperi was excessive, and should have been overturned by the district court. * * *

Janet Laaperi testified that on the night of the fire, she woke up and smelled smoke. She woke her friend who was sleeping in her room, and they climbed out to the icy roof of the house. Her father grabbed her from the roof and took her down a ladder. She was taken to the hospital. Although she was in "mild distress," she was found to be "alert, awake, [and] cooperative." Her chest was clear. She was diagnosed as having first and second degree burns of her right calf, both buttocks and heels, and her left lower back, or approximately 12 percent of her total body area. She also suffered from a burn of her tracheobronchial mucosa (i.e., the lining of her airway) due to smoke inhalation, and multiple superficial lacerations on her right hand.

The jury undoubtedly, and understandably, felt a great deal of sympathy for a young girl who, at the age of 13, lost three brothers in a tragic fire. But by law the jury was only permitted to compensate her for those damages associated with her own injuries. Her injuries included fright and pain at the time of and after the fire, a three-week hospital stay, some minor discomfort for several weeks after discharge, and a permanent scar on her lower back. Plaintiff has pointed to no cases, and we have discovered none, in which such a large verdict was sustained for such relatively minor injuries, involving no continuing disability.

The judgments in favor of Albin Laaperi in his capacity as administrator of the estates of his three sons are affirmed. In the action on behalf of Janet Laaperi, the verdict of the jury is set aside, the judgment of the district court vacated, and the cause remanded to that court for a new trial limited to the issue of damages.

Case Questions

1. The "C.A. 1" under the title of the case means it is a US Court of Appeals case from the First Circuit in Massachusetts. Why is this case in federal court?
2. Why does the court talk about its "sense of the current state of tort law in Massachusetts" and how this case "would be treated by the Massachusetts courts," as if it were not in the state at all but somehow outside?
3. What rule of law is in play here as to the defendants' liability?
4. This is a tragic case—three boys died in a house fire. Speaking dispassionately—if not heartlessly—though, did the fire actually cost Mr. Laaperi, or did he lose $3.4 million (in 2010 dollars) as the result of his sons' deaths? Does it make sense that he should become a millionaire as a result? Who ends up paying this amount? (The lawyers' fees probably took about half.)
5. Is it likely that smoke-alarm manufactures and sellers changed the instructions as a result of this case?

20.7 Summary and Exercises

Summary

Products liability describes a type of claim—for injury caused by a defective product—and not a separate theory of liability. In the typical case, three legal doctrines may be asserted: (1) warranty, (2) negligence, and (3) strict liability.

If a seller asserts that a product will perform in a certain manner or has certain characteristics, he has given an express warranty, and he will be held liable for damages if the warranty is breached—that is, if the goods do not live up to the warranty. Not every conceivable claim is an express warranty; the courts permit a certain degree of "puffing."

An implied warranty is one created by law. Goods sold by a merchant-seller carry an implied warranty of merchantability, meaning that they must possess certain characteristics, such as being of average quality for the type described and being fit for the ordinary purposes for which they are intended.

An implied warranty of fitness for a particular purpose is created whenever a seller knows or has reason to know that the buyer is relying on the seller's knowledge and skill to select a product for the buyer's particular purposes.

Under UCC Article 2, the seller also warrants that he is conveying good title and that the goods are free of any rightful claim by a third person.

UCC Article 2 permits sellers to exclude or disclaim warranties in whole or in part. Thus a seller may exclude express warranties. He may also disclaim many implied warranties—for example, by noting that the sale is "as is." The Magnuson-Moss Act sets out certain types of information that must be included in any written warranty. The act requires the manufacturer or seller to label the warranty as either "full" or "limited" depending on what types of defects are covered and what the customer must do to obtain repair or replacement. The act also abolishes "phantom warranties."

Privity once stood as a bar to recovery in suits brought by those one or more steps removed in the distribution chain from the party who breached a warranty. But the nearly universal trend in the state courts has been to abolish privity as a defense.

Because various impediments stand in the way of warranty suits, courts have adopted a tort theory of strict liability, under which a seller is liable for injuries resulting from the sale of any product in a defective condition if it is unreasonably dangerous to the user or consumer. Typical issues in strict liability cases are these: Is the defendant a seller engaged in the business of selling? Was the product sold in a defective condition? Was it unreasonably dangerous, either on its face or because of a failure to warn? Did the product reach the consumer in an unchanged condition? Strict liability applies regardless of how careful the seller was and regardless of his lack of contractual relation with the consumer or user.

Manufacturers can also be held liable for negligence—most often for faulty design of products and inadequate warnings about the hazards of using the product.

The products-liability revolution prompted many state legislatures to enact certain laws limiting to some degree the manufacturer's responsibility for defective products. These laws include statutes of repose and provide a number of other defenses.

Exercises

1. Ralph's Hardware updated its accounting system and agreed to purchase a computer system from a manufacturer, Bits and Bytes (BB). During contract negotiations, BB's sales representative promised that the system was "A-1" and "perfect." However, the written contract, which the parties later signed, disclaimed all warranties, express and implied. After installation the computer produced only random numbers and letters, rather than the desired accounting information. Is BB liable for breaching an express warranty? Why?
2. Kate owned a small grocery store. One day, John went to the store and purchased a can of chip dip that was, unknown to Kate or John, adulterated. John became seriously ill after eating the dip and sued Kate for damages on the grounds that she breached an implied warranty of merchantability. Is Kate liable? Why?
3. Carrie visited a neighborhood store to purchase some ham, which a salesperson cut by machine in the store. The next day, she made a ham sandwich. In eating the sandwich, Carrie bit into a piece of cartilage in the ham. As a result, Carrie lost a tooth, had to undergo root canal treatments, and must now wear a full-coverage crown to replace the tooth. Is the store liable for the damage? Why?
4. Clarence, a business executive, decided to hold a garage sale. At the sale, his neighbor Betty mentioned to Clarence that she was the catcher on her city-league baseball team and was having trouble catching knuckleball pitches, which required a special catcher's mitt. Clarence pulled an old mitt from a pile of items that were on sale and said, "Here, try this." Betty purchased the mitt but discovered during her next game that it didn't work. Has Clarence breached an express or implied warranty? Why?
5. Sarah purchased several elegant picture frames to hang in her dorm room. She also purchased a package of self-sticking hangers. Late one evening, while Sarah was studying business law in the library, the hangers came loose and her frames came crashing to the floor. After Sarah returned to her room and discovered the rubble, she examined the box in which the hangers were packaged and found the following language: "There are no warranties except for the description on this package and specifically there is NO IMPLIED WARRANTY OF MERCHANTABILITY." Assuming the hangers are not of fair, average, ordinary quality, would the hanger company be liable for breaching an implied warranty of merchantability? Why?
6. A thirteen-year-old boy received a Golfing Gizmo—a device for training novice golfers—as a gift from his mother. The label on the shipping carton and the cover of the instruction booklet urged players to "drive the ball with full power" and further stated: "COMPLETELY SAFE BALL WILL NOT HIT PLAYER." But while using the device, the boy was hit in the eye by the ball. Should lack of privity be a defense to the manufacturer? The manufacturer argued that the Gizmo was a "completely safe" training device only when the ball is hit squarely, and—the defendant argued—plaintiffs could not reasonably expect the Gizmo to be "completely safe" under all circumstances, particularly those in which the player hits beneath the ball. What legal argument is this, and is it valid?
7. A bank repossessed a boat and sold it to Donald. During the negotiations with Donald, Donald stated that he wanted to use the boat for charter service in Florida. The bank officers handling the sale made no representations concerning the boat during negotiations. Donald later discovered that the boat was defective and sued the bank for breach of warranty. Is the bank liable? Why?

8. Tom Anderson, the produce manager at the Thriftway Market in Pasco, Washington, removed a box of bananas from the top of a stack of produce. When he reached for a lug of radishes that had been under the bananas, a six-inch spider—*Heteropoda venatoria*, commonly called a banana spider—leaped from some wet burlap onto his left hand and bit him. Nine months later he died of heart failure. His wife brought an action against Associated Grocers, parent company of Thriftway Market, on theories of (1) strict products liability under Restatement, Section 402(a); (2) breach of the implied warranty of merchantability; and (3) negligence. The trial court ruled against the plaintiff on all three theories. Was that a correct ruling? Explain.
9. A broken water pipe flooded a switchboard at RCA's office. The flood tripped the switchboard circuit breakers and deactivated the air-conditioning system. Three employees were assigned to fix it: an electrical technician with twelve years on-the-job training, a licensed electrician, and an electrical engineer with twenty years of experience who had studied power engineering in college. They switched on one of the circuit breakers, although the engineer said he knew that one was supposed to test the operation of a wet switchboard before putting it back into use. There was a "snap" and everyone ran from the room up the stairs and a "big ball of fire" came after them up the stairs. The plaintiffs argued that the manufacturer of the circuit breaker had been negligent in failing to give RCA adequate warnings about the circuit breakers. How should the court rule, and on what theory should it rule?
10. Plaintiff's business was to convert vans to RVs, and for this purpose it had used a 3M adhesive to laminate carpeting to the van walls. This adhesive, however, failed to hold the fabric in place in hot weather, so Plaintiff approached Northern Adhesive Co., a manufacturer of adhesives, to find a better one. Plaintiff told Northern why it wanted the adhesive, and Northern—Defendant—sent several samples to Plaintiff to experiment with. Northern told Plaintiff that one of the adhesives, Adhesive 7448, was "a match" for the 3M product that previously failed. Plaintiff tested the samples in a cool plant and determined that Adhesive 7448 was better than the 3M product. Defendant had said nothing except that "what they would ship would be like the sample. It would be the same chemistry." Plaintiff used the adhesive during the fall and winter; by spring complaints of delamination came in: Adhesive 7448 failed just as the 3M product had. Over 500 vans had to be repaired. How should the court rule on Plaintiff's claims of breach of (1) express warranty, (2) implied warranty of merchantability, and (3) implied warranty of fitness for a particular purpose?

Self-Test Questions

1. In a products-liability case
   a. only tort theories are typically asserted
   b. both tort and contract theories are typically asserted
   c. strict liability is asserted only when negligence is not asserted
   d. breach of warranty is not asserted along with strict liability
2. An implied warranty of merchantability
   a. is created by an express warranty
   b. is created by law
   c. is impossible for a seller to disclaim
   d. can be disclaimed by a seller only if the disclaimer is in writing
3. A possible defense to breach of warranty is
   a. lack of privity
   b. absence of an express warranty
   c. disclaimer of implied warranties
   d. all of the above
4. Under the strict liability rule in Restatement, Section 402A, the seller is liable for all injuries resulting from a product

a. even though all possible care has been exercised
b. regardless of the lack of a contract with the user
c. in both of the above situations
d. in none of the above situations

5. An individual selling her car could be liable
   a. for breaching the implied warranty of merchantability
   b. under the strict liability theory
   c. for breaching the implied warranty of fitness
   d. under two of the above

Self-Test Answers

1. b
2. b
3. d
4. c
5. c

Endnotes

1. Upton Sinclair, *The Jungle* (New York: Signet Classic, 1963), 136.
2. FindLaw, AP reports.
3. US Consumer Product Safety Commission, *2009 Report to the President and the Congress*, accessed March 1, 2011, http://www.cpsc.gov/cpscpub/pubs/reports/2009rpt.pdf.
4. Matt Hamblen, "New Study Warns of Cell Phone Dangers," *Computerworld US*, August 9, 2009, accessed March 1, 2011, http://news.techworld.com/personal-tech/3200539/new-study-warns-of-cell-phone-dangers.
5. Michael Orey, "Taking on Toy Safety," *BusinessWeek*, March 6, 2009, accessed March 1, 2011, http://www.businessweek.com/managing/content/mar2009/ca2009036_271002.htm.
6. *Rhodes Pharmacal Co. v. Continental Can Co.*, 219 N.E.2d 726 (Ill. 1976).
7. *Wat Henry Pontiac Co. v. Bradley*, 210 P.2d 348 (Okla. 1949).
8. *Frederickson v. Hackney*, 198 N.W. 806 (Minn. 1924).
9. *Menzel v. List*, 246 N.E.2d 742 (N.Y. 1969).
10. A number of states have special laws that limit the use of the UCC implied warranty disclaimer rules in consumer sales. Some of these appear in amendments to the UCC and others are in separate statutes. The broadest approach is that of the nine states that prohibit the disclaimer of implied warranties in consumer sales (Massachusetts, Connecticut, Maine, Vermont, Maryland, the District of Columbia, West Virginia, Kansas, Mississippi, and, with respect to personal injuries only, Alabama). There is a difference in these states whether the rules apply to manufacturers as well as retailers.
11. *Spence v. Three Rivers Builders & Masonry Supply, Inc.*, 90 N.W.2d 873 (Mich. 1958).
12. C. Richard Newsome and Andrew F. Knopf, "Federal Preemption: Products Lawyers Beware," *Florida Justice Association Journal*, July 27, 2007, accessed March 1, 2011, http://www.newsomelaw.com/resources/articles/federal-preemption-products-lawyers-beware.
13. *Kaiser Steel Corp. v. Westinghouse Electric Corp.*, 127 Cal. Rptr. 838 (Cal. 1976).
14. Restatement (Second) of Contracts, Section 402A(i).
15. *Borel v. Fibreboard Paper Products Corp.*, 493 F.Zd 1076 (5th Cir. 1973).
16. *In re Johns-Manville Corp.*, 36 R.R. 727 (So. Dist. N.Y. 1984).
17. *Martin v. Ryder Rental, Inc.*, 353 A.2d 581 (Del. 1976).
18. *Idaho Power Co. v. Westinghouse Electric Corp.*, 596 F.2d 924, 9CA (1979).
19. *Eastman v. Stanley Works*, 907 N.E.2d 768 (Ohio App. 2009).
20. *Atlas Air v. General Electric*, 16 A.D.3d 444 (N.Y.A.D. 2005).
21. *Duffin v. Idaho Crop Imp. Ass'n*, 895 P.2d 1195 (Idaho 1995).
22. Quinlivan Wexler LLP, "The 3rd Restatement of Torts—Shaping the Future of Products Liability Law," June 1, 1999, accessed March 1, 2011, http://library.findlaw.com/1999/Jun/1/127691.html.
23. American Tort Reform Association website, accessed March 1, 2011, http://www.atra.org.
24. http://www.shragerlaw.com/html/legal_rights.html.
25. Uniform Commercial Code, Section 2-316.

CHAPTER 21

Bailments and the Storage, Shipment, and Leasing of Goods

Learning Objectives

After reading this chapter, you should understand the following:

1. What the elements of a bailment are.
2. What the bailee's liability is.
3. What the bailor's liability is.
4. What other rights and duties—compensation, bailee's liens, casualty to goods—arise.
5. What special types of bailments are recognized: innkeepers, warehousing.
6. What rules govern the shipment of goods.
7. How commodity paper is negotiated and transferred.

21.1 Introduction to Bailment Law

Learning Objectives

1. Understand what a bailment is, and why the law of bailment is important.
2. Recognize how bailments compare with sales.
3. Point out the elements required to create a bailment.

Finally, we turn to the legal relationships that buyers and sellers have with warehousers and carriers—the parties responsible for physically transferring goods from seller to buyer. This topic introduces a new branch of law—that of bailments; we'll examine it before turning directly to warehousers and carriers.

Overview of Bailments

A **bailment** is the relationship established when someone entrusts his property temporarily to someone else without intending to give up title. Although bailment has often been said to arise only through a contract, the modern definition does not require that there be an agreement. One widely quoted definition holds that a bailment is "the rightful possession of goods by one who is not the owner. It is the element of lawful possession, however created, and the duty to account for the thing as the property of another, that creates the bailment, regardless of whether such possession is based upon contract in the ordinary sense or not."[1]

bailment

A delivery of goods to one who does not have title.

bailee

The person to whom property is delivered to hold in bailment.

The word *bailment* derives from a Latin verb, *bajulare*, meaning "to bear a burden," and then from French, *bailler*, which means "to deliver" (i.e., into the hands or possession of someone). The one who bails out a boat, filling a bucket and emptying it overboard, is a water-bearer.The one who bails someone out of jail takes on the burden of ensuring that the one sprung appears in court to stand trial; he also takes on the risk of loss of bond money if the jailed party does not appear in court. The one who is a **bailee** takes on the burden of being responsible to return the goods to their owner.

The law of bailments is important to virtually everyone in modern society: anyone who has ever delivered a car to a parking lot attendant, checked a coat in a restaurant, deposited property in a safe-deposit box, rented tools, or taken items clothes or appliance in to a shop for repair. In commercial transactions, bailment law governs the responsibilities of warehousers and the carriers, such as UPS and FedEx, that are critical links in the movement of goods from manufacturer to the consumer. Bailment law is an admixture of common law (property and tort), state statutory law (in the Uniform Commercial Code; UCC), federal statutory law, and—for international issues—treaty.[2]

Bailments Compared with Sales

Bailment versus Sales

In a sale, the buyer acquires title and must pay for the goods. In a bailment, the bailee acquires possession and must return the identical object. In most cases the distinction is clear, but difficult borderline cases can arise. Consider the sad case of the leased cows: *Carpenter v. Griffen* (N.Y. 1841). Carpenter leased a farm for five years to Spencer. The lease included thirty cows. At the end of the term, Spencer was to give Carpenter, the owner, "cows of equal age and quality." Unfortunately, Spencer fell into hard times and had to borrow money from one Griffin. When the time came to pay the debt, Spencer had no money, so Griffin went to court to levy against the cows (i.e., he sought a court order giving him the cows in lieu of the money owed). Needless to say, this threatened transfer of the cows upset Carpenter, who went to court to stop Griffin from taking the cows. The question was whether Spencer was a bailee, in which case the cows would still belong to Carpenter (and Griffin could not levy against them), or a purchaser, in which case Spencer would own the cows and Griffin could levy against them. The court ruled that title had passed to Spencer—the cows were his. Why? The court reasoned that Spencer was not obligated to return the identical cows to Carpenter, hence Spencer was not a bailee.[3] Section 2-304(1) of the UCC confirms this position, declaring that whenever the price of a sale is payable in goods, each party is a seller of the goods that he is to transfer.

Note the implications that flow from calling this transaction a sale. Creditors of the purchaser can seize the goods. The risk of loss is on the purchaser. The seller cannot recover the goods (to make up for the buyer's failure to pay him) or sell them to a third party.

Fungible Goods

Fungible goods (goods that are identical, like grain in a silo) present an especially troublesome problem. In many instances the goods of several owners are mingled, and the identical items are not intended to be returned. For example, the operator of a grain elevator agrees to return an equal quantity of like-quality grain but not the actual kernels deposited there. Following the rule in Carpenter's cow case, this might seem to be a sale, but it is not. Under the UCC, Section 2-207, the depositors of fungible goods are "tenants in common" of the goods; in other words, the goods are owned by all. This distinction between a sale and a bailment is important. When there is a loss through natural causes—for example, if the grain elevator burns—the depositors must share the loss on a pro rata basis (meaning that no single depositor is entitled to take all his grain out; if 20 percent of the grain was destroyed, then each depositor can take out no more than 80 percent of what he deposited).

Elements of a Bailment

As noted, bailment is defined as "the rightful possession of goods by one who is not the owner." For the most part, this definition is clear (and note that it does not dictate that a bailment be created by contract). Bailment law applies to the delivery of goods—that is, to the delivery personal property. Personal property is usually defined as anything that can be owned other than real estate. As we have just seen in comparing bailments to sales, the definition implies a duty to return the identical goods when the bailment ends.

But one word in the definition is both critical and troublesome: possession. Possession requires both a physical and a mental element. We examine these in turn.

Possession: Physical Control

In most cases, physical control is proven easily enough. A car delivered to a parking garage is obviously within the physical control of the garage. But in some instances, physical control is difficult to conceptualize. For example, you can rent a safe-deposit box in a bank to store valuable papers, stock certificates, jewelry, and the like. The box is usually housed in the bank's vault. To gain access, you sign a register and insert your key after a bank employee inserts the bank's key. You may then inspect, add to, or remove contents of the box in the privacy of a small room maintained in the vault for the purpose. Because the bank cannot gain access to the box without your key and does not know what is in the box, it might be said to have no physical control. Nevertheless, the rental of a safe-deposit box is a bailment. In so holding, a New York court pointed out that if the bank was not in possession of the box renter's property "it is difficult to know who was. Certainly [the renter] was not, because she could not obtain access to the property without the consent and active participation of the defendant. She could not go into her safe unless the defendant used its key first, and then allowed her to open the box with her own key; thus absolutely controlling [her] access to that which she had deposited within the safe. The vault was the [company's] and was in its custody, and its contents were under the same conditions."[4] Statutes in some states, however, provide that the relationship is not a bailment but that of a landlord and tenant, and many of these statutes limit the bank's liability for losses.

Possession: Intent to Possess

In addition to physical control, the bailee must have had an intent to possess the goods; that is, to exercise control over them. This mental condition is difficult to prove; it almost always turns on the specific circumstances and, as a fact question, is left to the jury to determine. To illustrate the difficulty, suppose that one crisp fall day, Mimi goes to Sally Jane's Boutique to try on a jacket. The sales clerk hands Mimi a jacket and watches while Mimi takes off her coat and places it on a nearby table. A few minutes later, when Mimi is finished inspecting herself in the mirror, she goes to retrieve her coat, only to discover it is missing. Who is responsible for the loss? The answer depends on whether the store is a bailee. In some sense the boutique had physical control, but did it intend to exercise that control? In a leading case, the court held that it did, even though no one said anything about guarding the coat, because a store invites its patrons to come in. Implicit in the act of trying on a garment is the removal of the garment being worn. When the customer places it in a logical place, with the knowledge of and without objection from the salesperson, the store must exercise some care in its safekeeping.[5]

Now suppose that when Mimi walked in, the salesperson told her to look around, to try on some clothes, and to put her coat on the table. The salesperson was finished with her present customer, she said, she would be glad to help Mimi. So Mimi tried on a jacket and minutes later discovered her coat gone. Is this a bailment? Many courts, including the New York courts, would say no. The difference? The salesperson was helping another customer. Therefore, Mimi had a better opportunity to watch over her own coat and knew that the salesperson would not be looking out for it. This is a subtle distinction, but it has been sufficient in many cases to change the ruling.[6]

bailor

An owner of property who delivers it to another to hold in bailment.

Questions of intent and control frequently arise in parking lot cases. As someone once said, "The key to the problem is the key itself." The key is symbolic of possession and intent to possess. If you give the attendant your key, you are a **bailor** and he (or the company he works for) is the bailee. If you do not give him the key, no bailment arises. Many parking lot cases do not fall neatly within this rule, however. Especially common are cases involving self-service airport parking lots. The customer drives through a gate, takes a ticket dispensed by a machine, parks his car, locks it, and takes his key. He leaves, he retrieves the car himself, and pays at an exit gate. As a general rule, no bailment is created under these circumstances. The lot operator does not accept the vehicle nor intend to watch over it as bailee. In effect, the operator is simply renting out space.[7] But a slight change of facts can alter this legal conclusion. Suppose, for instance, that the lot had an attendant at the single point of entrance and exit, that the attendant jotted down the license number on the ticket, one portion of which he retained, and that the car owner must surrender the ticket when leaving or prove that he owns the car. These facts have been held to add up to an intention to exercise custody and control over the cars in the lot, and hence to have created a bailment.[8]

For a bailment to exist, the bailee must know or have reason to know that the property exists. When property is hidden within the main object entrusted to the bailee, lack of notice can defeat the bailment in the hidden property. For instance, a parking lot is not responsible for the disappearance of valuable golf clubs stored in the trunk of a car, nor is a dance hall cloak room responsible for the disappearance of a fur wrap inside a coat, if they did not know of their existence.[9] This result is usually justified by observing that when a person is unaware that goods exist or does not know their value, it is inequitable to hold him responsible for their loss since he cannot take steps to prevent it. This rule has been criticized: trunks are meant to hold things, and if the car was within the garage's control, surely its contents were too. Some courts soften the impact of the rule by holding that a bailee is responsible for goods that he might reasonably expect to be present, like gloves in a coat checked at a restaurant or ordinary baggage in a car checked at a hotel.

Key Takeaway

A bailment arises when one person (a bailee) rightfully holds property belonging to another (a bailor). The law of bailments addresses the critical links in the movement of goods from the manufacturer to the end user in a consumer society: to the storage and transportation of goods. Bailments only apply to personal property; a bailment requires that the bailor deliver physical control of the goods to the bailee, who has an intention to possess the goods and a duty to return them.

Exercises

1. Dennis takes his Mercedes to have the GPS system repaired. In the trunk of his car is a briefcase containing $5,000 in cash. Is the cash bailed goods?
2. Marilyn wraps up ten family-heirloom crystal goblets, packages them carefully in a cardboard box, and drops the box off at the local UPS store. Are the goblets bailed goods?
3. Bob agrees to help his friend Roger build a deck at Roger's house. Bob leaves some of his tools—without Bob's noticing—around the corner of the garage at the foot of a rhododendron bush. The tools are partly hidden. Are they bailed goods?

21.2 Liability of the Parties to a Bailment

Learning Objectives

1. Understand how the bailee's liability arises and operates.
2. Recognize the cases in which the bailee can disclaim liability, and what limits are put on such disclaimers.
3. Understand what duty and liability the bailor has.
4. Know other rights and duties that arise in a bailment.
5. Understand the extent to which innkeepers—hotel and motels—are liable for their guests' property.

Liability of the Bailee

Duty of Care

The basic rule is that the bailee is expected to return to its owner the bailed goods when the bailee's time for possession of them is over, and he is presumed liable if the goods are not returned. But that a bailee has accepted delivery of goods does not mean that he is responsible for their safekeeping no matter what. The law of bailments does not apply a standard of absolute liability: the bailee is not an insurer of the goods' safety; her liability depends on the circumstances.

The Ordinary Care Rule

Some courts say that the bailee's liability is the straightforward standard of "ordinary care under the circumstances." The question becomes whether the bailee exercised such care. If she did, she is not liable for the loss.

The Benefit-of-the-Bargain Rule

Most courts use a complex (some say annoying) tripartite division of responsibility. If the bailment is for the sole benefit of the owner (the bailor), the bailee is answerable only for gross neglect or fraud: the duty of care is slight. For example, imagine that your car breaks down on a dark night and you beg a passing motorist to tow it to a gas station; or you ask your neighbor if you can store your utility trailer in her garage.

On the other hand, if the goods are entrusted to the bailee for his sole benefit, then he owes the bailor extraordinary care. For example, imagine that your neighbor asks you to let him borrow your car to go to the grocery store downtown because his car is in the shop; or a friend asks if she can borrow your party canopy.

If the bailment is for the mutual benefit of bailee and bailor, then the ordinary negligence standard of care will govern. For example, imagine you park your car in a commercial parking lot, or you take your suit jacket to a dry cleaner (see Figure 21.1).

FIGURE 21.1 Duty of Care

Bailment for	Duty of Care
1. Benefit of Owner	Slight
2. Benefit of Bailee	Extraordinary
3. Mutual Benefit	Ordinary

One problem with using the majority approach is the inherent ambiguity in the standards of care. What constitutes "gross" negligence as opposed to "ordinary" negligence? The degree-of-care approach is further complicated by the tendency of the courts to take into account the value of the goods; the lesser the value of the goods, the lesser the obligation of the bailee to watch out for them. To some degree, this approach makes sense, because it obviously behooves a person guarding diamonds to take greater precautions against theft than one holding three paperback books. But the value of the goods ought not to be the whole story: some goods obviously have great value to the owner, regardless of any lack of intrinsic value.

Another problem in using the majority approach to the standard of care is determining whether or not a benefit has been conferred on the bailee when the bailor did not expressly agree to pay compensation. For example, a bank gives its customers free access to safe-deposit boxes. Is the bank a "gratuitous bailee" that owes its bailor only a slight degree of care, or has it made the boxes available as a commercial matter to hold onto its customers? Some courts cling to one theory, some to the other, suggesting the difficulty with the tripartite division of the standard of care. However, in many cases, whatever the formal theory, the courts look to the actual benefits to be derived. Thus when a customer comes to an automobile showroom and leaves her car in the lot while she test-drives the new car, most courts would hold that two bailments for mutual benefit have been created: (1) the bailment to hold the old car in the lot, with the customer as the bailor; and (2) the bailment to try out the new car, with the customer as the bailee.

Burden of Proof

In a bailment case, the plaintiff bailor has the burden of proving that a loss was caused by the defendant bailee's failure to exercise due care. However, the bailor establishes a prima facie ("at first sight"—on first appearance, but subject to further investigation) case by showing that he delivered the goods into the bailee's hands and that the bailee did not return them or returned them damaged. At that point, a presumption of negligence arises, and to avoid liability the defendant must rebut that presumption by showing affirmatively that he was not negligent. The reason for this rule is that the bailee usually has a much better opportunity to explain why the goods were not returned or were returned damaged. To put this burden on the bailor might make it impossible for him to win a meritorious case.

Liability of the Bailor

As might be expected, most bailment cases involve the legal liability of bailees. However, a body of law on the liability of bailors has emerged.

Negligence of Bailor

A bailor may be held liable for negligence. If the bailor receives a benefit from the bailment, then he has a duty to inform the bailee of known defects and to make a reasonable inspection for other defects. Suppose the Tranquil Chemical Manufacturing Company produces an insecticide that it wants the Plattsville Chemical Storage Company to keep in tanks until it is sold. One of the batches is defectively acidic and oozes out of the tanks. This acidity could have been discovered through a routine inspection, but Tranquil neglects to inspect the batch. The tanks leak and the chemical builds up on the floor until it explodes. Since Tranquil, the bailor, received a benefit from the storage, it had a duty to warn Plattsville, and its failure to do so makes it liable for all damages caused by the explosion.

If the bailor does not receive any benefit, however, then his only duty is to inform the bailee of known defects. Your neighbor asks to borrow your car. You have a duty to tell her that the brakes are weak, but you do not need to inspect the car beforehand for unknown defects.

Other Types of Liability

The theory of products liability discussed in Chapter 20 extends to bailors. Both warranty and strict liability theories apply. The rationale for extending liability in the absence of sale is that in modern commerce, damage can be done equally by sellers or lessors of equipment. A rented car can inflict substantial injury no less than a purchased one.

In several states, when an automobile owner (bailor) lends a vehicle to a friend (bailee) who causes an accident, the owner is liable to third persons injured in the accident. This liability is discussed in Chapter 38, which covers agency law.

Disclaimers of Liability

Bailee's Disclaimer

Bailees frequently attempt to disclaim their liability for loss or damage. But courts often refuse to honor the disclaimers, usually looking to one of two justifications for invalidating them.

Lack of Notice

The disclaimer must be brought to the attention of the bailor and must be unambiguous. Thus, posted notices and receipts disclaiming or limiting liability must set forth clearly and legibly the legal effects intended. Most American courts follow the rule that the defendant bailee must show that the bailor in fact knew about the disclaimer. Language printed on the back side of a receipt will not do.

Public Policy Exception

Even if the bailor reads the disclaimer, some courts will nevertheless hold the bailee liable on public policy grounds, especially when the bailee is a "business bailee," such as a warehouse or carrier. Indeed, to the extent that a business bailee attempts to totally disclaim liability, he will probably fail in every American jurisdiction. But the Restatement (Second) of Contracts, Section 195(2)(b), does not go quite this far for most nonbusiness bailees. They may disclaim liability as long as the disclaimer is read and does not relieve the bailee from wanton carelessness.

Bailor's Disclaimer

Bailors most frequently attempt to disclaim liability in rental situations. For example, in *Zimmer v. Mitchell and Ness*, the plaintiff went to the defendant's rental shop at the Camelback ski area to rent skis, boots, and poles.[10] He signed a rental agreement before accepting the ski equipment. He was a lessee and a bailee. Later, while descending the beginners' slope, he fell. The bindings on his skis did not release, thereby causing him to sustain numerous injuries. The plaintiff sued the defendant and Camelback Ski Corporation, alleging negligence, violation of Section 402A of the Restatement (Second) of Torts, and breach of warranty. The defendant filed an answer and claimed that the plaintiff signed a rental agreement that fully released the defendant from liability. In his reply, the plaintiff admitted signing the agreement but generally denied that it released the defendant from liability. The defendant won on summary judgment.

On appeal, the Pennsylvania Supreme Court held for the defendant and set out the law: "The test for determining the validity of exculpatory clauses, admittedly not favored in the law, is set out in [Citation]. The contract must not contravene any policy of the law. It must be a contract between individuals relating to their private affairs. Each party must be a free bargaining agent, not simply one drawn into an adhesion contract, with no recourse but to reject the entire transaction. We must construe the agreement strictly and against the party asserting it [and], the agreement must spell out the intent of the parties with the utmost particularity." The court here was satisfied with the disclaimer.

Other Rights and Duties

Compensation

If the bailor hires the bailee to perform services for the bailed property, then the bailee is entitled to compensation. Remember, however, that not every bailment is necessarily for compensation. The difficult question is whether the bailee is entitled to compensation when nothing explicit has been said about incidental expenses he has incurred to care for the bailed property—as, for example, if he were to repair a piece of machinery to keep it running. No firm rule can be given. Perhaps the best generalization that can be made is that, in the absence of an express agreement, ordinary repairs fall to the bailee to pay, but extraordinary repairs are the bailor's responsibility. An express agreement between the parties detailing the responsibilities would solve the problem, of course.

Bailee's Lien

lien

An encumbrance upon property to secure payment.

mechanic's lien

A claim allowed to one who furnishes labor, services, or materials to improve property.

Lien is from the French, originally meaning "line," "string," or "tie." In law a **lien** is the hold that someone has over the property of another. It is akin, in effect, to a security interest. A common type is the **mechanic's lien** ("mechanic" here means one who works with his or her hands). For example, a carpenter builds a room on your house and you fail to pay him; he can secure a lien on your house, meaning that he has a property interest in the house and can start foreclosure proceedings if you still fail to pay. Similarly, a bailee is said to have a lien on the bailed property in his possession and need not redeliver it to the bailor until he has been paid. Try to take your car out of a parking lot without paying and see what happens. The attendant's refusal to give you the car is entirely lawful under a common-law rule now more than a century and a half old. As the rule is usually stated, the common law confers the lien on the bailee if he has added value to the property through his labor, skill, or materials. But that statement of the rule is somewhat deceptive, since the person who has simply housed the goods is entitled to a lien, as is a person who has altered or repaired the goods without measurably adding value to them. Perhaps a better way of stating the rule is this: a lien is created when the bailee performs some special benefit to the goods (e.g., preserving them or repairing them).

Many states have enacted statutes governing various types of liens. In many instances, these have broadened the bailee's common-law rights. This book discusses two types of liens in great detail: the liens of warehousemen and those of common carriers. Recall that a *lease* creates a type of bailment: the lessor is the bailor and the lessee is the bailee. This book references the UCC's take on leasing in its discussion of the sale of goods.[11]

Rights When Goods Are Taken or Damaged by a Third Party

The general rule is that the bailee can recover damages in full if the bailed property is damaged or taken by a third party, but he must account in turn to the bailor. A delivery service is carrying parcels—bailed goods entrusted to the trucker for delivery—when the truck is struck from behind and blows up. The carrier may sue the third person who caused the accident and recover for the total loss, including the value of the packages. The bailor may also recover for damages to the parcels, but not if the bailee has already recovered a judgment. Suppose the bailee has sued and lost. Does the bailor have a right to sue independently on the same grounds? Ordinarily, the principle of res judicata would prevent a second suit, but if the bailor did not know of and cooperate in the bailee's suit, she probably has the right to proceed on his own suit.

Innkeepers' Liability

The liability of an innkeeper—a type of bailor—is thought to have derived from the warlike conditions that prevailed in medieval England, where brigands and bandits roamed the countryside and the innkeeper himself might not have been above stealing from his guests. The innkeeper's liability extended not merely to loss of goods through negligence. His was an insurer's liability, extending to any loss, no matter how occasioned, and even to losses that occurred in the guest's room, a place where the guest had the primary right of possession. The only exception was for losses due to the guest's own negligence.

Most states have enacted statutes providing exceptions to this extraordinarily broad common-law duty. Typically, the statutes exempt the hotel keeper from insurer's liability if the hotelier furnishes a safe in which the guests can leave their jewels, money, and other valuables and if a notice is posted a notice advising the guests of the safe's availability. The hotelier might face liability for valuables lost or stolen from the safe but not from the rooms.

Key Takeaway

If the bailee fails to redeliver the goods to the bailor, a presumption of negligence arises, but the bailee can rebut the presumption by showing that she exercised appropriate care. What is "appropriate care" depends on the test used in the jurisdiction: some courts use the "ordinary care under the circumstances," and some determine how much care the bailee should have exercised based on the extent to which she was benefited from the transaction compared to the bailor. The bailor can be liable too for negligently delivering goods likely to cause damage to the bailee. In either case reasonable disclaimers of liability are allowed. If the bailed goods need repair while in the bailee's possession, the usual rule is that ordinary repairs are the bailee's responsibility, extraordinary ones the bailor's. Bailees are entitled to liens to enforce payment owing to them. In common law, innkeepers were insurers of their guests' property, but hotels and motels today are governed mostly by statute: they are to provide a safe for their guests' valuables and are not liable for losses from the room.

Exercises

1. What is the "ordinary care under the circumstances" test for a bailee's liability when the bailed goods are not returned?
2. What is the tripartite test?

3. What liability does a bailor have for delivering defective goods to a bailee?
4. Under what circumstances are disclaimers of liability by the bailee or bailor acceptable?
5. Jason takes his Ford Mustang to a repair shop but fails to pay for the repairs. On what theory can the shop keep and eventually sell the car to secure payment?

21.3 The Storage and Shipping of Goods

Learning Objectives

1. Understand a warehouser's liability for losing goods, what types of losses a warehouser is liable for, and what rights the warehouser has concerning the goods.
2. Know the duties, liabilities, and exceptions to liability a carrier of freight has, and what rights the carrier has.
3. Understand the liability that is imposed on entities whose business it is to carry passengers.

Storage of Goods

Warehousing has been called the "second oldest profession," stemming from the biblical story of Joseph, who stored grain during the seven good years against the famine of the seven bad years. Whatever its origins, warehousing is today a big business, taking in billions of dollars to stockpile foods and other goods. As noted previously, the source of law governing warehousing is Article 7 of the UCC, but noncode law also can apply. Section 7-103 of the Uniform Commercial Code (UCC) specifically provides that any federal statute or treaty and any state regulation or tariff supersedes the provisions of Article 7. A federal example is the United States Warehouse Act, which governs receipts for stored agricultural products. Here we take up, after some definitions, the warehouser's liabilities and rights. A warehouser is a special type of bailee.

Definitions

warehouser

One whose business it is to store goods.

warehouse receipt

A written document for items warehoused, serving as evidence of title to the stored goods.

A **warehouser** is defined in UCC, Section 7-102(h), as "a person engaged in the business of storing goods for hire," and under Section 1-201(45) a **warehouse receipt** is any receipt issued by a warehouser. The warehouse receipt is an important document because it can be used to transfer title to the goods, even while they remain in storage: it is worth money. No form is prescribed for the warehouse receipt, but unless it lists in its terms the following nine items, the warehouser is liable to anyone who is injured by the omission of any of them:

1. Location of the warehouse
2. Date receipt was issued
3. Consecutive number of the receipt
4. Statement whether the goods will be delivered to bearer, to a specified person, or "to a specified person or his order"
5. The rate of storage and handling charges
6. Description of the goods or the packages containing them
7. Signature of the warehouser, which his or her authorized agent may make

8. The warehouser's ownership of the goods, if he or she has a sole or part ownership in them
9. The amount (if known, otherwise the fact) of advances made and liabilities incurred for which the warehouser claims a lien or security interest

General Duty of Care

The warehouser's general duty of care is embodied in the tort standard for measuring negligence: he is liable for any losses or injury to the goods caused by his failure to exercise "such care in regard to them as a reasonably careful man would exercise under like circumstances."[12] However, subsection 4 declares that this section does not repeal or dilute any other state statute that imposes a higher responsibility on a warehouser. Nor does the section invalidate contractual limitations otherwise permissible under Article 7. The warehouser's duty of care under this section is considerably weaker than the carrier's duty. Determining when a warehouser becomes a carrier, if the warehouser is to act as shipper, can become an important issue.

Limitation of Liability

The warehouser may limit the amount of damages she will pay by so stating in the warehouse receipt, but she must strictly observe that section's requirements, under which the limitation must be stated "per article or item, or value per unit of weight."[13] Moreover, the warehouser cannot force the bailor to accept this limitation: the bailor may demand in writing increased liability, in which event the warehouser may charge more for the storage. If the warehouser converts the goods to her own UCC, the limitation of liability does not apply.

Specific Types of Liability and Duties

Several problems recur in warehousing, and the law addresses them.

Nonreceipt or Misdescription

Under UCC Section 7-203, a warehouser is responsible for goods listed in a warehouse receipt that were not in fact delivered to the warehouse (or were misdescribed) and must pay damages to a good-faith purchaser of or party to a document of title. To avoid this liability, the issuer must conspicuously note on the document that he does not know whether the goods were delivered or are correctly described. One simple way is to mark on the receipt that "contents, condition, and quality are unknown."

Delivery to the Wrong Party

The bailee is obligated to deliver the goods to any person with documents that entitle him to possession, as long as the claimant pays any outstanding liens and surrenders the document so that it can be marked "cancelled" (or can be partially cancelled in the case of partial delivery). The bailee can avoid liability for no delivery by showing that he delivered the goods to someone with a claim to possession superior to that of the claimant, that the goods were lost or destroyed through no fault of the bailee, or that certain other lawful excuses apply.[14] Suppose a thief deposits goods he has stolen with a warehouse. Discovering the theft, the warehouser turns the goods over to the rightful owner. A day later the thief arrives with a receipt and demands delivery. Because the rightful owner had the superior claim, the warehouser is not liable in damages to the thief.

Now suppose you are moving and have placed your goods with a local storage company. A few weeks later, you accidentally drop your wallet, which contains the receipt for the goods and all your identification. A thief picks up the wallet and immediately heads for the warehouse, pretending to be you. Having no suspicion that anything is amiss—it's a large place and no one can be expected to remember what you look like—the warehouse releases the goods to the thief. This time you are probably out of luck. Section 7-404 says that "a bailee who in good faith including observance of reasonable commercial standards has received goods and delivered...them according to the terms of the document of title...is not liable." This rule is true even though the person to whom he made delivery had no authority to receive them, as in the case of the thief. However, if the warehouser had a suspicion and failed to take precautions, then he might be liable to the true owner.

Duty to Keep Goods Separate

Except for fungible goods, like grain, the warehouse must keep separate goods covered by each warehouse receipt. The purpose of this rule, which may be negated by explicit language in the receipt, is to permit the bailor to identify and take delivery of his goods at any time.

Rights of the Warehouser

The warehouser has certain rights concerning the bailed goods.

Termination

A warehouser is not obligated to store goods indefinitely. Many warehouse receipts will specify the period of storage. At the termination of the period, the warehouser may notify the bailor to pay and to recover her goods. If no period is fixed in the receipt or other document of title, the warehouser may give notice to pay and remove within no less than thirty days. The bailor's failure to pay and remove permits the warehouser to sell the goods for her fee. Suppose the goods begin to deteriorate. Sections 7-207(2) and 7-207(3) of the UCC permit the warehouser to sell the goods early if necessary to recover the full amount of her lien or if the goods present a hazard. But if the rightful owner demands delivery before such a sale, the warehouser is obligated to do so.

Liens

Section 7-209(1) of the UCC provides that a warehouser has a lien on goods covered by a warehouse receipt to recover the following charges and expenses: charges for storage or transportation, insurance, labor, and expenses necessary to preserve the goods. The lien is not discharged if the bailor transfers his property interest in the goods by negotiating a warehouse receipt to a purchaser in good faith, although the warehouser is limited then to an amount or a rate fixed in the receipt or to a reasonable amount or rate if none was stated. The lien attaches automatically and need not be spelled out in the warehouse receipt.

The warehouser may enforce the lien by selling the goods at a public or private sale, as long as she does so in a commercially reasonable manner, as defined in Section 7-210. All parties known to be claiming an interest in the goods must be notified of the sale and told the amount due, the nature of the sale, and its time and place. Any person who in good faith purchases the goods takes them free of any claim by the bailor, even if the warehouser failed to comply with the requirements of Section 7-210. However, her failure to comply subjects her to damages, and if she has willfully violated the provisions of this section she is liable to the bailor for conversion.

Shipment of Goods

Introduction and Terminology

The shipment of goods throughout the United States and abroad is a very big business, and many specialized companies have been established to undertake it, including railways, air cargo operations, trucking companies, and ocean carriers. Article 7 of the UCC applies to carriage of goods as it does to warehousing, but federal law is more important. The Federal Bill of Lading Act (FBLA) covers bills of lading issued by common carriers for transportation of goods in interstate or foreign commerce (i.e., from one state to another; in federal territory; or to foreign countries). The Carmack Amendment was enacted in 1906 as an amendment to the Interstate Commerce Act of 1887, and it is now part of the Interstate Commerce Commission Termination Act of 1995; it covers liability of interstate carriers for loss, destruction, and damage to goods. The **shipper** is the entity hiring the one who transports the goods: if you send your sister crystal goblets for her birthday, you are the shipper.

shipper

One who engages the services of a carrier.

Two terms are particularly important in discussing shipment of goods. One is common carrier; the **common carrier** is "one who undertakes for hire or reward to transport the goods of such as chooses to employ him, from place to place."[15] This definition contains three elements: (1) the carrier must hold itself out for all in common for hire—the business is not restricted to particular customers but is open to all who apply for its services; (2) it must charge for his services—it is for hire; (3) the service in question must be carriage. Included within this tripartite definition are numerous types of carriers: household moving companies, taxicabs, towing companies, and even oil and gas pipelines. Note that to be a common carrier it is not necessary to be in the business of carrying every type of good to every possible point; common carriers may limit the types of goods or the places to which they will transport them.

common carrier

A carrier that holds itself open to any member of the public for a fee.

A **bill of lading** is any document that evidences "the receipt of goods for shipment issued by a person engaged in the business of transporting or forwarding goods."[16] This is a comprehensive definition and includes documents used by contract carriers—that is, carriers who are not common carriers. An example of a bill of lading is depicted in Figure 21.2.

bill of lading

A document of title acknowledging receipt of goods by a carrier.

FIGURE 21.2 A Bill of Lading Form

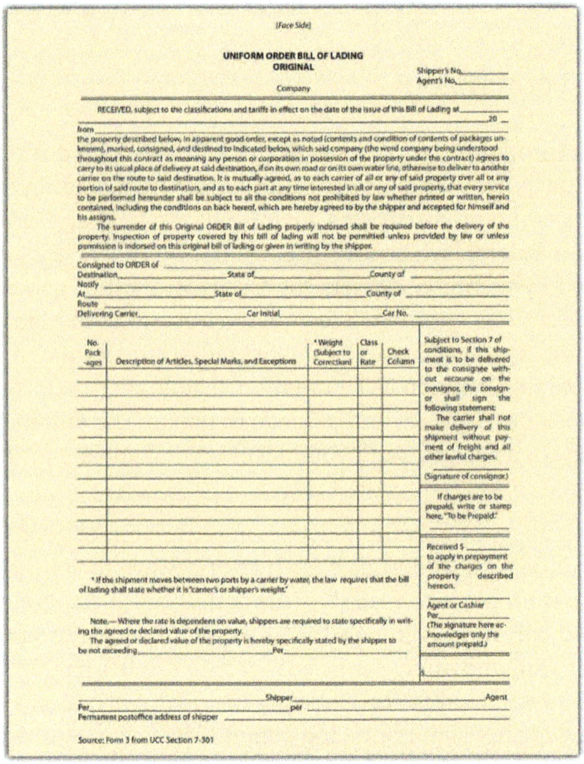

(Face Side)

UNIFORM ORDER BILL OF LADING
ORIGINAL

Shipper's No.________
Agent's No.________

Company

RECEIVED, subject to the classifications and tariffs in effect on the date of the issue of this Bill of Lading at________ 20 __

from________

the property described below, in apparent good order, except as noted (contents and condition of contents of packages unknown), marked, consigned, and destined to indicated below, which said company (the word company being understood throughout this contract as meaning any person or corporation in possession of the property under the contract) agrees to carry to its usual place of delivery at said destination, if on its own road or on its own water line, otherwise to deliver to another carrier on the route to said destination. It is mutually agreed, as to each carrier of all or any of said property over all or any portion of said route to destination, and as to each part at any time interested in all or any of said property, that every service to be performed hereunder shall be subject to all the conditions not prohibited by law whether printed or written, herein contained, including the conditions on back hereof, which are hereby agreed to by the shipper and accepted for himself and his assigns.

The surrender of this Original ORDER Bill of Lading properly indorsed shall be required before the delivery of the property. Inspection of property covered by this bill of lading will not be permitted unless provided by law or unless permission is indorsed on this original bill of lading or given in writing by the shipper.

Consigned to ORDER of ________
Destination________ State of________ County of ________
Notify ________
At________ State of________ County of ________
Route ________
Delivering Carrier________ Car Initial________ Car No. ________

No. Packages	Description of Articles, Special Marks, and Exceptions	*Weight (Subject to Correction)	Class or Rate	Check Column

Subject to Section 7 of conditions, if this shipment is to be delivered to the consignee without recourse on the consignor, the consignor shall sign the following statement:

The carrier shall not make delivery of this shipment without payment of freight and all other lawful charges.

(Signature of consignor.)

If charges are to be prepaid, write or stamp here, "To be Prepaid."

Received $________ to apply in prepayment of the charges on the property described hereon.

Agent or Cashier
Per________
(The signature here acknowledges only the amount prepaid.)

$________

*If the shipment moves between two ports by a carrier by water, the law requires that the bill of lading shall state whether it is "carrier's or shipper's weight."

Note.—Where the rate is dependent on value, shippers are required to state specifically in writing the agreed or declared value of the property.

The agreed or declared value of the property is hereby specifically stated by the shipper to be not exceeding________ Per________

________ Shipper________ Agent
Per________ per ________
Permanent postoffice address of shipper ________

Source: Form 3 from UCC Section 7-301

Duties and Liabilities

The transportation of goods has been an important part of all evolved economic systems for a long time, and certainly it is critical to the development and operation of any capitalistic system. The law regarding it is well developed.

Absolute Liability

Damage, destruction, and loss are major hazards of transportation for which the carrier will be liable. Who will assert the claim against the carrier depends on who bears the risk of loss. The rules governing risk of loss (examined in Chapter 18) determine whether the buyer or seller will be the plaintiff. But whoever is the plaintiff, the common carrier defendant faces absolute liability. With five exceptions explored two paragraphs on, the common carrier is an insurer of goods, and regardless of the cause of damage or loss—that is, whether or not the carrier was negligent—it must make the owner whole. This ancient common-law rule is codified in state law, in the federal Carmack Amendment, and in the UCC, Section 7-309(1), all of which hold the common carrier to absolute liability to the extent that the common law of the state had previously done so.

Absolute liability was imposed in the early cases because the judges believed such a rule was necessary to prevent carriers from conspiring with thieves. Since it is difficult for the owner, who was not on the scene, to prove exactly what happened, the judges reasoned that putting the burden of loss on the carrier would prompt him to take extraordinary precautions against loss (and would certainly preclude him from colluding with thieves). Note that the rules in this section govern only common carriers; contract carriers that do not hold themselves out for transport for hire are liable as ordinary bailees.

Exceptions to Absolute Liability

In general, the burden or proof rests on the carrier in favor of the shipper. The shipper (or consignee of the shipper) can make out a prima facie case by showing that it delivered the goods to the carrier in good condition and that the goods either did not arrive or arrived damaged in a specified amount. Thereafter the carrier has the burden of proving that it was not negligent and that the loss or damage was caused by one of the five following recognized exceptions to the rule of absolute liability.

Act of God

No one has ever succeeded in defining precisely what constitutes an act of God, but the courts seem generally agreed that it encompasses acts that are of sudden and extraordinary natural, as opposed to human, origin. Examples of acts of God are earthquakes, hurricanes, and fires caused by lightning against which the carrier could not have protected itself. Rapid River Carriers contracts to transport a refrigerated cargo of beef down the Mississippi River on the SS *Rapid*. When the ship is en route, it is hit by a tornado and sinks. This is an act of God. But a contributing act of negligence by a carrier overcomes the act of God exception. If it could be shown that the captain was negligent to set sail when the weather warned of imminent tornadoes, the carrier might be liable.

Act of Public Enemy

This is a narrow exception that applies only to acts committed by pirates at high sea or by the armed forces of enemies of the state to which the carrier owes allegiance. American ships at sea that are sunk during wartime by enemy torpedoes would not be liable for losses to the owners of cargo. Moreover, public enemies do not include lawless mobs or criminals listed on the FBI's Ten Most Wanted list, even if federal troops are required, as in the Pullman Strike of 1894, to put down the violence. After the Pullman Strike, carriers were held liable for property destroyed by violent strikers.

Act of Public Authority

When a public authority—a sheriff or federal marshal, for example—through lawful process seizes goods in the carrier's possession, the carrier is excused from liability. Imagine that federal agents board the SS *Rapid* in New Orleans and, as she is about to sail, show the captain a search warrant and seize several boxes of cargo marked "beef" that turn out to hold cocaine. The owner or consignee of this illegal cargo will not prevail in a suit against the carrier to recover damages. Likewise, if the rightful owner of the goods obtains a lawful court order permitting him to attach them, the carrier is obligated to permit the goods to be taken. It is not the carrier's responsibility to contest a judicial writ or to face the consequences of resisting a court order. The courts generally agree that the carrier must notify the owner whenever goods are seized.

Act of Shipper

When goods are lost or damaged because of the shipper's negligence, the shipper is liable, not the carrier. The usual situation under this exception arises from defective packing. The shipper who packs the goods defectively is responsible for breakage unless the defect is apparent and the carrier accepts the goods anyway. For example, if you ship your sister crystal goblets packed loosely in the box, they will inevitably be broken when driven in trucks along the highways. The trucker who knowingly accepts boxes in this condition is liable for the damage. Likewise, the carrier's negligence will overcome the exception and make him absolutely liable. A paper supplier ships several bales of fine stationery in thin cardboard boxes susceptible to moisture. Knowing their content, SS *Rapid* accepts the bales and exposes them to the elements on the upper deck. A rainstorm curdles the stationery. The carrier is liable.

Inherent Nature of the Goods

The fifth exception to the rule of absolute liability is rooted in the nature of the goods themselves. If they are inherently subject to deterioration or their inherent characteristics are such that they might be destroyed, then the loss must lie on the owner. Common examples are chemicals that can explode spontaneously and perishable fruits and vegetables. Of course, the carrier is responsible for seeing that foodstuffs are properly stored and cared for, but if they deteriorate naturally and not through the carrier's negligence, it is not liable.

Which Carrier Is Liable?

The transportation system is complex, and few goods travel from portal to portal under the care of one carrier only. In the nineteenth century, the shipper whose goods were lost had a difficult time recovering their value. Initial carriers blamed the loss on subsequent carriers, and even if the shipper could determine which carrier actually had possession of the goods when the damage or loss occurred, diverse state laws made proof burdensome. The Carmack Amendment ended the considerable confusion by placing the burden on the initial carrier; connecting carriers are deemed agents of the initial carrier. So the plaintiff, whether seller or buyer, need sue only the initial carrier, no matter where the loss occurred. Likewise, Section 7-302 of the UCC fastens liability on an initial carrier for damages or loss caused by connecting carriers.

When Does Carrier Liability Begin and End?

When a carrier's liability begins and ends is an important issue because the same company can act both to store the goods and to carry them. The carrier's liability is more stringent than the warehouser's. So the question is, when does a warehouser become a carrier and vice versa?

The basic test for the beginning of carrier liability is whether the shipper must take further action or give further instructions to the carrier before its duty to transport arises. Suppose that Cotton Picking Associates delivers fifty bales of cotton to Rapid River Carriers for transport on the SS *Rapid*. The SS *Rapid* is not due back to port for two more days, so Rapid River Carrier stores the cotton in its warehouse, and on the following day the warehouse is struck by lightning and burns to the ground. Is Rapid River Carriers liable in its capacity as a carrier or warehouse? Since nothing was left for the owner to do, and Rapid River was storing the cotton for its own convenience awaiting the ship's arrival, it was acting as a carrier and is liable for the loss. Now suppose that when Cotton Picking Associates delivered the fifty bales it said that another fifty bales would be coming in a week and the entire lot was to be shipped together. Rapid River stores the first fifty bales and lightning strikes. Since more remained for Cotton Picking to do before Rapid River was obligated to ship, the carrier was acting in its warehousing capacity and is not liable.

The carrier's absolute liability ends when it has delivered the goods to the consignee's residence or place of business, unless the agreement states otherwise (as it often does). By custom, certain carriers—notably rail carriers and carriers by water—are not required to deliver the goods to the consignee (since rail lines and oceans do not take the carrier to the consignee's door). Instead, consignees must take delivery at the dock or some other place mutually agreed on or established by custom.

When the carrier must make personal delivery to the consignee, carrier liability continues until the carrier has made reasonable efforts to deliver. An express trucking company cannot call on a corporate customer on Sunday or late at night, for instance. If reasonable efforts to deliver fail, it may store the goods in its own warehouse, in which case its liability reverts to that of a warehouser.

If personal delivery is not required (e.g., as in shipment by rail), the states use different approaches for determining when the carrier's liability terminates. The most popular intrastate approach provides that the carrier continues to be absolutely responsible for the goods until the consignee has been notified of their arrival and has had a reasonable opportunity to take possession of them.

Interstate shipments are governed by the Carmack Amendment, which generally provides that liability will be determined by language in the bill of lading. The typical bill of lading (or "BOL" and "B/L") provides that if the consignee does not take the goods within a stated period of time after receiving notice of their arrival, the carrier will be liable as warehouser only.

Disclaimers

The apparently draconian liability of the carrier—as an insurer of the goods—is in practice easily minimized. Under neither federal nor state law may the carrier disclaim its absolute liability, but at least as to commercial transactions it may limit the damages payable under certain circumstances. Both the Carmack Amendment and Section 7-309 of the UCC permit the carrier to set alternate tariffs, one costing the shipper more and paying full value, the other costing less and limited to a dollar per pound or some other rate less than full value. The shipper must have a choice; the carrier may not impose a lesser tariff unilaterally on the shipper, and the loss must not be occasioned by the carrier's own negligence.

Specific Types of Liability

The rules just discussed relate to the general liability of the carrier for damages to the goods. There are two specific types of liability worth noting.

Nonreceipt or Misdescription

Under the UCC, Section 7-301(1), the owner of the goods (e.g., a consignee) described in a bill of lading may recover damages from the issuer of the bill (the carrier) if the issuer did not actually receive the goods from the shipper, if the goods were misdescribed, or if the bill was misdated. The issuer may avoid liability by reciting in the bill of lading that she does not know whether the goods were received or if they conform to the description; the issuer may avoid liability also by marking the goods with such words as "contents or condition of contents unknown." Even this qualifying language may be ineffective. For instance, a common carrier may not hide behind language indicating that the description was given by the shipper; the carrier must actually count the packages of goods or ascertain the kind and quantity of bulk freight. Just because the carrier is liable to the consignee for errors in description does not mean that the shipper is free from blame. Section 7-301(5) requires the shipper to indemnify the carrier if the shipper has inaccurately described the goods in any way (including marks, labels, number, kind, quantity, condition, and weight).

Delivery to the Wrong Party

The rule just discussed for warehouser applies to carriers under both state and federal law: carriers are absolutely liable for delivering the goods to the wrong party. In the classic case of *Southern Express Co. v. C. L. Ruth & Son*, a clever imposter posed as the representative of a reputable firm and tricked the carrier into delivering a diamond ring.[17] The court held the carrier liable, even though the carrier was not negligent and there was no collusion. The UCC contains certain exceptions; under Section 7-303(1), the carrier is immune from liability if the holder, the consignor, or (under certain circumstances) the consignee gives instructions to deliver the goods to someone other than a person named in the bill of lading.

Carrier's Right to Lien and Enforcement of Lien

Just as the warehouser can have a lien, so too can the carrier. The lien can cover charges for storage, transportation, and preservation of goods. When someone has purchased a negotiable bill of lading, the lien is limited to charges stated in the bill, allowed under applicable tariffs, or, if none are stated, to a reasonable charge. A carrier who voluntarily delivers or unjustifiably refuses to deliver the goods loses its lien. The carrier has rights paralleling those of the warehouser to enforce the lien.

Passengers

In addition to shipping goods, common carriers also transport passengers and their baggage. The carrier owes passengers a high degree of care; in 1880 the Supreme Court described the standard as "the utmost caution characteristic of very careful prudent men."[18] This duty implies liability for a host of injuries, including mental distress occasioned by insults ("lunatic," "whore," "cheap, common scalawag") and by profane or indecent language. In *Werndli v. Greyhound*,[19] Mrs. Werndli deboarded the bus at her destination at 2:30 a.m.; finding the bus station closed, she walked some distance to find a bathroom. While doing so, she became the victim of an assault. The court held Greyhound liable: it should have known the station was closed at 2:30 a.m. and that it was located in a area that became dangerous after hours. The case illustrates the degree to which a carrier is responsible for its passengers' safety and comfort.

The baggage carrier is liable as an insurer unless the baggage is not in fact delivered to the carrier. A passenger who retains control over his hand luggage by taking it with him to his seat has not delivered the baggage to the carrier, and hence the carrier has no absolute liability for its loss or destruction. The carrier remains liable for negligence, however. When the passenger does deliver his luggage to the carrier, the question often arises whether the property so delivered is "baggage." If it is not, the carrier does not have an insurer's liability toward it. Thus, a person who transports household goods in a suitcase would not have given the carrier "baggage," as that term is usually defined (i.e., something transported for the passenger's personal use or convenience). At most, the carrier would be responsible for the goods as a gratuitous bailee.

Key Takeaway

The storage of goods is a special type of bailment. People who store goods can retrieve them or transfer ownership of them by transferring possession of the warehouse receipt: whoever has rightful possession of the receipt can take the goods, and the warehouser is liable for misdelivery or for mixing up goods. The warehouser has a right to a lien to secure his fee, enforceable by selling the goods in a commercially reasonable way. The shipping of goods is of course an important business. Common carriers (those firms that hire out their trucks, airplanes, ships, or trains to carry cargo) are strictly liable to ensure the proper arrival of the goods to their destination, with five exceptions (act of God, public enemy, public authority, shipper; inherent nature of the goods); the first carrier to receive them is liable—others who subsequently carry are that carrier's agents. The carrier may also store goods: if it does so for its own convenience it is liable as a carrier; if it does so for the shipper's convenience, it is liable as a warehouser. As with warehousers, the carrier is liable for misdelivery and is entitled to a lien to enforce payment. Carriers also carry people, and the standard of care they owe to passengers is very high. Carrying passengers' baggage, the carrier is liable as an insurer—it is strictly liable.

Exercises

1. How are warehousers any different from the more generic bailees?
2. How do the duties and liabilities of warehousers differ from those of carriers?
3. What rights do warehousers and carriers have to ensure their payment?
4. May a carrier limit its liability for losses not its fault?

21.4 Negotiation and Transfer of Documents of Title (or Commodity Paper)

Learning Objectives

1. Understand how commodity paper operates in the sale of goods.
2. Recognize when the transferee of a properly negotiated document of title gets better rights than her transferor had and the exceptions to this principle.

Overview of Negotiability

We have discussed in several places the concept of a **document of title** (also called **commodity paper**). That is a written description, identification, or declaration of goods authorizing the holder—usually a bailee—to receive, hold, and dispose of the document and the goods it covers. Examples of documents of title are warehouse receipts, bills of lading, and delivery orders. The document of title, properly negotiated (delivered), gives its holder ownership of the goods it represents. It is much easier to pass around a piece of paper representing the ownership interest in goods than it is to pass around the goods themselves.

document of title

A written description of goods authorizing its holder to have them.

commodity paper

A loan or cash advance secured by commodities, bills of lading, or warehouse receipts.

It is a basic feature of our legal system that a person cannot transfer more rights to property than he owns. It would follow here that no holder of a document of title has greater rights in the goods than the holder's transferor—the one from whom she got the document (and thus the goods). But there are certain exceptions to this rule; for example, Chapter 17 discusses the power of a merchant in certain circumstances to transfer title to goods, even though the merchant himself did not have title to them. A critically important exception to the general rule arises when certain types of paper are sold. Chapter 23 discusses this rule as it relates to commercial paper such as checks and notes. To conclude this chapter, we discuss the rule as it applies to documents of title, sometimes known as commodity paper.

The Elements and Effect of Negotiation

If a document of title is "negotiable" and is "duly negotiated," the purchaser can obtain rights greater than those of the storer or shipper. In the following discussion, we refer only to the Uniform Commercial Code (UCC), although federal law also distinguishes between negotiable and nonnegotiable documents of title (some of the technical details in the federal law may differ, but these are beyond the scope of this book).

Negotiable Defined

Any document of title, including a warehouse receipt and a bill of lading, is negotiable or becomes negotiable if by its terms the goods are to be delivered "to bearer or to the order of" a named person.[20] All other documents of title are nonnegotiable. Suppose a bill of lading says that the goods are consigned to Tom Thumb but that they may not be delivered unless Tom signs a written order that they be delivered. Under Section 7-104(2), that is not a negotiable document of title. A negotiable document of title must bear words such as "Deliver to the bearer" or "deliver to the order of Tom Thumb." These are the "magic words" that create a negotiable document.

Duly Negotiated

duly negotiated

The transfer of commercial paper to a legitimate transferee, usually by indorsement.

bearer paper

A negotiable instrument payable to whoever has possession.

holder

One who has legal possession of a negotiable instrument and who is entitled to payment.

To transfer title effectively through **negotiation** of the document of title, it must be "duly negotiated." In general terms, under Section 7-501 of the UCC, a negotiable document of title is **duly negotiated** when the person named in it indorses (signs it over—literally "on the back of") and delivers it to a holder who purchases it in good faith and for value, without any notice that someone else might have a claim against the goods, assuming the transaction is in the regular course of business or financing. Note that last part: assuming the transaction is in the regular course of business. If you gave your roommate a negotiable document of title in payment for a car you bought from her, your roommate would have something of value, but it would not have been duly negotiated. Paper made out "to bearer" (**bearer paper**) is negotiated by delivery alone; no indorsement is needed. A **holder** is anyone who possesses a document of title that is drawn to his order, indorsed to him, or made out "to bearer."

Effect

As a general rule, if these requirements are not met, the transferee acquires only those rights that the transferor had and nothing more. And if a nonnegotiable document is sold, the buyer's rights may be defeated. For example, a creditor of the transferor might be entitled to treat the sale as void.

Under Section 7-502 of the UCC, however, if the document is duly negotiated, then the holder acquires (1) title to the document, (2) title to the goods, (3) certain rights to the goods delivered to the bailee after the document itself was issued, and (4) the right to have the issuer of the document of title hold the goods or deliver the goods free of any defense or claim by the issuer.

To contrast the difference between sale of goods and negotiation of the document of title, consider the plight of Lucy, the owner of presidential campaign pins and other political memorabilia. Lucy plans to hold them for ten years and then sell them for many times their present value. She does not have the room in her cramped apartment to keep them, so she crates them up and takes them to a friend for safekeeping. The friend gives her a receipt that says simply: "Received from Lucy, five cartons; to be stored for ten years at $25 per year." Although a document of title, the receipt is not negotiable. Two years later, a browser happens on Lucy's crates, discovers their contents, and offers the friend $1,000 for them. Figuring Lucy will forget all about them, the friend sells them. As it happens, Lucy comes by a week later to check on her memorabilia, discovers what her former friend has done, and sues the browser for their return. Lucy would prevail. Now suppose instead that the friend, who has authority from Lucy to store the goods, takes the cartons to the Trusty Storage Company, receives a negotiable warehouse receipt ("deliver to bearer five cartons"), and then negotiates the receipt. This time Lucy would be out of luck. The bona fide purchaser from her friend would cut off Lucy's right to recover the goods, even though the friend never had good title to them.

A major purpose of the concept is to allow banks and other creditors to loan money with the right to the goods as represented on the paper as collateral. They can, in effect, accept the paper as collateral without fear that third parties will make some claim on the goods.

But even if the requirements of negotiability are met, the document of title still will confer no rights in certain cases. For example, when a thief forges the indorsement of the owner, who held negotiable warehouse receipts, the bona fide purchaser from the thief does not obtain good title. Only if the receipts were in bearer form would the purchaser prevail in a suit by the owner. Likewise, if the owner brought his goods to a repair shop that warehoused them without any authority and then sold the negotiable receipts received for them, the owner would prevail over the subsequent purchaser.

Another instance in which an apparent negotiation of a document of title will not give the bona fide purchaser superior rights occurs when a term in the document is altered without authorization. But if blanks are filled in without authority, the rule states different consequences for bills of lading and warehouse receipts. Under Section 7-306 of the UCC, any unauthorized filling in of a blank in a bill of lading leaves the bill enforceable only as it was originally. However, under Section 7-208, an unauthorized filling in of a blank in a warehouse receipt permits the good-faith purchaser with no notice that authority was lacking to treat the insertion as authorized, thus giving him good title. This section makes it dangerous for a warehouser to issue a receipt with blanks in it, because she will be liable for any losses to the owner if a good-faith purchaser takes the goods.

Finally, note that a purchaser of a document of title who is unable to get his hands on the goods—perhaps the document was forged—might have a breach of warranty action against the seller of the document. Under Section 7-507 of the UCC, a person who negotiates a document of title warrants to his immediate purchaser that the document is genuine, that he has no knowledge of any facts that would impair its validity, and that the negotiation is rightful and effective. Thus the purchaser of a forged warehouse receipt would not be entitled to recover the goods but could sue his transferor for breach of the warranty.

Key Takeaway

It is a lot easier to move pieces of paper around than goods in warehouses. Therefore commercial paper, or commodity paper, was invented: the paper represents the goods, and the paper is transferred from one person to another by negotiation. The holder signs on the back of the paper and indicates who its next holder should be (or foolishly leaves that blank); that person then has rights to the goods and, indeed, better rights. On due negotiation the transferee does not merely stand in the transferor's shoes: the transferee takes free of defects and defenses that could have been available against the transferor. For a document of title to be a negotiable one, it must indicate that the intention of it is that it should be passed on through commerce, with the words "to bearer" or "to the order of [somebody]," and it must be duly negotiated: signed off on by its previous holder (or without any signature needed if it was bearer paper).

Exercises

1. "George Baker deposited five cardboard boxes in my barn's loft, and he can pick them up when he wants." Is this statement a negotiable document of title?
2. "George Baker deposited five cardboard boxes in my barn's loft, and he or anybody to his order can pick them up." Is this statement a negotiable document of title?
3. Why is the concept of being a holder of duly negotiated documents of title important?

21.5 Cases

Bailments and Disclaimers of Bailee's Liability

Carr v. Hoosier Photo Supplies, Inc.

441 N.E.2d 450 (Ind. 1982)

Givan, J.

Litigation in this cause began with the filing of a complaint in Marion Municipal Court by John R. Carr, Jr. (hereinafter "Carr"), seeking damages in the amount of $10,000 [about $62,000 in 2016 dollars] from defendants Hoosier Photo Supplies, Inc. (hereinafter "Hoosier") and Eastman Kodak Company (hereinafter "Kodak"). Carr was the beneficiary of a judgment in the amount of $1,013.60 [about $6,200 in 2017 dollars]. Both sides appealed. The Court of Appeals affirmed the trial court in its entirety.

The facts were established by stipulation agreement between the parties and thus are not in dispute. In the late spring or early summer of 1970, Carr purchased some Kodak film from a retailer not a party to this action, including four rolls of Kodak Ektachrome-X 135 slide film that are the subject matter of this dispute. During the month of August, 1970, Carr and his family vacationed in Europe. Using his own camera, Carr took a great many photographs of the sites they saw, using among others the four rolls of film referred to earlier. Upon their return to the United States, Carr took a total of eighteen [18] rolls of exposed film to Hoosier to be developed. Only fourteen [14] of the rolls were returned to Carr after processing. All efforts to find the missing rolls or the pictures developed from them were unsuccessful. Litigation commenced when the parties were unable to negotiate a settlement.

The film Carr purchased, manufactured by Kodak, is distributed in boxes on which there is printed the following legend:

> *READ THIS NOTICE*
> *This film will be replaced if defective in manufacture, labeling, or packaging, or if damaged or lost by us or any subsidiary company even though by negligence or other fault. Except for such replacement, the sale, processing, or other handling of this film for any purpose is without other warranty of liability.*

In the stipulation of facts it was agreed though Carr never read this notice on the packages of film he bought, he knew there was printed on such packages "a limitation of liability similar or identical to the Eastman Kodak limitation of liability." The source of Carr's knowledge was agreed to be his years of experience as an attorney and as an amateur photographer.

When Carr took all eighteen [18] rolls of exposed film to Hoosier for processing, he was given a receipt for each roll. Each receipt contained the following language printed on the back side:

> *Although film price does not include processing by Kodak, the return of any film or print to us for processing or any other purpose, will constitute an agreement by you that if any such film or print is damaged or lost by us or any subsidiary company, even though by negligence or other fault, it will be replaced with an equivalent amount of Kodak film and processing and, except for such replacement, the handling of such film or prints by us for any purpose is without other warranty or liability.*

Again, it was agreed though Carr did not read this notice he was aware Hoosier "[gave] to their customers at the time of accepting film for processing, receipts on which there are printed limitations of liability similar or identical to the limitation of liability printed on each receipt received by Carr from Hoosier Photo."

It was stipulated upon receipt of the eighteen [18] rolls of exposed film only fourteen [14] were returned to Hoosier by Kodak after processing. Finally, it was stipulated the four rolls of film were lost by either Hoosier or Kodak. * * *

That either Kodak or Hoosier breached the bailment contract, by negligently losing the four rolls of film, was established in the stipulated agreement of facts. Therefore, the next issue raised is whether either or both, Hoosier or Kodak, may limit their liability as reflected on the film packages and receipts. * * *

[A] prerequisite to finding a limitation of liability clause in a contract unconscionable and therefore void is a showing of disparity in bargaining power in favor of the party whose liability is thus limited. * * * In the case at bar the stipulated facts foreclose a finding of disparate bargaining power between the parties or lack of knowledge or understanding of the liability clause by Carr. The facts show Carr is an experienced attorney who practices in the field of business law. He is hardly in a position comparable to that of the plaintiff in Weaver, supra. Moreover, it was stipulated he was aware of the limitation of liability on both the film packages and the receipts. We believe these crucial facts belie a finding of disparate bargaining power working to Carr's disadvantage.

Contrary to Carr's assertions, he was not in a "take it or leave it position" in that he had no choice but to accept the limitation of liability terms of the contract. As cross-appellants Hoosier and Kodak correctly point out, Carr and other photographers like him do have some choice in the matter of film processing. They can, for one, undertake to develop their film themselves. They can also go to independent film laboratories not a part of the Kodak Company. We do not see the availability of processing as limited to Kodak. * * *

We hold the limitation of liability clauses operating in favor of Hoosier and Kodak were assented to by Carr; they were not unconscionable or void. Carr is, therefore, bound by such terms and is limited in his remedy to recovery of the cost of four boxes of unexposed Kodak Ektachrome-X 135 slide film.

The Court of Appeals' opinion in this case is hereby vacated. The cause is remanded to the trial court with instructions to enter a judgment in favor of appellant, John R. Carr, Jr., in the amount of $13.60 [about $84.00 in 2016 dollars], plus interest. Each party is to bear its own costs.

Hunter and Pivarnik, JJ., concur. Prentice, J., concurs in result without opinion.

DeBruler, J., dissenting.

* * * As a general rule the law does not permit professional bailees to escape or diminish liability for their own negligence by posting signs or handing out receipts. [Citations] The statements on the film box and claim check used by Kodak and Hoosier Photo are in all respects like the printed forms of similar import which commonly appear on packages, signs, chits, tickets, tokens and receipts with which we are all bombarded daily. No one does, or can reasonably be expected, to take the time to carefully read the front, back, and sides of such things. We all know their gist anyway.

The distinguished trial judge below characterizes these statements before us as "mere notices" and concludes that plaintiff below did not "assent" to them so as to render them a binding part of the bailment contract. Implicit here is the recognition of the exception to the general rule regarding such notices, namely, that they may attain the dignity of a special contract limiting liability where the bailor overtly assents to their terms.[Citations] To assent to provisions of this sort requires more than simply placing the goods into the hands of the bailee and taking back a receipt or claim check. Such acts are as probative of ignorance as they are of knowledge. However, according to the agreed statement of facts, plaintiff Carr "knew" by past experience that the claim checks carried the limitation of liability statements, but he did not read them and was unaware of the specific language in them. There is nothing in this agreed statement that Carr recalled this knowledge to present consciousness at the time of these transactions. Obviously, we all know many things which we do not recall or remember at any given time. The assent required by law is more than this; it is, I believe, to perform an act of understanding. There is no evidence of that here.

The evidence presented tending to support the award of damages included an actual uncontroverted amount of $13.60 thereby precluding mere nominal damages. There was further evidence that 150 exposures were lost. The actual award of $1,014.60 amounted to between $6.00 and $7.00 per picture. Carr provided evidence that the pictures were of exceptional value to him, having been taken in a once-in-a-lifetime European trip costing $6,000 [about $33,000 in 2110 dollars], including visits arranged there before hand with relatives. The award was fair and just compensation for the loss of value to the owner and does not include sentimental or fanciful value.

The trial court judgment should be affirmed.

Case Questions

1. Four out of eighteen rolls of film were not returned to the bailor, Mr. Carr. The court here affirmed a judgment for about $6 per lost image. How could an image taken by an amateur photographer be worth $6 a piece?
2. The European trip cost him $6,000 in 1970; he asked for $10,000 (about $55,000 in 2016 dollars). Upon what basis could such damages be arrived? What did he apparently want?

3. What argument did the plaintiff make as to why the limitation of liability should not be enforced? What response did the court have to that?
4. Would it have made a difference if the plaintiff were not himself a business attorney? Why or why not?
5. Why did the dissent think the court of appeals' decision to award the plaintiff $1,000 was correct and the majority's opinion incorrect?

Bailed Goods of Sentimental Value

Mieske v. Bartell Drug Co.
593 P.2d 1308 (Wash. 1979)

Brachtenbach, J.

This case determines the measure of damages for personal property, developed movie film, which is destroyed, and which cannot be replaced or reproduced. It also decides the legal effect of a clause which purports to limit the responsibility of a film processor to replacement of film. A jury verdict of $7,500 [about $32,000 in 2016 dollars] was returned against the defendants.

The facts are that over a period of years the plaintiffs had taken movie films of their family activities. The films started with the plaintiffs' wedding and honeymoon and continued through vacations in Mexico, Hawaii and other places, Christmas gatherings, birthdays, Little League participation by their son, family pets, building of their home and irreplaceable pictures of members of their family, such as the husband's brother, who are now deceased.

Plaintiffs had 32 50-foot reels of such developed film which they wanted spliced together into four reels for convenience of viewing. Plaintiff wife visited defendant Bartell's camera department, with which she had dealt as a customer for at least 10 years. She was told that such service could be performed.

The films were put in the order which plaintiffs desired them to be spliced and so marked. They were then placed in four separate paper bags which in turn were placed in one large bag and delivered to the manager of Bartell. The plaintiff wife explained the desired service and the manner in which the films were assembled in the various bags. The manager placed a film processing packet on the bag and gave plaintiff wife a receipt which contained this language: "We assume no responsibility beyond retail cost of film unless otherwise agreed to in writing." There was no discussion about the language on the receipt. Rather, plaintiff wife told the manager, "Don't lose these. They are my life."

Bartell sent the film package to defendant GAF Corporation, which intended to send them to another processing lab for splicing. Plaintiffs assumed that Bartell did this service and were unaware of the involvement of two other firms.

The bag of films arrived at the processing lab of GAF. The manager of the GAF lab described the service ordered and the packaging as very unusual. Yet it is undisputed that the film was in the GAF lab at the end of one day and gone the next morning. The manager immediately searched the garbage disposal dumpster which already had been emptied. The best guess is that the plaintiffs' film went from GAF's lab to the garbage dumpster to a truck to a barge to an up-Sound landfill where it may yet repose.

After several inquiries to Bartell, plaintiff wife was advised to call GAF. Not surprisingly, after being advised of the complete absence and apparent fatality of plaintiffs' films, this lawsuit ensued.
* * *

Two main issues are raised: (1) the measure of damages and (2) the effect of the exclusionary clause appearing on the film receipt.

On damages, the defendants assign error to (a) the court's damages instruction and (b) the court's failure to give their proposed damages instruction.

The standard of recovery for destruction of personal property was summarized in [McCurdy]. We recognized in McCurdy that (1) personal property which is destroyed may have a market value, in which case that market value is the measure of damages; (2) if destroyed property has no market value but can be replaced or reproduced, then the measure is the cost of replacement or reproduction; (3) if the destroyed property has no market value and cannot be replaced or reproduced, then the value to the owner is to be the proper measure of damages. However, while not stated in McCurdy, we have held that in the third McCurdy situation, damages are not recoverable for the sentimental value which the owner places on the property. [Citations]

The defendants argue that plaintiffs' property comes within the second rule of McCurdy, i.e., the film could be replaced and that their liability is limited to the cost of replacement film. Their position is not well taken. Defendants' proposal would award the plaintiffs the cost of acquiring film without pictures imposed thereon. That is not what plaintiffs lost. Plaintiffs lost not merely film able to capture images by exposure but rather film upon which was recorded a multitude of frames depicting many significant events in their lives. Awarding plaintiffs the funds to purchase 32 rolls of blank film is hardly a replacement of the 32 rolls of images which they had recorded over the years. Therefore the third rule of McCurdy is the appropriate measure of damages, i.e., the property has no market value and cannot be replaced or reproduced.

The law, in those circumstances, decrees that the measure of damages is to be determined by the value to the owner, often referred to as the intrinsic value of the property. Restatement of Torts s. 911 (1939).

Necessarily the measure of damages in these circumstances is the most imprecise of the three categories. Yet difficulty of assessment is not cause to deny damages to a plaintiff whose property has no market value and cannot be replaced or reproduced. [Citations]

The fact that damages are difficult to ascertain and measure does not diminish the loss to the person whose property has been destroyed. Indeed, the very statement of the rule suggests the opposite. If one's destroyed property has a market value, presumably its equivalent is available on the market and the owner can acquire that equivalent property. However, if the owner cannot acquire the property in the market or by replacement or reproduction, then he simply cannot be made whole.

The problem is to establish the value to the owner. Market and replacement values are relatively ascertainable by appropriate proof. Recognizing that value to the owner encompasses a subjective element, the rule has been established that compensation for sentimental or fanciful values will not be allowed. [Citations] That restriction was placed upon the jury in this case by the court's damages instruction. * * *

Under these rules, the court's damages instruction was correct. In essence it allowed recovery for the actual or intrinsic value to the plaintiffs but denied recovery for any unusual sentimental value of the film to the plaintiffs or a fanciful price which plaintiffs, for their own special reasons, might place thereon. * * *

The next issue is to determine the legal effect of the exclusionary clause which was on the film receipt given plaintiff wife by Bartell. As noted above, it read: "We assume no responsibility beyond retail cost of film unless otherwise agreed to in writing."

Is the exclusionary clause valid? Defendants rely upon 2-719(3), a section of the Uniform Commercial Code, which authorizes a limitation or exclusion of consequential damages unless the limitation is unconscionable.

Plaintiffs, on the other hand, argue that the Uniform Commercial Code is not applicable to this transaction. * * * It is now clearly established that the reach of Article 2 goes considerably beyond the confines of that type transaction which the Code itself defines to be a "sale"; namely, the passing of title from a party called the seller to one denominated a buyer for a price. Chief opportunity for this expansion is found in Section 2-102, which states that the article applies to "transactions in goods." "Article 2 sections are finding their way into more and more decisions involving transactions which are not sales, but which are used as substitutes for a sale or which to a court appear to have attributes to which sales principles or at least some of them seem appropriate for application. * * * Most important of these is the application of the Article's warranty provisions to leases, bailments, or construction contracts. Of growing importance is the tendency of courts to find the Section on unconscionability, Section 2-302, appropriate to nonsales deals."

Application of the Uniform Commercial Code to this transaction leads to defendants' next two contentions. First, they urge that the code's recognition of course of dealings and trade usage validates the exclusionary clause. Second, defendants assign error to the grounds upon which the court found the clause to be unconscionable and therefore invalid.

Defendants contend that it is the uniform trade practice of film processors to impose an exclusionary clause similar to that contained in Bartell's film receipt. However, the existence of a trade usage is to be established as a fact [Citation]. It was proved as a usage among film processors, but not as between commercial film processors and their retail customers. * * * Consequently, defendants' reliance on trade usage to uphold the exclusionary clause is not well founded.

As to course of dealings, the record is clear that Mrs. Mieske and the Bartell manager never discussed the exclusionary clause. Mrs. Mieske had never read it, she viewed the numbered slip as merely a receipt. The manager was not "too clear on what it said." There was no showing what was the language on any other receipt given in prior dealings between the parties. In summary, defendants' proof fell short of that required by the express language of 1-205(3). Defendants contend we should apply a course of dealing standard as a matter of law, but cite no authority for such proposition. We decline the invitation.

Defendants next assert that the trial court held the exclusionary clause to be unconscionable without considering the rules laid down in *Schroeder v. Fageol Motors, Inc.*, 544 P.2d 20 (1975). In Schroeder, we recognized that the term unconscionable is not defined in the Uniform Commercial Code. We acknowledge that the code mandates the court to determine unconscionability as a matter of law, 2-302(1). Schroeder held that numerous factors enter into a determination of unconscionability. No one element is controlling. The court must examine all the circumstances surrounding the transaction, including conspicuousness of the clause, prior course of dealings between the parties, negotiations about the clause, the commercial setting and usage of the trade. Not each element will be applicable factually to every transaction. * * *

The real question is whether the court considered the necessary elements of Schroeder. A review of the record convinces us that it did. The court had the facts, the Schroeder case was argued, the criteria set forth therein were discussed by defendants' counsel both on objections and on exceptions. There was no error. Judgment affirmed.

Case Questions

1. This case presents pretty much the same fact situation as the previous one, but it comes out the other way. Why? What's the difference?
2. The court said there could be "recovery for the actual or intrinsic value to the plaintiffs but [not for] for any unusual sentimental value of the film to the plaintiffs or a fanciful price which plaintiffs, for their own special reasons, might place thereon." What actual value does a role of film have if not sentimental value, and if the court were not concerned about the sentimental value, why did it mention all the irreplaceable memories recorded on the film—what difference would it make what was on the film if it had an ascertainable "actual value"?
3. Determining that this bailment was governed by the UCC opened up three lines of argument for the defendant. What were they?
4. Why did the court here say the disclaimer was unconscionable?

Liability of Carrier; Limitations on Liability

Calvin Klein Ltd. v. Trylon Trucking Corp.
892 F.2d 191C.A.2 (N.Y. 1989)

Miner, J.

Defendant-appellant Trylon Trucking Corp. ("Trylon") appeals from a judgment...in favor of plaintiff-appellee Calvin Klein Ltd. ("Calvin Klein") for the full value of a lost shipment of clothing. The appeal presents a novel issue under New York law: whether a limitation of liability agreement between a shipper and a carrier is enforceable when the shipment is lost as a result of the carrier's gross negligence.

The district court held that the parties' customary limitation of liability agreement did not extend to the shipment at issue, due to the absence of assent and consideration. The court observed that, had there been such an agreement, the liability of the carrier for its gross negligence would be limited. For the reasons that follow, we reverse the judgment of the district court, find that the parties agreed to the limitation of liability, and determine that the agreement limits Trylon's liability for its gross negligence. * * *

Trylon is a New Jersey trucking firm which engaged in the business of transporting goods from New York City's airports for delivery to its customers' facilities. Calvin Klein, a New York clothing company, had used the services of Trylon for at least three years, involving hundreds of shipments, prior to the lost shipment at issue. In past deliveries Calvin Klein, through its customs broker, would contact Trylon to pick up the shipment from the airport for delivery to Calvin Klein's facility. After completing the carriage, Trylon would forward to Calvin Klein an invoice, which contained a limitation of liability provision as follows:

> *In consideration of the rate charged, the shipper agrees that the carrier shall not be liable for more than $50.00 on any shipment accepted for delivery to one consignee unless a greater value is declared, in writing, upon receipt at time of shipment and charge for such greater value paid, or agreed to be paid, by the shipper.*

A shipment of 2,833 blouses from Hong Kong arrived at John F. Kennedy International Airport for Calvin Klein on March 27, 1986. Calvin Klein arranged for Trylon to pick up the shipment and deliver it to Calvin Klein's New Jersey warehouse. On April 2, Trylon dispatched its driver, Jamahl Jefferson, to pick up this shipment. Jefferson signed a receipt for the shipment from Calvin Klein's broker. By April 2, the parties discovered that Jefferson had stolen Trylon's truck and its shipment. The shipment never was recovered. Calvin Klein sent a claim letter to Trylon for the full value of the lost blouses. In the absence of any response by Trylon, Calvin Klein filed this action * * * to recover $150,000 [about $327,000 in 2017 dollars], allegedly the value of the lost shipment.

In their stipulation in lieu of a jury trial, the parties agreed that Trylon is liable to Calvin Klein for the loss of the shipment and that Trylon was grossly negligent in the hiring and supervision of Jefferson. They also agreed that "[t]he terms and conditions of [Trylon]'s carriage [were] that liability for loss or damage to cargo is limited to $50 in accordance with the legend on Trylon's invoice forms." Calvin Klein conceded that it was aware of this limitation of liability, and that it did not declare a value on the blouses at the time of shipment.

The parties left at issue whether the limitation of liability clause was valid and enforceable. Calvin Klein argued in the district court, as it does here, that the limitation clause was not enforceable for two reasons: no agreement existed between Calvin Klein and Trylon as to the limitation of liability; and, if such an agreement existed, public policy would prevent its enforcement because of Trylon's gross negligence.

The district court applied New York law, finding that the carriage was exempt from the Interstate Commerce Commission's jurisdiction, being entirely within the New York City commercial zone. * * *

A common carrier * * * under New York law is strictly liable for the loss of goods in its custody. "Where the loss is not due to the excepted causes [that is, act of God or public enemy, inherent nature of goods, or shipper's fault], it is immaterial whether the carrier was negligent or not." [Citations] Even in the case of loss from theft by third parties, liability may be imposed up on a negligent common carrier. [Citation]

A shipper and a common carrier may contract to limit the carrier's liability in cases of loss to an amount agreed to by the parties [Citations], so long as the language of the limitation is clear, the shipper is aware of the terms of the limitation, and the shipper can change the terms by indicating the true value of the goods being shipped. [Citations] * * * [A similar scheme applies] under Interstate Commerce Act. Such a limitation agreement is generally valid and enforceable despite carrier negligence. The limitation of liability provision involved here clearly provides that, at the time of delivery, the shipper may increase the limitation by written notice of the value of the goods to be delivered and by payment of a commensurately higher fee.

The parties stipulated to the fact that the $50 limitation of liability was a term and condition of carriage and that Calvin Klein was aware of that limitation. This stipulated fact removes the first issue, namely whether an agreement existed as to a liability limitation between the parties, from this case. Calvin Klein's argument that it never previously acknowledged this limitation by accepting only $50 in settlement of a larger loss does not alter this explicit stipulation. "[A] stipulation of fact that is fairly entered into is controlling on the parties and the court is bound to enforce it." [Citations] Neither party here has argued that the stipulation was unfairly entered into. * * *

The remaining issue concerns the enforceability of the limitation clause in light of Trylon's conceded gross negligence. The district court considered that, assuming an agreement between the parties as to Trylon's liability, Trylon's gross negligence would not avoid the enforcement of a limitation clause.

The district court found that New York law, as opposed to federal interstate commerce law, applies in this case. The parties do not seriously contest this choice of law. With the choice thus unchallenged, we must apply both established New York law as well as our belief of how the New York Court of Appeals would rule if this case were before it. * * *

Although the New York Court of Appeals has addressed a limitation of liability provision in the context of a contract between an airline and a passenger, [Citation] (refusing to enforce unilateral limitation provision for death of passenger due to defendant's negligence), that court has never been called upon to enforce a limitation provision in the case of a grossly negligent common carrier of goods. The various departments of the Appellate Division of the New York State Supreme Court have addressed whether gross negligence bars enforcement of limitations of liability in the context of contracts for the installation, maintenance and monitoring of burglar alarm systems and are divided on the issue. Compare [Citation] (enforcing limitation despite gross negligence) and [Citation] (even if gross negligence were established, plaintiff's recovery would be limited by limitation clause) with [Citation] (limitation clause cannot limit liability for gross negligence) and [Citation] (finding "no significant distinction" between complete exculpation and limitation "to a nominal sum," therefore limitation is ineffective). The First Department distinguished between exculpatory provisions and limitation provisions, indicating that the latter would be effective even if the former are unenforceable due to the contracting party's gross negligence. [Citations]. * * * The other departments which have considered the question applied the holding of [Citation], that "[a]greements which purport to exempt a party from liability for willful or grossly negligent acts are contrary to public policy and are void." * * *

Absent a rule of decision formulated by the New York Court of Appeals, we are not bound by the opinions issued by the state's lower courts. * * *

In the absence of direct New York authority, we must make our best estimate as to how New York's highest court would rule in this case. In making that determination, we are free to consider all the resources the highest court of the state could use, including decisions reached in other jurisdictions. * * * We believe that the New York Court of Appeals would not differentiate between gross negligence and ordinary negligence in recognizing the validity of the limitation of liability in this case.

Since carriers are strictly liable for loss of shipments in their custody and are insurers of these goods, the degree of carrier negligence is immaterial. [Citation] The common carrier must exercise reasonable care in relation to the shipment in its custody. U.C.C. § 7-309(1). Carriers can contract with their shipping customers on the amount of liability each party will bear for the loss of a shipment, regardless of the degree of carrier negligence. See U.C.C. § 7-309(2) (allowing limitation of liability for losses from any cause save carrier conversion). Unlike the parachute school student, see [Citation], or the merchant acquiring a burglar alarm, the shipper can calculate the specific amount of its potential damages in advance, declare the value of the shipment based on that calculation, and pay a commensurately higher rate to carry the goods, in effect buying additional insurance from the common carrier.

In this case, Calvin Klein and Trylon were business entities with an on-going commercial relationship involving numerous carriages of Calvin Klein's goods by Trylon. Where such entities deal with each other in a commercial setting, and no special relationship exists between the parties, clear limitations between them will be enforced. [Citation]. Here, each carriage was under the same terms and conditions as the last, including a limitation of Trylon's liability. See [Citation] (court enforced limitation on shipper who possessed over five years of the carrier's manifests which included the $50 limitation). This is not a case in which the shipper was dealing with the common carrier for the first time or contracting under new or changed terms. Calvin Klein was aware of the terms and was free to adjust the limitation upon a written declaration of the value of a given shipment, but failed to do so with the shipment at issue here. Since Calvin Klein failed to adjust the limitation, the limitation applies here, and no public policy that dictates otherwise can be identified.

Calvin Klein now argues that the limitation is so low as to be void. * * * This amount is immaterial because Calvin Klein had the opportunity to negotiate the amount of coverage by declaring the value of the shipment. * * * Commercial entities can easily negotiate the degree of risk each party will bear and which party will bear the cost of insurance. That this dispute actually involves who will bear the cost of insurance is illustrated by the fact that this case has been litigated not by the principal parties, but by their insurers. Calvin Klein could have increased Trylon's coverage by declaring the value of its shipment, but did not do so. Calvin Klein had the opportunity to declare a higher value and we find all of its arguments relating to the unreasonableness of the limitation to be without merit.

We reverse and remand to the district court with instructions to enter judgment against defendant in the sum of $50.

Case Questions

1. Why is the federal court here trying to figure out what the New York high court would do if it had this case in front of it?
2. Did the federal court find direct New York State law to apply?
3. What is the legal issue here?

4. What argument did Calvin Klein make as to why the $50 limitation should not be valid?
5. The common-law rule was that carriers were strictly liable. Why didn't the court apply that rule?
6. Would this case have come out differently if the shipper (a) were an unsophisticated in matters of relevant business or (b) if it had never done business with Trylon before?
7. Why doesn't it make any difference if the negligence here were "normal" negligence or--as here--gross negligence? (The court said the limitation of damages would be okay in either situation.)

21.6 Summary and Exercises

Summary

Ownership and sale of goods are not the only important legal relationships involving goods. In a modern economy, possession of goods is often temporarily surrendered without surrendering title. This creates a bailment, which is defined as the lawful possession of goods by one who is not the owner.

To create a bailment, the goods must be in the possession of the bailee. Possession requires physical control and intent. Whether the owner or someone else must bear a loss often hinges on whether the other person is or is not a bailee.

The bailee's liability for loss depends on the circumstances. Some courts use a straightforward standard of ordinary care. Others use a tripartite test, depending on whether the bailment was for the benefit of the owner (the standard then is gross negligence), for the bailee (extraordinary care), or for both (ordinary care). Bailees may disclaim liability unless they have failed to give adequate notice or unless public policy prohibits disclaimers. A bailee who converts the property will be held liable as an insurer.

A bailor may have liability toward the bailee—for example, for negligent failure to warn of hazards in the bailed property and for strict liability if the injury was caused by a dangerous object in a defective condition.

Special bailments arise in the cases of innkeepers (who have an insurer's liability toward their guests, although many state statutes provide exceptions to this general rule), warehouses, carriers, and leases.

A warehouser is defined as a person engaged in the business of storing goods for hire. The general standard of care is the same as that of ordinary negligence. Many states have statutes imposing a higher standard.

A common carrier—one who holds himself out to all for hire to transport goods—has an insurer's liability toward the goods in his possession, with five exceptions: act of God, act of public enemy, act of public authority, negligence of shipper, and inherent nature of the goods. Because many carriers are involved in most commercial shipments of goods, the law places liability on the initial carrier. The carrier's liability begins once the shipper has given all instructions and taken all action required of it. The carrier's absolute liability ends when it has delivered the goods to the consignee's place of business or residence (unless the agreement states otherwise) or, if no delivery is required, when the consignee has been notified of the arrival of the goods and has had a reasonable opportunity to take possession.

Commodity paper—any document of title—may be negotiated; that is, through proper indorsements on the paper, title may be transferred without physically touching the goods. A duly negotiated document gives the holder title to the document and to the goods, certain rights to the goods delivered to the bailee after the document was issued, and the right to take possession free of any defense or claim by the issuer of the document of title. Certain rules limit the seemingly absolute right of the holder to take title better than that held by the transferor.

Exercises

1. Joe Andrews delivered his quarter horse I'll Call Ya (worth about $319,000 in 2010 dollars) to Harold Stone for boarding and stabling. Later he asked Stone if Stone could arrange for the horse's transportation some distance, and Stone engaged the services of the Allen brothers for that purpose. Andrews did not know the Allens, but Stone had previously done business with them. On the highway the trailer with I'll Call Ya in it became disengaged from the Allens' truck and rolled over. The mare, severely injured, "apparently lingered for several hours on the side of the road before she died without veterinary treatment." The evidence was that the Allens had properly secured the horse's head at the front of the trailer and used all other equipment that a reasonably prudent person would use to secure and haul the horse; that the ball was the proper size and in good condition; that the ball was used without incident to haul other trailers after the accident; that Ronny Allen was driving at a safe speed and in a safe manner immediately before the accident; that after the accident the sleeve of the trailer hitch was still in the secured position; and that they made a reasonable effort to obtain veterinary treatment for the animal after the accident. The court determined this was a mutual-benefit bailment. Are the Allens liable?[21]
2. Fisher Corporation, a manufacturer of electronic equipment, delivered VCRs to Consolidated Freightways' warehouse in California for shipment to World Radio Inc., an electronics retailer in Council Bluffs, Iowa. World Radio rejected the shipments as duplicative, and they were returned to Consolidated's terminal in Sarpy County, Nebraska, pending Fisher's instructions. The VCRs were loaded onto a trailer; the doors of the trailer were sealed but not padlocked, and the trailer was parked at the south end of the terminal. Padlocks were not used on any trailers so as not to call attention to a trailer containing expensive cargo. The doors of the trailer faced away from the terminal toward a cyclone fence that encircled the yard. Two weeks later, on Sunday, July 15, a supervisor checked the grounds and found nothing amiss. On Tuesday, July 17, Consolidated's employees discovered a 3 × 5 foot hole had been cut in the fence near the trailer, and half the VCRs were gone; they were never recovered. Consolidated received Fisher's return authorization after the theft occurred. If Consolidated is considered a carrier, it would be strictly liable for the loss; if it is considered a bailee, it is not liable unless negligent. Which is it?
3. Plaintiff purchased a Greyhound bus ticket in St. Petersburg, Florida, for a trip to Fort Meyers. The bus left at 11:30 p.m. and arrived at 4:15 a.m. When Plaintiff got off the bus, she noticed that the station and restrooms were darkened, closed, and locked. She left the terminal to cross at a lighted service station to use the bathroom. As she walked away from the terminal, she was attacked by an unknown person and injured. The terminal was located in a high-crime area of Fort Meyers. Is Greyhound liable?
4. Mrs. Carter, Plaintiff, took her fur coat to Reichlin Furriers for cleaning, glazing, and storage until the next winter season. She was given a printed receipt form on the front of which Furrier's employee had written "$100" as the coat's value, though Mrs. Carter did not discuss its value with the employee, did not know that such a value had been noted, and didn't read the receipt. A space for the customer's signature on the front of the receipt was blank; below this in prominent type was this notice: "see reverse side for terms and conditions." On the back was a statement that this was a storage contract and the customer would be bound by the terms unless contrary notice was given within ten days. There were fifteen conditions, one of which was the following: "Storage charges are based upon valuation herein declared by the depositor and amount recoverable for loss or damage shall not exceed...the depositor's valuation appearing in this receipt." Six months later, when Mrs. Carter sought to retrieve her coat, she was informed by Furrier that it was lost. Carter sued Furrier for $450 (about $2,200 in 2010 dollars); Furrier claimed its liability was limited to $100. Who wins and why?
5. Michael Capezzaro (Plaintiff) reported to the police that he had been robbed of $30,000 (in 2010 dollars) at gunpoint by a woman. The next day police arrested a woman with $9,800 in her possession. Plaintiff identified her as the woman who had robbed him, and the money was impounded as evidence. Two years later the case against her was dismissed because she was determined to have been insane when she committed the crime, and the money in the police property room was released to her. Plaintiff then sued the police department, which claimed it was "obligated to return the money to [the woman] as bailor." Who wins and why?

6. Harley Hightower delivered his Cadillac to Auto Auction, where it was damaged. Auto Auction defended itself against Hightower's claim that it was a negligent bailee by asserting (1) that he had not met the required burden of proof that a proximate cause of the injury was Auto Auction's negligence because it introduced evidence that negligence of a third party was a proximate cause of the damage to his car and (2) that it was entitled to judgment in the absence of evidence of specific acts of negligence of the bailee. There was evidence that a Mrs. Tune drove her automobile onto the lot to sell it and parked it where she was directed to; that the automobiles on said lot for sale were ordinarily lined up and numbered by Auto Auction; that Plaintiff's Cadillac was not so parked by the auction company but was parked so that if Mrs. Tune's automobile continued forward it would strike Hightower's Cadillac broadside; that when Mrs. Tune stopped her Buick and alighted, her car rolled down the incline on the lot toward Hightower's car; that she attempted to stop her car but it knocked her down and continued rolling toward appellee's Cadillac and, finally, struck and damaged it. Who wins and why?
7. Several student radicals led by Richard Doctor, ranked number three on the FBI's Ten Most Wanted list, destroyed a shipment of military cargo en route from Colorado to a military shipping facility in Washington State. Should the carrier be liable for the loss?
8. Everlena Mitchell contracted in writing with All American Van & Storage to transport and store her household goods and furnishings, and she was to pay all charges incurred on a monthly basis. As security she granted All American a warehouser's lien giving it the right to sell the property if the charges remained unpaid for three months and if, in the opinion of the company, such action would be necessary to protect accrued charges. Everlena fell eight months in arrears and on October 20 she received notice that the amount owed was to be paid by October 31, 1975. The notice also stated that if payment was not made, her goods and furnishings would be sold on November 7, 1975. Everlena had a pending claim with the Social Security Administration, and advised All American that she would be receiving a substantial sum of money soon from the Social Services Administration; this was confirmed by two government agents. However, All American would not postpone the sale. Everlena's property was sold on November 7, 1975, for $925.50. Near the end of November 1975, Everlena received approximately $5,500 (about $22,000 in 2010 dollars) from the United States as a disability payment under the Social Security Act, and she sued All American for improperly selling her goods. The trial court ruled for All American on summary judgment. What result should Everlena obtain on appeal?
9. Roland delivered a shipment of desks to Security Warehousers and received from Security a negotiable receipt. Peter broke into Roland's office, stole the document, and forged Roland's signature as an indorsement, making Peter himself the holder. Peter then indorsed the document over to Billings, who knew nothing of the theft. Does Billings get good title to the desks?
10. Baker's Transfer & Storage Company, Defendant, hauled household goods and personal effects by trucks "anywhere for hire." Its trucks did not travel on regular routes or between established terminals; it hauled household goods and personal effects on private contracts with the owners as and when the opportunity presented itself. Baker contracted to haul the Klein family's household goods from Bakersfield, California, to Hollywood. En route the goods were destroyed by fire without Baker's negligence. Baker's contract provided it would redeliver the property "damage by the elements excepted." If Baker were a common carrier, its liability would be statutorily limited to less than the amount ordered by the trial court; if it were a private carrier, its liability would be either based on ordinary negligence or as the parties' contract provided. Working with both points, what result obtains here?

Self-Test Questions

1. In a bailment, the bailee
    a. must return similar goods
    b. must return identical goods
    c. acquires title to the goods
    d. must pay for the goods

2. In a bailment for the benefit of a bailee, the bailee's duty of care is
   a. slight
   b. extraordinary
   c. ordinary
3. A disclaimer of liability by a bailee is
   a. never allowed
   b. sometimes allowed
   c. always allowed
   d. unheard of in business
4. A bailor may be held liable to the bailee on
   a. a negligence theory
   b. a warranty theory
   c. a strict liability theory
   d. all of the above
5. The highest duty of care is imposed on which of the following?
   a. a common carrier
   b. a lessee
   c. a warehouser
   d. an innkeeper

Self-Test Answers

1. b
2. b
3. b
4. d
5. a

Endnotes

1. *Zuppa v. Hertz*, 268 A.2d 364 (N.J. 1970).
2. Here is a link to a history of bailment law: Globusz Publishing, "Lecture v. the Bailee at Common Law," accessed March 1, 2011, http://www.globusz.com/ebooks/CommonLaw/00000015.htm.
3. *Carpenter v. Spencer & Griffin*, 37 Am. Dec. 396 (N.Y. 1841).
4. *Lockwood v. Manhattan Storage & Warehouse Co.*, 50 N.Y.S. 974 (N.Y. 1898).
5. *Bunnell v. Stern*, 25 N.E. 910 (N.Y. 1890).
6. *Wamser v. Browning, King & Co.*, 79 N.E. 861 (N.Y. 1907).
7. *Wall v. Airport Parking Co. of Chicago*, 244 N.E.2d 190 (Ill. 1969).
8. *Continental Insurance Co. v. Meyers Bros. Operations, Inc.*, 288 N.Y.S.2d 756 (Civ. Ct. N.Y. 1968).
9. *Samples v. Geary*, 292 S.W. 1066 (Mo. App. 1927).
10. *Zimmer v. Mitchell and Ness*, 385 A.2d 437 (Penn. 1978).
11. Uniform Commercial Code, Section 2A.
12. Uniform Commercial Code, Section 7-204(1).
13. Uniform Commercial Code, Section 7-204(2).
14. Uniform Commercial Code, Section 7-403(1).
15. *Ace High Dresses v. J. C. Trucking Co.*, 191 A. 536 (Conn. 1937).
16. Uniform Commercial Code, Section 1-206(6).
17. *Southern Express Co. v. C. L. Ruth & Son*, 59 So. 538 (Ala. Ct. App. 1912).
18. *Pennsylvania Co. v. Roy*, 102 US 451 (1880).
19. *Werndli v. Greyhound Corp.*, 365 So.2d 177 (Fla. Ct. App., 1978)
20. Uniform Commercial Code, Section 7-104(1)(a).
21. *Andrews v. Allen*, 724 S.W.2d 893 (Tex. Ct. App., 1987).

CHAPTER 22

Nature and Form of Commercial Paper

Learning Objectives

After reading this chapter, you should understand the following:

1. Why commercial paper is important in modern economic systems.
2. How the law of commercial paper has developed over the past four hundred years, and what role it plays in economics and finance.
3. What the types of commercial paper are, and who the parties to such paper are
4. What is required for paper to be negotiable.

Here we begin our examination of commercial paper, documents representing an obligation by one party to pay another money. You are familiar with one kind of commercial paper: a check.

22.1 Introduction to Commercial Paper

Learning Objectives

1. Understand why commercial paper is an important concept in modern finance.
2. Be familiar with the historical development of commercial paper.
3. Recognize how commercial paper is viewed in economics and finance.

The Importance of Commercial Paper

Because commercial paper is a vital invention for the working of our economic system, brief attention to its history and its function as a medium of exchange in economics and finance is appropriate.

The Central Role of Commercial Paper

Commercial paper is the collective term for various financial instruments, or tools, that include checks drawn on commercial banks, drafts (drawn on something other than a bank), certificates of deposit, and notes evidencing a promise to pay. Like money, commercial paper is a medium of exchange, but because it is one step removed from money, difficulties arise that require a series of interlocking rules to protect both sellers and buyers.

To understand the importance of commercial paper, consider the following example. It illustrates a distinction that is critical to the discussion in our four chapters on commercial paper.

Lorna Love runs a tennis club. She orders a truckload of new tennis rackets from Rackets, Inc., a manufacturer. The contract price of the rackets is $100,000. Rackets ships the rackets to Love. Rackets then sells for $90,000 its contract rights (rights to receive the payment from Love of $100,000) to First Bank (see Figure 22.1). Unfortunately, the rackets that arrive at Love's are warped and thus commercially worthless. Rackets files for bankruptcy.

FIGURE 22.1 Assignment of Contract Rights

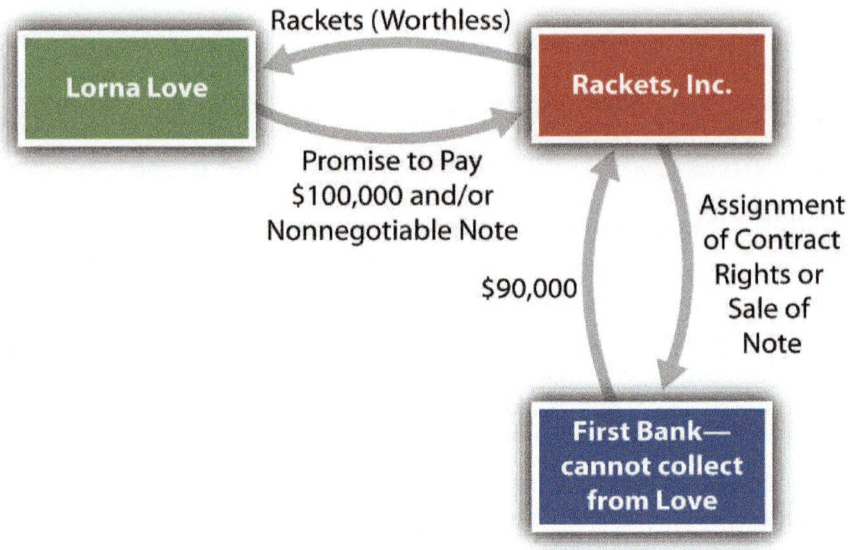

May the bank collect from Love $100,000, the value of the contract rights it purchased? No. Under the contract rule discussed in Chapter 14, an assignee—here, the bank—steps into the shoes of the assignor and takes the assigned rights subject to any defense of the obligor, Love. (Here, of course, Love's defense against paying is that the rackets are worthless.) The result would be the same if Love had given Rackets a nonnegotiable note, which Rackets proceeded to sell to the bank (By nonnegotiable we do not mean that the note cannot be sold but only that certain legal requirements, discussed in Section 3 of this chapter, have not been met.)

Now let us add one fact: In addition to signing a contract, Love gives Rackets a *negotiable* note in exchange for the rackets, and Rackets sells the note to the bank. By adding that the note is negotiable, the result changes significantly. Because the note is negotiable and because the bank, we assume, bought the note in good faith (i.e., unaware that the rackets were warped), the bank will recover the $100,000 (see Figure 22.2).

FIGURE 22.2 Sale of Negotiable Note

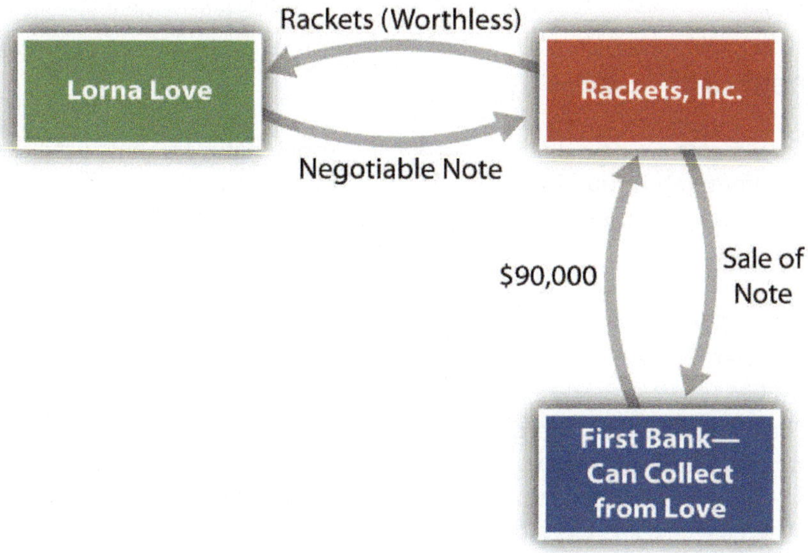

The key to the central role that commercial paper plays in modern finance is **negotiability**. *Negotiability* means that the paper is freely and unconditionally transferable from one person to another by delivery or by delivery and indorsement. ("Indorsement," not "endorsement," is the spelling used in the UCC, though the latter is more common in nonlegal usage.) Without the ability to pay and finance through commercial paper, the business world would be paralyzed. At bottom, negotiability is the means by which a person is empowered to transfer to another more than what the transferor himself possesses. In essence, this is the power to convey to a transferee the right in turn to convey clear title, when the original transferor does not have clear title.

negotiability

Transferable from one person to another by delivery or by delivery and indorsement.

Overview of Chapters on Commercial Paper

In this chapter, we examine the history and nature of commercial paper and define the types of parties (persons who have an interest in the paper) and the types of instruments. We then proceed to four fundamental issues that must be addressed to determine whether parties such as First Bank, in the preceding example, can collect:

1. Is the paper negotiable? That is, is the paper in the proper form? We explore that issue in this chapter.
2. Was the paper negotiated properly? See Chapter 23.
3. Is the purchaser of the paper a holder in due course? See Chapter 24.
4. Does the maker of the paper have available any defenses against even the holder in due course? See Chapter 24.

In most transactions, especially when the first three questions are answered affirmatively, the purchaser will have little trouble collecting. But when the purchaser is unable to collect, questions of liability arise. These questions, along with termination of liability, are discussed in Chapter 25.

Finally, in Chapter 26 we examine other legal aspects of banking, including letters of credit and electronic funds transfer.

History of Commercial Paper

Development of the Law

Negotiable instruments are no modern invention; we know that merchants used them as long ago as the age of Hammurabi, around 1700 BC. They fell into disuse after the collapse of the Roman Empire and then reappeared in Italy around the fourteenth century. They became more common as long-distance commerce spread. In an era before paper currency, payment in coins or bullion was awkward, especially for merchants who traveled great distances across national boundaries to attend the fairs at which most economic exchanges took place. Merchants and traders found it far more efficient to pay with paper.

Bills of exchange, today commonly known as *drafts*, were recognized instruments in the law merchant. (The "law merchant" was the system of rules and customs recognized and adopted by early-modern traders and is the basis of the UCC Article 3.) A draft is an unconditional order by one person (the drawer) directing another person (drawee or payor) to pay money to a named third person or to bearer; a check is the most familiar type of draft. The international merchant courts regularly enforced drafts and permitted them to be transferred to others by indorsement (again, the legal spelling of *endorsement*). By the beginning of the sixteenth century, the British common-law courts began to hear cases involving bills of exchange, but it took a half century before the courts became comfortable with them and accepted them as crucial to the growing economy.

Courts were also hesitant until the end of the seventeenth century about sanctioning a transferor's assignment of a promissory note if it meant that the transferee would have better title than the transferor. One reason for the courts' reluctance to sanction assignments stemmed from the law that permitted debtors to be jailed, a law that was not repealed until 1870. The buyer of goods might have been willing originally to give a promissory note because he knew that a particular seller would not attempt to jail him for default, but who could be sure that a transferee, probably a complete stranger, would be so charitable?

The inability to negotiate promissory notes prevented a banking system from fully developing. During the English civil wars in the seventeenth century, merchants began to deposit cash with the goldsmiths, who lent it out at interest and issued the depositors promissory notes, the forerunner of bank notes. But a judicial decision in 1703 declared that promissory notes were not negotiable, whether they were made payable to the order of a specific person or to the bearer. Parliament responded the following year with the Promissory Notes Act, which for the first time permitted an assignee to sue the note's maker.

Thereafter the courts in both England and the United States began to shape the modern law of negotiable instruments. By the late nineteenth century, Parliament had codified the law of negotiable instruments in England. Codification came later in the United States. In 1896, the National Conference of Commissioners on Uniform State Laws proposed the Negotiable Instruments Act, which was adopted in all states by 1924. That law eventually was superseded by the adoption of Articles 3 and 4 of the Uniform Commercial Code (UCC), which we study in these chapters.

In 1990, the American Law Institute and the National Conference of Commissioners on Uniform State Laws approved revised Article 3, entitled "Negotiable Instruments," and related amendments in Article 4. The revisions clarified and updated the law. All states except New York and North Carolina have adopted Articles 3 and 4.

The Future of Commercial Paper: Federal and International Preemption

State law governing commercial paper is vulnerable to federal preemption. This preemption could take two major forms. First, the Federal Reserve Board governs the activities of Federal Reserve Banks. As a result, Federal Reserve regulations provide important guidelines for the check collection process. Second, Article 3 of the UCC can be preempted by federal statutes. An important example is the Expedited Funds Availability Act, which became effective in 1988 (discussed in Chapter 26).

Federal preemption may also become intertwined with international law. In 1988, the United Nations General Assembly adopted the Convention on International Bills of Exchange and International Promissory Notes. Progress on the treaty emanating from the convention has been slow, however: the United States, Canada, and Russia have approved the convention (in 1989 and 1990) but have not ratified the treaty; Gabon, Guinea, Honduras, Liberia, and Mexico are the only countries to have ratified it.

Commercial Paper in Economics and Finance

Economics

To the economist, one type of commercial paper—the bank check—is the primary component of M1, the basic money supply. It is easy to see why. When you deposit cash in a checking account, you may either withdraw the currency—coins and bills—or draw on the account by writing out a check. If you write a check to "cash," withdraw currency, and pay a creditor, there has been no change in the money supply if you pay your creditor by check, the quantity of money has increased: the cash you deposited remains available, and your creditor deposits the check to his own account as though it were cash. (A more broadly defined money supply, M2, includes savings deposits at commercial banks.)

Finance

Commercial paper is defined more narrowly in finance than in law. To the corporate treasurer and other financiers, commercial paper ordinarily means short-term promissory notes sold by finance companies and large corporations for a fixed rate of interest. Maturity dates range from a low of three days to a high of nine months. It is an easy way for issuers to raise short-term money quickly. And although short-term notes are unsecured, historically they have been almost as safe as obligations of the U.S. government. By contrast, for legal purposes, commercial paper includes long-term notes (which are often secured), drafts, checks, and certificates of deposit.

Key Takeaway

Commercial paper is a medium of exchange used like cash but safer than cash; cash is rarely used today except for small transactions. The key to the success of this invention is the concept of negotiability: through this process, a person can pass on—in most cases—better title to receive payment than he had; thus the transferee of such paper will most likely get paid by the obligor and will not be subject to most defenses of any prior holders. The law of commercial paper has developed over the past four hundred years. It is now the Uniform Commercial Code that governs most commercial paper transactions in the United States, but federal or international preemption is possible in the future. Commercial paper is important in both economics and finance.

Exercises

1. If there were no such thing as commercial paper, real or virtual (electronic funds transfers), how would you pay your bills? How did merchants have to pay their bills four hundred years ago?

2. What is it about negotiability that it is the key to the success of commercial paper?
3. How could state law—the UCC—be preempted in regard to commercial paper?

22.2 Scope of Article 3 and Types of Commercial Paper and Parties

Learning Objectives

1. Understand the scope of Article 3 of the Uniform Commercial Code.
2. Recognize the types of commercial paper: drafts, checks, notes, and certificates of deposit.
3. Give the names of the various parties to commercial paper.

Scope of Article 3

Article 3 of the Uniform Commercial Code (UCC) covers commercial paper but explicitly excludes money, documents of title, and investment securities. Documents of title include bills of lading and warehouse receipts and are governed by Article 7 of the UCC. Investment securities are covered by Article 8. Instruments that fall within the scope of Article 3 may also be subject to Article 4 (bank deposits and collections), Article 8 (securities), and Article 9 (secured transactions). If so, the rules of these other articles supersede the provisions of Article 3 to the extent of conflict. Article 3 is a set of general provisions on negotiability; the other articles deal more narrowly with specific transactions or instruments.

Types of Commercial Paper

There are four types of commercial paper: drafts, checks, notes, and certificates of deposit.

Drafts

draft

A document ordering the payment of money; drawn by one person or bank on another.

A **draft** is an unconditional written order by one person (the drawer) directing another person (the drawee) to pay a certain sum of money on demand or at a definite time to a named third person (the payee) or to bearer. The draft is one of the two basic types of commercial paper; the other is the note. As indicated by its definition, the draft is a three-party transaction.

Parties to a Draft

The **drawer** is one who directs a person or an entity, usually a bank, to pay a sum of money stated in an instrument—for example, a person who makes a draft or writes a check. The drawer prepares a document (a form, usually)—the draft—ordering the drawee to remit a stated sum of money to the payee. The **drawee** is the person or entity that a draft is directed to and that is ordered to pay the amount stated on it. The most common drawee is a bank. The drawer, drawee, and payee need not be different people; the same person may have different capacities in a single transaction. For example, a drawer (the person asking that payment be made) may also be the payee (the person to whom the payment is to be made). A drawee who signs the draft becomes an **acceptor**: the drawee pledges to honor the draft as written. To accept, the drawee need only sign her name on the draft, usually vertically on the face, but anywhere will do. Words such as "accepted" or "good" are unnecessary. However, a drawee who indicates that she might refuse to pay will not be held to have accepted. Thus, in the archetypal case, the court held that a drawee who signed his name and appended the words "Kiss my foot" did not accept the draft.[1]

The drawer directs the funds to be drawn from—pulled from—the drawee, and the drawee pays the person entitled to payment as directed.

drawer

The person who makes out (draws) a check or draft.

drawee

The person (or bank) expected to pay a check or draft when it is presented for payment.

acceptor

A drawee who accepts a draft, agreeing to be primarily responsible for paying it.

Types of Drafts

Drafts can be divided into two broad subcategories: sight drafts and time drafts.

A **sight draft** calls for payment "on sight," that is, when presented. Recall from Section 1 that Lorna Love wished to buy tennis rackets from Rackets, Inc. Suppose Love had the money to pay but did not want to do so before delivery. Rackets, on the other hand, did not want to ship before Love paid. The solution: a sight draft, drawn on Love, to which would be attached an order bill of lading that Rackets received from the trucker when it shipped the rackets. The sight draft and bill of lading go to a bank in Love's city. When the tennis rackets arrive, the carrier notifies the bank, which presents the draft to Love for payment. When she has done so, the bank gives Love the bill of lading, entitling her to receive the shipment. The bank forwards the payment to Rackets' bank, which credits Rackets' account with the purchase amount.

sight draft

A draft or bill that is payable on demand or upon presentation. Also called demand draft.

A **time draft**, not surprisingly, calls for payment on a date specified in the draft. Suppose that Love will not have sufficient cash to pay until she has sold the rackets but that Rackets needs to be paid immediately. The solution: a common form of time draft known as a trade acceptance. Rackets, the seller, draws a draft on Love, who thus becomes a drawee. The draft orders Love to pay the purchase price to the order of Rackets, as payee, on a fixed date. Rackets presents the draft to Love, who accepts it by signing her name. Rackets then can indorse the draft (by signing it) and sell it, at a discount, to its bank or some other financial institution. Rackets thus gets its money right away; the bank may collect from Love on the date specified. See the example of a time draft in Figure 22.3.

time draft

Draft (bill of exchange) payable to a third party on a specified or determinable future date.

FIGURE 22.3 A Time Draft

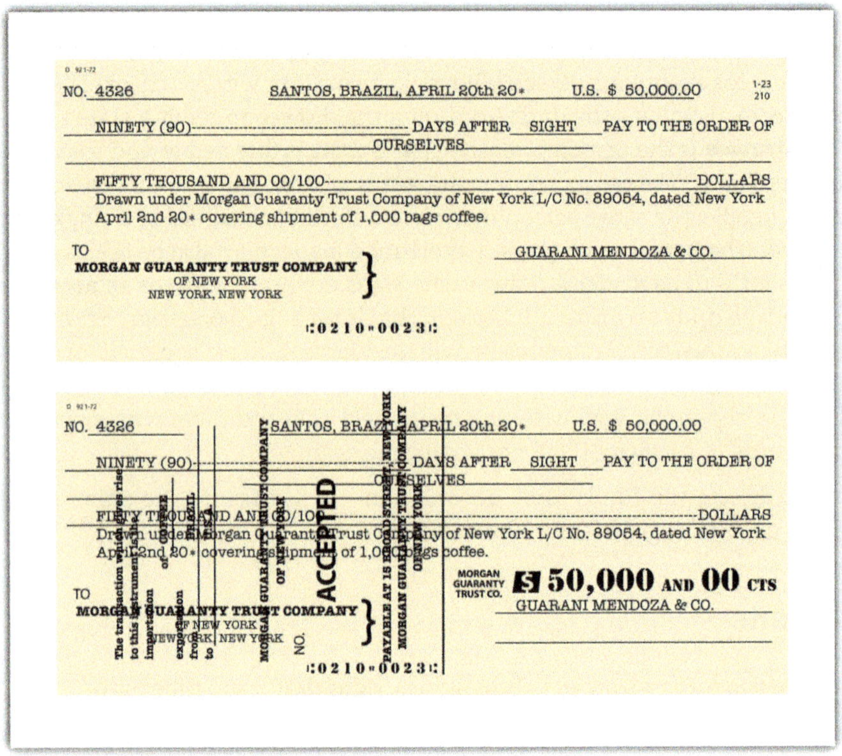
NO. 4326 SANTOS, BRAZIL, APRIL 20th 20* U.S. $ 50,000.00 1-23 210

NINETY (90) DAYS AFTER SIGHT PAY TO THE ORDER OF OURSELVES

FIFTY THOUSAND AND 00/100 DOLLARS

Drawn under Morgan Guaranty Trust Company of New York L/C No. 89054, dated New York April 2nd 20* covering shipment of 1,000 bags coffee.

TO MORGAN GUARANTY TRUST COMPANY OF NEW YORK NEW YORK, NEW YORK

GUARANI MENDOZA & CO.

⑆0210⑉0023⑆

NO. 4326 SANTOS, BRAZIL, APRIL 20th 20* U.S. $ 50,000.00

NINETY (90) DAYS AFTER SIGHT PAY TO THE ORDER OF OURSELVES

FIFTY THOUSAND AND 00/100 DOLLARS

Drawn under Morgan Guaranty Trust Company of New York L/C No. 89054, dated New York April 2nd 20* covering shipment of 1,000 bags coffee.

ACCEPTED

MORGAN GUARANTY TRUST CO. $ 50,000 AND 00 CTS

TO MORGAN GUARANTY TRUST COMPANY OF NEW YORK NEW YORK, NEW YORK

GUARANI MENDOZA & CO.

⑆0210⑉0023⑆

Drafts in International Trade

bill of exchange

A written order by one person to pay a sum of money to a third person.

banker's acceptance

A draft or bill of exchange accepted by a bank where the accepting institution guarantees payment. Used extensively in foreign trade transactions.

Drafts are an international convention. In England and the British Commonwealth, drafts are called bills of exchange. Like a draft, a **bill of exchange** is a kind of check or promissory note without interest. Used primarily in international trade, it is a written order by one person to pay another a specific sum on a specific date sometime in the future. If the bill of exchange is drawn on a bank, it is called a bank draft. If it is drawn on another party, it is called a trade draft. Sometimes a bill of exchange will simply be called a draft, but whereas a draft is always negotiable (transferable by endorsement), this is not necessarily true of a bill of exchange.

A widely used draft in international trade is the **banker's acceptance**. It is a short-term credit investment created by a nonfinancial firm and guaranteed by a bank. This instrument is used when an exporter agrees to extend credit to an importer.

Assume Love, the importer, is in New York; Rackets, the exporter, is in Taiwan. Rackets is willing to permit Love to pay ninety days after shipment. Love makes a deal with her New York bank to issue Rackets' bank in Taiwan a letter of credit. This tells the seller's bank that the buyer's bank is willing to accept a draft drawn on the buyer in accordance with terms spelled out in the letter of credit. Love's bank may insist on a security interest in the tennis rackets, or it may conclude that Love is creditworthy. On receipt of the letter of credit, Rackets presents its bank in Taiwan with a draft drawn on Love's bank. That bank antes up the purchase amount (less its fees and interest), paying Rackets directly. It then forwards the draft, bill of lading, and other papers to a correspondent bank in New York, which in turn presents it to Love's bank. If the papers are in order, Love's bank will "accept" the draft (sign it). The signed draft is the banker's acceptance (see Figure 22.3). It is returned to the bank in Taiwan, which can then discount the banker's acceptance if it wishes payment immediately or else wait the ninety days to present it to the New York bank for payment. After remitting to the Taiwanese bank, the New York bank then demands payment from Love.

Checks

A second type of commercial paper is the common bank check, a special form of draft. Section 3-104(2)(b) of the UCC defines a **check** as "a draft drawn on a bank and payable on demand." **Postdating** a check (putting in a future date) does not invalidate it or change its character as payable on demand. Postdating simply changes the first time at which the payee may demand payment. Checks are, of course, usually written on paper forms, but a check can be written on anything—a door, a shirt, a rock—though certainly the would-be holder is not obligated to accept it.

Like drafts, checks may be accepted by the drawee bank. Bank acceptance of a check is called **certification**; the check is said to be certified by stamping the word "certified" on the face of the check. When the check is certified, the bank guarantees that it will honor the check when presented. It can offer this guarantee because it removes from the drawer's account the face amount of the check and holds it for payment. The payee may demand payment from the bank but not from the drawer or any prior indorser of the check.

A certified check is distinct from a cashier's check. A **cashier's check** is drawn on the account of the bank itself and signed by an authorized bank representative in return for a cash payment to it from the customer. The bank guarantees payment of the cashier's check also.

check

A negotiable instrument drawn against deposited funds to pay a specified amount of money to a specific person upon demand.

Postdating

Putting a date on an instrument (e.g., a check) that is later than the actual date.

certification

The acceptance by a drawee of a check or draft.

cashier's check

A check guaranteed by a bank and so as good as cash.

Notes

A note—often called a **promissory note**—is a written promise to pay a specified sum of money on demand or at a definite time. There are two parties to a note: the **maker** (promisor), and the **payee** (promisee). For an example of a promissory note, see Figure 22.4. The maker might execute a promissory note in return for a money loan from a bank or other financial institution or in return for the opportunity to make a purchase on credit.

promissory note

A written promise to pay or repay a specified sum of money at a stated time or on demand.

maker

A party that signs a promissory note.

payee

The person who is to receive payment on a draft or note.

FIGURE 22.4 A Promissory Note

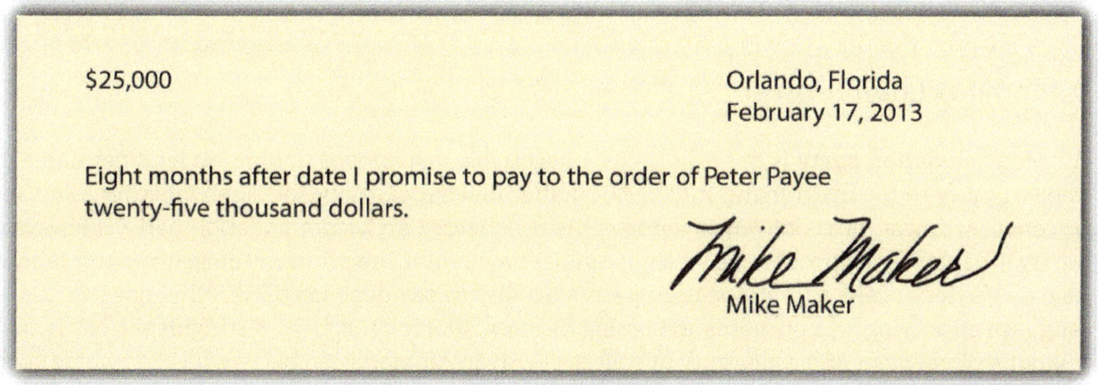
$25,000

Orlando, Florida
February 17, 2013

Eight months after date I promise to pay to the order of Peter Payee
twenty-five thousand dollars.

Mike Maker
Mike Maker

Certificates of Deposit

A fourth type of commercial paper is the **certificate of deposit**, commonly called a CD. The CD is a written acknowledgment by a bank that it has received money and agrees to repay it at a time specified in the certificate. The first negotiable CD was issued in 1961 by First National City Bank of New York (now Citibank); it was designed to compete for corporate cash that companies were investing in Treasury notes and other funds. Because CDs are negotiable, they can be traded easily if the holder wants cash, though their price fluctuates with the market.

certificate of deposit

A debt instrument issued by a bank; usually pays interest.

Other Parties to Commercial Paper

In addition to makers, drawees, and payees, there are five other capacities in which one can deal with commercial paper.

Indorser and Indorsee

indorser

The person who indorses.

indorsee

The person to whom a note or bill is indorsed, or assigned by indorsement.

The **indorser** (also spelled *endorser*) is one who transfers ownership of a negotiable instrument by signing it. A depositor indorses a check when presenting it for deposit by signing it on the back. The bank deposits its own funds, in the amount of the check, to the depositor's account. By indorsing it, the depositor transfers ownership of the check to the bank. The depositor's bank then can present it to the drawer's bank for repayment from the drawer's funds. The **indorsee** is the one to whom a draft or note is indorsed. When a check is deposited in a bank, the bank is the indorsee.

Holder

holder

One who has legal possession of a draft, note, or other negotiable instrument and who is entitled to payment.

A **holder** is "a person in possession of a negotiable that is payable either to bearer, or to an identified person that is the person in possession."[2] *Holder* is thus a generic term that embraces several of the specific types of parties already mentioned. An indorsee and a drawee can be holders. But a holder can also be someone unnamed whom the original parties did not contemplate by name—for example, the holder of a bearer note.

Holder in Due Course

holder in due course

Good-faith holder who has taken a negotiable instrument for value, without notice that it was overdue or had been dishonored or that there was any defense against or claim to it.

A **holder in due course** is a special type of holder who, if certain requirements are met, acquires rights beyond those possessed by the transferor (we alluded to this in describing the significance of Lorna Love's making of a negotiable—as opposed to a nonnegotiable—instrument). We discuss the requirements for a holder in due course in Chapter 24.

Accommodation Party

accommodation party

One who signs an instrument as drawer, indorser, or acceptor to help another raise money.

An **accommodation party** is one who signs a negotiable instrument in order to lend her name to another party to the instrument. It does not matter in what capacity she signs, whether as maker or comaker, drawer or codrawer, or indorser. As a signatory, an accommodation party is always a surety (Chapter 26; a surety is one who guarantees payment if the primarily obligated party fails to pay). The extent of the accommodation party's liability to pay depends on whether she has added language specifying her purposes in signing. Section 3-416 of the UCC distinguishes between a guaranty of payment and a guaranty of collection. An accommodation party who adds words such as "payment guaranteed" subjects herself to primary liability: she is guaranteeing that she will pay if the principal signatory fails to pay when the instrument is due. But if the accommodation party signs "collection guaranteed," the holder must first sue the maker and win a court judgment. Only if the judgment is unsatisfied can the holder seek to collect from the accommodation party. When words of guaranty do not specify the type, the law presumes a payment guaranty.

Key Takeaway

The modern law of commercial paper is, in general, covered by UCC Article 3. The two basic types of commercial paper are drafts and notes. The note is a two-party instrument whereby one person (maker) promises to pay money to a second person (payee). The draft is a three-party instrument whereby one person (drawer) directs a second (drawee) to pay money to the third (payee). Drafts may be sight drafts, payable on sight, or they may be time drafts, payable at a date specified on the draft. Checks are drafts drawn on banks. Other parties include indorser and indorsee, holder, holder in due course, and accommodation party.

Exercises

1. What are the two basic types of commercial paper?
2. What are the two types of drafts?
3. What kind of commercial paper is a check?

22.3 Requirements for Negotiability

Learning Objective

1. Know what is required for an instrument to be negotiable.

Overview

Whether or not a paper is negotiable is the first of our four major questions, and it is one that nonlawyers must confront. Auditors, retailers, and financial institutions often handle notes and checks and usually must make snap judgments about negotiability. Unless the required elements of Sections 3-103 and 3-104 of the Uniform Commercial Code (UCC) are met, the paper is not negotiable. Thus the paper meets the following criteria:

1. It must be in writing.
2. It must be signed by the maker or drawer.
3. It must be an unconditional promise or order to pay.
4. It must be for a fixed amount in money.
5. It must be payable on demand or at a definite time.
6. It must be payable to order or bearer, unless it is a check.

This definition states the basic premise of a negotiable instrument: the holder must be able to ascertain all essential terms from the face of the instrument.

Analysis of Required Elements

In Writing

Under UCC Section 1-201, "written" or "writing" includes "printing, typewriting or any other intentional reduction to tangible form." That definition is broad—so broad, in fact, that from time to time the newspapers report checks written on material ranging from a girdle (an Ohio resident wanted to make his tax payment stretch) to granite. Since these are tangible materials, the checks meet the writing requirement. The writing can be made in any medium: ink, pencil, or even spray paint, as was the case with the granite check. Of course, there is a danger in using pencil or an ink that can be erased, since the drawer might be liable for alterations. For example, if you write out in pencil a check for $10 and someone erases your figures and writes in $250, you may lose your right to protest when the bank cashes it.

Signed by the Maker or Drawer

Signature is not limited to the personal handwriting of one's name. "Any symbol executed or adopted by a party with present intention to authenticate a writing" will serve.[3] That means that a maker or drawer may make an impression of his signature with a rubber stamp or even an *X* if he intends that by so doing he has signed. It can be typed or by thumbprint. In some cases, an appropriate letterhead may serve to make the note or draft negotiable without any other signature. Nor does the position of the signature matter. Blackstone Kent's handwritten note, "Ten days from this note, I, Blackstone Kent, promise to pay $5,000 to the order of Webster Mews," is sufficient to make the note negotiable, even though there is no subsequent signature. Moreover, the signature may be in a trade name or an assumed name. (Note: special problems arise when an agent signs on behalf of a principal. We consider these problems in Chapter 25.)

Unconditional Promise or Order to Pay

Section 3-106(a) of the UCC provides that an instrument is *not* negotiable if it "states (i) an express condition to payment, (ii) that the promise or order is subject to or governed by another writing, or (iii) that rights or obligations with respect to the promise or order are stated in another writing. A reference to another writing does not of itself make the promise or order conditional." Under 3-106(b), a promise is not made conditional by "(i) reference to another writing for a statement of rights with respect to collateral, pre-payment, or acceleration, or (ii) because payment is limited to resort to a particular fund or source." As to "reference to another writing," see *Holly Hill Acres, Ltd. v. Charter Bank of Gainesville*, in Section 4.

The only permissible promise or order in a negotiable instrument is to pay a sum certain in money. Any other promise or order negates negotiability. The reason for this rule is to prevent an instrument from having an indeterminate value. The usefulness of a negotiable instrument as a substitute for money would be seriously eroded if the instrument's holder had to investigate whether a stipulation or condition had been met before the thing had any value (i.e., before the obligor's obligation to pay ripened).

Fixed Amount in Money

The value of the paper must be fixed (specific) so it can be ascertained, and it must be payable in money.

Fixed Amount

The instrument must recite an exact amount of money that is to be paid, although the exact amount need not be expressed in a single figure. For example, the note can state that the principal is $1,000 and the interest is 11.5 percent, without specifying the total amount. Or the note could state the amount in installments: twelve equal installments of $88.25. Or it could state different interest rates before and after a certain date or depending on whether or not the maker has defaulted; it could be determinable by a formula or by reference to a source described in the instrument.[4] It could permit the maker to take a discount if he pays before a certain date or could assess a penalty if he pays after the date. It could also provide for an attorney's fees and the costs of collection on default. If it is clear that interest is to be included but no interest amount is set, UCC Section 3-112 provides that it is "payable at the judgment rate in effect at the place of payment of the instrument and at the time interest first accrues." The fundamental rule is that for any time of payment, the holder must be able to determine, after the appropriate calculations, the amount then payable. See Section 4, *Centerre Bank of Branson v. Campbell*, for a case involving the "fixed amount" rule.

In Money

Section 1-201(24) of the UCC defines money as "a medium of exchange authorized or adopted by a domestic or foreign government as a part of its currency." As long as the medium of exchange was such at the time the instrument was made, it is payable in money, even if the medium of exchange has been abolished at the time the instrument is due. Section 3-107 provides the following as to payment in foreign currency: "Unless the instrument otherwise provides, an instrument that states the amount payable in foreign money may be paid in the foreign money or in an equivalent amount in dollars calculated by using the current bank-offered spot rate at the place of payment for the purchase of dollars on the day on which the instrument is paid."

Payable on Demand or at a Definite Time

An instrument that says it is payable on sight is payable on demand, as is one that states no time for payment. "Definite time" may be stated in several ways; it is not necessary to set out a specific date. For example, a note might say that it is payable on or before a stated date, at a fixed period after the date, at a fixed period after sight, at a definite time subject to acceleration, or at a definite time subject to extension at the option of the holder or automatically on or after the occurrence of a particular event. However, if the only time fixed is on the occurrence of a contingent event, the time is not definite, even though the event in fact has already occurred. An example of a valid acceleration clause is the following: "At the option of the holder, this note shall become immediately due and payable in the event that the maker fails to comply with any of the promises contained in this note or to perform any other obligation of the maker to the holder."

Is the note "Payable ten days after I give birth" negotiable? No, because the date the baby is due is uncertain. Is the note "Payable on January 1, but if the Yankees win the World Series, payable four days earlier" negotiable? Yes: this is a valid acceleration clause attached to a definite date.

One practical difference between a demand instrument and a time instrument is the date on which the statute of limitations begins to run. (A statute of limitations is a limit on the time a creditor has to file a lawsuit to collect the debt.) Section 3-118(1) of the UCC says that a lawsuit to enforce payment at a definite time "must be commenced within six years after the due date" (or the accelerated due date). For demand paper, an action must be brought "within six years after the demand."

Payable to Order or Bearer

An instrument payable to order is one that will be paid to a particular person or organization identifiable in advance. To be payable to order, the instrument must so state, as most ordinarily do, by placing the words "payable to order of" before the name of the payee. An instrument may be payable to the order of the maker, drawer, drawee, or someone else. It also may be payable to the order of two or more payees (together or in the alternative), to an estate, a trust, or a fund (in which case it is payable to the representative, to an office or officer, or to a partnership or unincorporated association). Suppose a printed form says that the instrument is payable both to order and to bearer. In that event, the instrument is payable only to order. However, if the words "to bearer" are handwritten or typewritten, then the instrument can be payable either to order or to bearer.

A negotiable instrument not payable to a particular person must be payable to bearer, meaning to any person who presents it. To be payable to bearer, the instrument may say "payable to bearer" or "to the order of bearer." It may also say "payable to John Doe or bearer." Or it may be made payable to cash or the order of cash.

Section 3-104(c) of the UCC excepts checks from the requirement that the instrument be "payable to bearer or order." Official Comment 2 to that section explains why checks are not required to have the "payable" wording: "Subsection (c) is based on the belief that it is good policy to treat checks, which are payment instruments, as negotiable instruments whether or not they contain the words 'to the order of.' These words are almost always pre-printed on the check form. . . . Absence of the quoted words can easily be overlooked and should not affect the rights of holders who may pay money or give credit for a check without being aware that it is not in the conventional form."

Also affecting this policy is the fact that almost all checks are now read by machines, not human beings. There is no one to see that the printed form does not contain the special words, and the significance of the words is recognized by very few people. In short, it doesn't matter for checks.

Missing and Ambiguous Terms

The rules just stated make up the conditions for negotiability. Dealing with two additional details—missing terms or ambiguous terms—completes the picture. Notwithstanding the presence of readily available form instruments, sometimes people leave words out or draw up confusing documents.

Incompleteness

An incomplete instrument—one that is missing an essential element, like the due date or amount—can be signed before being completed if the contents at the time of signing show that the maker or drawer intends it to become a negotiable instrument. Unless the date of an instrument is required to determine when it is payable, an undated instrument can still be negotiable.[5] Otherwise, to be enforceable, the instrument must first be completed—if not by the maker or drawer, then by the holder in accordance with whatever authority he has to do so.[6] See the case presented in Section 4, *Newman v. Manufacturers Nat. Bank of Detroit*.

Ambiguity

When it is unclear whether the instrument is a note or draft, the holder may treat it as either. Handwritten terms control typewritten and printed terms, and typewritten terms control printed terms. Words control figures, unless the words themselves are ambiguous, in which case the figures control. If the instrument contains a "conspicuous statement, however expressed, to the effect that the promise or order is not negotiable," its negotiability is destroyed, except for checks, and "an instrument may be a check even though it is described on its face by another term, such as 'money order.'"[7]

Key Takeaway

If an instrument is not negotiable, it generally will not be acceptable as payment in commercial transactions. The UCC requires that the value of a negotiable instrument be ascertainable on its face, without reference to other documents. Thus the negotiable instrument must be in writing, signed by the maker or drawer, an unconditional promise or order to pay, for a fixed amount in money, payable on demand or at a definite time, and payable to order or bearer, unless it is a check. If the instrument is incomplete or ambiguous, the UCC provides rules to determine what the instrument means.

Exercises

1. Why does the UCC require that the value of a negotiable instrument be ascertainable from its face, without extrinsic reference?
2. What are the six requirements for an instrument to meet the negotiability test?
3. Why are the words "pay to order" or "pay to bearer" or similar words required on negotiable instruments (except for checks—and why not for checks)?
4. If an instrument is incomplete, is it invalid?

22.4 Cases

Negotiability: Requires Unconditional Promise to Pay

Holly Hill Acres, Ltd. v. Charter Bank of Gainesville

314 So.2d 209 (Fla. App. 1975)

Scheb, J.

Appellant/defendant [Holly Hill] appeals from a summary judgment in favor of appellee/plaintiff Bank in a suit wherein the plaintiff Bank sought to foreclose a note and mortgage given by defendant.

The plaintiff Bank was the assignee from Rogers and Blythe of a promissory note and purchase money mortgage executed and delivered by the defendant. The note, executed April 28, 1972, contains the following stipulation:

> *This note with interest is secured by a mortgage on real estate, of even date herewith, made by the maker hereof in favor of the said payee, and shall be construed and enforced according to the laws of the State of Florida.* **The terms of said mortgage are by this reference made a part hereof.** *(emphasis added)*

Rogers and Blythe assigned the promissory note and mortgage in question to the plaintiff Bank to secure their own note. Plaintiff Bank sued defendant [Holly Hill] and joined Rogers and

Blythe as defendants alleging a default on their note as well as a default on defendant's [Holly Hill's] note.

Defendant answered incorporating an affirmative defense that fraud on the part of Rogers and Blythe induced the sale which gave rise to the purchase money mortgage. Rogers and Blythe denied the fraud. In opposition to plaintiff Bank's motion for summary judgment, the defendant submitted an affidavit in support of its allegation of fraud on the part of agents of Rogers and Blythe. The trial court held the plaintiff Bank was a holder in due course of the note executed by defendant and entered a summary final judgment against the defendant.

The note having incorporated the terms of the purchase money mortgage was not negotiable. The plaintiff Bank was not a holder in due course, therefore, the defendant was entitled to raise against the plaintiff any defenses which could be raised between the appellant and Rogers and Blythe. Since defendant asserted an affirmative defense of fraud, it was incumbent on the plaintiff to establish the non-existence of any genuine issue of any material fact or the legal insufficiency of defendant's affirmative defense. Having failed to do so, plaintiff was not entitled to a judgment as a matter of law; hence, we reverse.

The note, incorporating by reference the terms of the mortgage, did not contain the unconditional promise to pay required by [the UCC]. Rather, the note falls within the scope of [UCC 3-106(a)(ii)]: "A promise or order is unconditional unless it states that...it is subject to or governed by any other writing."

Plaintiff Bank relies upon *Scott v. Taylor* [Florida] 1912 [Citation], as authority for the proposition that its note is negotiable. *Scott*, however, involved a note which stated: "this note secured by mortgage." Mere reference to a note being secured by mortgage is a common commercial practice and such reference in itself does not impede the negotiability of the note. There is, however, a significant difference in a note stating that it is "secured by a mortgage" from one which provides, "the terms of said mortgage are by this reference made a part hereof." In the former instance the note merely refers to a separate agreement which does not impede its negotiability, while in the latter instance the note is rendered non-negotiable.

As a general rule the assignee of a mortgage securing a non-negotiable note, even though a bona fide purchaser for value, takes subject to all defenses available as against the mortgagee. [Citation] Defendant raised the issue of fraud as between himself and other parties to the note, therefore, it was incumbent on the plaintiff Bank, as movant for a summary judgment, to prove the non-existence of any genuinely triable issue. [Citation]

Accordingly, the entry of a summary final judgment is reversed and the cause remanded for further proceedings.

Case Questions

1. What was wrong with the promissory note that made it nonnegotiable?
2. How did the note's nonnegotiability—as determined by the court of appeals—benefit the defendant, Holly Hill?
3. The court determined that the bank was not a holder in due course; on remand, what happens now?

Negotiability: Requires Fixed Amount of Money

Centerre Bank of Branson v. Campbell
744 S.W.2d 490 (Mo. App. 1988)

Crow, J.

On or about May 7, 1985, appellants ("the Campbells") signed the following document:

FIGURE 22.5

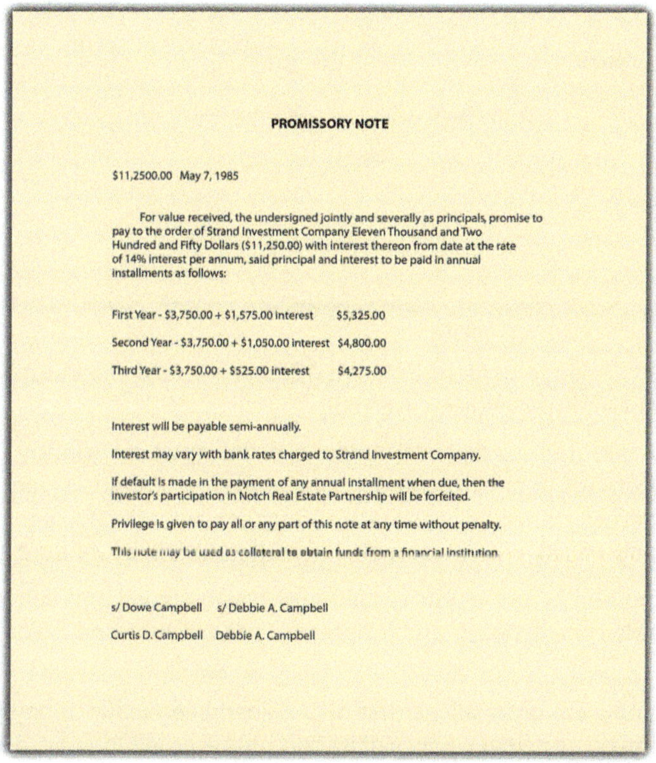
PROMISSORY NOTE

$11,2500.00 May 7, 1985

For value received, the undersigned jointly and severally as principals, promise to pay to the order of Strand Investment Company Eleven Thousand and Two Hundred and Fifty Dollars ($11,250.00) with interest thereon from date at the rate of 14% interest per annum, said principal and interest to be paid in annual installments as follows:

First Year - $3,750.00 + $1,575.00 interest $5,325.00

Second Year - $3,750.00 + $1,050.00 interest $4,800.00

Third Year - $3,750.00 + $525.00 interest $4,275.00

Interest will be payable semi-annually.

Interest may vary with bank rates charged to Strand Investment Company.

If default is made in the payment of any annual installment when due, then the investor's participation in Notch Real Estate Partnership will be forfeited.

Privilege is given to pay all or any part of this note at any time without penalty.

This note may be used as collateral to obtain funds from a financial institution

s/ Dowe Campbell s/ Debbie A. Campbell

Curtis D. Campbell Debbie A. Campbell

On May 13, 1985, the president and secretary of Strand Investment Company ("Strand") signed the following provision [see Figure 22.6] on the reverse side of the above [Figure 22.5] document:

FIGURE 22.6

I hereby Pledge and assign this promissory note in the amount $11,250.00 with recourse, dated this 13th day of May, 1985, to Centerre Bank of Branson, Branson, Mo.

s/ Ben P. Gaines
Strand Investment Co.
Ben P. Gaines, President

Attest:

s/ Betty Hawkins, Secretary, Betty Hawkins

On June 30, 1986, Centerre Bank of Branson ("Centerre") sued the Campbells. Pertinent to the issues on this appeal, Centerre's petition averred:

"1. ...on [May 7,] 1985, the [Campbells] made and delivered to Strand . . . their promissory note...and thereby promised to pay to Strand . . . or its order . . . ($11,250.00 [about $25,000 in 2016 dollars) with interest thereon from date at the rate of fourteen percent (14%) per annum; that a copy of said promissory note is attached here . . . and incorporated herein by reference.

2. That thereafter and before maturity, said note was assigned and delivered by Strand . . . to [Centerre] for valuable consideration and [Centerre] is the owner and holder of said promissory note."

Centerre's petition went on to allege that default had been made in payment of the note and that there was an unpaid principal balance of $9,000, plus accrued interest, due thereon. Centerre's petition prayed for judgment against the Campbells for the unpaid principal and interest.

[The Campbells] aver that the note was given for the purchase of an interest in a limited partnership to be created by Strand, that no limited partnership was thereafter created by Strand, and that by reason thereof there was "a complete and total failure of consideration for the said promissory note." Consequently, pled the answers, Centerre "should be estopped from asserting a claim against [the Campbells] on said promissory note because of such total failure of consideration for same."

The cause was tried to the court, all parties having waived trial by jury. At trial, the attorney for the Campbells asked Curtis D. Campbell what the consideration was for the note. Centerre's attorney interrupted: "We object to any testimony as to the consideration for the note because it's our position that is not a defense in this lawsuit since the bank is the holder in due course." * * *

The trial court entered judgment in favor of Centerre and against the Campbells for $9,000, plus accrued interest and costs. The trial court filed no findings of fact or conclusions of law, none having been requested. The trial court did, however, include in its judgment a finding that Centerre "is a holder in due course of the promissory note sued upon."

The Campbells appeal, briefing four points. Their first three, taken together, present a single hypothesis of error consisting of these components: (a) the Campbells showed "by clear and convincing evidence a valid and meritorious defense in that there existed a total lack and failure of consideration for the promissory note in question," (b) Centerre acquired the note subject to such defense in that Centerre was not a holder in due course, as one can be a holder in due course of a note only if the note is a negotiable instrument, and (c) the note was not a negotiable instrument inasmuch as "it failed to state a sum certain due the payee." * * *

We have already noted that if Centerre is not a holder in due course, the Campbells can assert the defense of failure of consideration against Centerre to the same degree they could have asserted it against Strand. We have also spelled out that Centerre cannot be a holder in due course if the note is not a negotiable instrument. The pivotal issue, therefore, is whether the provision that interest may vary with bank rates charged to Strand prevents the note from being a negotiable instrument. * * *

Neither side has cited a Missouri case applying [UCC 3-104(a)] to a note containing a provision similar to: "Interest may vary with bank rates charged to Strand." Our independent research has likewise proven fruitless. There are, however, instructive decisions from other jurisdictions.

In *Taylor v. Roeder*, [Citation, Virginia] (1987), a note provided for interest at "[t]hree percent (3.00%) over Chase Manhattan prime to be adjusted monthly." A second note provided for interest at "3% over Chase Manhattan prime adjusted monthly." Applying sections of the Uniform Commercial Code adopted by Virginia identical to [the Missouri UCC], the court held the notes were not negotiable instruments in that the amounts required to satisfy them could not be ascertained without reference to an extrinsic source, the varying prime rate of interest charged by Chase Manhattan Bank.

In *Branch Banking and Trust Co. v. Creasy*, [Citation, North Carolina] (1980), a guaranty agreement provided that the aggregate amount of principal of all indebtedness and liabilities at any one time for which the guarantor would be liable shall not exceed $35,000. The court, emphasizing that to be a negotiable instrument a writing must contain, among other things, an unconditional promise to pay a sum certain in money, held the agreement was not a negotiable instrument. The opinion recited that for the requirement of a sum certain to be met, it is necessary that at the time of payment the holder be able to determine the amount which is then payable from the instrument itself, with any necessary computation, without reference to any outside source. It is essential, said the court, for a negotiable instrument "to bear a definite sum so that subsequent holders may take and transfer the instrument without having to plumb the intricacies of the instrument's background. * * *

In *A. Alport & Son, Inc. v. Hotel Evans, Inc.*, [Citation] (1970), a note contained the notation "with interest at bank rates." Applying a section of the Uniform Commercial Code adopted by New York identical to [3-104(a)] the court held the note was not a negotiable instrument in that the amount of interest had to be established by facts outside the instrument.

In the instant case, the Campbells insist that it is impossible to determine from the face of the note the amount due and payable on any payment date, as the note provides that interest may vary with bank rates charged to Strand. Consequently, say the Campbells, the note is not a negotiable instrument, as it does not contain a promise to pay a "sum certain" [UCC 3-104(a)].

Centerre responds that the provision that interest may vary with bank rates charged to Strand is not "directory," but instead is merely "discretionary." The argument begs the question. Even if one assumes that Strand would elect not to vary the interest charged the Campbells if interest rates charged Strand by banks changed, a holder of the note would have to investigate such facts before determining the amount due on the note at any time of payment. We hold that under 3-104 and 3-106, supra, and the authorities discussed earlier, the provision that interest may vary with bank rates charged to Strand bars the note from being a negotiable instrument, thus no assignee thereof can be a holder in due course. The trial court therefore erred as a matter of law in ruling that Centerre was a holder in due course....

An alert reader will have noticed two other extraordinary features about the note, not mentioned in this opinion. First, the note provides in one place that principal and interest are to be paid in annual installments; in another place it provides that interest will be payable semiannually. Second, there is no acceleration clause providing that if default be made in the payment of any installment when due, then all remaining installments shall become due and payable immediately. It would have thus been arguable that, at time of trial, only the first year's installment of principal and interest was due. No issue is raised, however, regarding any of these matters, and we decline to consider them sua sponte [on our own].

The judgment is reversed and the cause is remanded for a new trial.

Case Questions

1. What was defective about this note that made it nonnegotiable?
2. What was the consequence to Centerre of the court's determination that the note was non-negotiable?
3. What did the Campbells give the note for in the first place, and why do they deny liability on it?

Undated or Incomplete Instruments

Newman v. Manufacturers Nat. Bank of Detroit

152 N.W.2d 564 (Mich. App. 1967)

Holbrook, J.

As evidence of [a debt owed to a business associate, Belle Epstein], plaintiff [Marvin Newman in 1955] drew two checks on the National Bank of Detroit, one for $1,000 [about $9,000 in 2016 dollars] and the other for $200 [about $1,800 in 2010 dollars]. The checks were left undated. Plaintiff testified that he paid all but $300 of this debt during the following next 4 years. Thereafter, Belle Epstein told plaintiff that she had destroyed the two checks. * * *

Plaintiff never notified defendant Bank to stop payment on the checks nor that he had issued the checks without filling in the dates. The date line of National Bank of Detroit check forms contained the first 3 numbers of the year but left the last numeral, month and day entries, blank, viz., "Detroit 1, Mich. _ _ 195_ _." The checks were cashed in Phoenix, Arizona, April 17, 1964, and the date line of each check was completed. * * * They were presented to and paid by Manufacturers National Bank of Detroit, April 22, 1964, under the endorsement of Belle Epstein. The plaintiff protested such payment when he was informed of it about a month later. Defendant Bank denied liability and plaintiff brought suit. * * *

The two checks were dated April 16, 1964. It is true that the dates were completed in pen and ink subsequent to the date of issue. However, this was not known by defendant. Defendant had a right to rely on the dates appearing on the checks as being correct. [UCC 3-113] provides in part as follows:

> *(a) An instrument may be antedated or postdated.*

Also, [UCC 3-114] provides in part as follows:

> *[T]ypewritten terms prevail over printed terms, handwritten terms prevail over both...*

Without notice to the contrary, defendant was within its rights to assume that the dates were proper and filled in by plaintiff or someone authorized by him. * * *

Plaintiff admitted at trial that defendant acted in good faith in honoring the two checks of plaintiff's in question, and therefore defendant's good faith is not in issue.

In order to determine if defendant bank's action in honoring plaintiff's two checks under the facts present herein constituted an exercise of proper procedure, we turn to article 4 of the UCC. * * * [UCC 4-401(d)] provides as follows:

> *A bank that in good faith makes payment to a holder may charge the indicated account of its customer according to:*
>
> *(1) the original tenor of his altered item; or*
>
> *(2) the tenor of his completed item, even though the bank knows the item has been completed unless the bank has notice that the completion was improper.*

* * * [W]e conclude it was shown that two checks were issued by plaintiff in 1955, filled out but for the dates which were subsequently completed by the payee or someone else to read April 16, 1964, and presented to defendant bank for payment, April 22, 1964. Applying the rules set forth in the UCC as quoted herein, the action of the defendant bank in honoring plaintiff's checks was in good faith and in accord with the standard of care required under the UCC.

Since we have determined that there was no liability under the UCC, plaintiff cannot succeed on this appeal.

Affirmed.

Case Questions

1. Why does handwriting control over printing or typing on negotiable instruments?
2. How could the plaintiff have protected himself from liability in this case?

22.5 Summary and Exercises

Summary

Commercial paper is the collective term for a variety of instruments—including checks, certificates of deposit, and notes—that are used to pay for goods; commercial paper is basically a contract to pay money. The key to the central role of commercial paper is negotiability, the means by which a person is empowered to transfer to another more than what the transferor himself possesses. The law regulating negotiability is Article 3 of the Universal Commercial Code.

Commercial paper can be divided into two basic types: the draft and the note. A draft is a document prepared by a drawer ordering the drawee to remit a stated sum of money to the payee. Drafts can be subdivided into two categories: sight drafts and time drafts. A note is a written promise to pay a specified sum of money on demand or at a definite time.

A special form of draft is the common bank check, a draft drawn on a bank and payable on demand. A special form of note is the certificate of deposit, a written acknowledgment by a bank that it has received money and agrees to repay it at a time specified in the certificate.

In addition to drawers, makers, drawees, and payees, one can deal with commercial paper in five other capacities: as indorsers, indorsees, holders, holders in due course, and accommodation parties.

A holder of a negotiable instrument must be able to ascertain all essential terms from its face. These terms are that the instrument (1) be in writing, (2) be signed by the maker or drawer, (3) contain an unconditional promise or order to pay (4) a sum certain in money, (5) be payable on demand or at a definite time, and (6) be payable to order or to bearer. If one of these terms is missing, the document is not negotiable, unless it is filled in before being negotiated according to authority given.

Exercises

1. Golf Inc. manufactures golf balls. Jack orders 1,000 balls from Golf and promises to pay $4,000 two weeks after delivery. Golf Inc. delivers the balls and assigns its contract rights to First Bank for $3,500. Golf Inc. then declares bankruptcy. May First Bank collect $3,500 from Jack? Explain.
2. Assume in problem 1 that Jack gives Golf Inc. a nonnegotiable note for $3,500 and Golf sells the note to the bank shortly after delivering the balls. May the bank collect the $3,500? Would the result be different if the note were negotiable? Explain.
3. George decides to purchase a new stereo system on credit. He signs two documents—a contract and a note. The note states that it is given "in payment for the stereo" and "if stereo is not delivered by July 2, the note is cancelled." Is the note negotiable? Explain.
4. Is the following instrument a note, check, or draft? Explain.

FIGURE 22.7

To: Robert Canon December 14, 2012

Five days after date pay to the order of: *Frances Sharp* the sum of $500.

Signed: *Dolores Jackson*

5. State whether the following provisions in an instrument otherwise in the proper form make the instrument nonnegotiable and explain why:
    a. A note stating, "This note is secured by a mortgage of the same date on property located at 1436 Dayton Street, Jameson, New York"
    b. A note for $25,000 payable in twenty installments of $1,250 each that provides, "In the event the maker dies all unpaid installments are cancelled"
    c. An instrument reading, "I.O.U., Rachel Donaldson, $3,000"
    d. A note reading, "I promise to pay Rachel Donaldson $3,000"
    e. A note stating, "In accordance with our telephone conversation of January 7th, I promise to pay Sally Wilkenson or order $1,500"
    f. An undated note for $1,500 "payable one year after date"
    g. A note for $1,500 "payable to the order of Marty Dooley, six months after Nick Solster's death"
    h. A note for $18,000 payable in regular installments also stating, "In the event any installment is not made as provided here, the entire amount remaining unpaid may become due immediately"
6. Lou enters into a contract to buy Alan's car and gives Alan an instrument that states, "This acknowledges my debt to Alan in the amount of $10,000 that I owe on my purchase of the 2008 Saturn automobile I bought from him today." Alan assigns the note to Judy for $8,000. Alan had represented to Lou that the car had 20,000 miles on it, but when Lou discovered the car had 120,000 miles he refused to make further payments on the note. Can Judy successfully collect from Lou? Explain.
7. The same facts as above are true, but the instrument Lou delivered to Alan reads, "I promise to pay to Alan or order $10,000 that I owe on my purchase of the 2008 automobile I bought from him today." Can Judy successfully collect from Lou? Explain.
8. Joe Mallen, of Sequim, Washington, was angry after being cited by a U.S. Fish and Wildlife Service for walking his dog without a leash in a federal bird refuge. He was also aggravated with his local bank because it held an out-of-state check made out to Mallen for ten days before honoring it. To vent his anger at both, Mallen spray painted a twenty-five-pound rock from his front yard with three coats of white paint, and with red paint, spelled out his account number, the bank's name, the payee, his leash law citation number, and his signature. Should the U.S. District Court in Seattle—the payee—attempt to cash the rock, would it be good? Explain.[8]

9. Raul Castana purchased a new stereo system from Eddington Electronics Store. He wrote a check on his account at Silver Bank in the amount of $1,200 and gave it to Electronics' clerk. David Eddington, the store owner, stamped the back of the check with his rubber indorsement stamp, and then wrote, "Pay to the order of City Water," and he mailed it to City Water to pay the utility bill. Designate the parties to this instrument using the vocabulary discussed in this chapter.
10. Would Castana's signed note made out to Eddington Electronics Store be negotiable if it read, "I promise to pay Eddington's or order $1,200 on or before May 1, 2012, but only if the stereo I bought from them works to my satisfaction"? Explain. And—disregarding negotiability for a moment—designate the parties to this instrument using the vocabulary discussed in this chapter.

Self-Test Questions

1. A negotiable instrument must
    a. be signed by the payee
    b. contain a promise to pay, which may be conditional
    c. include a sum certain
    d. be written on paper or electronically
2. The law governing negotiability is found in
    a. Article 3 of the UCC
    b. Article 9 of the UCC
    c. the Uniform Negotiability Act
    d. state common law
3. A sight draft
    a. calls for payment on a certain date
    b. calls for payment when presented
    c. is not negotiable
    d. is the same as a certificate of deposit
4. A note reads, "Interest hereon is 2% above the prime rate as determined by First National Bank in New York City." Under the UCC,
    a. the interest rate provision is not a "sum certain" so negotiability is destroyed
    b. the note is not negotiable because the holder must look to some extrinsic source to determine the interest rate
    c. the note isn't negotiable because the prime rate can vary before the note comes due
    d. variable interest rates are OK
5. A "maker" in negotiable instrument law does what?
    a. writes a check
    b. becomes obligated to pay on a draft
    c. is the primary obligor on a note
    d. buys commercial paper of dubious value for collection

Self-Test Answers

1. c
2. a

3. b
4. d
5. c

Endnotes

1. *Norton v. Knapp*, 19 N.W. 867 (IA 1884).
2. Uniform Commercial Code, Section 1-201(21).
3. Uniform Commercial Code, Section 1-201(39).
4. Uniform Commercial Code, Section 3-112(b).
5. Uniform Commercial Code, Section 3-113(b).
6. Uniform Commercial Code, Section 3-115.
7. Uniform Commercial Code, Section 3-104(d); Uniform Commercial Code, Section 3-104(f).
8. Joel Schwarz, "Taking Things for Granite," *Student Lawyer*, December 1981.

CHAPTER 23

Negotiation of Commercial Paper

Learning Objectives

After reading this chapter, you should understand the following:

1. The distinction between *transfer* and *negotiation* of commercial paper.
2. The liability of a person who transfers paper.
3. The types of indorsements and their effects.
4. Special problems that arise with forged indorsements.

In the previous chapter, we took up the requirements for paper to be negotiable. Here we take up negotiation.

23.1 Transfer and Negotiation of Commercial Paper

Learning Objectives

1. Understand what a transfer of commercial paper is.
2. Recognize the rights and liabilities of transferees and the liabilities of transferors.
3. Know how a transfer becomes a negotiation payable to order or to bearer.

Definitions, Rights, and Liabilities

Transfer means physical delivery of any instrument—negotiable or not—intending to pass title. Section 3-203(a) of the Uniform Commercial Code (UCC) provides that "an instrument is transferred when it is delivered by a person other than its issuer for the purpose of giving to the person receiving delivery the right to enforce the instrument."

Transfer

Delivery of an instrument by a person other than its issuer for the purpose of giving the transferee rights to enforce the instrument.

Negotiation and Holder

negotiation

The act of transferring commercial paper to a subsequent holder.

holder

Person in possession of an instrument drawn, issued, or indorsed to him or to his order, or to bearer, or in blank.

Section 3-201(a) of the UCC defines **negotiation** as "a transfer of possession, whether voluntary or involuntary, of an instrument to a person who thereby becomes its holder if possession is obtained from a person other than the issuer of the instrument." A **holder** is defined in Section 1-201(2) as "a person who is in possession of an instrument drawn, issued, or indorsed to him or his order or to bearer or in blank" ("in blank" means that no indorsement is required for negotiation). The original issuing or making of an instrument is not negotiation, though a holder can be the beneficiary of either a transfer or a negotiation. The Official Comment to 3-201(a) is helpful:

> *A person can become holder of an instrument when the instrument is issued to that person, or the status of holder can arise as the result of an event that occurs after issuance. "Negotiation" is the term used in article 3 to describe this post-issuance event. Normally, negotiation occurs as the result of a voluntary transfer of possession of an instrument by a holder to another person who becomes the holder as a result of the transfer. Negotiation always requires a change in possession of the instrument because nobody can be a holder without possessing the instrument, either directly or through an agent. But in some cases the transfer of possession is involuntary and in some cases the person transferring possession is not a holder.... [S]ubsection (a) states that negotiation can occur by an involuntary transfer of possession. For example, if an instrument is payable to bearer and it is stolen by Thief or is found by Finder, Thief or Finder becomes the holder of the instrument when possession is obtained. In this case there is an involuntary transfer of possession that results in negotiation to Thief or Finder.*[1]

In other words, to qualify as a holder, a person must possess an instrument that runs to her. An instrument "runs" to a person if (1) it has been issued to her or (2) it has been transferred to her by negotiation (negotiation is the "post-issuance event" cited in the comment). Commercially speaking, the status of the immediate person to whom the instrument was issued (the payee) is not very interesting; the thing of interest is whether the instrument is passed *on* by the payee *after* possession, through negotiation. Yes, the payee of an instrument is a holder, and can be a holder in due course, but the crux of negotiable instruments involves taking an instrument free of defenses that might be claimed by anybody against paying on the instrument; the payee would know of defenses, usually, so—as the comment puts it—"use of the holder-in-due-course doctrine by the payee of an instrument is not the normal situation....[r]ather, the holder in due course is an immediate or remote transferee of the payee."[2]

Liability of Transferors

We discuss liability in Chapter 25. However, a brief introduction to liability will help in understanding the types of indorsements discussed in this chapter. There are two types of liability affecting transferors: contract liability and warranty liability.

Contract Liability

Persons who sign the instrument—that is, makers, acceptors, drawers, indorsers—have signed a contract and are subject to contract liabilities. Drafts (checks) and notes are, after all, contracts. Makers and acceptors are *primary parties* and are unconditionally liable to pay the instrument. Drawers and indorsers are *secondary parties* and are conditionally liable. The conditions creating liability—that is, presentment, dishonor, and notice—are discussed in Chapter 25.

Warranty Liability

The transferor's *contract* liability is limited. It applies only to those who sign and only if certain additional conditions are met and, as will be discussed, can even be disclaimed. Consequently, a holder who has not been paid often must resort to a suit based on one of five warranties. These warranties are implied by law; UCC, Section 3-416, details them:

> *(A) A person who transfers an instrument for consideration warrants all of the following to the transferee and, if the transfer is by indorsement, to any subsequent transferee:*
>
> *(1) The warrantor is a person entitled to enforce the instrument.*
>
> *(2) All signatures on the instrument are authentic and authorized.*
>
> *(3) The instrument has not been altered.*
>
> *(4) The instrument is not subject to a defense or claim in recoupment of any party which can be asserted against the warrantor.*
>
> *(5) The warrantor has no knowledge of any insolvency proceeding commenced with respect to the maker or acceptor or, in the case of an unaccepted draft, the drawer.*

Breach of one of these warranties must be proven at trial if there is no general contract liability.

Liability of Transferees

The transferee takes by assignment; as an assignee, the new owner of the instrument has only those rights held by the assignor. Claims that could be asserted by third parties against the assignor can be asserted against the assignee. A negotiable instrument can be transferred in this sense without being negotiated. A payee, for example, might fail to meet all the requirements of negotiation; in that event, the instrument might wind up being merely transferred (assigned). When all requirements of negotiability and negotiation have been met, the buyer is a holder and may (if a holder in due course—see Chapter 24) collect on the instrument without having to prove anything more. But if the instrument was not properly negotiated, the purchaser is at most a transferee and cannot collect if defenses are available, even if the paper itself is negotiable.

How Negotiation Is Accomplished

Negotiation can occur with either bearer paper or order paper.

Negotiation of Instrument Payable to Bearer

An instrument payable to bearer—**bearer paper**—can be negotiated simply by delivering it to the transferee (see Figure 23.1; recall that "Lorna Love" is the proprietor of a tennis club introduced in Chapter 22): bearer paper runs to whoever is in possession of it, even a thief. Despite this simple rule, the purchaser of the instrument may require an indorsement on some bearer paper anyway. You may have noticed that sometimes you are requested to indorse your own check when you make it out to cash. That is because the indorsement increases the liability of the indorser if the holder is unable to collect. *Chung v. New York Racing Association* (Section 4) deals with issues involving bearer paper.

bearer paper

A negotiable instrument payable to whoever has possession.

FIGURE 23.1 Negotiation of Bearer Paper

Negotiation of Instrument Payable to Order

Order paper

Negotiable instrument that by its term is payable to a specified person or his or her assignee (as opposed to bearer paper).

Negotiation is usually voluntary, and the issuer usually directs payment "to order"—that is, to someone's order, originally the payee. **Order paper** is this negotiable instrument that by its term is payable to a specified person or his assignee. If it is to continue its course through the channels of commerce, it must be indorsed—signed, usually on the back—by the payee and passed on to the transferee. Continuing with the example used in Chapter 22, Rackets, Inc. (the payee) negotiates Lorna Love's check (Lorna is the issuer or drawer) drawn to the order of Rackets when an agent of Rackets "signs" the company's name on the reverse of the check and passes it to the indorsee, such as the bank or someone to whom Rackets owed money. (A company's signature is usually a rubber stamp for mere deposit, but an agent can sign the company name and direct the instrument elsewhere.) The transferee is a holder (see Figure 23.2). Had Rackets neglected to indorse the check, the transferee, though in physical possession, would not be a holder. Issues regarding indorsement are discussed in Section 2.

FIGURE 23.2 Negotiation of Order Paper

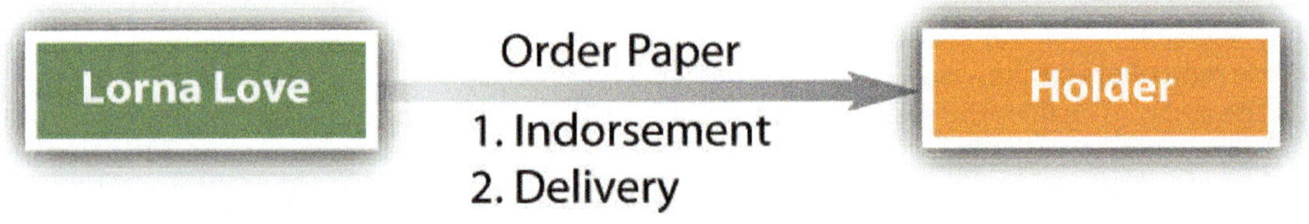

Key Takeaway

A transfer is the physical delivery of an instrument with the intention to pass title—the right to enforce it. A mere transferee stands in the transferor's shoes and takes the instrument subject to all the claims and defenses against paying it that burdened it when the transferor delivered it. Negotiation is a special type of transfer—voluntary or involuntary—to a holder. A holder is a person who has an instrument drawn, issued, or indorsed to him or his order or to bearer or in blank. If the instrument is order paper, negotiation is accomplished by indorsement and delivery to the next holder; if it is bearer paper or blank paper, delivery alone accomplishes negotiation. Transferors incur two types of liability: those who sign the instrument are contractually liable; those who sign or those who do not sign are liable to the transferee in warranty.

Exercises

1. What is a transfer of commercial paper, and what rights and liabilities has the transferee?
2. What is a negotiation of commercial paper?
3. What is a holder?
4. How is bearer paper negotiated?
5. How is order paper negotiated?

23.2 Indorsements

Learning Objectives

1. Understand the meaning of indorsement and its formal requirements.
2. Know the effects of various types of indorsements: no indorsement, partial, blank, special, restrictive, conditional, qualified.

Definition and Formal Requirements of Indorsement

Definition

Most commonly, paper is transferred by indorsement. The indorsement is evidence that the indorser intended the instrument to move along in the channels of commerce. An **indorsement** is defined by UCC Section 3-204(a) as

> *a signature, other than that of a signer as maker, drawer, or acceptor, that alone or accompanied by other words is made on an instrument for the purpose of (i) negotiating the instrument, (ii) restricting payment of the instrument, or (iii) incurring indorser's liability on the instrument, but regardless of the intent of the signer, a signature and its accompanying words is an indorsement unless the accompanying words, terms of the instrument, place of the signature, or other circumstances unambiguously indicated that the signature was made for a purpose other than indorsement.*

indorsement

The act of a payee, drawee, accommodation party, indorser, or holder of an instrument in writing his name on the back of same with the intention of negotiating it.

Placement of Indorsement

Indorse (or *endorse*) literally means "on the back of," as fish, say, have dorsal fins—fins on their backs. Usually indorsements are on the back of the instrument, but an indorsement could be on a piece of paper affixed to the instrument. Such an attachment is called an **allonge**—it comes along with the instrument (UCC, Section 3-204(a)).

allonge

A piece of paper firmly affixed to an instrument.

There are rules about where indorsements are placed. The Expedited Funds Availability Act was enacted in 1987 by Congress to standardize holding periods on deposits made to commercial banks and to regulate institutions' use of deposit holds—that is, how soon customers can access the money after they have deposited a check in the bank. The Federal Reserve Board subsequently adopted "Regulation CC, Check Endorsement Standards" to improve funds availability and expedite the return of checks. See Figure 23.3.

FIGURE 23.3 Indorsement Standard

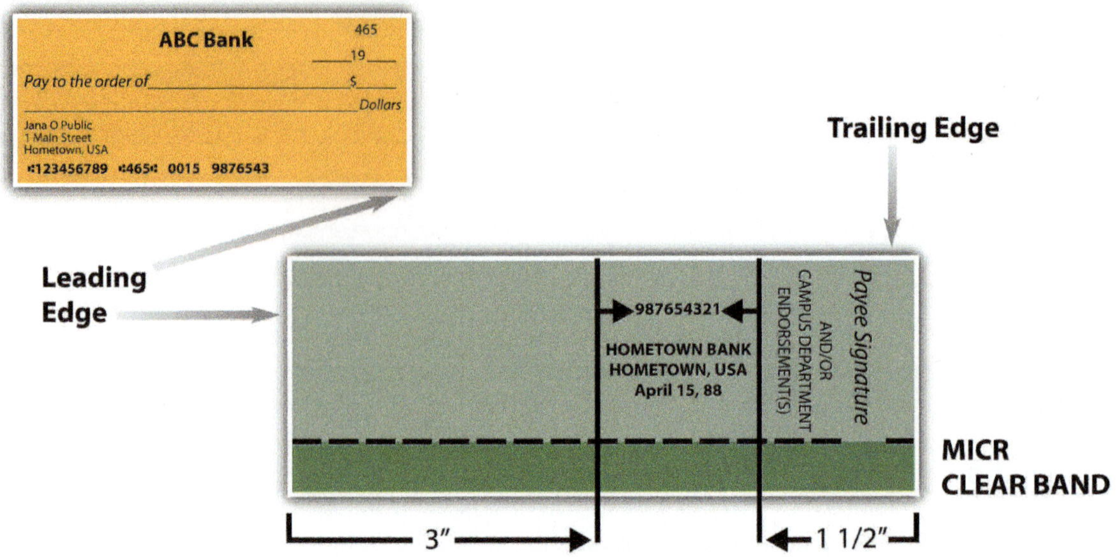

From UC Irvine Administrative Policies & Procedures, Business and Financial Affairs, Financial Services, Sec. 704-13: Check Endorsement Procedures, at http://www.policies.uci.edu/adm/procs/700/704-13.html.

As shown in Figure 23.3, specific implementing guidelines define criteria for the placement, content, and ink color of endorsement areas on the back of checks for the depositary bank (bank of first deposit), subsequent indorsers (paying banks), and corporate or payee indorsers. Indorsements must be made within 1½ inches of the trailing (left) edge of the back of the check; remaining space is for bank indorsements. There is no penalty for violating the standard—it is a guideline. The abbreviation "MICR" stands for magnetic ink character recognition. The "clear band" is a section of the back of the check that is not supposed to be intruded upon with any magnetic (machine-readable) printing that would interfere with machine reading on the front side (the bank routing numbers).

Sometimes an indorser adds words intended to strengthen the indorsement; for example, "I hereby assign all my right, title, and interest in this note to Carl Carpenter." Words of assignment such as these and also words of condition, waiver, guaranty, limitation, or disclaimer of liability do not negate the effect of an indorsement.

Misspelled or Incorrect Indorsements

When the instrument is made payable to a person under a misspelled name (or in a name other than his own), he may indorse in the wrong name or the right one or both. It is safer to sign in both names, and the purchaser of the instrument may demand a signature in both names (UCC, Section 3-204(d)).

Various Indorsements and Their Effects

A holder can indorse in a variety of ways; indorsements are not identical and have different effects.

No Indorsement

If the instrument requires a signature, transfer without indorsement is an assignment only. Bearer paper does not require indorsement, so it can be negotiated simply by delivering it to the transferee, who becomes a holder. The transferor has no contract liability on the instrument, however, because he has not signed it. He does remain liable on the warranties, but only to the person who receives the paper, not to subsequent transferees.

Because it is common practice for a depository bank (the bank into which a person makes a deposit) to receive unindorsed checks under so-called lockbox agreements from customers who receive a high volume of checks, a customer who is a holder can deposit a check or other instrument for credit to his account without indorsement. Section 4-205(1) of the UCC provides that a "depositary bank becomes a holder ... at the time it receives the item for collection if the customer at the time of delivery was a holder, whether or not the customer indorses the item."

Partial Indorsement

To be effective as negotiation, an indorsement must convey the entire instrument. An indorsement that purports to convey only a portion of the sum still due amounts to a partial assignment. If Rackets' agent signs the check "Rackets, Inc." together with the words "Pay half to City Water, /s/ Agent" and delivers the check to City Water, that does not operate as an indorsement, and City Water becomes an assignee, not a holder.

Blank Indorsement

A **blank indorsement** consists of the indorser's signature alone (see Figure 23.4, left). A blank indorsement converts the instrument into paper closely akin to cash. Since the indorsement does not specify to whom the instrument is to be paid, it is treated like bearer paper—assuming, of course, that the first indorser is the person to whom the instrument was payable originally. A paper with blank indorsement may be negotiated by delivery alone, until such time as a holder converts it into a *special indorsement* (discussed next) by writing over the signature any terms consistent with the indorsement. For example, a check indorsed by the payee (signed on the back) may be passed from one person to another and cashed in by any of them.

blank indorsement

Indorsement of a check or other negotiable paper without naming a further indorsee (usually simply the indorser's name).

FIGURE 23.4 Forms of Endorsement

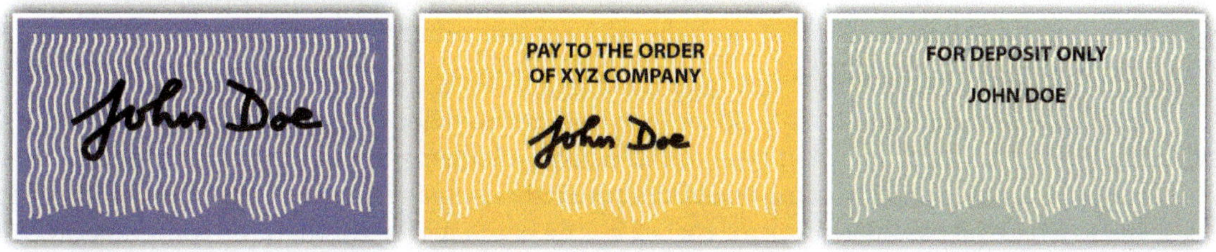

A blank indorsement creates conditional contract liability in the indorser: he is liable to pay if the paper is dishonored. The blank indorser also has warranty liability toward subsequent holders.

Special Indorsement

A **special indorsement**, sometimes known as an "indorsement in full," names the transferee-holder. The payee of a check can indorse it over to a third party by writing "Pay to the order of [name of the third party]" and then signing her name (see Figure 23.4, center). Once specially indorsed, the check (or other instrument) can be negotiated further only when the special indorsee adds his own signature. A holder may convert a blank indorsement into a special indorsement by writing above the signature of the indorser words of a contractual nature consistent with the character of the instrument.

special indorsement

Indorsement that names the transferee-holder.

So, for example, Lorna Love's check to Rackets, Inc., indorsed in blank (signed by its agent or stamped with Rackets' indorsement stamp—its name alone) and handed to City Water, is not very safe: it is bearer paper. If the check fell onto the floor, anybody could be a holder and cash it. It can easily be converted into a check with special indorsement: City Water's clerk need only add the words "Pay City Water" above Rackets' indorsement. (The magic words of negotiability—"pay to order of bearer"—are not required in an indorsement.) Before doing so, City Water could have negotiated it simply by giving it to someone (again, a blank indorsement acts as bearer paper). After converting it to a special indorsement, City Water must indorse it in order to transfer it by negotiation to someone else. The liabilities of a special indorser are the same as those of a blank indorser.

The dichotomy here of indorsement in blank or special indorsement is the indorser's way of indicating how the instrument can be subsequently negotiated: with or without further indorsing.

Restrictive Indorsement

restrictive indorsement

Indorsement specifying the use to which an instrument may be put; most common is "For deposit only."

A **restrictive indorsement** attempts to limit payment to a particular person or otherwise prohibit further transfer or negotiation. We say "attempts to limit" because a restrictive indorsement is generally invalid. Section 3-206(a) of the UCC provides that an attempt to limit payment to a particular person or prohibit further transfer "is not effective." Nor is "[a]n indorsement stating a condition to the right of the indorsee to receive payment"; the restriction may be disregarded. However, two legitimate restrictive indorsements are valid: collection indorsements and trust indorsements. *Wisner Elevator Company, Inc. v. Richland State Bank* (Section 4) deals with conditional and restrictive indorsements.

Collection Indorsement

collection indorsement

Indorsement restricting payment to collection or deposit.

It is very common for people and businesses to mail checks to their bank for deposit to their accounts. Sometimes mail goes astray or gets stolen. Surely it must be permissible for the customer to safeguard the check by restricting its use to depositing it in her account. A **collection indorsement**, such as "For deposit" or "For collection," is effective. Section 3-206(c) of the UCC provides that anybody other than a bank who purchases the instrument with such an indorsement converts the instrument—effectively steals it. A depositary bank that takes it must deposit it as directed, or the bank has converted it. A payor bank that is also the depositary bank that takes the instrument for immediate payment over the counter converts it: the check cannot be cashed; it must be deposited (see Figure 23.4).

To illustrate, suppose that Kate Jones indorses her paycheck "For deposit only, Kate Jones," which is by far the most common type of restrictive indorsement (see Figure 23.4, right). A thief steals the check, indorses his name below the restrictive indorsement, and deposits the check in Last Bank, where he has an account, or cashes it. The check moves through the collection process to Second Bank and then to First Bank, which pays the check. Kate has the right to recover only from Last Bank, which did not properly honor the indorsement by depositing the payment in her account.

Trust Indorsement

trust indorsement

An indorsement to a person who is to hold or use the funds for the benefit of the indorser or a third party.

A second legitimate restrictive indorsement is indorsement in trust, called a **trust indorsement** (sometimes *agency indorsement*). Suppose Paul Payee owes Carlene Creditor a debt. Payee indorses a check drawn to him by a third party, "Pay to Tina Attorney in trust for Carlene Creditor." Attorney indorses in blank and delivers it to (a) a holder for value, (b) a depository bank for collection, or (c) a payor bank for payment. In each case, these takers can safely pay Attorney so long as they have no notice under Section 3-307 of the UCC of any breach of fiduciary duty that Attorney may be committing. For example, under Section 3-307(b), these takers have notice of a breach of trust if the check was taken in any transaction known by the taker to be for Attorney's personal benefit. Subsequent transferees of the check from the holder or depositary bank are not affected by the restriction unless they have knowledge that Attorney dealt with the check in breach of trust (adapted from UCC, Section 3-206, Official Comment 4). (Of course Attorney should not indorse in blank; she should indorse "Tina Attorney, in trust for Carlene Creditor" and deposit the check in her trust account.)

The dichotomy here between restrictive and unrestrictive indorsements is the indorser's way of showing to what use the instrument may be put.

Conditional Indorsement

An indorser might want to condition the negotiation of an instrument upon some event, such as "Pay Carla Green if she finishes painting my house by July 15." Such a **conditional indorsement** is generally ineffective: the UCC, Section 3-206(b), says a person paying for value can disregard the condition without liability.

conditional indorsement

Indorsement that makes instrument's payment dependent on the occurrence of some event specified in the indorsement; generally invalid.

Qualified Indorsement

An indorser can limit his liability by making a **qualified indorsement**. The usual qualified indorsement consists of the words "**without recourse**," which mean that the indorser has no contract liability to subsequent holders if a maker or drawee defaults. A qualified indorsement does not impair negotiability. The qualification must be in writing by signature on the instrument itself. By disclaiming contract liability, the qualified indorser also limits his warranty liabilities, though he does not eliminate them. Section 3-415(a) of the UCC narrows the indorser's warranty that no defense of any party is good against the indorser. In its place, the qualified indorser warrants merely that he has no *knowledge* of any defense.

qualified indorsement

Wording designed to limit the indorser's contract liability; "without recourse" is the most frequently seen example.

without recourse

Language used in a qualified indorsement to limit indorser's contract liability.

"Without recourse" indorsements can have a practical impact on the balance sheet. A company holding a promissory note can obtain cash by discounting it—indorsing it over to a bank for maturity value less the bank's discount. As an indorser, however, the company remains liable to pay the amount to subsequent holders should the maker default at maturity. The balance sheet must reflect this possibility as a contingent liability. However, if the note is indorsed without recourse, the company need not account for any possible default of the maker as a contingent liability.

The dichotomy here between qualified and unqualified indorsements is the indorser's way of indicating what liability she is willing to incur to subsequent holders.

Key Takeaway

An indorsement is, usually, the signature of an instrument's holder on the back of the instrument, indicating an intention that the instrument should proceed through the channels of commerce. The Federal Reserve Board has recommendations for how instruments should be indorsed to speed machine reading of them. Indorsements are either blank or special; they are either restrictive or nonrestrictive; and they are either qualified or unqualified. These pairings show the indorser's intention as to *how* further negotiation may be accomplished, to *what uses* the instrument may be put, and *what liability* the indorser is willing to assume.

Exercises

1. If an instrument is not indorsed according to Federal Reserve Board standards, is it still valid?
2. Suppose that Indorsee signs an instrument in blank and drops it. Suppose that the instrument is found by Finder and that Finder delivers it to Third Person with the intention to sell it. Is this successful negotiation?
3. Why would a person make a restrictive indorsement? A qualified indorsement?

23.3 Problems and Issues in Negotiation

Learning Objectives

1. Recognize under what circumstances a negotiation is subject to rescission.
2. Know the effect of reacquisition of an instrument.
3. Understand how instruments made payable to two or more persons are negotiated.
4. Understand how the UCC treats forged indorsements, imposters, and other signatures in the name of the payee.

Common Issues Arising in Negotiation of Commercial Paper

A number of problems commonly arise that affect the negotiation of commercial paper. Here we take up three.

Negotiation Subject to Rescission

A negotiation—again, transfer of possession to a person who becomes a holder—can be effective even when it is made by a person without the capacity to sign. Section 3-202(a) of the UCC declares that negotiation is effective even when the indorsement is made by an infant or by a corporation exceeding its powers; is obtained by fraud, duress, or mistake; is part of an illegal transaction; or is made in breach of a duty.

However, unless the instrument was negotiated to a holder in due course, the indorsement can be rescinded or subjected to another appropriate legal remedy. The Official Comment to this UCC section is helpful:

> *Subsection (a) applies even though the lack of capacity or the illegality is of a character which goes to the essence of the transaction and makes it entirely void. It is inherent in the character of negotiable instruments that any person in possession of an instrument which by its terms is payable to that person or to bearer is a holder and may be dealt with by anyone as a holder. The principle finds its most extreme application in the well-settled rule that a holder in due course may take the instrument even from a thief and be protected against the claim of the rightful owner. The policy of subsection (a) is that any person to whom an instrument is negotiated is a holder until the instrument has been recovered from that person's possession.*[3]

So suppose a mentally incapacitated person under a guardianship evades her guardian, goes to town, and writes a check for a new car. Normally, contracts made by such persons are void. But the check is negotiable here. If the guardian finds out about the escapade before the check leaves the dealer's hands, the deal could be rescinded: the check could be retrieved and the car returned.

Effect of Reacquisition

A prior party who reacquires an instrument may reissue it or negotiate it further. But doing so discharges intervening parties as to the reacquirer and to later purchasers who are not holders in due course. Section 3-207 of the UCC permits the reacquirer to cancel indorsements unnecessary to his title or ownership; in so doing, he eliminates the liability of such indorsers even as to holders in due course.

Instruments Payable to Two or More Persons

A note or draft can be payable to two or more persons. In form, the payees can be listed in the alternative or jointly. When a commercial paper says "Pay to the order of Lorna Love or Rackets, Inc.," it is stated in the alternative. Either person may negotiate (or discharge or enforce) the paper without the consent of the other. On the other hand, if the paper says "Pay to the order of Lorna Love and Rackets, Inc." or does not clearly state that the payees are to be paid in the alternative, then the instrument is payable to both of them and may be negotiated (or discharged or enforced) only by both of them acting together. The case presented in Section 4, *Wisner Elevator Company, Inc. v. Richland State Bank*, deals, indirectly, with instruments payable to two or more persons.

Forged Indorsements, Imposters, and Fictitious Payees

The General Rule on Forged Indorsements

When a check already made out to a payee is stolen, an unscrupulous person may attempt to negotiate it by forging the payee's name as the indorser. Under UCC Section 1-201(43), a forgery is an "unauthorized signature." Section 3-403(a) provides that any unauthorized signature on an instrument is "ineffective except as the signature of the unauthorized signer." The consequence is that, generally, the loss falls on the first party to take the instrument with a forged or unauthorized signature because that person is in the best position to prevent the loss.

Lorna Love writes a check to Steve Supplier on her account at First State Bank, but the check goes astray and is found by Carl Crooks. Crooks indorses the check "Steve Supplier" and presents it for cash to a busy teller who fails to request identification. Two days later, Steve Supplier inquires about his check. Love calls First State Bank to stop payment. Too late—the check has been cashed. Who bears the loss—Love, Supplier, or the bank? The bank does, and it must recredit Love's account. The forged indorsement on the check was ineffective; the bank was not a holder, and the check should not have been allowed into the channels of commerce. This is why banks may retain checks for a while before allowing access to the money. It is, in part, what the Expedited Funds Availability Act (mentioned in Section 2, "Indorsements") addresses—giving banks time to assess the validity of checks.

Exceptions: Imposter, Fictitious Payee, and Dishonest Employee Rules

The loss for a forged indorsement usually falls on the first party to take the instrument with a forged signature. However, there are three important exceptions to this general rule: the imposter rule, the fictitious payee rule, and the dishonest employee rule.

The Imposter Rule

If one person poses as the named payee or as an agent of the named payee, inducing the maker or drawer to issue an instrument in the name of the payee to the imposter (or his confederate), the imposter's indorsement of the payee's name is effective. The paper can be negotiated according to the **imposter rule**.

imposter rule

Rule stating that if an impostor endorses a negotiable instrument and receives payment in good faith, the drawer of the instrument is responsible for the loss.

If the named payee is a real person or firm, the negotiation of the instrument by the imposter is good and has no effect on whatever obligation the drawer or maker has to the named payee. Lorna Love owes Steve Supplier $2,000. Knowing of the debt, Richard Wright writes to Love, pretending to be Steve Supplier, requesting her to send a check to Wright's address in Supplier's name. When the check arrives, Wright indorses it by signing "Pay to the order of Richard Wright, (signed) Steve Supplier," and then indorses it in his own name and cashes it. Love remains liable to Steve Supplier for the money that she owes him, and Love is out the $2,000 unless she can find Wright.

The difference between this case and the one involving the forger Carl Crooks is that in the second case the imposter (Wright) "induced the maker or drawer [Lorna Love] to issue the instrument ... by impersonating the payee of the instrument [Steve Supplier]" (UCC, Section 3-404(a)), whereas in the first case the thief did not induce Love to issue the check to him—he simply found it. And the rationale for making Lorna Love bear the loss is that she failed to detect the scam: she *intended* the imposter, Wright, to receive the instrument. Section 3-404(c) provides that the indorsement of the imposter (Wright, posing as Steve Supplier) is effective. The same rule applies if the imposter poses as an agent: if the check is payable to Supplier, Inc., a company whose president is Steve Supplier, and an impostor impersonates Steve Supplier, the check could be negotiated if the imposter indorses it as Supplier, Inc.'s, agent "Steve Supplier."[4]

Similarly, suppose Love is approached by a young man who says to her, "My company sells tennis balls, and we're offering a special deal this month: a can of three high-quality balls for $2 each. We'll send your order to you by UPS." He hands her a sample ball: it is substantial, and the price is good. Love has heard of the company the man says he represents; she makes out a check for $100 to "Sprocket Athletic Supply." The young man does not represent the company at all, but he cashes the check by forging the indorsement and the bank pays. Love takes the loss: surely she is more to blame than the bank.

The Fictitious Payee Rule

fictitious payee

A payee who has no existence or is intended to have no interest in the instrument.

Suppose Lorna Love has a bookkeeper, Abby Accountant. Abby presents several checks for Love to sign, one made out to Carlos Aquino. Perhaps there really is no such person, or perhaps he is somebody whom Love deals with regularly, but Accountant intends him to have no interest here. No matter: Love signs the check in the amount of $2,000. Accountant takes the check and indorses it: "Carlos Aquino, pay to the order of Abby Accountant." Then she signs her name as the next indorser and cashes the check at Love's bank. The check is good, even though it was never intended by Accountant that "Carlos Aquino"—the **fictitious payee**—have any interest in the instrument. The theory here is to "place the loss on the drawer of the check rather than on the drawee or the Depositary Bank that took the check for collection. ... The drawer is in the best position to avoid the fraud and thus should take the loss."[5] This is also known as "the padded-payroll rule."

In the *imposter* cases, Love drew checks made out to real names but gave them to the wrong person (the imposter); in the *fictitious payee* cases she wrote checks to a nonexistent person (or a real person who was not intended to have any interest at all).

The Dishonest Employee Rule

The UCC takes head-on the recurring problem of a dishonest employee. It says that if an employer "entrust[s] an employee with responsibility with respect to the instrument and the employee or a person acting in concert with the employee makes a fraudulent indorsement of the instrument, the indorsement is effective."[6] For example (adapted from UCC 3-405, Official Comment 3; the Comment does not use the names of these characters, of course), the duties of Abby Accountant, a bookkeeper, include posting the amounts of checks payable to Lorna Love to the accounts of the drawers of the checks. Accountant steals a check payable to Love, which was entrusted to Accountant, and forges Love's indorsement. The check is deposited by Accountant to an account in the depositary bank that Accountant opened in the same name as Lorna Love, and the check is honored by the drawee bank. The indorsment is effective as Love's indorsement because Accountant's duties include processing checks for bookkeeping purposes. Thus, Accountant is entrusted with "responsibility" with respect to the check. Neither the depositary bank nor the drawee bank is liable to Love for conversion of the check. The same result would follow if Accountant deposited the check in the account in the depositary bank without indorsement (UCC, Section 4-205(a)). Under Section 4-205(c), deposit in a depositary bank in an account in a name substantially similar to that of Lorna Love is the equivalent of an indorsement in the name of Lorna Love. If, say, the janitor had stolen the checks, the result would be different, as the janitor is not entrusted with responsibility regarding the instrument.

Negligence

Not surprisingly, though, if a person fails to exercise ordinary care and thereby substantially contributes to the success of a forgery, that person cannot assert "the alteration or the forgery against a person that, in good faith, pays the instrument or takes it for value."[7] If the issuer is also negligent, the loss is allocated between them based on comparative negligence theories. Perhaps the bank teller in the example about the tennis-ball scam should have inquired whether the young man had any authority to cash the check made out to Sprocket Athletic Supply. If so, the bank could be partly liable. Or suppose Lorna Love regularly uses a rubber signature stamp for her tennis club business but one day carelessly leaves it unprotected. As a result, the stamp and some checks are stolen; Love bears any loss for being negligent. Similarly liable is a person who has had previous notice that his signature has been forged and has taken no steps to prevent reoccurrences, as is a person who negligently mails a check to the wrong person, one who has the same name as the payee. The UCC provides that the negligence of two or more parties might be compared in order to determine whether each party bears a percentage of the loss, as illustrated in *Victory Clothing Co., Inc. v. Wachovia Bank, N.A.* (Section 4).

Key Takeaway

A negotiation is effective even if the transaction involving it is void or voidable, but the transferor—liable on the instrument—can regain its possession and rescind the deal (except as to holders in due course or a person paying in good faith without notice). Instruments may be made payable to two or more parties in the alternative or jointly and must be indorsed accordingly. Generally, a forged indorsement is ineffective, but exceptions hold for cases involving imposters, fictitious payees, and certain employee dishonesty. If a person's own negligence contributes to the forgery, that person must bear as much of the loss as is attributable to his or her negligence.

Exercises

1. A makes a check out to B for $200 for property both parties know is stolen. Is the check good?
2. What is the difference between (a) the imposter rule, (b) the fictitious payee rule, and (c) the dishonest employee rule?
3. How does comparative negligence work as it relates to forged indorsements?

23.4 Cases

Bearer Paper

(Note: this is a trial court's opinion.)

Chung v. New York Racing Ass'n
714 N.Y.S.2d 429 (N.Y. Dist. Ct. 2000)

Gartner, J.

A published news article recently reported that an investigation into possible money laundering being conducted through the racetracks operated by the defendant New York Racing Association was prompted by a small-time money laundering case in which a Queens bank robber used stolen money to purchase betting vouchers and then exchanged the vouchers for clean cash. [Citation] The instant case does not involve any such question of wrongdoing, but does raise a novel legal issue regarding the negotiability of those same vouchers when their possession is obtained by a thief or finder. The defendant concedes that "there are no cases on point."

The defendant is a private stock corporation incorporated and organized in New York as a non-profit racing association pursuant to [New York law]. The defendant owns and operates New York's largest thoroughbred racetracks—Belmont Park Racetrack, Aqueduct Racetrack, and Saratoga Racetrack—where it stages thoroughbred horse races and conducts pari-mutuel wagering on them pursuant to a franchise granted to the defendant by the State of New York.

The plaintiff was a Belmont Park Racetrack horse player. He attended the track and purchased from the defendant a voucher for use in SAMS machines. As explained in [Citation]:

In addition to accepting bets placed at parimutuel facility windows staffed by facility employees, [some] facilities use SAMS. SAMS are automated machines which permit a bettor to enter his bet by inserting money, vouchers or credit cards into the machine, thereby enabling him to select the number or combination he wishes to purchase. A ticket is issued showing those numbers.[8]

When a voucher is utilized for the purpose of placing a bet at a SAMS machine, the SAMS machine, after deducting the amount bet by the horse player during the particular transaction, provides the horse player with, in addition to his betting ticket(s), a new voucher showing the remaining balance left on the voucher.

In the instant case, the unfortunate horse player departed the SAMS machine with his betting tickets, but *without* his new voucher—showing thousands of dollars in remaining value—which he inadvertently left sitting in the SAMS machine. Within several minutes he realized his mistake and hurried back to the SAMS machine, only to find the voucher gone. He immediately notified a security guard. The defendant's personnel thereafter quickly confirmed the plaintiff as the original purchaser of the lost voucher. The defendant placed a computerized "stop" on the voucher. However, whoever had happened upon the voucher in the SAMS machine and taken it had acted even more quickly: the voucher had been brought to a nearby track window and "cashed out" within a minute or so of the plaintiff having mistakenly left it in the SAMS machine.

The plaintiff now sues the defendant, contending that the defendant should be liable for having failed to "provide any minimal protection to its customers" in checking the identity and ownership of vouchers prior to permitting their "cash out." The defendant, in response, contends that the voucher consists of "bearer paper," negotiable by anyone having possession, and that it is under no obligation to purchasers of vouchers to provide any such identity or ownership checks.

As opposed to instruments such as ordinary checks, which are typically made payable to the order of a specific person and are therefore known as "order paper," bearer paper is payable to the "bearer," *i.e.*, whoever walks in carrying (or "bearing") the instrument. Pursuant to [New York's UCC] "[a]n instrument is payable to bearer when by its terms it is payable to...(c) 'cash' or the order of 'cash', or any other indication which does not purport to designate a specific payee."

Each New York Racing Association voucher is labeled "Cash Voucher." Each voucher contains the legend "Bet Against the Value or Exchange for Cash." Each voucher is also encoded with certain computer symbols which are readable by SAMS machines. The vouchers do by their terms constitute "bearer paper."

There is no doubt that under the [1990 Revision] Model Uniform Commercial Code the defendant would be a "holder in due course" of the voucher, deemed to have taken it free from all defenses that could be raised by the plaintiff. As observed in 2 White & Summers, *Uniform Commercial Code* pp. 225–226, 152–153 (4th ed. 1995):

> *Consider theft of bearer instruments. . . . [T]he thief can make his or her transferee a holder simply by transfer to one who gives value in good faith. If the thief's transferee cashes the check and so gives value in good faith and without notice of any defense, that transferee will be a holder in due course under 3-302, free of all claims to the instrument on the part . . . of any person and free of all personal defenses of any prior party. Therefore, the holder in due course will not be liable in conversion to the true owner. . . . Of course, the owner of the check will have a good cause of action against the thief, but no other cause of action. . . .*
>
> *If an instrument is payable to bearer . . . the possessor of the instrument will be a holder and, if he meets the other tests, a holder in due course. This is so even though the instrument may have passed through the hands of a thief; the holder in due course is one of the few purchasers in Anglo-Saxon jurisprudence who may derive a good title from a chain of title that includes a thief in its links.*

However, the Model Uniform Commercial Code in its present form is not in effect in New York.[9] In 1990, the National Conference of Commissioners on Uniform State Laws and the American Law Institute approved a revised Article 3. This revised Article 3 has never been enacted in New York. Comment 1 to § 3-201 of the [1990] Uniform Commercial Code, commenting on the difference between it and its predecessor (which is still in effect in New York), states:

> *A person can become holder of an instrument . . . as the result of an event that occurs after issuance. "Negotiation" is the term used in Article 3 to describe this post-issuance event. . . . In defining "negotiation" former Section 3-202(1) used the word "transfer," an undefined term, and "delivery," defined in Section 1-201(14) to mean voluntary change of possession. Instead, subsections (a) and (b) [now] use the term "transfer of possession," and subsection (a) states that negotiation can occur by an involuntary transfer of possession. For example, if an instrument is payable to bearer and it is stolen by Thief or is found by Finder, Thief or Finder becomes the holder of the instrument when possession is obtained. In this case there is an involuntary transfer of possession that results in negotiation to Thief or Finder.*

Thus, it would initially appear that under the prior Model Uniform Commercial Code, still in effect in New York, a thief or finder of bearer paper, as the recipient of an involuntary transfer, could not become a "holder," and thus could not pass holder-in-due-course status, or good title, to someone in the position of the defendant.

This conclusion, however, is not without doubt. For instance, in 2 Anderson, *Uniform Commercial Code* § 3-202:35 (2nd ed., 1971), it was observed that:

> *The Code states that bearer paper is negotiated by "delivery." This is likely to mislead for one is not inclined to think of the acquisition of paper by a finder or a thief as a "voluntary transfer of possession."*

By stating that the Code's terminology was "misleading," the treatise appears to imply that despite the literal import of the words, the contrary was true—negotiation could be accomplished by involuntary transfer, *i.e.*, loss or theft.

In [Citation], the Appellate Division determined that the Tropicana Casino in New Jersey became a holder in due course of signed cashier's checks with blank payee designations which a thief had stolen from the defendant and negotiated to the casino for value after filling in the payee designation with his brother-in-law's name. The Appellate Division, assuming without discussion that the thief was a "holder" of the stolen instruments and therefore able to transfer good title, held the defendant obligated to make payment on the stolen checks. *Accord* [Citation] (check cashing service which unknowingly took for value from an intervening thief the plaintiff's check, which the plaintiff had endorsed in blank and thus converted to a bearer instrument, was a holder in due course of the check, having received good title from the thief).

Presumably, these results have occurred because the courts in New York have implicitly interpreted the undefined term "transfer" as utilized in [the pre-1990] U.C.C. § 3-202(1) as including the involuntary transfer of possession, so that as a practical matter the old Code (as still in effect in New York) has the same meaning as the new Model Uniform Commercial Code, which represents a clarification rather than a change in the law.

This result makes sense. A contrary result would require extensive verification procedures to be undertaken by all transferees of bearer paper. The problem with imposing an identity or ownership check requirement on the negotiation of bearer paper is that such a requirement would impede the free negotiability which is the essence of bearer paper. As held in [Citation (1970)],

> *[Where] the instrument entrusted to a dishonest messenger or agent was freely negotiable bearer paper . . . the drawee bank [cannot] be held liable for making payment to one presenting a negotiable instrument in bearer form who may properly be presumed to be a holder [citations omitted].*

* * * Moreover, the plaintiff in the instant case knew that the voucher could be "Exchange[d] for cash." The plaintiff conceded at trial that (1) when he himself utilized the voucher prior to its loss, no identity or ownership check was ever made; and (2) he nevertheless continued to use it. The plaintiff could therefore not contend that he had any expectation that the defendant had in place any safeguards against the voucher's unencumbered use, or that he had taken any actions in reliance on the same.

This Court is compelled to render judgment denying the plaintiff's claim, and in favor of the defendant.

Case Questions

1. Was the instrument in question a note or a draft?
2. How did the court determine it was bearer paper?

3. What would the racetrack have to have done if it wanted the machine to dispense order paper?
4. What confusion arose from the UCC's pre-1990 use of the words "transfer" and "delivery," which was clarified by the revised Article 3's use of the phrase "transfer of possession"? Does this offer any insight into why the change was made?
5. How had—have—the New York courts decided the question as to whether a thief could be a holder when the instrument was acquired from its previous owner involuntarily?

Forged Drawer's Signature, Forged Indorsements, Fictitious Payee, and Comparative Negligence

Victory Clothing Co., Inc. v. Wachovia Bank, N.A.

2006 WL 773020 (Penn. [Trial Court] 2006)

Abramson, J.

Background

This is a subrogation action brought by the insurance carrier for plaintiff Victory Clothing, Inc. ("Victory"), to recover funds paid to Victory under an insurance policy. This matter arises out of thefts from Victory's commercial checking account by its office manager and bookkeeper, Jeanette Lunny ("Lunny"). Lunny was employed by Victory for approximately twenty-four (24) years until she resigned in May 2003. From August 2001 through May 2003, Lunny deposited approximately two hundred (200) checks drawn on Victory's corporate account totaling $188,273.00 into her personal checking account at defendant Wachovia Bank ("Wachovia"). Lunny's scheme called for engaging in "double forgeries" (discussed infra). Lunny would prepare the checks in the company's computer system, and make the checks payable to known vendors of Victory (e.g., Adidas, Sean John), to whom no money was actually owed. The checks were for dollar amounts that were consistent with the legitimate checks to those vendors. She would then forge the signature of Victory's owner, Mark Rosenfeld ("Rosenfeld"), on the front of the check, and then forge the indorsement of the unintended payee (Victory's various vendors) on the reverse side of the check. The unauthorized checks were drawn on Victory's bank account at Hudson Bank (the "drawee bank" or "payor bank"). After forging the indorsement of the payee, Lunny either indorsed the check with her name followed by her account number, or referenced her account number following the forged indorsement. She then deposited the funds into her personal bank account at Wachovia (the "depositary bank" or "collecting bank").

At the time of the fraud by Lunny, Wachovia's policies and regulations regarding the acceptance of checks for deposit provided that "checks payable to a non-personal payee can be deposited ONLY into a non-personal account with the same name" [Emphasis in original].

Rosenfeld reviewed the bank statements from Hudson Bank on a monthly basis. However, among other observable irregularities, he failed to detect that Lunny had forged his signature on approximately two hundred (200) checks. Nor did he have a procedure to match checks to invoices.

In its Complaint, Victory asserted a claim against Wachovia pursuant to the Pennsylvania Commercial Code, [3-405] . . . [it] states, in relevant part:

Employer's responsibility for fraudulent indorsement by employee

(b) RIGHTS AND LIABILITIES. For the purpose of determining the rights and liabilities of a person who, in good faith, pays an instrument or takes it for value or for collection, if an employer entrusted an employee with responsibility with respect to the instrument and the employee or a person acting in concert with the employee makes a fraudulent indorsement of the instrument, the indorsement is effective as the indorsement of the person to whom the instrument is payable if it is made in the name of that person. If the person paying the instrument or taking it for value or for collection fails to exercise ordinary care in paying or taking the instrument and that failure substantially contributes to loss resulting from the fraud, the person bearing the loss may recover from the person failing to exercise ordinary care to the extent the failure to exercise ordinary care contributed to the loss.

In essence, Victory contends that Wachovia's actions in accepting the checks payable to various businesses for deposit into Lunny's personal account were commercially unreasonable, contrary to Wachovia's own internal rules and regulations, and exhibited a want of ordinary care.

Discussion

I. Double Forgeries

As stated supra, this case involves a double forgery situation. This matter presents a question of first impression in the Pennsylvania state courts, namely how should the loss be allocated in double forgery situations. A double forgery occurs when the negotiable instrument contains both a forged maker's [bank customer's] signature and a forged indorsement. The Uniform Commercial Code ("UCC" or "Code") addresses the allocation of liability in cases where either the maker's signature is forged or where the indorsement of the payee or holder is forged. [Citation] ("the Code accords separate treatment to forged drawer signatures...and forged indorsements"). However, the drafters of the UCC failed to specifically address the allocation of liability in double forgery situations. * * * Consequently, the courts have been left to determine how liability should be allocated in a double forgery case. * * *

II. The Effect of the UCC Revisions

In 1990, new revisions to Articles 3 and 4 of the UCC were implemented (the "revisions"). * * * The new revisions made a major change in the area of double forgeries. Before the revisions, the case law was uniform in treating a double forgery case as a forged drawer's signature case [only], with the loss falling [only] on the drawee bank. The revisions, however, changed this rule by shifting to a comparative fault approach. Under the revised version of the UCC, the loss in double forgery cases is allocated between the depositary and drawee banks based on the extent that each contributed to the loss. * * *

Specifically, revised § 3-405 of the UCC, entitled "Employer's Responsibility for Fraudulent Indorsement by Employee," introduced the concept of comparative fault as between the employer of the dishonest employee/embezzler and the bank(s). This is the section under which Victory sued Wachovia. Section 3-405(b) states, in relevant part:

> *If the person paying the instrument or taking it for value or for collection fails to exercise ordinary care in paying or taking the instrument and that failure substantially contributes to loss resulting from the fraud, the person bearing the loss may recover from the person failing to exercise ordinary care to the extent the failure to exercise ordinary care contributed to the loss.*

Wachovia argues that this section is applicable only in cases of forged indorsements, and not in double forgery situations. However, at least one court has found that the new revisions have made section 3-405 apply to double forgery situations. "Nothing in the [Revised UCC] statutory language indicates that, where the signature of the drawer is forged...the drawer is otherwise precluded from seeking recovery from a depositary bank under these sections" [Citation] * * * The Court finds the reasoning persuasive and holds that * * * Victory can maintain its cause of action against Wachovia.

III. The Fictitious Payee Rule

Lunny made the fraudulent checks payable to actual vendors of Victory with the intention that the vendors not get paid. Wachovia therefore argues that Victory's action against it should be barred by the fictitious payee rule under UCC 3-404 [which] states, in relevant part:

> *(b) Fictitious Payee. If a person . . . does not intend the person identified as payee to have any interest in the instrument or the person identified as payee of an instrument is a fictitious person, the following rules apply until the instrument is negotiated by special indorsement:*
>
> *(1) Any person in possession of the instrument is its holder.*
>
> *(2) An indorsement by any person in the name of the payee stated in the instrument is effective as the indorsement of the payee in favor of a person who, in good faith, pays the instrument or takes it for value or for collection....*

The theory under the rule is that since the indorsement is "effective," the drawee bank was justified in debiting the company's account. Therefore, [Wachovia argues] the loss should fall on the company whose employee committed the fraud.

* * * [However] under revised UCC §§ 3-404 and 3-405, the fictitious payee defense triggers principles of comparative fault, so a depositary bank's own negligence may be considered by the trier of fact. * * * Therefore, based on the foregoing reasons, the fictitious payee defense does not help Wachovia in this case.

IV. Allocation of Liability

As stated supra, comparative negligence applies in this case because of the revisions in the Code. In determining the liability of the parties, the Court has considered, *inter alia* [among other things], the following factors:

- At the time of the fraud by Lunny, Wachovia's policies and regulations regarding the acceptance of checks for deposit provided that "checks payable to a non-personal payee can be deposited ONLY into a non-personal account with the same name." [Emphasis in original].
- Approximately two hundred (200) checks drawn on Victory's corporate account were deposited into Lunny's personal account at Wachovia.

- The first twenty-three (23) fraudulent checks were made payable to entities that were not readily distinguishable as businesses, such as "Sean John." The check dated December 17, 2001 was the first fraudulent check made payable to a payee that was clearly a business, specifically "Beverly Hills Shoes, Inc."
- In 2001, Victory had approximately seventeen (17) employees, including Lunny.
- Lunny had been a bookkeeper for Victory from approximately 1982 until she resigned in May 2003. Rosenfeld never had any problems with Lunny's bookkeeping before she resigned.
- Lunny exercised primary control over Victory's bank accounts.
- Between 2001 and 2003, the checks that were generated to make payments to Victory's vendors were all computerized checks generated by Lunny. No other Victory employee, other than Lunny, knew how to generate the computerized checks, including Rosenfeld.
- The fraudulent checks were made payable to known vendors of Victory in amounts that were consistent with previous legitimate checks to those vendors.
- After forging the indorsement of the payee, Lunny either indorsed the check with her name followed by her account number, or referenced her account number following the forged indorsement.
- About ten (10) out of approximately three hundred (300) checks each month were forged by Lunny and deposited into her personal account.
- Rosenfeld reviewed his bank statements from Hudson Bank on a monthly basis.
- Rosenfeld received copies of Victory's cancelled checks from Hudson Bank on a monthly basis. However, the copies of the cancelled checks were not in their normal size; instead, they were smaller, with six checks (front and back side) on each page.
- The forged indorsements were written out in longhand, i.e., Lunny's own handwriting, rather than a corporate stamped signature.
- Victory did not match its invoices for each check at the end of each month.
- An outside accounting firm performed quarterly reviews of Victory's bookkeeping records, and then met with Rosenfeld. This review was not designed to pick up fraud or misappropriation.

Based on the foregoing, the Court finds that Victory and Wachovia are comparatively negligent.

With regard to Wachovia's negligence, it is clear that Wachovia was negligent in violating its own rules in repeatedly depositing corporate checks into Lunny's personal account at Wachovia. Standard commercial bank procedures dictate that a check made payable to a business be accepted only into a business checking account with the same title as the business. Had a single teller at Wachovia followed Wachovia's rules, the fraud would have been detected as early as December 17, 2001, when the first fraudulently created non-personal payee check was presented for deposit into Lunny's personal checking account. Instead, Wachovia permitted another one hundred and seventy-six (176) checks to be deposited into Lunny's account after December 17, 2001. The Court finds that Wachovia failed to exercise ordinary care, and that failure substantially contributed to Victory's loss resulting from the fraud. Therefore, the Court concludes that Wachovia is seventy (70) percent liable for Victory's loss.

Victory, on the other hand, was also negligent in its supervision of Lunny, and for not discovering the fraud for almost a two-year period. Rosenfeld received copies of the cancelled checks, albeit smaller in size, on a monthly basis from Hudson Bank. The copies of the checks displayed both the front and back of the checks. Rosenfeld was negligent in not recognizing his own forged signature on the front of the checks, as well as not spotting his own bookkeeper's name and/or account number on the back of the checks (which appeared far too many times and on various "payees" checks to be seen as regular by a non-negligent business owner).

Further, there were inadequate checks and balances in Victory's record keeping process. For example, Victory could have ensured that it had an adequate segregation of duties, meaning that more than one person would be involved in any control activity. Here, Lunny exercised primary control over Victory's bank accounts. Another Victory employee, or Rosenfeld himself, could have reviewed Lunny's work. In addition, Victory could have increased the amount of authorization that was needed to perform certain transactions. For example, any check that was over a threshold monetary amount would have to be authorized by more than one individual. This would ensure an additional control on checks that were larger in amounts. Furthermore, Victory did not match its invoices for each check at the end of each month. When any check was created by Victory's computer system, the value of the check was automatically assigned to a general ledger account before the check could be printed. The values in the general ledger account could have been reconciled at the end of each month with the actual checks and invoices. This would not have been overly burdensome or costly because Victory already had the computer system that could do this in place. Based on the foregoing, the Court concludes that Victory is also thirty (30) percent liable for the loss.

Conclusion

For all the foregoing reasons, the Court finds that Wachovia is 70% liable and Victory is 30% liable for the $188,273.00 loss. Therefore, Victory Clothing Company, Inc. is awarded $131,791.10.

Case Questions

1. How does the double-forgery scam work?
2. What argument did Wachovia make as to why it should not be liable for the double forgeries?
3. What argument did Wachovia make as to why it should not be liable under the fictitious payee rule?
4. What change in the revised UCC (from the pre-1990 version) made Wachovia's arguments invalid, in the court's opinion?
5. What factors appear to have caused the court to decide that Wachovia was more than twice as responsible for the embezzlement as Victory was?

Joint Payees and Conditional and Restrictive Indorsements

Wisner Elevator Company, Inc. v. Richland State Bank
862 So.2d 1112 (La. App. 2003)

Gaskins, J.

Wisner Elevator Company, Inc. [plaintiff] ("Wisner"), appeals from a summary judgment in favor of the defendant, Richland State Bank. At issue is the deposit of a check with a typed statement on the back directing that a portion of the funds be paid to a third party. We affirm the trial court judgment.

Facts

On July 13, 2001, the United States Treasury, through the Farm Service Agency, issued a check in the amount of $17,420.00, made payable to Chad E. Gill. On the back of the check the following was typed:

> *PAY TO THE ORDER OF RICHLAND STATE BANK FOR ISSUANCE OF A CASHIER'S CHECK PAYABLE TO WISNER ELEVATOR IN THE AMOUNT OF $13,200.50 AND PAY THE BALANCE TO CHAD GILL IN THE AMOUNT OF $4,219.50.*

On July 23, 2001, the check was deposited into Gill's checking account at Richland State Bank. Gill's signature is found on the back of the check below the typed paragraph. No cashier check to Wisner Elevator was issued; instead the entire amount was deposited into Gill's checking account as per Gill's deposit ticket.

* * * On May 28, 2002, Wisner filed suit against the bank, claiming that its failure to apply the funds as per the restrictive indorsement constituted a conversion of the portion of the check due to Wisner under UCC 3-206(c)(2) [that a depositary bank converts an instrument if it pays out on an indorsement "indicating a purpose of having the instrument collected for the indorser or for a particular account"].

[The bank] asserted that the indorsement on the back of the check was a conditional indorsement and ineffective under 3-206(b), [which states:]

> *An indorsement stating a condition to the right of the indorsee to receive payment does not affect the right of the indorsee to enforce the instrument. A person paying the instrument or taking it for value or collection may disregard the condition, and the rights and liabilities of that person are not affected by whether the condition has been fulfilled.*

* * * [T]he bank asserts the fault of the United States Treasury, * * * in failing to make the check payable to both Gill and Wisner. To the extent that the indorsement was conditional, the bank contends that it was unenforceable; to the extent that it was restrictive, it maintains that the restrictions were waived by the indorser when he deposited the full amount of the check into his own checking account.

Wisner * * * [stated that it] was owed $13,200.50 by Gill for seeds, chemicals, crop supplies and agricultural seed technology fees. [It] further stated that Gill never paid the $13,200.50 he owed and that Wisner did not receive a cashier's check issued in that amount by Richland State Bank. * * * According to [the bank teller], Gill asked to deposit the entire amount in his account. She further stated that the bank was unaware that the indorsement was written by someone other than Gill.

* * * The court found that the typed indorsement placed on the check was the indorsement of the maker, not Gill. However, when Gill signed below the indorsement, he made it his own indorsement. The court concluded that Gill had the legal power and authority to verbally instruct that the entire proceeds be deposited into his account. The court stated that as long as the indorsement was his own, whether it was restrictive or conditional, Gill had the power to ignore it, strike it out or give contrary instructions. The court further concluded that the bank acted properly when it followed the verbal instructions given by Gill to the teller and the written instructions on his deposit slip to deposit the entire proceeds into Gill's account. Consequently, the court gave summary judgment in favor of the bank. Wisner appeals. * * *

Discussion

Wisner contends that the trial court erred in holding that the bank could disregard what Wisner characterizes as a special and restrictive indorsement on the back of the check. It claims that under UCC 3-206, the amount paid by the bank had to be "applied consistently with" the indorsement and that the bank's failure to comply with the indorsement made it liable to Wisner. According to Wisner, Gill was not entitled to deposit the amount due to Wisner by virtue of his own special indorsement and the bank converted the check under 3-420 by crediting the full amount to Gill's account.

The bank argues that the indorsement was conditional and thus could be ignored pursuant to 3-206(b). It also asserts that nothing on the check indicated that the indorsement was written by someone other than Gill. Since the check was made payable to Gill, the indorsement was not necessary to his title and could be ignored, struck out or simply waived. The bank also claims that Wisner had no ownership interest in the check, did not receive delivery of the check, and had no claim for conversion under 3-420.

We agree with the bank that the true problem in this case is the failure of the government to issue the check jointly to Gill and Wisner as co-payees. Had the government done so, there would be no question as to Wisner's entitlement to a portion of the proceeds from the check.

Although the writing on the back of the check is referred to as an indorsement, we note that, standing alone, it does not truly conform to the definition found in 3-204(a) [which states]:

> *"Indorsement" means a signature, other than that of a signer as maker, drawer, or acceptor, that alone or accompanied by other words is made on an instrument for the purpose of (i) negotiating the instrument, (ii) restricting payment of the instrument, or (iii) incurring indorser's liability on the instrument, but regardless of the intent of the signer, a signature and its accompanying words is an indorsement unless the accompanying words, terms of the instrument, place of the signature, or other circumstances unambiguously indicate that the signature was made for a purpose other than indorsement.*

This paragraph was placed on the back of the check by the government as the maker or drawer of the check. Consequently, the bank argues that Gill as sole payee could waive, ignore or strike out the language.

Although the Louisiana jurisprudence contains no similar case dealing with the Uniform Commercial Code, we may look to other jurisdictions for guidance. * * * In [Citation, a New Jersey case] (1975), the drawer of a check placed instructions on the backs of several checks * * * that the instruments not be deposited until a specific future date. However, the payee presented some of the checks prior to the date specified on the back. The court found that the drawer did not have the capacity to indorse the instruments; as a result the typed instructions on the backs of the checks could not be indorsements. Instead, they were "merely requests to plaintiff who may or may not comply at its own pleasure. The instructions are neither binding on plaintiff nor the subsequent holders." In other words, the payee could ignore the instructions.

In the instant case, the payee did precisely that. Gill ignored the writing on the back of the check and instructed the teller at the defendant bank to do the same through verbal and written instructions.

Wisner argues that by affixing his signature under the writing on the back of the check, Gill made it his own indorsement. Furthermore, it asserts that it was a restrictive indorsement, not a conditional one which could be disregarded pursuant to 3-206. Wisner relies upon the provisions of 3-206 for the proposition that the check had a restrictive indorsement and that the bank converted the check because it failed to apply the amount it paid consistently with the indorsement. However, Comment 3 to 3-206 states, in pertinent part:

This Article does not displace the law of waiver as it may apply to restrictive indorsements. The circumstances under which a restrictive indorsement may be waived by the person who made it is not determined by this Article.

Not all jurisdictions recognize a doctrine of waiver of restrictive indorsements. [Citing cases from various jurisdictions in which a bank customer effectively requested the bank to disregard a restrictive indorsement; some cases affirmed the concept that the restriction could be waived (disregarded), others did not.]. * * *

In two cases arising under pre-UCC law, Louisiana recognized that indorsements could be ignored or struck out. In [Citation] (1925), the Louisiana Supreme Court held that the holder of a check could erase or strike out a restrictive indorsement on a check that was not necessary to the holder's title. In [Citation] (1967), the court stated that an erroneous indorsement could be ignored and even struck out as unnecessary to the plaintiff's title.

Like the trial court, we find that when Gill affixed his signature under the writing on the back of the check, he made it his own indorsement. We further find that the indorsement was restrictive, not conditional. As Gill's own restrictive indorsement, he could waive it and direct that the check, upon which he was designated as the sole payee, be deposited in his account in its entirety.

Affirmed.

Case Questions

1. Notice that the check was made payable to Chad Gill—he was the named payee on the front side of the check. To avoid the problems here, if the drawer (the U.S. government) wanted to control the uses to which the check could be put, how should it have named the payee?
2. The court held that when Gill "affixed his signature under the writing on the back of the check, he made it his own indorsement." But why wasn't it the indorsement of the drawer—the U.S. government?
3. If the language on the back was considered his own conditional indorsement (the instrument was not valid unless the stated conditions were met), how could the condition be disregarded by the bank?
4. If it was his own restrictive indorsement, how could it be disregarded by the bank?
5. What recourse does Wisner have now?

23.5 Summary and Exercises

Summary

Negotiation is the transfer of an instrument in such a form that the transferee becomes a holder. There are various methods for doing so; if the procedures are not properly adhered to, the transfer is only an assignment.

An instrument payable to the order of someone must be negotiated by indorsement and delivery to the transferee. The indorsement must convey the entire instrument. An instrument payable to bearer may be negotiated simply by delivery to the transferee.

Those who sign the instrument have made a contract and are liable for its breach. Makers and acceptors are primary parties and are liable to pay the instrument. Drawers and indorsers are secondary parties and are conditionally liable. Signatories are liable under a warranty theory.

Various forms of indorsement are possible: blank or special, restrictive or unrestrictive, qualified or unqualified.

Between drawer and drawee, liability for a forged instrument—one signed without authority—usually falls on the drawee who paid it. There are, however, several exceptions to this rule: where an imposter induces the maker or drawer to issue an instrument in the name of the payee, where the instrument is made to a fictitious payee (or to a real person who is intended to have no interest in it), and where the instrument is made by an employee authorized generally to deal in such paper.

Exercises

1. Mal, a minor, purchased a stereo from Howard for $425 and gave Howard a negotiable note in that amount. Tanker, a thief, stole the note from Howard, indorsed Howard's signature and sold the note to Betty. Betty then sold the note to Carl; she did not indorse it. Carl was unable to collect on the note because Mal disaffirmed the contract. Is Betty liable to Carl on a contract or warranty theory? Why?
2. Would the result in Exercise 1 be different if Betty had given a qualified indorsement? Explain.
3. Alphonse received a check one Friday from his employer and cashed the check at his favorite tavern, using a blank indorsement. After the tavern closed that evening, the owner, in reviewing the receipts for the evening, became concerned that if the check was stolen and cashed by a thief, the loss would fall on the tavern. Is this concern justified? What can the owner of the tavern do for protection?
4. Martha owns a sporting goods store. She employs a bookkeeper, Bob, who is authorized to indorse checks received by the store and to deposit them in the store's bank account at Second Bank. Instead of depositing all the checks, Bob cashes some of them and uses the proceeds for personal purposes. Martha sues the bank for her loss, claiming that the bank should have deposited the money in the store's account rather than paying Bob. Is the bank liable? Explain.
5. Daniel worked as a writer in order to support himself and his wife while she earned her MBA degree. Daniel's paychecks were important, as the couple had no other source of income. One day, Daniel drove to Old Faithful State Bank to deposit his paycheck. Standing at a counter, he indorsed the check with a blank indorsement and then proceeded to fill out a deposit slip. While he was completing the slip, a thief stole the check and cashed it. Whose loss is this? How could the loss be avoided?
6. You are the branch manager of a bank. A well-respected local attorney walks into the bank with a check for $100,000 that he wants to deposit in the general account his firm has at your bank. The payee on the check is an elderly widow, Hilda Jones, who received the check from the profit-sharing plan of her deceased husband, Horatio Jones. The widow indorsed the check "Pay to the order of the estate of Horatio Jones. Hilda Jones." The attorney produces court documents showing that he is the executor of the estate. After the attorney indorses the check, you deposit the check in the attorney's account. The attorney later withdraws the $100,000 and spends it on a pleasure trip, in violation of his duties as executor. Discuss the bank's liability.
7. Stephanie borrows $50,000 from Ginny and gives Ginny a negotiable note in that amount. Ginny sells the note to Roe for $45,000. Ginny's indorsement reads, "For valuable consideration, I assign all of my rights in this note to Roe. Ginny." When Stephanie refuses to pay the note and skips town, Roe demands payment from Ginny, claiming contract liability on the basis of her signature. Ginny argues that she is not liable because the indorsement is qualified by the language she used on the note. Who is correct? Explain.
8. The state of California issued a check that read, "To Alberto Cruz and Roberta Gonzales." Alberto endorsed it "Pay to the order of Olivia Cruz." What rights does Olivia get in the instrument?
9. a. Bill's weekly paycheck was stolen by a thief. The thief indorsed Bill's name and cashed the check at the drawee bank before Bill's employer had time to stop payment. May the drawee bank charge this payment against the drawer's account? Explain.

b. Would the result change in (a) if Bill had carelessly left his check where it could easily be picked up by the thief? Explain.
c. Would the result change in (a) if the bank had specific regulations that tellers were not to cash any check without examining the identification of the person asking for cash?
d. Would the result change if Bill's employer had carelessly left the check where it could be found by the thief?

Self-Test Questions

1. A person who signs a negotiable instrument with a blank endorsement has
   a. warranty liability
   b. contract liability
   c. both of the above
   d. neither of the above
2. "For deposit" is an example of
   a. a special indorsement
   b. a restrictive indorsement
   c. a qualified indorsement
   d. a blank indorsement
3. "Pay to the order of XYZ Company" is an example of
   a. a special indorsement
   b. a restrictive indorsement
   c. a qualified indorsement
   d. a blank indorsement
4. The indorser's signature alone is
   a. a special indorsement
   b. a restrictive indorsement
   c. a qualified indorsement
   d. a blank indorsement
5. Generally, liability for a forged instrument falls on
   a. the drawer
   b. the drawee
   c. both of the above
   d. neither of the above
6. State whether each of the following is (1) blank or special, (2) restrictive or nonrestrictive, or (3) qualified or unqualified:
   a. "Pay to David Murphy without recourse."
   b. "Ronald Jackson"
   c. "For deposit only in my account at Industrial Credit Union."
   d. "Pay to ABC Co."
   e. "I assign to Ken Watson all my rights in this note."

Self-Test Answers

1. c

2. b
3. a
4. d
5. b
6.
   a. special, nonrestrictive, qualified
   b. blank, nonrestrictive, unqualified
   c. special, nonrestrictive, unqualified
   d. special, restrictive, unqualified
   e. special, restrictive, unqualified

Endnotes

1. Uniform Commercial Code, Section 3-201, Official Comment.
2. Uniform Commercial Code, Section 3-302, Comment 4.
3. Uniform Commercial Code, Section 3-404, Official Comment 1.
4. Uniform Commercial Code, Section 3-404, Official Comment 1.
5. Uniform Commercial Code, Section 3-404, Comment 3.
6. Uniform Commercial Code, Section 3-405(B).
7. Uniform Commercial Code, Section 4-406(a).
8. Authors' note: Pari-mutuel betting (from the French *pari mutuel*, meaning mutual stake) is a betting system in which all bets of a particular type are placed together in a pool; taxes and a house take are removed, and payoff odds are calculated by sharing the pool among all winning bets.
9. Authors' note: As of 2016, New York is the sole remaining state yet to adopt the 1990 revisions to Articles 3 and 4. https://www.morganlewis.com/pubs/bf_lf_2014changestonyuniformcommercialcode_06jan15

CHAPTER 24
Holder in Due Course and Defenses

Learning Objectives

After reading this chapter, you should understand the following:

1. What a holder in due course is, and why that status is critical to commercial paper.
2. What defenses are good against a holder in due course.
3. How the holder-in-due-course doctrine is modified in consumer transactions.

In this chapter, we consider the final two questions that are raised in determining whether a holder can collect:

1. Is the holder a holder in due course?
2. What defenses, if any, can be asserted against the holder in due course to prevent collection on the instrument?

24.1 Holder in Due Course

Learning Objectives

1. Understand why the concept of holder in due course is important in commercial transactions.
2. Know what the requirements are for being a holder in due course.
3. Determine whether a payee may be a holder in due course.
4. Know what the shelter rule is and why the rule exists.

Overview of the Holder-in-Due-Course Concept

Importance of the Holder-in-Due-Course Concept

A holder is a person in possession of an instrument payable to bearer or to the identified person possessing it. But a holder's rights are ordinary, as we noted briefly in Chapter 22. If a person to whom an instrument is negotiated becomes nothing more than a holder, the law of commercial paper would not be very significant, nor would a negotiable instrument be a particularly useful commercial device. A mere holder is simply an assignee, who acquires the assignor's rights but also his liabilities; an ordinary holder must defend against claims and overcome defenses just as his assignor would. The holder in due course is really the crux of the concept of commercial paper and the key to its success and importance. What the holder in due course gets is an instrument free of claims or defenses by previous possessors. A holder with such a preferred position can then treat the instrument almost as money, free from the worry that someone might show up and prove it defective.

Requirements for Being a Holder in Due Course

Under Section 3-302 of the Uniform Commercial Code (UCC), to be a holder in due course (HDC), a transferee must fulfill the following:

1. Be a holder of a negotiable instrument;

2. Have taken it:

a) for value,

b) in good faith,

c) without notice

(1) that it is overdue or

(2) has been dishonored (not paid), or

(3) is subject to a valid claim or defense by any party, or

(4) that there is an uncured default with respect to payment of another instrument issued as part of the same series, or

(5) that it contains an unauthorized signature or has been altered, and

3. Have no reason to question its authenticity on account of apparent evidence of forgery, alteration, irregularity or incompleteness.

The point is that the HDC should honestly pay for the instrument and not know of anything wrong with it. If that's her status, she gets paid on it, almost no matter what.

Specific Analysis of Holder-in-Due-Course Requirements

Holder

Again, a holder is a person who possesses a negotiable instrument "payable to bearer or, the case of an instrument payable to an identified person, if the identified person is in possession."[1] An instrument is payable to an identified person if she is the named payee, or if it is indorsed to her. So a holder is one who possesses an instrument and who has all the necessary indorsements.

Taken for Value

Section 3-303 of the UCC describes what is meant by transferring an instrument "for value." In a broad sense, it means the holder has given something for it, which sounds like consideration. But "value" here is not the same as consideration under contract law. Here is the UCC language:

An instrument is issued or transferred for value if any of the following apply:

(1) The instrument is issued or transferred for a promise of performance, to the extent the promise has been performed.

(2) The transferee acquires a security interest or other lien in the instrument other than a lien obtained by judicial proceeding.

(3) The instrument is issued or transferred as payment of, or as security for, an antecedent claim against any person, whether or not the claim is due.

(4) The instrument is issued or transferred in exchange for a negotiable instrument.

(5) The instrument is issued or transferred in exchange for the incurring of an irrevocable obligation to a third party by the person taking the instrument.

1. *For a promise, to the extent performed*. Suppose A contracts with B: "I'll buy your car for $5,000." Under contract law, A has given consideration: the promise is enough. But this executory (not yet performed) promise given by A is not giving "value" to support the HDC status because the promise has not been performed.

Lorna Love sells her car to Paul Purchaser for $5,000, and Purchaser gives her a note in that amount. Love negotiates the note to Rackets, Inc., for a new shipment of tennis rackets to be delivered in thirty days. Rackets never delivers the tennis rackets. Love has a claim for $5,000 against Rackets, which is not an HDC because its promise to deliver is still executory. Assume Paul Purchaser has a defense against Love (a reason why he doesn't want to pay on the note), perhaps because the car was defective. When Rackets presents the note to Purchaser for payment, he refuses to pay, raising his defense against Love. If Rackets had been an HDC, Purchaser would be obligated to pay on the note regardless of the defense he might have had against Love, the payee. See *Carter & Grimsley v. Omni Trading, Inc.*, Section 3, regarding value as related to executory contracts.

A taker for value can be a partial HDC if the consideration was only partly performed. Suppose the tennis rackets were to come in two lots, each worth $2,500, and Rackets only delivered one lot. Rackets would be an HDC only to the extent of $2,500, and the debtor—Paul Purchaser—could refuse to pay $2,500 of the promised sum.

The UCC presents two exceptions to the rule that an executory promise is not value. Section 3-303(a)(4) provides that an instrument is issued or transferred for value if the issuer or transferor gives it in exchange for a negotiable instrument, and Section 3-303(5) says an instrument is transferred for value if the issuer gives it in exchange for an irrevocable obligation to a third party.

2. *Security interest*. Value is not limited to cash or the fulfillment of a contractual obligation. A holder who acquires a lien on, or a security interest in, an instrument other than by legal process has taken for value.

3. *Antecedent debt*. Likewise, taking an instrument in payment of, or as security for, a prior claim, whether or not the claim is due, is a taking for value. Blackstone owes Webster $1,000, due in thirty days. Blackstone unexpectedly receives a refund check for $1,000 from the Internal Revenue Service and indorses it to Webster. Webster is an HDC though he gave value in the past.

The rationale for the rule of value is that if the holder has not yet given anything of value in exchange for the instrument, he still has an effective remedy should the instrument prove defective: he can rescind the transaction, given the transferor's breach of warranty.

In Good Faith

good faith

Defined in the Uniform Commercial Code as "honesty in fact and the observance of reasonable commercial standards of fair dealing."

Section 3-103(4) of the UCC defines **good faith** as "honesty in fact and the observance of reasonable commercial standards of fair dealing."

Honesty in Fact

"Honesty in fact" is subjectively tested. Suppose Lorna Love had given Rackets, Inc., a promissory note for the tennis rackets. Knowing that it intended to deliver defective tennis rackets and that Love is likely to protest as soon as the shipment arrives, Rackets offers a deep discount on the note to its fleet mechanic: instead of the $1,000 face value of the note, Rackets will give it to him in payment of an outstanding bill of $400. The mechanic, being naive in commercial dealings, has no suspicion from the large discount that Rackets might be committing fraud. He has acted in good faith under the UCC test. That is not to say that no set of circumstances will ever exist to warrant a finding that there was a lack of good faith.

Observance of Reasonable Commercial Standards of Fair Dealing

Whether reasonable commercial standards were observed in the dealings is objectively tested, but buying an instrument at a discount—as was done in the tennis rackets example—is not commercially unreasonable, necessarily.

Without Notice

It obviously would be unjust to permit a holder to enforce an instrument that he knew—when he acquired it—was defective, was subject to claims or defenses, or had been dishonored. A purchaser with knowledge cannot become an HDC. But proving knowledge is difficult, so the UCC at Section 3-302(2) lists several types of notice that presumptively defeat any entitlement to status as HDC. Notice is not limited to receipt of an explicit statement; it includes an inference that a person should have made from the circumstances. The explicit things that give a person notice include those that follow.

Without Notice That an Instrument Is Overdue

The UCC provides generally that a person who has notice that an instrument is overdue cannot be an HDC. What constitutes notice? When an inspection of the instrument itself would show that it was due before the purchaser acquired it, notice is presumed. A transferee to whom a promissory note due April 23 is negotiated on April 24 has notice that it was overdue and consequently is not an HDC. Not all paper contains a due date for the entire amount, and demand paper has no due date at all. In Sections 3-302(a)(2) and 3-304, the UCC sets out specific rules dictating what is overdue paper.

Without Notice That an Instrument Has Been Dishonored

dishonor

Failure to pay or refusal to accept a note, a bill, or another commercial obligation.

Dishonor means that instrument is not paid when it is presented to the party who should pay it.

Without Notice of a Defense or Claim

A purchaser of an instrument cannot be an HDC if he has notice that there are any defenses or claims against it. A defense is a reason why the would-be obligor will not pay; a claim is an assertion of ownership in the instrument. If a person is fraudulently induced to issue or make an instrument, he has a claim to its ownership and a defense against paying.

Without Notice of Unauthorized Signature or Alteration

This is pretty clear: a person will fail to achieve the HDC status if he has notice of alteration or an unauthorized signature.

Without Reason to Question the Instrument's Authenticity Because of Apparent Forgery, Alteration, or Other Irregularity or Incompleteness as to Call into Question Its Authenticity

This also is pretty straightforward, though it is worth observing that a holder will flunk the HDC test if she has notice of unauthorized signature or alteration, or if she *should* have notice on account of apparent irregularity. So a clever forgery would not by itself defeat the HDC status, unless the holder had notice of it.

Payee as Holder in Due Course

The payee can be an HDC, but in the usual circumstances, a payee would have knowledge of claims or defenses because the payee would be one of the original parties to the instrument. Nevertheless, a payee may be an HDC if all the prerequisites are met. For instance, Blackstone fraudulently convinces Whitestone into signing a note as a co-maker, with Greenstone as the payee. Without authority, Blackstone then delivers the note for value to Greenstone. Having taken the note in good faith, for value, without notice of any problems, and without cause to question its validity because of apparent irregularities, Greenstone is an HDC. In any event, typically the HDC is not the payee of the instrument, but rather, is an immediate or remote transferee of the payee.

The Shelter Rule

There is one last point to mention before we get to the real nub of the holder-in-due-course concept (that the sins of her predecessors are washed away for an HDC). The **shelter rule** provides that the transferee of an instrument acquires the same rights that the transferor had. Thus a person who does not himself qualify as an HDC can still acquire that status if some previous holder (someone "upstream") was an HDC.

shelter rule

Under Article 3 of the Uniform Commercial Code, the transferee of an instrument acquires the same rights his or her transferor had.

On June 1, Clifford sells Harold the original manuscript of Benjamin Franklin's autobiography. Unknown to Harold, however, the manuscript is a forgery. Harold signs a promissory note payable to Clifford for $250,000 on August 1. Clifford negotiates the note to Betsy on July 1 for $200,000; she is unaware of the fraud. On August 2, Betsy gives the note to Al as a token of her affection. Al is Clifford's friend and knows about the scam (see Figure 24.1). May Al collect?

FIGURE 24.1 The Shelter Rule

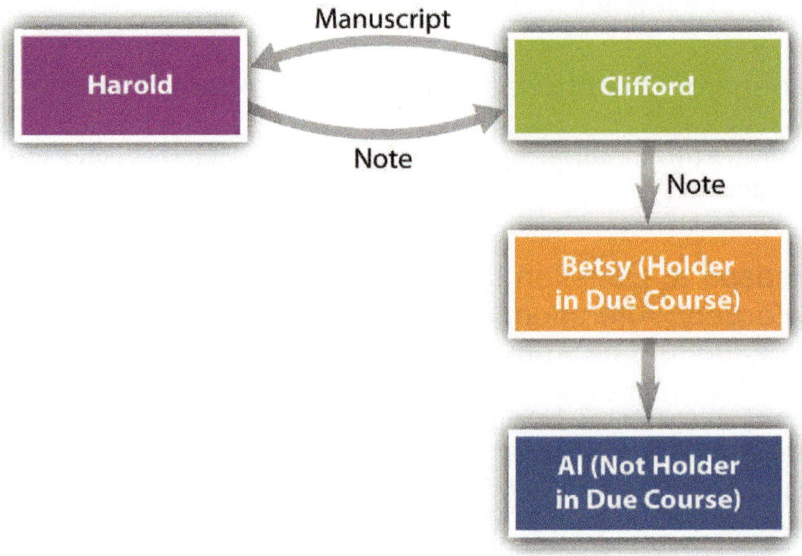

Begin the analysis by noting that Al is not an HDC. Why? For three reasons: he did not take the instrument for value (it was a gift), he did not take in good faith (he knew of the fraud), and he had notice (he acquired it after the due date). Nevertheless, Al is entitled to collect from Harold the full $250,000. His right to do so flows from UCC, Section 3-203(b): "Transfer of an instrument, whether or not the transfer is a negotiation, vests in the transferee any right of the transferor to enforce the instrument, including any right as a holder in due course, but the transferee cannot acquire rights of a holder in due course by a direct or indirect transfer from a holder in due course if the transferee engaged in fraud or illegality affecting the instrument."

By virtue of the shelter rule, Al as transferee from Betsy acquires all rights that she had as transferor. Clearly Betsy is an HDC: she paid for the instrument, she took it in good faith, had no notice of any claim or defense against the instrument, and there were no apparent irregularities. Since Betsy is an HDC, so is Al. His knowledge of the fraud does not undercut his rights as HDC because he was not a party to it and was not a prior holder. Now suppose that after negotiating the instrument to Betsy, Clifford repurchased it from her. He would not be an HDC—and would not acquire all Betsy's rights—because he had been a party to fraud and as a prior holder had notice of a defense. The purpose of the shelter rule is "to assure the holder in due course a free market for the paper."[2]

Key Takeaway

The holder-in-due-course doctrine is important because it allows the holder of a negotiable instrument to take the paper free from most claims and defenses against it. Without the doctrine, such a holder would be a mere transferee. The UCC provides that to be an HDC, a person must be a holder of paper that is not suspiciously irregular, and she must take it in good faith, for value, and without notice of anything that a reasonable person would recognize as tainting the instrument. A payee may be an HDC but usually would not be (because he would know of problems with it). The shelter rule says that a transferee of an instrument acquires the same rights her transferor had, so a person can have the rights of an HDC without satisfying the requirements of an HDC (provided she does not engage in any fraud or illegality related to the transaction).

Exercises

1. Summarize the requirements to be a holder in due course.
2. Why is the status of holder in due course important in commercial transactions?
3. Why is it unlikely that a payee would be a holder in due course?
4. What is the shelter rule, and why does it exist?

24.2 Defenses and Role in Consumer Transactions

Learning Objective

1. Know to what defenses the holder in due course is not subject.
2. Know to what defenses the holder in due course is subject.
3. Understand how the holder-in-due-course doctrine has been modified for consumer transactions and why.

Defenses

We mentioned in Section 1 that the importance of the holder-in-due-course status is that it promotes ready transferability of commercial paper by giving transferees confidence that they can buy and in turn sell negotiable instruments without concern that somebody upstream—previous holders in the chain of distribution—will have some reason not to pay. The holder-in-due-course doctrine makes the paper almost as readily transferable as cash. Almost, but not quite. We examine first the defenses to which the holder in due course (HDC) is *not subject* and then—the "almost" part—the defenses to which even HDCs *are* subject.

Holder in Due Course Is Not Subject to Personal Defenses

An HDC is *not* subject to the obligor's **personal defenses**. But a holder who is not an HDC is subject to them: he takes a negotiable instrument subject to the possible personal claims and defenses of numerous people.

personal defenses

In negotiable-instrument law, defenses that are not good against a holder in due course.

In general, the personal defenses—to which the HDC is *not* subject—are similar to the whole range of defenses for breach of simple contract: lack of consideration; failure of consideration;

duress, undue influence, and misrepresentation that does not render the transaction void; breach of warranty; unauthorized completion of an incomplete instrument; prior payment. Incapacity that does not render the transaction void (except infancy) is also a personal defense. As the Uniform Commercial Code (UCC) puts it, this includes "mental incompetence, guardianship, ultra vires acts or lack of corporate capacity to do business, or any other incapacity apart from infancy. If under the state law the effect is to render the obligation of the instrument entirely null and void, the defense may be asserted against a holder in due course. If the effect is merely to render the obligation voidable at the election of the obligor, the defense is cut off."[3] James White and Robert Summers, in their hornbook on the UCC, opine that unconscionability is almost always a personal defense, not assertable against an HDC.[4] But again, the HDC takes free only from personal defenses of parties with whom she has not dealt. So while the payee of a note can be an HDC, if he dealt with the maker, he is subject to the maker's defenses.

Holder in Due Course Is Subject to Real Defenses

real defenses

In negotiable-instrument law, defenses that are good against a holder in due course.

An HDC in a nonconsumer transaction is not subject to personal defenses, but he *is* subject to the so-called **real defenses** (or "universal defenses")—they are good against an HDC.

The real defenses good against any holder, including HDCs, are as follows (see Figure 24.2):

1. Unauthorized signature (forgery) (UCC, Section 3-401(a))
2. Bankruptcy (UCC, Section 3-305(a))
3. Infancy (UCC, Section 3-305(a))
4. Fraudulent alteration (UCC, Section 3-407(b) and (c))
5. Duress, mental incapacity, or illegality that renders the obligation void (UCC, Section 3-305(a))
6. Fraud in the execution (UCC, Section 3-305(a))
7. Discharge of which the holder has notice when he takes the instrument (UCC, Section 3-601)

FIGURE 24.2 Real Defenses

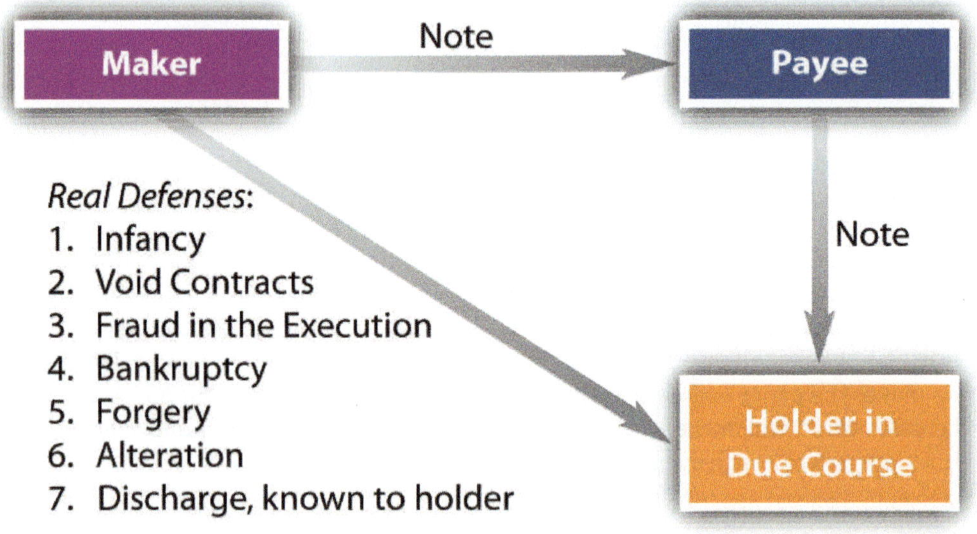

Analysis of the Real Defenses

Though most of these concepts are pretty clear, a few comments by way of analysis are appropriate.

Forgery

Forgery is a real defense to an action by an HDC. As we have noted, though, negligence in the making or handling of a negotiable instrument may cut off this defense against an HDC—as, for example, when a drawer who uses a rubber signature stamp carelessly leaves it unattended. And notice, too, that Section 3-308 of the UCC provides that signatures are presumed valid unless their validity is specifically denied, at which time the burden shifts to the person claiming validity. These issues are discussed in *Triffin v. Somerset Valley Bank*, in Section 3 of this chapter.

Bankruptcy

Drawers, makers, and subsequent indorsers are not liable to an HDC if they have been discharged in bankruptcy. If they were, bankruptcy would not serve much purpose.

Infancy

Whether an infant's signature on a negotiable instrument is a valid defense depends on the law of the state. In some states, for instance, an infant who misrepresents his age is estopped from asserting infancy as a defense to a breach of contract. In those states, infancy would not be available as a defense against the effort of an HDC to collect.

Fraudulent Alteration

Under Section 3-407 of the UCC, "fraudulent alteration" means either (1) an unauthorized change in an instrument that purports to modify in any respect the obligation of a party or (2) an unauthorized addition of words or numbers or other change to an incomplete instrument relating to the obligation of a party. An alteration fraudulently made discharges a party whose obligation is affected by the alteration unless that party assents or is precluded from asserting the alteration. But a nonfraudulent alteration—for example, filling in an omitted date or giving the obligor the benefit of a lower interest rate—does not discharge the obligor. In any case, the person paying or taking the instrument may pay or collect "according to its original terms, or in the case of an incomplete instrument that is altered by unauthorized completion, according to its terms as completed. If blanks are filled or an incomplete instrument is otherwise completed, subsection (c) places the loss upon the party who left the instrument incomplete by permitting enforcement in its completed form. This result is intended even though the instrument was stolen from the issuer and completed after the theft." A moral here: don't leave instruments lying around with blanks that could be filled in.

Void Contract

A void contract is distinguished from a voidable contract; only the former is a real defense.

Fraud in the Execution

You may recall that this is the rather unusual situation in which a person is tricked into signing a document. Able holds out a piece of paper for her boss and points to the signature line, saying, "This is a receipt for goods we received a little while ago." Baker signs it. It is not a receipt; it's the signature line on a promissory note. Able has committed fraud in the execution, and the note is void.

Discharge of Which the Holder Has Notice

If the holder knows that the paper—a note, say—has already been paid, she cannot enforce it. That's a good reason to take back any note you have made from the person who presents it to you for payment.

Consumer Transactions and Holders in Due Course

The holder-in-due-course doctrine often worked considerable hardship on the consumer, usually as the maker of an installment note.

factor

One that lends money to another, taking back a negotiable instrument as security.

For example, a number of students are approached by a gym owner who induces them to sign one-year promissory notes for $150 for a one-year gym membership. The owner says, "I know that right now the equipment in the gym is pretty rudimentary, but then, too, $150 is about half what you'd pay at the YMCA or Gold's Gym. And the thing is, as we get more customers signing up, we're going to use the money to invest in new equipment. So within several months we'll have a fully equipped facility for your use." Several students sign the notes, which the owner sells to a **factor** (one that lends money to another, taking back a negotiable instrument as security, usually at about a 20 percent discount). The factor takes as an apparent HDC, but the gym idea doesn't work and the owner declares bankruptcy. If this were a commercial transaction, the makers (the students) would still owe on the notes even if there was, as here, a complete failure of consideration (called "paying on a dead horse"). But the students don't have to pay.

Whether the gym owner here committed fraud is uncertain, but the holder-in-due-course doctrine did often work to promote fraud. Courts frequently saw cases brought by credit companies (factors) against consumers who bought machines that did not work and services that did not live up to their promises. The ancient concept of an HDC did not square with the realities of modern commerce, in which instruments by the millions are negotiated for uncompleted transactions. The finance company that bought such commercial paper could never have honestly claimed (in the sociological sense) to be wholly ignorant that many makers will have claims against their payees (though they could and did make the claim in the legal sense).

Acting to curb abuses, the Federal Trade Commission (FTC) in 1976 promulgated a trade regulation rule that in effect abolished the holder-in-due-course rule for consumer credit transactions. Under the FTC rule titled "Preservation of Consumers' Claims and Defenses,"[5] the creditor becomes a mere holder and stands in the shoes of the seller, subject to all claims and defenses that the debtor could assert against the seller. Specifically, the rule requires the seller to provide notice in any consumer credit contract that the debtor is entitled to raise defenses against any subsequent purchaser of the paper. It also bars the seller from accepting any outside financing unless the loan contract between the consumer and the outside finance company contains a similar notice. (The required notice, to be printed in no less than ten-point, boldface type, is set out in Figure 24.3.) The effect of the rule is to ensure that a consumer's claim against the seller will not be defeated by a transfer of the paper. The FTC rule has this effect because the paragraph to be inserted in the consumer credit contract gives the holder notice sufficient to prevent him from becoming an HDC.

consumer transaction

A transaction in which an individual incurs an obligation primarily for personal, family, or household purposes.

The rule applies only to consumer credit transactions. A **consumer transaction** is defined as a purchase of goods or services by a natural person, not a corporation or partnership, for personal, family, or household use from a seller in the ordinary course of business.[6] Purchases of goods or services for commercial purposes and purchases of interests in real property, commodities, or securities are not affected. The rule applies to any credit extended by the seller himself (except for credit card transactions) or to any "purchase money loan." This type of loan is defined as a cash advance to the consumer applied in whole or substantial part to a purchase of goods or services from a seller who either (a) refers consumers to the creditor or (b) is affiliated with the creditor. The purpose of this definition is to prevent the seller from making an end run around the rule by arranging a loan for the consumer through an outside finance company. The rule does not apply to a loan that the consumer arranges with an independent finance company entirely on his own.

The net effect of the FTC rule is this: the holder-in-due-course doctrine is virtually dead in consumer credit contracts. It remains alive and flourishing as a legal doctrine in all other business transactions.

FIGURE 24.3 Notice of Defense

NOTICE

ANY HOLDER OF THIS CONSUMER CREDIT CONTRACT IS SUBJECT TO ALL CLAIMS AND DEFENSES WHICH THE DEBTOR COULD ASSERT AGAINST THE SELLER OF GOODS OR SERVICES OBTAINED PURSUANT HERETO OR WITH THE PROCEEDS HEREOF. RECOVERY HEREUNDER BY THE DEBTOR SHALL NOT EXCEED AMOUNTS PAID BY THE DEBTOR HEREUNDER.

Key Takeaway

The privileged position of the HDC stands up against the so-called personal defenses, which are—more or less—the same as typical defenses to obligation on any contract, *not including*, however, the real defenses. Real defenses are good against any holder, including an HDC. These are infancy, void obligations, fraud in the execution, bankruptcy, discharge of which holder has notice, unauthorized signatures, and fraudulent alterations. While a payee may be an HDC, his or her rights as such are limited to avoiding defenses of persons the payee did not deal with. The shelter rule says that the transferee of an instrument takes the same rights that the transferor had. The Federal Trade Commission has abrogated the holder-in-due-course doctrine for consumer transactions.

Exercises

1. What purpose does the holder-in-due-course doctrine serve?
2. What defenses is an HDC not subject to? What defenses is an HDC subject to?
3. What is the Shelter Rule, and what purpose does it serve?
4. For what transactions has the FTC abolished the holder-in-due-course doctrine and why?
5. Under what circumstances is a forged signature valid?

24.3 Cases

Executory Promise as Satisfying "Value"

Carter & Grimsley v. Omni Trading, Inc.

716 N.E.2d 320 (Ill. App. 1999)

Lytton, J.

Facts

Omni purchased some grain from Country Grain, and on February 2, 1996, it issued two checks, totaling $75,000, to Country Grain. Country Grain, in turn, endorsed the checks over to Carter as a retainer for future legal services. Carter deposited the checks on February 5; Country Grain failed the next day. On February 8, Carter was notified that Omni had stopped payment on the checks. Carter subsequently filed a complaint against Omni * * * alleging that it was entitled to the proceeds of the checks, plus pre-judgment interest, as a holder in due course. * * * [Carter moved for summary judgment; the motion was denied.]

Discussion

Carter argues that its motion for summary judgment should have been granted because, as a holder in due course, it has the right to recover on the checks from the drawer, Omni.

The Illinois Uniform Commercial Code (UCC) defines a holder in due course as:

> *"the holder of an instrument if:*
>
> *(1) the instrument when issued does not bear such apparent evidence of forgery or alteration or is not otherwise so irregular or incomplete as to call into question its authenticity, and (2) the holder took the instrument (i) for value,...*

Section 3-303(a) of the UCC also states that:

> *(a) "An instrument is issued or transferred for value if: (1) the instrument is issued or transferred for a promise of performance,* **to the extent that the promise has been performed.** ** * *" (emphasis added)*

Carter contends that in Illinois a contract for future legal services should be treated differently than other executory contracts. It contends that when the attorney-client relationship is created by payment of a fee or retainer, the contract is no longer executory. Thus, Carter would achieve holder in due course status. We are not persuaded.

A retainer is the act of a client employing an attorney; it also denotes the fee paid by the client when he retains the attorney to act for him. [Citation] We have found no Illinois cases construing section 3-303(a) as it relates to a promise to perform future legal services under a retainer. The general rule, however, is that "an executory promise is not value." [Citation] "[T]he promise does not rise to the level of 'value' in the commercial paper market until it is actually performed." [Citation]

The UCC comment to section 303 gives the following example:

"Case # 2. X issues a check to Y in consideration of Y's promise to perform services in the future. Although the executory promise is consideration for issuance of the check it is value only to the extent the promise is performed.

We have found no exceptions to these principles for retainers. Indeed, courts in other jurisdictions interpreting similar language under section 3-303 have held that attorneys may be holders in due course only to the extent that they have actually performed legal services prior to acquiring a negotiable instrument. See [Citations: Pennsylvania, Florida, Massachusetts]. We agree.

This retainer was a contract for future legal services. Under section 3-303(a)(1), it was a "promise of performance," not yet performed. Thus, no value was received, and Carter is not a holder in due course.

Furthermore, in this case, no evidence was presented in the trial court that Carter performed any legal services for Country Grain prior to receiving the checks. Without an evidentiary basis for finding that Carter received the checks for services performed, the trial court correctly found that Carter failed to prove that it was a holder in due course. [Citations]

Conclusion

Because we have decided that Carter did not take the checks for value under section 3-303(a) of the UCC, we need not address its other arguments.

The judgment of the circuit court of Peoria County is affirmed.

Holdridge, J., dissenting.

I respectfully dissent. In a contractual relationship between attorney and client, the payment of a fee or retainer creates the relationship, and once that relationship is created the contract is no longer executory. [Citation] Carter's agreement to enter into an attorney-client relationship with Country Grain was the value exchanged for the checks endorsed over to the firm. Thus, the general rule cited by the majority that "an executory promise is not value" does not apply to the case at bar. On that basis, I would hold that the trial court erred in determining that Carter was not entitled to the check proceeds and I therefore dissent.

Case Questions

1. How did Carter & Grimsley obtain the two checks drawn by Omni?
2. Why—apparently—did Omni stop payments on the checks?
3. Why did the court determine that Carter was not an HDC?
4. Who is it that must have performed here in order for Carter to have been an HDC, Country Grain or Carter?
5. How could making a retainer payment to an attorney be considered anything other than payment on an executory contract, as the dissent argues?

The "Good Faith and Reasonable Commercial Standards" Requirement

Buckeye Check Cashing, Inc. v. Camp

825 N.E.2d 644 (Ohio App. 2005)

Donovan, J.

Defendant-appellant Shawn Sheth appeals from a judgment of the Xenia Municipal Court in favor of plaintiff-appellee Buckeye Check Cashing, Inc. ("Buckeye"). Sheth contends that the trial court erred in finding that Buckeye was a holder in due course of a postdated check drawn by Sheth and therefore was entitled to payment on the instrument despite the fact that Sheth had issued a stop-payment order to his bank.

In support of this assertion, Sheth argues that the trial court did not use the correct legal standard in granting holder-in-due-course status to Buckeye. In particular, Sheth asserts that the trial court used the pre-1990 Uniform Commercial Code ("UCC") definition of "good faith" as it pertains to holder-in-due-course status, which defined it as "honesty in fact." The definition of "good faith" was extended by the authors of the UCC in 1990 to also mean "the observance of reasonable commercial standards of fair dealing." The post-1990 definition was adopted by the Ohio legislature in 1994.

Sheth argues that while Buckeye would prevail under the pre-1990, "honesty in fact" definition of "good faith," it failed to act in a commercially reasonable manner when it chose to cash the postdated check drawn by Sheth. The lower court * * * adjudged Buckeye to be a holder in due course and, therefore, entitled to payment. We conclude that the trial court used the incorrect "good faith" standard when it granted holder-in-due-course status to Buckeye because Buckeye did not act in a commercially reasonable manner when it cashed the postdated check drawn by Sheth. Because we accept Sheth's sole assignment of error, the judgment of the trial court is reversed.

On or about October 12, 2003, Sheth entered into negotiations with James A. Camp for Camp to provide certain services to Sheth by October 15, 2003. To that end, Sheth issued Camp a check for $1,300. The check was postdated to October 15, 2003.

On October 13, 2003, Camp negotiated the check to Buckeye and received a payment of $1,261.31. Apparently fearing that Camp did not intend to fulfill his end of the contract, Sheth contacted his bank on October 14, 2003, and issued a stop-payment order on the check. Unaware of the stop-payment order, Buckeye deposited the check with its own bank on October 14, 2003, believing that the check would reach Sheth's bank by October 15, 2003. Because the stop-payment order was in effect, the check was ultimately dishonored by Sheth's bank. After an unsuccessful attempt to obtain payment directly from Sheth, Buckeye brought suit.

Sheth's sole assignment of error is as follows:

"The trial court erred by applying the incorrect legal standard in granting holder in due course status to the plaintiff-appellee because the plaintiff-appellee failed to follow commercially reasonable standards in electing to cash the check that gives rise to this dispute."

[UCC 3-302] outlines the elements required to receive holder-in-due-course status. The statute states:

...'holder in due course' means the holder of an instrument if both of the following apply:

"(1) The instrument when issued or negotiated to the holder does not bear evidence of forgery or alteration that is so apparent, or is otherwise so irregular or incomplete as to call into question its authenticity;

"(2) The holder took the instrument under all of the following circumstances:

(a) For value;

(b) **In good faith***;*

(c) Without notice that the instrument is overdue or has been dishonored or that there is an uncured default with respect to payment of another instrument issued as part of the same series;

(d) Without notice that the instrument contains an unauthorized signature or has been altered;

(e) Without notice of any claim to the instrument as described in [3-306];

(f) Without notice that any party has a defense or claim in recoupment described in [UCC 3-305(a); emphasis added].

At issue in the instant appeal is whether Buckeye acted in "good faith" when it chose to honor the postdated check originally drawn by Sheth. * * * UCC 1-201, defines "good faith" as "honesty in fact and the observance of reasonable commercial standards of fair dealing." Before the Ohio legislature amended UCC 1-201 in 1994, that section did not define "good faith"; the definition of "good faith" as "honesty in fact" in UCC 1-201 was the definition that applied[.] * * *

"Honesty in fact" is defined as the absence of bad faith or dishonesty with respect to a party's conduct within a commercial transaction. [Citation] Under that standard, absent fraudulent behavior, an otherwise innocent party was assumed to have acted in good faith. The "honesty in fact" requirement, also known as the "pure heart and empty head" doctrine, is a subjective test under which a holder had to subjectively believe he was negotiating an instrument in good faith for him to become a holder in due course. Maine [Citation, 1999].

In 1994, however, the Ohio legislature amended the definition of "good faith" to include not only the subjective "honesty in fact" test, but also an objective test: "the observance of reasonable commercial standards of fair dealing." UCC 1-201(20). A holder in due course must now satisfy both a subjective and an objective test of good faith. What constitutes "reasonable commercial standards of fair dealing" for parties claiming holder-in-due-course status, however, has not heretofore been defined in the state of Ohio.

In support of his contention that Buckeye is not a holder in due course, Sheth cites a decision from the Supreme Court of Maine, [referred to above] in which the court provided clarification with respect to the objective prong of the "good faith" analysis:

> *"The fact finder must therefore determine, first, whether the conduct of the holder comported with industry or 'commercial' standards applicable to the transaction and second, whether those standards were reasonable standards intended to result in fair dealing. Each of those determinations must be made in the context of the specific transaction at hand. If the fact finder's conclusion on each point is 'yes,' the holder will be determined to have acted in good faith even if, in the individual transaction at issue, the result appears unreasonable. Thus, a holder may be accorded holder in due course where it acts pursuant to those reasonable commercial standards of fair dealing—even if it is negligent—but may lose that status, even where it complies with commercial standards, if those standards are not reasonably related to achieving fair dealing." [Citation]*

Check cashing is an unlicensed and unregulated business in Ohio. [Citation] Thus, there are no concrete commercial standards by which check-cashing businesses must operate. Moreover, Buckeye argues that its own internal operating policies do not require that it verify the availability of funds, nor does Buckeye apparently have any guidelines with respect to the acceptance of postdated checks. Buckeye asserts that cashing a postdated check does not prevent a holder from obtaining holder-in-due-course status and cites several cases in support of this contention. All of the cases cited by Buckeye, however, were decided prior to the UCC's addition of the objective prong to the definition of "good faith."

Under a purely subjective "honesty in fact" analysis, it is clear that Buckeye accepted the check from Camp in good faith and would therefore achieve holder-in-due-course status. When the objective prong of the good faith test is applied, however, we find that Buckeye did not conduct itself in a commercially reasonable manner. While not going so far as to say that cashing a postdated check prevents a holder from obtaining holder-in-due-course status in every instance, the presentation of a postdated check should put the check cashing entity on notice that the check might not be good. Buckeye accepted the postdated check at its own peril. Some attempt at verification should be made before a check-cashing business cashes a postdated check. Such a failure to act does not constitute taking an instrument in good faith under the current objective test of "reasonable commercial standards" enunciated in [the UCC].

We conclude that in deciding to amend the good faith requirement to include an objective component of "reasonable commercial standards," the Ohio legislature intended to place a duty on the holders of certain instruments to act in a responsible manner in order to obtain holder-in-due-course status. When Buckeye decided to cash the postdated check presented by Camp, it did so without making any attempt to verify its validity. This court in no way seeks to curtail the free negotiability of commercial instruments. However, the nature of certain instruments, such as the postdated check in this case, renders it necessary for appellee Buckeye to take minimal steps to protect its interests. That was not done. Buckeye was put on notice that the check was not good until October 15, 2003. "Good faith," as it is defined in the UCC and the Ohio Revised Code, requires that a holder demonstrate not only honesty in fact but also that the holder act in a commercially reasonable manner. Without taking any steps to discover whether the postdated check issued by Sheth was valid, Buckeye failed to act in a commercially reasonable manner and therefore was not a holder in due course.

Based upon the foregoing, Sheth's single assignment of error is sustained, the judgment of the Xenia Municipal Court is reversed, and this matter is remanded to that court for further proceedings in accordance with law and consistent with this opinion.

Judgment reversed, and cause remanded.

Case Questions

1. Who was Camp? Why did Sheth give him a check? Why is the case titled *Buckeye v. Camp*?
2. How does giving someone a postdated check offer the drawer any protection? How does it give rise to any "notice that the check might not be good"?
3. If Camp had taken the check to Sheth's bank to cash it, what would have happened?
4. What difference did the court discern between the pre-1990 UCC Article 3 and the post-1990 Article 3 (that Ohio adopted in 1994)?

The Shelter Rule

Triffin v. Somerset Valley Bank
777 A.2d 993 (N.J. Ct. App. 2001)

Cuff, J.

This case concerns the enforceability of dishonored checks against the issuer of the checks under Article 3 of the Uniform Commercial Code (UCC), as implemented in New Jersey[.]

Plaintiff [Robert J. Triffin] purchased, through assignment agreements with check cashing companies, eighteen dishonored checks, issued by defendant Hauser Contracting Company (Hauser Co.). Plaintiff then filed suit * * * to enforce Hauser Co.'s liability on the checks. The trial court granted plaintiff's motion for summary judgment. Hauser Co. appeals the grant of summary judgment. * * * We affirm.

In October 1998, Alfred M. Hauser, president of Hauser Co., was notified by Edwards Food Store in Raritan and the Somerset Valley Bank (the Bank), that several individuals were cashing what appeared to be Hauser Co. payroll checks. Mr. Hauser reviewed the checks, ascertained that the checks were counterfeits and contacted the Raritan Borough and Hillsborough Police Departments. Mr. Hauser concluded that the checks were counterfeits because none of the payees were employees of Hauser Co., and because he did not write the checks or authorize anyone to sign those checks on his behalf. At that time, Hauser Co. employed Automatic Data Processing, Inc. (ADP) to provide payroll services and a facsimile signature was utilized on all Hauser Co. payroll checks.

Mr. Hauser executed affidavits of stolen and forged checks at the Bank, stopping payment on the checks at issue. Subsequently, the Bank received more than eighty similar checks valued at $25,000 all drawn on Hauser Co.'s account.

Plaintiff is in the business of purchasing dishonored negotiable instruments. In February and March 1999, plaintiff purchased eighteen dishonored checks from four different check cashing agencies, specifying Hauser Co. as the drawer. The checks totaled $8,826.42. Pursuant to assignment agreements executed by plaintiff, each agency stated that it cashed the checks for value, in good faith, without notice of any claims or defenses to the checks, without knowledge that any of the signatures were unauthorized or forged, and with the expectation that the checks would be paid upon presentment to the bank upon which the checks were drawn. All eighteen checks bore a red and green facsimile drawer's signature stamp in the name of Alfred M. Hauser. All eighteen checks were marked by the Bank as "stolen check" and stamped with the warning, "do not present again." * * *

Plaintiff then filed this action against the Bank, Hauser Co., * * * Plaintiff contended that Hauser Co. was negligent in failing to safeguard both its payroll checks and its authorized drawer's facsimile stamp, and was liable for payment of the checks.

The trial court granted plaintiff's summary judgment motion, concluding that no genuine issue of fact existed as to the authenticity of the eighteen checks at issue. Judge Hoens concluded that because the check cashing companies took the checks in good faith, plaintiff was a holder in due course as assignee. Judge Hoens also found that because the checks appeared to be genuine, Hauser Co. was required, but had failed, to show that plaintiff's assignor had any notice that the checks were not validly drawn. * * *

Hauser Co. argues that summary judgment was improperly granted because the court failed to properly address Hauser Co.'s defense that the checks at issue were invalid negotiable instruments and therefore erred in finding plaintiff was a holder in due course.

As a threshold matter, it is evident that the eighteen checks meet the definition of a negotiable instrument [UCC 3-104]. Each check is payable to a bearer for a fixed amount, on demand, and does not state any other undertaking by the person promising payment, aside from the payment of money. In addition, each check appears to have been signed by Mr. Hauser, through the use of a facsimile stamp, permitted by the UCC to take the place of a manual signature. [Section 3-401(b) of the UCC] provides that a "signature may be made manually or by means of a device or machine...with present intention to authenticate a writing." It is uncontroverted by Hauser Co. that the facsimile signature stamp on the checks is identical to Hauser Co.'s authorized stamp.

Hauser Co., however, contends that the checks are not negotiable instruments because Mr. Hauser did not sign the checks, did not authorize their signing, and its payroll service, ADP, did not produce the checks. Lack of authorization, however, is a separate issue from whether the checks are negotiable instruments. Consequently, given that the checks are negotiable instruments, the next issue is whether the checks are unenforceable by a holder in due course, because the signature on the checks was forged or unauthorized.

[Sections 3-203 and 3-302 of the UCC] discuss the rights of a holder in due course and the rights of a transferee of a holder in due course. Section 3-302 establishes that a person is a holder in due course if:

> *(1) the instrument when issued or negotiated to the holder does not bear such apparent evidence of forgery or alteration or is not otherwise so irregular or incomplete as to call into question its authenticity; and*
>
> *(2) the holder took the instrument for value, in good faith, without notice that the instrument is overdue or has been dishonored or that there is an uncured default with respect to payment of another instrument issued as part of the same series, without notice that the instrument contains an unauthorized signature or has been altered, without notice of any claim to the instrument described in 3-306, and without notice that any party has a defense or claim in recoupment described in subsection a. of 3-305.*

Section 3-203 deals with transfer of instruments and provides:

> *a. An instrument is transferred when it is delivered by a person other than its issuer for the purpose of giving to the person receiving delivery the right to enforce the instrument.*
>
> *b. Transfer of an instrument, whether or not the transfer is a negotiation, vests in the transferee any right of the transferor to enforce the instrument, including any right as a holder in due course, but the transferee cannot acquire rights of a holder in due course by a transfer, directly or indirectly, from a holder in due course if the transferee engaged in fraud or illegality affecting the instrument....*

Under subsection (b) a holder in due course that transfers an instrument transfers those rights as a holder in due course to the purchaser. The policy is to assure the holder in due course a free market for the instrument.

The record indicates that plaintiff has complied with the requirements of both sections 3-302 and 3-203. Each of the check cashing companies from whom plaintiff purchased the dishonored checks were holders in due course. In support of his summary judgment motion, plaintiff submitted an affidavit from each company; each company swore that it cashed the checks for value, in good faith, without notice of any claims or defenses by any party, without knowledge that any of the signatures on the checks were unauthorized or fraudulent, and with the expectation that the checks would be paid upon their presentment to the bank upon which the checks were drawn. Hauser Co. does not dispute any of the facts sworn to by the check cashing companies.

The checks were then transferred to plaintiff in accordance with section 3-303, vesting plaintiff with holder in due course status. Each company swore that it assigned the checks to plaintiff in exchange for consideration received from plaintiff. Plaintiff thus acquired the check cashing companies' holder in due course status when the checks were assigned to plaintiff. Moreover, pursuant to section 3-403(a)'s requirement that the transfer must have been made for the purpose of giving the transferee the right to enforce the instrument, the assignment agreements expressly provided plaintiff with that right, stating that "all payments [assignor] may receive from any of the referenced Debtors ... shall be the exclusive property of [assignee]." Again, Hauser Co. does not dispute any facts relating to the assignment of the checks to plaintiff.

Hauser Co. contends, instead, that the checks are per se invalid because they were fraudulent and unauthorized. Presumably, this argument is predicated on section 3-302. This section states a person is not a holder in due course if the instrument bears "apparent evidence of forgery or alteration" or is otherwise "so irregular or incomplete as to call into question its authenticity."

In order to preclude liability from a holder in due course under section 3-302, it must be apparent on the face of the instrument that it is fraudulent. The trial court specifically found that Hauser Co. had provided no such evidence, stating that Hauser Co. had failed to show that there was anything about the appearance of the checks to place the check cashing company on notice that any check was not valid. Specifically, with respect to Hauser Co.'s facsimile signature on the checks, the court stated that the signature was identical to Hauser Co.'s authorized facsimile signature. Moreover, each of the check cashing companies certified that they had no knowledge that the signatures on the checks were fraudulent or that there were any claims or defenses to enforcement of the checks. Hence, the trial court's conclusion that there was no apparent evidence of invalidity was not an abuse of discretion and was based on a reasonable reading of the record.

To be sure, section 3-308(a) does shift the burden of establishing the validity of the signature to the plaintiff, but only if the defendant specifically denies the signature's validity in the pleadings. The section states:

> *In an action with respect to an instrument, the authenticity of, and authority to make, each signature on the instrument is admitted unless specifically denied in the pleadings. If the validity of a signature is denied in the pleadings, the burden of establishing validity is on the person claiming validity, but the signature is presumed to be authentic and authorized unless the action is to enforce the liability of the purported signer and the signer is dead or incompetent at the time of trial of the issue of validity of the signature.*

Examination of the pleadings reveals that Hauser Co. did not specifically deny the factual assertions in plaintiff's complaint.

Hence, the trial court's conclusion that there was no apparent evidence of invalidity was not an abuse of discretion and was based on a reasonable reading of the record.

In conclusion, we hold that Judge Hoens properly granted summary judgment. There was no issue of material fact as to: (1) the status of the checks as negotiable instruments; (2) the status of the check cashing companies as holders in due course; (3) the status of plaintiff as a holder in due course; and (4) the lack of apparent evidence on the face of the checks that they were forged, altered or otherwise irregular. Moreover, Hauser Co.'s failure to submit some factual evidence indicating that the facsimile signature was forged or otherwise unauthorized left unchallenged the UCC's rebuttable presumption that a signature on an instrument is valid. Consequently, the trial court properly held, as a matter of law, that plaintiff was a holder in due course and entitled to enforce the checks. Affirmed.

Case Questions

1. Why did the plaintiff, Mr. Triffin, obtain possession of the dishonored checks? Regarding the plaintiff, consider this: http://caselaw.findlaw.com/nj-supreme-court/1332248.html.
2. Section 4-401 of the UCC says nobody is liable on an instrument unless the person signed it, and Section 4-403(a) provides that "an unauthorized signature is ineffective" (except as the signature of the unauthorized person), so how could Hauser Co. be liable at all? And why did the court never discuss plaintiff's contention that the defendant "was negligent in failing to safeguard both its payroll checks and its authorized drawer's facsimile stamp"?
3. Why didn't the Hauser Co. specifically deny the authenticity of the signatures?
4. Obviously, the plaintiff must have known that there was something wrong with the checks when he bought them from the check-cashing companies: they had been dishonored and were marked "Stolen, do not present again." Did he present them again?
5. While the UCC does not require that the transferee of an instrument acted in good faith in order to collect on the instrument as an HDC (though he can't have participated in any scam), it disallows a person from being an HDC if he takes an instrument with notice of dishonor. Surely the plaintiff had notice of that. What does the UCC require that transformed Mr. Triffin—via the shelter rule—into a person with the rights of an HDC?

6. If the plaintiff had not purchased the checks from the check-cashing companies, who would have taken the loss here?
7. What recourse does the defendant, Hauser Co., have now?

Authors' comment: How this scam unfolded is suggested in the following segment of an online guide to reducing financial transaction fraud.

> *Recommendations: It is clear from this case that if a thief can get check stock that looks genuine, your company can be held liable for losses that may occur from those counterfeit checks. Most companies buy check stock from vendors that sell the identical check stock entirely blank to other companies, totally uncontrolled, thus aiding the forgers. Many companies opt for these checks because they are less expensive than controlled, high security checks (excluding legal fees and holder in due course judgments). Forgers buy the check stock, and using a $99 scanner and Adobe Illustrator, create counterfeit checks that cannot be distinguished from the account holder's original checks. This is how legal exposure to a holder in due course claim can be and is created. Companies should use checks uniquely designed and manufactured for them, or buy from vendors such as SAFEChecks (http://www.safechecks.com) that customize every company's check and never sells check stock entirely blank without it first being customized for the end user.*[7]

24.4 Summary and Exercises

Summary

A holder is a holder in due course (HDC) if he takes the instrument without reason to question its authenticity on account of obvious facial irregularities, for value, in good faith, and without notice that it is overdue or has been dishonored, or that it contains a forgery or alteration, or that that any person has any defense against it or claim to it. The HDC takes the paper free of most defenses; an ordinary holder takes the paper as an assignee, acquiring only the rights of the assignor.

Value is not the same as consideration; hence, a promise will not satisfy this criterion until it has been performed. The HDC must have given something of value other than a promise to give.

Good faith means (1) honesty in fact in the conduct or transaction concerned and (2) the observance of reasonable commercial standards of fair dealing. Honesty in fact is a subjective test, but the observance of reasonable commercial standards is objective.

Notice is not limited to receipt of an explicit statement of defenses; a holder may be given notice through inferences that should be drawn from the character of the instrument. Thus an incomplete instrument, one that bears marks of forgery, or one that indicates it is overdue may give notice on its face. Certain facts do not necessarily give notice of defense or claim: that the instrument is antedated or postdated, that the instrument was negotiated in return for an executory promise, that any party has signed for accommodation, that an incomplete instrument has been completed, that any person negotiating the instrument is or was a fiduciary, or that there has been default in payment of interest or principal.

A person who could not have become an HDC directly (e.g., because he had notice of a defense or claim) may become so if he takes as transferee from an HDC as long as he was not a party to any fraud or illegality affecting the instrument or had not previously been a holder with notice of a defense or claim. This is the shelter rule.

Holders in due course are not immune from all defenses. A real, as opposed to a personal, defense may be asserted against the HDC. Personal defenses include fraud in the inducement, failure of consideration, nonperformance of a condition precedent, and the like. Real defenses consist of infancy, acts that would make a contract void (such as duress), fraud in the execution, forgery, and discharge in bankruptcy. A 1976 trade regulation rule of the Federal Trade Commission abolishes the holder-in-due-course rule for consumer transactions.

Exercises

1. Mike signed and delivered a note for $9,000 to Paul Payee in exchange for Paul's tractor. Paul transferred the note to Hilda, who promised to pay $7,500 for it. After Hilda had paid Paul $5,000 of the promised $7,500, Hilda learned that Mike had a defense: the tractor was defective. How much, if anything, can Hilda collect from Mike on the note, and why?
2. In Exercise 1, if Hilda had paid Paul $7,500 and then learned of Mike's defense, how much—if any of the amount—could she collect from Mike?
3. Tex fraudulently sold a boat, to which he did not have title, to Sheryl for $30,000 and received, as a deposit from her, a check in the amount of $5,000. He deposited the check in his account at First Bank and immediately withdrew $3,000 of the proceeds. When Sheryl discovered that Tex had no title, she called her bank (the drawee) and stopped payment on the check. Tex, in the meantime, disappeared. First Bank now wishes to collect the $3,000 from Sheryl, but she claims it is not an HDC because it did not give value for the check in that the payment to Tex was conditional: the bank retained the right to collect from Tex if it could not collect on the check. Is Sheryl correct? Explain.
4. Corporation draws a check payable to First Bank. The check is given to an officer of Corporation (known to Bank), who is instructed to deliver it to Bank in payment of a debt owed by Corporation to Bank. Instead, the officer, intending to defraud Corporation, delivers the check to Bank in payment of his personal debt. Bank has received funds of Corporation that have been used for the personal benefit of the officer. Corporation asserts a claim to the proceeds of the check against Bank. Is Bank an HDC of the check?
5. Contractor contracted with Betty Baker to install a new furnace in Baker's business. Baker wrote a check for $8,000 (the price quoted by Contractor) payable to Furnace Co., which Contractor delivered to Furnace Co. in payment of his own debt to it. Furnace Co. knew nothing of what went on between Contractor and Baker. When Contractor did not complete the job, Baker stopped payment on the check. Furnace Co. sued Baker, who defended by claiming failure of consideration. Is this a good defense against Furnace Co.?
6. Benson purchased a double-paned, gas-filled picture window for his house from Wonder Window, making a $200 deposit and signing an installment contract, which is here set out in its entirety:

   > *October 3, 2012*
   >
   > *I promise to pay to Wonder Window or order the sum of $1,000 in five equal installments of $200.*
   >
   > *[Signed] Benson*

   Wonder Window negotiated the installment contract to Devon, who took the instrument for value, in good faith, without notice of any claim or defense of any party, and without question of the instrument's authenticity. After Benson made three payments, the window fogged up inside and was unacceptable. Benson wants his money back from Wonder Window, and he wants to discontinue further payments. Can he do that? Explain.
7. The Turmans executed a deed of trust note (a note and mortgage) dated November 12, 2012, for $100,000 payable to Ward's Home Improvement, Inc. The note was consideration

for a contract: Ward was to construct a home on the Turmans' property. The same day, Ward executed a separate written assignment of the note to Robert L. Pomerantz, which specifically used the word "assigns." Ward did not endorse the note to Pomerantz or otherwise write on it. Ward did not complete the house; to do so would require the expenditure of an additional $42,000. Pomerantz maintained he is a holder in due course of the $100,000 note and demanded payment from the Turmans. Does he get paid? Explain.[8]

Self-Test Questions

1. Which defeats a person from being an HDC?
    a. She takes the paper in return for a promise by the maker or drawer to perform a service in the future.
    b. She subjectively takes it in good faith, but most people would recognize the deal as suspect.
    c. The instrument contains a very clever, almost undetectable forged signature.
    d. The instrument was postdated.
    e. All these are grounds to defeat the HDC status.
2. Personal defenses are
    a. good against all holders
    b. good against holders but not HDCs
    c. good against HDCs but not holders
    d. not good against any holder, HDC or otherwise
    e. sometimes good against HDCs, depending on the facts
3. Fraud in the inducement is a ______________ defense.
    a. real
    b. personal
4. A person would not be an HDC if she
    a. was notified that payment on the instrument had been refused
    b. knew that one of the prior indorsers had been discharged
    c. understood that the note was collateral for a loan
    d. purchased the note at a discount
5. Rock Industries agreed to sell Contractor gravel to repair an airport drain field. Contractor was uncertain how many loads of gravel would be needed, so he drew a check made out to "Rock Industries" as the payee but left the amount blank, to be filled in on the job site when the last load of gravel was delivered. Five truckloads, each carrying ten tons of gravel, were required, with gravel priced at $20 per ton. Thus Contractor figured he'd pay for fifty tons, or $1,000, but Rock Industries had apparently filled in the amount as $1,400 and negotiated it to Fairchild Truck Repair. Fairchild took it in good faith for an antecedent debt. Contractor will
    a. be liable to Fairchild, but only for $1,000
    b. be liable to Fairchild for $1,400
    c. not be liable to Fairchild because the check was materially altered
    d. not be liable to Fairchild because it did not give "value" for it to Rock Industries

Self-Test Answers

1. a

2. b
3. b
4. a
5. b

Endnotes

1. Uniform Commercial Code, Section 1-201(20).
2. Uniform Commercial Code, Section 3-203, Comment 2.
3. Uniform Commercial Code, Section 3-305, Comment 1.
4. James White and Robert Summers, Uniform Commercial Code, 2/e, 575 (1980).
5. 16 *Code of Federal Regulations*, Section 433.
6. Uniform Commercial Code, Section 2-201(11).
7. Frank Abagnale and Greg Litster, Holder in Due Course and Check Fraud, TransactionDirectory.com.
8. *Turman v. Ward's Home Imp., Inc.*, 1995 WL 1055769, Va. Cir. Ct. (1995).

CHAPTER 25

Liability and Discharge

Learning Objectives

After reading this chapter, you should understand the following:

1. The liability of an agent who signs commercial paper.
2. What contract liability is imposed when a person signs commercial paper.
3. What warranty liability is imposed upon a transferor.
4. What happens if there is payment or acceptance by mistake.
5. How parties are discharged from liability on commercial paper.

In Chapter 22, Chapter 23, and Chapter 24, we focused on the methods and consequences of negotiating commercial paper when all the proper steps are followed. For example, a maker gives a negotiable note to a payee, who properly negotiates the paper to a third-party holder in due course. As a result, this third party is entitled to collect from the maker, unless the latter has a real defense.

In this chapter, we begin by examining a question especially important to management: personal liability for signing company notes and checks. Then we look at the two general types of liability—contract and warranty—introduced in Chapter 23. We conclude the chapter by reviewing the ways in which parties are discharged from liability.

25.1 Liability Imposed by Signature: Agents, Authorized and Unauthorized

Learning Objectives

1. Recognize what a signature is under Article 3 of the Uniform Commercial Code.
2. Understand how a person's signature on an instrument affects liability if the person is an agent, or a purported agent, for another.

The liability of an agent who signs commercial paper is one of the most frequently litigated issues in this area of law. For example, Igor is an agent (treasurer) of Frank N. Stein, Inc. Igor signs a note showing that the corporation has borrowed $50,000 from First Bank. The company later becomes bankrupt. The question: Is Igor personally liable on the note? The unhappy treasurer might be sued by the bank—the immediate party with whom he dealt—or by a third party to whom the note was transferred (see Figure 25.1).

FIGURE 25.1 Signature by Representative

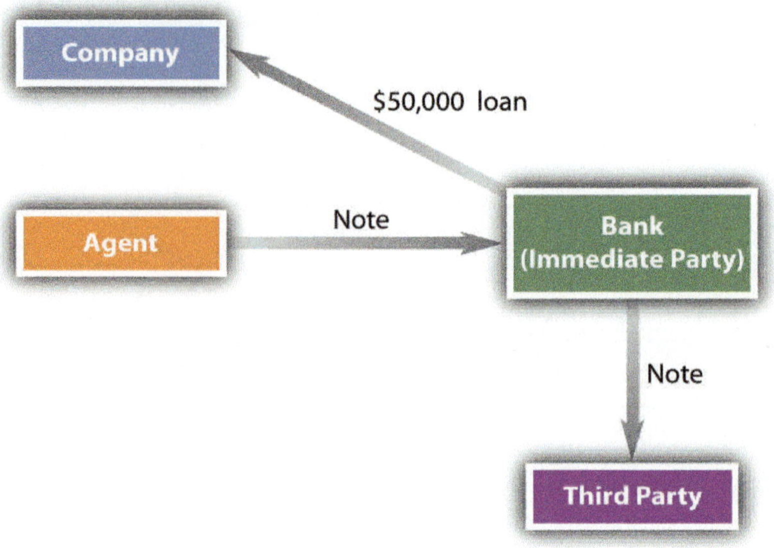

There are two possibilities regarding an agent who signs commercial paper: the agent was authorized to do so, or the agent was not authorized to do so. First, though, what is a signature?

A "Signature" under the Uniform Commercial Code

Section 3-401 of the Uniform Commercial Code (UCC) provides fairly straightforwardly that "a signature can be made (i) manually or by means of a device or machine, and (ii) by the use of any name, including any trade or assumed name, or by any word, mark, or symbol executed or adopted by a person with the present intention to authenticate a writing."

Liability of an Agent Who Has Authority to Sign

Agents often sign instruments on behalf of their principals, and—of course—because a corporation's existence is a legal fiction (you can't go up and shake hands with General Motors), corporations can only act through their agents.

The General Rule

Section 3-402(a) of the UCC provides that a person acting (or purporting to act) as an agent who signs an instrument binds the principal to the same extent that the principal would be bound if the signature were on a simple contract. The drafters of the UCC here punt to the common law of agency: if, under agency law, the principal would be bound by the act of the agent, the signature is the authorized signature of the principal. And the general rule in agency law is that the agent is not liable if he signs his own name and makes clear he is doing so as an agent. In our example, Igor should sign as follows: "Frank N. Stein, Inc., by Igor, Agent." Now it is clear under agency law that the corporation is liable and Igor is not.[1] Good job, Igor.

Incorrect Signatures

The problems arise where the agent, although authorized, signs in an incorrect way. There are three possibilities: (1) the agent signs only his own name—"Igor"; (2) the agent signs both names but without indication of any agency—"Frank N. Stein, Inc., / Igor" (the signature is ambiguous—are both parties to be liable, or is Igor merely an agent?); (3) the agent signs as agent but doesn't identify the principal—"Igor, Agent."

The UCC provides that in each case, the agent is liable to a holder in due course (HDC) who took the instrument without notice that the agent wasn't intended to be liable on the instrument. As to any other person (holder or transferee), the agent is liable unless she proves that the original parties to the instrument did not intend her to be liable on it. Section 3-402(c) says that, as to a *check*, if an agent signs his name without indicating agency status but the check has the principal's identification on it (that would be in the upper left corner), the authorized agent is not liable.

Liability of an "Agent" Who Has No Authority to Sign

A person who has no authority to sign an instrument cannot really be an "agent" because by definition an agent is a person or entity authorized to act on behalf of and under the control of another in dealing with third parties. Nevertheless, unauthorized persons not infrequently purport to act as agents: either they are mistaken or they are crooks. Are their signatures binding on the "principal"?

The General Rule

An unauthorized signature is not binding; it is—as the UCC puts it—"ineffective except as the signature of the unauthorized signer."[2] So, if Crook signs a Frank N. Stein, Inc., check with the name "Igor," the only person liable on the check is Crook.

The Exceptions

There are two exceptions. Section 4-403(a) of the UCC provides that an unauthorized signature may be ratified by the principal, and Section 3-406 says that if negligence contributed to an instrument's alteration or forgery, the negligent person cannot assert lack of authority against an HDC or a person who in good faith pays or takes the instrument for value or for collection. This is the situation where Principal leaves the rubber signature stamp lying about and Crook makes mischief with it, making out a check to Payee using the stamp. But if Payee herself failed to exercise reasonable care in taking a suspicious instrument, both Principal and Payee could be liable, based on comparative negligence principles.[3]

Key Takeaway

Under the UCC, a "signature" is any writing or mark used by a person to indicate that a writing is authentic. Agents often sign on behalf of principals, and when the authorized agent makes clear that she is so signing—by naming the principal and signing her name as "agent"—the principal is liable, not the agent. But when the agent signs incorrectly, the UCC says, in general, that the agent is personally liable to an HDC who takes the paper without notice that the agent is not intended to be liable. Unauthorized signatures (forgeries) are ineffective as to the principal: they are effective as the forger's signature, unless the principal or the person paying on the instrument has been negligent in contributing to, or in failing to notice, the forgery, in which case comparative negligence principles are applied.

Exercises

1. Able signs his name on a note with an entirely illegible squiggle. Is that a valid signature?

2. Under what circumstances is an agent clearly not personally liable on an instrument?
3. Under what circumstances is a forgery effective as to the person whose name is forged?

25.2 Contract Liability of Parties

Learning Objectives

1. Understand that a person who signs commercial paper incurs contract liability.
2. Recognize the two types of such liability: primary and secondary.
3. Know the conditions that must be met before secondary liability attaches.

Two types of liability can attach to those who deal in commercial paper: contract liability and warranty liability. Contract liability is based on a party's signature on the paper. For contract liability purposes, signing parties are divided into two categories: primary parties and secondary parties.

We discuss here the liability of various parties. You may recall the discussion in Chapter 22 about accommodation parties. An *accommodation party* signs a negotiable instrument in order to lend his name to another party to the instrument. The Uniform Commercial Code (UCC) provides that such a person "may sign the instrument as maker, drawer, acceptor, or indorser" and that in whatever capacity the person signs, he will be liable in that capacity.[4]

Liability of Primary Parties

Two parties are primarily liable: the maker of a note and the acceptor of a draft. They are required to pay by the terms of the instrument itself, and their liability is unconditional.

Maker

By signing a promissory note, the maker promises to pay the instrument—that's the maker's contract and, of course, the whole point to a note. The obligation is owed to a person entitled to enforce the note or to an indorser that paid the note.[5]

Acceptor

Recall that *acceptance* is the drawee's signed engagement to honor a draft as presented. The drawee's signature on the draft is necessary and sufficient to accept, and if that happens, the drawee as acceptor is primarily liable. The acceptance must be written on the draft by some means—any means is good. The signature is usually accompanied by some wording, such as "accepted," "good," "I accept." When a bank *certifies* a check, that is the drawee bank's acceptance, and the bank as acceptor becomes liable to the holder; the drawer and all indorsers prior to the bank's acceptance are discharged. So the holder—whether a payee or an indorsee—can look only to the bank, not to the drawer, for payment.[6] If the drawee varies the terms when accepting the draft, it is liable according to the terms as varied.[7]

Liability of Secondary Parties

Unlike primary liability, secondary liability is conditional, arising only if the primarily liable party fails to pay. The parties for whom these conditions are significant are the drawers and the indorsers. By virtue of UCC Sections 3-414 and 3-415, drawers and indorsers engage to pay the amount of an unaccepted draft to any subsequent holder or indorser who takes it up, again, *if* (this is the conditional part) the (1) the instrument is dishonored and, in some cases, (2) notice of dishonor is given to the drawer or indorser.

Drawer's Liability

If Carlos writes (more properly "draws") a check to his landlord for $700, Carlos does not expect the landlord to turn around and approach him for the money: Carlos's bank—the drawee—is supposed to pay from Carlos's account. But if the bank dishonors the check—most commonly because of insufficient funds to pay it—then Carlos is liable to pay according to the instrument's terms when he wrote the check or, if it was incomplete when he wrote it, according to its terms when completed (subject to some limitations).[8] Under the pre-1997 UCC, Carlos's liability was conditioned not only upon dishonor but also upon notice of dishonor; however, under the revised UCC, notice is not required for the drawer to be liable unless the draft has been accepted and the acceptor is not a bank. Most commonly, if a check bounces, the person who wrote it is liable to make it good.

The drawer of a noncheck draft may disclaim her contractual liability on the instrument by drawing "without recourse."[9]

Indorser's Liability

Under UCC Section 3-415, an indorser promises to pay on the instrument according to its terms if it is dishonored or, if it was incomplete when indorsed, according to its terms when completed. The liability here is conditioned upon the indorser's receipt of *notice of dishonor* (with some exceptions, noted in Section 2 on contract liability of parties. Indorsers may disclaim contractual liability by indorsing "without recourse."[10]

Conditions Required for Liability

We have alluded to the point that secondary parties do not become liable unless the proper conditions are met—there are conditions precedent to liability (i.e., things have to happen before liability "ripens").

Conditions for Liability in General

The conditions are slightly different for two classes of instruments. For an unaccepted draft, the drawer's liability is conditioned on (1) presentment and (2) dishonor. For an accepted draft on a non-bank, or for an indorser, the conditions are (1) presentment, (2) dishonor, and (3) notice of dishonor.

Presentment

Presentment occurs when a person entitled to enforce the instrument (creditor) demands *payment* from the maker, drawee, or acceptor, or when a person entitled to enforce the instrument (again, the creditor) demands *acceptance* of a draft from the drawee.[11]

presentment

A holder's demand for payment from a payor.

conversion

Wrongful possession or disposition of another's property as if it were one's own.

The common-law tort that makes a person who wrongfully takes another's property liable for that taking is **conversion**—it's the civil equivalent of theft. The UCC provides that "the law applicable to conversion of personal property applies to instruments."[12] Conversion is relevant here because if an instrument is presented for payment or acceptance and the person to whom it is presented refuses to pay, accept, or return it, the instrument is converted. An instrument is also converted if a person pays an instrument on a forged indorsement: a bank that pays a check on a forged indorsement has converted the instrument and is liable to the person whose indorsement was forged. There are various permutations on the theme of conversion; here is one example from the Official Comment:

> *A check is payable to the order of A. A indorses it to B and puts it into an envelope addressed to B. The envelope is never delivered to B. Rather, Thief steals the envelope, forges B's indorsement to the check and obtains payment. Because the check was never delivered to B, the indorsee, B has no cause of action for conversion, but A does have such an action. A is the owner of the check. B never obtained rights in the check. If A intended to negotiate the check to B in payment of an obligation, that obligation was not affected by the conduct of Thief. B can enforce that obligation. Thief stole A's property not B's.*[13]

Dishonor

Dishonor

Refusal to pay or accept an instrument when it is presented.

Dishonor generally means failure by the obligor to pay on the instrument when presentment for payment is made (but return of an instrument because it has not been properly indorsed does not constitute dishonor). The UCC at Section 3-502 has (laborious) rules governing what constitutes dishonor and when dishonor occurs for a note, an unaccepted draft, and an unaccepted documentary draft. (A documentary draft is a draft to be presented for acceptance or payment if specified documents, certificates, statements, or the like are to be received by the drawee or other payor before acceptance or payment of the draft.)

Notice of Dishonor

Again, when acceptance or payment is refused after presentment, the instrument is said to be dishonored. The holder has a right of recourse against the drawers and indorsers, but he is usually supposed to give notice of the dishonor. Section 3-503(a) of the UCC requires the holder to give notice to a party before the party can be charged with liability, unless such notice is excused, but the UCC exempts notice in a number of circumstances (Section 3-504, discussed in Section 2 on contract liability). The UCC makes giving notice pretty easy: it permits any party who may be compelled to pay the instrument to notify any party who may be liable on it (but each person who is to be charged with liability must actually be notified); notice of dishonor may "be given by any commercially reasonable means including an oral, written, or electronic communication"; and no specific form of notice is required—it is "sufficient if it reasonably identifies the instrument and indicates that the instrument has been dishonored or has not been paid or accepted."[14] Section 3-503(c) sets out time limits when notice of dishonor must be given for collecting banks and for other persons. An oral notice is unwise because it might be difficult to prove. Usually, notice of dishonor is given when the instrument is returned with a stamp ("NSF"—the dreaded "nonsufficient funds"), a ticket, or a memo.

Suppose—you'll want to graph this out—Ann signs a note payable to Betty, who indorses it to Carl, who in turn indorses it to Darlene. Darlene indorses it to Earl, who presents it to Ann for payment. Ann refuses. Ann is the only primary party, so if Earl is to be paid he must give notice of dishonor to one or more of the secondary parties, in this case, the indorsers. He knows that Darlene is rich, so he notifies only Darlene. He may collect from Darlene but not from the others. If

Darlene wishes to be reimbursed, she may notify Betty (the payee) and Carl (a prior indorser). If she fails to notify either of them, she will have no recourse. If she notifies both, she may recover from either. Carl in turn may collect from Betty, because Betty already will have been notified. If Darlene notifies only Carl, then she may collect only from him, but he must notify Betty or he cannot be reimbursed. Suppose Earl notified only Betty. Then Carl and Darlene are discharged. Why? Earl cannot proceed against them because he did not notify them. Betty cannot proceed against them because they indorsed subsequent to her and therefore were not contractually obligated to her. However, if, mistakenly believing that she could collect from either Carl or Darlene, Betty gave each notice within the time allowed to Earl, then he would be entitled to collect from one of them if Betty failed to pay, because they would have received notice. It is not necessary to receive notice from one to whom you are liable; Section 3-503(b) says that notice may be given by any person, so that notice operates for the benefit of all others who have rights against the obligor.

There are some deadlines for giving notice: on an instrument taken for collection, a bank must give notice before midnight on the next banking day following the day on which it receives notice of dishonor; a nonbank must give notice within thirty days after the day it received notice; and in all other situations, the deadline is thirty days after the day dishonor occurred.[15]

Waived or Excused Conditions

Presentment and notice of dishonor have been discussed as conditions precedent for imposing liability upon secondarily liable parties (again, drawers and indorsers). But the UCC provides circumstances in which such conditions may be waived or excused.

Presentment Waived or Excused

Under UCC Section 3-504(a), presentment is excused if (1) the creditor cannot with reasonable diligence present the instrument; (2) the maker or acceptor has repudiated the obligation to pay, is dead, or is in insolvency proceedings; (3) no presentment is necessary by the instrument's terms; (4) the drawer or indorsers waived presentment; (5) the drawer instructed the drawee not to pay or accept; or (6) the drawee was not obligated to the drawer to pay the draft.

Notice of Dishonor Excused

Notice of dishonor is not required if (1) the instrument's terms do not require it or (2) the debtor waived the notice of dishonor. Moreover, a waiver of presentment is also a waiver of notice of dishonor. Delay in giving the notice is excused, too, if it is caused by circumstances beyond the control of the person giving notice and she exercised reasonable diligence when the cause of delay stopped.[16]

In fact, in real life, presentment and notice of dishonor don't happen very often, at least as to notes. Going back to presentment for a minute: the UCC provides that the "party to whom presentment is made [the debtor] may require exhibition of the instrument, . . . reasonable identification of the person demanding payment, . . . [and] a signed receipt [from the creditor (among other things)]" (Section 3-501). This all makes sense: for example, certainly the prudent contractor paying on a note for his bulldozer wants to make sure the creditor actually still has the note (hasn't negotiated it to a third party) and is the correct person to pay, and getting a signed receipt when you pay for something is always a good idea. "Presentment" here is listed as a condition of liability, but in fact, most of the time there is no presentment at all:

> *[I]t's a fantasy. Every month millions of homeowners make payments on the notes that they signed when they borrowed money to buy their houses. Millions of college graduates similarly make payments on their student loan notes. And millions of drivers and boaters pay down the notes that they signed when they borrowed money to purchase automobiles or vessels. [Probably] none of these borrowers sees the notes that they are paying. There is no "exhibition" of the instruments as section 3-501 [puts it]. There is no showing of identification. In some cases . . . there is no signing of a receipt for payment. Instead, each month, the borrowers simply mail a check to an address that they have been given.*[17]

The Official Comment to UCC Section 5-502 says about the same thing:

> *In the great majority of cases presentment and notice of dishonor are waived with respect to notes. In most cases a formal demand for payment to the maker of the note is not contemplated. Rather, the maker is expected to send payment to the holder of the note on the date or dates on which payment is due. If payment is not made when due, the holder usually makes a demand for payment, but in the normal case in which presentment is waived, demand is irrelevant and the holder can proceed against indorsers when payment is not received.*

Key Takeaway

People who sign commercial paper become liable on the instrument by contract: they contract to honor the instrument. There are two types of liability: primary and secondary. The primarily liable parties are makers of notes and drawees of drafts (your bank is the drawee for your check), and their liability is unconditional. The secondary parties are drawers and indorsers. Their liability is conditional: it arises if the instrument has been presented for payment or collection by the primarily liable party, the instrument has been dishonored, and notice of dishonor is provided to the secondarily liable parties. The presentment and notice of dishonor are often unnecessary to enforce contractual liability.

Exercises

1. What parties have primary liability on a negotiable instrument?
2. What parties have secondary liability on a negotiable instrument?
3. Secondary liability is conditional. What are the conditions precedent to liability?
4. What conditions may be waived or excused, and how?

25.3 Warranty Liability of Parties

Learning Objectives

1. Understand that independent of contract liability, parties to negotiable instruments incur warranty liability.
2. Know what warranties a person makes when she transfers an instrument.
3. Know what warranties a person makes when he presents an instrument for payment or acceptance.
4. Understand what happens if a bank pays or accepts a check by mistake.

Overview of Warranty Liability

We discussed the contract liability of primary and secondary parties, which applies to those who sign the instrument. Liability arises a second way, too—by warranty. A negotiable instrument is a type of property that is sold and bought, just the way an automobile is, or a toaster. If you buy a car, you generally expect that it will, more or less, work the way cars are supposed to work—that's the implied warranty of merchantability. Similarly, when an instrument is transferred from A to B for consideration, the transferee (B) expects that the instrument will work the way such instruments are supposed to work. If A transfers to B a promissory note made by Maker, B figures that when the time is right, she can go to Maker and get paid on the note. So A makes some implied warranties to B—transfer warranties. And when B presents the instrument to Maker for payment, Maker assumes that B as the indorsee from A is entitled to payment, that the signatures are genuine, and the like. So B makes some implied warranties to Maker—presentment warranties. Usually, claims of breach of warranty arise in cases involving forged, altered, or stolen instruments, and they serve to allocate the loss to the person in the best position to have avoided the loss, putting it on the person (or bank) who dealt with the wrongdoer. We take up both transfer and presentment warranties.

Transfer Warranties

Transfer warranties are important because—as we've seen—contract liability is limited to those who have actually signed the instrument. Of course, secondary liability will provide a holder with sufficient grounds for recovery against a previous indorser who did not qualify his indorsement. But sometimes there is no indorsement, and sometimes the indorsement is qualified. Sometimes, also, the holder fails to make timely presentment or notice of dishonor, thereby discharging a previous indorsee. In such cases, the transferee-holder can still sue a prior party on one or more of the five implied warranties.

A person who receives consideration for transferring an instrument makes the five warranties listed in UCC Section 3-416. The warranty may be sued on by the immediate transferee or, if the transfer was by indorsement, by any subsequent holder who takes the instrument in good faith. The warranties thus run with the instrument. They are as follows:

1. *The transferor is entitled to enforce the instrument.* The transferor warrants that he is—or would have been if he weren't transferring it—entitled to enforce the instrument. As UCC Section 3-416, Comment 2, puts it, this "is in effect a warranty that there are no unauthorized or missing indorsements that prevent the transferor from making the transferee a person entitled to enforce the instrument." Suppose Maker makes a note payable to Payee; Thief steals the note, forges Payee's indorsement, and sells the note. Buyer is not a holder because he is not "a person in possession of an instrument drawn, issued, or indorsed to him, or to his order, or to bearer, or in blank," so he is not entitled to enforce it. "'Person entitled to enforce' means

(i) the holder, (ii) a non-holder in possession of the instrument who has the rights of a holder [because of the shelter rule]" (UCC, Section 3-301). Buyer sells the note to Another Party, who can hold Buyer liable for breach of the warranty: he was not entitled to enforce it.

2. *All signatures on the instrument are authentic and authorized.* This warranty would be breached, too, in the example just presented.
3. *The instrument has not been altered.*
4. *The instrument is not subject to a defense or claim in recoupment of any party that can be asserted against the warrantor.* "Recoupment" means to hold back or deduct part of what is due to another. The Official Comment to UCC Section 3-416 observes, "[T]he transferee does not undertake to buy an instrument that is not enforceable in whole or in part, unless there is a contrary agreement. Even if the transferee takes as a holder in due course who takes free of the defense or claim in recoupment, the warranty gives the transferee the option of proceeding against the transferor rather than litigating with the obligor on the instrument the issue of the holder-in-due-course status of the transferee."
5. *The warrantor has no knowledge of any insolvency proceeding commenced with respect to the maker or acceptor or, in the case of an unaccepted draft, the drawer.* The UCC Official Comment here provides the following: "The transferor does not warrant against difficulties of collection, impairment of the credit of the obligor or even insolvency [only knowledge of insolvency]. The transferee is expected to determine such questions before taking the obligation. If insolvency proceedings . . . have been instituted against the party who is expected to pay and the transferor knows it, the concealment of that fact amounts to a fraud upon the transferee, and the warranty against knowledge of such proceedings is provided accordingly."[18]

Presentment Warranties

A payor paying or accepting an instrument in effect takes the paper from the party who presents it to the payor, and that party has his hand out. In doing so, the presenter makes certain implied promises to the payor, who is about to fork over cash (or an acceptance). The UCC distinguishes between warranties made by one who presents an unaccepted draft for payment and warranties made by one who presents other instruments for payment. The warranties made by the presenter are as follows.[19]

Warranties Made by One Who Presents an Unaccepted Draft

1. *The presenter is entitled to enforce the draft or to obtain payment or acceptance.* This is "in effect a warranty that there are no unauthorized or missing indorsements."[20] Suppose Thief steals a check drawn by Drawer to Payee and forges Payee's signature, then presents it to the bank. If the bank pays it, the bank cannot charge Drawer's account because it has not followed Drawer's order in paying to the wrong person (except in the case of an imposter or fictitious payee). It can, though, go back to Thief (fat chance it can find her) on the claim that she breached the warranty of no unauthorized indorsement.
2. *There has been no alteration of the instrument.* If Thief takes a check and changes the amount from $100 to $1,000 and the bank pays it, the bank can recover from Thief $900, the difference between the amount paid by the bank and the amount Drawer (customer) authorized the bank to pay.[21] If the drawee accepts the draft, the same rules apply.
3. *The presenter has no knowledge that the signature of the drawer is unauthorized.* If the presenter doesn't know Drawer's signature is forged and the drawee pays out on a forged signature, the drawee bears the loss. (The bank would be liable for paying out over the forged drawer's signature: that's why it has the customer's signature on file.)

These rules apply—again—to warranties made by the presenter to a drawee paying out on an unaccepted draft. The most common situation would be where a person has a check made out to her and she gets it cashed at the drawer's bank.

Warranties Made by One Who Presents Something Other Than an Unaccepted Draft

In all other cases, there is only one warranty made by the presenter: that he or she is a person entitled to enforce the instrument or obtain payment on it.

This applies to the presentment of accepted drafts, to the presentment of dishonored drafts made to the drawer or an indorser, and to the presentment of notes. For example, Maker makes a note payable to Payee; Payee indorses the note to Indorsee, Indorsee indorses and negotiates the note to Subsequent Party. Subsequent Party presents the note to Maker for payment. The Subsequent Party warrants to Maker that she is entitled to obtain payment. If she is paid and is *not* entitled to payment, Maker can sue her for breach of that warranty. If the reason she isn't entitled to payment is because Payee's signature was forged by Thief, then Maker can go after Thief: the UCC says that "the person obtaining payment [Subsequent Party] and a prior transferor [Thief] warrant to the person making payment in good faith [Maker] that the warrantor [Subsequent Party] is entitled to enforce the instrument."[22] Or, again, Drawer makes the check out to Payee; Payee attempts to cash or deposit the check, but it is dishonored. Payee presents the check to Drawer to make it good: Payee warrants he is entitled to payment on it.

Warranties cannot be disclaimed in the case of checks (because, as UCC Section 3-417, Comment 7, puts it, "it is not appropriate to allow disclaimer of warranties appearing on checks that normally will not be examined by the payor bank"—they're machine read). But a disclaimer of warranties is permitted as to other instruments, just as disclaimers of warranty are usually OK under general contract law. The reason presentment warranties 2 and 3 don't apply to makers and drawers (they apply to drawees) is because makers and drawers are going to know their own signatures and the terms of the instruments; indorsers already warranted the wholesomeness of their transfer (transfer warranties), and acceptors should examine the instruments when they accept them.

Payment by Mistake

Sometimes a drawee pays a draft (most familiarly, again, a bank pays a check) or accepts a draft by mistake. The UCC says that if the mistake was in thinking that there was no stop-payment order on it (when there was), or that the drawer's signature was authorized (when it was not), or that there were sufficient funds in the drawer's account to pay it (when there were not), "the drawee may recover the amount paid...or in the case of acceptance, may revoke the acceptance."[23] Except—and it's a big exception—such a recovery of funds does not apply "against a person who took the instrument in good faith and for value."[24] The drawee in that case would have to go after the forger, the unauthorized signer, or, in the case of insufficient funds, the drawer. Example: Able draws a check to Baker. Baker deposits the check in her bank account, and Able's bank mistakenly pays it even though Able doesn't have enough money in his account to cover it. Able's bank cannot get the money back from Baker: it has to go after Able. To rephrase, in most cases, the remedy of restitution will not be available to a bank that pays or accepts a check because the person receiving payment of the check will have given value for it in good faith.

Key Takeaway

A transferor of a negotiable instrument warrants to the transferee five things: (1) entitled to enforce, (2) authentic and authorized signatures, (3) no alteration, (4) no defenses, and (5) no knowledge of insolvency. If the transfer is by delivery, the warranties run only to the immediate transferee; if by indorsement, to any subsequent good-faith holder. Presenters who obtain payment of an instrument and all prior transferors make three presenter's warranties: (1) entitled to enforce, (2) no alteration, (3) genuineness of drawer's signature. These warranties run to any good-faith payor or acceptor. If a person pays or accepts a draft by mistake, he or she can recover the funds paid out unless the payee took the instrument for value and in good faith.

Exercises

1. What does it mean to say that the transferor of a negotiable instrument warrants things to the transferee, and what happens if the warranties are breached? What purpose do the warranties serve?
2. What is a presenter, and to whom does such a person make warranties?
3. Under what circumstances would suing for breach of warranties be useful compared to suing on the contract obligation represented by the instrument?
4. Why are the rules governing mistaken payments not very often useful to a bank?

25.4 Discharge

Learning Objective

1. Understand how the obligations represented by commercial paper may be discharged.

Overview

Negotiable instruments eventually die. The obligations they represent are discharged (terminated) in two general ways: (1) according to the rules stated in Section 3-601 of the Uniform Commercial Code (UCC) or (2) by an act or agreement that would discharge an obligation to pay money under a simple contract (e.g., declaring bankruptcy).

Discharge under the Uniform Commercial Code

The UCC provides a number of ways by which an obligor on an instrument is discharged from liability, but notwithstanding these several ways, under Section 3-601, no discharge of any party provided by the rules presented in this section operates against a subsequent holder in due course unless she has notice when she takes the instrument.

Discharge in General

Discharge by Payment

A person primarily liable discharges her liability on an instrument to the extent of payment by paying or otherwise satisfying the holder, and the discharge is good even if the payor knows that another has claim to the instrument. However, discharge does not operate if the payment is made in bad faith to one who unlawfully obtained the instrument (and UCC Section 3-602(b) lists two other exceptions).

Discharge by Tender

A person who tenders full payment to a holder on or after the date due discharges any subsequent liability to pay interest, costs, and attorneys' fees (but not liability for the face amount of the instrument). If the holder refuses to accept the tender, any party who would have had a right of recourse against the party making the tender is discharged. Mario makes a note payable to Carol, who indorses it to Ed. On the date the payment is due, Mario (the maker) tenders payment to Ed, who refuses to accept the payment; he would rather collect from Carol. Carol is discharged: had she been forced to pay as indorser in the event of Mario's refusal, she could have looked to him for recourse. Since Mario did tender, Ed can no longer look to Carol for payment.[25]

Discharge by Cancellation and Renunciation

The holder may discharge any party, even without consideration, by marking the face of the instrument or the indorsement in an unequivocal way, as, for example, by intentionally canceling the instrument or the signature by destruction or mutilation or by striking out the party's signature. The holder may also renounce his rights by delivering a signed writing to that effect or by surrendering the instrument itself.[26]

Discharge by Material and Fraudulent Alteration

Under UCC Section 3-407, if a holder materially and fraudulently alters an instrument, any party whose contract is affected by the change is discharged. A payor bank or drawee paying a fraudulently altered instrument or a person taking it for value, in good faith, and without notice of the alteration, may enforce rights with respect to the instrument according to its original terms or, if the incomplete instrument was altered by unauthorized completion, according to its terms as completed.

- Example 1: Marcus makes a note for $100 payable to Pauline. Pauline fraudulently raises the amount to $1,000 without Marcus's negligence and negotiates it to Ned, who qualifies as a holder in due course (HDC). Marcus owes Ned $100.
- Example 2: Charlene writes a check payable to Lumber Yard and gives it to Contractor to buy material for a deck replacement. Contractor fills it in for $1,200: $1,000 for the decking and $200 for his own unauthorized purposes. Lumber Yard, if innocent of any wrongdoing, could enforce the check for $1,200, and Charlene must go after Contractor for the $200.

Discharge by Certification

As we have noted, where a drawee certifies a draft for a holder, the drawer and all prior indorsers are discharged.

Discharge by Acceptance Varying a Draft

If the holder assents to an acceptance varying the terms of a draft, the obligation of the drawer and any indorsers who do not expressly assent to the acceptance is discharged.[27]

Discharge of Indorsers and Accommodation Parties

The liability of indorsers and accommodation parties is discharged under the following three circumstances.[28]

Extension of Due Date

If the holder agrees to an extension of the due date of the obligation of the obligor, the extension discharges an indorser or accommodation party having a right of recourse against the obligor to the extent the indorser or accommodation party proves that the extension caused her loss with respect to the right of recourse.

Material Modification of Obligation

If the holder agrees to a material modification of the obligor's obligation, other than an extension of the due date, the modification discharges the obligation of an indorser or accommodation party having a right of recourse against the obligor to the extent the modification causes her loss with respect to the right of recourse.

Impairment of Collateral

If the obligor's duty to pay is secured by an interest in collateral and the holder impairs the value of the interest in collateral, the obligation of an indorser or accommodation party having a right of recourse against the obligor is discharged to the extent of the impairment.

The following explanatory paragraph from UCC Section 3-605, Official Comment 1, may be helpful:

> *Bank lends $10,000 to Borrower who signs a note under which she (in suretyship law, the "Principal Debtor") agrees to pay Bank on a date stated. But Bank insists that an accommodation party also become liable to pay the note (by signing it as a co-maker or by indorsing the note). In suretyship law, the accommodation party is a "Surety." Then Bank agrees to a modification of the rights and obligations between it and Principal Debtor, such as agreeing that she may pay the note at some date after the due date, or that she may discharge her $10,000 obligation to pay the note by paying Bank $3,000, or the Bank releases collateral she gave it to secure the note. Surety is discharged if changes like this are made by Bank (the creditor) without Surety's consent to the extent Surety suffers loss as a result. Section 3-605 is concerned with this kind of problem with Principal Debtor and Surety. But it has a wider scope: it also applies to indorsers who are not accommodation parties. Unless an indorser signs without recourse, the indorser's liability under section 3-415(a) is that of a surety. If Bank in our hypothetical case indorsed the note and transferred it to Second Bank, Bank has rights given to an indorser under section 3-605 if it is Second Bank that modifies rights and obligations of Borrower.*

Discharge by Reacquisition

Suppose a prior party reacquires the instrument. He may—but does not automatically—cancel any indorsement unnecessary to his title and may also reissue or further negotiate the instrument. Any intervening party is thereby discharged from liability to the reacquiring party or to any subsequent holder not in due course. If an intervening party's indorsement is cancelled, she is not liable even to an HDC.[29]

Discharge by Unexcused Delay in Presentment or Notice of Dishonor

If notice of dishonor is not excused under UCC Section 3-504, failure to give it discharges drawers and indorsers.

Key Takeaway

The potential liabilities arising from commercial paper are discharged in several ways. Anything that would discharge a debt under common contract law will do so. More specifically as to commercial paper, of course, payment discharges the obligation. Other methods include tender of payment, cancellation or renunciation, material and fraudulent alteration, certification, acceptance varying a draft, reacquisition, and—in some cases—unexcused delay in giving notice of presentment or dishonor. Indorsers and accommodation parties' liability may be discharged by the same means that a surety's liability is discharged, to the extent that alterations in the agreement between the creditor and the holder would be defenses to a surety because right of recourse is impaired to the surety.

Exercises

1. What is the most common way that obligations represented by commercial paper are discharged?
2. Parents loan Daughter $6,000 to attend college, and she gives them a promissory note in return. At her graduation party, Parents ceremoniously tear up the note. Is Daughter's obligation terminated?
3. Juan signs Roberta's note to Creditor as an accommodation party, agreeing to serve in that capacity for two years. At the end of that term, Roberta has not paid Creditor, who—without Juan's knowledge—gives Roberta an extra six months to pay. He fails to do so. Does Creditor still have recourse against Juan?

25.5 Cases

Breach of Presentment Warranties and Conduct Precluding Complaint about Such Breach

Bank of Nichols Hills v. Bank of Oklahoma

196 P.3d 984 (Okla. Civ. App. 2008)

Gabbard, J.

Plaintiff, Bank of Nichols Hills (BNH), appeals a trial court judgment for Defendant, Bank of Oklahoma (BOK), regarding payment of a forged check. The primary issue on appeal is whether BOK presented sufficient proof to support the trial court's finding that the [UCC] § 3-406 preclusion defense applied. We find that it did, and affirm.

Facts

Michael and Stacy Russell owned a mobile home in Harrah, Oklahoma. The home was insured by Oklahoma Farm Bureau Mutual Insurance Company (Farm Bureau). The insurance policy provided that in case of loss, Farm Bureau "will pay you unless another payee is named on the Declarations page," that "Loss shall be payable to any mortgagee named in the Declarations," and that one of

Farm Bureau's duties was to "protect the mortgagee's interests in the insured building." The Declarations page of the policy listed Conseco Finance as the mortgagee. Conseco had a mortgage security interest in the home.

In August 2002, a fire completely destroyed the mobile home. The Russells submitted an insurance claim to Farm Bureau. Farm Bureau then negotiated a $69,000 settlement with the Russells, issued them a check in this amount payable to them and Conseco jointly, and mailed the check to the Russells. Neither the Russells nor Farm Bureau notified Conseco of the loss, the settlement, or the mailing of the check.

The check was drawn on Farm Bureau's account at BNH. The Russells deposited the check into their account at BOK. The check contains an endorsement by both Russells, and a rubber stamp endorsement for Conseco followed by a signature of a Donna Marlatt and a phone number. It is undisputed that Conseco's endorsement was forged. Upon receipt, BOK presented the check to BNH. BNH paid the $69,000 check and notified Farm Bureau that the check had been paid from its account.

About a year later, Conseco learned about the fire and the insurance payoff. Conseco notified Farm Bureau that it was owed a mortgage balance of more than $50,000. Farm Bureau paid off the balance and notified BNH of the forgery. BNH reimbursed Farm Bureau the amount paid to Conseco. BNH then sued BOK.

Both banks relied on the Uniform Commercial Code. BNH asserted that under § 4-208, BOK had warranted that all the indorsements on the check were genuine. BOK asserted an affirmative defense under § 3-406, alleging that Farm Bureau's own negligence contributed to the forgery. After a non-jury trial, the court granted judgment to BOK, finding as follows:

- Conseco's endorsement was a forgery, accomplished by the Russells;
- Farm Bureau was negligent in the manner and method it used to process the claim and pay the settlement without providing any notice or opportunity for involvement in the process to Conseco;
- Farm Bureau's negligence substantially contributed to the Russells' conduct in forging Conseco's endorsement; and
- BOK proved its affirmative defense under § 3-406 by the greater weight of the evidence.

From this judgment, BNH appeals.

Analysis

It cannot be disputed that BOK breached its presentment warranty to BNH under § 4-208.[30] Thus the primary issue raised is whether BOK established a preclusion defense under 3-406 [that BNH is precluded from complaining about BOK's breach of presentment warranty because of its own negligence].[31] BNH asserts that the evidence fails to establish this defense because the mailing of its check to and receipt by the insured "is at most an event of opportunity and has nothing to do with the actual forgery."

Section 3-406 requires less stringent proof than the "direct and proximate cause" test for general negligence.[32] Conduct is a contributing cause of an alteration or forgery if it is a substantial factor in bringing it about, or makes it "easier for the wrongdoer to commit his wrong." The UCC Comment to § 3-406 notes that the term has the meaning as used by the Pennsylvania court in *Thompson* [Citation].

In *Thompson*, an independent logger named Albers obtained blank weighing slips, filled them out to show fictitious deliveries of logs for local timber owners, delivered the slips to the company, accepted checks made payable to the timber owners, forged the owners' signatures, and cashed the checks at the bank. When the company discovered the scheme, it sued the bank and the bank raised § 3-406 as a defense. The court specifically found that the company's negligence did not have to be the direct and proximate cause of the bank's acceptance of the forged checks. Instead, the defense applied because the company left blank logging slips readily accessible to haulers, the company had given Albers whole pads of blank slips, the slips were not consecutively numbered, haulers were allowed to deliver both the original and duplicate slips to the company's office, and the company regularly entrusted the completed checks to the haulers for delivery to the payees without the payees' consent. The court noted:

> *While none of these practices, in isolation, might be sufficient to charge the plaintiff [the company] with negligence within the meaning of § 3-406, the company's course of conduct, viewed in its entirety, is surely sufficient to support the trial judge's determination that it substantially contributed to the making of the unauthorized signatures. . . . [T]hat conduct was "no different than had the plaintiff simply given Albers a series of checks signed in blank for his unlimited, unrestrictive use."*

The UCC Comment to § 3-406 gives three examples of conduct illustrating the defense. One example involves an employer who leaves a rubber stamp and blank checks accessible to an employee who later commits forgery; another example involves a company that issues a ten dollar check but leaves a blank space after the figure which allows the payee to turn the amount into ten thousand dollars; and the third example involves an insurance company that mails a check to one policyholder whose name is the same as another policyholder who was entitled to the check. In each case, the company's negligence substantially contributed to the alterations or forgeries by making it easier for the wrongdoer to commit the malfeasance.

In the present case, we find no negligence in Farm Bureau's delivery of the check to the Russells. There is nothing in the insurance policy that prohibits the insurer from making the loss-payment check jointly payable to the Russells and Conseco. Furthermore, under § 3-420, if a check is payable to more than one payee, delivery to one of the payees is deemed to be delivery to all payees. The authority cited by BOK, in which a check was delivered to one joint payee who then forged the signature of the other, involve cases where the drawer knew or should have known that the wrongdoer was not entitled to be a payee in the first place. See [Citations].

We also find no negligence in Farm Bureau's violation of its policy provisions requiring the protection of the mortgage holder. Generally, violation of contract provisions and laxity in the conduct of the business affairs of the drawer do not per se establish negligence under this section. See [Citations].

However, evidence was presented that the contract provision merely reflected an accepted and customary commercial standard in the insurance industry. Failure to conform to the reasonable commercial standards of one's business has been recognized by a number of courts as evidence of negligence. See, e.g., [Citations].

Here, evidence was presented that Farm Bureau did not act in a commercially reasonable manner or in accordance with reasonable commercial standards of its business when it issued the loss check to the insured without notice to the mortgagee. BOK's expert testified that it is standard practice in the industry to notify the lender of a loss this size, in order to avoid exactly the result that occurred here. Mortgagees often have a greater financial stake in an insurance policy than do the mortgagors. That was clearly true in this case. While there was opinion testimony to the contrary, the trial court was entitled to conclude that Farm Bureau did not act in a commercially reasonably manner and that this failure was negligence which substantially contributed to the forgery, as contemplated by § 3-406.

We find the trial court's judgment supported by the law and competent evidence. Accordingly, the trial court's decision is affirmed. Affirmed.

Case Questions

1. How did BOK breach its presentment warranty to BNH?
2. What part of the UCC did BOK point to as why it should not be liable for that breach?
3. In what way was Farm Bureau Mutual Insurance Co. negligent in this case, and what was the consequence?

Presentment, Acceptance, Dishonor, and Warranties

Messing v. Bank of America
821 A.2d 22 (Md. 2003)

At some point in time prior to 3 August 2000, Petitioner, as a holder, came into possession of a check in the amount of Nine Hundred Seventy-Six Dollars ($976.00) (the check) from Toyson J. Burruss, the drawer, doing business as Prestige Auto Detail Center. Instead of depositing the check into his account at his own bank, Petitioner elected to present the check for payment at a branch of Mr. Burruss' bank, Bank of America, the drawee.[33] On 3 August 2000, Petitioner approached a teller at Bank of America * * * in Baltimore City and asked to cash the check. The teller, by use of a computer, confirmed the availability of funds on deposit, and placed the check into the computer's printer slot. The computer stamped certain data on the back of the check, including the time, date, amount of the check, account number, and teller number. The computer also effected a hold on the amount of $976.00 in the customer's account. The teller gave the check back to the Petitioner, who endorsed it. The teller then asked for Petitioner's identification. Petitioner presented his driver's license and a major credit card. The teller took the indorsed check from Petitioner and manually inscribed the driver's license information and certain credit card information on the back of the check.

At some point during the transaction, the teller counted out $976.00 in cash from her drawer in anticipation of completing the transaction. She asked if the Petitioner was a customer of Bank of America. The Petitioner stated that he was not. The teller returned the check to Petitioner and requested, consistent with bank policy when cashing checks for non-customers, that Petitioner place his thumbprint on the check. [The thumbprint identification program was designed by various banking and federal agencies to reduce check fraud.] Petitioner refused and the teller informed him that she would be unable to complete the transaction without his thumbprint.

* * * Petitioner presented the check to the branch manager and demanded that the check be cashed notwithstanding Petitioner's refusal to place his thumbprint on the check. The branch manager examined the check and returned it to the Petitioner, informing him that, because Petitioner was a non-customer, Bank of America would not cash the check without Petitioner's thumbprint on the instrument. * * * Petitioner left the bank with the check in his possession. * * *

Rather than take the check to his own bank and deposit it there, or returning it to Burruss, the drawer, as dishonored and demanding payment, Petitioner, * * * [sued] Bank of America (the Bank) * * *Petitioner claimed that the Bank had violated the Maryland Uniform Commercial Code (UCC) and had violated his personal privacy when the teller asked Petitioner to place an "inkless" thumbprint on the face of the check at issue. * * *

* * * [T]he Circuit Court heard oral arguments, * * * entered summary judgment in favor of the Bank, dismissing the Complaint with prejudice. [The special appeals court affirmed. The Court of Appeals—this court—accepted the appeal.]

[Duty of Bank on Presentment and Acceptance]

Petitioner argues that he correctly made "presentment" of the check to the Bank pursuant to § 3-111 and § 3-501(a), and demands that, as the person named on the instrument and thus entitled to enforce the check, the drawee Bank pay him. * * * In a continuation, Petitioner contends that the teller, by placing the check in the slot of her computer, and the computer then printing certain information on the back of the check, accepted the check as defined by § 3-409(a). * * * Thus, according to Petitioner, because the Bank's computer printed information on the back of the check, under § 3-401(b) the Bank "signed" the check, said "signature" being sufficient to constitute acceptance under § 3-409(a).

Petitioner's remaining arguments line up like so many dominos. According to Petitioner, having established that under his reading of § 3-409(a) the Bank accepted the check, Petitioner advances that the Bank is obliged to pay him, pursuant to § 3-413(a). * * * Petitioner extends his line of reasoning by arguing that the actions of the Bank amounted to a conversion under § 3-420, * * * Petitioner argues that because the Bank accepted the check, an act which, according to Petitioner, discharged the drawer, he no longer had enforceable rights in the check and only had a right to the proceeds. Petitioner's position is that the Bank exercised unauthorized dominion and control over the proceeds of the check to the complete exclusion of the Petitioner after the Bank accepted the check and refused to distribute the proceeds, counted out by the teller, to him.

We turn to the Bank's obligations, or lack thereof, with regard to the presentment of a check by someone not its customer. Bank argues, correctly, that it had no duty to the Petitioner, a non-customer and a stranger to the Bank, and that nothing in the Code allows Petitioner to force Bank of America to act as a depository bank. * * *

Absent a special relationship, a non-customer has no claim against a bank for refusing to honor a presented check. [Citations] This is made clear by § 3-408, which states:

> *A check or other draft does not of itself operate as an assignment of funds in the hands of the drawee available for its payment, and the drawee is not liable on the instrument until the drawee accepts it.*

Once a bank accepts a check, under § 3-409, it is obliged to pay on the check under § 3-413. Thus, the relevant question in terms of any rights Petitioner had against the Bank [regarding presentment] turns not on the reasonableness of the thumbprint identification, but rather upon whether the Bank accepted the check when presented as defined by § 3-409. As will be seen infra [below] the question of the thumbprint identification is relevant only to the issue of whether the Bank's refusal to pay the instrument constituted dishonor under § 3-502, a determination which has no impact in terms of any duty allegedly owed by the Bank to the Petitioner.

The statute clearly states that acceptance becomes effective when the presenter is notified of that fact. The facts demonstrate that at no time did the teller notify Petitioner that the Bank would pay on the check. Rather, the facts show that:

> *[T]he check was given back to [Petitioner] by the teller so that he could put his thumbprint signature on it, not to notify or give him rights on the purported acceptance. After appellant declined to put his thumbprint signature on the check, he was informed by both the teller and the branch manager that it was against bank policy to honor the check without a thumbprint signature. Indignant, [Petitioner] walked out of the bank with the check.*

As the intermediate appellate court correctly pointed out, the negotiation of the check is in the nature of a contract, and there can be no agreement until notice of acceptance is received. As a result, there was never acceptance as defined by § 3-409(a), and thus the Bank, pursuant to § 3-408 never was obligated to pay the check under § 3-413(a). Thus, the answer to Petitioner's second question [Did the lower court err in finding the Bank did not accept the...check at issue, as "acceptance" is defined in UCC Section 3-409?] is "no."

"Conversion" under § 3-420.

Because it never accepted the check, Bank of America argues that the intermediate appellate court also correctly concluded that the Bank did not convert the check or its proceeds under § 3-420. Again, we must agree. The Court of Special Appeals stated:

> *"Conversion," we have held, "requires not merely temporary interference with property rights, but the exercise of unauthorized dominion and control to the complete exclusion of the rightful possessor." [Citation] At no time did [Respondent] exercise "unauthorized dominion and control [over the check] to the complete exclusion of the rightful possessor," [Petitioner].*
>
> *[Petitioner] voluntarily gave the check to [Respondent's] teller. When [Petitioner] indicated to the teller that he was not an account holder, she gave the check back to him for a thumbprint signature in accordance with bank policy. After being informed by both [Respondent's] teller and branch manager that it was [Respondent's] policy not to cash a non-account holder's check without a thumbprint signature, [Petitioner] left the bank with the check in hand.*
>
> *Because [Petitioner] gave the check to the teller, [Respondent's] possession of that check was anything but "unauthorized," and having returned the check, within minutes of its receipt, to [Petitioner] for his thumbprint signature, [Respondent] never exercised "dominion and control [over it] to the complete exclusion of the rightful possessor," [Petitioner]. In short, there was no conversion.*

D. "Reasonable Identification" under § 3-501(b)(2)(ii) and "Dishonor" under § 3-502

We now turn to the issue of whether the Bank's refusal to accept the check as presented constituted dishonor under § 3-501 and § 3-502 as Petitioner contends. Petitioner's argument that Bank of America dishonored the check under § 3-502(d) fails because that section applies to dishonor of an accepted draft. We have determined, supra, [above] that Bank of America never accepted the draft. Nevertheless, the question remains as to whether Bank of America dishonored the draft under § 3-502(b). * * *

> *(2) Upon demand of the person to whom presentment is made, the person making presentment must (i) exhibit the instrument, (ii) give reasonable identification...*
>
> *(3) Without dishonoring the instrument, the party to whom presentment is made may (i) return the instrument for lack of a necessary indorsement, or (ii) refuse payment or acceptance for failure of the presentment to comply with the terms of the instrument, an agreement of the parties, or other applicable law or rule.*

The question is whether requiring a thumbprint constitutes a request for "reasonable identification" under § 3-501(b)(2)(ii). If it is "reasonable," then under § 3-501(b)(3)(ii) the refusal of the Bank to accept the check from Petitioner did not constitute dishonor. If, however, requiring a thumbprint is not "reasonable" under § 3-501(b)(2)(ii), then the refusal to accept the check may constitute dishonor under § 3-502(b)(2). The issue of dishonor is arguably relevant because Petitioner has no cause of action against any party, including the drawer, until the check is dishonored.

Respondent Bank of America argues that its relationship with its customer is contractual, [Citations] and that in this case, its contract with its customer, the drawer, authorizes the Bank's use of the Thumbprint Signature Program as a reasonable form of identification.

According to Respondent, this contractual agreement allowed it to refuse to accept the check, without dishonoring it pursuant to § 3-501(b)(3)(ii), because the Bank's refusal was based upon the presentment failing to comply with "an agreement of the parties." The intermediate appellate court agreed. We, however, do not.

* * * Bank and its customer cannot through their contract define the meaning of the term "reasonable" and impose it upon parties who are not in privity with that contract. Whether requiring a thumbprint constitutes "reasonable identification" within the meaning of § 3-501(b)(2)(ii) is therefore a broader policy consideration, and not, as argued in this case, simply a matter of contract. We reiterate that the contract does not apply to Petitioner and, similarly, does not give him a cause of action against the Bank for refusing to accept the check. This also means that the Bank cannot rely on the contract as a defense against the Petitioner, on the facts presented here, to say that it did not dishonor the check.

Petitioner, as noted, argues that requiring a thumbprint violates his privacy, and further argues that a thumbprint is not a reasonable form of identification because it does not prove contemporaneously the identity of an over the counter presenter at the time presentment is made. According to Petitioner, the purpose of requiring "reasonable identification" is to allow the drawee bank to determine that the presenter is the proper person to be paid on the instrument. Because a thumbprint does not provide that information at the time presentment and payment are made, Petitioner argues that a thumbprint cannot be read to fall within the meaning of "reasonable identification" for the purposes of § 3-501(b)(2)(ii).

Bank of America argues that the requirement of a thumbprint has been upheld, in other non-criminal circumstances, not to be an invasion of privacy, and is a reasonable and necessary industry response to the growing problem of check fraud. The intermediate appellate court agreed, pointing out that the form of identification was not defined by the statute, but that the Code itself recognized a thumbprint as a form of signature, § 1-201(39), and observing that requiring thumbprint or fingerprint identification has been found to be reasonable and not to violate privacy rights in a number of non-criminal contexts. * * *

We agree with [Petitioner] that a thumbprint cannot be used, in most instances, to confirm the identity of a non-account checkholder at the time that the check is presented for cashing, as his or her thumbprint is usually not on file with the drawee at that time. We disagree, however, with [Petitioner's] conclusion that a thumbprint signature is therefore not "reasonable identification" for purposes of § 3-501(b)(2).

Nowhere does the language of § 3-501(b)(2) suggest that "reasonable identification" is limited to information [Bank] can authenticate at the time presentment is made. Rather, all that is required is that the "person making presentment must * * * give reasonable identification." § 3-501(b)(2). While providing a thumbprint signature does not necessarily confirm identification of the checkholder at presentment—unless of course the drawee bank has a duplicate thumbprint signature on file—it does assist in the identification of the checkholder should the check later prove to be bad. It therefore serves as a powerful deterrent to those who might otherwise attempt to pass a bad check. That one method provides identification at the time of presentment and the other identification after the check may have been honored, does not prevent the latter from being "reasonable identification" for purposes of § 3-501(b)(2) [Citation].

[So held the lower courts.] We agree, and find this conclusion to be compelled, in fact, by our State's Commercial Law Article.

The reason has to do with warranties. The transfer of a check for consideration creates both transfer warranties (§ 3-416(a) and (c)) and presentment warranties (§ 3-417(a) and (e)) which cannot be disclaimed. The warranties include, for example, that the payee is entitled to enforce the instrument and that there are no alterations on the check. The risk to banks is that these contractual warranties may be breached, exposing the accepting bank to a loss because the bank paid over the counter on an item which was not properly payable. * * * In such an event, the bank would then incur the expense to find the presenter, to demand repayment, and legal expenses to pursue the presenter for breach of his warranties.

In short, when a bank cashes a check over the counter, it assumes the risk that it may suffer losses for counterfeit documents, forged endorsements, or forged or altered checks. Nothing in the Commercial Law Article forces a bank to assume such risks. *See* [Citations] To the extent that banks are willing to cash checks over the counter, with reasonable identification, such willingness expands and facilitates the commercial activities within the State....

Because the reduction of risk promotes the expansion of commercial practices, we * * * conclude that a bank's requirement of a thumbprint placed upon a check presented over the counter by a non-customer is reasonable. [Citations] As the intermediate appellate court well documented, the Thumbprint Program is part of an industry wide response to the growing threat of check fraud. Prohibiting banks from taking reasonable steps to protect themselves from losses could result in banks refusing to cash checks of non-customers presented over the counter at all, a result which would be counter to the direction of § 1-102(2)(b).

As a result of this conclusion, Bank of America in the present case did not dishonor the check when it refused to accept it over the counter. Under § 3-501(b)(3)(ii), Bank of America "refused payment or acceptance for failure of the presentment to comply with * * * other applicable law or rule." The rule not complied with by the Petitioner-presenter was § 3-502(b)(2)(ii), in that he refused to give what we have determined to be reasonable identification. Therefore, there was no dishonor of the check by Bank of America's refusal to accept it. The answer to Petitioner's third question is therefore "no," [Did Bank dishonor the check?] * * *

Judgment of the court of special appeals affirmed; costs to be paid by petitioner.

Eldridge, J., concurring in part and dissenting in part.

I cannot agree with the majority's holding that, after the petitioner presented his driver's license and a major credit card, it was "reasonable" to require the petitioner's thumbprint as identification.

Today, honest citizens attempting to cope in this world are constantly being required to show or give drivers' licenses, photo identification cards, Social Security numbers, the last four digits of social security numbers, mothers' "maiden names," 16-digit account numbers, etc. Now, the majority takes the position that it is "reasonable" for banks and other establishments to require, in addition, thumbprints and fingerprints. Enough is enough. The most reasonable thing in this case was petitioner's "irritation with the Bank of America's Thumbprint Signature Program." Chief Judge Bell has authorized me to state that he joins this concurring and dissenting opinion.

Case Questions

1. Petitioner claimed (a) he made a valid presentment, (b) Bank accepted the instrument, (c) Bank dishonored the acceptance, and (d) Bank converted the money and owes it to him. What did the court say about each assertion?
2. There was no dispute that there was enough money in the drawer's account to pay the check, so why didn't Petitioner just deposit it in his own account (then he wouldn't have been required to give a thumbprint)?
3. What part of UCC Article 3 became relevant to the question of whether it was reasonable for Bank to demand Petitioner's thumbprint?
4. How do the presentment and transfer warranties figure into the majority opinion?
5. What did the dissenting judges find fault with in the majority's opinion? What result would have obtained if the minority side had prevailed?

Breach of Transfer Warranties and the Bank's Obligation to Act in Good Faith

PNC Bank v. Robert L. Martin
2010 WL 3271725, U.S. Dist. Ct. (Ky. 2010)

Coffman, J.

This matter is before the court on plaintiff PNC Bank's motion for summary judgment. The court will grant the motion as to liability and damages, because the defendant, Robert L. Martin, fails to raise any genuine issue of material fact, and the evidence establishes that Martin breached his transfer warranties and account agreement with PNC....

I. Background

Martin, an attorney, received an e-mail message on August 16, 2008, from a person who called himself Roman Hidotashi. Hidotashi claimed that he was a representative of Chipang Lee Song Manufacturing Company and needed to hire a lawyer to collect millions of dollars from past-due accounts of North American customers. Martin agreed to represent the company.

On September 8, 2008, Martin received a check for $290,986.15 from a purported Chipang Lee Song Manufacturing Company customer, even though Martin had yet to commence any collections work. The check, which was drawn on First Century Bank USA, arrived in an envelope with a Canadian postmark and no return address. The check was accompanied by an undated transmittal letter. Martin endorsed the check and deposited it in his client trust account at PNC. Martin then e-mailed Hidotashi, reported that he had deposited the check, and stated that he would await further instructions.

Hidotashi responded to Martin's e-mail message on September 9, 2008. Hidotashi stated that he had an "immediate need for funds" and instructed Martin to wire $130,600 to a bank account in Tokyo. Martin went to PNC's main office in Louisville the next morning and met with representative Craig Friedman. According to Martin, Friedman advised that the check Martin deposited had cleared. Martin instructed Friedman to wire $130,600 to the Tokyo account.

Martin returned to PNC later the same day. According to Martin, Friedman accessed Martin's account information and said, "I don't understand this. The check was cleared yesterday. Let me go find out what is going on." Friedman returned with PNC vice president and branch manager Sherry Jennewein, who informed Martin that the check was fraudulent. According to Martin, Jennewein told him that she wished he had met with her instead of Friedman because she never would have authorized the wire transfer.

First Century Bank, on which the check was drawn, dishonored the check. PNC charged Martin's account for $290,986.15. PNC, however, could not recover the $130,600 the bank had wired to the Tokyo account. Martin's account, as a result, was left overdrawn by $124,313.01.

PNC commenced this action. PNC asserts one count for Martin's alleged breach of the transfer warranties provided in Kentucky's version of the Uniform Commercial Code and one count for breach of Martin's account agreement. PNC moves for summary judgment on both counts.

II. Discussion

A. Breach of transfer warranties

PNC is entitled to summary judgment on its breach-of-transfer-warranties claim because the undisputed facts establish Martin's liability.

Transfer warranties trigger when a person transfers an instrument for consideration. UCC § 3-416(a)). A transfer, for purposes of the statute, occurs when an instrument is delivered by a person other than its issuer for the purpose of giving to the person receiving delivery the right to enforce the instrument. § 3-203(a). Martin transferred an instrument to PNC when he endorsed the check and deposited it in his account, thereby granting PNC the right to enforce the check. [Citation] Consideration, for purposes of the statute, need only be enough to support a simple contract. [Citation] Martin received consideration from PNC because PNC made the funds provisionally available before confirming whether First Century Bank would honor the check.

As a warrantor, Martin made a number of representations to PNC, including representations that he was entitled to enforce the check and that all signatures on the check were authentic and authorized. [UCC] § 3-416(a). Martin breached his warranties twofold. First, he was not entitled to enforce the check because the check was a counterfeit and, as a result, Martin had nothing to enforce. Second, the drawer's signature was not authentic because the check was a counterfeit.

Martin does not dispute these facts. Instead, Martin argues, summary judgment is inappropriate because Friedman and Jennewein admitted that PNC made a mistake when Friedman said that he thought the check cleared and Jennewein said that she never would have authorized the wire transfer. Friedman's and Jennewein's statements are immaterial facts. The transfer warranties placed the risk of loss on Martin, regardless of whether PNC, Martin, or both of them were at fault. [Citation] Martin, in any event, fails to support Friedman's and Jennewein's statements with first-hand deposition testimony or affidavits, so the statements do not qualify as competent evidence. [Citation]

Martin claims that the risk of loss falls on the bank. But the cases Martin cites in support of that proposition suffer from two defects. First, all but one of the cases were decided before the Kentucky General Assembly adopted the Uniform Commercial Code. Martin fails to argue, much less demonstrate, that his cases are good law. Second, Martin's cases are inapposite even if they are good law. [UCC] § 3-416(a) addresses whether a transferor or transferee bears the risk of loss. Martin's cases address who bears the risk of loss as between other players: a drawee bank and a collecting agent [Citation]; a drawer and a drawee bank [Citation]; and an execution creditor and drawee bank [Citation—all of these cases are from 1910–1930]. The one modern case that Martin cites is also inapposite because the case involves a drawer and a drawee bank. [Citation]

In sum, the court must grant summary judgment in PNC's favor on the breach-of-transfer-warranties claim because the parties do not contest any material facts, which establish Martin's liability.

B. Breach of Contract

PNC is also entitled to summary judgment on its breach-of-contract claim because the undisputed facts establish Martin's liability.

To support its allegation that a contract existed, PNC filed copies of Martin's account agreement and Martin's accompanying signature card. Under the agreement's terms, Martin agreed to bind himself to the agreement by signing the signature card. Martin does not dispute that the account agreement was a binding contract, and he does not dispute the account agreement's terms.

Martin's account agreement authorized PNC to charge Martin's account for the value of any item returned to PNC unpaid or any item on which PNC did not receive payment. If PNC's charge-back created an overdraft, Martin was required to pay PNC the amount of the overdraft immediately.

The scam of which Martin was a victim falls squarely within the charge-back provision of the account agreement. The check was returned to PNC unpaid. PNC charged Martin's account, leaving it with an overdraft. Martin was obliged to pay PNC immediately.

As with the breach-of-transfer-warranties claim, Martin cannot defend against the breach-of-contract claim by arguing that PNC made a mistake. The account agreement authorized PNC to charge back Martin's account "even if the amount of the item has already been made available to you." The account agreement, as a result, placed the risk of loss on Martin. Any mistake on PNC's part was immaterial because PNC always had the right to charge back Martin's account. [Citation]

C. Martin's Counterclaims

Martin has asserted counterclaims for violations of various Uniform Commercial Code provisions; negligence and failure to exercise ordinary care; negligent misrepresentation; breach of contract and breach of the implied covenants of good faith and fair dealing; detrimental reliance; conversion; and negligent retention and supervision. Martin argues that "[t]o the extent that either party should be entitled to summary judgment in this case, it would be Martin with respect to his counterclaims against PNC." Martin, however, has not moved for summary judgment on his counterclaims, and the court does not address them on PNC's motion.

D. Damages

PNC's recovery under both theories of liability is contingent on PNC's demonstrating that it acted in good faith. PNC may recover for breach of the transfer warranties only if it took the check in good faith. § 3-416(b). Moreover, PNC must satisfy the implied covenant of good faith and fair dealing, which Kentucky law incorporates in the account agreement. [Citation] Good faith, under both theories, means honesty in fact and the observance of reasonable commercial standards of fair dealing. That means "contracts impose on the parties thereto a duty to do everything necessary to carry them out." [Citation]

The undisputed evidence establishes that PNC acted in good faith. PNC accepted deposit of Martin's check, attempted to present the check for payment at First Century Bank, and charged back Martin's account when the check was dishonored. Martin cannot claim that PNC lacked good faith and fair dealing when PNC took actions permitted under the contract. [Citation] Although PNC might have had the ability to investigate the authenticity of the check before crediting Martin's account, PNC bore no such obligation because Martin warranted that the check was authentic. [UCC] § 3-416(a). Friedman's and Jennewein's statements do not impute a lack of good faith to PNC, even if Martin could support the statements with competent evidence. The Uniform Commercial Code and the account agreement place the risk of loss on Martin, even if PNC made a mistake.

Martin suggests that an insurance carrier might have already reimbursed PNC for the loss. Martin, however, presents no evidence of reimbursement, which PNC, presumably, would have disclosed in discovery.

PNC, therefore, may recover from Martin the overdraft value of $124,313.01, which is the loss PNC suffered as a result of Martin's breach of the transfer warranties and breach of contract. [UCC] § 3-416(b)...

III. Conclusion

For the foregoing reasons, IT IS ORDERED that PNC's motion for summary judgment is granted...to the extent that...PNC is permitted to recover $124,313.01 from Martin....

Case Questions

1. How did Martin come to have an overdraft of $124,313.01 in his account?
2. Under what UCC provision did the court hold Martin liable for this amount?
3. The contract liability the court discusses was *not* incurred by Martin on account of his signature on the check (though he did indorse it); what was the contract liability?
4. If the bank had not taken the check in good faith (honesty in fact and observing reasonable commercial standards), what would the consequence have been, and why?
5. Is a reader really constrained here to say that Mr. Martin got totally scammed, or was his behavior reasonable under the circumstances?

25.6 Summary and Exercises

Summary

As a general rule, one who signs a note as maker or a draft as drawer is personally liable unless he or she signs in a representative capacity and either the instrument or the signature shows that the signing has been made in a representative capacity. Various rules govern the permutations of signatures when an agent and a principal are involved.

The maker of a note and the acceptor of a draft have primary contract liability on the instruments. Secondarily liable are drawers and indorsers. Conditions precedent to secondary liability are presentment, dishonor, and notice of dishonor. Under the proper circumstances, any of these conditions may be waived or excused.

Presentment is a demand for payment made on the maker, acceptor, or drawee, or a demand for acceptance on the drawee. Presentment must be made (1) at the time specified in the instrument unless no time is specified, in which case it must be at the time specified for payment, or (2) within a reasonable time if a sight instrument.

Dishonor occurs when acceptance or payment is refused after presentment, at which time a holder has the right of recourse against secondary parties if he has given proper notice of dishonor.

A seller-transferor of any commercial paper gives five implied warranties, which become valuable to a holder seeking to collect in the event that there has been no indorsement or the indorsement has been qualified. These warranties are (1) good title, (2) genuine signatures, (3) no material alteration, (4) no defenses by other parties to the obligation to pay the transferor, and (5) no knowledge of insolvency of maker, acceptor, or drawer.

A holder on presentment makes certain warranties also: (1) entitled to enforce the instrument, (2) no knowledge that the maker's or drawer's signature is unauthorized, and (3) no material alteration.

Among the ways in which the parties may be discharged from their contract to honor the instrument are the following: (1) payment or satisfaction, (2) tender of payment, (3) cancellation and renunciation, (4) impairment of recourse or of collateral, (5) reacquisition, (6) fraudulent and material alteration, (7) certification, (8) acceptance varying a draft, and (9) unexcused delay in presentment or notice of dishonor.

Exercises

1. Howard Corporation has the following instrument, which it purchased in good faith and for value from Luft Manufacturing, Inc.

FIGURE 25.2

To: McHugh Wholesalers, Inc. July 2, 2012

Pullman, WA

Pay to the order of Luft Manufacturing, Inc., one thousand seven hundred dollars ($1700), three months after acceptance.

Judith Glen, President

Luft Mfg., Inc.

Accepted July 12, 2010

McHugh Wholesalers, Inc, by Charles Towne, President

Judith Glen indorsed the instrument on the back in her capacity as president of Luft when it was transferred to Howard on July 15, 2012.

a. Is this a note or a draft?
b. What liability do McHugh and Luft have to Howard? Explain.

2. An otherwise valid negotiable bearer note is signed with the forged signature of Darby. Archer, who believed he knew Darby's signature, bought the note in good faith from Harding, the forger. Archer transferred the note without indorsement to Barker, in partial payment of a debt. Barker then sold the note to Chase for 80 percent of its face amount and delivered it without indorsement. When Chase presented the note for payment at maturity, Darby refused to honor it, pleading forgery. Chase gave proper notice of dishonor to Barker and to Archer.
   a. Can Chase hold Barker liable? Explain.
   b. Can Chase hold Archer liable? Explain.
   c. Can Chase hold Harding liable? Explain.
3. Marks stole one of Bloom's checks, already signed by Bloom and made payable to Duval, drawn on United Trust Company. Marks forged Duval's signature on the back of the check and cashed it at Check Cashing Company, which in turn deposited it with its bank, Town National. Town National proceeded to collect on the check from United. None of the parties was negligent. Who will bear the loss, assuming Marks cannot be found?
4. Robb stole one of Markum's blank checks, made it payable to himself, and forged Markum's signature on it. The check was drawn on the Unity Trust Company. Robb cashed the check at the Friendly Check Cashing Company, which in turn deposited it with its bank, the Farmer's National. Farmer's National proceeded to collect on the check from Unity. The theft and forgery were quickly discovered by Markum, who promptly notified Unity. None of the parties mentioned was negligent. Who will bear the loss, assuming the amount cannot be recovered from Robb? Explain.
5. Pat stole a check made out to the order of Marks, forged the name of Marks on the back, and made the instrument payable to herself. She then negotiated the check to Harrison for cash by signing her own name on the back of the instrument in Harrison's presence. Harrison was unaware of any of the facts surrounding the theft or forged indorsement and presented the check for payment. Central County Bank, the drawee bank, paid it. Disregarding Pat, who will bear the loss? Explain.
6. American Music Industries, Inc., owed Disneyland Records over $340,000. As evidence of the debt, Irv Schwartz, American's president, issued ten promissory notes, signing them

himself. There was no indication they were obligations of the corporation, American Music Industries, Inc., or that Irv Schwartz signed them in a representative capacity, but Mr. Schwartz asserted that Disneyland knew the notes were corporate obligations, not his personally. American paid four of the notes and then defaulted, and Disneyland sued him personally on the notes. He asserted he should be allowed to prove by parol evidence that he was not supposed to be liable. Is he personally liable? Explain.[34]

7. Alice Able hired Betty Baker as a bookkeeper for her seamstress shop. Baker's duties included preparing checks for Able to sign and reconciling the monthly bank statements. Baker made out several checks to herself, leaving a large space to the left of the amount written, which Able noticed when she signed the checks. Baker took the signed checks, altered the amount by adding a zero to the right of the original amount, and cashed them at First Bank, the drawee. Able discovered the fraud, Baker was sent to prison, and Able sued First Bank, claiming it was liable for paying out on altered instruments. What is the result?
8. Christina Reynolds borrowed $16,000 from First Bank to purchase a used Ford automobile. Bank took a note and a secured interest in the car (the car is collateral for the loan). It asked for further security, so Christina got her sister Juanita to sign the note as an accommodation maker. Four months later, Christina notified Bank that she wished to sell the Ford for $14,000 in order to get a four-wheel drive Jeep, and Bank released its security interest. When Christina failed to complete payment on the note for the Ford, Bank turned to Juanita. What, if anything, does Juanita owe?

Self-Test Questions

1. Drawers and indorsers have
   a. primary contract liability
   b. secondary liability
   c. no liability
   d. none of the above
2. Conditions(s) needed to establish secondary liability include
   a. presentment
   b. dishonor
   c. notice of dishonor
   d. all of the above
3. A demand for payment made on a maker, acceptor, or drawee is called
   a. protest
   b. notice
   c. presentment
   d. certification
4. An example of an implied warranty given by a seller of commercial paper includes a warranty
   a. of good title
   b. that there are no material alterations
   c. that signatures are genuine
   d. covering all of the above
5. Under UCC Article 3, discharge may result from
   a. cancellation
   b. impairment of collateral
   c. fraudulent alteration
   d. all of the above

Self-Test Answers

1. b
2. d
3. c
4. d
5. d

Endnotes

1. Uniform Commercial Code, Section 4-402(b)(1).
2. Uniform Commercial Code, Section 3-403.
3. Uniform Commercial Code, Section 3-406(b).
4. Uniform Commercial Code, Section 3-419.
5. Uniform Commercial Code, Section 3-412.
6. Uniform Commercial Code, Section 3-414(b).
7. Uniform Commercial Code, Section 3-413(a)(iii).
8. Uniform Commercial Code, Section 3-414.
9. Uniform Commercial Code, Section 3-414(d).
10. Uniform Commercial Code, Section 3-415(b).
11. Uniform Commercial Code, Section 3-501.
12. Uniform Commercial Code, Section 3-420.
13. Uniform Commercial Code, Section 3-420, Official Comment 1.
14. Uniform Commercial Code, Section 3-503(b).
15. Uniform Commercial Code, Section 3-503(c).
16. Uniform Commercial Code, Section 3-504.
17. Gregory E. Maggs, "A Complaint about Payment Law Under the U.C.C.: What You See Is Often Not What You Get," *Ohio State Law Journal* 68, no. 201, no. 207 (2007), http://ssrn.com/abstract=1029647.
18. Uniform Commercial Code, Section 3-416, Official Comment 4.
19. Uniform Commercial Code, Section 3-417.
20. Uniform Commercial Code, Section 3-417, Comment 2.
21. Uniform Commercial Code, Sections 3-417(2) and (b).
22. Uniform Commercial Code, Section 3-417(d).
23. Uniform Commercial Code, Section 3-418.
24. Uniform Commercial Code, Section 3-418(c).
25. Uniform Commercial Code, Section 3-603(b).
26. Uniform Commercial Code, Section 3-604.
27. Uniform Commercial Code, Section 3-410.
28. Uniform Commercial Code, Section 3-605.
29. Uniform Commercial Code, Section 3-207.
30. Section 4-208 provides as follows: "(a) If an unaccepted draft is presented [in this case, by BOK] to the drawee [BNH] for payment or acceptance and the drawee pays or accepts the draft,(i) the person obtaining payment or acceptance, at the time of presentment, and(ii) a previous transferor of the draft, at the time of transfer, warrant to the drawee that pays or accepts the draft in good faith, that:(1) The warrantor is, or was, at the time the warrantor transferred the draft, a person entitled to enforce the draft or authorized to obtain payment or acceptance of the draft on behalf of a person entitled to enforce the draft;(2) The draft has not been altered; and(3) The warrantor has no knowledge that the signature of the purported drawer of the draft is unauthorized.(b) A drawee making payment may recover from a warrantor damages for breach of warranty....(c) If a drawee asserts a claim for breach of warranty under subsection (a) of this section based on an unauthorized indorsement of the draft or an alteration of the draft, the warrantor may defend by proving that...the drawer [here, Farm Bureau] is precluded under Section 3-406 or 4-406 of this title from asserting against the drawee the unauthorized indorsement or alteration."
31. (a) A person whose failure to exercise ordinary care substantially contributes to an alteration of an instrument or to the making of a forged signature on an instrument is precluded from asserting the alteration or the forgery against a person who, in good faith, pays the instrument or takes it for value or for collection.
32. The parties do not address Section 3-406(b), which states that the person asserting preclusion may be held partially liable under comparative negligence principles for failing to exercise ordinary care in paying or taking the check. They also do not address any possible negligence by either bank in accepting the forged check without confirming the legitimacy of Conseco's indorsement.
33. Petitioner's choice could be viewed as an attempt at risk shifting. Petitioner, an attorney, may have known that he could have suffered a fee charged by his own bank if he deposited a check into his own account and then the bank on which it was drawn returned it for insufficient funds, forged endorsement, alteration, or the like. Petitioner's action, viewed against that backdrop, would operate as a risk-shifting strategy, electing to avoid the risk of a returned-check fee by presenting in person the check for acceptance at the drawee bank.
34. *Schwartz v. Disneyland Vista Records*, 383 So.2d 1117 (Fla. App. 1980).

CHAPTER 26

Legal Aspects of Banking

Learning Objectives

After reading this chapter, you should understand the following:

1. Banks' relationships with their customers for payment or nonpayment of checks.
2. Electronic funds transfers and how the Electronic Fund Transfer Act affects the bank-consumer relationship.
3. What a wholesale funds transfer is and the scope of Article 4A.
4. What letters of credit are and how they are used.

To this point, we have examined the general law of commercial paper as found in Article 3 of the UCC. Commercial paper—notwithstanding waves of digital innovation—still passes through bank collection processes by the ton every day, and Article 3 applies to this flow. But there is also a separate article in the UCC, Article 4, "Bank Deposits and Collections." In case of conflict with Article 3 rules, those of Article 4 govern.

A discussion of government regulation of the financial services industry is beyond the scope of this book. Our focus is narrower: the laws that govern the operations of the banking system with respect to its depositors and customers. Although histories of banking dwell on the relationship between banks and the national government, the banking law that governs the daily operation of checking accounts is state based—Article 4 of the UCC. The enormous increase in noncheck banking has given rise to the Electronic Fund Transfer Act, a federal law.

26.1 Banks and Their Customers

Learning Objectives

1. Understand how checks move, both traditionally and electronically.
2. Know how Article 4 governs the relationship between a bank and its customers.

The Traditional Bank Collection Process

The Traditional System in General

Once people mostly paid for things with cash: actual bills. That is obviously not very convenient or safe: a lost ten-dollar bill is almost certainly gone, and carrying around large quantities of cash is dangerous (probably only crooks do much of that). Today, though cash is still important as to overall transaction numbers, it represents only 14% of the value of total consumer transactions—cash is used for low-value payments. And while it is indisputable that electronic payment is replacing the paper check, the latter is still very significant.

FIGURE 26.1 Trends in Non-Cash Payments 2000-2015
Number of Transactions by Payment Instrument

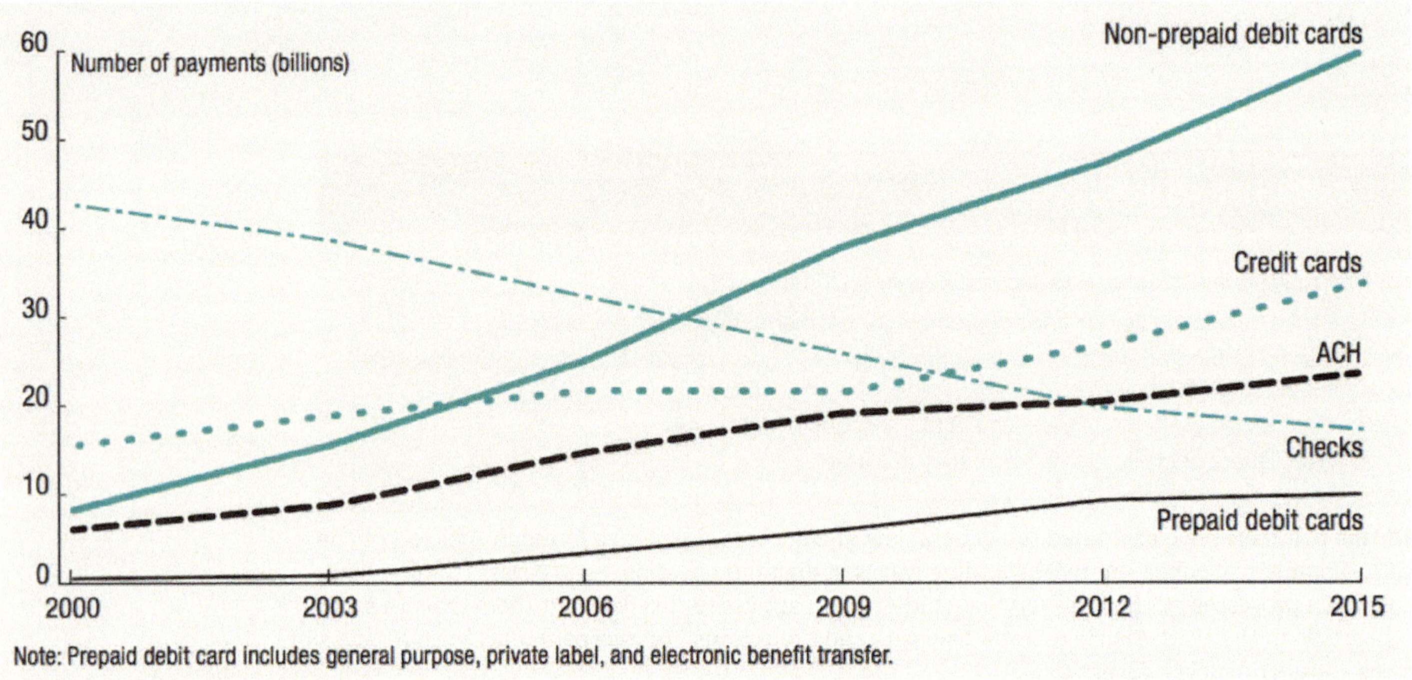

Federal Reserve's 2016 Payments Study at https://www.federalreserve.gov/newsevents/press/other/2016-payments-study-20161222.pdf

Some thirty billion checks were written in the U.S. in 2006.[1] Six years later that number wass down to less than twenty billion, according to the Federal Reserve (reporting on 2012 surveys).[2] But twenty billion—you can readily imagine how complex the bank collection process must be to cope with such a flood of paper. Every check written must eventually come back to the bank on which it is drawn, after first having been sent to the landlord, say, to pay rent, then to the landlord's bank, and from there through a series of intermediate banks and collection centers.

Terminology

To trace the traditional check-collection process, it is necessary to understand the terminology used. The bank upon which a check is written is the **payor bank** (it is also the drawee bank). The **depository bank** is the one the payee deposits the check into. Two terms are used to describe the various banks that may handle the check after it is written: collecting banks and intermediary banks. All banks that handle the check—except the payor bank—are **collecting banks** (including the depository bank); **intermediary banks** are all the collecting banks except the payor and depository banks. A bank can take on more than one role: Roger in Seattle writes a check on his account at Seattle Bank and mails it to Julia in Los Angeles in payment for merchandise; Julia deposits it in her account at Bank of L.A. Bank of L.A. is a depository bank and a collecting bank. Any other bank through which the check travels (except the two banks already mentioned) is an intermediary bank.

payor bank

The bank upon which a check is drawn; the drawee.

depository bank

The bank into which a check is deposited by its payee.

collecting banks

A bank that collects the amount of a check for its customer from the payor bank.

intermediary banks

A bank that handles checks, but not including payor and depository banks.

Collection Process between Customers of the Same Bank

If the depository bank is also the payor bank (about 30% of all checks), the check is called an "on-us" item and UCC 4-215(e)(2) provides that—if the check is not dishonored—it is available by the payee "at the opening of the bank's second banking day following receipt of the item." Roger writes a check to Matthew, both of whom have accounts at Seattle Bank; Matthew deposits the check on Monday. On Wednesday, the check is good for Matthew (he may have been given "provisional credit" before then, as discussed below, the bank could subtract the money from his account if Roger didn't have enough to cover the check).

Collection Process between Customers of Different Banks

Roger in Seattle writes a check on Seattle Bank payable to Julia in L.A. Julia deposits it in her account at L.A. Bank, the depository bank. L.A. Bank must somehow present the check to Seattle Bank either directly or through intermediary banks. If the collecting banks (again, all of them except Seattle Bank) act before the midnight deadline following receipt, they have acted "seasonably" according to UCC 4-202. When the payor bank—Seattle Bank—gets the check it must pay it, unless the check is dishonored or returned (UCC 4-302).

Physical Movement of Checks

The physical movement of checks—such as it still occurs—is handled by three possible systems.

The Federal Reserve System's regional branches process checks for banks holding accounts with them. The Feds charge for the service, and prior to 2004 it regularly included check collection, air transportation of checks to the Reserve Bank (hired out to private contractors) and ground transportation delivery of checks to paying banks. Reserve Banks handle about 27 percent of US checks, but the air service is decreasing with "Check 21," a federal law discussed below, that allows electronic transmission of checks.

correspondent banks

Those banks that form a partnership to exchange checks among themselves, bypassing the Federal Reserve and its fees.

clearinghouse corporation

An office where banks exchange checks and drafts and settle accounts, owned by the member banks participating.

Correspondent banks are banks that have formed "partnerships" with other banks in order to exchange checks and payments directly, bypassing the Federal Reserve and its fees. Outside banks may go through a correspondent bank to exchange checks and payments with one of its partners.

Correspondent banks may also form a **clearinghouse corporation**, in which members exchange checks and payments in bulk, instead of on a check-by-check basis, which can be inefficient considering that each bank might receive thousands of checks in a day. The clearinghouse banks save up the checks drawn on other members and exchange them on a daily basis. The net payments for these checks are often settled through Fedwire, a Federal Reserve Board electronic funds transfer (EFT) system that handles large-scale check settlement among US banks. Correspondent banks and clearinghouse corporations make up the private sector of check clearing, and together they handle about 43 percent of US checks.

The Electronic System: Check 21 Act

Rationale for the "Check Clearing for the 21st Century Act"

After the events of September 11, 2001, Congress felt with renewed urgency that banks needed to present and clear checks in a way not dependent upon the physical transportation of the paper instruments by air and ground, in case such transportation facilities were disrupted. The federal Check Clearing for the 21st Century Act (Public Law 108-100)—more commonly referred to as "Check 21 Act"—became effective in 2004.

Basic Idea of Check 21 Act

substitute check

A paper reproduction of an electronically copied check the image of which is transferred if requested, instead of the paper check.

Check 21 Act provides the legal basis for the electronic transportation of check data. A bank scans the check. The data on the check is already encoded in electronically readable numbers and the data, now separated ("truncated") from the paper instrument (which may be destroyed), is transmitted for processing. "The Act authorizes a new negotiable instrument, called a **substitute check**, to replace the original check. A substitute check is a paper reproduction of the original check that is suitable for automated processing in the same manner as the original check. The Act permits banks to provide substitute checks in place of original checks to subsequent parties in the check processing stream....Any financial institution in the check clearing process can truncate the original check and create a substitute check.[3] However, in the check collection process it is not required that the image be converted to a substitute check: the electronic image itself may suffice.

For example, suppose Roger in Seattle writes a check on Seattle Bank payable to Julia in L.A. and mails it to her. Julia deposits it in her account at L.A. Bank, the depository bank. L.A. Bank truncates the check (again, scans it and destroys the original) and transmits the data to Seattle Bank for presentation and payment. If for any reason Roger, or any appropriate party, wants a paper version, a substitute check will be created (see Figure 26.2). Most often, though, that is not necessary: Roger does not receive the actual cancelled checks he wrote in his monthly statement as he did formerly. He receives instead a statement listing paid checks he's written and a picture of the check (not a substitute check) is available to him online through his bank's website. Or he may receive his monthly statement itself electronically, with pictures of the checks he wrote available with a mouse click. Roger may also dispense with mailing the check to Julia entirely, as noted in the discussion of electronic funds transfers.

FIGURE 26.2 **Substitute Check Front and Back**

Front and back of a substitute check (not actual size).

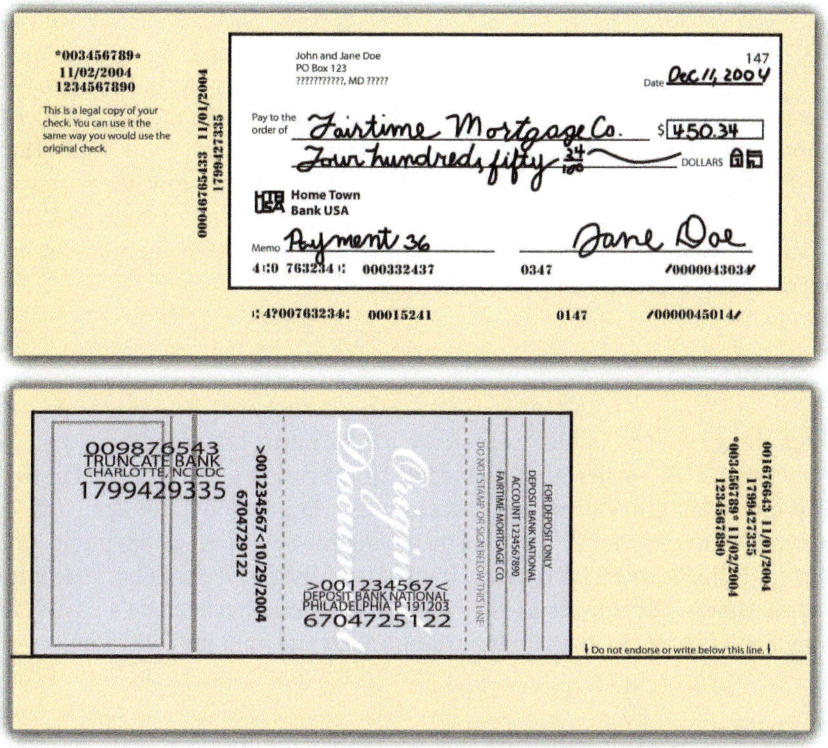

Images from Federal Reserve Board: http://www.federalreserve.gov/pubs/check21/consumer_guide

Substitute checks are legal negotiable instruments. The act provides certain warranties to protect recipients of substitute checks that are intended to protect recipients against losses associated with the check substitution process. One of these warranties provides that "[a] bank that transfers, presents, or returns a substitute check ... for which it receives consideration warrant ... that ... [t]he substitute check meets the requirements of legal equivalence" (12 CFR § 229.52(a)(1)). The Check 21 Act does not replace existing state laws regarding such instruments. The Uniform Commercial Code still applies, and we turn to it next.

Two notable consequences of the Check 21 Act are worth mentioning. The first is that a check may be presented to the payor bank for payment very quickly, perhaps in less than an hour: the customer's "float" time is abbreviated. That means be sure you have enough money in your account to cover the checks that you write. The second consequence of Check 21 Act is that it is now possible for anybody—you at home or the merchant from whom you are buying something—to scan a check and deposit it instantly. "Remote deposit capture" allows users to transmit a scanned image of a check for posting and clearing using a web-connected computer and a check scanner, or—most recently—by smart phone: take a picture of the front and back of the check with your smart phone and click to send the deposit to the desired existing bank account. Many merchants are using this system: that's why if you write a check at the hardware store you may see it scanned and returned immediately to you. The digital data is transmitted, and the scanned image may be retrieved, if needed, as a "substitute check." About 25% of financial institutions in the U.S. offered remote deposit capture in 2014, and the number is expected to grow, but there are restrictions and timing questions associated with the technology.[4]

UCC Article 4: Aspects of Bank Operations

Reason for Article 4

Over the years, the states had begun to enact different statutes to regulate the check collection process. Eighteen states adopted the American Bankers Association Bank Collection Code; many others enacted Deferred Posting statutes. Not surprisingly, a desire for uniformity was the principal reason for the adoption of UCC Article 4. Article 4 absorbed many of the rules of the American Bankers Association Code and of the principles of the Deferred Posting statutes, as well as court decisions and common customs not previously codified.

Banks Covered

Article 4 covers three types of banks: depository banks, payor banks, and collecting banks. These terms—already mentioned earlier—are defined in UCC Section 4-105. A depositary bank is the first bank to which an item is transferred for collection. Section 4-104 defines "item" as "an instrument or a promise or order to pay money handled by a bank for collection or payment[,]...not including a credit or debit card slip." A payor bank is any bank that must pay a check because it is drawn on the bank or accepted there—the drawee bank (a depositary bank may also be a payor bank). A collecting bank is any bank except the payor bank that handles the item for collection.

Technical Rules

Detailed coverage of Parts 2 and 3 of Article 4, the substantive provisions, is beyond the scope of this book. However, Article 4 answers several specific questions that bank customers most frequently ask.

1. What is the effect of a "pay any bank" indorsement? The moment these words are indorsed on a check, only a bank may acquire the rights of a holder. This restriction can be lifted whenever (a) the check has been returned to the customer initiating collection or (b) the bank specially indorses the check to a person who is not a bank (4-201).
2. May a depositary bank supply a missing indorsement? It may supply any indorsement of the customer necessary to title unless the check contains words such as "payee's indorsement required." If the customer fails to indorse a check when depositing it in his account, the bank's notation that the check was deposited by a customer or credited to his account takes effect as the customer's indorsement. (Section 4-205(1)).
3. Are any warranties given in the collection process? Yes. They are identical to those provided in Article 3, except that they apply only to customers and collecting banks (4-207(a)). The customer or collecting bank that transfers an item and receives a settlement or other consideration warrants (1) he is entitled to enforce the item; (2) all signatures are authorized authentic; (3) the item has not been altered; (4) the item is not subject to a defense or claim in recoupment; (5) he has no knowledge of insolvency proceedings regarding the maker or acceptor or in the case of an unaccepted draft, the drawer. These warranties cannot be disclaimed as to checks.
4. Does the bank have the right to a charge-back against a customer's account, or refund? The answer turns on whether the settlement was provisional or final. A settlement is the proper crediting of the amount ordered to be paid by the instrument. Someone writes you a check for $1,000 drawn on First Bank, and you deposit it in Second Bank. Second Bank will make a "provisional settlement" with you—that is, it will provisionally credit your account with $1,000, and that settlement will be final when First Bank debits the check writer's account and credits Second Bank with the funds. Under Section 4-212(1), as long as the settlement was still provisional, a collecting bank has the right to a "charge-back" or refund if the check "bounces" (is dishonored). However, if settlement was final, the bank cannot claim a refund.

What determines whether settlement is provisional or final? Section 4-213(1) spells out four events (whichever comes first) that will convert a payor bank's provisional settlement into final settlement: When it (a) pays the item in cash; (b) settles without reserving a right to revoke and without having a right under statute, clearinghouse rule, or agreement with the customer; finishes posting the item to the appropriate account; or (d) makes provisional settlement and fails to revoke the settlement in the time and manner permitted by statute, clearinghouse rule, or agreement. All clearinghouses have rules permitting revocation of settlement within certain time periods. For example an item cleared before 10 a.m. may be returned and the settlement revoked before 2 p.m. From this section it should be apparent that a bank generally can prevent a settlement from becoming final if it chooses to do so.

Relationship with Customers

The relationship between a bank and its customers is governed by UCC Article 4. However, Section 4-103(1) permits the bank to vary its terms, except that no bank can disclaim responsibility for failing to act in good faith or to exercise ordinary care. Most disputes between bank and customer arise when the bank either pays or refuses to pay a check. Under several provisions of Article 4, the bank is entitled to pay, even though the payment may be adverse to the customer's interest.

Common Issues Arising between Banks and Their Customers

Payment of Overdrafts

Suppose a customer writes a check for a sum greater than the amount in her account. May the bank pay the check and charge the customer's account? Under Section 4-401(1), it may. Moreover, it may pay on an altered check and charge the customer's account for the original tenor of the check, and if a check was completed it may pay the completed amount and charge the customer's account, assuming the bank acted in good faith without knowledge that the completion was improper.

Payment of Stale Checks

Section 4-404 permits a bank to refuse to pay a check that was drawn more than six months before being presented. Banks ordinarily consider such checks to be "stale" and will refuse to pay them, but the same section gives them the option to pay if they choose. A corporate dividend check, for example, will be presumed to be good more than six months later. The only exception to this rule is for certified checks, which must be paid whenever presented, since the customer's account was charged when the check was certified.

Post-dated checks

To post-date a check is to write a check but to put a future date on it. People do this intending that the recipient not deposit the check until a date later than when it was written. Joan's mortgage payment is due the first of the month. On June 20th, she writes a check to the bank holding the mortgage, putting the date "July 1" on the check. This is entirely fine. Except, if a person writes a post-dated check with the knowledge that when it is deposited it won't be honored, and with the intent to defraud its recipient, that is a criminal offense. It's a type of fraud.[5]

Payment of Deceased's or Incompetent's Checks

Suppose a customer dies or is adjudged to be incompetent. May the bank honor her checks? Section 4-405 permits banks to accept, pay, and collect an item as long as it has no notice of the death or declaration of incompetence, and has no reasonable opportunity to act on it. Even after notice of death, a bank has ten days to payor certify checks drawn on or prior to the date of death unless someone claiming an interest in the account orders it to refrain from doing so.

Stop Payment Orders

Section 4-403 expressly permits the customer to order the bank to "stop payment" on any check payable for her account, assuming the stop order arrives in enough time to reasonably permit the bank to act on it. An oral stop order is effective for fourteen days; a follow-up written confirmation within that time is effective for six months and can be renewed in writing. But if a stop order is not renewed, the bank will not be liable for paying the check, even one that is quite stale (e.g., *Granite Equipment Leasing Corp. v. Hempstead Bank*, 326 N.Y.S. 2d 881 (1971)).

Wrongful Dishonor

If a bank wrongfully dishonors an item, it is liable to the customer for all damages that are a direct consequence of ("proximately caused by") the dishonor. The bank's liability is limited to the damages actually proved; these may include damages for arrest and prosecution. See Section 4 under "Bank's Liability for Paying over Customer's 'Stop Payment' Order" (*Meade v. National Bank of Adams County*).

Customers' Duties

In order to hold a bank liable for paying out an altered check, the customer has certain duties under Section 4-406. Primarily, the customer must act promptly in examining her statement of account and must notify the bank if any check has been altered or her signature has been forged. If the customer fails to do so, she cannot recover from the bank for an altered signature or other term if the bank can show that it suffered a loss because of the customer's slowness. Recovery may also be denied when there has been a series of forgeries and the customer did not notify the bank within two weeks after receiving the first forged item. See Section 4 under "Customer's Duty to Inspect Bank Statements" (the *Planters Bank v. Rogers* case).

These rules apply to a payment made with ordinary care by the bank. If the customer can show that the bank negligently paid the item, then the customer may recover from the bank, regardless of how dilatory the customer was in notifying the bank—with two exceptions: (1) from the time she first sees the statement and item, the customer has one year to tell the bank that her signature was unauthorized or that a term was altered, and (2) she has three years to report an unauthorized indorsement.

The Expedited Funds Availability Act

In General

In addition to UCC Article 4 (again, state law), the federal Expedited Funds Availability Act—also referred to as "Regulation CC" after the Federal Reserve regulation that implements it—addresses an aspect of the relationship between a bank and its customers. It was enacted in 1988 in response to complaints by consumer groups about long delays before customers were allowed access to funds represented by checks they had deposited. It has nothing to do with electronic transfers, although the increasing use of electronic transfers does speed up the system and make it easier for banks to comply with Regulation CC.

The Act's Provisions

The act provides that when a customer deposits a cashier's check, certified check, or a check written on an account in the same bank, the funds must be available by the next business day. Funds from other local checks (drawn on institutions within the same Federal Reserve region) must be available within two working days, while there is a maximum five-day wait for funds from out-of-town checks. In order for these time limits to be effective, the customer must endorse the check in a designated space on the back side. The FDIC sets out the law at its website: http://www.fdic.gov/regulations/laws/rules/6500-3210.html.

Key Takeaway

The bank collection process is the method by which checks written on one bank are transferred by the collecting bank to a clearing house. Traditionally this has been a process of physical transfer by air and ground transportation from the depository bank to various intermediary banks to the payor bank where the check is presented. Since 2004 the Check 21 Act has encouraged a trend away from the physical transportation of checks to the electronic transportation of the check's data, which is truncated (stripped) from the paper instrument and transmitted. However, if a paper instrument is required, a "substitute check" will recreate it. The UCC's Article 4 deals generally with aspects of the bank-customer relationship, including warranties on payment or collection of checks, payment of overdrafts, stop orders, and customers' duties to detect irregularities. The Expedited Funds Availability Act is a federal law governing customer's access to funds in their accounts from deposited checks.

Exercises

1. Describe the traditional check-collection process, from the drawing of the check to its presentation for payment to the drawee (payor) bank.
2. Describe how the Check 21 Act has changed the check-collection process.
3. Why was Article 4 developed, and what is its scope of coverage?

26.2 Electronic Funds Transfers

Learning Objectives

1. Understand why electronic fund transfers have become prevalent.
2. Recognize some typical examples of EFTs.
3. Know that the EFT Act of 1978 protects consumers, and recognize what some of those protections—and liabilities—are.
4. Understand when financial institutions will be liable for violating the act, and some of the circumstances when the institutions will not be liable.

Background to Electronic Fund Transfers

In General

Drowning in the yearly flood of billions of checks, eager to eliminate the "float" that a bank customer gets by using her money between the time she writes a check and the time it clears, and recognizing that better customer service might be possible, financial institutions sought a way to computerize the check collection process. What has developed is electronic fund transfer (EFT), a system that has changed how customers interact with banks, credit unions, and other financial institutions. Paper checks have their advantages, but their use is decreasing in favor of EFT.

In simplest terms, EFT is a method of paying by substituting an electronic signal for checks. A "debit card," inserted in the appropriate terminal, will authorize automatically the transfer of funds from your checking account, say, to the account of a store whose goods you are buying.

Types of EFT

You are of course familiar with some forms of EFT:

- The automated teller machine (ATM) permits you to electronically transfer funds between checking and savings accounts at your bank with a plastic ID card and a personal identification number (PIN), and to obtain cash from the machine.
- Telephone transfers or computerized transfers allow customers to access the bank's computer system and direct it to pay bills owed to a third party or to transfer funds from one account to another.
- Point of sale terminals located in stores let customers instantly debit their bank accounts and credit the merchant's account.
- Preauthorized payment plans permit direct electronic deposit of paychecks, Social Security checks, and dividend checks.
- Preauthorized withdrawals from customers' bank accounts or credit card accounts allow paperless payment of insurance premiums, utility bills, automobile or mortgage payments, and property tax payments.

The "short circuit" that EFT permits in the check processing cycle is illustrated in Figure 26.3.

FIGURE 26.3 How EFT Replaces Checks

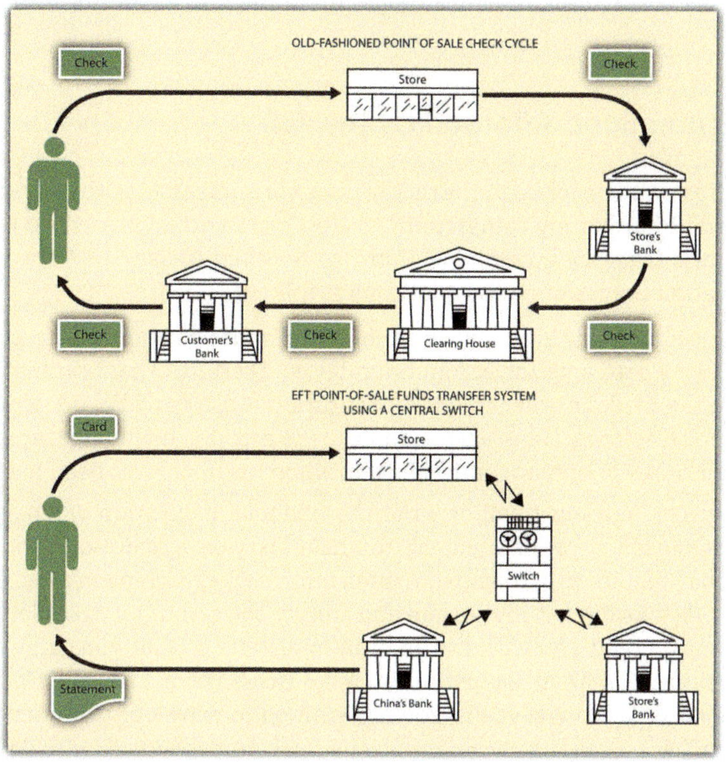

Unlike the old-fashioned check collection process, EFT is virtually instantaneous: at one instant a customer has a sum of money in her account; in the next, after insertion of a plastic card in a machine or the transmission of a coded message by telephone or computer, an electronic signal automatically debits her bank checking account and posts the amount to the bank account of the store where she is making a purchase. No checks change hands; no paper is written on. It is quiet, odorless, smudge proof. But errors are harder to trace than when a paper trail exists, and when the system fails ("our computer is down") the financial mess can be colossal. Obviously some sort of law is necessary to regulate EFT systems.

Electronic Fund Transfer Act of 1978

Purpose

Because EFT is a technology consisting of several discrete types of machines with differing purposes, its growth has not been guided by any single law or even set of laws. The most important law governing consumer transactions is the **Electronic Fund Transfer Act of 1978**,[6] whose purpose is "to provide a basic framework establishing the rights, liabilities, and responsibilities of participants in electronic fund transfer systems. The primary objective of [the statute], however, is the provision of individual consumer rights." This federal statute has been implemented and supplemented by the Federal Reserve Board's Regulation E, Comptroller of the Currency guidelines on EFT, and regulations of the Federal Home Loan Bank Board. (Wholesale transactions are governed by UCC Article 4A, which is discussed later in this chapter.)

Electronic Fund Transfer Act of 1978

Federal law that provides a basic framework establishing the rights, liabilities, and responsibilities of participants in electronic fund transfer systems.

The EFT Act of 1978 is primarily designed to disclose the terms and conditions of electronic funds transfers so the customer knows the rights, costs and liabilities associated with EFT, but it does not embrace every type of EFT system. Included are "point-of-sale transfers, automated teller machine transactions, direct deposits or withdrawal of funds, and transfers initiated by telephone or computer" (EFT Act Section 903(6)). Not included are such transactions as wire transfer services, automatic transfers between a customer's different accounts at the same financial institution, and "payments made by check, draft, or similar paper instrument at electronic terminals" (Reg. E, Section 205.2(g)).

Consumer Protections Afforded by the Act

Four questions present themselves to the mildly wary consumer facing the advent of EFT systems: (1) What record will I have of my transaction? (2) How can I correct errors? (3) What recourse do I have if a thief steals from my account? (4) Can I be required to use EFT? The EFT Act, as implemented by Regulation E, answers these questions as follows.

1. Proof of transaction. The electronic terminal itself must be equipped to provide a receipt of transfer, showing date, amount, account number, and certain other information. Perhaps more importantly, the bank or other financial institution must provide you with a monthly statement listing all electronic transfers to and from the account, including transactions made over the computer or telephone, and must show to whom payment has been made.
2. Correcting errors. You must call or write the financial institution whenever you believe an error has been made in your statement. You have sixty days to do so. If you call, the financial institution may require you to send in written information within ten days. The financial institution has forty-five days to investigate and correct the error. If it takes longer than ten days, however, it must credit you with the amount in dispute so that you can use the funds while it is investigating. The financial institution must either correct the error promptly or explain why it believes no error was made. You are entitled to copies of documents relied on in the investigation.
3. Recourse for loss or theft. If you notify the issuer of your EFT card within two business days after learning that your card (or code number) is missing or stolen, your liability is limited to \$50. If you fail to notify the issuer in this time, your liability can go as high as \$500. More daunting is the prospect of loss if you fail within sixty days to notify the financial institution of an unauthorized transfer noted on your statement: after sixty days of receipt, your liability is unlimited. In other words, a thief thereafter could withdraw all your funds and use up your line of credit and you would have no recourse against the financial institution for funds withdrawn after the sixtieth day, if you failed to notify it of the unauthorized transfer.
4. Mandatory use of EFT. Your employer or a government agency can compel you to accept a salary payment or government benefit by electronic transfer. But no creditor can insist that you repay outstanding loans or pay off other extensions of credit electronically. The act prohibits a financial institution from sending you an EFT card "valid for use" unless you specifically request one or it is replacing or renewing an expired card. The act also requires the financial institution to provide you with specific information concerning your rights and responsibilities (including how to report losses and thefts, resolve errors, and stop payment of preauthorized transfers). A financial institution may send you a card that is "not valid for use" and that you alone have the power to validate if you choose to do so, after the institution has verified that you are the person for whom the card was intended.

Liability of the Financial Institution

The financial institution's failure to make an electronic fund transfer, in accordance with the terms and conditions of an account, in the correct amount or in a timely manner when properly instructed to do so by the consumer makes it liable for all damages proximately caused to the consumer, except where

1) the consumer's account has insufficient funds;

2) the funds are subject to legal process or other encumbrance restricting such transfer;

3) such transfer would exceed an established credit limit;

4) an electronic terminal has insufficient cash to complete the transaction; or

5) a circumstance beyond its control, where it exercised reasonable care to prevent such an occurrence, or exercised such diligence as the circumstances required.

Enforcement of the Act

A host of federal regulatory agencies oversees enforcement of the act. These include the Comptroller of the Currency (national banks), Federal Reserve District Bank (state member banks), Federal Deposit Insurance Corporation regional director (nonmember insured banks), Federal Home Loan Bank Board supervisory agent (members of the FHLB system and savings institutions insured by the Federal Savings & Loan Insurance Corporation), National Credit Union Administration (federal credit unions), Securities & Exchange Commission (brokers and dealers), and the Federal Trade Commission (retail and department stores) consumer finance companies, all nonbank debit card issuers, and certain other financial institutions. Additionally, consumers are empowered to sue (individually or as a class) for actual damages caused by any EFT system, plus penalties ranging from $100 to $1,000. Section 4, under "Customer's Duty to Inspect Bank Statements" (*Commerce Bank v. Brown*), discusses the bank's liability under the act.

Key Takeaway

Eager to reduce paperwork for both themselves and for customers, and to speed up the check collection process, financial institutions have for thirty years been moving away from paper checks and toward electronic fund transfers. These EFTs are ubiquitous, including ATMs, point-of-sale systems, direct deposits and withdrawals and online banking of various kinds. Responding to the need for consumer protection, Congress adopted the Electronic Fund Transfers Act, effective in 1978. The act addresses many common concerns consumers have about using electronic fund transfer systems, sets out liability for financial institutions and customers, and provides an enforcement mechanism.

Exercises

1. Why have EFTs become very common?
2. What major issues are addressed by the EFTA?
3. If you lose your credit card, what is your liability for unauthorized charges?

26.3 Wholesale Transactions and Letters of Credit

Learning Objectives

1. Understand what a "wholesale transaction" is; recognize that UCC Article 4A governs such transactions, and recognize how the Article addresses three common issues.
2. Know what a "letter of credit" (LC) is, the source of law regarding LCs, and how such instruments are used.

Wholesale Funds Transfers

wholesale funds transfers

Transfers of large sums of money—tens of millions of dollars—between businesses or between businesses and financial institutions.

Another way that money is transferred is by commercial fund transfers or **wholesale funds transfers**, which is by far the largest segment of the US payment system measured in amounts of money transferred. It is trillions of dollars a day. Wholesale transactions are the transfers of funds between businesses or financial institutions.

Background and Coverage

It was in the development of commercial "wholesale wire transfers" of money in the nineteeth and early twentieth centuries that businesses developed the processes enabling the creation of today's consumer electronic funds transfers. Professor Jane Kaufman Winn described the development of uniform law governing commercial funds transfers:

> *Although funds transfers conducted over funds transfer facilities maintained by the Federal Reserve Banks were subject to the regulation of the Federal Reserve Board, many funds transfers took place over private systems, such as the Clearing House for Interbank Payment Systems ("CHIPS"). The entire wholesale funds transfer system was not governed by a clear body of law until U.C.C. Article 4A was promulgated in 1989 and adopted by the states shortly thereafter. The Article 4A drafting process resulted in many innovations, even though it drew heavily on the practices that had developed among banks and their customers during the 15 years before the drafting committee was established. While a consensus was not easy to achieve, the community of interests shared by both the banks and their customers permitted the drafting process to find workable compromises on many thorny issues.*[7]

All states and US territories have adopted Article 4A. Consistent with other UCC provisions, the rights and obligations under Article 4A may be varied by agreement of the parties. Article 4A does not apply if any step of the transaction is governed by the Electronic Fund Transfer Act. Although the implication may be otherwise, the rules in Article 4A apply to any funds transfer, not just electronic ones (i.e., transfers by mail are covered, too). Certainly, however, electronic transfers are most common, and—as the Preface to Article 4A notes—a number of characteristics of them influenced the Code's rules. These transactions are characterized by large amounts of money—multimillions of dollars; the parties are sophisticated businesses or financial institutions; funds transfers are completed in one day, they are highly efficient substitutes for paper delivery; they are usually low cost—a few dollars for the funds transfer charged by the sender's bank.

Operation of Article 4A

The UCC "Prefatory Note" to Article 4A observes that "the funds transfer that is covered by Article 4A is not a complex transaction." To illustrate the operation of Article 4A, assume that Widgets International has an account with First Bank. In order to pay a supplier, Supplies Ltd., in China, Widgets instructs First Bank to pay $6 million to the account of Supplies Ltd. in China Bank. In the terminology of Article 4A, Widgets' instruction to its bank is a "payment order." Widgets is the "sender" of the payment order, First Bank is the "receiving bank," and Supplies Ltd. is the "beneficiary" of the order.

When First Bank performs the purchase order by instructing China Bank to credit the account of Supplies Limited, First Bank becomes a sender of a payment order, China Bank becomes a receiving bank, and Supplies Ltd. is still the beneficiary. This transaction is depicted in Figure 26.4. In some transactions there may also be one or more "intermediary banks" between First and Second Bank.

FIGURE 26.4
Funds Transfer

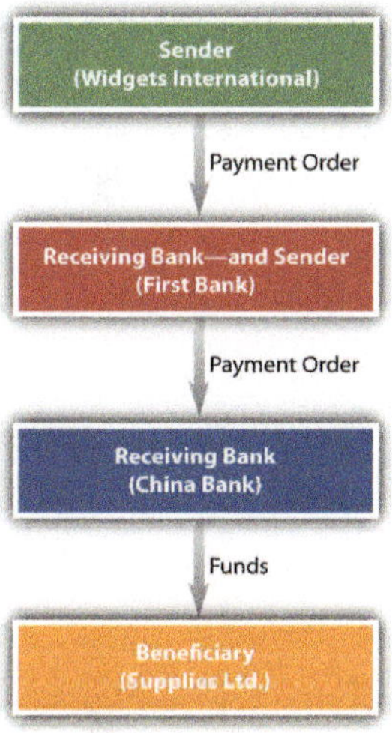

Frequently Occurring Legal Issues in Funds Transfers

Three legal issues that frequently arise in funds transfer litigation are addressed in Article 4A and might be mentioned here.

Responsibility for Unauthorized Payments

First, who is responsible for unauthorized payment orders? The usual practice is for banks and their customers to agree to security procedures for the verification of payment orders. If a bank establishes a commercially reasonable procedure, complies with that procedure, and acts in good faith and according to its agreement with the customer, the customer is bound by an unauthorized payment order. There is, however, an important exception to this rule. A customer will not be liable when the order is from a person unrelated to its business operations.

Error by Sender

Second, who is responsible when the sender makes a mistake—for instance, in instructing payment greater than what was intended? The general rule is that the sender is bound by its own error. But in cases where the error would have been discovered had the bank complied with its security procedure, the receiving bank is liable for the excess over the amount intended by the sender, although the bank is allowed to recover this amount from the beneficiary.

Bank Mistake in Transferring Funds

Third, what are the consequences when the bank makes a mistake in transferring funds? Suppose, for example, that Widgets (in the previous situation) instructed payment of $2 million but First Bank in turn instructed payment of $20 million. First Bank would be entitled to only $2 million from Widgets and would then attempt to recover the remaining $18 million from Supplies Ltd. If First Bank had instructed payment to the wrong beneficiary, Widgets would have no liability and the bank would be responsible for recovering the entire payment. Unless the parties agree otherwise, however, a bank that improperly executes a payment order is not liable for consequential damages.

Letters of Credit

Because international trade involves risks not usually encountered in domestic trade—government control of exports, imports, and currency; problems in verifying goods' quality and quantity; disruptions caused by adverse weather, war; and so on—merchants have over the years devised means to minimize these risks, most notably the letter of credit ("LC"). Here are discussed the definition of letters of credit, the source of law governing them, how they work as payments for exports and as payments for imports.

Definition

letter of credit

A statement by a bank (or other financial institution) that it will pay a specified sum of money to specific persons if certain conditions are met.

A **letter of credit** is a statement by a bank (or other financial institution) that it will pay a specified sum of money to specific persons if certain conditions are met. Or, to rephrase, it is a letter issued by a bank authorizing the bearer to draw a stated amount of money from the issuing bank (or its branches, or other associated banks or agencies). Originally, a letter of credit was quite literally that—a letter addressed by the buyer's bank to the seller's bank stating that the former could vouch for their good customer, the buyer, and that it would pay the seller in case of the buyer's default. An LC is issued by a bank on behalf of its creditworthy customers, whose application for the credit has been approved by that bank.

Source of Law

Letters of credit are governed by both international and US domestic law.

International Law

Many countries (including the United States) have bodies of law governing letters of credit. Sophisticated traders will agree among themselves by which body of law they choose to be governed. They can agree to be bound by the UCC, or they may decide they prefer to be governed by the Uniform Customs and Practice for Commercial Documentary Credits (UCP), a private code devised by the Congress of the International Chamber of Commerce. Suppose the parties do not stipulate a body of law for the agreement, and the various bodies of law conflict, what then? Julius is in New York and Rochelle is in Paris; does French law or New York law govern? The answer will depend on the particulars of the dispute. An American court must determine under the applicable principles of the law of "conflicts of law" whether New York or French law applies.

Domestic Law

The principal body of law applicable to the letter of credit in the United States is Article 5 of the UCC. Section 5-103 declares that Article 5 "applies to letters of credit and to certain rights and obligations arising out of transactions involving letters of credit." The Official Comment to 5-101 observes, "A letter of credit is an idiosyncratic form of undertaking that supports performance of an obligation incurred in a separate financial, mercantile, or other transaction or arrangement." And—as is the case in other parts of the Code—parties may, within some limits, agree to "variation by agreement in order to respond to and accommodate developments in custom and usage that are not inconsistent with the essential definitions and mandates of the statute." Although detailed consideration of Article 5 is beyond the scope of this book, a distinction between guarantees and letters of credit should be noted: Article 5 applies to the latter and not the former.

Letters of Credit as Payment for Exports

The following discussion presents how letters of credit work as payment for exports, and a sample letter of credit is presented at Figure 26.5.

FIGURE 26.5 A Letter of Credit

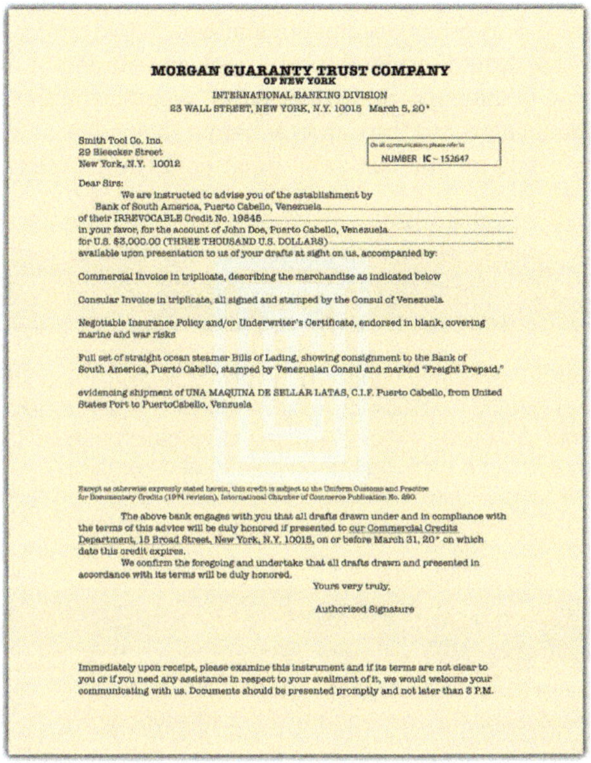

MORGAN GUARANTY TRUST COMPANY
OF NEW YORK
INTERNATIONAL BANKING DIVISION
23 WALL STREET, NEW YORK, N.Y. 10015 March 5, 20*

Smith Tool Co. Inc.
29 Bleecker Street
New York, N.Y. 10012

On all communications please refer to
NUMBER IC – 152647

Dear Sirs:

We are instructed to advise you of the astablishment by
Bank of South America, Puerto Cabello, Venezuela
of their IRREVOCABLE Credit No. 19846
in your favor, for the account of John Doe, Puerto Cabello, Venezuela
for U.S. $3,000.00 (THREE THOUSAND U.S. DOLLARS)
available upon presentation to us of your drafts at sight on us, accompanied by:

Commercial Invoice in triplicate, describing the merchandise as indicated below

Consular Invoice in triplicate, all signed and stamped by the Consul of Venezuela

Negotiable Insurance Policy and/or Underwriter's Certificate, endorsed in blank, covering marine and war risks

Full set of straight ocean steamer Bills of Lading, showing consignment to the Bank of South America, Puerto Cabello, stamped by Venezuelan Consul and marked "Freight Prepaid,"

evidencing shipment of UNA MAQUINA DE SELLAR LATAS, C.I.F. Puerto Cabello, from United States Port to PuertoCabello, Venzuela

Except as otherwise expressly stated herein, this credit is subject to the Uniform Customs and Practice for Documentary Credits (1974 revision), International Chamber of Commerce Publication No. 290.

The above bank engages with you that all drafts drawn under and in compliance with the terms of this advice will be duly honored if presented to our Commercial Credits Department, 15 Broad Street, New York, N.Y. 10015, on or before March 31, 20* on which date this credit expires.

We confirm the foregoing and undertake that all drafts drawn and presented in accordance with its terms will be duly honored.

Yours very truly,

Authorized Signature

Immediately upon receipt, please examine this instrument and if its terms are not clear to you or if you need any assistance in respect to your availment of it, we would welcome your communicating with us. Documents should be presented promptly and not later than 3 P.M.

Julius desires to sell fine quality magic wands and other stage props to Rochelle's Gallery in Paris. Rochelle agrees to pay by letter of credit—she will, in effect, get her bank to inform Julius that he will get paid if the goods are right. She does so by "opening" a letter of credit at her bank—the issuing bank—the Banque de Rue de Houdini where she has funds in her account, or good credit. She tells the bank the terms of sale, the nature and quantity of the goods, the amount to be paid, the documents she will require as proof of shipment, and an expiration date. Banque de Rue de Houdini then directs its correspondent bank in the United States, First Excelsior Bank, to inform Julius that the letter of credit has been opened: Rochelle is good for it. For Julius to have the strongest guarantee that he will be paid, Banque de Rou de Houdini can ask First Excelsior to confirm the letter of credit, thus binding both Banque de Rue de Houdini and Excelsior to pay according to the terms of the letter.

Once Julius is informed that the letter of credit has been issued and confirmed, he can proceed to ship the goods and draw a draft to present (along with the required documents such as commercial invoice, bill of lading, and insurance policy) to First Excelsior, which is bound to follow exactly its instructions from Banque de Rue de Houdini. Julius can present the draft and documents directly, through correspondent banks, or by a representative at the port from which he is shipping the goods. On presentation, First Excelsior may forward the documents to Banque de Rue de Houdini for approval and when First Excelsior is satisfied it will take the draft and pay Julius immediately on a sight draft or will stamp the draft "accepted" if it is a time draft (payable in thirty, sixty, or ninety days). Julius can discount an accepted time draft or hold it until it matures and cash it in for the full amount. First Excelsior will then forward the draft through international banking channels to Banque de Rue de Houdini to debit Rochelle's account.

As Payment for Imports

US importers—buyers—also can use the letter of credit to pay for goods bought from abroad. The importer's bank may require that the buyer put up collateral to guarantee it will be reimbursed for payment of the draft when it is presented by the seller's agents. Since the letter of credit ordinarily will be irrevocable, the bank will be bound to pay the draft when presented (assuming the proper documents are attached), regardless of deficiencies ultimately found in the goods. The bank will hold the bill of lading and other documents and could hold up transfer of the goods until the importer pays, but that would saddle the bank with the burden of disposing of the goods if the importer failed to pay. If the importer's credit rating is sufficient, the bank could issue a trust receipt. The goods are handed over to the importer before they are paid for, but the importer then becomes trustee of the goods for the bank and must hold the proceeds for the bank up to the amount owed

Key Takeaway

Wholesale funds transfers are a mechanism by which businesses and financial institutions can transmit large sums of money—millions of dollars—between each other, usually electronically, from and to their clients' accounts. Article 4A of the UCC governs these transactions. A letter of credit is a promise by a buyer's bank that upon presentation of the proper paperwork it will pay a specified sum to the identified seller. Letters of credit are governed by domestic and international law.

Exercises

1. What is a "wholesale funds transfer," and why would anybody want one?
2. A letter of credit is a letter issued by a bank to another bank (typically in a different country) to serve as a guarantee for payments made to a specified person under specified conditions. Why were letters of credit invented?

26.4 Cases

Bank's Liability for Paying over Customer's "Stop Payment" Order

Meade v. National Bank of Adams County

2002 WL 31379858 (Ohio App. 2002)

Kline, J.

The National Bank of Adams County appeals the Adams County Court's judgment finding that it improperly paid a check written by Denton Meade, and that Meade incurred $3,800 in damages as a result of that improper payment....

I.

Denton Meade maintained a checking account at the Bank. In 2001, Meade entered into an agreement with the Adams County Lumber Company to purchase a yard barn for $2,784 [about $3900 in 2017 dollars] and paid half the cost as a deposit. On the date of delivery, Friday, March 9, 2001, Meade issued a check to the Lumber Company for the remaining amount he owed on the barn, $1,406.79.

Meade was not satisfied with the barn. Therefore, at 5:55 p.m. on March 9, 2001, Meade called the Bank to place a stop payment order on his check. Jacqueline Evans took the stop payment order from Meade. She received all the information and authorization needed to stop payment on the check at that time.

Bank employees are supposed to enter stop payments into the computer immediately after taking them. However, Evans did not immediately enter the stop payment order into the computer because it was 6:00 p.m. on Friday, and the Bank closes at 6:00 p.m. on Fridays. Furthermore, the Bank's policy provides that any matters that are received after 2:00 p.m. on a Friday are treated as being received on the next business day, which was Monday, March 12, 2001 in this instance.

On the morning of Saturday, March 10, 2001, Greg Scott, an officer of the Lumber Company, presented the check in question for payment at the Bank. The Bank paid the check. On Monday, the Bank entered Meade's stop payment into the computer and charged Meade a $15 stop payment fee. Upon realizing that it already paid the check, on Tuesday the Bank credited the $15 stop payment fee back to Meade's account. On Thursday, the Bank deducted the amount of the check, $1,406.79, from Meade's account.

In the meanwhile, Meade contacted Greg Scott at the Lumber Company regarding his dissatisfaction with the barn. Scott sent workers to repair the barn on Saturday, March 10 and on Monday, March 12. However, Meade still was not satisfied. In particular, he was unhappy with the runners supporting the barn. Although his order with the Lumber Company specifically provided for 4 x 6" runner boards, the Lumber Company used 2 x 6" boards. The Lumber Company "laminated" the two by six-inch boards to make them stronger. However, carpenter Dennis Baker inspected the boards and determined that the boards were not laminated properly.

Meade hired Baker to repair the barn. Baker charged Meade approximately three hundred dollars to make the necessary repairs. Baker testified that properly laminated two by six-inch boards are just as strong as four by six-inch boards.

Meade filed suit against the Bank in the trial court seeking $5,000 in damages. The Bank filed a motion for summary judgment, which the trial court denied. At the subsequent jury trial the court permitted Meade to testify, over the Bank's objections, to the amount of his court costs, attorney fees, and deposition costs associated with this case. The Bank filed motions for directed verdict at the close of Meade's case and at the close of evidence, which the trial court denied.

The jury returned a general verdict finding the Bank liable to Meade in the amount of $3,800. The Bank filed motions for a new trial and for judgment notwithstanding the verdict, which the trial court denied. The Bank now appeals, asserting the following five assignments of error. * * *

II.

In its first assignment of error, the Bank contends that the trial court erred in denying its motion for summary judgment. Specifically, the Bank asserts that Meade did not issue the stop payment order within a reasonable time for the Bank to act upon it, and therefore that the trial court should have granted summary judgment in favor of the Bank.

Summary judgment is appropriate only when it has been established: (1) that there is no genuine issue as to any material fact; (2) that the moving party is entitled to judgment as a matter of law; and (3) that reasonable minds can come to only one conclusion, and that conclusion is adverse to the nonmoving party. [Citation]

[UCC 4-403(A)] provides that a customer may stop payment on any item drawn on the customer's account by issuing an order to the bank that describes the item with reasonable certainty and is received by the bank "at a time and in a manner that affords the bank a reasonable opportunity to act on it before any action by the bank with respect to the item." What constitutes a reasonable time depends upon the facts of the case. See *Chute v. Bank One of Akron*, (1983) [Citation]

In *Chute*, Bank One alleged that its customer, Mr. Chute, did not give it a reasonable opportunity to act upon his stop payment order when he gave an oral stop payment at one Bank One branch office, and a different Bank One branch office paid the check the following day. In ruling that Bank One had a reasonable opportunity to act upon Mr. Chute's order before it paid the check, the court considered the teller's testimony that stop payment orders are entered onto the computer upon receipt, where they are virtually immediately accessible to all Bank One tellers.

In this case, as in *Chute*, Meade gave notice one day, and the Bank paid the check the following day. Additionally, in this case, the same branch that took the stop payment order also paid the check. Moreover, Evans testified that the Bank's policy for stop payment orders is to enter them into the computer immediately, and that Meade's stop payment order may have shown up on the computer on Saturday if she had entered it on Friday. Based on this information, and construing the facts in the light most favorable to Meade, reasonable minds could conclude that Meade provided the Bank with the stop payment order within time for the Bank to act upon the stop payment order. Accordingly, we overrule the Bank's first assignment of error.

III.

In its second assignment of error, the Bank contends that the trial court erred in permitting Meade to testify regarding the amount he spent on court costs, attorney fees, and taking depositions. Meade contends that because he incurred these costs as a result of the Bank paying his check over a valid stop payment order, the costs are properly recoverable.

As a general rule, the costs and expenses of litigation, other than court costs, are not recoverable in an action for damages. [Citations]

In this case, the statute providing for damages, [UCC 4-403(c)], provides that a customer's recoverable loss for a bank's failure to honor a valid stop payment order "may include damages for dishonor of subsequent items * * *." The statute does not provide for recouping attorney fees and costs. Meade did not allege that the Bank acted in bad faith or that he is entitled to punitive damages. Additionally, although Meade argues that the Bank caused him to lose his bargaining power with the Lumber Company, Meade did not present any evidence that he incurred attorney fees or costs by engaging in litigation with the Lumber Company.

Absent statutory authority or an allegation of bad faith, attorney fees are improper in a compensatory damage award....Therefore, the trial court erred in permitting the jury to hear evidence regarding Meade's expenditures for his attorney fees and costs. Accordingly, we sustain the Bank's second assignment of error. * * *

IV.

In its third assignment of error, the Bank contends that the trial court erred when it overruled the Bank's motion for a directed verdict. The Bank moved for a directed verdict both at the conclusion of Meade's case and at the close of evidence.

The Bank first asserts that the record does not contain sufficient evidence to show that Meade issued a stop payment order that provided it with a reasonable opportunity to act as required by [the UCC]. Meade presented evidence that he gave the Bank his stop payment order prior to 6:00 p.m. on Friday, and that the Bank paid the check the following day. * * * We find that this constitutes sufficient evidence that Meade communicated the stop payment order to the Bank in time to allow the Bank a reasonable opportunity to act upon it.

The Bank also asserts that the record does not contain sufficient evidence that Meade incurred some loss resulting from its payment of the check. Pursuant to [UCC 4-403(c)] "[t]he burden of establishing the fact and amount of loss resulting from the payment of an item contrary to a stop payment order or order to close an account is on the customer." Establishing the fact and amount of loss, "the customer must show some loss other than the mere debiting of the customer's account." [Citation]

...Baker testified that he charged Meade between two hundred-eighty and three hundred dollars to properly laminate the runners and support the barn. Based upon these facts, we find that the record contains sufficient evidence that Meade sustained some loss beyond the mere debiting of his account as a result of the Bank paying his check. Accordingly, we overrule the Bank's third assignment of error.

V.

* * * [I]n its final assignment of error, the Bank contends that the trial court erred in denying its motions for judgment notwithstanding the verdict and for a new trial. * * *

[U]nlike our consideration of the Bank's motions for a directed verdict, in considering the Bank's motion for judgment notwithstanding the verdict, we also must consider whether the amount of the jury's award is supported by sufficient evidence. The Bank contends the jury's general verdict, awarding Meade $3,800, is not supported by evidence in the record.

A bank customer seeking damages for the improper payment of a check over a valid stop payment order carries the burden of proving "the fact and amount of loss." [UCC 4-403(C).] To protect banks and prevent unjust enrichment to customers, the mere debiting of the customer's account does not constitute a loss. [Citation]

In this case, the Bank's payment of Meade's $1,406.79 check to the Lumber Company discharged Meade's debt to the Lumber Company in the same amount. Therefore, the mere debiting of $1,406.79 from Meade's account does not constitute a loss.

Meade presented evidence that he incurred $300 in repair costs to make the barn satisfactory. Meade also notes that he never got the four by six-inch runners he wanted. However, Meade's carpenter, Baker, testified that since he properly laminated the two by six-inch runners, they are just as strong or stronger than the four by six-inch runners would have been.

Meade also presented evidence of his costs and fees. However, as we determined in our review of the Bank's second assignment of error, only the court may award costs and fees, and therefore this evidence was improperly admitted. Thus, the evidence cannot support the damage award. Meade did not present any other evidence of loss incurred by the Bank's payment of his check....Therefore, we find that the trial court erred in declining to enter a judgment notwithstanding the verdict on the issue of damages. Upon remand, the trial court should grant in part the Bank's motion for judgment notwithstanding the verdict as it relates to damages and consider the Bank's motion for a new trial only on the issue of damages [* * *]. Accordingly, we sustain the Banks fourth and fifth assignments of error in part.

VI.

In conclusion, we find that the trial court did not err in denying the Bank's motions for summary judgment and for directed verdict. However, we find that the trial court erred in permitting Meade to testify as to his court costs, attorney fees and deposition costs. Additionally, we find that the trial court erred in totally denying the Bank's motion for judgment notwithstanding the verdict, as the amount of damages awarded by the jury is not supported by sufficient evidence in the record. Accordingly, we affirm the judgment of the trial court as to liability, but reverse the judgment of the trial court as to the issue of damages, and remand this cause for further proceedings consistent with this opinion.

Case Questions

1. What did the bank do wrong here?
2. Why did the court deny Meade damages for his attorneys' fees?
3. Why did the court conclude that the jury-awarded damages were not supported by evidence presented at trial? What damages did the evidence support?

Customer's Duty to Inspect Bank Statements

Union Planters Bank, Nat. Ass'n v. Rogers
912 So.2d 116 (Miss. 2005)

Waller, J.

This appeal involves an issue of first impression in Mississippi—the interpretation of [Mississippi's UCC 4-406], which imposes duties on banks and their customers insofar as forgeries are concerned.

Facts

Neal D. and Helen K. Rogers maintained four checking accounts with the Union Planters Bank in Greenville, Washington County, Mississippi. * * * The Rogers were both in their eighties when the events which gave rise to this lawsuit took place.[8] After Neal became bedridden, Helen hired Jackie Reese to help her take care of Neal and to do chores and errands.

In September of 2000, Reese began writing checks on the Rogers' four accounts and forged Helen's name on the signature line. Some of the checks were made out to "cash," some to "Helen K. Rogers," and some to "Jackie Reese." The following chart summarizes the forgeries to each account:

Account Number	Beginning	Ending	Number of Checks	Amount of Checks
54282309	11/27/2000	6/18/2001	46	$16,635.00
0039289441	9/27/2000	1/25/2001	10	$2,701.00
6100110922	11/29/2000	8/13/2001	29	$9,297.00
6404000343	11/20/2000	8/16/2001	83	$29,765.00
Total			168	$58,398.00

Neal died in late May of 2001. Shortly thereafter, the Rogers' son, Neal, Jr., began helping Helen with financial matters. Together they discovered that many bank statements were missing and that there was not as much money in the accounts as they had thought. In June of 2001, they contacted Union Planters and asked for copies of the missing bank statements. In September of 2001, Helen was advised by Union Planters to contact the police due to forgeries made on her accounts. More specific dates and facts leading up to the discovery of the forgeries are not found in the record.

Subsequently, criminal charges were brought against Reese. (The record does not reveal the disposition of the criminal proceedings against Reese.) In the meantime, Helen filed suit against Union Planters, alleging conversion (unlawful payment of forged checks) and negligence. After a trial, the jury awarded Helen $29,595 [about $40,000 in 2017 dollars] in damages, and the circuit court entered judgment accordingly. From this judgment, Union Planters appeals.

Discussion

II. Whether Rogers' Delay in Detecting the Forgeries Barred Suit against Union Planters.

The relationship between Rogers and Union Planters is governed by Article 4 of the Uniform Commercial Code. [UCC] 4-406(a) and (c) provide that a bank customer has a duty to discover and report "unauthorized signatures"; i.e., forgeries. [The section] reflects an underlying policy decision that furthers the UCC's "objective of promoting certainty and predictability in commercial transactions." The UCC facilitates financial transactions, benefiting both consumers and financial institutions, by allocating responsibility among the parties according to whomever is best able to prevent a loss. Because the customer is more familiar with his own signature, and should know whether or not he authorized a particular withdrawal or check, he can prevent further unauthorized activity better than a financial institution which may process thousands of transactions in a single day....The customer's duty to exercise this care is triggered when the bank satisfies its burden to provide sufficient information to the customer. As a result, if the bank provides sufficient information, the customer bears the loss when he fails to detect and notify the bank about unauthorized transactions. [Citation]

A. Union Planters' Duty to Provide Information under 4-406(a).

The court admitted into evidence copies of all Union Planters statements sent to Rogers during the relevant time period. Enclosed with the bank statements were either the cancelled checks themselves or copies of the checks relating to the period of time of each statement. The evidence shows that all bank statements and cancelled checks were sent, via United States Mail, postage prepaid, to all customers at their "designated address" each month. Rogers introduced no evidence to the contrary. We therefore find that the bank fulfilled its duty of making the statements available to Rogers and that the remaining provisions of 4-406 are applicable to the case at bar. * * *

In defense of her failure to inspect the bank statements, Rogers claims that she never received the bank statements and cancelled checks. Even if this allegation is true,[9] it does not excuse Rogers from failing to fulfill her duties under 4-406(a) & (c) because the statute clearly states a bank discharges its duty in providing the necessary information to a customer when it "sends...to a customer a statement of account showing payment of items." * * * The word "receive" is absent. The customer's duty to inspect and report does not arise when the statement is received, as Rogers claims; the customer's duty to inspect and report arises when the bank sends the statement to the customer's address. A reasonable person who has not received a monthly statement from the bank would promptly ask the bank for a copy of the statement. Here, Rogers claims that she did not receive numerous statements. We find that she failed to act reasonably when she failed to take any action to replace the missing statements.

B. Rogers' Duty to Report the Forgeries under 4-406(d).

[Under UCC 4-406] a customer who has not promptly notified a bank of an irregularity may be precluded from bringing certain claims against the bank:

> *"(d) If the bank proves that the customer failed, with respect to an item, to comply with the duties imposed on the customer by subsection (c), the customer is precluded from asserting against the bank:*
>
> *(1) The customer's unauthorized signature . . . on the item, . . .*

Also, when there is a series of forgeries, 406(d)(2) places additional duties on the customer, [who is precluded from asserting against the bank]:

> *(2) The customer's unauthorized signature...by the same wrongdoer on any other item paid in good faith by the bank if the payment was made before the bank received notice from the customer of the unauthorized signature...and after the customer had been afforded a reasonable period of time, not exceeding thirty (30) days, in which to examine the item or statement of account and notify the bank.*

Although there is no mention of a specific date, Rogers testified that she and her son began looking for the statements in late May or early June of 2001, after her husband had died....When they discovered that statements were missing, they notified Union Planters in June of 2001 to replace the statements. At this time, no mention of possible forgery was made, even though Neal, Jr., thought that "something was wrong." In fact, Neal, Jr., had felt that something was wrong as far back as December of 2000, but failed to do anything. Neal, Jr., testified that neither he nor his mother knew that Reese had been forging checks until September of 2001.[10]

Rogers is therefore precluded from making claims against Union Planters because (1) under 4-406(a), Union Planters provided the statements to Rogers, and (2) under 4-406(d)(2), Rogers failed to notify Union Planters of the forgeries within 30 days of the date she should have reasonably discovered the forgeries. * * *

Conclusion

The circuit court erred in denying Union Planters' motion for JNOV because, under 4-406, Rogers is precluded from recovering amounts paid by Union Planters on any of the forged checks because she failed to timely detect and notify the bank of the unauthorized transactions and because she failed to show that Union Planters failed to use ordinary care in its processing of the forged checks. Therefore, we reverse the circuit court's judgment and render judgment here that Rogers take nothing and that the complaint and this action are finally dismissed with prejudice. Reversed.

Case Questions

1. If a bank pays out over a forged drawer's signature one time, and the customer (drawer) reports the forgery to the bank within thirty days, why does the bank take the loss?
2. Who forged the checks?
3. Why did Mrs. Rogers think she should not be liable for the forgeries?
4. In the end, who probably really suffered the loss here?

Customer's Duty to Inspect Bank Statements

Commerce Bank of Delaware v. Brown
2007 WL 1207171 (Del. Com. Pl. 2007)

I. Procedural Posture

Plaintiff, Commerce Bank/Delaware North America ("Commerce") initially filed a civil complaint against defendant Natasha J. Brown ("Brown") on October 28, 2005. Commerce seeks judgment in the amount of $4.020.11 plus costs and interest and alleges that Brown maintained a checking account with Commerce and has been unjustly enriched by $4,020.11. * * *

The defendant, Brown...denied all allegations of the complaint. As an affirmative defense Brown claims the transaction for which plaintiff seeks to recover a money judgment were made by means of an ATM Machine using a debit card issued by the defendant. On January 16, 2005 Brown asserts that she became aware of the fraudulent transactions and timely informed the plaintiff of the facts on January 16, 2005. Brown asserts that she also requested Commerce in her answer to investigate the matter and to close her account. Based upon these facts, Brown asserts a maximum liability on her own part from $50.00 to $500.00 in accordance with the Electronic Fund Transfer Act ("EFTA") 15 U.S.C. § 1693(g) and regulation (e), 12 CFR 205.6. [Commerce Bank withdrew its complaint at trial, leaving only the defendant's counter-claim in issue.]

Defendant Brown asserts [that] defendant failed to investigate and violated EFTA and is therefore liable to the plaintiff for money damages citing [EFTA].

II. The Facts

Brown was the only witness called at trial. Brown is twenty-seven years old and has been employed by Wilmington Trust as an Administrative Assistant for the past three years. Brown previously opened a checking account with Commerce and was issued a debit/ATM card by Commerce which was in her possession in December 2004. Brown, on or about January 14, 2005 went to Commerce to charge a $5.00 debit to the card at her lunch-break was informed that there was a deficiency balance in the checking account. Brown went to the Talleyville branch of Commerce Bank and spoke with "Carla" who agreed to investigate these unauthorized charges, as well as honor her request to close the account. Defendant's Exhibit No.: 1 is a Commerce Bank electronic filing and/or e-mail which details a visit by defendant on January 16, 2005 to report her card loss. The "Description of Claim" indicates as follows:

Customer came into speak with a CSR "Carla Bernard" on January 16, 2005 to report her card loss. At this time her account was only showing a negative $50.00 balance. She told Ms. Bernard that this was not her transaction and to please close this account. Ms. Bernard said that she would do this and that there would be an investigation on the unauthorized transactions. It was at this time also that she had Ms. Bernard change her address. In the meantime, several transactions posted to the account causing a balance of negative $3,948.11 and this amount has since been charged off on 1/27/05. Natasha Brown never received any notification of this until she received a letter from one of our collection agencies. She is now here to get this resolved.

On the back of defendant's Exhibit No.: 1 were 26 separate unauthorized transactions at different mercantile establishments detailing debits with the pin number used on Brown's debit card charged to Commerce Bank. The first charge was $501.75 on January 13, 2005....Brown asserts at trial that she therefore timely gave notice to Commerce to investigate and requested Commerce to close the debit checking account on January 16, 2005.

At trial Brown also testified she "never heard" from Commerce again until she received a letter in December 2005 citing a $4,000.00 deficiency balance....

On cross-examination Brown testified she received a PIN number from Commerce and "gave the PIN number to no other person." In December 2004 she resided with Charles Williams, who is now her husband. Brown testified on cross-examination that she was the only person authorized as a PIN user and no one else knew of the card, 'used the card,' or was provided orally or in writing of the PIN number. Brown spoke with Carla Bernard at the Commerce Bank at the Talleyville branch. Although Brown did not initially fill out a formal report, she did visit Commerce on January 16, 2005 the Talleyville branch and changed her address with Carla. Brown does not recall the last time she ever received a statement from Commerce Bank on her checking account. Brown made no further purchases with the account and she was unaware of all the "incidents of unauthorized debit charges on her checking account" until she was actually sued by Commerce Bank in the Court of Common Pleas.

III. The Law

15 U.S.C. § 1693(g). Consumer Liability:

(a) Unauthorized electronic fund transfers; limit. A consumer shall be liable for any unauthorized electronic fund transfer. . . . In no event, however, shall a consumer's liability for an unauthorized transfer exceed the lesser of—

(1) $ 50; or

(2) the amount of money or value of property or services obtained in such unauthorized electronic fund transfer prior to the time the financial institution is notified of, or otherwise becomes aware of, circumstances which lead to the reasonable belief that an unauthorized electronic fund transfer involving the consumer's account has been or may be affected. Notice under this paragraph is sufficient when such steps have been taken as may be reasonably required in the ordinary course of business to provide the financial institution with the pertinent information, whether or not any particular officer, employee, or agent of the financial institution does in fact receive such information.

15 U.S.C. § 1693(m) Civil Liability:

(a) [A]ction for damages; amount of award....[A]ny person who fails to comply with any provision of this title with respect to any consumer, except for an error resolved in accordance with section 908, is liable to such consumer in an amount equal to the sum of—

(1) any actual damage sustained by such consumer as a result of such failure;

(2) in the case of an individual action, an amount not less than $ 100 nor greater than $ 1,000; or . . .

(3) in the case of any successful action to enforce the foregoing liability, the costs of the action, together with a reasonable attorney's fee as determined by the court.

12 C.F.R. § 205.6 Liability of consumer for unauthorized transfers.

(b) Limitations on amount of liability. A consumer's liability for an unauthorized electronic fund transfer or a series of related unauthorized transfers shall be determined as follows:

(1) Timely notice given. If the consumer notifies the financial institution within two business days after learning of the loss or theft of the access device, the consumer's liability shall not exceed the lesser of $ 50 or the amount of unauthorized transfers that occur before notice to the financial institution.

(2) Timely notice not given. If the consumer fails to notify the financial institution within two business days after learning of the loss or theft of the access device, the consumer's liability shall not exceed the lesser of $ 500 or the sum of:

(i) $ 50 or the amount of unauthorized transfers that occur within the two business days, whichever is less; and

(ii) The amount of unauthorized transfers that occur after the close of two business days and before notice to the institution, provided the institution establishes that these transfers would not have occurred had the consumer notified the institution within that two-day period.

IV. Opinion and Order

The Court finds based upon the testimony presented herein that defendant in her counter-claim has proven by a preponderance of evidence damages in the amount of $1,000.00 plus an award of attorney's fees. Clearly, Commerce failed to investigate the unauthorized charges pursuant to 15 U.S.C. § 1693(h). Nor did Commerce close the account as detailed in Defendant's Exhibit No. 1. Instead, Commerce sued Brown and then withdrew its claim at trial. The Court finds $50.00 is the appropriate liability for Brown for the monies charged on her account as set forth within the above statute because she timely notified, in person, Commerce on January 16, 2005. Brown also requested Commerce to close her checking account. Based upon the trial record, defendant has proven by a preponderance of the evidence damages of $1,000.00 as set forth in the above statute, 15 U.S.C. § 1693(m).

Case Questions

1. Why—apparently—did the bank withdraw its complaint against Brown at the time of trial?
2. Why does the court mention Ms. Brown's occupation, and that she was at the time of the incident living with the man who was—at the time of trial—her husband?
3. What is the difference between the United States Code (USC) and the *Code of Federal Regulations* (CFR), both of which are cited by the court?
4. What did the bank do wrong here?
5. What damages did Ms. Brown suffer for which she was awarded $1,000? What else did she get by way of an award that is probably more important?

26.5 Summary and Exercises

Summary

Traditionally when a customer wrote a check (on the payor bank) and the payee deposited it into his account (at the depository bank), the check was physically routed by means of ground and air transportation to the various intermediary banks until it was physically presented to the payor bank for final settlement. The federal Check 21 Act (2004) promotes changes in this process by allowing banks to process electronic images of customers' checks instead of the actual paper instrument: the data on the check is truncated (stripped) from the instrument and the data are transmitted. The original check can be digitally recreated by the making of a "substitute check." Merchants—indeed, anyone with a check scanner and a computer—can also process electronic data from checks to debit the writer's account and credit the merchant's instantly.

In addition to Check 21 Act, the Electronic Fund Transfer Act of 1978 also facilitates electronic banking. It primarily addresses the uses of credit and debit cards. Under this law, the electronic terminal must provide a receipt of transfer. The financial institution must follow certain procedures on being notified of errors, the customer's liability is limited to $50 if a card or code number is wrongfully used and the institution has been notified, and an employer or government agency can compel acceptance of salary or government benefits by EFT.

Article 4 of the UCC—state law, of course—governs a bank's relationship with its customers. It permits a bank to pay an overdraft, to pay an altered check (charging the customer's account for the original tenor of the check), to refuse to pay a six-month-old check, to pay or collect an item of a deceased person (if it has no notice of death) and obligates it to honor stop payment orders. A bank is liable to the customer for damages if it wrongfully dishonors an item. The customer also has duties; primarily, the customer must inspect each statement of account and notify the bank promptly if the checks have been altered or signatures forged. The federal Expedited Funds Availability Act requires that, within some limits, banks make customers' funds available quickly.

Wholesale funds transactions, involving tens of millions of dollars, were originally made by telegraph ("wire transfers"). The modern law governing such transactions is, in the United States, UCC Article 4A.

A letter of credit is a statement by a bank or other financial institution that it will pay a specified sum of money to specified persons when certain conditions are met. Its purpose is to facilitate nonlocal sales transactions by ensuring that the buyer will not get access to the goods until the seller has proper access to the buyer's money. In the US letters of credit are governed by UCC Article 5, and in international transactions they may be covered by a different internationally recognized law.

Exercises

1. On March 20, Al gave Betty a check for $1,000. On March 25, Al gave Carl a check for $1,000, which Carl immediately had certified. On October 24, when Al had $1,100 in his account, Betty presented her check for payment and the bank paid her $1,000. On October 25, Carl presented his check for payment and the bank refused to pay because of insufficient funds. Were the bank's actions proper?
2. Winifred had a balance of $100 in her checking account at First Bank. She wrote a check payable to her landlord in the amount of $400. First Bank cashed the check and then attempted to charge her account. May it? Why?
3. Assume in Exercise 2 that Winifred had deposited $4,000 in her account a month before writing the check to her landlord. Her landlord altered the check by changing the amount from $400 to $4,000 and then cashed the check at First Bank. May the bank charge Winifred's account for the check? Why?
4. Assume in Exercise 2 that Winifred had deposited $5,000 in her account a month before writing the check but the bank misdirected her deposit, with the result that her account showed

a balance of $100. Believing the landlord's check to be an overdraft, the bank refused to pay it. Was the refusal justified? Why?

5. Assume in Exercise 2 that, after sending the check to the landlord, Winifred decided to stop payment because she wanted to use the $300 in her account as a down payment on a stereo. She called First Bank and ordered the bank to stop payment. Four days later the bank mistakenly paid the check. Is the bank liable to Winifred? Why?
6. Assume in Exercise 5 that the landlord negotiated the check to a holder in due course, who presented the check to the bank for payment. Is the bank required to pay the holder in due course after the stop payment order? Why?
7. On Wednesday, August 4, Able wrote a $1,000 check on his account at First Bank. On Saturday, August 7, the check was cashed, but the Saturday activity was not recorded by the bank until Monday, August 9. On that day at 8:00 a.m., Able called in a stop payment order on the check and he was told the check had not cleared; at 9:00 he went to the bank and obtained a printed notice confirming the stop payment, but shortly thereafter the Saturday activity was recorded—Able's account had been debited. He wants the $1,000 recredited. Was the stop payment order effective? Explain.
8. Alice wrote a check to Carl's Contracting for $190 on April 23, 2011. Alice was not satisfied with Carl's work. She called, leaving a message for him to return the call to discuss the matter with her. He did not do so, but when she reconciled her checks upon receipt of her bank statement, she noticed the check to Carl did not appear on the April statement. Several months went by. She figured Carl just tore the check up instead of bothering to resolve any dispute with her. The check was presented to Alice's bank for payment on March 20, 2012, and Alice's bank paid it. May she recover from the bank?
9. Fitting wrote a check in the amount of $800. Afterwards, she had second thoughts about the check and contacted the bank about stopping payment. A bank employee told her a stop payment order could not be submitted until the bank opened the next day. She discussed with the employee what would happen if she withdrew enough money from her account that when the $800 check was presented, there would be insufficient funds to cover it. The employee told her that in such a case the bank would not pay the check. Fitting did withdraw enough money to make the $800 an overdraft, but the bank paid it anyway, and then sued her for the amount of the overdraft. Who wins and why? *Continental Bank v. Fitting*, 559 P.2d 218 (1977).
10. Plaintiff's executive secretary forged plaintiff's name on number checks by signing his name and by using a rubber facsimile stamp of his signature: of fourteen checks that were drawn on her employer's account, thirteen were deposited in her son's account at the defendant bank, and one was deposited elsewhere. Evidence at trial was presented that the bank's system of comparing its customer's signature to the signature on checks was the same as other banks in the area. Plaintiff sued the bank to refund the amount of the checks paid out over a forged drawer's signature. Who wins and why? *Read v. South Carolina National Bank*, 335 S.E.2d 359 (S.C., 1965).
11. On Tuesday morning, Reggie discovered his credit card was not in his wallet. He realized he had not used it since the previous Thursday when he'd bought groceries. He checked his online credit card account register and saw that some $1,700 had been charged around the county on his card. He immediately notified his credit union of the lost card and unauthorized charges. For how much is Reggie liable?

Self-Test Questions

1. Article 4 of the UCC permits a bank to pay
   a. an overdraft
   b. an altered check
   c. an item of a deceased person if it has no notice of death
   d. all of the above
2. The type of banks covered by Article 4 include

a. depository banks
b. payor banks
c. both of the above
d. none of the above

3. A bank may
   a. refuse to pay a check drawn more than six months before being presented
   b. refuse to pay a check drawn more than sixty days before being presented
   c. not refuse to pay a check drawn more than six months before being presented
   d. do none of the above
4. Forms of electronic fund transfer include
   a. automated teller machines
   b. point of sale terminals
   c. preauthorized payment plans
   d. all of the above

Self-Test Answers

1. d
2. c
3. a
4. d

Endnotes

1. Scott Schuh, *Overview of the Survey of Consumer Payment Choice (SCPC) Program*, Federal Reserve Bank of Boston, p. 5 (May 2010). http://www.bos.frb.org/economic/cprc/presentations/2010/Schuh050610.pdf.
2. Barbara Bennett, et al., *Cash Continues to Play a Key Role in Consumer Spending: Evidence from the Diary of Consumer Payment Choice*, Federal Reserve Bank of San Francisco, April 2014. http://www.frbsf.org/cash/publications/fed-notes/2014/april/cash-consumer-spending-payment-diary#figure1.
3. United States Treasury, *The Check Clearing for the 21st Century Act: Frequently Asked Questions*, October 2004, http://www.justice.gov/ust/eo/private_trustee/library/chapter07/docs/check21/Check21FAQs-final.pdf.
4. Susan Tompor, *Know When the Check Clears with Smartphone Deposits*, *Detroit Free Press*, January 8, 2015. http://www.freep.com/story/money/personal-finance/susan-tompor/2015/01/08/mobile-check-deposit-smartphone-banking-susan-tompor/21410239/.
5. *Is it illegal to post-date a check?* Nolo, Law for All. http://www.nolo.com/legal-encyclopedia/is-illegal-post-date-check.html.
6. FDIC, "Electronic Fund Transfer Act of 1978," http://www.fdic.gov/regulations/laws/rules/6500-1350.html.
7. Jane Kaufman Winn, *Clash of the Titans: Regulating the Competition between Established and Emerging Electronic Payment Systems*, http://www.law.washington.edu/Directory/docs/Winn/Clash%20of%20the%20Titans.htm.
8. Neal Rogers died prior to the institution of this lawsuit. Helen Rogers died after Union Planters filed this appeal. We have substituted Helen's estate as appellee.
9. Since there was a series of forged checks, it is reasonable to assume that Reese intercepted the bank statements before Rogers could inspect them. However, Union Planters cannot be held liable for Reese's fraudulent concealment.
10. Actually, it was Union Planters that notified Rogers that there had been forgeries, as opposed to Rogers' discovering the forgeries herself.

CHAPTER 27

Consumer Credit Transactions

Learning Objectives

After reading this chapter, you should understand the following:

1. How consumers enter into credit transactions and what protections they are afforded when they do.
2. What rights consumers have after they have entered into a consumer transaction.
3. What debt collection practices third-party collectors may pursue.

This chapter and the three that follow are devoted to debtor-creditor relations. In this chapter, we focus on the consumer credit transaction. Chapter 28 and Chapter 29 explore different types of security that a creditor might require. Chapter 30 examines debtors' and creditors' rights under bankruptcy law.

The amount of consumer debt, or **household debt**, owed by Americans to mortgage lenders, stores, automobile dealers, and other merchants who sell on credit is difficult to ascertain. One reads that the average household *credit card* debt (not including mortgages, auto loans, and student loans) in 2014 was almost $16,000.[1] Or maybe it was $7,300.[2] Or maybe it was $2,700.[3] But probably focusing on the *average* household debt is not very helpful: 55 percent of households have no credit card debt at all, and the *median* debt is $1,000 for those in the lowest percentile of income-earners, and $7,900 for those in the top percentile of income.[4]

household debt

Debt owed by consumers.

In 2014, the total household debt owed by Americans was $11.8 trillion, according to the Federal Reserve Board. That is really an incomprehensible number: suffice it to say, then, that the availability of credit is an important factor in the U.S. economy, and not surprisingly, a number of statutes have been enacted over the years to protect consumers both before and after signing credit agreements.

The statutes tend to fall within three broad categories. First, several statutes are especially important when a consumer enters into a credit transaction. These include laws that regulate credit costs, the credit application, and the applicant's right to check a credit record. Second, after a consumer has contracted for credit, certain statutes give a consumer the right to cancel the contract and correct billing mistakes. Third, if the consumer fails to pay a debt, the creditor has several traditional debt collection remedies that today are tightly regulated by the government.

Following banking scandals and the accompanying "Great Recession" of 2008, in 2010 Congress created the Consumer Finance Protection Bureau to help—as the agency's name suggests—protect consumers against certain kinds of abusive commercial financial practices.

27.1 Entering into a Credit Transaction

Learning Objectives

1. Understand what statutes regulate the cost of credit, and the exceptions.
2. Know how the cost of credit is expressed in the Truth in Lending Act.
3. Recognize that there are laws prohibiting discrimination in credit granting.
4. Understand how consumers' credit records are maintained and may be corrected.

The Cost of Credit

Usury

Charging interest in excess of the legal limit.

Lenders, whether banks or retailers, are not necessarily free to charge whatever they wish for credit. **Usury** laws establish a maximum rate of lawful interest. The penalties for violating usury laws vary from state to state. The heaviest penalties are loss of both principal and interest, or loss of a multiple of the interest the creditor charged. The courts often interpret these laws stringently, so that even if the impetus for a usurious loan comes from the borrower, the contract can be avoided, as demonstrated in *Matter of Dane's Estate* (Section 3).

Some states have eliminated interest rate limits altogether. In other states, usury law is riddled with exceptions, and indeed, in many cases, the exceptions have pretty much eaten up the general rule. Here are some common exceptions:

- Business loans. In many states, businesses may be charged any interest rate, although some states limit this exception to incorporated businesses.
- Mortgage loans. Mortgage loans are often subject to special usury laws. The allowable interest rates vary, depending on whether a first mortgage or a subordinate mortgage is given, or whether the loan is insured or provided by a federal agency, among other variables.
- Second mortgages and home equity loans by licensed consumer loan companies.
- Credit card and other retail installment debt. The interest rate for these is governed by the law of the state where the credit card company does business. (That's why the giant Citibank, otherwise headquartered in New York City, runs its credit card division out of South Dakota, which has no usury laws for credit cards.)
- Consumer leasing.
- "Small loans" such as payday loans and pawnshop loans.
- Lease-purchases on personal property. This is the lease-to-own concept.
- Certain financing of mobile homes that have become real property or where financing is insured by the federal government.
- Loans a person takes from her tax-qualified retirement plan.
- Certain loans from stockbrokers and dealers.
- Interest and penalties on delinquent property taxes.
- Deferred payment of purchase price (layaway loans).
- Statutory interest on judgments.

And there are others. Moreover, certain charges are not considered interest, such as fees to record documents in a public office and charges for services such as title examinations, deed preparation, credit reports, appraisals, and loan processing. But a creditor may not use these devices to cloak what is in fact a usurious bargain; it is not the form but the substance of the agreement that controls.

As suggested, part of the difficulty here is that governments at all levels have for a generation attempted to promote consumption to promote production; production is required to maintain politically acceptable levels of employment. If consumers can get what they want on credit, consumerism increases. Also, certainly, tight limits on interest rates cause creditors to deny credit to the less creditworthy, which may not be helpful to the lower classes. That's the rationale for the usury exceptions related to pawnshop and payday loans.

Disclosure of Credit Costs

Setting limits on what credit costs—as usury laws do—is one thing. Disclosing the cost of credit is another.

The Truth in Lending Act

Until 1969, lenders were generally free to disclose the cost of money loaned or credit extended in any way they saw fit—and they did. Financing and credit terms varied widely, and it was difficult and sometimes impossible to understand what the true cost was of a particular loan, much less to comparison shop. After years of failure, consumer interests finally persuaded Congress to pass a national law requiring disclosure of credit costs in 1968. Officially called the Consumer Credit Protection Act, Title I of the law is more popularly known as the **Truth in Lending Act** (TILA). The act only applies to *consumer* credit transactions, and it only protects natural-person debtors—it does not protect business organization debtors.

Truth in Lending Act

A federal act ensuring that every individual who has need for consumer credit is given full disclosure of the terms and cost of the credit.

The act provides what its name implies: lenders must inform borrowers about significant terms of the credit transaction. The TILA does not establish maximum interest rates; these continue to be governed by state law. The two key terms that must be disclosed are the finance charge and the annual percentage rate. To see why, consider two simple loans of $1,000, each carrying interest of 10 percent, one payable at the end of twelve months and the other in twelve equal installments. Although the actual charge in each is the same—$100—the interest rate is not. Why? Because with the first loan you will have the use of the full $1,000 for the entire year; with the second, for much less than the year because you must begin repaying part of the principal within a month. In fact, with the second loan you will have use of only about half the money for the entire year, and so the actual rate of interest is closer to 15 percent. Things become more complex when interest is compounded and stated as a monthly figure, when different rates apply to various portions of the loan, and when processing charges and other fees are stated separately. The act regulates open-end credit (revolving credit, like charge cards) and closed-end credit (like a car loan—extending for a specific period), and—as amended later—it regulates consumer leases and credit card transactions, too.

FIGURE 27.1 Credit Disclosure Form

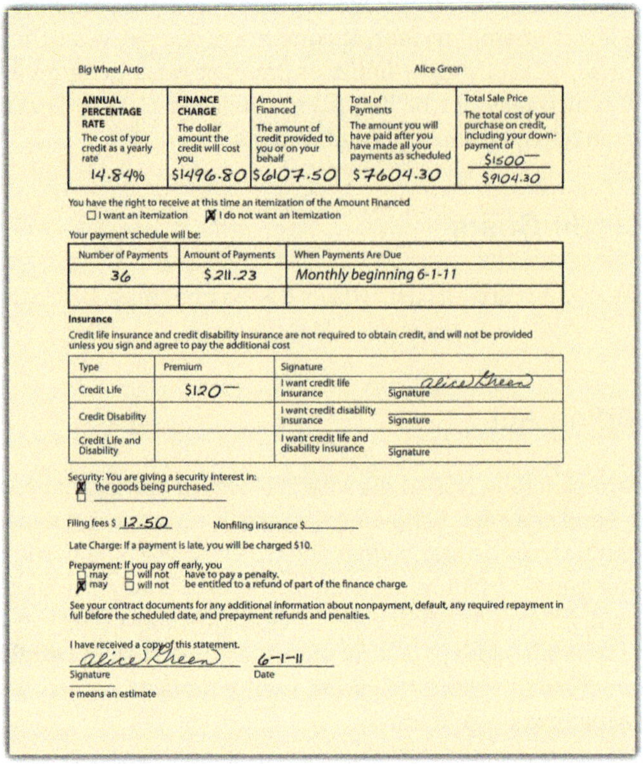

Big Wheel Auto Alice Green

ANNUAL PERCENTAGE RATE The cost of your credit as a yearly rate	FINANCE CHARGE The dollar amount the credit will cost you	Amount Financed The amount of credit provided to you or on your behalf	Total of Payments The amount you will have paid after you have made all your payments as scheduled	Total Sale Price The total cost of your purchase on credit, including your down-payment of $1500—
14.84%	$1496.80	$6107.50	$7604.30	$9104.30

You have the right to receive at this time an itemization of the Amount Financed
☐ I want an itemization ☒ I do not want an itemization

Your payment schedule will be:

Number of Payments	Amount of Payments	When Payments Are Due
36	$211.23	Monthly beginning 6-1-11

Insurance

Credit life insurance and credit disability insurance are not required to obtain credit, and will not be provided unless you sign and agree to pay the additional cost

Type	Premium	Signature
Credit Life	$120—	I want credit life insurance Signature Alice Green
Credit Disability		I want credit disability insurance Signature
Credit Life and Disability		I want credit life and disability insurance Signature

Security: You are giving a security interest in:
☒ the goods being purchased.
☐ ______________

Filing fees $ 12.50 Nonfiling insurance $______

Late Charge: If a payment is late, you will be charged $10.

Prepayment: If you pay off early, you
☐ may ☐ will not have to pay a penalty.
☒ may ☐ will not be entitled to a refund of part of the finance charge.

See your contract documents for any additional information about nonpayment, default, any required repayment in full before the scheduled date, and prepayment refunds and penalties.

I have received a copy of this statement.

Alice Green 6-1-11
Signature Date

e means an estimate

finance charge

The total cost of credit a customer must pay on a consumer loan, including interest.

By requiring that the finance charge and the annual percentage rate be disclosed on a uniform basis, the TILA makes understanding and comparison of loans much easier. The **finance charge** is the total of all money paid for credit; it includes the interest paid over the life of the loan and all processing charges. The annual percentage rate is the true rate of interest for money or credit actually available to the borrower. The annual percentage rate must be calculated using the total finance charge (including all extra fees). See Figure 27.1 for an example of a disclosure form used by creditors.

Consumer Leasing Act of 1988

The Consumer Leasing Act (CLA) amends the TILA to provide similar full disclosure for consumers who lease automobiles or other goods from firms whose business it is to lease such goods, if the goods are valued at $25,000 or less and the lease is for four months or more. All material terms of the lease must be disclosed in writing.

Fair Credit and Charge Card Disclosure

In 1989, the Fair Credit and Charge Card Disclosure Act went into effect. This amends the TILA by requiring credit card issuers to disclose in a uniform manner the annual percentage rate, annual fees, grace period, and other information on credit card applications.

Credit Card Accountability, Responsibility, and Disclosure Act of 2009

The 1989 act did make it possible for consumers to know the costs associated with credit card use, but the card companies' behavior over 20 years convinced Congress that more regulation was required. In 2009, Congress passed and President Obama signed the Credit Card Accountability,

Responsibility, and Disclosure Act of 2009 (the CARD Act). It is a further amendment of the TILA. Some of the salient parts of the act are as follows:

- Restricts all interest rate increases during the first year, with some exceptions. The purpose is to abolish "teaser" rates.
- Increases notice for rate increase on future purchases to 45 days.
- Preserves the ability to pay off on the old terms, with some exceptions.
- Limits fees and penalty interest and requires statements to clearly state the required due date and late payment penalty.
- Requires fair application of payments. Amounts in excess of the minimum payment must be applied to the highest interest rate (with some exceptions).
- Provides sensible due dates and time to pay.
- Protects young consumers. Before issuing a card to a person under the age of twenty-one, the card issuer must obtain an application that contains either the signature of a cosigner over the age of twenty-one or information indicating an independent means of repaying any credit extended.
- Restricts card issuers from providing tangible gifts to students on college campuses in exchange for filling out a credit card application.
- Requires colleges to publicly disclose any marketing contracts made with a card issuer.
- Requires enhanced disclosures.
- Requires issuers to disclose the period of time and the total interest it will take to pay off the card balance if only minimum monthly payments are made.
- Limits credit to young adults. No credit cards can be issued to anyone under 21 absent an adult co-signer, unless the young adult can show proof of enough income. Credit card companies must stay at least 1,000 feet from college campuses if they offer free food or other gifts as enticements to get students to apply for credit cards.
- Establishes gift card protections.[5]

Consumer credit cards are governed by the act, not those used for business, and not debit cards. The Consumer Financial Protection Bureau administers the CARD Act, and more information about the act is available at the CFPB's website: http://www.consumerfinance.gov/credit-cards/credit-card-act/feb2011-factsheet/.

Creditors who violate the TILA are subject to both criminal and civil sanctions. Of these, the most important are the civil remedies open to consumers. If a creditor fails to disclose the required information, a customer may sue to recover twice the finance charge, plus court costs and reasonable attorneys' fees, with some limitations. As to the Credit Card Act of 2009, the issuing companies were not happy with the reforms. Before the law went into effect, the companies—as one commentator put it—unleashed a "frenzy of retaliation,"[6] by repricing customer accounts, changing fixed rates to variable rates, lowering credit limits, and increasing fees.

State Credit Disclosure Laws

The federal TILA is not the only statute dealing with credit disclosures. A uniform state act, the Uniform Consumer Credit Code, as amended in 1974, is now on the books in twelve U.S. jurisdictions,[7] though its effect on the development of modern consumer credit law has been significant beyond the number of states adopting it. It is designed to protect consumers who buy goods and services on credit by simplifying, clarifying, and updating legislation governing consumer credit and usury.

Getting Credit

Disclosure of credit costs is a good thing. After discovering how much credit will cost, a person might decide to go for it: get a loan or a credit card. The potential creditor, of course, should want to know if the applicant is a good risk; that requires a credit check. And somebody who knows another person's creditworthiness has what is usually considered confidential information, the possession of which is subject to abuse, and thus regulation.

Equal Credit Opportunity Act

Through the 1960s, banks and other lending and credit-granting institutions regularly discriminated against women. Banks told single women to find a cosigner for loans. Divorced women discovered that they could not open store charge accounts because they lacked a prior credit history, even though they had contributed to the family income on which previous accounts had been based. Married couples found that the wife's earnings were not counted when they sought credit; indeed, families planning to buy homes were occasionally even told that the bank would grant a mortgage if the wife would submit to a hysterectomy! In all these cases, the premise of the refusal to treat women equally was the unstated—and usually false—belief that women would quit work to have children or simply to stay home.

By the 1970s, as women became a major factor in the labor force, Congress reacted to the manifest unfairness of the discrimination by enacting (as part of the Consumer Credit Protection Act) the Equal Credit Opportunity Act (ECOA) of 1974. The act prohibits any creditor from discriminating "against any applicant on the basis of sex or marital status with respect to any aspect of a credit transaction." In 1976, Congress broadened the law to bar discrimination (1) on the basis of race, color, religion, national origin, and age; (2) because all or a part of an applicant's income is from a public assistance program; or (3) because an applicant has exercised his or her rights under the Consumer Credit Protection Act.

Under the ECOA, a creditor may not ask a credit applicant to state sex, race, national origin, or religion. And unless the applicant is seeking a joint loan or account or lives in a community-property state, the creditor may not ask for a statement of marital status or, if you have voluntarily disclosed that you are married, for information about your spouse, nor may one spouse be required to cosign if the other is deemed independently creditworthy. All questions concerning plans for children are improper. In assessing the creditworthiness of an applicant, the creditor must consider all sources of income, including regularly received alimony and child support payments. And if credit is refused, the creditor must, on demand, tell you the specific reasons for rejection. See *Rosa v. Park West Bank & Trust Co.* in Section 3 for a case involving the ECOA.

The Home Mortgage Disclosure Act, 1975, and the Community Reinvestment Act (CRA), 1977, get at another type of discrimination: redlining. This is the practice by a financial institution of refusing to grant home loans or home-improvement loans to people living in low-income neighborhoods. The act requires that financial institutions within its purview report annually by transmitting information from their Loan Application Registers to a federal agency. From these reports it is possible to determine what is happening to home prices in a particular area, whether investment in one neighborhood lags compared with that in others, if the racial or economic composition of borrowers changed over time, whether minorities or women had trouble accessing mortgage credit, in what kinds of neighborhoods subprime loans are concentrated, and what types of borrowers are most likely to receive subprime loans, among others. "Armed with hard facts, users of all types can better execute their work: Advocates can launch consumer education campaigns in neighborhoods being targeted by subprime lenders, planners can better tailor housing policy to market conditions, affordable housing developers can identify gentrifying neighborhoods, and activists can confront banks with poor lending records in low income communities."[8] Under the CRA, federal regulatory agencies examine banking institutions for CRA compliance and take this information into consideration when approving applications for new bank branches or for mergers or acquisitions.

Fair Credit Reporting Act of 1970: Checking the Applicant's Credit Record

It is in the interests of all consumers that people who would be bad credit risks not get credit: if they do and they default (fail to pay their debts), the rest of us end up paying for their improvidence. Because credit is such a big business, a number of support industries have grown up around it. One of the most important is the credit-reporting industry, which addresses this issue of checking creditworthiness. Certain companies—**credit bureaus**—collect information about borrowers, holders of credit cards, store accounts, and installment purchasers. For a fee, this information—currently held on tens of millions of Americans—is sold to companies anxious to know whether applicants are creditworthy. If the information is inaccurate, it can lead to rejection of a credit application that should be approved, and it can wind up in other files where it can live to do more damage. In 1970, Congress enacted, as part of the Consumer Credit Protection Act, the Fair Credit Reporting Act (FCRA) to give consumers access to their credit files in order to correct errors.

credit bureau

A private firm that maintains consumer credit data files and provides credit information to authorized users for a fee.

Under this statute, an applicant denied credit has the right to be told the name and address of the credit bureau (called "consumer reporting agency" in the act) that prepared the report on which the denial was based. (The law covers reports used to screen insurance and job applicants as well as to determine creditworthiness.) The agency must list the nature and substance of the information (except medical information) and its sources (unless they contributed to an investigative-type report). A credit report lists such information as name, address, employer, salary history, loans outstanding, and the like. An investigative-type report is one that results from personal interviews and may contain nonfinancial information, like drinking and other personal habits, character, or participation in dangerous sports. Since the investigators rely on talks with neighbors and coworkers, their reports are usually subjective and can often be misleading and inaccurate.

The agency must furnish the consumer the information free if requested within thirty days of rejection and must also specify the name and address of anyone who has received the report within the preceding six months (two years if furnished for employment purposes).

If the information turns out to be inaccurate, the agency must correct its records; if investigative material cannot be verified, it must be removed from the file. Those to whom it was distributed must be notified of the changes. When the agency and the consumer disagree about the validity of the information, the consumer's version must be placed in the file and included in future distributions of the report. After seven years, any adverse information must be removed (ten years in the case of bankruptcy). A person is entitled to one free copy of his or her credit report from each of the three main national credit bureaus every twelve months. If a reporting agency fails to correct inaccurate information in a reasonable time, it is liable to the consumer for $1,000 plus attorneys' fees.

Under the FCRA, any person who obtains information from a credit agency under false pretenses is subject to criminal and civil penalties. The act is enforced by the Federal Trade Commission. See *Rodgers v. McCullough* in Section 3 for a case involving use of information from a credit report.

Key Takeaway

Credit is an important part of the U.S. economy, and there are various laws regulating its availability and disclosure. Usury laws prohibit charging excessive interest rates, though the laws are riddled with exceptions. The disclosure of credit costs is regulated by the Truth in Lending Act of 1969, the Consumer Leasing Act of 1988, the Fair Credit and Charge Card Disclosure Act of 1989, and the Credit Card Accountability, Responsibility, and Disclosure Act of 2009 (these latter three are amendments to the TILA). Some states have adopted the Uniform Consumer Credit Code as well. Two major laws prohibit invidious discrimination in the granting of credit: the Equal

Credit Opportunity Act of 1974 and the Home Mortgage Disclosure Act of 1975 (addressing the problem of redlining). The Fair Credit Reporting Act of 1970 governs the collection and use of consumer credit information held by credit bureaus.

Exercises

1. The penalty for usury varies from state to state. What are the two typical penalties?
2. What has the TILA done to the use of *interest* as a term to describe how much credit costs, and why?
3. What is redlining?
4. What does the Fair Credit Reporting Act do, in general?

27.2 Consumer Credit Protection Laws and Debt Collection Practices

Learning Objectives

1. Understand that consumers have the right to cancel some purchases made on credit.
2. Know how billing mistakes may be corrected.
3. Recognize that professional debt collectors are governed by some laws restricting certain practices.

Cancellation Rights

Ordinarily, a contract is binding when signed. But consumer protection laws sometimes provide an escape valve. For example, a Federal Trade Commission (FTC) regulation gives consumers three days to cancel contracts made with door-to-door salespersons. Under this cooling-off provision, the cancellation is effective if made by midnight of the third business day after the date of the purchase agreement. The salesperson must notify consumers of this right and supply them with two copies of a cancellation form, and the sales agreement must contain a statement explaining the right. The purchaser cancels by returning one copy of the cancellation form to the seller, who is obligated either to pick up the goods or to pay shipping costs. The three-day cancellation privilege applies only to sales of twenty-five dollars or more made either in the home or away from the seller's place of business; it does not apply to sales made by mail or telephone, to emergency repairs and certain other home repairs, or to real estate, insurance, or securities sales.

The Truth in Lending Act (TILA) protects consumers in a similar way. For certain big-ticket purchases (such as installations made in the course of major home improvements), sellers sometimes require a mortgage (which is subordinate to any preexisting mortgages) on the home. The law gives such customers three days to rescind the contract. Many states have laws similar to the FTC's three-day cooling-off period, and these may apply to transactions not covered by the federal rule (e.g., to purchases of less than twenty-five dollars and even to certain contracts made at the seller's place of business).

Correcting Billing Mistakes

Billing Mistakes

In 1975, Congress enacted the **Fair Credit Billing Act** as an amendment to the Consumer Credit Protection Act. It was intended to put to an end the phenomenon, by then a standard part of any comedian's repertoire, of the many ways a computer could insist that you pay a bill, despite errors and despite letters you might have written to complain. The act, which applies only to open-end credit and not to installment sales, sets out a procedure that creditors and customers must follow to rectify claimed errors. The customer has sixty days to notify the creditor of the nature of the error and the amount. Errors can include charges not incurred or those billed with the wrong description, charges for goods never delivered, accounting or arithmetic errors, failure to credit payments or returns, and even charges for which you simply request additional information, including proof of sale. During the time the creditor is replying, you need not pay the questioned item or any finance charge on the disputed amount.

Fair Credit Billing Act

A federal law (1975) to protect consumers from unfair billing practices and to provide a mechanism for addressing billing errors in open-end credit accounts, such as credit card or charge card accounts.

The creditor has thirty days to respond and ninety days to correct your account or explain why your belief that an error has been committed is incorrect. If you do turn out to be wrong, the creditor is entitled to all back finance charges and to prompt payment of the disputed amount. If you persist in disagreeing and notify the creditor within ten days, it is obligated to tell all credit bureaus to whom it sends notices of delinquency that the bill continues to be disputed and to tell you to whom such reports have been sent; when the dispute has been settled, the creditor must notify the credit bureaus of this fact. Failure of the creditor to follow the rules, an explanation of which must be provided to each customer every six months and when a dispute arises, bars it from collecting the first fifty dollars in dispute, plus finance charges, even if the creditor turns out to be correct.

Disputes about the Quality of Goods or Services Purchased

While disputes over the quality of goods are not "billing errors," the act does apply to unsatisfactory goods or services purchased by credit card (except for store credit cards); the customer may assert against the credit card company any claims or defenses he or she may have against the seller. This means that under certain circumstances, the customer may withhold payments without incurring additional finance charges. However, this right is subject to three limitations: (1) the value of the goods or services charged must be in excess of fifty dollars, (2) the goods or services must have been purchased either in the home state or within one hundred miles of the customer's current mailing address, and (3) the consumer must make a good-faith effort to resolve the dispute before refusing to pay. If the consumer does refuse to pay, the credit card company would acquiesce: it would credit her account for the disputed amount, pass the loss down to the merchant's bank, and that bank would debit the merchant's account. The merchant would then have to deal with the consumer directly.

Debt Collection Practices

Banks, financial institutions, and retailers have different incentives for extending credit—for some, a loan is simply a means of making money, and for others, it is an inducement to buyers. But in either case, credit is a risk because the consumer may default; the creditor needs a means of collecting when the customer fails to pay. Open-end credit is usually given without collateral. The creditor can, of course, sue, but if the consumer has no assets, collection can be troublesome. Historically, three different means of recovering the debt have evolved: garnishment, wage assignment, and confession of judgment.

Garnishment

garnishment

The attachment or seizure of personal wages through a court-assisted process.

Garnishment is a legal process by which a creditor obtains a court order directing the debtor's employer (or any party who owes money to the debtor) to pay directly to the creditor a certain portion of the employee's wages until the debt is paid. Until 1970, garnishment was regulated by state law, and its effects could be devastating—in some cases, even leading to suicide. In 1970, Title III of the Consumer Credit Protection Act asserted federal control over garnishment proceedings for the first time. The federal wage-garnishment law limits the amount of employee earnings that may be withheld in any one pay date to the lesser of 25 percent of disposable (after-tax) earnings or the amount by which disposable weekly earnings exceed thirty times the highest current federal minimum wage. The federal law covers everyone who receives personal earnings, including wages, salaries, commissions, bonuses, and retirement income (though not tips), but it allows courts to garnish above the federal maximum in cases involving support payments (e.g., alimony), in personal bankruptcy cases, and in cases where the debt owed is for state or federal tax.

The federal wage-garnishment law also prohibits an employer from firing any worker solely because the worker's pay has been garnished for one debt (multiple garnishments may be grounds for discharge). The penalty for violating this provision is a $1,000 fine, one-year imprisonment, or both. But the law does not say that an employee fired for having one debt garnished may sue the employer for damages. In a 1980 case, the Fifth Circuit Court of Appeals denied an employee the right to sue, holding that the statute places enforcement exclusively in the hands of the federal secretary of labor.[9]

The 1970 federal statute is not the only limitation on the garnishment process. Note that the states can also still regulate garnishment so long as the state regulation is not in conflict with federal law: North Carolina, Pennsylvania, South Carolina, and Texas prohibit most garnishments, unless it is the government doing the garnishment (as for child-support payments). And there is an important constitutional limitation as well. Many states once permitted a creditor to garnish the employee's wage even before the case came to court: a simple form from the clerk of the court was enough to freeze a debtor's wages, often before the debtor knew a suit had been brought. In 1969, the U.S. Supreme Court held that this prejudgment garnishment procedure was unconstitutional.[10]

Wage Assignment

wage assignment

A clause in a loan contract that allows the lender to obtain the borrower's wages in the case of a default.

A **wage assignment** is an agreement by an employee that a creditor may take future wages as security for a loan or to pay an existing debt. With a wage assignment, the creditor can collect directly from the employer. However, in some states, wage assignments are unlawful, and an employer need not honor the agreement (indeed, it would be liable to the employee if it did). Other states regulate wage assignments in various ways—for example, by requiring that the assignment be a separate instrument, not part of the loan agreement, and by specifying that no wage assignment is valid beyond a certain period of time (two or three years).

Confession of Judgment

confession of judgment

A written agreement in which the defendant in a lawsuit admits liability and accepts the amount of agreed-upon damages that must be paid to the plaintiff.

Because suing is at best nettlesome, many creditors have developed forms that allow them to sidestep the courthouse when debtors have defaulted. As part of the original credit agreement, the consumer or borrower waives his right to defend himself in court by signing a **confession of judgment**. This written instrument recites the debtor's agreement that a court order be automatically entered against him in the event of default. The creditor's lawyer simply takes the confession of judgment to the clerk of the court, who enters it in the judgment book of the court without ever consulting a judge. Entry of the judgment entitles the creditor to attach the debtor's assets to satisfy the debt. Like prejudgment garnishment, a confession of judgment gives the consumer no right to be heard, and it has been banned by statute or court decisions in many states.

Fair Debt Collection Practices Act of 1977

Many stores, hospitals, and other organizations attempt on their own to collect unpaid bills, but thousands of merchants, professionals, and small businesses rely on collection agencies to recover accounts receivable. The debt collection business employed some 216,000 people in 2007 and collected over $40 billion in debt.[11] For decades, some of these collectors used harassing tactics: posing as government agents or attorneys, calling at the debtor's workplace, threatening physical harm or loss of property or imprisonment, using abusive language, publishing a deadbeats list, misrepresenting the size of the debt, and telling friends and neighbors about the debt. To provide a remedy for these abuses, Congress enacted, as part of the Consumer Credit Protection Act, the Fair Debt Collection Practices Act (FDCPA) in 1977.

This law regulates the manner by which third-party collection agencies conduct their business. It covers collection of all personal, family, and household debts by collection agencies. It does not deal with collection by creditors themselves; the consumer's remedy for abusive debt collection by the creditor is in tort law.

Under the FDCPA, the third-party collector may contact the debtor only during reasonable hours and not at work if the debtor's employer prohibits it. The debtor may write the collector to cease contact, in which case the agency is prohibited from further contact (except to confirm that there will be no further contact). A written denial that money is owed stops the bill collector for thirty days, and he can resume again only after the debtor is sent proof of the debt. Collectors may no longer file suit in remote places, hoping for default judgments; any suit must be filed in a court where the debtor lives or where the underlying contract was signed. The use of harassing and abusive tactics, including false and misleading representations to the debtor and others (e.g., claiming that the collector is an attorney or that the debtor is about to be sued when that is not true), is prohibited. Unless the debtor has given the creditor her cell phone number, calls to cell phones (but not to landlines) are not allowed.[12] In any mailings sent to the debtor, the return address cannot indicate that it is from a debt collection agency (so as to avoid embarrassment from a conspicuous name on the envelope that might be read by third parties).

Communication with third parties about the debt is not allowed, except when the collector may need to talk to others to trace the debtor's whereabouts (though the collector may not tell them that the inquiry concerns a debt) or when the collector contacts a debtor's attorney, if the debtor has an attorney. The federal statute gives debtors the right to sue the collector for damages for violating the statute and for causing such injuries as job loss or harm to reputation.

The Consumer Finance Protection Bureau

Background. In July 2010, Congress, responding to the financial crisis and the "Great Recession," adopted the Dodd-Frank Wall Street Reform and Consumer Protection Act. The priorities of the Consumer Finance Protection Agency, created under the authority of this statute, are mortgages, credit cards, and student loans. The agency is an independent unit inside the U.S. Federal Reserve, and it works with state regulators.

The agency's website says CFPB's "central mission . . . is to make markets for consumer financial products and services work for Americans—whether they are applying for a mortgage, choosing among credit cards, or using any number of other consumer financial products."[13] And the website also provides that "The CFPB is an independent federal agency built to protect consumers. We write and enforce rules that keep banks and other financial companies operating fairly. We also educate and empower consumers, helping them make more informed choices to achieve their financial goals."

Activities

The agency has an accessible and informative website which allows consumers to submit complaints if they think they've been abused by a financial institution; the website has "consumer tools," "educational resources," "data and research," "policy and compliance," as well as "about us."

In the "policy and compliance" section is a sub-section on rulemaking, and within that (drill down) a statement of "Final Rules" issued by the Agency. To get a sense of what the agency has been doing since it opened its doors in 2010, here are some of the rules:

Electronic Fund Transfers (Regulation E); Amendments

Prepaid Accounts under the Electronic Fund Transfer Act (Regulation E) and the Truth In Lending Act (Regulation Z)

Status of New Uniform Residential Loan Application and Collection of Expanded Home Mortgage Disclosure Act Information about Ethnicity and Race in 2017 under Regulation B

In September, 2016, the CFPB fined Wells Fargo Bank $185 million for opening fraudulent bank-customer accounts. It appears some irregular banking practices remain notwithstanding the fire that burned through the financial industry in the middle of the second decade of the 21st century (http://www.wsj.com/articles/wells-fargo-to-pay-185-million-fine-over-account-openings-1473352548).

Key Takeaway

Several laws regulate practices after consumer credit transactions. The FTC provides consumers with a three-day cooling-off period for some in-home sales, during which time the consumer-purchaser may cancel the sale. The TILA and some state laws also have some cancellation provisions. Billing errors are addressed by the Fair Credit Billing Act, which gives consumers certain rights. Debt collection practices such as garnishment, wage assignments, and confessions of judgment are regulated (and in some states prohibited) by federal and state law. Debt collection practices for third-party debt collectors are constrained by the Fair Debt Collection Practices Act.

Exercises

1. Under what circumstances may a consumer have three days to avoid a contract?
2. How does the Fair Credit Billing Act resolve the problem that occurs when a consumer disputes a bill and "argues" with a computer about it?
3. What is the constitutional problem with garnishment as it was often practiced before 1969?
4. If Joe of Joe's Garage wants to collect on his own the debts he is owed, he is not constrained by the FDCPA. What limits are there on his debt collection practices?

27.3 Cases

Usury

Matter of Dane's Estate

390 N.Y.S.2d 249 (N.Y.A.D. 1976)

MAHONEY, J.

On December 17, 1968, after repeated requests by decedent [Leland Dane] that appellant [James Rossi] loan him $10,500 [about $72,000 in 2017 dollars] the latter drew a demand note in that amount and with decedent's consent fixed the interest rate at 7 1/2% per annum, the then maximum annual interest permitted being 7 1/4%. Decedent executed the note and appellant gave him the full amount of the note in cash. * * * [The estate] moved for summary judgment voiding the note on the ground that it was a usurious loan, the note having been previously rejected as a claim against the estate. The [lower court] granted the motion, voided the note, and enjoined any prosecution on it thereafter. Appellant's cross motion to enforce the claim was denied.

New York's usury laws are harsh, and courts have been reluctant to extend them beyond cases that fall squarely under the statutes [Citation]. [New York law] makes any note for which more than the legal rate of interests is 'reserved or taken' or 'agreed to be reserved or taken' void. [The law] commands cancellation of a note in violation of [its provisions]. Here, since both sides concede that the note evidences the complete agreement between the parties, we cannot aid appellant by reliance upon the presumption that he did not make the loan at a usurious rate [Citation]. The terms of the loan are not in dispute. Thus, the note itself establishes, on its face, clear evidence of usury. There is no requirement of a specific intent to violate the usury statute. A general intent to charge more than the legal rate as evidenced by the note, is all that is needed. If the lender intends to take and receive a rate in excess of the legal percentage at the time the note is made, the statute condemns the act and mandates its cancellation [Citation]. The showing, as here, that the note reserves to the lender an illegal rate of interest satisfies respondents' burden of proving a usurious loan.

Next, where the rate of interest on the face of a note is in excess of the legal rate, it cannot be argued that such a loan may be saved because the borrower prompted the loan or even set the rate. The usury statutes are for the protection of the borrower and [their] purpose would be thwarted if the lender could avoid its consequences by asking the borrower to set the rate. Since the respondents herein asserted the defense of usury, it cannot be said that the decedent waived the defense by setting or agreeing to the 7 1/2% Rate of interest.

Finally, equitable considerations cannot be indulged when, as here, a statute specifically condemns an act. The statute fixes the law, and it must be followed.

The order should be affirmed, without costs.

Case Questions

1. What is the consequence to the lender of charging usurious rates in New York?
2. The rate charged here was one-half of one percent in excess of the allowable limit. Who made the note, the borrower or the lender? That makes no difference, but should it?
3. What "equitable considerations" were apparently raised by the creditor?

Discrimination under the ECOA

Rosa v. Park West Bank & Trust Co.
214 F.3d 213, C.A.1 (Mass. 2000)

Lynch, J.

Lucas Rosa sued the Park West Bank & Trust Co. under the Equal Credit Opportunity Act (ECOA), 15 U.S.C. §§ 1691–1691f, and various state laws. He alleged that the Bank refused to provide him with a loan application because he did not come dressed in masculine attire and that the Bank's refusal amounted to sex discrimination under the Act. The district court granted the Bank's motion to dismiss the ECOA claim. * * *

I.

According to the complaint, which we take to be true for the purpose of this appeal, on July 21, 1998, Mr. Lucas Rosa came to the Bank to apply for a loan. A biological male, he was dressed in traditionally feminine attire. He requested a loan application from Norma Brunelle, a bank employee. Brunelle asked Rosa for identification. Rosa produced three forms of photo identification: (1) a Massachusetts Department of Public Welfare Card; (2) a Massachusetts Identification Card; and (3) a Money Stop Check Cashing ID Card. Brunelle looked at the identification cards and told Rosa that she would not provide him with a loan application until he "went home and changed." She said that he had to be dressed like one of the identification cards in which he appeared in more traditionally male attire before she would provide him with a loan application and process his loan request.

II.

Rosa sued the Bank for violations of the ECOA and various Massachusetts antidiscrimination statutes. Rosa charged that "[b]y requiring [him] to conform to sex stereotypes before proceeding with the credit transaction, [the Bank] unlawfully discriminated against [him] with respect to an aspect of a credit transaction on the basis of sex." He claims to have suffered emotional distress, including anxiety, depression, humiliation, and extreme embarrassment. Rosa seeks damages, attorney's fees, and injunctive relief.

Without filing an answer to the complaint, the Bank moved to dismiss....The district court granted the Bank's motion. The court stated:

> *[T]he issue in this case is not [Rosa's] sex, but rather how he chose to dress when applying for a loan. Because the Act does not prohibit discrimination based on the manner in which someone dresses, Park West's requirement that Rosa change his clothes does not give rise to claims of illegal discrimination. Further, even if Park West's statement or action were based upon Rosa's sexual orientation or perceived sexual orientation, the Act does not prohibit such discrimination.*

Price Waterhouse v. Hopkins (U.S. Supreme Court, 1988), which Rosa relied on, was not to the contrary, according to the district court, because that case "neither holds, nor even suggests, that discrimination based merely on a person's attire is impermissible."

On appeal, Rosa says that the district court "fundamentally misconceived the law as applicable to the Plaintiff's claim by concluding that there may be no relationship, as a matter of law, between telling a bank customer what to wear and sex discrimination." ...The Bank says that Rosa loses for two reasons. First, citing cases pertaining to gays and transsexuals, it says that the ECOA does not apply to crossdressers. Second, the Bank says that its employee genuinely could not identify Rosa, which is why she asked him to go home and change.

III.

* * * In interpreting the ECOA, this court looks to Title VII case law, that is, to federal employment discrimination law. * * * The Bank itself refers us to Title VII case law to interpret the ECOA.

The ECOA prohibits discrimination, "with respect to any aspect of a credit transaction[,] on the basis of race, color, religion, national origin, sex or marital status, or age." 15 U.S.C. § 1691(a). Thus to prevail, the alleged discrimination against Rosa must have been "on the basis of . . . sex." See [Citation.] The ECOA's sex discrimination prohibition "protects men as well as women."

While the district court was correct in saying that the prohibited bases of discrimination under the ECOA do not include style of dress or sexual orientation, that is not the discrimination alleged. It is alleged that the Bank's actions were taken, in whole or in part, "on the basis of... [the appellant's] sex." The Bank, by seeking dismissal under Rule 12(b)(6), subjected itself to rigorous standards. We may affirm dismissal "only if it is clear that no relief could be granted under any set of facts that could be proved consistent with the allegations." [Citations] Whatever facts emerge, and they may turn out to have nothing to do with sex-based discrimination, we cannot say at this point that the plaintiff has no viable theory of sex discrimination consistent with the facts alleged.

The evidence is not yet developed, and thus it is not yet clear why Brunelle told Rosa to go home and change. It may be that this case involves an instance of disparate treatment based on sex in the denial of credit. See [Citation]; ("'Disparate treatment'...is the most easily understood type of discrimination. The employer simply treats some people less favorably than others because of their...sex."); [Citation] (invalidating airline's policy of weight limitations for female "flight hostesses" but not for similarly situated male "directors of passenger services" as impermissible disparate treatment); [Citation] (invalidating policy that female employees wear uniforms but that similarly situated male employees need wear only business dress as impermissible disparate treatment); [Citation] (invalidating rule requiring abandonment upon marriage of surname that was applied to women, but not to men). It is reasonable to infer that Brunelle told Rosa to go home and change because she thought that Rosa's attire did not accord with his male gender: in other words, that Rosa did not receive the loan application because he was a man, whereas a similarly situated woman would have received the loan application. That is, the Bank may treat, for credit purposes, a woman who dresses like a man differently than a man who dresses like a woman. If so, the Bank concedes, Rosa may have a claim. Indeed, under *Price Waterhouse*, "stereotyped remarks [including statements about dressing more 'femininely'] can certainly be evidence that gender played a part." [Citation.] It is also reasonable to infer, though, that Brunelle refused to give Rosa the loan application because she thought he was gay, confusing sexual orientation with cross-dressing. If so, Rosa concedes, our precedents dictate that he would have no recourse under the federal Act. See [Citation]. It is reasonable to infer, as well, that Brunelle simply could not ascertain whether the person shown in the identification card photographs was the same person that appeared before her that day. If this were the case, Rosa again would be out of luck. It is reasonable to infer, finally, that Brunelle may have had mixed motives, some of which fall into the prohibited category.

It is too early to say what the facts will show; it is apparent, however, that, under some set of facts within the bounds of the allegations and non-conclusory facts in the complaint, Rosa may be able to prove a claim under the ECOA. * * *

We reverse and remand for further proceedings in accordance with this opinion.

Case Questions

1. Could the bank have denied Mr. Rosa a loan because he was gay?
2. If a woman had applied for loan materials dressed in traditionally masculine attire, could the bank have denied her the materials?
3. The Court offers up at least three possible reasons why Rosa was denied the loan application. What were those possible reasons, and which of them would have been valid reasons to deny him the application?
4. To what federal law does the court look in interpreting the application of the ECOA?
5. Why did the court rule in Mr. Rosa's favor when the facts as to why he was denied the loan application could have been interpreted in several different ways?

Uses of Credit Reports under the FCRA

Rodgers v. McCullough

296 F.Supp.2d 895 (W.D. Tenn. 2003)

Background

This case concerns Defendants' receipt and use of Christine Rodgers' consumer report. The material facts do not seem to be disputed. The parties agree that Ms. Rodgers gave birth to a daughter, Meghan, on May 4, 2001. Meghan's father is Raymond Anthony. Barbara McCullough, an attorney, represented Mr. Anthony in a child custody suit against Ms. Rodgers in which Mr. Anthony sought to obtain custody and child support from Ms. Rodgers. Ms. McCullough received, reviewed, and used Ms. Rodgers' consumer report in connection with the child custody case.

On September 25, 2001, Ms. McCullough instructed Gloria Christian, her secretary, to obtain Ms. Rodgers' consumer report. Ms. McCullough received the report on September 27 or 28 of 2001. She reviewed the report in preparation for her examination of Ms. Rodgers during a hearing to be held in juvenile court on October 23, 2001. She also used the report during the hearing, including attempting to move the document into evidence and possibly handing it to the presiding judge.

The dispute in this case centers around whether Ms. McCullough obtained and used Ms. Rodgers' consumer report for a purpose permitted under the Fair Credit Reporting Act (the "FCRA"). Plaintiff contends that Ms. McCullough, as well as her law firm, Wilkes, McCullough & Wagner, a partnership, and her partners, Calvin J. McCullough and John C. Wagner, are liable for the unlawful receipt and use of Ms. Rodgers' consumer report in violation 15 U.S.C. §§ 1681 *o* (negligent failure to comply with the FCRA) and 1681n (willful failure to comply with the FCRA or obtaining a consumer report under false pretenses). Plaintiff has also sued Defendants for the state law tort of unlawful invasion of privacy....

Analysis

Plaintiff has moved for summary judgment on the questions of whether Defendants failed to comply with the FCRA (i.e. whether Defendants had a permissible purpose to obtain Ms. Rodgers' credit report), whether Defendants' alleged failure to comply was willful, and whether Defendants' actions constituted unlawful invasion of privacy. The Court will address the FCRA claims followed by the state law claim for unlawful invasion of privacy.

A. Permissible Purpose under the FCRA

Pursuant to the FCRA, "A person shall not use or obtain a consumer report for any purpose unless (1) the consumer report is obtained for a purpose for which the consumer report is authorized to be furnished under this section...." [Citation.] Defendants do not dispute that Ms. McCullough obtained and used Ms. Rodgers' consumer report.

[The act] provides a list of permissible purposes for the receipt and use of a consumer report, of which the following subsection is at issue in this case:

[A]ny consumer reporting agency may furnish a consumer report under the following circumstances and no other:...

(3) To a person which it has reason to believe-

(A) intends to use the information in connection with a credit transaction involving the consumer on whom the information is to be furnished and involving the extension of credit to, or review or collection of an account of, the consumer...

[Citation.] Defendants concede that Ms. McCullough's receipt and use of Ms. Rodgers' consumer report does not fall within any of the other permissible purposes enumerated in [the act].

Ms. Rodgers requests summary judgment in her favor on this point, relying on the plain text of the statute, because she was not in arrears on any child support obligation at the time Ms. McCullough requested the consumer report, nor did she owe Ms. McCullough's client any debt. She notes that Mr. Anthony did not have custody of Meghan Rodgers and that an award of child support had not even been set at the time Ms. McCullough obtained her consumer report.

Defendants maintain that Ms. McCullough obtained Ms. Rodgers' consumer report for a permissible purpose, namely to locate Ms. Rodgers' residence and set and collect child support obligations. Defendants argue that 15 U.S.C. § 1681b(a)(3)(A) permits the use of a credit report in connection with "collection of an account" and, therefore, Ms. McCullough was permitted to use Ms. Rodgers' credit report in connection with the collection of child support.[14]

The cases Defendants have cited in response to the motion for summary judgment are inapplicable to the present facts. In each case cited by Defendants, the person who obtained a credit report did so in order to collect on an *outstanding* judgment or an *outstanding* debt. *See, e.g.*, [Citation] (finding that collection of a judgment of arrears in child support is a permissible purpose under [the act]; [Citation] (holding that defendant had a permissible purpose for obtaining a consumer report where plaintiff owed an outstanding debt to the company).

However, no such outstanding debt or judgment existed in this case. At the time Ms. McCullough obtained Ms. Rodgers' consumer report, Ms. Rodgers' did not owe money to either Ms. McCullough or her client, Mr. Anthony. Defendants have provided no evidence showing that Ms. McCullough believed Ms. Rodgers owed money to Mr. Anthony at the time she requested the credit report. Indeed, Mr. Anthony had not even been awarded custody of Meghan Rodgers at the time Ms. McCullough obtained and used the credit report. Ms. McCullough acknowledged each of the facts during her deposition. Moreover, in response to Plaintiff's request for admissions, Ms. McCullough admitted that she did not receive the credit report for the purpose of collecting on an account from Ms. Rodgers.

The evidence before the Court makes clear that Ms. McCullough was actually attempting, on behalf of Mr. Anthony, to secure custody of Meghan Rodgers and obtain a future award of child support payments from Ms. Rodgers by portraying Ms. Rodgers as irresponsible to the court. These are not listed as permissible purposes under [FCRA]. Defendants have offered the Court no reason to depart from the plain language of the statute, which clearly does not permit an individual to obtain a consumer report for the purposes of obtaining child custody and instituting child support payments. Moreover, the fact that the Juvenile Court later awarded custody and child support to Mr. Anthony does not retroactively provide Ms. McCullough with a permissible purpose for obtaining Ms. Rodgers' consumer report. Therefore, the Court GRANTS Plaintiff's motion for partial summary judgment on the question of whether Defendants had a permissible purpose to obtain Ms. Rodgers' credit report.

B. Willful Failure to Comply with the FCRA

Pursuant to [the FCRA], "Any person who willfully fails to comply with any requirement imposed under this subchapter with respect to any consumer is liable to that consumer" for the specified damages.

"To show willful noncompliance with the FCRA, [the plaintiff] must show that [the defendant] 'knowingly and intentionally committed an act in conscious disregard for the rights of others,' but need not show 'malice or evil motive.'" [Citation.] "Under this formulation the defendant must commit the act that violates the Fair Credit Reporting Act with knowledge that he is committing the act and with intent to do so, and he must also be conscious that his act impinges on the rights of others." "The statute's use of the word 'willfully' imports the requirement that the defendant know his or her conduct is unlawful." [Citation.] A defendant can not be held civilly liable under [the act] if he or she obtained the plaintiff's credit report "under what is believed to be a proper purpose under the statute but which a court...later rules to be impermissible legally under [Citation].

Ms. McCullough is an attorney who signed multiple service contracts with Memphis Consumer Credit Association indicating that the primary purpose for which credit information would be ordered was "to collect judgments." Ms. McCullough also agreed in these service contracts to comply with the FCRA. Her deposition testimony indicates that she had never previously ordered a consumer report for purposes of calculating child support. This evidence may give rise to an inference that Ms. McCullough was aware that she did not order Ms. Rodgers' consumer report for a purpose permitted under the FCRA.

Defendants argue in their responsive memorandum that if Ms. McCullough had suspected that she had obtained Ms. Rodgers' credit report in violation of the FCRA, it is unlikely that she would have attempted to present the report to the Juvenile Court as evidence during the custody hearing for Meghan Rodgers. Ms. McCullough also testified that she believed she had a permissible purpose for obtaining Ms. Rodgers' consumer report (i.e. to set and collect child support obligations).

Viewing the evidence in the light most favorable to the nonmoving party, Defendants have made a sufficient showing that Ms. McCullough may not have understood that she lacked a permissible purpose under the FCRA to obtain and use Ms. Rodgers' credit report.

If Ms. McCullough was not aware that her actions might violate the FCRA at the time she obtained and used Ms. Rodgers' credit report, she would not have willfully failed to comply with the FCRA. The question of Ms. McCullough's state of mind at the time she obtained and used Ms. Rodgers' credit report is an issue best left to a jury. [Citation] ("state of mind is typically not a proper issue for resolution on summary judgment"). The Court DENIES Plaintiff's motion for summary judgment on the question of willfulness under [the act].

C. Obtaining a Consumer Report under False Pretenses or Knowingly without a Permissible Purpose

* * * For the same reasons the Court denied Plaintiff's motion for summary judgment on the question of willfulness, the Court also DENIES Plaintiff's motion for summary judgment on the question of whether Ms. McCullough obtained and used Ms. Rodgers' credit report under false pretenses or knowingly without a permissible purpose.

[Discussion of the invasion of privacy claim omitted.]

Conclusion

For the foregoing reasons, the Court GRANTS Plaintiff's Motion for Partial Summary Judgment Regarding Defendants' Failure to Comply with the Fair Credit Reporting Act [having no permissible purpose]. The Court DENIES Plaintiff's remaining motions for partial summary judgment.

Case Questions

1. Why did the defendant, McCullough, order her secretary to obtain Ms. Rodgers's credit report? If Ms. McCullough is found liable, why would her law firm partners also be liable?
2. What "permissible purpose" did the defendants contend they had for obtaining the credit report? Why did the court determine that purpose was not permissible?
3. Why did the court deny the plaintiff's motion for summary judgment on the question of whether the defendant "willfully" failed to comply with the act? Is the plaintiff out of luck on that question, or can it be litigated further?

27.4 Summary and Exercises

Summary

Consumers who are granted credit have long received protection through usury laws (laws that establish a maximum interest rate). The rise in consumer debt in recent years has been matched by an increase in federal regulation of consumer credit transactions. The Truth in Lending Act requires disclosure of credit terms; the Equal Credit Opportunity Act prohibits certain types of discrimination in the granting of credit; the Fair Credit Reporting Act gives consumers access to their credit dossiers and prohibits unapproved use of credit-rating information. After entering into a credit transaction, a consumer has certain cancellation rights and may use a procedure prescribed by the Fair Credit Billing Act to correct billing errors. Traditional debt collection practices—garnishment, wage assignments, and confession of judgment clauses—are now subject to federal regulation, as are the practices of collection agencies under the Fair Debt Collection Practices Act. Following the banking scandals and accompanying "Great Recession" of 2008, Congress created the Consumer Finance Protection Bureau to help--as the agency's name suggests--protect consumers against certain kinds of abusive commercial financial practices.

Exercises

1. Carlene Consumer entered into an agreement with Rent to Buy, Inc., to rent a computer for $20 per week. The agreement also provided that if Carlene chose to rent the computer for fifty consecutive weeks, she would own it. She then asserted that the agreement was not a lease but a sale on credit subject to the Truth in Lending Act, and that Rent to Buy, Inc., violated the act by failing to state the annual percentage rate. Is Carlene correct?
2. Carlos, a resident of Chicago, was on a road trip to California when he heard a noise under the hood of his car. He took the car to a mechanic for repair. The mechanic overhauled the power steering unit and billed Carlos $600, which he charged on his credit card. Later that day, after Carlos drove about fifty miles, the car made the same noise. Carlos took it to another mechanic, who diagnosed the problem as a loose exhaust pipe connection at the manifold. Carlos was billed $300 for this repair, with which he was satisfied. Carlos returned

to Chicago and examined his credit card statement. What rights has he as to the $600 charge on his card?

3. Ken was the owner of Scrimshaw, a company that manufactured and sold carvings made from fossilized ivory. He applied for a loan from Bank. Bank found him creditworthy, but seeking additional security for repayment, it required his wife, Linda, to sign a guaranty as well. During a subsequent recession, demand for scrimshaw fell, and Ken's business went under. Bank filed suit against both Ken and Linda. What defense has Linda?
4. The FCRA requires that credit-reporting agencies "follow reasonable procedures to assure maximum possible accuracy of the information." In October of 1989, Renie Guimond became aware of, and notified the credit bureau TransUnion about, inaccuracies in her credit report: that she was married (and it listed a Social Security number for this nonexistent spouse), that she was also known as Ruth Guimond, and that she had a Saks Fifth Avenue credit card. About a month later, TransUnion responded to Guimond's letter, stating that the erroneous information had been removed. But in March of 1990, TransUnion again published the erroneous information it purportedly had removed. Guimond then requested the source of the erroneous information, to which TransUnion responded that it could not disclose the identity of the source because it did not know its source. The disputed information was eventually removed from Guimond's file in October 1990. When Guimond sued, TransUnion defended that she had no claim because no credit was denied to her as a result of the inaccuracies in her credit file. The lower court dismissed her case; she appealed. To what damages, if any, is Guimond entitled?
5. Plaintiff incurred a medical debt of $160. She received two or three telephone calls from Defendant, the collection agency; each time, she denied owing any money. Subsequently she received this letter:

   > *You have shown that you are unwilling to work out a friendly settlement with us to clear the above debt. Our field investigator has now been instructed to make an investigation in your neighborhood and to personally call on your employer.*
   >
   > *The immediate payment of the full amount, or a personal visit to this office, will spare you this embarrassment.*

   The top of the letter notes the creditor's name and the amount of the alleged debt. The letter was signed by a "collection agent." The envelope containing that letter presented a return address that included Defendant's full name: "Collection Accounts Terminal, Inc." What violations of the Fair Debt Collection Practices Act are here presented?
6. Eric and Sharaveen Rush filed a claim alleging violations of the Fair Credit Reporting Act arising out of an allegedly erroneous credit report prepared by a credit bureau from information, in part, from Macy's, the department store. The error causes the Rushes to be denied credit. Macy's filed a motion to dismiss. Is Macy's liable? Discuss.

Self-Test Questions

1. An example of a loan that is a common exception to usury law is
   a. a business loan
   b. a mortgage loan
   c. an installment loan
   d. all of the above
2. Under the Fair Credit Reporting Act, an applicant denied credit
   a. has a right to a hearing

   b. has the right to be told the name and address of the credit bureau that prepared the credit report upon which denial was based
   c. always must pay a fee for information regarding credit denial
   d. none of the above
3. Garnishment of wages
   a. is limited by federal law
   b. involves special rules for support cases
   c. is a legal process where a creditor obtains a court order directing the debtor's employer to pay a portion of the debtor's wages directly to the creditor
   d. involves all of the above
4. A wage assignment is
   a. an example of garnishment
   b. an example of confession of judgment
   c. an exception to usury law
   d. an agreement that a creditor may take future wages as security for a loan
5. The Truth-in-Truth in Lending Act requires disclosure of
   a. the annual percentage rate
   b. the borrower's race
   c. both of the above
   d. neither of the above

Self-Test Answers

1. d
2. b
3. d
4. d
5. a

Endnotes

1. Tim Chen, American Household Credit Card Debt Statistics: 2014. http://www.nerdwallet.com/blog/credit-card-data/average-credit-card-debt-household/.
2. Id.
3. Michele Lerner, Is Your Credit Card Debt Average? And What's Average? Daily Finance, Credit Center. http://www.dailyfinance.com/2014/06/11/is-your-credit-card-debt-average/.
4. Gerri Detweiler, What is the Average Credit Card Debt in America? http://www.credit.com/debt/average-credit-card-debt/.
5. Connie Prater, What the Credit Card Reform Act Means to You: A primer on how the Credit CARD Act has changed the rules. http://www.creditcards.com/credit-card-news/help/what-the-new-credit-card-rules-mean-6000.php#young.
6. Liz Pulliam Weston, "Credit Card Lenders Go on a Rampage," *MSN Money*, November 25, 2009.
7. States adopting the Uniform Consumer Credit Code are the following: Colorado, Idaho, Indiana, Iowa, Kansas, Maine, Oklahoma, South Carolina, Utah, Wisconsin, Wyoming, and Guam. Cornell University Law School, "Uniform Laws." http://www.law.cornell.edu/uniform/vol7.html#concc.
8. Kathryn L.S. Pettit and Audrey E. Droesch, "A Guide to Home Mortgage Disclosure Act Data," The Urban Institute, December 2008, http://www.urban.org/uploadedpdf/1001247_hdma.pdf.
9. *Smith v. Cotton Brothers Baking Co., Inc.*, 609 F.2d 738 (5th Cir. 1980).
10. *Sniadach v. Family Finance Corp.*, 395 U.S. 337 (1969).
11. PricewaterhouseCoopers LLP, *Value of Third-Party Debt Collection to the U.S. Economy in 2007: Survey And Analysis*, June 2008, http://www.acainternational.org/files.aspx?p=/images/12546/pwc2007-final.pdf.
12. Federal Communications Commission, "In the Matter of Rules and Regulations Implementing the Telephone Consumer Protection Act of 1991," http://fjallfoss.fcc.gov/edocs_public/attachmatch/FCC-07-232A1.txt. (This document shows up best with Adobe Acrobat.)
13. http://www.consumerfinance.gov/about-us/the-bureau/.
14. Defendants also admit that Ms. McCullough used the credit report to portray Ms. Rodgers as irresponsible, financially unstable, and untruthful about her residence and employment history to the Juvenile Court. Defendants do not allege that these constitute permissible purposes under the FCRA.

CHAPTER 28
Secured Transactions and Suretyship

Learning Objectives

After reading this chapter, you should understand the following:

1. The basic concepts of secured transactions.
2. The property subject to the security interest.
3. Creation and perfection of the security interest.
4. Priorities for claims on the security interest.
5. Rights of creditors on default.
6. The basic concepts of suretyship.
7. The relationship between surety and principal.
8. Rights among cosureties.

28.1 Introduction to Secured Transactions

Learning Objectives

1. Recognize, most generally, the two methods by which debtors' obligations may be secured.
2. Know the source of law for personal property security.
3. Understand the meaning of *security interest* and other terminology necessary to discuss the issues.
4. Know what property is subject to the security interest.
5. Understand how the security interest is created—"attached"—and perfected.

The Problem of Security

Creditors want assurances that they will be repaid by the debtor. An oral promise to pay is no security at all, and—as it is oral—it is difficult to prove. A **signature loan** is merely a written promise by the debtor to repay, but the creditor stuck holding a promissory note with a signature loan only—while he may sue a defaulting debtor—will get nothing if the debtor is insolvent. Again, that's no security at all. Real security for the creditor comes in two forms: by agreement with the debtor or by operation of law without an agreement.

signature loan

A loan for which no collateral is pledged.

By Agreement with the Debtor

Security obtained through agreement comes in three major types: (1) personal property security (the most common form of security); (2) suretyship—the willingness of a third party to pay if the primarily obligated party does not; and (3) mortgage of real estate.

By Operation of Law

lien

An encumbrance upon property to secure payment.

Security obtained through operation of law is known as a **lien**. Derived from the French for "string" or "tie," a *lien* is the legal hold that a creditor has over the property of another in order to secure payment or discharge an obligation.

In this chapter, we take up security interests in personal property and suretyship. In the next chapter, we look at mortgages and nonconsensual liens.

Basics of Secured Transactions

The law of secured transactions consists of five principal components: (1) the nature of property that can be the subject of a security interest; (2) the methods of creating the security interest; (3) the perfection of the security interest against claims of others; (4) priorities among secured and unsecured creditors—that is, who will be entitled to the secured property if more than one person asserts a legal right to it; and (5) the rights of creditors when the debtor defaults. After considering the source of the law and some key terminology, we examine each of these components in turn.

Here is the simplest (and most common) scenario: Debtor borrows money or obtains credit from Creditor, signs a note and security agreement putting up collateral, and promises to pay the debt or, upon Debtor's default, let Creditor (secured party) take possession of (repossess) the collateral and sell it. Figure 28.1 illustrates this scenario—the grasping *hand* is Creditor's reach for the collateral, but the hand will not close around the collateral and take it (repossess) unless Debtor defaults.

FIGURE 28.1 The Grasping Hand

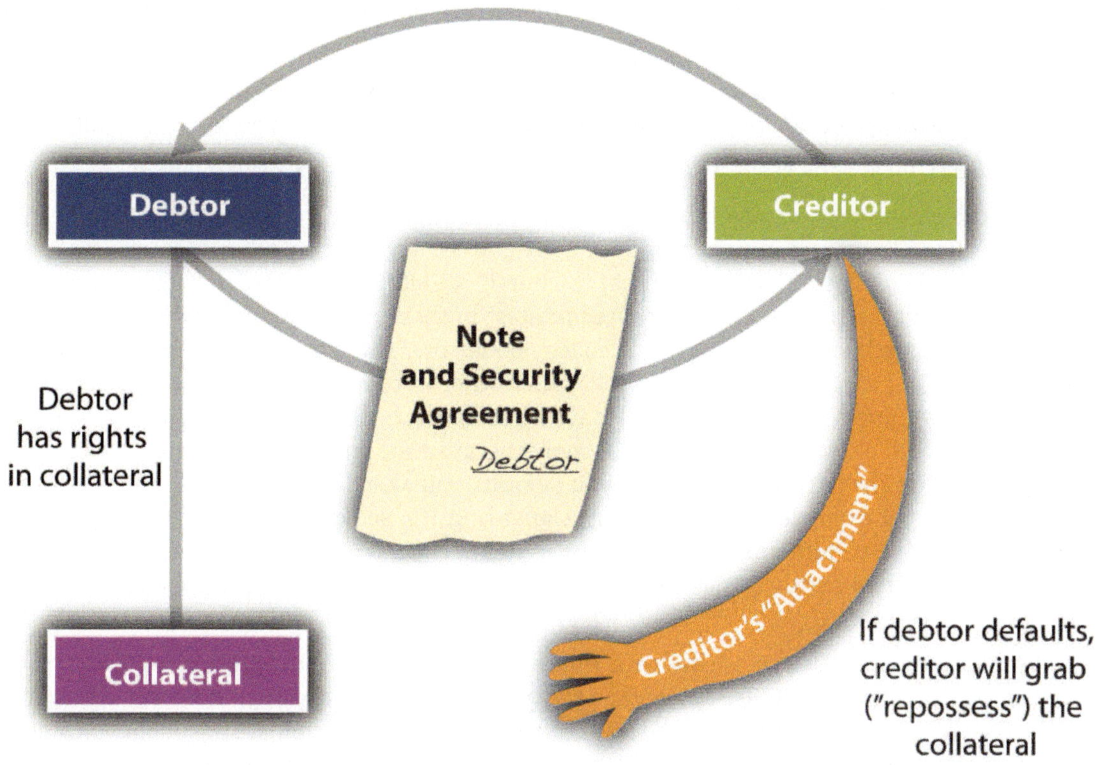

Source of Law and Definitions

Source of Law

Article 9 of the Uniform Commercial Code (UCC) governs security interests in personal property. The UCC defines the scope of the article (here slightly truncated):[1]

> *This chapter applies to the following:*
>
> 1. *A transaction, regardless of its form, that creates a security interest in personal property or fixtures by contract;*
> 2. *An agricultural lien;*
> 3. *A sale of accounts, chattel paper, payment intangibles, or promissory notes;*
> 4. *A consignment...*

Definitions

As always, it is necessary to review some definitions so that communication on the topic at hand is possible. The secured transaction always involves a debtor, a secured party, a security agreement, a security interest, and collateral.

security interest

Right in personal property to secure payment or performance of an obligation.

Security agreement

Agreement that grants a security interest.

collateral

Property given as security for a debt.

A purchase-money security interest

The security interest held by the seller of collateral to secure payment of all or part of the price.

Article 9 applies to any transaction "that creates a security interest." The UCC in Section 1-201(35) defines **security interest** as "an interest in personal property or fixtures which secures payment or performance of an obligation."

Security agreement is "an agreement that creates or provides for a security interest." It is the contract that sets up the debtor's duties and the creditor's rights in event the debtor defaults.[2]

Collateral "means the property subject to a security interest or agricultural lien."[3]

A purchase-money security interest (PMSI) is the simplest form of security interest. Section 9-103(a) of the UCC defines "purchase-money collateral" as "goods or software that secures a purchase-money obligation with respect to that collateral." A PMSI arises where the debtor gets credit to buy goods and the creditor takes a secured interest in those goods. Suppose you want to buy a big hardbound textbook on credit at your college bookstore. The manager refuses to extend you credit outright but says she will take back a PMSI. In other words, she will retain a security interest in the book itself, and if you don't pay, you'll have to return the book; it will be repossessed. Contrast this situation with a counteroffer you might make: because she tells you not to mark up the book (in the event that she has to repossess it if you default), you would rather give her some other collateral to hold—for example, your gold college signet ring. Her security interest in the ring is not a PMSI but a pledge; a PMSI must be an interest in the particular goods purchased. A PMSI would also be created if you borrowed money to buy the book and gave the lender a security interest in the book.

Whether a transaction is a lease or a PMSI is an issue that frequently arises. The answer depends on the facts of each case. However, a security interest is created if (1) the lessee is obligated to continue payments for the term of the lease; (2) the lessee cannot terminate the obligation; and (3) one of several economic tests, which are listed in UCC Section 1-201 (37), is met. For example, one of the economic tests is that "the lessee has an option to become owner of the goods for no additional consideration or nominal additional consideration upon compliance with the lease agreement."

The issue of lease versus security interest gets litigated because of the requirements of Article 9 that a security interest be perfected in certain ways (as we will see). If the transaction turns out to be a security interest, a lessor who fails to meet these requirements runs the risk of losing his property to a third party. And consider this example. Ferrous Brothers Iron Works "leases" a $25,000 punch press to Millie's Machine Shop. Under the terms of the lease, Millie's must pay a yearly rental of $5,000 for five years, after which time Millie's may take title to the machine outright for the payment of $1. During the period of the rental, title remains in Ferrous Brothers. Is this "lease" really a security interest? Since ownership comes at a nominal charge when the entire lease is satisfied, the transaction would be construed as one creating a security interest. What difference does this make? Suppose Millie's goes bankrupt in the third year of the lease, and the trustee in bankruptcy wishes to sell the punch press to satisfy debts of the machine shop. If it were a true lease, Ferrous Brothers would be entitled to reclaim the machine (unless the trustee assumed the lease). But if the lease is really intended as a device to create a security interest, then Ferrous Brothers can recover its collateral only if it has otherwise complied with the obligations of Article 9—for example, by recording its security interest, as we will see.

Now we return to definitions.

debtor

One who owes money or a duty of performance to another.

Obligor

One who owes an obligation.

Debtor is "a person (1) having an interest in the collateral other than a security interest or a lien; (2) a seller of accounts, chattel paper, payment intangibles, or promissory notes; or (3) a consignee."[4]

Obligor is "a person that, with respect to an obligation secured by a security interest in or an agricultural lien on the collateral, (i) owes payment or other performance of the obligation, (ii) has provided property other than the collateral to secure payment or other performance of the obligation, or (iii) is otherwise accountable in whole or in part for payment or other performance of the obligation."[5] Here is example 1 from the Official Comment to UCC Section 9-102: "Behnfeldt borrows money and grants a security interest in her Miata to secure the debt. Behnfeldt is a debtor and an obligor."

Behnfeldt is a debtor because she has an interest in the car—she owns it. She is an obligor because she owes payment to the creditor. Usually the debtor is the obligor.

A *secondary obligor* is "an obligor to the extent that: (a) [the] obligation is secondary; or (b) [the person] has a right of recourse with respect to an obligation secured by collateral against the debtor, another obligor, or property of either."[6] The secondary obligor is a guarantor (surety) of the debt, obligated to perform if the primary obligor defaults. Consider example 2 from the Official Comment to Section 9-102: "Behnfeldt borrows money and grants a security interest in her Miata to secure the debt. Bruno cosigns a negotiable note as maker. As before, Behnfeldt is the debtor and an obligor. As an accommodation party, Bruno is a secondary obligor. Bruno has this status even if the note states that her obligation is a primary obligation and that she waives all suretyship defenses."

Again, usually the debtor is the obligor, but consider example 3 from the same Official Comment: "Behnfeldt borrows money on an unsecured basis. Bruno cosigns the note and grants a security interest in her Honda to secure her [Behnfeldt's] obligation. Inasmuch as Behnfeldt does not have a property interest in the Honda, Behnfeldt is not a debtor. Having granted the security interest, Bruno is the debtor. Because Behnfeldt is a principal obligor, she is not a secondary obligor. Whatever the outcome of enforcement of the security interest against the Honda or Bruno's secondary obligation, Bruno will look to Behnfeldt for her losses. The enforcement will not affect Behnfeldt's aggregate obligations."

Secured party is "a person in whose favor a security interest is created or provided for under a security agreement," and it includes people to whom accounts, chattel paper, payment intangibles, or promissory notes have been sold; consignors; and others under Section 9-102(a)(72).

Chattel mortgage means "a debt secured against items of personal property rather than against land, buildings and fixtures."[7] Chattel mortgages are among the most common methods of obtaining loans against movable personal property. In the U.S., chattel mortgages are referred to as secured transactions.

secured party

The creditor who has a security interest in a debtor's collateral.

Chattel mortgage

A security device by which a mortgagee takes security interest in personal property of the mortgagor; mostly superseded by other security arrangements under UCC Article 9.

Property Subject to the Security Interest

Now we examine what property may be put up as security—collateral. Collateral is—again—property that is subject to the security interest. It can be divided into four broad categories: goods, intangible property, indispensable paper, and other types of collateral.

Goods

Tangible property as collateral is goods. *Goods* means "all things that are movable when a security interest attaches. The term includes (i) fixtures, (ii) standing timber that is to be cut and removed under a conveyance or contract for sale, (iii) the unborn young of animals, (iv) crops grown, growing, or to be grown, even if the crops are produced on trees, vines, or bushes, and (v) manufactured homes. The term also includes a computer program embedded in goods."[8] Goods are divided into several subcategories; six are taken up here.

Consumer Goods

These are "goods used or bought primarily for personal, family, or household purposes."[9]

Inventory

"Goods, other than farm products, held by a person for sale or lease or consisting of raw materials, works in progress, or material consumed in a business."[10]

Farm Products

"Crops, livestock, or other supplies produced or used in farming operations," including aquatic goods produced in aquaculture.[11]

Equipment

This is the residual category, defined as "goods other than inventory, farm products, or consumer goods."[12]

Fixtures

These are "goods that have become so related to particular real property that an interest in them arises under real property law."[13] Examples would be windows, furnaces, central air conditioning, and plumbing fixtures—items that, if removed, would be a cause for significant reconstruction.

Accession

These are "goods that are physically united with other goods in such a manner that the identity of the original goods is lost."[14] A new engine installed in an old automobile is an accession.

Intangible Property

Two types of collateral are neither goods nor indispensible paper: accounts and general intangibles.

Accounts

This type of intangible property includes accounts receivable (the right to payment of money), insurance policy proceeds, energy provided or to be provided, winnings in a lottery, health-care-insurance receivables, promissory notes, securities, letters of credit, and interests in business entities.[15] Often there is something in writing to show the existence of the right—such as a right to receive the proceeds of somebody else's insurance payout—but the writing is merely evidence of the right. The paper itself doesn't have to be delivered for the transfer of the right to be effective; that's done by assignment.

General Intangibles

General intangibles refers to "any personal property, including things in action, other than accounts, commercial tort claims, deposit accounts, documents, goods, instruments, investment property, letter-of-credit rights, letters of credit, money, and oil, gas, or other minerals before extraction." General intangibles include payment intangibles and software.[16]

Indispensable Paper

This oddly named category is the middle ground between goods—stuff you can touch—and intangible property. It's called "indispensable" because although the right to the value—such as a warehouse receipt—is embodied in a written paper, the paper itself is indispensable for the transferee to access the value. For example, suppose Deborah Debtor borrows $3,000 from Carl Creditor, and Carl takes a security interest in four designer chairs Deborah owns that are being stored in a warehouse. If Deborah defaults, Carl has the right to possession of the warehouse receipt: he takes it to the warehouser and is entitled to take the chairs and sell them to satisfy the obligation. The warehouser will not let Carl have the chairs without the warehouse receipt—it's indispensable paper. There are four kinds of indispensable paper.

Chattel Paper

Chattel is another word for goods. Chattel paper is a record (paper or electronic) that demonstrates both "a monetary obligation and a security interest either in certain goods or in a lease on certain goods."[17] The paper represents a valuable asset and can itself be used as collateral. For example, Creditor Car Company sells David Debtor an automobile and takes back a note and security agreement (this is a purchase-money security agreement; the note and security agreement is chattel paper). The chattel paper is not yet collateral; the automobile is. Now, though, Creditor Car Company buys a new hydraulic lift from Lift Co., and grants Lift Co. a security interest in Debtor's chattel paper to secure Creditor Car's debt to Lift Co. The chattel paper is now collateral. Chattel paper can be tangible (actual paper) or electronic.

Documents

This category includes documents of title—bills of lading and warehouse receipts are examples.

Instruments

An "instrument" here is "a negotiable instrument (checks, drafts, notes, certificates of deposit) or any other writing that evidences a right to the payment of a monetary obligation, is not itself a security agreement or lease, and is of a type that in the ordinary course of business is transferred by delivery with any necessary indorsement or assignment." "Instrument" does not include (i) investment property, (ii) letters of credit, or (iii) writings that evidence a right to payment arising out of the use of a credit or charge card or information contained on or for use with the card.[18]

Investment Property

This includes securities (stock, bonds), security accounts, commodity accounts, and commodity contracts.[19] Securities may be certified (represented by a certificate) or uncertified (not represented by a certificate).[20]

Other Types of Collateral

Among possible other types of collateral that may be used as security is the **floating lien**. This is a security interest in property that was not in the possession of the debtor when the security agreement was executed. The floating lien creates an interest that floats on the river of present and future collateral and proceeds held by—most often—the business debtor. It is especially useful in loans to businesses that sell their collateralized inventory. Without the floating lien, the lender would find its collateral steadily depleted as the borrowing business sells its products to its customers. Pretty soon, there'd be no security at all. The floating lien includes the following:

floating lien
A lien that is expanded to cover any additional property that is acquired by the debtor while the debt is outstanding.

- *After-acquired property*. This is property that the debtor acquires after the original deal was set up. It allows the secured party to enhance his security as the debtor (obligor) acquires more property subject to collateralization.

- *Sale proceeds*. These are proceeds from the disposition of the collateral. Carl Creditor takes a secured interest in Deborah Debtor's sailboat. She sells the boat and buys a garden tractor. The secured interest attaches to the garden tractor.
- *Future advances*. Here the security agreement calls for the collateral to stand for both present and future advances of credit without any additional paperwork.

  Here are examples of future advances:

  - Example 1: A debtor enters into a security agreement with a creditor that contains a future advances clause. The agreement gives the creditor a security interest in a $700,000 inventory-picking robot to secure repayment of a loan made to the debtor. The parties contemplate that the debtor will, from time to time, borrow more money, and when the debtor does, the machine will stand as collateral to secure the further indebtedness, without new paperwork.
  - Example 2: A debtor signs a security agreement with a bank to buy a car. The security agreement contains a future advances clause. A few years later, the bank sends the debtor a credit card. Two years go by: the car is paid for, but the credit card is in default. The bank seizes the car. "Whoa!" says the debtor. "I paid for the car." "Yes," says the bank, "but it was collateral for all future indebtedness you ran up with us. Check out your loan agreement with us and UCC Section 9-204(c), especially Comment 5."

See Figure 28.2.

FIGURE 28.2 Tangibles and Intangibles as Collateral

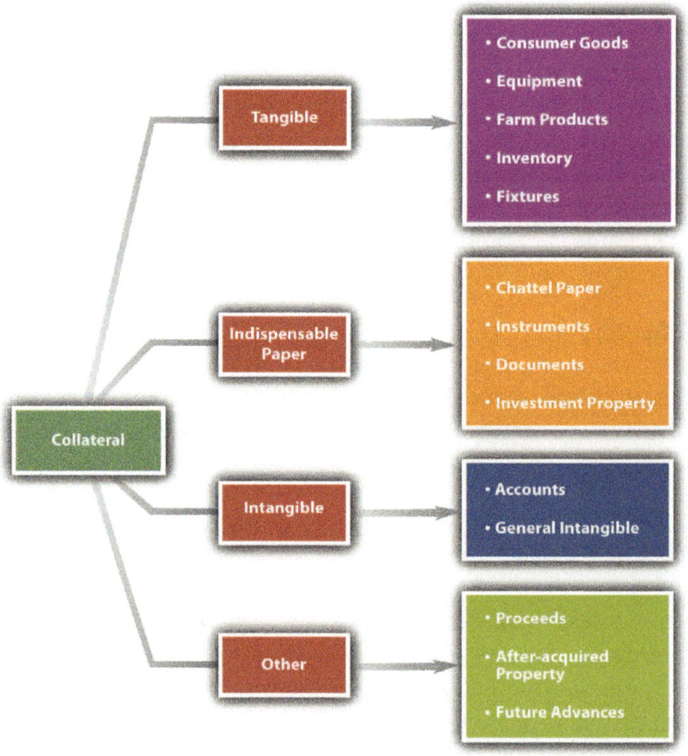

Attachment of the Security Interest

In General

Attachment is the term used to describe when a security interest becomes enforceable against the debtor with respect to the collateral. In Figure 28.1, "Attachment" is the outreached hand that is prepared, if the debtor defaults, to grasp the collateral.[21]

Attachment

The process by which a security interest becomes enforceable against the debtor with respect to the collateral.

Requirements for Attachment

There are three requirements for attachment: (1) the secured party gives value; (2) the debtor has rights in the collateral or the power to transfer rights in it to the secured party; (3) the parties have a security agreement "authenticated" (signed, usually) by the debtor, or the creditor has possession of the collateral.

Creditor Gives Value

The creditor, or secured party, must give "value" for the security interest to attach. The UCC, in Section 1-204, provides that

> *a person gives 'value' for rights if he acquires them*
>
> *(1) in return for a binding commitment to extend credit or for the extension of immediately available credit whether or not drawn upon and whether or not a charge-back is provided for in the event of difficulties in collection; or*
>
> *(2) as security for or in total or partial satisfaction of a pre-existing claim; or*
>
> *(3) by accepting delivery pursuant to a pre-existing contract for purchase; or*
>
> *(4) generally, in return for any consideration sufficient to support a simple contract.*

Suppose Deborah owes Carl $3,000. She cannot repay the sum when due, so she agrees to give Carl a security interest in her automobile to the extent of $3,000 in return for an extension of the time to pay. That is sufficient value.

Debtor's Rights in Collateral

The debtor must have rights in the collateral. Most commonly, the debtor owns the collateral (or has some ownership interest in it). The rights need not necessarily be the immediate right to possession, but they must be rights that can be conveyed.[22] A person can't put up as collateral property she doesn't own.

Security Agreement (Contract) or Possession of Collateral by Creditor

The debtor most often signs the written security agreement, or contract. The UCC says that "the debtor [must have] authenticated a security agreement that provides a description of the collateral. . . ." "Authenticating" (or "signing," "adopting," or "accepting") means to sign or, in recognition of electronic commercial transactions, "to execute or otherwise adopt a symbol, or encrypt or similarly process a record . . . with the present intent of the authenticating person to identify the person and adopt or accept a record." The "record" is the modern UCC's substitution for the term "writing." It includes information electronically stored or on paper.[23]

pledge

The delivery of goods to a creditor as security for the debt.

The "authenticating record" (the signed security agreement) is *not* required in some cases. It is not required if the debtor makes a **pledge** of the collateral—that is, delivers it to the creditor for the creditor to possess. For example, upon a creditor's request of a debtor for collateral to secure a loan of $3,000, the debtor offers up his stamp collection. The creditor says, "Fine, have it appraised (at your expense) and show me the appraisal. If it comes in at $3,000 or more, I'll take your stamp collection and lock it in my safe until you've repaid me. If you don't repay me, I'll sell it." A creditor could take possession of any goods and various kinds of paper, tangible or intangible. In commercial transactions, it would be common for the creditor to have possession of—actually or virtually—certified securities, deposit accounts, electronic chattel paper, investment property, or other such paper or electronic evidence of value.[24]

Again, Figure 28.1 diagrams the attachment, showing the necessary elements: the creditor gives value, the debtor has rights in collateral, and there is a security agreement signed (authenticated) by the debtor. If the debtor defaults, the creditor's "hand" will grab (repossess) the collateral.

Perfection of the Security Interest

Perfection

The process by which a secured party announces to the world her secured interest in particular goods.

As between the debtor and the creditor, attachment is fine: if the debtor defaults, the creditor will repossess the goods and—usually—sell them to satisfy the outstanding obligation. But unless an additional set of steps is taken, the rights of the secured party might be subordinated to the rights of other secured parties, certain lien creditors, bankruptcy trustees, and buyers who give value and who do not know of the security interest. **Perfection** is the secured party's way of announcing the security interest to the rest of the world. It is the secured party's claim on the collateral.

There are five ways a creditor may perfect a security interest: (1) by filing a financing statement, (2) by taking or retaining possession of the collateral, (3) by taking control of the collateral, (4) by taking control temporarily as specified by the UCC, or (5) by taking control automatically.

Perfection by Filing

"Except as otherwise provided . . . a financing statement must be filed to perfect all security agreements."[25]

The Financing Statement

financing statement

Filing of a notice in the appropriate state office to perfect a security interest.

A **financing statement** is a simple notice showing the creditor's general interest in the collateral. It is what's filed to establish the creditor's "dibs."

Contents of the Financing Statement

It may consist of the security agreement itself, as long as it contains the information required by the UCC, but most commonly it is much less detailed than the security agreement: it "indicates merely that a person may have a security interest in the collateral[.] . . . Further inquiry from the parties concerned will be necessary to disclose the full state of affairs."[26] The financing statement must provide the following information:

- The debtor's name. Financing statements are indexed under the debtor's name, so getting that correct is important. Section 9-503 of the UCC describes what is meant by "name of debtor."
- The secured party's name.
- An "indication" of what collateral is covered by the financing statement.[27] It may describe the collateral or it may "indicate that the financing statement covers all assets or all personal prop-

erty" (such generic references are not acceptable in the security agreement but are OK in the financing statement).[28] If the collateral is real-property-related, covering timber to be cut or fixtures, it must include a description of the real property to which the collateral is related.[29]

The form of the financing statement may vary from state to state, but see Figure 28.3 for a typical financing statement. Minor errors or omissions on the form will not make it ineffective, but the debtor's signature is required unless the creditor is authorized by the debtor to make the filing without a signature, which facilitates paperless filing.[30]

FIGURE 28.3 UCC-1 Financing Statement

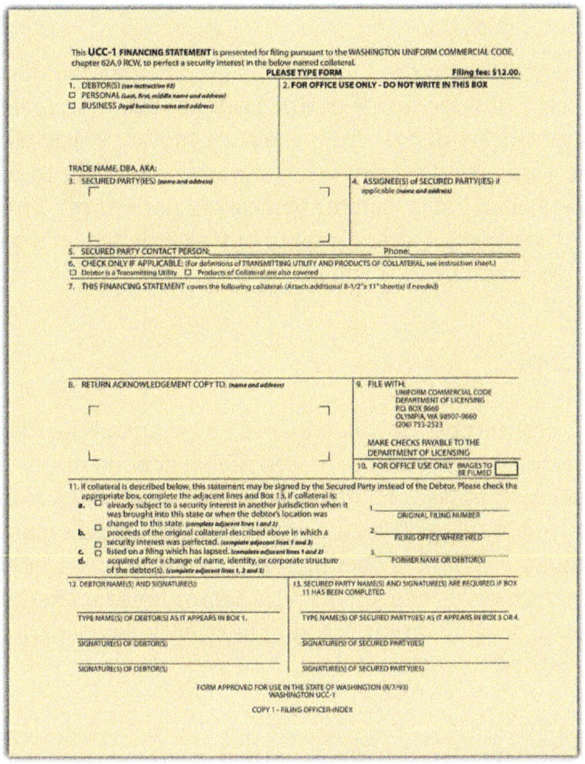
This **UCC-1 FINANCING STATEMENT** is presented for filing pursuant to the WASHINGTON UNIFORM COMMERCIAL CODE, chapter 62A.9 RCW, to perfect a security interest in the below named collateral.

PLEASE TYPE FORM **Filing fee: $12.00.**

1. DEBTOR(S) *(see instruction #3)*
☐ PERSONAL *(Last, first, middle name and address)*
☐ BUSINESS *(legal business name and address)*

TRADE NAME, DBA, AKA:

2. **FOR OFFICE USE ONLY - DO NOT WRITE IN THIS BOX**

3. SECURED PARTY(IES) *(name and address)*

4. ASSIGNEE(S) of SECURED PARTY(IES) if applicable *(name and address)*

5. SECURED PARTY CONTACT PERSON:______ Phone:______

6. CHECK ONLY IF APPLICABLE: (For definitions of TRANSMITTING UTILITY AND PRODUCTS OF COLLATERAL, see instruction sheet.)
☐ Debtor is a Transmitting Utility ☐ Products of Collateral are also covered

7. THIS FINANCING STATEMENT covers the following collateral: (Attach additional 8-1/2"x 11" sheet(s) if needed)

8. RETURN ACKNOWLEDGEMENT COPY TO: *(name and address)*

9. FILE WITH:
UNIFORM COMMERCIAL CODE
DEPARTMENT OF LICENSING
P.O. BOX 9660
OLYMPIA, WA 98507-9660
(206) 753-2523

MAKE CHECKS PAYABLE TO THE DEPARTMENT OF LICENSING

10. FOR OFFICE USE ONLY IMAGES TO BE FILMED ☐

11. If collateral is described below, this statement may be signed by the Secured Party instead of the Debtor. Please check the appropriate box, complete the adjacent lines and Box 13, if collateral is:
a. ☐ already subject to a security interest in another jurisdiction when it was brought into this state or when the debtor's location was changed to this state. *(complete adjacent lines 1 and 2)*
b. ☐ proceeds of the original collateral described above in which a security interest was perfected. *(complete adjacent lines 1 and 2)*
c. ☐ listed on a filing which has lapsed. *(complete adjacent lines 1 and 2)*
d. ☐ acquired after a change of name, identity, or corporate structure of the debtor(s). *(complete adjacent lines 1, 2 and 3)*

1.______ ORIGINAL FILING NUMBER
2.______ FILING OFFICE WHERE HELD
3.______ FORMER NAME OR DEBTOR(S)

12. DEBTOR NAME(S) AND SIGNATURE(S):
TYPE NAME(S) OF DEBTOR(S) AS IT APPEARS IN BOX 1.
SIGNATURE(S) OF DEBTOR(S)
SIGNATURE(S) OF DEBTOR(S)

13. SECURED PARTY NAME(S) AND SIGNATURE(S) ARE REQUIRED IF BOX 11 HAS BEEN COMPLETED.
TYPE NAME(S) OF SECURED PARTY(IES) AS IT APPEARS IN BOX 3 OR 4.
SIGNATURE(S) OF SECURED PARTY(IES)
SIGNATURE(S) OF SECURED PARTY(IES)

FORM APPROVED FOR USE IN THE STATE OF WASHINGTON (8/7/93)
WASHINGTON UCC-1

COPY 1 - FILING OFFICER-INDEX

Duration of the Financing Statement

Generally, the financing statement is effective for five years; a **continuation statement** may be filed within six months before the five-year expiration date, and it is good for another five years.[31] Manufactured-home filings are good for thirty years. When the debtor's obligation is satisfied, the secured party files a **termination statement** if the collateral was consumer goods; otherwise—upon demand—the secured party sends the debtor a termination statement.[32]

continuation statement

An amendment of a financing statement that identifies, by its file number, the initial financing statement to which it relates and that indicates that it is a continuation statement for, or that it is filed to continue the effectiveness of, the identified financing statement.

termination statement

The notice from a creditor that the debtor's obligations are discharged.

Debtor Moves out of State

The UCC also has rules for continued perfection of security interests when the debtor—whether an individual or an association (corporation)—moves from one state to another. Generally, an interest remains perfected until the earlier of when the perfection would have expired or for four months after the debtor moves to a new jurisdiction.[33]

Where to File the Financing Statement

For most real-estate-related filings—ore to be extracted from mines, agricultural collateral, and fixtures—the place to file is with the local office that files mortgages, typically the county auditor's office.[34] For other collateral, the filing place is as duly authorized by the state. In some states, that is the office of the Secretary of State; in others, it is the Department of Licensing; or it might be a private party that maintains the state's filing system.[35] The filing should be made in the state where the debtor has his or her primary residence for individuals, and in the state where the debtor is organized if it is a registered organization.[36] The point is, creditors need to know where to look to see if the collateral offered up is already encumbered. In any event, filing the statement in more than one place can't hurt. The filing office will provide instructions on how to file; these are available online, and electronic filing is usually available for at least some types of collateral.

Exemptions

Some transactions are exempt from the filing provision. The most important category of exempt collateral is that covered by state certificate of title laws. For example, many states require automobile owners to obtain a certificate of title from the state motor vehicle office. Most of these states provide that it is not necessary to file a financing statement in order to perfect a security interest in an automobile. The reason is that the motor vehicle regulations require any security interests to be stated on the title, so that anyone attempting to buy a car in which a security interest had been created would be on notice when he took the actual title certificate.[37]

Temporary Perfection

The UCC provides that certain types of collateral are automatically perfected but only for a while: "A security interest in certificated securities, or negotiable documents, or instruments is perfected without filing or the taking of possession for a period of twenty days from the time it attaches to the extent that it arises for new value given under an authenticated security agreement."[38] Similar temporary perfection covers negotiable documents or goods in possession of a bailee, and when a security certificate or instrument is delivered to the debtor for sale, exchange, presentation, collection, enforcement, renewal, or registration.[39] After the twenty-day period, perfection would have to be by one of the other methods mentioned here.

Perfection by Possession

A secured party may perfect the security interest by possession where the collateral is negotiable documents, goods, instruments, money, tangible chattel paper, or certified securities.[40] This is a pledge of assets (mentioned in the example of the stamp collection). No security agreement is required for perfection by possession.

field warehousing

Mortgage arrangement in which a lender secures its loan with a lien on items stored in a warehouse or at the debtor's place of business, with access to the items controlled by the lender, who releases goods as they are paid for by the borrower.

A variation on the theme of pledge is **field warehousing**. When the pawnbroker lends money, he takes possession of the goods—the watch, the ring, the camera. But when large manufacturing concerns wish to borrow against their inventory, taking physical possession is not necessarily so easy. The bank does not wish to have shipped to its Wall Street office several tons of copper mined in Colorado. Bank employees perhaps could go west to the mine and take physical control of the copper, but banks are unlikely to employ people and equipment necessary to build a warehouse on the spot. Thus, this so-called field pledge is rare.

More common is the field warehouse. The field warehouse can take one of two forms. An independent company can go to the site and put up a temporary structure—for example, a fence around the copper—thus establishing physical control of the collateral. Or the independent company can lease the warehouse facilities of the debtor and post signs indicating that the goods inside are within its sale custody. Either way, the goods are within the physical possession of the field warehouse service. The field warehouse then segregates the goods secured to the particular bank or finance company and issues a warehouse receipt to the lender for those goods. The lender is thus assured of a security interest in the collateral.

Perfection by Control

"A security interest in investment property, deposit accounts, letter-of-credit rights, or electronic chattel paper may be perfected by control of the collateral." [41] "Control" depends on what the collateral is. If it's a checking account, for example, the bank with which the deposit account is maintained has "control": the bank gets a security interest automatically because, as Official Comment 3 to UCC Section 9-104 puts it, "all actual and potential creditors of the debtor are always on notice that the bank with which the debtor's deposit account is maintained may assert a claim against the deposit account." "Control" of electronic chattel paper of investment property, and of letter-of-credit rights is detailed in Sections 9-105, 9-106, and 9-107. Obtaining "control" means that the creditor has taken whatever steps are necessary, given the manner in which the items are held, to place itself in a position where it can have the items sold, without further action by the owner.[42]

Automatic Perfection

The fifth mechanism of perfection is addressed in Section 9-309 of the UCC: there are several circumstances where a security interest is perfected upon mere attachment. The most important here is **automatic perfection** of a purchase-money security interest given in consumer goods. If a seller of consumer goods takes a PMSI in the goods sold, then perfection of the security interest is automatic. But the seller may file a financial statement and faces a risk if he fails to file and the consumer debtor sells the goods. Under Section 9-320(b), a buyer of consumer goods takes free of a security interest, even though perfected, if he buys without knowledge of the interest, pays value, and uses the goods for his personal, family, or household purposes—unless the secured party had first filed a financing statement covering the goods.

automatic perfection

Perfection by mere attachment.

FIGURE 28.4 Attachment and Perfection

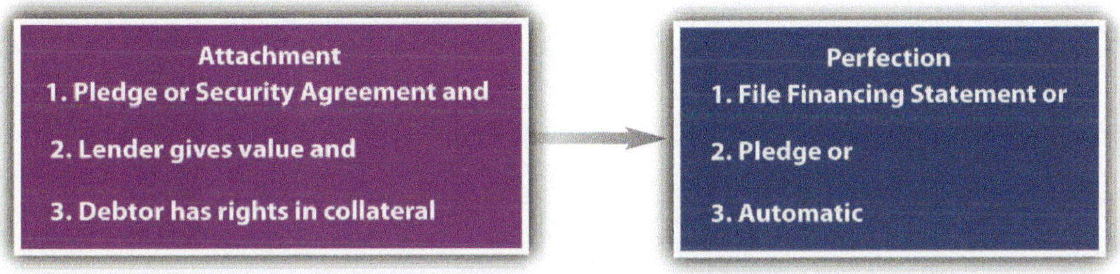

Key Takeaway

A creditor may be secured—allowed to take the debtor's property upon debtor's default—by agreement between the parties or by operation of law. The law governing agreements for personal property security is Article 9 of the UCC. The creditor's first step is to attach the security interest. This is usually accomplished when the debtor, in return for value (a loan or credit) extended from the creditor, puts up as collateral some valuable asset in which she has an interest and authenticates (signs) a security agreement (the contract) giving the creditor a security interest in collateral and allowing that the creditor may take it if the debtor defaults. The UCC lists various kinds of assets that can be collateralized, ranging from tangible property (goods), to assets only able to be manifested by paper (indispensable paper), to intangible assets (like patent rights). Sometimes no security agreement is necessary, mostly if the creditor takes possession of the collateral. After attachment, the prudent creditor will want to perfect the security interest to make sure no other creditors claim an interest in the collateral. Perfection is most often accomplished by filing a financing statement in the appropriate place to put the world on notice of the creditor's interest. Perfection can also be achieved by a pledge (possession by the secured creditor) or by "control" of certain assets (having such control over them as to be able to sell them if the debtor defaults). Perfection is automatic temporarily for some items (certified securities, instruments, and negotiable documents) but also upon mere attachment to purchase-money security interests in consumer goods.

Exercises

1. Why is a creditor ill-advised to be unsecured?
2. Elaine bought a computer for her use as a high school teacher, the school contributing one-third of its cost. Elaine was compelled to file for bankruptcy. The computer store claimed it had perfected its interest by mere attachment, and the bankruptcy trustee claimed the computer as an asset of Elaine's bankruptcy estate. Who wins, and why?
3. What is the general rule governing where financing statements should be filed?
4. If the purpose of perfection is to alert the world to the creditor's claim in the collateral, why is perfection accomplishable by possession alone in some cases?
5. Contractor pawned a power tool and got a $200 loan from Pawnbroker. Has there been a perfection of a security interest?

28.2 Priorities

Learning Objectives

1. Understand the general rule regarding who gets priority among competing secured parties.
2. Know the immediate exceptions to the general rule—all involving PMSIs.
3. Understand the basic ideas behind the other exceptions to the general rule.

Priorities: this is the money question. Who gets what when a debtor defaults? Depending on how the priorities in the collateral were established, even a secured creditor may walk away with the collateral or with nothing. Here we take up the general rule and the exceptions.

General Rule

The general rule regarding priorities is, to use a quotation attributed to a Southern Civil War general, the one who wins "gets there firstest with the mostest." The first to do the best job of perfecting wins. The Uniform Commercial Code (UCC) creates a race of diligence among competitors.

Application of the Rule

If both parties have perfected, the first to perfect wins. If one has perfected and one attached, the perfected party wins. If both have attached without perfection, the first to attach wins. If neither has attached, they are unsecured creditors. Let's test this general rule against the following situations:

1. Rosemary, without having yet lent money, files a financing statement on February 1 covering certain collateral owned by Susan—Susan's fur coat. Under UCC Article 9, a filing may be made before the security interest attaches. On March 1, Erika files a similar statement, also without having lent any money. On April 1, Erika loans Susan $1,000, the loan being secured by the fur coat described in the statement she filed on March 1. On May 1, Rosemary also loans

Susan $1,000, with the same fur coat as security. Who has priority? Rosemary does, since she filed first, even though Erika actually first extended the loan, which was perfected when made (because she had already filed). This result is dictated by the rule even though Rosemary may have known of Erika's interest when she subsequently made her loan.

2. Susan cajoles both Rosemary and Erika, each unknown to the other, to loan her $1,000 secured by the fur coat, which she already owns and which hangs in her coat closet. Erika gives Susan the money a week after Rosemary, but Rosemary has not perfected and Erika does not either. A week later, they find out they have each made a loan against the same coat. Who has priority? Whoever perfects first: the rule creates a race to the filing office or to Susan's closet. Whoever can submit the financing statement or actually take possession of the coat first will have priority, and the outcome does not depend on knowledge or lack of knowledge that someone else is claiming a security interest in the same collateral. But what of the rule that in the absence of perfection, whichever security interest first attached has priority? This is "thought to be of merely theoretical interest," says the UCC commentary, "since it is hard to imagine a situation where the case would come into litigation without [either party] having perfected his interest." And if the debtor filed a petition in bankruptcy, neither unperfected security interest could prevail against the bankruptcy trustee.

To rephrase: An attached security interest prevails over other unsecured creditors (unsecured creditors lose to secured creditors, perfected or unperfected). If both parties are secured (have attached the interest), the first to perfect wins.[43] If both parties have perfected, the first to have perfected wins.[44]

Exceptions to the General Rule

There are three immediate exceptions to the general rule, and several other exceptions, all of which—actually—make some straightforward sense even if it sounds a little complicated to explain them.

Immediate Exceptions

We call the following three exceptions "immediate" ones because they allow junior filers immediate priority to take their collateral before the debtor's other creditors get it. They all involve purchase-money security interests (PMSIs), so if the debtor defaults, the creditor repossesses the very goods the creditor had sold the debtor.

(1) *Purchase-money security interest in goods (other than inventory or livestock).* The UCC provides that "a perfected purchase-money security interest in goods other than inventory or livestock has priority over a conflicting security interest in the same goods . . . if the purchase-money security interest is perfected when debtor receives possession of the collateral or within 20 days thereafter."[45] The Official Comment to this UCC section observes that "in most cases, priority will be over a security interest asserted under an after-acquired property clause."

Suppose Susan manufactures fur coats. On February 1, Rosemary advances her $10,000 under a security agreement covering all Susan's machinery and containing an after-acquired property clause. Rosemary files a financing statement that same day. On March 1, Susan buys a new machine from Erika for $5,000 and gives her a security interest in the machine; Erika files a financing statement within twenty days of the time that the machine is delivered to Susan. Who has priority if Susan defaults on her loan payments? Under the PMSI rule, Erika has priority, because she had a PMSI. Suppose, however, that Susan had not bought the machine from Erika but had merely given her a security interest in it. Then Rosemary would have priority, because her filing was prior to Erika's.

What would happen if this kind of PMSI in noninventory goods (here, equipment) did not get priority status? A prudent Erika would not extend credit to Susan at all, and if the new machine is necessary for Susan's business, she would soon be out of business. That certainly would not inure to the benefit of Rosemary. It is, mostly, to Rosemary's advantage that Susan gets the machine: it enhances Susan's ability to make money to pay Rosemary.

(2) *Purchase-money security interest in inventory.* The UCC provides that a perfected PMSI in inventory has priority over conflicting interests in the same inventory, provided that the PMSI is perfected when the debtor receives possession of the inventory, the PMSI-secured party sends an authenticated notification to the holder of the conflicting interest and that person receives the notice within five years before the debtor receives possession of the inventory, and the notice states that the person sending it has or expects to acquire a PMSI in the inventory and describes the inventory.[46] The notice requirement is aimed at protecting a secured party in the typical situation in which incoming inventory is subject to a prior agreement to make advances against it. If the original creditor gets notice that new inventory is subject to a PMSI, he will be forewarned against making an advance on it; if he does not receive notice, he will have priority. It is usually to the earlier creditor's advantage that her debtor is able to get credit to "floor" (provide) inventory, without selling which, of course, the debtor cannot pay back the earlier creditor.

(3) *Purchase-money security interest in fixtures.* Under UCC Section 9-334(e), a perfected security in fixtures has priority over a mortgage if the security interest is a PMSI and the security interest is perfected by a fixture filing before the goods become fixtures or within twenty days after. A mortgagee is usually a bank (the mortgagor is the owner of the real estate, subject to the mortgagee's interest). The bank's mortgage covers the real estate and fixtures, even fixtures added after the date of the mortgage (after-acquired property clause). In accord with the general rule, then, the mortgagee/bank would normally have priority if the mortgage is recorded first, as would a fixture filing if made before the mortgage was recorded. But with the exception noted, the bank's interest is subordinate to the fixture-seller's later-perfected PMSI. Example: Susan buys a new furnace from Heating Co. to put in her house. Susan gave a bank a thirty-year mortgage on the house ten years before. Heating Co. takes back a PMSI and files the appropriate financing statement before or within twenty days of installation. If Susan defaults on her loan to the bank, Heating Co. would take priority over the bank. And why not? The mortgagee has, in the long run, benefited from the improvement and modernization of the real estate. (Again, there are further nuances in Section 9-334 beyond our scope here.) A non-PMSI in fixtures or PMSIs perfected more than twenty days after goods become a fixture loses out to prior recorded interests in the realty.

Other Exceptions

We have noted the three immediate exceptions to the general rule that "the firstest with the mostest" prevails. There are some other exceptions.

lien creditor

A creditor who is secured by a lien.

Think about how these other exceptions might arise: who might want to take property subject to a security agreement (not including thieves)? That is, Debtor gives Creditor a security interest in, say, goods, while retaining possession. First, *buyers* of various sorts might want the goods if they paid for them; they usually win. Second, *lien creditors* might want the goods (a **lien creditor** is one whose claim is based on operation of law—involuntarily against Debtor, and including a trustee in bankruptcy—as opposed to one whose claim is based on agreement); lien creditors may be statutory (landlords, mechanics, bailees) or judicial. Third, a *bankruptcy trustee* representing Debtor's creditors (independent of the trustee's role as a lien creditor) might want to take the goods to sell and satisfy Debtor's obligations to the creditors. Fourth, unsecured creditors; fifth, secured creditors; and sixth, secured and perfected creditors. We will examine some of the possible permutations but are compelled to observe that this area of law has many fine nuances, not all of which can be taken up here.

First we look at buyers who take priority over, or free of, unperfected security interests. Buyers who take delivery of many types of collateral covered by an *unperfected* security interest win out over the hapless secured party who failed to perfect if they give value and don't know of the security interest or agricultural lien.[47] A buyer who doesn't give value or who knows of the security interest will not win out, nor will a buyer prevail if the seller's creditor files a financing statement before or within twenty days after the debtor receives delivery of the collateral.

Now we look at buyers who take priority over *perfected* security interests. Sometimes people who buy things even covered by a perfected security interest win out (the perfected secured party loses).

- *Buyers in the ordinary course of business*. "A buyer in the ordinary course of business, other than [one buying farm products from somebody engaged in farming] takes free of a security interest created by the buyer's seller, even if the security interest is perfected and the buyer knows [it]."[48] Here the buyer is usually purchasing inventory collateral, and it's OK if he knows the inventory is covered by a security interest, but it's not OK if he knows "that the sale violates a term in an agreement with the secured party."[49] It would not be conducive to faith in commercial transactions if buyers of inventory generally had to worry whether their seller's creditors were going to repossess the things the buyers had purchased in good faith. For example (based on example 1 to the same comment, UCC 9-320, Official Comment 3), Manufacturer makes appliances and owns manufacturing equipment covered by a perfected security agreement in favor of Lender. Manufacturer sells the equipment to Dealer, whose business is buying and selling used equipment; Dealer, in turn, sells the stuff to Buyer, a buyer in the ordinary course. Does Buyer take free of the security interest? No, because Dealer didn't create it; Manufacturer did.
- Buyers of consumer goods purchased for personal, family, or household use take free of security interests, even if perfected, so long as they buy without knowledge of the security interest, for value, for their own consumer uses, and before the filing of any financing statement covering the goods. This—again—is the rub when a seller of consumer goods perfects by "mere attachment" (automatic perfection) and the buyer of the goods turns around and sells them. For example, Tom buys a new refrigerator from Sears, which perfects by mere attachment. Tom has cash flow problems and sells the fridge to Ned, his neighbor. Ned doesn't know about Sears's security interest and pays a reasonable amount for it (gives "value"). He puts it in his kitchen for home use. Sears cannot repossess the fridge from Ned. If it wanted to protect itself fully, Sears would have filed a financing statement; then Ned would be out the fridge when the repo men came.[50] The "value" issue is interestingly presented in the *Nicolosi* case (Section 5).
- *Buyers of farm products*. The UCC itself does not protect buyers of farm products from security interests created by "the person engaged in farming operations who is in the business of selling farm products," and the result was that sometimes the buyer had to pay twice: once to the farmer and again to the lender whom the farmer didn't pay. As a result, Congress included in its 1985 Farm Security Act, 7 USC 1631, Section 1324, this language: "A buyer who in the ordinary course of business buys a farm product from a seller engaged in farming operations shall take free of a security interest created by the seller, even though the security interest is perfected; and the buyer knows of the existence of such interest."

There are some other exceptions, beyond our scope here.

Lien Creditors

Persons (including bankruptcy trustees) who become lien creditors *before* the security interest is perfected win out—the unperfected security interest is subordinate to lien creditors. Persons who become lien creditors *after* the security interest is perfected lose (subject to some nuances in situations where the lien arises between attachment by the creditor and the filing, and depending upon the type of security interest and the type of collateral).[51] More straightforwardly, perhaps, a lien securing payment or performance of an obligation for services or materials furnished with respect to goods by a person in the ordinary course of business has priority over other security interests (unless a statute provides otherwise).[52] This is the bailee or "material man" (one who supplies materials, as to build a house) with a lien situation. Garage Mechanic repairs a car in which Owner has previously given a perfected security interest to Bank. Owner doesn't pay Bank. Bank seeks to repossess the car from Mechanic. It will have to pay the Mechanic first. And why not? If the car was not running, Bank would have to have it repaired anyway.

Bankruptcy Trustee

To what extent can the bankruptcy trustee take property previously encumbered by a security interest? It depends. If the security interest was not perfected at the time of filing for bankruptcy, the trustee can take the collateral.[53] If it was perfected, the trustee can't take it, subject to rules on preferential transfers: the Bankruptcy Act provides that the trustee can avoid a transfer of an interest of the debtor in property—including a security interest—(1) to or for the benefit of a creditor, (2) on or account of an antecedent debt, (3) made while the debtor was insolvent, (4) within ninety days of the bankruptcy petition date (or one year, for "insiders"—like relatives or business partners), (5) which enables the creditor to receive more than it would have in the bankruptcy.[54] There are further bankruptcy details beyond our scope here, but the short of it is that sometimes creditors who think they have a valid, enforceable security interest find out that the bankruptcy trustee has snatched the collateral away from them.

Deposit accounts perfected by control. A security interest in a deposit account (checking account, savings account, money-market account, certificate of deposit) takes priority over security interests in the account perfected by other means, and under UCC Section 9-327(3), a bank with which the deposit is made takes priority over all other conflicting security agreements.[55] For example, a debtor enters into a security agreement with his sailboat as collateral. The creditor perfects. The debtor sells the sailboat and deposits the proceeds in his account with a bank; normally, the creditor's interest would attach to the proceeds. The debtor next borrows money from the bank, and the bank takes a security interest in the debtor's account by control. The debtor defaults. Who gets the money representing the sailboat's proceeds? The bank does. The rationale: "this . . . enables banks to extend credit to their depositors without the need to examine [records] to determine whether another party might have a security interest in the deposit account."[56]

Key Takeaway

Who among competing creditors gets the collateral if the debtor defaults? The general rule on priorities is that the first to secure most completely wins: if all competitors have perfected, the first to do so wins. If one has perfected and the others have not, the one who perfects wins. If all have attached, the first to attach wins. If none have attached, they're all unsecured creditors. To this general rule there are a number of exceptions. Purchase-money security interests in goods and inventory prevail over previously perfected secured parties in the same goods and inventory (subject to some requirements); fixture financers who file properly have priority over previously perfected mortgagees. Buyers in the ordinary course of business take free of a security interest created by their seller, so long as they don't know their purchase violates a security agreement. Buyers of consumer goods perfected by mere attachment win out over the creditor who declined to file. Buyers in the ordinary course of business of farm products prevail over the farmer's creditors (under federal law, not the UCC). Lien creditors who become such before perfection win out; those who become such after perfection usually lose. Bailees in possession and material men have priority over previous perfected claimants. Bankruptcy trustees win out over unperfected security interests and over perfected ones if they are considered voidable transfers from the debtor to the secured party. Deposit accounts perfected by control prevail over previously perfected secured parties in the same deposit accounts.

Exercises

1. What is the general rule regarding priorities for the right to repossess goods encumbered by a security interest when there are competing creditors clamoring for that right?

2. Why does it make good sense to allow purchase-money security creditors in (1) inventory, (2) equipment, and (3) fixtures priority over creditors who perfected before the PMSI was perfected?
3. A buyer in the ordinary course of business is usually one buying inventory. Why does it make sense that such a buyer should take free of a security interest created by his seller?

28.3 Rights of Creditor on Default and Disposition after Repossession

Learning Objectives

1. Understand that the creditor may sue to collect the debt.
2. Recognize that more commonly the creditor will realize on the collateral—repossess it.
3. Know how collateral may be disposed of upon repossession: by sale or by strict foreclosure.

Rights of Creditor on Default

Upon default, the creditor must make an election: to sue, or to repossess.

Resort to Judicial Process

After a debtor's default (e.g., by missing payments on the debt), the creditor could ignore the security interest and bring suit on the underlying debt. But creditors rarely resort to this remedy because it is time consuming and costly. Most creditors prefer to repossess the collateral and sell it or retain possession in satisfaction of the debt.

Repossession

Section 9-609 of the Uniform Commercial Code (UCC) permits the secured party to take possession of the collateral on default (unless the agreement specifies otherwise):

> *(a) After default, a secured party may (1) take possession of the collateral; and (2) without removal, may render equipment unusable and dispose of collateral on a debtor's premises.*
>
> *(b) A secured party may proceed under subsection (a): (1) pursuant to judicial process; or (2) without judicial process, if it proceeds without breach of the peace.*

This language has given rise to the flourishing business of professional "repo men" (and women). "Repo" companies are firms that specialize in repossession collateral. They have trained car-lock pickers, in-house locksmiths, experienced repossession teams, damage-free towing equipment, and the capacity to deliver repossessed collateral to the client's desired destination. Some firms advertise that they have 360-degree video cameras that record every aspect of the repossession. They have "skip chasers"—people whose business it is to track down those who skip out on their obligations, and they are trained not to breach the peace.[57] See *Pantoja-Cahue v. Ford Motor Credit Co.*, a case discussing repossession, in Section 5.

The reference in Section 9-609(a)(2) to "render equipment unusable and dispose of collateral on a debtor's premises" gets to situations involving "heavy equipment [when] the physical removal from the debtor's plant and the storage of collateral pending disposition may be impractical or unduly expensive. . . . Of course . . . all aspects of the disposition must be commercially reasonable."[58] Rendering the equipment unusable would mean disassembling some critical part of the machine—letting it sit there until an auction is set up on the premises.

The creditor's agents—the repo people—charge for their service, of course, and if possible the cost of repossession comes out of the collateral when it's sold. A debtor would be better off voluntarily delivering the collateral according to the creditor's instructions, but if that doesn't happen, "self-help"—repossession—is allowed because, of course, the debtor said it would be allowed in the security agreement, so long as the repossession can be accomplished without breach of peace. "Breach of peace" is language that can cover a wide variety of situations over which courts do not always agree. For example, some courts interpret a creditor's taking of the collateral despite the debtor's clear oral protest as a breach of the peace; other courts do not.

Disposition after Repossession

After repossession, the creditor has two options: sell the collateral or accept it in satisfaction of the debt (see Figure 28.5).

FIGURE 28.5 Disposition after Repossession

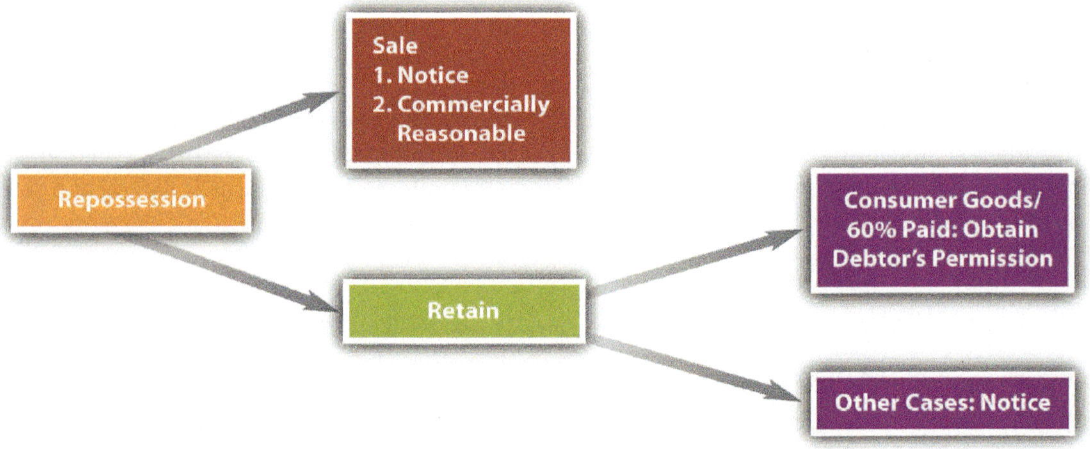

Sale

Sale is the usual method of recovering the debt. Section 9-610 of the UCC permits the secured creditor to "sell, lease, license, or otherwise dispose of any or all of the collateral in its present condition or following any commercially reasonable preparation or processing." The collateral may be sold as a whole or in parcels, at one time or at different times. Two requirements limit the creditor's power to resell: (1) it must send notice to the debtor and secondary obligor, and (unless consumer goods are sold) to other secured parties; and (2) all aspects of the sale must be "commercially reasonable."[59] Most frequently the collateral is auctioned off.

Section 9-615 of the UCC describes how the proceeds are applied: first, to the costs of the repossession, including reasonable attorney's fees and legal expenses as provided for in the security agreement (and it will provide for that!); second, to the satisfaction of the obligation owed; and third, to junior creditors. This again emphasizes the importance of promptly perfecting the security interest: failure to do so frequently subordinates the tardy creditor's interest to junior status. If there is money left over from disposing of the collateral—a surplus—the debtor gets that back. If there is still money owing—a deficiency—the debtor is liable for that. In Section 9-616, the UCC carefully explains how the surplus or deficiency is calculated; the explanation is required in a consumer goods transaction, and it has to be sent to the debtor after the disposition.

Strict Foreclosure

Because resale can be a bother (or the collateral is appreciating in value), the secured creditor may wish simply to accept the collateral in full satisfaction or partial satisfaction of the debt, as permitted in UCC Section 9-620(a). This is known as **strict foreclosure**. The debtor must consent to letting the creditor take the collateral without a sale in a "record authenticated after default," or after default the creditor can send the debtor a proposal for the creditor to accept the collateral, and the proposal is effective if not objected to within twenty days after it's sent.

strict foreclosure

The creditor takes the collateral, discharges the debtor, and has no right to seek any deficiency.

The strict foreclosure provisions contain a safety feature for consumer goods debtors. If the debtor has paid at least 60 percent of the debt, then the creditor may not use strict foreclosure—unless the debtor signs a statement after default renouncing his right to bar strict foreclosure and to force a sale.[60] A consumer who refuses to sign such a statement thus forces the secured creditor to sell the collateral under Section 9-610. Should the creditor fail to sell the goods within ninety days after taking possession of the goods, she is liable to the debtor for the value of the goods in a conversion suit or may incur the liabilities set forth in Section 9-625, which provides for minimum damages for the consumer debtor. Recall that the UCC imposes a duty to act in good faith and in a commercially reasonable manner, and in most cases with reasonable notification.[61] See Figure 28.5.

Foreclosure on Intangible Collateral

A secured party's repossession of inventory or equipment can disrupt or even close a debtor's business. However, when the collateral is intangible—such as accounts receivable, general intangibles, chattel paper, or instruments—collection by a secured party after the debtor's default may proceed without interrupting the business. Section 9-607 of the UCC provides that on default, the secured party is entitled to notify the third party—for example, a person who owes money on an account—that payment should be made to him. The secured party is accountable to the debtor for any surplus, and the debtor is liable for any deficiency unless the parties have agreed otherwise.

As always in parsing the UCC here, some of the details and nuances are necessarily omitted because of lack of space or because a more detailed analysis is beyond this book's scope.

Key Takeaway

Upon default, the creditor may bring a lawsuit against the debtor to collect a judgment. But the whole purpose of secured transactions is to avoid this costly and time-consuming litigation. The more typical situation is that the creditor repossesses the collateral and then either auctions it off (sale) or keeps it in satisfaction of the debt (strict foreclosure). In the former situation, the creditor may then proceed against the debtor for the deficiency. In consumer cases, the creditor cannot use strict foreclosure if 60 percent of the purchase price has been paid.

Exercises

1. Although a creditor could sue the debtor, get a judgment against it, and collect on the judgment, usually the creditor repossesses the collateral. Why is repossession the preferred method of realizing on the security?
2. Why is repossession allowed *so long as* it can be done without a breach of the peace?
3. Under what circumstances is strict foreclosure not allowed?

28.4 Suretyship

Learning Objectives

1. Understand what a surety is and why sureties are used in commercial transactions.
2. Know how suretyships are created.
3. Recognize the general duty owed by the surety to the creditor, and the surety's defenses.
4. Recognize the principal obligor's duty to the surety, and the surety's rights against the surety.
5. Understand the rights among cosureties.

Definition, Types of Sureties, and Creation of the Suretyship

Definition

Suretyship is the second of the three major types of consensual security arrangements noted at the beginning of this chapter (personal property security, suretyship, real property security)—and a common one. Creditors frequently ask the owners of small, closely held companies to guarantee their loans to the company, and parent corporations also frequently are guarantors of their subsidiaries' debts. The earliest sureties were friends or relatives of the principal debtor who agreed—for free—to lend their guarantee. Today most sureties in commercial transaction are insurance companies (but insurance is not the same as suretyship).

A **surety** is one who promises to pay or perform an obligation owed by the **principal debtor**, and, strictly speaking, the surety is primarily liable on the debt: the creditor can demand payment from the surety when the debt is due. The creditor is the person to whom the principal debtor (and the surety, strictly speaking) owes an obligation. Very frequently, the creditor requires first that the debtor put up collateral to secure indebtedness, and—in addition—that the debtor engage a surety to make extra certain the creditor is paid or performance is made. For example, David Debtor wants Bank to loan his corporation, David Debtor, Inc., $100,000. Bank says, "Okay, Mr. Debtor, we'll loan the corporation money, but we want its computer equipment as security, and we want you personally to guarantee the debt if the corporation can't pay." Sometimes, though, the surety and the principal debtor may have no agreement between each other; the surety might have struck a deal with the creditor to act as surety without the consent or knowledge of the principal debtor.

surety

One who promises to act or pay upon the default of another: a guarantor.

principal debtor

The person whose debt is guaranteed by a surety.

A **guarantor** also is one who guarantees an obligation of another, and for practical purposes, therefore, *guarantor* is usually synonymous with *surety*—the terms are used pretty much interchangeably. But here's the technical difference: a surety is usually a party to the original contract and signs her (or his, or its) name to the original agreement along with the surety; the consideration for the principal's contract is the same as the surety's consideration—she is bound on the contract from the very start, and she is also expected to know of the principal debtor's default so that the creditor's failure to inform her of it does not discharge her of any liability. On the other hand, a guarantor usually does not make his agreement with the creditor at the same time the principal debtor does: it's a separate contract requiring separate consideration, and if the guarantor is not informed of the principal debtor's default, the guarantor can claim discharge on the obligation to the extent any failure to inform him prejudices him. But, again, as the terms are mostly synonymous, *surety* is used here to encompass both.

guarantor

One who promises to pay or perform a contract obligation upon the default of another; a surety.

FIGURE 28.6 Defenses of Principal Debtor and Surety

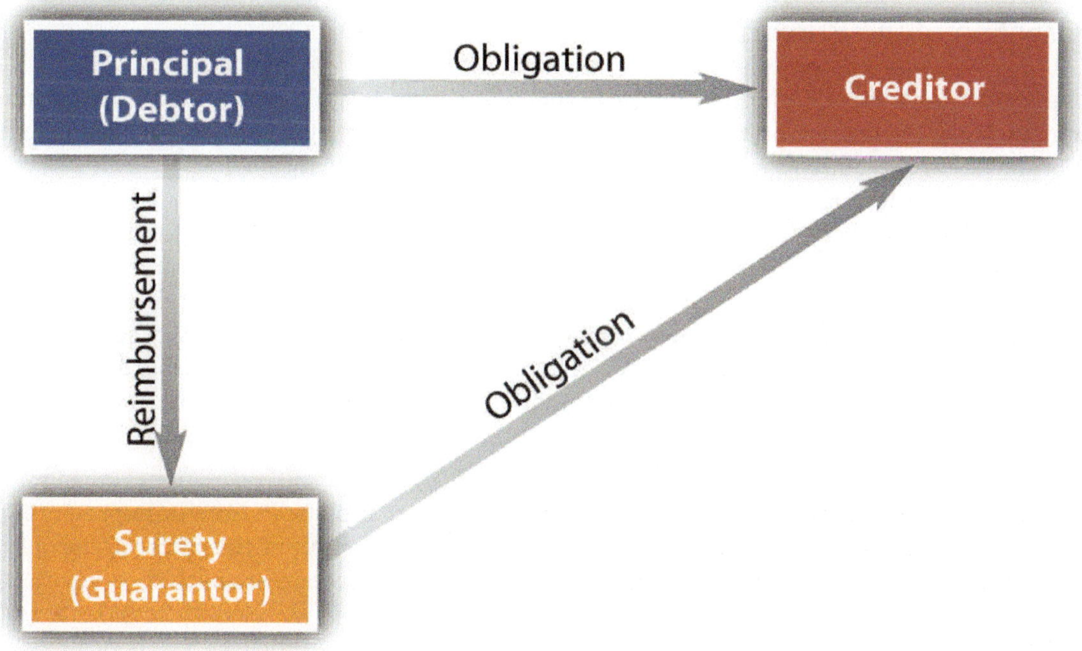

Types of Suretyship

performance bond

A surety bond that ensures a property owner (as a developer or municipality) of the completion of a construction contract or payment of actual damages to the extent of the bond in the event that the contractor fails to complete it.

judicial bond

A bond filed with the court as a guarantee. For example, a party to a court action may post a judicial bond to guarantee payment of a verdict while an appeal is being considered.

fidelity bond

An assurance, generally purchased by an employer, to cover employees who are entrusted with valuable property or funds.

Where there is an interest, public or private, that requires protection from the possibility of a default, sureties are engaged. For example, a landlord might require that a commercial tenant not only put up a security deposit but also show evidence that it has a surety on line ready to stand for three months' rent if the tenant defaults. Often, a municipal government will want its road contractor to show it has a surety available in case, for some reason, the contractor cannot complete the project. Many states require general contractors to have bonds, purchased from insurance companies, as a condition of getting a contractor's license; the insurance company is the surety—it will pay out if the contractor fails to complete work on the client's house. These are types of a **performance bond**. A judge will often require that a criminal defendant put up a bond guaranteeing his appearance in court—that's a type of suretyship where the bail-bonder is the surety—or that a plaintiff put up a bond indemnifying the defendant for the costs of delays caused by the lawsuit—a **judicial bond**. (A bail bond, generally, costs about 10% of the amount set as bail. Therefore, if your bail is set at $5,000, you can expect to pay about $500 in order to purchase a bail bond.) A bank will take out a bond on its employees in case they steal money from the bank—the bank teller, in this case, is the principal debtor (a **fidelity bond**). However, as we will see, sureties do not anticipate financial loss like insurance companies do: the surety expects, or hopes, to be repaid if it has to perform. The principal debtor goes to an insurance company and buys the bond—the suretyship policy. The cost of the premium depends on the surety company, the type of bond applied for, and the applicant's financial history. A sound estimate of premium costs is 1 percent to 4 percent, but if a surety company classifies an applicant as high risk, the premium falls between 5 percent and 20 percent of the bond amount. When the purchaser of real estate agrees to assume the seller's mortgage (promises to pay the mortgage debt), the seller then becomes a surety: unless the mortgagee releases the seller (not likely), the seller has to pay if the buyer defaults.

Creation of the Suretyship

Suretyship can arise only through contract. The general principles of contract law apply to suretyship. Thus a person with the general capacity to contract has the power to become a surety. Consideration is required for a suretyship contract: if Debtor asks a friend to act as a surety to induce Creditor to make Debtor a loan, the consideration Debtor gives Creditor also acts as the consideration Friend gives. A gratuitous surety's promise to perform to the creditor if the primary obligor defaults is bound to her promise based on promissory estoppel, even without consideration. Where the suretyship arises *after* Creditor has already extended credit, new consideration would be required (absent application of the doctrine of promissory estoppel[62]). You may recall from the chapters on contracts that the promise by one person to pay or perform for the debts or defaults of another must be evidenced by a writing under the statute of frauds (subject to the "main purpose" exception).

Suretyship contracts are affected to some extent by government regulation. Under a 1985 Federal Trade Commission Credit Practices Rule, creditors are prohibited from misrepresenting a surety's liability. Creditors must also give the surety a notice that explains the nature of the obligation and the potential liability that can arise if a person cosigns on another's debt.[63]

Duties and Rights of the Surety

Duties of the Surety

Upon the principal debtor's default, the surety is contractually obligated to perform unless the principal herself or someone on her behalf discharges the obligation. When the surety performs, it must do so in good faith. Because the principal debtor's defenses are generally limited, and because—as will be noted—the surety has the right to be reimbursed by the debtor, debtors not infrequently claim the surety acted in bad faith by doing things like failing to make an adequate investigation (to determine if the debtor really defaulted), overpaying claims, interfering with the contact between the surety and the debtor, and making unreasonable refusals to let the debtor complete the project. The case *Fidelity and Deposit Co. of Maryland v. Douglas Asphalt Co.*, in Section 5, is typical.

Rights of the Surety

The surety has four main rights stemming from its obligation to answer for the debt or default of the principal debtor.

Exoneration

If, at the time a surety's obligation has matured, the principal can satisfy the obligation but refuses to do so, the surety is entitled to **exoneration**—a court order requiring the principal to perform. It would be inequitable to force the surety to perform and then to have to seek **reimbursement** from the principal if all along the principal is able to perform.

exoneration

Relieving of liability.

reimbursement

The right of a surety to be repaid by the principal debtor.

Reimbursement

If the surety must pay the creditor because the principal has defaulted, the principal is obligated to reimburse the surety. The amount required to be reimbursed includes the surety's reasonable, good-faith outlays, including interest and legal fees.

Subrogation

Suppose the principal's duty to the creditor is fully satisfied and that the surety has contributed to this satisfaction. Then the surety is entitled to be subrogated to the rights of the creditor against the principal. In other words, the surety stands in the creditor's shoes and may assert against the principal whatever rights the creditor could have asserted had the duty not been discharged. The right of **subrogation** includes the right to take secured interests that the creditor obtained from the principal to cover the duty. Sarah's Pizzeria owes Martha $5,000, and Martha has taken a security interest in Sarah's Chevrolet. Eva is surety for the debt. Sarah defaults, and Eva pays Martha the $5,000. Eva is entitled to have the security interest in the car transferred to her.

subrogation

Substitution of one person for another who has a legal claim or right.

Contribution

Two or more sureties who are bound to answer for the principal's default and who should share between them the loss caused by the default are known as **cosureties**. A surety who in performing its own obligation to the creditor winds up paying more than its proportionate share is entitled to **contribution** from the cosureties.

cosureties

An arrangement where two or more surety companies directly participate on a bond.

contribution

The sharing of a loss or payment by two or more persons or sureties.

Defenses of the Parties

The principal and the surety may have defenses to paying.

Defenses of the Principal

The principal debtor may avail itself of any standard contract defenses as against the creditor, including impossibility, illegality, incapacity, fraud, duress, insolvency, or bankruptcy discharge.

However, the surety may contract with the creditor to be liable despite the principal's defenses, and a surety who has undertaken the suretyship with knowledge of the creditor's fraud or duress remains obligated, even though the principal debtor will be discharged. When the surety turns to the principal debtor and demands reimbursement, the latter may have defenses against the surety—as noted—for acting in bad faith.

One of the main reasons creditors want the promise of a surety is to avoid the risk that the principal debtor will go bankrupt: the debtor's bankruptcy is a defense to the debtor's liability, certainly, but that defense cannot be used by the surety. The same is true of the debtor's incapacity: it is a defense available to the principal debtor but not to the surety.

Defenses of the Surety

Generally, the surety may exercise defenses on a contract that would have been available to the principal debtor (e.g., creditor's breach; impossibility or illegality of performance; fraud, duress, or misrepresentation by creditor; statute of limitations; refusal of creditor to accept tender or performance from either debtor or surety). Beyond that, the surety has some defenses of its own. Common defenses raised by sureties include the following:

- *Release of the principal.* Whenever a creditor releases the principal, the surety is discharged, unless the surety consents to remain liable or the creditor expressly reserves her rights against the surety. The creditor's release of the surety, though, does not release the principal debtor because the debtor is liable without regard to the surety's liability.
- *Modification of the contract.* If the creditor alters the instrument sufficiently to discharge the principal, the surety is discharged as well. Likewise, when the creditor and principal modify their contract, a surety who has not consented to the modification is discharged if the surety's risk is materially increased (but not if it is decreased). Modifications include extension of the time of payment, release of collateral (this releases the surety to the extent of the impairment), change in principal debtor's duties, and assignment or delegation of the debtor's obligations to a third party. The surety may consent to modifications.
- *Creditor's failure to perfect.* A creditor who fails to file a financing statement or record a mortgage risks losing the security for the loan and might also inadvertently release a surety, but the failure of the creditor to resort first to collateral is no defense.
- *Statute of frauds.* Suretyship contracts are among those required to be evidenced by some writing under the statute of frauds, and failure to do so may discharge the surety from liability.
- *Creditor's failure to inform surety of material facts within creditor's knowledge affecting debtor's ability to perform* (e.g., that debtor has defaulted several times before).
- *General contract defenses.* The surety may raise common defenses like incapacity (infancy), lack of consideration (unless promissory estoppel can be substituted or unless no separate consideration is necessary because the surety's and debtor's obligations arise at the same time), and creditor's fraud or duress on surety. However, fraud by the principal debtor on the surety to induce the suretyship will not release the surety if the creditor extended credit in good faith; if the creditor knows of the fraud perpetrated by the debtor on the surety, the surety may avoid liability. See Figure 28.6.

The following are defenses of principal debtor *only:*

- Death or incapacity of principal debtor
- Bankruptcy of principal debtor
- Principal debtor's setoffs against creditor

The following are defenses of *both* principal debtor and surety:

- Material breach by creditor
- Lack of mutual assent, failure of consideration
- Creditor's fraud, duress, or misrepresentation of debtor

- Impossibility or illegality of performance
- Material and fraudulent alteration of the contract
- Statute of limitations

The following are defenses of surety *only*:

- Fraud or duress by creditor on surety
  - Illegality of suretyship contract
  - Surety's incapacity
  - Failure of consideration for surety contract (unless excused)
  - Statute of frauds
  - Acts of creditor or debtor materially affecting surety's obligations:
    - Refusal by creditor to accept tender of performance
    - Release of principal debtor without surety's consent
    - Release of surety
    - Release, surrender, destruction, or impairment of collateral
    - Extension of time on principal debtor's obligation
    - Modification of debtor's duties, place, amount, or manner of debtor's obligations

Key Takeaway

Creditors often require not only the security of collateral from the debtor but also that the debtor engage a surety. A contract of suretyship is a type of insurance policy, where the surety (insurance company) promises the creditor that if the principal debtor fails to perform, the surety will undertake good-faith performance instead. A difference between insurance and suretyship, though, is that the surety is entitled to reimbursement by the principal debtor if the surety pays out. The surety is also entitled, where appropriate, to exoneration, subrogation, and contribution. The principal debtor and the surety both have some defenses available: some are personal to the debtor, some are joint defenses, and some are personal to the surety.

Exercises

1. Why isn't collateral put up by the debtor sufficient security for the creditor—why is a surety often required?
2. How can it be said that sureties do not anticipate financial losses like insurance companies do? What's the difference, and how does the surety avoid losses?
3. Why does the creditor's failure to perfect a security interest discharge the surety from liability? Why doesn't failure of the creditor to resort first to perfected collateral discharge the surety?
4. What is the difference between a guarantor and a surety?

28.5 Cases

Perfection by Mere Attachment; Priorities

In re NICOLOSI

4 UCC Rep. 111 (Ohio 1966)

Preliminary Statement and Issues

This matter is before the court upon a petition by the trustee to sell a diamond ring in his possession free of liens. * * * Even though no pleadings were filed by Rike-Kumler Company, the issue from the briefs is whether or not a valid security interest was perfected in this chattel as consumer goods, superior to the * * * lien of the trustee in bankruptcy.

Findings of Fact

The [debtor] purchased from the Rike-Kumler Company, on July 7, 1964, the diamond ring in question, for $1,237.35 [about $9,600 in 2016 dollars], as an engagement ring for his fiancée. He executed a purchase money security agreement, which was not filed. Also, no financing statement was filed. The chattel was adequately described in the security agreement.

The controversy is between the trustee in bankruptcy and the party claiming a perfected security interest in the property. The recipient of the property has terminated her relationship with the [debtor—Mr. Nicolosi], and delivered the property to the trustee.

Conclusion of Law, Decision, and Order

If the diamond ring, purchased as an engagement ring by the bankrupt, cannot be categorized as consumer goods, and therefore exempted from the notice filing requirements of the Uniform Commercial Code as adopted in Ohio, a perfected security interest does not exist.

No judicial precedents have been cited in the briefs.

Under the commercial code, collateral is divided into tangible, intangible, and documentary categories. Certainly, a diamond ring falls into the tangible category. The classes of tangible goods are distinguished by the primary use intended. Under [the UCC] the four classes [include] "consumer goods," "equipment," "farm products" and "inventory."

The difficulty is that the code provisions use terms arising in commercial circles which have different semantical values from legal precedents. Does the fact that the purchaser bought the goods as a special gift to another person signify that it was not for his own "personal, family or household purposes" [and thus not "consumer goods"]? * * *

By a process of exclusion, a diamond engagement ring purchased for one's fiancée is not "equipment" bought or used in business, "farm products" used in farming operations, or "inventory" held for sale, lease or service contracts. When the [debtor] purchased the ring, therefore, it could only have been "consumer goods" bought "primarily for personal use." There could be no judicial purpose to create a special class of property in derogation of the statutory principles. * * *

By the foregoing summary analysis, it is apparent that the diamond ring, when the interest of the debtor attached, was consumer goods since it could have been no other class of goods. * * *

[Another problem is presented: If the fiancée could be considered to have given "value" for the ring, the perfection-by-mere-attachment is defeated, because a good faith purchaser of consumer goods takes free such "mere attachment" perfection.] Is a promise, as valid contractual consideration, included under the term "value"? In other words, was the ring given to his betrothed in consideration of marriage (promise for a promise)? If so, and "value" has been given, the transferee [the fiancée] is a "buyer" under traditional concepts.

The Uniform Commercial Code definition of "value" * * * very definitely covers a promise for a promise. The definition reads that "a person gives 'value' for rights if he acquires them . . . generally in return for any consideration sufficient to support a simple contract."

It would seem unrealistic, nevertheless, to apply contract law concepts historically developed into the law of marriage relations in the context of new concepts developed for uniform commercial practices. They are not, in reality, the same juristic manifold. The purpose of uniformity of the code should not be defeated by the obsessions of the code drafters to be all inclusive for secured creditors.

Even if the trustee, in behalf of the unsecured creditors, would feel inclined to insert love, romance and morals into commercial law [so that the fiancée was a "buyer for value," he is appearing in the wrong era, and possibly the wrong court.

Ordered, that the Rike-Kumler Company holds a perfected security interest in the diamond engagement ring, and the security interest attached to the proceeds realized from the sale of the goods by the trustee in bankruptcy.

Case Questions

1. Why didn't the jewelry store, Rike-Kumler, file a financing statement to protect its security interest in the ring?
2. How did the bankruptcy trustee get the ring?
3. What argument did the trustee make as to why the ring should not be considered "consumer goods" so that he—the trustee—should be able to take the ring as an asset belonging to the estate of the debtor? What did the court determine on this issue?
4. If Mr. Nicolosi's fiancée could have been considered to have given "value" for the ring, why would that defeat the jewelry store's claim? What did the court rule on this issue?

Repossession and Breach of the Peace

Pantoja-Cahue v. Ford Motor Credit Co.
872 N.E.2d 1039 (Ill. App. 2007)

Plaintiff Mario Pantoja-Cahue filed a six-count complaint seeking damages from defendant Ford Motor Credit Company for Ford's alleged breach of the peace and "illegal activities" in repossessing plaintiff's automobile from his locked garage. * * *

In August 2000, plaintiff purchased a 2000 Ford Explorer from auto dealer Webb Ford. Plaintiff, a native Spanish speaker, negotiated the purchase with a Spanish-speaking salesperson at Webb. Plaintiff signed what he thought was a contract for the purchase and financing of the vehicle, with monthly installment payments to be made to Ford. The contract was in English. Some years later, plaintiff discovered the contract was actually a lease, not a purchase agreement. Plaintiff brought suit against Ford and Webb on August 22, 2003, alleging fraud. Ford brought a replevin action against plaintiff asserting plaintiff was in default on his obligations under the lease. In the late night/early morning hours of March 11–12, 2004, repossession agents [from Doe Repossession Services] entered plaintiff's locked garage and removed the car. * * *

Plaintiff sought damages for Ford and Doe's "unlawful activities surrounding the wrongful repossession of Plaintiff's vehicle." He alleged Ford and Doe's breaking into plaintiff's locked garage to effectuate the repossession and Ford's repossession of the vehicle knowing that title to the car was the subject of ongoing litigation variously violated section 2A-525(3) of the [Uniform Commercial] Code (count I against Ford), the [federal] Fair Debt Collection Practices Act (count II against Doe), * * * Ford's contract with plaintiff (count V against Ford) and section 2A-108 of the Code (count VI against Ford and Doe). * * *

Uniform Commercial Code Section 2A-525(3)

In count I, plaintiff alleged "a breach of the peace occurred as [Ford]'s repossession agent broke into Plaintiff's locked garage in order to take the vehicle" and Ford's agent "repossessed the subject vehicle by, among other things, breaking into Plaintiff's locked garage and causing substantial damage to Plaintiff's personal property in violation of [section 2A-525(3)]":

"After a default by the lessee under the lease contract * * * or, if agreed, after other default by the lessee, the lessor has the right to take possession of the goods. * * *

The lessor *may proceed under subsection (2) without judicial process if it can be done without breach of the peace* or the lessor may proceed by action." [emphasis added.]

[U]pon a lessee's default, a lessor has the right to repossess the leased goods in one of two ways: by using the judicial process or, if repossession could be accomplished without a breach of the peace, by self-help [UCC Section 2A-525(3)]. "If a breach of the peace is likely, a properly instituted civil action is the appropriate remedy." [Citation] (interpreting the term "breach of the peace" in the context of section 9-503 of the Code, which provides for the same self-help repossession as section 2A-525 but for secured creditors rather than lessors).

Taking plaintiff's well-pleaded allegations as true, Ford resorted to self-help, by employing an agent to repossess the car and Ford's agent broke into plaintiff's locked garage to effectuate the repossession. Although plaintiff's count I allegations are minimal, they are sufficient to plead a cause of action for a violation of section 2A-525(3) if breaking into a garage to repossess a car is, as plaintiff alleged, a breach of the peace. Accordingly, the question here is whether breaking into a locked garage to effectuate a repossession is a breach of the peace in violation of section 2A-525(3).

There are no Illinois cases analyzing the meaning of the term "breach of the peace" as used in the lessor repossession context in section 2A-525(3). However, there are a few Illinois cases analyzing the term as used in section 9-503 of the Code, which contains a similar provision providing that a secured creditor may, upon default by a debtor, repossess its collateral either "(1) pursuant to judicial process; or (2) without judicial process, if it proceeds without breach of the peace." The seminal case, and the only one of any use in resolving the issue, is *Chrysler Credit Corp. v. Koontz*, 277 Ill.App.3d 1078, 214 Ill.Dec. 726, 661 N.E.2d 1171 (1996).

In *Koontz*, Chrysler, the defendant creditor, sent repossession agents to repossess the plaintiff's car after the plaintiff defaulted on his payments. The car was parked in the plaintiff's front yard. The plaintiff heard the repossession in progress and ran outside in his underwear shouting "Don't take it" to the agents. The agents did not respond and proceeded to take the car. The plaintiff argued the repossession breached the peace and he was entitled to the statutory remedy for violation of section 9-503, denial of a deficiency judgment to the secured party, Chrysler. * * *

After a thorough analysis of the term "breach of the peace," the court concluded the term "connotes conduct which incites or is likely to incite immediate public turbulence, or which leads to or is likely to lead to an immediate loss of public order and tranquility. Violent conduct is not a necessary element. The probability of violence at the time of or immediately prior to the repossession is sufficient." * * * [The *Koontz* court] held the circumstances of the repossession did not amount to a breach the peace.

The court then considered the plaintiff's argument that Chrysler breached the peace by repossessing the car under circumstances constituting criminal trespass to property. Looking to cases in other jurisdictions, the court determined that, "in general, a mere trespass, standing alone, does not automatically constitute a breach of the peace." [Citation] (taking possession of car from private driveway does not, without more, constitute breach of the peace), [Citation] (no breach of the peace occurred where car repossessed from debtor's driveway without entering "any gates, doors, or other barricades to reach" car), [Citation] (no breach of the peace occurred where car was parked partially under carport and undisputed that no door, "not even one to a garage," on the debtor's premises was opened, much less broken, to repossess the car), [Citation] (although secured party may not break into or enter homes or buildings or enclosed spaces to effectuate a repossession, repossession of vehicle from parking lot of debtor's apartment building was not breach of the peace), [Citation] (repossession of car from debtor's driveway without entering any gates, doors or other barricades was accomplished without breach of the peace). * * *

Although the evidence showed the plaintiff notified Chrysler prior to the repossession that it was not permitted onto his property, the court held Chrysler's entry onto the property to take the car did not constitute a breach of the peace because there was no evidence Chrysler entered through a barricade or did anything other than drive the car away. [Citation] "Chrysler enjoyed a limited privilege to enter [the plaintiff's] property for the sole and exclusive purpose of effectuating the repossession. So long as the entry was limited in purpose (repossession), and so long as no gates, barricades, doors, enclosures, buildings, or chains were breached or cut, no breach of the peace occurred by virtue of the entry onto his property."

* * * [W]e come to essentially the same conclusion: where a repossession is effectuated by an actual breaking into the lessee/debtor's premises or breaching or cutting of chains, gates, barricades, doors or other barriers designed to exclude trespassers, the likelihood that a breach of the peace occurred is high.

Davenport v. Chrysler Credit Corp., [Citation] (Tenn.App.1991), a case analyzing Tennessee's version of section 9-503 is particularly helpful, holding that "'[a] breach of the peace is almost certain to be found if the repossession is accompanied by the unauthorized entry into a closed or locked garage.'" * * * This is so because "public policy favors peaceful, non-trespassory repossessions when the secured party has a free right of entry" and "forced entries onto the debtor's property or into the debtor's premises are viewed as seriously detrimental to the ordinary conduct of human affairs." *Davenport* held that the creditor's repossession of a car by entering a closed garage and cutting a chain that would have prevented it from removing the car amounted to a breach of the peace, "[d]espite the absence of violence or physical confrontation" (because the debtor was not at home when the repossession occurred). *Davenport* recognized that the secured creditors' legitimate interest in obtaining possession of collateral without having to resort to expensive and cumbersome judicial procedures must be balanced against the debtors' legitimate interest in being free from unwarranted invasions of their property and privacy interests.

"Repossession is a harsh procedure and is, essentially, a delegation of the State's exclusive prerogative to resolve disputes. Accordingly, the statutes governing the repossession of collateral should be construed in a way that prevents abuse and discourages illegal conduct which might otherwise go unchallenged because of the debtor's lack of knowledge of legally proper repossession techniques" [Citation].

We agree with [this] analysis of the term "breach of the peace" in the context of repossession and hold, with regard to section 2A-525(3) of the Code, that breaking into a locked garage to effectuate a repossession may constitute a breach of the peace.

Here, plaintiff alleges more than simply a trespass. He alleges Ford, through Doe, broke into his garage to repossess the car. Given our determination that breaking into a locked garage to repossess a car may constitute a breach of the peace, plaintiff's allegation is sufficient to state a cause of action under section 2A-525(3) of the Code. The court erred in dismissing count I of plaintiff's second amended complaint and we remand for further proceedings.

Uniform Commercial Code Section 2A-108

In count VI, plaintiff alleged the lease agreement was unconscionable because it was formed in violation of [the Illinois Consumer Fraud Statute, requiring that the customer verify that the negotiations were conducted in the consumer's native language and that the document was translated so the customer understood it.] * * * Plaintiff does not quote [this] or explain how the agreement violates [it]. Instead, he quotes UCC section 2A-108 of the Code, as follows:

"With respect to a consumer lease, if the court as a matter of law finds that a lease contract or any clause of a lease contract has been induced by unconscionable conduct or that unconscionable conduct has occurred in the collection of a claim arising from a lease contract, the court may grant appropriate relief.

Before making a finding of unconscionability under subsection (1) or (2), the court, on its own motion or that of a party, shall afford the parties a reasonable opportunity to present evidence as to the setting, purpose, and effect of the lease contract or clause thereof, or of the conduct."

He then, in "violation one" under count VI, alleges the lease was made in violation of [the Illinois Consumer Fraud Statute] because it was negotiated in Spanish but he was only given a copy of the contract in English; he could not read the contract and, as a result, Webb Ford was able to trick him into signing a lease, rather than a purchase agreement; such contract was induced by unconscionable conduct; and, because it was illegal, the contract was unenforceable.

This allegation is insufficient to state a cause of action against Ford under section 2A-108. * * * First, Ford is an entirely different entity than Webb Ford and plaintiff does not assert otherwise. Nor does plaintiff assert that Webb Ford was acting as Ford's agent in inducing plaintiff to sign the lease. Plaintiff asserts no basis on which Ford can be found liable for something Webb Ford did. Second, there is no allegation as to how the contract violates [the statute], merely the legal conclusion that it does, as well as the unsupported legal conclusion that a violation of [it] is necessarily unconscionable. * * * [Further discussion omitted.]

For the reasons stated above, we affirm the trial court's dismissal of counts IV, V and VI of plaintiff's second amended complaint. We reverse the court's dismissal of count I and remand for further proceedings. Affirmed in part and reversed in part; cause remanded.

Case Questions

1. Under what circumstances, if any, would breaking into a locked garage to repossess a car *not* be considered a breach of the peace?
2. The court did *not* decide that a breach of the peace had occurred. What would determine that such a breach had occurred?
3. Why did the court dismiss the plaintiff's claim (under UCC Article 2A) that it was unconscionable of Ford to trick him into signing a lease when he thought he was signing a purchase contract? Would that section of Article 2A make breaking into his garage unconscionable?
4. What alternatives had Ford besides taking the car from the plaintiff's locked garage?
5. If it was determined on remand that a breach of the peace had occurred, what happens to Ford?

Defenses of the Principal Debtor as against Reimbursement to Surety

Fidelity and Deposit Co. of Maryland v. Douglas Asphalt Co.
338 Fed.Appx. 886, 11th Cir. Ct. (2009)

Per Curium:[64]

The Georgia Department of Transportation ("GDOT") contracted with Douglas Asphalt Company to perform work on an interstate highway. After Douglas Asphalt allegedly failed to pay its suppliers and subcontractors and failed to perform under the contract, GDOT defaulted and terminated Douglas Asphalt. Fidelity and Deposit Company of Maryland and Zurich American Insurance Company had executed payment and performance bonds in connection with Douglas Asphalt's work on the interstate, and after Douglas Asphalt's default, Fidelity and Zurich spent $15,424,798 remedying the default.

Fidelity and Zurich, seeking to recover their losses related to their remedy of the default, brought this suit against Douglas Asphalt, Joel Spivey, and Ronnie Spivey. The Spiveys and Douglas Asphalt had executed a General Indemnity Agreement in favor of Fidelity and Zurich.[65]

After a bench trial, the district court entered judgment in favor of Fidelity and Zurich for $16,524,798 [nearly $19 million in 2016 dollars]. Douglas Asphalt and the Spiveys now appeal.

Douglas Asphalt and the Spiveys argue that the district court erred in entering judgment in favor of Fidelity and Zurich because Fidelity and Zurich acted in bad faith in three ways.

First, Douglas Asphalt and the Spiveys argue that the district court erred in not finding that Fidelity and Zurich acted in bad faith because they claimed excessive costs to remedy the default. Specifically, Douglas Asphalt and the Spiveys argue that they introduced evidence that the interstate project was 98% complete, and that only approximately $3.6 million was needed to remedy any default. But, the district court found that the interstate project was only 90%–92% complete and that approximately $2 million needed to be spent to correct defective work already done by Douglas Asphalt. Douglas Asphalt and the Spiveys have not shown that the district court's finding was clearly erroneous, and accordingly, their argument that Fidelity and Zurich showed bad faith in claiming that the project was only 90% complete and therefore required over $15 million to remedy the default fails.

Second, Douglas Asphalt and the Spiveys argue that Fidelity and Zurich acted in bad faith by failing to contest the default. However, the district court concluded that the indemnity agreement required Douglas Asphalt and the Spiveys to request a contest of the default, and to post collateral security to pay any judgment rendered in the course of contesting the default. The court's finding that Douglas Asphalt and the Spiveys made no such request and posted no collateral security was not clearly erroneous, and the sureties had no independent duty to investigate a default. Accordingly, Fidelity and Zurich's failure to contest the default does not show bad faith.

Finally, Douglas Asphalt and the Spiveys argue that Fidelity and Zurich's refusal to permit them to remain involved with the interstate project, either as a contractor or consultant, was evidence of bad faith. Yet, Douglas Asphalt and the Spiveys did not direct the district court or this court to any case law that holds that the refusal to permit a defaulting contractor to continue working on a project is bad faith. As the district court concluded, Fidelity and Zurich had a contractual right to take possession of all the work under the contract and arrange for its completion. Fidelity and Zurich exercised that contractual right, and, as the district court noted, the exercise of a contractual right is not evidence of bad faith.

Finding no error, we affirm the judgment of the district court.

Case Questions

1. Why were Douglas Asphalt and the Spiveys supposed to pay the sureties nearly $15.5 million?
2. What did the plaintiffs claim the defendant sureties did wrong as relates to how much money they spent to cure the default?
3. What is a "contest of the default"?
4. Why would the sureties probably *not* want the principal involved in the project?

28.6 Summary and Exercises

Summary

The law governing security interests in personal property is Article 9 of the UCC, which defines a security interest as an interest in personal property or fixtures that secures payment or performance of an obligation. Article 9 lumps together all the former types of security devices, including the pledge, chattel mortgage, and conditional sale.

Five types of tangible property may serve as collateral: (1) consumer goods, (2) equipment, (3) farm products, (4) inventory, and (5) fixtures. Five types of intangibles may serve as collateral: (1) accounts, (2) general intangibles (e.g., patents), (3) documents of title, (4) chattel paper, and (5) instruments. Article 9 expressly permits the debtor to give a security interest in after-acquired collateral.

To create an enforceable security interest, the lender and borrower must enter into an agreement establishing the interest, and the lender must follow steps to ensure that the security interest first attaches and then is perfected. There are three general requirements for attachment: (1) there must be an authenticated agreement (or the collateral must physically be in the lender's possession), (2) the lender must have given value, and (3) the debtor must have some rights in the collateral. Once the interest attaches, the lender has rights in the collateral superior to those of unsecured creditors. But others may defeat his interest unless he perfects the security interest. The three common ways of doing so are (1) filing a financing statement, (2) pledging collateral, and (3) taking a purchase-money security interest (PMSI) in consumer goods.

A financing statement is a simple notice, showing the parties' names and addresses, the signature of the debtor, and an adequate description of the collateral. The financing statement, effective for five years, must be filed in a public office; the location of the office varies among the states.

Security interests in instruments and negotiable documents can be perfected only by the secured party's taking possession, with twenty-one-day grace periods applicable under certain circumstances. Goods may also be secured through pledging, which is often done through field warehousing. If a seller of consumer goods takes a PMSI in the goods sold, then perfection is automatic and no filing is required, although the lender may file and probably should, to avoid losing seniority to a bona fide purchaser of consumer goods without knowledge of the security interest, if the goods are used for personal, family, or household purposes.

The general priority rule is "first in time, first in right." Priority dates from the earlier of two events: (1) filing a financing statement covering the collateral or (2) other perfection of the security interest. Several exceptions to this rule arise when creditors take a PMSI, among them, when a buyer in the ordinary course of business takes free of a security interest created by the seller.

On default, a creditor may repossess the collateral. For the most part, self-help private repossession continues to be lawful but risky. After repossession, the lender may sell the collateral or accept it in satisfaction of the debt. Any excess in the selling price above the debt amount must go to the debtor.

Suretyship is a legal relationship that is created when one person contracts to be responsible for the proper fulfillment of another's obligation, in case the latter (the principal debtor) fails to fulfill it. The surety may avail itself of the principal's contract defenses, but under various circumstances, defenses may be available to the one that are not available to the other. One general defense often raised by sureties is alteration of the contract. If the surety is required to perform, it has rights for reimbursement against the principal, including interest and legal fees; and if there is more than one surety, each standing for part of the obligation, one who pays a disproportionate part may seek contribution from the others.

Exercises

1. Kathy Knittle borrowed $20,000 from Bank to buy inventory to sell in her knit shop and signed a security agreement listing as collateral the entire present and future inventory in the shop, including proceeds from the sale of inventory. Bank filed no financing statement. A month later, Knittle borrowed $5,000 from Creditor, who was aware of Bank's security interest. Knittle then declared bankruptcy. Who has priority, Bank or Creditor?
2. Assume the same facts as in Exercise 1, except Creditor—again, aware of Bank's security interest—filed a financing statement to perfect its interest. Who has priority, Bank or Creditor?
3. Harold and Wilma are married. First Bank has a mortgage on their house, and it covers after-acquired property. Because Harold has a new job requiring travel to neighboring cities, they purchase a second car for Wilma's normal household use, financed by Second Bank. They sign a security agreement; Second Bank files nothing. If they were to default on their house payments, First Bank could repossess the house; could it repossess the car, too?
4. a. Kathy Knittle borrowed $20,000 from Bank to buy inventory to sell in her knit shop and signed a security agreement listing her collateral—present and future—as security for the loan. Carlene Customer bought yarn and a tabletop loom from Knittle. Shortly thereafter, Knittle declared bankruptcy. Can Bank get the loom from Customer?
   b. Assume that the facts are similar to those in Exercise 4a, except that the loom that Knittle sold had been purchased from Larry Loomaker, who had himself given a secured interest in it (and the other looms he manufactured) from Fine Lumber Company (FLC) to finance the purchase of the lumber to make the looms. Customer bought the loom from Knittle (unaware of Loomaker's situation); Loomaker failed to pay FLC. Why can FLC repossess the loom from Customer?
   c. What recourse does Customer have now?
5. Creditor loaned Debtor $30,000 with the provision that the loan was callable by Creditor with sixty days' notice to Debtor. Debtor, having been called for repayment, asked for a ninety-day extension, which Creditor assented to, provided that Debtor would put up a surety to secure repayment. Surety agreed to serve as surety. When Debtor defaulted, Creditor turned to Surety for payment. Surety asserted that Creditor had given no consideration for Surety's promise, and therefore Surety was not bound. Is Surety correct?
6. a. Mrs. Ace said to University Bookstore: "Sell the books to my daughter. I'll pay for them." When University Bookstore presented Mrs. Ace a statement for $900, she refused to pay, denying she'd ever promised to do so, and she raised the statute of frauds as a defense. Is this a good defense?
   b. Defendant ran a stop sign and crashed into Plaintiff's car, causing $8,000 damage. Plaintiff's attorney orally negotiated with Defendant's insurance company, Goodhands Insurance, to settle the case. Subsequently, Goodhands denied liability and refused to pay, and it raised the statute of frauds as a defense, asserting that any promise by it to pay for its insured's negligence would have to be in writing to be enforceable under the statute's suretyship clause. Is Goodhands's defense valid?
7.

a. First Bank has a security interest in equipment owned by Kathy Knittle in her Knit Shop. If Kathy defaults on her loan and First Bank lawfully repossesses, what are the bank's options? Explain.
b. Suppose, instead, that First Bank had a security interest in Kathy's home knitting machine, worth $10,000. She paid $6,200 on the machine and then defaulted. Now what are the bank's options?

Self-Test Questions

1. Creditors may obtain security
    a. by agreement with the debtor
    b. through operation of law
    c. through both of the above
    d. through neither of the above
2. Under UCC Article 9, when the debtor has pledged collateral to the creditor, what other condition is required for attachment of the security interest?
    a. A written security agreement must be authenticated by the debtor.
    b. There must be a financing statement filed by or for the creditor.
    c. The secured party received consideration.
    d. The debtor must have rights in the collateral.
3. To perfect a security interest, one may
    a. file a financing statement
    b. pledge collateral
    c. take a purchase-money security interest in consumer goods
    d. do any of the above
4. Perfection benefits the secured party by
    a. keeping the collateral out of the debtor's reach
    b. preventing another creditor from getting a secured interest in the collateral
    c. obviating the need to file a financing statement
    d. establishing who gets priority if the debtor defaults
5. Creditor filed a security interest in inventory on June 1, 2012. Creditor's interest takes priority over which of the following?
    a. a purchaser in the ordinary course of business who bought on June 5
    b. mechanic's lien filed on May 10
    c. purchase-money security interest in after-acquired property who filed on May 15
    d. judgment lien creditor who filed the judgment on June 10

Self-Test Answers

1. c
2. d
3. d
4. d
5. d

Endnotes

1. Uniform Commercial Code, Section 9-109.
2. Uniform Commercial Code, Section 9-102(a)(73).
3. Uniform Commercial Code, Section 9-102(12).
4. Uniform Commercial Code, Section 9-102(a)(28).
5. Uniform Commercial Code, Section 9-102 (59).
6. Uniform Commercial Code, Section 9-102(a)(71).
7. Commercial Brokers, Inc., "Glossary of Real Estate Terms," http://www.cbire.com/index.cfm/fuseaction/terms.list/letter/C/contentid/32302EC3-81D5-47DF-A9CBA32FAE38B22A.
8. Uniform Commercial Code, Section 9-102(44).
9. Uniform Commercial Code, Section 9-102(a)(48).
10. Uniform Commercial Code, Section 9-102(a)(48).
11. Uniform Commercial Code, Section 9-102(a)(34).
12. Uniform Commercial Code, Section 9-102(a)(33).
13. Uniform Commercial Code, Section 9-102(a)(41).
14. Uniform Commercial Code, Section 9-102(a)(1).
15. Uniform Commercial Code, Section 9-102(a)(2).
16. Uniform Commercial Code, Section 9-102(42).
17. Uniform Commercial Code, Section 9-102(11).
18. Uniform Commercial Code, Section 9-102(a)(47).
19. Uniform Commercial Code, Section 9-102(a)(49).
20. Uniform Commercial Code, Section 8-102(a)(4) and (a)(18).
21. Uniform Commercial Code, Section 9-203(a).
22. Uniform Commercial Code, Section 9-203(b)(2).
23. Uniform Commercial Code, Section 9-102, Official Comment 9. Here is a free example of a security agreement online: Docstoc, "Free Business Templates—Sample Open-Ended Security Agreement," http://www.docstoc.com/docs/271920/Free-Business-Templates---Sample-Open-Ended-Security-Agreement.
24. Uniform Commercial Code, Section 9-203(b)(3)(B-D).
25. Uniform Commercial Code, Section 9-310(a).
26. Uniform Commercial Code, Section 9-502, Official Comment 2.
27. Uniform Commercial Code, Section 9-502(a).
28. Uniform Commercial Code, Section 9-504.
29. Uniform Commercial Code, Section 9-502(b).
30. Uniform Commercial Code, Section 9-506; Uniform Commercial Code, Section, 9-502, Comment 3.
31. Uniform Commercial Code, Section 9-515.
32. Uniform Commercial Code, Section 9-513.
33. Uniform Commercial Code, Section 9-316.
34. Uniform Commercial Code, Section 9-501.
35. Uniform Commercial Code, Section 9-501(a)(2).
36. Uniform Commercial Code, Section 9-307(b).
37. Uniform Commercial Code, Section 9-303.
38. Uniform Commercial Code, Section 9-312(o).
39. Uniform Commercial Code, Section 9-312(f) and (g).
40. Uniform Commercial Code, Section 9-313.
41. Uniform Commercial Code, Section 9-314.
42. Uniform Commercial Code, Section 8-106, Official Comment 1.
43. Uniform Commercial Code, Section 9-322(a)(2).
44. Uniform Commercial Code, Section 9-322(a)(1).
45. Uniform Commercial Code, Section 9-324(a).
46. Uniform Commercial Code, Section 9-324(b).
47. Uniform Commercial Code, Section 9-317(b).
48. Uniform Commercial Code, Section 9-320(a).
49. Uniform Commercial Code, Section 9-320, Comment 3.
50. Uniform Commercial Code, Section 9-320(b).
51. Uniform Commercial Code, Section 9-317(a)(2)(B) and 9-317(e).
52. Uniform Commercial Code, Section 9-333.
53. 11 United States Code, Section 544 (Bankruptcy Act).
54. United States Code, Section 547.
55. Uniform Commercial Code, Section 9-327(1).
56. Uniform Commercial Code, Section 9-328, Official Comment 3 and 4.
57. Here is an example of sophisticated online advertising for a repossession firm: SSR, "Southern & Central Coast California Repossession Services," http://www.simonsrecovery.com/index.htm.
58. Uniform Commercial Code, Section 9-609(a)(2), Official Comment 6.
59. Uniform Commercial Code, Section 9-611; Uniform Commercial Code, Section 9-610.
60. Uniform Commercial Code, 9-620(e); Uniform Commercial Code, Section 9-624.
61. Uniform Commercial Code, Section 1-203.
62. *American Druggists' Ins. Co. v. Shoppe*, 448 N.W.2d 103, Minn. App. (1989).
63. Here is an example of the required notice: Federal Trade Commission, "Facts for Consumers: The Credit Practices Rule," http://www.ftc.gov/bcp/edu/pubs/consumer/credit/cre12.shtm.
64. Latin for "by the court." A decision of an appeals court as a whole in which no judge is identified as the specific author.
65. They promised to reimburse the surety for its expenses and hold it harmless for further liability.

CHAPTER 29

Mortgages and Nonconsensual Liens

Learning Objectives

After reading this chapter, you should understand the following:

1. The basic concepts of mortgages.
2. How the mortgage is created.
3. Priorities with mortgages as security devices.
4. Termination of the mortgage.
5. Other methods of using real estate as security.
6. Nonconsensual liens.

29.1 Uses, History, and Creation of Mortgages

Learning Objectives

1. Understand the terminology used in mortgage transactions, and how mortgages are used as security devices.
2. Know a bit about the history of mortgages.
3. Understand how the mortgage is created.
4. Recognize that the 2010 federal Dodd-Frank Wall Street Reform and Consumer Protection Act regulates aspects of the mortgage transaction.

Having discussed in Chapter 28 security interests in personal property and suretyship—two of the three common types of consensual security arrangements—we turn now to the third type of consensual security arrangement, the mortgage. We also discuss briefly various forms of nonconsensual liens (see Figure 29.1).

FIGURE 29.1 Security Arrangements

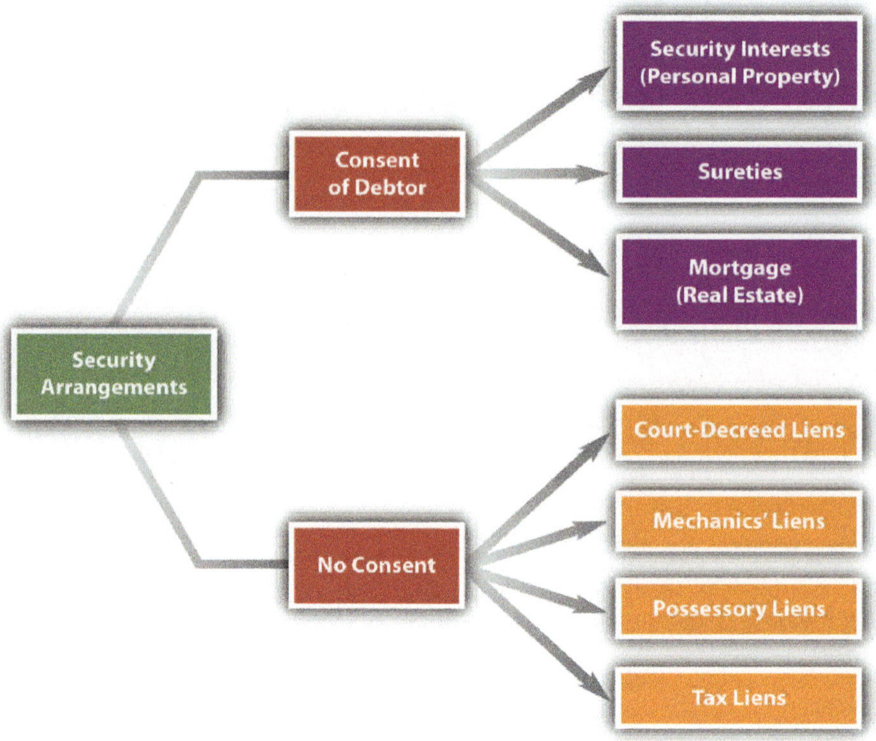

Definitions

mortgage

Security in which collateral is land.

mortgagor

One who gives a mortgage; the debtor.

mortgagee

The party who holds a mortgage; the creditor (such as a bank).

A **mortgage** is a means of securing a debt with real estate. A long time ago, the mortgage was considered an actual transfer of title, to become void if the debt was paid off. The modern view, held in most states, is that the mortgage is but a lien, giving the holder, in the event of default, the right to sell the property and repay the debt from the proceeds. The person giving the mortgage is the **mortgagor**, or borrower. In the typical home purchase, that's the buyer. The buyer needs to borrow to finance the purchase; in exchange for the money with which to pay the seller, the buyer "takes out a mortgage" with, say, a bank. The lender (bank) is the **mortgagee**, the person or institution holding the mortgage, with the right to foreclose on the property if the debt is not timely paid. Although the law of real estate mortgages is different from the set of rules in Article 9 of the Uniform Commercial Code (UCC) that we examined in Chapter 28, the circumstances are the same, except that the security is real estate rather than personal property (secured transactions) or the promise of another (suretyship).

The Uses of Mortgages

Most frequently, we think of a mortgage as a device to fund a real estate purchase: for a homeowner to buy her house, or for a commercial entity to buy real estate (e.g., an office building), or for a person to purchase farmland. But the value in real estate can be mortgaged for almost any purpose (a home equity loan): a person can take out a mortgage on land to fund a vacation. Indeed, during the period leading up to the recession in 2007–08, a lot of people borrowed money on their houses to buy things: boats, new cars, furniture, and so on. Unfortunately, it turned out that some of the real estate used as collateral was overvalued: when the economy weakened and people lost income or their jobs, they couldn't make the mortgage payments. And, to make things worse, the value of the real estate sometimes sank too, so that the debtors owed more on the property than it was worth (that's called being "underwater"). They couldn't sell without taking a loss, and they couldn't make the payments. Some debtors just walked away, leaving the banks with a large number of houses, commercial buildings, and even shopping centers on their hands.

Short History of Mortgage Law

The mortgage has ancient roots, but the form we know evolved from the English land law in the Middle Ages. Understanding that law helps to understand modern mortgage law. In the fourteenth century, the mortgage was a deed that actually transferred title to the mortgagee. If desired, the mortgagee (again, that's the one who lends the money—today usually a bank) could move into the house, occupy the property, or rent it out. But because the mortgage obligated him to apply to the mortgage debt whatever rents he collected, he seldom ousted the mortgagor. Moreover, the mortgage set a specific date (the "law day") on which the debt was to be repaid. If the mortgagor did so, the mortgage became void and the mortgagor was entitled to recover the property. If the mortgagor failed to pay the debt, the property automatically vested in the mortgagee. No further proceedings were necessary.

This law was severe. A day's delay in paying the debt, for any reason, forfeited the land, and the courts strictly enforced the mortgage. The only possible relief was a petition to the king, who over time referred these and other kinds of petitions to the courts of equity. At first fitfully, and then as a matter of course (by the seventeenth century), the equity courts would order the mortgagee to return the land when the mortgagor stood ready to pay the debt plus interest. Thus, a new right developed: the *equitable right of redemption*, known for short as the equity of redemption. In time, the courts held that this equity of redemption was a form of property right; it could be sold and inherited. This was a powerful right: no matter how many years later, the mortgagor could always recover his land by proffering a sum of money.

Understandably, mortgagees did not warm to this interpretation of the law, because their property rights were rendered insecure. They tried to defeat the equity rule allowing redemption by having mortgagors waive and surrender it to the mortgagees, but the courts voided waiver clauses as a violation of public policy. Hence a mortgage, once a transfer of title, became a security for debt. A mortgage as such can never be converted into a deed of title.

The law did not rest there. Mortgagees won a measure of relief in the development of the **foreclosure**. On default, the mortgagee would seek a court order giving the mortgagor a fixed time—perhaps six months or a year—within which to pay off the debt; under the court decree, failure meant that the mortgagor was forever foreclosed from asserting his right of redemption. This **strict foreclosure** gave the mortgagee (again, bank) outright title at the end of the time period.

In the United States today, most jurisdictions follow a somewhat different approach: the mortgagee forecloses by forcing a public sale at auction. Proceeds up to the amount of the debt are the mortgagee's to keep; surplus is paid over to the mortgagor. **Foreclosure by sale** is the usual procedure in the United States. At bottom, its theory is that a mortgage is a lien on land. (Foreclosure issues are further discussed in Section 2.)

Under statutes enacted in many states, the mortgagor has one last chance to recover his property, even after foreclosure. This statutory **right of redemption** extends the period to repay, often by one year.

foreclosure

To shut off the owner's interest in property and sell it upon default.

strict foreclosure

The creditor takes the collateral, discharges the debtor, and has no right to seek any deficiency.

Foreclosure by sale

To sell land upon buyer's default at a public auction.

right of redemption

After foreclosure, for a limited period, the debtor's right to reclaim the property sold, upon paying all costs and fees.

Creation of the Mortgage

Statutory Regulation

The decision whether to lend money and take a mortgage is affected by several federal and state regulations.

Consumer Credit Statutes Apply

Statutes dealing with consumer credit transactions (as discussed in Chapter 27) have a bearing on the mortgage, including state usury statutes, and the federal Truth in Lending Act and Equal Credit Opportunity Act.

Real Estate Settlement Procedures Act

Other federal statutes are directed more specifically at mortgage lending. One, enacted in 1974, is the Real Estate Settlement Procedures Act (RESPA), aimed at abuses in the settlement process—the process of obtaining the mortgage and purchasing a residence. The act covers all federally related first mortgage loans secured by residential properties for one to four families. It requires the lender to disclose information about settlement costs in advance of the closing day: it prohibits the lender from "springing" unexpected or hidden costs onto the borrower. The RESPA is a U.S. Department of Housing and Urban Development (HUD) consumer protection statute designed to help home buyers be better shoppers in the home-buying process, and it is enforced by HUD. It also outlaws what had been a common practice of giving and accepting kickbacks and referral fees. The act prohibits lenders from requiring mortgagors to use a particular company to obtain insurance, and it limits add-on fees the lender can demand to cover future insurance and tax charges.

Redlining

redlining

The alleged practice by lenders not to lend within certain geographic areas; considered discrimination.

Several statutes are directed to the practice of **redlining**—the refusal of lenders to make loans on property in low-income neighborhoods or impose stricter mortgage terms when they do make loans there. (The term derives from the supposition that lenders draw red lines on maps around ostensibly marginal neighborhoods.) The most important of these is the Community Reinvestment Act (CRA) of 1977.[1] The act requires the appropriate federal financial supervisory agencies to encourage regulated financial institutions to meet the credit needs of the local communities in which they are chartered, consistent with safe and sound operation. To enforce the statute, federal regulatory agencies examine banking institutions for CRA compliance and take this information into consideration when approving applications for new bank branches or for mergers or acquisitions. The information is compiled under the authority of the Home Mortgage Disclosure Act of 1975, which requires financial institutions within its purview to report annually by transmitting information from their loan application registers to a federal agency.

The Dodd-Frank Wall Street Reform and Consumer Protection Act of 2010 ("Dodd-Frank")

This legislation—2,300 pages—was signed into law by President Obama in July 2010 in response to the abuses and irregularities suffered by homeowners in the run-up to the recession of 2007–10. It is was said to be "one of the most significant regulatory reform measures since the Great Depression."[2] The act has several sections; Title XIV is the "Mortgage Reform and Anti-Predatory Lending Act of 2010." This part modifies the Truth in Lending Act to impose specific duties on the mortgage originator to act in the best interests of consumers. Consumers are supposed to have the ability to repay their loans, and the act requires that lenders ensure that they can, within reason. It prohibits unfair and deceptive lending practices, gives increased protection to high cost loan borrowers, and it requires fuller disclosures of the costs associated with variable-rate mortgages.

But Dodd-Frank has turned out to be less than some reformists had hoped it would. The left-leaning *Rolling Stone* magazine put it this way in 2012:

The fate of Dodd-Frank over the past two years is an object lesson in the government's inability to institute even the simplest and most obvious reforms, especially if those reforms happen to clash with powerful financial interests. From the moment it was signed into law, lobbyists and lawyers have fought regulators over every line in the rule making process. [3]

The Note and the Mortgage Documents

The note and the mortgage documents are the contracts that set up the deal: the mortgagor gets credit, and the mortgagee gets the right to repossess the property in case of default.

The Note

If the lender decides to grant a mortgage, the mortgagor signs two critical documents at the closing: the note and the mortgage. We cover notes in Chapter 22. It is enough here to recall that in a note (really a type of IOU), the mortgagor promises to pay a specified principal sum, plus interest, by a certain date or dates. The note is the underlying obligation for which the mortgage serves as security. Without the note, the mortgagee would have an empty document, since the mortgage would secure nothing. Without a mortgage, a note is still quite valid, evidencing the debtor's personal obligation.

One particular provision that usually appears in both mortgages and the underlying notes is the **acceleration clause**. This provides that if a debtor should default on any particular payment, the entire principal and interest will become due immediately at the lender's option. Why an acceleration clause? Without it, the lender would be powerless to foreclose the entire mortgage when the mortgagor defaulted but would have to wait until the expiration of the note's term. Although the acceleration clause is routine, it will not be enforced unless the mortgagee acts in an equitable and fair manner. The problem arises where the mortgagor's default was the result of some unconscionable conduct of the mortgagee, such as representing to the mortgagee that she might take a sixty-day "holiday" from having to make payments. In *Paul H. Cherry v. Chase Manhattan Mortgage Group* (Section 4), the equitable powers of the court were invoked to prevent acceleration.

acceleration clause

A contract clause providing that the entire amount owing in debt becomes due if one payment is missed.

The Mortgage

Under the statute of frauds, the mortgage itself must be evidenced by some writing to be enforceable. The mortgagor will usually make certain promises and warranties to the mortgagee and state the amount and terms of the debt and the mortgagor's duties concerning taxes, insurance, and repairs. A sample mortgage form is presented in Figure 29.2.

FIGURE 29.2 Sample Mortgage Form

Mortgage

This mortgage is made the___day of ______, 20__, between the mortgagor, [name of mortgagor], at [insert residence], and [name of mortgagee], mortgagee, at [insert residence].

To secure the payment of an indebtedness of $[numbers]____[written out]____dollars, to be paid on starting on the ___ day of ____, 20__ with interest to be computed from _____ at the rate of ___% per year, and to be paid monthly, according to the promissory note of today's date, the mortgagor hereby mortgages to the mortgagee.

[address and legal description of the property].

And the mortgagor promises the mortgagee as follows:

1. That the mortgagor will pay the debt as provided.
2. That the mortgagor will keep the buildings on the premises insured against loss by fire for the benefit of the mortgagee; that s/he will assign and deliver the policies to the mortgagee; and that s/he will reimburse the mortgagee for any premiums paid for insurance made by the mortgagee on the mortgagor's default in insuring the buildings.
3. That no building on the premises shall be removed or demolished without the consent of the mortgagee.
4. That the whole principal sum and interest shall become due at the option of the mortgagee:
    - after default in the payment of any installment of principal or of interest for ____ days;
    - or after default in the payment of any tax, water rate or assessment for ____ days, after notice and demand;
    - or after default after notice and demand either in assigning and delivering the policies insuring the buildings against loss by fire to the mortgagee;
    - or in reimbursing the mortgagee for premiums paid on such insurance, as provided here;
5. That the mortgagor will pay all taxes, assessments or water rates, and if s/he defaults, the mortgagee may pay instead.
6. That the mortgagor within ____ days upon request in person or ___ days upon request by mail will furnish a written statement, properly acknowledged, of the amount due on this mortgage and whether any offsets or defenses exist against the mortgage debt.
7. That any notice and demand or request shall be in writing and may be served in person or by mail.
9. That the mortgagor warrants the title to the premises.

As evidence of this agreement between the parties, this mortgage is signed below by them.

______________________________ Mortgagor.

______________________________ Mortgagee.

Key Takeaway

As a mechanism of security, a mortgage is a promise by the debtor (mortgagor) to repay the creditor (mortgagee) for the amount borrowed or credit extended, with real estate put up as security. If the mortgagor doesn't pay as promised, the mortgagee may repossess the real estate. Mortgage law has ancient roots and brings with it various permutations on the theme that even if the mortgagor defaults, she may nevertheless have the right to get the property back or at least be reimbursed for any value above that necessary to pay the debt and the expenses of foreclosure. Mortgage law is regulated by state and federal statute.

Exercises

1. What role did the right of redemption play in courts of equity changing the substance of a mortgage from an actual transfer of title to the mortgagee to a mere lien on the property?
2. What abuses did the federal RESPA address?
3. What are the two documents most commonly associated with mortgage transactions?

29.2 Priority, Termination of the Mortgage, and Other Methods of Using Real Estate as Security

Learning Objectives

1. Understand why it is important that the mortgagee (creditor) record her interest in the debtor's real estate.
2. Know the basic rule of priority—who gets an interest in the property first in case of default—and the exceptions to the rule.
3. Recognize the three ways mortgages can be terminated: payment, assumption, and foreclosure.
4. Be familiar with other methods (besides mortgages) by which real property can be used as security for a creditor.

Priorities in Real Property Security

You may recall from Chapter 28 how important it is for a creditor to perfect its secured interest in the goods put up as collateral. Absent perfection, the creditor stands a chance of losing out to another creditor who took its interest in the goods subsequent to the first creditor. The same problem is presented in real property security: the mortgagee wants to make sure it has first claim on the property in case the mortgagor (debtor) defaults.

The General Rule of Priorities

The general rule of priority is the same for real property security as for personal property security: the first in time to give notice of the secured interest is first in right. For real property, the notice is by **recording** the mortgage. Recording is the act of giving public notice of changes in interests in real estate. Recording was created by statute; it did not exist at common law. The typical recording statute calls for a transfer of title or mortgage to be placed in a particular county office, usually the auditor, recorder, or register of deeds.

recording

The official filing of a legal document (a mortgage or a deed) so as to inform the world of it.

A mortgage is valid between the parties whether or not it is recorded, but a mortgagee might lose to a third party—another mortgagee or a good-faith purchaser of the property—unless the mortgage is recorded.

Exceptions to the General Rule

There are exceptions to the general rule; two are taken up here.

Fixture Filing

The fixture-filing provision in Article 9 of the UCC is one exception to the general rule. As noted in Chapter 28, the UCC gives priority to purchase money security interests in fixtures if certain requirements are met.

Future Advances

A bank might make advances to the debtor after accepting the mortgage. If the future advances are obligatory, then the first-in-time rule applies. For example: Bank accepts Debtor's mortgage (and records it) and extends a line of credit on which Debtor draws, up to a certain limit. (Or, as in the construction industry, Bank might make periodic advances to the contractors as work progresses, backed by the mortgage.) Second Creditor loans Debtor money—secured by the same property—before Debtor began to draw against the first line of credit. Bank has priority: by searching the mortgage records, Second Creditor should have been on notice that the first mortgage was intended as security for the entire line of credit, although the line was doled out over time.

However, if the future advances are not obligatory, then priority is determined by notice. For example, a bank might take a mortgage as security for an original loan and for any future loans that the bank chooses to make. A later creditor can achieve priority by notifying the bank with the first mortgage that it is making an advance. Suppose Jimmy mortgages his property to a wealthy dowager, Mrs. Calabash, in return for an immediate loan of $20,000 and they agree that the mortgage will serve as security for future loans to be arranged. The mortgage is recorded. A month later, before Mrs. Calabash loans him any more money, Jimmy gives a second mortgage to Louella in return for a loan of $10,000. Louella notifies Mrs. Calabash that she is loaning Jimmy the money. A month later, Mrs. Calabash loans Jimmy another $20,000. Jimmy then defaults, and the property turns out to be worth only $40,000. Whose claims will be honored and in what order? Mrs. Calabash will collect her original $20,000, because it was recited in the mortgage and the mortgage was recorded. Louella will collect her $10,000 next, because she notified the first mortgage holder of the advance. That leaves Mrs. Calabash in third position to collect what she can of her second advance. Mrs. Calabash could have protected herself by refusing the second loan.

Termination of the Mortgage

The mortgagor's liability can terminate in three ways: payment, assumption (with a novation), or foreclosure.

Payment

Unless they live in the home for twenty-five or thirty years, the mortgagors usually pay off the mortgage when the property is sold. Occasionally, mortgages are paid off in order to refinance. If the mortgage was taken out at a time of high interest rates and rates later drop, the homeowner might want to obtain a new mortgage at the lower rates. In many mortgages, however, this entails extra closing costs and penalties for prepaying the original mortgage. Whatever the reason, when a mortgage is paid off, the discharge should be recorded. This is accomplished by giving the mortgagor a copy of, and filing a copy of, a Satisfaction of Mortgage document. In the *Paul H. Cherry v. Chase Manhattan Mortgage Group* case (Section 4), the bank *mistakenly* filed the Satisfaction of Mortgage document, later discovered its mistake, retracted the satisfaction, accelerated the loan because the mortgagor stopped making payments (the bank, seeing no record of an outstanding mortgage, refused to accept payments), and then tried to foreclose on the mortgage, meanwhile having lost the note and mortgage besides.

Assumption

The property can be sold without paying off the mortgage if the mortgage is assumed by the new buyer, who agrees to pay the seller's (the original mortgagor's) debt. This is a novation *if*, in approving the assumption, the bank releases the old mortgagor and substitutes the buyer as the new debtor.

The buyer need not assume the mortgage. If the buyer purchases the property without agreeing to be personally liable, this is a sale "subject to" the mortgage (see Figure 29.3). In the event of the seller's subsequent default, the bank can foreclose the mortgage and sell the property that the buyer has purchased, but the buyer is not liable for any deficiency.

FIGURE 29.3 "Subject to" Sales versus Assumption

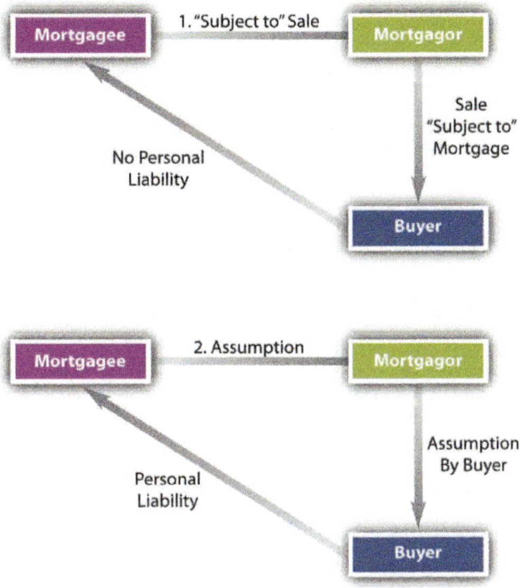

What if mortgage rates are high? Can buyers assume an existing low-rate mortgage from the seller rather than be forced to obtain a new mortgage at substantially higher rates? Banks, of course, would prefer not to allow that when interest rates are rising, so they often include in the mortgage a **due-on-sale clause**, by which the entire principal and interest become due when the property is sold, thus forcing the purchaser to get financing at the higher rates. The clause is a device for preventing subsequent purchasers from assuming loans with lower-than-market interest rates. Although many state courts at one time refused to enforce the due-on-sale clause, Congress reversed this trend when it enacted the Garn–St. Germain Depository Institutions Act in 1982.[4] The act preempts state laws and upholds the validity of due-on-sale clauses. When interest rates are low, banks have no interest in enforcing such clauses, and there are ways to work around the due-on-sale clause.

due-on-sale clause

A contract clause requiring the entire mortgage amount be paid to the mortgagee if the property is sold; it prevents any assumption.

Foreclosure

The third method of terminating the mortgage is by foreclosure when a mortgagor defaults. Even after default, the mortgagor has the right to exercise his equity of redemption—that is, to redeem the property by paying the principal and interest in full. If she does not, the mortgagee may foreclose the equity of redemption. Although strict foreclosure is used occasionally, in most cases the mortgagee forecloses by one of two types of sale (see Figure 29.4).

The first type is **judicial sale**. The mortgagee seeks a court order authorizing the sale to be conducted by a public official, usually the sheriff. The mortgagor is entitled to be notified of the proceeding and to a hearing. The second type of sale is that conducted under a clause called a **power of sale**, which many lenders insist be contained in the mortgage. This clause permits the mortgagee to sell the property at public auction without first going to court—although by custom or law, the sale must be advertised, and typically a sheriff or other public official conducts the public sale or auction.

judicial sale

A court-ordered sale of property by a public official, such as the sheriff.

power of sale

A term allowing the mortgagee to sell real estate upon mortgagor's default without going to court.

FIGURE 29.4 Foreclosure

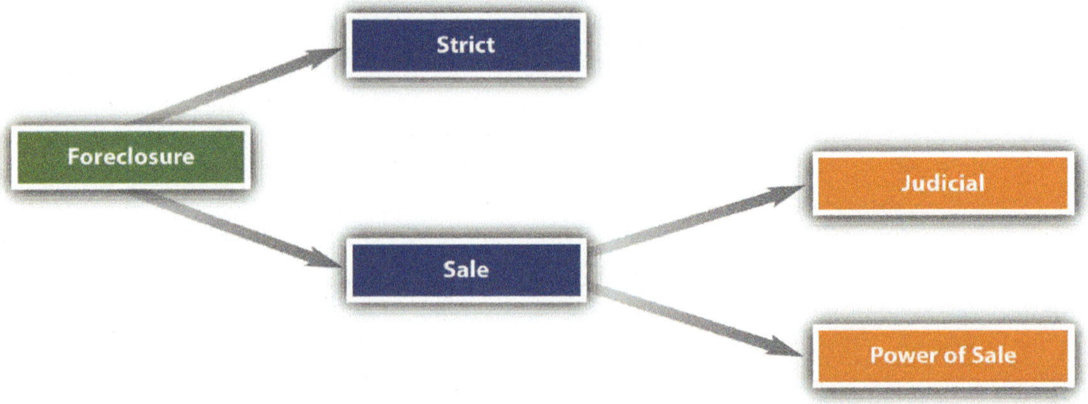

Once the property has been sold, it is deeded to the new purchaser. In about half the states, the mortgagor still has the right to redeem the property by paying up within six months or a year—the statutory redemption period. Thereafter, the mortgagor has no further right to redeem. If the sale proceeds exceed the debt, the mortgagor is entitled to the excess unless he has given second and third mortgages, in which case the junior mortgagees are entitled to recover their claims before the mortgagor. If the proceeds are less than the debt, the mortgagee is entitled to recover the deficiency from the mortgagor. However, some states have statutorily abolished deficiency judgments.

Other Methods of Using Real Estate as Security

Besides the mortgage, there are other ways to use real estate as security. Here we take up two: the deed of trust and the installment or land contract.

Deed of Trust

deed of trust

A type of mortgage where title to the property is nominally in a trustee, who sells if the buyer defaults; it provides for a nonjudicial foreclosure.

The **deed of trust** is a device for securing a debt with real property; unlike the mortgage, it requires three parties: the borrower, the trustee, and the lender. Otherwise, it is at base identical to a mortgage. The borrower conveys the land to a third party, the trustee, to hold in trust for the lender until the borrower pays the debt. (The trustee's interest is really a kind of legal fiction: that person is expected to have no interest in the property.) The primary benefit to the deed of trust is that it simplifies the foreclosure process by containing a provision empowering the trustee to sell the property on default, thus doing away with the need for any court filings. The disinterested third party making sure things are done properly becomes the trustee, not a judge. In thirty states and the District of Columbia—more than half of U.S. jurisdictions—the deed of trust is usually used in lieu of mortgages.[5]

But the deed of trust may have certain disadvantages as well. For example, when the debt has been fully paid, the trustee will not release the deed of trust until she sees that all notes secured by it have been marked canceled. Should the borrower have misplaced the canceled notes or failed to keep good records, he will need to procure a surety bond to protect the trustee in case of a mistake. This can be an expensive procedure. In many jurisdictions, the mortgage holder is prohibited from seeking a deficiency judgment if the holder chooses to sell the property through nonjudicial means.

Alpha Imperial Building, LLC v. Schnitzer Family Investment, LLC, Section 4, discusses several issues involving deeds of trust.

Installment or Land Contract

Under the **installment contract or land contract**, the purchaser takes possession and agrees to pay the seller over a period of years. Until the final payment, title belongs to the seller. The contract will specify the type of deed to be conveyed at closing, the terms of payment, the buyer's duty to pay taxes and insure the premises, and the seller's right to accelerate on default. The buyer's particular concern in this type of sale is whether the seller in fact has title. The buyers can protect themselves by requiring proof of title and title insurance when the contract is signed. Moreover, the buyer should record the installment contract to protect against the seller's attempt to convey title to an innocent third-party purchaser while the contract is in effect.

installment contract or land contract

The buyer makes installment payments on a real estate purchase, the title shifting when all payments are made.

The benefit to the land contract is that the borrower need not bank-qualify, so the pool of available buyers is larger, and buyers who have inadequate resources at the time of contracting but who have the expectation of a rising income in the future are good candidates for the land contract. Also, the seller gets all the interest paid by the buyer, instead of the bank getting it in the usual mortgage. The obvious disadvantage from the seller's point is that she will not get a big lump sum immediately: the payments trickle in over years (unless she can sell the contract to a third party, but that would be at a discount).

Key Takeaway

The general rule on priority in real property security is that the first creditor to record its interest prevails over subsequent creditors. There are some exceptions; the most familiar is that the seller of a fixture on a purchase-money security interest has priority over a previously recorded mortgagee. The mortgage will terminate by payment, assumption by a new buyer (with a novation releasing the old buyer), and foreclosure. In a judicial-sale foreclosure, a court authorizes the property's sale; in a power-of-sale foreclosure, no court approval is required. In most states, the mortgagor whose property was foreclosed is given some period of time—six months or a year—to redeem the property; otherwise, the sale is done, but the debtor may be liable for the deficiency, if any. The deed of trust avoids any judicial involvement by having the borrower convey the land to a disinterested trustee for the benefit of the lender; the trustee sells it upon default, with the proceeds (after expenses) going to the lender. Another method of real property security is a land contract: title shifts to the buyer only at the end of the term of payments.

Exercises

1. A debtor borrowed $350,000 to finance the purchase of a house, and the bank recorded its interest on July 1. On July 15, the debtor bought $10,000 worth of replacement windows from Window Co.; Window Co. recorded its purchase-money security interest that day, and the windows were installed. Four years later, the debtor, in hard financial times, declared bankruptcy. As between the bank and Windows Co., who will get paid first?
2. Under what interest rate circumstances would banks insist on a due-on-sale clause? Under what interest rate circumstance would banks not object to a new person assuming the mortgage?
3. What is the primary advantage of the deed of trust? What is the primary advantage of the land contract?
4. A debtor defaulted on her house payments. Under what circumstances might a court *not* allow the bank's foreclosure on the property?

29.3 Nonconsensual Lien

Learning Objectives

1. Understand the nonconsensual liens issued by courts—attachment liens and judgment liens—and how they are created.
2. Recognize other types of nonconsensual liens: mechanic's lien, possessory lien, and tax lien.

The security arrangements discussed so far—security interests, suretyship, mortgages—are all obtained by the creditor with the debtor's consent. A creditor may obtain certain liens without the debtor's consent.

Court-Decreed Liens

Some nonconsensual liens are issued by courts.

Attachment Lien

attachment lien

A judicial lien imposed to preserve property during litigation.

An **attachment lien** is ordered against a person's property—real or personal—to prevent him from disposing of it during a lawsuit. To obtain an attachment lien, the plaintiff must show that the defendant likely will dispose of or hide his property; if the court agrees with the plaintiff, she must post a bond and the court will issue a writ of attachment to the sheriff, directing the sheriff to seize the property. Attachments of real property should be recorded. Should the plaintiff win her suit, the court issues a writ of execution, directing the sheriff to sell the property to satisfy the judgment.

Judgment Lien

judgment lien

A lien imposed to secure payment of a judgment owing.

A **judgment lien** may be issued when a plaintiff wins a judgment in court if an attachment lien has not already been issued. Like the attachment lien, it provides a method by which the defendant's property may be seized and sold.

Mechanic's Lien

Overview

mechanic's lien

A claim allowed to one who furnishes labor, services, or materials to improve property.

The most common nonconsensual lien on real estate is the **mechanic's lien**. A mechanic's lien can be obtained by one who furnishes labor, services, or materials to improve real estate: this is statutory, and the statute must be carefully followed. The "mechanic" here is one who works with his or her hands, not specifically one who works on machines. An automobile mechanic could not obtain a mechanic's lien on a customer's house to secure payment of work he did on her car. (The lien to which the automobile mechanic is entitled is a "possessory lien" or "artisan's lien," considered in Section 3.) To qualify for a mechanic's lien, the claimant must file a sworn statement describing the work done, the contract made, or the materials furnished that permanently improved the real estate.

A particularly difficult problem crops up when the owner has paid the contractor, who in turn fails to pay his subcontractors. In many states, the subcontractors can file a lien on the owner's property, thus forcing the owner to pay them (see Figure 29.5)—and maybe twice. To protect themselves, owners can demand a sworn statement from general contractors listing the subcontractors used on the job, and from them, owners can obtain a waiver of lien rights before paying the general contractor.

Procedure for Obtaining a Mechanic's Lien

Anyone claiming a lien against real estate must record a lien statement stating the amount due and the nature of the improvement. The lienor (the person who wants to claim the lien interest) has a specified period of time (e.g., ninety days) to file from the time the work is finished. Recording as such does not give the lienor an automatic right to the property if the debt remains unpaid. All states specify a limited period of time, usually one year, within which the claimant must file suit to enforce the lien. Only if the court decides the lien is valid may the property be sold to satisfy the debt. Difficult questions sometimes arise when a lien is filed against a landlord's property as a result of improvements and services provided to a tenant, as discussed in *F & D Elec. Contractors, Inc. v. Powder Coaters, Inc.*, Section 4.

FIGURE 29.5 Subcontractors' Lien

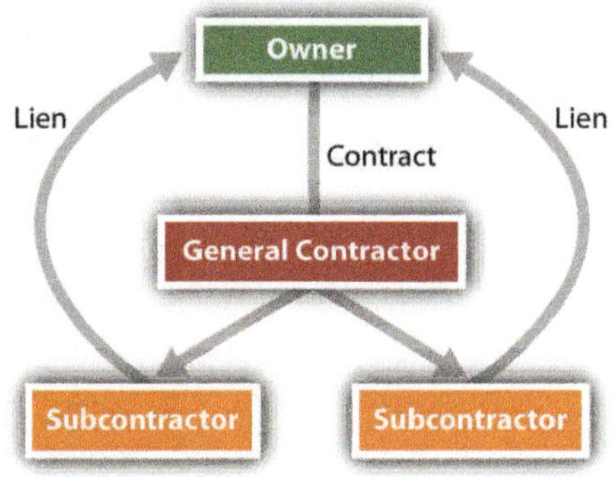

Mechanic's Liens Priorities

A mechanic's lien represents a special risk to the purchaser of real estate or to lenders who wish to take a mortgage. In most states, the mechanic's lien is given priority not from the date when the lien is recorded but from an earlier date—either the date the contractor was hired or the date construction began. Thus a purchaser or lender might lose priority to a creditor with a mechanic's lien who filed after the sale or mortgage. A practical solution to this problem is to hold back part of the funds (purchase price or loan) or place them in escrow until the period for recording liens has expired.

Possessory Lien

The most common nonconsensual lien on personal property (not real estate) is the **possessory lien**. This is the right to continue to keep the goods on which work has been performed or for which materials have been supplied until the owner pays for the labor or materials. The possessory lien arises both under common law and under a variety of statutes. Because it is nonconsensual, the possessory lien is not covered by Article 9 of the UCC, which is restricted to consensual security interests. Nor is it governed by the law of mechanic's liens, which are nonpossessory and relate only to work done to improve real property.

possessory lien
Lien imposed by one who has possession of goods to secure payment for improvements to them.

The common-law rule is that anyone who, under an express or implied contract, adds value to another's chattel (personal property) by labor, skill, or materials has a possessory lien for the value of the services. Moreover, the lienholder may keep the chattel until her services are paid. For example, the dry cleaner shop is not going to release the wool jacket that you took in for cleaning unless you make satisfactory arrangements to pay for it, and the chain saw store won't let you take the chain saw that you brought in for a tune-up until you pay for the labor and materials for the tune-up.

Tax Lien

An important statutory lien is the federal **tax lien**. Once the government assesses a tax, the amount due constitutes a lien on the owner's property, whether real or personal. Until it is filed in the appropriate state office, others take priority, including purchasers, mechanics' lienors, judgment lien creditors, and holders of security interests. But once filed, the tax lien takes priority over all subse-

tax lien
A lien imposed by the government to secure payment of taxes owing.

quently arising liens. Federal law exempts some property from the tax lien; for example, unemployment benefits, books and tools of a trade, workers' compensation, judgments for support of minor children, minimum amounts of wages and salary, personal effects, furniture, fuel, and provisions are exempt.

Local governments also can assess liens against real estate for failure to pay real estate taxes. After some period of time, the real estate may be sold to satisfy the tax amounts owing.

Key Takeaway

There are four types of nonconsensual liens: (1) court-decreed liens are attachment liens, which prevent a person from disposing of assets pending a lawsuit, and judgment liens, which allow the prevailing party in a lawsuit to take property belonging to the debtor to satisfy the judgment; (2) mechanics' liens are authorized by statute, giving a person who has provided labor or material to a landowner the right to sell the property to get paid; (3) possessory liens on personal property allow one in possession of goods to keep them to satisfy a claim for work done or storage of them; and (4) tax liens are enforced by the government to satisfy outstanding tax liabilities and may be assessed against real or personal property.

Exercises

1. The mortgagor's interests are protected in a judicial foreclosure by a court's oversight of the process; how is the mortgagor's interest protected when a deed of trust is used?
2. Why is the deed of trust becoming increasingly popular?
3. What is the rationale for the common-law possessory lien?
4. Mike Mechanic repaired Alice Ace's automobile in his shop, but Alice didn't have enough money to pay for the repairs. May Mike have a mechanic's lien on the car? A possessory lien?
5. Why does federal law exempt unemployment benefits, books and tools of a trade, workers' compensation, minimum amounts of wages and salary, personal effects, furniture, fuel, and other such items from the sweep of a tax lien?

29.4 Cases

Denial of Mortgagee's Right to Foreclose; Erroneous Filings; Lost Instruments

Paul H. Cherry v. Chase Manhattan Mortgage Group
190 F.Supp.2d 1330 (Fed. Dist. Ct. FL 2002)

Background

[Paul Cherry filed a complaint suing Chase for Fair Debt Collection Practices Act violations and slander of credit.] * * * Chase counter-claimed for foreclosure and reestablishment of the lost note....

* * * Chase held a mortgage on Cherry's home to which Cherry made timely payments until August 2000. Cherry stopped making payments on the mortgage after he received a letter from

Chase acknowledging his satisfaction of the mortgage. Cherry notified Chase of the error through a customer service representative. Cherry, however, received a check dated August 15, 2000, as an escrow refund on the mortgage. Chase subsequently recorded a Satisfaction of Mortgage into the Pinellas County public records on October 19, 2000. On November 14, 2000, Chase sent Cherry a "Loan Reactivation" letter with a new loan number upon which to make the payments. During this time, Cherry was placing his mortgage payments into a bank account, which subsequently were put into an escrow account maintained by his attorney. These payments were not, and have not, been tendered to Chase. As a result of the failure to tender, Chase sent Cherry an acceleration warning on November 17, 2000, and again on March 16, 2001. Chase notified the credit bureaus as to Cherry's default status and moved for foreclosure. In a letter addressed to Cherry's attorney, dated April 24, 2001, Chase's attorney advised Cherry to make the mortgage payments to Chase. Chase recorded a "vacatur, revocation, and cancellation of satisfaction of mortgage" (vacatur) [vacatur: an announcement filed in court that something is cancelled or set aside; an annulment] in the Pinellas County public records on May 3, 2001. Chase signed the vacatur on March 21, 2001, and had it notarized on March 27, 2001. Chase has also been unable to locate the original note, dated October 15, 1997, and deems it to be lost. * * *

Foreclosure

Chase accelerated Cherry's mortgage debt after determining he was in a default status under the mortgage provisions. Chase claims that the right to foreclose under the note and mortgage is "absolute," [Citation], and that this Court should enforce the security interest in the mortgage though Chase made an administrative error in entering a Satisfaction of Mortgage into the public records. * * *

Mortgage

* * * Chase relies on the Florida Supreme Court decision in *United Service Corp. v. Vi-An Const. Corp.*, [Citation] (Fla.1955), which held that a Satisfaction of Mortgage "made through a mistake may be canceled" and a mortgage reestablished as long as no other innocent third parties have "acquired an interest in the property." Generally the court looks to the rights of any innocent third parties, and if none exist, equity will grant relief to a mortgagee who has mistakenly satisfied a mortgage before fully paid. [Citation]. Both parties agree that the mortgage was released before the debt was fully paid. Neither party has presented any facts to this Court that implies the possibility nor existence of a third party interest. Although Cherry argues under *Biggs v. Smith*, 184 So. 106, 107 (1938), that a recorded satisfaction of mortgage is "prima facie evidence of extinguishment of a mortgage lien," Biggs does not apply this standard to mortgage rights affected by a mistake in the satisfaction.

Therefore, on these facts, this Court acknowledges that a vacatur is a proper remedy for Chase to correct its unilateral mistake since "equity will grant relief to those who have through mistake released a mortgage." [Citation.] Accordingly, this Court holds that an equity action is required to make a vacatur enforceable unless the parties consent to the vacatur or a similar remedy during the mortgage negotiation. * * *

Tender

Cherry has not made a mortgage payment to Chase since August 2000, but claims to have made these payments into an escrow account, which he claims were paid to the escrow account because Chase recorded a satisfaction of his mortgage and, therefore, no mortgage existed. Cherry also claims that representatives of Chase rejected his initial attempts to make payments because of a lack of a valid loan number. Chase, however, correctly argues that payments made to an escrow account are not a proper tender of payment. *Matthews v. Lindsay*, [Citation] (1884) (requiring tender to be made to the court). Nor did Cherry make the required mortgage payments to the court as provided by [relevant court rules], allowing for a "deposit with the court all or any part of such sum or thing, whether that party claims all or any part of the sum or thing." Further, Chase also correctly argues that Cherry's failure to tender the payments from the escrow account or make deposits with the court is more than just a "technical breach" of the mortgage and note. [Citation.]

Chase may, therefore, recover the entire amount of the mortgage indebtedness, unless the court finds a "limited circumstance" upon which the request may be denied. [Citation.] Although not presented by Chase in its discussion of this case, the Court may refuse foreclosure, notwithstanding that the defendant established a foreclosure action, if the acceleration was unconscionable and the "result would be inequitable and unjust." This Court will analyze the inequitable result test and the limited circumstances by which the court may deny foreclosure.

First, this Court does not find the mortgage acceleration unconscionable by assuming arguendo [for the purposes of argument] that the mortgage was valid during the period that the Satisfaction of Mortgage was entered into the public records. Chase did not send the first acceleration warning until November 14, 2000, the fourth month of non-payment, followed by the second acceleration letter on March 16, 2001, the eighth month of non-payment. Although Cherry could have argued that a foreclosure action was an "inequitable" and "unjust" result after the Satisfaction of Mortgage was entered on his behalf, the result does not rise to an unconscionable level since Cherry could have properly tendered the mortgage payments to the court.

Second, the following "limited circumstances" will justify a court's denial of foreclosure: 1) waiver of right to accelerate; 2) mortgagee estopped from asserting foreclosure because mortgagor reasonably assumed the mortgagee would not foreclose; 3) mortgagee failed to perform a condition precedent for acceleration; 4) payment made after default but prior to receiving intent to foreclose; or, 5) where there was intent to make to make timely payment, and it was attempted, or steps taken to accomplish it, but nevertheless the payment was not made due to a misunderstanding or excusable neglect, coupled with some conduct of the mortgagee which in a measure contributed to the failure to pay when due or within the grace period. [Citations.]

Chase fails to address this fifth circumstance in its motion, an apparent obfuscation of the case law before the court. This Court acknowledges that Cherry's facts do not satisfy the first four limited circumstances. Chase at no time advised Cherry that the acceleration right was being waived; nor is Chase estopped from asserting foreclosure on the mortgage because of the administrative error, and Cherry has not relied on this error to his detriment; and since Chase sent the acceleration letter to Cherry and a request for payment to his attorney, there can be no argument that Cherry believed Chase would not foreclose. Chase has performed all conditions precedent required by the mortgage provisions prior to notice of the acceleration; sending acceleration warnings on November 17, 2000, and March 16, 2001. Cherry also has no argument for lack of notice of intent to accelerate after default since he has not tendered a payment since July 2000, thus placing him in default of the mortgage provisions, and he admits receiving the acceleration notices.

This Court finds, however, that this claim fails squarely into the final limited circumstance regarding intent to make timely payments. Significant factual issues exist as to the intent of Cherry to make or attempt to make timely mortgage payments to Chase. Cherry claims that he attempted to make the payments, but was told by a representative of Chase that there was no mortgage loan number upon which to apply the payments. As a result, the mortgage payments were placed into an account and later into his counsel's trust account as a mortgage escrow. Although these payments should have, at a minimum, been placed with the court to ensure tender during the resolution of the mortgage dispute, Cherry did take steps to accomplish timely mortgage payments. Although Cherry, through excusable neglect or a misunderstanding as to what his rights were after the Satisfaction of Mortgage was entered, failed to tender the payments, Chase is also not without fault; its conduct in entering a Satisfaction of Mortgage into the Pinellas County public records directly contributed to Cherry's failure to tender timely payments. Cherry's attempt at making the mortgage payments, coupled with Chase's improper satisfaction of mortgage fits squarely within the limited circumstance created to justify a court's denial of a foreclosure. Equity here requires a balancing between Chase's right to the security interest encumbered by the mortgage and Cherry's attempts to make timely payments. As such, these limited circumstances exist to ensure that a foreclosure remains an action in equity. In applying this analysis, this Court finds that equity requires that Chase's request for foreclosure be denied at this juncture. * * *

Reestablishment of the Lost Note and Mortgage

Chase also requests, as part of the foreclosure counterclaim, the reestablishment of the note initially associated with the mortgage, as it is unable to produce the original note and provide by affidavit evidence of its loss. Chase has complied with the [necessary statutory] requirements[.] * * * This Court holds the note to be reestablished and that Chase has the lawful right to enforce the note upon the issuance of this order.

This Court also agrees that Chase may reestablish the mortgage through a vacatur, revocation, and cancellation of satisfaction of mortgage. [Citation] (allowing the Equity Court to reestablish a mortgage that was improperly canceled due to a mistake). However, this Court will deem the vacatur effective as of the date of this order. This Court leaves the status of the vacatur during the disputed period, and specifically since May 3, 2001, to be resolved in subsequent proceedings. * * * Accordingly, it is:

ORDERED that [Chase cannot foreclose and] the request to reestablish the note and mortgage is hereby granted and effective as of the date of this order. Cherry will tender all previously escrowed mortgage payments to the Court, unless the parties agree otherwise, within ten days of this order and shall henceforth, tender future monthly payments to Chase as set out in the reestablished note and mortgage.

Case Questions

1. When Chase figured out that it had issued a Satisfaction of Mortgage erroneously, what did it file to rectify the error?
2. Cherry had not made any mortgage payments between the time Chase sent the erroneous Satisfaction of Mortgage notice to him and the time of the court's decision in this case. The court listed five circumstances in which a mortgagee (Chase here) might be denied the right to foreclose on a delinquent account. Which one applied here? The court said Chase had engaged in "an apparent obfuscation of the case law before the court?" What obfuscation did it engage in?
3. What did Cherry do with the mortgage payments after Chase erroneously told him the mortgage was satisfied? What did the court say he should have done with the payments?

Mechanic's Lien Filed against Landlord for Payment of Tenant's Improvements

F & D Elec. Contractors, Inc. v. Powder Coaters, Inc.

567 S.E.2d 842 (S.C. 2002)

Factual/ Procedural Background

BG Holding f/k/a Colite Industries, Inc. ("BG Holding") is a one-third owner of about thirty acres of real estate in West Columbia, South Carolina. A warehouse facility is located on the property. In September 1996, Powder Coaters, Inc. ("Powder Coaters") agreed to lease a portion of the warehouse to operate its business. Powder Coaters was engaged in the business of electrostatically painting machinery parts and equipment and then placing them in an oven to cure. A signed lease was executed between Powder Coaters and BG Holding. Prior to signing the lease, Powder Coaters negotiated the terms with Mark Taylor, ("Taylor") who was the property manager for the warehouse facility and an agent of BG Holding.

The warehouse facility did not have a sufficient power supply to support Powder Coaters' machinery. Therefore, Powder Coaters contracted with F & D Electrical ("F & D") to perform electrical work which included installing two eight foot strip light fixtures and a two hundred amp load center. Powder Coaters never paid F & D for the services. Powder Coaters was also unable to pay rent to BG Holding and was evicted in February 1997. Powder Coaters is no longer a viable company.

In January 1997, F & D filed a Notice and Certificate of Mechanic's Lien and Affidavit of Mechanic's Lien. In February 1997, F & D filed this action against BG Holding foreclosing on its mechanic's lien pursuant to S.C. [statute]. * * *

A jury trial was held on September 2nd and 3rd, 1998. At the close of F & D's evidence, and at the close of all evidence, BG Holding made motions for directed verdicts, which were denied. The jury returned a verdict for F & D in the amount of $8,264.00. The court also awarded F & D attorneys' fees and cost in the amount of $8,264.00, for a total award of $16,528.00.

BG Holding appealed. The Court of Appeals, in a two to one decision, reversed the trial court, holding a directed verdict should have been granted to BG Holding on the grounds BG Holding did not consent to the electrical upgrade, as is required by the Mechanic's Lien Statute. This Court granted F & D's petition for certiorari, and the issue before this Court is:

> *Did the trial court err in denying BG Holding's motion for directed verdict because the record was devoid of any evidence of owner's consent to materialman's performance of work on its property as required by [the S.C. statute]?*

Law/Analysis

F & D argues the majority of the Court of Appeals erred in holding the facts of the case failed to establish that BG Holding consented to the work performed by F & D, as is required by the [South Carolina] Mechanic's Lien Statute. We agree. * * *

South Carolina's Mechanic's Lien Statute provides:

> *A person to whom a debt is due for labor performed or furnished or for materials furnished and actually used in the erection, alteration, or repair of a building . . . by virtue of an agreement with,* or by consent of, the owner of the building or structure, or a person having authority from, or rightfully acting for, the owner *in procuring or furnishing the labor or materials shall have a lien upon the building or structure and upon the interest of the owner of the building or structure . . . to secure the payment of the debt due. [emphasis added.]*

Both parties in this case concede there was no express "agreement" between F & D and BG Holding. Therefore, the issue in this appeal turns on the meaning of the word "consent" in the statute, as applied in the landlord-tenant context. This is a novel issue in South Carolina.

This Court must decide who must give the consent, who must receive consent, and what type of consent (general, specific, oral, written) must be given in order to satisfy the statute. Finally, the Court must decide whether the evidence in this case shows BG Holding gave the requisite consent.

A. Who Must Receive the Consent.

The Court of Appeals' opinion in this case contemplates the consent must be between the materialman (lien claimant) and the landlord (owner). "It is only logical . . . that consent under [the relevant section] must . . . be between the owner and the entity seeking the lien . . ." [Citation from Court of Appeals]. As stated previously, applying the Mechanic's Lien Statute in the landlord-tenant context presents a novel issue. We find the consent required by the statute does not have to be between the landlord/owner and the materialman, as the Court of Appeals' opinion indicates. A determination that the required consent must come from the owner to the materialman means the materialman can only succeed if he can prove an agreement with the owner. Such an interpretation would render meaningless the language of the statute that provides: "... by virtue of an agreement with, or by consent of the owner."

Therefore, it is sufficient for the landlord/owner or his agent to give consent to his tenant. The landlord/owner should be able to delegate to his tenant the responsibility for making the requested improvements. The landlord/owner may not want to have direct involvement with the materialman or sub-contractors, but instead may wish to allow the tenant to handle any improvements or upgrades himself. In addition, the landlord/owner may be located far away and may own many properties, making it impractical for him to have direct involvement with the materialman. We find the landlord/owner or his agent is free to enter into a lease or agreement with a tenant which allows the tenant to direct the modifications to the property which have been specifically consented to by the landlord/owner or his agent.

We hold a landlord/owner or his agent can give his consent to the lessee/tenant, as well as directly to the lien claimant, to make modifications to the leased premises.

B. What Kind of Consent Is Necessary.

This Court has already clearly held the consent required by [the relevant section] is "something more than a mere acquiescence in a state of things already in existence. It implies an agreement to that which, but for the consent, could not exist, and which the party consenting has a right to forbid." [Citations.] However, our Mechanics Lien Statute has never been applied in the landlord-tenant context where a third party is involved.

Other jurisdictions have addressed this issue. The Court of Appeals cited [a Connecticut case, 1987] in support of its holding. We agree with the Court of Appeals that the Connecticut court's reasoning is persuasive, especially since Connecticut has a similar mechanics lien statute....

The Connecticut courts have stated "the consent required from the owner or one acting under the owner's authority is more than the mere granting of permission for work to be conducted on one's property; or the mere knowledge that work was being performed on one's land." Furthermore, although the Connecticut courts have stated the statute does not require an express contract, the courts have required "consent that indicates an agreement that the owner of...the land shall be, or may be, liable for the materials or labor."...

The reasoning of [Connecticut and other states that have decided this issue] is persuasive. F & D's brief appears to argue that mere knowledge by the landowner that the work needed to be done, coupled with the landlord's general "permission" to perform the work, is enough to establish consent under the statute. Under this interpretation, a landlord who knew a tenant needed to improve, upgrade, or add to the leased premises would be liable to any contractor and/or subcontractor who performed work on his land. Under F & D's interpretation the landlord would not be required to know the scope, cost, etc. of the work, but would only need to give the tenant general permission to perform upgrades or improvements.

Clearly, if the landlord/owner or his agent gives consent directly to the materialman, a lien can be established. Consent can also be given to the tenant, but the consent needs to be specific. The landlord/owner or his agent must know the scope of the project (for instance, as the lease provided in the instant case, the landlord could approve written plans submitted by the tenant). The consent needs to be more than "mere knowledge" that the tenant will perform work on the property. There must be some kind of express or implied agreement that the landlord may be held liable for the work or material. The landlord/owner or his agent may delegate the project or work to his tenant, but there must be an express or implied agreement about the specific work to be done. A general provision in a lease which allows tenant to make repairs or improvements is not enough.

C. Evidence There Was No Consent

- The record is clear that no contract, express or implied, existed between BG Holding and F & G. BG Holding had no knowledge F & G would be performing the work.
- F & G's supervisor, David Weatherington, and Ray Dutton, the owner of F & D, both testified they never had a conversation with anyone from BG Holding. In fact, until Powder Coaters failed to pay under the contract, F & D did not know BG Holding was the owner of the building.
- Mark Taylor, BG Holding's agent, testified he never authorized any work by F & D, nor did he see any work being performed by them on the site.
- The lease specifically provided that all work on the property was to be approved in writing by BG Holding.
- David Weatherington of F & D testified he was looking to Powder Coaters, not BG Holding, for payment.
- Powder Coaters acknowledged it was not authorized to bind BG Holding to pay for the modifications.
- The lease states, "[i]f the Lessee should make any [alterations, modification, additions, or installations], the Lessee hereby agrees to indemnify, defend, and save harmless the Lessor from any liability..."

D. Evidence There Was Consent

- Bruce Houston, owner of Powder Coaters testified that during the lease negotiations, he informed Mark Taylor, BG Holding's property manager and agent, that electrical and gas upgrading would be necessary for Powder Coaters to perform their work.
- Houston testified Mark Taylor was present at the warehouse while F & D performed their work. [However, Taylor testified he did not see F & D performing any work on the premises.]
- Houston testified he would not have entered into the lease if he was not authorized to upgrade the electrical since the existing power source was insufficient to run the machinery needed for Powder Coaters to operate.
- Houston testified Mark Taylor, BG Holding's agent, showed him the power source for the building so Taylor could understand the extent of the work that was going to be required.
- Houston testified Paragraph 5 of the addendum to the lease was specifically negotiated. He testified the following language granted him the authority to perform the electrical upfit, so that he was not required to submit the plans to BG Holding as required by a provision in the lease: "Lessor shall allow Lessee to put Office Trailer in Building. All Utilities necessary to handle Lessee's equipment shall be paid for by the Lessee including, but not limited to electricity, water, sewer, and gas." (We note that BG Holding denies this interpretation, but insists it just requires the Lessee to pay for all utility bills.)
- Powder Coaters no longer occupies the property, and BG Holding possibly benefits from the work done.

In the instant case, there is some evidence of consent. However, it does not rise to the level required under the statute....

Viewing the evidence in the light most favorable to F & D, whether BG Holding gave their consent is a close question. However, we agree with the Court of Appeals, that F & D has not presented enough evidence to show: (1) BG Holding gave anything more than general consent to make improvements (as the lease could be interpreted to allow); or (2) BG Holding had anything more that "mere knowledge" that the work was to be done. Powder Coaters asserted the lease's addendum evidenced BG Holding's consent to perform the modifications; however, there is no evidence BG Holding expressly or implicitly agreed that it might be liable for the work. In fact, the lease between Powder Coaters and BG Holding expressly provided Powder Coaters was responsible for any alterations made to the property. Even Powder Coaters acknowledged it was not authorized to bind BG Holding....Therefore, it is impossible to see how the very general provision requiring Powder Coaters to pay for water, sewer, and gas can be interpreted to authorize Powder Coaters to perform an electrical upgrade. Furthermore, we agree with the Court of Appeals that the mere presence of BG Holding's agent at the work site is not enough to establish consent.

Conclusion

We hold consent, as required by the Mechanic's Lien Statute, is something more than mere knowledge work will be or could be done on the property. The landlord/owner must do more than grant the tenant general permission to make repairs or improvements to the leased premises. The landlord/owner or his agent must give either his tenant or the materialman express or implied consent acknowledging he may be held liable for the work.

The Court of Appeals' opinion is affirmed as modified.

Case Questions

1. Why did the lienor want to go after the landlord instead of the tenant?
2. Did the landlord here know that there were electrical upgrades needed by the tenant?
3. What kind of knowledge or acceptance did the court determine the landlord-owner needed to have or give before a material man could have a lien on the real estate?
4. What remedy has F & D (the material man) now?

Deeds of Trust; Duties of Trustee

Alpha Imperial Building, LLC v. Schnitzer Family Investment, LLC, II (SFI).
2005 WL 715940, (Wash. Ct. App. 2005)

Applewick, J.

Alpha Imperial LLC challenges the validity of a non-judicial foreclosure sale on multiple grounds. Alpha was the holder of a third deed of trust on the building sold, and contests the location of the sale and the adequacy of the sale price. Alpha also claims that the trustee had a duty to re-open the sale, had a duty to the junior lienholder, chilled the bidding, and had a conflict of interest. We find that the location of the sale was proper, the price was adequate, bidding was not chilled, and that the trustee had no duty to re-open the sale, [and] no duty to the junior lienholder....We affirm.

Facts

Mayur Sheth and another individual formed Alpha Imperial Building, LLC in 1998 for the purpose of investing in commercial real estate. In February 2000 Alpha sold the property at 1406 Fourth Avenue in Seattle (the Property) to Pioneer Northwest, LLC (Pioneer). Pioneer financed this purchase with two loans from [defendant Schnitzer Family Investment, LLC, II (SFI)]. Pioneer also took a third loan from Alpha at the time of the sale for $1.3 million. This loan from Alpha was junior to the two [other] loans[.]

Pioneer defaulted and filed for bankruptcy in 2002....In October 2002 defendant Blackstone Corporation, an entity created to act as a non-judicial foreclosure trustee, issued a Trustee's Notice of Sale. Blackstone is wholly owned by defendant Witherspoon, Kelley, Davenport & Toole (Witherspoon). Defendant Michael Currin, a shareholder at Witherspoon, was to conduct the sale on January 10, 2003. Currin and Witherspoon represented SFI and 4th Avenue LLC. Sheth received a copy of the Notice of Sale through his attorney.

On January 10, 2003, Sheth and his son Abhi arrived at the Third Avenue entrance to the King County courthouse between 9:30 and 9:45 a.m. They waited for about ten minutes. They noticed two signs posted above the Third Avenue entrance. One sign said that construction work was occurring at the courthouse and 'all property auctions by the legal and banking communities will be moved to the 4th Avenue entrance of the King County Administration Building.' The other sign indicated that the Third Avenue entrance would remain open during construction. Sheth and Abhi asked a courthouse employee about the sign, and were told that all sales were conducted at the Administration Building.

Sheth and Abhi then walked to the Administration Building, and asked around about the sale of the Property. [He was told Michael Currin, one of the shareholders of Blackstone—the trustee—was holding the sale, and was advised] to call Currin's office in Spokane. Sheth did so, and was told that the sale was at the Third Avenue entrance. Sheth and Abhi went back to the Third Avenue entrance.

In the meantime, Currin had arrived at the Third Avenue entrance between 9:35 and 9:40 a.m. The head of SFI, Danny Schnitzer (Schnitzer), and his son were also present. Currin was surprised to notice that no other foreclosure sales were taking place, but did not ask at the information desk about it. Currin did not see the signs directing auctions to occur at the Administration Building. Currin conducted the auction, Schnitzer made the only bid, for $2.1 million, and the sale was complete. At this time, the debt owed on the first two deeds of trust totaled approximately $4.1 million. Currin then left the courthouse, but when he received a call from his assistant telling him about Sheth, he arranged to meet Sheth back at the Third Avenue entrance. When they met, Sheth told Currin that the sales were conducted at the Administration Building. Currin responded that the sale had already been conducted, and he was not required to go to the Administration Building. Currin told Sheth that the notice indicated the sale was to be at the Third Avenue entrance, and that the sale had been held at the correct location. Sheth did not ask to re-open the bidding....

Sheth filed the current lawsuit, with Alpha as the sole plaintiff, on February 14, 2003. The lawsuit asked for declaratory relief, restitution, and other damages. The trial court granted the defendants' summary judgment motion on August 8, 2003. Alpha appeals.

Location of the Sale

Alpha argues that the sale was improper because it was at the Third Avenue entrance, not the Administration Building. Alpha points to a letter from a King County employee stating that auctions are held at the Administration Building. The letter also stated that personnel were instructed to direct bidders and trustees to that location if asked. In addition, Alpha argues that the Third Avenue entrance was not a 'public' place, as required by [the statute], since auction sales were forbidden there. We disagree. Alpha has not shown that the Third Avenue entrance was an improper location. The evidence shows that the county had changed its policy as to where auctions would be held and had posted signs to that effect. However, the county did not exclude people from the Third Avenue entrance or prevent auctions from being held there. Street, who frequented sales, stated that auctions were being held in both locations. The sale was held where the Notice of Sale indicated it would be. In addition, Alpha has not introduced any evidence to show that the Third Avenue entrance was not a public place at the time of the sale. The public was free to come and go at that location, and the area was 'open and available for all to use.' Alpha relies on *Morton v. Resolution Trust* (S.D. Miss. 1995) to support its contention that the venue of the sale was improper. [But] *Morton* is not on point.

Duty to Re-Open Sale

Alpha argues that Currin should have re-opened the sale. However, it is undisputed that Sheth did not request that Currin re-open it. The evidence indicates that Currin may have known about Sheth's interest in bidding prior to the day of the sale, due to a conversation with Sheth's attorney about Sheth's desire to protect his interest in the Property. But, this knowledge did not create in Currin any affirmative duty to offer to re-open the sale.

In addition, Alpha cites no Washington authority to support the contention that Currin would have been obligated to re-open the sale if Sheth had asked him to. The decision to continue a sale appears to be fully within the discretion of the trustee: "[t]he trustee may for any cause the trustee deems advantageous, continue the sale." [Citation.] Alpha's citation to *Peterson v. Kansas City Life Ins. Co.,* Missouri (1936) to support its contention that Currin should have re-opened the sale is unavailing. In Peterson, the Notice of Sale indicated that the sale would be held at the 'front' door of the courthouse. But, the courthouse had four doors, and the customary door for sales was the east door. The sheriff, acting as the trustee, conducted the sale at the east door, and then re-opened the sale at the south door, as there had been some sales at the south door. Alpha contends this shows that Currin should have re-opened the sale when learning of the Administration Building location, akin to what the sheriff did in Peterson. However, Peterson does not indicate that the sheriff had an affirmative duty to re-sell the property at the south door. This case is not on point.

Chilled Bidding

Alpha contends that Currin chilled the bidding on the Property by telling bidders that he expected a full credit sale price and by holding the sale at the courthouse. Chilled bidding can be grounds for setting aside a sale. *Country Express Stores, Inc. v. Sims,* [Washington Court of Appeals] (1997). The *Country Express* court explained the two types of chilled bidding:

The first is intentional, occurring where there is collusion for the purpose of holding down the bids. The second consists of inadvertent and unintentional acts by the trustee that have the effect of suppressing the bidding. To establish chilled bidding, the challenger must establish the bidding was actually suppressed, which can sometimes be shown by an inadequate sale price.

We hold that there was no chilling. Alpha has not shown that Currin engaged in intentional chilling. There is no evidence that Currin knew about the signs indicating auctions were occurring at the Administration Building when he prepared the Notice of Sale, such that he intentionally held the sale at a location from which he knew bidders would be absent. Additionally, Currin's statement to [an interested person who might bid on the property] that a full credit sale price was expected and that the opening bid would be $4.1 million did not constitute intentional chilling. SFI was owed $4.1 million on the Property. SFI could thus bid up to that amount at no cost to itself, as the proceeds would go back to SFI. Currin confirmed that SFI was prepared to make a full-credit bid. [It is common for trustees to] disclose the full-credit bid amount to potential third party bidders, and for investors to lose interest when they learn of the amount of indebtedness on property. It was therefore not a misrepresentation for Currin to state $4.1 million as the opening bid, due to the indebtedness on the Property. Currin's statements had no chilling effect—they merely informed [interested persons] of the minimum amount necessary to prevail against SFI. Thus, Currin did not intentionally chill the bidding by giving Street that information.

Alpha also argues that the chilled bidding could have been unintended by Currin.... [But the evidence is that] Currin's actions did not intentionally or unintentionally chill the bidding, and the sale will not be set aside.

Adequacy of the Sale Price

Alpha claims that the sale price was 'greatly inadequate' and that the sale should thus be set aside. Alpha submitted evidence that the property had an 'as is' value of $4.35 million in December 2002, and an estimated 2004 value of $5.2 million. The debt owed to SFI on the property was $4.1 million. SFI bought the property for $2.1 million. These facts do not suggest that the sale must be set aside.

Washington case law suggests that the price the property is sold for must be 'grossly inadequate' for a trustee's sale to be set aside on those grounds alone. In *Cox* [Citation, 1985], the property was worth between $200,000 and $300,000, and was sold to the beneficiary for $11,873. The Court held that amount to be grossly inadequate In *Steward* [Citation, 1988] the property had been purchased for approximately $64,000, and then was sold to a third party at a foreclosure sale for $4,870. This court held that $4,870 was not grossly inadequate. In *Miebach* [Citation] (1984), the Court noted that a sale for less than two percent of the property's fair market value was grossly inadequate. The Court in *Miebach* also noted prior cases where the sale had been voided due to grossly inadequate purchase price; the properties in those cases had been sold for less than four percent of the value and less than three percent of the value. In addition, the Restatement indicates that gross inadequacy only exists when the sale price is less than 20 percent of the fair market value—without other defects, sale prices over 20 percent will not be set aside. [Citation.] The Property was sold for between 40 and 48 percent of its value. These facts do not support a grossly inadequate purchase price.

Alpha cites *Miebach* for the proposition that 'where the inadequacy of price is great the sale will be set aside with slight indications of fraud or unfairness,' arguing that such indications existed here. However, the cases cited by the Court in *Miebach* to support this proposition involved properties sold for less than three and four percent of their value. Alpha has not demonstrated the slightest indication of fraud, nor shown that a property that sold for 40 to 48 percent of its value sold for a greatly inadequate price.

Duty to a Junior Lienholder

Alpha claims that Currin owed a duty to Alpha, the junior lienholder. Alpha cites no case law for this proposition, and, indeed, there is none—Division Two specifically declined to decide this issue in *Country Express* [Citation]. Alpha acknowledges the lack of language in RCW 61.24 (the deed of trust statute) regarding fiduciary duties of trustees to junior lienholders. But Alpha argues that since RCW 61.24 requires that the trustee follow certain procedures in conducting the sale, and allows for sales to be restrained by anyone with an interest, a substantive duty from the trustee to a junior lienholder can be inferred.

Alpha's arguments are unavailing. The procedural requirements in RCW 61.24 do not create implied substantive duties. The structure of the deed of trust sale illustrates that no duty is owed to the junior lienholder. The trustee and the junior lienholder have no relationship with each other. The sale is pursuant to a contract between the grantor, the beneficiary and the trustee. The junior lienholder is not a party to that contract. The case law indicates only that the trustee owes a fiduciary duty to the debtor and beneficiary: "a trustee of a deed of trust is a fiduciary for both the mortgagee and mortgagor and must act impartially between them." *Cox* [Citation]. The fact that a sale in accordance with that contract can extinguish the junior lienholder's interest further shows that the grantor's and beneficiary's interest in the deed of trust being foreclosed is adverse to the junior lienholder. We conclude the trustee, while having duties as fiduciary for the grantor and beneficiary, does not have duties to another whose interest is adverse to the grantor or beneficiary. Thus, Alpha's claim of a special duty to a junior lienholder fails....

Attorney Fees

...Defendants claim they are entitled to attorney fees for opposing a frivolous claim, pursuant to [the Washington statute]. An appeal is frivolous 'if there are no debatable issues upon which reasonable minds might differ and it is so totally devoid of merit that there was no reasonable possibility of reversal.' [Citation] Alpha has presented several issues not so clearly resolved by case law as to be frivolous, although Alpha's arguments ultimately fail. Thus, Respondents' request for attorney fees under [state law] is denied.

Affirmed.

Case Questions

1. Why did the plaintiff (Alpha) think the sale should have been set aside because of the location problems?
2. Why did the court decide the trustee had no duty to reopen bidding?
3. What is meant by "chilling bidding"? What argument did the plaintiff make to support its contention that bidding was chilled?
4. The court notes precedent to the effect that a "grossly inadequate" bid price has some definition. What is the definition? What percentage of the real estate's value in this case was the winning bid?
5. A trustee is one who owes a fiduciary duty of the utmost loyalty and good faith to another, the beneficiary. Who was the beneficiary here? What duty is owed to the junior lienholder (Alpha here)—any duty?
6. Why did the defendants not get the attorneys' fee award they wanted?

29.5 Summary and Exercises

Summary

A mortgage is a means of securing a debt with real estate. The mortgagor, or borrower, gives the mortgage. The lender is the mortgagee, who holds the mortgage. On default, the mortgagee may foreclose the mortgage, convening the security interest into title. In many states, the mortgagor has a statutory right of redemption after foreclosure.

Various statutes regulate the mortgage business, including the Truth in Lending Act, the Equal Credit Opportunity Act, the Real Estate Settlement Procedures Act, and the Home Mortgage Disclosure Act, which together prescribe a code of fair practices and require various disclosures to be made before the mortgage is created.

The mortgagor signs both a note and the mortgage at the closing. Without the note, the mortgage would secure nothing. Most notes and mortgages contain an acceleration clause, which calls for the entire principal and interest to be due, at the mortgagee's option, if the debtor defaults on any payment.

In most states, mortgages must be recorded for the mortgagee to be entitled to priority over third parties who might also claim an interest in the land. The general rule is "First in time, first in right," although there are exceptions for fixture filings and nonobligatory future advances. Mortgages are terminated by repayment, novation, or foreclosure, either through judicial sale or under a power-of-sale clause.

Real estate may also be used as security under a deed of trust, which permits a trustee to sell the land automatically on default, without recourse to a court of law.

Nonconsensual liens are security interests created by law. These include court-decreed liens, such as attachment liens and judgment liens. Other liens are mechanic's liens (for labor, services, or materials furnished in connection with someone's real property), possessory liens (for artisans working with someone else's personal properly), and tax liens.

Exercises

1. Able bought a duplex from Carr, who had borrowed from First Bank for its purchase. Able took title subject to Carr's mortgage. Able did not make mortgage payments to First Bank; the bank foreclosed and sold the property, leaving a deficiency. Which is correct?
    a. Carr alone is liable for the deficiency.
    b. Able alone is liable for the deficiency because he assumed the mortgage.
    c. First Bank may pursue either Able or Carr.
    d. Only if Carr fails to pay will Able be liable.
2. Harry borrowed $175,000 from Judith, giving her a note for that amount and a mortgage on his condo. Judith did not record the mortgage. After Harry defaulted on his payments, Judith began foreclosure proceedings. Harry argued that the mortgage was invalid because Judith had failed to record it. Judith counterargues that because a mortgage is not an interest in real estate, recording is not necessary. Who is correct? Explain.
3. Assume in Exercise 2 that the documents did not contain an acceleration clause and that Harry missed three consecutive payments. Could Judith foreclose? Explain.
4. Rupert, an automobile mechanic, does carpentry work on weekends. He built a detached garage for Clyde for $20,000. While he was constructing the garage, he agreed to tune up Clyde's car for an additional $200. When the work was completed, Clyde failed to pay him the $20,200, and Rupert claimed a mechanic's lien on the garage and car. What problems, if any, might Rupert encounter in enforcing his lien? Explain.
5. In Exercise 4, assume that Clyde had borrowed $50,000 from First Bank and had given the bank a mortgage on the property two weeks after Rupert commenced work on the garage but several weeks before he filed the lien. Assuming that the bank immediately recorded its mortgage and that Rupert's lien is valid, does the mortgage take priority over the lien? Why?
6. Defendant purchased a house from Seller and assumed the mortgage indebtedness to Plaintiff. All monthly payments were made on time until March 25, 1948, when no more were made. On October 8, 1948, Plaintiff sued to foreclose and accelerate the note. In February of 1948, Plaintiff asked to obtain a loan elsewhere and pay him off; he offered a discount if she would do so, three times, increasing the amount offered each time. Plaintiff understood that Defendant was getting a loan from the Federal Housing Administration (FHA), but she was confronted with a number of requirements, including significant property improvements, which—because they were neighbors—Plaintiff knew were ongoing. While the improvements were being made, in June or July, he said to her, "Just let the payments go and we'll settle everything up at the same time," meaning she need not make monthly payments until the FHA was consummated, and he'd be paid from the proceeds. But then "he changed his tune" and sought foreclosure. Should the court order it?

Self-Test Questions

1. The person or institution holding a mortgage is called
    a. the mortgagor
    b. the mortgagee
    c. the debtor
    d. none of the above

2. Mortgages are regulated by
    a. the Truth in Lending Act
    b. the Equal Credit Opportunity Act
    c. the Real Estate Settlement Procedures Act
    d. all of the above
3. At the closing, a mortgagor signs
    a. only a mortgage
    b. only a note
    c. either a note or the mortgage
    d. both a note and the mortgage
4. Mortgages are terminated by
    a. repayment
    b. novation
    c. foreclosure
    d. any of the above
5. A lien ordered against a person's property to prevent its disposal during a lawsuit is called
    a. a judgment lien
    b. an attachment lien
    c. a possessory lien
    d. none of the above

Self-Test Answers

1. b
2. d
3. d
4. d
5. b

Endnotes

1. 12 United States Code, Section 2901.
2. Steven J. Markovich, *The Dodd-Frank Act*, Council on Foreign Relations, http://www.cfr.org/united-states/dodd-frank-act/p28735?cid=ppc-google-grant-dodd_frank&gclid=CILEIPTwqMUCFUWVfgodRXYAwg
3. Matt Taibbi, "How Wall Street Killed Financial Reform," *Rolling Stone*, May 10, 2012. http://www.rollingstone.com/politics/news/how-wall-street-killed-financial-reform-20120510.
4. 12 United States Code, Section 1701-j.
5. The states using the deed of trust system are as follows: Alabama, Alaska, Arkansas, Arizona, California, Colorado, District of Columbia, Georgia, Hawaii, Idaho, Iowa, Michigan, Minnesota, Mississippi, Missouri, Montana, Nevada, New Hampshire, North Carolina, Oklahoma, Oregon, Rhode Island, South Dakota, Tennessee, Texas, Utah, Virginia, Washington, West Virginia, Wisconsin, and Wyoming.

CHAPTER 30
Bankruptcy

Learning Objectives

After reading this chapter, you should understand the following:

1. A short history of U.S. bankruptcy law.
2. An overview of key provisions of the 2005 bankruptcy act.
3. The basic operation of Chapter 7 bankruptcy.
4. The basic operation of Chapter 11 bankruptcy.
5. The basic operation of Chapter 13 bankruptcy.
6. What debtor's relief is available outside of bankruptcy.

30.1 Introduction to Bankruptcy and Overview of the 2005 Bankruptcy Act

Learning Objectives

1. Understand what law governs bankruptcy in the United States.
2. Know the key provisions of the law.

The Purpose of Bankruptcy Law

Bankruptcy law governs the rights of creditors and insolvent debtors who cannot pay their debts. In broadest terms, bankruptcy deals with the seizure of the debtor's assets and their distribution to the debtor's various creditors. The term derives from the Renaissance custom of Italian traders, who did their trading from benches in town marketplaces. Creditors literally "broke the bench" of a merchant who failed to pay his debts. The term *banco rotta* (broken bench) thus came to apply to business failures.

In the Victorian era, many people in both England and the United States viewed someone who became bankrupt as a wicked person. In part, this attitude was prompted by the law itself, which to a greater degree in England and to a lesser degree in the United States treated the insolvent debtor as a sort of felon. Until the second half of the nineteenth century, British insolvents could be imprisoned; jail for insolvent debtors was abolished earlier in the United States. And the entire administration of bankruptcy law favored the creditor, who could with a mere filing throw the financial affairs of the alleged insolvent into complete disarray.

Today a different attitude prevails. Bankruptcy is understood as a system that permits creditors to receive an equitable distribution of the bankrupt person's assets and promises new hope to debtors facing impossible financial burdens. Without such a law, we may reasonably suppose that the level of economic activity would be far less than it is, for few would be willing to risk being personally burdened forever by crushing debt. Bankruptcy gives the honest debtor a fresh start and resolves disputes among creditors.

History of the Bankruptcy System; Bankruptcy Courts and Judges

Constitutional Basis

The U.S. Constitution prohibits the states from impairing the "obligation of a contract." This means that no state can directly provide a means for discharging a debtor unless the debt has been entirely paid. But the Constitution in Article I, Section 8, does give the federal government such a power by providing that Congress may enact a uniform bankruptcy law.

Bankruptcy Statutes

Congress passed bankruptcy laws in 1800, 1841, and 1867. These lasted only a few years each. In 1898, Congress enacted the Bankruptcy Act, which together with the Chandler Act amendments in 1938, lasted until 1978. In 1978, Congress passed the Bankruptcy Reform Act, and in 2005, it adopted the current law, the Bankruptcy Abuse Prevention and Consumer Protection Act (BAPCPA). This law is the subject of our chapter.

At the beginning of the twentieth century, bankruptcies averaged fewer than 20,000 per year. Even in 1935, at the height of the Great Depression, bankruptcy filings in federal court climbed only to 69,000. At the end of World War II, in 1945, they stood at 13,000. From 1950 on, the statistics show a steep increase. During the decade before the 1978 changes, bankruptcy filings in court averaged 181,000 a year—reaching a high of 254,000 in 1975. They soared to over 450,000 filings per year in the 1980s and mostly maintained that pace until just before the 2005 law took effect (see U.S. Bankruptcies 1980-2014). The 2005 act—preceded by "massive lobbying largely by banks and credit card companies"[1]—was intended by its promoters to restore personal responsibility and integrity in the bankruptcy system. The law's critics said it was simply a way for the credit card industry to extract more money from consumers before their debts were wiped away. The title of the act, which includes the phrase "bankruptcy abuse protection" reflects the feeling in Congress that bankruptcy law was—well—being abused.

FIGURE 30.1 U.S. Non-Business Bankruptcy Filings 1994-2015

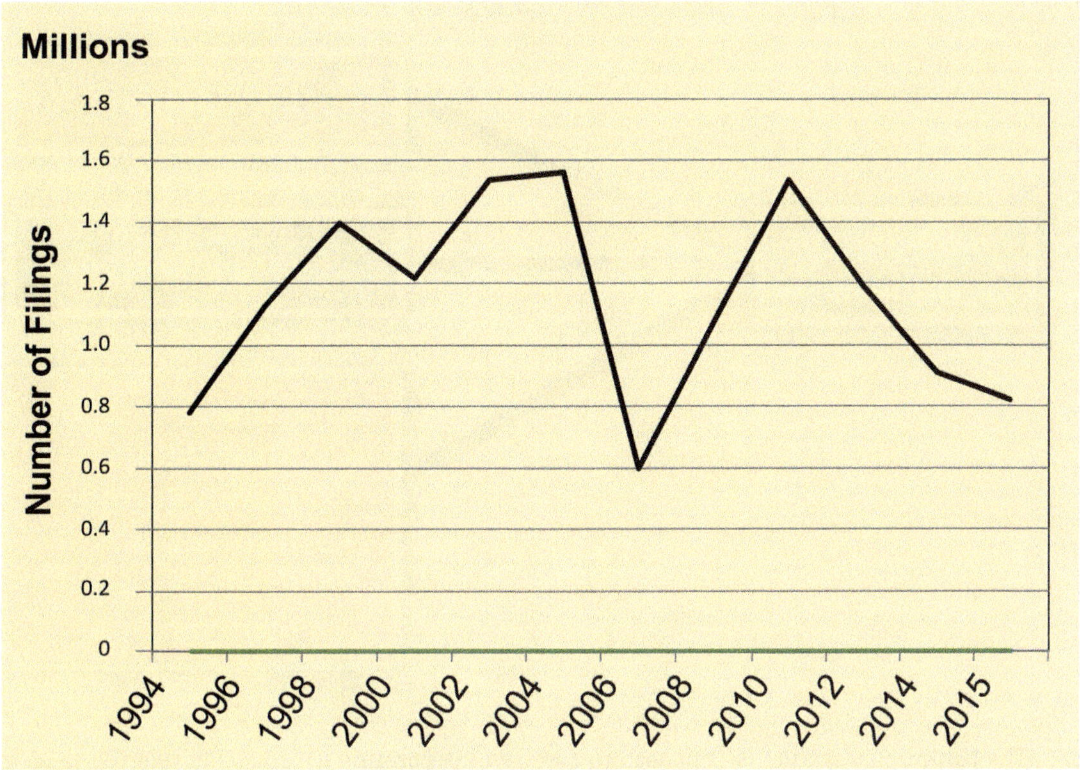

Source: Data from http://www.bankruptcyaction.com/USbankstats.htm

Bankruptcy Courts, Judges, and Costs

Each federal judicial district has a U.S. Bankruptcy Court, whose judges are appointed by U.S. Courts of Appeal. Unless both sides agree otherwise, bankruptcy judges are to hear only bankruptcy matters (called core proceedings). Bankruptcy trustees are government lawyers appointed by the U.S. Attorney General. They have administrative responsibilities in overseeing the proceedings.

The filing fee for a bankruptcy is about $350, depending upon the type of bankruptcy, and the typical lawyer's fee for uncomplicated cases is about $1,200–$1,400.

Overview of Bankruptcy Provisions

The BAPCPA provides for six different kinds of bankruptcy proceedings. Each is covered by its own chapter in the act and is usually referred to by its chapter number (see Figure 30.2).

FIGURE 30.2 Bankruptcy Options

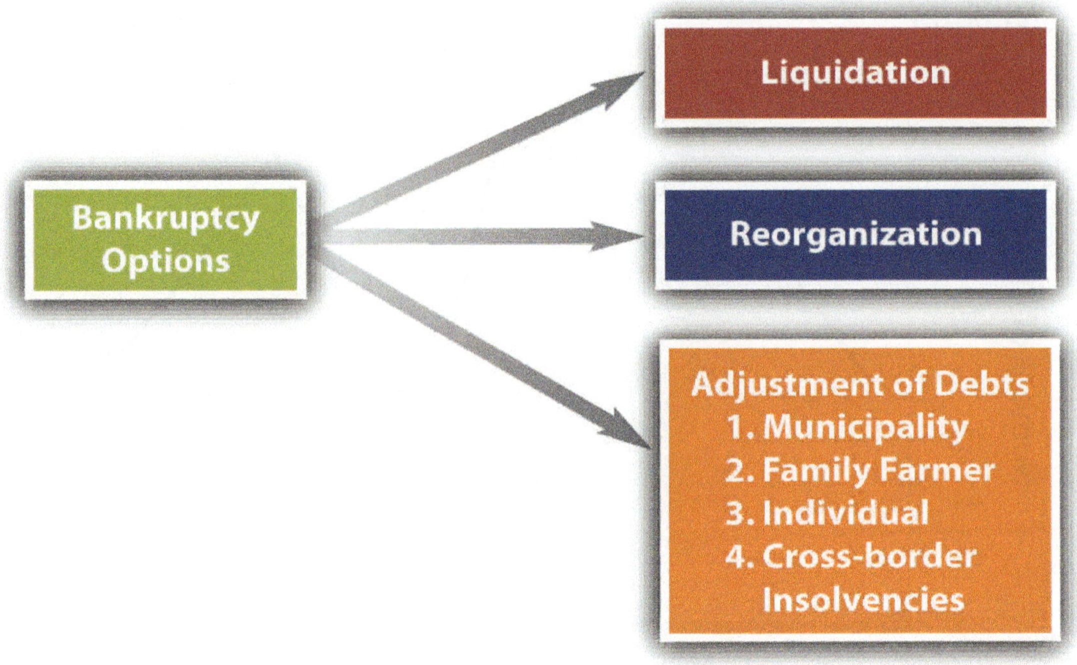

The bankruptcy statute (as opposed to case law interpreting it) is usually referred to as the bankruptcy *code*. The types of bankruptcies are as follows:

- Chapter 7, Liquidation: applies to all debtors except railroads, insurance companies, most banks and credit unions, and homestead associations.[2] A liquidation is a "straight" bankruptcy proceeding. It entails selling the debtor's nonexempt assets for cash and distributing the cash to the creditors, thereby discharging the insolvent person or business from any further liability for the debt. About 70 percent of all bankruptcy filings are Chapter 7. (Check out http://www.americanbar.org/content/dam/aba/migrated/publiced/practical/books/family_legal_guide/bankruptcy_7_13.authcheckdam.pdf.)
- Chapter 9, Adjustment of debts of a municipality: applies to municipalities that are insolvent and want to adjust their debts.[3] (The law does not suppose that a town, city, or county will go out of existence in the wake of insolvency. Detroit went bankrupt in 2013, with debt estimated at some $20 billion.[4])
- Chapter 11, Reorganization: applies to anybody who could file Chapter 7, plus railroads. It is the means by which a financially troubled company or individual can continue to operate while its financial affairs are put on a sounder basis. A business might liquidate following reorganization but will probably take on new life after negotiations with creditors on how the old debt is to be paid off. A company may voluntarily decide to seek Chapter 11 protection in court, or it may be forced involuntarily into a Chapter 11 proceeding. Compared to Chapters 7 and 13, Chapter 11 cases usually involve more money regarding the debts and assets.
- Chapter 12, Adjustment of debts of a family farmer or fisherman with regular annual income.[5] Many family farmers cannot qualify for reorganization under Chapter 13 because of the low debt ceiling, and under Chapter 11, the proceeding is often complicated and expensive. As a result, Congress created Chapter 12, which applies only to farmers whose total debts do not exceed $4,031,575 (a farming operation) or $1,868,200 for a commercial fishing operation).[6] Few cases are filed: in 2011 only 637 of the 1.4 million bankruptcy cases were Chapter 12.
- Chapter 13, Adjustment of debts of an individual with regular income: applies only to individuals (no corporations or partnerships) with unsecured debt not exceeding about $395,000, and secured debt not exceeding about $1.2 million.[7] This chapter permits an individual with regular income to establish a repayment plan, usually either a composition (an agreement among

creditors, discussed in Section 5, "Alternatives to Bankruptcy") or an extension (a stretch-out of the time for paying the entire debt).

- Chapter 15, Ancillary and other cross-border cases: incorporates the United Nations' Model Law on Cross-Border Insolvency to promote cooperation among nations involved in cross-border cases and is intended to create legal certainty for trade and investment. "Ancillary" refers to the possibility that a U.S. debtor might have assets or obligations in a foreign country; those non-U.S. aspects of the case are "ancillary" to the U.S. bankruptcy case.

The BAPCPA includes three chapters that set forth the procedures to be applied to the various proceedings. Chapter 1, "General Provisions," establishes who is eligible for relief under the act. Chapter 3, "Case Administration," spells out the powers of the various officials involved in the bankruptcy proceedings and establishes the methods for instituting bankruptcy cases. Chapter 5, "Creditors, the Debtor, and the Estate," deals with the debtor's "estate"—his or her assets. It lays down ground rules for determining which property is to be included in the estate, sets out the powers of the bankruptcy trustee to "avoid" (invalidate) transactions by which the debtor sought to remove property from the estate, orders the distribution of property to creditors, and sets forth the duties and benefits that accrue to the debtor under the act.

To illustrate how these procedural chapters (especially Chapter 3 and Chapter 5) apply, we focus on the most common proceeding: liquidation (Chapter 7). Most of the principles of bankruptcy law discussed in connection with liquidation apply to the other types of proceedings as well. However, some principles vary, and we conclude the chapter by noting special features of two other important proceedings—Chapter 13 and Chapter 11.

Key Takeaway

Bankruptcy law's purpose is to give the honest debtor a fresh start and to resolve disputes among creditors. The most recent amendments to the law were effective in 2005. Bankruptcy law provides relief to six kinds of debtors: (1) Chapter 7, straight bankruptcy—liquidation—applies to most debtors (except banks and railroads); (2) Chapter 9 applies to municipalities; (3) Chapter 11 is business reorganization; (4) Chapter 12 applies to farmers; (5) Chapter 13 is for wage earners; and (6) Chapter 15 applies to cross-border bankruptcies. The bankruptcy statutes also have several chapters that cover procedures of bankruptcy proceedings.

Exercises

1. Why is bankruptcy law required in a modern capitalistic society?
2. Who does the bankruptcy trustee represent?
3. The three most commonly filed bankruptcies are Chapter 7, 11, and 13. Who gets relief under those chapters?

30.2 Case Administration; Creditors' Claims; Debtors' Exemptions and Dischargeable Debts; Debtor's Estate

Learning Objectives

1. Understand the basic procedures involved in administering a bankruptcy case.
2. Recognize the basic elements of creditors' rights under the bankruptcy code.
3. Understand the fundamentals of what property is included in the debtor's estate.
4. Identify some of the debtor's exemptions—what property can be kept by the debtor.
5. Know some of the debts that cannot be discharged in bankruptcy.
6. Know how an estate is liquidated under Chapter 7.

Case Administration (Chapter 3 of the Bankruptcy Code)

Recall that the purpose of liquidation is to convert the debtor's assets—except those exempt under the law—into cash for distribution to the creditors and thereafter to discharge the debtor from further liability. With certain exceptions, any person may voluntarily file a petition to liquidate under Chapter 7. A "person" is defined as any individual, partnership, or corporation. The exceptions are railroads and insurance companies, banks, savings and loan associations, credit unions, and the like.

For a Chapter 7 liquidation proceeding, as for bankruptcy proceedings in general, the various aspects of case administration are covered by the bankruptcy code's Chapter 3. These include the rules governing commencement of the proceedings, the effect of the petition in bankruptcy, the first meeting of the creditors, and the duties and powers of trustees.

Commencement

The bankruptcy begins with the filing of a petition in bankruptcy with the bankruptcy court.

Voluntary and Involuntary Petitions

The individual, partnership, or corporation may file a voluntary petition in bankruptcy; 99 percent of bankruptcies are voluntary petitions filed by the debtor. But involuntary bankruptcy is possible, too, under Chapter 7 or Chapter 11. To put anyone into bankruptcy involuntarily, the petitioning creditors must meet conditions regarding the amount (about $15,000), the number of creditors joining in (at least three, usually), and the debt must be undisputed. If there is a dispute, the debtor can resist the involuntary filing, and if she wins the dispute, the creditors who pushed for the involuntary petition have to pay the associated costs. Persons owing less than $13,475, farmers, and charitable organizations cannot be forced into bankruptcy. Involuntary bankruptcy is rare.[8]

The Automatic Stay

The petition—voluntary or otherwise—operates as a **stay** against suits or other actions against the debtor to recover claims, enforce judgments, or create liens (but not alimony collection). In other words, once the petition is filed, the debtor is freed from worry over other proceedings affecting her finances or property. No more debt collection calls! Anyone with a claim, secured or unsecured, must seek relief in the bankruptcy court. This provision in the act can have dramatic consequences. Beset by tens of thousands of products-liability suits for damages caused by asbestos, UNR Industries and Manville Corporation, the nation's largest asbestos producers, filed (separate) voluntary bankruptcy petitions in 1982; those filings automatically stayed all pending lawsuits.

stay

Upon filing the bankruptcy, an automatic injunction that halts actions by creditors to collect debts.

First Meeting of Creditors

Once a petition in bankruptcy is filed, the court issues an **order of relief**, which determines that the debtor's property is subject to bankruptcy court control and creates the stay. The Chapter 7 case may be dismissed by the court if, after a notice and hearing, it finds that among other things (e.g., delay, nonpayment of required bankruptcy fees), the debts are primarily consumer debts and the debtor could pay them off—that's the 2005 act's famous "means test," discussed in Section 3.

order of relief

The court's order determining the debtor's property to be under the control of the bankruptcy court.

Assuming that the order of relief has been properly issued, the creditors must meet within a reasonable time. The debtor is obligated to appear at the meeting and submit to examination under oath. The judge does not preside and, indeed, is not even entitled to attend the meeting.

When the judge issues an order for relief, an interim trustee is appointed who is authorized initially to take control of the debtor's assets. The trustee is required to collect the property, liquidate the debtor's estate, and distribute the proceeds to the creditors. The trustee may sue and be sued in the name of the estate. Under every chapter except Chapter 7, the court has sole discretion to name the trustee. Under Chapter 7, the creditors may select their own trustee as long as they do it at the first meeting of creditors and follow the procedures laid down in the act.

Trustee's Powers and Duties

The act empowers the trustee to use, sell, or lease the debtor's property in the ordinary course of business or, after notice and a hearing, even if not in the ordinary course of business. In all cases, the trustee must protect any security interests in the property. As long as the court has authorized the debtor's business to continue, the trustee may also obtain credit in the ordinary course of business. She may invest money in the estate to yield the maximum, but reasonably safe, return. Subject to the court's approval, she may employ various professionals, such as attorneys, accountants, and appraisers, and may, with some exceptions, assume or reject executory contracts and unexpired leases that the debtor has made. The trustee also has the power to avoid many pre-bankruptcy transactions in order to recover property of the debtor to be included ("clawed back") in the liquidation.

Creditors' Claims, the Debtor, and the Estate (Chapter 5 of the Bankruptcy Code)

We now turn to the major matters covered in Chapter 5 of the bankruptcy act: creditors' claims, debtors' exemptions and discharge, and the property to be included in the estate. We begin with the rules governing proof of claims by creditors and the priority of their claims.

Claims and Creditors

A claim is defined as a right to payment, whether or not it is reduced to judgment, liquidated, unliquidated, fixed, contingent, matured, unmatured, disputed, undisputed, legal, equitable, secured, or unsecured. A creditor is defined as a person or entity with a claim that arose no later than when the court issues the order for relief. These are very broad definitions, intended to give the debtor the broadest possible relief when finally discharged.

Proof of Claims

proof of claim

The form used to file a claim by a creditor.

Before the trustee can distribute proceeds of the estate, unsecured creditors must file a **proof of claim**, prima facie evidence that they are owed some amount of money. They must do so within six months after the first date set for the first meeting of creditors. A creditor's claim is disallowed, even though it is valid, if it is not filed in a timely manner. A party in interest, such as the trustee or creditor, may object to a proof of claim, in which case the court must determine whether to allow it. In the absence of objection, the claim is "deemed allowed." The court will not allow some claims. These include unenforceable claims, claims for unmatured interest, claims that may be offset by debts the creditor owes the debtor, and unreasonable charges by an insider or an attorney. If it's a "no asset" bankruptcy—most are—creditors are in effect told by the court not to waste their time filing proof of claim.

Claims with Priority

The bankruptcy act sets out categories of claimants and establishes priorities among them. The law is complex because it sets up different orders of priorities.

First, *secured creditors* get their security interests before anyone else is satisfied, because the security interest is not part of the property that the trustee is entitled to bring into the estate. This is why being a secured creditor is important (as discussed in Chapter 28 and Chapter 29). To the extent that secured creditors have claims in excess of their collateral, they are considered unsecured or general creditors and are lumped in with general creditors of the appropriate class.

Second, of the six classes of claimants (see Figure 30.3), the first is known as that of "*priority claims.*" It is subdivided into ten categories ranked in order of priority. The highest-priority class within the general class of priority claims must be paid off in full before the next class can share in a distribution from the estate, and so on. Within each class, members will share pro rata if there are not enough assets to satisfy everyone fully. The priority classes, from highest to lowest, are set out in the bankruptcy code (11 USC Section 507) as follows:

gap creditors

Creditors giving credit, or lending money to a debtor, in the period between the filing of an involuntary bankruptcy petition and the entry of the order for relief.

(1) Domestic support obligations *("DSO"), which are claims for support due to the spouse, former spouse, child, or child's representative, and at a lower priority within this class are any claims by a governmental unit that has rendered support assistance to the debtor's family obligations.*

(2) Administrative expenses *that are required to administer the bankruptcy case itself. Under former law, administrative expenses had the highest priority, but Congress elevated domestic support obligations above administrative expenses with the passage of the BAPCPA. Actually, though, administrative expenses have a de facto priority over domestic support obligations, because such expenses are deducted before they are paid to DSO recipients. Since trustees are paid from the bankruptcy estate, the courts have allowed de facto top priority for administrative expenses because no trustee is going to administer a bankruptcy case for nothing (and no lawyer will work for long without getting paid, either).*

(3) Gap creditors. *Claims made by* ***gap creditors*** *in an involuntary bankruptcy petition under Chapter 7 or Chapter 11 are those that arise between the filing of an involuntary bankruptcy petition and the order for relief issued by the court. These claims are given priority because otherwise creditors would not deal with the debtor, usually a business, when the business has declared bankruptcy but no trustee has been appointed and no order of relief issued.*

(4) Employee wages *up to $10,950 for each worker, for the 180 days previous to either the bankruptcy filing or when the business ceased operations, whichever is earlier (180-day period).*

(5) Unpaid contributions to employee benefit plans *during the 180-day period, but limited by what was already paid by the employer under subsection (4) above plus what was paid on behalf of the employees by the bankruptcy estate for any employment benefit plan.*

(6) Any claims for grain from a grain producer or fish from a fisherman *for up to $5,400 each against a storage or processing facility.*

(7) Consumer layaway deposits *of up to $2,425 each.*

(8) Taxes owing to federal, state, and local governments *for income, property, employment and excise taxes. Outside of bankruptcy, taxes usually have a higher priority than this, which is why many times creditors—not tax creditors—file an involuntary bankruptcy petition against the debtor so that they have a higher priority in bankruptcy than they would outside it.*

(9) Allowed claims based on any commitment by the debtor to a federal depository institution *to maintain the capital of an insured depository institution.*

(10) Claims for death or personal injury from a motor vehicle or vessel that occurred while the debtor was legally intoxicated.

Third through sixth (after secured creditors and priority claimants), other claimants are attended to, but not immediately. The bankruptcy code (perhaps somewhat awkwardly) deals with who gets paid when in more than one place. Chapter 5 sets out priority *claims* as just noted; that order applies to *all* bankruptcies. Chapter 7, dealing with liquidation (as opposed to Chapter 11 and Chapter 13, wherein the debtor pays most of her debt), then lists the order of *distribution*. Section 726 of 11 United States Code provides: "Distribution of property of the estate. (1) First, in payment of claims of the kind specified in, and in the order specified in section 507..." (again, the priority of claims just set out). Following the order specified in the bankruptcy code, our discussion of the order of distribution is taken up in Section 3.

Debtor's Duties and Exemptions

The act imposes certain duties on the debtor, and it exempts some property that the trustee can accumulate and distribute from the estate.

Debtor's Duties

The debtor, reasonably enough, is supposed to file a list of creditors, assets, liabilities, and current income, and a statement of financial affairs. The debtor must cooperate with the trustee and be an "honest debtor" in general; the failure to abide by these duties is grounds for a denial of discharge.

The individual debtor (not including partnerships or corporations) also must show evidence that he or she attended an approved nonprofit budget and counseling agency within 180 days before the filing. The counseling may be "an individual or group briefing (including a briefing conducted by telephone or on the Internet) that outline[s] the opportunities for available credit counseling and assisted such individual in performing a related budget analysis."[9] In Section 111, the 2005 act describes who can perform this counseling, and a host of regulations and enforcement mechanisms are instituted, generally applying to persons who provide goods or services related to bankruptcy work for consumer debtors whose nonexempt assets are less than $150,000, in order to improve the professionalism of attorneys and others who work with debtors in, or contemplating, bankruptcy. A debtor who is incapacitated, disabled, or on active duty in a military zone doesn't have to go through the counseling.

Debtor's Exemptions

The bankruptcy act exempts certain property of the estate of an individual debtor so that he or she will not be impoverished upon discharge. Exactly what is exempt depends on state law.

Notwithstanding the Constitution's mandate that Congress establish "uniform laws on the subject of bankruptcies," bankruptcy law is in fact not uniform because the states persuaded Congress to allow nonuniform exemptions. The concept makes sense: what is necessary for a debtor in Maine to live a non-impoverished post-bankruptcy life might not be the same as what is necessary in southern California. The bankruptcy code describes how a person's residence is determined for claiming state exemptions, the point being to reduce "exemption shopping"—to reduce the incidences in which a person moves to a generous exemption state only to declare bankruptcy there.

Unless the state has opted out of the federal exemptions (a majority have), a debtor can choose which exemptions to claim.[10] There are also some exemptions not included in the bankruptcy code: veteran's, Social Security, unemployment, and disability benefits are outside the code, and alimony payments are also exempt under federal law. The federal exemptions can be doubled by a married couple filing together.

Here are the federal exemptions:[11]

Homestead

$23,675 as of 2016 (or $47,350 for a married couple filing a joint bankruptcy).

Personal Property:

- *Animals, crops, clothing, appliances and furnishings, books, household goods, and musical instruments up to $525 per item, and up to $10,775 total.*
- *Jewelry up to $1,600.*
- *$600 of any property, and $12,600 aggregate, and unused portion of homestead up to $10,125.*
- *Health aids.*
- *Wrongful death recovery for person you depended upon.*
- *Personal injury recovery up to $20,200 except for pain and suffering or for pecuniary loss.*
- *Lost earnings payments.*

Pensions:

- *Tax exempt retirement accounts; IRAs and Roth IRAs up to $1,095,000 per person.*

Public Benefits:

- *Public assistance, Social Security, veteran's benefits, unemployment compensation.*
- *Crime victim's compensation.*

Tools of Trade:

- *Implements, books, and tools of trade, up to $2,025.*

Alimony and Child Support:

- *Alimony and child support needed for support.*

Insurance:

- *Unmatured life insurance policy except credit insurance.*
- *Life insurance policy with loan value up to $10,775.*
- *Disability, unemployment, or illness benefits.*
- *Life insurance payments for a person you depended on, which you need for support.*

In the run-up to the 2005 changes in the bankruptcy law, there was concern that some states—especially Florida[12]—had gone too far in giving debtors' exemptions. The BAPCPA amended Section 522 to limit the amount of equity a debtor can exempt, even in a state with unlimited homestead exemptions, in certain circumstances. (Section 522(o) and (p) set out the law's changes.)

Secured Property

As already noted, secured creditors generally have priority, even above the priority claims. That's why banks and lending institutions almost always secure the debtor's obligations. But despite the general rule, the debtor can avoid certain types of security interests. Liens that attach to assets that the debtor is entitled to claim as exempt can be avoided to the extent the lien impairs the value of the exemption in both Chapter 13 and Chapter 7. To be avoidable, the lien must be a judicial lien (like a judgment or a garnishment), or a nonpossessory, non-purchase-money security interest in household goods or tools of the trade.

Tax liens (which are statutory liens, not judicial liens) aren't avoidable in Chapter 7 even if they impair exemptions; tax liens can be avoided in Chapter 13 to the extent the lien is greater than the asset's value.

Dischargeable and Nondischargeable Debts

The whole point of bankruptcy, of course, is for debtors to get relief from the press of debt that they cannot reasonably pay.

Dischargeable Debts

Once discharged, the debtor is no longer legally liable to pay any remaining unpaid debts (except nondischargeable debts) that arose before the court issued the order of relief. The discharge operates to void any money judgments already rendered against the debtor and to bar the judgment creditor from seeking to recover the judgment.

Nondischargeable Debts

Some debts are not dischargeable in bankruptcy. A bankruptcy discharge varies, depending on the type of bankruptcy the debtor files (Chapter 7, 11, 12, or 13). The most common nondischargeable debts listed in Section 523 include the following:

- All debts not listed in the bankruptcy petition
- Student loans—unless it would be an undue hardship to repay them (see Section 6, *In re Zygarewicz*)
- Taxes—federal, state, and municipal
- Fines for violating the law, including criminal fines and traffic tickets
- Alimony and child support, divorce, and other property settlements
- Debts for personal injury caused by driving, boating, or operating an aircraft while intoxicated
- Consumer debts owed to a single creditor and aggregating more than $550 for luxury goods or services incurred within ninety days before the order of relief
- Cash advances aggregating more than $825 obtained by an individual debtor within ninety days before the order for relief
- Debts incurred because of fraud or securities law violations
- Debts for willful injury to another's person or his or her property
- Debts from embezzlement

This is not an exhaustive list, and as noted in Section 3, there are some circumstances in which it is not just certain debts that aren't dischargeable: sometimes a discharge is denied entirely.

Reaffirmation

reaffirmation

To confirm again the validity of a promise that was discharged, as in bankruptcy.

A debtor may reaffirm a debt that was discharged. Section 524 of the bankruptcy code provides important protection to the debtor intent on doing so. No **reaffirmation** is binding unless the reaffirmation was made *prior* to the granting of the discharge; the reaffirmation agreement must contain a clear and conspicuous statement that advises the debtor that the agreement is not required by bankruptcy or nonbankruptcy law and that the agreement may be rescinded by giving notice of rescission to the holder of such claim at any time prior to discharge or within sixty days after the agreement is filed with the court, whichever is later.

A written agreement to reaffirm a debt must be filed with the bankruptcy court. The attorney for the debtor must file an affidavit certifying that the agreement represents a fully informed and voluntary agreement, that the agreement does not impose an undue hardship on the debtor or a dependent of the debtor, and that the attorney has fully advised the debtor of the legal consequences of the agreement and of a default under the agreement. Where the debtor is an individual who was not represented by an attorney during the course of negotiating the agreement, the reaffirmation agreement must be approved by the court, after disclosures to the debtor, and after the court finds that it is in the best interest of the debtor and does not cause an undue hardship on the debtor or a dependent.

Property Included in the Estate

When a bankruptcy petition is filed, a **debtor's estate** is created consisting of all the debtor's then-existing property interests, whether legal or equitable. In addition, the estate includes any bequests, inheritances, and certain other distributions of property that the debtor receives within the next 180 days. It also includes property recovered by the trustee under certain powers granted by the law. What is not exempt property will be distributed to the creditors.

debtor's estate

The intangible entity containing all the debtor's nonexempt property and liabilities.

The bankruptcy code confers on the trustee certain powers to recover property for the estate that the debtor transferred before bankruptcy.

One such power (in Section 544) is to act as a **hypothetical lien creditor**. This power is best explained by an example. Suppose Dennis Debtor purchases equipment on credit from Acme Supply Company. Acme fails to perfect its security interest, and a few weeks later Debtor files a bankruptcy petition. By virtue of the section conferring on the trustee the status of a hypothetical lien creditor, the trustee can act as though she had a lien on the equipment, with priority over Acme's unperfected security interest. Thus the trustee can avoid Acme's security interest, with the result that Acme would be treated as an unsecured creditor.

hypothetical lien creditor

The trustee acts as if he or she were a lien creditor with power to defeat any unperfected security interests.

Another power is to avoid transactions known as **voidable preferences**—transactions highly favorable to particular creditors.[13] A transfer of property is voidable if it was made (1) to a creditor or for his benefit, (2) on account of a debt owed before the transfer was made, (3) while the debtor was insolvent, (4) on or within ninety days before the filing of the petition, and (5) to enable a creditor to receive more than he would have under Chapter 7. If the creditor was an "insider"—one who had a special relationship with the debtor, such as a relative or general partner of the debtor or a corporation that the debtor controls or serves in as director or officer—then the trustee may void the transaction if it was made within one year of the filing of the petition, assuming that the debtor was insolvent at the time the transaction was made.

voidable preferences

Transfer of assets by a debtor filing a voluntary bankruptcy petition in favor of one creditor at the expense of other secured creditors.

Some prebankruptcy transfers that seem to fall within these provisions do not. The most important exceptions are (1) transfers made for new value (the debtor buys a refrigerator for cash one week before filing a petition; this is an exchange for new value and the trustee may not void it); (2) a transfer that creates a purchase-money security interest securing new value if the secured party perfects within ten days after the debtor receives the goods; (3) payment of a debt incurred in the ordinary course of business, on ordinary business terms; (4) transfers totaling less than $600 by an individual whose debts are primarily consumer debts; (5) transfers totaling less than $5,475 by a debtor whose debts are not primarily consumer debts; and (6) transfers to the extent the transfer was a bona fide domestic support obligation.

A third power of the trustee is to avoid **fraudulent transfers** made within two years before the date that the bankruptcy petition was filed.[14] This provision contemplates various types of fraud. For example, while insolvent, the debtor might transfer property to a relative for less than it was worth, intending to recover it after discharge. This situation should be distinguished from the voidable preference just discussed, in which the debtor pays a favored creditor what he actually owes but in so doing cannot then pay other creditors.

fraudulent transfers

The transfer of an asset for less than its fair value.

Key Takeaway

A bankruptcy commences with the filing of a petition of bankruptcy. Creditors file proofs of claim and are entitled to certain priorities: domestic support obligations and the costs of administration are first. The debtor has an obligation to file full and truthful schedules and to attend a credit counseling session, if applicable. The debtor has a right to claim exemptions, federal or state, that leave her with assets sufficient to make a fresh start: some home equity, an automobile, and clothing and personal effects, among others. The honest debtor is discharged of many debts, but some are nondischargeable, among them taxes, debt from illegal behavior (embezzlement, drunk driving), fines, student loans, and certain consumer debt. A debtor may, after proper counseling, reaffirm debt, but only before filing. The bankruptcy trustee takes over the nonexempt property of the debtor; he may act as a hypothetical lien creditor (avoiding unperfected security interests) and avoid preferential and fraudulent transfers that unfairly diminish the property of the estate.

Exercises

1. What is the automatic stay, and when does it arise?
2. Why are the expenses of claimants administering the bankruptcy given top priority (notwithstanding the nominal top priority of domestic support obligations)?
3. Why are debtor's exemptions not uniform? What sorts of things are exempt from being taken by the bankruptcy trustee, and why are such exemptions allowed?
4. Some debts are nondischargeable; give three examples. What is the rationale for disallowing some debts from discharge?
5. How does the law take care that the debtor is fully informed of the right *not* to reaffirm debts, and why is such care taken?
6. What is a hypothetical lien creditor? What is the difference between a preferential transfer and a fraudulent one? Why is it relevant to discuss these three things in the same paragraph?

30.3 Chapter 7 Liquidation

Learning Objectives

1. Recognize the grounds for a Chapter 7 case to be dismissed.
2. Be familiar with the BAPCPA's means-testing requirements before Chapter 7 discharge is granted.
3. Know under what circumstances a debtor will be denied discharge.
4. Understand the order of distribution of the debtor's estate under Chapter 7.

Trustee's Duties under Chapter 7; Grounds for Dismissal: The Means Test

Except as noted, the provisions discussed up until now apply to each type of bankruptcy proceeding. The following discussion is limited to certain provisions under Chapter 7.

Trustee's Duties

In addition to the duties already noted, the trustee has other duties under Chapter 7. He must sell the property for money, close up the estate "as expeditiously as is compatible with the best interests of parties in interest," investigate the debtor's financial affairs, examine proofs of claims, reject improper ones, oppose the discharge of the debtor where doing so is advisable in the trustee's opinion, furnish a creditor with information about the estate and his administration (unless the court orders otherwise), file tax reports if the business continues to be operated, and make a final report and file it with the court.

Conversion

Under Section 706 of the bankruptcy code, the debtor may convert a Chapter 7 case to Chapter 11, 12, or 13 at any time. The court may order a **conversion** to Chapter 11 at any time upon request of a party in interest and after notice and hearing. And, as discussed next, a case may be converted from Chapter 7 to Chapter 13 if the debtor agrees, or be dismissed if he does not, in those cases where the debtor makes too much money to be discharged without it being an "abuse" under the 2005 act.

conversion

In bankruptcy, changing the chapter number filed from one to another.

Dismissal

The court may dismiss a case for three general reasons.

The first reason is "for cause," after notice and a hearing for cause, including (1) unreasonable delay by the debtor that prejudices creditors, (2) nonpayment of any fees required, (3) failure to file required documents and schedules.

The second reason for dismissal (or, with the debtor's permission, conversion to Chapter 11 or 13) applies to debtors whose debt is primarily consumer debt: the court may—after notice and a hearing—dismiss a case if granting relief would be "an abuse of the provisions" of the bankruptcy code.

The third reason for dismissal is really the crux of the 2005 law: under it, the court will find that granting relief under Chapter 7 to a debtor whose debt is primarily consumer debt *is* "an abuse" if the debtor makes too much money. The debtor must pass a means test: If he's poor enough, he can go Chapter 7. If he is not poor enough (or if they are not, in case of a married couple), Chapter 13—making payments to creditors—is the way to go. Here is one practitioner's explanation of the means test:

To apply the means test, the courts will look at the debtor's average income for the 6 months prior to filing [not the debtor's income at the time of filing, when—say—she just lost her job] and compare it to the median income for that state. For example, the median annual income for a single wage-earner in California is $42,012. If the income is below the median, then Chapter 7 remains open as an option. If the income exceeds the median, the remaining parts of the means test will be applied.

The next step in the calculation takes monthly income less reasonable living expenses ["reasonable living expenses" are strictly calculated based on IRS standards; the figure excludes payments on the debts included in the bankruptcy], and multiplies that figure times 60. This represents the amount of income available over a 5-year period for repayment of the debt obligations.

If the income available for debt repayment over that 5-year period is $10,000 or more, then Chapter 13 will be required. In other words, anyone earning above the state median, and with at least $166.67 per month ($10,000 divided by 60) of available income, will automatically be denied Chapter 7. So for example, if the court determines that you have $200 per month income above living expenses, $200 times 60 is $12,000. Since $12,000 is above $10,000, you're stuck with Chapter 13.

What happens if you are above the median income but do NOT have at least $166.67 per month to pay toward your debts? Then the final part of the means test is applied. If the available income is less than $100 per month, then Chapter 7 again becomes an option. If the available income is between $100 and $166.66, then it is measured against the debt as a percentage, with 25% being the benchmark.

In other words, let's say your income is above the median, your debt is $50,000, and you only have $125 of available monthly income. We take $125 times 60 months (5 years), which equals $7,500 total. Since $7,500 is less than 25% of your $50,000 debt, Chapter 7 is still a possible option for you. If your debt was only $25,000, then your $7,500 of available income would exceed 25% of your debt and you would be required to file under Chapter 13.

To sum up, first figure out whether you are above or below the median income for your state—median income figures are available at http://www.new-bankruptcy-law-info.com. Be sure to account for your spouse's income if you are a two-income family. Next, deduct your average monthly living expenses from your monthly income and multiply by 60. If the result is above $10,000, you're stuck with Chapter 13. If the result is below $6,000, you may still be able to file Chapter 7. If the result is between $6,000 and $10,000, compare it to 25% of your debt. Above 25%, you're looking at Chapter 13 for sure.[15]

The law also requires that attorneys sign the petition (as well as the debtor); the attorney's signature certifies that the petition is well-grounded in fact and that the attorney has no knowledge after reasonable inquiry that the schedules and calculations are incorrect. Attorneys thus have an incentive to err in favor of filing Chapter 13 instead of Chapter 7 (perhaps that was part of Congress's purpose in this section of the law).

dismissal

An order terminating a case before its normal end.

If there's been a **dismissal**, the debtor and creditors have the same rights and remedies as they had prior to the case being commenced—as if the case had never been filed (almost). The debtor can refile immediately, unless the court orders a 120-day penalty (for failure to appear). In most cases, a debtor can file instantly for a Chapter 13 following a Chapter 7 dismissal.

Distribution of the Estate and Discharge; Denying Discharge

Distribution of the Estate

no-asset cases

A bankruptcy case with no nonexempt property.

The estate includes all his or her assets or all their assets (in the case of a married couple) broadly defined. From the estate, the debtor removes property claimed exempt; the trustee may recapture some assets improperly removed from the estate (preferential and fraudulent transfers), and what's left is the distributable estate. It is important to note that the vast majority of Chapter 7 bankruptcies are **no-asset cases**—90–95 percent of them, according to one longtime bankruptcy trustee.[16] That means creditors get nothing. But in those cases where there are assets, the trustee must distribute the estate to the remaining classes of claimants in this order:

1. Secured creditors, paid on their security interests
2. Claims with priority
3. Unsecured creditors who filed their claims on time
4. Unsecured creditors who were tardy in filing, if they had no notice of the bankruptcy
5. Unsecured creditors who were tardy and had notice, real or constructive
6. Claims by creditors for fines, penalties, and exemplary or punitive damages
7. Interest for all creditors at the legal rate
8. The debtor

FIGURE 30.3 Distribution of the Estate

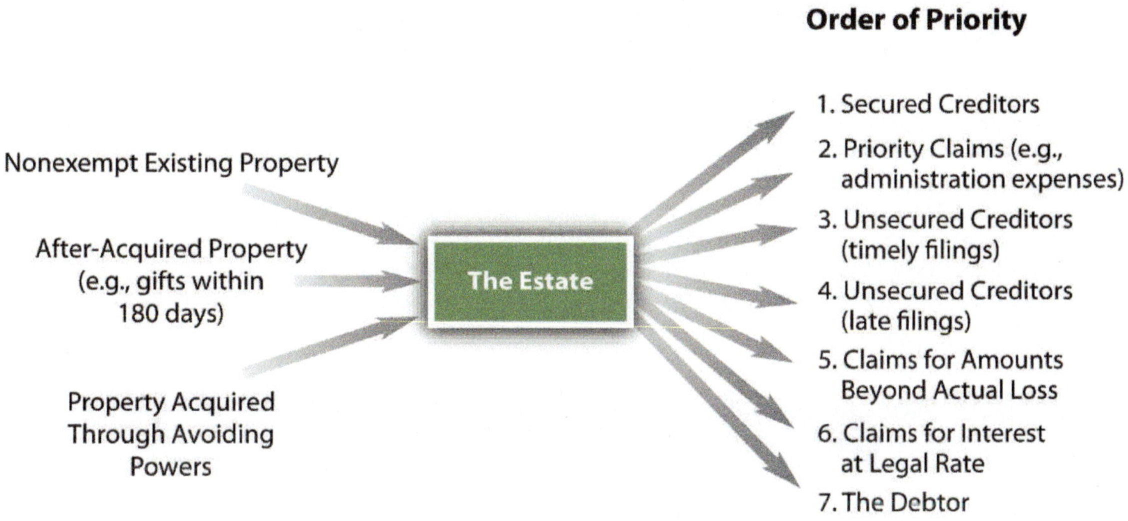

Discharge

Once the estate is distributed, the court will order the debtor discharged (except for nondischargeable debts) unless one of the following overall exceptions applies for denying **discharge** (i.e., relief from the debt). This list is not exhaustive:

discharge
The determination that debts are no longer owing.

1. The debtor is not an individual. In a Chapter 7 case, a corporation or partnership does not receive a bankruptcy discharge; instead, the entity is dissolved and its assets liquidated. The debts remain theoretically valid but uncollectible until the statute of limitations on them has run. Only an individual can receive a Chapter 7 discharge.[17]
2. The debtor has concealed or destroyed property with intent to defraud, hinder, or delay within twelve months preceding filing of the petition.
3. The debtor has concealed, destroyed, or falsified books and records
4. The debtor has lied under oath, knowingly given a false account, presented or used a false claim, given or received bribes, refused to obey court orders.
5. The debtor has failed to explain satisfactorily any loss of assets.
6. The debtor has declared Chapter 7 or Chapter 11 bankruptcy within eight years, or Chapter 13 within six years (with some exceptions).

7. The debtor failed to participate in "an instructional course concerning personal financial management" (unless that's excused).
8. An individual debtor has "abused" the bankruptcy process. A preferential transfer is not an "abuse," but it will be set aside. Making too much money to file Chapter 7 is "an abuse" that will deny discharge.

A discharge may be revoked if the debtor committed fraud during the bankruptcy proceedings, but the trustee or a creditor must apply for revocation within one year of the discharge.

discharge denied

Refusal of a bankruptcy court to allow discharge, usually because the debtor has acted in bad faith.

Having the **discharge denied** does not affect the administration of the bankruptcy case. The trustee can (and will) continue to liquidate any nonexempt assets of the debtor and pay the creditors, but the debtor still has to pay the debts left over.

As to any consequence of discharge, bankruptcy law prohibits governmental units from discriminating against a person who has gone through bankruptcy. Debtors are also protected from discrimination by private employers; for example, a private employer may not fire a debtor because of the bankruptcy. Certainly, however, the debtor's credit rating will be affected by the bankruptcy.

Key Takeaway

A Chapter 7 bankruptcy case may be dismissed for cause or because the debtor has abused the system. The debtor is automatically considered to have abused the system if she makes too much money. With the debtor's permission, the Chapter 7 may be converted to Chapter 11, 12, or 13. The law requires that the debtor pass a means test to qualify for Chapter 7. Assuming the debtor does qualify for Chapter 7, her nonexempt assets (if there are any) are sold by the trustee and distributed to creditors according to a priority set out in the law. A discharge may be denied, in general because the debtor has behaved dishonestly or—again—has abused the system.

Exercises

1. What is the difference between denial of a discharge for cause and denial for abuse?
2. What is the difference between a dismissal and a denial of discharge?
3. Which creditors get satisfied first in a Chapter 7 bankruptcy?

30.4 Chapter 11 and Chapter 13 Bankruptcies

Learning Objectives

1. Understand the basic concepts of Chapter 11 bankruptcies.
2. Understand the basic concepts of Chapter 13 bankruptcies.

Reorganization: Chapter 11 Bankruptcy

Overview

Chapter 11 provides a means by which corporations, partnerships, and other businesses, including sole proprietorships, can rehabilitate themselves and continue to operate free from the burden of debts that they cannot pay.

It is simple enough to apply for the protection of the court in Chapter 11 proceeding, and for many years, large financially ailing companies have sought shelter in Chapter 11. Well-known examples include General Motors, Texaco, K-Mart, Delta Airlines, and Northwest Airlines. An increasing number of corporations have turned to Chapter 11 even though, by conventional terms, they were solvent. Doing so enables them to negotiate with creditors to reduce debt. It also may even permit courts to snuff out lawsuits that have not yet been filed. Chapters 3 and 5, discussed in Section 2, apply to Chapter 11 proceedings also. Our discussion, therefore, is limited to special features of Chapter 11.

How It Works

Eligibility

Any person eligible for discharge in Chapter 7 proceeding (plus railroads) is eligible for a Chapter 11 proceeding, except stockbrokers and commodity brokers. Individuals filing Chapter 11 must take credit counseling; businesses do not. A company may voluntarily enter Chapter 11 or may be put there involuntarily by creditors. Individuals can file Chapter 11 particularly if they have too much debt to qualify for Chapter 13 and make too much money to qualify for Chapter 7; under the 2005 act, individuals must commit future wages to creditors, just as in Chapter 13.[18] Chapter 11 is most commonly used by corporate entities and partnerships.

Operation of Business

Unless a trustee is appointed, the debtor will retain possession of the business and may continue to operate with its own management. The court may appoint a trustee on request of any party in interest after notice and a hearing. The appointment may be made for cause—such as dishonesty, incompetence, or gross mismanagement—or if it is otherwise in the best interests of the creditors. Frequently, the same incompetent management that got the business into bankruptcy is left running it—that's a criticism of Chapter 11.

Creditors' Committee

The court must appoint a committee of unsecured creditors as soon as practicable after issuing the order for relief. The committee must consist of creditors willing to serve who have the seven largest claims, unless the court decides to continue a committee formed before the filing, if the committee was fairly chosen and adequately represents the various claims. The committee has several duties, including these: (1) to investigate the debtor's financial affairs, (2) to determine whether to seek appointment of a trustee or to let the business continue to operate, and (3) to consult with the debtor or trustee throughout the case.

The Reorganization Plan

The debtor may always file its own plan, whether in a voluntary or involuntary case. If the court leaves the debtor in possession without appointing a trustee, the debtor has the exclusive right to file a reorganization plan during the first 120 days. If it does file, it will then have another 60 days to obtain the creditors' acceptances. Although its exclusivity expires at the end of 180 days, the court may lengthen or shorten the period for good cause. At the end of the exclusive period, the creditors' committee, a single creditor, or a holder of equity in the debtor's property may file a plan. If the court does appoint a trustee, any party in interest may file a plan at any time.

The Bankruptcy Reform Act specifies certain features of the plan and permits others to be included. Among other things, the plan must (1) designate classes of claims and ownership interests; (2) specify which classes or interests are impaired—a claim or ownership interest is impaired if the creditor's legal, equitable, contractual rights are altered under the plan; (3) specify the treatment of any class of claims or interests that is impaired under the plan; (4) provide the same treatment of each claim or interests of a particular class, unless the holder of a particular claim or interest agrees to a less favorable treatment; and (5) provide adequate means for carrying out the plan. Basically, what the plan does is provide a process for rehabilitating the company's faltering business by relieving it from repaying part of its debt and initiating reforms so that the company can try to get back on its feet.

Acceptance of the Plan

The act requires the plan to be accepted by certain proportions of each impaired class of claims and interests. A class of claims accepts the plan if creditors representing at least two-thirds of the dollar amount of claims and more than one-half the number of allowed claims vote in favor. A class of property interests accepts the plan if creditors representing two-thirds of the dollar amount of the allowed ownership interests vote in favor. Unimpaired classes of claims and interest are deemed to have accepted the plan; it is unnecessary to solicit their acceptance.

Confirmation of the Plan

The final act necessary under Chapter 11 is confirmation by the court. Once the court confirms the plan, the plan is binding on all creditors. The rules governing confirmation are complex, but in essence, they include the following requirements:

1. The plan must have been proposed in good faith. Companies must also make a good-faith attempt to negotiate modifications in their collective bargaining agreements (labor union contracts).
2. All provisions of the act must have been complied with.
3. The court must have determined that the reorganized business will be likely to succeed and be unlikely to require further financial reorganization in the foreseeable future.
4. Impaired classes of claims and interests must have accepted the plan, unless the plan treats them in a "fair and equitable" manner, in which case consent is not required. This is sometimes referred to as the cram-down provision.
5. All members of every class must have received no less value than they would have in Chapter 7 liquidation.

Discharge, Conversion

The debtor gets discharged when all payments under the plan are completed. A Chapter 11 bankruptcy may be converted to Chapter 7, with some restrictions, if it turns out the debtor cannot make the plan work.

Adjustment of Debts of an Individual with Regular Income: Chapter 13 Bankruptcy

In General

Anyone with a steady income who is having difficulty paying off accumulated debts may seek the protection of a bankruptcy court in Chapter 13 proceeding (often called the wage earner's plan). Under this chapter, the individual debtor presents a payment plan to creditors, and the court appoints a trustee. If the creditors wind up with more under the plan presented than they would receive in Chapter 7 proceeding, then the court is likely to approve it. In general, a Chapter 13 repayment plan extends the time to pay the debt and may reduce it so that the debtor need not pay it all. Typically, the debtor will pay a fixed sum monthly to the trustee, who will distribute it to the creditors. The previously discussed provisions of Chapters 3 and 5 apply also to this chapter; therefore, the discussion that follows focuses on some unique features of Chapter 13.

People seek Chapter 13 discharges instead of Chapter 7 for various reasons: they make too much money to pass the Chapter 7 means test; they are behind on their mortgage or car payments and want to make them up over time and reinstate the original agreement; they have debts that can't be discharged in Chapter 7; they have nonexempt property they want to keep; they have co-debtors on a personal debt who would be liable if the debtor went Chapter 7; they have a real desire to pay their debts but cannot do so without getting the creditors to give them some breathing room. Chapter 7 cases may always be converted to Chapter 13.

How It Works

Eligibility

Chapter 13 is voluntary only. Anyone—sole proprietorships included—who has a regular income, unsecured debts of less than $336,000, and secured debts of less than $1,010,650 is eligible to seek its protection. The debts must be unpaid and owing at the time the debtor applies for relief. If the person has more debt than that, she will have to file Chapter 11. The debtor must attend a credit-counseling class, as in Chapter 7.

The Plan

Plans are typically extensions or compositions—that is, they extend the time to pay what is owing, or they are agreements among creditors each to accept something less than the full amount owed (so that all get something). Under Chapter 13, the stretch-out period is three to five three years. The plan must provide for payments of all future income or a sufficient portion of it to the trustee. Priority creditors are entitled to be paid in full, although they may be paid later than required under the original indebtedness. As long as the plan is being carried out, the debtor may enjoin any creditors from suing to collect the original debt.

Confirmation

Under Section 1325 of the bankruptcy code, the court must approve the plan if it meets certain requirements. These include (1) distribution of property to unsecured creditors whose claims are allowed in an amount no less than that which they would have received had the estate been liquidated under Chapter 7; (2) acceptance by secured creditors, with some exceptions, such as when the debtor surrenders the secured property to the creditor; and (3) proposal of the plan "in good faith." If the trustee or an unsecured creditor objects to confirmation, the plan must meet additional tests. For example, a plan will be approved if all of the debtor's disposable income (as defined in Section 1325) over the commitment period (three to five years) will be used to make payments under the plan.

Discharge

Once a debtor has made all payments called for in the plan, the court will discharge him from all remaining debts except certain long-term debts and obligations to pay alimony, maintenance, and support. Under former law, Chapter 13 was so broad that it permitted the court to discharge the debtor from many debts considered nondischargeable under Chapter 7, but 1994 amendments and the 2005 act made Chapter 13 less expansive. Debts dischargeable in Chapter 13, but not in Chapter 7, include debts for willful and malicious injury to property, debts incurred to pay nondischargeable tax obligations, and debts arising from property settlements in divorce or separation proceedings. (See Section 6, *In re Ryan*, for a discussion of what debts are dischargeable under Chapter 13 as compared with Chapter 7.)

Although a Chapter 13 debtor generally receives a discharge only after completing all payments required by the court-approved (i.e., "confirmed") repayment plan, there are some limited circumstances under which the debtor may request the court to grant a "hardship discharge" even though the debtor has failed to complete plan payments. Such a discharge is available only to a debtor whose failure to complete plan payments is due to circumstances beyond the debtor's control. A Chapter 13 discharge stays on the credit record for up to ten years.

A discharge may be denied if the debtor previously went through a bankruptcy too soon before filing Chapter 13, failed to act in good faith, or—with some exceptions—failed to complete a personal financial management course.

Key Takeaway

Chapter 11—frequently referred to as "corporate reorganization"—is most often used by businesses whose value as a going concern is greater than it would be if liquidated, but, with some exceptions, anyone eligible to file Chapter 7 can file Chapter 11. The business owners, or in some cases the trustee or creditors, develop a plan to pay the firm's debts over a three- to five-year period; the plan must be approved by creditors and the court. Chapter 13—frequently called the wage-earner's plan—is a similar mechanism by which a person can discharge some debt and have longer to pay debts off than originally scheduled. Under Chapter 13, people can get certain relief from creditors that they cannot get in Chapter 7.

Exercises

1. David Debtor is a freelance artist with significant debt that he feels a moral obligation to pay. Why is Chapter 11 his best choice of bankruptcy chapters to file under?
2. What is the practical difference between debts arising from property settlements in divorce or separation proceedings—which can be discharged under Chapter 13—and debts owing

for alimony (maintenance) and child support—which cannot be discharged under Chapter 13?

3. Why would a person want to go through the long grind of Chapter 13 instead of just declaring straight bankruptcy (Chapter 7) and being done with it?

30.5 Alternatives to Bankruptcy

Learning Objectives

1. Understand that there are nonbankruptcy alternatives for debtors who cannot pay their bills in a timely way: assignment for benefit of creditors, compositions, and receiverships.
2. Recognize the reasons why these alternatives might not work.

Alternatives to Bankruptcy: Overview

Bankruptcy is a necessary thing in a capitalist economic system. As already noted, without it, few people would be willing to take business risks, and the economy would necessarily operate at a lower level (something some people might not think is so bad overall). But bankruptcy, however "enlightened" society may have become about it since Victorian days, still carries a stigma (in 2016, presidential candidate Donald Trump was criticized for having had several bankruptcy filings—apparently six).[19] Bankruptcy filings are public information; the lists of people and businesses who declare bankruptcy are regularly published in monthly business journals. Bankruptcy is expensive, too, and both debtors and creditors become enmeshed in significantly complex federal law. For these reasons, among others, both parties frequently determine that it is in their best interests to find an alternative to bankruptcy. Here, we take up briefly three common alternatives.

In other parts of this book, other nonbankruptcy creditors' rights are discussed: under the Uniform Commercial Code (UCC), creditors have rights to reclaim goods sold and delivered but not paid for; under the UCC, too, creditors have a right to repossess personal property that has been put up as collateral for the debtor's loan or extension of credit; and mortgagees have the right to repossess real estate without judicial assistance in many circumstances. These nonbankruptcy remedies are governed mostly by state law.

The nonbankruptcy alternatives discussed here are governed by state law also.

Assignment for Benefit of Creditors; Compositions; Receivership

Assignment for Benefit of Creditors

Under a common-law **assignment for the benefit of creditors**, the debtor transfers some or all of his assets to a trustee—usually someone appointed by the adjustment bureau of a local credit managers' association—who sells the assets and apportions the proceeds in some agreed manner, usually pro rata, to the creditors. Of course, not every creditor need agree with such a distribution. Strictly speaking, the common-law assignment does not discharge the balance of the debt. Many state statutes attempt to address this problem either by prohibiting creditors who accept a partial payment of debt under an assignment from claiming the balance or by permitting debtors to demand a release from creditors who accept partial payment.

assignment for the benefit of creditors

The debtor assigns property to a trustee to sell for creditors.

Composition

composition

Creditors' agreement to accept less than the face amount owing.

A **composition** is simply an agreement by creditors to accept less than the full amount of the debt and to discharge the debtor from further liability. As a contract, composition requires consideration; the mutual agreement among creditors to accept a pro rata share of the proceeds is held to be sufficient consideration to support the discharge. The essential difference between assignment and composition lies in the creditors' agreement: an assignment implies no agreement among the creditors, whereas a composition does. Not all creditors of the particular debtor need agree to the composition for it to be valid. A creditor who does not agree to the composition remains free to attempt to collect the full sum owed; in particular, a creditor not inclined to compose the debt could attach the debtor's assets while other creditors are bargaining over the details of the composition agreement.

One advantage of the assignment over the composition is that in the former the debtor's assets—having been assigned—are protected from attachment by hungry creditors. Also, the assignment does not require creditors' consent. However, an advantage to the debtor of the assignment (compared with the composition) is that in the composition creditors cannot go after the debtor for any deficiency (because they agreed not to).

Receivership

receivership

A court action placing the debtor's property under control of a custodian so that it can be preserved or distributed for the benefit of all creditors.

A creditor may petition the court to appoint a receiver; **receivership** is a long-established procedure in equity whereby the receiver takes over the debtor's property under instructions from the court. The receiver may liquidate the property, continue to operate the business, or preserve the assets without operating the business until the court finally determines how to dispose of the debtor's property.

The difficulty with most of the alternatives to bankruptcy lies in their voluntary character: a creditor who refuses to go along with an agreement to discharge the debtor can usually manage to thwart the debtor and her fellow creditors because, at the end of the day, the U.S. Constitution forbids the states from impairing private citizens' contractual obligations. The only final protection, therefore, is to be found in the federal bankruptcy law.

Key Takeaway

Bankruptcy is expensive and frequently convoluted. Nonbankruptcy alternatives include assignment for the benefit of creditors (the debtor's assets are assigned to a trustee who manages or disposes of them for creditors), compositions (agreements by creditors to accept less than they are owed and to discharge the debtor from further liability), and receivership (a type of court-supervised assignment).

Exercises

1. What is an assignment for benefit of creditors?
2. What is a composition?
3. What is a receivership?
4. Why are these alternatives to bankruptcy often unsatisfactory?

30.6 Cases

Dischargeability of Student Loans under Chapter 7

In re Zygarewicz

423 B.R. 909 (Bkrtcy.E.D.Cal. 2010)

MCMANUS, BANKRUPTCY JUDGE.

Angela Zygarewicz, a Chapter 7 debtor and the plaintiff in this adversary proceeding, borrowed 16 government-guaranteed student [sic] loans totaling $81,429. The loans have been assigned to Educational Credit Management Corporation ("ECMC"). By September 2009, the accrual of interest on these student loans had caused the debt to balloon to more than $146,000. The debtor asks the court to declare that these student loans were discharged in bankruptcy.

The Bankruptcy Code provides financially distressed debtors with a fresh start by discharging most of their pre-petition debts. * * * However, under 11 U.S.C. § 523(a)(8), there is a presumption that educational loans extended by or with the aid of a governmental unit or nonprofit institution are nondischargeable unless the debtor can demonstrate that their repayment would be an undue hardship. See [Citation]. This exception to a bankruptcy discharge ensures that student loans, which are typically extended solely on the basis of the student's future earnings potential, cannot be discharged by recent graduates who then pocket all of the future benefits derived from their education. See [Citation].

The debtor bears the burden of proving by a preponderance of the evidence that she is entitled to a discharge of the student loan. See [Citation]. That is, the debtor must prove that repayment of student loans will cause an undue hardship.

The Bankruptcy Code does not define "the undue hardship." Courts interpreting section 523(a)(8), however, have concluded that undue hardship [and] is something more than "garden-variety hardship." [Citation.] Only cases involving "real and substantial" hardship merit discharges. See [Citation.]

The Ninth Circuit has adopted a three-part test to guide courts in their attempts to determine whether a debtor will suffer an undue hardship is required to repay a student loan:

- First, the debtor must establish "that she cannot maintain, based on current income and expenses, a 'minimal' standard of living for herself and her dependents if forced to repay the loans." * * *
- Second, the debtor must show "that additional circumstances exist indicating that this state of affairs is likely to persist for a significant portion of the repayment period of the student loans." * * *
- The third prong requires "that the debtor has made good faith efforts to repay the loans. * * *"

(*Pena*, citing *Brunner v. N.Y. State Higher Educ. Servs. Corp.*, [Citation]).

Debtor must satisfy all three parts of the *Brunner* test before her student loans can be discharged. Failure to prove any of the three prongs will defeat a debtor's case.

When this bankruptcy case was filed in September 2005, the debtor was a single woman and had no dependents. She is 39 years old.

Schedule I reported that the debtor was unemployed. The debtor's responses to the Statement of Financial Affairs revealed that she had received $5,500 in income during 2005 prior to the filing of the petition. Evidence at trial indicated that after the petition was filed, the debtor found work and earned a total of $9,424 in 2005. In 2004 and 2003, she earned $13,994 and $17,339, respectively.

Despite this modest income, the debtor did not immediately file an adversary proceeding to determine the dischargeability of her student loans. It was almost three years after the entry of her Chapter 7 discharge 'on January 3, 2006 that the debtor reopened her Chapter 7 case in order to pursue this adversary proceeding.'

In her complaint, the debtor admits that after she received a discharge, she found part-time work with a church and later took a full-time job as a speech therapist. During 2006, the debtor earned $20,009 and in 2007 she earned $37,314. Hence, while it is clear the debtor's income was very modest in the time period immediately prior to her bankruptcy petition, her financial situation improved during her bankruptcy case.

The court cannot conclude based on the evidence of the debtor's financial circumstances up to the date of the discharge, that she was unable to maintain a minimal standard of living if she was required to repay her students [sic] loans.

However, in January 2007, the debtor was injured in an automobile accident. Her injuries eventually halted the financial progress she had been making and eventually prevented her from working. She now subsists on social security disability payments.

The circumstance creating the debtor's hardship, the automobile accident, occurred after her Chapter 7 petition was filed, indeed, approximately one year after her discharge was entered. The debtor is maintaining that this post-petition, post-discharge circumstance warrants a declaration that her student loans were discharged effective from the petition date.

When must the circumstances creating a debtor's hardship arise: before the bankruptcy case is filed; after the case if filed but prior to the entry of a discharge; or at anytime, including after the entry of a discharge?

The court concludes that the circumstances causing a Chapter 7 debtor's financial hardship must arise prior to the entry of the discharge. If the circumstances causing a debtor's hardship arise after the entry of a discharge, those circumstances cannot form the basis of a determination that repayment of a student loan will be an undue hardship. * * *

[T]here is nothing in the Bankruptcy Code requiring that a complaint under section 523(a)(8) [to discharge student loans] be filed at any particular point in a bankruptcy case, whether it is filed under Chapter 7 or 13. [Relevant Federal Rules of Bankruptcy Procedure] permits such dischargeability complaints to be brought at any time, including after the entry of a discharge and the closing of the bankruptcy case. * * *

While a debtor's decision to file an action to determine the dischargeability of a student loan is not temporally constrained, this does not mean that a debtor's financial hardship may arise after a discharge has been entered. * * *

[The] Coleman [case, cited by debtor] deals with the ripeness of a dispute concerning the dischargeability of a student loan. [The Ninth Circuit held that it] is ripe for adjudication at any point during the case. The Ninth Circuit did not conclude, however, that a debtor could rely upon post-discharge circumstances to establish undue hardship. In fact, the court in Coleman made clear that the debtor could take a snapshot of the hardship warranting a discharge of a student loan any time prior to discharge. [Coleman was a Chapter 13 case.]

Here, the debtor was injured in an automobile accident on January 17, 2007, almost exactly one year after her January 3, 2006 Chapter 7 discharge. Because the accident had no causal link to the misfortune prompting the debtor to seek bankruptcy relief in the first instance, the accident cannot be relied on to justify the discharge of the student loans because repayment would be an undue hardship.

To hold otherwise would mean that a bankruptcy discharge is a perpetual license to discharge student loans based on events that occur years after the bankruptcy discharge is granted. If a discharged debtor suffers later financial misfortune, that debtor must consider seeking another discharge subject to the limitations imposed by [the sections of the code stipulating how often a person can petition for bankruptcy]. In the context of a second case, the debtor could then ask that the student loan be declared dischargeable under section 523(a)(8).

In this instance, the debtor is now eligible for a discharge in a Chapter 13 case. * * * She would not be eligible for a Chapter 7 discharge until September 19, 2013.

This is not to say that post-discharge events are irrelevant. The second and third prongs of the *Pena* test require the court to consider whether the circumstances preventing a debtor from repaying a student loan are likely to persist, and whether the debtor has made good faith efforts to repay the student loan. Post-discharge events are relevant to these determinations because they require the court to look into the debtor's financial future.

Unfortunately for the debtor, it is unnecessary to consider the second and third prongs because she cannot satisfy the first prong.

Case Questions

1. What is the rationale for making the bankruptcy discharge of student loans very difficult?
2. Petitioner argued that she should be able to use a postdischarge event (the auto accident) as a basis for establishing that she could not maintain a "minimal" standard of living, and thus she should get a retroactive discharge of her student loans. What benefit is there to her if she could successfully make the argument, given that she could—as the court noted—file for Chapter 13?
3. The court cites the *Coleman* case. That was a Chapter 13 proceeding. Here were the facts: Debtor had not yet completed her payments under her five-year repayment plan, and no discharge order had yet been entered; one year into the plan, she was laid off work. She had been trying to repay her student loans for several years, and she claimed she would suffer hardship in committing to the five-year repayment plan without any guarantee that her student loan obligations would be discharged, since she was required to commit all of her disposable income to payments under the plan and would likely be forced to pursue undue hardship issue pro se upon completion of the plan." In *Coleman,* the court held that Debtor could, postfiling but predischarge—one year into the five-year plan—bring up the hardship issue.

   Now, in the case here, after the auto accident, the petitioner "subsists" on Social Security disability payments, and she has almost $150,000 in debt, yet the court prohibited her from claiming a hardship discharge of student loans. Does this result really make sense? Is the court's concern that allowing this postdischarge relief would mean "that a bankruptcy discharge is a perpetual license to discharge student loans based on events that occur years after the bankruptcy discharge is granted" well founded? Suppose it is scheduled to take thirty years to pay off student loans; in year 4, the student-borrower, now Debtor, declares Chapter 7 bankruptcy, student loans not being discharged; in year 6, the person is rendered disabled. What public policy is offended if the person is allowed to "reopen" the bankruptcy and use the postbankruptcy event as a basis for claiming a hardship discharge of student loans?
4. The court suggests she file for Chapter 13. What if—because of timing—the petitioner was not eligible for Chapter 13? What would happen then?

Chapter 11 Bankruptcy

In re Johns-Manville Corp.

36 B.R. 727 (Bkrtcy. N.Y. 1984)

Lifland, Bankruptcy Judge.

Whether an industrial enterprise in the United States is highly successful is often gauged by its "membership" in what has come to be known as the "Fortune 500." Having attained this measure of financial achievement, Johns-Manville Corp. and its affiliated companies (collectively referred to as "Manville") were deemed a paradigm of success in corporate America by the financial community. Thus, Manville's filing for protection under Chapter 11 of Title 11 of the United States Code ("the Code or the Bankruptcy Code") on August 26, 1982 ("the filing date") was greeted with great surprise and consternation on the part of some of its creditors and other corporations that were being sued along with Manville for injuries caused by asbestos exposure. As discussed at length herein, Manville submits that the sole factor necessitating its filing is the mammoth problem of uncontrolled proliferation of asbestos health suits brought against it because of its substantial use for many years of products containing asbestos which injured those who came into contact with the dust of this lethal substance. According to Manville, this current problem of approximately 16,000 lawsuits pending as of the filing date is compounded by the crushing economic burden to be suffered by Manville over the next 20–30 years by the filing of an even more staggering number of suits by those who had been exposed but who will not manifest the asbestos-related diseases until some time during this future period ("the future asbestos claimants"). Indeed, approximately 6,000 asbestos health claims are estimated to have arisen in only the first 16 months since the filing date. This burden is further compounded by the insurance industry's general disavowal of liability to Manville on policies written for this very purpose.

It is the propriety of the filing by Manville which is the subject of the instant decision. Four separate motions to dismiss the petition pursuant to Section 1112(b) of the Code have been lodged before this Court. * * *

Preliminarily, it must be stated that there is no question that Manville is eligible to be a debtor under the Code's statutory requirements. Moreover, it should also be noted that neither Section 109 nor any other provision relating to voluntary petitions by companies contains any insolvency requirement. * * * Accordingly, it is abundantly clear that Manville has met all of the threshold eligibility requirements for filing a voluntary petition under the Code. * * *

A "principal goal" of the Bankruptcy Code is to provide "open access" to the "bankruptcy process." [Citation.] The rationale behind this "open access" policy is to provide access to bankruptcy relief which is as "open" as "access to the credit economy." Thus, Congress intended that "there should be no legal barrier to voluntary petitions." Another major goal of the Code, that of "rehabilitation of debtors," requires that relief for debtors must be "timely." Congress declared that it is essential to both the "open access" and "rehabilitation" goals that

> *[i]nitiating relief should not be a death knell. The process should encourage resort to it, by debtors and creditors, that cuts short the dissipation of assets and the accumulation of debts. Belated commencement of a case may kill an opportunity for reorganization or arrangement.*

Accordingly, the drafters of the Code envisioned that a financially beleaguered debtor with real debt and real creditors should not be required to wait until the economic situation is beyond repair in order to file a reorganization petition. The "Congressional purpose" in enacting the Code was to encourage resort to the bankruptcy process. This philosophy not only comports with the elimination of an insolvency requirement, but also is a corollary of the key aim of Chapter 11 of the Code, that of avoidance of liquidation. The drafters of the Code announced this goal, declaring that reorganization is more efficient than liquidation because "assets that are used for production in the industry for which they were designed are more valuable than those same assets sold for scrap." [Citation.] Moreover, reorganization also fosters the goals of preservation of jobs in the threatened entity. [Citation.]

In the instant case, not only would liquidation be wasteful and inefficient in destroying the utility of valuable assets of the companies as well as jobs, but, more importantly, liquidation would preclude just compensation of some present asbestos victims and all future asbestos claimants. This unassailable reality represents all the more reason for this Court to adhere to this basic potential liquidation avoidance aim of Chapter 11 and deny the motions to dismiss. Manville must not be required to wait until its economic picture has deteriorated beyond salvation to file for reorganization.

Clearly, none of the justifications for declaring an abuse of the jurisdiction of the bankruptcy court announced by these courts [in various cases cited] are present in the *Manville* case. In *Manville*, it is undeniable that there has been no sham or hoax perpetrated on the Court in that Manville is a real business with real creditors in pressing need of economic reorganization. Indeed, the Asbestos Committee has belied its own contention that Manville has no debt and no real creditors by quantifying a benchmark settlement demand approaching one billion dollars for compensation of approximately 15,500 pre-petition asbestos claimants, during the course of negotiations pitched toward achieving a consensual plan. This huge asserted liability does not even take into account the estimated 6,000 new asbestos health claims which have arisen in only the first 16 months since the filing date. The number of post-filing claims increases each day as "future claims back into the present." * * *

In short, Manville's filing did not in the appropriate sense abuse the jurisdiction of this Court and it is indeed, like the debtor in [Citation], a "once viable business supporting employees and unsecured creditors [that] has more recently been burdened with judgments [and suits] that threaten to put it out of existence." Thus, its petition must be sustained. * * *

In sum, Manville is a financially besieged enterprise in desperate need of reorganization of its crushing real debt, both present and future. The reorganization provisions of the Code were drafted with the aim of liquidation avoidance by great access to Chapter 11. Accordingly, Manville's filing does not abuse the jurisdictional integrity of this Court, but rather presents the same kinds of reasons that were present in [Citation] * * * [.]

[A]ll four of the motions to dismiss the Manville petition are denied in their entirety.

Case Questions

1. What did Manville want to do here, and why?
2. How does this case demonstrate the fundamental purpose of Chapter 11 as opposed to Chapter 7 filings?
3. The historical background here is that Manville knew from at least 1930 that asbestos—used in many industrial applications—was a deadly carcinogen, and it worked diligently for decades to conceal and obfuscate the fact.[20] What "good faith" argument was raised by the movants in this case?

Chapter 13: What Debts Are Dischargeable?

In re Ryan

389 B.R. 710 9th Cir. BAP, (Idaho, 2008)

On July 13, 1995, Ryan was convicted of possession of an unregistered firearm under 26 U.S.C. § 5861(d) in the United States District Court for the District of Alaska. Ryan was sentenced to fifty-seven months in prison followed by three years of supervised release. In addition, Ryan was ordered to pay a fine of $7,500, * * * costs of prosecution in the amount of $83,420, and a special assessment of $50.00. Ryan served his sentence. He also paid the $7,500 fine. The district court, following an appellate mandate, ultimately eliminated the restitution obligation.

On April 25, 2003, Ryan filed a petition for bankruptcy relief under chapter 7 in the District of Idaho. He received his Chapter 7 discharge on August 11, 2003. Shortly thereafter, Ryan filed a case under Chapter 13, listing as his only obligation the amount of unpaid costs of prosecution owed to the United States ("Government"). * * *

Ryan completed payments under the plan, and an "Order of Discharge" was entered on October 5, 2006. The Chapter 13 trustee's final report reflected that the Government received $2,774.89 from payments made by Ryan under his plan, but a balance of $77,088.34 on the Government's costs of prosecution claim remained unpaid. Ryan then renewed his request for determination of dischargeability. The bankruptcy court held that the unpaid portion of the Government's claim for costs of prosecution was excepted from discharge by § 1328(a)(3). Ryan appealed.

Section 1328(a)(3) provides an exception to discharge in chapter 13 for "restitution, or a criminal fine." It states, in pertinent part:

> *[A]s soon as practicable after the completion by the debtor of all payments under the plan, the court shall grant the debtor a discharge of all debts provided for by the plan or disallowed under section 502 of this title except any debt...*
>
> *(3) for restitution, or a criminal fine, included in a sentence on the debtor's conviction of a crime [.] [emphasis added].*

The essential question, then, is whether these costs of prosecution constitute a "criminal fine."

Statutory interpretation begins with a review of the particular language used by Congress in the relevant version of the law. [Citation.]

The term "criminal fine" is not defined in [Chapter 13] or anywhere else in the Bankruptcy Code. However, its use in § 1328(a)(3) implicates two important policies embedded in the Bankruptcy Code. First, in light of the objective to provide a fresh start for debtors overburdened by debts that they cannot pay, exceptions to discharge are interpreted strictly against objecting creditors and in favor of debtors. *See, e.g.* [Citations]. In Chapter 13, this principle is particularly important because Congress adopted the liberal "superdischarge" provisions of § 1328 as an incentive to debtors to commit to a plan to pay their creditors all of their disposable income over a period of years rather than simply discharging their debts in a Chapter 7 liquidation.

"[T]he dischargeability of debts in Chapter 13 that are not dischargeable in Chapter 7 represents a policy judgment that [it] is preferable for debtors to attempt to pay such debts to the best of their abilities over three years rather than for those debtors to have those debts hanging over their heads indefinitely, perhaps for the rest of their lives." [Citations.]

A second, countervailing policy consideration is a historic deference, both in the Bankruptcy Code and in the administration of prior bankruptcy law, to excepting criminal sanctions from discharge in bankruptcy. Application of this policy is consistent with a general recognition that, "[t]he principal purpose of the Bankruptcy Code is to grant a 'fresh start' to the '*honest* but unfortunate debtor.'" [Citation] (emphasis added [in original]).

The legislative history is clear that [in its 1994 amendments to the bankruptcy law] Congress intended to overrule the result in [of a 1990 Supreme Court case so that]: "[N]o debtor with criminal restitution obligations will be able to discharge them through any bankruptcy proceeding." * * *

The imposition on a defendant of the costs of a special prosecutor is different from ordering a defendant to pay criminal fines. Costs are paid to the entity incurring the costs; criminal fines are generally paid to a special fund for victims' compensation and assistance in the U.S. Treasury. * * *

To honor the principle that exceptions to discharge are to be construed narrowly in favor of debtors, particularly in Chapter 13, where a broad discharge was provided by Congress as an incentive for debtors to opt for relief under that chapter rather than under Chapter 7, it is not appropriate to expand the scope of the [Chapter 13] exception beyond the terms of the statute. Congress could have adopted an exception to discharge in Chapter 13 that mirrored [the one in Chapter 7]. It did not do so. In contrast, under [the 2005] BAPCPA, when Congress wanted to limit the Chapter 13 "superdischarge," it incorporated exceptions to discharge from [Chapter 7] wholesale. * * *

As a bottom line matter, Ryan served his time and paid in full the criminal fine that was imposed as part of his sentence for conviction of possession of an unregistered firearm. The restitution obligation that was included as part of his sentence was voided. Ryan paid the Government a total of $6,331.66 to be applied to the costs of prosecution awarded as part of his criminal judgment, including $2,774.89 paid under his Chapter 13 plan, leaving a balance of $77,088.34. We determine that the unpaid balance of the costs of prosecution award was covered by Ryan's Chapter 13 discharge.

Based on the foregoing analysis, we conclude that the exception to discharge included in [Chapter 13] for "restitution, or a criminal fine, included in a sentence on the debtor's conviction of a crime" does not cover costs of prosecution included in such a sentence, and we REVERSE.

Case Questions

1. What is the rationale for making some things dischargeable under Chapter 13 that are not dischargeable under Chapter 7?
2. What is the difference between "criminal restitution" (which in 1994 Congress said could not get discharged at all) and "the costs of prosecution"?
3. Why did the court decide that Ryan's obligation to pay "costs of prosecution" was not precluded by the limits on Chapter 13 bankruptcies imposed by Congress?

30.7 Summary and Exercises

Summary

The Constitution gives Congress the power to legislate on bankruptcy. The current law is the Bankruptcy Abuse Prevention and Consumer Protection Act of 2005, which provides for six types of proceedings: (1) liquidation, Chapter 7; (2) adjustment of debts of a municipality, Chapter 9; (3) reorganization, Chapter 11; (4) family farmers with regular income, Chapter 12; (5) individuals with regular income, Chapter 13; and (6) cross-border bankruptcies, Chapter 15.

With some exceptions, any individual, partnership, or corporation seeking liquidation may file a voluntary petition in bankruptcy. An involuntary petition is also possible; creditors petitioning for that must meet certain criteria.

A petition operates as a stay against the debtor for lawsuits to recover claims or enforce judgments or liens. A judge will issue an order of relief and appoint a trustee, who takes over the debtor's property and preserves security interests. To recover monies owed, creditors must file proof of claims. The trustee has certain powers to recover property for the estate that the debtor transferred before bankruptcy. These include the power to act as a hypothetical lien creditor, to avoid fraudulent transfers and voidable preferences.

The bankruptcy act sets out categories of claimants and establishes priority among them. After secured parties take their security, the priorities are (1) domestic support obligations, (2) administrative expenses, (3) gap creditor claims, (4) employees' wages, salaries, commissions, (5) contributions to employee benefit plans, (6) grain or fish producers' claims against a storage facility, (7) consumer deposits, (8) taxes owed to governments, (9) allowed claims for personal injury or death resulting from debtor's driving or operating a vessel while intoxicated. After these priority claims are paid, the trustee must distribute the estate in this order: (a) unsecured creditors who filed timely, (b) unsecured creditors who filed late, (c) persons claiming fines and the like, (d) all other creditors, (e) the debtor. Most bankruptcies are no-asset, so creditors get nothing.

Under Chapter 7's 2005 amendments, debtors must pass a means test to be eligible for relief; if they make too much money, they must file Chapter 13.

Certain property is exempt from the estate of an individual debtor. States may opt out of the federal list of exemptions and substitute their own; most have.

Once discharged, the debtor is no longer legally liable for most debts. However, some debts are not dischargeable, and bad faith by the debtor may preclude discharge. Under some circumstances, a debtor may reaffirm a discharged debt. A Chapter 7 case may be converted to Chapter 11 or 13 voluntarily, or to Chapter 11 involuntarily.

Chapter 11 provides for reorganization. Any person eligible for discharge in Chapter 7 is eligible for Chapter 11, except stockbrokers and commodity brokers; those who have too much debt to file Chapter 13 and surpass the means test for Chapter 7 file Chapter 11. Under Chapter 11, the debtor retains possession of the business and may continue to operate it with its own management unless the court appoints a trustee. The court may do so either for cause or if it is in the best interests of the creditors. The court must appoint a committee of unsecured creditors, who remain active throughout the proceeding. The debtor may file its own reorganization plan and has the exclusive right to do so within 120 days if it remains in possession. The plan must be accepted by certain proportions of each impaired class of claims and interests. It is binding on all creditors, and the debtor is discharged from all debts once the court confirms the plan.

Chapter 13 is for any individual with regular income who has difficulty paying debts; it is voluntary only; the debtor must get credit counseling. The debtor presents a payment plan to creditors, and the court appoints a trustee. The plan extends the time to pay and may reduce the size of the debt. If the creditors wind up with more in this proceeding than they would have in Chapter 7, the court is likely to approve the plan. The court may approve a stretch-out of five years. Some debts not dischargeable under Chapter 7 may be under Chapter 13.

Alternatives to bankruptcy are (1) composition (agreement by creditors to accept less than the face amount of the debt), (2) assignment for benefit of creditors (transfer of debtor's property to a trustee, who uses it to pay debts), and (3) receivership (a disinterested person is appointed by the court to preserve assets and distribute them at the court's direction). Because these are voluntary procedures, they are ineffective if all parties do not agree to them.

Exercises

1. David has debts of $18,000 and few assets. Because his debts are less than $25,000, he decides to file for bankruptcy using the state court system rather than the federal system. Briefly describe the procedure he should follow to file for bankruptcy at the state level.
2. Assume that David in Exercise 1 is irregularly employed and has developed a plan for paying off his creditors. What type of bankruptcy should he use, Chapter 7, 11, or 13? Why?
3. Assume that David owns the following unsecured property: a $3,000 oboe, a $1,000 piano, a $2,000 car, and a life insurance policy with a cash surrender value of $8,000. How much of this property is available for distribution to his creditors in a bankruptcy? Explain.
4. If David owes his ex-wife alimony (maintenance) payments and is obligated to pay $12,000 for an educational loan, what effect will his discharge have on these obligations?
5. Assume that David owns a corporation that he wants to liquidate under Chapter 7. After the corporate assets are distributed to creditors, there is still money owing to many of them. What obstacle does David face in obtaining a discharge for the corporation?

6. The famous retired professional football player—with a pension from the NFL—Orenthal James "O.J." Simpson was convicted of wrongful death in a celebrated Santa Monica, California, trial in 1997 and ordered to pay $33.5 million in damages to the families of the deceased. Mr. Simpson sold his California house, moved to Florida, and, from occasional appearances in the press, seemed to be living a high-style life with a big house, nice cars, and sharp clothing. He has never declared bankruptcy. Why hasn't he been forced into an involuntary Chapter 7 bankruptcy by his creditors?
7. a. A debtor has an automobile worth $5,000. The federal exemption applicable to her was $3,225. The trustee sells the car and gives the debtor the amount of the exemption. The debtor, exhausted by the bankruptcy proceedings, takes the $3,225 and spends it on a six-week vacation in Baja California. Is this an "abuse" of the bankruptcy system?
   b. A debtor has $500 in cash beyond what is exempt in bankruptcy. She takes the cash and buys new tires for her car, which is worth about $2,000. Is this an "abuse" of the bankruptcy system?

Self-Test Questions

1. Alternatives to bankruptcy include
   a. an assignment
   b. a composition
   c. receivership
   d. all of the above
2. A composition is
   a. a procedure where a receiver takes over the debtor's property
   b. an agreement by creditors to take less than the face value of their debt
   c. basically the same as an assignment
   d. none of these
3. The highest-priority class set out by the 2005 act is for
   a. employees' wages
   b. administrative expenses
   c. property settlements arising from divorce
   d. domestic support obligations
4. Darlene Debtor did the following within ninety days of filing for bankruptcy. Which could be set aside as a preferential payment?
   a. paid water and electricity bills
   b. made a gift to the Humane Society
   c. prepaid an installment loan on inventory
   d. borrowed money from a bank secured by a mortgage on business property
5. Donald Debtor sold his 1957 Chevrolet to his brother for one-fifth its value sixty days before filing for bankruptcy. The trustee wishes to avoid the transaction on the basis that it was
   a. a hypothetical lien
   b. a lease disguised as a sale
   c. a preferential payment
   d. a voidable preference
6. Acme Co. filed for bankruptcy with the following debts; which is their correct priority from highest to lowest?
   i. wages of $15,000 owed to employees
   ii. unpaid federal taxes

iii. balance owed to a creditor who claimed its security with a $5,000 deficiency owing

a. i, ii, iii
b. ii, iii, i
c. iii, ii, i
d. i, iii, ii

Self-Test Answers

1. d
2. b
3. d
4. c
5. d
6. a

Endnotes

1. CCH Bankruptcy Reform Act Briefing, "Bankruptcy Abuse Prevention and Consumer Protection Act of 2005," April 2005, http://www.cch.com/bankruptcy/bankruptcy_04-21.pdf.
2. 11 United States Code, Section 109(b).
3. 11 United States Code, Section 109(c).
4. Monica Davey and Mary Williams Walsh, "Billions in Debt, Detroit Tumbles into Bankruptcy," *The New York Times*, July 18, 2013. http://www.nytimes.com/2013/07/19/us/detroit-files-for-bankruptcy.html?pagewanted=all&_r=1.
5. 11 United States Code, Section 109(f).
6. http://www.uscourts.gov/services-forms/bankruptcy/bankruptcy-basics/chapter-12-bankruptcy-basics.
7. 11 United States Code, Section 109(e). http://wartchowlaw.com/2016/04/13/the-2016-chapter-13-debt-limits-effective-april-1-2016/.
8. http://thismatter.com/money/credit/bankruptcy/bankruptcy-petition.htm.
9. 11 United States Code, Section 109(h).
10. These states allow residents to chose either federal or state exemptions (the other states mandate the use of state exemptions only): Alaska, Arkansas, Connecticut, District of Columbia, Hawaii, Kentucky, Massachusetts, Michigan, Minnesota, New Hampshire, New Jersey, New Mexico, New York, Oregon, Pennsylvania, Rhode Island, Texas, Vermont, Washington, and Wisconsin.
11. 11 United States Code, Section 522.
12. The Florida homestead exemption is "[r]eal or personal property, including mobile or modular home and condominium, to unlimited value. Property cannot exceed: 1/2 acre in a municipality, or 160 acres elsewhere." The 2005 act limits the state homestead exemptions, as noted.
13. 11 United States Code, Section 547.
14. 11 United States Code, Section 548.
15. Charles Phelan, "The New Bankruptcy Means Test Explained in Plain English," *Buzzle.com*, http://www.buzzle.com/editorials/1-10-2006-85999.asp.
16. Eugene Crane, Hearing before the Subcommittee on Commercial and Administrative Law of the Committee on the Judiciary, House of Representatives, One Hundred Tenth Congress, Second Session, *Statement to the House Judiciary Sub-Committee,* September 16, 2008; http://judiciary.house.gov/hearings/printers/110th/44493.PDF.
17. 11 United States Code, Section 727(a)(1).
18. 11 United States Code, Sections 1115, 1123(a)(8), and 1129(a)(15).
19. http://www.politifact.com/truth-o-meter/statements/2016/jun/21/hillary-clinton/yep-donald-trumps-companies-have-declared-bankrupt/.
20. https://www.asbestos.com/asbestos/cover-up/.

CHAPTER 31

Introduction to Property: Personal Property and Fixtures

Learning Objectives

After reading this chapter, you should understand the following:

1. The difference between personal property and other types of property.
2. How rights in personal property are acquired and maintained.
3. How some kinds of personal property can become real property, and how to determine who has rights in fixtures that are part of real property.

In this chapter, we examine the general nature of property rights and the law relating to personal property—with special emphasis on acquisition and fixtures. In Chapter 32, we discuss intellectual property, a kind of personal property that is increasingly profitable. In Chapter 33 through Chapter 35, we focus on real property, including its nature and regulation, its acquisition by purchase (and some other methods), and its acquisition by lease (landlord and tenant law).

In Chapter 36 and Chapter 37, we discuss estate planning and insurance—two areas of the law that relate to both personal and real property.

31.1 The General Nature of Property Rights

Learning Objectives

1. Understand the elastic and evolving boundaries of what the law recognizes as property that can be bought or sold on the market.
2. Distinguish real property from personal property.

Definition of Property

Property, which seems like a commonsense concept, is difficult to define in an intelligible way; philosophers have been striving to define it for the past 2,500 years. To say that "property is what we own" is to beg the question—that is, to substitute a synonym for the word we are trying to define. Blackstone's famous definition is somewhat wordy: "The right of property is that sole and despotic dominion which one man claims and exercises over the external things of the world, in total exclusion of the right of any other individual in the universe. It consists in the free use, enjoyment, and disposal of all a person's acquisitions, without any control or diminution save only by the laws of the land." A more concise but perhaps too broad definition comes from the Restatement of the Law of Property, which defines property as the "legal relationship between persons with respect to a thing."

The Restatement's definition makes an important point: property is a *legal relationship*, the power of one person to use objects in ways that affect others, to exclude others from the property, and to acquire and transfer property. Still, this definition does not contain a specific list of those nonhuman "objects" that could be in such a relationship. We all know that we can own personal objects like iPods and DVDs, and even more complex objects like homes and minerals under the ground. Property also embraces objects whose worth is representative or symbolic: ownership of stock in a corporation is valued not for the piece of paper called a stock certificate but for dividends, the power to vote for directors, and the right to sell the stock on the open market. Wholly intangible things or objects like copyrights and patents and bank accounts are capable of being owned as property. But the list of things that can be property is not fixed, for our concept of property continues to evolve. Collateralized debt obligations (CDOs) and structured investment vehicles (SIVs), prime players in the subprime mortgage crisis, were not on anyone's list of possible property even fifteen years ago.

The Economist's View

Property is not just a legal concept, of course, and different disciplines express different philosophies about the purpose of property and the nature of property rights. To the jurist, property rights should be protected because it is just to do so. To an economist, the legal protection of property rights functions to create incentives to use resources efficiently. For a truly efficient system of property rights, some economists would require universality (everything is owned), exclusivity (the owners of each thing may exclude all others from using it), and transferability (owners may exchange their property). Together, they maintain, these aspects of property would lead to efficient production and distribution of goods. But the law of property does not entirely conform to the economic conception of the ownership of productive property by private parties; there remain many kinds of property that are not privately owned and some parts of the Earth that are considered part of "the commons." For example, large areas of the Earth's oceans are not "owned" by any one person or nation-state, and certain land areas (e.g., Yellowstone National Park) are not in private hands, nor is the air that we breathe. Interesting conflicts have arisen recently over what was agreed by treaty not to be owned by any nation: the Continent of Antarctica.[1]

Classification of Property

Property can be classified in various ways, including tangible versus intangible, private versus public, and personal versus real. **Tangible property** is that which physically exists, like a building, a popsicle stand, a hair dryer, or a steamroller. **Intangible property** is something without physical reality that entitles the owner to certain benefits; stocks, bonds, and intellectual property would be common examples. **Public property** is that which is owned by any branch of government; **private property** is that which is owned by anyone else, including a corporation.

Perhaps the most important distinction is between real and personal property. Essentially, **real property** is immovable; **personal property** is movable. At common law, personal property has been referred to as "chattels." When chattels become affixed to real property in a certain manner, they are called fixtures and are treated as real property. (For example, a bathroom cabinet purchased at Home Depot and screwed into the bathroom wall may be converted to part of the real property when it is affixed.) Fixtures are discussed in Section 3.

tangible property

That which physically exists, like a building, a popsicle stand, a hair dryer, or a steamroller.

intangible property

Something without physical reality that entitles the owner to certain benefits; stocks, bonds, and intellectual property would be common examples.

public property

That which is owned by any branch of government; private property is that which is owned by anyone else, including a corporation.

private property

All property, real or personal, that is not publicly owned or part of "the commons."

real property

Land and all structures and fixtures that have legally become part of the land.

personal property

Any property that is not real property.

Importance of the Distinction between Real and Personal Property

In our legal system, the distinction between real and personal property is significant in several ways. For example, the sale of personal property, but not real property, is governed by Article 2 of the Uniform Commercial Code (UCC). Real estate transactions, by contrast, are governed by the general law of contracts. Suppose goods are exchanged for realty. Section 2-304 of the UCC says that the transfer of the goods and the seller's obligations with reference to them are subject to Article 2, but not the transfer of the interests in realty nor the transferor's obligations in connection with them.

The form of transfer depends on whether the property is real or personal. Real property is normally transferred by a deed, which must meet formal requirements dictated by state law. By contrast, transfer of personal property often can take place without any documents at all.

Another difference can be found in the law that governs the transfer of property on death. A person's heirs depend on the law of the state for distribution of his property if he dies intestate—that is, without a will. Who the heirs are and what their share of the property will be may depend on whether the property is real or personal. For example, widows may be entitled to a different percentage of real property than personal property when their husbands die intestate.

Tax laws also differ in their approach to real and personal property. In particular, the rules of valuation, depreciation, and enforcement depend on the character of the property. Thus real property depreciates more slowly than personal property, and real property owners generally have a longer time than personal property owners to make good unpaid taxes before the state seizes the property.

Key Takeaway

Property is difficult to define conclusively, and there are many different classifications of property. There can be public property as well as private property, tangible property as well as intangible property, and, most importantly, real property as well as personal property. These are important distinctions, with many legal consequences.

Exercises

1. Kristen buys a parcel of land on Marion Street, a new and publicly maintained roadway. Her town's ordinances say that each property owner on a public street must also provide a sidewalk within ten feet of the curb. A year after buying the parcel, Kristen commissions a house to be built on the land, and the contractor begins by building a sidewalk in accordance with the town's ordinance. Is the sidewalk public property or private property? If it snows, and if Kristen fails to remove the snow and it melts and ices over and a pedestrian slips and falls, who is responsible for the pedestrian's injuries?
2. When can private property become public property? Does public property ever become private property?

31.2 Personal Property

Learning Objective

1. Explain the various ways that personal property can be acquired by means other than purchase.

Most legal issues about personal property center on its acquisition. Acquisition by purchase is the most common way we acquire personal property, but there are at least five other ways to legally acquire personal property: (1) possession, (2) finding lost or misplaced property, (3) gift, (4) accession, and (5) confusion.

Possession

It is often said that "possession is nine-tenths of the law." There is an element of truth to this, but it's not the whole truth. For our purposes, the more important question is, what is meant by "possession?" Its meaning is not intuitively obvious, as a moment's reflection will reveal. For example, you might suppose than you possess something when it is physically within your control, but what do you say when a hurricane deposits a boat onto your land? What if you are not even home when this happens? Do you possess the boat? Ordinarily, we would say that you don't, because you don't have physical control when you are absent. You may not even have the intention to control the boat; perhaps instead of a fancy speedboat in relatively good shape, the boat is a rust-bucket badly in need of repair, and you want it removed from your front yard. You may even insist that the "true owner" come and remove it at their expense.

Even the element of physical domination of the object may not be necessary. Suppose you give your new class ring to a friend to examine. Is it in the friend's possession? No: the friend has custody, not possession, and you retain the right to permit a second friend to take it from her hands. This is different from the case of a bailment, in which the bailor gives possession of an object to the bailee. For example, a garage (a bailee) entrusted with a car for the evening has the exclusive right to exclude others from the car, not the owner, during the period of the bailment. While it is in bailment, the owner could not demand that the garage attendants refrain from moving the car around as necessary.

From these examples, we can see that possession or physical control must usually be understood as the power to exclude others from using the personal property. Otherwise, anomalies arise from the difficulty of physically controlling certain objects. It is more difficult to exercise control over a one-hundred-foot television antenna than a diamond ring. Moreover, in what sense do you possess your household furniture when you are out of the house? Only, we suggest, in the power to exclude others. But this power is not purely a physical one: being absent from the house, you could not physically restrain anyone. Thus the concept of possession must be mixed with legal rules that apply to others who wish to use or control your property.

Possession confers ownership in a restricted class of cases only: when no person was the owner at the time the current owner took the object into his possession. The most obvious categories of objects to which this rule of possession applies are wild animals and abandoned goods. The rule requires that the would-be owner actually take possession of the animal or goods; the hunter who is pursuing a particular wild animal has no legal claim until he has actually captured it. Two hunters are perfectly free to pursue the same animal, and whoever actually grabs it will be the owner.

But even this simple rule is fraught with difficulties in the case of both wild animals and abandoned goods. We examine abandoned goods in Section 2. In the case of wild game, fish in a stream, and the like, the general rule is subject to the rights of the owner of the land on which the animals are caught. Thus even if the animals caught by a hunter are wild, as long as they are on another's land, the landowner's rights are superior to the hunter's. Suppose a hunter captures a wild animal, which subsequently escapes, and a second hunter thereafter captures it. Does the first hunter have a claim to the animal? The usual rule is that he does not, for once an animal returns to the wild, ownership ceases.

Lost or Misplaced Property

At common law, a technical distinction arose between lost and misplaced property. An object is lost if the owner inadvertently and unknowingly lets it out of his possession. It is merely misplaced if the owner intentionally puts it down, intending to recover it, even if he subsequently forgets to retrieve it. These definitions are important in considering the old saying "Finders keepers, losers weepers." This is a misconception that is, at best, only partially true, and more often false. The following hierarchy of ownership claims determines the rights of finders and losers.

First, the owner is entitled to the return of the property unless he has intentionally abandoned it. The finder is said to be a quasi-bailee for the true owner, and as bailee she owes the owner certain duties of care. The finder who knows the owner or has reasonable means of discovering the owner's identity commits larceny if she holds on to the object with the intent that it be hers. This rule applies only if the finder actually takes the object into her possession. For example, if you spot someone's wallet on the street you have no obligation to pick it up; but if you do pick it up and see the owner's name in it, your legal obligation is to return it to the rightful owner. The finder who returns the object is not automatically entitled to a reward, but if the loser has offered a reward, the act of returning it constitutes performance of a unilateral contract. Moreover, if the finder has had expenses in connection with finding the owner and returning the property, she is entitled to reasonable reimbursement as a quasi-bailee. But the rights of the owner are frequently subject to specific statutes, such as the one discussed in *Bishop v. Ellsworth* in Section 4.

Second, if the owner fails to claim the property within the time allowed by statute or has abandoned it, then the property goes to the owner of the real estate on which it was found if (1) the finder was a trespasser, (2) the goods are found in a private place (though what exactly constitutes a private place is open to question: is the aisle of a grocery store a private place? the back of the food rack? the stockroom?), (3) the goods are buried, or (4) the goods are misplaced rather than lost.

If none of these conditions apply, then the finder is the owner. These rules are considered in the *Bishop* case, (see Section 4).

Gift

gift

A voluntary transfer of property without consideration or compensation.

gift inter vivos

A gift made between living persons.

gift causa mortis

A gift made by someone in contemplating death in the near future.

A **gift** is a voluntary transfer of property without consideration or compensation. It is distinguished from a sale, which requires consideration. It is distinguished from a promise to give, which is a declaration of an intention to give in the future rather than a present transfer. It is distinguished from a testamentary disposition (will), which takes effect only upon death, not upon the preparation of the documents. Two other distinctions are worth noting. An **inter vivos** (enter VYE vos) gift is one made between living persons without conditions attached. A **causa mortis** (KAW zuh mor duz) gift is made by someone contemplating death in the near future.

Requirements

FIGURE 31.1 Gift Requirements

To make an effective gift inter vivos or causa mortis, the law imposes three requirements: (1) the donor must *deliver* a deed or object to the donee; (2) the donor must actually *intend* to make a gift, and (3) the donee must *accept* (see Figure 31.1).

Delivery

Although it is firmly established that the object be delivered, it is not so clear what constitutes delivery. On the face of it, the requirement seems to be that the object must be transferred to the donee's possession. Suppose your friend tells you he is making a gift to you of certain books that are lying in a locked trunk. If he actually gives you the trunk so that you can carry it away, a gift has been made. Suppose, however, that he had merely given you the key, so that you could come back the next day with your car. If this were the sole key, the courts would probably construe the transfer of the key as possession of the trunk. Suppose, instead, that the books were in a bank vault and the friend made out a legal document giving both you and him the power to take from the bank vault. This would not be a valid gift, since he retained power over the goods.

Intent

The intent to make a gift must be an intent to give the property at the present time, not later. For example, suppose a person has her savings account passbook put in her name and a friend's name, intending that on her death the friend will be able to draw out whatever money is left. She has not made a gift, because she did not intend to give the money when she changed the passbook. The intent requirement can sometimes be sidestepped if legal title to the object is actually transferred, postponing to the donee only the use or enjoyment of the property until later. Had the passbook been made out in the name of the donee only and delivered to a third party to hold until the death of the donor, then a valid gift may have been made. Although it is sometimes difficult to discern this distinction in practice, a more accurate statement of the rule of intent is this: Intention to give in the future does not constitute the requisite intent, whereas present gifts of future interests will be upheld.

Acceptance

In the usual case, the rule requiring acceptance poses no difficulties. A friend hands you a new book and says, "I would like you to have this." Your taking the book and saying "thank you" is enough to constitute your acceptance. But suppose that the friend had given you property without your knowing it. For example, a secret admirer puts his stock certificates jointly in your name and his without telling you. Later, you marry someone else, and the former admirer is not so enamored, and asks you to transfer the certificates back to his name. This is the first you have heard of the transaction. Has a gift been made? The usual answer is that even though you had not accepted the stock when the name change was made, the transaction was a gift that took effect immediately, subject to your right to repudiate when you find out about it. If you do not reject the gift, you have joint rights in the stock. But if you expressly refuse to accept a gift or indicate in some manner that you might not have accepted it, then the gift is not effective. For example, suppose you are running for office. A lobbyist whom you despise sends you a check for $50,000. If you refuse the money, no gift has been made.

Gifts Causa Mortis

Even though the requirements of delivery, intent, and acceptance apply to gifts causa mortis as well as inter vivos, a gift causa mortis (one made in contemplation of death) may be distinguished from a gift inter vivos on other grounds. The gift does not have to be made on the donor's death bed, but should be made in "contemplation" of death, or, where death is a strong possibility. Suppose that Gabriel is going to Afghanistan with the U.S. Army and expects to come under attack; a gift of personal property in contemplation of death (requiring delivery and acceptance) would vest title to the property in the donee. But with a gift causa mortis, the donor may revoke the gift before he dies.

Put differently, for the gift causa mortis to be irrevocable the donor must die. Since the law does not permit gifts that take place in the future contingent on some happening, how can it be that a gift causa mortis is effective? The answer lies in the nature of the transfer: the donee takes actual title when the gift is made; should the donor not in fact die or should she revoke the gift before he dies, then and only then will the donee lose title. The difference is subtle and amounts to the difference between saying "If I die, the watch is yours" (an impermissible contingent gift) and "The watch is yours, unless I survive." In the former case, sometimes known as a condition precedent, there is no valid gift; in the latter case, known as a condition subsequent, the gift is valid.

Gifts to Minors

Every state has adopted either the Uniform Gifts to Minors Act (UGMA) or the Uniform Transfers to Minors Act (UTMA), both of which establish the manner by which irrevocable gifts are made to minors. Under these acts, a custodian holds the gifts until the minor reaches the age of eighteen, twenty-one, or twenty-five, depending on state law. Gifts under UGMA are limited for the most part to money or securities, while UTMA allows other types of gifts as well, such as real estate or tangible personal property.

Gift Tax

The federal government and many states impose gift taxes on gifts above a certain dollar amount. We discuss gift taxes in connection with estate taxes in Chapter 36.

Accession

accession

Something that is added to what one already possesses.

An **accession** is something that is added to what one already possesses. In general, the rule is that the owner of the thing owns the additional thing that comes to be attached to it. For example, the owner of a cow owns her calves when she gives birth. But when one person adds value to another person's property, either through labor alone or by adding new materials, the rule must be stated somewhat differently. The general rule is this: when goods are added to goods, the owner of the principal goods becomes the owner of the enhanced product. For example, a garage uses its paint to repaint its customer's automobile. The car owner, not the painter, is the owner of the finished product.

When someone has wrongfully converted—that is, taken as her own—the property of another, the owner may sue for damages, either to recover his property or its value. But a problem arises when the converter has added to the value of that property. In general, the courts hold that when the conversion is willful, the owner is entitled to the full value of the goods as enhanced by the converter. Suppose that a carpenter enters a ten-acre forest that he knows belongs to his neighbor, cuts down one hundred trees, transports them to his shop, and cuts them up into standard lumber, thus increasing their market value. The owner is entitled to this full value, and the carpenter will get nothing for his trouble. Thus the willful converter loses the value of his labor or materials. If, on the other hand, the conversion was innocent, or at most negligent, the rule is somewhat more uncertain. Generally the courts will award the forest owner the value of the standing timber, giving the carpenter the excess attributable to his labor and transportation. A more favorable treatment of the owner is to give her the full value of the lumber as cut, remitting to the carpenter the value of his expenses.

Confusion

confusion

Where personal property is intermingled, negligently or intentionally, with the personal property of others.

In accession, the goods of one owner are transformed into a more valuable commodity or are inextricably united with the goods of another to form a constituent part. Still another type of joining is known as **confusion**, and it occurs when goods of different owners, while maintaining their original form, are commingled. A common example is the intermingling of grain in a silo. But goods that are identifiable as belonging to a particular person—branded cattle, for instance—are not confused, no matter how difficult it may be to separate herds that have been put together.

When the goods are identical, no particular problem of division arises. Assuming that each owner can show how much he has contributed to the confused mass, he is entitled to that quantity, and it does not matter which particular grains or kernels he extracts. So if a person, seeing a container of grain sitting on the side of the road, mistakes it for his own and empties it into a larger container in his truck, the remedy is simply to restore a like quantity to the original owner. When owners of like substances consent to have those substances combined (such as in a grain silo), they are said to be tenants in common, holding a proportional share in the whole.

In the case of willful confusion of goods, many courts hold that the wrongdoer forfeits all his property unless he can identify his particular property. Other courts have modified this harsh rule by shifting the burden of proof to the wrongdoer, leaving it up to him to claim whatever he can establish was his. If he cannot establish what was his, then he will forfeit all. Likewise, when the defendant has confused the goods negligently, without intending to do so, most courts will tend to shift to the defendant the burden of proving how much of the mass belongs to him.

Key Takeaway

Other than outright purchase of personal property, there are various ways in which to acquire legal title. Among these are possession, gift, accession, confusion, and finding property that is abandoned, lost, or mislaid, especially if the abandoned, lost, or mislaid property is found on real property that you own.

Exercises

1. Dan captures a wild boar on U.S. Forest Service land. He takes it home and puts it in a cage, but the boar escapes and runs wild for a few days before being caught by Romero, some four miles distant from Dan's house. Romero wants to keep the boar. Does he "own" it? Or does it belong to Dan, or to someone else?
2. Harriet finds a wallet in the college library, among the stacks. The wallet has $140 in it, but no credit cards or identification. The library has a lost and found at the circulation desk, and the people at the circulation desk are honest and reliable. The wallet itself is unique enough to be identified by its owner. (a) Who owns the wallet and its contents? (b) As a matter of ethics, should Harriet keep the money if the wallet is "legally" hers?

31.3 Fixtures

Learning Objective

1. Know the three tests for when personal property becomes a fixture and thus becomes real property.

Definition

A **fixture** is an object that was once personal property but that has become so affixed to land or structures that it is considered legally a part of the real property. For example, a stove bolted to the floor of a kitchen and connected to the gas lines is usually considered a fixture, either in a contract for sale, or for testamentary transfer (by will). For tax purposes, fixtures are treated as real property.

fixture

An object that was once personal property that has become so affixed to land or structures that it is legally a part of the real property.

Tests

FIGURE 31.2 Fixture Tests

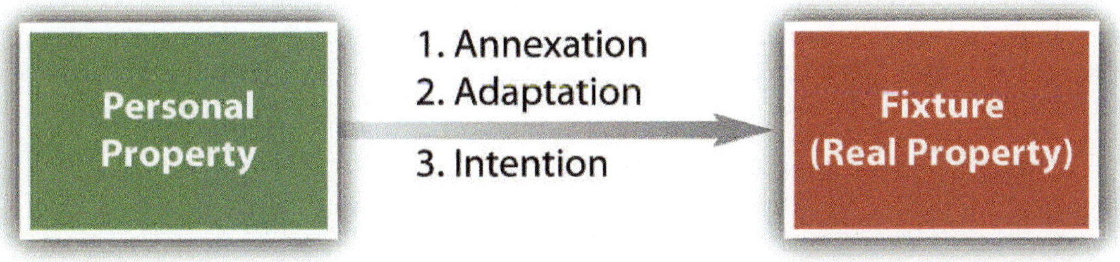

Obviously, no clear line can be drawn between what is and what is not a fixture. In general, the courts look to three tests to determine whether a particular object has become a fixture: annexation, adaptation, and intention (see Figure 31.2).

Annexation

The object must be annexed or affixed to the real property. A door on a house is affixed. Suppose the door is broken and the owner has purchased a new door made to fit, but the house is sold before the new door is installed. Athough it is not yet "annexed" or "affixed," most courts would consider that new door a fixture under a rule of "constructive annexation." Sometimes courts have said that an item is a fixture if its removal would damage the real property, but this test is not conclusive; ceiling fans, for example, can be removed and a decorative plate left over the hole, and there is no "damage" to real property, but the ceiling fan would nonetheless be a fixture. Must the object be attached with nails, screws, glue, bolts, or some other physical device? Not always; in one case, the court held that a four-ton statue was sufficiently affixed merely by its weight.[2]

Adaptation

Another test is whether the object is adapted to the use or enjoyment of the real property. Examples are home furnaces, power equipment in a mill, and computer systems in bank buildings.

Intention

Recent decisions suggest that the controlling test is whether the person who actually annexes the object intends by so doing to make it a permanent part of the real estate. The intention is usually deduced from the circumstances, not from what a person might later say her intention was. If an owner installs a heating system in her house, the law will presume she intended it as a fixture because the installation was intended to benefit the house; she would not be allowed to remove the heating system when she sold the house by claiming that she had not intended to make it a fixture.

Fixture Disputes

Because fixtures have a hybrid nature (once personal property, subsequently real property), they generate a large number of disputes. We have already examined two types of these disputes in other contexts: (1) disputes between mortgagees and secured parties (Chapter 28) and (2) disputes over whether the sale of property attached to real estate (such as crops or a structure) but about to be severed is a sale of goods or real estate (Chapter 17). Two other types of disputes remain.

Transfer of Real Estate

When a homeowner sells her house, the problem frequently crops up as to whether certain items in the home have been sold or may be removed by the seller. Is a refrigerator, which simply plugs into the wall, a fixture or an item of personal property? If a dispute arises, the courts will apply the three tests—annexation, adaptation, and intention. Of course, the simplest way of avoiding the dispute is to incorporate specific reference to questionable items in the contract for sale, indicating whether the buyer or the seller is to keep them.

Tenant's Fixtures

Tenants frequently install fixtures in the buildings they rent or the property they occupy. A company may install tens of thousands of dollars worth of equipment; a tenant in an apartment may bolt a bookshelf into the wall or install shades over a window. Who owns the fixtures when the tenant's lease expires? The older rule was that any fixture, determined by the usual tests, must remain with the landlord. Today, however, certain types of fixtures—known as **tenant's fixtures**—stay with the tenant. These fall into three categories: (1) trade fixtures—articles placed on the premises to enable the tenant to carry on his or her trade or business in the rented premises; (2) agricultural fixtures—devices installed to carry on farming activities (e.g., milling plants and silos); (3) domestic fixtures—items that make a tenant's personal life more comfortable (carpeting, screens, doors, washing machines, bookshelves, and the like).

tenant's fixtures

Fixtures added to rental property that become property of the owner.

The three types of tenant's fixtures remain personal property and may be removed by the tenant if the following three conditions are met: (1) They must be installed for the requisite purposes of carrying on the trade or business or the farming or agricultural pursuits or for making the home more comfortable, (2) they must be removable without causing substantial damage to the landlord's property, and (3) they must be removed before the tenant turns over possession of the premises to the landlord. Again, any debatable points can be resolved in advance by specifying them in the written lease.

Key Takeaway

Personal property is often converted to real property when it is affixed to real property. There are three tests that courts use to determine whether a particular object has become a fixture and thus has become real property: annexation, adaptation, and intention. Disputes over fixtures often arise in the transfer of real property and in landlord-tenant relations.

Exercises

1. Jim and Donna Stoner contract to sell their house in Rochester, Michigan, to Clem and Clara Hovenkamp. Clara thinks that the decorative chandelier in the entryway is lovely and gives the house an immediate appeal. The chandelier was a gift from Donna's mother, "to enhance the entryway" and provide "a touch of beauty" for Jim and Donna's house. Clem and Clara assume that the chandelier will stay, and nothing specific is mentioned about the chandelier in the contract for sale. Clem and Clara are shocked when they move in and find the chandelier is gone. Have Jim and Donna breached their contract of sale?
2. Blaine Goodfellow rents a house from Associated Properties in Abilene, Texas. He is there for two years, and during that time he installs a ceiling fan, custom-builds a bookcase for an alcove on the main floor, and replaces the screening on the front and back doors, saving the old screening in the furnace room. When his lease expires, he leaves, and the bookcase remains behind. Blaine does, however, take the new screening after replacing it with the old screening, and he removes the ceiling fan and puts back the light. He causes no damage to Associated Properties' house in doing any of this. Discuss who is the rightful owner of the screening, the bookcase, and the ceiling fan after the lease expires.

31.4 Case

Lost or Misplaced Property

Bishop v. Ellsworth

91 Ill. App.2d 386, 234 N.E. 2d 50 (1968)

OPINION BY: STOUDER, Presiding Justice

Dwayne Bishop, plaintiff, filed a complaint alleging that on July 21, 1965, defendants, Mark and Jeff Ellsworth and David Gibson, three small boys, entered his salvage yard premises at 427 Mulberry Street in Canton, without his permission, and while there happened upon a bottle partially embedded in the loose earth on top of a landfill, wherein they discovered the sum of $12,590 in U.S. currency [about $97,000 in 2017 dollars]. It is further alleged that said boys delivered the money to the municipal chief of police who deposited it with defendant, Canton State Bank. The complaint also alleges defendants caused preliminary notices to be given as required by Ill. Rev. Stats., chapter 50, subsections 27 and 28 (1965), but that such statute or compliance therewith does not affect the rights of the plaintiff. [The trial court dismissed the plaintiff's complaint.]

...It is defendant's contention that the provisions of Ill Rev Stats, chapter 50, subsections 27 and 28 govern this case. The relevant portions of this statute are as follows:

> *"27. Lost goods...If any person or persons shall hereafter find any lost goods, money, bank notes, or other choses in action, of any description whatever, such person or persons shall inform the owner thereof, if known, and shall make restitution of the same, without any compensation whatever, except the same shall be voluntarily given on the part of the owner. If the owner be unknown, and if such property found is of the value of $ 15 or upwards, the finder...shall, within five days after such finding...appear before some judge or magistrate...and make affidavit of the description thereof, the time and place when and where the same was found, that no alteration has been made in the appearance thereof since the finding of the same, that the owner thereof is unknown to him and that he has not secreted, withheld or disposed of any part thereof. The judge or magistrate shall enter the value of the property found as near as he can ascertain in his estray book together with the affidavit of the finder, and shall also, within ten days after the proceedings have been entered on his estray book, transmit to the county clerk a certified copy thereof, to be by him recorded in his estray book and to file the same in his office...28. Advertisement...If the value thereof exceeds the sum of $ 15, the county clerk, within 20 days after receiving the certified copy of the judge or magistrate's estray record shall cause an advertisement to be set up on the court house door, and in 3 other of the most public places in the county, and also a notice thereof to be published for 3 weeks successively in some public newspaper printed in this state and if the owner of such goods, money, bank notes, or other choses in action does not appear and claim the same and pay the finder's charges and expenses within one year after the advertisement thereof as aforesaid, the ownership of such property shall vest in the finder."*

* * *

We think it apparent that the statute to which defendants make reference provides a means of vesting title to lost property in the finder where the prescribed search for the owner proves fruitless. This statute does not purport to provide for the disposition of property deemed mislaid or abandoned nor does it purport to describe or determine the right to possession against any party other than the true owner. The plain meaning of this statute does not support plaintiff's position that common law is wholly abrogated thereby. The provisions of the statute are designed to provide a procedure whereby the discoverer of "lost" property may be vested with the ownership of said property even as against the true owner thereof, a right which theretofore did not exist at common law. In the absence of any language in the statute from which the contrary can be inferred it must be assumed that the term "lost" was used in its generally accepted legal sense and no extension of the term was intended. Thus, the right to possession of discovered property still depends upon the relative rights of the discoverer and the owner of the locus in quo and the distinctions which exist between property which is abandoned, mislaid, lost or is treasure trove. The statute assumes that the discoverer is in the rightful possession of lost property and proceedings under such statute are not a bar where the issue is a claim to the contrary. There is a presumption that the owner or occupant of land or premises has custody of property found on it or actually imbedded in the land. The ownership or possession of the locus in quo is related to the right to possession of property discovered thereon or imbedded therein in two respects. First, if the premises on which the property is discovered are private it is deemed that the property discovered thereon is and always has been in the constructive possession of the owner of said premises and in a legal sense the property can be neither mislaid nor lost. *Pyle v. Springfield Marine Bank*, 330 Ill App 1, 70 NE2d 257. Second, the question of whether the property is mislaid or lost in a legal sense depends upon the intent of the true owner. The ownership or possession of the premises is an important factor in determining such intent. If the property be determined to be mislaid, the owner of the premises is entitled to the possession thereof against the discoverer. It would also appear that if the discoverer is a trespasser such trespasser can have no claim to possession of such property even if it might otherwise be considered lost.

* * * The facts as alleged in substance are that the Plaintiff was the owner and in possession of real estate, that the money was discovered in a private area of said premises in a bottle partially imbedded in the soil and that such property was removed from the premises by the finders without any right or authority and in effect as trespassers. We believe the averment of facts in the complaint substantially informs the defendants of the nature of and basis for the claim and is sufficient to state a cause of action. [The trial court's dismissal of the Plaintiff's complaint is reversed and the case is remanded.]

Case Questions

1. What is the actual result in this case? Do the young boys get any of the money that they found? Why or why not?
2. Who is Dwayne Bishop, and why is he a plaintiff here? Was it Bishop that put the $12,590 in U.S. currency in a bottle in the landfill at the salvage yard? If not, then who did?
3. If Bishop is not the original owner of the currency, what are the rights of the original owner in this case? Did the original owner "lose" the currency? Did the original owner "misplace" the currency? What difference does it make whether the original owner "lost" or "misplaced" the currency? Can the original owner, after viewing the legal advertisement, have a claim superior to Dwayne Bishop's claim?

31.5 Summary and Exercises

Summary

Property is the *legal relationship* between persons with respect to things. The law spells out what can be owned and the degree to which one person can assert an interest in someone else's things. Property is classified in several ways: personal versus real, tangible versus intangible, private versus public. The first distinction, between real and personal, is the most important, for different legal principles often apply to each. Personal property is movable, whereas real property is immovable.

Among the ways personal property can be acquired are: by (1) possession, (2) finding, (3) gift, (4) accession, and (5) confusion.

Possession means the power to exclude others from using an object. Possession confers ownership only when there is no owner at the time the current owner takes possession. "Finders keepers, losers weepers" is not a universal rule; the previous owner is entitled to return of his goods if it is reasonably possible to locate him. If not, or if the owner does not claim his property, then it goes to the owner of the real estate on which it was found, if the finder was a trespasser, or the goods were buried, were in a private place, or were misplaced rather than lost. If none of these conditions applies, the property goes to the finder.

A gift is a voluntary transfer of property without consideration. Two kinds of gifts are possible: inter vivos and causa mortis. To make an effective gift, (1) the donor must make out a deed or physically deliver the object to the donee, (2) the donor must intend to make a gift, and (3) the donee must accept the gift. Delivery does not always require physical transfer; sometimes, surrender of control is sufficient. The donor must intend to give the gift now, not later.

Accession is an addition to that which is already owned—for example, the birth of calves to a cow owned by a farmer. But when someone else, through labor or by supplying material, adds value, the accession goes to the owner of the principal goods.

Confusion is the intermingling of like goods so that each, while maintaining its form, becomes a part of a larger whole, like grain mixed in a silo. As long as the goods are identical, they can easily enough be divided among their owners.

A fixture is a type of property that ceases to be personal property and becomes real property when it is annexed or affixed to land or buildings on the land and adapted to the use and enjoyment of the real property. The common-law rules governing fixtures do not employ clear-cut tests, and sellers and buyers can avoid many disputes by specifying in their contracts what goes with the land. Tenant's fixtures remain the property of the tenant if they are for the convenience of the tenant, do not cause substantial damage to the property when removed, and are removed before possession is returned to the landlord.

Exercises

1. Kate owns a guitar, stock in a corporation, and an antique bookcase that is built into the wall of her apartment. How would you classify each kind of property?
2. After her last business law class, Ingrid casually throws her textbook into a trash can and mutters to herself, "I'm glad I don't have to read that stuff anymore." Tom immediately retrieves the book from the can. Days later, Ingrid realizes that the book will come in handy, sees Tom with it, and demands that he return the book. Tom refuses. Who is entitled to the book? Why?
3. In Exercise 2, suppose that Ingrid had accidentally left the book on a table in a restaurant. Tom finds it, and chanting "Finders keepers, losers weepers," he refuses to return the book. Is Ingrid entitled to the book? Why?

4. In Exercise 3, if the owner of the book (Ingrid) is never found, who is entitled to the book—the owner of the restaurant or Tom? Why?
5. Matilda owned an expensive necklace. On her deathbed, Matilda handed the necklace to her best friend, Sadie, saying, "If I die, I want you to have this." Sadie accepted the gift and placed it in her safe-deposit box. Matilda died without a will, and now her only heir, Ralph, claims the necklace. Is he entitled to it? Why or why not?

Self-Test Questions

1. Personal property is defined as property that is
   a. not a chattel
   b. owned by an individual
   c. movable
   d. immovable
2. Personal property can be acquired by
   a. accession
   b. finding
   c. gift
   d. all of the above
3. A gift causa mortis is
   a. an irrevocable gift
   b. a gift made after death
   c. a gift made in contemplation of death
   d. none of the above
4. To make a gift effective,
   a. the donor must intend to make a gift
   b. the donor must either make out a deed or deliver the gift to the donee
   c. the donee must accept the gift
   d. all of the above are required
5. Tenant's fixtures
   a. remain with the landlord in all cases
   b. remain the property of the tenant in all cases
   c. remain the property of the tenant if they are removable without substantial damage to the landlord's property
   d. refer to any fixture installed by a tenant

Self-Test Answers

1. c
2. d
3. c
4. d
5. c

Endnotes

1. Matthew Teller, BBC, June 20, 2014: Why do so many nations want a piece of Antarctica? http://www.bbc.com/news/magazine-27910375.
2. *Snedeker v. Warring*, 12 N.Y. 170 (1854).

CHAPTER 32
Intellectual Property

Learning Objectives

After reading this chapter, you should understand the following:

1. The principal kinds of intellectual property.
2. The difference between patents and trade secrets, and why a company might choose to rely on trade secrets rather than obtain a patent.
3. What copyrights are, how to obtain them, and how they differ from trademarks.
4. Why some "marks" may not be eligible for trademark protection, and how to obtain trademark protection for those that are.

Few businesses of any size could operate without being able to protect their rights to a particular type of intangible personal property: **intellectual property**. The major forms of intellectual property are patents, copyrights, and trademarks. Unlike tangible personal property (machines, inventory) or real property (land, office buildings), intellectual property is formless. It is the product of the human intellect that is embodied in the goods and services a company offers and by which the company is known.

A **patent** is a grant from the government that gives an inventor the exclusive right to make, use, and sell an invention for a period of twenty years from the date of filing the application for a patent. A **copyright** is the right to exclude others from using or marketing certain forms of expression. A **trademark** is the right to prevent others from using a company's product name, slogan, or identifying design. Other forms of intellectual property are trade secrets (particular kinds of information of commercial use to a company that created it) and right of publicity (the right to exploit a person's name or image). Note that the property interest protected in each case is not the tangible copy of the invention or writing—not the machine with a particular serial number or the book lying on someone's shelf—but the invention or words themselves. That is why intellectual property is said to be intangible: it is a right to exclude any others from gaining economic benefit from your own intellectual creation. In this chapter, we examine how Congress, the courts, and the Patent and Trademark Office have worked to protect the major types of intellectual property.

intellectual property

Intangible personal property whose major forms are patents, copyrights, and trademarks.

patent

A grant from government that gives an inventor the exclusive right to make, use, and sell an invention for a period of twenty years from the date of filing the application for a patent.

copyright

The legal right given "authors" to prevent others from copying the expression embodied in a protected work.

trademark

Defined by the federal Lanham Act of 1946 as "any word, name, symbol, or device or any combination thereof adopted and used by a manufacturer or merchant to identify his goods and distinguish them from goods manufactured or sold by others."

32.1 Patents

Learning Objectives

1. Explain why Congress would grant exclusive monopolies (patents) for certain periods of time.
2. Describe what kinds of things may be patentable and what kinds of things may not be patentable.
3. Explain the procedures for obtaining a patent, and how patent rights may be an issue where the invention is created by an employee.
4. Understand who can sue for patent infringement, on what basis, and with what potential remedies.

Source of Authority and Duration

Patent and copyright law are federal, enacted by Congress under the power given by Article I of the Constitution "to promote the Progress of Science and useful Arts, by securing for limited Times to Authors and Inventors the exclusive Right to their respective Writings and Discoveries." Under current law, a patent gives an inventor exclusive rights to make, use, or sell an invention for twenty years. (If the patent is a design patent—protecting the appearance rather than the function of an item—the period is fourteen years.) In return for this limited monopoly, the inventor must fully disclose, in papers filed in the U.S. Patent and Trademark Office (PTO), a complete description of the invention.

Patentability

What May Be Patented

process

A "means devised for the production of a given result"—for example, a process for making steel.

machine

A particular apparatus for achieving a certain result or carrying out a distinct process—lathes, printing presses, motors, and the cotton gin are all examples of machines.

manufacture

An article or product, such as a television, automobile, telephone, and lightbulb.

composition of matter

A new arrangement of elements such that the resulting compound, such as a metal alloy, is not found in nature.

The patent law says that "any new and useful process, machine, manufacture, or composition of matter, or any new and useful improvement thereof" may be patented.[1] A **process** is a "process, art or method, and includes a new use of a known process, machine, manufacture, composition of matter, or material."[2] A process for making rolled steel, for example, qualifies as a patentable process under the statute. A **machine** is a particular apparatus for achieving a certain result or carrying out a distinct process—lathes, printing presses, motors, and the cotton gin are all examples of the hundreds of thousands of machines that have received US patents since the first Patent Act in 1790. A **manufacture** is an article or a product, such as a television, an automobile, a telephone, or a lightbulb. A **composition of matter** is a new arrangement of elements so that the resulting compound, such as a metal alloy, is not found in nature. In *Commissioner of Patents v. Chakrabarty*,[3] the Supreme Court said that even living organisms—in particular, a new "genetically engineered" bacterium that could "eat" oil spills—could be patented. The *Chakrabarty* decision has spawned innovation: a variety of small biotechnology firms have attracted venture capitalists and other investors.

Most of the above, whether "process," machine, composition of matter, chemical invention, electrical invention, or mechanical invention, are known as "utility patents." Always keep in mind that any such patent is not available just for an idea, but for its tangible, practical application. Laws of nature, scientific principles, mathematical algorithms and formulas are not patentable. Financial firms that use algorithms to make investment decisions can best protect these as trade secrets, not patents. Utility patents are distinguishable from two other kinds of patents: design patents and plant patents.[4] (In a design patent, it is not the article itself that is protected, but rather the design embodied in the article. That includes "ornamental designs of all kinds including surface ornamentation as well as configuration." Utility patents can cover such innovations as gene sequence patenting and other biological patenting, provided that the patent applicant has in some way modified what was a "naturally occurring" gene or gene sequence. In the 2013 case of *Association for Molecular Pathology v. Myriad Genetics*, the U.S. Supreme Court ruled unanimously that a naturally occurring DNA segment is a product of nature and not patent eligible merely because it has been isolated."[5] Yet an Australian high court had come to the opposite conclusion just months earlier.[6]

According to the PTO, gene sequences are patentable subject matter, provided they are isolated from their natural state and processed in a way that separates them from other molecules naturally occurring with them. Gene patenting, always controversial, generated new controversy when the PTO issued a patent to Human Genome Sciences, Inc. for a gene found to serve as a platform from which the AIDS virus can infect cells of the body. Critics faulted the PTO for allowing "ownership" of a naturally occurring human gene and for issuing patents without requiring a showing of the gene's utility. New guidelines from the PTO followed in 2000; these focused on requiring the applicant to make a strong showing on the utility aspect of patentability and somewhat diminished the rush of biotech patent requests.

What May Not Be Patented

Many things can be patented, but not (1) the laws of nature, (2) natural phenomena, and (3) abstract ideas, including algorithms (step-by-step formulas for accomplishing a specific task).

One frequently asked question is whether patents can be issued for computer software. The PTO was reluctant to do so at first, based on the notion that computer programs were not "novel"—the software program either incorporated automation of manual processes or used mathematical equations (which were not patentable). But in 1998, the Supreme Court held in *Diamond v. Diehr*[7] that patents could be obtained for a process that incorporated a computer program if the process itself was patentable.

A business process can also be patentable, as the U.S. Court of Appeals for the Federal Circuit ruled in 1998 in *State Street Bank and Trust v. Signature Financial Group, Inc.*[8] Signature Financial had a patent for a computerized accounting system that determined share prices through a series of mathematical calculations that would help manage mutual funds. State Street sued to challenge that patent. Signature argued that its model and process was protected, and the court of appeals upheld it as a "practical application of a mathematical, algorithm, formula, or calculation," because it produces a "useful, concrete and tangible result." Since *State Street*, many other firms have applied for business process patents. For example, Amazon.com obtained a business process patent for its "one-click" ordering system, a method of processing credit-card orders securely. (But see *Amazon.com v. Barnesandnoble.com*,[9] in which the court of appeals rejected Amazon's challenge to Barnesandnoble.com using its Express Land one-click ordering system.)

Tests for Patentability

Just because an invention falls within one of the categories of patentable subjects, it is not necessarily patentable. The Patent Act and judicial interpretations have established certain tests that must first be met. To approve a patent application, the PTO (as part of the Department of Commerce) will require that the invention, discovery, or process be novel, useful, and nonobvious in light of current technology.

Perhaps the most significant test of patentability is that of obviousness. The act says that no invention may be patented "if the differences between the subject matter sought to be patented and the prior art are such that the subject matter as a whole would have been obvious at the time the invention was made to a person having ordinary skill in the art to which said subject matter pertains." This provision of the law has produced innumerable court cases, especially over improvement patents, when those who wish to use an invention on which a patent has been issued have refused to pay royalties on the grounds that the invention was obvious to anyone who looked.

Procedures for Obtaining a Patent

In general, the United States (unlike many other countries) grants a patent right to the first person to invent a product or process rather than to the first person to file for a patent on that product or process. As a practical matter, however, someone who invents a product or process but does not file immediately should keep detailed research notes or other evidence that would document the date of invention. An inventor who fails to apply for a patent within a year of that date would forfeit the rights granted to an inventor who had published details of the invention or offered it for sale. But until the year has passed, the PTO may not issue a patent to X if Y has described the invention in a printed publication here or abroad or the invention has been in public use or on sale in this country.

specification

A description of the invention that gives enough detail so that one skilled in the art will be able to make and use the invention.

An inventor cannot obtain a patent automatically; obtaining a patent is an expensive and time-consuming process, and the inventor will need the services of a patent attorney, a highly specialized practitioner. The attorney will help develop the required **specification**, a description of the invention that gives enough detail so that one skilled in the art will be able to make and use the invention. After receiving an application, a PTO examiner will search the records and accept or reject the claim. Usually, the attorney will negotiate with the examiner and will rewrite and refine the application until it is accepted. A rejection may be appealed, first to the PTO's Board of Appeals and then, if that fails, to the federal district court in the District of Columbia or to the US Court of Appeals for the Federal Circuit, the successor court to the old US Court of Customs and Patent Appeals.

Once a patent application has been filed, the inventor or a company to which she has assigned the invention may put the words "patent pending" on the invention. These words have no legal effect. Anyone is free to make the invention as long as the patent has not yet been issued. But they do put others on notice that a patent has been applied for. Once the patent has been granted, infringers may be sued even if the infringed has made the product and offered it for sale before the patent was granted.

In today's global market, obtaining a US patent is important but is not usually sufficient protection. The inventor will often need to secure patent protection in other countries as well. Under the Paris Convention for the Protection of Industrial Property (1883), parties in one country can file for patent or trademark protection in any of the other member countries (172 countries as of 2011). The World Trade Organization's Agreement on Trade-Related Aspects of Intellectual Property Rights (TRIPS) established standards for protecting intellectual property rights (patents, trademarks, and copyrights) and provides that each member nation must have laws that protect intellectual property rights with effective access to judicial systems for pursuing civil and criminal penalties for violations of such rights.

Patent Ownership

The patent holder is entitled to make and market the invention and to exclude others from doing so. Because the patent is a species of property, it may be transferred. The inventor may assign part or all of his interest in the patent or keep the property interest and license others to manufacture or use the invention in return for payments known as royalties. The license may be exclusive with one licensee, or the inventor may license many to exploit the invention. One important limitation on the inventor's right to the patent interest is the so-called shop right. This is a right created by state courts on equitable grounds giving employers a nonexclusive royalty-free license to use any invention made by an employee on company time and with company materials. The shop right comes into play only when a company has no express or implied understanding with its employees. Most corporate laboratories have contractual agreements with employees about who owns the invention and what royalties will be paid.

Infringement and Invalidity Suits

Suits for patent infringement can arise in three ways: (1) the patent holder may seek damages and an injunction against the infringer in federal court, requesting damages for royalties and lost profits as well; (2) even before being sued, the accused party may take the patent holder to court under the federal Declaratory Judgment Act, seeking a court declaration that the patent is invalid; (3) the patent holder may sue a licensee for royalties claimed to be due, and the licensee may counterclaim that the patent is invalid. Such a suit, if begun in state court, may be removed to federal court.

In a federal patent infringement lawsuit, the court may grant the winning party reimbursement for attorneys' fees and costs. If the infringement is adjudged to be intentional, the court can triple the amount of damages awarded. Prior to 2006, courts were typically granting permanent injunctions to prevent future infringement. Citing *eBay, Inc. v. Merc Exchange, LLC*,[10] the Supreme

Court ruled that patent holders are not automatically entitled to a permanent injunction against infringement during the life of the patent. Courts have the discretion to determine whether justice requires a permanent injunction, and they may conclude that the public interest and equitable principles may be better satisfied with compensatory damages only.

Proving infringement can be a difficult task. Many companies employ engineers to "design around" a patent product—that is, to seek ways to alter the product to such an extent that the substitute product no longer consists of enough of the elements of the invention safeguarded by the patent. However, infringing products, processes, or machines need not be identical; as the Supreme Court said in *Sanitary Refrigerator Co. v. Winers*,[11] "one device is an infringement of another...if two devices do the same work in substantially the same way, and accomplish substantially the same result...even though they differ in name, form, or shape." This is known as the **doctrine of equivalents.** In an infringement suit, the court must choose between these two extremes: legitimate "design around" and infringement through some equivalent product.

doctrine of equivalents

The judicial doctrine that infringing products, processes, or machines need not be identical.

An infringement suit can often be dangerous because the defendant will almost always assert in its answer that the patent is invalid. The plaintiff patent holder thus runs the risk that his entire patent will be taken away from him if the court agrees. In ruling on validity, the court may consider all the tests, such as prior art and obviousness, discussed in Section 1 and rule on these independently of the conclusions drawn by the PTO.

Patent Misuse

Although a patent is a monopoly granted to the inventor or his assignee or licensee, the monopoly power is legally limited. An owner who misuses the patent may find that he will lose an infringement suit. One common form of misuse is to tie the patented good to some unpatented one—for example, a patented movie projector that will not be sold unless the buyer agrees to rent films supplied only by the manufacturer of the movie projector, or a copier manufacturer that requires buyers to purchase plain paper from it. As we will see in Chapter 48, various provisions of the federal antitrust laws, including, specifically, Section 3 of the Clayton Act, outlaw some of these so-called "tying arrangements." Another form of patent misuse is a provision in the licensing agreement prohibiting the manufacturer from also making competing products. Although the courts have held against several other types of misuse, the general principle is that the owner may not use his patent to restrain trade in unpatented goods.

Key Takeaway

Many different "things" are patentable, include gene sequences, business processes, and any other "useful invention." The US Patent and Trademark Office acts on initial applications and may grant a patent to an applicant. The patent, which allows a limited-time monopoly, is for twenty years. The categories of patentable things include processes, machines, manufactures, compositions of matter, and improvements. Ideas, mental processes, naturally occurring substances, methods of doing business, printed matter, and scientific principles cannot be patented. Patent holders may sue for infringement and royalties from an infringer user.

Exercises

1. Calera, Inc. discovers a way to capture carbon dioxide emissions at a California power plant and use them to make cement. This is a win for the power company, which needs to reduce its carbon dioxide emissions, and a win for Calera. Calera decides to patent this invention. What kind of patent would this be?

2. In your opinion, what is the benefit of allowing companies to isolate genetic material and claim a patent? What kind of patent would this be?
3. How could a "garage inventor," working on her own, protect a patentable invention while yet demonstrating it to a large company that could bring the invention to market?

32.2 Trade Secrets

Learning Objectives

1. Describe the difference between trade secrets and patents, and explain why a firm might prefer keeping a trade secret rather than obtaining a patent.
2. Understand the dimensions of corporate espionage and the impact of the federal Economic Espionage Act.

Definition of Trade Secrets

trade secret

A process, chemical formula, list, plan, or mechanism known only to an employer and those employees who need to know in order to use it in the business.

A patent is an invention publicly disclosed in return for a monopoly. A **trade secret** is a means to a monopoly that a company hopes to maintain by preventing public disclosure. Why not always take out a patent? There are several reasons. The trade secret might be one that is not patentable, such as a customer list or an improvement that does not meet the tests of novelty or nonobviousness. A patent can be designed around; but if the trade secret is kept, its owner will be the exclusive user of it. Patents are expensive to obtain, and the process is extremely time consuming. Patent protection expires in twenty years, after which anyone is free to use the invention, but a trade secret can be maintained for as long as the secret is kept.

However, a trade secret is valuable only so long as it is kept secret. Once it is publicly revealed, by whatever means, anyone is free to use it. The critical distinction between a patent and a trade secret is this: a patent gives its owner the right to enjoin anyone who infringes it from making use of it, whereas a trade secret is not public, as patents must be, and gives its "owner" the right to sue only the person who improperly took it or revealed it.

According to the Restatement of Torts, Section 757, Comment b, a trade secret may consist of

> *any formula, pattern, device or compilation of information which is used in one's business, and which gives him an opportunity to obtain an advantage over competitors who do not know or use it. It may be a formula for a chemical compound, a process of manufacturing, treating or preserving materials, a pattern for a machine or other device, or a list of customers....A trade secret is a process or device for continuous use in the operation of a business. Generally it relates to the production of goods, as, for example, a machine or formula for the production of an article.*

Other types of trade secrets are customer information, pricing data, marketing methods, sources of supply, and secret technical know-how.

Elements of Trade Secrets

To be entitled to protection, a trade secret must be (1) original and (2) secret.

Originality

The trade secret must have a certain degree of originality, although not as much as would be necessary to secure a patent. For example, a principle or technique that is common knowledge does not become a protectable trade secret merely because a particular company taught it to one of its employees who now wants to leave to work for a competitor.

Secrecy

Some types of information are obviously secret, like the chemical formula that is jealously guarded through an elaborate security system within the company. But other kinds of information might not be secret, even though essential to a company's business. For instance, a list of suppliers that can be gathered easily by reading through a telephone directory or a set of websites is not secret. Nor is a method secret simply because someone develops and uses it, if no steps are taken to guard it. A company that circulates a product description in its catalog may not claim a trade secret in the design of the product if the description permits someone to do "reverse engineering." A company that hopes to keep its processes and designs secret should affirmatively attempt to do so—for example, by requiring employees to sign a nondisclosure agreement covering the corporate trade secrets with which they work. However, a company need not go to every extreme to guard a trade secret.

Trade-secrets espionage has become a big business. To protect industrial secrets, US corporations spend billions on security arrangements. The line between competitive intelligence gathering and espionage can sometimes be difficult to draw. The problem is by no means confined to the United States; companies and nations all over the world have become concerned about theft of trade secrets to gain competitive advantage, and foreign governments are widely believed to be involved in espionage and cyberattacks.

Economic Espionage Act

The Economic Espionage Act (EEA) of 1996 makes the theft or misappropriation of a trade secret a federal crime. The act is aimed at protecting commercial information rather than classified national defense information. Two sorts of activities are criminalized. The first section of the act[12] criminalizes the misappropriation of trade secrets (including conspiracy to misappropriate trade secrets and the subsequent acquisition of such misappropriated trade secrets) with the knowledge or intent that the theft will benefit a foreign power. Penalties for violation are fines of up to US$500,000 per offense and imprisonment of up to fifteen years for individuals, and fines of up to US$10 million for organizations. In 2007, Xiadong Meng pleaded guilty to violating the Economic Espionage Act by possessing a trade secret belonging to Quantum3D, a San Jose company at which he was formerly employed. The prosecutor alleged that Meng intended and knew that this would benefit the People's Republic of China ("PRC") Navy Research Center. The trade secret, known as "Mantis," was a Quantum3D product used to simulate real world motion for military training purposes.

The second section[13] criminalizes the misappropriation of trade secrets related to or included in a product that is produced for or placed in interstate (including international) commerce, with the knowledge or intent that the misappropriation will injure the owner of the trade secret. Penalties for violation are imprisonment for up to ten years for individuals (no fines) and fines of up to

US$5 million for organizations. Timothy Kissane received a sentence for stealing computer source code form an employer; he had planned to sell it to the company's competitors.

In addition to these specific penalties, the fourth section of the EEA[14] also requires criminal forfeiture of (1) any proceeds of the crime and property derived from proceeds of the crime and (2) any property used, or intended to be used, in commission of the crime.

The EEA authorizes civil proceedings by the Department of Justice to enjoin violations of the act but does not create a private cause of action. This means that anyone believing they have been victimized must go through the U.S. attorney general in order to obtain an injunction.

The EEA is limited to the United States and has no extraterritorial application unless (1) the offender is a U.S. company, or, a citizen operating from abroad against a U.S. company or (2) an act in furtherance of the espionage takes place in the United States. Other nations lack such legislation, and some may actively support industrial espionage using both their national intelligence services. The U.S. Office of the National Counterintelligence Executive publishes an annual report, mandated by the U.S. Congress, on foreign economic collection and industrial espionage, which outlines these espionage activities of many foreign nations.

President Obama made cyber-hacking an issue with the People's Republic of China. In 2014, the Administration brought charges for the first time against a state actor for cyber-espionage including theft of trade secrets. The U.S. government has alleged that five Chinese Officials stole valuable information from a number of U.S. companies. The indictment included charges of stealing confidential and proprietary technical and design specifications for pipes, pipe supports, and pipe routing for a Westinghouse Power Plant; stealing confidential information from SolarWorld regarding their cash flow, manufacturing metrics, production line, and costs; installing malware on U.S. Steel computers in an attempt to identify and exploit vulnerable servers; stealing network credentials for nearly every ATI employee; stealing e-mails from senior USW employees containing sensitive information about USW strategies related to pending trade disputes with China; and stealing emails from Alcoa pertaining to an agreement between Alcoa and a Chinese State Owned Enterprise.

Right of Employees to Use Trade Secrets

A perennial source of lawsuits in the trade secrets arena is the employee who is hired away by a competitor, allegedly taking trade secrets along with him. Companies frequently seek to prevent piracy by requiring employees to sign confidentiality agreements. An agreement not to disclose particular trade secrets learned or developed on the job is generally enforceable. Even without an agreement, an employer can often prevent disclosure under principles of agency law. Sections 395 and 396 of the Restatement (Second) of Agency suggest that it is an actionable breach of duty to disclose to third persons information given confidentially during the course of the agency. However, every person is held to have a right to earn a living. If the rule were strictly applied, a highly skilled person who went to another company might be barred from using his knowledge and skills. The courts do not prohibit people from using elsewhere the general knowledge and skills they developed on the job. Only specific trade secrets are protected.

To get around this difficulty, some companies require their employees to sign agreements not to compete. But unless the agreements are limited in scope and duration to protect a company against only specific misuse of trade secrets, they are unenforceable.

Key Takeaway

Trade secrets, if they can be kept, have indefinite duration and thus greater potential value than patents. Trade secrets can be any formula, pattern, device, process, or compilation of information to be used in a business. Customer information, pricing data, marketing methods, sources of supply, and technical know-how could all be trade secrets. State law has protected trade secrets, and federal law has provided criminal sanctions for theft of trade secrets. With the importance of digitized information, methods of theft now include computer hacking; theft of corporate secrets is a burgeoning global business that often involves cyberattacks.

Exercises

1. Wu Dang, based in Hong Kong, hacks into the Hewlett-Packard database and "steals" plans and specifications for HP's latest products. The HP server is located in the United States. He sells this information to a Chinese company in Shanghai. Has he violated the US Economic Espionage Act?
2. What are the advantages of keeping a formula as a trade secret rather than getting patent protection?

32.3 Copyright

Learning Objectives

1. Describe and explain copyrights, how to obtain one, and how they differ from trademarks.
2. Explain the concept of fair use and describe its limits.

Definition and Duration

Copyright is the legal protection given to "authors" for their "writings." Copyright law is federal; like patent law, its source lies in the Constitution. Copyright protects the expression of ideas in some tangible form, but it does not protect the ideas themselves. For example, the basic idea in the films *Freaky Friday*, *Dream a Little Dream*, and *Like Father Like Son* is that there is a comedic "body swap" of some sort (sister and sister, or parent and child) but the expressions of this basic idea are different, and so there is no copyright infringement.

Under the 1976 Copyright Act as amended, a copyright in any work created after January 1, 1978, begins when the work is fixed in tangible form—for example, when a book is written down or a picture is painted—and generally lasts for the life of the author plus 70 years after his or her death. If there is co-authorship, the 70 years begins after the death of the second author. This is similar to copyright protection in many countries, but in some countries, the length of copyright protection is the life of the author plus 50 years.

For copyrights owned by corporations such as publishing houses, done as works for hire, common copyright expires 95 years from the date of publication or 120 years from the date of creation, whichever is first. For works created before 1978, such as many of Walt Disney's movies and cartoons, the U.S. Sonny Bono Copyright Term Extension Act of 1998 provided additional protection of up to 95 years from publication date. Thus, works created in 1923 by Disney would not enter the public domain until 2019 or after, unless the copyright had expired prior to 1998 or unless the Disney company released the work into the public domain. In general, after expiration of the copyright, the work enters the **public domain**.

public domain

Once a copyright has expired, the material enters the public domain, meaning that no one can claim exclusive rights in the material.

In 1989, the United States signed the Berne Convention, an international copyright treaty. This law eliminated the need to place the symbol © or the word *Copyright* or the abbreviation *Copr.* on the work itself. Copyrights can be registered with the U.S. Copyright Office in Washington, DC.

Protected Expression

The Copyright Act protects a variety of "writings," some of which may not seem written at all. These include literary works (books, newspapers, and magazines), music, drama, choreography, films, art, sculpture, and sound recordings. Since copyright covers the expression and not the material or physical object, a book may be copyrighted whether it is on paper, microfilm, tape, or computer disk.

Rights Protected by the Copyright Act

Preventing Copying

A copyright gives its holder the right to prevent others from copying his or her work. The copyright holder has the exclusive right to reproduce the work in any medium (paper, film, sound recording), to perform it (e.g., in the case of a play), or to display it (a painting or film). A copyright also gives its holder the exclusive right to prepare derivative works based on the copyrighted work. Thus a playwright could not adapt to the stage a novelist's book without the latter's permission.

Fair Use

fair use doctrine

Use of copyrighted material in criticism, comment, news reporting, teaching (including multiple copies for classroom use), scholarship, or research that does not significantly reduce the market for the copyrighted material.

One major exception to the exclusivity of copyrights is the **fair use doctrine**. Section 107 of the Copyright Act provides as follows:

> *Fair use of a copyrighted work, including such use by reproduction in copies or phonorecords or by any other means specified by section 106 of the copyright, for purposes such as criticism, comment, news reporting, teaching (including multiple copies for classroom use), scholarship, or research, is not an infringement of copyright. In determining whether the use made of a work in any particular case is a fair use, the factors to be considered shall include–*
>
> *(1) the purpose and character of the use, including whether such use is of a commercial nature or is for nonprofit educational purposes;*
>
> *(2) the nature of the copyrighted work;*
>
> *(3) the amount and substantiality of the portion used in relation to the copyrighted work as a whole; and*
>
> *(4) the effect of the use upon the potential market for or value of the copyrighted work.*[15]

These are broad guidelines. Any copying could potentially be an infringement, and fair use could become a question of fact on a case-by-case basis. In determining fair use, however, courts have often considered the fourth factor (effect of the use upon the potential market for the copyrighted work) to be the most important.

Clear examples of fair use would be when book reviewers or writers quote passages from copyrighted books. Without fair use, most writing would be useless because it could not readily be discussed. But the doctrine of fair use grew more troublesome with the advent of plain-paper copiers and is now even more troublesome with electronic versions of copyrighted materials that are easily copied and distributed. The 1976 act took note of the new copier technology, listing "teaching (including multiple copies for classroom use)" as one application of fair use. The Copyright Office follows guidelines specifying just how far the copying may go—for example, multiple copies of certain works may be made for classroom use, but copies may not be used to substitute for copyrighted anthologies.

Infringement

Verbatim use of a copyrighted work is easily provable. The more difficult question arises when the copyrighted work is altered in some way. As in patent law, the standard is one of substantial similarity. Courts may enjoin further infringement from the defendant, order destruction of the infringing material, and require the defendant/infringer to pay damages, profits earned, and attorney's fees.

Courts will look at four factors to determine the appropriate amount of statutory damages: (1) the infringer's profits and expenses saved because of the infringement; (2) the plaintiff's lost revenues; (3) the strong public interest in ensuring the integrity of copyright laws; and (4) whether the infringer acted willfully. In a case involving 12 photographic images of cats and dogs copyrighted by Getty Images, the defendant (who was offering web-based designs for veterinary clinics) was ordered to pay damages in excess of $200,000, largely because of willful infringement.

A copyright owner suing for infringement must show that the copyright is registered with the Copyright Office, or that the owner's nation is a member of the Berne Convention[16]. "Actual damages" or "statutory damages" may be recovered by the copyright owner where infringement is proven. Any actual damage can be increased by the amount of the gross profits the infringer has made. The infringer has the burden of proving any deductible expenses and any "elements of profit attributable to factors other than the copyrighted work."

The copyright owner may alternatively elect, at any time before a final judgment, a sum of not less than $750 nor more than $30,000, at the discretion of the presiding judge. In cases of "willful infringement," the court may also award additional statutory damages of not more than $150,000. But if the infringer can demonstrate that the infringement was not intentional, the court may reduce the award of statutory damages to a sum of not less than $200.

Aside from damages, copyright owners can also ask for injunctions and the impounding and possible destruction of infringing articles.

Copyrightability Standards

To be subject to copyright, the writing must be "fixed" in some "tangible medium of expression." A novelist who composes a chapter of her next book in her mind and tells it to a friend before putting it on paper could not stop the friend from rushing home, writing it down, and selling it (at least the federal copyright law would offer no protection; some states might independently offer a legal remedy, however).

The work also must be creative, at least to a minimal degree. Words and phrases, such as names, titles, and slogans, are not copyrightable; nor are symbols or designs familiar to the public. But an author who contributes her own creativity—like taking a photograph of nature—may copyright the resulting work, even if the basic elements of the composition were not of her making.

Finally, the work must be "original," which means simply that it must have originated with the author. The law does not require that it be novel or unique. This requirement was summarized by Judge Learned Hand: "If by some magic a man who had never known it were to compose anew Keats's "Ode on a Grecian Urn," he would be an author, and, if he copyrighted it, others might not copy that poem, though they might of course copy Keats's."[17] Sometimes the claim is made that a composer, for example, just happened to compose a tune identical or strikingly similar to a copyrighted song; rather than assume the unlikely coincidence that Judge Hand hypothesized, the courts will look for evidence that the alleged copier had access to the copyrighted song. If he did—for example, the song was frequently played on the air—he cannot defend the copying with the claim that it was unconscious, because the work would not then have been original. In 2016, a federal court decided that Led Zeppelin's use of certain thematic material from Spirit's song, "Taurus" was not a copyright infringement; in that case, there was plenty of evidence that Led Zeppelin had access—the band had done a cover of a song that was on the same Spirit album as Taurus—but still, the degree of similarity was not so close as to call for a copyright violation.[18]

Section 102 of the Copyright Act excludes copyright protection for any "idea, procedure, process, system, method of operation, concept, principle, or discovery, regardless of the form in which it is described, explained, illustrated, or embodied."[19]

Einstein copyrighted books and monographs he wrote on the theory of relativity, but he could not copyright the famous formula $E = mc^2$, nor could he prevent others from writing about the theory. But he could protect the particular way in which his ideas were expressed. In general, facts widely known by the public are not copyrightable, and mathematical calculations are not copyrightable. Compilations of facts may be copyrightable, if the way that they are coordinated or arranged results in a work that shows some originality. For example, compiled information about yachts listed for sale may qualify for copyright protection.[20]

One of the most troublesome recent questions concerning expression versus ideas is whether a computer program may be copyrighted. After some years of uncertainty, the courts have accepted the copyrightability of computer programs.[21] Now the courts are wrestling with the more difficult question of the scope of protection: what constitutes an "idea" and what constitutes its mere "expression" in a program.

How far the copyright law will protect particular software products is a hotly debated topic, sparked by a federal district court's ruling in 1990 that the "look and feel" of Lotus 1-2-3's menu system is copyrightable and was in fact infringed by Paperback Software's VP-Planner, a competing spreadsheet.[22] The case has led some analysts to "fear that legal code, rather than software code, is emerging as the factor that will determine which companies and products will dominate the 1990s."[23]

Who May Obtain a Copyright?

With one important exception, only the author may hold the initial copyright, although the author may assign it or license any one or more of the rights conveyed by the copyright. This is a simple principle when the author has written a book or painted a picture. But the law is unclear in the case of a motion picture or a sound recording. Is the author the script writer, the producer, the performer, the director, the engineer, or someone else? As a practical matter, all parties involved spell out their rights by contract.

The exception, which frequently covers the difficulties just enumerated, is for works for hire. Any person employed to write—a journalist or an advertising jingle writer, for example—is not the "author." For purposes of the statute, the employer is the author and may take out the copyright. When the employee is in fact an "independent contractor" and the work in question involves any one of nine types (book, movies, etc.) spelled out in the Copyright Act, the employer and the creator must spell out their entitlement to the copyright in a written agreement.[24]

Obtaining a Copyright

Until 1978, a work could not be copyrighted unless it was registered in the Copyright Office or was published and unless each copy of the work carried a copyright notice, consisting of the word *Copyright*, the abbreviation *Copr.*, or the common symbol ©, together with the date of first publication and the name of the copyright owner. Under the 1976 act, copyright became automatic whenever the work was fixed in a tangible medium of expression (e.g., words on paper, images on film or videotape, sound on tape or compact disc), even if the work remained unpublished or undistributed. However, to retain copyright protection, the notice had to be affixed once the work was "published" and copies circulated to the public. After the United States entered the Berne Convention, an international treaty governing copyrights, Congress enacted the Berne Implementation Act, declaring that, effective in 1989, notice, even after publication, was no longer required.

Notice does, however, confer certain benefits. In the absence of notice, a copyright holder loses the right to receive statutory damages (an amount stated in the Copyright Act and not required to be proved) if someone infringes the work. Also, although it is no longer required, an application and two copies of the work (for deposit in the Library of Congress) filed with the Copyright Office, in Washington, DC, will enable the copyright holder to file suit should the copyright be infringed. Unlike patent registration, which requires elaborate searching of Patent and Trademark Office (PTO) records, copyright registration does not require a reading of the work to determine whether it is an original creation or an infringement of someone else's prior work. But copyright registration does not immunize the holder from an infringement suit. If a second work has been unlawfully copied from an earlier work, the second author's copyright will not bar the infringed author from collecting damages and obtaining an injunction.

Computer Downloads and the Digital Millennium Copyright Act

The ubiquity of the Internet and the availability of personal computers with large capacities have greatly impacted the music business. Sharing of music files took off in the late 1990s with Napster, which lost a legal battle on copyright and had to cease doing business. By providing the means by which individuals could copy music that had been purchased, major record labels were losing substantial profits. Grokster, a privately owned software company based in the West Indies, provided peer-to-peer file sharing from 2001 to 2005 until the US Supreme Court's decision in *MGM Studios, Inc. v. Grokster, Ltd.*[25]

For computers with the Microsoft operating system, the Court disallowed the peer-to-peer file sharing, even though Grokster claimed it did not violate any copyright laws because no files passed through its computers. (Grokster had assigned certain user computers as "root supernodes" that acted as music hubs for the company and was not directly involved in controlling any specific music-file downloads.)

Grokster had argued, based on *Sony v. Universal Studios,*[26] that the sale of its copying equipment (like the Betamax videocassette recorders at issue in that case) did not constitute contributory infringement "if the product is widely used for legitimate, unobjectionable purposes." Plaintiffs successfully argued that the Sony safe-harbor concept requires proof that the noninfringing use is the primary use in terms of the product's utility.

The Digital Millennium Copyright Act (DMCA), passed into law in 1998, implements two 1996 treaties of the World Intellectual Property Organization. It criminalizes production and sale of devices or services intended to get around protective measures that control access to copyrighted works. In addition, the DMCA heightens the penalties for copyright infringement on the Internet. The DMCA amended Title 17 of the United States Code to extend the reach of copyright, while limiting the liability of the providers of online services for copyright infringement by their users.

Key Takeaway

Copyright is the legal protection given to "authors" for their "writings." It protects ideas in fixed, tangible form, not ideas themselves. Copyright protection can extend as long as 120 years from the date of creation or publication. Expression found in literary works, music, drama, film, art, sculpture, sound recordings, and the like may be copyrighted. The fair use doctrine limits the exclusivity of copyright in cases where scholars, critics, or teachers use only selected portions of the copyrighted material in a way that is unlikely to affect the potential market for or value of the copyrighted work.

Exercises

1. An author wrote a novel, *Brunch at Bruno's*, in 1961. She died in 1989, and her heirs now own the copyright. When do the rights of the heirs come to an end? That is, when does *Brunch at Bruno's* enter the public domain?
2. Keith Bradsher writes a series of articles on China for the *New York Times* and is paid for doing so. Suppose he wants to leave the employ of the *Times* and be a freelance writer. Can he compile his best articles into a book, *Changing Times in China*, and publish it without the *New York Times*'s permission? Does it matter that he uses the word *Times* in his proposed title?
3. What kind of file sharing of music is now entirely legal? Shaunese Collins buys a Yonder Mountain String Band CD at a concert at Red Rocks in Morrison, Colorado. With her computer, she makes a series of CDs for her friends. She does this six times. Has she committed six copyright violations?

32.4 Trademarks

Learning Objectives

1. Understand what a trademark is and why it deserves protection.
2. Know why some "marks" may not be eligible for trademark protection, and how to obtain trademark protection for those that are.
3. Explain what "blurring" and "tarnishment" are and what remedies are available to the holder of the mark.

Definitions of Trademarks

A trademark is defined in the federal Lanham Act of 1946 as "any word, name, symbol, or device or any combination thereof adopted and used by a manufacturer or merchant to identify his goods and distinguish them from goods manufactured or sold by others."[27]

Examples of well-known trademarks are Coca-Cola, Xerox, and Apple. A **service mark** is used in the sale or advertising of services to identify the services of one person and distinguish them from the services of others. Examples of service marks are McDonald's, BP, and Hilton. A **certification mark** is used in connection with many products "to certify regional or other origin, material, mode of manufacture, quality, accuracy or other characteristics of such goods or services or that the work or labor on the goods or services was performed by members of a union or other organization." Examples are the Good Housekeeping Seal of Approval and UL (Underwriters Laboratories, Inc., approval mark). Unlike other forms of trademark, the owner of the certification mark (e.g., Good Housekeeping, or the Forest Stewardship Council's FSC mark) is not the owner of the underlying product.

service mark

Used in the sale or advertising of services to identify the services of one person and distinguish them from the services of others.

certification mark

A mark placed on a product or used in connection with a service that signifies the product or service as having met the standard set by the certifying entity.

Extent of Trademark Protection

Kinds of Marks

Trademarks and other kinds of marks may consist of words and phrases, pictures, symbols, shapes, numerals, letters, slogans, and sounds. Trademarks are a part of our everyday world: the sounds of a radio or television network announcing itself (NBC, BBC), the shape of a whiskey bottle (Haig & Haig's Pinch Bottle), a series of initials (GE, KPMG, IBM), or an animal's warning growl (MGM's lion).

Limitations on Marks

Although trademarks abound, the law limits the subjects that may fall into one of the defined categories. Not every word or shape or symbol will be protected in an infringement action. To qualify for protection, a trademark must be used to identify and distinguish. The courts employ a four-part test: (1) Is the mark so arbitrary and fanciful that it merits the widest protection? (2) Is it "suggestive" enough to warrant protection without proof of secondary meaning? (3) Is it "descriptive," warranting protection if secondary meaning is proved? (4) Is the mark generic and thus unprotectable?

These tests do not have mechanical answers; they call for judgment. Some marks are wholly fanciful, clearly identify origin of goods, and distinguish them from others—Kodak, for example. Other marks may not be so arbitrary but may nevertheless be distinctive, either when adopted or as a result of advertising—for example, Crest, as the name of a toothpaste.

Marks that are merely descriptive of the product are entitled to protection only if it can be shown that the mark has acquired **secondary meaning**. This term reflects a process of identification on the mark in the public mind with the originator of the product. Holiday Inn was initially deemed too descriptive: an inn where people might go on holiday. But over time, travelers came to identify the source of the "Great Sign" and the name Holiday Inn as the Holiday Inn Corporation in Memphis, and secondary meaning was granted. Holiday Inn could thus protect its mark against other innkeepers, hoteliers, and such; however, the trademark protection for the words Holiday Inn was limited to the corporation's hotel and motel business, and no other.

secondary meaning

A descriptive or generic word or phrase that would otherwise not qualify for trademark protection may be eligible once it acquires secondary meaning—that is, that the origin of the goods or services becomes identified with a particular source or provider and the mark makes that connection in the public's mind.

Certain words and phrases may not qualify at all for trademark protection. These include generic terms like "straw broom" (for a broom made of straw) and ordinary words like "fast food." In one case, a federal appeals court held that the word "Lite" is generic and cannot be protected by a beer manufacturer to describe a low-calorie brew.[28] Donald Trump's effort to trademark "You're fired!" (from the television show, *The Apprentice*) and Paris Hilton's desire to trademark "That's hot!" were also dismissed as being generic.

Deceptive words will not be accepted for registration. Thus the US Patent and Trademark Office (PTO) denied registration to the word *Vynahyde* because it suggested that the plastic material to which it was applied came from animal skin. Geographic terms are descriptive words and may not be used as protected trademarks unless they have acquired a secondary meaning, such as Hershey when used for chocolates. (Hershey's chocolates are made in Hershey, Pennsylvania.) A design that reflects a common style cannot be protected in a trademark to exclude other similar designs in the same tradition. Thus the courts have ruled that a silverware pattern that is a "functional feature" of the "baroque style" does not qualify for trademark protection. Finally, the Lanham Act denies federal registration to certain marks that fall within categories of words and shapes, including the following: the flag; the name, portrait, or signature of any living person without consent, or of a deceased US president during the lifetime of his widow; and immoral, deceptive, or scandalous matter (in an earlier era, the phrase "Bubby Trap" for brassieres was denied registration).

Dilution, Tarnishment, and Blurring

Under the federal Trademark Dilution Act of 1995, companies with marks that dilute the value of a senior mark may be liable for damages. The act provides that owners of marks of significant value have property rights that should not be eroded, blurred, tarnished, or diluted in any way by another. But as a plaintiff, the holder of the mark must show (1) that it is a famous mark, (2) that the use of a similar mark is commercial, and (3) that such use causes dilution of the distinctive quality of the mark. Thus, a T-shirt maker who promotes a red-and-white shirt bearing the mark Buttweiser may be liable to Anheuser-Busch, or a pornographic site called Candyland could be liable to Parker Brothers, the board game company. Interesting cases have already been brought under this act, including a case brought by Victoria's Secret against a small adult store in Kentucky called Victor's Little Secret. Notice that unlike most prior trademark law, the purpose is not to protect the consumer from confusion as to the source or origin of the goods or services being sold; for example, no one going to the Candyland site would think that Parker Brothers was the source.

Acquiring Trademark Rights

In 1988, for the first time in over forty years, Congress changed the way in which trademarks can be secured. Under the Lanham Act, the fundamental means of obtaining a trademark was through use. The manufacturer or distributor actually must have placed the mark on its product—or on related displays, labels, shipping containers, advertisements, and the like—and then have begun selling the product. If the product was sold in interstate commerce, the trademark was entitled to protection under the Lanham Act (or if not, to protection under the common law of the state in which the product was sold).

opposition proceeding

Those who feel that their own marks would be hurt by registration of a proposed mark may file an opposition proceeding in the US Patent and Trademark Office.

Under the Trademark Law Revision Act of 1988, which went into effect in 1989, trademarks can be obtained in advance by registering with the PTO an intention to use the mark within six months (the applicant can gain extensions of up to thirty more months to put the mark into use). Once obtained, the trademark will be protected for ten years (before the 1988 revision, a federal trademark remained valid for twenty years); if after that time the mark is still being used, the registration can be renewed. Obtaining a trademark registration lies between obtaining patents and obtaining copyrights in difficulty. The PTO will not routinely register a trademark; it searches its records to ensure that the mark meets several statutory tests and does not infringe another mark. Those who feel that their own marks would be hurt by registration of a proposed mark may file an **opposition proceeding** with the PTO. Until 1990, the office received about 77,000 applications each year. With the change in procedure, some experts predicted that applications would rise by 30 percent.

In many foreign countries, use need not be shown to obtain trademark registration. It is common for some people in these countries to register marks that they expect to be valuable so that they can sell the right to use the mark to the company that established the mark's value. Companies that expect to market abroad should register their marks early.

Loss of Rights

Trademark owners may lose their rights if they abandon the mark, if a patent or copyright expires on which the mark is based, or if the mark becomes generic. A mark is abandoned if a company goes out of business and ceases selling the product. Some marks are based on design patents; when the patent expires, the patent holder will not be allowed to extend the patent's duration by arguing that the design or name linked with the design is a registrable trademark.

The most widespread difficulty that a trademark holder faces is the prospect of too much success: if a trademark comes to stand generically for the product itself, it may lose exclusivity in the mark. Famous examples are aspirin, escalator, and cellophane. The threat is a continual one. Trademark holders can protect themselves from their marks' becoming generic in several ways.

1. Use a descriptive term along with the trademark. Look on a jar of Vaseline and you will see that the label refers to the contents as Vaseline petroleum jelly.
2. Protest generic use of the mark in all publications by writing letters and taking out advertisements.
3. Always put the words Trademark, Registered Trademark, or the symbol ® (meaning "registered") next to the mark itself, which should be capitalized.

Key Takeaway

Trademark protection is federal, under the Lanham Act. Branding of corporate logos, names, and products is essential to business success, and understanding trademarks is pivotal to branding. A "mark" must be distinctive, arbitrary, or fanciful to merit protection: this means that it must not be generic or descriptive. Marks can be words, symbols, pictures, slogans, sounds, phrases, and even shapes. In the United States, rights to marks are obtained by registration and intent to use in commerce and must be renewed every ten years.

Exercises

1. How will Google protect its trademark, assuming that people begin using "Google" as a verb substitute for "Internet search," just like people began using the word "cellophane" for all brands of plastic wrap?
2. Do a small amount of web searching and find out what "trade dress" protection is, and how it differs from trademark protection.
3. LexisNexis is a brand for a database collection offered by Mead Data Central. Lexus is a high-end automobile. Can Lexus succeed in getting Mead Data Central to stop using "Lexis" as a mark?

32.5 Cases

Fair Use in Copyright

Elvis Presley Enterprises et al. v. Passport Video et al.
349 F.3d 622 (9th Circuit Court of Appeals, 2003)

TALLMAN, CIRCUIT JUDGE:

Plaintiffs are a group of companies and individuals holding copyrights in various materials relating to Elvis Presley. For example, plaintiff SOFA Entertainment, Inc., is the registered owner of several Elvis appearances on *The Ed Sullivan Show*. Plaintiff Promenade Trust owns the copyright to two television specials featuring Elvis: *The Elvis 1968 Comeback Special* and *Elvis Aloha from Hawaii*. * * * Many Plaintiffs are in the business of licensing their copyrights. For example, SOFA Entertainment charges $10,000 per minute for use of Elvis' appearances on *The Ed Sullivan Show*.

Passport Entertainment and its related entities (collectively "Passport") produced and sold *The Definitive Elvis*, a 16-hour video documentary about the life of Elvis Presley. *The Definitive Elvis* sold for $99 at retail. Plaintiffs allege that thousands of copies were sent to retail outlets and other distributors. On its box, *The Definitive Elvis* describes itself as an all-encompassing, in-depth look at the life and career of a man whose popularity is unrivaled in the history of show business and who continues to attract millions of new fans each year. * * *

The Definitive Elvis uses Plaintiffs' copyrighted materials in a variety of ways. With the video footage, the documentary often uses shots of Elvis appearing on television while a narrator or interviewee talks over the film. These clips range from only a few seconds in length to portions running as long as 30 seconds. In some instances, the clips are the subject of audio commentary, while in other instances they would more properly be characterized as video "filler" because the commentator is discussing a subject different from or more general than Elvis' performance on a particular television show. But also significant is the frequency with which the copyrighted video footage is used. *The Definitive Elvis* employs these clips, in many instances, repeatedly. In total, at least 5% to 10% of *The Definitive Elvis* uses Plaintiffs' copyrighted materials.

Use of the video footage, however, is not limited to brief clips. * * * Thirty-five percent of his appearances on *The Ed Sullivan Show* is replayed, as well as three minutes from *The 1968 Comeback Special*. * * *

Plaintiffs sued Passport for copyright infringement....Passport, however, asserts that its use of the copyrighted materials was "fair use" under 17 U.S.C. § 107. Plaintiffs moved for a preliminary injunction, which was granted by the district court after a hearing. The district court found that Passport's use of Plaintiffs' copyrighted materials was likely not fair use. The court enjoined Passport from selling or distributing *The Definitive Elvis*. Passport timely appeals.

* * *

We first address the purpose and character of Passport's use of Plaintiffs' copyrighted materials. Although not controlling, the fact that a new use is commercial as opposed to non-profit weighs against a finding of fair use. *Harper & Row Publishers, Inc. v. Nation Enters.*, 471 U.S. 539, 562, 85 L. Ed. 2d 588, 105 S.Ct. 2218 (1985). And the degree to which the new user exploits the copyright for commercial gain—as opposed to incidental use as part of a commercial enterprise—affects the weight we afford commercial nature as a factor. More importantly for the first fair-use factor, however, is the "transformative" nature of the new work. Specifically, we ask "whether the new work...merely supersedes the objects of the original creation, or instead adds something new, with a further purpose or different character, altering the first with new expression, meaning, or message...." The more transformative a new work, the less significant other inquiries, such as commercialism, become.

* * *

The district court below found that the purpose and character of *The Definitive Elvis* will likely weigh against a finding of fair use. We cannot say, based on this record, that the district court abused its discretion.

First, Passport's use, while a biography, is clearly commercial in nature. But more significantly, Passport seeks to profit directly from the copyrights it uses without a license. One of the most salient selling points on the box of *The Definitive Elvis* is that "Every Film and Television Appearance is represented." Passport is not advertising a scholarly critique or historical analysis, but instead seeks to profit at least in part from the inherent entertainment value of Elvis' appearances on such shows as *The Steve Allen Show*, *The Ed Sullivan Show*, and *The 1968 Comeback Special*. Passport's claim that this is scholarly research containing biographical comments on the life of Elvis is not dispositive of the fair use inquiry.

Second, Passport's use of Plaintiffs' copyrights is not consistently transformative. True, Passport's use of many of the television clips is transformative because the clips play for only a few seconds and are used for reference purposes while a narrator talks over them or interviewees explain their context in Elvis' career. But voice-overs do not necessarily transform a work....

It would be impossible to produce a biography of Elvis without showing some of his most famous television appearances for reference purposes. But some of the clips are played without much interruption, if any. The purpose of showing these clips likely goes beyond merely making a reference for a biography, but instead serves the same intrinsic entertainment value that is protected by Plaintiffs' copyrights.

* * *

The third factor is the amount and substantiality of the portion used in relation to the copyrighted work as a whole. This factor evaluates both the quantity of the work taken and the quality and importance of the portion taken. Regarding the quantity, copying "may not be excused merely because it is insubstantial with respect to the *infringing* work." *Harper & Row*, 471 U.S. at 565 (emphasis in original). But if the amount used is substantial with respect to the infringing work, it is evidence of the value of the copy-righted work.

Passport's use of clips from television appearances, although in most cases of short duration, were repeated numerous times throughout the tapes. While using a small number of clips to reference an event for biographical purposes seems fair, using a clip over and over will likely no longer serve a biographical purpose. Additionally, some of the clips were not short in length. Passport's use of Elvis' appearance on *The Steve Allen Show* plays for over a minute and many more clips play for more than just a few seconds.

Additionally, although the clips are relatively short when compared to the entire shows that are copyrighted, they are in many instances the heart of the work. What makes these copyrighted works valuable is Elvis' appearance on the shows, in many cases singing the most familiar passages of his most popular songs. Plaintiffs are in the business of licensing these copyrights. Taking key portions extracts the most valuable part of Plaintiffs' copyrighted works. With respect to the photographs, the entire picture is often used. The music, admittedly, is usually played only for a few seconds.

* * *

The last, and "undoubtedly the single most important" of all the factors, is the effect the use will have on the potential market for and value of the copyrighted works. *Harper & Row*, 471 U.S. at 566. We must "consider not only the extent of market harm caused by the particular actions of the alleged infringer, but also whether unrestricted and widespread conduct of the sort engaged in by the defendant...would result in a substantially adverse impact on the potential market for the original." *Campbell*, 510 U.S. at 590. The more transformative the new work, the less likely the new work's use of copyrighted materials will affect the market for the materials. Finally, if the purpose of the new work is commercial in nature, "the likelihood [of market harm] may be presumed." *A&M Records*, 239 F.3d at 1016 (quoting *Sony*, 464 U.S. at 451).

The district court found that Passport's use of Plaintiffs' copyrighted materials likely does affect the market for those materials. This conclusion was not clearly erroneous.

First, Passport's use is commercial in nature, and thus we can assume market harm. Second, Passport has expressly advertised that *The Definitive Elvis* contains the television appearances for which Plaintiffs normally charge a licensing fee. If this type of use became wide-spread, it would likely undermine the market for selling Plaintiffs' copyrighted material. This conclusion, however, does not apply to the music and still photographs. It seems unlikely that someone in the market for these materials would purchase *The Definitive Elvis* instead of a properly licensed product. Third, Passport's use of the television appearances was, in some instances, not transformative, and therefore these uses are likely to affect the market because they serve the same purpose as Plaintiffs' original works.

* * *

We emphasize that our holding today is not intended to express how we would rule were we examining the case *ab initio* as district judges. Instead, we confine our review to whether the district court abused its discretion when it weighed the four statutory fair-use factors together and determined that Plaintiffs would likely succeed on the merits. Although we might view this case as closer than the district court saw it, we hold there was no abuse of discretion in the court's decision to grant Plaintiffs' requested relief.

AFFIRMED.

Case Questions

1. How would you weigh the four factors in this case? If the trial court had found fair use, would the appeals court have overturned its ruling?
2. Why do you think that the fourth factor is especially important?
3. What is the significance of the discussion on "transformative" aspects of the defendant's product?

Trademark Infringement and Dilution

Playboy Enterprises v. Welles
279 F.3d 796 (9th Circuit Court of Appeals, 2001)

T. G. NELSON, Circuit Judge:

Terri Welles was on the cover of Playboy in 1981 and was chosen to be the Playboy Playmate of the Year for 1981. Her use of the title "Playboy Playmate of the Year 1981," and her use of other trademarked terms on her website are at issue in this suit. During the relevant time period, Welles' website offered information about and free photos of Welles, advertised photos for sale, advertised memberships in her photo club, and promoted her services as a spokesperson. A biographical section described Welles' selection as Playmate of the Year in 1981 and her years modeling for Playboy Enterprises Incorporated (PEI). The site included a disclaimer that read as follows: "This site is neither endorsed, nor sponsored, nor affiliated with Playboy Enterprises, Inc. PLAYBOY™, PLAYMATE OF THE YEAR™, and PLAYMATE OF THE MONTH™ are registered trademarks of Playboy Enterprises, Inc."

Wells used (1) the terms "Playboy "and "Playmate" in the metatags of the website; (2) the phrase "Playmate of the Year 1981" on the masthead of the website; (3) the phrases "Playboy Playmate of the Year 1981" and "Playmate of the Year 1981" on various banner ads, which may be transferred to other websites; and (4) the repeated use of the abbreviation "PMOY '81" as the watermark on the pages of the website. PEI claimed that these uses of its marks constituted trademark infringement, dilution, false designation of origin, and unfair competition. The district court granted defendants' motion for summary judgment. PEI appeals the grant of summary judgment on its infringement and dilution claims. We affirm in part and reverse in part.

A. Trademark Infringement

Except for the use of PEI's protected terms in the wallpaper of Welles' website, we conclude that Welles' uses of PEI's trademarks are permissible, nominative uses. They imply no current sponsorship or endorsement by PEI. Instead, they serve to identify Welles as a past PEI "Playmate of the Year."

We articulated the test for a permissible, nominative use in *New Kids On The Block v. New America Publishing, Inc.* The band, New Kids On The Block, claimed trademark infringement arising from the use of their trademarked name by several newspapers. The newspapers had conducted polls asking which member of the band New Kids On The Block was the best and most popular. The papers' use of the trademarked term did not fall within the traditional fair use doctrine. Unlike a traditional fair use scenario, the defendant newspaper was using the trademarked term to describe not its own product, but the plaintiff's. Thus, the factors used to evaluate fair use were inapplicable. The use was nonetheless permissible, we concluded, based on its nominative nature.

We adopted the following test for nominative use:

> *First, the product or service in question must be one not readily identifiable without use of the trademark; second, only so much of the mark or marks may be used as is reasonably necessary to identify the product or service; and third, the user must do nothing that would, in conjunction with the mark, suggest sponsorship or endorsement by the trademark holder.*

We group the uses of PEI's trademarked terms into three for the purpose of applying the test for nominative use.

1. Headlines and banner advertisements.

. . .

The district court properly identified Welles' situation as one which must... be excepted. No descriptive substitute exists for PEI's trademarks in this context....Just as the newspapers in *New Kids* could only identify the band clearly by using its trademarked name, so can Welles only identify herself clearly by using PEI's trademarked title.

The second part of the nominative use test requires that "only so much of the mark or marks may be used as is reasonably necessary to identify the product or service[.]" *New Kids* provided the following examples to explain this element: "[A] soft drink competitor would be entitled to compare its product to Coca-Cola or Coke, but would not be entitled to use Coca-Cola's distinctive lettering." Similarly, in a past case, an auto shop was allowed to use the trademarked term "Volkswagen" on a sign describing the cars it repaired, in part because the shop "did not use Volkswagen's distinctive lettering style or color scheme, nor did he display the encircled 'VW' emblem." Welles' banner advertisements and headlines satisfy this element because they use only the trademarked words, not the font or symbols associated with the trademarks.

The third element requires that the user do "nothing that would, in conjunction with the mark, suggest sponsorship or endorsement by the trademark holder." As to this element, we conclude that aside from the wallpaper, which we address separately, Welles does nothing in conjunction with her use of the marks to suggest sponsorship or endorsement by PEI. The marks are clearly used to describe the title she received from PEI in 1981, a title that helps describe who she is. It would be unreasonable to assume that the Chicago Bulls sponsored a website of Michael Jordan's simply because his name appeared with the appellation "former Chicago Bull." Similarly, in this case, it would be unreasonable to assume that PEI currently sponsors or endorses someone who describes herself as a "Playboy Playmate of the Year in 1981." The designation of the year, in our case, serves the same function as the "former" in our example. It shows that any sponsorship or endorsement occurred in the past.

For the foregoing reasons, we conclude that Welles' use of PEI's marks in her headlines and banner advertisements is a nominative use excepted from the law of trademark infringement.

2. Metatags

Welles includes the terms "playboy" and "playmate" in her metatags. Metatags describe the contents of a website using keywords. Some search engines search metatags to identify websites relevant to a search. Thus, when an internet searcher enters "playboy" or "playmate" into a search engine that uses metatags, the results will include Welles' site. Because Welles' metatags do not repeat the terms extensively, her site will not be at the top of the list of search results. Applying the three-factor test for nominative use, we conclude that the use of the trademarked terms in Welles' metatags is nominative.

As we discussed above with regard to the headlines and banner advertisements, Welles has no practical way of describing herself without using trademarked terms. In the context of metatags, we conclude that she has no practical way of identifying the content of her website without referring to PEI's trademarks. * * *

Precluding their use would have the unwanted effect of hindering the free flow of information on the internet, something which is certainly not a goal of trademark law. Accordingly, the use of trademarked terms in the metatags meets the first part of the test for nominative use....We conclude that the metatags satisfy the second and third elements of the test as well. The metatags use only so much of the marks as reasonably necessary and nothing is done in conjunction with them to suggest sponsorship or endorsement by the trademark holder. We note that our decision might differ if the metatags listed the trademarked term so repeatedly that Welles' site would regularly appear above PEI's in searches for one of the trademarked terms.

3. Wallpaper/watermark.

The background, or wallpaper, of Welles' site consists of the repeated abbreviation "PMOY '81," which stands for "Playmate of the Year 1981." Welles' name or likeness does not appear before or after "PMOY '81." The pattern created by the repeated abbreviation appears as the background of the various pages of the website. Accepting, for the purposes of this appeal, that the abbreviation "PMOY" is indeed entitled to protection, we conclude that the repeated, stylized use of this abbreviation fails the nominative use test.

The repeated depiction of "PMOY '81" is not necessary to describe Welles. "Playboy Playmate of the Year 1981" is quite adequate. Moreover, the term does not even appear to describe Welles—her name or likeness do not appear before or after each "PMOY '81." Because the use of the abbreviation fails the first prong of the nominative use test, we need not apply the next two prongs of the test.

Because the defense of nominative use fails here, and we have already determined that the doctrine of fair use does not apply, we remand to the district court. The court must determine whether trademark law protects the abbreviation "PMOY," as used in the wallpaper.

B. Trademark Dilution [At this point, the court considers and rejects PEI's claim for trademark dilution.]

Conclusion

For the foregoing reasons, we affirm the district court's grant of summary judgment as to PEI's claims for trademark infringement and trademark dilution, with the sole exception of the use of the abbreviation "PMOY." We reverse as to the abbreviation and remand for consideration of whether it merits protection under either an infringement or a dilution theory.

Case Questions

1. Do you agree with the court's decision that there is no dilution here?
2. If PMOY is not a registered trademark, why does the court discuss it?

3. What does nominative use mean in the context of this case?
4. In business terms, why would PEI even think that it was losing money, or could lose money, based on Welles's use of its identifying marks?

32.6 Summary and Exercises

Summary

The products of the human mind are at the root of all business, but they are legally protectable only to a certain degree. Inventions that are truly novel may qualify for a twenty-year patent; the inventor may then prohibit anyone from using the art (machine, process, manufacture, and the like) or license it on his own terms. A business may sue a person who improperly gives away its legitimate trade secrets, but it may not prevent others from using the unpatented trade secret once publicly disclosed. Writers or painters, sculptors, composers, and other creative artists may generally protect the expression of their ideas for the duration of their lives plus seventy years, as long as the ideas are fixed in some tangible medium. That means that they may prevent others from copying their words (or painting, etc.), but they may not prevent anyone from talking about or using their ideas. Finally, one who markets a product or service may protect its trademark or service or other mark that is distinctive or has taken on a secondary meaning, but may lose it if the mark becomes the generic term for the goods or services.

Exercises

1. Samuel Morse filed claims in the U.S. Patent Office for his invention of the telegraph and also for the "use of the motive power of the electric or galvanic current...however developed, for marking or printing intelligible characters, signs or letters at any distances." For which claim, if any, was he entitled to a patent? Why?
2. In 1957, an inventor dreamed up and constructed a certain new kind of computer. He kept his invention a secret. Two years later, another inventor who conceived the same machine filed a patent application. The first inventor, learning of the patent application, filed for his own patent in 1963. Who is entitled to the patent, assuming that the invention was truly novel and not obvious? Why?
3. A large company discovered that a small company was infringing one of its patents. It wrote the small company and asked it to stop. The small company denied that it was infringing. Because of personnel changes in the large company, the correspondence file was lost and only rediscovered eight years later. The large company sued. What would be the result? Why?
4. Clifford Witter was a dance instructor at the Arthur Murray Dance Studios in Cleveland. As a condition of employment, he signed a contract not to work for a competitor. Subsequently, he was hired by the Fred Astaire Dancing Studios, where he taught the method that he had learned at Arthur Murray. Arthur Murray sued to enforce the noncompete contract. What would be the result? What additional information, if any, would you need to know to decide the case?
5. Greenberg worked for Buckingham Wax as its chief chemist, developing chemical formulas for products by testing other companies' formulas and modifying them. Brite Products bought Buckingham's goods and resold them under its own name. Greenberg went to work for Brite, where he helped Brite make chemicals substantially similar to the ones it had been buying from Buckingham. Greenberg had never made any written or oral commitment to Buckingham restricting his use of the chemical formulas he developed. May Buckingham stop Greenberg from working for Brite? May it stop him from working on formulas learned while working at Buckingham? Why?

Self-Test Questions

1. Which of the following cannot be protected under patent, copyright, or trademark law?
    a. a synthesized molecule
    b. a one-line book title
    c. a one-line advertising jingle
    d. a one-word company name
2. Which of the following does not expire by law?
    a. a closely guarded trade secret not released to the public
    b. a patent granted by the US Patent and Trademark Office
    c. a copyright registered in the US Copyright Office
    d. a federal trademark registered under the Lanham Act
3. A sculptor casts a marble statue of a three-winged bird. To protect against copying, the sculptor can obtain which of the following?
    a. a patent
    b. a trademark
    c. a copyright
    d. none of the above
4. A stock analyst discovers a new system for increasing the value of a stock portfolio. He may protect against use of his system by other people by securing
    a. a patent
    b. a copyright
    c. a trademark
    d. none of the above
5. A company prints up its customer list for use by its sales staff. The cover page carries a notice that says "confidential." A rival salesman gets a copy of the list. The company can sue to recover the list because the list is
    a. patented
    b. copyrighted
    c. a trade secret
    d. none of the above

Self-Test Answers

1. b
2. a
3. c
4. d
5. c

Endnotes

1. 35 United States Code, Section 101.
2. 35 United States Code, Section 101.
3. *Commissioner of Patents v. Chakrabarty*, 444 U.S. 1028 (1980).
4. A plant patent is granted by the government to an inventor (or the inventor's heirs or assigns) who has invented or discovered and asexually reproduced a distinct and new variety of plant, other than a tuber propagated plant or a plant found in an uncultivated state.

5. Adam Liptak, "Justices, 9-0, Bar Patenting Human Genes," *New York Times*, June 13, 2013.
6. Amy Corderoy, "Landmark patent ruling over breast cancer gene BRCA1," *Sydney Morning Herald*, Feb. 15, 2013.
7. *Diamond v. Diehr*, 450 U.S. 175 (1981).
8. *State Street Bank and Trust v. Signature Financial Group, Inc.*, 149 F.3d 1368 (Fed. Cir. 1998).
9. *Amazon.com v. Barnesandnoble.com, Inc.*, 239 F.3d 1343 (Fed. Cir. 2001).
10. *eBay, Inc. v. Merc Exchange, LLC*, 546 U.S. 388 (2006).
11. *Sanitary Refrigerator Co. v. Winers*, 280 U.S. 30 (1929).
12. Economic Espionage Act, 18 United States Code, Section 1831(a) (1996).
13. Economic Espionage Act, 18 United States Code, Section 1832 (1996).
14. Economic Espionage Act, 18 United States Code, Section 1834 (1996).
15. 17 United States Code, Section 107.
16. Berne Convention: http://www.wipo.int/treaties/en/ip/berne/summary_berne.html
17. *Sheldon v. Metro-Goldwyn Pictures Corp.*, 81 F.2d 49 (2d Cir. 1936).
18. "Does it Matter If Led Zeppelin Stole 'Stairway to Heaven'?" *Rolling Stone*, June 23, 2016. http://www.rollingstone.com/music/news/does-it-matter-if-led-zeppelin-stole-stairway-to-heaven-20160614?page=2
19. 17 United States Code, Section 102.
20. *BUC International Corp. v. International Yacht Council, Ltd.*, 489 F.3d 1129 (11th Cir. 2007).
21. *Apple Computer, Inc. v. Franklin Computer Corp.*, 714 F.2d 1240 (3d Cir. 1983).
22. *Lotus Development Corp. v. Paperback Software International*, 740 F.Supp. 37 (D. Mass. 1990).
23. Peter H. Lewis, "When Computing Power Is Generated by the Lawyers," *New York Times*, July 22 1990.
24. *Community for Creative Non-Violence v. Reid*, 109 S.Ct. 2166 (1989).
25. *MGM Studios, Inc. v. Grokster, Ltd.*, 545 U.S. 913 (2005).
26. *Sony v. Universal Studios*, 464 U.S. 417 (1984).
27. 15 United States Code, Section 1127.
28. *Miller Brewing Co. v. Falstaff Brewing Corp.*, 655 F.2d 5 (1st Cir. 1981).

CHAPTER 33

The Nature and Regulation of Real Estate and the Environment

Learning Objectives

After reading this chapter, you should understand the following:

1. The various kinds of interests (or "estates") in real property.
2. The various rights that come with ownership of real property.
3. What easements are, how they are created, and how they function.
4. How ownership of real property is regulated by tort law, by agreement, and by the public interest (through eminent domain).
5. The various ways in which environmental laws affect the ownership and use of real property.

Real property is an important part of corporate as well as individual wealth. As a consequence, the role of the corporate real estate manager has become critically important within the corporation. The real estate manager must be aware not only of the value of land for purchase and sale but also of proper lease negotiation, tax policies and assessments, zoning and land development, and environmental laws.

In this chapter and in Chapter 34 and Chapter 35, we focus on regulation of land use and the environment (see Figure 33.1). We divide our discussion of the nature of real estate into three major categories: (1) estates; (2) rights that are incidental to the possession and ownership of land—for example, the right to air, water, and minerals; and (3) easements—the rights in lands of others.

33.1 Estates

Learning Objective

1. Distinguish between the various kinds of estates, or interests, in real property that the law recognizes.

In property law, an estate is an interest in real property, ranging from absolute dominion and control to bare possession. Ordinarily when we think of property, we think of only one kind: absolute ownership. The owner of a car has the right to drive it where and when she wants, rebuild it, repaint it, sell it, or scrap it. The thought that an owner might lose her property when something happens doesn't fit with our concepts of personal property. But real property is different. You would probably think it very odd if you were sold a used car subject to the condition that you not paint it a different color—and that if you did, you would automatically be stripped of ownership. But land can be sold that way. Land and other real property can be divided into many categories of interests, as we will see.

FIGURE 33.1 Chapter Overview

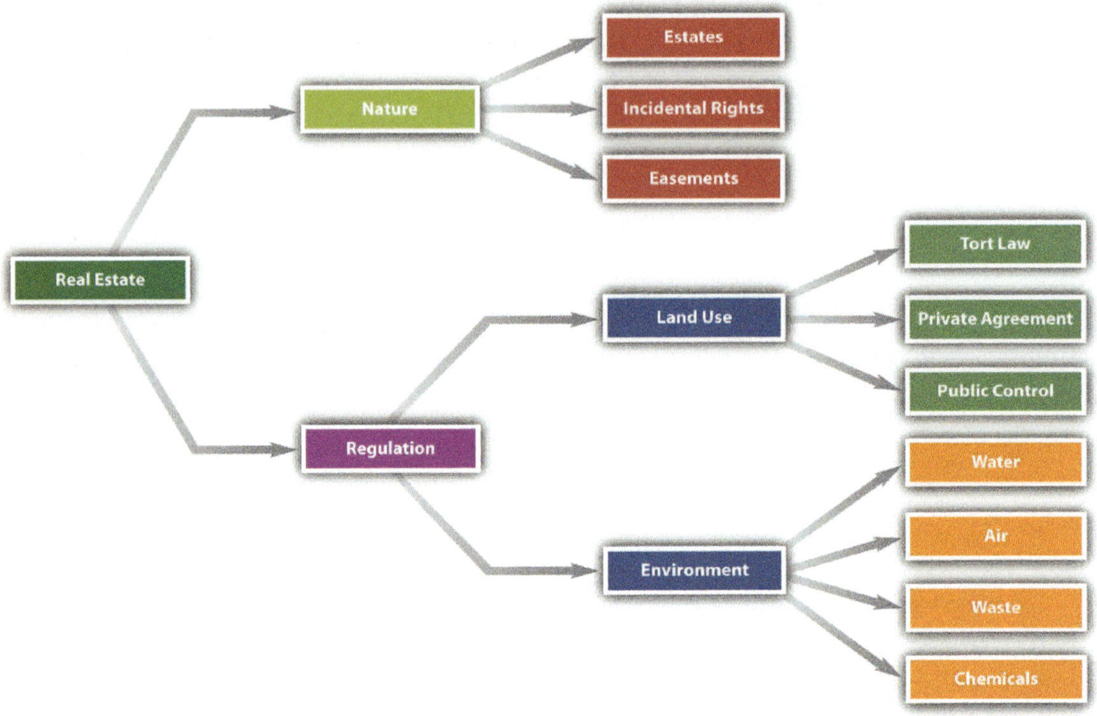

freehold estate

An interest in land that has an uncertain duration.

leasehold estate

An estate whose termination date is usually known—a one-year lease, for example.

The common law distinguishes estates along two main axes: (1) freeholds versus leaseholds and (2) present versus future interests. A **freehold estate** is an interest in land that has an uncertain duration. The freehold can be outright ownership—called the "fee simple absolute"—or it can be an interest in the land for the life of the possessor; in either case, it is impossible to say exactly how long the estate will last. A **leasehold estate** is one whose termination date is usually known. A one-year lease, for example, will expire at the time stated in the lease agreement.

A present estate is one that is currently owned and enjoyed; a future estate is one that will come into the owner's possession upon the occurrence of a particular event. In this chapter, we consider both present and future freehold interests; we save leasehold interests for Chapter 35.

Present Estates (Freeholds)

Fee Simple Absolute

fee simple absolute

The most extensive set of rights that can be conveyed in real property.

The strongest form of ownership is known as the **fee simple absolute** (or fee simple). This is what we think of when we say that someone "owns" the land. As one court put it, "The grant of a fee in land conveys to the grantee complete ownership, immediately and forever, with the right of possession from boundary to boundary and from the center of the Earth to the sky, together with all the lawful uses thereof."[1] Although the fee simple may be encumbered by a mortgage (you may borrow money against the equity in your home) or an easement (you may grant someone the right to walk across your backyard, or drive along one of its boundaries, or use water from a well on your land), the underlying control is in the hands of the owner. Though it was once a complex matter to determine whether a person had been given a fee simple interest, today the law presumes that the estate being transferred is a fee simple, unless the conveyance expressly states to the contrary. Suppose that in her will, Lady Gaga grants her five-thousand-acre ranch "to my screen idol, Tilda Swinton." On the death of Lady Gaga, Swinton takes ownership of the ranch outright in fee simple absolute.

Fee Simple Defeasible

Not every transfer of real property creates a fee simple absolute. Some transfers may limit the estate. Any transfer specifying that the ownership will terminate upon a particular happening is known as a **fee simple defeasible**. Suppose, for example, that Mr. Warbucks conveys a tract of land "to Miss Florence Nightingale, for the purpose of operating her hospital and for no other purpose. Conveyance to be good as long as hospital remains on the property." This grant of land will remain the property of Miss Nightingale and her heirs as long as she and they maintain a hospital. When they stop doing so, the land will automatically revert to Mr. Warbucks or his heirs, without their having to do anything to regain title. Note that the conveyance of land could be perpetual but is not absolute, because it will remain the property of Miss Nightingale only so long as she observes the conditions in the grant.

fee simple defeasible

Any transfer specifying that the ownership will terminate upon a particular happening.

Life Estates

A life estate is usually created by deed, but can also be created in a will. Among the living, for example, Sherry could divide her fee simple estate to Susannah by saying in a deed, "To Sherry, for life, remainder to my heirs." Sherry could do the same thing in a will (in a "testamentary capacity."

The **life tenant** may use the property as though he were the owner in fee simple absolute with this exception: she may not act so as to diminish the value of the property that will ultimately go to the remainderman—the person or persons who will become owner when the life estate terminates. In the above example, Susannah could not "waste" the or diminish the rights of the "remaindermen" (Sherry's heirs) during her life. The life tenant must pay for ordinary upkeep of the property, but the remaindermen are responsible for extraordinary repairs.

life tenant

Someone who holds an estate in land for his or her life or the life of another.

Some life estates are created by operation of law and are known as legal life estates. The most common form is a widow's interest in the real property of her husband. In about one-third of the states, a woman is entitled to **dower**, a right to a percentage (often one-third) of the property of her husband when he dies. Most of these states give a widower a similar interest in the property of his deceased wife. Dower is an alternative to whatever is bequeathed in the will; the widow has the right to elect to take either the share stated in the will or the share available under dower. To prevent the dower right from upsetting the interests of remote purchasers, the right may be waived on sale by having the spouse sign the deed.

dower

A statutory alternative to whatever is bequeathed in the will; the widow has the right to elect the share stated in the will or the share available under dower.

Future Estates

To this point, we have been considering present estates. But people also can have future interests in real property. Despite the implications of its name, the future interest is owned now but is not available to be used or enjoyed now. For the most part, future interests may be bought and sold, just as land held in fee simple absolute may be bought and sold. There are several classes of future interests, but in general there are two major types: reversion and remainder.

Reversion

reversion

A reversion arises whenever the estate transferred has a duration less than that originally owned by the transferor.

A **reversion** arises whenever the estate transferred has a duration less than that originally owned by the transferor. A typical example of a simple reversion is that which arises when a life estate is conveyed. The ownership conveyed is only for the life; when the life tenant dies, the ownership interest reverts to the grantor. Suppose the grantor has died before the death of the life tenant; who gets the reversion interest? Since the reversion is a class of property that is owned now, it can be inherited, and the grantor's heirs would take the reversion at the subsequent death of the life tenant. In our example above, if Sherry had simply said, "To Susannah, for life," and nothing else, whoever were her heirs at the time she pre-deceased Susannah would hold the remainder interest. Susannah

Remainder

remainder

The real property interest that remains after the life estate interest or other interest subject to defeasance.

As implied above, the owner who conveys less than fee simple ("the transferor) need not keep the reversion interest for himself. He can give that interest to someone else, in which case it is known as a **remainder** interest, because the remainder of the property is being transferred. Suppose the transferor conveys land with these words: "to Scarlett for life and then to Rhett." Scarlett has a life estate; the remainder goes to Rhett in fee simple absolute. Rhett is said to have a vested remainder interest, because on Scarlett's death, he or his heirs will automatically become owners of the property. Some remainder interests are contingent—and are therefore known as contingent remainder interests—on the happening of a certain event: "to my mother for her life, then to my sister if she marries Harold before my mother dies." The transferor's sister will become the owner of the property in fee simple only if she marries Harold while her mother is alive; otherwise, the property will revert to the transferor or his heirs. As you can now imagine, the number of permutations of reversions and remainders can become quite complex.

Key Takeaway

An estate is an interest in real property. Estates are of many kinds, but one generic difference is between ownership estates and possessory estates. Fee simple estates and life estates are ownership estates, while leasehold interests are possessory. Among ownership estates, the principal division is between present estates and future estates. An owner of a future estate has an interest that can be bought and sold and that will ripen into present possession at the end of a period of time, at the end of the life of another, or with the happening of some contingent event.

Exercises

1. Jessa owns a house and lot on 9th Avenue. She sells the house to the Hartley family, who wish to have a conveyance from her that says, "to Harriet Hartley for life, remainder to her son, Alexander Sandridge." Alexander is married to Chloe, and they have three children, Carmen, Sarah, and Michael. Who has a future interest, and who has a present interest? What is the correct legal term for Harriet's estate? Do Alexander, Carmen, Sarah, or Michael have any part of the estate at the time Jessa conveys to Harriet using the stated language?
2. After Harriet dies, Alexander wants to sell the property. Alexander and Chloe's children are all eighteen years of age or older. Can he convey the property by his signature alone? Who else needs to sign?

33.2 Rights Incident to Possession and Ownership of Real Estate

Learning Objective

1. Understand that property owners have certain rights in the airspace above their land, in the minerals beneath their land, and even in water that adjoins their land.

Rights to Airspace

The traditional rule was stated by Lord Coke: "Whoever owns the soil owns up to the sky." This traditional rule remains valid today, but its application can cause problems. A simple example would be a person who builds an extension to the upper story of his house so that it hangs out over the edge of his property line and thrusts into the airspace of his neighbor. That would clearly be an encroachment on the neighbor's property. But is it trespass when an airplane—or an earth satellite—flies over your backyard? Obviously, the courts must balance the general public's right to travel against landowners' rights. In *U.S. v. Causby*,[2] the Court determined that flights over private land may constitute a diminution in the property value if they are so low and so frequent as to be a direct and immediate interference with the enjoyment and use of land. The low-flying of drones over residential property may also create some interesting legal issues.[3]

Rights to the Depths

Lord Coke's dictum applies to the depths as well as the sky. The owner of the surface has the right to the oil, gas, and minerals below it, although this right can be severed and sold separately. Perplexing questions may arise in the case of oil and gas, which can flow under the surface. Some states say that oil and gas can be owned by the owner of the surface land; others say that they are not owned until actually extracted—although the property owner may sell the exclusive right to extract them from his land. But states with either rule recognize that oil and gas are capable of being "captured" by drilling that causes oil or gas from under another plot of land to run toward the drilled hole. Since the possibility of capture can lead to wasteful drilling practices as everyone nearby rushes to capture the precious commodities, many states have enacted statutes requiring landowners to share the resources.

Rights to Water

The right to determine how bodies of water will be used depends on basic property rules. Two different approaches to water use in the United States—eastern and western—have developed over time (see Figure 33.2). Eastern states, where water has historically been more plentiful, have adopted the so-called riparian rights theory, which itself can take two forms. *Riparian* refers to land that includes a part of the bed of a waterway or that borders on a public watercourse. A riparian owner is one who owns such land. What are the rights of upstream and downstream owners of riparian land regarding use of the waters? One approach is the "natural flow" doctrine: Each riparian owner is entitled to have the river or other waterway maintained in its natural state. The upstream owner may use the river for drinking water or for washing but may not divert it to irrigate his crops or to operate his mill if doing so would materially change the amount of the flow or the quality of the water. Virtually all eastern states today are not so restrictive and rely instead on a "reasonable use" doctrine, which permits the benefit to be derived from use of the waterway to be weighed against the gravity of the harm. This approach is illustrated in *Hoover v. Crane*, (see Section 6.[4]

FIGURE 33.2 Water Rights

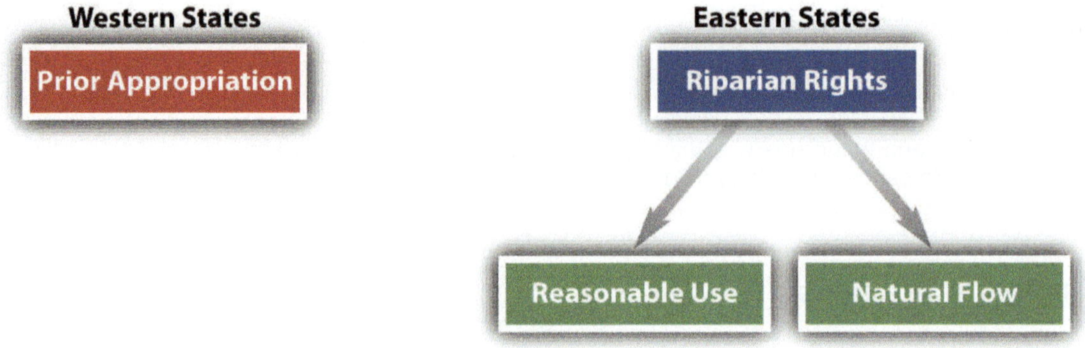

In contrast to riparian rights doctrines, western states have adopted the prior appropriation doctrine. This rule looks not to equality of interests but to priority in time: first in time is first in right. The first person to use the water for a beneficial purpose has a right superior to latecomers. This rule applies even if the first user takes all the water for his own needs and even if other users are riparian owners. This rule developed in water-scarce states in which development depended on incentives to use rather than hoard water. Today, the prior appropriation doctrine has come under criticism because it gives incentives to those who already have the right to the water to continue to use it profligately, rather than to those who might develop more efficient means of using it.

Key Takeaway

Property owners have certain rights in the airspace above their land. They also have rights in subsurface minerals, which include oil and gas. Those property owners who have bodies of water adjacent to their land will also have certain rights to withdraw or impound water for their own use. Regarding US water law, the reasonable use doctrine in the eastern states is distinctly different from the prior appropriation doctrine in western states.

Exercises

1. Steve Hannaford farms in western Nebraska. The farm has passed to succeeding generations of Hannafords, who use water from the North Platte River for irrigation purposes. The headlands of the North Platte are in Colorado, but use of the water from the North Platte by Nebraskans preceded use of the water by settlers in Colorado. What theory of water rights governs Nebraska and Colorado residents? Can the state of Colorado divert and use water in such a way that less of it reaches western Nebraska and the Hannaford farm? Why or why not?
2. Jamie Stoner decides to put solar panels on the south face of his roof. Jamie lives on a block of one- and two-bedroom bungalows in South Miami, Florida. In 2009, someone purchases the house next door and within two years decides to add a second and third story. This proposed addition will significantly decrease the utility of Jamie's solar array. Does Jamie have any rights that would limit what his new neighbors can do on their own land?

33.3 Easements: Rights in the Lands of Others

Learning Objectives

1. Explain the difference between an easement and a license.
2. Describe the ways in which easements can be created.

Definition

An **easement** is an interest in land created by agreement between land owners. An easement permits one person to make use of another's estate. Though the common law once distinguished between an easement and profit (the taking of something from another's land), today the distinction has faded, and profits are treated as a type of easement. An easement must be distinguished from a mere **license**, which is permission, revocable at the will of the owner, to make use of the owner's land. An easement is an estate; a license is personal to the grantee and is not assignable.

The two main types of easements are affirmative and negative. An affirmative easement gives a landowner the right to use the land of another (e.g., crossing it or using water from it), while a **negative easement**, by contrast, prohibits the landowner from using his land in ways that would affect the holder of the easement. For example, the builder of a solar home would want to obtain negative easements from neighbors barring them from building structures on their land that would block sunlight from falling on the solar home. With the growth of solar energy, some states have begun to provide stronger protection by enacting laws that regulate one's ability to interfere with the enjoyment of sunlight. These laws range from a relatively weak statute in Colorado, which sets forth rules for obtaining easements, to the much stronger statute in California, which says in effect that the owner of a solar device has a vested right to continue to receive the sunlight.

Another important distinction is made between easements appurtenant and easements in gross. An **easement appurtenant** benefits the owner of adjacent land. The easement is thus appurtenant to the holder's land. The benefited land is called the **dominant tenement**, and the burdened land—that is, the land subject to the easement—is called the **servient tenement** (see Figure 33.3). An easement in gross, in contrast, is granted to someone (or some firm) independent of that someone's ownership of land. It is simply an independent right—for example, the right granted to a boat owner to drive his boat and trailer across someone else's land to get to a certain marina. If Jeff owns the boat and Jackie refuses to let him cross her land for free, they may strike a deal where $2,000 gives Jeff the right to cross Jackie's land with his boat at least three times a week for the rest of Jeff's boat-owning life. Note that (1) Jeff's easement is not dependent on him owning real estate adjacent to Jackie's, and so is an easement in gross; (2) since all easements, even easements in gross, are "estates," that the payment of $2,000 will suffice to give Jeff the right to sell not only his boat, but the ability (the easement in gross) to go over Jackie's property, and (3) the easement, if it is to last more than a year, should be in writing so as to meet the requirements of the state's Statute of Frauds, and (4) whoever owns the land after Jackie will not be bound by the easement in gross unless it's not only in writing, but either placed on the public record or disclosed by Jackie to the new owner.

easement

An interest in land created by agreement that permits one person to make use of another's estate.

license

As opposed to an easement, a license is personal to the grantee and is not assignable.

negative easement

An easement that prohibits the owner of the land from using his or her land in ways that would affect the holder of the easement.

easement appurtenant

An easement that benefits the owner of adjacent land. The easement is thus appurtenant to the holder's land.

dominant tenement

The land that benefits from an easement.

servient tenement

The burdened land—that is, the land subject to the easement.

FIGURE 33.3 Easement Appurtenant

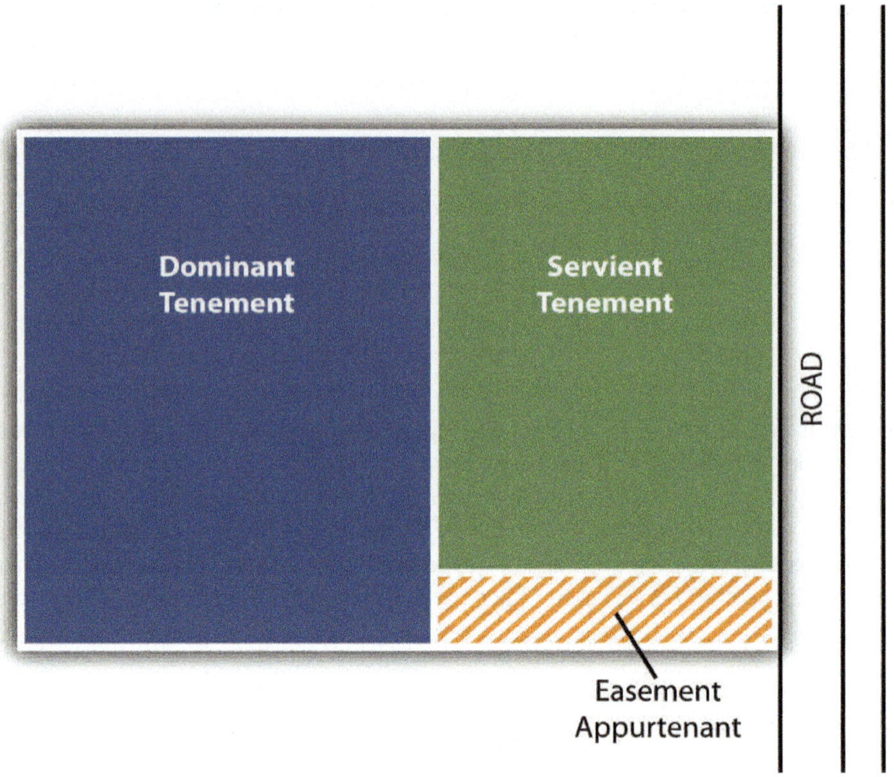

Unless it is explicitly limited to the grantee, an easement appurtenant "runs with the land." That is, when the dominant tenement is sold or otherwise conveyed, the new owner automatically owns the easement. Thus, if in 1923 a "shared driveway" easement was created by Mr. Hanks in favor of his neighbor, Ms. Collins, it becomes a matter of public record and Ms. Collins owns the "dominant tenement" which becomes part of her estate when she conveys to X, and when X conveys to Y, and so on. It "runs with the land" and can only be extinguished if and when Ms. Collins (or subsequent buyers of that land) explicitly sells the easement appurtenant back to the owner of the dominant tenement.

A commercial easement in gross may be transferred—for instance, easements to construct pipelines, telegraph and telephone lines, and railroad rights of way. However, most noncommercial easements in gross are not transferable, being deemed personal to the original owner of the easement. Ms. Harbin sells her friend Ms. Paradise—who does not own land adjacent to Ms. Harbin—an easement across her country farm to operate skimobiles during the winter. The easement is personal to Ms. Paradise; she could not sell the easement to anyone else.

Creation

Easements may be created by express agreement, either in deeds or in wills. The owner of the dominant tenement may buy the easement from the owner of the servient tenement or may reserve the easement for himself when selling part of his land. But courts will sometimes allow implied easements under certain circumstances. For instance, if the deed refers to an easement that bounds the premises—without describing it in any detail—a court could conclude that an easement was intended to pass with the sale of the property.

An easement can also be implied from prior use. Suppose a seller of land has two lots, with a driveway connecting both lots to the street. The only way to gain access to the street from the back lot is to use the driveway, and the seller has always done so. If the seller now sells the back lot, the buyer can establish an easement in the driveway through the front lot if the prior use was (1) apparent at the time of sale, (2) continuous, and (3) reasonably necessary for the enjoyment of the back lot. The rule of implied easements through prior use operates only when the ownership of the dominant and servient tenements was originally in the same person.

Use of the Easement

The servient owner may use the easement—remember, it is on or under or above his land—as long as his use does not interfere with the rights of the easement owner. Suppose you have an easement to walk along a path in the woods owned by your neighbor and to swim in a private lake that adjoins the woods. At the time you purchased the easement, your neighbor did not use the lake. Now he proposes to swim in it himself, and you protest. You would not have a sound case, because his swimming in the lake would not interfere with your right to do so. But if he proposed to clear the woods and build a mill on it, obliterating the path you took to the lake and polluting the lake with chemical discharges, then you could obtain an injunction to bar him from interfering with your easement.

The owner of the dominant tenement is not restricted to using his land as he was at the time he became the owner of the easement. The courts will permit him to develop the land in some "normal" manner. For example, an easement on a private roadway for the benefit of a large estate up in the hills would not be lost if the large estate were ultimately subdivided and many new owners wished to use the roadway; the easement applies to the entire portion of the original dominant tenement, not merely to the part that abuts the easement itself.

Key Takeaway

An easement appurtenant runs with the land and benefits the dominant tenement, burdening the servient tenement. An easement, generally, has a specific location or description within or over the servient tenement. Easements can be created by deed, by will, or by implication.

Exercise

1. Beth Delaney owns property next to Kerry Plemmons. The deed to Delaney's property notes that she has access to a well on the Plemmons property "to obtain water for household use." The well has been dry for many generations and has not been used by anyone on the Plemmons property or the Delaney property for as many generations. The well predated Plemmons's ownership of the property; as the servient tenement, the Plemmons property was burdened by this easement dating back to 1898. Plemmons hires a company to dig a very deep well near one of his outbuildings to provide water for his horses. The location is one hundred yards from the old well. Does the Delaney property have any easement to use water from the new well?

33.4 Regulation of Land Use

Learning Objectives

1. Compare the various ways in which law limits or restricts the right to use your land in any way that you decide is best for you.

2. Distinguish between regulation by common law and regulation by public acts such as zoning or eminent domain.
3. Understand that property owners may restrict the uses of land by voluntary agreement, subject to important public policy considerations.

Land use regulation falls into three broad categories: (1) restriction on the use of land through tort law, (2) private regulation by agreement, and (3) public ownership or regulation through the powers of eminent domain and zoning.

Regulation of Land Use by Tort Law

Tort law is used to regulate land use in two ways: (1) The owner may become liable for certain activities carried out on the real estate that affect others beyond the real estate. (2) The owner may be liable to persons who, upon entering the real estate, are injured.

Landowner's Activities

nuisance

A common-law nuisance is an interference with the use and enjoyment of one's land.

The two most common torts in this area are nuisance and trespass. A common-law **nuisance** is an interference with the use and enjoyment of one's land. Examples of nuisances are excessive noise (especially late at night), polluting activities, and emissions of noxious odors. But the activity must produce substantial harm, not fleeting, minor injury, and it must produce those effects on the reasonable person, not on someone who is peculiarly allergic to the complained-of activity. A person who suffered migraine headaches at the sight of croquet or badminton being played on a neighbor's lawn would not likely win a nuisance lawsuit. While the meaning of nuisance is difficult to define with any precision, this common-law cause of action is a primary means for landowners to obtain damages for invasive environmental harms.[5]

trespass

The wrongful physical invasion of or entry upon land possessed by another.

A **trespass** is the wrongful physical invasion of or entry upon land possessed by another. Loud noise blaring out of speakers in the house next door might be a nuisance but could not be a trespass, because noise is not a physical invasion. But spraying pesticides on your gladiolas could constitute a trespass on your neighbor's property if some of the pesticide drifts across the boundary.

Nuisance and trespass are complex theories, a full explanation of which could take up an entire chapter. What is important to remember is that these torts are two-edged swords. In some situations, the landowner himself will want to use these theories to sue trespassers or persons creating a nuisance, but in other situations, the landowner will be liable under these theories for his own activities.

Injury to Persons Entering the Real Estate

Traditionally, liability for injury has depended on the status of the person who enters the real estate.

Trespassers

If the person is an intruder without permission—a trespasser—the landowner owes him no duty of care unless he knows of the intruder's presence, in which case the owner must exercise reasonable care in his activities and warn of hidden dangers on his land of which he is aware. A known trespasser is someone whom the landowner actually sees on the property or whom he knows frequently intrudes on the property, as in the case of someone who habitually walks across the land. If a landowner knows that people frequently walk across his property and one day he puts a poisonous chemical on the ground to eliminate certain insects, he is obligated to warn those who continue to walk on the grounds. Intentional injury to known trespassers is not allowed, even if the trespasser is a criminal intent on robbery, for the law values human life above property rights.

Children

If the trespasser is a child, a different rule applies in most states. This is the doctrine of **attractive nuisance**. Originally this rule was enunciated to deal with cases in which something on the land attracted the child to it, like a swimming pool. In recent years, most courts have dropped the requirement that the child must have been attracted to the danger. Instead, the following elements of proof are necessary to make out a case of attractive nuisance (Restatement of Torts, Section 339):

attractive nuisance

A thing or condition on land that is attractive to small children and represents a distinct hazard to their health or well-being.

1. The child must have been injured by a structure or other artificial condition.
2. The possessor of the land (not necessarily the owner) must have known or should have known that young children would be likely to trespass.
3. The possessor must have known or should have known that the artificial condition exists and that it posed an unreasonable risk of serious injury.
4. The child must have been too young to appreciate the danger that the artificial condition posed.
5. The risk to the child must have far outweighed the utility of the artificial condition to the possessor.
6. The possessor did not exercise reasonable care in protecting the child or eliminating the danger.

Old refrigerators, open gravel pits, or mechanisms that a curious child would find inviting are all examples of attractive nuisance. Suppose Farmer Brown keeps an old buggy on his front lawn, accessible from the street. A five-year-old boy clambers up the buggy one day, falls through a rotted floorboard, and breaks his leg. Is Farmer Brown liable? Probably so. The child was too young to appreciate the danger posed by the buggy, a structure. The farmer should have appreciated that young children would be likely to come onto the land when they saw the buggy and that they would be likely to climb up onto the buggy. Moreover, he should have known, if he did not know in fact, that the buggy, left outside for years without being tended, would pose an unreasonable risk. The buggy's utility as a decoration was far overbalanced by the risk that it posed to children, and the farmer failed to exercise reasonable care.

Licensees

A nontrespasser who comes onto the land without being invited, or if invited, comes for purposes unconnected with any business conducted on the premises, is known as a **licensee**. This class of visitors to the land consists of (1) social guests (people you invite to your home for a party); (2) a salesman, not invited by the owner, who wishes to sell something to the owner or occupier of the property; and (3) persons visiting a building for a purpose not connected with the business on the land (e.g., students who visit a factory to see how it works). The landowner owes the same duty of care to licensees that he owes to known trespassers. That is, he must warn them against hidden dangers of which he is aware, and he must exercise reasonable care in his activities to ensure that they are not injured.

licensee

A noninvitee to the land, such as a social guest, a salesman not invited by the owner to the property, or someone else not on the property for an invited business purpose.

Invitees

invitee

A person who has been invited onto real property for purpose of potential economic benefit to the owner or occupier of the land.

A final category of persons entering land is that of **invitee**. This is one who has been invited onto the land, usually, though not necessarily, for a business purpose of potential economic benefit to the owner or occupier of the premises. This category is confusing because it sounds as though it should include social guests (who clearly are invited onto the premises), but traditionally social guests are said to be licensees.

Invitees include customers of stores, users of athletic and other clubs, customers of repair shops, strollers through public parks, restaurant and theater patrons, hotel guests, and the like. From the owner's perspective, the major difference between licensees and invitees is that he is liable for injuries resulting to the latter from hidden dangers that he should have been aware of, even if he is not actually aware of the dangers. How hidden the dangers are and how broad the owner's liability is depends on the circumstances, but liability sometimes can be quite broad. Difficult questions arise in lawsuits brought by invitees (or business invitees, as they are sometimes called) when the actions of persons other than the landowner contribute to the injury.

The foregoing rules dealing with liability for persons entering the land are the traditional rules at common law. In recent years, some courts have moved away from the rigidities and sometimes perplexing differences between trespassers, licensees, and invitees. By court decision, several states have now abolished such distinctions and hold the proprietor, owner, or occupier liable for failing to maintain the premises in a reasonably safe condition. According to the California Supreme Court,

> *A man's life or limb does not become less worthy of protection by the law nor a loss less worthy of compensation under the law because he has come upon the land of another without permission or with permission but without a business purpose. Reasonable people do not ordinarily vary their conduct depending upon such matters, and to focus upon the status of the injured party as a trespasser, licensee, or invitee in order to determine the question whether the landowner has a duty of care, is contrary to our modern social mores and humanitarian values. Where the occupier of land is aware of a concealed condition involving in the absence of precautions an unreasonable risk of harm to those coming in contact with it and is aware that a person on the premises is about to come in contact with it, the trier of fact can reasonably conclude that a failure to warn or to repair the condition constitutes negligence. Whether or not a guest has a right to expect that his host will remedy dangerous conditions on his account, he should reasonably be entitled to rely upon a warning of the dangerous condition so that he, like the host, will be in a position to take special precautions when he comes in contact with it.*[6]

Private Regulation of Land Use by Agreement

A restrictive covenant is an agreement regarding the use of land that "runs with the land." In effect, it is a contractual promise that becomes part of the property and that binds future owners. Violations of covenants can be redressed in court in suits for damages or injunctions but will not result in reversion of the land to the seller.

Usually, courts construe restrictive covenants narrowly—that is, in a manner most conducive to free use of the land by the ultimate owner (the person against whom enforcement of the covenant is being sought). Sometimes, even when the meaning of the covenant is clear, the courts will not enforce it. For example, when the character of a neighborhood changes, the courts may declare the covenant a nullity. Thus a restriction on a one-acre parcel to residential purposes was voided when in the intervening thirty years a host of businesses grew up around it, including a bowling alley, restaurant, poolroom, and sewage disposal plant.[7]

An important nullification of restrictive covenants came in 1947 when the US Supreme Court struck down as unconstitutional racially restrictive covenants, which barred blacks and other minorities from living on land so burdened. The Supreme Court reasoned that when a court enforces such a covenant, it acts in a discriminatory manner (barring blacks but not whites from living in a home burdened with the covenant) and thus violates the Fourteenth Amendment's guarantee of equal protection of the laws.[8]

Public Control of Land Use through Eminent Domain

The government may take private property for public purposes. Its power to do so is known as eminent domain. The power of eminent domain is subject to constitutional limitations. Under the Fifth Amendment, the property must be put to public use, and the owner is entitled to "just compensation" for his loss. These requirements are sometimes difficult to apply.

Public Use

The requirement of public use normally means that the property will be useful to the public once the state has taken possession—for example, private property might be condemned to construct a highway. Although not allowed in most circumstances, the government could even condemn someone's property in order to turn around and sell it to another individual, if a legitimate public purpose could be shown. For example, a state survey in the mid-1960s showed that the government owned 49 percent of Hawaii's land. Another 47 percent was controlled by seventy-two private landowners. Because this concentration of land ownership (which dated back to feudal times) resulted in a critical shortage of residential land, the Hawaiian legislature enacted a law allowing the government to take land from large private estates and resell it in smaller parcels to homeowners. In 1984, the US Supreme Court upheld the law, deciding that the land was being taken for a public use because the purpose was "to attack certain perceived evils of concentrated property ownership."[9] Although the use must be public, the courts will not inquire into the necessity of the use or whether other property might have been better suited. It is up to government authorities to determine whether and where to build a road, not the courts.

The limits of public use were amply illustrated in the Supreme Court's 2002 decision of *Kelo v. New London*,[10] in which Mrs. Kelo's house was condemned so that the city of New London, in Connecticut, could create a marina and industrial park to lease to Pfizer Corporation. The city's motives were to create a higher tax base for property taxes. The Court, following precedent in *Midkiff* and other cases, refused to invalidate the city's taking on constitutional grounds. Reaction from states was swift; many states passed new laws restricting the bases for state and municipal governments to use powers of eminent domain, and many of these laws also provided additional compensation to property owners whose land was taken.

Just Compensation

The owner is ordinarily entitled to the fair market value of land condemned under eminent domain. This value is determined by calculating the most profitable use of the land at the time of the taking, even though it was being put to a different use. The owner will have a difficult time collecting lost profits; for instance, a grocery store will not usually be entitled to collect for the profits it might have made during the next several years, in part because it can presumably move elsewhere and continue to make profits and in part because calculating future profits is inherently speculative.

Taking

The most difficult question in most modern cases is whether the government has in fact "taken" the property. This is easy to answer when the government acquires title to the property through condemnation proceedings. But more often, a government action is challenged when a law or regulation inhibits the use of private land. Suppose a town promulgates a setback ordinance, requiring owners along city sidewalks to build no closer to the sidewalk than twenty feet. If the owner of a small store had only twenty-five feet of land from the sidewalk line, the ordinance would effectively prevent him from housing his enterprise, and the ordinance would be a taking. Challenging such ordinances can sometimes be difficult under traditional tort theories because the government is immune from suit in some of these cases. Instead, a theory of inverse condemnation has developed, in which the plaintiff private property owner asserts that the government has condemned the property, though not through the traditional mechanism of a condemnation proceeding.

Public Control of Land Use through Zoning

zoning

A process by which a city or other municipality regulates the type of activity to be permitted.

Zoning is a technique by which a city or other municipality regulates the type of activity to be permitted in geographical areas within its boundaries. Though originally limited to residential, commercial, and industrial uses, today's zoning ordinances are complex sets of regulations. A typical municipality might have the following zones: residential with a host of subcategories (such as for single-family and multiple-family dwellings), office, commercial, industrial, agricultural, and public lands. Zones may be exclusive, in which case office buildings would not be permitted in commercial zones, or they may be cumulative, so that a more restricted use would be allowed in a less restrictive zone. Zoning regulations do more than specify the type of use: they often also dictate minimum requirements for parking, open usable space, setbacks, lot sizes, and the like, and maximum requirements for height, length of side lots, and so on.

Nonconforming Uses

When a zoning ordinance is enacted, it will almost always affect existing property owners, many of whom will be using their land in ways no longer permitted under the ordinance. To avoid the charge that they have thereby "taken" the property, most ordinances permit previous nonconforming uses to continue, though some ordinances limit the nonconforming uses to a specified time after becoming effective. But this permission to continue a nonconforming use is narrow; it extends only to the specific use to which the property was put before the ordinance was enacted. A manufacturer of dresses that suddenly finds itself in an area zoned residential may continue to use its sewing machines, but it could not develop a sideline in woodworking.

Variances

variance

Permission by zoning authorities to carry on a nonconforming use.

Sometimes an owner may desire to use his property in ways not permitted under an existing zoning scheme and will ask the zoning board for a **variance**—authority to carry on a nonconforming use. The board is not free to grant a variance at its whim. The courts apply three general tests to determine the validity of a variance: (1) The land must be unable to yield a reasonable return on the uses allowed by the zoning regulation. (2) The hardship must be unique to the property, not to property generally in the area. (3) If granted, the variance must not change the essential character of the neighborhood.

Key Takeaway

Land use regulation can mean (1) restrictions on the use of land through tort law, (2) private regulation—by agreement, or (3) regulation through powers of eminent domain or zoning.

Exercises

1. Give one example of the exercise of eminent domain. In order to exercise its power under eminent domain, must the government actually take eventual ownership of the property that is "taken"?
2. Felix Unger is an adult, trespassing for the first time on Alan Spillborghs's property. Alan has been digging a deep grave in his backyard for his beloved Saint Bernard, Maximilian, who has just died. Alan stops working on the grave when it gets dark, intending to return to the task in the morning. He seldom sees trespassers cutting through his backyard. Felix, in the dark, after visiting the local pub, decides to take a shortcut through Alan's yard and falls into the grave. He breaks his leg. What is the standard of care for Alan toward Felix or other infrequent trespassers? If Alan has no insurance for this accident, would the law make Felix responsible?
3. Atlantic Cement owns and operates a cement plant in New York State. Nearby residents are exposed to noise, soot, and dust and have experienced lowered property values as a result of Atlantic Cement's operations. Is there a common-law remedy for nearby property owners for losses occasioned by Atlantic's operations? If so, what is it called?

33.5 Environmental Law

Learning Objectives

1. Describe the major federal laws that govern business activities that may adversely affect air quality and water quality.
2. Describe the major federal laws that govern waste disposal and chemical hazards including pesticides.

In one sense, environmental law is very old. Medieval England had smoke control laws that established the seasons when soft coal could be burned. Nuisance laws give private individuals a limited control over polluting activities of adjacent landowners. But a comprehensive set of US laws directed toward general protection of the environment is largely a product of the past quarter-century, with most of the legislative activity stemming from the late 1960s and later, when people began to perceive that the environment was systematically deteriorating from assaults by rapid population growth and greatly increased automobile driving, vast proliferation of factories that generate waste products, and a sharp rise in the production of toxic materials. Two of the most significant developments in environmental law came in 1970, when the National Environmental Policy Act took effect and the Environmental Protection Agency became the first of a number of new federal administrative agencies to be established during the decade.

National Environmental Policy Act

Signed into law by President Nixon on January 1, 1970, the National Environmental Policy Act (NEPA) declared that it shall be the policy of the federal government, in cooperation with state and local governments, "to create and maintain conditions under which man and nature can exist in productive harmony, and fulfill the social, economic, and other requirements of present and future generations of Americans....The Congress recognizes that each person should enjoy a healthful environment and that each person has a responsibility to contribute to the preservation and enhancement of the environment."[11]

environmental impact statement

A statement mandated by the National Environmental Policy Act that is required of most federal agencies and includes an assessment of whether the agency's actions will significantly affect environmental quality.

The most significant aspect of NEPA is its requirement that federal agencies prepare an **environmental impact statement** in every recommendation or report on proposals for legislation and whenever undertaking a major federal action that significantly affects environmental quality. The statement must (1) detail the environmental impact of the proposed action, (2) list any unavoidable adverse impacts should the action be taken, (3) consider alternatives to the proposed action, (4) compare short-term and long-term consequences, and (5) describe irreversible commitments of resources. Unless the impact statement is prepared, the project can be enjoined from proceeding. Note that NEPA does not apply to purely private activities but only to those proposed to be carried out in some manner by federal agencies.

Environmental Protection Agency

The Environmental Protection Agency (EPA) has been in the forefront of the news since its creation in 1970. Charged with monitoring environmental practices of industry, assisting the government and private business to halt environmental deterioration, promulgating regulations consistent with federal environmental policy, and policing industry for violations of the various federal environmental statutes and regulations, the EPA has had a pervasive influence on American business. *Business Week* noted the following in 1977: "Cars rolling off Detroit's assembly line now have antipollution devices as standard equipment. The dense black smokestack emissions that used to symbolize industrial prosperity are rare, and illegal, sights. Plants that once blithely ran discharge water out of a pipe and into a river must apply for permits that are almost impossible to get unless the plants install expensive water treatment equipment. All told, the EPA has made a sizable dent in man-made environmental filth."[12]

The EPA is especially active in regulating water and air pollution and in overseeing the disposition of toxic wastes and chemicals. To these problems we now turn.

Water Pollution

Clean Water Act

Legislation governing the nation's waterways goes back a long time. The first federal water pollution statute was the Rivers and Harbors Act of 1899. Congress enacted new laws in 1948, 1956, 1965, 1966, and 1970. But the centerpiece of water pollution enforcement is the Clean Water Act of 1972 (technically, the Federal Water Pollution Control Act Amendments of 1972), as amended in 1977 and by the Water Quality Act of 1987. The Clean Water Act is designed to restore and maintain the "chemical, physical, and biological integrity of the Nation's waters."[13] It operates on the states, requiring them to designate the uses of every significant body of water within their borders (e.g., for drinking water, recreation, commercial fishing) and to set water quality standards to reduce pollution to levels appropriate for each use.

Congress only has power to regulate interstate commerce, and so the Clean Water Act is applicable only to "navigable waters" of the United States. This has led to disputes over whether the act can apply, say, to an abandoned gravel pit that has no visible connection to navigable waterways, even if the gravel pit provides habitat for migratory birds. In *Solid Waste Agency of Northern Cook County v. Army Corps of Engineers*, the US Supreme Court said no.[14]

Private Industry

The Clean Water Act also governs private industry and imposes stringent standards on the discharge of pollutants into waterways and publicly owned sewage systems. The act created an effluent permit system known as the National Pollutant Discharge Elimination System. To discharge any pollutants into navigable waters from a "point source" like a pipe, ditch, ship, or container, a company must obtain a certification that it meets specified standards, which are continually being tightened. For example, until 1983, industry had to use the "best practicable technology" currently available, but after July 1, 1984, it had to use the "best available technology" economically achievable. Companies must limit certain kinds of "conventional pollutants" (such as suspended solids and acidity) by "best conventional control technology."

Other EPA Water Activities

Federal law governs, and the EPA regulates, a number of other water control measures. Ocean dumping, for example, is the subject of the Marine Protection, Research, and Sanctuaries Act of 1972, which gives the EPA jurisdiction over wastes discharged into the oceans. The Clean Water Act gives the EPA and the US Army Corps of Engineers authority to protect waters, marshlands, and other wetlands against degradation caused by dredging and fills. The EPA also oversees state and local plans for restoring general water quality to acceptable levels in the face of a host of non-point-source pollution. The Clean Water Act controls municipal sewage systems, which must ensure that wastewater is chemically treated before being discharged from the sewage system.

Obviously, of critical importance to the nation's health is the supply of drinking water. To ensure its continuing purity, Congress enacted the Safe Drinking Water Act of 1974, with amendments passed in 1986 and 1996. This act aims to protect water at its sources: rivers, lakes, reservoirs, springs, and groundwater wells. (The act does not regulate private wells that serve fewer than twenty-five individuals.) This law has two strategies for combating pollution of drinking water. It establishes national standards for drinking water derived from both surface reservoirs and underground aquifers. It also authorizes the EPA to regulate the injection of solid wastes into deep wells (as happens, for instance, by leakage from underground storage tanks).

Air Pollution

The centerpiece of the legislative effort to clean the atmosphere is the Clean Air Act of 1970 (amended in 1975, 1977, and 1990). Under this act, the EPA has set two levels of National Ambient Air Quality Standards (NAAQS). The primary standards limit the ambient (i.e., circulating) pollution that affects human health; secondary standards limit pollution that affects animals, plants, and property. The heart of the Clean Air Act is the requirement that subject to EPA approval, the states implement the standards that the EPA establishes. The setting of these pollutant standards was coupled with directing the states to develop state implementation plans (SIPs), applicable to appropriate industrial sources in the state, in order to achieve these standards. The act was amended in 1977 and 1990 primarily to set new goals (dates) for achieving attainment of NAAQS since many areas of the country had failed to meet the deadlines.

Beyond the NAAQS, the EPA has established several specific standards to control different types of air pollution. One major type is pollution that mobile sources, mainly automobiles, emit. The EPA requires new cars to be equipped with catalytic converters and to use unleaded gasoline to eliminate the most noxious fumes and to keep them from escaping into the atmosphere. To minimize pollution from stationary sources, the EPA also imposes uniform standards on new industrial plants and those that have been substantially modernized. And to safeguard against emissions from older plants, states must promulgate and enforce SIPs.

The Clean Air Act is even more solicitous of air quality in certain parts of the nation, such as designated wilderness areas and national parks. For these areas, the EPA has set standards to prevent significant deterioration in order to keep the air as pristine and clear as it was centuries ago.

The EPA also worries about chemicals so toxic that the tiniest quantities could prove fatal or extremely hazardous to health. To control emission of substances like asbestos, beryllium, mercury, vinyl chloride, benzene, and arsenic, the EPA has established or proposed various National Emissions Standards for Hazardous Air Pollutants.

Concern over acid rain and other types of air pollution prompted Congress to add almost eight hundred pages of amendments to the Clean Air Act in 1990. (The original act was fifty pages long.) As a result of these amendments, the act was modernized in a manner that parallels other environmental laws. For instance, the amendments established a permit system that is modeled after the Clean Water Act. And the amendments provide for felony convictions for willful violations, similar to penalties incorporated into other statutes.

The amendments include certain defenses for industry. Most important, companies are protected from allegations that they are violating the law by showing that they were acting in accordance with a permit. In addition to this "permit shield," the law also contains protection for workers who unintentionally violate the law while following their employers' instructions.

Waste Disposal

Though pollution of the air by highly toxic substances like benzene or vinyl chloride may seem a problem removed from that of the ordinary person, we are all in fact polluters. Every year, the United States generates approximately 230 million tons of "trash"—about 4.6 pounds per person per day. Less than one-quarter of it is recycled; the rest is incinerated or buried in landfills. But many of the country's landfills have been closed, either because they were full or because they were contaminating groundwater. Once groundwater is contaminated, it is extremely expensive and difficult to clean it up. In the 1965 Solid Waste Disposal Act and the 1970 Resource Recovery Act, Congress sought to regulate the discharge of garbage by encouraging waste management and recycling. Federal grants were available for research and training, but the major regulatory effort was expected to come from the states and municipalities.

But shocking news prompted Congress to get tough in 1976. The plight of homeowners near Love Canal in upstate New York became a major national story as the discovery of massive underground leaks of toxic chemicals buried during the previous quarter century led to evacuation of hundreds of homes. Next came the revelation that Kepone, an exceedingly toxic pesticide, had been dumped into the James River in Virginia, causing a major human health hazard and severe damage to fisheries in the James and downstream in the Chesapeake Bay. The rarely discussed industrial dumping of hazardous wastes now became an open controversy, and Congress responded in 1976 with the Resource Conservation and Recovery Act (RCRA) and the Toxic Substances Control Act (TSCA) and in 1980 with the Comprehensive Environmental Response, Compensation, and Liability Act (CERCLA).

Resource Conservation and Recovery Act

The RCRA expresses a "cradle-to-grave" philosophy: hazardous wastes must be regulated at every stage. The act gives the EPA power to govern their creation, storage, transport, treatment, and disposal. Any person or company that generates hazardous waste must obtain a permit (known as a "manifest") either to store it on its own site or ship it to an EPA-approved treatment, storage, or disposal facility. No longer can hazardous substances simply be dumped at a convenient landfill. Owners and operators of such sites must show that they can pay for damage growing out of their operations, and even after the sites are closed to further dumping, they must set aside funds to monitor and maintain the sites safely.

This philosophy can be severe. In 1986, the Supreme Court ruled that bankruptcy is not a sufficient reason for a company to abandon toxic waste dumps if state regulations reasonably require protection in the interest of public health or safety. The practical effect of the ruling is that trustees of the bankrupt company must first devote assets to cleaning up a dump site, and only from remaining assets may they satisfy creditors.[15] Another severity is RCRA's imposition of criminal liability, including fines of up to $25,000 a day and one-year prison sentences, which can be extended beyond owners to individual employees, as discussed in *U.S. v. Johnson & Towers, Inc., et al.*, (see Section 6).

Comprehensive Environmental Response, Compensation, and Liability Act

The CERCLA, also known as the Superfund, gives the EPA emergency powers to respond to public health or environmental dangers from faulty hazardous waste disposal, currently estimated to occur at more than seventeen thousand sites around the country. The EPA can direct immediate removal of wastes presenting imminent danger (e.g., from train wrecks, oil spills, leaking barrels, and fires). Injuries can be sudden and devastating; in 1979, for example, when a freight train derailed in Florida, ninety thousand pounds of chlorine gas escaped from a punctured tank car, leaving 8 motorists dead and 183 others injured and forcing 3,500 residents within a 7-mile radius to be evacuated. The EPA may also carry out "planned removals" when the danger is substantial, even if immediate removal is not necessary.

The EPA prods owners who can be located to voluntarily clean up sites they have abandoned. But if the owners refuse, the EPA and the states will undertake the task, drawing on a federal trust fund financed mainly by taxes on the manufacture or import of certain chemicals and petroleum (the balance of the fund comes from general revenues). States must finance 10 percent of the cost of cleaning up private sites and 50 percent of the cost of cleaning up public facilities. The EPA and the states can then assess unwilling owners' punitive damages up to triple the cleanup costs.

Cleanup requirements are especially controversial when applied to landowners who innocently purchased contaminated property. To deal with this problem, Congress enacted the Superfund Amendment and Reauthorization Act in 1986, which protects innocent landowners who—at the time of purchase—made an "appropriate inquiry" into the prior uses of the property. The act also requires companies to publicly disclose information about hazardous chemicals they use. We now turn to other laws regulating chemical hazards.

Chemical Hazards

Toxic Substances Control Act

Chemical substances that decades ago promised to improve the quality of life have lately shown their negative side—they have serious adverse side effects. For example, asbestos, in use for half a century, causes cancer and asbestosis, a debilitating lung disease, in workers who breathed in fibers decades ago. The result has been crippling disease and death and more than thirty thousand asbestos-related lawsuits filed nationwide. Other substances, such as polychlorinated biphenyls (PCBs) and dioxin, have caused similar tragedy. Together, the devastating effects of chemicals led to enactment of the TSCA, designed to control the manufacture, processing, commercial distribution, use, and disposal of chemicals that pose unreasonable health or environmental risks. (The TSCA does not apply to pesticides, tobacco, nuclear materials, firearms and ammunition, food, food additives, drugs, and cosmetics—all are regulated by other federal laws.)

The TSCA gives the EPA authority to screen for health and environmental risks by requiring companies to notify the EPA ninety days before manufacturing or importing new chemicals. The EPA may demand that the companies test the substances before marketing them and may regulate them in a number of ways, such as requiring the manufacturer to label its products, to keep records on its manufacturing and disposal processes, and to document all significant adverse reactions in people exposed to the chemicals. The EPA also has authority to ban certain especially hazardous substances, and it has banned the further production of PCBs and many uses of asbestos.

Both industry groups and consumer groups have attacked the TSCA. Industry groups criticize the act because the enforcement mechanism requires mountainous paperwork and leads to widespread delay. Consumer groups complain because the EPA has been slow to act against numerous chemical substances. The debate continues.

Pesticide Regulation

The United States is a major user of pesticides, substances that eliminate troublesome insects, rodents, fungi, and bacteria, consuming more than a billion pounds a year in the form of thirty-five thousand separate chemicals. As useful as they can be, like many chemical substances, pesticides can have serious side effects on humans and plant and animal life. Beginning in the early 1970s, Congress enacted major amendments to the Federal Insecticide, Fungicide, and Rodenticide Act of 1947 and the Federal Food, Drug, and Cosmetic Act (FFDCA) of 1906.

These laws direct the EPA to determine whether pesticides properly balance effectiveness against safety. If the pesticide can carry out its intended function without causing unreasonable adverse effects on human health or the environment, it may remain on the market. Otherwise, the EPA has authority to regulate or even ban its distribution and use. To enable the EPA to carry out its functions, the laws require manufacturers to provide a wealth of data about the way individual pesticides work and their side effects. The EPA is required to inspect pesticides to ensure that they conform to their labeled purposes, content, and safety, and the agency is empowered to certify pesticides for either general or restricted use. If a pesticide is restricted, only those persons certified in approved training programs may use it. Likewise, under the Pesticide Amendment to the FFDCA, the EPA must establish specific tolerances for the residue of pesticides on feed crops and both raw and processed foods. The Food and Drug Administration (for agricultural commodities) and the US Department of Agriculture (for meat, poultry, and fish products) enforce these provisions.

Other Types of Environmental Controls

Noise Regulation

Under the Noise Regulation Act of 1972, Congress has attempted to combat a growing menace to US workers, residents, and consumers. People who live close to airports and major highways, workers who use certain kinds of machinery (e.g., air compressors, rock drills, bulldozers), and consumers who use certain products, such as power mowers and air conditioners, often suffer from a variety of ailments. The Noise Regulation Act delegates to the EPA power to limit "noise emissions" from these major sources of noise. Under the act, manufacturers may not sell new products that fail to conform to the noise standards the EPA sets, and users are forbidden from dismantling noise control devices installed on these products. Moreover, manufacturers must label noisy products properly. Private suits may be filed against violators, and the act also permits fines of up to $25,000 per day and a year in jail for those who seek to avoid its terms.

Radiation Controls

The terrifying effects of a nuclear disaster became frighteningly clear when the Soviet Union's nuclear power plant at Chernobyl exploded in early 1986, discharging vast quantities of radiation into the world's airstream and affecting people thousands of miles away. In the United States, the most notorious nuclear accident occurred at the Three Mile Island nuclear utility in Pennsylvania in 1979, crippling the facility for years because of the extreme danger and long life of the radiation. Primary responsibility for overseeing nuclear safety rests with the Nuclear Regulatory Commission, but many other agencies and several federal laws (including the Clean Air Act; the Federal Water Pollution Control Act; the Safe Drinking Water Act; the Uranium Mill Tailings Radiation Control Act; the Marine Protection, Research, and Sanctuaries Act; the Nuclear Waste Policy Act of 1982; the CERCLA; and the Ocean Dumping Act) govern the use of nuclear materials and the storage of radioactive wastes (some of which will remain severely dangerous for thousands of years). Through many of these laws, the EPA has been assigned the responsibility of setting radiation guidelines, assessing new technology, monitoring radiation in the environment, setting limits on release of radiation from nuclear utilities, developing guidance for use of X-rays in medicine, and helping to plan for radiation emergencies.

Key Takeaway

Laws limiting the use of one's property have been around for many years; common-law restraints (e.g., the law of nuisance) exist as causes of action against those who would use their property to adversely affect the life or health of others or the value of their neighbors' property. Since the 1960s, extensive federal laws governing the environment have been enacted. These include laws governing air, water, chemicals, pesticides, solid waste, and nuclear activities. Some laws include criminal penalties for noncompliance.

Exercises

1. Who is responsible for funding CERCLA? That is, what is the source of funds for cleanups of hazardous waste?
2. Why is it necessary to have criminal penalties for noncompliance with environmental laws?
3. What is the role of states in setting standards for clean air and clean water?
4. Which federal act sets up a "cradle-to-grave" system for handling waste?
5. Why are federal environmental laws necessary? Why not let the states exclusively govern in the area of environmental protection?

33.6 Cases

Reasonable Use Doctrine

Hoover v. Crane

362 Mich. 36, 106 N.W.2d 563 (1960)

EDWARDS, JUSTICE

This appeal represents a controversy between plaintiff cottage and resort owners on an inland Michigan lake and defendant, a farmer with a fruit orchard, who was using the lake water for irrigation. The chancellor who heard the matter ruled that defendant had a right to reasonable use of lake water. The decree defined such reasonable use in terms which were unsatisfactory to plaintiffs who have appealed.

The testimony taken before the chancellor pertained to the situation at Hutchins Lake, in Allegan county, during the summer of 1958. Defendant is a fruit farmer who owns a 180-acre farm abutting on the lake. Hutchins Lake has an area of 350 acres in a normal season. Seventy-five cottages and several farms, including defendant's, abut on it. Defendant's frontage is approximately 1/4 mile, or about 10% of the frontage of the lake.

Hutchins Lake is spring fed. It has no inlet but does have an outlet which drains south. Frequently in the summertime the water level falls so that the flow at the outlet ceases.

All witnesses agreed that the summer of 1958 was exceedingly dry and plaintiffs' witnesses testified that Hutchins Lake's level was the lowest it had ever been in their memory. Early in August, defendant began irrigation of his 50-acre pear orchard by pumping water out of Hutchins Lake. During that month the lake level fell 6 to 8 inches—the water line receded 50 to 60 feet and cottagers experienced severe difficulties with boating and swimming.

* * *

The tenor of plaintiffs' testimony was to attribute the 6- to 8-inch drop in the Hutchins Lake level in that summer to defendant's irrigation activities. Defendant contended that the decrease was due to natural causes, that the irrigation was of great benefit to him and contributed only slightly to plaintiff's discomfiture. He suggests to us:

> *One could fairly say that because plaintiffs couldn't grapple with the unknown causes that admittedly occasioned a greater part of the injury complained of, they chose to grapple mightily with the defendant because he is known and visible.*

The circuit judge found it impossible to determine a normal lake level from the testimony, except that the normal summer level of the lake is lower than the level at which the lake ceases to drain into the outlet. He apparently felt that plaintiffs' problems were due much more to the abnormal weather conditions of the summer of 1958 than to defendant's irrigation activities.

His opinion concluded:

> *Accepting the reasonable use theory advanced by plaintiffs it appears to the court that the most equitable disposition of this case would be to allow defendant to use water from the lake until such time when his use interferes with the normal use of his neighbors. One quarter inch of water from the lake ought not to interfere with the rights and uses of defendant's neighbors and this quantity of water ought to be sufficient in time of need to service 45 acres of pears. A meter at the pump, sealed if need be, ought to be a sufficient safeguard. Pumping should not be permitted between the hours of 11 p.m. and 7 a.m. Water need be metered only at such times as there is no drainage into the outlet.*
>
> *The decree in this suit may provide that the case be kept open for the submission of future petitions and proofs as the conditions permit or require.*

Michigan has adopted the reasonable-use rule in determining the conflicting rights of riparian owners to the use of lake water.

In 1874, Justice COOLEY said:

> *It is therefore not a diminution in the quantity of the water alone, or an alteration in its flow, or either or both of these circumstances combined with injury, that will give a right of action, if in view of all the circumstances, and having regard to equality of right in others, that which has been done and which causes the injury is not unreasonable. In other words, the injury that is incidental to a reasonable enjoyment of the common right can demand no redress.* Dumont v. Kellogg, *29 Mich 420, 425.*

And in *People* v. *Hulbert*, the Court said:

> *No statement can be made as to what is such reasonable use which will, without variation or qualification, apply to the facts of every case. But in determining whether a use is reasonable we must consider what the use is for; its extent, duration, necessity, and its application; the nature and size of the stream, and the several uses to which it is put; the extent of the injury to the one proprietor and of the benefit to the other; and all other facts which may bear upon the reasonableness of the use.* Red River Roller Mills v. Wright, *30 Minn 249, 15 NW 167, and cases cited.*

The Michigan view is in general accord with 4 Restatement, Torts, §§ 851–853.

We interpret the circuit judge's decree as affording defendant the total metered equivalent in pumpage of 1/4 inch of the content of Hutchins Lake to be used in any dry period in between the cessation of flow from the outlet and the date when such flow recommences. Where the decree also provides for the case to be kept open for future petitions based on changed conditions, it would seem to afford as much protection for plaintiffs as to the future as this record warrants.

Both resort use and agricultural use of the lake are entirely legitimate purposes. Neither serves to remove water from the watershed. There is, however, no doubt that the irrigation use does occasion some water loss due to increased evaporation and absorption. Indeed, extensive irrigation might constitute a threat to the very existence of the lake in which all riparian owners have a stake; and at some point the use of the water which causes loss must yield to the common good.

The question on this appeal is, of course, whether the chancellor's determination of this point was unreasonable as to plaintiffs. On this record, we cannot overrule the circuit judge's view that most of plaintiffs' 1958 plight was due to natural causes. Nor can we say, if this be the only irrigation use intended and the only water diversion sought, that use of the amount provided in the decree during the dry season is unreasonable in respect to other riparian owners.

Affirmed.

Case Questions

1. If the defendant has caused a diminution in water flow, an alteration of the water flow, and the plaintiff is adversely affected, why would the Supreme Court of Michigan not provide some remedy?
2. Is it possible to define a use that is "not unreasonable"?
3. Would the case even have been brought if there had not been a drought?

Criminal Liability of Employees under RCRA

U.S. v. Johnson & Towers, Inc., Jack W. Hopkins, and Peter Angel

741 F.2d 662 (1984)

SLOVITER, Circuit Judge

Before us is the government's appeal from the dismissal of three counts of an indictment charging unlawful disposal of hazardous wastes under the Resource Conservation and Recovery Act. In a question of first impression regarding the statutory definition of "person," the district court concluded that the Act's criminal penalty provision imposing fines and imprisonment could not apply to the individual defendants. We will reverse.

The criminal prosecution in this case arose from the disposal of chemicals at a plant owned by Johnson & Towers in Mount Laurel, New Jersey. In its operations the company, which repairs and overhauls large motor vehicles, uses degreasers and other industrial chemicals that contain chemicals such as methylene chloride and trichlorethylene, classified as "hazardous wastes" under the Resource Conservation and Recovery Act (RCRA), 42 U.S.C. §§ 6901–6987 (1982) and "pollutants" under the Clean Water Act, 33 U.S.C. §§ 1251–1376 (1982). During the period relevant here, the waste chemicals from cleaning operations were drained into a holding tank and, when the tank was full, pumped into a trench. The trench flowed from the plant property into Parker's Creek, a tributary of the Delaware River. Under RCRA, generators of such wastes must obtain a permit for disposal from the Environmental Protection Agency (E.P.A.). The E.P.A. had neither issued nor received an application for a permit for Johnson & Towers' operations.

The indictment named as defendants Johnson & Towers and two of its employees, Jack Hopkins, a foreman, and Peter Angel, the service manager in the trucking department. According to the indictment, over a three-day period federal agents saw workers pump waste from the tank into the trench, and on the third day observed toxic chemicals flowing into the creek.

Count 1 of the indictment charged all three defendants with conspiracy under 18 U.S.C. § 371 (1982). Counts 2, 3, and 4 alleged violations under the RCRA criminal provision, 42 U.S.C. § 6928(d) (1982). Count 5 alleged a violation of the criminal provision of the Clean Water Act, 33 U.S.C. § 1319(c) (1982). Each substantive count also charged the individual defendants as aiders and abettors under 18 U.S.C. § 2 (1982).

The counts under RCRA charged that the defendants "did knowingly treat, store, and dispose of, and did cause to be treated, stored and disposed of hazardous wastes without having obtained a permit...in that the defendants discharged, deposited, injected, dumped, spilled, leaked and placed degreasers...into the trench...." The indictment alleged that both Angel and Hopkins "managed, supervised and directed a substantial portion of Johnson & Towers' operations...including those related to the treatment, storage and disposal of the hazardous wastes and pollutants" and that the chemicals were discharged by "the defendants and others at their direction." The indictment did not otherwise detail Hopkins' and Angel's activities or responsibilities.

Johnson & Towers pled guilty to the RCRA counts. Hopkins and Angel pled not guilty, and then moved to dismiss counts 2, 3, and 4. The court concluded that the RCRA criminal provision applies only to "owners and operators," i.e., those obligated under the statute to obtain a permit. Since neither Hopkins nor Angel was an "owner" or "operator," the district court granted the motion as to the RCRA charges but held that the individuals could be liable on these three counts under 18 U.S.C. § 2 for aiding and abetting. The court denied the government's motion for reconsideration, and the government appealed to this court under 18 U.S.C. § 3731 (1982).

* * *

The single issue in this appeal is whether the individual defendants are subject to prosecution under RCRA's criminal provision, which applies to:

> any person *who*— . . .
>
> *(2) knowingly treats, stores, or disposes of any hazardous waste identified or listed under this subchapter either—*
>
> *(A) without having obtained a permit under section 6925 of this title...or*
>
> *(B) in knowing violation of any material condition or requirement of such permit.*

42 U.S.C. § 6928(d) (emphasis added). The permit provision in section 6925, referred to in section 6928(d), requires "each person owning or operating a facility for the treatment, storage, or disposal of hazardous waste identified or listed under this subchapter to have a permit" from the E.P.A.

The parties offer contrary interpretations of section 6928(d)(2)(A). Defendants consider it an administrative enforcement mechanism, applying only to those who come within section 6925 and fail to comply; the government reads it as penalizing anyone who handles hazardous waste without a permit or in violation of a permit. Neither party has cited another case, nor have we found one, considering the application of this criminal provision to an individual other than an owner or operator.

As in any statutory analysis, we are obliged first to look to the language and then, if needed, attempt to divine Congress' specific intent with respect to the issue.

First, "person" is defined in the statute as "an individual, trust, firm, joint stock company, corporation (including a government corporation), partnership, association, State, municipality, commission, political subdivision of a State, or any interstate body." 42 U.S.C. § 6903(15) (1982). Had Congress meant in section 6928(d)(2)(A) to take aim more narrowly, it could have used more narrow language. Since it did not, we attribute to "any person" the definition given the term in section 6903(15).

Second, under the plain language of the statute the only explicit basis for exoneration is the existence of a permit covering the action. Nothing in the language of the statute suggests that we should infer another provision exonerating persons who knowingly treat, store or dispose of hazardous waste but are not owners or operators.

Finally, though the result may appear harsh, it is well established that criminal penalties attached to regulatory statutes intended to protect public health, in contrast to statutes based on common law crimes, are to be construed to effectuate the regulatory purpose. * * *

Congress enacted RCRA in 1976 as a "cradle-to-grave" regulatory scheme for toxic materials, providing "nationwide protection against the dangers of improper hazardous waste disposal." H.R. Rep. No. 1491, 94th Cong., 2d Sess. 11, *reprinted in* 1976 U.S. Code Cong. & Ad. News 6238, 6249. RCRA was enacted to provide "a multifaceted approach toward solving the problems associated with the 3–4 billion tons of discarded materials generated each year, and the problems resulting from the anticipated 8% annual increase in the volume of such waste." *Id.* at 2, 1976 U.S. Code Cong. & Ad. News at 6239. The committee reports accompanying legislative consideration of RCRA contain numerous statements evincing the Congressional view that improper disposal of toxic materials was a serious national problem.

The original statute made knowing disposal (but not treatment or storage) of such waste without a permit a misdemeanor. Amendments in 1978 and 1980 expanded the criminal provision to cover treatment and storage and made violation of section 6928 a felony. The fact that Congress amended the statute twice to broaden the scope of its substantive provisions and enhance the penalty is a strong indication of Congress' increasing concern about the seriousness of the prohibited conduct.

We conclude that in RCRA, no less than in the Food and Drugs Act, Congress endeavored to control hazards that, "in the circumstances of modern industrialism, are largely beyond self-protection." *United States v. Dotterweich*, 320 U.S. at 280. It would undercut the purposes of the legislation to limit the class of potential defendants to owners and operators when others also bear responsibility for handling regulated materials. The phrase "without having obtained a permit *under section 6925*" (emphasis added) merely references the section under which the permit is required and exempts from prosecution under section 6928(d)(2)(A) anyone who has obtained a permit; we conclude that it has no other limiting effect. Therefore we reject the district court's construction limiting the substantive criminal provision by confining "any person" in section 6928(d)(2)(A) to owners and operators of facilities that store, treat or dispose of hazardous waste, as an unduly narrow view of both the statutory language and the congressional intent.

Case Questions

1. The district court (trial court) accepted the individual defendants' argument. What was that argument?
2. On what reasoning did the appellate court reject that argument?
3. If employees of a company that is violating the RCRA carry out disposal of hazardous substances in violation of the RCRA, they would presumably lose their jobs if they didn't. What is the moral justification for applying criminal penalties to such employees (such as Hopkins and Angel)?

33.7 Summary and Exercises

Summary

An estate is an interest in real property; it is the degree to which a thing is owned. Freehold estates are those with an uncertain duration; leaseholds are estates due to expire at a definite time. A present estate is one that is currently owned; a future estate is one that is owned now but not yet available for use.

Present estates are (1) the fee simple absolute; (2) the fee simple defeasible, which itself may be divided into three types, and (3) the life estate.

Future estates are generally of two types: reversion and remainder. A reversion arises whenever a transferred estate will endure for a shorter time than that originally owned by the transferor. A remainder interest arises when the transferor gives the reversion interest to someone else.

Use of air, earth, and water are the major rights incident to ownership of real property. Traditionally, the owner held "up to the sky" and "down to the depths," but these rules have been modified to balance competing rights in a modern economy. The law governing water rights varies with the states; in general, the eastern states with more plentiful water have adopted either the natural flow doctrine or the reasonable use doctrine of riparian rights, giving those who live along a waterway certain rights to use the water. By contrast, western states have tended to apply the prior appropriation doctrine, which holds that first in time is first in right, even if those downstream are disadvantaged.

An easement is an interest in land—created by express agreement, prior use, or necessity—that permits one person to make use of another's estate. An affirmative easement gives one person the right to use another's land; a negative easement prevents the owner from using his land in a way that will affect another person's land. In understanding easement law, the important distinctions are between easements appurtenant and in gross, and between dominant and servient owners.

The law not only defines the nature of the property interest but also regulates land use. Tort law regulates land use by imposing liability for (1) activities that affect those off the land and (2) injuries caused to people who enter it. The two most important theories relating to the former are nuisance and trespass. With respect to the latter, the common law confusingly distinguishes among trespassers, licensees, and invitees. Some states are moving away from the perplexing and rigid rules of the past and simply require owners to maintain their property in a reasonably safe condition.

Land use may also be regulated by private agreement through the restrictive covenant, an agreement that "runs with the land" and that will be binding on any subsequent owner. Land use is also regulated by the government's power under eminent domain to take private land for public purposes (upon payment of just compensation), through zoning laws, and through recently enacted environmental statutes, including the National Environmental Policy Act and laws governing air, water, treatment of hazardous wastes, and chemicals.

Exercises

1. Dorothy deeded an acre of real estate that she owns to George for the life of Benny and then to Ernie. Describe the property interests of George, Benny, Ernie, and Dorothy.
2. In Exercise 1, assume that George moves into a house on the property. During a tornado, the roof is destroyed and a window is smashed. Who is responsible for repairing the roof and window? Why?
3. Dennis likes to spend his weekends in his backyard, shooting his rifle across his neighbor's yard. If Dennis never sets foot on his neighbor's property, and if the bullets strike neither persons nor property, has he violated the legal rights of the neighbor? Explain.
4. Wanda is in charge of acquisitions for her company. Realizing that water is important to company operations, Wanda buys a plant site on a river, and the company builds a plant that uses all of the river water. Downstream owners bring suit to stop the company from using any water. What is the result? Why?
5. Sunny decides to build a solar home. Before beginning construction, she wants to establish the legal right to prevent her neighbors from constructing buildings that will block the sunlight. She has heard that the law distinguishes between licenses and easements, easements appurtenant and in gross, and affirmative and negative easements. Which of these interests would you recommend for Sunny? Why?

Self-Test Questions

1. A freehold estate is defined as an estate
    - a. with an uncertain duration
    - b. due to expire at a definite time
    - c. owned now but not yet available for use
    - d. that is leased or rented
2. A fee simple defeasible is a type of
    - a. present estate
    - b. future estate
    - c. life estate
    - d. leasehold estate
3. A reversion is
    - a. a present estate that prevents transfer of land out of the family
    - b. a form of life estate

c. a future estate that arises when the estate transferred has a duration less than that originally owned by the transferor
d. identical to a remainder interest

4. An easement is an interest in land that may be created by
    a. express agreement
    b. prior use
    c. necessity
    d. all of the above
5. The prior appropriation doctrine
    a. tends to be applied by eastern states
    b. holds that first in time is first in right
    c. gives those that live along a waterway special rights to use the water
    d. all of the above

Self-Test Answers

1. a
2. a
3. c
4. d
5. b

Endnotes

1. *Magnolia Petroleum Co. v. Thompson*, 106 F.2d 217 (8th Cir. 1939).
2. *U.S. v. Causby*, 328 U.S. 256 (1946).
3. Gary Wickert, Drone Wars: Airspace and Legal Rights in the Age of Drones. http://www.claimsjournal.com/news/national/2015/07/02/264216.htm.
4. *Hoover v. Crane*, 362 Mich. 36, 106 N.W.2d 563 (1960).
5. See http://tort.laws.com/nuisance.
6. *Rowland v. Christian*, 443 P.2d 561 (Cal. 1968).
7. *Norris v. Williams*, 54 A.2d 331 (Md. 1947).
8. *Shelley v. Kraemer*, 334 U.S. 1 (1947).
9. *Hawaii Housing Authority v. Midkiff*, 467 U.S. 229 (1984).
10. *Kelo v. New London*, 545 U.S. 469 (2005).
11. 42 United States Code, Section 4321 et seq.
12. "The Tricks of the Trade-off," *Business Week*, April 4, 1977, 72.
13. 33 United States Code, Section 1251.
14. *Solid Waste Agency of Northern Cook County v. Army Corps of Engineers*, 531 U.S. 159 (2001).
15. *Midlantic National Bank v. New Jersey*, 474 U.S. 494 (1986).

CHAPTER 34

The Transfer of Real Estate by Sale

Learning Objectives

After reading this chapter, you should understand the following:

1. The various forms of real estate ownership, including fee simple, tenancy in common, and joint tenancy.
2. The mechanics of finding, financing, and closing a real estate transaction.
3. How adverse possession may sometimes vest title in real property despite the nonconsent of the owner.

This chapter follows the steps taken when real estate is transferred by sale.

1. The buyer selects a form of ownership.
2. The buyer searches for the real estate to be purchased. In doing so, the buyer will usually deal with real estate brokers.
3. After a parcel is selected, the seller and buyer will negotiate and sign a sales agreement.
4. The seller will normally be required to provide proof of title.
5. The buyer will acquire property insurance.
6. The buyer will arrange financing.
7. The sale and purchase will be completed at a closing.

During this process, the buyer and seller enter into a series of contracts with each other and with third parties such as brokers, lenders, and insurance companies. In this chapter, we focus on the unique features of these contracts, with the exception of mortgages (Chapter 29) and property insurance (Chapter 37). We conclude by briefly examining adverse possession—a method of acquiring property for free.

34.1 Forms of Ownership

Learning Objectives

1. Be familiar with the various kinds of legal interests in real property.
2. Know the ways that two or more people can own property together.
3. Understand the effect of marriage, divorce, and death on various forms of property ownership.

Overview

severalty

Ownership by one individual.

The transfer of property begins with the buyer's selection of a form of ownership. Ownership by one individual is known to lawyers as ownership "in **severalty**." That's the simplest form of ownership. But buyers often make it a bit more complicated by grouping together—because of marriage, close friendship, or simply in order to finance the purchase more easily.

When purchasers group together for investment purposes, they often use the various forms of organization discussed in Chapter 40, Chapter 41, Chapter 42, and Chapter 43—corporations, partnerships, limited partnerships, joint ventures, and business trusts. The most popular of these forms of organization for owning real estate is the limited partnership. A real estate limited partnership is designed to allow investors to take substantial deductions that offset current income from the partnership and other similar investments, while at the same time protecting the investor from personal liability if the venture fails.

But you do not have to form a limited partnership or other type of business in order to acquire property with others; many other forms are available for personal or investment purposes. To these we now turn.

Joint Tenancy

Joint tenancy is an estate in land owned by two or more persons. It is distinguished chiefly by the right of survivorship. If two people own land as joint tenants, then either becomes the sole owner when the other dies. For land to be owned jointly, four unities must coexist:

unity of time

The interests of the joint owners must begin at the same time.

unity of title

The joint tenants must acquire their title in the same conveyance—that is, the same will or deed.

unity of interest

Each owner must have the same interest in the property; for example, one may not hold a life estate and the other the remainder interest.

unity of possession

Where all parties have an equal right to possession of the property.

1. **Unity of time**. The interests of the joint owners must begin at the same time.
2. **Unity of title**. The joint tenants must acquire their title in the same conveyance—that is, the same will or deed.
3. **Unity of interest**. Each owner must have the same interest in the property; for example, one may not hold a life estate and the other the remainder interest.
4. **Unity of possession**. All parties must have an equal right to possession of the property (see Figure 34.1).

FIGURE 34.1 Forms of Ownership and Unities

Unities	Joint Tenancy	Tenancy by Entirety	Tenancy in Common
Time	✓	✓	
Title	✓	✓	
Interest	✓	✓	
Possession	✓	✓	✓
Person		✓	

Suppose a woman owns real property and upon marriage wishes to own it jointly with her husband. She deeds it to herself and her husband "as joint tenants and not tenants in common." (Strictly speaking, the common law would deny that the resulting form of ownership was joint because the unities of title and time were missing. The wife owned the property first and originally acquired title under a different conveyance. But the modern view in most states is that an owner may convey directly to herself and another in order to create a joint estate.)

When one or more of the unities is destroyed, however, the joint tenancy lapses. Suppose Fritz and Ahmed own a farm as joint tenants. Fritz decides to sell his interest to Julia. Julia and Ahmed would hold as tenants in common and not as joint tenants.

Suppose Fritz and Ahmed own as joint tenants, and Fritz had made out his will, leaving his interest in the farm to Reuben. On Fritz's death, would the unities be destroyed, leaving Ahmed and Reuben as tenants in common? No, because Ahmed, as joint tenant, would own the entire farm on Fritz's death, leaving nothing behind for Reuben to inherit.

Tenancy by the Entirety

About half the states permit husbands and wives to hold property as **tenants by the entirety**. This form of ownership is similar to joint tenancy, but is restricted to husbands and wives. This is sometimes described as the unity of person. In most of the states permitting tenancy by the entirety, acquisition by husband and wife of property as joint tenants automatically becomes a tenancy by the entirety. The fundamental importance of tenancy by the entirety is that neither spouse individually can terminate it; only a joint decision to do so will be effective. One spouse alone cannot sell or lease an interest in such property without consent of the other, and in many states a creditor of one spouse cannot seize the individual's separate interest in the property, because the interest is indivisible.

tenants by the entirety

When spouses own property jointly and all unities are applicable.

Tenancy in Common

Two or more people can hold property as **tenants in common** when the unity of possession is present, that is, when each is entitled to occupy the property. None of the other unities—of time, title, or interest—is necessary, though their existence does not impair the common ownership. Note that the tenants in common do not own a specific portion of the real estate; each has an undivided share in the whole, and each is entitled to occupy the whole estate. One tenant in common may sell, lease, or mortgage his undivided interest. When a tenant in common dies, his interest in the property passes to his heirs, not to the surviving tenants in common.

tenants in common

When the unity of possession is present—that is, when each is entitled to occupy the property. None of the other unities—of time, title, or interest—is necessary, though their existence does not impair the common ownership.

Because tenancy in common does not require a unity of interest, it has become a popular form of "mingling," by which unrelated people pool their resources to purchase a home. If they were joint tenants, each would be entitled to an equal share in the home, regardless of how much each contributed, and the survivor would become sole owner when the other owner dies. But with a tenancy-in-common arrangement, each can own a share in proportion to the amount invested.

Community Property

community property

There are differences among community property states, but the general theory is that, with certain exceptions, each spouse has an undivided equal interest in property acquired while the husband and wife are married to each other.

separate property

Property acquired by gift of inheritance or owned before the marriage.

In ten states—Alaska, Arizona, California, Idaho, Louisiana, Nevada, New Mexico, Texas, Washington, and Wisconsin—property acquired during a marriage is said to be **community property**. There are differences among these states, but the general theory is that with certain exceptions, each spouse has an undivided equal interest in property acquired while the husband and wife are married to each other. The major exception is for property acquired by gift or inheritance during the marriage. (By definition, property owned by either spouse before the marriage is not community property.) Property acquired by gift of inheritance or owned before the marriage is known as **separate property**. Community property states recognize other forms of ownership; specifically, husbands and wives may hold property as joint tenants, permitting the survivor to own the whole.

The consequence of community property laws is that either the husband or the wife may manage the community property, borrow against it, and dispose of community personal property. Community real estate may only be sold or encumbered by both jointly. Each spouse may bequeath only half the community property in his or her will. In the absence of a will, the one-half property interest will pass in accordance with the laws of intestate succession. If the couple divorces, the states generally provide for an equal or near-equal division of the community property, although a few permit the court in its discretion to divide in a different proportion.

Condominiums

In popular parlance, a condominium is a kind of apartment building, but that is not its technical legal meaning. Condominium is a form of ownership, not a form of structure, and it can even apply to space—for example, to parking spaces in a garage. The word *condominium* means joint ownership or control, and it has long been used whenever land has been particularly scarce or expensive. Condominiums were popular in ancient Rome (especially near the Forum) and in the walled cities of medieval Europe.

In its modern usage, *condominium* refers to a form of housing involving two elements of ownership. The first is the living space itself, which may be held in common, in joint tenancy, or in any other form of ownership. The second is the common space in the building, including the roof, land under the structure, hallways, swimming pool, and the like. The common space is held by all purchasers as tenants in common. The living space may not be sold apart from the interest in the common space.

Two documents are necessary in a condominium sale—the master deed and the bylaws. The master deed (1) describes the condominium units, the common areas, and any restrictions that apply to them; (2) establishes the unit owner's interest in the common area, his number of votes at owners' association meetings, and his share of maintenance and operating expenses (sometimes unit owners have equal shares, and sometimes their share is determined by computing the ratio of living area or market price or original price of a single unit to the whole); and (3) creates a board of directors to administer the affairs of the whole condominium. The bylaws usually establish the owners' association, set out voting procedures, list the powers and duties of the officers, and state the obligations of the owners for the use of the units and the common areas.

Cooperatives

Another popular form of owning living quarters with common areas is the cooperative. Unlike the person who lives in a condominium, the tenant of a cooperative does not own a particular unit. Instead, he owns a share of the entire building. Since the building is usually owned by a corporation (a cooperative corporation, hence the name), this means that the tenant owns stock in the corporation. A tenant occupies a unit under a lease from the corporation. Together, the lease and stock in the building corporation are considered personal, not real, property.

In a condominium, an owner of a unit who defaults in paying monthly mortgage bills can face foreclosure on the unit, but neighbors in the building suffer no direct financial impact, except that the defaulter probably has not paid monthly maintenance charges either. In a cooperative, however, a tenant who fails to pay monthly charges can jeopardize the entire building, because the mortgage is on the building as a whole; consequently, the others will be required to make good the payments or face foreclosure.

Time-Shares

A time-share is an arrangement by which several people can own the same property while being entitled to occupy the premises exclusively at different times on a recurring basis. In the typical vacation property, each owner has the exclusive right to use the apartment unit or cottage for a specified period of time each year—for example, Mr. and Mrs. Smith may have possession from December 15 through December 22, Mr. and Mrs. Jones from December 23 through December 30, and so on. The property is usually owned as a condominium but need not be. The sharers may own the property in fee simple, hold a joint lease, or even belong to a vacation club that sells time in the unit.

Time-share resorts have become popular in recent years. But the lure of big money has brought unscrupulous contractors and salespersons into the market. Sales practices can be unusually coercive, and as a result, most states have sets of laws specifically to regulate time-share sales. Almost all states provide a cooling-off period, or rescission period; these periods vary from state to state and provide a window where buyers can change their minds without forfeiting payments or deposits already made.

Key Takeaway

Property is sometimes owned by one person or one entity, but more often two or more persons will share in the ownership. Various forms of joint ownership are possible, including joint tenancies, tenancy by the entirety, and tenancy in common. Married persons should be aware of whether the state they live in is a community property state; if it is, the spouse will take some interest in any property acquired during the marriage. Beyond traditional landholdings, modern real estate ownership may include interests in condominiums, cooperatives, or time-shares.

Exercises

1. Miguel and Maria Ramirez own property in Hendersonville, North Carolina as tenants by the entirety. Miguel is a named defendant in a lawsuit that alleges defamation, and an award is made for $245,000 against Miguel. The property he owns with Maria is worth $320,000 and is owned free of any mortgage interest. To what extent can the successful plaintiff recover damages by forcing a sale of the property?
2. Miguel and Maria Ramirez own property in Hendersonville, N.C. as tenants by the entirety. They divorce. At the time of the divorce, there are no new deeds signed or recorded. Are they now tenants in common or joint tenants?

34.2 Brokers, Contracts, Proof of Title, and Closing

Learning Objectives

1. Know the duties of the real estate broker and how brokers are licensed.
2. Be able to discuss the impact of constitutonal and statutory law on real estate sellers and brokers.
3. Describe the various kinds of listing contracts and their import.
4. Know the elements of a sales agreement and the various types of deeds to real estate.
5. Understand the closing process and how "good title" is obtained through the title search and insurance process.

listing agreement

An agreement between the owner of real property and a real estate broker.

Once the buyer (or buyers) knows what form of ownership is most desirable, the search for a suitable property can begin. This search often involves contact with a broker hired by the seller. The seller's contract with the broker, known as the **listing agreement**, is the first of the series of contracts in a typical real estate transaction. As you consider these contracts, it is important to keep in mind that despite the size of the transaction and the dire financial consequences should anything go awry, the typical person (buyer or seller) usually acts as his or her own attorney. An American Bar Association committee has noted the following:

> *It is probably safe to say that in a high percentage of cases the seller is unrepresented and signs the contracts of brokerage and sale on the basis of his faith in the broker. The buyer does not employ a lawyer. He signs the contract of sale without reading it and, once financing has been obtained, leaves all the details of title search and closing to the lender or broker. The lender or broker may employ an attorney but, where title insurance is furnished by a company maintaining its own title plant, it is possible that no lawyer, not even house counsel, will appear.*

This being so, the material that follows is especially important for buyers and sellers who are not represented in the process of buying or selling real estate.

Regulation of the Real Estate Business

State Licensing

Real estate brokers, and the search for real estate generally, are subject to state and federal government regulation. Every state requires real estate brokers to be licensed. To obtain a license, the broker must pass an examination covering the principles of real estate practice, transactions, and instruments. Many states additionally insist that the broker take several courses in finance, appraisal, law, and real estate practice and apprentice for two years as a salesperson in a real estate broker's office.

Civil Rights Act

Two federal civil rights laws also play an important role in the modern real estate transaction. These are the Civil Rights Act of 1866 and the Civil Rights Act of 1968 (Fair Housing Act). In *Jones v. Alfred H. Mayer Co.*,[1] the Supreme Court upheld the constitutionality of the 1866 law, which expressly gives all citizens of the United States the same rights to inherit, purchase, lease, sell, hold, and convey real and personal property. A minority buyer or renter who is discriminated against may sue for relief in federal court, which may award damages, stop the sale of the house, or even direct the seller to convey the property to the plaintiff.

The 1968 Fair Housing Act prohibits discrimination on the grounds of race, color, religion, sex, national origin, handicap, or family status (i.e., no discrimination against families with children) by any one of several means, including the following:

1. Refusing to sell or rent to or negotiate with any person
2. Discriminating in the terms of sale or renting
3. Discriminating in advertising
4. Denying that the housing is available when in fact it is
5. "Blockbusting" (panicking owners into selling or renting by telling them that minority groups are moving into the neighborhood)
6. Creating different terms for granting or denying home loans by commercial lenders
7. Denying anyone the use of real estate services

However, the 1968 act contains several exemptions:

1. Sale or rental of a single-family house if the seller
    a. owns less than four such houses,
    b. does not use a broker,
    c. does not use discriminatory advertising,
    d. within two years sells no more than one house in which the seller was not the most recent occupant.
    e. Rentals in a building occupied by the owner as long as it houses fewer than five families and the owner did not use discriminatory advertising
    f. Sale or rental of space in buildings or land restricted by religious organization owners to people of the same religion (assuming that the religion does not discriminate on the basis of race, color, or national origin)
    g. Private clubs, if they limit their noncommercial rentals to members

The net impact of these laws is that discrimination based on color or race is flatly prohibited and that other types of discrimination are also barred unless one of the enumerated exemptions applies.

Hiring the Broker: The Listing Agreement

When the seller hires a real estate broker, he will sign a listing agreement. (In several states, the Statute of Frauds says that the seller must sign a written agreement; however, he should do so in all states in order to provide evidence in the event of a later dispute.) This listing agreement sets forth the broker's commission, her duties, the length of time she will serve as broker, and other terms of her agency relationship. Whether the seller will owe a commission if he or someone other than the broker finds a buyer depends on which of three types of listing agreements has been signed.

Exclusive Right to Sell

exclusive right to sell

If the seller agrees to an exclusive-right-to-sell agency, he will owe the broker the stated commission regardless of who finds the buyer.

If the seller agrees to an **exclusive-right-to-sell** agency, he will owe the broker the stated commission regardless of who finds the buyer. Language such as the following gives the broker an exclusive right to sell: "Should the seller or anyone acting for the seller (including his heirs) sell, lease, transfer, or otherwise dispose of the property within the time fixed for the continuance of the agency, the broker shall be entitled nevertheless to the commission as set out herein."

Exclusive Agency

exclusive agency

The broker has the exclusive right to sell and will be entitled to the commission if anyone other than the seller finds the buyer (in other words, the seller will owe no commission if he finds a buyer).

open listing

Calls for payment to the broker only if the broker was instrumental in finding the buyer; the broker is not entitled to her commission if anyone else, seller or otherwise, locates the buyer.

Somewhat less onerous from the seller's perspective (and less generous from the broker's perspective) is the **exclusive agency**. The broker has the exclusive right to sell and will be entitled to the commission if anyone other than the seller finds the buyer (i.e., the seller will owe no commission if he finds a buyer). Here is language that creates an exclusive agency: "A commission is to be paid the broker whether the purchaser is secured by the broker or by any person other than the seller."

Open Listing

The third type of listing, relatively rarely used, is the open listing, which authorizes "the broker to act as agent in securing a purchaser for my property." The **open listing** calls for payment to the broker only if the broker was instrumental in finding the buyer; the broker is not entitled to her commission if anyone else, seller or otherwise, locates the buyer.

Suppose the broker finds a buyer, but the seller refuses at that point to sell. May the seller simply change his mind and avoid having to pay the broker's commission? The usual rule is that when a broker finds a buyer who is "ready, willing, and able" to purchase or lease the property, she has earned her commission. Many courts have interpreted this to mean that even if the buyers are unable to obtain financing, the commission is owed nevertheless once the prospective buyers have signed a purchase agreement. To avoid this result, the seller should insist on either a "no deal, no commission" clause in the listing agreement (entitling the broker to payment only if the sale is actually consummated) or a clause in the purchase agreement making the purchase itself contingent on the buyer's finding financing.

Broker's Duties

Once the listing agreement has been signed, the broker becomes the seller's agent—or, as occasionally happens, the buyer's agent, if hired by the buyer. A broker is not a general agent with broad authority. Rather, a broker is a special agent with authority only to show the property to potential buyers. Unless expressly authorized, a broker may not accept money on behalf of the seller from a prospective buyer. Suppose Eunice hires Pete's Realty to sell her house. They sign a standard exclusive agency listing, and Pete cajoles Frank into buying the house. Frank writes out a check for $10,000 as a down payment and offers it to Pete, who absconds with the money. Who must bear the loss? Ordinarily, Frank would have to bear the loss, because Pete was given no authority to accept money. If the listing agreement explicitly said that Pete could accept the down payment from a buyer, then the loss would fall on Eunice.

Although the broker is but a special agent, she owes the seller, her principal, a **fiduciary duty**. (See Chapter 38 on relations between principal and agent.) A fiduciary duty is a duty of the highest loyalty and trust. It means that the broker cannot buy the property for herself through an intermediary without full disclosure to the seller of her intentions. Nor may the broker secretly receive a commission from the buyer or suggest to a prospective buyer that the property can be purchased for less than the asking price.

fiduciary duty

A fiduciary duty is a duty of the highest loyalty and trust. It means that the broker cannot buy the property for himself through an intermediary without full disclosure to the seller.

The Sales Agreement

Once the buyer has selected the real estate to be acquired, an agreement of sale will be negotiated and signed. Contract law in general is discussed in Chapter 8; our discussion here will focus on specific aspects of the real estate contract. The Statute of Frauds requires that contracts for sale of real estate must be in writing. The writing must contain certain information.

Names of Buyers and Sellers

The agreement must contain the names of the buyers and sellers. As long as the parties sign the agreement, however, it is not necessary for the names of buyers and sellers to be included within the body of the agreement.

Real Estate Description

The property must be described sufficiently for a court to identify the property without having to look for evidence outside the agreement. The proper address, including street, city, and state, is usually sufficient.

Price

The price terms must be clear enough for a court to enforce. A specific cash price is always clear enough. But a problem can arise when installment payments are to be made. To say "$50,000, payable monthly for fifteen years at 12 percent" is not sufficiently detailed, because it is impossible to determine whether the installments are to be equal each month or are to be equal principal payments with varying interest payments, declining monthly as the balance decreases.

Signature

As a matter of prudence, both buyer and seller should sign the purchase agreement. However, the Statute of Frauds requires only the signature of the party against whom the agreement is to be enforced. So if the seller has signed the agreement, he cannot avoid the agreement on the grounds that the buyer has not signed it. However, if the buyer, not having signed, refuses to go to closing and take title, the seller would be unable to enforce the agreement against him.

Easements and Restrictive Covenants

Unless the contract specifically states otherwise, the seller must deliver **marketable title**. A marketable title is one that is clear of restrictions to which a reasonable buyer would object. Most buyers would refuse to close the deal if there were potential third-party claims to all or part of the title. But a buyer would be unreasonable if, at closing, he refused to consummate the transaction on the basis that there were utility easements for the power company or a known and visible driveway easement that served the neighboring property. As a precaution, a seller must be sure to say

marketable title

A marketable title is one that can be transferred to a new owner without the likelihood that claims will be made on it by another party.

in the contract for sale that the property is being sold "subject to easements and restrictions of record." A buyer who sees only such language should insist that the particular easements and restrictive covenants be spelled out in the agreement before he signs.

Risk of Loss

Suppose the house burns down after the contract is signed but before the closing. Who bears the loss? Once the contract is signed, most states apply the rule of equitable conversion, under which the buyer's interest (his executory right to enforce the contract to take title to the property) is regarded as real property, and the seller's interest is regarded as personal property. The rule of equitable conversion stems from an old maxim of the equity courts: "That which ought to be done is regarded as done." That is, the buyer ought to have the property and the seller ought to have the money. A practical consequence of this rule is that the loss of the property falls on the buyer. Because most buyers do not purchase insurance until they take title, eleven states have adopted the Uniform Vendor and Purchaser Risk Act, which reverses the equitable conversion rule and places risk of loss on the seller. The parties may themselves reverse the application of the rule; the buyer should always insist on a clause in a contract stating that risk of loss remains with the seller until a specified date, such as the closing.

Earnest Money

As protection against the buyer's default, the seller usually insists on a down payment known as earnest money. This is intended to cover such immediate expenses as proof of marketable title and the broker's commission. If the buyer defaults, he forfeits the earnest money, even if the contract does not explicitly say so.

Contingencies

Performance of most real estate contracts is subject to various contingencies—that is, it is conditioned on the happening of certain events. For example, the buyer might wish to condition his agreement to buy the house on his ability to find a mortgage or to find one at a certain rate of interest. Thus the contract for sale might read that the buyer "agrees to buy the premises for $50,000, subject to his obtaining a $40,000 mortgage at 5 percent." The person protected by the contingency may waive it; if the lowest interest rate the buyer could find was 5.5 percent, he could either refuse to buy the house or waive the condition and buy it anyway.

Times for Performance

A frequent difficulty in contracting to purchase real estate is the length of time it takes to receive an acceptance to an offer. If the acceptance is not received in a reasonable time, the offeror may treat the offer as rejected. To avoid the uncertainty, an offeror should always state in his offer that it will be held open for a definite period of time (five working days, two weeks, or whatever). The contract also ought to spell out the times by which the following should be done: (1) seller's proof that he has title, (2) buyer's review of the evidence of title, (3) seller's correction of title defects, (4) closing date, and (5) possession by the buyer. The absence of explicit time provisions will not render the contract unenforceable—the courts will infer a reasonable time—but their absence creates the possibility of unnecessary disputes.

Types of Deeds

Most real estate transactions involve two kinds of deeds, the general warranty deed and the quitclaim deed.

1. **General warranty deed.** In a warranty deed, the seller warrants to the buyer that he possesses certain types of legal rights in the property. In the **general warranty deed**, the seller warrants that (a) he has good title to convey, (b) the property is free from any encumbrance not stated in the deed (the warranty against encumbrances), and (c) the property will not be taken by someone with a better title (the warranty of quiet enjoyment). Breach of any of these warranties exposes the seller to damages.
2. **Quitclaim deed.** The simplest form of deed is the **quitclaim deed**, in which the seller makes no warranties. Instead, he simply transfers to the buyer whatever title he had, defects and all. A quitclaim deed should not be used in the ordinary purchase and sale transaction. It is usually reserved for removing a cloud on the title—for instance, a quitclaim deed by a widow who might have a dower interest in the property.

   If the purchase agreement is silent about the type of deed, courts in many states will require the seller to give the buyer a quitclaim deed. In the contract, the buyer should therefore specify that the seller is to provide a warranty deed at closing.

general warranty deed

A deed in which the seller warrants that (a) he has good title to convey, (b) the property is free from any encumbrance not stated in the deed (the warranty against encumbrances), and (c) the property will not be taken by someone with a better title (the warranty of quiet enjoyment).

quitclaim deed

A deed in which the seller makes no warranties.

When buyers move in after the closing, they frequently discover defects (the boiler is broken, a pipe leaks, the electrical power is inadequate). To obtain recourse against such an eventuality, the buyer could attempt to negotiate a clause in the contract under which the seller gives a warranty covering named defects. However, even without an express warranty, the law implies two warranties when a buyer purchases a new house from a builder. These are warranties that (1) the house is habitable and (2) the builder has completed the house in a workmanlike manner. Most states have refused to extend these warranties to subsequent purchasers—for example, to the buyer from a seller who had bought from the original builder. However, a few states have begun to provide limited protection to subsequent purchasers—in particular, for defects that a reasonable inspection will not reveal but that will show up only after purchase.

Proof of Title

Contracts are often formed and performed simultaneously, but in real estate transactions there is more often a gap between contract formation and performance (the closing). The reason is simple: the buyer must have time to obtain financing and to determine whether the seller has marketable title. That is not always easy; at least, it is not as straightforward as looking at a piece of paper. To understand how title relates to the real estate transaction, some background on recording statutes will be useful.

Recording Statutes

Suppose Slippery Sam owned Whispering Pines, a choice resort hotel on Torch Lake, Michigan. On October 1, Slippery deeded Whispering Pines to Lorna for $5,575,000. Realizing the profit potential, Slippery decided to sell it again, and did so on October 6, to Malvina. But he did not tell Malvina that he had already sold it to Lorna. He then departed for a long sailing trip to the British Virgin Islands.

recording statutes

Statutes that award title to the person who has complied with the requirement to place the deed in a public registry, usually a county Register of Deeds office.

When Malvina and her helpers arrive at Whispering Pines, they find Lorna already tidying up. Who should prevail in the litigation over the title that will surely follow? At common law, the first deed prevailed over subsequent deeds. So if this were a pure common-law state, Lorna would have title and Malvina would be out of luck, stuck with a worthless piece of paper. Her only recourse, probably futile, would be to search out and sue Slippery Sam for fraud. Most states, however, have enacted **recording statutes**, which award title to the person who has complied with the requirement to place the deed in a publicly available file in a public office in the county, often called the recorder's office or the register of deeds.

Notice Statute

Under the most common type of recording statute, called a notice statute, a deed must be recorded in order for the owner to prevail against a subsequent purchaser. Again, in a common law state with no recording statute, the first deed (to Lorna) would grant defensible title to the grantee (Lorna). But suppose that Lorna took her time recording her deed, recording it on October 10th, so that at the time of the second sale to Malvina there was no notice on the public record of a deed from Sam to Lorna. In that case, if Malvina promptly records her deed, she will prevail, even if Lorna records her deed five minutes later.

What if Malvina is "in" with Sam on swindling Lorna? For most notice statute rules to apply, Malvina must have been a bona fide purchaser, meaning that she must have (1) paid valuable consideration, (2) bought in good faith, and (3) had no notice of the earlier sale. If Malvina were in possession and Lorna has to bring a lawsuit to "quiet title," the burden will be on Lorna to prove any of the three conditions above. Without all three, Malvina will lose the lawsuit.

constructive notice

A buyer is on constructive notice of anything put in the public records, whether or not she actually notices.

Assuming Malvina is not conspiring with Sam, and meets all three conditions, she will lose the litigation with Lorna if Lorna records promptly, putting Malvina (and all others) on notice that she owns the property as a result of being Sam's purchaser/grantee. Malvina should have checked the public records before closing the deal with Sam; lawyers and judges would say that the prior recorded deed put subsequent purchasers on **constructive notice** of the deal between Sam and Lorna.

constructive notice

A buyer is on constructive notice of anything put in the public records, whether or not she actually notices.

Lorna had recorded before Malvina took the deed, Lorna would prevail if Malvina did not in fact check the public records; she should have checked, and the recorded deed is said to put subsequent purchasers on **constructive notice**.

Race-Notice Statute

Another common type of recording statute is the race-notice statute. To gain priority under this statute, the subsequent bona fide purchaser must also record—that is, win the race to the recorder's office before the earlier purchaser. But the second purchaser must also be a bona fide purchaser (having no knowledge of the earlier sale and paying fair value for the property). So in our example, in a notice-race jurisdiction, Lorna would only prevail if she records before Malvina does, or if she can prove that Malvina either knew of her deal with Sam or paid less than fair value.

Race Statute

A third, relatively uncommon type is the race statute, which gives title to whoever records first, even if the subsequent purchaser is not bona fide and has actual knowledge of the prior sale. Suppose that when she received the deed, Malvina knew of the earlier sale to Lorna. Malvina got to the recording office the day she got the deed, October 6, and Lorna came in the following day. In a race-statute jurisdiction, Malvina would take title.

Chain of Title

Given the recording statutes, the buyer must check the deed on record to determine (1) whether the seller ever acquired a valid deed to the property—that is, whether a chain of title can be traced from earlier owners to the seller—and (2) whether the seller has already sold the property to another purchaser, who has recorded a deed. There are any number of potential "clouds" on the title that would defeat a fee simple conveyance: among others, there are potential judgments, liens, mortgages, and easements that might affect the value of the property. There are two ways to protect the buyer: the abstract of title and opinion, and title insurance.

Abstract and Opinion

An abstract of title is a summary of the chain of title, listing all previous deeds, mortgages, tax liens, and other instruments recorded in the county land records office. The abstract is prepared by either an attorney or a title company. Since the list itself says nothing about whether the recorded instruments are legally valid, the buyer must also have the opinion of an attorney reviewing the abstract, or must determine by doing his own search of the public records, that the seller has valid title. The attorney's opinion is known as a title opinion or certificate of title. The problem with this method of proving title is that the public records do not reveal hidden defects. One of the previous owners might have been a minor or an incompetent person who can still void his sale, or a previous deed might have been forged, or a previous seller might have claimed to be single when in fact he was married and his wife failed to sign away her dower rights. A search of the records would not detect these infirmities.

Title Insurance

To overcome these difficulties, the buyer should obtain **title insurance**. This is a one-premium policy issued by a title insurance company after a search through the same public records. When the title company is satisfied that title is valid, it will issue the insurance policy for a premium that could be as high as 1 percent of the selling price. When the buyer is taking out a mortgage, he will ordinarily purchase two policies, one to cover his investment in the property and the other to cover the mortgagee lender's loan. In general, a title policy protects the buyer against losses that would occur if title (1) turns out to belong to someone else; (2) is subject to a lien, encumbrance, or other defect; or (3) does not give the owner access to the land. A preferred type of title policy will also insure the buyer against losses resulting from an unmarketable title.

title insurance

A one-premium policy issued by a title insurance company after a search through the public records. Title insurance is usually provided to both the buyer and the buyer's lender. It guarantees against defects in the title rather than any physical aspects of the property.

Note that in determining whether to issue a policy, the title company goes through the process of searching through the public records again. The title policy as such does not guarantee that title is sound. A buyer could conceivably lose part or all of the property someday to a previous rightful owner, but if he does, the title insurance company must reimburse him for his losses.

Although title insurance is usually a sound protection, most policies are subject to various exclusions and exceptions. For example, they do not provide coverage for zoning laws that restrict use of the property or for a government's taking of the property under its power of eminent domain. Nor do the policies insure against defects created by the insured or known by the insured but unknown to the company. Some companies will not provide coverage for mechanics' liens, public utility easements, and unpaid taxes. (If the accrued taxes are known, the insured will be presented with a list, and if he pays them on or before the closing, they will be covered by the final policy.) Furthermore, as demonstrated in *Title and Trust Co. of Florida v. Barrows*, (see Section 4), title insurance covers title defects only, not physical defects in the property.

The Closing

Closing can be a confusing process because in most instances several contracts are being performed simultaneously:

1. The seller and purchaser are performing the sales contract.
2. The seller is paying off a mortgage, while the buyer is completing arrangements to borrow money and mortgage the property.
3. Title and other insurance arrangements will be completed.
4. The seller will pay the broker.
5. If buyer and seller are represented, attorneys for each party will be paid.

FIGURE 34.2 Closing Process

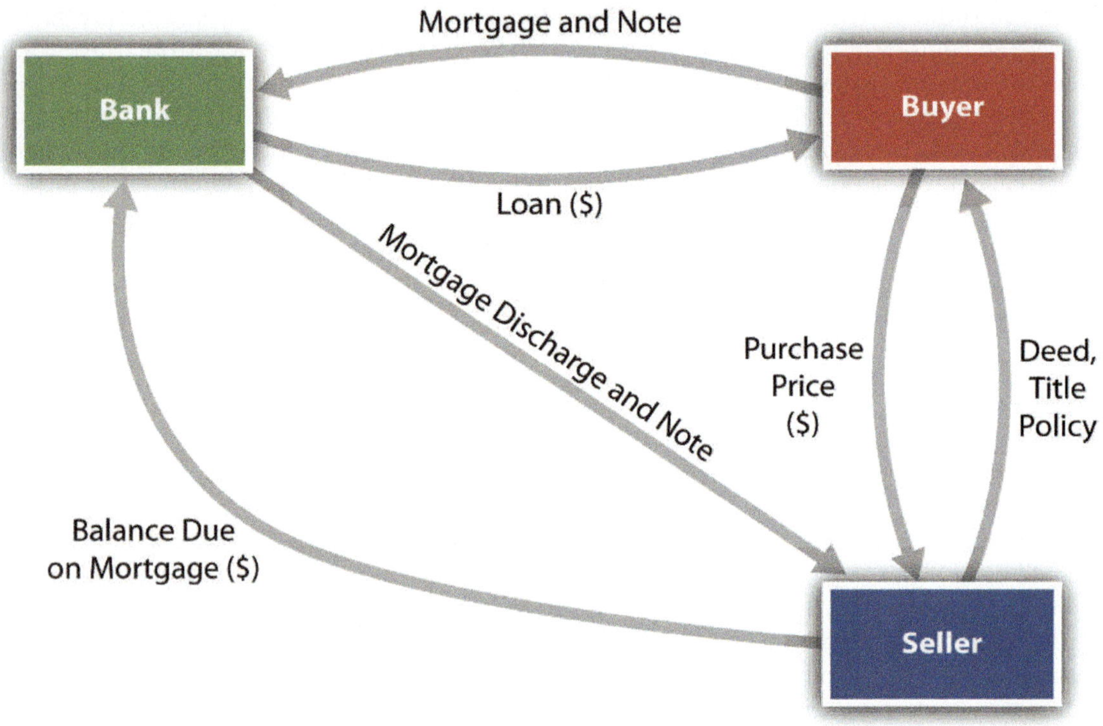

Despite all these transactions, the critical players are the seller, the purchaser, and the bank. To place the closing process in perspective, assume that one bank holds the existing (seller's) mortgage on the property and is also financing the buyer's purchase. We can visualize the three main players sitting at a table, ready to close the transaction. The key documents and the money will flow as illustrated in Figure 34.2.

Form of the Deed

The deed must satisfy two fundamental legal requirements: it must be in the proper form, and there must be a valid delivery. Deeds are usually prepared by attorneys, who must include not only information necessary for a valid deed but also information required in order to be able to record the deed. The following information is typically required either for a valid deed or by the recording statutes.

Grantor

The grantor—the person who is conveying the property—must be designated in some manner. Obviously, it is best to give the grantor's full name, but it is sufficient that the person or persons conveying the deed are identifiable from the document. Thus "the heirs of Lockewood Filmer" is sufficient identification if each of the heirs signs the deed.

Grantee

Similarly, the deed should identify the grantee—the person to whom the property is being conveyed. It does not void the deed to misspell a person's name or to omit part of a name, or even to omit the name of one of the grantees (as in "Lockewood Filmer and wife"). Although not technically necessary, the deed ought to detail the interests being conveyed to each grantee in order to avoid considerable legal difficulty later. "To Francis Lucas, a single man, and Joseph Lucas and Matilda Lucas, his wife" was a deed of unusual ambiguity. Did each party have a one-third interest? Or did Joseph and Matilda hold half as tenants by the entirety and Francis have a one-half interest as a tenant in common? Or perhaps Francis had a one-third interest as a tenant in common and Joseph and Matilda held two-thirds as tenants by the entirety? Or was there some other possible combination? The court chose the second interpretation, but considerable time and money could have been saved had the deed contained a few simple words of explanation.[2]

Addresses

Addresses of the parties should be included, although their absence will not usually invalidate the deed. However, in some states, failure to note the addresses will bar the deed from being recorded.

Words of Conveyance

The deed must indicate that the grantor presently intends to convey his interest in the property to the grantee. The deed may recite that the grantor "conveys and warrants" the property (warranty deed) or "conveys and quitclaims" the property (quitclaim deed). Some deeds use the words "bargain and sell" in place of convey.

Description

The deed must contain an accurate description of the land being conveyed, a description clear enough that the land can be identified without resorting to other evidence. Four general methods are used.

1. **The US government survey.** This is available west of the Mississippi (except in Texas) and in Alabama, Florida, Illinois, Indiana, Michigan, Mississippi, Ohio, and Wisconsin. With this survey, it is possible to specify with considerable exactitude any particular plot of land in any township in these states.
2. **Metes and bounds.** The description of metes and bounds begins with a particular designated point (called a monument)—for example, a drainpipe, an old oak tree, a persimmon stump—and then defines the boundary with distances and angles until returning to the monument. As you can tell, using monuments that are biological (like trees and stumps) will have a limited utility as time goes on. Most surveyors put in stakes (iron pins), and the metes and bounds description will go from points where stakes have been put in the ground.
3. **Plats.** Many land areas have been divided into numbered lots and placed on a map called a plat. The plats are recorded. The deed, then, need only refer to the plat and lot number—for

example, "Lot 17, Appledale Subdivision, record in Liber 2 of Plats, page 62, Choctaw County Records."

4. **Informal description.** If none of the preceding methods can be used, an informal description, done precisely enough, might suffice. For instance, "my home at 31 Fernwood Street, Maplewood, Idaho" would probably pass muster.

Statement of Consideration

Statutes usually require that some consideration be stated in the deed, even though a grantor may convey property as a gift. When there is a selling price, it is easy enough to state it, although the actual price need not be listed. When land is being transferred as a gift, a statement of nominal consideration—for example, one dollar—is sufficient.

Date

Dates are customary, but deeds without dates will be enforced.

Execution

The deed must be signed by the grantor and, in some states, witnesses, and these signatures must be acknowledged by a notary public in order to make the deed eligible for recording. If someone is signing for the grantor under a power of attorney, a written instrument authorizing one person to sign for another, the instrument must be recorded along with the deed.

Delivery

delivery

Entails (1) physical delivery to the grantee, (2) an intention by the grantor to convey title, and (3) acceptance of title by the grantee.

To validly convey title to the property, the deed must not only be in proper form but also be delivered. This technical legal requirement is sometimes misunderstood. **Delivery** entails (1) physical delivery to the grantee, (2) an intention by the grantor to convey title, and (3) acceptance of title by the grantee. Because the grantor must intend to convey title, failure to meet the other two elements during the grantor's lifetime will void title on his death (since at that point he of course cannot have an intention). Thus when a grantee is unaware of the grantor's intention to deed the property to him, an executed deed sitting in a safe-deposit box will be invalid if discovered after the grantor's death.

Delivery to Grantee

If the deed is physically delivered to the grantee or recorded, there is a rebuttable presumption that legal delivery has been made. That is, the law presumes, in the absence of evidence to the contrary, that all three conditions have been met if delivery or recording takes place. But this presumption can be rebutted, as shown in *Havens v. Schoen*, (see Section 4).

Delivery to Third Party (Commercial Escrow)

The grantor may deliver the deed to a third party to hold until certain conditions have been met. Thus to avoid the problem of the deed sitting in the grantor's own safe-deposit box, he could deliver it to a third party with instructions to hold it until his death and then to deliver it to the grantee. This would be an effective delivery, even though the grantee could not use the property until the grantor died. For this method to be effective, the grantor must lose all control over the deed, and the third party must be instructed to deliver the deed when the specified conditions occur.

This method is most frequently used in the commercial escrow. **Escrow** is a method by which a third party holds a document or money or both until specified conditions have been met. A typical example would be a sale in which the buyer is afraid of liens that might be filed after the closing. A contractor that has supplied materials for the building of a house, for example, might file a lien against the property for any amounts due but unpaid under the contract. The effectiveness of the lien would relate back to the time that the materials were furnished. Thus, at closing, all potential liens might not have been filed. The buyer would prefer to pay the seller after the time for filing materialmen's liens has lapsed. But sellers ordinarily want to ensure that they will receive their money before delivering a deed. The solution is for the buyer to pay the money into escrow (e.g., to a bank) and for the seller to deliver the deed to the same escrow agent. The bank would be instructed to hold both the money and the deed until the time for filing mechanics' liens has ended. If no materialmen's liens have been filed, then the money is paid out of escrow to the seller and the deed is released to the buyer. If a lien has been filed, then the money will not be paid until the seller removes the lien (usually by paying it off).

escrow

A method by which a third party holds a document or money or both until specified conditions have been met.

Key Takeaway

Most real estate is bought and sold through real estate brokers, who must be licensed by the state. Brokers have different kinds of agreements with clients, including exclusive right to sell, exclusive agency, and open listing. Brokers will usually arrange a sales agreement that includes standard provisions such as property description, earnest money, and various contingencies. A deed, usually a warranty deed, will be exchanged at the closing, but not before the buyer has obtained good proof of title, usually by getting an abstract and opinion and paying for title insurance. The deed will typically be delivered to the buyer and recorded at the county courthouse in the register of deeds' office.

Exercises

1. Deepak Abhishek, a single man, lives in a race-notice state. He contracts to buy a large parcel of land from his friend, Ron Khurana, for the sum of $280,000. Subsequent to the contract, Khurana finds another buyer, who is willing to pay $299,000. Khurana arranges for two closings on the same day, within two hours of each other. At 10 a.m., he sells the property to Beverly Hanks and her husband, John, for $299,000. The Hanks are not represented by an attorney. Khurana hands them the deed at closing, but he takes it back from them and says, "I will record this at the courthouse this afternoon." The Hankses take a copy of the deed with them and are satisfied that they have bought the property; moreover, Khurana gives them a commitment from Lawyer's Title Company that the company will insure that they are receiving fee simple title from Khurana, subject to the deed's being recorded in the county register of deeds' office.

   At noon, Khurana has a closing with Abhishek, who is represented by an attorney. The attorney went to the courthouse earlier, at 11:30 a.m., and saw nothing on record that would prevent Khurana from conveying fee simple title. As the deal closes, and as Khurana prepares to leave town, Abhishek's attorney goes to the courthouse and records the deed at 1:15 p.m. At 2:07 p.m., on his way out of town, Khurana records the deed to the Hankses.

   a. Who has better claim to the property—the Hankses or Deepak Abhishek?
   b. Does it matter if the state is a notice jurisdiction or a notice-race jurisdiction?
   c. A warranty deed is given in both closings. What would be the best remedy for whichever buyer did not get the benefit of clear title from these two transactions?
2. Kitty Korniotis is a licensed real estate broker. Barney Woodard and his wife, Carol, sign an exclusive agency listing with Kitty to sell their house on Woodvale Avenue. At a social gathering, Carol mentions to a friend, Helen Nearing, that the house on Woodvale is for sale. The next day, Helen drives by the property and calls the number on Kitty's sign. Helen and Scott

Nearing sign a contract to buy the house from the Woodards. Is Kitty entitled to the commission?

34.3 Adverse Possession

Learning Objective

1. Explain how it is possible to own land without paying for it.

adverse possession

Title may pass to someone who occupies the lands of another for a certain (statutorily prescribed) period of time in an open, notorious, and hostile manner.

In some instances, real property can be acquired for free—or at least without paying the original owner anything. (Considerable cost may be involved in meeting the requisite conditions.) This method of acquisition—known as **adverse possession**—is effective when five conditions are met: (1) the person claiming title by adverse possession must assert that he has a right to possession hostile to the interest of the original owner, (2) he must actually possess the property, (3) his possession must be "open and notorious," (4) the possession must be continuous, and (5) the possession must be exclusive.

Hostile Possession

Suppose Jean and Jacques are tenants in common of a farm. Jean announces that he no longer intends to pursue agricultural habits and leaves for the city. Jacques continues to work on the land, making improvements and paying taxes and the mortgage. Years later, Jacques files suit for title, claiming that he now owns the land outright by adverse possession. He would lose, since his possession was not hostile to Jacques. To be hostile, possession of the land must be without permission and with the intention to claim ownership. Possession by one cotenant is deemed permissive, since either or both are legally entitled to possession. Suppose, instead, that Jean and Jacques are neighboring farmers, each with title to his own acreage, and that Jean decides to fence in his property. Just to be on the safe side, he knowingly constructs the fence twenty feet over on Jacques's side. This is adverse possession, since it is clearly hostile to Jacques's possession of the land.

Actual Possession

Not only must the possession be hostile but it must also be actual. The possessor must enter onto the land and make some use of it. Many state statutes define the permissible type of possession—for example, substantial enclosure or cultivation and improvement. In other states, the courts will look to the circumstances of each case to determine whether the claimant had in fact possessed the land (e.g., by grazing cattle on the land each summer).

Open and Notorious Possession

The possessor must use the land in an open way, so that the original owner could determine by looking that his land was being claimed and so that people in the area would know that it was being used by the adverse possessor. In the melodramatic words of one court, the adverse possessor "must unfurl his flag on the land, and keep it flying so that the owner may see, if he will, that an enemy has invaded his domains, and planted the standard of conquest."[3] Construction of a building on the owner's property would be open and notorious; development of a cave or tunnel under the owner's property would not be.

Continuous Possession

The adverse possessor must use the land continuously, not intermittently. In most states, this continuous period must last for at least twenty years. If the adverse possession is passed on to heirs or the interest is sold, the successor adverse possessors may tack on the time they claim possession to reach the twenty years. Should the original owner sell his land, the time needed to prove continuous possession will not lapse. Of course, the original owner may interrupt the period—indeed, may terminate it—by moving to eject the adverse possessor any time before the twenty years has elapsed.

Exclusive Possession

The adverse possessor must claim exclusive possession of the land. Sharing the land with the owner is insufficient to ground a claim of legal entitlement based on adverse possession, since the sharing is not fully adverse or hostile. Jean finds a nice wooded lot to enjoy weekly picnics. The lot belongs to Jacques, who also uses it for picnics. This use would be insufficient to claim adverse possession because it is neither continuous nor exclusive.

If the five tests are met, then the adverse possessor is entitled to legal title. If any one of the tests is missing, the adverse possession claim will fail.

Key Takeaway

Real property can be acquired without paying the lawful owner if five conditions of adverse possession are met: (1) the person claiming title by adverse possession must assert that he has a right to possession hostile to the interest of the original owner, (2) he must actually possess the property, (3) his possession must be "open and notorious," (4) the possession must be continuous, and (5) the possession must be exclusive.

Exercise

1. Tyler decides to camp out on a sandy beach lot near Isle of Palms, South Carolina. The owner, who had hoped to build a large house there, lived out of state. Tyler made no secret of his comings and goings, and after several weeks, when no one challenged his right to be there, he built a sturdy lean-to. After a while, he built a "micro house" and put a propane tank next to it. Although there was no running water, Tyler was plenty comfortable. His friends came often, they partied on the beach, and life was good. Five years after he first started camping out there, an agent of the owner came and told him to deconstruct his shelter and "move on." Does Tyler have any rights in the property? Why or why not?

34.4 Cases

Title Insurance

Title and Trust Co. of Florida v. Barrows

381 So.2d 1088 (Fla. App. 1979)

McCORD, ACTING CHIEF JUDGE.

This appeal is from a final judgment awarding money damages to appellees (Barrows) for breach of title insurance policy. We reverse.

Through a realtor, the Barrowses purchased, for $ 12,500 [about $47,000 in 2017 dollars], a lot surrounded on three sides by land owned by others, all of which is a part of a beach subdivision. The fourth side of their lot borders on a platted street called Viejo Street, the right-of-way for which has been dedicated to and accepted by St. Johns County. The right-of-way line opposite their lot abuts a Corps of Engineers' right-of-way in which there is a stone breakwater. The intracoastal waterway flows on the other side of the breakwater.

The realtor who sold the lot to the Barrows represented to them that the county would build a road in the right-of-way along Viejo Street when they began plans for building on their lot. There have been no street improvements in the dedicated right-of-way, and St. Johns County has no present plans for making any improvements. The "road" is merely a continuation of a sandy beach.

A year after purchasing the land the Barrowses procured a survey which disclosed that the elevation of their lot is approximately one to three feet above the mean high water mark. They later discovered that their lot, along with the Viejo Street right-of-way abutting it, is covered by high tide water during the spring and fall of each year.

At the time appellees purchased their lot, they obtained title insurance coverage from appellant. The title policy covered:

> *Any defect in or lien or encumbrance on the title to the estate or title covered hereby...or a lack of a right of access to and from the land . . .*

Appellees' complaint of lack of right of access was founded on the impassable condition of the platted street. After trial without a jury, the trial court entered final judgment finding that appellees did not have access to their property and, therefore, were entitled to recover $ 12,500 from appellant the face amount of the policy.

Appellant and Florida Land Title Association, appearing as amicus curiae, argue that appellant cannot be held liable on grounds of "lack of right of access to and from the land" since there is no defect shown by the public record as to their right of access; that the public record shows a dedicated and accepted public right-of-way abutting the lot. They contend that title insurance does not insure against defects in the physical condition of the land or against infirmities in legal right of access not shown by the public record. *See Pierson v. Bill*, 138 Fla. 104, 189 So. 679 (1939). They argue that defects in the physical condition of the land such as are involved here are not covered by title insurance. We agree. Title insurance only insures against title defects.

The Supreme Court of North Carolina in *Marriott Financial Services, Inc. v. Capitol Funds, Inc.*, 288 N.C. 122, 217 S.E.2d 551 (1975), construed "right of access" to mean the right to go to and from the public right-of-way without unreasonable restrictions. *Compare Hocking v. Title Insurance & Trust Company*, 37 Cal.2d 644, 234 P.2d 625 (1951), where, in ruling that the plaintiff failed to state a cause of action in a suit brought under her title policy, the court said:

> *She appears to possess fee simple title to the property for whatever it may be worth; if she has been damaged by false representations in respect to the condition and value of the land her remedy would seem to be against others than the insurers of the title she acquired.*

In *Mafetone, et al., v. Forest Manor Homes, Inc., et al.*, 34 A.D.2d 566, 310 N.Y.S.2d 17 (N.Y.1970), the plaintiff brought an action against a title insurance company for damages allegedly flowing from a change in the grade of a street. There the court said:

> *The title company is not responsible to plaintiffs for the damages incurred by reason of the change in elevating the abutting street to its legal grade, since the provisions of the standard title insurance policy here in question are concerned with matters affecting title to property and do not concern themselves with physical conditions of the abutting property absent a specific request by the person ordering a title report and policy....*

In *McDaniel v. Lawyers' Title Guaranty Fund*, 327 So.2d 852 (Fla. 2 D.C.A. 1976), our sister court of the Second District said:

> *The man on the street buys a title insurance policy to insure against defects in the record title. The title insurance company is in the business of guaranteeing the insured's title to the extent it is affected by the public records.*

In the case here before us, there is no dispute that the public record shows a legal right of access to appellant's property via the platted Viejo Street. The title insurance policy only insured against record title defects and not against physical infirmities of the platted street.

Reversed.

Case Questions

1. Do you think that the seller (or the seller's agent) actually took the Barrowses to see the property when it was underwater? Why or why not?
2. Before buying, should the Barrowses have actually gone to the property to see for themselves "the lay of the land" or made inquiries of neighboring lot owners?
3. Assuming that they did not make inspection of the property or make other inquiries, do you think the seller or the seller's agent made any misrepresentations about the property that would give the Barrowses any remedies in law or equity?

Delivery of a Deed

Havens v. Schoen
108 Mich. App. 758; 310 N.W.2d 870 (Mich. App. 1981)

[Norma Anderson Havens, the owner of certain farm property in Marlette, Michigan, in contemplation of her death executed a quit-claim deed to the property to her only daughter, Linda Karen Anderson. The deed was subsequently recorded. Subsequently, Linda Karen Anderson married and became Linda Karen Adams and died. Thereafter, Norma Anderson Havens and Norman William Scholz, a nephew of Havens who has an interest in the property as the beneficiary of a trust, brought a suit in Sanilac Circuit Court against Ernest E. Schoen, Administrator of the estate of Linda Karen Adams, deceased, and other heirs of James W. Anderson, the ex-husband of Norma Anderson Havens, seeking to set aside the deed or to impose a constructive trust on the farm property which was the subject of the deed. Arthur E. Moore, J., found no cause of action and entered judgment for defendants. The plaintiffs appeal alleging error because there never was a delivery of the deed or an intent by Havens to then presently and unconditionally convey an interest in the property.]

PER CURIAM.

In 1962, plaintiff Dr. [Norma Anderson] Havens purchased the Scholz family farm from the estate of her twin brother, Norman Scholz. She gave a deed of trust to her other brother Earl Scholz in 1964, naming her daughter Linda Karen Adams as the principal beneficiary. In 1969, she filed suit against Earl and Inez Scholz and, in settlement of that suit, the property was conveyed to Dr. Havens and her daughter, now deceased. On August 13, 1969, Dr. Havens executed a quit-claim deed to her daughter of her remaining interest in the farm. It is this deed which Dr. Havens wishes to set aside.

The trial court found that plaintiffs failed to meet the burden of proving an invalid conveyance. Plaintiffs claim that there was never a delivery or an intent to presently and unconditionally convey an interest in the property to the daughter. The deed was recorded but defendants presented no other evidence to prove delivery. The recording of a deed raises a presumption of delivery. *Hooker v Tucker*, 335 Mich 429, 434; 56 NW2d 246 (1953). The only effect of this presumption is to cast upon the opposite party the burden of moving forward with the evidence. *Hooker v Tucker, supra*. The burden of proving delivery by a preponderance of the evidence remains with the party relying on the deed. *Camp v Guaranty Trust Co*, 262 Mich 223, 226; 247 NW 162 (1933). Acknowledging that the deed was recorded, plaintiffs presented substantial evidence showing no delivery and no intent to presently and unconditionally convey an interest in the property. The deed, after recording, was returned to Dr. Havens. She continued to manage the farm and pay all expenses for it. When asked about renting the farm, the daughter told a witness to ask her mother. Plaintiffs presented sufficient evidence to dispel the presumption. We find that the trial court erred when it stated that plaintiffs had the burden of proof on all issues. The defendants had the burden of proving delivery and requisite intent.

In *Haasjes v Woldring*, 10 Mich App 100; 158 NW2d 777 (1968), *leave denied* 381 Mich 756 (1968), two grandparents executed a deed to property to two grandchildren. The grandparents continued to live on the property, pay taxes on it and subsequent to the execution of the deed they made statements which this Court found inconsistent with a prior transfer of property. These circumstances combined with the fact that the deed was not placed beyond the grantors' control led the *Haasjes* Court to conclude that a valid transfer of title had not been effected. The *Haasjes* Court, citing *Wandel v Wandel*, 336 Mich 126; 57 NW2d 468 (1953), and *Resh v Fox*, 365 Mich 288, 112 NW2d 486 (1961), held that in considering whether there was a present intent to pass title, courts may look to the subsequent acts of the grantor.

This Court reviews *de novo* the determinations of a trial court sitting in an equity case. *Chapman v Chapman*, 31 Mich App 576, 579; 188 NW2d 21 (1971). Having reviewed the evidence presented by the defendants to prove delivery, we find that the defendants failed to meet their burden of proof. Under the circumstances, the recording itself and the language of the deed were not persuasive proof of delivery or intent. Defendants presented no evidence of possession of the deed by anyone but the grantor and presented no evidence showing knowledge of the deed by the grantee. No evidence was presented showing that the daughter was ever aware that she owned the property. The showing made by defendants was inadequate to carry their burden of proof. The deed must be set aside.

Plaintiffs alleged none of the grounds which have traditionally been recognized as justifying the imposition of a constructive trust. See *Chapman v Chapman, supra*. A constructive trust is imposed only when it would be inequitable to do otherwise. *Arndt v Vos*, 83 Mich App 484; 268 NW2d 693 (1978). Although plaintiffs claim relief for a mutual mistake, plaintiffs have presented no facts suggesting a mistake on the part of the grantee. Creation of a constructive trust is not warranted by the facts as found by the trial court. There has been no claim that those findings are erroneous.

We remand to the trial court to enter an order setting aside the August 13, 1969, deed from Norma Anderson Havens to Linda Karen Anderson Adams purporting to convey the interest of Dr. Havens in the farm. The decision of the trial court finding no justification for imposing a trust upon the property is affirmed.

Affirmed in part, reversed in part, and remanded.

DISSENT BY:

MacKenzie, J. *(dissenting)*.

I respectfully dissent. The deed was recorded with the knowledge and assent of the grantor, which creates a presumption of delivery. See *Schmidt v Jennings*, 359 Mich 376, 383; 102 NW2d 589 (1960), *Reed v Mack*, 344 Mich 391, 397; 73 NW2d 917 (1955). Crucial evidence was conflicting and I would disagree that the trial court's findings were clearly erroneous.

In *Reed v Mack*, the Court affirmed the trial court's finding that there had been delivery where the grantor defendant, who had owned the property with her husband, recorded a deed conveying a property jointly to herself and the two other grantees, stating:

"We are in agreement with the trial court. The defendant-appellant, a grantor in the deed, caused the recording of the deed, the delivery of which she attacks. The recording of a warranty deed may, under some circumstances, be effectual to show delivery. A delivery to one of several joint grantees, in absence of proof to the contrary, is delivery to all. *Mayhew v Wilhelm*, 249 Mich 640 [229 NW 459 (1930)]. While placing a deed on record does not in itself necessarily establish delivery, the recording of a deed raises a presumption of delivery, and the whole object of delivery is to indicate an intent by the grantor to give effect to the instrument." [Citations]

In *McMahon v Dorsey*, 353 Mich 623, 626; 91 NW2d 893 (1958), the significance of delivery was characterized as the manifestation of the grantor's intent that the instrument be a completed act.

* * *

The evidence herein indicates that plaintiff Norma Anderson Havens, after she had been told she was dying from cancer, executed a quit-claim deed on August 16, 1969, to her daughter, Linda Karen Anderson. Plaintiff Havens testified that the reason she executed the deed was that she felt "if something should happen to me, at least Karen would be protected". The deed was recorded the same day by plaintiff Havens's attorney. Plaintiff Havens either knew that the deed was recorded then or learned of the recording shortly thereafter. Although plaintiff Havens testified that she intended only a testamentary disposition, she apparently realized that the deed was effective to convey the property immediately because her testimony indicated an intention to execute a trust agreement. Linda Karen lived on the farm for five years after the deed was recorded until her death in 1974, yet plaintiff Havens did not attempt to have Linda Karen deed the farm back to her so she could replace the deed with a trust agreement or a will. Plaintiff Havens testified that she approached her attorneys regarding a trust agreement, but both attorneys denied this. The trial judge specifically found the testimony of the attorneys was convincing and he, of course, had the benefit of observing the witnesses.

Haasjes v Woldring, 10 Mich App 100; 158 NW2d 777 (1968), relied upon by the majority, involved unrecorded deeds which remained in a strongbox under control of the grantors until after their deaths. The grantors continued to live alone on the property and pay taxes thereon. Based on the lack of recording, I find *Haasjes* distinguishable from the present case.

In *Hooker v Tucker*, 335 Mich 429; 56 NW2d 246 (1953), delivery was held not to have occurred where the grantor handed her attorney a copy of a deed containing a legal description of property she wished included in a will to be drawn by him and he subsequently mailed the deed to the grantee without the grantor's knowledge or permission. The purported delivery by mailing being unauthorized distinguishes *Hooker* from this case where there was no indication the recording was done without the grantor's authorization.

The majority relies on the grantee's purported lack of knowledge of the conveyance but the record is not at all clear in this regard. Further, if a deed is beneficial to the grantee, its acceptance is presumed. *Tackaberry v Monteith*, 295 Mich 487, 493; 295 NW 236 (1940), see also *Holmes v McDonald*, 119 Mich 563; 78 NW 647 (1899). While the burden of proving delivery is on the person relying upon the instrument, the burden shifts upon its recordation so that the grantor must go forward with the evidence of showing nondelivery, once recordation and beneficial interest have been shown. *Hooker v Tucker, supra*, and *Tackaberry, supra*. The trial court properly found that plaintiffs failed to go forward with the evidence and found that the deed conveyed title to the farm.

Factually, this is a difficult case because plaintiff Havens executed a deed which she intended to be a valid conveyance at the time it was executed and recorded. Subsequently, when her daughter unexpectedly predeceased her, the deed created a result she had not foreseen. She seeks to eradicate the unintended *result* by this litigation.

I am reluctant to set aside an unambiguous conveyance which was on record and unchallenged for five years on the basis of the self-serving testimony of the grantor as to her intent at the time she executed the deed and authorized its recordation.

I would affirm.

Case Question

1. Which opinion, the majority or the dissenting opinion, do you agree with, and why?

34.5 Summary and Exercises

Summary

Real property can be held in various forms of ownership. The most common forms are tenancy in common, joint tenancy, and tenancy by the entirety. Ten states recognize the community property form of ownership.

In selling real property, various common-law and statutory provisions come into play. Among the more important statutory provisions are the Civil Rights Acts of 1866 and 1968. These laws control the manner in which property may be listed and prohibit discrimination in sales. Sellers and buyers must also be mindful of contract and agency principles governing the listing agreement. Whether the real estate broker has an exclusive right to sell, an exclusive agency, or an open listing will have an important bearing on the fee to which the broker will be entitled when the property is sold.

The Statute of Frauds requires contracts for the sale of real property to be in writing. Such contracts must include the names of buyers and sellers, a description of the property, the price, and signatures. Unless the contract states otherwise, the seller must deliver marketable title, and the buyer will bear the loss if the property is damaged after the contract is signed but before the closing. The seller will usually insist on being paid earnest money, and the buyer will usually protect himself contractually against certain contingencies, such as failure to obtain financing. The contract should also specify the type of deed to be given to the buyer.

To provide protection to subsequent buyers, most states have enacted recording statutes that require buyers to record their purchases in a county office. The statutes vary: which of two purchasers will prevail depends on whether the state has a notice, notice-race, or race statute. To protect themselves, buyers usually purchase an abstract and opinion or title insurance. Although sale is the usual method of acquiring real property, it is possible to take legal title without the consent of the owner. That method is adverse possession, by which one who openly, continuously, and exclusively possesses property and asserts his right to do so in a manner hostile to the interest of the owner will take title in twenty years in most states.

Exercises

1. Rufus enters into a contract to purchase a lot in Oshkosh from Sharpy. The contract provides that Sharpy is to give Rufus a quitclaim deed at the closing. After the closing, Rufus learns that Sharpy did not own the property and sues him for violating the terms of the deed. What is the result? Why?
2. Pancho and Cisco decide to purchase ten acres of real estate. Pancho is to provide 75 percent of the purchase price, Cisco the other 25 percent. They want to use either a joint tenancy or tenancy in common form of ownership. What do you recommend? Why?
3. Suppose in Exercise 2 that a friend recommends that Pancho and Cisco use a tenancy by the entirety. Would this form of ownership be appropriate? Why?
4. Richard and Elizabeth, a married couple, live in a community property state. During their marriage, they save $500,000 from Elizabeth's earnings. Richard does not work, but during the marriage, he inherits $500,000. If Richard and Elizabeth are divorced, how will their property be divided? Why?
5. Jack wants to sell his house. He hires Walter, a real estate broker, to sell the house and signs an exclusive-right-to-sell listing agreement. Walter finds a buyer, who signs a sales contract with Jack. However, the buyer later refuses to perform the contract because he cannot obtain financing. Does Jack owe a commission to Walter? Why?
6. Suppose in Exercise 5 that Jack found the buyer, the buyer obtained financing, and the sale was completed. Does Jack owe a commission to Walter, who provided no assistance in finding the buyer and closing the deal? Why?
7. Suppose in Exercise 5 that Jack's house is destroyed by fire before the closing. Who bears the loss—Jack or the buyer? Must Jack pay a commission to Walter? Why?
8. Suppose in Exercise 5 that the buyer paid $15,000 in earnest money when the contract was signed. Must Jack return the earnest money when the buyer learns that financing is unavailable? Why?

Self-Test Questions

1. A contract for a sale of property must include
   a. a description of the property
   b. price
   c. signatures of buyer and seller
   d. all of the above

2. If real property is damaged after a contract for sale is signed but before closing, it is generally true that the party bearing the loss is
   a. the seller
   b. the buyer
   c. both parties, who split the loss evenly
   d. none of the above
3. The following deeds extend warranties to the buyer:
   a. quitclaim and special warranty
   b. quitclaim and general warranty
   c. general and special warranty
   d. all of the above
4. Under a notice-race statute,
   a. whoever records first is given title, regardless of the good faith of the purchaser
   b. whoever records first and is a bona fide purchaser is given title
   c. either of the above may be acceptable
   d. none of the above is acceptable
5. The elements of adverse possession do not include
   a. actual possession
   b. open and notorious use
   c. consent of the owner
   d. continuous possession

Self-Test Answers

1. d
2. b
3. c
4. b
5. c

Endnotes

1. *Jones v. Alfred H. Mayer Co.*, 392 U.S. 409 (1968).
2. *Heatter v. Lucas*, 80 A.2d 749 (Pa. 1951).
3. *Robin v. Brown*, 162 A. 161 (Pa. 1932).

CHAPTER 35

Landlord and Tenant Law

Learning Objectives

After reading this chapter, you should understand the following:

1. The various types of leasehold estates.
2. How leasehold states are created and extended.
3. The rights and duties of landlords.
4. The rights and duties of tenants.
5. The potential tort liability of landlords.

35.1 Types and Creation of Leasehold Estates

Learning Objectives

1. Distinguish between the different types of leasehold estates.
2. Describe how leasehold states can be created, both orally and in writing, and the requirements for creating leases that last for more than one year.

In Chapter 33 we noted that real property can be divided into two types of interests: freehold estates and leasehold estates. The freehold estate is characterized by indefinite duration, and the owner has title and the right to possess. The **leasehold estate**, by contrast, lasts for a specific period. The owner of the leasehold estate—the tenant—may take possession but does not have title to the underlying real property. When the period of the leasehold ends, the right to possession reverts to the landlord—hence the landlord's interest during the tenant's possession is known as a **reversionary interest**. Although a leasehold estate is said to be an interest in real property, the leasehold itself is in fact personal property. The law recognizes three types of leasehold estates: the estate for years, the periodic tenancy, and the tenancy at will.

leasehold estate

An estate whose termination date is usually known—a one-year lease, for example.

Types of Leasehold Estates

Estate for Years

The **estate for years** is characterized by a definite beginning and a definite end. When you rent an apartment for two years, beginning September 1 and ending on the second August 31st, you are the owner of an estate for years. Virtually any period will do; although it is called an estate "for years," it can last but one day or extend ninety-nine years. Some statutes declare that any estate for years longer than a specified period—one hundred years in Massachusetts, for instance—is a fee simple estate.

estate for years

A leasehold in which the tenant has possession for a fixed term.

lease

The agreement that creates the leasehold interest.

Unless the **lease**—the agreement creating the leasehold interest—provides otherwise, the estate for years terminates automatically at midnight of the last day specified in the lease. The lease need not refer explicitly to calendar dates. It could provide that "the tenant may occupy the premises for six months to commence one week from the date of signing." Suppose the landlord and tenant sign on June 23. Then the lease term begins at 12:00 a.m. on July 1 and ends just before midnight of December 31. Unless a statute provides otherwise, the landlord is not obligated to send the tenant a notice of termination. Should the tenant die before the lease term ends, her property interest can be inherited under her will along with her other personal property or in accordance with the laws of intestate succession.

Periodic Tenancy

periodic tenancy

A tenancy for a period of time that is renewed automatically until either landlord or tenant notifies the other that it will end.

As its name implies, a **periodic tenancy** lasts for a period that is renewed automatically until either landlord or tenant notifies the other that it will end. The periodic tenancy is sometimes called an estate from year to year (or month to month, or week to week). The lease may provide explicitly for the periodic tenancy by specifying that at the expiration of, say, a one-year lease, it will be automatically renewed for another year unless one party notifies the other to the contrary within six months prior to the expiration of the term. The periodic tenancy may also be created by implication: if the lease fails to state a term or is defective in some other way, but the tenant takes possession and pays rent. The usual method of creating a periodic tenancy occurs when the tenant remains on the premises ("holds over") when an estate for years has ended. In a hold over situation, the landlord can accept the implied offer by the tenant to rent under a periodic tenancy by taking the tenant's money. But if she rejects the implied offer, the landlord may take legal action to eject the tenant. If she accepts the offer, the original lease determines the rent and length of the renewable period, except that no periodic tenancy may last longer than from year to year—that is, the renewable period may never be any longer than twelve months.

At common law, a party was required to give notice at least six months prior to the end of a year-to-year tenancy, and notice equal to the term for any other periodic tenancy. In most states today, the time period for giving notice is regulated by statute. Usually, a year-to-year tenancy will requires a month's notice, and shorter tenancies require notice equal to the term. To illustrate: suppose Simone rents from Anita on a month-to-month tenancy beginning September 15. On March 30, Simone passes the orals for her doctorate and decides to leave town. How soon may she cancel her tenancy? If she calls Anita that afternoon, she will be two weeks shy of a full month's notice for the period ending April 15. Calling Anita on March 30 to give the full month's notice tells Anita that the month ending May 15 will be her last; that is, the earliest she can finish her obligation to pay rent is May 15. (Anita can, of course, agree to let Simone vacate immediately, pay through April 15, and prepare for a new tenant starting April 16. This will work if the demand for rentals is high.) Suppose Simone's term had been from the first of each month. On April 1, she notifies Anita of her intention to leave at the end of April, but she is stuck until the end of May, because notice on the first of the month is not notice for a full month. She would have had to notify Anita by March 31 to terminate the tenancy by April 30.

Tenancy at Will

tenancy at will

A tenancy that will last only so long as the landlord and tenant desire.

If the landlord and tenant agree that the lease will last only as long as both want it to, then they have created a **tenancy at will**. Statutes in most states require some notice of intention to terminate. Simone comes to the university to study, and Anita gives her a room to stay in her house for $50 per night. The arrangement is a tenancy at will, and it will continue as long as both want it to. One Friday night, after dinner with classmates, Simone decides she would rather move in with Bob. She goes back to her apartment, packs her suitcase, and tells Anita she's leaving. The tenancy at will terminates that day.

Creation of Leasehold Estates

Oral Leases

Leases can be created orally, unless the term of the lease exceeds the period specified by the Statute of Frauds. In most states, that period is one year. Any oral lease for a period longer than the statutory period is invalid. Suppose that Simone, in a state with a one-year Statute of Frauds period, orally agrees with Anita to rent Anita's apartment for two years, at a monthly rent of $750. The lease is invalid, and either could repudiate it.

Written Leases

A lease required to be in writing under the Statute of Frauds must contain the following items or provisions: (1) it must identify the parties, (2) it must identify the premises, (3) it must specify the duration of the lease, (4) it must state the rent to be paid, and (5) it must be signed by the party against whom enforcement is sought (known as "the party to be charged").

The provisions need not be perfectly stated. As long as they satisfy the five requirements, they will be adequate to sustain the lease under the Statute of Frauds. For instance, the parties need not necessarily be named in the lease itself. Suppose that the prospective tenant gives the landlord a month's rent in advance and that the landlord gives the tenant a receipt listing the property and the terms of the lease but omitting the name of the tenant. The landlord subsequently refuses to let the tenant move in. Who would prevail in court? Since the tenant had the receipt in her possession, that would be sufficient to identify her as the tenant to whom the terms of the lease were meant to apply. Likewise, the lease need not specify every aspect of the premises to be enjoyed. Thus the tenant who rents an apartment in a building will be entitled to the use of the common stairway, the roof, and so on, even though the lease is silent on these points. And as long as a specific amount is ascertainable, the rent may be stated in other than absolute dollar terms. For example, it could be expressed in terms of a cost-of-living index or as a percentage of the tenant's dollar business volume.

Key Takeaway

A leasehold estate, unlike a freehold estate, has a definite duration. The landlord's interest during the term of a leasehold estate is a reversionary interest. Leasehold estates can last for short terms or very long terms; in the case of long-term leases, a property right is created that can be passed to heirs. The usual landlord-tenant relationship is a periodic tenancy, which carries with it various common-law and statutory qualifications regarding renewal and termination. In a tenancy at will, either landlord or tenant can end the leasehold estate as soon as notice is provided by either party.

Exercises

1. What is the difference between a periodic tenancy and a tenancy at will?
2. What are the essential terms that must be in a written lease?

35.2 Rights and Duties of Landlords and Tenants

Learning Objectives

1. Itemize and explain the rights and duties of landlords.
2. List and describe the rights and duties of tenants.
3. Understand the available remedies for tenants when a landlord is in breach of his or her duties.

Rights and Duties of Landlords

The law imposes a number of duties on the landlord and gives the tenant a number of corresponding rights. These include (1) possession, (2) habitable condition, and (3) noninterference with use.

Possession

The landlord must give the tenant the right of possession of the property. This duty is breached if, at the time the tenant is entitled to take possession, someone else has a superior title (also known as "paramount title") to the property and is in possession of the premises.

If the tenant has already taken possession and then discovers the paramount title, the landlord is not automatically in breach. But if the tenant thereafter is evicted from the premises by the holder of the paramount title, then the landlord is in breach. A more likely scenario on possession is that a landlord rents a house to a medical doctor for ten years, knowing also that the lot is restricted to residential uses only. The doctor moves in. The landlord is not yet in default. But the landlord will be in default if a neighbor obtains an injunction against maintaining the office. But if the landlord did not know (and could not reasonably have known) that the doctor intended to use his home for an office, then the landlord would not be in default under the lease, since the property could have been put to normal—that is, residential—use without jeopardizing the tenant's right to possession.

Warranty of Habitability

caveat emptor

"Let the buyer beware." At common law, once the tenant has signed the lease, she must take the premises as she finds them.

implied warranty of habitability

The landlord's duty to provide conditions suitable for residential use.

As applied to leases, the old common-law doctrine of **caveat emptor** said that once the tenant has signed the lease, she must take the premises as she finds them. Since she could inspect them before signing the lease, she should not complain later. Moreover, if hidden defects come to light, they ought to be easy enough for the tenant herself to fix. Today this rule no longer applies, at least to residential rentals. Unless the parties specifically agree otherwise, the landlord is in breach of his lease if the conditions are unsuitable for residential use when the tenant is due to move in. The landlord is held to an **implied warranty of habitability**.

The change in the rule is due in part to the conditions of the modern urban setting: tenants have little or no power to walk away from an available apartment in areas where housing is scarce. It is also due to modem construction and technology: few tenants are capable of fixing most types of defects. A US court of appeals has said the following:

> *Today's urban tenants, the vast majority of whom live in multiple dwelling houses, are interested not in the land, but solely in "a house suitable for occupation." Furthermore, today's city dweller usually has a single, specialized skill unrelated to maintenance work; he is unable to make repairs like the "jack-of-all-trades" farmer who was the common law's model of the lessee. Further, unlike his agrarian predecessor who often remained on one piece of land for his entire life, urban tenants today are more mobile than ever before. A tenant's tenure in a specific apartment will often not be sufficient to justify efforts at repairs. In addition, the increasing complexity of today's dwellings renders them much more difficult to repair than the structures of earlier times. In a multiple dwelling, repairs may require access to equipment and areas in control of the landlord. Low and middle income tenants, even if they were interested in making repairs, would be unable to obtain financing for major repairs since they have no long-term interest in the property.*[1]

At common law, the landlord was not responsible if the premises became unsuitable once the tenant moved in. This rule was often harshly applied, even for unsuitable conditions caused by a sudden act of God, such as a tornado. Even if the premises collapsed, the tenant would be liable to pay the rent for the duration of the lease. Today, however, many states have statutorily abolished the tenant's obligation to pay the rent if a non-man-made force renders the premises unsuitable. Moreover, most states today impose on the landlord, after the tenant has moved in, the responsibility for maintaining the premises in a safe, livable condition, consistent with the safety, health, and housing codes of the jurisdiction.

These rules apply only in the absence of an express agreement between the parties. The landlord and tenant may allocate in the lease the responsibility for repairs and maintenance. But it is unlikely that any court would enforce a lease provision waiving the landlord's implied warranty of habitability for residential apartments, especially in areas where housing is relatively scarce.

Noninterference with Use

In addition to maintaining the premises in a physically suitable manner, the landlord has an obligation to the tenant not to interfere with a permissible use of the premises. Suppose Simone moves into a building with several apartments. One of the other tenants consistently plays music late in the evening, causing Simone to lose sleep. She complains to the landlord, who has a provision in the lease permitting him to terminate the lease of any tenant who persists in disturbing other tenants. If the landlord does nothing after Simone has notified him of the disturbance, he will be in breach. This right to be free of interference with permissible uses is sometimes said to arise from the landlord's implied **covenant of quiet enjoyment**.

covenant of quiet enjoyment

An implied right in most leases—the right to be free of interference with permissible uses.

Tenant's Remedies

When the landlord breaches one of the foregoing duties, the tenant has a choice of three basic remedies: **termination**, damages, or rent adjustment.

termination

A remedy for a tenant, but requiring notice to the landlord and compliance with previously agreed on terms or statutory requirements for terminating the leasehold estate.

In virtually all cases where the landlord breaches, the tenant may terminate the lease, thus ending her obligation to continue to pay rent. To terminate, the tenant must (1) actually vacate the premises during the time that she is entitled to terminate and (2) either comply with lease provisions governing the method of terminating or else take reasonable steps to ensure that the landlord knows she has terminated and why.

constructive eviction

Conditions that interfere substantially enough with the tenant's permissible use that it is tantamount to eviction.

When the landlord physically deprives the tenant of possession, he has evicted the tenant; wrongful eviction permits the tenant to terminate the lease. Even if the landlord's conduct falls short of actual eviction, it may interfere substantially enough with the tenant's permissible use so that they are tantamount to eviction. This is known as **constructive eviction**, and it covers a wide variety of actions by both the landlord and those whose conduct is attributable to him, as illustrated by *Fidelity Mutual Life Insurance Co. v Kaminsky*, (see Section 5).

Damages

Another traditional remedy is money damages, available whenever termination is an appropriate remedy. Damages may be sought after termination or as an alternative to termination. Suppose that after the landlord had refused Simone's request to repair the electrical system, Simone hired a contractor to do the job. The cost of the repair work would be recoverable from the landlord. Other recoverable costs can include the expense of relocating if the lease is terminated, moving costs, expenses connected with finding new premises, and any increase in rent over the period of the terminated lease for comparable new space. A business may recover the loss of anticipated business profits, but only if the extent of the loss is established with reasonable certainty. In the case of most new businesses, it would be almost impossible to prove loss of profits.

In all cases, the tenant's recovery will be limited to damages that would have been incurred by a tenant who took all reasonable steps to mitigate losses. That is, the tenant must take reasonable steps to prevent losses attributable to the landlord's breach, to find new space if terminating, to move efficiently, and so on.

Rent Remedies

independent covenants

Under an old common-law rule, the landlord's obligation to provide the tenant with habitable space and the tenant's obligation to pay rent.

rent adjustment

One remedy among several for tenants where the landlord has breached one or more duties. Rent adjustment may involve withholding the rent until the landlord complies, depositing payments in escrow, or applying withheld rent to the problem that the landlord has not fixed.

Under an old common-law rule, the landlord's obligation to provide the tenant with habitable space and the tenant's obligation to pay rent were **independent covenants**. If the landlord breached, the tenant was still legally bound to pay the rent; her only remedies were termination and suit for damages. But these are often difficult remedies for the tenant. Termination means the aggravation of moving, assuming that new quarters can be found, and a suit for damages is time consuming, uncertain, and expensive. The obvious solution is to permit the tenant to withhold rent, or what we here call **rent adjustment**. The modern rule, adopted in several states (but not yet in most), holds that the mutual obligations of landlord and tenant are dependent. States following this approach have developed three types of remedies: rent withholding, rent application, and rent abatement.

The simplest approach is for the tenant to withhold the rent until the landlord remedies the defect. In some states, the tenant may keep the money. In other states, the rent must be paid each month into an escrow account or to the court, and the money in the escrow account becomes payable to the landlord when the default is cured.

Several state statutes permit the tenant to apply the rent money directly to remedy the defect or otherwise satisfy the landlord's performance. Thus Simone might have deducted from her rent the reasonable cost of hiring an electrician to repair the electrical system.

In some states, the rent may be reduced or even eliminated if the landlord fails to cure specific types of defects, such as violations of the housing code. The abatement will continue until the default is eliminated or the lease is terminated.

Rights and Duties of Tenants

In addition to the duties of the tenant set forth in the lease itself, the common law imposes three other obligations: (1) to pay the rent reserved (stated) in the lease, (2) to refrain from committing waste (damage), and (3) not to use the premises for an illegal purpose.

Duty to Pay Rent

What constitutes rent is not necessarily limited to the stated periodic payment usually denominated "rent." The tenant may also be responsible for such assessments as taxes and utilities, payable to the landlord as rent. Simone's lease calls for her to pay taxes of $500 per year, payable in quarterly installments. She pays the rent on the first of each month and the first tax bill on January 1. On April 1, she pays the rent but defaults on the next tax bill. She has failed to pay the rent reserved in the lease.

The landlord in the majority of states is not obligated to mitigate his losses should the tenant abandon the property and fail thereafter to pay the rent. As a practical matter, this means that the landlord need not try to rent out the property but instead can let it sit vacant and sue the defaulting tenant for the balance of the rent as it becomes due. However, the tenant might notify the landlord that she has abandoned the property or is about to abandon it and offer to surrender it. If the landlord accepts the surrender, the lease then terminates. Unless the lease specifically provides for it, a landlord who accepts the surrender will not be able to recover from the tenant the difference between the amount of her rent obligation and the new tenant's rent obligation.

Many leases require the tenant to make a **security deposit**—a payment of a specific sum of money to secure the tenant's performance of duties under the lease. If the tenant fails to pay the rent or otherwise defaults, the landlord may use the money to make good the tenant's performance. Whatever portion of the money is not used to satisfy the tenant's obligations must be repaid to the tenant at the end of the lease. In the absence of an agreement to the contrary, the landlord must pay interest on the security deposit when he returns the sum to the tenant at the end of the lease.

security deposit

A payment of a specific sum of money to secure the tenant's performance of duties under the lease.

Alteration and Restoration of the Premises

In the absence of a specific agreement in the lease, the tenant is entitled to physically change the premises in order to make the best possible permissible use of the property, but she may not make structural alterations or damage (waste) the property. A residential tenant may add telephone lines, put up pictures, and affix bookshelves to the walls, but she may not remove a wall in order to enlarge a room.

The tenant must restore the property to its original condition when the lease ends, but this requirement does not include normal wear and tear. Simone rents an apartment with newly polished wooden floors. Because she likes the look of oak, she decides against covering the floors with rugs. In a few months' time, the floors lose their polish and become scuffed. Simone is not obligated to refinish the floors, because the scuffing came from normal walking, which is ordinary wear and tear.

Use of the Property for an Illegal Purpose

It is a breach of the tenant's obligation to use the property for an illegal purpose. A landlord who found a tenant running a numbers racket, for example, or making and selling moonshine whisky could rightfully evict her.

Landlord's Remedies

tenant at sufferance

When a tenant improperly overstays his or her lease.

self-help

Entering the premises to regain possession and remove a holdover tenant's belongings—must be peaceful, must not cause physical harm or even convey the expectation of harm to the tenant or anyone on the premises with the tenant's permission, and must not result in unreasonable damage to the tenant's property.

In general, when the tenant breaches any of the three duties imposed by the common law, the landlord may terminate the lease and seek damages. One common situation deserves special mention: the holdover tenant. When a tenant improperly overstays her lease, she is said to be a **tenant at sufferance**, meaning that she is liable to eviction. Some cultures, like the Japanese, exhibit a considerable bias toward the tenant, making it exceedingly difficult to move out holdover tenants who decide to stay. But in the United States, landlords may remove tenants through summary (speedy) proceedings available in every state or, in some cases, through **self-help**. Self-help is a statutory remedy for landlords or incoming tenants in some states and involves the peaceful removal of a holdover tenant's belongings. If a state has a statute providing a summary procedure for removing a holdover tenant, neither the landlord nor the incoming tenant may resort to self-help, unless the statute specifically allows it. A provision in the lease permitting self-help in the absence of statutory authority is unenforceable. Self-help must be peaceful, must not cause physical harm or even the expectation of harm to the tenant or anyone on the premises with his permission, and must not result in unreasonable damage to the tenant's property. Any clause in the lease attempting to waive these conditions is void.

Self-help can be risky, because some summary proceeding statutes declare it to be a criminal act and because it can subject the landlord to tort liability. Suppose that Simone improperly holds over in her apartment. With a new tenant scheduled to arrive in two days, the landlord knocks on her door the evening after her lease expires. When Simone opens the door, she sees the landlord standing between two 450-pound Sumo wrestlers with menacing expressions. He demands that she leave immediately. Fearing for her safety, she departs instantly. Since she had a reasonable expectation of harm had she not complied with the landlord's demand, Simone would be entitled to recover damages in a tort suit against her landlord, although she would not be entitled to regain possession of the apartment.

Besides summary judicial proceedings and self-help, the landlord has another possible remedy against the holdover tenant: to impose another rental term. In order to extend the lease in this manner, the landlord need simply notify the holdover tenant that she is being held to another term, usually measured by the periodic nature of the rent payment. For example, if rent was paid each month, then imposition of a new term results in a month-to-month tenancy. One year is the maximum tenancy that the landlord can create by electing to hold the tenant to another term.

Key Takeaway

Both landlords and tenants have rights and duties. The primary duty of a landlord is to meet the implied warranty of habitability: that the premises are in a safe, livable condition. The tenant has various remedies available if the landlord fails to meet that duty, or if the landlord fails to meet the implied covenant of quiet enjoyment. These include termination, damages, and withholding of rent. The tenant has duties as well: to pay the rent, refrain from committing waste, and not use the property for an illegal purpose.

Exercises

1. Consistent with the landlord's implied warranty of habitability, can the landlord and tenant agree in a lease that the tenant bear any and all expenses to repair the refrigerator, the stove, and the microwave?
2. Under what conditions is it proper for a tenant to withhold rent from the landlord?

35.3 Transfer of Landlord's or Tenant's Interest

Learning Objectives

1. Explain how the landlord's reversionary interest works and how it may be assigned.
2. Describe the two ways in which a tenant's leasehold interest may be transferred to another party.

General Rule

At common law, the interests of the landlord and tenant may be transferred freely unless (1) the tenancy is at will; (2) the lease requires either party to perform significant personal services, which would be substantially less likely to be performed if the interest was transferred; or (3) the parties agree that the interest may not be transferred.

Landlord's Interest

When the landlord sells his interest, the purchaser takes subject to the lease. If there are tenants with leases in an apartment building, the new landlord may not evict them simply because he has taken title. The landlord may divide his interest as he sees fit, transferring all or only part of his entire interest in the property. He may assign his right to the rent or sell his reversionary interest in the premises. For instance, Simone takes a three-year lease on an apartment near the university. Simone's landlord gives his aged uncle his reversionary interest for life. This means that Simone's landlord is now the uncle, and she must pay him rent and look to him for repairs and other performances owed under the lease. When Simone's lease terminates, the uncle will be entitled to rent the premises. He does so, leasing to another student for three years. One year later, the uncle dies. His nephew (Simone's original landlord) has the reversionary interest and so once again becomes the landlord. He must perform the lease that the uncle agreed to with the new student, but when that lease expires, he will be free to rent the premises as he sees fit.

Tenant's Interest

Why would a tenant be interested in transferring her leasehold interest? For at least two reasons: she might need to move before her lease expired, or she might be able to make money on the leasehold itself. In recent years, many companies in New York have discovered that their present leases were worth far more to them by moving out than staying in. They had signed long-term leases years ago when the real estate market was glutted and were paying far less than current market prices. By subletting the premises and moving to cheaper quarters, they could pocket the difference between their lease rate and the market rate they charged their subtenants.

The tenant can transfer her interest in the lease by assigning or by subletting. In an **assignment**, the tenant transfers all interest in the premises and all obligations. Thus the assignee-tenant is duty bound to pay the landlord the periodic rental and to perform all other provisions in the lease. If the assignee defaults, however, the original tenant would remain liable to the landlord. In short, with an assignment, both assignor and assignee are liable under the lease unless the landlord releases the assignor. By contrast, a **sublease** is a transfer of something less than the entire leasehold interest (see Figure 35.1). For instance, the tenant might have five years remaining on her lease and sublet the premises for two years, or she might sublet the ground floor of a four-story building. Unlike an assignee, the subtenant does not step into the shoes of the tenant and is not

assignment

The tenant transfers all interest in the premises, along with all obligations.

sublease

A transfer of something less than the entire leasehold interest.

liable to the landlord for performance of the tenant's duties. The subtenant's only obligations are to the tenant. What distinguishes the assignment from the sublease is not the name but whether or not the entire leasehold interest has been transferred. If not, the transfer is a sublease.

FIGURE 35.1 Assignment vs. Sublease

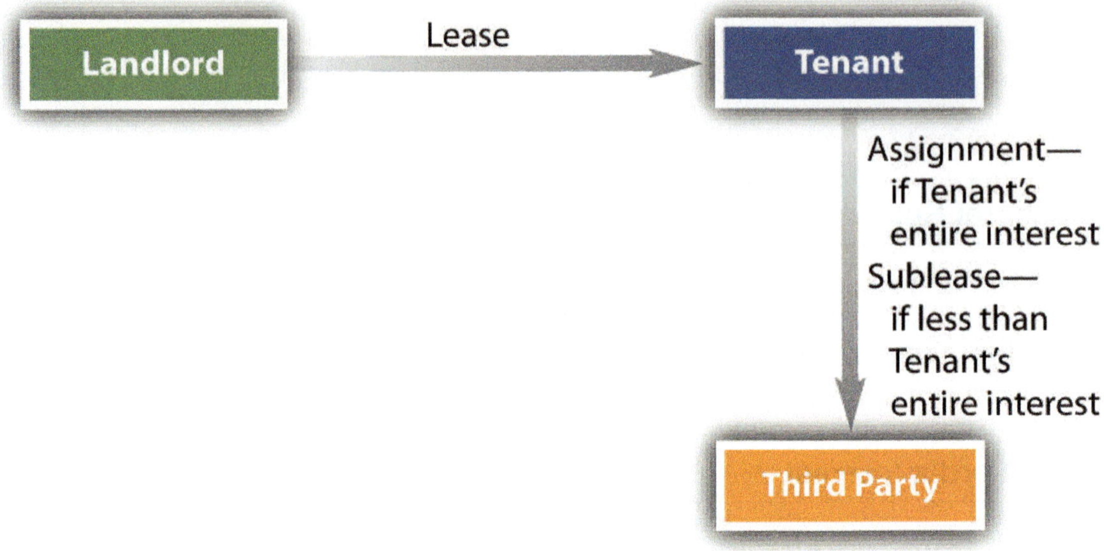

Many landlords include clauses in their leases prohibiting assignments or subleases, and these clauses are generally upheld. But the courts construe them strictly, so that a provision barring subleases will not be interpreted to bar assignments.

Key Takeaway

The interests of landlords and tenants can be freely transferred unless the parties agree otherwise or unless there is a tenancy at will. If the tenant assigns her leasehold interest, she remains liable under the lease unless the landlord releases her. If less than the entire leasehold interest is transferred, it is a sublease rather than an assignment. But the original lease may prohibit either or both.

Exercises

1. What is the difference between an assignment and a sublease?
2. Are the duties of the tenant any different if the reversionary interest is assigned? Suppose that Simone is in year one of a three-year lease and that Harry is the landlord. If Harry assigns his reversionary interest to Louise, can Louise raise the rent for the next two years beyond what is stated in the original lease?

35.4 Landlord's Tort Liability

Learning Objectives

1. State the general common-law rule as to the liability of the landlord for injuries occurring on the leased premises.
2. State the exceptions to the general rule, and explain the modern trend toward increased liability of the landlord.

In Chapter 33 we discussed the tort liability of the owner or occupier of real estate to persons injured on the property. As a general rule, when injury occurs on premises rented to a tenant, it is the tenant—an occupier—who is liable. The reason for this rule seems clear: The landlord has given up all but a reversionary interest in the property; he has no further control over the premises. Indeed, he is not even permitted on the property without the tenant's permission. But over the years, certain exceptions have developed to the rule that the landlord is not liable. The primary reason for this change is the recognition that the landlord is better able to pay for repairs to his property than his relatively poorer tenants and that he has ultimate control over the general conditions surrounding the apartment or apartment complex.

Exceptions to the General Rule

Hidden Dangers Known to Landlord

The landlord is liable to the tenant, her family, or guests who are injured by hidden and dangerous conditions that the landlord knew about or should have known about but failed to disclose to the tenant.

Dangers to People off the Premises

The landlord is liable to people injured outside the property by defects that existed when the lease was signed. Simone rents a dilapidated house and agrees with the landlord to keep the building repaired. Yet she neglects to hire contractors to repair the cracked and sagging wall next to the street. The building soon collapses, damaging several automobiles parked alongside. Simone can be held responsible but so can the landlord; the tenant's contractual agreement to maintain the property is not sufficient to shift the liability away from the landlord. In a few cases, the landlord has even been held liable for activities carried on by the tenant, but only because he knew about them when the lease was signed and should have known that the injuries were probable results.

Premises Leased for Admitting the Public

A landlord is responsible for injuries caused by dangerous conditions on property to be used by the public if the danger existed when the lease was made. Thus an uneven floor that might cause people to trip, or a defective elevator that stops a few inches below the level of each floor would be sufficiently dangerous to pin liability on the landlord.

Landlord Retaining Control of Premises

Frequently, a landlord will retain control over certain areas of the property—for example, the common hallways and stairs in an apartment building. When injuries occur as a result of faulty and careless maintenance of these areas, the landlord will be responsible. In more than half the states, the landlord is liable for failure to remove ice and snow from a common walkway and stairs at the entrance. In one careless maintenance case, the tenant recovered damages for a broken hip caused when she fell in fright from seeing a mouse that jumped out of her stove; she successfully charged the landlord with negligence in failing to prevent mice from entering the dwelling in areas under his control.

Faulty Repair of Premises

Landlords often have a duty to repair the premises. The duty may be statutory or may rest on an agreement in the lease. In either case, the landlord will be liable to a tenant or others for injury resulting from defects that should have been repaired. No less important, a landlord will be liable even if he has no duty to repair but negligently makes repairs that themselves turn out to be dangerous.

Key Takeaway

At common law, injuries taking place on leased premises were the responsibility of the tenant. There were notable exceptions, including situations where hidden dangers were known to the landlord but not the tenant, where the premises' condition caused injury to people off the premises, or where faulty repairs caused the injuries. The modern trend is to adopt general negligence principles to determine landlord liability. Thus where the landlord does not use reasonable care and subjects others to an unreasonable risk of harm, there may be liability for the landlord. This varies from state to state.

Exercises

1. What was the basic logic of the common law in having tenants be responsible for all injuries that took place on leased premises?
2. Does the modern trend of applying general negligence principles to landlords make more sense? Explain your answer.

35.5 Cases

Constructive Eviction

Fidelity Mutual Life Insurance Co. v. Kaminsky

768 S.W.2d 818 (Tx. Ct. App. 1989)

MURPHY, JUSTICE

The issue in this landlord-tenant case is whether sufficient evidence supports the jury's findings that the landlord and appellant, Fidelity Mutual Life Insurance Company ["Fidelity"], constructively evicted the tenant, Robert P. Kaminsky, M.D., P.A. ["Dr. Kaminsky"] by breaching the express covenant of quiet enjoyment contained in the parties' lease. We affirm.

Dr. Kaminsky is a gynecologist whose practice includes performing elective abortions. In May 1983, he executed a lease contract for the rental of approximately 2,861 square feet in the Red Oak Atrium Building for a two-year term which began on June 1, 1983. The terms of the lease required Dr. Kaminsky to use the rented space solely as "an office for the practice of medicine." Fidelity owns the building and hires local companies to manage it. At some time during the lease term, Shelter Commercial Properties ["Shelter"] replaced the Horne Company as managing agents. Fidelity has not disputed either management company's capacity to act as its agent.

The parties agree that: (1) they executed a valid lease agreement; (2) Paragraph 35 of the lease contains an express covenant of quiet enjoyment conditioned on Dr. Kaminsky's paying rent when due, as he did through November 1984; Dr. Kaminsky abandoned the leased premises on or about December 3, 1984 and refused to pay additional rent; anti-abortion protestors began picketing at the building in June of 1984 and repeated and increased their demonstrations outside and inside the building until Dr. Kaminsky abandoned the premises.

When Fidelity sued for the balance due under the lease contract following Dr. Kaminsky's abandonment of the premises, he claimed that Fidelity constructively evicted him by breaching Paragraph 35 of the lease. Fidelity apparently conceded during trial that sufficient proof of the constructive eviction of Dr. Kaminsky would relieve him of his contractual liability for any remaining rent payments. Accordingly, he assumed the burden of proof and the sole issue submitted to the jury was whether Fidelity breached Paragraph 35 of the lease, which reads as follows:

> *Quiet Enjoyment*
> *Lessee, on paying the said Rent, and any Additional Rental, shall and may peaceably and quietly have, hold and enjoy the Leased Premises for the said term.*

A constructive eviction occurs when the tenant leaves the leased premises due to conduct by the landlord which materially interferes with the tenant's beneficial use of the premises. Texas law relieves the tenant of contractual liability for any remaining rentals due under the lease if he can establish a constructive eviction by the landlord.

The protests took place chiefly on Saturdays, the day Dr. Kaminsky generally scheduled abortions. During the protests, the singing and chanting demonstrators picketed in the building's parking lot and inner lobby and atrium area. They approached patients to speak to them, distributed literature, discouraged patients from entering the building and often accused Dr. Kaminsky of "killing babies." As the protests increased, the demonstrators often occupied the stairs leading to Dr. Kaminsky's office and prevented patients from entering the office by blocking the doorway. Occasionally they succeeded in gaining access to the office waiting room area.

Dr. Kaminsky complained to Fidelity through its managing agents and asked for help in keeping the protestors away, but became increasingly frustrated by a lack of response to his requests. The record shows that no security personnel were present on Saturdays to exclude protestors from the building, although the lease required Fidelity to provide security service on Saturdays. The record also shows that Fidelity's attorneys prepared a written statement to be handed to the protestors soon after Fidelity hired Shelter as its managing agent. The statement tracked TEX. PENAL CODE ANN. §30.05 (Vernon Supp. 1989) and generally served to inform trespassers that they risked criminal prosecution by failing to leave if asked to do so. Fidelity's attorneys instructed Shelter's representative to "have several of these letters printed up and be ready to distribute them and verbally demand that these people move on and off the property." The same representative conceded at trial that she did not distribute these notices. Yet when Dr. Kaminsky enlisted the aid of the Sheriff's office, officers refused to ask the protestors to leave without a directive from Fidelity or its agent. Indeed, an attorney had instructed the protestors to remain *unless* the landlord or its representative ordered them to leave. It appears that Fidelity's only response to the demonstrators was to state, through its agents, that it was aware of Dr. Kaminsky's problems.

Both action and lack of action can constitute "conduct" by the landlord which amounts to a constructive eviction....

This case shows ample instances of Fidelity's failure to act in the fact of repeated requests for assistance despite its having expressly covenanted Dr. Kaminsky's quiet enjoyment of the premises. These instances provided a legally sufficient basis for the jury to conclude that Dr. Kaminsky abandoned the leased premises, not because of the trespassing protestors, but because of Fidelity's lack of response to his complaints about the protestors. Under the circumstances, while it is undisputed that Fidelity did not "encourage" the demonstrators, its conduct essentially allowed them to continue to trespass.

[The trial court judgment is affirmed.]

Case Questions

A constructive eviction occurs when the tenant leaves the leased premises because of conduct by the landlord that materially interferes with the tenant's beneficial use of the premises.

1. At the trial, who concluded that Fidelity's "conduct" constituted constructive eviction? Is this a question of fact, an interpretation of the contract, or both?
2. How can failure to act constitute "conduct"?

Landlord's Tort Liability

Stephens v. Stearns

106 Idaho 249; 678 P.2d 41 (Idaho Sup. Ct. 1984)

Donaldson, Chief Justice

Plaintiff-appellant Stephens filed this suit on October 2, 1978, for personal injuries she sustained on July 15, 1977, from a fall on an interior stairway of her apartment. Plaintiff's apartment, located in a Boise apartment complex, was a "townhouse" consisting of two separate floors connected by an internal stairway.

The apartments were built by defendant Koch and sold to defendant Stearns soon after completion in 1973. Defendant Stearns was plaintiff's landlord from the time she moved into the apartment in 1973 through the time of plaintiff's fall on July 15, 1977. Defendant Albanese was the architect who designed and later inspected the apartment complex.

* * *

When viewed in the light most favorable to appellant, the facts are as follows: On the evening of July 15, 1977, Mrs. Stephens went to visit friends. While there she had two drinks. She returned to her apartment a little past 10:00 p.m. Mrs. Stephens turned on the television in the living room and went upstairs to change clothes. After changing her clothes, she attempted to go downstairs to watch television. As Mrs. Stephens reached the top of the stairway, she either slipped or fell forward. She testified that she "grabbed" in order to catch herself. However, Mrs. Stephens was unable to catch herself and she fell to the bottom of the stairs. As a result of the fall, she suffered serious injury. The evidence further showed that the stairway was approximately thirty-six inches wide and did not have a handrail although required by a Boise ordinance.

* * *

In granting defendant Stearns' motion for directed verdict, the trial judge concluded that there was "an absolute lack of evidence" and that "to find a proximate cause between the absence of the handrail and the fall suffered by the plaintiff would be absolutely conjecture and speculation." (Although the trial judge's conclusion referred to "proximate cause," it is apparent that he was referring to factual or actual cause. *See Munson v. State, Department of Highways*, 96 Idaho 529, 531 P.2d 1174 (1975).) We disagree with the conclusion of the trial judge.

We have considered the facts set out above in conjunction with the testimony of Chester Shawver, a Boise architect called as an expert in the field of architecture, that the primary purpose of a handrail is for user safety. We are left with the firm conviction that there is sufficient evidence from which reasonable jurors could have concluded that the absence of a handrail was the actual cause of plaintiff's injuries; *i.e.*, that plaintiff would not have fallen, or at least would have been able to catch herself, had there been a handrail available for her to grab.

In addition, we do not believe that the jury would have had to rely on conjecture and speculation to find that the absence of the handrail was the actual cause. To the contrary, we believe that reasonable jurors could have drawn legitimate inferences from the evidence presented to determine the issue. This comports with the general rule that the factual issue of causation is for the jury to decide. *McKinley v. Fanning*, 100 Idaho 189, 595 P.2d 1084 (1979); *Munson v. State, Department of Highways, supra*. In addition, courts in several other jurisdictions, when faced with similar factual settings, have held that this issue is a question for the jury.

* * *

Rather than attempt to squeeze the facts of this case into one of the common-law exceptions, plaintiff instead has brought to our attention the modern trend of the law in this area. Under the modern trend, landlords are simply under a duty to exercise reasonable care under the circumstances. The Tennessee Supreme Court had the foresight to grasp this concept many years ago when it stated: "The ground of liability upon the part of a landlord when he demises dangerous property has nothing special to do with the relation of landlord and tenant. It is the ordinary case of liability for personal misfeasance, which runs through all the relations of individuals to each other." *Wilcox v. Hines*, 100 Tenn. 538, 46 S.W. 297, 299 (1898). Seventy-five years later, the Supreme Court of New Hampshire followed the lead of *Wilcox*. *Sargent v. Ross*, 113 N.H. 388, 308 A.2d 528 (1973). The *Sargent* court abrogated the common-law rule and its exceptions, and adopted the reasonable care standard by stating:

> *We thus bring up to date the other half of landlord-tenant law. Henceforth, landlords as other persons must exercise reasonable care not to subject others to an unreasonable risk of harm....A landlord must act as a reasonable person under all of the circumstances including the likelihood of injury to others, the probable seriousness of such injuries, and the burden of reducing or avoiding the risk.*

Id. at 534 [Citations]

Tennessee and New Hampshire are not alone in adopting this rule. As of this date, several other states have also judicially adopted a reasonable care standard for landlords.

* * *

In commenting on the common-law rule, A. James Casner, Reporter of Restatement (Second) of Property—Landlord and Tenant, has stated: "While continuing to pay lip service to the general rule, the courts have expended considerable energy and exercised great ingenuity in attempting to fit various factual settings into the recognized exceptions." Restatement (Second) of Property—Landlord and Tenant ch. 17 Reporter's Note to Introductory Note (1977). We believe that the energies of the courts of Idaho should be used in a more productive manner. Therefore, after examining both the common-law rule and the modern trend, we today decide to leave the common-law rule and its exceptions behind, and we adopt the rule that a landlord is under a duty to exercise reasonable care in light of all the circumstances.

We stress that adoption of this rule is not tantamount to making the landlord an insurer for all injury occurring on the premises, but merely constitutes our removal of the landlord's common-law cloak of immunity. Those questions of hidden danger, public use, control, and duty to repair, which under the common-law were prerequisites to the consideration of the landlord's negligence, will now be relevant only inasmuch as they pertain to the elements of negligence, such as foreseeability and unreasonableness of the risk. We hold that defendant Stearns did owe a duty to plaintiff Stephens to exercise reasonable care in light of all the circumstances, and that it is for a jury to decide whether that duty was breached. Therefore, we reverse the directed verdict in favor of defendant Stearns and remand for a new trial of plaintiff's negligence action against defendant Stearns.

Case Questions

1. Does it mean anything at all to say, as the court does, that persons (including landlords) must "exercise reasonable care not to subject others to an unreasonable risk of harm?" Is this a rule that gives very much direction to landlords who may wonder what the limit of their liabilities might be?
2. What is the importance of the architect and landlord's failure to follow the city ordinance regarding handrails on stairways?

35.6 Summary and Exercises

Summary

A leasehold is an interest in real property that terminates on a certain date. The leasehold itself is personal property and has three major forms: (1) the estate for years, (2) the periodic tenancy, and (3) the tenancy at will. The estate for years has a definite beginning and end; it need not be measured in years. A periodic tenancy—sometimes known as an estate from year to year or month to month—is renewed automatically until either landlord or tenant notifies the other that it will end. A tenancy at will lasts only as long as both landlord and tenant desire. Oral leases are subject to the Statute of Frauds. In most states, leases to last longer than a year must be in writing, and the lease must identify the parties and the premises, specify the duration, state the rent, and be signed by the party to be charged.

The law imposes on the landlord certain duties toward the tenant and gives the tenant corresponding rights, including the right of possession, habitable condition, and noninterference with use. The right of possession is breached if a third party has paramount title at the time the tenant is due to take possession. In most states, a landlord is obligated to provide the tenant with habitable premises not only when the tenant moves in but also during the entire period of the lease. The landlord must also refrain from interfering with a tenant's permissible use of the premises.

If the landlord breaches an obligation, the tenant has several remedies. He may terminate the lease, recover damages, or (in several states) use a rent-related remedy (by withholding rent, by applying it to remedy the defect, or by abatement).

The tenant has duties also. The tenant must pay the rent. If she abandons the property and fails to pay, most states do not require the landlord to mitigate damages, but several states are moving away from this general rule. The tenant may physically change the property to use it to her best advantage, but she may not make structural alterations or commit waste. The tenant must restore the property to its original condition when the lease ends. This rule does not include normal wear and tear.

Should the tenant breach any of her duties, the landlord may terminate the lease and seek damages. In the case of a holdover tenant, the landlord may elect to hold the tenant to another rental term.

The interest of either landlord or tenant may be transferred freely unless the tenancy is at will, the lease requires either party to perform significant personal services that would be substantially less likely to be performed, or the parties agree that the interest may not be transferred.

Despite the general rule that the tenant is responsible for injuries caused on the premises to outsiders, the landlord may have significant tort liability if (1) there are hidden dangers he knows about, (2) defects that existed at the time the lease was signed injure people off the premises, (3) the premises are rented for public purposes, (4) the landlord retains control of the premises, or (5) the landlord repairs the premises in a faulty manner.

Exercises

1. Lanny orally agrees to rent his house to Tenny for fifteen months, at a monthly rent of $1,000. Tenny moves in and pays the first month's rent. Lanny now wants to cancel the lease. May he? Why?
2. Suppose in Exercise 1 that Tenny had an option to cancel after one year. Could Lanny cancel before the end of the year? Why?
3. Suppose in Exercise 1 that Lanny himself is a tenant and has leased the house for six months. He subleases the house to Tenny for one year. The day before Tenny is to move into the house, he learns of Lanny's six-month lease and attempts to terminate his one-year lease. May he? Why?
4. Suppose In Exercise 3 that Tenny learned of Lanny's lease the day after he moved Into the house. May he terminate? Why?
5. Simon owns a four-story building and rents the top floor to a college student. Simon is in the habit of burning refuse in the backyard, and the smoke from the refuse is so noxious that it causes the student's eyes to water and his throat to become raw. Has Simon breached a duty to the student? Explain.
6. In Exercise 5, if other tenants (but not Simon) were burning refuse in the backyard, would Simon be in breach? Why?
7. Assume in Exercise 5 that Simon was in breach. Could the student move out of the apartment and terminate the lease? What effect would this have on the student's duty to pay rent? Explain.

Self-Test Questions

1. An estate for years
   a. has a definite beginning and end
   b. is a leasehold estate
   c. usually terminates automatically at midnight of the last day specified in the lease
   d. includes all of the above
2. Not included among the rights given to a tenant is
   a. paramount title

b. possession
c. habitable condition
d. noninterference with use

3. The interest of either landlord or tenant may be transferred freely
   a. unless the tenancy is at will
   b. unless the lease requires significant personal services unlikely to be performed by someone else
   c. unless either of the above apply
   d. under no circumstances
4. When injuries are caused on the premises to outsiders,
   a. the tenant is always liable
   b. the landlord is always liable
   c. the landlord may be liable if there are hidden dangers the landlord knows about
   d. they have no cause of action against the landlord or tenant since they have no direct contractual relationship with either party
5. Legally a tenant may
   a. commit waste
   b. make some structural alterations to the property
   c. abandon the property at any time
   d. physically change the property to suit it to her best advantage, as long as no structural alterations are made

Self-Test Answers

1. d
2. a
3. c
4. c
5. d

Endnotes

1. *Javins v. First National Realty Corp.*, 428 F.2d 1071, 1078-79 (D.C. Cir.), *cert. denied*, 400 U.S. 925 (1970).

CHAPTER 36

Estate Planning: Wills, Estates, and Trusts

Learning Objectives

After reading this chapter, you should understand the following:

1. How property, both real and personal, can be devised and bequeathed to named heirs in a will.
2. What happens to property of a decedent when there is no will.
3. The requirements for "testamentary capacity"—what it takes to make a valid will that can be admitted to probate.
4. The steps in the probate and administration of a will.
5. How a will is distinguished from a trust, and how a trust is created, how it functions, and how it may come to an end.
6. The various kinds of trusts, as well as factors that affect both estates and trusts.

Broadly defined, **estate planning** is the process by which someone decides how his assets are to be passed on to others at his death. Estate planning has two general objectives: to ensure that the assets are transferred according to the owner's wishes and to minimize state and federal taxes.

estate planning

The process by which an owner over the course of his life decides how his assets are to be passed on to others at his death.

People have at their disposal four basic estate planning tools: (1) wills, (2) trusts, (3) gifts, and (4) joint ownership (see Figure 36.1). The rules governing gifts are discussed in Chapter 31, and joint ownership is treated in Chapter 33. Consequently, we focus on the first two tools here. In addition to these tools, certain assets, such as insurance (discussed in Chapter 37), are useful in estate planning.

FIGURE 36.1 Estate Planning

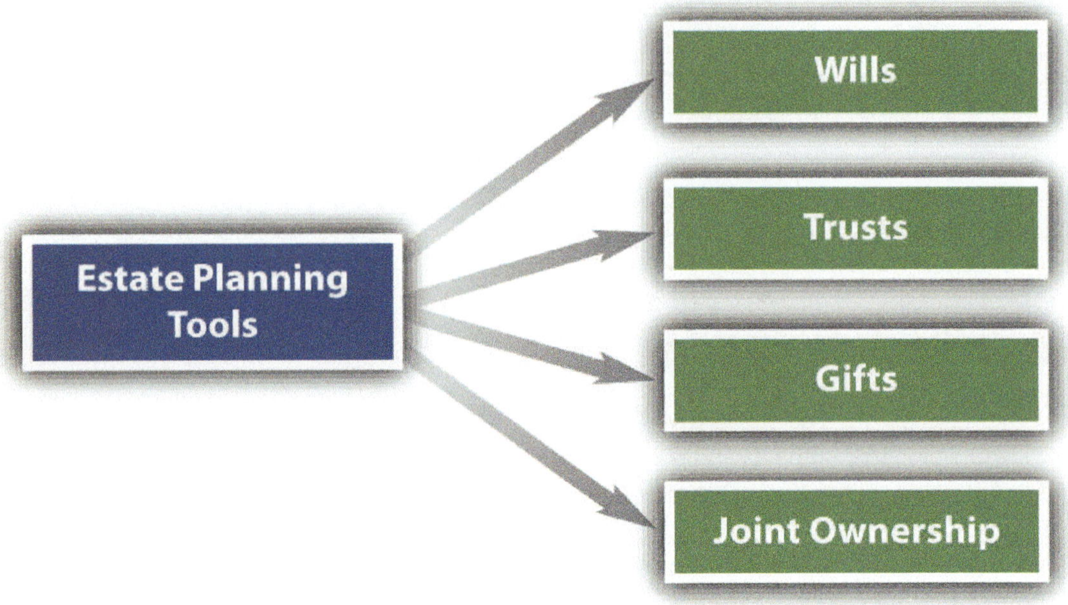

Estate planning not only provides for the spouses and children, other relatives and friends, the children's education, payoff of the mortgage, and so on, but also serves as the principal means by which liquidity can be guaranteed for taxes, expenses for administering the estate, and the like, while preserving the assets of the estate. And whenever a business is formed, estate planning consequences should always be considered, because the form and structure of the business can have important tax ramifications for the individual owners.

36.1 Wills and Estate Administration

Learning Objectives

1. Describe how property, both real and personal, can be devised and bequeathed to named heirs in a will.
2. Understand what happens to property of a decedent when there is no will.
3. Explain the requirements for "testamentary capacity"—what it takes to make a valid will that can be admitted to probate.
4. Describe the steps in the probate and administration of a will.

Definition

will

The declaration of a person's wishes (the testator) about the disposition of his assets on his death.

A **will** is the declaration of a person's wishes about the disposition of his assets on his death. Normally a written document, the will names the persons who are to receive specific items of real and personal property. Unlike a contract or a deed, a will is not binding as long as the person making the will lives. He may revoke it at any time. Wills have served their present function for virtually all of recorded history. The earliest known will is from 1800 BC (see Figure 36.2). Even if somewhat different in form, it served the same basic function as a modern will.

FIGURE 36.2 An Ancient Will

> **[Will of Uah] “I, Uah, devise to my wife Sheftu, the woman of Gesab called Teta, daughter of Sat Sepdu, all properties given to me by my brother Ankh-ren. She shall give it to whomsoever she may see fit of her issue born to me.**
>
> **"I devise to her the Eastern slaves, 4 persons, that my brother Ankh-ren gave me. She shall give them to whomsoever she may see fit of her children.**
>
> **“As to my tomb, let me be buried in it with my wife alone.**
>
> **"Moreover, as to the house built for me by my brother Ankh-ren, my wife shall dwell therein and shall not be evicted by any person.**
>
> **“The deputy Sebu shall act as guardian of my son. Done in the presence of these witnesses:**
>
> **"Kemen, Decorator of Columns,**
>
> **“Apu, Doorkeeper of the Temple,**
>
> **"Senb, son of Senb, Doorkeeper of the Temple.”**

Source: John H. Wigmore, A Panorama of the World's Legal Systems, vol. 1, p. 22.

Although most wills are written in a standardized form, some special types of wills are enforceable in many states.

1. A *nuncupative will* is one that is declared orally in front of witnesses. In states where allowed, the statutes permit it to be used only when the testator is dying as he declares his will. (A testator is one who dies with a will.)
2. A *holographic will* is one written entirely by the testator's hand and not witnessed. At common law, a holographic will was invalid if any part of the paper on which it was written contained printing. Modern statutes tend to validate holographic wills, even with printing, as long as the testator who signs it puts down material provisions in his own hand.
3. *Soldiers' and sailors' wills* are usually enforceable, no matter how informal the document, if made while the soldier is on service or the sailor is at sea (although they cannot usually transfer real property without observing certain formalities).
4. A *conditional will* is one that will take effect only on the happening of a particular named event. For example, a man intending to marry might write, “This will is contingent on my marrying Alexa Jansey.” If he and Ms. Jansey do not marry, the will can have no operational effect.
5. A *joint will* is one in which two (or more) people use the same instrument to dispose of their assets. It must be signed by each person whose assets it is to govern.
6. *Mutual* or *reciprocal wills* are two or more instruments with reciprocal terms, each written by a person who intends to dispose of his or her assets in favor of the others.

The Uniform Probate Code

probate

The process by which a deceased's estate is managed under the supervision of a court.

Probate is the process by which a deceased's estate is managed under the supervision of a court. In most states, the court supervising this process is a specialized one and is often called the probate court. Probate practices vary widely from state to state, although they follow a general pattern in which the assets of an estate are located, added up, and disbursed according to the terms of the will or, if there is no will, according to the law of intestate succession. To attempt to bring uniformity into the conflicting sets of state laws the National Conference of Commissioners on Uniform State Laws issued the Uniform Probate Code (UPC) in 1969, and by 2011 it had been adopted in its entirety in sixteen states. Several other states have adopted significant parts of the UPC, which was revised in 2006. Our discussion of wills and estate administration is drawn primarily from the UPC, but you should note that there are variations among the states in some of the procedures standardized in the UPC.

Will Requirements and Interpretation

Capacity

Any person who is over eighteen and of "sound mind" may make a will. One who is insane may not make an enforceable will, although the degree of mental capacity necessary to sustain a will is generally said to be a "modest level of competence" and is lower than the degree of capacity people must possess to manage their own affairs during their life. In other words, a court might order a guardian to manage the affairs of one who is mentally deficient but will uphold a will that the person has written. Insanity is not the only type of mental deficiency that will disqualify a will; medication of a person for serious physical pain might lead to the conclusion that the person's mind was dulled and he did not understand what he was doing when writing his will. The case *Estate of Seymour M. Rosen*, (see Section 4), considers just such a situation.

Writing

bequest

Gift of personal property by will.

devise

Gift of real property by will.

Under the UPC, wills must be in writing. The will is not confined to the specific piece of paper called "will" and signed by the testator. It may incorporate by reference any other writing in existence when the will is made, as long as the will sufficiently identifies the other writing and manifests an intent to incorporate it. Although lawyers prepare neatly typed wills, the document can be written in pencil or pen and on any kind of paper or even on the back of an envelope. Typically, the written will has the following provisions: (1) a "publication clause," listing the testator's name and his or her intention to make a will; (2) a "revocation clause," revoking all previously made wills; (3) burial instructions; (4) debt payments, listing specific assets to be used; (5) **bequests**, which are gifts of personal property by will; (6) **devises**, which are gifts of real property by will; (7) a "residuary clause," disposing of all property not covered by a specific bequest or devise; (8) a "penalty clause," stating a penalty for anyone named in the will who contests the will; (9) the name of minor children's guardian; and (10) the name of the executor. The executor's job is to bring in all the assets of an estate, pay all just claims, and make distribution to beneficiaries in accord with the testator's wishes. Beginning with California in 1983, several states have adopted statutory wills—simple fill-in-the-blank will forms that can be completed without consulting an attorney.

Signature

The testator must sign the will, and the proper place for the signature is at the end of the entire document. The testator need not sign his full name, although that is preferable; his initials or some other mark in his own hand, intended as an execution of the document, will suffice. The UPC permits someone else to sign for the testator as long as the signing is done in the testator's presence and by his or her direction.

Witnesses

Most states require two or three witnesses to sign the will. The UPC requires two witnesses. The witnesses should observe the testator sign the will and then sign it themselves in the presence of each other. Since the witnesses might be asked to attest in court to the testator's signature, it is sound practice to avoid witnesses who are unduly elderly and to use an extra witness or two. Most states forbid a person who has an interest in the will—that is, one who is a beneficiary under the will—from witnessing.

In some states, a beneficiary who serves as a witness will lose his or her right to a bequest or devise. The UPC differs from the usual rule: no will or any provision of a will is invalid because an interested party witnesses it, nor does the interested witness forfeit a bequest or devise.

Revocation and Modification

Since wills are generally effective only at death, the testator may always revoke or amend a will during his lifetime. He may do so by tearing, burning, obliterating, or otherwise destroying it. A subsequent will has the effect of revoking an inconsistent prior will, and most wills expressly state that they are intended to revoke all prior wills. A written modification of or supplement to a prior will is called a **codicil**. The codicil is often necessary, because circumstances are constantly changing. The testator may have moved to a new state where he must meet different formal requirements for executing the will; one of his beneficiaries may have died; his property may have changed. Or the law, especially the tax law, may have changed.

codicil

A written modification of or supplement to a prior will.

One exception to the rule that wills are effective only at death is the so-called **living will**. Beginning with California in 1976, most states have adopted legislation permitting people to declare that they refuse further treatment should they become terminally ill and unable to tell physicians not to prolong their lives if they can survive only by being hooked up to life-preserving machines. This living will takes effect during the patient's life and must be honored by physicians unless the patient has revoked it. The patient may revoke at any time, even as he sees the doctor moving to disconnect the plug.

living will

A will that takes effect during life in cases of terminal illness, directing that physicians and others take no life-prolonging measures.

In most states, a later marriage revokes a prior will, but divorce does not. Under the UPC, however, a divorce or annulment revokes any disposition of property bequeathed or devised to the former spouse under a will executed prior to the divorce or annulment. A will is at least partially revoked if children are born after it is executed, unless it has either provided for subsequently born children or stated the testator's intention to disinherit such children.

Abatement

Specific bequests listed in a will might not be available in the estate when the testator or testatrix dies. **Abatement** of a bequest happens when there are insufficient assets to pay the bequest. Suppose the testatrix leaves $10,000 each to "my four roommates," but when she dies, her estate is worth only $20,000. The gift to each of the roommates is said to have abated, and each will take only $5,000.

abatement

A proportional reduction of the amount payable under a will when the funds are no longer available to pay in full.

Abatement can pose a serious problem in wills not carefully drafted. Since circumstances can always change, a general provision in a father's will, providing "my dear daughter with all the rest, residue, and remainder of my estate," will do her little good if business setbacks mean that the $10,000 bequest to the local hospital exhausts the estate of its assets—even though at the time the will was made, the testator had assets of $1 million and supposed his daughter would be getting the bulk of it. Since specific gifts must be paid out ahead of general bequests or devises, abatement can cause the residual legatee (the person taking all assets not specifically distributed to named individuals) to suffer.

Ademption

Ademption

Revocation or cancellation of a legatee's rights under a will by the actions of the testator during his life, often by his having given away assets that the will says are to go to the legatee.

Suppose that a testator bequeathed her 1923 Rolls Royce to "my faithful secretary," but that the car had been sold and she owned only a 1980 Volkswagen when she died. Since the Rolls was not part of the estate, it is said to have adeemed (to have been taken away). **Ademption** of a gift in a will means that the intended legatee (the person named in the will) forfeits the object because it no longer exists as part of the estate. An object used as a substitute by the testator will not pass to the legatee unless it is clear that she intended the legatee to have it.

Intestacy

Intestacy

Dying without a will.

Intestacy means dying without a will. Intestacy happens all too frequently; even those who know the consequences for their heirs often put off making a will until it is too late—Abraham Lincoln, for one, who as an experienced lawyer knew very well the hazards to heirs of dying intestate. On his death, Lincoln's property was divided, with one-third going to his widow, one-third to a grown son, and one-third to a twelve-year-old son. Statistics show that in New York, about one-third of the people who die with estates of $5,000 or more die without wills. In every state, statutes provide for the disposition of property of decedents dying without wills. If you die without a will, the state has already made one out for you. Although the rules vary by statute from state to state, a common distribution pattern prevails.

Unmarried Decedent

escheat

Property of decedents that have no known heirs will "escheat" to the state.

At common law, parents of an intestate decedent could not inherit his property. Today, however, many states provide that parents will share in the property. If the parents have already died, then the estate will pass to collateral heirs (siblings, nieces, nephews, aunts, and uncles). If there are no collateral heirs, most state laws provide that the next surviving kin of equal degree will share the property equally (e.g., first cousins). If there are no surviving kin, the estate **escheats** (es CHEETS) to the state, which is then the sole owner of the assets of the estate.

Married with No Children

In some states, the surviving spouse without children will inherit the entire estate. In other states, the spouse must share the property with the decedent's parents or, if they are deceased, with the collateral heirs.

Married with Children

per stirpes

By representation; in a distribution per stirpes, each class of individuals takes the share to which their deceased would have been entitled.

In general, the surviving spouse will be entitled to one-third of the estate, and the remainder will pass in equal shares to living children of the decedent. The share of any child who died before the decedent will be divided equally among that child's offspring. These grandchildren of the decedent are said to take **per stirpes** (per STIR peas), meaning that they stand in the shoes of their parent. Suppose that the decedent left a wife, three children, and eight grandchildren (two children each of the three surviving children and two children of a fourth child who predeceased the decedent), and that the estate was worth $300,000. Under a typical intestate succession law, the widow would receive property worth $100,000. The balance of the property would be divided into four equal parts, one for each of the four children. The three surviving children would each receive $50,000.

The two children of the fourth child would each receive $25,000. The other grandchildren would receive nothing.

A system of distribution in which all living descendants share equally, regardless of generation, is said to be a distribution **per capita**. In the preceding example, after the widow took her share, the remaining sum would be divided into eleven parts, three for the surviving children and eight for the surviving grandchildren.

per capita

According to the number of individuals, share and share alike; in a distribution per capita, each person named will receive an equal share.

Unmarried with Children

If the decedent was a widow or widower with children, then the surviving children generally will take the entire estate.

Estate Administration

To carry on the administration of an estate, a particular person must be responsible for locating the estate property and carrying out the decedent's instructions. If named in the will, this person is called an **executor**. When a woman serves, she is still known in many jurisdictions as an **executrix**. If the decedent died intestate, the court will appoint an administrator (or administratrix, if a woman), usually a close member of the family. The UPC refers to the person performing the function of executor or administrator as a personal representative. Unless excused by the will from doing so, the personal representative must post a bond, usually in an amount that exceeds the value of the decedent's personal property.

executor

The administrator of an estate, named in the will by the testator.

executrix

The female administrator of an estate, named in the will by the testator.

The personal representative must immediately become familiar with the decedent's business, preserve the assets, examine the books and records, check on insurance, and notify the appropriate banks.

When confirmed by the court (if necessary), the personal representative must offer the will in probate—that is, file the will with the court, prove its authenticity through witnesses, and defend it against any challenges. Once the court accepts the will, it will enter a formal decree admitting the will to probate.

Traditionally, a widow could make certain elections against the will; for example, she could choose dower and homestead rights. The right of **dower** entitled the widow to a life estate in one-third of the husband's inheritable land, while a **homestead right** is the right to the family home as measured by an amount of land (e.g., 160 acres of rural land or 1 acre of urban land in Kansas) or a specific dollar amount. In some states, this amount is quite low (e.g., $4,000 in Kansas) where the legislature has not upwardly adjusted the dollar amount for many years.

dower

A right given to a widow to a life estate in one-third of the husband's inheritable land.

homestead right

The right to the family home (as measured by an amount of land or a specific dollar amount) to be free of all claims of creditors.

Today, most states have eliminated traditional dower rights. These states give the surviving spouse (widow or widower) the right to reject provisions made in a will and to take a share of the decedent's estate instead.

Once the will is admitted to probate, the personal representative must assemble and inventory all assets. This task requires the personal representative to collect debts and rent due, supervise the decedent's business, inspect the real estate, store personal and household effects, prove the death and collect proceeds of life insurance policies, take securities into custody, and ascertain whether the decedent held property in other states. Next, the assets must be appraised as of the date of death. When inventory and appraisal are completed, the personal representative must decide how and when to dispose of the assets by answering the following sorts of questions: Should a business be liquidated, sold, or allowed to continue to operate? Should securities be sold, and if so, when? Should the real estate be kept intact under the will or sold? To whom must the personal effects be given?

The personal representative must also handle claims against the estate. If the decedent had unpaid debts while alive, the estate will be responsible for paying them. In most states, the personal representative is required to advertise that the estate is in probate. When all claims have been gathered and authenticated, the personal representative must pay just claims in order of priority. In general (though by no means in every state), the order of priority is as follows: (1) funeral expenses, (2) administration expenses (cost of bond, advertising expenses, filing fees, lawsuit costs, etc.), (3) family allowance, (4) claims of the federal government, (5) hospital and other expenses associated with the decedent's last illness, (6) claims of state and local governments, (7) wage claims, (8) lien claims, (9) all other debts. If the estate is too small to cover all these claims, every claim in the first category must be satisfied before the claims in the second category may be paid, and so on.

estate taxes

Taxes imposed by the federal government on large estates.

Before the estate can be distributed, the personal representative must take care of all taxes owed by the estate. She will have to file returns for both estate and income taxes and pay from assets of the estate the taxes due. (She may have to sell some assets to obtain sufficient cash to do so.) **Estate taxes**—imposed by the federal government and based on the value of the estate—are nearly as old as the Republic; they date back to 1797. They were instituted originally to raise revenue, but in our time they serve also to break up large estates.

As of 2011, the first $1 million of an estate is exempt from taxation, lowering the threshold from an earlier standard. The Tax Policy Institute of the Brookings Institution estimates that 108,200 estates of people dying in 2011 will file estate tax returns, and 44,200 of those estates will pay taxes totaling $34.4 billion.

Although a unified tax is imposed on gifts during life and transfers at death, everyone is permitted to give away $14,000 per donee each year without paying any tax on the gift. A tax on sizable gifts is imposed to prevent people with large estates from giving away during their lives portions of their estate in order to escape estate taxes. Thus two grandparents with two married children and four grandchildren may give away $28,000 ($14,000 from each grandparent) to their eight descendants (children, spouses, grandchildren) each year, for a total of $224,000, without paying any tax.

inheritance taxes

State taxes on an heir's right to receive the property.

State governments also impose taxes at death. In many states, these are known as **inheritance taxes** and are taxes on the heir's right to receive the property. The tax rate depends on the relationship to the decedent: the closer the relation, the smaller the tax. Thus a child will pay less than a nephew or niece, and either of them will pay less than an unrelated friend who is named in the will.

final accounting

Done by the executor to close out an estate in probate. After taxes and debts are paid, an accounting must be prepared, showing the remaining principal, income, and disbursements to beneficiaries.

Once the taxes are paid, a **final accounting** must be prepared, showing the remaining principal, income, and disbursements. Only at this point may the personal representative actually distribute the assets of the estate according to the will.

Key Takeaway

Any person with the requisite capacity may make a will and bequeath personal property to named heirs. A will can also devise real property. Throughout the United States, there are fairly common requirements to be met for a will to qualify for probate.

Intestacy statutes will govern where there is no will, and an administrator will be appointed by the probate court. Intestacy statutes will dictate which relatives will get what portion of the decedent's estate, portions that are likely to differ from what the decedent would have done had he or she left a valid will. Where there are no heirs, the decedent's property escheats to the state.

An executor (or executrix) is the person named in the will to administer the estate and render a final accounting. Estate and inheritance taxes may be owed if the estate is large enough.

Exercises

1. Dennis Trent is married to Irene Trent, but they divorce. Dennis neglects to change his will, which leaves everything to Irene. If he were to die before remarrying, would the will still be valid?

2. Tom Tyler, married to Tina Tyler, dies without a will. There are two children. If his legal state of residence is California, how will his estate be distributed? (This will require a small amount of Internet browsing.)
3. Suppose Tom Tyler is very wealthy. When he dies at age sixty-three, there are two wills: one leaves everything to his wife and family, and the other leaves everything to his alma mater, the University of Colorado. The family wishes to dispute the validity of the second (later in time) will. What, in general, are the bases on which a will can be challenged so that it does not enter into probate?

36.2 Trusts

Learning Objectives

1. Distinguish a will from a trust, and describe how a trust is created, how it functions, and how it may come to an end.
2. Compare the various kinds of trusts, as well as factors that affect both estates and trusts.

Definitions

When the legal title to certain property is held by one person while another has the use and benefit of it, a relationship known as a **trust** has been created. The trust developed centuries ago to get around various nuances and complexities, including taxes, of English real property law. The trustee has legal title and the beneficiary has "equitable title," since the courts of equity would enforce the obligations of the trustee to honor the terms by which the property was conveyed to him. A typical trust might provide for the trustee to manage an estate for the grantor's children, paying out income to the children until they are, say, twenty-one, at which time they would become legal owners of the property.

trust

The holding of legal title by one party for the benefit of another.

Trusts may be created by bequest in a will, by agreement of the parties, or by a court decree. However created, the trust is governed by a set of rules that grew out of the courts of equity. Every trust involves specific property, known as the *res* (rez or rees; Latin for "thing"), and three parties, though the parties may be the same person.

Settlor or Grantor

Anyone who has legal capacity to make a contract may create a trust. The creator is known as the **settlor** or grantor. Trusts are created for many reasons; for example, so that a minor can have the use of assets without being able to use them up too quickly, or so that a person can have a professional manage her money.

settlor

Grantor; the one who creates a trust.

Trustee

The trustee is the person or legal entity that holds the legal title to the *res*. Many banks have trust departments that serve as trustees. If the settlor should neglect to name a trustee, a court may name one if the issue comes before a court. The trustee is a fiduciary of the trust's beneficiary and will be held to the highest standard of loyalty and due care. Not even an appearance of impropriety toward the trust property will be permitted. Thus, a trustee may not loan trust property to friends, to a corporation of which he is a principal, or to himself, even if he is scrupulous to account for every penny and pays the principal back with interest. The trustee must act prudently in administering the trust.

Beneficiary

The beneficiary is the person, institution, or other thing for which the trust has been created. Beneficiaries are not limited to one's children or close friends; an institution, a corporation, or some other organization, such as a charity, can be a beneficiary of a trust, as can one's pet dogs, cats, and the like. The beneficiary may usually sell or otherwise dispose of his interest in a trust, and that interest likewise can usually be reached by creditors. Note that the settlor may create a trust of which he is the beneficiary, just as he may create a trust of which he is the trustee.

Continental Bank & Trust Co. v. Country Club Mobile Estates, Ltd., (see Section 4), considers a basic element of trust law: the settlor's power over the property once he has created the trust.

Express Trusts

testamentary trusts

A trust made during the settlor's life that takes effect on his death.

***inter vivos* (or living) trusts**

A trust that takes effect during the life of the settlor.

Trusts are divided into two main categories: express and implied. Express trusts include **testamentary trusts** and ***inter vivos* (or living) trusts**. The testamentary trust is one created by will. It becomes effective on the testator's death. The inter vivos trust is one created during the lifetime of the grantor. It can be revocable or irrevocable (see Figure 36.3).

FIGURE 36.3 Express Trusts

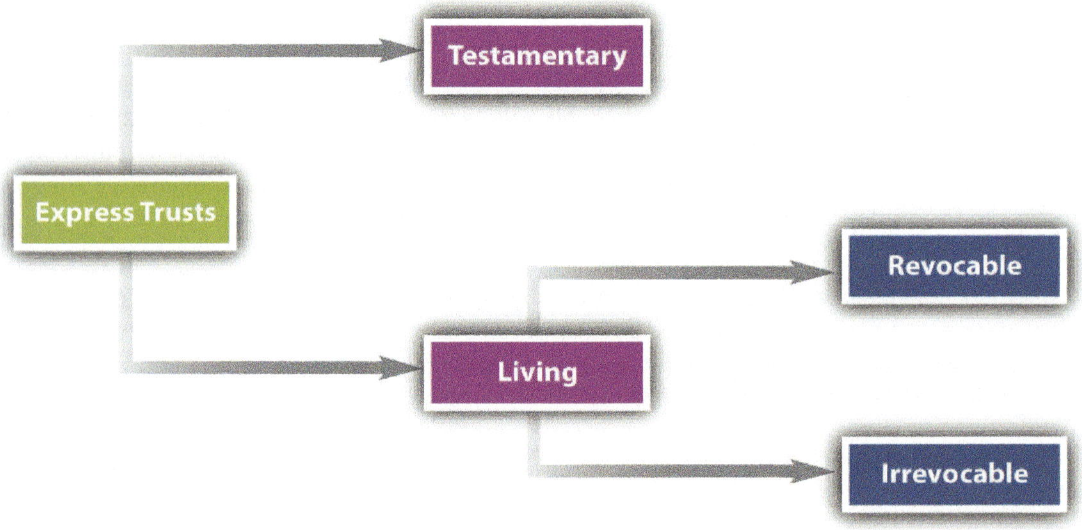

revocable trust

A trust that the settlor can terminate at his option.

irrevocable trust

A trust that the settlor cannot terminate at his option.

A **revocable trust** is one that the settlor can terminate at his option. On termination, legal title to the trust assets returns to the settlor. Because the settlor can reassert control over the assets whenever she wishes, the income they generate is taxed to her.

By contrast, an **irrevocable trust** is permanent, and the settlor may not revoke or modify its terms. All income to the trust must be accumulated in the trust or be paid to the beneficiaries in accordance with the trust agreement. Because income does not go to the settlor, the irrevocable trust has important income tax advantages, even though it means permanent loss of control over the assets, at least beyond the control the settlor provides in the instructions for the trustee in the trust agreement. A hybrid form is the reversionary trust: until the end of a fixed period, the trust is irrevocable and the settlor may not modify its terms, but thereafter the trust assets revert to the settlor. The reversionary trust combines tax advantages with ultimate possession of the assets.

Of the possible types of express trusts, five are worth examining briefly: (1) Totten trusts, (2), blind trusts, (3) Clifford trusts, (4) charitable trusts, and (5) spendthrift trusts. The use of express trusts in business will also be noted.

Totten Trust

The Totten trust, which gets its name from a New York case, *In re Totten*,[1] is a tentative trust created when someone deposits funds in a bank as trustee for another person as beneficiary. (Usually, the account will be named in the following form: "Mary, in trust for Ed.") During the beneficiary's lifetime, the grantor-depositor may withdraw funds at his discretion or revoke the trust altogether. But if the grantor-depositor dies before the beneficiary and had not revoked the trust, then the beneficiary is entitled to whatever remains in the account at the time of the depositor's death.

Blind Trust

In a blind trust, the grantor transfers assets—usually stocks and bonds—to trustees who hold and manage them for the grantor as beneficiary. The trustees are not permitted to tell the grantor how they are managing the portfolio. The blind trust is used by high government officials who are required by the Ethics in Government Act of 1978 to put their assets in blind trusts or abstain from making decisions that affect any companies in which they have a financial stake. Once the trust is created, the grantor-beneficiary is forbidden from discussing financial matters with the trustees or even to give the trustees advice. All that the grantor-beneficiary sees is a quarterly statement indicating by how much the trust net worth has increased or decreased.

Clifford Trust

The Clifford trust, named after the settlor in the Supreme Court case of *Helvering v. Clifford*,[2] is reversionary: the grantor establishes a trust irrevocable for at least ten years and a day. By so doing, the grantor shifts the tax burden to the beneficiary. So a person in a higher bracket can save considerable money by establishing a Clifford trust to benefit, say, his or her children. The tax savings will apply as long as the income from the trust is not devoted to needs of the children that the grantor is legally required to supply. At the expiration of the express period in the trust, legal title to the *res* reverts to the grantor. However, the Tax Reform Act of 1986 removed the tax advantages for Clifford trusts established after March 1986. As a result, all income from such trusts is taxed to the grantor. Existing Clifford trusts were not affected by the 1986 tax law.

Charitable Trust

A charitable trust is one devoted to any public purpose. The definition is broad; it can encompass funds for research to conquer disease, to aid battered wives, to add to museum collections, or to permit a group to proselytize on behalf of a particular political or religious doctrine. The law in all states recognizes the benefits to be derived from encouraging charitable trusts, and states use the *cy pres* (pronounced as "see press," meaning as near as possible) doctrine to further the intent of the grantor. The most common type of trust is the charitable remainder trust. You would donate property—usually intangible property such as stock—in trust to an approved charitable organization, usually one that has tax-exempt 501(c)(3) status from the IRS. The organization serves as trustee during your life and provides you or someone you designate with a specified level of income from the property that you donated. This could be for a number of years or for your lifetime. After your death or the period that you set, the trust ends and the charitable organization owns the assets that were in the trust.

There are important tax reasons why people set up charitable trusts. The trustor gets five years' worth of tax deductions for the value of the assets in the charitable trust. Capital gains are treated favorably, as well: charitable trusts are irrevocable, which means that the person setting up the trust (the "trustor") permanently gives up control of the assets to the charitable organization. Thus, the charitable organization could sell an asset in the trust that would ordinarily incur significant capital gains taxes, but since the trustor no longer owns the asset, there is no capital gains tax: as a tax-exempt organization, the charity will not pay capital gains, either.

Spendthrift Trust

A spendthrift trust is established when the settlor believes that the beneficiary is not to be trusted with whatever rights she might possess to assign the income or assets of the trust. By express provision in a trust instrument, the settlor may ensure that the trustees are legally obligated to pay only income to the beneficiary; no assignment of the assets may be made, either voluntarily by the beneficiary or involuntarily by operation of law. Hence the spendthrift beneficiary cannot gamble away the trust assets nor can they be reached by creditors to pay her gambling (or other) debts.

Express Trusts in Business

In addition to their use in estate planning, express trusts are also created for business purposes. The business trust was popular late in the nineteenth century as a way of getting around state limitations on the corporate form and is still used today. By giving their shares to a voting trust, shareholders can ensure that their agreement to vote as a bloc will be carried out. But voting trusts can be dangerous. As discussed in Chapter 48 agreements that result in price fixing or other restraints of trade violate the antitrust laws; for example, companies are in violation when they act collusively to fix prices by pooling voting stock under a trust agreement, as happened frequently at the turn of the century.

Implied Trusts

constructive trust

Created by courts to redress fraud or prevent unjust enrichment.

resulting trust

Created by courts to give effect to the intent of the parties.

Trusts can be created by courts without any intent by a settlor to do so. For various reasons, a court will declare that particular property is to be held by its owner in trust for someone else. Such trusts are implied trusts and are usually divided into two types: **constructive trusts** and **resulting trusts**. A constructive trust is one created usually to redress a fraud or to prevent unjust enrichment. Suppose you give $1 to an agent to purchase a lottery ticket for you, but the agent buys the ticket in his own name instead and wins $1,000,000, payable into an account in amounts of $50,000 per year for twenty years. Since the agent had violated his fiduciary obligation and unjustly enriched himself, the court would impose a constructive trust on the account, and the agent would find himself holding the funds as trustee for you as beneficiary. By contrast, a resulting trust is one imposed to carry out the supposed intent of the parties. You give an agent $100,000 to purchase a house for you. Title is put in your agent's name at the closing, although it is clear that since she was paid for her services, you did not intend to give the house to her as a gift. The court would declare that the house was to be held by the agent as trustee for you during the time that it takes to have the title put in your name.

Key Takeaway

A trust can be created during the life of the settlor of the trust. A named trustee and beneficiary are required, as well as some assets that the trustee will administer. The trustee has a fiduciary duty to administer the trust with the utmost care. Inter vivos trusts can be revocable or irrevocable. Testamentary trusts are, by definition, not revocable, as they take effect on the death of the settlor.

Exercises

1. Karen Vreeland establishes a testamentary trust for her son, Brian, who has a gambling addiction. What kind of trust should she have established?
2. A group of ten coworkers "invests" in the Colorado Lottery when the jackpot reaches $200 million. Each puts in $10 for five tickets. Dan Connelly purchases fifty Colorado Lottery tickets on behalf of the group and holds them. As luck would have it, one of the tickets is a winner. Dan takes the ticket, claims the $200 million, quits his job, and refuses to share. Do the coworkers have any legal recourse? Was a trust created in this situation?
3. Laura Sarazen has two sisters, Lana and Linda. Laura deposits $50,000 at the Bank of America and creates an account that names her sister, Linda, in the following form: "Laura Sarazen, in trust for Linda Sarazen." Laura dies two years later and has not withdrawn funds from the bank. The executrix wants to include those funds in the estate. Can she?

36.3 Factors Affecting Estates and Trusts

Learning Objectives

1. Know how principal and income are distinguished in administering a trust.
2. Explain how estates and trusts are taxed, and the utility of powers of appointment.

Principal and Income

Often, one person is to receive income from a trust or an estate and another person, the remainderman, is to receive the remaining property when the trust or estate is terminated. In thirty-six states, a uniform act, the Uniform Principal and Income Act (UPIA), defines principal and income and specifies how expenses are to be paid. If the trust agreement expressly gives the trustee power to determine what is income and what is principal, then his decision is usually not reviewable by a court. If the agreement is silent as to what is principal and what is income, the trustee is bound by the provisions of the UPIA.

The general rule is that ordinary receipts are income, whereas extraordinary receipts are additions to principal. Ordinary receipts are defined as the return of money or property derived from the use of the principal, including rent, interest, and cash dividends. Extraordinary receipts include stock dividends, revenues or other proceeds from the sale or exchange of trust assets, proceeds from insurance on assets, all income accrued at the testator's death, proceeds from the sale or redemption of bonds, and awards or judgments received in satisfaction of injuries to the trust property. Expenses or obligations incurred in producing or preserving income—including ordinary repairs and ordinary taxes—are chargeable to income. Expenses incurred in making permanent improvements to the property, in investing the assets, and in selling or purchasing trust property are chargeable to principal, as are all obligations incurred before the decedent's death.

Taxation

Estates and trusts are taxable entities under the federal income tax statute. The general rule is that all income paid out to the beneficiaries is taxable to the beneficiaries and may be deducted from the trust's or estate's gross income in arriving at its net taxable income. The trust or estate is then taxed on the balance left over—that is, on any amounts accumulated. This is known as the conduit rule, because the trust or estate is seen as a conduit for the income.

Power of Appointment

A power of appointment is the authority given by one person (the donor) to another (the donee) to dispose of the donor's property according to whatever instructions the donor provides. A power of appointment can be created in a will, in a trust, or in some other writing. The writing may imply the power of appointment rather than specifically calling it a power of appointment. In a will, a devise of real property or a bequest of personal property to X that allows X to receive it or transfer it gives that person a power of appointment. The person giving the power is the donor, and the person receiving it is the donee.

There are three classes of powers of appointment. General powers of appointment give donees the power to dispose of the property in any way they see fit. Limited powers of appointment, also known as special powers of appointment, give donees the power to transfer the property to a specified class of persons identified in the instrument creating the power. Testamentary powers of appointment are powers of appointment created by wills.

If properly used, the power of appointment is an important tool, because it permits the donee to react flexibly to circumstances that the donor could not have foreseen. Suppose you desire to benefit your children when they are thirty-five or forty according to whether they are wealthy or poor. The poorer children will be given more from the estate or trust than the wealthier ones. Since you will not know when you write the will or establish the trust which children will be poorer, a donee with a power of appointment will be able to make judgments impossible for the donor to make years or decades before.

Key Takeaway

Administering either an estate or a trust requires knowing the distinction between principal and income in a variety of situations. For example, knowing which receipts are ordinary and which are extraordinary is essential to knowing whether to allocate the receipts as income or as an addition to principal. Knowing which expenses are chargeable to principal and which are chargeable to income is also important. Both estates and trusts are taxable entities, subject to federal and state laws on estate and trust taxation. Powers of appointment can be used in both trusts and estates in order to give flexibility to named donees.

Exercises

1. In his will, Hagrid leaves his pet dragon, Norberta, to Ron Weasley as donee with power of appointment. He intends to restrict Ron's power as donee to give or sell Norberta only to wizards or witches. What kind of power of appointment should Hagrid use?
2. In a testamentary trust, Baxter Black leaves Hilda Garde both real and personal property to administer as she sees fit as trustee "for the benefit of the Michigan Militia." Hilda intends

to sell the house, but meanwhile she rents it out at $1,200 a month and incurs repairs to the property to prepare it for sale in the amount of $4,328.45. Is the expense chargeable to income or principal? Is the rent to be characterized as ordinary receipts or extraordinary receipts?

36.4 Cases

Testamentary Capacity

Estate of Seymour M. Rosen
Supreme Judicial Court of Maine
447 A.2d 1220 (1982)

GODFREY, JUSTICE

Phoebe Rosen and Jeffrey Rosen, widow and son of the decedent, Seymour M. Rosen, appeal from an order of the Knox County Probate Court admitting the decedent's will to probate. Appellants argue that the decedent lacked the testamentary capacity necessary to execute a valid will and that the Probate Court's finding that he did have the necessary capacity is clearly erroneous. On direct appeal from the Probate Court pursuant to section 1-308 of the Probate Code (18-A M.R.S.A. § 1-308), this Court reviews for clear error the findings of fact by the Probate Court. *Estate of Mitchell*, Me., 443 A.2d 961 (1982). We affirm the judgment.

Decedent, a certified public accountant, had an accounting practice in New York City, where he had been married to Phoebe for about thirty years. Their son, Jeffrey, works in New York City. In 1973, the decedent was diagnosed as having chronic lymphatic leukemia, a disease that, as it progresses, seriously impairs the body's ability to fight infection. From 1973 on, he understood that he might die within six months. In June, 1978, he left his home and practice and moved to Maine with his secretary of two months, Robin Gordon, the appellee. He set up an accounting practice in Camden.

The leukemia progressed. The decedent was on medication and was periodically hospitalized for infections, sometimes involving septic shock, a condition described by the treating physician as akin to blood poisoning. The infections were treated with antibiotics with varying degrees of success. Despite his medical problems, the decedent continued his accounting practice, working usually three days a week, until about two months before his death on December 4, 1980. Robin Gordon lived with him and attended him until his death.

While living in New York, the decedent had executed a will leaving everything to his wife or, if she should not survive him, to his son. In November, 1979, decedent employed the services of Steven Peterson, a lawyer whose office was in the same building as decedent's, to execute a codicil to the New York will leaving all his Maine property to Robin. At about this time, decedent negotiated a property settlement with his wife, who is now living in Florida. He executed the will at issue in this proceeding on July 25, 1980, shortly after a stay in the hospital with a number of infections, and shortly before a hospitalization that marked the beginning of the decedent's final decline. This will, which revoked all earlier wills and codicils, left all his property, wherever located, to Robin, or to Jeffrey if Robin did not survive him.

The court admitted the 1980 will to probate over the objections of Phoebe and son, making extensive findings to support its conclusion that "the decedent clearly had testamentary capacity when he executed his Will."

The Probate Court applied the standard heretofore declared by this Court for determining whether a decedent had the mental competence necessary to execute a valid will:

> *A 'disposing mind' involves the exercise of so much mind and memory as would enable a person to transact common and simple kinds of business with that intelligence which belongs to the weakest class of sound minds; and a disposing memory exists when one can recall the general nature, condition and extent of his property, and his relations to those to whom he gives, and also to those from whom he excludes, his bounty. He must have active memory enough to bring to his mind the nature and particulars of the business to be transacted, and mental power enough to appreciate them, and act with sense and judgment in regard to them. He must have sufficient capacity to comprehend the condition of his property, his relations to the persons who were or should have been the objects of his bounty, and the scope and bearing of the provisions of his will. He must have sufficient active memory to collect in his mind, without prompting, the particulars or elements of the business to be transacted, and to hold them in his mind a sufficient length of time to perceive at least their obvious relations to each other, and be able to form some rational judgment in relation to them. [Citations.]*

Appellants portray the decedent as "a man ravaged by cancer and dulled by medication," and it is true that some evidence in the record tends to support this characterization. However, the law as set out in *In re Leonard* requires only a modest level of competence ("the weakest class of sound minds"), and there is considerable evidence of record that the decedent had at least that level of mental ability and probably more:

1. The three women who witnessed the will all testified that decedent was of sound mind. They worked in the same building as the decedent, knew him, and saw him regularly. Such testimony is admissible to show testamentary capacity. *In re Leonard*, 321 A.2d at 489.
2. Lawyer Peterson, who saw the decedent daily, testified that he was of sound mind. Peterson used the decedent as a tax adviser, and the decedent did accounting work for Peterson's clients. Peterson had confidence in the decedent's tax abilities and left the tax aspects of the will to the decedent's own consideration.
3. Dr. Weaver, the treating physician, testified that although the decedent would be mentally deadened for a day or two while in shock in the hospital, he would then regain "normal mental function." Though on medication, the decedent was able to conduct his business until soon before his death. Dr. Weaver testified without objection that on one occasion he had offered a written opinion that the decedent was of sound mind.

Appellants' principal objection to the will is that the decedent lacked the necessary knowledge of "the general nature, condition and extent of his property." *In re Leonard*, 321 A.2d at 488. The record contains testimony of Robin Gordon and lawyer Peterson that decedent did not know what his assets were or their value. However, there is other evidence, chiefly Peterson's testimony about his discussions with the decedent preliminary to the drafting of the 1980 will and, earlier, when the 1979 codicil to the New York will was being prepared, that the decedent did have knowledge of the contents of his estate. He knew that he had had a Florida condominium, although he was unsure whether this had been turned over to his wife as part of the recent property settlement; he knew that he had an interest in an oil partnership, and, although he was unable to place a value on that interest, he knew the name of an individual who could supply further information about it; he knew he had stocks and bonds, two motor vehicles, an account at the Camden National Bank, and accounts receivable from his accounting practice.

The law does not require that a testator's knowledge of his estate be highly specific in order for him to execute a valid will. It requires only that the decedent be able to recall "the general nature, condition and extent of his property." *In re Leonard*, 321 A.2d at 488. Such knowledge of one's property is an aspect of mental soundness, not an independent legal requirement as the appellants seem to suggest. Here, there was competent evidence that the decedent had a general knowledge of his estate. The Probate Court was justified in concluding that, in the circumstances, the decedent's ignorance of the precise extent of his property did not establish his mental incompetence. The decedent's uncertainty about his property was understandable in view of the fact that some of his property had been transferred to his wife in the recent property negotiations in circumstances rendering it possible that the decedent might have wanted to put the matter out of his mind. Also, there was evidence from which the court could have inferred that much of the property was of uncertain or changing value.

On the evidence of record, this Court cannot hold that the findings of the Probate Court were clearly erroneous. Where, as here, there is a choice between two permissible views of the weight of the evidence, the findings of the Probate Court must stand. *Estate of Mitchell*, Me., 443 A.2d 961 (1982).

Case Questions

1. Based on what is written in this opinion, did the decedent's widow get nothing as a result of her husband's death? What did she get, and how?
2. If Phoebe Rosen's appeal had resulted in a reversal of the probate court, what would happen?
3. Is it possible that Seymour Rosen lacked testamentary capacity? Could the probate court have ruled that he did and refuse to admit the will to probate? If so, what would happen, using the court's language and cited opinions?

Settlor's Limited Power over the Trust

Continental Bank & Trust Co. v. Country Club Mobile Estates, Ltd.
632 P.2d 869 (Utah 1981)

Oaks, Justice

The issue in this appeal is whether a settlor who has created a trust by conveying property that is subject to an option to sell can thereafter extend the period of the option without the participation or consent of the trustee. We hold that he cannot. For ease of reference, this opinion will refer to the plaintiff-appellant, Continental Bank & Trust Co., as the "trustee," to defendant-respondent, Country Club Mobile Estates, Ltd., as the "lessee-optionee," and to Marshall E. Huffaker, deceased, as the "settlor."

The sequence of events is critical. On September 29, 1965, the settlor gave the lessee-optionee a fifty-year lease and an option to purchase, during the sixth year of the lease, the 31 acres of land at issue in this litigation. On March 1, 1971, the settlor granted the lessee-optionee a five-year extension of its option, to September 29, 1976. On December 6, 1973, the settlor conveyed the subject property to the trustee in trust for various members of his family, signing a trust agreement and conveying the property to the trustee by a warranty deed, which was promptly recorded. The lessee-optionee had actual as well as constructive notice of the creation of this trust by at least April, 1975, when it began making its monthly lease payments directly to the trustee. On March 1, 1976, the settlor signed an instrument purporting to grant the lessee-optionee another five-year extension of its option, to September 29, 1981. The trustee was unaware of this action and did not participate in it. On October 30, 1978, approximately one week after the settlor's death, the trustee learned of the March 1, 1976, attempted extension and demanded and obtained a copy of the instrument.

On July 3, 1979, the trustee brought this action against the lessee-optionee and other interested parties to quiet title to the 31 acres of trust property and to determine the validity of the attempted extension of the option. Both parties moved for summary judgment on the issue of the validity of the extended option. The district court denied the trustee's motion and granted the lessee-optionee's motion, and the trustee appealed. We reverse.

A settlor admittedly could reserve power to extend the duration of an option on trust property, and do so without the consent or involvement of the trustee. The question is whether this settlor did so. The issue turns on the terms of the trust instrument, which, in this case, gave the trustee broad powers, including the power to grant options, but also reserved to the settlor the right to revoke the trust or to direct the trustee to sell trust property. The relevant clauses are as follows:

> *ARTICLE IV.*
> *To carry out the Trust purposes of the Trust created hereby...the Trustee is vested with the following powers...:*
>
> *B. To manage, control, sell, convey...; to grant options...*
>
> *K....The enumeration of certain powers of the Trustee herein shall not be construed as a limitation of the Trustee's power, it being intended that the Trustee shall have all rights, powers and privileges that an absolute owner of the property would have.*

> *ARTICLE V.*
> *The Trustor by an instrument in writing filed with the Trustee may modify, alter or revoke this Agreement in whole or in part, and may withdraw any property subject to the agreement;...*
>
> *There is hereby reserved to the Trustor the power to direct the trustee, in writing, from time to time, to retain, sell, exchange or lease any property of the trust estate....Upon receipt of such directions, the Trustee shall comply therewith.*

A trust is a form of ownership in which the legal title to property is vested in a trustee, who has equitable duties to hold and manage it for the benefit of the beneficiaries. *Restatement of Trusts, Second*, § 2 (1959). It is therefore axiomatic in trust law that the trustee under a valid trust deed has exclusive control of the trust property, subject only to the limitations imposed by law or the trust instrument, and that once the settlor has created the trust he is no longer the owner of the trust property and has only such ability to deal with it as is expressly reserved to him in the trust instrument. *Boone v. Davis*, 64 Miss. 133, 8 So. 202 (1886); *Marvin v. Smith*, 46 N.Y. 571 (1871). As stated in Bogert, *Trusts & Trustees*, §42 (2d ed. 1965):

> *After a settlor has completed the creation of a trust he is, with small exceptions noted below, and except as expressly provided otherwise by the trust instrument or by statute, not in any legal relationship with the beneficiaries or the trustee, and has no liabilities or powers with regard to the trust administration.*

The lessee-optionee argues, and the district court held, that in the foregoing provisions of the trust agreement the settlor reserved the power to direct the trustee in regard to the leased property, and that the effect of his executing the extension of the option on March 1, 1976, was to direct the trustee to sell the property to the lessee-optionee upon its exercise of the option. We disagree. We are unable to find an exercise of the "power to direct the trustee, in writing," in an act that was not intended to communicate and did not in fact communicate anything to the trustee. We are likewise unable to construe the extension agreement signed by the settlor and the lessee-optionee as "an instrument in writing filed with the Trustee" to "modify, alter or revoke this Agreement. ..." Nor can we agree with the dissent's argument for "liberal construction ... to the reserved powers of a settlor" in a trust agreement which expressly vests **the trustee** with the power "to grant options" and explicitly states its intention that **the trustee** "shall have all rights, powers and privileges that an absolute owner of the property would have." Article IV, quoted above. (emphases in original)

None of the exceptions identified by Bogert applies in this case.

This is a case where a settlor created a trust and then chose to ignore it. He could have modified or revoked the trust, or directed the trustee in writing to sell or lease the trust property, but he took neither of these actions. Instead, more than two years after the creation and recording of the trust, and without any direction or notice to the trustee, the settlor gave the lessee-optionee a signed instrument purporting to extend its option to buy the trust property for another five years. The trustee did not learn of this instrument until two and one-half years later, immediately following the death of the settlor.

An extension of the option to buy would obviously have a limiting effect on the value of the reversion owned by the trust (and thus on the rights of the trust beneficiaries), which the trustee has a duty to protect. Even a revocable trust clothes beneficiaries, for the duration of the trust, with a legally enforceable right to insist that the terms of the trust be adhered to. If we gave legal effect to the settlor's extension of this option in contravention of the existence and terms of the trust, we would prejudice the interests of the beneficiaries, blur some fundamental principles of trust law, and cast doubt upon whether it is the trustee or the settlor who is empowered to manage and dispose of the trust property in a valid revocable trust.

The judgment of the district court is reversed and the cause is remanded with instructions to enter judgment for the plaintiff. Costs to appellant.

HOWE, Justice: (Dissenting)

I dissent. The majority opinion has overlooked the cardinal principle of construction of a trust agreement which is that the settlor's intent should be followed. See *Leggroan v. Zion's Savings Bank & Trust Co.*, 120 Utah 93, 232 P.2d 746 (1951). Instead, the majority places a strict and rigid interpretation on the language of the trust agreement which defeats the settlor's intent and denies him an important power he specifically reserved to himself. All of this is done in a fact situation where there is no adverse interest asserted and no one will be prejudiced in any way by following the undisputed and obvious intent of the settlor.

Unlike the situation found with many trusts, Huffaker in establishing his trust reserved to himself broad powers in Article V.:

> *ARTICLE V.*
> *The Trustor by an instrument in writing filed with the Trustee* may modify, alter or revoke this Agreement *in whole or in part, and* may withdraw any property subject to the Agreement; *Provided, however, that the duties, powers and limitations of the Trustee shall not be substantially changed without its written consent, except as to revocation or withdrawal. (emphasis added)*
>
> * * * *
>
> *There is hereby reserved to the Trustor the power to* direct the trustee, in writing, *from time to time,* to retain, sell, exchange or lease any property of the Trust estate, *to invest Trust funds, or to purchase for the Trust any property which they [sic] may designate and which is acceptable to the Trustee.* Upon receipt of such directions, the Trustee shall comply therewith. *(emphasis added)*

Thus while Huffaker committed the property into the management and control of the trustee, he retained the right in Article V. to direct the trustee from time to time with regard to the property, and the trustee agreed that upon receipt of any such directions it would comply. It is significant that the consent of the trustee was not required. These broad reserved powers in effect gave him greater power over the property than the trustee possessed since he had the final word.

The property in question was subject to defendant's option when it was placed in trust. The trustee took title subject to that option and subject to future directions from Huffaker. The extension granted by Huffaker to the defendant was in effect a directive that the trustee sell the property to the defendant if and when it elected to purchase the property. At that time, the defendant could deliver the directive to the trustee which held legal title and the sale could be consummated. Contrary to what is said in the majority opinion, the extension was intended to communicate and did communicate to the trustee the settlor's intention to sell to the defendant. The trustee does not claim to have any doubt as to what the settlor intended.

There was no requirement in the trust agreement as to when the directive to sell had to be delivered to the trustee nor was there any requirement that the settlor must himself deliver the direction to sell to the trustee rather than the buyer deliver it. The majority opinion concedes that Huffaker had the power to extend the option but denies him that power because he did not communicate his intention to exercise that power to the trustee at the time he extended the option. It ignores the fact that the lessee had five years to decide whether it wanted to buy the property, at which time it could deliver the direction to sell to the trustee. The majority opinion reads into the trust agreement rigidity and strictness which is unwarranted.

The majority opinion contains a quote from Bogert, *Trust and Trustees*, § 42, for authority that after a settlor has completed the creation of a trust he is not in any legal relationship with the beneficiaries or the trustee, and has no liabilities or power with regard to the trust administration. However, as will be seen in that quote, it is there recognized that those rules do not apply where it has been expressly provided otherwise by the trust instrument. Such is the case here where the settlor reserved extensive powers and was himself the primary beneficiary.

Huffaker's extension agreement apparently would not have been challenged by his trustee if he had given written directions to the trustee to extend the option instead of executing the extension with the defendant himself, and apparently would not have been challenged had he not died. Yet, although the trustee did not itself extend the option nor receive a copy of the agreement until after Huffaker's death, it had not in the meantime dealt with third parties concerning the property or made any commitments that were inconsistent with Huffaker's action. Since there were no intervening third-party rights and it is not unfair to the trust beneficiaries to require them to abide by the intention of their donor and benefactor, I see no justification for the refusal of the trustee to accept the extension agreement as a valid direction to sell the property as provided for by the terms of the trust. This is not a case where the trustee in ignorance of the action of the settlor in granting an option had also granted an option or dealt with the property in a manner inconsistent with the actions of the settlor so that there are conflicting claims of innocent third-parties presented. In such a case there would be some justification for applying a strict construction so that there can be orderliness in trust administration. After all, the reason for the provisions of the trust agreement defining the powers of the trustee and the reserved powers of the settlor was to provide for the exercise of those powers in a manner that would be orderly and without collision between the trustee and settlor. In the instant case the trustee has not even suggested how it will be prejudiced by following Huffaker's directions. The majority opinion makes reference to protecting the interest of the contingent beneficiaries but overlooks that Huffaker was not only the settlor but also the primary beneficiary both when the trust was established and when the option was extended.

The majority opinion treats the relationship between Huffaker and his trustee as an adversary relationship instead of recognizing that the trustee was Huffaker's fiduciary to *assist* him in managing *his* property. Therefore, there is no reason to construe the trust agreement as if it were meant to deal with a relationship between two adverse parties.

My view that a liberal construction should be given to the reserved powers of a settlor under these circumstances finds support in a decision of the Supreme Judicial Court of Massachusetts, *Trager v. Schwartz*, 345 Mass. 653, 189 N.E.2d 509 (1963). There the settlor on July 15, 1942, executed as donor a declaration of trust. The property was 65 shares of stock and 4 lots of land. In that instrument he reserved the right to alter, amend or revoke the instrument in whole or in part. However, it was specifically provided in the declaration of trust that "any such alterations, amendments or revocations of this trust shall be by an instrument in writing signed by the donor, and shall become effective only upon being recorded in the South District Registry of Deeds for Middlesex County."

Later, on February 4, 1954, the trustor executed a document entitled "Modification and Amendment of Trust" whereby he withdrew the 65 shares of stock from the trust and sold them to his son and told him that he had arranged for the recording of that instrument by his lawyer. However, he did not record the document nor instruct his attorney to do so. On August 25, 1960, the settlor executed a document entitled "Revocation of Declaration of Trust," in which he revoked in whole the declaration of trust of July 15, 1942. This revocation was recorded on August 26th. He thereupon directed the trustees to deliver to him the 65 shares of stock and the 4 lots of real estate. His son received notice of the revocation on August 30, 1960, and recorded the following day the modification and amendment dated February 4, 1954, by which he had obtained the 165 shares of stock.

In a suit brought by the settlor to regain ownership of the stock, he contended that the recording of his complete revocation on August 26, 1960, rendered ineffective the recording of the partial revocation on August 31, 1960. He relied upon the principle that "A valid trust once created cannot be revoked or altered except by the exercise of a reserve power to do so, which must be exercised in strict conformity to its terms." The court upheld the earlier sale of stock stating:

> *The provision of the declaration of trust that amendments and revocations 'shall become effective only upon being recorded' shall not be interpreted, where there are no intervening rights of third-parties, as preventing the carrying out of the earlier amendment once it has been recorded. This should be the result, particularly where there was an express undertaking by one of the parties to see to the recording.*

In the instant case, defendant will be greatly prejudiced, and the settlor's intention thwarted, as a result of following the majority opinion's interpretation of the trust terms as they relate to a written direction to the trustee to sell trust property. Defendant gave up the opportunity to purchase the property within the original option period in reliance on Huffaker's execution of the extension agreement, a document prepared by his attorney. I am not persuaded that because defendant was making its rental payments to the trustee it was unreasonable in obtaining the extension of the option, which previously had been granted it by Huffaker, to again deal with him and rely on him since he was the final power respecting his property, and since neither he nor his attorney who had full and complete knowledge of the trust apparently raised any question as to the propriety of what they were doing. Just as the settlor in *Trager v. Schwartz*, supra, was not permitted to gain advantage by his failure to record as required by the trust agreement, I think the settlor's beneficiaries in the instant case should not gain by Huffaker's omissions and to the extreme prejudice of defendant.

The trustee has based its arguments on cases and principles that are distinguishable or inapplicable to the instant case. It regards the trust agreement as expressly allowing only it, as trustee and holder of the legal title to the property, to sell, option, or otherwise dispose of it. But the language of the trust regarding powers retained by Huffaker is inclusive enough to encompass his action in this case, for he expressly retained the right to direct the plaintiff to sell the property, a right that is compatible with his granting of the option extension.

The trustee also asserts that the written instrument received after Huffaker's death was ineffective as a directive to the trustee. Plaintiff cites authority for the principle that a revocable trust can only be modified during the settlor's lifetime, e.g., *Chase National Bank of City of N.Y. v. Tomagno*, 172 Misc. 63, 14 N.Y.S.2d 759 (1939). We are not dealing with an attempted testamentary disposition in this case, however. The option extension agreement was executed during Huffaker's lifetime, and the fact that it was received by plaintiff only after he died does not deprive it of its effect.

I would affirm the judgment below.

Case Questions

1. Does the decision effectively deprive Country Club Mobile Estates, Ltd. of anything? What?
2. Why would the trustee (Continental Bank & Trust Co.) object to giving Country Club Mobile Estates, Ltd. another two and a half years to exercise an option to buy the 31 acres?
3. Which opinion seems better reasoned—the majority or the dissent? Why do you think so?

36.5 Summary and Exercises

Summary

Estate planning is the process by which an owner decides how her property is to be passed on to others. The four basic estate planning tools are wills, trusts, gifts, and joint ownership. In this chapter, we examined wills and trusts. A will is the declaration of a person's wishes about the disposition of her assets on her death. The law of each state sets forth certain formalities, such as the number of witnesses, to which written wills must adhere. Wills are managed through the probate process, which varies from state to state, although many states have now adopted the Uniform Probate Code. In general, anyone over eighteen and of sound mind may make a will. It must be signed by the testator, and two or three others must witness the signature. A will may always be modified or revoked during the testator's lifetime, either expressly through a codicil or through certain actions, such as a subsequent marriage and the birth of children, not contemplated by the will. Wills must be carefully drafted to avoid abatement and ademption. The law provides for distribution in the case of intestacy. The rules vary from state to state and depend on whether the decedent was married when she died, had children or parents who survived her, or had collateral heirs.

Once a will is admitted to probate, the personal representative must assemble and inventory all assets, have them appraised, handle claims against the estate, pay taxes, prepare a final accounting, and only then distribute the assets according to the will.

A trust is a relationship in which one person holds legal title to certain property and another person has the use and benefit of it. The settlor or grantor creates the trust, giving specific property (the res) to the trustee for the benefit of the beneficiary. Trusts may be living or testamentary, revocable or irrevocable. Express trusts come in many forms, including Totten trusts, blind trusts, Clifford trusts, charitable trusts, and spendthrift trusts. Trusts may also be imposed by law; constructive and resulting trusts are designed to redress frauds, prevent unjust enrichment, or see to it that the intent of the parties is carried out.

Exercises

1. Seymour deposits $50,000 in a bank account, ownership of which is specified as "Seymour, in trust for Fifi." What type of trust is this? Who is the settlor? The beneficiary? The trustee? May Seymour spend the money on himself? When Seymour dies, does the property pass under the laws of intestacy, assuming he has no will?
2. Seymour, a resident of Rhode Island, signed a will in which he left all his property to his close friend, Fifi. Seymour and Fifi then moved to Alabama, where Seymour eventually died. Seymour's wife Hildegarde, who stayed behind in Rhode Island and who was not named in the will, claimed that the will was revoked when Seymour moved from one state to another. Is she correct? Why?
3. Assume in Exercise 2 that Seymour's Rhode Island will is valid in Alabama. Is Hildegarde entitled to a part of Seymour's estate? Explain.
4. Assume in Exercise 2 that Seymour's Rhode Island will is valid in Alabama. Seymour and Hildegarde own, as tenants by the entirety, a cottage on the ocean. In the will, Seymour specifically states that the cottage goes to Fifi on his death. Does Fifi or Hildegarde get the cottage? Or do they share it? Explain?
5. Assume in Exercise 2 that Seymour's Rhode Island will is not valid. Seymour's only relative besides Hildegarde is his nephew, Chauncey, whom Seymour detests. Who is entitled to Seymour's property when he dies—Fifi, Hildegarde, or Chauncey? Explain.
6. Scrooge is in a high tax bracket. He has set aside in a savings account $100,000, which he eventually wants to use to pay the college expenses of his tiny son, Tim, who is three. The account earns $10,000 a year, of which $5,000 goes to the government in taxes. How could Scrooge lower the tax payments while retaining control of the $100,000?
7. Assume in Exercise 6 that Scrooge considers placing the $100,000 in trust for Tim. But he is worried that when Tim comes of age, he might sell his interest in the trust. Could the trust be structured to avoid this possibility? Explain.
8. Assume that Scrooge has a substantial estate and no relatives. Is there any reason for him to consider a will or trust? Why? If he dies without a will, what will happen to his property?

Self-Test Questions

1. A will written by the testator's hand and not witnessed is called
    a. a conditional will
    b. a nuncupative will
    c. a holographic will
    d. a reciprocal will
2. A written modification or supplement to a prior will is called
    a. a revocation clause
    b. an abatement
    c. a codicil
    d. none of the above

3. A trust created by will is called
    a. an inter vivos trust
    b. a reversionary trust
    c. a Totten trust
    d. a testamentary trust
4. Trustees are not permitted to tell the grantor how they are managing their portfolio of assets in
    a. a Clifford trust
    b. a spendthrift trust
    c. a blind trust
    d. a voting trust
5. An example of an implied trust is
    a. a spendthrift trust
    b. a Clifford trust
    c. a resulting trust
    d. none of the above

Self-Test Answers

1. c
2. c
3. d
4. c
5. c

Endnotes

1. *In re Totten*, 71 N.E. 748 (N.Y. 1904).
2. *Helvering v. Clifford*, 309 U.S. 331 (1940).

CHAPTER 37

Insurance

Learning Objectives

After reading this chapter, you should understand the following:

1. The basic terms and distinctions in the law of insurance.
2. The basic types of insurance for property, liability, and life.
3. The basic defenses to claims against insurance companies by the insured: representation, concealment, and warranties.

We conclude our discussions about property with a focus on insurance law, not only because insurance is a means of compensating an owner for property losses but also because the insurance contract itself represents a property right. In this chapter, we begin by examining regulation of the insurance industry. We then look at legal issues relating to specific types of insurance. Finally, we examine defenses that insurance companies might raise to avoid making payments under insurance policies.

37.1 Definitions and Types of Insurance

Learning Objectives

1. Know the basic types of insurance for individuals.
2. Name and describe the various kinds of business insurance.

Insurance

A contract of reimbursement.

insurer

The entity that agrees to provide insurance for the risk of certain kinds of losses, usually life, property, health, and liability claims.

insured

The person or firm insured by a contract of insurance.

policy

The contract for the insurance sought by the insured.

risks

Potential losses that may be covered by policies of insurance.

perils

Risks that are insured against.

Insurance is a contract of reimbursement. For example, it reimburses for losses from specified perils, such as fire, hurricane, and earthquake. An **insurer** is the company or person who promises to reimburse. The **insured** (sometimes called the assured) is the one who receives the payment, except in the case of life insurance, where payment goes to the beneficiary named in the life insurance contract. The **premium** is the consideration paid by the insured—usually annually or semiannually—for the insurer's promise to reimburse. The contract itself is called the **policy**. The events insured against are known as **risks** or **perils**.

Regulation of insurance is left mainly in the hands of state, rather than federal, authorities. Under the McCarran-Ferguson Act, Congress exempted state-regulated insurance companies from the federal antitrust laws. Every U.S. state now has an insurance department that oversees insurance rates, policy standards, reserves, and other aspects of the industry. Over the years, these departments have come under fire in many states for being either ineffective, or being "captives" of the industry. Large insurance companies operate in many states, and both they and consumers must contend with fifty different state regulatory schemes that provide very different degrees of protection. From time to time, attempts have been made to bring insurance under federal regulation, but none have been successful.

We will begin with an overview of the types of insurance, from both a consumer and a business perspective. Then we will examine in greater detail, in Section 37.2, the three most important types of insurance: property, liability, and life.

Public and Private Insurance

Sometimes a distinction is made between public and private insurance. Public (or social) insurance includes Social Security, Medicare, temporary disability insurance, and the like, funded through government plans. Private insurance plans, by contrast, are all types of coverage offered by private corporations or organizations. The focus of this chapter is private insurance.

Types of Insurance for the Individual

Life Insurance

term insurance

Life insurance with a death benefit but no accumulated savings.

whole-life insurance

Provides savings as well as insurance and can let the insured collect before death.

Life insurance provides for your family or some other named beneficiaries on your death. Two general types are available: **term insurance** provides coverage only during the term of the policy and pays off only on the insured's death; **whole-life insurance** provides savings as well as insurance and can let the insured collect before death.

Health Insurance

Health insurance covers the cost of hospitalization, visits to the doctor's office, and prescription medicines. The most useful policies, provided by many employers, are those that cover 100 percent of the costs of being hospitalized and 80 percent of the charges for medicine and a doctor's services. Usually, the policy will contain a deductible amount; the insurer will not make payments until after the deductible amount has been reached. Twenty years ago, the deductible might have been the first $100 or $250 of charges; today, it is often much higher.

Disability Insurance

A disability policy pays a certain percentage of an employee's wages (or a fixed sum) weekly or monthly if the employee becomes unable to work through illness or an accident. Premiums are lower for policies with longer waiting periods before payments must be made: a policy that begins to pay a disabled worker within thirty days might cost twice as much as one that defers payment for six months.

Homeowner's Insurance

A homeowner's policy provides insurance for damages or losses due to fire, theft, and other named perils. No policy routinely covers all perils. The homeowner must assess his needs by looking to the likely risks in his area—earthquake, hailstorm, flooding, and so on. Homeowner's policies provide for reduced coverage if the property is not insured for at least 80 percent of its replacement costs. In inflationary times, this requirement means that the owner must adjust the policy limits upward each year or purchase a rider that automatically adjusts for inflation. Where property values have dropped substantially, the owner of a home (or a commercial building) might find savings in lowering the policy's insured amount.

Automobile Insurance

Automobile insurance is perhaps the most commonly held type of insurance. Automobile policies are required in at least minimum amounts for general liability coverage in all states. The typical automobile policy covers the driver's legal liability for bodily injury and property damage, medical payments, damage to or loss of the car itself, and attorneys' fees in case of a lawsuit.

Other Liability Insurance

In this litigious society, a person can be sued for just about anything: a slip on the walk, a harsh and untrue word spoken in anger, an accident on the ball field. A personal liability policy covers many types of these risks and can give coverage in excess of that provided by homeowner's and automobile insurance. Such umbrella coverage is usually fairly inexpensive, perhaps $250 a year for $1 million in liability.

Types of Business Insurance

Workers' Compensation

Almost every business in every state must insure against injury to workers on the job. Some may do this through self-insurance—that is, by setting aside certain reserves for this contingency. Most smaller businesses purchase workers' compensation policies, available through commercial insurers, trade associations, or state funds.

Automobile Insurance

Any business that uses motor vehicles should maintain at least a minimum automobile insurance policy on the vehicles, covering personal injury, property damage, and general liability.

Property Insurance

No business should take a chance of leaving unprotected its buildings, permanent fixtures, machinery, inventory, and the like. Various property policies cover damage or loss to a company's own property or to property of others stored on the premises.

Malpractice Insurance

Professionals such as doctors, lawyers, and accountants will often purchase malpractice insurance to protect against claims made by disgruntled patients or clients. For doctors, the cost of such insurance has been rising over the past thirty years, largely because of larger jury awards against physicians who are negligent in the practice of their profession.

Business Interruption Insurance

Depending on the size of the business and its vulnerability to losses resulting from damage to essential operating equipment or other property, a company may wish to purchase insurance that will cover loss of earnings if the business operations are interrupted in some way—by a strike, loss of power, loss of raw material supply, and so on.

Liability Insurance

Businesses face a host of risks that could result in substantial liabilities. Many types of policies are available, including policies for owners, landlords, and tenants (covering liability incurred on the premises); for manufacturers and contractors (for liability incurred on all premises); for a company's products and completed operations (for liability that results from warranties on products or injuries caused by products); for owners and contractors (protective liability for damages caused by independent contractors engaged by the insured); and for contractual liability (for failure to abide by performances required by specific contracts).

Some years ago, different types of individual and business coverage had to be purchased separately and often from different companies. Today, most insurance is available on a package basis, through single policies that cover the most important risks. These are often called multi-peril policies.

Key Takeaway

Although insurance is a need for every US business, and many businesses operate in all fifty states, regulation of insurance has remained at the state level. There are several forms of public insurance (Social Security, disability, Medicare) and many forms of private insurance. Both individuals and businesses have significant needs for various types of insurance, to provide protection for health care, for their property, and for legal claims made against them by others.

Exercises

1. Anthony Villa has just signed a franchise agreement with Papa Luigi's Pizza and will be operating his own Papa Luigi's store in Lubbock, Texas. The franchise agreement requires that he personally contract for "all necessary insurance" for the successful operation of the franchise. He expects to have twelve employees, five full-time and seven part-time (the delivery people), at his location, which will be on a busy boulevard in Lubbock and will offer take-out only. Pizza delivery employees will be using their own automobiles to deliver orders. What kinds of insurance will be "necessary"?
2. Theresa Conley is joining the accounting firm of Hunter and Patton in Des Moines, Iowa. She is a certified public accountant. What kind of insurance will she (or the firm, on her behalf) need to buy because of her professional activities?

37.2 Property Insurance, Liability Insurance, and Life Insurance

Learning Objectives

1. Distinguish and define the basic types of insurance for property, liability, and life.
2. Explain the concepts of subrogation and assignment.

We turn now to a more detailed discussion of the law relating to the three most common types of insurance: property, liability, and life insurance.

Property Insurance

It is sometimes said that property is the foundation for a system of free market capitalism. If so, then protecting property is a necessary part of being part of that system, whether as an individual or as a business entity.

Coverage

As we have noted, property insurance provides coverage for real and personal property owned by a business or an individual. Property insurance is also part of automobile policies covering damage to the car caused by an accident (collision coverage) or by other events such as vandalism or fire (comprehensive coverage). Different levels of coverage are available. For example, many basic homeowners' policies cover damage resulting from the following types of perils only: fire and lightning, windstorm and hail, explosions, riots and civil commotions, aircraft and vehicular accidents, smoke, vandalism and malicious mischief, theft, and breakage of glass that is part of a building.

A broader policy, known as broad coverage, also includes these perils: falling objects; weight of ice, snow, and sleet; collapse of buildings; sudden and accidental damage to heating systems; accidental discharge from plumbing, heating, or air-conditioning systems; freezing of heating, plumbing, and air conditioning systems; and sudden and accidental injury from excess currents to electrical appliances and wiring. Even with the broadest form of coverage, known as comprehensive, which covers all perils except for certain named exclusions, the homeowner can be left without protection. For example, comprehensive policies do not usually cover damage resulting from flooding, earthquakes, war, or nuclear radiation. The homeowner can purchase separate coverage for these perils but usually at a steep premium.

Insurable Interest in Property

To purchase property insurance, the would-be insured must have an **insurable interest** in the property. Insurable interest is a real and substantial interest in specific property such that a loss to the insured would ensue if the property were damaged. You could not, for instance, take out an insurance policy on a motel down the block with which you have no connection. If a fire destroyed it, you would suffer no economic loss. But if you helped finance the motel and had an investment interest in it, you would be permitted to place an insurance policy on it. This requirement of an insurable interest stems from the public policy against wagering. If you could insure anything, you would in effect be betting on an accident.

insurable interest

A sufficiently substantial interest in property or someone's life to support a contract to insure it.

To insure property, therefore, you must have a legal interest and run the risk of a pecuniary loss. Any legal interest is sufficient: a contractual right to purchase, for instance, or the right of possession (a bailee may insure). This insurable interest must exist both at the time you take out the policy and at the time the loss occurs. Moreover, coverage is limited to the extent of the interest. As a mortgagee, you could ensure only for the amount still due.

Prior to the financial meltdown of 2008, many investment banks took insurance against possible losses from collateralized debt obligations (CDOs) and other financial products based on subprime loans. The principal insurer was American International Group, Inc. (AIG), which needed a US government bailout when the risks covered by AIG turned out to be riskier than AIG's models had projected.

Subrogation

FIGURE 37.1 Subrogation

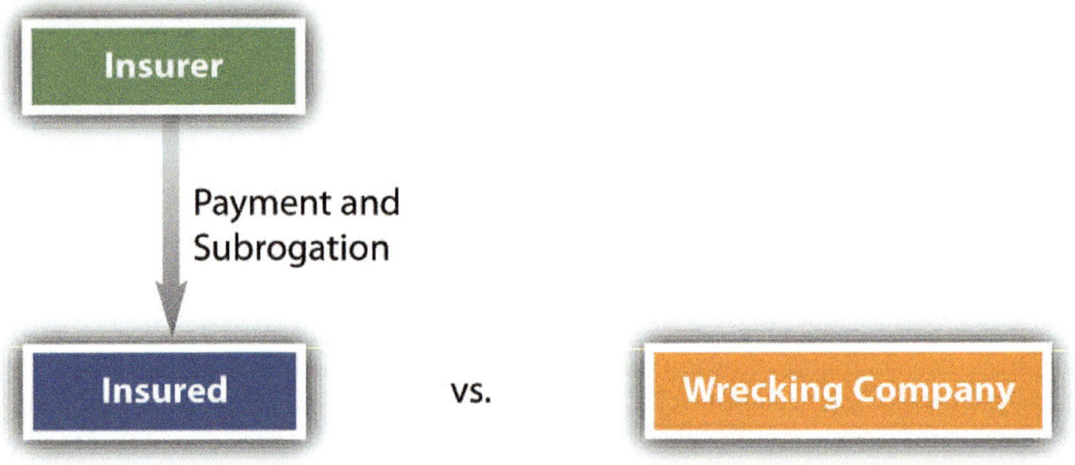

subrogation

Substitution of one person for another who has a legal claim or right.

Subrogation is the substitution of one person for another in pursuit of a legal claim. When an insured is entitled to recover under a policy for property damage, the insurer is said to be subrogated to the insured's right to sue any third party who caused the damage. For example, a wrecking company negligently destroys an insured's home, mistaking it for the building it was hired to tear down. The insured has a cause of action against the wrecking company. If the insured chooses instead to collect against a homeowner's policy, the insurance company may sue the wrecking company in the insured's place to recover the sum it was obligated to pay out under the policy (see Figure 37.1).

Assignment

assignment

The transfer of any rights in a contract of insurance.

Assignment is the transfer of any property right to another. In property insurance, a distinction is made between assignment of the coverage and assignment of the proceeds. Ordinarily, the insured may not assign the policy itself without the insurer's permission—that is, he may not commit the insurer to insure someone else. But the insured may assign any claims against the insurer—for example, the proceeds not yet paid out on a claim for a house that has already burned down.

Intentional Losses

Insurance is a means of spreading risk. It is economically feasible because not every house burns down and not every car is stolen. The number that do burn down or that are stolen can be calculated and the premium set accordingly. Events that will certainly happen, like ordinary wear and tear and the destruction of property through deliberate acts such as arson, must be excluded from such calculations. The injury must result from accidental, not deliberate, causes.

Coinsurance Clause

Most commercial property policies contain a so-called **coinsurance clause**, which requires the insured to maintain insurance equal to a specified percentage of the property value. It is often 80 percent but may be higher or lower. If the property owner insures for less than that percentage, the recovery will be reduced. In effect, the owner becomes a coinsurer with the insurance company. The usual formula establishes the proportion that the insurer must pay by calculating the ratio of (1) the amount of insurance actually taken to (2) the coinsurance percentage multiplied by the total dollar value of the property. Suppose a fire causes $160,000 damage to a plant worth $1,000,000. The plant should have been insured for 80 percent ($800,000), but the insured took out only a $500,000 policy. He will recover only $100,000. To see why, multiply the total damages of $160,000 by the coinsurance proportion of five-eighths ($500,000 of insurance on the required minimum of $800,000). Five-eighths of $160,000 equals $100,000, which would be the insured's recovery where the policy has a coinsurance clause.

coinsurance clause

In property insurance, a clause that requires the insured to maintain insurance equal to a specified percentage of the property value.

Liability Insurance

Liability insurance has taken on great importance for both individuals and businesses in contemporary society. Liability insurance covers specific types of legal liabilities that a homeowner, driver, professional, business executive, or business itself might incur in the round of daily activities. A business is always at risk in sending products into the marketplace. Doctors, accountants, real estate brokers, insurance agents, and lawyers should obtain liability insurance to cover the risk of being sued for malpractice. A prudent homeowner will acquire liability insurance as part of homeowner's policy and a supplemental umbrella policy that insures for liability in excess of a limit of, say, $100,000 in the regular homeowner's policy. And businesses, professionals, and individuals typically acquire liability insurance for driving-related activities as part of their automobile insurance. In all cases, liability policies cover not only any settlement or award that might ultimately have to be paid but also the cost of lawyers and related expenses in defending any claims.

Liability insurance is similar in several respects to property insurance and is often part of the same package policy. As with property insurance, subrogation is allowed with liability insurance, but assignment of the policy is not allowed (unless permission of the insurer is obtained), and intentional losses are not covered. For example, an accountant who willfully helps a client conceal fraud will not recover from his malpractice insurance policy if he is found guilty of participating in the fraud.

No-Fault Trends

The major legal development of the century relating to liability insurance has been the elimination of liability in the two areas of greatest exposure: in the workplace and on the highway. In the next unit on agency law, we discuss the no-fault system of workers' compensation, under which a worker receives automatic benefits for workplace injuries and gives up the right to sue the employer under common-law theories of liability. Here we will look briefly at the other major type of no-fault system: recovery for damages stemming from motor vehicle accidents.

"No-fault" means that recovery for damages in an accident no longer depends on who was at fault in causing it. A motorist will file a claim to recover his actual damages (medical expenses, income loss) directly from his own insurer. The no-fault system dispenses with the costly and uncertain tort system of having to prove negligence in court. Many states have adopted one form or another of no-fault automobile insurance, but even in these states the car owner must still carry other insurance. Some no-fault systems have a dollar "threshold" above which a victim may sue for medical expenses or other losses. Other states use a "verbal threshold," which permits suits for "serious" injury, defined variously as "disfigurement," "fracture," or "permanent disability." These thresholds have prevented no-fault from working as efficiently as theory predicts. Inflation has reduced the power of dollar thresholds (in some states as low as $200) to deter lawsuits, and the verbal thresholds have standards that can only be defined in court, so much litigation continues.

No state has adopted a "pure" no-fault system. A pure no-fault system trades away entirely the right to sue in return for the prompt payment of "first-party" insurance benefits—that is, payment by the victim's own insurance company instead of traditional "third-party" coverage, in which the victim collects from the defendant's insurance company.

Among the criticisms of no-fault insurance is the argument that it fails to strengthen the central purpose of the tort system: to deter unsafe conduct that causes accidents. No-fault lessens, it is said, the incentive to avoid accidents. In any event, no-fault automobile insurance has been a major development in the insurance field since 1970 and seems destined to be a permanent fixture of insurance law.

Life Insurance

Insurable Interest

The two types of life insurance mentioned in Section 1, term and whole-life policies, are important both to individuals and to businesses (insurance for key employees). As with property insurance, whoever takes out a life insurance policy on a person's life must have an insurable interest. Everyone has an insurable interest in his own life and may name whomever he pleases as beneficiary; the beneficiary need not have an insurable interest. But the requirement of insurable interest restricts those who may take out insurance on someone else's life. A spouse or children have an insurable interest in a spouse or parent. Likewise, a parent has an insurable interest in any minor child. That means that a wife, for example, may take out a life insurance policy on her husband without his consent. But she could not take out a policy on a friend or neighbor. As long as the insurable interest existed when the policy was taken out, the owner may recover when the insured dies, even if the insurable interest no longer exists. Thus a divorced wife who was married when the policy was obtained may collect when her ex-husband dies as long as she maintained the payments. Likewise, an employer has an insurable interest in his key employees and partners; such insurance policies help to pay off claims of a partner's estate and thus prevent liquidation of the business.

Subrogation

Unlike property insurance, life insurance does not permit subrogation. The insurer must pay the claim when the insured dies and may not step into the shoes of anyone entitled to file a wrongful death claim against a person who caused the death. Of course, if the insured died of natural causes, there would be no one to sue anyway.

Change of Beneficiary and Assignment

Unless the insured reserves the right to change beneficiaries, his or her initial designation is irrevocable. These days, however, most policies do reserve the right if certain formalities are observed, including written instructions to the insurer's home office to make the change and endorsement of the policy. The insured may assign the policy, but the beneficiary has priority to collect over the assignee if the right to change beneficiaries has not been reserved. If the policy permits beneficiaries to be changed, then the assignee will have priority over the original beneficiary.

Intentional Losses

Two types of intentional losses are especially important in life insurance: suicide and murder of the insured by the beneficiary.

Suicide

In a majority of states, in the absence of a suicide clause in the policy, when an insured commits suicide, the insurer need not pay out if the policy is payable to the insured's estate. However, if the policy is payable to a third person (e.g., the insured's company), payment will usually be allowed. And if an insured kills himself while insane, all states require payment, whether to the estate or a third party. Most life insurance policies today have a provision that explicitly excepts suicide from coverage for a limited period, such as two years, after the policy is issued. In other words, if the insured commits suicide within the first two years, the insurer will refund the premiums to his estate but will not pay the policy amount. After two years, suicide is treated as any other death would be.

Murder

Under the law in every state, a beneficiary who kills the insured in order to collect the life insurance is barred from receiving it. But the invocation of that rule does not absolve the insurer of liability to pay the policy amount. An alternate beneficiary must be found. Sometimes the policy will name contingent beneficiaries, and many, but not all, states require the insurer to pay the contingent beneficiaries. When there are no contingent beneficiaries or the state law prohibits paying them, the insurer will pay the insured's estate. Not every killing is murder; the critical question is whether the beneficiary intended his conduct to eliminate the insured in order to collect the insurance.

The willful, unlawful, and felonious killing of the insured by the person named as beneficiary in a life policy results in the forfeiture of all rights of such person therein. It is unnecessary that there should be an express exception in the contract of insurance forbidding a recovery in favor of such a person in such an event. On considerations of public policy, the death of the insured, willfully and intentionally caused by the beneficiary of the policy, is an excepted risk so far as the person thus causing the death is concerned.

Key Takeaway

Many kinds of insurance are available for individuals and businesses. For individuals, life insurance, homeowner's insurance, and automobile insurance are common, with health insurance considered essential but often expensive. Businesses with sufficient employees will obtain workers' compensation insurance, property insurance, and liability insurance, and auto insurance for any employees driving company vehicles. Insurance companies will often pay a claim for their insured and take over the insured's claim against a third party.

Liability insurance is important for individuals, companies, and licensed professionals. A trend toward no-fault in liability insurance is seen in claims for work-related injuries (workers' compensation) and in automobile insurance. Life insurance is common for most families and for businesses that want to protect against the loss of key employees.

Exercises

1. Helen Caldicott raises a family and then begins a career as a caterer. As her business grows, she hires several employees and rents space near downtown that has a retail space, parking, and a garage for the three vehicles that bear her business's name. What kinds of insurance does Helen need for her business?
2. One of Helen's employees, Bob Zeek, is driving to a catered event when another car fails to stop at a red light and severely injures Bob and nearly totals the van Bob was driving. The police issue a ticket for careless and reckless driving to the other driver, who pleads guilty to the offense. The other driver is insured, but Helen's automobile insurance carrier goes ahead and pays for the damages to the company vehicle. What will her insurance company likely do next?
3. The health insurance provider for Helen's employees pays over $345,000 of Bob's medical and hospitalization bills. What will Helen's insurance company likely do next?
4. Many homeowners live on floodplains but have homeowner's insurance nonetheless. Must insurance companies write such policies? Do homeowners on floodplains pay more in premiums? If insurance companies are convinced that global climate change is happening, with rising sea levels and stronger storms, can they simply avoid writing policies for homes and commercial buildings in coastal areas?

37.3 Insurer's Defenses

Learning Objectives

1. Understand the principal defenses available to insurers when claims are made.
2. Recognize that despite these defenses, insurance companies must act in good faith.

Types of Defenses

It is a common perception that because insurance contracts are so complex, many insureds who believe they are covered end up with uninsured losses. In other words, the large print giveth, and the "fine print" taketh away. Carefully crafted by lawyers for insurance companies who wish to limit their own risk while offering insurance, the fine print may detail exceptions and exclusions that the average consumer does not fully realize. For example, damage from sinkholes, earthquakes, and mudflows are generally excluded from homeowners' policies. Also, insurance companies will use three common defenses, all of which relate to a duty of good faith on the part of the insured: (1) representation, (2) concealment, and (3) warranties.

Representation

representation

Statements made by the insured in the application process.

A **representation** is a statement made by someone seeking an insurance policy—for example, a statement that the applicant did (or did not) consult a doctor for any illness during the previous five years. An insurer has grounds to avoid the contract if the applicant makes a false representation. The misrepresentation must have been material; that is, a false description of a person's hair coloring should not defeat a claim under an automobile accident policy. But a false statement, even if innocent, about a material fact—for instance, that no one in the family uses the car to go to work, when unbeknownst to the applicant, his wife uses the car to commute to a part-time job she hasn't told him about—will at the insurer's option defeat a claim by the insured to collect under the policy.

The accident need not have arisen out of the misrepresentation to defeat the claim. In the example given, the insurance company could refuse to pay a claim for any accident in the car, even one occurring when the car was driven by the husband to go to the movies, if the insurer discovered that the car was used in a manner in which the insured had declared it was not used. This chapter's case, *Mutual Benefit Life Insurance Co. v. JMR Electronics Corp.*, (see Section 4), illustrates what happens when an insured misrepresents his smoking habits.

Concealment

An insured is obligated to volunteer to the insurer all material facts that bear on insurability. The failure of an insured to set forth such information is a **concealment**, which is, in effect, the mirror image of a false representation. But the insured must have had a fraudulent intent to conceal the material facts. For example, if the insured did not know that gasoline was stored in his basement, the insurer may not refuse to pay out on a fire insurance policy.

concealment

The failure of an insured to set forth all the material facts in applying for insurance.

Warranties

Many insurance policies covering commercial property will contain warranties. For example, a policy may have a warranty that the insured bank has installed or will install a particular type of burglar alarm system. Until recently, the rule was strictly enforced: any breach of a warranty voided the contract, even if the breach was not material. A nonmaterial breach might be, for example, that the bank obtained the alarm system from a manufacturer other than the one specified, even though the alarm systems are identical. In recent years, courts or legislatures have relaxed the application of this rule. But a material breach still remains absolute grounds for the insurer to avoid the contract and refuse to pay.

Incontestable Clause

In life insurance cases, the three common defenses often are unavailable to the insurer because of the so-called **incontestable clause**. This states that if the insured has not died during a specified period of time in which the life insurance policy has been in effect (usually two years), then the insurer may not refuse to pay even if it is later discovered that the insured committed fraud in applying for the policy. Few nonlife policies contain an incontestable clause; it is used in life insurance because the effect on many families would be catastrophic if the insurer claimed misrepresentation or concealment that would be difficult to disprove years later when the insured himself would no longer be available to give testimony about his intentions or knowledge.

incontestable clause

A clause in a life insurance policy that limits the insurance carrier's right to contest insurability after a certain number of years of premium payments on the policy.

Requirement of Insurer's Good Faith

Like the insured, the insurer must act in good faith. Thus defenses may be unavailable to an insurer who has waived them or acted in such a manner as to create an estoppel. Suppose that when an insured seeks to increase the amount on his life insurance policy, the insurance company learns that he lied about his age on his original application. Nevertheless, the company accepts his application for an increase. The insured then dies, and the insurer refuses to pay his wife any sum. A court would hold that the insurer had waived its right to object, since it could have cancelled the policy when it learned of the misrepresentation. Finally, an insurer that acts in bad faith by denying a claim that it knows it should pay may find itself open to punitive damage liability.

Key Takeaway

Some claims by insured parties can be legally denied by insurance companies where the insured has made a material misrepresentation. Some claims can be legally denied if the insured has deliberately concealed important matters in applying for insurance coverage. Because insurance coverage is by contract, courts often strictly construe the contract language, and if the language does not cover the insured, the courts will typically not bend the language of the contract to help the insured.

Exercises

1. Amir Labib gets a reduced rate from his auto insurance company because he represents in his application that he commutes less than ten miles a day to work. Three years later, he and his wife buy a new residence, farther away from work, and he begins a fifteen-mile-a-day commute. The rate would be raised if he were to mention this to his insurance company. The insurance company sees that he has a different address, because they are mailing invoices to his new home. But the rate remains the same. Amir has a serious accident on a vacation to Yellowstone National Park, and his automobile is totaled. His insurance policy is a no-fault policy as it relates to coverage for vehicle damage. Is the insurance company within its rights to deny any payment on his claim? How so, or why not?
2. In 2009, Peter Calhoun gets a life insurance policy from Northwest Mutual Life Insurance Company, and the death benefit is listed as $250,000. The premiums are paid up when he dies in 2011 after a getaway car being chased by the police slams into his car at fifty miles per hour on a street in suburban Chicago. The life insurance company gets information that he smoked two packs of cigarettes a day, whereas in his application in 2009, he said he smoked only one pack a day. In fact, he had smoked about a pack and a half every day since 1992. Is the insurance company within its rights to deny any payment on his claim? How so, or why not?

37.4 Case

Misrepresentation to Insurer

Mutual Benefit Life Insurance Co. v. JMR Electronics Corp.

848 F.2d 30 (2nd Cir. 1988)

PER CURIAM

JMR Electronics Corporation ("JMR") appeals from a judgment of the District Court for the Southern District of New York (Robert W. Sweet, Judge) ordering rescission of a life insurance policy issued by plaintiff-appellant The Mutual Benefit Life Insurance Company ("Mutual") and dismissing JMR's counterclaim for the policy's proceeds. Judge Sweet ruled that a misrepresentation made in the policy application concerning the insured's history of cigarette smoking was material as a matter of law. Appellant contends that the misrepresentation was not material because Mutual would have provided insurance—albeit at a higher premium rate—even if the insured's smoking history had been disclosed. We agree with the District Court that summary judgment was appropriate and therefore affirm.

The basic facts are not in dispute. On June 24, 1985, JMR submitted an application to Mutual for a $ 250,000 "key man" life insurance policy on the life of its president, Joseph Gaon, at the non-smoker's discounted premium rate. Mutual's 1985 Ratebook provides: "The Non-Smoker rates are available when the proposed insured is at least 20 years old and has not smoked a cigarette for at least twelve months prior to the date of the application." Question 13 of the application inquired about the proposed insured's smoking history. Question 13(a) asked, "Do you smoke cigarettes? How many a day?" Gaon answered this question, "No." Question 13(b) asked, "Did you ever smoke cigarettes? " Gaon again answered, "No." Based on these representations, Mutual issued a policy on Gaon's life at the non-smoker premium rate.

Gaon died on June 22, 1986, within the period of contestability contained in policy, *see* N.Y. Ins. Law § 3203 (a)(3) (McKinney 1985). Upon routine investigation of JMR's claim for proceeds under the policy, Mutual discovered that the representations made in the insurance application concerning Gaon's smoking history were untrue. JMR has stipulated that, at the time the application was submitted, Gaon in fact "had been smoking one-half of a pack of cigarettes per day for a continuous period of not less than 10 years." Mutual brought this action seeking a declaration that the policy is void. Judge Sweet granted Mutual's motion for summary judgment, dismissed JMR's counterclaim for the proceeds of the policy, and ordered rescission of the insurance policy and return of JMR's premium payments, with interest.

Under New York law, which governs this diversity suit, "it is the rule that even an innocent misrepresentation as to [the applicant's medical history], if material, is sufficient to allow the insurer to avoid the contract of insurance or defeat recovery thereunder." *Process Plants Corp. v. Beneficial National Life Insurance Co.*, 366 N.E.2d 1361 (1977). A "misrepresentation" is defined by statute as a false "statement as to past or present fact, made to the insurer...at or before the making of the insurance contract as an inducement to the making thereof." N.Y. Ins. Law § 3105(a) (McKinney 1985). A misrepresentation is "material" if "knowledge by the insurer of the facts misrepresented would have led to a refusal by the insurer to make such contract." *Id.* § 3105(b). Case law has somewhat broadened the materiality inquiry: "The question. . . is not whether the company might have issued the policy even if the information had been furnished; the question in each case is whether the company has been induced to accept an application which it might otherwise have refused. . . The materiality determination normally presents an issue of fact for the jury, but where the evidence concerning the materiality is clear and substantially uncontradicted, the matter is one of law for the Court to determine." *Process Plants Corp. v. Beneficial National Life Insurance Co., supra*, at 310-11.

In the present case JMR has stipulated that Gaon's smoking history was misrepresented in the insurance application. However, JMR disputes that this misrepresentation is material as a matter of law. JMR argues that under New York law a misrepresentation is not material unless the insurer can demonstrate that, had the applicant provided complete and accurate information, coverage either would have been refused or at the very least withheld pending a more detailed underwriting examination. In JMR's view summary judgment was inappropriate on the facts of this case because a jury could reasonably have found that even "had appellee been aware of Gaon's smoking history, a policy at the smoker's premium rate would have been issued." JMR takes the position that the appropriate remedy in this situation is to permit recovery under the policy in the amount that the premium actually paid would have purchased for a smoker.

We agree with Judge Sweet that this novel theory is without basis in New York law. The plain language of the statutory definition of "materiality," found in section 3105(b), permits avoidance of liability under the policy where "knowledge by the insurer of the facts misrepresented would have led to a refusal by the insurer to make *such contract*." (emphasis added) Moreover, numerous courts have observed that the materiality inquiry under New York law is made with respect to the particular policy issued in reliance upon the misrepresentation.

* * *

There is no doubt that Mutual was induced to issue the non-smoker, discounted-premium policy to JMR precisely as a result of the misrepresentations made by Gaon concerning his smoking history. That Mutual might not have refused the risk on *any* terms had it known the undisclosed facts is irrelevant. Most risks are insurable at some price. The purpose of the materiality inquiry is not to permit the jury to rewrite the terms of the insurance agreement to conform to the newly disclosed facts but to make certain that the risk insured was the risk covered by the policy agreed upon. If a fact is material to the risk, the insurer may avoid liability under a policy if that fact was misrepresented in an application for that policy whether or not the parties might have agreed to some other contractual arrangement had the critical fact been disclosed. As observed by Judge Sweet, a contrary result would reward the practice of misrepresenting facts critical to the underwriter's task because the unscrupulous (or merely negligent) applicant "would have everything to gain and nothing to lose" from making material misrepresentations in his application for insurance. Such a claimant could rest assured not only that he may demand full coverage should he survive the contestability period, N.Y. Ins. Law § 3203 (a)(3), but that even in the event of a contested claim, he would be entitled to the coverage that he might have contracted for had the necessary information been accurately disclosed at the outset. New York law does not permit this anomalous result. The judgment of the District Court is affirmed.

Case Questions

1. When you read this case, did you assume that Gaon died from lung cancer or some other smoking-related cause? Does the court actually say that?
2. Can you reasonably infer from the facts here that Gaon himself filled out the form and signed it? That is, can you know with some degree of certainty that he lied to the insurance company? Would it make any difference if he merely signed a form that his secretary filled out? Why or why not?
3. What if Gaon died of causes unrelated to smoking (e.g., he was in a fatal automobile accident), and the insurance company was looking for ways to deny the claim? Does the court's opinion and language still seem reasonable (e.g., the statement "there is no doubt that Mutual was induced to issue the non-smoker, discounted-premium policy to JMR precisely as a result of the misrepresentations made by Gaon concerning his smoking history")?
4. If Gaon had accurately disclosed his smoking history, is it clear that the insurance company would have refused to write any policy at all? Why is this question important?

37.5 Summary and Exercises

Summary

Insurance is an inescapable cost of doing business in a modern economy and an important service for any individual with dependents or even a modest amount of property. Most readers of this book will someday purchase automobile, homeowner's, and life insurance, and many readers will deal with insurance in the course of a business career.

Most insurance questions are governed by contract law, since virtually all insurance is voluntary and entered into through written agreements. This means that the insured must pay careful attention to the wording of the policies to determine what is excluded from coverage and to ensure that he makes no warranties that he cannot keep and no misrepresentations or concealments that will void the contract. But beyond contract law, some insurance law principles—such as insurable interest and subrogation rights—are important to bear in mind. Defenses available to an insurance company may be based upon representation, concealment, or warranties, but an insurer that is overzealous in denying coverage may find itself subject to punitive damages.

Exercises

1. Martin and Williams, two business partners, agreed that each would insure his life for the benefit of the other. On his application for insurance, Martin stated that he had never had any heart trouble when in fact he had had a mild heart attack some years before. Martin's policy contained a two-year incontestable clause. Three years later, after the partnership had been dissolved but while the policy was still in force, Martin's car was struck by a car being negligently driven by Peters. Although Martin's injuries were superficial, he suffered a fatal heart attack immediately after the accident—an attack, it was established, that was caused by the excitement. The insurer has refused to pay the policy proceeds to Williams. Does the insurer have a valid defense based on Martin's misrepresentation? Explain.
2. In Exercise 1, was it necessary for Williams to have an insurable interest in Martin's life to recover under the policy? Why?
3. In Exercise 1, if Williams had taken out the policy rather than Martin, could the insurer defend the claim on the ground that at the time of Martin's death, Williams had no insurable interest? Why?
4. If Williams had no insurable interest, would the incontestable clause prevent the company from asserting this defense? Why?
5. If the insurer pays Williams's claim, may it recover from Peters? Why?
6. Skidmore Trucking Company decided to expand its operations into the warehousing field. After examining several available properties, it decided to purchase a carbarn for $100,000 from a local bus company and to convert it into a warehouse. The standard contract for a real estate purchase was signed by the parties. The contract obligated Skidmore to pay the seller on an apportioned basis for the prepaid premiums on the existing fire insurance policy ($100,000 extended coverage). The policy expired two years and one month from the closing date. At the closing, the seller duly assigned the fire insurance policy to Skidmore in return for the payment of the apportioned amount of the prepaid premiums, but Skidmore failed to notify the insurance company of the change in ownership. Skidmore took possession of the premises and, after extensive renovation, began to use the building as a warehouse. Soon afterward, one of Skidmore's employees negligently dropped a lighted cigarette into a trash basket and started a fire that totally destroyed the building. Was the assignment of the policy to Skidmore valid? Why?
7. In Exercise 6, assuming the assignment is valid, would the insurer be obligated to pay for the loss resulting from the employee's negligence? Why?

Self-Test Questions

1. The substitution of one person for another in pursuit of a legal claim is called
    a. assignment
    b. coinsurance
    c. subrogation
    d. none of the above
2. Most insurance questions are covered by
    a. tort law
    b. criminal law
    c. constitutional law
    d. contract law
3. Common defenses used by insurance companies include
    a. concealment
    b. false representation

c. breach of warranty
d. all of the above

4. A coinsurance clause
    a. requires the insured to be insured by more than one policy
    b. requires the insured to maintain insurance equal to a certain percentage of the property's value
    c. allows another beneficiary to be substituted for the insured
    d. is none of the above
5. Property insurance typically covers
    a. ordinary wear and tear
    b. damage due to theft
    c. intentional losses
    d. damage due to earthquakes

Self-Test Answers

1. c
2. d
3. d
4. b
5. b

CHAPTER 38

Relationships between Principal and Agent

Learning Objectives

After reading this chapter, you should understand the following:

1. Why agency is important, what an agent is, and the types of agents.
2. What an independent contractor is.
3. The duties owed by the agent to the principal.
4. The duties owed by the principal to the agent.

38.1 Introduction to Agency and the Types of Agents

Learning Objectives

1. Understand why agency law is important.
2. Recognize the recurring legal issues in agency law.
3. Know the types of agents.
4. Understand how the agency relationship is created.

Introduction to Agency Law

Why Is Agency Law Important, and What Is an Agent?

An agent is a person who acts in the name of and on behalf of another, having been given and assumed some degree of authority to do so. Most organized human activity—and virtually all commercial activity—is carried on through agency. No corporation would be possible, even in theory, without such a concept. We might say "General Motors is building cars in China," for example, but we can't shake hands with General Motors. "The General," as people say, exists and works through agents. Likewise, partnerships and other business organizations rely extensively on agents to conduct their business. Indeed, it is not an exaggeration to say that agency is the cornerstone of enterprise organization. In a partnership each partner is a general agent, while under corporation law the officers and all employees are agents of the corporation.

The existence of agents does not, however, require a whole new law of torts or contracts. A tort is no less harmful when committed by an agent; a contract is no less binding when negotiated by an agent. What does need to be taken into account, though, is the manner in which an agent acts on behalf of his principal and toward a third party.

Recurring Issues in Agency Law

Several problematic fact scenarios recur in agency, and law has developed in response.

John Alden

Consider John Alden (1599–1687), one of the most famous agents in American literature. He is said to have been the first person from the *Mayflower* to set foot on Plymouth Rock in 1620; he was a carpenter, a cooper (barrel maker), and a diplomat. His agency task—of interest here—was celebrated in Henry Wadsworth Longfellow's "The Courtship of Miles Standish." He was to woo Priscilla Mullins (d. 1680), "the loveliest maiden of Plymouth," on behalf of Captain Miles Standish, a valiant soldier who was too shy to propose marriage. Standish turned to John Alden, his young and eloquent protégé, and beseeched Alden to speak on his behalf, unaware that Alden himself was in love with Priscilla. Alden accepted his captain's assignment, despite the knowledge that he would thus lose Priscilla for himself, and sought out the lady. But Alden was so tongue-tied that his vaunted eloquence fell short, turned Priscilla cold toward the object of Alden's mission, and eventually led her to turn the tables in one of the most famous lines in American literature and poetry: "Why don't you speak for yourself, John?" John eventually did: the two were married in 1623 in Plymouth.

Recurring Issues in Agency

Let's analyze this sequence of events in legal terms—recognizing, of course, that this example is an analogy and that the law, even today, would not impose consequences on Alden for his failure to carry out Captain Standish's wishes. Alden was the captain's agent: he was specifically authorized to speak in his name in a manner agreed on, toward a specified end, and he accepted the assignment in consideration of the captain's friendship. He had, however, a conflict of interest. He attempted to carry out the assignment, but he did not perform according to expectations. Eventually, he wound up with the prize himself. Here are some questions to consider, the same questions that will recur throughout the discussion of agency:

- How extensive was John's authority? Could he have made promises to Priscilla on the captain's behalf—for example, that Standish would have built her a fine house?
- Could he, if he committed a tort, have imposed liability on his principal? Suppose, for example, that he had ridden at breakneck speed to reach Priscilla's side and while en route ran into and injured a pedestrian on the road. Could the pedestrian have sued Standish?
- Suppose Alden had injured himself on the journey. Would Standish be liable to Alden?
- Is Alden liable to Standish for stealing the heart of Priscilla—that is, for taking the "profits" of the enterprise for himself?

As these questions suggest, agency law often involves three parties—the principal, the agent, and a third party. It therefore deals with three different relationships: between principal and agent, between principal and third party, and between agent and third party. These relationships can be summed up in a simple diagram (see Figure 38.1).

FIGURE 38.1 Agency Relationships

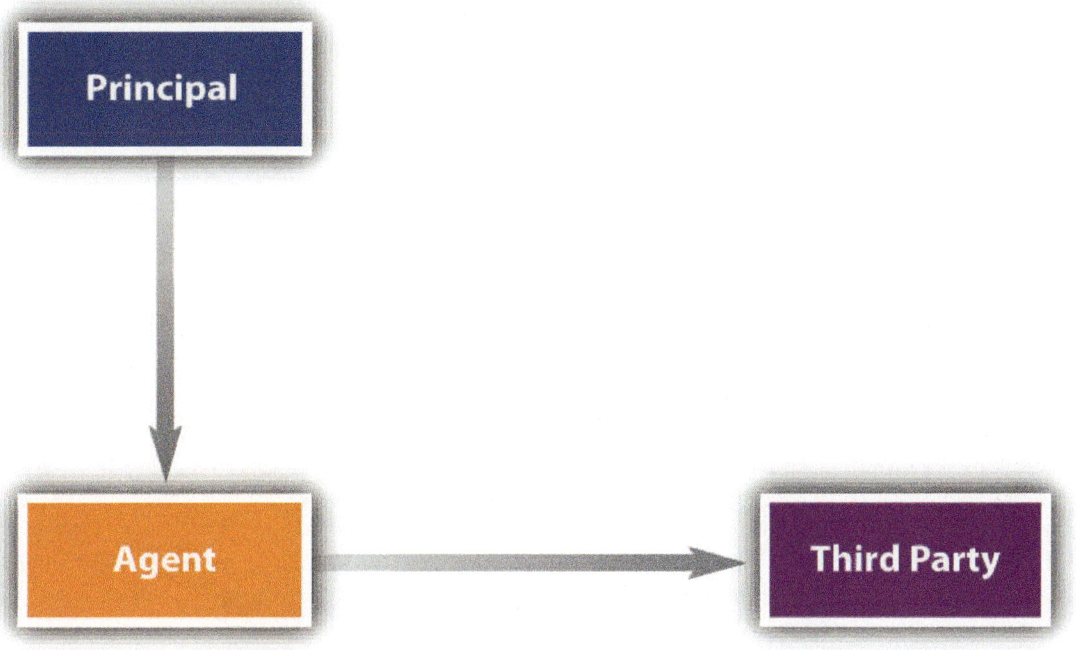

In this chapter, we will consider the principal-agent side of the triangle. In the next chapter we will turn to relationships involving third parties.

Types of Agents

There are five types of agents.

General Agent

The **general agent** possesses the authority to carry out a broad range of transactions in the name and on behalf of the principal. The general agent may be the manager of a business or may have a more limited but nevertheless ongoing role—for example, as a purchasing agent or as a life insurance agent authorized to sign up customers for the home office. In either case, the general agent has authority to alter the principal's legal relationships with third parties. One who is designated a general agent has the authority to act in any way required by the principal's business. To restrict the general agent's authority, the principal must spell out the limitations explicitly, and even so the principal may be liable for any of the agent's acts in excess of his authority.

general agent
Someone authorized to transact every kind of business for the principal.

Normally, the general agent is a business agent, but there are circumstances under which an individual may appoint a general agent for personal purposes. One common form of a personal general agent is the person who holds another's power of attorney. This is a delegation of authority to another to act in his stead; it can be accomplished by executing a simple form, such as the one shown in Figure 38.2. Ordinarily, the power of attorney is used for a special purpose—for example, to sell real estate or securities in the absence of the owner. But a person facing a lengthy operation and recuperation in a hospital might give a general power of attorney to a trusted family member or friend.

FIGURE 38.2 General Power of Attorney

General Power of Attorney

I, ______________________, of (address) ___________________, hereby appoint ______________________, of (address) _______________, to be my agent and attorney in fact. I grant my agent full authority and power to act on my behalf to do anything I could do if I were personally present.

Signed________________________; date ___________________.

In witness:

____

____

{Acknowledgement by notary}

Special Agent

special agent

An agent hired by contract to carry out specifically stated activities.

The **special agent** is one who has authority to act only in a specifically designated instance or in a specifically designated set of transactions. For example, a real estate broker is usually a special agent hired to find a buyer for the principal's land. Suppose Sam, the seller, appoints an agent Alberta to find a buyer for his property. Alberta's commission depends on the selling price, which, Sam states in a letter to her, "in any event may be no less than $150,000." If Alberta locates a buyer, Bob, who agrees to purchase the property for $160,000, her signature on the contract of sale will not bind Sam. As a special agent, Alberta had authority only to find a buyer; she had no authority to sign the contract.

Agency Coupled with an Interest

agency coupled with an interest

An agency in which the agent has an interest in the property regarding which he or she is acting on the principal's behalf.

An agent whose reimbursement depends on his continuing to have the authority to act as an agent is said to have an **agency coupled with an interest** if he has a property interest in the business. A literary or author's agent, for example, customarily agrees to sell a literary work to a publisher in return for a percentage of all monies the author earns from the sale of the work. The literary agent also acts as a collection agent to ensure that his commission will be paid. By agreeing with the principal that the agency is coupled with an interest, the agent can prevent his own rights in a particular literary work from being terminated to his detriment.

Subagent

subagents

The agent of an agent.

To carry out her duties, an agent will often need to appoint her own agents. These appointments may or may not be authorized by the principal. An insurance company, for example, might name a general agent to open offices in cities throughout a certain state. The agent will necessarily conduct her business through agents of her own choosing. These agents are **subagents** of the principal if the general agent had the express or implied authority of the principal to hire them. For legal purposes, they are agents of both the principal and the principal's general agent, and both are liable for the subagent's conduct although normally the general agent agrees to be primarily liable (see Figure 38.3).

FIGURE 38.3 Subagent

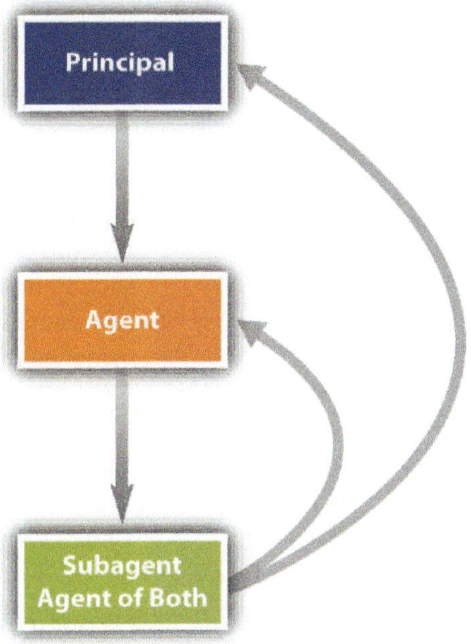

Servant

The final category of agent is the **servant**. Until the early nineteenth century, any employee whose work duties were subject to an employer's control was called a servant; we would not use that term so broadly in modern English. The Restatement (Second) of Agency, Section 2, defines a servant as "an agent employed by a master [employer] to perform service in his affairs whose physical conduct in the performance of the service is controlled or is subject to the right to control by the master."

Independent Contractor

Not every contract for services necessarily creates a master-servant relationship. There is an important distinction made between the status of a servant and that of an **independent contractor**. According to the Restatement (Second) of Agency, Section 2, "an independent contractor is a person who contracts with another to do something for him but who is not controlled by the other nor subject to the other's right to control with respect to his physical conduct in the performance of the undertaking." As the name implies, the independent contractor is legally autonomous. A plumber salaried to a building contractor is an employee and agent of the contractor. But a plumber who hires himself out to repair pipes in people's homes is an independent contractor. If you hire a lawyer to settle a dispute, that person is not your employee or your servant; she is an independent contractor. The terms "agent" and "independent contractor" are not necessarily mutually exclusive. In fact, by definition, "... an independent contractor is an agent in the broad sense of the term in undertaking, at the request of another, to do something for the other. As a general rule the line of demarcation between an independent contractor and a servant is not clearly drawn."[1]

servant

An employee.

independent contractor

A person who is hired to accomplish a result but is not subject to specific control by the one hiring.

This distinction between agent and independent contractor has important legal consequences for taxation, workers' compensation, and liability insurance. For example, employers are required to withhold income taxes from their employees' paychecks. But payment to an independent contractor, such as the plumber for hire, does not require such withholding. Deciding who is an independent contractor is not always easy; there is no single factor or mechanical answer. In *Robinson v. New York Commodities Corp.*, an injured salesman sought workers' compensation benefits, claiming to be an employee of the New York Commodities Corporation.[2] But the state workmen's compensation board ruled against him, citing a variety of factors. The claimant sold canned meats, making rounds in his car from his home. The company did not establish hours for him, did not control his movements in any way, and did not reimburse him for mileage or any other expenses or withhold taxes from its straight commission payments to him. He reported his taxes on a form for the self-employed and hired an accountant to prepare it for him. The court agreed with the compensation board that these facts established the salesman's status as an independent contractor.

The factual situation in each case determines whether a worker is an employee or an independent contractor. Neither the company nor the worker can establish the worker's status by agreement. As the North Dakota Workmen's Compensation Bureau put it in a bulletin to real estate brokers, "It has come to the Bureau's attention that many employers are requiring that those who work for them sign 'independent contractor' forms so that the employer does not have to pay workmen's compensation premiums for his employees. Such forms are meaningless if the worker is in fact an employee." *Vizcaino v. Microsoft Corporation*, discussed in Section 3, examines the distinction.

In addition to determining a worker's status for tax and compensation insurance purposes, it is sometimes critical for decisions involving personal liability insurance policies, which usually exclude from coverage accidents involving employees of the insureds. *General Accident Fire & Life Assurance Corp v. Pro Golf Association*[3] involved such a situation. The insurance policy in question covered members of the Professional Golfers Association. Gerald Hall, a golf pro employed by the local park department, was afforded coverage under the policy, which excluded "bodily injury to any employee of the insured arising out of and in the course of his employment by the insured." That is, no employee of Hall's would be covered (rather, any such person would have coverage under workers' compensation statutes). Bradley Martin, age thirteen, was at the golf course for junior league play. At Hall's request, he agreed to retrieve or "shag" golf balls to be hit during a lesson Hall was giving; he was—as Hall put it—to be compensated "either through golf instructions or money or hotdogs or whatever." During the course of the lesson, a golf ball hit by Hall hit young Martin in the eye. If Martin was an employee, the insurance company would be liable; if he was not an employee, the insurance company would not liable. The trial court determined he was not an employee. The evidence showed: sometimes the boys who "shagged" balls got paid, got golfing instructions, or got food, so the question of compensation was ambiguous. Martin was not directed in how to perform (the admittedly simple) task of retrieving golf balls, no control was exercised over him, and no equipment was required other than a bag to collect the balls: "We believe the evidence is susceptible of different inferences. . . . We cannot say that the decision of the trial court is against the manifest weight of the evidence."

Creation of the Agency Relationship

The agency relationship can be created in two ways: by agreement (expressly) or by operation of law (constructively or impliedly).

Agency Created by Agreement

Most agencies are created by contract. Thus, the general rules of contract law covered in Chapter 8 through Chapter 16 govern the law of agency. But agencies can also be created without contract, by agreement. Therefore, three contract principles are especially important: the first is the requirement for consideration, the second for a writing, and the third concerns contractual capacity.

Consideration

gratuitous agency

An agency where the agent receives no compensation.

Agencies created by consent—agreement—are not necessarily contractual. It is not uncommon for one person to act as an agent for another without consideration. For example, Abe asks Byron to run some errands for him: to buy some lumber on his account at the local lumberyard. Such a **gratuitous agency** gives rise to no different results than the more common contractual agency.

Formalities

Most oral agency contracts are legally binding; the law does not require that they be reduced to writing. In practice, many agency contracts are written to avoid problems of proof. And there are situations where an agency contract must be in writing: (1) if the agreed-on purpose of the agency cannot be fulfilled within one year or if the agency relationship is to last more than one year; (2) in many states, an agreement to pay a commission to a real estate broker; (3) in many states, authority given to an agent to sell real estate; and (4) in several states, contracts between companies and sales representatives.

Even when the agency contract is not required to be in writing, contracts that agents make with third parties often must be in writing. Thus, Section 2-201 of the Uniform Commercial Code specifically requires contracts for the sale of goods for the price of five hundred dollars or more to be in writing and "signed by the party against whom enforcement is sought or by his authorized agent."

Capacity

A contract is void or voidable when one of the parties lacks capacity to make one. If both principal and agent lack capacity—for example, a minor appoints another minor to negotiate or sign an agreement—there can be no question of the contract's voidability. But suppose only one or the other lacks capacity. Generally, the law focuses on the principal. If the principal is a minor or otherwise lacks capacity, the contract can be avoided even if the agent is fully competent. There are, however, a few situations in which the capacity of the agent is important. Thus, a mentally incompetent agent cannot bind a principal.

Agency Created by Operation of Law

Most agencies are made by contract, but agency also may arise impliedly or apparently.

Implied Agency

In areas of social need, courts have declared an agency to exist in the absence of an agreement. The agency relationship then is said to have been implied "by operation of law." Children in most states may purchase necessary items—food or medical services—on the parent's account. Long-standing social policy deems it desirable for the head of a family to support his dependents, and the courts will put the expense on the family head in order to provide for the dependents' welfare. The courts achieve this result by supposing the dependent to be the family head's agent, thus allowing creditors to sue the family head for the debt.

Implied agencies also arise where one person behaves as an agent would and the "principal," knowing that the "agent" is behaving so, acquiesces, allowing the person to hold himself out as an agent. Such are the basic facts in *Weingart v. Directoire Restaurant, Inc.* in Section 3.

Apparent Agency

Suppose Arthur is Paul's agent, employed through October 31. On November 1, Arthur buys materials at Lumber Yard—as he has been doing since early spring—and charges them to Paul's account. Lumber Yard, not knowing that Arthur's employment terminated the day before, bills Paul. Will Paul have to pay? Yes, because the termination of the agency was not communicated to Lumber Yard. It *appeared* that Arthur was an authorized agent. This issue is discussed further in Chapter 39.

Key Takeaway

An agent is one who acts on behalf of another. Many transactions are conducted by agents so acting. All corporate transactions, including those involving governmental organizations, are so conducted because corporations cannot themselves actually act; they are legal fictions. Agencies may be created expressly, impliedly, or apparently. Recurring issues in agency law include whether the "agent" really is such, the scope of the agent's authority, and the duties among the parties. The five types of agents include: general agent, special agent, subagent, agency coupled with an interest, and servant (or employee). The independent contractor is not an employee; her activities are not specifically controlled by her client, and the client is not liable for payroll taxes, Social Security, and the like. But it is not uncommon for an employer to claim workers are independent contractors when in fact they are employees, and the cases are often hard-fought on the facts.

Exercises

1. Why is agency law especially important in the business and government context?
2. What are the five types of agents?
3. What distinguishes an employee from an independent contractor?
4. Why do employers frequently try to pass off employees as independent contractors?

38.2 Duties between Agent and Principal

Learning Objectives

1. Understand that the agent owes the principal two types of duties: a special duty—the fiduciary duty—and other general duties as recognized in agency law.
2. Recognize that the principal owes the agent duties: contract, tort, and workers' compensation.

Agent's Duty to Principal

The agent owes the principal duties in two categories: the fiduciary duty and a set of general duties imposed by agency law. But these general duties are not unique to agency law; they are duties owed by any employee to the employer.

Fiduciary Duty

In a non-agency contractual situation, the parties' responsibilities terminate at the border of the contract. There is no relationship beyond the agreement. This literalist approach is justified by the more general principle that we each should be free to act unless we commit ourselves to a particular course.

fiduciary duty

The duty of an agent to act always in the best interest of the principal, to avoid self-dealing.

But the agency relationship is more than a contractual one, and the agent's responsibilities go beyond the border of the contract. Agency imposes a higher duty than simply to abide by the contract terms. It imposes a **fiduciary duty**. The law infiltrates the contract creating the agency relationship and reverses the general principle that the parties are free to act in the absence of agreement. As a fiduciary of the principal, the agent stands in a position of special trust. His responsibility is to subordinate his self-interest to that of his principal. The fiduciary responsibility is imposed by law. The absence of any clause in the contract detailing the agent's fiduciary duty does not relieve him of it. The duty contains several aspects.

Duty to Avoid Self-Dealing

A fiduciary may not lawfully profit from a conflict between his personal interest in a transaction and his principal's interest in that same transaction. A broker hired as a purchasing agent, for instance, may not sell to his principal through a company in which he or his family has a financial interest. The penalty for breach of fiduciary duty is loss of compensation and profit and possible damages for breach of trust.

Duty to Preserve Confidential Information

To further his objectives, a principal will usually need to reveal a number of secrets to her agent—how much she is willing to sell or pay for property, marketing strategies, and the like. Such information could easily be turned to the disadvantage of the principal if the agent were to compete with the principal or were to sell the information to those who do. The law therefore prohibits an agent from using for his own purposes or in ways that would injure the interests of the principal, information confidentially given or acquired. This prohibition extends to information gleaned from the principal though unrelated to the agent's assignment: "[A]n agent who is told by the principal of his plans, or who secretly examines books or memoranda of the employer, is not privileged to use such information at his principal's expense."[4] Nor may the agent use confidential information after resigning his agency. Though he is free, in the absence of contract, to compete with his former principal, he may not use information learned in the course of his agency, such as trade secrets and customer lists. Section 3, *Bacon v. Volvo Service Center, Inc.*, deals with an agent's breach of the duty of confidentiality.

Other Duties

In addition to fiduciary responsibility (and whatever special duties may be contained in the specific contract) the law of agency imposes other duties on an agent. These duties are not necessarily unique to agents: a nonfiduciary employee could also be bound to these duties on the right facts.

Duty of Skill and Care

An agent is usually taken on because he has special knowledge or skills that the principal wishes to tap. The agent is under a legal duty to perform his work with the care and skill that is "standard in the locality for the kind of work which he is employed to perform" and to exercise any special skills, if these are greater or more refined than those prevalent among those normally employed in the community. In short, the agent may not lawfully do a sloppy job.[5]

Duty of Good Conduct

In the absence of an agreement, a principal may not ordinarily dictate how an agent must live his private life. An overly fastidious florist may not instruct her truck driver to steer clear of the local bar on his way home from delivering flowers at the end of the day. But there are some jobs on which the personal habits of the agent may have an effect. The agent is not at liberty to act with impropriety or notoriety, so as to bring disrepute on the business in which the principal is engaged. A lecturer at an antialcohol clinic may be directed to refrain from frequenting bars. A bank cashier who becomes known as a gambler may be fired.

Duty to Keep and Render Accounts

The agent must keep accurate financial records, take receipts, and otherwise act in conformity to standard business practices.

Duty to Act Only as Authorized

This duty states a truism but is one for which there are limits. A principal's wishes may have been stated ambiguously or may be broad enough to confer discretion on the agent. As long as the agent acts reasonably under the circumstances, he will not be liable for damages later if the principal ultimately repudiates what the agent has done: "Only conduct which is contrary to the principal's manifestations to him, interpreted in light of what he has reason to know at the time when he acts, . . . subjects the agent to liability to the principal."[6]

Duty Not to Attempt the Impossible or Impracticable

The principal says to the agent, "Keep working until the job is done." The agent is not obligated to go without food or sleep because the principal misapprehended how long it would take to complete the job. Nor should the agent continue to expend the principal's funds in a quixotic attempt to gain business, sign up customers, or produce inventory when it is reasonably clear that such efforts would be in vain.

Duty to Obey

As a general rule, the agent must obey reasonable directions concerning the manner of performance. What is reasonable depends on the customs of the industry or trade, prior dealings between agent and principal, and the nature of the agreement creating the agency. A principal may prescribe uniforms for various classes of employees, for instance, and a manufacturing company may tell its sales force what sales pitch to use on customers. On the other hand, certain tasks entrusted to agents are not subject to the principal's control; for example, a lawyer may refuse to permit a client to dictate courtroom tactics.

Duty to Give Information

Because the principal cannot be every place at once—that is why agents are hired, after all—much that is vital to the principal's business first comes to the attention of agents. If the agent has actual notice or reason to know of information that is relevant to matters entrusted to him, he has a duty to inform the principal. This duty is especially critical because information in the hands of an agent is, under most circumstances, imputed to the principal, whose legal liabilities to third persons may hinge on receiving information in timely fashion. Service of process, for example, requires a defendant to answer within a certain number of days; an agent's failure to communicate to the principal that a summons has been served may bar the principal's right to defend a lawsuit. The imputation to the principal of knowledge possessed by the agent is strict: even where the agent is acting adversely to the principal's interests—for example, by trying to defraud his employer—a third party may still rely on notification to the agent, unless the third party knows the agent is acting adversely.

"Shop Rights" Doctrine

In *Grip Nut Co. v. Sharp*, Sharp made a deal with Grip Nut Company that in return for a salary and bonuses as company president, he would assign to the company any inventions he made.[7] When the five-year employment contract expired, Sharp continued to serve as chief executive officer, but no new contract was negotiated concerning either pay or rights to inventions. During the next ten years, Sharp invented a number of new products and developed new machinery to manufacture them; patent rights went to the company. However, he made one invention with two other employees and they assigned the patent to him. A third employee invented a safety device and also assigned the patent to Sharp. At one time, Sharp's son invented a leakproof bolt and a process to manufacture it; these, too, were assigned to Sharp. These inventions were developed in the company's plants at its expense.

When Sharp died, his family claimed the rights to the inventions on which Sharp held assignments and sued the company, which used the inventions, for patent infringement. The family reasoned that after the expiration of the employment contract, Sharp was employed only in a managerial capacity, not as an inventor. The court disagreed and invoked the **shop rights doctrine**, under which an invention "developed and perfected in [a company's] plant with its time, materials, and appliances, and wholly at its expense" may be used by the company without payment of royalties: "Because the servant uses his master's time, facilities and materials to attain a concrete result, the employer is entitled to use that which embodies his own property and to duplicate it as often as he may find occasion to employ similar appliances in his business." The company would have been given complete ownership of the patents had there been an express or implied (e.g., the employee is hired to make inventions) contract to this effect between Sharp and the company.

shop rights doctrine

The rights of a company to exploit inventions made by employees on company time and resources.

Principal's Duty to Agent

In this category, we may note that the principal owes the agent duties in contract, tort, and—statutorily—workers' compensation law.

Contract Duties

The fiduciary relationship of agent to principal does not run in reverse—that is, the principal is not the agent's fiduciary. Nevertheless, the principal has a number of contractually related obligations toward his agent.

General Contract Duties

These duties are analogues of many of the agent's duties that we have just examined. In brief, a principal has a duty "to refrain from unreasonably interfering with [an agent's] work."[8] The principal is allowed, however, to compete with the agent unless the agreement specifically prohibits it. The principal has a duty to inform his agent of risks of physical harm or pecuniary loss that inhere in the agent's performance of assigned tasks. Failure to warn an agent that travel in a particular neighborhood required by the job may be dangerous (a fact unknown to the agent but known to the principal) could under common law subject the principal to a suit for damages if the agent is injured while in the neighborhood performing her job. A principal is obliged to render accounts of monies due to agents; a principal's obligation to do so depends on a variety of factors, including the degree of independence of the agent, the method of compensation, and the customs of the particular business. An agent's reputation is no less valuable than a principal's, and so an agent is under no obligation to continue working for one who sullies it.

Employment at Will

Under the traditional "employment-at-will" doctrine, an employee who is not hired for a specific period can be fired at any time, for any reason (except bad reasons: an employee cannot be fired, for example, for reporting that his employer's paper mill is illegally polluting groundwater). This doctrine, which has been much criticized, is discussed in Chapter 51.

Duty to Indemnify

Agents commonly spend money pursuing the principal's business. Unless the agreement explicitly provides otherwise, the principal has a duty to indemnify or reimburse the agent. A familiar form of indemnity is the employee expense account.

Tort and Workers' Compensation Duties

The employer owes the employee—any employee, not just agents—certain statutorily imposed tort and workers' compensation duties.

Background to Workers' Compensation

Andy, who works in a dynamite factory, negligently stores dynamite in the wrong shed. Andy warns his fellow employee Bill that he has done so. Bill lights up a cigarette near the shed anyway, a spark lands on the ground, the dynamite explodes, and Bill is injured. May Bill sue his employer to recover damages? At common law, the answer would be no—three times no. First, the "fellow-servant" rule would bar recovery because the employer was held not to be responsible for torts committed by one employee against another. Second, Bill's failure to heed Andy's warning and his decision to smoke near the dynamite amounted to contributory negligence. Hence, even if the dynamite had been negligently stored by the employer rather than by a fellow employee, the claim would have been dismissed. Third, the courts might have held that Bill had "assumed the risk": since he was aware of the dangers, it would not be fair to saddle the employer with the burden of Bill's actions.

workers' compensation

Laws imposing strict employer liability for injuries sustained by employees in the scope of employment.

The three common-law rules just mentioned ignited intense public fury by the turn of the twentieth century. In large numbers of cases, workers who were mutilated or killed on the job found themselves and their families without recompense. Union pressure and grass roots lobbying led to **workers' compensation** acts—statutory enactments that dramatically overhauled the law of torts as it affected employees.

The System in General

Workers' compensation is a no-fault system. The employee gives up the right to sue the employer (and, in some states, other employees) and receives in exchange predetermined compensation for a job-related injury, regardless of who caused it. This trade-off was felt to be equitable to employer and employee: the employee loses the right to seek damages for pain and suffering—which can be a sizable portion of any jury award—but in return he can avoid the time-consuming and uncertain judicial process and assure himself that his medical costs and a portion of his salary will be paid—and paid promptly. The employer must pay for all injuries, even those for which he is blameless, but in return he avoids the risk of losing a big lawsuit, can calculate his costs actuarially, and can spread the risks through insurance.

Most workers' compensation acts provide 100 percent of the cost of a worker's hospitalization and medical care necessary to cure the injury and relieve him from its effects. They also provide for payment of lost wages and death benefits. Even an employee who is able to work may be eligible to receive compensation for specific injuries. Check out New York State's workers' compensation page—interesting and well done: http://www.wcb.ny.gov/content/main/Workers/ScheduledLossUse.jsp. And here is a page from the state of Kansas workers' comp benefit schedule:

Kansas Workers' Compensation Benefits for Specific Injuries

Article 5.—Workers' Compensation
44-510d. Compensation for certain permanent partial disabilities; schedule. If there is an award of permanent disability as a result of the injury there shall be a presumption that disability existed immediately after the injury and compensation is to be paid for not to exceed the number of weeks allowed in the following schedule:

(1) For loss of a thumb, 60 weeks.

(2) For the loss of a first finger, commonly called the index finger, 37 weeks.

(3) For the loss of a second finger, 30 weeks.

(4) For the loss of a third finger, 20 weeks.

(5) For the loss of a fourth finger, commonly called the little finger, 15 weeks.

(6) Loss of the first phalange of the thumb or of any finger shall be considered to be equal to the loss of 1/2 of such thumb or finger, and the compensation shall be 1/2 of the amount specified above. The loss of the first phalange and any part of the second phalange of any finger, which includes the loss of any part of the bone of such second phalange, shall be considered to be equal to the loss of 2/3 of such finger and the compensation shall be 2/3 of the amount specified above. The loss of the first phalange and any part of the second phalange of a thumb which includes the loss of any part of the bone of such second phalange, shall be considered to be equal to the loss of the entire thumb. The loss of the first and second phalanges and any part of the third proximal phalange of any finger, shall be considered as the loss of the entire finger. Amputation through the joint shall be considered a loss to the next higher schedule.

(7) For the loss of a great toe, 30 weeks.

(8) For the loss of any toe other than the great toe, 10 weeks.

(9) The loss of the first phalange of any toe shall be considered to be equal to the loss of 1/2 of such toe and the compensation shall be 1/2 of the amount above specified.

(10) The loss of more than one phalange of a toe shall be considered to be equal to the loss of the entire toe.

(11) For the loss of a hand, 150 weeks.

(12) For the loss of a forearm, 200 weeks.

(13) For the loss of an arm, excluding the shoulder joint, shoulder girdle, shoulder musculature or any other shoulder structures, 210 weeks, and for the loss of an arm, including the shoulder joint, shoulder girdle, shoulder musculature or any other shoulder structures, 225 weeks.

(14) For the loss of a foot, 125 weeks.

(15) For the loss of a lower leg, 190 weeks.

(16) For the loss of a leg, 200 weeks.

(17) For the loss of an eye, or the complete loss of the sight thereof, 120 weeks.

Source: *http://www.kslegislature.org/li/statute/044_000_0000_chapter/044_005_0000_article/044_005_0010d_section/044_005_0010d_k/.*

The injured worker is typically entitled to two-thirds his or her average pay, not to exceed some specified maximum, for two hundred weeks. If the loss is partial (like partial loss of sight), the recovery is decreased by the percentage still usable.

Coverage

Although workers' compensation laws are on the books of every state, in two states—New Jersey and Texas—they are not compulsory. In those states the employer may decline to participate, in which event the employee must seek redress in court. But in those states permitting an employer election, the old common-law defenses (fellow-servant rule, contributory negligence, and assumption of risk) have been statutorily eliminated, greatly enhancing an employee's chances of winning a suit. The incentive is therefore strong for employers to elect workers' compensation coverage.

Those frequently excluded are farm and domestic laborers and public employees; public employees, federal workers, and railroad and shipboard workers are covered under different but similar laws. The trend has been to include more and more classes of workers. Approximately half the states now provide coverage for household workers, although the threshold of coverage varies widely from state to state. Some use an earnings test; other states impose an hours threshold. People who fall within the domestic category include maids, baby-sitters, gardeners, and handymen but generally not plumbers, electricians, and other independent contractors.

Paying for Workers' Compensation

There are three general methods by which employers may comply with workers' compensation laws. First, they may purchase employer's liability and workers' compensation policies through private commercial insurance companies. These policies consist of two major provisions: payment by the insurer of all claims filed under workers' compensation and related laws (such as occupational disease benefits) and coverage of the costs of defending any suits filed against the employer, including any judgments awarded. Since workers' compensation statutes cut off the employee's right to sue, how can such a lawsuit be filed? The answer is that there are certain exceptions to the ban: for instance, a worker may sue if the employer deliberately injures an employee.

The second method of compliance with workers' compensation laws is to insure through a state fund established for the purpose. The third method is to self-insure. The laws specify conditions under which companies may resort to self-insurance, and generally only the largest corporations qualify to do so. In short, workers' compensation systems create a tax on employers with which they are required (again, in most states) to buy insurance. The amount the employer has to pay for the insurance depends on the number and seriousness of claims made—how dangerous the work is. For example, Washington State's 2017 proposed hourly rates for employers to purchase insurance include these items: for egg and poultry farms, $1.40 per hour; shake and shingle mills (non automated), $19.05 per hour; asphalt paving, $2.20 per hour; lawn care maintenance, $1.54 per hour; plastic products manufacturing, $0.89 per hour; freight handling, $1.79 per hour; supermarkets, $0.74; restaurants, $0.41; entertainers and dancers, $7.60; colleges and universities, $0.34.[9]

Recurring Legal Issues

There are a number of legal issues that recur in workers' compensation cases. The problem is, from the employer's point of view, that the cost of buying insurance is tied to the number of claims made. The employer therefore has reason to assert the injured employee is not eligible for compensation. Recurring legal issues include the following:

- Is the injury work related? As a general rule, on-the-job injuries are covered no matter what their relationship to the employee's specific duties. Although injuries resulting from drunkenness or fighting are not generally covered, there are circumstances under which they will be, as Section 3 shows.
- Is the injured person an employee? Courts are apt to be liberal in construing statutes to include those who might not seem to be employed. In *Betts v. Ann Arbor Public Schools*, a University of Michigan student majoring in physical education was a student teacher in a junior high school.[10] During a four-month period, he taught two physical education courses. On the last day of his student teaching, he walked into the locker room and thirty of his students grabbed him and tossed him into the swimming pool. This was traditional, but he "didn't feel like going in that morning" and put up a struggle that ended with a whistle on an elastic band hitting him in the eye, which he subsequently lost as a result of the injury. He filed a workers' compensation claim. The school board argued that he could not be classified as an employee because he received no pay. Since he was injured by students—not considered agents of the

school—he would probably have been unsuccessful in filing a tort suit; hence the workers' compensation claim was his only chance of recompense. The state workers' compensation appeal board ruled against the school on the ground that payment in money was not required: "Plaintiff was paid in the form of training, college credits towards graduation, and meeting of the prerequisites of a state provisional certificate." The state supreme court affirmed the award.

- How palpable must the "injury" be? A difficult issue is whether a worker is entitled to compensation for psychological injury, including cumulative trauma. Until the 1970s, insurance companies and compensation boards required physical injury before making an award. Claims that job stresses led to nervous breakdowns or other mental disorders were rejected. But most courts have liberalized the definition of injury and now recognize that psychological trauma can be real and that job stress can bring it on, as shown by the discussion of *Wolfe v. Sibley, Lindsay & Curr Co.* in Section 3.

Key Takeaway

The agent owes the principal two categories of duties: fiduciary and general. The fiduciary duty is the duty to act always in the interest of the principal; the duty here includes that to avoid self-dealing and to preserve confidential information. The general duty owed by the agent encompasses the sorts of obligations any employee might have: the duty of skill and care, of good conduct, to keep and render accounts, to not attempt the impossible or impracticable, to obey, and to give information. The shop rights doctrine provides that inventions made by an employee using the employer's resources and on the employer's time belong to the employer.

The principal owes the agent duties too. These may be categorized as contract and tort duties. The contract duties are to warn the agent of hazards associated with the job, to avoid interfering with the agent's performance of his job, to render accounts of money due the agent, and to indemnify the agent for business expenses according to their agreement. The tort duty owed by the principal to the agent—employee—is primarily the statutorily imposed duty to provide workers' compensation for injuries sustained on the job. In reaction to common-law defenses that often exonerated the employer from liability for workers' injuries, the early twentieth century saw the rise of workers' compensation statutes. These require the employer to provide no-fault insurance coverage for any injury sustained by the employee on the job. Because the employer's insurance costs are claims rated (i.e., the cost of insurance depends on how many claims are made), the employer scrutinizes claims. A number of recurring legal issues arise: Is the injury work related? Is the injured person an employee? What constitutes an "injury"?

Exercises

1. Judge Learned Hand, a famous early-twentieth-century jurist (1872–1961), said, "The fiduciary duty is not the ordinary morals of the marketplace." How does the fiduciary duty differ from "the ordinary morals of the marketplace"? Why does the law impose a fiduciary duty on the agent?
2. What are the nonfiduciary duties owed by the agent to the principal?
3. What contract duties are owed by the principal to the agent?
4. Why were workers' compensation statutes adopted in the early twentieth century?
5. How do workers' compensation statutes operate, and how are the costs paid for?

38.3 Cases

Creation of Agency: Apparent Authority

Weingart v. Directoire Restaurant, Inc.
333 N.Y.S.2d 806 (N.Y., 1972)

KASSEL, J.

The issue here is whether defendant restaurant by permitting an individual to park patrons' cars thereby held him out as its "employee" for such purposes. Admittedly, this individual, one Buster Douglas, is not its employee in the usual sense but with the knowledge of defendant, he did station himself in front of its restaurant, wore a doorman's uniform and had been parking its customers' autos. The parties stipulated that if he were held to be defendant's employee, this created a bailment between the parties [and the "employer" would have to rebut a presumption of negligence if the customer's property was not returned to the customer].

On April 20, 1968, at about 10 P.M., plaintiff drove his 1967 Cadillac Coupe de Ville to the door of the Directoire Restaurant at 160 East 48th Street in Manhattan. Standing in front of the door was Buster Douglas, dressed in a self-supplied uniform, comprised of a regular doorman's cap and matching jacket. Plaintiff gave the keys to his vehicle to Douglas and requested that he park the car. He gave Douglas a $1.00 tip [about $6.90 in 2016 dollars] and received a claim check. Plaintiff then entered defendant's restaurant, remained there for approximately 45 minutes and when he departed, Douglas was unable to locate the car which was never returned to plaintiff.

At the time of this occurrence, the restaurant had been open for only nine days, during which time plaintiff had patronized the restaurant on at least one prior occasion.

Defendant did not maintain any sign at its entrance or elsewhere that it would provide parking for its customers (nor, apparently, any sign warning to the contrary).

Buster Douglas parked cars for customers of defendant's restaurant and at least three or four other restaurants on the block. He stationed himself in front of each restaurant during the course of an evening and was so engaged during the evening of April 20, 1968. Defendant clearly knew of and did not object to Douglas' activities outside its restaurant. Defendant's witness testified at an examination before trial:

Q. Did anybody stand outside your restaurant in any capacity whatsoever?

A. There was a man out there parking cars for the block, but he was in no way connected with us or anything like that. He parked cars for the Tamburlaine and also for the Chateau Madrid, Nepentha and a few places around the block.

Q. Did you know that this gentleman was standing outside your restaurant?

A. Yes, I knew he was there.

Q. How did you know that he was standing outside your restaurant?

A. Well, I knew the man's face because I used to work in a club on 55th Street and he was there. When we first opened up here, we didn't know if we would have a doorman or have parking facilities or what we were going to do at that time. We just let it hang and I told this Buster, Buster was his name, that you are a free agent and you do whatever you want to do. I am tending bar in the place and what you do in the street is up to you, I will not stop you, but we are not hiring you or anything like that, because at that time, we didn't know what we were going to use the parking lot or get a doorman and put on a uniform or what.

These facts establish to the court's satisfaction that, although Douglas was not an actual employee of the restaurant, defendant held him out as its authorized agent or "employee" for the purpose of parking its customers' cars, by expressly consenting to his standing, in uniform, in front of its door to receive customers, to park their cars and issue receipts therefor—which services were rendered without charge to the restaurant's customers, except for any gratuity paid to Douglas. Clearly, under these circumstances, apparent authority has been shown and Douglas acted within the scope of this authority.

Plaintiff was justified in assuming that Douglas represented the restaurant in providing his services and that the restaurant had placed him there for the convenience of its customers. A restaurateur knows that this is the impression created by allowing a uniformed attendant to so act. Facility in parking is often a critical consideration for a motorist in selecting a restaurant in midtown Manhattan, and the Directoire was keenly aware of this fact as evidenced by its testimony that the management was looking into various other possibilities for solving customers' parking problems.

There was no suitable disclaimer posted outside the restaurant that it had no parking facilities or that entrusting one's car to any person was at the driver's risk. It is doubtful that any prudent driver would entrust his car to a strange person on the street, if he thought that the individual had no authorization from the restaurant or club or had no connection with it, but was merely an independent operator with questionable financial responsibility.

The fact that Douglas received no compensation directly from defendant is not material. Each party derived a benefit from the arrangement: Douglas being willing to work for gratuities from customers, and the defendant, at no cost to itself, presenting the appearance of providing the convenience of free parking and doorman services to its patrons. In any case, whatever private arrangements existed between the restaurant and Douglas were never disclosed to the customers.

Even if such person did perform these services for several restaurants, it does not automatically follow that he is a freelance entrepreneur, since a shared employee working for other small or moderately sized restaurants in the area would seem a reasonable arrangement, in no way negating the authority of the attendant to act as doorman and receive cars for any one of these places individually.

The case most analogous to the instant one is *Klotz v. El Morocco* [Citation, 1968], and plaintiff here relies on it. That case similarly involved the theft of a car parked by a uniformed individual standing in front of defendant's restaurant who, although not employed by it, parked vehicles for its patrons with the restaurant's knowledge and consent. Defendant here attempts to distinguish this case principally upon the ground that the parties in El Morocco *stipulated* that the "doorman" was an agent or employee of the defendant acting within the scope of his authority. However, the judge made an express finding to that effect: * * * "there was sufficient evidence in plaintiff's case on which to find DiGiovanni, the man in the uniform, was acting within the scope of his authority as agent of defendant." Defendant here also points to the fact that in *Klotz* DiGiovanni placed patrons' car keys on a rack inside El Morocco; however, this is only one fact to be considered in finding a bailment and is, to me, more relevant to the issue of the degree of care exercised.

When defendant's agent failed to produce plaintiff's automobile, a presumption of negligence arose which now requires defendant to come forward with a sufficient explanation to rebut this presumption. [Citation] The matter should be set down for trial on the issues of due care and of damages.

Case Questions

1. Buster Douglas was not the restaurant's employee. Why did the court determine his negligence could nevertheless be imputed to the restaurant?
2. The plaintiff in this case relied on *Klotz*, very similar in facts, in which the car-parking attendant *was* found to be an employee. The defendant, necessarily, needed to argue that the cases were not very similar. What argument did the defendant make? What did the court say about that argument?
3. The restaurant here is a bailee—it has rightful possession of the plaintiff's (bailor's) property, the car. If the car is not returned to the plaintiff a rebuttable presumption of negligence arises. What does that mean?

Employee versus Independent Contractor

Vizcaino v. Microsoft Corp.

97 F.3d 1187 (9th Cir. 1996)

Reinhardt, J.

Large corporations have increasingly adopted the practice of hiring temporary employees or independent contractors as a means of avoiding payment of employee benefits, and thereby increasing their profits. This practice has understandably led to a number of problems, legal and otherwise. One of the legal issues that sometimes arises is exemplified by this lawsuit. The named plaintiffs, who were classified by Microsoft as independent contractors, seek to strip that label of its protective covering and to obtain for themselves certain benefits that the company provided to all of its regular or permanent employees. After certifying the named plaintiffs as representatives of a class of "common-law employees," the district court granted summary judgment to Microsoft on all counts. The plaintiffs . . . now appeal as to two of their claims: a) the claim that they are entitled to savings benefits under Microsoft's Savings Plus Plan (SPP); and b) that they are entitled to stock-option benefits under Microsoft's Employee Stock Purchase Plan (ESPP). In both cases, the claims are based on their contention that they are common-law employees.

Microsoft, one of the country's fastest growing and most successful corporations and the world's largest software company, produces and sells computer software internationally. It employs a core staff of permanent employees. It categorizes them as "regular employees" and offers them a wide variety of benefits, including paid vacations, sick leave, holidays, short-term disability, group health and life insurance, and pensions, as well as the two benefits involved in this appeal. Microsoft supplements its core staff of employees with a pool of individuals to whom it refuses to pay fringe benefits. It previously classified these individuals as "independent contractors" or "freelancers," but prior to the filing of the action began classifying them as "temporary agency employees." Freelancers were hired when Microsoft needed to expand its workforce to meet the demands of new product schedules. The company did not, of course, provide them with any of the employee benefits regular employees receive.

The plaintiffs performed services as software testers, production editors, proofreaders, formatters and indexers. Microsoft fully integrated the plaintiffs into its workforce: they often worked on teams along with regular employees, sharing the same supervisors, performing identical functions, and working the same core hours. Because Microsoft required that they work on site, they received admittance card keys, office equipment and supplies from the company.

Freelancers and regular employees, however, were not without their obvious distinctions. Freelancers wore badges of a different color, had different electronic-mail addresses, and attended a less formal orientation than that provided to regular employees. They were not permitted to assign their work to others, invited to official company functions, or paid overtime wages. In addition, they were not paid through Microsoft's payroll department. Instead, they submitted invoices for their services, documenting their hours and the projects on which they worked, and were paid through the accounts receivable department.

The plaintiffs were told when they were hired that, as freelancers, they would not be eligible for benefits. None has contended that Microsoft ever promised them any benefits individually. All eight named plaintiffs signed [employment agreements] when first hired by Microsoft or soon thereafter. [One] included a provision that states that the undersigned "agrees to be responsible for all federal and state taxes, withholding, social security, insurance and other benefits." The [other one] states that "as an Independent Contractor to Microsoft, you are self-employed and are responsible to pay all your own insurance and benefits." Eventually, the plaintiffs learned of the various benefits being provided to regular employees from speaking with them or reading various Microsoft publications concerning employee benefits.

In 1989 and 1990, the Internal Revenue Service (IRS)[,] * * * applying common-law principles defining the employer-employee relationship, concluded that Microsoft's freelancers were not independent contractors but employees for withholding and employment tax purposes, and that Microsoft would thereafter be required to pay withholding taxes and the employer's portion of Federal Insurance Contribution Act (FICA) tax. Microsoft agreed. * * *

After learning of the IRS rulings, the plaintiffs sought various employee benefits, including those now at issue: the ESPP and SPP benefits. The SPP * * * is a cash or deferred salary arrangement under § 401k of the Internal Revenue Code that permits Microsoft's employees to save and invest up to fifteen percent of their income through tax-deferred payroll deductions. * * * Microsoft matches fifty percent of the employee's contribution in any year, with [a maximum matching contribution]. The ESPP * * * permits employees to purchase company stock [with various rules].

Microsoft rejected the plaintiffs' claims for benefits, maintaining that they were independent contractors who were personally responsible for all their own benefits. * * *

The plaintiffs brought this action, challenging the denial of benefits.

Microsoft contends that the extrinsic evidence, including the [employment agreements], demonstrates its intent not to provide freelancers or independent contractors with employee benefits[.] * * * We have no doubt that the company did not intend to provide freelancers or independent contractors with employee benefits, and that if the plaintiffs had in fact been freelancers or independent contractors, they would not be eligible under the plan. The plaintiffs, however, were not freelancers or independent contractors. They were common-law employees, and the question is what, if anything, Microsoft intended with respect to persons who were actually common-law employees but were not known to Microsoft to be such. The fact that Microsoft did not intend to provide benefits to persons who it thought were freelancers or independent contractors sheds little or no light on that question. * * *

Microsoft's argument, drawing a distinction between common-law employees on the basis of the manner in which they were paid, is subject to the same vice as its more general argument. Microsoft regarded the plaintiffs as independent contractors during the relevant period and learned of their common-law-employee status only after the IRS examination. They were paid through the accounts receivable department rather than the payroll department because of Microsoft's mistaken view as to their legal status. Accordingly, Microsoft cannot now contend that the fact that they were paid through the accounts receivable department demonstrates that the company intended to deny them the benefits received by all common-law employees regardless of their actual employment status. Indeed, Microsoft has pointed to no evidence suggesting that it ever denied eligibility to any employees, whom it *understood* to be common-law employees, by paying them through the accounts receivable department or otherwise.

We therefore construe the ambiguity in the plan against Microsoft and hold that the plaintiffs are eligible to participate under the terms of the SPP.

[Next, regarding the ESPP] we hold that the plaintiffs * * * are covered by the specific provisions of the ESPP. We apply the "objective manifestation theory of contracts," which requires us to "impute an intention corresponding to the reasonable meaning of a person's words and acts." [Citation] Through its incorporation of the tax code provision into the plan, Microsoft manifested an objective intent to make all common-law employees, and hence the plaintiffs, eligible for participation. The ESPP specifically provides:

> *It is the intention of the Company to have the Plan qualify as an "employee stock purchase plan" under Section 423 of the Internal Revenue Code of 1954.* The provisions of the Plan shall, accordingly, be construed so as to extend and limit participation in a manner consistent with the requirements of that Section of the Code. *(emphasis added)*

[T]he ESPP, when construed in a manner consistent with the requirements of § 423, extends participation to all common-law employees not covered by one of the express exceptions set forth in the plan. Accordingly, we find that the ESPP, through its incorporation of § 423, expressly extends eligibility for participation to the plaintiff class and affords them the same options to acquire stock in the corporation as all other employees.

Microsoft next contends that the [employment agreements] signed by the plaintiffs render them ineligible to participate in the ESPP. First, the label used in the instruments signed by the plaintiffs does not control their employment status. Second, the employment instruments, if construed to exclude the plaintiffs from receiving ESPP benefits, would conflict with the plan's express incorporation of § 423. Although Microsoft may have generally intended to exclude individuals who were in fact independent contractors, it could not, consistent with its express intention to extend participation in the ESPP to all common-law employees, have excluded the plaintiffs. Indeed, such an exclusion would defeat the purpose of including § 423 in the plan, because the exclusion of common-law employees not otherwise accepted would result in the loss of the plan's tax qualification.

Finally, Microsoft maintains that the plaintiffs are not entitled to ESPP benefits because the terms of the plan were never communicated to them and they were therefore unaware of its provisions when they performed their employment services. * * * In any event, to the extent that knowledge of an offer of benefits is a prerequisite, it is probably sufficient that Microsoft publicly promulgated the plan. In [Citation], the plaintiff was unaware of the company's severance plan until shortly before his termination. The Oklahoma Supreme Court concluded nonetheless that publication of the plan was "the equivalent of constructive knowledge on the part of *all* employees not specifically excluded."

We are not required to rely, however, on the [this] analysis or even on Microsoft's own unwitting concession. There is a compelling reason, implicit in some of the preceding discussion, that requires us to reject the company's theory that the plaintiffs' entitlement to ESPP benefits is defeated by their previous lack of knowledge regarding their rights. It is "well established" that an optionor may not rely on an optionee's failure to exercise an option when he has committed any act or failed to perform any duty "calculated to cause the optionee to delay in exercising the right." [Citation] "[T]he optionor may not make statements or representations calculated to cause delay, [or] fail to furnish [necessary] information. . . . " Similarly, "[I]t is a principle of fundamental justice that if a promisor is himself the cause of the failure of performance, either of an obligation due him or of a condition upon which his own liability depends, he cannot take advantage of the failure." [Citation] * * *

Applying these principles, we agree with the magistrate judge, who concluded that Microsoft, which created a benefit to which the plaintiffs were entitled, could not defend itself by arguing that the plaintiffs were unaware of the benefit, when its own false representations precluded them from gaining that knowledge. Because Microsoft misrepresented both the plaintiffs' actual employment status and their eligibility to participate in the ESPP, it is responsible for their failure to know that they were covered by the terms of the offer. It may not now take advantage of that failure to defeat the plaintiffs' rights to ESPP benefits. Thus, we reject Microsoft's final argument.

Conclusion

For the reasons stated, the district court's grant of summary judgment in favor of Microsoft and denial of summary judgment in favor of the plaintiffs is REVERSED and the case REMANDED for the determination of any questions of individual eligibility for benefits that may remain following issuance of this opinion and for calculation of the damages or benefits due the various class members.

Case Questions

1. In a 1993 *Wall Street Journal* article, James Bovard asserted that the IRS "is carrying out a sweeping campaign to slash the number of Americans permitted to be self-employed—and to punish the companies that contract with them . . . IRS officials indicate that more than half the nation's self-employed should no longer be able to work for themselves." Why did Microsoft want these employees to "be able to work for themselves"?
2. Why did the employees accept employment as independent contractors?
3. It seems unlikely that the purpose of the IRS's campaign was really to keep people from working for themselves, despite Mr. Bovard's assumption. What was the purpose of the campaign?
4. Why did the IRS and the court determine that these "independent contractors" were in fact employees?

Breach of Fiduciary Duty

Bacon v. Volvo Service Center, Inc.

597 S.E.2d 440 (Ga. App. 2004)

Smith, J.

[This appeal is] taken in an action that arose when two former employees left an existing business and began a new, competing business. * * * Bacon and Johnson, two former employees of Volvo Service Center, Inc. (VSC), and the new company they formed, South Gwinnett Volvo Service, Ltd. (SGVS), appeal from the trial court's denial of their motion for judgment notwithstanding the jury's verdict in favor of VSC. * * *

VSC filed suit against appellants, alleging a number of claims arising from the use by Bacon, who had been a service technician at VSC, of VSC's customer list, and his soliciting Johnson, a service writer, and another VSC employee to join SGVS. SGVS moved for a directed verdict on certain claims at the close of plaintiff's evidence and at the close of the case, which motions were denied. The jury was asked to respond to specific interrogatories, and it found for VSC and against all three appellants on VSC's claim for misappropriation of trade secrets. The jury also found for plaintiff against Bacon for breach of fiduciary duty, * * * tortious interference with business relations, employee piracy, and conversion of corporate assets. The jury awarded VSC attorney fees, costs, and exemplary damages stemming from the claim for misappropriation of trade secrets. Judgment was entered on the jury's verdict, and appellants' motion for j.n.o.v. was denied. This appeal ensued. We find that VSC did not meet its burden of proof as to the claims for misappropriation of trade secrets, breach of fiduciary duty, or employee piracy, and the trial court should have granted appellants' motion for j.n.o.v.

Construed to support the jury's verdict, the evidence of record shows that Bacon was a technician at VSC when he decided to leave and open a competing business. Before doing so, he printed a list of VSC's customers from one of VSC's two computers. Computer access was not password restricted, was easy to use, and was used by many employees from time to time.

About a year after he left VSC, Bacon gave Johnson and another VSC employee an offer of employment at his new Volvo repair shop, which was about to open. Bacon and Johnson advertised extensively, and the customer list was used to send flyers to some VSC customers who lived close to the new shop's location. These activities became the basis for VSC's action against Bacon, Johnson, and their new shop, SGVS....

1. The Georgia Trade Secrets Act of 1990, [Citation], defines a "trade secret" as

> *information, without regard to form, including, but not limited to, . . . a list of actual or potential customers or suppliers which is not commonly known by or available to the public and which information:*
>
> *(A) Derives economic value, actual or potential, from not being generally known to, and not being readily ascertainable by proper means by, other persons who can obtain economic value from its disclosure or use; and*
>
> *(B) Is the subject of efforts that are reasonable under the circumstances to maintain its secrecy.*

If an employer does not prove both prongs of this test, it is not entitled to protection under the Act. Our Supreme Court held in [Citation, 1991] for instance, that information was not a trade secret within the meaning of the Act because no evidence showed that the employer "made reasonable efforts under the circumstances . . . to maintain the confidentiality of the information it sought to protect."

While a client list may be subject to confidential treatment under the Georgia Trade Secrets Act, the information itself is not inherently confidential. Customers are not trade secrets. Confidentiality is afforded only where the customer list is not generally known or ascertainable from other sources and was the subject of reasonable efforts to maintain its secrecy. * * *

Here, VSC took *no* precautions to maintain the confidentiality of its customer list. The information was on both computers, and it was not password-protected. Moreover, the same information was available to the technicians through the repair orders, which they were permitted to retain indefinitely while Bacon was employed there. Employees were not informed that the information was confidential. Neither Bacon nor Johnson was required to sign a confidentiality agreement as part of his employment.

Because no evidence was presented from which the jury could have concluded that VSC took any steps, much less reasonable ones, to protect the confidentiality of its customer list, a material requirement for trade secret status was not satisfied. The trial court should have granted appellants' motion for j.n.o.v.

2. To prove tortious interference with business relations, "a plaintiff must show defendant: (1) acted improperly and without privilege, (2) acted purposely and with malice with the intent to injure, (3) induced a third party or parties not to enter into or continue a business relationship with the plaintiff, and (4) caused plaintiff financial injury." [Citation] But "[f]air competition is always legal." [Citations] Unless an employee has executed a valid non-compete or non-solicit covenant, he is not barred from soliciting customers of his former employer on behalf of a new employer. [Citation]

No evidence was presented that Bacon acted "improperly," that any of VSC's former customers switched to SGVS because of any improper act by Bacon, or that these customers would have continued to patronize VSC but for Bacon's solicitations. Therefore, it was impossible for a jury to calculate VSC's financial damage, if any existed.

3. With regard to VSC's claim for breach of fiduciary duty, "[a]n employee breaches no fiduciary duty to the employer simply by making plans to enter a competing business while he is still employed. Even before the termination of his agency, he is entitled to make arrangements to compete and upon termination of employment immediately compete." [Citation] He cannot solicit customers for a rival business or do other, similar acts in direct competition with his employer's business before his employment ends. But here, no evidence was presented to rebut the evidence given by Bacon and Johnson that they engaged in no such practices before their employment with VSC ended. Even assuming, therefore, that a fiduciary relationship existed, no evidence was presented showing that it was breached.

4. The same is true for VSC's claim for employee piracy. The evidence simply does not show that any employees of VSC were solicited for SGVS before Bacon left VSC's employ. * * *

Judgment reversed.

Case Questions

1. Why was it determined that the defendants were not liable for any breach of trade secrecy?
2. What would have been necessary to show tortious interference with business relations?
3. The evidence was lacking that there was any breach of fiduciary duty. What would have been necessary to show that?
4. What is "employee piracy"? Why was it not proven?

Workers' Compensation: What "Injuries" Are Compensable?

Wolfe v. Sibley, Lindsay & Curr Co.
330 N.E.2d 603 (N.Y. 1975)

Wachtler, J.

This appeal involves a claim for workmen's compensation benefits for the period during which the claimant was incapacitated by severe depression caused by the discovery of her immediate supervisor's body after he had committed suicide.

The facts as adduced at a hearing before the Workmen's Compensation Board are uncontroverted. The claimant, Mrs. Diana Wolfe, began her employment with the respondent department store, Sibley, Lindsay & Curr Co. in February, 1968. After working for some time as an investigator in the security department of the store she became secretary to Mr. John Gorman, the security director. It appears from the record that as head of security, Mr. Gorman was subjected to intense pressure, especially during the Christmas holidays. Mrs. Wolfe testified that throughout the several years she worked at Sibley's Mr. Gorman reacted to this holiday pressure by becoming extremely agitated and nervous. She noted, however, that this anxiety usually disappeared when the holiday season was over. Unfortunately, Mr. Gorman's nervous condition failed to abate after the 1970 holidays. * * *

Despite the fact that he followed Mrs. Wolfe's advice to see a doctor, Mr. Gorman's mental condition continued to deteriorate. On one occasion he left work at her suggestion because he appeared to be so nervous. This condition persisted until the morning of June 9, 1971 when according to the claimant, Mr. Gorman looked much better and even smiled and 'tousled her hair' when she so remarked.

A short time later Mr. Gorman called her on the intercom and asked her to call the police to room 615. Mrs. Wolfe complied with this request and then tried unsuccessfully to reach Mr. Gorman on the intercom. She entered his office to find him lying in a pool of blood caused by a self-inflicted gunshot wound in the head. Mrs. Wolfe became extremely upset and was unable to continue working that day.

She returned to work for one week only to lock herself in her office to avoid the questions of her fellow workers. Her private physician perceiving that she was beset by feelings of guilt referred her to a psychiatrist and recommended that she leave work, which she did. While at home she ruminated about her guilt in failing to prevent the suicide and remained in bed for long periods of time staring at the ceiling. The result was that she became unresponsive to her husband and suffered a weight loss of 20 pounds. Her psychiatrist, Dr. Grinols diagnosed her condition as an acute depressive reaction.

After attempting to treat her in his office Dr. Grinols realized that the severity of her depression mandated hospitalization. Accordingly, the claimant was admitted to the hospital on July 9, 1971 where she remained for two months during which time she received psychotherapy and medication. After she was discharged, Dr. Grinols concluded that there had been no substantial remission in her depression and ruminative guilt and so had her readmitted for electroshock treatment. These treatments lasted for three weeks and were instrumental in her recovery. She was again discharged and, in mid-January, 1972, resumed her employment with Sibley, Lindsay & Curr.

Mrs. Wolfe's claim for workmen's compensation was granted by the referee and affirmed by the Workmen's Compensation Board. On appeal the Appellate Division reversed citing its opinions in [Citations], [concluding] * * * that mental injury precipitated solely by psychic trauma is not compensable as a matter of law. We do not agree with this conclusion.

Workmen's compensation, as distinguished from tort liability which is essentially based on fault, is designed to shift the risk of loss of earning capacity caused by industrial accidents from the worker to industry and ultimately the consumer. In light of its beneficial and remedial character the Workmen's Compensation Law should be construed liberally in favor of the employee [Citation].

Liability under the act is predicated on accidental injury arising out of and in the course of employment. * * * Applying these concepts to the case at bar we note that there is no issue raised concerning the causal relationship between the occurrence and the injury. The only testimony on this matter was given by Dr. Grinols who stated unequivocally that the discovery of her superior's body was the competent producing cause of her condition. Nor is there any question as to the absence of physical impact. Accordingly, the focus of our inquiry is whether or not there has been an accidental injury within the meaning of the Workmen's Compensation Law.

Since there is no statutory definition of this term we turn to the relevant decisions. These may be divided into three categories: (1) psychic trauma which produces physical injury, (2) physical impact which produces psychological injury, and (3) psychic trauma which produces psychological injury. As to the first class our court has consistently recognized the principle that an injury caused by emotional stress or shock may be accidental within the purview of the compensation law. [Citation] Cases falling into the second category have uniformly sustained awards to those incurring nervous or psychological disorders as a result of physical impact [Citation]. As to those cases in the third category the decisions are not as clear. * * *

We hold today that psychological or nervous injury precipitated by psychic trauma is compensable to the same extent as physical injury. This determination is based on two considerations. First, as noted in the psychiatric testimony there is nothing in the nature of a stress or shock situation which ordains physical as opposed to psychological injury. The determinative factor is the particular vulnerability of an individual by virtue of his physical makeup. In a given situation one person may be susceptible to a heart attack while another may suffer a depressive reaction. In either case the result is the same—the individual is incapable of functioning properly because of an accident and should be compensated under the Workmen's Compensation Law.

Secondly, having recognized the reliability of identifying psychic trauma as a causative factor of injury in some cases and the reliability by identifying psychological injury as a resultant factor in other cases, we see no reason for limiting recovery in the latter instance to cases involving physical impact. There is nothing talismanic about physical impact.

We would note in passing that this analysis reflects the view of the majority of jurisdictions in this country and England. [Citations] * * *

Accordingly, the order appealed from should be reversed and the award to the claimant reinstated, with costs.

Case Questions

1. Why did the appeals court deny workers' compensation benefits for Wolfe?
2. On what reasoning did the New York high court reverse?
3. There was a dissent in this case (not included here). Judge Breitel noted that the evidence was that Mrs. Wolfe had a psychological condition such that her trauma "could never have occurred unless she, to begin with, was extraordinarily vulnerable to severe shock at or away from her place of employment or one produced by accident or injury to those close to her in employment or in her private life." The judge worried that "one can easily call up a myriad of commonplace occupational pursuits where employees are often exposed to the misfortunes of others which may in the mentally unstable evoke precisely the symptoms which this claimant suffered." He concluded, "In an era marked by examples of overburdening of socially desirable programs with resultant curtailment or destruction of such programs, a realistic assessment of impact of doctrine is imperative. An overburdening of the compensation system by injudicious and open-ended expansion of compensation benefits, especially for costly, prolonged, and often only ameliorative psychiatric care, cannot but threaten its soundness or that of the enterprises upon which it depends." What is the concern here?

38.4 Summary and Exercises

Summary

An agent is one who acts on behalf of another. The law recognizes several types of agents, including (1) the general agent, one who possesses authority to carry out a broad range of transactions in the name of and on behalf of the principal; (2) the special agent, one with authority to act only in a specifically designated instance or set of transactions; (3) the agent whose agency is coupled with an interest, one who has a property interest in addition to authority to act as an agent; (4) the subagent, one appointed by an agent with authority to do so; and (5) the servant ("employee" in modern English), one whose physical conduct is subject to control of the principal.

A servant should be distinguished from an independent contractor, whose work is not subject to the control of the principal. The difference is important for purposes of taxation, workers' compensation, and liability insurance.

The agency relationship is usually created by contract, and sometimes governed by the Statute of Frauds, but some agencies are created by operation of law.

An agent owes his principal the highest duty of loyalty, that of a fiduciary. The agent must avoid self-dealing, preserve confidential information, perform with skill and care, conduct his personal life so as not to bring disrepute on the business for which he acts as agent, keep and render accounts, and give appropriate information to the principal.

Although the principal is not the agent's fiduciary, the principal does have certain obligations toward the agent—for example, to refrain from interfering with the agent's work and to indemnify. The employer's common-law tort liability toward his employees has been replaced by the workers' compensation system, under which the employee gives up the right to sue for damages in return for prompt payment of medical and job-loss expenses. Injuries must have been work related and the injured person must have been an employee. Courts today allow awards for psychological trauma in the absence of physical injury.

Exercises

1. A woman was involved in an automobile accident that resulted in the death of a passenger in her car. After she was charged with manslaughter, her attorney agreed to work with her insurance company's claims adjuster in handling the case. As a result of the agreement, the woman gave a statement about the accident to the claims adjuster. When the prosecuting attorney demanded to see the statement, the woman's attorney refused on the grounds that the claims adjuster was his—the attorney's—agent, and therefore the statement was covered by the attorney-client privilege. Is the attorney correct? Why?
2. A local hotel operated under a franchise agreement with a major hotel chain. Several customers charged the banquet director of the local hotel with misconduct and harassment. They sued the hotel chain (the franchisor) for acts committed by the local hotel (the franchisee), claiming that the franchisee was the agent of the franchisor. Is an agency created under these circumstances? Why?
3. A principal hired a mortgage banking firm to obtain a loan commitment of $10,000,000 from an insurance company for the construction of a shopping center. The firm was promised a fee of $50,000 for obtaining the commitment. The firm was successful in arranging for the loan, and the insurance company, without the principal's knowledge, agreed to pay the firm a finder's fee. The principal then refused to pay the firm the promised $50,000, and the firm brought suit to recover the fee. May the firm recover the fee? Why?
4. Based on his experience working for the CIA, a former CIA agent published a book about certain CIA activities in South Vietnam. The CIA did not approve of the publication of the book although, as a condition of his employment, the agent had agreed not to publish any information relating to the CIA without specific approval of the agency. The government brought suit against the agent, claiming that all the agent's profits from publishing the book should go to the government. Assuming that the government suffered only nominal damages because the agent published no classified information, will the government prevail? Why?
5. Upon graduation from college, Edison was hired by a major chemical company. During the time when he was employed by the company, Edison discovered a synthetic oil that could be manufactured at a very low cost. What rights, if any, does Edison's employer have to the discovery? Why?
6. A U.S. company hired MacDonald to serve as its resident agent in Bolivia. MacDonald entered into a contract to sell cars to Bolivia and personally guaranteed performance of the contract as required by Bolivian law. The cars delivered to Bolivia were defective, and Bolivia

recovered a judgment of $83,000 from MacDonald. Must the U.S. company reimburse MacDonald for this amount? Explain.

7. According to the late Professor William L. Prosser, "The theory underlying the workmen's compensation acts never has been stated better than in the old campaign slogan, 'The cost of the product should bear the blood of the workman.'" What is meant by this statement?
8. An employee in a Rhode Island foundry inserted two coins in a coin-operated coffee machine in the company cafeteria. One coin stuck in the machine, and the worker proceeded to "whack" the machine with his right arm. The arm struck a grate near the machine, rupturing the biceps muscle and causing a 10 percent loss in the use of the arm. Is the worker entitled to workers' compensation? Explain.
9. Paulson engaged Arthur to sell Paul's restored 1948 Packard convertible to Byers for $23,000. A few days later, Arthur saw an advertisement showing that Collector was willing to pay $30,000 for a 1948 Packard convertible in "restored" condition. Arthur sold the car to Byers, and subsequently Paulson learned of Collector's interest. What rights, if any, has Paulson against Arthur?

Self-Test Questions

1. One who has authority to act only in a specifically designated instance or in a specifically designated set of transactions is called
   a. a subagent
   b. a general agent
   c. a special agent
   d. none of the above
2. An agency relationship may be created by
   a. contract
   b. operation of law
   c. an oral agreement
   d. all of the above
3. An agent's duty to the principal includes
   a. the duty to indemnify
   b. the duty to warn of special dangers
   c. the duty to avoid self dealing
   d. all of the above
4. A person whose work is not subject to the control of the principal, but who arranges to perform a job for him is called
   a. a subagent
   b. a servant
   c. a special agent
   d. an independent contractor
5. An employer's liability for employees' on-the-job injuries is generally governed by
   a. tort law
   b. the workers' compensation system
   c. Social Security
   d. none of the above

Self-Test Answers

1. c
2. d
3. c
4. d
5. b

Endnotes

1. *Flick v. Crouch*, 434 P.2d 256, 260 (OK, 1967).
2. *Robinson v. New York Commodities Corp.*, 396 N.Y.S.2d 725, App. Div. (1977).
3. *General Accident Fire & Life Assurance Corp v. Pro Golf Association*, 352 N.E.2d 441 (Ill. App. 1976).
4. Restatement (Second) of Agency, Section 395.
5. Restatement (Second) of Agency, Section 379.
6. Restatement (Second) of Agency, Section 383.
7. *Grip Nut Co. v. Sharp*, 150 F.2d 192 (7th Cir. 1945).
8. Restatement (Second) of Agency, Section 434.
9. Washington State Department of Labor & Industries, *Rates for Workers' Compensation, Proposed 2011 Rates*, http://www.lni.wa.gov/ClaimsIns/Insurance/RatesRisk/Check/RatesHistory.
10. *Betts v. Ann Arbor Public Schools*, 271 N.W.2d 498 (Mich. 1978).

CHAPTER 39

Liability of Principal and Agent; Termination of Agency

Learning Objectives

After reading this chapter, you should understand the following:

1. The principal's liability in contract.
2. The principal's liability in tort.
3. The principal's criminal liability.
4. The agent's personal liability in tort and contract.
5. How agency relationships are terminated.

In Chapter 38, we considered the relationships between agent and principal. Now we turn to relationships between third parties and the principal or agent. When the agent makes a contract for his principal or commits a tort in the course of his work, is the principal liable? What is the responsibility of the agent for torts committed and contracts entered into on behalf of his principal? How may the relationship be terminated so that the principal or agent will no longer have responsibility toward or liability for the acts of the other? These are the questions addressed in this chapter.

39.1 Principal's Contract Liability

Learning Objectives

1. Understand that the principal's liability depends on whether the agent was authorized to make the contract.
2. Recognize how the agent's authority is acquired: expressly, impliedly, or apparently.
3. Know that the principal may also be liable—even if the agent had no authority—if the principal ratifies the agent's contract after the fact.

Principal's Contract Liability Requires That Agent Had Authority

The key to determining whether a principal is liable for contracts made by his agent is authority: was the agent authorized to negotiate the agreement and close the deal? Obviously, it would not be sensible to hold a contractor liable to pay for a whole load of lumber merely because a stranger wandered into the lumberyard saying, "I'm an agent for ABC Contractors; charge this to their account." To be liable, the principal must have authorized the agent in some manner to act in his behalf, and that authorization must be communicated to the third party by the principal.

Types of Authority

There are three types of authority: express, implied, and apparent (see Figure 39.1). We will consider each in turn.

Express Authority

express authority

Contractually given authority to the agent from the principal, orally or in writing, communicated to the third party.

The strongest form of authority is that which is expressly granted, often in written form. The principal consents to the agent's actions, and the third party may then rely on the document attesting to the agent's authority to deal on behalf of the principal. One common form of **express authority** is the standard signature card on file with banks allowing corporate agents to write checks on the company's credit. The principal bears the risk of any wrongful action of his agent, as demonstrated in *Allen A. Funt Productions, Inc. v. Chemical Bank*.[1] Allen A. Funt submitted to his bank through his production company various certificates permitting his accountant to use the company's checking accounts.[2] In fact, for several years the accountant embezzled money from the company by writing checks to himself and depositing them in his own account. The company sued its bank, charging it with negligence, apparently for failing to monitor the amount of money taken by the accountant. But the court dismissed the negligence complaint, citing a state statute based on the common-law agency principle that a third party is entitled to rely on the express authorization given to an agent; in this case, the accountant drew checks on the account within the monetary limits contained in the signature cards on file with the bank. Letters of introduction and work orders are other types of express authority.

FIGURE 39.1 Types of Authority

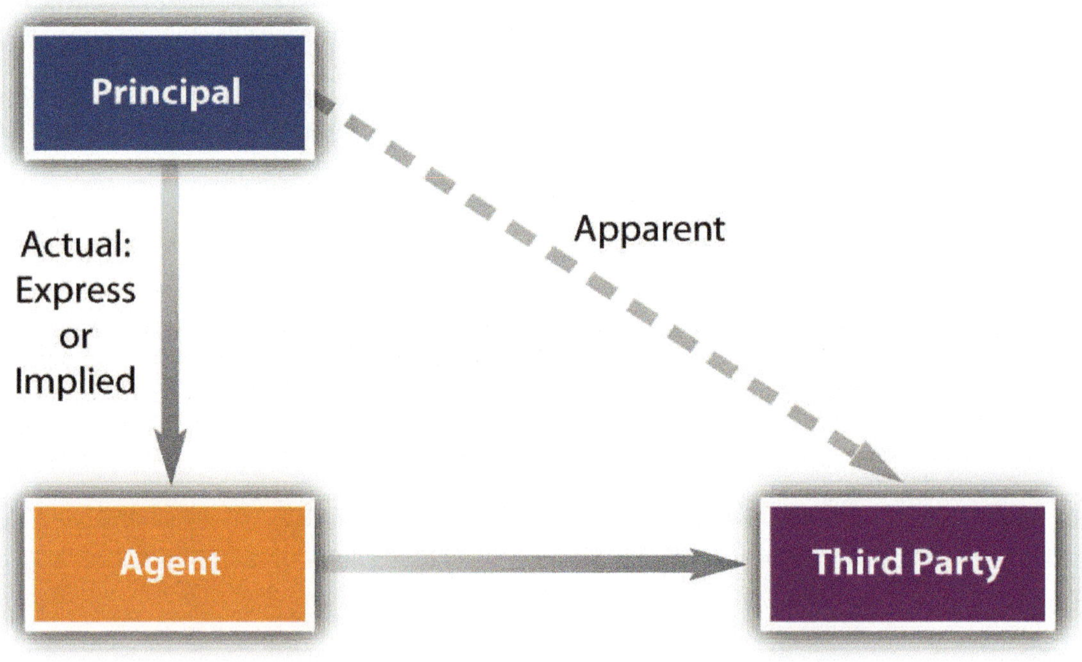

Implied Authority

Not every detail of an agent's work can be spelled out. It is impossible to delineate step-by-step the duties of a general agent; at best, a principal can set forth only the general nature of the duties that the agent is to perform. Even a special agent's duties are difficult to describe in such detail as to leave him without discretion. If express authority were the only valid kind, there would be no efficient way to use an agent, both because the effort to describe the duties would be too great and because the third party would be reluctant to deal with him.

But the law permits authority to be "implied" by the relationship of the parties, the nature and customs of the business, the circumstances surrounding the act in question, the wording of the agency contract, and the knowledge that the agent has of facts relevant to the assignment. The general rule is that the agent has implied or "incidental" authority to perform acts incidental to or reasonably necessary to carrying out the transaction. Thus, if a principal instructs her agent to "deposit a check in the bank today," the agent has authority to drive to the bank unless the principal specifically prohibits the agent from doing so.

The theory of **implied authority** is especially important to business in the realm of the business manager, who may be charged with running the entire business operation or only a small part of it. In either event, the business manager has a relatively large domain of implied authority. He can buy goods and services; hire, supervise, and fire employees; sell or junk inventory; take in receipts and pay debts; and in general, direct the ordinary operations of the business. The full extent of the manager's authority depends on the circumstances—what is customary in the particular industry, in the particular business, and among the individuals directly concerned.

implied authority

The authority of an agent to perform acts that are reasonably necessary to accomplish the purpose of the agency.

On the other hand, a manager does not have implicit authority to undertake unusual or extraordinary actions on behalf of his principal. In the absence of express permission, an agent may not sell part of the business, start a new business, change the nature of the business, incur debt (unless borrowing is integral to the business, as in banking, for example), or move the business premises. For example, the owner of a hotel appoints Andy manager; Andy decides to rename the hotel and commissions an artist to prepare a new logo for the hotel's stationery. Andy has no implied authority to change the name or to commission the artist, though he does have implied authority to engage a printer to replenish the stationery supply—and possibly to make some design changes in the letterhead.

Even when there is no implied authority, in an emergency the agent may act in ways that would in the normal course require specific permission from the principal. If unforeseen circumstances arise and it is impracticable to communicate with the principal to find out what his wishes would be, the agent may do what is reasonably necessary in order to prevent substantial loss to his principal. During World War II, Eastern Wine Corporation marketed champagne in a bottle with a diagonal red stripe that infringed the trademark of a French producer. The French company had granted licenses to an American importer to market its champagne in the United States. The contract between producer and importer required the latter to notify the French company whenever a competitor appeared to be infringing its rights and to recommend steps by which the company could stop the infringement. The authority to institute suit was not expressly conferred, and ordinarily the right to do so would not be inferred. Because France was under German occupation, however, the importer was unable to communicate with the producer, its principal. The court held that the importer could file suit to enjoin Eastern Wine from continuing to display the infringing red diagonal stripe, since legal action was "essential to the preservation of the principal's property."[3]

The rule that a person's position can carry with it implied authority is fundamental to American business practice. But outside the United States this rule is not applicable, and the business executive traveling abroad should be aware that in civil-law countries it is customary to present proof of authority to transact corporate business—usually in the form of a power of attorney. This is not always an easy task. Not only must the power of the traveling executive be shown but the right of the corporate officer back in the United States to delegate authority must also be proven.

Apparent Authority

In the agency relationship, the agent's actions in dealing with third parties will affect the legal rights of the principal. What the third party knows about the agency agreement is irrelevant to the agent's legal authority to act. That authority runs from principal to agent. As long as an agent has authorization, either express or implied, she may bind the principal legally. Thus, the seller of a house may be ignorant of the buyer's true identity; the person he supposes to be the prospective purchaser might be the agent of an undisclosed principal. Nevertheless, if the agent is authorized to make the purchase, the seller's ignorance is not a ground for either seller or principal to void the deal.

apparent authority

In agency, the situation in which a principal leads a third party to believe that an agent has authority to bind the principal, even where the agent lacks the actual authority to bind the principal.

But if a person has no authority to act as an agent, or an agent has no authority to act in a particular way, is the principal free from all consequences? The answer depends on whether or not the agent has **apparent authority**—that is, on whether or not the third person reasonably believes from the principal's words, written or spoken, or from his conduct that he has in fact consented to the agent's actions. Apparent authority is a manifestation of authority communicated to the third person; it runs from principal to third party, not to the agent.

Apparent authority is sometimes said to be based on the principle of estoppel. Estoppel is the doctrine that a person will not now be allowed to deny a promise or assertion she previously made where there has been detrimental reliance on that promise or assertion. Estoppel is commonly used to avoid injustice. It may be a substitute for the requirement of consideration in contract (making the promise of a gift enforceable where the donee has relied upon the promise), and it is sometimes available to circumvent the requirement of a writing under the Statute of Frauds.

Apparent authority can arise from prior business transactions. On July 10, Meggs sold to Buyer his business, the right to use the trade name Rose City Sheet Metal Works, and a list of suppliers he had used. Three days later, Buyer began ordering supplies from Central Supply Company, which was on Meggs's list but with which Meggs had last dealt four years before. On September 3, Central received a letter from Meggs notifying it of Meggs's sale of the business to Buyer. Buyer failed to pay Central, which sued Meggs. The court held that Rose City Sheet Metal Works had apparent authority to buy on Meggs's credit; Meggs was liable for supplies purchased between July 10 and September 3.[4] In such cases, and in cases involving the firing of a general manager, actual notice should be given promptly to all customers. See the discussion of *Kanavos v. Hancock Bank & Trust Company* in Section 4.

Ratification

Even if the agent possessed no actual authority and there was no apparent authority on which the third person could rely, the principal may still be liable if he ratifies or adopts the agent's acts before the third person withdraws from the contract. Ratification usually relates back to the time of the undertaking, creating authority after the fact as though it had been established initially. Ratification is a voluntary act by the principal. Faced with the results of action purportedly done on his behalf but without authorization and through no fault of his own, he may affirm or disavow them as he chooses. To ratify, the principal may tell the parties concerned or by his conduct manifest that he is willing to accept the results as though the act were authorized. Or by his silence he may find under certain circumstances that he has ratified. Note that ratification does not require the usual consideration of contract law. The principal need be promised nothing extra for his decision to affirm to be binding on him. Nor does ratification depend on the position of the third party; for example, a loss stemming from his reliance on the agent's representations is not required. In most situations, ratification leaves the parties where they expected to be, correcting the agent's errors harmlessly and giving each party what was expected.

Key Takeaway

The principal is liable on an agent's contract only if the agent was authorized by the principal to make the contract. Such authority is express, implied, or apparent. *Express* means made in words, orally or in writing; *implied* means the agent has authority to perform acts incidental to or reasonably necessary to carrying out the transaction for which she has express authority. *Apparent authority* arises where the principal gives the third party reason to believe that the agent had authority. The reasonableness of the third party's belief is based on all the circumstances—all the facts. Even if the agent has no authority, the principal may, after the fact, ratify the contract made by the agent.

Exercises

1. Could express authority be established by silence on the part of the principal?
2. Why is the concept of implied authority very important in business situations?
3. What is the rationale for the doctrine of apparent authority—that is, why would the law impose a contract on a "principal" when in fact there was no principal-agent relationship with the "agent" at all?

39.2 Principal's Tort and Criminal Liability

Learning Objectives

1. Understand in what circumstances a principal will be vicariously liable for torts committed by employees.
2. Recognize the difference between agents whose tort and criminal liability may be imputed to the employer and those whose liability will not be so imputed.
3. Know when the principal will be vicariously liable for intentional torts committed by the agent.
4. Explain what is meant by "the scope of employment," within which the agent's actions may be attributed to the principal and without which they will not.
5. Name special cases of vicarious liability.
6. Describe the principal's liability for crimes committed by the agent.

Principal's Tort Liability

The Distinction between Direct and Vicarious Liability

When is the principal liable for injuries that the agent causes another to suffer?

Direct Liability

There is a distinction between torts prompted by the principal himself and torts of which the principal was innocent. If the principal directed the agent to commit a tort or knew that the consequences of the agent's carrying out his instructions would bring harm to someone, the principal is liable. This is an application of the general common-law principle that one cannot escape liability by delegating an unlawful act to another. The syndicate that hires a hitman is as culpable of murder as the man who pulls the trigger. Similarly, a principal who is negligent in his use of agents will be held liable for their negligence. This rule comes into play when the principal fails to supervise employees adequately, gives faulty directions, or hires incompetent or unsuitable people for a particular job. Imposing liability on the principal in these cases is readily justifiable since it is the principal's own conduct that is the underlying fault; the principal here is directly liable.

Vicarious Liability

respondeat superior

The Latin term for the master-servant doctrine.

master-servant doctrine

A doctrine under which the employer is liable for torts committed by the employee in the scope of employment.

vicarious liability

Liability incurred indirectly through the actions of another.

But the principle of liability for one's agent is much broader, extending to acts of which the principal had no knowledge, that he had no intention to commit nor involvement in, and that he may in fact have expressly prohibited the agent from engaging in. This is the principle of **respondeat superior** ("let the master answer") or the **master-servant doctrine**, which imposes on the principal **vicarious liability** (*vicarious* means "indirectly, as, by, or through a substitute") under which the principal is responsible for acts committed by the agent within the scope of the employment (see Figure 39.2).

FIGURE 39.2 Principal's Tort Liability

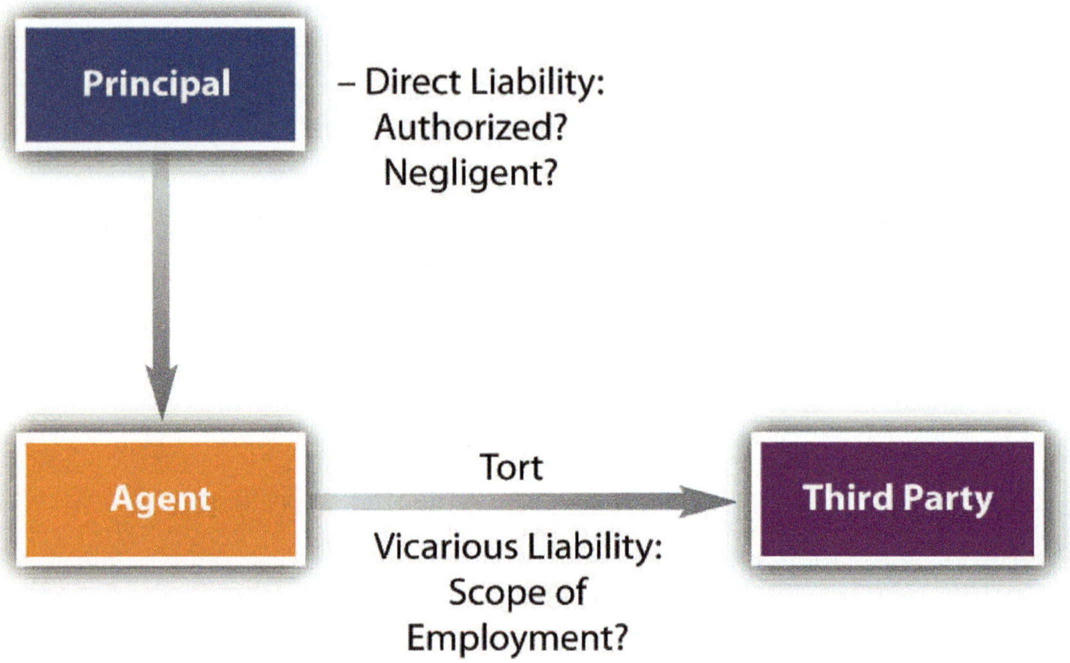

The modern basis for vicarious liability is sometimes termed the "deep pocket" theory: the principal (usually a corporation) has deeper pockets than the agent, meaning that it has the wherewithal to pay for the injuries traceable one way or another to events it set in motion. A million-dollar industrial accident is within the means of a company or its insurer; it is usually not within the means of the agent—employee—who caused it.

The "deep pocket" of the defendant-company is not always very deep, however. For many small businesses, in fact, the principle of respondeat superior is one of life or death. One example was the closing in San Francisco of the much-beloved Larraburu Brothers Bakery—at the time, the world's second largest sourdough bread maker. The bakery was held liable for $2 million in damages after one of its delivery trucks injured a six-year-old boy. The bakery's insurance policy had a limit of $1.25 million, and the bakery could not absorb the excess. The Larraburus had no choice but to cease operations. (See http://www.outsidelands.org/larraburu.php.)

Respondeat superior raises three difficult questions: (1) What type of agents can create tort liability for the principal? (2) Is the principal liable for the agent's intentional torts? (3) Was the agent acting within the scope of his employment? We will consider these questions in turn.

Agents for Whom Principals Are Vicariously Liable

In general, the broadest liability is imposed on the master in the case of tortious physical conduct by a servant, as discussed in Chapter 38. If the servant acted within the scope of his employment—that is, if the servant's wrongful conduct occurred while performing his job—the master will be liable to the victim for damages unless, as we have seen, the victim was another employee, in which event the workers' compensation system will be invoked. Vicarious tort liability is primarily a function of the employment relationship and not agency status.

Ordinarily, an individual or a company is not vicariously liable for the tortious acts of independent contractors. The plumber who rushes to a client's house to repair a leak and causes a traffic accident does not subject the homeowner to liability. But there are exceptions to the rule. Generally, these exceptions fall into a category of duties that the law deems nondelegable. In some situations, one person is obligated to provide protection to or care for another. The failure to do so results in liability whether or not the harm befell the other because of an independent contractor's wrongdoing. Thus, a homeowner has a duty to ensure that physical conditions in and around the home are not unreasonably dangerous. If the owner hires an independent contracting firm to dig a sewer line and the contractor negligently fails to guard passersby against the danger of falling into an open trench, the homeowner is liable because the duty of care in this instance cannot be delegated. (The contractor is, of course, liable to the homeowner for any damages paid to an injured passerby.)

Liability for Agent's Intentional Torts

In the nineteenth century, a principal was rarely held liable for intentional wrongdoing by the agent if the principal did not command the act complained of. The thought was that one could never infer authority to commit a willfully wrongful act. Today, liability for intentional torts is imputed to the principal if the agent is acting to further the principal's business. See the very disturbing *Lyon v. Carey* in Section 4.

Deviations from Employment

The general rule is that a principal is liable for torts only if the servant committed them "in the scope of employment." But determining what this means is not easy.

The "Scope of Employment" Problem

It may be clear that the person causing an injury is the agent of another. But a principal cannot be responsible for every act of an agent. If an employee is following the letter of his instructions, it will be easy to determine liability. But suppose an agent deviates in some way from his job. The classic test of liability was set forth in an 1833 English case, *Joel v. Morrison*.[5] The plaintiff was run over on a highway by a speeding cart and horse. The driver was the employee of another, and inside was a fellow employee. There was no question that the driver had acted carelessly, but what he and his fellow employee were doing on the road where the plaintiff was injured was disputed. For weeks before and after the accident, the cart had never been driven in the vicinity in which the plaintiff was walking, nor did it have any business there. The suggestion was that the employees might have gone out of their way for their own purposes. As the great English jurist Baron Parke put it, "If the servants, being on their master's business, took a detour to call upon a friend, the master will be responsible. ... But if he was going on a frolic of his own, without being at all on his master's business, the master will not be liable." In applying this test, the court held the employer liable.

The test is thus one of degree, and it is not always easy to decide when a detour has become so great as to be transformed into a frolic. For a time, a rather mechanical rule was invoked to aid in making the decision. The courts looked to the servant's purposes in "detouring." If the servant's mind was fixed on accomplishing his own purposes, then the detour was held to be outside the scope of employment; hence the tort was not imputed to the master. But if the servant also intended to accomplish his master's purposes during his departure from the letter of his assignment, or if he committed the wrong while returning to his master's task after the completion of his frolic, then the tort was held to be within the scope of employment.

This test is not always easy to apply. If a hungry deliveryman stops at a restaurant outside the normal lunch hour, intending to continue to his next delivery after eating, he is within the scope of employment. But suppose he decides to take the truck home that evening, in violation of rules, in order to get an early start the next morning. Suppose he decides to stop by the beach, which is far away from his route. Does it make a difference if the employer knows that his deliverymen do this?

The Zone of Risk Test

Court decisions in the last forty years have moved toward a different standard, one that looks to the foreseeability of the agent's conduct. By this standard, an employer may be held liable for his employee's conduct even when devoted entirely to the employee's own purposes, as long as it was foreseeable that the agent might act as he did. This is the "zone of risk" test. The employer will be within the zone of risk for vicarious liability if the employee is where she is supposed to be, doing—more or less—what she is supposed to be doing, and the incident arose from the employee's pursuit of the employer's interest (again, more or less). That is, the employer is within the zone of risk if the servant is in the place within which, if the master were to send out a search party to find a missing employee, it would be reasonable to look. See Section 4, *Cockrell v. Pearl River Valley Water Supply Dist.*

Special Cases of Vicarious Liability

Vicarious liability is not limited to harm caused in the course of an agency relationship. It may also be imposed in other areas, including torts of family members, and other torts governed by statute or regulation. We will examine each in turn.

Use of Automobiles

A problem commonly arises when an automobile owner lends his vehicle to a personal friend, someone who is not an agent, and the borrower injures a third person. Is the owner liable? In many states, the owner is not liable; in other states, however, two approaches impose liability on the owner.

The first approach is legislative: **owner's consent statutes** make the owner liable when the automobile is being driven with his consent or knowledge. The second approach to placing liability on the owner is judicial and known as the **family purpose doctrine**. Under this doctrine, a family member who negligently injures someone with the car subjects the owner to liability if the family member was furthering family purposes. These are loosely defined to include virtually every use to which a child, for example, might put a car. In a Georgia case, *Dixon v. Phillips*, the father allowed his minor son to drive the car but expressly forbade him from letting anyone else do so.[6] Nevertheless, the son gave the wheel to a friend and a collision occurred while both were in the car. The court held the father liable because he made the car available for the pleasure and convenience of his son and other family members.

owner's consent statutes

Doctrine under which the owner of an automobile is liable for damages caused by the driver who has permission to use the car.

family purpose doctrine

A doctrine under which an owner of an automobile is liable for damages to others incurred while members of his family are driving the vehicle, under the theory that the vehicle is owned for family purposes.

Torts of Family Members

At common law, the husband was liable for the torts of his wife, not because she was considered an agent but because she was considered to be an extension of him. "Husband and wife were only one person in law,"[7] says Holmes, and any act of the wife was supposed to have been done at the husband's direction (to which Mr. Dickens's Mr. Bumble responded, in the memorable line, "If the law supposes that, the law is a ass—a idiot"[8]). This ancient view has been abrogated by statute or by court ruling in all the states, so that now a wife is solely responsible for her own torts unless she in fact serves as her husband's agent.

Unlike wives, children are not presumed at common law to be agents or extensions of the father so that normally parents are not vicariously liable for their children's torts. However, they can be held liable for failing to control children known to be dangerous.

Most states have statutorily changed the common-law rule, making parents responsible for willful or malicious tortious acts of their children whether or not they are known to be mischief-makers. Thus, the Illinois Parental Responsibility Law provides the following: "The parent or legal guardian of an unemancipated minor who resides with such parent or legal guardian is liable for actual damages for the willful or malicious acts of such minor which cause injury to a person or property."[9] Several other states impose a monetary limit on such liability.

Other Torts Governed by Statute or Regulation

There are certain types of conduct that statutes or regulation attempt to control by placing the burden of liability on those presumably in a position to prevent the unwanted conduct. An example is the "Dramshop Act," which in many states subjects the owner of a bar to liability if the bar continues to serve an intoxicated patron who later is involved in an accident while intoxicated. Another example involves the sale of adulterated or short-weight foodstuffs: the employer of one who sells such may be liable, even if the employer did not know of the sales.

Principal's Criminal Liability

As a general proposition, a principal will not be held liable for an agent's unauthorized criminal acts if the crimes are those requiring specific intent. Thus, a department store proprietor who tells his chief buyer to get the "best deal possible" on next fall's fashions is not liable if the buyer steals clothes from the manufacturer. A principal will, however, be liable if the principal directed, approved, or participated in the crime. Cases here involve, for example, a corporate principal's liability for agents' activity in antitrust violations—price-fixing is one such violation.

There is a narrow exception to the broad policy of immunity. Courts have ruled that under certain regulatory statutes and regulations, an agent's criminality may be imputed to the principal, just as civil liability is imputed under Dramshop Acts. These include pure food and drug acts, speeding ordinances, building regulations, child labor rules, and minimum wage and maximum hour legislation. Misdemeanor criminal liability may be imposed upon corporations and individual employees for the sale or shipment of adulterated food in interstate commerce, notwithstanding the fact that the defendant may have had no actual knowledge that the food was adulterated at the time the sale or shipment was made.

Key Takeaway

The principal will be liable for the employee's torts in two circumstances: first, if the principal was directly responsible, as in hiring a person the principal knew or should have known was incompetent or dangerous; second, if the employee committed the tort in the scope of business for the principal. This is the master-servant doctrine or respondeat superior. It imposes vicarious liability on the employer: the master (employer) will be liable if the employee was in the zone of activity creating a risk for the employer ("zone of risk" test), that is—generally—if the employee was where he was supposed to be, when he was supposed to be there, and the incident arose out of the employee's interest (however perverted) in promoting the employer's business.

Special cases of vicarious liability arise in several circumstances. For example, the owner of an automobile may be liable for torts committed by one who borrows it, or if it is—even if indirectly—used for family purposes. Parents are, by statute in many states, liable for their children's torts. Similarly by statute, the sellers and employers of sellers of alcohol or adulterated or short-weight foodstuffs may be liable. The employer of one who commits a crime is not usually liable unless the employer put the employee up to the crime or knew that a crime was being committed. But some prophylactic statutes impose liability on the employer for the employee's crime—even if the employee had no intention to commit it—as a means to force the employer to prevent such actions.

Exercises

1. What is the difference between direct and vicarious employer tort liability?
2. What is meant by the "zone of risk" test?
3. Under what circumstances will an employer be liable for intentional torts of the employee?
4. When will the employer be liable for an employee's criminal acts?

39.3 Agent's Personal Liability for Torts and Contracts; Termination of Agency

Learning Objectives

1. Understand the agent's personal liability for tort.
2. Understand the agent's personal liability for contract.
3. Recognize the ways the agency relationship is terminated.

Agent's Personal Liability for Torts and Contracts

Tort Liability

That a principal is held vicariously liable and must pay damages to an injured third person does not excuse the agent who actually committed the tortious acts. A person is always liable for his or her own torts (unless the person is insane, involuntarily intoxicated, or acting under extreme duress). The agent is personally liable for his wrongful acts and must reimburse the principal for any damages the principal was forced to pay, as long as the principal did not authorize the wrongful conduct. The agent directed to commit a tort remains liable for his own conduct but is not obliged to repay the principal. Liability as an agent can be burdensome, sometimes perhaps more burdensome than as a principal. The latter normally purchases insurance to cover against wrongful acts of agents, but liability insurance policies frequently do not cover the employee's personal liability if the employee is named in a lawsuit individually. Thus, doctors' and hospitals' malpractice policies protect a doctor from both her own mistakes and those of nurses and others that the doctor would be responsible for; nurses, however, might need their own coverage. In the absence of insurance, an agent is at serious risk in this lawsuit-conscious age. The risk is not total. The agent is not liable for torts of other agents unless he is personally at fault—for example, by negligently supervising a junior or by giving faulty instructions. For example, an agent, the general manager for a principal, hires Brown as a subordinate. Brown is competent to do the job but by failing to exercise proper control over a machine negligently injures Ted, a visitor to the premises. The principal and Brown are liable to Ted, but the agent is not.

Contract Liability

It makes sense that an agent should be liable for her own torts; it would be a bad social policy indeed if a person could escape tort liability based on her own fault merely because she acted in an agency capacity. It also makes sense that—as is the general rule—an agent is not liable on contracts she makes on the principal's behalf; the agent is not a party to a contract made by the agent on behalf of the principal. No public policy would be served by imposing liability, and in many cases it would not make sense. Suppose an agent contracts to buy $25 million of rolled aluminum for a principal, an airplane manufacturer. The agent personally could not reasonably perform such contract, and it is not intended by the parties that she should be liable. (Although the rule is different in England, where an agent residing outside the country is liable even if it is clear that he is signing in an agency capacity.) But there are three exceptions to this rule: (1) if the agent is undisclosed or partially disclosed, (2) if the agent lacks authority or exceeds it, or (3) if the agent entered into the contract in a personal capacity. We consider each situation.

Agent for Undisclosed or Partially Disclosed Principal

An agent need not, and frequently will not, inform the person with whom she is negotiating that she is acting on behalf of a principal. The secret principal is usually called an "undisclosed principal." Or the agent may tell the other person that he is acting as an agent but not disclose the principal's name, in which event the principal is "partially disclosed." To understand the difficulties that may occur, consider the following hypothetical but common example. A real estate developer known for building amusement parks wants to acquire several parcels of land to construct a new park. He wants to keep his identity secret to hold down the land cost. If the landowners realized that a major building project was about to be launched, their asking price would be quite high. So the developer obtains two options to purchase land by using two secret agents—Betty and Clem.

Betty does not mention to sellers that she is an agent; therefore, to those sellers the developer is an undisclosed principal. Clem tells those with whom he is dealing that he is an agent but refuses to divulge the developer's name or his business interest in the land. Thus, the developer is, to the latter sellers, a partially disclosed principal. Suppose the sellers get wind of the impending construction and want to back out of the deal. Who may enforce the contracts against them?

The developer and the agents may sue to compel transfer of title. The undisclosed or partially disclosed principal may act to enforce his rights unless the contract specifically prohibits it or there is a representation that the signatories are not signing for an undisclosed principal. The agents may also bring suit to enforce the principal's contract rights because, as agents for an undisclosed or partially disclosed principal, they are considered parties to their contracts.

Now suppose the developer attempts to call off the deal. Whom may the sellers sue? Both the developer and the agents are liable. That the sellers had no knowledge of the developer's identity—or even that there was a developer—does not invalidate the contract. If the sellers first sue agent Betty (or Clem), they may still recover the purchase price from the developer as long as they had no knowledge of his identity prior to winning the first lawsuit. The developer is discharged from liability if, knowing his identity, the plaintiffs persist in a suit against the agents and recover a judgment against them anyway. Similarly, if the seller sues the principal and recovers a judgment, the agents are relieved of liability. The seller thus has a "right of election" to sue either the agent or the undisclosed principal, a right that in many states may be exercised any time before the seller collects on the judgment.

Lack of Authority in Agent

An agent who purports to make a contract on behalf of a principal, but who in fact has no authority to do so, is liable to the other party. The theory is that the agent has warranted to the third party that he has the requisite authority. The principal is not liable in the absence of apparent authority or ratification. But the agent does not warrant that the principal has capacity. Thus, an agent for a minor is not liable on a contract that the minor later disavows unless the agent expressly warranted that the principal had attained his majority. In short, the implied warranty is that the agent has authority to make a deal, not that the principal will necessarily comply with the contract once the deal is made.

Agent Acting on Own Account

An agent will be liable on contracts made in a personal capacity—for instance, when the agent personally guarantees repayment of a debt. The agent's intention to be personally liable is often difficult to determine on the basis of his signature on a contract. Generally, a person signing a contract can avoid personal liability only by showing that he was in fact signing as an agent. If the contract is signed "Jones, Agent," Jones can introduce evidence to show that there was never an intention to hold him personally liable. But if he signed "Jones" and neither his agency nor the principal's name is included, he will be personally liable. This can be troublesome to agents who routinely indorse checks and notes. There are special rules governing these situations, which are discussed in Chapter 25 dealing with commercial paper.

Termination of Agency

The agency relationship is not permanent. Either by action of the parties or by law, the relationship will eventually terminate.

By Act of the Parties

Certainly the parties to an agency contract can terminate the agreement. As with the creation of the relationship, the agreement may be terminated either expressly or implicitly.

Express Termination

Many agreements contain specified circumstances whose occurrence signals the end of the agency. The most obvious of these circumstances is the expiration of a fixed period of time ("agency to terminate at the end of three months" or "on midnight, December 31"). An agreement may also terminate on the accomplishment of a specified act ("on the sale of the house") or following a specific event ("at the conclusion of the last horse race").

revocation

The principal's unilateral termination of the agency relationship.

renunciation of agency

The agent's unilateral termination of the agency relationship.

Mutual consent between the parties will end the agency. Moreover, the principal may revoke the agency or the agent may renounce it; such a **revocation** or **renunciation of agency** would be an express termination. Even a contract that states the agreement is irrevocable will not be binding, although it can be the basis for a damage suit against the one who breached the agreement by revoking or renouncing it. As with any contract, a person has the *power* to breach, even in absence of the *right* to do so. If the agency is coupled with an interest, however, so that the authority to act is given to secure an interest that the agent has in the subject matter of the agency, then the principal lacks the power to revoke the agreement.

Implied Termination

There are a number of other circumstances that will spell the end of the relationship by implication. Unspecified events or changes in business conditions or the value of the subject matter of the agency might lead to a reasonable inference that the agency should be terminated or suspended; for example, the principal desires the agent to buy silver but the silver market unexpectedly rises and silver doubles in price overnight. Other circumstances that end the agency include disloyalty of the agent (e.g., he accepts an appointment that is adverse to his first principal or embezzles from the principal), bankruptcy of the agent or of the principal, the outbreak of war (if it is reasonable to infer that the principal, knowing of the war, would not want the agent to continue to exercise authority), and a change in the law that makes a continued carrying out of the task illegal or seriously interferes with it.

By Operation of Law

Aside from the express termination (by agreement of both or upon the insistence of one), or the necessary or reasonable inferences that can be drawn from their agreements, the law voids agencies under certain circumstances. The most frequent termination by operation of law is the death of a principal or an agent. The death of an agent also terminates the authority of subagents he has appointed, unless the principal has expressly consented to the continuing validity of their appointment. Similarly, if the agent or principal loses capacity to enter into an agency relationship, it is suspended or terminated. The agency terminates if its purpose becomes illegal.

Even though authority has terminated, whether by action of the parties or operation of law, the principal may still be subject to liability. Apparent authority in many instances will still exist; this is called **lingering authority**. It is imperative for a principal on termination of authority to notify all those who may still be in a position to deal with the agent. The only exceptions to this requirement are when termination is effected by death, loss of the principal's capacity, or an event that would make it impossible to carry out the object of the agency.

lingering authority

Authority that arises where actual authority has been terminated, but third parties are led by the principal's negligence to believe it still exists.

Key Takeaway

A person is always liable for her own torts, so an agent who commits a tort is liable; if the tort was in the scope of employment the principal is liable too. Unless the principal put the agent up to committing the tort, the agent will have to reimburse the principal. An agent is not generally liable for contracts made; the principal is liable. But the agent will be liable if he is undisclosed or partially disclosed, if the agent lacks authority or exceeds it, or, of course, if the agent entered into the contract in a personal capacity.

Agencies terminate expressly or impliedly or by operation of law. An agency terminates expressly by the terms of the agreement or mutual consent, or by the principal's revocation or the agent's renunciation. An agency terminates impliedly by any number of circumstances in which it is reasonable to assume one or both of the parties would not want the relationship to continue. An agency will terminate by operation of law when one or the other party dies or becomes incompetent, or if the object of the agency becomes illegal. However, an agent may have apparent lingering authority, so the principal, upon termination of the agency, should notify those who might deal with the agent that the relationship is severed.

Exercises

1. Pauline, the owner of a large bakery business, wishes to expand her facilities by purchasing the adjacent property. She engages Alice as an agent to negotiate the deal with the property owner but instructs her not to tell the property owner that she—Alice—is acting as an agent because Pauline is concerned that the property owner would demand a high price. A reasonable contract is made. When the economy sours, Pauline decides not to expand and cancels the plan. Who is liable for the breach?
2. Peter, the principal, instructs his agent, Alice, to tour England and purchase antique dining room furniture for Peter's store. Alice buys an antique bed set. Who is liable, Peter or Alice? Suppose the seller did not know of the limit on Alice's authority and sells the bed set to Alice in good faith. What happens when Peter discovers he owes the seller for the set?
3. Under what circumstances will the agency terminate expressly?

4. Agent is hired by Principal to sell a new drug, Phobbot. Six months later, as it becomes apparent that Phobbot has nasty side effects (including death), the Food and Drug Administration orders the drug pulled from the shelves. Agent's agency is terminated; what terminology is appropriate to describe how?
5. Principal engages Agent to buy lumber, and in that capacity Agent deals with several large timber owners. Agent's contract ends on July 31; on August 1, Agent buys $150,000 worth of lumber from a seller with whom he had dealt previously on Principal's behalf. Who is liable and why?

39.4 Cases

Implied Authority

Kanavos v. Hancock Bank & Trust Company

439 N.E.2d 311 (Mass. 1982)

KASS, J.

At the close of the plaintiff's evidence, the defendant moved for a directed verdict, which the trial judge allowed. The judge's reason for so doing was that the plaintiff, in his contract action, failed to introduce sufficient evidence tending to prove that the bank officer who made the agreement with which the plaintiff sought to charge the bank had any authority to make it. Upon review of the record we are of opinion that there was evidence which, if believed, warranted a finding that the bank officer had the requisite authority or that the bank officer had apparent authority to make the agreement in controversy. We therefore reverse the judgment.

For approximately ten years prior to 1975, Harold Kanavos and his brother borrowed money on at least twenty occasions from the Hancock Bank & Trust Company (the Bank), and, during that period, the loan officer with whom Kanavos always dealt was James M. Brown. The aggregate loans made by the Bank to Kanavos at any given time went as high as $800,000.

Over that same decade, Brown's responsibilities at the Bank grew, and he had become executive vice-president. Brown was also the chief loan officer for the Bank, which had fourteen or fifteen branches in addition to its head office. Physically, Brown's office was at the head office, toward the rear of the main banking floor, opposite the office of the president—whose name was Kelley. Often Brown would tell Kanavos that he had to check an aspect of a loan transaction with Kelley, but Kelley always backed Brown up on those occasions. * * *

[The plaintiff, Harold Kanavos, entered into an agreement with the defendant Bank whereby stock owned by the Kanavos brothers was sold to the Bank and the plaintiff was given an option to repurchase the stock. Kanavos' suit against the Bank was based on an amendment to the agreement offered by Brown.]

Kanavos was never permitted to introduce in evidence the terms of the offer Brown made. That offer was contained in a writing, dated July 16, 1976, on bank letterhead, which read as follows: "This letter is to confirm our conversation regarding your option to re-purchase the subject property. In lieu of your not exercising your option, we agree to pay you $40,000 representing a commission upon our sale of the subject property, and in addition, will give you the option to match the price of sale of said property to extend for a 60-day period from the time our offer is received." Brown signed the letter as executive vice-president. The basis of exclusion was that the plaintiff had not established the authority of Brown to make with Kanavos the arrangement memorialized in the July 16, 1976, letter.

Whether Brown's job description impliedly authorized the right of last refusal or cash payment modification is a question of how, in the circumstances, a person in Brown's position could reasonably interpret his authority. Whether Brown had apparent authority to make the July 16, 1976, modification is a question of how, in the circumstances, a third person, e.g., a customer of the Bank such as Kanavos, would reasonably interpret Brown's authority in light of the manifestations of his principal, the Bank.

Titles of office generally do not establish apparent authority. Brown's status as executive vice-president was not, therefore, a badge of apparent authority to modify agreements to which the Bank was a party.

Trappings of office, e.g., office and furnishing, private secretary, while they may have some tendency to suggest executive responsibility, do not without other evidence provide a basis for finding apparent authority. Apparent authority is drawn from a variety of circumstances. Thus, in *Federal Nat. Bank v. O'Connell* * * * (1940), it was held apparent authority could be found because an officer who was a director, vice-president and treasurer took an active part in directing the affairs of the bank in question and was seen by third parties talking with customers and negotiating with them. In *Costonis v. Medford Housing Authy.* * * * (1961), the executive director of a public housing authority was held to have apparent authority to vary specifications on the basis of the cumulative effect of what he had done and what the authority appeared to permit him to do.

In the instant case there was evidence of the following variety of circumstances: Brown's title of executive vice-president; the location of his office opposite the president; his frequent communications with the president; the long course of dealing and negotiations; the encouragement of Kanavos by the president to deal with Brown; the earlier amendment of the agreement by Brown on behalf of the Bank on material points, namely the price to be paid by the Bank for the shares and the repurchase price; the size of the Bank (fourteen or fifteen branches in addition to the main office); the secondary, rather than fundamental, nature of the change in the terms of the agreement now repudiated by the Bank, measured against the context of the overall transaction; and Brown's broad operating authority * * * all these added together would support a finding of apparent authority. When a corporate officer, as here, is allowed to exercise general executive responsibilities, the "public expectation is that the corporation should be bound to engagements made on its behalf by those who presume to have, and convincingly appear to have, the power to agree." [Citation] This principle does not apply, of course, where in the business context, the requirement of specific authority is presumed, e.g., the sale of a major asset by a corporation or a transaction, which by its nature commits the corporation to an obligation outside the scope of its usual activity. The modification agreement signed by Brown and dated July 16, 1976, should have been admitted in evidence, and a verdict should not have been directed.

Judgment reversed.

Case Questions

1. Why are "titles of office" insufficient to establish apparent authority?
2. Why are "trappings of office" insufficient to establish apparent authority?
3. What is the relationship between apparent authority and estoppel? Who is estopped to do what, and why?

Employer's Liability for Employee's Intentional Torts: Scope of Employment

Lyon v. Carey

533 F.2d 649 (Cir. Ct. App. DC 1976)

McMillan, J.:

Corene Antoinette Lyon, plaintiff, recovered a $33,000.00 verdict [about $160,000 in 2016 dollars] in the United States District Court for the District of Columbia before Judge Barrington T. Parker and a jury, against the corporate defendants, George's Radio and Television Company, Inc., and Pep Line Trucking Company, Inc. The suit for damages arose out of an assault, including rape, committed with a knife and other weapons upon the plaintiff on May 9, 1972, by Michael Carey, a nineteen-year-old deliveryman for Pep Line Trucking Company, Inc. Three months after the trial, Judge Parker set aside the verdict and rendered judgment for both defendants notwithstanding the verdict. Plaintiff appealed. * * *

Although the assault was perhaps at the outer bounds of respondeat superior, the case was properly one for the jury. Whether the assault in this case was the outgrowth of a job-related controversy or simply a personal adventure of the deliveryman, was a question for the jury. This was the import of the trial judge's instructions. The verdict as to Pep Line should not have been disturbed.

Irene Lyon bought a mattress and springs for her bed from the defendant George's Radio and Television Company, Inc. The merchandise was to be delivered on May 9, 1972. Irene Lyon had to be at work and the plaintiff [Irene's sister] Corene Lyon, had agreed to wait in her sister's apartment to receive the delivery.

A C.O.D. balance of $13.24 was due on the merchandise, and Irene Lyon had left a check for $13.24 to cover that balance. Plaintiff had been requested by her sister to "wait until the mattress and the springs came and to check and make sure they were okay."

Plaintiff, fully clothed, answered the door. Her description of what happened is sufficiently brief and unqualified that it will bear repeating in full. She testified, without objection, as follows:

> *I went to the door, and I looked in the peephole, and I asked who was there. The young man told me he was a delivery man from George's. He showed me a receipt, and it said, "George's." He said he [needed cash on delivery—COD], so I let him in, and I told him to bring the mattress upstairs and he said, "No," that he wasn't going to lug them upstairs, and he wanted the COD first, and I told him I wanted to see the mattress and box springs to make sure they were okay, and he said no, he wasn't going to lug them upstairs [until he got the check].*
>
> *So this went back and forwards and so he was getting angry, and I told him to wait right here while I go get the COD. I went to the bedroom to get the check, and I picked it up, and I turned around and he was right there.*
>
> *And then I was giving him the check and then he told me that his boss told him not to accept a check, that he wanted cash money, and that if I didn't give him cash money, he was going to take it on my ass, and he told me that he was no delivery man, he was a rapist and then he threw me on the bed.*
>
> *[The Court] Talk louder, young lady, the jury can't hear you.*
>
> *[The witness] And then he threw me on the bed, and he had a knife to my throat.*
>
> *[Plaintiff's attorney] Then what happened?*
>
> *And then he raped me.*

Plaintiff's pre-trial deposition was a part of the record on appeal, and it shows that Carey raped plaintiff at knife point; that then he chased her all over the apartment with a knife and scissors and cut plaintiff in numerous places on her face and body, beat and otherwise attacked her. All of the physical injury other than the rape occurred after rather than before the rape had been accomplished. * * *

[Carey was convicted of rape and sent to prison. The court determined that George's was properly dismissed because Pep Line, Carey's employer, was an independent contractor over which George's had no control.]

The principal question, therefore, is whether the evidence discloses any other basis upon which a jury could reasonably find Pep Line, the employer of Carey, liable for the assault.

Michael Carey was in the employment of the defendant Pep Line as a deliveryman. He was authorized to make the delivery of the mattress and springs plaintiff's sister had bought. He gained access to the apartment only upon a showing of the delivery receipt for the merchandise. His employment contemplated that he visit and enter that particular apartment. Though the apartment was not owned by nor in the control of his employer, it was nevertheless a place he was expected by his employer to enter.

After Carey entered, under the credentials of his employment and the delivery receipt, a dispute arose naturally and immediately between him and the plaintiff about two items of great significance in connection with his job. These items were the request of the plaintiff, the customer's agent, to inspect the mattress and springs before payment (which would require their being brought upstairs before the payment was made), and Carey's insistence on getting cash rather than a check.

The dispute arose out of the very transaction which had brought Carey to the premises, and, according to the plaintiff's evidence, out of the employer's instructions to get cash only before delivery.

On the face of things, Pep Line Trucking Company, Inc. is liable, under two previous decisions of the Court of Appeals for the District of Columbia Circuit. [Citation (1953)] held a taxi owner liable for damages (including a broken leg) sustained by a customer who had been run over by the taxi in pursuit of a dispute between the driver and the customer about a fare. [Citation (1939)], held a restaurant owner liable to a restaurant patron who was beaten with a stick by a restaurant employee, after a disagreement over the service. The theory was that:

> *It is well established that an employer may be held responsible in tort for assaults committed by an employee while he is acting within the scope of his employment, even though he may act wantonly and contrary to his employer's instructions. [Citations] ". . . . having placed [the employee] in charge and committed the management of the business to his care, defendants may not escape liability either on the ground of his infirmity of temperament or because, under the influence of passion aroused by plaintiff's threat to report the circumstances, he went beyond the ordinary line of duty and inflicted the injury shown in this case. [Citations]"*

Munick v. City of Durham ([Citation], Supreme Court of North Carolina, 1921), though not a binding precedent, is informative and does show that the theory of liability advanced by the plaintiff is by no means recent in origin. The plaintiff, Munick, a Russian born Jew, testified that he went to the Durham, North Carolina city water company office on April 17, 1919, and offered to pay his bill with "three paper dollars, one silver dollar, and fifty cents in pennies." The pennies were in a roll "like the bank fixes them." The clerk gave a receipt and the plaintiff prepared to leave the office. The office manager came into the room, saw the clerk counting the pennies, became enraged at the situation, shoved the pennies onto the floor and ordered Munick to pick them up. Bolton, the manager, "locked the front door and took me by the jacket and called me 'God damned Jew,' and said, 'I want only bills.' I did not say anything and he hit me in the face. I did not resist, and the door was locked and I could not get out. ... " With the door locked, Bolton then repeatedly choked and beat the plaintiff, finally extracted a bill in place of the pennies, and ordered him off the premises with injuries including finger marks on his neck that could be seen for eight or ten days. Bolton was convicted of unlawful assault [but the case against the water company was dismissed].

The North Carolina Supreme Court (Clark, C. J.) reversed the trial court's dismissal and held that the case should have gone to the jury. The court * * * said [Citation]:

*"It is now fully established that corporations may be held liable for negligent and malicious torts, and that responsibility will be imputed whenever such wrongs are committed by their employees and agents in the course of their employment and within its scope * * * in many of the cases, and in reliable textbooks * * * 'course of employment' is stated and considered as sufficiently inclusive; but, whether the one or the other descriptive term is used, they have the same significance in importing liability on the part of the principal when the agent is engaged in the work that its principal has employed or directed him to do and * * * in the effort to accomplish it. When such conduct comes within the description that constitutes an actionable wrong, the corporation principal, as in other cases of principal and agent, is liable not only for 'the act itself, but for the ways and means employed in the performance thereof.'"*

In 1 Thompson, Negligence, s 554, it is pointed out that, unless the above principle is maintained:

"It will always be more safe and profitable for a man to conduct his business vicariously than in his own person. He would escape liability for the consequences of many acts connected with his business, springing from the imperfections of human nature, because done by another, for which he would be responsible if done by himself. Meanwhile, the public, obliged to deal or come in contact with his agent, for injuries done by them must be left wholly without redress. He might delegate to persons pecuniarily irresponsible the care of large factories, of extensive mines, of ships at sea, or of railroad trains on land, and these persons, by the use of the extensive power thus committed to them, might inflict wanton and malicious injuries on third persons, without other restraint than that which springs from the imperfect execution of the criminal laws. A doctrine so fruitful of mischief could not long stand unshaken in an enlightened jurisprudence.' This court has often held the master liable, even if the agent was willful, provided it was committed in the course of his employment. [Citation]"

"The act of a servant done to effect some independent purpose of his own and not with reference to the service in which he is employed, or while he is acting as his own master for the time being, is not within the scope of his employment so as to render the master liable therefor. In these circumstances the servant alone is liable for the injury inflicted." [Citation]. ..." The general idea is that the employee at the time of doing the wrongful act, in order to fix liability on the employer, must have been acting in behalf of the latter and not on his own account [Citation]."

The principal physical (as opposed to psychic) damage to the plaintiff is a number of disfiguring knife wounds on her head, face, arms, breasts and body. If the instrumentalities of assault had not included rape, the case would provoke no particular curiosity nor interest because it comes within all the classic requirements for recovery against the master. The verdict is not attacked as excessive, and could not be excessive in light of the physical injuries inflicted.

It may be suggested that [some of the cases discussed] are distinguishable because in each of those cases the plaintiff was a business visitor on the defendant's "premises." * * * Home delivery customers are usually in their homes, sometimes alone; and deliveries of merchandise may expose householders to one-on-one confrontations with deliverymen. It would be a strange rule indeed which, while allowing recovery for assaults committed in "the store," would deny a master's liability for an assault committed on a lone woman in her own home, by a deliveryman required by his job to enter the home. * * *

If, as in [one case discussed], the assault was not motivated or triggered off by anything in the employment activity but was the result of only propinquity and lust, there should be no liability. However, if the assault, sexual or otherwise, was triggered off or motivated or occasioned by a dispute over the conduct then and there of the employer's business, then the employer should be liable.

It is, then, a question of fact for the trier of fact, rather than a question of law for the court, whether the assault stemmed from purely and solely personal sources or arose out of the conduct of the employer's business; and the trial judge so instructed the jury.

It follows that, under existing decisions of the District of Columbia Circuit, plaintiff has made out a case for the jury against Pep Line Trucking, Inc. unless the sexual character of one phase of the assault bars her from recovery for damages from all phases of the assault.

We face, then, this question: Should the entire case be taken from the jury because, instead of a rod of wood (as in [one case]), in addition to weapons of steel (as in [one case, a knife]); and in addition to his hands (as in [the third case, regarding the dispute about the pennies]), Carey also employed a sexual weapon, a rod of flesh and blood in the pursuit of a job-related controversy?

The answer is, No. It is a jury's job to decide how much of plaintiff's story to believe, and how much if any of the damages were caused by actions, including sexual assault, which stemmed from job-related sources rather than from purely personal origins. * * *

The judgment is affirmed as to the defendant George's and reversed as to the defendant Pep Line Trucking Company, Inc.

Case Questions

1. What triggered the dispute here?
2. The court observes, "On the face of things, Pep Line Trucking Company, Inc. is liable." But there are two issues that give the court cause for more explanation. (1) Why does the court discuss the point that the assault did not occur on the employer's premises? (2) Why does the court mention that the knife assault happened *after* the rape?
3. It is difficult to imagine that a sexual assault could be anything other than some "purely and solely personal" gratification, unrelated to the employer's business. How did the court address this?
4. What is the controlling rule of law as to the employer's liability for intentional torts here?
5. What does the court mean when it says, "the assault was perhaps at the outer bounds of respondeat superior"?
6. Would the jury think about who had the "deep pocket" here? Who did have it?

Employer's Liability for Employee's Intentional Torts: Scope of Employment

Cockrell v. Pearl River Valley Water Supply Dist.

865 So.2d 357 (Miss. 2004)

The Pearl River Valley Water Supply District ("District") was granted summary judgment pursuant to the Mississippi Tort Claims Act (MTCA) dismissing with prejudice all claims asserted against it by Sandra Cockrell. Cockrell appeals the ruling of the circuit court citing numerous errors. Finding the motion for summary judgment was properly granted in favor of the District, this Court affirms the final judgment entered by the Circuit Court of Rankin County.

Facts and Proceedings in the Trial Court

On June 28, 1998, Sandra Cockrell was arrested for suspicion of driving under the influence of alcohol by Officer Joey James who was employed as a security patrol officer with the Reservoir Patrol of the Pearl River Valley Water Supply District. Officer James then transported Cockrell to the Reservoir Patrol office and administered an intoxilyzer test. The results of the test are not before us; however, we do know that after the test was administered, Officer James apologized to Cockrell for arresting her, and he assured her that he would prepare her paperwork so that she would not have to spend much time in jail. As they were leaving the Reservoir Patrol office, Officer James began asking Cockrell personal questions such as where she lived, whether she was dating anyone and if she had a boyfriend. Officer James then asked Cockrell for her cell phone number so that he could call and check on her. As they were approaching his patrol car for the trip to the Rankin County jail, Officer James informed Cockrell that she should be wearing handcuffs; however, he did not handcuff Cockrell, and he allowed her to ride in the front seat of the patrol car with him. In route to the jail, Cockrell became emotional and started crying. As she was fixing her makeup using the mirror on the sun visor, Officer James pulled his patrol car into a church parking lot and parked the car. He then pulled Cockrell towards him in an embrace and began stroking her back and hair telling her that things would be fine. Cockrell told Officer James to release her, but he continued to embrace her for approximately five minutes before continuing on to the jail.

On June 30, 1998, Cockrell returned to the Reservoir Patrol office to retrieve her driver's license. Officer James called Cockrell into his office and discussed her DUI charge with her. As she was leaving, Officer James grabbed her from behind, turned her around, pinned both of her arms behind her and pulled her to his chest. When Officer James bent down to kiss her, she ducked her head, thus causing Officer James to instead kiss her forehead. When Officer James finally released Cockrell, she ran out of the door and drove away. [Subsequently, Cockrell's attorney threatened civil suit against Patrol; James was fired in October 1998.]

On September 22, 1999, Cockrell filed a complaint for damages against the District alleging that on the nights of June 28 and June 30, 1998, Officer James was acting within the course and scope of his employment with the District and that he acted with reckless disregard for her emotional well-being and safety. * * * On April 2, 2002, the District filed its motion for summary judgment alleging that there was no genuine issue of material fact regarding Cockrell's claim of liability. The motion alleged that the conduct described by Cockrell was outside the course and scope of Officer James's public employment as he was intending to satisfy his lustful urges. Cockrell responded to the motion arguing that the misconduct did occur in the course and scope of Officer James's employment with the District and also that the misconduct did not reach the level of a criminal offense such that the District could be found not liable under the MTCA.

The trial court entered a final judgment granting the District's motion for summary judgment and dismissing the complaint with prejudice. The trial court found that the District could not be held liable under the MTCA for the conduct of Officer James which was both criminal and outside the course and scope of his employment. Cockrell * * * appeal[ed].

Discussion

Summary judgment is granted in cases where there is "no genuine issue as to any material fact and that the moving party is entitled to a judgment as a matter of law." * * *

Cockrell contends there is a genuine issue of material of fact regarding whether Officer James was acting in the course and scope of his employment with the District during the incidents which occurred on the nights of June 28 and June 30, 1998. Cockrell argues Officer James's conduct, although inappropriate, did not rise to the level of criminal conduct. Cockrell contends Officer James's action of hugging Cockrell was similar to an officer consoling a victim of a crime. Cockrell does admit that Officer James's action of kissing her is more difficult to view as within the course and scope of his employment. * * *

The District argues that although Officer James acted within the course and scope of his duties when he arrested Cockrell, his later conduct, which was intended to satisfy his lustful desires, was outside the scope of his employment with it. * * *

"Mississippi law provides that an activity must be in furtherance of the employer's business to be within the scope and course of employment." [Citation] To be within the course and scope of employment, an activity must carry out the employer's purpose of the employment or be in furtherance of the employer's business. [Citations] Therefore, if an employee steps outside his employer's business for some reason which is not related to his employment, the relationship between the employee and the employer "is temporarily suspended and this is so 'no matter how short the time and the [employer] is not liable for [the employee's] acts during such time.'" "An employee's personal unsanctioned recreational endeavors are beyond the course and scope of his employment." [Citation]

[In one case cited,] Officer Kerry Collins, a Jackson Police officer, was on duty when he came upon the parked car of L.T., a minor, and her boyfriend, who were about to engage in sexual activity. [Citation] Officer Collins instructed L.T. to take her boyfriend home, and he would follow her to make sure she followed his orders. After L.T. dropped off her boyfriend, Officer Collins continued to follow her until he pulled L.T. over. Officer Collins then instructed L.T. to follow him to his apartment or else he would inform L.T.'s parents of her activities. L.T. followed Officer Collins to his apartment where they engaged in sexual activity. Upon returning home, L.T. told her parents everything that had happened. L.T. and her parents filed suit against Officer Collins, the City of Jackson and the Westwood Apartments, where Officer Collins lived rent free in return for his services as a security guard. * * * The district court granted summary judgment in favor of the City finding that Officer Collins acted outside the course and scope of his employment with the Jackson Police Department. [Citation]

In [Citation] the plaintiff sued the Archdiocese of New Orleans for damages that allegedly resulted from his sexual molestation by a Catholic priest. The Fifth Circuit found that the priest was not acting within the course and scope of his employment. The Fifth Circuit held that "smoking marijuana and engaging in sexual acts with minor boys" in no way furthered the interests of his employer.

The Southern District of Mississippi and the Fifth Circuit, applying Mississippi law, have held that sexual misconduct falls outside the course and scope of employment. There is no question that Officer James was within the course and scope of his employment when he first stopped Cockrell for suspicion of driving under the influence of alcohol. However, when Officer James diverted from his employment for personal reasons, he was no longer acting in the furtherance of his employer's interests. * * * Therefore, the District cannot be held liable * * * for the misconduct of Officer James which occurred outside the course and scope of his employment.

Affirmed.

Case Questions

1. How can this case and *Lyon v. Carey* (Section 4) be reconciled? Both involve an agent's unacceptable behavior—assault—but in *Lyon* the agent's actions were imputed to the principal, and in *Cockrell* the agent's actions were not imputed to the principal.
2. What is the controlling rule of law governing the principal's liability for the agent's actions?
3. The law governing the liability of principals for acts of their agents is well settled. Thus the cases turn on the facts. Who decides what the facts are in a lawsuit?

39.5 Summary and Exercises

Summary

A contract made by an agent on behalf of the principal legally binds the principal. Three types of authority may bind the principal: (1) express authority—that which is actually given and spelled out, (2) implied authority—that which may fairly be inferred from the parties' relationship and which is incidental to the agent's express authority, and (3) apparent authority—that which reasonably appears to a third party under the circumstances to have been given by the principal. Even in the absence of authority, a principal may ratify the agent's acts.

The principal may be liable for tortious acts of the agent but except under certain regulatory statutes may not be held criminally liable for criminal acts of agents not prompted by the principal. Under the doctrine of respondeat superior, a principal is generally liable for acts by a servant within the scope of employment. A principal usually will not be held liable for acts of nonservant agents that cause physical damage, although he will be held liable for nonphysical torts, such as misrepresentation. The principal will not be held liable for tortious acts of independent contractors, although the principal may be liable for injuries resulting from his failure to act in situations in which he was not legally permitted to delegate a duty to act. Whenever an agent is acting to further the principal's business interests, the principal will be held vicariously liable for the agent's intentional torts. What constitutes scope of employment is not easy to determine; the modern trend is to hold a principal liable for the conduct of an agent if it was foreseeable that the agent might act as he did.

Most states have special rules of vicarious liability for special situations; for example, liability of an automobile owner for use by another. Spouses are not vicariously liable for each other, nor are parents for children, except for failing to control children known to be dangerous.

In general, an agent is not personally liable on contracts he has signed on behalf of a principal. This general rule has several exceptions recognized in most states: (1) when the agent is serving an undisclosed or partially disclosed principal, (2) when the agent lacks authority or exceeds his authority, and (3) if the agent entered into the contract in a personal capacity.

The agency relationship may be terminated by mutual consent, by express agreement of the parties that the agency will end at a certain time or on the occurrence of a certain event, or by an implied agreement arising out of the circumstances in each case. The agency may also be unilaterally revoked by the principal—unless the agency is coupled with an interest—or renounced by the agent. Finally, the agency will terminate by operation of law under certain circumstances, such as death of the principal or agent.

Exercises

1. Parke-Bernet Galleries, acting as agent for an undisclosed principal, sold a painting to Weisz. Weisz later discovered that the painting was a forgery and sued Parke-Bernet for breach of contract. In defense, Parke-Bernet argued that as a general rule, agents are not liable on contracts made for principals. Is this a good defense? Explain.
2. Lynch was the loan officer at First Bank. Patterson applied to borrow $25,000. Bank policy required that Lynch obtain a loan guaranty from Patterson's employer, a milk company. The manager of the milk company visited the bank and signed a guaranty on behalf of the company. The last paragraph of the guaranty stated, "This guaranty is signed by an officer having legal right to bind the company through authorization of the Board of Directors." Should Lynch be satisfied with this guaranty? Would he be satisfied if the president of the milk company, who was also a director, affirmed that the manager had authority to sign the guaranty? Explain.
3. Ralph owned a retail meat market. Ralph's agent Sam, without authority but purporting to act on Ralph's behalf, borrowed $7,500 from Ted. Although he never received the money, Ralph repaid $700 of the alleged loan and promised to repay the rest. If Sam had no authority to make the loan, is Ralph liable? Why?
4. A guest arrived early one morning at the Hotel Ohio. Clemens, a person in the hotel office who appeared to be in charge, walked behind the counter, registered the guest, gave him a key, and took him to his room. The guest also checked valuables (a diamond pin and money) with Clemens, who signed a receipt on behalf of the hotel. Clemens in fact was a roomer at the hotel, not an employee, and had no authority to act on behalf of the hotel. When Clemens absconded with the valuables, the guest sued the hotel. Is the hotel liable? Why?
5. A professional basketball player punched an opposing player in the face during the course of a game. The opponent, who was seriously injured, sued the owner of the team for damages.

A jury awarded the player $222,000 [about $800,000 in 2010 dollars] for medical expenses, $200,000 [$700,000] for physical pain, $275,000 [$963,000] for mental anguish, $1,000,000 [$3.5 million] for lost earnings, and $1,500,000 [$5.2 million] in punitive damages (which was $500,000 more than requested by the player). The jury also awarded $50,000 [$150,000] to the player's wife for loss of companionship. If we assume that the player who threw the punch acted out of personal anger and had no intention to further the business, how could the damage award against his principal be legally justified?

6. A doctor in a University of Chicago hospital seriously assaulted a patient in an examining room. The patient sued the hospital on the theory that the doctor was an agent or employee of the hospital and the assault occurred within the hospital. Is the hospital liable for the acts of its agent? Why?
7. Hector was employed by a machine shop. One day he made a delivery for his employer and proceeded back to the shop. When he was four miles from the shop and on the road where it was located, he turned left onto another road to visit a friend. The friend lived five miles off the turnoff. On the way to the friend's house, Hector caused an accident. The injured person sued Hector's employer. Is the employer liable? Discuss.
8. A fourteen-year-old boy, who had no driver's license, took his parents' car without permission and caused an automobile accident. A person injured in the accident sued the boy's parents under the relevant state's Parental Responsibility Law (mentioned in Section 2). Are the parents liable? Discuss.
9. In the past decades the Catholic Church has paid out hundreds of millions of dollars in damage awards to people—mostly men—who claimed that when they were boys and teenagers they were sexually abused by their local parish priests, often on Church premises. That is, the men claimed they had been victims of child rape. Obviously, such behavior is antithetical to any reasonable standard of clergy behavior: the priests could not have been in the scope of employment. How is the Church liable?

Self-Test Questions

1. Authority that legally may bind the principal includes
   a. implied authority
   b. express authority
   c. apparent authority
   d. all of the above
2. As a general rule, a principal is not
   a. liable for tortious acts of an agent, even when the principal is negligent
   b. liable for acts of a servant within the scope of employment
   c. criminally liable for acts of the agent
   d. liable for nondelegable duties performed by independent contractors
3. An agent may be held personally liable on contracts signed on behalf of a principal when
   a. the agent is serving an undisclosed or partially disclosed principal
   b. the agent exceeds his authority
   c. the agent entered into the contract in a personal capacity
   d. all of the above are true
4. An agency relationship may be terminated by
   a. an implied agreement arising out of the circumstances
   b. mutual consent of parties
   c. death of the principal or agent
   d. all of the above
5. The principal's liability for the agent's acts of which the principal had no knowledge or intention to commit is called

a. contract liability
b. implied liability
c. respondeat superior
d. all of the above

Self-Test Answers

1. d
2. c
3. d
4. c
5. b

Endnotes

1. *Allen A. Funt Productions, Inc. v. Chemical Bank*, 405 N.Y.S.2d 94 (1978).
2. Allen Funt (1914–99) was an American television producer, director, and writer, best known as the creator and host of *Candid Camera* from the 1940s to 1980s, which was broadcast as either a regular show or a series of specials. Its most notable run was from 1960 to 1967 on CBS.
3. *G. H. Mumm Champagne v. Eastern Wine Corp.*, 52 F.Supp. 167 (S.D.N.Y. 1943).
4. *Meggs v. Central Supply Co.*, 307 N.E.2d 288 (Ind. App. 1974).
5. *Joel v. Morrison*, 6 Carrington & Payne 501.
6. *Dixon v. Phillips*, 217 S.E.2d 331 (Ga. 1975).
7. O.W. Holmes, *Agency*, 4 Harvard Law Rev. 353 (1890–91).
8. Charles Dickens, *Oliver Twist*, (London: 1838), chap 51.
9. Ill. Rev. Stat. (2005), chapter 70, paragraph 51. http://law.justia.com/illinois/codes/2005/chapter57/2045.html.

CHAPTER 40

Partnerships: General Characteristics and Formation

Learning Objectives

After reading this chapter, you should understand the following:

1. The importance of partnership and the present status of partnership law.
2. The extent to which a partnership is an entity.
3. The tests that determine whether a partnership exists.
4. Partnership by estoppel.
5. Partnership formation.

40.1 Introduction to Partnerships and Entity Theory

Learning Objectives

1. Describe the importance of partnership.
2. Understand partnership history.
3. Identify the entity characteristics of partnerships.

Importance of Partnership Law

It would be difficult to conceive of a complex society that did not operate its businesses through organizations. In this chapter we study partnerships, limited partnerships, and limited liability companies, and we touch on joint ventures and business trusts.

When two or more people form their own business or professional practice, they usually consider becoming partners. Partnership law defines a **partnership** as "the association of two or more persons to carry on as co-owners a business for profit . . . whether or not the persons intend to form a partnership."[1] Back in 2011, there were more than three million business firms in the United States as partnerships (see Table 40.1, showing data to 2006), and partnerships are a common form of organization among accountants, lawyers, doctors, and other professionals. When we use the word *partnership*, we are referring to the *general business partnership*. There are also limited partnerships and limited liability partnerships, which are discussed in Chapter 42.

partnership

Two or more persons carrying on a business as co-owners for profit.

TABLE 40.1 Selected Data: Number of U.S. Partnerships, Limited Partnerships, and Limited Liability Companies

	2003	2004	2005	2006
Total number of active partnerships	2,375,375	2,546,877	2,763,625	2,947,116
Number of partners	14,108,458	15,556,553	16,211,908	16,727,803
Number of limited partnerships	378,921	402,238	413,712	432,550
Number of partners	6,262,103	7,023,921	6,946,986	6,738,737
Number of limited liability companies	1,091,502	1,270,236	1,465,223	1,630,161
Number of partners	4,226,099	4,949,808	5,640,146	6,361,958

Source: IRS, http://www.irs.gov/pub/irs-soi/09sprbul.pdf.

Partnerships are also popular as investment vehicles. Partnership law and tax law permit an investor to put capital into a limited partnership and realize tax benefits without liability for the acts of the general partners.

Even if you do not plan to work within a partnership, it can be important to understand the law that governs it. Why? Because it is possible to become someone's partner without intending to or even realizing that a partnership has been created. Knowledge of the law can help you avoid partnership liability.

History of Partnership Law

Through the Twentieth Century

Partnership is an ancient form of business enterprise, and special laws governing partnerships date as far back as 2300 BC, when the Code of Hammurabi explicitly regulated the relations between partners. Partnership was an important part of Roman law, and it played a significant role in the law merchant, the international commercial law of the Middle Ages.

In the nineteenth century, in both England and the United States, partnership was a popular vehicle for business enterprise. But the law governing it was jumbled. Common-law principles were mixed with equitable standards, and the result was considerable confusion. Parliament moved to reduce the uncertainty by adopting the Partnership Act of 1890, but codification took longer in the United States. The Commissioners on Uniform State Laws undertook the task at the turn of the twentieth century. The Uniform Partnership Act (UPA), completed in 1914, and the Uniform Limited Partnership Act (ULPA), completed in 1916, were the basis of partnership law for many decades. UPA and ULPA were adopted by all states except Louisiana.

The Current State of Partnership Law

Despite its name, UPA was not enacted uniformly among the states; moreover, it had some shortcomings. So the states tinkered with it, and by the 1980s, the National Conference of Commissioners on Uniform Laws (NCCUL) determined that a revised version was in order. An amended UPA appeared in 1992, and further amendments were promulgated in 1993, 1994, 1996, and 1997. The NCCUL reports that thirty-nine states have adopted some version of the revised act. This chapter will discuss the Revised Uniform Partnership Act (RUPA) as promulgated in 1997, but because not all jurisdictions have not adopted it, where RUPA makes significant changes, the original 1914 UPA will also be considered.[2] The NCCUL observes in its "prefatory note" to the 1997 act: "The Revised Act is largely a series of 'default rules' that govern the relations among partners in situations they have not addressed in a partnership agreement. The primary focus of RUPA is the small, often informal, partnership. Larger partnerships generally have a partnership agreement addressing, and often modifying, many of the provisions of the partnership act."[3]

Entity Theory

Meaning of "Legal Entity"

A significant difference between a partnership and most other kinds of business organization relates to whether, and the extent to which, the business is a legal entity. A legal entity is a person or group that the law recognizes as having legal rights, such as the right to own and dispose of property, to sue and be sued, and to enter into contracts; the **entity theory** is the concept of a business firm as a legal person, with existence and accountability separate from its owners. When individuals carry out a common enterprise as partners, a threshold legal question is whether the partnership is a legal entity. The common law said no. In other words, under the common-law theory, a partnership was but a convenient name for an aggregate of individuals, and the rights and duties recognized and imposed by law are those of the individual partners. By contrast, the mercantile theory of the law merchant held that a partnership is a legal entity that can have rights and duties independent of those of its members.

entity theory

The concept of a business firm as a legal person, with existence and accountability separate from its owners.

During the drafting of the 1914 UPA, a debate raged over which theory to adopt. The drafters resolved the debate through a compromise. In Section 6(1), UPA provides a neutral definition of partnership ("an association of two or more persons to carry on as co-owners a business for profit") and retained the common-law theory that a partnership is an aggregation of individuals—the **aggregate theory**.

aggregate theory

The theory that a business firm is not an entity but rather a collection of individual owners who bind themselves together to share profits.

RUPA moved more toward making partnerships entities. According to the NCCUL, "The Revised Act enhances the entity treatment of partnerships to achieve simplicity for state law purposes, particularly in matters concerning title to partnership property. RUPA does not, however, relentlessly apply the entity approach. The aggregate approach is retained for some purposes, such as partners' joint and several liability."[4] Section 201(a) provides, "A partnership is an entity distinct from its partners."[5]

Entity Characteristics of a Partnership

Under RUPA, then, a partnership has entity characteristics, but the partners remain guarantors of partnership obligations, as always—that is the partners' joint and several liability noted in the previous paragraph (and discussed further in Chapter 41). This is a very important point and a primary weakness of the partnership form: all partners are, and each one of them is, ultimately personally liable for the obligations of the partnership, without limit, which includes personal and unlimited liability. This personal liability is very distasteful, and it has been abolished, subject to some exceptions, with limited partnerships and limited liability companies, as discussed in Chapter 42. And, of course, the owners of corporations are also not generally liable for the corporation's obligations, which is a major reason for the corporate form's popularity.

For Accounting Purposes

Under both versions of the law, the partnership may keep business records as if it were a separate entity, and its accountants may treat it as such for purposes of preparing income statements and balance sheets.

For Purposes of Taxation

Under both versions of the law, partnerships are *not* taxable entities, so they do not pay income taxes. Instead, each partner's distributive share, which includes income or other gain, loss, deductions, and credits, must be included in the partner's personal income tax return, whether or not the share is actually distributed.

For Purposes of Litigation

In litigation, the aggregate theory causes some inconvenience in naming and serving partnership defendants: under UPA, lawsuits to enforce a partnership contract or some other right must be filed in the name of all the partners. Similarly, to sue a partnership, the plaintiff must name and sue each of the partners. This cumbersome procedure was modified in many states, which enacted special statutes expressly permitting suits by and against partnerships in the firm name. In suits on a claim in federal court, a partnership may sue and be sued in its common name. The move by RUPA to make partnerships entities changed very little. Certainly it provides that "a partnership may sue and be sued in the name of the partnership"—that's handy where the plaintiff hopes for a judgment against the partnership, without recourse to the individual partners' personal assets.[6] But a plaintiff must still name the partnership and the partners individually to have access to both estates, the partnership and the individuals': "A judgment against a partnership is not by itself a judgment against a partner. A judgment against a partnership may not be satisfied from a partner's assets unless there is also a judgment against the partner."[7]

For Purposes of Owning Real Estate

Aggregate theory concepts bedeviled property co-ownership issues, so UPA finessed the issue by stating that partnership property, real or personal, could be held in the name of the partners as "tenants in partnership"—a type of co-ownership—or it could be held in the name of the partnership.[8] Under RUPA, "property acquired by the partnership is property of the partnership and not of the partners."[9] But RUPA is no different from UPA in practical effect. The latter provides that "property originally brought into the partnership stock or subsequently acquired by purchase...on account of the partnership, is partnership property."[10] Under either law, a partner may bring onto the partnership premises her own property, not acquired in the name of the partnership or with its credit, and it remains her separate property. Under neither law can a partner unilaterally dispose of partnership property, however labeled, for the obvious reason that one cannot dispose of another's property or property rights without permission.[11] And keep in mind that partnership law is the default: partners are free to make up partnership agreements as they like, subject to some limitations. They are free to set up property ownership rules as they like.

For Purposes of Bankruptcy

Under federal bankruptcy law—state partnership law is preempted—a partnership is an entity that may voluntarily seek the haven of a bankruptcy court or that may involuntarily be thrust into a bankruptcy proceeding by its creditors. The partnership cannot discharge its debts in a liquidation proceeding under Chapter 7 of the bankruptcy law, but it can be rehabilitated under Chapter 11 (see Chapter 30).

Key Takeaway

Partnership law is very important because it is the way most small businesses are organized and because it is possible for a person to become a partner without intending to. Partnership law goes back a long way, but in the United States, most states—but not all—have adopted the Revised Uniform Partnership Act (RUPA, 1997) over the previous Uniform Partnership Act, originally promulgated in 1914. One salient change made by RUPA is to directly announce that a partnership is an entity: it is like a person for purposes of accounting, litigation, bankruptcy, and owning real estate. Partnerships do not pay taxes; the individual partners do. But in practical terms, what RUPA does is codify already-existing state law on these matters, and partners are free to organize their relationship as they like in the partnership agreement.

Exercises

1. When was UPA set out for states to adopt? When was RUPA promulgated for state adoption?
2. What does it mean to say that the partnership act is the "default position"? For what types of partnership is UPA (or RUPA) likely to be of most importance?
3. What is the aggregate theory of partnership? The entity theory?

40.2 Partnership Formation

Learning Objectives

1. Describe the creation of an express partnership.
2. Describe the creation of an implied partnership.
3. Identify tests of partnership existence.
4. Understand partnership by estoppel.

Creation of an Express Partnership

Creation in General

The most common way of forming a partnership is expressly—that is, in words, orally or in writing. Such a partnership is called an **express partnership**. If parties have an express partnership with no partnership agreement, the relevant law—the Uniform Partnership Act (UPA) or the Revised Uniform Partnership Act (RUPA)—applies the governing rules.

express partnership

A partnership intentionally created and recognized, orally or in writing.

Assume that three persons have decided to form a partnership to run a car dealership. Able contributes $250,000. Baker contributes the building and space in which the business will operate. Carr contributes his services; he will manage the dealership.

The first question is whether Able, Baker, and Carr must have a partnership agreement. As should be clear from the foregoing discussion, no agreement is necessary as long as the tests of partnership are met. However, they *ought* to have an agreement in order to spell out their rights and duties among themselves.

The agreement itself is a contract and should follow the principles and rules spelled out in Chapter 8 through Chapter 16 of this book. Because it is intended to govern the relations of the partners toward themselves and their business, every partnership contract should set forth clearly the following terms: (1) the name under which the partners will do business; (2) the names of the partners; (3) the nature, scope, and location of the business; (4) the capital contributions of each partner; (5) how profits and losses are to be divided; (6) how salaries, if any, are to be determined; (7) the responsibilities of each partner for managing the business; (8) limitations on the power of each partner to bind the firm; (9) the method by which a given partner may withdraw from the partnership; (10) continuation of the firm in the event of a partner's death and the formula for paying a partnership interest to his heirs; and (11) method of dissolution.

Specific Issues of Concern

In forming a partnership, three of these items merit special attention. And note again that if the parties do not provide for these in their agreement, RUPA will do it for them as the default.

Who Can Be a Partner?

As discussed earlier in this chapter, a partnership is not limited to a direct association between human beings but may also include an association between other entities, such as corporations or even partnerships themselves.[12] Family members can be partners, and partnerships between parents and minor children are lawful, although a partner who is a minor may disaffirm the agreement.

Written versus Oral Agreements

If the business cannot be performed within one year from the time that the agreement is entered into, the partnership agreement should be in writing to avoid invalidation under the Statute of Frauds. Most partnerships have no fixed term, however, and are partnerships "at will" and therefore not covered by the Statute of Frauds.

Validity of the Partnership Name

Able, Baker, and Carr decide that it makes good business sense to choose an imposing, catchy, and well-known name for their dealership—General Motors Corporation. There are two reasons why they cannot do so. First, their business is a partnership, not a corporation, and should not be described as one. Second, the name is deceptive because it is the name of an existing business. Furthermore, if not registered, the name would violate the assumed or fictitious name statutes of most states. These require that anyone doing business under a name other than his real name register the name, together with the names and addresses of the proprietors, in some public office. (Often, the statutes require the proprietors to publish this information in the newspapers when the business is started.) As *Loomis v. Whitehead* in Section 3 shows, if a business fails to comply with the statute, it could find that it will be unable to file suit to enforce its contracts.

Creation of Implied Partnership

implied partnership

A partnership that arises where parties' behavior objectively manifests an intention to create a relationship that the law recognizes as a partnership.

An **implied partnership** exists when in fact there are two or more persons carrying on a business as co-owners for profit. For example, Carlos decides to paint houses during his summer break. He gathers some materials and gets several jobs. He hires Wally as a helper. Wally is very good, and pretty soon both of them are deciding what jobs to do and how much to charge, and they are splitting the profits. They have an implied partnership, without intending to create a partnership at all.

Tests of Partnership Existence

But how do we know whether an implied partnership *has* been created? Obviously, we know if there is an express agreement. But partnerships can come into existence quite informally, indeed, without any formality—they can be created accidentally. In contrast to the corporation, which is the creature of statute, partnership is a catchall term for a large variety of working relationships, and frequently, uncertainties arise about whether or not a particular relationship is that of partnership. The law can reduce the uncertainty in advance only at the price of severely restricting the flexibility of people to associate. As the chief drafter of the Uniform Partnership Act (UPA, 1914) explained,

> *All other business associations are statutory in origin. They are formed by the happening of an event designated in a statute as necessary to their formation. In corporations this act may be the issuing of a charter by the proper officer of the state; in limited partnerships, the filing by the associates of a specified document in a public office. On the other hand, an infinite number of combinations of circumstances may result in co-ownership of a business. Partnership is the residuum, including all forms of co-ownership, of a business except those business associations organized under a specific statute.*[13]

FIGURE 40.1 Partnership Tests

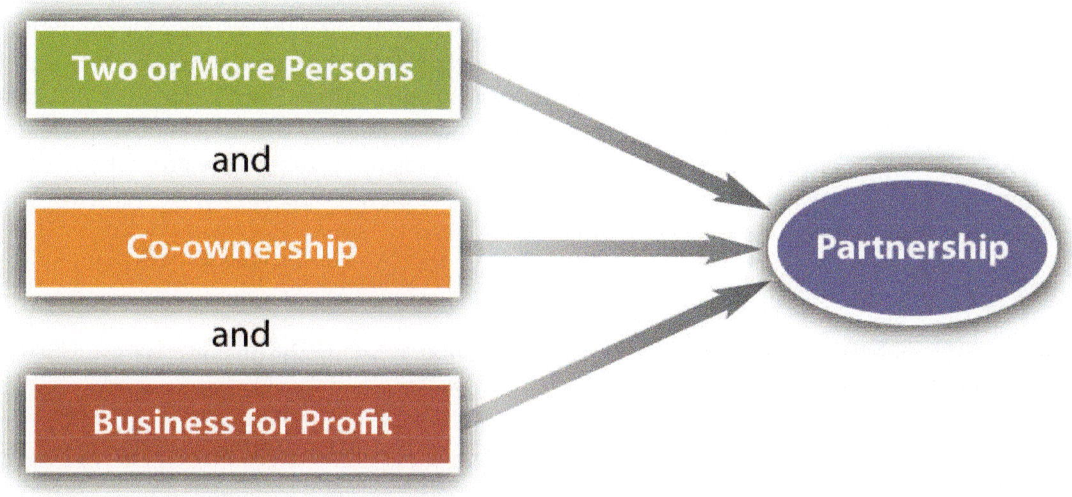

Because it is frequently important to know whether a partnership exists (as when a creditor has dealt with only one party but wishes to also hold others liable by claiming they were partners, see Section 3, *Chaiken v. Employment Security Commission*), a number of tests have been established that are clues to the existence of a partnership (see Figure 40.1). We return to the definition of a partnership: "the association of two or more persons to carry on as co-owners a business for profit[.]" The three elements are (1) the association of persons, (2) as co-owners, (3) for profit.

Association of Persons

This element is pretty obvious. A partnership is a contractual agreement among persons, so the persons involved need to have *capacity* to contract. But RUPA does not provide that only *natural* persons can be partners; it defines *person* as follows: "'Person' means an individual, corporation, business trust, estate, trust, partnership, association, joint venture, government, governmental subdivision, agency, or instrumentality, or any other legal or commercial entity."[14] Thus unless state law precludes it, a corporation can be a partner in a partnership. The same is true under UPA.

Co-owners of a Business

If what two or more people own is clearly a business—including capital assets, contracts with employees or agents, an income stream, and debts incurred on behalf of the operation—a partnership exists. A tougher question arises when two or more persons co-own property. Do they automatically become partners? The answer can be important: if one of the owners while doing business pertinent to the property injures a stranger, the latter could sue the other owners if there is a partnership.

Co-ownership comes in many guises. The four most common are joint tenancy, tenancy in common, tenancy by the entireties, and community property. In joint tenancy, the owners hold the property under a single instrument, such as a deed, and if one dies, the others automatically become owners of the deceased's share, which does not descend to his heirs. Tenancy in common has the reverse rule: the survivor tenants do not take the deceased's share. Each tenant in common has a distinct estate in the property. The tenancy by the entirety and community property (in community-property states) forms of ownership are limited to spouses, and their effects are similar to that of joint tenancy. These concepts are discussed in more detail in relation to real property in Chapter 34.

Suppose a husband and wife who own their home as tenants by the entirety (or community property) decide to spend the summer at the seashore and rent their home for three months. Is their co-ownership sufficient to establish that they are partners? The answer is no. By UPA Section 7(2) and RUPA Section 202(b)(1), the various forms of joint ownership by themselves do not establish partnership, whether or not the co-owners share profits made by the use of the property. To establish a partnership, the ownership must be of a business, not merely of property.

Sharing of Profits

There are two aspects to consider with regard to profits: first, whether the business is for-profit, and second, whether there is a sharing of the profit.

Business for Profit

Unincorporated nonprofit organizations (UNAs) cannot be partnerships. The paucity of coherent law governing these organizations gave rise in 2005 to the National Conference of Commissioners of Uniform Laws' promulgation of the Revised Uniform Unincorporated Nonprofit Association Act (RUUNAA). The prefatory note to this act says, "RUUNAA was drafted with small informal associations in mind. These informal organizations are likely to have no legal advice and so fail to consider legal and organizational questions, including whether to incorporate. The act provides better answers than the common law for a limited number of legal problems. . . . There are probably hundreds of thousands of UNAs in the United States including unincorporated nonprofit philanthropic, educational, scientific and literary clubs, sporting organizations, unions, trade associations, political organizations, churches, hospitals, and condominium and neighborhood associations."[15] At least twelve states have adopted RUUNAA or its predecessor.

Sharing the Profit

While co-ownership does not establish a partnership unless there is a business, a business by itself is not a partnership unless co-ownership is present. Of the tests used by courts to determine co-ownership, perhaps the most important is sharing of profits. Section 202(c) of RUPA provides that "a person who receives a share of the profits of a business is presumed to be a partner in the business," but this presumption can be rebutted by showing that the share of the profits paid out was (1) to repay a debt; (2) wages or compensation to an independent contractor; (3) rent; (4) an annuity, retirement, or health benefit to a representative of a deceased or retired partner; (5) interest on a loan, or rights to income, proceeds, or increase in value from collateral; or (5) for the sale of the goodwill of a business or other property. Section 7(4) of UPA is to the same effect.

Other Factors

Courts are not limited to the profit-sharing test; they also look at these factors, among others: the right to participate in decision making, the duty to share liabilities, and the manner in which the business is operated. Section 3, *Chaiken v. Employment Security Commission*, illustrates how these factors are weighed in court.

Creation of Partnership by Estoppel

Ordinarily, if two people are not legally partners, then third parties cannot so regard them. For example, Mr. Tot and Mr. Tut own equal shares of a house that they rent but do not regard it as a business and are not in fact partners. They do have a loose "understanding" that since Mr. Tot is mechanically adept, he will make necessary repairs whenever the tenants call. On his way to the house one day to fix its boiler, Mr. Tot injures a pedestrian, who sues both Mr. Tot and Mr. Tut. Since they are not partners, the pedestrian cannot sue them as if they were; hence, Mr. Tut has no partnership liability.

Suppose that Mr. Tot and Mr. Tut happened to go to a lumberyard together to purchase materials that Mr. Tot intended to use to add a room to the house. Short of cash, Mr. Tot looks around and espies Mr. Tat, who greets his two friends heartily by saying within earshot of the salesman who is debating whether to extend credit, "Well, how are my two partners this morning?" Messrs. Tot and Tut say nothing but smile faintly at the salesman, who mistakenly but reasonably believes that the two are acknowledging the partnership. The salesman knows Mr. Tat well and assumes that since Mr. Tat is rich, extending credit to the "partnership" is a "sure thing." Tot and Tut fail to pay. The lumberyard is entitled to collect from Mr. Tat, even though he may have forgotten completely about the incident by the time suit is filed. Under Uniform Partnership Act Section 16(1), Mr. Tat would be liable for the debt as being part of a **partnership by estoppel**. The Revised Uniform Partnership Act is to the same effect:

partnership by estoppel

Partnership arising when in fact none exists, where one allows himself or herself to be represented as a partner, thus incurring partnership liability.

> *Section 308. Liability of Purported Partner.*
>
> *(a) If a person, by words or conduct, purports to be a partner, or consents to being represented by another as a partner, in a partnership or with one or more persons not partners, the purported partner is liable to a person to whom the representation is made, if that person, relying on the representation, enters into a transaction with the actual or purported partnership.*

Partnership by estoppel has two elements: (1) a representation to a third party that there is in fact a partnership and (2) reliance by the third party on the representation. See Section 3, *Chavers v. Epsco, Inc.*, for an example of partnership by estoppel.

Key Takeaway

A partnership is any two or more persons—including corporate persons—carrying on a business as co-owners for profit. A primary test of whether a partnership exists is whether there is a sharing of profits, though other factors such as sharing decision making, sharing liabilities, and how the business is operated are also examined.

Most partnerships are expressly created. Several factors become important in the partnership agreement, whether written or oral. These include the name of the business, the capital contributions of each partner, profit sharing, and decision making. But a partnership can also arise by implication or by estoppel, where one has held herself as a partner and another has relied on that representation.

Exercises

1. Why is it necessary—or at least useful—to have tests to determine whether a partnership exists?
2. What elements of the business organization are examined to make this determination?
3. Jacob rents farmland from Davis and pays Davis a part of the profits from the crop in rent. Is Davis a partner? What if Davis offers suggestions on what to plant and when? Now is he a partner?
4. What elements should be included in a written partnership agreement?
5. What is an implied partnership?
6. What is a partnership by estoppel, and why are its "partners" estopped to deny its existence?

40.3 Cases

Tests of Partnership Existence

Chaiken v. Employment Security Commission

274 A.2d 707 (Del. 1971)

STOREY, J.

The Employment Security Commission, hereinafter referred to as the Commission, levied an involuntary assessment against Richard K. Chaiken, complainant, hereinafter referred to as Chaiken, for not filing his unemployment security assessment report. Pursuant to the same statutory section, a hearing was held and a determination made by the Commission that Chaiken was the employer of two barbers in his barber shop and that he should be assessed as an employer for his share of unemployment compensation contributions. Chaiken appealed the Commission's decision. * * *

Both in the administrative hearing and in his appeal brief Chaiken argues that he had entered into partnership agreements with each of his barbers and, therefore, was and is not subject to unemployment compensation assessment. The burden is upon the individual assessed to show that he is outside the ambit of the statutory sections requiring assessment. If Chaiken's partnership argument fails he has no secondary position and he fails to meet his burden.

Chaiken contends that he and his "partners":

1. properly registered the partnership name and names of partners in the prothonotary's office, in accordance with [the relevant statute],[16]
2. properly filed federal partnership information returns and paid federal taxes quarterly on an estimated basis, and
3. duly executed partnership agreements.

Of the three factors, the last is most important. Agreements of "partnership" were executed between Chaiken and Mr. Strazella, a barber in the shop, and between Chaiken and Mr. Spitzer, similarly situated. The agreements were nearly identical. The first paragraph declared the creation of a partnership and the location of business. The second provided that Chaiken would provide barber chair, supplies, and licenses, while the other partner would provide tools of the trade. The paragraph also declared that upon dissolution of the partnership, ownership of items would revert to the party providing them. The third paragraph declared that the income of the partnership would be divided 30% for Chaiken, 70% for Strazella; 20% for Chaiken and 80% for Spitzer. The fourth paragraph declared that all partnership policy would be decided by Chaiken, whose decision was final. The fifth paragraph forbade assignment of the agreement without permission of Chaiken. The sixth paragraph required Chaiken to hold and distribute all receipts. The final paragraph stated hours of work for Strazella and Spitzer and holidays.

The mere existence of an agreement labeled "partnership" agreement and the characterization of signatories as "partners" docs not conclusively prove the existence of a partnership. Rather, the intention of the parties, as explained by the wording of the agreement, is paramount.

A partnership is defined as an association of two or more persons to carry on as co-owners a business for profit. As co-owners of a business, partners have an equal right in the decision making process. But this right may be abrogated by agreement of the parties without destroying the partnership concept, provided other partnership elements are present.

Thus, while paragraph four reserves for Chaiken all right to determine partnership policy, it is not standing alone, fatal to the partnership concept. Co-owners should also contribute valuable consideration for the creation of the business. Under paragraph two, however, Chaiken provides the barber chair (and implicitly the barber shop itself), mirror, licenses and linen, while the other partners merely provide their tools and labor—nothing more than any barber-employee would furnish. Standing alone, however, mere contribution of work and skill can be valuable consideration for a partnership agreement.

Partnership interests may be assignable, although it is not a violation of partnership law to prohibit assignment in a partnership agreement. Therefore, paragraph five on assignment of partnership interests does not violate the partnership concept. On the other hand, distribution of partnership assets to the partners upon dissolution is only allowed after all partnership liabilities are satisfied. But paragraph two of the agreement, in stating the ground rules for dissolution, makes no declaration that the partnership assets will be utilized to pay partnership expenses before reversion to their original owners. This deficiency militates against a finding in favor of partnership intent since it is assumed Chaiken would have inserted such provision had he thought his lesser partners would accept such liability. Partners do accept such liability, employees do not.

Most importantly, co-owners carry on "a business for profit." The phrase has been interpreted to mean that partners share in the profits and the losses of the business. The intent to divide the profits is an indispensable requisite of partnership. Paragraph three of the agreement declares that each partner shall share in the income of the business. There is no sharing of the profits, and as the agreement is drafted, there are no profits. Merely sharing the gross returns does not establish a partnership. Nor is the sharing of profits prima facie evidence of a partnership where the profits received are in payment of wages.

The failure to share profits, therefore, is fatal to the partnership concept here.

Evaluating Chaiken's agreement in light of the elements implicit in a partnership, no partnership intent can be found. The absence of the important right of decision making or the important duty to share liabilities upon dissolution individually may not be fatal to a partnership. But when both are absent, coupled with the absence of profit sharing, they become strong factors in discrediting the partnership argument. Such weighing of the elements against a partnership finding compares favorably with *Fenwick v. Unemployment Compensation Commission*, which decided against the partnership theory on similar facts, including the filing of partnership income tax forms.

In addition, the total circumstances of the case taken together indicate the employer-employee relationship between Chaiken and his barbers. The agreement set forth the hours of work and days off—unusual subjects for partnership agreements. The barbers brought into the relationship only the equipment required of all barber shop operators. And each barber had his own individual "partnership" with Chaiken. Furthermore, Chaiken conducted all transactions with suppliers, and purchased licenses, insurance, and the lease for the business property in his own name. Finally, the name "Richard's Barber Shop" continued to be used after the execution of the so-called partnership agreements. [The Commission's decision is affirmed.]

Case Questions

1. Why did the unemployment board sue Chaiken?
2. Why did Chaiken set up this "partnership"?
3. What factors did the court examine to determine whether there was a partnership here? Which one was the most important?
4. Why would it be unusual in a partnership agreement to set forth the hours of work and days off?

Creation of a Partnership: Registering the Name

Loomis v. Whitehead

183 P.3d 890 (Nev. 2008)

Per Curiam.

In this appeal, we address whether [Nevada Revised Statute] NRS 602.070 bars the partners of an unregistered fictitious name partnership from bringing an action arising out of a business agreement that was not made under the fictitious name. [The statute] prohibits persons who fail to file an assumed or fictitious name certificate from suing on any contract or agreement made under the assumed or fictitious name. We conclude that it does not bar the partners from bringing the action so long as the partners did not conduct the business or enter into an agreement under the fictitious name or otherwise mislead the other party into thinking that he was doing business with some entity other than the partners themselves.

Background Facts

Appellants Leroy Loomis and David R. Shanahan raised and sold cattle in Elko County, Nevada. Each of the appellants had certain responsibilities relating to the cattle business. Loomis supplied the livestock and paid expenses, while Shanahan managed the day-to-day care of the cattle. Once the cattle were readied for market and sold, Loomis and Shanahan would share the profits equally. While Loomis and Shanahan often called themselves the 52 Cattle Company, they had no formal partnership agreement and did not file an assumed or fictitious name certificate in that name. Loomis and Shanahan bring this appeal after an agreement entered into with respondent Jerry Carr Whitehead failed.

In the fall of 2003, Shanahan entered into a verbal agreement with Whitehead, a rancher, through Whitehead's ranch foreman to have their cattle wintered at Whitehead's ranch. Neither Loomis nor Whitehead was present when the ranch foreman made the deal with Shanahan, but the parties agree that there was no mention of the 52 Cattle Company at the time they entered into the agreement or anytime during the course of business thereafter. Shanahan and Loomis subsequently alleged that their cattle were malnourished and that a number of their cattle died from starvation that winter at Whitehead's ranch. Whitehead denied these allegations.

Suit against Whitehead

The following summer, Shanahan and Loomis sued Whitehead, claiming negligence and breach of contract. Later, well into discovery, Whitehead was made aware of the existence of the 52 Cattle Company when Shanahan stated in his deposition that he did not actually own any of the cattle on Whitehead's ranch. In his deposition, he described the partnership arrangement. At about the same time, Whitehead learned that the name "52 Cattle Company" was not registered with the Elko County Clerk.

Whitehead then filed a motion for partial summary judgment, asserting that, pursuant to NRS 602.070, Loomis and Shanahan's failure to register their fictitiously named partnership with the county clerk barred them from bringing a legal action. The district court agreed with Whitehead, granted the motion, and dismissed Loomis and Shanahan's claims. Loomis and Shanahan timely appealed.

Discussion

The district court found that Loomis and Shanahan conducted business under a fictitious name without filing a fictitious name certificate with the Elko County Clerk as required by NRS 602.010.[17] The district court therefore concluded that, pursuant to NRS 602.070, they were barred from bringing an action against Whitehead because they did not file a fictitious name certificate for the 52 Cattle Company.[18]

Loomis and Shanahan contend that the district court erred in granting partial summary judgment because they did not enter into a contract with Whitehead under the name of the 52 Cattle Company, and they did not conduct business with Whitehead under that name. Loomis and Shanahan argue that NRS 602.070 is not applicable to their action against Whitehead because they did not mislead Whitehead into thinking that he was doing business with anyone other than them. We agree. * * *

When looking at a statute's language, this court is bound to follow the statute's plain meaning, unless the plain meaning was clearly not intended. Here, in using the phrase "under the assumed or fictitious name," the statute clearly bars bringing an action when the claims arise from a contract, transaction, or business conducted beneath the banner of an unregistered fictitious name. However, NRS 602.070 does not apply to individual partners whose transactions or business with another party were not performed under the fictitious name.

Here, Whitehead knew that Shanahan entered into the oral contract under his own name. He initially thought that Shanahan owned the cattle and Loomis had "some type of interest." Shanahan did not enter into the contract under the fictitious "52 Cattle Company" name. Moreover, Whitehead does not allege that he was misled by either Loomis or Shanahan in any way that would cause him to think he was doing business with the 52 Cattle Company. In fact, Whitehead did not know of the 52 Cattle Company until Shanahan mentioned it in his deposition. Under these circumstances, when there simply was no indication that Loomis and Shanahan represented that they were conducting business as the 52 Cattle Company and no reliance by Whitehead that he was doing business with the 52 Cattle Company, NRS 602.070 does not bar the suit against Whitehead.

We therefore reverse the district court's partial summary judgment in this instance and remand for trial because, while the lawsuit between Loomis and Whitehead involved partnership business, the transaction at issue was not conducted and the subsequent suit was not maintained under the aegis of the fictitiously named partnership.

Case Questions

1. The purpose of the fictitious name statute might well be, as the court here describes it, "to prevent fraud and to give the public information about those entities with which they conduct business." But that's not what the statute says; it says nobody can sue on a cause of action arising out of business conducted under a fictitious name if the name is not registered. The legislature determined the consequence of failure to register. Should the court disregard the statute's plain, unambiguous meaning?
2. That was one of two arguments by the dissent in this case. The second one was based on this problem: Shanahan and Loomis agreed that the cattle at issue were partnership cattle bearing the "52" brand. That is, the cows were *not* Shanahan's; they were the partnership's. When Whitehead moved to dismiss Shanahan's claim—again, because the cows weren't Shanahan's—Shanahan conceded that but for the existence of the partnership he would have no claim against Whitehead. If there is no claim against the defendant except insofar as he harmed the partnership business (the cattle), how could the majority assert that claims against Whitehead did not arise out of "the business" conducted under 52 Cattle Company? Who has the better argument, the majority or the dissent?
3. Here is another problem along the same lines but with a different set of facts and a Uniform Partnership Act (UPA) jurisdiction (i.e., pre-Revised Uniform Partnership Act [RUPA]). Suppose the plaintiffs had a partnership (as they did here), but the claim by one was that the other partner had stolen several head of cattle, and UPA was in effect so that the partnership property was owned as "tenant in partnership"—the cattle would be owned by the partners as a whole. A person who steals his own property cannot be criminally liable; therefore, a partner cannot be guilty of stealing (or misappropriating) firm property. Thus, under UPA there arise anomalous cases, for example, in *People v. Zinke*, 555 N.E.2d 263 (N.Y. 1990), which is a criminal case, Zinke embezzled over a million dollars from his own investment firm but the prosecutor's case against him was dismissed because, the New York court said, "partners cannot be prosecuted for stealing firm property." If the partnership is a legal entity, as under RUPA, how is this result changed?

Partnership by Estoppel

Chavers v. Epsco, Inc.
98 S.W.3d 421 (Ark. 2003)

Hannah, J.

Appellants Reggie Chavers and Mark Chavers appeal a judgment entered against them by the Craighead County Circuit Court. Reggie and Mark argue that the trial court erred in holding them liable for a company debt based upon partnership by estoppel because the proof was vague and insufficient and there was no detrimental reliance on the part of a creditor. We hold that the trial court was not clearly erroneous in finding liability based upon partnership by estoppel. Accordingly, we affirm.

Facts

Gary Chavers operated Chavers Welding and Construction ("CWC"), a construction and welding business, in Jonesboro. Gary's sons Reggie Chavers and Mark Chavers joined their father in the business after graduating from high school. Gary, Mark, and Reggie maintain that CWC was a sole proprietorship owned by Gary, and that Reggie and Mark served only as CWC employees, not as CWC partners.

In February 1999, CWC entered into an agreement with Epsco, Inc. ("Epsco"), a staffing service, to provide payroll and employee services for CWC. Initially, Epsco collected payments for its services on a weekly basis, but later, Epsco extended credit to CWC. Melton Clegg, President of Epsco, stated that his decision to extend credit to CWC was based, in part, on his belief that CWC was a partnership.

CWC's account with Epsco became delinquent, and Epsco filed a complaint against Gary, Reggie, and Mark, individually, and doing business as CWC, to recover payment for the past due account. Gary discharged a portion of his obligation to Epsco due to his filing for bankruptcy. Epsco sought to recover CWC's remaining debt from Reggie and Mark. After a hearing on March 7, 2002, the trial court issued a letter opinion, finding that Reggie and Mark "represented themselves to [Epsco] as partners in an existing partnership and operated in such a fashion to give creditors in general, and Epsco in particular, the impression that such creditors/potential creditors were doing business with a partnership." On May 21, 2002, the trial court entered an order stating that Reggie and Mark were partners by estoppel as relates to Epsco. The trial court found that Reggie and Mark were jointly and severally liable for the debt of CWC in the amount of $80,360.92 [about $108,000 in 2016 dollars]'. In addition, the trial court awarded Epsco pre-judgment interest at the rate of six percent, post-judgment interest at the rate of ten percent, and attorney's fees in the amount of $8,036.92.

[The relevant Arkansas statute provides]:

> *(1) When a person, by words spoken or written or by conduct, represents himself, or consents to another representing him to any one, as a partner in an existing partnership or with one (1) or more persons not actual partners, he is liable to any person to whom such representation has been made, who has, on the faith of such representation, given credit to the actual or apparent partnership, and if he has made such representation or consented to its being made in a public manner, he is liable to that person, whether the representation has or has not been made or communicated to that person so giving credit by or with the knowledge of the apparent partner making the representation or consenting to it being made.*
>
> *(a) When a partnership liability results, he is liable as though he were an actual member of the partnership.*

We have long recognized the doctrine of partnership by estoppel. [Citation, 1840], the court stated that

> *they who hold themselves out to the world as partners in business or trade, are to be so regarded as to creditors and third persons; and the partnership may be established by any evidence showing that they so hold themselves out to the public, and were so regarded by the trading community.*

Further, we have stated that "[p]artnerships may be proved by circumstantial evidence; and evidence will sometimes fix a joint liability, where persons are charged as partners, in a suit by a third person, when they are not, in fact, partners as between themselves." [Citation, 1843.]

In [Citation, 1906], the court noted that

> *[a] person who holds himself out as a partner of a firm is estopped to deny such representation, not only as to those as to whom the representation was directly made, but as to all others who had knowledge of such holding out and in reliance thereon sold goods to the firm. . . .*

In addition, "if the party himself puts out the report that he is a partner, he will be liable to all those selling goods to the firm on the faith and credit of such report." [Citation] When a person holds himself out as a member of partnership, any one dealing with the firm on the faith of such representation is entitled to assume the relation continues until notice of some kind is given of its discontinuance. [Citations]

In [Citation, 1944], the court wrote:

> *It is a thoroughly well-settled rule that persons who are not as between themselves partners, or as between whom there is in fact no legal partnership, may nevertheless become subject to the liabilities of partners, either by holding themselves out as partners to the public and the world generally or to particular individuals, or by knowingly or negligently permitting another person to do so. All persons who hold themselves out, or knowingly permit others to hold them out, to the public as partners, although they are not in partnership, become bound as partners to all who deal with them in their apparent relation.*
>
> *The liability as a partner of a person who holds himself out as a partner, or permits others to do so, is predicated on the doctrine of estoppel and on the policy of the law seeking to prevent frauds on those who lend their money on the apparent credit of those who are held out as partners. One holding himself out as a partner or knowingly permitting himself to be so held out is estopped from denying liability as a partner to one who has extended credit in reliance thereon, although no partnership has in fact existed.*

In the present case, the trial court cited specific examples of representations made by Reggie and Mark indicating that they were partners of CWC, including correspondence to Epsco, checks written to Epsco, business cards distributed to the public, and credit applications. We will discuss each in turn.

The Faxed Credit References

Epsco argues that Plaintiff's Exhibit # 1, a faxed list of credit references, clearly indicates that Gary was the owner and that Reggie and Mark were partners in the business. The fax lists four credit references, and it includes CWC's contact information. The contact information lists CWC's telephone number, fax number, and federal tax number. The last two lines of the contact information state: "Gary Chavers Owner" and "Reggie Chavers and Mark Chavers Partners."

Gary testified that he did not know that the list of credit references was faxed to Epsco. In addition, he testified that his signature was not at the bottom of the fax. He testified that his former secretary might have signed his name to the fax; however, he stated that he did not authorize his secretary to sign or fax a list of credit references to Epsco. Moreover, Gary testified that the first time he saw the list of credit references was at the bench trial.

This court gives deference to the superior position of the trial judge to determine the credibility of the witnesses and the weight to be accorded their testimony. [Citations] Though there was a dispute concerning whether Gary faxed the list to Epsco, the trial court found that Epsco received the faxed credit references from CWC and relied on CWC's statement that Reggie and Mark were partners. The trial court's finding is not clearly erroneous.

The Fax Cover Sheet

At trial, Epsco introduced Plaintiff's Exhibit # 2, a fax cover sheet from "Chavers Construction" to Epsco. The fax cover sheet was dated July 19, 2000. The fax cover sheet contained the address, telephone number, and fax number of the business. Listed under this information was "Gary, Reggie, or Mark Chavers." Epsco argues that Gary, Reggie, and Mark are all listed on the fax cover sheet, and that this indicates that they were holding themselves out to the public as partners of the business. The trial court's finding that the fax cover sheet indicated that Reggie and Mark were holding themselves out as partners of CWC is not clearly erroneous.

The Epsco Personnel Credit Application

Epsco introduced Plaintiff's Exhibit # 9, a personnel credit application, which was received from CWC. Adams testified that the exhibit represented a completed credit application that she received from CWC. The type of business checked on the credit application is "partnership." Adams testified that the application showed the company to be a partnership, and that this information was relied upon in extending credit. Clegg testified that he viewed the credit application which indicated that CWC was a partnership, and that his decision to extend credit to CWC was based, in part, on his belief that CWC was a partnership. Gary denied filling out the credit application form.

It was within the trial court's discretion to find Adams's and Clegg's testimony more credible than Gary's testimony and to determine that Epsco relied on the statement of partnership on the credit application before extending credit to CWC. The trial court's finding concerning the credit application is not clearly erroneous.

The Checks to Epsco

Epsco argues that Plaintiff's Exhibit # 3 and Plaintiff's Exhibit # 11, checks written to Epsco showing the CWC account to be in the name of "Gary A. or Reggie J. Chavers," indicates that Reggie was holding himself out to be a partner of CWC. Plaintiff's Exhibit # 3 was signed by Gary, and Plaintiff's Exhibit # 11 was signed by Reggie. The checks are evidence that Reggie was holding himself out to the public as a partner of CWC, and Epsco could have detrimentally relied on the checks before extending credit to CWC. The trial court was not clearly erroneous in finding that the checks supported a finding of partnership by estoppel.

The Business Card

Epsco introduced Plaintiff's Exhibit # 4, a business card that states "Chavers Welding, Construction & Crane Service." Listed on the card as "owners" are Gary Chavers and Reggie Chavers. Gary testified that the business cards were printed incorrectly, and that Reggie's name should not have been included as an owner. He also testified that some of the cards might have been handed out, and that it was possible that he might have given one of the cards to a business listed as one of CWC's credit references on Plaintiff's Exhibit # 1.

The business card listing Reggie as an owner indicates that Reggie was holding himself out as a partner. As we stated in [Citation] when a person holds himself out as a member of partnership, any one dealing with the firm on the faith of such representation is entitled to assume the relation continues until notice of some kind is given of its discontinuance. There is no indication that Reggie ever informed any person who received a business card that the business relationship listed on the card was incorrect or had been discontinued. The trial court's finding concerning the business card is not clearly erroneous.

The Dealership Application

Epsco introduced Plaintiff's Exhibit # 5, an application form from "Chavers Welding," signed by Reggie, seeking a dealership from Sukup Manufacturing. The application, dated January 23, 1997, lists "Gary & Reggie Chavers" as owners of "Chavers Welding." The application is signed by Reggie. Reggie admits that he signed the dealership application and represented that he was an owner of "Chavers Welding," but he dismisses his statement of ownership as mere "puffery" on his part. Epsco argues that instead, the application shows that Reggie was holding himself out to the public as being a partner. The trial court's determination that Reggie's dealership application supports a finding of partnership by estoppel is not clearly erroneous.

In sum, the trial court was not clearly erroneous in finding that Reggie and Mark held themselves out as partners of CWC and that Epsco detrimentally relied on the existence of the partnership before extending credit to CWC. The appellants argue that even if we find Reggie liable based upon partnership by estoppel, there was scant proof of Mark being liable based upon partnership by estoppel. We disagree. We are aware that some examples of holding out cited in the trial court's order pertain only to Reggie. However, the representations attributed to both Reggie and Mark are sufficient proof to support the trial court's finding that both Reggie and Mark are estopped from denying liability to Epsco.

Affirmed.

Case Questions

1. What is the rationale for the doctrine of partnership by estoppel?
2. Gary and Reggie claimed the evidence brought forth to show the existence of a partnership was unconvincing. How credible were their claims?

40.4 Summary and Exercises

Summary

The basic law of partnership is found in the Uniform Partnership Act and Revised Uniform Partnership Act. The latter has been adopted by thirty-five states. At common law, a partnership was not a legal entity and could not sue or be sued in the partnership name. Partnership law defines a partnership as "an association of two or more persons to carry on as co-owners a business for profit." The Uniform Partnership Act (UPA) assumes that a partnership is an aggregation of individuals, but it also applies a number of rules characteristic of the legal entity theory. The Revised Uniform Partnership Act (RUPA) assumes a partnership is an entity, but it applies one crucial rule characteristic of the aggregate theory: the partners are ultimately liable for the partnership's obligations. Thus, a partnership may keep business records as if it were a legal entity, may hold real estate in the partnership name, and may sue and be sued in federal court and in many state courts in the partnership name.

Partnerships may be created informally. Among the clues to the existence of a partnership are (1) co-ownership of a business, (2) sharing of profits, (3) right to participate in decision making, (4) duty to share liabilities, and (5) manner in which the business is operated. A partnership may also be formed by implication; it may be formed by estoppel when a third party reasonably relies on a representation that a partnership in fact exists.

No special rules govern the partnership agreement. As a practical matter, it should sufficiently spell out who the partners are, under what name they will conduct their business, the nature and scope of the business, capital contributions of each partner, how profits are to be divided, and similar pertinent provisions. An oral agreement to form a partnership is valid unless the business cannot be performed wholly within one year from the time that the agreement is made. However, most partnerships have no fixed terms and hence are "at-will" partnerships not subject to the Statute of Frauds.

Exercises

1. Able, Baker, and Carr own, as partners, a warehouse. The income from the warehouse during the current year is $300,000, two-thirds of which goes to Able. Who must file a tax return listing this as income, the partnership or Able? Who pays the tax, the partnership or Able?
2. The Havana Club operated in Salt Lake City under a lease running to defendant Dale Bowen, who owned the equipment, furnishings, and inventory. He did not himself work in operating the club. He made an oral agreement with Frances Cutler, who had been working for him as a bartender, that she take over the management of the club. She was to have the authority and the responsibility for the entire active management and operation: to purchase the supplies, pay the bills, keep the books, hire and fire employees, and do whatever else was necessary to run the business. As compensation, the arrangement was for a down-the-middle split; each was to receive $300 per week plus one half of the net profits. This went on for four years until the city took over the building for a redevelopment project. The city offered Bowen $30,000 as compensation for loss of business while a new location was found for the club. Failing to find a suitable location, the parties decided to terminate the business. Bowen then contended he was entitled to the entire $30,000 as the owner, Cutler being an employee only. She sued to recover half as a partner. What was the result? Decide and discuss.
3. Raul, a business student, decided to lease and operate an ice cream stand during his summer vacation. Because he could not afford rent payments, his lessor agreed to take 30 percent of the profits as rent and provide the stand and the parcel of real estate on which it stood. Are the two partners?
4. Able, Baker, and Carr formed the ABC Partnership in 2001. In 2002 Able gave her three sons, Duncan, Eldon, and Frederick, a gift of her 41 percent interest in the partnership to provide money to pay for their college expenses. The sons reported income from the part-

nership on their individual tax returns, and the partnership reported the payment to them on its information return. The sons were listed as partners on unaudited balance sheets in 2003, and the 2004 income statement listed them as partners. The sons never requested information about the management of the firm, never attended any meetings or voted, and never attempted to withdraw the firm's money or even speak with the other partners about the firm. Two of the sons didn't know where the firm was located, but they all once received "management fees" totaling $3,000, without any showing of what the "fees" were for. In 2005, the partnership incurred liability for pension-fund contributions to an employee, and a trustee for the fund asserted that Able's sons were personally liable under federal law for the money owing because they were partners. The sons moved for summary judgment denying liability. How should the court rule?

5. The Volkmans wanted to build a house and contacted David McNamee for construction advice. He told them that he was doing business with Phillip Carroll. Later the Volkmans got a letter from McNamee on stationery that read "DP Associates," which they assumed was derived from the first names of David and Phillip. At the DP Associates office McNamee introduced Mr. Volkman to Carroll, who said to Volkman, "I hope we'll be working together." At one point during the signing process a question arose and McNamee said, "I will ask Phil." He returned with the answer to the question. After the contract was signed but before construction began, Mr. Volkman visited the DP Associates office where the two men chatted; Carroll said to him, "I am happy that we will be working with you." The Volkmans never saw Carroll on the construction site and knew of no other construction supervised by Carroll. They understood they were purchasing Carroll's services and construction expertise through DP Associates. During construction, Mr. Volkman visited the DP offices several times and saw Carroll there. During one visit, Mr. Volkman expressed concerns about delays and expressed the same to Carroll, who replied, "Don't worry. David will take care of it." But David did not, and the Volkmans sued DP Associates, McNamee, and Carroll. Carroll asserted he could not be liable because he and McNamee were not partners. The trial court dismissed Carroll on summary judgment; the Volkmans appealed. How should the court rule on appeal?
6. Wilson and VanBeek want to form a partnership. Wilson is seventeen and VanBeek is twenty-two. May they form a partnership? Explain.
7. Diane and Rachel operate a restaurant at the county fair every year to raise money for the local 4-H Club. They decide together what to serve, what hours to operate, and generally how to run the business. Do they have a partnership?

Self-Test Questions

1. The basic law of partnership is currently found in
    a. common law
    b. constitutional law
    c. statutory law
    d. none of the above
2. Existence of a partnership may be established by
    a. co-ownership of a business for profit
    b. estoppel
    c. a formal agreement
    d. all of the above
3. Which is false?
    a. An oral agreement to form a partnership is valid.
    b. Most partnerships have no fixed terms and are thus not subject to the Statute of Frauds.
    c. Strict statutory rules govern partnership agreements.
    d. A partnership may be formed by estoppel.

4. Partnerships
   a. are not taxable entities
   b. may buy, sell, or hold real property in the partnership name
   c. may file for bankruptcy
   d. have all of the above characteristics
5. Partnerships
   a. are free to select any name not used by another partnership
   b. must include the partners' names in the partnership name
   c. can be formed by two corporations
   d. cannot be formed by two partnerships

Self-Test Answers

1. c
2. d
3. c
4. d
5. c

Endnotes

1. Revised Uniform Partnership Act, Section 202(a).
2. NCCUSL, Uniform Law Commission, "Acts: Partnership Act," http://www.nccusl.org/Act.aspx?title=Partnership Act. The following states *have* adopted the RUPA: Alabama, Alaska, Arizona, Arkansas, California, Colorado, Delaware, District of Columbia, Florida, Hawaii, Idaho, Illinois, Iowa, Kansas, Kentucky, Maine, Maryland, Minnesota, Mississippi, Montana, Nebraska, Nevada, New Jersey, New Mexico, North Dakota, Oklahoma, Oregon, Puerto Rico, South Dakota (substantially similar), Tennessee, Texas (substantially similar), US Virgin Islands, Vermont, Virginia, and Washington. Connecticut, West Virginia, and Wyoming adopted the 1992 or 1994 version. Here are the states that have *not* adopted RUPA (Louisiana never adopted UPA at all): Georgia, Indiana, Massachusetts, Michigan, Mississippi, New Hampshire, New York, North Carolina, Ohio, Pennsylvania, Rhode Island, and Wisconsin.
3. University of Pennsylvania Law School, Biddle Law Library, "Uniform Partnership Act (1997)," NCCUSL Archives, http://www.law.upenn.edu/bll/archives/ulc/fnact99/1990s/upa97fa.pdf.
4. University of Pennsylvania Law School, Biddle Law Library, "Uniform Partnership Act (1997)," NCCUSL Archives, http://www.law.upenn.edu/bll/archives/ulc/fnact99/1990s/upa97fa.pdf.
5. RUPA, Section 201(a).
6. RUPA, Section 307(a).
7. RUPA, Section 307(c).
8. Uniform Partnership Act, Section 25(1); UPA, Section 8(3).
9. RUPA, Section 203.
10. UPA, Section 8(1).
11. UPA, Sections 9(3)(a) and 25; RUPA, Section 302.
12. A joint venture—sometimes known as a joint adventure, coadventure, joint enterprise, joint undertaking, syndicate, group, or pool—is an association of persons to carry on a particular task until completed. In essence, a joint venture is a "temporary partnership." In the United States, the use of joint ventures began with the railroads in the late 1800s. Throughout the middle part of the twentieth century joint ventures were common in the manufacturing sector. By the late 1980s, they increasingly appeared in both manufacturing and service industries as businesses looked for new, competitive strategies. They are aggressively promoted on the Internet: "Joint Ventures are in, and if you're not utilizing this strategic weapon, chances are your competition is, or will soon be, using this to their advantage....possibly against you!" (Scott Allen, "Joint Venturing 101," About.com Entrepreneurs, http://entrepreneurs.about.com/od/beyondstartup/a/jointventures.htm).As a risk-avoiding device, the joint venture allows two or more firms to pool their differing expertise so that neither needs to "learn the ropes" from the beginning; neither needs the entire capital to start the enterprise.Partnership rules generally apply, although the relationship of the joint venturers is closer to that of special than general agency as discussed in Chapter 38. Joint venturers are fiduciaries toward one another. Although no formality is necessary, the associates will usually sign an agreement. The joint venture need have no group name, though it may have one. Property may be owned jointly. Profits and losses will be shared, as in a partnership, and each associate has the right to participate in management. Liability is unlimited.Sometimes two or more businesses will form a joint venture to carry out a specific task—prospecting for oil, building a nuclear reactor, doing basic scientific research—and will incorporate the joint venture. In that case, the resulting business—known as a "joint venture corporation"—is governed by corporation law, not the law of partnership, and is not a joint venture in the sense described here. Increasingly, companies are forming joint ventures to do business abroad; foreign investors or governments own significant interests in these joint ventures. For example, in 1984 General Motors entered into a joint venture with Toyota to revive GM's shuttered Fremont, California, assembly plant to create New United Motor Manufacturing, Inc. (NUMMI). For GM the joint venture was an opportunity to learn about lean manufacturing from the Japanese company, while Toyota gained its first manufacturing base in North America and a chance to test its production system in an American labor environment. Until May 2010, when the copartnership ended and the plant closed, NUMMI built an average of six thousand vehicles a week, or nearly eight million cars and trucks. These vehicles were the Chevrolet Nova (1984–88), the Geo Prizm (1989–97), the Chevrolet Prizm (1998–2002), and the Hilux (1991–95, predecessor of the Tacoma), as well as the Toyota Voltz, the Japanese right-hand-drive version of the Pontiac Vibe. The latter two were based on the Toyota Matrix. Paul Stenquist, "GM and Toyota's Joint Venture Ends in California," *New York Times*, April 2, 2010, http://wheels.blogs.nytimes.com/2010/04/02/g-m-and-toyotas-joint-venture-ends-in-california.
13. W. D. Lewis, "The Uniform Partnership Act," *Yale Law Journal* 24 (1915): 617, 622.
14. RUPA, Section 101(10).
15. Revised Uniform Unincorporated Nonprofit Associations Act, http://www.abanet.org/intlaw/leadership/policy/RUUNAA_Final_08.pdf.

16. The word *prothonotary* means first notary of the court. The prothonotary is the keeper of the civil records for the court system. The office is responsible for the creation, maintenance, and certification of matters pending or determined by the court. The office is also responsible for certain reporting and collection duties to state agencies.
17. NRS 602.010(1): "Every person doing business in this state under an assumed or fictitious name that is in any way different from the legal name of each person who owns an interest in the business must file with the county clerk of each county in which the business is being conducted a certificate containing the information required by NRS 602.020."
18. NRS 602.070: "No action may be commenced or maintained by any person…upon or on account of any contract made or transaction had under the assumed or fictitious name, or upon or on account of any cause of action arising or growing out of the business conducted under that name, unless before the commencement of the action the certificate required by NRS 602.010 has been filed."

CHAPTER 41

Partnership Operation and Termination

Learning Objectives

After reading this chapter, you should understand the following:

1. The operation of a partnership, including the relations among partners and relations between partners and third parties.
2. The dissolution and winding up of a partnership.

41.1 Operation: Relations among Partners

Learning Objectives

1. Recognize the duties partners owe each other: duties of service, loyalty, care, obedience, information, and accounting.
2. Identify the rights that partners have, including the rights to distributions of money, to management, to choice of copartners, to property of the partnership, to assign partnership interest, and to enforce duties and rights.

Most of the rules discussed in this section apply unless otherwise agreed, and they are really intended for the small firm.[1] The Uniform Partnership Act (UPA) and the Revised Uniform Partnership Act (RUPA) do not dictate what the relations among partners must be; the acts supply rules in the event that the partners have not done so for themselves. In this area, it is especially important for the partners to elaborate their agreement in writing. If the partners should happen to continue their business beyond the term fixed for it in their agreement, the terms of the agreement continue to apply.

Duties Partners Owe Each Other

Among the duties partners owe each other, six may be called out here: (1) the duty to serve, (2) the duty of loyalty, (3) the duty of care, (4) the duty of obedience, (5) the duty to inform copartners, and (6) the duty to account to the partnership. These are all very similar to the duty owed by an agent to the principal, as partnership law is based on agency concepts.[2]

Duty to Serve

Unless otherwise agreed, expressly or impliedly, a partner is expected to work for the firm. The partnership, after all, is a profit-making co-venture, and it would not do for one to loaf about and still expect to get paid. For example, suppose Joan takes her two-week vacation from the horse-stable partnership she operates with Sarah and Sandra. Then she does not return for four months because she has gone horseback riding in the Southwest. She might end up having to pay if the partnership hired a substitute to do her work.

Duty of Loyalty

fiduciary duty

The highest duty of good faith and trust, imposed on partners as to each other and the firm.

In general, this requires partners to put the firm's interests ahead of their own. Partners are *fiduciaries* as to each other and as to the partnership, and as such, they owe a **fiduciary duty** to each other and the partnership. Judge Benjamin Cardozo, in an often-quoted phrase, called the fiduciary duty "something stricter than the morals of the market place. Not honesty alone, but the punctilio of an honor the most sensitive, is then the standard of behavior."[3] Breach of the fiduciary duty gives rise to a claim for compensatory, consequential, and incidental damages; recoupment of compensation; and—rarely—punitive damages. See Section 4, *Gilroy v. Conway*, for an example of breach of fiduciary duty.

Application of the Fiduciary Standard to Partnership Law

Under UPA, all partners are fiduciaries of each other—they are all principals and agents of each other—though the word *fiduciary* was not used except in the *heading* to Section 21. The section reads, "Every partner must account to the partnership for any benefit, and hold as trustee for it any profits derived by him without the consent of the other partners from any transaction connected with the formation, conduct, or liquidation of the partnership or from any use by him of its property."

Section 404 of RUPA specifically provides that a partner has a fiduciary duty to the partnership and other partners. It imposes the fiduciary standard on the duty of loyalty in three circumstances:

> *(1) to account to the partnership and hold as trustee for it any property, profit, or benefit derived by the partner in the conduct and winding up of the partnership business or derived from a use by the partner of partnership property, including the appropriation of a partnership opportunity;*
>
> *(2) to refrain from dealing with the partnership in the conduct or winding up of the partnership business as or on behalf of a party having an interest adverse to the partnership; and*
>
> *(3) to refrain from competing with the partnership in the conduct of the partnership business before the dissolution of the partnership.*

Limits on the Reach of the Fiduciary Duty

This sets out a fairly limited scope for application of the fiduciary standard, which is reasonable because partners do not delegate open-ended control to their copartners. Further, there are some specific limits on how far the fiduciary duty reaches (which means parties are held to the lower standard of "good faith"). Here are two examples. First, RUPA—unlike UPA—does not extend to the *formation* of the partnership; Comment 2 to RUPA Section 404 says that would be inappropriate because then the parties are "really dealing at arm's length." Second, fiduciary duty doesn't apply to a dissociated partner (one who leaves the firm—discussed in Section 3) who can immediately begin competing without the others' consent; and it doesn't apply if a partner violates the standard "merely because the partner's conduct furthers the partner's own interest."[4] Moreover, the partnership agreement may eliminate the duty of loyalty so long as that is not "manifestly unreasonable."[5]

Activities Affected by the Duty of Loyalty

The duty of loyalty means, again, that partners must put the firm's interest above their own. Thus, it is held that a partner

- may not compete with the partnership,
- may not make a secret profit while doing partnership business,
- must maintain the confidentiality of partnership information.

This is certainly not a comprehensive list, and courts will determine on a case-by-case basis whether the duty of loyalty has been breached.

Duty of Care

Stemming from its roots in agency law, partnership law also imposes a duty of care on partners. Partners are to faithfully serve to the best of their ability. Section 404 of RUPA imposes the fiduciary standard on the duty of care, but rather confusingly: how does the "punctilio of an honor the most sensitive"—as Judge Cardozo described that standard—apply when under RUPA Section 404(c) the "the duty of care . . . is limited to refraining from engaging in grossly negligent or reckless conduct, intentional misconduct, or a knowing violation of law"? Recognize that a person can attend to business both loyally and negligently. For example, Alice Able, a partner in a law firm who is not very familiar with the firm's computerized bookkeeping system, attempts to trace a missing check and in so doing erases a month's worth of records. She has not breached her duty of care: maybe she was negligent, but not grossly negligent under RUPA Section 404(c). The partnership agreement may reduce the duty of care so long as it is not "unreasonably reduce[d]"; it may increase the standard too.[6]

Duty of Obedience

The partnership is a contractual relationship among the partners; they are all agents and principals of each other. Expressly or impliedly that means no partner can disobey the partnership agreement or fail to follow any properly made partnership decision. This includes the duty to act within the authority expressly or impliedly given in the partnership agreement, and a partner is responsible to the other partners for damages or losses arising from unauthorized activities.

Duty to Inform Copartners

As in the agency relationship, a partner is expected to inform copartners of notices and matters coming to her attention that would be of interest to the partnership.

Duty to Account

The partnership—and necessarily the partners—have a duty to allow copartners and their agents access to the partnership's books and records and to provide "any information concerning the partnership's business and affairs reasonably required for the proper exercise of the partner's rights and duties under the partnership agreement [or this Act]."[7] The fiduciary standard is imposed upon the duty to account for "any property, profit, or benefit derived by [a] partner," as noted in RUPA Section 404.[8]

The Rights That Partners Have in a Partnership

Necessarily, for every duty owed there is a correlative right. So, for example, if a partner has a duty to account, the other partners and the partnership have a right to an accounting. Beyond that, partners have recognized rights affecting the operation of the partnership.

Here we may call out the following salient rights: (1) to distributions of money, (2) to management, (3) to choose copartners, (4) to property of the partnership, (5) to assign partnership interest, and (6) to enforce duties and rights.

Rights to Distributions

The purpose of a partnership is ultimately to distribute "money or other property from a partnership to a partner in the partner's capacity."[9] There are, however, various types of money distributions, including profits (and losses), indemnification, capital, and compensation.

Right to Profits (and Losses)

Profits and losses may be shared according to any formula on which the partners agree. For example, the partnership agreement may provide that two senior partners are entitled to 35 percent each of the profit from the year and the two junior partners are entitled to 15 percent each. The next year the percentages will be adjusted based on such things as number of new clients garnered, number of billable hours, or amount of income generated. Eventually, the senior partners might retire and each be entitled to 2 percent of the firm's income, and the previous junior partners become senior, with new junior partners admitted.

If no provision is stated, then under RUPA Section 401(b), "each partner is entitled to an equal share of the partnership profits and is chargeable with a share of the partnership losses in proportion to the partner's share of the profits." Section 18(a) of the Uniform Partnership Act is to the same effect. The right to share in the profits is the reason people want to "make partner": a partner will reap the benefits of other partners' successes (and pay for their failures too). A person working for the firm who is not a partner is an associate and usually only gets only a salary.

Right to Indemnification

A partner who incurs liabilities in the normal course of business or to preserve its business or property is entitled to indemnification (UPA Section 18(b), RUPA Section 401(c)). The liability is a loan owing to the partner by the firm.

Right to Return of Capital Contribution

When a partner joins a partnership, she is expected to make a capital contribution to the firm; this may be deducted from her share of the distributed profit and banked by the firm in its capital account. The law provides that "the partnership must reimburse a partner for an advance of funds beyond the amount of the partner's agreed capital contribution, thereby treating the advance as a loan."[10] A partner may get a return of capital under UPA after creditors are paid off if the business is wound down and terminated.[11]

Right to Compensation

Section 401(d) of RUPA provides that "a partner is not entitled to remuneration for services performed for the partnership, except for reasonable compensation for services rendered in winding up the business of the partnership"; UPA Section 18(f) is to the same effect. A partner gets his money from the firm by sharing the profits, *not* by a salary or wages.

Right to Management

All partners are entitled to share equally in the management and conduct of the business, unless the partnership agreement provides otherwise.[12] The partnership agreement could be structured to delegate more decision-making power to one class of partners (senior partners) than to others (junior partners), or it may give more voting weight to certain individuals. For example, perhaps those with the most experience will, for the first four years after a new partner is admitted, have more voting weight than the new partner.

Right to Choose Partners

A business partnership is often analogized to a marriage partnership. In both there is a relationship of trust and confidence between (or among) the parties; in both the poor judgment, negligence, or dishonesty of one can create liabilities on the other(s). In a good marriage or good partnership, the partners are friends, whatever else the legal relationship imposes. Thus, no one is compelled to accept a partner against his or her will. Section 401(i) of RUPA provides, "A person may become a partner only with the consent of all of the partners." UPA Section 18(g) is to the same effect; the doctrine is called **delectus personae**. The freedom to select new partners, however, is not absolute. In 1984, the Supreme Court held that Title VII of the Civil Rights Act of 1964—which prohibits discrimination in employment based on race, religion, national origin, or sex—applies to partnerships.[13]

delectus personae

The theory that a new partner can only be admitted to a firm with the unanimous consent of all.

Right to Property of the Partnership

Partners are the owners of the partnership, which might not include any physical property; that is, one partner could contribute the building, furnishings, and equipment and rent those to the partnership (or those could count as her partnership capital contribution and become the partnership's). But partnership property consists of all property originally advanced or contributed to the partnership or subsequently acquired by purchase or contribution. Unless a contrary intention can be shown, property acquired with partnership funds is partnership property, not an individual partner's: "Property acquired by a partnership is property of the partnership and not of the partners individually."[14]

Rights in Specific Partnership Property: UPA Approach

Suppose that Able, who contributed the building and grounds on which the partnership business is conducted, suddenly dies. Who is entitled to her share of the specific property, such as inventory, the building, and the money in the cash register—her husband and children, or the other partners, Baker and Carr? Section 25(1) of UPA declares that the partners hold the partnership property as **tenants in partnership**. As spelled out in Section 25(2), the specific property interest of a tenant in partnership vests in the surviving partners, not in the heirs. But the heirs are entitled to the deceased partner's interest in the partnership itself, so that while Baker and Carr may use the partnership property for the benefit of the partnership without consulting Able's heirs, they must account to her heirs for her proper share of the partnership's profits.

tenants in partnership

Under UPA, how partnership property is held by the partners: jointly.

Rights in Specific Property: RUPA Approach

Section 501 of RUPA provides, "A partner is not a co-owner of partnership property and has no interest in partnership property which can be transferred, either voluntarily or involuntarily." Partnership property is owned by the entity; UPA's concept of tenants in partnership is abolished in favor of adoption of the entity theory. The result, however, is not different.

Right to Assign Partnership Interest

One of the hallmarks of the capitalistic system is that people should be able to dispose of their property interests more or less as they see fit. Partnership interests may be assigned to some extent.

Voluntary Assignment

At common law, assignment of a partner's interest in the business—for example, as a mortgage in return for a loan—would result in a legal dissolution of the partnership. Thus, in the absence of UPA, which changed the law, Baker's decision to mortgage his interest in the car dealership in return for a $20,000 loan from his bank would mean that the three—Able, Baker, and Carr—were no longer partners. Section 27 of UPA declares that assignment of an interest in the partnership neither dissolves the partnership nor entitles the assignee "to interfere in the management or administration of the partnership business or affairs, or to require any information or account of partnership transactions, or to inspect the partnership books." The assignment merely entitles the assignee to receive whatever profits the assignor would have received—this is the assignor's transferable interest.[15] Under UPA, this interest is assignable.[16]

Under RUPA, the same distinction is made between a partner's interest in the partnership and a partner's transferable interest. The Official Comment to Section 101 reads as follows: "'Partnership interest' or 'partner's interest in the partnership' is defined to mean all of a partner's interests in the partnership, including the partner's transferable interest and all management and other rights. A partner's 'transferable interest' is a more limited concept and means only his share of the profits and losses and right to receive distributions, that is, the partner's economic interests."[17]

This transferable interest is assignable under RUPA 503 (unless the partners agree to restrict transfers, Section 103(a)). It does not, by itself, cause the dissolution of the partnership; it does not entitle the transferee to access to firm information, to participate in running the firm, or to inspect or copy the books. The transferee is entitled to whatever distributions the transferor partner would have been entitled to, including, upon dissolution of the firm, the net amounts the transferor would have received had there been no assignment.

RUPA Section 101(b)(3) confers standing on a transferee to seek a judicial dissolution and winding up of the partnership business as provided in Section 801(6), thus continuing the rule of UPA Section 32(2). But under RUPA 601(4)(ii), the other partners may by unanimous vote expel a partner who has made "a transfer of all or substantially all of that partner's transferable interest in the partnership, other than a transfer for security purposes [as for a loan]." Upon a creditor's *foreclosure* of the security interest, though, the partner may be expelled.

Involuntary Assignment

It may be a misnomer to describe an involuntary assignment as a "right"; it might better be thought of as a consequence of the right to own property. In any event, if a partner is sued in his personal capacity and a judgment is rendered against him, the question arises: may the judgment creditor seize partnership property? Section 28 of UPA and RUPA Section 504 permit a judgment creditor to obtain a **charging order**, which charges the partner's interest in the partnership with obligation to satisfy the judgment. The court may appoint a receiver to ensure that partnership proceeds are paid to the judgment creditor. But the creditor is not entitled to specific partnership property. The partner may always pay off the debt and redeem his interest in the partnership. If the partner does not pay off the debt, the holder of the charging order may acquire legal ownership of the partner's interest. That confers upon the judgment creditor an important power: he may, if the partnership is one at will, dissolve the partnership and claim the partner's share of the assets. For that reason, the copartners might wish to redeem the interest—pay off the creditor—in order to preserve the partnership. As with the voluntary assignment, the assignee of an involuntary assignment does not become a partner. See Figure 41.1.

charging order

A court order directing a partnership to pay a partner's judgment creditor the distribution that the partner would normally receive.

FIGURE 41.1 Property Rights

	Specific Property	Interest
1. At Death	To Surviving Partners	To Estate
2. Assignment by One Partner?	No	Yes
3. Claims by a Partner's Creditors?	No	Yes

Right to Enforce Partnership Rights

The rights and duties imposed by partnership law are, of course, valueless unless they can be enforced. Partners and partnerships have mechanisms under the law to enforce them.

Right to Information and Inspection of Books

We noted in Section 1 of this chapter that partners have a duty to account; the corollary right is the right to access books and records, which is usually very important in determining partnership rights. Section 403(b) of RUPA provides, "A partnership shall provide partners and their agents and attorneys access to its books and records. It shall provide former partners and their agents and attorneys access to books and records pertaining to the period during which they were partners. The right of access provides the opportunity to inspect and copy books and records during ordinary business hours. A partnership may impose a reasonable charge, covering the costs of labor and material, for copies of documents furnished."[18]

Section 19 of UPA is basically in accord. This means that without demand—and for any purpose—the partnership must provide any information concerning its business and affairs reasonably required for the proper exercise of the partner's rights and duties under the partnership agreement or the act; and on demand, it must provide any other information concerning the partnership's business and affairs, unless the demand is unreasonable or improper.[19] Generally, the partnership agreement cannot deny the right to inspection.

The duty to account mentioned in Section 1 of this chapter normally means that the partners and the partnership should keep reasonable records so everyone can tell what is going on. A formal accounting under UPA is different.

Under UPA Section 22, any partner is entitled to a formal account (or accounting) of the partnership affairs under the following conditions:

1. If he is wrongfully excluded from the partnership business or possession of its property by his copartners;
2. If the right exists under the terms of any agreement;
3. If a partner profits in violation of his fiduciary duty (as per UPA 22); and
4. Whenever it is otherwise just and reasonable.

At common law, partners could not obtain an accounting except in the event of dissolution. But from an early date, equity courts would appoint a referee, auditor, or special master to investigate the books of a business when one of the partners had grounds to complain, and UPA broadened considerably the right to an accounting. The court has plenary power to investigate all facets of the business, evaluate claims, declare legal rights among the parties, and order money judgments against any partner in the wrong.

Under RUPA Section 405, this "accounting" business is somewhat modified. Reflecting the entity theory, the *partnership* can sue a partner for wrongdoing, which is not allowed under UPA. Moreover, to quote from the Official Comment, RUPA "provides that, during the term of the partnership, partners may maintain a variety of legal or equitable actions, including an action for an accounting, as well as a final action for an accounting upon dissolution and winding up. It reflects a new policy choice that partners should have access to the courts during the term of the partnership to resolve claims against the partnership and the other partners, leaving broad judicial discretion to fashion appropriate remedies [and] an accounting is not a prerequisite to the availability of the other remedies a partner may have against the partnership or the other partners."[20]

Key Takeaway

Partners have important duties in a partnership, including (1) the duty to serve—that is, to devote herself to the work of the partnership; (2) the duty of loyalty, which is informed by the fiduciary standard: the obligation to act always in the best interest of the partnership and not in one's own best interest; (3) the duty of care—that is, to act as a reasonably prudent partner would; (4) the duty of obedience not to breach any aspect of the agreement or act without authority; (5) the duty to inform copartners; and (6) the duty to account to the partnership.

Partners also have rights. These include the rights (1) to distributions of money, including profits (and losses), indemnification, and return of capital contribution (but not a right to compensation); (2) to management; (3) to choose copartners; (4) to property of the partnership, and no partner has any rights to specific property; (5) to assign (voluntarily or involuntarily) the partnership interest; and (6) to enforce duties and rights by suits in law or equity. (Under RUPA, a formal accounting is not first required.)

Exercises

1. What is the "fiduciary duty," and why is it imposed on some partners' actions with the partnership?
2. Distinguish between ownership of partnership property under UPA as opposed to under RUPA.
3. Carlos obtained a judgment against Pauline, a partner in a partnership, for negligently crashing her car into Carlos's while she was not in the scope of partnership business. Carlos wants to satisfy the judgment from her employer. How can Carlos do that?

4. What is the difference between the duty to account and a formal partnership accounting?
5. What does it mean to say a partnership interest has been involuntarily assigned?

41.2 Operation: The Partnership and Third Parties

Learning Objectives

1. Understand the partners' and partnership's contract liability.
2. Understand the partners' and partnership's tort and criminal liability.
3. Describe the partners' and partnership's tax liability.

By express terms, the law of agency applies to partnership law. Every partner is an agent of the partnership for the purpose of its business. Consequently, the following discussion will be a review of agency law, covered in Chapter 40 as it applies to partnerships. The Revised Uniform Partnership Act (RUPA) adds a few new wrinkles to the liability issue.

Contract Liability

Liability of the Partnership

Recall that an agent can make contracts on behalf of a principal under three types of authority: express, implied, and apparent. *Express authority* is that explicitly delegated to the agent, *implied authority* is that necessary to the carrying out of the express authority, and *apparent authority* is that which a third party is led to believe has been conferred by the principal on the agent, even though in fact it was not or it was revoked. When a partner has authority, the partnership is bound by contracts the partner makes on its behalf. Section 4, *Hodge v. Garrett*, discusses all three types of authority.

The General Rule

Section 305 of RUPA restates agency law: "A partnership is liable for loss or injury, or for a penalty incurred, as a result of a wrongful act or omission, or other actionable conduct, of a partner acting in the ordinary course"[21] of partnership business or with its authority. The ability of a partner to bind the partnership to contract liability is problematic, especially where the authority is apparent: the firm denies liability, lawsuits ensue, and unhappiness generally follows.

But the firm is not liable for an act not apparently in the ordinary course of business, unless the act was authorized by the others.[22] Section 401(j) of RUPA requires the unanimous consent of the partners for a grant of authority outside the ordinary course of business, unless the partnership agreement provides otherwise.

Under the Uniform Partnership Act (UPA) Section 9(3), the firm is not liable for five actions that no single partner has implied or apparent authority to do, because they are not "in the ordinary course of partnership." These actions are: (1) assignment of partnership property for the benefit of creditors, (2) disposing of the firm's goodwill (selling the right to do business with the firm's clients to another business), (3) actions that make it impossible to carry on the business, (4) confessing a judgment against the partnership, and (5) submitting a partnership claim or liability. RUPA omits that section, leaving it to the courts to decide the outer limits of the agency power of a partner. In any event, unauthorized actions by a partner may be ratified by the partnership.

Partnership "Statements"

New under RUPA is the ability of partnerships, partners, or even non-partners to issue and file "statements" that announce to the world the establishment or denial of authority. The goal here is to control the reach of apparent authority. There are several kinds of statements authorized.

statement of partnership authority

A public filing setting out or limiting partners' authority.

statement of denial

A public filing that a partner has no authority to perform some act(s) on the firm's behalf or that a person is not a partner.

statement of dissociation

A public filing that a partner is withdrawing from the firm.

A **statement of partnership authority** is allowed by RUPA Section 303. It specifies the names of the partners authorized, or not authorized, to enter into transactions on behalf of the partnership and any other matters. The most important goal of the statement of authority is to facilitate the transfer of real property held in the name of the partnership. A statement must specify the names of the partners authorized to execute an instrument transferring that property.

A **statement of denial**, RUPA Section 304, operates to allow partners (and persons named as partners) an opportunity to deny any fact asserted in a statement of partnership authority.

A **statement of dissociation**, RUPA Section 704, may be filed by a partnership or a dissociated partner, informing the world that the person is no longer a partner. This tells the world that the named person is no longer in the partnership.

There are three other statements authorized: a *statement of qualification* establishes that the partnership has satisfied all conditions precedent to the qualification of the partnership as a limited liability partnership; a *statement of foreign qualification* means a limited liability partnership is qualified and registered to do business in a state other than that in which it is originally registered; and a *statement of amendment or cancellation* of any of the foregoing.[23] Limited liability partnerships are taken up in Chapter 42.

Generally, RUPA Section 105 allows partnerships to file these statements with the state secretary of state's office; those affecting real estate need to be filed with (or also with) the local county land recorder's office. The notices bind those who know about them right away, and they are constructive notice to the world after ninety days as to authority to transfer real property in the partnership's name, as to dissociation, and as to dissolution. However, as to other grants or limitations of authority, "only a third party who knows or has received a notification of a partner's lack of authority in an ordinary course transaction is bound."[24]

Since RUPA is mostly intended to provide the rules for the small, unsophisticated partnership, it is questionable whether these arcane "statements" are very often employed, or very useful.

Personal Liability of Partners, in General

It is clear that the *partnership* is liable for contracts by authorized partners, as discussed in the preceding paragraphs. The bad thing about the partnership as a form of business organization is that it imposes liability on the partners *personally and without limit*. Section 306 of RUPA provides that "all partners are liable jointly and severally for all obligations of the partnership unless otherwise agreed by the claimant or provided by law."[25] Section 13 of UPA is in accord.

Liability of Existing Partners

Contract liability is joint and several: that is, all partners are liable ("joint") and each is "several." (We usually do not use *several* in modern English to mean "each"; it's an archaic usage.) But—and here's the intrusion of entity theory—generally RUPA requires the judgment creditor to exhaust the partnership's assets before going after the separate assets of a partner. Thus, under RUPA the partners are *guarantors* of the partnership's liabilities.[26]

Under UPA, contract liability is joint only, not also several. This means the partners must be sued in a joint action brought against them all. A partner who is not named cannot later be sued by a creditor in a separate proceeding, though the ones who were named could see a proportionate contribution from the ones who were not.

Liability of Incoming Partners

Under RUPA Section 306(b), a new partner has no personal liability to existing creditors of the partnership, and only her capital investment in the firm is at risk for the satisfaction of existing partnership debts. Sections 17 and 41(7) of UPA are in accord. But, again, under either statute a new partner's personal assets are at risk with respect to partnership liabilities incurred after her admission as a partner. This is a daunting prospect, and it is the reason for the invention of hybrid forms of business organization: limited partnerships, limited liability companies, and limited liability partnerships. The corporate form, of course, also (usually) obviates the owners' personal liability.

Tort and Criminal Liability

Partnership Liability for Torts

The rules affecting partners' tort liability (discussed in Section 2) and those affecting contract liability are the same. Section 13 of UPA says the partnership is liable for "any wrongful act or omission of any partner acting in the ordinary course of the business of the partnership or with the authority of his co-partners."[27] A civil "wrongful act" is necessarily either a tort or a breach of contract, so no distinction is made between them. (Section 305 of RUPA changed the phraseology slightly by adding after *any wrongful act or omission* the words *or other actionable conduct*; this makes the partnership liable for its partner's no-fault torts.) That the principal should be liable for its agents' wrongdoings is of course basic agency law. RUPA does expand liability by allowing a partner to sue during the term of the partnership without first having to get out of it, as is required under UPA.

For tortious acts, the partners are said to be jointly and severally liable under both UPA and RUPA, and the plaintiff may separately sue one or more partners. Even after winning a judgment, the plaintiff may sue other partners unnamed in the original action. Each and every partner is separately liable for the entire amount of the debt, although the plaintiff is not entitled to recover more than the total of his damages. The practical effect of the rules making partners personally liable for partnership contracts and torts can be huge. In his classic textbook *Economics*, Professor Paul Samuelson observed that unlimited liability "reveals why partnerships tend to be confined to small, personal enterprises. . . . When it becomes a question of placing their personal fortunes in jeopardy, people are reluctant to put their capital into complex ventures over which they can exercise little control. . . . In the field of investment banking, concerns like JPMorgan Chase used to advertise proudly 'not incorporated' so that their creditors could have extra assurance. But even these concerns have converted themselves into corporate entities."[28]

Partners' Personal Liability for Torts

Of course, a person is always liable for his own torts. All partners are also liable for any partner's tort committed in the scope of partnership business under agency law, and this liability is—again—personal and unlimited, subject to RUPA's requirement that the judgment creditor exhaust the partnership's assets before going after the separate assets of the partners. The partner who commits a tort or breach of trust must indemnify the partnership for losses paid to the third party.[29]

Liability for Crimes

Criminal liability is generally personal to the miscreant. Nonparticipating copartners are ordinarily not liable for crimes if guilty intent is an element. When guilty intent is not an element, as in certain regulatory offenses, all partners may be guilty of an act committed by a partner in the course of the business.

Liability for Taxes

conduit theory

The theory that a business entity does not itself owe taxes on income; it only acts as a pass-through for its members to receive income.

Corporate income gets taxed twice under federal law: once to the corporation and again to the shareholders who receive income as dividends. However, the partnership's income "passes through" the partnership and is distributed to the partners under the **conduit theory**. When partners get income from the firm they have to pay tax on it, but the partnership pays no tax (it files an information return). This is perceived to be a significant advantage of the partnership form.

Key Takeaway

The partnership is generally liable for any contract made by a partner with authority express, implied, or apparent. Under RUPA the firm, partners, or even nonpartners may to some extent limit their liability by filing "statements" with the appropriate state registrar; such statements only affect those who know of them, except that a notice affecting the right of a partner to sell real estate or regarding dissociation or dissolution is effective against the world after ninety days.

All partners are liable for contracts entered into and torts committed by any partner acting in or apparently in the normal course of business. This liability is personal and unlimited, joint and several (although under UPA contract liability it is only joint). Incoming partners are not liable, in contract or in tort, for activities predating their arrival, but their capital contribution is at risk. Criminal liability is generally personal unless the crime requires no intention.

Exercises

1. What is the partnership's liability for contracts entered into by its partners?
2. What is the personal liability of partners for breach of a contract made by one of the partnership's members?
3. Why would people feel more comfortable knowing that JPMorgan Bank—Morgan was at one time the richest man in the United States—was a partnership and not a corporation?
4. What is the point of RUPA's "statements"? How can they be of use to a partner who has, for example, retired and is no longer involved in the firm?
5. Under what circumstances is the partnership liable for crimes committed by its partners?
6. How is a partnership taxed more favorably than a corporation?

41.3 Dissolution and Winding Up

Learning Objectives

1. Understand the dissolution of general partnerships under the Uniform Partnership Act (UPA).

2. Understand the dissociation and dissolution of general partnerships under the Revised Uniform Partnership Act (RUPA).
3. Explain the winding up of partnerships under UPA and RUPA.

It is said that a partnership is like a marriage, and that extends to its ending too. It's easier to get into a partnership than it is to get out of it because legal entanglements continue after a person is no longer a partner. The rules governing "getting out" of a partnership are different under the Revised Uniform Partnership Act (RUPA) than under the Uniform Partnership Act (UPA). We take up UPA first.

Dissolution of Partnerships under UPA

Dissolution, in the most general sense, means a separation into component parts.

Meaning of Dissolution under UPA

People in business are sometimes confused about the meaning of **dissolution**. It does not mean the termination of a business. It has a precise legal definition, given in UPA Section 29: "The dissolution of a partnership is the change in the relation of the partners caused by any partner ceasing to be associated in the carrying on as distinguished from the winding up of the business." The partnership is not necessarily terminated on dissolution; rather, it continues until the winding up of partnership affairs is completed, and the remaining partners may choose to continue on as a new partnership if they want.[30] But, again, under UPA the partnership dissolves upon the withdrawal of any partner.

dissolution

A legal severance or breaking up; under UPA the change in relations caused by a partner's withdrawal from the firm.

Causes of Dissolution

Partnerships can dissolve for a number of reasons.[31]

In Accordance with the Agreement

The term of the partnership agreement may have expired or the partnership may be at will and one of the partners desires to leave it. All the partners may decide that it is preferable to dissolve rather than to continue. One of the partners may have been expelled in accordance with a provision in the agreement. In none of these circumstances is the agreement violated, though its spirit surely might have been. Professor Samuelson calls to mind the example of William Dean Howells's Silas Lapham, who forces his partner to sell out by offering him an ultimatum: "You may buy me out or I'll buy you out." The ultimatum was given at a time when the partner could not afford to buy Lapham out, so the partner had no choice.

In Violation of the Agreement

Dissolution may also result from violation of the agreement, as when the partners decide to discharge a partner though no provision permits them to do so, or as when a partner decides to quit in violation of a term agreement. In the former case, the remaining partners are liable for damages for wrongful dissolution, and in the latter case, the withdrawing partner is liable to the remaining partners the same way.

By Operation of Law

A third reason for dissolution is the occurrence of some event, such as enactment of a statute, that makes it unlawful to continue the business. Or a partner may die or one or more partners or the entire partnership may become bankrupt. Dissolution under these circumstances is said to be by operation of law.[32]

By Court Order

Finally, dissolution may be by court order. Courts are empowered to dissolve partnerships when "on application by or for a partner" a partner is shown to be a lunatic, of unsound mind, incapable of performing his part of the agreement, "guilty of such conduct as tends to affect prejudicially the carrying on of the business," or otherwise behaves in such a way that "it is not reasonably practicable to carry on the business in partnership with him." A court may also order dissolution if the business can only be carried on at a loss or whenever equitable. In some circumstances, a court will order dissolution upon the application of a purchaser of a partner's interest.[33]

Effect of Dissolution on Authority

For the most part, dissolution terminates the authority of the partners to act for the partnership. The only significant exceptions are for acts necessary to wind up partnership affairs or to complete transactions begun but not finished at the time of dissolution.[34] Notwithstanding the latter exception, no partner can bind the partnership if it has dissolved because it has become unlawful to carry on the business or if the partner seeking to exercise authority has become bankrupt.

After Dissolution

After a partnership has dissolved, it can follow one of two paths. It can carry on business as a new partnership, or it can wind up the business and cease operating (see Figure 41.2).

FIGURE 41.2 Alternatives Following UPA Dissolution

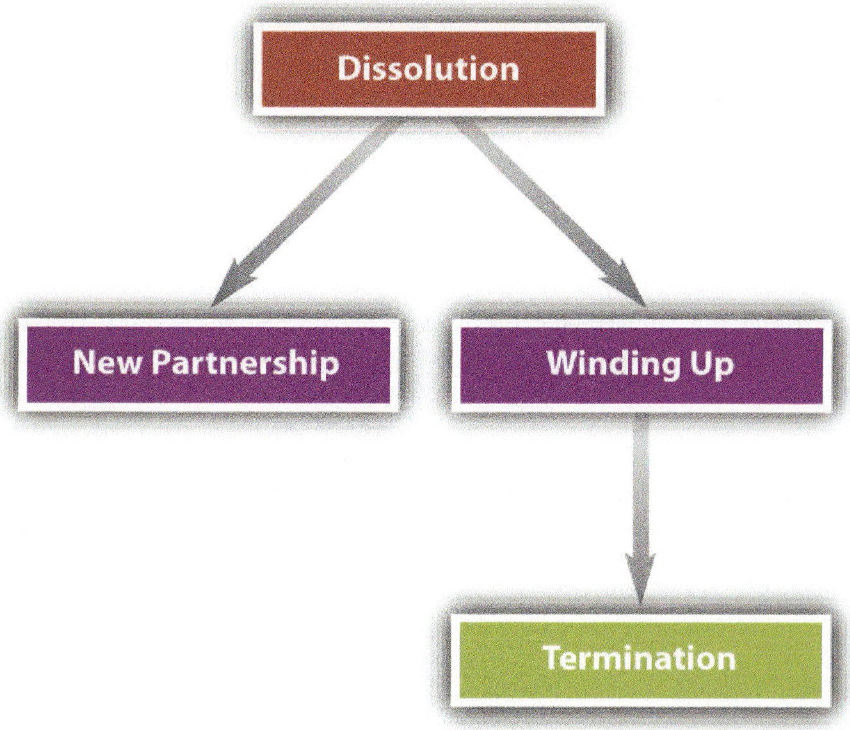

Forming a New Partnership

In order to carry on the business as a new partnership, there must be an agreement—preferably as part of the original partnership agreement but maybe only after dissolution (and maybe oral)—that upon dissolution (e.g., if a partner dies, retires, or quits) the others will regroup and carry on.

Under UPA the remaining partners have the right to carry on when (1) the dissolution was in contravention of the agreement, (2) a partner was expelled according to the partnership agreement, or (3) all partners agree to carry on.[35]

Whether the former partner dies or otherwise quits the firm, the noncontinuing one or his, her, or its legal representative is entitled to an accounting and to be paid the value of the partnership interest, less damages for wrongful dissolution.[36] The firm may need to borrow money to pay the former partner or her estate; or, in the case of a deceased partner, the money to pay the former partner is obtained through a life insurance buyout policy.

Partnerships routinely insure the lives of the partners, who have no ownership interests in the insurance policies. The policies should bear a face amount equal to each partner's interest in the partnership and should be adjusted as the fortunes of the partnership change. Proceeds of the insurance policy are used on death to pay the purchase price of the interest inherited by the deceased's estate. If the insurance policy pays out more than the interest at stake, the partnership retains the difference. If the policy pays out less, the partnership agrees to pay the difference in installments.

Another set of issues arises when the partnership changes because an old partner departs and a new one joins. Suppose that Baker leaves the car dealership business and his interest is purchased by Alice, who is then admitted to the partnership. Assume that when Baker left, the business owed Mogul Parts Company $5,000 and Laid Back Upholsterers $4,000. After Baker left and Alice joined, Mogul sells another $5,000 worth of parts to the firm on credit, and Sizzling Radiator Repair, a new creditor, advances $3,000 worth of radiator repair parts. These circumstances pose four questions.

First, do creditors of the old partnership remain creditors of the new partnership? Yes.[37]

Second, does Baker, the old partner, remain liable to the creditors of the old partnership? Yes.[38] That could pose uncomfortable problems for Baker, who may have left the business because he lost interest in it and wished to put his money elsewhere. The last thing he wants is the threat of liability hanging over his head when he can no longer profit from the firm's operations. That is all the more true if he had a falling out with his partners and does not trust them. The solution is given in UPA Section 36(2), which says that an old partner is discharged from liability if the creditors and the new partnership agree to discharge him.

Third, is Alice, the new partner, liable to creditors of the old partnership? Yes, but only to the extent of her capital contribution.[39]

Fourth, is Baker, the old partner, liable for debts incurred after his withdrawal from the partnership? Surprisingly, yes, unless Baker takes certain action toward old and new creditors. He must provide actual notice that he has withdrawn to anyone who has extended credit in the past. Once he has done so, he has no liability to these creditors for credit extended to the partnership thereafter. Of course, it would be difficult to provide notice to future creditors, since at the time of withdrawal they would not have had a relationship with the partnership. To avoid liability to new creditors who knew of the partnership, the solution required under UPA Section 35(l)(b)(II) is to advertise Baker's departure in a general circulation newspaper in the place where the partnership business was regularly carried on.

Winding Up and Termination

Because the differences between UPA's and RUPA's provisions for winding up and termination are not as significant as those between their provisions for dissolution, the discussion for winding up and termination will cover both acts at once, following the discussion of dissociation and dissolution under RUPA.

Dissociation and Dissolution of Partnerships under RUPA

Comment 1 to RUPA Section 601 is a good lead-in to this section. According to the comment, RUPA dramatically changes the law governing partnership breakups and dissolution. An entirely new concept, "dissociation," is used in lieu of UPA term "dissolution" to denote the change in the relationship caused by a partner's ceasing to be associated in the carrying on of the business. "Dissolution" is retained but with a different meaning. The entity theory of partnership provides a conceptual basis for continuing the firm itself despite a partner's withdrawal from the firm.

Under UPA, the partnership is an aggregate, a collection of individuals; upon the withdrawal of any member from the collection, the aggregate dissolves. But because RUPA conforms the partnership as an entity, there is no conceptual reason for it to dissolve upon a member's withdrawal. "Dissociation" occurs when any partner ceases to be involved in the business of the firm, and "dissolution" happens when RUPA requires the partnership to wind up and terminate; dissociation does not necessarily cause dissolution.

Dissociation

Dissociation, as noted in the previous paragraph, is the change in relations caused by a partner's withdrawal from the firm's business.

dissociation

Under RUPA, the withdrawal of a partner from the firm.

Causes of Dissociation

Dissociation is caused in ten possible ways: (1) a partner says she wants out; (2) an event triggers dissociation as per the partnership agreement; (3) a partner is expelled as per the agreement; (4) a partner is expelled by unanimous vote of the others because it is unlawful to carry on with that partner, because that partner has transferred to a transferee all interest in the partnership (except for security purposes), or because a corporate partner's or partnership partner's existence is effectively terminated; (5) by a court order upon request by the partnership or another partner because the one expelled has been determined to have misbehaved (engaged in serious wrongful conduct, persists in abusing the agreement, acts in ways making continuing the business impracticable); (6) the partner has declared bankruptcy; (7) the partner has died or had a guardian appointed, or has been adjudicated as incompetent; (8) the partner is a trust whose assets are exhausted; (9) the partner is an estate and the estate's interest in the partnership has been entirely transferred; (10) the partner dies or, if the partner is another partnership or a corporation trust or estate, that entity's existence is terminated.[40]

Effect of Dissociation

After a partner dissociates, the partner's right to participate in management terminates. (However, if the dissociation goes on to dissolution and winding up, partners who have not wrongfully caused the dissociation may participate in winding-up activities.)[41] The dissociated partner's duty of loyalty and care terminates; the former partner may compete with the firm, except for matters arising before the dissociation.[42]

When partners come and go, as they do, problems may arise. What power does the dissociated partner have to bind the partnership? What power does the partnership have to impose liability on the dissociated one? RUPA provides that the dissociated partner loses any actual authority upon dissociation, and his or her apparent authority lingers for not longer than two years if the dissociated one acts in a way that would have bound the partnership before dissociation, provided the other party (1) reasonably believed the dissociated one was a partner, (2) did not have notice of the dissociation, and (3) is not deemed to have constructive notice from a filed "statement of dissociation."[43] The dissociated partner, of course, is liable for damages to the partnership if third parties had cause to think she was still a partner and the partnership became liable because of that; she is liable to the firm as an unauthorized agent.[44]

A partner's dissociation does nothing to change that partner's liability for predissociation obligations.[45] For postdissociation liability, exposure is for two years if at the time of entering into the transaction the other party (1) reasonably believed the dissociated one was a partner, (2) didn't have notice of the dissociation, and (3) is not deemed to have constructive notice from a filed "statement of dissociation." For example, Baker withdraws from the firm of Able, Baker, and Carr. Able contracts with HydroLift for a new hydraulic car lift that costs $25,000 installed. HydroLift is not aware at the time of contracting that Baker is disassociated and believes she is still a partner. A year later, the firm not having been paid, HydroLift sues Able, Baker, and Carr and the partnership. Baker has potential liability. Baker could have protected herself by filing a "statement of dissociation," or—better—the partnership agreement should provide that the firm would file such statements upon the dissociation of any partner (and if it does not, it would be liable to her for the consequences).

Dissolution

Dissociation does not necessarily cause dissolution (see the discussion later in this section of how the firm continues after a dissociation); dissolution and winding up happen only for the causes stated in RUPA Section 801, discussed in the following paragraphs.

Causes of Dissolution

There are three causes of dissolution: (1) by act of the partners—some dissociations do trigger dissolution; (2) by operation of law; or (3) by court order. The partnership agreement may change or eliminate the dissolution trigger as to (1); dissolution by the latter two means cannot be tinkered with.[46]

at-will partnership

A partnership with no stated term of continuation or existence.

term partnership

A partnership with a time period for its duration expressed.

(1) Dissolution by *act of the partners* may occur as follows:

- Any member of an **at-will partnership** can dissociate at any time, triggering dissolution and liquidation. The partners who wish to continue the business of a **term partnership**, though, cannot be forced to liquidate the business by a partner who withdraws prematurely in violation of the partnership agreement. In any event, common agreement formats for dissolution will provide for built-in dispute resolution, and enlightened partners often agree to such mechanisms in advance to avoid the kinds of problems listed here.
- Any partnership will dissolve upon the happening of an event the partners specified would cause dissolution in their agreement. They may change their minds, of course, agree to continue, and amend the partnership agreement accordingly.
- A term partnership may be dissolved before its term expires in three ways. First, if a partner dissociated by death, declaring bankruptcy, becoming incapacitated, or wrongfully dissociates, the partnership will dissolve if within ninety days of that triggering dissociation at least half the remaining partners express their will to wind it up. Second, the partnership may be dissolved if the term expires. Third, it may be dissolved if all the partners agree to amend the partnership agreement by expressly agreeing to dissolve.

(2) Dissolution will happen in some cases by *operation of law* if it becomes illegal to continue the business, or substantially all of it. For example, if the firm's business was the manufacture and distribution of trans fats and it became illegal to do that, the firm would dissolve.[47] This cause of dissolution is not subject to partnership agreement.

(3) *Dissolution by court order* can occur on application by a partner. A court may declare that it is, for various reasons specified in RUPA Section 801(5), no longer reasonably practicable to continue operation. Also, a court may order dissolution upon application by a transferee of a partner's transferable interest or by a purchaser at a foreclosure of a charging order if the court determines it is equitable. For example, if Creditor gets a charging order against Paul Partner and the obligation cannot reasonably be paid by the firm, a court could order dissolution so Creditor would get paid from the liquidated assets of the firm.

Effect of Dissolution

A partnership continues after dissolution only for the purpose of winding up its business. The partnership is terminated when the winding up of its business is completed.[48] However, before winding up is completed, the partners—except any wrongfully dissociating—may agree to carry on the partnership, in which case it resumes business as if dissolution never happened.[49]

Continuing after Dissociation

Dissociation, again, does not necessarily cause dissolution. In an at-will partnership, the death (including termination of an entity partner), bankruptcy, incapacity, or expulsion of a partner will not cause dissolution.[50] In a term partnership, the firm continues if, within ninety days of an event triggering dissociation, fewer than half the partners express their will to wind up. The partnership agreement may provide that RUPA's dissolution-triggering events, including dissociation, will not trigger dissolution. However, the agreement cannot change the rules that dissolution is caused by the business becoming illegal or by court order. Creditors of the partnership remain as before, and the dissociated partner is liable for partnership obligations arising before dissociation.

Section 701 of RUPA provides that if the firm continues in business after a partner dissociates, without winding up, then the partnership must purchase the dissociated partner's interest; RUPA Section 701(b) explains how to determine the buyout price. It is the amount that would have been distributed to the dissociated partner if, on the date of dissociation, the firm's assets were sold "at a price equal to the greater of the liquidation value or the value based on a sale of the entire business as a going concern," minus damages for wrongful dissociation. A wrongful dissociater may have to wait a while to get paid in full, unless a court determines that immediate payment "will not cause an undue hardship to the partnership," but the longest nonwrongful dissociaters need to wait is 120 days.[51] A dissociated partner can sue the firm to determine the buyout price and the court may assess attorney's, appraiser's, and expert's fees against a party the court finds "acted arbitrarily, vexatiously, or in bad faith."[52]

Winding Up the Partnership under UPA and RUPA

If the partners decide not to continue the business upon dissolution, they are obliged to wind up the business. The partnership continues after dissolution only for the purpose of winding up its business, after which it is terminated.[53] **Winding up** entails concluding all unfinished business pending at the date of dissolution and payment of all debts. The partners must then settle accounts among themselves in order to distribute the remaining assets. At any time after dissolution and before winding up is completed, the partners (except a wrongfully dissociated one) can stop the process and carry on the business.

Winding up

Finishing the business at hand, settling accounts, and terminating a firm.

UPA and RUPA are not significantly different as to winding up, so they will be discussed together. Two issues are discussed here: who can participate in winding up and how the assets of the firm are distributed on liquidation.

Who Can Participate in Winding Up

The partners who have not wrongfully dissociated may participate in winding up the partnership business. On application of any partner, a court may for good cause judicially supervise the winding up.[54]

Settlement of Accounts among Partners

Determining the priority of liabilities can be problematic. For instance, debts might be incurred to both outside creditors and partners, who might have lent money to pay off certain accounts or for working capital.

An agreement can spell out the order in which liabilities are to be paid, but if it does not, UPA Section 40(a) and RUPA Section 807(1) rank them in this order: (1) to creditors other than partners, (2) to partners for liabilities other than for capital and profits, (3) to partners for capital contributions, and finally (4) to partners for their share of profits (see Figure 41.3). However, RUPA eliminates the distinction between capital and profits when the firm pays partners what is owed to them; RUPA Section 807(b) speaks simply of the right of a partner to a liquidating distribution.

FIGURE 41.3 Priority Partnership Liabilities under RUPA

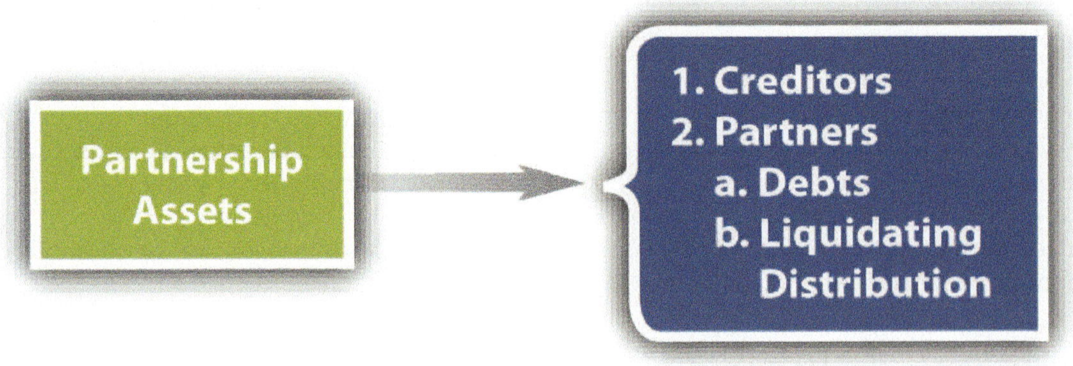

Partners are entitled to share equally in the profits and surplus remaining after all liabilities, including those owed to partners, are paid off, although the partnership agreement can state a different share—for example, in proportion to capital contribution. If after winding up there is a net loss, whether capital or otherwise, each partner must contribute toward it in accordance with his share in the profits, had there been any, unless the agreement states otherwise. If any of the partners is insolvent or refuses to contribute and cannot be sued, the others must contribute their own share to pay off the liabilities and in addition must contribute, in proportion to their share of the profits, the additional amount necessary to pay the liabilities of their defaulting partners.

In the event of insolvency, a court may take possession of both partnership property and individual assets of the partners; this again is a big disadvantage to the partnership form.

The estate of a deceased partner is credited or liable as that partner would have been if she were living at the time of the distribution.

Key Takeaway

Under UPA, the withdrawal of any partner from the partnership causes dissolution; the withdrawal may be caused in accordance with the agreement, in violation of the agreement, by operation of law, or by court order. Dissolution terminates the partners' authority to act for the partnership, except for winding up, but remaining partners may decide to carry on as a new partnership or may decide to terminate the firm. If they continue, the old creditors remain as creditors of the new firm, the former partner remains liable for obligations incurred while she was a partner (she may be liable for debts arising after she left, unless proper notice is given to creditors), and the former partner or her estate is entitled to an accounting and payment for the partnership interest. If the partners move to terminate the firm, winding up begins.

Under RUPA, a partner who ceases to be involved in the business is dissociated, but dissociation does not necessarily cause dissolution. Dissociation happens when a partner quits, voluntarily or involuntarily; when a partner dies or becomes incompetent; or on request by the firm or a partner upon court order for a partner's wrongful conduct, among other reasons. The dissociated partner loses actual authority to bind the firm but remains liable for pre-dissociation obligations and may have lingering authority or lingering liability for two years provided the other party thought the dissociated one was still a partner; a notice of dissociation will, after ninety days, be good against the world as to dissociation and dissolution. If the firm proceeds to termination (though partners can stop the process before its end), the next step is dissolution, which occurs by acts of partners, by operation of law, or by court order upon application by a partner if continuing the business has become untenable. After dissolution, the only business undertaken is to wind up affairs. However, the firm may continue after dissociation; it must buy out the dissociated one's interest, minus damages if the dissociation was wrongful.

If the firm is to be terminated, winding up entails finishing the business at hand, paying off creditors, and splitting the remaining surplus or liabilities according the parties' agreement or, absent any, according to the relevant act (UPA or RUPA).

Exercises

1. Under UPA, what is the effect on the partnership of a partner's ceasing to be involved in the business?
2. Can a person no longer a partner be held liable for partnership obligations after her withdrawal? Can such a person incur liability to the partnership?
3. What obligation does a partnership or its partners owe to a partner who wrongfully terminates the partnership agreement?
4. What bearing does RUPA's use of the term *dissociate* have on the entity theory that informs the revised act?
5. When a partnership is wound up, who gets paid first from its assets? If the firm winds up toward termination and has inadequate assets to pay its creditors, what recourse, if any, do the creditors have?

41.4 Cases

Breach of Partnership Fiduciary Duty

Gilroy v. Conway

391 N.W. 2d 419 (Mich. App. 1986)

PETERSON, J.

Defendant cheated his partner and appeals from the trial court's judgment granting that partner a remedy.

Plaintiff was an established commercial photographer in Kalamazoo who also had a partnership interest in another photography business, Colonial Studios, in Coldwater. In 1974, defendant became plaintiff's partner in Colonial Studios, the name of which was changed to Skylight Studios. Under the partnership agreement, defendant was to be the operating manager of the partnership, in return for which he would have a guaranteed draw. Except for the guaranteed draw, the partnership was equal in ownership and the sharing of profits.

Prior to defendant's becoming a partner, the business had acquired a small contractual clientele of schools for which the business provided student portrait photographs. The partners agreed to concentrate on this type of business, and both partners solicited schools with success. Gross sales, which were $40,000 in 1974, increased every year and amounted to $209,085 in 1980 [about $606,000 in 2016 dollars].

In the spring of 1981, defendant offered to buy out plaintiff and some negotiations followed. On June 25, 1981, however, plaintiff was notified by the defendant that the partnership was dissolved as of July 1, 1981. Plaintiff discovered that defendant: had closed up the partnership's place of business and opened up his own business; had purchased equipment and supplies in preparation for commencing his own business and charged them to the partnership; and had taken with him the partnership employees and most of its equipment.

Defendant had also stolen the partnership's business. He had personally taken over the business of some customers by telling them that the partnership was being dissolved; in other cases he simply took over partnership contracts without telling the customers that he was then operating on his own. Plaintiff also learned that defendant's deceit had included the withdrawal, without plaintiff's knowledge, of partnership funds for defendant's personal use in 1978 in an amount exceeding $11,000 [about $41,000 in 2011 dollars].

The trial judge characterized the case as a "classic study of greed" and found that defendant had in effect appropriated the business enterprise, holding that defendant had "knowingly and willfully violated his fiduciary relationship as a partner by converting partnership assets to his use and, in doing so, literally destroying the partnership." He also found that the partnership could have been sold as a going business on June 30, 1981, and that after a full accounting, it had a value on that date of $94,596 less accounts payable of $17,378.85, or a net value of $77,217.15. The division thereof after adjustments for plaintiff's positive equity or capital resulted in an award to plaintiff for his interest in the business of $53,779.46 [about $140,000 in 2016 dollars]. * * *

Plaintiff also sought exemplary [punitive] damages. Count II of the complaint alleged that defendant's conduct constituted a breach of defendant's fiduciary duty to his partner under §§ 19-22 of the Uniform Partnership Act, and Count III alleged conversion of partnership property. Each count contained allegations that defendant's conduct was willful, wanton and in reckless disregard of plaintiff's rights and that such conduct had caused injury to plaintiff's feelings, including humiliation, indignity and a sense of moral outrage. The prayer for relief sought exemplary damages therefore.

Plaintiff's testimony on the point was brief. He said:

> *The effect of really the whole situation, and I think it was most apparent when I walked into the empty building, was extreme disappointment and really total outrage at the fact that something that I had given the utmost of my talent and creativity, energy, and whatever time was necessary to build, was totally destroyed and there was just nothing of any value that was left.... My business had been stolen and there wasn't a thing that I could do about it. And to me, that was very humiliating that one day I had something that I had worked 10 years on, and the next day I had absolutely nothing of any value.*

As noted above, the trial judge found that defendant had literally destroyed the partnership by knowingly and willfully converting partnership assets in violation of his fiduciary duty as a partner. He also found that plaintiff had suffered a sense of outrage, indignity and humiliation and awarded him $10,000 [$23,000 in 2016 dollars] as exemplary damages.

Defendant appeals from that award, asserting that plaintiff's cause of action arises from a breach of the partnership contract and that exemplary damages may not be awarded for breach of that contract. * * *

If it were to be assumed that a partner's breach of his fiduciary duty or appropriation of partnership equipment and business contract to his own use and profit are torts, it is clear that the duty breached arises from the partnership contract. One acquires the property interest of a co-tenant in partnership only by the contractual creation of a partnership; one becomes a fiduciary in partnership only by the contractual undertaking to become a partner. There is no tortious conduct here existing independent of the breach of the partnership contract.

Neither do we see anything in the Uniform Partnership Act to suggest that an aggrieved partner is entitled to any remedy other than to be made whole economically. The act defines identically the partnership fiduciary duty and the remedy for its breach, i.e., to account:

> *Sec. 21. (1) Every partner must account to the partnership for any benefit, and hold as trustee for it any profits derived by him without the consent of the other partners from any transaction connected with the formation, conduct, or liquidation of the partnership or from any use by him of its property.*

So, the cases involving a partner's breach of the fiduciary duty to their partners have been concerned solely with placing the wronged partners in the economic position that they would have enjoyed but for the breach.

[Judgment for plaintiff affirmed, as modified with regard to damages.]

Case Questions

1. For what did the court award the plaintiff $53,000?
2. The court characterizes the defendant as having "cheated his partner"—that is, Conway committed fraud. (Gilroy said his business had been "stolen.") Fraud is a tort. Punitive damages may be awarded against a tortfeasor, even in a jurisdiction that generally disallows punitive damages in contract. In fact, punitive damages are sometimes awarded for breach of the partnership fiduciary duty. In *Cadwalader, Wickersham & Taft v. Beasley*, 728 So.2d 253 (Florida Ct. App., 1998), a New York law firm was found to have wrongfully expelled a partner lawyer, Beasley, from membership in its Palm Beach, Florida, offices. New York law controlled. The trial court awarded Beasley $500,000 in punitive damages. The appeals court, construing the same UPA as the court construed in *Gilroy*, said:

   > *Under New York law, the nature of the conduct which justifies an award of punitive damages is conduct having a high degree of moral culpability, or, in other words, conduct which shows a "conscious disregard of the rights of others or conduct so reckless as to amount to such disregard." . . . [S]ince the purpose of punitive damages is to both punish the wrongdoer and deter others from such wrongful behavior, as a matter of policy, courts have the discretion to award punitive damages[.] . . . [The defendant] was participating in a clandestine plan to wrongfully expel some partners for the financial gain of other partners. Such activity cannot be said to be honorable, much less to comport with the "punctilio of an honor." Because these findings establish that [the defendant] consciously disregarded the rights of Beasley, we affirm the award of punitive damages.*

   As a matter of social policy, which is the better ruling, the Michigan court's in *Gilroy* or the Florida court's in *Cadwalader*?

Partnership Authority, Express or Apparent

Hodge v Garrett

614 P.2d 420 (Idaho 1980)

Bistline, J.

[Plaintiff] Hodge and defendant-appellant Rex E. Voeller, the managing partner of the Pay-Ont Drive-In Theatre, signed a contract for the sale of a small parcel of land belonging to the partnership. That parcel, although adjacent to the theater, was not used in theater operations except insofar as the east 20 feet were necessary for the operation of the theater's driveway. The agreement for the sale of land stated that it was between Hodge and the Pay-Ont Drive-In Theatre, a partnership. Voeller signed the agreement for the partnership, and written changes as to the footage and price were initialed by Voeller. (The trial court found that Hodge and Voeller had orally agreed that this 20 foot strip would be encumbered by an easement for ingress and egress to the partnership lands.)

Voeller testified that he had told Hodge prior to signing that Hodge would have to present him with a plat plan which would have to be approved by the partners before the property could be sold. Hodge denied that a plat plan had ever been mentioned to him, and he testified that Voeller did not tell him that the approval of the other partners was needed until after the contract was signed. Hodge also testified that he offered to pay Voeller the full purchase price when he signed the contract, but Voeller told him that that was not necessary.

The trial court found that Voeller had actual and apparent authority to execute the contract on behalf of the partnership, and that the contract should be specifically enforced. The partners of the Pay-Ont Drive-In Theatre appeal, arguing that Voeller did not have authority to sell the property and that Hodge knew that he did not have that authority.

At common law one partner could not, "without the concurrence of his copartners, convey away the real estate of the partnership, bind his partners by a deed, or transfer the title and interest of his copartners in the firm real estate." [Citation] This rule was changed by the adoption of the Uniform Partnership Act. * * * [citing the statute].

The meaning of these provisions was stated in one text as follows:

> *"If record title is in the partnership and a partner conveys in the partnership name, legal title passes. But the partnership may recover the property (except from a bona fide purchaser from the grantee) if it can show (A) that the conveying partner was not apparently carrying on business in the usual way or (B) that he had in fact no authority and the grantee had knowledge of that fact. The burden of proof with respect to authority is thus on the partnership." [Citation]*

Thus this contract is enforceable if Voeller had the actual authority to sell the property, or, even if Voeller did not have such authority, the contract is still enforceable if the sale was in the usual way of carrying on the business and Hodge did not know that Voeller did not have this authority.

As to the question of actual authority, such authority must affirmatively appear, "for the authority of one partner to make and acknowledge a deed for the firm will not be presumed. * * * " [Citation] Although such authority may be implied from the nature of the business, or from similar past transactions [Citation], nothing in the record in this case indicates that Voeller had express or implied authority to sell real property belonging to the partnership. There is no evidence that Voeller had sold property belonging to the partnership in the past, and obviously the partnership was not engaged in the business of buying and selling real estate.

The next question, since actual authority has not been shown, is whether Voeller was conducting the partnership business in the usual way in selling this parcel of land such that the contract is binding under [the relevant section of the statute] i.e., whether Voeller had apparent authority. Here the evidence showed, and the trial court found:

1. "That the defendant, Rex E. Voeller, was one of the original partners of the Pay-Ont Drive In Theatre; that the other defendants obtained their partnership interest by inheritance upon

the death of other original partners; that upon the death of a partner the partnership affairs were not wound up, but instead, the partnership merely continued as before, with the heirs of the deceased partner owning their proportionate share of the partnership interest.

2. "That at the inception of the partnership, and at all times thereafter, Rex E. Voeller was the exclusive, managing partner of the partnership and had the full authority to make all decisions pertaining to the partnership affairs, including paying the bills, preparing profit and loss statements, income tax returns and the ordering of any goods or services necessary to the operation of the business."

The court made no finding that it was customary for Voeller to sell real property, or even personal property, belonging to the partnership. Nor was there any evidence to this effect. Nor did the court discuss whether it was in the usual course of business for the managing partner of a theater to sell real property. Yet the trial court found that Voeller had apparent authority to sell the property. From this it must be inferred that the trial court believed it to be in the usual course of business for a partner who has exclusive control of the partnership business to sell real property belonging to the partnership, where that property is not being used in the partnership business. We cannot agree with this conclusion. For a theater, "carrying on in the usual way the business of the partnership," [Citation to relevant section of the statute] means running the operations of the theater; it does not mean selling a parcel of property adjacent to the theater. Here, the contract of sale stated that the land belonged to the partnership, and, even if Hodge believed that Voeller as the exclusive manager had authority to transact all business for the firm, Voeller still could not bind the partnership through a unilateral act which was not in the usual business of the partnership. We therefore hold that the trial court erred in holding that this contract was binding on the partnership.

Judgment reversed. Costs to appellant.

Case Questions

1. What was the argument that Voeller had actual authority? What did the court on appeal say about that argument?
2. What was the argument that Voeller had apparent authority? What did the court on appeal say about that argument? To rephrase the question, what facts would have been necessary to confer on Voeller apparent authority?

Partnership Bound by Contracts Made by a Partner on Its Behalf; Partners' Duties to Each Other; Winding Up

Long v. Lopez

115 S.W.3d 221 (Texas App. 2003)

Holman, J.

Wayne A. Long [plaintiff at the trial court] sued Appellee Sergio Lopez to recover from him, jointly and severally, his portion of a partnership debt that Long had paid. After a bench trial, the trial court ruled that Long take nothing from Appellee. We reverse and render, and remand for calculation of attorney's fees in this suit and pre- and post-judgment interest.

Long testified that in September 1996, Long, Lopez, and Don Bannister entered into an oral partnership agreement in which they agreed to be partners in Wood Relo ("the partnership"), a trucking business located in Gainesville, Texas. Wood Relo located loads for and dispatched approximately twenty trucks it leased from owner-operators. * * *

The trial court found that Long, Lopez, and Bannister formed a partnership, Wood Relo, without a written partnership agreement. Lopez does not contest these findings.

Long testified that to properly conduct the partnership's business, he entered into an office equipment lease with IKON Capital Corporation ("IKON") on behalf of the partnership. The lease was a thirty-month contract under which the partnership leased a telephone system, fax machine, and photocopier at a rate of $577.91 per month. The lease agreement was between IKON and Wood Relo; the "authorized signer" was listed as Wayne Long, who also signed as personal guarantor.

Long stated that all three partners were authorized to buy equipment for use by the partnership. He testified that the partners had agreed that it was necessary for the partnership to lease the equipment and that on the day the equipment was delivered to Wood Relo's office, Long was the only partner at the office; therefore, Long was the only one available to sign the lease and personal guaranty that IKON required. [The partnership disintegrated when Bannister left and he later filed for bankruptcy.] * * * Long testified that when Bannister left Wood Relo, the partnership still had "quite a few" debts to pay, including the IKON lease. * * *

Eventually, IKON did repossess all the leased equipment. Long testified that he received a demand letter from IKON, requesting payment by Wood Relo of overdue lease payments and accelerating payment of the remaining balance of the lease. IKON sought recovery of past due payments in the amount of $2,889.55 and accelerated future lease payments in the amount of $11,558.20, for a total of $14,447.75, plus interest, costs, and attorney's fees, with the total exceeding $16,000. Long testified that he advised Lopez that he had received the demand letter from IKON.

Ultimately, IKON filed a lawsuit against Long individually and d/b/a Wood Relo, but did not name Lopez or Bannister as parties to the suit. Through his counsel, Long negotiated a settlement with IKON for a total of $9,000. An agreed judgment was entered in conjunction with the settlement agreement providing that if Long did not pay the settlement, Wood Relo and Long would owe IKON $12,000.

After settling the IKON lawsuit, Long's counsel sent a letter to Lopez and Bannister regarding the settlement agreement, advising them that they were jointly and severally liable for the $9,000 that extinguished the partnership's debt to IKON, plus attorney's fees. * * *

The trial court determined that Long was not entitled to reimbursement from Lopez because Long was not acting for the partnership when he settled IKON's claim against the partnership. The court based its conclusion on the fact that Long had no "apparent authority with respect to lawsuits" and had not notified Lopez of the IKON lawsuit.

Analysis

To the extent that a partnership agreement does not otherwise specify, the provisions of the Texas Revised Partnership Act govern the relations of the partners and between the partners and the partnership. [Citations] Under the Act, each partner has equal rights in the management and conduct of the business of a partnership. With certain inapplicable exceptions, all partners are liable jointly and severally for all debts and obligations of the partnership unless otherwise agreed by the claimant or provided by law. A partnership may be sued and may defend itself in its partnership name. Each partner is an agent of the partnership for the purpose of its business; unless the partner does not have authority to act for the partnership in a particular matter and the person with whom the partner is dealing knows that the partner lacks authority, an act of a partner, including the execution of an instrument in the partnership name, binds the partnership if "the act is for apparently carrying on in the ordinary course: (1) the partnership business." [Citation] If the act of a partner is not apparently for carrying on the partnership business, an act of a partner binds the partnership only if authorized by the other partners. [Citation]

The extent of authority of a partner is determined essentially by the same principles as those measuring the scope of the authority of an agent. [Citation] As a general rule, each partner is an agent of the partnership and is empowered to bind the partnership in the normal conduct of its business. [Citation] Generally, an agent's authority is presumed to be coextensive with the business entrusted to his care. [Citations] An agent is limited in his authority to such contracts and acts as are incident to the management of the particular business with which he is entrusted. [Citation]

Winding Up the Partnership

A partner's duty of care to the partnership and the other partners is to act in the conduct and winding up of the partnership business with the care an ordinarily prudent person would exercise in similar circumstances. [Citation] During the winding up of a partnership's business, a partner's fiduciary duty to the other partners and the partnership is limited to matters relating to the winding up of the partnership's affairs. [Citation]

Long testified that he entered into the settlement agreement with IKON to save the partnership a substantial amount of money. IKON's petition sought over $16,000 from the partnership, and the settlement agreement was for $9,000; therefore, Long settled IKON's claim for 43% less than the amount for which IKON sued the partnership.

Both Long and Lopez testified that the partnership "fell apart," "virtually was dead," and had to move elsewhere. * * * The inability of the partnership to continue its trucking business was an event requiring the partners to wind up the affairs of the partnership. See [Citation] * * *

The Act provides that a partner winding up a partnership's business is authorized, to the extent appropriate for winding up, to perform the following in the name of and for and on behalf of the partnership:

(1) prosecute and defend civil, criminal, or administrative suits;
(2) settle and close the partnership's business;
(3) dispose of and convey the partnership's property;
(4) satisfy or provide for the satisfaction of the partnership's liabilities;
(5) distribute to the partners any remaining property of the partnership; and
(6) perform any other necessary act. [Citation]

Long accrued the IKON debt on behalf of the partnership when he secured the office equipment for partnership operations, and he testified that he entered into the settlement with IKON when the partnership was in its final stages and the partners were going their separate ways. Accordingly, Long was authorized by the Act to settle the IKON lawsuit on behalf of the partnership. * * *

Lopez's Liability for the IKON Debt

If a partner reasonably incurs a liability in excess of the amount he agreed to contribute in properly conducting the business of the partnership or for preserving the partnership's business or property, he is entitled to be repaid by the partnership for that excess amount. [Citation] A partner may sue another partner for reimbursement if the partner has made such an excessive payment. [Citation]

With two exceptions not applicable to the facts of this case, all partners are liable jointly and severally for all debts and obligations of the partnership unless otherwise agreed by the claimant or provided by law. Because Wood Relo was sued for a partnership debt made in the proper conduct of the partnership business, and Long settled this claim in the course of winding up the partnership, he could maintain an action against Lopez for reimbursement of Long's disproportionate payment. [Citations]

Attorneys' Fees

Long sought to recover the attorney's fees expended in defending the IKON claim, and attorney's fees expended in the instant suit against Lopez. Testimony established that it was necessary for Long to employ an attorney to defend the action brought against the partnership by IKON; therefore, the attorney's fees related to defending the IKON lawsuit on behalf of Wood Relo are a partnership debt for which Lopez is jointly and severally liable. As such, Long is entitled to recover from Lopez one-half of the attorney's fees attributable to the IKON lawsuit. The evidence established that reasonable and necessary attorney's fees to defend the IKON lawsuit were $1725. Therefore, Long is entitled to recover from Lopez $862.50.

Long also seeks to recover the attorney's fees expended pursuing the instant lawsuit. See [Texas statute citation] (authorizing recovery of attorney's fees in successful suit under an oral contract); see also [Citation] (holding attorney's fees are recoverable by partner under because action against other partner was founded on partnership agreement, which was a contract). We agree that Long is entitled to recover reasonable and necessary attorney's fees incurred in bringing the instant lawsuit. Because we are remanding this case so the trial court can determine the amount of pre- and post-judgment interest to be awarded to Long, we also remand to the trial court the issue of the amount of attorney's fees due to Long in pursuing this lawsuit against Lopez for collection of the amount paid to IKON on behalf of the partnership.

Conclusion

We hold the trial court erred in determining that Long did not have authority to act for Wood Relo in defending, settling, and paying the partnership debt owed by Wood Relo to IKON. Lopez is jointly and severally liable to IKON for $9,000, which represents the amount Long paid IKON to defend and extinguish the partnership debt. We hold that Lopez is jointly and severally liable to Long for $1,725, which represents the amount of attorney's fees Long paid to defend against the IKON claim. We further hold that Long is entitled to recover from Lopez reasonable and necessary attorney's fees in pursuing the instant lawsuit.

We reverse the judgment of the trial court. We render judgment that Lopez owes Long $5362.50 (one-half of the partnership debt to IKON plus one-half of the corresponding attorney's fees). We remand the case to the trial court for calculation of the amount of attorney's fees owed by Lopez to Long in the instant lawsuit, and calculation of pre- and post-judgment interest.

Case Questions

1. Why did the trial court determine that Lopez owed Long nothing?
2. Absent a written partnership agreement, what rules control the operation and winding up of the partnership?
3. Why did the appeals court determine that Long did have authority to settle the lawsuit with IKON?
4. Lopez was not named by IKON when it sued Long and the partnership. Why did the court determine that did not matter, that Lopez was still liable for one-half the costs of settling that case?
5. Why was Long awarded compensation for the attorneys' fees expended in dealing with the IKON matter and in bringing this case?

Dissolution under RUPA

Horizon/CMS Healthcare Corp. v. Southern Oaks Health Care, Inc.
732 So.2d 1156 (Fla. App. 1999)

Goshorn, J.

Horizon is a large, publicly traded provider of both nursing home facilities and management for nursing home facilities. It wanted to expand into Osceola County in 1993. Southern Oaks was already operating in Osceola County[.] * * * Horizon and Southern Oaks decided to form a partnership to own the proposed [new] facility, which was ultimately named Royal Oaks, and agreed that Horizon would manage both the Southern Oaks facility and the new Royal Oaks facility. To that end, Southern Oaks and Horizon entered into several partnership and management contracts in 1993.

In 1996, Southern Oaks filed suit alleging numerous defaults and breaches of the twenty-year agreements. * * * [T]he trial court found largely in favor of Southern Oaks, concluding that Horizon breached its obligations under two different partnership agreements [and that] Horizon had breached several management contracts. Thereafter, the court ordered that the partnerships be dissolved, finding that "the parties to the various agreements which are the subject of this lawsuit are now incapable of continuing to operate in business together" and that because it was dissolving the partnerships, "there is no entitlement to future damages. * * * " In its cross appeal, Southern Oaks asserts that because Horizon unilaterally and wrongfully sought dissolution of the partnerships, Southern Oaks should receive a damage award for the loss of the partnerships' seventeen remaining years' worth of future profits. We reject its argument.

Southern Oaks argues Horizon wrongfully caused the dissolution because the basis for dissolution cited by the court is not one of the grounds for which the parties contracted. The pertinent contracts provided in section 7.3 "Causes of Dissolution": "In addition to the causes for dissolution set forth in Section 7.2(c), the Partnership shall be dissolved in the event that:...(d) upon thirty (30) days prior written notice to the other Partner, either Partner elects to dissolve the Partnership on account of an Irreconcilable Difference which arises and cannot, after good faith efforts, be resolved. ..."

Southern Oaks argues that what Horizon relied on at trial as showing irreconcilable differences—the decisions of how profits were to be determined and divided—were not "good faith differences of opinion," nor did they have "a material and adverse impact on the conduct of the Partnerships' Business." Horizon's refusal to pay Southern Oaks according to the terms of the contracts was not an "irreconcilable difference" as defined by the contract, Southern Oaks asserts, pointing out that Horizon's acts were held to be breaches of the contracts. Because there was no contract basis for dissolution, Horizon's assertion of dissolution was wrongful, Southern Oaks concludes.

Southern Oaks contends further that not only were there no contractual grounds for dissolution, dissolution was also wrongful under the Florida Statutes. Southern Oaks argues that pursuant to section [of that statute] Horizon had the power to dissociate from the partnership, but, in the absence of contract grounds for the dissociation, Horizon wrongfully dissociated. It asserts that it is entitled to lost future profits under Florida's partnership law. * * *

We find Southern Oaks' argument without merit. First, the trial court's finding that the parties are incapable of continuing to operate in business together *is* a finding of "irreconcilable differences," a permissible reason for dissolving the partnerships under the express terms of the partnership agreements. Thus, dissolution was not "wrongful," assuming there can be "wrongful" dissolutions, and Southern Oaks was not entitled to damages for lost future profits. Additionally, the partnership contracts also permit dissolution by "judicial decree." Although neither party cites this provision, it appears that pursuant thereto, the parties agreed that dissolution would be proper if done by a trial court for whatever reason the court found sufficient to warrant dissolution.

Second, even assuming the partnership was dissolved for a reason not provided for in the partnership agreements, damages were properly denied. Under RUPA, it is clear that wrongful *dissociation* triggers liability for lost future profits. *See* [RUPA:] "A partner who wrongfully dissociates is liable to the partnership and to the other partners for damages caused by the dissociation. The liability is in addition to any other obligation of the partner to the partnership or to the other partners." However, RUPA does *not* contain a similar provision for dissolution; RUPA does not refer to the dissolutions as rightful or wrongful. [RUPA sets out] "Events causing dissolution and winding up of partnership business," [and] outlines the events causing dissolution without any provision for liability for damages. * * * [RUPA] recognizes judicial dissolution:

> *A partnership is dissolved, and its business must be wound up, only upon the occurrence of any of the following events:...*
>
> *(5) On application by a partner, a judicial determination that:*
>
> *(a) The economic purpose of the partnership is likely to be unreasonably frustrated;*
>
> *(b) Another partner has engaged in conduct relating to the partnership business which makes it not reasonably practicable to carry on the business in partnership with such partner; or*
>
> *(c) It is not otherwise reasonably practicable to carry on the partnership business in conformity with the partnership agreement[.]...*

Paragraph (5)(c) provides the basis for the trial court's dissolution in this case. While "reasonably practicable" is not defined in RUPA, the term is broad enough to encompass the inability of partners to continue working together, which is what the court found.

Certainly the law predating RUPA allowed for recovery of lost profits upon the wrongful dissolution of a partnership. *See e.g.*, [Citation]: "A partner who assumes to dissolve the partnership before the end of the term agreed on in the partnership articles is liable, in an action at law against him by his co-partner for the breach of the agreement, to respond in damages for the value of the profits which the plaintiff would otherwise have received."

However, RUPA brought significant changes to partnership law, among which was the adoption of the term "dissociation." Although the term is undefined in RUPA, dissociation appears to have taken the place of "dissolution" as that word was used pre-RUPA. "Dissolution" under RUPA has a different meaning, although the term is undefined in RUPA. It follows that the pre-RUPA cases providing for future damages upon wrongful dissolution are no longer applicable to a partnership dissolution. In other words, a "wrongful dissolution" referred to in the pre-RUPA case law is now, under RUPA, known as "wrongful dissociation." Simply stated, under [RUPA], only when a partner *dissociates* and the dissociation is wrongful can the remaining partners sue for damages. When a partnership is *dissolved*, RUPA ... provides the parameters of liability of the partners upon dissolution. * * *

[Citation]: "Dissociation is not a condition precedent to dissolution. * * * Most dissolution events are dissociations. On the other hand, it is not necessary to have a dissociation to cause a dissolution and winding up."

Southern Oaks' attempt to bring the instant dissolution under the statute applicable to dissociation is rejected. The trial court ordered dissolution of the partnership, not the dissociation of Horizon for wrongful conduct. There no longer appears to be "wrongful" dissolution—either dissolution is provided for by contract or statute or the dissolution was improper and the dissolution order should be reversed. In the instant case, because the dissolution either came within the terms of the partnership agreements or [RUPA] (judicial dissolution where it is not reasonably practicable to carry on the partnership business), Southern Oaks' claim for lost future profits is without merit. Affirmed.

Case Questions

1. Under RUPA, what is a dissociation? What is a dissolution?
2. Why did Southern Oaks claim there was no contractual basis for dissolution, notwithstanding the determination that Horizon had breached the partnership agreement and the management contract?
3. Given those findings, what did Southern Oaks *not* get at the lower-court trial that it wanted on this appeal?
4. Why didn't Southern Oaks get what it wanted on this appeal?

41.5 Summary and Exercises

Summary

Most of the Uniform Partnership Act (UPA) and Revised Uniform Partnership Act (RUPA) rules apply only in the absence of agreement among the partners. Under both, unless the agreement states otherwise, partners have certain duties: (1) the duty to serve—that is, to devote themselves to the work of the partnership; (2) the duty of loyalty, which is informed by the fiduciary standard: the obligation to act always in the best interest of the partnership and not in one's own best interest; (3) the duty of care—that is, to act as a reasonably prudent partner would; (4) the duty of obedience not to breach any aspect of the agreement or act without authority; (5) the duty to inform copartners; and (6) the duty to account to the partnership. Ordinarily, partners operate through majority vote, but no act that contravenes the partnership agreement itself can be undertaken without unanimous consent.

Partners' rights include rights (1) to distributions of money, including profits (and losses) as per the agreement or equally, indemnification, and return of capital contribution (but not a right to compensation); (2) to management as per the agreement or equally; (3) to choose copartners; (4) to property of the partnership, but no partner has any rights to specific property (under UPA the partners own property as tenants in partnership; under RUPA the partnership as entity owns property, but it will be distributed upon liquidation); (5) to assign (voluntarily or involuntarily) the partnership interest; the assignee does not become a partner or have any management rights, but a judgment creditor may obtain a charging order against the partnership; and (6) to enforce duties and rights by suits in law or equity (under RUPA a formal accounting is not required).

Under UPA, a change in the relation of the partners dissolves the partnership but does not necessarily wind up the business. Dissolution may be voluntary, by violation of the agreement, by operation of law, or by court order. Dissolution terminates the authority of the partners to act for the partnership. After dissolution, a new partnership may be formed.

Under RUPA, a change in the relation of the partners is a dissociation, leaving the remaining partners with two options: continue on; or wind up, dissolve, and terminate. In most cases, a partnership may buy out the interest of a partner who leaves without dissolving the partnership. A term partnership also will not dissolve so long as at least one-half of the partners choose to remain. When a partner's dissociation triggers dissolution, partners are allowed to vote subsequently to continue the partnership.

When a dissolved partnership is carried on as a new one, creditors of the old partnership remain creditors of the new one. A former partner remains liable to the creditors of the former partnership. A new partner is liable to the creditors of the former partnership, bur only to the extent of the new partner's capital contribution. A former partner remains liable for debts incurred after his withdrawal unless he gives proper notice of his withdrawal; his actual authority terminates upon dissociation and apparent authority after two years.

If the firm is to be terminated, it is wound up. The assets of the partnership include all required contributions of partners, and from the assets liabilities are paid off (1) to creditors and (2) to partners on their accounts. Under RUPA, nonpartnership creditors share equally with unsatisfied partnership creditors in the personal assets of their debtor-partners.

Exercises

1. Anne and Barbara form a partnership. Their agreement specifies that Anne will receive two-thirds of the profit and Barbara will get one-third. The firm suffers a loss of $3,000 the first year. How are the losses divided?
2. Two lawyers, Glenwood and Higgins, formed a partnership. Glenwood failed to file Client's paperwork on time in a case, with adverse financial consequences to Client. Is Higgins liable for Glenwood's malpractice?
3. When Client in Exercise 2 visited the firm's offices to demand compensation from Glenwood, the two got into an argument. Glenwood became very agitated; in an apparent state of rage, he threw a law book at Client, breaking her nose. Is Higgins liable?
4. Assume Glenwood from Exercise 2 entered into a contract on behalf of the firm to buy five computer games. Is Higgins liable?
5. Grosberg and Goldman operated the Chatham Fox Hills Shopping Center as partners. They agreed that Goldman would deposit the tenants' rental checks in an account in Grosberg's name at First Bank. Without Grosberg's knowledge or permission, Goldman opened an account in both their names at Second Bank, into which Goldman deposited checks payable to the firm or the partners. He indorsed each check by signing the name of the partnership or the partners. Subsequently, Goldman embezzled over $100,000 of the funds. Second Bank did not know Grosberg and Goldman were partners. Grosberg then sued Second Bank for converting the funds by accepting checks on which Grosberg's or the partnership's indorsement was forged. Is Second Bank liable? Discuss.
6. Pearson Collings, a partner in a criminal defense consulting firm, used the firm's phones and computers to operate a side business cleaning carpets. The partnership received no compensation for the use of its equipment. What claim would the other partners have against Collings?
7. Follis, Graham, and Hawthorne have a general partnership, each agreeing to split losses 20 percent, 20 percent, and 60 percent, respectively. While on partnership business, Follis negligently crashes into a victim, causing $100,000 in damages. Follis declares bankruptcy, and the firm's assets are inadequate to pay the damages. Graham says she is liable for only $20,000 of the obligation, as per the agreement. Is she correct?
8. Ingersoll and Jackson are partners; Kelly, after much negotiation, agreed to join the firm effective February 1. But on January 15, Kelly changed his mind. Meanwhile, however, the other two had already arranged for the local newspaper to run a notice that Kelly was joining the firm. The notice ran on February 1. Kelly did nothing in response. On February 2, Creditor, having seen the newspaper notice, extended credit to the firm. When the firm did not pay, Creditor sought to have Kelly held liable as a partner. Is Kelly liable?

Self-Test Questions

1. Under UPA, a partner is generally entitled to a formal accounting of partnership affairs
    a. whenever it is just and reasonable
    b. if a partner is wrongfully excluded from the business by copartners

c. if the right exists in the partnership agreement
d. all of the above

2. Donners, Inc., a partner in CDE Partnership, applies to Bank to secure a loan and assigns to Bank its partnership interest. After the assignment, which is true?
    a. Bank steps into Donners's shoes as a partner.
    b. Bank does not become a partner but has the right to participate in the management of the firm to protect its security interest until the loan is paid.
    c. Bank is entitled to Donners's share of the firm's profits.
    d. Bank is liable for Donners's share of the firm's losses.
    e. None of these is true.
3. Which of these requires unanimous consent of the partners in a general partnership?
    a. the assignment of a partnership interest
    b. the acquisition of a partnership debt
    c. agreement to be responsible for the tort of one copartner
    d. admission of a new partner
    e. agreement that the partnership should stand as a surety for a third party's obligation
4. Paul Partner (1) bought a computer and charged it to the partnership's account; (2) cashed a firm check and used the money to buy a computer in his own name; (3) brought from home a computer and used it at the office. In which scenario does the computer become partnership property?
    a. 1 only
    b. 1 and 2
    c. 1, 2, and 3
5. That partnerships are entities under RUPA means they have to pay federal income tax in their own name.
    a. true
    b. false
6. That partnerships are entities under RUPA means the partners are not personally liable for the firm's debts beyond their capital contributions.
    a. true
    b. false

Self-Test Answers

1. d
2. c
3. d
4. b
5. a
6. b

Endnotes

1. "The basic mission of RUPA is to serve the small firm. Large partnerships can fend for themselves by drafting partnership agreements that suit their special needs." Donald J. Weidner, "RUPA and Fiduciary Duty: The Texture of Relationship," *Law and Contemporary Problems* 58, no. 2 (1995): 81, 83.
2. Revised Uniform Partnership Act, Section 404, Comment 3: "Indeed, the law of partnership reflects the broader law of principal and agent, under which every agent is a fiduciary."
3. *Meinhard v. Salmon*, 164 N.E. 545 (N.Y. 1928).

4. RUPA, Section 503(b)(2); RUPA, Section 404 (e).
5. RUPA, Section 103(2)(c).
6. RUPA, Section 103(2)(d); RUPA, Section 103.
7. UPA, Sections 19 and 20; RUPA, Section 403.
8. RUPA, Section 404(1).
9. RUPA, Section 101(3).
10. UPA, Section 18(c); RUPA, Section 401(d).
11. UPA, Section 40(b); RUPA, Section 807(b).
12. UPA, Section 18(e); RUPA, Section 401(f).
13. *Hishon v. King & Spalding*, 467 U.S. 69 (1984).
14. RUPA, Section 203; UPA, Sections 8(1) and 25.
15. UPA, Section 26.
16. UPA, Section 27.
17. RUPA, Official Comment to Section 101.
18. RUPA Section 403(b).
19. RUPA, Section 403(c)(1); RUPA, Section 403(c)(2).
20. RUPA Official Comment 2, Section 405(b).
21. RUPA Section 305.
22. RUPA, Section 301(2); UPA, Section 9(2).
23. RUPA, Section 1001(d); RUPA, Section 1102.
24. RUPA, Section 303, Comment 3.
25. RUPA, Section 306.
26. RUPA Section 306.
27. UPA, Section 13.
28. Paul A. Samuelson, *Economics* (New York: McGraw-Hill, 1973), 106.
29. RUPA, Section 405(a).
30. UPA, Section 30.
31. UPA, Section 31.
32. UPA, Section 31.
33. UPA, Section 32.
34. UPA, Section 33.
35. UPA, Sections 37 and 38.
36. UPA, Section 38.
37. UPA, Section 41(1).
38. UPA, Section 36(1).
39. UPA, Section 17.
40. RUPA, Section 601.
41. RUPA. Sections 603(b) and 804(a).
42. RUPA, Section 603(b)(3).
43. RUPA, Section 603(b)(1).
44. RUPA, Section 702.
45. RUPA, Section 703(a).
46. RUPA, Section 103.
47. Trans fats are hydrogenated vegetable oils; the process of hydrogenation essentially turns the oils into semisolids, giving them a higher melting point and extending their shelf life but, unfortunately, also clogging consumers' arteries and causing heart disease. California banned their sale effective January 1, 2010; other jurisdictions have followed suit.
48. RUPA, Section 802.
49. RUPA, Section 802(b).
50. RUPA, Sections 601 and 801.
51. RUPA, Section 701(e).
52. RUPA, Section 701(h)(4)(i).
53. UPA, Section 30; RUPA, Section 802(a).
54. UPA, Section 37; RUPA, Section 803(a).

CHAPTER 42

Hybrid Business Forms

Learning Objectives

After reading this chapter, you should understand the following:

1. The limited partnership.
2. The limited liability company.
3. Other hybrid business forms: the sub-S corporation, limited liability partnerships, and limited liability limited partnerships.

This chapter provides a bridge between the partnership and the corporate form. It explores several types of associations that are hybrid forms—that is, they share some aspects of partnerships and some of corporations. Corporations afford the inestimable benefit of limited liability, partnerships the inestimable benefit of limited taxation. Businesspeople always seek to limit their risk and their taxation.

At base, whether to allow businesspeople and investors to grasp the holy grail of limited liability is a political issue. When we say a person is "irresponsible," it means he (or she, or it) does not take responsibility for his harmful actions; the loss is borne by others. Politically speaking, there is an incentive to allow businesspeople insulation from liability: it encourages them to take risks and invest, thus stimulating economic activity and forestalling unemployment. So the political trade-off with allowing various inventive forms of business organization is between providing business actors with the security that they will lose only their calculable investment, thus stimulating the economy, versus the "moral hazard" of allowing them to emerge mostly unscathed from their own harmful or foolish activities, thus externalizing resulting losses upon others. Some people feel that during the run-up to the "Great Recession" of 2007–09, the economic system allowed too much risk taking. When the risky investments collapsed, though, instead of forcing the risk takers to suffer loss, the government intervened—it "bailed them out," as they say, putting the consequences of the failed risks on the taxpayer.

The risk-averseness and inventiveness of businesspeople is seemingly unlimited, as is investors' urge to make profits through others' efforts with as little risk as possible. The rationale for the invention of these hybrid business forms, then, is (1) risk reduction and (2) tax reduction. Here we take up the most common hybrid types first: limited partnerships and limited liability companies. Then we cover them in the approximate chronological order of their invention: sub-S corporations, limited liability partnerships, and limited liability limited partnerships. All these forms are entities.

42.1 Limited Partnerships

Learning Objectives

Understand the following aspects of the limited partnership:

1. Governing law and definition.

2. Creation and capitalization.
3. Control and compensation.
4. Liabilities.
5. Taxation.
6. Termination.

Governing Law and Definition

The limited partnership is attractive because of its treatment of taxation and its imposition of limited liability on its limited partners.

Governing Law

The original source of limited partnership law is the Uniform Limited Partnership Act (ULPA), which was drafted in 1916. It was—like the UPA—a codification of common-law concepts. A revised version, the Revised Uniform Limited Partnership Act (RULPA), was adopted by the National Conference of Commissioners on Uniform Laws in 1976 and further amended in 1985 and in 2001.

The 2001 act was

> *drafted for a world in which limited liability partnerships and limited liability companies can meet many of the needs formerly met by limited partnerships. This Act therefore targets two types of enterprises that seem largely beyond the scope of LLPs and LLCs: (i) sophisticated, manager-entrenched commercial deals whose participants commit for the long term, and (ii) estate planning arrangements (family limited partnerships). The Act accordingly assumes that, more often than not, people utilizing it will want (1) strong centralized management, strongly entrenched, and (2) passive investors with little control over or right to exit the entity. The Act's rules, and particularly its default rules, have been designed to reflect these assumptions.*[1]

All states except Louisiana adopted the 1976 or 1985 act—most opting for the 1985 version—and sixteen states have adopted the 2001 version. The acts may be properly referred to with a hyphen: "ULPA-1985," or "ULPA-2001"; the word *revised* has been dropped. Here, we mainly discuss ULPA-1985. The Uniform Partnership Act (UPA) or the Revised Uniform Partnership Act (RUPA) also applies to limited partnerships except where it is inconsistent with the limited partnership statutes. The ULPA-2001 is not so much related to UPA or RUPA as previous versions were.

Definition

limited partnership

A partnership formed by two or more persons under state law and having one or more general partners and one or more limited partners.

A **limited partnership** (LP) is defined as "a partnership formed by two or more persons under the laws of a State and having one or more general partners and one or more limited partners."[2] The form tends to be attractive in business situations that focus on a single or limited-term project, such as making a movie or developing real estate; it is also widely used by private equity firms.

Creation and Capitalization

Unlike a general partnership, a limited partnership is created in accordance with the state statute authorizing it. There are two categories of partners: limited and general. The limited partners capitalize the business and the general partners run it.

Creation

The act requires that the firm's promoters file a **certificate of limited partnership** with the secretary of state; if they do not, or if the certificate is substantially defective, a general partnership is created. The certificate must be signed by all general partners. It must include the name of the limited partnership (which must include the words *limited partnership* so the world knows there are owners of the firm who are not liable beyond their contribution) and the names and business addresses of the general partners. If there are any changes in the general partners, the certificate must be amended. The general partner may be, and often is, a corporation. Having a general partner be a corporation achieves the goal of limited liability for everyone, but it is somewhat of a "clunky" arrangement. That problem is obviated in the limited liability company, discussed in Section 2. Here is an example of a limited partnership operating agreement: http://www.wyopa.com/Articles of limited partnership.htm.

certificate of limited partnership

The document filed with the appropriate state authority that, when approved, marks the legal existence of the limited partnership.

Any natural person, partnership, limited partnership (domestic or foreign), trust, estate, association, or corporation may become a partner of a limited partnership.

Capitalization

The money to capitalize the business typically comes mostly from the **limited partners**, who may themselves be partnerships or corporations. That is, the limited partners use the business as an investment device: they hope the managers of the firm (the general partners) will take their contributions and give them a positive return on it. The contributions may be money, services, or property, or promises to make such contributions in the future.

limited partners

A member of a limited partnership who is not involved in running the firm but rather stands as a passive investor.

Control and Compensation

Control

Control is *not* generally shared by both classes of partners.

General Partners

The control of the limited partnership is in the hands of the general partners, which may—as noted—be partnerships or corporations.

Limited Partners

Under ULPA-1985 and its predecessors, a limited partner who exercised any significant control would incur liability like a general partner as to third parties who believed she was one (the "control rule"). However, among the things a limited partner could do that would *not* risk the loss of insulation from personal liability were these "safe harbors":

- Acting as an agent, employee, or contractor for the firm; or being an officer, director, or shareholder of a corporate general partner

- Consulting with the general partner of the firm
- Requesting or attending a meeting of partners
- Being a surety for the firm
- Voting on amendments to the agreement, on dissolution or winding up the partnership, on loans to the partnership, on a change in its nature of business, on removing or admitting a general or limited partner

However, see Section 3 for how this "control rule" has been abolished under ULPA-2001.

General partners owe fiduciary duties to other general partners, the firm, and the limited partners; limited partners who do not exercise control do not owe fiduciary duties. See Figure 42.1.

FIGURE 42.1 The Limited Partnership under ULPA-1985

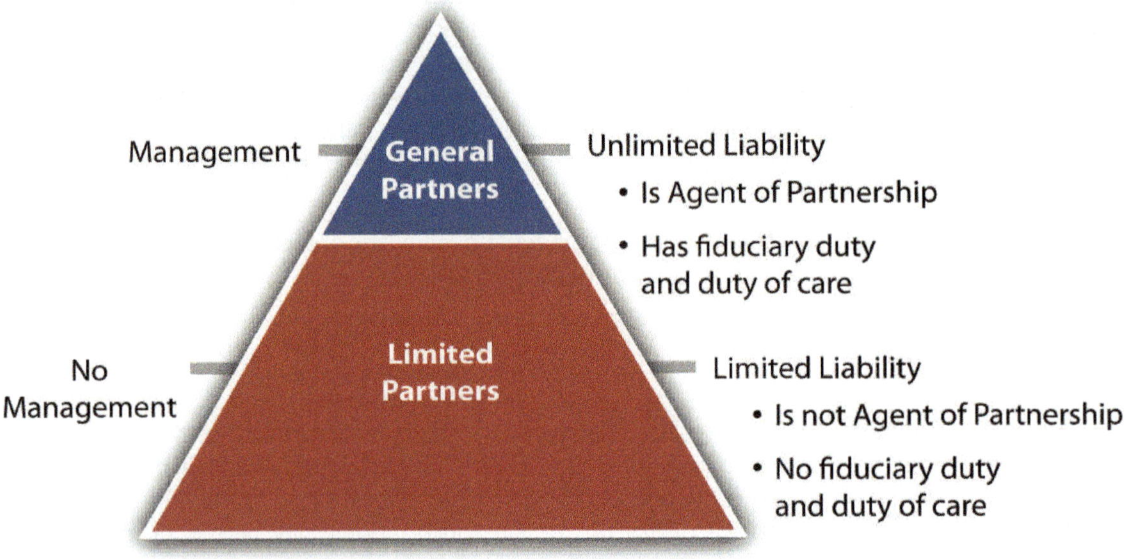

The partnership agreement may specify which general or limited partners have the right to vote on any matter, but if the agreement grants limited partners voting rights beyond the "safe harbor," a court may abolish that partner's limited liability.

Assignment of Partnership Rights

Limited partnership interests may be assigned in whole or in part; if in whole, the assignor ceases to be a partner unless otherwise agreed. An assignment is usually made as security for a loan. The assignee becomes a new limited partner only if all the others consent or if provided for in the certificate; the assignment does not cause dissolution. The happy ease with which a limited partner can divest himself of the partnership interest makes the investment in the firm here more like that in a corporation than in a general partnership.

Inspection of Books

Limited partners have the right to inspect the firm's books and records, they may own competing interests, they may be creditors of the firm, and they may bring derivative suits on the firm's behalf. They may not withdraw their capital contribution if that would impair creditors' rights.

Addition of New Partners

Unless the partnership agreement provides otherwise (it usually does), the admission of additional limited partners requires the written consent of all. A general partner may withdraw at any time with written notice; if withdrawal is a violation of the agreement, the limited partnership has a right to claim of damages. A limited partner can withdraw any time after six months' notice to each general partner, and the withdrawing partner is entitled to any distribution as per the agreement or, if none, to the fair value of the interest based on the right to share in distributions.

Compensation

We noted in discussing partnerships that the partners are not entitled to "compensation," that is, payment for their work; they are entitled to a share of the profits. For limited partnerships, the rule is a bit different.

General Partners

Often, general partners are paid for their management work on a sliding scale, receiving a greater share of each dollar of cash flow as the limited partners' cash distributions rise, thus giving the general partner an incentive to increase limited-partner distributions.

Limited Partners

Profits or losses are shared as agreed in the certificate or, if there is no agreement, in accordance with the percentages of capital contributions made.

Liabilities

Liability is not shared.

General Partners

The general partners are liable as in a general partnership, and they have the same fiduciary duty and duty of care as partners in a general partnership. However, see the discussion in Section 3 of the newest type of LP, the limited liability limited partnership (triple LP), where the general partner is also afforded limited liability under ULPA-2001.

Limited Partners

The limited partners are only liable up to the amount of their capital contribution, provided the surname of the limited partner does not appear in the partnership name (unless his name is coincidentally the same as that of one of the general partners whose name does appear) and provided the limited partner does not participate in control of the firm. See Section 4 for a case that highlights liability issues for partners.

We have been discussing ULPA-1985 here. But in a world of limited liability companies, limited liability partnerships, and limited liability limited partnerships, "the control rule has become an anachronism"; ULPA-2001 provides a full, status-based liability shield for each limited partner, "even if the limited partner participates in the management and control of the limited partnership."[3] The section thus eliminates the so-called control rule with respect to personal liability for entity obligations and brings limited partners into parity with LLC members, LLP partners and corporate shareholders."[4] And as will be noted in Section 3 under ULPA-2001 the *general* partner is also shielded from liability.

Taxation

Assuming the limited partnership meets a minimum number of criteria related to limited liability, centralized management, duration, and transferability of ownership, it can enjoy the benefits of pass-through taxation; otherwise it will be taxed as a corporation. Pass-through ("conduit") taxation is usually very important to partners.

Termination

The limited partnership's termination involves the same three steps as in a general partnership: (1) dissolution, (2) winding up, and (3) termination.

Dissolution

Dissolution of a limited partnership is the first step toward termination (but termination does not necessarily follow dissolution). The limited partners have no power to dissolve the firm except on court order, and the death or bankruptcy of a limited partner does not dissolve the firm. The following events may cause dissolution: (1) termination of the partnership as per the certificate's provisions; (2) termination upon an event specified in the partnership agreement; (3) the unanimous written consent of the partners; (4) the withdrawal of a general partner, unless at least one remains and the agreement says one is enough, or if within ninety days all partners agree to continue; (5) an event that causes the business to be illegal; and (6) judicial decree of dissolution when it is not reasonable to carry on. If the agreement has no term, its dissolution is not triggered by some agreed-to event, and none of the other things listed cause dissolution.

Dissolution requires the filing of a certificate of cancellation with the state if winding up commences.

Winding Up

General partners who have not wrongfully dissolved the partnership may wind it up, and so may the limited partners if all the general partners have wrongfully dissolved the firm. Any partner or that person's legal representative can petition a court for winding up, with cause.

Upon winding up, the assets are distributed (1) to creditors, including creditor-partners, not including liabilities for distributions of profit; (2) to partners and ex-partners to pay off unpaid distributions; (3) to partners as return of capital contributions, unless otherwise agreed; and (4) to partners for partnership interests in proportion as they share in distributions, unless otherwise agreed. No distinction is made between general and limited partners—they share equally, unless otherwise agreed. When winding up is completed, the firm is terminated.

It is worth reiterating the part about "unless otherwise agreed": people who form any kind of a business organization—partnership, a hybrid form, or corporations—can to a large extent choose to structure their relationship as they see fit. Any aspect of the company's formation, operation, or ending that is not included in an agreement flops into the default provisions of the relevant law.

Key Takeaway

A limited partnership is a creature of statute: it requires filing a certificate with the state because it confers on some of its members the marvel of limited liability. It is an investment device composed of one or more general partners and one or more limited partners; limited partners may leave with six months' notice and are entitled to an appropriate payout. The general partner is liable as a partner is a general partnership; the limited partners' liability is limited to the loss of their investment, unless they exercise so much control of the firm as to become general partners. The general partner is paid, and the general and limited partners split profit as per the agreement or, if none, in the proportion as they made capital contributions. The firm is usually taxed like a general partnership: it is a conduit for the partners' income. The firm is dissolved upon the end of its term, upon an event specified in the agreement, or in several other circumstances, but it may have indefinite existence.

Exercises

1. Why does the fact that the limited liability company provides limited liability for some of its members mean that a state certificate must be filed?
2. What liability has the general partner? The limited partner?
3. How easy is it for the limited partner to dispose of (sell) her partnership interest?

42.2 Limited Liability Companies

Learning Objectives

1. Understand the history and law governing limited liability companies (LLCs).
2. Identify the creation and capitalization of an LLC.
3. Understand control and compensation of a firm.
4. Recognize liabilities in the LLC form.
5. Explain the taxation of an LLC.
6. Identify how LLCs are terminated.

History and Law Governing Limited Liability Companies

History of the Limited Liability Company

limited liability company

An unincorporated organization of one or more persons or entities established in accordance with applicable state laws and whose members may actively participate in the organization without being personally liable for the debts, obligations, or liabilities of the organization.

The **limited liability company** (LLC) gained sweeping popularity in the late twentieth century because it combines the best aspects of partnership and the best aspects of corporations: it allows all its owners (members) insulation from personal liability and pass-through (conduit) taxation. The first efforts to form LLCs were thwarted by IRS rulings that the business form was too much like a corporation to escape corporate tax complications. Tinkering by promoters of the LLC concept and flexibility by the IRS solved those problems in interesting and creative ways.

Corporations have six characteristics: (1) associates, (2) an objective to carry on a business and divide the gains, (3) continuity of life, (4) centralized management, (5) limited liability, and (6) free transferability of interests. Partnerships also, necessarily, have the first two corporate characteristics; under IRS rulings, if the LLC is *not* to be considered a corporation for tax purposes, it must lack at least one-half of the remaining four characteristics of a corporation: the LLC, then, must lack two of these corporate characteristics (otherwise it will be considered a corporation): (1) limited liability, (2) centralized management, (3) continuity of life, or (4) free transferability of interests. But limited liability is essential and centralized management is necessary for passive investors who don't want to be involved in decision making, so pass-through taxation usually hinges on whether an LLC has continuity of life and free transferability of accounts. Thus, it is extremely important that the LLC promoters avoid the corporate characteristics of continuity of life and free transferability of interests.

We will see how the LLC can finesse these issues.

Governing Law

All states have statutes allowing the creation of LLCs, and while a Uniform Limited Liability Company Act has been promulgated, not all states have adopted it as of November, 2016. The Uniform Law Commission (the people that make up uniform laws), observes: "The existing state LLC statutes, however, are far from uniform and many have been amended on a patchwork basis and have not kept up with the LLC cases and other legal developments."[5] Whether state law is uniform or not, the LLC has become the entity of choice for many businesses.

Creation and Capitalization

Creation of the LLC

An LLC is created according to the statute of the state in which it is formed. It is required that the LLC members file a "certificate of organization" with the secretary of state, and the name must indicate that it is a limited liability company. Partnerships and limited partnerships may convert to LLCs; the partners' previous liability under the other organizational forms is not affected, but going forward, limited liability is provided. The members' operating agreement spells out how the business will be run; it is subordinate to state and federal law. Unless otherwise agreed, the operating agreement can be amended only by unanimous vote. The LLC is an entity. Foreign LLCs (this means from a different state, not from a foreign country) must register with the secretary of state before doing business in a "foreign" state, or they cannot sue in state courts.

As compared with corporations, the LLC is not a good form if the owners expect to have multiple investors or to raise money from the public. The typical LLC has relatively few members (six or seven at most), all of whom usually are engaged in running the firm.

Most early LLC statutes, at least, prohibited their use by professionals. That is, practitioners who need professional licenses, such as certified public accountants, lawyers, doctors, architects, chiropractors, and the like, could not use this form because of concern about what would happen to the standards of practice if such people could avoid legitimate malpractice claims. For that reason, the limited liability partnership was invented.

Capitalization

Capitalization is like a partnership: members contribute capital to the firm according to their agreement. As in a partnership, the LLC property is not specific to any member, but each has a personal property interest in general. Contributions may be in the form of cash, property or services rendered, or a promise to render them in the future.

Control and Compensation

Control

The LLC operating agreement may provide for either a member-managed LLC or a manager-managed (centralized) LLC. If the former, all members have actual and apparent authority to bind the LLC to contracts on its behalf, as in a partnership, and all members' votes have equal weight unless otherwise agreed. Member-managers have duty of care and a fiduciary duty, though the parameters of those duties vary from state to state. If the firm is manager managed, only managers have authority to bind the firm; the managers have the duty of care and fiduciary duty, but the non-manager members usually do not. Some states' statutes provide that voting is based on the financial interests of the members. Most statutes provide that any extraordinary firm decisions be voted on by all members (e.g., amend the agreement, admit new members, sell all the assets prior to dissolution, merge with another entity). Members can make their own rules without the structural requirements (e.g., voting rights, notice, quorum, approval of major decisions) imposed under state corporate law.

If the firm has a centralized manager system, it gets a check in its "corporate-like" box, so it will need to make sure there are enough noncorporate-like attributes to make up for this one. If it looks too much like a corporation, it will be taxed like one.

One of the real benefits of the LLC as compared with the corporation is that no annual meetings are required, and no minutes need to be kept. Often, owners of small corporations ignore these formalities to their peril, but with the LLC there are no worries about such record keeping.

Compensation

Distributions are allocated among members of an LLC according to the operating agreement; managing partners may be paid for their services. Absent an agreement, distributions are allocated among members in proportion to the values of contributions made by them or required to be made by them. Upon a member's dissociation that does not cause dissolution, a dissociating member has the right to distribution as provided in the agreement, or—if no agreement—the right to receive the fair value of the member's interest within a reasonable time after dissociation. No distributions are allowed if making them would cause the LLC to become insolvent.

Liability

The great accomplishment of the LLC is, again, to achieve limited liability for all its members: no general partner hangs out with liability exposure. Ta-da!

Liability to Outsiders

Members are not liable to third parties for contracts made by the firm or for torts committed in the scope of business (but of course a person is always liable for her own torts), regardless of the owner's level of participation—unlike a limited partnership, where the general partner is liable. Third parties' only recourse is as against the firm's property. See *Puleo v. Topel*, (see Section 4), for an analysis of owner liability in an LLC.

Internal Liabilities

Unless the operating agreement provides otherwise, members and managers of the LLC are generally not liable to the firm or its members except for acts or omissions constituting gross negligence, intentional misconduct, or knowing violations of the law. Members and managers, though, must account to the firm for any personal profit or benefit derived from activities not consented to by a majority of disinterested members or managers from the conduct of the firm's business or member's or managers use of firm property—which is the same as in partnership law.

Taxation

Assuming the LLC is properly formed so that it is not too much like a corporation, it will—upon its members' election—be treated like a partnership for tax purposes. This is considered a big advantage.

Termination

Termination, loosely speaking, refers either to how the entity's life as a business ends (continuity of life) or to how a member's interest in the firm ends—that is, how freely the interest is transferable.

Continuity of Life

The first step in the termination of the LLC is dissolution, though dissolution is not necessarily followed by termination.

Dissolution and Winding Up

The IRS has determined that continuity of life does *not* exist "if the death, insanity, bankruptcy, retirement, resignation, or expulsion of any member will cause a dissolution of the organization,"[6] and that if one of these events occurs, the entity may continue only with the members' unanimous consent. Dissolution may occur even if the business is continued by the remaining members.

The typical LLC statute provides that an LLC will dissolve upon (1) expiration of the LLC's term as per its agreement; (2) events specified in the agreement; (3) written consent of all members; (4) an "event of dissociation" of a member, unless within ninety days of the event all remaining members agree to continue, or the right to continue is stated in the LLC; (5) the entry of a judicial decree of dissolution; (6) a change in membership that results in there being fewer than two members; or (7) the expiration of two years after the effective date of administrative dissolution.

And an "event of dissociation" is typically defined as (1) a member's voluntary withdrawal, (2) her assignment of the entire LLC interest, (3) her expulsion, (4) her bankruptcy, (5) her becoming incompetent, (6) dissolution of an entity member (as an LLC, limited partnership, or corporation), or (7) any other event specified in the agreement.

Thus under most statutes' default position, if a member dies, becomes insane or bankrupt, retires, resigns, or is expelled, the LLC will dissolve *unless* within ninety days the rest of the members unanimously agree to continue. And by this means the firm does *not* have continuity of life. Some states provide opportunities for even more flexibility regarding the "unanimous" part. In the mid-1990s, the IRS issued revenue rulings (as opposed to regulations) that it would be enough if a "majority in interest" of remaining partners agreed to continue the business, and the "flexible" statute states adopted this possibility (the ones that did not are called "bulletproof" statutes). "Majority in interests" means a majority of profits and capital.

If the firm does dissolve, some states require public filings to that effect. If dissolution leads to winding up, things progress as in a general partnership: the business at hand is finished, accounts are rendered, bills paid, assets liquidated, and remaining assets are distributed to creditors (including member and manager creditors, but not for their shares in profits); to members and past members for unpaid distributions; to members for capital contributions; and to members as agreed or in proportion to contributions made. Upon dissolution, actual authority of members or managers terminates except as needed to wind up; members may have apparent authority, though, unless the third party had notice of the dissolution.

Free Transferability of Interest

Again, the problem here is that if a member's interest in the LLC is as freely transferable as a shareholder's interest in a corporation (an owner can transfer all attributes of his interest without the others' consent), the LLC will probably be said to have a check mark in the "corporate-like" box: too many of those and the firm will not be allowed pass-through taxation. Thus, the trick for the LLC promoters is to limit free transferability enough to pass the test of not being a corporation, but not limit so much as to make it really difficult to divest oneself of the interest (then it's not a very liquid or desirable investment).

Some states' LLC statutes have as the default rule that the remaining members must unanimously consent to allow an assignee or a transferee of a membership interest to participate in managing the LLC. Since this prevents a member from transferring *all* attributes of the interest (the right to participate in management isn't transferred or assigned), the LLC formed under the default provision will not have "free transferability of interest." But if the LLC agreement allows *majority* consent for the transfer of all attributes, that also would satisfy the requirement that there not be free transferability of interests. Then we get into the question of how to define "majority": by number of members or by value of their membership? And what if only the managing partners need to consent? Or if there are two classes of membership and the transfer of interests in one class requires the consent of the other? The point is that people keep pushing the boundaries to see how close their LLC can come to corporation-like status without being called a corporation.

Statutes for LLCs allow other business entities to convert to this form upon application.

Key Takeaway

The limited liability company has become the entity of choice for many businesspeople. It is created by state authority that, upon application, issues the "certificate of organization." It is controlled either by managers or by members, it affords its members limited liability, and it is taxed like a partnership. But these happy results are obtained only if the firm lacks enough corporate attributes to escape being labeled as a corporation. To avoid too much "corporateness," the firm's certificate usually limits its continuity of life and the free transferability of interest. The ongoing game is to finesse these limits: to make them as non-constraining as possible, to get right up to the line to preserve continuity, and to make the interest as freely transferable as possible.

Exercises

1. What are the six attributes of a corporation? Which are automatically relevant to the LLC? Which two corporate attributes are usually dropped in an LLC?
2. Why does the LLC not want to be treated like a corporation?
3. Why does the name of the LLC have to include an indication that it is an LLC?
4. How did LLCs finesse the requirement that they not allow too-free transferability of the interest?

42.3 Other Forms

Learning Objective

1. Recognize other business forms: sub-S corporations, limited liability partnerships, and limited liability limited partnerships.

Sub-S Corporation

History

S corporation

A corporation whose owners elect to have it treated as a partnership for tax purposes.

The sub-S corporation or the **S corporation** gets its name from the IRS Code, Chapter 1, Subchapter S. It was authorized by Congress in 1958 to help small corporations and to stem the economic and cultural influence of the relatively few, but increasingly powerful, huge multinational corporations. According to the website of an S corporation champion, "a half century later, S corporations are the most popular corporate structure in America. The IRS estimates that there were 4.6 million S corporation owners in the United States in 2014—about twice the number of C [standard] corporations."[7]

Creation and Capitalization

The S corporation is a regular corporation created upon application to the appropriate secretary of state's office and operated according to its bylaws and shareholders' agreements. There are, however, some limits on how the business is set up, among them the following:

- It must be incorporated in the United States.
- It cannot have more than one hundred shareholders (a married couple counts as one shareholder).
- The only shareholders are individuals, estates, certain exempt organizations, or certain trusts.
- Only U.S. citizens and resident aliens may be shareholders.
- The corporation has only one class of stock.
- With some exceptions, it cannot be a bank, thrift institution, or insurance company.
- All shareholders must consent to the S corporation election.
- It is capitalized as is a regular corporation.

Liability

The owners of the S corporation have limited liability.

Taxation

Taxation is the crux of the matter. The S corporation pays no corporate income tax (unless it has a lot of passive income). The S corporation's shareholders include on their personal income statements, and pay tax on, their share of the corporation's separately stated items of income, deduction, and loss. That is, the S corporation avoids the dreaded double taxation of corporate income.

Transferability of Ownership

S corporations' shares can be bought or sold via share purchase agreements, and all changes in the ownership are reflected in the share ledger in the corporate minute book.

Limited Liability Partnerships

Background

In 1991, Texas enacted the first **limited liability partnership** (LLP) statute, largely in response to the liability that had been imposed on partners in partnerships sued by government agencies in relation to massive savings and loan failures in the 1980s.[8] (Here we see an example of the legislature allowing business owners to externalize the risks of business operation.) More broadly, the success of the limited liability company attracted the attention of professionals like accountants, lawyers, and doctors who sought insulation from personal liability for the mistakes or malpractice of their partners. Their wish was granted with the adoption in all states of statutes authorizing the creation of the limited liability partnership in the early 1990s. Most partnership law under the Revised Uniform Partnership Act applies to LLPs.

limited liability partnership

A partnership in which some or all partners (depending on the jurisdiction) have limited liability.

Creation

Members of a partnership (only a majority is required) who want to form an LLP must file with the secretary of state; the name of the firm must include "limited liability partnership" or "LLP" to notify the public that its members will not stand personally for the firm's liabilities.

Liability

As noted, the purpose of the LLP form of business is to afford insulation from liability for its members. A typical statute provides as follows: "Any obligation of a partnership incurred while the partnership is a limited liability partnership, whether arising in contract, tort or otherwise, is solely the obligation of the partnership. A partner is not personally liable, directly or indirectly, by way of indemnification, contribution, assessment or otherwise, for such an obligation solely by reason of being or so acting as a partner."[9]

However, the statutes vary. The early ones only allowed limited liability for negligent acts and retained unlimited liability for other acts, such as malpractice, misconduct, or wrongful acts by partners, employees, or agents. The second wave eliminated all these as grounds for unlimited liability, leaving only breaches of ordinary contract obligation. These two types of legislation are called *partial shield* statutes. The third wave of LLP legislation offered *full shield* protection—no unlimited liability at all. Needless to say, the full-shield type has been most popular and most widely adopted. Still, however, many statutes require specified amounts of professional malpractice insurance, and partners remain fully liable for their own negligence or for wrongful acts of those in the LLP whom they supervise.

In other respects, the LLP is like a partnership.

Limited Liability Limited Partnerships

limited liability limited partnership

A limited partnership that has chosen to limit the liability of the general partnership under state law.

The progress toward achieving limited liability continues. A **limited liability limited partnership** (LLLP, or triple LP) is the latest invention. It is a limited partnership that has invoked the LLLP provisions of its state partnership law by filing with a specified public official the appropriate documentation to become an LLLP. This form completely eliminates the automatic personal liability of the general partner for partnership obligations and, under most statutes, also eliminates the "control rule" liability exposure for all limited partners. It is noteworthy that California law does not allow for an LLLP to be formed in California; however, it does recognize LLLPs formed in other states. A "foreign" LLLP doing business in California must register with the secretary of state. As of November 2016, twenty-one states allow the formation of LLLPs.

The 2001 revision of the Uniform Limited Partnership Act (ULPA) provides this definition of an LLLP: "'Limited liability limited partnership' . . . means a limited partnership whose certificate of limited partnership states that the limited partnership is a limited liability limited partnership."[10] Section 404(c) gets to the point: "An obligation of a limited partnership incurred while the limited partnership is a limited liability limited partnership, whether arising in contract, tort, or otherwise, is solely the obligation of the limited partnership. A general partner is not personally liable, directly or indirectly, by way of contribution or otherwise, for such an obligation solely by reason of being or acting as a general partner. This subsection applies despite anything inconsistent in the partnership agreement that existed immediately before the consent required to become a limited liability limited partnership[.]"[11]

In the discussion of limited partnerships, we noted that ULPA-2001 eliminates the "control rule" so that limited partners who exercise day-to-day control are *not* thereby liable as general partners. Now, in the section quoted in the previous paragraph, the *general partner's* liability for partnership obligations is vaporized too. Hooray for encouraging entrepreneurship, maybe not so much cheering for the "moral hazard" then encouraged--see below. (Of course, the general partner is liable for its, his, or her own torts.) The preface to ULPA-2001 explains, "In a limited liability limited partnership ('LLLP'), no partner—whether general or limited—is liable on account of partner status for the limited partnership's obligations. Both general and limited partners benefit from a full, status-based liability shield that is equivalent to the shield enjoyed by corporate shareholders, LLC members, and partners in an LLP."

Presumably, most existing limited partnerships will switch over to LLLPs. The ULPA-2001 provides that "the Act makes LLLP status available through a simple statement in the certificate of limited partnership."

Ethical Concerns

There was a reason that partnership law imposed personal liability on the partners: people tend to be more careful when they are personally liable for their own mistakes and bad judgment. Many government programs reflect peoples' interest in adverting risk: federal deposit insurance, Social Security, and bankruptcy, to name three. And of course corporate limited liability has existed for two hundred years.[12] Whether the movement to allow almost anybody the right to a business organization that affords limited liability will encourage entrepreneurship and business activity or whether it will usher in a new era of **moral hazard**—people being allowed to escape the consequences of their own irresponsibility—is yet to be seen.

moral hazard

The lack of incentive to guard against a risk when a person is protected against it, as by being afforded limited liability.

Key Takeaway

Businesspeople always prefer to reduce their risks. The partnership form imposes serious potential risk: unlimited personal liability. The corporate form eliminates that risk but imposes some onerous formalities and double taxation. Early on, then, the limited partnership form was born, but it still imposed unlimited liability on the general partner and on the limited partner if she became too actively involved. Congress was induced in the mid-1950s to allow certain small U.S. corporations the right to single taxation, but the sub-S corporation still suffered from various limitations on its structure. In the 1980s, the limited liability company was invented; it has become the entity of choice for many businesspeople, but its availability for professionals was limited. In the late 1980s, the limited liability partnership form gained favor, and in the early 2000s, the limited liability limited partnership finished off unlimited liability for limited partnerships.

Exercises

1. The principal disadvantage of the general partnership is that it imposes unlimited personal liability on the partners. What is the disadvantage of the corporate form?
2. Why isn't the limited partnership an entirely satisfactory solution to the liability problem of the partnership?
3. Explain the issue of "moral hazard" and the business organization form.

42.4 Cases

Limited Partnerships: Limited Partners' Liability for Managing Limited Partnership

Frigidaire Sales Corp. v. Union Properties, Inc.

562 P.2d 244 (Wash. 1977)

Plaintiff [Frigidaire] entered into a contract with Commercial Investors (Commercial), a limited partnership. Defendants, Leonard Mannon and Raleigh Baxter, were limited partners of Commercial. Defendants were also officers, directors, and shareholders of Union Properties, Inc., the only general partner of Commercial. Defendants controlled Union Properties, and through their control of Union Properties they exercised the day-to-day control and management of Commercial. Commercial breached the contract, and Plaintiff brought suit against Union Properties and Defendants. The trial court concluded that Defendants did not incur general liability for Commercial's obligations by reason of their control of Commercial, and the Court of Appeals affirmed.

[Plaintiff] does not contend that Defendants acted improperly by setting up the limited partnership with a corporation as the sole general partner. Limited partnerships are a statutory form of business organization, and parties creating a limited partnership must follow the statutory requirements. In Washington, parties may form a limited partnership with a corporation as the sole general partner. [Citations]

Plaintiff's sole contention is that Defendants should incur general liability for the limited partnership's obligations under RCW 25.08.070, because they exercised the day-to-day control and management of Commercial. Defendants, on the other hand, argue that Commercial was controlled by Union Properties, a separate legal entity, and not by Defendants in their individual capacities. [RCW 25.08.070 then read: "A limited partner shall not become liable as a general partner unless, in addition to the exercise of his rights and powers as limited partner, he takes part in the control of the business."]

* * * The pattern of operation of Union Properties was to investigate and conceive of real estate investment opportunities and, when it found such opportunities, to cause the creation of limited partnerships with Union Properties acting as the general partner. Commercial was only one of several limited partnerships so conceived and created. Defendants did not form Union Properties for the sole purpose of operating Commercial. Hence, their acts on behalf of Union Properties were not performed merely for the benefit of Commercial. * * *

[P]etitioner was never led to believe that Defendants were acting in any capacity other than in their corporate capacities. The parties stipulated at the trial that Defendants never acted in any direct, personal capacity. When the shareholders of a corporation, who are also the corporation's officers and directors, conscientiously keep the affairs of the corporation separate from their personal affairs, and no fraud or manifest injustice is perpetrated upon third persons who deal with the corporation, the corporation's separate entity should be respected. [Citations]

For us to find that Defendants incurred general liability for the limited partnership's obligations under RCW 25.08.070 would require us to apply a literal interpretation of the statute and totally ignore the corporate entity of Union Properties, when Plaintiff knew it was dealing with that corporate entity. There can be no doubt that Defendants, in fact, controlled the corporation. However, they did so only in their capacities as agents for their principal, the corporate general partner. Although the corporation was a separate entity, it could act only through its board of directors, officers, and agents. [Citations] Plaintiff entered into the contract with Commercial. Defendants signed the contract in their capacities as president and secretary-treasurer of Union Properties, the general partner of Commercial. In the eyes of the law it was Union Properties, as a separate corporate entity, which entered into the contract with Plaintiff and controlled the limited partnership.

Further, because Defendants scrupulously separated their actions on behalf of the corporation from their personal actions, Plaintiff never mistakenly assumed that Defendants were general partners with general liability. [Citations] Plaintiff knew Union Properties was the sole general partner and did not rely on Defendants' control by assuming that they were also general partners. If Plaintiff had not wished to rely on the solvency of Union Properties as the only general partner, it could have insisted that Defendants personally guarantee contractual performance. Because Plaintiff entered into the contract knowing that Union Properties was the only party with general liability, and because in the eyes of the law it was Union Properties, a separate entity, which controlled the limited partnership, there is no reason for us to find that Defendants incurred general liability for their acts done as officers of the corporate general partner.

The decision of the Court of Appeals is affirmed.

Case Questions

1. Frigidaire entered into a contract with Commercial Investors, a limited partnership. The general partner in the limited partnership was Union Properties, Inc., a corporation. Who were the limited partners in the limited partnership? Who were the controlling principals of the corporate general partner?
2. Why is it common for the general partner in a limited partnership to be a corporation?
3. Why does the court reiterate that the plaintiff knew it was dealing with a limited partnership that had a corporate general partner?
4. What could the plaintiff have done in this case to protect itself?
5. Why was it significant that Union Properties was the general partner is several limited partnerships, of which Commercial Investors, LP, was only one?
6. The court ruled in favor of the defendants, but is this setup kind of a scam? What is the "moral hazard" problem lurking in this case?

Liability Issues in LLCs

Puleo v. Topel
856 N.E.2d 1152 (Ill. App. 2006)

Plaintiffs Philip Puleo [and others] * * * appeal the order of the circuit court dismissing their claims against defendant Michael Topel.

The record shows that effective May 30, 2002, Thinktank, a limited liability company (LLC) primarily involved in web design and web marketing, was involuntarily dissolved by the Illinois Secretary of State * * * due to Thinktank's failure to file its 2001 annual report as required by the Illinois Limited Liability Company Act (the Act) [Citation].

[In December 2002], plaintiffs, independent contractors hired by Topel, filed a complaint against Topel and Thinktank in which they alleged breach of contract, unjust enrichment, and claims under the account stated theory. Those claims stemmed from plaintiffs' contention that Topel, who plaintiffs alleged was the sole manager and owner of Thinktank, knew or should have known of Thinktank's involuntary dissolution, but nonetheless continued to conduct business as Thinktank from May 30, 2002, through the end of August 2002. They further contended that on or about August 30, 2002, Topel informed Thinktank employees and independent contractors, including plaintiffs, that the company was ceasing operations and that their services were no longer needed. Thinktank then failed to pay plaintiffs for work they had performed. * * *

On September 2, 2003, the circuit granted plaintiffs' motion for judgment on the pleadings against Thinktank. Thereafter, on October 16, 2003, plaintiffs filed a separate motion for summary judgment against Topel [personally]. Relying on [Citation], plaintiffs contended that Topel, as a principal of Thinktank, an LLC, had a legal status similar to a shareholder or director of a corporation, who courts have found liable for a dissolved corporation's debts. Thus, plaintiffs argued that Topel was personally liable for Thinktank's debts. * * *

The circuit court denied plaintiffs' motion for summary judgment against Topel. * * * In doing so, the circuit court acknowledged that Topel continued to do business as Thinktank after its dissolution and that the contractual obligations at issue were incurred after the dissolution.

However * * * the court entered a final order dismissing all of plaintiffs' claims against Topel with prejudice. * * * The court stated in pertinent part:

> *Based upon the Court's . . . finding that the Illinois Legislature did not intend to hold a member of a Limited Liability Company liable for debts incurred after the Limited Liability Company had been involuntarily dissolved, the Court finds that all of Plaintiffs' claims against Defendant Topel within the Complaint fail as a matter of law, as they are premised upon Defendant Topel's alleged personal liability for obligations incurred in the name of Thinktank LLC after it had been involuntarily dissolved by the Illinois Secretary of State.*

Plaintiffs now appeal that order * * * [contending] that * * * the circuit court erred in dismissing their claims against Topel. In making that argument, plaintiffs acknowledge that the issue as to whether a member or manager of an LLC may be held personally liable for obligations incurred by an involuntarily dissolved LLC appears to be one of first impression under the Act. That said, plaintiffs assert that it has long been the law in Illinois that an officer or director of a dissolved corporation has no authority to exercise corporate powers and thus is personally liable for any debts he incurs on behalf of the corporation after its dissolution. [Citations] Plaintiffs reason that Topel, as managing member of Thinktank, similarly should be held liable for debts the company incurred after its dissolution.

We first look to the provisions of the Act as they provided the trial court its basis for its ruling. * * *

> *(a) Except as otherwise provided in subsection (d) of this Section, the debts, obligations, and liabilities of a limited liability company, whether arising in contract, tort, or otherwise, are solely the debts, obligations, and liabilities of the company. A member or manager is not personally liable for a debt, obligation, or liability of the company solely by reason of being or acting as a member or manager....*
>
> *(c) The failure of a limited liability company to observe the usual company formalities or requirements relating to the exercise of its company powers or management of its business is not a ground for imposing personal liability on the members or managers for liabilities of the company.*
>
> *(d) All or specified members of a limited liability company are liable in their capacity as members for all or specified debts, obligations, or liabilities of the company if:*
>
> *(1) a provision to that effect is contained in the articles of organization; and*
>
> *(2) a member so liable has consented in writing to the adoption of the provision or to be bound by the provision.*
>
> *[Another relevant section provides]:*
>
> *(a) A limited liability company is bound by a member or manager's act after dissolution that:*
>
> *(1) is appropriate for winding up the company's business; or*
>
> *(2) would have bound the company before dissolution, if the other party to the transaction did not have notice of the dissolution.*
>
> *(b) A member or manager who, with knowledge of the dissolution, subjects a limited liability company to liability by an act that is not appropriate for winding up the company's business is liable to the company for any damage caused to the company arising from the liability.*

[The statute] clearly indicates that a member or manager of an LLC is not personally liable for debts the company incurs unless each of the provisions in subsection (d) is met. In this case, plaintiffs cannot establish either of the provisions in subsection (d). They have not provided this court with Thinktank's articles of organization, much less a provision establishing Topel's personal liability, nor have they provided this court with Topel's written adoption of such a provision. As such, under the express language of the Act, plaintiffs cannot establish Topel's personal liability for debts that Thinktank incurred after its dissolution. * * * *

In 1998, * * * the legislature amended [the LLC statute] * * * and in doing so removed language which explicitly provided that a member or manager of an LLC could be held personally liable for his or her own actions or for the actions of the LLC to the same extent as a shareholder or director of a corporation could be held personally liable [which would include post-dissolution acts undertaken without authority]. As we have not found any legislative commentary regarding that amendment, we presume that by removing the noted statutory language, the legislature meant to shield a member or manager of an LLC from personal liability. [Citation] "When a statute is amended, it is presumed that the legislature intended to change the law as it formerly existed."

Nonetheless, plaintiffs ask this court to disregard the 1998 amendment and to imply a provision into the Act similar to * * * the Business Corporation Act. We cannot do so. * * * When the legislature amended section [the relevant section] it clearly removed the provision that allowed a member or manager of an LLC to be held personally liable in the same manner as provided in section 3.20 of the Business Corporation Act. Thus, the Act does not provide for a member or manager's personal liability to a third party for an LLC's debts and liabilities, and no rule of construction authorizes this court to declare that the legislature did not mean what the plain language of the statute imports.

We, therefore, find that the circuit court did not err in concluding that the Act did not permit it to find Topel personally liable to plaintiffs for Thinktank's debts and liabilities. We agree with plaintiff that the circuit court's ruling does not provide an equitable result. However, the circuit court, like this court, was bound by the statutory language.

Accordingly, we affirm the judgment of the circuit court of Cook County.

Case Questions

1. Is it possible the defendant did not know his LLC had been involuntarily dissolved because it failed to file its required annual report? Should he have known it was dissolved?
2. If Topel's business had been a corporation, he would not have had insulation from liability for postdissolution contracts—he would have been liable. Is the result here equitable? Is it fraud?
3. Seven months after the LLC's existence was terminated by the state, the defendant hired a number of employees, did not pay them, and then avoided liability under the LLC shield. How else could the court have ruled here? It is possible that the legislature's intent was simply to eliminate compulsory piercing (see Chapter 43 under corporate law principles and leave the question of LLC piercing to the courts. If so was the court's decision was correct? The current LLC act language is similar to the Model Business Corporation Act, which surely permits piercing (see Chapter 43).

Defective Registration as a Limited Liability Partnership

Campbell v. Lichtenfels
2007 WL 447919 (Conn. Super. 2007)

This case concerns the aftermath of the dissolution of the parties' law practice. Following a hearing on January 2 and 3, 2007, this court issued a memorandum of decision on January 5, 2007 granting the plaintiff a prejudgment remedy in the amount of $15,782.01. The plaintiff has now moved for reargument, contending that the court improperly considered as a setoff one-half of a malpractice settlement paid personally by the defendant, which sum the court found to be a debt of a partnership. [The defendant was sued for malpractice by a third party; he paid the entire claim personally and when the law firm dissolved, the plaintiff's share from the liquidated assets was reduced by one-half to account for the amount the defendant had paid.]

In support of his motion to reargue, the plaintiff relies on General Statutes Sec. 34-427(c) and, in that motion, italicizes those portions which he believes apply to his request for reargument. That section states (with emphasis as supplied in the plaintiff's motion) that:

> *a partner in a registered limited liability partnership is not liable directly or indirectly,* including by way of indemnification, contribution or otherwise, *for any debts, obligations and liabilities of or chargeable* to the partnership or another partner *or partners,* whether arising in *contract,* tort, *or otherwise, arising in the course of the partnership business while the partnership is a registered limited liability partnership. (emphasis in original)*

While italicizing the phases that appear to suit his purposes, the plaintiff completely ignores the most important phrase: "a partner in a registered limited liability partnership." At the hearing, neither party presented any evidence at the hearing that tended to prove that the nature of the business relationship between the parties was that of a "registered limited liability partnership." To the contrary, the testimony presented at the hearing revealed that the parties had a general partnership in which they had orally agreed to share profits and losses equally and that they never signed a partnership agreement. There was certainly no testimony or tangible evidence to the effect that the partnership had filed "a certificate of limited liability partnership with the Secretary of the State, stating the name of the partnership, which shall conform to the requirements of [the statute]; the address of its principal office; * * * a brief statement of the business in which the partnership engages; any other matters the partnership may determine to include; and that the partnership therefore applies for status as a registered limited liability partnership." [Citation]

It is true that certain of the exhibits, such as copies of checks and letters written on the law firm letterhead, refer to the firm as "Campbell and Lichtenfels, LLP." These exhibits, however, were not offered for the purpose of establishing the partnership's character, and merely putting the initials "LLP" on checks and letterhead is not, in and of itself, proof of having met the statutory requirements for registration as a limited liability partnership. The key to establishing entitlement to the protections offered by [the limited liability partnership statute] is proof that the partnership has filed "a certificate of limited liability partnership with the Secretary of the State," and the plaintiff presented no such evidence to the court.

Because the evidence presented at the hearing does not support a claim that the nature of the relationship between the parties to this case was that of partners in a registered limited liability partnership, the provisions of [the limited liability partnership statute] do not apply. Rather, this partnership is governed by the provisions of [the Uniform Partnership Act] which states: "Except as otherwise provided . . . all partners are liable jointly and severally for all obligations of the partnership unless otherwise agreed by the claimant or provided by law." Because there has been no evidence that this partnership falls within [any exceptions] the court finds Campbell and Lichtenfels to have been a general partnership in which the plaintiff shares the liability for the malpractice claim, even if he was not the partner responsible for the alleged negligence that led to that claim.

The plaintiff correctly points out that reargument is appropriate when the court has "overlooked" a "* * * principle of law which would have a controlling effect * * * " on the outcome of the case at hand. [Citation] The principle of law now raised by the plaintiff was "overlooked" by the court at the time of the hearing for two good reasons. First, it was not brought to the court's attention at the time of the hearing. Second, and more importantly, the plaintiff presented no evidence that would have supported the claim that the principle of law in question, namely the provisions of [the limited liability partnership] was applicable to the facts of this case. Because the provisions of [that statute] are inapplicable, they are quite obviously not "controlling." The principle of law which does control this issue is found in [general partnership law] and that principle makes the plaintiff liable for his share of the malpractice settlement, as the court has previously found. The motion for reargument is therefore denied.

Case Questions

1. If the parties had been operating as a limited liability partnership, how would that have changed the result?
2. Why did the court find that there was no limited liability partnership?
3. How does general partnership law treat a debt by one partner incurred in the course of partnership business?
4. Here, as in the case in Section 4, there really is no inequitable result. Why is this true?

42.5 Summary and Exercises

Summary

Between partnerships and corporations lie a variety of hybrid business forms: limited partnerships, sub-S corporations, limited liability companies, limited liability partnerships, and limited liability limited partnerships. These business forms were invented to achieve, as much as possible, the corporate benefits of limited liability, centralized control, and easy transfer of ownership interest with the tax treatment of a partnership.

Limited partnerships were recognized in the early twentieth century and today are governed mostly by the Uniform Limited Partnership Act (ULPA-1985 or ULPA-2001). These entities, not subject to double taxation, are composed of one or more general partners and one or more limited partners. The general partner controls the firm and is liable like a partner in a general partnership (except under ULPA-2001 liability is limited); the limited partners are investors and have little say in the daily operations of the firm. If they get too involved, they lose their status as limited partners (except this is not so under ULPA-2001). The general partner, though, can be a corporation, which finesses the liability problem. A limited partnership comes into existence only when a certificate of limited partnership is filed with the state.

In the mid-twentieth century, Congress was importuned to allow small corporations the benefit of pass-through taxation. It created the sub-S corporation (referring to a section of the IRS code). It affords the benefits of taxation like a partnership and limited liability for its members, but there are several inconvenient limitations on how sub-S corporations can be set up and operate.

The 1990s saw the limited liability company become the entity of choice for many businesspeople. It deftly combines limited liability for all owners—managers and nonmanagers—with pass-through taxation and has none of the restrictions perceived to hobble the sub-S corporate form. Careful crafting of the firm's bylaws and operating certificate allow it to combine the best of all possible business forms. There remained, though, one fly in the ointment: most states did not allow professionals to form limited liability companies (LLCs).

This last barrier was hurtled with the development of the limited liability partnership. This form, though mostly governed by partnership law, eschews the vicarious liability of nonacting partners for another's torts, malpractice, or partnership breaches of contract. The extent to which such exoneration from liability presents a moral hazard—allowing bad actors to escape their just liability—is a matter of concern.

Having polished off liability for all owners with the LLC and the LLP, the next logical step occurred when eyes returned to the venerable limited partnership. The invention of the limited liability limited partnership in ULPA-2001 not only abolished the "control test" that made limited partners liable if they got too involved in the firm's operations but also eliminated the general partner's liability.

TABLE 42.1 Comparison of Business Organization Forms

Type of Business Form	Formation and Ownership Rules	Funding	Management	Liability	Taxes	Dissolution
Limited partnership	Formal filing of articles of partnership; unlimited number of general and limited partners	General and limited partners contribute capital	General partner	General partner personally liable; limited partners to extent of contribution[13]	Flow-through as in partnership	Death or termination of general partner, unless otherwise agreed
S corporation	Formal filing of articles of incorporation; up to 100 shareholders allowed but only one class of stock	Equity (sell stock) or debt funding (issue bonds); members share profits and losses	Board of directors, officers	Owners not personally liable absent piercing corporate veil (see Chapter 43)	Flow-through as in partnership	Only if limited duration or shareholders vote to dissolve
Limited liability company	Formal filing of articles of organization; unlimited "members"	Members make capital contributions, share profits and losses	Member managed or manager managed	Limited liability	Flow-through as in partnership.	Upon death or bankruptcy, unless otherwise agreed
Limited liability partnership (LLP)	Formal filing of articles of LLP	Members make capital contributions, share profits and losses	All partners or delegated to managing partner	Varies, but liability is generally on partnership; nonacting partners have limited liability	Flow-through as in partnership	Upon death or bankruptcy, unless otherwise agreed
Limited liability limited partnership (LLLP)	Formal filing of articles of LLP; choosing LLLP form	Same as above	Same as above	Liability on general partner abolished: all members have limited liability	Flow-through as in partnership	Same as above

Exercises

1. Yolanda and Zachary decided to restructure their small bookstore as a limited partnership, called "Y to Z's Books, LP." Under their new arrangement, Yolanda contributed a new infusion of $300; she was named the general partner. Zachary contributed $300 also, and he was named the limited partner: Yolanda was to manage the store on Monday, Wednesday, and Friday, and Zachary to manage it on Tuesday, Thursday, and Saturday. Y to Z Books, LP failed to pay $800 owing to Vendor. Moreover, within a few weeks, Y to Z's Books became insolvent. Who is liable for the damages to Vendor?
2. What result would be obtained in Exercise 1 if Yolanda and Zachary had formed a limited liability company?

3. Suppose Yolanda and Zachary had formed a limited liability partnership. What result would be obtained then?
4. Jacobsen and Kelly agreed to form an LLC. They filled out the appropriate paperwork and mailed it with their check to the secretary of state's office. However, they made a mistake: instead of sending it to "Boston, MA"—Boston, Massachusetts—they sent it to "Boston, WA"—Boston, Washington. There is a town in Washington State called "Little Boston" that is part of an isolated Indian reservation. The paperwork got to Little Boston but then was much delayed. After two weeks, Jacobsen and Kelly figured the secretary of state in Boston, MA, was simply slow to respond. They began to use their checks, business cards, and invoices labeled "Jacobsen and Kelly, LLC." They made a contract to construct a wind turbine for Pablo; Kelly did the work but used guy wires that were too small to support the turbine. During a modest wind a week after the turbine's erection, it crashed into Pablo's house. The total damages exceeded $35,000. Pablo discovered Jacobsen and Kelly's LLC was defectively created and sought judgment against them personally. May Pablo proceed against them both personally?
5. Holden was the manager of and a member of Frost LLLP, an investment firm. In that capacity, he embezzled $30,000 from one of the firm's clients, Backus. Backus sued the firm and Holden personally, but the latter claimed he was shielded from liability by the firm. Is Holden correct?
6. Bellamy, Carlisle, and Davidson formed a limited partnership. Bellamy and Carlisle were the general partners and Davidson the limited partner. They contributed capital in the amounts of $100,000, $100,000, and $200,000, respectively, but then could not agree on a profit-sharing formula. At the end of the first year, how should they divide their profits?

Self-Test Questions

1. Peron and Quinn formed P and Q Limited Partnership. Peron made a capital contribution of $20,000 and became a general partner. Quinn made a capital contribution of $10,000 and became a limited partner. At the end of the first year of operation, a third party sued the partnership and both partners in a tort action. What is the potential liability of Peron and Quinn, respectively?
    a. $20,000 and $10,000
    b. $20,000 and $0
    c. unlimited and $0
    d. unlimited and $10,000
    e. unlimited and unlimited
2. A limited partnership
    a. comes into existence when a certificate of partnership is filed.
    b. always provides limited liability to an investor.
    c. gives limited partners a say in the daily operation of the firm.
    d. is not likely to be the business form of choice if a limited liability limited partnership option is available.
    e. two of these (specify).
3. Puentes is a limited partner of ABC, LP. He paid $30,000 for his interest and he also loaned the firm $20,000. The firm failed. Upon dissolution and liquidation,
    a. Puentes will get his loan repaid pro rata along with other creditors.
    b. Puentes will get repaid, along with other limited partners, in respect to his capital and loan after all other creditors have been paid.
    c. if any assets remain, the last to be distributed will be the general partners' profits.
    d. if Puentes holds partnership property as collateral, he can resort to it to satisfy his claim if partnership assets are insufficient to meet creditors' claims.

4. Reference to "moral hazard" in conjunction with hybrid business forms gets to what concern?
    a. that general partners in a limited partnership will run the firm for their benefit, not the limited partners' benefit
    b. that the members of a limited liability company or limited liability partnership will engage in activities that expose themselves to potential liability
    c. that the trend toward limited liability gives bad actors little incentive to behave ethically because the losses caused by their behavior are mostly not borne by them
    d. that too few modern professional partnerships will see any need for malpractice insurance
5. One of the advantages to the LLC form over the sub-S form is
    a. in the sub-S form, corporate profits are effectively taxed twice.
    b. the sub-S form does not provide "full-shield" insulation of liability for its members.
    c. the LLC cannot have a "manager-manager" form of control, whereas that is common for sub-S corporations.
    d. the LLC form requires fewer formalities in its operation (minutes, annual meetings, etc.).

Self-Test Answers

1. d
2. e (that is, a and d)
3. d (Choice a is wrong because as a secured creditor Puentes can realize on the collateral without regard to other creditors' payment.)
4. c
5. d

Endnotes

1. "Uniform Limited Partnership Act (2001), Prefatory Note," NCCUSL Archives, http://www.law.upenn.edu/bll/archives/ulc/ulpa/final2001.pdf.
2. ULPA, Section 102(11).
3. ULPA-2001, Section 303.
4. Official Comment to Uniform Limited Partnership Act 2001, Section 303.
5. http://www.uniformlaws.org/Narrative.aspx?title=Why States Should Adopt RULLCA. This website offers an accessible presentation of LLC law.
6. Treasury Regulation, § 301.7701-2(b)(1).
7. "The History and Challenges of America's Dominant Business Structure," *S Corp: Defending America's Small and Family-Owned Businesses*, http://www.s-corp.org/our-history.
8. Christine M. Przybysz, "Shielded Beyond State Limits: Examining Conflict-Of-Law Issues In Limited Liability Partnerships," *Case Western Reserve Law Review* 54, no. 2 (2003): 605.
9. Revised Code of Washington (RCW), Section 25.05.130.
10. "Uniform Limited Partnership Act (2001)," NCCUSL Archives, http://www.law.upenn.edu/bll/archives/ulc/ulpa/final2001.htm; ULPA Section, 102(9).
11. ULPA Section, 404(c).
12. See, for example, David A. Moss, "Risk, Responsibility, and the Role of Government," *Drake Law Review* 56, no. 2 (2008): 541.
13. Under ULPA-2001, the general partner has limited liability.

CHAPTER 43

Corporation: General Characteristics and Formation

Learning Objectives

After reading this chapter, you should understand the following:

1. The historical background of the corporation.
2. How partnerships compare with corporations.
3. What the corporation is as a legal entity, and how corporate owners can lose limited liability by certain actions.
4. How corporations are classified.

The corporation is the dominant form of the business enterprise in the modern world. As a legal entity, it is bound by much of the law discussed in the preceding chapters. However, as a significant institutional actor in the business world, the corporation has a host of relationships that have called forth a separate body of law.

43.1 Historical Background

Learning Objectives

1. Comprehend the historical significance of corporate formation.
2. Learn about key court decisions and their effect on interstate commerce and corporate formation.
3. Become acquainted with how states formed their corporate laws.

A Fixture of Every Major Legal System

Like partnership, the corporation is an ancient concept, recognized in the Code of Hammurabi, and to some degree a fixture in every other major legal system since then. The first corporations were not business enterprises; instead, they were associations for religious and governmental ends in which perpetual existence was a practical requirement. Thus, until relatively late in legal history, kings, popes, and jurists assumed that corporations could be created only by political or ecclesiastical authority and that corporations were creatures of the state or church. By the seventeenth century, with feudalism on the wane and business enterprise becoming a growing force, kings extracted higher taxes and intervened more directly in the affairs of businesses by refusing to per-

concession theory

Incorporation was a concession given by royal grant of a sovereign.

mit them to operate in corporate form except by royal grant. This came to be known as the **concession theory**, because incorporation was a concession from the sovereign.

joint-stock companies

Companies in which stock or company funds are held jointly.

The most important concessions, or charters, were those given to the giant foreign trading companies, including the Russia Company (1554), the British East India Company (1600), Hudson's Bay Company (1670, and still operating in Canada under the name "the Bay"), and the South Sea Company (1711). These were **joint-stock companies**—that is, individuals contributed capital to the enterprise, which traded on behalf of all the stockholders. Originally, trading companies were formed for single voyages, but the advantages of a continuing fund of capital soon became apparent. Also apparent was the legal characteristic that above all led shareholders to subscribe to the stock: limited liability. They risked only the cash they put in, not their personal fortunes.

Some companies were wildly successful. The British East India Company paid its original investors a fourfold return between 1683 and 1692. But perhaps nothing excited the imagination of the British more than the discovery of gold bullion aboard a Spanish shipwreck; 150 companies were quickly formed to salvage the sunken Spanish treasure. Though most of these companies were outright frauds, they ignited the search for easy wealth by a public unwary of the risks. In particular, the South Sea Company promised the sun and the moon: in return for a monopoly over the slave trade to the West Indies, it told an enthusiastic public that it would retire the public debt and make every person rich.

In 1720, a fervor gripped London that sent stock prices soaring. Beggars and earls alike speculated from January to August; and then the bubble burst. Without considering the ramifications, Parliament had enacted the highly restrictive Bubble Act, which was supposed to do away with unchartered **joint-stock** companies. When the government prosecuted four companies under the act for having fraudulently obtained charters, the public panicked and stock prices came tumbling down, resulting in history's first modern financial crisis.

As a consequence, corporate development was severely retarded in England. Distrustful of the chartered company, Parliament issued few corporate charters, and then only for public or quasi-public undertakings, such as transportation, insurance, and banking enterprises. Corporation law languished: William Blackstone devoted less than 1 percent of his immensely influential *Commentaries on the Law of England* (1765) to corporations and omitted altogether any discussion of limited liability. In *The Wealth of Nations* (1776), Adam Smith doubted that the use of corporations would spread. England did not repeal the Bubble Act until 1825, and then only because the value of true incorporation had become apparent from the experience of its former colonies.

U.S. Corporation Formation

The United States remained largely unaffected by the Bubble Act. Incorporation was granted only by special acts of state legislatures, even well into the nineteenth century, but many such acts were passed. Before the Revolution, perhaps fewer than a dozen business corporations existed throughout the thirteen colonies. During the 1790s, two hundred businesses were incorporated, and their numbers swelled thereafter. The theory that incorporation should not be accomplished except through special legislation began to give way. As industrial development accelerated in the mid-1800s, it was possible in many states to incorporate by adhering to the requirements of a general statute. Indeed, by the late nineteenth century, all but three states constitutionally *forbade* their legislatures from chartering companies through special enactments.

foreign corporations

A company incorporated outside the state in which it is doing business.

The U.S. Supreme Court contributed importantly to the development of corporate law. In *Gibbons v. Ogden*,[1] a groundbreaking case, the Court held that the Commerce Clause of the U.S. Constitution (Article I, Section 8, Clause 3) granted Congress the power to regulate interstate commerce. However, in *Paul v. Virginia*,[2] the Court said that a state could prevent corporations not chartered there—that is, **out-of-state** or **foreign corporations**—from engaging in what it considered the local, and not interstate, business of issuing insurance policies. The inference made by many was that states could not bar foreign corporations engaged in *interstate* business from their borders.

This decision brought about a competition in corporation laws. The early general laws had imposed numerous restrictions. The breadth of corporate enterprise was limited, ceilings were placed on total capital and indebtedness, incorporators were required to have residence in the state, the duration of the company often was not perpetual but was limited to a term of years or until a particular undertaking was completed, and the powers of management were circumscribed. These restrictions and limitations were thought to be necessary to protect the citizenry of the chartering legislature's own state. But once it became clear that companies chartered in one state could operate in others, states began in effect to "sell" incorporation for tax revenues.

New Jersey led the way in 1875 with a general incorporation statute that greatly liberalized the powers of management and lifted many of the former restrictions. The Garden State was ultimately eclipsed by Delaware, which in 1899 enacted the most liberal corporation statute in the country, so that to the present day there are thousands of "Delaware corporations" that maintain no presence in the state other than an address on file with the secretary of state in Dover and the appointment of a registered agent (often a lawyer) for the company to receive service of process in the event it is sued.

During the 1920s, the National Conference of Commissioners on Uniform State Laws drafted a Uniform Business Corporation Act, the final version of which was released in 1928. It was not widely adopted, but it did provide the basis during the 1930s for revisions of some state laws, including those in California, Illinois, Michigan, Minnesota, and Pennsylvania. By that time, in the midst of the Great Depression, the federal government for the first time intruded into corporate law in a major way by creating federal agencies, most notably the Securities and Exchange Commission in 1934, with power to regulate the interstate issuance of corporate stock.

Corporate Law Today

Following World War II, most states revised their general corporation laws. A significant development for states was the preparation of the Model Business Corporation Act by the American Bar Association's Committee on Corporate Laws. About half of the states have adopted all or major portions of the act. The 2005 version of this act, the Revised Model Business Corporation Act (RMBCA), will be referred to throughout our discussion of corporation law.

Key Takeaway

Corporations have their roots in political and religious authority. The concept of limited liability and visions of financial rewards fueled the popularity of joint-stock companies, particularly trading companies, in late-seventeenth- and early eighteenth-century England. The English Parliament successfully enacted the Bubble Act in 1720 to curb the formation of these companies; the restrictions weren't loosened until over one hundred years later, after England viewed the success of corporations in its former colonies. Although early corporate laws in the United States were fairly restrictive, once states began to "sell" incorporation for tax revenues, the popularity of liberal and corporate-friendly laws caught on, especially in Delaware beginning in 1899. A corporation remains a creature of the state—that is, the state in which it is incorporated. Delaware remains the state of choice because more corporations are registered there than in any other state.

Exercises

1. If the English Parliament had not enacted the Bubble Act in 1720, would the "bubble" have burst? If so, what would have been the consequences to corporate development?

2. What were some of the key components of early U.S. corporate laws? What was the rationale behind these laws?
3. Why are so many corporations attracted to Delaware?

43.2 Partnerships versus Corporations

Learning Objectives

1. Distinguish basic aspects of partnership formation from those of corporate formation.
2. Explain ownership and control in partnerships and in publicly held and closely held corporations.
3. Know how partnerships and corporations are taxed.

Let us assume that three people have already formed a partnership to run a bookstore business. Bob has contributed $160,000. Carol has contributed a house in which the business can lawfully operate. Ted has contributed his services; he has been managing the bookstore, and the business is showing a slight profit. A friend has been telling them that they ought to incorporate. What are the major factors they should consider in reaching a decision?

Ease of Formation

Partnerships are easy to form. If the business is simple enough and the partners are few, the agreement need not even be written down. Creating a corporation is more complicated because formal documents must be placed on file with public authorities. Bob, Ted, and Carol must pay for the relevant legal time and advice, not only on formation, but during the life of the venture.

Ownership and Control

All general partners have equal rights in the management and conduct of the business. By contrast, ownership and control of corporations are, in theory, separated. In the **publicly held corporation**, which has many shareholders, the separation is real. Ownership is widely dispersed because millions of shares are outstanding and it is rare that any single shareholder will own more than a tiny percentage of stock. It is difficult under the best of circumstances for shareholders to exert any form of control over corporate operations. However, in the **closely held corporation**, which has few shareholders, the officers or senior managers are usually also the shareholders, so the separation of ownership and control may be less pronounced or even nonexistent. Practically, then, with the three former partners becoming shareholders, the business operations may feel similar to when the partnership existed, although one person will have to be the president ("CEO"), and each former partner will not necessarily have a "veto" over the others.

publicly held corporation

A firm that is traded publicly through the sale of stock subscriptions, has many shareholders and widely dispersed ownership, and in which shareholders have little control.

closely held corporation

A corporation with few shareholders, so that separation of ownership and control may be less pronounced than in a publicly held corporation or even nonexistent.

Transferability of Interests

Transferability of an interest in a partnership is a problem because a transferee cannot become a member unless all partners consent. The problem can be addressed and overcome in the partnership agreement. **Transfer of interest** in a corporation, through a sale of stock, is much easier; but for the stock of a small corporation, there might not be a market or there might be contractual restrictions on transfer. For Carol, Bob, and Ted, an agreement must be reached to have an accountant or some trusted professional appraise the value of their respective shares at the time one of them wishes to sell to the other two. Or, one who wishes to sell could find a buyer for his or her shares; this could not happen in a partnership. With a sale to the remaining shareholders/owners, liquidity is a likely issue; if Bob wants out, the business will probably not have the amount of his contribution ($160,000 plus any accrued value if the business is successful) on hand. Some form of promissory note would be required, but if this is not possible, the business would have to be sold as a whole. But this would not be much different if the three were still partners: if one partner wants to dissolve a general partnership, s/he can.

Transfer of interest

Transferring an ownership interest through the sale of stock from one person to the next.

Financing

Partners have considerable flexibility in financing. They can lure potential investors by offering interests in profits and, in the case of general partnerships, control. Corporations can finance by selling freely transferable stock to the public or by incurring debt. Different approaches to the financing of corporations are discussed in Chapter 44. For Bob, Carol, and Ted, however, being a small, closely held corporation will not raise their chances of selling more stock to others.

Taxation

The partnership is a conduit for income and is not taxed as a separate entity. Individual partners are taxed, and although limited by the 1986 Tax Reform Act, they can deduct partnership losses. Corporate earnings, on the other hand, are subject to double taxation. The corporation is first taxed on its own earnings as an entity. Then, when profits are distributed to shareholders in the form of dividends, the shareholders are taxed again. (A small corporation, with no more than one hundred shareholders, can elect S corporation status. Because S corporations are taxed as partnerships, they avoid double taxation.) However, incorporating brings several tax benefits. For example, the corporation can take deductions for life, medical, and disability insurance coverage for its employees, whereas partners or sole proprietors cannot.

Key Takeaway

Partnerships are easier to form than corporations, especially since no documents are required. General partners share both ownership and control, but in publicly held corporations, these functions are separated. Additional benefits for a partnership include flexibility in financing, single taxation, and the ability to deduct losses. Transfer of interest in a partnership can be difficult if not addressed in the initial agreement, since all partners must consent to the transfer.

Exercises

1. Provide an example of when it would be best to form a partnership, and cite the advantages and disadvantages of doing so.
2. Provide an example of when it would be best to form a corporation, and cite the advantages and disadvantages of doing so.

43.3 The Corporate Veil: The Corporation as a Legal Entity

Learning Objectives

1. Know what rights a corporate "person" and a natural person have in common.
2. Recognize when a corporate "veil" is pierced and shareholder liability is imposed.
3. Identify other instances when a shareholder will be held personally liable.

In comparing partnerships and corporations, there is one additional factor that ordinarily tips the balance in favor of incorporating: the corporation is a legal entity in its own right, one that can provide a "veil" that protects its shareholders from personal liability.

FIGURE 43.1 The Corporate Veil: Shielding Shareholders

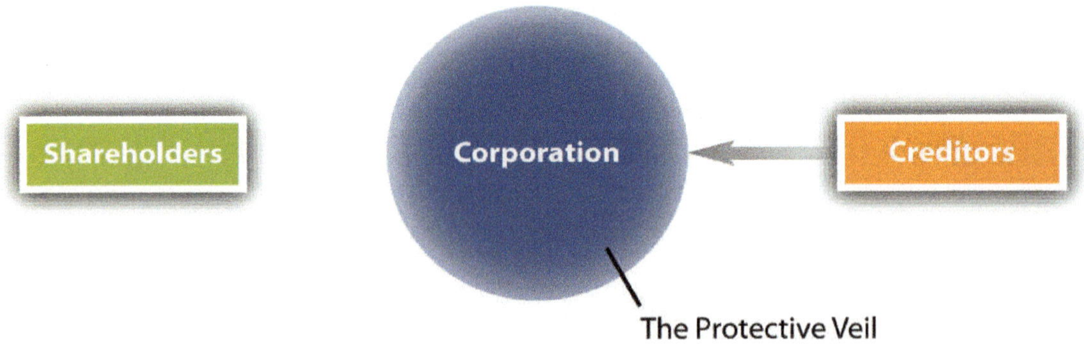

This crucial factor accounts for the development of much of corporate law. Unlike the individual actor in the legal system, the corporation is difficult to deal with in conventional legal terms. The business of the sole proprietor and the sole proprietor herself are one and the same. When a sole proprietor makes a decision, she risks her own capital. When the managers of a corporation take a corporate action, they are risking the capital of others—the shareholders. Thus accountability is a major theme in the system of law constructed to cope with legal entities other than natural persons.

The Basic Rights of the Corporate "Person"

To say that a **corporation is a "person"** does not automatically describe what its rights are, for the courts have not accorded the corporation every right guaranteed a natural person. Yet the Supreme Court recently affirmed in *Citizens United v. Federal Election Commission* (2010) that the government may not suppress the First Amendment right of political speech because the speaker is a corporation rather than a natural person. According to the Court, "No sufficient governmental interest justifies limits on the political speech of nonprofit or for-profit corporations."[3]

corporation is a "person"

When corporations are granted the same rights as natural persons.

The courts have also concluded that corporations are entitled to the essential constitutional protections of due process and equal protection. They are also entitled to Fourth Amendment protection against unreasonable search and seizure; in other words, the police must have a search warrant to enter corporate premises and look through files. Warrants, however, are not required for highly regulated industries, such as those involving liquor or guns. The Double Jeopardy Clause applies to criminal prosecutions of corporations: an acquittal cannot be appealed nor can the case be retried. For purposes of the federal courts' diversity jurisdiction, a corporation is deemed to be a citizen of both the state in which it is incorporated and the state in which it has its principal place of business (often, the corporate "headquarters").

Until relatively recently, few cases had tested the power of the state to limit the right of corporations to spend their own funds to speak the "corporate mind." Most cases involving corporate free speech address advertising, and few states have enacted laws that directly impinge on the freedom of companies to advertise. But those states that have done so have usually sought to limit the ability of corporations to sway voters in public referenda. In 1978, the Supreme Court finally confronted the issue head on in *First National Bank of Boston v. Bellotti* (Section 7). The ruling in *Bellotti* was reaffirmed by the Supreme Court in *Citizens United v. Federal Election Commission*. In *Citizens United*, the Court struck down the part of the McCain-Feingold Act[4] that prohibited all corporations, both for-profit and not-for-profit, and unions from broadcasting "electioneering communications."

Absence of Rights

Corporations lack certain rights that natural persons possess. For example, corporations do not have the privilege against self-incrimination guaranteed for natural persons by the Fifth and Fourteenth Amendments. In any legal proceeding, the courts may force a corporation to turn over incriminating documents, even if they also incriminate officers or employees of the corporation. As we explore in Chapter 47, corporations are not citizens under the Privileges and Immunities Clause of the Constitution, so that the states can discriminate between domestic and foreign corporations. And the corporation is not entitled to federal review of state criminal convictions, as are many individuals.

Piercing the Corporate Veil

piercing the corporate veil

The protection of the corporation (the veil) is set aside for litigation purposes, and liability can be imposed on individual shareholders or entities that exist behind the corporation.

Given the importance of the corporate entity as a veil that limits shareholder liability, it is important to note that in certain circumstances, the courts may reach beyond the wall of protection that divides a corporation from the people or entities that exist behind it. This is known as **piercing the corporate veil**, and it will occur in two instances: (1) when the corporation is used to commit a fraud or an injustice and (2) when the corporation does not act as if it were one.

Fraud

The Felsenthal Company burned to the ground. Its president, one of the company's largest creditors and also virtually its sole owner, instigated the fire. The corporation sued the insurance company to recover the amount for which it was insured. According to the court in the Felsenthal case, "The general rule of law is that the willful burning of property by a stockholder in a corporation is not a defense against the collection of the insurance by the corporation, and...the corporation cannot be prevented from collecting the insurance because its agents willfully set fire to the property without the participation or authority of the corporation or of all of the stockholders of the corporation."[5] But because the fire was caused by the beneficial owner of "practically all" the stock, who also "has the absolute management of [the corporation's] affairs and its property, and is its president," the court refused to allow the company to recover the insurance money; allowing the company to recover would reward fraud.[6]

Failure to Act as a Corporation

personal liability of individual shareholders

A failure to follow corporate formalities—for example, inadequate capitalization or commingling of assets—can subject stockholders to personal liability.

In other limited circumstances, individual stockholders may also be found personally liable. Failure to follow corporate formalities, for example, may subject stockholders to **personal liability**. This is a special risk that small, especially one-person, corporations run. Particular factors that bring this rule into play include inadequate capitalization, omission of regular meetings, failure to record minutes of meetings, failure to file annual reports, and commingling of corporate and personal assets. Where these factors exist, the courts may look through the corporate veil and pluck out the individual stockholder or stockholders to answer for a tort, contract breach, or the like. The classic case is the taxicab operator who incorporates several of his cabs separately and services them through still another corporation. If one of the cabs causes an accident, the corporation is usually "judgment proof" because the corporation will have few assets (practically worthless cab, minimum insurance). The courts frequently permit plaintiffs to proceed against the common owner on the grounds that the particular corporation was inadequately financed.

FIGURE 43.2 The Subsidiary as a Corporate Veil

Can a wholly owned subsidiary serve to shield a parent company against creditors?

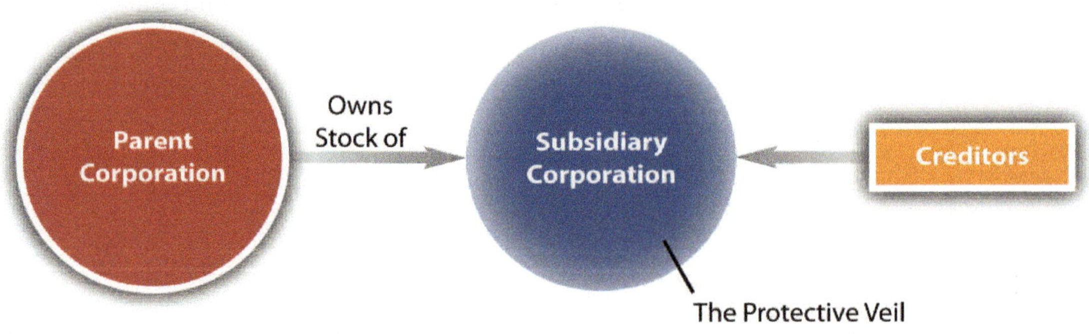

When a corporation owns a subsidiary corporation, the question frequently arises whether the subsidiary is acting as an independent entity (see Figure 43.2). The Supreme Court addressed this question of derivative versus direct liability of the corporate parent vis-à-vis its subsidiary in *United States v. Bestfoods*, (see Section 7).

Other Types of Personal Liability

Even when a corporation is formed for a proper purpose and is operated as a corporation, there are instances in which individual shareholders will be personally liable. For example, if a shareholder involved in company management commits a tort or enters into a contract in a personal capacity, he will remain personally liable for the consequences of his actions. In some states, statutes give employees special rights against shareholders. For example, a New York statute permits employees to recover wages, salaries, and debts owed them by the company from the ten largest shareholders of the corporation. (Shareholders of public companies whose stock is traded on a national exchange or over the counter are exempt.) Likewise, federal law permits the IRS to recover from the "responsible persons" any withholding taxes collected by a corporation but not actually paid over to the U.S. Treasury.

Key Takeaway

Corporations have some of the legal rights of a natural person. They are entitled to the constitutional protections of due process and equal protection, Fourth Amendment protection against unreasonable search and seizure, and First Amendment protection of free speech and expression. For purposes of the federal courts' diversity jurisdiction, a corporation is deemed to be a citizen of both the state in which it is incorporated and the state in which it has its principal place of business. However, corporations do not have the privilege against self-incrimination guaranteed for natural persons by the Fifth and Fourteenth Amendments. Further, a corporation's shareholders are not always free from civil liability. Courts will pierce the corporate veil and hold a corporation liable when the corporation is used to perpetrate fraud or when it fails to act as a corporation.

Exercises

1. Do you think that corporations should have rights similar to those of natural persons? Should any of these rights be curtailed?
2. What is an example of speaking the "corporate mind"?

43.4 Classifications of Corporations

Learning Objectives

1. Distinguish the "public," or municipal, corporation from the publicly held corporation.
2. Explain how the tax structure for professional corporations evolved.
3. Define the two types of business corporations.

Nonprofit Corporations

nonprofit corporation

A corporation in which no part of the income is distributable to its members, directors, or officers.

One of the four major classifications of corporations is the **nonprofit corporation** (also called not-for-profit corporation). It is defined in the American Bar Association's Model Non-Profit Corporation Act as "a corporation no part of the income of *which* is distributable to its members, directors or officers." Nonprofit corporations may be formed under this law for charitable, educational, civil, religious, social, and cultural purposes, among others.

Public Corporations

municipal corporation

A governmental entity; also called a public corporation.

The true public corporation is a governmental entity. It is often called a **municipal corporation**, to distinguish it from the publicly held corporation, which is sometimes also referred to as a "public" corporation, although it is in fact private (i.e., it is not governmental). Major cities and counties, and many towns, villages, and special governmental units, such as sewer, transportation, and public utility authorities, are incorporated. These corporations are not organized for profit, do not have shareholders, and operate under different statutes than do business corporations.

Professional Corporations

professional corporation

A corporation of lawyers, doctors, accountants, or other professionals who enjoy the same benefits in corporate form as do other corporations.

Until the 1960s, lawyers, doctors, accountants, and other professionals could not practice their professions in corporate form. Most often, these professionals would form partnerships. The lack of corporate form for professionals was financially disadvantageous. Under the federal income tax laws then in effect, corporations could establish far better pension plans than could partners or the self-employed. During the 1960s, the states began to let professionals incorporate, but the IRS balked, denying them many tax benefits. In 1969, the IRS finally conceded that it would tax a **professional corporation** just as it would any other corporation, so that professionals could, from that time on, place a much higher proportion of tax-deductible income into a tax-deferred pension. That decision led to a burgeoning number of professional corporations.

Business Corporations

The Two Types

business corporation

In contrast to public (municipal), professional, or nonprofit corporations, business corporations are of two types: publicly held and closely held, referring to how the stock is held within the corporation.

It is the **business corporation** proper that we focus on in this unit. There are two broad types of business corporations: publicly held (or public) and closely held (or private) corporations. Again, both types are private in the sense that they are not governmental.

The publicly held corporation is one in which stock is widely held or available for wide public distribution through such means as trading on a national or regional stock exchange. Its managers, if they are also owners of stock, usually constitute a small percentage of the total number of shareholders and hold a small amount of stock relative to the total shares outstanding. Few shareholders of public corporations know their fellow shareholders.

By contrast, the shareholders of the closely held corporation are fewer in number. Shares in a closely held corporation could be held by one person, and usually by no more than thirty. Shareholders of the closely held corporation often share family ties or have some other association that permits each to know the others.

Though most closely held corporations are small, no economic or legal reason prevents them from being large. Some are huge, having annual sales of several billion dollars each. Roughly 90 percent of U.S. corporations are closely held.

The giant publicly held companies with more than $1 billion in assets and sales, such as Apple, Inc. or IBM, constitute an exclusive group. Publicly held corporations outside this elite class fall into two broad (nonlegal) categories: those that are quoted on stock exchanges and those whose stock *is* too widely dispersed to be called closely held but is not traded on exchanges.

Key Takeaway

There are four major classifications of corporations: (1) nonprofit, (2) municipal, (3) professional, and (4) business. Business corporations are divided into two types, publicly held and closely held corporations.

Exercises

1. What are the main advantages of professionals being able to incorporate?
2. Distinguish a publicly held corporation from a closely held one.
3. Are most corporations in the U.S. publicly or closely held? Are closely held corporations subject to different provisions than publicly held ones?

43.5 Corporate Organization

Learning Objectives

1. Recognize the steps to issue a corporate charter.
2. Know the states' rights in modifying a corporate charter.
3. Discuss factors to consider in selecting a state in which to incorporate.
4. Explain the functions and liability of a promoter.
5. Understand the business and legal requirements in executing and filing the articles of incorporation.

As discussed in Section 4, corporate status offers companies many protections. If the owners of a business decide to incorporate after weighing the pros and cons of incorporation, they need to take the steps explained in this section.

The Corporate Charter

Function of the Charter

The ultimate goal of the incorporation process is issuance of a **corporate charter**. The term used for the document varies from state to state. Most states call the basic document filed in the appropriate public office the "articles of incorporation" or "certificate of incorporation," but there are other variations. There is no legal significance to these differences in terminology.

corporate charter

The basic document of incorporation filed in the appropriate public office, also referred to as articles of incorporation.

Chartering is basically a state prerogative. Congress has chartered several enterprises, including national banks (under the National Banking Act), federal savings and loan associations, national farm loan associations, and the like, but virtually all business corporations are chartered at the state level.

Originally a legislative function, chartering is now an administrative function in every state. The secretary of state issues the final indorsement to the articles of incorporation, thus giving them legal effect.

Charter as a Contract

The charter is a contract between the state and the corporation. Under the Contracts Clause of Article I of the Constitution, no state can pass any law "impairing the obligation of contracts." In 1816, the question arose whether a state could revoke or amend a corporate charter once granted. The corporation in question was Dartmouth College. The New Hampshire legislature sought to turn the venerable private college, operating under an old royal charter, into a public institution by changing the membership of its board. The case wound up in the Supreme Court. Chief Justice John Marshall ruled that the legislature's attempt was unconstitutional, because to amend a charter is to impair a contract.[7]

This decision pleased incorporators because it implied that once a corporation had been created, the state could never modify the powers it had been granted. But, in addition, the ruling seemed to favor monopolies. The theory was that by granting a charter to, say, a railroad corporation, the state was barred from creating any further railroad corporations. Why? Because, the lawyers argued, a competitor would cut into the first company's business, reducing the value of the charter, hence impairing the contract. Justice Joseph Story, concurring in the *Dartmouth* case, had already suggested the way out for the states: "If the legislature mean to claim such an authority [to alter or amend the charter], it must be reserved in the grant. The charter of Dartmouth College contains no such reservation...." The states quickly picked up on Justice Story's suggestion and wrote into the charter explicit language giving legislatures the authority to modify corporations' charters at their pleasure. So the potential immutability of corporate charters had little practical chance to develop.

Selection of a State

Where to Charter

Choosing the particular venue in which to incorporate is the first critical decision to be made after deciding to incorporate. Some corporations, though headquartered in the United States, choose to incorporate offshore to take advantage of lenient taxation laws. Advantages of an offshore corporation include not only lenient tax laws but also a great deal of privacy as well as certain legal protections. For example, the names of the officers and directors can be excluded from documents filed. In the United States, over half of the *Fortune* 500 companies hold Delaware charters for reasons related to Delaware's having a lower tax structure, a favorable business climate, and a legal system—both its statutes and its courts—seen as being up to date, flexible, and often pro-business. Delaware's success has led other states to compete, and the political realities have caused the Revised Model Business Corporation Act (RMBCA), which was intentionally drafted to balance the interests of all significant groups (management, shareholders, and the public), to be revised from time to time so that it is more permissive from the perspective of management.

Why Choose Delaware?

Delaware remains the most popular state in which to incorporate for several reasons, including the following: (1) low incorporation fees; (2) only one person is needed to serve the incorporator of the corporation; the RMBC requires three incorporators; (3) no minimum capital requirement; (4) favorable tax climate, including no sales tax; (5) no taxation of shares held by nonresidents; and (5) no corporate income tax for companies doing business outside of Delaware. In addition,

Delaware's Court of Chancery, a court of equity, is renowned as a premier business court with a well-established body of corporate law, thereby affording a business a certain degree of predictability in judicial decision making.

The Promoter

Functions

Once the state of incorporation has been selected, it is time for **promoters**, the midwives of the enterprise, to go to work. Promoters are the individuals who take the steps necessary to form the corporation, and they often will receive stock in exchange for their efforts. They have four principal functions: (1) to seek out or discover business opportunities, (2) to raise capital by persuading investors to sign stock subscriptions, (3) to enter into contracts on behalf of the corporation to be formed, (4) and to prepare the articles of incorporation.

promoters
An individual who takes the initial steps needed to form a corporation.

Promoters have acquired an unsavory reputation as fast talkers who cajole investors out of their money. Though some promoters fit this image, it is vastly overstated. Promotion is difficult work often carried out by the same individuals who will manage the business.

Contract Liability

Promoters face two major legal problems. First, they face possible liability on contracts made on behalf of the business before it is incorporated. For example, suppose Bob is acting as promoter of the proposed BCT Bookstore, Inc. On September 15, Bob enters into a contract with Computogram Products to purchase computer equipment for the corporation to be formed. If the incorporation never takes place, or if the corporation is formed but the corporation refuses to accept the contract, Bob remains liable.

Now assume that the corporation is formed on October 15, and on October 18 it formally accepts all the contracts that Bob signed prior to October 15. Does Bob remain liable? In most states, he does. The ratification theory of agency law will not help in many states that adhere strictly to agency rules, because there was no principal (the corporation) in existence when the contract was made; without a principal, Bob cannot be an agent, and hence he as promoter must remain liable. To avoid this result, Bob should seek an express novation (see Chapter 15), although in some states, a novation will be implied. The intention of the parties should be stated as precisely as possible in the contract, as the promoters learned in *RKO-Stanley Warner Theatres, Inc. v. Graziano*, (see Section 7).

The promoters' other major legal concern is the duty owed to the corporation. The law is clear that promoters owe a fiduciary duty to the corporation. For example, the transfer by a promoter to the corporation of real estate worth at most $250,000, in exchange for $750,000 worth of stock would be liable for $500,000 for breach of fiduciary duty.

Preincorporation Stock Subscriptions

One of the promoter's jobs is to obtain **preincorporation stock subscriptions** to line up offers by would-be investors to purchase stock in the corporation to be formed. These stock subscriptions are agreements to purchase, at a specified price, a certain number of shares of stock of a corporation, which is to be formed at some point in the future. The contract, however, actually comes into existence *after* formation, once the corporation itself accepts the offer to subscribe. Suppose Alice agrees with Bob to invest $10,000 in the BCT Bookstore, Inc. for one thousand shares. The agreement is treated as an offer to purchase. The offer is deemed accepted at the moment the bookstore is incorporated.

preincorporation stock subscriptions
Offers by would-be investors to purchase stock in a corporation that is not as yet formed.

One problem for the corporation is an attempt by subscribers to revoke their offers. A basic rule of contract law is that offers are revocable before acceptance. Under RMBCA, Section 6.20, however, a subscription for shares is irrevocable for six months unless the subscription agreement itself provides otherwise or unless all the subscribers consent to revocation. In many states that have not adopted the model act, the contract rule applies and the offer is always revocable. Other states use various common-law devices to prevent revocation. For example, the subscription by one investor is held as consideration for the subscription of another, so that a binding contract has been formed.

Execution and Filing of the Articles of Incorporation

Once the business details are settled, the promoters, now known as incorporators, must sign and deliver the articles of incorporation to the secretary of state. The articles of incorporation typically include the following: the corporate name; the address of the corporation's initial registered office; the period of the corporation's duration (usually perpetual); the company's purposes; the total number of shares, the classes into which they are divided, and the par value of each; the limitations and rights of each class of shareholders; the authority of the directors to establish preferred or special classes of stock; provisions for preemptive rights; provisions for the regulation of the internal affairs of the corporation, including any provision restricting the transfer of shares; the number of directors constituting the initial board of directors and the names and addresses of initial members; and the name and address of each incorporator. Although compliance with these requirements is largely a matter of filling in the blanks, two points deserve mention.

First, the choice of a name is often critical to the business. Under RMBCA, Section 4.01, the name must include one of the following words (or abbreviations): corporation, company, incorporated, or limited (Corp., Co., Inc., or Ltd.). The name is not allowed to deceive the public about the corporation's purposes, nor may it be the same as that of any other company incorporated or authorized to do business in the state.

These legal requirements are obvious; the business requirements are much harder. If the name is not descriptive of the business or does not anticipate changes in the business, it may have to be changed, and the change can be expensive. For example, when Standard Oil Company of New Jersey changed its name to Exxon in 1972, the estimated cost was over $100 million. (And even with this expenditure, some shareholders grumbled that the new name sounded like a laxative.)

The second point to bear in mind about the articles of incorporation is that drafting the clause stating corporate purposes requires special care, because the corporation will be limited to the purposes set forth. In one famous case, the charter of Cornell University placed a limit on the amount of contributions it could receive from any one benefactor. When Jennie McGraw died in 1881, leaving to Cornell the carillon that still plays on the Ithaca, New York, campus, she also bequeathed to the university her residuary estate valued at more than $1 million. This sum was greater than the ceiling placed in Cornell's charter. After lengthy litigation, the university lost in the U.S. Supreme Court, and the money went to her family.[8] Most incorporators include the broadest possible language, usually something like "for all lawful purposes."

Some states require the purpose clauses to be specific, but the usual approach is to permit a broad statement of purposes. Section 3.01 of the RMBCA goes one step further in providing that a corporation automatically "has the purpose of engaging in any lawful business" unless the articles specify a more limited purpose. Once completed, the articles of incorporation are delivered to the secretary of state for filing. The existence of a corporation begins once the articles have been filed.

Organizational Meeting of Directors

The first order of business, once the certificate of incorporation is issued, is a meeting of the board of directors named in the articles of incorporation. They must adopt bylaws, elect officers, and transact any other business that may come before the meeting (RMBCA, Section 2.05). Other business would include accepting (ratifying) promoters' contracts, calling for the payment of stock subscriptions, and adopting bank resolution forms, giving authority to various officers to sign checks drawn on the corporation.

Section 10.20 of the RMBCA vests in the directors the power to alter, amend, or repeal the bylaws adopted at the initial meeting, subject to repeal or change by the shareholders. The articles of incorporation may reserve the power to modify or repeal exclusively to the shareholders. The bylaws may contain any number of provisions, but no provisions may conflict with the articles of incorporation or the law of the state.

Typical provisions in the bylaws include fixing the place and time at which annual stockholders' meetings will be held, fixing a quorum, setting the method of voting, establishing the method of choosing directors, creating committees of directors, setting down the method by which board meetings may be called and the voting procedures to be followed, determining the offices to be filled by the directors and the powers with which each officer shall be vested, fixing the method of declaring dividends, establishing a fiscal year, setting out rules governing issuance and transfer of stock, and establishing the method of amending the bylaws.

Section 2.07 of the RMBCA provides that the directors may adopt bylaws that will operate during an emergency. An emergency is a situation in which "a quorum of the corporation's directors cannot readily be assembled because of some catastrophic event."

Key Takeaway

Articles of incorporation represent a corporate charter—that is, a contract between the corporation and the state. Filing these articles, or "chartering," is accomplished at the state level. The secretary of state's final approval gives these articles legal effect. A state cannot change a charter unless it reserves the right when granting the charter.

In selecting a state in which to incorporate, a corporation looks for a favorable corporate climate. Delaware remains the state of choice for incorporation, particularly for publicly held companies. Most closely held companies choose to incorporate in their home states.

Following the state selection, the promoter commences his or her functions, which include entering into contracts on behalf of the corporation to be formed (for which he or she can be held liable) and preparing the articles of incorporation.

The articles of incorporation must include the corporation's name and its corporate purpose, which can be broad. Finally, once the certificate of incorporation is issued, the corporation's board of directors must hold an organizational meeting.

Exercises

1. Does the Contracts Clause of the Constitution, which forbids a state from impeding a contract, apply to corporations?
2. What are some of the risks that a promoter faces for his or her actions on behalf of the corporation? Can he or she limit these risks?
3. What are the dangers of limiting a corporation's purpose?
4. What is the order of business at the first board of directors' meeting?

43.6 Effect of Organization

Learning Objectives

1. Distinguish between a de jure and a de facto corporation.
2. Define the doctrine of corporation by estoppel.

De Jure and De Facto Corporations

de jure corporation

A corporation that exists in law, having met all of the necessary legal requirements.

If promoters meet the requirements of corporate formation, a **de jure corporation**, considered a legal entity, is formed. Because the various steps are complex, the formal prerequisites are not always met. Suppose that a company, thinking its incorporation has taken place when in fact it hasn't met all requirements, starts up its business. What then? If three conditions exist, a court might decide that a *de facto* corporation has been formed; that is, the business will be recognized as a corporation. The state then has the power to force the *de facto* corporation to correct the defect(s) so that a *de jure* corporation will be created.

The three traditional conditions are the following: (1) a statute must exist under which the corporation could have been validly incorporated, (2) the promoters must have made a *bona fide* attempt to comply with the statute, and (3) corporate powers must have been used or exercised.

A frequent cause of defective incorporation is the promoters' failure to file the articles of incorporation in the appropriate public office. The states are split on whether a *de facto* corporation results if every other legal requirement is met.

Corporation by Estoppel

corporation by estoppel

Use of the equitable principle of estoppel by a court to treat a business as a corporation.

Even if the incorporators omit important steps, it is still possible for a court, under estoppel principles, to treat the business as a corporation. Assume that Bob, Carol, and Ted have sought to incorporate the BCT Bookstore, Inc., but have failed to file the articles of incorporation. At the initial directors' meeting, Carol turns over to the corporation a deed to her property. A month later, Bob discovers the omission and hurriedly submits the articles of incorporation to the appropriate public office. Carol decides she wants her land back. It is clear that the corporation was not *de jure* at the time she surrendered her deed, and it was probably not *de facto* either. Can she recover the land? Under equitable principles, the answer is no. She is estopped from denying the existence of the corporation, because it would be inequitable to permit one who has conducted herself as though there were a corporation to deny its existence in order to defeat a contract into which she willingly entered. As *Cranson v. International Business Machines Corp.* indicates (Section 7), the doctrine of **corporation by estoppel** can also be used by the corporation against one of its creditors.

Key Takeaway

A court will find that a corporation might exist under fact (*de facto*), and not under law (*de jure*) if the following conditions are met: (1) a statute exists under which the corporation could have been validly incorporated, (2) the promoters must have made a *bona fide* attempt to comply with the statute, and (3) corporate powers must have been used or exercised. A de facto corporation may also be found when a promoter fails to file the articles of incorporation. In the alternative, the court may look to estoppel principles to find a corporation.

Exercises

1. What are some of the formal prerequisites to forming a de jure corporation?
2. Are states in agreement over what represents a de facto corporation if a promoter fails to file the articles of incorporation?
3. What is the rationale for corporation by estoppel?

43.7 Cases

Corporate First Amendment Rights

First National Bank of Boston v. Bellotti

435 U.S. 765 (1978)

MR. JUSTICE POWELL delivered the opinion of the Court.

In sustaining a state criminal statute that forbids certain expenditures by banks and business corporations for the purpose of influencing the vote on referendum proposals, the Massachusetts Supreme Judicial Court held that the First Amendment rights of a corporation are limited to issues that materially affect its business, property, or assets. The court rejected appellants' claim that the statute abridges freedom of speech in violation of the First and Fourteenth Amendments. The issue presented in this context is one of first impression in this Court. We postponed the question of jurisdiction to our consideration of the merits. We now reverse.

The statute at issue, Mass. Gen. Laws Ann., Ch. 55, § 8 (West Supp. 1977), prohibits appellants, two national banking associations and three business corporations, from making contributions or expenditures "for the purpose of...influencing or affecting the vote on any question submitted to the voters, other than one materially affecting any of the property, business or assets of the corporation." The statute further specifies that "[no] question submitted to the voters solely concerning the taxation of the income, property or transactions of individuals shall be deemed materially to affect the property, business or assets of the corporation." A corporation that violates § 8 may receive a maximum fine of $50,000; a corporate officer, director, or agent who violates the section may receive a maximum fine of $10,000 or imprisonment for up to one year, or both. Appellants wanted to spend money to publicize their views on a proposed constitutional amendment that was to be submitted to the voters as a ballot question at a general election on November 2, 1976. The amendment would have permitted the legislature to impose a graduated tax on the income of individuals. After appellee, the Attorney General of Massachusetts, informed appellants that he intended to enforce § 8 against them, they brought this action seeking to have the statute declared unconstitutional.

The court below framed the principal question in this case as whether and to what extent corporations have First Amendment rights. We believe that the court posed the wrong question. The Constitution often protects interests broader than those of the party seeking their vindication. The First Amendment, in particular, serves significant societal interests. The proper question therefore is not whether corporations "have" First Amendment rights and, if so, whether they are coextensive with those of natural persons. Instead, the question must be whether § 8 abridges expression that the First Amendment was meant to protect. We hold that it does. The speech proposed by appellants is at the heart of the First Amendment's protection.

The freedom of speech and of the press guaranteed by the Constitution embraces at the least the liberty to discuss publicly and truthfully all matters of public concern without previous restraint or fear of subsequent punishment. Freedom of discussion, if it would fulfill its historic function in this nation, must embrace all issues about which information is needed or appropriate to enable the members of society to cope with the exigencies of their period. *Thornhill v. Alabama*, 310 U.S. 88, 101-102 (1940).

The referendum issue that appellants wish to address falls squarely within this description. In appellants' view, the enactment of a graduated personal income tax, as proposed to be authorized by constitutional amendment, would have a seriously adverse effect on the economy of the State. The importance of the referendum issue to the people and government of Massachusetts is not disputed. Its merits, however, are the subject of sharp disagreement.

We thus find no support in the First or Fourteenth Amendment, or in the decisions of this Court, for the proposition that speech that otherwise would be within the protection of the First Amendment loses that protection simply because its source is a corporation that cannot prove, to the satisfaction of a court, a material effect on its business or property. The "materially affecting" requirement is not an identification of the boundaries of corporate speech etched by the Constitution itself. Rather, it amounts to an impermissible legislative prohibition of speech based on the identity of the interests that spokesmen may represent in public debate over controversial issues and a requirement that the speaker have a sufficiently great interest in the subject to justify communication.

Section 8 permits a corporation to communicate to the public its views on certain referendum subjects—those materially affecting its business—but not others. It also singles out one kind of ballot question—individual taxation as a subject about which corporations may never make their ideas public. The legislature has drawn the line between permissible and impermissible speech according to whether there is a sufficient nexus, as defined by the legislature, between the issue presented to the voters and the business interests of the speaker.

In the realm of protected speech, the legislature is constitutionally disqualified from dictating the subjects about which persons may speak and the speakers who may address a public issue. If a legislature may direct business corporations to "stick to business," it also may limit other corporations—religious, charitable, or civic—to their respective "business" when addressing the public. Such power in government to channel the expression of views is unacceptable under the First Amendment. Especially where, as here, the legislature's suppression of speech suggests an attempt to give one side of a debatable public question an advantage in expressing its views to the people, the First Amendment is plainly offended.

Because that portion of § 8 challenged by appellants prohibits protected speech in a manner unjustified by a compelling state interest, it must be invalidated. The judgment of the Supreme Judicial Court is reversed.

Case Questions

1. According to the court, does § 8 abridge a freedom that the First Amendment is intended to protect? If so, which freedom(s)?
2. Must a corporation prove a material effect on its business or property to maintain protection under the First Amendment?
3. Can a state legislature dictate the subjects on which a corporation may "speak"?

Piercing the Corporate Veil

United States v. Bestfoods
113 F.3d 572 (1998)

SOUTER, JUSTICE

The United States brought this action under §107(a)(2) of the Comprehensive Environmental Response, Compensation, and Liability Act of 1980 (CERCLA) against, among others, respondent CPC International, Inc., the parent corporation of the defunct Ott Chemical Co. (Ott II), for the costs of cleaning up industrial waste generated by Ott II's chemical plant. Section 107(a)(2) authorizes suits against, among others, "any person who at the time of disposal of any hazardous substance owned or operated any facility." The trial focused on whether CPC, as a parent corporation, had "owned or operated" Ott II's plant within the meaning of §107(a)(2). The District Court said that operator liability may attach to a parent corporation both indirectly, when the corporate veil can be pierced under state law, and directly, when the parent has exerted power or influence over its subsidiary by actively participating in, and exercising control over, the subsidiary's business during a period of hazardous waste disposal. Applying that test, the court held CPC liable because CPC had selected Ott II's board of directors and populated its executive ranks with CPC officials, and another CPC official had played a significant role in shaping Ott II's environmental compliance policy.

The Sixth Circuit reversed. Although recognizing that a parent company might be held directly liable under §107(a)(2) if it actually operated its subsidiary's facility in the stead of the subsidiary, or alongside of it as a joint venturer, that court refused to go further. Rejecting the District Court's analysis, the Sixth Circuit explained that a parent corporation's liability for operating a facility ostensibly operated by its subsidiary depends on whether the degree to which the parent controls the subsidiary and the extent and manner of its involvement with the facility amount to the abuse of the corporate form that will warrant piercing the corporate veil and disregarding the separate corporate entities of the parent and subsidiary. Applying Michigan veil-piercing law, the court decided that CPC was not liable for controlling Ott II's actions, since the two corporations maintained separate personalities and CPC did not utilize the subsidiary form to perpetrate fraud or subvert justice.

Held:

1. When (but only when) the corporate veil may be pierced, a parent corporation may be charged with derivative CERCLA liability for its subsidiary's actions in operating a polluting facility. It is a general principle of corporate law that a parent corporation (so-called because of control through ownership of another corporation's stock) is not liable for the acts of its subsidiaries. CERCLA does not purport to reject this bedrock principle, and the Government has indeed made no claim that a corporate parent is liable as an owner or an operator under §107(a)(2) simply because its subsidiary owns or operates a polluting facility. But there is an equally fundamental principle of

corporate law, applicable to the parent-subsidiary relationship as well as generally, that the corporate veil may be pierced and the shareholder held liable for the corporation's conduct when, *inter alia*, the corporate form would otherwise be misused to accomplish certain wrongful purposes, most notably fraud, on the shareholder's behalf. CERCLA does not purport to rewrite this well-settled rule, either, and against this venerable common-law backdrop, the congressional silence is audible. Cf. *Edmonds* v. *Compagnie Generale Transatlantique*, 443 U.S. 256, 266-267. CERCLA's failure to speak to a matter as fundamental as the liability implications of corporate ownership demands application of the rule that, to abrogate a common-law principle, a statute must speak directly to the question addressed by the common law. *United States* v. *Texas*, 507 U.S. 529, 534.

2. A corporate parent that actively participated in, and exercised control over, the operations of its subsidiary's facility may be held directly liable in its own right under §107(a)(2) as an operator of the facility.

(a) Derivative liability aside, CERCLA does not bar a parent corporation from direct liability for its own actions. Under the plain language of §107(a)(2), any person who operates a polluting facility is directly liable for the costs of cleaning up the pollution, and this is so even if that person is the parent corporation of the facility's owner. Because the statute does not define the term "operate," however, it is difficult to define actions sufficient to constitute direct parental "operation." In the organizational sense obviously intended by CERCLA, to "operate" a facility ordinarily means to direct the workings of, manage, or conduct the affairs of the facility. To sharpen the definition for purposes of CERCLA's concern with environmental contamination, an operator must manage, direct, or conduct operations specifically related to the leakage or disposal of hazardous waste, or decisions about compliance with environmental regulations.

(b) The Sixth Circuit correctly rejected the direct liability analysis of the District Court, which mistakenly focused on the relationship between parent and subsidiary, and premised liability on little more than CPC's ownership of Ott II and its majority control over Ott II's board of directors. Because direct liability for the parent's operation of the facility must be kept distinct from derivative liability for the subsidiary's operation of the facility, the analysis should instead have focused on the relationship between CPC and the facility itself, *i.e.*, on whether CPC "operated" the facility, as evidenced by its direct participation in the facility's activities. That error was compounded by the District Court's erroneous assumption that actions of the joint officers and directors were necessarily attributable to CPC, rather than Ott II, contrary to time-honored common-law principles. The District Court's focus on the relationship between parent and subsidiary (rather than parent and facility), combined with its automatic attribution of the actions of dual officers and directors to CPC, erroneously, even if unintentionally, treated CERCLA as though it displaced or fundamentally altered common-law standards of limited liability. The District Court's analysis created what is in essence a relaxed, CERCLA-specific rule of derivative liability that would banish traditional standards and expectations from the law of CERCLA liability. Such a rule does not arise from congressional silence, and CERCLA's silence is dispositive.

(c) Nonetheless, the Sixth Circuit erred in limiting direct liability under CERCLA to a parent's sole or joint venture operation, so as to eliminate any possible finding that CPC is liable as an operator on the facts of this case. The ordinary meaning of the word "operate" in the organizational sense is not limited to those two parental actions, but extends also to situations in which, *e.g.*, joint officers or directors conduct the affairs of the facility on behalf of the parent, or agents of the parent with no position in the subsidiary manage or direct activities at the subsidiary's facility. Norms of corporate behavior (undisturbed by any CERCLA provision) are crucial reference points, both for determining whether a dual officer or director has served the parent in conducting operations at the facility, and for distinguishing a parental officer's oversight of a subsidiary from his control over the operation of the subsidiary's facility. There is, in fact, some evidence that an agent of CPC alone engaged in activities at Ott II's plant that were eccentric under accepted norms of parental oversight of a subsidiary's facility: The District Court's opinion speaks of such an agent who played a conspicuous part in dealing with the toxic risks emanating from the plant's operation. The findings in this regard are enough to raise an issue of CPC's operation of the facility, though this Court draws no ultimate conclusion, leaving the issue for the lower courts to reevaluate and resolve in the first instance.

113 F.3d 572, vacated and remanded.

Case Questions

1. In what ways can operator liability attach to a parent corporation? How did the Sixth Circuit Court disagree with the district court's analysis?
2. How does the court in this case distinguish between direct liability and derivative liability?

Corporate Promoter

RKO-Stanley Warner Theatres, Inc. v. Graziano
355 A.2d. 830 (1976)

EAGEN, JUSTICE.

On April 30, 1970, RKO-Stanley Warner Theatres, Inc. [RKO], as seller, entered into an agreement of sale with Jack Jenofsky and Ralph Graziano, as purchasers. This agreement contemplated the sale of the Kent Theatre, a parcel of improved commercial real estate located at Cumberland and Kensington Avenues in Philadelphia, for a total purchase price of $70,000. Settlement was originally scheduled for September 30, 1970, and, at the request of Jenofsky and Graziano, continued twice, first to October 16, 1970, and then to October 21, 1970. However, Jenofsky and Graziano failed to complete settlement on the last scheduled date.

Subsequently, on November 13, 1970, RKO filed a complaint in equity seeking judicial enforcement of the agreement of sale. Although Jenofsky, in his answer to the complaint, denied personal liability for the performance of the agreement, the chancellor, after a hearing, entered a decree nisi granting the requested relief sought by RKO. ... This appeal ensued.

At the time of the execution of this agreement, Jenofsky and Graziano were engaged in promoting the formation of a corporation to be known as Kent Enterprises, Inc. Reflecting these efforts, Paragraph 19 of the agreement, added by counsel for Jenofsky and Graziano, recited:

It is understood by the parties hereto that it is the intention of the Purchaser to incorporate. Upon condition that such incorporation be completed by closing, all agreements, covenants, and warranties contained herein shall be construed to have been made between Seller and the resultant corporation and all documents shall reflect same.

In fact, Jenofsky and Graziano did file Articles of Incorporation for Kent Enterprises, Inc., with the State Corporation Bureau on October 9, 1971, twelve days prior to the scheduled settlement date. Jenofsky now contends the inclusion of Paragraph 19 in the agreement and the subsequent filing of incorporation papers, released him from any personal liability resulting from the non-performance of the agreement.

The legal relationship of Jenofsky to Kent Enterprises, Inc., at the date of the execution of the agreement of sale was that of promoter. As such, he is subject to the general rule that a promoter, although he may assume to act on behalf of a projected corporation and not for himself, will be held personally liable on contracts made by him for the benefit of a corporation he intends to organize. This personal liability will continue even after the contemplated corporation is formed and has received the benefits of the contract, unless there is a novation or other agreement to release liability.

The imposition of personal liability upon a promoter where that promoter has contracted on behalf of a corporation is based upon the principle that one who assumes to act for a nonexistent principal is himself liable on the contract in the absence of an agreement to the contrary.

[T]here [are] three possible understandings that parties may have when an agreement is executed by a promoter on behalf of a proposed corporation:

When a party is acting for a proposed corporation, he cannot, of course, bind it by anything he does, at the time, but he may (1) take on its behalf an offer from the other which, being accepted after the formation of the company, becomes a contract; (2) make a contract at the time binding himself, with the stipulation or understanding, that if a company is formed it will take his place and that then he shall be relieved of responsibility; or (3) bind himself personally without more and look to the proposed company, when formed, for indemnity.

Both RKO and Jenofsky concede the applicability of alternative No. 2 to the instant case. That is, they both recognize that Jenofsky (and Graziano) was to be initially personally responsible with this personal responsibility subsequently being released. Jenofsky contends the parties, by their inclusion of Paragraph 19 in the agreement, manifested an intention to release him from personal responsibility upon the mere formation of the proposed corporation, provided the incorporation was consummated prior to the scheduled closing date. However, while Paragraph 19 does make provision for recognition of the resultant corporation as to the closing documents, it makes no mention of any release of personal liability. Indeed, the entire agreement is silent as to the effect the formation of the projected corporation would have upon the personal liability of Jenofsky and Graziano. Because the agreement fails to provide expressly for the release of personal liability, it is, therefore, subject to more than one possible construction.

In *Consolidated Tile and Slate Co. v. Fox*, 410 Pa. 336,339,189 A.2d 228, 229 (1963), we stated that where an agreement is ambiguous and reasonably susceptible of two interpretations, "it must be construed most strongly against those who drew it." ... Instantly, the chancellor determined that the intent of the parties to the agreement was to hold Jenofsky personally responsible until such time as a corporate entity was formed and until such time as that corporate entity adopted the agreement. We believe this construction represents the only rational and prudent interpretation of the parties' intent.

As found by the court below, this agreement was entered into on the financial strength of Jenofsky and Graziano, alone as individuals. Therefore, it would have been illogical for RKO to have consented to the release of their personal liability upon the mere formation of a resultant corporation prior to closing. For it is a well-settled rule that a contract made by a promoter, even though made for and in the name of a proposed corporation, in the absence of a subsequent adoption (either expressly or impliedly) by the corporation, will not be binding upon the corporation. If, as Jenofsky contends, the intent was to release personal responsibility upon the mere incorporation prior to closing, the effect of the agreement would have been to create the possibility that RKO, in the event of non-performance, would be able to hold no party accountable: there being no guarantee that the resultant corporation would ratify the agreement. Without express language in the agreement indicating that such was the intention of the parties, we may not attribute this intention to them.

Therefore, we hold that the intent of the parties in entering into this agreement was to have Jenofsky and Graziano personally liable until such time as the intended corporation was formed and ratified the agreement. [And there is no evidence that Kent Enterprises ratified the agreement. The decree is affirmed.]

Case Questions

1. Does a promoter's personal liability continue even after the corporation is formed? Can he or she look to the corporation for indemnity after the corporation is formed?
2. In what instance(s) is a contract made by a promoter not binding on a corporation?
3. In whose favor does a court construe an ambiguous agreement?

De Jure and De Facto Corporations

Cranson v. International Business Machines Corp.
234 Md. 477, 200 A.2d 33 (1964)

HORNEY, JUDGE

On the theory that the Real Estate Service Bureau was neither a *de jure* nor a *de facto* corporation and that Albion C. Cranson, Jr., was a partner in the business conducted by the Bureau and as such was personally liable for its debts, the International Business Machines Corporation brought this action against Cranson for the balance due on electric typewriters purchased by the Bureau. At the same time it moved for summary judgment and supported the motion by affidavit. In due course, Cranson filed a general issue plea and an affidavit in opposition to summary judgment in which he asserted in effect that the Bureau was a *de facto* corporation and that he was not personally liable for its debts.

The agreed statement of facts shows that in April 1961, Cranson was asked to invest in a new business corporation which was about to be created. Towards this purpose he met with other interested individuals and an attorney and agreed to purchase stock and become an officer and director. Thereafter, upon being advised by the attorney that the corporation had been formed under the laws of Maryland, he paid for and received a stock certificate evidencing ownership of shares in the corporation, and was shown the corporate seal and minute book. The business of the new venture was conducted as if it were a corporation, through corporate bank accounts, with auditors maintaining corporate books and records, and under a lease entered into by the corporation for the office from which it operated its business. Cranson was elected president and all transactions conducted by him for the corporation, including the dealings with I.B.M., were made as an officer of the corporation. At no time did he assume any personal obligation or pledge his individual credit to I.B.M. Due to an oversight on the part of the attorney, of which Cranson was not aware, the certificate of incorporation, which had been signed and acknowledged prior to May 1, 1961, was not filed until November 24, 1961. Between May 17 and November 8, the Bureau purchased eight typewriters from I.B.M., on account of which partial payments were made, leaving a balance due of $4,333.40 [about $36,000 in 2017 dollars], for which this suit was brought.

Although a question is raised as to the propriety of making use of a motion for summary judgment as the means of determining the issues presented by the pleadings, we think the motion was appropriate. Since there was no genuine dispute as to the material facts, the only question was whether I.B.M. was entitled to judgment as a matter of law. The trial court found that it was, but we disagree.

The fundamental question presented by the appeal is whether an officer of a defectively incorporated association may be subjected to personal liability under the circumstances of this case. We think not.

Traditionally, two doctrines have been used by the courts to clothe an officer of a defectively incorporated association with the corporate attribute of limited liability. The first, often referred to as the doctrine of *de facto* corporations, has been applied in those cases where there are elements showing: (1) the existence of law authorizing incorporation; (2) an effort in good faith to incorporate under the existing law; and (3) actual use or exercise of corporate powers. The second, the doctrine of estoppel to deny the corporate existence, is generally employed where the person seeking to hold the officer personally liable has contracted or otherwise dealt with the association in such a manner as to recognize and in effect admit its existence as a corporate body.

* * *

There is, as we see it, a wide difference between creating a corporation by means of the *de facto* doctrine and estopping a party, due to his conduct in a particular case, from setting up the claim of no incorporation. Although some cases tend to assimilate the doctrines of incorporation *de facto* and by estoppel, each is a distinct theory and they are not dependent on one another in their application. Where there is a concurrence of the three elements necessary for the application of the *de facto* corporation doctrine, there exists an entity which is a corporation *de jure* against all persons but the state.

On the other hand, the estoppel theory is applied only to the facts of each particular case and may be invoked even where there is no corporation *de facto*. Accordingly, even though one or more of the requisites of a *de facto* corporation are absent, we think that this factor does not preclude the application of the estoppel doctrine in a proper case, such as the one at bar.

I.B.M. contends that the failure of the Bureau to file its certificate of incorporation debarred *all* corporate existence. But, in spite of the fact that the omission might have prevented the Bureau from being either a corporation *de jure* or *de facto*, *Jones v. Linden Building Ass'n*, we think that I.B.M. having dealt with the Bureau as if it were a corporation and relied on its credit rather than that of Cranson, is estopped to assert that the Bureau was not incorporated at the time the typewriters were purchased. In 1 Clark and Marshall, Private Corporations, § 89, it is stated:

> *The doctrine in relation to estoppel is based upon the ground that it would generally be inequitable to permit the corporate existence of an association to be denied by persons who have represented it to be a corporation, or held it out as a corporation, or by any persons who have recognized it as a corporation by dealing with it as such; and by the overwhelming weight of authority, therefore, a person may be estopped to deny the legal incorporation of an association which is not even a corporation* de facto.

In cases similar to the one at bar, involving a failure to file articles of incorporation, the courts of other jurisdictions have held that where one has recognized the corporate existence of an association, he is estopped to assert the contrary with respect to a claim arising out of such dealings.

Since I.B.M. is estopped to deny the corporate existence of the Bureau, we hold that Cranson was not liable for the balance due on account of the typewriters.

Judgment reversed; the appellee to pay the costs.

Case Questions

1. What is the fundamental question presented by the case?
2. What are the differences between creating a corporation de facto and by estoppel?

43.8 Summary and Exercises

Summary

The hallmark of the corporate form of business enterprise is limited liability for its owners. Other features of corporations are separation of ownership and management, perpetual existence, and easier transferability of interests. In the early years of the common law, corporations were thought to be creatures of sovereign power and could be created only by state grant. But by the late nineteenth century, corporations could be formed by complying with the requirements of general corporation statutes in virtually every state. Today the standard is the Revised Model Business Corporation Act.

The corporation, as a legal entity, has many of the usual rights accorded natural persons. The principle of limited liability is broad but not absolute: when the corporation is used to commit a fraud or an injustice or when the corporation does not act as if it were one, the courts will pierce the corporate veil and pin liability on stockholders.

Besides the usual business corporation, there are other forms, including not-for-profit corporations and professional corporations. Business corporations are classified into two types: publicly held and closely held corporations.

To form a corporation, the would-be stockholders must choose the state in which they wish to incorporate. The goal of the incorporation process is issuance of a corporate charter. The charter is a contract between the state and the corporation. Although the Constitution prohibits states from impairing the obligation of contracts, states reserve the right to modify corporate charters.

The corporation is created by the incorporators (initially, "promoters"), who raise capital, enter into contracts on behalf of the corporation to be formed, and prepare the articles of incorporation. The promoters are personally liable on the contracts they enter into before the corporation is formed. Incorporators owe a fiduciary duty to each other, to investors, and to the corporation.

The articles of incorporation typically contain a number of features, including the corporate name, corporate purposes, total number of shares and classes into which they are divided, par value, and the like. The name must include one of the following words (or abbreviations): corporation, company, incorporated, or limited (Corp., Co., Inc., or Ltd.). The articles of incorporation must be filed with the secretary of state. Once they have been filed, the board of directors named in the articles must adopt bylaws, elect officers, and conduct other necessary business. The directors are empowered to alter the bylaws, subject to repeal or change by the shareholders.

Even if the formal prerequisites to incorporation are lacking, a de facto corporation will be held to have been formed if (1) a statute exists under which the corporation could have been validly incorporated, (2) the promoters made a bona fide attempt to comply with the statute, and (3) a corporate privilege was exercised. Under appropriate circumstances, a corporation will be held to exist by estoppel.

Exercises

1. Two young business school graduates, Key and Peele, form a consulting firm. In deciding between the partnership and corporation form of organization, they are especially concerned about personal liability for giving bad advice to their clients; that is, in the event they are sued, they want to prevent plaintiffs from taking their personal assets to satisfy judgments against the firm. Which form of organization would you recommend? Why?
2. Assume that Key and Peele in Exercise 1 must negotiate a large loan from a local bank in order to finance their firm. A friend advises them that they should incorporate in order to avoid personal liability for the loan. Is this good advice? Why?
3. Assume that Key and Peele decide to form a corporation. Before the incorporation process is complete, Key enters into a contract on behalf of the corporation to purchase office furniture and equipment for $20,000. After the incorporation process has been completed, the

corporation formally accepts the contract made by Key. Is Key personally liable on the contract before corporate acceptance? After corporate acceptance? Why?

4. Assume that Key and Peele have incorporated their business. One afternoon, an old college friend visits Peele at the office. Peele and hisr friend decide to go out for dinner to discuss old times. Peele, being short of cash, takes money from a petty cash box to pay for dinner. (He first obtains permission from Key, who has done the same thing many times in the past.) Over dinner, Peele learns that her friend is now an IRS agent and is investigating Peele corporation. What problems does Peele face in the investigation? Why?
5. Assume that Key and Peele prepare articles of incorporation but forget to send the articles to the appropriate state office. A few months after they begin to operate their consulting business as a corporation, Key visits a client. After her meeting, in driving out of a parking lot, Key inadvertently backs his car over the client, causing serious bodily harm. Is Peele liable for the accident? Why?
6. Ralph, a resident of Oklahoma, was injured when using a consumer product manufactured by a corporation whose principal offices were in Tulsa. Since his damages exceeded $10,000, he filed a products-liability action against the company, which was incorporated in Delaware, in federal court. Does the federal court have jurisdiction? Why?
7. Alice is the president and only shareholder of a corporation. The IRS is investigating Alice and demands that she produce her corporate records. Alice refuses, pleading the Fifth Amendment privilege against self-incrimination. May the IRS force Alice to turn over her corporate records? Why?

Self-Test Questions

1. In comparing partnerships with corporations, the major factor favoring the corporate form is
    a. ease of formation
    b. flexible financing
    c. limited liability
    d. control of the business by investors
2. A corporation with no part of its income distributable to its members, directors, or officers is called
    a. a publicly held corporation
    b. a closely held corporation
    c. a professional corporation
    d. a nonprofit corporation
3. A corporation in which stock is widely held or available through a national or regional stock exchange is called
    a. a publicly held corporation
    b. a closely held corporation
    c. a public corporation
    d. none of the above
4. Essential to the formation of a de facto corporation is
    a. a statute under which the corporation could have been validly incorporated
    b. promoters who make a bona fide attempt to comply with the corporation statute
    c. the use or exercise of corporate powers
    d. each of the above
5. Even when incorporators miss important steps, it is possible to create
    a. a corporation by estoppel
    b. a de jure corporation

c. an S corporation
d. none of the above

Self-Test Answers

1. c
2. d
3. a
4. d
5. a

Endnotes

1. *Gibbons v. Ogden*, 22 U.S. 1 (1824).
2. *Paul v. Virginia*, 75 U.S. 168 (1868).
3. *Citizens United v. Federal Election Commission*, 558 U.S. 310 (2010).
4. The Bipartisan Campaign Reform Act of 2002 (BCRA, McCain–Feingold Act, Pub.L. 107-155, 116 Stat. 81, enacted March 27, 2002, H.R. 2356).
5. *D. I. Felsenthal Co. v. Northern Assurance Co., Ltd.*, 284 Ill. 343, 120 N.E. 268 (1918).
6. *Felsenthal Co. v. Northern Assurance Co., Ltd.*, 120 N.E. 268 (Ill. 1918).
7. *Trustees of Dartmouth College v. Woodward*, 17 U.S. 518 (1819).
8. *Cornell University v. Fiske*, 136 U.S. 152 (1890).

CHAPTER 44

Legal Aspects of Corporate Finance

Learning Objectives

After reading this chapter, you should understand the following:

1. The general sources of corporate funds.
2. The basics of corporate bonds and other debt leveraging.
3. What the various types of stocks are.
4. Initial public offerings and consideration for stock.
5. What dividends are.
6. Some of the modern trends in corporate finance.

A corporation requires money for many reasons. In this chapter, we look at the methods available to a corporation for raising funds, focusing on how firms generate large amounts of funds and finance large projects, such as building a new factory.

One major method of finance is the sale of stock. A corporation sells shares of stock, often in an initial public offering. In exchange for consideration—usually cash—the purchaser acquires stock in the corporation. This stock may give the owner a share in earnings, the right to transfer the stock, and, depending on the size of the corporation and the number of shares, power to exercise control. Other methods of corporate finance include bank financing and bonds. We also discuss some more modern financing methods, such as private equity and venture capital. Additional methods of corporate finance, such as commercial paper (see Chapter 22 and Chapter 23), are discussed elsewhere in this book.

44.1 General Sources of Corporate Funds

Learning Objectives

1. Discuss the main sources for raising corporate funds.
2. Examine the reinvestment of earnings to finance growth.
3. Review debt and equity as methods of raising funds.
4. Consider private equity and venture capital, and compare their utility to other forms of financing.

Sources

To finance growth, any ongoing business must have a source of funds. Apart from bank and trade debt, the principal sources are plowback, debt securities, equity securities, and private equity.

Plowback

Plowback

Reinvesting corporate earnings in the corporation as a method of raising funds.

A significant source of new funds that corporations spend on capital projects is earnings. Rather than paying out earnings to shareholders, the corporation plows those earnings back into the business. **Plowback** is simply reinvesting earnings in the corporation. It is an attractive source of capital because it is subject to managerial control. No approval by governmental agencies is necessary for its expenditure, as it is when a company seeks to sell securities, or stocks and bonds. Furthermore, stocks and bonds have costs associated with them, such as the interest payments on bonds (discussed in Section 1). Retaining profits avoids these costs.

Debt Securities

bond

A debt security to raise corporate funds where the corporation pays periodic interest (the coupon rate) and the face value at maturity.

A second source of funds is borrowing through debt securities. A corporation may take out a debt security such as a loan, commonly evidenced by a note and providing security to the lender. This is covered in Chapter 28 and Chapter 29. A common type of corporate debt security is a **bond**, which is a promise to repay the face value of the bond at maturity and make periodic interest payments called the coupon rate. For example, a bond may have a face value of $10,000 (the amount to be repaid at maturity) and a coupon rate of 4 percent paid annually; the corporation pays $400 interest on such a bond each year. Bondholders have priority over stockholders because a bond is a debt, and in the event of bankruptcy, creditors have priority over equity holders.

Equity Securities

stock

An ownership interest in a corporation (synonymous with *shares*).

equity

Ownership interest, such as stock, in property or a business.

The third source of new capital funds is equity securities—namely, **stock**. **Equity** is an ownership interest in property or a business. Stock is the smallest source of new capital but is of critical importance to the corporation in launching the business and its initial operations. Stock gives the investor a bundle of legal rights—ownership, a share in earnings, transferability and, to some extent, the power to exercise control through voting. The usual way to acquire stock is by paying cash or its equivalent as consideration. Both stock and consideration are discussed in more detail in Section 3 and Section 4.

Other Forms of Finance

private equity

Finance conducted through private investors, either individuals or firms.

venture capital

Financial capital provided to early-stage, high-potential, high-risk start-up companies by investors who often expect a return on the investment by an eventual sale of the company or by taking the firm public.

Stock, debt securities, and reinvested profits are the most common types of finance for major corporations (particularly publicly traded corporations), but smaller corporations or start-ups cannot (or do not want to) avail themselves of these financing options. Instead, they seek to raise funds through **private equity**, which involves private investors providing funds to a company in exchange for an interest in the company. A private equity firm is a group of investors who pool their money together for investment purposes, usually to invest in other companies. Looking to private equity firms is an option for start-ups—companies newly formed or in the process of being formed—that cannot raise funds through the bond market or that wish to avoid debt or a public stock sale. Start-ups need money to begin operations, expand, or conduct further research and development. A private equity firm might provide **venture capital** financing for these start-ups. Generally, private equity firms that provide a lot of venture capital must be extremely savvy about the start-up plans of new businesses and must ask the start-up entrepreneurs numerous challenging and pertinent questions. Such private equity firms expect a higher rate of return on their investment than would be available from established companies. Today, venture capital is often used to finance entrepreneurial start-ups in biotechnology and clean technology.

Sometimes, a private equity firm will buy all the publicly traded shares of a company—a process commonly termed "going private." Private equity may also be involved in providing financing to established firms.

Another source of private equity is angel investors, affluent individuals who operate like venture capitalists, providing capital for a business to get started in exchange for repayment with interest or an ownership interest. The main difference between an angel investor and a venture capitalist is the source of funds: an angel investor invests his or her own money, while venture capitalists use pooled funds.

Private equity firms may also use a **leveraged buyout (LBO)** to finance the acquisition of another firm. Discussed further in Chapter 47 on Corporate Expansion, in the realm of private equity, an LBO is a financing option using debt to acquire another firm. In an LBO, private equity investors use the assets of the target corporation as collateral for a loan to purchase that target corporation. Such investors may pursue an LBO as a debt acquisition option since they do not need to use much—or even any—of their own money in order to finance the acquisition.

leveraged buyout (LBO)

The acquisition of another company using a significant amount of borrowed money to pay for the acquisition. Often, the assets of the company being acquired may be used as collateral for the loans.

A major drawback to private equity, whether through a firm or through venture capital, is the risk versus return trade-off. Private equity investors may demand a significant interest in the firm, or a high return, to compensate them for the riskiness of their investment. They may demand a say in how the firm is operated or a seat on the board of directors.

Key Takeaway

There are four main sources of corporate finance. The first is plowback, or reinvesting profits in the corporation. The second is borrowing, commonly through a bond issue. A corporation sells a bond, agreeing to periodic interest payments and repayment of the face value of the bond at maturity. The third source is equity, usually stock, whereby a corporation sells an ownership interest in the corporation. The fourth source is private equity and venture capital.

Exercises

1. What are the main sources of corporate finance?
2. What are some of the legal rights associated with stock ownership?
3. Explain why many "start-ups"would typically use private equity rather than issue debt or offer stock to the public.

44.2 Bonds

Learning Objectives

1. Discuss the basics of corporate bonds.
2. Review the advantages and disadvantages to the corporation of issuing bonds.

Basics of Corporate Bonds

Corporations often raise money through debt. This can be done through loans or bank financing but is often accomplished through the sale of bonds. Large corporations, in particular, use the bond market. Private equity is not ideal for established firms because of the high cost to them, both monetarily and in terms of the potential loss of control.

face value

The amount that a corporation pays a bondholder at the bond's maturity.

coupon payment

The interest payment made by a corporation to the holder of a bond.

For financing, many corporations sell corporate bonds to investors. A bond is like an IOU. When a corporation sells a bond, it owes the bond purchaser periodic interest payments as well as a lump sum at the end of the life of the bond (the maturity date). A typical bond is issued with a face value, also called the par value, of $1,000 or some multiple of $1,000. The **face value** is the amount that the corporation must pay the purchaser at the end of the life of the bond. Interest payments, also called **coupon payments**, are usually made on a biannual basis but could be of nearly any duration. There are even zero coupon bonds, which pay only the face value at maturity.

Advantages and Disadvantages of Bonds

One advantage of issuing bonds is that the corporation does not give away ownership interests. When a corporation sells stock, it changes the ownership interest in the firm, but bonds do not alter the ownership structure. Bonds provide flexibility for a corporation: it can issue bonds of varying durations, value, payment terms, convertibility, and so on. Bonds also expand the number of investors available to the corporation. For investors, bonds are generally less risky than stock. Most corporate bonds are given ratings—a measurement of the risk associated with holding a particular bond. Therefore, risk-averse investors who would not purchase a corporation's stock could seek lower-risk returns in highly rated corporate bonds (usually with lower interest rates than riskier bonds). Investors are also drawn to bonds because the bond market is much larger than the stock market and bonds are highly liquid and less risky than many other types of investments.

Another advantage to the corporation is the ability to make bonds "callable"—the corporation can force the investor to sell bonds back to the corporation before the maturity date. Often, there is an additional cost to the corporation (a call premium) that must be paid to the bondholder, but the call provision provides another level of flexibility for the corporation. Perhaps the most important advantage to issuing bonds is from a taxation standpoint: the interest payments made to the bondholders may be deductible from the corporation's taxes.

A key disadvantage of bonds is that they are debt. The corporation must make its bond interest payments. If a corporation cannot make its interest payments, the bondholders can force it into bankruptcy. In bankruptcy, the bondholders have a liquidation preference over investors with ownership—that is, the shareholders. Additionally, being highly leveraged can be risky: a corporation could load itself up with too much debt and not be able to make its interest payments or face-value payments. Another major consideration is the "cost" of debt. When interest rates are high, corporations must offer higher interest rates to attract investors.

Key Takeaway

Corporations often raise capital and finance operations through debt. Bank loans are one source of debt, but large corporations often turn to bonds for financing. Bonds are an IOU, whereby the corporation sells a bond to an investor; agrees to make periodic interest payments, such as 5 percent of the face value of the bond annually; and at the maturity date, pays the face value of the bond to the investor. There are several advantages to the corporation in using bonds as a financial instrument: the corporation does not give up ownership in the firm, it attracts more investors, it increases its flexibility, and it can deduct the interest payments from corporate taxes. Bonds do have some disadvantages: they are debt and can hurt a highly leveraged company, the corporation must pay the interest and principal when they are due, and the bondholders have a preference over shareholders upon liquidation.

Exercises

1. Describe a bond.

2. What are some advantages to the corporation in issuing bonds?
3. What are some disadvantages to the corporation in using bonds?

44.3 Types of Stock

Learning Objectives

1. Understand the basic features of corporate stock.
2. Be familiar with the basic terminology of corporate stock.
3. Discuss preferred shares and the rights of preferred shareholders.
4. Compare common stock with preferred stock.
5. Describe treasury stock, and explain its function.
6. Analyze whether debt or equity is a better financing option.

Stocks, or **shares**, represent an ownership interest in a corporation. Traditionally, stock was the original capital paid into a business by its founders. This stock was then divided into shares, or fractional ownership of the stock. In modern usage, the two terms are used interchangeably, as we will do here. Shares in closely held corporations are often identical: each share of stock in BCT Bookstore, Inc. carries with it the same right to vote, to receive dividends, and to receive a distribution of the net assets of the company upon liquidation. Many large corporations do not present so simple a picture. Large corporations may have many different types of stock: different classes of common stock, preferred stock, stock with par value and no-par stock, voting and nonvoting stock, outstanding stock, and treasury stock. To find out which types of stock a company has issued, look at the shareholders' (or stockholders') equity section of the company's balance sheet.

Stocks

An ownership interest in a corporation (synonymous with *shares*).

shares

An ownership interest in a corporation (synonymous with *stock*).

Authorized, Issued, and Outstanding Stock

Stocks have different designations depending on who holds them. The articles of incorporation spell out how many shares of stock the corporation may issue: these are its **authorized shares**. The corporation is not obliged to issue all authorized shares, but it may not issue more than the total without amending the articles of incorporation. The total of stock sold to investors is the issued stock of the corporation; the issued stock in the hands of all shareholders is called outstanding stock. For example Amazon's corporate charter allows authorized stock of 5 billion shares of common stock and 500 million shares of preferred stock.

authorized shares

The maximum number of shares of stock that a company can issue, although management will typically keep the amount higher than those actually issued.

Par Value and No-Par Stock

Par value is the face value of stock. Par value, though, is not the market value; it is a value placed on the stock by the corporation but has little to do with the buying and selling value of that stock on the open market.

par value

The face value of a stock.

When a value is specified on a stock certificate, it is said to be par value. Par value is established in the articles of incorporation and is the floor price of the stock; the corporation may not accept less than par value for the stock.

Companies in most states can also issue no-par shares. No-par stock may be sold for whatever price is set by the board of directors or by the market—unless the shareholders themselves are empowered to establish the price. But many states permit (and some states require) no-par stock to have a stated value. Corporations issue no-par stock to reduce their exposure to liability: if the par value is greater than the market value, the corporation may be liable for that difference.

Once the universal practice, issuance of par value common stock is now limited. However, preferred stock usually has a par value, which is useful in determining dividend and liquidation rights.

surplus

The excess of net assets of a corporation over its stated capital.

The term *stated capital* describes the sum of the par value of the issued par value stock and the consideration received (or stated value) for the no-par stock. The excess of net assets of a corporation over stated capital is its **surplus**. Surplus is divided into earned surplus (essentially the company's retained earnings) and capital surplus (all surpluses other than earned surplus). We will return to these concepts in our discussion of dividends.

Preferred Stock

preferred stock

A variety of stock that differs from common stock in provisions for dividends and/or preference upon liquidation.

The term *preferred* has no set legal meaning, but shareholders of **preferred stock** often have different rights than shareholders of common stock. Holders of preferred stock must look to the articles of incorporation to find out what their rights are. Preferred stock has elements of both stock (equity) and bonds (debt). Thus, corporations issue preferred stock to attract more conservative investors: common stock is riskier than preferred stock, so corporations can attract more investors if they have both preferred and common stock.

Preference to Dividends

A dividend is a payment made to stockholders from corporate profits. Assume that one class of preferred stock is entitled to a 7 percent dividend. The percentage applies to the par value; if par value is $100, each share of preferred is entitled to a dividend of $7 per year. Assuming the articles of incorporation say so, this 7 percent preferred stock has preference over other classes of shares for dividend payments.

Liquidation Preference

An additional right of preferred shareholders is the right to share in the distribution of assets in the event of liquidation, after having received assets under a liquidation preference—that is, a preference, according to a predetermined formula, to receive the assets of the company on liquidation ahead of other classes of shareholders.

Convertible Shares

With one exception, the articles of incorporation may grant the right to convert any class of stock into any other at the holder's option according to a fixed ratio. Alternatively, the corporation may force a conversion of a shareholder's convertible stock. Thus, if permitted, a preferred shareholder may convert his or her preferred shares into common stock, or vice versa. The exception bars conversion of stock into a class with an asset liquidation preference, although some states permit even that type of so-called upstream conversion to a senior security. Convertible preferred shares can be used as a poison pill (a corporate strategy to avoid a hostile takeover): when an outsider seeks to gain control, convertible shareholders may elect to convert their preferred shares into common stock, thus increasing the number of common shares and increasing the number of shares the outsider must purchase in order to gain control.

Redeemable Shares

The articles of incorporation may provide for the redemption of shares, unless in doing so the corporation would become insolvent. Redemption may be either at an established price and time or by election of the corporation or the shareholder. Redeemed stock is called cancelled stock. Unless the articles of incorporation prohibit it, the shares are considered authorized but unissued and can be reissued as the need arises. If the articles of incorporation specifically make the cancellation permanent, then the total number of authorized shares is reduced, and new shares cannot be reissued without amending the articles of incorporation. In this case, the redeemed shares cannot be reissued and must be marked as cancelled stock.

Voting Rights

Ordinarily, the articles of incorporation provide that holders of preferred shares do not have a voting right. Or they may provide for contingent voting rights, entitling preferred shareholders to vote on the happening of a particular event—for example, the nonpayment of a certain number of dividends. The articles may allow class voting for directors, to ensure that the class of preferred stockholders has some representation on the board.

Common Stock

Common stock is different from preferred stock. Common stock represents an ownership interest in a corporation. Unless otherwise provided in the articles of incorporation, common stockholders have the following rights:

common stock

A security that represents ownership in a corporation and allows the holder to elect a board of directors.

1. Voting rights. This is a key difference: preferred shareholders usually do not have the right to vote. Common shareholders express their ownership interest in the corporation by voting. Votes are cast at meetings, typically the annual meetings, and the shareholders can vote for directors and on other important corporate decisions (e.g., there has been a recent push to allow shareholders to vote on executive compensation).
2. The right to ratable participation in earnings (i.e., in proportion to the total shares) and/or the right to ratable participation in the distribution of net assets on liquidation. Bondholders and other creditors have seniority upon liquidation, but if they have been satisfied, or the corporation has no debt, the common shareholders may ratably recover from what is left over in liquidation.
3. Some shares may give holders preemptive rights to purchase additional shares. This right is often invoked in two instances. First, if a corporation is going to issue more shares, a shareholder may invoke this right so that his or her total percentage ownership is not diluted. Second, the right to purchase additional shares can be invoked to prevent a hostile takeover (a poison pill, discussed in Section 3).

Corporations may issue different classes of shares (including both common and preferred stock). This permits a corporation to provide different rights to shareholders. For example, one class of common stock may give holders more votes than another class of common stock. Stock is a riskier investment for its purchasers compared with bonds and preferred stock. In exchange for this increased risk and junior treatment, common stockholders have the rights noted here.

Treasury Shares

Treasury shares

Stock that was issued and then later reacquired by a company (a buyback) or that was never sold to the public in the first place and simply retained by the company.

buyback

A process whereby a corporation reacquires or repurchases its shares (the shares then become treasury shares).

Treasury shares are those that were originally issued and then reacquired by the company (such as in a buyback, discussed next) or, alternatively, never sold to the public in the first place and simply retained by the corporation. Thus, treasury shares are shares held or owned by the corporation. They are considered to be issued shares but not outstanding shares.

Buyback

Corporations often reacquire their shares, for a variety of reasons, in a process sometimes called a **buyback**. If the stock price has dropped so far that the shares are worth considerably less than book value, the corporation might wish to buy its shares to prevent another company from taking it over. The company might decide that investing in itself is a better strategic decision than making other potential expenditures or investments. And although it is essentially an accounting trick, buybacks improve a company's per-share earnings because profits need to be divided into fewer outstanding shares.

Buybacks can also be used to go private. Private equity may play a role in going-private transactions, as discussed in Section 1. The corporation may not have sufficient equity to buy out all its public shareholders and thus will partner with private equity to finance the stock buyback to go private. For example, in early 2011, Playboy Enterprises, Inc., publisher of *Playboy* magazine, went private. Hugh Hefner, the founder of Playboy, teamed up with private equity firm Rizvi Traverse Management to buy back the public shares. Hefner said that the transaction "will give us the resources and flexibility to return Playboy to its unique position and to further expand our business around the world."[1]

Corporations may go private to consolidate control, because of a belief that the shares are undervalued, to increase flexibility, or because of a tender offer or hostile takeover. Alternatively, an outside investor may think that a corporation is not being managed properly and may use a tender offer to buy all the public shares.

Stocks and Bonds, Bulls and Bears, Oh My!

Suppose that BCT Bookstore, Inc. has become a large, well-established corporation after a round of private equity and bank loans (since repaid) but needs to raise capital. What is the best method? There is no one right answer. Much of the decision will depend on the financial and accounting standing of the corporation: if BCT already has a lot of debt, it might be better to issue stock rather than bring on more debt. Alternatively, BCT could wish to remain a privately held corporation, and thus a stock sale would not be considered, as it would dilute the ownership. The economy in general could impact the decision: a bear market could push BCT more toward using debt, while a bull market could push BCT more toward an initial public offering (discussed in Section 4) or stock sale. If interest rates are low, offering bonds may create more value for the company. Additionally, public stock sales can be risky for the corporation: the corporation could undervalue its stock in the initial sale, selling the stock for less than what the marketplace thinks it is worth, missing out on additional funds because of this undervaluation. Debt may also be beneficial because of the tax treatment of interest payments—the corporation can deduct the interest payments from corporate profits. Thus, there are many factors a corporation must consider when deciding whether to finance through debt or equity.

Key Takeaway

Stock, or shares (equity), express an ownership interest in a corporation. Shares have different designations, depending on who holds the shares. The two main types of stock are preferred stock and common stock, each with rights that often differ from the rights of the other. Preferred stock has elements of both debt and equity. Holders of preferred shares have a dividend preference and have a right to share in the distribution of assets in liquidation. Holders of common stock have a different set of rights, namely, the right to vote on important corporate decisions such as the election of directors. A corporation may purchase some of its shares from its shareholders in a process called a buyback. Stock in the hands of the corporation is called treasury stock. There are a variety of factors that a corporation must consider in determining whether to raise capital through bonds or through stock issuance.

Exercises

1. What are some key rights of holders of preferred shares?
2. What is the major difference between preferred stock and common stock?
3. Why would a corporation buy back its own shares?

44.4 Initial Public Offerings and Consideration for Stock

Learning Objectives

1. Understand what an initial public offering is and under what circumstances one is usually done.
2. Examine the various requirements of selling stock.
3. Discuss what adequate and valid consideration is in exchange for stock.

Sale of stock

Rather than using debt to finance operations, a corporation may instead sell stock. This is most often accomplished through an **initial public offering (IPO)**. An IPO represents the first time a corporation offers stock for sale to the public. The sale of securities, such as stock, is governed by the Securities Act of 1933. In particular, Section 5 of the 1933 act governs the specifics of the sale of securities. To return to BCT Bookstore, Inc., suppose the company wishes to sell stock on the New York Stock Exchange (NYSE) for the first time. That would be an IPO. The company would partner with securities lawyers and investment banks to accomplish the sale. The banks underwrite the sale of the securities: in exchange for a fee, the bank will buy the shares from BCT and then sell them. The company and its team prepare a registration statement, which contains required information about the IPO and is submitted to the Securities and Exchange Commission (SEC). The SEC reviews the registration statement and makes the decision whether to permit or prohibit BCT's IPO. Once the SEC approves the IPO, BCT's investment banks purchase the shares in the primary market and then resell them to investors on the secondary market on the NYSE. (For a further discussion of these two markets, see Chapter 46). Stock sales are not limited to an IPO—publicly

initial public offering (IPO)

The first time a corporation offers stock for sale to the public.

traded corporations may sell stock several times after going public. The requirements of the 1933 act remain but are loosened for well-known corporations (well-known seasoned issuers).

An IPO or stock sale has several advantages. A corporation may have too much debt and would prefer to raise funds through a sale of stock rather than increasing its debt. The total costs of selling stock are often lower than financing through debt: the IPO may be expensive, but debt costs can vastly exceed the IPO cost because of the interest payments on the debt. Also, IPOs are a popular method of increasing a firm's exposure, bringing the corporation many more investors and increasing its public image. Issuing stock is also beneficial for the corporation because the corporation can use shares as compensation; for example, employment compensation may be in the form of stock, such as in an employee stock ownership plan. Investors also seek common stock, whether in an IPO or in the secondary market. While common stock is a riskier investment than a bond, stock ownership can have tremendous upside—after all, the sky is the limit on the price of a stock. On the other hand, there is the downside: the price of the stock can plummet, causing the shareholder significant monetary loss.

Certainly, an IPO has some disadvantages. Ownership is diluted: BCT had very few owners before its IPO but may have millions of owners after the IPO. As mentioned, an IPO can be expensive. An IPO can also be undervalued: the corporation and its investment banks may undervalue the IPO stock price, causing the corporation to lose out on the difference between its determined price and the market price. Being a public corporation also places the corporation under the purview of the SEC and requires ongoing disclosures. Timing can be problematic: the registration review process can take several weeks. The stock markets can change drastically over that waiting period. Furthermore, the offering could have insufficient purchasers to raise sufficient funds; that is, the public might not have enough interest in purchasing the company's stock to bring in sufficient funds to the corporation. Finally, a firm that goes public releases information that is available to the public, which could be useful to competitors (trade secrets, innovations, new technology, etc.).

As mentioned, one of the main disadvantages of going public is the SEC review and disclosure requirements. The Securities Exchange Act of 1934 governs most secondary market transactions. The 1934 act places certain requirements on corporations that have sold securities. Both the 1933 and 1934 acts require corporations to disseminate information to the public and/or its investors. These requirements were strengthened after the collapse of Enron in 2001. The SEC realized that its disclosure requirements were not strong enough, as demonstrated by the accounting tricks and downfall of Enron and its accountant, Arthur Andersen.[2]

As a result of Enron's accounting scandal, as well as problems with other corporations, Congress tightened the noose by passing the Sarbanes-Oxley Act of 2002.[3] This act increased the disclosure of financial information, increased transparency, and required the dissemination of information about what a corporation was doing. For example, Section 302 of Sarbanes-Oxley requires that a corporation's chief executive officer and chief financial officer certify annual and quarterly reports and state that the report does not contain any material falsehoods and that the financial data accurately reflect the corporation's condition.

Nature of the Consideration

consideration

The surrender of any legal right (a detriment) in return for the promise of some benefit in return.

Consideration is property or services exchanged for stock. While cash is commonly used to purchase stock, a stock purchaser may pay with something other than cash, such as property, whether tangible or intangible, or services or labor performed for the corporation. In most states, promissory notes and contracts for future services are not lawful forms of consideration. The case *United Steel Industries, Inc. v. Manhart*, (see Section 7), illustrates the problems that can arise when services or promises of future delivery are intended as payment for stock.

Evaluating the Consideration: Watered Stock

In *United Steel Industries* (Section 7), assume that Griffitts's legal services had been thought by the corporation to be worth $6,000 but in fact were worth $1,000, and that he had received stock with par value of $6,000 (i.e., 6,000 shares of $1 par value stock) in exchange for his services. Would Griffitts be liable for the $5,000 difference between the actual value of his services and the stock's par value? This is the problem of **watered stock**: the inflated consideration is in fact less than par value. The term itself comes from the ancient fraud of farmers and ranchers who increased the weight of their cattle (also known as stock) by forcing them to ingest excess water.

watered stock

When consideration is inflated such that the property given for consideration in exchange for shares is in fact less than par value.

The majority of states follow the **good-faith rule**. As noted near the end of the *United Steel Industries* case, in the absence of fraud, "the judgment of the board of directors 'as to the value of consideration received for shares' is conclusive." In other words, if the directors or shareholders conclude in good faith that the consideration does fairly reflect par value, then the stock is not watered and the stock buyer cannot be assessed for the difference. This is in line with the business judgment rule, discussed in Chapter 45. If the directors concluded in good faith that the consideration provided by Griffitts's services accurately reflected the value of the shares, they would not be liable. The minority approach is the true value rule: the consideration must in fact equal par value by an objective standard at the time the shares are issued, regardless of the board's good-faith judgment.

good-faith rule

Directors' judgment as to the value of consideration received for shares is deemed conclusive.

A shareholder may commence a derivative lawsuit (a suit by a shareholder, on behalf of the corporation, often filed against the corporation; see Chapter 45). In a watered stock lawsuit, the derivative suit is filed against a shareholder who has failed to pay full consideration under either rule to recover the difference between the value received by the corporation and the par value.

Key Takeaway

Corporations may raise funds through the sale of stock. This can be accomplished through an initial public offering (IPO)—the first time a corporation sells stock—or through stock sales after an IPO. The SEC is the regulatory body that oversees the sale of stock. A sale of stock has several benefits for the corporation, such as avoiding the use of debt, which can be much more expensive than selling stock. Stock sales also increase the firm's exposure and attract investors who prefer more risk than bonds. On the other hand, stock sales have some disadvantages, namely, the dilution of ownership of the corporation. Also, the corporation may undervalue its shares, thus missing out on additional capital because of the undervaluation. Being a publicly traded company places the corporation under the extensive requirements of the SEC and the 1933 and 1934 securities acts, such as shareholder meetings and annual financial reports. The Sarbanes-Oxley Act adds yet more requirements that a corporation may wish to avoid.

Consideration is property or services exchanged for stock. Most investors will exchange money for stock. Certain forms of consideration are not permitted. Finally, a corporation may be liable if it sells watered stock, where consideration received by the corporation is less than the stock par value.

Exercises

1. Describe the process of conducting an IPO.
2. What are some advantages of selling stock?
3. What are some disadvantages of selling stock?
4. What is consideration? What are some types of consideration that may not be acceptable?

44.5 Dividends

Learning Objectives

1. Discuss several types of dividends.
2. Review legal limitations on distributing dividends.
3. Define the duties of directors when paying dividends.

Types of Dividends

dividend

A share of a corporation's profits.

A **dividend** is a share of profits, a dividing up of the company's earnings. The law does not require a corporation to give out a specific type of dividend.

Cash Dividend

If a company's finances are such that it can declare a dividend to stockholders, a cash dividend always is permissible. It is a payment (by check, ordinarily) to the stockholders of a certain amount of money per share. Under current law, qualified dividends are taxed as a long-term capital gain (usually 15 percent, but the figure can be as low as zero percent under current law). These rules are set to expire in 2013, when dividends will be taxed as ordinary income (i.e., at the recipient's ordinary income tax rate).

Stock Dividend

Next to cash, the most frequent type of dividend is stock itself. Normally, the corporation declares a small percentage dividend (between 1 and 10 percent), so that a holder of one hundred shares would receive four new shares on a 4 percent dividend share. Although each shareholder winds up with more stock, he realizes no personal net gain at that moment, as he would with a cash dividend, because each stockholder has the same relative proportion of shares and has not sold or otherwise transferred the shares or dividend. The total outstanding stock represents no greater amount of assets than before. The corporation may issue share dividends either from treasury stock or from authorized but unissued shares.

Property Dividend

Rarely, corporations pay dividends in property rather than in cash. Armand Hammer, the legendary financier and CEO of Occidental Petroleum Corporation, recounts how during World War II he founded a liquor business by buying shares of the American Distilling Company. American Distilling was giving out one barrel of whiskey per share as a dividend. Whiskey was in short supply during the war, so Hammer bought five thousand shares and took five thousand barrels of whiskey as a dividend.

Stock Split

A stock dividend should be distinguished from a stock split. In a **stock split**, one share is divided into more shares—for example, a two-for-one split means that for every one share the stockholder owned before the split, he now has two shares. In a reverse stock split, shares are absorbed into one. In a one-for-two reverse split, the stockholder will get one share in place of the two he held before the split.

stock split

Increasing the number of a firm's outstanding shares by issuing more shares to current shareholders, adjusting the price to keep the firm's market capitalization the same.

The stock split has no effect on the assets of the company, nor is the interest of any shareholder diluted. No transfer from surplus into stated capital is necessary. The only necessary accounting change is the adjustment of par value and stated value. Because par value is being changed, many states require not only the board of directors but also the shareholders to approve a stock split.

Why split? The chief reason is to reduce the current market price of the stock in order to make it affordable to a much wider class of investors. For example, in 1978, IBM, whose stock was then selling for around $284, split four for one, reducing the price to about $70 a share. That was the lowest IBM's stock had been since 1932. Stock need not sell at stratospheric prices to be split, however; for example, American Telnet Corporation, whose stock had been selling at $0.4375 a share, declared a five-for-one split in 1980. Apparently the company felt that the stock would be more affordable at $0.0875 a share. At the opposite end of the spectrum are Class A shares of Warren Buffett's Berkshire Hathaway, which routinely trade for more than $100,000 a share. Buffett has rebuffed efforts to split the Class A shares, but in 2010, shareholders approved a fifty-for-one split of Class B shares.[4]

Legal Limitations on Dividends

The law imposes certain limitations on cash or property dividends a corporation may disburse. Dividends may not be paid if (1) the business is insolvent (i.e., unable to pay its debts as they become due), (2) paying dividends would make it insolvent, or (3) payment would violate a restriction in the articles of incorporation. Most states also restrict the funds available for distribution to those available in earned surplus. Under this rule, a corporation that ran a deficit in the current year could still declare a dividend as long as the total earned surplus offset the deficit.

A few states—significantly, Delaware is one of them—permit dividends to be paid out of the net of current earnings and those of the immediately preceding year, both years taken as a single period, even if the balance sheet shows a negative earned surplus. Such dividends are known as nimble dividends. See *Weinberg v. Baltimore Brick Co.*[5]

Distribution from Capital Surplus

Assets in the form of cash or property may be distributed from capital surplus if the articles of incorporation so provide or if shareholders approve the distribution. Such distributions must be identified to the shareholders as coming from capital surplus.

Record Date, Payment Date, Rights of Stockholders

Under the securities exchange rules, the board of directors cannot simply declare a dividend payable on the date of the board meeting and instruct the treasurer to hand out cash. The board must fix two dates: a record date and a payment date. By the first, the board declares a dividend for shareholders of record as of a certain future date—perhaps ten days hence. Actual payment of the dividend is postponed until the payment date, which could be a month after the record date.

The board's action creates a debtor-creditor relationship between the corporation and its shareholders. The company may not revoke a cash dividend unless the shareholders consent. It may revoke a share dividend as long as the shares have not been issued.

Discretion of Directors to Pay Dividends

When Directors Are Too Stingy

In every state, dividends are normally payable only at the discretion of the directors. Courts will order distribution only if they are expressly mandatory or if it can be shown that the directors abused their discretion by acting fraudulently or in a manner that was manifestly unreasonable. *Dodge v. Ford Motor Co.*, (see Section 7), involves Henry Ford's refusal in 1916 to pay dividends in order to reinvest profits; it is often celebrated in business annals because of Ford's testimony at trial, although, as it turned out, the courts held his refusal to be an act of miserliness and an abuse of discretion. Despite this ruling, many corporations today do not pay dividends. Corporations may decide to reinvest profits in the corporation rather than pay a dividend to its shareholders, or to just sit on the cash. For example, Apple Computer, Inc., maker of many popular computers and consumer electronics, saw its share price skyrocket in the late 2000s. Apple also became one of the most valuable corporations in the world. Despite an immense cash reserve, Apple has refused to pay a dividend, choosing instead to reinvest in the business, stating that they require a large cash reserve as a security blanket for acquisitions or to develop new products. Thus, despite the ruling in *Dodge v. Ford Motor Co.*, courts will usually not intercede in a corporation's decision not to pay dividends, following the business judgment rule and the duties of directors. (For further discussion of the duties of directors, see Chapter 45).

When Directors Are Too Generous

Directors who vote to declare and distribute dividends in excess of those allowed by law or by provisions in the articles of incorporation personally may become jointly and severally liable to the corporation (but liability may be reduced or eliminated under the business judgment rule). Shareholders who receive a dividend knowing it is unlawful must repay any directors held liable for voting the illegal dividend. The directors are said to be entitled to contribution from such shareholders. Even when directors have not been sued, some courts have held that shareholders must repay dividends received when the corporation is insolvent or when they know that the dividends are illegal.

Key Takeaway

A dividend is a payment made from the corporation to its shareholders. A corporation may pay dividends through a variety of methods, although money and additional shares are the most common. Corporations may increase or decrease the total number of shares through either a stock split or a reverse stock split. A corporation may decide to pay dividends but is not required to do so and cannot issue dividends if the corporation is insolvent. Directors may be liable to the corporation for dividend payments that violate the articles of incorporation or are illegal.

Exercises

1. What is a dividend, and what are the main types of dividends?
2. Is a corporation required to pay dividends? Under what circumstances is a corporation barred from paying dividends?
3. You have ten shares of BCT, valued at $10 each. The company engages in a two-for-one stock split. How many shares do you now have? What is the value of each share, and what is the total value of all of your BCT shares?

44.6 The Winds of Change

Learning Objectives

1. Know the modern changes to corporate finance terminology and specific requirements imposed by states.
2. Compare the application of the Uniform Commercial Code to corporate finance with the applicability of the 1933 and 1934 federal securities acts.

Changes in the Revised Model Business Corporation Act

Perhaps the most dramatic innovations incorporated into the Revised Model Business Corporation Act (RMBCA) are the financial provisions. The revisions recommend eliminating concepts such as par value stock, no-par stock, stated capital, capital surplus, earned surplus, and treasury shares. It was felt that these concepts—notably par value and stated capital—no longer serve their original purpose of protecting creditors.

A key definition under the revisions is that of *distributions*—that is, any transfer of money or property to the shareholders. In order to make distributions, a corporation must meet the traditional insolvency test and balance sheet tests. Under the balance sheet test, corporate assets must be greater than or equal to liabilities and liquidation preferences on senior equity. The RMBCA also provides that promissory notes and contracts for future services may be used in payment for shares.

The RMBCA is only advisory. But at least 28 states have eliminated the concepts of par value, stated capital, and capital surplus; Delaware is quite permissive with its requirements:

> *Every corporation may issue 1 or more classes of stock or 1 or more series of stock within any class thereof, any or all of which classes may be of stock with par value or stock without par value and which classes or series may have such voting powers, full or limited, or no voting powers, and such designations, preferences and relative, participating, optional or other special rights, and qualifications, limitations or restrictions thereof, as shall be stated and expressed in the certificate of incorporation or of any amendment thereto, or in the resolution or resolutions providing for the issue of such stock adopted by the board of directors pursuant to authority expressly vested in it by the provisions of its certificate of incorporation.*[6]

Because some states grant more favorable tax treatment to par value stock, some companies will issue low par value stock, providing almost the same flexibility as no par stock.

Introduction to Article 8 of the Uniform Commercial Code

Partial ownership of a corporation would be an awkward investment if there were no ready means of transfer. The availability of paper certificates as tangible evidence of the ownership of equity securities solves the problem of what to transfer, but since a corporation must maintain records of its owners, a set of rules is necessary to spell out how transfers are to be made. That set of rules is Article 8 of the Uniform Commercial Code (UCC). Article 8 governs certificated securities, uncertificated securities, registration requirements, transfer, purchase, and other specifics of securities. Article 8 can be viewed at http://www.law.cornell.edu/ucc/8/overview.html.

The UCC and the 1933 and 1934 Securities Acts

The Securities Act of 1933 requires the registration of securities that are sold or offered to be sold using interstate commerce. The Securities Exchange Act of 1934 governs the secondary trading of securities, such as stock market sales. The UCC also governs securities, through Articles 8 and 9. The key difference is that the 1933 and 1934 acts are federal law, while the UCC operates at the state level. The UCC was established to standardize state laws governing sales and commercial transactions. There are some substantial differences, however, between the two acts and the UCC. Without going into exhaustive detail, it is important to note a few of them. For one, the definition of *security* in the UCC is different from the definition in the 1933 and 1934 acts. Thus, a security may be governed by the securities acts but not by the UCC. The definition of a private placement of securities also differs between the UCC and the securities acts. Other differences exist.[7] The UCC, as well as state-specific laws, and the federal securities laws should all be considered in financial transactions.

Key Takeaway

The RMBCA advises doing away with financial concepts such as stock par value. Despite this suggestion, these concepts persist. Corporate finance is regulated through a variety of mechanisms, most notably Articles 8 and 9 of the Uniform Commercial Code and the 1933 and 1934 securities acts.

Exercises

1. What suggested changes are made by the RMBCA?
2. What does UCC Article 8 govern?

44.7 Cases

Consideration in Exchange for Stock

United Steel Industries, Inc. v. Manhart

405 S.W.2d 231 (Tex. 1966)

MCDONALD, CHIEF JUSTICE

This is an appeal by defendants, United Steel Industries, Inc., J. R. Hurt and W. B. Griffitts, from a judgment declaring void and cancelling 5,000 shares of stock in United Steel Industries, Inc. issued to Hurt, and 4,000 shares of stock in such corporation issued to Griffitts.

Plaintiffs Manhart filed this suit individually and as major stockholders against defendants United Steel Industries, Inc., Hurt, and Griffitts, alleging the corporation had issued Hurt 5,000 shares of its stock in consideration of Hurt agreeing to perform CPA and bookkeeping services for the corporation for one year in the future; and had issued Griffitts 4,000 shares of its stock in consideration for the promised conveyance of a 5 acre tract of land to the Corporation, which land was never conveyed to the Corporation. Plaintiffs assert the 9,000 shares of stock were issued in violation of Article 2.16 Business Corporation Act, and prayed that such stock be declared void and cancelled.

Trial was before the Court without a jury which, after hearing, entered judgment declaring the 5,000 shares of stock issued to Hurt, and the 4,000 shares issued to Griffitts, issued without valid consideration, void, and decreeing such stock cancelled.

* * *

The trial court found (on ample evidence) that the incorporators of the Corporation made an agreement with Hurt to issue him 5,000 shares in consideration of Hurt's agreement to perform bookkeeping and accounting services for the Corporation for the first year of its operation. The Corporation minutes reflect the 5,000 shares issued to Hurt "in consideration of labor done, services in the incorporation and organization of the Corporation." The trial court found (on ample evidence) that such minutes do not reflect the true consideration agreed upon, and that Hurt performed no services for the Corporation prior to February 1, 1965. The Articles of Incorporation were filed on January 28, 1965, and the 5,000 shares were issued to Hurt on May 29, 1965. There is evidence that Hurt performed some services for the Corporation between January and May 29, 1965; but Hurt himself testified the "5,000 (shares) were issued to me for services rendered or to be rendered for the first year in keeping the books...."

The situation is thus one where the stock was issued to Hurt both for services already performed and for services to be rendered in the future.

The trial court concluded the promise of future services was not a valid consideration for the issuance of stock under Article 2.16 Business Corporation Act; that the issuance was void; and that since there was no apportionment of the value of future services from the value of services already rendered, the entire 5000 shares were illegally issued and void.

Article 12, Section 6, Texas Constitution, provides: "No corporation shall issue stock...except for money paid, labor done, or property actually received...." And Article 2.16 Texas Business Corporation Act provides: "Payment for Shares.

> *"A. The consideration paid for the issuance of shares shall consist of money paid, labor done, or property actually received. Shares may not be issued until the full amount of the consideration, fixed as provided by law, has been paid. ...*
>
> *"B. Neither promissory notes nor the promise of future services shall constitute payment or part payment for shares of a corporation.*
>
> *"C. In the absence of fraud in the transaction, the judgment of the board of directors...as to the value of the consideration received for shares shall be conclusive."*

The Fifth Circuit in Champion v. CIR, 303 Fed. 2d 887 construing the foregoing constitutional provision and Article 2.16 of the Business Corporation Act, held:

> *Where it is provided that stock can be issued for labor done, as in Texas ... the requirement is not met where the consideration for the stock is work or services to be performed in the future. ... The situation is not changed by reason of the provision that the stock was to be given ... for services rendered as well as to be rendered, since there was no allocation or apportionment of stock between services performed and services to be performed."*

The 5000 shares were issued before the future services were rendered. Such stock was illegally issued and void.

Griffitts was issued 10,000 shares partly in consideration for legal services to the Corporation and partly in exchange for the 5 acres of land. The stock was valued at $1 per share and the land had an agreed value of $4,000. The trial court found (upon ample evidence) that the 4,000 shares of stock issued to Griffitts was in consideration of his promise to convey the land to the Corporation; that Griffitts never conveyed the land; and the issuance of the stock was illegal and void.

The judgment of the board of directors "as to the value of consideration received for shares" is conclusive, but such does not authorize the board to issue shares contrary to the Constitution, for services to be performed in the future (as in the case of Hurt), or for property not received (as in the case of Griffitts).

The judgment is correct. Defendants' points and contentions are overruled.

AFFIRMED.

Case Questions

1. What was wrong with the consideration in the transaction between United Steel and Hurt?
2. What if Hurt had completed one year of bookkeeping prior to receiving his shares?
3. What was wrong with the consideration Griffitts provided for the 4,000 shares he received?

Payment of Dividends

Dodge v. Ford Motor Co.

204 Mich. 459, 170 N.W. 668 (Mich. 1919)

[Action by plaintiffs John F. Dodge and Horace E. Dodge against defendant Ford Motor Company and its directors. The lower court ordered the directors to declare a dividend in the amount of $19,275,385.96 [about $367 million in 2017 dollars]. The court also enjoined proposed expansion of the company. The defendants appealed.]

[T]he case for plaintiffs must rest upon the claim, and the proof in support of it, that the proposed expansion of the business of the corporation, involving the further use of profits as capital, ought to be enjoined because it is inimical to the best interests of the company and its shareholders, and upon the further claim that in any event the withholding of the special dividend asked for by plaintiffs is arbitrary action of the directors requiring judicial interference.

The rule which will govern courts in deciding these questions is not in dispute. It is, of course, differently phrased by judges and by authors, and, as the phrasing in a particular instance may seem to lean for or against the exercise of the right of judicial interference with the actions of corporate directors, the context, or the facts before the court, must be considered.

* * *

In 1 Morawetz on Corporations (2d Ed.), § 447, it is stated:

Profits earned by a corporation may be divided among its shareholders; but it is not a violation of the charter if they are allowed to accumulate and remain invested in the company's business. The managing agents of a corporation are impliedly invested with a discretionary power with regard to the time and manner of distributing its profits. They may apply profits in payment of floating or funded debts, or in development of the company's business; and so long as they do not abuse their discretionary powers, or violate the company's charter, the courts cannot interfere.

But it is clear that the agents of a corporation, and even the majority, cannot arbitrarily withhold profits earned by the company, or apply them to any use which is not authorized by the company's charter....

Mr. Henry Ford is the dominant force in the business of the Ford Motor Company. No plan of operations could be adopted unless he consented, and no board of directors can be elected whom he does not favor. One of the directors of the company has no stock. One share was assigned to him to qualify him for the position, but it is not claimed that he owns it. A business, one of the largest in the world, and one of the most profitable, has been built up. It employs many men, at good pay.

"My ambition," said Mr. Ford, "is to employ still more men, to spread the benefits of this industrial system to the greatest possible number, to help them build up their lives and their homes. To do this we are putting the greatest share of our profits back in the business."

"With regard to dividends, the company paid sixty per cent on its capitalization of two million dollars, or $1,200,000, leaving $58,000,000 to reinvest for the growth of the company. This is Mr. Ford's policy at present, and it is understood that the other stockholders cheerfully accede to this plan."

He had made up his mind in the summer of 1916 that no dividends other than the regular dividends should be paid, "for the present."

"Q. For how long? Had you fixed in your mind any time in the future, when you were going to pay—

"A. No.

"Q. That was indefinite in the future?

"A. That was indefinite, yes, sir."

The record, and especially the testimony of Mr. Ford, convinces that he has to some extent the attitude towards shareholders of one who has dispensed and distributed to them large gains and that they should be content to take what he chooses to give. His testimony creates the impression, also, that he thinks the Ford Motor Company has made too much money, has had too large profits, and that although large profits might be still earned, a sharing of them with the public, by reducing the price of the output of the company, ought to be undertaken. We have no doubt that certain sentiments, philanthropic and altruistic, creditable to Mr. Ford, had large influence in determining the policy to be pursued by the Ford Motor Company—the policy which has been herein referred to.

* * *

The difference between an incidental humanitarian expenditure of corporate funds for the benefit of the employees, like the building of a hospital for their use and the employment of agencies for the betterment of their condition, and a general purpose and plan to benefit mankind at the expense of others, is obvious. There should be no confusion (of which there is evidence) of the duties which Mr. Ford conceives that he and the stockholders owe to the general public and the duties which in law he and his codirectors owe to protesting, minority stockholders. A business corporation is organized and carried on primarily for the profit of the stockholders. The powers of the directors are to be employed for that end. The discretion of directors is to be exercised in the choice of means to attain that end and does not extend to a change in the end itself, to the reduction of profits or to the nondistribution of profits among stockholders in order to devote them to other purposes.

* * *

We are not, however, persuaded that we should interfere with the proposed expansion of the business of the Ford Motor Company. In view of the fact that the selling price of products may be increased at any time, the ultimate results of the larger business cannot be certainly estimated. The judges are not business experts. It is recognized that plans must often be made for a long future, for expected competition, for a continuing as well as an immediately profitable venture. The experience of the Ford Motor Company is evidence of capable management of its affairs. It may be noticed, incidentally, that it took from the public the money required for the execution of its plan and that the very considerable salaries paid to Mr. Ford and to certain executive officers and employees were not diminished. We are not satisfied that the alleged motives of the directors, in so far as they are reflected in the conduct of the business, menace the interests of shareholders. It is enough to say, perhaps, that the court of equity is at all times open to complaining shareholders having a just grievance.

[The court affirmed the lower court's order that the company declare a dividend and reversed the lower court's decision that halted company expansion].

Case Questions

1. What basis does the court use to order the payment of dividends?
2. Does the court have a positive view of Mr. Ford?
3. How do you reconcile 1 Morawetz on Corporations (2d Ed.), § 447 ("Profits earned by a corporation may be divided among its shareholders; but it is not a violation of the charter if they are allowed to accumulate and remain invested in the company's business") with the court's decision?

44.8 Summary and Exercises

Summary

Corporations finance through a variety of mechanisms. One method is to reinvest profits in the corporation. Another method is to use private equity. Private equity involves financing from private investors, whether individuals (angel investors) or a private equity firm. Venture capital is often used as a fundraising mechanism by businesses that are just starting operations.

A third method is to finance through debt, such as a loan or a bond. A corporation sells a bond and agrees to make interest payments over the life of the bond and to pay the face value of the bond at the bond's maturity.

The final important method of raising capital is by the sale of stock. The articles of incorporation govern the total number of shares of stock that the corporation may issue, although it need not issue the maximum. Stock in the hands of shareholders is said to be authorized, issued, and outstanding. Stock may have a par value, which is usually the floor price of the stock. No-par shares may be sold for any price set by the directors.

Preferred stock (1) may have a dividend preference, (2) takes preference upon liquidation, and (3) may be convertible. Common stock normally has the right to (1) ratable participation in earnings, (2) ratable participation in the distribution of net assets on liquidation, and (3) ratable vote.

Ordinarily, the good-faith judgment of the directors concerning the fair value of the consideration received for stock is determinative. A minority of states adhere to a true value rule that holds to an objective standard.

A corporation that sells shares for the first time engages in an initial public offering (IPO). The Securities Act of 1933 governs most IPOs and initial stock sales. A corporation that has previously issued stock may do so many times afterward, depending on the corporation's needs. The Securities Exchange Act of 1934 governs most secondary market stock sales. The Sarbanes-Oxley Act of 2002 adds another layer of regulation to the financial transactions discussed in this chapter.

A dividend is a share of a corporation's profits. Dividends may be distributed as cash, property, or stock. The law imposes certain limitations on the amount that the corporation may disburse; most states restrict the cash or property available for distribution to earned surplus. However, a few states, including Delaware, permit dividends to be paid out of the net of current earnings and those of the immediately preceding year, both years taken as a single period; these are known as nimble dividends. The directors have discretion, within broad limits, to set the level of dividends; however, they will be jointly and severally liable if they approve dividends higher than allowed by law or under the articles of incorporation.

With several options available, corporations face many factors to consider in deciding how to raise funds. Each option is not available to every corporation. Additionally, each option has advantages and disadvantages. A corporation must carefully weigh the pros and cons of each before making a decision to proceed on a particular financing path.

Exercises

1. Ralph and Alice have decided to incorporate their sewer cleaning business under the name R & A, Inc. Their plans call for the authorization and issuance of 5,000 shares of par value stock. Ralph argues that par value must be set at the estimated market value of the stock, while Alice feels that par value is the equivalent of book value—that is, assets divided by the number of shares. Who is correct? Why?
2. In Exercise 1, Ralph feels that R & A should have an IPO of 1 million shares of common stock, to be sold on the New York Stock Exchange (NYSE). What are the pros and cons of conducting an IPO?
3. Assume that Ralph and Alice decide to issue preferred stock. What does this entail from R & A's standpoint? From the standpoint of a preferred stock purchaser?
4. Alice changes her mind and wants to sell bonds in R & A. What are the pros and cons of selling bonds?
5. Assume that Ralph and Alice go on to consider options other than financing through an IPO or through the sale of bonds. They want to raise $5 million to get their business up and running, to purchase a building, and to acquire machines to clean sewers. What are some other options Ralph and Alice should consider? What would you suggest they do? Would your suggestion be different if Ralph and Alice wanted to raise $500 million? $50,000?

Self-Test Questions

1. Corporate funds that come from earnings are called
    a. equity securities
    b. depletion
    c. debt securities
    d. plowback
2. When a value is specified on a stock certificate, it is said to be
    a. par value
    b. no-par
    c. an authorized share
    d. none of the above
3. Common stockholders normally
    a. have the right to vote ratably
    b. do not have the right to vote ratably
    c. never have preemptive rights
    d. hold all of the company's treasury shares
4. Preferred stock may be
    a. entitled to cumulative dividends
    b. convertible
    c. redeemable
    d. all of the above
5. When a corporation issues stock to the public for the first time, the corporation engages in
    a. a distribution
    b. an initial public offering
    c. underwriting
    d. a stock split

Self-Test Answers

1. d
2. a
3. a
4. d
5. b

Endnotes

1. Dawn C. Chmielewski and Robert Channick, "Hugh Hefner Reaches Deal to Take Playboy Private," *Los Angeles Times*, January 11, 2011. http://articles.latimes.com/2011/jan/11/business/la-fi-ct-playboy-hefner-20110111.
2. For a full discussion of Enron, see Bethany McLean and Peter Elkind, *Enron: The Smartest Guys in the Room* (New York: Portfolio, 2004).
3. Sarbanes-Oxley Act can be viewed at University of Cincinnati, "The Sarbanes-Oxley Act of 2002," *Securities Lawyer's Deskbook*, http://taft.law.uc.edu/CCL/SOact/toc.html.
4. *BusinessWeek* covers many stock splits and reverse splits in its finance section, available at http://www.businessweek.com/finance.
5. *Weinberg v. Baltimore Brick Co.*, 35 Del. Ch. 225; 114 A.2d 812 (Del. 1955).
6. Del. Code Ann. tit. 8, § 151 (2011).
7. See Lynn Soukup, "Securities Law and the UCC: When Godzilla Meets Bambi," *Uniform Commercial Code Law Journal* 38, no. 1 (Summer 2005): 3–28.

CHAPTER 45

Corporate Powers and Management

Learning Objectives

After reading this chapter, you should understand the following:

1. The powers of a corporation to act.
2. The rights of shareholders.
3. The duties, powers, and liability of officers and directors.

Power within a corporation is present in many areas. The corporation itself has powers, although with limitations. There is a division of power between shareholders, directors, and officers. Given this division of power, certain duties are owed among the parties. We focus this chapter on these powers and on the duties owed by shareholders, directors, and officers. In Chapter 46, we will continue discussion of officers' and directors' liability within the context of securities regulation and insider trading.

45.1 Powers of a Corporation

Learning Objectives

1. Understand the two types of corporate power.
2. Consider what happens when a corporation acts outside its prescribed powers.
3. Review legal issues surrounding corporate actions.

Two Types of Corporate Powers

A corporation generally has three groups that share power and control: directors, officers, and shareholders. Directors are the managers of the corporation, and officers control the day-to-day decisions and work more closely with the employees. The shareholders at any given time are considered as "owners" of the corporation, but they have only limited authority under most state corporate laws. The corporation itself has powers; while a corporation is not the same as a person (e.g., a corporation cannot be put in prison), it is allowed to conduct certain activities and has been granted certain rights.

Express Powers

express powers

Powers granted to a corporation through statute and its articles of incorporation.

The corporation may exercise all powers expressly given it by statute and by its articles of incorporation. Section 3.02 of the Revised Model Business Corporation Act (RMBCA) sets out a number of **express powers**, including the following: to sue and be sued in the corporate name; to purchase, use, and sell land and dispose of assets to the same extent a natural person can; to make contracts, borrow money, issue notes and bonds, lend money, invest funds, make donations to the public welfare, and establish pension plans; and to join in partnerships, joint ventures, trusts, or other enterprises. These powers do not need to be explicitly named in the articles of incorporation.

Implied Powers

implied powers

Corporate powers that extend beyond those powers explicitly defined as express powers.

Corporate powers beyond those explicitly established are **implied powers**. For example, suppose BCT Bookstore, Inc.'s statement of purpose reads simply, "to operate a bookstore." The company may lawfully conduct all acts that are necessary or appropriate to running a bookstore—hiring employees, advertising special sales, leasing trucks, and so forth. Could Ted, its vice president and general manager, authorize the expenditure of funds to pay for a Sunday afternoon lecture on the perils of nuclear war or the adventures of a professional football player? Yes—if the lectures are relevant to current books on sale or serve to bring people into the store, they comply with the corporation's purpose.

The Ultra Vires Doctrine

ultra vires doctrine

A doctrine holding that certain legal consequences attach to an attempt by a corporation to carry out acts that are outside its lawful powers.

The law places limitations upon what acts a corporation may undertake. Corporations cannot do anything they wish, but rather, must act within the prescribed rules as laid out in corporation statutes, case law, their articles of incorporation, and their bylaws. Sometimes, though, a corporation will act in ways that are not explicitly or implicity allowed. The **ultra vires doctrine** (literally "beyond the powers)holds that certain legal consequences attach to an attempt by a corporation to carry out acts that are outside its lawful powers. The ultra vires doctrine (literally "beyond the powers") is not limited to illegal acts; it encompasses actions barred by statute as well as by the corporate charter. Under the traditional approach, either the corporation or the other party could assert ultra vires as a defense when refusing to abide by a contract that has not been fully executed. The ultra vires doctrine loses much of its significance when corporate powers are broadly stated in a corporation's articles. Furthermore, RMBCA Section 3.04 states that "the validity of corporate action may not be challenged on the ground that the corporation lacks or lacked power to act."

Nonetheless, ultra vires acts are still challenged in courts today. For example, particularly in the area of environmental law, plaintiffs are challenging corporate environmental actions as ultra vires. Delaware corporation law states that the attorney general shall revoke the charter of a corporation for illegal acts. Additionally, the Court of Chancery of Delaware has jurisdiction to forfeit or revoke a corporate charter for abuse of corporate powers.[1] See Adam Sulkowski's "Ultra Vires Statutes: Alive, Kicking, and a Means of Circumventing the Scalia Standing Gauntlet."[2]

In essence, ultra vires retains force in three ways:

1. Shareholders may bring suits against the corporation to enjoin it from acting beyond its powers.
2. The corporation itself, through receivers, trustees, or shareholders, may sue incumbent or former officers or directors for causing the corporation to act ultra vires.
3. The state attorney general may assert the doctrine in a proceeding to dissolve the corporation or to enjoin it from transacting unauthorized business (see Figure 45.1).

FIGURE 45.1 Attacks on Ultra Vires Acts

Shareholders, the Attorney General of the corporation's home state, and the corporation itself - through shareholders and others - have standing to challenge corporate acts that are beyond its powers.

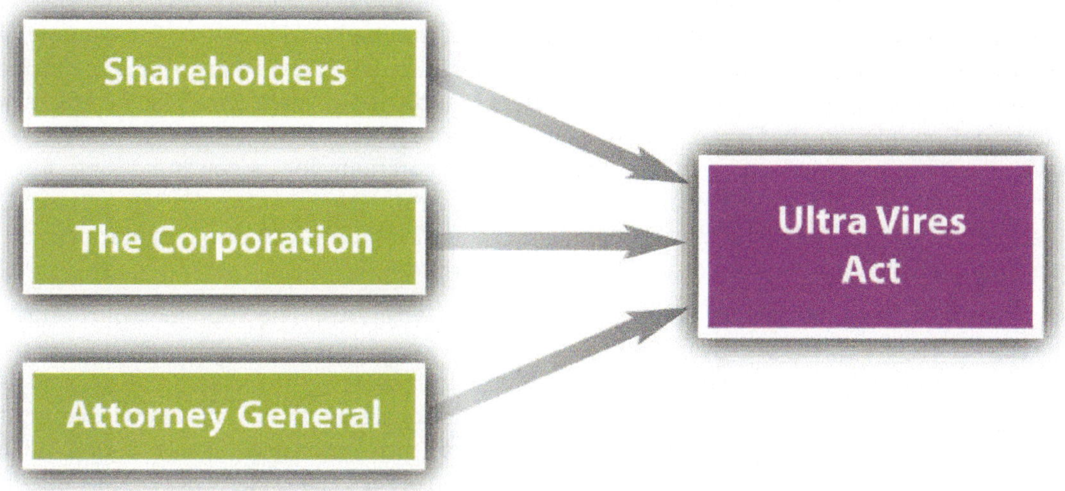

Suppose an incorporated luncheon club refuses to admit women as club members or guests. What happens if this action is ultra vires? *Cross v. The Midtown Club, Inc.* (see Section 5), focuses on this issue. An ultra vires act is not necessarily criminal or tortious. However, every crime and tort is in some sense ultra vires because a corporation never has legal authority to commit crimes or torts. They raise special problems, to which we now turn.

Criminal, Tortious, and Other Illegal Acts

The early common law held that a corporation could not commit a crime because it did not have a mind and so could not have the requisite intent. Also, it isn't possible to actually imprison an entire corporation. But modern law is not so constricting. Illegal acts of its agents may be imputed to the corporation. Thus, if the board of directors specifically authorizes the company to carry out a criminal scheme, or the president instructs his employees to break a regulatory law for the benefit of the company, the corporation itself may be convicted and fined. Often, because criminal law requires "proof beyond a reasonable doubt," state and federal prosecutors will pursue civil suits for what might be criminal offenses. The U.S. Department of Justice, for example, brought a number of civil prosecutions against financial firms in the wake of the 2008 financial meltdown. [3]

It is rare for people in a corporate setting to admit their criminal intentions, so in most cases courts determine the corporation's liability by deciding whether an employee's crime was part of a job-related activity. The individuals within the corporation are much more likely to be held legally liable, but the corporation may be as well. In rare and extreme cases, a court could order the dissolution of the corporation; revoke some or all of its ability to operate, such as by revoking a license the corporation may hold; or prevent the corporation from engaging in a critical aspect of its business, such as acting as a trustee or engaging in securities transactions. But these cases are extremely rare.

That a corporation is found guilty of a violation of the law does not excuse company officials who authorized or carried out the illegal act. They, too, can be prosecuted and sent to jail. Legal punishments are being routinely added to the newer federal regulatory statutes, such as the Occupational Safety and Health Act, and the Toxic Substances Control Act—although prosecution depends mainly on whether and where a particular administration wishes to spend its enforcement dollars. Additionally, state prosecuting attorneys have become more active in filing criminal charges against management when employees are injured or die on the job. For instance, a trial court judge in Chicago sentenced a company president, plant manager, and foreman to twenty-five years in prison after they were convicted of murder following the death of a worker as a result of unsafe working conditions at a plant;[4] the punishments were later overturned, but the three pled guilty several years later and served shorter sentences of varying duration.

Federal prosecutors have been expanding their prosecutions of corporations and developing methodologies to evaluate whether a corporation has committed a criminal act; for example, U.S. Deputy Attorney General Paul McNulty revised "Principles of Federal Prosecutions of Business Organizations" in 2006 to further guide prosecutors in indicting corporations. The Securities and Exchange Commission, the Department of Justice, other regulatory bodies, and legal professionals have increasingly sought legal penalties against both corporations for money laundering, foreign corrupt practices, and the Racketeer Influenced and Corrupt Organizations (RICO) statute.[5] See Exercise 2 at the end of this section to consider the legal ramifications of a corporation and its employees for the drunk-driving death of one of its patrons.

In certain cases, the liability of an executive can be "'vicarious." The Supreme Court affirmed the conviction of a chief executive who had no personal knowledge of a violation by his company of regulations promulgated by the Food and Drug Administration. In this case, an officer was held strictly liable for his corporation's violation of the regulations, regardless of his knowledge, or lack thereof, of the actions (see Chapter 6).[6] This stands in contrast to the general rule that an individual must know, or should know, of a violation of the law in order to be liable. Strict liability does not require knowledge. Thus, a corporation's top managers can be found criminally responsible even if they did not directly participate in the illegal activity. Employees directly responsible for violation of the law can also be held liable, of course. In short, violations of tort law, criminal law, and regulatory law can result in negative consequences for both the corporation and its employees.

Key Takeaway

A corporation has two types of powers: express powers and implied powers. When a corporation is acting outside its permissible power, it is said to be acting ultra vires. A corporation engages in ultra vires acts whenever it engages in illegal activities, such as criminal acts.

Exercises

1. What is an ultra vires act?
2. A group of undergraduate students travel from their university to a club. The club provides dinner and an open bar. One student becomes highly intoxicated and dies as the result of an automobile collision caused by the student. Can the club be held liable for the student's death? See *Commonwealth v. Penn Valley Resorts.*[7]

45.2 Rights of Shareholders

Learning Objectives

1. Explain the various parts of the corporate management structure and how they relate to one another.
2. Describe the processes and practices of typical corporate meetings, including annual meetings.

3. Explain the standard voting process in most U.S. corporations and what the respective roles of management and shareholders are.
4. Understand what corporate records can be reviewed by a shareholder and under what circumstances.

General Management Functions

In the modern publicly held corporation, ownership and control are separated. The shareholders "own" the company through their ownership of its stock, but power to manage is vested in the directors. In a large publicly traded corporation, most of the ownership of the corporation is diluted across its numerous shareholders, many of whom have no involvement with the corporation other than through their stock ownership. On the other hand, the issue of separation and control is generally irrelevant to the closely held corporation, since ordinarily the shareholders are the same people who manage and work for the corporation.

Shareholders do retain some degree of control. For example, they elect the directors, although only a small fraction of shareholders control the outcome of most elections because of the diffusion of ownership and modern proxy rules; proxy fights are extremely difficult for insurgents to win. Shareholders also may adopt, amend, and repeal the corporation's bylaws; they may adopt resolutions ratifying or refusing to ratify certain actions of the directors. And they must vote on certain extraordinary matters, such as whether to amend the articles of incorporation, merge, or liquidate.

Meetings

In most states, the corporation must hold at least one meeting of shareholders each year. The board of directors or shareholders representing at least 10 percent of the stock may call a special shareholders' meeting at any time unless a different threshold number is stated in the articles or bylaws. Timely notice is required: not more than sixty days nor less than ten days before the meeting, under Section 7.05 of the Revised Model Business Corporation Act (RMBCA). Shareholders may take actions without a meeting if every shareholder entitled to vote consents in writing to the action to be taken. This option is obviously useful to the closely held corporation but not to large, publicly held companies.

Right to Vote

Who Has the Right to Vote?

Through its bylaws or by resolution of the board of directors, a corporation can set a "record date." Only the shareholders listed on the corporate records on that date receive notice of the next shareholders' meeting and have the right to vote. Every share is entitled to one vote unless the articles of incorporation state otherwise.

The one-share, one-vote principle, commonly called **regular voting** or statutory voting, is not required, and many U.S. companies have restructured their voting rights in an effort to repel corporate raiders. For instance, a company might decide to issue both voting and nonvoting shares (as discussed in Chapter 45), with the voting shares going to insiders who thereby control the corporation. In response to these new corporate structures, the Securities and Exchange Commission (SEC) adopted a one-share, one-vote rule in 1988 that was designed to protect a shareholder's right to vote. In 1990, however, a federal appeals court overturned the SEC rule on the grounds that voting rights are governed by state law rather than by federal law.[8]

regular voting

The principle of one share, one vote. Also called statutory voting.

Quorum

shareholder quorum

Minimum number of shareholders needed to have a valid vote. Also, when a simple majority of the shares entitled to vote is sufficient to effectuate a meeting.

When the articles of incorporation are silent, a **shareholder quorum** is a simple majority of the shares entitled to vote, whether represented in person or by proxy, according to RMBCA Section 7.25. Thus, if there are 1 million shares, 500,001 must be represented at the shareholder meeting. A simple majority of those represented shares is sufficient to carry any motion, so 250,001 shares are enough to decide upon a matter other than the election of directors (governed by RMBCA, Section 7.28). The articles of incorporation may decree a different quorum, but not less than one-third of the total shares entitled to vote.

Cumulative Voting

Cumulative voting

Shareholder voting method permitting the holder to distribute his total votes in any manner that he chooses—all for one candidate or several shares for different candidates.

With cumulative voting, each shareholder has a total number of votes equal to the number of shares that he owns multiplied by the number of directors to be elected. **Cumulative voting** means that a shareholder may distribute his total votes in any manner that he chooses—all for one candidate or several shares for different candidates. Thus, if a shareholder has 1,000 shares and there are five directors to be elected, the shareholder has 5,000 votes, and he may vote those shares in a manner he desires (all for one director, or 2,500 each for two directors, etc.). Some states permit this right unless the articles of incorporation deny it. Other states deny it unless the articles of incorporation permit it. Several states have constitutional provisions requiring cumulative voting for corporate directors.

Cumulative voting is meant to provide minority shareholders with representation on the board. Assume that Bob and Carol each owns 2,000 shares, which they have decided to vote as a block, and Ted owns 6,000 shares. At their annual shareholder meeting, they are to elect five directors. Without cumulative voting, Ted's slate of directors would win: under statutory voting, each share represents one vote available for each director position. With this method, by placing as many votes as possible for each director, Ted could cast 6,000 votes for each of his desired directors. Thus each of Ted's directors would receive 6,000 votes, while each of Bob and Carol's directors would receive only 4,000. Under cumulative voting, however, each shareholder has as many votes as there are directors to be elected. Hence with cumulative voting Bob and Carol could strategically distribute their 20,000 votes (4,000 votes multiplied by five directors) among the candidates to ensure representation on the board. By placing 10,000 votes each on two of their candidates, they would be guaranteed two positions on the board. (The candidates from the two slates are not matched against each other on a one-to-one basis; instead, the five candidates with the highest number of votes are elected.) Various formulas and computer programs are available to determine how votes should be allocated, but the principle underlying the calculations is this: cumulative voting is democratic in that it allows the shareholders who own 40 percent of the stock—Bob and Carol—to elect 40 percent of the board.

RMBCA Section 8.08 provides a safeguard against attempts to remove directors. Ordinarily, a director may be removed by a majority vote of the shareholders. Cumulative voting will not aid a given single director whose ouster is being sought because the majority obviously can win on a straight vote. So Section 8.08 provides, "If cumulative voting is authorized, a director may not be removed if the number of votes sufficient to elect him under cumulative voting is voted against his removal."

Voting Arrangements to Concentrate Power

Shareholders use three types of arrangements to concentrate their power: proxies, voting agreements, and voting trusts.

Proxies

A **proxy** is the representative of the shareholder. A proxy may be a person who stands in for the shareholder or may be a written instrument by which the shareholder casts her votes before the shareholder meeting. Modern proxy voting allows shareholders to vote electronically through the Internet. Proxies are usually solicited by and given to management, either to vote for proposals or people named in the proxy or to vote however the proxy holder wishes. Through the proxy device, management of large companies can maintain control over the election of directors. Proxies must be signed by the shareholder and are valid for eleven months from the time they are received by the corporation unless the proxy explicitly states otherwise. Management may use reasonable corporate funds to solicit proxies if corporate policy issues are involved, but misrepresentations in the solicitation can lead a court to nullify the proxies and to deny reimbursement for the solicitation cost. Only the last proxy given by a particular shareholder can be counted.

proxy

A method whereby a shareholder elects a representative, commonly another individual or a written document, through which the shareholder casts his vote at the annual meeting.

Proxy solicitations are regulated by the SEC. For instance, SEC rules require companies subject to the Securities Exchange Act of 1934 to file proxy materials with the SEC at least ten days before proxies are mailed to shareholders. Proxy statements must disclose all material facts, and companies must use a proxy form on which shareholders can indicate whether they approve or disapprove of the proposals.

Dissident groups opposed to management's position are entitled to solicit their own proxies at their own expense. The company must either furnish the dissidents with a list of all shareholders and addresses or mail the proxies at corporate expense. Since management usually prefers to keep the shareholder list private, dissidents can frequently count on the corporation to pay for the mailing.

Voting Agreements

Unless they intend to commit fraud on a minority of stockholders, shareholders may agree in advance to vote in specific ways. Such a **voting agreement**, often called a shareholder agreement, is generally legal. Shareholders may agree in advance, for example, to vote for specific directors; they can even agree to vote for the dissolution of the corporation in the event that a predetermined contingency occurs. A voting agreement is easier to enter into than a voting trust (discussed next) and can be less expensive, since a trustee is not paid to administer a voting agreement. A voting agreement also permits shareholders to retain their shares rather than turning the shares over to a trust, as would be required in a voting trust.

voting agreement

An agreement made in advance among shareholders to vote in a particular manner. Also called shareholder agreement.

Voting Trusts

To ensure that shareholder agreements will be honored, shareholders in most states can create a **voting trust**. By this device, voting shares are given to voting trustees, who are empowered to vote the shares in accordance with the objectives set out in the trust agreement. Section 7.30 of the RMBCA limits the duration of voting trusts to ten years. The voting trust is normally irrevocable, and the shareholders' stock certificates (or their electronic equivalents) are physically transferred to the voting trustees for the duration of the trust. The voting trust agreement must be on file at the corporation, open for inspection by any shareholder.

voting trust

A trust created among shareholders where the shareholders elect a trust agreement, the provisions of which are effectuated by a voting trustee.

Inspection of Books and Records

Shareholders are legally entitled to inspect the records of the corporation in which they hold shares. These records include the articles of incorporation, bylaws, and corporate resolutions. As a general rule, shareholders who want certain records (such as minutes of a board of directors' meeting or accounting records) must also have a "proper purpose," such as to determine the propriety of the company's dividend policy or to ascertain the company's true financial worth. Improper purposes include uncovering trade secrets for sale to a competitor or compiling mailing lists for personal business purposes. A shareholder's motivation is an important factor in determining whether the purpose is proper, as the courts attempt to balance the rights of both the shareholders and the corporation. For example, a Minnesota court applied Delaware law in finding that a shareholder's request to view the corporation's shareholder ledger to identify shareholders and communicate with them about the corporation's involvement in the Vietnam War was improper. A desire to communicate with the other corporate shareholders was found to be insufficient to compel inspection.[9] Contrast that finding with a Delaware court's finding that a shareholder had a proper purpose in requesting a corporation's shareholder list in order to communicate with them about the economic risks of the firm's involvement in Angola.[10]

Preemptive Rights

Assume that BCT Bookstore has outstanding 5,000 shares with par value of ten dollars and that Carol owns 1,000. At the annual meeting, the shareholders decide to issue an additional 1,000 shares at par and to sell them to Alice. Carol vehemently objects because her percentage of ownership will decline. She goes to court seeking an injunction against the sale or an order permitting her to purchase 200 of the shares (she currently has 20 percent of the total). How should the court rule?

preemptive rights

The rights of shareholders to protect dilution of their percentage of share ownership.

The answer depends on the statutory provision dealing with **preemptive rights**—that is, the right of a shareholder to be protected from dilution of her percentage of ownership. In some states, shareholders have no preemptive rights unless expressly declared in the articles of incorporation, while other states give shareholders preemptive rights unless the articles of incorporation deny it. Preemptive rights were once strongly favored, but they are increasingly disappearing, especially in large publicly held companies where ownership is already highly diluted.

Derivative Actions

derivative action

Lawsuit brought on behalf of the corporation by a shareholder when the directors refuse to act.

Suppose Carol discovers that Ted has been receiving kickbacks from publishers and has been splitting the proceeds with Bob. At a directors' meeting, Carol might demand that the corporation file suit to recover the sums they pocketed, but Bob and Ted outvote her. Carol has another remedy. She can file a **derivative action** against them. A derivative lawsuit is one brought on behalf of the corporation by a shareholder when the directors refuse to act. Although the corporation is named as a defendant in the suit, the corporation itself is the so-called real party in interest—the party entitled to recover if the plaintiff wins.

disinterested director

A director who has no interest in the disputed transaction.

While derivative actions can potentially be abused by plaintiffs' attorneys seeking settlements that pay their fees, safeguards have been built into the law. At least ninety days before starting a derivative action, for instance, shareholders must demand in writing that the corporation take action. Shareholders may not commence derivative actions unless they were shareholders at the time of the wrongful act. Derivative actions may be dismissed if disinterested directors decide that the proceeding is not in the best interests of the corporation. (A **disinterested director** is a director who has no interest in the disputed transaction.) Derivative actions are discussed further in Chapter 45.

Key Takeaway

In large publicly traded corporations, shareholders own the corporation but have limited power to affect decisions. The board of directors and officers exercise much of the power. Shareholders exercise their power at meetings, typically through voting for directors. Statutes, bylaws, and the articles of incorporation determine how voting occurs—such as whether a quorum is sufficient to hold a meeting or whether voting is cumulative. Shareholders need not be present at a meeting—they may use a proxy to cast their votes or set up voting trusts or voting agreements. Shareholders may view corporate documents with proper demand and a proper purpose. Some corporations permit shareholders preemptive rights—the ability to purchase additional shares to ensure that the ownership percentage is not diluted. A shareholder may also file suit on behalf of the corporation—a legal proceeding called a derivative action.

Exercises

1. Explain cumulative voting. What is the different between cumulative voting and regular voting? Who benefits from cumulative voting?
2. A shareholder will not be at the annual meeting. May that shareholder vote? If so, how?
3. The BCT Bookstore is seeking an additional store location. Ted, a director of BCT, knows of the ideal building that would be highly profitable for BCT and finds out that it is for sale. Unbeknownst to BCT, Ted is starting a clothing retailer. He purchases the building for his clothing business, thereby usurping a corporate opportunity for BCT. Sam, a BCT shareholder, finds out about Ted's business deal. Does Sam have any recourse? See RMBCA Section 8.70.

45.3 Duties and Powers of Directors and Officers

Learning Objectives

1. Examine the responsibility of directors and the delegation of operating authority to management.
2. Discuss the qualifications, election, and removal of directors.
3. Determine what requirements are placed on directors for meetings and compensation.

General Management Responsibility of the Directors

Directors derive their power to manage the corporation from statutory law. Section 8.01 of the Revised Model Business Corporation Act (RMBCA) states that "all corporate powers shall be exercised by or under the authority of, and the business and affairs of the corporation managed under the direction of, its board of directors." A director is a **fiduciary**, a person to whom power is entrusted for another's benefit, and as such, as the RMBCA puts it, must perform his duties "in good faith, with the care an ordinarily prudent person in a like position would exercise under similar circumstances" (Section 8.30). A director's main responsibilities include the following: (1) to protect shareholder investments, (2) to select and remove officers, (3) to delegate operating authority to the managers or other groups, and (4) to supervise the company as a whole.

fiduciary

A person to whom power is entrusted for the benefit of another.

Delegation to Committees

Under RMBCA Section 8.25, the board of directors, by majority vote, may delegate its powers to various committees. This authority is limited to some degree. For example, only the full board can determine dividends, approve a merger, and amend the bylaws. The delegation of authority to a committee does not, by itself, relieve a director from the duty to exercise due care.

Delegation to Officers

FIGURE 45.2 The Corporate Governance Model

The distribution of power and responsibility throughout the corporation.

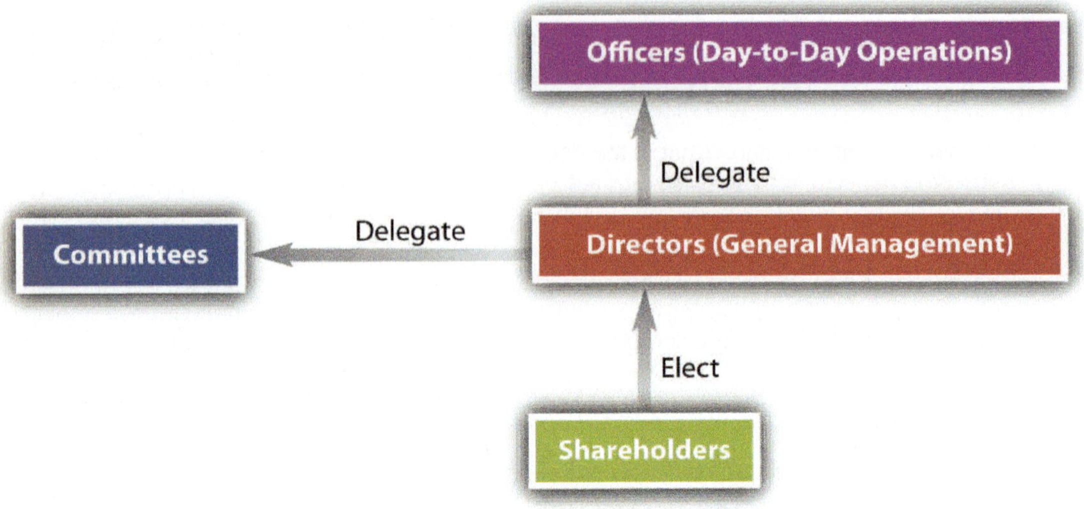

The directors often delegate to officers the day-to-day authority to execute the policies established by the board and to manage the firm (see Figure 45.2). Normally, the president is the chief executive officer (CEO) to whom all other officers and employees report, but sometimes the CEO is also the chairman of the board.

Number and Election of Directors

Section 8.03 of the RMBCA provides that there must be one director, but there may be more, the precise number to be fixed in the articles of incorporation or bylaws. The initial members of the board hold office until the first annual meeting, when elections occur. (The initial board members are permitted to succeed themselves.) Directors are often chosen to serve one-year terms and must be elected or reelected by the shareholders annually, unless there are nine or more directors. In that case, if the articles of incorporation so provide, the board may be divided into two or three roughly equal classes and their terms staggered, so that the second class is elected at the second annual meeting and the third at the third annual meeting. A staggered board allows for the continuity of directors or as a defense against a hostile takeover.

Directors' Qualifications and Characteristics

The statutes do not catalog qualifications that directors are expected to possess. In most states, directors need not be residents of the state or shareholders of the corporation unless required by the articles of incorporation or bylaws, which may also set down more precise qualifications if desired.

Until the 1970s, directors tended to be a homogeneous lot: white male businessmen or lawyers. Political change—rising consumer, environmental, and public interest consciousness—and embarrassment stemming from disclosures made in the wake of Securities and Exchange Commission (SEC) investigations growing out of Watergate[11] prompted companies to diversify their boardrooms. Today, members of minority groups and women are being appointed in increasing numbers, although their proportion to the total is still small. Outside directors (directors who are not employees, officers, or otherwise associated with the corporation; they are also called nonexecutive directors) are becoming a potent force on corporate boards. The trend to promote the use of outside directors has continued—the Sarbanes-Oxley Act of 2002 places emphasis on the use of outside directors to provide balance to the board and protect the corporation's investors.

Removal of Directors and Officers

In 1978, one week before he was scheduled to unveil the 1979 Mustang to trade journalists in person, Lee Iacocca, president of the Ford Motor Company, was summarily fired by unanimous vote of the board of directors, although his departure was billed as a resignation. Iacocca was reported to have asked company chairman Henry Ford II, "What did I do wrong?" To which Ford was said to have replied, "I just don't like you."[12] To return to our usual example: BCT Bookstore is set to announce its acquisition of Borders Group, Inc., a large book retailer that is facing bankruptcy. Alice, one of BCT's directors, was instrumental in the acquisition. One day prior to the announcement of the acquisition, BCT's board relieved Alice of her directorship, providing no reason for the decision. The story raises this question: May a corporate officer, or director for that matter, be fired without cause?

Yes. Many state statutes expressly permit the board to fire an officer with or without cause. However, removal does not defeat an officer's rights under an employment contract. Shareholders may remove directors with or without cause at any meeting called for the purpose. A majority of the shares entitled to vote, not a majority of the shares represented at the meeting, are required for removal.

Meetings

Directors must meet, but the statutes themselves rarely prescribe how frequently. More often, rules prescribing time and place are set out in the bylaws, which may permit members to participate in any meeting by conference telephone. In practice, the frequency of board meetings varies.

The board or committees of the board may take action without meeting if all members of the board or committee consent in writing. A majority of the members of the board constitutes a quorum, unless the bylaws or articles of incorporation specify a larger number. Likewise, a majority present at the meeting is sufficient to carry any motion unless the articles or bylaws specify a larger number.

Compensation

In the past, directors were supposed to serve without pay, as shareholder representatives. The modern practice is to permit the board to determine its own pay unless otherwise fixed in the articles of incorporation. Directors' compensation has risen sharply in recent years. The Dodd-Frank Wall Street Reform and Consumer Protection Act of 2010, however, has made significant changes to compensation, allowing shareholders a "say on pay," or the ability to vote on compensation.

Key Takeaway

The directors exercise corporate powers. They must exercise these powers with good faith. Certain decisions may be delegated to a committee or to corporate officers. There must be at least one director, and directors may be elected at once or in staggered terms. No qualifications are required, and directors may be removed without cause. Directors, just like shareholders, must meet regularly and may be paid for their involvement on the board.

Exercises

1. How would a staggered board prevent a hostile takeover?
2. How can a director be replaced?

45.4 Liability of Directors and Officers

Learning Objectives

1. Examine the fiduciary duties owed by directors and officers.
2. Consider constituency statutes.
3. Discuss modern trends in corporate compliance and fiduciary duties.

Nature of the Problem

Not so long ago, boards of directors of large companies were quiescent bodies, virtual rubber stamps for their friends among management who put them there. By the late 1970s, with the general increase in the climate of litigiousness, one out of every nine companies on the *Fortune* 500 list saw its directors or officers hit with claims for violation of their legal responsibilities.[13] In a seminal case, the Delaware Supreme Court found that the directors of TransUnion were grossly negligent in accepting a buyout price of $55 per share without sufficient inquiry or advice on the adequacy of the price, a breach of their duty of care owed to the shareholders. The directors were held liable for $23.5 million for this breach.[14] Thus serving as a director or an officer was never free of business risks. Today, the task is fraught with legal risk as well.

Two main fiduciary duties apply to both directors and officers: one is a duty of loyalty, the other the duty of care. These duties arise from responsibilities placed upon directors and officers because of their positions within the corporation. The requirements under these duties have been refined over time. Courts and legislatures have both narrowed the duties by defining what is or is not a breach of each duty and have also expanded their scope. Courts have further refined the duties, such as laying out tests such as in the *Caremark* case, outlined in Section 4. Additionally, other duties have been developed, such as the duties of good faith and candor.

Duty of Loyalty

As a fiduciary of the corporation, the director owes his primary loyalty to the corporation and its stockholders, as do the officers and majority shareholders. This responsibility is called the **duty of loyalty**. When there is a conflict between a director's personal interest and the interest of the corporation, he is legally bound to put the corporation's interest above his own. This duty was mentioned in Exercise 3 of Section 2 when Ted usurped a corporate opportunity and will be discussed later in this section.

duty of loyalty

Fiduciary obligation requiring loyalty of directors and officers to the corporation and its shareholders.

FIGURE 45.3 Common Conflict Situations

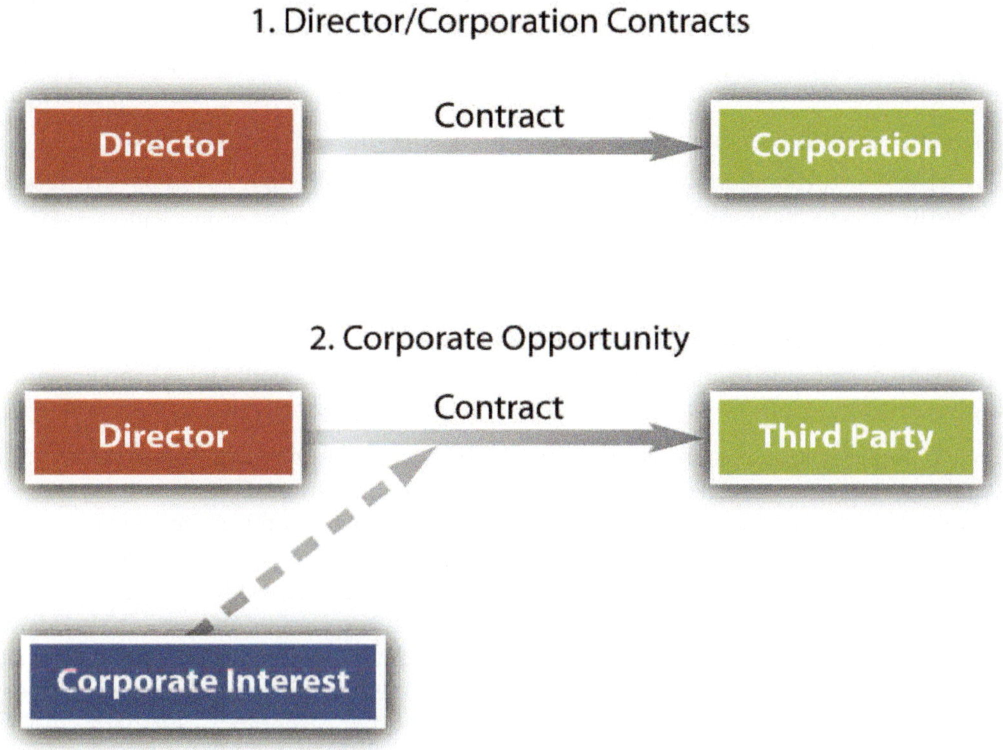

Two situations commonly give rise to the director or officer's duty of loyalty: (1) contracts with the corporation and (2) corporate opportunity (see Figure 45.3).

Contracts with the Corporation

The law does not bar a director from contracting with the corporation he serves. However, unless the contract or transaction is "fair to the corporation," Sections 8.61, 8.62, and 8.63 of the Revised Model Business Corporation Act (RMBCA) impose on him a stringent duty of disclosure. In the absence of a fair transaction, a contract between the corporation and one of its directors is voidable. If the transaction is unfair to the corporation, it may still be permitted if the director has made full disclosure of his personal relationship or interest in the contract and if disinterested board members or shareholders approve the transaction.

Corporate Opportunity

Whenever a director or officer learns of an opportunity to engage in a variety of activities or transactions that might be beneficial to the corporation, his first obligation is to present the opportunity to the corporation. The rule encompasses the chance of acquiring another corporation, purchasing property, and licensing or marketing patents or products. This duty of disclosure was placed into legal lexicon by Judge Cardozo in 1928 when he stated that business partners owe more than a general sense of honor among one another; rather, they owe "the punctilio of honor most sensitive."[15] Thus, when a corporate opportunity arises, business partners must disclose the opportunity, and a failure to disclose is dishonest—a breach of the duty of loyalty.

Whether a particular opportunity is a corporate opportunity can be a delicate question. For example, BCT owns a golf course and a country club. A parcel of land adjacent to their course comes on the market for sale, but BCT takes no action. Two BCT officers purchase the land personally, later informing the BCT board about the purchase and receiving board ratification of their purchase. Then BCT decides to liquidate and enters into an agreement with the two officers to sell both parcels of land. A BCT shareholder brings a derivative suit against the officers, alleging that purchasing the adjacent land stole a corporate opportunity. The shareholder would be successful in his suit. In considering *Farber v. Servan Land Co., Inc.*,[16] a case just like the one described, the *Farber* court laid out four factors in considering whether a corporate opportunity has been usurped:

1. Whether there is an actual corporate opportunity that the firm is considering
2. Whether the corporation's shareholders declined to follow through on the opportunity
3. Whether the board or its shareholders ratified the purchase and, specifically, whether there were a sufficient number of disinterested voters
4. What benefit was missed by the corporation

In considering these factors, the *Farber* court held that the officers had breached a duty of loyalty to the corporation by individually purchasing an asset that would have been deemed a corporate opportunity.

direct interlock

A situation where one person sits on the board of directors of two different companies.

indirect interlock

A situation where directors of two different companies serve jointly on the board of a third company.

When a director serves on more than one board, the problem of corporate opportunity becomes even more complex, because he may be caught in a situation of conflicting loyalties. Moreover, multiple board memberships pose another serious problem. A **direct interlock** occurs when one person sits on the boards of two different companies; an **indirect interlock** happens when directors of two different companies serve jointly on the board of a third company. The Clayton Act prohibits interlocking directorates between direct competitors. Despite this prohibition, as well as public displeasure, corporate board member overlap is commonplace. According to an analysis by *USA Today* and The Corporate Library, eleven of the fifteen largest companies have at least two board members who also sit together on the board of another corporation. Furthermore, CEOs of one corporation often sit on the boards of other corporations. Bank board members may sit on the boards of other corporations, including the bank's own clients. This web of connections has both pros and cons.[17]

Duty of Care

duty of care

Fiduciary obligation upon directors and officers to act with the care an ordinarily prudent person in a like position would exercise under similar circumstances.

The second major aspect of the director's responsibility is that of **duty of care**. Section 8.30 of RMBCA calls on the director to perform his duties "with the care an ordinarily prudent person in a like position would exercise under similar circumstances." An "ordinarily prudent person" means one who directs his intelligence in a thoughtful way to the task at hand. Put another way, a director must make a reasonable effort to inform himself before making a decision, as discussed in the next paragraph. The director is not held to a higher standard required of a specialist (finance, marketing) unless he is one. A director of a small, closely held corporation will not necessarily be held to the same standard as a director who is given a staff by a large, complex, diversified company. The standard of care is that which an ordinarily prudent person would use who is in "a like position" to the director in question. Moreover, the standard is not a timeless one for all people in the same position. The standard can depend on the circumstances: a fast-moving situation calling for a snap decision will be treated differently later, if there are recriminations because it was the wrong decision, than a situation in which time was not of the essence.

What of the care itself? What kind of care would an ordinarily prudent person in any situation be required to give? Unlike the standard of care, which can differ, the care itself has certain requirements. At a minimum, the director must pay attention. He must attend meetings, receive and digest information adequate to inform him about matters requiring board action, and monitor the performance of those to whom he has delegated the task of operating the corporation. Of course, documents can be misleading, reports can be slanted, and information coming from self-interested management can be distorted. To what heights must suspicion be raised? Section 8.30 of the RMBCA forgives directors the necessity of playing detective whenever information, including financial data, is received in an apparently reliable manner from corporate officers or employees or from experts such as attorneys and public accountants. Thus, the director does not need to check with another attorney once he has received financial data from one competent attorney.

A New Jersey Supreme Court decision considered the requirements of fiduciary duties, particularly the duty of care. Pritchard & Baird was a reissuance corporation owned by Pritchard and having four directors: Pritchard, his wife, and his two sons. Pritchard and his sons routinely took loans from the accounts of the firm's clients. After Pritchard died, his sons increased their borrowing, eventually sending the business into bankruptcy. During this time, Mrs. Pritchard developed a fondness for alcohol, drinking heavily and paying little attention to her directorship responsibilities. Creditors sued Mrs. Pritchard for breaches of her fiduciary duties, essentially arguing that the bankruptcy would not have occurred had she been acting properly. After both the trial court and appellate court found for the creditors, the New Jersey Supreme Court took up the case. The court held that a director must have a basic understanding of the business of the corporation upon whose board he or she sits. This can be accomplished by attending meetings, reviewing and understanding financial documents, investigating irregularities, and generally being involved in the corporation. The court found that Mrs. Pritchard's being on the board because she was the spouse was insufficient to excuse her behavior, and that had she been performing her duties, she could have prevented the bankruptcy.[18]

business judgment rule

Presumption given by the courts to corporate directors that their actions were informed and done with good faith and with an honest belief that the actions were in the best interests of the corporation.

Despite the fiduciary requirements, in reality a director does not spend all his time on corporate affairs, is not omnipotent, and must be permitted to rely on the word of others. Nor can directors be infallible in making decisions. Managers work in a business environment, in which risk is a substantial factor. No decision, no matter how rigorously debated, is guaranteed. Accordingly, courts will not second-guess decisions made on the basis of good-faith judgment and due care. This is the **business judgment rule**, mentioned in previous chapters. The business judgment rule was coming into prominence as early as 1919 in *Dodge v. Ford*, discussed in Chapter 44. It has been a pillar of corporate law ever since. As described by the Delaware Supreme Court: "The business judgment rule is an acknowledgment of the managerial prerogatives of Delaware directors....It is a presumption that in making a business decision the directors of a corporation acted on an informed basis, in good faith and in the honest belief that the action taken was in the best interests of the company."[19]

Under the business judgment rule, the actions of directors who fulfill their fiduciary duties will not be second-guessed by a court. The general test is whether a director's decision or transaction was so one sided that no businessperson of ordinary judgment would reach the same decision. The business judgment rule has been refined over time. While the business judgment rule may seem to provide blanket protection for directors (the rule was quite broad as outlined by the court in *Dodge v. Ford*), this is not the case. The rule does not protect every decision made by directors, and they may face lawsuits, a topic to which we now turn. For further discussions of the business judgment rule, see *Cede & Co. v. Technicolor, Inc.*,[20] *In re The Walt Disney Co. Derivative Litigation*,[21] and *Smith v. Van Gorkom*.[22]

If a shareholder is not pleased by a director's decision, that shareholder may file a derivative suit. The derivative suit may be filed by a shareholder on behalf of the corporation against directors or officers of the corporation, alleging breach of their fiduciary obligations. However, a shareholder, as a prerequisite to filing a derivative action, must first demand that the board of directors take action, as the actual party in interest is the corporation, not the shareholder (meaning that if the shareholder is victorious in the lawsuit, it is actually the corporation that "wins"). If the board refuses, is its decision protected by the business judgment rule? The general rule is that the board may refuse to file a derivative suit and will be protected by the business judgment rule. And even when a derivative suit is filed, directors can be protected by the business judgment rule for decisions even the judge considers to have been poorly made. See *In re The Walt Disney Co. Derivative Litigation*, (see Section 5).

In a battle for control of a corporation, directors (especially "inside" directors, who are employees of the corporation, such as officers) often have an inherent self-interest in preserving their positions, which can lead them to block mergers that the shareholders desire and that may be in the firm's best interest. As a result, Delaware courts have modified the usual business judgment presumption in this situation. In *Unocal Corp. v. Mesa Petroleum*,[23] for instance, the court held that directors who adopt a defensive mechanism "must show that they had reasonable grounds for believing that a danger to corporate policy and effectiveness existed. ... [T]hey satisfy that burden 'by showing good faith and reasonable investigation.'" The business judgment rule clearly does not protect every decision of the board. The *Unocal* court developed a test for the board: the directors may only work to prevent a takeover when they can demonstrate a threat to the policies of the corporation and that any defensive measures taken to prevent the takeover were reasonable and proportional given the depth of the threat. The *Unocal* test was modified further by requiring a finding, before a court steps in, that the actions of a board were coercive, a step back toward the business judgment rule.[24]

In a widely publicized case, the Delaware Supreme Court held that the board of Time, Inc. met the *Unocal* test—that the board reasonably concluded that a tender offer by Paramount constituted a threat and acted reasonably in rejecting Paramount's offer and in merging with Warner Communications.[25]

The specific elements of the fiduciary duties are not spelled out in stone. For example, the Delaware courts have laid out three factors to examine when determining whether a duty of care has been breached:[26]

1. The directors knew, or should have known, that legal breaches were occurring.
2. The directors took no steps to prevent or resolve the situation.
3. This failure caused the losses about which the shareholder is complaining in a derivative suit.

duty of good faith

Fiduciary duty to act honestly and avoid violations of corporate norms and business practices.

Thus the court expanded the duty of oversight (which is included under the umbrella of the duty of care; these duties are often referred to as the *Caremark* duties). Furthermore, courts have recognized a **duty of good faith**—a duty to act honestly and avoid violations of corporate norms and business practices.[27] Therefore, the split in ownership and decision making within the corporate structure causes rifts, and courts are working toward balancing the responsibilities of the directors to their shareholders with their ability to run the corporation.

Constituency Statutes and Corporate Social Responsibility

Until the 1980s, the law in all the states imposed on corporate directors the obligation to advance shareholders' economic interests to ensure the long-term profitability of the corporation. Other groups—employees, local communities and neighbors, customers, suppliers, and creditors—took a back seat to this primary responsibility of directors. Of course, directors could consider the welfare of these other groups if in so doing they promoted the interests of shareholders. But directors were not legally permitted to favor the interests of others over shareholders. The prevailing rule was, and often still is, that maximizing shareholder value is the primary duty of the board. Thus in *Revlon, Inc. v. MacAndrews & Forbes Holdings, Inc.*,[28] the Delaware Supreme Court held that Revlon's directors had breached their fiduciary duty to the company's shareholders in response to a hostile tender offer from Pantry Pride. While the facts of the case are intricate, the general gist is that the Revlon directors thwarted the hostile tender by adopting a variation of a poison pill involving a tender offer for their own shares in exchange for debt, effectively eliminating Pantry Pride's ability to take over the firm. Pantry Pride upped its offer price, and in response, Revlon began negotiating with a leveraged buyout by a third party, Forstmann Little. Pantry Pride publicly announced it would top any bid made by Forstmann Little. Despite this, the Revlon board negotiated a deal with Forstmann Little. The court noted an exception to the general rule that permitted directors to consider the interests of other groups as long as "there are rationally related benefits accruing to the stockholders." But when a company is about to be taken over, the object must be to sell it to the highest bidder, Pantry Pride in this case. It is then, said the court, in situations where the corporation is to be sold, that "concern for nonstockholder interests is inappropriate," thus giving rise to what are commonly called the Revlon duties.

constituency statutes

Statutes that permit corporate directors to take into account interests other than maximizing shareholder value.

Post-*Revlon*, in response to a wave of takeovers in the late 1980s, some states have enacted laws to give directors legal authority to take account of interests other than those of shareholders in deciding how to defend against hostile mergers and acquisitions. These laws are known as **constituency statutes**, because they permit directors to take account of the interests of other constituencies of corporations. These do not permit a corporation to avoid its Revlon duties (that when a corporation is up for sale, it must be sold to the highest bidder) but will allow a corporation to consider factors other than shareholder value in determining whether to make charitable donations or reinvest profits. This ability has been further expanding as the concept of corporate social responsibility has grown, as discussed later in this section.

Although the other constituency statutes are not identically worded, they are all designed to release directors from their formal legal obligation to keep paramount the interests of shareholders. The Pennsylvania and Indiana statutes make this clear; statutes in other states are worded a bit more ambiguously, but the intent of the legislatures in enacting these laws seems clear: directors may give voice to employees worried about the loss of jobs or to communities worried about the possibility that an out-of-state acquiring company may close down a local factory to the detriment of the local economy. So broadly worded are these laws that although the motive for enacting them was to give directors a weapon in fighting hostile tender offers, in some states the principle applies to any decision by a board of directors. So, for example, it is possible that a board might legally decide to give a large charitable grant to a local community—a grant so large that it would materially decrease an annual dividend, contrary to the general rule that at some point the interests of shareholders in dividends clearly outweighs the board's power to spend corporate profits on "good works."

Critics have attacked the constituency statutes on two major grounds: first, they substitute a clear principle of conduct for an amorphous one, because they give no guidance on how directors are supposed to weigh the interests of a corporation's various constituencies. Second, they make it more difficult for shareholders to monitor the performance of a company's board; measuring decisions against the single goal of profit maximization is far easier than against the subjective goal of "balancing" a host of competing interests. Constituency statutes run contrary to the concept of shareholders as owners, and of the fiduciary duties owed to them, effectively softening shareholder power. Nevertheless, since many states now have constituency statutes, it is only reasonable to expect that the traditional doctrine holding shareholder interests paramount will begin to give way, even as the shareholders challenge new decisions by directors that favor communities, employees, and others with an important stake in the welfare of the corporations with which they deal. For a more complete discussion of constituency statutes, see "Corporate Governance and the Sarbanes-Oxley Act: Corporate Constituency Statutes and Employee Governance."[29]

Many modern corporations have begun to promote socially responsible behavior. While dumping toxic waste out the back door of the manufacturing facility rather than expending funds to properly dispose of the waste may result in an increase in value, the consequences of dumping the waste can be quite severe, whether from fines from regulatory authorities or from public backlash. Corporate social responsibility results from internal corporate policies that attempt to self-regulate and fulfill legal, ethical, and social obligations. Thus, under corporate social responsibility, corporations may make donations to charitable organizations or build environmentally friendly or energy-efficient buildings. Socially irresponsible behavior can be quite disastrous for a corporation. Nike, for example, was hit by consumer backlash due to its use of child labor in other countries, such as India and Malaysia. British Petroleum (BP) faced public anger as well as fines and lawsuits for a massive oil spill in the Gulf of Mexico. This spill had serious consequences for BP's shareholders—BP stopped paying dividends, its stock price plummeted, and it had to set aside significant amounts of money to compensate injured individuals and businesses.

Many businesses try to fulfill what is commonly called the triple bottom line, which is a focus on profits, people, and the planet. For example, Ben and Jerry's, the ice cream manufacturer, had followed a triple bottom line practice for many years. Nonetheless, when Ben and Jerry's found itself the desired acquisition of several other businesses, it feared that a takeover of the firm would remove this focus, since for some firms, there is only one bottom line—profits. Unilever offered $43.60 per share for Ben and Jerry's. Several Ben and Jerry's insiders made a counteroffer at $38 per share, arguing that a lower price was justified given the firm's focus. Ultimately, in a case like this, the Revlon duties come into play: when a corporation is for sale, corporate social responsibility goes out the window and only one bottom line exists—maximum shareholder value. In the case of Ben and Jerry's, the company was acquired in 2000 for $326 million by Unilever, the Anglo-Dutch corporation that is the world's largest consumer products company.

Sarbanes-Oxley and Other Modern Trends

The Sarbanes-Oxley Act of 2002, enacted following several accounting scandals, strengthens the duties owed by the board and other corporate officers. In particular, Title III contains corporate responsibility provisions, such as requiring senior executives to vouch for the accuracy and completeness of their corporation's financial disclosures. While the main goal of Sarbanes-Oxley is to decrease the incidents of financial fraud and accounting tricks, its operative goal is to strengthen the fiduciary duties of loyalty and care as well as good faith.

The modern trend has been to impose more duties. Delaware has been adding to the list of fiduciary responsibilities other than loyalty and care. As mentioned previously, the Delaware judicial system consistently recognizes a duty of good faith. The courts have further added a duty of candor with shareholders when the corporation is disseminating information to its investors. Particular duties arise in the context of mergers, acquisitions, and tender offers. As mentioned previously in the *Revlon* case, the duty owed to shareholders in situations of competing tender offers is that of maximum value. Other duties may arise, such as when directors attempt to retain their positions on the board in the face of a hostile tender offer. Trends in fiduciary responsibilities, as well as other changes in the business legal field, are covered extensively by the American Bar Association at http://www.americanbar.org/groups/business_law.html.

Liability Prevention and Insurance

Alice, the director of BCT, has been charged with breaching her duty of care. Is she personally liable for a breach of the duty of care? How can a director avoid liability? Of course, she can never avoid defending a lawsuit, for in the wake of any large corporate difficulty—from a thwarted takeover bid to a bankruptcy—some group of shareholders will surely sue. But the director can immunize herself ultimately by carrying out her duties of loyalty and care. In practice, this often means that she should be prepared to document the reasonableness of her reliance on information from all sources considered. Second, if the director dissents from action that she considers mistaken or unlawful, she should ensure that her negative vote is recorded. Silence is construed as assent to any proposition before the board, and assent to a woefully mistaken action can be the basis for staggering liability.

Corporations, however, are permitted to limit or eliminate the personal liability of its directors. For example, Delaware law permits the articles of incorporation to contain a provision eliminating or limiting the personal liability of directors to the corporation, with some limitations.[30]

Beyond preventive techniques, another measure of protection from director liability is **indemnification** (reimbursement). In most states, the corporation may agree under certain circumstances to indemnify directors, officers, and employees for expenses resulting from litigation when they are made party to suits involving the corporation. In third-party actions (those brought by outsiders), the corporation may reimburse the director, officer, or employee for all expenses (including attorneys' fees), judgments, fines, and settlement amounts. In derivative actions, the corporation's power to indemnify is more limited. For example, reimbursement for litigation expenses of directors adjudged liable for negligence or misconduct is allowed only if the court approves. In both third-party and derivative actions, the corporation must provide indemnification expenses when the defense is successful.

indemnification

A method of protecting directors and officers whereby the corporation agrees to pay legal expenses incurred by the directors or officers.

Whether or not they have the power to indemnify, corporations may purchase liability insurance for directors, officers, and employees (for directors and officers, the insurance is commonly referred to as D&O insurance). But insurance policies do not cover every act. Most exclude "willful negligence" and criminal conduct in which intent is a necessary element of proof. Furthermore, the cost of liability insurance has increased dramatically in recent years, causing some companies to cancel their coverage. This, in turn, jeopardizes the recent movement toward outside directors because many directors might prefer to leave or decline to serve on boards that have inadequate liability coverage. As a result, most states have enacted legislation that allows a corporation, through a charter amendment approved by shareholders, to limit the personal liability of its outside directors for failing to exercise due care. In 1990, Section 2.02 of the RMBCA was amended to provide that the articles of incorporation may include "a provision eliminating or limiting the liability of a director to the corporation or its shareholders for money damages. ..." This section includes certain exceptions; for example, the articles may not limit liability for intentional violations of criminal law. Delaware Code Section 102(b)(7), as mentioned previously, was enacted after *Smith v. Van Gorkom* (discussed in Section 4) and was prompted by an outcry about the court's decision. As a result, many corporations now use similar provisions to limit director liability. For example, Delaware and California permit the limitation or abolition of liability for director's breach of the duty of care except in instances of fraud, bad faith, or willful misconduct.

Key Takeaway

Directors and officers have two main fiduciary duties: the duty of loyalty and the duty of care. The duty of loyalty is a responsibility to act in the best interest of the corporation, even when that action may conflict with a personal interest. This duty commonly arises in contracts with the corporation and with corporate opportunities. The duty of care requires directors and officers to act with the care of an ordinarily prudent person in like circumstances. The business judgment rule may protect directors and officers, since courts give a presumption to the corporation that its personnel are informed and act in good faith. A shareholder may file a derivative lawsuit on behalf of the corporation against corporate insiders for breaches of these fiduciary obligations or other actions that harm the corporation. While directors and officers have obligations to the corporation and its shareholders, they may weigh other considerations under constituency statutes. In response to recent debacles, state and federal laws, such as Sarbanes-Oxley, have placed further requirements on officers and directors. Director and officer expenses in defending claims of wrongful acts may be covered through indemnification or insurance.

Exercises

1. What are the two major fiduciary responsibilities that directors and officers owe to the corporation and its shareholders?
2. What are some benefits of having interlocking directorates? What are some disadvantages?
3. Is there any connection between the business judgment rule and constituency statutes?

45.5 Cases

Ultra Vires Acts

Cross v. The Midtown Club, Inc.

33 Conn. Supp. 150; 365 A.2d 1227 (Conn. 1976)

STAPLETON, JUDGE.

The following facts are admitted or undisputed: The plaintiff is a member in good standing of the defendant nonstock Connecticut corporation. Each of the individual defendants is a director of the corporation, and together the individual defendants constitute the entire board of directors. The certificate of incorporation sets forth that the sole purpose of the corporation is "to provide facilities for the serving of luncheon or other meals to members." Neither the certificate of incorporation nor the bylaws of the corporation contain any qualifications for membership, nor does either contain any restrictions on the luncheon guests members may bring to the club. The plaintiff sought to bring a female to lunch with him, and both he and his guest were refused seating at the luncheon facility. The plaintiff wrote twice to the president of the corporation to protest the action, but he received no reply to either letter. On three different occasions, the plaintiff submitted applications for membership on behalf of a different female, and only on the third of those occasions did the board process the application, which it then rejected. Shortly after both of the above occurrences, the board of directors conducted two separate pollings of its members, one by mail, the other by a special meeting held to vote on four alternative proposals for amending the bylaws of corporation concerning the admission of women members and guests. None of these proposed amendments to the bylaws received the required number of votes for adoption. Following that balloting, the plaintiff again wrote to the president of the corporation and asked that the directors stop interfering with his rights as a member to bring women guests to the luncheon facility and to propose women for membership. The president's reply was that "the existing bylaws, house rules and customs continue in effect, and therefore [the board] consider[s] the matter closed."

* * *

In addition to seeking a declaratory judgment which will inform him of his rights vis-à-vis the corporation and its directors, the plaintiff is also seeking injunctive relief, orders directing the admission of the plaintiff's candidate to membership and denying indemnity to the directors, money damages, and costs and expenses including reasonable attorney's fees. It should be noted at the outset that the plaintiff is not making a claim under either the federal or state civil rights or equal accommodations statutes, but that he is solely asserting his membership rights under the certificate of incorporation, the bylaws, and the statutes governing the regulation of this nonstock corporation. As such, this is a case of first impression in Connecticut.

* * *

Connecticut has codified the common-law right of a member to proceed against his corporation or its directors in the event of an ultra vires act. In fact, it has been done specifically under the Nonstock Corporation Act.

No powers were given to the defendant corporation in its certificate of incorporation, only a purpose, and as a result the only incidental powers which the defendant would have under the common law are those which are necessary to effect its purpose, that being to serve lunch to its members. Since the club was not formed for the purpose of having an exclusively male luncheon club, it cannot be considered necessary to its stated purpose for the club to have the implied power at common law to exclude women members.

Under the Connecticut Nonstock Corporation Act, the corporation could have set forth in its certificate of incorporation that its purpose was to engage in any lawful activity permitted that corporation. That was not done. Its corporate purposes were very narrowly stated to be solely for providing "facilities for the serving of luncheon or other meals to members." The certificate did not restrict the purpose to the serving of male members. Section 33-428 of the General Statutes provides that the corporate powers of a nonstock corporation are those set forth in the Nonstock Corporation Act, those specifically stated in the certificate of incorporation, neither of which includes the power to exclude women members, and the implied power to "exercise all legal powers necessary or convenient to effect any or all of the purposes stated in its certificate of incorporation. ..."

We come, thus, to the nub of this controversy and the basic legal question raised by the facts in this case: Is it necessary or convenient to the purpose for which this corporation was organized for it to exclude women members? This court concludes that it is not. While a corporation might be organized for the narrower purpose of providing a luncheon club for men only, this one was not so organized. Its stated purpose is broader and this court cannot find that it is either necessary or convenient to that purpose for its membership to be restricted to men. It should be borne in mind that this club is one of the principal luncheon clubs for business and professional people in Stamford. It is a gathering place where a great many of the civic, business, and professional affairs of the Stamford community are discussed in an atmosphere of social intercourse. Given the scope of the entry of women today into the business and professional life of the community and the changing status of women before the law and in society, it would be anomalous indeed for this court to conclude that it is either necessary or convenient to the stated purpose for which it was organized for this club to exclude women as members or guests.

While the bylaws recognize the right of a member to bring guests to the club, the exclusion of women guests is nowhere authorized and would not appear to be any more necessary and convenient to the purpose of the club than the exclusion of women members. The bylaws at present contain no restrictions against female members or guests and even if they could be interpreted as authorizing those restrictions, they would be of no validity in light of the requirement of § 33-459 (a) of the General Statutes, that the bylaws must be "reasonable [and] germane to the purposes of the corporation...."

The court therefore concludes that the actions and policies of the defendants in excluding women as members and guests solely on the basis of sex is ultra vires and beyond the power of the corporation and its management under its certificate of incorporation and the Nonstock Corporation Act, and in derogation of the rights of the plaintiff as a member thereof. The plaintiff is entitled to a declaratory judgment to that effect and one may enter accordingly.

Case Questions

1. What is the basis of the plaintiff's claim?
2. Would the club have had a better defense against the plaintiff's claim if its purpose was "to provide facilities for the serving of luncheon or other meals to male members"?
3. Had the corporation's purpose read as it does in Question 2, would the plaintiff have had other bases for a claim?

Business Judgment Rule

In re The Walt Disney Co. Derivative Litigation
907 A.2d 693 (Del. Ch. 2005)

JACOBS, Justice:

[In 1995, the Walt Disney Company hired Michael Ovitz as its executive president and as a board member for five years. This was done after lengthy compensation negotiations regarding Ovitz's compensation, negotiations done by its then CEO Michael Eisner and two of the members of the compensation committee (a four-member panel). The terms of Ovitz's compensation were then presented to the full board. In a meeting lasting around one hour, where a variety of topics were discussed, the board approved Ovitz's compensation after reviewing only a term sheet rather than the full contract. The full contract was extremely generous to Ovitz, and included termination payments that would give Ovitz $10 million [about $16 million in 2017 dollars] plus $7.5 million for each year remaining on his five year contract as well as a vesting of stock options.

Ovitz's time at Disney was tumultuous and short-lived.] * * * In December 1996, only fourteen months after he commenced employment, Ovitz was terminated without cause, resulting in a severance payout to Ovitz valued at approximately $130 million [about $202 million in 2017 dollars]. Under the original employment contract, Ovitz was entitled to this under a "no fault termination," with $39 million due under the remainder of his contract, and the stock options' vesting–with a value of $101 million.

Because Ovitz time in office had been so dismal for Disney, and the severance package was so generous, Disney shareholders then filed derivative actions on behalf of Disney against Ovitz and the directors of Disney (the "Disney defendants"), claiming that the $130 million severance payout was the product of fiduciary duty and contractual breaches by Ovitz and of breaches of fiduciary duty by the Disney defendants and a waste of assets. The Chancellor found in favor of the defendants. The plaintiff appealed.

We next turn to the claims of error that relate to the Disney defendants. Those claims are subdivisible into two groups: (A) claims arising out of the approval of the OEA [Ovitz employment agreement] and of Ovitz's election as President; and (B) claims arising out of the NFT [nonfault termination] severance payment to Ovitz upon his termination. We address separately those two categories and the issues that they generate. ...

... [The due care] argument is best understood against the backdrop of the presumptions that cloak director action being reviewed under the business judgment standard. Our law presumes that "in making a business decision the directors of a corporation acted on an informed basis, in good faith, and in the honest belief that the action taken was in the best interests of the company." Those presumptions can be rebutted if the plaintiff shows that the directors breached their fiduciary duty of care or of loyalty or acted in bad faith. If that is shown, the burden then shifts to the director defendants to demonstrate that the challenged act or transaction was entirely fair to the corporation and its shareholders. ...

The appellants' first claim is that the Chancellor erroneously (i) failed to make a "threshold determination" of gross negligence, and (ii) "conflated" the appellants' burden to rebut the business judgment presumptions, with an analysis of whether the directors' conduct fell within the 8 *Del. C.* § 102(b)(7) provision that precludes exculpation of directors from monetary liability "for acts or omissions not in good faith." The argument runs as follows: *Emerald Partners v. Berlin* required the Chancellor first to determine whether the business judgment rule presumptions were rebutted based upon a showing that the board violated its duty of care, *i.e.*, acted with gross negligence. If gross negligence were established, the burden would shift to the directors to establish that the OEA was entirely fair. Only if the directors failed to meet that burden could the trial court then address the directors' Section 102(b)(7) exculpation defense, including the statutory exception for acts not in good faith.

This argument lacks merit. To make the argument the appellants must ignore the distinction between (i) a determination of bad faith for the threshold purpose of rebutting the business judgment rule presumptions, and (ii) a bad faith determination for purposes of evaluating the availability of charter-authorized exculpation from monetary damage liability after liability has been established. Our law clearly permits a judicial assessment of director good faith for that former purpose. Nothing in *Emerald Partners* requires the Court of Chancery to consider only evidence of lack of due care (*i.e.* gross negligence) in determining whether the business judgment rule presumptions have been rebutted. * * *

The appellants argue that the Disney directors breached their duty of care by failing to inform themselves of all material information reasonably available with respect to Ovitz's employment agreement. ... [but the] only properly reviewable action of the entire board was its decision to elect Ovitz as Disney's President. In that context the sole issue, as the Chancellor properly held, is "whether [the remaining members of the old board] properly exercised their business judgment and acted in accordance with their fiduciary duties when they elected Ovitz to the Company's presidency." The Chancellor determined that in electing Ovitz, the directors were informed of all information reasonably available and, thus, were not grossly negligent. We agree.

* * * [The court turns to good faith.] The Court of Chancery held that the business judgment rule presumptions protected the decisions of the compensation committee and the remaining Disney directors, not only because they had acted with due care but also because they had not acted in bad faith. That latter ruling, the appellants claim, was reversible error because the Chancellor formulated and then applied an incorrect definition of bad faith.

* * * Their argument runs as follows: under the Chancellor's 2003 definition of bad faith, the directors must have "*consciously and intentionally disregarded their responsibilities*, adopting a 'we don't care about the risks' attitude concerning a material corporate decision." Under the 2003 formulation, appellants say, "directors violate their duty of good faith if they are making material decisions without adequate information and without adequate deliberation[,]" but under the 2005 post-trial definition, bad faith requires proof of a subjective bad motive or intent. This definitional change, it is claimed, was procedurally prejudicial because appellants relied on the 2003 definition in presenting their evidence of bad faith at the trial. * * *

Second, the appellants claim that the Chancellor's post-trial definition of bad faith is erroneous substantively. They argue that the 2003 formulation was (and is) the correct definition, because it is "logically tied to board decision-making under the duty of care." The post-trial formulation, on the other hand, "wrongly incorporated substantive elements regarding the rationality of the decisions under review rather than being constrained, as in a due care analysis, to strictly procedural criteria." We conclude that both arguments must fail.

The appellants' first argument—that there is a real, significant difference between the Chancellor's pre-trial and post-trial definitions of bad faith—is plainly wrong. We perceive no substantive difference between the Court of Chancery's 2003 definition of bad faith—a "conscious and intentional disregard [of] responsibilities, adopting a we don't care about the risks' attitude..."—and its 2005 post-trial definition—an "intentional dereliction of duty, a conscious disregard for one's responsibilities." Both formulations express the same concept, although in slightly different language.

The most telling evidence that there is no substantive difference between the two formulations is that the appellants are forced to contrive a difference. Appellants assert that under the 2003 formulation, "directors violate their duty of good faith if they are making material decisions without adequate information and without adequate deliberation." For that *ipse dixit* they cite no legal authority. That comes as no surprise because their verbal effort to collapse the duty to act in good faith into the duty to act with due care, is not unlike putting a rabbit into the proverbial hat and then blaming the trial judge for making the insertion.

* * * The precise question is whether the Chancellor's articulated standard for bad faith corporate fiduciary conduct—intentional dereliction of duty, a conscious disregard for one's responsibilities—is legally correct. In approaching that question, we note that the Chancellor characterized that definition as "*an* appropriate (*although not the only*) standard for determining whether fiduciaries have acted in good faith." That observation is accurate and helpful, because as a matter of simple logic, at least three different categories of fiduciary behavior are candidates for the "bad faith" pejorative label.

The first category involves so-called "subjective bad faith," that is, fiduciary conduct motivated by an actual intent to do harm. That such conduct constitutes classic, quintessential bad faith is a proposition so well accepted in the liturgy of fiduciary law that it borders on axiomatic. * * * The second category of conduct, which is at the opposite end of the spectrum, involves lack of due care—that is, fiduciary action taken solely by reason of gross negligence and without any malevolent intent. In this case, appellants assert claims of gross negligence to establish breaches not only of director due care but also of the directors' duty to act in good faith. Although the Chancellor found, and we agree, that the appellants failed to establish gross negligence, to afford guidance we address the issue of whether gross negligence (including a failure to inform one's self of available material facts), without more, can also constitute bad faith. The answer is clearly no.

* * * [I]ssues of good faith are (to a certain degree) inseparably and necessarily intertwined with the duties of care and loyalty. * * * " But, in the pragmatic, conduct-regulating legal realm which calls for more precise conceptual line drawing, the answer is that grossly negligent conduct, without more, does not and cannot constitute a breach of the fiduciary duty to act in good faith. The conduct that is the subject of due care may overlap with the conduct that comes within the rubric of good faith in a psychological sense, but from a legal standpoint those duties are and must remain quite distinct. * * *

The Delaware General Assembly has addressed the distinction between bad faith and a failure to exercise due care (*i.e.*, gross negligence) in two separate contexts. The first is Section 102(b)(7) of the DGCL, which authorizes Delaware corporations, by a provision in the certificate of incorporation, to exculpate their directors from monetary damage liability for a breach of the duty of care. That exculpatory provision affords significant protection to directors of Delaware corporations. The statute carves out several exceptions, however, including most relevantly, "for acts or omissions not in good faith. * * * " Thus, a corporation can exculpate its directors from monetary liability for a breach of the duty of care, but not for conduct that is not in good faith. To adopt a definition of bad faith that would cause a violation of the duty of care automatically to become an act or omission "not in good faith," would eviscerate the protections accorded to directors by the General Assembly's adoption of Section 102(b)(7).

A second legislative recognition of the distinction between fiduciary conduct that is grossly negligent and conduct that is not in good faith, is Delaware's indemnification statute, found at 8 *Del. C.* § 145. To oversimplify, subsections (a) and (b) of that statute permit a corporation to indemnify (*inter alia*) any person who is or was a director, officer, employee or agent of the corporation against expenses * * * where (among other things): (i) that person is, was, or is threatened to be made a party to that action, suit or proceeding, and (ii) that person "acted in good faith and in a manner the person reasonably believed to be in or not opposed to the best interests of the corporation. * * * " Thus, under Delaware statutory law a director or officer of a corporation can be indemnified for liability (and litigation expenses) incurred by reason of a violation of the duty of care, but not for a violation of the duty to act in good faith.

Section 145, like Section 102(b)(7), evidences the intent of the Delaware General Assembly to afford significant protections to directors (and, in the case of Section 145, other fiduciaries) of Delaware corporations. To adopt a definition that conflates the duty of care with the duty to act in good faith by making a violation of the former an automatic violation of the latter, would nullify those legislative protections and defeat the General Assembly's intent. There is no basis in policy, precedent or common sense that would justify dismantling the distinction between gross negligence and bad faith.

That leaves the third category of fiduciary conduct, which falls in between the first two categories of (1) conduct motivated by subjective bad intent and (2) conduct resulting from gross negligence. This third category is what the Chancellor's definition of bad faith—intentional dereliction of duty, a conscious disregard for one's responsibilities—is intended to capture. The question is whether such misconduct is properly treated as a non-exculpable, non-indemnifiable violation of the fiduciary duty to act in good faith. In our view it must be, for at least two reasons.

First, the universe of fiduciary misconduct is not limited to either disloyalty in the classic sense (*i.e.*, preferring the adverse self-interest of the fiduciary or of a related person to the interest of the corporation) or gross negligence. Cases have arisen where corporate directors have no conflicting self-interest in a decision, yet engage in misconduct that is more culpable than simple inattention or failure to be informed of all facts material to the decision. To protect the interests of the corporation and its shareholders, fiduciary conduct of this kind, which does not involve disloyalty (as traditionally defined) but is qualitatively more culpable than gross negligence, should be proscribed. A vehicle is needed to address such violations doctrinally, and that doctrinal vehicle is the duty to act in good faith. The Chancellor implicitly so recognized in his Opinion, where he identified different examples of bad faith as follows:

The good faith required of a corporate fiduciary includes not simply the duties of care and loyalty, in the narrow sense that I have discussed them above, but all actions required by a true faithfulness and devotion to the interests of the corporation and its shareholders. A failure to act in good faith may be shown, for instance, where the fiduciary intentionally acts with a purpose other than that of advancing the best interests of the corporation, where the fiduciary acts with the intent to violate applicable positive law, or where the fiduciary intentionally fails to act in the face of a known duty to act, demonstrating a conscious disregard for his duties. There may be other examples of bad faith yet to be proven or alleged, but these three are the most salient.

* * * Second, the legislature has also recognized this intermediate category of fiduciary misconduct, which ranks between conduct involving subjective bad faith and gross negligence. Section 102(b)(7)(ii) of the DGCL expressly denies money damage exculpation for "acts or omissions not in good faith or which involve intentional misconduct or a knowing violation of law." By its very terms that provision distinguishes between "intentional misconduct" and a "knowing violation of law" (both examples of subjective bad faith) on the one hand, and "acts * * * not in good faith," on the other. Because the statute exculpates directors only for conduct amounting to gross negligence, the statutory denial of exculpation for "acts * * * not in good faith" must encompass the intermediate category of misconduct captured by the Chancellor's definition of bad faith.

For these reasons, we uphold the Court of Chancery's definition as a legally appropriate, although not the exclusive, definition of fiduciary bad faith. We need go no further. To engage in an effort to craft (in the Court's words) "a definitive and categorical definition of the universe of acts that would constitute bad faith" would be unwise and is unnecessary to dispose of the issues presented on this appeal. * * *

For the reasons stated above, the judgment of the Court of Chancery is affirmed.

Case Questions

1. Did the Court here find that the Directors had breached the duty of due care? What do you think? (Were they grossly negligent?)
2. If the Directors that approved the OEA (Ovitz employment agreement) were not grossly negligent, can the shareholders possibly win this derivative litigation?
3. What remedies do shareholders have, other than a shareholders' derivative lawsuit?
4. Does this court recognize two different formulations of "bad faith," one from 2003 and one from the "post trial 2005 definition"?
5. What are the "three categories" of "bad faith" that would be recognizable as breaches of directors' fiduciary duties?

45.6 Summary and Exercises

Summary

A corporation may exercise two types of powers: (1) express powers, set forth by statute and in the articles of incorporation, and (2) implied powers, necessary to carry out its stated purpose. The corporation may always amend the articles of incorporation to change its purposes. Nevertheless, shareholders may enjoin their corporation from acting ultra vires, as may the state attorney general. However, an individual stockholder, director, or officer (except in rare instances under certain regulatory statutes) may not be held vicariously liable if he did not participate in the crime or tort.

Because ownership and control are separated in the modern publicly held corporation, shareholders generally do not make business decisions. Shareholders who own voting stock do retain the power to elect directors, amend the bylaws, ratify or reject certain corporate actions, and vote on certain extraordinary matters, such as whether to amend the articles of incorporation, merge, or liquidate.

In voting for directors, various voting methodologies may be used, such as cumulative voting, which provides safeguards against removal of minority-shareholder-supported directors. Shareholders may use several voting arrangements that concentrate power, including proxies, voting agreements, and voting trusts. Proxies are regulated under rules promulgated by the Securities and Exchange Commission (SEC).

Corporations may deny preemptive rights—the rights of shareholders to prevent dilution of their percentage of ownership—by so stating in the articles of incorporation. Some states say that in the absence of such a provision, shareholders do have preemptive rights; others say that there are no preemptive rights unless the articles specifically include them.

Directors have the ultimate authority to run the corporation and are fiduciaries of the firm. In large corporations, directors delegate day-to-day management to salaried officers, whom they may fire, in most states, without cause. The full board of directors may, by majority, vote to delegate its authority to committees.

Directors owe the company a duty of loyalty and of care. A contract between a director and the company is voidable unless fair to the corporation or unless all details have been disclosed and the disinterested directors or shareholders have approved. Any director or officer is obligated to inform fellow directors of any corporate opportunity that affects the company and may not act personally on it unless he has received approval. The duty of care is the obligation to act "with the care an ordinarily prudent person in a like position would exercise under similar circumstances." Other fiduciary duties have also been recognized, and constituency statutes permit the corporation to consider factors other than shareholders in making decisions. Shareholders may file derivative suits alleging breaches of fiduciary responsibilities. The duties have been expanded. For example, when the corporation is being sold, the directors have a duty to maximize shareholder value. Duties of oversight, good faith, and candor have been applied.

The corporation may agree, although not in every situation, to indemnify officers, directors, and employees for litigation expenses when they are made party to suits involving the corporation. The corporation may purchase insurance against legal expenses of directors and officers, but the policies do not cover acts of willful negligence and criminal conduct in which intent is a necessary element of proof. Additionally, the business judgment rule may operate to protect the decisions of the board.

The general rule is to maximize shareholder value, but over time, corporations have been permitted to consider other factors in decision making. Constituency statutes, for example, allow the board to consider factors other than maximizing shareholder value. Corporate social responsibility has increased, as firms consider things such as environmental impact and consumer perception in making decisions.

Exercises

1. First Corporation, a Massachusetts company, decides to expend $100,000 to publicize its support of a candidate in an upcoming presidential election. A Massachusetts statute forbids corporate expenditures for the purpose of influencing the vote in elections. Chauncey, a shareholder in First Corporation, feels that the company should support a different presidential candidate and files suit to stop the company's publicizing efforts. What is the result? Why?
2. Assume in Exercise 1 that Chauncey is both an officer and a director of First Corporation. At a duly called meeting of the board, the directors decide to dismiss Chauncey as an officer and a director. If they had no cause for this action, is the dismissal valid? Why?
3. A book publisher that specializes in children's books has decided to publish pornographic literature for adults. Amanda, a shareholder in the company, has been active for years in an antipornography campaign. When she demands access to the publisher's books and records, the company refuses. She files suit. What arguments should Amanda raise in the litigation? Why?
4. The CEO of First Bank, without prior notice to the board, announced a merger proposal during a two-hour meeting of the directors. Under the proposal, the bank was to be sold to an acquirer at $55 per share. (At the time, the stock traded at $38 per share.) After the CEO discussed the proposal for twenty minutes, with no documentation to support the adequacy of the price, the board voted in favor of the proposal. Senior management approved the proposal, and it was eventually approved by the stockholders, with 70 percent in favor and 7 percent opposed. A group of stockholders later filed a class action, claiming that the directors were personally liable for the amount by which the fair value of the shares exceeded $55—an amount allegedly in excess of $100 million. Are the directors personally liable? Why or why not?

Self-Test Questions

1. Acts that are outside a corporation's lawful powers are considered
    a. ultra vires
    b. express powers
    c. implied powers
    d. none of the above
2. Powers set forth by statute and in the articles of incorporation are called
    a. implied powers
    b. express powers
    c. ultra vires
    d. incorporation by estoppel
3. The principle that mistakes made by directors on the basis of good-faith judgment can be forgiven
    a. is called the business judgment rule
    b. depends on whether the director has exercised due care
    c. involves both of the above
    d. involves neither of the above

4. A director of a corporation owes
    a. a duty of loyalty
    b. a duty of care
    c. both a duty of loyalty and a duty of care
    d. none of the above
5. A corporation may purchase indemnification insurance
    a. to cover acts of simple negligence
    b. to cover acts of willful negligence
    c. to cover acts of both simple and willful negligence
    d. to cover acts of criminal conduct

Self-Test Answers

1. a
2. b
3. c
4. c
5. a

Endnotes

1. Del. Code Ann., Title 8, Section 284 (2011).
2. Adam Sulkowski, "Ultra Vires Statutes: Alive, Kicking, and a Means of Circumventing the Scalia Standing Gauntlet," *Journal of Environmental Law and Litigation* 14, no. 1 (2009): 75.
3. http://www.pbs.org/wgbh/frontline/article/too-big-to-jail-the-top-10-civil-cases-against-the-banks/.
4. *People v. O'Neil*, 550 N.E. 2d 1090 (Ill. App. 1990).
5. https://www.nolo.com/legal-encyclopedia/content/rico-act.html.
6. *United States v. Park*, 421 U.S. 658 (1975).
7. *Commonwealth v. Penn Valley Resorts*, 494 A.2d 1139 (Pa. Super. 1985).
8. *Business Roundtable v. SEC*, 905 F.2d 406 (D.C. Cir. 1990).
9. *Pillsbury v. Honeywell*, 291 Minn. 322; 191 N.W.2d 406 (Minn. 1971).
10. *The Conservative Caucus Research, Analysis & Education Foundation, Inc. v. Chevron*, 525 A.2d 569 (Del. 1987). See Del. Code Ann., Title 8, Section 220 (2011).
11. http://www.historycommons.org/timeline.jsp?timeline=nixon_and_watergate_tmln&nixon_and_watergate_tmln_other=nixon_and_watergate_tmln_itt_and_dita_beard
12. "Friction Triggers Iacocca Ouster," *Michigan Daily*, July 15, 1978.
13. "D & O Claims Incidence Rises," *Business Insurance*, November 12, 1979, 18.
14. *Smith v. Van Gorkom*, 488 A.2d 858 (Del. 1985).
15. *Meinhard v. Salmon*, 164 N.W. 545 (N.Y. 1928).
16. *Farber v. Servan Land Co., Inc.*, 662 F.2d 371 (5th Cir. 1981).
17. For a further discussion of board member connectedness, see Matt Krant, "Web of Board Members Ties Together Corporation America," at http://www.usatoday.com/money/companies/management/2002-11-24-interlock_x.htm.
18. *Francis v. United Jersey Bank*, 87 N.J. 15, 432 A.2d 814 (N.J. 1981).
19. *Aronson v. Lewis*, 473 A.2d 805, 812 (Del. 1984).
20. *Cede & Co. v. Technicolor, Inc.*, 634 A.2d 345 (Del. 1993).
21. *In re The Walt Disney Co. Derivative Litigation*, 906 A.2d 27 (Del. 2006).
22. *Smith v. Van Gorkom*, 488 A.2d 858 (Del. 1985).
23. *Unocal Corp. v. Mesa Petroleum*, 493 A.2d 946 (Del. 1985).
24. *Unitrin v. American General Corp.*, 651 A.2d 1361 (Del. 1995).
25. *Paramount Communications, Inc. v. Time, Inc.*, 571 A.2d 1140 (Del. 1989).
26. *In re Caremark International Inc. Derivative Litigation*, 698 A.2d 959 (Del. Ch. 1996).
27. For more information, see Melvin Eisenberg, "The Duty of Good Faith in Corporate Law," 31 *Delaware Journal of Corporate Law*, 1 (2005).
28. *Revlon, Inc. v. MacAndrews & Forbes Holdings, Inc.*, 506 A.2d 173 (Del. 1986).
29. Brett H. McDonnell, "Corporate Governance and the Sarbanes-Oxley Act: Corporate Constituency Statutes and Employee Governance," *William Mitchell Law Review* 30 (2004): 1227.
30. Del. Code Ann., Title 8, Section 102(b)(7) (2011).

CHAPTER 46

Securities Regulation

Learning Objectives

After reading this chapter, you should understand the following:

1. The nature of securities regulation.
2. The Securities Act of 1933 and the Securities Exchange Act of 1934.
3. Liability under securities laws.
4. What insider trading is and why it's unlawful.
5. Civil and criminal penalties for violations of securities laws.

In Chapter 44, we examined state law governing a corporation's issuance and transfer of stock. In Chapter 45, we covered the liability of directors and officers. This chapter extends and ties together the themes raised in Chapter 44 and Chapter 45 by examining government regulation of securities and insider trading. Both the registration and the trading of securities are highly regulated by the Securities and Exchange Commission (SEC). A violation of a securities law can lead to severe criminal and civil penalties. But first we examine the question, Why is there a need for securities regulation?

46.1 The Nature of Securities Regulation

Learning Objectives

1. Recognize that the definition of *security* encompasses a broad range of interests.
2. Understand the functions of the Securities and Exchange Commission and the penalties for violations of the securities laws.
3. Understand which companies the Securities Exchange Act of 1934 covers.
4. Explore the purpose of state Blue Sky Laws.
5. Know the basic provisions of the Dodd-Frank Wall Street Reform and Consumer Protection Act.

What we commonly refer to as "**securities**" are essentially worthless pieces of paper. Their inherent value lies in the interest in property or an ongoing enterprise that they represent. This disparity between the tangible property—the stock certificate, for example—and the intangible interest it represents gives rise to several reasons for regulation. First, there is need for a mechanism to inform the buyer accurately what it is he is buying. Second, laws are necessary to prevent and provide remedies for deceptive and manipulative acts designed to defraud buyers and sellers. Third, the evolution of stock trading on a massive scale has led to the development of numerous types of specialists and professionals, in dealings with whom the public can be at a severe disadvantage, and so the law undertakes to ensure that they do not take unfair advantage of their customers.

The **Securities Act of 1933** and the **Securities Exchange Act of 1934** are two federal statutes that are vitally important, having virtually refashioned the law governing corporations during the past half century. In fact, it is not too much to say that although they deal with securities, they have become the general federal law of corporations. This body of federal law has assumed special importance in recent years as the states have engaged in a race to the bottom in attempting to compete with Delaware's permissive corporation law (see Chapter 43).

What Is a Security?

security

Any note, stock, treasury stock, bond, debenture, evidence of indebtedness, certificate of interest or participation in any profit-sharing agreement, collateral-trust certificate, or subscription, transferable share, investment contract, voting-trust certificate, certificate of deposit for a security, fractional undivided interest in oil, gas, or other mineral rights, or, in general, any interest or instrument commonly known as a security.

investment contract

A commitment of money or capital to purchase financial instruments as a means to gain profitable returns in the form of income, interest, or the appreciation of the value of the instrument itself. It can be interpreted by the courts to be a security for purposes of the federal securities laws.

Securities law questions are technical and complex and usually require professional counsel. For the nonlawyer, the critical question on which all else turns is whether the particular investment or document is a **security**. If it is, anyone attempting any transaction beyond the routine purchase or sale through a broker should consult legal counsel to avoid the various civil and criminal minefields that the law has strewn about.

The definition of *security*, which is set forth in the Securities Act of 1933, is comprehensive, but it does not on its face answer all questions that financiers in a dynamic market can raise. Under Section 2(1) of the act, "security" includes "any note, stock, treasury stock, bond, debenture, evidence of indebtedness, certificate of interest or participation in any profit-sharing agreement, collateral-trust certificate, preorganization certificate or subscription, transferable share, investment contract, voting-trust certificate, certificate of deposit for a security, fractional undivided interest in oil, gas, or other mineral rights, or, in general, any interest or instrument commonly known as a 'security,' or any certificate of interest or participation in, temporary or interim certificate for, receipt for, guarantee of, or warrant or right to subscribe to or purchase, any of the foregoing."

Under this definition, an investment may not be a security even though it is so labeled, and it may actually be a security even though it is called something else. For example, does a service contract that obligates someone who has sold individual rows in an orange orchard to cultivate, harvest, and market an orange crop involve a security subject to regulation under federal law? Yes, said the Supreme Court in *Securities & Exchange Commission v. W. J. Howey Co.*[1] The Court said the test is whether "the person invests his money in a common enterprise and is led to expect profits solely from the efforts of the promoter or a third party." Under this test, courts have liberally interpreted "**investment contract**" and "certificate of interest or participation in any profit-sharing agreement" to be securities interests in such property as real estate condominiums and cooperatives, commodity option contracts, and farm animals.

The Supreme Court ruled that notes that are not "investment contracts" under the *Howey* test can still be considered securities if certain factors are present, as discussed in *Reves v. Ernst & Young*, (see Section 3). These factors include (1) the motivations prompting a reasonable seller and buyer to enter into the transaction, (2) the plan of distribution and whether the instruments are commonly traded for speculation or investment, (3) the reasonable expectations of the investing public, and (4) the presence of other factors that significantly reduce risk so as to render the application of the Securities Act unnecessary.

The Securities and Exchange Commission

Functions

The **Securities and Exchange Commission** (SEC) is over eighty years old, having been created by Congress in the Securities Exchange Act of 1934. It is an independent regulatory agency, subject to the rules of the Administrative Procedure Act (see Chapter 5). The commission is composed of five members, who have staggered five-year terms. Every June 5, the term of one of the commissioners expires. Although the president cannot remove commissioners during their terms of office, he does have the power to designate the chairman from among the sitting members. The SEC is bipartisan: not more than three commissioners may be from the same political party.

Securities and Exchange Commission

An independent federal regulatory agency whose primary task is to investigate complaints or other possible violations of the law in securities transactions and to bring enforcement proceedings when it believes that violations have occurred.

The SEC's primary task is to investigate complaints or other possible violations of the law in securities transactions and to bring enforcement proceedings when it believes that violations have occurred. It is empowered to conduct information inquiries, interview witnesses, examine brokerage records, and review trading data. If its requests are refused, it can issue subpoenas and seek compliance in federal court. Its usual leads come from complaints of investors and the general public, but it has authority to conduct surprise inspections of the books and records of brokers and dealers. Another source of leads is price fluctuations that seem to have been caused by manipulation rather than regular market forces.

Among the violations the commission searches out are these: (1) unregistered sale of securities subject to the registration requirement of the Securities Act of 1933, (2) fraudulent acts and practices, (3) manipulation of market prices, (4) carrying out of a securities business while insolvent, (5) misappropriation of customers' funds by brokers and dealers, and (4) other unfair dealings by brokers and dealers.

When the commission believes that a violation has occurred, it can take one of three courses. First, it can refer the case to the Justice Department with a recommendation for **criminal prosecution** in cases of fraud or other willful violation of law.

criminal prosecution

The process of bringing a legal action against a defendant for criminal behavior.

Second, the SEC can seek a **civil injunction** in federal court against further violations. As a result of amendments to the securities laws in 1990 (the Securities Enforcement Remedies and Penny Stock Reform Act), the commission can also ask the court to impose **civil penalties**. The maximum penalty is $100,000 for each violation by a natural person and $500,000 for each violation by an entity other than a natural person. Alternatively, the defendant is liable for the gain that resulted from violating securities law if the gain exceeds the statutory penalty. The court is also authorized to bar an individual who has committed securities fraud from serving as an officer or a director of a company registered under the securities law.

civil injunction

A judicial process or order requiring a person or entity to do a particular act or to refrain from doing a particular act.

civil penalties

A term used to describe when a state entity, government agency, or private party seeks monetary relief, fines, and/or restitution for wrongdoing by another.

Third, the SEC can proceed administratively—that is, hold its own hearing, with the usual due process rights, before an **administrative law judge**. If the commissioners by majority vote accept the findings of the administrative law judge after reading briefs and hearing oral argument, they can impose a variety of sanctions: suspend or expel members of exchanges; deny, suspend, or revoke the registrations of broker-dealers; censure individuals for misconduct; and bar censured individuals (temporarily or permanently) from employment with a registered firm. The 1990 securities law amendments allow the SEC to impose civil fines similar to the court-imposed fines described. The amendments also authorize the SEC to order individuals to cease and desist from violating securities law.

administrative law judge

The presiding officer of an administrative hearing.

Fundamental Mission

The SEC's fundamental mission is to ensure adequate disclosure in order to facilitate informed investment decisions by the public. However, whether a particular security offering is worthwhile or worthless is a decision for the public, not for the SEC, which has no legal authority to pass on the merits of an offering or to bar the sale of securities if proper disclosures are made.

One example of SEC's regulatory mandate with respect to disclosures involved the 1981 sale of $274 million in limited partnership interests in a company called Petrogene Oil & Gas Associates, New York. The Petrogene offering was designed as a tax shelter. The company's filing with the SEC stated that the offering involved "a high degree of risk" and that only those "who can afford the complete loss of their investment" should contemplate investing. Other disclosures included one member of the controlling group having spent four months in prison for conspiracy to commit securities fraud; that he and another principal were the subject of a New Mexico cease and desist order involving allegedly unregistered tax-sheltered securities; that the general partner, brother-in-law of one of the principals, had no experience in the company's proposed oil and gas operations (Petrogene planned to extract oil from plants by using radio frequencies); that one of the oils to be produced was potentially carcinogenic; and that the principals "stand to benefit substantially" whether or not the company fails and whether or not purchasers of shares recovered any of their investment. The prospectus went on to list specific risks. Despite this daunting compilation of troublesome details, the SEC permitted the offering because all disclosures were made (*Wall Street Journal*, December 29, 1981). It is the business of the marketplace, not the SEC, to determine whether the risk is worth taking.

The SEC enforces securities laws through two primary federal acts: The Securities Act of 1933 and The Securities Exchange Act of 1934.

Securities Act of 1933

Goals

The **Securities Act of 1933** is the fundamental "truth in securities" law. Its two basic objectives, which are written in its preamble, are "to provide full and fair disclosure of the character of securities sold in interstate and foreign commerce and through the mails, and to prevent frauds in the sale thereof."

Securities Act of 1933

The first law enacted by Congress to regulate the securities market. This act regulates the public offering of new securities and provides for securities registration requirements, and prevention of fraudulent conduct.

registration statement

A set of documents that a company must file with the SEC before it proceeds with an initial public offering.

prospectus

A document that provides details about an investment offering for sale to the public—the facts an investor needs to make an informed decision.

Registration

The primary means for realizing these goals is the requirement of registration. Before securities subject to the act can be offered to the public, the issuer must file a **registration statement** and **prospectus** with the SEC, laying out in detail relevant and material information about the offering as set forth in various schedules to the act. If the SEC approves the registration statement, the issuer must then provide any prospective purchaser with the prospectus. Since the SEC does not pass on the fairness of price or other terms of the offering, it is unlawful to state or imply in the prospectus that the commission has the power to disapprove securities for lack of merit, thereby suggesting that the offering is meritorious.

The SEC has prepared special forms for registering different types of issuing companies. All call for a description of the registrant's business and properties and of the significant provisions of the security to be offered, facts about how the issuing company is managed, and detailed financial statements certified by independent public accountants.

Once filed, the registration and prospectus become public and are open for public inspection. Ordinarily, the effective date of the registration statement is twenty days after filing. Until then, the offering may not be made to the public. Section 2(10) of the act defines *prospectus* as any "notice, circular, advertisement, letter, or communication, written or by radio or television, which offers any security for sale or confirms the sale of any security." (An exception: brief notes advising the public of the availability of the formal prospectus.) The import of this definition is that any communication to the public about the offering of a security is unlawful unless it contains the requisite information.

The SEC staff examines the registration statement and prospectus, and if they appear to be materially incomplete or inaccurate, the commission may suspend or refuse the effectiveness of the registration statement until the deficiencies are corrected. Even after the securities have gone on sale, the agency has the power to issue a stop order that halts trading in the stock.

Section 5(c) of the act bars any person from making any sale of any security unless it is first registered. Nevertheless, there are certain classes of exemptions from the registration requirement. Perhaps the most important of these is Section 4(3), which exempts "transactions by any person other than an issuer, underwriter or dealer." Section 4(3) also exempts most transactions of dealers. So the net is that trading in outstanding securities (the secondary market) is exempt from registration under the Securities Act of 1933: you need not file a registration statement with the SEC every time you buy or sell securities through a broker or dealer, for example. Other exemptions include the following: (1) private offerings to a limited number of persons or institutions who have access to the kind of information registration would disclose and who do not propose to redistribute the securities; (2) offerings restricted to the residents of the state in which the issuing company is organized and doing business; (3) securities of municipal, state, federal and other government instrumentalities, of charitable institutions, of banks, and of carriers subject to the Interstate Commerce Act; (4) offerings not in excess of certain specified amounts made in compliance with regulations of the Commission...: and (5) offerings of "small business investment companies" made in accordance with rules and regulations of the Commission.

Penalties

Section 24 of the Securities Act of 1933 provides for fines not to exceed $10,000 and a prison term not to exceed five years, or both, for willful violations of any provisions of the act. This section makes these criminal penalties specifically applicable to anyone who "willfully, in a registration statement filed under this title, makes any untrue statement of a material fact or omits to state any material fact required to be stated therein or necessary to make the statements therein not misleading."

Sections 11 and 12 provide that anyone injured by false declarations in registration statements, prospectuses, or oral communications concerning the sale of the security—as well as anyone injured by the unlawful failure of an issuer to register—may file a civil suit to recover the net consideration paid for the security or for damages if the security has been sold.

Although these civil penalty provisions apply only to false statements in connection with the registration statement, prospectus, or oral communication, the Supreme Court held, in *Case v. Borak*,[2] that there is an "**implied private right of action**" for damages resulting from a violation of SEC rules under the act. The Court's ruling in *Borak* opened the courthouse doors to many who had been defrauded but were previously without a practical remedy.

implied private right of action

A ruling by the Supreme Court that allows individuals who have been defrauded to seek damages resulting from a violation of SEC rules.

Securities Exchange Act of 1934

Companies Covered

primary market

The market in which the money or capital for the security is received by the issuer of the security directly from investors (such as in an initial public offering transaction).

secondary market

The market in which securities are bought and sold subsequent to original issuance and are typically held by one investor selling them to another investor.

Securities Exchange Act of 1934

A law that was enacted to provide governance of securities transactions on the secondary market and to regulate the exchanges and broker-dealers in order to protect the investing public. This act also established the SEC.

proxy solicitation

An attempt by a group or delegation to obtain the authorization from other individuals to vote on their behalf.

The Securities Act of 1933 is limited, as we have just seen, to new securities issues—that is the **primary market**. The trading that takes place in the **secondary market** is far more significant, however. In a normal year, trading in outstanding stock totals some twenty times the value of new stock issues.

To regulate the secondary market, Congress enacted the **Securities Exchange Act of 1934**. This law, which created the SEC, extended the disclosure rationale to securities listed and registered for public trading on the national securities exchanges. Amendments to the act have brought within its ambit every corporation whose equity securities are traded over the counter if the company has at least $10 million in assets and five hundred or more shareholders.

Reporting Proxy Solicitation

Any company seeking listing and registration of its stock for public trading on a national exchange—or over the counter, if the company meets the size test—must first submit a registration application to both the exchange and the SEC. The registration statement is akin to that filed by companies under the Securities Act of 1933, although the Securities Exchange Act of 1934 calls for somewhat fewer disclosures. Thereafter, companies must file annual and certain other periodic reports to update information in the original filing.

The Securities Exchange Act of 1934 also covers **proxy solicitation**. Whenever management, or a dissident minority, seeks votes of holders of registered securities for any corporate purpose, disclosures must be made to the stockholders to permit them to vote yes or no intelligently.

Penalties

The logic of the *Borak* case (discussed in Section 1) also applies to this act, so that private investors may bring suit in federal court for violations of the statute that led to financial injury. Violations of any provision and the making of false statements in any of the required disclosures subject the defendant to a maximum fine of $5 million and a maximum twenty-year prison sentence, but a defendant who can show that he had no knowledge of the particular rule he was convicted of violating may not be imprisoned. The maximum fine for a violation of the act by a person other than a natural person is $25 million. Any issuer omitting to file requisite documents and reports is liable to pay a fine of $100 for each day the failure continues.

Blue Sky Laws

blue sky law

A state law that regulates the offering and sale of securities to protect the public from fraud.

merit review laws

Laws that regulate the disclosure and the substantive merits and fairness of the securities offerings to investors.

Long before congressional enactment of the securities laws in the 1930s, the states had legislated securities regulations. Today, every state has enacted a **blue sky law**, so called because its purpose is to prevent "speculative schemes which have no more basis than so many feet of 'blue sky.'"[3] The federal Securities Act of 1933, discussed in Section 1, specifically preserves the jurisdiction of states over securities.

Blue sky laws are divided into three basic types of regulation. The simplest is that which prohibits fraud in the sale of securities. Thus at a minimum, issuers cannot mislead investors about the purpose of the investment. All blue sky laws have antifraud provisions; some have no other provisions. The second type calls for registration of broker-dealers, and the third type for registration of securities. Some state laws parallel the federal laws in intent and form of proceeding, so that they overlap; other blue sky laws empower state officials (unlike the SEC) to judge the merits of the offerings, often referred to as **merit review laws.** As part of a movement toward deregulation, several states have recently modified or eliminated merit provisions.

Many of the blue sky laws are inconsistent with each other, making national uniformity difficult. In 1956, the National Conference of Commissioners on Uniform State Laws approved the Uniform Securities Act. It has not been designed to reconcile the conflicting philosophies of state regulation but to take them into account and to make the various forms of regulation as consistent as possible. States adopt various portions of the law, depending on their regulatory philosophies. The Uniform Securities Act has antifraud, broker-dealer registration, and securities registration provisions. More recent acts have further increased uniformity. These include the National Securities Markets Improvement Act of 1996, which preempted differing state philosophies with regard to registration of securities and regulation of brokers and advisors, and the Securities Litigation Uniform Standards Act of 1998, which preempted state law securities fraud claims from being raised in class action lawsuits by investors.

Dodd-Frank Wall Street Reform and Consumer Protection Act

In 2010, Congress passed the **Dodd-Frank Wall Street Reform and Consumer Protection Act**, which is the largest amendment to financial regulation in the United States since the Great Depression. This amendment was enacted in response to the economic recession of the late 2000s for the following purposes: (1) to promote the financial stability of the United States by improving accountability and transparency in the financial system, (2) to end "too big to fail" institutions, (3) to protect the American taxpayer by ending bailouts, and (4) to protect consumers from abusive financial services practices. The institutions most affected by the regulatory changes include those involved in monitoring the financial system, such as the Federal Deposit Insurance Corporation (FDIC) and the SEC. Importantly, the amendment ended the exemption for investment advisors who previously were not required to register with the SEC because they had fewer than fifteen clients during the previous twelve months and did not hold out to the public as investment advisors. This means that in practice, numerous investment advisors, as well as hedge funds and private equity firms, are now subject to registration requirements.[4]

Dodd-Frank Wall Street Reform and Consumer Protection Act

A federal law aimed at financial reform and designed to promote financial stability, it was established to enhance the power of regulatory agencies and add additional enforcement agencies.

Key Takeaway

The SEC administers securities laws to prevent the fraudulent practices in the sales of securities. The definition of *security* is intentionally broad to protect the public from fraudulent investments that otherwise would escape regulation. The Securities Act of 1933 focuses on the issuance of securities, and the Securities Exchange Act of 1934 deals predominantly with trading in issued securities. Numerous federal and state securities laws are continuously created to combat securities fraud, with penalties becoming increasingly severe.

Exercises

1. What differentiates an ordinary investment from a security? List all the factors.
2. What is the main objective of the SEC?
3. What are the three courses of action that the SEC may take against one who violates a securities law?
4. What is the difference between the Securities Act of 1933 and the Securities Exchange Act of 1934?
5. What do blue sky laws seek to protect?

46.2 Liability under Securities Law

Learning Objectives

1. Understand how the Foreign Corrupt Practices Act prevents American companies from using bribes to enter into contracts or gain licenses from foreign governments.
2. Understand the liability for insider trading for corporate insiders, "tippees," and secondary actors under Sections 16(b) and 10(b) of the 1934 Securities Exchange Act.
3. Recognize how the Sarbanes-Oxley Act has amended the 1934 act to increase corporate regulation, transparency, and penalties.

Corporations may be found liable if they engage in certain unlawful practices, several of which we explore in this section.

The Foreign Corrupt Practices Act

Foreign Corrupt Practices Act (FCPA)

A US law, enacted 1977, that in part prohibits US firms from bribing foreign officials to obtain or retain business.

Investigations by the Securities and Exchange Commission (SEC) and the Watergate Special Prosecutor in the early 1970s turned up evidence that hundreds of companies had misused corporate funds, mainly by bribing foreign officials to induce them to enter into contracts with or grant licenses to U.S. companies. Companies paying bribes routinely hid the payments in various accounts; revealing the bribes would defeat the secret purpose of the bribe, and, if revealed, could be expected to stir up immense criticism from competitors, NGOs, and political groups. As a result, one of many statutes enacted in the aftermath of Watergate, the **Foreign Corrupt Practices Act (FCPA)** of 1977, was incorporated into the 1934 Securities Exchange Act. Business gained through bribery puts a premium on stealth, influence, and money, rather than goods and services that compete on their own price and merit. The SEC's legal interest in the matter, however, is not premised on the morality of bribery but rather on the falsity of the financial statements that are being filed, statements that seldom spoke the truth about the money being used to bribe.

Yet Congress's response (the FCPA) to the hiding of these transactions in financial reporting was much broader than necessary to treat the violations that were uncovered. The FCPA prohibits an issuer (i.e., any U.S. business enterprise), a stockholder acting on behalf of an issuer, and "any officer, director, employee, or agent" of an issuer from using either the mails or interstate commerce corruptly to offer, pay, or promise to pay anything of value to foreign officials, foreign political parties, or candidates if the purpose is to gain business by inducing the foreign official to influence an act of the government to render a decision favorable to the U.S. corporation.

Not all payments are illegal. Under 1988 amendments to the FCPA, payments may be made to expedite routine governmental actions, such as obtaining a visa or getting perishable goods promptly put through customs. And payments are allowed if they are lawful under the written law of a foreign country. More important than the foreign-bribery provisions, the act includes accounting provisions, which broaden considerably the authority of the SEC. These provisions are discussed in *SEC v. World-Wide Coin Investments, Ltd.*,[5] the first accounting provisions case brought to trial.

Insider Trading

Corporate insiders—directors, officers, or important shareholders—can have a substantial trading advantage if they are privy to important confidential information. Learning bad news (such as financial loss or cancellation of key contracts) in advance of all other stockholders will permit the privileged few to sell shares before the price falls. Conversely, discovering good news (a major oil find or unexpected profits) in advance gives the insider a decided incentive to purchase shares before the price rises.

Because of the unfairness to those who are ignorant of inside information, federal law prohibits **insider trading**. Two provisions of the 1934 Securities Exchange Act are paramount: **Section 16(b)** and 10(b).

Recapture of Short-Swing Profits: Section 16(b)

The Securities Exchange Act assumes that any director, officer, or shareholder owning 10 percent or more of the stock in a corporation is using inside information if he or any family member makes a profit from trading activities, either buying and selling or selling and buying, during a six-month period. Section 16(b) penalizes any such person by permitting the corporation or a shareholder suing on its behalf to recover the **short-swing profits**. The law applies to any company with more than $10 million in assets and at least five hundred or more shareholders of any class of stock.

Suppose that on January 1, Bob (a company officer) purchases one hundred shares of stock in BCT Bookstore, Inc., for $60 a share. On September 1, he sells them for $100 a share. What is the result? Bob is in the clear, because his $4,000 profit was not realized during a six-month period. Now suppose that the price falls, and one month later, on October 1, he repurchases one hundred shares at $30 a share and holds them for two years. What is the result? He will be forced to pay back $7,000 in profits even if he had no inside information. Why? In August, Bob held one hundred shares of stock, and he did again on October 1—within a six-month period. His net gain on these transactions was $7,000 ($10,000 realized on the sale less the $3,000 cost of the purchase).

As a consequence of Section 16(b) and certain other provisions, trading in securities by directors, officers, and large stockholders presents numerous complexities. For instance, the law requires people in this position to make periodic reports to the SEC about their trades. As a practical matter, directors, officers, and large shareholders should not trade in their own company stock in the short run without legal advice.

corporate insider

A corporate director, officer, or shareholder with more than 10 percent of a registered security who through influence of position obtains knowledge that may be used to gain an unfair advantage to the detriment of others. The definition has been broadened to include relatives and others.

insider trading

Buying or selling securities of a publicly held company by those who have privileged access to information concerning a company's financial condition or plans.

Section 16(b)

A section of the 1934 Securities Exchange Act that allows shareholders to sue corporate officers, directors, or owners of more than 10% of the company's shares for any profits made by insider trading. 16(b) is not enforced by the SEC,but by private parties, and covers profits made within a "short swing" (six month) period.

short-swing profits

Any profits made from the purchase and sale of company stock if both transactions occur within a six-month period; insiders are required to return any profits made from the purchase and sale of company stock if both transactions occur within a six-month period.

Insider Trading: Section 10(b) and Rule 10b-5

Section 10(b)

A section of the Securities Exchange Act of 1934 that prohibits any person from using the mails or facilities of interstate commerce "to use or employ, in connection with the purchase or sale of any security...any manipulative or deceptive device..."

Rule 10b-5

A rule by the SEC that applies to any person who purchases or sells any security and that prohibits fraud related to securities trading.

Section 10(b) of the Securities Exchange Act of 1934 prohibits any person from using the mails or facilities of interstate commerce "to use or employ, in connection with the purchase or sale of any security ... any manipulative or deceptive device or contrivance in contravention of such rules and regulations as the Commission may prescribe as necessary or appropriate in the public interest or for the protection of investors." In 1942, the SEC learned of a company president who misrepresented the company's financial condition in order to buy shares at a low price from current stockholders. So the commission adopted a rule under the authority of Section 10(b). **Rule 10b-5**, as it was dubbed, has remained unchanged for more than forty years and has spawned thousands of lawsuits and SEC proceedings. It reads as follows:

> *It shall be unlawful for any person, directly or indirectly, by the use of any means or instrumentality of interstate commerce, or of the mails, or of any facility of any national securities exchange,*
>
> *(1) to employ any device, scheme, or artifice to defraud,*
>
> *(2) to make any untrue statement of a material fact or to omit to state a material fact necessary in order to make the statements made, in the light of circumstances under which they were made, not misleading, or*
>
> *(3) to engage in any act, practice, or course of business which operates or would operate as a fraud or deceit upon any person, in connection with the purchase or sale of any security.*

Rule 10b-5 applies to any person who purchases or sells any security. It is not limited to securities registered under the 1934 Securities Exchange Act. It is not limited to publicly held companies. It applies to any security issued by any company, including the smallest closely held company. In substance, it is an antifraud rule, enforcement of which seems, on its face, to be limited to action by the SEC. But over the years, the courts have permitted people injured by those who violate the statute to file private damage suits. This sweeping rule has at times been referred to as the "federal law of corporations" or the "catch everybody" rule.

Insider trading ran headlong into Rule 10b-5 beginning in 1964 in a series of cases involving Texas Gulf Sulphur Company (TGS). On November 12, 1963, the company discovered a rich deposit of copper and zinc while drilling for oil near Timmins, Ontario. Keeping the discovery quiet, it proceeded to acquire mineral rights in adjacent lands. By April 1964, word began to circulate about TGS's find.

Newspapers printed rumors, and the Toronto Stock Exchange experienced a wild speculative spree. On April 12, an executive vice president of TGS issued a press release downplaying the discovery, asserting that the rumors greatly exaggerated the find and stating that more drilling would be necessary before coming to any conclusions. Four days later, on April 16, TGS publicly announced that it had uncovered a strike of 25 million tons of ore. In the months following this announcement, TGS stock doubled in value.

tippees

Someone who receives and acts on insider information.

The SEC charged several TGS officers and directors with having purchased or told their friends, so-called **tippees**, to purchase TGS stock from November 12, 1963, through April 16, 1964, on the basis of material inside information. The SEC also alleged that the April 12, 1964, press release was deceptive. The U.S. Court of Appeals, in *SEC v. Texas Gulf Sulphur Co.*,[6] decided that the defendants who purchased the stock before the public announcement had violated Rule 10b-5. According to the court, "anyone in possession of material inside information must either disclose it to the investing public, or, if he is disabled from disclosing to protect a corporate confidence, or he chooses not to do so, must abstain from trading in or recommending the securities concerned while such inside information remains undisclosed." On remand, the district court ordered certain defendants to pay

$148,000 into an escrow account to be used to compensate parties injured by the insider trading.

The court of appeals also concluded that the press release violated Rule 10b-5 if "misleading to the reasonable investor." On remand, the district court held that TGS failed to exercise "due diligence" in issuing the release. Sixty-nine private damage actions were subsequently filed against TGS by shareholders who claimed they sold their stock in reliance on the release. The company settled most of these suits in late 1971 for $2.7 million.

Following the TGS episode, the Supreme Court refined Rule 10b-5 on several fronts. First, in *Ernst & Ernst v. Hochfelder*,[7] the Court decided that proof of **scienter**—defined as "mental state embracing intent to deceive, manipulate, or defraud"—is required in private damage actions under Rule 10b-5. In other words, negligence alone will not result in Rule 10b-5 liability. The Court also held that scienter, which is an intentional act, must be established in SEC injunctive actions.[8]

scienter

A legal term that refers to having intent or knowledge of wrongdoing.

The Supreme Court has placed limitations on the liability of tippees under Rule 10b-5. In 1980, the Court reversed the conviction of an employee of a company that printed tender offer and merger prospectuses. Using information obtained at work, the employee had purchased stock in target companies and later sold it for a profit when takeover attempts were publicly announced. In *Chiarella v. United States*, the Court held that the employee was not an insider or a fiduciary and that "a duty to disclose under Section 10(b) does not arise from the mere possession of nonpublic market information."[9] Following *Chiarella*, the Court ruled in *Dirks v. Securities and Exchange Commission* (see Section 3), that tippees are liable if they had reason to believe that the tipper breached a fiduciary duty in disclosing confidential information and the tipper received a personal benefit from the disclosure.

The Supreme Court has also refined Rule 10b-5 as it relates to the duty of a company to disclose **material information**, as discussed in *Basic, Inc. v. Levinson*, 485 U.S. 224 (1998). Basic was engaged in merger talks, suspended trading on the NYSE, and made a public statement that it was not engaged in any merger talks. Many Basic shareholders, Levinson among them, relied to their detriment on the CEO's public statements. The Court used a fraud-on-the-market theory, based on the notion that stock prices are a function of all material information about the company and its business. It applies in open and developed securities markets, where it can be assumed that all material information is available to investors. The fraud-on-the-market theory states that under these conditions, there is a causal link between any misstatement and any stock purchaser, because the misstatements defraud the entire market and thus affect the price of the stock. The *Levinson* case is also important in its discussion of the degree of reliance investors must prove to support a Rule 10b-5 action.

material information

Information that would be likely to affect a stock's price once it became known to the public.

In 2000, the SEC enacted **Rule 10b5-1**, which defines trading "on the basis of" inside information as any time a person trades while aware of material nonpublic information. Therefore, a defendant is not saved by arguing that the trade was made independent of knowledge of the nonpublic information. However, the rule also creates an affirmative defense for trades that were planned prior to the person's receiving inside information.

Rule 10b5-1

A provision that defines when a purchase or sale constitutes trading "on the basis of" material nonpublic information as any time a person trades while aware of material nonpublic information.

misappropriation theory

A theory based on the act of stealing, or misappropriating, confidential information and then trading securities based on the misappropriated insider knowledge.

Rule 10b5-2

A provision that includes a nonexclusive definition of circumstances and that establishes a duty of trust or confidence for purposes of the misappropriation theory of insider trading.

In addition to its decisions relating to intent (*Ernst & Ernst*), tippees (*Dirks*), materiality (*Basic*), and awareness of nonpublic information (10b5-1), the Supreme Court has considered the **misappropriation theory**, under which a person who misappropriates information from an employer faces insider trading liability. In a leading misappropriation theory case, the Second Circuit Court of Appeals reinstated an indictment against employees who traded on the basis of inside information obtained through their work at investment banking firms. The court concluded that the employees' violation of their fiduciary duty to the firms violated securities law.[10] The U.S. Supreme Court upheld the misappropriation theory in *United States v. O'Hagan*,[11] and the SEC adopted the theory as new **Rule 10b5-2**. Under this new rule, the duty of trust or confidence exists when (1) a person agrees to maintain information in confidence; (2) the recipient knows or should have known through history, pattern, or practice of sharing confidences that the person communicating the information expects confidentiality; and (3) a person received material nonpublic information from his or her spouse, parent, child, or sibling.

In 1987, in *Carpenter v. United States*,[12] the Supreme Court affirmed the conviction of a *Wall Street Journal* reporter who leaked advanced information about the contents of his "Heard on the Street" column. The reporter, who was sentenced to eighteen months in prison, had been convicted on both mail and wire fraud and securities law charges for misappropriating information. The Court upheld the mail and wire fraud conviction by an 8–0 vote and the securities law conviction by a 4–4 vote. (In effect, the tie vote affirmed the conviction.)[13]

Beyond these judge-made theories of liability, Congress had been concerned about insider trading, and in 1984 and 1988, it substantially increased the penalties. A person convicted of insider trading now faces a maximum criminal fine of $1 million and a possible ten-year prison term. A civil penalty of up to three times the profit made (or loss avoided) by insider trading can also be imposed. This penalty is in addition to liability for profits made through insider trading. For example, financier Ivan Boesky, who was sentenced in 1987 to a three-year prison term for insider trading, was required to disgorge $50 million of profits and was liable for another $50 million as a civil penalty. In 2003, Martha Stewart was indicted on charges of insider trading but was convicted for obstruction of justice, serving only five months. More recently, in 2009, billionaire founder of the Galleon Group, Raj Rajaratnam, was arrested for insider trading; he was convicted in May 2011 of all 14 counts of insider trading. For the SEC release on the Martha Stewart case, see http://www.sec.gov/news/press/2003-69.htm.

Companies that knowingly and recklessly fail to prevent insider trading by their employees are subject to a civil penalty of up to three times the profit gained or loss avoided by insider trading or $1 million, whichever is greater. Corporations are also subject to a criminal fine of up to $2.5 million.

Secondary Actor

secondary actors

A ruling by the Supreme Court stating that "aiders and abettors" of fraud cannot be held secondarily liable under 10(b) for a private cause of action.

In *Stoneridge Investment Partners v. Scientific-Atlanta*,[14] the U.S. Supreme Court held that "aiders and abettors" of fraud cannot be held secondarily liable under 10(b) for a private cause of action. This means that **secondary actors**, such as lawyers and accountants, cannot be held liable unless their conduct satisfies all the elements for 10(b) liability.

For an overview of insider trading, go to http://www.sec.gov/answers/insider.htm.

Sarbanes-Oxley Act

Congress enacted the Sarbanes-Oxley Act in 2002 in response to major corporate and accounting scandals, most notably those involving Enron, Tyco International, Adelphia, and WorldCom. The act created the **Public Company Accounting Oversight Board**, which oversees, inspects, and regulates accounting firms in their capacity as auditors of public companies. As a result of the act, the SEC may include civil penalties to a disgorgement fund for the benefit of victims of the violations of the Securities Act of 1933 and the Securities Exchange Act of 1934.

Public Company Accounting Oversight Board

A body created by Sarbanes-Oxley that oversees, inspects, and regulates accounting firms in their capacity as auditors of public companies.

Key Takeaway

Corrupt practices, misuse of corporate funds, and insider trading unfairly benefit the minority and cost the public billions. Numerous federal laws have been enacted to create liability for these bad actors in order to prevent fraudulent trading activities. Both civil and criminal penalties are available to punish those actors who bribe officials or use inside information unlawfully.

Exercises

1. Why is the SEC so concerned with bribery? What does the SEC really aim to prevent through the FCPA?
2. What are short-swing profits?
3. To whom does Section 16(b) apply?
4. Can a secondary actor (attorney, accountant) be liable for insider trading? What factors must be present?

46.3 Cases

What Is a Security?

Reves v. Ernst & Young

494 U.S. 56, 110 S.Ct. 945 (1990)

JUSTICE MARSHALL delivered the opinion of the Court.

This case presents the question whether certain demand notes issued by the Farmer's Cooperative of Arkansas and Oklahoma are "securities" within the meaning of § 3(a)(10) of the Securities and Exchange Act of 1934. We conclude that they are.

The Co-Op is an agricultural cooperative that, at the same time relevant here, had approximately 23,000 members. In order to raise money to support its general business operations, the Co-Op sold promissory notes payable on demand by the holder. Although the notes were uncollateralized and uninsured, they paid a variable rate of interest that was adjusted monthly to keep it higher than the rate paid by local financial institutions. The Co-Op offered the notes to both members and nonmembers, marketing the scheme as an "Investment Program." Advertisements for the notes, which appeared in each Co-Op newsletter, read in part: "YOUR CO-OP has more than

$11,000,000 in assets to stand behind your investments. The Investment is not Federal [sic] insured but it is...Safe...Secure...and available when you need it." App. 5 (ellipses in original). Despite these assurances, the Co-Op filed for bankruptcy in 1984. At the time of the filing, over 1,600 people held notes worth a total of $10 million.

After the Co-Op filed for bankruptcy, petitioners, a class of holders of the notes, filed suit against Arthur Young & Co., the firm that had audited the Co-Op's financial statements (and the predecessor to respondent Ernst & Young). Petitioners alleged, inter alia, that Arthur Young had intentionally failed to follow generally accepted accounting principles in its audit, specifically with respect to the valuation of one of the Co-Op's major assets, a gasohol plant. Petitioners claimed that Arthur Young violated these principles in an effort to inflate the assets and net worth of the Co-Op. Petitioners maintained that, had Arthur Young properly treated the plant in its audits, they would not have purchased demand notes because the Co-Op's insolvency would have been apparent. On the basis of these allegations, petitioners claimed that Arthur Young had violated the antifraud provisions of the 1934 Act as well as Arkansas' securities laws.

Petitioners prevailed at trial on both their federal and state claims, receiving a $6.1 million judgment. Arthur Young appealed, claiming that the demand notes were not "securities" under either the 1934 Act or Arkansas law, and that the statutes' antifraud provisions therefore did not apply. A panel of the Eighth Circuit, agreeing with Arthur Young on both the state and federal issues, reversed. *Arthur Young & Co. v. Reves*, 856 F.2d 52 (1988). We granted certiorari to address the federal issue, 490 U.S. 1105, 109 S.Ct. 3154, 104 L.Ed.2d 1018 (1989), and now reverse the judgment of the Court of Appeals.

* * *

The fundamental purpose undergirding the Securities Acts is "to eliminate serious abuses in a largely unregulated securities market." *United Housing Foundation, Inc. v. Forman*, 421 U.S. 837, 849, 95 S.Ct. 2051, 2059, 44 L.Ed.2d 621 (1975). In defining the scope of the market that it wished to regulate, Congress painted with a broad brush. It recognized the virtually limitless scope of human ingenuity, especially in the creation of "countless and variable schemes devised by those who seek the use of the money of others on the promise of profits," *SEC v. W.J. Howey Co.*, 328 U.S. 293, 299, 66 S.Ct. 1100, 1103, 90 L.Ed. 1244 (1946), and determined that the best way to achieve its goal of protecting investors was "to define 'the term "security" in sufficiently broad and general terms so as to include within that definition the many types of instruments that in our commercial world fall within the ordinary concept of a security.'" Forman, supra, 421 U.S., at 847-848, 95 S.Ct., at 2058-2059 (quoting H.R.Rep. No. 85, 73d Cong., 1st Sess., 11 (1933)). Congress therefore did not attempt precisely to cabin the scope of the Securities Acts. Rather, it enacted a definition of "security" sufficiently broad to encompass virtually any instrument that might be sold as an investment.

* * *

[In deciding whether this transaction involves a "security," four factors are important.] First, we examine the transaction to assess the motivations that would prompt a reasonable seller and buyer to enter into it. If the seller's purpose is to raise money for the general use of a business enterprise or to finance substantial investments and the buyer is interested primarily in the profit the note is expected to generate, the instrument is likely to be a "security." If the note is exchanged to facilitate the purchase and sale of a minor asset or consumer good, to correct for the seller's cash-flow difficulties, or to advance some other commercial or consumer purpose, on the other hand, the note is less sensibly described as a "security." Second, we examine the "plan of distribution" of the instrument to determine whether it is an instrument in which there is "common trading for speculation or investment." Third, we examine the reasonable expectations of the investing public: The Court will consider instruments to be "securities" on the basis of such public expectations, even where an economic analysis of the circumstances of the particular transaction might suggest that the instruments are not "securities" as used in that transaction. Finally, we examine whether some factor such as the existence of another regulatory scheme significantly reduces the risk of the instrument, thereby rendering application of the Securities Acts unnecessary.

* * *

[We] have little difficulty in concluding that the notes at issue here are "securities."

Case Questions

1. What are the four factors the court uses to determine whether or not the transaction involves a security?
2. How does the definition of security in this case differ from the definition in *Securities & Exchange Commission v. W. J. Howey*?

Tippee Liability

Dirks v. Securities and Exchange Commission

463 U.S. 646 (1983)

POWELL, J., delivered the opinion of the Court, in which BURGER, C. J., and WHITE, REHNQUIST, STEVENS, and O'CONNOR, JJ., joined.

[A] tippee assumes a fiduciary duty to the shareholders of a corporation not to trade on material nonpublic information only when the insider has breached his fiduciary duty to the shareholders by disclosing the information to the tippee and the tippee knows or should know that there has been a breach.

* * *

Whether disclosure is a breach of duty therefore depends in large part on the purpose of the disclosure. This standard was identified by the SEC itself in Cady, Roberts: a purpose of the securities laws was to eliminate "use of inside information for personal advantage." Thus, the test is whether the insider personally will benefit, directly or indirectly, from his disclosure. Absent some personal gain, there has been no breach of duty to stockholders. And absent a breach by the insider, there is no derivative breach.

* * *

Under the inside-trading and tipping rules set forth above, we find that there was no actionable violation by Dirks. It is undisputed that Dirks himself was a stranger to Equity Funding, with no preexisting fiduciary duty to its shareholders. He took no action, directly, or indirectly, that induced the shareholders or officers of Equity Funding to repose trust or confidence in him. There was no expectation by Dirk's sources that he would keep their information in confidence. Nor did Dirks misappropriate or illegally obtain the information about Equity Funding. Unless the insiders breached their Cady, Roberts duty to shareholders in disclosing the nonpublic information to Dirks, he breached no duty when he passed it on to investors as well as to the Wall Street Journal.

* * *

It is clear that neither Secrist nor the other Equity Funding employees violated their Cady, Roberts duty to the corporation's shareholders by providing information to Dirks. The tippers received no monetary or personal benefit for revealing Equity Funding's secrets, nor was their purpose to make a gift of valuable information to Dirks. As the facts of this case clearly indicate, the tippers were motivated by a desire to expose the fraud. In the absence of a breach of duty to shareholders by the insiders, there was no derivative breach by Dirks. Dirks therefore could not have been "a participant after the fact in [an] insider's breach of a fiduciary duty." Chiarella, 445 U.S., at 230, n. 12.

* * *

We conclude that Dirks, in the circumstances of this case, had no duty to abstain from the use of the inside information that he obtained. The judgment of the Court of Appeals therefore is reversed.

BLACKMUN, J., filed a dissenting opinion, in which BRENNAN and MARSHALL, JJ., joined

In disclosing inside information to Dirks, Secrist intended that Dirks would disseminate the information to his clients, those clients would unload their Equity Funding securities on the market, and the price would fall precipitously, thereby triggering a reaction from the authorities.

Dirks complied with his informant's wishes. Instead of reporting that information to the Securities and Exchange Commission (SEC or Commission) or to other regulatory agencies, Dirks began to disseminate the information to his clients and undertook his own investigation.

Dirks' attempts to disseminate the information to non-clients were feeble, at best. On March 12, he left a message for Herbert Lawson, the San Francisco bureau chief of *The Wall Street Journal*. Not until March 19 and 20 did he call Lawson again, and outline the situation. William Blundell, a Journal investigative reporter based in Los Angeles, got in touch with Dirks about his March 20 telephone call. On March 21, Dirks met with Blundell in Los Angeles. Blundell began his own investigation, relying in part on Dirks' contacts, and on March 23 telephoned Stanley Sporkin, the SEC's Deputy Director of Enforcement. On March 26, the next business day, Sporkin and his staff interviewed Blundell and asked to see Dirks the following morning. Trading was halted by the New York Stock Exchange at about the same time Dirks was talking to Los Angeles SEC personnel. The next day, March 28, the SEC suspended trading in Equity Funding securities. By that time, Dirks' clients had unloaded close to $15 million of Equity Funding stock and the price had plummeted from $26 to $15. The effect of Dirks' selective dissemination of Secrist's information was that Dirks' clients were able to shift the losses that were inevitable due to the Equity Funding fraud from themselves to uninformed market participants.

. . . .

No one questions that Secrist himself could not trade on his inside information to the disadvantage of uninformed shareholders and purchasers of Equity Funding securities. Unlike the printer in Chiarella, Secrist stood in a fiduciary relationship with these shareholders.

The Court also acknowledges that Secrist could not do by proxy what he was prohibited from doing personally. But this is precisely what Secrist did. Secrist used Dirks to disseminate information to Dirks' clients, who in turn dumped stock on unknowing purchasers. Secrist thus intended Dirks to injure the purchasers of Equity Funding securities to whom Secrist had a duty to disclose. Accepting the Court's view of tippee liability, it appears that Dirks' knowledge of this breach makes him liable as a participant in the breach after the fact.

. . . .

The Court holds, however, that Dirks is not liable because Secrist did not violate his duty; according to the Court, this is so because Secrist did not have the improper purpose of personal gain. In so doing, the Court imposes a new, subjective limitation on the scope of the duty owed by insiders to shareholders. The novelty of this limitation is reflected in the Court's lack of support for it.

The insider's duty is owed directly to the corporation's shareholders. 7 See Langevoort, Insider Trading and the Fiduciary Principle: A Post-Chiarella Restatement, 70 Calif. L. Rev. 1, 5 (1982); 3A W. Fletcher, Cyclopedia of the Law of Private Corporations 1168.2, pp. 288-289 (rev. ed. 1975). As Chiarella recognized, it is based on the relationship of trust and confidence between the insider and the shareholder. 445 U.S., at 228. That relationship assures the shareholder that the insider may not take actions that will harm him unfairly. The affirmative duty of disclosure protects against this injury. See *Pepper v. Litton*, 308 U.S. 295, 306 (1939); see also Chiarella, 445 U.S., at 228.

. . .

The fact that the insider himself does not benefit from the breach does not eradicate the shareholder's injury. . . It makes no difference to the shareholder whether the corporate insider gained or intended to gain personally from the transaction; the shareholder still has lost because of the insider's misuse of nonpublic information. The duty is addressed not to the insider's motives, 10 but to his actions and their consequences on the shareholder. Personal gain is not an element of the breach of this duty.

This conclusion is borne out by the Court's decision in *Mosser v. Darrow*, 341 U.S.267 (1951). There, the Court faced an analogous situation: a reorganization trustee engaged two employee-promoters of subsidiaries of the companies being reorganized to provide services that the trustee considered to be essential to the successful operation of the trust. In order to secure their services, the trustee expressly agreed with the employees that they could continue to trade in the securities of the subsidiaries. The employees then turned their inside position into substantial profits at the expense both of the trust and of other holders of the companies' securities.

The Court acknowledged that the trustee neither intended to nor did in actual fact benefit from this arrangement; his motives were completely selfless and devoted to the companies. Id., at 275. The Court, nevertheless, found the trustee liable to the estate for the activities of the employees he authorized. The Court described the trustee's defalcation as "a willful and deliberate setting up of an interest in employees adverse to that of the trust." Id. at 272. The breach did not depend on the trustee's personal gain, and his motives in violating his duty were irrelevant; like Secrist, the trustee intended that others would abuse the inside information for their personal gain.

As Mosser demonstrates, the breach consists in taking action disadvantageous to the person to whom one owes a duty. In this case, Secrist owed a duty to purchasers of Equity Funding shares. The Court's addition of the bad-purpose element to a breach-of-fiduciary-duty claim is flatly inconsistent with the principle of Mosser. I do not join this limitation of the scope of an insider's fiduciary duty to shareholders.

In my view, Secrist violated his duty to Equity Funding shareholders by transmitting material nonpublic information to Dirks with the intention that Dirks would cause his clients to trade on that information. Dirks, therefore, was under a duty to make the information publicly available or to refrain from actions that he knew would lead to trading. Because Dirks caused his clients to trade, he violated 10(b) and Rule 10b-5. Any other result is a disservice to this country's attempt to provide fair and efficient capital markets. I dissent.

Case Questions

1. When does a tippee assume a fiduciary duty to shareholders of a corporation?
2. Did Dirks violate any insider trading laws? Why or why not?
3. How does this case re-define Rule 10b-5?

Tippee Liability

United States vs. Newman and Chiasson (2014)

Second Circuit Court of Appeals, 773 F.3d 438.

Barrington D. Parker, Circuit Judge

[Todd Newman and Anthony Chiasson were convicted in the Southern District of New York, on May 9, 2013, for conspiracy to commit insider trading and insider trading in Dell and NVIDIA securities. Newman and Chiasson—both hedge fund managers—were three and four steps removed, respectively, from the corporate insiders who allegedly had the fiduciary duty to maintain the confidentiality of the company information at issue.

The defendants did not know the insiders, much less the circumstances under which either insider allegedly had shared material, non-public information. The Government, however, argued that it need only prove that Newman and Chiasson were aware of the insiders' breach of fiduciary duty and did not need to prove that they knew the tippers had received a personal benefit in exchange for sharing the inside information. The lower court agreed, charging the jury on this basis, and the jury convicted. Newman and Chiasson then appealed.]

Opinion by BARRINGTON D. PARKER, Circuit Judge: * * *

At the close of evidence, Newman and Chiasson moved for a judgment of acquittal pursuant to Federal Rule of Criminal Procedure 29. They argued that there was no evidence that the corporate insiders provided inside information in exchange for a personal benefit which is required to establish tipper liability under *Dirks v. S.E.C.*, 463 U.S. 646 (1983). Because a tippee's liability derives from the liability of the tipper, Newman and Chiasson argued that they could not be found guilty of insider trading. Newman and Chiasson also argued that, even if the corporate insiders had received a personal benefit in exchange for the inside information, there was no evidence that they knew about any such benefit. Absent such knowledge, appellants argued, they were not aware of, or participants in, the tippers' fraudulent breaches of fiduciary duties to Dell or NVIDIA, and could not be convicted of insider trading under Dirks. In the alternative, appellants requested that the court instruct the jury that it must find that Newman and Chiasson knew that the corporate insiders had disclosed confidential information for personal benefit in order to find them guilty. * * *

In accepting [a] theory of insider trading [in Dirks that requires a breach of the insider's fiduciary duty toward shareholders], the Supreme Court explicitly rejected the notion of "a general duty between all participants in market transactions to forgo actions based on material, nonpublic information." Id. at 233. Instead, the Court limited the scope of insider trading liability to situations where the insider had "a duty to disclose arising from a relationship of trust and confidence between parties to a transaction," such as that between corporate officers and shareholders. Chiarella, [Citation].

The insider trading case law, however, is not confined to insiders or misappropriators who trade for their own accounts. Id. at 285. Courts have expanded insider trading liability to reach situations where the insider or misappropriator in possession of material nonpublic information (the "tipper") does not himself trade but discloses the information to an outsider (a "tippee") who then trades on the basis of the information before it is publicly disclosed. See Dirks, 463 U.S. at 659.

In reviewing the appeal, the Court articulated the general principle of tipping liability: "Not only are insiders forbidden by their fiduciary relationship from personally using undisclosed corporate information to their advantage, but they may not give such information to an outsider for the same improper purpose of exploiting the information for their personal gain." Id. at 659 (citation omitted). The test for determining whether the corporate insider has breached his fiduciary duty "is whether the insider personally will benefit, directly or indirectly, from his disclosure. Absent some personal gain, there has been no breach of duty. . . ." Id. at 662 (emphasis added).

In Dirks, the corporate insider provided the confidential information in order to expose a fraud in the company and not for any personal benefit, and thus, the Court found that the insider had not breached his duty to the company's shareholders and that Dirks could not be held liable as tippee.

. . . the Government cites Dirks for the proposition that the Supreme Court only required that the "tippee know that the tipper disclosed information in breach of a duty." Id. at 40 (citing Dirks, 463 U.S. at 660) (emphasis added).

While we have not yet been presented with the question of whether the tippee's knowledge of a tipper's breach requires knowledge of the tipper's personal benefit, the answer follows naturally from Dirks. Dirks counsels us that the exchange of confidential information for personal benefit is not separate from an insider's fiduciary breach; it is the fiduciary breach that triggers liability for securities fraud under Rule 10b-5. For purposes of insider trading liability, the insider's disclosure of confidential information, standing alone, is not a breach. Thus, without establishing that the tippee knows of the personal benefit received by the insider in exchange for the disclosure, the Government cannot meet its burden of showing that the tippee knew of a breach. * * *

....

For the foregoing reasons, we vacate the convictions and remand for the district court to dismiss the indictment with prejudice as it pertains to Newman and Chiasson.

Exercises

1. What would the dissenting Justices in *Dirks v. SEC* say to the Newman court?
2. Do you think the Newman court was correct in the way it relied on *Dirks v. SEC* as a precedent?

46.4 Summary and Exercises

Summary

Beyond state corporation laws, federal statutes—most importantly, the Securities Act of 1933 and the Securities Exchange Act of 1934—regulate the issuance and trading of corporate securities. The federal definition of *security* is broad, encompassing most investments, even those called by other names.

The law does not prohibit risky stock offerings; it bans only those lacking adequate disclosure of risks. The primary means for realizing this goal is the registration requirement: registration statements, prospectuses, and proxy solicitations must be filed with the Securities and Exchange Commission (SEC). Penalties for violation of securities law include criminal fines and jail terms, and damages may be awarded in civil suits by both the SEC and private individuals injured by the violation of SEC rules. A 1977 amendment to the 1934 act is the Foreign Corrupt Practices Act, which prohibits an issuer from paying a bribe or making any other payment to foreign officials in order to gain business by inducing the foreign official to influence his government in favor of the U.S. company. This law requires issuers to keep accurate sets of books reflecting the dispositions of their assets and to maintain internal accounting controls to ensure that transactions comport with management's authorization.

The Securities Exchange Act of 1934 presents special hazards to those trading in public stock on the basis of inside information. One provision requires the reimbursement to the company of any profits made from selling and buying stock during a six-month period by directors, officers, and shareholders owning 10 percent or more of the company's stock. Under Rule 10b-5, the SEC and private parties may sue insiders who traded on information not available to the general public, thus gaining an advantage in either selling or buying the stock. Insiders include company employees.

The Sarbanes-Oxley Act amended the 1934 act, creating more stringent penalties, increasing corporate regulation, and requiring greater transparency.

Exercises

1. Anne operated a clothing store called Anne's Rags, Inc. She owned all of the stock in the company. After several years in the clothing business, Anne sold her stock to Louise, who personally managed the business. Is the sale governed by the antifraud provisions of federal securities law? Why?
2. While waiting tables at a campus-area restaurant, you overhear a conversation between two corporate executives who indicate that their company has developed a new product that will revolutionize the computer industry. The product is to be announced in three weeks. If you

purchase stock in the company before the announcement, will you be liable under federal securities law? Why?

3. Eric was hired as a management consultant by a major corporation to conduct a study, which took him three months to complete. While working on the study, Eric learned that someone working in research and development for the company had recently made an important discovery. Before the discovery was announced publicly, Eric purchased stock in the company. Did he violate federal securities law? Why?
4. While working for the company, Eric also learned that it was planning a takeover of another corporation. Before announcement of a tender offer, Eric purchased stock in the target company. Did he violate securities law? Why?
5. The commercial lending department of First Bank made a substantial loan to Alpha Company after obtaining a favorable confidential earnings report from Alpha. Over lunch, Heidi, the loan officer who handled the loan, mentioned the earnings report to a friend who worked in the bank's trust department. The friend proceeded to purchase stock in Alpha for several of the bank's trusts. Discuss the legal implications.
6. In Exercise 6, assume that after work one day, Heidi told her friend in the trust department that Alpha was Beta's takeover target. The friend proceeded to purchase additional stock in Alpha for a bank trust he administered. Discuss the legal implications.

Self-Test Questions

1. The issuance of corporate securities is governed by
   a. various federal statutes
   b. state law
   c. both of the above
   d. neither of the above
2. The law that prohibits the payment of a bribe to foreign officials to gain business is called
   a. the Insider Trading Act
   b. the blue sky law
   c. the Foreign Corrupt Practices Act
   d. none of the above
3. The primary means for banning stock offerings that inadequately disclose risks is
   a. the registration requirement
   b. SEC prohibition of risky stock offerings
   c. both of the above
   d. neither of the above
4. To enforce its prohibition under insider trading, the SEC requires reimbursement to the company of any profits made from selling and buying stock during any six-month period by directors owing
   a. 60 percent or more of company stock
   b. 40 percent or more of company stock
   c. 10 percent or more of company stock
   d. none of the above
5. Under Rule 10b-5, insiders include
   a. all company employees
   b. any person who possesses nonpublic information
   c. all tippees
   d. none of the above
6. The purpose of the Dodd-Frank Act is to

a. promote financial stability
b. end “too big to fail”
c. end bailouts
d. protect against abusive financial services practices
e. all of the above

Self-Test Answers

1. c
2. c
3. a
4. d
5. a
6. e

Endnotes

1. *Securities & Exchange Commission v. W. J. Howey Co.*, 328 U.S. 293 (1946).
2. *Case v. Borak*, 377 U.S. 426 (1964).
3. *Hall v. Geiger-Jones Co.*, 242 U.S. 539 (1917).
4. For more information on the Dodd-Frank Wall Street Reform and Consumer Protection Act (Pub.L. 111-203, H.R. 4173), see Thomas, “Major Actions,” Bill Summary & Status 111th Congress (2009–2010) H.R.4173, http://thomas.loc.gov/cgi-bin/bdquery/z?d111:HR04173:@@@L&summ2=m&#major%20actions.
5. *SEC v. World-Wide Coin Investments, Ltd.*, 567 F.Supp. 724 (N.D. Ga. 1983).
6. *SEC v. Texas Gulf Sulphur Co.*, 401 F.2d 833 (2d Cir. 1968).
7. *Ernst & Ernst v. Hochfelder*, 425 U.S. 185 (1976).
8. *Aaron v. SEC*, 446 U.S. 680 (1980).
9. *Chiarella v. United States*, 445 U.S. 222 (1980).
10. *United States v. Newman*, 664 F.2d 12 (2d Cir. 1981).
11. *United States v. O’Hagan*, 521 U.S. 642 (1997).
12. *Carpenter v. United States*, 484 U.S. 19 (1987).
13. *Carpenter v. United States*, 484 U.S. 19 (1987).
14. *Stoneridge Investment Partners v. Scientific-Atlanta*, 552 U.S. 148 (2008).

CHAPTER 47

Corporate Expansion, State and Federal Regulation of Foreign Corporations, and Corporate Dissolution

Learning Objectives

After reading this chapter, you should understand the following:

1. How a corporation can expand by purchasing assets of another company without purchasing stock or otherwise merging with the company whose assets are purchased.
2. The benefits of expanding through a purchase of assets rather than stock.
3. Both the benefits and potential detriments of merging with another company.
4. How a merger differs from a stock purchase or a consolidation.
5. Takeovers and tender offers.
6. Appraisal rights.
7. Foreign corporations and the requirements of the U.S. Constitution.
8. The taxation of foreign corporations.
9. Corporate dissolution and its various types.

This chapter begins with a discussion of the various ways a corporation can expand. We briefly consider successor liability—whether a successor corporation, such as a corporation that purchases all of the assets of another corporation, is liable for debts, lawsuits, and other liabilities of the purchased corporation. We then turn to appraisal rights, which are a shareholder's right to dissent from a corporate expansion. Next, we look at several aspects, such as jurisdiction and taxation, of foreign corporations—corporations that are incorporated in a state that is different from the one in which they do business. We conclude the chapter with dissolution of the corporation.

47.1 Corporate Expansion

Learning Objective

1. Understand the four methods of corporate expansion: purchase of assets other than in the regular course of business, merger, consolidation, and purchase of stock in another corporation.

merger

Any type of corporate expansion by which one corporation acquires part or all of another corporation.

In popular usage, "**merger**" often is used to mean any type of expansion by which one corporation acquires part or all of another corporation. But in legal terms, merger is only one of four methods of achieving expansion other than by internal growth.

Antitrust law—an important aspect of corporate expansion—will be discussed in Chapter 48. There, in the study of Section 7 of the Clayton Act, we will see the possible antitrust hazards of merging or consolidating with a competing corporation.

Purchase of Assets

purchase of assets

One corporation purchases the assets of another corporation in order to expand.

One method of corporate expansion is the **purchase of assets** of another corporation. Suppose ABC Corporation wishes to expand, and the assets of XYZ Corporation are attractive to ABC. So ABC purchases the assets of XYZ, resulting in the expansion of ABC. After the purchase, XYZ may remain in corporate form or may cease to exist, depending on how many of its assets were purchased by ABC.

There are several advantages to an asset purchase, most notably, that the acquiring corporation can pick which assets and liabilities it wishes to acquire. Furthermore, XYZ may avoid a shareholder vote if it is not selling all or substantially all of its assets. (This has important qualifiers, as discussed further on in this chapter).

For example, after several years of successful merchandising, a corporation formed by Bob, Carol, and Ted (BCT Bookstore, Inc.) has opened three branch stores around town and discovered its transportation costs mounting. Inventory arrives in trucks operated by the Flying Truckman Co., Inc. The BCT corporation concludes that the economics of delivery do not warrant purchasing a single truck dedicated to hauling books for its four stores alone. Then Bob learns that the owners of Flying Truckman might be willing to part with most of their assets, because it has not been earning money lately. If BCT could reorganize Flying Truckman's other routes, it could reduce its own shipping costs while making a profit on other lines of business.

Under the circumstances, the simplest way to acquire Flying Truckman is by purchasing its assets. That way BCT would own the trucks and whatever routes it chooses, without taking upon itself any reputational baggage associated with Flying Truckman, and could even stop using the name Flying Truckman.

In most states, the board of directors of both the seller and the buyer must approve a transfer of assets. Shareholders of the selling corporation must also consent by majority vote, but shareholders of the acquiring company need not be consulted; if Bob likes the idea, it will require both Ted and Carol to oppose it as directors. See Figure 47.1. (When inventory is sold in bulk, the acquiring company must also comply with the law governing bulk transfers; see Chapter 18.) By purchasing the assets—trucks, truck routes, and the trademark Flying Truckman (to prevent anyone else from using it) — the acquiring corporation can carry on the functions of the acquired company without carrying on its business as such.[1]

FIGURE 47.1 Purchase of Assets

Who must approve the sale of assets for cash from one company to another?

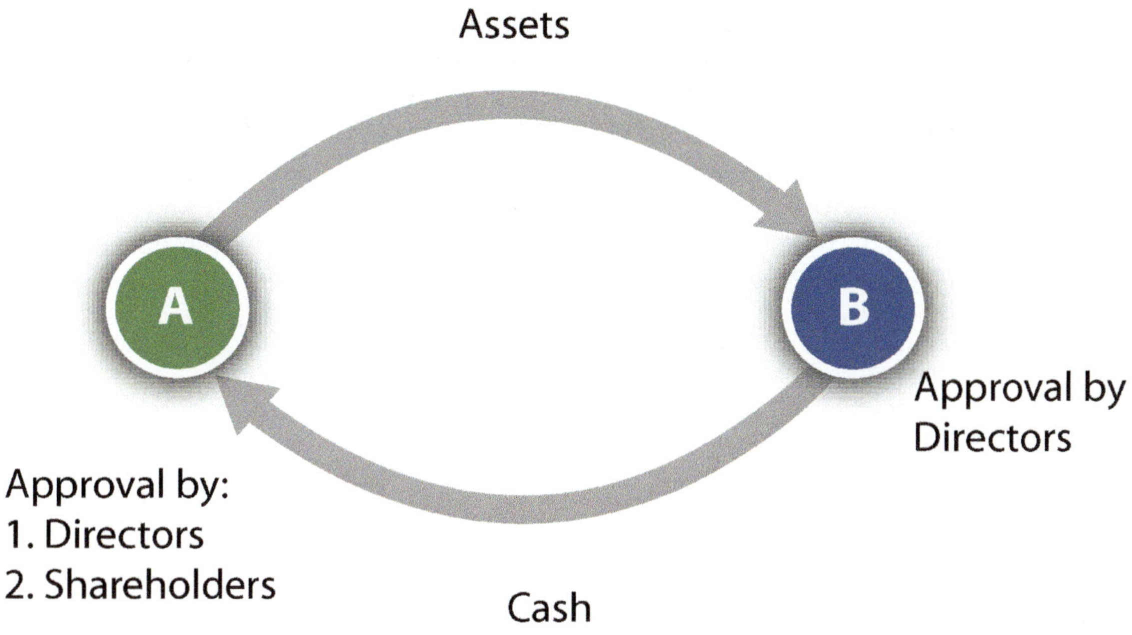

Successor Liability

One of the principal advantages of this method of expansion is that the acquiring company generally is not liable for the debts and/or lawsuits of the corporation whose assets it purchased, generally known as **successor liability**. Suppose BCT paid Flying Truckman $250,000 for its trucks, routes, and name. With that cash, Flying Truckman paid off several of its creditors. Its shareholders then voted to dissolve the corporation, leaving one creditor unsatisfied. The creditor can no longer sue Flying Truckman since it does not exist. So he sues BCT. Unless certain circumstances exist, as discussed in *Ray v. Alad Corporation* (in 47.4, Cases), BCT is not liable for Flying Truckman's debts.

successor liability

The liability of an acquiring company for the debts and/or lawsuits of the corporation whose assets it purchased.

Several states, although not a majority, have adopted the Ray product-line exception approach to successor liability. The general rule is that the purchasing corporation does not take the liabilities of the acquired corporation. Several exceptions exist, as described in *Ray*, the principal exception being the product-line approach. This minority exception has been further limited in several jurisdictions by applying it solely to cases involving products liability. Other jurisdictions also permit a continuity-of-enterprise exception, whereby the court examines how closely the acquiring corporation's business is to the acquired corporation's business (e.g., see *Turner v. Bituminous Casualty Co.*).[2]

Merger

When the assets of a company are purchased, the selling company itself may or may not go out of existence. By contrast, in a merger, the acquired company goes out of existence by being absorbed into the acquiring company. In the example, Flying Truck would merge into BCT, resulting in Flying Truckman, losing its corporate existence entirely. The acquiring company receives all of the acquired company's assets, including physical property and intangible property such as contracts and goodwill. The acquiring company also assumes all debts of the acquired company.

A merger begins when two or more corporations negotiate an agreement outlining the specifics of a merger, such as which corporation survives and who will run the company after the merger. There are two main types of merger: a cash merger and a non-cash merger. In a cash merger, the shareholders of the disappearing corporation surrender their shares for cash. After the buy out of their shares, these shareholders retain no interest in the surviving corporation. This is often called a freeze-out merger.

In a noncash merger, the shareholders of the disappearing corporation retain an interest in the surviving corporation. The shareholders of the disappearing corporation trade their shares for shares in the surviving corporation; thus they retain an interest in the surviving corporation when they become shareholders of that surviving corporation.

Unless the articles of incorporation state otherwise, majority approval of the merger by both boards of directors and both sets of shareholders is necessary (see Figure 47.2). The shareholder majority must be of the total shares eligible to vote, not merely of the total actually represented at the special meeting called for the purpose of determining whether to merge.

FIGURE 47.2 Merger
Who must approve a merger when corporation A merges with corporation B?

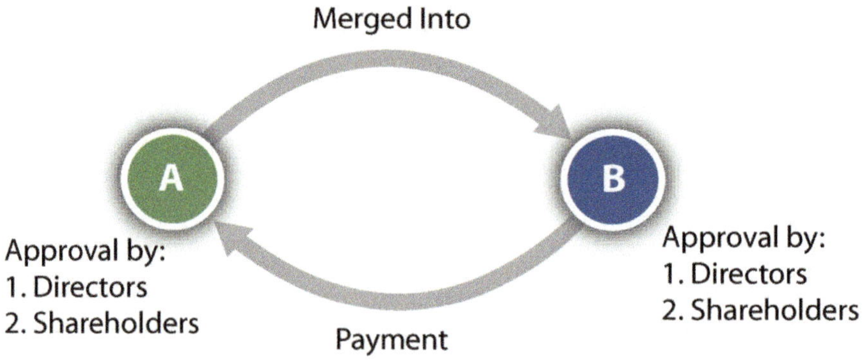

Consolidation

Consolidation

A corporate expansion similar to a merger but resulting in an entity that is an entirely new corporation.

Consolidation operates much like a merger, except that when the companies merge, the resulting entity is a new corporation. For example, BCT and Flying Truckman could consolidate and form a new corporation. As with mergers, the boards and shareholders must approve the consolidation by majority votes (see Figure 47.3). The resulting corporation becomes effective when the secretary of state issues a certificate of merger or incorporation.

FIGURE 47.3 Consolidation
What happens in a consolidation?

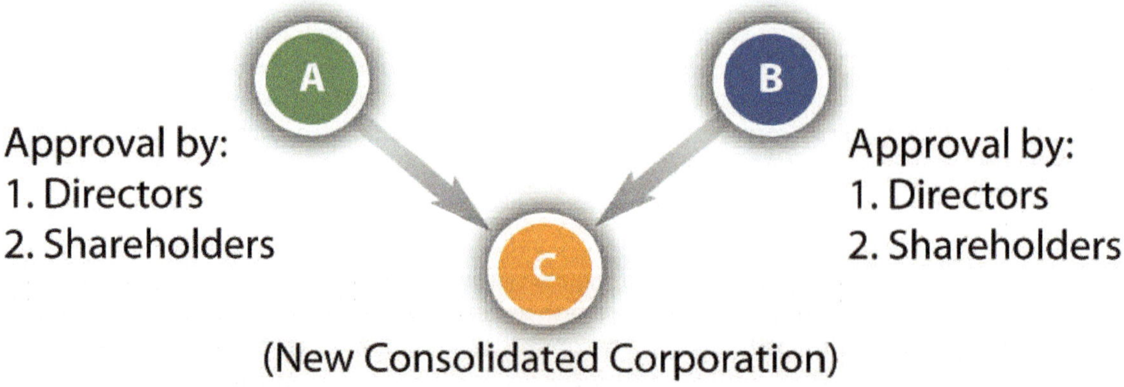

For more information on mergers and consolidation under Delaware law, see Del. Code Ann., Title 8, Sections 251–267 (2011), at http://delcode.delaware.gov/title8/index.shtml#TopOfPage.

Purchase of Stock

Takeovers

The fourth method of expanding, purchase of a company's stock, is more complicated than the other methods. The takeover has become a popular method for gaining control because it does not require an affirmative vote by the target company's board of directors. In a **takeover**, often called a "hostile takeover" when the target company's board and management resist, the acquiring company will appeal directly to the target's shareholders. This is done by offering either money or other securities, often at a premium over market value, in exchange for shares of the target company. The acquiring company usually doesn't need to purchase 100 percent of the shares; if the shares are numerous and widely enough dispersed, control can be achieved by acquiring less than half the outstanding stock. In our example, if Flying Truckman has shareholders, BCT would make an offer directly to those shareholders to acquire their shares.

takeover

An appeal directly to the shareholders of a target corporation by offering money or other securities in exchange for the shareholders' shares.

Tender Offers

In the case of closely held corporations, it is possible for a company bent on takeover to negotiate with each stockholder individually, making a direct offer to purchase his or her shares. That is impossible in the case of large publicly held companies since it is impracticable and/or too expensive to reach each individual shareholder. To reach all shareholders, the acquiring company must make a tender offer, which is a public offer to purchase shares. In fact, the tender offer is not really an offer at all in the technical sense; the **tender offer** is an invitation to shareholders to sell their shares at a stipulated price. The tender offer might express the price in cash or in shares of the acquiring company. Ordinarily, the offeror will want to purchase only a controlling interest, so it will limit the tender to a specified number of shares and reserve the right not to purchase any above that number. It will also condition the tender offer on receiving a minimum number of shares so that it need buy none if stockholders do not offer a threshold number of shares for purchase.

tender offer

An invitation to the shareholders of a target corporation to tender their shares for a stipulated price. Often used when a target has many shareholders.

Leveraged Buyouts

A tender offer or other asset purchase can be financed as a **leveraged buyout (LBO)**, a purchase financed by debt. A common type of LBO involves investors who are members of the target corporation and/or outsiders who wish to take over the target or retain a controlling interest. These purchasers use the assets of the target corporation, such as its real estate or a manufacturing plant, as security for a loan to purchase the target. The purchasers also use other types of debt, such as the issuance of bonds or a loan, to implement the LBO.

For more information about tender offers and mergers, see *Unocal v. Mesa*[3] and *Revlon v. MacAndrews & Forbes*.[4]

leveraged buyout (LBO)

The acquisition of another company using a significant amount of borrowed money to pay for the acquisition. Often, the assets of the company being acquired may be used as collateral for the loans.

State versus Federal Regulation of Takeovers

Under the federal Williams Act, whenever this is a tender offer for more than 5 percent of the target's stock, the offeror must file a statement with the Securities and Exchange Commission (SEC) stating the source of funds to be used in making the purchase, the purpose of the purchase, and the extent of its holdings in the target company. Even when a tender offer has not been made, the Williams Act requires any person who acquires more than 5 percent ownership of a corporation to file a statement with the SEC within ten days. The US Constitution is also implicated in the regulation of foreign corporations. The Commerce Clause of Article I, Section 8, of the Constitution provides that Congress has power "to regulate Commerce...among the several States."

Because officers and directors of target companies have no legal say in whether stockholders will tender their shares, many states began, in the early 1970s, to enact takeover laws. The first generation of these laws acted as delaying devices by imposing lengthy waiting periods before a tender offer could be put into effect. Many of the laws expressly gave management of the target companies a right to a hearing, which could go on for weeks or months, giving the target time to build up a defense. The political premise of the laws was the protection of incumbent managers from takeover by out-of-state corporations, although the "localness" of some managers was mostly a polite fiction. One such law was enacted in Illinois. It required notifying the Illinois secretary of state and the target corporation of the intent to make a tender offer twenty days prior to the offer. During that time, the corporation seeking to make the tender offer could not spread information about the offer. Finally, the secretary of state could delay the tender offer by ordering a hearing and could even deny the offer if it was deemed inequitable. In 1982, the Supreme Court, in *Edgar v. Mite Corp.*, struck down the Illinois takeover law because it violated the Commerce Clause, which prohibits states from unduly burdening the flow of interstate commerce, and also was preempted by the Williams Act.[5]

Following the *Mite* decision, states began to enact a second generation of takeover laws. In 1987, in *CTS Corporation v. Dynamics Corporation of America*, the Supreme Court upheld an Indiana second-generation statute that prevents an offeror who has acquired 20 percent or more of a target's stock from voting unless other shareholders (not including management) approve. The vote to approve can be delayed for up to fifty days from the date the offeror files a statement reporting the acquisition. The Court concluded that the Commerce Clause was not violated nor was the Williams Act, because the Indiana law, unlike the Illinois law in *Mite*, was consistent with the Williams Act, since it protects shareholders, does not unreasonably delay the tender offer, and does not discriminate against interstate commerce.[6]

Emboldened by the *CTS* decision, almost half the states have adopted a third-generation law that requires a bidder to wait several years before merging with the target company unless the target's board agrees in advance to the merger. Because in many cases a merger is the reason for the bid, these laws are especially powerful. In 1989, the Seventh Circuit Court of Appeals upheld Wisconsin's third-generation law, saying that it did not violate the Commerce Clause and that it was not preempted by the Williams Act. The Supreme Court decided not to review the decision.[7]

Short-Form Mergers

If one company acquires 90 percent or more of the stock of another company, it can merge with the target company through the so-called **short-form merger**. Only the parent company's board of directors need approve the merger; consent of the shareholders of either company is unnecessary.

short-form merger

If the one company acquires 90 percent or more of the stock of another company, it can initiate a merger without the consent of the shareholders.

Appraisal Rights

Because shareholders have the right to vote on a corporate plan to merge, consolidate, or sell all or substantially all of its assets, those shareholders also have the right to dissent and invoke **appraisal rights**. Returning again to BCT, suppose that Bob and Carol, as shareholders, are anxious to acquire Flying Truckman, but Ted has serious doubts, and actually believes that the cost of the acquisition outweigh the financial benefits to BCT. He could invoke his appraisal rights to dissent from an expansion involving Flying Truckman. The law requires the shareholder to file with the corporation, before the vote, a notice of intention to demand the fair value of his shares. If the plan is approved and the shareholder does not vote in favor, the corporation must send a notice to the shareholder specifying procedures for obtaining payment, and the shareholder must demand payment within the time set in the notice, which cannot be less than thirty days. Fair value means the

appraisal rights

If a shareholder has the right to vote on a corporate plan to merge, consolidate, or sell all or substantially all of its assets, that shareholder has the right to dissent and demand compensation.

value of shares immediately before the effective date of the corporate action to which the shareholder has objected. Appreciation and depreciation in anticipation of the action are excluded, unless the exclusion is unfair.

If the shareholder and the company cannot agree on the fair value, the shareholder must file a petition requesting a court to determine the fair value. The method of determining fair value depends on the circumstances. When there is a public market for stock traded on an exchange, fair value is usually the price quoted on the exchange. In some circumstances, other factors, especially net asset value and investment value—for example, earnings potential—assume greater importance.

See *Hariton v. Arco Electronics, Inc.*[8] and *M.P.M. Enterprises, Inc. v. Gilbert*[9] for further discussion of appraisal rights and when they may be invoked.

Key Takeaway

There are four main methods of corporate expansion. The first involves the purchase of assets not in the ordinary course of business. Using this method, the purchase expands the corporation. The second and third methods, merger and consolidation, are very similar: two or more corporations combine. In a merger, one of the merging companies survives, and the other ceases to exist. In a consolidation, the merging corporations cease to exist when they combine to form a new corporation. The final method is a stock purchase, accomplished via a tender offer, takeover, or leveraged buyout. Federal and state regulations play a significant role in takeovers and tender offers, particularly the Williams Act. A shareholder who does not wish to participate in a stock sale may invoke his appraisal rights and demand cash compensation for his shares.

Exercises

1. What are some benefits in purchasing the assets of another corporation? What dangers might there be in purchasing the assets of another corporation?
2. What are some possible rationales behind statutes such as the Williams Act and state anti-takeover statutes?
3. When may a shareholder invoke appraisal rights?

47.2 Foreign Corporations

Learning Objectives

1. Discuss state-imposed conditions on the admission of foreign corporations.
2. Discuss state court jurisdiction over foreign corporations.
3. Explain how states may tax foreign corporations.
4. Apply the US Constitution to foreign corporations.

A **foreign corporation** is a company incorporated outside the state in which it is doing business. A Delaware corporation, operating in all states, is a foreign corporation in forty-nine of them.

foreign corporation

A company incorporated outside the state in which it is doing business.

Conditions on Admission to Do Business

A state can impose conditions on foreign corporations wishing to do business in its territory, as long as certain constitutional conditions are met. One such condition is the Privileges and Immunities Clause in Article IV, Section 2, of the Constitution. It says that "citizens shall be entitled to all privileges and immunities of citizens in the several states." The Supreme Court has interpreted this to mean that states may not discriminate in favor of their own citizens relative to those from other states. For example, the Court voided a tax New Hampshire imposed on out-of-state commuters on the grounds that "the tax falls exclusively on the incomes of nonresidents."[10] But the Court has also held that corporaints are not to be treated as "citizens" for purposes of this clause; thus, the states may impose burdens on foreign corporations that they do not put upon companies incorporated under their laws.

Other constitutional rights of the corporation or its members may also come into play when states attempt to license foreign corporations. Arkansas sought to revoke the license of a Missouri construction company to do business within the state, because the company had gone to federal court with a dispute that had taken place in Arkansas, rather than use the state courts of Arkansas. The Supreme Court held that the state had acted unconstitutionally (violating Article III, Section 2, of the U.S. Constitution) in conditioning the license on a waiver of the right to remove a case from the state courts to the federal courts.[11]

The Court said: "The principle established by the more recent decisions of this Court is that a state may not, in imposing conditions upon the privilege of a foreign corporation's doing business in the state, exact from it a waiver of the exercise of its constitutional right to resort to the federal courts, or thereafter withdraw the privilege of doing business because of its exercise of such right, whether waived in advance or not."

Typical Requirements for Foreign Corporations

Certain preconditions for doing business are common to most states. Foreign corporations must get a certificate of authority to do business from the secretary of state. Any foreign corporation also must maintain a registered office with a registered agent who works there. (This is a requirement of all corporations, foreign or domestic, as potential plaintiffs need to know who and where to serve a summons and complaint against the company.) Once provided with a certificate of authority, foreign corporations are generally granted every right and privilege enjoyed by domestic corporations.

transacting business

A minimum level of corporate activities required for a corporation to need a certificate of authority.

These requirements must be met whenever the corporation transacts business within the state. Some activities do not fall within the definition of **transacting business** and may be carried on even if the foreign corporation has not obtained a certificate of authority. These include defending a lawsuit, holding meetings of directors or shareholders, maintaining bank accounts, selling through independent contractors, soliciting orders through agents or employees (but only if the orders become binding contracts upon acceptance outside the state), creating or acquiring security interests in real or personal property, securing or collecting debts, transacting any business in interstate commerce, and "conducting an isolated transaction that is completed within 30 days and that is not one in the course of repeated transactions of a like nature" (Revised Model Business Corporation Act, Section 15.01). Notice that any or all of these do not require having a fixed place of business within the state; if BCT as a Delaware corporation wanted to have an office in DesMoines, Iowa, or open a chain of bookstores in Iowa, it would need to have a certificate of authority from Iowa's Secretary of State.

Penalties for Failure to Comply with a Statute

A corporation may not sue in the state courts to enforce its rights until it obtains a certificate of authority. It may defend any lawsuits brought against it, however. The state attorney general has authority to collect civil penalties that vary from state to state. Other sanctions in various states include fines and penalties on taxes owed; fines and imprisonment of corporate agents, directors, and officers; nullification of corporate contracts; and personal liability on contracts by officers and directors. In some states, contracts made by a corporation that has failed to qualify are void.

Jurisdiction over Foreign Corporations

Whether corporations are subject to state court jurisdiction depends on the extent to which they are operating within the state. If the corporation is qualified to do business within the state and has a certificate of authority or license, then state courts have jurisdiction and process may be served on the corporation's registered agent. If the corporation has failed to name an agent or is doing business without a certificate, the plaintiff may serve the secretary of state on the corporation's behalf.

Even if the corporation is not transacting enough business within the state to be required to qualify for a certificate or license, it may still be subject to suit in state courts under long-arm statutes. These laws permit state courts to exercise personal jurisdiction over a corporation that has sufficient contacts with the state.

The major constitutional limitation on long-arm statutes is the Due Process Clause. The Supreme Court upheld the validity of long-arm statutes applied to corporations in *International Shoe Co. v. Washington*.[12] But the long-arm statute will only be constitutionally valid where there are minimum contacts—that is, for a state to exercise personal jurisdiction over a foreign corporation, the foreign corporation must have at least "minimum contacts" the state. That jurisdictional test is still applied many years after the *International Shoe* decision was handed down.[13] Since *International Shoe*, the nationalization of commerce has given way to the internationalization of commerce. This change has resulted in difficult jurisdictional questions that involve conflicting policy considerations.[14]

Some of the most difficult jurisdictional questions are raised in the context of global contracts and trade, which we will consider in Chapter 51, International Law.

Taxing Authority

May a state tax foreign corporations on income earned by its operations in that state? Since a state can clearly tax its domestic corporations, the question might seem surprising. Why should a state ever be barred from taxing foreign corporations licensed to do business in the state? If the foreign corporation was engaged in purely local, intrastate business, no quarrel would arise. The constitutional difficulty is allocating what portion of the company's income is attributable to intra-state activities, and whether the tax is an unreasonable burden on the company's interstate business. That would be a violation of the Constitution's **Commerce Clause**. The basic approach, illustrated in *D. H. Holmes Co., Ltd. v. McNamara* (see Section 4), is that a state can impose a tax on activities for which the state gives legal protection, so long as the tax does not unreasonably burden interstate commerce.

Commerce Clause

Provision in the US Constitution that gives Congress the power to regulate commerce between the states.

State taxation of corporate income raises special concerns. In the absence of ground rules, a company doing business in many states could be liable for paying income tax to several different states on the basis of its total earnings. A company doing business in all fifty states, for example, would pay five times its earnings in income taxes if each state were to charge a 10 percent tax on those earnings. Obviously, such a result would seriously burden interstate commerce. The courts have long held, therefore, that the states may only tax that portion of the company's earnings attributable to the business carried on in the state. To compute the proportion of a company's total earnings subject to tax within the state, most states have adopted a formula based on the local percentage of the company's total sales, property, and payroll.

Key Takeaway

A foreign corporation is a company incorporated outside of the state in which it is doing business. States can place reasonable limitations upon foreign corporations subject to constitutional requirements. A foreign corporation must do something that is sufficient to rise to the level of transacting business within a state in order to fall under the jurisdiction of that state. These transactions must meet the minimum-contacts requirement for jurisdiction under long-arm statutes. A state may tax a foreign corporation as long as it does not burden interstate commerce.

Exercises

1. What are some typical requirements that a corporation must meet in order to operate in a foreign state?
2. Provide examples of business activities that rise to the level of minimum contacts such as that a state may exercise jurisdiction over a foreign corporation.
3. What are some possible jurisdictional problems that arise from increasing globalization and from many corporations providing input for a particular product? For more information, see the *Asahi Metal* and *Pavlovich* court cases, cited in endnotes 13 and 14.

47.3 Dissolution

Learning Objectives

1. Define and distinguish dissolution and liquidation.
2. Discuss the different types of dissolution and liquidation.
3. Discuss claims against a dissolved corporation.

Dissolution

The end of the existence of a corporation.

liquidation

The process of paying creditors and distributing the assets of a corporation.

Dissolution is the end of the legal existence of the corporation. It is, basically, "corporate death." It is not the same as **liquidation**, which is the process of paying the creditors and distributing the assets. Until dissolved, a corporation endures, despite the ups and downs of the economy or the corporation's internal affairs. As Justice Cardozo said while serving as chief judge of the New York Court of Appeals: "Neither bankruptcy...nor cessation of business...nor dispersion of stockholders, nor the absence of directors...nor all combined, will avail without more to stifle the breath of juristic personality. The corporation abides as an ideal creation, impervious to the shocks of these temporal vicissitudes. Not even the sequestration of the assets at the hands of a receiver will terminate its being."[15]

See http://www.irs.gov/businesses/small/article/0,,id=98703,00.html for the Internal Revenue Service's checklist of closing and dissolving a business. State and local government regulations may also apply.

Voluntary Dissolution

Any corporation may be dissolved with the unanimous written consent of the shareholders; this is a **voluntary dissolution**. This provision applies primarily to closely held corporations. Dissolution can also be accomplished even if some shareholders dissent. The directors must first adopt a resolution by majority vote recommending the dissolution. The shareholders must then have an opportunity to vote on the resolution at a meeting after being notified of its purpose. A majority of the outstanding voting shares is necessary to carry the resolution. Although this procedure is most often used when a company has been inactive, nothing bars its use by large corporations. In 1979, UV Industries, then number 357 on the *Fortune* 500 list, with profits of $40 million annually, voted to dissolve and to distribute some $500 million to its stockholders. In part, this was done to fend off a hostile takeover. *Fortune* magazine referred to it as "a company that's worth more dead than alive."[16]

voluntary dissolution

Dissolution of a corporation by unanimous written consent of its shareholders.

Once dissolution has been approved, the corporation may dissolve by filing a certificate or articles of dissolution with the secretary of state. The certificate may be filed as the corporation begins to wind up its affairs or at any time thereafter. The process of winding up is called "liquidation." The company must notify all creditors of its intention to liquidate. It must collect and dispose of its assets, discharge all obligations, and distribute any remainder to its stockholders.

Involuntary Dissolution

In certain cases, a corporation can face **involuntary dissolution**. A state may bring an action to dissolve a corporation on one of five grounds: failure to file an annual report or pay taxes, fraud in procuring incorporation, exceeding or abusing authority conferred, failure for thirty days to appoint and maintain a registered agent, and failure to notify the state of a change of registered office or agent. State-specific differences exist as well. Delaware permits its attorney general to involuntarily dissolve a corporation for abuse, misuse, or nonuse of corporate powers, privileges, or franchise.[17] California, on the other hand, permits involuntary dissolution for abandonment of a business, board deadlocks, internal strife and deadlocked shareholders, mismanagement, fraud or abuse of authority, expiration of term of corporation, or protection of a complaining shareholder if there are fewer than thirty-five shareholders.[18] California permits the initiation of involuntary dissolution by vote of half of the directors in office or by a third of shareholders.

involuntary dissolution

A state action to dissolve a corporation.

Judicial Liquidation

Action by Shareholder

A shareholder may file suit to have a court dissolve the company on a showing that the company is being irreparably injured because the directors are deadlocked in the management of corporate affairs and the shareholders cannot break the deadlock. Shareholders may also sue for liquidation if corporate assets are being misapplied or wasted, or if directors or those in control are acting illegally, oppressively, or fraudulently.

Claims against a Dissolved Corporation

Under Sections 14.06 and 14.07 of the Revised Model Business Corporation Act, a dissolved corporation must provide written notice of the dissolution to its creditors. The notice must state a deadline, which must be at least 120 days after the notice, for receipt of creditors' claims. Claims not received by the deadline are barred. The corporation may also publish a notice of the dissolution in a local newspaper. Creditors who do not receive written notice or whose claim is not acted on have five years to file suit against the corporation. If the corporate assets have been distributed, shareholders are personally liable, although the liability may not exceed the assets received at liquidation.

Bankruptcy

As an alternative to dissolution, a corporation in financial trouble may look to federal bankruptcy law for relief. A corporation may use liquidation proceedings under Chapter 7 of the Bankruptcy Reform Act or may be reorganized under Chapter 11 of the act. Both remedies are discussed in detail in Chapter 30.

Key Takeaway

Dissolution is the end of the legal existence of a corporation. It usually occurs after liquidation, which is the process of paying debts and distributing assets. There are several methods by which a corporation may be dissolved. The first is voluntary dissolution, which is an elective decision to dissolve the entity. A second is involuntary dissolution, which occurs upon the happening of statute-specific events such as a failure to pay taxes. Last, a corporation may be dissolved judicially, either by shareholder or creditor lawsuit. A dissolved corporation must provide notice to its creditors of upcoming dissolution.

Exercises

1. What are the main types of dissolution?
2. What is the difference between dissolution and liquidation?
3. What are the rights of a stockholder to move for dissolution?

47.4 Cases

Successor Liability

Ray v. Alad Corporation

19 Cal. 3d 22; 560 P2d 3; 136 Cal. Rptr. 574 (Cal. 1977)

Claiming damages for injury from a defective ladder, plaintiff asserts strict tort liability against defendant Alad Corporation (Alad II), which neither manufactured nor sold the ladder but, prior to plaintiff's injury, had succeeded to the business of the ladder's manufacturer, the now dissolved "Alad Corporation" (Alad I), through a purchase of Alad I's assets for adequate cash consideration. Upon acquiring Alad I's plant, equipment, inventory, trade name, and good will, Alad II continued to manufacture the same line of ladders under the "Alad" name, using the same equipment, designs, and personnel, and soliciting Alad I's customers through the same sales representatives with no outward indication of any change in the ownership of the business. The trial court entered summary judgment for Alad II and plaintiff appeals....

Our discussion of the law starts with the rule ordinarily applied to the determination of whether a corporation purchasing the principal assets of another corporation assumes the other's liabilities. As typically formulated, the rule states that the purchaser does not assume the seller's liabilities unless (1) there is an express or implied agreement of assumption, (2) the transaction amounts to a consolidation or merger of the two corporations, (3) the purchasing corporation is a mere continuation of the seller, or (4) the transfer of assets to the purchaser is for the fraudulent purpose of escaping liability for the seller's debts.

If this rule were determinative of Alad II's liability to plaintiff it would require us to affirm the summary judgment. None of the rule's four stated grounds for imposing liability on the purchasing corporation is present here. There was no express or implied agreement to assume liability for injury from defective products previously manufactured by Alad I. Nor is there any indication or contention that the transaction was prompted by any fraudulent purpose of escaping liability for Alad I's debts.

With respect to the second stated ground for liability, the purchase of Alad I's assets did not amount to a consolidation or merger. This exception has been invoked where one corporation takes all of another's assets without providing any consideration that could be made available to meet claims of the other's creditors or where the consideration consists wholly of shares of the purchaser's stock which are promptly distributed to the seller's shareholders in conjunction with the seller's liquidation. In the present case the sole consideration given for Alad I's assets was cash in excess of $207,000 [about $833,000 in 2017 dollars]. Of this amount Alad I was paid $70,000 when the assets were transferred and at the same time a promissory note was given to Alad I for almost $114,000. Shortly before the dissolution of Alad I the note was assigned to the Hamblys, Alad I's principal stockholders, and thereafter the note was paid in full. The remainder of the consideration went for closing expenses or was paid to the Hamblys for consulting services and their agreement not to compete. There is no contention that this consideration was inadequate or that the cash and promissory note given to Alad I were not included in the assets available to meet claims of Alad I's creditors at the time of dissolution. Hence, the acquisition of Alad I's assets was not in the nature of a merger or consolidation for purposes of the aforesaid rule.

Plaintiff contends that the rule's third stated ground for liability makes Alad II liable as a mere continuation of Alad I in view of Alad II's acquisition of all Alad I's operating assets, its use of those assets and of Alad I's former employees to manufacture the same line of products, and its holding itself out to customers and the public as a continuation of the same enterprise. However, California decisions hold that a corporation acquiring the assets of another corporation is only liable for its debts where (1) no adequate consideration was given for the predecessor corporation's assets and made available for meeting the claims of its unsecured creditors; (2) one or more persons were officers, directors, or stockholders of both corporations. * * *

We therefore conclude that the general rule governing succession to liabilities does not require Alad II to respond to plaintiff's claim. * * *

[However], we must decide whether the policies underlying strict tort liability for defective products call for a special exception to the rule that would otherwise insulate the present defendant from plaintiff's claim.

The purpose of the rule of strict tort liability "is to insure that the costs of injuries resulting from defective products are borne by the manufacturers that put such products on the market rather than by the injured persons who are powerless to protect themselves." However, the rule does not rest on the analysis of the financial strength or bargaining power of the parties to the particular action. It rests, rather, on the proposition that 'The cost of an injury and the loss of time or health may be an overwhelming misfortune to the person injured, and a needless one, for the risk of injury can be insured by the manufacturer and distributed among the public as a cost of doing business. [Citation.] Thus, "the paramount policy to be promoted by the rule is the protection of otherwise defenseless victims of manufacturing defects and the *spreading throughout society* of the cost of compensating them." Justification for imposing strict liability upon a *successor* to a manufacturer under the circumstances here presented rests upon (1) the virtual destruction of the plaintiff's remedies against the original manufacturer caused by the successor's acquisition of the business, (2) the successor's ability to assume the original manufacturer's risk-spreading role, and (3) the fairness of requiring the successor to assume a responsibility for defective products that was a burden necessarily attached to the original manufacturer's good will being enjoyed by the successor in the continued operation of the business.

We therefore conclude that a party which acquires a manufacturing business and continues the output of its line of products under the circumstances here presented assumes strict tort liability for defects in units of the same product line previously manufactured and distributed by the entity from which the business was acquired.

The judgment is reversed.

Case Questions

1. What is the general rule regarding successor liability?
2. How does the *Ray* court deviate from this general rule?
3. What is the court's rationale for this deviation?
4. What are some possible consequences for corporations considering expansion?

Constitutional Issues Surrounding Taxation of a Foreign Corporation

D. H. Holmes Co. Ltd. V. McNamara

486 U.S. 24; 108 S.Ct. 1619, 100 L. Ed. 2d 21 (1988)

Appellant D. H. Holmes Company, Ltd., is a Louisiana corporation with its principal place of business and registered office in New Orleans. Holmes owns and operates 13 department stores in various locations throughout Louisiana that employ about 5,000 workers. It has approximately 500,000 credit card customers and an estimated 1,000,000 other customers within the State.

In 1979–1981, Holmes contracted with several New York companies for the design and printing of merchandise catalogs. The catalogs were designed in New York, but were actually printed in Atlanta, Boston, and Oklahoma City. From these locations, 82% of the catalogs were directly mailed to residents of Louisiana; the remainder of the catalogs was mailed to customers in Alabama, Mississippi, and Florida, or was sent to Holmes for distribution at its flagship store on Canal Street in New Orleans. The catalogs were shipped free of charge to the addressee, and their entire cost (about $ 2 million for the 3-year period) [about $6.7 million in 2017 dollars], including mailing, was borne by Holmes. Holmes did not, however, pay any sales tax where the catalogs were designed or printed.

Although the merchandise catalogs were mailed to selected customers, they contained instructions to the postal carrier to leave them with the current resident if the addressee had moved, and to return undeliverable catalogs to Holmes' Canal Street store. Holmes freely concedes that the purpose of the catalogs was to promote sales at its stores and to instill name recognition in future buyers. The catalogs included inserts which could be used to order Holmes' products by mail.

The Louisiana Department of Revenue and Taxation, of which appellee is the current Secretary, conducted an audit of Holmes' tax returns for 1979–1981 and determined that it was liable for delinquent use taxes on the value of the catalogs. The Department of Revenue and Taxation assessed the use tax pursuant to La. Rev. Stat. Ann. §§ 47:302 and 47:321. Together, they impose a use tax of 3% on all tangible personal property used in Louisiana. "Use," as defined elsewhere in the statute, is the exercise of any right or power over tangible personal property incident to ownership, and includes consumption, distribution, and storage. The use tax is designed to compensate the State for sales tax that is lost when goods are purchased out-of-state and brought for use into Louisiana, and is calculated on the retail price the property would have brought when imported.

When Holmes refused to pay the use tax assessed against it, the State filed suit in Louisiana Civil District Court to collect the tax. [The lower courts held for the State.] * * *

The Commerce Clause of the Constitution, Art. I, § 8, cl. 3, provides that Congress shall have the power "to regulate Commerce with foreign Nations, and among the several States, and with the Indian Tribes." Even where Congress has not acted affirmatively to protect interstate commerce, the Clause prevents States from discriminating against that commerce. The "distinction between the power of the State to shelter its people from menaces to their health or safety and from fraud, even when those dangers emanate from interstate commerce, and its lack of power to retard, burden or constrict the flow of such commerce for their economic advantage, is one deeply rooted in both our history and our law." *[Citation].*

One frequent source of conflict of this kind occurs when a State seeks to tax the sale or use of goods within its borders. This recurring dilemma is exemplified in what has come to be the leading case in the area. *Complete Auto Transit, Inc. v. Brady, 430 U.S. 274, (1977).* In *Complete Auto*, Mississippi imposed a tax on appellant's business of in-state transportation of motor vehicles manufactured outside the State. We found that the State's tax did not violate the Commerce Clause, because appellant's activity had a substantial nexus with Mississippi, and the tax was fairly apportioned, did not discriminate against interstate commerce, and was fairly related to benefits provided by the State.

Complete Auto abandoned the abstract notion that interstate commerce "itself" cannot be taxed by the States. We recognized that, with certain restrictions, interstate commerce may be required to pay its fair share of state taxes. Accordingly, in the present case, it really makes little difference for Commerce Clause purposes whether Holmes' catalogs "came to rest" in the mailboxes of its Louisiana customers or whether they were still considered in the stream of interstate commerce. * * *

In the case before us, then, the application of Louisiana's use tax to Holmes' catalogs does not violate the Commerce Clause if the tax complies with the four prongs of *Complete Auto*. We have no doubt that the second and third elements of the test are satisfied. The Louisiana taxing scheme is fairly apportioned, for it provides a credit against its use tax for sales taxes that have been paid in other States. Holmes paid no sales tax for the catalogs where they were designed or printed; if it had, it would have been eligible for a credit against the use tax exacted. Similarly, Louisiana imposed its use tax only on the 82% of the catalogs distributed in-state; it did not attempt to tax that portion of the catalogs that went to out-of-state customers.

The Louisiana tax structure likewise does not discriminate against interstate commerce. The use tax is designed to compensate the State for revenue lost when residents purchase out-of-state goods for use within the State. It is equal to the sales tax applicable to the same tangible personal property purchased in-state; in fact, both taxes are set forth in the same sections of the Louisiana statutes.

Complete Auto requires that the tax be fairly related to benefits provided by the State, but that condition is also met here. Louisiana provides a number of services that facilitate Holmes' sale of merchandise within the State: It provides fire and police protection for Holmes' stores, runs mass transit and maintains public roads which benefit Holmes' customers, and supplies a number of other civic services from which Holmes profits. To be sure, many others in the State benefit from the same services; but that does not alter the fact that the use tax paid by Holmes, on catalogs designed to increase sales, is related to the advantages provided by the State which aid Holmes' business.

Finally, we believe that Holmes' distribution of its catalogs reflects a substantial nexus with Louisiana. To begin with, Holmes' contention that it lacked sufficient control over the catalogs' distribution in Louisiana to be subject to the use tax verges on the nonsensical. Holmes ordered and paid for the catalogs and supplied the list of customers to whom the catalogs were sent; any catalogs that could not be delivered were returned to it. Holmes admits that it initiated the distribution to improve its sales and name recognition among Louisiana residents. Holmes also has a significant presence in Louisiana, with 13 stores and over $100 million in annual sales in the State. The distribution of catalogs to approximately 400,000 Louisiana customers was directly aimed at expanding and enhancing its Louisiana business. There is "nexus" aplenty here. [Judgment affirmed.]

Case Questions

1. What is the main constitutional issue in this case?
2. What are the four prongs to test whether a tax violates the Constitution, as laid out in *Complete Auto?*
3. Does this case hold for the proposition that a state may levy any tax upon a foreign corporation?

47.5 Summary and Exercises

Summary

Beyond the normal operations of business, a corporation can expand in one of four ways: (1) purchase of assets, (2) merger, (3) consolidation, and (4) purchase of another corporation's stock.

A purchase of assets occurs when one corporation purchases some or all of the assets of another corporation. When assets are purchased, the purchasing corporation is not generally liable for the debts of the corporation whose assets were sold. There are several generally recognized exceptions, such as when the asset purchase is fraudulent or to avoid creditors. Some states have added additional exceptions, such as in cases involving products liability.

In a merger, the acquired company is absorbed into the acquiring company and goes out of business. The acquiring corporation assumes the other company's debts. Unless the articles of incorporation say otherwise, a majority of directors and shareholders of both corporations must approve the merger. There are two main types of merger: a cash merger and a noncash merger. A consolidation is virtually the same as a merger, except that the resulting entity is a new corporation.

A corporation may take over another company by purchasing a controlling interest of its stock, commonly referred to as a takeover. This is accomplished by appealing directly to the target company's shareholders. In the case of a large publicly held corporation, the appeal is known as a tender offer, which is not an offer but an invitation to shareholders to tender their stock at a stated price. A leveraged buyout involves using the target corporation's assets as security for a loan used to purchase the target.

A shareholder has the right to fair value for his stock if he dissents from a plan to merge, consolidate, or sell all or substantially all of the corporate assets, referred to as appraisal rights. If there is disagreement over the value, the shareholder has the right to a court appraisal. When one company acquires 90 percent of the stock of another, it may merge with the target through a short-form merger, which eliminates the requirement of consent of shareholders and the target company's board.

Certain federal regulations are implicated in corporate expansion, particularly the Williams Act. States may impose conditions on admission of a foreign corporation to do business of a purely local nature but not if its business is exclusively interstate in character, which would violate the Commerce Clause. Among the requirements are obtaining a certificate of authority from the secretary of state and maintaining a registered office with a registered agent. But certain activities do not constitute doing business, such as filing lawsuits and collecting debts, and may be carried on even if the corporation is not licensed to do business in a state. Under long-arm statutes, state courts have jurisdiction over foreign corporations as long as the corporations have minimum contacts in the state. States may also tax corporate activities as long as the tax does not unduly burden interstate commerce.

Dissolution is the legal termination of a corporation's existence, as distinguished from liquidation, the process of paying debts and distributing assets. A corporation may be dissolved by shareholders if they unanimously agree in writing, or by majority vote of the directors and shareholders. A corporation may also be dissolved involuntarily on one of five grounds, including failure to file an annual report or to pay taxes. Shareholders may sue for judicial liquidation on a showing that corporate assets are being wasted or directors or officers are acting illegally or fraudulently.

Exercises

1. Preston Corporation sold all of its assets to Adam Corporation in exchange for Adam stock. Preston then distributed the stock to its shareholders, without paying a debt of $150,000 owed to a major supplier, Corey. Corey, upon discovery that Preston is now an empty shell, attempts to recover the debt from Adam. What is the result? Why?
2. Would the result in Exercise 1 be different if Corey had a products-liability claim against Preston? Why? What measures might you suggest to Adam to prevent potential losses from such claims?
3. In Exercise 1, assuming that Preston and Adam had merged, what are the rights of Graham, a shareholder who opposed the merger? Explain the procedure for enforcing his rights.
4. A bus driver from Massachusetts was injured when his seat collapsed while he was driving his bus through Maine. He brought suit in Massachusetts against the Ohio corporation that manufactured the seat. The Ohio corporation did not have an office in Massachusetts but occasionally sent a sales representative there and delivered parts to the state. Assuming that process was served on the company at its Ohio office, would a Massachusetts court have jurisdiction over the Ohio corporation? Why?

Self-Test Questions

1. In a merger, the acquired company
    a. goes out of existence
    b. stays in existence
    c. is consolidated into a new corporation
    d. does none of the above
2. An offer by an acquiring company to buy shareholders' stock at a stipulated price is called
    a. an appraisal
    b. a short-form merger
    c. a tender offer
    d. none of the above
3. The legal termination of a corporation's existence is called
    a. liquidation
    b. bankruptcy
    c. extinguishment
    d. dissolution
4. The most important constitutional provision relating to a state's ability to tax foreign corporations is
    a. the Commerce Clause

b. the First Amendment
c. the Due Process Clause
d. the Privileges and Immunities Clause

5. An act that is considered to be a corporation's "transacting business" in a state is
   a. collecting debts
   b. holding directors' meetings
   c. filing lawsuits
   d. none of the above

Self-Test Answers

1. a
2. c
3. d
4. a
5. d

Endnotes

1. For a discussion of asset purchases see *Airborne Health v. Squid Soap*, 984 A.2d 126 (Del. 2010).
2. *Turner v. Bituminous Casualty Co.*, 244 N.W.2d 873 (Mich. 1976).
3. *Unocal Corp. v. Mesa Petroleum*, 493 A.2d 946 (Del. 1985).
4. *Revlon, Inc. v. MacAndrews & Forbes Holdings, Inc.*, 506 A.2d 173 (Del. 1985).
5. *Edgar v. Mite Corp.*, 457 U.S. 624 (1982).
6. *CTS Corporation v. Dynamics Corporation of America*, 481 U.S. 69 (1987).
7. *Amanda Acquisition Corp. v. Universal Foods Corp.*, 877 F.2d 496 (7th Cir. 1989).
8. *Hariton v. Arco Electronics, Inc.*, 40 Del. Ch. 326; 182 A.2d 22 (Del. 1962).
9. *M.P.M. Enterprises, Inc. v. Gilbert*, 731 A.2d 790 (Del. 1999).
10. *Austin v. New Hampshire*, 420 U.S. 656 (1975).
11. *Terral v. Burke Construction Co.*, 257 U.S. 529 (1922).
12. *International Shoe Co. v. Washington*, 326 U.S. 310 (1945).
13. *Judas Priest v. District Court*, 104 Nev. 424; 760 P.2d 137 (Nev. 1988); *Pavlovich v. Superior Court*, 29 Cal. 4th 262; 58 P.3d 2 (Cal. 2002).
14. *Asahi Metal Industry v. Superior Court of California*, 480 U.S. 102, 107 S.Ct. 1026, 94 L. Ed. 92 (1987).
15. *Petrogradsky Mejdunarodny Kommerchesky Bank v. National City Bank*, 170 N.E. 479, 482 (N.Y. 1930).
16. *Fortune*, February 26, 1979, 42–44.
17. Del. Code Ann. tit. 8, § 282 (2011).
18. Cal. Corp. Code § 1800 et seq. (West 2011).

CHAPTER 48

Antitrust Law

Learning Objectives

After reading this chapter, you should understand the following:

1. The history and basic framework of antitrust laws on horizontal restraints of trade.
2. The distinction between vertical restraints of trade and horizontal restraints of trade.
3. The various exemptions from antitrust law that Congress has created.
4. Why monopolies pose a threat to competitive markets, and what kinds of monopolies are proscribed by the Sherman Act and the Clayton Act.

This chapter will describe the history and current status of federal laws to safeguard the U.S. market from anticompetitive practices, especially those of very large companies that may have a **monopoly**. Companies that have a monopoly in any market segment have the potential to exercise **monopoly power** in ways that are harmful to consumers and competitors. Economic theory assures us that for the most part, competition is good: that sound markets will offer buyers lots of choices and good information about products and services being sold and will present few barriers to entry for buyers and sellers. By encouraging more, rather than fewer, competitors in a given segment of the market, U.S. antitrust law attempts to preserve consumer choice and to limit barriers to entry, yet it does allow some businesses to achieve considerable size and market share on the belief that size can create efficiencies and pass along the benefits to consumers.

monopoly

A company has a monopoly where it has a large enough percentage of a given market segment to exercise monopoly power in a manner that would adversely affect competition.

monopoly power

The ability of a monopoly to dictate prices and other characteristics in a given market segment.

48.1 History and Basic Framework of Antitrust Laws in the United States

Learning Objectives

1. Know the history and basic framework of antitrust laws in the United States.
2. Understand how US antitrust laws may have international application.
3. Explain how US antitrust laws are enforced and what kinds of criminal and civil penalties may apply.

In this chapter, we take up the origins of the federal antitrust laws and the basic rules governing restraints of trade.[1] We also look at concentrations of market power: monopoly and acquisitions and mergers.[2] In Chapter 49, we explore the law of deceptive acts and unfair trade practices, both as administered by the Federal Trade Commission (FTC) and as regulated at common law.

FIGURE 48.1 An Antitrust Schematic

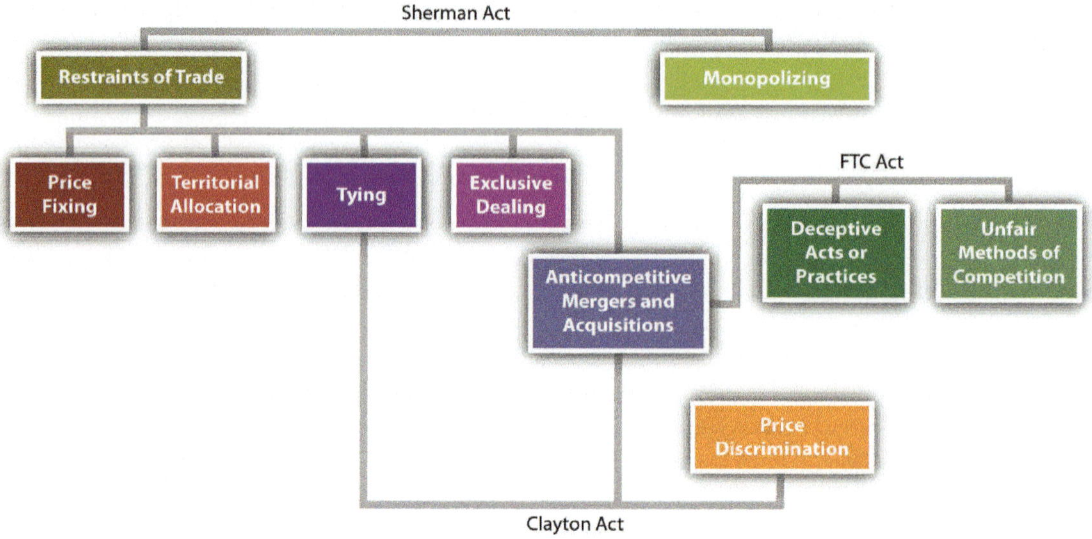

The antitrust laws are aimed at maintaining competition as the driving force of the U.S. economy. The very word *antitrust* implies opposition to the giant trusts that began to develop after the Civil War. Until then, the economy was largely local; manufacturers, distributors, and retailers were generally small. The Civil War demonstrated the utility of large-scale enterprise in meeting the military's ferocious production demands, and business owners were quick to understand the advantage of size in attracting capital. For the first time, immense fortunes could be made in industry, and adventurous entrepreneurs were quick to do so in an age that lauded the acquisitive spirit.

The first great business combinations were the railroads. To avoid ruinous price wars, railroad owners made private agreements, known as "pools," through which they divided markets and offered discounts to favored shippers who agreed to ship goods on certain lines. The pools discriminated against particular shippers and certain geographic regions, and public resentment grew.

Farmers felt the effects first and hardest, and they organized politically to express their opposition. In time, they persuaded many state legislatures to pass laws regulating railroads. In *Munn v. Illinois*, the Supreme Court rejected a constitutional attack on a state law regulating the transportation and warehousing of grain; the court declared that the "police powers" of the states permit the regulation of property put to public uses.[3] But over time, many state railroad laws were struck down because they interfered with interstate commerce, which only Congress may regulate constitutionally. The consequence was federal legislation: the Interstate Commerce Act of 1887, establishing the first federal administrative agency, the Interstate Commerce Commission.

In the meantime, the railroads had discovered that their pools lacked enforcement power. Those who nominally agreed to be bound by the pooling arrangement could and often did cheat. The corporate form of business enterprise allowed for potentially immense accumulations of capital to be under the control of a small number of managers; but in the 1870s and 1880s, the corporation was not yet established as the dominant legal form of operation. To overcome these disadvantages, clever lawyers for John D. Rockefeller organized his Standard Oil of Ohio as a common-law *trust*. Trustees were given corporate stock certificates of various companies; by combining numerous corporations into the trust, the trustees could effectively manage and control an entire industry. Within a decade, the Cotton Trust, Lead Trust, Sugar Trust, and Whiskey Trust, along with oil, telephone, steel, and tobacco trusts, had become, or were in the process of becoming, monopolies.

Consumers howled in protest. The political parties got the message: In 1888, both Republicans and Democrats put an antitrust plank in their platforms. In 1889, the new president, Republican Benjamin Harrison, condemned monopolies as "dangerous conspiracies" and called for legislation to remedy the tendency of monopolies that would "crush out" competition.

The result was the Sherman Antitrust Act of 1890, sponsored by Senator John Sherman of Ohio. Its two key sections forbade combinations in restraint of trade and monopolizing. Senator Sherman and other sponsors declared that the act had roots in a common-law policy that frowned on monopolies. To an extent, it did, but it added something quite important for the future of business and the US economy: the power of the federal government to enforce a national policy against monopoly and restraints of trade. Nevertheless, passage of the Sherman Act did not end the public clamor, because fifteen years passed before a national administration began to enforce the act, when President Theodore Roosevelt—"the Trustbuster"—sent his attorney general after the Northern Securities Corporation, a transportation holding company.

During its seven years, the Roosevelt administration initiated fifty-four antitrust suits. The pace picked up under the Taft administration, which in only four years filed ninety antitrust suits. But the pressure for further reform did not abate, especially when the Supreme Court, in the *Standard Oil* case of 1911,[4] declared that the Sherman Act forbids only "unreasonable" restraints of trade. A congressional investigation of US Steel Corporation brought to light several practices that had gone unrestrained by the Sherman Act. It also sparked an important debate, one that has echoes in our own time, about the nature of national economic policy: should it enforce competition or regulate business in a partnership kind of arrangement?

Big business was firmly on the side of regulation, but Congress opted for the policy followed waveringly to the present: competition enforced by government, not a partnership of government and industry, must be the engine of the economy. Accordingly, in 1914, at the urging of President Woodrow Wilson, Congress enacted two more antitrust laws, the Clayton Act and the Federal Trade Commission Act. The Clayton Act outlawed price discrimination, exclusive dealing and tying contracts, acquisition of a company's competitors, and interlocking directorates. The FTC Act outlawed "unfair methods" of competition, established the FTC as an independent administrative agency, and gave it power to enforce the antitrust laws alongside the Department of Justice.

The Sherman, Clayton, and FTC Acts remain the basic texts of antitrust law. Over the years, many states have enacted antitrust laws as well; these laws govern intrastate competition and are largely modeled on the federal laws. The various state antitrust laws are beyond the scope of this textbook.

Two additional federal statutes were adopted during the next third of a century as amendments to the Clayton Act. Enacted in the midst of the Depression in 1936, the Robinson-Patman Act prohibits various forms of price discrimination. The Celler-Kefauver Act, strengthening the Clayton Act's prohibition against the acquisition of competing companies, was enacted in 1950 in the hopes of stemming what seemed to be a tide of corporate mergers and acquisitions. We will examine these laws in turn.

The Sherman Act

Section 1 of the Sherman Act declares, "Every contract, combination in the form of trust or otherwise, or conspiracy, in restraint of trade or commerce among the several states, or with foreign nations, is declared to be illegal." This is sweeping language. What it embraces seems to depend entirely on the meaning of the words "restraint of trade or commerce." Whatever they might mean, *every* such restraint is declared unlawful. But in fact, as we will see, the proposition cannot be stated quite so categorically, for in 1911 the Supreme Court limited the reach of this section to *unreasonable* restraints of trade.

What does "restraint of trade" mean? The Sherman Act's drafters based the act on a common-law policy against monopolies and other infringements on competition. But common law regarding restraints of trade had been developed in only rudimentary form, and the words have come to mean whatever the courts say they mean. In short, the antitrust laws, and the Sherman Act in particular, authorize the courts to create a federal "common law" of competition.

Section 2 of the Sherman Act prohibits monopolization: "Every person who shall monopolize, or attempt to monopolize, or combine or conspire with any other person or persons, to monopolize any part of the trade or commerce among the several states, or with foreign nations, shall be deemed guilty of a misdemeanor." In 1976, Congress upped the ante: violations of the Sherman Act are now felonies. Unlike Section 1, Section 2 does not require a combination between two or more people. A single company acting on its own can be guilty of monopolizing or attempting to monopolize.

The Clayton Act

The Clayton Act was enacted in 1914 to plug what many in Congress saw as loopholes in the Sherman Act. Passage of the Clayton Act was closely linked to that of the FTC Act. Unlike the Sherman Act, the Clayton Act is not a criminal statute; it merely declares certain defined practices as unlawful and leaves it to the government or to private litigants to seek to enjoin those practices. But unlike the FTC Act, the Clayton Act does spell out four undesirable practices. Violations of the Sherman Act require an *actual* adverse impact on competition, whereas violations of the Clayton Act require merely a *probable* adverse impact. Thus the enforcement of the Clayton Act involves a prediction that the defendant must rebut in order to avoid an adverse judgment.

The four types of proscribed behavior are these:

1. Discrimination in prices charged different purchasers of the same commodities.
2. Conditioning the sale of one commodity on the purchaser's refraining from using or dealing in commodities of the seller's competitors.[5]
3. Acquiring the stock of a competing corporation.[6] Because the original language did not prohibit various types of acquisitions and mergers that had grown up with modem corporate law and finance, Congress amended this section in 1950 (the Celler-Kefauver Act) to extend its prohibition to a wide variety of acquisitions and mergers.
4. Membership by a single person on more than one corporate board of directors if the companies are or were competitors.[7]

The Federal Trade Commission Act

Like the Clayton Act, the FTC Act is a civil statute, involving no criminal penalties. Unlike the Clayton Act, its prohibitions are broadly worded. Its centerpiece is Section 5, which forbids "unfair methods of competition in commerce, and unfair or deceptive acts or practices in commerce." We examine Section 5 in Chapter 49.

Enforcement of Antitrust Laws

General Enforcement

There are four different means of enforcing the antitrust laws.

First, the US Department of Justice may bring civil actions to enjoin violations of any section of the Sherman and Clayton Acts and may institute criminal prosecutions for violations of the Sherman Act. Both civil and criminal actions are filed by the offices of the US attorney in the appropriate federal district, under the direction of the US attorney general. In practice, the Justice Department's guidance comes through its Antitrust Division in Washington, headed by an assistant attorney general. With several hundred lawyers and dozens of economists and other professionals, the Antitrust Division annually files fewer than one hundred civil and criminal actions combined. On average, far more criminal cases are filed than civil cases. In 2006, thirty-four criminal cases and twelve civil cases were filed; in 2007, forty criminal cases and six civil cases; in 2008, fifty-four criminal cases and nineteen civil cases; and in 2009, seventy-two criminal cases and nine civil cases.

The number of cases can be less important than the complexity and size of a particular case. For example, *U.S. v. American Telephone & Telegraph* and *U.S. v. IBM* were both immensely complicated, took years to dispose of, and consumed tens of thousands of hours of staff time and tens of millions of dollars in government and defense costs.

Second, the FTC hears cases under the Administrative Procedure Act, as described in Chapter 5. The commission's decisions may be appealed to the US courts of appeals. The FTC may also promulgate "trade regulation rules," which define fair practices in specific industries. The agency has some five hundred lawyers in Washington and a dozen field offices, but only about half the lawyers are directly involved in antitrust enforcement. The government's case against Microsoft was, like the cases against AT&T and IBM, a very complex case that took a large share of time and resources from both the government and Microsoft.

Third, in the Antitrust Improvements Act of 1976, Congress authorized state attorneys general to file antitrust suits in federal court for damages on behalf of their citizens; such a suit is known as a *parens patriae* claim. Any citizen of the state who might have been injured by the defendant's actions may opt out of the suit and bring his or her own private action. The states have long had the authority to file antitrust suits seeking injunctive relief on behalf of their citizens.

Fourth, private individuals and companies may file suits for damages or injunctions if they have been directly injured by a violation of the Sherman or Clayton Act. Private individuals or companies may not sue under the FTC Act, no matter how unfair or deceptive the behavior complained of; only the FTC may do so. In the 1980s, more than 1,500 private antitrust suits were filed in the federal courts each year, compared with fewer than 100 suits filed by the Department of Justice. More recently, from 2006 to 2008, private antitrust suits numbered above 1,000 but dropped significantly, to 770, in 2009. The pace was even slower for the first half of 2010. Meanwhile, the Department of Justice filed 40 or fewer criminal antitrust cases from 2006 to 2008; that pace has quickened under the Obama administration (72 cases in 2009).

Enforcement in International Trade

The Sherman and Clayton Acts apply when a company's activities affect US commerce. This means that these laws apply to US companies that agree to fix the price of goods to be shipped abroad and to the acts of a US subsidiary of a foreign company. It also means that non–US citizens and business entities can be prosecuted for violations of antitrust laws, even if they never set foot in the United States, as long as their anticompetitive activities are aimed at the US market. For example, in November of 2010, a federal grand jury in San Francisco returned an indictment against three former executives in Taiwan. They had conspired to fix prices on color display tubes (CDTs), a type of cathode-ray tube used in computer monitors and other specialized applications.

The indictment charged Seung-Kyu "Simon" Lee, Yeong-Ug "Albert" Yang, and Jae-Sik "J. S." Kim with conspiring with unnamed coconspirators to suppress and eliminate competition by fixing prices, reducing output, and allocating market shares of CDTs to be sold in the United States and elsewhere. Lee, Yang, and Kim allegedly participated in the conspiracy during various time periods between at least as early as January 2000 and as late as March 2006. The conspirators met in Taiwan, Korea, Malaysia, China, and elsewhere, but not in the United States. They allegedly met for the purpose of exchanging CDT sales, production, market share, and pricing information for the purpose of implementing, monitoring, and enforcing their agreements. Because the intended effects of their actions were to be felt in the United States, the US antitrust laws could apply.

Criminal Sanctions

Until 1976, violations of the Sherman Act were misdemeanors. The maximum fine was $50,000 for each count on which the defendant was convicted (only $5,000 until 1955), and the maximum jail sentence was one year. But in the CDT case just described, each of the three conspirators was charged with violating the Sherman Act, which carries a maximum penalty of ten years in prison and a $1 million fine for individuals. The maximum fine may be increased to twice the gain derived from the crime or twice the loss suffered by the victims if either of those amounts is greater than the statutory maximum fine of $1 million.

Forfeitures

One provision in the Sherman Act, not much used, permits the government to seize any property in transit in either interstate or foreign commerce if it was the subject of a contract, combination, or conspiracy outlawed under Section 1.

Injunctions and Consent Decrees

divestiture

A remedy, occasionally used, to break up a firm into smaller, independent units, where the firm has exercised its monopoly power in ways that harm competition. For example, the breakup of AT&T was a divestiture.

The Justice Department may enforce violations of the Sherman and Clayton Acts by seeking injunctions in federal district court. The injunction can be a complex set of instructions, listing in some detail the practices that a defendant is to avoid and even the way in which it will be required to conduct its business thereafter. Once an injunction is issued and affirmed on appeal, or the time for appeal has passed, it confers continuing jurisdiction on the court to hear complaints by those who say the defendant is violating it. In a few instances, the injunction or a consent decree is in effect the basic "statute" by which an industry operates. A 1956 decree against American Telephone & Telegraph Company (AT&T) kept the company out of the computer business for a quarter-century, until the government's monopoly suit against AT&T was settled and a new decree issued in 1983. The federal courts also have the power to break up a company convicted of monopolizing or to order **divestiture** when the violation consists of unlawful mergers and acquisitions.

The FTC may issue cease and desist orders against practices condemned under Section 5 of the FTC Act—which includes violations of the Sherman and Clayton Acts—and these orders may be appealed to the courts.

consent decree

A judicial order entered into by defendants in lieu of litigating, in which they admit their guilt but agree to not carry on certain activities complained of. Failure to comply with the terms will result in fines. Similar to an injunction or a cease and desist order.

Rather than litigate a case fully, defendants may agree to **consent decrees**, in which, without admitting guilt, they agree not to carry on the activity complained of. Violations of injunctions, cease and desist orders, and consent decrees subject companies to a fine of $10,000 a day for every day the violation continues. Companies frequently enter into consent decrees—and not just because they wish to avoid the expense and trouble of trial. Section 5 of the Clayton Act says that whenever an antitrust case brought by the federal government under either the Clayton Act or the Sherman Act goes to final judgment, the judgment can be used, in a private suit in which the same facts are at issue, as prima facie evidence that the violation was committed. This is a powerful provision, because it means that a private plaintiff need prove only that the violation in fact injured him. He need not prove that the defendant committed the acts that amount to antitrust violations. Since this provision makes it relatively easy for private plaintiffs to prevail in subsequent suits, defendants in government suits have a strong inducement to enter into consent decrees, because these are not considered judgments. Likewise, a guilty plea in a criminal case gives the plaintiff in a later private civil suit prima facie evidence of the defendant's liability. However, a plea of nolo contendere will avoid this result. Section 5 has been the spur for a considerable proportion of all private antitrust suits. For example, the government's price-fixing case against the electric equipment industry that sent certain executives of General Electric to jail in the 1950s led to more than 2,200 private suits.

Treble Damages

The crux of the private suit is its unique damage award: any successful plaintiff is entitled to collect *three times* the amount of damages actually suffered—treble damages, as they are known—and to be paid the cost of his attorneys. These fees can be huge: defendants have had to pay out millions of dollars for attorneys' fees alone in single cases. The theory of **treble damages** is that they will serve as an incentive to private parties to police industry for antitrust violations, thus saving the federal government the immense expense of maintaining an adequate staff for that job.

treble damages

For private lawsuits, successful plaintiffs may collect three times the amount of damages actually suffered.

Class Actions

One of the most important developments in antitrust law during the 1970s was the rise of the class action. Under liberalized rules of federal procedure, a single plaintiff may sue on behalf of the entire class of people injured by an antitrust violation. This device makes it possible to bring numerous suits that would otherwise never have been contemplated. A single individual who has paid one dollar more than he would have been charged in a competitive market obviously will not file suit. But if there are ten million consumers like him, then in a class action he may seek—on behalf of the entire class, of course—$30 million ($10 million trebled), plus attorneys' fees. Critics charge that the class action is a device that in the antitrust field benefits only the lawyers, who have a large incentive to find a few plaintiffs willing to have their names used in a suit run entirely by the lawyers. Nevertheless, it is true that the class action permits antitrust violations to be rooted out that could not otherwise be attacked privately. During the 1970s, suits against drug companies and the wallboard manufacturing industry were among the many large-scale antitrust class actions.

Interpreting the Laws

Vagueness

The antitrust laws, and especially Section 1 of the Sherman Act, are exceedingly vague. As Chief Justice Charles Evans Hughes once put it, "The Sherman Act, as a charter of freedom, has a generality and adaptability comparable to that found to be desirable in constitutional provisions."[8] Without the sweeping but vague language, the antitrust laws might quickly have become outdated. As written, they permit courts to adapt the law to changing circumstances. But the vagueness can lead to uncertainty and uneven applications of the law.

The "Rule of Reason"

Section 1 of the Sherman Act says that "every" restraint of trade is illegal. But is a literal interpretation really possible? No, for as Justice Louis Brandeis noted in 1918 in one of the early price-fixing cases, "Every agreement concerning trade, every regulation of trade restrains. To bind, to restrain, is of their very essence."[9] When a manufacturing company contracts to buy raw materials, trade in those goods is restrained: no one else will have access to them. But to interpret the Sherman Act to include such a contract is an absurdity. Common sense says that "every" cannot really mean *every* restraint.

Throughout this century, the courts have been occupied with this question. With the hindsight of thousands of cases, the broad outlines of the answer can be confidently stated. Beginning with *Standard Oil Co. of New Jersey v. United States*, the Supreme Court has held that only *unreasonable* restraints of trade are unlawful.[10]

rule of reason

A judicial test balancing the positive effects of an agreement against its potentially anticompetitive effects.

Often called the **rule of reason**, the interpretation of Section 1 made in *Standard Oil* itself has two possible meanings, and they have been confused over the years. The rule of reason could mean that a restraint is permissible only if it is *ancillary* to a legitimate business purpose. The standard example is a covenant not to compete. Suppose you decide to purchase a well-regarded bookstore in town. The proprietor is well liked and has developed loyal patrons. He says he is going to retire in another state. You realize that if he changed his mind and stayed in town to open another bookstore, your new business would suffer considerably. So you negotiate as a condition of sale that he agrees not to open another bookstore within ten miles of the town for the next three years. Since your intent is not to prevent him from going into business—as it would be if he had agreed never to open a bookstore anywhere—but merely to protect the value of your purchase, this restraint of trade is ancillary to your business purpose. The rule of reason holds that this is not an unlawful restraint of trade.

Another interpretation of the rule of reason is even broader. It holds that agreements that might directly impair competition are not unlawful unless the particular impairment itself is unreasonable. For example, several retailers of computer software are distraught at a burgeoning price war that will possibly reduce prices so low that they will not be able to offer their customers proper service. To avert this "cutthroat competition," the retailers agree to set a price floor—a floor that, under the circumstances, is reasonable. Chief Justice Edward White, who wrote the *Standard Oil* opinion, might have found that such an agreement was reasonable because, in view of its purposes, it was not *unduly* restrictive and did not unduly restrain trade.

But this latter view is not the law. Almost any business agreement could enhance the market power of one or more parties to the agreement, and thus restrain trade. "The true test of legality," Justice Brandeis wrote in 1918 in *Chicago Board of Trade*, "is whether the restraint imposed is such as merely regulates and perhaps thereby promotes competition or whether it is such as may suppress or even destroy competition."[11] Section 1 violations analyzed under the rule of reason will look at several factors, including the purpose of the agreement, the parties' power to implement the agreement to achieve that purpose, and the effect or potential effect of the agreement on competition. If the parties could have used less restrictive means to achieve their purpose, the Court would more likely have seen the agreement as unreasonable.[12]

"Per Se" Rules

per se illegal

Unlawful on its face. Applies to acts that by their very nature are regarded as impairing competition. For example, price-fixing is said to be per se illegal under the Sherman Act.

price-fixing

Agreements, usually among competitors, that directly set prices, exchange price information, control output, or regulate competitive benefits.

Not every act or commercial practice needs to be weighed by the rule of reason. Some acts have come to be regarded as intrinsically or necessarily impairing competition, so that no further analysis need be made if the plaintiff can prove that the defendant carried them out or attempted or conspired to do so. Price-fixing is an example. Price-fixing is said to be **per se illegal** under the Sherman Act—that is, unlawful on its face. The question in a case alleging **price-fixing** is not whether the price was reasonable or whether it impaired or enhanced competition, but whether the price in fact *was* fixed by two sellers in a market segment. Only that question can be at issue.

Under the Clayton Act

The rule of reason and the per se rules apply to the Sherman Act. The Clayton Act has a different standard. It speaks in terms of acts that may tend substantially to lessen competition. The courts must construe these terms too, and in the sections that follow, we will see how they have done so.

Key Takeaway

The preservation of competition is an important part of public policy in the United States. The various antitrust laws were crafted in response to clear abuses by companies that sought to claim easier profits by avoiding competition through the exercise of monopoly power, price-fixing, or territorial agreements. The Department of Justice and the Federal Trade Commission have substantial criminal and civil penalties to wield in their enforcement of the various antitrust laws.

Exercises

1. Why did industries become so much larger after the U.S. Civil War, and how did this lead to abusive practices? What role did politics play in creating U.S. laws fostering competition?
2. Go to the Department of Justice website and see how many antitrust enforcement actions have taken place since 2008.
3. Consider whether the U.S. government should break up the biggest U.S. banks. Why or why not? If the United States does so, and other nations have very large government banks, or have very large private banks, can U.S. banks remain competitive?

48.2 Horizontal Restraints of Trade: Sherman Act, Section 1

Learning Objectives

1. Know why competitors are the likely actors in horizontal restraints of trade.
2. Explain what it means when the Supreme Court declares a certain practice to be a per se violation of the antitrust laws.
3. Describe at least three ways in which otherwise competing parties can fix prices.
4. Recognize why dividing territories is a horizontal restraint of trade.

Classification of antitrust cases and principles is not self-evident because so many cases turn on complex factual circumstances. One convenient way to group the cases is to look to the relationship of those who have agreed or conspired. If the parties are competitors—whether competing manufacturers, wholesalers, retailers, or others—there could be a **horizontal restraint of trade**. If the parties are at different levels of the distribution chain—for example, manufacturer and retailer—their agreement is said to involve a **vertical restraint of trade**. These categories are not airtight: a retailer might get competing manufacturers to agree not to supply a competitor of the retailer. This is a vertical restraint with horizontal effects.

horizontal restraint of trade

An agreement that in some way restrains competition between rival firms competing in the same market.

vertical restraint of trade

Any restraint on trade created by agreements between firms at different levels in the manufacturing and distribution process.

Price-Fixing

Direct Price-Fixing Agreements

Price-fixing agreements are per se violations of Section 1 of the Sherman Act. The per se rule was announced explicitly in *United States v. Trenton Potteries*.[13] In that case, twenty individuals and twenty-three corporations, makers and distributors of 82 percent of the vitreous pottery bathroom fixtures used in the United States, were found guilty of having agreed to establish and adhere to a price schedule. On appeal, they did not dispute that they had combined to fix prices. They did argue that the jury should have been permitted to decide whether what they had done was reasonable. The Supreme Court disagreed, holding that any fixing of prices is a clear violation of the Sherman Act.

Twenty-four years later, the Court underscored this categorical per se rule in *Kiefer-Stewart Co. v. Joseph E. Seagram & Sons*.[14] The defendants were distillers who had agreed to sell liquor only to those wholesalers who agreed to resell it for no more than a *maximum* price set by the distillers. The defendants argued that setting maximum prices did not violate the Sherman Act because such prices promoted rather than restrained competition. Again, the Supreme Court disagreed: "[S]uch agreements, no less than those to fix minimum prices, cripple the freedom of traders and thereby restrain their ability to sell in accordance with their own judgment."

In 2012, the U.S. Department of Justice sued five major book publishers and Apple, Inc. The government charged that the defendants had conspired to fix the prices of e-books. Strong competition had reduced e-book prices to $9.99 per book, a price that cut into profits by the defendants. The five publishers settled, but Apple went to trial and lost; the court found compelling evidence that Apple had conspired to fix prices in violation of the Sherman Act.[15]

The per se prohibition against price-fixing is not limited to agreements that directly fix prices. Hundreds of schemes that have the effect of controlling prices have been tested in court and found wanting, some because they were per se restraints of trade, others because their effects were unreasonable—that is, because they impaired competition—under the circumstances. In the following sections, we briefly examine some of these cases.

Exchanging Price Information

Knowledge of competitors' prices can be an effective means of controlling prices throughout an industry. Members of a trade association of hardwood manufacturers adopted a voluntary "open competition" plan. About 90 percent of the members adhered to the plan. They accounted for one-third of the production of hardwood in the United States. Under the plan, members reported daily on sales and deliveries and monthly on production, inventory, and prices. The association, in turn, sent out price, sales, and production reports to the participating members. Additionally, members met from time to time to discuss these matters, and they were exhorted to refrain from excessive production in order to keep prices at profitable levels. In *American Column and Lumber Company v. United States*, the Supreme Court condemned this plan as a per se violation of Section 1 of the Sherman Act.[16]

Not every exchange of information is necessarily a violation, however. A few years after *American Column and Lumber*, in *Maple Flooring Manufacturers' Association v. United States*, the Court refused to find a violation in the practice of an association of twenty-two hardwood-floor manufacturers in circulating a list to all members of average costs and freight rates, as well as summaries of sales, prices, and inventories.[17] The apparent difference between *American Column and Lumber* and *Maple Flooring* was that in the latter, the members did not discuss prices at their meetings, and their rules permitted them to charge individually whatever they wished. It is not unlawful, therefore, for members of an industry to meet to discuss common problems or to develop statistical information about the industry through a common association, as long as the discussions do not border on price or on techniques of controlling prices, such as by restricting output. Usually, it takes evidence of collusion to condemn the exchange of prices or other data.

Controlling Output

Competitors also fix prices by controlling an industry's output. For example, competitors could agree to limit the amount of goods each company makes or by otherwise limiting the amount that comes to market. This latter technique was condemned in *United States v. Socony-Vacuum Oil Co.*[18] To prevent oil prices from dropping, dominant oil companies agreed to and did purchase from independent refiners surplus gasoline that the market was forcing them to sell at distress prices. By buying up this gasoline, the large companies created a price floor for their own product. This conduct, said the Court, is a per se violation.

In the global oil markets, of course, OPEC has at times been able to control output, thus raising prices for oil. This would not be a violation of U.S. anti-trust law, since (a) the Sherman Act has only limited application to global markets, and (b) suing sovereign states is difficult, even where they are engaged in "commercial activity." (See Chapter 51, section 3).

Regulating Competitive Methods

Many companies may want to end offering discounts or premiums, but don't because they fear their competitors will continue those offers, and thereby gain market share. So why not just forge agreements with competitors who may also want to end these practices? In most instances, such agreements are unlawful when they affect the product's price. Still, not all agreed-on restraints or standards are necessarily unlawful. Companies might decide that it would serve their customers' interests as well as their own if the product could be standardized, so that certain names or marks would come to signify a grade or quality of product. When no restriction is placed on what grades are to be sold or at what prices, no restraint of trade has occurred.

In *National Society of Professional Engineers v. United States*, Section 8, a canon of ethics of the National Society of Professional Engineers had prohibited its members from making competitive bids. This type of prohibition was once common in the codes of ethics of all kinds of groups that claimed professional status. Lawyers in a certain county, for example, would keep a price list for standard kinds of services, so that potential clients found it pointless to "shop around" on the basis of price. The professional groups usually justified such lists by saying they insured quality and kept practitioners from offering cut-rate services that weren't professional enough.

Nonprice Restraints of Trade

Allocating Territories

Suppose four ice-cream manufacturers decided one day that their efforts to compete in all four corners of the city were costly and destructive. Why not simply strike a bargain: each will sell ice cream to retail shops in only one quadrant of the city. This is not a pricing arrangement; each is free to sell at whatever price it desires. But it is a restraint of trade, for in carving up the territory in which each may sell, they make it impossible for grocery stores to have a choice among all four manufacturers. This becomes obvious if the same kind of agreement is put on a national scale: e.g., suppose Ford and Toyota agreed that Ford would not sell its cars in New York and Toyota would not sell Toyotas in California.

Most cases of **territorial allocation** are examples of vertical restraints in which manufacturers and distributors strike bargains. But some cases deal with horizontal allocation of territories. In *United States v. Sealy*, the defendant company licensed manufacturers to use the Sealy trademark on beds and mattresses and restricted the territories in which the manufacturers could sell.[19] The evidence showed that the licensees, some thirty small bedding manufacturers, actually owned the licensor and were using the arrangement to allocate the territory. It was held to be unlawful per se.

territorial allocation

Horizontal allocations of territory are per se illegal under Section 1 of the Sherman Act. But producers may wish to assign dealers an exclusive area within which to sell their products. For these vertical allocations of territory, the rule of reason is followed.

Exclusionary Agreements

As mentioned earlier, manufacturers—through a trade association—can legally establish certain quality standards for the convenience of the public. As long as these standards are not exclusionary and do not reflect any control over price, they might not inhibit competition. The UL mark on electrical and other equipment—a mark to show that the product conforms to specifications of the private Underwriters Laboratory—is an example. But suppose that certain widget producers establish the Scientific Safety Council, a membership association whose staff ostensibly assigns quality labels, marked SSC, to those manufacturers who meet certain engineering and safety standards. In fact, however, the manufacturers are using the widespread public acceptance of the SSC mark to keep the market to themselves by refusing to let nonmembers join and by refusing to let nonmembers use the SSC mark, even if their widgets conform to the announced standards. This subterfuge would be a violation of Section 1 of the Sherman Act.

Boycotts

Agreements by competitors to boycott (i.e., refuse to deal with) those who engage in undesirable practices are unlawful. In an early case, a retailers' trade association circulated a list of wholesale distributors who sold directly to the public. The intent was to warn member retailers not to buy from those wholesalers. Although each member was free to act however it wanted, the Court saw in this blacklist a plan to promote a boycott.[20]

This policy remains true even if the objective of the boycott is to prevent unethical or even illegal activities. Members of a garment manufacturers association agreed with a textile manufacturers association not to use any textiles that had been "pirated" from designs made by members of the textile association. The garment manufacturers also pledged, among other things, not to sell their goods to any retailer who did not refrain from using pirated designs. The argument that this was the only way to prevent unscrupulous design pirates from operating fell on deaf judicial ears; the Supreme Court held the policy unlawful under Section 5 of the Federal Trade Commission (FTC) Act, the case having been brought by the FTC.[21]

Proof of Agreement

It is vital for business managers to realize that once an agreement or a conspiracy is shown to have existed, they or their companies can be convicted of violating the law even if neither agreement nor conspiracy led to concrete results. Suppose the sales manager of Extremis Widget Company sits down over lunch with the sales manager of De Minimis Widget Company and says, "Why are we working so hard? I have a plan that will let us both relax." He explains that their companies can put into operation a data exchange program that will stabilize prices. The other sales manager does not immediately commit himself, but after lunch, he goes to the stationery store and purchases a notebook in which to record the information he will get from a telephone test of the plan. That action is probably enough to establish a conspiracy to fix prices, and the government could file criminal charges at that point. Discussion with your competitors of prices, discounts, production quotas, rebates, bid rigging, trade-in allowances, commission rates, salaries, advertising, and the like is exceedingly dangerous. It can lead to criminal conduct and potential jail terms.

Proof of Harm

It is unnecessary to show that the public is substantially harmed by a restraint of trade as long as the plaintiff can show that the restraint injured him. In *Klor's, Inc. v. Broadway-Hale Stores*, the plaintiff was a small retail appliance shop in San Francisco.[22] Next door to the shop was a competing appliance store, one of a chain of stores run by Broadway-Hale. Klor's alleged that Broadway-Hale, using its "monopolistic buying power," persuaded ten national manufacturers and their distributors, including GE, RCA, Admiral, Zenith, and Emerson, to cease selling to Klor's or to sell at discriminatory prices. The defendants did not dispute the allegations. Instead, they moved for summary judgment on the ground that even if true, the allegations did not give rise to a legal claim because the public could not conceivably have been injured as a result of their concerted refusal to deal. As evidence, they cited the uncontradicted fact that within blocks of Klor's, hundreds of household appliance retailers stood ready to sell the public the very brands Klor's was unable to stock as a result of the boycott. The district court granted the motion and dismissed Klor's complaint. The court of appeals affirmed. But the Supreme Court reversed, saying as follows:

This combination takes from Klor's its freedom to buy appliances in an open competitive market and drives it out of business as a dealer in the defendants' products. It deprives the manufacturers and distributors of their freedom to sell to Klor's....It interferes with the natural flow of interstate commerce. It clearly has, by its "nature" and "character," a "monopolistic tendency." As such it is not to be tolerated merely because the victim is just one merchant whose business is so small that his destruction makes little difference to the economy. Monopoly can surely thrive by the elimination of such small businessmen, one at a time, as it can by driving them out in large groups.

Note, however, that the Klor's case was decided in 1944. A shift in the Court's anti-trust philosophy began in the 1980s, and has tended to give more weight to consumer injury than injury to competition itself. There have been no cases comparable to Klor's since then, but it's far from clear that the current Court would follow Klor's where the restraint injured a competitor rather than consumers generally.

We have been exploring the Sherman Act as it applies to horizontal restraints of trade—that is, restraints of trade between competitors. We now turn our attention to vertical restraints—those that are the result of agreements or conspiracies between different levels of the chain of distribution, such as manufacturer and wholesaler or wholesaler and retailer.

Key Takeaway

Competitors can engage in horizontal restraints of trade by various means of price-fixing. They can also engage in horizontal price restraints of trade by allocating territories or by joint boycotts (refusals to deal). These restraints need not be substantial in order to be actionable as a violation of US antitrust laws.

Exercises

1. The NFL includes 32 separately owned football teams. Each team has its own logo, colors, and owns intellectual property (copyrights and trademarks) that it markets through National Football League properties (NFLP). Until 2000, the NFL granted a number of nonexclusive licenses to several vendors, licenses to manufacture and sell apparel with NFL team insignias. One of the licensees was American Needle, Incorporated. In 2000, the teams authorized the NFLP to grant exclusive licenses. The NFLP granted Reebok International an exclusive ten-year license to manufacture and sell trademarked headwear for all 32 teams. At the same time, it declined to renew American Needle's nonexclusive license. American Needle sued under the Sherman Act section 1. What is the result?
2. Suppose that JPMorgan Chase, the Bank of England, and the Bank of China agree that they will not compete for investment services, and that JPMorgan Chase is given an exclusive right to North and South America, Bank of England is given access rights to Europe, and Bank of China is given exclusive rights to Asia, India, and Australia. Is there a violation of U.S. antitrust law here? If not, why not? If so, what act does it violate, and how?
3. "It's a free country." Why are agreements by competitors to boycott (to refuse to deal with) certain others considered a problem that needs to be dealt with by law? Doesn't the law interfere with the competitors' "freedom"?

48.3 Vertical Restraints of Trade

Learning Objectives

1. Distinguish vertical restraints of trade from horizontal restraints of trade.
2. Describe exclusive dealing, and explain why exclusive dealing is anticompetitive in any way.
3. Explain how tying one product's sale to that of another could be anticompetitive.

We have looked at the Sherman Act as it applies to restraints that are created between competitors ("horizontal" restraints). We turn now to vertical restraints—those that result from agreements between different levels of the chain of distribution, such as manufacturer and wholesaler or wholesaler and retailer.

Resale Price Maintenance

resale price maintenance agreement

An agreement between a manufacturer and a retailer in which the manufacturer specifies what the retail prices of its products must be.

Is it permissible for manufacturers to require distributors or retailers to sell products at a set price? Generally, the answer is no, but the strict per se rule against any kind of **resale price maintenance** has been somewhat relaxed.

But why would a manufacturer want to fix the price at which the retailer sells its goods? There are several possibilities. For instance, sustained, long-term sales of many branded appliances and other goods depend on reliable servicing by the retailer. Unless the retailer can get a fair price, it will not provide good service. Anything less than good service will ultimately hurt the brand name and lead to fewer sales. Another possible argument for resale price maintenance is that unless all retailers must abide by a certain price, some goods will not be stocked at all. For instance, the argument runs, bookstores will not stock slow-selling books if they cannot be guaranteed a good price on best sellers. Stores free to discount best sellers will not have the profit margin to stock other types of books. To guarantee sales of best sellers to bookstores carrying many lines of books, it is necessary to put a floor under the price of books. Still another argument is that brand-name goods are inviting targets for loss-leader sales; if one merchant drastically discounts Extremis Widgets, other merchants may not want to carry the line, and the manufacturer may experience unwanted fluctuations in sales.

None of these reasons has completely appeased the critics of price fixing, including the most important critics—the U.S. federal judges. As long ago as 1910, in *Dr. Miles Medical Co. v. John D. Park & Sons Co.*, the Supreme Court declared vertical price-fixing (what has come to be called resale price maintenance) unlawful under the Sherman Act. Dr. Miles Medical Company required wholesalers that bought its proprietary medicines to sign an agreement in which they agreed not to sell below a certain price and not to sell to retailers who did not have a "retail agency contract" with Dr. Miles. The retail agency contract contained a price floor. Dr. Miles argued that since it was free to make or not make the medicines, it should be free to dictate the prices at which purchasers could sell them. The Court said that Dr. Miles's arrangement with more than four hundred jobbers (wholesale distributors) and twenty-five thousand retailers was no different than if the wholesalers or retailers agreed among themselves to fix the price. Dr. Miles, "having sold its product at prices satisfactory to itself, the public is entitled to whatever advantage may be derived from a competition in the subsequent traffic."[23]

In *Dr. Miles*, the company's restrictions impermissibly limited the freedom of choice of other drug distributors and retailers. Society was therefore deprived of various benefits it would have received from unrestricted distribution of the drugs. But academics and some judges argue that most vertical price restraints do not limit competition among competitors, and manufacturers retain the power to restrict output, and the power to raise prices. Arguably, vertical price restraints help to ensure economic efficiencies and maximize consumer welfare. Some of the same arguments noted in this section—such as the need to ensure good service for retail items—continue to be made in support of a rule of reason.

The Supreme Court has not accepted these arguments with regard to minimum prices but has increased the plaintiff's burden of proof by requiring evidence of an agreement on specific price levels. Where a discounter is terminated by a manufacturer, it will probably not be told exactly why, and very few manufacturers would be leaving evidence in writing that insists on dealers agreeing to minimum prices.

The "rule of reason" finally won out in *State Oil Company v. Khan*. In that case, the Supreme Court held that "vertical maximum price fixing, like the majority of commercial arrangements subject to the antitrust laws, should be evaluated under the rule of reason."[24] Vertical maximum price-fixing is not legal per se but should be analyzed under a rule of reason "to identify the situations in which it amounts to anti-competitive conduct."

Exclusive Dealing and Tying

We move now to nonprice vertical forms of restraint. Suppose you went to the grocery store intent on purchasing a bag of potato chips to satisfy a late-night craving. Imagine your surprise—and indignation—if the store manager waved a paper in your face and said, "I'll sell you this bag only on the condition that you sign this agreement to buy all of your potato chips in the next five years from me." Or if he said, "I'll sell only if you promise never to buy potato chips from my rival across the street." This is an **exclusive dealing agreement**, and if the effect may be to lessen competition substantially, it is unlawful under Section 3 of the Clayton Act. It also may be unlawful under Section 1 of the Sherman Act and Section 5 of the Federal Trade Commission (FTC) Act. Another form of exclusive dealing, known as a **tying contract**, is also prohibited under Section 3 of the Clayton Act and under the other statutes. A tying contract results when you are forced to take a certain product in order to get the product you are really after: "I'll sell you the potato chips you crave, but only if you purchase five pounds of my Grade B liver."

exclusive dealing agreement

A contract—as between buyer and seller—where the parties agree only to deal with each other.

tying contract

A form of exclusive dealing, prohibited under Section 3 of the Clayton Act, forcing you to take an additional product in order to get the product you really want.

Section 3 of the Clayton Act declares it unlawful for any person engaged in commerce

> *to lease or make a sale or contract for sale of goods, wares, merchandise, machinery, supplies or other commodities, whether patented or unpatented, for use, consumption or resale...or fix a price charged therefore, or discount from or rebate upon, such price,* **on the condition...that the lessee or purchaser...shall not use or deal in the goods, wares, merchandise, machinery, supplies, or other commodities of a competitor or competitors of the lessor or seller**, *where the effect of such lease, sale, or contract for sale or such condition ... may be to substantially lessen competition or tend to erect a monopoly in any line of commerce. (emphasis added)*

Under Section 3, the potato chip example is not unlawful, for you would not have much of an effect on competition nor tend to create a monopoly if you signed with your corner grocery. But the Clayton Act has serious ramifications for a producer who might wish to require a dealer to sell only its products—such as a fast-food franchisee that can carry cooking ingredients bought only from the franchisor (Chapter 49), an appliance store that can carry only one national brand of refrigerators, or an ice-cream parlor that must buy ice-cream supplies from the supplier of its machinery.

A situation like the one in the ice-cream example came under review in *International Salt Co. v. United States*.[25] International Salt was the largest US producer of salt for industrial uses. It held patents on two machines necessary for using salt products; one injected salt into foodstuffs during canning. It leased most of these machines to canners, and the lease required the lessees to purchase from International Salt all salt to be used in the machines. The case was decided on summary judgment; the company did not have the chance to prove the reasonableness of its conduct. The Court held that it was not entitled to. International Salt's valid patent on the machines did not confer on it the right to restrain trade in unpatented salt. Justice Tom Clark said that doing so was a violation of both Section 1 of the Sherman Act and Section 3 of the Clayton Act:

> *Not only is price-fixing unreasonable,* per se, *but also it is unreasonable,* per se, *to foreclose competitors from any substantial market. The volume of business affected by these contracts cannot be said to be insignificant or insubstantial, and the tendency of the arrangement to accomplishment of monopoly seems obvious. Under the law, agreements are forbidden which "tend to create a monopoly," and it is immaterial that the tendency is a creeping one rather than one that proceeds at full gallop; nor does the law await arrival at the goal before condemning the direction of the movement.*

In a case involving the sale of newspaper advertising space (to purchase space in the morning paper, an advertiser would have to take space in the company's afternoon paper), the government lost because it could not use the narrower standards of Section 3 and could not prove that the defendant had monopoly power over the sale of advertising space. (Another afternoon newspaper carried advertisements, and its sales did not suffer.) In the course of his opinion, Justice Clark set forth the rule for determining legality of tying arrangements under both the Clayton and Sherman Acts:

> *When the seller enjoys a monopolistic position in the market for the "tying" product [i.e., the product that the buyer wants] or if a substantial volume of commerce in the "tied" product [i.e., the product that the buyer does not want] is restrained, a tying arrangement violates the narrower standards expressed in section 3 of the Clayton Act because from either factor the requisite potential lessening of competition is inferred. And because for even a lawful monopolist it is "unreasonable* per se *to foreclose competitors from any substantial market" a tying arrangement is banned by section 1 of the Sherman Act wherever both conditions are met.*[26]

This rule was broadened in a Sherman Act case in 1958 involving the Northern Pacific Railroad Company. Northern Pacific had received forty million acres of land from Congress in the late nineteenth century in return for building a rail line from the Great Lakes to the Pacific. For decades, Northern Pacific leased or sold the land on condition that the buyer or lessee use Northern Pacific to ship any crops grown on the land or goods manufactured there. To no avail, the railroad argued that unlike International Salt's machines, the railroad's "tying product" (its land) was not patented, and that the land users were free to ship on other lines if they could find cheaper rates. Wrote Justice Hugo Black,

> *[A] tying arrangement may be defined as an agreement by a party to sell one product but only on the condition that the buyer also purchases a different (or tied) product, or at least agrees that he will not purchase that product from any other supplier. Where such conditions are successfully exacted competition on the merits with respect to the tied product is inevitably curbed. ... They deny competitors free access to the market for the tied product, not because the party imposing the tying requirements has a better product or a lower price but because of his power or leverage in another market. At the same time buyers are forced to forego their free choice between competing products. ...* **They are unreasonable in and of themselves whenever a party has sufficient economic power with respect to the tying product to appreciably restrain free competition in the market for the tied product and a "not insubstantial" amount of interstate commerce is affected.** *In this case ... the undisputed facts established beyond any genuine question that the defendant possessed substantial economic power by virtue of its extensive landholdings which it used as leverage to induce large numbers of purchasers and lessees to give it preference.*[27] *(emphasis in original)*

Taken together, the tying cases suggest that anyone with certain market power over a commodity or other valuable item (such as a trademark) runs a serious risk of violating the Clayton Act or Sherman Act or both if he insists that the buyer must also take some other product as part of the bargain. Microsoft learned about the perils of "tying" in a case brought by the United States, nineteen individual states, and the District of Columbia. The allegation was that Microsoft had tied together various software programs on its operating system, Microsoft Windows. Windows came prepackaged with Microsoft's Internet Explorer (IE), its Windows Media Player, Outlook Express, and Microsoft Office. The United States claimed that Microsoft had bundled (or "tied") IE to sales of Windows 98, making IE difficult to remove from Windows 98 by not putting it on the Remove Programs list.

The government alleged that Microsoft had designed Windows 98 to work "unpleasantly" with Netscape Navigator and that this constituted an illegal tying of Windows 98 and IE. Microsoft argued that its web browser and mail reader were just parts of the operating system, included with other personal computer operating systems, and that the integration of the products was technologically justified. The United States Court of Appeals for the District of Columbia Circuit rejected Microsoft's claim that IE was simply one facet of its operating system, but the court held that the tie between Windows and IE should be analyzed deferentially under the rule of reason. The case settled before reaching final judicial resolution. (See *United States v. Microsoft*.[28])

Nonprice Vertical Restraints: Allocating Territory and Customers

With horizontal restraints of trade, we have already seen that it is a per se violation of Section 1 of the Sherman Act for competitors to allocate customers and territory. But a vertical allocation of customers or territory is only illegal if competition to the markets as a whole is adversely affected. The key here is distinguishing intrabrand competition from interbrand competition. Suppose that Samsung electronics has relationships with ten different retailers in Gotham City. If Samsung decides to limit its contractual relationships to only six retailers, the market for consumer electronics in Gotham City is still competitive in terms of interbrand competition. Intrabrand competition, however, is now limited. It could be that consumers will pay slightly higher prices for Samsung electronics with only six different retailers selling those products in Gotham City. That is, intrabrand competition is lowered, but interbrand competition remains strong.

Notice that it is unlikely that the six remaining retailers will raise their prices substantially, since there is still strong interbrand competition. If the retailer only deals in Samsung electronics, it is unlikely to raise prices that much, given the strength of interbrand competition.

If the retailer carries Samsung and other brands, it will also not want to raise prices too much, for then its inventory of Samsung electronics will pile up, while its inventory of other electronics products will move off the shelves.

Why would Samsung want to limit its retail outlets in Gotham City at all? It may be that Samsung has decided that by firming up its dealer network, it can enhance service, offer a wider range of products at each of the remaining retailers, ensure improved technical and service support, increase a sense of commitment among the remaining retail outlets, or other good business reasons. Where the retailer deals in other electronic consumer brands as well, making sure that well-trained sales and service support is available for Samsung products can promote interbrand competition in Gotham City. Thus vertical allocation of retailers within the territory is not a per se violation of the Sherman Act. It is instead a rule of reason violation, or the law will intervene only if Samsung's activities have an anticompetitive effect on the market as a whole. Notice here that the only likely objections to the new allocation would come from those dealers who were contractually terminated and who are then effectively restricted from selling Samsung electronics.

There are other potentially legitimate territorial restrictions, and limits on what kind of customer the retailer can sell to will prevent a dealer or distributor from selling outside a certain territory or to a certain class of customers. Samsung may reduce its outlets in Iowa from four to two, and it may also impose limits on those retail outlets from marketing beyond certain areas in and near Iowa.

Suppose that a Monsanto representative selling various kinds of fertilizers and pesticides was permitted to sell only to individual farmers and not to co-ops or retail distributors, or was limited to the state of Iowa. The Supreme Court has held that such vertical territorial or customer searches are not per se violations of Section 1 of the Sherman Act, as the situations often increase "interbrand competition." Thus the rule of reason will apply to vertical allocation of customers and territory.

Nonprice Vertical Restraints: Exclusive Dealing Agreements

Often, a distributor or retailer agrees with the manufacturer or supplier not to carry the products of any other supplier. This is not in itself (per se) illegal under Section 1 of the Sherman Act or Section 3 of the Clayton Act. Only if these **exclusive dealing contracts** have an anticompetitive effect will there be an antitrust violation. Ideally, in a competitive market, there are no significant barriers to entry. In the real world, however, various deals are made that can and do restrict entry. Suppose that on his farm in Greeley, Colorado, Richard Tucker keeps goats, and he creates a fine, handcrafted goat cheese for the markets in Denver, Fort Collins, and Boulder, Colorado, and Cheyenne, Wyoming. In these markets, if Safeway, Whole Foods, Albertsons, and King Soopers already have suppliers, and the suppliers have gained exclusive dealing agreements, Tucker will be effectively barred from the market.

Suppose that Billy Goat Cheese is a nationally distributed brand of goat cheese and has created exclusive dealing arrangements with the four food chains in the four cities. Tucker could sue Billy Goat for violating antitrust laws if he finds out about the arrangements. But the courts will not assume a per se violation has taken place. Instead, the courts will look at the number of other distributors available, the portion of the market foreclosed by the exclusive dealing arrangements, the ease with which new distributors could enter the market, the possibility that Tucker could distribute the product himself, and legitimate business reasons that led the distributors to accept exclusive dealing contracts from Billy Goat Cheese.

Key Takeaway

Vertical restraints of trade can be related to price, can be in the form of tying arrangements, and can be in the form of allocating customers and territories. Vertical restraints can also come in the form of exclusive dealing agreements.

Exercises

1. Explain how a seller with a monopoly in one product and tying the sale of that product to a new product that has no such monopoly is in any way hurting competition. How "free" is the buyer to choose a product different from the seller's?
2. If your company wants to maintain its image as a high-end product provider, is it legal to create a floor for your product's prices? If so, under what circumstances?

48.4 Price Discrimination: The Robinson-Patman Act

Learning Objectives

1. Understand why Congress legislated against price-cutting by large companies.
2. Recognize why price discrimination is not per se illegal.
3. Identify and explain the defenses to a Robinson-Patman price discrimination charge.

If the relatively simple and straightforward language of the Sherman Act can provide litigants and courts with interpretive headaches, the law against price discrimination—the Robinson-Patman Act—can strike the student with a crippling migraine. Technically, Section 2 of the Clayton Act [the Robinson-Patman Act] has been verbally abused almost since its enactment in 1936. It has been called the "Typhoid Mary of Antitrust," a "grotesque manifestation of the scissors and paste-pot method" of draftsmanship. Critics carp at more than its language; many have asserted over the years that the act is anticompetitive because it prevents many firms from lowering their prices to attract more customers.

Despite this rhetoric, the Robinson-Patman Act has withstood numerous attempts to modify or repeal it, and it can come into play in many situations. Although in recent years the Justice Department has declined to enforce it, leaving government enforcement efforts to the Federal Trade Commission (FTC), *private* plaintiffs are actively seeking treble damages in numerous cases. So whether it makes economic sense or not, the act is a living reality for marketers. This section introduces certain problems that lurk in deciding how to price goods and how to respond to competitors' prices.

The Clayton Act's original Section 2, enacted in 1914, was aimed at the price-cutting practice of the large trusts, which would reduce the price of products below cost where necessary in a particular location to wipe out smaller competitors who could not long sustain such losses. But the original Clayton Act exempted from its terms any "discrimination in price...on account of differences in the quantity of the commodity sold." This was a gaping loophole that made it exceedingly difficult to prove a case of price discrimination.

Not until the Depression in the 1930s did sufficient cries of alarm over price discrimination force Congress to act. The alarm was centered on the practices of large grocery chains. Their immense buying power was used as a lever to pry out price discounts from food processors and wholesalers. Unable to extract similar price concessions, the small mom-and-pop grocery stores found that they could not offer the retail customer the lower food prices set by the chains. The small shops began to fail. In 1936, Congress strengthened Section 2 by enacting the Robinson-Patman Act. Although prompted by concern about how large buyers could use their purchasing power, the act in fact places most of its restrictions on the pricing decisions of sellers.

The Statutory Framework

The heart of the act is Section 2(a), which reads in pertinent part as follows: "[I]t shall be unlawful for any person engaged in commerce … to discriminate in price between different purchasers of commodities of like grade and quality … where the effect of such discrimination may be substantially to lessen competition or tend to create a monopoly in any line of commerce, or to injure, destroy or prevent competition with any person who either grants or knowingly receives the benefit of such discrimination, or with customers of either of them."

This section provides certain defenses to a charge of price discrimination. For example, differentials in price are permissible whenever they "make only due allowances for differences in the cost of manufacture, sale, or delivery resulting from the differing methods or quantities in which such commodities are to such purchasers sold or delivered." This section also permits sellers to change prices in response to changing marketing conditions or the marketability of the goods—for example, if perishable goods begin to deteriorate, the seller may drop the price in order to move the goods quickly.

Section 2(b) provides the major defense to price discrimination: any price is lawful if made in good faith to meet competition.

Discrimination by the Seller

Preliminary Matters

Simultaneous Sales

To be discriminatory, the different prices must have been charged in sales made at the same time or reasonably close in time. What constitutes a reasonably close time depends on the industry and the circumstances of the marketplace. The time span for dairy sales would be considerably shorter than that for sales of mainframe computers, given the nature of the product, the frequency of sales, the unit cost, and the volatility of the markets.

Identity of Purchaser

Another preliminary issue is the identity of the actual purchaser. A supplier who deals through a dummy wholesaler might be charged with price discrimination even though on paper only one sale appears to have been made. Under the "indirect purchaser" doctrine, a seller who deals with two or more retail customers but passes their orders on to a single wholesaler and sells the total quantity to the wholesaler in one transaction, can be held to have violated the act. The retailers are treated as indirect purchasers of the supplier.

Sales of Commodities

The act applies only to *sales of commodities*. A lease, a rental, or a license to use a product does not constitute a sale; hence price differentials under one of those arrangements cannot be unlawful under Robinson-Patman. Likewise, since the act applies only to commodities—tangible things—the courts have held that it does not apply to the sale of intangibles, such as rights to license or use patents, shares in a mutual fund, newspaper or television advertising, or title insurance.

Goods of Like Grade and Quality

Only those sales involving goods of "like grade and quality" can be tested under the act for discriminatory pricing. What do these terms mean? The leading case is *FTC v. Borden Co.*, in which the Supreme Court ruled that trademarks and labels do not, for Robinson-Patman purposes, distinguish products that are otherwise the same.[29] Grade and quality must be determined "by the characteristics of the product itself." When the products are physically or chemically identical, they are of like grade and quality, regardless of how imaginative marketing executives attempt to distinguish them. But physical differences that affect marketability can serve to denote products as being of different grade and quality, even if the differences are slight and do not affect the seller's cost in manufacturing or marketing.

Competitive Injury

To violate the Robinson-Patman Act, the seller's price discrimination must have an anticompetitive effect. The usual Clayton Act standard for measuring injury applies to Robinson-Patman violations—that is, a violation occurs when the effect may be substantially to lessen competition or tend to create a monopoly in any line of commerce. But because the Robinson-Patman Act has a more specific test of competitive injury, the general standard is rarely cited.

The more specific test measures the impact on particular persons affected. Section 2(a) says that it is unlawful to discriminate in price where the effect is "to injure, destroy, or prevent competition with any person who grants or knowingly receives the benefit of such discrimination or to customers of either of them." The effect—injury, destruction, or prevention of competition—is measured against three types of those suffering it: (1) competitors of the seller or supplier (i.e., competitors of the person who "grants" the price discrimination), (2) competitors of the buyer (i.e., competitors of the buyer who "knowingly receives the benefit" of the price differential), and (3) customers of either of the two types of competitors. As we will see, the third category presents many difficulties.

For purposes of our discussion, assume the following scenario: Ace Brothers Widget Company manufactures the usual sizes and styles of American domestic widgets. It competes primarily with National Widget Corporation, although several smaller companies make widgets in various parts of the country. Ace Brothers is the largest manufacturer and sells throughout the United States. National sells primarily in the western states. The industry has several forms of distribution. Many retailers buy directly from Ace and National, but several regional and national wholesalers also operate, including Widget Jobbers, Ltd. and Widget Pushers, LLC. The retailers in any particular city compete directly against each other to sell to the general public. Jobbers and Pushers are in direct competition. Jobbers also sells directly to the public, so that it is in direct competition with retailers as well as Widget Pushers. As everyone knows, widgets are extremely price sensitive, being virtually identical in physical appearance and form.

Primary-Line Injury

primary-line injury

Price discrimination under the Robinson-Patman Act that directly injures a competitor, in violation of Section 2(a).

Now consider the situation in California, Oregon, and Wisconsin. The competing manufacturers, Ace Brothers and National Widgets, both sell to wholesalers in California and Oregon, but only Ace has a sales arm in Wisconsin. Seeing an opportunity, Ace drops its prices to wholesalers in California and Oregon and raises them in Wisconsin, putting National at a competitive disadvantage. This situation, illustrated in Figure 48.2, is an example of **primary-line injury**—the injury is done directly to a competitor of the company that differentiates its prices. This is price discrimination, and it is prohibited under Section 2(a).

FIGURE 48.2 Primary-Line Injury

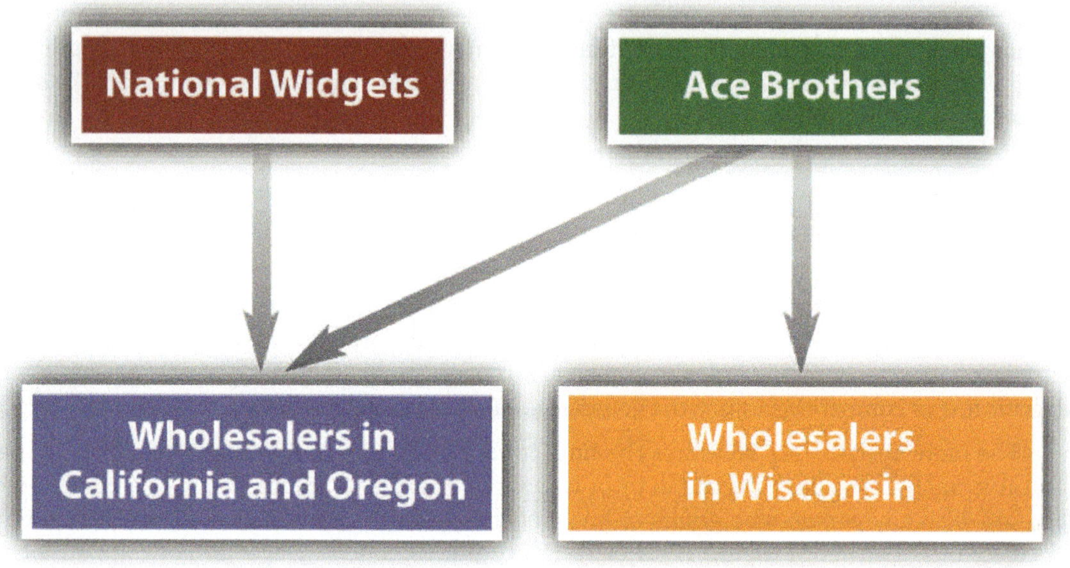

Most forms of primary-line injury have a geographical basis, but they need not. Suppose National sells exclusively to Jobbers in northern California, and Ace Brothers sells both to Jobbers and several other wholesalers. If Ace cuts its prices to Jobbers while charging higher prices to the other wholesalers, the effect is also primary-line injury to National. Jobbers will obviously want to buy more from Ace at lower prices, and National's reduced business is therefore a direct injury. If Ace intends to drive National out of business, this violation of Section 2(a) could also be an attempt to monopolize in violation of Section 2 of the Sherman Act.

Secondary-Line Injury

secondary-line injury

Price discrimination under the Robinson-Patman act that injures a competitor of a buyer, in violation of Section 2(a).

Next, we consider injury done to competing buyers. Suppose that Ace Brothers favors Jobbers—or that Jobbers, a powerful and giant wholesaler, induces Ace to act favorably by threatening not to carry Ace's line of widgets otherwise. Although Ace continues to supply both Jobbers and Widget Pushers, it cuts its prices to Jobbers. As a result, Jobbers can charge its retail customers lower prices than can Pushers, so that Pushers's business begins to slack off. This is **secondary-line injury** at the buyer's level. Jobbers and Pushers are in direct competition, and by impairing Pushers's ability to compete, the requisite injury has been committed. This situation is illustrated in Figure 48.3.

FIGURE 48.3 Secondary-Line Injury

Potential injury to horizontal competitor in the wholesale widget business.

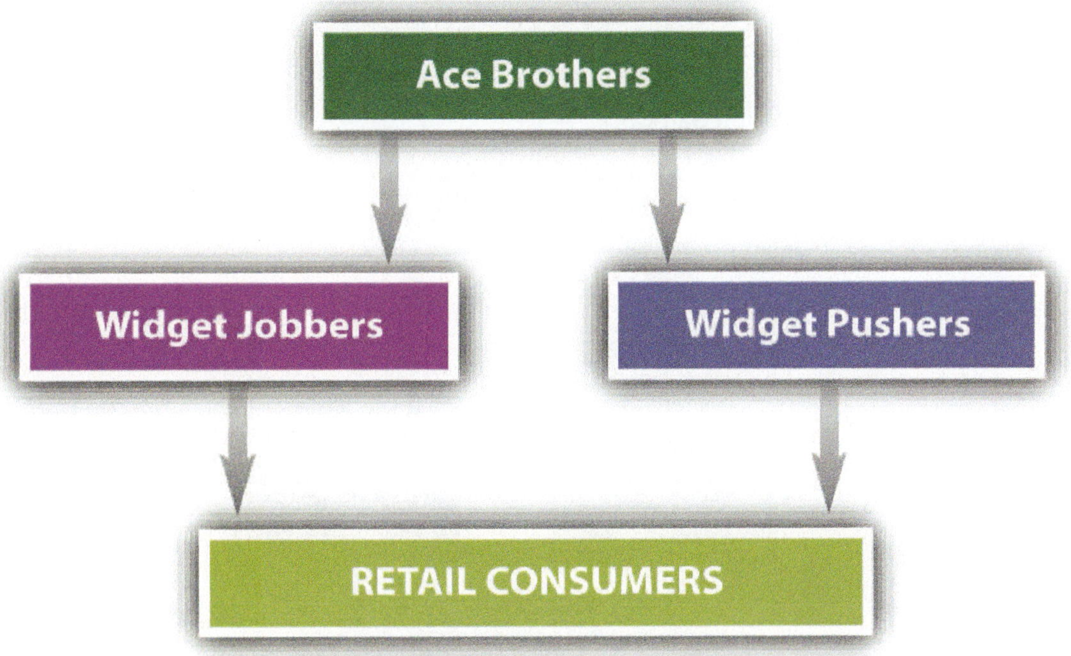

Variations on this secondary-line injury are possible. Assume Ace Brothers sells directly to Fast Widgets, a retail shop, and also to Jobbers. Jobbers sells to retail shops that compete with Fast Widgets and also directly to consumers. The situation is illustrated in Figure 48.4).

FIGURE 48.4 Variation on Secondary-Line Injury

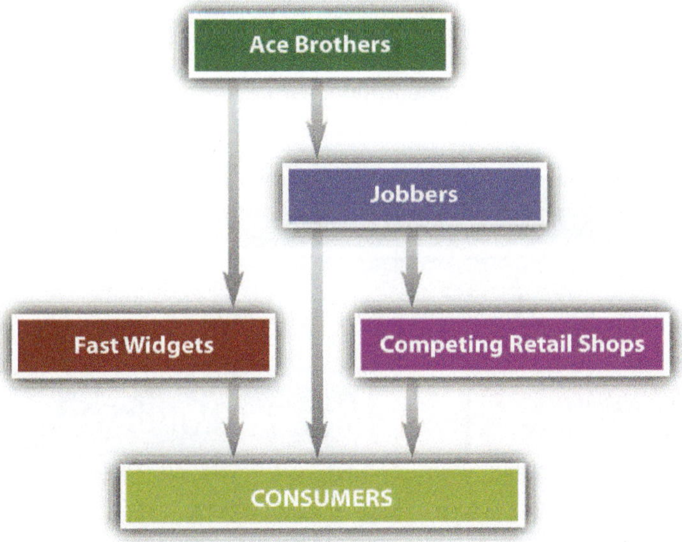

If Ace favors Jobbers by cutting its prices, discriminating against Fast Widgets, the transaction is unlawful, even though Jobbers and Fast Widgets do not compete for sales to other retailers. Their competition for the business of ultimate consumers is sufficient to establish the illegality of the discrimination. A variation on this situation was at issue in the first important case to test Section 2(a) as it affects buyers. Morton Salt sold to both wholesalers and retailers, offering quantity discounts. Its pricing policy was structured to give large buyers great savings, computed on a yearly total, not on shipments made at any one time. Only five retail chains could take advantage of the higher discounts, and as a result, these chains could sell salt to grocery shoppers at a price below that at which the chains' retail competitors could buy it from their wholesalers. See Figure 48.5 for a schematic illustration. In this case, *FTC v. Morton Salt Co.*, the Supreme Court for the first time declared that the impact of the discrimination does not have to be actual; it is enough if there is a "reasonable possibility" of competitive injury.[30]

FIGURE 48.5 Variation: Morton Salt Co.

In order to make out a case of secondary-line injury, it is necessary to show that the buyers purchasing at different prices are in fact competitors. Suppose that Ace Brothers sells to Fast Widgets, the retailer, and also to Boron Enterprises, a manufacturer that incorporates widgets in most of its products. Boron does not compete against Fast Widgets, and therefore Ace Brothers may charge different prices to Boron and Fast without fearing Robinson-Patman repercussions. Figure 48.6 shows the Boron-Fast schematic.

FIGURE 48.6 Variation: Boron-Fast Schematic

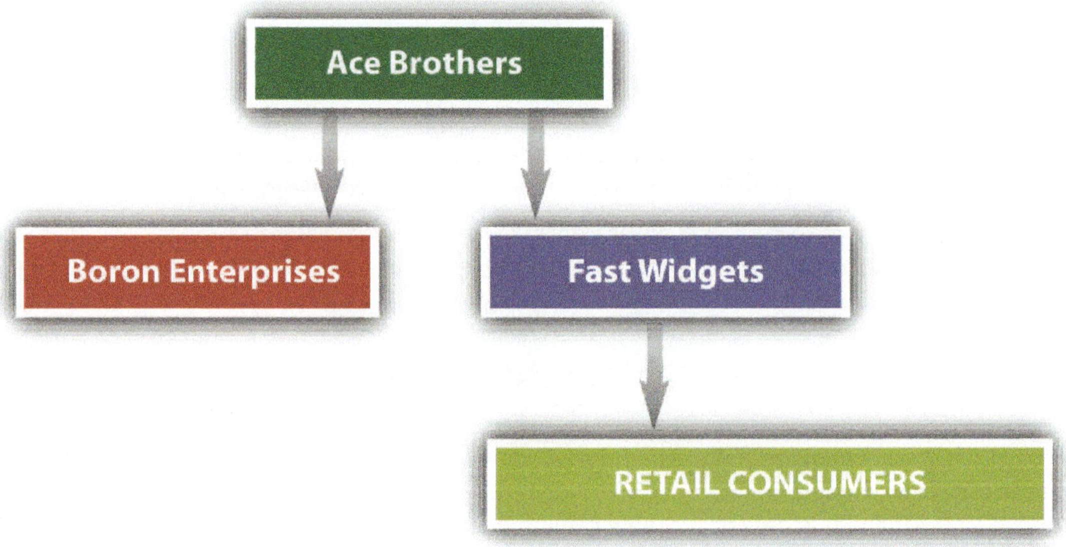

Seller's Defenses

Price discrimination is not per se unlawful. The Robinson-Patman Act allows the seller two general defenses: (1) cost justification and (2) meeting competition. If the seller can demonstrate that sales to one particular buyer are cheaper than sales to others, a price differential is permitted if it is based entirely on the cost differences. For example, if one buyer is willing to have the goods packed in cheaper containers or larger crates that save money, that savings can be passed along to the buyer. Similarly, a buyer who takes over a warehousing function formerly undertaken by the seller is entitled to have the cost saving reflected in the selling price. Suppose the buyer orders its entire requirements for the year from the manufacturer, a quantity many times greater than that taken by any other customer. This large order permits the manufacturer to make the goods at a considerably reduced unit cost. May the manufacturer pass those savings along to the quantity buyer? It may, as long as it does not pass along the entire savings but only that attributable to the particular buyer, for other buyers add to its total production run and thus contribute to the final unit production cost. The marketing manager should be aware that the courts strictly construe cost-justification claims, and few companies have succeeded with this defense.

Meeting Competition

Lowering a price to meet competition is a complete defense to a charge of price discrimination. Assume Ace Brothers is selling widgets to retailers in Indiana and Kentucky at $100 per dozen. National Widgets suddenly enters the Kentucky market and, because it has lower manufacturing costs than Ace, sells widgets to the four Kentucky widget retailers at $85 per dozen. Ace may lower its price to that amount in Kentucky without lowering its Indiana price. However, if National's price violated the Robinson-Patman Act and Ace knew or should have known that it did, Ace may not reduce its price.

The defense of meeting competition has certain limitations. For example, the seller may not use this defense as an excuse to charge different customers a price differential over the long run. Moreover, if National's lower prices result from quantity orders, Ace may reduce its prices only for like quantities. Ace may not reduce its price for lesser quantities if National charges more for smaller orders. And although Ace may meet National's price to a given customer, Ace may not legally charge less.

Section 2(c) prohibits payment of commissions by one party in a transaction to the opposite party (or to the opposite party's agent) in a sale of goods unless services are actually rendered for them. Suppose the buyer's broker warehouses the goods. May the seller pass along this cost to the broker in the form of a rebate? Isn't that "services rendered"? Although it might seem so, the courts have said no, because they refuse to concede that a buyer's broker or agent can perform services for the seller. Because Section 2(c) of the Robinson-Patman Act stands on its own, the plaintiff need prove only that a single payment was made. Further proof of competitive impact is unnecessary. Hence Section 2(c) cases are relatively easy to win once the fact of a brokerage commission is uncovered.

Allowances for Merchandising and Other Services

Sections 2(d) and 2(e) of the Robinson-Patman Act prohibit sellers from granting discriminatory allowances for merchandising and from performing other services for buyers on a discriminatory basis. These sections are necessary because price alone is far from the only way to offer discounts to favored buyers. Allowances and services covered by these sections include advertising allowances, floor and window displays, warehousing, return privileges, and special packaging.

Key Takeaway

Under the Robinson-Patman Act, it is illegal to charge different prices to different purchasers if the items are the same and the price discrimination lessens competition. It is legal, however, to charge a lower price to a specific buyer if the cost of serving that buyer is lower or if the seller is simply "meeting competition."

Exercises

1. Nikon sells its cameras to retailers at 5 percent less in the state of California than in Nevada or Arizona. Without knowing more, can you say that this is illegal?
2. Tysons Foods sells its chicken wings to GFS and other very large distributors at a price per wing that is 10 percent less than it sells to most grocery store chains. The difference is attributable to transportation costs, since GFS and others accept shipments in very large containers, which cost less to deliver than smaller containers. Is the price differential legal?
3. Your best customer, who has high volume with your company, asks you for a volume discount. Actually, he demands this, rather than just asking. Under what circumstances, if any, can you grant this request without violating antitrust laws?

48.5 Exemptions

Learning Objective

1. Know and describe the various exemptions from U.S. antitrust law.

Organized Labor

In the Clayton Act, Congress explicitly exempted labor unions from the antitrust laws in order to permit workers to band together. Section 6 says that "the labor of a human being is not a commodity or article of commerce. Nothing contained in the antitrust laws shall be construed to forbid the existence and operation of labor...organizations,...nor shall such organizations, or the members thereof, be held or construed to be illegal combinations or conspiracies in restraint of trade, under the antitrust laws." This provision was included to reverse earlier decisions of the courts that had applied the Sherman Act more against labor than business. Nevertheless, the immunity is not total, and unions have run afoul of the laws when they have combined with nonlabor groups to achieve a purpose unlawful under the antitrust laws. Thus, a union could not bargain with an employer to sell its products above a certain price floor.

Insurance Companies

Under the McCarran-Ferguson Act of 1945, insurance companies are not covered by the antitrust laws to the extent that the states regulate the business of insurance. Whether or not the states adequately regulate insurance and the degree to which the exemption applies are complex questions, and there has been some political pressure to repeal the insurance exemption.

State Action

In 1943, the Supreme Court ruled in *Parker v. Brown* that when a valid state law regulates a particular industry practice and the industry members are bound to follow that law, then they are exempt from the federal antitrust laws.[31] Such laws include regulation of public power and licensing and regulation of the professions. This exemption for "state action" has proved troublesome and, like the other exemptions, a complex matter to apply. But it is clear that the state law must require or compel the action and not merely permit it. No state law would be valid if it simply said, "Bakers in the state may jointly establish tariffs for the sale of cookies."

The recent trend of Supreme Court decisions is to construe the exemption as narrowly as possible. A city, county, or other subordinate unit of a state is not immune under the *Parker* doctrine. A municipality can escape the consequences of antitrust violations—for example, in its operation of utilities—only if it is carrying out express policy of the state. Even then, a state-mandated price-fixing scheme may not survive a federal antitrust attack. New York law required liquor retailers to charge a certain minimum price, but because the state itself did not actively supervise the policy it had established, it fell to the Supreme Court's antitrust axe.

Group Solicitation of Government

Suppose representatives of the railroad industry lobby extensively and eventually successfully for state legislation that hampers truckers, the railroads' deadly enemies. Is this a combination or conspiracy to restrain trade? In *Eastern Railroad President's Conference v. Noerr Motor Freight, Inc.*, the Supreme Court said no.[32] What has come to be known as the *Noerr* doctrine holds that applying the antitrust laws to such activities would violate First Amendment rights to petition the government. One exception to this rule of immunity for soliciting action by the government comes when certain groups seek to harass competitors by instituting state or federal proceedings against them if the claims are baseless or known to be false. Nor does the *Noerr* doctrine apply to horizontal boycotts even if the object is to force the government to take action. In *FTC v. Superior Court Trial Lawyers Assn.*, the Supreme Court held that a group of criminal defense lawyers had clearly violated the Sherman Act when they agreed among themselves to stop handling cases on behalf of indigent defendants to force the local government to raise the lawyers' fees.[33] The Court rejected their claim that they had a First Amendment right to influence the government through a boycott to pay a living wage so that indigent defendants could be adequately represented.

Baseball

Baseball, the Supreme Court said back in 1923, is not "in commerce." Congress has never seen fit to overturn this doctrine. Although some inroads have been made in the way that the leagues and clubs may exercise their power, the basic decision stands. Some things are sacred.

Key Takeaway

For various reasons over time, certain industries and organized groups have been exempted from the operation of US antitrust laws. These include organized labor, insurance companies, and baseball. In addition, First Amendment concerns allow trade groups to solicit both state and federal governments, and state law may sometimes provide a "state action" exemption.

Exercise

1. Do a little Internet research. Find out why Curt Flood brought an antitrust lawsuit against Major League Baseball and what the Supreme Court did with his case.

48.6 Sherman Act, Section 2: Concentrations of Market Power

Learning Objectives

1. Understand the ways in which monopoly power can be injurious to competition.
2. Explain why not all monopolies are illegal under the Sherman Act.
3. Recognize the importance of defining the relevant market in terms of both geography and product.
4. Describe the remedies for Sherman Act Section 2 violations.

Introduction

Large companies, or any company that occupies a large portion of any market segment, can thwart competition through the exercise of **monopoly power**. Indeed, monopoly means the lack of competition, or at least of effective competition. As the Supreme Court has long defined it, **monopoly** is "the power to control market prices or exclude competition."[34] Public concern about the economic and political power of the large trusts, which tended to become monopolies in the late nineteenth century, led to Section 2 of the Sherman Act in 1890 and to Section 7 of the Clayton Act in 1914. These statutes are not limited to the giants of American industry, such as ExxonMobil, Microsoft, Google, or AT&T. A far smaller company that dominates a relatively small geographic area or that merges with another company in an area where few others compete can also violate Sections 2 or 7. These laws should therefore be of concern to all businesses, not just those on the *Fortune* 500 list. In this section, we will consider how the courts have interpreted both the Section 2 prohibition against monopolizing and the Section 7 prohibition against mergers and acquisitions that tend to lessen competition or to create monopolies.

Section 2 of the Sherman Act reads as follows: "Every person who shall monopolize, or attempt to monopolize, or combine or conspire with any other person or persons, to monopolize any part of the trade or commerce among the several states, or with foreign nations, shall be deemed guilty of a [felony]."

We begin the analysis of Section 2 with the basic proposition that a monopoly is not per se unlawful. Section 2 itself makes this proposition inescapable: it forbids the act of *monopolizing*, not the condition or attribute of *monopoly*. Why should that be so? If monopoly power is detrimental to a functioning competitive market system, why shouldn't the law ban the very existence of a monopoly?

The answer is that we cannot hope to have "perfect competition" but only "workable competition." Any number of circumstances might lead to monopolies that we would not want to eliminate. Demand for a product might be limited to what one company could produce, there thus being no incentive for any competitor to come into the market. A small town may be able to support only one supermarket, newspaper, or computer outlet. If a company is operating efficiently through economies of scale, we would not want to split it apart and watch the resulting companies fail. An innovator may have a field all to himself, yet we would not want to penalize the inventor for his very act of invention. Or a company might simply be smarter and more efficient, finally coming to stand alone through the very operation of competitive pressures. It would be an irony indeed if the law were to condemn a company that was forged in the fires of competition itself. As the Supreme Court has said, the Sherman Act was designed to protect competition, not competitors.

A company that has had a monopoly position "thrust upon it" is perfectly lawful. The law penalizes not the monopolist as such but the competitor who gains his monopoly power through illegitimate means with an intent to become a monopolist, or who after having become a monopolist acts illegitimately to maintain his power.

A Section 2 case involves three essential factors:

1. What is the **relevant market** for determining dominance? The question of relevant market has two aspects: a geographic market dimension and a **relevant product market** dimension. It makes a considerable difference whether the company is thought to be a competitor in ten states or only one. A large company in one state may appear tiny matched against competitors operating in many states. Likewise, if the product itself has real substitutes, it makes little sense to brand its maker a monopolist. For instance, Coca-Cola is made by only one company, but that does not make the Coca-Cola Company a monopoly, for its soft drink competes with many in the marketplace.
2. How much monopoly power is too much? What share of the market must a company have to be labeled a monopoly? Is a company with 50 percent of the market a monopoly? 75 percent? 90 percent?
3. What constitutes an illegitimate means of gaining or maintaining monopoly power?

These factors are often closely intertwined, especially the first two. This makes it difficult to examine each separately, but to the extent possible, we will address each factor in the order given.

relevant market

For a court to determine if a firm has a dominant market share, it must first define the relevant market, which consists of two elements: a relevant product market and a relevant geographic market.

relevant product market

The market that includes all products that have identical attributes or are reasonably interchangeable. If customers treat different products as acceptable substitutes for one another, the products are reasonably interchangeable.

Relevant Markets: Product Market and Geographic Market

Product Market

The monopolist never exercises power in the abstract. When exercised, monopoly power is used to set prices or exclude competition in the market for a particular product or products. Therefore, it is essential in any Section 2 case to determine what products to include in the relevant market.

The Supreme Court looks at "cross-elasticity of demand" to determine the relevant market. That is, to what degree can a substitute be found for the product in question if the producer sets the price too high? If consumers stay with the product as its price rises, moving to a substitute only at a very high price, then the product is probably in a market by itself. If consumers shift to another product with slight rises in price, then the product market is "elastic" and must include all such substitutes.

Geographic Market

A company doesn't have to dominate the world market for a particular product or service in order to be held to be a monopolist. The Sherman Act speaks of "any part" of the trade or commerce. The Supreme Court defines this as the "area of effective competition." Ordinarily, the smaller the part the government can point to, the greater its chances of prevailing, since a company usually will have greater control over a single marketplace than a regional or national market. Because of this, alleged monopolists will usually argue for a broad geographic market, while the government tries to narrow it by pointing to such factors as transportation costs and the degree to which consumers will shop outside the defined area.

Monopoly Power

After the relevant product and geographic markets are defined, the next question is whether the defendant has sufficient power within them to constitute a monopoly. The usual test is the market share the alleged monopolist enjoys, although no rigid rule or mathematical formula is possible. In *United States v. Aluminum Company of America*, presented in Section 8 of this chapter, Judge Learned Hand said that Alcoa's 90 percent share of the ingot market was enough to constitute a monopoly but that 64 percent would have been doubtful.[35] In a case against DuPont many years ago, the court looked at a 75 percent market share in cellophane but found that the relevant market (considering the cross-elasticity of demand) was not restricted to cellophane.

Monopolization: Acquiring and Maintaining a Monopoly

Once a company has been found to have monopoly power in a relevant market, the final question is whether it either acquired its monopoly power in an unlawful way or has acted unlawfully to maintain it. This additional element of "deliberateness" does not mean that the government must prove that the defendant *intended* monopolization, in the sense that what it *desired* was the complete exclusion of all competitors. It is enough to show that the monopoly would probably result from its actions, for as Judge Hand put it, "No monopolist monopolizes unconscious of what he is doing."

What constitutes proof of unlawful acquisition or maintenance of a monopoly? In general, proof is made by showing that the defendant's acts were aimed at or had the probable effect of excluding competitors from the market. Violations of Section 1 or other provisions of the antitrust laws are examples. "Predatory pricing"—charging less than cost—can be evidence that the defendant's purpose was monopolistic, for small companies cannot compete with large manufacturers that can sustain continued losses until the competition folds up and ceases operations.

In *United States v. Lorain Journal Company*, the town of Lorain, Ohio, could support only one newspaper.[36] With a circulation of twenty thousand, the *Lorain Journal* reached more than 99 percent of the town's families. The *Journal* had thus lawfully become a monopoly. But when a radio station was set up, the paper found itself competing directly for local and national advertising. To retaliate, the *Journal* refused to accept advertisements unless the advertiser agreed not to advertise on the local station. The Court agreed that this was an unlawful attempt to boycott and hence was a violation of Section 2 because the paper was using its monopoly power to exclude a competitor. (Where was the *interstate* commerce that would bring the activity under federal law? The Court said that the radio station was in interstate commerce because it broadcast national news supported by national advertising.)

Practices that help a company acquire or maintain its monopoly position need not be unlawful in themselves. In the *Aluminum Company* case, Alcoa claimed its monopoly power was the result of superior business skills and techniques. These superior skills led it to constantly build plant capacity and expand output at every opportunity. But Judge Hand thought otherwise, given that for a quarter of a century other producers could not break into the market because Alcoa acted at every turn to make it impossible for them to compete, even as Alcoa increased its output by some 800 percent. Judge Hand's explanation remains the classic exposition.

Innovation as Evidence of Intent to Monopolize

During the 1970s, several monopolization cases seeking huge damages were filed against a number of well-known companies, including Xerox, International Business Machines (IBM), and Eastman Kodak. In particular, IBM was hit with several suits as an outgrowth of the Justice Department's lawsuit against the computer maker. (*United States v. IBM* was filed in 1969 and did not terminate until 1982, when the government agreed to drop all charges, a complete victory for the company.) The plaintiffs in many of these suits—SCM Corporation against Xerox, California Computer Products Incorporated against IBM (the *Calcomp* case), Berkey Photo Incorporated against Kodak—charged that the defendants had maintained their alleged monopolies by strategically introducing key product innovations that rendered competitive products obsolete. For example, hundreds of computer companies manufacture peripheral equipment "plug-compatible" with IBM computers. Likewise, Berkey manufactured film usable in Kodak cameras. When the underlying products are changed—mainframe computers, new types of cameras—the existing manufacturers are left with unusable inventory and face a considerable time lag in designing new peripheral equipment. In some of these cases, the plaintiffs managed to obtain sizable treble damage awards—SCM won more than $110 million, IBM initially lost one case in the amount of $260 million, and Berkey bested Kodak to the tune of $87 million. Had these cases been sustained on appeal, a radical new doctrine would have been imported into the antitrust laws—that innovation for the sake of competing is unlawful.

None of these cases withstood appellate scrutiny. The Supreme Court has not heard cases in this area, so the law that has emerged is from decisions of the federal courts of appeals. A typical case is *ILC Peripherals Leasing Corp. v. International Business Machines* (the *Memorex* case).[37] Memorex argued that among other things, IBM's tactic of introducing a new generation of computer technology at lower prices constituted monopolization. The court disagreed, noting that other companies could "reverse engineer" IBM equipment much more cheaply than IBM could originally design it and that IBM computers and related products were subject to intense competition to the benefit of plug-compatible equipment users. The actions of IBM undoubtedly hurt Memorex, but they were part and parcel of the competitive system, the very essence of competition. "This kind of conduct by IBM," the court said, "is precisely what the antitrust laws were meant to encourage....Memorex sought to use the antitrust laws to make time stand still and preserve its very profitable position. This court will not assist it and the others who would follow after in this endeavor."

The various strands of the innovation debate are perhaps best summed up in *Berkey Photo, Inc. v. Eastman Kodak Company*, Section 8.

Attempts to Monopolize

Section 2 prohibits not only actual monopolization but also attempts to monopolize. An attempt need not succeed to be unlawful; a defendant who tries to exercise sway over a relevant market can take no legal comfort from failure. In any event, the plaintiff must show a specific intent to monopolize, not merely an intent to commit the act or acts that constitute the attempt.

Remedies

Since many of the defendant's acts that constitute Sherman Act Section 2 monopolizing are also violations of Section 1 of the Clayton Act, why should plaintiffs resort to Section 2 at all? What practical difference does Section 2 make? One answer is that not every act of monopolizing is a violation of another law. Leasing and pricing practices that are perfectly lawful for an ordinary competitor may be unlawful only because of Section 2. But the more important reason is the remedy provided by the Sherman Act: divestiture. In the right case, the courts may order the company broken up.

In the *Standard Oil* decision of 1911, the Supreme Court held that the Standard Oil Company constituted a monopoly and ordered it split into separate companies. Several other trusts were similarly dealt with. In many of the early cases, doing so posed no great difficulties, because the companies themselves essentially consisted of separate manufacturing plants knit together by financial controls. But not every company is a loose confederation of potentially separate operating companies.

The *Alcoa* case (Section 8) was fraught with difficult remedial issues. Judge Hand's opinion came down in 1945, but the remedial side of the case did not come up until 1950. By then the industry had changed radically, with the entrance of Reynolds and Kaiser as effective competitors, reducing Alcoa's share of the market to 50 percent. Because any aluminum producer needs considerable resources to succeed and because aluminum production is crucial to national security, the later court refused to order the company broken apart. The court ordered Alcoa to take a series of measures that would boost competition in the industry. For example, Alcoa stockholders had to divest themselves of the stock of a closely related Canadian producer in order to remove Alcoa's control of that company; and the court rendered unenforceable a patent-licensing agreement with Reynolds and Kaiser that required them to share their inventions with Alcoa, even though neither the Canadian tie nor the patent agreements were in themselves unlawful.

Although the trend has been away from breaking up the monopolist, it is still employed as a potent remedy. In perhaps the largest monopolization case ever brought—*United States v. American Telephone & Telegraph Company*—the government sought divestiture of several of AT&T's constituent companies, including Western Electric and the various local operating companies. To avoid prolonged litigation, AT&T agreed in 1982 to a consent decree that required it to spin off all its operating companies, companies that had been central to AT&T's decades-long monopoly.

Key Takeaway

Aggressive competition is good for consumers and for the market, but if the company has enough power to control a market, the benefits to society decrease. Under Section 2 of the Sherman Act, it is illegal to monopolize or attempt to monopolize the market. If the company acquires a monopoly in the wrong way, using wrongful tactics, it is illegal under Section 2. Courts will look at three questions to see if a company has illegally monopolized a market: (1) What is the relevant market? (2) Does the company control the market? and (3) How did the company acquire or maintain its control?

Exercises

1. Mammoth Company, through three subsidiaries, controls 87 percent of the equipment to operate central station hazard-detecting devices; these devices are used to prevent burglary and detect fires and to provide electronic notification to police and fire departments at a central location. In an antitrust lawsuit, Mammoth Company claims that there are other means of protecting against burglary and it therefore does not have monopoly power. Explain how the Justice Department may be able to prove its claim that Mammoth Company is operating an illegal monopoly.
2. Name the sanctions used to enforce Section 2 of the Sherman Act.
3. Look at any news database or the Department of Justice antitrust website for the past three years and describe a case involving a challenge to the exercise of a US company's monopoly power.

48.7 Acquisitions and Mergers under Section 7 of the Clayton Act

Learning Objectives

1. Distinguish the three kinds of mergers.
2. Describe how the courts will define the relevant market in gauging the potential anticompetitive effects of mergers and acquisitions.

Neither Section 1 nor Section 2 of the Sherman Act proved particularly useful in barring mergers or acquisitions that would tend to reduce competition. As originally written, neither did the Clayton Act, which prohibited only mergers accomplished through the sale of stock, not mergers or acquisitions carried out through acquisition of assets. In 1950, Congress amended the Clayton Act to close the loophole concerning acquisition of assets. It also narrowed the search for relevant markets; under the 1950 amendment, if competition might be lessened *in any line of commerce in any section of the country*, the merger is unlawful.

As amended, the pertinent part of Section 7 of the Clayton Act reads as follows:

> *[N]o corporation engaged in commerce shall acquire, directly or indirectly, the whole or any part of the stock or other share capital and no corporation subject to the jurisdiction of the Federal Trade Commission shall acquire the whole or any part of the assets of another corporation engaged also in commerce, where in any line of commerce in any section of the country, the effect of such acquisition may be substantially to lessen competition, or to tend to create a monopoly.*
>
> *No corporation shall acquire, directly or indirectly, the whole or any part of the stock or other share capital and no corporation subject to the jurisdiction of the Federal Trade Commission shall acquire the whole or any part of the assets of one or more corporations engaged in commerce, where in any line of commerce in any section of the country, the effect of such acquisition, of such stock or assets, or of the use of such stock by the voting or granting of proxies or otherwise, may be substantially to lessen competition, or to tend to create a monopoly.*

Definitions

Mergers and Acquisitions

For the sake of brevity, we will refer to both mergers and acquisitions as mergers. Mergers are usually classified into three types: horizontal, vertical, and conglomerate.

Horizontal

horizontal merger

A merger between competitors—for example, between two bread manufacturers or two grocery chains competing in the same locale.

A **horizontal merger** is one between competitors—for example, between two bread manufacturers or two grocery chains competing in the same locale.

Vertical

vertical merger

A merger between a supplier and a customer. If the customer acquires the supplier, it is backward vertical integration; if the supplier acquires the customer, it is forward vertical integration.

A **vertical merger** will combine a supplier and a customer. If the customer acquires the supplier, it is known as backward vertical integration; if the supplier acquires the customer, it is forward vertical integration. For example, a book publisher that buys a paper manufacturer has engaged in backward vertical integration. Its purchase of a bookstore chain would be forward vertical integration.

Conglomerate Mergers

Conglomerate mergers

A merger between companies whose businesses are not directly related.

Conglomerate mergers do not have a standard definition but generally are taken to be mergers between companies whose businesses are not directly related. Commentators have subdivided this category into three types. In a "pure" conglomerate merger, the businesses are not related, as when a steel manufacturer acquires a movie distributor. In a product-extension merger, the manufacturer of one product acquires the manufacturer of a related product—for instance, a producer of household cleansers, but not of liquid bleach, acquires a producer of liquid bleach. In a market-extension merger, a company in one geographic market acquires a company in the same business in a different location. For example, suppose a bakery operating only in San Francisco buys a bakery operating only in Palo Alto. Since they had not competed before the merger, this would not be a horizontal merger.

General Principles

As in monopolization cases, a relevant product market and geographic market must first be marked out to test the effect of the merger. But Section 7 of the Clayton Act has a market definition different from the Sherman Act's Section 2. Section 7 speaks of "*any line* of commerce in any *section* of the country" (emphasis added). And its test for the effect of the merger is the same as that which we have already seen for exclusive dealing cases governed by Section 3 of the Clayton Act: that is, that the effect of the merger "may be substantially to lessen competition or to tend to create a monopoly."

relevant geographic market

The market that is the territory or territories within which a company markets its products or services.

Taken together, this language makes it easier to condemn an unlawful merger than an unlawful monopoly. The relevant product market is any *line* of commerce, and the courts have taken this language to permit the plaintiff to prove the existence of "submarkets" in which the relative effect of the merger is greater. The **relevant geographic market** is any *section of the country*, which means that the plaintiff can show the appropriate effect in a city or a particular region and not worry about having to show the effect in a national market. Moreover, as we have seen, the effect is one of probability, not actuality. Thus, the question is, *Might* competition be substantially lessened? rather than, *Was* competition in fact substantially lessened? Likewise, the question is, Did the merger *tend* to create a monopoly? rather than, Did the merger in fact create a monopoly?

In *United States v. du Pont*, the government charged that du Pont's "commanding position as General Motors' supplier of automotive finishes and fabrics" was not achieved on competitive merit alone but because du Pont had acquired a sizable block of GM stock, and the "consequent close intercompany relationship led to the insulation of most of the General Motors' market from free competition," in violation of Section 7.[38] Between 1917 and 1919, du Pont took a 23 percent stock interest in GM. The district court dismissed the complaint, partly on the grounds that at least before the 1950 amendment to Section 7, the Clayton Act did not condemn vertical mergers and partly on the grounds that du Pont had not dominated GM's decision to purchase millions of dollars' worth of automotive finishes and fabrics. The Supreme Court disagreed with this analysis and sent the case back to trial. The Court specifically held that even though the stock acquisition had occurred some thirty-five years earlier, the government can resort to Section 7 whenever it appears that the result of the acquisition will violate the competitive tests set forth in the section.

Defining the Market

In the seminal *Brown Shoe* case, the Supreme Court said that the outer boundaries of broad markets "are determined by the reasonable interchangeability of use or the cross elasticity of demand between the product itself and substitutes for it" but that narrower "well defined submarkets" might also be appropriate lines of commerce.[39] In drawing market boundaries, the Court said, courts should realistically reflect "[c]ompetition where, in fact, it exists." Among the factors to consider are "industry or public recognition of the submarket as a separate economic entity, the product's peculiar characteristics and uses, unique production facilities, distinct customers, distinct prices, sensitivity to price changes and specialized vendors." To select the geographic market, courts must consider both "the commercial realities" of the industry and the economic significance of the market.

The Failing Company Doctrine

One defense to a Section 7 case is that one of the merging companies is a failing company. In *Citizen Publishing Company v. United States*, the Supreme Court said that the defense is applicable if two conditions are satisfied.[40] First, a company must be staring bankruptcy in the face; it must have virtually no chance of being resuscitated without the merger. Second, the acquiring company must be the only available purchaser, and the failing company must have made bona fide efforts to search for another purchaser.

Beneficial Effects

That a merger might produce beneficial effects is not a defense to a Section 7 case. As the Supreme Court said in *United States v. Philadelphia National Bank*, "[A] merger, the effect of which 'may be substantially to lessen competition' is not saved because, on some ultimate reckoning of social or economic debits or credits, it may be deemed beneficial."[41] And in *FTC v. Procter & Gamble Co.*, the Court said, "Possible economies cannot be used as a defense to illegality."[42] Congress was also aware that some mergers which lessen competition may also result in economies but it struck the balance in favor of protecting competition.

Tests of Competitive Effect

Horizontal Mergers

Three factors are critical in assessing whether a horizontal merger may substantially lessen competition: (1) the market shares of the merging companies, (2) the concentration ratios, and (3) the trends in the industry toward concentration.

The first factor is self-evident. A company with 10 percent or even 5 percent of the market is in a different position from one with less than 1 percent. A concentration ratio indicates the number of firms that constitute an industry. An industry with only four firms is obviously much more concentrated than one with ten or seventy firms. Concentration trends indicate the frequency with which firms in the relevant market have been merging. The first merger in an industry with a low concentration ratio might be predicted to have no likely effect on competition, but a merger of two firms in a four-firm industry would obviously have a pronounced effect.

In the *Philadelphia National Bank* case, the court announced this test in assessing the legality of a horizontal merger: "[A] merger which produces a firm controlling an undue percentage share of the relevant market, and results in a significant increase in the concentration of firms in that market is so inherently likely to lessen competition substantially that it must be enjoined in the absence of evidence clearly showing that the merger is not likely to have such anticompetitive effects." In this case, the merger led to a 30 percent share of the commercial banking market in a four-county region around Philadelphia and an increase in concentration by more than one-third, and the court held that those numbers amounted to a violation of Section 7. The court also said that "if concentration is already great, the importance of preventing even slight increases in concentration and so preserving the possibility of eventual de-concentration is correspondingly great."

The Hart-Scott-Rodino Antitrust Improvements Act of 1976 requires certain companies to notify the Justice Department before actually completing mergers or acquisitions, whether by private negotiation or by public tender offer. When one of the companies has sales or assets of $100 million or more and the other company $10 million or more, premerger notification must be provided at least thirty days prior to completion of the deal—or fifteen days in the case of a tender offer of cash for publicly traded shares if the resulting merger would give the acquiring company $50 million worth or 15 percent of assets or voting securities in the acquired company. The rules are complex, but they are designed to give the department time to react to a merger before it has been secretly accomplished and then announced. The 1976 act gives the department the authority to seek an injunction against the completion of any such merger, which of course greatly simplifies the remedial phase of the case should the courts ultimately hold that the merger would be unlawful. (Note: Section 7 is one of the "tools" in the kit of the lawyer who defends companies against unwelcomed takeover attempts: if the target company can point to lines of its business in which it competes with the acquiring company, it can threaten antitrust action in order to block the merger.)

Vertical Mergers

To prove a Section 7 case involving a vertical merger, the plaintiff must show that the merger forecloses competition "in a substantial share of" a substantial market. But statistical factors alone do not govern in a vertical merger. To illustrate, we see that in *Ford Motor Co. v. United States*, the merger between Ford and Autolite (a manufacturer of spark plugs) was held unlawful because it eliminated Ford's potential entry into the market as an independent manufacturer of spark plugs and because it foreclosed Ford "as a purchaser of about ten percent of total industry output" of spark plugs.[43] This decision underscores the principle that a company may serve to enhance competition simply by waiting in the wings as a potential entrant to a market. If other companies feel threatened by a company the size of Ford undertaking to compete where it had not done so before, the existing manufacturers will likely keep their prices low so as not to tempt the giant in. Of course, had Ford entered the market on its own by independently manufacturing spark plugs, it might ultimately have caused weak competitors to fold. As the Court said, "Had Ford taken the internal-expansion route, there would have been no illegality; not, however, because the result necessarily would have been commendable, but simply because that course has not been proscribed."

Conglomerate Mergers

Recall the definition of a conglomerate merger given in Section 7. None of the three types listed has a direct impact on competition, so the test for illegality is more difficult to state and apply than for horizontal or vertical mergers. But they are nonetheless within the reach of Section 7. In the late 1960s and early 1970s, the government filed a number of divestiture suits against conglomerate mergers. It did not win them all, and none reached the Supreme Court; most were settled by consent decree, leading in several instances to divestiture either of the acquired company or of another division of the acquiring company. Thus International Telephone & Telegraph Company agreed to divest itself of Canteen Corporation and either of the following two groups: (1) Avis, Levin & Sons, and Hamilton Life Insurance Company; or (2) Hartford Fire Insurance Company. Ling-Temco-Vought agreed to divest itself of either Jones & Laughlin Steel or Braniff Airways and Okonite Corporation. In these and other cases, the courts have looked to specific potential effects, such as raising the barriers to entry into a market and eliminating potential competition, but they have rejected the more general claim of "the rising tide of economic concentration in American industry."

Entrenching Oligopoly

One way to attack conglomerate mergers is to demonstrate that by taking over a dominant company in an oligopolistic industry, a large and strong acquiring company will further entrench the oligopoly. In an oligopolistic industry, just a few major competitors so dominate the industry that competition is quelled. In *FTC v. Procter & Gamble Co.*, the government challenged Procter & Gamble's (P&G's) acquisition of Clorox. P&G was the leading seller of household cleansers, with annual sales of more than $1 billion.[44] In addition, it was the "nation's largest advertiser," promoting its products so heavily that it was able to take advantage of substantial advertising discounts from the media. Clorox had more than 48 percent of national sales for liquid bleach in a heavily **concentrated industry**. Since all liquid bleach is chemically identical, advertising and promotion plays the dominant role in selling the product. Prior to the merger, P&G did not make or sell liquid bleach; hence it was a product-extension merger rather than a horizontal one.

concentrated industry

An industry in which a large percentage of market sales is controlled by either a single firm or a small number of firms.

The Supreme Court concluded that smaller firms would fear retaliation from P&G if they tried to compete in the liquid bleach market and that "a new entrant would be much more reluctant to face the giant Procter than it would have been to face the smaller Clorox." Hence, "the substitution of the powerful acquiring firm for the smaller, but already dominant firm may substantially reduce the competitive structure of the industry by raising entry barriers and by dissuading the smaller firms from aggressively competing." The entrenchment theory probably applies only to highly concentrated industries and dominant firms, however. Many subsequent cases have come out in favor of the defendants on a variety of grounds—that the merger led simply to a more efficient acquired firm, that the existing competitors were strong and able to compete, or even that the acquiring firm merely gives the acquired company a deep pocket to better finance its operations.

Eliminating Potential Competition

This theory holds that but for the merger, the acquiring company might have competed in the acquired company's market. In *Procter & Gamble*, for example, P&G might have entered the liquid bleach market itself and thus given Clorox a run for its money. An additional strong company would then have been in the market. When P&G bought Clorox, however, it foreclosed that possibility. This theory depends on proof of some probability that the acquiring company would have entered the market. When the acquired company is small, however, a Section 7 violation is unlikely; these so-called toehold mergers permit the acquiring company to become a competitive force in an industry without necessarily sacrificing any preexisting competition.

Reciprocity

Many companies are both heavy buyers and heavy sellers of products. A company may buy from its customers as well as sell to them. This practice is known in antitrust jargon as reciprocity. Reciprocity is the practice of a seller who uses his volume of purchases from the buyer to induce the buyer to purchase from him. The clearest example arose in *FTC v. Consolidated Foods Corp.*[45] Consolidated owned wholesale grocery outlets and retail food stores. It wanted to merge with Gentry, which made dehydrated onions and garlic. The Supreme Court agreed that the merger violated

Section 7 because of the possibility of reciprocity: Consolidated made bulk purchases from several food processors, which were purchasers of dehydrated onions and garlic from Gentry and others. Processors who did not buy from Gentry might feel pressured to do so in order to keep Consolidated as a customer for their food supplies. If so, other onion and garlic processors would be foreclosed from competing for sales. A merger that raises the mere possibility of reciprocity is not per se unlawful, however. The plaintiff must demonstrate that it was probable the acquiring company would adopt the practice—for example, by conditioning future orders for supplies on the receipt of orders for onions and garlic—and that doing so would have an anticompetitive effect given the size of the reciprocating companies and their positions in the market.

Joint Ventures

Section 7 can also apply to joint ventures, a rule first announced in 1964. Two companies, Hooker and American Potash, dominated sales of sodium chlorate in the Southeast, with 90 percent of the market. Pennsalt Chemicals Corporation produced the rest in the West and sold it in the Southeast through Olin Mathieson Chemical Corporation. The latter two decided to team up, the better to compete with the giants, and so they formed Penn-Olin, which they jointly owned. The district court dismissed the government's suit, but the Supreme Court reinstated it, saying that a joint venture can serve to blunt competition, or at least potential competition, between the parent companies. The Court said that the lower court must look to a number of factors to determine whether the joint venture was likely to lessen competition substantially:

> *The number and power of the competitors in the relevant market; the background of their growth; the power of the joint venturers; the relationship of their lines of commerce; competition existing between them and the power of each in dealing with the competitors of the other; the setting in which the joint venture was created; the reasons and necessities for its existence; the joint venture's line of commerce and the relationship thereof to that of its parents; the adaptability of its line of commerce to non-competitive practices; the potential power of the joint venture in the relevant market; and appraisal of what the competition in the relevant market would have been if one of the joint venturers had entered it alone instead of through Penn-Olin; the effect, in the event of this occurrence, of the other joint venturer's potential competition; and such other factors as might indicate potential risk to competition in the relevant market.*[46]

These numerous factors illustrate how the entire economic environment surrounding the joint venture and mergers in general must be assessed to determine the legalities.

Remedies

The Clayton Act provides that the government may seek divestiture when an acquisition or a merger violates the act. Until relatively recently, however, it was unresolved whether a private plaintiff could seek divestiture after proving a Clayton Act violation. In 1990, the Supreme Court unanimously agreed that divestiture is an available remedy in private suits, even in suits filed by a state's attorney general on behalf of consumers.[47] This ruling makes it more likely that antimerger litigation will increase in the future.

During the years of the Reagan administration in the 1980s, the federal government became far less active in prosecuting antitrust cases, especially merger cases, than it had been in previous decades. Many giant mergers went unchallenged, like the merger between two oil behemoths, Texaco and Getty, resulting in a company with nearly $50 billion in assets in 1984. With the arrival of the first Bush administration in 1989, the talk in Washington antitrust circles was of a renewed interest in antitrust enforcement. The arrival of the second Bush administration in 2000 brought about an era of less antitrust enforcement than had been undertaken during the Clinton administration. Whether the Obama administration reinvigorates antitrust enforcement remains to be seen.

Key Takeaway

Section 7 prohibits mergers or acquisitions that might tend to lessen competition in any line of commerce in any section of the country. Mergers and acquisitions are usually classified in one of three ways: horizontal (between competitors), vertical (between different levels of the distribution chain), or conglomerate (between businesses that are not directly related). The latter may be divided into product-extension and market-expansion mergers. The relevant market test is different than in monopolization cases; in a Section 7 action, relevance of market may be proved.

In assessing horizontal mergers, the courts will look to the market shares of emerging companies, industry concentration ratios, and trends toward concentration in the industry. To prove a Section 7 case, the plaintiff must show that the merger forecloses competition "in a substantial share of" a substantial market. Conglomerate merger cases are harder to prove and require a showing of specific potential effects, such as raising barriers to entry into an industry and thus entrenching monopoly, or eliminating potential competition. Joint ventures may also be condemned by Section 7. The Hart-Scott-Rodino Antitrust Improvements Act of 1976 requires certain companies to get premerger notice to the Justice Department.

Exercises

1. Sirius Satellite radio and XM satellite radio proposed to merge. Was this a horizontal merger, a vertical merger, or a conglomerate merger? How is the market defined, in terms of both product or service and geographic area?
2. In 2010, Live Nation and Ticketmaster proposed to merge. Was this a horizontal merger, a vertical merger, or a conglomerate merger? How should the market be defined, in terms of both product or service and geographic area? Should the U.S. government approve the merger?

48.8 Cases

Horizontal Restraints of Trade

National Society of Professional Engineers v. United States

435 U.S. 679 (1978)

MR. JUSTICE STEVENS delivered the opinion of the Court.

This is a civil antitrust case brought by the United States to nullify an association's canon of ethics prohibiting competitive bidding by its members. The question is whether the canon may be justified under the Sherman Act, 15 U.S. c. § 1 et seq. (1976 ed.), because it was adopted by members of a learned profession for the purpose of minimizing the risk that competition would produce inferior engineering work endangering the public safety. The District Court rejected this justification without making any findings on the likelihood that competition would produce the dire consequences foreseen by the association. The Court of Appeals affirmed. We granted certiorari to decide whether the District Court should have considered the factual basis for the proffered justification before rejecting it. Because we are satisfied that the asserted defense rests on a fundamental misunderstanding of the Rule of Reason frequently applied in antitrust litigation, we affirm.

Engineering is an important and learned profession. There are over 750,000 graduate engineers in the United States, of whom about 325,000 are registered as professional engineers. Registration requirements vary from State to State, but usually require the applicant to be a graduate engineer with at least four years of practical experience and to pass a written examination. About half of those who are registered engage in consulting engineering on a fee basis. They perform services in connection with the study, design, and construction of all types of improvements to real property—bridges, office buildings, airports, and factories are examples. Engineering fees, amounting to well over $2 billion each year, constitute about 5% of total construction costs. In any given facility, approximately 50% to 80% of the cost of construction is the direct result of work performed by an engineer concerning the systems and equipment to be incorporated in the structure.

The National Society of Professional Engineers (Society) was organized in 1935 to deal with the nontechnical aspects of engineering practice, including the promotion of the professional, social, and economic interests of its members. Its present membership of 69,000 resides throughout the United States and in some foreign countries. Approximately 12,000 members are consulting engineers who offer their services to governmental, industrial, and private clients. Some Society members are principals or chief executive officers of some of the largest engineering firms in the country.

The charges of a consulting engineer may be computed in different ways. He may charge the client a percentage of the cost of the project, may charge fixed rates per hour for different types of work, may perform an assignment for a specific sum, or he may combine one or more of these approaches....This case...involves a charge that the members of the Society have unlawfully agreed to refuse to negotiate or even to discuss the question of fees until after a prospective client has selected the engineer for a particular project. Evidence of this agreement is found in § II(c) of the Society's Code of Ethics, adopted in July 1964.

The District Court found that the Society's Board of Ethical Review has uniformly interpreted the "ethical rules against competitive bidding for engineering services as prohibiting the submission of any form of price information to a prospective customer which would enable that customer to make a price comparison on engineering services." If the client requires that such information be provided, then § II(c) imposes an obligation upon the engineering firm to withdraw from consideration for that job.

[P]etitioner argues that its attempt to preserve the profession's traditional method of setting fees for engineering services is a reasonable method of forestalling the public harm which might be produced by unrestrained competitive bidding. To evaluate this argument it is necessary to identify the contours of the Rule of Reason and to discuss its application to the kind of justification asserted by petitioner.

* * *

The test prescribed in Standard Oil is whether the challenged contracts or acts "were unreasonably restrictive of competitive conditions." Unreasonableness under that test could be based either (1) on the nature or character of the contracts, or (2) on surrounding circumstances giving rise to the inference or presumption that they were intended to restrain trade and enhance prices. Under either branch of the test, the inquiry is confined to a consideration of impact on competitive conditions.

* * *

Price is the "central nervous system of the economy," *United States v. Socony-Vacuum Oil Co.*, 310 U.S. 150, 226 n. 59, and an agreement that "interfere[s] with the setting of price by free market forces" is illegal on its face, *United States v. Container Corp.*, 393 U.S. 333,337. In this case we are presented with an agreement among competitors to refuse to discuss prices with potential customers until after negotiations have resulted in the initial selection of an engineer. While this is not price fixing as such, no elaborate industry analysis is required to demonstrate the anticompetitive character of such an agreement. It operates as an absolute ban on competitive bidding, applying with equal force to both complicated and simple projects and to both inexperienced and sophisticated customers. As the District Court found, the ban "impedes the ordinary give and take of the market place," and substantially deprives the customer of "the ability to utilize and compare prices in selecting engineering services." On its face, this agreement restrains trade within the meaning of § 1 of the Sherman Act.

The Society's affirmative defense confirms rather than refutes the anticompetitive purpose and effect of its agreement. The Society argues that the restraint is justified because bidding on engineering services is inherently imprecise, would lead to deceptively low bids, and would thereby tempt individual engineers to do inferior work with consequent risk to public safety and health. The logic of this argument rests on the assumption that the agreement will tend to maintain the price level; if it had no such effect, it would not serve its intended purpose. The Society nonetheless invokes the Rule of Reason, arguing that its restraint on price competition ultimately inures to the public benefit by preventing the production of inferior work and by insuring ethical behavior. As the preceding discussion of the Rule of Reason reveals, this Court has never accepted such an argument.

It may be, as petitioner argues, that competition tends to force prices down and that an inexpensive item may be inferior to one that is more costly. There is some risk, therefore, that competition will cause some suppliers to market a defective product. Similarly, competitive bidding for engineering projects may be inherently imprecise and incapable of taking into account all the variables which will be involved in the actual performance of the project. Based on these considerations, a purchaser might conclude that his interest in quality—which may embrace the safety of the end product—outweighs the advantages of achieving cost savings by pitting one competitor against another. Or an individual vendor might independently refrain from price negotiation until he has satisfied himself that he fully understands the scope of his customers' needs. These decisions might be reasonable; indeed, petitioner has provided ample documentation for that thesis. But these are not reasons that satisfy the Rule; nor are such individual decisions subject to antitrust attack.

The Sherman Act does not require competitive bidding; it prohibits unreasonable restraints on competition. Petitioner's ban on competitive bidding prevents all customers from making price comparisons in the initial selection of an engineer, and imposes the Society's views of the costs and benefits of competition on the entire marketplace. It is this restraint that must be justified under the Rule of Reason, and petitioner's attempt to do so on the basis of the potential threat that competition poses to the public safety and the ethics of its profession is nothing less than a frontal assault on the basic policy of the Sherman Act.

The Sherman Act reflects a legislative judgment that ultimately competition will produce not only lower prices, but also better goods and services. "The heart of our national economic policy long has been faith in the value of competition." *Standard Oil Co. v. FTC*, 340 U.S. 231, 248. The assumption that competition is the best method of allocating resources in a free market recognizes that all elements of a bargain—quality, service, safety, and durability—and not just the immediate cost, are favorably affected by the free opportunity to select among alternative offers. Even assuming occasional exceptions to the presumed consequences of competition, the statutory policy precludes inquiry into the question whether competition is good or bad.

* * *

In sum, the Rule of Reason does not support a defense based on the assumption that competition itself is unreasonable. Such a view of the Rule would create the "sea of doubt" on which Judge Taft refused to embark in Addyston, 85 F. 271 (1898), at 284, and which this Court has firmly avoided ever since.

* * *

The judgment of the Court of Appeals is affirmed.

Case Questions

1. What kinds of harms are likely if there is unrestrained competitive bidding among engineering firms?
2. By what other means (i.e., *not* including deliberate nondisclosure of price information up to the time of contracting) could the National Society of Professional Engineers protect the public from harm?

Acquiring and Maintaining a Monopoly

United States v. Aluminum Company of America

148 F.2d 416 (2d Cir. 1945)

JUDGE LEARNED HAND

It does not follow because "Alcoa" had such a monopoly that it "monopolized" the ingot market: it may not have achieved monopoly; monopoly may have been thrust upon it. If it had been a combination of existing smelters which united the whole industry and controlled the production of all aluminum ingot, it would certainly have "monopolized" the market....We may start therefore with the premise that to have combined ninety percent of the producers of ingot would have been to "monopolize" the ingot market; and, so far as concerns the public interest, it can make no difference whether an existing competition is put an end to, or whether prospective competition is prevented....

Nevertheless, it is unquestionably true that from the very outset the courts have at least kept in reserve the possibility that the origin of a monopoly may be critical in determining its legality; and for this they had warrant in some of the congressional debates which accompanied the passage of the Act....This notion has usually been expressed by saying that size does not determine guilt; that there must be some "exclusion" of competitors; that the growth must be something else than "natural" or "normal"; that there must be a "wrongful intent," or some other specific intent; or that some "unduly" coercive means must be used. At times there has been emphasis upon the use of the active verb, "monopolize," as the judge noted in the case at bar.

A market may, for example, be so limited that it is impossible to produce at all and meet the cost of production except by a plant large enough to supply the whole demand. Or there may be changes in taste or in cost which drive out all but one purveyor. A single producer may be the survivor out of a group of active competitors, merely by virtue of his superior skill, foresight, and industry. In such cases a strong argument can be made that, although the result may expose the public to the evils of monopoly, the Act does not mean to condemn the resultant of those very forces which it is its prime object to foster: finis opus coronal. The successful competitor, having been urged to compete, must not be turned upon when he wins.

* * *

[As] Cardozo, J., in *United States v. Swift & Co.*, 286 U.S. 106, p. 116, 52 S. Ct. 460, 463, 76 L.Ed. 999,...said, "Mere size...is not an offense against the Sherman Act unless magnified to the point at *which* it amounts to a monopoly...but size carries with it an opportunity for abuse that is not to be ignored when the opportunity is proved to have been utilized in the past." "Alcoa's" size was "magnified" to make it a "monopoly"; indeed, it has never been anything else; and its size not only offered it an "opportunity for abuse," but it "utilized" its size for "abuse," as can easily be shown.

It would completely misconstrue "Alcoa's" position in 1940 to hold that it was the passive beneficiary of a monopoly, following upon an involuntary elimination of competitors by automatically operative *economic* forces. Already in 1909, when its last lawful monopoly ended, it sought to strengthen its position by unlawful practices, and these concededly continued until 1912. In that year it had two plants in New York, at which it produced less than 42 million pounds of ingot; in 1934 it had five plants (the original two, enlarged; one in Tennessee; one in North Carolina; one in Washington), and its production had risen to about 327 million pounds, an increase of almost eight-fold. Meanwhile not a pound of ingot had been produced by anyone else in the United States. This increase and this continued and undisturbed control did not fall undesigned into "Alcoa's" lap; obviously it could not have done so. It could only have resulted, as it did result, from a persistent determination to maintain the control, with which it found itself vested in 1912. There were at least one or two abortive attempts to enter the industry, but "Alcoa" effectively anticipated and forestalled all competition, and succeeded in holding the field alone. True, it stimulated demand and opened new uses for the metal, but not without making sure that it could supply what it had evoked. There is no dispute as to this; "Alcoa" avows it as evidence of the skill, energy and initiative with which it has always conducted its business: as a reason why, having won its way by fair means, it should be commended, and not dismembered. We need charge it with no moral derelictions after 1912; we may assume that all its claims for itself are true. The only question is whether it falls within the exception established in favor of those who do not seek, but cannot avoid, the control of a market. It seems to us that that question scarcely survives its statement. It was not inevitable that it should always anticipate increases in the demand for ingot and be prepared to supply them. Nothing compelled it to keep doubling and redoubling its capacity before others entered the field. It insists that it never excluded competitors; but we can think of no more effective exclusion than progressively to embrace each new opportunity as it opened, and to face every newcomer with new capacity already geared into a great organization, having the advantage of experience, trade connections and the elite of personnel. Only in case we interpret "exclusion" as limited to maneuvers not honestly industrial, but actuated solely by a desire to prevent competition, can such a course, indefatigably pursued, be deemed not "exclusionary." So to limit it would in our judgment emasculate the Act; would permit just such consolidations as it was designed to prevent.

We disregard any question of "intent." Relatively early in the history of the Act—1905—Holmes, J., in *Swift & Co. v. United States*, explained this aspect of the Act in a passage often quoted. Although the primary evil was monopoly, the Act also covered preliminary steps, which, if continued, would lead to it. These may do no harm of themselves; but if they are initial moves in a plan or scheme which, carried out, will result in monopoly, they are dangerous and the law will nip them in the bud....In order to fall within § 2, the monopolist must have both the power to monopolize, and the intent to monopolize. To read the passage as demanding any "specific," intent, makes nonsense of it, for no monopolist monopolizes unconscious of what he is doing. So here, "Alcoa" meant to keep, and did keep, that complete and exclusive hold upon the ingot market with which it started. That was to "monopolize" that market, however innocently it otherwise proceeded. So far as the judgment held that it was not within § 2, it must be reversed.

Case Questions

1. Judge Learned Hand claims there would be no violation of the Sherman Act in any case where a company achieves monopoly through "natural" or "normal" operation of the market.
    a. What language in the Sherman Act requires the plaintiff to show something more than a company's monopoly status?
    b. What specifics, if any, does Judge Hand provide that indicate that Alcoa not only had market dominance but sought to increase its dominance and to exclude competition?
2. Can you think of a single producer in a given product or geographic market that has achieved that status because of "peer skill, foresight, and industry"? Is there anything wrong with

Alcoa's selling the concept of aluminum products to an ever-increasing set of customers and then also ensuring that it had the capacity to meet the increasing demand?

3. To stimulate interbrand competition, would you recommend that Congress change Section 2 so that any company that had over 80 percent of market share would be "broken up" to ensure competition? Why is this a bad idea? Or why do you think it is a good idea?

Innovation and Intent to Monopolize

Berkey Photo, Inc. v. Eastman Kodak Company
603 F.2d 263 (2d Cir. 1979)

IRVING R. KAUFMAN, CHIEF JUDGE

To millions of Americans, the name Kodak is virtually synonymous with photography....It is one of the giants of American enterprise, with international sales of nearly $6 billion in 1977 and pre-tax profits in excess of $1.2 billion.

This action, one of the largest and most significant private antitrust suits in history, was brought by Berkey Photo, Inc., a far smaller but still prominent participant in the industry. Berkey competes with Kodak in providing photofinishing services—the conversion of exposed film into finished prints, slides, or movies. Until 1978, Berkey sold cameras as well. It does not manufacture film, but it does purchase Kodak film for resale to its customers, and it also buys photofinishing equipment and supplies, including color print paper, from Kodak.

The two firms thus stand in a complex, multifaceted relationship, for Kodak has been Berkey's competitor in some markets and its supplier in others. In this action, Berkey claims that every aspect of the association has been infected by Kodak's monopoly power in the film, color print paper, and camera markets, willfully acquired, maintained, and exercised in violation of § 2 of the Sherman Act, 15 U.S.C. § 2....Berkey alleges that these violations caused it to lose sales in the camera and photofinishing markets and to pay excessive prices to Kodak for film, color print paper, and photofinishing equipment.

* * *

[T]he jury found for Berkey on virtually every point, awarding damages totalling $37,620,130. Judge Frankel upheld verdicts aggregating $27,154,700 for lost camera and photofinishing sales and for excessive prices on film and photofinishing equipment....Trebled and supplemented by attorneys' fees and costs pursuant to § 4 of the Clayton Act, 15 U.S.C. § 15, Berkey's judgment reached a grand total of $87,091,309.47, with interest, of course, continuing to accrue.

Kodak now appeals this judgment.

The principal markets relevant here, each nationwide in scope, are amateur conventional still cameras, conventional photographic film, photofinishing services, photofinishing equipment, and color print paper.

The "amateur conventional still camera" market now consists almost entirely of the so-called 110 and 126 instant-loading cameras. These are the direct descendants of the popular "box" cameras, the best-known of which was Kodak's so-called "Brownie." Small, simple, and relatively inexpensive, cameras of this type are designed for the mass market rather than for the serious photographer.

Kodak has long been the dominant firm in the market thus defined. Between 1954 and 1973 it never enjoyed less than 61% of the annual unit sales, nor less than 64% of the dollar volume, and in the peak year of 1964, Kodak cameras accounted for 90% of market revenues. Much of this success is no doubt due to the firm's history of innovation.

Berkey has been a camera manufacturer since its 1966 acquisition of the Keystone Camera Company, a producer of movie cameras and equipment. In 1968 Berkey began to sell amateur still cameras made by other firms, and the following year the Keystone Division commenced manufacturing such cameras itself. From 1970 to 1977, Berkey accounted for 8.2% of the sales in the camera market in the United States, reaching a peak of 10.2% in 1976. In 1978, Berkey sold its camera division and thus abandoned this market.

* * *

One must comprehend the fundamental tension—one might almost say the paradox—that is near the heart of § 2....

The conundrum was indicated in characteristically striking prose by Judge Hand, who was not able to resolve it. Having stated that Congress "did not condone 'good trusts' and condemn 'bad' ones; it forbad all," he declared with equal force, "The successful competitor, having been urged to compete, must not be turned upon when he wins."...We must always be mindful lest the Sherman Act be invoked perversely in favor of those who seek protection against the rigors of competition.

* * *

In sum, although the principles announced by the § 2 cases often appear to conflict, this much is clear. The mere possession of monopoly power does not *ipso facto* condemn a market participant. But, to avoid the proscriptions of § 2, the firm must refrain at all times from conduct directed at smothering competition. This doctrine has two branches. Unlawfully acquired power remains anathema even when kept dormant. And it is no less true that a firm with a legitimately achieved monopoly may not wield the resulting power to tighten its hold on the market.

* * *

As Kodak had hoped, the 110 system proved to be a dramatic success. In 1972—the system's first year—the company sold 2,984,000 Pocket Instamatics, more than 50% of its sales in the amateur conventional still camera market. The new camera thus accounted in large part for a sharp increase in total market sales, from 6.2 million units in 1971 to 8.2 million in 1972....

Berkey's Keystone division was a late entrant in the 110 sweepstakes, joining the competition only in late 1973. Moreover, because of hasty design, the original models suffered from latent defects, and sales that year were a paltry 42,000. With interest in the 126 dwindling, Keystone thus suffered a net decline of 118,000 unit sales in 1973. The following year, however, it recovered strongly, in large part because improvements in its pocket cameras helped it sell 406,000 units, 7% of all 110s sold that year.

Berkey contends that the introduction of the 110 system was both an attempt to monopolize and actual monopolization of the camera market.

* * *

It will be useful at the outset to present the arguments on which Berkey asks us to uphold its verdict: Kodak, a film and camera monopolist, was in a position to set industry standards. Rivals could not compete effectively without offering products similar to Kodak's. Moreover, Kodak persistently refused to make film available for most formats other than those in which it made cameras. Since cameras are worthless without film, this policy effectively prevented other manufacturers from introducing cameras in new formats. Because of its dominant position astride two markets, and by use of its film monopoly to distort the camera market, Kodak forfeited its own right to reap profits from such innovations without providing its rivals with sufficient advance information to enable them to enter the market with copies of the new product on the day of Kodak's introduction. This is one of several "predisclosure" arguments Berkey has advanced in the course of this litigation.

* * *

Through the 1960s, Kodak followed a checkered pattern of predisclosing innovations to various segments of the industry. Its purpose on these occasions evidently was to ensure that the industry would be able to meet consumers' demand for the complementary goods and services they would need to enjoy the new Kodak products. But predisclosure would quite obviously also diminish Kodak's share of the auxiliary markets. It was therefore, in the words of Walter Fallon, Kodak's chief executive officer, "a matter of judgment on each and every occasion" whether predisclosure would be for or against Kodak's self-interest. Kodak decided not to release advance information about the new film and format. The decision was evidently based on the perception of Dr. Louis K. Eilers, Kodak's chief executive officer at that time, that Kodak would gain more from being first on the market for the sale of all goods and services related to the 110 system than it would lose from the inability of other photofinishers to process Kodacolor II.

Judge Frankel did not decide that Kodak should have disclosed the details of the 110 to other camera manufacturers prior to introduction. Instead, he left the matter to the jury....We hold that this instruction was in error and that, as a matter of law, Kodak did not have a duty to predisclose information about the 110 system to competing camera manufacturers.

As Judge Frankel indicated, and as Berkey concedes, a firm may normally keep its innovations secret from its rivals as long as it wishes, forcing them to catch up on the strength of their own efforts after the new product is introduced. It is the possibility of success in the marketplace, attributable to superior performance, that provides the incentives on which the proper functioning of our competitive economy rests....

Withholding from others advance knowledge of one's new products, therefore, ordinarily constitutes valid competitive conduct. Because, as we have already indicated, a monopolist is permitted, and indeed encouraged, by § 2 to compete aggressively on the merits, any success that it may achieve through "the process of invention and innovation" is clearly tolerated by the antitrust laws.

* * *

Moreover, enforced predisclosure would cause undesirable consequences beyond merely encouraging the sluggishness the Sherman Act was designed to prevent. A significant vice of the theory propounded by Berkey lies in the uncertainty of its application. Berkey does not contend, in the colorful phrase of Judge Frankel, that "Kodak has to live in a goldfish bowl," disclosing every innovation to the world at large. However predictable in its application, such an extreme rule would be insupportable. Rather, Berkey postulates that Kodak had a duty to disclose limited types of information to certain competitors under specific circumstances. But it is difficult to comprehend how a major corporation, accustomed though it is to making business decisions with antitrust considerations in mind, could possess the omniscience to anticipate all the instances in which a jury might one day in the future retrospectively conclude that predisclosure was warranted. And it is equally difficult to discern workable guidelines that a court might set forth to aid the firm's decision. For example, how detailed must the information conveyed be? And how far must research have progressed before it is "ripe" for disclosure? These inherent uncertainties would have an inevitable chilling effect on innovation. They go far, we believe, towards explaining why no court has ever imposed the duty Berkey seeks to create here.

* * *

We do not perceive, however, how Kodak's introduction of a new format was rendered an unlawful act of monopolization in the camera market because the firm also manufactured film to fit the cameras. "The 110 system was in substantial part a camera development...."

Clearly, then, the policy considerations militating against predisclosure requirements for monolithic monopolists are equally applicable here. The first firm, even a monopolist, to design a new camera format has a right to the lead time that follows from its success. The mere fact that Kodak manufactured film in the new format as well, so that its customers would not be offered worthless cameras, could not deprive it of that reward.

* * *

Conclusion We have held that Kodak did not have an obligation, merely because it introduced film and camera in a new format, to make any predisclosure to its camera-making competitors. Nor did the earlier use of its film monopoly to foreclose format innovation by those competitors create of its own force such a duty where none had existed before. In awarding Berkey $15,250,000, just $828,000 short of the maximum amount demanded, the jury clearly based its calculation of lost camera profits on Berkey's central argument that it had a right to be "at the starting line when the whistle blew" for the new system. The verdict, therefore, cannot stand.

Case Questions

1. Consider patent law. Did Kodak have a legal monopoly on the 110 system (having invented it) for seventeen years? Did it have any legal obligation to share the technology with others?
2. Might it have been better business strategy to give predisclosure to Berkey and others about the necessary changes in film that would come about with the introduction of the 110 camera? How so, or why not? Is there any way that some sort of predisclosure to Berkey and others would maintain or sustain good relations with competitors?

48.9 Summary and Exercises

Summary

Four basic antitrust laws regulate the competitive activities of U.S. business: the Sherman Act, the Clayton Act, the Federal Trade Commission Act, and the Robinson-Patman Act. The Sherman Act prohibits restraints of trade and monopolizing. The Clayton Act prohibits a variety of anticompetitive acts, including mergers and acquisitions that might tend to lessen competition. The Federal Trade Commission Act prohibits unfair methods of competition and unfair and deceptive acts or practices in commerce. The Robinson-Patman Act prohibits a variety of price discriminations. (This act is actually an amendment to the Clayton Act.) These laws are enforced in four ways: (1) by the U.S. Department of Justice, Antitrust Division; (2) by the Federal Trade Commission; (3) by state attorneys general; and (4) by private litigants.

The courts have interpreted Section 1 of the Sherman Act, prohibiting every contract, combination, or conspiracy in restraint of trade, by using a "rule of reason." Thus, reasonable restraints that are ancillary to legitimate business practices are lawful. But some acts are *per se* unreasonable, such as price-fixing, and will violate Section 1. Section 1 restraints of trade include both horizontal and vertical restraints of trade. Vertical restraints of trade include resale price maintenance, refusals to deal, and unreasonable territorial restrictions on distributors. Horizontal restraints of trade include price-fixing, exchanging price information when doing so permits industry members to control prices, controlling output, regulating competitive methods, allocating territories, exclusionary agreements, and boycotts.

Exclusive dealing contracts and tying contracts whose effects may be to substantially lessen competition violate Section 3 of the Clayton Act and may also violate both Section 1 of the Sherman Act and Section 5 of the Federal Trade Commission Act. Requirements and supply contracts are unlawful if they tie up so much of a commodity that they tend substantially to lessen competition or might tend to do so.

The Robinson-Patman Act (Section 2 of the Clayton Act) prohibits price discrimination for different purchasers of commodities of like grade and quality if the effect may be substantially to (1) lessen competition or tend to create a monopoly in any line of commerce or (2) impair competition with (a) any person who grants or (b) knowingly receives the benefit of the discrimination, or (c) with customers of either of them.

Some industries and groups are insulated from the direct reach of the antitrust laws. These include industries separately regulated under federal law, organized labor, insurance companies, activities mandated under state law, group solicitation government action, and baseball.

Section 2 of the Sherman Act prohibits monopolizing or attempting to monopolize any part of interstate or foreign trade or commerce. The law does not forbid monopoly as such but only acts or attempts or conspiracies to monopolize. The prohibition includes the monopolist who has acquired his monopoly through illegitimate means.

Three factors are essential in a Section 2 case: (1) relevant market for determining dominance, (2) the degree of monopoly power, and (3) the particular acts claimed to be illegitimate.

The issue of "relevant market" has two dimensions: product market and geographic market. Since many goods have close substitutes, the courts look to the degree to which consumers will shift to other goods or suppliers if the price of the commodity or service in question is priced in a monopolistic way. If the "cross-elasticity of demand" is high—meaning that consumers will readily shift—then the other goods or services must be included in the product market definition, thus reducing the share of the market that the defendant will be found to have. The geographic market is not the country as a whole, because Section 2 speaks in terms of "any part" of trade or commerce. Usually the government or private plaintiff will try to show that the geographic market is small, since that will tend to give the alleged monopolist a larger share of it.

Market power in general means the share of the relevant market that the alleged monopolist enjoys. The law does not lay down fixed percentages, though various decisions seem to suggest that two-thirds of the market might be too low but three-quarters high enough to constitute monopoly power.

Acts that were aimed at or had the probable effect of excluding competitors from the market are acts of monopolizing. Examples are predatory pricing and boycotts. Despite repeated claims during the 1970s and 1980s by smaller competitors, large companies have prevailed in court against the argument that innovation suddenly sprung on the market without notice is per se evidence of intent to monopolize.

Remedies for Sherman Act Section 2 violations include damages, injunction, and **divestiture**. These remedies are also available in Clayton Act Section 7 cases.

Section 7 prohibits mergers or acquisitions that might tend to lessen competition in any line of commerce in any section of the country. Mergers and acquisitions are usually classified in one of three ways: horizontal (between competitors), vertical (between different levels of the distribution chain), or conglomerate (between businesses that are not directly related). The latter may be divided into product-extension and market-expansion mergers. The relevant market test is different than in monopolization cases; in a Section 7 action, relevance of market may be proved.

In assessing horizontal mergers, the courts will look to the market shares of emerging companies, industry concentration ratios, and trends toward concentration in the industry. To prove a Section 7 case, the plaintiff must show that the merger forecloses competition "in a substantial share of" a substantial market. Conglomerate merger cases are harder to prove and require a showing of specific potential effects, such as raising barriers to entry into an industry and thus entrenching monopoly, or eliminating potential competition. Joint ventures may also be condemned by Section 7. The Hart-Scott-Rodino Antitrust Improvements Act of 1976 requires certain companies to get premerger notice to the Justice Department.

Exercises

1. To protect its state's businesses against ruinous price wars, a state legislature has passed a law permitting manufacturers to set a "suggested resale price" on all goods that they make and sell direct to retailers. Retailers are forbidden to undercut the resale price by more than 10 percent. A retailer who violates the law may be sued by the manufacturer for treble damages: three times the difference between the suggested resale price and the actual selling price. But out-of-state retailers are bound by no such law and are regularly discounting the goods between 35 and 40 percent. As the general manager of a large discount store located within a few miles of a city across the state line, you wish to offer the public a price of only 60 percent of the suggested retail price on items covered by the law in order to compete with the out-of-state retailers to which your customers have easy access. May you lower your price in order to compete? How would you defend yourself if sued by a manufacturer whose goods you discounted in violation of the law?

2. Twenty-five local supermarket chains banded together as Topco Associates Incorporated to sell groceries under a private label. Topco was formed in 1940 to compete with the giant chains, which had the economic clout to sell private-label merchandise unavailable to the smaller chains. Topco acted as a purchasing agent for the members. By the late 1960s, Topco's members were doing a booming business: $1.3 billion in retail sales, with market share ranging from 1.5 percent to 16 percent in the markets that members served. Topco-brand groceries accounted for no more than 10 percent of any store's total merchandise. Under Topco's rules, members were assigned exclusive territories in which to sell Topco-brand goods. A member chain with stores located in another member's exclusive territory could not sell Topco-brand goods in those stores. Topco argued that the market division was necessary to give each chain the economic incentive to advertise and develop brand consciousness and thus to be able to compete more effectively against the large nonmember supermarkets' private labels. If other stores in the locality could also carry the Topco brand, then it would not be a truly "private" label and there would be no reason to tout it; it would be like any national brand foodstuff, and Topco members did not have the funds to advertise the brand nationally. Which, if any, antitrust laws has Topco violated? Why?

3. In 1983, Panda Bears Incorporated, a small manufacturer, began to sell its patented panda bear robot dolls (they walk, smile, and eat bamboo shoots) to retail toy shops. The public took an immediate fancy to panda bears, and the company found it difficult to meet the demand. Retail shops sold out even before their orders arrived. In order to allocate the limited supply fairly while it tooled up to increase production runs, the company announced to its distributors that it would not sell to any retailers that did not also purchase its trademarked Panda Bear's Bambino Bamboo Shoots. It also announced that it would refuse to supply any retailer that sold the robots for less than $59.95. Finally, it said that it would refuse to sell to retailers unless they agreed to use the company's repair services exclusively when customers brought bears back to repair malfunctions in their delicate, patented computerized nervous system. By the following year, with demand still rising, inferior competitive panda robots and bamboo shoots began to appear. Some retailers began to lower the Panda Bear price to meet the competition. The company refused to resupply them. Panda Bears Incorporated also decreed that it would refuse to sell to retailers who carried any other type of bamboo shoot. What antitrust violations, if any, has Panda Bear Incorporated committed? What additional information might be useful in helping you to decide?

4. Elmer has invented a new battery-operated car. The battery, which Elmer has patented, functions for five hundred miles before needing to be recharged. The car, which he has named The Elmer, is a sensation when announced, and his factory can barely keep up with the orders. Worried about the impact, all the other car manufacturers ask Elmer for a license to use the battery in their cars. Elmer refuses because he wants the car market all to himself. Banks are eager to lend him the money to expand his production, and within three years he has gained a 5 percent share of the national market for automobiles. During these years, Elmer has kept the price of The Elmer high, to pay for his large costs in tooling up a factory. But then it dawns on him that he can expand his market much more rapidly if he drops his price, so he prices the car to yield the smallest profit margin of any car being sold in the country. Its retail price is far lower than that of any other domestic car on the market. Business begins to boom. Within three more years, he has garnered an additional 30 percent of the market, and he announces at a press conference

that he confidently expects to have the market "all to myself" within the next five years. Fighting for their lives now, the Big Three auto manufacturers consult their lawyers about suing Elmer for monopolizing. Do they have a case? What is Elmer's defense?

5. National Widget Company is the dominant manufacturer of widgets in the United States, with 72 percent of the market for low-priced widgets and 89 percent of the market for high-priced widgets. Dozens of companies compete with National in the manufacture and sale of compatible peripheral equipment for use with National's widgets, including countertops, holders, sprockets and gear assemblies, instruction booklets, computer software, and several hundred replacements parts. Revenues of these peripherals run upwards of $100 million annually. Beginning with the 1981 model year, National Widget sprang a surprise: a completely redesigned widget that made most of the peripheral equipment obsolete. Moreover, National set the price for its peripherals below that which would make economic sense for competitors to invest in new plants to tool up for producing redesigned peripherals. Five of the largest peripheral-equipment competitors sued National under Section 2 of the Sherman Act. One of these, American Widget Peripherals, Inc., had an additional complaint: on making inquiries in early 1980, American was assured by National's general manager that it would not be redesigning any widgets until late 1985 at the earliest. On the basis of that statement, American invested $50 million in a new plant to manufacture the now obsolescent peripheral equipment, and as a result, it will probably be forced into bankruptcy. What is the result? Why? How does this differ, if at all, from the *Berkey Camera* case?

6. In 1959, The Aluminum Company of America (Alcoa) acquired the stock and assets of the Rome Cable Corporation. Alcoa and Rome both manufactured bare and insulated aluminum wire and cable, used for overhead electric power transmission lines. Rome, but not Alcoa, manufactured copper conductor, used for underground transmissions. Insulated aluminum wire and cable is quite inferior to copper, but it can be used effectively for overhead transmission, and Alcoa increased its share of annual installations from 6.5 percent in 1950 to 77.2 percent in 1959. During that time, copper lost out to aluminum for overhead transmission. Aluminum and copper conductor prices do not respond to one another; lower copper conductor prices do not put great pressure on aluminum wire and cable prices. As the Supreme Court summarized the facts in *United States v. Aluminum Co. of America*,

In 1958—the year prior to the merger—Alcoa was the leading producer of aluminum conductor, with 27.8% of the market; in bare aluminum conductor, it also led the industry with 32.5%. Alcoa plus Kaiser controlled 50% of the aluminum conductor market and, with its three leading competitors, more than 76%. Only nine concerns (including Rome with 1.3%) accounted for 95.7% of the output of aluminum conductor, Alcoa was third with 11.6%, and Rome was eighth with 4.7%. Five companies controlled 65.4% and four smaller ones, including Rome, added another 22.8%.

The Justice Department sued Alcoa-Rome for violation of Section 7 of the Clayton Act. What is the government's argument? What is the result?

7. Quality Graphics has been buying up the stock of companies that manufacture billboards. Quality now owns or controls 23 of the 129 companies that make billboards, and its sales account for 3.2 percent of the total national market of $72 million. In Texas, Quality has acquired 27 percent of the billboard market, and in the Dallas–Ft. Worth area alone, about 25 percent. Billboard advertising accounts for only 0.001 percent of total national advertising sales; the majority goes to newspaper, magazine, television, and radio advertising. What claims could the Justice Department assert in a suit against Quality? What is Quality's defense? What is the result?

Self-Test Questions

1. A company with 95 percent of the market for its product is
    a. a monopolist
    b. monopolizing
    c. violating Section 2 of the Sherman Act
    d. violating Section 1 of the Sherman Act
2. Which of the following may be evidence of an intent to monopolize?

a. innovative practices
b. large market share
c. pricing below cost of production
d. low profit margins

3. A merger that lessens competition in any line of commerce is prohibited by
    a. Section 1 of the Sherman Act
    b. Section 2 of the Sherman Act
    c. Section 7 of the Clayton Act
    d. none of the above
4. Which of the following statements is true?
    a. A horizontal merger is always unlawful.
    b. A conglomerate merger between companies with unrelated products is always lawful.
    c. A vertical merger violates Section 2 of the Sherman Act.
    d. A horizontal merger that unduly increases the concentration of firms in a particular market is always unlawful.
5. A line of commerce is a concept spelled out in
    a. Section 7 of the Clayton Act
    b. Section 2 of the Sherman Act
    c. Section 1 of the Sherman Act
    d. none of the above

Self-Test Answers

1. a
2. c
3. c
4. d
5. d

Endnotes

1. Sherman Act, Section 1; Clayton Act, Section 3.
2. Sherman Act, Section 2; Clayton Act, Section 7.
3. *Munn v. Illinois*, 94 U.S. 113 (1877).
4. *Standard Oil Co. of New Jersey v. United States*, 221 U.S. 1 (1911).
5. Clayton Act, Section 3.
6. Clayton Act, Section 7.
7. Clayton Act, Section 8.
8. *Appalachian Coals v. United States*, 288 U.S. 344, 359 (1933).
9. *Chicago Board of Trade v. United States*, 246 U.S. 231 (1918).
10. *Standard Oil Co. of New Jersey v. United States*, 221 U.S. 1 (1911).
11. *Chicago Board of Trade v. United States*, 246 U.S. 231 (1918).
12. *Chicago Board of Trade v. United States*, 246 U.S. 231 (1918).
13. *United States v. Trenton Potteries*, 273 U.S. 392 (1927).
14. *Kiefer-Stewart Co. v. Joseph E. Seagram & Sons*, 340 U.S. 211 (1951).
15. *U.S. v. Apple, Inc.* 952 F.Supp. 2d 638 (S.D.N.Y. 2013). See http://www.nysd.uscourts.gov/cases/show.php?db=special&id=306.
16. *American Column and Lumber Company v. United States*, 257 U.S. 377 (1921).
17. *Maple Flooring Manufacturers' Association v. United States*, 268 U.S. 563 (1925).
18. *United States v. Socony-Vacuum Oil Co.*, 310 U.S. 150 (1940).
19. *United States v. Sealy*, 388 U.S. 350 (1967).
20. *Eastern State Lumber Dealers' Association v. United States*, 234 U.S. 600 (1914).
21. *Fashion Originators' Guild of America v. Federal Trade Commission*, 312 U.S. 457 (1941).
22. *Klor's, Inc. v. Broadway-Hale Stores*, 359 U.S. 207 (1959).

23. *Dr. Miles Medical Co. v. John D. Park & Sons Co.*, 220 U.S. 373 (1910).
24. *State Oil Company v. Khan*, 522 U.S. 3 (1997).
25. *International Salt Co. v. United States*, 332 U.S. 392 (1947).
26. *Times-Picayune Publishing Co. v. United States*, 345 U.S. 594 (1953).
27. *Northern Pacific Railway Co. v. United States*, 356 U.S. 1 (1958).
28. *United States v. Microsoft*, 253 F.3d 34 (D.C. Cir. 2001).
29. *FTC v. Borden Co.*, 383 U.S. 637 (1966).
30. *FTC v. Morton Salt Co.*, 334 U.S. 37 (1948).
31. *Parker v. Brown*, 317 U.S. 341 (1943).
32. *Eastern Railroad President's Conference v. Noerr Motor Freight, Inc.*, 365 U.S. 127 (1961).
33. *FTC v. Superior Court Trial Lawyers Assn.*, 493 U.S. 411 (1990).
34. *United States v. Grinnell Corp.*, 384 U.S. 563, 571 (1966).
35. *United States v. Aluminum Co. of America*, 148 F.2d 416 (2d Cir. 1945).
36. *United States v. Lorain Journal Company*, 342 U.S. 143 (1951).
37. *ILC Peripherals Leasing Corp. v. International Business Machines*, 458 F.Supp. 423 (N.D. Cal. 1978).
38. *United States v. du Pont*, 353 U.S. 586 (1957).
39. *Brown Shoe Co., Inc. v. United States*, 370 U.S. 294 (1962).
40. *Citizen Publishing Company v. United States*, 394 U.S. 131 (1969).
41. *United States v. Philadelphia National Bank*, 374 U.S. 321, 371 (1963).
42. *FTC v. Procter & Gamble Co.*, 386 U.S. 568, 580 (1967).
43. *Ford Motor Co. v. United States*, 405 U.S. 562 (1972).
44. *FTC v. Procter & Gamble Co.*, 386 U.S. 568 (1967).
45. *FTC v. Consolidated Foods Corp.*, 380 U.S. 592 (1965).
46. *United States v. Penn-Olin Chemical Co.*, 378 U.S. 158 (1964).
47. *California v. American Stores*, 58 U.S.L.W. 4529 (1990).

CHAPTER 49
Unfair Trade Practices, the Federal Trade Commission, and Consumer Protection Laws

Learning Objectives

After reading this chapter, you should understand the following:

1. The general powers of the Federal Trade Commission.
2. The general principles of law that govern deceptive acts and practices.
3. Several categories of deceptive acts and practices, with examples.
4. The remedies that the Federal Trade Commission has at its disposal to police unfair trade practices.
5. Some of the other federal and state consumer protection laws.

49.1 The Federal Trade Commission: Powers and Law Governing Deceptive Acts

Learning Objectives

1. Describe the general powers of the Federal Trade Commission.
2. Describe the general principles that guide laws and regulations against unfair and deceptive trade practices.

General Powers of the Federal Trade Commission

Common law prohibited a variety of trade practices that were unfair, either to competitors or to consumers. These included passing off one's products as though they were made by someone else, using a trade name confusingly similar to that of another, stealing trade secrets, and various forms of misrepresentation. In the Federal Trade Commission Act of 1914, Congress for the first time empowered a federal agency to investigate and deter acts of unfair competition—the common law only allowed remedies after the harm was caused.

Section 5 of the act gave the Federal Trade Commission (FTC) power to enforce a law that said "unfair methods of competition in commerce are hereby declared unlawful." By "unfair methods of competition," Congress originally intended acts that constituted violations of the Sherman and Clayton Antitrust Acts. But from the beginning, the commissioners of the FTC took a broader view of their mandate. Specifically, they were concerned about the problem of false and deceptive advertising and promotional schemes. But the original Section 5 was confining; it seemed to authorize FTC action only when the deceptive advertising injured a competitor of the company. In 1931, the Supreme Court ruled that this was indeed the case: an advertisement that deceived the public was not within the FTC's jurisdiction unless a competitor was injured by the misrepresentation also. Congress responded in 1938 with the Wheeler-Lea Amendments to the FTC Act. To the words "unfair methods of competition" were added these words: "unfair or deceptive acts or practices in commerce." Now it became clear that the FTC had a broader role to play than as a second agency enforcing the antitrust laws. Henceforth, the FTC would be the guardian also of consumers.

Deceptive practices that the FTC has prosecuted can also be remedied using the common law. A tire manufacturer who advertises that his "special tire" is "new" when it is actually a retread has committed a common-law misrepresentation, and the buyer could sue for rescission of the contract or for damages. But having a few buyers sue for misrepresentation does not stop the determined fraudster. Moreover, such lawsuits are expensive to bring, and the amount of damages awarded is usually small; thus, law actions alone cannot adequately address deliberately fraudulent practices.

Through Section 5, however, the FTC can seek far-reaching remedies against fraudulent business practices; it is not limited to proving damages to individual customers case by case. The FTC can issue cease and desist orders and has other sanctions to wield as well. So do its counterpart agencies at the state level.

trade regulation rules

Made by the FTC, these rules have the same force and effect as a federal statute. Each rule must pass through a long process, including publication of the proposed rule in the *Federal Register*, hearings or written comments, and final publication in the *Code of Federal Regulations*.

As an administrative agency, the FTC has broader powers than those vested in the ordinary prosecutorial authority, such as the Department of Justice. It can initiate administrative proceedings in accordance with the Administrative Procedure Act to enforce the several statutes that it administers. In addition to issuing cease and desist orders and getting them enforced in court, the FTC can seek temporary and permanent injunctions, fines, and monetary damages and promulgate **trade regulation rules** (TRRs). Although the FTC's authority to issue TRRs had long been assumed (and was approved by the US court of appeals in Washington in 1973), Congress formalized it in 1975 in the FTC Improvement Act (part of the Magnuson-Moss Warranty Act), which gives the FTC explicit authority to prescribe rules defining unfair or deceptive acts or practices.

A TRR is like a statute. It is a detailed statement of procedures and substantive dos and don'ts. Before promulgating a TRR, the commission must publish its intention to do so in the *Federal Register* and must hold open hearings on its proposals. Draft versions of a TRR must be published to allow the public to comment. Once issued, the final version is published as part of the *Code of Federal Regulations* and becomes a permanent part of the law unless modified or repealed by the FTC itself or by Congress—or overturned by a court on grounds of arbitrariness, lack of procedural regularity, or the like. A violation of a TRR is treated exactly like a violation of a federal statute. Once the FTC proves that a defendant violated a TRR, no further proof is necessary that the defendant's act was unfair or deceptive. Examples of TRRs include the Retail Food Store Advertising and Marketing Practices Rule, Games of Chance in the Food Retailing and Gasoline Industries Rule, Care Labeling of Textile Wearing Apparel Rule, Mail Order Merchandise Rule, Cooling-Off Period for Door-to-Door Sales Rule, and Use of Negative Option Plans by Sellers in Commerce.

General Principles of Law Governing Deceptive Acts and Practices

With a staff of some sixteen hundred and ten regional offices, the FTC is, at least from time to time, an active regulatory agency. The FTC's enforcement vigor waxes and wanes with the economic climate. Critics have often charged that what the FTC chooses to investigate defies common sense because so many of the cases seem to involve trivial, or at least relatively unimportant, offenses: Does the nation really need a federal agency to guard us against pronouncements by singer Pat Boone on the efficacy of acne medication or to ensure the authenticity of certain crafts sold to tourists in Alaska as "native"? One answer is that through such cases, important principles of law are declared and ratified.

To be sure, most readers of this book, unlikely to be gulled by false claims, may see a certain Alice-in-Wonderland quality to FTC enforcement. But the first principle of FTC action is that it gauges deceptive acts and practices as interpreted by the general public, not by the more sophisticated. As a U.S. court of appeals once said, the FTC Act was not "made for the protection of experts, but for the public—that vast multitude which includes the ignorant, the unthinking, and the credulous." The deceptive statement or act need not actually deceive. Before 1983, it was sufficient that the statement had a "capacity to deceive." According to a standard adopted in 1983, however, the FTC will take action against deceptive advertising "if there is a representation, omission or practice that is likely to mislead the consumer acting reasonably in the circumstances, to the consumer's detriment." Critics of the new standard have charged that it will be harder to prove deception because an advertisement must be "likely to mislead" rather than merely have a "capacity to deceive." The FTC might also be put to the burden of showing that consumers reasonably interpreted the ad and that they relied on the ad.

The FTC also has the authority to proceed against "unfair...acts or practices." These need not be deceptive but, instead, of such a character that they offend a common sense of propriety, basic fairness, or an honest way of acting. See Figure 49.1 for a diagram of the unfair and deceptive practices discussed in this chapter.

FIGURE 49.1 Unfair and Deceptive Practices Laws

Areas of regulatory interest for the Federal Trade Commission

Key Takeaway

Although common law still serves to prohibit certain kinds of trade practices, the FTC has far more extensive powers to police unfair and deceptive trade practices. The FTC's rules, once passed through the processes defined in the Administrative Procedure Act, have the same authority as a federal statute. Trade regulation rules issued by the FTC, if violated, can trigger injunctions, fines, and other remedial actions.

Exercise

1. Go to the FTC website and look at its most recent annual report. Find a description of a loan modification scam, and discuss with another student why a regulatory agency is needed. Ask yourselves whether leaving it up to individual consumers to sue the scammers, using common law, would create greater good for society.

49.2 Deceptive Acts and Practices

Learning Objective

1. Name the categories of deceptive acts and practices that the Federal Trade Commission has found, and give examples.

Failure to Disclose Pertinent Facts

Businesses are under no general obligation to disclose everything. Advertisers may put a bright face on their products as long as they do not make a direct material misrepresentation or misstatement. But a business may be required to disclose things it would prefer not to, so as not to engage in unfair or deceptive acts and practices. For example, failure to state the cost of a service might constitute deception. Thus, a federal court has ruled that it is deceptive for a telephone service to fail to disclose that it cost fifteen dollars per call for customers dialing a special 900 number listed in newspaper advertisements offering jobs.[1] Likewise, if a fact not disclosed might have a material bearing on a consumer's decision whether to purchase the product, its omission might be judicially regarded as deception, as *J. B. Williams Co. v. FTC* (see Section 5), suggests. Suppose you're planning a vacation and you find a glowing review about a resort on a blog. If you knew the blogger had been given a couple of days' free stay at the resort, that might influence your thoughts on the validity of the endorsement. The FTC requires disclosure. Here is the relevant federal regulation, http://www.ecfr.gov/cgi-bin/text-idx?SID=de10601c673ac6ac7500291dbfecca38&mc=true&node=pt16.1.255&rgn=div5.

Descriptions of Products

Certain words are considered mere "puffery" (*greatest, best*). Other words with more precise connotations can cause trouble if they are misused. One example is the word *new*. In most cases, the Federal Trade Commission (FTC) has held that if a product is more than six months old, it is not new and may not lawfully be advertised as such.

The efficacy of products is perhaps their most often advertised aspect. An ad stating that a product will do more than it can is almost always deceptive if the claim is specific. Common examples that the FTC continues to do battle over are claims that a cream, pill, or other substance will "rejuvenate" the body, "cure" baldness, "permanently remove" wrinkles, or "restore" the vitality of hair.

The composition of goods is another common category of deceptive claims. For example, a product advertised as "wool" had better be 100 percent wool; a mixture of wool and synthetic fabrics cannot be advertised as wool. The FTC has lists of dozens of descriptive words with appropriate definitions.

Labeling of certain products is strictly regulated by specific statutes. Under the Food, Drug, and Cosmetic Act, artificial colors and flavors must be disclosed. Other specific federal statutes include the Wool Products Labeling Act, the Textile Fiber Products Identification Act, the Fur Products Labeling Act, and the Flammable Fabrics Act; these acts are enforced by the FTC. In 1966, Congress enacted the Fair Packaging and Labeling Act. It governs most consumer products and gives the FTC authority to issue regulations for proper labeling of most of them. In particular, the statute is designed to help standardize quantity descriptions ("small," "medium," and "large") and enable shoppers to compare the value of competing goods in the stores.

Misleading Price and Savings Claims

"Buy one, get another for half price." "Suggested retail price: $25. Our price: $5.95." "Yours for only $95. You save $50." Claims like these assault us daily. Unless these ads are strictly true, they are violations of Section 5 of the FTC Act. To regulate deceptive price and savings claims, the FTC has issued a series of *Guides against Deceptive Pricing* that set forth principles the commission uses to judge the merits of price claims. These guides are not themselves law, but they are important clues to how the FTC will act when faced with a price claim case and they may even provide guidance to state courts hearing claims of deceptive pricing ads.

In general, the guides deal with five claims, as follows:

- **Comparisons of the sale price to a former price.** The former price must have been offered for a substantial period of time in the near past for a seller to be justified in referring to it. A product that once had a price tag of $50, but that never actually sold for more than $40, cannot be hawked at "the former price of $50." Under the FTC guides, a reduction of at least 10 percent is necessary to make the claim true.
- **Comparable products.** "This same mattress and box spring would cost you $450 at retail." The advertisement is true only if the seller is in fact offering the same merchandise and if the price quoted is genuine.
- **"Suggested" retail price.** The same rules apply as those just mentioned. But in the case of a "manufacturer's suggested" price, an additional wrinkle can occur: the manufacturer might help the retailer deceive by listing a "suggested" price that is in fact considerably greater than the going price in the retailer's trading area. Whether it is the manufacturer who is doing his own selling or the retailer who takes advantage of the "list price" ticket on the goods, the resulting claim of a bargain is deceptive if the product does not sell for the list price in any market or in the market of the retailer.
- **Bargain based on the purchase of something else.** The usual statement in these cases is "Buy one, get one free" (or at some percentage of the usual selling price). Again, the watchwords are *literal accuracy*. If the package of batteries normally sells in the advertiser's store for ninety-nine cents, and two packages are now selling for that price, then the advertisement is unexceptionable. But advertisers are often tempted to raise the original selling price or reduce the size or quantity of the bargain product; doing so is deceptive.
- **False claims to explain a "sale" price.** "Giant clearance sale" or "going out of business" or "limited offer" are common advertising gimmicks. If true, they are legitimate, but it takes very little to make them deceptive. A "limited offer" that goes on forever (or a sale price charged beyond the date on which a sale is said to end) is deceptive. Likewise, false claims that imply the manufacturer is charging the customer a small price are illegitimate. These include claims like "wholesale price," "manufacturer's close-outs," "irregulars," or "seconds."

Bait-and-Switch Advertisements

A common sales pitch in retail is the **bait and switch**. The retailer "baits" the prospective customer by dangling an alluring offer, but the offer either disappears or is disparaged once the customer arrives. Suppose someone sees this advertisement: "Steinway Grand Piano—only $1,000." But when the customer arrives at the store, he finds that the advertised product has "sold out." The retailer then tries to sell the disappointed customer a higher priced product. Or the salesperson may have the product, but she will disparage it—pointing out that it does not really live up to the advertised expectations—and will exhort the customer to buy the "better," more expensive model. These and related tactics are all violations of Section 5 of the FTC Act. In its *Guides Against Bait Advertising*, the FTC lists several such unfair practices, including the following: (1) refusing to demonstrate the advertised product, (2) disparaging the product (e.g., by exhibiting a visibly inferior grade of product next to higher-priced merchandise), (3) failing to stock enough of the advertised product to meet anticipated demand (although the advertiser may say "supplies limited," if that is the case), (4) stat-

bait and switch

A sales pitch where the retailer "baits" the prospective customer by dangling a very attractive offer, which disappears or is disparaged once the customer arrives in the store.

ing that delivery of the advertised product will take an inordinate amount of time, (5) demonstrating a defective product, and (6) deliberately discouraging the would-be buyer from purchasing the advertised product.

Free Offers

Careless advertisers will discover that *free*, perhaps the most powerful word in advertising, comes at a cost. As just noted, a product is not free if it is conditional on buying another product and the price of the "free" product is included in the purchased product ("Buy one tube and get another tube free"). Just how far the commission is prepared to take this rule is clear from *F.T.C. v. Mary Carter Paint Co.*[2] In that case, the company offered, from the time it began business, to sell on a two-for-one basis: "every second can FREE, gallon or quart." The problem was that it had never priced and sold single cans of paint, so the FTC assumed that the price of the second can was included in the first, even though Mary Carter claimed it had established single-can prices that were comparable to those for paint of comparable quality sold by competing manufacturers. The Supreme Court sustained the commission's finding of deception.

Product Comparisons and Disparagements

Product disparagement

Saying defamatory things about a competitor's product. It is a tort of defamation under common law but is actionable under Section 5 of the FTC Act where any specific untrue statement is made about a competitor's product.

Product disparagement—saying defamatory things about a competitor's product—is a common-law tort, actionable under state law. It is also actionable under Section 5 of the FTC Act. The FTC brands as disparagement the making of specific untrue statements about a competitor's product. The agency labels an indirect form of disparagement "comparative misrepresentation"—making false claims of superiority of one's own product. Again, the common-law puffing rule would permit the manufacturer of an over-the-counter pain reliever to make the general statement "Our pill is the best." But the claim that a pill "works three times as fast as the leading competitor's" violates Section 5 if the claim is not true.

Truth has always been a defense to claims of product disparagement, but even that common-law rule has been eroded in recent years with the application of the *significance* doctrine. A statement may be technically true but insignificant and made in such a way as to be misleading. For example, *P. Lorillard Co. v. Federal Trade Commission* (Section 5) concerned a comparative study published in *Reader's Digest* of tar and nicotine in cigarettes. The article suggested that the differences were inconsequential to health, but the company making the cigarette with the smallest amount of tar and nicotine touted the fact anyway.

During the 1970s, to help enforce its rules against comparative misrepresentations, the FTC began to insist that advertisers fully document any quantitative claims that their products were superior to others. This meant that the advertiser should have proof of accuracy not only if the commission comes calling; the advertiser should collect the information beforehand. If it does not, the claim will be held presumptively deceptive.

The FTC Act and state laws against misleading advertising are not the only statutes aimed at product comparisons. One important federal law is the Trademark Law Revision Act of 1988, amending the original Lanham Act that protects trademarks as intellectual property (see Chapter 32). For many years, the federal courts had ruled that a provision in the Lanham Act prohibiting false statements in advertisements was limited to an advertiser's false statements about its own goods or services only. The 1988 amendments overturned that line of court cases, broadening the rule to cover false statements about someone else's goods or services as well. The amendments also prohibit false or misleading claims about another company's commercial activities, such as the nature of its warranties. The revised Lanham Act now permits a company injured by a competitor's false advertising to sue directly in federal court.

Endorsements

How wonderful to have a superstar (or maybe yesterday's superstar) appear on television drooling over your product. Presumably, millions of people would buy a throat spray if Lady Gaga swore by it, or a pair of jeans if Justin Bieber wore them, or a face cream if Kim Kardashian blessed it. In more subtle ways, numerous products are touted every day with one form of testimonial or another: "Three out of four doctors recommend ..." or "Drivers across the country use. ..." In this area, there are endless opportunities for deception.

It is not a deception for a well-known personality to endorse a product without disclosing that she is being paid to do so. But the person giving the testimonial must in fact use the product; if she does not, the endorsement is deceptive. In the following consent decree, singer Pat Boone (very popular in the 1950s) endorsed a product that his daughters had apparently used, but given the large number of complaints (over 13,000) about the ineffectiveness of Acne-Statin, he was required to have made "reasonable inquiry" as to its effectiveness, and ordered to make contributions toward any restitution that might be ordered by the commission or a court.

FIGURE 49.2 The FTC and Pat Boone
Consent Decree: Pat Boone and Cooga Mooga, Inc.

COOGA MOOGA, INC. Trade Reg. REp. (CCH)

21,247 (FTC, 1978)

The FTC issued a complaint alleging that Karr Preventative Medica Products, Inc (KPMP), Beverly Hills, Calif., and its controlling officer, Atida H. Karr, M.D. have made false and unsubstansiated claims for Acne-Statin, a mail order preperation advertised for the treatment of acne ....

The FTC also accepted an agreement containing a consent order entered into by Charles E. "Pat" Boone and Cooga Mooga, Inc., Los Angeles, Calif., of which Mr. Boone is president. Mr. Boone appeared in print and television advertisements for Acne-Statin in which he provided an endorsement for the product. Key provisions of the consent agreement require that Mr. Boone make a reasonable inquiry before endorsing products in the future and that he pay part of any restitution that may be ordered in this matter.

The Commission's administrative complaint against KPMP and Dr. Karr alleges in part that : (1) Acne-Statin neither will cure acne nor can eliminate its cause, as claimed; (2) thay have falsely advertised that Acne-Statin is superior to all other acne preperations and to soap in the anti-bacterial treatment of acne; (3) contrary to other claims, there are time and quantity limitations on the money-back guarantee for Acne-Statin; and (4) there was no reasonable basis for claims that Acne-Statin will cure acne and result in skin free of acne blemishes or for various other performance claims.

Under the agreed-to order, ML Boone and Cooga Mooga, nc. must have a reaonable basis when making any claim relating to the efficacy, performance, and characteristic or property, or the result of use of any product. Also, they must make a reasonable inquiry into the truthfulness of any proposed endorsement of this nature.

Mr. Boone must also pay his pro rata share of any restitution which might be orderd by the Commission or by a court.

The consent agreement, among other things, prohibits misrepresentations of (a) the benefits Boone family members have derived from any product; (b) product tests or product test results; and (c) the efficacy, use or performance of any product where the use or misuse could affect the user's health and safety.

According to Albert H. Kramer, Director, Bureau of Consumer Protection, the negotiated order, while not a binding legal precedent, stands for the pronciple that an endorser must verify the claims made about the advertised product before the first commercial goes on the air or appears in print, or else risk FTC action. Unless the endorser is an expert on the subject, the endorser must look to independent reliable sources to validate claims, tests, or studies supplied by the advertiser. Failure to make a reasonable effort at independent evaluation could result in personal liability for the endorser.

That a particular consumer-endorser is enthusiastic or even ecstatic about a product does not save a false statement: it is deceptive to present this glowing testimonial to the public if there are no facts to back up the customer's claim. The assertion "I was cured by apricot pits" to market a cancer remedy would not pass FTC muster. Nor may an endorser give a testimonial involving subjects known only to experts if the endorser is not himself that kind of expert, as shown in the consent decree negotiated by the FTC with singer Pat Boone (Figure 49.2).

Pictorial and Television Advertising

Pictorial representations create special problems because the picture can belie the caption or the announcer's words. A picture showing an expensive car may be deceptive if the dealer does not stock those cars or if the only readily available cars are different models. The ways of deceiving by creating false inferences through pictures are limited only by imagination. White-coated "doctors," seals of the British monarchy, and plush offices can connote various things about a product, even if the advertisement never says that the man in the white coat is a doctor, that the product is related to the British crown, or that the company has its operations in the building depicted.

Television demonstrations may also suggest nonexistent properties or qualities in a product. In one case, the commission ordered the manufacturer of a liquid cleaner to cease showing it in use near hot stoves and candles, implying falsely that it was nonflammable. A commercial showing a knife cutting through nails is deceptive if the nails were pre-cut and different knives were used for the before and after shots.

Key Takeaway

A variety of fairly common acts and practices have been held by the FTC to be deceptive (and illegal). These include the failure to disclose pertinent facts, misleading price and savings claims, bait and switch advertisements, careless use of the word "free," and comparative misrepresentation—making misleading comparisons between your product and the product of another company.

Exercises

1. Look around this week for an example of a merchant offering something for "free." Do you think there is anything deceptive about the merchant's offer? If they offer "free shipping," how do you know that the shipping cost is not hidden in the price? In any case, why do consumers need protection from an agency that polices merchant offerings that include the word *free*?
2. Find the FTC's guide against deceptive pricing (http://www.ftc.gov/bcp/guides/decptprc.htm). Can you find any merchants locally that appear to be in violation of the FTC's rules and principles?

49.3 Unfair Trade Practices

Learning Objectives

1. Explain how unfair trade practices are different from deceptive trade practices.
2. Name three categories of unfair trade practices, and give examples.

We turn now to certain practices that not only have deceptive elements but also operate unfairly in ways beyond mere deception. In general, three types of unfair practices will be challenged: (1) failing to substantiate material representations in advertisements before publishing them or putting them on the air, (2) failing to disclose certain material information necessary for consumers to make rational comparisons of price and quality of products, and (3) taking unconscionable advantage of certain consumers or exploiting their weakness. The Federal Trade Commission (FTC) has enjoined many ads of the first type. The second type of unfairness has led the commission to issue a number of trade regulation rules (TRRs) setting forth what must be disclosed—for example, octane ratings of gasoline. In this section, we focus briefly on the third type.

Contests and Sweepstakes

In 1971, the FTC obtained a consent order from *Reader's Digest* barring it from promoting a mail-order sweepstakes—a sweepstakes in which those responding had a chance to win large monetary or other prizes by returning numbered tickets—unless the magazine expressly disclosed how many prizes would be awarded and unless all such prizes were in fact awarded. *Reader's Digest* had heavily promoted the size and number of prizes, but few of the winning tickets were ever returned, and consequently few of the prizes were ever actually awarded.[3] In a more recent case, 26 states brought their own unfair trade practice claims, using state laws, against Publisher's Clearing House. For years, PCH had promoted magazines, tapes, figurines, and collectibles with a "sweepstakes" contest that used fake personalities and misleading statements to promote its merchandise. The case settled for $34 million.[4]

Beginning in the 1960s, the retail food and gasoline industries began to heavily promote games of chance. Investigations by the FTC and a U.S. House of Representatives small business subcommittee showed that the games were rigged: winners were "picked" early by planting the winning cards early on in the distribution, winning cards were sent to geographic areas most in need of the promotional benefits of announcing winners, not all prizes were awarded before many games terminated, and local retailers could spot winning cards and cash them in or give them to favored customers. In 1969, as a result of these investigations, the FTC issued its Trade Regulation Rule for Games of Chance in the Food Retailing and Gasoline Industries, strictly regulating how the games may operate and be promoted.

Many marketers use contests, as opposed to sweepstakes, in merchandising their products. In a contest, the consumer must actually do something other than return a ticket, such as fill in a bingo card or come up with certain words. It is an unfair practice for the sponsoring company not to abide by its own rules in determining winners.

Door-to-Door, Direct Mail, and Unsolicited Merchandise

In 1974, the FTC promulgated a TRR requiring a three-day cooling-off period within which any door-to door sales contract can be cancelled. The contract must state the buyer's right to the cooling-off period.

For many years, certain unscrupulous distributors would mail unsolicited merchandise to consumers and demand payment through a series of dunning letters and bills. In 1970, Congress enacted legislation that declares any unsolicited mailing and subsequent dunning to be an unfair trade practice under Section 5 of the FTC Act. Under this law, if you receive an unsolicited product in the mail, you may treat it as a gift and use it; you are under no obligation to return it or pay for it.

Another regulation of mail-order sales is the FTC's TRR concerning mail-order merchandise. Any direct-mail merchandiser must deliver the promised goods within thirty days or allow the buyer to accept delayed delivery or get a prompt refund of his money. If the order has not been prepaid, the customer has the right to cancel without penalty.

Negative-Option Plans

The "negative option" was devised in the 1920s by the Book-of-the-Month Club. It is a marketing device through which the consumer responds to the seller only if she wishes *not* to receive the product. As used by book clubs and other distributors of goods that are sent out periodically, the customer agrees, when "joining," to accept and pay for all items unless she specifically indicates, before they arrive, that she wishes to reject them. If she does nothing, she must pay. Difficulties arise when the negative-option notice arrives late in the mail or when a member quits and continues to receive the monthly notices. Internet users will recognize this negative option as the "opt out" process, where you are "in" unless you notice what's going on and specifically opt out.

In 1974, the FTC issued a TRR governing use of negative-option plans by sellers. The TRR laid down specific notice requirements. Among other things, a subscriber is entitled to ten days in which to notify sellers that she has rejected the particular item about to be sent. If a customer has cancelled hers membership, the seller must take back and pay the former member's mailing expenses for any merchandise mailed after cancellation. The former member may treat any shipments beyond one after cancellation as unsolicited merchandise and keep it without having to pay for it or return it.

Breach of Contract

Sometimes, a company's willful breach of contract can be an unfair trade practice, thus violating section 5 of the FTC Act. In one typical case, a termite and pest exterminating company signed contracts with its customers guaranteeing "lifetime" protection against termite damage to structures that the company treated. The contract required a customer to renew the service each year by paying an unchanging annual fee. Five years after signing these contracts, the company notified 207,000 customers that it was increasing the annual fee because of inflation. The FTC challenged the fee hike on the ground that it was a breach of contract amounting to an unfair trade practice. The FTC's charges were sustained on appeal. The eleventh circuit approved the FTC's three-part test for determining unfairness: (1) the injury "must be substantial," (2) "it must not be outweighed by countervailing benefits to consumers," and (3) "it must be an injury that consumers themselves could not reasonably have avoided." In the termite case, all three parts were met: consumers were forced to pay substantially higher fees, they received no extra benefits, and they could not have anticipated or prevented the price hike, since the contract specifically precluded such hikes.[5]

Other FTC Initiatives

The rise of mobile communications is a new field for scammers. Recent FTC initiatives include creation of a "Mobile Technology Unit" to help it keep apace of current developments such as cramming, mobile tracking in stores, and issues involving privacy and security. In July 2014, the agency sued T-Mobile for cramming bogus charges on consumers' bills. In January 2014, the "Commission reached a settlement with mobile platform provider Apple, Inc., for allegedly billing consumers for millions of dollars of charges incurred by children in mobile apps without their parents' consent." And it continues, as it has for years, to go after phony diet and weight-loss products.[6]

The FTC has been waging a kind of war against tobacco manufacturers since 1967. Its March 2015 "Cigarette Report" is available here (it reviews the year 2012): https://www.ftc.gov/reports/federal-trade-commission-cigarette-report-2012.

Key Takeaway

Market efficiency and fairness are premised on buyers being able to make rational choices about their purchases. Where sellers fail to substantiate material representations or fail to disclose material information that is necessary for buyers to act rationally, the FTC may find an unfair trade practice. In addition, some sellers will take "unconscionable advantage" of certain buyers or exploit their weakness. This takes place in various contests and sweepstakes, door-to-door and mail-order selling, and negative-option plans. The FTC has issued a number of TRRs to combat some of these unfair practices.

Exercises

1. The FTC receives over ten thousand complaints every year about sweepstakes and prizes. Using the Internet or conversations with people you know, name two ways that sweepstakes or contests can be unfair to consumers.
2. As economic hard times return, many scam artists have approached people in debt or people who are in danger of losing their homes. Describe some of the current practices of such people and companies, and explain why they are unfair.
3. With regard to Exercise 2, discuss and decide whether government serves a useful public function by protecting consumers against such scam artists or whether use of the common law—by the individuals who have been taken advantage of—would create greater good for society.

49.4 Remedies

Learning Objectives

1. Describe the various remedies the Federal Trade Commission has used against unfair and deceptive acts and practices.
2. Understand that the states also have power to regulate unfair and deceptive trade practices and often do.

The Federal Trade Commission (FTC) has a host of weapons in its remedial arsenal. It may issue cease and desist orders against unfair and deceptive acts and practices and let the punishment fit the crime. For instance, the FTC can order a company to remove or modify a deceptive trade name. It may order companies to substantiate their advertising. Or if a company fails to disclose facts about a product, the commission may order the company to affirmatively disclose the facts in future advertising. In the *J. B.Williams* case (Section 5), the court upheld the commission's order that the company tell consumers in future advertising that the condition Geritol is supposed to treat—iron-poor blood—is only rarely the cause of symptoms of tiredness that Geritol would help cure.

corrective advertising

A rarely used power of the FTC to require a company to correct previously misleading advertising. It does so by requiring the company to pay for further advertising that admits to the deception and makes corrected statements that are not misleading.

The FTC has often exercised its power to order affirmative disclosures during the past decade, but its power to correct advertising deceptions is even broader. In *Warner Lambert Co. v. Federal Trade Commission*, the U.S. court of appeals in Washington approved the FTC's order for **corrective advertising**. Warner Lambert had challenged the commission's power to order a company to *correct* in future advertisements its former misleading and deceptive statements; in this case, the product was Listerine, and the claims for it were many, and the corrective advertising requirement only applied if the company chose to continue advertising Listerine.[7] The court also approved the FTC's formula for determining how much the company must spend: an amount equal to the average annual expenditure on advertising the mouthwash during the ten years preceding the case.

In addition to its injunctive powers, the FTC may seek civil penalties of $10,000 for violations of final cease and desist orders, and if the violation is a continuing one—e.g., an advertising campaign that lasts for weeks or months—each day is considered a separate violation. The commission may also sue for up to $10,000 per violation, as just described, for violations of its trade regulation rules (TRRs). Under the FTC Improvement Act of 1975, the commission is authorized to seek injunctions and collect monetary damages on behalf of injured consumers in cases involving violations of TRRs. It may also seek restitution for consumers in cases involving cease and desist orders if the party continuing to commit the unfair or deceptive practice should have known that it would be dishonest or fraudulent to continue doing so. The exact reach of this power to seek restitution, which generally had not been available before 1975, remains to be tested in the courts. As for *private* parties, though they have rights under the antitrust statutes, they have no right to sue under Section 5 of the FTC Act.

Other Federal Consumer Protection Agencies

There are several other federal agencies that address consumer protection.

- Food and Drug Administration. The oldest consumer-protection agency, the FDA was created in 1906. It regulates the safety and purity of food (including dietary supplements), drugs (prescription and non-prescription), biologics (vaccines, blood and blood products, tissue and tissue products), medical devices, electronic products that give off radiation (microwaves, x-ray and laser equipment, sunlamps), cosmetics, veterinary products (food, drugs and devices), and tobacco products.[8]
- National Highway Traffic Safety Administration, 1970. NHTSA ("Nit-suh") is "dedicated to achieving the highest standards of excellence in motor vehicle and highway safety. It works daily to help prevent crashes and their attendant costs, both human and financial."[9]
- Consumer Product Safety Commission. This agency was created in 1972 with the passage of the Consumer Product Safety Act. The act gives CPSC the power to develop safety standards for consumer goods and pursue recalls for products that present unreasonable or substantial risks of injury or death to consumers. It has jurisdiction over more than 15,000 products (not including what the FDA regulates, and not including firearms, motor vehicles, pesticides, aircraft, and boats, which are regulated by various other agencies). In 2014, the CPSA was amended to protect whistleblowers who raise concerns about consumer product safety. The CPSC has a colorful, accessible website, including news of products that have been recalled because they are dangerous for consumers: http://www.cpsc.gov/en/.
- Consumer Financial Protection Bureau. Created in 2010, Congress established the CFPB to protect consumers by carrying out federal consumer financial laws. Among other things, the Bureau:
    - Writes rules, supervises companies, and enforces financial protection laws.
    - Restricts unfair, deceptive, or abusive acts or practices in regard to consumer financial transactions.
    - Takes consumer complaints.
    - Promotes financial education.

- Researches consumer behavior.
- Monitors financial markets for new risks to consumers.
- Enforces prohibitions against discrimination and other unfair treatment in consumer finance.[10]

We have also considered consumer protection issues in other contexts: product liability (Chapter 20), the purchase of real estate (Chapter 34), landlord-tenant law (Chapter 35), and, as related, to the liability of accountants (Chapter 53).

Little FTC Acts

Even when consumers have no direct remedy under federal law for unfair or deceptive acts and practices, they may have recourse under state laws modeled on the FTC Act, known as little FTC acts. All states have some sort of consumer protection act, and these acts are often more liberal than the federal unfair trade rules; they permit consumers—and in several states, even aggrieved businesses—to sue when injured by a host of "immoral, unethical, oppressive, or unscrupulous" commercial acts. Often, a successful plaintiff can recover treble damages and attorneys' fees. Previously, we noted how 26 states sued Publisher's Clearing House using "little FTC Acts."

The acts are helpful to consumers because common-law fraud is difficult to prove. Its elements are rigorous and unyielding: an intentional misrepresentation of material facts, reliance by the recipient, causation, and damages. Many of these elements are omitted from consumer fraud statutes. While most statutes require some aspect of willfulness, some do not. In fact, many states relax or even eliminate the element of reliance, and some states do not even require a showing of causation or injury.

Key Takeaway

The FTC has many weapons to remedy unfair and deceptive trade practices. These include civil penalties, cease and desist orders, restitution for consumers, and corrective advertising. States have supplemented common law with their own consumer protection acts, known as little FTC acts. Remedies are similar for state statutes, and private parties may bring lawsuits directly.

Exercise

1. Doan's Pills are an over-the-counter medicine for low back pain. Using the Internet, find out what claims Doan's was making and why the FTC thought corrective advertising was necessary.

49.5 Cases

False and Misleading Representations

J. B. Williams Co. v. FTC

381 F.2d 884 (6th Cir. 1967)

CELEBREEZE, CIRCUIT JUDGE

The question presented by this appeal is whether Petitioners' advertising of a product, Geritol, for the relief of iron deficiency anemia, is false and misleading so as to violate Sections 5 and 12 of the Federal Trade Commission Act.

The J. B. Williams Company, Inc. is a New York corporation engaged in the sale and distribution of two products known as Geritol liquid and Geritol tablets. Geritol liquid was first marketed in August, 1950; Geritol tablets in February, 1952. Geritol is sold throughout the United States and advertisements for Geritol have appeared in newspapers and on television in all the States of the United States.

Parkson Advertising Agency, Inc. has been the advertising agency for Williams since 1957. Most of the advertising money for Geritol is spent on television advertising. * * *

The Commission's Order requires that not only must the Geritol advertisements be expressly limited to those persons whose symptoms are due to an existing deficiency of one or more of the vitamins contained in the preparation, or due to an existing deficiency of iron, but also the Geritol advertisements must affirmatively disclose the negative fact that a great majority of persons who experience these symptoms do not experience them because they have a vitamin or iron deficiency; that for the great majority of people experiencing these symptoms, Geritol will be of no benefit. Closely related to this requirement is the further requirement of the Order that the Geritol advertisements refrain from representing that the symptoms are generally reliable indications of iron deficiency.

* * *

The main thrust of the Commission's Order is that the Geritol advertising must affirmatively disclose the negative fact that a great majority of persons who experience these symptoms do not experience them because there is a vitamin or iron deficiency.

The medical evidence on this issue is conflicting and the question is not one which is susceptible to precise statistical analysis.

* * *

While the advertising does not make the affirmative representation that the majority of people who are tired and rundown are so because of iron deficiency anemia and the product Geritol will be an effective cure, there is substantial evidence to support the finding of the Commission that most tired people are not so because of iron deficiency anemia, and the failure to disclose this fact is false and misleading because the advertisement creates the impression that the tired feeling is caused by something which Geritol can cure.

* * *

Here the advertisements emphasize the fact that if you are often tired and run-down you will feel stronger fast by taking Geritol. The Commission, in looking at the overall impression created by the advertisements on the general public, could reasonably find these advertisements were false and misleading. The finding that the advertisements link common, non-specific symptoms with iron deficiency anemia, and thereby create a false impression because most people with these symptoms are not suffering from iron deficiency anemia, is both reasonable and supported by substantial evidence. The Commission is not bound to the literal meaning of the words, nor must the Commission take a random sample to determine the meaning and impact of the advertisements.

Petitioners argue vigorously that the Commission does not have the legal power to require them to state the negative fact that "in the great majority of persons who experience such symptoms, these symptoms are not caused by a deficiency of one or more of the vitamins contained in the preparation or by iron deficiency or iron deficiency anemia"; and "for such persons the preparation will be of no benefit."

We believe the evidence is clear that Geritol is of no benefit in the treatment of tiredness except in those cases where tiredness has been caused by a deficiency of the ingredients contained in Geritol. The fact that the great majority of people who experience tiredness symptoms do not suffer from any deficiency of the ingredients in Geritol is a "material fact" under the meaning of that term as used in Section 15 of the Federal Trade Commission Act and Petitioners' failure to reveal this fact in this day when the consumer is influenced by mass advertising utilizing highly developed arts of persuasion, renders it difficult for the typical consumer to know whether the product will in fact meet his needs unless he is told what the product will or will not do....

* * *

The Commission forbids the Petitioners' representation that the presence of iron deficiency anemia can be self-diagnosed or can be determined without a medical test. The danger to be remedied here has been fully and adequately taken care of in the other requirements of the Order. We can find no Congressional policy against self-medication on a trial and error basis where the consumer is fully informed and the product is safe as Geritol is conceded to be. In fact, Congressional policy is to encourage such self-help. In effect the Commission's Order l(f) tends to place Geritol in the prescription drug field. We do not consider it within the power of the Federal Trade Commission to remove Geritol from the area of proprietary drugs and place it in the area of prescription drugs. This requirement of the Order will not be enforced. We also find this Order is not unduly vague and fairly apprises the Petitioners of what is required of them. Petition denied and, except for l(f) of the Commission's Order, enforcement of the Order will be granted.

Video: Geritol: "Keep Women in Line," 1960 Ad

View the video online at: http://www.youtube.com/embed/pni9ZePXR-w?rel=0

Case Questions

1. Did the defendant actually make statements that were false? If so, what were they? Or, rather than being clearly false, were the statements deceptive? If so, how so?
2. Whether or not you feel that you have "tired blood" or "iron-poor blood," you may be amused by a Geritol ad from 1960. See Video 49.1. Do the disclaimers at the start of the ad that "the majority of tired people don't feel that way because of iron-poor blood" sound like corrective advertising? Is the ad still deceptive in some way? If so, how? If not, why not?

Product Comparisons

P. Lorillard Co. v. Federal Trade Commission

186 F.2d 52 (4th Cir. 1950)

Parker, Chief Judge

This is a petition to set aside an order of the Federal Trade Commission which directed that the P. Lorillard Company cease and desist from making certain representations found to be false in the advertising of its tobacco products. The Commission has filed an answer asking that its order be enforced. The company was ordered to cease and desist "from representing by any means directly or indirectly":

That Old Gold cigarettes or the smoke therefrom contains less nicotine, or less tars and resins, or is less irritating to the throat than the cigarettes or the smoke therefrom of any of the six other leading brands of cigarettes.

* * *

Laboratory tests introduced in evidence show that the difference in nicotine, tars and resins of the different leading brands of cigarettes is insignificant in amount; and there is abundant testimony of medical experts that such difference as there is could result in no difference in the physiological effect upon the smoker. There is expert evidence, also, that the slight difference in the nicotine, tar and resin content of cigarettes is not constant between different brands, but varies from place to place and from time to time, and that it is a practical impossibility for the manufacturer of cigarettes to determine or to remove or substantially reduce such content or to maintain constancy of such content in the finished cigarette. This testimony gives ample support to the Commission's findings.

* * *

The company relies upon the truth of the advertisements complained of, saying that they merely state what had been truthfully stated in an article in the Reader's Digest. An examination of the advertisements, however, shows a perversion of the meaning of the Reader's Digest article which does little credit to the company's advertising department—a perversion which results in the use of the truth in such a way as to cause the reader to believe the exact opposite of what was intended by the writer of the article. A comparison of the advertisements with the article makes this very plain. The article, after referring to laboratory tests that had been made on cigarettes of the leading brands, says:

"The laboratory's general conclusion will be sad news for the advertising copy writers, but good news for the smoker, who need no longer worry as to which cigarette can most effectively nail down his coffin. For one nail is just about as good as another. Says the laboratory report: 'The differences between brands are, practically speaking, small, and no single brand is so superior to its competitors as to justify its selection on the ground that it is less harmful.' How small the variations are may be seen from the data tabulated on page 7."

The table referred to in the article was inserted for the express purpose of showing the insignificance of the difference in the nicotine and tar content of the smoke from the various brands of cigarettes. It appears therefrom that the Old Gold cigarettes examined in the test contained less nicotine, tars and resins than the others examined, although the difference, according to the uncontradicted expert evidence, was so small as to be entirely insignificant and utterly without meaning so far as effect upon the smoker is concerned. The company proceeded to advertise this difference as though it had received a citation for public service instead of a castigation from the Reader's Digest. In the leading newspapers of the country and over the radio it advertised that the Reader's Digest had had experiments conducted and had found that Old Gold cigarettes were lowest in nicotine and lowest in irritating tars and resins, just as though a substantial difference in such content had been found. The following advertisement may be taken as typical:

OLD GOLDS FOUND LOWEST IN NICOTINE

OLD GOLDS FOUND LOWEST IN

THROAT-IRRITATING TARS AND RESINS

"See Impartial Test by Reader's Digest July Issue." See How Your Brand Compares with Old Gold.

"Reader's Digest assigned a scientific testing laboratory to find out about cigarettes. They tested seven leading cigarettes and Reader's Digest published the results.

"The cigarette whose smoke was lowest in nicotine was Old Gold. The cigarette with the least throat-irritating tars and resins was Old Gold.

"On both these major counts Old Gold was best among all seven cigarettes tested.

"Get July Reader's Digest. Turn to Page 5. See what this highly respected magazine reports.

"You'll say, 'From now on, my cigarette is Old Gold.' Light one? Note the mild, interesting flavor. Easier on the throat? Sure: And more smoking pleasure: Yes, it's the new Old Gold—finer yet, since 'something new has been added'."

The fault with this advertising was not that it did not print all that the Reader's Digest article said, but that it printed a small part thereof in such a way as to create an entirely false and misleading impression, not only as to what was said in the article, but also as to the quality of the company's cigarettes. Almost anyone reading the advertisements or listening to the radio broadcasts would have gained the very definite impression that Old Gold cigarettes were less irritating to the throat and less harmful than other leading brands of cigarettes because they contained substantially less nicotine, tars and resins, and that the Reader's Digest had established this fact in impartial laboratory tests; and few would have troubled to look up the Reader's Digest to see what it really had said. The truth was exactly the opposite. There was no substantial difference in Old Gold cigarettes and the other leading brands with respect to their content of nicotine, tars and resins and this was what the Reader's Digest article plainly said. The table whose meaning the advertisements distorted for the purpose of misleading and deceiving the public was intended to prove that there was no practical difference and did prove it when properly understood. To tell less than the whole truth is a well-known method of deception; and he who deceives by resorting to such method cannot excuse the deception by relying upon the truthfulness per se of the partial truth by which it has been accomplished.

In determining whether or not advertising is false or misleading within the meaning of the statute regard must be had, not to fine spun distinctions and arguments that may be made in excuse, but to the effect which it might reasonably be expected to have upon the general public. "The important criterion is the net impression which the advertisement is likely to make upon the general populace." As was well said by Judge Coxe in *Florence Manufacturing Co. v. J. C Dowd & Co.*, with reference to the law relating to trademarks: "The law is not made for the protection of experts, but for the public—that vast multitude which includes the ignorant, the unthinking and the credulous, who, in making purchases, do not stop to analyze, but are governed by appearances and general impressions."

* * *

For the reasons stated, the petition to set aside the order will be denied and the order will be enforced.

Case Questions

1. From a practical perspective, what (if anything) is wrong with caveat emptor—"let the buyer beware"? The careful consumer could have looked at the *Reader's Digest* article; the magazine was widely available in libraries and newsstands.
2. Why isn't this just an example of "puffing" the company's wares? (Puffing presents opinions rather than facts; statements like "This car is a real winner" and "Your wife will love this watch" constitute puffing.)

Corrective Advertising

United States v. Phillip Morris, et al.

U.S. Court of Appeals for the District of Columbia (May 22, 2015)

TATEL, Circuit Judge:

In this appeal, the fifth in this long-running RICO case against the nation's cigarette manufacturers, defendants challenge a district court order requiring that they add two statements to their cigarette packages and advertisements: an announcement that a federal court has ruled that they "deliberately deceived the American public" about the dangers of cigarettes; and a declaration that they "intentionally designed cigarettes" to maximize addiction. * * *

[Fifteen years after the U.S. first sued the tobacco companies], supported by more than 4,000 findings of fact detailing the cigarette manufacturers' "pervasive scheme to defraud consumers and potential consumers of cigarettes," carried out "over the course of more than 50 years," the district court entered final judgment against the defendants. Finding that they joined together to "maximize their profits" through "false and fraudulent statements, representations, and promises" about "the devastating health effects of smoking," the court concluded that the manufacturers operated an illegal racketeering enterprise in violation of RICO.

[After further proceedings] the district court set about drafting the required corrective disclosures . . . which we reproduce . . . for the reader's benefit:

"A Federal Court has ruled that Altria, R.J. Reynolds Tobacco, Lorillard, and Philip Morris USA deliberately deceived the American public about the health effects of smoking, and has ordered those companies to make this statement. Here is the truth:

- Smoking kills, on average, 1,200 Americans. Every day.
- More people die every year from smoking than from murder, AIDS, suicide, drugs, car crashes, and alcohol, combined.
- Smoking causes heart disease, emphysema, acute myeloid leukemia, and cancer of the mouth, esophagus, larynx, lung, stomach, kidney, bladder, and pancreas.
- Smoking also causes reduced fertility, low birth weight in newborns, and cancer of the cervix.

A Federal Court has ruled that [the cigarette companies] deliberately deceived the American public about the addictiveness of smoking and nicotine, and has ordered those companies to make this statement. Here is the truth:

- Smoking is highly addictive. Nicotine is the addictive drug in tobacco.
- Cigarette companies intentionally designed cigarettes with enough nicotine to create and sustain addiction. * * *
- Defendant tobacco companies intentionally designed cigarettes to make them more addictive.
- Cigarette companies control the impact and delivery of nicotine in many ways, including designing filters and selecting cigarette paper to maximize the ingestion of nicotine, adding

ammonia to make the cigarette taste less harsh, and controlling the physical and chemical make-up of the tobacco blend. * * *

[As to second-hand smoke] A Federal Court has ruled that [the defendants] deliberately deceived the American public about the health effects of secondhand smoke, and has ordered those companies to make this statement. Here is the truth:

- Secondhand smoke kills over 38,000 Americans each year.
- Secondhand smoke causes lung cancer and coronary heart disease in adults who do not smoke.
- Children exposed to secondhand smoke are at an increased risk for sudden infant death syndrome (SIDS), acute respiratory infections, ear problems, severe asthma, and reduced lung function.
- There is no safe level of exposure to secondhand smoke." * * *

[W]e turn to the manufacturers' claim that the district court exceeded the bounds of its remedial power under RICO when it ordered them to disseminate the corrective disclosures listed above. The manufacturers principally challenge . . . (1) the statements . . . which reveal that they "intentionally designed cigarettes" to ensure addiction, and (2) the preambles announcing that a federal court has ruled they "deliberately deceived the American public" about the dangers of cigarettes. . . . [T]he manufacturers maintain that these disclosures "force Defendants to vilify and shame themselves for past wrongdoing," rather than "reveal the previously hidden truth" about cigarettes as required by our prior decisions. * * *

[In a previous decision on this matter] we held that disseminating corrective statements *on the proposed topic* would prevent future RICO violations by "requiring Defendants to reveal the previously hidden truth about their products" [citation]. But unlike the bulleted statements, which do just that, the preambles reveal nothing about cigarettes; instead, they disclose defendants' prior deceptive *conduct*. * * *

Were this an enforcement proceeding brought by the FTC . . . the preamble might well represent a proper exercise of the court's remedial power. But this is a civil RICO case, and as we have explained, that statute empowers district courts to issue injunctions for one purpose and only one purpose: to prevent and restrain future RICO violations. Correcting consumer misinformation, which focuses on remedying the effects of past conduct, is thus an impermissible objective under RICO. Seeking to *prevent* consumer deception is similarly impermissible because, although forward-looking, it focuses not on restraining the RICO violator, but on safeguarding *consumers* against RICO violations

To be sure, although the district court's reasoning was largely consumer focused, . . . it did at one point suggest that the preambles might also discourage the manufacturers from again violating RICO. "By ensuring that consumers know that Defendants have misled the public in the past on the issue of secondhand smoke . . . ," the district court stated, "Defendants will be less likely to attempt to argue in the future that such a consensus does not exist." But even were we to extend this deterrence rationale beyond secondhand smoke to every corrective statement, our case law makes clear that when it comes to RICO remedies, it fails. [As we previously explained], district courts may order injunctions under [RICO] only to "prevent and restrain" RICO violations, not to *discourage* such violations through "any remedy that inflicts pain."

So too here. Even if the preambles would discourage cigarette manufacturers from falsely marketing cigarettes by arming consumers against misinformation, thus making RICO violations unprofitable—something the government never even attempted to prove—"[s]uch a remedy [would] reach[] beyond the bounds of [RICO], which authorizes the district court to order injunctions [only] to prevent and restrain fraudulent statements about smoking and health and addiction." The bulleted statements will achieve this goal because they "reveal the previously hidden truth about [the manufacturers'] products." The preambles, however, do no such thing and may not be justified on grounds of general deterrence.

* * *

For the reasons set forth above, we affirm in part, reverse in part, and remand for further proceedings consistent with this opinion.

Case Questions

1. Why did tobacco companies lie to the American people for sixty years about the adverse health consequences of cigarette smoking?
2. The appeals court overturned the lower court order directing the companies to advertise that they had "intentionally designed cigarettes to ensure addiction" and "deliberately deceived the American public." Why did it rule this way?
3. Would you say peddling an addictive poison—what cigarettes are—is an ethical business?

49.6 Summary and Exercises

Summary

Section 5 of the Federal Trade Commission (FTC) Act gives the FTC the power to enforce a provision prohibiting "unfair methods of competition and unfair or deceptive acts or practices in commerce." Under this power, the FTC may bring enforcement proceedings against companies on a case-by-case basis or may promulgate trade regulation rules.

A deceptive act or practice need not actually deceive as long as it is "likely to mislead." An unfair act or practice need not deceive at all but must offend a common sense of propriety or justice or of an honest way of acting. Among the proscribed acts or practices are these: failure to disclose pertinent facts, false or misleading description of products, misleading price and savings claims, bait-and-switch advertisements, free-offer claims, false product comparisons and disparagements, and endorsements by those who do not use the product or who have no reasonable basis for making the claims. Among the unfair trade practices that the FTC has sought to deter are certain types of contests and sweepstakes, high-pressure door-to-door and mail-order selling, and certain types of negative-option plans.

The FTC has a number of remedial weapons: cease and desist orders tailored to the particular deception or unfair act (including affirmative disclosure in advertising and corrections in future advertising), civil monetary penalties, and injunctions, damages, and restitution on behalf of injured consumers. Only the FTC may sue to correct violations of Section 5; private parties have no right to sue under Section 5, but they can sue for certain kinds of false advertising under the federal trademark laws.

In addition to the Federal Trade Commission, several other federal agencies are involved in consumer protection regulation.

Exercises

1. Icebox Ike, a well-known tackle for a professional football team, was recently signed to a multimillion-dollar contract to appear in a series of nationally televised advertisements touting the pleasures of going to the ballet and showing him in the audience watching a ballet. In fact, Icebox has never been to a ballet, although he has told his friends that he "truly believes" ballet is a "wonderful thing." The FTC opens an investigation to determine whether there are grounds to take legal action against Icebox and the ballet company ads. What advice can you give Icebox Ike? What remedies can the FTC seek?
2. Door-to-door salespersons of an encyclopedia company offer a complete set of encyclopedias to "selected" customers. They tell customers that their only obligation is to pay for

a ten-year updating service. In fact, the price of the updating service includes the cost of the encyclopedias. The FTC sues, charging deception under Section 5 of the FTC Act. The encyclopedia company defends itself on the ground that no one could possibly have been misled because everyone must have understood that no company could afford to give away a twenty-volume set of books for free. What is the result?

3. Vanessa Cosmetics takes out full-page advertisements in the local newspaper stating that "this Sunday only" the Vanessa Makeup Kit will be "reduced to only $25." In fact, the regular price has been $25.50. Does this constitute deceptive advertising? Why?
4. Lilliputian Department Stores advertises a "special" on an electric carrot slicer, priced "this week only at $10." When customers come to the store, they find the carrot slicer in frayed boxes, and the advertised special is clearly inferior to a higher-grade carrot slicer priced at $25. When customers ask about the difference, the store clerk tells them, "You wouldn't want to buy the cheaper one; it wears out much too fast." What grounds, if any, exist to charge Lilliputian with violations of the FTC Act?
5. A toothpaste manufacturer advertises that special tests demonstrate that use of its toothpaste results in fewer cavities than a "regular toothpaste." In fact, the "regular" toothpaste was not marketed but was merely the advertiser's brand stripped of its fluoride. Various studies over the years have demonstrated, however, that fluoride in toothpaste will reduce the number of cavities a user will get. Is this advertisement deceptive under Section 5 of the FTC Act?
6. McDonald's advertises a sweepstakes through a mailing that says prizes are to be reserved for 15,610 "lucky winners." The mailing further states, "You may be [a winner] but you will never know if you don't claim your prize. All prizes not claimed will never be given away, so hurry." The mailing does not give the odds of winning. The FTC sues to enjoin the mailing as deceptive. What is the result?

Self-Test Questions

1. Section 5 of the Federal Trade Commission Act is enforceable by
   a. a consumer in federal court
   b. a consumer in state court
   c. the FTC in an administrative proceeding
   d. the FTC suing in federal court
2. The FTC
   a. is an independent federal agency
   b. is an arm of the Justice Department
   c. supersedes Congress in defining deceptive trade practices
   d. speaks for the president on consumer matters
3. A company falsely stated that its competitor's product "won't work." Which of the following statements is false?
   a. The competitor may sue the company under state law.
   b. The competitor may sue the company for violating the FTC Act.
   c. The competitor may sue the company for violating the Lanham Act.
   d. The FTC may sue the company for violating the FTC Act.
4. The FTC may order a company that violated Section 5 of the FTC Act by false advertising
   a. to go out of business
   b. to close down the division of the company that paid for false advertising
   c. to issue corrective advertising
   d. to buy back from its customers all the products sold by the advertising
5. The ingredients in a nationally advertised cupcake must be disclosed on the package under

a. state common law
b. a trade regulation rule promulgated by the FTC
c. the federal Food, Drug, and Cosmetic Act
d. an executive order of the president

Self-Test Answers

1. c
2. a
3. b
4. c
5. b

Endnotes

1. *FTC v. Transworld Courier Services, Inc.*, 59 A&TR Rpt. 174 (N.D. Ga. 1990).
2. *F.T.C. v. Mary Carter Paint Co.*, 382 U.S. 46 (1965).
3. *Reader's Digest Assoc.*, 79 F.T.C. 599 (1971).
4. http://abcnews.go.com/Business/story?id=88032&page=1
5. *Orkin Exterminating Co. v. FTC*, 849 F.2d 1354 (11th Cir. 1988), *cert. denied*, 488 U.S. 1041 (1989).
6. Dan Hansell and Charles Dixon, "Current FTC Enforcement Initiatives in the Consumer Protection Arena," p. 26. http://www.corporatelivewire.com/CorporateLiveWireExpertGuides/CompAntiTrust2014/flipviewerxpress.html?pn=24
7. *Warner Lambert Co. v. Federal Trade Commission*, 562 F.2d 749 (D.C. Cir. 1977), *cert. denied*, 435 U.S. 950 (1978).
8. http://www.fda.gov/AboutFDA/Transparency/Basics/ucm194879.htm.
9. http://www.nhtsa.gov/About.
10. http://www.consumerfinance.gov/.

CHAPTER 50
Employment Law

Learning Objectives

After reading this chapter, you should understand the following:

1. How the common-law doctrine of employment at will has been modified by courts, federal statutes, and state statutes.
2. That many (but not all) kinds of employment discrimination are prohibited under Title VII of the Federal Civil Rights Act (and by Executive Order).
3. How labor unions came to be an important part of American employment law, what rights labor laws grants to employees (and employers), and how unions have more recently become apparently less important.
4. That various other protections for employees are imposed by federal statute, including the Age Discrimination in Employment Act (ADEA) and the Americans with Disabilities Act (ADA).

In this chapter, we will examine both the federal laws that govern the relationship between the employer and the employee who belongs, or wants to belong, to a union, and also to the broader state and federal laws that govern employer-employee relationships outside of unions. There are a number of laws dealing with employment discrimination. Beyond discrimination, the law also governs other issues, such as the extent to which an employer may terminate the relationship itself. We examine these issues.

Even before statutes governing collective bargaining (labor unions) and various state and federal discrimination laws, the common law set boundaries for employer-employee relationships. The basic rule that evolved prior to the twentieth century was "employment at will," which we examine. But as we go through the key statutes on employment law and employment discrimination, bear in mind that these statutes stand as an important set of exceptions to the basic common-law rule of **employment at will**. That rule holds that in the absence of a contractual agreement otherwise, an employee is free to leave employment at any time and for any reason; similarly, an employer is free to fire employees at any time and for any reason.

employment at will

The common-law doctrine that allows employers to discharge an employee at any time and for any reason or for no reason. Courts have created exceptions for "bad reasons."

50.1 Federal Employment Discrimination Laws

Learning Objectives

1. Know the various federal discrimination laws and how they are applied in various cases.
2. Distinguish between disparate impact and disparate treatment cases.
3. Understand the concept of affirmative action and its limits in employment law.

employment discrimination

Treating employees or job applicants unequally on the basis of race, color, national origin, religion, sex (gender), age, or disability; prohibited by federal statutes and many state statutes.

As we look at federal **employment discrimination** laws, bear in mind that most states also have laws that prohibit discriminatory practices in employment. Until the 1960s, Congress had legislated only a little in how businesses hired, promted, and fired employees; the exception was in collective bargaining law. A business could refuse to hire members of racial minorities, exclude women from promotions, or pay men more than women for the same work. But with the rise of the civil rights movement in the early 1960s, Congress (and many states) began to legislate away the employer's power to discriminate. The most important statutes are Title VII of the Civil Rights Act of 1964, the Equal Pay Act of 1963, the Age Discrimination in Employment Act of 1967, and the Americans with Disabilities Act of 1990.

Title VII of the Civil Rights Act of 1964

The most basic anti-discrimination law in employment is Title VII of the federal Civil Rights Act of 1964. The key prohibited discrimination is that based on race, but Congress also included sex, religion, national origin, and color as prohibited bases for hiring, promotion, layoff, and discharge decisions. To put the Civil Rights Act in its proper context, a short history of racial discrimination in the United States follows.

The passage of the Civil Rights Act of 1964 was the culmination of a long history that dated back to slavery, the founding of the U.S. legal system, the Civil War, and many historical and political developments over the ninety-nine years from the end of the Civil War to the passage of the act. The years prior to 1964 had seen a remarkable rise of civil disobedience, led by many in the civil rights movement but most prominently by Dr. Martin Luther King Jr. Peaceful civil disobedience was sometimes met with violence, and television cameras were there to record most of it.

Video: Birmingham protests, 1963

Martin Luther King, Jr. and the civil rights protests in Birmingham, met with police violence.

View the video online at: http://www.youtube.com/embed/joc3CRL6x4E?rel=0

While the Civil War had addressed slavery and the secession of Southern states, the Thirteenth, Fourteenth, and Fifteenth Amendments, ratified just after the war, provided for equal protection under the law, guaranteed citizenship, and protected the right to vote for African Americans. The amendments also allowed Congress to enforce these provisions by enacting appropriate, specific legislation.

But during the Reconstruction Era, many of the Southern states resisted the laws that were passed in Washington to bolster civil rights. To a significant extent, decisions rendered by the U.S. Supreme Court in this era—such as *Plessy v. Ferguson*, condoning "separate but equal" facilities for different races—greatly restricted the utility of the new Constitutional provisions. The states effectively controlled the public treatment of African Americans, and a period of neglect set in that lasted until after World War II. The state laws essentially mandated segregated facilities for blacks (restaurants, hotels, schools, water fountains, public bathrooms), facilities that were usually inferior.

Along with these "Jim Crow" laws in the South, the Ku Klux Klan was very strong, and lynchings (hangings without any sort of public due process) by the Klan and others were designed to limit the civil and economic rights of the former slaves and their descendants. The hatred of blacks from that era by many whites in America has only gradually softened since 1964. Even as the civil rights bill was being debated in Congress in 1964, some Young Americans for Freedom in the right wing of the GOP would clandestinely chant "Be a man, join the Klan" and sing "We will hang Earl Warren from a sour apple tree," to the tune of "Battle Hymn of the Republic." This was in anger over

Chief Justice Warren's presiding over *Brown v. Board of Education*, which reversed *Plessy v. Ferguson*, and determined that segregated schools could not, in fact, be separate but equal.

But just a few years earlier, the public service and heroism of many black military units and individuals in World War II had created a perceptual shift in U.S. society; men of many races who had served together in the war against the Axis powers (fascism in Europe and the Japanese emperor's rule in the Pacific) began to understand their common humanity. Major migrations of blacks from the South to industrial cities of the North also gave impetus to the civil rights movement.

Bills introduced in Congress regarding employment policy brought the issue of civil rights to the attention of representatives and senators. In 1945, 1947, and 1949, the House of Representatives voted to abolish the poll tax. The poll tax was a method used in many states to confine voting rights to those who could pay a tax, and often, blacks could not. The Senate did not go along, but these bills signaled a growing interest in protecting civil rights through federal action. The executive branch of government, by presidential order, likewise became active by ending discrimination in the nation's military forces, in federal employment, and in work done under government contract.

The Supreme Court gave impetus to the civil rights movement in its reversal of the "separate but equal" doctrine in the *Brown v. Board of Education* decision. In its 1954 decision, the Court said, "To separate black children from others of similar age and qualifications solely because of their race generates a feeling of inferiority as to their status in the community that may affect their hearts and minds in a way never to be undone. ... We conclude that in the field of public education the doctrine of separate but equal has no place. Separate educational facilities are inherently unequal."

This decision meant that white and black children could not be forced to attend separate public schools. By itself, however, this decision did not create immediate gains, either in public school desegregation or in the desegregation of other public facilities. There were memorable standoffs between federal agents and state officials in Little Rock, Arkansas; the Democratic governor of Arkansas personally blocked young black students from entering Little Rock's Central High School, and it was only President Eisenhower's order to have federal marshals accompany the students that forced integration. The year was 1957.

But resistance to public school integration was widespread, and other public facilities were not governed by the *Brown* ruling. Restaurants, hotels, and other public facilities were still largely segregated. Segregation kept blacks from using public city buses, park facilities, and restrooms on an equal basis with whites. Along with inferior schools, workplace practices throughout the South and also in many Northern cities sharply limited African Americans' ability to advance economically. Civil disobedience began to grow.

The bus protests in Montgomery, Alabama, were particularly effective. Planned by civil rights leaders, Rosa Parks's refusal to give up her seat to a white person and sit at the back of the public bus led to a boycott of the Montgomery bus system by blacks and, later, a boycott of white businesses in Montgomery. There were months of confrontation and some violence; finally, the city agreed to end its long-standing rules on segregated seating on buses.

There were also protests at lunch counters and other protests on public buses, where groups of Northern protesters—Freedom Riders—sometimes met with violence. In 1962, James Meredith's attempt to enroll as the first African American at the University of Mississippi generated extreme hostility; two people were killed and 375 were injured as the state resisted Meredith's admission. The murders of civil rights workers Medgar Evers and William L. Moore added to the inflamed sentiments, and whites in Birmingham, Alabama, killed four young black girls who were attending Sunday school when their church was bombed.

These events were all covered by the nation's news media, whose photos—and television was particularly important here—showed beatings and the use of fire hoses and police dogs on peaceful protesters. Social tensions were reaching a postwar high by 1964. According to the government, there were nearly one thousand civil rights demonstrations in 209 cities in a three-month period beginning May 1963. Representatives and senators could not ignore the impact of social protest. But the complicated political history of the Civil Rights Act of 1964 also tells us that the legislative result was anything but a foregone conclusion.[1]

In Title VII of the Civil Rights Act of 1964, Congress for the first time outlawed discrimination in employment based on race, religion, sex, or national origin. Title VII declares: "It shall be an unlawful employment practice for an employer to fail or refuse to hire or to discharge any individual, or otherwise to discriminate against any individual with respect to his compensation, terms, conditions, or privileges of employment, because of such individual's race, color, religion, sex, or national origin." Title VII applies to (1) employers with fifteen or more employees whose business affects interstate commerce, (2) all employment agencies, (3) labor unions with fifteen or more members, (4) state and local governments and their agencies, and (5) most federal government employment.

In 1984, the Supreme Court said that Title VII applies to partnerships as well as corporations when ruling that it is illegal to discriminatorily refuse to promote a female lawyer to partnership status in a law firm. This applies, by implication, to other fields, such as accounting.[2] The remedy for unlawful discrimination is back pay and hiring, reinstatement, or promotion.

Title VII established the Equal Employment Opportunity Commission (EEOC) to investigate violations of the act. A victim of discrimination who wishes to file suit must first file a complaint with the EEOC to permit that agency to attempt conciliation of the dispute. The EEOC has filed a number of lawsuits to prove statistically that a company has systematically discriminated on one of the forbidden bases. The EEOC has received perennial criticism for its extreme slowness in filing suits and for failure to handle the huge backlog of complaints with which it has had to wrestle.

The courts have come to recognize two major types of Title VII cases:

disparate treatment

A form of employment discrimination that results when an employer intentionally discriminates against employees who are members of protected classes.

disparate impact

A form of employment discrimination resulting from employer practices that appear to be neutral but that have a discriminatory impact on protected classes.

1. Cases of **disparate treatment**
    - In this type of lawsuit, the plaintiff asserts that because of race, sex, religion, or national origin, he or she has been treated less favorably than others within the organization. To prevail in a disparate treatment suit, the plaintiff must show that the company *intended* to discriminate because of one of the factors the law forbids to be considered. Thus, in *McDonnell Douglas Corp. v. Green*, the Supreme Court held that the plaintiff had shown that the company intended to discriminate by refusing to rehire him because of his race.[3] In general, there are two types of disparate treatment cases: (1) pattern-and-practice cases, in which the employee asserts that the employer systematically discriminates on the grounds of race, religion, sex, or national origin; and (2) reprisal or retaliation cases, in which the employee must show that the employer discriminated against him or her because that employee asserted his or her Title VII rights.
2. Cases of **disparate impact**
    - In this second type of Title VII case, the employee need not show that the employer intended to discriminate but only that the effect, or impact, of the employer's action was discriminatory. Usually, this impact will be upon an entire class of employees. The plaintiff must demonstrate that the reason for the employer's conduct (such as refusal to promote) was not job related. Disparate impact cases often arise out of practices that appear to be neutral or nondiscriminatory on the surface, such as educational requirements and tests administered to help the employer choose the most qualified candidate. In the seminal case of *Griggs v. Duke Power Co.*, the Supreme Court held that under Title VII, an employer is not free to use any test it pleases; the test must bear a genuine relationship to job performance.[4] *Griggs* stands for the proposition that Title VII "prohibits employment practices that have discriminatory effects as well as those that are intended to discriminate."

FIGURE 50.1 A Checklist of Employment Law

Employers have a complex set of state and federal laws to observe in hiring, firing, promotion, pensions, labor standards, and workers' compensation for on the job injuries.

- ✓ Employment discrimination laws
  - Title VII, Civil Rights Act of 1964
  - Civil Rights Act of 1866
  - Equal Pay Act of 1963
  - Age Discrimination Act of 1967
  - Pregnancy Discrimination Act of 1978
  - Rehabilitation Act of 1973
  - Americans with Disabilities Act of 1990
- ✓ Common law of employment at will
- ✓ Contract law
- ✓ Tort law
- ✓ Agency law
- ✓ Worker Adjustment and Retraining Notification Act
- ✓ Polygraph Protection Act
- ✓ Occupational Safety and Health Act
- ✓ Employee Retirement Income Security Act
- ✓ Fair Labor Standards Act
- ✓ Workers' Compensation laws

Discrimination Based on Religion

An employer who systematically refuses to hire Catholics, Jews, Buddhists, or members of any other religious group engages in unlawful disparate treatment under Title VII. But refusal to deal with someone because of his or her religion is not the only type of violation under the law. Title VII defines religion as including religious observances and practices as well as belief and requires the employer to "reasonably accommodate to an employee's or prospective employee's religious observance or practice" unless the employer can demonstrate that a reasonable accommodation would work an "undue hardship on the conduct of the employer's business." Thus, a company that refused to allow a Sikh to wear a turban on the job would violate Title VII.

But the company need not make an accommodation that would impose more than a minimal cost. For example, an employee in an airline maintenance department, open twenty-four hours a day, wished to avoid working on his Sabbath. The employee belonged to a union, and under the collective bargaining agreement, a rotation system determined by seniority would have put the worker into a work shift that fell on his Sabbath. The Supreme Court held that the employer was not required to pay premium wages to someone whom the seniority system assigned to work on that day, and could discharge the employee if he refused the assignment.[5]

Title VII permits religious organizations to give preference in employment to individuals of the same religion. Obviously, a synagogue looking for a spiritual leader would hire a rabbi and not a priest.

Sex Discrimination

A refusal to hire or promote a woman simply because she is female is a clear violation of Title VII. Under the Pregnancy Act of 1978, Congress declared that discrimination because of pregnancy is also a form of sex discrimination. Equal pay for equal or comparable work has also been an issue in sex (or gender) discrimination. *Barbano v. Madison County* (see Section 5), presents a straightforward case of sex discrimination. In that case, notice how the plaintiff has the initial burden of proving discriminatory intent and how the burden then shifts to the defendant to show a plausible, nondiscriminatory reason for its hiring decision.

sexual harassment

Demands for sexual favors in return for job promotions or other benefits, or language or conduct so sexually offensive that it creates a hostile work environment, disadvantaging the employee on the basis of sex.

The late 1970s brought another problem of sex discrimination to the fore: **sexual harassment**. There is much fear and ignorance about sexual harassment among both employers and employees. Many men think they cannot compliment a woman on her appearance without risking at least a warning by the human resources department. Many employers have spent significant time and money trying to train employees about sexual harassment, so as to avoid lawsuits. Put simply, sexual harassment involves unwelcome sexual advances, requests for sexual favors, and other verbal or physical conduct of a sexual nature that creates a hostile work environment or requires the employee to tolerate such conduct in order to keep his or her job or be promotable.

There are two major categories of sexual harassment: (1) quid pro quo and (2) hostile work environment.

Quid pro quo comes from the Latin phrase "one thing in return for another." If any part of a job is made conditional on sexual activity, there is quid pro quo sexual harassment. Here, one person's power over another is essential; a coworker, for example, is not usually in a position to make sexual demands on someone at his same level, unless he has special influence with a supervisor who has power to hire, fire, promote, or change work assignments. A supervisor, on the other hand, typically has those powers or the power to influence those kinds of changes. For example, when the male foreman says to the female line worker, "I can get you off of the night shift if you'll sleep with me," there is quid pro quo sexual harassment.

In *Harris v. Forklift Systems, Inc.*[6] and in *Meritor v. Vinson*,[7] we see examples of hostile work environment. Hostile work environment claims are more frequent than quid pro quo claims and so are more worrisome to management. An employee has a valid claim of sexual harassment if sexual talk, imagery, or behavior becomes so pervasive that it interferes with the employee's ability to work to her best capacity. On occasion, courts have found that offensive jokes, if sufficiently frequent and pervasive in the workplace, can create a hostile work environment. Likewise, comments about body parts or public displays of pornographic pictures can also create a hostile work environment. In short, the plaintiff can be detrimentally offended and hindered in the workplace even if there are no measurable psychological injuries.

In the landmark hostile work environment case of *Meritor v. Vinson*, the Supreme Court held that Title VII's ban on sexual harassment encompasses more than the trading of sexual favors for employment benefits. Unlawful sexual harassment also includes the creation of a hostile or offensive working environment, subjecting both the offending employee and the company to damage suits even if the victim was in no danger of being fired or of losing a promotion or raise.

In recalling *Harris v. Forklift Systems* (Chapter 1, Chapter 1.6), we see that the "reasonable person" standard is declared by the court as follows: "So long as the environment would reasonably be perceived, and is perceived, as hostile or abusive there is no need for it also to be psychologically injurious." Following the Harris decision, in 2002, the 8th Circuit Court in *Duncan v. General Motors Corporation* determined that the jury verdict in favor of the plaintiff (for over 1 million dollars) should be reversed because the court believed the sexual harassment she suffered was not severe or pervasive enough to unreasonably interfere with her work. The Supreme Court declined to review the case.

Sex discrimination in terms of wages and benefits is common enough that a number of sizeable class actions have been brought. A class action is generally initiated by one or more people who believe that they, along with a group of other people, have been wronged in similar ways. Class actions for sexual harassment have been successful in the past. On June 11, 1998, the EEOC reached a $34 million settlement with Mitsubishi over allegations of widespread sexual harassment at the Normal, Illinois, auto plant. The settlement involved about five hundred women who split the $34 million, although only seven received the maximum $300,000 allowed by law. The others received amounts ranging from $8,000 to $225,000.

Class actions involve specific plaintiffs (called class plaintiffs or class representatives) who are named in the class action lawsuit to assert the claims of the unnamed or absent members of the class; thus, all those with a common complaint need not file their own separate lawsuit. From the point of view of plaintiffs who may have lost only a few thousand dollars annually as a result of the discrimination, a class action is advantageous: almost no lawyer would take a complicated civil case that had a potential gain of only a few thousand dollars. But if there are thousands of plaintiffs with very similar claims, the judgment could be well into the millions. Defendants can win the procedural battle by convincing a court that the proposed class of plaintiffs does not present common questions of law or of fact.

In the Wal-Mart class action decided by the Supreme Court in 2011, three named plaintiffs (Dukes, Arana, and Kwapnoski) represented a proposed class of 1.5 million current or former Wal-Mart employees. The plaintiffs' attorneys asked the trial court in 2001 to certify as a class all women employed at any Wal-Mart domestic retail store at any time since December of 1998. As the case progressed through the judicial system, the class grew in size. If the class were certified, and discrimination proven, Wal-Mart could have been liable for over $1 billion in back pay. So Wal-Mart argued that as plaintiffs, the cases of the 1.5 million women did not present common questions of law or of fact—that is, that the claims were different enough that the Court should not allow a single class action lawsuit to present such differing kinds of claims. Initially, a federal judge disagreed, finding the class sufficiently coherent for purposes of federal civil procedure. The U.S. Court of Appeals for the Ninth Circuit upheld the trial judge on two occasions.

But the U.S. Supreme Court agreed with Wal-Mart. In the majority opinion, Justice Scalia discussed the commonality condition for class actions.

> *Quite obviously, the mere claim by employees of the same company that they have suffered a Title VII injury, or even a disparate impact Title VII injury, gives no cause to believe that all their claims can productively be litigated at once. Their claims must depend upon a common contention—for example, the assertion of discriminatory bias on the part of the same supervisor. That common contention, moreover, must be of such a nature that it is capable of classwide resolution—which means that determination of its truth or falsity will resolve an issue that is central to the validity of each one of the claims in one stroke.*[8]

Finding that there was no common contention, the Supreme Court reversed the lower courts. Many commentators, and four dissenting Justices, believed that the majority opinion has created an unnecessarily high hurdle for class action plaintiffs in Title VII cases.

An additional barrier to class actions for employment discrimination claims has been created by Supreme Court decisions that enforce arbitration clauses in employment contracts. These clauses specifically forbid employees from using any dispute resolution other than individual arbitration with the employer. See *AT&T v. Conception* in section 50.6 (cases). In general, the use of arbitration has become a convenient way for the courts to limit the number of cases it hears. Some have argued, with considerable force, that the use of arbitration has begun to erode the rights of employees, franchisees, and many others to their "day in court."[9]

Discrimination Based on Race, Color, and National Origin

Title VII was primarily enacted to prohibit employment discrimination based on race, color, and national origin. Race refers to broad categories such as black, Caucasian, Asian, and Native American. Color simply refers to the color of a person's skin, and national origin refers to the country of the person's ancestry.

Exceptions to Title VII

Merit

Employers are allowed to select on merit and promote on merit without offending title VII's requirements. Merit decisions are usually based on work, educational experience, and ability tests. All requirements, however, must be job related. For example, the ability to lift heavy cartons of sixty pounds or more is appropriate for certain warehouse jobs but is not appropriate for all office workers. The ability to do routine maintenance (electrical, plumbing, construction) is an appropriate requirement for maintenance work but not for a teaching position. Requiring someone to have a high school degree, as in *Griggs vs. Duke Power Co.*, is not appropriate as a qualification for common labor.

Seniority

Employers may also maintain seniority systems that reward workers who have been with the company for a long time. Higher wages, benefits, and choice of working hours or vacation schedules are examples of rewards that provide employees with incentives to stay with the company. If they are not the result of intentional discrimination, they are lawful. Where an employer is dealing with a union, it is typical to see seniority systems in place.

Bona Fide Occupational Qualification (BFOQ)

bona fide occupational qualifications (BFOQs)

Employers may require that employees be of a certain religion, sex, or national origin where that requirement is made in good faith and goes to the essence of the business. Race and color cannot be BFOQs.

For certain kinds of jobs, employers may impose **bona fide occupational qualifications (BFOQs)**. Under the express terms of Title VII, however, a bona fide (good faith) occupational qualification of race or color is never allowed. In the area of religion, as noted earlier, a group of a certain religious faith that is searching for a new spiritual leader can certainly limit its search to those of the same religion. With regard to sex (gender), allowing women to be locker room attendants only in a women's gym is a valid BFOQ, or casting men only in a movie about, say, life in a Korean-war era prisoner of war camp would make such discrimination against women a BFOQ. One important test that the courts employ in evaluating an employer's BFOQ claims is the "essence of the business" test.

In *Diaz v. Pan American World Airways, Inc.*, the airline maintained a policy of exclusively hiring females for its flight attendant positions.[10] The essence of the business test was established with the court's finding that "discrimination based on sex is valid only when the essence of the business operation would be undermined by not hiring members of one sex exclusively." Although the court acknowledged that females might be better suited to fulfill the required duties of the position, this was not enough to fulfill the essence of the business test:

> *The primary function of an airline is to transport passengers safely from one point to another. While a pleasant environment, enhanced by the obvious cosmetic effect that female stewardesses provide as well as...their apparent ability to perform the non-mechanical functions of the job in a more effective manner than most men, may all be important, they are tangential to the essence of the business involved. No one has suggested that having male stewards will so seriously affect the operation of an airline as to jeopardize or even minimize its ability to provide safe transportation from one place to another.*[11]

The reason that airlines now use the gender-neutral term *flight attendant* is a direct result of Title VII. In the 1990s, Hooters had some difficulty convincing the EEOC and certain male plaintiffs that only women could be hired as waitstaff in its restaurants. With regard to national origin, directors of movies and theatrical productions would be within their Title VII BFOQ rights to restrict the roles of fictional Asians to those actors whose national origin was Asian, but could also permissibly hire Caucasian actors made up in "yellow face."

Independent Contractors

One potentially troublesome area here involves independent contractors. Title VII generally does not apply to them: if they really are independent contractors, they have no claim for discrimination because the law only protects *employees*. For example, suppose a well-known national magazine wanted to hire a freelance writer for a particular project. Could the magazine legally refuse to hire a writer because she was a woman, or because he was Catholic? Yes. Could the magazine refuse to hire a black plumber for a repair job in its employee lounge? Yes, at least as far as federal employment anti-discrimination laws go. An *employee* is, so to say, "trapped" in the job and cannot usually quit easily. Harassment and discrimination are types of abuse of power. Independent contractors are, usually, not likely to be as powerless as employees: they can move on to another job. "The price of freedom is protecting yourself against the lechery, bigotry, and general idiocies of [your] clients; the benefit is not being bossed around."[12]

Defenses in Sexual Harassment Cases

In 1977, the U.S. Supreme Court issued two decisions that provide an affirmative defense in some sexual harassment cases. In *Faragher v. City of Boca Raton*[13] and in *Burlington Industries, Inc. v. Ellerth*,[14] female employees sued for sexual harassment. In each case, they proved that their supervisors had engaged in unconsented-to touching as well as verbal sexual harassment. In both cases, the plaintiff quit her job and, after going through the EEOC process, got a right-to-sue letter and sued for sexual harassment. In *Faragher*, the employer had never disseminated the policy against sexual harassment to its employees. But in the second case, *Burlington Industries*, the employer had a policy that was made known to employees. Moreover, a complaints system had been established that was not used by the female employee.

Both opinions rejected the notion of strict or automatic liability for employers when agents (employees) engage in sexual harassment. But the employer can have a valid defense to liability if it can prove (1) that it exercised reasonable care to prevent and correct any sexual harassment behaviors and (2) that the plaintiff employee unreasonably failed to take advantage of any preventive or corrective opportunities provided by the employer or to otherwise avoid harm. As with all affirmative defenses, the employer has the burden of proving this defense.

Affirmative Action

Affirmative action is mentioned in the statutory language of Title VII, as courts have the power to order affirmative action as a remedy for the effects of past discrimination. In addition to court-ordered affirmative action, employers may voluntarily use an affirmative action plan to remedy the effects of past practices or to achieve diversity within the workforce to reflect the diversity in their community. In *Johnson v. Santa Clara County Transportation Agency*,[15] the agency had an affirmative action plan. A woman was promoted from within to the position of dispatcher, even though a male candidate had a slightly higher score on a test that was designed to measure aptitude for the job. The man brought a lawsuit alleging sex discrimination. The Court found that voluntary affirmative action was not reverse discrimination in this case, but employers should be careful in hiring and firing and layoff decisions versus promotion decisions. It is in the area of promotions that affirmative action is more likely to be upheld.

Affirmative action

Actions by an employer, either court-ordered or voluntary, that are designed to make up for past discrimination by hiring or promoting previously disadvantaged classes of workers.

In government contracts, President Lyndon Johnson's Executive Order 11246 prohibits private discrimination by federal contractors. This is important: millions of U.S. workers are employed by companies that do business with the federal government. Because of this executive order, many companies that do business with the government have adopted voluntary affirmative action programs. In 1995, the Supreme Court limited the extent to which the government could require contractors to establish affirmative action programs. The Court said that such programs are permissible only if they serve a "compelling national interest" and are "narrowly tailored" so that they minimize the harm to white males. To make a requirement for contractors, the government must show that the programs are needed to remedy past discrimination, that the programs have time limits, and that nondiscriminatory alternatives are not available.[16]

The Age Discrimination in Employment Act

The Age Discrimination in Employment Act (ADEA) of 1967 (amended in 1978 and again in 1986) prohibits discrimination based on age, and recourse to this law has been growing at a faster rate than any other federal antibias employment law. In particular, the act protects workers over forty years of age and prohibits forced retirement in most jobs because of age. Until 1987, federal law had permitted mandatory retirement at age seventy, but the 1986 amendments that took effect January 1, 1987, abolished the age ceiling except for a few jobs, such as firefighters, police officers, tenured university professors, and executives with annual pensions exceeding $44,000 (mind you, annual *pensions*, not salary). Like Title VII, the law has a BFOQ exception—for example, employers may set reasonable age limitations on certain high-stress jobs requiring peak physical condition.

There are important differences between the ADEA and Title VII, as *Gross v. FBL Financial Services, Inc.* (Section 5) makes clear. It is now more difficult to prove an age discrimination claim than a claim under Title VII.

Disabilities: Discrimination against the Handicapped

The 1990 Americans with Disabilities Act (ADA) prohibits employers from discriminating on the basis of disability. A disabled person is someone with a physical or mental impairment that substantially limits a major life activity or someone who is regarded as having such an impairment. This definition includes people with mental illness, epilepsy, visual impairment, dyslexia, and AIDS. It also covers anyone who has recovered from alcoholism or drug addiction. It specifically does not cover people with sexual disorders, pyromania, kleptomania, exhibitionism, or compulsive gambling.

Employers cannot disqualify an employee or job applicant because of disability as long as he or she can perform the essential functions of the job, with reasonable accommodation. Reasonable accommodation might include installing ramps for a wheelchair, establishing more flexible working hours, creating or modifying job assignments, and the like.

Reasonable accommodation means that there is no undue hardship for the employer. The law does not offer uniform standards for identifying what may be an undue hardship other than the imposition on the employer of a "significant difficulty or expense." Cases will differ: the resources and situation of each particular employer relative to the cost or difficulty of providing the accommodation will be considered; relative cost, rather than some definite dollar amount, will be the issue.

As with other areas of employment discrimination, job interviewers cannot ask questions about an applicant's disabilities before making a job offer; the interviewer may only ask whether the applicant can perform the work. Requirements for a medical exam are a violation of the ADA unless the exam is job related and required of all applicants for similar jobs. Employers may, however, use drug testing, although public employers are to some extent limited by the Fourth Amendment requirements of reasonableness.

The ADA's definition of disability is very broad. However, the Supreme Court has issued several important decisions that narrow the definition of what constitutes a disability under the act.

Two kinds of narrowing decisions stand out: one deals with "correctable conditions," and the other deals with repetitive stress injuries. In 1999, the Supreme Court reviewed a case that raised an issue of whether severe nearsightedness (which can be corrected with lenses) qualifies as a disability under the ADA.[17] The Supreme Court ruled that disability under the ADA will be measured according to how a person functions with corrective drugs or devices and not how the person functions without them. In *Orr v. Wal-Mart Stores, Inc.*, a federal appellate court held that a pharmacist who suffered from diabetes did not have a cause of action against Wal-Mart under the ADA as long as the condition could be corrected by insulin.[18]

The other narrowing decision deals with repetitive stress injuries. For example, carpal tunnel syndrome—or any other repetitive stress injury—could constitute a disability under the ADA. By compressing a nerve in the wrist through repetitive use, carpal tunnel syndrome causes pain and weakness in the hand. In 2002, the Supreme Court determined that while an employee with carpal tunnel syndrome could not perform all the manual tasks assigned to her, her condition did not constitute a disability under the ADA because it did not "extensively limit" her major life activities. (See [Content Removed: #mayer_1.0-ch50_s04_s04].) Check out the U.S. Department of Labor's website: http://www.dol.gov/dol/topic/disability/ada.htm.

Equal Pay Act

The Equal Pay Act of 1963 protects both men and women from pay discrimination based on sex. The act covers all levels of private sector employees and state and local government employees but not federal workers. The act prohibits disparity in pay for jobs that require equal skill and equal effort. Equal skill means equal experience, and equal effort means comparable mental and/or physical exertion. The act prohibits disparity in pay for jobs that require equal responsibility, such as equal supervision and accountability, or similar working conditions.

In making their determinations, courts will look at the stated requirements of a job as well as the actual requirements of the job. If two jobs are judged to be equal and similar, the employer cannot pay disparate wages to members of different sexes. Along with the EEOC enforcement, employees can also bring private causes of action against an employer for violating this act. There are four criteria that can be used as defenses in justifying differentials in wages: seniority, merit, quantity or quality of product, and any factor other than sex. The employer will bear the burden of proving any of these defenses.

A defense based on merit will require that there is some clearly measurable standard that justifies the differential. In terms of quantity or quality of product, there may be a commission structure, piecework structure, or quality-control-based payment system that will be permitted. Factors "other than sex" do not include so-called market forces. In *Glenn v. General Motors Corp.*, the U.S. Court of Appeals for the Eleventh Circuit rejected General Motor's argument that it was justified in paying three women less than their male counterparts on the basis of "the market force theory" that women will work for less than a man.[19]

Sexual Orientation, Gender Orientation

Sixteen states have laws prohibiting employment discrimination against gays or lesbians (sexual orientation) and gender orientation (trans-gender people). Three states have such laws prohibiting employment discrimination against sexual orientation, but not including gender orientation.[20] In July of 2014, President Obama signed an executive order making it illegal for federal contractors (businesses that contract with the federal government, like Boeing or a military backpack manufacturer) to discriminate fire or harass their employees based on their sexual orientation or gender identities, and it explicitly bans discrimination against transgender employees of the federal government. The part targeting federal contractors affects 24,000 companies employing roughly 28 million workers, or about one-fifth of the nation's workforce. It is expected that more states will bar discrimination on account of these factors.

Key Takeaway

Starting with employment at will as a common-law doctrine, we see many modifications by statute, particularly after 1960. Title VII of the Civil Rights Act of 1964 is the most significant, for it prohibits employers engaged in interstate commerce from discriminating on the basis of race, color, sex, religion, or national origin.

Sex discrimination, especially sexual harassment, has been a particularly fertile source of litigation. There are many defenses to Title VII claims: the employer may have a merit system or a seniority system in place, or there may be bona fide occupational qualifications in religion, gender, or national origin. In addition to Title VII, federal statutes limiting employment discrimination are the ADEA, the ADA, and the Equal Pay Act. In the last five years, several states have banned discrimination against gays, lesbians, and trans-gendered people, and under a 2014 Executive Order, federal contractors are prohibited from such discrimination.

Exercises

1. Go to the EEOC website. Describe the process by which an employee or ex-employee who wants to make a Title VII claim obtains a right-to-sue letter from the EEOC.
2. Again, looking at the EEOC website, find the statistical analysis of Title VII claims brought to the EEOC. What kind of discrimination is most frequent?
3. According to the EEOC website, what is "retaliation"? How frequent are retaliation claims relative to other kinds of claims?
4. Greg Connolly is a member of the Church of God and believes that premarital sex and abortion are sinful. He works as a pharmacist for Wal-Mart, and at many times during the week, he is the only pharmacist available to fill prescriptions. One product sold at his Wal-Mart is the morning-after pill (RU 468). Based on his religious beliefs, he tells his employer that he will refuse to fill prescriptions for the morning-after pill. Must Wal-Mart make a reasonable accommodation to his religious beliefs?

50.2 Employment at Will

Learning Objectives

1. Understand what is meant by employment at will under common law.
2. Explain the kinds of common-law (judicially created) exceptions to the employment-at-will doctrine, and provide examples.

At common law, an employee without a contract guaranteeing a job for a specific period was an employee at will and could be fired at any time and for any reason, or for no reason at all. After all, the employee without a contract can also quit work at will. The various federal statutes we examine in this chapter have made inroads on the at-will doctrine: yes, an employer can discharge an at-will employee for any reason, or no reason, but not for a *bad* reason. Employers cannot discharge employees for reasons now prohibited by Title VII, among other statutes, or for exercising their employment-law rights.

But beyond the prohibition against discharging at-will employees for exercising their rights, the courts and legislatures in more than forty states have made big changes in the at-will doctrine. They have done so under three theories: tort, contract, and duty of good faith and fair dealing. We will first consider the tort of wrongful discharge.

Courts have created a major exception to the employment-at-will rule by allowing the tort of wrongful discharge. *Wrongful discharge* means firing a worker for a bad reason—touched on previously. What is a bad reason? A bad reason can be (1) discharging an employee for refusing to violate a law, (2) discharging an employee for exercising a legal right, (3) discharging an employee for performing a legal duty, and (4) discharging an employee in a way that violates public policy.

Discharging an Employee for Refusing to Violate a Law

Some employers will not want employees to testify truthfully at trial. In one case, a nurse refused a doctor's order to administer a certain anesthetic when she believed it was wrong for that particular patient; the doctor, angry at the nurse for refusing to obey him, then administered the anesthetic himself. The patient soon stopped breathing. The doctor and others could not resuscitate him soon enough, and he suffered permanent brain damage. When the patient's family sued the hospital, the hospital told the nurse she would be in trouble if she testified. She did testify according to her oath in the court of law (i.e., truthfully), and after several months of harassment, was finally fired on a pretext. The hospital was held liable for the tort of wrongful discharge. As a general rule, you should not fire an employee for refusing to break the law.

Discharging an Employee for Exercising a Legal Right

Suppose Bob Berkowitz files a claim for workers' compensation for an accident at Pacific Gas & Electric, where he works and where the accident that injured him took place. He is fired for doing so, because the employer does not want to have its workers' comp premiums increased. In this case, the right exercised by Berkowitz is supported by public policy: he has a legal right to file the claim, and if he can establish that his discharge was caused by his filing the claim, he will prove the tort of wrongful discharge.

Discharging an Employee for Performing a Legal Duty

Courts have long held that an employee may not be fired for serving on a jury. This is so even though courts do recognize that many employers have difficulty replacing employees called for jury duty. Jury duty is an important civic obligation, and employers are not permitted to undermine it.

Discharging an Employee in a Way That Violates Public Policy

This is probably the most controversial basis for a tort of wrongful discharge. There is an inherent vagueness in the phrase "basic social rights, duties, or responsibilities." This is similar to the exception in contract law: the courts will not enforce contract provisions that violate public policy. (For the most part, public policy is found in statutes and in cases.) But what constitutes public policy is an important decision for state courts. In *Wagenseller v. Scottsdale Memorial Hospital*,[21] for example, a nurse who refused to "play along" with her coworkers on a rafting trip was discharged. The group of coworkers had socialized at night, drinking alcohol; when the partying was near its peak, the plaintiff refused to be part of a group that bared their buttocks to the tune of "Moon River" (a composition by Henry Mancini that was popular in the 1970s). The court, at great length, considered that "mooning" was a misdemeanor under Arizona law and that therefore her employer could not discharge her for refusing to violate a state law.

Other courts have gone so far as to include professional oaths and codes as part of public policy. In *Rocky Mountain Hospital and Medical Services v. Diane Mariani*, the Colorado Supreme Court determined that an at-will CPA could not be fired for refusing to "cook the books" as her employer insisted she do (that is, plug in numbers and results that did not reflect the true situation, using processes that were not in accord with her training).[22]

The court noted that the stated purpose of the licensing and registration of certified public accountants was to "provide for the maintenance of high standards of professional conduct by those so licensed and registered as certified public accountants." Further, the relevant CPA standard proclaimed that "A certificate holder shall not in the performance of professional services knowingly misrepresent facts, nor subordinate his judgment to others." The fact that Mariani's employer asked her to knowingly misrepresent facts was a sufficient basis in public policy to make her discharge wrongful.

Contract Modification of Employment at Will

Contract law can modify employment at will. Oral promises made in the hiring process may be enforceable even though the promises are not approved by top management. Employee handbooks may create implied contracts that specify personnel processes and statements that the employees can be fired only for a "just cause" or only after various warnings, notice, hearing, or other procedures.

Good Faith and Fair Dealing Standard

A few states, among them Massachusetts and California, have modified the at-will doctrine in a far-reaching way by holding that every employer has entered into an implied covenant of good faith and fair dealing with its employees. That means, the courts in these states say, that it is "bad faith" and therefore unlawful to discharge employees to avoid paying commissions or pensions due them. Under this implied covenant of fair dealing, any discharge without good cause—such as incompetence, corruption, or habitual tardiness—is actionable. This is not the law in most states, however.

Key Takeaway

Although employment at will is still the law, numerous exceptions have been established by judicial decision. Employers can be liable for the tort of wrongful discharge if they discharge an employee for refusing to violate a law, for exercising a legal right or performing a legal duty, or in a way that violates basic public policy.

Exercises

1. Richard Mudd, an employee of Compuserve, is called for jury duty in Wayne County, Michigan. His immediate supervisor, Harvey Lorie, lets him know that he "must" avoid jury duty at all costs. Mudd tells the judge of his circumstances and his need to be at work, but the judge refuses to let Mudd avoid jury duty. Mudd spends the next two weeks at trial. He sends regular e-mails and texts to Lorie during this time, but on the fourth day gets a text message from Lorie that says, "Don't bother to come back." When he does return, Lorie tells him he is fired. Does Mudd have a cause of action for the tort of wrongful discharge?
2. Olga Monge was a schoolteacher in her native Costa Rica. She moved to New Hampshire and attended college in the evenings to earn U.S. teaching credentials. At night, she worked at the Beebe Rubber Company after caring for her husband and three children during the day. When she applied for a better job at the plant, the foreman offered to promote her if

she would be "nice" and go out on a date with him. She refused, and he assigned her to a lower-wage job, took away her overtime, made her clean the washrooms, and generally ridiculed her. She finally collapsed at work, and he fired her. Does Monge have any cause of action?

50.3 Labor-Management Relations

Learning Objectives

After reading this section, you should understand the following:

1. A bit of the history of U.S. labor law: how unions were resisted for many years in the United States, the common-law principles used by employers and courts to do that, and how political and economic changes resulted in legalization of labor unions.
2. How and why labor-union representation has declined in the United States since the 1980s.
3. The four major federal labor laws in the United States.
4. The organization and functioning of the National Labor Relations Board.
5. What is meant by "unfair labor practices" under modern law.

A Brief History of American Labor Law

Here we briefly examine the history of American labor law, followed by a short examination of the laws themselves.

Over one hundred years, the federal law of labor relations has developed out of four basic statutes into an immense body of cases and precedents that regulate the formation and governance of labor unions, and the relationships among employers, unions, and union members. Like antitrust law, labor law is a complex subject that has spawned many specialized practitioners. Though specialized, it is a subject that no employer of any size can ignore, for labor law—despite more than four decades of decline in unionization—still has a pervasive influence on how business is conducted throughout the United States.

It is important to note at the outset that legal rights for laborers in the United States came about through physical and political struggles. The right of collective bargaining and the right to strike (and corresponding rights for employers, such as the lockout) were hard-won and incremental. The legislation described in this chapter began only after many years of labor-management strife, including judicial opposition to unions and violent and deadly confrontations between pro-union workers and management.

In 1806, the union of Philadelphia Journeymen Cordwainers was convicted of and bankrupted by charges of criminal conspiracy after a strike for higher wages, setting a precedent by which the U.S. government would combat unions for years to come. Andrew Jackson became a strike-breaker in 1834 when he sent troops to the construction sites of the Chesapeake and Ohio Canal. In 1877, a general strike halted the movement of U.S. railroads. In the following days, strike riots spread across the United States. The next week, federal troops were called out to force an end to the nationwide strike. At the Battle of the Viaduct in Chicago, federal troops (recently returned from massacring Native Americans) killed thirty workers and wounded over one hundred. Numerous other violent confrontations marked the post–Civil War period in America, including the violent rail strikes of 1877, when President Rutherford B. Hayes sent troops to prevent obstruction of the mails. President Grover Cleveland used soldiers to break the Pullman strike of 1894. Not until the anthracite coal strikes in Pennsylvania in 1902 did the U.S. government become a mediator between labor and management rather than an enforcer for industry.

Many U.S. labor historians see the first phase of the labor movement in terms of the struggles in the private sector that led to the labor legislation of the New Deal, described previously. The second phase of the movement, post-World War II, saw less violent confrontation and more peaceful resolution of labor issues in collective bargaining. Yet right-to-work states in the southern part of the United States as well as globalization weakened unions in the private sector. Right-to-work states provided a haven for certain kinds of manufacturing operations that wanted no part of bargaining with unions. Globalization meant that companies could (realistically) threaten to relocate outside the United States entirely. Unions in the public sector of the United States began to grow stronger relative to unions in the private sector: governments could not relocate as companies could, and over the last half century, there has been a gradual but significant decline in private sector unionism and growth in public sector unionism. However, as President-Elect, Donald Trump announced plans to curb the power of union workers in the federal government.[23]

Republicans elected with Tea Party support in 2010, most notably Scott Walker of Wisconsin, have launched major efforts against public sector unions, especially teachers' unions. States with higher levels of union membership tend to have higher median incomes. The International Monetary Fund has stated that rising inequality in the United States is directly related to the decline of the labor movement and union membership.

Labor and the Common Law in the Nineteenth Century

Labor unions appeared in modern form in the United States in the 1790s in Boston, New York, and Philadelphia. Early in the nineteenth century, employers began to seek injunctions against union organizing and other activities. Two doctrines were employed: (1) *common-law conspiracy* and (2) *common-law restraint of trade*. The first doctrine held that workers who joined together were acting criminally as conspirators, regardless of the means chosen or the objectives sought.

The second doctrine—common-law restraint of trade—was also a favorite theory used by the courts to enjoin unionizing and other joint employee activities. Workers who banded together to seek better wages or working conditions were, according to this theory, engaged in concerted activity that restrained trade in their labor. This theory made sense when conventional wisdom held that an employer was entitled to buy labor as cheaply as possible—the price would obviously rise if workers were allowed to bargain jointly rather than if they were required to offer their services individually on the open market.

Labor in the Early 20th Century

By 1912, labor had organized widely; it played a pivotal role in electing Woodrow Wilson and giving him a Democratic Congress, which responded in 1914 with the Clayton Act's "labor exemption." Section 6 of the Clayton Act effectively reversed judicial determinations that labor unions' activities were a violation of antitrust laws; it provides that labor unions are not "illegal combinations or conspiracies in restraint of trade, under the antitrust laws." Section 20 forbids courts from issuing injunctions in cases involving strikes, boycotts, and other concerted union activities (which were declared to be lawful) as long as they arose out of disputes between employer and employees over the terms of employment.

But even the Clayton Act proved of little lasting value to the unions. In 1921, the Supreme Court again struck out against a secondary boycott that crippled the significance of the Clayton Act provisions. In the case, a machinists' union staged a boycott against an employer (by whom the members were not employed) in order to pressure the employer into permitting one of its factories to be unionized. The Court ruled that the Clayton Act exemptions applied only in cases involving an employer and its own employees.[24] Without the ability to boycott under those circumstances, and with the threat of antitrust prosecutions or treble-damage actions, labor would be hard-pressed to unionize many companies. More antiunion decisions followed.

Moves toward Modern Labor Legislation

In 1926, Congress enacted the Railway Labor Act. This statute imposed a duty on railroads to bargain in good faith with their employees' elected representatives. The act also established the National Mediation Board to mediate disputes that were not resolved in contract negotiations. The stage was set for more comprehensive national labor laws. These would come with the Great Depression.

The Norris-LaGuardia Act, 1932

The first labor law of the Great Depression was the Norris–La Guardia Act of 1932. It dealt with the propensity of federal courts to issue preliminary injunctions, often ex parte (i.e., after hearing only the plaintiff's argument), against union activities. Even though the permanent injunction might later have been denied, the effect of the vaguely worded preliminary injunction would have been sufficient to destroy the attempt to unionize. The Norris–La Guardia Act forbids federal courts from temporarily or permanently enjoining certain union activities, such as peaceful picketing and strikes. The act is applicable toward any "labor dispute," defined as embracing "any controversy concerning terms or conditions of employment, or concerning the association or representation of persons in negotiating, fixing, maintaining, changing, or seeking to arrange terms or conditions of employment, regardless of whether or not the disputants stand in the proximate relation of employer and employee." This language thus permitted the secondary boycott that had been held as a violation of the antitrust laws in the 1921 case of *Duplex Printing Press v. Deering*.[25] The act also bars the courts from enforcing so-called yellow-dog contracts—agreements that employees made with their employer not to join unions.

The National Labor Relations Act (the Wagner Act), 1935

In 1935, Congress finally enacted a comprehensive labor statute. The National Labor Relations Act (NLRA), often called the Wagner Act after its sponsor, Senator Robert F. Wagner, declared in Section 7 that workers in interstate commerce "have the right to self-organization, to form, join or assist labor organizations, to bargain collectively through representatives of their own choosing, and to engage in concerted activities for the purpose of collective bargaining or other mutual aid or protection." Section 8 sets out five key **unfair labor practices**:

unfair labor practices

Acts that violate the National Labor Relations Act, such as failing to bargain in good faith. Unfair labor practices can be committed by employers and by unions.

1. Interference with the rights guaranteed by Section 7.
2. Interference with the organization of unions, or domination by the employer of union administration (this section thus outlaws "company unions"—sham unions run by the employer).
3. Discrimination against employees who belong to unions.
4. Discharging or otherwise discriminating against employees who seek relief under the act.
5. Refusing to bargain collectively, in good faith, with union representatives. The NLRB requires employers and unions to bargain over "terms and condition of employment." Wages, hours, and working conditions—whether workers must wear uniforms, when the lunch hour begins, the type of safety equipment on hand—are well-understood terms and conditions of employment. But the statutory phrase is vague, and the cases abound with debates over whether a term insisted on by union or management is within the statutory phrase.

The procedures for forming a union to represent employees in an appropriate "bargaining unit" are set out in the act. Finally, the Wagner Act established the National Labor Relations Board (NLRB) as an independent federal administrative agency, with power to investigate and remedy unfair labor practices.

The Supreme Court upheld the constitutionality of the act in 1937 in a series of five cases. In the first, *NLRB v. Jones & Laughlin Steel Corp.*, the Court ruled that congressional power under the Commerce Clause extends to activities that might affect the flow of interstate commerce, as labor relations certainly did.[26] Through its elaborate mechanisms for establishing collective bargaining as a basic national policy, the Wagner Act had a profound effect on interstate commerce in the mid-20th century.

The Taft-Hartley Act (Labor-Management Relations Act), 1947

The Wagner Act did not attempt to restrict union activities in any way. For a dozen years, opponents of unions sought some means of curtailing the breadth of opportunity opened up to unions by the Wagner Act. After failing to obtain relief in the Supreme Court, they took their case to Congress and finally succeeded after World War II. In 1947, for the first time in 17 years, Congress had Republican majorities in both houses. Congress responded to critics of "big labor" with the Taft-Hartley Act, passed over President Truman's veto. Taft-Hartley—known formally as the Labor-Management Relations Act—did not repeal the protections given employees and unions under the NLRA. Instead, it balanced union power with a declaration of rights of employers. In particular, Taft-Hartley lists six unfair labor practices of unions, including secondary boycotts, strikes aimed at coercing an employer to fire an employee who refuses to join a union, and so-called jurisdictional strikes over which union should be entitled to do specified jobs at the work site.

closed shop

A firm where potential employees must belong to a union before being hired and must remain a member during employment.

In addition to these provisions, Taft-Hartley contains several others that balance the rights of unions and employers. For example, the act guarantees both employers and unions the right to present their views on unionization and collective bargaining. Like employers, unions became obligated to bargain in good faith. The act outlaws the **closed shop** (where a worker must belong to a union before being hired), gives federal courts the power to enforce collective bargaining agreements, and permits private parties to sue for damages arising out of a secondary boycott. The act also created the Federal Mediation and Conciliation Service to cope with strikes that create national emergencies, and it declared strikes by federal employees to be unlawful. It was this provision that President Reagan invoked in 1981 to fire air traffic controllers who walked off the job for higher pay.

The Landrum-Griffin Act, 1959

Congressional hearings in the 1950s brought to light union corruption and abuses and led in 1959 to the last of the major federal labor statutes, the Landrum-Griffin Act (Labor-Management Reporting and Disclosure Act). It established a series of controls on internal union procedures, including the method of electing union officers and the financial controls necessary to avoid the problems of corruption that had been encountered. Landrum-Griffin also restricted union picketing under various circumstances, narrowed the loopholes in Taft-Hartley's prohibitions against secondary boycotts, and banned "hot cargo" agreements.

Labor law in the 21st Century

Only about 9% of non-agricultural workers are members of unions in 2015. This represents a steady decline in union membership since its heydays in the 1950s. There are a number of reasons:

1. Automation, including robots, continues to displace workers.
2. American businesses—in order to stay competitive with foreign labor—have moved jobs to states that have weak unions or, again, have set up shop in foreign countries where unions are weak or illegal.
3. Unions have achieved many of the basic goals they had one hundred years ago. The eight-hour day is now pretty much standard, and the minimum wage, paltry as it is, is—with various

federal welfare programs—sufficient to keep most people from starvation (though 25% of children in the U.S. have "food insecurity"—they don't know for sure they will have enough to eat tomorrow[27]).

4. After President Ronald Reagan denounced the Air Traffic Controllers' union in 1981 (following an illegal strike) and the union was decertified, it became much more politically palatable for management to "cut the fat" from their organizations and resist unionization.
5. Labor unions tend to be out-gunned in the campaign finance merry-go-round: capital (businesses) have more money to influence politics than labor does.

There is much talk recently about the inequality of income distribution in the United States. The rich control a very significantly disproportionate share of wealth—in 2015, the distribution is nearly the same as it was in 1929. Some commentators see the decline of labor unions as a part of the reason. The following chart plots the middle-class income and union membership rates.

As union membership declines, share of income going to middle class shrinks

FIGURE 1

As union membership declines, the share of income going to the middle class shrinks

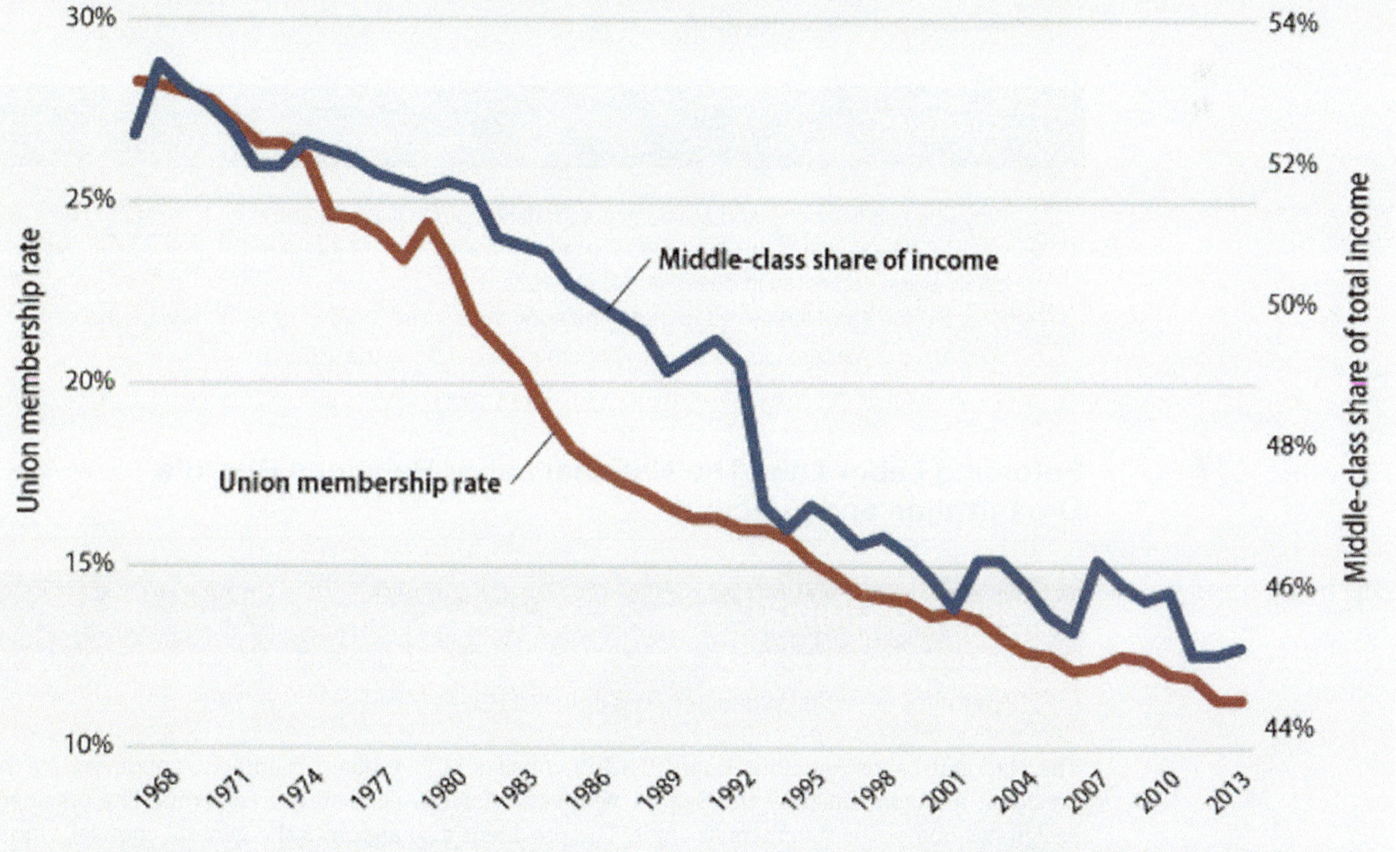

Source: Center for American Progress Action Fund analysis based on union membership rates from updated Barry T. Hirsch, David A. MacPherson, and Wayne G. Vroman, "Estimates of Union Density by State," *Monthly Labor Review* 124 (7) (2001): 51–55, available at http://unionstats.gsu.edu/MonthlyLaborReviewArticle.htm. Middle-class share of total income is from Bureau of the Census, Table H-2. *Share of Aggregate Income Recieved by Each Fifth and Top 5 Percent of Households* (2013), available at http://www.census.gov/hhes/www/income/data/historical/household.

Although union membership has decreased significantly, the basic laws remain on the books. If workers feel strongly enough that they are not getting a fair share of the economy's productivity, unions may well rise again. The threat that they might is probably not lost on employers (for example, Wal-Mart announced in early 2015 that it would raise its minimum wage to $9.00 per hour, 24% higher than the federal minimum.[28])

Key Takeaway

Common-law doctrines were used in the early history of the labor movement to enjoin unionizing and other joint employee activities. These were deemed to be restraints of trade that violated antitrust laws. In addition, common-law conspiracy charges provided criminal enforcement against joint employee actions and agreements. Politically, the labor movement gained some traction in 1912 and got an antitrust-law exemption in the Clayton Act. But it was not until the Great Depression and the New Deal that the right of collective bargaining was recognized by federal statute in the National Labor Relations Act. Subsequent legislation (Taft-Hartley and Landrum-Griffin) added limits to union activities and controls over unions in their internal functions.

In the 21st century, the percentage of employees who are unionized continues to decline (except among government workers). Some have suggested that this phenomena and the hollowing-out of the middle class are related. In any event, the laws remain on the books. Given the proper conditions, unions may rise again.

Exercises

1. Why were early labor-union advocates sometimes put in jail or prison?
2. What did the Norris-LaGuardia Act of 1932 do to address the problem (in labor-union advocates' eyes) presented in question #1, above?
3. How did the Taft-Hartley Act of 1947 "balance the scales" more in favor of management?
4. Why has the percentage of union members declined since the 1950s?

Enforcing Labor Law: The National Labor Relations Board's Organization and Functions

Learning Objective

1. Explain the organization and functions of the NLRB.

The National Labor Relations Board (NLRB) consists of five board members, appointed by the president and confirmed by the Senate, who serve for five-year, staggered terms. The president designates one of the members as chair. The president also appoints the general counsel, who is in charge of the board's investigatory and prosecutorial functions and who represents the NLRB when it goes (or is taken) to court. The general counsel also oversees the thirty-three regional offices scattered throughout the country, each of which is headed by a regional director.

The NLRB serves two primary functions: (1) it may, as appropriate, oversee union elections to make sure employees can freely select the appropriate union to represent them, and (2) it investigates allegations of unfair labor practices and provides remedies as required. Parties—whether employer or union—may appeal to the federal court of appeals if they feel a ruling by the NLRB is improper.

A union gets voted in as the employees' bargaining representative after it wins an election. The election must be fair: the employer cannot interfere with the employees' free choice. If it does interfere, the NLRB may declare the action an unfair labor practice and set aside the election results. These elections can be high-stakes affairs, and both sides hire specialized advisers (most often lawyers) who can guide the thrust and parry of the antagonists.

The results of all the electioneering are worth noting. In the 1980s, some 20 percent of the total U.S. workforce was unionized. As of 2009, the union membership rate was 12.3 percent, and more union members were public employees than private sector employees. Fairly or unfairly, public employee unions were under attack as of 2014, as their wages generally exceeded the average wages of other categories of workers by some 15%. That's good news for the employees, but maybe not such good news for the employer who has to deal with non-unionized competition, either nationally or internationally.

Key Takeaway

The National Labor Relations Board is a federal administrative agency charged with the responsibility to enforce the National Labor Relations Act (all of the major federal labor laws consist of the NLRA). It investigates charges of unfair labor practices and, as appropriate, oversees the fairness of union elections.

Exercises

1. What control does the U.S. president have over labor law, and how is that control exercised?
2. Who suffers when public-employee union members succeed in getting good pay and benefit packages? Who could object to that?

50.4 Other Employment-Related Laws

Learning Objective

1. Understand the various federal and state statutes that affect employers in the areas of plant closings, pensions, workers' compensation, use of polygraphs, and worker safety.

The Federal Plant-Closing Act

Because programs to support dislocated workers depend heavily on the giving of advance notice, a national debate on the issue in the late 1980s culminated in 1988 in Congress's enactment of the Worker Adjustment and Retraining Notification (WARN) Act, the formal name of the federal plant-closing act. Under this law (with some exceptions), businesses with 100 or more employees must give employees or their local bargaining units, along with the local city or county government, at least sixty days' notice whenever (1) at least 50 employees in a single plant or office facility will lose their jobs or face long-term layoffs or a reduction of more than half their working hours as the result of a shutdown and (2) a shutdown will require long-term layoffs of 500 employees or at least a third of the workforce. An employer who violates the act is liable to employees for back pay that they would have received during the notice period and may be liable to other fines and penalties.

The Employee Polygraph Protection Act

Studies calling into question the reliability of various forms of lie detectors led Congress in 1988 to legislate against their use by private businesses. The Employee Polygraph Protection Act forbids private employers from using lie detectors (including such devices as voice stress analyzers) for any reason. Neither employees nor applicants for jobs may be required or even asked to submit to them. (The act has some exceptions for public employers, defense and intelligence businesses, private companies in the security business, and manufacturers of controlled substances.)

Occupational Safety and Health Act

In a heavily industrialized society, workplace safety is a major concern. Hundreds of studies for more than a century have documented the gruesome toll taken by hazardous working conditions in mines, on railroads, and in factories from tools, machines, treacherous surroundings, and toxic chemicals and other substances. Studies in the late 1960s showed that more than 14,000 workers were killed and 2.2 million were disabled annually—at a cost of more than $8 billion (about $53 billion in 2014 dollars) and a loss of more than 250 million worker days. Congress responded in 1970 with the Occupational Safety and Health Act, the primary aim of which is "to assure so far as possible every working man and woman in the Nation safe and healthful working conditions."

The act imposes on each employer a general duty to furnish a place of employment free from recognized hazards likely to cause death or serious physical harm to employees. It also gives the secretary of labor the power to establish national health and safety standards. The standard-making power has been delegated to the Occupational Safety and Health Administration (OSHA), an agency within the U.S. Department of Labor. The agency has the authority to inspect workplaces covered by the act whenever it receives complaints from employees or reports about fatal or multiple injuries. The agency may assess penalties and proceed administratively to enforce its standards. Criminal provisions of the act are enforced by the Justice Department.

Employee Retirement Income Security Act

The Employee Retirement Income Security Act of 1974 (ERISA) is a federal law that sets minimum standards for pension plans in private industry. ERISA does not require any employer to establish a pension plan. It only requires that those who establish plans must meet certain minimum standards. The law generally does not specify how much money a participant must be paid as a benefit. ERISA requires plans to regularly provide participants with information about the plan including information about plan features and funding; sets minimum standards for participation, vesting, benefit accrual and funding; requires accountability of plan fiduciaries; and gives participants the right to sue for benefits and breaches of fiduciary duty. ERISA also guarantees payment of certain benefits through the Pension Benefit Guaranty Corporation, a federally chartered corporation, if a defined plan is terminated. The Department of Labor's (DOL) Employee Benefits Security Administration (EBSA) enforces ERISA.

Fair Labor Standards Act

In the midst of the Depression, Congress enacted at President Roosevelt's urging a national minimum wage law, the Fair Labor Standards Act of 1938 (FLSA). The act prohibits most forms of child labor and established a scale of minimum wages for the regular workweek and a higher scale for overtime. (The original hourly minimum was twenty-five cents, although the administrator of the Wage and Hour Division of the U.S. Department of Labor, a position created by the act, could raise the minimum rate industry by industry.) The act originally was limited to certain types of work: that which was performed in transporting goods in interstate commerce or in producing goods for shipment in interstate commerce.

Employers quickly learned that they could limit the minimum wage by, for example, separating the interstate and intrastate components of their production. Within the next quarter century, the scope of the FLSA was considerably broadened, so that it now covers all workers in businesses that do a particular dollar-volume of goods that move in interstate commerce, regardless of whether a particular employee actually works in the interstate component of the business. It now covers between 80 and 90 percent of all persons privately employed outside of agriculture, and a lesser but substantial percentage of agricultural workers and state and local government employees. Violations of the act are investigated by the administrator of the Wage and Hour Division, who has authority to negotiate back pay on the employee's behalf. If no settlement is reached, the Labor Department may sue on the employee's behalf, or the employee, armed with a notice of the administrator's calculations of back wages due, may sue in federal or state court for back pay. Under the FLSA, a successful employee will receive double the amount of back wages due.

The federal minimum wage is, as of July, 2015, $7.25 per hour. It is a shamefully low wage rate; it amounts to $14,500 per year (40 hours a week for 50 weeks). You could not live on $14,500 per year. As Congress has been remarkably unresponsive, state and local governments have stepped in. In May of 2015, Los Angeles became the largest city in the U.S. to raise the minimum wage. "San Francisco, Chicago, Seattle, and Oakland, Calif., have already approved increases, and dozens more are considering doing the same. In 2014, a number of Republican-leaning states like Alaska and and South Dakota raised their state-level minimum wage by ballot initiative."[29]

FIGURE 50.2 Real Value of the Federal Minimum Wage in Constant 2013 Dollars

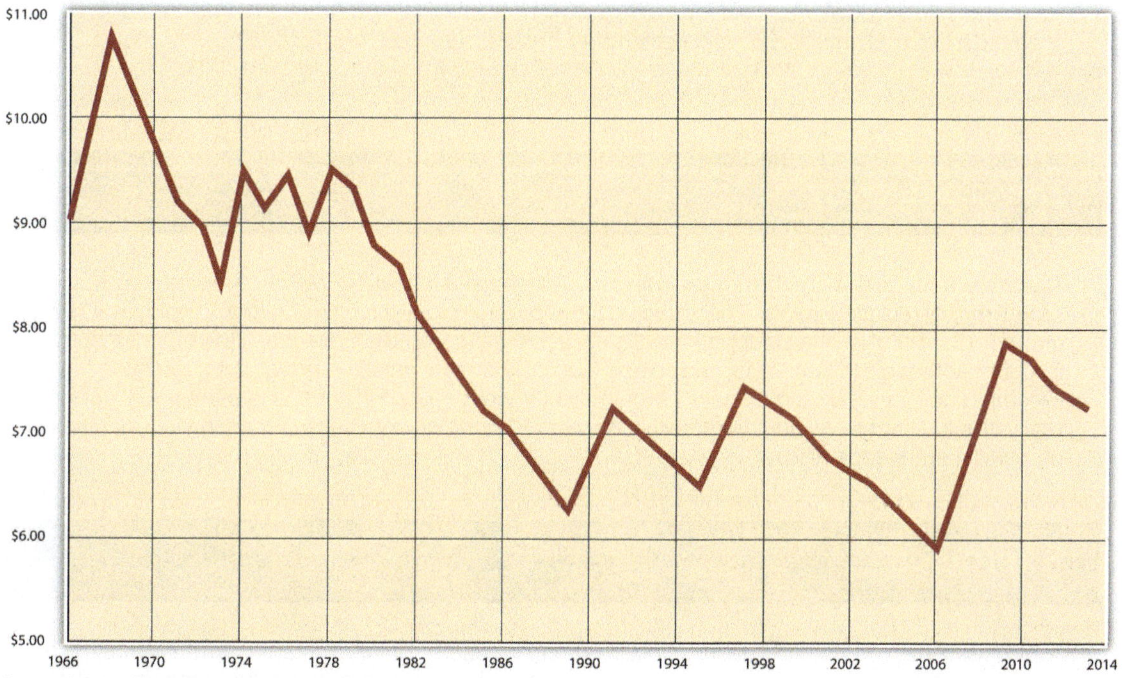

Source: National Employment Law Project at http://campaign.nelp.org/page/-/rtmw/uploads/Minimum-Wage-2013-new.png

Workers' Compensation Laws

Since the beginning of the twentieth century, work-related injuries or illnesses have been covered under state workers' compensation laws that provide a set amount of weekly compensation for disabilities caused by accidents and illnesses suffered on the job. The compensation plans also pay hospital and medical expenses necessary to treat workers who are injured by, or become ill from, their work, and it provides pensions for employees who cannot work, or for family members of employees who are killed in industrial accidents. In assuring workers of compensation, the plans eliminate the hazards and uncertainties of lawsuits by eliminating the need to prove fault. Employers fund the compensation plans by paying into statewide plans or purchasing insurance.

Other State Laws

Although it may appear that most employment law is federal, employment discrimination is largely governed by state law because Congress has so declared it. The Civil Rights Act of 1964 tells federal courts to defer to state agencies to enforce anti-discrimination provisions of parallel state statutes with remedies similar to those of the federal law. Moreover, many states have gone beyond federal law in banning certain forms of discrimination. Thus, well before enactment of the Americans with Disabilities Act, more than forty states prohibited such discrimination in private employment. More than a dozen states ban employment discrimination based on marital status, a category not covered by federal law. Two states have laws that protect those that may be considered "overweight."

In late June of 2015, the United States Supreme Court declared that same-sex couples have a constitutional right to marry, but that ruling does not guarantee gays and lesbian people won't be discriminated in employment. In March 2015, the Human Rights Campaign observed:

> *"Qualified, hardworking Americans are denied job opportunities, fired or otherwise discriminated against just because they are lesbian, gay, bisexual or transgender (LGBT). There is no federal law that consistently protects LGBT individuals from employment discrimination; there are no state laws in 29 states that explicitly prohibit discrimination based on sexual orientation, and in 32 states that do so based on gender identity. As a result, LGBT people face serious discrimination in employment, including being fired, being denied a promotion and experiencing harassment on the job."*[30]

Key Takeaway

There are a number of important federal employment laws affecting things other than collective bargaining or discrimination. These include the federal plant-closing act, the Employee Polygraph Protection Act, the Occupational Safety and Health Act, the Employee Retirement Income Security Act, and the Fair Labor Standards Act. At the state level, workers' compensation laws preempt common-law claims against employers for work-related injuries, and state equal opportunity employment laws provide remedies for certain kinds of workplace discrimination that have no parallel at the federal level.

Exercises

1. United Artists is a corporation doing business in Texas. United Pension Fund is a defined-contribution employee pension benefit plan sponsored by United Artists for employees. Each employee has his or her own individual pension account, but plan assets are pooled for investment purposes. The plan is administered by the board of trustees. From 1977 to 1986, seven of the trustees made a series of loans to themselves from the plan. These trustees did not (1) require the borrowers to submit a written application for the loans, (2) assess the prospective borrower's ability to repay loans, (3) specify a period in which the loans were to be repaid, or (4) call the loans when they remained unpaid. The trustees also charged less than fair-market-value interest for the loans. The secretary of labor sued the trustees, alleging that they had breached their fiduciary duty in violation of ERISA. Who won?[31]
2. Arrow Automotive Industries remanufactures and distributes automobile and truck parts. Its operating plants produce identical product lines. The company is planning to open a new facility in Santa Maria, California. The employees at the Arrow plant in Hudson, Massachusetts, are represented by a union, the United Automobile, Aerospace, and Agricultural

Implement Workers of America. The Hudson plant has a history of unprofitable operations. The union called a strike when the existing collective bargaining agreement expired and a new agreement could not be reached. After several months, the board of directors of the company voted to close the striking plant. The closing would give Arrow a 24 percent increase in gross profits and free capital and equipment for the new Santa Maria plant. In addition, the existing customers of the Hudson plant could be serviced by the Spartanburg, South Carolina, plant, which is currently being underutilized. What would have to be done if the plant-closing act applied to the situation?[32]

50.5 Cases

Disparate Treatment: Burdens of Proof

Barbano v. Madison County

922 F.2d 139 (2d Cir. 1990)

Factual Background

At the Madison County (New York State) Veterans Service Agency, the position of director became vacant. The County Board of Supervisors created a committee of five men to hold interviews for the position. The committee interviewed Maureen E. Barbano and four others. When she entered the interview room, she heard someone say, "Oh, another woman." At the beginning of the interview, Donald Greene said he would not consider "some woman" for the position. Greene also asked Barbano some personal questions about her family plans and whether her husband would mind if she transported male veterans. Ms. Barbano answered that the questions were irrelevant and discriminatory. However, Greene replied that the questions were relevant because he did not want to hire a woman who would get pregnant and quit. Another committee member, Newbold, agreed that the questions were relevant, and no committee member said the questions were not relevant.

None of the interviewers rebuked Greene or objected to the questions, and none of them told Barbano that she need not answer them. Barbano did state that if she decided to have a family she would take no more time off than medically necessary. Greene once again asked whether Barbano's husband would object to her "running around the country with men" and said he would not want his wife to do it. Barbano said she was not his wife. The interview concluded after Barbano asked some questions about insurance.

After interviewing several other candidates, the board hired a man. Barbano sued the county for sex discrimination in violation of Title VII, and the district court held in her favor. She was awarded $55,000 in back pay (about $117,000 in 2015 dollars), prejudgment interest, and attorney's fees. Madison County appealed the judgment of Federal District Judge McAvoy; Barbano cross-appealed, asking for additional damages.

The court found that Barbano had established a prima facie case of discrimination under Title VII, thus bringing into issue the appellants' purported reasons for not hiring her. [A prima facie case of discrimination is where the plaintiff has sufficient evidence to prove discrimination; then the employer has the burden to show discrimination was not the reason for the action complained of, and if the employer cannot, the employee victim will likely win.] The appellants provided four reasons why they chose Wagner over Barbano, which the district court rejected either as unsupported by the record or as a pretext for discrimination in light of Barbano's interview. The district court then found that because of Barbano's education and experience in social services, the appellants had failed to prove that absent the discrimination, they still would not have hired Barbano. Accordingly, the court awarded Barbano back pay, prejudgment interest, and attorney's fees. Subsequently, the court denied Barbano's request for front pay and a mandatory injunction ordering her appointment as director upon the next vacancy. This appeal and cross-appeal followed.

From the Opinion of FEINBERG, CIRCUIT JUDGE

Appellants argue that the district court erred in finding that Greene's statements during the interview showed that the Board discriminated in making the hiring decision, and that there was no direct evidence of discrimination by the Board, making it improper to require that appellants prove that they would not have hired Barbano absent the discrimination. Barbano in turn challenges the adequacy of the relief awarded to her by the district court.

* * *

B. The Employer's Burden

Having found that Barbano carried her burden of proving discrimination, the district court then placed the burden on appellants to prove by a preponderance of the evidence that, absent the discrimination, they would not have hired Barbano for the position. Appellants argue that this burden is only placed on an employer if the plaintiff proves discrimination by direct evidence, and since Barbano's evidence of discrimination was merely circumstantial, the district court erred by placing the burden of proof on them. Appellants, however, misapprehend the nature of Barbano's proof and thus the governing legal standard.

The burden is properly placed on the defendant "once the plaintiff establishes by direct evidence that an illegitimate factor played a motivating or substantial role in an employment decision." [Citation.] Thus, the key inquiry on this aspect of the case is whether the evidence is direct, that is, whether it shows that the impermissible criterion played some part in the decision-making process. If plaintiff provides such evidence, the fact-finder must then determine whether the evidence shows that the impermissible criterion played a motivating or substantial part in the hiring decision. [Citation.]

As we found above, the evidence shows that Barbano's gender was clearly a factor in the hiring decision. That the discrimination played a substantial role in that decision is shown by the importance of the recommendation to the Board. As Rafte testified, the Board utilizes a committee system, and so the Board "usually accepts" a committee's recommendation, as it did here when it unanimously voted to appoint Wagner [another candidate]. Had the Board distanced itself from Barbano's allegations of discrimination and attempted to ensure that it was not relying upon illegitimate criteria in adopting the Committee's recommendation, the evidence that discrimination played a substantial role in the Board's decision would be significantly weakened. The Board showed no inclination to take such actions, however, and in adopting the discriminatory recommendation allowed illegitimate criteria to play a substantial role in the hiring decision.

The district court thus properly required appellants to show that the Board would not have hired Barbano in the absence of discrimination. "The employer has not yet been shown to be a violator, but neither is it entitled to the . . . presumption of good faith concerning its employment decisions. At this point the employer may be required to convince the fact-finder that, despite the smoke, there is no fire." [Citation.]

[The court reviewed the reasons the employer gave for choosing another candidate—a man—instead of Barbano.] * * *

To be sure, both candidates were qualified for the Director's position, and it is not our job—nor was it the district court's—to decide which one was preferable. However, there is nothing to indicate that [the lower court judge] misconceived his function in this phase of the case, which was to decide whether appellants failed to prove by a preponderance of the evidence that they would not have hired Barbano even if they had not discriminated against her. The judge found that defendants had not met that burden. We must decide whether that finding was clearly erroneous, and we cannot say that it was.

Case Questions

1. Madison County contended that Barbano needed to provide "direct evidence" of discrimination that had played a motivating or substantial part in the decision. What would such evidence look like? Is it likely that most plaintiffs who are discriminated against because of their gender would be able to get "direct evidence" that gender was a motivating or substantial factor?
2. The "clearly erroneous" standard is applied here, as it is in many cases where appellate courts review trial court determinations. State the test, and say why the appellate court believed that the trial judge's ruling was not "clearly erroneous."

Title VII and Hostile Work Environment

Duncan v. General Motors Corporation
300 F.3d 928 (8th Cir. 2002)

OPINION BY HANSEN, Circuit Judge.

The Junior College District of St. Louis (the College) arranged for Diana Duncan to provide in-house technical training at General Motors Corporation's (GMC) manufacturing facility in Wentzville, Missouri. Throughout her tenure at GMC, Duncan was subjected to unwelcome attention by a GMC employee, James Booth, which culminated in Duncan's resignation. Duncan subsequently filed this suit under Title VII of the Civil Rights Act and the Missouri Human Rights Act * * * alleging that she was sexually harassed and constructively discharged. A jury found in favor of Duncan and awarded her $4,600 in back pay, $700,000 [about $96,000 in 2017 dollars] in emotional distress damages on her sexual harassment claim, and $300,000 in emotional distress damages on her constructive discharge claim. GMC appeals from the district court's denial of its post trial motion for judgment as a matter of law, and the district court's award of attorneys' fees attendant to the post trial motion. We reverse.

I. [Facts]

Diana Duncan worked as a technical training clerk in the high-tech area at GMC as part of the College's Center for Business, Industry, and Labor program from August 1994 until May 1997. Duncan provided in-house training support to GMC employees.

Duncan first learned about the College's position at GMC from Booth, a United Auto Workers Union technology training coordinator for GMC. Booth frequented the country club where Duncan worked as a waitress and a bartender. Booth asked Duncan if she knew anyone who had computer and typing skills and who might be interested in a position at GMC. Duncan expressed interest in the job. Booth brought the pre-employment forms to Duncan at the country club, and he forwarded her completed forms to Jerry Reese, the manager of operations, manufacturing, and training for the College. * * * Duncan began work at GMC in August 1994. Two weeks after Duncan began working at GMC, Booth requested an off-site meeting with her at a local restaurant. Booth explained to Duncan that he was in love with a married coworker and that his own marriage was troubled. Booth then propositioned Duncan by asking her if she would have a relationship with him. Duncan rebuffed his advance and left the restaurant. The next day Duncan mentioned the incident to the paint department supervisor Joe Rolen, who had no authority over Booth. Duncan did not report Booth's conduct to either Reese (her supervisor) at the College or Ish (Booth's management counterpart) at GMC. However, she did confront Booth, and he apologized for his behavior. He made no further such "propositions." Duncan stated that Booth's manner toward her after she declined his advance became hostile, and he became more critical of her work. For example, whenever she made a typographical error, he told her that she was incompetent and that he should hire a "Kelly Services" person to replace her. Duncan admitted that Booth's criticisms were often directed at other employees as well, including male coworkers.

Duncan testified to numerous incidents of Booth's inappropriate behavior. Booth directed Duncan to create a training document for him on his computer because it was the only computer with the necessary software. The screen saver that Booth had selected to use on his computer was a picture of a naked woman. Duncan testified to four or five occasions when Booth would unnecessarily touch her hand when she handed him the telephone. In addition, Booth had a planter in his office that was shaped like a slouched man wearing a sombrero. The planter had a hole in the front of the man's pants that allowed for a cactus to protrude. The planter was in plain view to anyone entering Booth's office. Booth also kept a child's pacifier that was shaped like a penis in his office that he occasionally showed to his coworkers and specifically to Duncan on two occasions.

In 1995, Duncan requested a pay increase and told Booth that she would like to be considered for an illustrator's position. Booth said that she would have to prove her artistic ability by drawing his planter. Duncan objected, particularly because previous applicants for the position were required to draw automotive parts and not his planter. Ultimately, Duncan learned that she was not qualified for the position because she did not possess a college degree.

Additionally in 1995, Booth and a College employee created a "recruitment" poster that was posted on a bulletin board in the high-tech area. The poster portrayed Duncan as the president and CEO of the Man Hater's Club of America. It listed the club's membership qualifications as: "Must always be in control of: (1) Checking, Savings, all loose change, etc.; (2) (Ugh) Sex; (3) Raising children our way!; (4) Men must always do household chores; (5) Consider T.V. Dinners a gourmet meal."...

On May 5, 1997, Booth asked Duncan to type a draft of the beliefs of the "He-Men Women Hater's Club." The beliefs included the following:

> *—Constitutional Amendment, the 19th, giving women [the] right to vote should be repealed. Real He-Men indulge in a lifestyle of cursing, using tools, handling guns, driving trucks, hunting and of course, drinking beer.*
>
> *—Women really do have coodies [sic] and they can spread.*
>
> *—Women [are] the cause of 99.9 per cent of stress in men.*
>
> *—Sperm has a right to live.*
>
> *—All great chiefs of the world are men.*
>
> *—Prostitution should be legalized.*

Duncan refused to type the beliefs and resigned two days later.

Duncan testified that she complained to anyone who would listen to her about Booth's behavior, beginning with paint department supervisor Joe Rolen after Booth propositioned her in 1994. Duncan testified that between 1994 and 1997 she complained several times to Reese at the College about Booth's behavior, which would improve at least in the short term after she spoke with Reese.

...

Duncan filed a charge of sex discrimination with the Equal Employment Opportunity Commission (EEOC) on October 30, 1997. The EEOC issued Duncan a right to sue notice on April 17, 1998. Alleging sexual harassment and constructive discharge, Duncan filed suit against the College and GMC under both Title VII of the Civil Rights Act and the Missouri Human Rights Act. Duncan settled with the College prior to trial. After the jury found in Duncan's favor on both counts against GMC, GMC filed a post-trial motion for judgment as a matter of law or, alternatively, for a new trial. The district court denied the motion. The district court also awarded Duncan attorneys' fees in conjunction with GMC's post-trial motion. GMC appeals.

II. [Analysis]

A. Hostile Work Environment

GMC argues that it was entitled to judgment as a matter of law on Duncan's hostile work environment claim because she failed to prove a prima facie case. We agree. * * *

It is undisputed that Duncan satisfies the first two elements of her prima facie case: she is a member of a protected group and Booth's attention was unwelcome. We also conclude that the harassment was based on sex....Although there is some evidence in the record that indicates some of Booth's behavior, and the resulting offensive and disagreeable atmosphere, was directed at both male and female employees, GMC points to ten incidents when Booth's behavior was directed at Duncan alone. GMC concedes that five of these ten incidents could arguably be based on sex: (1) Booth's proposition for a "relationship"; (2) Booth's touching of Duncan's hand; (3) Booth's request that Duncan sketch his planter; (4) the Man Hater's Club poster; and (5) Booth's request that Duncan type the He-Men Women Haters beliefs. "A plaintiff in this kind of case need not show...that only women were subjected to harassment, so long as she shows that women were the primary target of such harassment." We conclude that a jury could reasonably find that Duncan and her gender were the overriding themes of these incidents. The evidence is sufficient to support the jury finding that the harassment was based on sex.

We agree, however, with GMC's assertion that the alleged harassment was not so severe or pervasive as to alter a term, condition, or privilege of Duncan's employment. ... To clear the high threshold of actionable harm, Duncan has to show that "the workplace is permeated with discriminatory intimidation, ridicule, and insult." *Harris v. Forklift Systems, Inc.* (U.S. 1993). "Conduct that is not severe or pervasive enough to create an objectively hostile or abusive work environment—an environment that a reasonable person would find hostile or abusive—is beyond Title VII's purview." Thus, the fourth part of a hostile environment claim includes both objective and subjective components: an environment that a reasonable person would find hostile and one that the victim actually perceived as abusive. [Citing *Harris*.] In determining whether the conduct is sufficiently severe or pervasive, we look to the totality of the circumstances, including the "frequency of the discriminatory conduct; its severity; whether it is physically threatening or humiliating, or a mere offensive utterance; and whether it unreasonably interferes with an employee's work performance." * * * These standards are designed to "filter out complaints attacking the ordinary tribulations of the workplace, such as the sporadic use of abusive language, gender-related jokes, and occasional teasing." [*Citing Faragher v. City of Boca Raton*, U.S. 1998.]

The evidence presented at trial illustrates that Duncan was upset and embarrassed by the posting of the derogatory poster and was disturbed by Booth's advances and his boorish behavior; but, as a matter of law, she has failed to show that these occurrences in the aggregate were so severe and extreme that a reasonable person would find that the terms or conditions of Duncan's employment had been altered. ... Numerous cases have rejected hostile work environment claims premised upon facts equally or more egregious than the conduct at issue here. See, e.g., *Shepherd v. Comptrol-*

ler of Pub. Accounts, (5th Cir.) (holding that several incidents over a two-year period, including the comment "your elbows are the same color as your nipples," another comment that plaintiff had big thighs, repeated touching of plaintiff's arm, and attempts to look down the plaintiff's dress, were insufficient to support hostile work environment claim); *Adusumilli v. City of Chicago* (7th Cir. 1998) (holding conduct insufficient to support hostile environment claim when employee teased plaintiff, made sexual jokes aimed at her, told her not to wave at police officers "because people would think she was a prostitute," commented about low-necked tops, leered at her breasts, and touched her arm, fingers, or buttocks on four occasions); *Black v. Zaring Homes, Inc.*, (6th Cir.) (reversing jury verdict and holding behavior merely offensive and insufficient to support hostile environment claim when employee reached across plaintiff, stating "nothing I like more in the morning than sticky buns" while staring at her suggestively; suggested to plaintiff that parcel of land be named "Hootersville," "Titsville," or "Twin Peaks"; and asked "weren't you there Saturday night dancing on the tables?" while discussing property near a biker bar); *Weiss v. Coca-Cola Bottling Co.*, (7th Cir. 1993) (holding no sexual harassment when plaintiff's supervisor asked plaintiff for dates, asked about her personal life, called her a "dumb blonde," put his hand on her shoulder several times, placed "I love you" signs at her work station, and attempted to kiss her twice at work and once in a bar).

Booth's actions were boorish, chauvinistic, and decidedly immature, but we cannot say they created an objectively hostile work environment permeated with sexual harassment. Construing the evidence in the light most favorable to Duncan, she presented evidence of four categories of harassing conduct based on her sex: a single request for a relationship, which was not repeated when she rebuffed it, four or five isolated incidents of Booth briefly touching her hand, a request to draw a planter, and teasing in the form of a poster and beliefs for an imaginary club. It is apparent that these incidents made Duncan uncomfortable, but they do not meet the standard necessary for actionable sexual harassment. It is worth noting that Duncan fails to even address this component of her prima facie case in her brief. We conclude as a matter of law that she did not show a sexually harassing hostile environment sufficiently severe or pervasive so as to alter the conditions of her employment, a failure that dooms Duncan's hostile work environment claim. See *Meritor Sav. Bank, FSB v. Vinson*, 477 U.S. 57, 67, 91 L. Ed. 2d 49, 106 S. Ct. 2399 (1986). Reversed.

[There was a heated dissent in this case, ripping apart the majority's ruling. To read it, go here: http://caselaw.findlaw.com/us-8th-circuit/1435580.html, and begin reading at III, starting with the second paragraph. The United States Supreme Court declined to take the case.]

Case Questions

1. Is the majority opinion persuasive? How would you have ruled, and why?
2. "Numerous cases have rejected hostile work environment claims premised upon facts equally or more egregious than the conduct at issue here." By what standard or criteria does the majority opinion conclude that Duncan's experiences were no worse than those mentioned in the other cases?
3. Should the majority on the appeals court substitute its judgment for that of the jury?

Age Discrimination: Burden of Persuasion

Gross v. FBL Financial Services, Inc.

557 U.S. 167 (2009)

JUSTICE CLARENCE THOMAS delivered the opinion of the court.

I

Petitioner Jack Gross began working for respondent FBL Financial Group, Inc. (FBL), in 1971. As of 2001, Gross held the position of claims administration director. But in 2003, when he was 54 years old, Gross was reassigned to the position of claims project coordinator. At that same time, FBL transferred many of Gross' job responsibilities to a newly created position—claims administration manager. That position was given to Lisa Kneeskern, who had previously been supervised by Gross and who was then in her early forties. Although Gross (in his new position) and Kneeskern received the same compensation, Gross considered the reassignment a demotion because of FBL's reallocation of his former job responsibilities to Kneeskern.

In April 2004, Gross filed suit in District Court, alleging that his reassignment to the position of claims project coordinator violated the ADEA, which makes it unlawful for an employer to take adverse action against an employee "because of such individual's age." [Citation to statute.] The case proceeded to trial, where Gross introduced evidence suggesting that his reassignment was based at least in part on his age. FBL defended its decision on the grounds that Gross' reassignment was part of a corporate restructuring and that Gross' new position was better suited to his skills.

At the close of trial, and over FBL's objections, the District Court instructed the jury that it must return a verdict for Gross if he proved, by a preponderance of the evidence, that FBL "demoted [him] to claims projec[t] coordinator" and that his "age was a motivating factor" in FBL's decision to demote him. The jury was further instructed that Gross' age would qualify as a "'motivating factor,' if [it] played a part or a role in [FBL]'s decision to demote [him]." The jury was also instructed regarding FBL's burden of proof. According to the District Court, the "verdict must be for [FBL]...if it has been proved by the preponderance of the evidence that [FBL] would have demoted [Gross] regardless of his age." *Ibid.* The jury returned a verdict for Gross, awarding him $46,945 in lost compensation. FBL challenged the jury instructions on appeal. The United States Court of Appeals for the Eighth Circuit reversed and remanded for a new trial, holding that the jury had been incorrectly instructed under the standard established in *Price Waterhouse* v. *Hopkins*, 490 U. S. 228 (1989).
* * *

Because Gross conceded that he had not presented direct evidence of discrimination, the Court of Appeals held that the District Court should not have given the mixed-motives instruction. Rather, Gross should have been held to the burden of persuasion applicable to typical, non-mixed-motives claims; the jury thus should have been instructed only to determine whether Gross had carried his burden of "prov[ing] that age was the determining factor in FBL's employment action."

We * * * now vacate the decision of the Court of Appeals.

II

The parties have asked us to decide whether a plaintiff must "present direct evidence of discrimination in order to obtain a mixed-motive instruction in a non-Title VII discrimination case." Before reaching this question, however, we must first determine whether the burden of persuasion ever shifts to the party defending an alleged mixed-motives discrimination claim brought under the ADEA. We hold that it does not.

A

Petitioner relies on this Court's decisions construing Title VII for his interpretation of the ADEA. Because Title VII is materially different with respect to the relevant burden of persuasion, however, these decisions do not control our construction of the ADEA.

In *Price Waterhouse*, a plurality of the Court and two Justices concurring in the judgment determined that once a "plaintiff in a Title VII case proves that [the plaintiff's membership in a protected class] played a motivating part in an employment decision, the defendant may avoid a finding of liability only by proving by a preponderance of the evidence that it would have made the same decision even if it had not taken [that factor] into account." But as we explained in *Desert Palace, Inc.* v. *Costa* (2003), Congress has since amended Title VII by explicitly authorizing discrimination claims in which an improper consideration was "a motivating factor" for an adverse employment decision (providing that "an unlawful employment practice is established when the complaining party demonstrates that race, color, religion, sex, or national origin was *a motivating factor* for any employment practice, even though other factors also motivated the practice" (emphasis added)). * * *

This Court has never held that this burden-shifting framework applies to ADEA claims. And, we decline to do so now. When conducting statutory interpretation, we "must be careful not to apply rules applicable under one statute to a different statute without careful and critical examination." Unlike Title VII, the ADEA's text does not provide that a plaintiff may establish discrimination by showing that age was simply a motivating factor. Moreover, Congress neglected to add such a provision to the ADEA when it amended Title VII to add §§2000e–2(m) and 2000e–5(g)(2)(B), even though it contemporaneously amended the ADEA in several ways. * * *

We cannot ignore Congress' decision to amend Title VII's relevant provisions but not make similar changes to the ADEA. When Congress amends one statutory provision but not another, it is presumed to have acted intentionally. ... As a result, the Court's interpretation of the ADEA is not governed by Title VII decisions such as *Desert Palace* and *Price Waterhouse.*

B

The ADEA provides, in relevant part, that "[i]t shall be unlawful for an employer ... to fail or refuse to hire or to discharge any individual or otherwise discriminate against any individual with respect to his compensation, terms, conditions, or privileges of employment, *because of* such individual's age." 29 U. S. C. §623(a)(1) (emphasis added).

The words "because of" mean "by reason of: on account of." * * * The ordinary meaning of the ADEA's requirement that an employer took adverse action "because of" age is that age was the "reason" that the employer decided to act. * * *

It follows, then, that under §623(a)(1), the plaintiff retains the burden of persuasion to establish that age was the "but-for" cause of the employer's adverse action. Indeed, we have previously held that the burden is allocated in this manner in ADEA cases. . . . And nothing in the statute's text indicates that Congress has carved out an exception to that rule for a subset of ADEA cases. Where the statutory text is "silent on the allocation of the burden of persuasion," we "begin with the ordinary default rule that plaintiffs bear the risk of failing to prove their claims." *Schaffer* v. *Weast*, 546 U. S. 49, 56 (2005) ...

Hence, the burden of persuasion necessary to establish employer liability is the same in alleged mixed-motives cases as in any other ADEA disparate-treatment action. A plaintiff must prove by a preponderance of the evidence (which may be direct or circumstantial), that age was the "but-for" cause of the challenged employer decision.

* * *

[Section III is omitted.]

IV

We hold that a plaintiff bringing a disparate-treatment claim pursuant to the ADEA must prove, by a preponderance of the evidence, that age was the "but-for" cause of the challenged adverse employment action. The burden of persuasion does not shift to the employer to show that it would have taken the action regardless of age, even when a plaintiff has produced some evidence that age was one motivating factor in that decision. Accordingly, we vacate the judgment of the Court of Appeals and remand the case for further proceedings consistent with this opinion.

It is so ordered.

Case Questions

1. What is the practical effect of this decision? Will plaintiffs with age-discrimination cases find it harder to win after *Gross*?
2. As Justice Thomas writes about it, does "but-for" cause here mean the "sole cause"? Must plaintiffs now eliminate any other possible cause in order to prevail in an ADEA lawsuit?
3. Based on this opinion, if the employer provides a nondiscriminatory reason for the change in the employee's status (such as "corporate restructuring" or "better alignment of skills"), does the employer bear any burden of showing that those are not just words but that, for example, the restructuring really does make sense or that the "skills" really do line up better in the new arrangement?
4. If the plaintiff was retained at the same salary as before, how could he have a "discrimination" complaint, since he still made the same amount of money?
5. The case was decided by a 5-4 majority. A dissent was filed by Justice Stevens, and a separate dissent by Justice Breyer, joined by Justices Ginsburg and Souter. You can access those at http://www.law.cornell.edu/supct/pdf/08-441P.ZD1.

50.6 Summary and Exercises

Summary

For the past fifty years, Title VII of the Civil Rights Act of 1964 has prohibited employment discrimination based on race, religion, sex, or national origin. Any employment decision, including hiring, promotion, and discharge, based on one of these factors is unlawful and subjects the employer to making an award of back pay, promotion, or reinstatement. The Equal Employment Opportunity Commission (EEOC) may file suit, as may the employee—after the commission screens the complaint.

Two major types of discrimination suits are those for disparate treatment (in which the employer intended to discriminate) and disparate impact (in which, regardless of intent, the impact of a particular non-job-related practice has a discriminatory effect). In matters of religion, the employer is bound not only to refrain from discrimination based on an employee's religious beliefs or preferences but also to accommodate the employee's religious practices to the extent that the accommodation does not impose an undue hardship on the business.

Sex discrimination, besides refusal to hire a person solely on the basis of sex, includes discrimination based on pregnancy. Sexual harassment is a form of sex discrimination, and it includes the creation of a hostile or offensive working environment. A separate statute, the Equal Pay Act, mandates equal pay for men and women assigned to the same job.

One major exception to Title VII permits hiring people of a particular religion, sex, or nationality if that feature is a bona fide occupational qualification. There is no bona fide occupational qualification (BFOQ) exception for race, nor is a public stereotype a legitimate basis for a BFOQ. Also notable is the independent contractor exception: the act only applies to employees.

Affirmative action plans, permitting or requiring employers to hire on the basis of race to make up for past discrimination or to bring up the level of minority workers, have been approved, even though the plans may seem to conflict with Title VII. But affirmative action plans have not been permitted to overcome bona fide seniority or merit systems.

The Age Discrimination in Employment Act protects workers over forty from discharge solely on the basis of age. Amendments to the law have abolished the age ceiling for retirement, so that most people working for employers covered by the law cannot be forced to retire.

The Americans with Disabilities Act of 1990 prohibits discrimination based on disability and applies to most jobs in the private sector.

At common law, an employer was free to fire an employee for any reason or for no reason at all. In recent years, the employment-at-will doctrine has been seriously eroded. Many state courts have found against employers on the basis of implied contracts, tortious violation of public policy, or violations of an implied covenant of good faith and fair dealing.

After a century of labor-union agitation, Congress passed in 1935 the major federal legislation affecting labor-management relations. The National Labor Relations Act (the Wagner Act) basically does two things: (1) it provides that employees have a right to join unions and management must recognize and bargain with the union in good faith, and (2) it established the National Labor Relations Board with the power to hear complaints that management—and with the Taft-Hartley Act amendments of 1947, unions too—have committed Unfair Labor Practices. The Board may fashion appropriate remedies if it finds a ULP has been committed. The percent of employees who are unionized has declined very significantly in the last fifty years (except in the government sector), but basic laws allowing unionization remain effective if employees can find the interest, will, and organization to make use of them.

Beyond antidiscrimination law, several other statutes have an impact on the employment relationship. These include the plant-closing law, the Employee Polygraph Protection Act, the Occupational Safety and Health Act, the Employee Retirement Income Security Act, and the Fair Labor Standards Act.

Exercises

1. Rainbow Airlines, a new air carrier headquartered in Chicago with routes from Rome to Canberra, extensively studied the psychology of passengers and determined that more than 93 percent of its passengers felt most comfortable with female flight attendants between the ages of twenty-one and thirty-four. To increase its profitability, the company issued a policy of hiring only such people for jobs in the air but opened all ground jobs to anyone who could otherwise qualify. The policy made no racial distinction, and, in fact, nearly 30 percent of the flight attendants hired were black. What violations of federal law has Rainbow committed, if any?

2. Tex Olafson worked for five years as a messenger for Pressure Sell Advertising Agency, a company without a unionized workforce. On his fifth anniversary with the company, Tex was called in to the president's office, was given a 10 percent raise, and was complimented on his diligence. The following week, a new head of the messenger department was hired. He wanted to appoint his nephew to a messenger job but discovered that a company-wide hiring freeze prevented him from adding another employee to the messenger ranks. So he fired Tex and hired his nephew. What remedy, if any, does Tex have? What additional facts might change the result?

3. Ernest lost both his legs in combat in Vietnam. He has applied for a job with Excelsior Products in the company's quality control lab. The job requires inspectors to randomly check products coming off the assembly line for defects. Historically, all inspectors have stood two-hour shifts. Ernest proposes to sit in his wheelchair. The company refuses to hire him because it says he will be less efficient. Ernest's previous employment record shows him to be a diligent, serious worker. Does Ernest have a legal right to be hired? What additional facts might you want to know in deciding?

4. Charlie Goodfellow works for Yum-burger and has always commanded respect at the local franchise for being the fastest server. One day, he undergoes a profound religious experience, converts to Sikhism, and changes his name to Sanjay Singh. The tenets of his religion require him to wear a beard and a turban. He lets his beard grow, puts on a turban, and his fellow workers tease him. When a regional vice president sees that Sanjay is not wearing the prescribed Yum-Burger uniform, he fires him. What rights of Sanjay, if any, has Yum-burger violated? What remedies are available to him?

5. Employees are required to undergo security checks before leaving the Amazon.com warehouse after work. It takes about 25 minutes a day. The FLSA exempts employers from FLSA liability for claims based on "activities which are preliminary to or postliminary to" the perfor-

mance of the principal activities that an employee is employed to perform. Is security screening "preliminary or postliminary" to the employees' usual work, and thus not compensable? (*Integrity Staffing Solutions, Inc., v. Busk*, U.S. 2014).

6. Acme industries designates a group of 100 employees as "independent contractors," although their duties are the same as its regular employees. It pays them less, provides no benefits, and it refuses to hire women. What remedy is available to them?

7. Beta Company had an opening for a job and considered two candidates: Alice Able and Betty Baker. Able was just out of college, 25 years old. She was obviously technologically savvy, confident, and had high expectations, but Beta thought she was likely overindulged, impatient, and self-absorbed. So the company decided to hire Baker, who was 42. Neither had directly relevant work experience. Does Able have a remedy for age discrimination? (*General Dynamics v. Cline*, U.S. 2004.)

Self-Test Questions

1. Affirmative action in employment
    a. is a requirement of Title VII of the Civil Rights Act of 1964
    b. is prohibited by Title VII of the Civil Rights Act of 1964
    c. is a federal statute enacted by Congress
    d. depends on the circumstances of each case for validity
2. The Age Discrimination in Employment Act protects
    a. all workers of any age
    b. all workers up to age seventy
    c. most workers over forty
    d. no workers over seventy
3. Federal laws barring discrimination against the handicapped and disabled
    a. apply to all disabilities
    b. apply to most disabilities in private employment
    c. apply to all disabilities in public employment
    d. apply to most disabilities in public employment
4. Under Title VII, a bona fide occupational qualification exception may never apply to cases involving
    a. racial discrimination
    b. religious discrimination
    c. sex discrimination
    d. age discrimination
5. The employment-at-will doctrine derives from
    a. Title VII of the Civil Rights Act of 1964
    b. employment contracts
    c. the common law
    d. liberty of contract under the Constitution

Self-Test Answers

1. d
2. c

3. b
4. a
5. c

Endnotes

1. See CongressLink, "Major Features of the Civil Rights Act of 1964," at http://www.congresslink.org/print_basics_histmats_civilrights64text.htm.
2. *Hishon v. King & Spalding*, 467 U.S. 69 (1984).
3. *McDonnell Douglas Corp. v. Green*, 411 U.S. 792 (1973).
4. *Griggs v. Duke Power Co.*, 401 U.S. 424 (1971).
5. *Trans World Airlines v. Hardison*, 432 U.S. 63 (1977).
6. *Harris v. Forklift Systems, Inc.*, 510 U.S. 17 (1993).
7. *Meritor v. Vinson*, 477 U.S. 57 (1986).
8. 564 U.S. ___ (2011).
9. Economic Policy Institute, 2015, "The Arbitration Epidemic." http://www.epi.org/publication/the-arbitration-epidemic/.
10. *Diaz v. Pan American World Airways, Inc.*, 442 F.2d 385 (5th Cir. 1971).
11. *Diaz v. Pan American World Airways, Inc.*, 442 F.2d 385 (5th Cir. 1971).
12. Wendy Kaminer, "Sexual Harassment and the Independent Contractor," *The Atlantic*, August 24, 2010. http://www.theatlantic.com/national/archive/2010/08/sexual-harassment-and-the-independent-contractor/61976/.
13. *Faragher v. City of Boca Raton*, 524 U.S. 775 (1998).
14. *Burlington Industries v. Ellerth*, 524 U.S. 742 (1988).
15. *Johnson v. Santa Clara County Transportation Agency*, 480 U.S. 616 (1987).
16. *Adarand Constructors, Inc. v. Pena*, 515 U.S. 200 (1995).
17. *Sutton v. United Airlines, Inc.*, 527 U.S. 471 (1999).
18. *Orr v. Wal-Mart Stores, Inc.*, 297 F.3d 720 (8th Cir. 2002).
19. *Glenn v. General Motors Corp.*, 841 F.2d 1567 (1988).
20. https://www.aclu.org/map/non-discrimination-laws-state-state-information-map.
21. *Wagenseller v. Scottsdale Memorial Hospital*, 147 Ariz. 370; 710 P.2d 1025 (1085).
22. *Rocky Mountain Hospital and Medical Services v. Diane Mariani*, 916 P.2d 519 (Colo. 1996).
23. "Trump has a plan for government workers, and they are not going to like it." *Washington Post*, Nov. 21, 2016. https://www.washingtonpost.com/news/powerpost/wp/2016/11/21/trump-republicans-plan-to-target-government-workers-benefits-and-job-security/?tid=pm_politics_pop.
24. *Duplex Printing Press Co. v. Deering*, 254 U.S. 443 (1921).
25. https://supreme.justia.com/cases/federal/us/254/443/.
26. *NLRB v. Jones & Laughlin Steel Corp.*, 301 U.S. 1 (1937).
27. http://www.feedingamerica.org/hunger-in-america/our-research/map-the-meal-gap/child-food-insecurity-executive-summary.html.
28. Hiroko Tabuchi, "Walmart Raising Wage to at Least $9," *The New York Times*, February 19, 2015. http://www.nytimes.com/2015/02/20/business/walmart-raising-wage-to-at-least-9-dollars.html?_r=0.
29. Jennifer Medina and Noam Scheiber, "Los Angeles Lifts Its Minimum Wage to $15 Per Hour," *The New York Times*, May 19, 2015. Available at http://www.nytimes.com/2015/05/20/us/los-angeles-expected-to-raise-minimum-wage-to-15-an-hour.html?_r=0.
30. The Human Rights Campaign, *Employment Non-Discrimination Act*, http://www.hrc.org/resources/entry/employment-non-discrimination-act.
31. *Mc Laughlin v. Rowley*, 69 F.Supp. 1333 (N.D. Tex. 1988).
32. *Arrow Automotive Industries, Inc. v. NLRB*, 853 F.2d 233 (4th Cir. 1989).

CHAPTER 51

International Law

Learning Objectives

After reading this chapter, you should understand the following:

1. The concepts of sovereignty, self-determination, failed states, and failing states.
2. The sources of international law, and examples of treaties, conventions, and customary international law.
3. How civil-law disputes between the parties from different nation-states can be resolved through national court systems or arbitration.
4. The well-recognized bases for national jurisdiction over various parties from different nation-states.
5. The doctrines of *forum non conveniens*, sovereign immunity, and act of state.

51.1 Introduction to International Law

Learning Objectives

1. Explain what "sovereignty" is and why it is fundamental to international law.
2. Describe what national sovereigns do within their territories in terms of law making and law enforcing.
3. Understand how international law can be "law" with only national sovereigns.

J. L. Austin, the legal realist, famously defined law as "the command of a sovereign." He had in mind the fact that legal enforcement goes beyond negotiation and goodwill, and may ultimately have to be enforced by some agent of the government. For example, if you fail to answer a summons and complaint, a default judgment will be entered against you; if you fail to pay the judgment, the sheriff (or U.S. marshal) will actually seize assets to pay the judgment, and will come armed with force, if necessary.

The force and authority of a government in any given territory is fundamental to sovereignty. Historically, that was understood to mean a nation's "right" to issue its own currency, make and enforce laws within its borders without interference from other nations (the "right of self-determination" that is noted in the Charter of the United Nations), and to defend its territory with military force, if necessary. In a nation at relative peace, sovereignty can be exercised without great difficulty. But many countries are in civil war, and others experience "breakaway" areas where force must be used to assert continued sovereignty. In some countries, civil war may lead to the formation of new nation-states, such as in Sudan in 2011.

In the United States, there was a Civil War from 1860 to 1864, and even now, there are separatist movements, groups who refuse to recognize the authority of the local, state, or national governments. From time to time, these groups will declare their independence of the sovereign, raise their own flag, refuse to pay taxes, and resist government authority with arms. In the United States, the federal government typically responds to these "mini-secessionist" movements with force.

failing state

A nation-state where substantial parts of the geographic territory in that nation are no longer effectively controlled by the central government.

In Canada, the province of Quebec has considered separating from Canada, and this came close to reality in 1995 on a referendum vote for secession that gained 49.4 percent of the votes. Away from North America, claims to exclusive political and legal authority within some geographic area are often the stuff of civil and regional wars. Consider Kosovo's violent secession from Yugoslavia, or Chechnya's attempted secession from Russia. At stake in all these struggles is the uncontested right to make and enforce laws within a certain territory. In some nation-states, government control has failed to achieve effective control over substantial areas, leaving factions, tribal groups, or armed groups in control. For such nations, the phrase "failed states" or "failing states" has sometimes been used. A **failing state** usually has some combination of lack of control over much of its territory, failure to provide public services, widespread corruption and criminality, and sharp economic decline. Somalia, Chad, and Afghanistan, among others, head the list as of 2011.

In a functioning state, the right to make and enforce law is not contested or in doubt. But in the international arena, there is no sovereign lawgiver and law enforcer. If a criminal burglarizes your house and is caught, the legal authorities in your state have little difficulty bringing him to justice. But suppose a dictator or military-run government oppresses some of the citizenry, depriving these citizens of the chance to speak freely, to carry on a trade or profession, to own property, to be educated, or to have access to water and a livable environment, or routinely commits various atrocities against ethnic groups (forced labor, rape, pillage, murder, torture). Who will bring the dictator or government to justice, and before what tribunal?

There is still no forum (court or tribunal) that is universally accepted as a place to try to punish such people. The International Criminal Court has wide support and has prosecuted several individuals for crimes, but the United States has still not agreed to its jurisdiction.

During the 1990s, the United States selectively "policed" certain conflicts (Kosovo, Haiti, Somalia), but it cannot consistently serve over a long period of time as the world's policeman. The United States has often allowed human rights to be violated in many nations without much protest, particularly during the Cold War with the Union of Soviet Socialist Republics (USSR), where alliances with dictatorships and nondemocratic regimes were routinely made for strategic reasons.

Still, international law is no myth. As we shall see, there are enforceable treaties and laws that most nations abide by, even as they are free to defect from these treaties. Yet the recent retreat by the United States from pending international agreements (the Kyoto Protocol, the International Criminal Court, and others) may be a sign that multilateralism is on the wane or that other nations and regional groupings (the European Union, China) will take a more prominent role in developing binding multilateral agreements among nations.

Key Takeaway

International law is based on the idea of the nation-state that has sovereignty over a population of citizens within a given geographical territory. In theory, at least, this sovereignty means that nation-states should not interfere with legal and political matters within the borders of other nation-states.

Exercises

1. Using news sources, find at least one nation in the world where other nations are officially commenting on or objecting to what goes on within that nation's borders. Are such objections or comments amounting to an infringement of the other nation's sovereignty?

2. Using news sources, find at least one nation in the world that is engaged in trying to change the political and legal landscape of another nation. What is it doing, and why? Is this an infringement of the other nation's sovereignty?
3. What is a failed state? What is a failing state? What is the difference? Is either one a candidate for diplomatic recognition of its sovereignty? Discuss.

51.2 Sources and Practice of International Law

Learning Objectives

1. Explain what a treaty is and how it differs from a convention.
2. Understand that a treaty can be a voluntary relinquishment of some aspects of sovereignty.
3. Describe customary international law, and explain how it is different from treaties as a source of international law.
4. Describe some of the difficulties in enforcing one nation's judicial judgments in another nation.

In this section, we shall be looking at a number of different sources of international law. These sources include treaties and conventions, decisions of courts in various countries (including decisions in your own state and nation), decisions of regional courts (such as the European Court of Justice), the World Trade Organization (WTO), resolutions of the United Nations (UN), and decisions by regional trade organizations such as the North American Free Trade Agreement (NAFTA). These sources are different from most of the cases in your textbook, either because they involve parties from different nations or because the rule makers or decision makers affect entities beyond their own borders.

In brief, the sources of international law include everything that an international tribunal might rely on to decide international disputes. International disputes include arguments between nations, arguments between individuals or companies from different nations, and disputes between individuals or companies and a foreign nation-state. Article 38(1) of the Statute of the International Court of Justice (ICJ) lists four sources of international law: treaties and conventions, custom, general principles of law, and judicial decisions and teachings.

The ICJ only hears lawsuits between nation-states. Its jurisdiction is not compulsory, meaning that both nations in a dispute must agree to have the ICJ hear the dispute.

Treaties and Conventions

Even after signing a treaty or convention, a nation is always free to go it alone and repudiate all regional or international bodies, or refuse to obey the dictates of the United Nations or, more broadly and ambiguously, "the community of nations." The United States *could* repudiate NAFTA, *could* withdraw from the UN, and *could* let the WTO know that it would no longer abide by the post–World War II rules of free trade embodied in the General Agreement on Tariffs and Trade (GATT). The United States would be within its rights as a sovereign to do so, since it owes allegiance to no global or international sovereign. Why, however, does it not do so? Why is the United States so involved with the "entangling alliances" that George Washington warned about? Simply put, nations will give away part of their sovereignty if they think it's in their self-interest to do so. For example, if Latvia joins the European Union (EU), it gives up its right to have its own currency but believes it has more to gain.

treaty

An agreement between two or more nation-states. In US law, a treaty has the same standing as a federal statute.

nation-state

Under international law, the common term for a country or a nation.

conventions

Multilateral treaties that are sponsored by an international agency or institution (e.g., the United Nations).

A **treaty** is nothing more than an agreement between two sovereign nations. In international law, a nation is usually called a state or **nation-state**. This can be confusing, since there are fifty U.S. states, none of which has power to make treaties with other countries. It may be helpful to recall that the thirteen original states under the Articles of Confederation were in fact able to have direct relations with foreign states. Thus, New Jersey (for a few brief years) could have had an ambassador to France or made treaties with Spain. Such a decentralized confederation did not last long. Under the present Constitution, states gave up their right to deal directly with other countries and vested that power in the federal government.

There are many treaties to which the United States is a party. Some of these are **conventions**, which are treaties on matters of common concern, usually negotiated on a regional or global basis, sponsored by an international organization, and open to adoption by many nations. For example, as of 2011, there were 192 parties (nation-states) that had signed on to the Charter of the UN, including the United States, Uzbekistan, Ukraine, Uganda, United Arab Emirates, United Kingdom of Great Britain and Northern Ireland, and Uruguay (just to name a few of the nations starting with *U*).

The most basic kind of treaty is an agreement between two nation-states on matters of trade and friendly relations. Treaties of friendship, commerce, and navigation (FCN treaties) are fairly common and provide for mutual respect for each nation-state's citizens in (1) rights of entry, (2) practice of professions, (3) right of navigation, (4) acquisition of property, (5) matters of expropriation or nationalization, (6) access to courts, and (7) protection of patent rights. Bilateral investment treaties (BITs) are similar but are more focused on commerce and investment. The commercial treaties may deal with a specific product or product group, investment, tariffs, or taxation.

Nation-states customarily enter not only into FCN treaties and BITs but also into peace treaties or weapons limitations treaties, such as the US-Russia Strategic Arms Reduction Talks (START) treaty. Again, treaties are only binding as long as each party continues to recognize their binding effect. In the United States, the procedure for ratifying a treaty is that the Senate must approve it by a two-thirds vote (politically, an especially difficult number to achieve). Once ratified, a treaty has the same force of law within the United States as any statute that Congress might pass.

Custom

Custom between nations is another source of international law. Custom is practice followed by two or more nations in the course of dealing with each other. These practices can be found in diplomatic correspondence, policy statements, or official government statements. To become custom, a consistent and recurring practice must go on over a significant period of time, and nations must recognize that the practice or custom is binding and must follow it because of legal obligation and not mere courtesy. Customs may become codified in treaties.

General Principles of Law, or Customary International Law

Even without treaties, there would be some international law, since not all disputes are confined to the territory of one nation-state. For example, in *In re the Bremen*, a U.S. company's disagreement with a German company was heard in U.S. courts. The U.S. courts had to decide *where* the dispute would properly be heard. In giving full effect to a forum-selection clause, the U.S. Supreme Court set out a principle that it hoped would be honored by courts of other nations—namely, that companies from different states should honor any **forum-selection clause** in their contract to settle disputes at a specific place or court. (See the *Bremen* case, Section 5). If that principle is followed by enough national court systems, it could become a principle of **customary international law**. As an example, consider that for many years, courts in many nations believed that **sovereign immunity** was an established principle of international law.

forum-selection clause

In a contract, national or international, the parties may specify the court where any disputes between the parties will be settled. See the *Bremen* case.

customary international law

Rules of law derived from the consistent conduct of nation-states acting out of the belief that the law required them to act that way.

sovereign immunity

A long-standing doctrine under customary international law that recognizes a nation-state's immunity from legal claims. Although absolute sovereign immunity was widely held through the greater part of the twentieth century, a more restrictive doctrine began to take hold after World War II, one that denied sovereign immunity for a sovereign's commercial or private acts.

Judicial Decisions in International Tribunals; Scholarly Teachings

The Statute of the International Court of Justice recognizes that international tribunals may also refer to the teachings of preeminent scholars on international law. The ICJ, for example, often referred to the scholarly writings of Sir Hersh Lauterpacht in its early decisions. Generally, international tribunals are not bound by stare decisis (i.e., they may decide each case on its merits). However, courts such as the ICJ do refer to their own past decisions for guidance.

There are many international tribunals, including the European Court of Justice, the ICJ, and the International Criminal Court. Typically, however, disputes between corporations or between individuals that cross national boundaries must be resolved in national court systems or in arbitration. In other words, there is no international civil court, and much complexity in international law derives from the fact that national court systems must often choose from different sources of law, using different legal traditions in order to resolve international disputes. For example, a court in one nation may have some difficulty accepting the judgment of a foreign nation's court system, as we see in *Koster v. Automark* (see Section 5).

Due Process and Recognition of Foreign Judgments

Issues surrounding recognition of foreign judgments arise when one nation's courts have questions about the fairness of procedures used in foreign courts to acquire the judgment. Perhaps the defendant was not notified or did not have ample time in which to prepare a defense, or perhaps some measure of damages was assessed that seemed distinctly unfair. If a foreign state makes a judgment against a U.S. company, the judgment will not be recognized and enforced in the United States unless the U.S. court believes that the foreign judgment provided the U.S. company with due process. But skepticism about a foreign judgment works the other way, as well. For example, if a U.S. court were to assess punitive damages against a Belgian company, and the successful plaintiff were to ask for enforcement of the U.S. judgment in Belgium, the Belgian court would reject that portion of the award based on punitive damages. Compensatory damages would be allowed, but as Belgian law does not recognize punitive damages, it might not recognize that portion of the U.S. court's award.

Concerns about notice, service of process, and the ability to present certain defenses are evident in *Koster v. Automark*. Many such concerns are eliminated with the use of forum-selection clauses. The classic case in U.S. jurisprudence is the *Bremen* case, which resolves difficult questions of where the case should be tried between a U.S. and German company by approving the use of a forum-selection clause indicating that a court in the United Kingdom would be the only forum that could hear the dispute.

Part of what is going on in *Bremen* is the Supreme Court's concern that due process should be provided to the U.S. company. What is fair (procedurally) is the dominant question in this case. One clear lesson is that issues of fairness regarding personal jurisdiction can be resolved with a forum-selection clause—if both parties agree to a forum that would have subject matter jurisdiction, at least minimal fairness is evident, because both parties have "consented" to have the forum decide the case.

Arbitration

The idea that a forum-selection clause could, by agreement of the parties, take a dispute out of one national court system and into another court system is just one step removed from the idea that the parties can select a fair resolution process that does not directly involve national court systems. In international arbitration, parties can select, either before or after a dispute arises, an arbitrator or arbitral panel that will hear the dispute. As in all arbitration, the parties agree that the arbitrator's decision will be final and binding. Arbitration is generally faster, can be less expensive, and is always private, being a proceeding not open to media scrutiny.

Typically, an arbitration clause in the contract will specify the arbitrator or the means of selecting the arbitrator. For that purpose, there are many organizations that conduct international arbitrations, including the American Arbitration Association, the International Chamber of Commerce, the International Centre for Settlement of Investment Disputes, and the United Nations Commission on International Trade Law. Arbitrators need not be judges or lawyers; they are usually business people, lawyers, or judges who are experienced in global commercial transactions. The arbitration clause is thus in essence a forum-selection clause and usually includes a choice of law for the arbitrator or arbitral panel to follow.

An arbitral award is not a judgment. If the losing party refuses to pay the award, the winning party must petition a court somewhere to enforce it. Fortunately, almost every country that is engaged in international commerce has ratified the United Nations Convention on the Recognition and Enforcement of Arbitral Awards, sometimes known as the New York Convention. The United States adopted this convention in 1970 and has amended the Federal Arbitration Act accordingly. Anyone who has an arbitral award subject to the convention can attach property of the loser located in any country that has signed the convention.

Key Takeaway

Treaties and conventions, along with customary international law, are the primary sources of what we call international law. Disputes involving parties from different nation-states are resolved in national (federal) court systems, and one nation's recognition and enforcement of another nation's judicial orders or judgments will require reciprocal treaties or some review that the order or judgment was fairly obtained (that there was due process in the determination of the order or judgment).

Exercises

1. At the U.S. Senate website, read about the history of treaties in the United States. What is an "executive agreement," and why has the use of executive agreements grown so fast since World War II?
2. Is NAFTA a treaty or an executive agreement? What practical difference does it make if it is one rather than the other?

51.3 Important Doctrines of Nation-State Judicial Decisions

Learning Objectives

1. Define and describe the three traditional bases for a nation's jurisdiction over those individuals and entities from other nation-states.
2. Explain *forum non conveniens* and be able to apply that in a case involving citizens from two different nation-states.
3. Describe and explain the origins of both sovereign immunity and the act-of-state doctrine, and be able to distinguish between the two.

Bases for National Jurisdiction under International Law

A nation-state has jurisdiction to make and enforce laws (1) within its own borders, (2) with respect to its citizens (nationals") wherever they might be, and (3) with respect to actions taking place outside the territory but having an objective or direct impact within the territory. In the Restatement (Third) of Foreign Relations Law, these three jurisdictional bases are known as (1) the territorial principle, (2) the nationality principle, and (3) the objective territoriality principle.

As we have already seen, many difficult legal issues involve jurisdictional problems. When can a court assert authority over a person? (That's the personal jurisdiction question.) When can a court apply its own law rather than the law of another state? When is it obligated to respect the legal decisions of other states? All these problems have been noted in the context of U.S. domestic law, with its state-federal system; the resolution of similar problems on a global scale are only slightly more complicated.

The **territorial principle** is fairly simple. Anything that happens within a nation's borders is subject to its laws. A German company that makes direct investment in a plant in Spartanburg, South Carolina, is subject to South Carolina law and U.S. law as well.

territorial principle

A nation-state has the power to make and enforce laws with regard to events taking place within its political/geographic territory.

Nationality jurisdiction often raises problems. The citizens of a nation-state are subject to its laws while within the nation and beyond. The United States has passed several laws that govern the conduct of U.S. nationals abroad. United States companies may not, for example, bribe public officials of foreign countries in order to get contracts (Foreign Corrupt Practices Act of 1976). Title VII of the Civil Rights Act also applies extraterritorially—where a U.S. citizen is employed abroad by a U.S. company.

Nationality jurisdiction

Under customary international law, nation-states may exercise jurisdiction over their citizens (nationals) even when the citizens' actions in question take place beyond their borders.

For example, suppose Jennifer Stanley (a U.S. citizen) is discriminated against on the basis of gender by Aramco (a U.S.-based company) in Saudi Arabia, and she seeks to sue under Title VII of the Civil rights Act of 1964. The extraterritorial reach of U.S. law seems odd, especially if Saudi Arabian law or custom conflicts with U.S. law. Indeed, in *EEOC v. Arabian American Oil Co.*, the Supreme Court was hesitant to say that U.S. law would "reach" across the globe to dictate proper corporate conduct.[1] Later that year, Congress made it clear by amending Title VII so that its rules would in fact reach that far, at least where U.S. citizens were the parties to a dispute. But if Saudi Arabian law directly conflicted with U.S. law, principles of customary international law would require that territorial jurisdiction would trump nationality jurisdiction.

Note that where the U.S. laws conflict with local or host country laws, we have potential conflict in the extraterritorial application of US law to activities in a foreign land. See, for example, *Kern v. Dynalectron.*[2] In *Kern*, a Baptist pilot (U.S. citizen) wanted to work for a company that provided emergency services to those Muslims who were on a pilgrimage to Mecca. The job required helicopter pilots to occasionally land to provide emergency services. However, Saudi law required that all who set foot in Mecca must be Muslim. Saudi law provided for death to violators. Kern (wanting the job) tried to convert but couldn't give up his Baptist roots. He sued Dynalectron (a U.S. company) for discrimination under Title VII, claiming that he was denied the job because of his religion. Dynalectron did not deny that they had discriminated on the basis of his religion but argued that because of the Saudi law, they had no viable choice. Kern lost on the Title VII claim (his religion was a bona fide occupational qualification). The court understood that U.S. law would apply extraterritorially because of his nationality and the U.S. nationality of his employer.

objective territoriality

Under customary international law, nation-states may exercise jurisdiction over noncitizens when the actions of those noncitizens have a direct and foreseeable impact on the nation-state claiming jurisdiction.

The principle of **objective territoriality** is fairly simple: acts taking place within the borders of one nation can have a direct and foreseeable impact in another nation. International law recognizes that nation-states act appropriately when they make and enforce law against actors whose conduct has such direct effects. A lawsuit in the United States against Osama bin Laden and his relatives in the Middle East was based on objective territoriality. (Based in Afghanistan, the Al Qaeda leader who claimed credit for attacks on the United States on September 11, 2001.)

Where a defendant is not a U.S. national or is not located in the United States when prosecution or a civil complaint is filed, there may be conflicts between the United States and the country of the defendant's nationality. One of the functions of treaties is to map out areas of agreement between nation-states so that when these kinds of conflicts arise, there is a clear choice of which law will govern. For example, in an extradition treaty, two nation-states will set forth rules to apply when one country wants to prosecute someone who is present in the other country. In general, these treaties will try to give priority to whichever country has the greater interest in taking jurisdiction over the person to be prosecuted.

forum non conveniens

A common-law doctrine used in cases where two different federal court systems have both subject matter jurisdiction and personal jurisdiction over the parties. Using *forum non conveniens*, a court may refuse to hear a case if there is an alternative forum that is available and adequate and if public and private interest factors point to the other nation's legal system as the proper venue.

act-of-state doctrine

A US judicial doctrine that avoids making any determination on the merits of the case if doing so would cause the court to sit in judgment of the legal validity of public acts by a foreign sovereign.

Once jurisdiction is established in U.S. courts in cases involving parties from two different nations, there are some important limiting doctrines that business leaders should be aware of. These are **forum non conveniens**, sovereign immunity, and the **act-of-state doctrine**. Just as conflicts arise over the proper venue in U.S. court cases where two states' courts may claim jurisdiction, so do conflicts occur over the proper forum when the court systems of two nation-states have the right to hear the case.

Forum Non Conveniens; Forum-Selection Clauses

Forum non conveniens is a judicial doctrine that tries to determine the proper forum when the courts of two different nation-states can claim jurisdiction. For example, when Union Carbide's plant in Bhopal, India, exploded and killed or injured thousands of workers and local citizens, the injured Indian plaintiffs could sue Union Carbide in India (since Indian negligence law had territorial effect in Bhopal and Union Carbide was doing business in India) or Union Carbide in the United States (since Union Carbide was organized and incorporated in the United States, which would thus have both territorial and nationality bases for jurisdiction over Union Carbide). Which nation's courts should take a primary role? Note that *forum non conveniens* comes into play when courts in two different nation-states both have subject matter and personal jurisdiction over the matter. Which nation's court system should take the case? That, in essence, is the question that the *forum non conveniens* doctrine tries to answer.

In the *Bremen* case (Section 5), the German contractor (Unterweser) had agreed to tow a drilling rig owned by Zapata from Galveston, Texas, to the Adriatic Sea. The drilling rig was towed by Unterweser's vessel, The Bremen. An accident in the Gulf damaged the drilling rig, and Zapata sued in U.S. district court in Florida. Unterweser argued that London was a "better," or more convenient, forum for the resolution of Zapata's claim against Unterweser, but the district court rejected that claim. Had it not been for the forum-selection clause, the claim would have been resolved in Tampa, Florida. The *Bremen* case, although it does have a *forum non conveniens* analysis, is better known for its holding that in cases where sophisticated parties engage in arms-length bargaining and select a forum in which to settle their disputes, the courts will not second-guess that selection unless there is fraud or unless one party has overwhelming bargaining power over the other.

In short, parties to an international contract can select a forum (a national court system and even a specific court within that system, or an arbitral forum) to resolve any disputes that might arise. In the *Bremen* case, Zapata was held to its choice; this tells you that international contracting requires careful attention to the forum-selection clause. Since the *Bremen* case, the use of arbitration clauses in international contracting has grown exponentially. The arbitration clause is just like a forum-selection clause; instead of the party's selecting a judicial forum, the arbitration clause points to resolution of the dispute by an arbitrator or an arbitral panel.

Where there is no forum-selection clause, as in most tort cases, corporate defendants often find it useful to invoke *forum non conveniens* to avoid a lawsuit in the United States, knowing that the lawsuit elsewhere cannot as easily result in a dollar-value judgment. Consider the case of *Gonzalez v. Chrysler Corporation* (see Section 5).

Sovereign Immunity

For many years, sovereigns enjoyed complete immunity for their own acts. A king who established courts for citizens (subjects) to resolve their disputes would generally not approve of judges who allowed subjects to sue the king (the sovereign) and collect money from the treasury of the realm. If a subject sued a foreign sovereign, any judgment would have to be collectible in the foreign realm, and no king would allow another king's subjects to collect on his treasury, either. In effect, claims against sovereigns, domestic or foreign (at home or abroad), just didn't get very far. Judges, seeing a case against a sovereign, would generally dismiss it on the basis of "sovereign immunity." This became customary international law.

In the twentieth century, the rise of communism led to state-owned companies that began trading across national borders. But when a state-owned company failed to deliver the quantity or quality of goods agreed upon, could the disappointed buyer sue? Many tried, but sovereign immunity was often invoked as a reason why the court should dismiss the lawsuit. Indeed, most lawsuits were dismissed on this basis. Gradually, however, a few courts began distinguishing between governmental acts and commercial acts: where a state-owned company was acting like a private, commercial entity, the court would not grant immunity. This became known as the "restrictive" version of sovereign immunity, in contrast to "absolute" sovereign immunity. In U.S. courts, decisions as to sovereign immunity after World War II were often political in nature, with the U.S. State Department giving advisory letters on a case-by-case basis, recommending (or not recommending) that the court grant immunity to the foreign state. Congress moved to clarify matters in 1976 by passing the Foreign Sovereign Immunities Act, which legislatively recognized the restrictive theory. Note, especially, Section 1605(a)(2).

Jurisdictional Immunities of Foreign States

28 USCS § 1602 (1998)

§ 1602. Findings and declaration of purpose

The Congress finds that the determination by United States courts of the claims of foreign states to immunity from the jurisdiction of such courts would serve the interests of justice and would protect the rights of both foreign states and litigants in United States courts. Under international law, states are not immune from the jurisdiction of foreign courts insofar as their commercial activities are concerned, and their commercial property may be levied upon for the satisfaction of judgments rendered against them in connection with their commercial activities. Claims of foreign states to immunity should henceforth be decided by courts of the United States and of the States in conformity with the principles set forth in this chapter [28 USCS §§ 1602 et seq.].

§ 1603. Definitions

For purposes of this chapter [28 USCS §§ 1602 et seq.]—

(a) A "foreign state", except as used in section 1608 of this title, includes a political subdivision of a foreign state or an agency or instrumentality of a foreign state as defined in subsection (b).

(b) An "agency or instrumentality of a foreign state" means any entity—

(1) which is a separate legal person, corporate or otherwise, and

(2) which is an organ of a foreign state or political subdivision thereof, or a majority of whose shares or other ownership interest is owned by a foreign state or political subdivision thereof, and

(3) which is neither a citizen of a State of the United States as defined in section 1332(c) and (d) of this title nor created under the laws of any third country.

(c) The "United States" includes all territory and waters, continental or insular, subject to the jurisdiction of the United States.

(d) A "commercial activity" means either a regular course of commercial conduct or a particular commercial transaction or act. The commercial character of an activity shall be determined by reference to the nature of the course of conduct or particular transaction or act, rather than by reference to its purpose.

(e) A "commercial activity carried on in the United States by a foreign state" means commercial activity carried on by such state and having substantial contact with the United States.

§ *1604.* Immunity of a foreign state from jurisdiction

Subject to existing international agreements to which the United States is a party at the time of enactment of this Act [enacted Oct. 21, 1976] a foreign state shall be immune from the jurisdiction of the courts of the United States and of the States except as provided in sections 1605 to 1607 of this chapter.

§ *1605.* General exceptions to the jurisdictional immunity of a foreign state

(a) A foreign state shall not be immune from the jurisdiction of courts of the United States or of the States in any case—

(1) in which the foreign state has waived its immunity either explicitly or by implication, notwithstanding any withdrawal of the waiver which the foreign state may purport to effect except in accordance with the terms of the waiver;

(2) in which the action is based upon a commercial activity carried on in the United States by the foreign state; or upon an act performed in the United States in connection with a commercial activity of the foreign state elsewhere; or upon an act outside the territory of the United States in connection with a commercial activity of the foreign state elsewhere and that act causes a direct effect in the United States;

(3) in which rights in property taken in violation of international law are in issue and that property or any property exchanged for such property is present in the United States in connection with a commercial activity carried on in the United States by the foreign state; or that property or any property exchanged for such property is owned or operated by an agency or instrumentality of the foreign state and that agency or instrumentality is engaged in a commercial activity in the United States;

(4) in which rights in property in the United States acquired by succession or gift or rights in immovable property situated in the United States are in issue;

(5) not otherwise encompassed in paragraph (2) above, in which money damages are sought against a foreign state for personal injury or death, or damage to or loss of property, occurring in the United States and caused by the tortious act or omission of that foreign state or of any official or employee of that foreign state while acting within the scope of his office or employment; except this paragraph shall not apply to—

(A) any claim based upon the exercise or performance or the failure to exercise or perform a discretionary function regardless of whether the discretion be abused, or

(B) any claim arising out of malicious prosecution, abuse of process, libel, slander, misrepresentation, deceit, or interference with contract rights;

Act of State

A foreign country may expropriate private property and be immune from suit in the United States by the former owners, who might wish to sue the country directly or seek an order of attachment against property in the United States owned by the foreign country. In the United States, the government may constitutionally seize private property under certain circumstances, but under the Fifth Amendment, it must pay "just compensation" for any property so taken. Frequently, however, foreign governments have seized the assets of U.S. corporations without recompensing them for the loss. Sometimes the foreign government seizes all private property in a certain industry, sometimes only the property of U.S. citizens. If the seizure violates the standards of international law—as, for example, by failing to pay just compensation—the question arises whether the former owners may sue in U.S. courts. One problem with permitting the courts to hear such claims is that by time of suit, the property may have passed into the hands of bona fide purchasers, perhaps even in other countries.

The Supreme Court has enunciated a doctrine governing claims to recover for acts of expropriation. This is known as the act-of-state doctrine. As the Supreme Court put it in 1897, "Every sovereign State is bound to respect the independence of every other sovereign State, and the courts of one country will not sit in judgment on ... [and thereby adjudicate the legal validity of] the acts of the government of another done within its own territory."[3] This means that U.S. courts will "reject private claims based on the contention that the damaging act of another nation violates either U.S. or international law."[4] Sovereign immunity and the act-of-state doctrine rest on different legal principles and have different legal consequences. The doctrine of sovereign immunity bars a suit altogether: once a foreign-government defendant shows that sovereign immunity applies to the claims the plaintiff has raised, the court has no jurisdiction even to consider them and must dismiss the case. By contrast, the act-of-state doctrine does not require dismissal in a case properly before a court; indeed, the doctrine may be invoked by plaintiffs as well as defendants. Instead, it precludes anyone from arguing against the legal validity of an act of a foreign government. In a simple example, suppose a widow living in the United States is sued by her late husband's family to prevent her from inheriting his estate. They claim she was never married to the deceased. She shows that while citizens of another country, they were married by proclamation of that country's legislature. Although legislatures do not marry people in the United States, the act-of-state doctrine would bar a court from denying the legal validity of the marriage entered into in their home country.

The Supreme Court's clearest statement came in a case growing out of the 1960 expropriation of U.S. sugar companies operating in Cuba. A sugar broker had entered into contracts with a wholly owned subsidiary of Compania Azucarera Vertientes-Camaguey de Cuba (C.A.V.), whose stock was principally owned by U.S. residents. When the company was nationalized, sugar sold pursuant to these contracts had been loaded onto a German vessel still in Cuban waters. To sail, the skipper needed the consent of the Cuban government. That was forthcoming when the broker agreed to sign contracts with the government that provided for payment to a Cuban bank rather than to C.A.V. The Cuban bank assigned the contracts to Banco Nacional de Cuba, an arm of the Cuban government. However, when C.A.V. notified the broker that in its opinion, C.A.V. still owned the sugar, the broker agreed to turn the process of the sale over to Sabbatino, appointed under New York law as receiver of C.A.V.'s assets in the state. Banco Nacional de Cuba then sued Sabbatino, alleging that the broker's refusal to pay Banco the proceeds amounted to common-law conversion.

The federal district court held for Sabbatino, ruling that if Cuba had simply failed to abide by its own law, C.A.V.'s stockholders would have been entitled to no relief. But because Cuba had violated international law, the federal courts did not need to respect its act of appropriation. The violation of international law, the court said, lay in Cuba's motive for the expropriation, which was retaliation for President Eisenhower's decision to lower the quota of sugar that could be imported into the United States, and not for any public purpose that would benefit the Cuban people; moreover, the expropriation did not provide for adequate compensation and was aimed at U.S. interests only, not those of other foreign nationals operating in Cuba. The U.S. court of appeals affirmed the lower court's decision, holding that federal courts may always examine the validity of a foreign country's acts.

But in *Banco Nacional de Cuba v. Sabbatino*, the Supreme Court reversed, relying on the act-of-state doctrine.[5] This doctrine refers, in the words of the Court, to the "validity of the public acts a recognized foreign sovereign power commit[s] within its own territory." If the foreign state exercises its own jurisdiction to give effect to its public interests, however the government defines them, the expropriated property will be held to belong to that country or to bona fide purchasers. For the act-of-state doctrine to be invoked, the act of the foreign government must have been completely executed within the country—for example, by having enacted legislation expropriating the property. The Supreme Court said that the act-of-state doctrine applies even though the United States had severed diplomatic relations with Cuba and even though Cuba would not reciprocally apply the act-of-state doctrine in its own courts.

Despite its consequences in cases of expropriations, the act-of-state doctrine is relatively narrow. As *W. S. Kirkpatrick Co., Inc. v. Environmental Tectonics Co.* (Section 5) shows, it does not apply merely because a judicial inquiry in the United States might embarrass a foreign country or even interfere politically in the conduct of U.S. foreign policy.

Key Takeaway

Each nation-state has several bases of jurisdiction to make and enforce laws, including the territorial principle, nationality jurisdiction, and objective territoriality. However, nation-states will not always choose to exercise their jurisdiction: the doctrines of *forum non conveniens*, sovereign immunity, and act of state limit the amount and nature of judicial activity in one nation that would affect nonresident parties and foreign sovereigns.

Exercises

1. Argentina sells bonds on the open market, and buyers all around the world buy them. Five years later, Argentina declares that it will default on paying interest or principal on these bonds. Assume that Argentina has assets in the United States. Is it likely that a bondholder in the United States can bring an action in U.S. courts that will not be dismissed for lack of subject matter jurisdiction?
2. During the Falkland Island war between Argentina and Great Britain, neutral tanker traffic was at risk of being involved in hostilities. Despite diplomatic cables from the United States assuring Argentina of the vessels' neutrality, an oil tanker leased by Amerada Hess, traveling from Puerto Rico to Valdez, Alaska, was repeatedly bombed by the Argentine air force. The ship had to be scuttled, along with its contents. Will a claim by Amerada Hess be recognized in U.S. courts?

51.4 Regulating Trade

Learning Objectives

1. Understand why nation-states have sometimes limited imports but not exports.
2. Explain why nation-states have given up some of their sovereignty by lowering tariffs in agreement with other nation-states.

Before globalization, nation-states traded with one another, but they did so with a significant degree of protectiveness. For example, one nation might have imposed very high tariffs (taxes on imports from other countries) while not taxing exports in order to encourage a favorable "balance of trade." The balance of trade is an important statistic for many countries; for many years, the U.S. balance of trade has been negative because it imports far more than it exports (even though the United States, with its very large farms, is the world's largest exporter of agricultural products). This section will explore import and export controls in the context of the global agreement to reduce import controls in the name of free trade.

Export Controls

The United States maintains restrictions on certain kinds of products being sold to other nations and to individuals and firms within those nations. For example, the Export Administration Act of 1985 has controlled certain exports that would endanger national security, drain scarce materials from the U.S. economy, or harm foreign policy goals. The U.S. secretary of commerce has a list of controlled commodities that meet any of these criteria.

More specifically, the Arms Export Control Act permits the president to create a list of controlled goods related to military weaponry, and no person or firm subject to U.S. law can export any listed item without a license. When the United States has imposed sanctions, the International Emergency Economic Powers Act (IEEPA) has often been the legislative basis; and the act gives the president considerable power to impose limitations on trade. For example, in 1979, President Carter, using IEEPA, was able to impose sanctions on Iran after the diplomatic hostage crisis. The United States still imposes travel restrictions and other sanctions on Cuba, North Korea, and many other countries.

Import Controls and Free Trade

Nation-states naturally wish to protect their domestic industries. Historically, protectionism has come in the form of import taxes, or tariffs, also called duties. The tariff is simply a tax imposed on goods when they enter a country. Tariffs change often and vary from one nation-state to another. Efforts to implement free trade began with the General Agreement on Tariffs and Trade (GATT) and are now enforced through the World Trade Organization (WTO); the GATT and the WTO have sought, through successive rounds of trade talks, to decrease the number and extent of tariffs that would hinder the free flow of commerce from one nation-state to another. The theory of comparative advantage espoused by David Ricardo is the basis for the gradual but steady of tariffs, from early rounds of talks under the GATT to the Uruguay Round, which established the WTO.

The GATT was a huge multilateral treaty negotiated after World War II and signed in 1947. After various "rounds" of re-negotiation, the Uruguay Round ended in 1994 with the United States and 125 other nation-states signing the treaty that established the WTO. In 1948, the worldwide average tariff on industrial goods was around 40 percent. That number is now more like 4 percent as globalization has taken root. Free-trade proponents claim that globalization has increased general well-being, while opponents claim that free trade has brought outsourcing, industrial decline, and the hollowing-out of the U.S. manufacturing base. The same kinds of criticisms have been directed at the North American Free Trade Agreement (NAFTA).

The Uruguay Round was to be succeeded by the Doha Round. But that round has not concluded because developing countries have not been satisfied with the proposed reductions in agricultural tariffs imposed by the more developed economies; developing countries have been resistant to further agreements unless and until the United States and the European Union lower their agricultural tariffs.

There are a number of regional trade agreements other than NAFTA. The European Union, formerly the Common Market, provides for the free movement of member nations' citizens throughout the European Union (EU) and sets union-wide standards for tariffs, subsidies, transportation, human rights, and many other issues. Another regional trade agreement is Mercosur—an organization formed by Brazil, Argentina, Uruguay, and Paraguay to improve trade and commerce among those South American nations. Almost all trade barriers between the four nations have been eliminated, and the organization has also established a broad social agenda focusing on education, culture, the environment, and consumer protection.

Key Takeaway

Historically, import controls were more common than export controls; nation-states would typically impose tariffs (taxes) on goods imported from other nation-states. Some nation-states, such as the United States, nevertheless maintain certain export controls for national security and military purposes. Most nation-states have voluntarily given up some of their sovereignty in order to gain the advantages of bilateral and multilateral trade and investment treaties. The most prominent example of a multilateral trade treaty is the GATT, now administered by the WTO. There are also regional free-trade agreements, such as NAFTA and Mercosur, that provide additional relaxation of tariffs beyond those agreed to under the WTO.

Exercises

1. Look at various sources and describe, in one hundred or fewer words, why the Doha Round of WTO negotiations has not been concluded.
2. What is the most recent bilateral investment treaty (BIT) that has been concluded between the United States and another nation-state? What are its key provisions? Which U.S. businesses are most helped by this treaty?

51.5 Cases

Forum-selection clauses

In re the Bremen

407 U.S. 1 (1972)

MR. CHIEF JUSTICE BURGER delivered the opinion of the Court.

We granted certiorari to review a judgment of the United States Court of Appeals for the Fifth Circuit declining to enforce a forum-selection clause governing disputes arising under an international towage contract between petitioners and respondent. The circuits have differed in their approach to such clauses. For the reasons stated hereafter, we vacate the judgment of the Court of Appeals.

In November 1967, respondent Zapata, a Houston-based American corporation, contracted with petitioner Unterweser, a German corporation, to tow Zapata's ocean-going, self-elevating drilling rig Chaparral from Louisiana to a point off Ravenna, Italy, in the Adriatic Sea, where Zapata had agreed to drill certain wells.

Zapata had solicited bids for the towage, and several companies including Unterweser had responded. Unterweser was the low bidder and Zapata requested it to submit a contract, which it did. The contract submitted by Unterweser contained the following provision, which is at issue in this case:

Any dispute arising must be treated before the London Court of Justice.

In addition the contract contained two clauses purporting to exculpate Unterweser from liability for damages to the towed barge. After reviewing the contract and making several changes, but without any alteration in the forum-selection or exculpatory clauses, a Zapata vice president executed the contract and forwarded it to Unterweser in Germany, where Unterweser accepted the changes, and the contract became effective.

On January 5, 1968, Unterweser's deep sea tug Bremen departed Venice, Louisiana, with the Chaparral in tow bound for Italy. On January 9, while the flotilla was in international waters in the middle of the Gulf of Mexico, a severe storm arose. The sharp roll of the Chaparral in Gulf waters caused its elevator legs, which had been raised for the voyage, to break off and fall into the sea, seriously damaging the Chaparral. In this emergency situation Zapata instructed the Bremen to tow its damaged rig to Tampa, Florida, the nearest port of refuge.

On January 12, Zapata, ignoring its contract promise to litigate "any dispute arising" in the English courts, commenced a suit in admiralty in the United States District Court at Tampa, seeking $3,500,000 damages against Unterweser in personam and the Bremen *in rem*, alleging negligent towage and breach of contract. Unterweser responded by invoking the forum clause of the towage contract, and moved to dismiss for lack of jurisdiction or on forum non conveniens grounds, or in the alternative to stay the action pending submission of the dispute to the "London Court of Justice." Shortly thereafter, in February, before the District Court had ruled on its motion to stay or dismiss the United States action, Unterweser commenced an action against Zapata seeking damages for breach of the towage contract in the High Court of Justice in London, as the contract provided. Zapata appeared in that court to contest jurisdiction, but its challenge was rejected, the English courts holding that the contractual forum provision conferred jurisdiction.

In the meantime, Unterweser was faced with a dilemma in the pending action in the United States court at Tampa. The six-month period for filing action to limit its liability to Zapata and other potential claimants was about to expire, but the United States District Court in Tampa had not yet ruled on Unterweser's motion to dismiss or stay Zapata's action. On July 2, 1968, confronted with difficult alternatives, Unterweser filed an action to limit its liability in the District Court in Tampa. That court entered the customary injunction against proceedings outside the limitation court, and Zapata refiled its initial claim in the limitation action.

It was only at this juncture, on July 29, after the six-month period for filing the limitation action had run, that the District Court denied Unterweser's January motion to dismiss or stay Zapata's initial action. In denying the motion, that court relied on the prior decision of the Court of Appeals in *Carbon Black Export, Inc.* In that case the Court of Appeals had held a forum-selection clause unenforceable, reiterating the traditional view of many American courts that "agreements in advance of controversy whose object is to oust the jurisdiction of the courts are contrary to public policy and will not be enforced."

* * *

Thereafter, on January 21, 1969, the District Court denied another motion by Unterweser to stay the limitation action pending determination of the controversy in the High Court of Justice in London and granted Zapata's motion to restrain Unterweser from litigating further in the London court. The District Judge ruled that, having taken jurisdiction in the limitation proceeding, he had jurisdiction to determine all matters relating to the controversy. He ruled that Unterweser should be required to "do equity" by refraining from also litigating the controversy in the London court, not only for the reasons he had previously stated for denying Unterweser's first motion to stay Zapata's action, but also because Unterweser had invoked the United States court's jurisdiction to obtain the benefit of the Limitation Act.

On appeal, a divided panel of the Court of Appeals affirmed, and on rehearing *en banc* the panel opinion was adopted, with six of the 14 *en banc* judges dissenting.[6] As had the District Court, the majority rested on the *Carbon Black* decision, concluding that "at the very least" that case stood for the proposition that a forum-selection clause "will not be enforced unless the selected state would provide a more convenient forum than the state in which suit is brought." From that premise the Court of Appeals proceeded to conclude that, apart from the forum-selection clause, the District Court did not abuse its discretion in refusing to decline jurisdiction on the basis of *forum non conveniens*. It noted that (1) the flotilla never "escaped the Fifth Circuit's mare nostrum, and the casualty occurred in close proximity to the district court"; (2) a considerable number of potential witnesses, including Zapata crewmen, resided in the Gulf Coast area; (3) preparation for the voyage and inspection and repair work had been performed in the Gulf area; (4) the testimony of the Bremen crew was available by way of deposition; (5) England had no interest in or contact with the controversy other than the forum-selection clause. The Court of Appeals majority further noted that Zapata was a United States citizen and "[t]he discretion of the district court to remand the case to a foreign forum was consequently limited"—especially since it appeared likely that the English courts would enforce the exculpatory clauses. In the Court of Appeals' view, enforcement of such clauses would be contrary to public policy in American courts under *Bisso v. Inland Waterways Corp.*, 349 U.S. 85 (1955), and *Dixilyn Drilling Corp. v. Crescent Towing & Salvage Co.*, 372 U.S. 697 (1963). Therefore, "[t]he district court was entitled to consider that remanding Zapata to a foreign forum, with no practical contact with the controversy, could raise a bar to recovery by a United States citizen which its own convenient courts would not countenance."

We hold, with the six dissenting members of the Court of Appeals, that far too little weight and effect were given to the forum clause in resolving this controversy. For at least two decades we have witnessed an expansion of overseas commercial activities by business enterprises based in the United States. The barrier of distance that once tended to confine a business concern to a modest territory no longer does so. Here we see an American company with special expertise contracting with a foreign company to tow a complex machine thousands of miles across seas and oceans. The expansion of American business and industry will hardly be encouraged if, not-withstanding solemn contracts, we insist on a parochial concept that all disputes must be resolved under our laws and in our courts. Absent a contract forum, the considerations relied on by the Court of Appeals would be persuasive reasons for holding an American forum convenient in the traditional sense, but in an era of expanding world trade and commerce, the absolute aspects of the doctrine of the Carbon Black case have little place and would be a heavy hand indeed on the future development of international commercial dealings by Americans. We cannot have trade and commerce in world markets and international waters exclusively on our terms, governed by our laws, and resolved in our courts.

Forum-selection clauses have historically not been favored by American courts. Many courts, federal and state, have declined to enforce such clauses on the ground that they were "contrary to public policy," or that their effect was to "oust the jurisdiction" of the court. Although this view apparently still has considerable acceptance, other courts are tending to adopt a more hospitable attitude toward forum-selection clauses. This view ... is that such clauses are prima facie valid and should be enforced unless enforcement is shown by the resisting party to be "unreasonable" under the circumstances.

We believe this is the correct doctrine to be followed by federal district courts sitting in admiralty. It is merely the other side of the proposition recognized by this Court in *National Equipment Rental, Ltd. v. Szukhent*, 375 U.S. 311 (1964), holding that in federal courts a party may validly consent to be sued in a jurisdiction where he cannot be found for service of process through contractual designation of an "agent" for receipt of process in that jurisdiction. In so holding, the Court stated: "[I]t is settled ... that parties to a contract may agree in advance to submit to the jurisdiction of a given court, to permit notice to be served by the opposing party, or even to waive notice altogether."

This approach is substantially that followed in other common-law countries including England. It is the view advanced by noted scholars and that adopted by the Restatement of the Conflict of Laws. It accords with ancient concepts of freedom of contract and reflects an appreciation of the expanding horizons of American contractors who seek business in all parts of the world. Not surprisingly, foreign businessmen prefer, as do we, to have disputes resolved in their own courts, but if that choice is not available, then in a neutral forum with expertise in the subject matter. Plainly, the courts of England meet the standards of neutrality and long experience in admiralty litigation. The choice of that forum was made in an arm's-length negotiation by experienced and sophisticated businessmen, and absent some compelling and countervailing reason it should be honored by the parties and enforced by the courts.

* * *

The judgment of the Court of Appeals is vacated and the case is remanded for further proceedings consistent with this opinion.

Vacated and remanded.

MR. JUSTICE DOUGLAS, dissenting.

The Limitation Court is a court of equity and traditionally an equity court may enjoin litigation in another court where equitable considerations indicate that the other litigation might prejudice the proceedings in the Limitation Court. Petitioners' petition for limitation [407 U.S. 1, 23] subjects them to the full equitable powers of the Limitation Court.

Respondent is a citizen of this country. Moreover, if it were remitted to the English court, its substantive rights would be adversely affected. Exculpatory provisions in the towage control provide (1) that petitioners, the masters and the crews "are not responsible for defaults and/or errors in the navigation of the tow" and (2) that "[d]amages suffered by the towed object are in any case for account of its Owners." Under our decision in *Dixilyn Drilling Corp v. Crescent Towing & Salvage Co.*, 372 U.S. 697, 698, "a contract which exempts the tower from liability for its own negligence" is not enforceable, though there is evidence in the present record that it is enforceable in England. That policy was first announced in *Bisso v. Inland Waterways Corp.*, 349 U.S. 85; and followed in *Boston Metals Co. v. The Winding Gulf*, 349 U.S. 122.

* * *

Moreover, the casualty occurred close to the District Court, a number of potential witnesses, including respondent's crewmen, reside in that area, and the inspection and repair work were done there. The testimony of the tower's crewmen, residing in Germany, is already available by way of depositions taken in the proceedings. [407 U.S. 1, 24]

All in all, the District Court judge exercised his discretion wisely in enjoining petitioners from pursuing the litigation in England.

I would affirm the judgment below.

Case Questions

1. Without a forum-selection clause, would the court in England have personal jurisdiction over either party?
2. Under *forum non conveniens*, there will be two courts, both of which have subject matter and personal jurisdiction—and the court will defer jurisdiction to the more "convenient" forum. If there were no forum-selection clause here, could the U.S. court defer jurisdiction to the court in London?
3. Will Zapata recover anything if the case is heard in London?
4. Is it "fair" to let Unterweser excuse itself from liability? If not, under what ethical perspective does it "make sense" or "seem reasonable" for the court to allow Zapata to go to London and recover very little or nothing?

Due process in the enforcement of judgments

Koster v. Automark
640 F.2d 77 (N.D. Ill. 1980)

MARVIN E. ASPEN, District Judge:

On November 23, 1970, plaintiff Koster and defendant Automark Industries Incorporated ("Automark") consummated a five-month course of negotiation by entering into an agreement whereby Automark promised to purchase 600,000 valve cap gauges during 1971. As a result of Automark's alleged breach of this agreement, plaintiff brought an action for damages in the District Court in Amsterdam, 3rd Lower Chamber A. On October 16, 1974, plaintiff obtained a default judgment in the amount of Dutch Florins 214,747,50—$66,000 in American currency at the rate of exchange prevailing on December 31, 1971—plus costs and interest. Plaintiff filed this diversity action on January 27, 1978, to enforce that foreign judgment.

The case now is before the Court on plaintiff's motion for summary judgment pursuant to Federal Rules of Civil Procedure (Fed.R.Civ.P) 56(a). Defendant contests this motion on three grounds: (1) that service was inadequate, (2) that defendant lacked the minimum contacts necessary to render it subject to in personam jurisdiction in Amsterdam, and (3) that defendant has meritorious defenses to the action which it could not present in the foreign proceeding. For the reasons that follow, however, the Court finds defendant's contentions unavailing.

[Note: The discussion on inadequate service has been omitted from what follows.]

As the court noted in Walters...service of process cannot confer personal jurisdiction upon a court in the absence of minimum contacts. The requirement of minimum contacts is designed to ensure that it is reasonable to compel a party to appear in a particular forum to defend against an action. *Shaffer v. Heitner*, 433 U.S. 186 (1977); *International Shoe Co. v. Washington*, 326 U.S. 317 (1945). Here, it is undisputed that Automark initiated the negotiations by a letter to plaintiff dated June 25, 1970. The five-month period of negotiations, during which time defendant sent several letters and telegrams to plaintiff in Amsterdam, led to the agreement of November 23, 1970. Moreover, although there is no evidence as to the contemplated place of performance, plaintiff attests—without contradiction—that the payment was to be made in Amsterdam.

On facts not dissimilar from these, the Illinois courts have found the existence of minimum contacts sufficient to justify long-arm personal jurisdiction under the Illinois statute. Ill.Rev.Stat. Ch. 110, § 17(a)(1). In *Colony Press, Inc. v. Fleeman*, 17 Ill.App.3d 14, 308 N.E.2d 78 (1st Dist. 1974), the court found that minimum contacts existed where the defendant had initiated the negotiations by submitting a purchase order to an Illinois company and the contract was to be performed in Illinois. And in *Cook Associates, Inc. v. Colonial Broach & Machine Co.*, 14 Ill.App.3d 965, 304 N.E.2d 27 (1st Dist. 1973), the court found that a single telephone call into Illinois initiating a business transaction that was to be performed in Illinois by an Illinois agency was enough to establish personal jurisdiction in Illinois. Thus, the Court finds that the Amsterdam court had personal jurisdiction over Automark.

Finally, defendant suggests that it has meritorious defenses which it could not present because of its absence at the judicial proceeding in Amsterdam; specifically, that there was no binding agreement and, alternatively, that its breach was justified by plaintiff's failure to perform his end of the bargain. It is established beyond question, however, that a default judgment is a conclusive and final determination that is accorded the same *res judicata* effect as a judgment after a trial on the merits. Such a judgment may be attacked collaterally only on jurisdictional grounds, or upon a showing that the judgment was obtained by fraud or collusion. Thus, defendant is foreclosed from challenging the underlying merits of the judgment obtained in Amsterdam.

[In a footnote, the court says:] *"Again, even assuming that defendant could attack the judgment on the merits, it has failed to raise any genuine issue of material fact....An affidavit by defendant's secretary states only that "to the best of [his] knowledge" there was no contract with anyone in Amsterdam. Yet, there is no affidavit from the party who negotiated and allegedly contracted with plaintiff; nor is there any explanation why such an affidavit was not filed. In the face of the copy of a letter of agreement provided by plaintiff, this allegation is insufficient to create a factual question. Moreover, defendant offers no extrinsic material in support of its allegation of non-performance by plaintiff. Thus, even were the Court to consider defendant's alleged defenses to the contract action, it would grant summary judgment for plaintiff on the merits."*

Accordingly, the Court finds that plaintiff is entitled to enforcement of the foreign judgment. Thus, plaintiff's motion for summary judgment is granted. It is so ordered.

Case Questions

1. Why do you think Automark did not go to Amsterdam to contest this claim by Koster?
2. Why does the Illinois court engage in a due process analysis of personal jurisdiction?
3. What if the letter of agreement had an arbitration clause? Would the court in Amsterdam have personal jurisdiction over Automark?

Forum non conveniens

Gonzalez v. Chrysler Corporation

301 F.3d 377 (5th Cir. 2002)

[Note: Although the court's opinion was appealed to the Supreme Court, no writ of certiorari was issued, so the following decision stands as good precedent in *forum non conveniens* cases.]

Opinion by E. GRADY JOLLY, Circuit Judge.

In this forum non conveniens case, we first consider whether the cap imposed by Mexican law on the recovery of tort damages renders Mexico an inadequate forum for resolving a tort suit by a Mexican citizen against an American manufacturer and an American designer of an air bag. Holding that Mexico—despite its cap on damages—represents an adequate alternative forum, we next consider whether the district court committed reversible error when it concluded that the private and public interest factors so strongly pointed to Mexico that Mexico, instead of Texas, was the appropriate forum in which to try this case. Finding no reversible error, we affirm the district court's judgment dismissing this case on the ground of forum non conveniens.

In 1995, while in Houston, the plaintiff, Jorge Luis Machuca Gonzalez ("Gonzalez") saw several magazine and television advertisements for the Chrysler LHS. The advertisements sparked his interest. So, Gonzalez decided to visit a couple of Houston car dealerships. Convinced by these visits that the Chrysler LHS was a high quality and safe car, Gonzalez purchased a Chrysler LHS upon returning to Mexico.

On May 21, 1996, the wife of the plaintiff was involved in a collision with another moving vehicle while driving the Chrysler LHS in Atizapan de Zaragoza, Mexico. The accident triggered the passenger-side air bag. The force of the air bag's deployment instantaneously killed Gonzalez's three-year-old son, Pablo.

Seeking redress, Gonzalez brought suit in Texas district court against (1) Chrysler, as the manufacturer of the automobile; (2) TRW, Inc. and TRW Vehicle Safety Systems, Inc., as the designers of the front sensor for the air bag; and (3) Morton International, Inc., as designer of the air bag module. Gonzalez asserted claims based on products liability, negligence, gross negligence, and breach of warranty. As noted, Gonzalez chose to file his suit in Texas. Texas, however, has a tenuous connection to the underlying dispute. Neither the car nor the air bag module was designed or manufactured in Texas. The accident took place in Mexico, involved Mexican citizens, and only Mexican citizens witnessed the accident. Moreover, Gonzalez purchased the Chrysler LHS in Mexico (although he shopped for the car in Houston, Texas). Because of these factors, the district court granted the defendants' identical motions for dismissal on the ground of forum non conveniens. Gonzalez now appeals.

II. A

The primary question we address today involves the threshold inquiry in the forum non conveniens analysis: Whether the limitation imposed by Mexican law on the award of damages renders Mexico an inadequate alternative forum for resolving a tort suit brought by a Mexican citizen against a United States manufacturer.

We should note at the outset that we may reverse the grant or denial of a motion to dismiss on the ground of forum non conveniens only "where there has been a clear abuse of discretion." *Baumgart v. Fairchild Aircraft Corp.*, 981 F.2d 824, 835 (5th Cir. 1993).

The forum non conveniens inquiry consists of four considerations. First, the district court must assess whether an alternative forum is available. See *Alpine View Co. Ltd. v. Atlas Copco AB*, 205 F.3d 208, 221 (5th Cir. 2000). An alternative forum is available if "the entire case and all parties can come within the jurisdiction of that forum." In re *Air Crash Disaster Near New Orleans*, La. on July 9, 1982, 821 F.2d 1147, 1165 (5th Cir. 1987) (en banc), vacated on other grounds sub nom., *Pan Am. World Airways, Inc. v. Lopez*, 490 U.S. 1032, 104 L. Ed. 2d 400, 109 S. Ct. 1928 (1989). Second, the district court must decide if the alternative forum is adequate. See Alpine View, 205 F.3d at 221. An alternative forum is adequate if "the parties will not be deprived of all remedies or treated unfairly, even though they may not enjoy the same benefits as they might receive in an American court." In re *Air Crash*, 821 F.2d at 1165 (internal citation omitted).

If the district court decides that an alternative forum is both available and adequate, it next must weigh various private interest factors. See *Baumgart*, 981 F.2d at 835-36. If consideration of these private interest factors counsels against dismissal, the district court moves to the fourth consideration in the analysis. At this stage, the district court must weigh numerous public interest factors. If these factors weigh in the moving party's favor, the district court may dismiss the case. Id. at 837.

B. 1

The heart of this appeal is whether the alternative forum, Mexico, is adequate. (The court here explains that Mexico is an amenable forum because the defendants have agreed to submit to the jurisdiction of the Mexican courts.) The jurisprudential root of the adequacy requirement is the Supreme Court's decision in *Piper Aircraft Co. v. Reyno*, 454 U.S. 235, 70 L. Ed. 2d 419, 102 S. Ct. 252 (1981). The dispute in Piper Aircraft arose after several Scottish citizens were killed in a plane crash in Scotland. A representative for the decedents filed a wrongful death suit against two American aircraft manufacturers. The Court noted that the plaintiff filed suit in the United States because "[US] laws regarding liability, capacity to sue, and damages are more favorable to her position than are those of Scotland." Id. The Court further noted that "Scottish law does not recognize strict liability in tort." Id. This fact, however, did not deter the Court from reversing the Third Circuit. In so doing, the Court held that "although the relatives of the decedent may not be able to rely on a strict liability theory, and although their potential damage award may be smaller, there is no danger that they will be deprived of any remedy or treated unfairly [in Scotland]." Thus, the Court held that Scotland provided an adequate alternative forum for resolving the dispute, even though its forum provided a significantly lesser remedy. In a footnote, however, Justice Marshall observed that on rare occasions this may not be true:

At the outset of any forum non conveniens inquiry, the court must determine whether there exists an alternative forum. Ordinarily, this requirement will be satisfied when the defendant is "amenable to process" in the other jurisdiction. In rare circumstances, however, where the remedy offered by the other forum is clearly unsatisfactory, the other forum may not be an adequate alternative, and the initial requirement may not be satisfied. Thus, for example, dismissal would not be appropriate where the alternative forum does not permit litigation of the subject matter of the dispute. * * *

....

Citing the language from this footnote, Gonzalez contends that a Mexican forum would provide a clearly unsatisfactory remedy because (1) Mexican tort law does not provide for a strict liability theory of recovery for the manufacture or design of an unreasonably dangerous product and (2) Mexican law caps the maximum award for the loss of a child's life at approximately $2,500 (730 days' worth of wages at the Mexican minimum wage rate). Thus, according to Gonzalez, Mexico provides an inadequate alternative forum for this dispute.

B.2

(a) Gonzalez's first contention may be quickly dismissed based on the explicit principle stated in Piper Aircraft. As noted, there the Supreme Court held that Scotland's failure to recognize strict liability did not render Scotland an inadequate alternative forum. Id. at 255. There is no basis to distinguish the absence of a strict products liability cause of action under Mexican law from that of Scotland. Piper Aircraft therefore controls. Accordingly, we hold that the failure of Mexican law to allow for strict liability on the facts of this case does not render Mexico an inadequate forum.

(b) Gonzalez's second contention—that the damage cap renders the remedy available in a Mexican forum "clearly unsatisfactory"—is slightly more problematic. Underlying this contention are two distinct arguments: First, Gonzalez argues that if he brings suit in Mexico, the cap on damages will entitle him to a *de minimis* recovery only—a clearly unsatisfactory award for the loss of a child. Second, Gonzalez argues that because of the damage cap, the cost of litigating this case in Mexico will exceed the potential recovery. As a consequence, the lawsuit will never be brought in Mexico. Stated differently, the lawsuit is not economically viable in Mexico. It follows, therefore, that Mexico offers no forum (much less an adequate forum) through which Gonzalez can (or will) seek redress. We address each argument in turn.

(b)(i)

In addressing Gonzalez's first argument, we start from basic principles of comity. Mexico, as a sovereign nation, has made a deliberate choice in providing a specific remedy for this tort cause of action. In making this policy choice, the Mexican government has resolved a trade-off among the competing objectives and costs of tort law, involving interests of victims, of consumers, of manufacturers, and of various other economic and cultural values. In resolving this trade-off, the Mexican people, through their duly-elected lawmakers, have decided to limit tort damages with respect to a child's death. It would be inappropriate—even patronizing—for us to denounce this legitimate policy choice by holding that Mexico provides an inadequate forum for Mexican tort victims. In another forum non conveniens case, the District Court for the Southern District of New York made this same point observing (perhaps in a hyperbolic choice of words) that "to retain the litigation in this forum, as plaintiffs request, would be yet another example of imperialism, another situation in which an established sovereign inflicted its rules, its standards and values on a developing nation." In re *Union Carbide Corp. Gas Plant Disaster* at Bhopal, India in December, 1984, 634 F. Supp. 842, 867 (S.D.N.Y. 1986), aff'd as modified, 809 F.2d 195 (2d Cir. 1987). In short, we see no warrant for us, a United States court, to replace the policy preference of the Mexican government with our own view of what is a good policy for the citizens of Mexico.

Based on the considerations mentioned above, we hold that the district court did not err when it found that the cap on damages did not render the remedy available in the Mexican forum clearly unsatisfactory.

(b) (ii) We now turn our attention to Gonzalez's "economic viability" argument—that is, because there is no economic incentive to file suit in the alternative forum, there is effectively no alternative forum.

The practical and economic realities lying at the base of this dispute are clear. At oral argument, the parties agreed that this case would never be filed in Mexico. In short, a dismissal on the ground of forum non conveniens will determine the outcome of this litigation in Chrysler's favor. We nevertheless are unwilling to hold as a legal principle that Mexico offers an inadequate forum simply because it does not make economic sense for Gonzalez to file this lawsuit in Mexico. Our reluctance arises out of two practical considerations.

First, the plaintiff's willingness to maintain suit in the alternative (foreign) forum will usually depend on, *inter alia*, (1) whether the plaintiff's particular injuries are compensable (and to what extent) in that forum; (2) not whether the forum recognizes some cause of action among those applicable to the plaintiff's case, but whether it recognizes his most provable and compensable action; (3) similarly, whether the alternative forum recognizes defenses that might bar or diminish recovery; and (4) the litigation costs (i.e., the number of experts, the amount of discovery, geographic distances, attorney's fees, etc.) associated with bringing that particular case to trial. These factors will vary from plaintiff to plaintiff, from case to case. Thus, the forum of a foreign country might be deemed inadequate in one case but not another, even though the only difference between the two cases might be the cost of litigation or the recovery for the plaintiff's particular type of injuries. In sum, we find troublesome and lacking in guiding principle the fact that the adequacy determination could hinge on constantly varying and arbitrary differences underlying the "economic viability" of a lawsuit.

Second, if we allow the economic viability of a lawsuit to decide the adequacy of an alternative forum, we are further forced to engage in a rudderless exercise of line drawing with respect to a cap on damages: At what point does a cap on damages transform a forum from adequate to inadequate? Is it, as here, $2,500? Is it $50,000? Or is it $100,000? Any recovery cap may, in a given case, make the lawsuit economically unviable. We therefore hold that the adequacy inquiry under Piper Aircraft does not include an evaluation of whether it makes economic sense for Gonzalez to file this lawsuit in Mexico.

C.

Having concluded that Mexico provides an adequate forum, we now consider whether the private and public interest factors nonetheless weigh in favor of maintaining this suit in Texas. As noted, the district court concluded that the public and the private interest factors weighed in favor of Mexico and dismissed the case on the ground of forum non conveniens. Our review of this conclusion is restricted to abuse of discretion. See Alpine View, 205 F.3d at 220.

The district court found that almost all of the private and public interest factors pointed away from Texas and toward Mexico as the appropriate forum. It is clear to us that this finding does not represent an abuse of discretion. After all, the tort victim was a Mexican citizen, the driver of the Chrysler LHS (Gonzalez's wife) is a Mexican citizen, and the plaintiff is a Mexican citizen. The accident took place in Mexico. Gonzalez purchased the car in Mexico. Neither the car nor the air bag was designed or manufactured in Texas. In short, there are no public or private interest factors that would suggest that Texas is the appropriate forum for the trial of this case.

III.

For the foregoing reasons, the district court's dismissal of this case on the ground of forum non conveniens is

AFFIRMED.

Case Questions

1. How can an alternative forum be "adequate" if no rational lawyer would take Gonzalez's case to file in a Mexican state court?
2. To what extent does it strike you as "imperialism" for a U.S. court to make a judgment that a Mexican court is not "adequate"?

Act of State

W. S. Kirkpatrick Co., Inc. v. Environmental Tectonics Co.

493 U.S. 400 (1990)

Justice Scalia delivered the Court's opinion.

In 1981, Harry Carpenter, who was then Chairman of the Board and Chief Executive Officer of petitioner W. S. Kirkpatrick & Co., Inc. (Kirkpatrick) learned that the Republic of Nigeria was interested in contracting for the construction and equipment of an aeromedical center at Kaduna Air Force Base in Nigeria. He made arrangements with Benson "Tunde" Akindele, a Nigerian Citizen, whereby Akindele would endeavor to secure the contract for Kirkpatrick. It was agreed that in the event the contract was awarded to Kirkpatrick, Kirkpatrick would pay to two Panamanian entities controlled by Akindele an amount equal to 20% of the contract price, which would in turn be given as a bribe to officials of the Nigerian government. In accordance with this plan, the contract was awarded to petitioner W. S. Kirkpatrick & Co., International (Kirkpatrick International), a wholly owned subsidiary of Kirkpatrick; Kirkpatrick paid the promised "commission" to the appointed Panamanian entities; and those funds were disbursed as bribes. All parties agree that Nigerian law prohibits both the payment and the receipt of bribes in connection with the award of a government contract.

Respondent Environmental Tectonics Corporation, International, an unsuccessful bidder for the Kaduna contract, learned of the 20% "commission" and brought the matter to the attention of the Nigerian Air Force and the United States Embassy in Lagos. Following an investigation by the Federal Bureau of Investigation, the United States Attorney for the District of New Jersey brought charges against both Kirkpatrick and Carpenter for violations of the Foreign Corrupt Practices Act of 1977 and both pleaded guilty.

Respondent then brought this civil action in the United States District Court of the District of New Jersey against Carpenter, Akindele, petitioners, and others, seeking damages under the Racketeer Influenced and Corrupt Organizations Act, the Robinson-Patman Act, and the New Jersey Anti-Racketeering Act. The defendants moved to dismiss the complaint under Rule 12(b)(6) of the Federal Rules of Civil Procedure on the ground that the action was barred by the act of state doctrine.

The District Court concluded that the act of state doctrine applies "if the inquiry presented for judicial determination includes the motivation of a sovereign act which would result in embarrassment to the sovereign or constitute interference in the conduct of foreign policy of the United States." Applying that principle to the facts at hand, the court held that respondents suit had to be dismissed because in order to prevail respondents would have to show that "the defendants or certain other than intended to wrongfully influenced the decision to award the Nigerian contract by payment of a bribe, that the government of Nigeria, its officials or other representatives knew of the offered consideration forewarning the Nigerian contract to Kirkpatrick, that the bribe was actually received or anticipated and that but for the payment or anticipation of the payment of the bribed, ETC would have been awarded the Nigerian contract."

The Court of Appeals for the Third Circuit reversed.

This Courts' description of the jurisprudential foundation for the act of state doctrine has undergone some evolution over the years. We once viewed the doctrine as an expression of international law, resting upon "the highest considerations of international comity and expediency," Oetjen v. Central Leather Co., 246 U.S. 297, 303-304 (1918). We have more recently described it, however, as a consequence of domestic separation of powers, reflecting "the strong sense of the Judicial Branch that its engagement in the task of passing on the validity of foreign acts of state may hinder" the conduct of foreign affairs, Banco Nacional de Cuba v. Sabbatino, 376 U.S. 398, 423 (1964). Some Justices have suggested possible exceptions to application of the doctrine, where one or both of the foregoing policies would seemingly not be served: an exception, for example, for acts of state that consist of commercial transactions, since neither modern international comity nor the current position of our Executive Branch accorded sovereign immunity to such acts...or an exception for cases in which the executive branch has represented that it has no objection to denying validity to the foreign sovereign act, since then the court should be impeding no foreign-policy goals.

We find it unnecessary, however, to pursue those inquiries, since the factual predicate for application of the act of state doctrine does not exist. Nothing in the present suit requires the court to declare invalid, and thus ineffective as "a rule of decision for the courts of this country," the official act of a foreign sovereign.

In every case in which we have held the act of state doctrine applicable, the relief sought or the defense interposed would have required a court in the United States to declare invalid the official acts of a foreign sovereign performed within its own territory. * * * In *Sabbatino*, upholding the defendant's claim to the funds would have required a holding that Cuba's expropriation of goods located in Havana was null and void. In the present case, by contrast, neither the claim nor any asserted defense requires a determination that Nigeria's contract with Kirkpatrick International was, or, was not effective.

Petitioners point out, however, that the facts necessary to establish respondent's claim will also establish that the contract was unlawful. Specifically, they note that in order to prevail respondent must prove that petitioner Kirkpatrick made, and Nigerian officials received, payments that violate Nigerian law, which would, they assert, support a finding that the contract is invalid under Nigerian law. Assuming that to be true, it still does not suffice. The act of state doctrine is not some vague doctrine of abstention but a "principle *of decision* binding on federal and state courts alike." As we said in *Ricaud*, "the act within its own boundaries of one sovereign State...becomes a rule of decision for the courts of this country." Act of state issues only arise when a court *must* decide—that is, when the outcome of the case turns upon—the effect of official action by a foreign sovereign. When that question is not in the case, neither is the act of state doctrine. This is the situation here. Regardless of what the court's factual findings may suggest as to the legality of the Nigerian contract, its legality is simply not a question to be decided in the present suit, and there is thus no occasion to apply the rule of decision that the act of state doctrine requires.

* * *

The short of the matter is this: Courts in the United States have the Power, and ordinarily the obligation, to decide cases and controversies properly presented to them. The act of state doctrine does not establish an exception for cases and controversies that may embarrass foreign governments, but merely requires that; in the process of deciding, the acts of foreign sovereigns taken within their own jurisdictions shall be deemed valid: That doctrine has no application to the present case because the validity of no foreign sovereign act is at issue.

The judgment of the Court for the Third Circuit is affirmed.

Case Questions

1. Why is this case not about sovereign immunity?
2. On what basis does the U.S. court take jurisdiction over an event or series of events that takes place in Nigeria?
3. If the court goes on to the merits of the case and determines that an unlawful bribe took place in Nigeria, is it likely that diplomatic relations between the United States and Nigeria will be adversely affected?

51.6 Summary and Exercises

Summary

International law is not like the domestic law of any one country. The sovereign, or lawgiver, in any particular nation-state has the power to make and enforce laws within its territory. But globally, there is no single source of law or law enforcement. Thus international law is a collection of agreements between nation-states (treaties and conventions), customary international law (primarily based on decisions of national court systems), and customary practice between nation-states. There is an international court of justice, but it only hears cases between nation-states. There is no international court for the resolution of civil disputes, and no regional courts for that purpose, either.

The lack of unified law and prevalence of global commerce means that local and national court systems have had to devise ways of forcing judgments from one national court system or another to deal with claims against sovereigns and to factor in diplomatic considerations as national judicial systems encounter disputes that involve (directly or indirectly) the political and diplomatic prerogatives of sovereigns. Three doctrines that have been devised are sovereign immunity, act of state, and *forum non conveniens*. The recognition of forum-selection clauses in national contracting has also aided the use of arbitration clauses, making international commercial-dispute resolution more efficient. Arbitral awards against any individual or company in most nations engaged in global commerce are more easily enforceable than judgments from national court systems.

In terms of regulating trade, the traditional practice of imposing taxes (tariffs) on imports from other countries (and not taxing exports to other countries) has been substantially modified by the emergence of the General Agreement on Tariffs and Trade (GATT) rules as now enforced by the World Trade Organization (WTO). The United States has a practice of regulating exports, however, to take into account national security and other foreign policy considerations. For example, the Export Administration Act of 1985 has controlled certain exports that would endanger national security, drain scarce materials from the U.S. economy, or harm foreign policy goals. The U.S. secretary of commerce has a list of controlled commodities that meet any of these criteria.

Exercises

1. Assume that the United States enters into a multilateral treaty with several third-world countries under which then-existing private claims to molybdenum and certain other minerals in the United States are assigned to an international agency for exploitation. When the owner of a U.S. mine continues to dig for ore covered by the treaty, the Justice Department sues to enjoin further mining. What is the result? Why?
2. A foreign government enters into a contract with a U.S. company to provide computer equipment and services for the intelligence arm of its military forces. After the equipment has been supplied, the foreign government refuses to pay. The U.S. company files suit in federal court

in the United States, seeking to attach a U.S. bank account owned by the foreign government. The foreign government claims that the U.S. court has no jurisdiction and that even if it does, the government is immune from suit. What is the result?

3. Would the result in Exercise 2 be any different if the U.S. company had maintained its own equipment on a lease basis abroad and the foreign government had then expropriated the equipment and refused to pay the U.S. company its just value?
4. Canada and Russia have competing claims over fishing and mining rights in parts of the Arctic Ocean. Assuming they cannot settle their competing claims through diplomatic negotiation, where might they have their dispute settled?

Self-Test Questions

1. International law derives from
    a. the U.S. Constitution
    b. the common law
    c. treaties
    d. customary international law
    e. c and d
2. Foreign nations are immune from suit in U.S. courts for governmental acts because of
    a. the international sovereign immunity treaty
    b. a United Nations law forbidding suits against foreign sovereigns
    c. the Foreign Sovereign Immunities Act
    d. precedent created by the U.S. Supreme Court
3. A foreign government's expropriation of private assets belonging to a nonresident is
    a. a violation of international law
    b. a violation of the U.S. Constitution
    c. permitted by the domestic law of most nation states
    d. in violation of the act-of-state doctrine
4. Arbitration of business disputes is
    a. frowned upon by courts for replacing public dispute resolution with private dispute resolution
    b. permissible when a country's laws permit it
    c. permissible if the parties agree to it
    d. a and b
    e. b and c

Self-Test Answers

1. d
2. a
3. c
4. e

Endnotes

1. *EEOC v. Arabian American Oil Co.* 499 U.S. 244 (1991).
2. *Kern v. Dynalectron*, 746 F.2d 810 (1984).
3. *Underhill v. Hernandez*, 168 U.S. 250, 252 (1897).
4. *Mannington Mills, Inc. v. Congoleum Corp.*, 595 F.2d 1287 (3d Cir. 1979).
5. *Banco Nacional de Cuba v. Sabbatino*, 376 U.S. 398 (1964).

6. The term *en banc* means that all the judges of a circuit court of appeals heard oral arguments and voted to decide the outcome of the case.

CHAPTER 52
Liability and Regulation of Accountants

Learning Objectives

After reading this chapter, you should understand the following:

1. Why regulation of accountants is necessary.
2. Accountants' common law liability.
3. Federal statutory regulation of accountants.
4. State laws regulating accountants.
5. Other duties that accountants owe to their clients.

52.1 Why Regulation of Accountants is Necessary

Learning Objectives

1. Understand why the law has developed regulation of the accounting profession.
2. Recognize that cheating and malpractice by accounting professionals is not uncommon.

Let us recount some accounting scandals from the last forty years:

1. 1970s. Lockheed Airlines: investigations revealed a series of bribes and contributions, amounting to tens of millions of dollars, made by officials of U.S. aerospace company Lockheed from the late 1950s to the 1970s in the process of negotiating the sale of aircraft.[1]
2. 1988. Barry Minkow, who as a teenager founded the ZZZZ Best carpet-cleaning company, was sentenced to twenty five years in prison and ordered to pay $26 million restitution for fraud. The "boy wonder" of Wall Street created a $200 million company that existed only on paper.[2] The accounting firm of Ernst & Whinney (now part of Ernst and Young) was implicated in the scandal.
3. 1993. Paul Polishan, the former chief financial officer of The Leslie Fay Companies, received a nine-year prison sentence for fraudulently misrepresenting Leslie Fay's financial statements in the early 1990s. Among the defendants in a large class-action lawsuit stemming from the fraud was the company's audit firm, BDO Seidman.
4. 1993. "Crazy Eddie" Antar oversaw a profitable chain of consumer electronics stores on the East Coast during the 1970s and 1980s. After new owners discovered that the company's financial data had been grossly misrepresented to the tune of $80 million, Antar fled the country, leaving behind thousands of angry stockholders and creditors.
5. 1999. In the fall of 1999, just a few months after reporting a record profit for fiscal 1998, Just for FEET, Inc. collapsed and filed for bankruptcy. Subsequent investigations by law enforcement authorities revealed a massive accounting fraud that had grossly misrepresented the

company's reported operating results. Key features of the fraud at the retail footware chain were improper accounting for "vendor allowances."

6. 2002. Arthur Andersen (1913 to 2002) spent decades as a leading accounting and consulting firm. Founded in 1913, it was once a member of the "Big 8" accounting firms, which later became the "Big 5."[3] Unfortunately, the firm's association with one client, Enron Corporation, abruptly ended Andersen's long and proud history in the public accounting profession. The firm was implicated in a vast accounting scandal, and though a criminal conviction was overturned, the firm's reputation was ruined.
7. 2005. In January, Thomas Trauger became the first partner of a major accounting firm to be sent to prison for violating the criminal provisions of the Sarbanes-Oxley Act of 2002.
8. 2007. The collapse of New Century Financial Corporation in April 2007 signaled the beginning of the subprime mortgage crisis in the United States, a crisis that destabilized securities and credit markets around the globe, provoking "the Great Recession." A federal bankruptcy examiner maintained that New Century's independent audits were inadequate.
9. 2008. Wall Street was stunned in September 2008 when this iconic investment banking firm filed for bankruptcy. Lehman Brothers Holdings' bankruptcy examiner charged that the company had engaged in tens of billions of dollars of "accounting-motivated" transactions to enhance its apparent financial condition.[4]
10. 2009. As an adolescent, Bernie Madoff dreamed of becoming a "key player" on Wall Street. Madoff realized his dream by overseeing the world's largest and possibly longest running Ponzi scheme. Madoff's auditor pled guilty to various criminal charges for his role in that fraud, and Madoff was sentenced to 150 years in prison. His son Mark committed suicide in 2010. Losses to investors as a result of the scheme were around $13 billion.[5]
11. 2014. Citigroup—one of the world's largest banks, headquartered in New York City—agreed to pay $7 billion in fines and other costs. The firm knew, or should have known, that in the run-up to the 2008 financial crisis it had sold fraudulent mortgage-backed securities.[6]

Back in the early 1990s, one of our co-authors wrote the following:

> *The largest financial scandal in American history unfolded in the early 1990s—the collapse of hundreds, possibly thousands, of overextended savings and loan associations. The cost to taxpayers, it has been estimated, may rise to the staggering sum of $500 billion or more, as federal deposit insurance is paid to cover the bankruptcies of the S&Ls. Blame for these bank failures must no doubt be widely shared. Executives and managers stand in the front ranks: There is considerable evidence of widespread "looting" and wildly careless lending policies. Despite the criminality and gross negligence of many of the principals, the regulatory establishment might have stanched the flow of red ink far sooner if major portions of it had not been asleep—or deliberately averting its eyes—and if several U.S. senators and members of Congress, taking large contributions from influential S&L executives, had not prevailed on the regulators to go slow. But as federal agencies, prosecutors, and others finally began their investigations, a third group of culprits began to emerge: the professionals—accountants, lawyers, and other advisers—who collaborated with the S&Ls in their vast and irresponsible overextension of credit. One of the major questions in the aftermath of the S&L collapse, therefore, is the extent to which professionals will be held liable, both criminally and civilly, for their part in the debacle.*

Although new laws have emerged from the never-ending scandals to provide greater accountability in banking, by both bankers and the professionals without whom they could not do business, existing federal and state law has long regulated the conduct of advisers to business. In this chapter we examine the liability of professionals and the role of regulation in policing professional conduct. We use public accounting as the illustrative case, in part because accounting is more directly subject to regulations than other professions, and in part because it is inextricably linked to business.

Of course, a public accountant, in a non-professional capacity, has the same responsibilities as any nonprofessional. A certified public accountant (CPA), who while driving to work carelessly strikes a pedestrian, is liable for negligence, just as anyone else would be. Unlike other people, however, a CPA has additional legal responsibilities and liabilities arising from the practice of accounting. We examine first the common law theories of liability—breach of contract and tort—and then the effect of federal law and government regulation on public accounting practice.

Key Takeaway

Unfortunately, neither lawyers nor accountants are immune from the lure of money. As a result of wave after wave of accounting scandal, federal and state law regulates accountants. So too, certainly, does the common law.

Exercises

1. If an honorable accountant were asked by her boss or client to "cook the books," why would she ever consider going along with the scam?
2. Could government regulation or the threat of liability "cure" dishonorable accountants from accounting scams?
3. Who--besides the immediately affected people (accountants and their clients) is likely to benefit or to suffer from accounting chicanery and scamming?

52.2 Common Law Liability

Learning Objectives

1. Understand that accountants may be liable for breach of contract.
2. Explain accountants' liability in tort and negligence.
3. Recognize that accountants may be liable in negligence for failure to detect fraud.
4. Understand that accountants may be liable for negligence even to third parties with whom they never dealt.

Breach of Contract

The ordinary rules of contract law apply to agreements accountants make with clients. Failure to carry out the performance required under a contract is a breach, and the client is entitled to refuse payment. Suppose the accountant performed defectively. Some courts hold that defective performance, like nonperformance, is a breach, whereas others consider it to be negligence, a tort. The difference can be significant in some cases, since tort and contract cases are governed by different statutes of limitations, remedies, measures of damages, and standards of proof.

Tort Liability

The two usual grounds of tort liability are negligence and fraud. Negligence is usually the basis for the malpractice actions against professionals.

Negligence. In judging whether a professional has acted carelessly, the courts will hold the professional to a higher standard than that of the mythical "reasonable person." Professional conduct will be measured by the knowledge, skills, and judgment requisite to the discipline in question. An accountant who fails to follow a generally accepted accounting principle, without good reason, in auditing a company's books is liable for the harm to stockholders and others who depend on the audit, but a nonnegligent mistake is not by itself actionable. A surgeon need not guarantee that the operation will be successful, nor must an accountant guarantee the complete accuracy of her work. Her duty is simply to avoid being careless.

The public accountant's duties are therefore variable: they depend on the nature of the assignment and the developing art and practice of accounting. In this regard, one of the most vexing problems for the CPA is the degree to which she is required to ferret out fraud. Must she go behind every transaction that is recorded on the books to assure all who read her opinion that there is no possibility of fraud having been committed? At common law, no. As a British jurist said in an 1896 case: "An auditor is not bound to be a detective, or as was said, to approach his work with suspicion or with a foregone conclusion that there is something wrong. He is a watch-dog, but not a bloodhound."[7] But if 19th century common law did not impose a duty on the auditor to detect fraud, modern professional standards do. These in turn are now absorbed into common law. The Public Company Accounting Oversight Board (PCAOB, created by Congress in the Sarbanes-Oxley Act in 2002) has established certain standards; they include detective work:

> *Under generally accepted auditing standards, [auditors] have the responsibility, within the inherent limitations of the auditing process, to design [the] audit to provide reasonable assurance that errors and irregularities that have a material effect on the financial statements will be detected, and to exercise due care in the conduct of [the] audit.*[8]

As in any negligence suit, causation must be shown: the professional's failure to conform to the requisite standard of professional conduct must be the cause of the injury that the plaintiff has suffered.

Fraud

Because they deal with facts and figures that are subject to falsification, accountants are vulnerable to the charges that they have committed the intentional tort of fraud. Fraud has four elements: (1) scienter; (2) false representation; (3) reliance; and (4) injury or damages. The third and fourth elements are obvious enough: the plaintiff must have justifiably relied on the false representation (plaintiff's independent knowledge of the facts is a defense to a charge of fraud) and, as with negligence, damages must have occurred as a result of the plaintiff's reliance (or else there would be no case in any event).

Scienter
An intention to do wrong.

The first two points are a bit more subtle. **Scienter** is an intention to mislead, consisting either of knowing the telling of a falsity or the making of statements with reckless disregard for whether or not they are true. Scienter exists whether or not the person making the false representation desires that the falsehood be communicated or relied upon; the intention is present if he knows the statement to be false or says it oblivious of its possible falsehood. It is no excuse that he honestly believes the statement to be true if he has no basis for the belief.

A **false representation** is not limited to a direct lie. Concealing facts that, if known, would correct a misimpression can amount to a false representation in the eyes of the law. It is sometimes said that a false statement of an opinion is not actionable as a misrepresentation, but that conclusion does not apply to charges of fraud resulting from the expression of a professional opinion. A professional opinion is precisely what a client is paying for. The plaintiff seeks a professional opinion because she is unable to form one of her own. To say that "in my opinion, the balance sheet fairly reflects the assets and liabilities of the company" is actionable if that is not, in fact, the CPA's opinion or if he has no reasonable basis to offer it.

false representation

Lying, concealing the truth, failure to correct a misimpression, including actions or inactions by a professional that might be considered an opinion.

A fraud suit against an accountant may even be based on nondisclosure or complete silence. Silence can be deceit when previous statements stand uncorrected, despite the discovery of facts that negate them (this is the general common-law rule, not limited to cases involving accountants).

Accountants' Liability to Third Parties for Fraud or for Negligence

Granted that an accountant may commit fraud or negligence, to whom is the accountant liable? Circulation of a CPA's report is rarely restricted to the corporate or other business client. Among those with a direct interest in reading audit results are current and potential owners, creditors, suppliers, managers, employees, customers, business management, and taxing authorities. Those with a less direct, but nonetheless substantial interest, are financial analysts, securities exchanges, government regulators, the press, unions, and trade associations. If the auditor makes a mistake, is he liable to all of them for ensuing damages?

Contract law makes clear that the auditor is liable to her direct clients and any intended third-party beneficiaries. But these are usually the smaller portion of the total class likely to be harmed. The investing public does not hire the auditor, but millions of shareholders can be damaged by an erroneous statement made in an audit report. Under older principles of common law, those not "in privity of contract" (those not party to the contract) had no rights and hence no remedies against the auditor.

Liability for fraud. Today, courts are in agreement that the auditor guilty of *fraud* is liable to *all* third parties who might reasonably have been presumed to rely on a certified financial statement.

Liability for negligence. There remains disagreement in cases in which the accountant was not deceitful but merely negligent. Three different tests are used by different courts. For many years, the leading case was *Ultramares Corp. v. Touche,*[9] which held that accountants are not liable to third parties for ordinary negligence. Chief Judge Cardozo explained that the defendant accountants

> *owed to their employer a duty imposed by law to make their certificate [that the balance sheet was accurate] without fraud, and a duty growing out of contract to make it with the care and caution proper to their calling. Fraud includes the pretense of knowledge when knowledge there is none. To creditors and investors to whom the employer exhibited the certificate, the defendants owed a like duty to make it without fraud, since there was notice in the circumstances of its making that the employer did not intend to keep it to himself. A different question develops when we ask whether they owed a duty to these to make it without negligence. If liability for negligence exists, a thoughtless slip or blunder, the failure to detect a theft or forgery beneath the cover of deceptive entries, may expose accountants to a liability in an indeterminate amount for an indeterminate time to an indeterminate class. The hazards of a business conducted on these terms are so extreme as to enkindle doubt whether a flaw may not exist in the implication of a duty that exposes to these consequences.*

primary-benefit test

A professional's liability for negligence extends only to those in privity with the professional or third parties who are intended beneficiaries of the professional's client.

foreseen users (or foreseen class of users)

A professional's liability for negligence extends to those who the professional knew would use the work or those who would be likely to use it for the purpose for which the work was developed.

reasonably foreseeable plaintiffs

Imposes liability on a negligent professional in favor of anybody who might reasonably be foreseen as relying upon the work product, even if the professional did not specifically know that such reliance would occur.

Today, the *Ultramares* rule is called the **primary-benefit test**. It holds that a professional is liable only for negligence to third parties who are in privity of contract or privity-like relationships with the professional. The primary-benefit test provides the narrowest standard for holding professionals liable to third parties for negligence. Again, the idea here is that the only third parties who can sue an accountant for professional negligence are those who were specifically intended by the client *and* the accountant to benefit by the accountant's work.

A majority of states have abandoned the Ultramares rule and have adopted the **foreseen users (or foreseen class of users)** test, the rule also taken up by Section 552 of the Restatement (Second) of Torts; it expands liability to those the accountant knew would use the work or those who would be likely to use it for the purposes for which the work was developed (for example, a bank reviewing whether to extend a loan).

Some states have adopted a third rule, the **reasonably foreseeable plaintiffs** test; it is the most expansive. It imposes liability against a negligent accountant to anybody who might reasonably be foreseen as relying upon the work product. Notice the difference between the second and third tests: in the second one, the users must be *foreseen*; in the third one, the users must only be *foreseeable*.

For example, suppose Acme Excelsior Corporation wishes to establish a bank credit line of $3 million and hires Riemann & Lobachevsky Company, a certified public accounting firm, to prepare an audit. Acme Excelsior tells Riemann & Lobachevsky that it intends to negotiate with the First National Bank of Centerville. Riemann & Lobachevsky neglects to consider accounts payable and thus fails to spot Acme's probable insolvency. Under the *primary-benefit test*, certainly First National Bank may sue the accounting firm for negligence. Suppose, without telling its accountants, Acme negotiates instead with the Second National Bank of Centerville. Under *the foreseen users test*, Second Bank would have a valid suit against the accountants: although the audit was not prepared specifically for Second National Bank, it was prepared for a bank to use in determining whether to extend credit. And what difference does it make which bank gets "burned" by relying on the defective audit?

Key Takeaway

Accountants may be liable to their clients for both breach of contract and—probably more important—for tort liability. One type of tort liability arises in cases where the accountant has committed fraud. In fraud cases, the accountant's liability is very far reaching: anyone who might reasonably have been expected to rely on the accountant's work has standing to sue. The range of persons who have standing to sue the accountant in tort for negligence is more complex. Some jurisdictions require that the plaintiff be in privity with the accountant or that the plaintiff be an intended beneficiary of the accountant-client contract; other jurisdictions allow standing for more attenuated relationships between the account and the plaintiff.

Exercises

1. What are the common-law causes of actions against accountants whose bad work causes a client loss?
2. Describe the three tests used to determine the extent of a negligent accountant's scope of liability.

52.3 Federal Statutory Liability

Learning Objectives

1. Recognize that in addition to common-law liability, accountants may be civilly and criminally liable under federal law.
2. Understand the basics of accountants' liability under the following statutes:
   - the Securities Act of 1933;
   - the Securities Exchange Act of 1934;
   - the Private Securities Litigation Reform Act of 1995 (an amendment to the '34 Act); and
   - the Sarbanes-Oxley Act of 2002 (also an amendment to the '34 Act).
3. Know that other federal laws may also impose liability on accountants, including antitrust laws, RICO (the Racketeer Influenced and Corrupt Organizations Act) and federal Revenue Acts.

Accountants have, over hundreds of years, been found liable for breach of contract, fraud, and negligence. These are standard common-law causes of action. But common-law liability does not exhaust the perils of malpractice for the modern practitioner. Federal statutes considerably broaden their potential liability: more than fifteen separate statutory provisions in securities law relate to the liability of public accountants. We focus on only the most important ones, and also look briefly at antitrust liability and the liability of tax preparers.

Liability under the Securities Act of 1933

For accountants concerned about liability, the two key provisions of the Securities Act of 1933 are Sections 11 and 12(2).

Liability under Section 11—Registration Statements

You may recall from your study of securities regulations that (with some exceptions) before a security can be sold in interstate commerce it must be registered with the Securities and Exchange Commission, a federal regulatory agency. **Section 11 of the Securities Act** imposes third-party liability on an accountant who makes or certifies in a registration statement "an untrue statement of a material fact or [omits] to state a material fact required to be stated therein or necessary to make the statements therein not misleading." This provision applies only to registration statements and to reports and valuations used in connection with the registration statements. Registration statements are filed only for new public offerings, so the liability under this section is relatively limited. Only purchasers of the specific securities offered through the registration statement acquire rights to sue accountants; subsequent purchasers do not.

Except in one limited instance, the investor need not show reliance on the materially false statement. In other words, a purchaser who sees his investment go sour need not ever have read the registration statement. (Notice this is different from common-law liability for fraud or misrepresentation, where reliance is a required element of liability.) The purchaser can win a suit against the accountants by showing that the registration statement contained a misstatement or an omission of a fact that the average reasonable investor would consider important in determining whether to invest in the offering company's securities. The plaintiff must show reliance when he has made the purchase more than a year following the effective date of the registration statement and the company has issued an earnings statement covering a period of at least twelve months after the effective date.

The accountant's liability is neither strict nor absolute: she can prevail in a lawsuit by demonstrating that she has exercised due diligence. Through the due diligence defense, the accountant shows that she made a "reasonable investigation" and as a result had "reasonable ground to believe and did believe" that the statements contained in the registration document were true and that no material omissions had been made. Section 11 sets forth as the standard of reasonableness "that required of a prudent man [or woman] in the management of his own property." If the accountant fails the due diligence test, he is liable for the difference between the amount the investor paid for the stock and its market value at the time of suit, assuming the stock has not been sold. When the plaintiff has sold the stock prior to suit, he can recover the difference between what he paid and the sale price, but the initial offering price is a ceiling on the amount recoverable. Section 11 gives the plaintiff an incentive to sell the stock prior to suit by limiting recovery to market value at the time of filing suit. Should she subsequently sell the stock for a price even lower than that prevailing at the time of filing, she is barred from recovering the decrease. Moreover, if the stock has risen in price after filing, the defendant accountant is permitted to take that rise into account in calculating her financial exposure should she lose the suit. Plaintiffs have one year, measured from the time they discovered the false filing, to sue; in no case may a suit be filed more than three years after the security was first offered for public sale.

The best way to view the accountant's duties under the act is to scrutinize the facts in the *Escott* case (Case 52-1). It is the leading federal case on due diligence.

Liability under Section 12(2)—Prospectuses and Communications

Section 12(2) of the Securities Act imposes liability based on negligence for people who sell securities by making untrue material statements or omitting material facts. Since the provision applies to sellers, accountants ordinarily are not affected by it. However, some courts have found accountants to be culpable for aiding and abetting the seller when the accountant knew or should have known of material misrepresentations on which investors were likely to rely.[10] Under Section 12(2), plaintiffs are entitled to return the securities for the purchase price plus interest, or to be made whole if the securities have already been sold.

Liability under the Securities Exchange Act of 1934

The 1933 Act (what we just discussed) deals with "going public"—that is, the first time a security is offered for sale. But of course the vast majority of sales are of already-existing securities that are exchanged between seller and buyer on the market. This is what the Security Exchange Act of 1934 polices. The Act governs their sale on national exchanges, regulates proxy solicitations (among other things), and requires periodic reporting of corporate and other developments.

In General

Under the '34 act, accountants are made liable to investors, creditors, and others who rely on financial statements that the accountants are required to sign. The accountant's duty is less to the client than to the investing public for certifying the accuracy of the reports. More 1934 act lawsuits are filed under **Section 10(b) of the Securities and Exchange Act of 1934** and the corresponding **SEC Rule 10b-5**[11] than under any other provisions. Section 10(b) and the related rules prohibit the use of manipulative and deceptive devices to defraud anyone in connection with the sale of securities through national securities exchanges, the mails, or other instrumentalities of interstate commerce. Rule 10b-5 is used against insider trading, and it is also used as the basis for suits against accountants, who are generally charged with "aiding and abetting" others, such as insiders, who have violated the law. Accountants who accept from corporate insiders financial information that contains material errors, without undertaking some sort of investigation into its probable truth, and without then correcting or disclosing the errors, may be held liable under Rule 10b-5 if the errors find their way into reports filed with the SEC, whether or not the accountant has been asked to carry out a full-scale audit.

Section 10(b) of the Securities and Exchange Act of 1934

That section of the federal securities law that makes illegal "any manipulative or deceptive device or contrivance in contravention of such rules and regulations as the Commission may prescribe as necessary or appropriate in the public interest or for the protection of investors" in the purchase or sale of securities.

SEC Rule 10b-5

A rule promulgated by the SEC under the authority granted to it by Section 10(b) of the '34 Act. It prohibits any act or omission resulting in fraud or deceit in connection with the purchase or sale of any security.

During the 1970s, accountants became concerned that they could be held liable for aiding and abetting fraud even though they had no knowledge of it and even though their failure to detect it was thus simple negligence. Finally, the Supreme Court settled the matter by ruling in the landmark *Ernst & Ernst v. Hochfelder* case (Case 53-2) that there can be no private action for damages under Rule 10b-5 in the absence of a charge that the defendant intended to deceive, manipulate, or defraud. The Supreme Court later held that the SEC must establish scienter in civil enforcement actions to enjoin violations of Rule 10b-5.[12]

Sanctions

Hochfelder, then, reduced the potential for accountant liability by requiring that scienter be shown in Rule 10b-5 cases. That aside, potential liability for violation of the Act is heavy duty.

Section 18 imposes civil liability on an accountant who makes or causes to be made any false or misleading statement regarding any material fact in any document filed with the SEC under the '34 Act. As noted above, this liability is broad: it extends to anybody who purchased or sold a security without knowledge that a statement was false or misleading. Basically, if a plaintiff wins against an accountant, the accountant has to make the plaintiff whole, and if there are a lot of such plaintiffs, the damages can run into the millions. In addition to private suits that investors can file, the accountant is subject to both civil and criminal proceedings by the government. The 1933 and 1934 acts empower the SEC to seek injunctions and civil penalties in federal court against anyone who is about to engage in or is currently engaged in violating any of the federal statutory or regulatory provisions. The SEC can refer serious cases to the U.S. Attorney for criminal prosecution that can lead to jail sentences and large monetary fines (a fine up to $5 million, prison up to twenty years, or both, and an accounting firm can be liable up to $25 million).

The SEC also has an often overlooked but important administrative sanction: the **Rule 2(e) proceeding**. Under Rule 2(e), the SEC may discipline errant accountants and other professionals by disqualifying them from practicing before the Commission. The SEC must give notice to the accused and hold a due process hearing before it can disqualify an accountant from practice, either temporarily or permanently. Under certain circumstances, such as conviction of a felony or revocation or suspension of a license to practice accounting, the Commission may suspend the right without a hearing. Among the reasons for disqualification are unethical or improper behavior, willful violations of the securities laws, and a finding that the auditor does not "possess the requisite qualifications to represent others" or is "lacking in character or integrity."

Rule 2(e) proceeding

A hearing undertaken by the SEC to determine whether a person allegedly engaged in securities fraud should be barred from practicing before the SEC. It is similar to the disbarment of an attorney.

Although Rule 2(e) mentions only disqualification and censure, the SEC has actively devised a wide range of innovative sanctions against auditors. Many involve agreements by the auditors to employ new procedures to control their auditing practices, and to submit to independent compliance reviews. The sanctions have included peer reviews, continuing education programs, merger with larger firms, suspension of a partner from acting as such, and notification to new securities clients that the auditing firm is subject to sanction and why.

The Private Securities Litigation Reform Act of 1995

Private Securities Litigation Reform Act (PSLRA)

Requires auditors, in some circumstances, to "blow the whistle" on their clients if the auditor opines they are manipulating the firm's books and records; auditors must state whether they feel the firm they audit is viable as a "going concern" for the next year; requires that plaintiffs make a prima facie showing that the defendant engaged in fraudulent activities when filing suit (as opposed to suing and then trying to discover irregularities).

Under the '34 Act, accountants can be subject to serious criminal and civil penalties (have good malpractice insurance!). In December of 1995, over President Clinton's veto, Congress passed the **Private Securities Litigation Reform Act (PSLRA)**. Basically, the act does two things. First, it imposes a significant set of obligations upon auditors, requiring them to establish procedures to detect material illegal acts, to notify the issuer's management about such findings, and to make sure the board of directors knows about it. The board must then see that the SEC and the auditor are notified that it has received the auditor's report, and if no such notice is forthcoming, the auditor must give a copy of the report to the SEC (and the auditor will almost always resign). Also, the auditor must determine whether there is doubt about the firm's ability to act as a going concern for the next year. The Reform Act exonerates auditors from private civil liability for conclusions made in the report, but the SEC can impose civil penalties on the auditor if that person fails to furnish a report to the SEC. So, all of this is an additional—and pretty scary—burden on auditors.

But the act does a second thing: before the PSLRA, plaintiffs could file a lawsuit simply because a stock price changed significantly and hope that the discovery process would reveal potential fraud. And this discovery process could be very onerous, involving hundreds of thousands of pages of material that plaintiffs' lawyers would look through to find some irregularity. But since the PSLRA, plaintiffs are required to bring forth particular fraudulent statements made by the defendant, to allege that the fraudulent statements were reckless or intentional and to prove that they suffered a financial loss as a result of the alleged fraud.[13] The act also discourages class actions for frivolous purposes and awards costs and attorneys' fees against parties who fail to fulfill these pleading requirements.

Sarbanes-Oxley Act, 2002

Sarbanes-Oxley Act

Regulates auditors and accountants. Top management must individually certify the accuracy of financial information. In addition, penalties for fraudulent financial activity were enhanced severely. Also, SOX increased the oversight role of boards of directors and the independence of the outside auditors who review the accuracy of corporate financial information.

In response to vast accounting scandals in the 1990s, Congress adopted and President Bush signed into law the **Sarbanes-Oxley Act** in 2002[14] (the act is named for its Congressional sponsors, and is usually referred to as SOX).

Background. At base this is how it shook out: in order to increase their pay, which was pegged to their firms' stock price, executives at a number of big firms took advice from financial consultants and effectively manipulated the books to make it look like the firms were making money, lots of money. That made the stock price go up, and the executives' pay too. Auditors, who should have reported the inaccuracies, were in on the scam. During the '80s and '90s, accounting firms began to profit more from their audit clients by providing tax services, investment advice, human resource services, and other consulting than from auditing alone. So, the accounting firms did both: auditing and consulting; the auditor folks worried that if they did "clean" audits properly critical of their own colleagues' consulting advice, their clients might fire the consultants. That would be a huge financial blow to the accounting firm (and to the auditors), whose profits the auditor branch shared with the consultant branch. So the auditors acquiesced, at least, in cooking the books. Scandal followed. The Enron Company, once the seventh largest firm on the Fortune 500 list, went bankrupt. The debacle was one of the biggest business scandals of the twentieth century: thousands of people lost their jobs, their pensions, their security; millions suffered loss of their investments. (Of course, most accountants would never be party to such a scam, but some—with eyes on the money and not wanting to be seen as "not a team player"—played along with the scam.) SOX is generally recognized as the most significant change to federal securities laws since the 1930s.

Basic provisions. SOX applies to accountants who audit issuers of securities, and to relevant lawyers, consultants, and company employees. The act created a new class of federal crimes involving willful non-retention of audit work papers. Such papers must be retained for five years (sometimes seven); the act makes it illegal to destroy or falsify records to impede investigations; it provides for fines and/or imprisonment for up to twenty years. It is illegal for a CPA firm to provide any non-audit (consulting) services to the same company for which it is providing audit services; it is illegal for a CPA firm member to take a job with a company for which she had provided accounting services for a period of one year after quitting as the CPA. There are further provisions affecting corporate responsibilities for financial reports, for insider trading, rules for attorneys, disclosure statements, restrictions on personal loans for executives, rules for management of internal controls, criminal fraud accountability sections, and for protection of whistle-blowers. SOX created a new federal nonprofit corporation, the Public Company Accounting Oversight Board, which has five members. It regulates firms that audit SEC registrants, not other accounting firms; it conducts annual inspections of accounting firms. The SEC is also authorized to make new, tougher regulations regarding accounting standards.

SOX, as noted, applies directly only to publicly traded firms and those that plan to become publicly traded. But private companies are affected too because many in the business world view the SOX requirements to be the standard by which companies will be judged.

The outlook. To a large extent, SOX was really a restatement, more specific in many cases, of the standards of professional conduct already detailed in other legislation or regulation. Whether it will clean up "the corporate mess" is frankly doubtful. For one thing, the big accounting firms have a lot of influence about what regulations the SEC adopts—there is considerable "corporate capture" in the accounting profession (the regulated industry "captures" the regulatory agency).[15] And it is obvious that SOX hasn't stopped greed and recklessness in financial transactions: only six years later there was another financial calamity—the "Great Recession" of 2008—caused by flakey accounting and corporate malfeasance. Probably until the measure of success changes from "being rich" to "being decent," people will always be attracted to big-corporate scams: there is just too much money to be made in the system to avoid tempting those whose main measure of self-worth is money. Nonetheless, honest accountants—that's most of them—play a critical role in maintaining as much integrity in the system as possible.

Key Takeaway

The Securities Act of 1933 imposes civil liability on accountants if the paperwork they prepare for a registration statement contains any false or misleading statement or if it omits any material fact. A defense for the accountant is due diligence. For willful violations, fines and imprisonment may be imposed.

The Securities Exchange Act of 1934 imposes civil liability on an accountant who knowingly makes false or misleading statements in any document filed with the SEC; under Rule 10b-5, an accountant is civilly liable if she acts with scienter in making oral or written misstatements of material fact in connection with the purchase or sale of a security. Criminal liability may be imposed in cases of willful violation, and under Rule 2(e) accountants may be subject to various kinds of administrative oversight, or be disallowed to practice before the SEC.

The Private Securities Litigation Reform Act requires that auditors establish procedures capable of detecting material illegal acts; it empowers auditors to act as whistle-blowers; it requires that auditors determine—and report on—whether a firm can be considered a "going concern" for the next year.

The Sarbanes-Oxley Act (SOX) establishes a regulatory body to oversee public-firm auditors; it makes auditors more independent from their clients, and imposes direct responsibility for the audit relationship on audit committees.

Exercises

1. What's the difference between what an accountant did wrong if she is found liable under the Securities Act of 1933 compared to what she did if found liable under the act of 1934?
2. Does the Private Securities Litigation Reform Act allow for the suspension of an accountant's right to practice accounting?
3. How do the provisions of SOX attempt to address the behavior that gave rise to the Enron scandal?

Other Federal Laws Affecting Accountants

Antitrust liability. Until the mid-1970s, it had long been assumed that the "learned professions" were exempt from prosecution under the Sherman Act and that agreements fixing the price of services, as opposed to products put on the market, were likewise not subject to the antitrust laws. In 1975, in *Goldfarb v. Virginia State Bar,*[16] the U.S. Supreme Court struck down a Virginia State Bar fee schedule to which lawyers in the state were expected to adhere. The Court held that the practice of law is within the Sherman Act's meaning of "trade or commerce." Subsequent decisions have made clear that other acts also violate the antitrust laws: attempts by professionals—here we are concerned about accountants—either directly or through their professional associations and codes of ethics to fix fees, regulate advertising, set product or service standards that could exclude some practitioners from the market, and otherwise interfere with the right of individual practitioners to carry on their business in the marketplace.

Liability of tax preparers. The federal Revenue Acts of 1976 and 1978 established standards and liabilities for anyone, including accountants, who for compensation prepares federal tax returns for others, or who hires preparers to do so. Under these laws, the preparer must personally sign all returns he has done for compensation and include his special preparer's identification number and address. He must give a completed copy of the return or refund claim to the taxpayer no later than the moment when the preparer submits a copy to the taxpayer for signing. Employers of preparers must maintain lists of their employees, addresses, and identification numbers, and preparers themselves must maintain lists of taxpayers whose returns they filed, including taxable year, type of return or claim, and identification numbers. These lists must be kept for three years.

RICO. Accountants have also been held liable under the Racketeer Influenced and Corrupt Organizations Act (RICO).[17] RICO generally makes it unlawful for any person employed by or associated with an enterprise to conduct or participate in the conduct of the enterprise's affairs through "a pattern of racketeering activity." The statute defines a "pattern of racketeering activity" to be at least two acts of racketeering activity within ten years of each other. "Racketeering activity" in turn is defined to include offenses such as murder, kidnapping, gambling, arson, robbery, bribery, extortion, drug dealing and obstruction of justice, as well as mail fraud, wire fraud, and "fraud in the sale of securities." Of course securities fraud is already illegal. The kicker here is that RICO then goes on to provide a treble damage remedy to "any person injured in his business or property by reason of" the conduct of an enterprise through a pattern of racketeering activity.

Key Takeaway

Professionals—including accountants and accounting associations—may be liable under antitrust laws for price fixing, regulation of advertising, or maintaining unreasonable barriers to practice. Tax preparers are subject to federal regulation, and accountants may be considered racketeers if they engage in or are associated with wire fraud, mail fraud, or securities fraud. Racketeers are subject to treble damages.

52.4 State Regulation Affecting Accountants, and Other Duties Owed to Clients

Learning Objectives

1. Recognize that states have securities regulations similar to federal regulations, and accountants may be liable for violations of them.
2. Note that states, more than the federal government, regulate the practice of public accounting by licensing and certification requirements.
3. Understand the significant limits to the account-client privilege.
4. Recognize the legal significance of the accountant's working papers.

The accountant and state securities laws. State securities regulation also affects accountants. The Uniform Securities Act, adopted in many states, has a provision virtually identical to SEC Rule 10b-5. Although in many states this provision cannot be used as the basis for a suit for damages, other statutory provisions make available to private plaintiffs the right to file suits for damages for fraud and misrepresentation in the sale, purchase, and exchange of securities. These provisions are relevant to securities transactions not within federal securities laws (e.g., purely intrastate sales, sales to sophisticated investors, small offerings).

State regulation of accountants' privilege to practice. Perhaps more important, the states, far more so than the federal government, closely regulate the practice of public accounting. Most states have licensing and certification provisions that restrict the right to hold oneself out as a certified public accountant to those who meet specified standards of training and knowledge. Certification as a public accountant is not a vested right: a state may revoke a license or certificate for "unprofessional conduct of the holder of such certificate or for other sufficient cause," and may issue a set of regulations that detail the proper forms of conduct and the nature of such disabling acts as conflicts of interest.

The accountant-client privilege. Accountants have professional obligations to preserve the confidentiality of communications with clients. For the most part, the confidentiality of client communications is a matter of professional ethics and is not protected by federal or state common law. However, several statutes do recognize the so-called accountant-client privilege (akin to the lawyer-client privilege) and permit the accountant to refuse to testify in court, or in another legal proceeding, about what he has learned from the client of the client's business. Even in states recognizing the privilege, however, the communication is considered confidential only if it was intended to be confidential at the time it was made and if the client has not subsequently waived confidentiality. A communication is not considered to be intended as confidential if an outsider is present during the discussion between client and accountant; confidentiality is waived if the client subsequently volunteers any portions of the communication. The Internal Revenue Service Restructuring and Reform Act (1998), however, has this provision:

> *With respect to tax advice, the same common law protections of confidentiality which apply to a communication between a taxpayer and an attorney shall also apply to a communication between a taxpayer and any federally authorized tax practitioner to the extent the communication would be considered a privileged communication if it were between a taxpayer and an attorney.*

Working papers

Documents, notes of interviews and audits, and other papers that the auditor prepares in the course of working for a client; they belong to the auditor, not the client.

Working papers. **Working papers** are the documents, notes of interviews and audits, and other papers that the auditor prepares in the course of his work for a client. In the absence of a statute or contractual agreement to the contrary, the auditor owns these papers and need not accede to a client's demand, for example, that they be transferred to a new accountant at the termination of the relationship with the original auditor. One reason that accountants are permitted to keep their working papers is to defend themselves against potential charges of malpractice or other dereliction of duty.

In states where the confidential nature of the client-auditor relationship is recognized, consent of the client is ordinarily required before the auditor can give working papers on his own to another accountant or to any other outside party. Federal law recognizes no general right to the confidentiality of working papers. In 1984, for instance, the Supreme Court decided that an auditor's working papers are subject to subpoena by the Internal Revenue Service.[18]

Key Takeaway

States have securities laws similar to federal laws; securities transactions not subject to federal jurisdiction may give rise to state law liabilities for accountants. States also regulate who can be a CPA. While accountants have an ethical obligation to keep their clients' confidences, and while some states explicitly recognize an accountant-client privilege, this privilege is not universally recognized in state law and—with a limited exception for some tax advice—it does not apply under federal law. Generally speaking, an accountant's working papers belong to the accountant, not to the client.

Exercises

1. Why would an accountant doing securities work in the state of X need to be concerned about securities-law liability if the securities are exempt from federal jurisdiction?
2. Describe the reach of the account-client privilege under state and federal law.
3. Coleen Client has used Arthur Accountant's services for twenty years. She decides to retire from her job and move 500 miles to live near her daughter. She asks Arthur for her file. Whose file is it?

52.5 Cases

Liability and Defenses under the Securities Act of 1933

Escott v. BarChris Construction Co., 283 F. Supp 643 (SDNY, 1968)

MCLEAN, DISTRICT JUDGE.

This is an action by purchasers of debentures [these people loaned the corporation money; a debenture is like corporate bond, but not secured by specific property of the corporation] of Barchris Corporation. Plaintiffs purport to sue on their own behalf and "on behalf of all other present and former holders" of the debentures. When the action was begun on October 25, 1962, there were nine plaintiffs. Others were subsequently permitted to intervene. At the time of the trial, there were over sixty.

The action is brought under Section II of the Securities Act of 1933 . Plaintiffs allege that the registration statement with respect to these debentures filed with the Securities and Exchange Commission, which became effective on May 16, 1961, contained material false statements and material omissions.

Defendants fall into three categories: (1) the persons who signed the registration statement; (2) the underwriters, consisting of eight investment banking firms, led by Drexel & Co. (Drexel); and (3) BarChris's auditors, Peat, Marwick, Mitchell & Co. (Peat, Marwick).

At the time relevant here, BarChris was engaged primarily in the construction of bowling alleys, somewhat euphemistically referred to as "bowling centers." These were rather elaborate affairs. They contained not only a number of alleys or "lanes," but also, in most cases, bar and restaurant facilities.

By early 1961, BarChris needed additional working capital. The proceeds of the sale of the debentures involved in this action were to be devoted, in part at least, to fill that need. The registration statement of the debentures, in preliminary form, was filed with the Securities and Exchange Commission on March 30, 1961. A first amendment was filed on May 11 and a second on May 16. The registration statement became effective on May 16. The closing of the financing took place on May 24. On that day, BarChris received the net proceeds of the financing. By that time BarChris was experiencing difficulties in collecting amounts due from some of its customers. Some of them were in arrears in payments due to factors on their discounted notes. As time went on, those difficulties increased. Although BarChris continued to build alleys in 1961 and 1962, it became increasingly apparent that the industry was overbuilt. Operators of alleys, often inadequately financed, began to fail. Precisely when the tide turned is a matter of dispute, but at any rate, it was painfully apparent in 1962.

In October 1962, BarChris came to the end of the road. On October 29, 1962, it filed in this court a petition for an arrangement under Chapter 11 of the Bankruptcy Act. BarChris defaulted in the payment of the interest due on November I, 1962 on the debentures.

Section 11(b) [of the Securities Act of 1933] provides:

Notwithstanding the provisions of subsection (a) no person . . . shall be liable as provided therein who shall sustain the burden of proof—(3) that . . . (B) as regards any part of the registration statement purporting to be made upon his authority as an expert . . . (i) he had, after reasonable investigation, reasonable ground to believe and did believe, at the time such part of the registration statement became effective, that the statements therein were true and that there was no omission to state a material fact required to be stated therein or necessary to make the statements therein not misleading. . . .

This defines the due diligence defense for an expert. Peat, Marwick has pleaded it.

Peat, Marwick's work was in general charge of a member of the firm. Most of the actual work was performed by a senior accountant, Berardi, who had junior assistants, one of whom was Kennedy. Berardi was then about thirty years old. He was not yet a CPA. He had had no previous experience with the bowling industry. This was his first job as a senior accountant. He could hardly have been given a more difficult assignment.

The purpose of reviewing events subsequent to the date of a certified balance sheet (referred to as an S-1 review when made with reference to a registration statement) is to ascertain whether any material change has occurred in the company's financial position which should be disclosed in order to prevent the balance sheet figures from being misleading. The scope of such a review, under generally accepted auditing standards, is limited. It does not amount to a complete audit. Peat, Marwick prepared a written program for such a review. I find that this program conformed to generally accepted auditing standards. * * *

Berardi made the S-I review in May 1961. He devoted a little over two days to it, a total of 20.5 hours. He did not discover any of the errors or omissions pertaining to the state of affairs in 1961, all of which were material. The question is whether, despite his failure to find out anything, his investigation was reasonable within the meaning of the statute.

What Berardi did was to look at a consolidating trial balance as of March 31, 1961 which had been prepared by BarChris, compare it with the audited December 31, 1960 figures, discuss certain unfavorable developments which the comparison disclosed, and read certain minutes. He did not examine any "important financial records" other than the trial balance. As to minutes, he read only what minutes [were given] him, which consisted only of the board of directors' minutes of BarChris. He did not read such minutes as there were of the executive committee. He did not know that there was an executive committee, hence he did not discover that [there were] notes of executive committee minutes which had not been written up. He did not read the minutes of any subsidiary. He asked questions, he got answers which he considered satisfactory, and he did nothing to verify them. * * *

Accountants should not be held to a standard higher than that recognized in their profession. I do not do so here. Berardi's review did not come up to that standard. He did not take some of the steps which Peat, Marwick's written program prescribed. He did not spend an adequate amount of time on a task of this magnitude. Most important of all, he was too easily satisfied with glib answers to his inquiries.

This is not to say that he should have made a complete audit. But there were enough danger signals in the materials which he did examine to require some further investigation on his part. Generally accepted accounting standards required such further investigation under these circumstances. It is not always sufficient merely to ask questions.

Here again, the burden of proof is on Peat, Marwick. I find that that burden has not been satisfied. I conclude that Peat, Marwick has not established its due diligence defense.

Case Questions

1. What is an "investment banking firm"? Who was Escott?
2. BarChris borrowed money and gave the lenders a written promise that it would repay them. What did it want the money for, and what happened that caused it to be unable to repay them?
3. Why didn't the lenders just sue BarChris instead of suing Peat, Marwick?
4. What defense did the accounting firm raise? How did the court rule on the defense, and why?

Accountants' Liability Under the Act of 1934 for Aiding and Abetting Fraud

Ernst & Ernst v. Hochfelder, 425 US 185 (1976)

MR. JUSTICE POWELL delivered the opinion of the Court.

Petitioner, Ernst & Ernst, is an accounting firm. From 1946 through 1967 it was retained by First Securities Company of Chicago (First Securities), a small brokerage firm and member of the Midwest Stock Exchange and of the National Association of Securities Dealers, to perform periodic audits of the firm's books and records. In connection with these audits, Ernst & Ernst prepared for filing with the Securities and Exchange Commission (Commission) the annual reports required of First Securities under §17(a) of the 1934 Act. It also prepared for First Securities responses to the financial questionnaires of the Midwest Stock Exchange (Exchange).

Respondents were customers of First Securities who invested in a fraudulent securities scheme perpetrated by Leston B. Nay, president of the firm and owner of 92 percent of its stock. Nay induced the respondents to invest funds in "escrow" accounts that he represented would yield a high rate of return. Respondents did so from 1942 through 1966 with the majority of the transactions occurring in the 1950s. In fact, there were no escrow accounts as Nay converted respondents' funds to his own use immediately upon receipt. These transactions were not in the customary form of dealings between First Securities and its customers. The respondents drew their personal checks payable to Nay or a designated bank for his account. No such escrow accounts were reflected on the books and records of First Securities, and none was shown on its periodic accounting to respondents in connection with their other investments. Nor were they included in First Securities' filings with the Commission or the Exchange.

This fraud came to light in 1968 when Nay committed suicide, leaving a note that described First Securities as bankrupt and the escrow accounts as "spurious." The complaint charged that Nay's escrow scheme violated §10(b) and Commission Rule 10b-5, and that Ernst & Ernst had "aided and abetted" Nay's violations by its "failure" to conduct proper audits of First Securities. As revealed through discovery, respondents' cause of action rested on a theory of negligent nonfeasance. The premise was that Ernst & Ernst had failed to utilize "appropriate auditing procedures" in its audits of First Securities, thereby failing to discover internal practices of the firm said to prevent an effective audit. The practice principally relied on was Nay's rule that only he could open mail addressed to him at First Securities or addressed to First Securities to his attention, even if it arrived in his absence. Respondents contended that if Ernst & Ernst had conducted a proper audit, it would have discovered this "mail rule." The existence of the rule then would have been disclosed in reports to the Exchange and to the Commission by Ernst & Ernst as an irregular procedure that prevented an effective audit. This would have led to an investigation of Nay that would have revealed the fraudulent scheme. Respondents specifically disclaimed the existence of fraud or intentional misconduct on the part of Ernst & Ernst.

The Court of Appeals for the Seventh Circuit [held] that one who breaches a duty of inquiry and disclosure owed another is liable in damages for aiding and abetting a third party's violation of Rule 10b-5 if the fraud would have been discovered or prevented but for the breach.

We granted certiorari to resolve the question whether a private cause of action for damages will lie under §10(b) and Rule 10b-5 in the absence of any allegation of "scienter"—intent to deceive, manipulate, or defraud. We conclude that it will not and therefore we reverse.

Section 10(b) makes unlawful the use or employment of "any manipulative or deceptive device or contrivance" in contravention of Commission rules. The words "manipulative or deceptive" used in conjunction with "device or contrivance" strongly suggest that §10(b) was intended to proscribe knowing or intentional misconduct.

In its amicus curiae brief, however, the Commission contends that nothing in the language "manipulative or deceptive device or contrivance" limits its operation to knowing or intentional practices. In support of its view, the Commission cites the overall congressional purpose in the 1933 and 1934 Acts to protect investors against false and deceptive practices that might injure them. The Commission then reasons that since the "effect" upon investors of given conduct is the same regardless of whether the conduct is negligent or intentional, Congress must have intended to bar all such practices and not just those done knowingly or intentionally. The logic of this effect oriented approach would impose liability for wholly faultless conduct where such conduct results in harm to investors, a result the Commission would be unlikely to support. But apart from where its logic might lead, the Commission would add a gloss to the operative language of the statute quite different from its commonly accepted meaning. The argument simply ignores the use of the words "manipulative," "device," and "contrivance"—terms that make unmistakable a congressional intent to proscribe a type of conduct quite different from negligence. Use of the word "manipulative" is especially significant. It is and was virtually a term of art when used in connection with securities markets. It connotes intentional or willful conduct designed to deceive or defraud investors by controlling or artificially affecting the price of securities.

We have addressed, to this point, primarily the language and history of §10b. The Commission contends, however, that subsections (b) and (c) of Rule 10b-5 are cast in language which—if standing alone—could encompass both intentional and negligent behavior. These subsections respectively provide that it is unlawful "[t]o make any untrue statement of a material fact or to omit to state a material fact necessary in order to make the statements made, in the light of the circumstances under which they were made, not misleading . . . " and "[t]o engage in any act, practice, or course of business which operates or would operate as a fraud or deceit upon any person . . ."

Viewed in isolation the language of subsection (b), and arguably that of subsection (c), could be read as proscribing, respectively, any type of material misstatement or omission, and any course of conduct, that has the effect of defrauding investors, whether the wrongdoing was intentional or not.

We note first that such a reading cannot be harmonized with the administrative history of the Rule, a history making clear that when the Commission adopted the Rule it was intended to apply only to activities that involved scienter. More importantly, Rule 10b-5 was adopted pursuant to authority granted the Commission under §10(b). The rulemaking power granted to an administrative agency charged with the administration of a federal statute is not the power to make law. Rather it is "the power to adopt regulations to carry into effect the will of Congress as expressed by the statute." Thus, despite the broad view of the Rule advanced by the Commission in this case, its scope cannot exceed the power granted the Commission by Congress under §10(b). For the reasons stated above, we think the Commission's original interpretation of Rule 10b-5 was compelled by the language and history of §10(b) and related sections of the Acts. When a statute speaks so specifically in terms of manipulation and deception, and of implementing devices and contrivances—the commonly understood terminology of intentional wrongdoing—and when its history reflects no more expansive intent, we are quite unwilling to extend the scope of the statute to negligent conduct.

The judgment of the Court of Appeals is reversed.

Case Questions

1. Who wrote section 10(b) and who wrote Rule 10b-5?
2. What did the plaintiffs accuse the defendant of doing wrong?
3. Whose side was the Securities and Exchange Commission on here?
4. Why did the Court rule in favor of the defendant?

52.6 Summary and Exercises

Summary

Accountants, like other professionals, are subject to liability under both common law and federal statutes. Thus, an accountant who fails to follow generally accepted accounting principles is guilty of malpractice, and is liable for the harm to stockholders and others. But by itself, an unintentional, non-negligent mistake is not actionable.

An auditor guilty of fraud is liable to third parties who might reasonably have been presumed to rely on certified financial statements. In several states, an accountant who is merely negligent is liable only to direct clients and third-party beneficiaries, but not to the total class who might have been harmed. However, many states have adopted a rule that pins liability on the negligent accountant for losses suffered by any person (1) to whom the audit has been supplied for benefit or guidance, or with whom the auditor knew her client would share the information, and (2) who relied on it in a transaction which the accountant intended the information to influence.

Liability may be imposed on accountants under several federal statutes. Among them:

1. Section 11, Securities Act of 1933: liability to third parties for untrue statements in registration statements. To avoid liability, the accountant must show due diligence.
2. Section 12(2), Securities Act of 1933: liability to purchasers for aiding and abetting sellers in making untrue statements in prospectuses and communications.
3. Section 10(b), Securities Exchange Act of 1934: liability to investors, creditors, and others who rely on financial statements that accountants are required to sign and file with the SEC. But there can be no private suits under Rule 10b-5 against an accountant for damages for negligence, unless the accountant can be charged with intent to deceive, manipulate, or defraud.
4. Sherman Act: liability for attempting to restrain trade by fixing fees, regulating advertising, or excluding practitioners from the profession.
5. Private Securities Litigation Reform Act: for failure of auditors to have established procedures capable of detecting material illegal acts or for failure to evaluate whether an issuer of securities is able to continue as a going concern; the act requires that the auditor inform the firm of irregularities, and if the board does not inform the SEC, the auditor must do so.
6. SOX: willful violation of a rule made by the Public Company Oversight Board (a subagency under the SEC) is considered a violation of the 1934 Act; accounting firms may not perform certain non-audit services for audit clients; auditors must report directly to the firm's audit committee.

In addition to private suits, accountants are subject to sanction by the government under the securities laws. In particular, the SEC may, through a Rule 2(e) proceeding, discipline accountants by disqualifying them from practice before the Commission.

Although the professional ethics of accountants require them to maintain the confidentiality of client communications, most states do not protect this confidentiality by law. Likewise, although accountants' working papers are the property of accountants under the laws of many states, there is no federal privilege against disclosure and, if subpoenaed, the accountant will be required to turn these papers over to federal investigators.

Exercises

1. First Corporation hired Marie, a CPA, to write up its books and records. In performing the write-up, Marie noticed suspicious circumstances, such as missing invoices, but failed to inform the company. Assuming that Marie was not hired to audit the company's books and records, but merely to perform the writeup, would she be liable to First Corporation for negligence? Why?

2. Suppose in Exercise 1 that the suspicious circumstances noted by Marie were the result of First Corporation's negligence. Would Marie be liable for negligence if the company's contributory negligence could be proven? Why?
3. Assume in Exercise 1 that Marie was also hired to do First Corporation's tax returns. Marie gave the corporation a guarantee that, if she made a mistake, she would pay all penalties and interest. Is this guarantee enforceable? Why?
4. Suppose in Example 1 that Marie is also hired to certify First Corporation's balance sheet. First Corporation tells Marie that it will use the balance sheet in an attempt to obtain a loan from Fifth Bank only. If the company, without telling Marie, uses the balance sheet to negotiate a loan with Sixth Bank instead of Fifth Bank, and if Marie is negligent in certifying the balance sheet, would she be liable to Sixth Bank? Why?
5. Suppose in Exercise 4 that First Corporation had told Marie that it expected to negotiate a bank loan but did not name the bank. Would Marie be liable for negligence to Sixth Bank? Why?
6. Suppose in Exercise 4 that First Corp did not tell Marie that it was going to use the balance sheet to obtain a bank loan. Would Marie be liable for negligence to Sixth Bank? Why?

Self-Test Questions

1. The standards of the American Institute of Certified Public Accountants (AICPA):
    a. derive from a federal statute enacted by Congress
    b. derive from a model state code, enacted by various state legislatures
    c. derive from the AICPA and may be the basis of common-law liability
    d. derive from regulations adopted by the Securities and Exchange Commission
2. Scienter is an element of:
    a. negligence
    b. fraud
    c. malpractice
    d. restraint of trade
3. In some states, auditors are liable to:
    a. direct clients
    b. third-party beneficiaries of the audit
    c. third parties that might reasonably have relied on certified financial statements
    d. all of the above
4. For mistakes in a registration statement filed with the SEC, an accountant is:
    a. liable only for negligence
    b. absolutely liable
    c. strictly liable
    d. liable only for gross negligence
5. Due diligence requires an accountant to:
    a. exhaustively search every document in the files of the business audited
    b. reasonably investigate the books and records of the business audited
    c. investigate only those books and records specified by the client
    d. none of the above

Self-Test Answers

1. c
2. b
3. d
4. a
5. b

Endnotes

1. Lockheed executives admitted paying millions in bribes over more than a decade to the Dutch (Prince Bernhard, husband of Queen Juliana, in particular), to key Japanese and West German politicians, to Italian officials and generals, and to other highly placed figures from Hong Kong to Saudi Arabia, in order to get them to buy airplanes. Kelly (Clarence "Kelly" Johnson, first team leader of the Lockheed Skunk Works) was so sickened by these revelations that he had almost quit, even though the top Lockheed management implicated in the scandal resigned in disgrace. Ben R. Rich, and Leo Janos, *Skunk Works: A Personal Memoir of My Years at Lockheed.* (New York, NY: Little Brown & Co., 1994) p. 10.[1].
2. Michael Knapp, *Contempory Auditing: Real Issues and Cases, 7e* (Mason, OH: South-Western Cengage Learning, 2010). Used with permission.
3. "15 Most Memorable Companies that Vanished," accessed 2014, http://www.nbcnews.com/id/41027460/ns/business-us_business/t/most-memorable-companies-vanished/#.
4. These summaries of accounting scandals (1-9) are excerpted from Michael C. Knapp, *Contemporary Auditing: Real Issues and Cases,* 7e, (Mason, OH: South-Western Cengage Learning, 2010). Used with permission.
5. Michael Corkery, "Citibank Settles Mortgage Inquiry for $7 Billion," *The New York Times,* July 14, 2014. Available at http://dealbook.nytimes.com/2014/07/14/citigroup-and-u-s-reach-7-billion-mortgage-settlement/.
6. Michael Corkery, "Citigroup Settles Mortgage Inquiry for $7 Billion," *The New York Times,* July 14, 2014. Accessed at http://dealbook.nytimes.com/2014/07/14/citigroup-and-u-s-reach-7-billion-mortgage-settlement/. Here is an entertaining look at ten huge accounting scandals: http://www.accounting-degree.org/scandals/.
7. Re: *Kingston Cotton Mill Company*, 2 Ch. 279 (C.A. 1896).
8. PCAOB, AU Section 9339A.06.
9. *Ultramares Corp. v. Touche,* 174 N.E. 441 (N.Y. 1931).
10. *Sandusky Land, Ltd. v. Uniplan Groups, Inc.,* 400 F.Supp. 440 (N.D. Ohio 1975).
11. The underlying statute here is the Securities Exchange Act of 1934. In section 10b of that act, Congress declared illegal "fraudulent, deceptive, or manipulative acts or practices in the sale or exchange of securities," and Congress delegated some of that authority to go after such practices to the SEC (Securities Exchange Commission), which then promulgated its Rule 10b-5. Under the rule it is illegal "To make any untrue statement of a material fact or to omit to state a material fact necessary in order to make the statements made, in the light of the circumstances under which they were made, not misleading, or to engage in any act, practice, or course of business which operates or would operate as a fraud or deceit upon any person, in connection with the purchase or sale of any security."
12. *Aaron V. SEC,* 446 U.S. 680 (1980).
13. Investopedia, http://www.investopedia.com/terms/p/pslra.asp.
14. Paul D. Kimmel, PhD, CPA, Jerry J. Weygandt, PhD, CPA, Donal E. Kieso, PhD, CPA. *Financial Accounting, 6th Edition.* (Wiley, 2011).
15. "Signaling that the flag of reform has now been officially struck from the agency [the SEC] and replaced by the flags of the corporations it is charged with overseeing, the SEC recently capitulated on one of its key reforms. . . . It would've required that the boards of directors that supposedly serve as a check on CEO actions not be entirely chosen by CEOs. Instead, in board elections, large shareholders would be allowed to put forth their own independent nominees for a couple of board seats . . . [CEOs of major corporations] mounted a massive lobbying campaign with [President G.W.] Bush and Congress to get the SEC to stop this . . . encroachment. In February [2005], the SEC officials meekly ruled that this proposed reform had become "stale" with the passage of time, so they dropped it." Jim Hightower, "SEC Surrenders," *The Progressive Populist* (March 15, 2005): 3.
16. *Goldfarb v. Virginia State Bar,* 421 U.S. 773 (1975).
17. RICO, 18 U.S.C. §§ 1961-68.
18. *United States v. Arthur Young & Co.*, 465 U.S. 805 (1984).

Index